THE

Ellen G. White

ENCYCLOPEDIA

THE *Ellen G. White* ENCYCLOPEDIA

Editors
Denis Fortin
Jerry Moon

Assistant Editor
Michael W. Campbell

Consulting Editor
George R. Knight

Review and Herald® Publishing Association
Hagerstown, Maryland

Review and Herald® titles may be purchased in bulk for educational, business, fund-raising, or sales promotional use. For information, e-mail specialmarkets@reviewandherald.com

The Review and Herald® Publishing Association publishes biblically based materials for spiritual, physical, and mental growth and Christian discipleship.

Scripture quotations marked NASB are from the *New American Standard Bible,* copyright © 1960, 1962, 1963, 1968, 1971, 1972, 1973, 1975, 1977, 1995 by The Lockman Foundation. Used by permission.

Scripture quotations credited to NIV are from the *Holy Bible, New International Version.* Copyright © 1973, 1978, 1984, 2011 by Biblica, Inc. Used by permission. All rights reserved worldwide.

Texts credited to NKJV are from the New King James Version. Copyright © 1979, 1980, 1982 by Thomas Nelson, Inc. Used by permission. All rights reserved.

Bible texts credited to NRSV are from the New Revised Standard Version of the Bible, copyright © 1989 by the Division of Christian Education of the National Council of the Churches of Christ in the U.S.A. Used by permission.

Bible texts credited to RSV are from the Revised Standard Version of the Bible, copyright © 1946, 1952, 1971, by the Division of Christian Education of the National Council of the Churches of Christ in the U.S.A. Used by permission.

Texts credited to RV are from *The Holy Bible,* Revised Version, Oxford University Press, 1911.

Art Direction: Bryan Gray
Cover Design: Mark Bond

PRINTED IN U.S.A.

17 16 15 14 13   5 4 3 2 1

Library of Congress Control Number: 2013952459.

ISBN 978-0-8280-2504-1

CONTRIBUTORS

 **Denis Fortin** served as dean of the Seventh-day Adventist Theological Seminary from 2006 to 2013, where he currently is a professor of theology. He is an expert on Ellen White's life and work and since 1995 has shared with Jerry Moon the teaching of an influential course on issues in Ellen White studies. His previous books include *Adventism in Quebec: The Dynamic of Rural Church Growth, 1830-1910.* Denis and his wife, Kristine Knutson, reside in Berrien Springs, Michigan, where they raised their three children.

 Like Denis Fortin, **Jerry Moon** is an expert in Adventist studies and topics related to Ellen White. His Ph.D. dissertation dealt with the interaction of W. C. White and Ellen White. Moon is currently the chair of the Church History Department of the Seventh-day Adventist Theological Seminary. His previous books include *W. C. White and Ellen G. White: The Relationship Between the Prophet and Her Son* and *The Trinity* (with Woodrow Whidden and John Reeve). Jerry and his wife, Sue, are longtime residents of Berrien Springs, Michigan.

CONTRIBUTORS

Terrie Aamodt, Ph.D., professor of history and English, Walla Walla University, College Place, Washington.

Karen K. Abrahamson, Ph.D., managing editor, *Andrews University Seminary Studies,* Andrews University, Berrien Springs, Michigan.

Roy Adams, Ph.D., former associate editor of *Adventist Review* and *Adventist World,* General Conference of Seventh-day Adventists, Silver Spring, Maryland.

Gregory J. Allen, Th.D., associate professor of religion, Oakwood University, Huntsville, Alabama.

Reuel Almocera, D.P.S., associate dean of the seminary and professor of church ministry, Adventist International Institute of Advanced Studies, Silang, Cavite, Philippines.

Lewis O. Anderson, Ph.D., retired college Bible teacher, Allendale, Michigan.

David T. Arthur, Ph.D., professor emeritus of history, Aurora University, Aurora, Illinois. Died in 2005.

Warren S. Ashworth, Ph.D., former professor of religion, Pacific Union College, Angwin, California.

Daniel E. Augsburger, M.A., writer and speaker on practical Christianity, Berrien Springs, Michigan.

Delbert W. Baker, Ph.D., vice president, General Conference of Seventh-day Adventists, Silver Spring, Maryland.

Glen M. Baker, Ed.D., former principal and business manager, Glendale Adventist Academy, Glendale, California.

John T. Baldwin, Ph.D., professor emeritus of theology, Seventh-day Adventist Theological Seminary, Andrews University, Berrien Springs, Michigan.

Nigel Barham, Ph.D., former professor of history and political science, Oakwood University, Huntsville, Alabama.

Bruce L. Bauer, D.Miss., professor of world mission and chair, Department of World Mission, Seventh-day Adventist Theological Seminary, Andrews University, Berrien Springs, Michigan.

Stephen Bauer, Ph.D., professor of theology and ethics, Southern Adventist University, Collegedale, Tennessee.

Skip Bell, D.Min., professor of Christian ministry; director, Doctor of Ministry program, Seventh-day Adventist Theological Seminary, Andrews University, Berrien Springs, Michigan.

Jack J. Blanco, Ph.D., former dean and professor emeritus of theology, Southern Adventist University, Collegedale, Tennessee.

Arkadiusz Bojko, M.Div., pastor, Polish Seventh-day Adventist Church, Chicago, Illinois.

Tyler Bower, M.Div., pastor, Forth Worth First Seventh-day Adventist Church, Fort Worth, Texas.

Russell Burrill, D.Min., professor emeritus of evangelism and church growth, Seventh-day Adventist Theological Seminary, Andrews University, Berrien Springs, Michigan.

Merlin D. Burt, Ph.D., associate professor of church history; director, Center for Adventist Research, Andrews University, Berrien Springs, Michigan.

Aecio Cairus, Ph.D., retired professor of theology and chair, Department of Theological-Historical Studies, Adventist International Institute of Advanced Studies, Silang, Cavite, Philippines.

Heidi Olson Campbell, B.A., Adventist International Institute of Advanced Studies, Silang, Cavite, Philippines.

Michael W. Campbell, Ph.D., assistant professor of church history, Adventist International Institute of Advanced Studies, Silang, Cavite, Philippines.

Fernando Canale, Ph.D., professor emeritus of theology and philosophy, Seventh-day Adventist Theological Seminary, Andrews University, Berrien Springs, Michigan.

Erik C. Carter, D.Min., Ph.D. candidate, Claremont School of Theology, Claremont, California.

Wellington S. Chapi, D.Min., lecturer, Rusangu University, Monze, Zambia.

Jerry Chase, M.Div., pastor, First Seventh-day Adventist Church, Akron, Ohio.

Ron E. M. Clouzet, D.Min., professor of Christian ministry and pastoral theology; director, North American Division Evangelism Institute, Seventh-day Adventist Theological Seminary, Andrews University, Berrien Springs, Michigan.

Norma J. Collins, former associate director, Ellen G. White Estate, General Conference of Seventh-day Adventists, Silver Spring, Maryland.

Roger W. Coon, Ed.D., former associate director, Ellen G. White Estate, General Conference of Seventh-day Adventists, Silver Spring, Maryland. Died in 2011.

Winston J. Craig, Ph.D., professor of nutrition and wellness, Andrews University, Berrien Springs, Michigan.

Larry Crews, M.Div., support specialist, Ellen G. White Estate, General Conference of Seventh-day Adventists, Silver Spring, Maryland.

Rajmund L. Dabrowski, M.A., former director, Communication Department, General Conference of Seventh-day Adventists, Silver Spring, Maryland.

P. Gerard Damsteegt, Th.D., M.P.H., associate professor of church history, Seventh-day Adventist Theological Seminary, Andrews University, Berrien Springs, Michigan.

Jo Ann Davidson, Ph.D., professor of theology, Seventh-day Adventist Theological Seminary, Andrews University, Berrien Springs, Michigan.

Richard M. Davidson, Ph.D., J. N. Andrews professor of Old Testament interpretation, Seventh-day Adventist Theological Seminary, Andrews University, Berrien Springs, Michigan.

Jean Davis, local historian, Battle Creek, Michigan.

Kathleen Demsky, M.L.S., librarian, Architecture Resource Center, Andrews University, Berrien Springs, Michigan.

Lester D. Devine, Ph.D., former director, Ellen G. White Research Center, Avondale College of Higher Education, Australia.

Kwabena Donkor, Ph.D., associate director, Biblical Research Institute, General Conference of Seventh-day Adventists, Silver Spring, Maryland.

Herbert E. Douglass, Th.D., former president, Atlantic Union College; editor and author, Lincoln, California.

Jacques Doukhan, Th.D., professor of Hebrew and Old Testament exegesis, Seventh-day Adventist Theological Seminary, Andrews University, Berrien Springs, Michigan.

Lilianne Doukhan, Ph.D., professor of music and French, and chair, Department of Music, Andrews University, Berrien Springs, Michigan.

Ron du Preez, Th.D., director, Department of Communication, Michigan Conference of Seventh-day Adventists, Lansing, Michigan.

Roger Dudley, Ed.D., professor emeritus of Christian ministry, Seventh-day Adventist Theological Seminary, Andrews University, Berrien Springs, Michigan.

Cristian Dumitrescu, Ph.D., assistant professor of world mission, Adventist International Institute of Advanced Studies, Cavite, Silang, Philippines.

Eugene F. Durand, Ph.D., retired assistant editor, *Adventist Review,* Silver Spring, Maryland.

Jon L. Dybdahl, Ph.D., former president, Walla Walla University; adjunct professor of mission and Christian spirituality, Seventh-day Adventist Theological Seminary, Andrews University, Berrien Springs, Michigan.

Sylvia M. Fagal, M.S., adjunct professor of nutrition, Washington Adventist University, Takoma Park, Maryland.

William A. Fagal, M.Div., associate director, Ellen G. White Estate, General Conference of Seventh-day Adventists, Silver Spring, Maryland.

Teofilo Ferreira, Ph.D., former associate director, Ellen G. White Estate, General Conference of Seventh-day Adventists, Silver Spring, Maryland.

Herbert Ford, M.A., professor emeritus of journalism, Pacific Union College, and founder-director, Pitcairn Islands Study Center, Pacific Union College, Angwin, California.

Denis Fortin, Ph.D., dean and professor of theology, Seventh-day Adventist Theological Seminary, Andrews University, Berrien Springs, Michigan.

Anna Galeniece, D.Min., assistant professor of applied theology, Adventist University of Africa, Nairobi, Kenya.

Eriks Galenieks, Ph.D., assistant professor of Old Testament, Adventist University of Africa, Nairobi, Kenya.

Barry Gane, D.Min., Ph.D., head of school, Department of Ministry and Theology, Avondale College of Higher Education, South Pacific Division of Seventh-day Adventists, Australia.

Roy Gane, Ph.D., professor of Hebrew Bible and ancient Near Eastern languages, Seventh-day Adventist Theological Seminary, Andrews University, Berrien Springs, Michigan.

Paul A. Gordon, M.A., former director, Ellen G. White Etate, General Conference of Seventh-day Adventists, Silver Spring, Maryland. Died in 2009.

Helena R. Gregor, Ph.D., director, Seminary Distance Learning Center, Seventh-day Adventist Theological Seminary, Andrews University, Berrien Springs, Michigan.

Paul Z. Gregor, Ph.D., associate professor of Old Testament and biblical archaeology, Seventh-day Adventist Theological Seminary, Andrews University, Berrien Springs, Michigan.

Norman R. Gulley, Ph.D., professor emeritus of systematic theology, Southern Adventist University, Collegedale, Tennessee.

Donna J. Habenicht, Ed.D., professor emerita of counseling psychology, Andrews University, Berrien Springs, Michigan.

Herald A. Habenicht, M.D., retired physician, Berrien Springs, Michigan.

Mary Ann Hadley, B.A., former director, Ellen G. White Research Center, Southwestern Adventist University, Keene, Texas.

Martin F. Hanna, Ph.D., associate professor of historical theology, Seventh-day Adventist Theological Seminary, Andrews University, Berrien Springs, Michigan.

Mervyn G. Hardinge, M.D., professor emeritus and founder, School of Public Health, Loma Linda University, Loma Linda, California. Died in 2010.

Frank M. Hasel, Ph.D., dean, Theological Seminary, and professor of systematic theology and biblical hermeneutics, Bogenhofen Seminary, Austria.

Michael G. Hasel, Ph.D., professor of Near Eastern studies and archaeology; director, Institute of Archaeology, Southern Adventist University, Collegedale, Tennessee.

Daniel Heinz, Ph.D., director, European Archives for Seventh-day Adventist History, Friedensau Adventist University, Friedensau, Germany.

Hans (Johann) Heinz, Th.D., professor emeritus of systematic theology and former dean, Adventist Theological Seminary, Marienhoehe, Germany.

Stanley D. Hickerson, M.Div., letter and manuscript annotation editor, Center for Adventist Research, Andrews University,

Berrien Springs, Michigan.

B. Russell Holt, M.Div., former book editor and vice president for product development, Pacific Press Publishing Association, Nampa, Idaho.

Milton Hook, Ed.D., retired pastor, Sydney, Australia.

Darius Jankiewicz, Ph.D., professor of theology and chair, Department of Theology and Christian Philosophy, Seventh-day Adventist Theological Seminary, Andrews University, Berrien Springs, Michigan.

Warren H. Johns, Ph.D., associate professor, University Libraries, Loma Linda University, Loma Linda, California.

Del L. Johnson, M.H.A., administrator, Adventist Retirement, General Conference of Seventh-day Adventists, Silver Spring, Maryland.

Doug Johnson, M.Div., vice president for administration, Upper Columbia Conference, Spokane, Washington.

R. Clifford Jones, Ph.D., D.Min., associate dean and professor of Christian ministry, Seventh-day Adventist Theological Seminary, Andrews University, Berrien Springs, Michigan.

Meredith Jones Gray, Ph.D., professor of English, Andrews University, Berrien Springs, Michigan.

Kenneth Jorgensen, lecturer in Haderslev, Denmark, and Ph.D. candidate, Seventh-day Adventist Theological Seminary, Andrews University, Berrien Springs, Michigan.

Denis Kaiser, Ph.D. candidate, Seventh-day Adventist Theological Seminary, Andrews University, Berrien Springs, Michigan.

Roland Karlman, Ph.D., former director, Ellen G. White Research Center, Newbold College, Bracknell, England.

S. Joseph Kidder, D.Min., professor of Christian ministry, Seventh-day Adventist Theological Seminary, Andrews University, Berrien Springs, Michigan.

Miroslav M. Kiš, Ph.D., professor of ethics, Seventh-day Adventist Theological Seminary, Andrews University, Berrien Springs, Michigan.

Robert Kistler, Ph.D., professor emeritus of sociology, Andrews University, Berrien Springs, Michigan.

George R. Knight, Ed.D., professor emeritus of church history, Seventh-day Adventist Theological Seminary, Andrews University.

Bill Knott, Ph.D., editor, *Adventist Review* and *Adventist World,* General Conference of Seventh-day Adventists, Silver Spring, Maryland.

Ronald A. Knott, B.A., director, Andrews University Press, Berrien Springs, Michigan.

Johannes Kovar, D.E.S.T., professor of Greek and New Testament, Bogenhofen Seminary, Austria.

Howard Krug, M.A., high school history teacher and local historian, Rochester, New York.

Kathleen M. Liwidjaja-Kuntaraf, M.D., associate director, Health Ministries Department, General Conference of Seventh-day Adventists, Silver Spring, Maryland.

Jud Lake, D.Min., Th.D., professor of homiletics and Adventist studies, Southern Adventist University, Collegedale, Tennessee.

Gary Land, Ph.D., professor emeritus of history, Andrews University, Berrien Springs, Michigan.

Theodore Levterov, Ph.D., director, Ellen G. White Estate Branch Office and Heritage Awareness Office, Loma Linda University, Loma Linda, California.

Kathy Lewis, M.Div., hospital chaplain, Phoenix, Arizona.

Adelino T. Libato, Ph.D., former professor of education, Adventist International Institute of Advanced Studies; board chair, California Prep International School, Saraburi, Thailand, and Anglo Singapore International School, Bangkok, Thailand.

Allan G. Lindsay, Ed.D., historian, lecturer, and former director, Ellen G. White Research Center, Avondale College, Cooranbong, Australia.

Donald E. Mansell, B.A., assistant editor, *Seventh-day Adventist Encyclopedia*; former associate book editor, Review and Herald Publishing Association; former assistant secretary of the Ellen G. White Estate, former associate book editor, Pacific Press Publishing Association, Nampa, Idaho.

Medardo Marroquin, Ph.D., pastor, San Diego Spanish church, San Diego, California.

Mario Martinelli, D.Min., former vice president, Review and Herald Publishing Association, Hagerstown, Maryland.

Randy Maxwell, M.A., former associate editor, Pacific Press Publishing Association, Nampa, Idaho; pastor, Seventh-day Adventist church, Kuna, Idaho.

Don May, M.A., associate dean, College of Arts and Sciences, Andrews University, Berrien Springs, Michigan.

Alberta Mazat, M.S.W., Christian marriage and family therapist; former chair, Department of Marriage and Family Counseling, Division of Behavioral Sciences, Loma Linda University, Loma Linda, California.

Benjamin McArthur, Ph.D., vice president for academic administration, Southwestern Adventist University, Keene, Texas.

Alfred C. McClure, M.Div., former president, North American Division of Seventh-day Adventists. Died 2006.

John K. McVay, Ph.D., president, Walla Walla University, Walla Walla, Washington.

Julian Melgosa, Ph.D., dean, School of Education and Psychology, Walla Walla University, Walla Walla, Washington.

Nicholas Miller, J.D., Ph.D., associate professor of church history; director, International Religious Liberty Institute, Seventh-day Adventist Theological Seminary, Andrews University, Berrien Springs, Michigan.

Jerry Moon, Ph.D., professor of church history and chair, Department of Church History, Seventh-day Adventist Theological Seminary, Andrews University, Berrien Springs, Michigan.

A. Leroy Moore, Ph.D., professor emeritus of religion, Weimar College, Weimar, California.

Douglas Morgan, Ph.D., professor of history, Washington Adventist University, Takoma Park, Maryland.

Jiří Moskala, Ph.D., dean and professor of Old Testament exegesis and theology, Seventh-day Adventist Theological Seminary, Andrews University, Berrien Springs, Michigan.

Eike Mueller, Th.D. candidate, Seventh-day Adventist Theological Seminary, Andrews University, Berrien Springs, Michigan.

Ekkehart Mueller, Th.D., deputy director, Biblical Research Institute, General Conference of Seventh-day Adventists, Silver Spring, Maryland.

Shirley Mulkern, M.A., former rights and permissions coordinator, Review and Herald Publishing Association, Hagerstown, Maryland.

Juhyeok (Julius) Nam, Ph.D., associate professor, School of Religion, Loma Linda University, Loma Linda, California.

Marla Samaan Nedelcu, Ph.D. candidate, Seventh-day Adventist Theological Seminary, Andrews University, Berrien Springs, Michigan.

Craig H. Newborn, Ph.D., director of Sabbath school and Spirit of Prophecy ministries, South Central Conference of Seventh-day Adventists, Nashville, Tennessee.

James R. Nix, M.Div., director, Ellen G. White Estate, General Conference of Seventh-day Adventists, Silver Spring, Maryland.

Barry D. Oliver, Ph.D., president, South Pacific Division of Seventh-day Adventists, Wahroonga, Australia.

Robert W. Olson, Ph.D., former director, Ellen G. White Estate, General Conference of Seventh-day Adventists, Silver Spring, Maryland.

Lawrence W. Onsager, M.L.S., dean of libraries and associate professor of library science, Andrews University, Berrien Springs, Michigan.

Trevor O'Reggio, Ph.D., professor of church history, Seventh-day Adventist Theological Seminary, Andrews University, Berrien Springs, Michigan.

Arthur N. Patrick, D.Min., Ph.D., honorary senior research fellow, Avondale College of Higher Education, Cooranbong, Australia. Died in 2013.

Jon Paulien, Ph.D., dean, School of Religion, Loma Linda University, Loma Linda, California.

Michael D. Pearson, pastor, Meridian and Parma Seventh-day Adventist churches, Nampa, Idaho; Ph.D. candidate, Seventh-day Adventist Theological Seminary, Andrews University, Berrien Springs, Michigan.

Dennis Pettibone, Ph.D., chair, History Department, Southern Adventist University, Collegedale, Tennessee.

Gerhard Pfandl, Ph.D., former associate director, Biblical Research Institute, General Conference of Seventh-day Adventists, Silver Spring, Maryland.

Bob Pickle, apologist and researcher, Halstad, Minnesota.

Danel Oscar Plenc, Ph.D., director, Ellen G. White Research Center and Theology Graduate Studies, River Plate Adventist University, Entre Rios, Argentina.

Tim Poirier, M.Div., vice director and archivist, Ellen G. White Estate, General Conference of Seventh-day Adventists, Silver Spring, Maryland.

Martin Pröbstle, Ph.D., professor of Hebrew Bible, Bogenhofen Seminary, Austria.

Humberto M. Rasi, Ph.D., former director, Education Department,

Table of Contents

13 PREFACE

15 ABBREVIATIONS

GENERAL ARTICLES

18 Jerry Moon and Denis Kaiser: For Jesus and Scripture: The Life of Ellen G. White

96 Photos

104 Maps

112 Robert W. Olson and Roger W. Coon: Ellen G. White: A Chronology

121 George R. Knight: Ellen G. White's Writings

141 Tim Poirier: Archival Resources and Finding Aids

148 Merlin D. Burt: Bibliographic Essay on Publications About Ellen G. White

214 Jud Lake and Jerry Moon: Current Science and Ellen White: Twelve Controversial Statements

241 Denis Fortin: The Theology of Ellen G. White

ALPHABETICAL ENTRIES

287 Biographical Section

575 Topical Section

APPENDICES

1298 A. Genealogy Chart

1300 B. Chart of Relationships Between Early Books

1303 C. List of Ellen G. White's Letters

1407 D. List of Ellen G. White's Manuscripts

PREFACE

THE PUBLICATION OF THIS *ELLEN G. WHITE ENCYCLOPEDIA* represents approximately 15 years of dreaming, planning, and work. The project was begun in the late 1990s by our consulting editor George Knight. He saw *The C. S. Lewis Encyclopedia* and determined to prepare a similar work treating Ellen White, one of the most remarkable women of the nineteenth century. Despite thousands of pages published by and about her, there was no comprehensive source to which a new reader could turn for easy access to specific information. She was a prolific writer, successful health reformer, and cofounder of the Seventh-day Adventist Church, a global religious movement that now claims some 20 million adult adherents, yet she remains largely unknown to the general public.

The purpose of this book is to provide an easy-to-use standard reference that is readily comprehensible to a person without previous knowledge of the subject, yet informative enough to be useful to a specialist. Written by some 180 contributing authors from around the world, the *Encyclopedia* not only provides a concise yet comprehensive guide to the abundant resources already published about Ellen White, but also presents a considerable amount of new research. Both new and longtime readers will find reliable information, often presented from fresh new perspectives. To ensure the accuracy of the data presented, the entire manuscript was peer-reviewed by reputable scholars, further revised by the editors, and finally reedited by the publishers.

How to Use the *Encyclopedia*

The *Ellen G. White Encyclopedia* is organized into three major sections, easily distinguishable by the reader. The first section includes major introductory articles on Ellen White, including her life story, the major themes of her writings, principles of interpretation, her theology, research resources, and a bibliography of secondary sources. The first section is easily recognizable by the longer articles set in single-column format with endnotes.

The second section is the biographical section, including people Ellen White interacted with, corresponded with, or wrote about. A few historical figures that were *not* her contemporaries, such as Martin Luther and John Calvin, are found in the *topical* section with a discussion of their theological relationship to Ellen White. Thumbing through the book, one can recognize the second section by its mostly short articles about individuals.

The third section, the largest, contains articles on a great diversity of topics, which vary in length from several thousand words to under 100. Arranged alphabetically and set in double-column format, this section includes entries on themes or doctrines of Ellen White, books she wrote, historical events and places, and institutions she was connected with.

Each article in the topical or biographical sections is arranged alphabetically by a **boldface heading**. Within each article, references are given in parentheses, using standard abbreviations to the writings of Ellen White (see Abbreviations). For parenthetical references to other authors, see the full reference after the heading *Further reading* at the end of the article. Asterisks (*) identify topics or individuals on which there is a separate article in this *Encyclopedia*. Some articles also contain *See also* cross-references. Each article concludes with the name of the author. Unsigned articles are by the editors. The majority of the unsigned articles in the biographical section are by assistant editor Michael W. Campbell. For further information about authors, see Contributors.

Despite utmost care by authors and editors, readers will find mistakes. If those who do will kindly notify the editors, we will make corrections in the second printing. Corrections may be sent by postal mail to Department of Church History, SDA Theological Seminary, 4145 E. Campus Circle Drive, Berrien Springs, Michigan 49104-1515.

Acknowledgments

A work of this magnitude could not have been accomplished without the support and help of many people. We are grateful to Fran McMullen, administrative assistant in the department of Church History, for her support in many ways, especially entering editorial corrections in most of the manuscript. Graduate assistants Steven Toscano, Cyril Marshall, and Denis Kaiser proofread manuscripts and checked quotations from Ellen White's publications.

Our assistant editor, Michael Campbell, played a crucial role in the early years of the project while he earned his Ph.D. in Adventist studies. He helped us compile a list of topics and of possible contributors and contacted many of them regarding their interest in this project. Furthermore, he himself contributed many substantial articles and did the original research and writing of the vast majority of the small unsigned articles.

Although George Knight passed the idea for the project to us in its early stages, he remained a major contributor and consultant during the duration of the project. We are thankful to him and to Merlin Burt, Herbert Douglass, Stan Hickerson, Jim Nix, Tim Poirier, Wilfred Stuyvesant, Alden Thompson, and Woody Whidden for reviewing various sections of the manuscript.

Academic research would be impossible without the invaluable services of librarians and archivists. We are especially indebted to the staff of the Center for Adventist Research in the James White Library at Andrews University. The directors and associates at the Ellen G. White Estate in Silver Spring, Maryland, were always prompt in responding to urgent editorial inquiries. The Office of Archives and Statistics at the General Conference of Seventh-day Adventists, also in Silver Spring, Maryland, was another indispensable, priceless resource, always available through their online periodical, book, and document collections.

The editorial staff at the Review and Herald Publishing Association, especially Jeannette Johnson and Gerald Wheeler, have been a delight to work with, and we appreciate their encouragement and expertise during all the stages of this project. We are also grateful to the Office of Research and Creative Scholarship at Andrews University for research grants that enabled us to employ graduate students during the start-up years, and to the administration of Andrews University for providing financial support and time for research and writing.

Beyond providing ready access to much information about Ellen White, we hope that by our systematizing present knowledge this work will stimulate a new wave of interest in and research about this influential religious leader and writer of the nineteenth century.

ABBREVIATIONS

AA	*The Acts of the Apostles*, 1911
AG	*God's Amazing Grace*, 1973
AH	*The Adventist Home*, 1952
ApM	*An Appeal to Mothers*, 1864
AY	*An Appeal to the Youth*, 1864
1BC, 2BC, etc.	*The Seventh-day Adventist Bible Commentary*, Ellen G. White Comments. 7 vols. plus supplement (vol. 7-A), 1953-1957
BCL	*Battle Creek Letters*, 1928
CC	*Conflict and Courage*, 1970
Cch	*Counsels for the Church*, 1957
CD	*Counsels on Diet and Foods*, 1938
CE	*Christian Education*, 1893
CET	*Christian Experiences and Teachings of Ellen G. White*, 1922
CG	*Child Guidance*, 1954
CH	*Counsels on Health*, 1923
ChS	*Christian Service*, 1925
ChL	*Christian Leadership*, 1974
CL	*Country Living*, 1946
CM	*Colporteur Ministry*, 1953
CME	*A Call to Medical Evangelism and Health Education*, 1933
COL	*Christ's Object Lessons*, 1900
Con	*Confrontation*, 1971
CS	*Counsels on Stewardship*, 1940
CSW	*Counsels on Sabbath School Work*, 1938
CT	*Counsels to Parents, Teachers, and Students*, 1913
CTBH	*Christian Temperance and Bible Hygiene*, 1890
CTr	*Christ Triumphant*, 1999
CW	*Counsels to Writers and Editors*, 1946
DA	*The Desire of Ages*, 1898
DG	*Daughters of God*, 1998
EW	*Early Writings of Ellen G. White*, 1882
Ed	*Education*, 1903
1888 Materials	*The Ellen G. White 1888 Materials*. 4 vols., 1987
Ev	*Evangelism*, 1946
ExV	*A Sketch of the Christian Experience and Views of Ellen G. White*, 1851
ExV54	*Supplement to the Christian Experience and Views of Ellen G. White*, 1854
FE	*Fundamentals of Christian Education*, 1923
FLB	*The Faith I Live By*, 1958
FBS	*The Fannie Bolton Story*, 1982, 1990
FW	*Faith and Works*, 1979
GC, GC88	*The Great Controversy Between Christ and Satan*, 1911, 1888
GW, GW92	*Gospel Workers*, 1915, 1892
HFM	*The Health Food Ministry*, 1970
HL	*Healthful Living*, 1897
HP	*In Heavenly Places*, 1967
HS	*Historical Sketches of the Foreign Missions of the Seventh-day Adventists*, 1886
KC	*The Kress Collection*, 1985
LDE	*Last Day Events*, 1992
LHU	*Lift Him Up*, 1988
LLM	*Loma Linda Messages*, 1981
LP	*Sketches From the Life of Paul*, 1883
LS, LS80, LS88	*Life Sketches of Ellen G. White*, 1915, 1880, 1888
Lt	letter
LYL	*Letters to Young Lovers*, 1983
Mar	*Maranatha: The Lord Is Coming*, 1976
MB	*Thoughts From the Mount of Blessing*, 1896
MC	*Manual for Canvassers*, 1902
1MCP, 2MCP	*Mind, Character, and Personality*. 2 vols., 1977
MH	*The Ministry of Healing*, 1905
ML	*My Life Today*, 1952

MM	*Medical Ministry,* 1932
1MR, 2MR, etc.	*Manuscript Releases.* 21 vols., 1981-1993
Ms	manuscript
MYP	*Messages to Young People,* 1930
1NL, 2NL	*Notebook Leaflets From the Elmshaven Library,* 1985
OFC	*Our Father Cares,* 1991
OHC	*Our High Calling,* 1961
PaM	*Pastoral Ministry,* 1995
PC	*The Paulson Collection of Ellen G. White Letters,* 1985
PCO	*A Place Called Oakwood,* 2007
PCP	*Peter's Counsel to Parents,* 1981
PH	pamphlet
PK	*Prophets and Kings,* 1917
PM	*The Publishing Ministry,* 1983
PP	*Patriarchs and Prophets,* 1890
RC	*Reflecting Christ,* 1985
RY	*The Retirement Years,* 1990
SA	*A Solemn Appeal,* 1870
1SAT, 2SAT	*Sermons and Talks,* 1990, 1994
SC	*Steps to Christ,* 1892
SD	*Sons and Daughters of God,* 1955
1SG, 2SG, etc.	*Spiritual Gifts.* 4 vols., 1858, 1860, 1864
SJ	*Story of Jesus,* 1896
SL	*The Sanctified Life,* 1956
1SM, 2SM, 3SM	*Selected Messages,* 1958, 1980
1SP, 2SP, etc.	*The Spirit of Prophecy.* 4 vols., 1870, 1877, 1878, 1884
SpM	*Spalding and Magan's Unpublished Manuscript Testimonies of Ellen G. White,* 1915-1916
SpTA	*Special Testimonies, Series A*
SpTB	*Special Testimonies, Series B*
SpTEd	*Special Testimonies on Education,* c. 1897
SR	*The Story of Redemption,* 1947
SW	*The Southern Work,* 1898, 1901
SW (date)	*The Southern Watchman*
1T, 2T, etc.	*Testimonies for the Church.* 9 vols., 1855-1909
TA	*The Truth About Angels,* 1996
TDG	*This Day With God,* 1979
Te	*Temperance,* 1949
TM	*Testimonies to Ministers and Gospel Workers,* 1923
TMK	*That I May Know Him,* 1964
TSA	*Testimonies to Southern Africa,* 1977
TSB	*Testimonies on Sexual Behavior, Adultery, and Divorce,* 1989
TSDF	*Testimony Studies on Diet and Foods,* 1926
TSS	*Testimonies on Sabbath-School Work,* 1900
1TT, 2TT, 3TT	*Testimony Treasures,* 1949
UL	*The Upward Look,* 1982
VSS	*The Voice in Speech and Song,* 1988
WLF	*A Word to the "Little Flock,"* 1847
WM	*Welfare Ministry,* 1952
YRP	*Ye Shall Receive Power,* 1995

Other Abbreviations Used in the *Ellen G. White Encyclopedia*

AGD	Arthur G. Daniells
AHC	Adventist Heritage Center, Andrews University
AR	*Adventist Review*
art.	article
AU	Andrews University
AUG	*Atlantic Union Gleaner*
AUP	Andrews University Press
AUSS	*Andrews University Seminary Studies*
b.	born
BE	*Bible Echo and Signs of the Times*
1Bio, 2Bio, etc.	Arthur L. White, *Ellen G. White.* 6 vols., 1981-1986
Bk	Book, an archival category designating letter books in the General Conference Archives

BRI	Biblical Research Institute, General Conference of Seventh-day Adventists
BSL	*Bible Students' Library*
BTS	*Bible Training School*
Bx	Box, an archival category in the Center for Adventist Research, Andrews University
c.	*circa,* "about"
CAR	Center for Adventist Research, Andrews University, Berrien Springs, Michigan
Coll	Collection, an archival category in the Adventist Heritage Center, Andrews University
CUR	*Central Union Reaper*
CUV	*Columbia Union Visitor*
d.	died
DF	Document File, an archival category in the Ellen G. White Research Centers
DS	*The Day-Star*
EGW	Ellen G. White
EGWE	Ellen G. White Estate
EGWE-GC	Ellen G. White Estate main office, General Conference of SDA, Silver Spring, Maryland
EGWE-LLU	Ellen G. White Estate branch office/archives, Loma Linda University, California
EGWEnc	*Ellen G. White Encyclopedia*
EGWEur	*Ellen G. White in Europe,* 1975
EGWRC-AV	Ellen G. White Research Centre, Avondale College, Australia
fl.	flourished
Fld	Folder, an archival category in the General Conference Archives and in the Adventist Heritage Center, Andrews University
GCAr	General Conference Archives, General Conference of SDA, Silver Spring, Maryland
GCB, GCDB	*General Conference Bulletin, General Conference Daily Bulletin*
GCC Min	General Conference Executive Committee Minutes
GH	*Gospel Herald*
GIB	George I. Butler
HM	*The Home Missionary*
HR	*Health Reformer*
JATS	*Journal of the Adventist Theological Society*
JNA	John N. Andrews
JNL	John N. Loughborough
JW	James White
LLU	Loma Linda University, Loma Linda, California
LUH	*Lake Union Herald*
MMiss	*Medical Missionary*
MMM	*Manuscripts and Memories of Minneapolis,* 1988
MRmnt	*Ellen G. White—Messenger to the Remnant,* 1954, 1969
NPUG	*North Pacific Union Gleaner*
NUR	*Northern Union Reaper*
obit.	obituary
PPPA	Pacific Press Publishing Association
PT	*Present Truth*
PUC	Pacific Union College
PUR	*Pacific Union Recorder*
RG	Record Group, an archival category in the General Conference Archives
RH	*Review and Herald; Advent Review and Sabbath Herald*
RHPA	Review and Herald Publishing Association
SDoc	Shelf Document, one of a series of publications and research documents produced and distributed by the Ellen G. White Estate
SDA	Seventh-day Adventist
SDB	Seventh Day Baptist
SHM, SHM65	*The Story of Our Health Message,* 1943, 1965
SPA	Southern Publishing Association
SSW	*Sabbath School Worker*
ST	*Signs of the Times*
UCR (Australasian)	*Union Conference Record*
UM	University of Michigan
WB	*Workers' Bulletin*
WCW	William (Willie) C. White
1WCW, 2WCW, etc.	William C. White letter book
WL	Willard Library, Battle Creek, Michigan
YI	*Youth's Instructor*

For Jesus and Scripture: The Life of Ellen G. White

Jerry Moon and Denis Kaiser

ELLEN GOULD (HARMON) WHITE (1827-1915) was one of the most remarkable women in nineteenth-century America. Her lasting significance is attested by various well-documented accomplishments. First, she was the cofounder (with Joseph Bates and James White) of a denomination that at its establishment in 1863 had 3,500 members, but has grown to a global church of some 16 million baptized members.[1] By 2010 it was the twelfth-largest religious body worldwide and the sixth-largest highly international religious body.[2]

Second, Ellen White was a literary phenomenon. By the time of her death on July 16, 1915, her literary corpus included 26 books, approximately 200 tracts and pamphlets, more than 5,000 periodical articles, 6,000 typewritten letters and general manuscripts, plus diaries and journals, totaling approximately 100,000 pages of material from her 70-year ministry (1844-1915).[3] Today, including compilations, more than 126 titles are available in English. More impressive than the quantity of her literary productivity is the variety of subjects she addressed. She not only focused on religious matters, such as biblical prophecy, children's ministry, evangelistic methods, homiletics, the role of women in the church, spirituality, and theology, but wrote multiple works on health and education. She also wrote articles on such diverse topics as church-state relationships, ethics and morals, family life, history, leadership, literature, marriage, medicine, mental health, public speaking, and social relationships.

Third, she succeeded in founding worldwide systems of education, medical work, and publishing. By following her advice on health, Seventh-day Adventists became a population group much studied by health scientists.[4]

While historians document her achievements,[5] Seventh-day Adventists have a general explanation for her literary contributions, her insights on health, and her leadership in establishing institutions. They believe that the Bible foretold a renewal of the true gift of prophecy within Christianity prior to the second coming of Christ to earth, and that Ellen White's life and ministry represented at least a partial fulfillment of that biblical prediction. During the 70 years of her ministry she received an estimated 2,000 visions and prophetic dreams, ranging from less than a minute to nearly four hours in length. Although only an estimated 2 percent of her writings dealt with predictions of the future, many of her predictions were fulfilled, some during her own lifetime, others after her death in 1915, and a few are still being realized as trends she spoke about continue to unfold.[6]

At a conference of American historians in 2009, a perceptive question was raised: "What motivated Ellen White . . . to work tirelessly for the cause? What was it that made her so unique? Do her words reveal something more about her intentions and motivations?"[7] This article seeks to uncover the primary motivations of Ellen G. White by an investigation of her personal journey as a nineteenth-century woman—daughter, wife, mother, and friend—to complement the data elsewhere in this encyclopedia about her life as a church founder and public figure.[8] In this article Ellen White's life is divided into five periods.

1. Childhood and Teenage Years (1827-1844)
2. A New Vision—Raising a Church (1844-1863)
3. Shaping the Church and Its Mission (1863-1881)

4. Contending for the Gospel in Foreign Countries (1881-1900)

5. Senior Churchwoman (1900-1915)

The transition points of these periods are events that brought major changes either in her personal life or in the experience of Seventh-day Adventists—the disappointment of October 22, 1844; the founding of the Seventh-day Adventist Church in 1863; the death of Ellen White's husband, James White, in 1881; the return of Ellen White from Australia to North America in 1900; and her death in 1915—though there were certainly also other events of major importance.

Childhood and Teenage Years
(1827-1844)

When the twins Ellen and Elizabeth (Lizzie) were born on November 26, 1827,[9] their parents Robert F. Harmon, Sr. (1786-1866), and Eunice Gould Harmon (1787-1863) already had two sons and four daughters.[10] Both Robert and Eunice were deeply religious people; the fact that three of their six daughters married ministers may be an indication of the positive spirituality that characterized the home.[11]

Robert and Eunice Harmon grew up at the convergence of two historic epochs—the unprecedented optimism of the religious, economic, and political freedom of the new nation, and the most vigorous phase of Methodism, which by 1855 became the largest denomination in North America.[12] While in his teens, Harmon broke with family tradition by leaving the Congregational Church to become a Methodist (LS80 130). At age 24 he married Eunice Gould from Portland, Maine, who was a year younger and also a Methodist. She was a woman of both character and spirituality. In matters of principle she served God, leaving the consequences to Him (*ibid.* 234, 235).

Her ability to think rapidly and clearly made Eunice Harmon a firm and wise disciplinarian. Ellen remembered that as a young girl she sometimes left the room with a muttered complaint when her mother asked her to do something. But her mother would call her back, requiring Ellen to repeat what she had said. Ellen recalled her mother taking up that remark and showing her that she "was a part of the family, a part of the firm; and that it was as much [Ellen's] duty to carry [her] part of the responsibility as it was [her] parents' duty" to take care of their children. "I had my times now and then for amusement," Ellen later recalled, but "there was no idleness in my home, and there was no disobedience there that was not taken in hand at once" (Ms 82, 1901, in 1Bio 21). Eunice Harmon had high ideals for her children, and knew how to motivate them to those ideals.

Robert Harmon alternated between farming in Poland and Gorham and operating a hat business in Portland. Shortly after the birth of the twins—Ellen and Elizabeth—the family moved from Gorham to Portland. In 1829 the family relocated to Poland, before returning to Portland in 1833.[13] Portland was a rapidly growing city, the largest in Maine.[14] The climate of this shipbuilding center was cold, with high temperatures in midwinter hovering around 20°F (–7°C) and in the warmest part of the summer seldom above 60-70°F (16-21°C).

Ellen's Early Religious Experience

Since Ellen grew up in a devout Methodist home, it is no surprise that she early felt "the necessity of having [her] sins forgiven and washed away," lest she be "for ever miserable." She recalled her "praying parents, who felt great anxiety for the welfare of their children." She confessed "trying to appear perfectly indifferent before them, for fear they would think I was under conviction, while I bore an aching heart, and night and day was troubled, fearing death might come upon me while in sin"(YI, Dec. 1, 1852).[15] Ellen remembered that she "often" heard her mother pray "for her unconverted children." One night she overheard her mother, intensely "distressed," praying for her children. As Ellen eavesdropped, Eunice Harmon blurted out, "O! Will they wade through so many prayers, to destruction and misery?" Those words haunted Ellen "day and night," but she gave no indication to her mother (*ibid.*).

Ellen may have begun school in the fall of 1833, two months before her sixth birthday.[16] Brackett Street School was only one block from her home. She advanced rapidly and was soon called on to read to the younger students. Years later, while traveling by train, Ellen was reading to her husband when a passenger behind them asked, "Aren't you Ellen Harmon?"

"Yes," Ellen replied, "but how did you know me?"

"By your voice," the woman answered. "I attended school on Brackett Street in Portland, and you used to come and read our lessons to us" (1Bio 25, 26).

The schoolrooms in Portland typically included uncomfortable desks, poor lighting, inadequate heat and ventilation, too long hours, and too little exercise for young bodies—children often began primary school at 4 years of age. Teachers believed in corporal punishment and sometimes dished it out with impulsive violence. One such incident made a vivid impression on young Ellen. More than 50 years later she told it to a group of teachers as an example of how not to treat students.

"I have sat in school with a pupil sitting by my side, when the master sent a ruler to hit that student upon the head, but it hit me, and gave me a wonderful wound. I rose from my seat and left the room. When I left the schoolhouse and was on the way home, he ran after me and said, 'Ellen, I made a mistake; won't you forgive me?' Said I, 'Certainly I will, but where is the mistake?' 'I did not mean to hit you.' 'But,' said I, 'it is a mistake that you should hit anybody. I would just as soon have this gash in my forehead as to have another injured'" (9 MR 57).

The community schools taught not only the "virtues of hard work and obedience" but Protestant Christian theology as well. School rules required every student who could read to own a New Testament, from which teachers and students read verses at the opening and closing of each school day (1Bio 26). During the late 1830s and early 1840s the Chestnut Street Methodist Church, where the Harmons were members, was the largest Methodist church in Maine. It had a library of Christian books for children, including some about a girl named Ellen.[17] Ellen reported reading "many" of these "religious biographies" of virtuous and faultless children. "But far from encouraging me in my efforts to become a Christian, these books were as stumbling blocks to my feet," she recalled. "I despaired of ever attaining to the perfection of the youthful characters in those stories who lived the lives of saints and were free from all the doubts, and sins, and weaknesses under which I staggered." She reasoned that if those stories "really presented a correct picture of a child's Christian life," then "I can never be a Christian. I can never hope to be like those children" (LS80 146, 147).

Probably in 1836, as Ellen was on her way to school, she picked up "a scrap of paper containing an account of a man in England, who was preaching that the earth would be consumed in about thirty years [1866] from that time." She was so fascinated by that paper that she read it to her family. Yet when she contemplated the predicted event, she was seized with "great terror" because she had been taught that Christ's second coming would be preceded by a millennium of peace. The "little paragraph on the waste scrap of paper" made such an impression on her mind that she "could scarcely sleep for several nights, and prayed continually to be ready when Jesus came" (*ibid.* 136, 137; LS 20, 21).[18]

Maybe it was this fear of Christ's coming that motivated her to start reading the Bible, but despite her interest she did not want her parents to know it. When "I was reading my Bible," Ellen recalled, "and my parents would be coming into the room, I would hide it for shame" (YI, Dec. 1, 1852). She probably wanted to avoid attracting her parents' attention to her religious feelings. Despite her "great terror" of being lost, and the deep impression made by her mother's prayers, she still tried to put on a brave front to conceal her anxiety about salvation, and steadfastly refused to confide her troubles to her mother (*ibid.*). Perhaps this was one aspect of the "pride" that she later said characterized her life before her conversion (see 2SG 21; ST, Feb. 24, 1876; LS80 161; 1T 32; LS 39). However, despite recurrent worries about her spiritual condition, there were doubtless also days and weeks of relative respite as she applied herself to her schoolwork and all the other activities of an active 8-year-old.

The Accident
Probably in the late fall of 1836 Ellen's life took a traumatic turn.[19] Ellen, her twin sister Lizzie, and a classmate had a hostile encounter with an older girl from their school. Their parents had taught them that in case of such a conflict they should stop arguing and hurry home. They tried to follow that advice and get home as fast as possible, but the angry girl hurled a rock at the retreating younger girls (1T 9).[20] Just as Ellen looked back to see how close their pursuer was, the rock hit Ellen full in the face. She was immediately knocked "senseless." After regaining consciousness, she found herself in the store of a merchant. Her clothes were "covered with blood, which was pouring from [her] nose and streaming over the floor." A stranger offered to take her to her parents' home in his carriage, but she declined his offer and set out to walk home. After walking a short distance, however, she "grew faint and dizzy" and had to be carried home by Lizzie and their schoolmate. Ellen had no recollection of anything that happened afterward; she lay in a delirium for three weeks. No one but her mother thought that she would survive (2SG 7, 8; LS80 131, 132; LS 18).

When Ellen became aware of her surroundings, she thought she had been asleep. She could not remember the accident or the cause of her condition. At one point she overheard conversations between her mother and visiting friends. Ellen's curiosity was aroused by such remarks as "What a pity! I should not know her." When she asked for a mirror, she was shocked at her appearance, for "every feature of [her] face seemed changed." Her nose was totally smashed,[21] and she "was reduced almost to a skeleton." She recounted later that the sight of her own face was more than she could bear, and "the idea of carrying my misfortune through life" was insufferable. Finding no happiness in her existence, she did not want to live, but dared not die unprepared (2SG 9; LS80 132; LS 18).

Ellen Harmon's Conversion[22]

Convinced she was dying, Ellen "desired to become a Christian," and "prayed earnestly for the forgiveness of [her] sins." As a result, she felt a peace of mind and "loved every one, feeling desirous that all should have their sins forgiven and love Jesus" as she did. Another indication of her attitude became apparent when she witnessed a spectacular aurora borealis, perhaps on the night of January 25, 1837. [23] She remembered that "one night in winter when the snow was on the ground, the heavens were lighted up, the sky looked red and angry, and seemed to open and shut, while the snow looked like blood. The neighbors were very much frightened. Mother took me out of bed in her arms and carried me to the window. I was happy; I thought Jesus was coming, and I longed to see Him. My heart was full, I clapped my hands for joy, and thought my sufferings were ended. But I was disappointed; the singular appearance faded away from the heavens, and the next morning the sun arose the same as usual" (2SG 9, 10; LS80 133; 1T 11).[24]

Robert, her father, had not been at home when the accident happened, for he was on one of his business trips to Georgia—Maine had plenty of beaver fur that, made into hats, could be sold for a good price in the South. When he returned home, he embraced Ellen's siblings. Then he inquired for Ellen, but when his wife pointed at her, he did not recognize her. Robert could hardly believe that this was "his little Ellen, whom he had left only a few months before a healthy, happy child." She felt deeply hurt, yet she attempted to appear happy although her heart almost seemed to break (LS80 133; 1T 12).[25]

During her preteen and teen years, when physical appeal is so important to social relationships, Ellen was feeble, underweight, and unattractive in the eyes of her peers. This led to the loss of social acceptance. "I was forced to learn this bitter lesson," she wrote later, "that looks make a difference in the feelings of many. . . . How changeable the friendship of my young companions. A pretty face, dress, or good looks, are thought much of. But let misfortune take some of these away, and the friendship is broken" (2 SG 10, 11; 1T 12). She tried to escape by searching for "a lonely place," where she could "gloomily" ponder "over the trials [she] was doomed daily to bear." Only in Jesus could she find consolation and the assurance that she was loved (1T 12).

Yet that did not change her physical condition. For two years she could not breathe through her nose. Her health was so poor that she could attend school only a little, and it was hard for her to study and remember what she had learned. The girl that had thrown the rock at her was appointed by the teacher to assist her in writing and to make sure that she got her lessons. She was sorry for what she had done and was tender and patient with Ellen, seeing how hard she labored to get an education. But when Ellen tried to write, her hand would tremble. While trying to read, the letters would "run together," she would perspire excessively, and become "dizzy and faint." In addition, Ellen's persistent coughing—considered a sign of developing tuberculosis—prevented her from attending school. The teacher suggested finally that it would be better for Ellen to drop out of school until her health improved. Her recollection shows how difficult it was for her to make that decision: "It was the hardest struggle of my young life to yield to my feebleness and decide that I must leave my studies and give up the hope of gaining an education" (1T 13; 2SG 11, 12; LS 18, 19).

Then, in the fall of 1839, Ellen attempted to pick up her schoolwork again, enrolling in a female seminary. However, she was physically unable to cope with the strain, and she also felt that she could hardly maintain her religious experience in such a large seminary. At this point she gave up all attempts to gain a formal education. Her ambition for education "had been very great," she confessed, "and when I pondered over my disappointed hopes, and the thought that I was to be an invalid for life, I was unreconciled to my lot and at times murmured against the providence of God in thus afflicting me." As she blamed God, she lost her peace of mind and slipped back into her old fear of eternal damnation. Yet she continued to conceal her feelings from everyone near her, fearful they might even reinforce her gloomy presentiments (2SG 14; LS80 135, 148; 1T 13, 16).[26]

Some months after finally leaving school, Ellen with her family attended the first course of lectures that William Miller held in Portland, Maine, March 11-23, 1840 (LS80 136; 1T 14).[27] The conviction that Christ would come very soon—Miller said that Christ would come "about the year 1843"[28]—only intensified her fears. "My hope was so small, and my faith so weak," she later wrote, "that I feared if another took a similar view of my condition, it would plunge me into despair. Yet I longed for someone to tell me what I should do to be saved." One night, when Ellen was walking home with her brother Robert from the meeting, she confided for the first time in another human being the burden she carried. He responded sympathetically, but at only 14 he lacked the knowledge and experience to help her substantially. Hence her spiritual depression continued (1T 16).

The Buxton Camp Meeting

A breakthrough came in late summer 1841 at a Methodist camp meeting in Buxton, Maine.[29] Ellen heard a presentation on salvation, based on Esther 4:16, "I will go to the king, which is against the law; and if I perish, I perish" (NKJV). The minister encouraged those who feared that God would not accept them to go to Him anyway. First, they had nothing to lose, because if they did not go to God they would certainly perish as sinners. But second, they had nothing to fear. If the ruthless king of Persia had mercy on Esther, how much more would a loving God have mercy on the repentant believer. When the minister urged his hearers not to wait, hoping to "make themselves more worthy," but to come to God as they were, Ellen went forward and within a short time found peace, then joy. "Again and again" she said to herself, "Can this be religion? Am I not mistaken?" "I felt that the Savior had blessed me and pardoned my sins." Here Ellen experienced the second stage of her conversion by gaining a clearer understanding of justification, by believing that her sins were forgiven despite her continuing to "fall short" of perfection. She had been reborn, and Jesus, her Savior, was clearly at work in her life (LS80 142, 143; 1T 17, 18; LS 23, 24).[30]

On September 20, 1841, shortly after the camp meeting and two months before her fourteenth birthday, Ellen was accepted into the Methodist Church on a customary six months' probation before baptism. Her independent turn of mind was seen in her intense interest in the doctrine of baptism. Despite attempts by some of the church women to persuade her "that sprinkling was Bible baptism," she "could see but one mode of baptism authorized by the Scriptures," and insisted on being baptized by immersion. The church voted to recommend her for baptism on May 23, 1842, eight months after she was accepted as a candidate on probation. Another month passed before she was actually baptized in Casco Bay on June

26, 1842.[31] Thus a full nine months had elapsed between her first commitment to baptism and the actual administration of "the solemn ordinance"—long enough, unfortunately, for the experience of the Buxton camp meeting to wane, and long enough for a sea change in the attitude of the local church toward Millerite sympathizers. Ellen's baptism was the "last official act" of the more open-minded Pastor John Hobart at the Chestnut Street Methodist Church; he was replaced with William F. Farrington, who proceeded to subdue or expel the Millerites in the Chestnut Street congregation.[32]

Finding Assurance of Salvation

Ellen's conversion had begun with a deathbed repentance in 1836/1837. In 1841, at the Buxton camp meeting, she gained a deeper understanding of justification. But by the time of her baptism in 1842, she was already on the verge of a third religious crisis. Just two weeks before her baptism William Miller had visited Portland a second time, June 4-12, 1842. By now Ellen was an ardent believer in the Millerite message that "Jesus was soon to come in the clouds of heaven," but she was acutely "anxious" about her lack of readiness to meet Him.[33] Early Methodist belief defined sanctification as a "second blessing" through which one would receive at one point in time, holiness of heart resulting in victory over sin.[34] Ellen would later reject the emphasis on sanctification being instantaneous, insisting that it was rather the "work of a lifetime." But as a Methodist, she had heard sermons that only the "sanctified" would be saved, whereas she felt that she could claim only justification but not sanctification. Thus she "longed above all things to obtain this great blessing, and feel that [she] was entirely accepted of God," but she did not know how it could happen (LS80 149, 150; 1T 22, 23; LS 27, 28).[35]

As the year 1843 grew nearer, she became more concerned over her failure to experience sanctification, and her anxiety further intensified in view of the doctrine of the eternal torment of the lost, which preachers had vividly pictured from the pulpit. "While listening to these terrible descriptions," she recalled, "my imagination would be so wrought upon that the perspiration would start from every pore, and it was difficult to suppress a cry of anguish, for I seemed to already feel the pains of perdition." Consequently, she could not avoid the perception that God was a "tyrant, who delighted in the agonies of the condemned."

"When the thought took possession of my mind that God delighted in the torture of His creatures, who were formed in His image, a wall of darkness seemed to separate me from Him. When I reflected that the Creator of the universe would plunge the wicked into hell, there to burn through the ceaseless rounds of eternity, my heart sank with fear, and I despaired that so cruel and tyrannical a being would ever condescend to save me from the doom of sin" (ST, Feb. 10, 1876; LS80 151, 152; 1T 22-25; LS 28-31).

Thus the three issues—her conscious lack of sanctification, her terror of eternal torment, and her consequent inability to love and trust God—all combined to again bring "condemnation," "despair," "gloom," "anguish," and "hopelessness." Stressed to the point of weight loss and illness, she still feared to confide in anyone (LS80 152; 1T 23, 26).

After "three long weeks" of this depression she had two dreams. In the first, she dreamed of "a temple, to which many persons were flocking," for "only those who took refuge in that temple would be saved when time should close." Within the temple was "a lamb all mangled and bleeding," which those present knew "had been torn and bruised on [their] account. All who entered the temple must come before it and confess their sins." Many were entering the temple despite fierce opposition and harassment from the onlooking "multitudes." In her dream Ellen feared ridicule and was ashamed to publicly "humble" herself, so she "thought best to wait" until the crowds "dispersed" or she could somehow slip in before the lamb un-noticed. However, she delayed too long, "a trumpet sounded, the temple shook, shouts of triumph arose." Then "all was intense darkness," and she was "left alone in the silent horror of night." She felt as if her "doom was fixed," and that the "Spirit of the Lord had left [her], never to return" (1T 27, 28).

In her second dream she was sitting "in abject despair" with her face in her hands. "If Jesus were upon earth, I would go to Him, throw myself at His feet, and tell Him all my suf-ferings. He would not turn away from me, He would have mercy upon me, and I would love and serve Him always." Then a being "of beautiful form and countenance" asked her, "Do you wish to see Jesus? He is here, and you can see Him if you desire it. Take everything you possess and follow me." "With unspeakable joy" Ellen "gathered up all [her] little posses-sions, every treasured trinket," and followed. The guide led her up a "steep and apparently frail stairway." At the top she was directed to "leave all the things that [she] had brought" with her, and she "cheerfully laid them down." Then the door opened, and she "stood before Jesus. There was no mistaking that beautiful countenance. That expression of benevolence and majesty could belong to no other. As His gaze rested upon me," she continued, "I tried to shield myself from His gaze, feeling unable to endure His searching eyes, but He drew near with a smile, and, laying His hand upon my head, said: 'Fear not.' The sound of His sweet voice thrilled my heart with a happiness it had never before experienced. I was too joyful to utter a word, but, overcome with emotion, sank prostrate at His feet. . . . I seemed to have reached the safety and peace of heaven. At length my strength returned, and I arose. The loving eyes of Jesus were still upon me, and His smile filled my soul with gladness. His presence filled me with a holy reverence and an inexpressible love."

The guide again opened the door and invited her to take up the things she had laid there. Then he gave her "a green cord coiled up closely," which he told her to keep next to her heart. Whenever she "wished to see Jesus," she should take out the cord and "stretch it to the utmost. He cautioned [her] not to let it remain coiled for any length of time, lest it should become knotted and difficult to straighten. I placed the cord near my heart," she said, "and joyfully descended the narrow stairs, praising the Lord and telling all whom I met where they could find Jesus." This dream gave her hope. The green cord seemed to represent faith, and "the beauty and simplicity of trusting in God began to dawn" upon her mind (*ibid.* 28, 29).

This dream so increased her hope that she found the courage to confide in her mother, who referred her to Levi Stockman, a Methodist-Millerite minister in whom Ellen had "great confidence, for he was a devoted servant of Christ." She told Elder Stockman everything. With tears in his eyes he assured her that she had not committed any unpardonable sin. He described "the love of God for His erring children, that instead of rejoicing in their destruc-tion, He longed to draw them to Himself in simple faith and trust." He observed that her accident "was indeed a grievous affliction" but encouraged her to believe "that the hand of a loving Father had not been withdrawn" from her. In the future, he assured her, she would "discern the wisdom of the providence" that had so far seemed so cruel and inexplicable. "Go free, Ellen," he concluded. "Return to your home trusting in Jesus, for He will not withhold His love from any true seeker." She later wrote that the "few minutes" she had spent with Levi Stockman gave her "more knowledge" of "God's love and pitying tenderness than all the sermons and exhortations to which I had ever listened" (*ibid.* 29, 30). She commented on her experience as follows: "I felt an inexpressible love for God, and had the witness of His Spirit that my sins were pardoned. My views of the Father were changed. I now looked upon Him as a kind and tender parent, rather than a stern tyrant compelling men to a blind obedience. My heart went out toward Him in a deep and fervent love. Obedience to His will seemed a joy, it was a pleasure to be in His service. . . . I felt the assurance of an indwelling Savior.[36]

Early Public Witnessing

In this new perception of God's love for her, she again sensed a nudging toward "the same duty" she had so long refused—to pray in public—and she resolved to "take up [her] cross" at the earliest opportunity. That very evening—after the conversation with Levi Stockman—there was a prayer meeting at the home of her uncle. "I bowed trembling during the prayers," she remembered. "After a few had prayed, I lifted up my voice in prayer before I was aware of it, and in that moment the promises of God appeared to me like so many precious pearls that were to be received only for the asking. As I prayed, the burden and agony of soul that I had endured so long, left me, and the blessing of the Lord descended upon me like the gentle dew. I praised God from the depths of my heart. Everything seemed shut out from me but Jesus and His glory, and I lost consciousness of what was passing around me. When I again awoke to realization, I found myself cared for in the house of my uncle."

It was not until the next day that she had "recovered sufficiently to go home," but when she did, she felt she was "hardly the same person" that had left her father's house the previous evening. "My peace and happiness," she testified, were "in such marked contrast with my former gloom and anguish that it seemed to me as if I had been rescued from hell and transported to heaven" (LS80 159, 160; 1T 31).

The experience Ellen referred to as "blessing" corresponds with what Methodists called the "second blessing"[37]—sanctification following justification. She did not regard it as a state of sinless perfection but as one of right intentions and perfect love. Further, she felt a deep urging to relate her experience. Thus the very next evening after "receiving so great a blessing," she attended a Millerite meeting and shared her experience. "Not a thought had entered my mind of what I should say," she recalled, "but the simple story of Jesus' love to me fell from my lips with perfect freedom. . . . Tears of gratitude . . . choked utterance as I told of the wondrous love that Jesus had shown for me" (1T 32). Commenting upon the testimony that she gave at a conference meeting of the Freewill Baptists shortly afterward, she said: "I felt not only great freedom of expression, but happiness, in telling my simple story of the love of Jesus and the joy of being accepted of God. As I spoke, with subdued heart and tearful eyes, my soul seemed drawn toward heaven in thanksgiving" (*ibid.* 33).

Of her own experience of transformation she wrote, "The reality of true conversion seemed so plain to me that I felt like helping my young friends into the light, and at every opportunity exerted my influence toward this end." She had great empathy for those who, as she had been, were struggling under the sense of God's displeasure because of sin. She "arranged meetings" with her friends, including some who were "considerably older" than she and already "married." Many of them, she found, were "vain and thoughtless; my experience sounded to them like an idle tale, and they did not heed my entreaties," she recalled. But she "determined" not to cease her efforts until these loved ones "yielded to God." She spent "several entire nights" in prayer while she continued to urge them to seek salvation. Some of them thought she was beside herself to be so persistent, "especially when they manifested no concern on their own part." Yet Ellen kept up her "little meetings," where she "continued to exhort and pray for each one separately," until "every one" of them "yielded to Jesus" and "was converted to God." Then she began to have dreams about other specific individuals who needed Christ, and as she sought them out and prayed with them, "in every instance but one these persons yielded themselves to the Lord." Some older Christians criticized her for being "too zealous," but Ellen dared not accept their advice.

She had a clear understanding of the plan of salvation, and felt it to be her duty to continue her "efforts for the salvation of precious souls and to pray and confess Christ at every opportunity." "For six months not a shadow clouded my mind, nor did I neglect one known duty." Ellen felt so full of "love to God" that she "loved to meditate and to pray." In this experience of "perfect bliss," she "longed to tell the story of Jesus' love, but felt no disposition to engage in common conversation with anyone." She recognized that without the accident and the subsequent afflictions, she would probably not have given her heart to Jesus. Yet, now Ellen could even praise God for her misfortune, and she recalled that with "the smiles of Jesus brightening my life, and the love of God in my heart, I went on my way with a joyful spirit" (*ibid.* 34; cf. ST, Feb. 24, 1876).

Expulsion From the Methodist Church

Ironically, Ellen's experience of the long-sought "blessing" and assurance of salvation led directly to her expulsion from the Chestnut Street Methodist Church. In the Methodist class meeting she testified of her "great suffering under the conviction of sin, [and] how [she] had at length received the blessing so long sought, an entire conformity to the will of God" (1T 35). When she stated that it was the belief in Christ's second coming that had caused her to search more earnestly for the sanctification of the Holy Spirit, the class leader suddenly interrupted her, insisting that she had "received sanctification through Methodism" rather than "through an erroneous theory." Ellen disagreed, reiterating that she had found "peace, joy, and perfect love" through the acceptance of the truth concerning "the personal appearance of Jesus." This testimony was the last that she was to bear in that class (LS80 168; 2SG 22, 23). On February 6, 1843, the Chestnut Street church had already formed the first committee to discipline the Harmon family; further committees followed throughout the spring of that year. On June 5 the church appointed a committee to "keep order" in meetings and "prosecute all offenders if necessary." Ellen's "last testimony" as a Methodist probably occurred about this time. On July 19 the Maine Methodist Annual Conference in Bath, Maine, voted to suspend all members who persisted in advocating Millerism. The expulsion of most of the members of the Harmon family was announced at the

Chestnut Street church on August 21, and became final on September 2 when their appeal of the decision was rejected.[38]

Despite the break with the Methodists, Ellen G. White's concept of the way of salvation remained essentially Wesleyan-Arminian throughout her life. While her later writings on sanctification were nuanced differently than the Methodist teaching—she described sancti-fication as a lifelong process, not an instantaneous event—nevertheless, she fully endorsed John Wesley's view of justification and found much more to affirm than to deny in the Methodist understanding of the way of salvation (GC88 256).[39] Like Wesley she insisted that assurance of salvation is positively "essential" to "true conversion" (RH, June 3, 1880; Lt 1, 1889; RH, Nov. 1, 1892; TM 440, 441).[40]

The Nonimmortality of the Soul

Sometime between 1841 and 1843 (LS80 169, 170)[41] Eunice Harmon and another woman heard a discourse on the subject of the nonimmortality of the soul, and were dis-cussing the biblical texts it had been based on.[42] Up to this point Ellen had been certain of an eternally burning hell for the unrepentant. This belief, in fact, was at the root of her great fear of Christ's second coming. She was shocked, then, to hear her own mother en-dorsing the idea that the soul had no natural immortality. She later recounted the follow-ing conversation with her mother:

"I listened to these new ideas with an intense and painful interest. When alone with my mother, I inquired if she really believed that the soul was not immortal? Her reply was she feared we had been in error on that subject as well as upon some others.

" 'But mother,' said I, 'do you really believe that the soul sleeps in the grave until the resurrection? Do you think that the Christian, when he dies, does not go immediately to heaven, nor the sinner to hell?'

"She answered, 'The Bible gives us no proof that there is an eternally burning hell. If there is such a place, it should be mentioned in the Sacred Book.'

" 'Why, mother!' cried I, in astonishment, 'This is strange talk for you! If you believe this strange theory, do not let anyone know of it, for I fear that sinners would gather security from this belief and never desire to seek the Lord.'

" 'If this is sound Bible truth,' she replied, 'instead of preventing the salvation of sin-ners, it will be a means of winning them to Christ. If the love of God will not induce the rebel to yield, the terrors of an eternal hell will not drive him to repentance. Besides, it does not seem a proper way to win souls to Jesus, by appealing to one of the lowest attributes of the mind, abject fear. The love of Jesus attracts; it will subdue the hardest heart.' "

Eunice Harmon not only referred to the plain teaching of the Bible concerning this sub-ject, but she carried it also beyond the details of death to its implications for the gospel, urg-ing the superiority of a religious experience based on love over one merely driven by "abject fear." Had Ellen known that truth years earlier, it would have spared her much worry, fear, and sleepless nights. As she studied the subject for herself, she found a new world opening to her young mind. So many other biblical teachings—the sleep of the dead, the resurrec-tion of the body, the significance of the final judgment, and Christ's second coming—made more sense now (LS80 170-172; 1T 39, 40).

The Happiest Year of Her Life

Ellen would later describe the period from late 1843 to the autumn of 1844 as "the happiest year of my life," as she lived in "glad expectation" of soon seeing Jesus (LS80 168). The "Jewish year" 1843 was thought to end about March 21 or April 21, 1844, depending on which method of calculation was used.[43] Nothing unusual happened on either of those dates, but because the Millerites had not yet focused on a single day, the "spring disappointment" was not as acute as the later "great disappointment."

The explanation of the spring disappointment that became most compelling to the Millerites was popularized by Samuel S. Snow at a Millerite camp meeting at Exeter, New Hampshire, August 12-18, 1844.[44] Building on Miller's well-known exposition that the 2300 days of Daniel 8:14 represented years and extended from 457 B.C. to A.D. 1843, Snow introduced into Miller's system two refinements. First, Snow argued that if the period of 2300 years had started at the beginning of the year 457 B.C., it would have expired at the end of the year A.D. 1843. However, since the period of 2300 years started not at the beginning of the year 457 B.C. but in the autumn of 457 B.C., the end of the time period would extend the same number of months beyond the end of 1843 to the autumn of 1844. Second, Snow showed that in the typology of Leviticus 23, the spring festivals—Passover, First Fruits, and Feast of Weeks—foreshadowed and were precisely fulfilled in Christ's death, His resurrection, and the outpouring at Pentecost, each of which occurred on the exact date of its type in Leviticus 23. Extending the parallel, Snow argued that the fall festivals of Leviticus 23, particularly the Day of Atonement, should also be fulfilled on the exact date of the Levitical type. If this reasoning was correct, the "cleansing of the sanctuary" of Daniel 8:14 should begin on the Day of Atonement in the fall of 1844, which he calculated to be October 22, 1844[45]—then less than nine weeks away. That message, known as the "true Midnight Cry,"[46] spread through the Millerite ranks with great rapidity.

During that time Ellen was visiting families and praying with those whose faith was wavering. Believing that God would answer her prayers, she and those for whom she prayed experienced "the blessing and peace of Jesus." She appeared to have the signs of terminal tuberculosis—poor health, seriously affected lungs, and failing of the voice. Yet nothing was more important than having a right relationship with Jesus.

With diligent searching of hearts and humble confessions we came prayerfully up to the time of expectation. Every morning we felt that it was our first business to secure the evidence that our lives were right before God. We realized that if we were not advancing in holiness we were sure to retrograde. Our interest for each other increased; we prayed much with and for one another. We assembled in the orchards and groves to commune with God and to offer up our petitions to Him, feeling more clearly in His presence when surrounded by His natural works. The joys of salvation were more necessary to us than our food and drink. If clouds obscured our minds we dared not rest or sleep till they were swept away by the consciousness of our acceptance with the Lord" (LS80 188, 189).

When the time approached, the Millerite believers hoped that their Savior would come and complete their joys. However, the time passed again, "unmarked by the advent of Jesus." They had laid down their secular employments and businesses. "It was a bitter disappointment that fell upon the little flock whose faith had been so strong and whose hope had been so high" (*ibid.* 189). Many had recognized that the Holy Spirit had been active in the movement of the "true Midnight Cry" but after the passing of the time a general perplexity prevailed.[47] Recalling the experience of October 22, 1844, Hiram Edson wrote, "Our fondest hopes and expectations were blasted, and such a spirit of weeping came over us as I never experienced before. It seemed that the loss of all earthly friends could have been no comparison. We wept and wept, till the day dawn."[48] Another former Millerite recounted: "The passing of the time was a bitter disappointment. True believers had given up all for Christ, and had shared His presence as never before. The love of Jesus filled every soul; and with inexpressible desire they prayed, 'Come, Lord Jesus, and come quickly;' but He did not come. And now, to turn again to the cares, perplexities, and dangers of life, in full view of jeering and reviling unbelievers who scoffed as never before, was a terrible trial of faith and patience. When Elder Himes visited Waterbury, Vermont, a short time after the passing of the time, and stated that the brethren should prepare for another cold winter, my feelings were almost uncontrollable. I left the place of meeting and wept like a child."[49]

Yet despite the "bitter disappointment," Ellen White remembered that they "were surprised that [they] felt so free in the Lord, and were so strongly sustained by His strength and grace." She said, "We were disappointed but not disheartened" (*ibid.* 189, 190). The reason for the absence of the expected event had nevertheless still to be found.

A New Vision—Raising a Church
(1844-1863)

Though Ellen felt spiritually "sustained" through the "bitter disappointment," her physical health "rapidly failed." A physician diagnosed her case as "dropsical consumption" (tuberculosis), predicting she could not live long, and "might die suddenly at any time." Because she could hardly breathe when lying down, she spent her nights propped up to "almost a sitting posture, and was frequently wakened by coughing and bleeding" from her lungs. In this condition Ellen went to stay for a while at the home of Elizabeth Haines in Portland, Maine, probably to give her mother, Eunice Harmon, some respite from caring for her (LS80 192, 193).

First Vision and Call to Ministry

It was in that home in late December 1844, about a month after Ellen's seventeenth birthday, that she and four other women bowed for morning prayers. "While I was praying," Ellen later described, "the power of God came upon me as I had never felt it before" (EW 13). She was not unacquainted with supernatural spiritual manifestations.[50] But this was the first of what she would refer to as visions.[51] She reported: "While I was praying, the Holy Ghost fell upon me, and I seemed to be rising higher and higher, far above the dark world. I turned to look for the Advent people in the world, but could not find them, when a voice said to me, 'Look again, and look a little higher.' At this I raised my eyes, and saw a straight and narrow path, cast up high above the world. On this path the Advent people were traveling to the city, which was at the farther end of the path. They had a bright light set up behind them at the beginning of the path, which an angel told me was the midnight cry.[52] This light shone all along the path. . . . If they kept their eyes fixed on Jesus, who was just before them, leading them to the city, they were safe. But soon some grew weary, and said the city was a great way off, and they expected to have entered it before. Then Jesus would encourage them by raising His glorious right arm, and from His arm came a light which waved over the Advent band, and they shouted, 'Alleluia!' Others rashly denied the light behind them and said that it was not God that had led them out so far. The light behind them went out, leaving their feet in perfect darkness, and they stumbled and lost sight of the mark and of Jesus, and fell off the path down into the dark and wicked world below" (*ibid.* 14, 15; see also 2SG 30, 31).

Then she saw the second coming of Christ, the resurrection of the believers who had died, the arrival of the saved ones in heaven, and the heavenly city. When she related her experience to the Adventists in Portland, they "fully believed it to be of God. The Spirit of the Lord attended the testimony, and the solemnity of eternity rested upon us." Ellen remembered being filled with "an unspeakable awe," that she, "so young and feeble, should be chosen as the instrument by which God would give light to His people. While under the power of the Lord I was so inexpressibly happy, seeming to be surrounded by radiant angels in the glorious courts of heaven, . . . that it was a sad and bitter change to wake up to the unsatisfying realities of mortal life" (2SG 31-35; LS80 193; EW 15-17). That vision, later called the Midnight Cry vision, was of great importance for the group of believers. Like most other Millerites, Ellen had already given up belief that October 22, 1844, fulfilled any prophecy, though they still looked for the soon second coming of Christ (WLF 22; Lt 3, 1847).[53] The vision led her to accept again the date and readopt for a time the Millerite concept of the "shut door," though the vision itself did not say that sinners could no longer be converted (see article Shut Door). [54]

About a week later, probably in January 1845, Ellen received a second vision, showing her that she must tell others what God had revealed to her; that she would "meet with great opposition, and suffer anguish of spirit. Said the angel, 'The grace of God is sufficient for you; He will sustain you'" (2SG 35). The call to a public ministry was profoundly troubling. Her youth, her physical frailty, and her inexperience—all seemed insurmountable obstacles.[55] She especially dreaded violating custom on the proper role of women.[56] "The idea of a female traveling from place to place caused me to draw back. I looked with desire into the grave. Death appeared to me preferable to the responsibilities I should have to bear" (*ibid.* 36). Ellen's love for her father led her to confide in him about the command to tell others the vision. While Robert Harmon, Sr., could not accompany her because of his family and business, he "repeatedly assured [her] that if God had called [her] to labor in other places, He would not fail to open the way." Yet despite "these words of encouragement," Ellen's path seemed blocked by insurmountable difficulties, to the point that instead of fearing death from tuberculosis, she "coveted death as a release from the responsibilities" that faced her (LS80 194, 195).[57] For days she struggled with that call, feeling that the peace and favor of God had left her. This agony continued until Ellen "felt willing to make every sacrifice if only the favor of God might be restored." She begged the angel in the vision to preserve her "from undue exaltation" when she would relate to other people what God had shown her. She was assured that her prayer was answered (*ibid.* 195, 196; see also 2SG 36, 37).

Initial Public Labors

Trusting that promise, she committed herself to go wherever the Lord would send her. Soon the way opened for her to go with her brother-in-law Samuel Foss to her sisters in Poland, Maine, some 30 miles northwest of Portland. She wondered how she could do it, because, as she explained later, "for three months my throat and lungs had been so diseased that I could talk but little," in a "low and husky tone." At the meeting in Poland she began "speaking in a whisper," but after about five minutes "the soreness and obstruction" left her throat and lungs, her "voice became clear and strong," and she "spoke with perfect ease and freedom for nearly two hours." When her message was ended, her voice was gone until she stood before the people again, when the same singular restoration was repeated (LS80 197; 1T 65). [58]

Soon after Ellen returned to Portland, one of the local Adventists, William Jordan, needed to go to Orrington, Maine, "on business," and since his sister Sarah planned to accompany him, they invited Ellen Harmon to go also. "I felt somewhat reluctant," Ellen confessed, "but as I had promised the Lord to walk in the path he opened before me, I dared not refuse" (LS80 197). At Orrington she met James White, a young minister in the Christian Connection who had also accepted the Millerite message. [59] While working in Portland in the summer and fall of 1844, he had been impressed with Ellen, but she did not remember noticing him before the meeting at Orrington (2SG 38). [60] He considered Ellen Harmon as "a Christian of the most devoted type" who, at age 16, was already "a laborer in the cause of Christ in public and from house to house." He also noted that she was a "decided Adventist," that is, she did not downplay her Millerite beliefs. But even though not all agreed with her Adventist beliefs, James reported that "her experience was so rich and her testimony so powerful that ministers and leading men of different churches sought her labors as an exhorter in their several congregations" (LS80 126). It was at Orrington that James first heard Ellen tell her visions (2SG 38). Since they were both true-believer Millerites, and since he already admired her as a remarkable Christian, it did not take him long to conclude that her visions were from God. He noted her physical frailty and ill health, in a world of sometimes-violent anti-Millerite prejudices, and promptly offered to organize her meetings and provide his horse and sleigh for transportation. William Jordan had to return to Portland, but Sarah could stay and travel with Ellen for a while.

For three months, with various young women as chaperones, James and Ellen traveled together, holding meetings "almost every day," until they had "visited most of the Advent bands in Maine and eastern New Hampshire." [61] In many of these meetings they had a cordial reception, but once they barely escaped a mob. At Exeter, Maine, they encountered fanatics who abstained from work and crawled about on the floor in "groveling exercises" referred to as "voluntary humility (Lt 2, 1874)" [62] Ellen believed God had specifically called her to confront these fanatics, in order to remove the "stain" of their influence and to save some who were sincerely deceived (*ibid.*). At Atkinson, Maine, her attempt to minister among the congregation of Israel Damman led to allegations of misconduct between her and James White (see article Israel Damman). Back in Portland, Ellen's mother heard rumors of these adventures and dispatched a letter begging Ellen to "return home, for false reports were being circulated"—evidently concerning her association with James White.

"As for marriage," Ellen wrote, "we never thought of it, because we thought the Lord would come very soon" (1Bio 84). James reported later that "most of our brethren who believed with us that the second advent movement was the work of God were opposed to marriage" because it seemed a "denial" of their "faith" that Christ was coming soon.[63] However, several factors changed their attitude toward marriage. Despite their taking care never to travel without a chaperone, rumors began to circulate. "As our thus traveling subjected us to the reproaches of the enemies of the Lord and His truth," James wrote later, "duty seemed very clear that the one who had so important a message to the world should have a legal protector, and that we should unite our labors." A second reason was that James saw more and more clearly that as a young minister pioneering in uncharted waters, he needed the divine guidance that God was giving to her. On August 30, 1846, James White and Ellen Harmon were married in a civil ceremony in Portland, Maine (LS80 126, 238).

"We entered upon this work penniless, with few friends, and broken in health," wrote James later, "without a paper, and without books." The "congregations were small" and they had "no houses of worship," so most of their meetings were held in homes. Only "seldom" did any others than Adventists come to their meetings, "unless they were attracted by curiosity to hear a woman speak." The usual pattern of their meetings was that James White "would give a doctrinal discourse," then Ellen White would "give an exhortation of considerable length melting her way into the tenderest feelings of the congregation." His part was to plant the seed, her part was "to water it," and God gave "the increase" (*ibid.* 127).

Soon after their marriage they began to observe the seventh-day Sabbath. Joseph Bates had earlier preached to them about the Sabbath, without convincing them of its importance. For her part, Ellen thought Bates "erred in dwelling upon the fourth commandment more than upon the other nine" (1T 76). However, after reading Joseph Bates' first pamphlet[64] in August 1846 the Whites reconsidered the biblical evidence and began to "observe the Bible Sabbath, and to teach and defend it" (*ibid.* 75, 76).

At this time Bates had still serious doubts about Ellen's visions. In November he attended a conference in Topsham, Maine, where Ellen and James were also present. During one of the meetings she "was wrapt up in a vision of God's glory, and for the first time had a view of other planets." While in vision she started to describe some of the planets she was seeing. Bates, who had some knowledge of astronomy, thought he recognized such planets as Jupiter, Saturn, Uranus, and the "opening heavens." When he realized that Ellen knew nothing about astronomy, he became excited and concluded, "This is of the Lord." Ellen White never wrote out in detail what she had seen, nor did she ever specify the names of the planets, but the vision convinced Joseph Bates that her visions were of supernatural origin (WLF 22; LS80 239).[65] From this point onward Joseph Bates and the Whites united in their labors.

The Integration of Adventist Core Beliefs

In December 1846 Bates shared his insights on the seventh-day Sabbath with Hiram Edson, Owen R. L. Crosier, and Franklin B. Hahn at a meeting in Port Gibson, New York. Bates had already become convinced about their new light on Christ's two-phase ministry in the heavenly sanctuary, and at this meeting they accepted his view of the seventh-day Sabbath. In January 1847 Bates published the second edition of his *Seventh Day Sabbath: A Perpetual Sign*, which "not only highlighted the importance of the Sabbath, but also integrated it with his Bible-based understanding of the Second Coming, the heavenly sanctuary, and the three angels' messages of Revelation 14."[66] By this time the Whites, Joseph Bates, Hiram Edson, and a few others had become settled on four biblical doctrines that would become known as "landmarks" or "pillars" of Sabbatarian Adventism. These included (1) a premillennial second advent, (2) Christ's two-phase ministry in the heavenly sanctuary, (3) the seventh-day Sabbath, and (4) the nonimmortality of the wicked, all in the context of the three angels' messages of Revelation 14:6-12 (CW 30, 31).[67]

The role of Ellen White's visions in relation to these core doctrines was not to originate them, but to corroborate and confirm them in the thinking of Millerite Adventists; that is, to convince the Millerites that these doctrines were true. The Millerites in 1843 and 1844 had ventured out on an understanding of Bible prophecy that was not shared by any of the Christian denominations of the time. When their expectation turned to ridicule and humiliation, the majority simply accepted that Miller was wrong and tried to forget the whole experience. Later the studies of Bates on Revelation 14 and Crosier on the sanctuary offered biblical explanations for the Millerite experience. In the aftermath of the disappointment, however, there was such a plethora of divergent views that many sincere Millerites felt bewildered and unable to determine who to believe. Here is where the visions came in. When the Millerites witnessed Ellen White in vision, they noted the physical phenomena that accompanied the visions, saw predictions fulfilled, secrets revealed, and miracles of healing. When sincere seekers questioned the core beliefs, the visions revealed Bible passages that settled their disagreements. They saw that the visions and the Scripture were in perfect harmony, and over a period of time became convinced that God had provided dependable guidance out of their confusion and discouragement.

It is easy to demonstrate that Ellen White's visions, which began in December 1844, did not originate the "landmark" doctrines. The doctrine of the literal, visible, premillennial second advent of Christ had been rediscovered from Scripture by William Miller in 1818.[68] The seventh-day Sabbath had been observed and taught by Seventh Day Baptists since 1650.[69] The doctrine of conditional immortality (involving death as a sleep and the eventual annihilation of the wicked) has had supporters throughout Christian history, but was notably revived and promulgated from Scripture by George Storrs in 1841.[70] The sanctuary doctrine, the only biblical doctrine unique to Seventh-day Adventists, was given its first systematic biblical articulation by O.R.L. Crosier in 1846, completely apart from any influence from White.[71] The integrating framework for these doctrines was the prophecy of the three angels' messages of Revelation 14, which Joseph Bates worked out in detail in 1845, again before Ellen White had any vision on the topic.[72] All these doctrines were included in Bates' *Seventh-day Sabbath: A Perpetual Sign*, published in January 1847.

Four months later James White published *A Word to the "Little Flock,"* including sections by Joseph Bates and Ellen White. This publication and Bates' books ignited a publishing war between the "seventh-day" and "first-day" Adventists that led to a complete break between the two groups of former Millerites.[73]

Becoming a Mother

Meanwhile, on August 26, 1847, Ellen White gave birth to her and James' first son, Henry

Nichols White, at the home of Ellen's parents in Gorham, Maine, where the Whites still lived when they were not traveling. The Whites, however, had no income to contribute to the expenses of the Harmon home, and further, the Whites also insisted on Saturday rest, which the Harmons had not yet accepted. Both factors strained the relationship, and by October Ellen and James accepted the invitation of the Stockbridge Howland family to occupy a part of their house in Topsham, Maine (1T 82). The entrance of the baby into their lives brought another painful dilemma. Should Ellen travel with an infant? Should she stay at home with the baby, and allow her love for Henry to prevent her obedience to God's call to travel and preach?

For about six months they stayed with the Howlands, until Henry became sick, fell into unconsciousness, and did not respond to any therapy. Then James and Ellen realized that they had made their little son "an excuse for not traveling and laboring for the good of others." When they pledged to God that they would go wherever He would lead them if He would spare their child's life, the fever turned, and Henry began to recover. Not long afterward, in April 1848, they were invited to attend a conference of Sabbatarian Adventists in Rocky Hill, Connecticut. They accepted the invitation and took little Henry with them (1Bio 135, 136). Ellen traveled with him for a few months, probably until he was weaned. Then she left him with the Howlands in Topsham for about five years. She remarked later on that experience: "The greatest sacrifice I was called to make in connection with the work was to leave my children to the care of others" (1T 101; LS 165).[74]

Sabbatarian Bible Conferences

When the periodicals of first-day Adventists closed their columns to the Sabbath message, the Sabbatarian Adventists launched a series of evangelistic conferences designed to gather in as many as possible of those still undecided on the Sabbath question. This period of uniting people on a common biblical foundation became known as the "gathering time," superseding the "scattering time" since the disappointment. Over the next three years (1848-1850) some 23 of these conferences took place, beginning with the meeting in Rocky Hill, Connecticut, April 20-24, 1848 (2SG 93; LS80 245). At a second conference in Volney, New York, in August there were "hardly two" who "agreed" among the 35 people present. "Each was strenuous for his views, declaring that they were according to the Bible. All were anxious for an opportunity to advance their sentiments, or to preach to us. They were told that we had not come so great a distance to hear them, but had come to teach them the truth" (2SG 97, 98).

Ellen White noted a persistent frustration of hers at these conferences: "During this whole time I could not understand the reasoning of the brethren. My mind was locked, as it were, and I could not comprehend the meaning of the scriptures we were studying. This was one of the greatest sorrows of my life. I was in this condition of mind until all the principal points of our faith were made clear to our minds, in harmony with the Word of God. The brethren knew that when not in vision, I could not understand these matters, and they accepted as light direct from heaven the revelations given" (SpTB02 57; 1SM 207).

The period of time that Ellen White's mind remained "locked to an understanding of the Scriptures" extended for some "two or three years," from late 1846 to September 1849. (See article Sabbatarian Bible Conferences.)

The visions "confirmed" the core doctrines to the believers in at least four ways during these conferences. First, the visions corrected doctrinal errors, not by asserting extrabiblical authority, but by revealing Bible passages that had been overlooked. Second, those present at the conferences witnessed that Ellen White, when not in vision, was unable to contribute to the doctrinal studies or answer objections to the core doctrines. Yet they also observed that her visions revealed Bible passages that resolved seemingly intractable disagreements. This they saw as evidence that the information that came through the visions was not ultimately from her, but from a higher source.

A third factor that "confirmed" believers' confidence was their observation and documentation of the physical symptoms of Ellen White in vision, such as not breathing for long periods; having her eyes open, but being unaware of her surroundings; and having extreme physical weakness, sometimes replaced by supernatural strength. As they compared these to the records of biblical prophets, they concluded that genuine supernatural prophetic revelation was taking place.[75] Finally, the visions identified interrelationships between the core doctrines, showing that they formed an integral system of truth. A conference at Otis Nichols' home in Dorchester, Massachusetts, in November 1848 focused Bible study on the seal of God in Revelation 7 and 14. At that meeting Ellen White received a vision that connected the seal of God with the Sabbath, and also called on the group to publish it. After this "streams of light" vision, she told her husband: "I have a message for you. You must begin to print a little paper and send it out to the people. Let it be small at first; but as the people read, they will send you means with which to print, and it will be a success from the first. From this small beginning it was shown to me to be like streams of light that went clear round the world" (LS125).[76]

The Publishing Work

Poverty deterred James from starting immediately, but by July 1849 he brought out the first issue of *The Present Truth*. The title referred especially to the seventh-day Sabbath, in its last-day context of the seal of God, the mark of the beast, the temple in heaven, and the messages of the three angels. On July 28, 1849, Ellen White gave birth to their second son, James Edson White. In December 1849 James announced the publication of the first Sabbatarian Adventist hymnbook,[77] but financial support for the *Present Truth* was so weak that James was strongly tempted to discontinue the little periodical.[78] However, a vision Ellen White received January 10, 1850, declared "the paper should go," "that God did not want James to stop yet; but he must *write, write, write, write,* and speed the message and let it go. I saw that it would go where God's servants cannot go" (1Bio 172). James followed the advice and continued publishing the periodical. In August 1850 James started a second periodical, *The Advent Review*. Its purpose was to review the prophetic evidences taught by Millerite Adventists before the disappointment, together with the newly discovered biblical explanation of the disappointment, in the hope of reviving the faith of former Millerites. In November James merged the *Present Truth* and the *Advent Review* into the *Second Advent Review and Sabbath Herald*, later called *Review and Herald*, first published in Paris, Maine.[79] On December 24, 1850, Ellen White received a vision calling for "gospel order," that is, an organizational structure for the growing group of Sabbatarian Adventists (ExV54 15-23; EW 97-104).[80] During the 1850s, however, it was very difficult to convince even prominent leaders in the Sabbatarian Adventist movement of the need of organization.[81]

From 1850 to 1855 the *Review and Herald* published no direct reports of Ellen White's visions. Later those years would be called her "silent years." A hint of the absence of any visionary material in that magazine is found in a *Review and Herald Extra* published on July 21, 1851. There James White stated that many were "prejudiced against visions," which is why he chose to leave out of "the regular paper" anything related to visions. Hence he published the *Extra* for the purpose of communicating his wife's visions to a more select audience. Though he planned to publish an extra issue for that purpose "once in two weeks," the July 21 issue remained the only one.[82] Ellen's first book, *A Sketch of the Christian Experience and Views of Ellen G. White*, containing much of the content of the *Extra,* came out later the same month.[83] Her book concluded: "I recommend to you, dear reader, the Word of God as the rule of your faith and practice. By that Word we are to be judged. God has, in that Word, promised to give visions in the 'last days'; not for a new rule of faith, but for the comfort of His people, and to correct those who err from Bible truth" (ExV 64). Thus Ellen began a lifelong practice of pointing people to the Bible as the source of doctrine, faith, and practice.

In August 1851 the Whites relocated to Saratoga Springs, New York, where James continued to publish the *Review and Herald* until March 1852. In April, responding to the growing needs of "the cause," they moved to Rochester, New York, where they rented a home that also housed the press, the first one owned by Sabbatarian Adventists, which printed the *Review and Herald* and *The Youth's Instructor* (2SG 160; LS80 287; 1T 90).[84] For four years they lived and worked in Rochester, establishing a substantial congregation and the beginnings of publishing and administrative institutions. Staff members and workers lived together in that rented home. The living conditions become apparent in the report that Ellen gave to some friends.

"You would smile could you look in upon us and see our furniture. We have bought two old bedsteads for twenty-five cents each. My husband brought me home six old chairs, no two of them alike, for which he paid one dollar, and soon he presented me with four more old chairs without seating, for which he paid sixty-two cents. The frames are strong, and I have been seating them with drilling. Butter is so high that we do not purchase it, neither can we afford potatoes. We use sauce in the place of butter, and turnips for potatoes. Our first meals were taken on a fireboard placed upon two empty flour barrels" (1T 90; 2SG 160, 161; LS80 287).

Working there together as a group, they accomplished a lot in those years. However, it almost seemed that one after another they would all be wiped out by tuberculosis. On May 6, 1853, James' brother Nathaniel White died at the age of 22. James Edson, who was still a little boy, came down with the disease, but was healed in answer to prayer. Luman Masten became sick, was healed in answer to prayer, but then became sick again and died at the age of 25 on March 1, 1854. Then Anna White, James White's sister and editor of the *Youth's Instructor*, died of tuberculosis on November 30, 1854. Finally, Annie Smith also died of tuberculosis on July 26, 1855, at the age of 27.[85]

It was in the midst of that traumatic period—on August 24, 1854—that the White family welcomed a third son, William Clarence, who, as Ellen put it, "took my mind somewhat from the troubles around me" (2SG 192).[86] A year later, in November 1855, they moved with the publishing plant to Battle Creek, Michigan.

Time to Commence the Sabbath

Shortly after their arrival in Battle Creek they led in a conference from November 16 to 19, to study the "time to commence the Sabbath." While most of the Adventists began and ended the Sabbath at 6:00 p.m., there were some who believed that the Sabbath began at sunrise. When James White asked J. N. Andrews to study the matter, Andrews proved that "even" and "evening" of the Sabbath referred to sunset. The 6:00 p.m. time was in principle not incorrect, since it positioned the beginning of the Sabbath in the evening, yet the crux of the matter was in the detail—it was only at the equator that sunset occurred at 6:00 p.m.; north and south of it there were increasing deviations. The biblical evidence convinced everyone present except two—Joseph Bates and Ellen White.[87] Ellen wondered why a change should be necessary now, when the previous practice had been blessed by God for nine years. However, on November 20 Ellen "was taken off in vision," during which an angel called her attention to Leviticus 23:32: "From even unto even, shall ye celebrate your Sabbath." She agreed that the Sabbath should be celebrated "from even unto even," whereupon the angel instructed her: "Take the Word of God, read it, understand, and ye cannot err. Read carefully, and ye shall there find *what* even is, and *when* it is." It is significant that the angel did not just tell her when the Sabbath began, but pointedly referred her to Scripture. Then she understood that the "new" position did not contradict her vision of 1847, but that she and the others had too quickly assumed that "even" meant 6:00 p.m. Then the angel explained to her that God is displeased when people consciously reject revealed light, but not when they just need more time to fully understand. Then she saw "that the servants of God must draw together, press together," that is, all begin the Sabbath at the same time (4bSG 3, 4; cf. 1T 116).

The records of the conference in the December 4, 1855, issue of the *Review and Herald* also acknowledged that Adventists had been too reticent about confessing their faith in Ellen White's visions. To avoid criticism, the *Review and Herald* had not published any of her visions for five years. Believing that this policy was the cause of the visions becoming "less and less frequent," the delegates decided to change the policy. Two weeks later the December 18 *Review* contained an article titled "The Testimony of Jesus," by James White, defending the occurrence of the spirit of prophecy in the remnant church.[88] About this time appeared also the first 16-page pamphlet of Ellen White's *Testimonies for the Church*.[89]

The Great Controversy Vision

On the weekend of March 13 and 14, 1858, James and Ellen White stayed with the young church at Lovett's Grove, Ohio, where they held meetings in the public schoolhouse. On Sunday James was invited to preach at a funeral held in that schoolhouse. Afterward, Ellen also testified of the Christian's hope of resurrection. At some point during her testimony she was "wrapt in a vision of God's glory," which lasted for two hours. It became known as the great controversy vision because in it she was shown an overview of the cosmic battle between Christ and Satan, as it began in heaven and continued on earth. The theme of this vision would dominate her writings for the remainder of her life. On the way home two days later Ellen suffered a stroke that left her partly paralyzed. After earnest prayer was offered in her behalf, she recovered some ability to move her arm and leg. Although she continued the journey to Battle Creek the next day, on arrival home she was unable to climb the stairs, so occupied a first-floor bedroom. At first she was able to write only one page a day and then rest for three days. Another vision three months later informed her that Satan had attempted to kill her through that stroke, in order to prevent her from publishing the content of the great controversy vision (2SG 266, 271, 272). The new book, *Spiritual Gifts: The Great Controversy Between Christ and His Angels, and Satan and His Angels,* came out in September 1858.[90]

Systematic Benevolence

The Sabbatarian Adventist movement was growing, but there was yet no church organization or treasury. The personal finances of the ministers were so strained that between 1857 and 1858 several ministers were forced to drop out of the ministry and find other work to support their families.[91] By then it became evident that a permanent plan had to be found to provide financial resources for "the work of the ministry." Thus, in early January 1859, J. N. Andrews and others came to Battle Creek to study what the Scriptures have to say in regard to finances. On January 16 a plan on "systematic benevolence" was presented to the Battle Creek Church, and two weeks later the church adopted the plan by a unanimous vote. On the first weekend in June a large conference was held in Battle Creek with many Adventists coming from the "east, west, north, and south." The plan already adopted by the Battle Creek Church in January was read and freely discussed. The plan was "unanimously adopted" by the people present at the conference.[92] Ellen White, sick and discouraged, felt too miserable to attend the meeting. When J. N. Andrews and J. N. Loughborough came and earnestly prayed for her, she was given a vision in which she was shown that Satan had tried to drive her into despair, that the Laodicean message would need more time than just a few months to arouse the people of God, and that the plan of systematic benevolence was "pleasing to God" (1T 185-190).

Church Organization

Throughout the 1850s James and Ellen White called for "gospel order," or church organization. It was difficult, however, to convince the believers that organization would be something positive. Many still remembered how the established churches in 1843 and 1844 had opposed the message of Christ's second coming. Those churches were regarded as part of "Babylon," and thus church organization was considered a sign of apostasy. Even the idea of choosing a corporate name was considered a sign of Babylon. Yet Ellen White understood organization as a means to "effective mission outreach."[93] James saw also another dimension, namely legal implications. He was aware of some cases in other Adventist groups where church buildings built on private property had been lost to the church when the owner left the group. That is why he was calling for a legal status of the Sabbatarian Adventist movement, because only legal entities could own property. The church, rather than an individual church member, should own the property. He saw especially the need to establish an organization for the publishing house, which at that time legally belonged to him.[94]

The concept of organization was viewed negatively by many, but after extensive debates and discussions it was decided on September 30, 1860, to recommend "the organization of a publishing association that may legally hold the Review office."[95] Since it was now settled that the publishing house needed a legal organization, it was necessary to find a name for that organization. On October 1, 1860, the church chose the name "Seventh-day Adventist." When Ellen White heard the news, she was pleased. "The name, Seventh-day Adventist," she later wrote, "carries the true features of our faith in front, and will convict the inquiring mind. Like an arrow from the Lord's quiver, it will wound the transgressors of God's law, and will lead to repentance toward God, and faith in our Lord Jesus Christ" (4bSG 55).

The Nameless One

The reason Ellen White was not present for the vote on the denominational name, was that just 11 days earlier she had given birth to her and James' fourth son (2SG 294).[96] The boy, however, was still waiting for a name. Then James White left for meetings in Wisconsin, leaving his wife and boys in Battle Creek, and for two months the parents' correspondence referred to the baby as "the little nameless one" (Lts 10, 11, 1860, in 1Bio 426).[97] During the night of November 19 the baby became very sick (Lt 15, 1860). James started for home as soon as he learned of the baby's illness, but three weeks later, on December 14, the boy died. Sometime before the funeral they named him John Herbert White, and he was buried at Oak Hill Cemetery in Battle Creek, on December 17, 1860. Ellen fainted at the funeral, and when she returned home with her family, she felt that her "home seemed lonely" (Lt 17, 1861; 2SG 296).[98] The death of her baby really cut her heart as evidenced in a letter she wrote shortly afterward. "For weeks I had watched over my suffering child with agonizing feelings which I cannot describe and at last I witnessed its death struggle, the closing of its little eyes, but could find no relief by weeping. My heart was full to bursting, but could not shed a tear. His little coffin was near me in the meeting house. My eye rested upon it with such feelings of loneliness as none but a mother bereft of an infant can feel" (Lt 1, 1861).

The Threat of War

Less than a month later, in January 1861, Ellen White participated in the dedication of a new church building at Parkville, Michigan. Her prayer was interrupted by a vision that lasted 20 minutes. When she came out of the vision, she recounted what she had seen.

"There is not a person in this house who has even dreamed of the trouble that is coming upon this land. People are making sport of the secession ordinance of South Carolina, but I have just been shown that a large number of States are going to join that State, and there will be a most terrible war. In this vision I have seen large armies of both sides gathered on the field of battle. I heard the booming of the cannon, and saw the dead and dying on every hand. Then I saw them rushing up engaged in hand-to-hand fighting [bayoneting one another]. Then I saw the field after the battle, all covered with the dead and dying. Then I was carried to prison, and saw the suffering of those in want, who were wasting away. Then I was taken to the homes of those who had lost husbands, sons, or brothers in the war. I saw there distress and anguish.[99]

Then she looked at those who were present in the church building, and she said: "There are those in this house who will lose sons in that war." Although by this time four of the Southern states had seceded, hardly anyone thought it would lead to war. Those who favored military action to bring the seceding states back into line thought the conflict would be short and decisive. Some who heard her that day doubted it would be as bad as she predicted, but several families in the Parkville congregation lost sons in the Civil War.[100]

Organizing Conferences and the General Conference

After the delegates of the conference in 1860 had chosen a name for the church and decided to give the publishing house legal status, various local churches began to enter some form of organization in 1861. The churches in the state of Michigan went even further and united "in one conference with the name of the Michigan Conference of Seventh-day Adventists."[101] Other states followed in organizing state conferences. On May 20, 1863, a general conference took place, with delegates coming from all the state conferences. In that meeting, the state conferences were "bound together in a unified organization" called the General Conference of Seventh-day Adventists. On the first ballot James White was unanimously elected president, but he declined, lest anyone think his push for organization had been motivated by personal ambition. On the second ballot John Byington was elected as the first president of the General Conference.[102]

Shaping the Church and Its Mission
(1863-1881)

The major focus of Ellen White's visions in the second half of the 1840s was guiding the little group of believers toward a biblical foundation for their faith. During the 1850s, her counsels encouraged the publishing work and church organization. After the establishment of the General Conference of Seventh-day Adventists on May 21, 1863, her visions focused on other aspects of preparing the church for a worldwide mission.

The Comprehensive Health Reform Vision

Just 15 days after the organization of the General Conference, on the evening of Friday, June 5, while visiting the Aaron Hilliard family in Otsego, Michigan, Ellen White received a vision, known as the comprehensive health reform vision. Earlier visions in 1848 and 1854 had pointed out health hazards in tobacco, tea, and coffee, but the 1863 vision inaugurated a comprehensive health message as an aid to intellectual and spiritual growth (Ms 1, 1863; 4aSG 153; RH, Oct. 8, 1867; RH, Apr. 2, 1914; RH, Apr. 30, 1914).[103]

"I saw that it was a sacred duty to attend to our health, and arouse others to their duty, and yet not take the burden of their case upon us. Yet we have a duty to speak, to come out against intemperance of every kind—intemperance in working, in eating, in drinking, and in drugging—and then point them to God's great medicine, water, pure soft water, for diseases, for health, for cleanliness, and for a luxury. . . . I saw that we should not be silent upon the subject of health, but should wake up minds to the subject" (Ms 1, 1863, in 5MR 105, 106).

She emphasized that health reform was not only a personal matter but also had social and mission implications.[104] "The more perfect our health, the more perfect will be our labor" (*ibid.*). This vision called the church to become educated about the laws of health and the connection between health and spirituality. The early Adventists did not claim that the physical reforms recommended were original, but their view that caring for one's health was a *religious* responsibility was new to most people of the time.[105] Consequently the Whites began to practice the health reform in their own family. Though they made exceptions when traveling and in other emergencies, they adopted a lacto-ovo vegetarian diet at home.

In late November 1863 the Whites were bereaved of another son. Their eldest son Henry caught a cold that soon turned into "lung fever" (pneumonia). A physician was called and medicine administered, but Henry died on December 8, 1863. Ellen recollected: "When our noble Henry died, at the age of sixteen; when our sweet singer was borne to the grave, and we no more heard his early song, ours was a lonely home. Both parents and the two remaining sons felt the blow most keenly" (1T 103; LS 165, 166). While Henry's Christian experience had not always been satisfying, it had fortunately been revitalized during his last year.[106]

Only two months later their third son Willie contracted the same disease. This time they called no physician. Instead, Ellen determined to nurse him herself, using "hydropathy" (hydrotherapy) and constant prayer until the crisis was past (4aSG 151-153).[107] This success in her first direct experiment with water cure no doubt encouraged her to continue writing out what she had seen in the vision on June 5, 1863. Her first comprehensive publication of the message of that vision was a 32-page section of *Spiritual Gifts,* volume 4, in 1864 (4aSG 120-151).

Military Service and the Civil War

With the onset of the American Civil War, April 12, 1861, troubles and perplexities increased. The "war fever" diminished public interest in evangelistic meetings, and the question of Adventists' participation in the war became a major dilemma.

Adventists were against slavery, but they also believed in keeping the Sabbath and that it was wrong to take someone else's life. From August 12 through October 21, 1862, the denominational paper, the *Review and Herald*, published pro and con views about Adventist participation in the war.[108] In January 1863 Ellen White sent out to the churches *Testimony* no. 9, regarding "the war and our duty in relation to it."[109] There she predicted that the North would eventually win the war. She rebuked those who, facing threats, imprisonment, or death, claimed they would rather die than to submit to the draft. She asserted that this would be not an act of faith but "only fanatical presumption" (1T 357). It would be better to say little, pray for wisdom, and, if questioned, simply to answer that they do not sympathize with the rebellion. It would be their duty to obey the laws of the land as long as these do not conflict with the laws of God. However, there was no draft as yet; neither was there any legal provision for noncombatants or Sabbathkeepers.

When a draft law was passed in 1863, it still contained the option of either furnishing a substitute volunteer or paying a commutation fee of $300. While Adventists were willing to help each other in paying this fee, it became increasingly difficult to do so. On July 4, 1864, Congress passed an amendment to the draft law, revoking the exemption clause of the commutation fee except for those "conscientiously opposed to bearing arms." Now it was necessary for Seventh-day Adventists to act and become recognized as noncombatants. This could first be secured in the state of Michigan, and then in other states. From then on Adventists, as far as possible, served in noncombatant functions in the army. Yet the situation turned out to be more and more difficult. Thus the General Conference set aside March 1-4, 1865, for "earnest and importunate prayer." On those days business was to be suspended, church services held daily at 1:00 p.m., and two services were held on Sabbath. About a month later the war was virtually over.[110]

The Education of Edson and Willie

While Ellen White was a prophetic leader, prolific writer, and a powerful public speaker, she also had the everyday responsibilities of a mother.[111] A diary entry from January 28, 1868, shows how her household tasks competed with her writing.

"Brother [J. O.] Corliss [a young convert] helped me prepare breakfast. Everything we touched was frozen. All things in our cellar were frozen. We prepared frozen turnips and potatoes. . . . I baked eight pans of gems, swept rooms, washed dishes, helped Willie put snow in boiler, which requires many tubsful. We have no well water or cistern. Arranged my clothes press [closet]. Felt weary; rested a few minutes. Got dinner for Willie and me. Just as we got through my husband and Brother Andrews drove up. Had had no dinner. I started cooking again. Soon got them something to eat. Nearly all day has thus been spent—not a line written. I feel sad about this. Am exceedingly weary. My head is tired" (Ms 12, 1868).[112]

She deeply loved her children, and wanted to make her home "the pleasantest place of any" to them.[113] During the early years of her motherhood that was difficult because the family was extremely poor (they did not occupy a house by themselves until the mid-1850s), and they had to leave their children in the care of others, sometimes for six, eight, or 10 weeks at a time. In the midst of this hectic life, the salvation of her children was her ultimate concern.[114] In 1858 she wrote, "Many times I ask myself the question, Will my dear children be saved in the kingdom?" (Lt 3, 1858, in AY 44).

She commented to a friend about Edson at age 5, "You have seen Henry; well, Edson has more life and roughery than Henry, so you must know my hands are full" (Lt 5, 1854, in 6MR 297). However, it was not Edson's energy that caused her grief, but his "disposition to disobedience" and deception (Lt 4, 1865, in 4MR 173).[115] As Edson entered his teenage years she had additional reasons to be concerned. She noticed that even in church he played the rebel by fixing "himself in an easy position" and taking "a nap when he should be listening to the instruction given from the Word of God" (Lt 21, 1861, in 13MR 35).[116] Since Edson was the older of James and Ellen's two remaining sons, he had a strong influence on his younger brother Willie.

When she tried talking to Edson, he "seemed at a distance" from her, as though her "words were useless" (Lt 15, 1868, in 3MR 129). Besides his disobedience and deceptiveness, he was also a spendthrift. As a teenager he bought a new coat, just to wear to the Review and Herald office, for a price that equaled the monthly salary of a worker in that day. His mother later acknowledged that, apart from Edson's wrong behavior, parental mistakes at crucial points in his life had also hindered his development (Ms 12, 1868; Lt 12, 1878).[117]

When she was home, Ellen often laid aside her church work to spend time with her boys—reading to them, gardening with them, and much more.[118] When she traveled, they were on her mind. When Edson was 17, she sent him "comfortable clothing for winter" in the fall, saying: "I hope they will give you as much pleasure in wearing them as I have taken pleasure in making them for you. I have sat up late and arisen early, before anyone was astir, to work upon them. Prayers that you may be clothed with Christ's righteousness are stitched into these garments" (Lt 5, 1866, in 2Bio 155).

Further Developments on Health

In August 1864 Ellen White's fourth volume of *Spiritual Gifts*, including a 32-page section on health, had come from the press (4aSG 120-151). Shortly afterward, together with her husband, she visited Our Home on the Hillside, a health reform institution in Dansville, New York, operated by Dr. James C. Jackson. James White described the reason for their visit as follows: "In the month of September, 1864, Mrs. [White] and self spent three weeks at the health institution at Dansville, [Livingston] County, New York, called 'Our Home.' Our object in this visit was not to take treatment, as we were enjoying better health than usual; but to see what we could see, and hear what we could hear, so as to be able to give to many inquiring friends a somewhat definite report."[119]

One of the physicians was Dr. Horatio S. Lay, a Seventh-day Adventist with whom Ellen White had talked soon after her health reform vision in 1863. Encouraged by the vision, Dr. Lay took his ill wife to Dansville so that she could be treated and he could study the therapies used there. Soon he was taken onto the staff, which gave him even better opportunities to get acquainted with everything. When James and Ellen came to Dansville in 1864, they took treatments, dined at the institution's tables, observed the clothing of the women there, and talked freely with Dr. Jackson. Both were pleased with the "general atmosphere, the dietary program, and the courses of treatments." They spent three weeks at Dansville and found a "practical application of the principles of healthful living that would fit them" to be teachers of health reform. In subsequent weeks James and Ellen visited churches and spoke on diseases, their causes, and reforms of the habits of life.[120] In the early months of 1865 James White edited and published six pamphlets with the title *Health: or How to Live*.[121] Besides six articles from Ellen White's pen, these pamphlets also contained chapters from many contemporary health reformers, showing that the Whites were not uninformed about the larger health reform movement of their time.[122] In Ellen's sixth and last article, "Disease and Its Causes," she stated, "My sisters, there is need of a dress reform among us. There are many errors in the present style of female dress" (HR, Feb. 1, 1872). She found fault with the common dress styles of the day for reasons of health, modesty, and influence.[123]

The Whites' second visit to Dansville was precipitated when, on August 16, 1865, James White suffered the first of several strokes, the effects of which would plague him the rest of his life. By September 14 the Whites were bound for Dr. Jackson's "Our Home" at Dansville,[124] accompanied by J. N. Andrews, who was also ill. They stayed at the institution for three months. Ellen did not comply with some of the rules and restrictions of the institute, for they were not in harmony with the principles revealed to her in vision. For example, Dr. Jackson required his patients who had been under mental strain to take complete rest. Instead of any kind of work, he recommended such amusements as "dancing, card-playing, theater going"

(RH, Feb 20, 1866).[125] Since salt was considered a poison, its use was prohibited as well. Andrews complied with the rules and refused to use any salt. One day Ellen White sprinkled some salt on her unsalted mush. When Andrews saw what she was doing, he said in a solemn voice: "Sister White, don't you know that salt is a mineral substance, which should never be taken into the human body?" In equally solemn tones she replied: "My Bible says that salt is good." That ended the discussion.[126] Further, the physicians advised James to discontinue praying because they thought his religion was the source of the stress that broke his health. Yet, Ellen White could not agree with this reasoning. She believed, rather, that James needed useful physical work, opportunities to use his brain, and an active faith in God in order to recover (Ms 1, 1867).[127] Consequently, they decided to leave Dansville.

Health Institute Vision

Sometime in December they traveled to the home of friends near Rochester, New York. There on Christmas Day, 1865, Ellen received a vision instructing her how to bring about James' recovery. The vision also directed Adventists to establish a health-care institution, medically similar to the one in Dansville but without the amusements that she was shown were detrimental to spiritual well-being, and which therefore made the Dansville institution less than ideal for long-term patronage by Adventists (1T 485, 489, 494). The need for a healthier way of living was not difficult to recognize because most of the Adventist ministers were sick or disabled that year. The executive committee of the newly organized General Conference was not meeting for lack of a quorum—two of its three members were too ill to function.[128] However, the 1865 Christmas vision also integrated health reform with religion because "the health reform . . . is a part of the third angel's message and is just as closely connected with it as are the arm and hand with the human body." Further, the health message was to be instrumental in preparing Adventists "for the loud cry of the third angel" and for Christ's second coming (1T 486). Hence "health reform was to be a means to an end rather than an end in itself."[129] Some people had apparently missed this point, and that is why Ellen had to clarify in 1867 that "the health reform is closely connected with the work of the third message, yet it is not the message. Our preachers should teach the health reform, yet they should not make this the leading theme in the place of the message." It is rather a piece of the "preparatory work to meet the events brought to view by the message" (*ibid.* 559). This explains why she put so much emphasis on the right balance, and why she repeatedly warned against going to extremes.

Implementing the health instructions would be her dominant priority for the coming year (2Bio 118-125, 128-144, 154-159).[130] At the General Conference session in May 1866, Ellen White emphasized the need of a health-care institution. The young denomination accepted the twin challenge of health education and treatment. By August 1866 Adventists had launched a new journal, *The Health Reformer*, and in September they opened the Western Health Reform Institute in Battle Creek.[131]

Improving James' Health

Thus by December 1866 the church had achieved a major goal of the Christmas Day vision of 1865—the founding of the Western Health Reform Institute. Yet, for Ellen there seemed to be little progress in the battle for James White's health. His attitude had become more passive, and she feared that if he were not soon stimulated to use both mind and muscles, he would lose the potential for recovery. After much prayer she determined to take him on a preaching tour, even though it was winter, hoping that the activity would halt his mental decline. On December 19, during a driving snowstorm, against the advice of almost all, Ellen took her husband and their son Willie in an open carriage to Wright, Michigan, where they immediately began revival meetings. Over the next six weeks Ellen preached 20 times and James 12 times. But first she had to persuade him to enter the pulpit. "After much entreaty," she recalled, "he was prevailed upon to stand in the desk and speak to the people. My heart was full of gladness, but I could but weep aloud. The victory, I knew, was gained, the moral sensibilities and powers were aroused. My husband was saved" (Ms 1, 1867).[132] His health responded so well to the change of surroundings that by April 1867 they had purchased a farm and were building a home in Greenville, Michigan. They built through the spring and farmed through the summer, and by fall James had regained relative health, as Ellen devised all kinds of ways to involve her husband in physical exercise (*ibid.*). [133]

In September 1867 the Whites left on a 20-week itinerary,[134] during which they traveled 3,200 miles by railroad, 600 miles by horse and buggy, and held 140 meetings. James reported that "in more than 100 of these meetings," Ellen had "spoken from half an hour to two hours."[135] During 1867 Ellen preached almost twice as often as James. Arthur White observed that James White's invalidism "drove Ellen into unabashed public speaking, to the point where she could go into a church and address the audience at the worship service on a Sabbath morning" (2Bio 185). In January 1868 the Whites returned to Greenville. For the next three months they attended to writing during the week, and traveling on weekends to preach in churches within a day's drive of Greenville. Thus Ellen confirmed by experience what she had learned through her visions—that she and James needed to balance their strenuous life of ministry with physical exercise, adequate sleep, and interludes of rest and relaxation.

When James White returned to work in the early summer of 1868, he met with the workers of the Review and Herald. He led out in prayer, asking God to bless the publishing house, to make each page of the periodical a means to save souls, and to let every printer, editor, and worker see the fruits of their labor in the new earth. During his prayer James broke down and wept. Uriah Smith, then the editor of the periodical, recollected: "For a season we all wept together in silence, save the audible sobs, and the hearty response from those present."[136]

While James and Ellen resumed their travels, visiting almost every Adventist camp meeting in North America every year or two, they now began to include vacations in their plans. At the "turn of the year" 1870 they purchased a cottage in Washington, Iowa, for a "hideout" where they could "relax and pursue their writing." They spent a week there in early June, before attending the Iowa camp meeting, followed by camp meetings in Illinois, Minnesota, and Wisconsin in successive weeks (2Bio 290).[137] It was also in 1870 that the first volume of *The Spirit of Prophecy* was published.[138]

The Wedding of James Edson and Emma

In the summer of 1869 James and Ellen learned that Edson, who was not quite 20 years of age, was thinking of getting married. Neither of his parents was pleased about that news. Ellen wrote him: "Father weeps over your case. But we are both at a loss to know what to say or do in your case. We view it just alike. You are at present not fitted to have a family, for in judgment you are a child—in self-control a child." Yet she did not want to give up on him, despite her feeling of hopelessness. "My heart bleeds for you. I cannot give you up" (Lt 6, 1869).[139] The marriage of Edson White and Emma McDearmon took place in Battle Creek on July 28, 1870, Edson's twenty-first birthday. James conducted the wedding, which also provided the family with a break in the busy camp meeting schedule. Then James, Ellen, Willie, and Lucinda Hall, Ellen's best female friend and, at this time, general household and literary assistant, boarded the train for camp meetings in New York and Massachusetts.[140] Although Edson and Emma had no children, their marriage was successful, lasting until Emma died in 1916.

Summer in the Rocky Mountains

In 1872 James White's health was again failing, so James, Ellen, Willie, and Lucinda Hall set out for California (Lt 5, 1872; 2Bio 341; Lt 10, 1872; Lt 11, 1872; Ms 4, 1872).[141] Leaving Battle Creek June 23, they hoped to reach California within a week, but stops in Missouri and Kansas delayed their arrival, so that they had already been traveling for three weeks when they reached Denver, Colorado. James was so feeble that he fainted in the train depot. Too weak to walk, he rested on the floor while Willie hunted for his cousin, Ellen's sister's daughter, Louisa Walling. Her husband, William Walling, brought a carriage and invited the Whites and Lucinda to stay in Denver for a while. With James in no condition to continue the journey, they decided to rest immediately and "try the mountain air" in the high Rockies, then largely untouched by the amenities of modern civilization. A variety of holiday experiences—camping, hunting, fishing, horseback riding, mountain climbing, picking raspberries and gooseberries—made the summer pass quickly (Lt 30, 1872).[142]

Counsels on Educational Reform

It was while in the Rockies that Ellen described the ideals of Adventist education that she had seen in an earlier vision. The counsels were first issued under the title "Proper Education" in her *Testimony* no. 22. Later they were published in six parts in the *Health Reformer* (HR, December 1872; HR, April 1873; HR, May 1873; Hr, June 1873; HR, July 1873; HR, September 1873).[143] She began with the words: "It is the nicest [most delicate] work ever assumed by men and women to deal with youthful minds." Proper education, as she saw it, "embraces more than merely having a knowledge of books." Instead, she suggested a balanced and wholistic approach to education, one that "takes in everything that is good, virtuous, righteous, and holy," and "the practice of temperance, godliness, brotherly kindness, and love to God and to one another." This could be accomplished only by giving attention to "the physical, mental, moral, and religious education of children" (3T 131, 132). While Ellen White's educational suggestions and programs were not unique when compared with the ideas and programs of other educational reformers of her time, "her concepts were ahead of the general educational practices of the day."[144] Thus she suffered no illusion when she said, "We are reformers." However, the principle of synergizing mental labor and physical occupations was not caused by anti-intellectualism as is sometimes found among conservative Christians.

Rather she declared: "Ignorance will not increase the humility or spirituality of any professed follower of Christ. The truths of the divine word can be best appreciated by an intellectual Christian. Christ can be best glorified by those who serve Him intelligently" (*ibid.* 159, 160).

A winter of intensive labor in California climaxed with the organizing of the Caliornia Conference. In March the Whites returned to Battle Creek to attend the 1873 General Conference session and to promote the school that would become Battle Creek College (*ibid.* 371). Six weeks of hectic activity in Battle Creek climaxed with James White's fourth stroke of paralysis, April 22, 1873, and a fifth one on May 13. The pair of strokes was the signal to escape from the pressures of headquarters to the now familiar getaway spots in Iowa and Colorado. James and Ellen both preached at the Iowa camp meeting and planned to attend three other meetings. But a few days at their "hideaway home" in Washington, Iowa, convinced them that they should skip the camp meetings and go straight to Colorado (2Bio 381-384; Ms 8, 1873).[145]

The summer of 1873 the Whites stayed in Colorado more than four months. James and Ellen devoted themselves to resting and writing. Willie enjoyed boating, fishing, and hunting. Ellen reported one evening excursion that turned into an all-night adventure. "Brother Glover and Willie went out one night to fish, but the wind was so strong they . . . were obliged to camp out across the lake all night." They built a campfire and kept it going through the night. "We felt very anxious about them," Ellen wrote to Edson and Emma, "until they came home to [the] camp the next morning. As yet, all the fish we have caught have been with a silver bait. Brother Glover has now gone, evening after the Sabbath, to try his luck again" (Lt 13, 1873). A week later the person who was to have replenished their food supply did not show up, and the campers were running out of food. Ellen reported in her diary: "Our provisions have been very low for some days. Many of our supplies have gone—no butter, no sauce of any kind, no corn meal or graham flour. We have a little fine flour and that is all. We expected supplies three days ago certainly, but none has come. Willie went to the lake for water. We heard his gun and found that he had shot two ducks. This is really a blessing, for we need something to live upon" (Ms 12, 1873). As they were thinking what they "could do if no help came that day, Mr. Walling rode up" with some limited provisions. "He brought us butter, and fine flour." Willie added to the supplies that night by catching what Ellen described as "fourteen of the largest trout I had seen" (*ibid.*).[146]

During part of that time James invited Dudley M. and Lucretia Canright to join them in the mountains. Three weeks in an overcrowded cabin climaxed with an argument between James and Dudley. Canright later said that Ellen's siding with her husband on that occasion was the beginning of his loss of faith in her leadership. (See articles Colorado and Dudley M. Canright.)

The Whites stayed in the Rockies until early November, returned to Battle Creek for a General Conference session, and finally reached California in December.

Founding Pacific Press

Through a rainy California winter, waiting restlessly for James' health to improve, the Whites studied and prayed about their next steps. On April 1, 1874, Ellen had a vision about the power of the press, challenging church leaders not to have "too limited ideas of the work," but to "take broader views." She foresaw an expansion of the Adventist work in the western United States as well as overseas (LS208, 209).[147] As they counseled together about this message, they became convinced that they should publish a weekly paper in Oakland, California. Hence the Whites moved there in April, started tent meetings in May, and by June 4 founded the Pacific Press Publishing Association and brought out the initial issue of *Signs of the Times*. Immersing himself again in publishing, as he had earlier, James renewed his zest for life. Yet the financial obstacles were great. As they prayed for solutions, Ellen reported that "it was as if an audible voice said, 'Go to the churches and solicit money from those whom I have made stewards of means.'" At the same time she saw an angel pointing east across the Rocky Mountains. She "waited for [her] husband's consent," which was tearfully given because he could not leave the new paper. Fearing that he would change his mind, she hastily packed and left the same day the new paper came out. Traveling alone until Willie met her a few days later, she spoke at four camp meetings—Iowa, Illinois, Wisconsin, and Minnesota. After the Minnesota camp meeting Ellen and Willie spent a few days at the home in Washington, Iowa, before returning to Battle Creek July 3 (ST, June 4, 1874; Ms 4, 1874; 2Bio 419, 420; Lts 34, 36, 38, 40, 1874).[148]

When Ellen addressed a mass temperance meeting in Battle Creek on July 14, Willie escorted her on the platform. Ellen reported to James, "Willie waited upon me up in the desk and took a seat there with me, and placed my fur around my shoulders after I ceased speaking. He seems to understand his part" (Lt 43, 1874). Willie's assistance included accompanying her on personal calls and providing secretarial or even editorial assistance. To James she wrote, "We have just finished *Sufferings of Christ*. Willie has helped me, and now we take it to the office for Uriah [Smith] to criticize it. It will, I think, make a thirty-two-page tract" (Lts 41, 44, 1874). In August James joined her again for the Michigan camp meeting and the opening of the college.

The First Adventist College

Battle Creek College officially opened August 24, 1874. It had developed from the school that Goodloe Harper Bell had begun with 12 students in the summer of 1872. At the beginning of the school year 1873, the school committee replaced Bell with the 28-year-old Sidney Brownsberger, who had a master's degree from the University of Michigan. The Whites were unquestionably committed to the idea of a college that would train denominational workers. However, James and Ellen were not happy about the location chosen for the college. A close reading of Ellen's article "Proper Education" shows that a rural location would be preferable to a city like Battle Creek. Yet other considerations weighed more heavily in the final decision of the campus. In the fall of the year she read "Proper Education" to the college board, emphasizing the need to combine physical labor and mental studies. Brownsberger admitted that he had no knowledge and experience with that kind of education, but the board considered his academic degree too valuable to discard in favor of the suggested innovations. Ellen White was deeply disappointed, but she and James "continued to support the college and to work for its success."[149] She recognized the importance of the "sciences," a reference to the other academic courses, but insisted that "the Bible should be central to all instruction."[150] Three years later she reiterated the purpose of the school: "The college at Battle Creek was established for the purpose of teaching the sciences and at the same time leading the students to the Savior, whence all true knowledge flows. Education acquired without Bible religion is disrobed of its true brightness and glory. . . . The great object in the establishment of our college was to give correct views, showing the harmony of science and Bible religion" (4T 274).

During the summer and fall of 1874 a new building had been raised, and in December the school could move into it. The dedication of the college was planned for January 5, 1875, but Ellen White was very ill with influenza. When J. H. Waggoner, Uriah Smith, and James White came and prayed for her, she was given a vision, after which[151] "she . . . told her hearers that the time was not far distant when we should send ministers to many foreign lands, that God would bless their labors, and that there would be in many places a work of publishing the present truth. She said that in the vision, she had seen printing presses running in many foreign lands, printing periodicals, tracts, and books containing truths regarding the sacredness of the Sabbath, and the soon coming of Jesus. At this point, father interrupted and said, 'Ellen, can you tell us the names of those countries?' She hesitated a moment, and then said, 'No, I do not know the names. The picture of the places and of the printing presses is very clear, and if I should ever see them, I would recognize them. But I did not hear the names of the places. Oh, yes, I remember one, the angel said, "Australia." ' "[152] At that time the denomination had two publishing houses and one health institution, and was about to dedicate its first college. The church had just sent J. N. Andrews to Europe, but it would be years before the Adventist Church had printing presses in Europe, or work of any kind in Australia.

Difficulties With Her Husband

James and Ellen White had an unusual partnership for nineteenth-century America. The normal stresses of team ministry—often being together almost 24 hours a day, seven days a week—were heightened by the potential conflict between his authority as General Conference president and hers as a prophet. (See articles Marriage of James and Ellen White and Women's Issues.)[153]

James was a tremendously energetic, talented, dedicated, and persevering personality. Without his drive and leadership there would probably be "no Seventh-day Adventist Church as we know it today." His energy and persistence led in implementing the "publishing, administrative, medical, and educational" branches of Adventism's program. However, his dominant personality, combined with poor health after 1865 (he eventually experienced at least five strokes of paralysis), made him a person who was often difficult to live with. After his first stroke, "his inability to trust others, slow down, or delegate authority colored the remainder of his life."[154] While at times he suffered from depression and made "ill-advised statements and accusations," he continued to "make major contributions" to the church, accomplishing "more than three or four other men combined." Yet his problems affected his relationships with other church leaders as well as with his wife and children.[155]

One period of severe stress on their marriage began in the spring of 1874, when the Whites were in Oakland, California. Ellen felt strongly called to travel east and lead out in camp meetings, but was reluctant to do so without James. He, however, was intent on launching the new periodical, *Signs of the Times*. Further, his moods were so unpredictable that Ellen did not think he was suited for the public stresses of the camp meeting circuit.

When James realized a severe lack of funds at Pacific Press, Ellen proposed to attend the camp meetings and use that opportunity to raise funds for Pacific Press. James did not want to see her go, but when the impasse was framed in this way, he consented, and she left the same day (June 4) before he could change his mind. (See earlier section Founding Pacific Press.) Over the next month she wrote him a letter or postcard daily. By July 7 James was feeling much better, and on August 4 he rejoined her in Battle Creek, where they resumed their team ministry. They had worked separately for just two months.

A similar period of tension occurred in the spring of 1876. This time Ellen was the one who was comfortably settled into some rare weeks of uninterrupted writing on the "Life of Christ" manuscript, which she had begun in 1872 (3Bio 22). By putting much of her time into writing, she was able in the next two years to publish *The Spirit of Prophecy*, volumes 2 and 3, which cover large parts of Jesus' life on earth.[156]

James, on the other hand, left March 22, 1876, for Battle Creek administrative responsibilities, followed by camp meetings. He repeatedly urged Ellen to join him, but she wanted to continue her writing on the life of Christ. She felt that under the current circumstances it was better for them to be separate. Ellen could not explain the sudden changes in her husband's moods and feelings. She confided to her close friend, Lucinda Hall, that James frequently became angry, and would complain, fret, censure, and criticize. She had the impression that he wanted to dictate to her as though she was a "child." When in such a mood, he would speak so harshly that she did "not feel happy in his society," and really doubted that her husband desired her company. She no longer felt the "freedom with him in prayer" that they had previously enjoyed. She was obviously exhausted when she wrote to Lucinda Hall: "I have not lost my love for my husband, but I cannot explain things" (Lts 64, 65, 67, 1876, in DG 266-268, 271; 3Bio 22).

She wrote to her husband daily, but kept at her work. On May 14 she told him that her first volume on the life of Christ (*The Spirit of Prophecy,* vol. 2) would be finished in four weeks and then she would join him at the Minnesota camp meeting. But just one week after writing this note, she packed up her writing and took the train east to meet her husband at the Kansas camp meeting, May 27. They spent the rest of the summer speaking at camp meetings—14 in all. She worked on the book while they traveled, and finished it in November (Lts 26, 27, 1876, in DG 271).[157]

The Groveland Camp Meeting

One of the camp meetings in the summer season of 1877 stood out for several reasons. The logistical management of the meeting in Groveland, Massachusetts, was certainly a masterful performance. The campsite was a grove of pine and oak trees with train tracks of the Boston and Maine Railroad running along one side of the grove. Since the place was also near a river, it was possible during daylight hours to bring people to the meetings via ferry boats.[158] On Sunday morning, August 26, Ellen White spoke on the topic of Christian temperance to the largest group she had ever talked to at one time—20,000 people. Each day 18 trains ran, stopping at the campground to bring and take people. The train at 2:30 p.m. on Sunday had 15 cars, packed with people. One newspaper reported that "this lady [Ellen White] is a forcible and impressive speaker, and holds the crowd with her clear utterances and convincing logic."[159]

Salvation Through Jesus Christ

In June 1878 Ellen White traveled by steamship from San Francisco to Portland, Oregon. After she had distributed some Adventist publications, she heard a minister talking to a group of people in response to her tracts. He insisted that it is impossible to keep the law, and he stated: "Mrs. White is all law, law; she believes that we must be saved by the law, and no one can be saved unless they keep the law. Now *I* believe in Christ. He is *my* Savior, Christ alone can save us, and without Him we cannot be saved." The charge that she depended on the law for salvation, she could not ignore. "That is a false statement," she declared. "Mrs. White has never occupied that position. I will speak for myself and for our people. We have always taken the position that there was no power in the law to save a single transgressor of that law. The law convicts and condemns the sinner, but it is not in its province to pardon the least or greatest sin. If we sin we have an Advocate with the Father, Jesus Christ the righteous" (ST, July 18, 1878).[160] After a thorough explanation of the relationship between the law and the gospel, she concluded with the request that her critic "never again make the misstatement that we [Adventists] do not rely on Jesus Christ for salvation, but trust in the law to be saved" (*ibid.*).

This was a battle she fought over and over throughout her life, both outside and inside her denomination. Her understanding of salvation was thoroughly Wesleyan, emphasizing the "great truths" of "justification through faith in the atoning blood of Christ, and the renewing power of the Holy Spirit upon the heart, bringing forth fruit in a life conformed to the example of Christ" (GC 256). Because of her insistence that live faith and real conversion would always bring forth fruit in a Christlike life, she was accused of legalism. But she steadfastly maintained that the only way to salvation is to "rely upon the merits of the blood of Christ and claim His saving strength." When times of doubt and hopelessness would arise, she counseled believers "to trust, to depend on the sole merits of the atonement, and in all our helpless unworthiness cast ourselves upon the merits of the crucified and risen Savior. We shall never perish while we do this—*never!*" (RH, Apr. 22, 1862). James shared that conviction.[161] Both of them strongly argued that justification is through grace alone by faith, and that sanctification is the fruit of that faith.[162]

Vacation in Colorado and Winter in Texas

In August 1878 James was on vacation with Willie in Colorado. Ellen wrote him and expressed her hope that both would be "cheerful and happy" in the mountains. She suggested to James: "Lay aside your work. . . . Get all the pleasure you can out of this little season." Then she added that he and Willie should try to "be as free as the birds of the air. . . . The few days you now have together, improve. Roam about, camp out, fish, hunt, go to places that you have not seen, rest as you go, and enjoy everything. Then come back to your work fresh and vigorous" (Lt 1, 1878, in 9MR 317).[163]

During the fall and winter of 1878-1879 the Whites spent several months in Texas holding meetings and doing evangelistic outreach. The 21-year-old Arthur G. Daniells had come to Texas to help in tent evangelism. Soon he was assisting James White as a secretary, and his wife, Mary Daniells, was working in the White home as a cook.

James White was then president of the General Conference, president of several publishing, medical, and educational organizations, as well as the chief editor of both the *Review and Herald* and the *Signs of the Times*. It was difficult for James to let go of some responsibilities and make room for others in leadership. Little did he know that he and Ellen were just then mentoring a young minster—A. G. Daniells—who would lead the church for 21 years (3Bio 98-108).[164] (See articles Texas and Wagon Train.)

The Dime Tabernacle—James White's Last Major Project

On Sunday afternoon, April 20, 1879, the Battle Creek church dedicated its fourth church building. The "Dime Tabernacle" was the largest Adventist church building ever constructed to that date. It could seat 3,200 people, and "was 105 x 130 feet in size with an impressive 108 foot high clock and bell tower over the main entrance." The name of the church was derived from the method of funding its construction. Each church member was asked to "contribute a dime a month for a year to pay for it." It was this novel way of fund-raising that brought about the name of the church, "Dime Tabernacle."[165] Since at that time the membership of the entire church worldwide was less than 15,000 it can be expected that not a few people criticized the ambitious project. When the criticism became too loud, Uriah Smith, editor of the *Review and Herald*, wrote an editorial in response:

"The topic of their discourse is now the new tabernacle—'We don't believe in building great big meeting houses!' What have been their texts in times past?—They have been these: 'We don't believe in organization;' 'we don't believe in systematic benevolence;' 'we don't believe in large publishing houses with power presses;' 'we don't believe in camp-meetings;' 'we don't believe in establishing a Health Institute;' 'we don't believe in founding a college;' 'we don't believe in tract and missionary operations;' and now, 'we don't believe in building tabernacles,' and if we do, 'we don't believe in Christmas trees to raise means to pay for them;' and if ever these dear 'don't-believes' get through to the kingdom, we expect to hear them say, as the great multitudes come up from land and sea, 'We don't believe in such a great big crowd;' 'we don't believe in making such a stir to establish the kingdom of God.'"[166]

Smith eventually asked the consequent question: "Where would the cause have been now, if the views and feelings of these persons had prevailed?" However, James White did not know that the building of the Dime Tabernacle would be the last major project of his life.

James White's Last Year

As James' health continued to decline, his periods of rest were succeeded by recurring overwork and further breakdown of physical and mental health. In the early months of 1881 Ellen shared with Willie her perplexities about James: "Father has been in such a state of mind I feared he would lose his reason. But he is concluding to lay off the burdens of office matters and go to writing. I hope he will do so. . . . I am at times in such perplexity and distress of mind I covet retirement or death, but then I gather courage again" (Lt 1a, 1881). By mid-May 1881 Ellen was being so bitterly criticized in Battle Creek that even her closest friends were affected. She lamented that even Lucinda Hall "does not come near me any more than if we had been merely casual acquaintances. . . . A great gulf is between us" (Lt 4a, 1881). W. C. White later admitted that there were times when even he did not want to be too closely associated with his mother because of the way she was criticized.[167] She had been criticized before, but this time it was entirely different.

During 1881, in the months just before James White's death, the criticism of Ellen was the fiercest she ever remembered up to that time (Lt 4a, 1881; Lt 5a, 1881; Lt 8a, 1881).[168] People claimed that Ellen could not be trusted because she was "influenced" by various persons close to her. Nearly exhausted, she explained to Willie and Mary that James White was using her writings to undercut G. I. Butler and S. N. Haskell, who were serving as president and secretary of the General Conference since James' stroke-related retirement. Then a conflict was going on between her husband and J. H. Kellogg, with both using her words as verbal ammunition. The doctor would even come to her "to obtain expressions from [her] in regard to matters of the cause" in which she "could not sustain" her husband, only to turn these against James to destroy his influence (Lt 5a, 1881). In a dream that she had the year before, she saw Kellogg gathering stones—"the mistakes of Elder White"—to stone him "to death," and James gathered a similar pile to stone the doctor (Ms 2, 1880, in 12MR 10, 11). In short, leading individuals were using Ellen White's testimonies to justify themselves, while doubting the validity of her words as quoted by others. She said, "This lack of harmony is killing me. I have to keep my own counsel and have confidence in no one" in Battle Creek, she decided. Instead everyone should "labor for harmony. Let there be no divisions among us. We must present a united front to our enemies and to our people. This pulling apart is all the work of Satan. We must close the door to Satan's devices. We must cherish affection and love. We are growing hard, unsympathizing. . . . God is not pleased with this hard, critical, cast-iron measure among us as a people. It is time this matter came to an end, and another spirit more like Christ was cherished. We need Jesus in us every moment to warm our hearts and make us kind, pitiful, and courteous" (Lt 5a, 1881).

For months Ellen felt "crushed and heartbroken," but eventually she was able to commit her burden to Jesus and find peace. On the afternoon or evening of July 16, 1881, she privately read a "large number of pages" to Kellogg and her husband. Three days later she called together "all the responsible men of church and institutions," and again read the document concerning J. H. Kellogg and James White.[169] The result of those and other meetings held over a week's period was a dramatic breakthrough in the Battle Creek church (Lt 8a, 1881).[170] The entire situation had been a conflict of surmised "influence." When Ellen rebuked existing wrongs, some people surmised that she was influenced by her husband, whereas her husband assumed that others had prejudiced her against him when she reproved him for his wrongs (ibid.).[171] About this time James had some premonitions of a major change, and it was in that state of mind that he said to Ellen: "I confess my errors, and ask your forgiveness for any word or act that has caused you sorrow. There must be nothing to hinder our prayers. Everything must be right between us, and between ourselves and God" (Ms 6, 1881, in PH168 47).

On Sabbath, July 30, James "opened the services" in the Battle Creek church "with singing and prayer," and Ellen preached the sermon. Two days later, August 1, James suffered a severe chill, thought to be malarial fever. On Wednesday he was taken to the Battle Creek Sanitarium, and one day later he had another stroke. He died about 5:00 p.m. on Sabbath, August 6, 1881, two days after his sixtieth birthday (ibid. 50, 52).[172] To give Willie and Mary, who were in Oakland, California, the chance to attend the funeral, it was set for Sabbath, August 13. The week after the funeral Ellen spoke once more at the tabernacle. Then she and her daughters-in-law left for Colorado, leaving Willie and Edson to close out James White's financial affairs

(3Bio 181, 182).[173] Certain of Ellen's "friends" wanted to erect a "broken shaft as a monument" on James' grave in token of the fact that he died at a mere 60 years of age. "Never! Never!" she retorted. "He has done, singlehanded, the work of three men. Never shall a broken monument be placed over his grave!" (Ms 8, 1904, in 1SM 105).[174] Regardless of the challenges they experienced in their marriage after his strokes, James and Ellen had mutual love for one another. A year before his death, he wrote that Ellen had been his "crown of rejoicing" throughout their married life (LS80 126, 127). Five weeks after James' death she wrote, "I am fully of the opinion that my life was so entwined or interwoven with my husband's that it is about impossible for me to be of any great account without him" (Lt 17, 1881).[175] Eighteen years later she wrote: "How I miss him! How I long for his words of counsel and wisdom! How I long to hear his prayers blending with my prayers for light and guidance, for wisdom to know how to plan and lay out the work!" (Lt 196, 1899).[176] She felt that James was "the best man that ever trod shoe leather" (Ms 131, 1906, in 1Bio 84).

Contending for the Gospel in Foreign Countries
(1881-1900)

James White had accompanied Ellen for 36 years—an era had now come to an end. Together they had laid the theological foundation of the Adventist movement (1840s) and started its flourishing publishing work (1850s). Together they had emphasized the need for church organization, and eventually established it (1850s and early 1860s). Adventist lifestyle had changed through their influence (1860s), and together they had urged the necessity of educating church members to fulfill the mission of the church (1860s and 1870s). Through her books on the great controversy theme—*Spiritual Gifts*, volume 1; *The Spirit of Prophecy*, volumes 1-3—Ellen had pointed her church to the Scriptures, to the grand cosmic battle that rages in the universe, and to God's love and passion for humanity. Her husband's illnesses increasingly pushed her into public speaking. His death brought this period to an abrupt end.[177] Now she would have to walk the path of life without him.

Assistance in Literary Work and Business Affairs
During the year following James White's death in August 1881, the twin blows of grief and physical illness brought his widow so low that she expected her life to end soon. In this state of ill health she decided to attend the camp meeting held from October 5 through 17, 1882, in Healdsburg, California. According to several corroborating accounts, she experienced sudden healing, visible to all, as she stood before the congregation (ST, Nov. 2, 1882; Lt 82, 1906).[178] Shortly afterward, Ellen had a night vision in which she was told of God's provision for someone to assist her with her work in the absence of her husband.

"The Mighty Healer said, 'Live. I have put My Spirit upon your son, W. C. White, that he may be your counselor. I have given him the spirit of wisdom, and a discerning, perceptive mind. He will have wisdom in counsel, and if he walks in My way, and works out My will, he will be kept, and will be enabled to help you bring before My people the light I will give you for them. . . . I will be with your son, and will be his counselor. . . . He will have wisdom to defend the truth; for I will take charge of his mind, and will give him sound judgment in the councils that he attends in connection with the work. . . . Your son will be perplexed over many things that are to come before my people, but he is to wait and watch and pray, and let the words of God come to the people, even though he cannot always immediately discern the purpose of God' " (Lt 348, 1906, in PH116 19-24).

Already in late 1881 she had begun to express her desire to have W. C. White unite with her work on a regular basis. "Edson cannot attend the camp meetings with me, for his business requires his presence," she wrote in August 1884. "I am glad he feels inclined to stick to his business," she continued, "but . . . it would give character [dignity] to my work if one of my sons could attend me as I journey" (Lt 49, 1884). One of her urgent and continuing needs after the loss of her husband in 1881 was for someone with whom she could have spiritual and intellectual exchange, someone who understood and appreciated her viewpoints and with whom she could speak confidentially. At various times during this decade her expressed need for "counsel" was linked with her condition of being "alone." To Edson she wrote: "As far as anyone to consult with is concerned, I am alone" (Lt 14a, 1889, in 1888 Materials 293). To Willie and Mary she explained why at one point things did not move more efficiently. "I have, as you well know, not one soul to counsel with. I am obliged to go forward as best I can and lay my plans and do my business as well as I am able" (Lt 79, 1888). Because Edson was unavailable, she came to depend on Willie for help and advice on the whole spectrum of her personal and business affairs. She also depended on him as her liaison with the publishing houses. Negotiating royalties was just one of a variety of questions that he cared for with the publishing houses. Everything from illustrations to page size and binding, and much more, was his responsibility to arrange in consultation with her and with the publishers.[179]

By 1881 she also had begun to develop a staff of full-time "literary assistants" to help with typing and editing her manuscripts. Willie acted as the general supervisor; Mary K. White and Marian Davis worked under him as trusted and experienced editorial assistants, editing minor details. Through the years, other assistants included J. H. Waggoner, Sara McEnterfer, and Jenny Ings. Colleagues who were not connected with Ellen White's personal staff, but who were occasionally asked to help, included Uriah Smith, editor of the *Review and Herald*; C. H. Jones, manager of the Pacific Press; E. J. Waggoner and A. T. Jones, coeditors of the *Signs of the Times*; and J. H. Kellogg, medical superintendent of the Battle Creek Sanitarium (Lt 64a, 1889).

Problems at Battle Creek College

The school year 1881-1882 marked the lowest point of Battle Creek College. Sidney Brownsberger had left the school, and the college board had chosen Alexander McLearn, a potential convert to Adventism, as president. McLearn held a Doctor of Divinity degree, but was new to Adventist ideals and not particularly interested in educational reform. Since the leadership and the educators of the church did not fully understand the problems of traditional education or how to put into practice the educational reform, "Battle Creek College developed into a classics-oriented traditional school that failed to implement Ellen White's reform program."[180] The circumstances at the school called for Ellen White's forceful message "Our College." It was read to the leading workers of the General Conference and the college in December 1881. There she declared that, though the study of the arts and sciences was necessary, "the study of the Scripture should have the first place in our system of education"(5T 21). Yet the situation at the college became even worse in early 1882, so that the board of the school decided to close the college for the school year of 1882-1883. Before reopening the school, the trustees voted to run the school "upon a plan which shall harmonize in all respects with the light which God has given us . . . through the *Testimonies*."[181] Although greater efforts would be made to operate the reestablished college on the principles set forth by Ellen White, it failed to a significant extent. The workers involved were certainly honest in their efforts, but they did not fully understand "the radical nature of the needed reforms."[182] In addition, quite a number of leading officers were not pleased by her confrontational messages, and there were also "many among" the church members who did "not believe the visions."[183] These problems would frequently surface in subsequent years.

Reasserting Salvation Through Faith in Christ

At the General Conference session held from November 7 to 20, 1883, Ellen White opened a passionate attack on Adventist legalism and the doubts, fears, and unbelief that are its natural consequence. In 14 sermons she gave some of the clearest presentations on the gospel that had been heard in Adventism to that time.[184] Confronting some ministers, delegates at the conference, who were "talking fears and doubts" as to whether they would be saved, she challenged, "Brethren, you have expressed many doubts; but have you followed your Guide? You must dispense with Him before you can lose your way; for the Lord has hedged you in on every side" (RH, Apr. 15, 1884). When some testified that they did not have assurance of salvation, she reminded them that "such testimonies express only unbelief and darkness." Then she probed: "Are you expecting that your merit will recommend you to the favor of God, and that you must be free from sin before you trust his power to save? If this is the struggle going on in your mind, I fear you will gain no strength, and will finally become discouraged. As the brazen serpent was lifted up in the wilderness, so was Christ lifted up to draw all men unto him. All who looked upon that serpent, the means that God had provided, were healed; so in our sinfulness, in our great need, we must 'look and live.' While we realize our helpless condition without Christ, we must not be discouraged; we must rely upon the merits of a crucified and risen Savior. Poor sin-sick, discouraged soul, look and live. Jesus has pledged His word; He will save all who come unto Him. Then let us come confessing our sins, bringing forth fruits meet for repentance. Jesus is our Savior today. He is pleading for us in the most holy place of the heavenly sanctuary, and He will forgive our sins. It makes all the difference in the world with us spiritually whether we rely upon God without doubt, as upon a sure foundation, or whether we are seeking to find some righteousness in ourselves before we come to Him. Look away from self to the Lamb of God, that taketh away the sin of the world. It is a sin to doubt. The least unbelief, if cherished in the heart, involves the soul in guilt, and brings great darkness and discouragement" (RH, Apr. 22, 1884).

During the same year, she made an even more compelling statement through a picture on the way of salvation. She commissioned the reengraving of a lithograph that was originally designed by M. E. Kellogg in 1873 and revised by James White in 1876 and 1880. Kellogg's

The Way of Life From Paradise Lost to Paradise Restored showed side by side in the center of the picture the law of God hung upon a tree and Jesus hanging upon the cross. James White in 1876 left the picture essentially the same except that he had the all-seeing eye removed from within the tree upon which the law of God was hung. About 1880 James began plans to revise the lithograph with a further change in emphasis, but his involvement in the project terminated with his death on August 6, 1881. Two years later Ellen had the picture reengraved, placing Christ central to the picture and removing the equal position of the law of God. The picture also received a new title; she called it *Christ, the Way of Life.*[185] (See article *Christ, the Way of Life* Prints.)

The Revision of the Testimonies

Between 1855 and 1881 Ellen White wrote and published 31 consecutive numbers of *Testimonies for the Church,* which were reissued several times in varying formats. At the General Conference session in November 1883 the delegates recommended to republish all numbers of the *Testimonies* "in such a form as to make four volumes of seven or eight hundred pages each." Ellen White felt that many of the *Testimonies* had been written "under the most unfavorable circumstances" so that she was not able to "devote critical thought to the grammatical perfection of the writings." Thus these "imperfections" were allowed "to pass uncorrected." Therefore, she expressed her desire that appropriate editorial revisions be made now. The delegates noted that Adventists "believe the light given by God to His servants is by the enlightenment of the mind, thus imparting the thoughts, and not (except in rare cases) the very words in which the ideas should be expressed." Therefore they resolved "that in the republication of these volumes such verbal changes be made as to remove the above-named imperfections, as far as possible, without in any measure changing the thought."[186] When discussions arose during the following months as to the possibility of revising Ellen White's writings, she explained that God had shown her years ago that she "should not delay publishing the important light" given to her just because she was "not [able to] prepare the matter perfectly," but that she should present the matter in the best possible way. Later, with more time and better developed abilities, she should "improve everything, as far as possible bringing it to perfection, that it might be accepted by intelligent minds." She expressed her displeasure regarding the delay of the revision work to Uriah Smith who had been reticent in the matter (Lt 11, 1884, in 3SM 96-98). By 1885 the editorial work was accomplished, and the *Testimonies* were published as proposed in four volumes.

Camp Meetings in the East

During the summer of 1884 Ellen White received "many urgent calls" to visit camp meetings in the eastern United States. The organizers arranged the meetings and Ellen's speaking responsibilities so that she "could go from one [meeting] to the other without loss of time." She was, however, not very pleased with this arrangement and wrote to G. I. Butler and S. N. Haskell: "One meeting laps over on to the other, and I do not admire your judgment in this arrangement. Better have a set of camp meetings one year full and thorough, in selected places, and then next year take up the places left, and have those well manned, full and thorough. . . . But should I attend your meetings, I remember I am 56 years old, instead of

25 or 35, and no provision is made for me to rest, but to rush from one [camp meeting] to the other as fast as the cars will take me. I do not think your plans very flattering to me. I am not immortal yet, and have cause to remember this every day of my life. If you wish to finish me up this year, I think you have planned excellently for it. I think my best course is to remain in California and not trust myself to your mercies" (Lt 21, 1884, in 9MR 136).

Thus, although Ellen White was a welcome speaker at camp meetings and other church conventions, she was also an inconvenient one because she spoke up when convinced that it was necessary to do so. Denominational leaders were glad when much-needed counsel came, but they were not so pleased when they received correction for a certain path they wanted to take.

Missionary Work in Europe

On May 31, 1884, the European Missionary Council extended "a hearty and urgent invitation" to Ellen White to visit the various European fields, and to her son W. C. White to "render . . . assistance in the publishing work" in Europe.[187] The invitation was renewed by a memorandum that the council directed to the delegates of the General Conference session in 1884.[188] The presence of Ellen White in Europe was needed, not only for the counsel she might give but also that new believers might be able to become personally acquainted with her, something that could not be accomplished merely through her writings. While she was very much interested in the work in Europe, Adventists' greatest mission field at that time, she was not enthusiastic about the long journey to Europe.[189] By that time she had crossed the United States between east and west by train about 24 times, but the journey to the "old country" would be even more difficult (Ms 16, 1885).[190] Eventually, in the summer of 1885, she decided to at least "prepare for the trip," trusting in the "judgment of the brethren." During the journey from California to the East a change in her attitude became visible, a move "from depression and doubt about the wisdom of the journey to a state of perfect contentment and absolute certainty" (ibid.).[191]

Ellen White and her party boarded ship in Boston on Friday, August 7, and disembarked in Liverpool, England, on Tuesday evening, August 18 (HS 159-173). Initially she thought that her stay in Europe would last only for a few months, but she ended up staying for almost two years. While she made her home at the Adventist headquarters in Basel, Switzerland, she also traveled extensively in northwestern Italy (48 days) and in Scandinavia—three times in Norway (47 days), Sweden (30 days), and Denmark (26 days) respectively.[192] During her visits to Italy she was primarily in the Waldensian valleys.[193] Since the Adventist work in France and Germany was just beginning, it is understandable that she spent merely 18 days in France and five days in Germany.[194] Further, she arrived in and left from England, and remained there for almost a month in 1886 (53 days in total) (EGWEur 13-15).

As Ellen White visited historical sites of the Protestant Reformation, she recalled many things that she had already seen in vision, and determined to add as much material as possible to her next update of *The Spirit of Prophecy*, volume 4, to make it more persuasive to people from those countries. The fourth volume had already been published in September 1884, and completed *The Spirit of Prophecy* series, which was the first major expansion of *Spiritual Gifts*, volume 1. It was the first illustrated Ellen White book that was sold by literature evangelists. The colporteur edition of 1884-1888 first bore the title *The Great Controversy.* It went through 10 editions and 50,000 copies between 1884 and 1888 (see Lt 57, 1911).[195]

Another important book project accomplished while Ellen White was in Europe was an adapted one-volume edition of *The Spirit of Prophecy*, volumes 2 and 3, published under the new title *The Life of Christ*, in Danish-Norwegian, Swedish, German, French, and Finnish between 1885 and the late 1890s. In this book she articulated, more precisely than she had before, the relationship between justification and sanctification, the work of Christ *for* us and the work of Christ *in* us. Her ministry in Europe strongly emphasized both the law and the gospel, both the objective basis of salvation and the subjective change in the lives of those who believe. With that she also combined a major emphasis on the unity and love that are the fruit of faith when people of different nationalities, languages, and cultures put ethnic pride and personal self-will aside and consent for their lives to be possessed by the only perfect human, Jesus Christ. Some examples show her emphasis on salvation through Jesus.

On November 3, 1885, she was invited to speak in the town of Drammen, Norway. The best place that could be found was a hall used for balls and concerts. Since there was no pulpit, six beer tables were brought together from an adjoining room to form a platform. Ellen commented later: "We doubt if the hall or beer tables were ever put to so good use before. The people came and filled the seats, the galleries, and all the standing room, and listened with the best of attention while I spoke to them of the love of Christ, and his life of sacrifice" (HS 207).

During her last year in Europe she visited two churches in Germany—at Vohwinkel and Gladbach (May 27-31, 1887). Friday night she dreamed she was watching a congregation as a stranger entered the room, unnoticed. There was an atmosphere of disagreement and strife among the church members; there was a lack of true Christian love. Before the end of the meeting the stranger arose and directly addressed that lack. When he was done with his admonitions, everyone recognized that it was Jesus Christ. Each one confessed his sins to God and his neighbor. Ellen White described the result as follows: "There was weeping, for the hearts seemed to be broken, and then there was rejoicing and the room was filled with the mellow light of heaven. The musical voice of Jesus said, 'Peace be with you.' And His peace was" (Ms 32, 1887, in 2MR 127; EGWEur 276-278; 3Bio 364, 365). The next morning she talked to the congregation at Vohwinkel about the need for unity, harmony, love, mutual acceptance, and forgiveness. To Ludwig Richard Conradi, the minister who also interpreted for her, she suggested that he introduce a social meeting into the church since this would give them the possibility to share their experiences (EGWEur 279). She reported: "I felt much freedom, although weak for want of food which I could not take upon my stomach. Brother Conradi labored with them faithfully, and I think with good success. There was a healing of their difficulties, except with one brother who left the meeting. Brother Conradi went after him and labored with him until 2:00 a.m., with a good prospect of the difficulties being healed" (Ms 32, 1887, in 2MR 123).[196]

Ellen White had already packed all her things together at Basel before she left for Germany. Then she took a last tour through Denmark, Norway, and Sweden, before finally going to England. After a few days she left from Liverpool, crossing the ocean in a week to New York, where she arrived on August 11, 1885 (EGWEur 15).

The Saddest Experience of Her Life—The 1888 General Conference Session

Of all of the events that Ellen White attended during her lifetime, probably none impacted her—and her church—more powerfully than the General Conference session in Minneapolis, Minnesota, in the fall of 1888, which she called "the hardest and most incomprehensible tug-of-war we ever had among our people." Before the conference, she dreaded the confrontation, because she foresaw that in the controversy some would lose their faith. But she insisted that because unrecognized legalism was so widespread among Adventists, it must be met and exposed or the whole church would be poisoned by it. Heartsick and utterly dispirited, Ellen White purposed to leave Minneapolis in the midst of the session when "the angel of the Lord stood by my side and said, 'Not so; God has a work for you to do in this place.'" And though she later called it "one of the saddest chapters" in Adventist history, she believed that in the end it would "result in great good." She emphasized, "We are not the least discouraged. . . . The truth will triumph, and we mean to triumph with it" (Lt 82, 1888, in 1888 Materials 182, 184; Lt 2a, 1892, in 14MR 108; Lt 179, 1902, in 1MR 142). What had happened that caused so much regret?

While she was in Europe the gospel-oriented writing of E. J. Waggoner in the United States brought him and his colleague A. T. Jones into direct conflict with the entrenched theological leaders of the denomination, G. I. Butler and Uriah Smith.[197] Butler, Smith, and others taught that forgiveness for past sins is a free gift of grace through faith, but that present and future salvation depends on the believer's obedience, thus turning the believers' eyes from Christ to their own performance.[198]

The final confrontation took place at the General Conference session in 1888. While, on the surface, the discussion focused on the identity of the law in Paul's Epistle to the Galatians, the answer to that question was connected to varying views on justification. Butler regretted to find in Waggoner's book "the much-vaunted doctrine of justification by faith," to which Waggoner could only reply that "it is *impossible to overestimate the doctrine of justification by faith.*"[199] Butler insisted that the law in Galatians 3 was the ceremonial law, whereas Waggoner saw it as the moral law of the Ten Commandments. Ellen White pointed out later that both laws point humans to Christ, who alone can justify them (Gal. 3:24) (Lt 96, 1896, in 1SM 234, 235; Ms 87, 1900, in 1SM 233, 234). Yet a greater problem than the difference of opinion over the law was that the spirit exhibited during the meeting "was not the spirit of Jesus" (Lt 50, 1889, in 1888 Materials 294; cf. Ms 55, 1890, in 1888 Materials 839-845). Criticism of Waggoner and Jones broadened into resistance of the message of "Christ our righteousness." This was the tragedy that caused Ellen White such anguish at Minneapolis. She observed that the message from Jesus had "not been received, but despised," "resisted," and by many, "rejected" (Ms 30, 1890, in 1888 Materials 912-916; cf. 1888 Materials 955, 1019, 1025, 1030).

During the following two years Ellen White conducted revival meetings with E. J. Waggoner and A. T. Jones across North America, pointing out the sad results of the defective theology, and seeking to unify the church on the doctrine of righteousness by faith. "As a people we have preached the law until we are as dry as the hills of Gilboa that had neither dew nor rain," she pleaded. "We must preach *Christ in the law*, and there will be sap and nourishment in the preaching that will be as food to the famishing flock of God" (RH, Mar. 11, 1890; italics supplied).

"The thought that the righteousness of Christ is imputed to us, not because of any merit on our part, but as a free gift from God, [is] a precious thought. The enemy of man and God is not willing that this truth should be clearly presented; for he knows that if the people receive it fully, his power will be broken. If he can control minds so that doubt and unbelief and darkness shall compose the experience of those who claim to be the children of God, he can overcome them with temptation. That simple faith that takes God at His word should be encouraged" (RH, Sept. 3, 1889; cf. GW 161).

"The law and the gospel," she declared, go "hand in hand." She recognized that Seventh-day Adventists had promulgated "the commandments of God," but she contended that "the faith of Jesus has not been proclaimed . . . as of equal importance." While the faith of Jesus was "talked of," it was "not understood." Then she asked the question "What constitutes the faith of Jesus?" The answer to that question was, in her understanding: "Jesus becoming our sin-bearer that He might become our sin-pardoning Savior. He was treated as we deserve to be treated. He came to our world and took our sins that we might take His righteousness. Faith in the ability of Christ to save us amply and fully and entirely is the faith of Jesus" (Ms 24, 1888, in 1888 Materials 217).

In the summer of 1891 the church held an educational convention in Harbor Springs, Michigan. Ellen White talked on the necessity of a personal relationship with Jesus, the need for spiritual revival among the educators of the church, and "the centrality of the Christian message to education." The convention focused also on the place of the Bible in education.[200]

Drawing Her Sister Lizzie

Ellen White's twin sister Elizabeth—or Lizzie, as she was called—did not profess Christianity during her adult life. In 1843 Lizzie had made a commitment to Jesus and was anticipating baptism, but her young experience was interrupted by the Harmon family's expulsion from the Methodist Church for their Millerite beliefs. In 1844 she had joined her sisters in raising money to spread the Millerite message, and at least once in later years she attended a camp meeting with Ellen. But after the disappointment of 1844, and Lizzie's marriage to Reuben Bangs, her own home was "prayerless," and she did not have much interest in religion. Yet throughout the years Ellen tried to keep in touch with her sister; they wrote each other once in a while, and whenever possible, Ellen visited her. But Lizzie took "no open stand," and that is why Ellen felt the need to appeal to her sister and lead her to a decision (Lts 50, 50b, 1874).[201] When Lizzie's daughter died, Ellen described how at the second coming of Jesus "little infants" come forth from the graves and fly into their mother's arms, "nevermore to part." Then she continued, "But many of the little ones have no mother there. We listen in vain for the rapturous song of triumph from the mother. The angels receive the motherless infants and conduct them to the tree of life. . . . God grant that the dear mother of 'Eva' may be there, that her little wings may be folded upon the glad bosom of her mother" (YI, April 1858).

In 1891 Ellen sent her twin another powerful expression of God's love for Lizzie: "I love to speak of Jesus and His matchless love. I have not one doubt of the love of God and His care and His mercy and ability to save to the uttermost all who come unto Him. . . . Don't you believe on Jesus, Lizzie? Do you not believe He is your Savior? That He has evidenced

His love for you in giving His own precious life that you might be saved? All that is required of you is to take Jesus as your own precious Savior. I pray most earnestly that the Lord Jesus shall reveal Himself to you and to Reuben. . . . Dear sister, it is no wonderful thing that you have to do. You feel poor, suffering, and afflicted, and Jesus invites all of this class to come to Him. . . . Friends may feel sorrowful, but they cannot save you. Your physician cannot save you. But there is One who died that you might live through eternal ages. Just believe that Jesus will hear your confession, receive your penitence, and forgive every sin and make you children of God. . . . Will you give yourself in trusting faith to Jesus? I long to take you in my arms and lay you on the bosom of Jesus Christ. . . . With Jesus as your blessed Friend you need not fear to die, for it will be to you like closing your eyes here and opening them in heaven. Then we shall meet nevermore to part" (Lt 61, 1891).[202] Just 10 months after Ellen wrote this letter, Lizzie died, on December 21, 1891, in Gorham, Maine, the place of her birth, and it is not known if she ever gave her heart to Jesus.[203] That same year Ellen White was invited to visit Australia.

Beginning Service in Australia

As when she was called to Europe, six years earlier, again she wondered if it was really necessary for her, at 64 years of age, to do pioneer work in a foreign country. She prayed about it, but received no light as to God's will. But then she went. "I followed the voice of the [General] Conference, as I have ever tried to do at times when I had no clear light myself" (Ms 19, 1892, in 2SM 239).[204] She had just turned 64, and her son W. C. White was 37 years of age.

Adventists had begun formal work in Australia in the 1880s. By 1891 there were only a few churches and 729 members in Australia and New Zealand. The only denominational institution was a small publishing house in Melbourne (LS333; BE, Jan. 1, 1892).[205] Australia was, moreover, suffering under a severe economic depression that became a panic in 1893. Many of the church members were unemployed and in poverty.[206] As the decade wore on, the economic situation in the United States worsened, giving American Seventh-day Adventists their own financial problems. By 1895 the General Conference president, O. A. Olsen, lamented that declining tithes and offerings had left the General Conference treasury "virtually empty," which is why the church consequently found little money to send abroad.[207]

Ellen White and her son W. C. White disembarked in Sydney, Australia, December 8, 1891.[208] Their first major meeting was the fourth annual session of the Australian Conference, which convened in Melbourne from December 27, 1891, through January 1, 1892. Significant actions included the election of Arthur G. Daniells as conference president and resolutions to establish a Seventh-day Adventist college for Australasia. While the plans for a "permanent" school were being matured, work on a temporary school began immediately. Thus on August 24, 1892, the Australasian Bible School opened in rented quarters in Melbourne. W. C. White was elected to the conference executive committee and was made chair of a committee of seven on organization and plans for the Australasian Bible School.[209] He and his mother lived in Melbourne from December 1891 through August 1894. For 11 months of their stay in Melbourne she was seriously ill with malarial fever and inflammatory rheumatism (Ms 75, 1893).[210] During this time she experienced "the most terrible suffering" of her "whole life," but said that the suffering had nevertheless "a cheerful side."

"My Savior seemed to be close beside me. I felt His sacred presence in my heart, and I was thankful. These months of suffering were the happiest months of my life, because of the companionship of my Savior. . . . I am so thankful that I had this experience, because I am better acquainted with my precious Lord and Savior. His love filled my heart. All through my sickness His love, His tender compassion, was my comfort, my continual consolation" (*ibid.*).[211]

It was during those months of severe suffering that her book *Steps to Christ* was published by Fleming H. Revell in Chicago, Illinois.[212] The first edition of the book opened with the chapter "The Sinner's Need of Christ." To a later edition, she added the chapter "God's Love for Man."[213] *Steps to Christ,* on practical Christian living, came to be her most translated and most widely published book. One contemporary non-Adventist reviewer commented on the book as follows: "The treatment in every case has a freshness, a blood-streak of experience, and a sanctified purpose about it, which are appetizing. Her words and constructions are simple, straightforward, fluent. The tone is that of a bright, sweet, mature, Christian woman. Generally her theology seems correct. She is saturated with the Bible and uses her knowledge with tact. A good book for the inquirer, and for a child of God anywhere in the course of his ups and downs."[214]

The Conversion of James Edson White

Despite the spiritual impact Ellen White had on other people, she apparently had little influence on her son Edson. Throughout his 44 years he had not shown signs of a thorough conversion in his life and business dealings, but his mother had not given up on him. In May 1893 he wrote his mother that he had "no religious inclinations now in the least," and was considering leaving the church altogether. Ellen White was shocked to read that her son was turning his back on everything she had tried to teach him during the years.[215] In reply she wrote him that a "scene [was] presented before me. You and four other young men were upon the beach. You all seemed too careless—unconcerned, yet in great danger. . . . The waves were rolling up nearer and still nearer and then would roll back with a sullen roar. Gestures and warnings were given by the anxious ones looking on, but in answer to all their warnings you were presumptuous. Someone placed his hand on my shoulder. 'Did you know that is your son Edson? He cannot hear your voice, but he can see your motions. Tell him to come at once. He will not disobey his mother.' I reached out my hands. I did all I could do to warn. I cried with all my power of voice, You have not a moment to lose! The undertow! The undertow! I knew that once you were in the power of the treacherous undertow no human power could avail. A strong rope was brought and fastened securely around the body of a strong young man who ventured to risk his own life to save you. You seemed to be making light of the whole performance. I saw the merciless undertow embrace you and you were battling with the waves. I awoke as I heard a fearful shriek from you. I prayed most earnestly in your behalf and arose and am writing these lines."

She told him that sometimes she lay awake entire nights, thinking about mistakes she may have made in his education. She was worried that she had "brought a son into the world" who would help "to swell the rebel's ranks, to stand in defiance against God" (Lt 123, 1893).[216] When her letter from Australia reached Edson a month later, his attitude began to change. On August 10 he reported to his mother that he had begun to put away the "amusements and pleasures" that had previously made up the sum of his "enjoyments."[217] A few weeks later he discovered in Battle Creek a copy of her call to the church for evangelism and education among the Blacks in the South.[218] Now he was thinking about going to the South to work among the former slaves.[219] On August 11 he wrote his brother Willie, saying: "I have made a start in the way of life everlasting, and have found my Savior."[220] What had happened? What had brought about the change in his attitude? A few weeks later Edson described his experience: "One Sabbath I decided, while listening to a very dull sermon, that I might just as well be enjoying [the] blessing of my Savior RIGHT THEN as to wait for some more favorable opportunity. . . . I took this step AT ONCE, and 'He took me.' . . . Since then HE HAS NEVER LEFT ME."[221] When Ellen White read his letter, she was overjoyed and wrote: "This day we received your letter and were very glad that you had indeed made the surrender to God. I am glad more than I can express that you have, in the simplicity of faith, accepted Jesus and I am not surprised that you found something to do at once" (Lt 120, 1893).[222] While Edson continued to have his troubles, he remained committed to God. His greatest contribution was the evangelistic work among the Blacks in the South, which proved to be a "blessing to the people he worked for, to the church, and to his mother, who thrilled at his mission of faith in a neglected field." Edson was, through his changed life, a testimony to the "anguish, love, and perseverance" of his mother.[223]

The Visions of Anna C. Phillips

In 1892 a young woman named Anna Phillips who lived in Battle Creek came to believe that her impressions and dreams were prophetic revelations of the Holy Spirit.[224] When A. T. Jones read an unpublished testimony on the last Sabbath of 1893, which marked the close of the Week of Prayer, the congregation responded in a remarkable way by donating gold watches, chains, rings, bracelets, pins, etc. Yet, regardless of the results of the reading of that testimony, it had come, not from the pen of Ellen White, but from Anna Phillips. Phillips felt encouraged by this endorsement of her testimony as a divinely inspired communication. Her messages had received support from A. T. Jones and W. W. Prescott.[225] Other leading workers advised caution, an attitude that Phillips perceived as Satan's opposition to her message. Ellen White, however, neither sanctioned this new prophet, nor had "the least confidence in her claims, or the claims any one has made in her behalf." She became even clearer: "The Lord has not laid upon her [Phillips] the work of accusing, of judging, of reproving, of condemning and flattering others" (Lt 54, 1893, in 14MR 181, 182).

Phillips was initially confused about Ellen White's rejection of her work, but reasoned that White probably meant to criticize not Phillips' "gift" and "testimonies," but the public way certain people had used and interpreted them.[226] But when letters came from Ellen White in Australia to A. T. Jones and others, directly rebuking them for taking the position they did, they immediately recognized and acknowledged their mistake.[227] Anna Phillips and the church in general accepted Ellen White's reproof, and Phillips' supposed visions stopped immediately.[228] She later became a trusted Bible instructor, serving the denomination for many years.[229]

W. C. White Called to Assist His Mother

After James White's death, Ellen White repeatedly asked her son W. C. White, then 27, to connect with her as a full-time assistant, but he preferred administrative work and dreaded the criticism that seemed especially targeted at those closely connected with his mother.[230] She had also urged her other son, Edson, to join her staff (Lts 64, 79, 84, 1894; Lt 149, 1897).[231] "The light has always been given me," she wrote in 1894, that "Willie, his mother, and Edson should be connected in the work as a three-fold cord, one helping the other" (Lt 141, 1894).[232]

Ellen White sent Willie a key communication in July 1895. He was to be "free to help his mother get out her books and to accompany her in her journeying from place to place." She added: "You must not allow your brethren to make duties for you" that "so occupy your time and energies" that none are left for preaching. Because "your brethren have taken it for granted that another business line of work was your talent" and "have not encouraged you" to preach, she told him, "the Lord has seen fit to send a message to you and to them to lay fewer details of work on you that you may take your position in the work of ministering." "Reduce your board meetings," she urged him, "and increase your talents of speaking the Word of the Lord." "There are stormy times before you," she cautioned, "and you should become familiar with the work of feeding the flock of God." She clearly emphasized that his line of work was somewhere else.

"This work [communication in the foreign missionary work] has improved your talent as a speaker to the point [of being a concise communicator]. You have had nearly a worldwide theatre of operation, and you will be led and taught of God as you take up your long-neglected work in ministerial lines. You have been willing to toil in various lines irrespective of honors or gains, and now the Lord would have you stand more to the front in the place He has appointed you as a minister of the gospel, prepared to take the burden largely from me while my faculties are good, [so] that I can oversee and understand the things that are prepared for the press" (Lt 131, 1895).[233]

This letter, just 18 months after he had accepted the presidency of the Australasian Union Conference, clearly articulated her understanding of the divine will for her son. It basically called him to delegate the administrative and financial details to others and reduce his committee time so that he could develop his abilities as a preacher and also aid his mother in her book work. It called him to consider her work rather than conference work as his primary vocation. While he did not reject that call, it still took him several years to make the transition.

Wedding Bells and More Grandchildren

W. C. White's first wife, Mary Kelsey, had died of tuberculosis in 1890. They had married in 1876, and had two daughters—Ella May (born 1882) and Mabel Eunice (born 1886). When Willie's daughters grew up, they lived most of the time near his mother. She enjoyed and loved her granddaughters, but she also longed for grandsons. When in December 1894 his mother had an opening for a household employee, Willie urged her to hire May Lacey, a student whom he had met at her father's home in Tasmania. Ellen White "soon learned why Willie was anxious for May Lacey." May reminded him of his first wife, Mary; he was very much attracted to her, and he wanted the opportunity for his mother to become better acquainted with her (Lt 117, 1895, in 3MR 298, 299). As time went on, he proposed marriage and enthusiastically informed his brother of her acceptance. "I shall send you a photo as soon as I can get some," he promised Edson. "Do not look for a little sallow pinched-up body, nor for a 'stuck-up lady.' She is a good big wholesome woman, as full of life and goodness as can be. May is as tall as I am, and weighs a few pounds more. I tip the scale at 148; and she, at 153. Her vitals have not been crushed by corsets, nor her spirits by idle ambitions. Wherever she is, there is sunshine and comfort, and peace."[234]

The wedding took place at her father's home in Tasmania on May 9, 1895. Ellen White sent Edson and Emma a succinct summary of the occasion: "Last Thursday Willie and May Lacey were united in marriage. Everything passed off pleasantly. The children seemed very earnest that Mother should pray on the occasion, and I complied with their request. The blessing of the Lord was present. Every movement was conducted with the greatest solemnity. . . . All, every member of the family, dote on May, and they feel highly honored to take in Willie to their family circle. They all highly esteem Willie. He is 40 years old and May is 21. There was no sentimentalism in their courtship and marriage. Immediately after their engagement, Willie was called to Auckland, New Zealand, camp meeting, and he spent three months visiting the churches. . . . Willie planned for two weeks' vacation, but did not have any at all. They were married in the afternoon, and Willie had to attend a committee meeting in the evening" (Lt 120, 1895, in 4Bio 195).[235]

A dinner reception at 5:00 p.m. followed the wedding, and when Willie's committee meeting let out, he and May and Ellen White boarded the 8:30 train for Launceston. They spent two weeks in Melbourne with union conference committee meetings and other business. Finally on May 29 they left for their home in Granville near Sydney, where Willie was reunited with his daughters Ella and Mabel, who had arrived from America on May 5. The next year the family of four became six with the birth of Herbert and Henry on April 6, 1896. A fifth child, Evelyn Grace, was born June 1, 1900 (Lt 120, 1895).[236]

Avondale School for Christian Workers

The founding of the Avondale School—the forerunner of Avondale College—was a remarkable enterprise.[237] Both Ellen and W. C. White were involved in the selection and purchase of the land, the planning and erection of buildings, and the formative stages of developing a curriculum and faculty. When Ellen White was invited, on August 30, 1894, to meet with the school location committee, she warned them against comparing the soil of the Cooranbong land to that of Iowa. She commented in her diary that she had no question about the land, but that A. G. Daniells and L. J. Rousseau, the two who had farmed the black soil of Iowa, were "very firm and decided" in their opposition (Ms 77, 1894, in 8MR 361). Both of them felt further that in view of the financial situation of the colonies and the conferences, that it might be better to purchase "40 or 50 acres, one half to be reserved for campus and for cultivation for the school," and the rest to be sold "as village lots" to Adventists who would locate near the school, rather than buying 1,500 acres, which was favored by Ellen White (Ms 77, 1894).[238] She instead strongly opposed this "mistake," which would constitute an almost identical compromise to the one made in Battle Creek 20 years earlier.[239] At the August 30 meeting, she urged the committee to purchase the Cooranbong land without delay, promising that "if they decided that it was not the place they should have," she would purchase it herself (Lt 3, 1898; cf. Lt 54a, 1894). Frustrated with her inability to convince them to move ahead, she sought to move herself out of the conflict, urging the committee members involved to "seek the Lord" for themselves. When the brethren sought the Lord, they were individually convicted that the land she had designated was indeed the best choice of all the locations they had looked at. They still saw the land as having some deficiencies, but concluded that considering their financial limitations and other circumstances it was the best choice they had. That was all that she had claimed from the beginning (Lt 153, 1894, in 20MR 238; Lt 126, 1895).[240]

Thus, by the end of 1894, the land had been purchased. In early March 1895 W. C. White inaugurated a "manual training department" as the first department of the new school. Twenty-six students accepted the offer to receive "board, lodging, and tuition in two branches" of academic instruction, in exchange for their spending six hours per day in manual labor, clearing land, draining swamps, and "building roads and bridges."[241] Despite opposition, the program was successful. Ellen White felt vindicated by students who said they could "learn as much in the six hours of study as in giving their whole time to their books. More than this, the manual labor department is a success healthwise for the students," she exulted (Lt 126, 1895, in 8MR 150).

Ellen White moved to the Coorangbong property in December 1895, living in a tent while her house was being built. In the surrounding neighborhood lived some 250 descendants of three convict families; they were not only notorious thieves but also disinclined toward hard work. Ellen White and Sara McEnterfer, one of her literary assistants, tried to care for them in any possible way.[242]

On October 5, 1896, the "corner brick" of the first building of the Avondale School was laid. The Avondale School was to serve as a "pattern" school, as a second beginning, for Seventh-day Adventist education worldwide. To her son W. C. White she emphasized pointedly that "no breezes from Battle Creek are to be wafted in. I see I must watch before and behind and on every side to permit nothing to find entrance that has been presented before me as injuring our schools in America" (Lt 138, 1897, in 20MR 215).[243] During the initial years at Avondale she received visions on how to develop that school, and much of this instruction found its way into several books on education that she published by the end of her life; *Special Testimonies on Education* (1897) was the first of these. W. C. White remarked in 1899: "During the last two years I think Mother has written more upon the principles of education, the importance of Bible study, and the importance of combining labor with study, and the value of agriculture . . . than in all the years before. I think she has written more largely upon it than any other branch of our work."[244]

Books on the Life of Christ

When the foreign-language editions of the *Life of Christ* had been published in the 1880s, Ellen White had expressed her desire to enlarge the manuscript before publishing a new edition in English. Throughout her time in Australia she did much writing on that project. Her personal diary and her correspondence reflect her strong emotions and the depth of her feelings toward Jesus:[245]

"Oh, how inefficient, how incapable I am of expressing the things which burn in my soul in reference to the mission of Christ! . . . I know not how to speak or trace with pen the large subject of the atoning sacrifice. I know not how to present subjects in the living power in which they stand before me. I tremble for fear lest I shall belittle the great plan of salvation by cheap words" (Lt 40, 1892, in 4Bio 382).

"My whole being longs after the Lord, I am not content to be satisfied with occasional flashes of light. I must have more" (Ms 34, 1892, in 19MR 292).

"In writing upon the life of Christ I am deeply wrought upon. I forget to breathe as I should. I cannot endure the intensity of feeling that comes over me as I think of what Christ has suffered in our world" (Ms 70, 1897, in 3SM 118, 119).

"I awoke at three o'clock a.m. I feel deeply the need of casting my helpless soul upon Jesus Christ. He is my helper. He is my all and in all. I am weak as water without the Holy Spirit of God to help me" (Ms 177, 1897).

"I find tears running down my cheeks when I think of what the Lord is to His children, and when I contemplate His goodness, His mercy, [and] His tender compassion."[246]

The manuscript was eventually divided into three parts and published as *Thoughts From the Mount of Blessing* in 1896, *The Desire of Ages* in 1898, and *Christ's Object Lessons* in 1900. The first book (218 pages) is an exposition of Christ's sermon on the mount, while *Christ's Object Lessons* (436 pages) covers the parables. Ellen White donated the proceeds of the latter book to retiring the debts of Adventist educational institutions.[247] *The Desire of Ages* (866 pages) constitutes her final masterpiece on the life of Christ. She had begun to develop this theme already in *Spiritual Gifts*, volume 1 (pp. 28-87), in 1858, while she unfolded the topic more in volumes 2 and 3 of *The Spirit of Prophecy* in 1877 and 1878. Already in 1892 she had published *Steps to Christ*, which explained how one can come to Christ and remain in fellowship with Him. It is apparent that Ellen White saw the particular need in the 1890s to put more emphasis on the life and character of Christ, as well as on the gospel themes. Yet the subject of the life of Christ and salvation of humanity also forms the center of her writings on the great controversy theme. Her 1888 edition of *The Great Controversy* ended with the same words that began the book *Patriarchs and Prophets* in 1890—"God is love." Ellen White's book *Steps to Christ* starts out with the chapter "God's Love for Man," and this chapter begins with the words: "Nature and revelation alike testify of God's love." Hence while all these books point their readers to the Bible, they also emphasize clearly that God loves each individual.

The Desire of Ages had a remarkable impact on Seventh-day Adventist theology in at least two respects. In this book Ellen White made clearer statements on the eternal divinity of Christ and the personhood of the Holy Spirit than any other Adventist writer of her time. She stated, for example, that Christ "announced Himself to be the self-existent One, He who had been promised to Israel, 'whose goings forth have been from of old, from the days of eternity' " (DA 470). "In Christ is life, original, unborrowed, underived" (*ibid.* 530). In regard to the Holy Spirit, she pointed out that "He" was "the third person of the Godhead" (*ibid.* 671). Those statements eventually influenced leading Adventists of all age groups worldwide.[248]

W. C. White Accepts His Mother's Call

In March 1900 Ellen White "reasoned and prayed" for two successive nights until she decided that it was her "duty," as soon as she could "adjust matters, to go to America without delay." She wanted to "secure the very best kind of help possible" to get out a revised edition of *Christian Temperance* and further volumes of *Testimonies for the Church*. The "consuming desire to get out the works" was too much for her, and she wanted to proceed with this work as soon and as fast as possible. Then she wrote to Willie: "You have done the best you could under the circumstances, but it is not required that you should carry so many responsibilities. Therefore I will not press my work upon you, but say, Do whatever you feel is your duty and that you do not seem able to avoid. But my duty seems now to be made more plain and clear, . . . and go I must as it now appears" (Lt 196, 1900).

Two days later she sent another letter to him in which she essentially insisted that he make a decision as to which track he would follow (Lt 198, 1900). Would he, or would he not, devote himself wholeheartedly to her work? This "ultimatum" got his attention. When she suggested leaving him in Australia to sit on his committees while she would return to America and get Daniells and Haskell and Edson White to do the work he had neglected, W. C. White finally saw things in something closer to her perspective. From this point onward, he began to see the divestiture of his administrative responsibilities as more of a privilege than a sacrifice. "I have been shaking myself free from some of the responsibilities here," he wrote to G. A. Irwin. "I feel much blessed in the change, and I think it is better for the work" because responsibilities would now be borne by individuals who had previously depended on White to carry them.[249] But it was not until they sailed for America that W. C. White was fully able to free himself of his other responsibilities. Never again would he become so entangled in outside commitments as to be unavailable to his mother. "All my workers and W. C. White himself understand," she wrote upon arriving in the United States, "that in leaving Australia W. C. W. laid off every official duty that he might help me in my book work. I employ him as my general helper in this work" (Lt 139, 1900, in 1888 Materials 1714; Lt 371, 1907, in PH116 10-16). From 1900 until her death in 1915, he would be her spokesman, liaison, and chief of staff. In the process, he would prepare to be the primary custodian of her writings after her death.

Senior Churchwoman
(1900-1915)

When Ellen White returned to North America in 1900, she was 72.[250] Before 1891 she had maintained a rather high-profile approach to her leadership role, characterized by long, strenuous itineraries of speaking engagements at camp meetings and other convocations. During the Australian years and continuing into the early 1900s she gradually reduced the frequency of her public appearances and the quantity of her personal correspondence. In her latest years she wrote less and less new material of any kind and concentrated her waning strength on revising and arranging for publication the materials she had previously written.

Establishing a Residence
Ellen White first thought of returning to the home she still owned in Healdsburg, California,

but W. C. White argued against living "near any school." They thought of locating near the Pacific Press in Oakland, but after a few days they concluded that the prices were too high and the climate of Oakland "too cold and foggy" for her health at nearly 73 years (Lt 121, 1900, in 1888 Materials 1707, 1708; Lt 146, 1900; Lt 158, 1900). Taking a break from house hunting, they visited old friends at the St. Helena Sanitarium. As Ellen White described to Jenny L. Ings her disappointment in "house hunting," Mrs. Ings replied: "Well, there is a place under the hill that will suit you." Investigating, she discovered a farm with orchards, vineyards, barn, stable, and, best of all, "a house furnished throughout," ready for occupancy. She had received enough for her place in Australia to purchase the place in St. Helena. Thus within a week of her arrival in the United States she found a house ready for her to move into. "This place was none of my seeking," she exulted in a letter to Stephen and Hetty Haskell. "It has come to me without a thought or purpose of mine. The Lord is so kind and gracious to me. I can trust my interests with Him who is too wise to err and too good to do me harm" (Lt 132, 1900, in 21MR 126, 127; 5Bio 30-34). She took possession of the house on October 16, 1900. About three months later she named it Elmshaven for the large elm trees that then stood in front of the house (Lt 127, 1900; 5Bio 34-36, 46).[251] Shortly after settling down there, she published the sixth volume of *Testimonies for the Church* as well as the book *Testimonies on Sabbath School Work*. The *Testimonies* series would eventually be completed in 1909 with the ninth volume. Volumes 7 and 8 were published in 1902 and 1904, respectively.

General Conference Session of 1901

For a number of leading delegates, the effective opening of the 1901 General Conference session occurred the day before the official call to order. On April 1 Ellen White addressed a large group of denominational leaders in the Battle Creek College library, setting before them the challenges facing the church. Without specifying exactly how the work should be done, she called for a thorough reorganization of denominational structure (Ms 43, 1901).[252]

The session was officially called to order by incumbent president G. A. Irwin on April 2. Following Irwin's brief address, Ellen White took the speaker's stand and challenged the delegates to do a work "that should have been done . . . ten years ago." In the session of 1891 "the brethren assented to the light God had given," she said, "but no special change was made to bring about such a condition of things that the power of God could be revealed among His people." Now she renewed the call for personal reconversion and denominational restructuring. "What we want now is a reorganization," she declared. "We want to begin at the foundation and build upon a different principle" (GCB, Apr. 3, 1901).[253]

While she did not specify "just how" this reorganization was "to be accomplished," she did insist that the heavy responsibilities of leadership should rest on a larger group of men. "There are to be more than one or two or three men to consider the whole vast field. The work is great, and there is no one human mind that can plan for the work which needs to be done." She urged the delegates to take seriously the work to be done at the conference. "Let every one of you go home, not to chat, chat, chat, but to pray. . . . Go home and plead with God to mold you after the divine similitude" (*ibid.*). In this vein she emphasized each one's personal assurance of salvation. "Each one of you may know for yourself that you have a living Savior, that He is your helper and your God. You need not stand where you say, 'I do not know whether I am saved.' Do you believe in Christ as your personal Savior? If you do, then rejoice. We do not rejoice half as much as we should" (*ibid.*, Apr. 10, 1901).

The first motion to be placed before the assembly was by A. G. Daniells, who had chaired the meeting in the college library the day before. Speaking for "many" who had been present in that meeting, he moved to suspend "the usual rules and precedents for arranging and transacting the business of the conference," and that a broadly representative "general or central committee" be appointed to grapple with the challenges of reorganization and to prepare proposals to come before the delegates. After some discussion in which both Ellen and W. C. White participated, the motion was unanimously passed. The central committee came to be called the committee on counsel, and Daniells was elected its chair (*ibid.*, Apr. 3, 1901).[254] On April 12 a vote was taken to move Battle Creek College to a rural location near Berrien Springs, Michigan.[255] "It is time to get out now," said Ellen White to Percy T. Magan, "for great things will soon be happening in Battle Creek" (5Bio 92). During the last week of the session Ellen White confronted the "holy flesh" movement that had taken root in the Indiana Conference over the previous three years. At the 5:30 a.m. meeting, Wednesday, April 17, she repudiated the teaching that human beings may attain "holy flesh" in the present life. "Let this phase of doctrine be carried a little further," she warned, "and it will lead to the claim that its advocates cannot sin, that since they have holy flesh, their actions are all holy. What a door of temptation would thus be opened!" She labeled the teaching a "dangerous delusion" and said that those who had "sustained this fanaticism . . . might far better be engaged in secular labor," where they would not be "dishonoring the Lord and imperiling His people" (GCB, Apr. 23, 1901).

Relationship to Arthur G. Daniells

The years of working together in Australia had cemented a three-way relationship between Ellen White, her son Willie, and Arthur G. Daniells. When the latter became a local conference president, he "began to communicate regularly" with Ellen White, not especially for advice from her, but "simply to keep her informed of committee decisions and sundry news reports." Daniells sent reports to her regularly for almost two years before he began to specifically ask for her counsel. Then to spare her the burden of additional correspondence he formed the habit of sending his communications to her through W. C. White. While W. C. White was traveling to the United States for the 1897 General Conference session, Daniells began to "consult directly" with Ellen White rather than through her son. Upon W. C. White's return, Daniells again resumed communicating to Ellen White through him, out of respect for her heavy load of writing and other literary work.[256] By the time Daniells became the defacto General Conference president in 1901, there was a rather well-established three-way relationship between him and the Whites. Between 1901 and 1915 he wrote very frequently and at length about virtually every issue of importance with which he needed to deal. W. C. White shared these concerns with his mother and then reported to Daniells her responses. Thus by 1908 Daniells could assert to W. C. White: "I think the man who has the greatest influence over me is the one I am now addressing."[257]

Burning of the Battle Creek Sanitarium

On February 18, 1902, the Whites received word via telegraph that the main buildings of the Battle Creek Sanitarium had burned to the ground. Ellen White's first response was to caution against any hasty fixing of blame (Ms 76, 1903, in SpTB06 5-10). She feared that some people might "put their own construction on this accident," and start to condemn J. H. Kellogg (Lt 29, 1902, in 5Bio 151). She herself withheld judgment while she waited to see how Kellogg would respond to the emergency. The immediate questions facing the medical leaders concerned whether or not to rebuild at the same location and how large and expensive a new building should be. Ellen White, Daniells, and others favored moving the Battle Creek Sanitarium away from its urban environment (Lt 110, 1902).[258] Whatever passing thought Kellogg may have given to the option of moving out of Battle Creek, within a week he announced in the *Review and Herald* his plan to rebuild in Battle Creek. By the end of March the General Conference committee had approved Kellogg's plan. The sanitarium's insurance policy had paid $154,000, the citizens of Battle Creek had raised some $80,000 in cash and pledges, and the city had promised perpetual exemption from taxes. These promises of support, together with Kellogg's enthusiasm, convinced the committee to approve the rebuilding in Battle Creek. Daniells reported accepting an architect's plans for a "plain, but dignified" building, "absolutely fireproof," that when "finished, furnished, and fully equipped," would cost "between $250,000 and $300,000. But the board is determined that no debt shall be incurred by the erection of this building."[259] Daniells' determination not to incur additional debt would become a main focus of conflict between him and Kellogg before the year was out.

The Beginning of the Kellogg Crisis

Kellogg developed the "grand proposition" to donate the manuscript and the publishing costs of a new book, *The Living Temple*, and furnish to the General Conference 400,000 copies "free," provided the General Conference would "take up the sale of the book, and have the entire proceeds go to the Sanitariums" to cover the existing debts and to pay for the new building (Ms 123, 1902).[260] Daniells reported to Kellogg in April that Adventists in various places were enthusiastic about "selling something like half a million copies" of *The Living Temple*. Plans were being laid to release German and Scandinavian language editions "simultaneously with the English edition." Yet Daniells felt "anxious" about one aspect of the plan. "You know," he confided to Kellogg, "there are some who fear that you are grazing about very close to pantheism. In fact, some have felt from your talks about God in man that you are practically a pantheist. I do not believe this," Daniells assured him. "I should never report from anything I have heard in your talks on this topic that you are a pantheist. And yet some get this impression. Now I feel anxious that your thoughts [in *The Living Temple*] shall be so carefully and wisely and clearly stated that there will be no ground for misunderstanding and criticism."[261] He reasoned that, intentionally or not, none would want to "disseminate error," and it would be difficult to convince church members to sell the book if it already had a "black eye from the start."[262] When Kellogg laid the cornerstone for the new sanitarium, he eulogized it as a "temple" to truth, comparing it to the temple of Jerusalem. Kellogg's rhetoric was an exact inversion of the counsel Ellen White had written him 10 days earlier, that his proposed building was too ostentatious and that "Battle Creek [was] not to be made a Jerusalem" (Lt 125, 1902, in 5Bio 154).[263]

The Fall Council of the General Conference Committee, which convened in November 1902, discussed the question of finances, and decided that all enterprises in the name of the church were to "be conducted on a strictly cash basis."[264] Further, the use of Kellogg's new book *The Living Temple* as a means of raising funds for the new building was discussed. A committee of three appointed to evaluate *The Living Temple* made its report. J. H. Kellogg and David Paulson recommended the book's acceptance for the fund-raising campaign. W. W. Prescott, in a minority report, assessed the theological portions of the book as "tending to harm rather than to good" and expressed the "hope" that it would "never be published." As the ensuing discussion revealed that the council leaned toward the minority report, Kellogg withdrew the book from consideration for the fund-raising campaign. Thus Kellogg's two preferences—financial policy and the publication of *The Living Temple*—were rejected.[265] It soon became clear that Kellogg was not about to surrender on either of these points. He intensified his efforts to secure the acceptance of *The Living Temple* and began to campaign for the overthrow of A. G. Daniells.

About six weeks later Kellogg sat down to dictate a letter to Ellen White. "I have just finished a 75-page letter to send you," he explained, "stating the truth as I see it in relation to the matters which have been under controversy." Before sending it, he prepared an "abstract" to accompany it so that she could "get the gist of the matter" without having to read all of it, yet have the "complete statement to refer to if necessary." The second paragraph in Kellogg's cover letter announced that "last night [December 30, 1902] the main building of the Review and Herald was burned to the ground and everything in it burned up, an experience exactly parallel with that of the sanitarium."[266]

The General Conference Session in 1903

By January 1903 Kellogg's well-laid plan to remove Daniells from the presidency appeared to be gathering momentum. The 1901 constitution, by omitting the title of General Conference president and giving the General Conference Committee (instead of the General Conference session) the authority to elect its own chair, had made such an ouster a distinct possibility. Kellogg tried to make "every possible effort" to overthrow Daniells and "make A. T. Jones the president" during the 1903 General Conference session. At the same time, there was a "very persistent" rumor going out from Battle Creek that Ellen White had condemned Prescott and Daniells for their role in the Autumn Council.[267]

The session opened in Oakland, California, on Friday, March 27, 1903. In her Sabbath morning sermon, Ellen White set all the perplexing issues that faced the conference within one context—that of personal devotion to God and the finishing of the work of the gospel on earth. She saw the erecting of "mammoth buildings" as a "snare," a diversion that gave glory to men and ultimately hindered the work of God they were intended to advance (GCB, Mar. 30, 1903). "God is watching His people," she declared in another address Monday afternoon. "We should seek to find out what He means when He sweeps away our sanitarium and our publishing house. . . . [God] wants us to seek for the meaning of the calamities that have overtaken us, that we may not tread in the footsteps of Israel, and say, 'The temple of the Lord, the temple of the Lord are we,' when we are not this at all" (GCB, Apr. 1, 1903).

She spoke of what "might have been" at the 1901 General Conference session if the delegates had not only accepted new organizational structures but had also "confessed their sins" and "made a break" from the spiritual status quo. Had they done this, "the power of God would have gone through the meeting, and we should have had a Pentecostal season" (*ibid.*). From the records of this General Conference session stems one of the few printed prayers of Ellen White. She addressed God not so much as "our Father", rather she regularly used such phrases as "my heavenly Father," "O my Father," and "my Savior" (GCB, Apr. 2, 1903; GCB, Apr. 6, 1903). For her, even public prayers were obviously not just conventional exercises but an "opening of the heart to God as to a friend" (SC 93).

On April 2 the Committee on Plans and Constitution recommended that both the Review and Herald publishing house and the General Conference headquarters be moved out of Battle Creek. In speaking to this issue, Ellen White made an eloquent appeal for fair treatment of J. H. Kellogg. "Many souls have been converted," she declared, and "many wonderful cures have been wrought" through the work of Kellogg and the Battle Creek Sanitarium. She decried the opposition he had received. Some had tried "to make the work of Dr. Kellogg as hard as possible, in order to build themselves up," and many had rejected and ridiculed the health reform principles he taught. "God gave the light on health reform," she affirmed, "and those who rejected it rejected God. One and another who knew better said it all came from Dr. Kellogg, and they made war upon him" (GCB, Apr. 3, 1903; GCB, Apr. 6, 1903). Yet, while she pleaded for a supportive attitude toward Kellogg and toward the newly rebuilt sanitarium, she refused to endorse his theological theories and called for study as to how the Battle Creek Sanitarium could be directly owned by the General Conference. She was unequivocal in her support of moving the publishing house out of Battle Creek. "Never lay a stone or brick in Battle Creek to rebuild the Review office there," she said. "God has a better place for it" (GCB, Apr. 6, 1903). A committee to investigate suitable locations for relocating the Review office and the General Conference headquarters was authorized.

The 1903 General Conference session revised the constitution to restore the office of president, reelected Daniells, and endorsed his no-debt policy. The session also passed a resolution that the International Medical Missionary and Benevolent Association should "so arrange its constituency, and its constitution" to become "a department of the General Conference of Seventh-day Adventists." It was also voted to move the denominational headquarters and the Review and Herald publishing house out of Battle Creek to a location not yet determined (GCB, Apr. 14, 1903).

Moving the General Conference and the Publishing House to Washington, D.C.

As early as April 24, 1903, W. C. White had conveyed to Daniells the conviction of Ellen White that Daniells should "go straight forward" with "the removal of the General Conference headquarters from Battle Creek. Many things which cannot be done in a hurry will naturally follow this move. Let there be no delay in this." By mid-June news was coming to Elmshaven about prospective sites near Fishkill, New York, and Washington, D.C. Willie informed Daniells on June 19 that "Mother grows more and more in earnest about our duty to give Washington favorable consideration at this time."[268] Unlike Kellogg, who plunged ahead with his plans hoping Ellen White would not interfere, Daniells made frequent contact with her, pleading with her for guidance.[269] She recommended to "arrange as quickly as possible for the General Conference headquarters to be located in Washington, D.C.," and to move the Review and Herald to the same place.[270] Shortly after that, W. C. White went to Battle Creek to meet Daniells, and together they traveled to Washington to negotiate the purchase of the key property.[271] While Daniells and White were purchasing property on the East Coast, Prescott in Battle Creek was preparing to move the Review and Herald. He reported on August 6 that all of the "furniture, machinery, and printing outfit which we can take from here" had been loaded into four boxcars. The last of these left Battle Creek August 6. Within days Prescott and his staff would begin publishing the *Review and Herald* from rented quarters in downtown Washington, D.C.[272]

The Climax of the Kellogg Crisis

The Fall Council of the General Conference convened October 7-21, 1903, at Washington, D.C. The question of the Battle Creek situation and *The Living Temple* was not on the agenda. But despite the 1902 Fall Council's rejection of the book for fund-raising purposes, Kellogg had proceeded with plans for publication. When the initial printing plates were destroyed in the Review and Herald fire of December 30, 1902, Kellogg gave the manuscript to another printer in Battle Creek, who produced the book early in 1903. By autumn it had been widely read among Seventh-day Adventists. The arrival at the Washington council of several physicians from Battle Creek again propelled the issue to the forefront. A leader among this group of physicians was David Paulson, who in 1904 with his wife, Mary Paulson, also a physician, would found the Hinsdale Sanitarium in suburban Chicago.[273] On October 13 the issue of *The Living Temple* was discussed at the council, but no conclusions were reached. Late that evening Paulson accompanied Daniells from the meeting, arguing for the correctness of the views in *The Living Temple*.[274] Arriving home that night, Daniells found two letters waiting for him from Ellen G. White. The next morning he would read them to the assembled council. In them she warned against the teachings of the book.[275] Unsure what to believe, Paulson spent several hours talking and praying with Dr. Kellogg; a conversation that convinced Kellogg to give credit to Ellen White's testimony. Four days later Kellogg told the council that he would "revise the book," and desired to "work in harmony with the General Conference"—but his change of attitude was transitory.[276]

Shortly afterward Daniells received another letter from Ellen G. White entitled "Decided Action to Be Taken Now." In it she explained the story behind the timing of the testimonies sent to the Autumn Council. The letter would be a major point of reference for Daniells and Prescott during the next four years. "Shortly before I sent the testimonies that you said arrived just in time," Ellen White wrote to Daniells, "I had read an incident about a ship in a fog meeting an iceberg. For several nights I slept but little. I seemed to be bowed down as a cart beneath sheaves. One night a scene was clearly presented before me. A vessel was upon the waters, in a heavy fog. Suddenly the lookout cried, 'Iceberg just ahead!' There, towering high above the ship, was a gigantic iceberg. An authoritative voice cried out, 'Meet it!' There was not a moment's hesitation. It was a time for instant action. The engineer put on full steam, and the man at the wheel steered the ship straight into the iceberg. With a crash she struck the ice. There was a fearful shock, and the iceberg broke into many pieces, falling with a noise like thunder upon the deck. The passengers were violently shaken by the force of the collision, but no lives were lost. The vessel was injured, but not beyond repair. She rebounded from the contact, trembling from stem to stern, like a living creature. Then she moved forward on her way. Well I knew the meaning of this representation. I had my orders. I had heard the words, like a living voice from our Captain, 'Meet it!' I knew what my duty was, and that there was not a moment to lose. The time for decided action had come. I must without delay obey the command, 'Meet it!' This is why you received the testimonies when you did. That night I was up at one o'clock, writing as fast as my hand could pass over the paper. We have all stood at our posts like faithful sentinels, working early and late to send to the council instruction that we thought would help you" (Lt 238, 1903, in 5Bio 301).

Daniells was deeply grateful for that message. The storm was not over, but he felt greatly strengthened.[277]

Six months later came the session of the Lake Union Conference at Berrien Springs, Michigan. Ellen White's first address to the session Wednesday evening dealt with pantheism and *The Living Temple*. Prescott was scheduled to speak Friday night and intended to follow her opening with another sermon against pantheism, evidently in the spirit of "meeting [the] iceberg." Friday morning Ellen White told Prescott to "go ahead" with his intended topic. But after the conversation with Prescott, she sent him a note saying she had changed her mind. She had already addressed the pantheism issue and felt "deeply impressed" that for Prescott to take up the same topic would cause some "to think that Dr. Kellogg is receiving a thrashing." Instead she advised Prescott to speak on a topic that would "touch and tender hearts" and "bring in faith and love and unity." She asked W. C. White to hand the one-page note to Prescott, but he asked and received her permission not to deliver it. Not having received Ellen White's note, Prescott on Friday night preached against Kellogg's pantheism. As Ellen White had feared, Prescott's thrust provoked a counterattack. At the 5:45 a.m. meeting on Monday A. T. Jones launched a six-hour tirade against Prescott, seeking to prove that Prescott had taught pantheism before Kellogg (Lt 165, 1904, in SpTB02 30-35).[278]

The entire crisis had several major dimensions. The theological dimension was epitomized in the debate over *The Living Temple*, which lost influence in the denomination after its condemnation by Ellen White in the autumn of 1903. The organizational conflict between the General Conference and the International Medical Missionary and Benevolent Association virtually ended with the dissolution of the IMMBA—a legal process begun in 1904 and completed in 1905—and the creation of the General Conference Medical Department in 1905.[279] The removal of the Review and Herald Publishing Association and the General Conference offices from Battle Creek served to reinforce the separation that had taken place and to diminish Kellogg's continuing influence in denominational affairs.

The Establishment of New Institutions

In the spring of 1904 Ellen White, Mrs. J. Gotzian, and E. S. Ballenger purchased a failed health resort near National City, California, that would become the Paradise Valley Sanitarium.[280] Several months later, after the session of the Lake Union Conference, she went to Tennessee, joining her sons on Edson's steamboat, the *Morning Star*. The three Whites, with E. A. Sutherland and P. T. Magan, spent a few days resting and sailing the Cumberland River in search of land on which to found the school that would eventually become Madison College.[281]

Back in California, she also pushed strongly for the purchase of the Glendale Hotel, near Los Angeles, which reopened in 1905 as the Glendale Sanitarium (now Glendale Adventist Medical Center). Through W. C. White she kept in touch with the developing Paradise Valley and Glendale (California) sanitariums.[282]

Early in 1905 W. C. White made four visits to the new Pacific Press plant in Mountain View, California, where he was arranging the publishing details for *The Ministry of Healing*, Ellen White's new book on the principles of health. She donated the proceeds from that book to retire the debts on Adventist health-care institutions.

It was about this time that Ellen White, on the basis of visions, had commissioned John A. Burden to search diligently in the vicinity of Redlands, California, for a property suitable for a third southern California sanitarium. He had found a resort hotel called Loma Linda on 76 acres, but the price was too high. However, when repeated reductions had brought the price down to 27 percent of its original amount, Burden wrote letters to Ellen White and to G. W. Reaser, Southern California Conference president who were both at the General Conference session in Washington, D.C. Ellen's son vividly described the session milieu into which Burden's letters came. It was an atmosphere of high financial tension and concern over indebtedness. W. C. recalled: "I remember well the day when mother received and read Elder Burden's letter. She read it aloud to me, and then she said that she believed this place was one that had been presented to her in vision several years before. Its description answered more closely to what had been presented to her than anything she had ever seen. And as the Lord had been moving on her mind to appeal to our people to do something immediately in establishing a sanitarium in Redlands and Riverside, and as this place described by Elder Burden seemed to be so perfectly in accord with our needs, . . . she said we must take action at once."[283]

Although Reaser was initially against the purchase, Ellen White strongly urged to buy the property. Shortly afterward the conference constituency and executive committee voted to accept the responsibility for purchasing and operating the Loma Linda Sanitarium. John Burden, manager of the Glendale Sanitarium, was requested to take up similar responsibilities at Loma Linda, tentatively set to open in September 1905.[284] On April 15, 1906, Loma Linda Sanitarium, what would later become Loma Linda University Medical Center, was dedicated debt-free. Thus within one year three new Adventist sanitariums had been established in southern California through Ellen White's direct counsel. All three were purchased for small fractions of their construction cost.[285] Soon it became evident that these were important steps to compensate the loss of the Battle Creek Sanitarium, which was disconnected from the denomination through J. H. Kellogg's expulsion from the church in 1907.[286]

Elmshaven Councils

A pattern that became common in Ellen White's final years was that instead of her making the arduous train trip east, General Conference leaders would come to her home at Elmshaven. One such council meeting, on Sunday, January 26, 1908, considered the theological conflict over "the daily" in Daniel 8:12, 13, and parallel passages. A. G. Daniells and W. W. Prescott represented those who favored the "new view," whereas J. N. Loughborough, S. N. Haskell, and Hetty Haskell were present to give the defenders of the "old view" a voice. W. C. White, C. C. Crisler, and D. E. Robinson were present as well. They were open to the new view but hopeful of mediating some agreement between the two groups and thus precluding divisive conflict.[287] In another Elmshaven meeting shortly afterward, Prescott, Crisler, Robinson, and W. C. White spent parts of January 27 and 28 and February 2 studying possible responses to a contemporary Adventist publication critical of her work.[288]

The 1909 General Conference and the Debate Over Loma Linda

The 1909 General Conference session, the last that Ellen White attended, convened from May 13 through June 6. The main meetings were held in a large tent pitched on the campus of the Washington [D.C.] Foreign Mission Seminary (now Washington Adventist University). Ellen White gave 11 addresses, including three of the Sabbath morning sermons (6Bio 194).[289] Afterward she spent about a week in her girlhood home, Portland, Maine, where she spoke several times at a camp meeting.

Of high concern to church leaders in 1909 were the questions of whether or not the Loma Linda College of Evangelists should seek state approval, and whether it should provide a four-year medical course, or only the first two years, leaving the students to finish at other schools. These questions were on the agenda of the 1909 Autumn Council at College View, Nebraska, October 5-15. As the council approached, John Burden, superintendent of the Loma Linda institution, wrote to Ellen White for advice.[290] Her reply opposed the idea of a two-year program, which would force Loma Linda graduates to "complete their medical education in worldly colleges (Lt 132, 1909, in PC 301)." Regarding the issue of complying with state requirements, she set forth three principles. First, she said, "We cannot submit to regulations" involving "the sacrifice of principle, . . . for this would imperil the soul's salvation." Second, she cautioned, on the other hand, that Adventists should not seek exemption from legitimate regulations. "Whenever we can comply with the law of the land without putting ourselves in a false position, we should do so," she advised. Third, she observed that some requirements might fall between the two extremes, and such might be solved by negotiation. "We must carefully consider what is involved in these matters. If there are conditions to which we could not subscribe, we should endeavor to have these matters adjusted, so that there would not be strong opposition against our physicians. The Savior bids us to be wise as serpents, and harmless as doves" (Lt 140, 1909, in MM 84).

Her letter of October 11 reached Burden at College View, where the committee recommended to the "board of management of the Loma Linda College of Evangelists to secure a charter for the school, that it may develop as the opening providences and the instruction of the Spirit of God may indicate."[291] Following this action, the Loma Linda school applied to the State of California for legal authority to grant degrees in medicine. The school was chartered December 9, 1909, under the new name, College of Medical Evangelists.[292]

The 1911 Edition of *The Great Controversy*

In January 1910 the Whites received word that the printing plates used for printing *The*

Great Controversy since 1888 were badly worn, and the type needed to be reset. Ellen White saw this as an opportunity to improve the volume. "I determined," she wrote to F. M. Wilcox, "that we would have everything closely examined, to see if the truths it contained were stated in the very best manner, to convince those not of our faith that the Lord had guided and sustained me in the writing of its pages" (Lt 56, 1911, in 3SM 123). Consequently a rather wide circle of individuals was invited "to call our attention to any passages that needed to be considered in connection with the resetting of the book." [293] One of these individuals was W. W. Prescott, who returned in April a 39-page catalog of suggestions, first of which was that all citations to historical authorities ought to be identified with quotation marks and properly credited. On May 23, 1910, A. G. Daniells and Homer Salisbury, president of Washington Missionary College, joined W. C. White and others at Elmshaven to consider all the suggestions that had been received from various individuals. When Ellen White was asked what should be done about the historical references, "she was prompt and clear in her opinion" that "proper credit" should be given wherever possible. The matter of verifying the historical quotations would become a major research project, in the course of which Clarence Crisler would collect "several hundred pages of historical data." Much of 1910 and the first half of 1911 would be consumed in this work (6Bio 302-337). [294] The first copies of the new edition were received at Elmshaven on July 17, 1911. On October 30 at the Fall Council in Washington, D.C., W. C. White made some significant remarks about its preparation. [295] In the same year she also published the fourth volume of her Conflict of the Ages Series—*The Acts of the Apostles*.

Time Running Out (1912-1915)

On February 9, 1912, Ellen White signed the final edition of her will and was hurrying to publish as much of her writings as she could while still able to supervise the process. During that summer Ellen White worked with great urgency on a new book on Old Testament history, as yet untitled. She hoped to finish it for distribution at the General Conference session in 1913, but the process took longer than expected. [296] By 1914 Clarence Crisler was giving "nearly all his time" to the manuscript on Old Testament history, then titled *The Captivity and Restoration of Israel: The Conflict of the Ages Illustrated in the Lives of Prophets and Kings*. [297]

In mid-May 1914 Ellen White apparently suffered a light stroke that paralyzed her "right side for a day or two." She had some "trouble" with "her right foot for a week," and with "her right hand for two weeks." [298] October 6, 1914, found Willie leaving California en route to the Autumn Council in Washington, D.C. Typing on the train, he gave directions to the staff at home in Elmshaven: Clarence Crisler was to "forge ahead" on the last chapters of *Captivity and Restoration*, while D. E. Robinson, Maggie Hare Bree, Mary Steward, and Minnie Hawkins Crisler were to "concentrate their labors on perfecting for the printer" the manuscript of *Gospel Workers*.

While W. C. White was gone, Crisler reported from Elmshaven that Ellen White had taken "one of the most marked changes for the worse since your departure—the inability at times to grasp surrounding circumstances, and to realize that she is where she is. But even when thus confused as regards minor and local matters, she seems to be very clear on spiritual topics," he added. "Her hand continues somewhat swollen, and we do not like this unnatural condition, as we fear it presages a repetition of that which came over her a couple of months or so ago," evidently a reference to the stroke.[299] "Sister White seemed quite clear-minded on Friday," Crisler reported two weeks later, "and I was able to read her a few pages of advance work on the Old Testament articles. . . . Today I have read half a dozen pages with her of advance chapters, and she seems able to grasp the various lines of thought quite well. She makes a good many comments, but we cannot get much in addition to that which is on file. In general, she is today about as usual. She is still more or less confused as to her whereabouts. Miss Walling tells me that your mother spends a good deal of the time, nights, in prayer, evidently mostly in her sleep. Sometimes she seems to be holding prayer meetings. The other night she preached for an hour, and as she was using her voice in full strength, Miss Walling at last thought to suggest that she had preached long enough, and that now she should rest and sleep, which she did. . . . I write you thus freely, that you may know just how your mother is on these minor matters at times. This sort of thing is on the increase. . . . On the other hand, when we touch spiritual topics, the mind seems lifted above confusion. When a scripture is partially quoted, she very often finishes it. I have tried this over and over again, especially when repeating the promises. And . . . Jeremiah and other Old Testament scriptures seem very familiar to her, and she catches them up, and comments on them, and goes forward with the quotations, as of old. I regard this as a special providence in our favor just now."[300]

The above letter is typical of Crisler's almost daily reports to W. C. White regarding his mother's condition. "She says," he reported two weeks later, that "she does not wish to make any great noise about having courage continually, although she has [courage]; and she adds that the very fact that members of the household are waked up at times hearing her repeating the promises of God and claiming them as her own is proof that she still has battles of her own to fight against Satan. The enemy is still in the land of the living, and we must needs plead the promises; but we may have strong faith in God's power to deliver, and our hearts may be filled with courage.[301]

Meanwhile, Crisler informed W. C. White that he was "in the midst of the final work on the first four of the six lacking chapters" of *Captivity and Restoration of Israel: The Conflict of the Ages Illustrated in the Lives of Prophets and Kings*. When the book was published in 1917, it carried this title initially, but would later be known by the last words of that title, *Prophets and Kings*. On December 17 he reported having read to her two of the Daniel chapters. Her "frailty . . . is becoming more and still more manifest, and we know not how it may end," Crisler observed on December 23. "We are glad, profoundly glad, [that] she seems to keep clear on spiritual subjects, even when brain-weary, and that apparently she enjoys going over her books, over the pages of the *Review*, and over chapters presented for consideration." Nevertheless, Crisler urged Willie in Nashville to shorten his journey homeward. "If you have matters of paramount importance that you feel you must have her counsel on, every day gained during the return journey may count for much. I am sure you are determined in your own mind not to presume on the goodness of God in sustaining your mother so remarkably." W. C. White still planned to visit Chicago, New York City, Philadelphia, Washington, D.C., Nashville, and College View before coming home.[302] When White arrived home on January 27, he "was immediately called to Loma Linda for a week." Then he attended other meetings in Oakland and Mountain View, California. On Friday, February 12, he reached home again, and spent a few minutes of the afternoon with his mother outdoors in the yard, "walking about in the bright sunshine, and talking about the progress of the message in all the world."[303]

Ellen White's Last Months

The next day, February 13, 1915—a Sabbath morning—as Ellen White was "entering her study from the hallway," she tripped and fell, suffering a hip fracture of the left femur.[304] It was now clearly evident that she could not live much longer. The editorial staff at Elmshaven accelerated their work on a final edition of *Life Sketches of Ellen G. White* and on biographical information, photographs, and obituary materials to be released to the news media upon the event of her death.[305] She would be confined to her bed and wheelchair for the next five months, though suffering little or no pain. As she neared the end she was often unconscious. When she was awake, her conversations with friends and relatives during the final weeks bespoke an attitude of cheerfulness, a sense of having faithfully performed the work God had entrusted to her 70 years before, and a confident assurance that God's cause would "triumph gloriously." On Friday night, July 9, she had a severe spell of vomiting, after which the attending physician "stopped the treatments." On Friday, July 16, 1915, she "fell asleep without a struggle" at 3:40 p.m. at the age of 87.[306] She was surrounded by her immediate family and colleagues. Her last words were "I know in whom I have believed" (LS449). Writing to David Lacey four days later, her son Willie described her death: "It was like the burning out of a candle, so quiet."[307]

Memorial services were held in three locations. The first took place "under the elm trees, just [in] front of her house," Sunday afternoon, July 18. Her neighbors remembered her as "the little old lady with white hair, who always spoke so lovingly about Jesus."[308] The next morning a second service was held at the California Conference camp meeting then in progress in Richmond, a suburb of Oakland. The third funeral was conducted in the Battle Creek Tabernacle on Sabbath, July 24, 1915. Her gravesite is in Battle Creek's Oak Hill Cemetery (6Bio 441).

Conclusion

The life of Ellen G. White is inseparably connected to the origin and development of the Seventh-day Adventist Church. Without the vision, leadership, and personal sacrifice of Ellen White—besides the efforts of her husband James White, and Joseph Bates—"there would be no Seventh-day Adventist Church today."[309] Although the doctrines of the denomination were discovered in the Bible, it was through her guidance that the Sabbatarian Adventists were preserved from numerous doctrinal pitfalls. Her emphasis on the publishing work and the organization of the scattered Sabbatarian Adventist groups led to the establishment of a mission-focused denomination. Then Ellen White proceeded to stress the need of health education, health institutions, and educational institutions, which profoundly shaped the development of the denomination into a thriving worldwide church.

While her contemporaries described her as a "uniformly pleasant, cheerful, and courageous" person who "was never careless, flippant, or in any way cheap in conversation or manner of life," she herself always directed people to imitate the ultimate example—Jesus

Christ. Ellen White emphasized that God was the source of the guidance and the counsels she gave. She was convinced that God had called her to a special ministry. When she attended her last General Conference session in 1909, she held up her Bible before the assembled delegates and said, "Brethren and sisters, I commend unto you this Book."[310] She was passionate about the Bible, and throughout her life she referred people to the Scriptures as the only rule of faith and practice. The written Word reveals Jesus Christ as the living Word. A reader of Ellen White's writings can hardly miss that she was also passionate about Jesus. She left no doubt that "God is love," and that His love is unconditionally poured out on humanity. As a person who enjoyed a close personal and loving relationship with Jesus, she saw it as her mission to call people to accept Jesus as their own personal Savior and Lord of their lives. Thus her passion for Jesus and Scripture led her to work tirelessly for people in the Adventist community and outside it.

Yet, while Ellen White influenced people in her own lifetime and through them the development of the Seventh-day Adventist Church as well as the world—hospitals, medical centers, educational institutions, and lifestyle, to name some—her influence did not cease with her death. In view of her own mortality she wrote, "My writings will constantly speak, and their work will go forward as long as time shall last. My writings are kept on file in the office, and even though I should not live, these words that have been given to me by the Lord will still have life and will speak to the people." She commissioned the trustees of her estate to publish her writings "in the English language first, and afterward to secure their translation and publication in many other languages" (Lt 371, 1907, in PH116 13, 14). This task has been carried out since her death, and millions have been blessed through her writings.

A 1980 survey on church growth among Adventists in North America discovered that regardless of respondents' ethnic background, there was a direct correlation between spiritual attitudes and practices and the study of Ellen White's works. Researchers found that those who read her writings on a regular basis "have a closer relationship with Christ, more certainty of their standing with God, and are more likely to have identified their spiritual gifts. They are more in favor of spending for public evangelism and contribute more heavily to local missionary projects. They feel more prepared for witnessing and actually engage in more witnessing and outreach programs. They are more likely to study the Bible daily, to pray for specific people, to meet in fellowship groups, and to have daily family worship. They view their church more positively. They actually bring more people into the church." While that does not prove that reading Ellen White's writings directly causes "all of these spiritual benefits," it indicates that the regular reading of her writings "does make a positive difference in Christian life and witness."[311]

Another example of the impact of her books is a nationwide survey conducted by the Barna Group, which asked pastors of churches "to identify the three books that had been most helpful to them as a ministry leader during the past three years." Protestant pastors under the age of 40 identified "nineteenth "century Seventh-day Adventist icon Ellen White" as one of the authors they regarded as most helpful to their ministry.[312]

Such an impact on the Christian life and witness of Adventists and non-Adventists alike is consistent with the conviction of many that Ellen White's writings are deeply spiritual and saturated with her love for Jesus and Scripture. Her books truly were and are "a lesser light to lead men and women to the greater light"—Jesus and Scripture (RH, Jan. 20, 1903). Thus the words of the Protestant educator Irmgard Simon are both an assessment and an appeal: "Seventh-day Adventists still live on the spirit of Ellen G. White, and only as long as they pass on this heritage in accordance with this spirit do they have a future."[313]

---

[1] *147th Annual Statistical Report—2009* (Silver Spring, Md.: General Conference of Seventh-day Adventists, 2010), p. 4.

[2] *Religious Bodies of the World With at Least 1 Million Adherents* (2007); www.adherents.com/adh_rb.html.

[3] George E. Rice, "Spiritual Gifts," in Raoul Dederen, ed. *Handbook of Seventh-day Adventist Theology* (RHPA, 2000), 636; A. L. White, *Ellen White: Woman of Vision* (RHPA, 2000). *Ellen White: Woman of Vision* is a one-volume condensation of A. L. White, *Ellen G. White* (RHPA, 1981-1986).

[4] See Gary E. Fraser, *Diet, Life Expectancy, and Chronic Disease: Studies of Seventh-day Adventists and Other Vegetarians* (Oxford: Oxford University Press, 2003); Dan Buettner, "The Secrets of Long Life," *National Geographic*, November 2005; idem, *The Blue Zones: Lessons for Living Longer From the People Who've Lived the Longest* (Washington, D.C.: National Geographic Society, 2008); see also Martin Doblmeier, *The Adventists: Abiding Faith, Cutting-edge Medicine, Longer, Healthier Life* (Alexandria, Va.: Journey Films, 2010).

[5] Ronald Numbers, Gary Land, Terry Aamodt, and Julius Nam, eds., *Ellen White: American Prophet* (London and New York: Oxford University Press, forthcoming).

[6] Rice, "Spiritual Gifts," p. 633; A. L. White, *Ellen White: Woman of Vision*, p. 5.

[7] Randall J. Stephens, "Comments on Jerry Moon, 'Ellen White as a Denomination Builder,'" (response paper presented at a working conference entitled "Ellen White: American Prophet," Portland, Maine, Oct. 24, 2009).

[8] For more comprehensive biographies of Ellen White's life, see EGW, *A Sketch of the Christian Experience and Views of Ellen G. White* (Saratoga Springs, N.Y.: JW, 1851); idem, *Spiritual Gifts* (Battle Creek, Mich.: JW, 1860), vol. 2; JW, *Life Sketches: Ancestry, Early Life, Christian Experience, and Extensive Labors of Elder James White, and His Wife Mrs. Ellen G. White* (Battle Creek, Mich.: Steam Press, 1880); EGW, *Testimonies for the Church* (PPPA, 1948), vol. 1, pp. 9-112; idem, *Life Sketches of Ellen G. White* (PPPA, 1915); D. A. Delafield, *Ellen G. White in Europe, 1885-1887* (RHPA, 1975); A. L. White, *Ellen G. White*; George R. Knight, *Meeting Ellen White: A Fresh Look at Her Life, Writings, and Major Themes* (RHPA, 1996); idem, *Walking With Ellen White: The Human Interest Story* (RHPA, 1999); A. L. White, *Ellen G. White: Woman of Vision*.

[9] It is possible that the twins were born in 1826. Ellen White's father was not a careful recordkeeper, and she herself expressed some uncertainty about the year of their birth. See Lt 308, 1907.

[10] On the older siblings, see articles Caroline Harmon Clough, Harriet Harmon McCann, John B. Harmon, Mary P. Harmon Foss, Sarah B. Harmon Belden, and Robert F. Harmon, Jr. See also article on ancestry of Ellen White, and James R. Nix, "Ellen White's Racial Background," *Ellen G. White and Current Issues Symposium* 1 (2005): 30-45.

[11] Caroline and Harriet married Methodist ministers, and Ellen married a Sabbatarian Adventist minister.

[12] Nathan O. Hatch, *The Democratization of American Christianity* (New Haven, Conn.: Yale University Press, 1989), pp. 251, 254.

[13] Stanley D. Hickerson, "The Homes of James and Ellen White," *Ellen White and Current Issues Symposium* 5 (2009): 97. For information on places in New York and New England see Merlin D. Burt, *Adventist Pioneer Places: New York and New England* (RHPA, 2011).

[14] Frederick Hoyt, "Ellen White's Hometown: Portland, Maine, 1827-1846," in *The World of Ellen G. White*, ed. Gary Land (RHPA, 1987), p. 14.

[15] The phrase "under conviction" was used in Methodist and Evangelical circles as referring to an acute awareness of one's sinfulness.

[16] The public schools in Portland regularly accepted 4-year-olds. See Hoyt, "Ellen White's Hometown," p. 16. However, since it was not until 1833 that the Harmons returned to Portland, it is more reasonable that Ellen started school at 5 years. This also fits the chronology of the accident, which occured when Ellen was 9, near the end of the fall semester of her fourth year of school.

[17] *Catalogue of Books in the Sunday School Library of the Methodist Episcopal Church, Chestnut Street, Portland, Me.* (Portland, Maine: Staples and Lunt, 1854), cited in Merlin D. Burt, "Ellen G. Harmon's Three-Step Conversion Between 1836 and 1843 and the Harmon Family Methodist Experience" (research paper, AU, 1998), p. 13, CAR.

[18] JW, "Mrs. Ellen G. White—Her Life, Christian Experience, and Labors," ST, Jan. 20, 1876.

[19] The latest possible date for the accident would be January 3, 1837, because when Ellen witnessed the au-

rora borealis on January 25, 1837, she had already emerged from unconsciousness. Further, since the accident happened on a school day, and school would not have met from Christmas through New Year's Day, it seems probable that the accident took place before the Christmas break. Since she was already 9 when the accident happened, the earliest possible date for the accident would have been November 26, 1836, her ninth birthday; but no sources mention her birthday in connection with the accident. Thus the accident may have occurred in early to mid-December 1836.

[20] This incident was not an isolated one, as a report in Portland's *Eastern Argus* in November 1838 suggests: "A boy about 8 or 10 years of age threw a stone at another boy . . . knocking him down, and leaving him senseless . . . [and] seriously injured." Quoted in Hoyt, "Ellen White's Hometown," p. 18. Some bullies even used knives and pistols in schoolyard fights, although such extreme measures seemed to be rather uncommon. See *ibid.*, p. 17. Yet that would explain why Ellen's parents advised their children to stay out of conflicts and to hurry home immediately if any should occur.

[21] The extent of the initial damage is not obvious in her photographs because the first existing photographs of Ellen White come from more than 20 years later. However, a comparison between her nose line and that of her (not identical) twin sister shows an obvious difference, even on pictures from later years. The remaining traces of the injury were a general flattening of her nose and a slight dip at the bridge.

[22] The most thorough treatment of Ellen's three-step conversion is found in Burt, "Ellen G. Harmon's Three-Step Conversion"; cf. Burt, "My Burden Left Me," AR, Oct. 25, 2001.

[23] Denison Olmsted, "Observations of the Aurora Borealis of January 25, 1837," *American Journal of Science and Arts* 32 (1837): 176; *The American Almanac and Repository of Useful Knowledge for the Year 1838* (Boston: Charles Bowen, 1837), pp. 80-83; John Lee Comstock, *A Treatise on Mathematical and Physical Geography* (Hartford: Packard and Brown, 1837), pp. 274, 275; Joseph Comstock, *The Tongue of Time, and Star of the States: A System of Human Nature, With the Phenomena of the Heavens and Earth* (New York: n.p., 1838), pp. 158-160. There was also an aurora borealis November 13 and 14, 1837, that was probably more spectacular. See R. M. Devens, *Our First Century* [1776-1876] (Chicago: Heron, 1879), pp. 379-385.

[24] JW, "Mrs. Ellen G. White—Her Life, Christian Experience, and Labors," ST, Jan. 6, 1876.

[25] *Idem,* "Mrs. Ellen G. White—Her Life, Christian Experience, and Labors," ST, Jan. 13, 1876; *idem,* "Life Sketches, Chapter V: Parentage and Early Life," Mar. 28, 1878.

[26] *Idem,* "Mrs. Ellen G. White," ST, Jan. 13, 1876. Her mother, however, was a wise and careful woman who did not allow Ellen to grow up in ignorance. Ellen learned at home many of the practical lessons needed in preparation for life. She also studied in the school of nature, for the spacious Deering's Oaks Park was within walking distance, over the hill, from her home. Later she reported: "I have spent many pleasant hours in the woods at that place." See Lt 193, 1903.

[27] *Idem,* "Mrs. Ellen G. White," ST, Jan. 20, 1876. For biographical information on William Miller, see, for example: Sylvester Bliss, *Memoirs of William Miller*, Adventist Classic Library, reprint (AUP, 2005); George R. Knight, *William Miller and the Rise of Adventism* (PPPA, 2010), pp. 21-55; David L. Rowe, *God's Strange Work: William Miller and the End of the World* (Grand Rapids: William B. Eerdmans, 2008).

[28] William Miller, *Evidences From Scripture and History of the Second Coming of Christ About the Year A.D. 1843, and of His Personal Reign of 1000 Years* (Brandon, Vt.: Vermont Telegraph Office, 1833); *idem, Miller's Works: Views of the Prophecies and Prophetic Chronology* (Boston: Joshua V. Himes, 1842), vol. 1, p. 35; *idem, Miller's Works: Evidence From Scripture and History of the Second Coming of Christ About the Year 1843* (Boston: Joshua V. Himes, 1842), vol. 2.

[29] A camp meeting in the 1840s was a rural gathering where hundreds or even thousands converged to seek religious conversion or revival. Attendees lived in primitive tents for a week or more and listened to a succession of speakers on themes of repentance, confession, forgiveness of sin, and the new birth. See entry Camp Meeting.

[30] JW, "Mrs. Ellen G. White—Her Life, Christian Experience, and Labors," ST, Jan. 27, 1876.

[31] The date of baptism is verified by the Leader's Meeting Minutes and membership records of the Portland, Maine, Chestnut Street Methodist Episcopal Church. See Burt, "Ellen G. Harmon's Three-Step Conversion"; Burt, "My Burden Left Me," AR, Oct. 25, 2001. www.adventistreview.org/thisweek/archives2001.html.

[32] Pastor Hobart's term as pastor of the Chestnut Street Methodist Church terminated on June 30, 1842. Three weeks later, on July 20, the Maine Methodist Annual Conference meeting in Gardiner took action against Gershom F. Cox, the pro-Millerite presiding elder in Portland since 1839. He was transferred to Orrington, Maine, and replaced by Charles Baker as the presiding elder of the Portland district. Though Ellen's sister Lizzie Harmon had been approved to be baptized October 31, 1842, the ordinance never took place.

[33] JW, "Mrs. Ellen G. White—Her Life, Christian Experience, and Labors," ST, Feb. 3, 1876.

[34] John Wesley, *The Works of the Reverend John Wesley, A.M.* (New York: B. Waugh and T. Mason for the Methodist Episcopal Church, 1835), vol. 4, p. 140; Wesley, *A Plain Account of Christian Perfection* (New York: G. Lane and P. P. Sandford, 1844), pp. 3, 8, 10, 21, 22, 37, 56.

[35] JW, "Mrs. Ellen G. White," ST, Feb. 3, 1876.

[36] Quoted in JW, "Life Sketches, Chapter V—Continued: Parentage and Early Life," ST, Apr. 18, 1878.

[37] Cf. Catherine A. Brekus, *Strangers and Pilgrims: Female Preaching in America, 1740-1845* (Chapel Hill, N.C.: University of North Carolina Press, 1998), p. 180.

[38] Information on the trial of the Harmon family is found in the Leader's Meeting Minutes of the Portland, Maine, Chestnut Street Methodist Episcopal Church records. See Burt, "Ellen G. Harmon's Three Step Conversion"; Burt, "My Burden Left Me."

[39] See also W. W. Whidden, *Ellen White on Salvation: A Chronological* Study (RHPA, 1995). On Arminianism, see Roger E. Olson, *Arminian Theology: Myths and Realities* (Downers Grove, Ill.: InterVarsity Press, 2006), pp. 12-43.

[40] Cf. Kenneth J. Collins, *A Real Christian: The Life of John Wesley* (Nashville: Abingdon, 1999), pp. 108, 126-136.

[41] This development is associated with events after the Harmons' expulsion from the Methodist Church.

[42] George Storrs began to promote the subject in 1841. See, e.g., [George Storrs,] *An Inquiry: Are the Souls of the Wicked Immortal? In Three Letters* (Montpelier, Vt.: n.p., 1841); George Storrs, *An Inquiry: Are the Souls of the Wicked Immortal? In Six Sermons* (Albany, N.Y.: W. and A. White, and J. Vischer, 1842).

[43] The Rabbinic reckoning followed a solar year while the Karaite reckoning (see article) followed a lunar year, which in some years resulted in festival dates one month later than by Rabbinic reckoning. See also R. Winter, "England—Letter From Bro. Winter," *Advent Herald and Signs of the Times Reporter*, June 5, 1844.

[44] Joseph Bates, *Second Advent Way Marks and High Heaps: Or a Connected View of the Fulfillment of Prophecy, by God's Peculiar People, From the Year 1840 to 1847* (New Bedford, Mass.: Benjamin Lindsey, 1847), pp. 72, 73; *idem, The Autobiography of Elder Joseph Bates* (Battle Creek, Mich.: Seventh-day Adventist Pub. Assn., 1868), pp. 297, 298. See also JW, *Life Incidents: In Connection With the Great Advent Movement as Illustrated by the Three Angels of Revelation XIV* (Battle Creek, Mich: Seventh-day Adventist Pub. Assn., 1868), pp. 153, 157.

[45] See Clifford Goldstein, *1844 Made Simple* (PPPA, 1988); *idem, Graffiti in the Holy of Holies* (PPPA, 2003); C. Mervyn Maxwell, *Magnificent Disappointment: What Really Happened in 1844 and Its Meaning for Today* (PPPA, 1994), pp. 47-57.

[46] George Storrs, "The Tenth Day of the Seventh Month," *Advent Herald and Signs of the Times Reporter*, Oct. 9, 1844; Thomas M. Preble, "Dear Bro. Bliss," *Advent Herald and Signs of the Times Reporter*, Oct. 9, 1844; George Storrs, "The Tenth Day of the Seventh Month," *Advent Herald and Signs of the Times Reporter*, Oct. 16, 1844; "The Present Movement—Its Rise, Progress, and Characteristics," *Advent Herald and Signs of the Times Reporter*, Oct. 16, 1844; "The History of the Late Movement," *Advent Herald and Signs of the Times Reporter*, Oct. 30, 1844; cf. Bates, *Second Advent Way Marks*, pp. 72, 73; WLF 5. On Aug. 22, 1844, Snow began to publish this message in a small paper titled *The True Midnight Cry*. See also Knight, *William Miller and the Rise of Adventism*, pp. 159-183.

[47] See, for example, the reports and letters in the issue of October 30, 1844, of the *Advent Herald and Signs of the Times Reporter*.

[48] Hiram Edson, handwritten manuscript fragment, p. 8a, CAR. This manuscript currently has four double pages missing at the beginning and an unknown number from the end of the manuscript. The extant portion was reprinted in George R. Knight, comp. and ed., *1844 and the Rise of Sabbatarian Adventism* (RHPA, 1994), pp. 123-126. Some earlier sources knew parts of the manuscript that have since been lost. See, e.g., Herbert M. Kelley, "The Spirit of 1844," RH, June 23, 1921.

[49] Washington Morse, "Remembrance of Former Days," RH, May 7, 1901. For further reports, see Francis D. Nichol, *The Midnight Cry: A Defense of the Character and Conduct of William Miller and the Millerites, Who Mistakenly Believed That the Second Coming of Christ Would Take Place in the Year 1844* (RHPA, 1944), pp. 263-276; Knight, *William Miller and the Rise of Adventism*, pp. 184-200.

[50] In the prayer meeting where she received the "blessing" that climaxed her conversion process, she had been overcome by an unexplained power. Her unbelieving uncle thought to send for a physician, but Eunice Harmon and other "experienced Christians" immediately recognized it as the power of God, for similar experiences were well known in the evangelical camp meetings of the time as well as among the Millerites. See LS80 159.

[51] The first published account of that vision was "Letter From Sister Harmon, Portland, Me., Dec. 20, 1845," in the *Day-Star*, Jan. 24, 1846. She gave more details in a second edition, "Letter From Sister Harmon, Falmouth, Mass., Feb. 15, 1846," in the *Day-Star*, Mar. 14, 1846. The entire text of the vision appears in 2SG 30-35 and EW 13-17. When such experiences came during waking hours, she typically referred to them as "visions" or "views." Those received during sleeping hours she called "dreams." Cf. Angel Manuel Rodríguez, "Ellen G. White's Inaugural Vision: Prophetic Call, Commission, and Role," *Ellen White and Current Issues Symposium* 4 (2008): 61-82.

[52] The "midnight cry" (Matt. 25:10) was a term used by the Millerites for the message that the prophecy of Daniel 8:14 would be fulfilled and Christ would appear on October 22, 1844.

[53] Cf. Merlin D. Burt, "Ellen White and the Shut Door," *Ellen White and Current Issues Symposium* 1 (2005): 73-75, 80.

[54] She emphasized this point later: "For a time after the disappointment in 1844, I did hold, in common

with the advent body, that the door of mercy was then forever closed to the world. This position was taken before my first vision was given me." See Ms 4, 1883. "With my brothers and sisters, after the time passed in '44, I did believe no more sinners could be converted. But I never had a vision that no more sinners could be converted." See Lt 2, 1874, in 8MR 228. It is important to note that the word "sinners" referred to those who had rejected the light God had given them and were rebellious against God, but not to "those who were walking in the light they had received." See Burt, "Ellen White and the Shut Door," pp. 74, 75.

⁵⁵ As a prospective public speaker in 1845, Ellen was acutely vulnerable in at least four ways. 1. Her most fundamental handicap was simply being a woman in a public world that was virtually the exclusive domain of males. 2. In addition, she was single. By the standards of that day she was expected to be accompanied by a friend or relative, preferably a male relative, whenever she ventured beyond her home town. 3. She was physically debilitated; physicians had essentially given her up to die. 4. Finally, she was only 17, "small and frail, unused to society," and "so timid and retiring that it was painful" for her to "meet strangers." See LS 80 192-195; Brekus, pp. 53, 174, 179, 181, 184, 185, 190, 192, 193, 214.

⁵⁶ For a modern reader it may be almost incomprehensible that in the 1840s society in general was opposed to women speaking to a "promiscuous" audience—i.e. a mixed audience of both men and women. See Hoyt, "Ellen White's Hometown," p. 22; Brekus, pp. 179, 262, 283. The more respectable and socially conservative churches extended the ban on women speaking in public to prohibit even female participation in public prayer (Brekus, p. 153). Upper-class churches and people considered it a "sin against nature" for a woman to preach (ibid., 291). Some lower-class churches, such as Methodists, African Methodists, Freewill Baptists, and Christian Connectionists, encouraged women to pray and testify and even allowed them to "exhort" and preach. Yet, all the churches held that there was no biblical precedent for women "ruling" as the ordained pastor over a congregation (See ibid., pp. 7, 133, 153, 411). By the 1830s, however, many Methodists were upwardly mobile and becoming socially respectable. While the denomination still professed that a woman could have an "extraordinary call" to preach, many members were skeptical about anyone who actually claimed such a call. The congregation into which Ellen Harmon was baptized, the Chestnut Street Methodist Church in Portland, was the largest Methodist church in the state of Maine and may have been tending toward the upper-class culture. The rise of secular feminism in 1848 triggered a backlash by the churches, which passed "a flurry of resolutions" limiting women's participation in public worship. Many churches voted absolute prohibitions against any female participation in public worship, not even "praying aloud" (ibid., p. 281).

⁵⁷ Her reticence was not uncommon. The most prominent male leaders among the Millerites, including William Miller, Josiah Litch, and Charles Fitch, had each resisted the call of God for a time, and that was even before the 1844 disappointment. Ellen would later, at her visit to Poland, Maine, in early January 1845, learn from the lips of Hazen Foss, brother-in-law to her sister Mary Harmon Foss, that when he was told to relate a vision he received, his fear of social ostracism was so great that he had wished himself dead. Cf. 1 Bio 66, 67.

⁵⁸ It was at this meeting that Ellen had a conversation with *Hazen Foss who told her he had received a visioon identical to hers but had refused to tell it. After several repetitions of the vision and his repeated refusals to tell others what he had seen, God told him it was taken from him and given to "the weakest of the weak," apparently referring to Ellen Harmon. See 1Bio 66.

⁵⁹ For more biographical information on JW, see: JW, Life Incidents; idem, Life Sketches; Uriah Smith et al., In Memoriam: A Sketch of the Last Sickness and Death of Elder James White, Who Died at Battle Creek, Michigan, Aug. 6, 1881, Together With the Discourse at His Funeral (Battle Creek, Mich.: Review and Herald Press, 1881); Margaret Rossiter Thiele, By Saddle and Sleigh: A Story of James White's Youth (RHPA, 1965); Virgil E. Robinson, James White (RHPA, 1976); Andrew Gordon Mustard, James White and SDA Organization: Historical Development, 1844-1881, Andrews University Seminary Doctoral Dissertation Series (AUP, 1988), vol. 12; Gerald Wheeler, James White: Innovator and Overcomer (RHPA, 2003).

⁶⁰ JW, Life Incidents, pp. 104, 107, 157, 181.

⁶¹ Otis Nichols to William Miller, Apr. 20, 1846, EGWE; cf. 1Bio 74, 75; 2SG 38.

⁶² The laws of Maine made each town responsible for any poor within its borders; so people who refused to work were a genuine threat to the local economy. Their "inconsistent, fanatical course caused unbelievers to hate them" and brought "disrepute" on all "who bore the Advent name" (Lt 2, 1874).

⁶³ In reporting this some years later, James added, "We state the fact as it existed without pleading the correctness of the position." See LS80 126.

⁶⁴ Joseph Bates, The Seventh Day Sabbath: A Perpetual Sign From the Beginning to the Entering Into the Gates of the Holy City According to the Commandment (New Bedford, Mass.: Benjamin Lindsey, 1846). Sabbath controversies among Protestants in England, beginning in 1595, led to the emergence of Seventh Day Baptists as a distinct denomination in the 1650s. By the 1840s Seventh Day Baptists had already been keeping this true Sabbath for two centuries. Some Millerites began to observe it in 1844, though it was not accepted by the majority. See Don A. Sanford, A Choosing People: The History of Seventh Day Baptists (Nashville: Broadman, 1992), pp. 45-57.

⁶⁵ JNL, The Great Second Advent Movement: Its Rise and Progress (RHPA, 1905), p. 258; cf. 1Bio 113, 114.

⁶⁶ Knight, Meeting Ellen White, p. 25; Knight, Joseph Bates: The Real Founder of Seventh-day Adventism (RHPA, 2004), pp. 99, 100.

[67] Knight, *Joseph Bates*, pp. 102, 103, 110-117.

[68] William Miller, *Apology and Defence* (Boston: J. V. Himes, 1845), pp. 11, 12.

[69] Sanford, *A Choosing People: The History of Seventh Day Baptists*, pp. 44, 57-64.

[70] LeRoy Edwin Froom, *The Conditionalist Faith of Our Fathers* (RHPA, 1965-1966), vol. 1, pp. 17-25, 681-702.

[71] O.R.L. Crosier, "The Law of Moses," *Day-Star Extra*, Feb. 7, 1846.

[72] See article Three Angels' Messages.

[73] Merlin Burt, "The Historical Background, Interconnected Development, and Integration of the Doctrines of the Sanctuary, the Sabbath, and Ellen G. White's Role in Sabbatarian Adventism From 1844 to 1849" (Ph.D. diss., AU, 2002), pp. 325, 326, 352.

[74] In December 1850 she told friends how happy she was to see her oldest boy (Lt 30, 1850).

[75] Herbert E. Douglass, *Messenger of the Lord* (PPPA, 1998), pp. 26-28. See also Num. 24:2-4; Dan. 7:1, 10:7-11, 15-18; Eze. 8:1-4; Acts 9:3-7; 2 Cor. 12:2-4; Rev. 1:17.

[76] Cf. 1Bio 150, 151; Knight, *Meeting Ellen White*, pp. 51, 52.

[77] JW, *Hymns for God's Peculiar People, That Keep the Commandments of God and the Faith of Jesus* (Oswego, N.Y.: Richard Oliphant, 1849); JW, "Hymns for God's Peculiar People," *Present Truth,* December 1849.

[78] JW, "The Paper," *Present Truth,* December 1849; JW to Leonard Hastings, Jan. 3 and 10, 1849, EGWE; cf. 1Bio 171, 172.

[79] For reprints of the *Present Truth* and the *Advent Review,* see *Earliest Seventh-day Adventist Periodicals,* Adventist Classic Library (AUP, 2005). For reprints of other important Millerite and early Sabbatarian Adventist documents, see Knight, *1844 and the Rise of Sabbatarian Adventism.* See also, A. L. White, *Ellen White: Woman of Vision,* p. 53.

[80] Cf. Knight, *Meeting Ellen White*, p. 46.

[81] *Ibid.* Ellen White had a vision on church organization in September 1852. See EW 97-104. James White wrote several articles on that topic through the years. See JW, "Gospel Order," RH, Dec. 13, 1853; *idem*, "Gospel Order," RH, Dec. 20, 1853.

[82] JW, "This Sheet," RH Extra, July 21, 1851.

[83] Ellen G. White, *A Sketch of the Christian Experience and Views of Ellen G. White* (Saratoga Springs, N.Y.: JW, 1851).

[84] It was only when the Whites had moved to Rochester that they were able to bring Henry back to live with them. See JW, "Eastern Tour," RH, Nov. 1, 1853.

[85] Lumen V. Masten, "Experience of Bro. Masten," RH, Sept. 30, 1852; "Obituary," RH, Mar. 14, 1854; cf. Paul A. Gordon and James R. Nix, *Laughter and Tears of the Pioneers* (Silver Spring, Md.: Adventist Heritage Ministry, 2001), pp. 17-19.

[86] For the relationship between Ellen White and W. C. White during his childhood years, see Jerry Allen Moon, *W. C. White and Ellen G. White: The Relationship Between the Prophet and Her Son,* Andrews University Seminary Doctoral Dissertation Series (AUP, 1993), vol. 19, pp. 1-4, 34-47.

[87] A. L. White, *Ellen White: Woman of Vision,* pp. 61, 72; cf. Joseph Bates, J. H. Waggoner, and M. E. Cornell, "Address of the Conference Assembled at Battle Creek, Mich., Nov. 16th, 1855," RH, Dec. 4, 1855.

[88] JW, "A Test," RH, Oct. 16, 1855; Bates, Waggoner, and Cornell; JW, "The Testimony of Jesus," RH, Dec. 18, 1855; EGW, "Communication From Sister White," RH, Jan. 10, 1856.

[89] Throughout the years she added many more "testimonies." By 1909 they had accumulated to nine volumes, with almost 5,000 total pages.

[90] JW, "Spiritual Gifts," RH, Sept. 9, 1858. The subtitle of the book is reminiscent of H. L. Hastings' *The Great Controversy Between God and Man: Its Origin, Progress, and Termination* (Rochester, N.Y.: the author, 1858), but a comparison of the two books shows that the approach and the breadth of coverage are very different. Cf. Uriah Smith, "Book Notice: The Great Controversy Between God and Man," RH, Mar. 18, 1858.

[91] A. L. White, *Ellen G. White: Woman of Vision*, p. 68.

[92] JW, "General Conference," RH, Apr. 21, 1859; Joseph Bates and Uriah Smith, "Business Proceedings of the General Conference of June 3-6, 1859," RH, June 9, 1859, 20; cf. A. L. White, *Ellen White: Woman of Vision,* pp. 68-70.

[93] Knight, *Meeting Ellen White*, p. 46.

[94] JW, "Borrowed Money," RH, Feb. 23, 1860.

[95] R. F. Cottrell, "Making Us a Name," RH, Mar. 22, 1860; Joseph Bates and Uriah Smith, "Business Proceedings of B.C. Conference," RH, Oct. 9, 1860; Joseph Bates and Uriah Smith, "Business Proceedings of B.C. Conference," RH, Oct. 16, 1860; Joseph Bates and Uriah Smith, "Business Proceedings of B.C. Conference," RH, Oct. 23, 1860; cf. A. L. White, *Ellen White: Woman of Vision,* pp. 75, 76.

[96] John Herbert White was born September 20 and died December 14, 1860.

[97] JW to EGW, Nov. 4, 1860, EGWE.

[98] Cf. "It's a Boy!" AR, Oct. 21, 2010.

[99] Quoted in JNL, "The Study of the Testimonies—No. 4," GCDB, Feb. 1, 1893. As the war progressed, Ellen had further visions on it. See 1T 253-268, 355-368.

[100] JNL, "The Study of the Testimonies—No. 4," p. 61. See also A. L. White, *Ellen White: Woman of Vision*, pp. 86, 87.

[101] JW, "Michigan General Conference," RH, Oct. 8, 1861; Joseph Bates and Uriah Smith, "Doings of the Battle Creek Conference, Oct. 5 and 6, 1861," RH, Oct. 8, 1861; cf. A. L. White, *Ellen White: Woman of Vision*, pp. 81-83.

[102] A. L. White, *Ellen White: Woman of Vision*, pp. 83-85.

[103] Cf. SHM 75-85.

[104] Knight, *Meeting Ellen White*, p. 48.

[105] J. H. Waggoner, "Present Truth," RH, Aug. 7, 1866.

[106] Knight, *Walking With Ellen White*, pp. 83, 84. See also AY 28.

[107] Adelia P. Patten, "Brief Narrative of the Life, Experience, and Last Sickness of Henry N. White," in AY 16, 24.

[108] JW, "The Nation," RH, Aug. 12, 1862; JW, "To Correspondents," RH, Sept. 9, 1862; JW, "Our Duty in Reference to the War," RH, Sept. 16, 1862; J. H. Waggoner, "Our Duty and the Nation," RH, Sept. 23, 1862; R. F. Cottrell, "Non-resistance," RH, Oct. 14, 1862; B. F. Snook, "The War and Our Duty," RH, Oct. 14, 1862; JW, "The War Question," RH, Oct. 14, 1862; M. E. Cornell, "Extremes," RH, Oct. 21, 1862; Henry E. Carver, "The War," RH, Oct. 21, 1862; JW, "Letter to Bro. Carver," RH, Oct. 21, 1862.

[109] RH, Jan. 6, 1863, published in 1T 355-368.

[110] *The Views of Seventh-day Adventists Relative to Bearing Arms, Together With the Opinion of the Governor of Michigan and a Portion of the Enrollment Law* (Battle Creek, Mich.: Steam Press, 1864); *Compilation of Extracts From the Publications of Seventh-day Adventists, Setting Forth Their Views of the Sinfulness of War, Referred to in the Annexed Affidavits* (Battle Creek, Mich.: Steam Press, 1865); cf. WCW, "Sketches and Memories of James and Ellen G. White: XXXVIII—The Civil War Crisis," RH, Nov. 26, 1936; Francis M. Wilcox, *Seventh-day Adventists in Time of War* (Washington, D.C.: RHPA, 1936); "Chronology of Establishment of Noncombatancy by Seventh-day Adventists—1860-1865" (n.p., n.d.), EGWE; WCW, "The Civil War Crisis" (n.p., [1936]), EGWE; WCW, D. E. Robinson, and Arthur L. White, "The Spirit of Prophecy and Military Service" (Washington, D.C.: Ellen G. White Publications, June 15, 1956); Roger Guion Davis, "Conscientious Cooperators: The Seventh-day Adventists and Military Service, 1860-1945" (Ph.D. diss., George Washington University, 1970), pp. 45-100; Ron Graybill, "This Perplexing War: Why Adventists Avoided Military Service in the Civil War," Insight, Oct. 10, 1978; Wheeler, pp. 143-146; Douglas Morgan, ed., *The Peacemaking Remnant: Essays and Historical Documents* (Silver Spring, Md.: Adventist Peace Fellowship, 2005), pp. 93-98.

[111] Knight, *Walking With Ellen White*, p. 79.

[112] In *ibid.*, p. 119.

[113] WCW, "Sketches and Memories of James and Ellen G. White: XXXII—Jottings From Ellen G. White's Diary of 1859," RH, Feb. 27, 1936.

[114] Knight, *Walking With Ellen White*, p. 79.

[115] Cf. *ibid.*, p. 84.

[116] Cf. *ibid.*, p. 85.

[117] One example of James White's harsh treatment of his older surviving son occurred in 1880 when James, under the effects of his illness, removed Edson from a leadership position at the Pacific Press Publishing Association, replacing him with his younger brother Willie. See Lt 391, 1906.

[118] Knight, *Walking With Ellen White*, p. 85.

[119] JW, *Health: or How to Live* (Battle Creek, Mich.: Steam Press of the Seventh-day Adventist Pub. Assn., 1865), no. 1, p. 12.

[120] A. L. White, *Ellen White: Woman of Vision*, pp. 106, 108.

[121] JW, ed., *Health: or How to Live* (Battle Creek, Mich.: Steam Press of the Seventh-day Adventist Pub. Assn., 1865). The six pamphlets were probably published between the end of February and the end of July, and as a bound copy they totaled about 400 pages. See Isaac D. Van Horn and Dudley M. Canright, "Idolatry," RH, Mar. 7, 1865; Harriet I. Wescott, "From Sister Wescott," RH, May 16, 1865; Daniel T. Bourdeau, "How to Live," RH, Aug. 8, 1865.

[122] Knight, *Meeting Ellen White*, p. 51. Several scholars have pointed out that although some of the principles and methods suggested by Ellen White are also found in the writings of her contemporary health reformers, it is a masterly performance to select only the right principles from the overall mass of erroneous concepts of her contemporaries. See George W. Reid, "The Foundations and Early Development of the Health Emphasis Among Seventh-day Adventists" (Th.D. diss., Southwestern Baptist Theological Seminary, 1976), pp. 202-240; Robert D. Fetrick, "Erroneous Health Concepts of Health Reformers Contemporary With Ellen G. White" (term paper, AU, 1977); Don S. McMahon, *Acquired or Inspired? Exploring the Origins of the Adventist Lifestyle* (Warburton, Australia: Signs of the Times, 2005); *idem*, "The Nature of Inspiration in the Health Writings of Ellen White," *Ellen White and Current Issues Symposium* 4 (2008): 5-37.

[123] SHM 112-130, 441-445.

[124] Knight, *Walking With Ellen White*, p. 37.

[125] See Gordon and Nix, p. 54; Knight, *Walking With Ellen White*, p. 37.

[126] In Gordon and Nix, p. 54. She wrote later: "I use some salt, and always have, because from the light given me by God, this article, in the place of being deleterious, is actually essential for the blood. The whys and wherefores of this I know not, but I give you the instruction as it is given me" (Lt 37, 1901, in 12MR 173).

[127] Knight, *Walking With Ellen White*, pp. 37-39.

[128] Cf. Knight, *Meeting Ellen White*, p. 50.

[129] Knight, *Meeting Ellen White*, p. 49.

[130] V. E. Robinson, *James White*, pp. 169-171, 174.

[131] Knight, *Meeting Ellen White*, p. 50.

[132] In Gordon and Nix, pp. 41, 42.

[133] Cf. V. E. Robinson, p. 177; 2Bio 158, 159, 172; Knight, *Walking With Ellen White*, pp. 38-40.

[134] Moon, p. 10.

[135] JW, "Brief Summary of Labors," RH, Jan. 14, 1868.

[136] Quoted in Richard J. Hammond, "The Life and Work of Uriah Smith" (M.A. thesis, Seventh-day Adventist Theological Seminary, 1944), p. 44; Gordon and Nix, pp. 13, 14.

[137] WCW, "Trip to California," YI, October 1872.

[138] This volume was the forerunner of the 1890 book *Patriarchs and Prophets*.

[139] Cf. Knight, *Walking With Ellen White*, p. 86.

[140] V. E. Robinson, p. 232; General Conference Committee, "Appointments: Camp-Meetings," RH, July 19, 1870.

[141] WCW, "Trip to California," YI, October 1872; cf. Moon, pp. 13, 14.

[142] WCW, "Trip to California—No. 5," YI, March 1873; cf. Knight, *Walking With Ellen White*, pp. 26-29.

[143] Republished in 3T 131-160; CE 5-23. See also YI, Apr. 23, 1879; RH, July 14, 1885.

[144] Knight, *Meeting Ellen White*, p. 56; cf. Floyd Greenleaf, *In Passion for the World: A History of Seventh-day Adventist Education* (PPPA, 2005), pp. 21-24.

[145] V. E. Robinson, p. 241.

[146] See also 2Bio 405, 406; Roger W. Coon, *Ellen White and Vegetarianism: Did She Practice What She Preached?* (PPPA, 1986).

[147] Cf. Knight, *Meeting Ellen White*, pp. 52, 53.

[148] Cf. WCW to JW, EGW, Mar. 10, 1874, EGWE; Moon, p. 21.

[149] Greenleaf, pp. 24-26.

[150] *Ibid.*, p. 27.

[151] A. L. White, *Ellen White: Woman of Vision*, pp. 157, 158.

[152] WCW, "A Comprehensive Vision—II: Sketches and Memories of James and Ellen G. White," RH, Feb. 17, 1938.

[153] See 2Bio 443.

[154] Knight, *Walking With Ellen White*, p. 73.

[155] *Ibid.*, p. 74; cf. Gordon and Nix, pp. 46, 47.

[156] The second volume of *The Spirit of Prophecy* and the first half of the third volume were forerunners of the later book on Christ's life with the title *The Desire of Ages* (1898). The second part of the third volume formed the basis for the book *Acts of the Apostles* (1911).

[157] Cf. A. L. White, *Ellen White: Woman of Vision*, pp. 183-185; 3Bio 35-38; DG 233, 234, 260-275.

[158] Gordon and Nix, pp. 9, 10.

[159] Haverhill *Daily Bulletin*, Aug. 27, 1877, quoted in 3Bio 67; Knight, *Walking With Ellen White*, p. 129.

[160] During this trip it became apparent that Ellen White loved the sea, the waves, the wind, etc. See Knight, *Walking With Ellen White*, pp. 29, 30. On her visits in the northwest, see also Doug R. Johnson, *Adventism in the Northwestern Frontier* (Berrien Springs, Mich.: Oronoko Books, 1996), pp. 37-45.

[161] JW, "The Third Angel's Message," PT, April 1850; *idem, Life Incidents*, p. 354; *idem, The Law and the Gospel: A Treatise on the Relation Existing Between the Two Dispensations* (London: International Tract Society, n.d.), p. 11.

[162] See, for example, EGW, *Redemption* (Battle Creek, Mich.: Steam Press of the Seventh-day Adventist Pub. Assn., 1877-1878); see also Knight, *Joseph Bates*, pp. 83-88.

[163] Knight, *Walking With Ellen White*, p. 24.

[164] A. L. White, *Ellen White: Woman of Vision*, pp. 187-190.

[165] Gordon and Nix, p. 32; cf. JW and Uriah Smith, "The Dime Tabernacle," RH, July 11, 1878, quoted in 3Bio 91.

[166] Uriah Smith, "The Don't-Believes," RH, Apr. 3, 1879.

[167] WCW to EGW, Sept. 29, 1894, EGWE; WCW to James Edson White, Feb. 15, 1921, CAR.

[168] Moon, pp. 28-31.

[169] The original document is no longer extant, but Authur L. White believed that the dream mentioned above formed the content of those pages. See 3Bio 161, 162, 165, 167.

[170] Uriah Smith, "Meetings in Battle Creek," RH, July 19, 1881, pp. 56, 57; cf. Moon, p. 30.

[171] Cf. Moon, p. 31.

[172] James Edson White to WCW, Aug. 4, 1881, cited in V. E. Robinson, p. 297; John Harvey Kellogg, "Dr. J. H. Kellogg's Statement," in Uriah Smith et al., *In Memoriam: A Sketch of the Last Sickness and Death of Elder James White*, pp. 17-20; cf. Knight, *Walking With Ellen White*, pp. 77, 109, 110; idem, *Meeting Ellen White*, p. 60.

[173] Smith et al., *In Memoriam*, p. 21.

[174] Mary K. White to WCW, Aug. 27, 1881, EGWE.

[175] Quoted in Knight, *Walking With Ellen White*, p. 77.

[176] Quoted in *ibid.*

[177] Knight, *Meeting Ellen White*, p. 78.

[178] WCW, "Mrs. White's Healing at Healdsburg" (unpublished manuscript), EGWE; [J. H. Waggoner], "California Camp-Meeting," ST, Oct. 26, 1882; Uriah Smith, "Editorial Correspondence," RH, Oct. 31, 1882; cf. Moon, p. 72.

[179] See, for example, WCW to EGW, Jan. 12, 1885; idem to Mary K. White, Jan. 17, 1885; Lt 2, 1889); all at the EGWE; cf. Knight, *Meeting Ellen White*, p. 78.

[180] Knight, *Meeting Ellen White*, p. 56; Emmett K. Vande Vere, *The Wisdom Seekers*, (SPA, 1972), p. 42.

[181] A. B. Oyen and GIB, "S. D. A. Educational Society," RH, Jan. 2, 1883.

[182] Knight, *Meeting Ellen White*, p. 57.

[183] GIB, RH Supplement, Aug. 14, 1883; cf. Knight, *Meeting Ellen White*, p. 37; idem, *Walking With Ellen White*, p. 47.

[184] The addresses were published in the *Review and Herald* from March 4 through July 22, 1884 (not every issue), and later excerpted in 1SM 350-354 and FW 35-39.

[185] Merlin D. Burt, "Ellen White's Passion for Jesus and Scripture" (paper presented at the Oregon Conference Convocation, 2010), pp. 8, 9, CAR.

[186] GIB and A. B. Oyen, "General Conference Proceedings," RH, Nov. 27, 1883; *The Seventh-day Adventist Yearbook 1884, Containing Statistics of the General Conference and Other Organizations of the Denomination, With the Business Proceedings of the Anniversary Meetings Held at Battle Creek, Michigan, Nov. 8-20, 1883* (Battle Creek, Mich.: Seventh-day Adventist Pub. Assn., 1884), p. 43; cf. Knight, *Meeting Ellen White*, pp. 40, 41.

[187] GIB and A. B. Oyen, "European Council of Seventh-day Adventists—Second Session," RH, June 24, 1884; HS 113. For more information on the time Ellen White spent in Europe see Lewis H. Christian, *Pioneers and Builders of the Advent Cause in Europe* (PPPA, 1937), pp. 37-45; EGWEur; 3Bio 287-373; Pierre Winandy, ed., *Centennial Symposium: Ellen G. White and Europe, 1885/1887-1987* (Bracknell, Eng.: EGWRC-AV, 1987); Moon, pp. 75-78; Thomas Eißner, "Der Heilige Geist wird Einheit schaffen: Der Besuch von Ellen G. White in Europa," *AdventEcho*, March 2009.

[188] B. L. Whitney, A. C. Bourdeau, and D. T. Bourdeau, "To the Brethren Assembled in General Conference at Battle Creek, Mich., Oct. 30, 1884," RH, Nov. 11, 1884.

[189] Robert W. Olson, "Ellen White Goes to Europe," in Pierre Winandy, ed., *Centennial Symposium: Ellen G. White and Europe, 1885/1887-1987*, pp. 1, 2; Knight, *Walking With Ellen White*, p. 121.

[190] Knight, *Walking With Ellen White*, p. 120; Olson, p. 3.

[191] Olson, pp. 3, 4.

[192] On the history of Seventh-day Adventism in Switzerland see, for example, A. Buser-Wyss et al., *Chronik zum Andenken an das Wirken der Pioniere des Adventwerkes in Basel* (Basel, Switz.: E. and C. Spittler, 1964); Jean R. Zürcher and Robert W. Olson, *Ellen G. White in der Schweiz, 1885-1887* (Krattigen, Switz.: Advent-Verlag, n.d.); Karl Waber, *Streiflichter aus der Geschichte der Siebenten-Tags-Adventisten in der Schweiz* (Krattigen, Switz.: Advent-Verlag, 1995, 1999). For more information on the development of the Adventist Church in the Scandinavian countries, see Ragnar Svenson, *Stockholms Adventist församling 90 år jubileumsskrift* (Gävle, Sweden: Skandinaviska Bokförlagets Tryckeri, 1974); Hans Jørgen Schantz, *Ellen G. White i Danmark: En beskrivelse af Ellen Gould Whites tre besøg i Danmark, 1885-1887, og deres betydning* (Odense, Den.: Dansk Bogforlag, 1987); Bjorgvin Martin Hjelvik Snorrason, "The Origin, Development, and History of the Norwegian Seventh-day Adventist Church From the 1840s to 1889" (Ph.D. diss., AU 2010).

[193] She visited Torre Pellice, Villar Pellice, Luserna San Giovanni, Angrogna, San Germano Chisone, Bobbio, Turin, and Milan. See EGWEur 13, 14. For more information on Seventh-day Adventism in Italy, see Giuseppe de Meo, *Granel di sale: Un secolo di storia della Chiesa Cristiana Avventista del 7° Giorno in Italia (1864-1964)* (Turin, Italy: Editrice Claudiana, 1980); Ignazio Barbuscia, *Organizzazione della Chiesa Cristiana Avventista Italiana: Cenni storici, delibere, statistiche, progetti* (Rome: the author, 1984).

[194] For more information on the history of the Adventist Church in France and Germany, see Claude Hutin, *Les origines du mouvement Adventiste en France* (jusqu'en 1920-1921) (Collonges-sous-Salève, France: Séminaire Adventiste du Salève, 1966); Miroslav M. Kis, "Beginnings of Seventh-day Adventism in France, 1884-1901" (research paper, AU, 1975); Gerhard Padderatz, *Conradi und Hamburg: Die Anfänge der deutschen Adventgemeinde (1889 bis 1914) unter besonderer Berücksichtigung der organisatorischen, finanziellen und sozialen Aspekte* (Kiel, Germany: the author, 1978); Baldur E. Pfeiffer, *Die Siebenten-Tags-Adventisten in Deutschland: Bilddokumentation* (Hamburg: Advent-Verlag, 1989); Johannes Hartlapp, *Siebenten-Tags-Adventisten im Nationalsozialismus: Unter Berücksichtigung der geschichtlichen und theologischen Entwicklung*

in Deutschland von 1875 bis 1950, Kirche—Konfession—Religion (Göttingen, Germany: Vandenhoeck and Ruprecht, 2008), vol. 53. Quite a number of studies have been done on Seventh-day Adventists in the Third Reich (1933-1945) that are not listed here.

[195] It was translated into Danish, Swedish, and German. See EGW, *Den store Strid mellem Kristus og Satan: i den kristne tidsalder* (Battle Creek, Mich.: Internationale Traktatforening, 1890); *idem, Den Stora Striden mellan Kristus och Satan: i den Kristna Tidsåldern* (Stockholm: Skandinaviska Förlagsexpeditionen, 1896); *idem, Licht und Finsternis: oder, Der grosse Streit zwischen Christo und Satan wahrend des christlichen Zeitalters*, 1st ed. (Basel, Switz.: Internationale Traktat-Gesellschaft, 1890).

[196] Cf. Eißner, pp. 27, 28.

[197] Dudley M. Canright, who was involved in that conflict and became an early casualty of it, mentioned it in his *Seventh-day Adventism Renounced: After an Experience of Twenty-eight Years by a Prominent Minister and Writer of That Faith* (Kalamazoo, Mich.: Kalamazoo Publishing, 1888), p. 156.

[198] Knight, *Joseph Bates*, pp. 86, 87.

[199] GIB, *The Law in the Book of Galatians: Is it the Moral Law, or Does it Refer to That System of Laws Peculiarly Jewish?* (Battle Creek, Mich.: RHPA, 1886), p. 78; E. J. Waggoner, *The Gospel in the Book of Galatians: A Review* (Oakland, Calif.: n.p., 1888), p. 71. See also Knight, *Meeting Ellen White*, pp. 62-64.

[200] Knight, *Meeting Ellen White*, p. 65.

[201] Knight, *Walking With Ellen White*, pp. 64, 65.

[202] Cf. Knight, *Walking With Ellen White*, pp. 133-135; Burt, "Ellen White's Passion for Jesus and Scripture," p. 10.

[203] Knight, *Walking With Ellen White*, p. 135.

[204] Cf. *ibid.*, p. 121.

[205] *Seventh-day Adventist Yearbook 1892* (Battle Creek, Mich.: Review and Herald Pub. Co., 1892), p. 79.

[206] Alwyn Fraser, "The Australian 1890s," in *The World of Ellen G. White*, ed. Gary Land, pp. 227-230.

[207] O. A. Olsen to C. H. Jones, Sept. 11, 1893; *idem* to S. N. Haskell, Dec. 11, 1895; *idem* to W. W. Prescott, Aug. 31, 1896; all from GCAr.

[208] For more information on the history of the Adventist Church in Australia and New Zealand, see Milton F. Krause, "The Seventh-day Adventist Church in Australia, 1885-1900" (M.A. thesis, Univ. of Sydney, 1968); Sydney Goldstone Ross, *The Angel Said Australia* (Warburton, Australia: Signs Publishing, 1980); *Symposium on Adventist History in the South Pacific, 1885-1918*, ed. Arthur J. Ferch (Wahroonga, Australia: South Pacific Division of Seventh-day Adventists, 1986); Milton Raymond Hook, *Entry Into the Australian Colonies: Beginnings of Adventism in Australia*, Seventh-day Adventist Heritage Series, no. 2 (Wahroonga, Australia: South Pacific Division Department of Education, n.d.); *idem, Church in a Convict Gaol: Early Adventism on Norfolk Island*, Seventh-day Adventist Heritage Series, no. 9 (Wahroonga, Australia: South Pacific Division Department of Education, n.d.).

[209] G. C. Tenney and G. Foster, "Minutes of the S.D.A. Conference," BE, Jan. 15, 1892.

[210] WCW, "From Melbourne to Napier," BE, May 1, 1892; WCW to O. A. Olsen, July 9, 1893, CAR; Gary Krause, "White, Ellen Gould (1827-1915)," in *Australian Dictionary of Biography* (Melbourne, Australia: Melbourne Univ. Press, 1990), vol. 12, pp. 465, 466.

[211] Quoted in Knight, *Walking With Ellen White*, p. 108.

[212] The book was published in early 1892. See "Book Notices: Steps to Christ," RH, Feb. 23, 1892; "[Advertisement:] Steps to Christ," *American Sentinel*, Mar. 3, 1892; "[Notice on Steps to Christ]," BE, Apr. 1, 1892.

[213] F. H. Revell held North American rights to *Steps to Christ*, but Ellen White reserved international rights. In 1893 the British Publishing House requested that she add one more chapter on the love of God, which she did. That chapter was translated and published in other European languages even before the next English edition came out. (See, for example, the Danish-Norwegian translation: *idem, Vejen til Kristus* [Kristiana, Norway: Den skandinaviske Forlags- og Trykkeriforening, 1895].) The next English edition was *Steps to Christ* (RHPA, 1896).

[214] T. C. Johnson, "Book Review: *Steps to Christ*, by Mrs. E. G. White," *Union Seminary Magazine* 4, no. 1 (1892): 148.

[215] Knight, *Walking With Ellen White*, p. 86.

[216] Quoted in *ibid.*, pp. 86, 87.

[217] James Edson White to EGW, Aug. 10, 1893, quoted in Knight, *Meeting Ellen White*, p. 69.

[218] EGW, "Our Duty to the Colored People," Mar. 20, 1891, published in SW 9-19.

[219] Knight, *Walking With Ellen White*, p. 88. For more information on his work in the South, see Clayton Robinson Pritchett, "James Edson White and the *Morning Star*" (research paper, AU, 1967); Ronald D. Graybill, *Mission to Black America: The True Story of Edson White and the Riverboat* Morning Star (Mountain View, Calif.: PPPA, 1971).

[220] James Edson White to WCW, Aug. 11, 1893, quoted in Knight, *Walking With Ellen White*, p. 87.

[221] James Edson White to WCW, Sept. 6, 1893, quoted in Knight, *Walking With Ellen White*, p. 87.

[222] Quoted in Knight, *Walking With Ellen White*, 88.

[223] *Ibid.*

[224] The information in this section is largely taken from Glen Baker, "Anna Phillips—A Second Prophet?" AR, Feb. 6, 1986; *idem*, "Anna Phillips—Not Another Prophet," AR, Feb. 20, 1986.

[225] See, for example, A. T. Jones to Anna C. Phillips, Jan. 3, 1894, cited in Baker, "Anna Phillips—A Second Prophet?"; "Sabbath, Jan. 27," RH, Jan. 30, 1894; "Sabbath, Feb. 3," RH, Feb. 6, 1894.

[226] See A. T. Jones to Anna C. Phillips, Jan. 3, 1894, cited in Baker, "Anna Phillips—A Second Prophet?"

[227] Lt 37, 1894, EGWE; O. A. Olsen to EGW, Mar. 29, 1894; F. M. Wilcox to Dan T. Jones, Feb. 27, 1894; S. N. Haskell to EGW, Mar. 9, 1894; *idem* to EGW, Mar. 31, 1894; all quoted in Baker, "Anna Phillips—Not Another Prophet."

[228] S. N. Haskell to EGW, Mar. 31, 1894, cited in Baker, "Anna Phillips—Not Another Prophet."

[229] Baker, "Anna Phillips—Not Another Prophet."

[230] WCW to James Edson White, Oct. 24, 1905, EGWE.

[231] WCW to James Edson White, June 17, 1894, Oct. 19, 1894, June 21, 1899, July 3, 1899, and Sept. 12 and 24, 1899, EGWE.

[232] Cf. Moon, p. 244.

[233] Cf. *ibid.*, pp. 244-246.

[234] WCW to James Edson White, Feb. 22, 1895, CAR.

[235] Cf. Moon, p. 168.

[236] WCW to Ella May White, May 13, 1895, EGWE; WCW to A. W. Semmens, Apr. 9, 1896, EGWE; Ed Christian, "Life With My Mother-in-law: An Interview With Ethel May Lacey White Currow," AR, July 7, 1983; cf. Knight, *Walking With Ellen White*, pp. 22, 90-93.

[237] For more information on the history of Avondale College, see Milton Raymond Hook, "The Avondale School and Adventist Educational Goals, 1894-1900" (Ed.D. diss., AU, 1978); Allan G. Lindsay, "The Influence of Ellen White Upon the Development of the Seventh-day Adventist School System in Australia, 1891-1900" (M.Ed. thesis, Univ. of Newcastle, 1978); Milton Raymond Hook, *Avondale: Experiment on the Dora* (Cooranbong, Australia: Avondale Academic Press, 1998); *idem, An Experiment at Cooranbong: Pioneering Avondale College*, Seventh-day Adventist Heritage Series, no. 12 (Wahroonga, Australia: South Pacific Division Department of Education, n.d.); Stephen J. Currow, *Revisioning Mission: Avondale's Greater Vision: Papers Presented at the 1999 A. H. Piper Memorial Conference* (Cooranbong, Australia: Avondale Academic Press, 2000).

[238] W. W. Prescott to O. A. Olsen, Oct. 13, 1895, GCAr, Silver Spring, Md.; WCW to O. A. Olsen, Sept. 27, 1894, EGWE.

[239] Vande Vere, pp. 21, 22; WCW to James and Ellen White, Jan. 1, 1873 [1874], EGWE; GIB, "Our New School Grounds," RH, Jan. 6, 1874.

[240] Cf. Moon, pp. 200-202.

[241] WCW to James Edson White, Aug. 3, 1895, EGWE; L. J. Rousseau to All Our Brethren in New Zealand and Australia, Feb. 25, 1895, CAR.

[242] Knight, *Walking With Ellen White*, pp. 53-58.

[243] Knight, *Meeting Ellen White*, p. 66.

[244] WCW to C. M. Christiansen, Sept. 25, 1899, quoted in Knight, *Meeting Ellen White*, p. 67.

[245] Burt, "Ellen White's Passion for Jesus and Scripture," pp. 9, 10.

[246] EGW, Interview with C. C. Crisler, July 21, 1914, EGWE.

[247] Knight, *Walking With Ellen White*, p. 98.

[248] See Denis Kaiser, "The Reception of Ellen G. White's Trinitarian Statements by Her Contemporaries, 1897-1915," AUSS 50 (Spring 2012): 25-38.

[249] WCW to G. A. Irwin, July 17, 1900, EGWE.

[250] For some humorous experiences on the journey from Australia to California, see Gordon and Nix, p. 44; Knight, *Walking With Ellen White*, p. 20.

[251] R. M. Pratt, "Specifications of Labor and Material Required for the Erection and Completion of Frame Building for W. C. White" [July 14, 1901], EGWE; WCW to Mr. E. Jeffreys, timber merchant, July 14, 1901, EGWE; cf. Knight, *Walking With Ellen White*, p. 33.

[252] Cf. Knight, *Meeting Ellen White*, p. 70.

[253] Cf. AGD, "A Brief Glance at the Work of Reorganization," GCB, Third Quarter, 1901, 513.

[254] Cf. Knight, *Meeting Ellen White*, pp. 70, 71.

[255] Cf. Gordon and Nix, p. 26. The college was relocated to Berrien Springs, Michigan, in the summer of 1901 and renamed Emmanuel Missionary College. In 1959 it became Andrews University.

[256] AGD to WCW, Oct. 8, 1912, EGWE; Milton R. Hook, "The Interrelationships Between A. G. Daniells and E. G. White During Their Years in Australasia," in *Symposium on Adventist History in the South Pacific, 1885-1918*, pp. 94, 95, 98, 103; John J. Robertson, "Arthur Grosvenor Daniells: The Effect of Australasia Upon the Man and His Work as Revealed Through Correspondence With W. C. White and Ellen G. White" (M.A. thesis, AU, 1966), pp. 91, 113-115, 125; cf. Gilbert M. Valentine, "AGD, Administrator, and the Development of Conference Organization in Australia," in *Symposium on Adventist History in the South Pacific, 1885-1918*, pp. 78, 79.

[257] Robertson, "Arthur Grosvenor Daniells," pp. 113, 114; AGD to WCW, June 25, 1908, EGWE.

[258] S.P.S. Edwards, "Story of a Meeting" (unpublished manuscript, n.d.), CAR; AGD to W. W. Prescott, Feb. 25, 1902, GCAr.

[259] J. H. Kellogg, "The Battle Creek Sanitarium Fire," RH, Feb. 25, 1902; AGD to WCW, Mar. 25, 1902, EGWE.

[260] AGD, "How the Denomination Was Saved From Pantheism" (unpublished manuscript, copy B, n.d.), p. 2, EGWE; idem to WCW, Mar. 25, 1902, CAR.

[261] AGD to J. H. Kellogg, Apr. 14, 1902, GCAr.

[262] Ibid.

[263] Leon A. Smith, "The Laying of the Cornerstone of the New Sanitarium," RH, May 20, 1902. Given mail time from California to Battle Creek, Kellogg probably did not receive Ellen White's letter until after his speech.

[264] GCC Min, Nov. 20, 1902, GCAr.

[265] GCC Min, Nov. 22, 1902, GCAr; AGD to G. A. Irwin, Dec. 12, 1902, GCAr.

[266] J. H. Kellogg to EGW, Dec. 31, 1902, CAR; quoted in Moon, p. 289.

[267] W. W. Prescott to AGD, Jan. 25 and 26, 1903, GCAr; J. H. Kellogg to GIB, Feb. 8, 1903, CAR; idem to WCW, Mar. 18, 1903, EGWE.

[268] WCW to AGD, Apr. 24, 1903, GCAr; idem to AGD, June 19, 1903, CAR.

[269] AGD to WCW, June 21, 1903, GCAr.

[270] WCW to Dear Brethren, June 27, 1903, EGWE.

[271] WCW to M. H. Brown, June 30, 1903, CAR.

[272] William W. Prescott to WCW, Aug. 6, 1903, GCAr.

[273] GCC Min, Oct. 7, 1903, GCAr; 5Bio 294.

[274] [W. W. Prescott], "The Council," RH, Oct. 22, 1903; AGD, The Abiding Gift of Prophecy (PPPA, 1936), pp. 336, 337.

[275] Ibid.; GCC Min, Oct. 14, 1903, 9:00 a.m., GCAr.

[276] David Paulson to Frank E. Belden, Dec. 7, 1913, EGWE-LLU; GCC Min, Oct. 18, 1903; J. H. Kellogg to Dear Friend and Colleague, Dec. 16, 1903, EGWE-LLU; I. H. Evans to AGD, Jan. 24, 1904, GCAr.

[277] AGD to WCW, Nov. 20, 1903, EGWE.

[278] WCW to Percy T. Magan, May 19, 1904; WCW to W. S. Sadler, July 13, 1906; both in EGWE; cf. George R. Knight, From 1888 to Apostasy: The Case of A. T. Jones (RHPA, 1987), pp. 212, 213.

[279] A. T. Jones to AGD, Jan. 27, 1905, GCAr.

[280] WCW to James Edson White, Mar. 30, 1904; idem to EGW, Apr. 12, 1904; idem and E. R. Palmer, "Minutes of Meeting Held in San Diego, Cal., April 12[-13], 1904"; all in EGWE.

[281] WCW to Friends at Home, June 10, 1904; idem to AGD, June 15, 1904; idem to George A. Hare, June 16, 1904; idem to AGD, July 3, 1904; idem to J. R. Scott, July 11, 1904; idem to AGD, Aug. 21, 1904; all in EGWE.

[282] WCW to GIB, Jan. 19, 1905; idem to EGW, Feb. 16 and 26, 1905; idem to Dearest May, Apr. 10, 1905; idem to EGW, Apr. 18, 1905; idem to T. H. Robinson, Apr. 23, 1905; idem to C. C. Crisler, Apr. 18, 1905; all in EGWE.

[283] WCW to C. W. Irwin, Sept. 19, 1905, EGWE.

[284] WCW to J. A. Burden, E. S. Ballenger, and G. A. Reaser, June 5, 1905; idem to L. F. Starr and J. E. Coloran, June 5, 1905; idem to James Edson White, June 25, 1905; idem to W. A. Reaser, June 25, 1905; idem to R. Eason, June 25, 1905; idem to T. J. Evans, June 30, 1905; idem to AGD, June 30, 1905; all in EGWE.

[285] Seventh-day Adventist Encyclopedia (1996), vol. 10, pp. 613-615, 940-954; vol. 11, pp. 299-301.

[286] J. T. Case and Roy V. Ashley, stenographers, "Interview at Dr. J. H. Kellogg's House, October 7, 1907, Between Geo. W. Amadon, Eld. A. C. Bordeau, and Dr. J. H. Kellogg," CAR; Richard W. Schwarz, ed., "Kellogg vs. the Brethren: His Last Interview as an Adventist—October 7, 1907," Spectrum 20, no. 3 (1990): 46-62; idem, "Kellogg Snaps, Crackles, and Pops: His Last Interview as an Adventist—Part 2," Spectrum 20, no. 4 (1990): 37-61; cf. Knight, Meeting Ellen White, pp. 71-73.

[287] See article Daily; see also [C. C. Crisler], "MS. K.: An Introductory Statement," GCAr.

[288] See article Blue Book. See also WCW, Diary, Jan. 27-Feb. 6, 1908; W. W. Prescott to WCW, Feb. 21, 1908; WCW to AGD and F. Griggs, Feb. 6, 1908; all in EGWE.

[289] "Delegates to the General Conference," GCB, May 14, 1909; AGD and W. A. Spicer, "General Conference Proceedings: First Meeting," GCB, May 14, 1909; Knight, Walking With Ellen White, p. 122.

[290] G. A. Irwin, "Introductory Statement," PUR, Feb. 3, 1910; J. A. Burden to EGW, Sept. 20, 1909, EGWE; idem to EGW, Oct. 4, 1909, EGWE.

[291] J. A. Burden to the Officers of the General Conference Committee, and the Secretaries of the Medical and Educational Departments, Oct. 15, 1909, EGWE; G. A. Irwin, "Introductory Statement," PUR, Feb. 3, 1910.

[292] Seventh-day Adventist Encyclopedia, vol. 10, pp. 940-954.

[293] WCW to Our General Missionary Agents, July 24, 1911, EGWE.

[294] W. W. Prescott to WCW, Apr. 26, 1910, EGWE; WCW to W. W. Prescott, May 30, 1910, EGWE; idem to AGD, June 20, 1910, EGWE; idem to AGD, Sept. 8, 1911, EGWE.

[295] WCW to Dear Brethren, Jan. 20, 1911, EGWE; idem to Our General Missionary Agents, July 24, 1911,

EGWE; *idem*, "*The Great Controversy—*1911 Edition: A Statement Made before the General Conference Council, October 30, 1911," quoted in 3SM 433, 444; cf. Moon, pp. 427-436.

[296] WCW to AGD, Aug. 15, 1912, EGWE.

[297] Moon, pp. 337, 342, 343.

[298] WCW to AGD, Aug. 4, 1914, EGWE; James Edson White to WCW, Apr. 13, 1914, EGWE; *idem* to WCW, May 14, 1914, EGWE; WCW to James Edson White, Dec. 15, 1914; C. C. Crisler to WCW, Dec. 23, 1914, EGWE. Ellen White wrote her last letter on June 14, 1914. See EGW to Sister, June 14, 1914 (Lt 2, 1914), EGWE.

[299] C. C. Crisler to WCW, Nov. 7, 1914, EGWE.

[300] C. C. Crisler to WCW, Nov. 22, 1914, EGWE.

[301] C. C. Crisler to WCW, Dec. 2, 1914, EGWE.

[302] C. C. Crisler to WCW, Nov. 23, Dec. 17 and 23, 1914, EGWE; *idem* to WCW, Jan. 5, 1915, EGWE; WCW to EGW, Jan. 10, 1915, EGWE.

[303] D. E. Robinson to S. N. and Hattie Haskell, Feb. 10, 1915, EGWE; WCW to Dear Friend, Feb. 15, 1915, EGWE.

[304] WCW to Dear Friend, Feb. 15, 1915; cf. Knight, *Meeting Ellen White*, p. 80.

[305] C. C. Crisler to W. L. Burgan, Apr. 29, 1915, EGWE; *idem* to C. H. Jones, June 6, 1915, EGWE.

[306] WCW to E. E. Andross, July 11, 1915, EGWE; *idem* to David Lacey, July 20, 1915, EGWE.

[307] WCW to David Lacey, July 20, 1915.

[308] Quoted in Richard A. Schaefer, *Legacy: Daring to Care* (Loma Linda, Calif.: Legacy Pub. Assn., 2005), p. 89. For reasons now unknown, her casket was not interred until Aug. 23, 1915.

[309] Knight, *Meeting Ellen White*, p. 59.

[310] Quoted in W. A. Spicer, *The Spirit of Prophecy in the Advent Movement* (Washington, D.C.: RHPA, 1937), p. 30; cf. EW 78; RH, Jan. 20, 1903; 2SM 30.

[311] Roger L. Dudley and Des Cummings, Jr., "Who Reads Ellen White?" *Ministry*, October 1982.

[312] The Barna Group, "Survey Reveals the Books and Authors That Have Most Influenced Pastors," May 30, 2005; www.barna.org/barna-update/article/5-barna-update/178. For the interest in Ellen White's writings in the Catholic community see, e.g., Beatrice Short Neall, "Mother, Ellen White, and the Priests," AR, Mar. 2, 1989.

[313] Irmgard Simon, *Die Gemeinschaft der Siebenten-Tags-Adventisten in volkskundlicher Sicht*, Schriften der Volkskundlichen Kommission des Landschaftsverbandes Westfalen-Lippe (Münster, Germany: Aschendorff, 1965), vol. 16, pp. 62, 63; cf. "The Story Behind This Research: An Interview With Warren L. Johns, Chief Counsel of the Office of General Counsel, General Conference of SDA," AR, Sept. 17, 1981.

THE EARLIEST KNOWN PHOTO OF
JAMES AND ELLEN WHITE, C. 1857

ONE OF THE EARLIEST PHOTOS OF JAMES AND ELLEN
WHITE, AND THEIR SON WILLIE, C. 1857

Ellen G. White, c. 1864

James and Ellen White in 1864

James and Ellen White with two of their
sons, Willie (left) and Edson, c. 1865

ELLEN G. WHITE IN 1872

ELLEN G. WHITE, C. 1875

ELLEN G. WHITE, C. 1875

ELLEN G. WHITE IN 1878

ELLEN G. WHITE, C. 1878

ELLEN G. WHITE, C. 1899

The White family, c. 1905. Left to right: standing, Ella White-Robinson, Dores Robinson, Wilfred Workman, Mabel White-Workman; seated, Ethel May Lacey-White, Ellen G. White, William C. White; seated on rug, J. Henry White, Evelyn Grace White, Herbert C. White.

Ellen White at Madison, Tennessee, in 1909, with the founders of the Madison school. Left to right, seated: W. C. White, Ellen G. White, Emma White, J. E. White; standing: C. C. Crisler, P. T. Magan, Minnie Hawkins, Nellie Druillard, E. A. Sutherland, Sara McEnterfer.

ELLEN WHITE ADDRESSING LOCAL CHURCH SCHOOL
CHILDREN, JUNE 15, 1913, SANITARIUM, CALIFORNIA;
ONE OF THE LAST PHOTOS OF ELLEN WHITE.

ELLEN WHITE WITH HER OFFICE AND HOUSEHOLD STAFF, 1913. LEFT TO RIGHT: SEATED,
DORES E. ROBINSON, RALPH W. MUNSON, ELLEN G. WHITE, WILLIAM C. WHITE,
CLARENCE C. CRISLER; STANDING: HAROLD BREE, MAGGIE HARE-BREE, MARY STEWARD,
PAUL MASON, ARTHUR W. SPALDING, HELEN GRAHAM, TESSIE WOODBURY,
ALFRED CARTER, MAY WALLING, EFFIE JAMES.

ELLEN G. WHITE WITH A GROUP OF ELMSHAVEN STAFF IN 1913. LEFT TO RIGHT: STANDING,
MAY WALLING, TESSIE WOODBURY, EFFIE JAMES, DORES E. ROBINSON, SARA MCENTERFER,
MARY STEWARD, MAGGIE HARE-BREE, MINNIE HAWKINS CRISLER, CLARENCE C. CRISLER; SEATED,
M. S. REPPE, O A. OLSEN, ELLEN G. WHITE, WILLIAM C. WHITE, A. BOETTCHER.

ELLEN WHITE WITH FAMILY AND OFFICE AND HOUSEHOLD STAFF AT ELMSHAVEN IN 1913.

THE WHITE FAMILY AT ELMSHAVEN IN 1913. LEFT TO RIGHT: STANDING, MABEL WHITE-WORKMAN, WILFRED WORKMAN, HENRY WHITE, HERBERT WHITE; SEATED, DORES ROBINSON, ELLA WHITE-ROBINSON, ELLEN G. WHITE, MAY WHITE, WILLIAM WHITE; SEATED ON GROUND, VIRGIL ROBINSON, MABEL ROBINSON, ARTHUR WHITE, GRACE WHITE.

MICHIGAN

LAKE MICHIGAN

LAKE HURON

CANADA

Bay City •

• Wright   • Greenville
• Coopersville
● Grand Rapids   Flint ●   • Lapeer

◉ Lansing

• Monterey   • Potterville   Tyrone
● Allegan   Plymouth •
                                            ● Detroit
Battle Creek
Kalamazoo   • Jackson
       • Parkville   • Sylvan
Berrien Springs   • Three Rivers   • Hillsdale
  ● Buchanan
                                    • Madrid   • West Bangor
                                  • Buck's Bridge

                                                    Vergennes

LAKE ONTARIO
                          • Adams Center   Dresden •

                                                        Hampton
                          Oswego •   • Boonville
              Dexterville • • Volney
                    Roosevelt • • West   ● Rome   Saratoga Sprin
Rochester ●   Monroe   ● Utica   Ballston Spa •
                    • Port Gibson   ● Syracuse
● Buffalo   Canandaigua •   • Brookfield

                    N E W   Y O R K   Albany ◉
Dansville •

Salamanca •

• Elmira

P E N N S Y L V A N I A

Bridgep

104

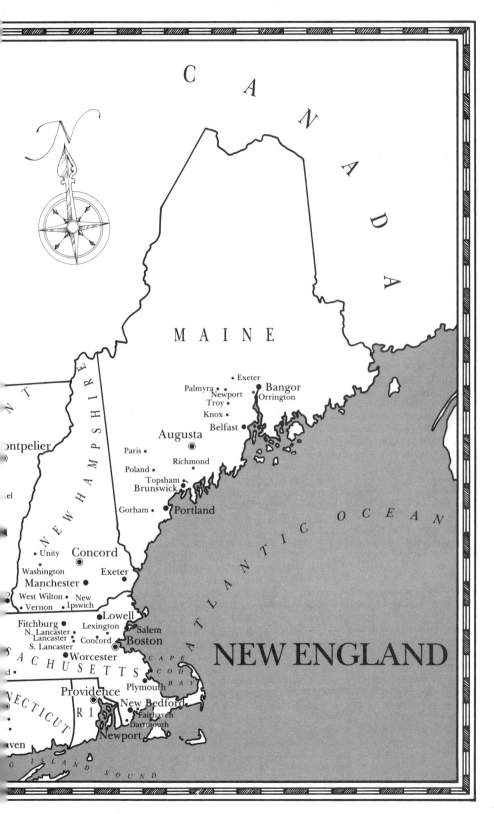

CANADA

MAINE

• Exeter
Palmyra • Newport   • Bangor
Troy •   Orrington
Knox •
Belfast •

Augusta ◉

Paris •
          Richmond
Poland •
       Topsham
       Brunswick •

Gorham • ● Portland

ATLANTIC OCEAN

• Unity Concord ◉
Washington •
Manchester ●   Exeter •
West Wilton • New •
• Vernon Ipswich •
         Lowell ●
Fitchburg ● Lexington • Salem
N. Lancaster •   Concord • Boston
S. Lancaster •
● Worcester

NEW ENGLAND

ASSACHUSETTS

CAPE
COD
BAY

Providence ◉   Plymouth •

NECTICUT R I New Bedford
                • Fairhaven
              • Dartmouth
aven   Newport •

G ISLAND SOUND

ontpelier

NEW HAMPSHIRE

105

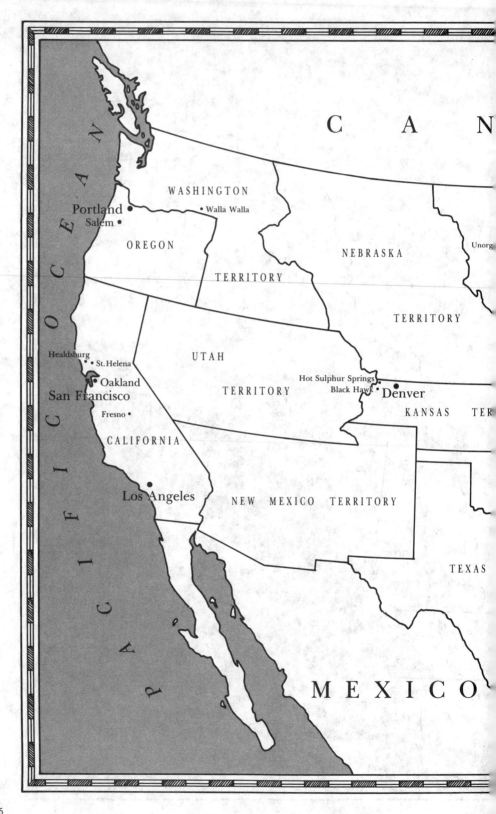

THE
UNITED STATES
IN
1860

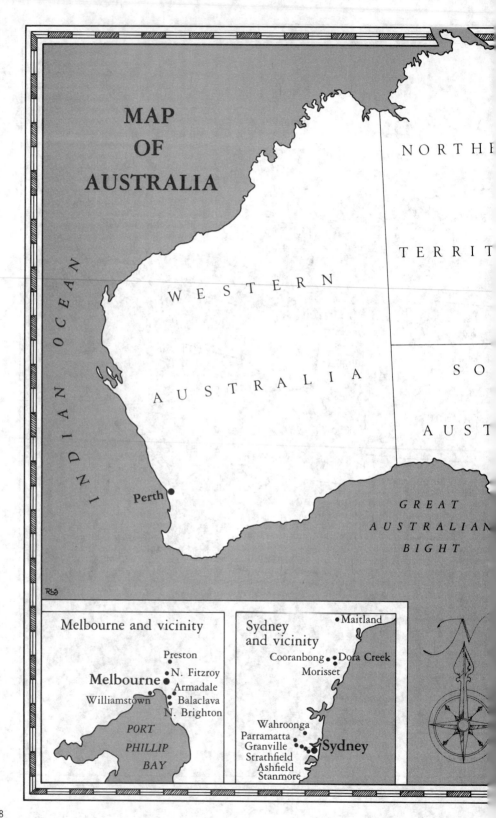

MAP
OF
AUSTRALIA

INDIAN OCEAN

NORTHE

TERRIT

WESTERN

AUSTRALIA

SO

AUST

Perth

*GREAT
AUSTRALIAN
BIGHT*

RbS

Melbourne and vicinity

Preston

N. Fitzroy

Melbourne

Armadale

Williamstown

Balaclava

N. Brighton

*PORT
PHILLIP
BAY*

Sydney
and vicinity

• Maitland

Cooranbong •• Dora Creek

Morisset

Wahroonga
Parramatta
Granville
Strathfield
Ashfield
Stanmore

Sydney

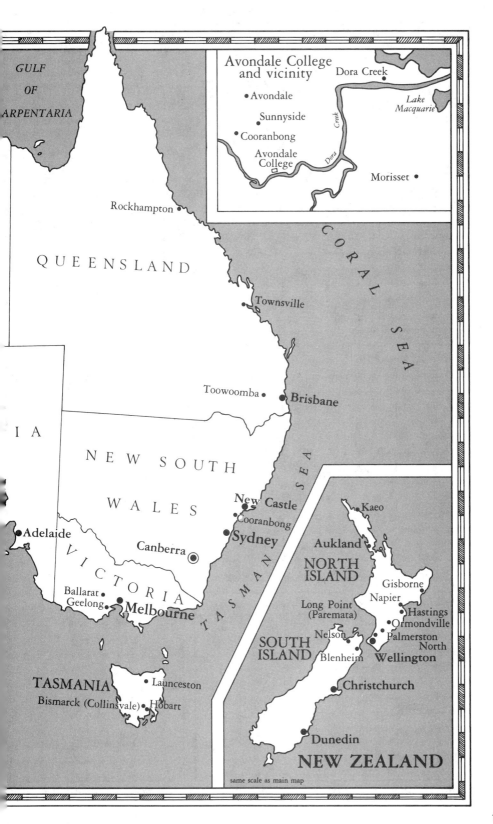

Avondale College
and vicinity

- Avondale
- Sunnyside
- Cooranbong
- Avondale College

Dora Creek

Lake Macquarie

Dora Creek

- Morisset

GULF
OF
CARPENTARIA

QUEENSLAND

- Rockhampton

CORAL SEA

- Townsville

- Toowoomba
- Brisbane

NEW SOUTH
WALES

- New Castle
- Cooranbong
- Sydney

- Adelaide
- Canberra

TASMAN SEA

VICTORIA

- Ballarat
- Geelong
- Melbourne

TASMANIA
- Launceston
- Bismarck (Collinsvale)
- Hobart

NORTH ISLAND

- Kaeo
- Aukland
- Gisborne
- Napier
- Hastings
- Ormondville
- Palmerston North

SOUTH ISLAND

Long Point (Paremata)
- Nelson
- Blenheim
- Wellington
- Christchurch

- Dunedin

NEW ZEALAND

same scale as main map

109

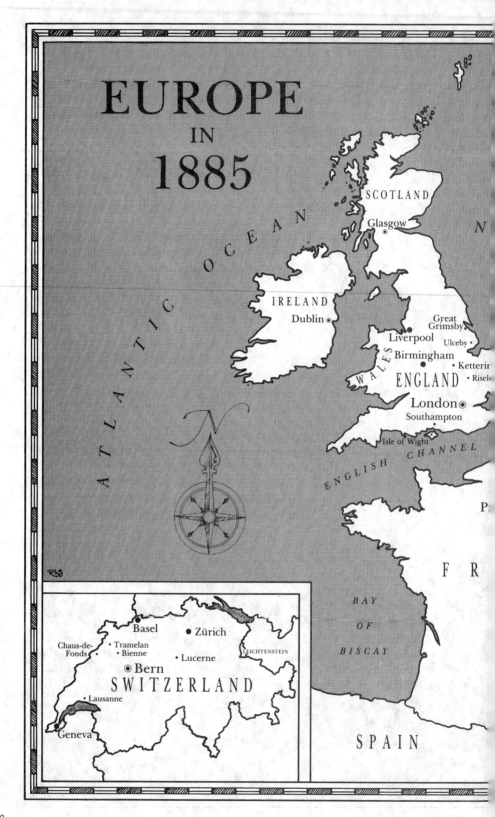

EUROPE
IN
1885

ATLANTIC OCEAN

SCOTLAND

Glasgow

N

IRELAND

Dublin

Great Grimsby

Liverpool · Ulceby ·

Birmingham · Kettering

WALES · Risel

ENGLAND

London

Southampton

Isle of Wight

ENGLISH CHANNEL

BAY

OF

BISCAY

P

F R

SPAIN

Basel · Zürich

Chaus-de-Fonds · · Tramelan
· Bienne · Lucerne

LEICHTENSTEIN

Bern

SWITZERLAND

· Lausanne

LAKE GENEVA

Geneva

NORWAY

Christiania
(Oslo) ◉

Dramen ●
Moss

Kopparberg
Grythyttehed ●

Stockholm ◉

● Örebro

Göteborg ●

SWEDEN

BALTIC SEA

RUSSIAN-

Frederickshavn ●

T H

Copenhagen ◉
● Malmö

DENMARK

E A

Kiel ●

● Hamburg

EMPIRE

Warsaw ●

erdam
◉
NETHERLANDS

◉ Berlin

G E R M A N Y

Brussels
◉

BELGIUM

● Vohwinkel
● Gladbach
● Cologne

● Frankfurt

A U S T R I A -

◉ Vienna

C   E

Basel
Zürich ●
◉ Bern
SWITZERLAND
(see inset)

Geneva

H U N G A R Y

Lyons ●

● Milan

● Valence

● Turin
● Torre
Pellice   ● Genoa

ADRIATIC

ies ●

Nice ●

I T A L Y

SEA

DITERRANEAN   SEA

◉ Rome

Ellen G. White: A Chronology

Robert W. Olson and Roger W. Coon

1786	Feb. 28	Birth of Robert Harmon, Sr.
1787		Birth of Eunice Gould; United States Constitution written.
1791		Death of John Wesley in England; Bill of Rights added to U.S. Constitution.
1810	July 11	Marriage of Robert Harmon and Eunice Gould.
1827	Nov. 26	Twins Ellen and Elizabeth born near Gorham, Maine, the last of eight children of Robert and Eunice Harmon.
1836	Nov. 26	Ninth birthday of Ellen Harmon.
	Dec.	Broken nose/concussion injury at Portland, Maine, effectively terminated her formal education. Through a deathbed conversion she found forgiveness, love, and peace.
1837	Jan. 25	Clapped her hands for joy while watching a dramatic aurora borealis, because she thought it was the Second Coming. She had regained consciousness after three weeks in delirium, but was still bedfast, which confirms the December date of the accident.
1840	Mar. 11-23	First heard William Miller in Portland, Maine.
1841	Sept.	Methodist camp meeting, Buxton, Maine.
1842	Mar. 22	Elizabeth Harmon taken into Methodist Church on probation.
	May 23	Ellen Harmon recommended for baptism.
	June 4-12	Miller's second course of lectures in Portland.
	June 26	Ellen G. Harmon baptized in Casco Bay, Portland, Maine, into the Chestnut Street Methodist Church. Pastor John N. Hobart presiding.
	June-July	Millerite meetings continued at Casco Street Christian Church; Ellen in anxiety.
	June 30	End of Pastor Hobart's term as pastor of the Chestnut Street church.

	July 20	Maine Methodist Annual Conference meeting in Gardiner; Gershom F. Cox, the pro-Millerite presiding elder in Portland since 1839, transferred to Orrington, Maine. Charles Baker replaced Cox as Portland district presiding elder. William F. Farrington replaced John N. Hobart as pastor of the Chestnut Street church.
	Oct. 31	Elizabeth Harmon approved for baptism. Farrington now the pastor; Elizabeth's baptism never took place.
late 1842- early 1843		Ellen was convicted of the duty to pray in public, resisted for "three long weeks" (LS80 154), then had two dreams, visited with Levi Stockman, finally received the "blessing," and testified of it publicly all over Portland.
1843	Feb. 6	Chestnut Street church forms first committee to discipline Harmons.
	Mar. 27	Second committee appointed to deal with Harmons.
	Apr. 23	Third committee appointed to deal with Harmons.
	May 1	Action taken to "induce . . . delinquent members to attend class meetings." This may have been the impetus for Ellen and Robert Harmon, Jr., to testify in class meeting. This was some time after Ellen's "blessing," but "not long" before her "last testimony" to Methodists (1T 35-37).
	May 29	Fourth committee appointed to deal with Harmons.
	June 5	Committee appointed to "keep order" in meetings and "prosecute all offenders if necessary." Ellen's "last testimony" as a Methodist probably occurred about this time (LS80 168; 2SG 22, 23).
	July 19	Maine Methodist Annual Conference in Bath, Maine, voted to suspend all members who persisted in advocating Millerism.
	Aug. 14	Fifth and last committee appointed to deal with Harmons.
	Aug. 21	Expulsion announced at Chestnut Street church.
	Sept. 2	Decision appealed to the quarterly meeting, but "expulsion sustained." Harmon family expelled from Methodist Church for their Adventist beliefs.

| 1843 | Sept.- | Harmons discover the nonimmortality of the soul, after their expulsion from Methodist Church and before the end of [Jewish year] 1843 (LS80 169, 170). |
| 1844 | Mar. | |

| 1844 Mar. 21-Apr. 21 | | Spring Disappointment; end of Jewish year 1843. |

| | Oct. 22 | The Great Disappointment, when, on a specific date, the Second Coming did not occur. |

| | Dec. | Ellen Harmon's first vision, Portland, Maine. |

| 1844 | Dec./ | A second vision directed her to tell others what she had seen. |
| 1845 | Jan. | |

| 1845 | Jan./Feb. | Ellen described her visions to Adventists gathered in the home of her sister, Mary Harmon Foss, at Megquier Hill in Poland, Maine. This was her first public presentation outside of Portland. |

| | spring | Trip to eastern Maine to visit believers; met future husband, James White. |

| 1846 | Apr. 6 | First publication by Ellen Harmon, "To the Little Remnant Scattered Abroad." Broadside; 250 copies. |

| | Aug. 30 | Marriage of James White, 25, and Ellen Harmon, 18. When not traveling, they lived with her parents. |

| | fall | Soon after their marriage James and Ellen began to observe the seventh-day Sabbath, on basis of Bible evidence presented in Joseph Bates' tract. |

| | Nov. | Formative conference with Joseph Bates in Topsham, Maine. Ellen's vision on the "opening heavens" convinced Bates that her visions were of more than human origin. From this time Bates and the Whites began united labors. See Sabbatarian Bible Conferences. |

| | Nov.-Dec. | Formative conference at the home of Hiram Edson, Port Gibson, New York, to which Bates and James White were invited. White was unable to come, but Bates convinced Edson and others of the Sabbath, while they convinced him about their new light on Christ's ministry in the heavenly sanctuary (Knight, *Joseph Bates* [RHPA, 2004], p. 100). |

| 1847 | Jan. | Bates published *The Seventh Day Sabbath: A Perpetual Sign,* 2nd ed. By this time the Whites, Joseph Bates, Hiram Edson, and a few others had become settled on four biblical doctrines that would become the |

"landmarks" of Sabbatarian Adventism (CW 30, 31). These included (1) a premillennial Second Advent, (2) Christ's two-phase ministry in the heavenly sanctuary, (3) the seventh-day Sabbath, and (4) the non-immortality of the wicked, all in the context of the three angels' messages of Revelation 14:6-12 (Knight, *Joseph Bates,* pp. 102, 103, 110-117).

Mar. 6	Formative conference with Whites and Joseph Bates in Fairhaven, Massachusetts.
Apr. 3	Formative conference in Topsham, Maine. Vision of law of God in heavenly sanctuary, with halo of light about fourth commandment. This was the first vision confirming the Sabbath-observance doctrine, seven months after the Whites began to observe it on the basis of Scripture (WLF 18, 19; EW 32, 33).
May	*A Word to the "Little Flock,"* by James White, Joseph Bates, and Ellen White, summarized the foundational doctrines of Sabbatarian Adventists.
summer-fall	The publication of *The Seventh Day Sabbath: A Perpetual Sign* and *A Word to the "Little Flock"* ignited a six-month publishing war over the Sabbath doctrine, culminating in complete schism between Sabbathkeeping and Sundaykeeping Adventists. The Sabbathkeepers' response to this general rejection was to launch a series of evangelistic conferences designed to gather in as many as possible of those still undecided on the Sabbath. See Sabbatarian Bible Conferences.
Aug. 26	Birth of James and Ellen White's first son, Henry Nichols White, at the home of her parents, Robert and Eunice Harmon, Gorham, Maine (1T 82).
Oct.	James and Ellen White set up housekeeping with the Howland family in Topsham, Maine (*ibid.*).
1848 Apr. 20-24	"The first general meeting of the Seventh-day Adventists" (James White, *Life Incidents,* p. 271), in Rocky Hill, Connecticut. This was first of some 23 overtly evangelistic Sabbatarian Bible Conferences in 1848-1850.
Aug. 18, 19	Conference in Volney, New York, with some 35 present. James White and Joseph Bates led out, and Ellen White had two visions.
Aug. 27, 28	Conference in Port Gibson, New York, in Hiram Edson's barn.
Sept. 8, 9	Conference in Rocky Hill, Connecticut.

	Oct. 20-22	Conference in Topsham, Maine.
	Nov. 17-19	Conference in Dorchester, Massachusetts (now part of Boston). "Seal of God" vision clarified eschatology and "streams of light" vision prompted beginnings of Sabbatarian Adventist publishing work.
1849	July	First of 11 issues of *Present Truth* published.
	July 28	Birth of the Whites' second son, James Edson White.
1850	summer	First four issues of the *Advent Review* published, Auburn, New York.
	Nov. 17	*Present Truth* and *Advent Review* merged into *Second Advent Review and Sabbath Herald,* Paris, Maine.
	Dec. 24	First vision calling for formal church organization, Paris, Maine
1851	Apr.	The Whites rent their first home at 124 Mount Hope Ave., Rochester, New York, which also housed the first Seventh-day Adventist-owned press, which printed the *Review and Herald* and the *Youth's Instructor*.
	July	Her first book, *A Sketch of the Christian Experience and Views of Ellen G. White* (64 pages).
1854	Aug. 29	Birth of the Whites' third son, William Clarence White.
1855	Nov.	Whites moved, with the publishing plant, to Battle Creek, Michigan.
	Dec.	*Testimony for the Church,* no. 1, a 16-page pamphlet, began what became, by 1909, a nine-volume set of books.
1856	spring	White family moved into the cottage on Wood Steet, Battle Creek, Michigan, the first home they owned.
1858	Mar. 14	Two-hour-long "great controversy" vision interrupted a funeral at Lovett's Grove, Ohio (now part of Bowling Green, Ohio).
	Mar. 16	On the way home from Ohio, Ellen suffered a stroke of paralysis at the home of Daniel and Abigail Palmer, Jackson, Michigan. Her next vision informed her that the stroke was an attack by Satan to prevent her from publishing the contents of the great controversy vision.

	Sept.	Great controversy vision published in *Spiritual Gifts,* volume 1 (219 pages), forerunner of her Conflict of the Ages Series (five volumes, 3,772 pages).
1860		*Spiritual Gifts,* volume 2, published; her first autobiography.
	May 13	First legally organized Seventh-day Adventist Church established, Parkville, Michigan.
	Sept. 20	Birth of fourth son, John Herbert White.
	Dec. 14	Death of John Herbert White.
1860	Oct. 1	Denomination name, Seventh-day Adventist, officially adopted at Battle Creek conference, in order to give a legal name to the publishing house.
1861	Jan. 12	Parkville, Michigan, church building dedicated; a 20-minute vision forecasted a long, costly American civil war, contrary to popular expectations that the war would be brief and decisive.
	Oct. 5, 6	First state conference organized in Michigan.
1863	May 20-23	General Conference of Seventh-day Adventists organized with eight state conferences.
	June 6	Comprehensive health reform vision, Otsego, Michigan.
	Dec. 8	Death of Whites' eldest son, Henry, age 16, at Topsham, Maine.
1864	summer	*Spiritual Gifts,* volume 4, published, with 30-page article on health.
1865	Dec. 25	Health institution vision at Rochester, New York, directed Adventists to establish a health-care institution (1T 485, 489, 494).
1866	Aug.	*Health Reformer* journal inaugurated.
	Sept.	Western Health Reform Institute opened; name changed in 1877 to Medical and Surgical Sanitarium, but commonly called Battle Creek Sanitarium.
1872		Whites make the first of many trips west to California.

1874	Apr. 1	Vision in Oakland, California, directed Adventists to expand their work in the western U.S. and overseas; it led to the founding of the Pacific Press publishing house and the periodical *Signs of the Times* in Oakland.
	Aug. 24	Battle Creek College opened.
1875	Jan. 3	In a vision in Battle Creek, Ellen White was shown publishing houses all over the world.
1876	Aug. 27	Ellen White spoke on temperance to the largest audience of her life (about 20,000) at a camp meeting in Groveland, Massachusetts.
1878-1879		Whites wintered in Texas with young minister A. G. Daniells and his wife.
1879	Apr. 20	Battle Creek Dime Tabernacle dedicated, seated about 4,000; last major project undertaken by James White before his death.
1881	Aug. 6	Death of James White bifurcates his wife's life; she was married 35 years and widowed 34.
1884	summer	Vision at the Portland, Oregon, camp meeting, thought to be her last public vision; during her later years more of her visions came through prophetic dreams at night.
	Sept.	*The Spirit of Prophecy,* volume 4 published (enlarged version of *The Great Controversy* account); 50,000 copies sold in three years.
1885-1887		Ministry in Europe; headquarters at Basel, Switzerland; see articles on Europe, Denmark, England, France, Germany, Italy, Norway, Sweden, and Switzerland.
1888	fall	*The Great Controversy* revised and enlarged to essentially its present form; she would update it once more in 1911.
	Oct.-Nov.	General Conference session, Minneapolis, Minnesota. The doctrine of righteousness by faith was vigorously debated—the first time Ellen White was publicly opposed by clergy of her own church.
1889-1891		Revivals conducted across America with E. J. Waggoner and A. T. Jones.

1891-1900		Ministry in Australia, New Zealand, South Pacific; counseled W. C. White and A. G. Daniells in developing union conference system of organization.
1892		*Steps to Christ* published by Fleming H. Revell, Chicago.
	Aug. 24	Australasian Bible School opened in rented quarters in Melbourne; later relocated to Cooranbong and renamed Avondale School for Christian Workers.
1895		Moved to Cooranbong, New South Wales, Australia, to supervise development of Avondale School; lived in a tent while her house was being built.
1896		Published *Thoughts From the Mount of Blessings,* an exposition of Christ's sermon on the mount.
	Oct.	Laid the "corner brick" of the first Avondale School building.
1897	Apr. 28	Avondale School opened as a "pattern" school for Seventh-day Adventist education worldwide; forerunner of Avondale College.
1898		Published *The Desire of Ages,* 866 pages on the life of Christ.
1900		Published *Christ's Object Lessons,* 436 pages on the parables of Christ. Proceeds donated to retiring debt on Adventist schools.
1901	Apr. 2-21	Major denominational reorganization at General Conference, Battle Creek.
	summer	Battle Creek College relocated to Berrien Springs, Michigan, and renamed Emmanuel Missionary College (became Andrews University in 1959).
1902	Feb. 18	Battle Creek Sanitarium destroyed by fire.
1902	Oct. 19	Vision at St. Helena, California, saved Southern Publishing Association from premature closure during a time of financial crisis.
	Dec. 30	Review and Herald publishing house destroyed by fire.
1903		Published *Education.*

	Oct.	General Conference relocated from Battle Creek to Takoma Park, Maryland, in the suburbs of Washington, D.C.
1905		*The Ministry of Healing* published; proceeds donated to retiring debt on Adventist health-care institutions.
	May 26	Ellen White directed John Burden to purchase property for a medical institution in Loma Linda, California.
1906	Apr. 15	Dedicated Loma Linda Sanitarium, forerunner of Loma Linda University Medical Center.
1909	May 15-June 6	Ellen White gave 11 addresses at her last General Conference session, Takoma Park, Maryland.
1914	June 14	Ellen White's last writing before her death.
1915	Feb. 13	Ellen White broke her hip in her Elmshaven home near St. Helena, California, precipitating her final decline.
	July 16	Death at Elmshaven, age 87.
	July 18	Funeral at Elmshaven, near St. Helena, California.
	July 19	Funeral at Richmond, California, camp meeting.
	July 24	Funeral at Battle Creek Tabernacle. Burial in Oak Hill Cemetery, Battle Creek.

Ellen G. White's Writings

George R. Knight

IN 1907 ELLEN WHITE PREDICTED that her writings would "constantly speak, and their work will go forward as long as time shall last. . . . Even though I should not live, these words that have been given to me by the Lord will still have life and will speak to the people" (1SM 55).

More than 100 years later it appears that those sentiments are accurate. In fact, the amount of published material from the pen of Ellen White is constantly increasing. Even her unpublished letters and manuscripts, since the opening of the Ellen White branch offices and research centers around the world, are being increasingly studied and heard.

The sheer bulk of Ellen White's writings is likely to intimidate the beginner. This article will describe the basic categories of her writings so that those interested in them will have some grasp of the various types and the content of each. Such an understanding has several values. First, it will help people to get some sense of how the various parts of her corpus relate to the whole. Second, it will serve as a general guide as to where to look for certain types of material. And third, it will provide beginning readers of Ellen White with some priorities as to where to begin their reading of her writings.

The most basic division in Ellen White's writings is between her published works and those that were largely unpublished at the time of her death—her letters and manuscripts. We will spend the bulk of our time describing her published works, since they most adequately set forth her basic ideas. The last sections of the article will deal with her letters and manuscripts and electronic publishing.

The contents of her corpus of writings can be divided in the following manner:

I. Published Writings
   A. Books and Compilations
      1. A Note on the Difference Between Books and Topical Compilations
      2. Books Related to the Conflict of the Ages Theme
      3. The Testimony Format
      4. Books on Christ, Salvation, and Related Issues
      5. Books Specifically Devoted to End-time Events
      6. Autobiographical Works
      7. The Counsel Books
         a. Books on Ministry
         b. Books on Education
         c. Books on Family Life
         d. Books Related to Health
         e. Books on Publishing
         f. Book on Race Relations
      8. The Devotional Books
   B. Periodical Articles

II. Unpublished Writings
    A. The Letter and Manuscript File
    B. Publications from the Letter and Manuscript File
III. The Electronic Publishing of Ellen White's Writings

I. Published Writings

A. Books and Compilations

The most important publications of Ellen White are her many books. At the time of her death she had more than 20 books in print. Since that time the number has more than quadrupled, with nearly all of the posthumous volumes being topical compilations from her manuscripts, letters, and published writings.

1. A Note on the Difference Between Books and Topical Compilations

At this point it is important to examine the difference between a book published by Ellen White in her lifetime and the topical compilations developed from her writings. While most of the topical compilations were developed after her death (according to authorization and guidelines in her will) by the Ellen G. White Estate, some were produced before that time. There is a sense in which both categories are books, but there are also differences that we should recognize.

The topical compilations generally consist of large numbers of short quotations on a given subject taken from such existing works as Ellen White's letters, unpublished manuscripts, diaries, and published articles and books. The compiler (generally the staff of the White Estate for "official" compilations) places the short quotations in logical order, supplies them with headings, and groups them into chapters. Thus the quotations in a topical compilation are necessarily removed from their literary and historical contexts. That is a potential disadvantage, since the context usually helps the reader understand more fully the author's intent and complete meaning. In order to moderate that disadvantage and provide access to the context, the original source for each statement has been supplied in all official compilations published since Ellen White's death.

Topical compilations are valuable because they seek to present in one place all of the most important counsel on a subject. But in spite of the best efforts of the compiler, compilations still risk not being as balanced as they might have been had Ellen White been able personally to round out the material or modify statements written to meet extreme situations, and are thus susceptible to misinterpretation. Compilers are restricted in their work to existing quotations and cannot generate new material that may answer aspects of a topic that Ellen White never discussed.

By way of contrast, because of her direct involvement many of Ellen White's books published during her lifetime tend to cover their topics with more balance in terms of well-rounded, principle-based treatment. They also set forth their material in its literary (and often historical) context.

Even though many of the books produced by Ellen White herself were themselves composed largely of material selected from her earlier writings, they generally present a more satisfactory and well-balanced approach to a topic than do the topical compilations of her material. That is because she had direct personal supervision over the process and was able to provide additional material as needed. Thus readers should read her well-thought-out book on a subject (in those fields where one is available) before they go to a topical compilation on the same subject. For example, a person interested in healthful living is well advised to read *The Ministry of Healing before delving into *Counsels on Diet and Foods. The reader should also remember when using quotations from topical compilations that the counsel generally went to specific individuals or groups with quite specific problems. No reader has all those problems, and he or she may or may not be facing the exact same difficulty as the original recipient of the counsel. As a result, it is best to seek out the general principles undergirding the counsel on a given topic rather than "running wild" with this or that quotation.

Beyond the "official" compilations published by the White Estate, there exist large numbers of topical compilations put out by individuals and special interest groups who have a burden to emphasize one point or another and who believe that they will be more successful if it appears that Ellen White had the same burden or interpretation. Not only are such compilations produced without the safeguards set up by the White Estate to ensure the most accurate representation of her original meaning, but they often present a biased or distorted view of their topic.

Needless to say, while all topical compilations need to be read with an awareness of their purpose and limitations, those put out by special interest groups demand great caution. Throughout her ministry Ellen White had to confront "those who will," as she put it, "select from the testimonies the strongest expressions and, without bringing in or making any account of the circumstances under which the cautions and warnings are given, make them of force in every case. Thus they produce unhealthy impressions upon the minds of the people. There are always those who are ready to grasp anything of a character which they can use to rein up people to a close, severe test, and who . . . work elements of their own characters into the reforms." Such people, she noted, "disgust rather than win souls" (3SM 285, 286).

Midway between Ellen White's books and topical compilations of her material are such works as the nine volumes of *Testimonies for the Church and the three books of *Selected Messages. These works generally consist of "chapter length" selections and thus have the advantage of providing more context than do the topical compilations. In actuality, quite a few of Ellen White's works fit into this intermediate category. Such volumes as *Fundamentals of Christian Education, *The Sanctified Life, and *Faith and Works are representative. The chapters in these works are made up in most cases of entire articles or sermons rather than bits and pieces of counsel from here and there.

2. Books Related to the Conflict of the Ages Theme

Perhaps Ellen White's most important books have been those developing the Conflict of the Ages theme, which deals with the great controversy between God and Satan, good and evil, down through history. In its mature form the Conflict of the Ages Series consists of five books that trace the struggle between God and Satan from the rebellion in heaven before the creation of Adam and Eve up through the end of the millennium.

Those five volumes provide the theological framework for everything else Ellen White has to say. An understanding of the great themes they highlight is foundational to understanding her other writings. Therefore, anyone with an interest in Ellen White's thought needs to read these volumes *early* in their study of her works.

The development of the Conflict of the Ages theme in Ellen White's writings went through three progressive stages of development. The first stage is found in the four volumes entitled *Spiritual Gifts.

Volume 1 of *Spiritual Gifts* (1858) carried the subtitle of *The Great Controversy Between Christ and His Angels and Satan and His Angels* and set the tone for her lifelong expansion on the Conflict of the Ages theme. Volume 1 treated the fall of Satan in heaven, the fall of Adam and Eve, the work of Christ, the apostolic church, the great apostasy, the Reformation, and the period running from the rise of Millerism up through the end of the millennium. The first half of volume 1 of *Spiritual Gifts* was published as the second half of *Early Writings* in 1882.

The material covered in volumes 3 (1864) and 4 (1864) of *Spiritual Gifts* was much more restricted, with volume 3 recounting Bible history from Creation to the giving of the Mosaic law. The first part of volume 4 continues that history from the building of the wilderness tabernacle up to the time of Christ. Thus in essence volumes 1, 3, and 4 cover the entire time of the conflict. The treatment, however, is not even in coverage, nor does it have the depth of her later contributions to the Conflict of the Ages theme.

The second stage in the development of the conflict theme centers on the four volumes entitled *The Spirit of Prophecy. Volume 1 (1870) opens with the fall of Lucifer and deals with biblical history to the time of Solomon. It is largely an amplification of the material presented in *Spiritual Gifts*, volumes 3 and 4. It would later be amplified to become *Patriarchs and Prophets* (1890).

The second volume of *The Spirit of Prophecy* (1877) covers the life of Christ from His birth to the triumphal entry into Jerusalem. It is largely an expanded version of the material found in the first half of *Spiritual Gifts*, volume 1. The material would later be amplified to become part of *The Desire of Ages* (1898).

The third volume of *The Spirit of Prophecy* (1878) has 20 chapters dealing with the last days of the ministry of Christ and 11 chapters covering the life and work of the apostles. As with volume 2, this one is also an amplification of materials found in the first volume of *Spiritual Gifts*. The treatment would later be greatly expanded to form the final portion of *The Desire of Ages* and *The Acts of the Apostles* (1911).

Volume 4 of *The Spirit of Prophecy* (1884) covered the period from the destruction of Jerusalem to the end of the millennium and is an expansion of the materials found in the second half of the first volume of *Spiritual Gifts*. In 1885 *The Spirit of Prophecy*, volume 4, was formatted for colporteur sale to the non-Adventist public and its subtitle became its title: *The Great Controversy Between Christ and Satan During the Christian Dispensation*. Under that title the book would be revised in 1888 and again in 1911 to become volume 5 in the Conflict of the Ages Series.

Simultaneously, with the publication of *The Spirit of Prophecy*, volumes 2 and 3, the denomination's Battle Creek publishing house released much of the same material arranged topically and somewhat modified to form eight small books with the collective title of *Redemption*. The subtitles are descriptive of the content of each volume:

Redemption, or The First Advent of Christ With His Life and Ministry (1877)

Redemption, or The Temptation of Christ in the Wilderness (first published as a stand-alone volume in 1874)

Redemption, or The Miracles of Christ the Mighty One (1877)

Redemption, or The Teachings of Christ the Anointed One (1877)

Redemption, or The Sufferings of Christ, His Trial and Crucifixion (1877)

Redemption, or The Resurrection of Christ and His Ascension (1877)

Redemption, or The Ministry of Peter and the Conversion of Saul (1878)

Redemption, or The Teachings of Paul and His Mission to the Gentiles (1878)

The third and final stage in the development of the Conflict of the Ages Series had five volumes, building upon but greatly amplifying the materials previously developed in the *Spiritual Gifts* and *Spirit of Prophecy* volumes.

The first volume in the Conflict series is *Patriarchs and Prophets* (1890). It carries the story of the struggle between God and Satan from the rebellion in heaven up through the reign of David. *Prophets and Kings* (1917) picks up the story with Solomon and continues through to the end of the Old Testament period.

Many people consider the third volume, *The Desire of Ages* (1898), to be Ellen White's finest work. It covers the life, death, and resurrection of Jesus. The preparation of *The Desire of Ages* was a labor of love that took the better part of a decade. Ellen White wrote that "God would be pleased to see *The Desire of Ages* in every home" (CM 126).

Her son Edson developed a simplified version of *The Desire of Ages* for children as *Christ Our Saviour* in 1896. In 1949 it was retitled *Story of Jesus*. A contemporary adaptation of *The Desire of Ages* entitled *Messiah* was produced by Jerry D. Thomas in 2002.

The Acts of the Apostles (1911) is the fourth volume of the Conflict of the Ages Series. It traces the struggle between good and evil from the book of Acts up through John's Revelation. The years between the publication of *The Spirit of Prophecy*, volume 3, in 1878 and the publication of *The Acts of the Apostles* saw Ellen White publish *Sketches From the Life of Paul* (1883). That 32-chapter work provided the basis for the later development of *The Acts of the Apostles*.

The fifth volume in the Conflict of the Ages Series is *The Great Controversy*. That volume, as we noted above, was first published as volume 4 of *The Spirit of Prophecy* in 1884. But since it became a book sold to the general non-Adventist public in 1885, Ellen White and the publishers thought it best to modify it for that larger audience in 1888. Another revision at Ellen White's request was published in 1911. That final edition corrected certain factual material of a historical nature and supplied credits to the authorities cited. The twentieth century would see *The Great Controversy* receive wide circulation under several different titles, perhaps the most well known being *The Triumph of God's Love* (1950). *The Great Controversy* develops the struggle between Christ and Satan during the postbiblical period. It begins with the destruction of Jerusalem in A.D. 70, runs through the course of church history, and climaxes with the events predicted in Scripture to be connected with the second coming of Christ. The final chapters of *The Great Controversy* also place Millerism and Seventh-day Adventism in the flow of prophetic history.

The Great Controversy rivals *The Desire of Ages* as being Ellen White's most important work. Ellen White said that she appreciated it "above silver or gold" (CM 128). She also wrote that she was "more anxious to see a wide circulation for this book than for any others I have written; for in *The Great Controversy*, the last message of warning to the world is given more distinctly than in any of my other books" (*ibid.* 127).

Ellen White developed the five-volume Conflict of the Ages Series with both Adventist and non-Adventist readers in mind. She desired these books to be sold widely so that she could get her message before the public. Used in conjunction with Bible study, the volumes have led many to a closer walk with God and a better understanding of His Word. There is no better place to become acquainted with Ellen White's writings than with a reading of the Conflict series.

All three sets of books in the great controversy sequence are still in print. They all set forth a theme Ellen White claims was first revealed to her in vision about 1848 and reinforced through an expanded vision at Lovett's Grove, Ohio, in the spring of 1858. Beyond the visions, Ellen White studied both the Bible and church history in order to fill in the outline of the history of the conflict between good and evil provided by the visions (see GC xi, xii).

Writing out the great controversy story extended across Ellen White's long ministry. Aspects of it show up in her private letters, articles, sermons, and unpublished manuscripts. The pulling together of that previously written material by Ellen White and her literary assistants provided a starting place for much of what she had to say in the Conflict of the Ages Series. The expanding storehouse of material in her files also did much to make each of the three stages in the development of the conflict story progressively more insightful and complete.

A final volume to note that deals specifically with the history of the great controversy is *The Story of Redemption* (1947). That volume traces Ellen White's early treatment of the great controversy theme. All material in *The Story of Redemption* had previously appeared in *Early Writings*, the *Spirit of Prophecy* volumes, or the *Signs of the Times*. The book's major contribution is that it provides a concise account of Ellen White's early thought on the topic that is compact enough to be widely translated into other languages.

3. The Testimony Format

A second influential set of books from Ellen White's pen are the nine volumes of *Testimonies for the Church*. This series, consisting of nearly 5,000 pages, has a significantly different purpose from the Conflict of the Ages volumes. Whereas the five-volume Conflict series traces the struggle between good and evil down the corridor of history, the *Testimonies* contain letters, articles, sermons, records of visions, and instruction regarding the everyday affairs of life. And while the five-volume Conflict series is aimed at both the church and those outside of the church, the *Testimonies* specifically target the members of the Seventh-day Adventist Church.

The *Testimonies* found their genesis in 1855 when a question arose among the leading Adventists as how best to circulate one of Ellen White's visions. They voted, after some discussion, that it should be published and distributed in tract form to the entire body of believers.

Thus was born Ellen White's first published *Testimony for the Church*—a document of 16 pages. This method of distributing Ellen White's visions and counsel was so successful that a second 16-page *Testimony* appeared in 1856. By 1864 she had produced 10 such consecutively numbered pamphlets. They contained not only general counsel to the church at large, but specific counsel to individuals, since Ellen White realized that the instruction to one person would help others in similar circumstances.

As Ellen White put it: "In rebuking the wrongs of one, He [God] designs to correct many. . . . He makes plain the wrongs of some that others may thus be warned and fear and shun those errors" (5T 659). "I was then directed to bring out general principles . . . and at the same time specify the dangers, errors, and sins of some individuals, that all might be warned, reproved, and counseled. I saw that all should search their own hearts and lives closely to see if they had not made the same mistakes for which others were corrected. . . . If so, they should feel that the counsel and reproofs were given especially for them and should make as practical an application of them as though they were especially addressed to themselves" (*ibid.* 660).

Ellen White developed the practice of deleting personal names from her published *Testimonies* in order to protect the privacy of the individuals to whom they were first written. Thus a student of the published *Testimonies* reads about Brother A or Sister C.

With the passage of time the earlier testimony pamphlets went out of print. But since there was still a demand for them, she had the first 10 of them reprinted in 1864 as the last section of *Spiritual Gifts*, volume 4. Other updated collections of the early *Testimonies* were republished in bound volumes in 1871 and 1879. Finally in 1883 the General Conference session voted to publish all the *Testimonies* up to that time (30 in all) in four volumes of 700 or 800 pages each. As a result, *Testimonies for the Church*, volumes 1-4, came off the press in 1885. Comprising a republication (with some editing) of the entire contents of *Testimonies* 1-30, these 2,619 pages provided the church with the entire collection of published testimonies up through 1881, plus a 100-page autobiographical sketch by Ellen White at the beginning of volume 1.

These four volumes have remained the standard since that time. Their pagination has remained the same, and the table of contents for each volume still contains the original *Testimony* numbers and the date of initial publication for each.

But Ellen White's work was far from over in 1885. As a result, the fifth volume of *Testimonies for the Church* appeared in 1889. It included *Testimonies* 31 to 33. Then in 1900 she published the nearly 500 pages of *Testimony* 34 as volume 6. But by that time things had greatly changed in Adventism. The fledgling movement of the 1850s had reached early adulthood and not only had more members but also an ever-expanding number of institutions. Beyond that, a great deal of published Ellen White counsel on various topics already existed in volumes 1-5 and other formats.

Those changed circumstances brought about a major change in the shape of volumes 6-9. For one thing, Ellen White felt no need to replicate counsel already given in earlier volumes. In addition, given the sheer bulk of her writing during these years, much more care had to be taken in selecting appropriate material. And finally, the volumes were more carefully edited and arranged so that the table of contents for each of volumes 6-9 reflects more of a topical than a chronological arrangement. The *Testimonies for the Church* series came to a close in 1909 with the publication of volume 9.

The nine volumes of the *Testimonies* have been invaluable to the church. While most people tend to use them as reference works, they can be profitably read chronologically from beginning to end. Such readers not only glimpse the flow of Ellen White's counsel across time, but also catch the flavor of Adventist history as it develops through its first six decades. Such readers might find it valuable to keep a book on denominational history and the six volumes of Arthur White's biography of Ellen White handy for reference and contextualization as they read through the *Testimonies*. Other helpful sources of information on historical points are the two-volume *Seventh-day Adventist Encyclopedia* and the *Ellen G. White Encyclopedia*.

Adventists around the world eventually desired to have the *Testimonies* in their own language, but the cost of translating and publishing all the material was prohibitive. As a result, several attempts have been made to abridge the nine volumes without losing any of the essential lines of content.

One early abridgment was the three-volume *Selections From the Testimonies,* published in 1936 in inexpensive form largely to meet the needs of North American Adventists during the Depression years. An abridgment with a broader purpose was the three volumes of *Testimony Treasures* published in 1949. It was hoped that *Testimony Treasures* would become the basis for foreign language translations of the *Testimonies*, as well as providing a more abbreviated collection for those who wanted to read them through in English.

Testimony Treasures contain approximately one third of the content of the nine-volume *Testimonies*, presenting the essential counsels for the world church without the repetition of subject matter that was inevitable in a collection published over a 55-year period. The articles are arranged in their natural chronological order. In addition to selections from *Testimonies for the Church* "there have also been included a few important articles of a testimony character, dealing with vital topics not represented in the *Testimonies*, but which appear elsewhere in the English editions of the E. G. White books not available in other languages" (1TT 7).

A similar abridgment project resulted in *Counsels for the Church* (1991). Unlike the *Testimony Treasures*, this volume does not restrict itself largely to an abridgment of the *Testimonies*. Rather, *Counsels for the Church* seeks to provide a one-volume abridgment of Ellen White's entire corpus of counsels that can be economically translated into those languages where believers are few and funds are short. The volume aims at presenting the essential core of Ellen White's writings.

Another line of development in the tradition of the *Testimonies* is the series consisting of the three *Selected Messages* books. The first two books were published in 1958 and are made up of general instruction on many topics that are of perennial interest and importance. The material was drawn from unpublished manuscripts as well as out-of-print pamphlets and periodical articles. The first two books of *Selected Messages* were the first volumes of general testimony from Ellen White's pen to be issued since volume 9 of *Testimonies for the Church* in 1909.

A third book of *Selected Messages* was published in 1980. Certain needs that had arisen in the church stimulated the new volume. Its format is the same as for books 1 and 2.

Like the *Testimonies*, in contrast to the topical compilation format, the *Selected Messages* books generally present the majority of the selections with most of their literary context intact so that the reader has either the largest part or all of each document rather than a collection of short quotations from various sources. The *Selected Messages* volumes have proven to be some of the most helpful and valuable works by Ellen White published since her death.

In addition to the nine volumes of *Testimonies for the Church*, over Ellen White's extended ministry many other works were published with the word "testimony" in the title. Many of those were pamphlets, such as *Testimony for the Battle Creek Church* (1882). Some of those stand-alone pamphlets eventually found their way into one of the collections of her writings. Two collections of the stand-alone, testimony-like pamphlets deserve special mention. *Special Testimonies, Series B,* consists of 19 Ellen White pamphlets (comprising more than 750 pages) issued between 1903 and 1913 to meet special situations of a local or temporary character. Much of the material in *Series B* that has permanent interest and value has been incorporated into such volumes as *Testimonies for the Church,* *Counsels on Health,* *Counsels on Stewardship,* and *Selected Messages.*

Series B had been preceded by *Special Testimonies to Ministers and Workers,* which became known as *Series A* after the publication of *Series B.* Made up originally of 11 pamphlets published between 1892 and 1897, a twelfth one was added in 1905. Much of the material in *Series A* was republished in 1923 in *Testimonies to Ministers and Gospel Workers* (described later under "The Counsel Books: Books on Ministry").

4. Books on Christ, Salvation, and Related Issues

A third grouping of Ellen White books is one that presents Christ's teachings and topics related to salvation through Him as its exclusive subject matter. At the very center of this grouping is *The Desire of Ages* (1898), the third volume in the Conflict of the Ages Series. *The Desire of Ages,* a life of Christ that extends from the Incarnation through His resurrection, is the book that provides the setting and context for all other Ellen White works dealing with the life and teachings of Jesus. (For a discussion of books related to *The Desire of Ages* in subject matter, see the earlier treatment "Books Related to the Conflict of the Ages Theme.")

Two spin-offs from Ellen White's study and writing for *The Desire of Ages* are *Thoughts From the Mount of Blessing* (1896) and *Christ's Object Lessons* (1900). The first of those books is a six-chapter, verse-by-verse discussion of the lessons taught in Matthew's version of the Sermon on the Mount. *Christ's Object Lessons* covers the parables of Jesus and their lessons, which for space reasons could not be included in *The Desire of Ages.* *Christ's Object Lessons* has also been widely distributed under the title of *Highways to Heaven* (1952) and *He Taught Love* (abridged, 1997), while *Thoughts From the Mount of Blessing* forms the second half of a publication titled *Love Unlimited* (1958), with *Steps to Christ* being the first half.

A fourth classic in this segment of Ellen White's books is *Steps to Christ* (1892). That slim volume, first published by the non-Adventist publishing house of Fleming H. Revell (Dwight L. Moody's brother-in-law), is perhaps Ellen White's best on salvation in Christ. Along with *Thoughts From the Mount of Blessing* and *Christ's Object Lessons*, the *Testimonies*, and the Conflict series, *Steps to Christ* stands at the center of the Ellen White corpus of writings. Its content reflects all the essential elements in personal salvation, such as the sinner's need, repentance, confession, consecration, faith and acceptance, growth in Christ, knowing God, prayer, and rejoicing in the Lord.

Two other Ellen White books dealing with salvation are *The Sanctified Life* (1937) and *Faith and Works* (1979). Those two volumes are collections of articles and/or sermons on their respective topics. Thus, unlike the topical compilations, they present their subject matter in its context.

The Sanctified Life is a reprint of a series of 11 articles that first appeared in the *Review and Herald* in 1881. In 1889 they were drawn together and published as a pamphlet titled *Bible Sanctification*, which appeared as number one of the Bible Students' Library. *The Sanctified Life* is a reprinting of the earlier book in its entirety, with one paragraph added from *Prophets and Kings*. Its basic subject matter centers on the elements of true sanctification and the contrast between true and false ideas of the topic.

Faith and Works is made up of 18 presentations selected from unpublished sermon manuscripts and articles in the *Review and Herald* and *Signs of the Times* dated 1881 to 1902. Thus they span the years surrounding the crucial 1888 General Conference session. The chapters are arranged in an "unstructured chronological sequence" (FW 11). They deal with Christ's righteousness and various aspects of justification and sanctification.

Two other works related to salvation are the topical compilations titled *The Truth About Angels* (1996) and *Prayer* (2002). The *Angels* volume is largely a chronological presentation of the ministry of angels across history from before the entrance of sin up through the earth made new. Many of the readings, as might be expected, reflect the role of angels in the Christian's journey toward God's kingdom. *Prayer* is a focused study of the topic in the Christian's personal experience.

5. Books Specifically Devoted to End-time Events

The Great Controversy is the volume most people think of first in this category (for a fuller discussion see the "Books Related to the Conflict of the Ages Theme" section discussed earlier). That volume provides the larger context for her other works specifically dealing with end-time events.

An important contribution to this sector of Ellen White's corpus is *Last Day Events*, a topical compilation published in 1992. That volume takes a thematic approach to the various events related to the end of time. Thus one will find chapters on Sunday laws, the shaking, the latter rain, the close of probation, and so on. Closely related to some of the topics presented in *Last Day Events* is a short topical compilation entitled *The Remnant Church* (1950), which deals with God's church in the days before the Second Advent. Many of the chapters in *Early Writings* (1882) also deal with material specifically related to events to take place just before the Second Advent.

6. Autobiographical Works

Ellen White's earliest books were autobiographical. July 1851 saw the publication of *A Sketch of the Christian Experience and Views of Ellen G. White*. This book contains a brief autobiographical sketch along with descriptions of many of her early visions and the circumstances in which they took place. Some of the reports of the visions had been published previously as broadsides and other of the material had been published in *Present Truth* and the *Review and Herald*.

Three years later Ellen White published her *Supplement to the Experience and Views of Ellen G. White* (1854). That slim volume presented some explanations of the material in her 1851 *Sketch* and also provided some fresh material that had previously been set forth in the *Review and Herald*. Both the *Sketch* and the *Supplement* were republished in 1882 in *Early Writings*. There were some additions and editorial changes made in the 1882 printing.

These early treatments of her life not only report the contents of Ellen White's first visions, but also provide a great deal of information on her early experience and thought. In addition they enable us to get a glimpse of the theology of Sabbatarian Adventism in the post-1844 period and Ellen White's contribution to that theology.

The second step in Ellen White's autobiographical writing came in 1860 with the publication of the second volume of *Spiritual Gifts*, which was subtitled *My Christian Experience, Views and Labors in Connection With the Rise and Progress of the Third Angel's Message*. The autobiographical material in *Spiritual Gifts* begins with her childhood and runs through 1860. It is much more detailed than that found in her earlier writings on the topic. "I have felt it my duty," she penned in the preface, "to give to my friends and to the world a sketch of my Christian experience, visions, and labors in connection with the rise and progress" of Adventism (2SG iii). She was, she points out, "under great disadvantages" in developing the manuscript "as I have had to depend in many instances, on memory, having kept no journal till within a few years" *(ibid.)*. Her treatment, however, is invaluable for both understanding Ellen White as a person and comprehending the development of early Adventism. The *Spiritual Gifts* treatment would form the starting point for her later autobiographical sketches. It does, however, contain details not found elsewhere.

The third stage of Ellen White's autobiographical writing took place in the 1880s. In 1880 she and her husband published *Life Sketches: Ancestry, Early Life, Christian Experience, and Extensive Labors of Elder James White, and His Wife Mrs. Ellen G. White*. That volume contains James's autobiography, first published in his *Life Incidents* (1868) but now updated to 1880, along with Ellen's most recent autobiographical update. The combined *Life Sketches* of the Whites came out in a new edition in 1888. The 1888 version was largely the same as that of 1880, except that it contained a record of James White's last illness and death. While the Ellen White autobiographical section in the 1880 and 1888 *Life Sketches* drew heavily upon volume 2 of *Spiritual Gifts*, the material was recast and much new material was added.

Another major autobiographical sketch from the 1880s was published in *Testimonies for the Church*, volume 1, in 1885. Much of the material parallels that in the 1880s versions of *Life Sketches*, but once again the material has been reformatted and some additional information is provided.

The final step in Ellen White's autobiographical writing came in 1915 with the publication of *Life Sketches of Ellen G. White: Being a Narrative of Her Experience to 1881 as Written by Herself; With a Sketch of Her Subsequent Labors and of Her Last Sickness Compiled From Original Sources*. Thus the book covers the entire span of her life from childhood up through her funeral.

As noted in the subtitle, the 1915 *Life Sketches* (the volume most people think of when they hear the title) is sharply divided into two halves, with only the years up to 1881 coming directly from Ellen White's pen. Those 41 chapters were penned in the first person and drew heavily upon the autobiographical accounts in *Spiritual Gifts*, volume 2 (1860), the *Life Sketches of James and Ellen White* (1880, 1888), and *Testimonies for the Church*, volume 1 (1885).

The last half of the book might better be characterized as biography rather than autobiography. The last 20 chapters were developed by C. C. Crisler with the help of W. C. White and D. E. Robinson, all from Ellen White's office staff. Those chapters, however, rely heavily on her writings.

Two other books need to be introduced before we move away from Ellen White's autobiographical writings. The first is *Christian Experience and Teachings of Ellen G. White* (1922). This volume was designed to introduce the life and teachings of Ellen White to new converts to Adventism. Its content is drawn mainly from *Life Sketches* (1915), *Early Writings*, and the *Testimonies*. The two informative appendix chapters on the prophetic gift were written by R. W. Munson and D. E. Robinson in 1914. Closely related to *Christian Experience* is *Life and Teachings of Ellen G. White* (1933), a work developed for use by evangelists, but one not widely used since all of its content was available elsewhere.

Historical Sketches of the Foreign Missions of the Seventh-day Adventists: With Reports of the European Missionary Councils of 1883, 1884, and 1885, and a Narrative by Mrs. E. G. White of Her Visit and Labors in These Missions (1886) also contains significant autobiographical material. The Ellen White portion of *Historical Sketches* consists of three types of material. First, "Notes of Travel," tracing her journey from California to Europe and some of her accounts of her visits to European countries, drawn largely from her reports published in the *Review and Herald*. Second, 13 "Practical Addresses," given at the European council she attended in 1885. And, third, four concluding chapters presenting "Appeals for Our Missions." Needless to say, much of the material found in Ellen White's sections to *Historical Sketches* (along with many other reports of her travels published at various times in the *Review and Herald*) is not found in any of her standard autobiographical works.

7. The Counsel Books

We now move into an area of Ellen White's works that is both extensive and often quite subject matter-specific. These volumes contain the bulk of the topical compilations from Ellen White's writings. The counsel books fall into six basic categories: (1) ministry, (2) education, (3) family life, (4) health, (5) publishing, and (6) race relations. Those six categories, it should be noted, include the four main branches of the organized Adventist work, along with family and race relations—the latter categories undergirding the health of every other aspect of Adventism. In these books one finds a great deal of counsel that applies to the denomination's institutions, as well as to lifestyle and daily Christian living.

The reader will notice two sorts of volumes in several of the counsel categories: (1) broad-based books developed during Ellen White's lifetime on the topic under consideration and (2) topical compilations that are quite specific as to their subject matter. The titles of the compilation volumes generally illustrate their subject matter. When exploring these areas of Ellen White's thought, it is best to read the broad-based book on the subject (where one is available) before the narrower topical compilations.

a. Books on Ministry. The earliest Ellen White book on ministry was a topical compilation published in 1892 as *Gospel Workers. That early version of the book included counsels on the topic up to the year 1890, selected largely from the first five volumes of *Testimonies for the Church* and other available sources. A closing section of 61 pages presents 13 Ellen White morning talks given to the ministers at the 1883 General Conference session.

A second work, published near the end of the century, was *Special Testimonies to Ministers and Workers* (a title that would later have *Series A* attached to it as a subtitle). This publication was a collection of 11 pamphlets issued by the General Conference between 1892 and 1897. It made available to ministers many special messages of counsel sent from *Australia during Ellen White's years there.

Those two early works would both be reformulated early in the twentieth century. The 1915 edition of *Gospel Workers* (the edition in current use) was a major revision and enlargement of the 1892 edition. It incorporated much of the material of the former edition, but also included important material written during Ellen White's final 25 years of ministry. A complete reorganization of the book made it possible to delete general material and items especially aimed at colporteurs, thus providing more space for the inclusion of counsels aimed specifically at those engaged in pastoral ministry.

Testimonies to Ministers and Gospel Workers appeared in 1923. It is made up largely of material published as *Special Testimonies, Series A*, but it also contains material from *Series B* as well as other related material. The larger part of the content of this volume was written between 1890 and 1898.

While there is no Ellen White book specifically written to provide a comprehensive introduction to the field of ministry and Christian service, the collections of material set forth in *Gospel Workers* (1915) and *Testimonies to Ministers* are very helpful in providing a general context in which to read the more topically specific compilations.

Evangelism (1946) and *Pastoral Ministry* (1995) are topical compilations whose titles adequately set forth their content. The material in both comes from unpublished manuscripts, periodical articles, out-of-print books, and pamphlets related to evangelism and the pastoral function. Though these are focused compilations in terms of their topics, they cover a broad range of material within those topics.

More specifically focused toward one area of ministry is *Counsels on Sabbath School Work* (1938). That topical compilation had been preceded by *Selections From the Testimonies Bearing on Sabbath School Work* in 1900. That earlier work was largely a chronological arrangement of articles from the *Sabbath School Worker* that were supplemented by selections from the *Testimonies*. The 1938 volume contained most of the earlier work, but is arranged topically rather than chronologically, and has been enriched by material from other Ellen White sources.

Of a more general nature are the topical compilations entitled *Instruction for Effective Christian Service* (1947, generally referred to as *Christian Service*) and *Welfare Ministry* (1952). The first of those volumes is designed as a handbook for community outreach, while the second presents Ellen White's counsel on "the delicate work of reaching hearts and winning souls through neighborly kindness" (WM 9). Both provide topically arranged counsel relating to work in the local community, and both are aimed at both laity and clergy, as opposed to *Gospel Workers* and *Testimonies to Ministers*, which are more tilted toward the "professional" aspects of the work of evangelists and ministers. *Christian Service* is composed entirely of material that had previously been published, whereas *Welfare Ministry* uses both published and unpublished sources.

Daughters of God: Messages Especially for Women (1998) is unique in Ellen White's corpus in that it is aimed specifically at women. A topical compilation, it presents an overview of women's ministry in the Bible as well as chapters on the various opportunities for women in ministry in the modern world. Of special interest are the appendices dealing with Ellen White's public ministry, items related to the ordination of women, and Ellen White's relationship with her husband.

More loosely related to ministry and Christian service than some of the volumes in this section are *Counsels on Stewardship* (1940) and *The Voice in Speech and Song* (1988). Both are topical compilations with direct implications for the performance of ministry in its various manifestations.

b. Books on Education. The central book in this category is the insightful volume entitled *Education* (1903). That book stands among the very best of the counsel volumes. A well-balanced treatment of education developed within the framework of the great controversy between good and evil, it sets forth human nature and human need as the focal point of education. True education is equated with redemption. The book takes a larger view of education as being lifelong and much more than schooling. The various aspects of the educative experience (such as recreation and discipline) are integrally related to the overall great controversy philosophy of the book. Because of its comprehensive philosophical framework, all of Ellen White's other works on education should be read within the framework of the concepts set forth in *Education*.

The earliest Ellen White collections on education were published in the 1890s. *Christian Education* was published in 1893, with *Special Testimonies on Education* following in 1897, largely being a collection of instruction written after the publication of *Christian Education*. The material in those two collections would be reprinted in *Education, Fundamentals of Christian Education* (1923), and *Counsels to Teachers, Parents, and Students Regarding Christian Education* (1913). The title of the latter was reworded *Counsels to Parents, Teachers, and Students* (1943), but the short form *Counsels to Teachers* has persisted in popular usage.

Counsels to Teachers is a topically arranged collection of Ellen White's writings that supplement the book *Education*. Based upon the same philosophy, it does much to fill out Ellen White's thought on the topic. A second supplement to *Education* was published 10 years after *Counsels to Teachers* as *Fundamentals of Christian Education*. That last volume is a chronologically arranged collection of published articles and unpublished manuscripts on education. Its publication largely rounded out and made available the main writings of

Ellen White on education. It should be noted that even though *Counsels to Teachers* and *Fundamentals* are collections from Ellen White's writings, they differ from most topical compilations in that nearly all the material is set forth in longer, "chapter-length" excerpts from her writings.

Two other books round out Ellen White's corpus on education. First, *Counsels on Education* (1968), which reprints in chronological order the major sections on education found in the nine volumes of *Testimonies for the Church*. Second, *True Education* (2000), which is an adapted version of *Education* for twenty-first-century readers.

c. Books on Family Life. Unlike the first two categories, this one has no flagship volume. All the books currently in print in the area of family life are topical compilations of short quotations. Even though Ellen White never wrote a broad-based book in the area of family life, she did pen an abundance of counsel in the field.

Her earliest books regarding family life were published in 1864. *An Appeal to the Youth* contains Uriah Smith's funeral sermon for Henry White (her oldest son), a narrative of his life by Adelia Patton, and 40 pages of letters from Ellen White to Henry. That same year saw the publication of *Appeal to Mothers Relative to the Great Cause of the Physical, Mental, and Moral Ruin of Many of the Children of Our Time*, a small volume dealing with the issue of "secret vice" (masturbation). It was reprinted by James in 1870 in *A Solemn Appeal*. *Appeal to Mothers* was also drawn on heavily for the "Preserving Moral Integrity" section in *Child Guidance*.

A Solemn Appeal Relative to Solitary Vice and the Abuses and Excesses of the Marriage Relation (1870), edited by James White, has 111 of its 272 pages from the pen of Ellen White. Among the Ellen White material is a reprint of *Appeal to Mothers*; three Ellen White chapters titled "The Marriage Relation," "The Care of Children," and "Errors in Education," drawn from *Health, or How to Live* (1865); and three chapters drawn from *Testimonies for the Church*, volume 2. The Ellen White materials from the 1870 edition were extracted and republished by themselves in 1890 with the shortened title of *A Solemn Appeal*.

Of the Ellen White books in print, the three central volumes in the area of family life are *The Adventist Home* (1952), *Child Guidance* (1954), and *Messages to Young People* (1930). Combined, they set forth Ellen White's basic thought on their respective topics. Each is a topical compilation, and each has a very broad coverage of the various aspects of its general topic. In 2002 *A Call to Stand Apart* was published as a book that is aimed at speaking to contemporary youth in language adapted to the twenty-first century.

Testimonies on Sexual Behavior, Adultery, and Divorce (1989) and *The Retirement Years* (1990) have their own specific niches in the realm of Ellen White's overall counsel on family life. Both volumes deal with the breadth of Ellen White's counsel on their respective topics. Of special interest in *The Retirement Years*, outside of Ellen White's counsel on the topic, is an extended year-by-year summary of Ellen White's extensive activities after age 65—demonstrating that life's contributions don't end at the typical retirement age.

d. Books Related to Health. The flagship book in this category is *The Ministry of Healing* (1905). It stands in a place analogous to that of *Education* in its area of interest. *The Ministry of Healing* is Ellen White's only broad-based treatment of health. Thus it provides the all-important context for reading the compilations on the topic. An added value of

The Ministry of Healing is that it sets forth its material in relationship to the healing ministry of Jesus.

The Ministry of Healing presents in a general way Ellen White's philosophy of health. It begins with an extended treatment of Christ's healing ministry and then moves on to the work of Christian physicians and medical missionaries. It also has major sections on the care of the sick, health principles, the role of the home in health, the essential knowledge on the topic, and needed characteristics in health workers. Over the years *The Ministry of Healing* has been published under more than one title, one of the most popular being *Your Home and Health* (1943), which was developed for colporteur sales and contains about three fifths of the original book.

Ellen White began writing on health-related topics in the 1860s. The year 1864, as we noted earlier under books on family life, saw the publication of *Appeal to Mothers*, with its discussion of the physical, mental, and moral results of masturbation. More central to her ongoing discussion of health issues was her 32-page presentation on the topic in the fourth volume of *Spiritual Gifts* (1864). That chapter is the first comprehensive presentation of the health message as given to Ellen White in her June 6, 1863, vision on the topic. That material would be amplified in 1865 to become the six Ellen White chapters published in a series of pamphlets bound together as *Health, or How to Live*.

Health, or How to Live (1865) is a composite book put together by James White that contains both Ellen White's writings and those of contemporary health reformers. Ellen White's material represents 86 of the book's 296 pages. The six Ellen White articles deal with (1) diet; (2) marriage and child care; (3) drugs; (4) fresh air, exercise, and general hygiene; (5) proper dress for children; and (6) proper dress for women. That material was republished in 1958 as *Selected Messages*, book 2, pages 409-479.

The 1890s saw the next generation of books on health. *Christian Temperance and Bible Hygiene,* by Ellen and James White, was published in 1890, with Ellen's part being the *Christian Temperance* chapters (155 of the work's 268 pages). The preface declares that "this book is not a new presentation . . . but is simply a compilation, and in some sense an abstract, of the various writings of Mrs. White upon this subject [health], to which have been added several articles, by Elder James White, elucidating the same principles" (CTBH iv).

Instruction Relating to the Principles of Healthful Living (usually referred to as *Healthful Living*) came off the press in 1897. This work, compiled by Dr. David Paulson, set forth "in the most concise and condensed form possible the various teachings upon the subject of health, health reform, and allied matters, which are to be found in the writings of Mrs. E. G. White" (HL 3).

The beginning of the twentieth century witnessed the publication of *The Ministry of Healing* (1905), a book that superseded all of her previous works on the topic. The twentieth century would also see the development of four topical compilations on health-related topics.

Counsels on Diet and Foods (1938) is a topically arranged reference volume embodying the full range of counsels on the subject drawn from both published and unpublished sources. *Temperance* (1949) deals not only with the philosophy of temperance, but also with Ellen White's counsel on alcohol, tobacco, and other stimulants and narcotics. In addition, it treats issues dealing with rehabilitation, prevention, and the work of temperance delegated to the church.

Counsels on Health (1923) contains a more general approach to the topic, whereas *Counsels on Diet and Foods* and *Temperance* are quite specific in their treatment of diet and substance abuse. *Counsels on Health* also differs from the other two volumes in that it contains sections that deal specifically with the work of health professionals. That topic, along with material speaking to Adventist health institutions, is also the subject of *Medical Ministry* (1932). That volume has the distinction of being the first posthumous Ellen White book to consist largely of previously unpublished materials.

Closely related to Ellen White's concern with physical health is the two-volume topical compilation titled *Mind, Character, and Personality: Guidelines to Mental and Spiritual Health* (1977). The purpose of that extensive, 882-page compilation "is to bring the Ellen G. White statements in this broad, important, and sometimes controversial field together for convenient study" (MCP [i]). This collection sought to be comprehensive in the sense that it aimed to bring together all known statements relevant to the topics covered.

e. Books on Publishing. Another area of Ellen White counsel books has to do with Adventist publishing. Like the family category, this one has no specifically written Ellen White book on the topic. All the volumes in this category are topical compilations.

The earliest of those compilations came out in 1902 as *Manual for Canvassers*, a pocket-sized volume of 73 pages that provided literature evangelists with Ellen White's counsels on book distribution. In 1920 the *Manual* was enlarged and issued as The *Colporteur Evangelist*. Then in 1953 the book was once more enlarged and published as *Colporteur Ministry*.

A second area to be represented by a topical compilation was counsel relevant to those who employ the written and spoken word in proclaiming the Adventist message through the public press, radio, and the visual media. *Counsels to Writers and Editors* was published in 1946, even though it had been released in a limited edition in 1939.

But the material in *Colporteur Ministry* and *Counsels to Writers and Editors* did not include large segments of Ellen White's counsel on publishing. As a result, The *Publishing Ministry* (1983) was developed to deal with the various aspects of publishing and the establishment, operation, and management of publishing houses. Thus The *Publishing Ministry* is the most comprehensive of Ellen White's statements on the topic and in a sense provides the context in which her more narrow works on the subject should be read.

f. Book on Race Relations. While this segment of Ellen White's writings has not been as fully developed with topical compilations as have the other five sections, it does have one small but significant book. *The Southern Work* (1898, 1966) was published by Ellen White's son James Edson in 1898 to promote missionary activity in the South.

The Southern Work is a compilation of Ellen White materials depicting conditions at the time and calling for missionary activity among the Blacks in the Southern states. It is made up of four sections. Opening the volume is an appeal made to church leaders by Ellen White in 1891 titled "Our Duty to the Colored People." The second section presents nine Ellen White articles published in the *Review and Herald* between November 1895 and February 1896. The reprint edition (1966) includes a tenth *Review and Herald* article from April 2, 1895, that was evidently overlooked in the initial compilation. The last two sections present some selected Ellen White counsels and cautions concerning the topic.

8. The Devotional Books

Every year since the 1940s the Seventh-day Adventist Church has published a daily devotional book with 365 readings. The first Ellen White volume to come out as a daily devotional was *Radiant Religion* in 1946. Its compilers prepared it entirely from previously published works, but subsequent Ellen White devotionals contain both published materials and selections from the letter and manuscript files. The various devotionals each focus on a topic for the year. As of 2005 there had been 19 Ellen White devotional books published. Most of them have remained in print.

Radiant Religion (1946)
*With God at Dawn (1949)
*My Life Today (1952)
*Sons and Daughters of God (1955)
*The Faith I Live By (1958)
*Our High Calling (1961, 2000)
*That I May Know Him (1964)
*In Heavenly Places (1967)
*Conflict and Courage (1970)
*God's Amazing Grace (1973)
*Maranatha: The Lord Is Coming (1976)
*This Day With God (1979)
*The Upward Look (1982)
*Reflecting Christ (1985)
*Lift Him Up (1988)
*Our Father Cares (1992)
*Ye Shall Receive Power (1995)
*Christ Triumphant (1999)
*To Be Like Jesus (2004)

B. PERIODICAL ARTICLES

During her many years of ministry Ellen White published more than 5,000 articles in Seventh-day Adventist periodicals. The largest number of those articles appeared in the *Review and Herald* and the *Signs of the Times*. During the last quarter century of her life, they each generally had a piece from her pen every week.

Ellen White also published in dozens of other periodicals, such as the *Youth's Instructor*, the *Health Reformer*, and the *General Conference Bulletin*. For many years one could read those articles only at the few institutions that had sets of the various periodicals. But that has changed.

In 1962 the Ellen G. White Estate reprinted in facsimile form all of Ellen White's *Present Truth* and *Review and Herald* articles in six large volumes. Since that time the White Estate has made available her articles in the *Signs of the Times* (four volumes, 1974) and the *Youth's Instructor* (1986). More recently (1990) her articles from periodicals that she was published in less frequently have also begun to be released in a series entitled *Ellen White Periodical Resource Collection.*

Her articles cover a broad range of topics, from notes on her travel and remarks on current issues to the needs of the church. But most of them deal with devotional or theological issues, often issues of contemporary pertinence to the church at the time they were published. The articles, as might be expected, have produced much of the material for the compilations and devotionals.

II. Unpublished Writings

A. LETTER AND MANUSCRIPT FILE

The amount of Ellen White's literary output is staggering. In addition to her published works, there are some 8,000 letters and manuscripts. The letters are generally to church leaders, family members, or personal friends. While many of them discuss the issues of daily life, nearly all of them deal with spiritual matters. Many of them were "testimonies" or messages from God to the church or various individuals.

The manuscripts are often sermons, testimonies to various groups, or diary materials. The total number of typewritten pages in this category is about 60,000. Several carbon copies were usually made of each document.

While all known Ellen White material has been put in a typed format, many handwritten manuscripts have also been preserved. The manuscripts and letters are kept in an integrated file. The master collection is located at the headquarters of the General Conference of Seventh-day Adventists, but the Ellen G. White Estate branch offices and research centers around the world also have complete sets of her unpublished writings.

B. PUBLICATIONS FROM THE LETTER AND MANUSCRIPT FILE

Up until recently one had to travel to an Ellen G. White office or research center in order to read her unpublished writings. But that has begun to change.

The White Estate took a major step forward in making previously unpublished material available when it began to publish all those sections that had already been released to the public for various uses since Ellen White's death. The first *Manuscript Releases* volume came off the press in 1981. Since that time 21 volumes have been published. *The Ellen G. White 1888 Materials* (four volumes, 1987) and the *Sermons and Talks* series (begun in 1990) represent two other efforts to get Ellen White's letters and manuscripts before the public.

III. Electronic Publication of Ellen White's Writings

In 1990 the Ellen G. White Estate published a *CD-ROM that contained all of Ellen White's published works. *The Published Ellen G. White Writings on Compact Disc* included every known book, article, and pamphlet written by Ellen White during her 70-year ministry, as well as the many thousands of pages that had been put into print from unpublished manuscripts between 1915 and 1990. Also included on the disc was *Ellen G. White*, the six-volume biography by Arthur L. White, D. A. Delafield's *Ellen G. White in Europe*, and a summary of the scope of Ellen White's ministry and the development of her major writings.

In 1998 the White Estate brought out a new edition of the CD-ROM entitled *The Complete Published Ellen G. White Writings*. At the same time it published *Legacy of Light*, a two-volume CD collection that not only included *The Complete Published Ellen G. White Writings* disc, but had a second disc with such features as interactive time lines, a photo gallery, video vignettes relating to the life and ministry of Ellen White, and a learning center to help children learn about Adventist history and Ellen White's ministry.

As of 2003 the unpublished writings had also been readied for electronic publication. That CD-ROM project had not been released at the time of the writing of this article, since it was believed that the material would be of more value to the average user if it was accompanied by some historical comment on the various people and events connected to the different letters and manuscripts. Efforts are being made to compile that background material. With the release of the CD-ROM of the unpublished material, all of Ellen White's writings will be available to the public in machine-readable form.

Archival Resources and Finding Aids

Tim Poirier

Ellen White's estimated total literary output is 100,000 pages. With such a large amount of material, how can one discover what she taught about a given topic, or how can one locate that key quotation that now seems so hard to find? This article reviews the finding aids and archival resources that have been created to help readers in their study of this important collection of materials. It first describes the various research aids, and then provides an example of how to use those aids in the study of a specific topic—prayer.

I. Published Resources

Comprehensive Index to the Writings of Ellen G. White, 4 volumes, 1962, 1992. Robert L. Odom, Theodore E. Wade, Jr., editors. For more than a generation Seventh-day Adventists have consulted the *Comprehensive Index* as the single most useful finding aid in the study of Ellen White's writings. Even after the release of *The Complete Published Writings of Ellen G. White* on CD-ROM in 1990, the *Comprehensive Index* remains the best topical research aid available.

A project that was six years in the making, the *Comprehensive Index* was initially released in 1962 as three volumes and covered the 51 books available as of 1958 when work on forming the index entries closed.* In 1992 the White Estate released a fourth volume, a supplement covering the previously unindexed portions of an additional 27 books published up to that time. All combined, the 4,251 pages of the *Index* include more than 300,000 index entries divided into three parts: Scripture Index, Topical Index, and Quotation Index.

Scripture Index. Scripture is pervasive in the writings of Ellen White, whether she included it by direct quotation or by allusion. An estimated 40,000 citations to Scripture are referenced in the 1962 Scripture Index, with thousands more added in the 1992 *Supplement*. Where Ellen White refers to or uses a particular text more than six times, the references considered to make the larger contribution appear in boldface type, less-significant references are given normal type, and references that quote or repeat the same statement appear in parentheses. Indication is also given in cases in which a version of the Scriptures other than the King James Version is used.

Research tip: Because many of the citations refer to passages of Scripture rather than a single verse, such as Luke 7:36-50, the *Comprehensive Index* user needs to survey the references surrounding the specific text being researched so as not to miss comments made in those larger contexts. (The Scripture Index in the *Supplement* also references the key texts used at the beginning of each reading in the devotional books, but as these were selected by the compilers, such references are designated with a "k" with the paragraph.)

Topical Index. The primary research aid of the *Comprehensive Index* is the Topical Index, consisting of phrase-length entries that summarize the main thought of the indexed passage. Larger topics, such as Diet or Schools, are further subdivided to aid in narrowing the range of relevant references. As in the Scripture Index, references that are repeated exactly, but found in different books, are included within parentheses.

Research tips: Because some topics may be categorized under more than one heading or have related themes, researchers should always take note of the "See also" references at the end of many topics. There are also certain topical headings that provide unique information worth taking note of. Under "Christ, Appellations of," one finds an impressive alphabetical list of hundreds of names and titles for Christ found in Ellen White's writings. Under "White, Ellen G." there are three major divisions: biographical data, general information, and visions of. The biographical entries provide month, day, and year for Ellen White's travels and personal incidents related in her works. The "visions of" entries provide in chronological order references to her published visions. There is no other list of Ellen White's visions as complete as this list, but it should be borne in mind that it includes only those visions referenced in her published works.

Quotation Index. Volume 3 of the *Comprehensive Index* includes a Quotation Index (pp. 3105-3176) designed to provide quick access to familiar and often-used Ellen White statements. When looking for a specific statement on a topic, the researcher will often save considerable time by checking this index first.

Appendix. An underutilized but valuable section of the *Comprehensive Index* is its five-part Appendix, beginning on page 3179. We will list these below, with brief explanations:

Appendix A—Glossary of Proper Names. Concise identifications of key persons, titles, and institutions that one may encounter in reading Ellen White's counsels, e.g., *Bible Echo* or Pacific Health Retreat.

Appendix B—Glossary of Obsolete and Little-used Words and Terms With Altered Meanings. Definitions for archaic expressions such as "lung fever," "magnetic healer," and "gruel."

Appendix C—Apocryphal Quotations. A collection of statements mistakenly attributed to Ellen White. Additional statements may be found on the White Estate's Web site: www.WhiteEstate.org.

Appendix D—Editions of Ellen G. White Books. A chronological, bibliographical listing of Ellen White's principal works, including posthumous compilations published through 1961.

Appendix E—Helpful Points in the Interpretation and Use of the Ellen G. White Writings. Twenty-one hermeneutical principles that readers of Ellen White's writings would do well to review.

Subject Index to the Ellen G. White Periodical Articles, 1977, Ellen G. White Estate, Inc., 1072 pp. This now-out-of-print index is the only topical index to Ellen White's articles in the *Review and Herald, Signs of the Times, Youth's Instructor, General Conference Bulletin, Health Reformer*, and a few other selected resources. Its less-than-desirable format and thoroughness is explained by its origins. The index is the result of the retyping of a card index prepared over many years by various individuals connected with the White Estate. In spite of its deficiencies, the White Estate made the index available in this form so that access would not be limited only to those able to visit the White Estate or its research centers.

The Ellen White CD-ROM has largely replaced the need for this index, although its topical nature still has usefulness when researching broad subjects.

The Complete Published Ellen G. White Writings on CD-ROM, 1990-2009, Ellen G. White Estate, Inc. Researching Ellen White's writings entered the computer age when, in 1990, the White Estate released its first edition of Ellen White's published works on CD-ROM. The CD included not only her currently printed and out-of-print books and pamphlets, but also her more than 5,000 periodical articles and other manuscript collections—approximately 75,000 pages of searchable text. In 1999 Version 3.0 added the *Comprehensive Index* (less the Quotation Index and Appendix) so that topical searches could be added to the full-text search features. In 2009 the *Comprehensive Research Edition* was issued, adding the extensive resources of the Adventist Pioneer Library. (See article CD-ROM for more information.)

II. Internet Resources

White Estate Web site. In 1995 the White Estate placed a duplicate copy of the contents of its CD-ROM on its Web site in a searchable database. The interface was updated and enhanced in 2002, and while the CD-ROM offers advanced features for research unavailable on the Web, the online version provides Internet users with free access to search and browse all of Ellen White's published works. The Archives section contains specialized databases that will be further described later.

Bibliographic listings. A bibliography of Ellen White book and pamphlet titles is maintained by Loma Linda University's Del E. Web Library. An online searchable database may be accessed at: www.llu.edu/webapps/univ_library/specolls/EGWBibliographySearch.php. The Heritage Room at Pacific Union College's Nelson Memorial Library has produced bibliographies for Ellen White-related studies, including lists of major research papers, theses, and dissertations. These bibliographies are updated periodically, and are available online on the Web site of Pacific Union College: http://library.puc.edu/heritage/bib-index.shtml.

III. Unpublished Resources and Finding Aids

A. THE ELLEN G. WHITE LETTERS AND MANUSCRIPTS

At the time of this writing, all of Ellen White's correspondence and manuscripts are being prepared for publication with historical annotation. Even after that project is completed, however, it is important to recognize a distinction between materials published under Ellen White's supervision and those published after her death. Ellen White cautioned her readers in 1889, "If you desire to know what the Lord has revealed through her, read her *published works*" (5T 696; italics supplied). What Ellen White chose to put into print during her lifetime—taken as a whole—represents her considered teachings, while individual letters or manuscripts addressing specific situations may or may not express ideas as thoroughly as those she intended for general circulation. For that reason, priority should always be given to Ellen White's published works when studying her counsels.

The White Estate vault contains approximately 50,000 pages of Ellen White's letters and manuscripts. Photocopies of these documents are located in each of the research centers. Of the roughly 8,100 documents, 5,500 are letters and 2,600 are manuscripts. About one fourth of the letters are addressed to members of the White family, with S. N. Haskell and J. H. Kellogg, respectively, receiving the next-highest number of letters.

While the entire collection is commonly referred to as the "manuscript file," Ellen White's secretaries made a distinction in their filing between "letters" and "manuscripts."

"Letters" consist of:

(a) testimonies addressed to individuals, churches, or institutions

(b) letters to associates in the church and acquaintances

(c) letters to family members

"Manuscripts" consist of:

(a) stenographic reports of many of her sermons

(b) reports of interviews in which she actively participated

(c) her day-to-day diary or journal entries

(d) her initial writing on topics that might form the basis for
chapters in her books, or articles in church journals

(e) other writings not specifically addressed to individuals or groups

Indexes to Letters and Manuscripts. There are two card indexes to the letters and manuscripts, dating back to the time of the Elmshaven staff. The first is called the Addressee Index. For every Ellen White letter to an individual or institution there is an index card giving a brief summary of the letter's content. The cards are arranged alphabetically by name, and then chronologically under that particular name. The second index is the Letter/Manuscript Subject Index. This is arranged alphabetically by topic. Larger subjects, such as "angels," "sin," "Christ," may be divided into subheadings.

Research tip: It is important to remember that names of individuals and institutions are also indexed in the Letter/Manuscript Subject Index; this will often provide references to persons and places mentioned in documents not specifically addressed to them. (The Addressee Index indexes letters addressed only to those persons or places.)

Biographical Index. Another unique White Estate resource, prepared as an aid for the preparation of Ellen White's biography, is the Ellen White Biographical Index. So far as there is documentation, every day of Ellen White's active ministry has been indexed chronologically. Each year has a summary card at the beginning, followed by individual cards for daily activities. Information on Ellen White's activities has been gleaned from her diaries and letters, and from published reports.

B. Non-Ellen White Materials

Question-and-answer file. This file contains hundreds of letters written by the White Estate staff, including W. C. White and Arthur L. White, pertaining to questions commonly asked regarding Ellen White, her books, teachings, or personal life. While not significantly updated since the early 1970s, most of the files contain definitive responses to questions that periodically resurface, such as certain statements attributed to Ellen White, her view on renting Seventh-day Adventist churches to other denominations, and a host of other subjects not directly addressed in her published books. The research centers contain photocopies of representative responses drawn from the original file in Silver Spring, Maryland.

Document File. Begun by C. C. Crisler about 1900, the Document File consists of more than 1,000 folders on topics related to Ellen White's life, teachings, and writings; historical records pertaining to the church's institutions; collections of source material on Ellen White-related topics; and archival files of the White Estate Corporation. In the 1970s files deemed to be of research value were photocopied for each research center. In addition many of the research centers have expanded their collections to include major research papers prepared by students at their respective universities.

W. C. White letters. Included in this collection are approximately 15,000 letters written by Ellen White's son W. C. White between 1867 and 1915, with those from the 1880s to 1909 filed in 57 letter books ranging from 500 to 1,000 pages each. W. C. White's letters from 1916 up to his death in 1937 are uninventoried, but are filed as part of the incoming correspondence (see below). The White Estate Web site contains a searchable database of W. C. White's letters up through 1915. The research centers contain microfilm copies of all of the inventoried letters (through 1915).

James White letters. This collection consists of letters written by James White from 1846 to 1880. An inventory of the letters may be searched on the White Estate Web site, and the entire collection is duplicated on microfilm at each research center.

James Edson White letters. The White Estate archives also contains uninventoried letters written by Ellen White's son Edson White—most of which were written to his mother and to his brother W. C. White—between 1860 and 1927.

Incoming correspondence. Ellen White preserved many thousands of letters written by church leaders, ministers, and laypersons alike to herself, James, and/or her office staff. While it is known that probably 90 percent of the letters she received were not preserved, the more than 35,000 that are extant provide an invaluable and unique window into nineteenth- and early-twentieth-century Adventism. More specifically, these letters often give us the background to messages Ellen White wrote to these individuals and/or their responses to her testimonies.

Letters through the end of 1915, the year of Ellen White's death, have been inventoried, and the listing is available for searching on the White Estate Web site. But the White Estate collection also includes the correspondence records of the Elmshaven office through W. C. White's death in 1937, and, of course, the White Estate's own archives up to the present time.

Research centers possess microfilm copies of all of the inventoried correspondence from the 1840s to 1915.

Photographs. The White Estate photograph file consists of approximately 1,500 original prints of persons and places associated with the White family. These include photographs of church workers and leaders, institutions, and places of historical interest. Most of the collection has been digitized, and a searchable database may be accessed on the White Estate Web site. Other photograph files are also available at the Loma Linda University Heritage Room and at the Andrews University James White Library Center for Adventist Research.

Web resources. As noted above, the White Estate Web site, www.WhiteEstate.org, contains an Archives section in which researchers may search the inventories of the W. C. White and incoming letters through 1915. The database of digitized photographs may be searched in the Photographs section, and all of Ellen White's published works may be searched and browsed in the Search the Writings section. The site's Online Books section includes significant books relating to Ellen White's ministry that are now out of print.

IV. Using the Resources for Topical Research: A Tutorial

The purpose of this section is to provide an illustration of how the described resources may be used in researching a topic, in contrast to looking for a specific quotation. Let's suppose that our interest is to learn Ellen White's perspective on perseverance in prayer.

Anyone familiar with Ellen White's writings knows that she wrote an enormous amount of material on the subject of prayer. In this technological age our first instinct might be to simply do a search of the word "prayer" in the Ellen White CD-ROM. But when the computer retrieves more than 20,000 paragraphs containing "prayer" and its various forms ("pray," "praying," "prayfulness," etc.), one may be sufficiently discouraged from pursuing any further research on this theme. How, then, might one approach such a study?

1. Check whether any official compilations have already been prepared on the topic

Referring to the Ellen White Bibliography (http://search.llu.edu/heritage/EGWBiblio graphy.htm), we find that a 320-page Ellen White book on prayer was published by Pacific Press in 2003. Depending on how exhaustive you wish to be in your research, scanning the table of contents and index of the book *Prayer* may lead you to just what you are looking for. But what if you want more?

2. Consult the four-volume *Comprehensive Index to the Writings of Ellen G. White* (print or CD-ROM edition)

Particularly on a broad subject, such as prayer, the *Comprehensive Index* is invaluable because it subdivides major headings into narrower topics. While "Prayer" as a subject fills 23 pages of entries (plus another eight in the *Supplement*), these are divided into 19 categories. Our interest is perseverence in prayer, and subentry 3 (Earnest or Fervent) appears to focus most closely on this aspect. That reduces our searching to only about one and a half pages of entries. But we also see subentry 7 (Kinds of). This, too, turns out to be a promising subcategory, with multiple references on persevering or persistent prayer. But what if you want more?

3. Check the *Subject Index to the Ellen G. White Periodical Articles*

This index contains eight more pages of references—first to the general topic of prayer—but then with several subcategories, as in the *Comprehensive Index*. One of the subheadings is "Prayer (Perseverance—Importunity in)." Again, we find helpful references not indexed in the four-volume series. But what if you want more?

4. Search the CD-ROM

Now we are better prepared to narrow our search using the Ellen White CD-ROM. Rather than scanning the 20,000-plus references that refer to prayer in general, our use of the indexes above provides us with associated words used by Ellen White that will help to focus our results on our main interest—perseverance in prayer. For example, we can combine the word "prayer" with the word "persistent" or the word "importunate." To be as inclusive as possible, we can use the search operator ["pray"] rather than "prayer" so as to find occurrences of any form of the word starting with "pray."[*] And we can use proximity searching (explained in the CD-ROM tutorial) to find records in which the search terms are closer to each other. Finally, the *Comprehensive Index* often suggests alternative terms for what we are looking for, such as "intercession," "communion," "petition," or "supplication."

5. Be creative

Computer databases rely on exact words, but topical searching involves concepts. Thinking of instances in the Bible in which persevering prayer was demonstrated is another way to approach the topic in Ellen White's writings. For example, researching the stories of Jacob wrestling with the angel, or Christ's parable of the importunate widow (and others with similar lessons) will yield passages that might be overlooked by using only direct verbal approaches. But what if you want more?

6. Visit a research center

If the published sources have been exhausted, a research visit to one of the Ellen G. White Adventist Research Centers may be profitable. There one can consult the Letter/Manuscript Subject Card Index on prayer (and its related subtopics) for any additional references that may supplement the published statements. (Full text computer searching of the letters and manuscripts is still in development.) The Document File may also contain collections on the topic that other researchers have found valuable. The staff at the research center is prepared to assist in locating any other relevant material.

---

[*] Earlier indexes included: *Index to the Scripture References and Quotations Contained in the Writings of Mrs. E. G. White* (Battle Creek, Mich.: International Tract Society, 1896), 114 pp.; *Scriptural and Subject Index to the Writings of Mrs. Ellen G. White* (PPPA, 1926), 865 pp., with *Supplement* (c. 1940), 97 pp.

Bibliographic Essay on Publications About Ellen G. White

Merlin D. Burt

SINCE 1845 THERE HAVE BEEN HUNDREDS of monograph publications and thousands of periodical articles written on Ellen G. White and her prophetic ministry. Her spiritual experience, the visions she received, and the subsequent counsels she gave over a period of 70 years greatly influenced the origin and development of the Seventh-day Adventist Church. Her distinctive experience of receiving divine revelation through visions protected the Sabbatarian movement and then the Seventh-day Adventist Church from fanatical extremes, enriched its Bible-based doctrinal development, gave support and guidance for organizational issues, provided the initiative to define its major ministries, mediated church conflicts, and gave personal counsel to individuals and groups across the Seventh-day Adventist spectrum. Yet, with this remarkable influence, she was not a controlling voice for the movement, and always pointed the church to the Bible as the foundation of faith and practice. Her visions played the role of a "lesser light" to lead people to the "greater light." Also, central to her life and work were Jesus, the plan of salvation, and the loving character of God. Her focus on the broader issues of the battle between good and evil gave a substantive biblical perspective to the church.

Naturally, her varied experiences and activities led to published comments both positive and negative. Publications regarding Ellen White and her experience are largely contextual to the Adventist movement. This essay divides publications regarding Ellen White into eras. These are somewhat arbitrary, though they do generally relate to experiences and events regarding the Seventh-day Adventist Church or Ellen White's life.

The six periods defined in this essay are:

1. The Early Years—1845-1865
2. Organized Opposition—1866-1883
3. Canright, Kellogg, and the New Opposition—1884-1919
4. Era of Serious Promotion—1920-1975
5. Reassessing Ellen White's Life and Ministry—1976-2008
6. Expanding Resources and Increasing Understanding—2009-present

This essay will include the more important publications that deal predominately with Ellen White and her prophetic ministry. Nearly every historical account of the Seventh-day Adventist Church has a chapter or more on Ellen White. These works will not generally be discussed unless the discussion of the prophetic gift and ministry of Ellen White is an important part of the publication history or provides significant new insights. While this essay has attempted to be comprehensive, it is not exhaustive. It traces the broader development through the year 2008.

There have been many periodical articles relating to Ellen White. As a general rule, this essay is limited to book publications, though it will discuss some significant periodical articles on Ellen White's life and prophetic ministry. Major Adventist periodicals together with certain periodicals with a focus on Ellen White during the period from 1976 through

2008 will receive more detailed treatment. As a general rule, less substantive articles or monographs that relate to Ellen White in terms of topical subjects, such as doctrines, lifestyle, etc., will not be included.

Similarly, since the twentieth century, many unpublished dissertations have been written that relate in some way to Ellen White. Most are oriented toward topics, individuals, institutions, general Adventist history, or theology in relation to Ellen White or her ministry. A selection are footnoted but not included in this essay.[1]

A few general observations are in order. As one evaluates the entire period from 1845 to the present, it is remarkable how much of the literary landscape is filled with opposing and apologetic works on Ellen White and her ministry. During her lifetime nearly all church-related publications were apologetic in nature or at least driven by apologetic concerns. Usually they answered individuals or groups and their particular ideas. The back-and-forth nature of the published material often resulted in somewhat scattered conclusions. Only in recent decades have more fundamental and systematic presentations on prophetic studies and the related issues of revelation and inspiration appeared.

Certain repetitive patterns appear among Ellen White's opponents. First, those who reject her visions usually reject the idea of modern prophetic special revelation. Second, they hold to a more verbal view of inspiration and reject the idea of progressive or unfolding revelation. They typically do not allow the prophetic messenger to grow in his/her understanding of God's revelation over time and with repetition. Third, the rejection of Ellen White's prophetic gift is often linked to a rejection of distinctive Adventist doctrines such as the Sabbath, the heavenly sanctuary ministry of Jesus, and the prophetic nature of the Advent movement and its organization. Fourth, some who opposed Ellen White during her lifetime had received a personal testimony they refused to accept. Similarly, since her death, many who have opposed her writings and ministry have manifested a negative disposition toward her instructions and counsels because they incorrectly viewed her as mean-spirited, inflexible, and legalistic.

A growing number of historians and scientists in recent years have abandoned the presuppositions of the Christian faith or are secular in their perspective. Hence they examine Ellen White from only a secular and/or naturalistic perspective, deny the possibility of divine revelation, and even question the existence of God. This essay is written from the perspective that there is a God who does reveal Himself, through special revelation using the prophetic gift, at various times throughout history as divine wisdom sees fit.

1. The Early Years—1845-1865

During the first two decades of Ellen White's prophetic experience, references to her prophetic gift are relatively sparse and usually brief. Nevertheless, James White and Joseph Bates established a baseline understanding of the role of visions in the movement. Opposing works are generally limited to dissident Sabbatarian Adventists or those from other branches of Adventism, such as the Advent Christian Church. Materials written by advocates of Ellen White's prophetic gift were largely apologetic in nature. One exception is the relatively frequent biblical studies on the "perpetuity of spiritual gifts" or the legitimacy of the modern manifestation of the gift of prophecy in the church.

The earliest published reference to Ellen White was within the context of conflict or interaction with extreme Millerites. In March of 1845 her name was mentioned in a reporter's account of the trial of Israel Dammon in Dover, Maine.[2] Ellen Harmon (later White) was mentioned by witnesses for both the prosecution and the defense. Little information is given beyond the events surrounding Dammon's arrest in the home of James Ayer. During that evening she was observed reclining on the floor, presumably in vision.[3]

During 1845 Ellen Harmon frequently found herself objecting to positions held by extreme Millerites—particularly mesmerism and the spiritualizing view of the second coming of Jesus. Her principle opponent during this period was Joseph Turner. Though a copy of his document on her visions is not extant, Ellen White recollected that he circulated a signed statement against her during the late summer or early fall of 1845. Turner was involved in mesmerism, and when Ellen Harmon opposed him, he turned against her.

The second extant published reference to Ellen Harmon is in an article by James White in the September 6, 1845, *Day-Star,* written on August 19, 1845.[4] He wrote of Harmon's first Midnight Cry vision (December 1844) and applied her figurative view of Adventists falling off the path to various fanatics and those who had rejected the Midnight Cry.

The first published material by Ellen White is found in two letters written to Enoch Jacobs, editor of the *Day-Star.* They were published in early 1846 and contain an account of her first major visions. These letters were published on April 6, 1846, in a broadside titled *To the Little Remnant Scattered Abroad.*[5] A year later in April 1847 Joseph Bates published *A Vision,* containing a letter from Ellen White describing a recent vision.[6] Both Bates and James White were clear that Ellen White's visions were subject to biblical authority. Bates also wanted to emphasize that Ellen White's gift was not a replacement, substitute, or addition to the Bible. In his comments, originally published in *A Vision,* he wrote of the Bible: "I do not publish the above vision thinking to add or diminish from the 'sure word of prophecy.' That will stand the test of men and wreck of worlds! 'It is written that man shall not live by bread alone, but by every word of God.' Amen."[7] James White republished his comments less than two months later in *A Word to the "Little Flock."*[8] To show the harmony between her visions and the Bible, he added 84 biblical and seven apocryphal references to her two articles. James White wrote explicitly that his wife's writings were not additional scripture or a source of doctrine. He also gave a defense for modern prophets: "The bible is a perfect, and complete revelation. It is our only rule of faith and practice. But this is no reason, why God may not show the past, present, and future fulfilment of his word, in these *last days,* by dreams and visions; according to Peter's testimony. True visions are given to lead us to God, and his written word; but those that are given for a new rule of faith and practice, separate from the bible, cannot be from God, and should be rejected."[9]

James White discussed whether her visions were simply enthusiasm or "reveries" or whether they were a product of special revelation.[10] Bates gave a further supportive explanation of Ellen White's prophetic gift, in his book on the seal of God, during January 1849, with quotations of her comments while in vision.[11] These early comments by Bates and James White established a baseline for future explanations of Ellen White's visions. Ellen

White herself shared this view, and on the last page of her first published tract she wrote: "I recommend to you, dear reader, the Word of God as the rule of your faith and practice. By that Word we are to be judged. God has, in that Word, promised to give visions in the 'last days;' not for a new rule of faith, but for the comfort of His people, and to correct those who err from Bible truth."[12] Thus the three principle founders of the Seventh-day Adventist Church affirmed the principle of *sola scriptura* while retaining belief in the modern manifestation of the prophetic gift.

One additional reference to Ellen White of a poetic nature needs to be mentioned. During 1845 Ellen White had a vision of the new earth that countered the spiritualizing views of some Bridegroom Adventists who said that Jesus had already come and that the saints were living spiritually in the New Jerusalem. In her vision she described in tangible terms the living green grass, flowers, people, houses, and food of the new earth. William H. Hyde, a teenage peer of Ellen White, observed the vision and composed a poem based on her description. This poetic reference to her new earth vision was set to music and widely published as a hymn, "We Have Heard From the Bright, the Holy Land."[13] It has been retained in Adventist hymnals to this day.[14]

As Sabbatarian Adventism rapidly grew during the early 1850s James White mostly refrained from publishing material by or about Ellen White's prophetic ministry in the regular *Review and Herald*. A limited-circulation extra issue of the *Review and Herald* in 1851 explained the reason: "We do not design this extra for so general circulation as the regular paper, for the reason that strong prejudice exists in many minds against a portion of its contents. . . . But as many are prejudiced against visions, we think best at present not to insert anything of the kind in the regular paper. We will therefore publish the visions by themselves for the benefit, of those who believe that God can fulfill his word and give visions '*in the last days.'* "[15] Thus until the end of 1855 James White generally avoided publicizing or defending Ellen White's writings in print. Nevertheless his careful attempt to present a biblical basis for the Adventist faith did not prevent opposition.

A. N. Seymour and the *Advent Harbinger*

The first significant published opposition to Ellen White from dissident Sabbatarian Adventists originated in Jackson, Michigan, and the *Messenger* Party. Just previous to this short-lived movement an article appeared in the *Advent Harbinger* attacking Ellen White based on her 1851 tract, *Experience and Views*. A. N. Seymour attempted to ridicule Ellen White based on her description of the Father and Son moving to the Most Holy Place of the heavenly sanctuary. He argued that it was inconsistent for Ellen White to write that she could not see the Father's person and then to write that she saw him rise from the throne. He also refused to see the metaphorical nature of Satan taking Jesus' place after the throne was moved to the Most Holy Place. "O what a blasphemous vision!" he wrote. "The Devil in the New Jerusalem! No wonder the sanctuary there, as they teach, needs cleansing!" Based on these observations, he concluded: "This vision is sufficient to stamp the rest as fabulous."[16] Seymour went on to criticize the whole idea that the "true midnight cry" was proclaimed in 1844. He did, though, accept the idea of a shut door but placed it in the future, when "Christ comes, and all the virgins that are ready enter in."[17]

Ellen White responded to this challenge by Seymour. "I really think that Mr. S. has manifested a disposition to catch at words, and will leave it for others to judge whether such a course becomes a minister of Christ." She went on to draw attention to what she had actually written. "Satan *appeared* to be by the throne, trying to carry on the work of God." She then declared that she had never thought that "individuals were actually in the New Jerusalem" or that "Satan was actually in the New Jerusalem." Finally Ellen White observed that even John the revelator saw a "great red dragon in heaven."[18] Thus ended this particular exchange, but not the antagonism to Ellen White and the Sabbatarian Adventists. At this time Joseph Marsh, the publisher of the *Advent Harbinger*, and James White, the publisher of the *Review and Herald,* were both publishing in Rochester, New York.

The *Messenger* Party

In 1853 the *Messenger* Party conflict began with a dispute over whether to censure Abigail Palmer, the wife of a prominent member in the Jackson church. In connection with the incident, Ellen White had two visions on June 3, 1853. The first rebuked Palmer for her attitude. H. S. Chase and C. P. Russell, two local ministers, were urging church discipline and strongly supported the vision. That same evening Ellen White had a second vision, which rebuked Case and Russell for being too harsh and unkind. When Ellen White shared the content of her second vision, Abigail Palmer repented, but the two men rejected the validity of the vision.[19] Before the year had ended, both Case and Russell were removed from membership in the Jackson church. By 1854 they, together with other discontented Sabbatarians, began publication of the *Messenger of Truth.* The three extant issues demonstrate that the purpose of the paper, at least initially, was to give their side of what happened in the above-described incident, to oppose James White's leadership, and to reject the visions of Ellen White.[20] They attempted to show inconsistencies or inaccurate details in the visions, but overall the extant articles do not develop theological or historical challenges to Ellen White's visions. They appear rather to be a collection of negative impressions concerning James and Ellen White.

First Supportive Monographs

The first published monographs written solely to address Ellen White's prophetic gift were R. F. Cottrell's *Spiritual Gifts* and M. E. Cornell's *Miraculous Powers*.[21] Cottrell's 16-page tract was published in 1858 and then appeared as a preface to Ellen White's *Spiritual Gifts*, volume 1.[22] Cornell's 143-page tract included material by James White and was published in 1862. The central purpose of these tracts was to argue that the gift of prophecy was not only legitimate beyond the Apostolic Era but was also prophetically predicted for the last days. Though the tracts were written to defend her visions, Ellen White remains unnamed. The second edition of Cornell's tract, published in 1875, did not include James White's remarks, but instead added an appendix that specifically explained the prophetic character of Ellen White's ministry.[23]

Summary: 1845-1865

The early years provided a baseline understanding of the prophetic gift for Sabbatarian Adventists. The limited early publications provided clarification on the relationship between Ellen White's writings and the Bible, the biblical basis for modern prophets, and a response to the first opposition to Ellen White's prophetic gift.

2. Organized Opposition—1866-1883

The year 1866 marked the beginning of a more systematic and focused opposition to Ellen White's prophetic gift by dissident Sabbatarian and non-Sabbatarian Adventists.

B. F. Snook and W. H. Brinkerhoff

B. F. Snook and W. H. Brinkerhoff produced a publication that set the course for a movement of opposition to Ellen White and the Seventh-day Adventist Church.[24] This first dissident movement of the Seventh-day Adventist Church continues to this day as the Church of God (Seventh Day). The Snook and Brinkerhoff tract titled *The Visions of E. G. White, Not of God* contained a series of 26 objections to Ellen White's visions. Each objection was specific, and many continue to serve as a starting point for Ellen White's modern opponents. Before beginning their formal objections, they proposed that Ellen White's visions could not be a fulfillment of Joel 2:28 because Ellen White was not a "young man" and was thus "from the wrong sex." They further set up an arbitrary requirement, previously rejected by James White, that her writings had "an equality with the Bible."[25] Building upon these presuppositions, they charged that she taught a shut door for sinners from 1844-1851 and that James White had suppressed the evidence. They argued that her writings contained doctrinal errors, internal inconsistencies, historical inaccuracies, false predictions, and nothing that was really new or supernatural. They further attacked her integrity and claimed she fabricated visions to accomplish her own purposes.

William Sheldon

Snook and Brinkerhoff's tract encouraged non-Sabbatarian Adventists to intensify their opposition to Ellen White and Seventh-day Adventists. In September 1866 William Sheldon announced his plan to write a series of articles against Ellen White.[26] J. V. Himes, in Buchanan, Michigan, published them during January and February 1867.[27] Sheldon's articles became the basis for a 64-page tract titled *The Visions and Theories of the Prophetess Ellen G. White in Conflict With the Bible*.[28] Sheldon is the first non-Sabbatarian to publish a monograph against Ellen White's visions. He served as one of the three members of the publishing committee for the *Voice of the West* and was a frequent contributor to the paper. Sheldon's articles and tract mixed contrasting arguments. First, he rejected that prophets can grow in their understanding or progressively unfold new ideas over time. He observed that Ellen White did not accept the Sabbath until after she had received several visions and then saw it as the "*seal* of the living God." He questioned how "this prophetess, so often enwrapped in visions, and so often receiving instruction for the Advent people, never once saw that God was displeased with our [other Millerites] having the 'mark of the beast.'"[29] Second, Sheldon expanded on Snook and Brinkerhoff's argument that Ellen White's writings were not supernatural because they presented nothing new. In his opinion Ellen White followed the lead of others and did not originate new ideas. "Why," he wrote, "could not God have revealed these items [such as the time to begin the Sabbath, church organization, systematic benevolence, and the shut door] to her, instead of waiting till men had devised the plans, and then sanction them?"[30] Throughout his tract Sheldon presented what he considered inconsistencies between Ellen White's writings and the Bible or reason. Some of his arguments were directed as much against Seventh-day Adventist doctrine as they were against Ellen White's views.

Adventist Responses to Snook, Brinkerhoff, and Sheldon

James White responded to both Snook and Brinkerhoff and Sheldon regarding both Ellen White's role in Seventh-day Adventist doctrinal development and progressive revelation: "It does not appear to be the design of the Lord to teach his people by the gifts of the Spirit on Bible questions until his servants have diligently searched his word."[31] He illustrated the progressive way in which God leads His people with the shut-door concept: "Some of this people did believe in the shut door, in common with the Adventists generally, soon after the passing of time. Some of us held fast this position longer than those did who gave up their Advent experience, and drew back in the direction of perdition. And God be thanked that we did hold fast to that position till the matter was explained by light from the heavenly sanctuary."[32]

For early Seventh-day Adventists the Bible took the lead in doctrinal and theological discussions, rather than Ellen White's visions. Early (and later) opponents failed or refused to recognize this distinction.

The tracts published by Snook and Brinkerhoff and Sheldon led to the first direct Seventh-day Adventist apologetic of Ellen White's visions. Uriah Smith initially published a series of articles in the *Review and Herald*[33] responding to Snook and Brinkerhoff. This material was then expanded to include objections made by Sheldon and published as a 144-page book, *The Visions of Mrs. E. G. White: A Manifestation of Spiritual Gifts According to the Scriptures.*[34] Smith's book gave important insight into early Sabbatarian Adventist thinking on inspiration, the relationship of Ellen White's writings to the Bible, background on her role in doctrinal development, an early response to the shut-door issue, and the charge that some early visions were suppressed. The tract concluded with a testimony by Worcester Ball and the 1865 confessions of Snook and Brinkerhoff before they hardened in their opposing positions. Smith further answered the charges against Ellen White's integrity and the authenticity of her visions with biblical and historical explanations.

Henry E. Carver

In 1870 Henry E. Carver, publisher of the *Hope of Israel* in Marion, Iowa, and an associate of Brinkerhoff, wrote *Mrs. E. G. White's Claims to Divine Inspiration Examined.*[35] The 108-page book shared many of Snook and Brinkerhoff's arguments but added a history of their separation from the Seventh-day Adventist Church and some additional "objections." Carver concluded that her visions were from "human frailty" and resulted from a combination of influences including her accident at the age of 9, the influence of Methodist demonstrative experience, and Millerite confusion after 1844.[36] In 1877 Carver published a second edition with essentially the same content but a more detailed conclusion. He modified some of his arguments in light of Seventh-day Adventist responses to the first edition of his book. He followed the line of previous opponents when he wrote: "The visions have brought out no new points of faith held by Seventh-day Adventists," including the Sabbath, the Second Coming, the unconscious state of the dead, the sanctuary and its cleansing after 1844, and the prophetic periods.[37] He attributed Ellen White's visions to mental illness and claimed: "As Mrs. White's health has improved the visions have become less frequent."[38]

H. C. Blanchard

In 1877 H. C. Blanchard, also associated with Brinkerhoff in Marion, Iowa, published *The Testimonies of Mrs. E. G. White Compared With the Bible*.[39] His tract was devoted to the subject of diet. Blanchard became a Seventh-day Adventist in 1861, before Ellen White's 1863 vision on health. He rejected her health vision's promotion of vegetarianism as inconsistent with Scripture. He pressed the issue in the Kansas and Missouri Conference and in 1876 lost his ministerial credentials.[40] The tract traced the history of meat eating from the 1850s, when James and Ellen White and even Uriah Smith had publicly taught that pork was an acceptable food.[41] Blanchard then presented the classic argument in favor of eating any meat and the abolishment of the distinction between clean and unclean (Mark 7:15; 1 Tim. 4:4; Acts 10 and 15; Rom. 14; Gal. 2; etc.) and charged that Ellen White's visions were out of harmony with Scripture. He compared the diet issue with dress reform and suggested that Seventh-day Adventists were inconsistent in strictly applying diet reform and not enforcing a shorter style of dress for women. The tract ended abruptly with a few additional arguments. Blanchard appears to be a casualty of the progressive nature of Seventh-day Adventist understanding and teaching on diet.

Miles Grant and the *World's Crisis*

Miles Grant, editor of the *World's Crisis*, was the second major non-Sabbatarian opponent of Ellen White. Arguably the most prominent and controversial Advent Christian during the 1870s, his publication in 1874, *The True Sabbath: Which Day Shall We Keep? An Examination of Mrs. Ellen White's Visions,* gave wide exposure to arguments against Ellen White.[42] Whereas William Sheldon, the first major non-Sabbatarian opponent of Ellen White, was located in the pioneering West of the Wisconsin territory, Grant was in refined Boston and the settled Eastern seaboard. Grant's 104-page book against the Sabbath included about 40 pages directed against Ellen White. The book was reprinted in 1877 and 1890.[43] Grant cited a then-recent vote of the General Conference endorsing "her as a true prophetess of the Lord" as his reason for publishing a critique of Ellen White's writings.[44] He gave several lengthy excerpts from Carver's booklet.

Previous to publishing the book, Grant ran a series of articles in the *World's Crisis* presenting his side of a Sabbath debate with D. M. Canright in Napa, California.[45] Grant then followed up with articles against Ellen White.[46] After publishing his book, he continued to write articles based on its content.[47]

A *Review and Herald Extra* issue traced Grant's public opposition-1866 and the aftermath of a debate between J. N. Andrews and T. M. Preble on the Sabbath. The *World's Crisis* had issued a challenge for Seventh-day Adventists to "risk" a published debate. J. N. Andrews accepted the challenge, but the *World's Crisis* refused to publish any articles. A question of justice and integrity continued to stand between Grant and Andrews for a number of years.[48]

The content of Grant's charges against Ellen White's prophetic gift was first gathered from other opponents. In 1871 Grant published an article drawing from Carver's book. He accused Ellen White of being an oracle for Seventh-day Adventists and compared her with Ann Lee and the Shakers.[49] This and other altercations culminated in his 1874 publication.

Grant's opposition focused almost exclusively on the shut-door issue. He included a number of testimonies by those who had associated with Ellen White during the early years of her experience. Like Snook, Brinkerhoff, Sheldon, and Carver, he argued that Ellen White's visions taught that probation or the "door of mercy" had closed for the world. These accusations brought a response from Ellen White. "With my brothers and sisters after the time passed in '44," she wrote, "I did believe no more sinners could be converted. But I never had a vision that no more sinners would be converted."[50]

During 1874 Isaac Wellcome published an extensive early history of Millerite Adventism. Following the mood of publications against Ellen White, Wellcome presented her as being a key proponent of the shut-door view. D. M. Canright challenged some of Wellcome's assertions, including his claim of seeing Ellen White in vision.[51] An April 14, 1874, *Review and Herald Extra* presented a history of the interactions between Miles Grant and Seventh-day Adventists.[52] This important publication also contained an article on the biblical basis for the perpetuity of spiritual gifts.[53] Negative articles and references continued in the *World's Crisis*, *Voice of the West*, and other papers during the last half of the 1870s.

1870s Seventh-day Adventist Publications on the Gift of Prophecy

During the 1870s Seventh-day Adventists prepared new publications presenting the Seventh-day Adventist view on the gift of prophecy. In 1877 J. H. Waggoner published *The Spirit of God: Its Offices and Manifestations, to the End of the Christian Age*, tracing prophetic and supernatural activities in the post-Apostolic Era and particularly during the eighteenth and nineteenth centuries.[54] Adventists continued to reprint and expand M. E. Cornell's *Miraculous Powers*.[55] Cornell's name was removed, perhaps because it also contained material written by others. In 1878 James White published another substantive tract titled *Spirit of Prophecy*.[56] Later it was slightly enlarged and revised with the title *The Spirit of Prophecy or Perpetuity and Object of the Gifts*.[57] The two editions of this tract covered similar ground as those written by Cottrell, Cornell, and Waggoner. It did incorporate a new general phrase for Ellen White's writing—"Spirit of Prophecy"—which also appeared on the title of her multivolume series on the great controversy between Christ and Satan.

Charges of Suppression and the Reprinting of *Early Writings*

In the fall of 1882 *Early Writings* appeared as a response to many requests for Ellen White's earlier materials and to silence the charge of suppression.[58] The book was published as a second edition to her 1851 *Christian Experience and Views* tract, though it contained additional material, including volume 1 of *Spiritual Gifts*. The preface claimed that "no shadow of change" was made "in any idea or sentiment of the original work."[59] In noticing the publication of *Early Writings* in the *Review and Herald*, G. I. Butler, perhaps unwisely, challenged the opponents that now Seventh-day Adventists could not be charged with suppressing Ellen White's early writings.[60]

The preface and Butler's statement was treated as a challenge by the Marion Party, and led to a new round of exchanges. The charge of suppression was urged with new vigor as Ellen White's statements from *A Word to the "Little Flock"* in 1847 and the 1851 edition of *Christian Experience and Views* were compared with the 1882 edition of *Early Writings*. This time A. C. Long led the attack through an article in the *Advent and Sabbath Advocate*, which was then published as a 16-page tract titled *Comparison of the Early Writings of Mrs. White With Later Publications*. Long claimed that 59 lines of text were removed from the 1851 edition of *Experience and Views*, though he acknowledged that the 1882 edition was a "correct reprint" of the 1851 tract.[61]

As in previous publications from Marion, Iowa, the shut door was the central focus. The crucial presupposition of Long's tract was a verbal view of inspiration. He denied the dynamic nature of the inspiration process and charged that to be inspired Ellen White's writings could not be altered. For her to change or omit any of the content was, in his view, to "suppress portions of God's word."[62] Joining Long were J. S. Green, a Seventh-day Adventist attorney from Battle Creek and Alexander McLearn, the recent past president of Battle Creek College. McLearn had participated in the conflict that had led to the closure of Battle Creek College in 1882.[63] One additional activity of the Marion Party was the 1884 third edition publication of Brinkerhoff's tract against Ellen White.[64]

In responding to Long's charge, Butler said that the reason the earlier material had not been published was because of its not being available to the publishers.[65] He further noted in 1883 that he had only recently become aware of the existence of *A Word to the "Little Flock."*[66] Ellen White herself in privately responding to Long's charges wrote that she had "lost all trace" of her "first published works." She did not even have a personal copy of her 1851 *Experience and Views*. She then appealed for anyone who had copies of her "first view, as published prior-1851," to send them so she could make a copy.[67] Butler further reported that a reprint of Ellen White's visions in *A Word to the "Little Flock"* was available for those who were interested.[68] It might be noted that even Long did not have the original *Day-Star* articles or the early broadsides when he wrote his 1883 tract.[69] Today researchers can peruse all of the original documents.

1883 *Review and Herald Supplement*

The August 14, 1883, *Review and Herald Supplement* and Uriah Smith's 1866 booklet *The Visions of Mrs. E. G. White* are the most important early publications that answered Ellen White's opponents and presented a position on how to interpret her writings. The 16-page supplement contains many substantive articles—including two by G. I. Butler and one by W. H. Littlejohn. Two of these three articles—Butler's "The Visions" and the one by Littlejohn—moved beyond apologetics. Butler's article continued for six columns and addressed how the visions of Ellen White were viewed by Adventists. He argued that people who accepted the visions demonstrated in their lives good fruits. He further argued that Adventists maintained the Bible as the "highest authority" to judge whether a prophet was true or not. He concluded by denying that the "visions" were "a test of fellowship."[70] Butler's brief article "Testimonies Public and Private" defined the difference between public and private testimonies.[71] Littlejohn's nine-column article is perhaps the most significant. He developed a biblical argument for modern-day prophets beyond the "perpetuity of spiritual gifts" argument that had already been widely promoted. In an exegetical study using Revelation 12:17, Revelation 14:9-12, and Revelation 19:10, he argued that the "last generation of Christians are to have the spirit of prophecy." He further connected Revelation 12:17 to the commandments of God and the Sabbath to argue that two distinctive marks of God's remnant people are the gift of prophecy and keeping all the commandments, including the Sabbath.[72]

Seldom did Ellen White publicly acknowledge criticisms against her visions or enter into argument with her opponents. Her August 28, 1883, article in the *Review and Herald*, titled "Our Present Position," gave her reason: "Many ask, why do you not contradict these reports? Why allow them to be circulated? The same question has been asked again and again for the last forty years. My answer is, in the language of one of old, I am doing a great work, and I cannot come down."[73]

Summary: 1866-1883

One of the more common characteristics of those who were opposed to Ellen White was a static view of prophetic revelation and inspiration that did not allow for growth in understanding by the prophetic messenger. Snook and Brinkerhoff both argued that because Ellen White believed in a shut door after receiving her first vision, she could not be a true prophet.[74] The next year William Sheldon, the first non-Sabbatarian Adventist published opponent of Ellen White, argued that she could not be a true prophet because she did not believe the Sabbath until more than a year and a half after receiving her first vision and then in later years considered keeping the first day of the week as the "mark of the beast." Carver continued the same arguments and Blanchard became a casualty when he would not accept the emergent health reform message. These early antagonists refused to acknowledge that though God is always careful to make sure that His intended revelation is understood and correctly communicated by His messenger, He does not require them to have personal infallibility of understanding or perspective.

The last few years of the period of organized opposition were transitional. The years 1881 and 1882 and the fiasco that led to the temporary closing of Battle Creek College brought significant developments. Uriah Smith rejected Ellen White's testimony to him and began to differentiate between what she was actually "shown" in vision and the letters she wrote. For several years he believed that her letters expressed her own opinions that were often influenced by others. When Alexander McLearn left the presidency of Battle Creek College, he associated himself with the Church of God challengers in Marion, Iowa. Perhaps his association with them and the troubles that had developed in Battle Creek influenced them to renew their challenge of Seventh-day Adventists and particularly Ellen White. The little tract by A. C. Long seems to have had greater influence because of the Battle Creek College difficulties.

Perhaps the person most affected by Smith's doubts of Ellen White was D. M. Canright. He left the ministry for a time during 1883, returned for a few years, and then finally left for good in 1887. He became the most significant adversary of the Seventh-day Adventist Church and Ellen White through the remainder of his life. To this day his publications continue to exert an influence.

3. Canright, Kellogg, and the New Opposition—1884-1919

During the last decades of Ellen White's life, much of the published material about her was generated by a new assortment of opponents. The Marion Party continued to agitate controversial issues but was eclipsed by the work of D. M. Canright, a longtime church leader, and those associated with John Harvey Kellogg, a leading physician and medical director of Battle Creek Sanitarium.

D. M. Canright

Soon after abandoning his Adventist faith in early 1887, Canright began to publish articles in various Michigan religious and secular newspapers against the teachings of his former colleagues. His most widely distributed book, *Seventh-Day Adventism Renounced*, went through 14 editions between 1889 and 1914.[75] The basic content was drawn from a series of articles published in the *Michigan Christian Advocate*, a Methodist paper published in Detroit. Canright's book is an extensive critical review of the history and teachings of Seventh-day Adventists. It did not mainly focus on Ellen White, though antagonistic remarks regarding her prophetic gift and influence thread throughout the book, and a chapter was devoted to the topic.[76] Articles by Canright also appeared in various other periodicals, such as the *Christian Oracle* of Des Moines, Iowa, the *World's Crisis*, Kalamazoo *Daily Telegraph*, Otsego *Union*, and the Detroit *Christian Herald*.[77] These articles led to a lengthy response through a *Review and Herald Extra* issue on November 22, 1887. This 20-page *Extra*, together with a second four-page *Extra* on February 21, 1888, was reprinted in 1888 and 1895 as a booklet entitled *Replies to Elder Canright's Attacks on Seventh-day Adventists*.[78]

Canright went on to publish other works against Adventist teachings, such as *Adventism Refuted in a Nutshell* (a 10-tract series), *The Complete Testimony of the Early Fathers*, and *The Lord's Day From Neither Catholics Nor Pagans*.[79] From 1887 until the end of his life, in 1919, D. M. Canright published and preached against the teachings of the Seventh-day Adventist Church and Ellen White.

Canright preserved correspondence from both James White and Uriah Smith that he believed cast doubt on the content and the manner in which Ellen White shared her testimonies.[80] These letters, together with early publications, such as *A Word to the "Little Flock,"* were important documents for Canright. After his death they continued to be used by E. S. Ballenger and those who published the *Gathering Call*. The originals are now located at the Center for Adventist Research, in the James White Library, in Berrien Springs, Michigan, as a part of the Ballenger/Mote Collection.

Canright's *Life of Mrs. E. G. White*

The most important publication from Canright was his 291-page book *Life of Mrs. E. G. White, Seventh-Day Adventist Prophet: Her False Claims Refuted*, published in 1919.[81] Most arguments against Ellen White's visions and prophetic gift published since then find a point of reference in *Life of Mrs. E. G. White*. It remains the most extensive negative response to Ellen White's prophetic gift.

Canright admitted that he had received help from other former Adventist ministers. "Several Advent ministers have rendered valuable aid in preparing these pages. Once they were believers in Mrs. White's divine inspiration, but plain facts finally compelled them to renounce faith in her dreams."[82] One of these was William Allen Colcord, who became embittered in a 1913 conflict with A. G. Daniells over a royalties issue with the Review and Herald. His 1934 confession included "assisting D. M. Canright in the writing of his book, 'Life of Mrs. E. G. White.' "[83]

The long-standing influence of Canright's book requires that a brief overview be given. The introduction of the book compares Ellen White to other prophetic claimants: Emanuel Swedenborg, Ann Lee, Joanna Southcott, Joseph Smith, Mary Baker Eddy, Charles Russell, and Alexander Dowie. In the first chapter the author argued that Ellen White's writings were placed "on a level with the Bible" and that they are accepted by Seventh-day Adventists as "the word of God."[84] The second chapter continued the theme of the first and concluded that if Ellen White's writings are inspired like the Bible, then they must be a part of the Adventist "Bible." He further asserted that Adventists deceptively hide this fact in their publications.[85] Canright, who had been a Seventh-day Adventist Church leader, chose to present a position that as an Adventist he had known to be false. He refused to recognize that Seventh-day Adventists and Ellen White herself saw her writings as subject to the Bible and for the purpose of leading people to the Bible. Though Seventh-day Adventists have always believed Ellen White's writings to be prophetically inspired, they have never considered them canonical. The Bible remains the basis of faith and practice and defines Seventh-day Adventist doctrine. One of the chapters of *Life of Mrs. E. G. White* is a sketch of her life. Canright intentionally slanted his descriptions of Ellen White to be pejorative. In describing her as a girl he used such adjectives as "feeble, sickly, uneducated, impressible, and abnormally religious and excitable." His conclusion was that Ellen White's visions were merely religious impressions and that were it not for the encouragement and support of her husband, James White, and other leaders, she would have probably given up her visions as a mistake.[86] This led to the next assertion that others influenced her writings.[87] He suggested that after her husband's death she gained more influence but still depended upon others to prepare her messages. Canright asserted that during the last years of her life "she often did not know her nearest friends, nor even some of her attendants whom she saw almost daily." He questioned her "supervision" of her books and argued that it was really her assistants that did the writing.[88] The chapter ends by claiming that Ellen White was "self-centered, and, on occasion, boastful," "naturally fanatical," and "inclined to take extreme views"; that she "would never tolerate any question of her authority" (which stirred in her "utmost wrath"); that she "[tampered] with the messages she says God gave her" and that she never did "[write] them just right"; and finally, that she was "inclined to be cutting and severe." For Canright, the "general effect of the 'testimonies'" was to create among her "followers a spirit of spying, faultfinding, criticizing, and judging one another" that led to a "narrow, bigoted, hostile" attitude toward those who were not Seventh-day Adventists. [89] For others who knew Ellen White well and those who have closely examined her life, these descriptions are strange and completely out of character with her life, experience, and ministry. Through the rest of the book, Canright had topical chapters discussing such issues as the shut door, suppressed writings, her visions caused by epileptic fits, plagiarism, enriching herself through her visions, and her simpleness and historical inaccuracies. Overall the author uses incomplete illustrations, innuendo, generalization, and assertions while failing to clearly address such fundamental theological issues as revelation and inspiration, the humanity of the prophet in the inspiration process, and hermeneutics. The one theological issue he did superficially address—Ellen White and Scripture—was incorrectly represented. He saw her writings as additional scripture for Seventh-day Adventists.

Limited Publications During the 1890s

There was a hiatus in published materials about Ellen White during the 1890s. This is perhaps a result of her extended mission service in the South Pacific and Australia. She left the United States in the fall of 1891, at the age of 64, for a nine-year sojourn. She maintained an active correspondence with church leaders in the United States and wrote *The Desire of Ages*, her well-known book on the life of Christ. There was an index to Scripture references in the writings of Ellen White published in 1896. The preface clearly stated that the writings of Ellen White were not intended to "take the place of the Bible, but to call attention to, and to stimulate a careful study of, the principles it contains."[90]

J. H. Kellogg, Frank Belden, A. T. Jones, and the Ballenger Brothers

Another prominent opponent of Ellen White from this era was J. H. Kellogg and those associated with him. The years Ellen White was in the South Pacific made it impossible for her to meet personally with many church and medical leaders. Her active correspondence and written counsel was disconnected from direct in-person communication. As the nineteenth century waned, Kellogg began to believe that Ellen White was more influenced by what people were telling her than by her visions, particularly in the testimonies she wrote him. His response was much like that of Uriah Smith during the 1880s over the Battle Creek College crisis and the 1888 Minneapolis General Conference session conflict. Kellogg's theological disagreements over the nature and personality of God and attempts to control Adventist medical institutions finally resulted in his removal from Seventh-day Adventist Church membership in 1907.

Conflict developed about the time of the two major fires in Battle Creek that destroyed the buildings of both the Battle Creek Sanitarium and the Review and Herald. Kellogg's supporters and others were critical of leaders at the Review and Herald and the General Conference. Among these was Ellen White's nephew Frank Belden. About 1903 his conflict with the Review and Herald increased over various matters but perhaps most over the refusal of the Review and Herald to publish his book manuscript "Conscience in Every Age." He had incurred significant expense in developing the illustrations, and received wages against future royalty from the book. When the book was not published, he appealed to his aunt Ellen White. His correspondence is strongly worded against various workers at the Review and Herald and General Conference leadership. He assumed that Ellen White would support him since she had written of problems at the Review and Herald and about the danger of "kingly power" in church leadership.[91] He came to believe that W. C. White and others had withheld his letters from Ellen White, and when he finally received rebuke from Ellen White he assumed that her son and others influenced her.[92] This played a factor in his rejection of his aunt's prophetic gift, and until the end of his life he was a bitter antagonist against her and his cousin W. C. White. He republished with comment some early church periodicals in an attempt to demonstrate Ellen White's shut-door belief.[93] He also cooperated with other antagonists.

The controversy surrounding the Kellogg conflict evoked collateral publications antagonistic to Ellen White and her prophetic ministry. In 1906 A. T. Jones challenged Ellen White's representation of events surrounding the conflict in Battle Creek over church organization and the medical work.[94] The Seventh-day Adventist General Conference Committee gave a response a few months later.[95] In the midst of this conflict Ellen White was impressed in vision to offer answers to sincere questions from medical workers in regard to her testimonies.[96] Soon many questions came, and she or her staff gave answers. The White Estate files contain more than 30 letters written by Ellen White between April and October 1906, dealing with these questions.[97] The most extensive collection of questions was published by C. E. Stewart in an 89-page tract that became known as "The Blue Book."[98] The book was seen as an attack on Ellen White couched in the form of questions rather than meeting her objective of answering sincere misunderstandings. She treated Stewart's book like other opposing publications, which she had refused to answer in previous years. Much capital was gained by Stewart and others when she refused to answer the publication. Ellen White wrote that "as fast as one [opposing question] is cleared away, another will be proffered. I have been instructed to say, 'The Lord would not have my mind thus employed.' "[99] The Stewart tract was later reprinted (with an index) by E. S. Ballenger.[100]

As Ellen White neared the end of her life, there were those who argued that she no longer had the prophetic gift because of her aged condition. In a tract written about 1910, E. T. Russell answered A. T. Jones' charges that others had either manipulated Ellen White's writings or influenced her, particularly her statements in regard to whether Seventh-day Adventists should refrain from work on Sunday to avoid offense.[101] Besides his lengthy response to this charge, Russell also succinctly defended Ellen White's prophetic gift and provided some new biblical arguments in her defense. He specifically addressed three questions: 1. Did her aged condition disqualify her as a prophetic messenger? 2. Since she has had no open visions for many years, was she still receiving special revelation? 3. Was she manipulated by others? Russell used such examples as Jacob, Ahijah, and the apostle John to demonstrate that God continued to use some prophets to the end of their lives. Russell then gave biblical examples of prophets who were guided by dreams of the night and illustrated that for Ellen White's dreams of the night, the supernatural character of the messages remained. He particularly focused on *Testimonies for the Church*, volume 9, for illustrations and compared it with what she had written in previous decades.

In 1913 the *Gathering Call* began in Alderson, Oklahoma, with Lee Eylar as editor. The energy behind the movement that the paper represented came from A. F. Ballenger, G. G. Rupert, and A. T. Jones. The purpose of the paper was to gather those who had either left or been expelled from the Seventh-day Adventist Church. It also was opposed to 1844, to an end-time atonement of Jesus in the Most Holy Place of the heavenly sanctuary, and to the inspiration of Ellen White's writings. Within two years the editorial office moved to Riverside, California, with A. F. Ballenger as editor and A. T. Jones and Lee Eylar as contributing editors.[102]

Ballenger defined his position on Ellen White in a series of articles during 1914.[103] These were slightly modified and compiled into a tract titled *The Spirit of Prophecy and the Gift to Prophesy*.[104] It was first advertised in the *Gathering Call* in June 1916. This tract went through various editions during the twentieth century. A fundamental premise was that the "spirit of prophecy" equated with the "testimony of Jesus" in Revelation 19:10 was not the same as the "gift of prophecy" as manifest in the Bible.[105] He wrote: "But there are *two classes* of prophets, and two classes of prophesying brought to view in the Scriptures. One class includes those prophets through whom God has given the *original* prophecy, the original testimony of Jesus which is found in the Bible. This class of prophesying is complete. There will be no more of that class of prophesying. There will be no additions to the Bible. . . . But there is another class of prophets, and another class of prophesying that will continue to the end. These are they who prophesy, or *testify* [to] the *original* prophecies of Jesus that are written in the book, as 'meat in due season' to the world."[106]

In the month Ellen White died, Ballenger wrote: "We believe she was sincere, but mistaken, in believing that her work was a fulfillment of Rev. 12:17 and 19:10, where a remnant is represented as keeping the commandments of God and having the testimony of Jesus, which is the spirit of prophecy. The mistake was made in thinking that the spirit of prophecy is the same as the gift to prophesy. With this wrong interpretation, it was easy to fall into the error that Mrs. White's work was a fulfillment of that prophecy."[107]

Others such as W. W. Fletcher and John I. Easterly followed Ballenger's interpretation that the spirit of prophecy and the testimony of Jesus referred to what the Holy Spirit does in every Christian's life to give a testimony regarding Jesus.[108]

After the death of Ellen White, Ballenger and Jones emphasized that since there was no living prophet in the Seventh-day Adventist Church, they could no longer claim to have the Spirit of Prophecy.[109] A. F. Ballenger gave emphasis to the work of the Holy Spirit and the power of the Spirit to heal and give Pentecostal power. After he died in 1921, his brother E. S. Ballenger became the editor of the *Gathering Call*.[110] E. S. continued as editor until his death in 1955.[111] He adopted a more strident posture in the paper than his brother had. The *Gathering Call* office published many tracts and booklets in opposition to Ellen White and the Seventh-day Adventist sanctuary doctrine.[112] They also cooperated with other denominations and groups who had shared views.

For a few years Donald E. Mote assisted John Easterly in continuing the *Gathering Call,* and in 1961 he became the editor. Mote continued the paper in a similar manner as Ballenger. Support for the publication eventually began to dwindle, and the last issue appeared in 1994. Mote sold the files and library of the *Gathering Call* to Andrews University, where it is a part of the Center for Adventist Research.

Other Publications From 1900 to 1915

Besides antagonistic materials developed by those connected with Kellogg, A. T. Jones and A. F. Ballenger, there were a number of other opponents that published on Ellen White and Seventh-day Adventist doctrine between 1900 and 1915. There was a wide spectrum of attitudes among non-Adventists or former Adventists. Aaron Nyman, a businessman of Chicago, Illinois, wrote a large work of more than 400 pages to refute the prophetic interpretations of both Seventh-day Adventists and of Charles T. Russell. A good portion of the book analyzes Ellen White and her visions.[113] Nyman also wrote a supplemental tract exclusively on Ellen White.[114]

A unique tract from 1912, written as an open letter from professed prophet Helge T. Nelson, strongly condemned Ellen White, using his own "visions" as the basis of his communication.[115]

This era is overwhelmed with negative publications. Besides those mentioned, there are perhaps another dozen written by various individuals, including Charles Barr, L. R. Conradi, David Hughes, E. B. Jones, Charles Stewart, Will Trowbridge, and F. E. Washburn.[116] Some of these authors continued to be published into the next era. There were a few supportive works. Two smaller works were written by G. A. Irwin and Mary McReynolds.[117]

A tract by J. Franklin Coon, an osteopathic physician, used Ellen White's writings extensively in an attempt to prove that she supported osteopathic practice as the correct demonstration of the Adventist health ministry. He further suggested that Jesus used osteopathic methods in His healing (Luke 13:10-13).[118] Ellen White rejected his use of her writings to support osteopathic theory and practice.[119]

J. N. Loughborough and *The Prophetic Gift*

Perhaps the most important positive publication from this period was *The Prophetic Gift in the Gospel Church,* by J. N. Loughborough, in the 1901 Bible Students' Library.[120] Totaling 120 pages, it was divided into two parts. The first part looked at the gift of prophecy in biblical and postbiblical times, and the second examined Ellen White's prophetic experience. Loughborough observed that since 1884 she had not received public or "open visions," but instead had received "night visions."[121] He built his argument by demonstrating that Bible prophets also experienced night visions or dreams. In the second part he gave seven "rules" to judge whether a prophet's claim is true and then applied them to Ellen White. A revised second edition appeared in 1911.[122] Loughborough also wrote other histories of the Seventh-day Adventist Church that extensively treated other issues related to Ellen White.[123]

When Ellen White died on July 16, 1915, several surveys of her life were published that considered her contribution to the Seventh-day Adventist Church and to the broader society.[124]

Summary: 1884-1919

The three and a half decades of this era were marked by a multitude of opposing publications against Ellen White and her prophetic gift. At the same time there were relatively few supportive publications. Ellen White's major opponents were D. M. Canright, J. H. Kellogg, A. T. Jones, and A. F. Ballenger. Many of their publications were of book length and in a long-published periodical, the *Gathering Call*. The few Adventist publications were tracts that inadequately answered the challenges of Ellen White's opponents.

Ellen White's challengers were usually shallow in their research, and frequently used false accusations, attacks on her character, innuendo, and debating techniques. None adequately addressed theological issues, such as how special revelation worked and the process of inspiration. Precious little was written about the role of Ellen White's visions in Adventist doctrine and practice or in counsel and church mission.

4. Era of Serious Promotion—1920-1975

The mid-twentieth century brought a steady progression of lengthy works on Ellen White and the prophetic gift. The Seventh-day Adventist Church finally began to seriously address Ellen White's prophetic gift in book-length publications.[125] The scales tipped from the previous era, and many book-length publications were developed to answer the arguments of opponents and give a theological and historical basis for Ellen White visions and prophetic guidance. In the first years after Ellen White's death, a few antagonistic books appeared continuing the trend of publications from the last years of her life.[126] The mid-twentieth century also saw the emergence of new scholarship in the area of Ellen White and Adventist history.

Adventist Books on Ellen White During the 1920s and 1930s

Book-length publications about Ellen White by Seventh-day Adventists began in 1922 with the publication of *Divine Predictions*, a 464-page compilation by F. C. Gilbert, with input from J. N. Loughborough, S. N. Haskell, W. C. White, and G. B. Starr.[127] Previously the largest work devoted exclusively to Ellen White and her ministry was D. M. Canright's 291-page *Life of Mrs. E. G. White*. Gilbert's book remained the largest volume for the next couple of decades. *Divine Predictions* is a biography of Ellen White and her contributions to the development of the Seventh-day Adventist Church and is written from a providential perspective of history with a focus on Ellen White's fulfilled prophecies.

Nine years later, in 1931, the first extensive biblical treatise on the gift of prophecy was published by Adventist evangelist Carlyle B. Haynes. *The Gift of Prophecy* was enlarged in a second edition in 1946 and was subsequently translated into other languages.[128] This volume was a significant resource for a generation of Adventists. It addressed classic issues, such as how God communicates with humans, biblical tests of true prophetic manifestation, and the supernatural nature of visions and dreams.

Three other reference volumes appeared during the 1930s: *The Testimony of Jesus* (1934), by *Review and Herald* editor F. M. Wilcox, and books by two former General Conference presidents: *The Abiding Gift of Prophecy* (1936), by A. G. Daniells, and *The Spirit of Prophecy and the Advent Movement* (1937), by W. A. Spicer. Wilcox addressed difficult questions, such as Ellen White's human limitations, verbal inspiration, the shut door, and her writings as a test of membership. His volume was reprinted in 1944, because of high demand.[129] Daniells' *Abiding Gift of Prophecy* gave a sweep of history demonstrating that the gift of prophecy has been operative since the patriarchal age. The last third of the book explained how the gift of prophecy has guided the Seventh-day Adventist Church.[130] Spicer's volume covered material similar to that of Haynes and Wilcox, though his goal was to show the influence of prophetic guidance on the history and development of the Seventh-day Adventist Church.[131] The providential nature of the Advent movement was a favorite theme for Spicer.[132] Spicer also published tracts on similar themes and a response to the writings of D. M. Canright.[133]

In 1933 William H. Branson wrote a 319-page comprehensive response to D. M. Canright's *Seventh-day Adventism Renounced* (which had continued in print long after Canright's death). Branson's book included a chapter regarding the work of Ellen White.[134] The underlying point of the volume was that Canright rejected not only Seventh-day Adventist teaching but "also fundamental teachings of the great Protestant churches concerning the law of God."[135] Branson responded to Canright's charge that Ellen White's writings were another Bible. He used Canright's 1877 testimony written while he was still a Seventh-day Adventist to show that he had understood that the Bible was the foundation of Adventist faith and not Ellen White's writings.[136]

In 1939 Ruth Wheeler published *His Messenger*, the first storybook on Ellen White intended for young people and a popular audience.[137] The book has had a long life and was reprinted most recently in 2001.[138] Many other storybooks on Ellen White would follow in succeeding years.

Adventist Publications on Ellen White During the 1940s

The 1940s brought several significant publications related to Ellen White. In 1943 Dores E. Robinson, who had been a secretary for Ellen White, published *The Story of Our Health Message*. To date, there have been three editions, and a fourth has been contemplated.[139] Robinson's well-researched and comprehensive study of the Adventist health message makes extensive reference to Ellen White and her role in the development of the Adventist health emphasis. In 1945 the Ellen G. White Estate published *Notebook Leaflets,* which was largely material by Ellen White. It included several miscellaneous leaflets to aid the reader in understanding Ellen White's vision, the work of the White Estate, and other important topics.[140] Most of the material was developed at Elmshaven during the 1920s and 1930s.[141]

In 1946 George K. Abbott, a physician who authored textbooks on hydrotherapy and was closely associated with the Seventh-day Adventist medical work, presented a series of health evangelism studies at Pacific Union College in California. The materials were presented in a printed syllabus manuscript titled *Studies in the Testimonies and Science*.[142] The next year it was published as a book and titled *The Witness of Science to the Testimonies of the Spirit of Prophecy*.[143] In 1948 it was published by Pacific Press and widely distributed among Adventists.[144]

In 1947 Lewis Christian wrote, from a providential perspective, about the role of Ellen White's visions and their influence on the development of the Seventh-day Adventist Church.[145] He also provided background information on the prophetic gift from Scripture with an examination of the legitimacy of Ellen White's visions.

Adventist Publications on Ellen White During the 1950s

The most comprehensive and significant publication to date on Ellen White and the prophetic gift was Francis D. Nichol's *Ellen G. White and Her Critics*.[146] As editor of the *Review and Herald*, and as general editor of the soon-to-be-published *Seventh-day Adventist Bible Commentary*, Nichol was one of the most influential and credible Adventist writers of his day. His scholarly book on the Millerite movement, *The Midnight Cry*, had nearly banished long-standing myths regarding William Miller and the Adventists who joined his movement.[147] Nichol's 703-page tome *Ellen G. White and Her Critics* was the definitive Adventist answer to Canright's *Life of Mrs. E. G. White*. Nichol recognized that Canright's book "most fully set forth in print the major accusations against Mrs. White" and that others "largely copied from him."[148] Nichol demonstrated the importance of the topic by identifying the manifestation of the prophetic gift as a "distinguishing mark" for Seventh-day Adventists. Though now somewhat dated, Nichol's work provides detailed answers to a wide spectrum of challenges against Ellen White's prophetic gift. In 1964 Nichol wrote a conversational and popular book for general audiences to present Ellen White and her prophetic ministry in *Why I Believe in Mrs. E. G. White*.[149] This volume was not written in an apologetic style; instead it offered a brief positive presentation that addressed questions and issues of concern to Seventh-day Adventists.

In 1952 W. E. Read published his Bible-based volume on the gift of prophecy. His book title reflected three ways through which God "has chosen to make Himself known to men": *The Bible, the Spirit of Prophecy, and the Church*.[150] *A Prophet Among You*, a 505-page, indexed college textbook by T. Housel Jemison, appeared in 1955.[151] Jemison's book was worthy of note because it addressed in some detail the theological and biblical issues relating to the prophetic gift. Of similar content, though not in textbook format, was Denton E. Rebok's *Believe His Prophets*. Originally published in India as *Divine Guidance*, it became a Christian Home Library reference work for Seventh-day Adventists and has had an extended influence.[152]

In 1953 Arthur W. Spalding published a popular story of Ellen White with highlights from her life in *There Shines a Light*.[153] In the same year Gladys King-Taylor published an examination of the clearness, force, and beauty of Ellen White's rhetorical style in writing her five-volume Conflict of the Ages Series.[154] King-Taylor's book, *Literary Beauty of Ellen G. White's Writings*, drew on the theories and applications of literary criticism as understood by various rhetoricians of the day, particularly John Franklin Genung.

The White Estate published two reference volumes on understanding and interpreting Ellen White's writings and a volume of *Notes and Papers* used by Arthur White for teaching seminary classes. These have remained an important reference over the years. *Ellen G. White, Messenger to the Remnant*, published in 1954 and revised in 1969,[155] was based on five White Estate pamphlets by Arthur White[156] originally published as articles in *Ministry*. The *Spirit of Prophecy Treasure Chest*, prepared as a textbook for the Prophetic Guidance Correspondence Course of the Voice of Prophecy, contained material from Arthur White, D. A. Delafield, and others.[157] In 1956 Arthur White prepared a collection of materials for the prophetic guidance class he taught for the Seventh-day Adventist Theological Seminary. *Notes and Papers* continued to be published and revised over the years and is still currently available from the White Estate.[158] In 1963 D. A. Delafield wrote a 90-page tract for new inquirers about Ellen White titled *Ellen G. White and the Seventh-day Adventist Church.*[159]

Evangelical Examination of Ellen White in Connection With *Questions on Doctrine*

The years 1955 and 1956 brought discussions between Seventh-day Adventist leaders and evangelicals Donald Grey Barnhouse and Walter Martin. The background of these meetings was correspondence between T. E. Unruh, an Adventist conference president, and Barnhouse, who was editor of *Eternity* magazine and an important conservative evangelical leader. About 1950 Unruh sent a copy of Ellen White's *Steps to Christ* to Barnhouse, who reviewed the book in *Eternity,* with the conclusion that it was "false in all its parts."[160] In 1954 Barnhouse and Zondervan Publishing asked a young evangelical scholar associated with *Eternity* magazine, Walter Martin, to write a book on Seventh-day Adventists. Martin then contacted Unruh, who arranged a meeting with LeRoy Froom, W. E. Read, and, later, R. A. Anderson, from the General Conference of Seventh-day Adventists. The result of this and other meetings was remarkable. Suspicion on both sides was replaced by genuine respect. The final result was the publication of the book *Seventh-day Adventists Answer Questions on Doctrine* and a declaration by Barnhouse and Martin that Seventh-day Adventists were indeed "redeemed brethren and members of the Body of Christ."[161] The reaction to this declaration and a similar position taken in 1960 by Martin in his book *The Truth About Seventh-day Adventism* led to a flurry of discussion by evangelicals as to whether Adventists were indeed orthodox in Christian essentials.[162] Martin diverged from many other evangelical critics of Adventism in attempting to correctly understand Adventist doctrines and treat them honestly and fairly. He included a chapter on Ellen White in his book and concluded: "Christians of all denominations may heatedly disagree with the Seventh-day Adventist attitude toward Mrs. White, but all that she wrote on such subjects as salvation or Christian living characterizes her as a Christian in every sense of the term."[163] Barnhouse and Martin did not accept that Ellen White manifested the prophetic gift, and rejected many of her views. Still the discussion and subsequent publications by these men started a new trend in Protestant circles that has strengthened over the years. Today a number of Seventh-day Adventist scholars attend the annual Evangelical Theological Society meetings, and in recent years the Adventist Theological Society has hosted a section and regularly presented papers. *Ministry* magazine, Adventist religious liberty publications, and scholarly publications of Andrews University Press have also been made available in various ways to evangelicals and a broad spectrum of Christian pastors and scholars.

While more evangelicals since the 1980s have somewhat warmed to Seventh-day Adventists, during the 1960s many of the published reactions to *Questions on Doctrine* and Martin's *The Truth About Seventh-day Adventism* were negative. Most negative responses directly pointed to Ellen White and her professed prophetic experience as a reason for rejecting Seventh-day Adventists as Christians and asserting that they were a cult or very nearly so. Julius Nam's carefully written dissertation documented the various published reactions by evangelicals to the book *Questions on Doctrine* and the positions of Barnhouse and Martin.[164]

The first published periodical response to *Questions on Doctrine* was authored by M. R.

DeHaan and appeared in *The King's Business* in March 1958.[165] DeHaan concluded that the book was "just a justification of their [Adventists] unaltered position and a defense of Mrs. Ellen White, their prophetess."[166]

Harold Lindsell of Fuller Theological Seminary weighed in on the issue in *Christianity Today*. Like DeHaan, his response was focused on Ellen White and her role in relationship to the Bible. Lindsell asserted that Adventists believed in the "immaculate nature of Mrs. White's teachings and life." He then claimed that evangelicals would never hold such a view of the "writings of Augustine, Calvin, Luther, and so forth." He concluded, "Mrs. Ellen G. White is the SDA's leading light, being regarded as its authoritative and final voice." F. D. Nichol responded to Lindsell and rejected the notion that Adventists held Ellen White to be "immaculate," claiming instead that they saw her as a "frail human being as well as one who received revelations from God."[167]

In *Christianity Today* Herbert S. Bird reacted to *Questions on Doctrine,* saying that Adventists settled their "doctrinal issues" through the revelations of Ellen White. He concluded: "Is any other conclusion possible than that her writings are in a real sense to be equated with Holy Scripture?"[168] Bird went a step further and published a book against Ellen White.[169] He affirmed the evangelical view of a verbally inspired, infallible biblical revelation. He wrote: "When God speaks, he speaks infallibly; the God of truth descends to no such equivocation as that implied in the Adventists' exposition of the character of Mrs. White's authority. That is to say, if in her writings 'it is God and not an erring mortal who has spoken,' there is no reason whatever for denying to them the qualities—including infallibility."[170] In a more detailed response to *Questions on Doctrine* and Walter Martin's *The Truth About Seventh-day Adventism*, Bird published *Theology of Seventh-Day Adventism*. His 137-page book rejected Seventh-day Adventists as orthodox Christians. His fundamental conclusion, in terms of Ellen White, included recognition that Adventists accepted the inspiration of Scripture. But he denied that they believed in the "sufficiency" of the Bible. For him, Ellen White's prophetic role violated the "*scriptura sola* principle" of the Westminster Confession of Faith.[171] He did not see any differentiation between canonical and noncanonical writings. Thus the "utterances of such people as Agabus or the daughters of Philip, or the written messages of Iddo the Seer, came to those to whom they were addressed with precisely the same authority as the canonical Scriptures came to the church today."[172] For Bird, the authority and role of Ellen White's writings must be the same as Scripture if they were inspired by God. Though he did not explicitly say it, Bird's line of reasoning suggests that since the canon of Scripture is closed, modern-day prophets cannot be legitimate without undermining Scripture. He finally rejected the Seventh-day Adventist Church as a Christian denomination. The two beliefs that tilted him in that direction were Ellen White's prophetic gift and the sanctuary doctrine. He saw both as a "serious corruption of the gospel."[173] Martin reviewed Bird's book in 1962 and concluded that his exegetical rebuttal of Adventist doctrine was the "best," but that he failed to review enough contemporary Adventist sources. He also made the challenge that Bird was not fair in accusing Adventists of "Galatianism" or a faulty Christology.[174] Quite a number of other books appeared during the 1960s that rejected Seventh-day Adventists as being a cult or nearly a cult.[175]

Publications on Ellen White During the 1960s and Early 1970s

By the 1960s many of those who had worked closely with Ellen White were passing away. Relatives of Ellen White and the Ellen G. White Estate developed publications that gave insight into what type of person Ellen White was with biographical insights and answers to questions. These include *"I'd Like to Ask Sister White . . . ,"* which was published as a companion volume to Ruth Wheeler's *His Messenger.*[176] Ella Robinson, Arthur White's half sister and Ellen White's oldest grandchild, wrote *Stories of My Grandmother* in 1967.[177] It was such a beloved book by Adventists that the Review and Herald republished it in 1995.[178] After Ella Robinson's death in 1977, her son Virgil compiled and organized additional firsthand and secondhand recollections of Ellen White's life into *Over My Shoulder,* published in 1982.[179]

In 1971 the White Estate published a small booklet comparing Ellen White's writings with modern medical science.[180] It maintained that her teachings on health and nutrition were well in advance of her day.

Arthur L. White, secretary of the Ellen G. White Estate, published two books on Ellen White—*Ellen G. White: The Human Interest Story* and *The Ellen G. White Writings.*[181] The first was a brief work that portrayed, through story and picture, aspects of her life, including those of homemaker, writer, counselor, and God's messenger. The second carefully dealt with issues of inspiration, authority, integrity, and hermeneutics in Ellen White's writings. While covering several substantive topics, Arthur White acknowledged and explained Ellen White's use of literary sources in the area of history, though he did not extend his explanation to theology and medical science. It was in these less-covered areas, and particularly medical science, that the greatest challenge would come a few years later.

In 1974 D. A. Delafield, an associate secretary and board trustee of the Ellen G. White Estate, wrote *Ellen G. White in Europe: 1885-1887.*[182] It used both White Estate resources and European historical resources and remains the definitive study on this period of Ellen White's life.

In 1973 a compendium of personal testimonies by church leaders from Seventh-day Adventist history was compiled and edited by Herbert E. Douglass.[183] *What Ellen White Has Meant to Me* intermingled contemporary and earlier writers to demonstrate the effect of Ellen White's writings on the personal experience of Adventists down through the years and their belief regarding Ellen White's prophetic gift.

Another smaller compilation appeared a year later, in 1974, but with a different purpose. It included a 32-page systematic reading guide by Ronald E. Ruskjer and was titled *Ellen G. White: Prophet of the Last Days.*[184] The reading guide was enriched by brief articles from some 21 Adventist authors, including H.M.S. Richards, George Vandeman, E. E. Cleveland, Ruth Murdoch, and S. Douglas Waterhouse. White Estate workers and others were included—Arthur White, Grace Jacques, Kenneth Wood, and Paul Gordon. The complementary articles comprised 62 pages.

Although not written about Ellen White, *Prophets Are People,* by Bobbie Jane Van Dolson, portrayed the humanness of Bible prophets, which indirectly suggested that the same would apply to Ellen White.[185]

Rene Noorbergen's *Ellen G. White: Prophet of Destiny,* published in 1972, was written in a popular and sympathetic style for the general public.[186] A Scandinavian with a Seventh-day Adventist background, Noorbergen was known as a reporter, editor, and author. He had gained some notoriety by coauthoring with Jean Dixon a best-selling book about her life titled *My Life and Prophecies*.[187] Additionally he had written a volume on David Bubar, a well-known psychic.[188] Noorbergen contrasted Ellen White with these and others who experienced paranormal phenomena. He laid out 10 biblical tests of a true prophet and reviewed her life and teachings—particularly in the area of health and the great controversy theme. His treatment of Ellen White was generally consistent with the Seventh-day Adventist perspective.

Opposing Publications

Some opposing publications appeared from traditional critics. Ballenger and Mote continued to publish their paper and tracts and circulate them as widely as possible. Some denominations, such as the Nazarene and Seventh Day Baptist, also published opposing materials. The Advent Christian Church had occasional articles in their church papers against Ellen White and Seventh-day Adventists. Of particular note were the five-part series and a later follow-up article by Arthur V. Fox, in the *World's Crisis* during 1947 and 1948, critiquing the Seventh-day Adventist Church and Ellen White.[189]

Summary: 1920-1975

During this era many books and tracts were written and published by Seventh-day Adventists. A few publications addressed theological and hermeneutical issues, though not in a systematic way. This era was in marked contrast to the previous era, which was dominated by opponents. Yet during the 1970s the rise of secularism, along with the activism of the 1960s, set the stage for a resurgence of critical evaluation of Ellen White's life, ministry, and writings.

5. Reassessing Ellen White's Life and Ministry—1976-2008

Since the 1970s there has been an intense and detailed examination of Ellen G. White and her prophetic experience. A perusal of recent publications on Ellen White reveals a heightened interest in her life and ministry. It also reveals a continuing lack of clarity by Seventh-day Adventists on a wide spectrum of fundamental issues, including revelation, inspiration, hermeneutics, authority, biography, and theology. Because of the extensive number of publications and documents that have been developed during the past 35 years, the modern era will be divided into three subsections: (1) 1976 through 1984, secular challenges and renewed opposition; (2) 1985 through 1994, moving toward resolution; and (3) since 1995, accomplishments and challenges.

Secular Challenges and Renewed Opposition: 1976 Through 1984

Ronald Numbers' 1976 *Prophetess of Health* is the most important publication rejecting Ellen White's special revelation and inspiration authority since Canright's *Life of Mrs.*

E. G. White.[190] Numbers wrote his book while serving as a Loma Linda University history professor. He attributed most of Ellen White's ideas on health to her contemporaries, and suggested that she had covered up this dependency. Numbers' a priori was to marginalize the supernatural in Ellen White's health visions and teachings.[191] He revised and enlarged his book *Prophetess of Health* in 1992 and again in 2008, but his fundamental orientation remained unchanged.[192]

In 1976 the staff of the Ellen G. White Estate prepared a 127-page critique of Numbers' book with appendices containing primary source material.[193] *A Critique of the Book Prophetess of Health* concluded that Numbers held "naturalistic" presuppositions. In his preface Numbers acknowledged that Ellen White's "disciples" believed she received "genuine revelations from God" and "accorded her a status equal to the biblical prophets." In attempting to be objective, Numbers "refrained from using divine inspiration as a historical explanation." In rejecting various providential "presuppositions" he adopted a historical-critical approach to Ellen White's writings similar to the approach of secular historians and many modern biblical scholars who critique the Bible.[194]

Protestant evangelicals would largely adopt Numbers' conclusions concerning Ellen White, though not all of his secular presuppositions. It was William B. Eerdmans, a Protestant and historically evangelical publisher, who printed Numbers' third edition of *Prophetess of Health*.

The mid-1970s brought a new evangelicalism to the Adventist Church. The principal activists for this perspective were Robert Brinsmead and Desmond Ford. Their emphasis on forensic justification restricted the atonement to Jesus' death on the cross. They defined salvation as a strictly legal and vicarious event, apart from sanctification or personal experience. Brinsmead evaluated Ellen White's writings through the lens of his "righteousness by faith" perspective and progressed through three stages in his interpretation of Ellen White's writings. These stages are reflected in three publications. The first, in 1975, was *The Theology of Ellen G. White and an Evangelical Reflection.*[195] Having abandoned his "awakening" view of the miraculous end-time perfection of God's people with many Ellen White statements, Brimsmead now argued that Ellen White held to a strictly forensic justification and vicarious atonement view of salvation.[196] Four years later, in 1979, he published *1844 Re-Examined* and argued that the distinctive elements of the Seventh-day Adventist investigative judgment and sanctuary doctrine were opposed to vicarious atonement, not based on Scripture, and dependent upon Ellen White's writings.[197] His view on Ellen White was split. While he affirmed Ellen White as being evangelical in her views on salvation, he rejected her sanctuary views. Brinsmead largely followed Desmond Ford's apotelesmatic principle that saw 1844 as a restoration of the New Testament evangelical gospel as he defined it. *1844 Re-Examined* was an intermediate position that soon transitioned in 1980 to the view that Ellen White's writings were necessary to establish Seventh-day Adventist doctrine. *Judged by the Gospel* abandoned any attempt to harmonize Brinsmead's gospel of forensic substitutionary atonement with Adventist and Ellen White positions on the sanctuary doctrine.[198] He considered the October 22, 1844, expectation a "fiasco" and an "apocalyptic fantasy."[199] Brinsmead questioned Ellen White's ethics in her use of sources and could not harmonize her practice with his view of inspiration.

Desmond Ford and the 1980 Glacier View Ranch, Colorado, meeting was a major shaking experience for the Seventh-day Adventist Church.[200] Scores of ministers left the church in its aftermath because they could not harmonize Ellen White's writings and Adventist sanctuary views with the gospel. Since then most opponents of Ellen White have mistakenly believed that her writings and not the Bible are the basis for distinctive Seventh-day Adventist doctrines. The Daniel and Revelation Committee and the Biblical Research Institute have in the intervening years published a number of volumes to establish the Bible basis for the Adventist sanctuary doctrine. Volume 5 of the seven-volume Daniel and Revelation Committee Series provided a survey of the history of the sanctuary doctrine in early Adventism and a response to Desmond Ford's Glacier View document.[201] Besides this volume, other chapters were published that address Ellen White and doctrinal or interpretive issues.[202] A separate 1981 Biblical Research Institute publication addressed sanctuary and atonement issues from a biblical, theological, and historical perspective.[203] A careful study of the development of Seventh-day Adventist theology shows that Ellen White did not originate any Adventist doctrines. Still, it is true that her first visions supported the continued importance of the prophetic periods described in Daniel based on a historicist model. Throughout her life, her writings and ministry were inseparably linked to the Adventist prophetic framework.

Donald R. McAdams was a more patient and conciliatory scholar than Ron Numbers and others who pressed their conclusions irrespective of the consequences. McAdams sought to work within the structures of the Seventh-day Adventist Church and the White Estate to bring a better understanding of Ellen White's use of sources in *The Great Controversy*. He was given access to White Estate materials and prepared a study that documented Ellen White's use of other historical sources. McAdams believed that higher education, and particularly Andrews University, where he taught, could effect positive change. His research materials were distributed only to trusted academics, church leaders, and the White Estate staff. His materials and correspondence were sealed at his request at the Andrews University Adventist Heritage Center. He also personally retained some materials. Finally in 2008, Benjamin McArthur, a history professor at Southern Adventist University, recounted, with McAdams' permission, more details on the history of his research and experience in the early and mid-1970s.[204]

In 1982 Walter Rea, a Seventh-day Adventist pastor in southern California, published *The White Lie*, which further expanded on Numbers' assertion that Ellen White was largely dependent on other authors and used material without giving credit. Rea's book demonstrated literary parallels between Ellen White and contemporary authors. He concluded that she largely plagiarized what she wrote.[205] The underlying assumption of this book is that inspiration essentially works independent of external uninspired sources. Therefore, since Ellen White "extensively" used literary sources, her authority is not based on special revelation but rather on the writings of others. Additionally, Rea argued that she unethically covered up her use of sources and attributed them to her visions. Numbers and Rea did demonstrate that Ellen White had drawn more heavily on literary sources than most had realized. Subsequent research, though, such as Fred Veltman's thorough "Life of Christ Research Project,"[206] has demonstrated that Ellen White clearly developed her own independent ideas and lines of thought and was not as extensively dependent on literary sources in *The Desire of Ages* as Rea had proposed. Some study has been given to the literary milieu of Ellen White's time. But more work is needed in regard to the characteristics and interdependence of nineteenth-century pietistic literature.

The influence and publications of four individuals, Numbers, Brinsmead, Ford, and Rea, brought a new focus to Ellen White studies. A number of publications and White Estate shelf documents appeared as a response to the concepts presented by these men. In March 1981 Robert W. Olson published his widely read and influential *One Hundred and One Questions on the Sanctuary and on Ellen White*.[207] Olson's booklet addressed a wide spectrum of issues related to the charges of Brinsmead and Ford. In 1983 George Rice, later an associate secretary of the Ellen G. White Estate, published *Luke, a Plagiarist?*[208] In this volume he proposed a model of biblical inspiration based on the Gospel of Luke. He argued that Luke was essentially an inspired compiler who drew from various sources and that if the Lukan model were understood, the "charges of plagiarism leveled at Ellen White today may not have arisen."[209] Even before Rea had published his book, John Robertson, another minister in southern California, published *The White Truth*. Though the author never intended the book to be a response to *The White Lie*, it was titled and adapted by the publishing house to respond to articles in the public press and the presentations made by Rea.[210]

Through the 1980s regular church papers and the White Estate responded to various issues through numerous shelf documents and publications[211] on Ellen White-related subjects. These included such issues as Ellen White and the sanctuary issues;[212] how Ellen White wrote, literary sources, and plagiarism;[213] the shut door;[214] Ellen White and Scripture;[215] Ellen White and Seventh-day Adventist doctrine;[216] inspiration and authority issues;[217] and hermeneutics.[218] White Estate shelf documents were for the most part not published, but they were made generally available and thus are treated as publications for the purpose of this essay.

Many of the articles and shelf documents dated to 1982 were produced in connection with the 1982 International Prophetic Guidance Conference held at the General Conference. The White Estate, under Robert Olson's direction, compiled relevant periodical articles and titled it *Periodical Articles Concerning Inspiration, Ellen G. White, and Adventist History*.[219] Roger Coon, who taught the Writings of Ellen G. White class at the Seventh-day Adventist Theological Seminary at Andrews University during the 1980s and 1990s, developed a two-volume anthology of published articles on current issues. This helpful resource covered the period between 1980 and 1992.[220] Coon also published a helpful volume describing Ellen White's most important visions, and three other tracts.[221]

In 1983 Ron Graybill completed his dissertation on Ellen White and religious founders in the nineteenth century.[222] As one of the most able researchers in the White Estate and an effective writer, he developed a number of valuable studies that continue to be used to this day. Unfortunately he misrepresented the content of his dissertation to hide his unauthorized use of unreleased materials from the Lucinda Hall collection. The White Estate had, not long before, purchased the Hall collection on the open market. Because the letters revealed marital tensions between James and Ellen White, they were for a time kept out of the regular file system. For a time there were different versions of Graybill's dissertation being read by those at the White Estate and his dissertation committee at Johns Hopkins University. This dissimulation resulted in Graybill's termination from employment by the White Estate.

By far the most extensive biography on Ellen White was Arthur L. White's definitive six-volume *Ellen G. White*. In all it includes 2,917 pages and was published between 1981 and 1986.[223] These volumes were abridged into a single volume in 2000 in part to facilitate translation into other languages.[224] This biography remains the best general source on the life of Ellen White. It effectively connects her story to the development of the Seventh-day Adventist Church to 1915.

The most recent biography of Ellen White is written by Ciro Sepulveda, a history professor at Oakwood University. *Ellen White: The Troubles and Triumphs of an American Prophet*, written in a popular style, gave emphasis to Ellen White's role in the development of ministry for African-Americans and Oakwood University against the background of American history.[225]

Seeking Understanding and Resolution: 1985 Through 1994

The decade from 1985 to 1995 brought a new succession of books on Ellen White issues that were informed by the challenges of the mid-1970s to mid-1980s. In 1987 Gary Land, a professor of history at Andrews University, edited a volume that examined the nineteenth-century historical background in which Ellen White lived. *The World of Ellen G. White* addressed such topics as the Civil War, racial tension, transportation, religious liberty, temperance, health care, education, and entertainment.[226]

George Knight, church history professor at the Seventh-day Adventist Theological Seminary at Andrews University, became the most prolific and influential author in the area of Adventist and Ellen White studies. In 1985 he published his widely read book *Myths in Adventism: An Interpretive Study of Ellen White*.[227] Knight's doctoral training was in the area of education, and the illustrations in the book had a slant toward education. Knight presented information on myths that had grown regarding Ellen White and her writings and added helpful principles of interpretation. Between the 1980s and his recent retirement Knight advised numerous doctoral students for future service in American church history and Adventist studies. Many of the current generation of Adventist studies scholars have been significantly influenced by him. Most of Knight's books on Adventist historical themes have dynamically interacted with Ellen White topics.

In 1987 and 1988 a reporter's transcript of the trial of Israel Dammon in Dover, Maine, February 14, 1845, brought to light Ellen Harmon's close association with seemingly fanatical Adventists in Atkinson, Maine.[228] Rediscovered independently by Bruce Weaver and Frederick Hoyt, this transcript was evaluated and discussed in *Adventist Currents* and *Spectrum*.[229] Though still unpublished, the most complete overview to date of Israel Dammon's life and the 1845 trial was provided by James Nix in February 2004.[230]

During this decade new doctoral dissertations were published that addressed Ellen White's life and ministry and issues relating to her influence on Adventism. A few will be mentioned. In 1985 Roy E. Graham published his dissertation on Ellen White's life, showing her role in the development of Seventh-day Adventism in such areas as race relations and ecumenism.[231] In 1989 Woodrow W. Whidden II defended his dissertation, titled "The Soteriology of Ellen G. White: The Persistent Path to Perfection, 1836-1902," at Drew University. This dissertation led to the publication of two volumes, one on Ellen White and soteriology and the other on Ellen White and the human nature of Christ.[232] Jerry Moon's dissertation is the definitive study of W. C. White and his relationship to his mother.[233] Zoltan Szalos-Farkas published his dissertation on Ellen White and Adventist spirituality in 2005.[234] Mention might also be made of the publication of *Ellen G. White and Europe* based on the 1987 Centennial Symposium held at Newbold, College in England.[235] I. J. van Zyl, longtime Ellen G. White Research Center director and professor at Helderberg College in South Africa, published several volumes on Ellen White, including two in English.[236]

A controversial study that related to Ellen White during this decade was Alden Thompson's 1991 *Inspiration: Hard Questions, Honest Answers.*[237] Though Thompson wrote more in terms of biblical interpretation, his perspective found application in Ellen White's writings. He suggested that the Bible be interpreted not as a "codebook" of rules but rather as a "casebook" of stories that teach eternal principles. Thompson was practical in his approach and used illustrations to demonstrate his point. A teacher with a pastor's heart, he sought to make biblical and Ellen White themes relevant and faith-building. In 2005 he wrote a testimonial volume titled *Escape From the Flames: How Ellen White Grew From Fear to Joy—and Helped Me Do It Too.*[238] Some took issue with his views on inspiration. Thompson's view of a "maturing" prophet functionally resulted in a "degrees of inspiration" perspective in Ellen White's writings. He saw Ellen White's later writings as more trustworthy in the areas of theology and soteriology. The Adventist Theological Society published a multiauthored volume in response to *Inspiration.*[239]

Accomplishments and Challenges: 1995-2008

Since the early 1990s there has been an unprecedented polarization of views on Ellen White in publications. Fortunately, helpful resources have been developed that clarify Ellen White-related issues.

A balanced and broad general treatment on Ellen White's life and ministry, with interpretive principles, is a college textbook written by well-known writer and theologian Herbert Douglass. Douglass' 1998 book, *Messenger of the Lord: The Prophetic Ministry of Ellen G. White*, was written with support from the White Estate and the editorial assistance of Kenneth Wood.[240] This 587-page reference work gives broad coverage of many issues relating to Ellen White's writings and ministry. To date, with Arthur White's six-volume biographical series, it remains the most extensive treatment in print on Ellen White. In 2006 Douglass published *They Were There*, a series of 24 stories on how individuals and the church were helped by Ellen White's prophetic gift.[241] The next year he published another book, *Dramatic Prophecies of Ellen White*, that connected important visions with historical developments such as the Civil War, spiritualism, racism, the United States in prophecy and the great controversy worldview.[242]

Equally balanced and more succinct are George Knight's four brief volumes on Ellen White written between 1996 and 1999. Knight carefully and clearly examined Ellen White as a person, her writings, how to understand her writings, and the world she lived in.[243]

Knight's work was enhanced by his decision to invite Ellen G. White Estate staff to serve as readers for these books. They continue to receive a wide circulation and are often used in classroom settings. Particularly appreciated is his 1997 *Reading Ellen White* that develops important hermeneutical principles in a simple and clear manner.

A sometimes-overlooked volume is Juan Carlos Viera's 1998 *The Voice of the Spirit*.[244] Viera, then director of the Ellen G. White Estate, provided a succinct overview of different models of inspiration within the dynamics of special revelation, as revealed in the Bible. He gave particular emphasis to how the divine and the human interfaced in the inspiration process and demonstrated that there is correspondence between models of biblical inspiration and what Ellen White experienced.

Arthur N. Patrick has written and spoken often on Ellen White-related themes. He has also published various materials on the Internet. An Australian Adventist scholar, he wrote an unpublished master's thesis, "Ellen Gould White and the Australian Woman, 1891-1900," and his published doctoral thesis *Christianity and Culture in Colonial Australia: Selected Catholic, Anglican, Wesleyan, and Adventist Perspectives, 1891-1900*.[245] He has published various connected articles including "Ellen White: Mother of the Church in the South Pacific," in *Adventist Heritage*, historiographic information that situates Ellen White studies within Adventist studies, and articles on Ellen White's present and future role in Adventism.[246]

Beginning in 2005, the Center for Adventist Research and White Estate Branch Office at Andrews University has organized, in cooperation with the Church History Department of the Seventh-day Adventist Theological Seminary, a symposium on Ellen White and current issues. The papers presented at these meetings have been published annually. Most of the articles are relevant to Ellen White issues and topics, with a goal to develop new scholarship.[247]

A prolific author and publisher has been Vance Ferrell, an independent commentator on Adventist faith and experience. He has published apologetic works on Ellen White.[248] Ferrell wrote respectfully of Ellen White and frankly of his opinion on people and ideas, though he remains controversial because of his personal challenges against prominent and respected Adventists.

The past decade has seen an increase in non-Seventh-day Adventist publications on Ellen White topics. Former Adventist pastors who left the Seventh-day Adventist Church during or following the Ford controversy in the 1980s have in recent years more actively produced materials directly in opposition to Ellen White and the Seventh-day Adventist Church.[249] In 1996 Dale Ratzlaff published *The Cultic Doctrine of Seventh-day Adventists: An Evangelical Resource, an Appeal to SDA Leadership*.[250] Ratzlaff's book, Rea's *White Lie*, Numbers' *Prophetess of Health*, and Canright's *Life of Mrs. E. G. White* are the most extensive and influential antagonistic works on Ellen White. Another widely distributed book by Ratzlaff in opposition to the seventh-day Sabbath was published between 1989 through 2003.[251] Ratzlaff and Life Assurance Ministries, Inc., have published since 2000 a periodical (*Proclamation!*) devoted to convincing Seventh-day Adventists to abandon their distinctive beliefs and as a communication tool with evangelicals. Edited in 2008 by Ratzlaff and Colleen Tinker, *Proclamation!* has published various opposing articles on Ellen White.[252] In

1999 and 2001 Dirk Anderson published *White Out* as an exposé on Ellen White. Between 1993 and 1999 Sydney G. Cleveland published multiple editions of *White-Washed: Uncovering the Myths of Ellen G. White*.[253]

In 1999 a video was released titled *Seventh-day Adventism, the Spirit Behind the Church*. It was produced by Grace Upon Grace and distributed through Jeremiah Films in Hemet, California. The executive producer was J. Mark Martin, a former Seventh-day Adventist minister who now pastors the Calvary Community Church in Phoenix, Arizona. The film was presented in a documentary style and featured five former Adventist pastors, Mark Martin, Sydney Cleveland, David Snyder, Dan Snyder, and Dale Ratzlaff, and other former Adventists. The video is clearly oriented to convince evangelicals that the Seventh-day Adventist Church and Ellen White are cultic. Certain misrepresentations, such as the charge that Seventh-day Adventists have their own Bible, have made the video less effective in influencing active Seventh-day Adventists. Bob Pickle published the most extensive response to the content of the video.[254]

While antagonistic books and video productions have had their effect, the greatest impact has been through the Internet. Easy access to information on the Internet through Google, Yahoo, and other search engines has made Web sites critical of Ellen White more easily available. Most challenging has been http://ellenwhiteexposed.com. Initially developed by Dirk Anderson as a supportive Web site, it has in recent years been devoted to undermining Ellen White's ministry under the guise of "objective research." In theological terms the opposing videos, Internet sites, and books have developed few new arguments and engaged in little serious scholarship. The adversarial video, books, and Internet sites seem to have had their greatest effect on those at the margins of Adventist faith. These have also impacted many active Adventists who are unfamiliar with or uncertain regarding Ellen White's writings and life. There are several other Internet sites with a similar orientation to that of http://ellenwhiteexposed.com.

The official White Estate Internet site (http://whiteestate.org) was slow in developing answers to Ellen White issues. During recent years many new shelf documents, the White Estate Document File, the Question and Answer File, and other resources have been added. It is an important site that usually receives more search hits than any other Ellen White-related Web site. This is mostly because of the searchable Ellen White published writings and a new dynamic interface. Many significant new primary resources are in preparation for inclusion on the Internet site. With the growth of negative Web sites there has been a corresponding growth in various supportive sites.

Seventh-day Adventists have produced several helpful educational videos, DVDs, and multimedia CDs to educate and inform people on Ellen White's life and ministry. The 1989 multivideo *Adventist Heritage Series: Keepers of the Flame*, narrated by Allan Lindsay, was produced by Media Centre Productions in Sydney, Australia. This widely viewed series included two significant episodes on Ellen White's life that were republished by the Review and Herald in 1996 as a part of the Ellen G. White Estate Video Library Series and titled *Meet Ellen White*. In 1982 a group of Adventist laymen copyrighted the first electronic *Ellen G. White Concordance* on five large Scotch Videodiscs.[255] In 1998 the White Estate first produced a well-received multimedia CD called *Legacy of Light*. During 2003, in connection with a young adult paraphrase of Ellen White material, *A Call to Stand Apart*, the White Estate produced a 23-minute video titled like the book. It provided a new look at Ellen White and contained testimonies from prominent Adventists.[256] On November 11 and 12, 2005, the Oregon Conference of Seventh-day Adventists hosted an Ellen White summit with presenters George Knight, Jud Lake, Craig Newborn, and Jon Paulien.[257] The presentations were distributed in a DVD format. Most recently in 2006 the South Pacific Division produced a five-episode DVD on Ellen White issues, titled *Prophetic Inspiration: The Holy Spirit at Work*. The DVD included additional resource documents in a PDF format.[258]

Pacific Union College and *Adventist Today* jointly published the controversial DVD *Red Books: Our Search for Ellen White* in 2008. It was an interview-based theater presentation that explored Seventh-day Adventist perspectives on Ellen White. First presented at Pacific Union College, the dramatic production was also presented at other locations. *Spectrum* and *Adventist Today* both published articles reporting on its production.[259] Julius Nam, a religion teacher for a time at Pacific Union College, was mentioned several times in the play and was influential in the script. The DVD production had a postmodern orientation toward Ellen White and how people reacted to her. It concluded with a potluck-type approach to Ellen White, with each actor bringing a different dish and presenting a conclusion on how they viewed her.

Four other recent developments need to be mentioned before the conclusion. There has been a rapid growth in storybooks for children about Ellen White, controversy has been stirred regarding Ellen White's racial background, there has been cutting-edge research in the area of Ellen White's counsels on health, and there have been books published about Ellen White that represent confused interpretive perspectives.

Publications that informed children about Ellen White began in 1950 with *Stories of Little Ellen and the Message,* by Helen Johnson and Evelyn Dinsmore, and Arthur Spalding's *Sister White: A Life of Ellen G. White for Primary Children.*[260] In 1975 the first color-illustrated book on Ellen White was printed titled *Tell Me About Ellen White,* by Marye Trim, with Vernon Nye as the artist.[261] Since 1975 publications for children on Ellen White have been particularly dominated by Paul B. Ricchiuti.[262] He has written book-length stories and shorter illustrated stories for children and for easy reading. Other authors include Carolyn Byers,[263] Miriam Hardinge,[264] Tom Kohls,[265] Eileen E. Lantry,[266] Mabel R. Miller,[267] Dorothy Nelson,[268] Becky Ponder,[269] Ella M. Robinson,[270] Norma Youngberg,[271] and Bernadine Irwin.[272] In 2007 the White Estate began publication of an online magazine about Ellen White for kids titled *Ellen G. White Visionary for Kids* under the leadership of Cindy Tutsch.[273] This periodical has been well received and widely read by Internet-savvy children. Tutsch, the White Estate associate director responsible for youth ministry, has been active in promoting Adventist Heritage and Ellen White issues among children and youth.[274] In 2008 the White Estate teamed with the *Adventist Review* to emphasize Adventist Church history for children through *KidsView*, a periodic supplement for the periodical. *KidsView* is circulated to Adventist elementary school students in grades 3-6.[275]

In *The Genealogy of Ellen Gould Harmon White* (1999) Charles Dudley argued that Ellen White was of Black ancestry through her mother, Eunice Gould.[276] He continued his argument in a second volume, *Thou Who Hast Brought Us Thus Far on Our Way* (2000).[277] The White Estate hired professional genealogical assistance to research the family line in question.[278] The genealogist concluded that there was no definitive link that confirmed that Ellen White had Black ancestry. The White Estate issued a brief statement on the subject.[279]

In a new research development Don S. McMahon, a physician from Australia, published *Acquired or Inspired: Exploring the Origins of the Adventist Lifestyle* (2005).[280] McMahon compared Ellen White's counsels on health with accepted findings of modern medical science. He made an innovative distinction between two categories of health writings that he calls the "whats" and the "whys." He found Ellen White remarkably accurate and more advanced than others in her day when she gave specific counsel on what should or should not be done in the area of health. At the same time McMahon demonstrated that when Ellen White gave a physiological or scientific rationale for certain practices, she was comparable to her contemporaries in accuracy. This argument fits with an Adventist understanding of inspiration. God must give direction to people in the context of their own time and knowledge or it will not be understandable. Leonard Brand and McMahon partnered to also publish *The Prophet and Her Critics*. This volume had similar content as *Acquired or Inspired* but added an examination of the scientific research methods used by Numbers and Rea.[281] Both Numbers and T. Joe Willey have responded to Brand and McMahon, arguing that their work is not scientifically defensible.[282]

In another helpful publication on Ellen White and health, Mervyn Hardinge did a careful contextual study of Ellen White's counsel on drugs and medicinals in *A Physician Explains Ellen White's Counsel on Drugs, Herbs, and Natural Remedies* (2001).[283]

Recent authorship of books on Ellen White from within the church reveal the polarity of thought between the old verbalist school of thought and a new evangelical interpretive model. This is demonstrated by the publications of the Standish brothers and Graeme Bradford. In 2002 Bradford, an Australian evangelist and lecturer, published *Prophets Are Human* as an extended Bible study between fictional personalities Dr. Smithurst and a couple named Doug and Jean. While being readable and evangelistic, the book gave a theologically and historically loose presentation with particular emphasis on the human dimension of Ellen White's experiences. Bradford diffused her prophetic authority by taking a more illumination-based rather than special-revelation approach to her inspiration.[284] For some the imprecision of information was justified by the popular purpose of the book. In 2006 he published *People Are Human*, which continued the hypothetical Bible study between Dr. Smithurst and Doug and Jean.[285]

In 2006 Bradford published a more formal examination of Ellen White's prophetic gift in *More Than a Prophet: How We Lost and Found Again the Real Ellen White.*[286] This book received wide promotion through its publisher, Samuele Bacchiocchi. It gave a more careful explanation of Bradford's view on the prophetic ministry of Ellen White. Following in part the views of Wayne Grudem, D. A. Carson, and Ben Witherington III on New Testament prophets, he argued for different categories of the gift of prophecy with different degrees of authority.[287] Since he saw Ellen White as having prophetic characteristics from different levels (Old Testament prophets/New Testament apostle and New Testament prophets), it followed that the reader was left to determine which level of authority to apply to her writings.[288]

In 2004 independent reformist writers Russell and Colin Standish published a response to Bradford's book *Prophets Are Human* and to other publications in *The Greatest of All the Prophets*.[289] The Standish brothers took a broad swipe at church leaders across the theological spectrum but were particularly strident in their opposition to recent developments in Australia. They presented a functionally verbalist approach to inspiration that was widely critical of Seventh-day Adventist teachers, authors, and leaders, and, in some cases, factually inaccurate. They concluded that "one particle of error destroys truth irrespective of the quantity of truth remaining" and argued that even historical details in Ellen White's writings were without error. They asserted that the participants of the 1919 Bible Conference set a course of "overt and covert attacks on the Spirit of Prophecy" and "wholesale destruction" of Seventh-day Adventist faith.[290]

Selected Significant Periodicals

Several issues-oriented periodicals have appeared that feature articles on Ellen White. The first, which began in 1969, was *Spectrum*, a journal of the Association of Adventist Forums. As various issues arose regarding Ellen White, it often published articles and reports.[291] So extensive has been the discussion on Ellen White that Gary Shearer published a bibliography of articles appearing in *Spectrum* on Ellen White.[292] The editor as of 2008 was Bonnie Dwyer. A second more news- and issues-oriented publication, *Adventist Today*, has published on such controversial issues as 1844, creationism, church polity, lifestyle, and Ellen White, and has tended to lean against traditional Adventist positions. Edited variously over the years by Raymond F. Cottrell, James Walters, John McLarty, Ervin Taylor, David Newman, and Andy Nash, it has contained frequent articles that are less news and more substantive.[293] In response to a naturalistic historical-critical approach to the Bible as sometimes perceived in *Spectrum* and within the Adventist Society of Religious Studies, the Adventist Theological Society was formed. Its scholarly publication, the *Journal of the Adventist Theological Society* (JATS), began publication in 1990. Though focused mostly on biblical themes, it has contained various articles supportive of Ellen White.[294] Related to JATS is the less-formal *Perspective Digest,* which has also contained articles on Ellen White-related issues.[295] *Adventists Affirm* was published in response to "liberal" trends in the church. It has particularly addressed the women's ordination issue and Adventist lifestyle. First published in 1987, *Adventists Affirm*, edited variously by William Fagal, C. Mervyn Maxwell, Lawrence Maxwell, and Jerry A. Stevens, has published some articles that were particularly focused toward Ellen White interpretive issues.[296] These periodicals were viable in 2008 and will undoubtedly continue to comment on Ellen White issues in the future.

The periodical *Adventist Heritage* was published between 1974 and 1998. As its title indicates, it was dedicated to examining the history and story of Adventism. Illustrated and with well-written articles, it provided a contribution to understanding the historical background of the Advent movement and Seventh-day Adventist Church. As might be expected, it also contained articles on Ellen White.[297] The Spring 1982 issue included the best-published photograph collection on Ellen White thus far.[298]

Ministry Magazine

Church papers such as the *Adventist Review* and *Ministry* published many articles on Ellen White between the years 1976 and 2008. The *Adventist Review* as a general church paper is oriented toward the membership at large, while *Ministry* is designed for clergy.

From the mid-1970s through the 1980s J. Robert Spangler was at the helm of *Ministry* magazine.[299] Those years saw many significant and traumatic developments in the Seventh-day Adventist Church. Issues relating to Ellen White remained integral to most of the theological struggles of the decade. While articles regarding Ellen White appeared regularly, there were periods of particular emphasis that related to broader developments, such as the publications and activities of Numbers, Ford, Brinsmead, and Rea. Spangler attempted to provide information and guidance to pastors through the pages of *Ministry* magazine.

In 1990 J. David Newman became the new editor of *Ministry*. He observed that when he was initially called to be associate editor, Spangler told him to "cover church issues that are often left to independent journals" and made the observation, "Why shouldn't church papers discuss issues confronting the church?"[300] Newman sought to continue this legacy of editorial leadership through *Ministry*, but with even more candor. Hence, issues relating to Ellen White and various points of tension in the church continued to be addressed by the magazine, though with slightly less frequency and less intensity.

The late 1970s and early 1980s brought a new resurgence of Bible study on distinctive Adventist subjects, such as righteousness by faith, the Sabbath, the sanctuary, Ellen White, and the prophetic worldwide mission of the Seventh-day Adventist Church. These years saw new research and publications from the Biblical Research Institute and the White Estate, as well as such committees as the Daniel and Revelation Committee, which produced significant new publications. This essay will give particular emphasis to those *Ministry* publications that were more directly related to Ellen White topics.

Ministry published a multiauthored supplement to the July 1977 issue that addressed the issue of modern prophets.[301] Between 1977 and 1980 a number of articles appeared on the subject of righteousness by faith that broadly interfaced with Ellen White's teachings, with additional articles on her writing and use of sources. A special double-size issue of *Ministry* was published in October 1980 to address the various issues raised by Desmond Ford and the Glacier View Conference. The Sanctuary Review Committee particularly addressed the role of Ellen G. White's writing in doctrinal matters on August 14, 1980. A consensus document was prepared to state the church's position.[302] A guide to additional materials on biblical and Ellen White issues was provided, including White Estate shelf documents.[303]

The next issue of *Ministry* largely dedicated to Ellen White issues was that of June 1982. The issue was titled "Ellen White: Prophet or Plagiarist?" Though not directly stated, it was a response to Walter Rea's *White Lie*.[304] As in October 1980, a list of shelf documents by the White Estate was provided for further study.[305] As a follow-up to the June 1982 issue, *Ministry* published a 16-page White Estate insert in the August 1982 issue that continued as a White Estate shelf document titled *The Truth About the White Lie*.[306] Besides providing a substantive response to Rea's book, it offered 25 additional shelf documents that addressed the issue of literary borrowing.

Also in the August 1982 issue of *Ministry* was an important and influential "statement of present understanding" on inspiration and the authority of Ellen White's writings prepared by an ad hoc committee of the General Conference.[307] Important elements included an affirmation that the Bible is the "foundation of faith" and "final authority in matters of doctrine and practice." It further affirmed the validity of Ellen White's prophetic gift and authority of her writings for Seventh-day Adventists. In answer to the issue of literary sources and assistants, it affirmed that "parallels" similar to Ellen White occur in "some of the writings of the Bible." The statement included several significant denials. It denied that the quality or degree of inspiration in Ellen White's writings was different than the Bible. It denied that her writings are an addition to the canon of sacred Scripture or that they should serve a similar purpose to Scripture, which "is the sole foundation and final authority of Christian faith." It denied that Ellen White's writings were to be "used as a basis of doctrine" or "to replace the study of Scripture." It continued by explicitly denying that the Bible could be understood only through her writings, denying that they "exhaust the meaning of Scripture," and denying that they are "essential for the proclamation of the truths of Scripture to society at large." The statement concluded: "A correct understanding of the inspiration and authority of Ellen White will avoid two extremes: (1) regarding these writings as functioning on the canonical level identical with Scripture, or (2) considering them as ordinary Christian literature." The 1982 statement was refined, though unchanged in its essentials, and republished in February 1983. Though not a "voted statement," the Biblical Research Institute affirmed that the "worldwide participation in its development" made it "a reflection of the views of the church" on Ellen White's inspiration and authority in relation to the Bible.[308]

The next issue of *Ministry* that had dominant content closely related to Ellen White was the February 1988 issue commemorating the centennial of the 1888 Minneapolis General Conference session and righteousness by faith. Though most of the articles were historical, theological, or practical, a few interfaced more closely with Ellen White issues.[309]

In 1990 *Ministry* published a two-part series by Fred Veltman on *The Desire of Ages* research project to determine the degree of Ellen White's literary dependence upon other authors. An interview with Robert Olson, then recently retired from the White Estate, was included.[310] Veltman's personal conclusion was that Ellen White was "not guilty" of plagiarism, though she did have literary parallels to other authors in *The Desire of Ages*. Robert Olson followed up the discussion in *Ministry* with another article on Ellen White's denials that she depended upon the published work of others. After examining 10 of her denials, he concluded that she "borrowed materials from books that she herself urged Adventists to buy and read"; "she acknowledged her use of historical and theological materials written by others"; in 1890 J. H. Kellogg acknowledged that Ellen White used the health writings of others; and Ellen White's literary borrowing was openly discussed at the 1899 General Conference session. Thus Olson believed that many of her contemporaries knew of Ellen White's use of sources, even though she discouraged detailed discussion of this because of her concern that people would be distracted from her message.[311]

During the early 1990s independent ministries and events such as the Branch Davidian confrontation at Waco, Texas, brought a greater perception of a liberal-conservative polarity in the church. This led to further discussion on the dynamic rather than static nature of Adventist experience and theology. The October 1993 issue of *Ministry* was titled "Adventists and Change: The Dynamic Nature of Present Truth." Articles in that issue sought to situate Ellen White in the discussion of how to relate to the essential character of early Adventist distinctive doctrines and God's continued leadership in the church.[312]

In October 1994 *Ministry* published a special issue on the sanctuary doctrine and 1844. It is important to note that this issue, unlike previous special issues, did not directly address Ellen White's role but rather examined the topic from a biblical, topical, and historical perspective.

During the editorship of Willmore D. Eva in the mid-1990s to 2005, and since that time with Nikolaus Satelmajer as editor of *Ministry*, Ellen White issues received lighter treatment. The frequency of articles would indicate the church had moved into a period of less discussion and activity. Notice was given in *Ministry* to the republication of *Questions on Doctrine* with a new introduction and annotations by George R. Knight. This led to two responding articles.[313] In connection with this, a 1970 supplement was reprinted in August 2003, which included material on perfection, including two articles focused particularly on Ellen White.[314] The discussion of *Questions on Doctrine* came to a new level of communication in the church with a conference held at Andrews University, October 24-27, 2007, for the fiftieth anniversary of its original publication. The scholarly interaction and perspectives presented recognized differences of opinion but allowed for fellowship and understanding.

Review and Herald

In 1976 the *Review and Herald* was edited by Kenneth H. Wood, who would later become longtime chair of the White Estate board of trustees. During Wood's era the *Review and Herald* largely integrated Ellen White issues and counsels and Adventist history topics throughout the paper, and it is difficult to single out specific articles relating to Ellen White issues. Besides frequent articles, the *Review and Herald* often addressed Ellen White issues through editorials.

During 1976, the bicentennial year for the United States, the church paper addressed Ellen White issues relating to health, science, race relations, righteousness by faith, inerrancy, and Ronald Numbers' book *Prophetess of Health* as reported in *Time* magazine, August 2, 1976.[315] During 1977 the *Review and Herald* addressed hermeneutical principles, biographical accounts with practical applications, and theological comparisons regarding interpreting Ellen White's writings and the Bible.[316] In 1978 the name of the church paper was changed to *Adventist Review,* and a four-part series on Ellen White and inspiration, by Arthur White, was published.[317] Few other articles on Ellen White appeared until the summer of 1979, when new emphasis was given to Ellen White issues. Kenneth Wood introduced a six-part series by Arthur White by giving four points on inspiration and revelation.[318] Arthur White addressed how Ellen White did her writing, and examined issues of inspiration and literary sources. Besides this series, other articles on Ellen White-related themes that were often linked to Adventist distinctive doctrines such as the sanctuary and the Sabbath continued to appear.[319] Editorials also regularly appeared affirming distinctive Adventist doctrines.[320] Of particular value to many *Adventist Review* readers were the personal testimonies and reflections of the editors. The frank and heartfelt statements by William Johnsson, as associate editor and editor, had a particular influence on Adventist readers.[321] The September 4, 1980, issue was largely devoted to presenting the Glacier View meetings addressing Desmond Ford's understanding of the sanctuary doctrine. It had similar aspects to what was presented in *Ministry*, but with more general information.[322] The *Adventist Review* also gave particular emphasis to the sanctuary doctrine in its editorials and articles during 1979 and 1980. As a follow-up to the Glacier View discussions, a two-part series on the sanctuary, originally produced by the White Estate in connection with the book *Christ in His Sanctuary,* was published.[323] A comparison of articles in *Ministry* and the *Adventist Review* with White Estate shelf documents reveals that there was close interaction between these church papers and the White Estate. The June 4, 1981, issue of the *Adventist Review* contained a supplement on Ellen White. It was a reprint of an August 1933 document prepared by W. C. White and D. E. Robinson.[324] Again in September 1981 the report by Attorney Vincent L. Ramik was discussed. After spending 300 hours researching the case, he determined that, by nineteenth-century standards, Ellen White was not guilty of plagiarism.[325]

On October 14, 1982, the *Adventist Review* published for the annual Week of Prayer a series of presentations by various church leaders and scholars on the gift of prophecy. This issue contained messages regarding the prophetic gift from various church leaders and scholars.[326] Then on September 15, 1983, the *Adventist Review* had a special issue on Adventist history that included material on Ellen White.[327]

In November 1982 Kenneth Wood concluded 16 years as editor of the *Review and Herald* and *Adventist Review*. William G. Johnsson, who began as associate editor in 1980, then launched his long tenure as editor, which continued until his retirement in 2006. William Knott, who began as an associate editor in 1998, became the next editor. Church papers largely followed church trends on issues relating to Ellen White. William Johnsson, after his retirement, gave helpful reflective overviews of issues he faced as editor.[328] The later 1980s and early 1990s included fewer publications regarding Ellen White.[329] There were informational articles on the White Estate and how to understand Ellen White and apply her writings accurately. The challenge of independent ministries diverting tithe from the church led to a 1991 supplement by Roger W. Coon on Ellen White's counsel and practice on tithing.[330] Overall, during these years the discussion of Ellen White in the *Adventist Review* was more measured and less intense than in previous years.

In 1992 the *Adventist Review* began a long-running emphasis on the understanding and personal application of various aspects of Adventist doctrine and faith that was titled "AnchorPoints—Exploring Our Faith." As the feature began, readers were specifically invited to submit brief responses on their faith, particularly concerning Christ's ministry in the heavenly sanctuary and how Ellen White's writings nurtured members' spiritual life.[331] The June 4, 1992, issue gave emphasis to Ellen White. In a direct, personal, and instructive way, Roy Adams, associate editor of the *Adventist Review*, gave his view on Ellen White. He published editorials to follow up his article and continued to give attention to Ellen White-related issues until 1995.[332] Again in 1994, at the 150th anniversary of the 1844 disappointment, AnchorPoints articles gave emphasis to Ellen White.[333] The year included many Adventist-history-related articles and features that sometimes included a review of stories and places connected to Ellen White. Even some articles for the children's story feature "People of the Past" were on Ellen White's early experience.[334] The year culminated with the special October issue commemorating the 150 years since 1844. The entire issue looked at the history and importance of the Adventist experience and included an article on Ellen White and a foldout picture from the White Estate featuring a mural by Elfred Lee based on Ellen White's first vision.[335]

Perhaps the most important connected event in 1994 was the October 20-22, 150-year commemoration of the Millerite disappointment at the William Miller farm. This event had the long-term effect of reawakening in Adventist leaders an appreciation of the importance of Adventist heritage and a desire to recapture the spirit and passion of Adventist pioneers.[336] The emphasis of the *Adventist Review* played a role in building this enthusiasm. An appreciation of and faith in Ellen White's prophetic gift is linked to the foundation of Bible prophecy that brought the Seventh-day Adventist Church into existence. The stimulus provided by the 1994 celebration and regular articles in church papers led to an expansion of Adventist Heritage Ministry, including the establishment of the Historic Adventist Village in Battle Creek, Michigan.[337] It also inspired the North American Division to hold its 1995 year-end meeting at the Historic Adventist Village.[338] Again, in 2004, the NAD year-end session delegates revisited the Historic Adventist Village and offered strong support for the promotion of Adventist heritage in the church.[339] The tours and presentations at Adventist historic sites did much to inform people and build faith in Ellen White and her writings.[340]

The years 1995 through 1997 were quiet years, with almost no articles about Ellen White except for a special issue on Ellen White on May 30, 1996. Discussions about Ellen White during these years was in connection with other issues, such as women's ordination and Adventist history.[341] The 1996 special issue was not answering any particular issue in the church, but rather was intended to draw the attention of Adventists back to the blessing and value of Ellen White's writings.[342]

Beginning in 1998, articles about Ellen White did appear on a somewhat regular basis.[343] These were most often familiarization or promotional articles rather than addressing issues. In July 1999 the *Adventist Review* published a heritage issue that looked back at its work and history over 150 years. The special issue blended discussions about Ellen White with the history of the *Adventist Review*.[344] Then on June 20, 2002, excerpts from two Ellen White rewritten or paraphrased books were published under a cover article titled "Ellen White for Us." The two books were *Messiah*, by Jerry Thomas, and the White Estate-developed publication *A Call to Stand Apart*.[345] These articles evoked reader correspondence to the *Adventist Review* with several sets of published letters, some of which were opposed to rewriting or paraphrasing her writings. This led James R. Nix, director of the White Estate, to write a response in support of modern language adaptations, rewrites, paraphrases, and condensations. Nix claimed the White Estate never envisioned changing any Ellen White reference books. The new publications were intended to introduce a new generation to Ellen White and her writings in a way that would lead to an increased reading of her books and an appreciation of her prophetic ministry. Some reader comments were positive toward modernizing Ellen White's phraseology to increase readability.[346]

In September 2007 the Seventh-day Adventist Church began publication of a new periodical, *Adventist World*, intended to communicate monthly with each world division of the Seventh-day Adventist Church.[347] Its circulation was vastly larger than the *Adventist Review*, with multiple international printing presses and an audience in the millions. *Adventist World* gave a new emphasis to Adventist beliefs, heritage, and the gift of prophecy. While the *Adventist Review* had reduced its focus on Ellen White during the 1990s and the new millennium, the new paper devoted space in each issue to an article by Ellen White with other supplemental materials. There were additional articles related to Adventist heritage and the gift of prophecy.[348]

6. Expanding Resources and Understanding—2009-Present

During the first decade of the twenty-first century significant new Ellen White-related resources were in development. The new publications represent a new day for Ellen White studies. The breadth and depth of materials provide new resources and details for understanding Ellen White's life and contribution.

The most important medium for new resources in the present and future is the Internet and digitization. This resource grew slowly at first in the 1980s and early 1990s, but at the present is poised to explode in growth and result in a whole new paradigm for accessing materials about Ellen White. A brief review and present developments are provided.

During the 1970s and 1980s the White Estate established research centers around the world on the campuses of Seventh-day Adventist colleges and universities. At these centers were placed a comprehensive collection of Ellen White's writings, including her unpublished letters and manuscripts and a generous collection of other White Estate materials, including the Question and Answer File, significant portions of the White Document File, microfilm materials, such as the incoming correspondence to Ellen White's office, the W. C. White letter books, shelf documents, and significant Ellen White-related publications. From the research centers has grown a further expansion of study centers that contain a rich collection of Ellen White resources, though not the unpublished letters and manuscripts. Many other Seventh-day Adventist institutional and church entities have established the more limited study centers. In some parts of the world a further subdivision has occurred with the establishment of mini centers in local churches and conferences. Scores of study centers, 16 (and increasing) research centers around the world, together with three branch offices and the main office of the Ellen G. White Estate at the General Conference of Seventh-day Adventists located in Silver Spring, Maryland, U.S.A., constitute the most extensive and important resource to provide local resources about Ellen White.

In 1994 the first Ellen White resources were placed on the Internet. William Fagal, at the White Estate branch office located at Andrews University, established a text-based site that included a number of Ellen White books, and in 1995 the entire published writings of Ellen White were made available. At the same time, the General Conference established a CompuServe forum titled "SDAs Online" with the help of Ralph Blodgett. It contained a number of key White Estate shelf documents and provided a place for discussion regarding

Ellen White issues. Other forums, not operated by the church, were also active during this time to discuss Ellen White issues in a less-supervised environment.

In 1999 the White Estate launched its graphical interface version of Ellen White's writings on the Internet. This included some shelf documents. New electronic resources remained limited until Darryl Thompson joined the White Estate in 2002. He was tasked to complete the *Legacy of Light* project, and develop electronic resources.

Electronic indexes to key Ellen White and related resources were developed during the mid-1990s and were first made available on the Internet through the Loma Linda University branch office. Other databases were also made available in electronic format, including the more than 1,200 White Estate photographs, a bibliographic listing of books in Ellen White's private and office libraries, and a new photo database of images at the Loma Linda University, Department of Archives and Special Collections. Soon the Andrews University Adventist Heritage Center began digitizing their photo collection for access on the Internet. Digitization of visual resources has continued since that time.

With the establishment of the Center for Adventist Research at Andrews University, digitization projects began to expand further. In 2005 the center began to archive Adventist Internet sites based on the *Seventh-day Adventist Yearbook* but including additional sites related to Adventists. In 2007 they began digitizing their extensive audio recordings. At the present (2009) they are beginning to scan for access their extensive book collection. Though not directly Ellen White-related, they contain and will contain many resources that will support Ellen White studies.

Other church entities have also developed important electronic resources. About the year 2000 the General Conference Archives began scanning the *Review and Herald* and other church resources. These resources first became available on the Internet in 2001. The scanning project expanded to include other periodicals, monographs, and church resources. The site www.adventistarchives.org has grown to be a significant electronic resource of Seventh-day Adventist materials. At their 2009 meeting held at Andrews University, the International Association of Seventh-day Adventist Librarians (ASDAL) voted to develop an integrated Adventist resource site to include electronic resources from many Seventh-day Adventist libraries and church entities.

At the board of trustees consultation in January 2008 the White Estate launched an extensive plan to expand their electronic resources on the Internet. Three students at Bogenhofen Seminary in Austria—Stefan Serena, Markus Kutzschbach, and Denis Kaiser—initiated a project to scan the materials in the Question and Answer File and the White Document File. They spent the summer of 2007 at the White Estate office in Silver Spring, Maryland, to complete their scanning. During this time they envisioned the launch of an interactive White Estate Internet site. Through the help of external donations, Serena and Kutzschbach were hired on a contract basis to develop the new Internet interface. In 2009 the White Estate added to their Internet site a searchable database (www.drc.whiteestate.org) that included the Question and Answer File, the White Document File, and extensive e-mail correspondence answers to questions since the mid-1990s, drawn largely from answers provided by William Fagal.

In 2008, though published in early 2009, the White Estate made available a new research edition of the published writings of Ellen White that included *Words of Pioneers* and other extensive resources at a very reasonable price. This collection of materials together with the General Conference Archives resources, the expanding electronic resources at the White Estate, and the digitization initiatives at Seventh-day Adventist universities is shifting the focus of Adventist and Ellen White resources toward an electronic and Internet-based access.

As electronic resources expand, paper resources remain significant. The publication of the *Ellen G. White Encyclopedia* is the most extensive publication to date on Ellen White. It includes articles from more than 180 authors in more than 1,400 pages and will make a lasting contribution to understanding Ellen White. It includes articles on most of the people who corresponded with Ellen White, as well as historical, theological, human interest, and contextual material.

Appearing at about the same time is the Ellen G. White Estate-produced *Ellen G. White Letters and Manuscripts With Annotation*. This significant multivolume publication will put in print, in annotated form, the roughly 50,000 pages of previously unpublished correspondence and manuscript material by Ellen G. White. The first phase of this publication project contains material up to 1860. Ably annotated by Roland Karlman, it gives important background information to assist researchers in understanding the historical context and theological issues relating to the letters and manuscripts. The volume also includes articles on issues relating to Ellen White and the 1840s and 1850s. The many volumes required in publishing the entire corpus of the correspondence and manuscripts will likely continue to appear in succeeding years.

An anthology on Ellen White and interpretive issues, edited by Merlin D. Burt, will contain chapters by more than a dozen scholars on issues ranging from inspiration, revelation, and illumination to literary borrowing, relationship to Scripture, and the 1919 Bible Conference.

Also in preparation is an academic publication on Ellen White from diverse perspectives edited by Gary Land and Ron Numbers. This book, to be published by Oxford University Press, brings together chapters from both Adventist and non-Adventist scholars on many aspects of Ellen White's impact on American history. Though varying in its posture toward Ellen White, this publication demonstrates an interest in Ellen White studies beyond the orbit of the Seventh-day Adventist Church.

Hopefully the future will allow Ellen White studies to expand beyond the traditional apologetic or antagonistic approaches. Adventists have increased the number of publications and papers that look at Ellen White from a biblical and historical perspective, with a broad view of Ellen White and her life, religious activities, and writings. Undoubtedly there will continue to be publications that further address issues and topics raised over the decades, particularly since the 1970s. Hopefully there will continue to be research and writing that provides in-depth information for researchers in order to gain an accurate and comprehensive understanding.

Proposing eras of further research is usually somewhat arbitrary. The future will undoubtedly continue to have carryover from the previous periods. In 2008 Ron Numbers published a third revised edition of his *Prophetess of Health: A Study of Ellen G. White*.[349]

In his preface to the third edition, Numbers gave his historiography on developments since the initial publication of *Prophetess of Health*. His approach remains naturalistically biased but accurately portrays how secularists who reject divinely initiated prophetic experience might interpret data developed since the late 1960s. He credits his book and influence as bringing Ellen White into the mainstream of American religious history studies. Numbers has attained a place of stature in the broader academic community and will continue to provide an influential secular perspective on Ellen White.

Conclusion

So how does one assess the history represented in Ellen White-related publications?[350] As one examines the whole history of publications about Ellen White, a number of obvious conclusions become apparent. First, there are a large number of publications that have appeared over the years. Second, most of the written discussion on Ellen White and her visions has been framed in an antagonistic versus apologetic orientation. Third, the passage of time has brought different developments. For example, during the period from 1884 to about 1920, opponents were most active and the church was less responsive; then between 1920 and 1975 the church was very aggressive in promoting and explaining Ellen White's prophetic ministry. Since the mid-1970s both the church and its opponents have been equally active, with a modest increase in interest by secular scholars. And fourth, there has been, over the years, substantial confusion and/or disagreement on fundamental issues of interpretation in terms of prophetic special revelation, inspiration, illumination, hermeneutics, and the relationship between Ellen White's writings and the Bible. The three decades from 1976 to about 2006 were particularly chaotic. Perspectives have ranged from fundamentalist-like views to an a priori that denies divine revelation. While important issues have been better addressed through some church publications, pervasive ignorance and confusion within the church and traditional Canright-like attacks from outside of the church continue.

The church stumbled into a more detailed examination of these topics through the publications and positions of Numbers, Brinsmead, Ford, and Rea. As one examines the shelf documents by the White Estate during the 1980s, it is obvious that a majority were devoted to topics related to the cluster of issues discussed by these men. Beyond shelf documents there have been numerous publications generated in connection with the White Estate or the denomination that address similar issues.

The Seventh-day Adventist Church formally studied the issues of 1844, sanctuary, and atonement through the work of DARCOM (Daniel and Revelation Committee of the Biblical Research Institute) and the continuing work of BRICOM (Biblical Research Institute Committee). But many had left the church before controversial issues could be addressed. Many who remained in the church never engaged in the discussions and remain confused.

The situation in the church regarding Ellen White's prophetic gift and ministry has been even more problematic. Many had grown up in an environment in which Ellen White was used in a manner that seemed legalistic and judgmental. "Ellen White said" and various private compilations too often presented a functional verbalism, confused hermeneutics, and subordinated scripture to Ellen White's writings. When these difficulties were combined with the challenges of Numbers and Rea regarding plagiarism, some lost faith and others decided to lay aside Ellen White's writings. Many of the children and now even the grand-children of these Adventists and former Adventists have remained functionally illiterate regarding Ellen White's writings and ministry.

When one examines the various documents and publications by the White Estate, it becomes clear that the White Estate staff and other church leaders have prepared defen-sible answers to various critical issues about Ellen White, such as revelation, inspiration, authority, use of literary sources, and hermeneutics. But even with the various documents and publications, many Adventists, most people in the broader Christian community, and interested secularists have not understood the Adventist view on these topics.

An examination of the publications regarding Ellen White reveal that there has been less research and writing on Ellen White in the greater academic community. Even with the many extensive publications, as outlined in this essay, Ellen White remains less widely known among non-Seventh-day Adventist historians and academics from other disciplines than many other American religious thought leaders of the nineteenth century.

The future will undoubtedly bring new carefully researched and scholarly publications as well as popular publications from the various orientations described in this essay. One unfortunate side effect of the strong polemical approach to Ellen White and her writings over the past century and a half has been a neglect of important aspects of biblical, theo-logical, social, ecclesiological, and historical understanding relating to Ellen White and the topic of prophetic manifestation.

The present and future is bringing important changes in information technology with expanded electronic access to Ellen White's writings and information about her. This will allow for more convenient and detailed study than in the past. New Internet resources and a broad digitization of searchable materials will provide simplified access to past publications and newly developed resources. The extensive digitization programs in broader society and within the Seventh-day Adventist Church should facilitate more widespread research and reading. Hopefully this will reduce confusion and illiteracy and bring greater understand-ing and appreciation of Ellen White, her Christian experience, and her contribution to the Seventh-day Adventist Church and beyond.

---

[1] Horace John Shaw, "A Rhetorical Analysis of the Speaking of Mrs. Ellen G. White, a Pioneer Leader and Spokeswoman of the Seventh-day Adventist Church" (Ph.D. diss., Michigan State University, 1959); Frederick E. J. Harder, "Revelation: A Source of Knowledge, as Conceived by Ellen G. White" (Ph.D. diss., New York University, 1960); Joseph Norman Barnes, "The Mind-Body Concept in the Thinking of Ellen G. White" (Ph.D. diss., New York University, 1965); Gil G. Fernandez, "Ellen G. White's Philosophy of History" (M.A. thesis, Philippine Union College, 1968); Charles Ashur Oliphant, "Seventh-day Adventist Publishing and Ellen G. White's Journalistic Principles" (Ph.D. diss., University of Iowa, 1968); William Richard Lesher, "Ellen G. White's Concept of Sanctification" (Ph.D. diss., New York University, 1970); Gil Gutierrez Fernandez, "Ellen G. White: The Doctrine of the Person of Christ" (Ph.D. diss., Drew University, 1978); Arthur LeRoy Moore, "Ellen G. White's Concept of Righteousness by Faith as It Relates to Contemporary SDA Issues" (Ph.D. diss., New York University, 1980); Masao Yamagata "Ellen G. White and American Premillennialism" (Ph.D. diss., Pennsylvania State University, 1983); Robert Wolfgramm, "Charismatic Delegitimation in a Sect: Ellen White and Her Critics" (M.A. thesis, Chisholm Institute of Technology, 1983); Arthur Nelson Patrick, "Ellen Gould White and the Australian Woman, 1891-1900" (M. L. thesis, University of New England, Armidale, New South Wales, 1984); Dennis E. Waite, "A Psychoanalytic and Archetypal Examination of Two Seminal

Dreams and Visions of Ellen G. White" (E.D. diss., Western Michigan University, 1993); Yoahio Murakami, "Ellen G. White's Views on the Sabbath in the Historical, Religious, and Social Context of Nineteenth-Century America" (Ph.D. diss., Drew University, 1994); Merlin D. Burt, "The Historical Background, Interconnected Development, and Integration of the Doctrines of the Sanctuary, the Sabbath, and Ellen G. White's Role in Sabbatarian Adventism From 1844 to 1849" (Ph.D. diss., Andrews University, 2002).

[2] "Trial of Elder I. Dammon: Reported for the Piscataquis Farmer," Piscataquis *Farmer*, Mar. 7, 1845.

[3] For additional information on the Dammon trial, see James R. Nix, "Another Look at Israel Dammon," Ellen G. White Summit (Avondale College, Cooranbong, Australia, 2004); Merlin D. Burt, "The Historical Background, Interconnected Development, and Integration of the Doctrines of the Sanctuary, the Sabbath, and Ellen G. White's Role in Sabbatarian Adventism From 1844 to 1849," pp. 132-140; Bruce Weaver, "Incident in Atkinson: Arrest and Trial of Israel Dammon," *Adventist Currents*, Apr. 1988.

[4] James White, "Letter From Bro. White," *Day-Star*, Sept. 6, 1845.

[5] Ellen G. Harmon, "Letter From Sister Harmon," *Day-Star*, Jan. 24, 1846; Ellen G. Harmon, "Letter From Sister Harmon," *Day-Star*, Mar. 14, 1846; Ellen G. Harmon, *To the Little Remnant Scattered Abroad*, Apr. 6, 1846, broadside.

[6] Joseph Bates and Ellen G. White, *A Vision*, Apr. 7, 1847, broadside.

[7] James White, ed., *A Word to the "Little Flock"* (May 30, 1847), p. 21.

[8] *Ibid.*, p. 22.

[9] *Ibid.*, p. 13.

[10] *Ibid.*, pp. 13, 22.

[11] Joseph Bates, *A Seal of the Living God: A Hundred Forty-Four Thousand, of the Servants of God Being Sealed in 1849* (New Bedford, Mass.: Benjamin Lindsey, 1849), pp. 24-32.

[12] Ellen G. White, *A Sketch of the Christian Experience and Views of Ellen G. White* (Saratoga Springs, N.Y.: James White, 1851), p. 64.

[13] First published in 1849 in *The Advent Harp: Designed for Believers in the Speedy Coming of Christ* (Boston: J. V. Himes, 1849), pp. 452, 453; James White, comp., *Hymns for God's Peculiar People That Keep the Commandments of God and the Faith of Jesus* (Oswego, N.Y.: Richard Oliphant, 1849), no. 9.

[14] *The Seventh-day Adventist Hymnal* (Hagerstown, Md.: Review and Herald Pub. Assn., 1985), no. 453.

[15] James White, "This Sheet," *Review and Herald Extra*, July 21, 1851.

[16] A. N. Seymour, "Delusion: E. White's Visions," *Advent Harbinger and Bible Advocate*, Mar. 26, 1853, p. 323.

[17] *Ibid.*

[18] Ellen G. White, "Dear Brethren and Sisters," *Review and Herald*, Apr. 14, 1853; see Rev. 12:3.

[19] Brian Strayer, "Early Adventist Waymarks in Jackson, Michigan: Parts I and II" (1984), pp. 10-14.

[20] *Messenger of Truth* 1, no. 3 (Oct. 19, 1854); *Messenger of Truth* 1, no. 4 (Nov. 2, 1854); *Messenger of Truth* 1, no. 5 (Nov. 30, 1854).

[21] R. F. Cottrell, *Spiritual Gifts* (Battle Creek, Mich.: Uriah Smith, 1858); M. E. Cornell, *Miraculous Powers: The Scripture Testimony of the Perpetuity of Spiritual Gifts, Illustrated by Narratives of Incidents and Sentiments Carefully Compiled From the Eminently Pious and Learned of Various Denominations* (Battle Creek, Mich.: Seventh-day Adventist Pub. Assn., 1862).

[22] Ellen G. White, *Spiritual Gifts: The Great Controversy, Between Christ and His Angels, and Satan and His Angels* (Battle Creek, Mich.: James White, 1858), vol. 1, pp. 5-16.

[23] M. E. Cornell, *Miraculous Powers: The Scripture Testimony of the Perpetuity of Spiritual Gifts, Illustrated by Narratives of Incidents and Sentiments Carefully Compiled From the Eminently Pious and Learned of Various Denominations*, second rev. ed. (Battle Creek, Mich.: Seventh-day Adventist Pub. Assn., 1875).

[24] B. F. Snook and W. H. Brinkerhoff, *The Visions of E. G. White, Not of God* (Cedar Rapids, Iowa: Cedar Valley Times Book and Job Print, 1866).

[25] *Ibid.*, p. 2.

[26] William Sheldon, "Ellen's Visions," *Voice of the West*, Sept. 18, 1866.

[27] William Sheldon, "The Visions and Theories of the Prophetess Ellen G. White in Conflict With the Bible," *Voice of the West*, Jan. 1, 1867; idem, "The Visions and Theories of the Prophetess Ellen G. White in Conflict with the Bible," *Voice of the West*, Feb. 5, 1867.

[28] William Sheldon, *The Visions and Theories of the Prophetess Ellen G. White in Conflict With the Bible* (Buchanan, Mich.: W.A.C.P. Assn., 1867).

[29] *Ibid.*, p. 3.

[30] *Ibid.*, p. 4.

[31] James White, "Time to Commence the Sabbath," *Review and Herald*, Feb. 25, 1868; see also Uriah Smith, *The Visions of Mrs. E. G. White: A Manifestation of Spiritual Gifts According to the Scriptures* (Battle Creek, Mich.: Seventh-day Adventist Pub. Assn., 1868), pp. 90-92.

[32] James White, *Life Incidents in Connection With the Great Second Advent Movement, as Illustrated by the Three Angels of Revelation 14* (Battle Creek, Mich.: Review and Herald Pub. Assn., 1868), p. 207.

[33] Uriah Smith, "The Visions—Objections Answered," *Review and Herald*, June 12, 1866; idem, *Review and Herald*, July 31, 1866.

[34] Uriah Smith, *The Visions of Mrs. E. G. White.*

[35] H. E. Carver, *Mrs. E. G. White's Claims to Divine Inspiration Examined* (Marion, Iowa: published at the "Hope of Israel" office, 1870).

[36] *Ibid.*, pp. 106-108.

[37] Henry E. Carver, *Mrs. E. G. White's Claims to Divine Inspiration Examined*, second ed. (Marion, Iowa: Advent and Sabbath Advocate, 1877), pp. 73, 74.

[38] *Ibid.*, p. 79.

[39] H. C. Blanchard, *The Testimonies of Mrs. E. G. White Compared With the Bible* (Marion, Iowa: Advent and Sabbath Advocate, 1877).

[40] *Ibid.*, pp. 2-5.

[41] *Ibid.*, pp. 18-21.

[42] Miles Grant, *The True Sabbath: Which Day Shall We Keep? An Examination of Mrs. Ellen White's Visions* (Boston: Advent Christian Publication Society, 1874), pp. 61-104.

[43] Miles Grant, *The True Sabbath: Which Day Shall We Keep? An Examination of Mrs. Ellen White's Visions* (Boston: Advent Christian Publication Society, 1877); *idem, The True Sabbath: Which Day Shall We Keep? An Examination of Mrs. Ellen White's Visions* (Boston: Advent Christian Publication Society, 1890).

[44] Grant, *The True Sabbath* (1874), p. 65.

[45] Miles Grant, "Sabbath Discussion," *World's Crisis,* Apr. 15, 1874; *idem,* "Sabbath Discussion," *World's Crisis,* Apr. 22, 1875; *idem,* "Sabbath Discussion," *World's Crisis,* Apr. 29, 1874; *idem,* "Sabbath Discussion," *World's Crisis,* May 6, 1874; *idem,* "Sabbath Discussion," *World's Crisis,* May 13, 1874; *idem,* "Sabbath Discussion," *World's Crisis,* May 20, 1874; *idem,* "Sabbath Discussion," *World's Crisis,* May 27, 1874.

[46] Miles Grant, "Visions and Prophecies," *World's Crisis,* June 10, 1874; *idem,* "Visions and Prophecies," *World's Crisis,* July 1, 1874; *idem,* "Visions and Prophecies," *World's Crisis,* July 8, 1874; *idem,* "Visions and Prophecies," *World's Crisis,* July 22, 1874; *idem,* "Visions and Prophecies," *World's Crisis,* Sept. 9, 1874.

[47] Miles Grant, "Visions and Prophecies," *World's Crisis,* Jan. 20, 1875; *idem,* "Visions and Prophecies," *World's Crisis,* Jan. 27, 1874; *idem,* "Visions and Prophecies," *World's Crisis,* Feb. 3, 1874.

[48] "Elder Grant's Injustice toward Seventh-day Adventists," *Review and Herald Extra,* Apr. 14, 1874.

[49] Miles Grant, *World's Crisis,* July 5, 1871.

[50] Ellen G. White to J. N. Loughborough, Aug. 24, 1874, letter 2, 1874, in Ellen G. White, *Selected Messages* (Washington, D.C.: Review and Herald Pub. Assn., 1958, 1980), book 1, p. 74.

[51] Isaac C. Wellcome, *History of the Second Advent Message and Mission, Doctrine and People* (Yarmouth, Maine: I. C. Wellcome, 1874), pp. 401-408; D. M. Canright, "Reply," *Review and Herald Extra,* Apr. 14, 1874.

[52] *Review and Herald Extra,* Apr. 14, 1874.

[53] "Our Views of Spiritual Gifts," *Review and Herald Extra,* Apr. 14, 1874.

[54] J. H. Waggoner, *The Spirit of God: Its Offices and Manifestations, to the End of the Christian Age* (Battle Creek, Mich.: Seventh-day Adventist Pub. Assn., 1877).

[55] M. E. Cornell, *Miraculous Powers,* second rev. ed. (1875).

[56] James White, *Spirit of Prophecy* (Battle Creek, Mich.: Review and Herald Pub. Assn., 1878).

[57] James White, *The Spirit of Prophecy or Perpetuity and Object of the Gifts* (Battle Creek, Mich.: Seventh-day Adventist Pub. Assn., c. 1880).

[58] G. I. Butler, "'Early Writings' and 'Suppression,'" *Review and Herald Supplement,* Aug. 14, 1883.

[59] Ellen G. White, *Early Writings of Mrs. White: Experience and Views and Spiritual Gifts,* second ed. (Battle Creek, Mich.: Review and Herald Pub. Assn., 1882), vol. 1, p. iv.

[60] G. I. Butler, "A Book Long Desired," *Review and Herald,* Dec. 26, 1882.

[61] A. C. Long, *Comparison of the Early Writings of Mrs. White With Later Publications* (Marion, Iowa: Advent and Sabbath Advocate, 1883), p. 11.

[62] *Ibid.*, p. 12.

[63] See Arthur L. White, *Ellen G. White: The Lonely Years, 1876-1891* (Washington, D.C.: Review and Herald Pub. Assn., 1984), vol. 3, p. 222.

[64] Jacob Brinkerhoff, *The Seventh-day Adventists and Mrs. White's Visions,* third ed. (Marion, Iowa: Advent and Sabbath Advocate, 1884).

[65] G. I. Butler, "'Early Writings' and 'Suppression.'"

[66] G. I. Butler, "A Venerable Document," *Review and Herald Supplement,* Aug. 14, 1883.

[67] Ellen G. White, "Suppression and the Shut Door," manuscript 4, 1883, in *Selected Messages,* book 2, pp. 59-73.

[68] Butler, "A Venerable Document"; Ellen G. White, *To the Remnant Scattered Abroad* (n.p., n.d.).

[69] Ellen G. Harmon, *To the Little Remnant Scattered Abroad,* Apr. 6, 1846; *idem,* "Dear Bro. Bates," *A Vision,* Apr. 7, 1847; *idem, To Those Who Are Receiving the Seal of the Living God,* Jan. 31, 1849; *idem,* "Letter From Sister Harmon," *Day-Star,* Jan. 24, 1846; *idem,* "Letter From Sister Harmon," *Day-Star,* Mar. 14, 1846.

[70] G. I. Butler, "The Visions: How They Are Held Among S. D. Adventists," *Review and Herald Supplement,* Aug. 14, 1883.

[71] G. I. Butler, "Testimonies, Public and Private," *Review and Herald Supplement,* Aug. 14, 1883.

[72] W. H. Littlejohn, "Seventh-day Adventists and the Testimony of Jesus Christ," *Review and Herald Supplement,* Aug. 14, 1883.

[73] Ellen G. White, "Our Present Position," *Review and Herald,* Aug. 28, 1883.

[74] Snook and Brinkerhoff, *The Visions of E. G. White, Not of God* (1866) pp. 3ff.

[75] D. M. Canright, *Seventh-Day Adventism Renounced After an Experience of Twenty-eight Years: By a Prominent Minister and Writer of That Faith* (Kalamazoo, Mich.: Kalamazoo Publishing, 1889); *idem, Seventh-Day Adventism Renounced After an Experience of Twenty-eight Years: By a Prominent Minister and Writer of That Faith,* fourteenth ed. (New York: Fleming H. Revell, 1914).

[76] Canright, *Seventh-Day Adventism Renounced* (1914), pp. 129-165.

[77] Uriah Smith, "Assumptions Vs. Facts," *Review and Herald Extra,* Nov. 22, 1887.

[78] "Elder Canright's Reply to *Extra* No. 1, and Our Rejoinder," *Advent Review Extra,* No. 2, Feb. 21, 1888; *Replies to Elder Canright's Attacks on Seventh-day Adventists* (Battle Creek, Mich.: Review and Herald Pub. Assn., 1888); *Replies to Elder Canright's Attacks on Seventh-day Adventists* (Battle Creek, Mich.: Review and Herald Pub. Assn., 1895).

[79] D. M. Canright, *Adventism Refuted in a Nutshell,* 10 tract series (n.p., 1889); *idem, The Complete Testimony of the Early Fathers: Proving the Universal Observance of Sunday in the First Centuries* (New York: Fleming H. Revell, 1916); *idem, The Lord's Day From Neither Catholics Nor Pagans: An Answer to Seventh-day Adventism on This Subject,* second ed. (New York: Fleming H. Revell, 1915).

[80] James White to D. M. Canright, May 24, 1881; James White to D. M. Canright, July 13, 1881; Uriah Smith to D. M. Canright, Mar. 22, 1883; Uriah Smith to D. M. Canright, Apr. 6, 1883; Uriah Smith to D. M. Canright, July 31, 1883; Uriah Smith to D. M. Canright, Aug. 7, 1883; Uriah Smith to D. M. Canright, Oct. 2, 1883. Center for Adventist Research, Andrews University, Berrien Springs, Mich. See also Uriah Smith, "Personal," *Review and Herald Extra,* Nov. 22, 1887.

[81] D. M. Canright, *Life of Mrs. E. G. White, Seventh-Day Adventist Prophet: Her False Claims Refuted* (Cincinnati: Standard Publishing, 1919).

[82] *Ibid.,* p. 15.

[83] Willard Allen Colcord, "A Statement and Confession," *Review and Herald,* Feb. 8, 1934.

[84] Canright, *Life of E. G. White,* pp. 34, 38.

[85] *Ibid.,* pp. 38, 45.

[86] *Ibid.,* pp. 57-60.

[87] *Ibid.,* pp. 77-79.

[88] *Ibid.,* p. 85.

[89] *Ibid.,* p. 86.

[90] *Index to the Scripture References and Quotations Contained in the Writings of Mrs. E. G. White* (Battle Creek, Mich.: International Tract Society, 1896).

[91] Frank Belden to Ellen G. White, Jan. 1, 1903; *idem,* Jan. 5, 1903; *idem,* Feb. 24, 1903; Frank Belden to W. C. White, Oct. 28 to Nov. 20, 1905 (84 pp.). See other correspondence in the Frank Belden Collection, Ellen G. White Estate Branch Office, Berrien Springs, Michigan.

[92] Frank Belden to Ellen G. White, Sept. 12, 1905, Ellen G. White Estate Branch Office, Berrien Springs, Michigan.

[93] Frank E. Belden, photographic reproduction with tip-in and comments (Battle Creek, Mich.: n.p., n.d.) of *The Advent Review* (Auburn, N.Y.: Henry Oliphant, 1850); *idem, A Word to the "Little Flock."*

[94] Alonzo T. Jones, *Some History, Some Experience, and Some Facts* (Washington, D.C.: Review and Herald Pub. Assn., 1906).

[95] *A Statement Refuting Charges Made by A. T. Jones Against the Spirit of Prophecy and the Plan of Organization of Seventh-day Adventist Denomination* (Washington, D.C.: General Conference Committee, May 1906).

[96] Ellen G. White, "To Those Who Are Perplexed Regarding the Testimonies Relating to the Medical Missionary Work," Mar. 30, 1906. Letter 120, 1906, Ellen G. White Estate, Silver Spring, Maryland.

[97] Tim Poirier, "To Those Who Are Perplexed . . ." (n.d.), Document File 213, Ellen G. White Estate Branch Office, Andrews University, Berrien Springs, Michigan.

[98] C. E. Stewart, *A Response to an Urgent Testimony From Mrs. Ellen G. White Concerning Contradictions, Inconsistencies and Other Errors in Her Writings* (Battle Creek, Mich.: Liberty Missionary Society, 1907).

[99] Ellen G. White to "To the Elders of the Battle Creek Church, July 17, 1906. Letter 244, 1906, Ellen G. White Estate, Silver Spring, Maryland.

[100] C. E. Stewart, *A Response to an Urgent Testimony From Mrs. Ellen G. White Concerning Contradictions, Inconsistencies and Other Errors in Her Writings* second ed. (Riverside, Calif.: E. S. Ballenger, n.d.).

[101] E. T. Russell, *Despise Not Prophesyings or Truth Vindicated* (College View, Nebr.: International Publishing, c. 1910); Ellen G. White, *Testimonies for the Church* (Mountain View, Calif.: Pacific Press Pub. Assn., 1948), vol. 9, pp. 232-238; A. T. Jones, *Ten Commandments for Sunday Observance* (Battle Creek, Mich.: A. T. Jones, 1909); *idem, An Appeal for Evangelical Christianity,* 1909, pp. 60-69; see also George Knight, *From 1888 to Apostasy: The Case of A. T. Jones* (Washington, D.C.: Review and Herald Pub. Assn., 1987), pp. 246-249.

[102] See Calvin W. Edwards and Gary Land, *Seeker After Light* (Berrien Springs, Mich.: Andrews University Press, 2000).

[103] A. F. Ballenger, "What Is the Spirit of Prophecy?" *Gathering Call*, April 1914; *idem,* "The Spirit of Prophecy: Who Has It, Who Has Had It, Who Will Have It?" *Gathering Call*, June 1914; *idem,* "The Spirit of Prophecy: Who Has It, Who Has Had It, Who Will Have It?" *Gathering Call*, July 1914; *idem,* "The Spirit of Prophecy Not the Gift of Prophecy," *Gathering Call*, August 1914; *idem,* The Spirit of Prophecy and the Gift of Prophecy," *Gathering Call*, Sept. 1914; *idem,* "Prophets and Prophesying," *Gathering Call*, Oct. 1914; *idem,* "Proving the Prophecy or Trying the Testimony," *Gathering Call*, Nov. 1914; *idem,* "The Spirit of Prophecy the Only Infallible Interpreter," *Gathering Call*, Dec. 1914.

[104] A. F. Ballenger, *The Spirit of Prophecy and the Gift to Prophesy*, third ed. (Riverside, Calif.: Gathering Call, n.d.).

[105] A. F. Ballenger, "Notes by the Way," *Gathering Call*, Mar. 1916.

[106] A. F. Ballenger, *The Spirit of Prophecy and the Gift to Prophesy*, p. 19.

[107] A. F. Ballenger, "Friday, July 16, Mrs. E. G. White," *Gathering Call*, July 1915.

[108] W. W. Fletcher, *"The Testimony of Jesus"* (Sydney, Australia: W. W. Fletcher, n.d.); John I. Easterly, *The Testimony of Jesus* (Santa Rosa, Calif.: John I. Easterly, n.d.).

[109] A. T. Jones, "Where Now Is the Spirit of Prophecy?" *Gathering Call*, September 1915.

[110] "In Loving Remembrance," *Gathering Call*, September-October 1921.

[111] "Elder Edward Stroud Ballenger," *Gathering Call*, November-December 1955.

[112] G. G. Rupert, *A Positive Appeal and Challenge to Seventh Day Adventists and All Others in Error to Correct Wrong Teaching* (Britton, Okla.: Union Pub. Co., n.d.); A. F. Ballenger, *The Spirit of Prophecy and the Gift of Prophecy*, fourth ed. (Riverside, Calif.: Gathering Call, n.d.); *idem, Events That Must Take Place Before Armageddon* (Riverside, Calif.: Gathering Call, 1918); *idem, Cast Out for the Cross of Christ* (Tropico, Calif.: by the author, n.d.); E. S. Ballenger, *What About the Testimonies?* (Riverside, Calif.: Gathering Call, n.d.); *idem, The Beginnings of Seventh-day Adventists* (Riverside, Calif.: E. S. Ballenger, n.d.); *idem, Facts About Seventh Day Adventists* (Riverside, Calif.: E. S. Ballenger, n.d.); *idem, The Centennial Supplement: A Compilation of Important Facts Relating to the Early History of the Seventh-day Adventist Church* (Riverside, Calif.: 1944); *idem, Seventh-day Adventists Weighed in the Balance of Honesty and Found Wanting* (Riverside, Calif.: E. S. Ballenger, n.d.); *idem, Important Facts About the Seventh-day Adventist Creed That Need Attention* (Riverside, Calif.: E. S. Ballenger, n.d.); *idem, Interesting Old Letters* (Riverside, Calif.: E. S. Ballenger, n.d.); *idem, Then Shall the Sanctuary Be Cleansed* (Riverside, Calif.: E. S. Ballenger, n.d.); *idem, Examining Seventh-day Adventism* (Riverside, Calif.: E. S. Ballenger, n.d.); *idem, The Reform Dress* (Riverside, Calif.: Gathering Call, n.d.); *idem, Valuable Helps on the Sabbath School Lessons, Second Quarter, 1948* (Riverside, Calif.: E. S. Ballenger, 1948); A. T. Jones, *A Letter From A. T. Jones to Mrs. E. G. White* (Riverside, Calif.: Gathering Call, n.d.).

[113] Aaron Nyman, *Astounding Errors: The Prophetic Message of the Seventh-day Adventists and the Chronology of Pastor C. T. Russell in the Light of History and Bible Knowledge* (Chicago: Aaron Nyman, 1914).

[114] Aaron Nyman, *Mrs. Ellen G. White Under the Microscope: The Prophetess of the Seventh-day Adventists, Weighed in the Balance of Biblical Truth and Found Wanting* (Chicago: n.p., c. 1915).

[115] Helge Nelson, *An Open Letter to Mrs. Ellen G. White* (Chicago: n.p., 1912).

[116] Charles H. Barr, *Adventism Unveiled or the Claims and Calling of Wm. Miller and Mrs. E. G. White Examined* (the author, 1900); L. R. Conradi, *Seventh Day Baptists and Seventh Day Adventists: How They Differ* (Plainfield, N.J.: American Sabbath Tract Society, 1934); David Hughes, *The Twentieth Century Pharisees: Seventh-day Adventism Exposed* (Hammondsport, N.Y.: Armon Publishing, 1915); E. B. Jones, *Did Mrs. E. G. White, the Professed Messenger of Seventh-day Adventism, Possess the Prophetic Gift?* (Minneapolis, Minn.: the author, n.d.); E. B. Jones, *Forty Bible-supported Reasons Why You Should Not Be a Seventh-day Adventist* (Minneapolis: Wilson Press, 1943); M. E. Kern, *Some Facts Regarding E. B. Jones* (c. 1942); A. C. Long, *Comparison of the Early Writings of Mrs. White With Later Publications*, second ed. (Stanberry, Mo.: Church of God, 1911); Charles E. Stewart, *A Response to an Urgent Testimony From Mrs. E. G. White Concerning Contradictions, Inconsistencies, and Other Errors in Her Writings* (Battle Creek, Mich.: Liberty Missionary Society, 1907); Will S. Trowbridge, *The Sabbath, the Law, and the Visions* (Oakland, Calif.: Messiah's Advocate, 1916); F. E. Washburn, *The "Testimonies" of Mrs. White, Seventh-day Adventist Prophetess: The Bible Rewritten* (Waterloo, Iowa: the author, n.d.).

[117] G. A. Irwin, *The Spirit of Prophecy: Its Relation to the Law of God and Its Place in the Plan of Salvation* (Washington, D.C.: Review and Herald Pub. Assn., 1907); Mary C. McReynolds, *The Gift of Prophecy*, second ed. (Angwin, Calif.: the author, 1900).

[118] J. Franklin Coon, *The Search Light* (n.p., n.d.), p. 23.

[119] Ellen G. White to Brother Coon, Oct. 10, 1911 (letter 108, 1911, and manuscript 67, 1911). Ellen G. White Estate, Silver Spring, Maryland.

[120] J. N. Loughborough, *The Prophetic Gift in the Gospel Church*, Bible Students' Library, no. 164 (Oakland, Calif.: Pacific Press Pub. Assn., 1901).

[121] *Ibid.,* pp. iii, iv.

[122] J. N. Loughborough, *The Prophetic Gift in the Gospel Church*, second rev. ed. (Oakland, Calif.: Pacific Press Pub. Assn., 1911).

[123] J. N. Loughborough, *Rise and Progress of the Seventh-day Adventists* (Battle Creek, Mich.: General Conference Association of the Seventh-day Adventists, 1892); *idem, The Great Second Advent Movement: Its Rise and Progress* (Washington, D.C.: Review and Herald Pub. Assn., 1905, 1909).

[124] A. G. Daniells, "The Life and Labors of Mrs. Ellen G. White," *Review and Herald,* July 29, 1915; F. M. Wilcox, "The Final Funeral Services of Mrs. Ellen G. White," *Review and Herald,* Aug. 5, 1915; *Signs of the Times* Memorial Issue, pp. 466-480; "Adventists' Founder Passes," Sacramento *Bee,* July 17, 1915; "Death Claims Founder of Adventists," San Bernardino *Sun,* July 17, 1915; "Passing of Ellen G. White, Adventist Founder," Richmond *Record Herald,* July 19, 1915; "Mrs. E. G. White, Eminent Seventh-day Adventist, Dead," Mountain View *Register-Leader,* July 23, 1915; "Leader of Adventists Dead," St. Helena *Star,* July 23, 1915; "Four Thousand at Funeral Services of Mother White, Battle Creek *Evening Star,* July 24, 1915; "Mrs. White Had No Idea of Successor," Battle Creek *Enquirer,* July 25, 1915; "An American Prophetess," *The Independent,* Aug. 23, 1915.

[125] George Knapp Abbott, *The Witness of Science to the Testimonies of the Spirit of Prophecy,* rev. ed. (Mountain View, Calif.: Pacific Press Pub. Assn., 1948); William H. Branson, *In Defense of the Faith: A Reply to Canright* (Washington, D.C.: Review and Herald Pub. Assn., 1933); Lewis Harrison Christian, *The Fruitage of Spiritual Gifts; The Influence and Guidance of Ellen G. White in the Advent Movement* (Washington, D.C.: Review and Herald Pub. Assn., 1947); Arthur G. Daniells, *The Abiding Gift of Prophecy* (Mountain View, Calif.: Pacific Press Pub. Assn., 1936); Everett Dick, *Founders of the Message* (Washington, D.C.: Review and Herald Pub. Assn., 1938); F. C. Gilbert, comp., *Divine Predictions of Mrs. Ellen G. White Fulfilled* (South Lancaster, Mass.: Good Tidings, 1922); Carlyle B. Haynes, *The Gift of Prophecy: The Teachings of the Bible Regarding the Voice of God Among His People From the Beginning of His Work on Earth, and Particularly the Manifestation of His Divine Leadership in Connection With the Closing Message of the Gospel; an Account of the Prophetic Gift, Its Removal, Because of Apostasy, and Its Restoration to the Remnant Church* (Nashville: Southern Pub. Assn., 1931); T. Housel Jemison, *A Prophet Among You* (Mountain View, Calif.: Pacific Press Pub. Assn., 1955); Gladys King-Taylor, *Literary Beauty of Ellen G. White's Writings* (Mountain View, Calif.: Pacific Press Pub. Assn., 1953); Francis D. Nichol, *Ellen G. White and Her Critics* (Washington, D.C.: Review and Herald Pub. Assn., 1951); Denton E. Rebok, *Believe His Prophets* (Washington, D.C.: Review and Herald Pub. Assn., 1956); Dores Eugene Robinson, *The Story of Our Health Message,* third ed. (Nashville: Southern Pub. Assn., 1965); William A. Spicer, *The Gift of Prophecy in the Advent Movement: A Gift That Builds Up* (Washington, D.C.: Review and Herald Pub. Assn., 1937); F. M. Wilcox, *The Testimony of Jesus: A Review of the Work and Teachings of Mrs. Ellen Gould White* (Washington, D.C.: Review and Herald Pub. Assn., 1934); Arthur L. White, *"I'd Like to Ask Sister White . . .": The Questions You Might Ask, Answered From Statements Selected From the Writings of Ellen G. White* (Washington, D.C.: Review and Herald Pub. Assn., 1965).

[126] W. S. Trowbridge, *The Sabbath, the Law, and the Visions* (Oakland, Calif.: Messiah's Advocate, 1916).

[127] Gilbert, *Divine Predictions,* p. 9.

[128] Haynes, *The Gift of Prophecy,* 1931; *idem, The Gift of Prophecy: The Teachings of the Bible Regarding the Voice of God Among His People From the Beginning of His Work on Earth, and Particularly the Manifestation of His Divine Leadership in Connection With the Closing Message of the Gospel; an Account of the Prophetic Gift, Its Removal, Because of Apostasy, and Its Restoration to the Remnant Church,* rev. (Nashville: Southern Pub. Assn., 1946).

[129] F. M. Wilcox, *The Testimony of Jesus: A Review of the Work and Teachings of Mrs. Ellen Gould White* (Washington, D.C.: Review and Herald Pub. Assn., 1944).

[130] Daniells, *The Abiding Gift of Prophecy,* pp. 253-378.

[131] Spicer, *The Gift of Prophecy in the Advent Movement.*

[132] For examples, see W. A. Spicer, *Certainties of the Advent Movement* (Washington, D.C.: Review and Herald Pub. Assn., 1929); *idem, The Hand of God in History: Notes on Important Eras of Fulfilling Prophecy* (Washington, D.C.: Review and Herald Pub. Assn., 1913); *idem, The Hand That Intervenes* (Washington, D.C.: Review and Herald Pub. Assn., 1918); *idem, Pioneer Days of the Advent Movement With Notes on Pioneer Workers and Early Experiences* (Washington, D.C.: Review and Herald Pub. Assn., 1941).

[133] W. A. Spicer, *God's Special Gift to the Remnant Church* (Washington, D.C.: General Conference of Seventh-day Adventists, n.d.).

[134] William H. Branson, *Reply to Canright: The Truth About Seventh-day Adventists* (Washington, D.C.: Review and Herald Pub. Assn., 1933), pp. 261-293.

[135] *Ibid.,* p. 8.

[136] *Ibid.,* p. 265.

[137] Ruth Wheeler, *His Messenger* (Washington, D.C.: Review and Herald Pub. Assn., 1939).

[138] Ruth Wheeler, *His Messenger,* rev. (Nampa, Idaho: Pacific Press Pub. Assn., 2001).

[139] Doris Eugene Robinson, *The Story of Our Health Message: The Origin Character, and Development of Health Education in the Seventh-day Adventist Church* (Nashville: Southern Pub. Assn., 1943); *idem, The Story of Our Health Message: The Origin, Character, and Development of Health Education in the Seventh-day*

Adventist Church, second ed. (Nashville: Southern Pub. Assn., 1955); *idem, The Story of Our Health Message: The Origin, Character, and Development of Health Education in the Seventh-day Adventist Church*, third ed., rev. and enl. (Nashville: Southern Pub. Assn., 1965).

[140] Ellen G. White, *Notebook Leaflets* (Washington, D.C.: Review and Herald Pub. Assn., 1945), vol. 1.

[141] Martha D. Amadon, "Mrs. E. G. White in Vision" (1925); W. C. White, "The Work at the Elmshaven Office" (1932); W. C. White, "A Brief Statement Regarding the Publication of the Writings of Ellen G. White" (1929); C. C. Crisler, "A Sure Basis of Belief"; Ellen G. White Estate, "The Story of 'Steps to Christ'" (1935).

[142] George K. Abbott, *Studies in the Testimonies and Science* (Angwin, Calif.: Pacific Union College, 1946).

[143] George Knapp Abbott, *The Witness of Science to the Testimonies of the Spirit of Prophecy* (published by the author, 1947).

[144] George Knapp Abbott, *The Witness of Science to the Testimonies of the Spirit of Prophecy*, rev. ed. (Mountain View, Calif.: Pacific Press Pub. Assn., 1948).

[145] Lewis Harrison Christian, *The Fruitage of Spiritual Gifts: The Influence and Guidance of Ellen G. White in the Advent Movement* (Washington, D.C.: Review and Herald Pub. Assn., 1947).

[146] Francis D. Nichol, *Ellen G. White and Her Critics: An Answer to the Major Charges That Critics Have Brought Against Mrs. Ellen G. White* (Washington, D.C.: Review and Herald Pub. Assn., 1951).

[147] Francis D. Nichol, *The Midnight Cry: A Defense of William Miller and the Millerites* (Takoma Park, D.C.: Review and Herald Pub. Assn., 1944).

[148] Nichol, *Ellen G. White and Her Critics*, pp. 16, 17.

[149] Francis D. Nichol, *Why I Believe in Mrs. E. G. White: Some Reasons Why Seventh-day Adventists Believe That Ellen G. White Possessed the Gift of "the Spirit of Prophecy"* (Washington, D.C.: Review and Herald Pub. Assn., 1964).

[150] W. E. Read, *The Bible, the Spirit of Prophecy, and the Church* (Washington, D.C.: Review and Herald Pub. Assn., 1952), p. 3.

[151] T. Housel Jemison, *A Prophet Among You* (Mountain View, Calif.: Pacific Press Pub. Assn., 1955).

[152] Denton Edward Rebok, *Believe His Prophets* (Washington, D.C.: Review and Herald Pub. Assn., 1956); *idem, Divine Guidance in the Remnant of God's Church* (Poona, India: Oriental Watchman, 1955).

[153] Arthur W. Spalding, *There Shines a Light: The Life and Work of Ellen G. White* (Nashville: Southern Pub. Assn., 1953).

[154] Gladys King-Taylor, *Literary Beauty of Ellen G. White's Writings* (Mountain View, Calif.: Pacific Press Pub. Assn., 1953).

[155] Arthur L. White, *Ellen G. White, Messenger to the Remnant* (Washington, D.C.: Ellen G. White Publications, 1954; rev. ed. 1969).

[156] The five titles are *The Prophetic Gift in Action; Prophetic Guidance in Early Days; The Ellen G. White Books; The Custody and Use of the Ellen G. White Writings; Ellen G. White: The Human-Interest Story*.

[157] *The Spirit of Prophecy Treasure Chest: An Advent Source Collection of Materials Relating to the Gift of Prophecy in the Remnant Church and the Life and Ministry of Ellen G. White* (Glendale, Calif.: Prophetic Guidance School, 1960).

[158] *Notes and Papers Concerning Ellen G. White and the Spirit of Prophecy*, rev. (Washington, D.C.: Ellen G. White Estate, 1974).

[159] D. A. Delafield, *Ellen G. White and the Seventh-day Adventist Church* (Mountain View, Calif.: Pacific Press Pub. Assn., 1963).

[160] Donald Grey Barnhouse, "Spiritual Discernment, or How to Read Religious Books," *Eternity*, June 1950, pp. 9, 42-44.

[161] *Seventh-day Adventists Answer Questions on Doctrine: An Explanation of Certain Major Aspects of Seventh-day Adventist Belief* (Washington, D.C.: Review and Herald Pub. Assn., 1957); Donald Grey Barnhouse, "Are Seventh-day Adventists Christians? Another Look at Seventh-day Adventism," *Eternity*, September 1956.

[162] Walter R. Martin, *The Truth About Seventh-day Adventism* (Grand Rapids: Zondervan Publishing, 1960).

[163] *Ibid.*, p. 113.

[164] Nam, "Reactions to the Seventh-day Adventist Evangelical Conferences and Questions on Doctrine, 1955-1971" (Ph.D. diss., Andrews University, 2005); see also the recent annotated edition of *Seventh-day Adventists Answer Questions on Doctrine*, with notes and historical and theological introduction by George R. Knight (Berrien Springs, Mich.: Andrews University, 2003), pp. xiii-xxxvi.

[165] M. R. DeHaan, "Questions on Doctrine," *The King's Business*, March 1958; see also *idem,* "What Do Seventh-day Adventists Believe Today?" *The King's Business*, October 1959.

[166] *Ibid.,* quoted in Nam, p. 149.

[167] Harold Lindsell, "What of Seventh-day Adventism? Part I," *Christianity Today*, Mar. 31, 1958; *idem,* "What of Seventh-day Adventism? Part II," *Christianity Today*, Apr. 14, 1958; F. D. Nichol, "Adventists and Others," *Christianity Today*, May 14, 1858; see also Frank H. Yost, "A Seventh-day Adventist Speaks Back," *Christianity Today*, July 31, 1958.

[168] Herbert S. Bird, "SDA and the Evangelicals," *Christianity Today*, Apr. 14, 1958; *idem,* "Another Look at Adventism," *Christianity Today*, Apr. 28, 1958.

[169] Herbert S. Bird, *Theology of Seventh-day Adventism* (Grand Rapids: Wm. B. Eerdmans, 1961).

[170] Herbert S. Bird, "Reply to An Adventist," *Christianity Today*, Aug. 18, 1958.

[171] Bird, *Theology of Seventh-Day Adventism*, pp. 26, 27.

[172] *Ibid.*, p. 37.

[173] *Ibid.*, pp. 130-132.

[174] Walter R. Martin, "Years Too Late," *Christianity Today*, Mar. 2, 1962.

[175] John Gerstner, *The Theology of the Major Sects* (Grand Rapids: Baker, 1960); Norman F. Douty, *Another Look at Seventh-day Adventism* (Grand Rapids: Baker, 1962); Russell P. Spittler, *Cults and Isms* (Grand Rapids: Baker, 1962); J. Oswald Sanders, *Heresies and Cults* (London: Marshall, Morgan, and Scott, 1962); Jan Karel van Baalen, *The Chaos of Cults,* fourth rev. and expanded ed. (Grand Rapids: Eerdmans, 1962); Anthony A. Hoekema, *The Four Major Cults* (Grand Rapids: Eerdmans, 1963); Gordon R. Lewis, *Confronting the Cults* (Grand Rapids: Baker, 1966); Irvine Robertson, *What the Cults Believe* (Chicago: Moody, 1966).

[176] *"I'd Like to Ask Sister White . . .": The Questions You Might Ask Answered From Statements Selected From the Writings of Ellen G. White* (Washington, D.C.: Review and Herald Pub. Assn., 1965).

[177] Ella M. Robinson, *Stories of My Grandmother* (Nashville: Southern Pub. Assn., 1967).

[178] Ella M. Robinson, *Stories of My Grandmother* (Hagerstown, Md.: Review and Herald Pub. Assn., 1995).

[179] Ella White Robinson, *Over My Shoulder* (Washington, D.C.: Review and Herald Pub. Assn., 1982).

[180] *Medical Science and the Spirit of Prophecy* (Washington, D.C.: Review and Herald Pub. Assn., 1971); Roger W. Coon, "E. G. White, M.D.?: Current Research Evaluates Her Counsels on Health," *Dialogue* 3, no. 1 (1991): 11-13, 28.

[181] Arthur L. White, *Ellen G. White: The Human Interest Story* (Washington, D.C.: Review and Herald Pub. Assn., 1972); *idem, The Ellen G. White Writings* (Washington, D.C.: Review and Herald Pub. Assn., 1973).

[182] D. A. Delafield, *Ellen G. White in Europe: 1885-1887* (Washington, D.C.: Review and Herald Pub. Assn., 1975).

[183] Herbert E. Douglass, ed., *What Ellen White Has Meant to Me* (Washington, D.C.: Review and Herald Pub. Assn., 1973).

[184] Ronald E. Ruskjer, comp. and ed., *Ellen G. White: Prophet of the Last Days With Guide to Systematic Reading* (Mountain View, Calif.: Pacific Press Pub. Assn., 1974).

[185] Bobbie Jane Van Dolson, *Prophets Are People: Believe It or Not* (Washington, D.C.: Review and Herald Pub. Assn., 1974).

[186] Rene Noorbergen, *Ellen G. White: Prophet of Destiny* (New Canaan, Conn.: Keats Publishing, 1972).

[187] Jean Dixon, *My Life and Prophecies: Her Own Story as Told to Rene Noorbergen* (New York: William Morrow and Company, Inc., 1969).

[188] Rene Noorbergen, *You Are Psychic: The Incredible Story of David N. Buber* (New York: Morrow, 1971).

[189] Arthur V. Fox, "What Is Truth?" *World's Crisis*, Dec. 10, 1947; *idem,* "To Err Is Human," *World's Crisis*, Dec. 17, 1947; *idem,* "Seventh-day Adventists vs. Roman Catholics, *World's Crisis*, Dec. 31, 1947; *idem,* "Investigative Judgment," *World's Crisis*, Jan. 7, 1947; *idem,* "The True Foundation: Should We Keep the Seventh Day?" *World's Crisis*, Jan. 14, 1948; *idem,* "Inspiration," *World's Crisis*, May 26, 1948.

[190] D. M. Canright, *Life of Mrs. E. G. White, Seventh-day Adventist Prophet: Her False Claims Refuted* (Cincinnati: Standard Publishing, 1919).

[191] Ronald L. Numbers, *Prophetess of Health: A Study of Ellen G. White* (New York: Harper and Row, 1976).

[192] Ronald L. Numbers, *Prophetess of Health: Ellen G. White and the Origins of Seventh-day Adventist Health Reform*, rev. and enl. (Knoxville: University of Tennessee, 1992); *idem, Prophetess of Health: A Study of Ellen G. White*, third ed. (Grand Rapids: William B. Eerdmans Publishing, 2008).

[193] *A Critique of the Book Prophetess of Health* (Washington, D.C.: Ellen G. White Estate, 1976); see also *A Discussion and Review of Prophetess of Health* (Washington, D.C.: Ellen G. White Estate, 1976).

[194] Numbers, *Prophetess of Health* (1976), pp. ix, xi; for a more detailed explanation of Numbers' philosophical approach, see Ronald L. Numbers, "In Defense of Secular History," *Spectrum*, Spring 1969.

[195] Robert D. Brinsmead, *The Theology of Ellen G. White and an Evangelical Reflection* (Fallbrook, Calif.: Present Truth, 1975).

[196] Robert D. Brinsmead, *God's Eternal Purpose*, second ed. (Conway, Mo.: Ministry of Healing Health Centers, n.d.), pp. 196-212; *idem, Dear Brethren* (Baker, Oreg.: n.p., May 20, 1961); *idem, Perfection in the Light of the Judgment and the Second Advent* (Conway, Mo.: Gems of Truth, 1966).

[197] Robert D. Brinsmead, *1844 Re-Examined Syllabus* (Fallbrook, Calif.: I. H. I., 1979).

[198] Robert D. Brinsmead, *Judged by the Gospel: A Review of Adventism* (Fallbrook, Calif.: Verdict Publications, 1980), pp. 326, 327.

[199] *Ibid.*, p. 351.

[200] Desmond Ford, *1844, The Day of Atonement and the Investigative Judgment* (Casselberry, Fla.: Euangelion Press, 1980). In 1980, the same year Desmond Ford met with church leaders and scholars at Glacier View to examine his views on prophecy and the heavenly sanctuary, he published *Physicians of the Soul: God's Prophets Through the Ages* (Nashville: Southern Pub. Assn., 1980). The book is an overview of his views on doctrinal topics set in the framework of selected Bible prophets and ending with Ellen White. Ford shared a personal

testimony of how Ellen White's writings had positively impacted his life. The book is significant more for when it was published than for containing position-defining content.

[201] Frank B. Holbrook, ed., *Doctrine of the Sanctuary: A Historical Survey (1845-1863)* (Silver Spring, Md.: Biblical Research Institute, 1989).

[202] George E. Rice, "Ellen G. White's Use of Daniel and Revelation," in *Symposium on Revelation: Introductory and Exegetical Studies, Book 1,* ed. Frank B. Holbrook (Silver Spring, Md.: Biblical Research Institute, 1992), pp. 145-161; Jon Paulien, "The Interpreter's Use of the Writings of Ellen G. White," in *Symposium on Revelation, Book 1,* pp. 163-172; *idem,* "Ellen G. White and Revelation 4-6," in *Symposium on Revelation, Book 1,* pp. 363-373; Gerhard Pfandl, "The Remnant Church and the Spirit of Prophecy," in *Symposium on Revelation: Introductory and Exegetical Studies, Book 2,* ed. Frank B. Holbrook (Silver Spring, Md.: Biblical Research Institute, 1992), pp. 295-333.

[203] C. Mervyn Maxwell, "Sanctuary and Atonement in SDA Theology," in *The Sanctuary and the Atonement: Biblical, Historical, and Theological Studies,* ed. Arnold V. Wallenkampf and W. Richard Lesher (Washington, D.C.: Review and Herald Pub. Assn., 1981), pp. 516-544; *idem,* "The Investigative Judgment: Its Early Development," in *The Sanctuary and the Atonement,* pp. 545-581; Arnold V. Wallenkampf, "A Brief Review of Some of the Internal and External Challengers to the SDA Teachings on the Sanctuary and Atonement," in *The Sanctuary and the Atonement,* pp. 582-603; John W. Wood, "'We Must All Appear': The Investigative Judgment Theme in the Writings of Ellen G. White," in *The Sanctuary and the Atonement,* pp. 640-666; *idem,* "The Mighty Opposites: The Atonement of Christ in the Writings of Ellen G. White, Part I and Part II," in *The Sanctuary and the Atonement,* pp. 694-730.

[204] Benjamin McArthur, "Point of the Spear: Adventist Liberalism and the Study of Ellen White in the 1970s," *Spectrum,* Spring 2008.

[205] Walter T. Rea, *The White Lie* (Turlock, Calif.: M and R Publications, 1982).

[206] Fred Veltman, "Full Report of the Life of Christ Research Project" (Silver Spring, Md.: Ellen G. White Estate, November 1988). Research was reviewed and distributed by the Life of Christ Research Project Review Committee, comprising: Charles R. Taylor, chair; Alden Thompson, secretary; B. B. Beach; W. T. Clark; R. R. Hegstad; W. G. Johnsson; R. W. Nixon; R. W. Olson; G. W. Reid; G. W. Rice; F. W. Wernick; K. H. Wood.

[207] Robert W. Olson, *One Hundred and One Questions on the Sanctuary and on Ellen White* (Washington, D.C.: Ellen G. White Estate, 1981).

[208] George E. Rice, *Luke, a Plagiarist?* (Mountain View, Calif.: Pacific Press Pub. Assn., 1983).

[209] *Ibid.,* p. 15.

[210] John J. Robertson, *The White Truth* (Mountain View, Calif.: Pacific Press Pub. Assn., 1981). The White Estate staff also wrote a response to Rea's book, "The Truth About the White Lie," *Ministry* insert, August 1982, reprinted as a shelf document.

[211] Robert W. Olson, *Doctrinal Discussions: Brief Studies on Current Issues* (Washington, D.C.: Ellen G. White Estate, January 1982); Roger W. Coon, comp., *Sourcebook of Documents and Study Outlines of Selected Issues in Prophetic Guidance* (for the Writings of Ellen G. White class GSEM 534) (Berrien Springs, Mich.: Andrews University, 1992). A complete listing of articles about Ellen White in regular church papers is not included in this bibliographic essay.

[212] Robert W. Olson, "The Investigative Judgment in the Writings of Ellen G. White" (Ellen G. White Estate [EGWE], Feb. 25, 1980, shelf document [SDoc]); Paul A. Gordon, "The Pioneers and the Sanctuary" (EGWE, n.d., SDoc); *idem,* comp., "Pioneer Articles on the Sanctuary, Daniel 8:14, the Judgment, 2300 Days, Year-day Principle, Atonement: 1846-1905" (EGWE, 1983, SDoc).

[213] Ron Graybill, "The Making of *The Ministry of Healing,*" *Insight,* July 10, 1979; Raymond F. Cottrell, "The Literary Relationship between *The Desire of Ages,* by Ellen G. White, and *The Life of Christ,* by William Hanna" (EGWE, Nov. 1, 1979, SDoc); D. E. Robinson, "How the E. G. White Books Were Written," *Ministry,* February 1980; Walter F. Specht, "The Literary Relationship Between *The Desire of Ages,* by Ellen G. White, and *The Life of Christ,* by William Hanna, Part II" (EGWE, n.d., SDoc); Robert W. Olson, "Ellen G. White's Use of Uninspired Sources" (EGWE, Apr. 10, 1980, SDoc); J. R. Spangler, "Ellen White and Literary Dependency," *Ministry,* June 1980; Paul A. Gordon, "Sources or Aids—Why Did Ellen G. White Borrow?" (EGWE, May 1981, SDoc); Ron Graybill, "Ellen White as a Reader and a Writer," *Insight,* May 19, 1981; Neal C. Wilson, "The Ellen G. White Writings and the Church," *Adventist Review,* July 9, 1981; Ron Graybill, *Analysis of E. G. White's Luther Manuscript* (Washington, D.C.: Review and Herald Pub. Assn., 1981); Vincent L. Ramik, "The Ramik Report: Memorandum of Law Literary Property Rights, 1790-1915" (EGWE, Aug. 14, 1981, SDoc); [Roger W. Coon], "Was Ellen G. White a Plagiarist?" from articles in *Adventist Review* (EGWE, Sept. 17, 1981, SDoc); Kenneth H. Wood, "This Work Is of God, or It Is Not," *Adventist Review,* Sept, 17, 1981; Ron Graybill, "E. G. White's Literary Work: An Update," from General Conference worship (EGWE, Nov. 15-19, 1981, SDoc); Niels-Erik Andreasen, "From Vision to Prophecy," *Adventist Review,* Jan. 28, 1982; "The Fannie Bolton Story: A Collection of Source Documents" (EGWE, April 1982, SDoc); Ron Graybill, Warren H. Johns, Tim Poirier, comps., "Henry Melvill and Ellen G. White: A Study in Literary and Theological Relationships" (EGWE, May 1982, SDoc); Warren H. Johns, "Ellen White: Prophet or Plagiarist? Closed Windows or Open Doors?" *Ministry,* June 1982; *idem,* "Literary Thief or God's Messenger?" *Ministry,* June 1982; *idem,* "Human Thoughts

or Divine Truths?" *Ministry*, June 1982; Ron Graybill, "The 'I Saw' Parallels in Ellen White's Writings," *Adventist Review*, July 29, 1982; Delmer A. Johnson, "The Sources of Inspired Writings," *Adventist Review*, Dec. 30, 1982; George E. Rice, "Luke: Healer of Bodies and Souls, "*Adventist Review*, Mar. 17, 1983; Gerald Wheeler, "God Speaks With a Human Accent," *Adventist Review*, July 14, 1983; Robert W. Olson, "Ellen G. White's Use of Historical Sources in *The Great Controversy*," *Adventist Review*, Feb. 23, 1984; Tim Crosby, "Does Inspired Mean Original?" *Ministry*, February 1986; Tim Poirier, "Did James White Attempt a 'Cover-up' of Ellen White's Literary Borrowing?: An Explanation of His Statements in *Life Sketches* (1880), pp. 328, 329" (EGWE, Aug. 15, 1986, SDoc); Robert W. Olson, "The Literary Borrowing Issue" (EGWE, June 1, 1986, SDoc); Warren H. Johns, Tim Poirier, Ron Graybill, comps., *A Bibliography of Ellen G. White's Private and Office Libraries*, third rev. ed. (Silver Spring, Md.: Ellen G. White Estate, April 1993).

[214] Robert W. Olson, "The Shut Door Documents: Statements Relating to the 'Shut Door,' the Door of Mercy, and the Salvation of Souls by Ellen G. White and Other Early Adventists Arranged in a Chronological Setting from 1844 to 1851" (EGWE, Apr. 11, 1982, SDoc); Arthur L. White, "Ellen G. White and the Shut Door Question: A Review of the Experience of Early Seventh-day Adventist Believers in Its Historical Context" (EGWE, May 9, 1982, SDoc). Other treatments on the shut door include: Rolf J. Poehler, "'. . . And the Door Was Shut': Seventh-day Adventists and the Shut-Door Doctrine in the Decade after the Great Disappointment" (term paper, Andrews University, 1978, Berrien Springs, Mich.); P. Gerard Damsteegt, *Foundations of the Seventh-day Adventist Message and Mission* (Grand Rapids: Eerdmans, 1977; reprint: Berrien Springs, Mich.: Andrews University Press, 1995), pp. 104-124; Herbert E. Douglass, *Messenger of the Lord: The Prophetic Ministry of Ellen G. White* (Nampa, Idaho: Pacific Press Pub. Assn., 1998), pp. 500-512, 549-569; Merlin D. Burt, "The Historical Background, Interconnected Development, and Integration of the Doctrines of the Sanctuary, the Sabbath, and Ellen G. White's Role in Sabbatarian Adventism from 1844 to 1849" (Ph.D. diss., Andrews University, 2002).

[215] Raoul Dederen, "Ellen White's Doctrine of Scripture," *Ministry* (supp.), July 1977; T. H. Blincoe, "The Prophets Were Until John," *Ministry* (supp.), July 1977; Arthur L. White, "Comments on the SDA Forum Presentation at Pacific Union College," Oct. 27, 1979; Eric Livingstone, "Inquire of the Lord," *Ministry*, April 1981; Roger W. Coon, "Inspiration/Revelation: What It Is and How It Works, Part 3: The Relationship Between the Ellen G. White Writings and the Bible," *Journal of Adventist Education*, February-March 1982; Richard Hammill, "Spiritual Gifts in the Church Today," *Ministry*, July 1982; Roy Graham, "How the Gift of Prophecy Relates to God's Word," *Adventist Review*, Oct. 14, 1982; "The Inspiration and Authority of the Ellen G. White Writings," *Adventist Review*, Dec. 23, 1982; Alfred S. Jorgensen, "The Holy Spirit and His Gifts, Part I," *Australasian Record*, Feb. 11, 1984; *idem*, "The Holy Spirit and His Gifts, Part II," *Australasian Record*, Feb. 18, 1984; Robert W. Olson, comp., "The Relationship Between Ellen G. White and the Bible" (EGWE, July 7, 1986, SDoc).

[216] D. F. Neufeld, "How Seventh-day Adventists Adopted the Sanctuary Doctrine," *Adventist Review*, Jan. 3, 1980; *idem*, "Aftermath of Autumn Disappointment," *Adventist Review*, Jan. 10, 1980; *idem*, "Edson's October 23 Experience," *Adventist Review*, Jan. 17, 1980; *idem*, "Ellen White and Crosier's *Day-Star* Article," *Adventist Review*, Jan. 24, 1980; *idem*, "A Significant Early Vision," *Adventist Review*, Jan. 31, 1980; *idem*, "The Investigative Judgment—1," *Adventist Review*, Feb. 7, 1980; *idem*, "The Investigative Judgment—2," *Adventist Review*, Feb. 14, 1980; *idem*, "A Basis for Confidence—1," *Adventist Review*, Feb. 21, 1980; *idem*, "A Basis for Confidence—2," *Adventist Review*, Feb. 28, 1980; W. Richard Lesher, "Landmark Truth Versus 'Specious Error,'" *Adventist Review*, Mar. 6, 1980; *idem*, "Truth Stands Forever," *Adventist Review*, Mar. 13, 1980; "The Role of the Ellen G. White Writings in Doctrinal Matters," *Ministry*, October 1980; J. R. Spangler, "Ellen White's Role in Doctrinal Matters," *Ministry*, October 1980; V. N. Olsen, "Ellen White's Defense Against Error and Apostasy," *Adventist Review*, Oct. 14, 1982; Richard Hammill, "Ellen White and Change," *Adventist Review*, Jan. 13, 1983; Arthur L. White, "The Certainty of Basic Doctrinal Positions," *Adventist Review*, July 26, 1984.

[217] Arthur L. White, "The Importance of Understanding Inspiration," *Adventist Review*, Feb. 2, 1978; White Estate staff, "Ellen G. White, Dates, and Biblical Chronology" (EGWE, May 17, 1978, SDoc); Alfred S. Jorgensen, "Hallmarks of Inspiration," *Australasian Record*, Aug. 14, 1978; Arthur L. White, "Inspiration and the Ellen G. White Writings," from reprinted articles in the *Adventist Review* (EGWE, 1978, 1979, SDoc); Robert W. Olson, "The 1919 Bible Conference and Bible and History Teachers' Council" (EGWE, Sept. 24, 1979, SDoc); "Study Documents on Inspiration and Creation," *Adventist Review*, Jan. 17, 1980; Arthur L. White, "The Prescott Letter to W. C. White, Apr. 6, 1915" (EGWE, June 15, 1981, SDoc); William G. Johnsson, "How Does God Speak?" *Ministry*, October 1981; Robert W. Olson, "The Question of Inerrancy in Inspired Writings" (EGWE, Apr. 12, 1982, SDoc); R. J. Wieland, "Ellen White's Inspiration, Authentic and Profound," *Australasian Record*, May 31, 1882; Robert W. Olson, comp., "The Salamanca Vision and the 1890 Diary" (EGWE, Oct. 12, 1983, SDoc); Wadie Farag, "Inspiration in Islam and Christianity," *Adventist Review*, June 21, 1984; C. R. Stanley, "Visions: The Prophet's Credentials," *Australian Record*, Aug. 25, 1984; Alden Thompson, "Improving the *Testimonies* Through Revisions," *Adventist Review*, Sept. 12, 1985; Robert W. Olson, "Evidence of Inspiration" (EGWE, July 7, 1986, SDoc); Tim Poirier, "The 1907 Interview With John Harvey Kellogg" (EGWE, May 17, 1987, SDoc).

[218] Roger W. Coon, "Inspiration/Revelation: What It Is and How It Works," reprinted from three-part article in *Journal of Adventist Education* (EGWE, 1981, 1982, SDoc); George R. Knight, "The Myth of the Inflexible Prophet," *Adventist Review*, Apr. 3, 1986; Roger W. Coon, "Hermeneutics: Interpreting a Nineteenth-Century Prophet in the Space Age," reprinted from article in *Journal of Adventist Education* (EGWE, Summer 1988, SDoc); Robert W. Olson, "Hermeneutics: Guiding Principles in the Interpretation of the Bible and the Writings of Ellen G. White" (EGWE, June 1, 1986, SDoc); Herbert E. Douglass, "Basic Principles of Understanding Ellen G. White's Writings" (EGWE, SDoc); Herbert E. Douglass, "Basic Rules of Interpretation—Internal and External" (EGWE, SDoc).

[219] *Periodical Articles Concerning Inspiration, Ellen G. White, and Adventist History* (Washington, D.C.: Ellen G. White Estate, General Conference of Seventh-day Adventists, June 1986); relevant articles from this publication are included on topics listed above.

[220] Roger W. Coon, comp., *Anthology of Recently Published Articles on Selected Issues in Prophetic Guidance: 1980-1992* (for the Writings of Ellen G. White class GSEM 534) (Berrien Springs, Mich.: Andrews University, 1992); the articles contained in the anthology are not listed here.

[221] Roger W. Coon, *The Great Visions of Ellen G. White* (Hagerstown, Md.: Review and Herald Pub. Assn., 1992), vol. 1; *idem, A Gift of Light* (Hagerstown, Md.: Review and Herald Pub. Assn., 1983); *idem, Ellen G. White and Vegetarianism: Did She Practice What She Preached?* (Boise, Idaho: Pacific Press Pub. Assn., 1986); *idem, Heralds of New Light: Another Prophet to the Remnant?* (Boise, Idaho: Pacific Press Pub. Assn., 1987).

[222] Ron Graybill, "The Power of Prophecy: "Ellen G. White and the Women Religious Founders of the Nineteenth Century" (Ph.D. diss., Johns Hopkins University, 1983).

[223] Arthur L. White, *Ellen G. White: The Early Years, 1827-1862* (Washington, D.C.: Review and Herald Pub. Assn., 1985); *idem, Ellen G. White: The Progressive Years, 1863-1875* (Washington, D.C.: Review and Herald Pub. Assn., 1986); *idem, Ellen G. White: The Lonely Years, 1876-1891* (Washington, D.C.: Review and Herald Pub. Assn., 1984); *idem, Ellen G. White: The Australian Years, 1891-1900* (Washington, D.C.: Review and Herald Pub. Assn., 1983); *idem, Ellen G. White: The Early Elmshaven Years, 1900-1905* (Washington, D.C.: Review and Herald Pub. Assn., 1981); *idem, Ellen G. White: The Later Elmshaven Years, 1905-1915* (Washington, D.C.: Review and Herald Pub. Assn., 1982).

[224] Arthur L. White, *Ellen White: Woman of Vision* (Hagerstown, Md.: Review and Herald Pub. Assn., 2000).

[225] Ciro Sepulveda, *Ellen White: The Troubles and Triumphs of an American Prophet* (Huntsville, Ala.: Oakwood College, 2002).

[226] Gary Land, ed., *The World of Ellen G. White* (Washington, D.C.: Review and Herald Pub. Assn., 1987).

[227] George R. Knight, *Myths in Adventism: An Interpretive Study of Ellen White, Education, and Related Issues* (Washington, D.C.: Review and Herald Pub. Assn., 1985).

[228] "Trial of Elder I. Dammon: Reported for the *Piscataquis Farmer*," *Piscataquis Farmer*, Mar. 7, 1845.

[229] Bruce Weaver, "Incident in Atkinson: The Arrest and Trial of Israel Dammon," *Adventist Currents*, April 1988. For additional dialogue on the Dammon trial, see Rennie Schoepflin, ed., Jonathan Butler, Ronald Graybill, and Frederick Hoyt, "Scandal or Rite of Passage? Historians on the Dammon Trail," *Spectrum*, August 1987; Robert W. Olson to White Estate Board of Trustees, White Estate staff, Research Centers, Oct. 21, 1987, White Estate Branch Office, Loma Linda, Calif.

[230] James R. Nix, "Another Look at Israel Dammon" (EGWE, February 2005, SDoc). See also Merlin D. Burt, "Historical Background" (2002), pp. 132-140.

[231] Roy E. Graham, *Ellen G. White: Cofounder of the Seventh-day Adventist Church*, in American University Studies, Series VII: Theology and Religion (New York: Peter Lang, 1985), vol. 12; *idem*, "Ellen G. White: An Examination of Her Position and Role in the Seventh-day Adventist Church" (Ph.D. diss., University of Birmingham, 1977).

[232] Woodrow W. Whidden II, *Ellen White on Salvation: A Chronological Study* (Hagerstown, Md.: Review and Herald Pub. Assn., 1995); *idem, Ellen White on the Humanity of Christ: A Chronological Study* (Hagerstown, Md.: Review and Herald Pub. Assn., 1997); *idem*, "The Soteriology of Ellen G. White: The Persistent Path to Perfection, 1836-1902" (Ph.D. diss., Drew University, 1989).

[233] Jerry Allen Moon, *W. C. White and Ellen G. White: The Relationship Between the Prophet and Her Son* (Berrien Springs, Mich.: Andrews University Press, 1993).

[234] See Zoltan Szalos-Farkas, *The Rise and Development of Seventh-day Adventist Spirituality: The Impact of the Charismatic Guidance of Ellen G. White* (Cernica, Romania: Editura Institutului Teologic Adventist, 2005).

[235] *Ellen G. White and Europe: Symposium Papers* (Bracknell, Eng.: Ellen G. White Research Center, Newbold College, 1987).

[236] I. J. van Zyl, *Ellen G. White and Her Critics* (South Africa: Esdea Books, 1994); *idem, Ellen G. White the Writer* (South Africa: Esdea Books, 1997).

[237] Alden Thompson, *Inspiration: Hard Questions, Honest Answers* (Hagerstown, Md.: Review and Herald Pub. Assn., 1991).

[238] Alden Thompson, *Escape From the Flames: How Ellen White Grew From Fear to Joy—and Helped Me Do It Too* (Nampa, Idaho: Pacific Press Pub. Assn., 2005).

[239] Frank Holbrook and Leo Van Dolson, eds., *Issues in Revelation and Inspiration* (Berrien Springs, Mich.: Adventist Theological Society, 1992). Chapter authors included Raoul Dederen, Samuel Koranteng-Pipim, Norman R. Gulley, Richard A. Davidson, Gerhard F. Hasel, Randall W. Younker, Frank M. Hasel, and Miroslav M. Kis.

[240] Herbert E. Douglass, *Messenger of the Lord: The Prophetic Ministry of Ellen G. White* (Nampa, Idaho: Pacific Press Pub. Assn., 1998). For Douglass the great controversy theme was the integrating theological framework in Ellen White's writings. See *idem,* "Ellen White and the Adventist Theology," *Dialogue* 10, no. 1 (1998): 13-15, 19.

[241] Herbert E. Douglass, *They Were There: Stories of Those Who Witnessed Ellen White's Prophetic Gift—and Believed* (Nampa, Idaho: Pacific Press Pub. Assn., 2006).

[242] Herbert E. Douglass, *Dramatic Prophecies of Ellen White: Stories of World Events Divinely Foretold* (Nampa, Idaho: Pacific Press Pub. Assn., 2007).

[243] George R. Knight, *Meeting Ellen White: A Fresh Look at Her Life, Writings, and Major Themes* (Hagerstown, Md.: Review and Herald Pub. Assn., 1996); *idem, Reading Ellen White: How to Understand and Apply Her Writings* (Hagerstown, Md.: Review and Herald Pub. Assn., 1997); *idem, Ellen White's World: A Fascinating Look at the Times in Which She Lived* (Hagerstown, Md.: Review and Herald Pub. Assn., 1998); *idem, Walking With Ellen White: The Human Interest Story* (Hagerstown, Md.: Review and Herald Pub. Assn., 1999).

[244] Juan Carlos Viera, *The Voice of the Spirit: How God Has Led His People Through the Gift of Prophecy* (Nampa, Idaho: Pacific Press Pub. Assn., 1998).

[245] Arthur N. Patrick, "Ellen Gould White and the Australian Woman, 1891-1900 (M.Litt. thes., University of New England, 1994); *idem, Christianity and Culture in Colonial Australia: Selected Catholic, Anglican, Wesleyan, and Adventist Perspectives, 1891-1900* (Sydney: Fast Books, 1993).

[246] Arthur N. Patrick, "Seventh-day Adventists in the South Pacific: A Review of Sources," *Journal of Religious History,* June 1987; *idem,* "Re-Visioning the Role of Ellen White Beyond the Year 2000," *Adventist Today,* March-April 1998, with an enlarged article on the same theme published on the Internet; *idem,* "Ellen White: Mother of the Church in the South Pacific," *Adventist Heritage,* Spring 1993.

[247] *"Ellen White and Current Issues" Symposium* (Berrien Springs, Mich.: Center for Adventist Research, 2005, 2006, 2007, 2008), vols. 1-4.

[248] Vance Ferrell, *The Editions of Great Controversy* (Beersheba Springs, Tenn.: Pilgrims Books, 1994); *idem, Prophet of the End* (Altamont, Tenn.: Pilgrim's Rest, 1984).

[249] Maurice Barnett published a 70-page booklet titled *Ellen G. White and Inspiration* (Louisville, Ky.: Gospel Anchor Publishing, 1983) primarily to inform non-Adventists on Ellen White. Barnett also wrote books on Jehovah's Witnesses and Mormons.

[250] Dale Ratzlaff, *The Cultic Doctrine of Seventh-day Adventists: An Evangelical Resource, an Appeal to SDA Leadership* (Sedona, Ariz.: Life Assurance Ministries, 1996).

[251] Dale Ratzlaff, *Sabbath in Crisis* (Applegate, Calif.: Life Assurance Ministries, 1989, 1990); *idem, Sabbath in Christ* (Glendale, Ariz.: Life Assurance Ministries, 2003).

[252] (Anonymous), "Ellen White: An Unreliable Prophet," *Proclamation!* November/December 2002; Walter Rea, "Walter Rea on Ellen White," *Proclamation!* May/June 2003; Dennis L. Palmer, "Whose Authority Shall We Follow?" *Proclamation!* September-December 2003; Richard Goyne, "A Word (or Two) From God," *Proclamation!* September/October 2004; Esther Shu, "I Stand Alone on the Word of God," *Proclamation!* November/December 2004; Walter Rea, "Recant No!: I Stand Firm," *Proclamation!* November/December 2004; Verle Streifling, "The Bible Inerrant?: Adventist Claims of Bible Contradictions and Errors," *Proclamation!* May/June 2006; Russell Kelly, "Biblical Inspiration and Ellen G. White," *Proclamation!* May/June 2006; Dale Ratzlaff, "The Ellen White Summit: A Response to Jud Lake," *Proclamation!* November/December 2006; *idem,* "The Christ Event and the Spirit of Prophecy," *Proclamation!* March /April 2007.

[253] Dirk Anderson, *White Out: How a Prophetess's Failed Visions, Mistaken Prophecies, and Embarrassing Blunders Were Covered Up and Concealed by Her Followers* (Glendale, Ariz.: Life Assurance Ministries, 2001); Sydney Cleveland, *White-Washed: Uncovering the Myths of Ellen G. White* (Greenwood, Ind.: Sydney Cleveland, 1999).

[254] Bob Pickle, *A Response to Video: "Seventh-day Adventism, The Spirit Behind the Church"* (Halstad, Mich.: Pickle Publishing, 2002).

[255] *Ellen G. White Concordance* (St. Paul: Select Video Products, 1982).

[256] Ellen G. White, *A Call to Stand Apart: Challenging Young Adults to Make an Eternal Difference* (Silver Spring, Md.: Ellen G. White Estate, 2002).

[257] George R. Knight, Jud Lake, Craig Newborn, and Jon Paulien, *Ellen White Summit 2005: November 11, 12, 2005,* DVD (Enumclaw, Wash.: A and J Enterprises, 2005).

[258] Allan Lindsay, narrator, *Prophetic Inspiration: The Holy Spirit at Work* (Wahroonga, Australia: ampm, 2006).

[259] Eryck Chairez, writer, Mei Ann Toe, director, *Red Books: Our Search for Ellen White* (Pacific Union College, *Adventist Today,* 2008); "Red Books Play Tours Southern California, DVD Next," *Adventist Today,*

January/February 2008; Adrian Zytkoskee, "Red Books: Our Search for Ellen White," *Spectrum*, Spring 2007; A. Gregory Schneider, "Inside Red Books: A View of Loss, and Maybe, Recovery," *Spectrum*, Summer 2008.

[260] Helen M. Johnson and Evelyn Roose Dinsmore, *Stories of Little Ellen and the Message* (Mountain View, Calif.: Pacific Press Pub. Assn., 1950); Arthur Whitefield Spalding, *Sister White: A Life of Ellen G. White for Primary Children* (Washington, D.C.: Review and Herald Pub. Assn., 1950).

[261] Marye Trim, *Tell Me About Ellen White,* illustrated by Vernon Nye (Washington, D.C.: Review and Herald Pub. Assn., 1975).

[262] Paul B. Ricchiuti, *Ellen: Trial and Triumph on the American Frontier* (Mountain View, Calif.: Pacific Press Pub. Assn., 1977); idem, *Ellen White: Friend of Angels, Stories From Her Amazing Adventures, Travels, and Relationships* (Nampa, Idaho: Pacific Press Pub. Assn., 1999); idem, *Ellen White: Trailblazer for God: More Stories From Her Amazing Adventures, Travels, and Relationships* (Nampa, Idaho: Pacific Press Pub. Assn., 2003); idem, *Charlie Horse/Mrs. White's Secret Sock,* illustrated by James Converse (Hagerstown, Md.: Review and Herald Pub. Assn., 1992); idem, *Where's Moo Cow?/Tig's Tale* (Hagerstown, Md.: Review and Herald Pub. Assn., 1995); idem, *The Little Girl Who Giggled/Camp Meeting Angel* (Hagerstown, Md.: Review and Herald Pub. Assn., 1998); idem, *Mr. Squirrel's Treasure/Ellen's Miracle Horse,* illustrated by Marcus Mashburn (Hagerstown, Md.: Review and Herald Pub. Assn., 2002); idem, *Four Boys in the White House: The Children of James and Ellen White* (Grantham, Eng.: Stanborough Press, 2008).

[263] Carolyn Byers, *Good Night Too Soon: The Story of the Brief Life of Henry Nichols White, Son of James and Ellen White* (Washington, D.C.: Review and Herald Pub. Assn., 1980).

[264] Miriam Hardinge, *Long Ago Stories: Stories of Ellen White and Other SDA Pioneers for Parents to Read to Children* (Hagerstown, Md.: Review and Herald Pub. Assn., 1986).

[265] Tom Kohls, *Gathering Fruit* (Boise, Idaho: Pacific Press Pub. Assn., 1987); idem, *The Green Cord* (Boise, Idaho: Pacific Press Pub. Assn., 1987); idem, *The Missing Hairnet* (Boise, Idaho: Pacific Press Pub. Assn., 1987); idem, *A Trip to Heaven* (Boise, Idaho: Pacific Press Pub. Assn., 1987).

[266] Eileen E. Lantry, *Miss Marian's Gold* (Mountain View, Calif.: Pacific Press Pub. Assn., 1981); idem, *Why Me, Lord? The Story of Ellen White* (Boise, Idaho: Pacific Press Pub. Assn., 1988).

[267] Mabel R. Miller, *Ellen: The Girl With Two Angels* (Boise, Idaho: Pacific Press Pub. Assn., 1996); idem, *Grandma Ellen and Me* (Nampa, Idaho: Pacific Press Pub. Assn., 2000).

[268] Dorothy Nelson, *God Spoke to a Girl* (Nampa, Idaho: Pacific Press Pub. Assn., 1998).

[269] Becky Ponder, *Jeanie Meets Ellen White* (Mountain View, Calif.: Pacific Press Pub. Assn., 1978).

[270] Ella M. Robinson, *Over My Shoulder* (Washington, D.C.: Review and Herald Pub. Assn., 1982).

[271] Norma Youngberg, *The Spirit of Prophecy Emphasis Stories* (Washington, D.C.: Ellen G. White Estate and General Conference Department of Education, 1979-1985).

[272] Bernadine Irwin, *Ellen White: We Never Knew You* (Colorado Springs, Colo.: 1999). Irwin's book, while not really a children's book, was written in a popular story style. It constructed stories using fictional scenarios that are sometimes inconsistent with historical sources.

[273] "EGW Estate Launches New Web Magazine for Kids," *Adventist Review*, May 17, 2007. Though not related to children's ministry, Tutsch published the results of her Doctor of Ministry dissertation. Cindy Tutsch, *Ellen White on Leadership: Guidance for Those Who Influence Others* (Nampa, Idaho: Pacific Press Pub. Assn., 2008); Bonnie McLean, "*Ellen White on Leadership* Reveals Pioneer's Insights," *Adventist Review*, June 19, 2008.

[274] Cindy Tutsch, "Back to Our Future: Why Adventist Heritage Should Matter to Our Kids," *Adventist Review*, July 24, 2008. See also Arthur W. Spalding, "Meeting the Needs of Children," *Adventist World*, Dec. 2007.

[275] Ansel Oliver, "Historical Focus Can Shape Future Adventist Generations," *Adventist Review*, Aug. 26, 2008; Ella May Robinson, "Stories of My Grandmother," *KidsView*, Sept. 18, 2008.

[276] Charles Edward Dudley, Sr., *The Genealogy of Ellen Gould Harmon White: The Prophetess of the Seventh-day Adventist Church, and the Story of the Growth and Development of the Seventh-day Adventist Denomination as It Relates to African-Americans* (Nashville: Dudley Publishing, 1999), vol. 2.

[277] Charles Edward Dudley, Sr., *Thou Who Hast Brought Us Thus Far on Our Way: The Development of Seventh-day Adventist Denomination Among African-Americans* (Nashville: Dudley Publications, 2000), vol. 3.

[278] Roger D. Joslyn, "Gould Ancestry of Ellen Gould (Harmon) White," 2002, updated Apr. 9, 2003.

[279] "The Genealogy of Ellen G. White: An Update" (Ellen G. White Estate, April 2003).

[280] Don S. McMahon, *Acquired or Inspired: Exploring the Origins of the Adventist Lifestyle* (Victoria, Australia: Signs Publishing, 2005).

[281] Leonard Brand and Don S. McMahon, *The Prophet and Her Critics: A Striking New Analysis Refutes the Charges That Ellen G. White "Borrowed" the Health Message* (Nampa, Idaho: Pacific Press Pub. Assn., 2005).

[282] T. Joe Willey, "Natural or Supernatural: Can Science Establish the Supernatural in the Health Writings of Ellen G. White? *Adventist Today*, September/October 2008 (includes a response by Leonard Brand and Don McMahon; Numbers, *Prophetess of Health* [2008], p. xxiv).

[283] Mervyn G. Hardinge, *A Physician Explains Ellen White's Counsel on Drugs, Herbs, and Natural Remedies* (Hagerstown, Md.: Review and Herald Pub. Assn., 2001).

[284] Graeme S. Bradford, *Prophets Are Human* (Victoria, Australia: Signs Publishing, 2004); see also Denis Fortin, "Ellen G. White as Messenger of the Lord: What Else Could Dr. Smithurst Say?" *Ellen White and Current Issues Symposium* (Center for Adventist Research, 2005), pp. 10-29.

[285] Graeme S. Bradford, *People Are Human: Look What They Did to Ellen White* (Victoria, Australia: Signs Publishing, 2005).

[286] Graeme S. Bradford, *More Than a Prophet: How We Lost and Found Again the Real Ellen White* (Berrien Springs, Mich.: Biblical Perspectives, 2006); *idem,* books and articles on CD-ROM including a live lecture (Berrien Springs, Mich.: Biblical Perspectives, 2006).

[287] Wayne Grudem, *The Gift of Prophecy in the New Testament and Today*, rev. ed. (Wheaton, Ill.: Crossway Books, 2000); D. A. Carson, *Showing the Spirit—A Theological Exposition of 1 Corinthians 12-14* (Homebush West, Australia: Lancer Books, 1988); Ben Witherington III, *Jesus the Seer* (Peabody, Mass.: Hendrickson, 1999); Bradford, *More Than a Prophet*, pp. 70, 71.

[288] Bradford, *More Than a Prophet*, p. 113.

[289] Russell R. Standish and Colin D. Standish, *The Greatest of All the Prophets* (Narbethong, Australia: Highwood Books, 2004), p. 12.

[290] *Ibid.,* pp. 101, 198.

[291] Jonathan Butler, "Ellen G. White and the Chicago Mission," *Spectrum*, Winter 1970; Roy Branson and Herold D. Weiss, "Ellen White: A Subject for Adventist Scholarship," *Spectrum*, Autumn 1970; Frederick E. J. Harder, "Divine Revelation: A Review of Some of Ellen White's Concepts," *Spectrum,* Autumn 1970; William S. Peterson, "A Textual and Historical Study of Ellen White's Account of the French Revolution, *Spectrum,* Autumn 1970; Richard Lewis, "The 'Spirit of Prophecy,'" *Spectrum,* Autumn 1970; W. Paul Bradley, "Ellen G. White and Her Writings," *Spectrum*, Spring 1971; William S. Peterson, "Ellen White's Literary Indebtedness," *Spectrum*, Autumn 1971; Arthur L. White, "Ellen G. White the Person," *Spectrum*, Spring 1972; Ronald Graybill, "How Did Ellen White Choose and Use Historical Sources?" *Spectrum*, Summer 1972; Stanley G. Sturges, "Ellen White's Authority and the Church," *Spectrum*, Summer 1972; Ingemar Linden, Norval F. Pease, Jonathan M. Butler, "The Prophet of Destiny?" *Spectrum* 6, nos. 1, 2 (1974); Stephen T. Hand, "The Conditionality of Ellen White's Writings," *Spectrum* 6, nos. 3, 4 (1974); W. Frederick Norwood, Ellen G. White Estate, Fawn M. Brodie, Ernest R. Sandeen, Richard Schwarz, Fritz Guy, Ronald L. Numbers, "Commentary on *Prophetess of Health: A Study of Ellen G. White*, by Ronald L. Numbers," *Spectrum*, January 1977; Joseph J. Battistone, "Ellen White's Authority as Bible Commentator," *Spectrum*, January 1977; Gary Land, "Faith, History, and Ellen White," *Spectrum*, March 1978; Eric Anderson, "Ellen White and Reformation Historians," *Spectrum*, July 1978; Jonathan Butler, "The World of E. G. White and the End of the World," *Spectrum*, August 1979; "Chuck and Marianne Scriven, "Another Look at Ellen White on Music," *Spectrum*, August 1979; Douglas Hackleman, "GC Committee Studies Ellen White's Sources," *Spectrum*, March 1980; Harold E. Fagal, Thomas A. Norris, W. Larry Richards, Jonathan Butler, "Butler on Ellen White's Eschatology," *Spectrum*, July 1980; Carlyle Manous, Jeanne Fleming, Martha Ford, Russell Stafford, B. E. Seton, Charles and Marianne Scriven, "Scrivens on Music," *Spectrum*, July 1980; Sanctuary Review Committee, "The Role of the Ellen G. White Writings in Doctrinal Matters," *Spectrum*, November 1980; Donald Casebolt, "Ellen White, the Waldenses, and Historical Interpretation," *Spectrum*, February 1981; *idem,* "Is Ellen White's Interpretation of Biblical Prophecy Final? *Spectrum*, June 1982; "Gordon Shigley, "Amalgamation of Man and Beast: What Did Ellen White Mean?" *Spectrum*, June 1982; Bert Haloviak with Gary Land, "Ellen White and Doctrinal Conflict: Context of the 1919 Bible Conference," *Spectrum*, June 1982; Jonathan Butler, "*The White Lie*, by Walter Rea," *Spectrum*, June 1982; Ronald Numbers, "The Psychological World of Ellen White," *Spectrum*, August 1983; Bonnie L. Casey, "Graybill's Exit: Turning Point at the White Estate," *Spectrum*, March 1984; Donald R. McAdams, "The Scope of Ellen White's Authority," *Spectrum*, August 1985; Herold Weiss, "Formative Authority—Yes, Canonization—No," *Spectrum*, August 1985; Arthur L. White, "In Defense of Compilations," *Spectrum*, August 1985; Jean Zurcher, "A Vindication of Ellen White as Historian," *Spectrum*, August 1985; Lourdes Morales-Gudmundsson, "Pleasing the Senses: Ellen White Wouldn't Object," *Spectrum*, May 1987; Tim Poirier, "Black Forerunner to Ellen White: William E. Foy," *Spectrum*, August 1987; Frederick Hoyt, ed., "Trial of Elder I. Dammon: Reported for the *Piscataquis Farmer*," *Spectrum*, August 1987; Rennie Schoepflin, ed., "Scandal or Rite of Passage? Historians on the Dammon Trial," *Spectrum*, August 1987; Rolf J. Poehler, "Adventism and 1844: Shut Door or Open Mind?" *Spectrum*, August 1988; Bert Haloviak, "Ellen White Endorsed Adventist Women Ministers," *Spectrum*, July 1989; Gary Land, "Adventists in Plain Dress," *Spectrum*, December 1989; James Walters, "Ellen White in a New Key," *Spectrum*, December 1991; Jonathan Butler, "The Historian as Heretic," *Spectrum*, August 1993; David Thiele, "Is Conservatism a Heresy?" *Spectrum*, January 1994; Kathleen Joyce, "Illness as a Refuge and Strength," *Spectrum*, April 1995; Woodrow Whidden, "Ellen White and John Wesley," *Spectrum*, September 1996; "A Conversation With Herbert Douglass About Ellen White," *Spectrum*, Winter 1999; Alden Thompson, "Review of *Messenger of the Lord*," *Spectrum*, Winter 1999; Ronald D. Graybill, "That 'Great African-American Woman,' Ellen Gould Harmon White," *Spectrum*, Autumn 2000; A. Gragory Schneider, "The Shouting Ellen White: A Review of Ann Taves' Book," *Spectrum*, Autumn 2001; Gary Land, "An Ambiguous Legacy: A Retrospective Review of *Prophetess of Health*," *Spectrum*, Winter 1999; Herbert E. Douglass,

"Reexamining the Way God Speaks to His Messengers: Rereading *Prophetess of Health*," *Spectrum*, Winter 1999; Douglas Morgan, "A New Era of Ellen G. White Studies?" *Spectrum*, Autumn 2002; Richard Rice, "The Great Controversy and the Problem of Evil," *Spectrum*, Winter 2004; Arthur Patrick, "South Pacific Division Convenes Ellen White Summit," *Spectrum*, Spring 2004; Arthur Patrick, "Prophets Are Human! Are Humans Prophets?" *Spectrum*, Spring 2005; Alexander Carpenter, "That Embarrassing Voice of Prophecy," *Spectrum*, Winter 2006; John Hoyt, "Danish Cheese and American Gothic: Thoughts on Depicting the Prophet," *Spectrum*, Spring 2006; Bert Haloviak, "Ellen White, the Australasian Ministers, and the Role of Women Preachers," *Spectrum*, Spring 2006; Malcolm Bull and Keith Lockhart, "Authority and Identity," *Spectrum*, Fall 2006; Bonnie Dwyer and Graeme Bradford, "Saving Ellen White," *Spectrum*, Spring 2007; Daneen Akers, "Writing a Prophet: A Behind-the-Scenes Look at Red Books, a New Play About Ellen White," *Spectrum*, Spring 2007; Benjamin McArthur, "Point of the Spear: Adventist Liberalism and the Study of Ellen White in the 1970s," *Spectrum*, Spring 2008; Alita Byrd and Ronald L. Numbers, "Prophetess of Health Reappears," *Spectrum*, Summer 2008; David H. Thiele, "Straitjacket or Flight Suit? Ellen White's Role in the Adventist Theology of the Twenty-first Century," *Spectrum*, Summer 2008.

[292] Gary Shearer, "A Bibliography of Sources About Ellen White in *Spectrum*," *Spectrum*, Winter 1999.

[293] Alden Thompson, "The *Great Controversy* Is Dated But True," *Adventist Today*, September/October 1993; Fred Veltman, "Text and Community in Dynamic Relationship," *Adventist Today*, September/October 1993; Steven P. Vitrano, "Prophecy: A Blessing and a Danger," *Adventist Today*, September/October 1993; Bert B. Haloviak, "Ellen White: 75 More Years of Role Confusion," *Adventist Today*, November/December 1994; Bruce Heinrich, "Ellen G. White: Will Her Writings Stand in the Light of Truth?" *Adventist Today*, March /April 1998; Max Phillips, "Cultic Doctrine: Powerful But Also Unfair," *Adventist Today*, March /April 1998; James Walters, "Ellen G. White and Truth-telling: An Ethical Analysis of Literary Dependency," *Adventist Today*, March /April 1998; Arthur Patrick, "Re-Visioning the Role of Ellen White Beyond the Year 2000," *Adventist Today*, March / April 1998; John A. Ramirez, Jr., and Eva Paschal, "Quest for the Historical Ellen White: Numbers Speaks for Richard Hammill Memorial Lecture," *Adventist Today*, May/June 2001; Randy A. Croft, "Is Ellen an Option?" *Adventist Today*, November/December 2002; Kenneth Richards, "Two Authorities or One?" *Adventist Today*, March/April 2003; Michael Scofield, "A Response to Kenneth Richards on the Authority of Ellen White," *Adventist Today*, May/June 2003; John Thomas McLarty, "The Five Books of Adventist Theology," *Adventist Today*, September/October 2003; James Stirling, "Ellen G. White Updated?" *Adventist Today*, September/ October 2003; Frederick G. Hoyt, "Wrestling With Venerable Manuscripts," *Adventist Today*, May/June 2004; Jenann Elias, "Exposing Ellen White," *Adventist Today*, May/June 2005; Jim Moyers, "Ellen White and Adventism: Beyond the True/False Prophet Debate," *Adventist Today*, July/August 2005; Frederick G. Hoyt, "Ellen White, Mary Baker Eddy, and Mesmerism," *Adventist Today*, July/August 2005; Rick Williams (pseudonym), "The Lost Manuscript: A Dream," *Adventist Today*, July/August 2005; Max Gordon Phillips, "A Little Girl Who Had a Little Curl: Coming to Terms With the Prophet Ellen," *Adventist Today*, March /April 2007; Jim Walters, "Posner Is Wrong on Plagiarism," *Adventist Today*, May/June 2007; T. Joe Willey, "The Specter of Plagiarism Haunting Adventism," *Adventist Today*, May/June 2007; David Conklin, "The Specter of Plagiarism Haunting Adventism: A Comment and Response," *Adventist Today*, September/October 2007 (includes a response by T. Joe Willey); George [R.] Knight, "Visions of the Word: The Authority of Ellen White in Relation to the Authority of Scripture in the Seventh-day Adventist Movement, Part I," *Adventist Today*, November/December 2007; *idem,* "Visions of the Word: The Authority of Ellen White in Relation to the Authority of Scripture in the Seventh-day Adventist Movement, Part II," *Adventist Today*, November/December 2007; Ciro Sepulveda, "Why Ellen White and Leadership Didn't Get Along," *Adventist Today*, March /April 2008.

[294] Paul A. Gordon, "Ellen White's Role in Ministering to God's End-time Remnant," *Journal of the Adventist Theological Society* (JATS), Autumn 1991; P. Gerard Damsteegt, "Ellen White on Theology, Its Methods, and the Use of Scripture," JATS, Autumn 1993; *idem,* "The Inspiration of Scripture in the Writings of Ellen G. White," JATS, Spring 1994; Alberto R. Timm, "History of Inspiration in the Adventist Church (1844-1915)," JATS, Spring 1994; P. Gerard Damsteegt, "Ellen White, Lifestyle, and Scripture Interpretation," JATS, Autumn 1996; Alberto Timm, "Ellen G. White: Side Issues or Central Message?" JATS, Autumn 1996; Warren S. Ashworth, "The Lesser and the Greater Lights: Ellen White and the Bible," JATS, Spring-Autumn 1998; Denis Fortin, "Ellen G. White's Understanding of the Sanctuary and Hermeneutics," JATS, Spring-Autumn 1998; Alberto R. Timm, "A History of Seventh-day Adventist Views on Biblical and Prophetic Inspiration (1844-2000)," JATS, Spring-Autumn 1999; Gerhard Pfandl, "Ellen G. White and Earth Science," JATS, Spring 2003; Denis Fortin, "The Cross of Christ: Theological Differences Between Joseph H. Waggoner and Ellen G. White," JATS, Autumn 2003; Fernando Canale, "From Vision to System: Finishing the Task of Adventist Theology, Part I, Historical Review," JATS, Autumn 2004; Thomas A. Davis, "Was Ellen White Confused About Justification?" JATS, Autumn 2006; Jerry Moon, "The Quest for a Biblical Trinity: Ellen White's 'Heavenly Trio,'" JATS, Spring 2006; Denis Fortin, "Ellen White's Interpretation and Use of the Seven Letters of Revelation," JATS, Autumn 2007; Don Leo M. Garilva, "The Development of Ellen G. White's Concept of Babylon in *The Great Controversy*," JATS, Autumn 2007.

[295] Roger W. Coon, "A 'Testimony' From the 'Other Side,'" *Perspective Digest* 2, no. 2 (1997): 42-47; Roland R. Hegstad, "A Hell That Burns Out—the Doctrine That Alarmed Ellen White," *Perspective Digest* 2, no. 4

(1997): 8-10; Paul A. Gordon, "Warning: Don't Tell the Prophet What to Preach!" *Perspective Digest* 3, no. 1 (1998): 56-58; Roland R. Hegstad, "The Tale of Two Magazines," *Perspective Digest* 4, no. 3 (1999): 47-56; Denis Fortin, "The Dollhouse," *Perspective Digest* 4, no. 4 (1999): 52-58; Herbert E. Douglass, "The Great Controversy Theme," *Perspective Digest* 5, no. 2 (2000): 26-31; Hans K. LaRondelle, "Adventist at the Heart of the Gospel," *Perspective Digest* 7, no. 2 (2002): 39-46; Warren S. Ashworth, "Why Dad Left Church Confused," *Perspective Digest* 8, no. 2 (2003): 28-37; Roland R. Hegstad, "A Lesson in Right Thinking," *Perspective Digest* 9, no. 3 (2004): 7-9; *idem*, "Should Our Prophetic Schema Be Revised?" *Perspective Digest* 9, no. 3 (2004): 34-46; Gerhard Pfandl, "Seventh-day Adventists and Christmas," *Perspective Digest* 11, no. 4 (2006): 52-54; Warren S. Ashworth, "The Lesser and the Greater Light," *Perspective Digest* 12, no. 1 (2007): 4-14; Frank M. Hasel, "Ellen White and Creation," *Perspective Digest* 12, no. 1 (2007): 40-49; Alberto R. Timm, "Adventist Views on Inspiration," *Perspective Digest* 13, no. 3 (2008): 24-39; Thomas A. Davis, "Was Ellen White Confused About Justification?" *Perspective Digest* 13, no. 3 (2008): 40-49; Alberto R. Timm, "Adventist Views on Inspiration," *Perspective Digest* 13, no. 4 (2008): 29-49.

[296] Alberto R. Timm, "Responding Rightly to the Prophets," *Adventists Affirm*, Fall 2000; Samuel Koranteng-Pipin, "Understanding the Spirit of Prophecy: Some Key Questions and Principles," *Adventists Affirm*, Fall 2000; William Fagal, "Ellen G. White: Prophet or Plagiarist?" *Adventists Affirm*, Spring 2001; Jan Voerman, "Errors in Inspired Writings, Part I: How Ancient Were the Waldenses?" *Adventists Affirm*, Spring 2001; *idem*, "Errors in Inspired Writings, Part II: Historical, Chronological and Theological 'Errors'?" *Adventists Affirm*, Spring 2001; Allan G. Lindsay, "The Word and Ellen White," *Adventists Affirm*, Fall 2006.

[297] Ron and Gerte Graybill, "Ellen White in Copenhagen," *Adventist Heritage*, July 1974; Eric D. Anderson, "Ellen White and Jim Crow," *Adventist Heritage*, July 1974; Ron Graybill, "The Lucinda Abbey Hall Collection," *Adventist Heritage*, Winter 1975; Larry White, "Margaret W. Rowen: Prophetess of Reform and Doom," *Adventist Heritage*, Summer 1979; Jonathan Butler, "The First Book of the Chronicles," *Adventist Heritage*, Fall 1982; Arthur N. Patrick, "A Fourth Book of Chronicles," *Adventist Heritage*, Fall 1985; *idem*, "Founding Mothers: Women and the Adventist Work in the South Pacific Division," *Adventist Heritage*, Fall 1986; Roger W. Coon, "Council to a Nervous Bridegroom," *Adventist Heritage*, Summer 1990; Ron Graybill, "Letter to Elizabeth," *Adventist Heritage*, Summer 1990; Ron Graybill, "The Whites Come to Battle Creek: A Turning Point in Adventist History," *Adventist Heritage*, Fall 1992; Lila Jo Peck, "Relationships Among the White, Harmon, and MacDearman Families," *Adventist Heritage*, Winter 1993.

[298] Ron D. Graybill, "Heirloom: Leaves From Ellen White's Family Album," *Adventist Heritage*, Spring 1982.

[299] D. A. Delafield, "Why Ellen White Called for Help," *Ministry*, April 1976; J. Wayne McFarland and D. A. Delafield, "Celebrate the Bicentennial With 'The Story of Our Health Message,'" *Ministry*, April 1976; J. R. Spangler with Paul Bradley, "Does the White Estate Suppress Secret Documents?" *Ministry*, June 1976; N. R. Dower, "Righteousness by Faith," *Ministry*, August 1976; J. R. Spangler with H.M.S. Richards, "The Editor Interviews H.M.S. Richards," *Ministry*, October 1976; Joseph J. Battistone, "The Great Controversy Theme in Jesus' Parables," *Ministry*, October 1976; Robert H. Pearson, "The Alpha of Apostasy," *Ministry*, August 1977; Warren H. Johns, "Ellen G. White and Subterranean Fires, Part I: Does Borrowing of Literary Passages and Terms Constitute Borrowing of Concepts?" *Ministry*, August 1977; Leo R. Van Dolson, "Profiting From His Prophet: What Are We Waiting For?" *Ministry*, August 1977; Robert H. Pearson, "The Omega of Apostasy," *Ministry*, October 1977; Warren H. Johns, "Ellen G. White and Subterranean Fires, Part II: Does Borrowing of Literary Passages and Terms Constitute Borrowing of Concepts?" *Ministry*, October 1977; Gordon M. Hyde, "Righteousness by Faith Symposium in Washington," *Ministry*, October 1978; Arthur L. White, "How the E. G. White Books Were Written," *Ministry*, June 1979; *idem*, "How the E. G. White Books Were Written—2," *Ministry*, August 1979; *idem*, "How the E. G. White Books Were Written—3," *Ministry*, October 1979; *idem*, "How the E. G. White Books Were Written—4," *Ministry*, December 1979; *idem*, "How the E. G. White Books Were Written—5," *Ministry*, February 1980; Roger W. Coon, "How Near Is the Omega?" *Ministry*, April 1980; Neal C. Wilson, "This I Believe About Ellen G. White," *Ministry*, April 1980; "The Shaking Up of Adventism?" *Ministry*, May 1980; J. R. Spangler with Robert W. Olson and Ron Graybill, "Ellen White and Literary Dependency," *Ministry*, June 1980; J. R. Spangler, "Persecuting the Prophets," *Ministry*, February 1981; "Ellen G. White—Plagiarist?" *Ministry*, March 1981; Eric Livingston, "Inquire of the Lord," *Ministry*, April 1981; S.M.I. Henry [reprint from *Gospel of Health*], "My Telescope," *Ministry*, June 1981; Elbio Pereyra, "Prophetic Ministry," *Ministry*, August 1981; William G. Johnsson, "How Does God Speak?" *Ministry*, October 1981; Ron Graybill, "Ellen White's Role in Doctrinal Formation," *Ministry*, October 1981; J. R. Spangler, "What's So Unique About Adventism?" *Ministry*, December 1981; J. R. Spangler with Arthur L. White, "EGW: A Biography," February 1982; Richard Hammill, "This We Believe—9: Spiritual Gifts in the Church Today," *Ministry*, July 1982; Roger L. Dudley and Des Cummings, Jr., "Who Reads Ellen White?" *Ministry*, October 1982; Morris L. Venden, "What Jesus Said About the Prophets," *Ministry*, November 1982; Erwin R. Gane, "Within the Veil: Where Did Christ Go?" *Ministry*, December 1983; Warren H. Johns, "Ellen G. White and Biblical Chronology," *Ministry*, April 1984; "Ellen G. White and Epilepsy," *Ministry*, August 1984; Tim Crosby, "Does Inspired Mean Original?" *Ministry*, February 1986; Roger W. Coon, "Ellen G. White and Vegetarianism," *Ministry*, April 1986; J. R. Spangler, "The Gift of Prophecy and 'Thought Voices,'" *Ministry*, June 1986; George E. Rice, "How to Write a Bible," *Ministry*, June 1986; *idem*, "How to Write a Bible," *Ministry*, August 1986; Tim

Crosby, "Why I Don't Believe in *Sola Scriptura*," *Ministry*, October 1987; George W. Reid, "*Sola Scriptura*: A Response," *Ministry*, October 1987; George E. Rice, "The Church: Voice of God?" *Ministry*, December 1987; David C. Nieman, "Do Sports Belong in SDA Schools?" *Ministry*, August 1988; Ronald D. Graybill, "Health Reform and Adventists in the Nineteenth Century," *Ministry*, October 1988; William Fagal, "Did Ellen White Call for Ordaining Women?" *Ministry*, December 1988; *idem*, "Did Ellen White Support the Ordination of Women?" *Ministry*, February 1989; Gerald Wheeler, "The Historical Basis of Adventist Standards," *Ministry*, October 1989; Tim Poirier, "Sources Clarify Ellen White's Christology," *Ministry*, December 1989; George R. Knight, "Crisis in Authority," *Ministry*, February 1991; Arthur N. Patrick, "Does Our Past Embarrass Us?" *Ministry*, April 1991; Alden Thompson, "God's Word: Casebook or Codebook?" *Ministry*, July 1991; Ronald D. Graybill, "Enthusiasm in Early Advent Worship," *Ministry*, October 1991; George W. Reid, "Is the Bible Our Final Authority?" *Ministry*, November 1991; Woodrow Whidden, "The *Way of Life* Engravings: Harbingers of Minneapolis?" *Ministry*, October 1992; Russell L. Staples, "Understanding Adventism," *Ministry*, September 1993; Ron Graybill, "Visions and Revisions, Part 1," *Ministry*, February 1994; Alberto Timm, "Ellen G. White and Tithe," *Ministry*, February 1994; Ron Graybill, "Visions and Revisions, Part II," *Ministry*, April 1994; Arthur N. Patrick, "Are Adventists Evangelical? The Case of Ellen White in the 1890s," *Ministry*, February 1995; J. R. Spangler, "Believe in the Lord, Believe in His Prophets," *Ministry*, July/August 1995; George R. Knight, "Proving More Than Intended," *Ministry*, March 1996; Woodrow W. Whidden, "Ellen White and the Basics of Salvation," *Ministry*, June 1997; George R. Knight, "The Case of the Overlooked Postscript: A Footnote on Inspiration," *Ministry*, August 1997; Roy Naden, "Contemporary Manifestations of the Prophecy Gift," *Ministry*, June 1999; Alberto Timm, "Understanding Inspiration: The Symphonic and Wholistic Nature of Scripture," *Ministry*, August 1999; Graeme S. Bradford, "The Prophets Are Human Too!" *Ministry*, August 1999; Richard W. Coffen, "A Fresh Look at the Dynamics of Inspiration, Part 1," *Ministry*, December 1999; *idem*, "Thy Word Is a Light Unto My Feet, Part 2," *Ministry*, February 2000; Ekkehardt Mueller, "The Revelation, Inspiration, and Authority of Scripture," *Ministry*, April 2000; James A. Cress, "The Gift That Keeps Giving," *Ministry*, April 2000; Will Eva, "What's a Theologian After All?" *Ministry*, October 2000; Walter M. Booth, "Ellen White, Theologian?" *Ministry*, October 2000; Paul McGraw, "Without a Living Prophet," *Ministry*, December 2000; Woodrow W. Whidden, "Ellen White, Inerrancy, and Interpretation," *Ministry*, December 2002; Gilbert Valentine, "A Slice of History: The Difficulties of Imposing Orthodoxy," *Ministry*, February 2003; *idem*, "Developing Truth and Changing Perspectives," *Ministry*, April 2003; Alberto Timm, "Ellen G. White: Prophetic Voice for the Last Days," *Ministry*, January 2004; Alden Thompson, "Response to Dale Ratzlaff," *Ministry*, January 2004; Woodrow W. Whidden, "The Adventist 'Pioneer' Theological Heritage," *Ministry*, February 2005; Gilbert Valentine, "A Slice of History: How a Clearer View of Jesus Developed in the Adventist Church," *Ministry*, May 2005; Kevin L. Morgan with David J. Conklin, "Plagiarism: A Historical and Cultural Survey," *Ministry*, August 2007; *idem*, "Plagiarism: Alternate Explanations?" *Ministry*, October 2007; *idem*, "Was Ellen White a Plagiarist?" *Ministry*, December 2007.

[300] J. David Newman, "How Candid Should Ministry Be?" *Ministry*, December 1991.

[301] J. R. Spangler, "Are There Prophets in the Modern Church?" *Ministry*, July 1977; La Vonne Neff, "Ellen G. White—A Brief Life Sketch," in *Are There Prophets in the Modern Church?* supplement to *Ministry*, July 1977; Raoul Dederen, "Ellen White's Doctrine of Scripture," in *Are There Prophets in the Modern Church?* supplement to *Ministry*, July 1977; T. H. Blincoe, "The Prophets Were Until John," in *Are There Prophets in the Modern Church?* supplement to *Ministry*, July 1977; Mervyn A. Warren, "Christology and Soteriology in the Writings of Ellen White," in *Are There Prophets in the Modern Church?* supplement to *Ministry*, July 1977; Hedwig Jemison, "Looking Ahead Through the Eyes of Prophecy," in *Are There Prophets in the Modern Church?* supplement to *Ministry*, July 1977.

[302] "Questions Studied and Answered by the Sanctuary Review Committee," *Ministry*, October 1980; "Consensus Document: Christ in the Heavenly Sanctuary," *Ministry*, October 1980; "Consensus Document: The Role of Ellen G. White Writings in Doctrinal Matters," *Ministry*, October 1980; "Questions and Answers on Doctrinal Issues: 4. Ellen White's Role in Doctrinal Matters," *Ministry*, October 1980; "Questions and Answers on Doctrinal Issues: 5. Methodology," *Ministry*, October 1980.

[303] "Additional Study Materials Available," *Ministry*, October 1980.

[304] W. T. Rea, *The White Lie*; J. R. Spangler, "The Two Mind-sets," *Ministry*, June 1982; Warren H. Johns, "Ellen White: Prophet or Plagiarist?"

[305] "For Further Study," *Ministry*, June 1982.

[306] *Ministry* insert, *The Truth About the White Lie*, August 1982.

[307] "The Inspiration and Authority of the Ellen G. White Writings: A Statement of Present Understanding as Revised June 14, 1982," *Ministry*, August 1982.

[308] "The Inspiration and Authority of the Ellen G. White Writings: A Statement of Present Understanding," *Ministry*, February 1983.

[309] Robert W. Olson, "1888: Issues, Outcomes, Lessons," *Ministry*, February 1988; C. Mervyn Maxwell, "What Is the 1888 Message?" *Ministry*, February 1988; George E. Rice, "Corporate Repentance," *Ministry*, February 1988; Alden Thompson, "Must We Agree?" *Ministry*, February 1988.

[310] Fred Veltman, "The *Desire of Ages* Project: The Data, Part I," *Ministry*, October 1990; *idem*, "The *Desire*

of Ages Project: The Conclusions," *Ministry*, December 1990; David C. Jarnes with Robert W. Olson, "Olson Discusses the Veltman Study," *Ministry*, December 1990.

[311] Robert W. Olson, "Ellen White's Denials," *Ministry*, February 1991.

[312] Martin Weber, "Rejoicing Despite Apostasy," *Ministry*, October 1993; Woodrow Whidden, "Essential Adventism or Historic Adventism?" *Ministry*, October 1993; George R. Knight, "Adventists and Change," *Ministry*, October 1993.

[313] *Seventh-day Adventists Answer Questions on Doctrine*, annotated with notes by George R. Knight in the *Adventist Classic Series* (Berrien Springs, Mich.: Andrews University Press, 2003); Woodrow W. Whidden, "*Questions on Doctrine*: Then and Now," *Ministry*, August 2003; Herbert E. Douglass, "Thoughts on the Republished *Questions on Doctrine*," *Ministry*, August 2004.

[314] Erwin R. Gane, "Christ and Human Perfection in the Writings of E. G. White," *Ministry* supplement, August 2003; Robert W. Olson, "Outline Studies on Christian Perfection and Original Sin," *Ministry* supplement, August 2003.

[315] E. W. Nash, "Ellen G. White and Health," *Review and Herald*, Feb. 19, 1976; Merton E. Sprengel and Dowell E. Martz, "Orion Revisited: Two Seventh-day Adventist Scientists Discuss 'the Open Space in Orion' to which Ellen White Referred in an 1848 Vision, Part 1," *Review and Herald*, Mar. 25, 1976; *idem*, "How Open Is Orion's Open Space? Part 2," *Review and Herald*, Apr. 1, 1976; *idem*, "Does the 'Open Space' Exist Today? Part 3," *Review and Herald*, Apr. 8, 1976; Robert W. Olson, "The Spirit of 1876," *Review and Herald*, Apr. 22, 1976; "Christ Our Righteousness" statement, *Review and Herald*, May 27, 1976; Kenneth H. Wood, "Battle Over Inerrancy," *Review and Herald*, June 17, 1976; *idem*, "The Divine-Human Word," *Review and Herald*, June 24, 1976; Joseph J. Battistone, "Interpreting Ellen G. White's Writings," *Review and Herald*, July 1, 1976; W. Paul Bradley, "Race and the Ellen G. White Counsels," *Review and Herald*, July 15, 1976; Ernest Lloyd, "I Heard Mrs. White Say It," *Review and Herald*, Aug. 5, 1976; Kenneth H. Wood, "An Important Challenge to the Faith? Part 1," *Review and Herald*, Aug. 19, 1976; *idem*, "Inspired Persons, Ancient and Modern, Part 2," *Review and Herald*, Aug. 26, 1976; *idem*, "Dealing With 'Facts,' Part 3," *Review and Herald*, Sept. 2, 1976; Thomas H. Blincoe, "A Remnant Foretold: The Seventh-day Adventist Church Meets the Biblical Specifications for the Remnant Church," *Review and Herald*, Oct. 14, 1976.

[316] Charles Mitchell, "Why I Accepted the Spirit of Prophecy," *Review and Herald*, January 20, 1977; Raymond F. Cottrell, "The Historical Method of Interpretation," *Review and Herald*, Apr. 7, 1977; Alta Robinson, "Ellen White's 'Daughters,'" *Review and Herald*, Apr. 14, 1977; D. A. Delafield, "Are the Testimonies Negative?" *Review and Herald*, June 30, 1977; Don F. Neufeld, "Faith and Practice Versus Prophetic Fulfillment," *Review and Herald*, Aug. 11, 1977; Kenneth H. Wood, "Stoning God's Prophets," *Review and Herald*, Sept. 15, 1977; Robert H. Pierson, "The Testimony of Jesus," *Review and Herald*, Oct. 7, 1977; Alta Robinson, "Ellen G. White, Born November 26, 1827," *Review and Herald*, Nov. 24, 1977; Joseph J. Battistone, "Spiritual Gifts to the Remnant," *Review and Herald*, Dec. 1, 1977.

[317] Arthur L. White, "Toward an Adventist Concept of Inspiration," Part 1, *Adventist Review*, Jan. 12, 1978; *idem*, "The Prophet Bears Testimony," Part 2, *Adventist Review*, Jan. 19, 1978; *idem*, "The Question of Infallibility," Part 3, *Adventist Review*, Jan. 26, 1978; *idem*, "The Importance of Understanding Inspiration," Part 4, *Adventist Review*, Feb. 2, 1978.

[318] Kenneth H. Wood, "An Important Series About Ellen G. White," *Adventist Review*, July 12, 1979; Arthur L. White, "Ellen G. White's Sources for the Conflict Series Books, Part 1," *Adventist Review*, July 12, 1979; *idem*, "Rewriting and Amplifying the Controversy Story, Part 2," *Adventist Review*, July 19, 1979; *idem*, "Historical Sources and the Conflict Series, Part 3," *Adventist Review*, July 26, 1979; *idem*, "Writing on the Life of Christ, Part 4," *Adventist Review*, Aug. 2, 1979; *idem*, "Preparing *The Desire of Ages*, Part 5," *Adventist Review*, Aug. 9, 1979; *idem*, "Completing the Work on *The Desire of Ages*, Part 6," *Adventist Review*, Aug. 16, 1979; *idem*, "Completing *The Desire of Ages*," *Adventist Review*, Aug. 23, 1979.

[319] Clarence Dunbebin, "How Ellen White Disciplined Her Sons," *Adventist Review*, Mar. 15, 1979; D. A. Delafield, "Are Seventh-day Adventists a Cult?" *Adventist Review*, Apr. 26, 1979; Earl C. Mercill, "What About a 'Pantdress'?" *Adventist Review*, July 19, 1979; Milton Murray, "Ellen White, Printing, and I," *Adventist Review*, July 26, 1979; "Study Documents on Inspiration and Creation," *Adventist Review*, Jan. 17, 1980; Harold L. Calkins, "How Inspiration Works," *Adventist Review*, Feb. 14, 1980; Richard Lesher, "Landmark Truth Versus 'Specious Error'—1," *Adventist Review*, Mar. 6, 1980; *idem*, "Truth Stands Forever—2," *Adventist Review*, Mar. 13, 1980; Neal C. Wilson, "This I Believe About Ellen G. White," *Adventist Review*, Mar. 20, 1980; Ron Graybill, "Dramatic New Painting Exalts Christ," *Adventist Review*, Apr. 20, 1980; Kenneth G. Hance, "A Non-Adventist Viewpoint on Ellen G. White," *Adventist Review*, May 29, 1980; Ron Graybill, "What Academy Students Think of Ellen White," *Adventist Review*, June 26, 1980; Harold Baasch, "My 'Special Hand,'" *Adventist Review*, July 3, 1980; "Tape on EGW Literary Sources," *Adventist Review*, Nov. 20, 1980; Arthur L. White, "Ellen G. White and Her Writings," *Adventist Review*, Nov. 27, 1980; Clive M. McCay, "A Nutrition Authority Discusses Ellen G. White—1," *Adventist Review*, Jan. 8, 1981; *idem*, "Science Confirms Adventist Health Teachings—2," *Adventist Review*, Jan. 15, 1981; Robert G. Wearner, "Ellen White and Little Elias," *Adventist Review*, Feb. 26, 1981; Ron Graybill, "Did Mrs. White 'Borrow' in Reporting a Vision?" *Adventist Review*, Apr. 2, 1981; Arthur L. White, "Ellen White's Last Four Books—Part 1," *Adventist*

Review, June 11, 1981; *idem,* "More Than 'One More Book'—Part 2," *Adventist Review,* June 18, 1981; *idem,* "The Story of *Prophets and Kings*—Part 3," *Adventist Review,* June 25, 1981; J. N. Hunt, "Ellen White Books Bring Understanding to Readers," *Adventist Review,* June 25, 1981; Lewis Walton, "Omega," *Adventist Review,* July 2, 1981; Neal C. Wilson, "The Ellen G. White Writings and the Church," *Adventist Review,* July 9, 1981; Norman R. Gulley, "She Beheld Him and Was Changed," *Adventist Review,* Oct. 1, 1981; E. R. Gane, "The Great Physician's Prescription," *Adventist Review,* Dec. 17, 1981; Alden Thompson, "Ellen White's Pilgrimage to Golgotha," *Adventist Review,* Dec. 24, 1981; Clyde R. Bradley, "Inspiration: God's Filtration System," *Adventist Review,* Dec. 31, 1981; Alden Thompson, "The Theology of Ellen G. White: The Great Controversy Story," *Adventist Review,* Dec. 31, 1981; Roger W. Coon with Arthur L. White, "I Live With the Project 24 Hours a Day," *Adventist Review,* Jan. 21, 1982; Niels-Erik Andreasen, "From Vision to Prophecy," *Adventist Review,* Jan. 28, 1982; W. R. May, "Are We Guilty of Discrediting the Spirit of Prophecy?" *Adventist Review,* Apr. 22, 1982; Robert W. Olson, "People With the Spirit of Prophecy," *Adventist Review,* Friendship Issue, May 6, 1982; Roger W. Coon, "First International Prophetic Guidance Workshop Is Held," *Adventist Review,* May 20, 1982; Geoffrey E. Garne, "Are the *Testimonies* Legalistic?" *Adventist Review,* July 1, 1982; Alden Thompson, "The Prodigal Son Revisited," *Adventist Review,* July 1, 1982; J. T. McDuffie, "The Prodigal Son Rebutted," *Adventist Review,* July 1, 1982; "The Inspiration and Authority of the Ellen G. White Writings: Statement of Present Understanding, as Revised June 14, 1982," *Adventist Review,* July 15, 1982; Yvonne Hendley Hanson, "After 81 Years, a Visit 'Down Under,'" *Adventist Review,* July 15, 1982; Ron Graybill, "The 'I Saw' Parallels in Ellen White's Writings," *Adventist Review,* July 29, 1982; Robert G. Wearner, "Ellen White in Brazil," *Adventist Review,* Aug. 12, 1982; Roy Adams, "A Testimony," *Adventist Review,* Nov. 4, 1982; "The Inspiration and Authority of the Ellen G. White Writings: A Statement of Present Understanding," *Adventist Review,* Dec. 23, 1982; Delmer A. Johnson, "The Sources of Inspired Writings," *Adventist Review,* Dec. 30, 1982; Neal C. Wilson, "*Desire of Ages* Researcher Gives Progress Report," *Adventist Review,* Dec. 30, 1982; Richard Hammill, "Change and the SDA Church—1," *Adventist Review,* Jan. 6, 1983; *idem,* "Ellen White and Change," *Adventist Review,* Jan. 13, 1983; Ernest Lloyd, "Ellen White's Personal Work," *Adventist Review,* Jan. 13, 1983; D. A. Delafield, "In Times of Testing and Doubting," *Adventist Review,* Feb. 10, 1983; Neal C. Wilson, "White Biography Project Moves Forward," *Adventist Review,* Feb. 10, 1983; George I. Butler, "A Voice From the Past," *Adventist Review,* Apr. 21, 1983; Albert E. Hirst, "Ellen White's Criticism of Nineteenth-Century Medicine—1," *Adventist Review,* June 30, 1983; Ed Christian with Ethel May Lacey, "Life With My Mother-in-Law," *Adventist Review,* July 7, 1983; Albert E. Hirst, "Would Ellen White Favor Medicines Used Today?—2," *Adventist Review,* July 7, 1983; *idem,* "Ellen White's Attitude Toward Medical Progress," *Adventist Review,* July 14, 1983; Paul A. Gordon, "Ellen White's Birthplace Commemorated," *Adventist Review,* July 21, 1983; R. W. Olson, "White Estate Staffer Explains Dissertation," *Adventist Review,* Nov. 24, 1983; Neal C. Wilson, "White Estate Staffer Reassigned," *Adventist Review,* Feb. 2, 1984; Robert W. Olson, "Ellen G. White's Use of Historical Sources in *The Great Controversy*," *Adventist Review,* Feb. 23, 1984; Kenneth H. Wood, "The 1909 General Conference Session: Flashback," *Adventist Review,* May 24, 1984; *idem,* "The 1909 Session: Delegates Challenged," *Adventist Review,* May 31, 1984; Arthur L. White, "Why Seventh-day Adventists Have No Creed," *Adventist Review,* July 12, 1984; *idem,* "How Basic Doctrines Came to Adventists," July 17, 1984; *idem,* "The Certainty of Basic Doctrinal Positions," *Adventist Review,* July 26, 1984; Robert W. Olson, "Physicians Say Ellen White's Visions Not Result of Epilepsy," *Adventist Review,* Aug. 16, 1984; Earnest Lloyd, "Why Ellen G. White Practiced Economy," *Adventist Review,* Nov. 22, 1984; Paul Gordon, "Letters to Young Lovers," *Adventist Review,* Mar. 28, 1985; Nathaniel Krum, "The First Adventist Poem," *Adventist Review,* Apr. 18, 1985; Jocelyn R. Fay, "I Remember Ellen White," *Adventist Review,* June 6, 1985; Arthur L. White, "With Ellen G. White in Europe," *Adventist Review*; Alden Thompson, "Adventists and Inspiration," *Adventist Review,* Sept. 5, 1985; *idem,* "Improving the *Testimonies* Through Revision," *Adventist Review,* Sept. 12, 1985; *idem,* "Questions and Perplexities Without End," *Adventist Review,* Sept. 19, 1985; *idem,* "Letting the Bible Speak for Itself," *Adventist Review,* Sept. 26, 1985; Richard W. Coffen, "Checklist for Self-Proclaimed Prophets," *Adventist Review,* Jan. 30, 1986; Glen Baker, "Anna Phillips—A Second Prophet?" *Adventist Review,* Feb. 6, 1986; B. Vincent Tibbets, "Charlie's Angel," *Adventist Review,* Feb. 6, 1986; Glen Baker, "Anna Phillips—Not Another Prophet," *Adventist Review,* Feb. 20, 1986; George R. Knight, "The Myth of the Inflexible Prophet," *Adventist Review,* Apr. 3, 1986; Tim Crosby, "The Law and the Prophet—1," *Adventist Review,* May 8, 1986; W. C. White, "Her Never-Give-Up Kind of Love," *Adventist Review,* May 8, 1986; Paul A. Gordon, "Elmshaven: Home of Ellen G. White From 1900 to 1915," *Adventist Review,* May 8, 1986; Tim Crosby, "Using the Law to No Profit—2," *Adventist Review,* May 15, 1986; *idem,* "The Law of the Prophet—3," *Adventist Review,* May 22, 1986; *idem,* "A Law Without Profit—4," *Adventist Review,* May 29, 1986; James R. Nix, "The Unrecorded Earthquake Vision," *Adventist Review,* June 19, 1986; Fritz Guy, "A Frank Look at Ellen White," *Adventist Review,* July 10, 1986; James R. Nix, "The Third Prophet Spoke Forth," *Adventist Review,* Dec. 4, 1986; Kenneth H. Wood, "What the Gift of Prophecy Means to Me," *Adventist Review,* Jan. 8, 1987; Glen Baker, "The Humor of Ellen White," *Adventist Review,* Apr. 30, 1987; Edward Heppenstall, "The Inspired Witness of Ellen White," *Adventist Review,* May 7, 1987.

[320] Don F. Neufeld, "The Advent Delayed," *Adventist Review,* Oct. 25, 1979; *idem,* "Ellen White and Crosier's *Day-Star* Article," *Adventist Review,* Jan. 24, 1980; *idem,* "A Significant Early Vision," *Adventist Review,* Jan. 31,

1980; *idem,* "The 144,000," *Adventist Review,* Feb. 14, 1980; *idem,* "A Basis of Confidence—1," *Adventist Review,* Feb. 21, 1980; *idem,* "A Basis of Confidence—2," *Adventist Review,* Feb. 28, 1980; Kenneth H. Wood, "As Others See Us," *Adventist Review,* Mar. 13, 1980; Leo R. Van Dolson, "Understanding Inspiration," *Adventist Review,* Feb. 5, 1981; Kenneth H. Wood, "Visions, True and False," *Adventist Review,* Feb. 12, 1981; *idem,* "The 'Bright Light,'" *Adventist Review,* Apr. 16, 1981; William G. Johnsson, "What the Sanctuary Doctrine Means Today," *Adventist Review,* May 14, 1981; Kenneth H. Wood, "Confidence in Inspired Writings and Persons," *Adventist Review,* Oct. 21, 1982; William G. Johnsson, "Three Years After Glacier View," *Adventist Review,* Sept. 22, 1983; Eugene F. Durand, "The Story of a Story," *Adventist Review,* Feb. 14, 1985; *idem,* "The Story of a Story—2," *Adventist Review,* Feb. 21, 1985; *idem,* "The Story of a Story—3," *Adventist Review,* Mar. 14, 1985.

[321] William G. Johnsson, "Reflections on Ellen White's Inspiration," *Adventist Review,* Nov. 27, 1980; *idem,* "Liberated From Ellen White?" *Adventist Review,* Jan. 27, 1983; *idem,* "Ellen White in Perspective," *Adventist Review,* Aug. 16, 1984; *idem,* "Ellen White's Role in Adventism," *Adventist Review,* Feb. 28, 1985.

[322] Neal C. Wilson, "Update on the Church's Doctrinal Discussions," *Adventist Review,* July 3, 1980; William G. Johnsson, "Overview of a Historic Meeting, the Sanctuary Review Committee," *Adventist Review,* Sept. 4, 1980; "Statement on Desmond Ford Document," *Adventist Review,* Sept. 4, 1980; "Christ in the Heavenly Sanctuary," *Adventist Review,* Sept. 4, 1980; William G. Johnsson, "Looking Beyond Glacier View," *Adventist Review,* Oct. 16, 1980; Lawrence T. Geraty, "First Adventist Theological Consultation Between Administrators and Scholars," *Adventist Review,* Oct. 16, 1980; Kenneth H. Wood, "F.Y.I.," *Adventist Review,* Nov. 20, 1980.

[323] Ellen G. White, *Christ in His Sanctuary* (Mountain View, Calif.: Pacific Press Pub. Assn., 1969); "The Sanctuary Truth—1," *Adventist Review,* Nov. 6, 1980; "The Sanctuary Truth—2," *Adventist Review,* Nov. 13, 1980.

[324] W. C. White and D. E. Robinson, "Brief Statements Regarding the Writings of Ellen G. White, Aug. 1933," *Adventist Review supplement,* June 4, 1981; Kenneth H. Wood, "About the Insert in This Issue," *Adventist Review,* June 4, 1981.

[325] "Ellen White's Use of Sources," *Adventist Review,* Sept. 17, 1981; Vincent L. Ramik, interviewed, "There Simply Is No Case," *Adventist Review,* Sept. 17, 1981; Warren L. Johns, interviewed, "The Story Behind This Research," *Adventist Review,* Sept. 17, 1981; Kenneth H. Wood, "This Work Is of God, or It Is Not," *Adventist Review,* Sept. 17, 1981.

[326] C. E. Bradford, "God Speaks Through His Prophets," *Adventist Review,* Oct. 14, 1982; William G. Johnsson, " 'Fire . . . in My Bones'—the Prophetic Gift," *Adventist Review,* Oct. 14, 1982; Gerhard F. Hasel, "The Integrity of the Prophetic Gift," *Adventist Review,* Oct. 14, 1982; V. Norskov Olsen, "Ellen White: Defense Against Error and Apostasy," *Adventist Review,* Oct. 14, 1982; Fernando Chaij, "Prophecy Identifies the Remnant Church," *Adventist Review,* Oct. 14, 1982; Roy E. Graham, "How the Gift of Prophecy Relates to God's Word," *Adventist Review,* Oct. 14, 1982; Ellen G. White, "A Message of Comfort and Hope," *Adventist Review,* Oct. 14, 1982; Neal C. Wilson, "Believe His Prophets," *Adventist Review,* Oct. 14, 1982; Virginia D. Cason, "Children's Messages for the Week of Prayer: God's Special Love," *Adventist Review,* Oct. 14, 1982.

[327] Eugene F. Durand, "Following Prophetic Guidance," *Adventist Review,* Sept. 15, 1983.

[328] William Johnsson, "Crossroads in Adventism: An Inside Perspective on the Modern Seventh-day Adventist Church," *"Ellen White and Current Issues" Symposium* 4 (2008): 38-60; *idem, Embrace the Impossible* (Hagerstown, Md.: Review and Herald Pub. Assn., 2008).

[329] "White Estate Opens All Files," *Adventist Review,* May 28, 1987; Roger W. Coon, "What's the White Estate Attempting to Hide?" *Adventist Review,* July 2, 1987; Thomas Siebold, "Ellen White Speaks to a New Generation: How Relevant Is a Nineteenth-Century Prophet?" *Adventist Review,* July 16, 1987; Ron Graybill, "Glory! Glory! Glory!" *Adventist Review,* Oct. 1, 1987; Delbert Baker, "William Foy: Messenger to the Advent Believers," *Adventist Review,* Jan. 14, 1988; George E. Rice, "Steps to the Holy Spirit," *Adventist Review,* Feb. 18, 1988; Calvin Rock, "Did Ellen White Downplay Social Work?" *Adventist Review,* May 5, 1988; Tim Poirier, "The White Estate Answers Your Questions," *Adventist Review,* June 9, 1988; Paul A. Gordon, *"Great Controversy* Edition Achieves 100 Years," *Adventist Review,* Aug. 25, 1988; Richard Nixon, *"The Desire of Ages* Study Completed," *Adventist Review,* Sept. 22, 1988; Tim Poirier, "Did Ellen White Say That?" *Adventist Review,* Oct. 6, 1988; Martin Weber, "How We Survived 1888," Oct. 13, 1988; Myron Widmer with Walt Hamerslough and Jim Roy, "Yes-No: Interscholastic Sports and Competition," *Adventist Review,* Oct. 13, 1988; James R. Nix, "The Earthquake Vision," *Adventist Review,* Dec. 8, 1988; Beatrice Short Neall, "Mother, Ellen White, and the Priests," *Adventist Review,* Mar. 2, 1989; Robert W. Olson, "White Estate Uses Modern Technology," *Adventist Review,* May 25, 1989; Tim Poirier, "Did Ellen White Say . . . ?" *Adventist Review,* Aug. 31, 1989; Steven Daily, "Are We a Non-Prophet Organization?" *Adventist Review,* Oct. 12, 1989; Robert W. Olson, Ralph Willard, E. L. Becker, "Letters: Prophets and Others," *Adventist Review,* Nov. 30, 1989; Eileen E. Lantry, "Ellen White's Johnstown Flood Adventure," *Adventist Review,* Jan. 18, 1990; Ritchie Way, "My Burial and Resurrection of Ellen White," *Adventist Review,* Mar. 22, 1990; James R. Nix, "The Great Controversy Vision," *Adventist Review,* Apr. 12, 1990; "Ellen White Writings Now Available on Compact Disk," *Adventist Review,* June 28, 1990; Robert W. Olson, "Ellen G. White Estate," July 26-Aug. 2, 1990; Kenneth H. Wood, "Ellen G. White: A Noble Record," *Adventist Review,* Aug. 9, 1990; George E. Rice, "Perils and Possibilities,"

Adventist Review, Aug. 30, 1990; James R. Nix, "Arthur L. White, 1907-1991," *Adventist Review,* Feb. 28, 1991; C. David Wingate, "Is There Anything Mrs. White Doesn't Say?" *Adventist Review,* May 9, 1991; William G. Johnsson and Myron Widmer, "A Conversation With the Editor," *Adventist Review,* June 6, 1991; Ron Graybill, "Beyond the Bonnet's Brim," *Adventist Review,* July 18, 1991; Gary Patterson, "The Quest for Truth," *Adventist Review,* Sept. 26, 1991; Arthur Patrick, "Ellen White in Australia," *Adventist Review,* Dec. 12, 1991; Paul A. Gordon, "Messengers of Error," *Adventist Review,* Mar. 5, 1992; Helen Pearson, "The Woman Who Mothered the Church," *Adventist Review,* Apr. 2, 1992; Tim Poirier, "A Century of *Steps [to Christ],*" *Adventist Review,* May 14, 1992; Robert W. Olson, "How to Interpret Ellen G. White," *Adventist Review,* Aug. 20, 1992; Paul A. Gordon, "Ellen G. White Writings—1: How They Were Created," *Adventist Review,* Nov. 12, 1992; *idem,* "Ellen G. White Writings—2: Can We Legitimately Change, Abridge, or Simplify Them?" *Adventist Review,* Nov. 19, 1992; Adriel Chilson, "Pentecostalism in Early Adventism," *Adventist Review,* Dec. 10, 1992; "Church Aids Translation of E. G. White Books," *Adventist Review,* Mar. 25, 1993; Roger W. Coon, "Were Ellen White's Health Writings Unique? Does a Prophet Have to Say It First?" *Adventist Review,* Apr. 8, 1993; Myron Widmer, "Ellen G. White and the Ark of the Covenant," *Adventist Review,* Aug. 25, 1993; Robert S. Folkenberg, "Reading Ellen G. White: The Need for Balance," *Adventist Review,* Sept. 2, 1993; James Coffin, "How Long Until the Sunday Law?" *Adventist Review,* Oct. 21, 1993; Norman R. Gulley, "Ellen White and the End-Time," *Adventist Review,* Oct. 21, 1993; William G. Johnsson, "Ellen White Letter Comes to Light," *Adventist Review,* Feb. 17, 1994; Robert S. Folkenberg, "Needed: Preaching the Distinctives," *Adventist Review,* May 5, 1994.

[330] Roger W. Coon, "Ellen G. White's Counsel and Practice: Tithe," *Adventist Review Supplement,* Nov. 7, 1991.

[331] "Your Response Invited," *Adventist Review,* Feb. 6, 1992.

[332] Roy Adams, "A Prophet for Our Time: Sizing Up Ellen G. White," *Adventist Review,* June 4, 1992; "Voices of Adventist Faith: How Do Ellen White's Writings Nurture Your Spiritual Life?" *Adventist Review,* June 4, 1992; Roy Adams, "Abusing Ellen G. White," *Adventist Review,* Aug. 20, 1992; *idem,* "What Did She Mean?" *Adventist Review,* Sept. 3, 1992; *idem,* "Seventh-day Activists," *Adventist Review,* Feb. 4, 1993; *idem,* "Divided, We Crawl," *NAD Adventist Review,* February 1995.

[333] William G. Johnsson, "Present Truth: Walking in God's Light," *Adventist Review,* Jan. 5, 1994; Kyna D. Hinson, "Current, Contemporary, Up-to-date: A Fresh Look at Ellen G. White," *Adventist Review,* Apr. 7, 1994; "Voices of Adventist Faith: What Have You Found Most Helpful in the Writings of Ellen White?" *Adventist Review,* Apr. 7, 1994.

[334] Brian Jones, "Easy for Ellen?" *Adventist Review,* Mar. 10, 1994; *idem,* "Ellen Finds Jesus," *Adventist Review,* Mar. 17, 1994; *idem,* "Ellen's First Vision," *Adventist Review,* Apr. 14, 1994; *idem,* "Ellen's First Vision—2," *Adventist Review,* Apr. 21, 1994.

[335] Kit Watts, "Ellen White, Gift to the Church," *Adventist Review,* Oct. 6, 1994; "Special Poster Commemorating 150 Years of Adventist History," *Adventist Review,* Oct. 6, 1994.

[336] Myron Widmer, "150th Anniversary Draws 2,200 to Adventism's Birthplace," *NAD Adventist Review,* November 1994; *idem,* "October 22 Commemoration: Vignettes of Hope," *NAD Adventist Review,* December 1994.

[337] James R. Nix, "Historic Adventist Village Slated for Battle Creek," *NAD Adventist Review,* January 1995.

[338] "Battle Creek Commemoration Set for October," *NAD Adventist Review,* June 1995; Richard Dower, "North America Plans Battle Creek Celebration," *NAD Adventist Review,* September 1995; Carlos Medley, "Historic Assembly Brings Many Changes," *NAD Adventist Review,* November 1995; William G. Johnsson, "Battle Creek Soliloquy," *Adventist Review,* Nov. 23, 1995; Jack Stenger, "Back to Our Roots," *NAD Adventist Review,* December 1995.

[339] Sandra Blackmer, "NAD Session Delegates Revisit Their Roots," *NAD Adventist Review,* December 2004.

[340] James R. Nix, "Adventist Heritage Ministry Turns 25," *Adventist Review,* Apr. 26, 2007.

[341] James R. Nix, "Kellogg's Counsel to Church Critics," *Adventist Review,* May 25, 1995; Kit Watts, "Keeping Ellen White Current," *NAD Adventist Review,* March 1997.

[342] William G. Johnsson, "Meet Ellen White for Yourself," *Adventist Review,* May 30, 1996; Kenneth H. Wood, "She Called Herself 'Messenger,'" *Adventist Review,* May 30, 1996; James R. Nix, "Oh, Jesus, How I Love You!" *Adventist Review,* May 30, 1996; Mabel Miller, "A Letter From Grandma," *Adventist Review,* May 30, 1996; Andy Nash, "For Myself," *Adventist Review,* May 30, 1996; Rosa Taylor Banks, "Sisters in Service," *Adventist Review,* May 30, 1996; Karen Carlton, "A Typical Day, an Extraordinary Life," *Adventist Review,* May 30, 1996; Arthur L. White, "The Meeting a 14-Year-Old Girl Never Forgot," *Adventist Review,* May 30, 1996; Juan Carlos Viera, "The Dynamics of Inspiration," *Adventist Review,* May 30, 1996; Charles E. Bradford, "Ellen White and the Black Experience," *Adventist Review,* May 30, 1996; Alex Bryan, "Beyond Sound Bites," *Adventist Review,* May 30, 1996; George R. Knight, "Joseph Smith, Ellen White, and the Great Gulf," *Adventist Review,* May 30, 1996; Joe Engelkemier, "The Use—and Misuse—of a Precious Gift," *Adventist Review,* May 30, 1996; Michelle Nash, "Why Didn't You Tell Me?" *Adventist Review,* May 30, 1996.

[343] Calvin B. Rock, "Present Rewards and Future Glory," *Adventist Review,* Jan. 8, 1998; Roger W. Coon, "The Ghost Mrs. White," *Adventist Review,* Jan. 15, 1998; Calvin B. Rock, "Practical Assistance," *Adventist Review,* Mar. 12, 1998; Dwain N. Esmond, "They're Studying What?" *Adventist Review,* Feb. 19, 1998; Bill

Knott, "The Vision Glorious: Adventism's Unique Understanding of Human History," *Adventist Review*, May 28, 1998; Kenneth H. Wood, "Standard Bearers Old and New," *Adventist Review*, June 11, 1998; Jerry Moon, "Wrestling Till Dawn," *Adventist Review*, July 9, 1998; Richard Dower, "Battle Creek Cereal Attraction Features Ellen White and the Adventist Church," *Adventist Review*, Oct. 22, 1998; Clifford Goldstein, "The Reasonable Observer," *Adventist Review*, Nov. 26, 1998; George R. Knight, "Messenger of the Lord: The Prophetic Ministry of Ellen G. White," book review, *Adventist Review*, Dec. 17, 1998; Norma Collins, "A Century of Blessing," *Adventist Review*, Dec. 24, 1998; Esther F. Ramharacksingh Knott, "She Keeps Me Reading," *Adventist Review*, Mar. 4, 1999; Myrna Tetz, "Don't Read What Ellen White Wrote Unless . . ." *Adventist Review*, Mar. 19, 1999; Roger W. Coon, "Ellen White's Disturbing Disclaimer of 1904," *Adventist Review*, May 13, 1999; Calvin B. Rock, "Knowing for Sure," *Adventist Review*, July 8, 1999; Leslie N. Pollard, "The Cross-Culture," *NAD Adventist Review*, February 2000; Calvin B. Rock, "Roles and Relationships," *NAD Adventist Review*, March 2000; W. C. White, "Memories and Records of Early Experiences," *Adventist Review*, June 30, 2000; Richard Osborn, "Finding Middle C," *NAD Adventist Review*, August 2000; Roger W. Coon, "How Soon Is 'Soon'?" *Adventist Review*, Oct. 26, 2000; Lyndon K. McDowell, "Book Mark: A Search for Identity," *Adventist Review*, Feb. 22, 2001; Hyveth Williams, "The Prophetic Foundation of Adventist Faith," *Adventist Review*, Mar. 29, 2001; Oliver Jacques, "Driven by a Dream," *Adventist Review*, May 24, 2001; Merlin D. Burt, "My Burden Left Me: Ellen White's Conversion Story," *Adventist Review*, Oct. 25, 2001; George R. Knight, "Another Look at City Mission," *NAD Adventist Review*, December 2001; Roy Adams, "What Kind of Person This Ellen White?" *Adventist Review*, Jan. 24, 2002; Benjamin Baker, "The Woman Who Wouldn't Be Quiet: A Fresh Look at Ellen White and Racism," *Adventist Review*, Feb. 21, 2002; Denis Fortin, "Sixty-six Books—or Eighty-one?" *Adventist Review*, Mar. 28, 2002; John B. Hoehn, "The Adventist Drug Problem: Must All Remedies Be 'Natural'?" *Adventist Review*, Apr. 25, 2002; Clifford Goldstein, "1888 and All That . . ." *Adventist Review*, Apr. 25, 2002; Leslie N. Pollard, "More Than a Day," *NAD Adventist Review*, May 2002; William G. Johnsson, "Sharing the Gift," *Adventist Review*, Feb. 27, 2003; Ellen G. White, "Rocky Mountain Adventure: Diary Notes From a Memorable Vacation," *Adventist Review*, July 23, 2003; William G. Johnsson, "The Last Words of Ellen White," *Adventist Review*, Nov. 13, 2003; Terrie Dopp Aamodt, "Just How Hard Is It to Be a Prophet?" *Adventist Review*, June 24, 2004; *idem,* "It's Hard Being a Prophet," *KidsView,* in *Adventist Review*, June 24, 2004; James R. Nix, "The Light Still Shines," *Adventist Review*, July 22, 2004; Stoy Proctor, "True When Tried," *Adventist Review*, Dec. 30, 2004; Ken McFarland, "Beautiful Hill: The Beginnings of a Dream—a Vision—Come True," *Adventist Review*, Mar. 31, 2005; James R. Nix, "The Ministry of Healing: The History Behind Ellen White's Classic Work on Health," *Adventist Review*, Mar. 31, 2005; Stephen Chavez, "To Be Understood," *Adventist Review*, June 23, 2005; Limoni Manu, "Nonvegetarians Will Not Enter Heaven? Guidelines for Interpreting Ellen White on the Topic of Health," *Adventist Review*, Aug. 25, 2005; Clifford Goldstein, "Objective Truth," *Adventist Review*, Jan. 26, 2006; *idem,* "Deductions," *Adventist Review*, Feb. 23, 2006; Roy Adams, "A Perspective From the Writings of Ellen G. White," *Adventist Review*, May 11, 2006; Allan R. Handysides and Peter N. Landless, "Is Cows' Milk Safe to Drink?" *Adventist Review*, Nov. 23, 2006; Stephen Chavez, "Are We Still Protestant?" *Adventist Review*, Mar. 22, 2007; Douglas Morgan, "Following the Prince of Peace in a Time of War: How the Adventist Pioneers Dealt With Issues of War, Peace, and Military Service," *Adventist Review*, June 14, 2007; Jerry Stevens, "O Zion, Haste," *Adventist Review*, Jan. 17, 2008; James R. Nix, "A Monumental Vision," *Adventist Review*, Mar. 20, 2008; *idem,* "Telling the Story," *Adventist Review*, Mar. 20, 2008; Allan R. Handysides and Peter N. Landless, "Are Medications Safe to Take?" *Adventist Review*, Aug. 28, 2008; Mark A. Kellner, "How Would Ellen White Vote?" *Adventist Review*, Sept. 11, 2008.

[344] *Adventist Review Special Anniversary Issue,* July 29, 1999.

[345] Jerry Thomas, "Days at Capernaum" and "Social Justice," *Adventist Review*, June 20, 2002.

[346] "Letters," *Adventist Review*, Aug. 15, 2002; James R. Nix, "Ellen for Us (Revisited)," *Adventist Review*, Sept. 19, 2002; "Letters," *Adventist Review*, Oct. 10, 2002.

[347] Bill Knott, "And There Was Light," *Adventist World*, November 2008.

[348] Angel Manuel Rodríguez, "Prophets, True and False," *Adventist World*, September 2005; Nathaniel D. Faulkhead, "Confident in the Gift," *Adventist World*, February 2006; Norma J. Collins, "Blistered Hands, Square Truths," *Adventist World*, June 2006; Juan Carlos Viera, "God's Guiding Gift: The Work of the Prophet in the Life of the Church," *Adventist World*, December 2006; Michele Solomon, "The Oakwood Experience, Then and Now," *Adventist World*, February 2007; Arthur G. Daniells, "Believing His Prophets," *Adventist World*, October 2007; R. Steven Norman III, "Salvation and Social Action: Edson White's Southern Work Remembered," *Adventist World*, February 2008; Hubert Cisneros, "A Vision of Hope," *Adventist World*, May 2008; Alberto R. Timm, "He Still Speaks," *Adventist World*, July 2008; Gerhard Pfandl, "Foundations of Ellen White's Prophetic Call," *Adventist World*, September 2008; Denis Fortin, "Ellen White and the Bible," *Adventist World*, November 2008.

[349] Ronald L. Numbers, *Prophetess of Health: A Study of Ellen G. White* (Grand Rapids: William B. Eerdmans Publishing, 2008).

[350] There have been a number of other studies on various topics as they relate to Ellen White. A review of these publications is beyond the scope of this essay. Examples include: Ellen G. White, *E. G. White and Church Race Relations* (Washington, D.C.: Review and Herald Pub. Assn., 1970); Joseph Battistone, *The*

Great Controversy Theme in E. G. White Writings (Berrien Springs, Mich.: Andrews University Press, 1978); R. Edward Turner, *Proclaiming the Word: The Concept of Preaching in the Thought of Ellen G. White* (Berrien Springs, Mich.: Andrews University Press, 1980); Delbert W. Baker, *The Unknown Prophet* (Washington, D.C.: Review and Herald Pub. Assn., 1987); Ralph E. Neall, *How Long, O Lord: What Did Ellen White Really Say About the Problem of Our Long Wait for Christ's Soon Return?* (Washington, D.C.: Review and Herald Pub. Assn., 1988); Donald I. Peterson, *Visions and Seizures: Was Ellen White a Victim of Epilepsy?* (Boise, Idaho: Pacific Press Pub. Assn., 1988); Ciro Sepulveda, ed., *Ellen White on the Color Line: The Idea of Race in a Christian Community* (Biblos Press, 1997); Martin Frederick Hanna, *The Cosmic Christ of Scripture: How to Read God's Three Books Comparing Biblical Perspectives With the Writings of Ellen White* (Berrien Springs, Mich.: Cosmic Christ Connections, 2006).

Current Science and Ellen White:
Twelve Controversial Statements

Jud Lake and Jerry Moon*

BOTH ELLEN WHITE'S WRITINGS AND HER ACTIONS displayed a positive attitude toward science. She encouraged believers "to gain a knowledge of the sciences" (2MR 301). She urged and aided John Harvey Kellogg to receive proper scientific medical training. She even urged that ministers in preparation should "first receive a suitable degree of mental training" to "successfully meet the strange forms of error, religious and philosophical combined, to expose which requires a knowledge of scientific as well as Scriptural truth" (GW 81).

White is unsparing, however, in her denunciation of those who make "the truth of God . . . appear as a thing uncertain before the records of science. These false educators exalt nature above nature's God, and above the Author of all true science" (FE 328, 329). Her condemnation was particularly focused on geology where it contradicted the biblical record: "Inferences erroneously drawn from facts observed in nature have, however, led to supposed conflict between science and revelation; and in the effort to restore harmony, interpretations of Scripture have been adopted that undermine and destroy the force of the Word of God. Geology has been thought to contradict the literal interpretation of the Mosaic record of the creation. Millions of years, it is claimed, were required for the evolution of the earth from chaos; and in order to accommodate the Bible to this supposed revelation of science, the days of creation are assumed to have been vast, indefinite periods, covering thousands or even millions of years. Such a conclusion is wholly uncalled for" (Ed 128, 129). For a discussion of her statements on creation, see the article "Bible and Earth Sciences."

Ellen White also criticized nineteenth-century medicine—as practiced then, it could hardly be called "medical science." A few examples will show that it was not called "heroic medicine" for nothing. A commonly prescribed laxative was calomel, chloride of mercury. Calomel produced immediate and violent bowel movements, but the inevitable side effect was mercury poisoning. Tartrate of antimony, also a "lethal poison," was given to induce vomiting. For patients who were debilitated, doctors prescribed such "tonics" as arsenic, strychnine, quinine, or opium.[1] Ellen White denounced most of these by name, correctly pointing out that "preparations of mercury and calomel taken into the system ever retain their poisonous strength as long as there is a particle of it left in the system" (4aSG 139).

Instead she encouraged a healthy lifestyle and the use of harmless remedies. "Pure air, sunlight, abstemiousness [temperance], rest, exercise, proper diet, the use of water, trust in divine power—these are the true remedies" (MH 127). Most of Ellen White's health teachings enjoy broader scientific support now than they did when first written. For example, she denounced tobacco as a malignant poison (4aSG 128). She recommended whole grains as

---

Roger W. Coon laid the foundations of this article in the Seventh-day Adventist Theological Seminary at Andrews University course Writings of Ellen G. White, which he taught from about 1978 to 1995. His lecture "Ellen G. White, Science, and Faith: Part I: the 'Problem' Statements" (rev. May 9, 1995, CAR) formed the starting point for this revision and updating. Timothy G. Standish contributed the first three paragraphs of the article and, with Michael Campbell, much of the section on amalgamation.

nutritionally preferable to refined flour, vegetable oils as healthier than animal fats, and a balanced, varied vegetarian diet as preferable to a diet including flesh food. Some other statements, however, seem quite incredible from the perspective of twenty-first-century science.

This article addresses 12 statements by Ellen White that are in direct or partial conflict with current understandings in the natural sciences. These statements can be divided into three groups. The first group of statements were considered sound advice at the time they were given, and would still be considered sound advice under the same circumstances—but circumstances have changed. This group includes her warnings about wigs, "wasp-waist" corsets, toxic cosmetics, and cheese (statements 1-4).

The second group includes statements on which there is partial or tentative scientific support, such as warnings about disease from "miasma," a connection between pork-eating and leprosy, the influence of a wet nurse on a nursing infant, and risks associated with extreme age differences between spouses (statements 5-8).

The third group includes statements that were widely thought to be true at the time she wrote them, but that have been largely or wholly rejected by current scientific opinion, such as the dynamics of volcanoes, the height of the antediluvians, amalgamation of humans and animals, and the physical effects of masturbation (statements 9-12).

These topics will be evaluated on the basis of three interpretive premises, grounded in Scripture and consistent with the writings of Ellen White.

First Premise: Infallible God, but Fallible Prophets

The first interpretive premise is that Scripture portrays an infallible God speaking through prophets who were neither infallible nor inerrant (see Gen. 20:7; 2 Sam. 7:3-13). The variety of writing styles among the biblical writers supports the view that God revealed concepts to the prophets, but that the prophets' human individuality played a part in the choice of specific words by which the divinely revealed concepts were expressed. For a thorough, biblical exposition of this topic, see "Revelation and Inspiration."

Ellen White's position, in brief, was that revelation-inspiration is not verbal (word-for-word dictation), except on rare occasions, but in general represents "a union of the divine and the human" in which divinely revealed truths are "expressed," "embodied," and "conveyed through the imperfect expression of human language" (GC v-vii). The phrase "imperfect expression" acknowledges that supernaturally *revealed truth* (truth inaccessible to humans apart from direct revelation) may be adequately conveyed even through human language that is approximate or imprecise regarding factual details. Discrepancies of detail in biblical writings (compare the sequence of Christ's temptations in Matthew 4 and Luke 4) show the human individuality and/or fallibility of the biblical writers and imply that *revealed truth* does not exclude the human element in the process of revelation-inspiration.

A corollary to the human fallibility of the biblical prophets is that in communicating the truth revealed to them they drew on their entire stock of knowledge, including that gained by experience, study, and research (*common knowledge*) (Dan. 9:2; Luke 1:1-4; 1 Cor. 1:11-17). The biblical prophets cited many extrabiblical sources in support of their inspired messages (see Joshua 10:13; 2 Sam. 1:17-27; 2 Chron. 9:29; 12:15; 20:34). Under inspiration, fragments of information from these extrabiblical sources became integrated into Scripture.

Ellen White did not claim the authority of a canonical prophet, but she did claim to be inspired by the *same Spirit* in the *same way* as were the canonical prophets (see GC viii, x-xii).[2] Yet in writing out what she had seen in vision, she did not hesitate to use ordinary human sources for supplemental details, illustrations, and other kinds of support (see 3SM 445-465). In personal letters she amplified revealed counsel with facts received from common sources (1SM 38, 39). In expounding Scripture she used Bible dictionaries, chronologies, and other resources to expand her knowledge. In advocating health principles she utilized the writings of contemporary reformers and physicians (see, for example, HR, April 1871; HR, May 1871; HR, October 1871). In writing on historical subjects she consulted the histories, chronologies, and geographies available to her at the time, even sending assistants to search university libraries for needed information (6Bio 308, 318, 319; 3SM 439, 440). Further, she was willing in later editions to revise historical details when other sources were shown to be more reliable than the ones she had used (3SM 445-465).[3] Some alleged discrepancies she did not accept as discrepancies, but others she acknowledged and revised (see 6Bio 303-306). Such was the use of *common knowledge* in her writings.

The relationship between *revealed truth, inspired writings,* and *common knowledge* may be illustrated by a horizontal baseline intersected with a vertical line, as follows:

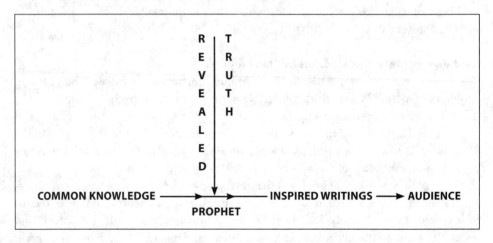

The point of intersection represents the mind of the prophet, and at the far right end of the baseline is the prophet's audience. The vertical line with downward arrow represents the descent of *revealed truth,* knowledge ordinarily inaccessible to humans. The left end of the baseline, with arrow toward the intersection, represents the input of *common knowledge* to the prophet's mind. Divinely revealed knowledge is of higher authority than common knowledge, but does not replace it; rather, it complements it. God does not usually reveal to humans supernaturally what He has given them ability to learn for themselves. [4] The right end of the baseline, with arrow toward the audience, represents *inspiration,* which is the work of the Holy Spirit in guiding the horizontal communication from the prophet's mind to the audience. Note that this communication is a product of the union of *revealed truth* and *common knowledge.*[5]

One example of the combination of revealed and common knowledge in Ellen White's writings is a letter she wrote regarding a minister in California (Ms 107, 1909, in 1SM 38, 39; italics supplied): "I am pained to see him denying the testimonies as a whole because of what seems to him an inconsistency—a statement made by me in regard to the number of rooms in the Paradise Valley Sanitarium. Brother A [E. S. Ballenger] says that in a letter written to one of the brethren in southern California, *the statement was made by me that the sanitarium contained forty rooms, when there were really only thirty-eight.* This, Brother A gives to me as the reason why he has lost confidence in the testimonies. . . .

"The information given concerning the number of rooms in the Paradise Valley Sanitarium was given, *not as a revelation from the Lord, but simply as a human opinion.* There has never been revealed to me the exact number of rooms in any of our sanitariums; and *the knowledge I have obtained of such things I have gained by inquiring of those who were supposed to know.* In my words, *when speaking upon these common subjects,* there is nothing to lead minds to believe that I receive my knowledge in a vision from the Lord and am stating it as such."

She explained that in response to God's call, "I gave myself, my whole being, to God, to obey His call in everything, and since that time my life has been spent in *giving the message, with my pen and in speaking before large congregations. It is not I who controls my words and actions at such times* [a reference to revelation-inspiration].

"*But there are times when common things must be stated, common thoughts must occupy the mind, common letters must be written and information given that has passed from one to another of the workers. Such words, such information, are not given under the special inspiration of the Spirit of God.* Questions are asked at times that are not upon religious subjects at all, and these questions must be answered. We converse about houses and lands, trades to be made, and locations for our institutions, their advantages and disadvantages." Her son W. C. White set forth a most careful exposition of this combination of revealed truth and common knowledge as found in her writings—an exposition that she approved in writing.

Revealed Truth and Common Knowledge in the Writings of Ellen White

The controversy that called out W. C. White's comments concerned her writings, not on science, but on history. However, the basic issue was the same: how Ellen White made use of *common knowledge* in communicating revealed truth. Thus his comments about her use of historical knowledge are relevant to the question of her use of scientific knowledge, which also progresses over time.

In connection with Ellen White's 1911 revision of *The Great Controversy,* her son W. C. White presented to his denomination's Autumn Council a rather comprehensive report on "the latest English edition of *Great Controversy.*"[6] Pertinent to the present study are his words about Ellen White as an authority on history. That he accurately expressed her views on this topic is not in doubt, for in a letter to F. M. Wilcox, Ellen White specifically endorsed this manuscript by W. C. White (Lt 57, 1911).

"Mother has never claimed to be an authority on history," W. C. White asserted. "The things which she has written out are descriptions of flashlight pictures[7] and other representations given her"—an obvious reference to her visions.

"In . . . writing out . . . these views, she has made use of good and clear historical statements to help make plain to the reader the things which she is endeavoring to present. When I was a mere boy, I heard her read D'Aubigne's *History of the Reformation* to my father. . . . She has read other histories of the Reformation. This has helped her to locate and describe many of the events and the movements presented to her in vision."[8]

W. C. White cited similar experiences in support of his belief that her descriptions of historical events were based on pictorial visions, but that dates, geographical relationships, and other details were derived from standard works on history and chronology. One such experience occurred during the years she and her son spent in Europe between 1885 and 1887. One Sabbath, at Basel, Switzerland, W. C. White was reading James Wylie's *History of Protestantism* to Ellen White. He later recalled that "she interrupted me and told me a lot of things in the pages ahead, and told me many things not in the book at all. She said, 'I have never read about it, but that scene has been presented to me over and over again.'" When he asked her, "Why did you not put it into your book [*The Great Controversy*]?" she replied, "I did not know where to put it."[9] By these statements W. C. White showed his understanding that while the controlling content of her historical writings was derived from visions, she was dependent on common sources for geographical and chronological connections.

A year after the 1911 presentation W. C. White reiterated more fully his understanding about the use of his mother's writings as authority for the details of history. S. N. Haskell and W. W. Eastman had relayed to W. C. White some questions raised by W. W. Prescott about the accuracy of certain dates in *The Great Controversy*.[10] W. C. White prepared a first draft of a response and took it to Ellen White for her criticism. That she approved is certain, because at the end of the letter appears a note in her own handwriting: "I approve of the remarks made in this letter. Ellen G. White."[11]

This letter to Haskell contains a rather detailed statement of W. C. White's understanding of the use of Ellen White as an authority on history. "Regarding Mother's writings," he began, "she has never wished our brethren to treat them as authority on history. When *Great Controversy* was first written, she oftentimes gave a partial description of some scene presented to her, and when Sister Davis made inquiry regarding time and place, Mother referred her to what was already written in the books [*Thoughts on Daniel* and *Thoughts on Revelation*] of Elder [Uriah] Smith and in secular histories. When *Controversy* was written, Mother never thought that the readers would take it as an authority on historical dates and use it to settle controversies, and she does not now feel that it ought to be used in that way. Mother regards with the greatest respect those faithful historians who have given their [lives] to the study of the working out in this world's history of God's great plan, and who have found in this study a correspondence of the history with prophecy. . . .

"It seems to me that there is a danger of placing altogether too much stress upon chronology. If it had been essential to the salvation of men that he [i.e., man] should have a clear and harmonious understanding of the chronology of the world, the Lord would not have permitted the disagreements and discrepancies which we find in the writings of the Bible historians, and it seems to me that in these last days there ought not to be so much controversy regarding dates. . . .

"I believe, Brother Haskell, that there is danger of our injuring Mother's work by claiming for it more than she claims for it, more than Father ever claimed for it, more than Elder [J. N.] Andrews, [J. H.] Waggoner, or [Uriah] Smith ever claimed for it. I cannot see consistency in our putting forth a claim of verbal inspiration when Mother does not make any such claim, and I certainly think we will make a great mistake if we lay aside historical research and endeavor to settle historical questions by the use of Mother's books as an authority when she herself does not wish them to be used in any such way."[12]

As noted above, W. C. White submitted this letter to Ellen White for her approval. Probably on the basis of conversation with her at the same time, he then prepared a second draft in which he refined his statement somewhat. The thematic sentence from the first letter was "Regarding Mother's writings, she has never wished our brethren to treat them as authority on history." In the second draft W. C. White rephrased this to the more careful construction "she has never wished our brethren to treat them as authority *on the dates or details of* history." This second draft of the letter to Haskell became the prototype for a letter of the same date to W. W. Eastman in which White continued to develop his exposition.[13] The third draft began, "Regarding Mother's writings and their use as authority on points of history and chronology, *Mother has never wished our brethren to treat them as authority regarding the details of history or historical dates.* . . . When writing out the chapters for *Great Controversy,* she sometimes gave a partial description of an important historical event, and when her copyist who was preparing the manuscripts for the printer made inquiry regarding time and place, Mother would say . . . those things are recorded by conscientious historians. Let the dates used by those historians be inserted. . . . When *Controversy* was written, Mother never thought that the readers would take it as authority on historical dates or use it to settle controversy regarding details of history, and she does not now feel that it should be used in that way. Mother regards with great respect the work of those faithful historians who devoted years of time to the study of God's great plan as presented in the prophecy, and the outworking of that plan as recorded in history."[14]

Much of the letter to Eastman follows the general outline of the Haskell letters. In concluding the letter, however, White went beyond the previous letters to Haskell. "Regarding Mother's writings, I have overwhelming evidence and conviction that they are the description and delineation of what God has revealed to her in vision, and where she has followed the description of historians or the exposition of Adventist writers, I believe that God has given her discernment to use that which is correct and in harmony with truth *regarding all matters essential to salvation.* If it should be found by faithful study that she has followed some expositions of prophecy which in some detail regarding dates we cannot harmonize with our understanding of secular history, it does not influence my confidence in her writings as a whole any more than my confidence in the Bible is influenced by the fact that I cannot harmonize many of the [biblical] statements regarding chronology."[15]

Thus White claimed to have "overwhelming evidence and conviction" that God had given his mother "discernment" to select from the available sources "that which is correct and in harmony with truth regarding all matters essential to salvation." He was confident that she accurately set forth the "big picture"[16] of salvific truth. At the same time, knowing that in many instances she had derived dates, quotations, and chronological information from standard historians, he could not agree that those details were ultimately authoritative. If they were, there would be no room for the kind of historical investigation, verification, and correction of quotations that went into the 1911 edition of *The Great Controversy*.[17]

In summary, W. C. White believed that the primary source of his mother's writings was divine revelation-inspiration, and that belief was the basic presupposition for all his dealings with her writings. Though he did not believe that God had directly revealed in vision every detail needed to make a connected historical narrative, he did believe that God had guided her in the selection of the historical sources she used to supply details not given in vision. And while he believed her historical writings were inspired, he did not hold that they were infallible. Against those who wanted to attribute to revelation every detail in her historical narratives, he argued (in a letter his mother approved) that she had not derived every detail from revelation and did not intend her writings to be used to prove historical details.

Finally, while W. C. White refused to attach infallibility to his mother's writings, he also rejected the opposite extreme. Against the flat statement that she was neither a theologian nor a historian, he argued that in the broader sense of those terms, she wrote much practical theology and practical history. He believed that in her theological concepts and broad historical themes she was both inspired and authoritative.

What Her Writings on History Imply About Her Writings on Science

It can be argued that her use of scientific and medical literature fits the same three-part pattern as her use of historical literature. 1. She derived her "big picture"[18] and enduring *principles* from *revealed truth*. 2. She buttressed that "big picture" with the most convincing factual evidence she could find in the sources (*common knowledge*) available to her. 3. Finally, she often modified what she learned from *common* sources to harmonize with what she knew from *revealed truth*.[19]

For example, David Neff has pointed out that Ellen White borrowed from Calvin Stowe some of his theological language, but she then modified that language to express her own concepts, which did not fully agree with Stowe's. Note the similarities and the differences between Stowe and Ellen White:

C. E. Stowe, *Origin and History of the Books of the Bible,* p. 20.	E. G. White, *Selected Messages,* book 1, p. 21.
"It is not the words of the Bible that were inspired, it is not the thoughts of the Bible that were inspired; it is the men who wrote the Bible that were inspired. "Inspiration was not on the man's words, not on the man's thoughts, but on the man himself; that he, by his own spontaneity, under the impulse of the Holy Ghost, conceives certain thoughts."	"It is not the words of the Bible that are inspired, but the men that were inspired. "Inspiration acts not on the man's words or his expressions but on the man himself, who, under the influence of the Holy Ghost, is imbued with thoughts."

Because Ellen White evaluated her *common knowledge* on the basis of the *revealed truth* given to her, she felt free, before publishing a new book, to submit it to qualified persons who could give her feedback on it (Lt 49, 1894, in 10MR 12, 13). There were times that, based on her visions, she rejected the views of her contemporaries, and other times that she modified her writings based on what she learned through dialogue with her readers (6Bio 302-337). She believed that in the selection of her sources and her peer reviewers she was led by God, but she did not believe that made either her or them infallible or inerrant. Nevertheless, she believed that through the superintendence of the Holy Spirit, what she wrote was true to the "big picture" and therefore reliable for the purposes for which it was given.[20]

In her writings on health, she believed that she had been inspired to write *revealed principles* in the *language of her time*. Therefore her advice was authoritative and trustworthy regarding the "practical purposes"[21] it was given for, but it was not intended to preclude further research and growth in knowledge. And twenty-first-century readers should not be surprised that since her death, knowledge has continued to advance. This first premise is foundational to this article.

Therefore, the purpose of this article is not to prove that she was infallible or inerrant in everything she wrote.[22] It is, however, the purpose of this article to show that certain statements she made in the nineteenth century, which today are being held up for ridicule, were, in fact, sound and sensible advice at the time and in the context in which they were originally given. She was simply using the best *human knowledge* available to her at the time to corroborate and communicate the *revealed truth* given her in vision. As Don S. McMahon, M.D., has shown, the suggestion that her whole health message could have been derived merely from contemporary health reformers is statistically inadequate to account for the accuracy of her health advice. Her health instruction was statistically so much more accurate than that of her contemporaries individually or collectively that it cannot be explained by luck or superior intellect, but demands that she had some superior source of information guiding her on what to agree with and what to reject.[23] And while science and technology have made gigantic advances in the past 150 years, that increase in knowledge has not undermined any of her basic health principles. The principles she gave in 1864 were so accurate that those who follow them in a commonsense way in the twenty-first century have measurably better health and a longer life span than almost everyone else on the planet.[24]

Second Major Premise: Both Science and Revelation Must Be Read in Historical Context

A second major interpretive premise is that human knowledge in all fields is incomplete but increasing. In White's terms, "human knowledge of both material and spiritual things is partial and imperfect" (GC 522; cf. 1 Cor. 8:2; 13:9-12), and "knowledge is progressive" (*ibid.* 677, 678). Individual religious experience is also "progressive" (CT 281; Ev 355; FW 85), as is education (CSW 103; Ev 105). In matters of revelation, new truth amplifies old truth without contradicting it,[25] but the human *understanding* of divine revelation is certainly subject to correction by further revelation. Both science and revelation, therefore, must be read in historical context.[26]

In the Bible both the instruction and the explanation were tailored to the historical context of the people to whom it was addressed. For example, in the regulations about clean and unclean flesh foods in Leviticus 11, the instruction is clear: "You may eat any animal that has a divided hoof and that chews the cud. There are some that only chew the cud or only have a divided hoof, but you must not eat them" (Lev. 11:3, 4, NIV). While the instruction is clear, the explanation that follows is adapted to the practical use of the common people: "The rabbit, though it chews the cud, does not have a divided hoof; it is unclean for you" (verse 6, NIV). Advancing knowledge has shown that rabbits only appear to chew the cud; they are not ruminants like cattle, sheep, and deer. [27] But the terminology of Leviticus 11 was clear to the people for whom it was given, and still enables anyone who reads it to make choices in harmony with the will of God.

Bible writers usually couched their messages in language that made sense to the original audience. For example, the assertion that God "suspends the earth over nothing" (Job 26:7, NIV) was factual in denying various ancient theories about what the earth rested on, but it was also incomplete, in that it made no attempt to suggest a theory of how the physical universe works. Another example is Psalm 58:8, which compares the wicked to "a snail which melts away as it goes" (NKJV). This poetically describes the snail's appearance, but a snail does not literally melt away as it moves, but rather secretes a film of mucus on which it travels.

A similar example in the experience of Ellen White occurred in 1846 at Topsham, Maine, where she had a vision on the "opening heavens." Present at the meeting was Joseph Bates, a sea captain, navigator, and amateur astronomer, who believed Ellen White to be a sincere Christian but thought her visions were merely a product of her long-term ill health. This vision changed his mind, because while in vision she described several planets. *Neither during this vision, nor at any subsequent time, did she herself identify by name which planets she had seen.* But her description was sufficiently accurate for Bates to identify the planets, and to express his astonishment that the number of moons she ascribed to each planet represented exactly the latest discoveries of Lord John Rosse, a leading British astronomer of the day. Because the vision gave information previously unknown to Ellen White, but that Bates recognized as in accord with the latest astronomy, he became a believer in the supernatural origin of her visions (1Bio 113, 114). Regarding the scientific accuracy of the vision, the development of more powerful telescopes has led to the discovery of additional moons for each of those planets, but had the vision revealed details not discovered by science until the twenty-first century, Bates could not have recognized their accuracy. This is an example of information that apparently would not have achieved its purpose had it been too far in advance of current knowledge at the time it was given.

Third Premise: Differentiating Principles and Explanations

It appears to be helpful in some situations to distinguish between principles and explanations. Because *principles* express God's will regarding human beings, *principles* are as enduring as human nature—even though the historical *explanations* were expressed in language and thought forms adapted to the time in which the instruction was given. For example, Scripture often describes physical causes and effects in terms of sin and penalty (see Ex. 15:26; Rom. 1:27; 1 Cor. 6:18; Heb. 2:2). Thus in Exodus 15:26 the precise wording could suggest that the diseases of the Egyptians were sent on them by God as punishment for their disobedience and that healing from disease is a divine reward for obedience. But modern science strongly affirms that obedience or disobedience to laws of health stands in a direct cause-and-effect relationship to the incidence of health or disease. Likewise in Leviticus, consumption of animal fat or blood was absolutely prohibited on penalty of death or banishment (Lev. 3:17; 7:23-25). Eating the flesh of certain species, including swine, was also prohibited (Lev. 11:4-8). The *explanation* given was simply that it is "unclean for you" (verse 8, NIV) and must be avoided, lest you "make yourselves abominable" or "defile yourselves" (verse 43, RSV). The *principle* was "Ye shall be holy; for I am holy" (verse 44). That principle of holiness is still valid, though many today might not think of physical health as an aspect of holiness. But when these *principles* were reiterated through Ellen White in the nineteenth century, she emphasized health consequences—a scientific explanation—as a compelling motive for not consuming animal fat, blood, or "unclean" flesh (CH 228, 229; CD 374, 375, 393, 394).

Some scholars have suggested the possibility of differentiating between *instruction* and *explanation* in some of the health writings of Ellen White, based on what she said about the use of salt. "I use some salt, and always have," she wrote, "because from the light given me by God, this article, in the place of being deleterious, is actually essential for the blood. The whys and wherefores of this I know not, but I give you the *instruction* as it is given me" (CD 344). Here she differentiates between the "instruction" and the "whys and wherefores," or explanation, of the instruction.[28]

Don S. McMahon's research indicates that while advances in scientific knowledge have not confirmed all of Ellen White's *explanations*, those same advances have produced a continually increasing accumulation of support for the *principles* of her basic *instruction*.[29] It has already been shown that Ellen White did not claim infallibility. For that reason she did *not* believe that the *revelation* to her through visions gave inspired authority to every piece of *common knowledge* she referred to in support of that revelation (see Ms 107, 1909, in 1SM 38, 39).

Twelve Statements That May Include Data From Common Knowledge

In several of the 12 topics to be considered, Ellen White is clearly utilizing information obtained from common sources, in which there was "nothing to lead minds to believe" that she received it "in a vision from the Lord" (*ibid.* 38). Four of the 12 statements (1, 2, 3, and 7) come from a period in 1871 in which, to help her overworked husband, she had agreed to be in charge of a "department" (column) in the *Health Reformer* and supply a certain quantity of health-related material for publication every month. In these articles she drew material from her travels, personal experience, and contemporary health publications to illustrate and reinforce the health principles she was teaching. It is evident that some of these statements are a combination of instruction based on visions and explanations gleaned from contemporary publications, which she added because, at the time, they gave additional force and credibility to the instruction. This interpretation is consistent with the recognition of spiritual and intellectual growth in a prophet. Based on the foregoing premises, therefore, we might expect to find revealed principles of enduring value, combined with explanations that made sense and provided motivation for the readers to whom the counsel was originally given.[30] As noted at the beginning of the article, the 12 statements will be considered in three groups.

First Group, Statements 1-4: Sound Advice at the Time They Were Given

The first group of statements includes those that were sound advice at the time they were given, and would still be sound advice if the same conditions still prevailed. This category includes her warnings about wigs, toxic cosmetics, the effects of "wasp-waist" corsets, and possible problems with cheese.

Statement 1, lethal wigs: "Artificial hair and pads covering the base of the brain, heat and excite the spinal nerves," producing "congestion" in the brain, loss of natural hair, and even insanity (HR, October 1871). Wigmaking in 1871 was vastly different from that of today. Whereas wigs today are of lightweight material, with an open-weave base that allows the scalp to breathe, wigs in Ellen White's day were of heavy materials—natural hair, cotton, sea grass, wool, Spanish moss, etc. (HR, July 1867)—and rather than lightweight and elastic, they bound the head so tightly as to cut off circulation, confine body heat in the head, and trap perspiration, all of which produced persistent headaches, according to a physician whom Ellen White quoted in her article.

When jute was the material used, a further hazard presented itself. The jute harbored small insects—jute bugs—that burrowed under the scalp of the wearer. Again Ellen White quotes from a contemporary physician who advised against wearing "switches, or jutes, or chignons, because they breed pestiferous vermin, whose life is fed by their drain on the small blood vessels of the scalp" (HR, October 1871).A "switch" of hair was a generic term for a hairpiece that could be made of various materials. "Jutes" referred to "jute switches," hairpieces made of dark, fibrous jute bark (HR, January 1871). "Chignons" could be made of human hair, of either local or imported origin (HR, July 1867).[31] The physician White quoted believed that the tight-fitting, heat-confining construction of the wig was a greater hazard to health than the possibility of insects (HR, October 1871). Another hazard of hairpieces was human hair harvested from plague victims in China, then shipped through Hong Kong to New York, where it was manufactured into "switches," i.e., hairpieces. The boiling and chemical soaking processes were presumed sufficient to kill the plague-carrying microbes, except that dirty and clean hair were "thoroughly mixed" in the tenement workrooms and "passed through the same combs."[32]

There is no indication in this article that Ellen White received a specific vision on the health effects of nineteenth-century hairpieces. She evidently derived her insights from the biblical principles of health (1 Cor. 6:19, 20; 10:31) and modesty (1 Tim. 2:9; 1 Peter 3:3), from the "big picture" of health presented to her in vision, and from the writings of others on the topic.[33] Whatever the level of precision in the details of Ellen White's description or in the physician's reports she quoted, her instruction to avoid such wigs made good sense at the time. The wearing of wigs adversely affected the health and happiness of those who wore them.[34]

Statement 2, toxic cosmetics: "Many are ignorantly injuring their health and endangering their life by using cosmetics. They are robbing the cheeks of the glow of health, and then to supply the deficiency use cosmetics. When they become heated in the dance the poison is absorbed by the pores of the skin, and is thrown into the blood. Many lives have been sacrificed by this means alone" (HR, October 1871).

In support of her warning against toxic cosmetics, White again quotes a physician who describes the contemporary women's fashion of painting the face with enamel or lacquer to give the skin the appearance of "fine porcelain." Whatever the supposed fashionable appearance, the physician declared, "the seeds of death or paralysis" are "hidden in every pot and jar of those mixtures," causing severe illness, sudden paralysis, or even death. The description suggests a white lead-based cosmetic, and the symptoms described are those of acute lead poisoning.[35] The physician continues: "Some who use them will suddenly have a severe illness; and receiving a private warning from the family physician, will cease the use of the cause of their disorder, and recovering, go through life with an extremely bad complexion" (ibid.). "Others will drop suddenly, with their features twisted on one side, and perhaps deprived of the use of their limbs. Others will die outright, no one guessing why" (ibid.).[36]

Lead, a highly toxic element, was often an ingredient in cosmetics.[37] Lead poisoning causes peripheral neuropathy (such as foot-drop and wrist-drop) and sleep disturbances.[38] The initial symptoms are irritability, headache, and nausea, according to Julian Chisholm, an expert on lead poisoning.[39] Thus the symptoms cited by Ellen White were entirely typical of lead poisoning.

In the 1870s there was no governmental agency to monitor the cosmetic industry. Ellen White herself was poisoned by applying a hair restorer to her husband's bald head (ibid.). Further evidence that her advice was practical is the fact that even with governmental oversight, cosmetics still contained dangerous poisons in the late twentieth century. A 1988 U.S. congressional investigation led by Congressman Ron Wyden found that "of the 3,000 most commonly used chemicals" in the cosmetics industry, "more than a third are toxic." Of these, "314 are reported to cause biological mutation, 218 are reported to cause reproductive complications, 778 are capable of causing acute toxicity, 146 are reported to cause tumors, and 376 ingredients are reported to cause skin and eye irritations."[40] Presently the cosmetics industry is changing but still uses harmful ingredients.[41]

Statement 3, "wasp-waist" corsets: "Some women have naturally small waists. But rather than regard such forms as beautiful, they should be viewed as defective. These wasp waists *may* have been transmitted to them from their mothers, as the result of their indulgence in the sinful practice of tight-lacing, and in consequence of imperfect breathing" (HR, November 1871; italics supplied). A few lines later she quotes from a contemporary periodical, *The Household*: " 'But my waist is naturally slender,' says one woman. She means that she has inherited small lungs. Her ancestors, more or less of them, compressed their lungs in the same way that we do, and it has become in her case a congenital deformity" (ibid.).

Ellen White's unsparing denunciation of the nineteenth-century fashion of "tight-lacing" the female abdomen to produce a "wasp waist" is certainly supported by all current evidence, but the notion that such acquire deformities can be transmitted genetically is completely inconsistent with scientific knowledge during most of the twentieth century. However, the second statement about the possibility of "small lungs" being "inherited" as a "congenital deformity" is not from her pen, but is a quotation from a contemporary periodical. Ellen White's own expression stops short of full assertion. "These wasp waists *may* have been transmitted to them from their mothers," she comments. The word "may" indicates her uncertainty about the reliability of a contemporary source she quoted.

As another illustration of the evils of tight-lacing of the female abdomen, Ellen White quoted a report from another contemporary publication, *Home and Health*. At a leading hospital in Paris, France, an internationally known physician, Dr. Gilbert Breschet, examined an 18-year-old female patient. The girl had on the right side of her throat something Breschet called a "tumor of variable size" that reached "from the collarbone as high as the thyroid cartilage. When pressed downward, it wholly disappeared; but as soon as the pressure was removed, it was indolent, soft, and elastic. It was observed to be largest when the chest was tightly laced with corsets. . . . The poor girl had been laced so tightly," said *Home and Health*, that her lungs were squeezed out of their natural position and were "forcing their way up along the neck" (HR, December 1871). It seems obvious from the description that this condition was not what would today be called a "tumor," but an air-filled sac produced by the extreme restriction of the lungs. Ellen White makes no comment whatsoever on this report. She simply quotes it as an example of the evils of tight-lacing.

Ellen White's purpose for writing on this topic was to warn her readers that tight-lacing constricted the lungs and disfigured the human body. In this she was correct. In support of her message, she quoted contemporary authorities but remained tentative about certain assertions, such as the possibility of inheriting a "wasp waist."

The possibility that acquired characteristics could be passed on to offspring was rejected by science during the twentieth century, but is now receiving renewed interest, because "studies in the field of epigenetics have highlighted the possible inheritance of behavioral traits acquired by the previous generation."[42]

Statement 4, dangers in eating cheese (see also separate article, Cheese): "Cheese should never be introduced into the stomach," wrote Ellen White in 1868, her first mention of the subject (2T 68). Her last mention of cheese (in 1905) said: "Cheese is still more objectionable [than butter]; it is wholly unfit for food" (MH 302). To understand why she would write such a statement requires consideration of several historical factors.

Perhaps the aspect of American cheese technology most relevant to Ellen White's comments was the difficulty of arresting the aging process to keep cheese from spoiling once it was "ripe." Curt Wohleber reported that in the nineteenth century cheese sales and consumption in America lagged far behind that of Europe for one simple reason: American cheese spoiled so rapidly on the grocery shelf that consumers often became sick from eating it. "Even a master cheesemaker couldn't consistently produce batch after batch of top quality," but homemade cheese production was even more erratic. Not until 1916—the year after Ellen White's death—did James L. Kraft receive the first American patent on a process that gave cheese a virtually indefinite shelf life. "Early advertisements played up Kraft cheese's nutritional value—a subtle way of saying that it wouldn't give you food poisoning."[43] This history goes far to explain Ellen White's advice that the substance commonly referred to as cheese in nineteenth-century America was indeed "unfit for food."

Another factor conditioning White's counsel on cheese was the unhealthful state of milk production in her day. Dairies were notoriously unsanitary; rampant disease in cows was transmitted to milk and cheese, and all these problems were made worse by the lack of refrigeration.[44] Pasteurization (heating milk to a certain temperature to reduce microbial contamination) did not become commercially available until 1882, and it was some years beyond that before cheesemakers figured out how to integrate pasteurization into cheese manufacture without interfering with the fermentation that is integral to the cheesemaking process.[45]

In that context, the word "cheese," without any qualifying adjectives, referred to common yellow cheese, which, without pasteurization or refrigeration, swiftly progressed from ripe to rancid. White mentioned accepting, on rare occasions, a bit of ripened cheese when it was served to her, but did not "think of making [ripened] cheese an article of diet, much less of buying it (15MR 246 [1873]; cf. 3SM 287 [1881]; 5MR 406 [1901]; CD 491 [1903]). In contrast, she regarded the *unripened* cheeses, cottage cheese and cream cheese, as wholesome foods that Ellen White regularly served at her own table.[46]

When *The Ministry of Healing* was being translated into German in 1906, the translators wrote to Ellen White, asking for clarification of her statement that cheese is "wholly unfit for food" (MH 302). Did she mean to condemn *all* cheese foods without exception? In reply, she authorized them to substitute, for the English word "cheese," the phrase "strong cheese" and to *entirely omit* the sentence "It is wholly unfit for food." Thus she clarified her intention to limit her criticism to a certain category of cheese. W. C. White's explanation confirms that spoilage was at least part of the problem. "If strong is not the term you use [in German] to designate the ordinary cheese of commerce, which is old and full of poison, please designate by the proper term." Following this counsel, the translators wrote: "Strong, sharp cheese should not be eaten."[47] She also advised moderation, common sense, and respect for each individual's conscience (CD 198, 206, 353).

In summary, White's cautions against cheese must be read in the context of the time and circumstances under which they were given. What she wrote was good general advice for the time in which she wrote it. Cheese can still be high in animal protein, saturated fat, cholesterol, and salt. Further, tyramine compounds in ripened cheese can trigger allergic reactions, hypertension, or mind-altering effects on brain cells, all of which are relieved when cheese is removed from the diet.[48]

Ironically, the technological advances resolving the problems of contamination and spoilage have led to an eightfold increase in per capita cheese consumption, now averaging more than 30 pounds per person per year in North America.[49]

Second Group, Statements 5-8: Partly or Tentatively Supported

A second group of statements includes those for which her explanations are partly or tentatively, and some increasingly, supported by current science. These include the danger of disease from "miasma"; a connection between pork-eating and leprosy; the influence of a wet nurse on a nursing infant; and large age differences between marriage partners. In some of these her counsel seems clearly to have been in advance of the findings of scientific research.

Statement 5, dangers of disease from miasma, an unpleasant or unhealthy vapor: "If we would have our homes the abiding place of health and happiness, we must place them above the miasma and fog of the lowlands. . . . Dispense with heavy curtains, open the windows and the blinds, allow no vines, however beautiful, to shade the windows, and permit no trees to stand so near the house as to shut out the sunshine. . . . Shade trees and shrubbery close and dense around a house make it unhealthful, for they prevent the free circulation of air and shut out the rays of the sun. In consequence, a dampness gathers in the house, especially in wet seasons" (AH 149; cf. MH 274, 275; 4aSG 144). The practical or "commonsense" reading of this counsel simply indicates that high, dry ground, with ample circulation of pure air, affords a healthier environment for a home than poorly drained or swampy surroundings. The gases and vapors [miasma] from decaying material in swampy ground do not provide the pure, fresh air that encourages deep breathing, oxygenates the blood, and invigorates the entire body.

The question about this statement concerns the technical explanation of how disease is transmitted. Some have ridiculed this statement as attributing illness to mere bad odors. But twenty-first-century knowledge of the role of mold and mildew in human diseases fully corroborates her cautions. Mold and mildew flourish in persistently damp conditions. In northern climates, with short summers and severe winters, the chill of cold weather is intensified by persistent dampness. All of these factors are either explicit or implied in White's several statements on this topic (2SM 463, 464; MH 274, 275).

The element missing from her counsel that a more recent perspective would certainly include is the role of mosquitoes in transmitting disease. Her warning about stagnant water near the house certainly describes the conditions in which mosquitoes breed and proliferate (4aSG 144), though she does not mention mosquitoes (3SG 243; HR, August 1872). However, her practical counsel remains perfectly valid in the light of today's scientific knowledge. Gases and vapors from decaying materials, the consequent lack of fresh air, the presence of mold and mildew, and possibly other airborne contaminants, are recognized today as aggravating to allergies and threats to health. The cold-weather chill that is exacerbated by persistent dampness may be less of an issue among the middle and upper classes in developed countries where homes are comfortably heated in cold weather, but in the nineteenth century, especially for those in poverty, the dangers of a cold, damp climate were not to be taken lightly.

Statement 6, leprosy from eating pork: "The eating of pork has produced scrofula, leprosy, and cancerous humors" (4aSG 146; 2SM 417). "God did not prohibit the Hebrews from eating swine's flesh merely to show His authority, but because it was not a proper article of food for man. It would fill the system with scrofula [a form of tuberculosis that caused swelling of the lymph glands and inflammation of the joints], and especially in that warm climate produced leprosy, and disease of various kinds. Its influence upon the system in that climate was far more injurious than in a colder climate" (2SM 417).[50]

There are two parts to this issue: the identity of the biblical leprosy and whether pork-eating contributes to its spread. Regarding the relation of biblical leprosy to modern leprosy, authorities are divided, but there is evidence that biblical leprosy included a broader range of ailments (such as fungus infections) than is included in the modern use of the term.[51] Biblical scholar Roland K. Harrison provides a persuasive argument that the symptoms of Hansen's disease (modern leprosy) correspond to the symptoms of biblical leprosy described in Leviticus 13.[52]

This is another example where Ellen White appears to have used commonly accepted ideas to reinforce sound health counsel. The linking of swine's flesh with leprosy—especially in hot climates—has a long history in ancient and especially Jewish tradition,[53] and is also reflected in older Christian commentaries. For example, Jamieson, Fausset, and Brown's *Commentary, Critical and Explanatory, on the Whole Bible* comments on Leviticus 11:7: "In hot climates indulgence in swine's flesh is particularly liable to produce leprosy, scurby, and various cutaneous eruptions." The wording of this quotation is so similar to Ellen White's as to suggest that she was familiar with their comment or a similar one. [54] If the connection between pork-eating and leprosy was unquestioned in her day—and she had no special light to the contrary—it is understandable that she would include this recognized risk along with the others she enumerated as one more reason pork should be excluded from the diet.

Regarding scientific evidence linking pork-eating and leprosy, there is one published study in which mice fed a pork diet showed a significantly greater predisposition to leprosy than those on a nonpork diet.[55] Additionally, there is some evidence that humans can contract leprosy by eating the meat of an infected armadillo, an animal 20 times more susceptible than humans to Hansen's disease.[56] Whether or not it can be proved that pork consumption increases the risk of leprosy under the circumstances Ellen White suggested, her counsel to avoid eating pork was certainly sound and biblical advice (Lev. 11:7, 8).[57]

Statement 7, choosing a wet nurse: Ellen White strongly recommended breast-feeding of an infant by its own mother in preference to bottle-feeding (CD 227). A third option widely practiced in her day was having another woman nurse the baby. White warned that if this is necessary, the wet nurse needed to be physically and mentally healthy, because she "imparts her temper and her temperament to the nursing child" (HR, September 1871). White continues: "The child's life is linked to hers. If the hireling is a coarse type of woman, passionate, and unreasonable; if she is not careful in her morals, the nursling will be, in all probability, of the same, or a similar type. The same coarse quality of blood, coursing in the veins of the hireling nurse, is in that of the child." Some question the suggestion of the wet nurse affecting the moral character of the nursing child. The mechanisms by which moral or immoral character may be passed from parent to child are areas that scientific research is only beginning to explore.[58]

Statement 8, great difference in age of marriage partners: Marriages between "old men" and "young wives" result in men living longer, but the wife's life may be shortened by the burden of caring for an aging husband (2SM 423, 424). This first counsel seems to be little more than attaching moral responsibility to issues of common sense. In the case of the husband being markedly older than the wife, men live longer when happily married and well cared for. The burden of caring for an elderly husband is often extremely wearing on the wife, and she can age more rapidly under this stress.

In a related counsel, Ellen White says that when young men marry older women, their children may be born with physical and mental weaknesses (*ibid.* 424).[59] This was not as widely recognized in the nineteenth century, but is abundantly documented today. As a woman's age at childbearing increases, the likelihood of birth defects also increases. Down syndrome, whose characteristics mirror Ellen White's description, is now recognized to occur at a higher frequency in children born to older mothers. Other congenital problems, along with such issues as autism, appear at higher frequencies in children born to older parents.[60]

What is remarkable in this passage is that White links the detrimental effects on children with both combinations—older women who bear children by younger men and older men who father children by younger women. *Only since the turn of the twenty-first century has it been scientifically established that an aged father increases the risk of birth defects.*[61] A study published in *Human Reproduction* (July 2005) found that compared to a man below age 30, a man of 45 is almost three times more likely to father a child with Down syndrome. A man over 50 is almost five times more likely to father a Down's child and is twice as likely to have a child with a cleft lip. The risk begins to rise when the father's age is between 35 and 40.[62] It is now established that "advanced paternal age has been linked to a variety of diseases" and "congenital malformations."[63] On this topic White's counsel appears to have been in advance of scientific knowledge.

It should be noted that the statement about spouses of widely different ages does not suggest that such marriages are always ill-advised, but cautions that they should not be entered into hastily without carefully considering the potential results. The fact that she specifically approved three marriages of people close to her, despite rather wide differences in age, suggests that some other factors can outweigh the issue of age differences. *S. N. Haskell was 64 when he married *Hetty Hurd, 40 (RY 114, 115). *G. I. Butler at 68 desired to marry Lorena Waite, 33, and Ellen White favored the planned marriage. Others did not, however, and thwarted Butler's intentions (*ibid.* 115-120). Five years later, at 73, he married *Elizabeth Work Grainger, 61. It is probably significant that neither the Haskells nor the Butlers had children from their second marriage. On the other hand, *W. C. White was 40 when he married Ethel May Lacey, 21, and she bore him five children, the last when she was 38 and he was 59.[64]

Group Three, Statements 9-12: Partly or Largely Unconfirmed

The third group of statements to be considered are those that agreed with commonly accepted thinking at the time they were given but that remain partially or wholly unconfirmed by science in the twenty-first century, such as the causes of volcanoes, the height of antediluvians, amalgamation of humans and animals, and the physical effects of masturbation.

Statement 9, causes of earthquakes and volcanic eruptions: This item was written regarding the residual effects of the Noachian flood. "Immense forests," "buried in the earth," have since "become coal" and oil. When the subterranean coal and oil ignited, "rocks are intensely heated, limestone is burned, and iron ore melted. Water and fire under the surface of the earth meet. The action of water upon the limestone adds fury to the intense heat, and causes earthquakes, volcanoes, and fiery issues" (3SG 79, 80). No current theories of volcanism are known to support the precise geological mechanisms she describes, although there is support for several of her assertions. For instance, O. Stutzer's *Geology of Coal* documents that "subterranean fires in coal beds are ignited through spontaneous combustion, resulting in the melting of nearby rocks that are classed as pseudovolcanic deposits." Stutzer lists several examples, including "a burning mountain," an outcrop that "lasted over 150 years," and "the heat from one burning coal bed [that] was used for heating greenhouses in that area from 1837 to 1868."[65] More recently Glenn Stracher argued in *Geology of Coal Fires:*

Case Studies From Around the World that coal fires beneath the earth start through a spontaneous combustion process. The coal is exposed to air at low temperatures, and, through a slow oxidation process, eventually heats. As the temperature of the coal rises, the oxidation process speeds up exponentially and is likely to result in a full-scale coal fire.[66] Here she appears to have supported her message with information that was commonly accepted in her day, but that is now known to be incorrect in important particulars.

Statement 10, height of antediluvians and giant fossils: In 1864 White wrote that Adam was more than twice the height of modern men (3SG 34). The parallel passage in *Patriarchs and Prophets* (1890) makes the more moderate claim that Adam's height was "much greater" than that of men who now inhabit the earth (PP 45). These assertions were made on the basis of her visions. Later she added that "geologists claim" to have found "bones of men and animals, as well as instruments of warfare, petrified trees, et cetera, much larger than any that now exist," from which these geologists infer the existence of "a race of beings vastly superior in size" to humans today (*ibid.* 112). This appears to be an example of her using commonly accepted contemporary knowledge to make more vivid and credible what she had already asserted on the basis of her visions. However, the statement about fossil evidence is not asserted on the basis of revelation, but only reports the claims of contemporary geologists. Claims of evidence for giant fossils and humans are still made on the Internet today by serious researchers, and vehemently disputed by others. [67] For her views on creation and evolution, see the separate article "Bible and Earth Sciences."

Statement 11, amalgamation of man and beast (see also entry Amalgamation):[68] "If there was one sin above another which called for the destruction of the race by the flood, it was the base crime of amalgamation of man and beast which defaced the image of God, and caused confusion everywhere." Further: "The confused species which God did not create, which were the result of amalgamation, were destroyed by the flood. Since the flood there has been amalgamation of man and beast, as may be seen in the almost endless varieties of species of animals, and in certain races of men" (3SG 63, 75). These statements were reprinted in 1870 (1SP 69, 78), but omitted in 1890 when the section was revised for *Patriarchs and Prophets* (PP 81, 82; cf. 3SM 452).

The grammatical construction of these statements, their context, and Ellen White's other uses of the term "amalgamation" allow several possible interpretations. Amalgamation of man [with] beast implies (1) bestiality, a crime requiring the death of both humans and animals involved and was referred to in the King James Version as "confusion" (Lev. 20:15, 16; 18:23); and/or (2) genetic combination of human and animal genomes to create chimeras. Ellen White's reference to amalgamation as a "base crime," causing "confusion" of species, correlates closely with the KJV terminology and fulfills the main criteria of the immediate literary context.

F. D. Nichol has argued for an alternative grammatical reading, "amalgamation of man[,] and [amalgamation of] beast," referring on the human level to (3) mingling of races of men, specifically, the pre-Flood intermarriage of the righteous descendents of Seth with the "ungodly race of Cain" (3SG 60); and on the animal level to (4) production of "confused species" of animals "which God did not create" and which did not survive the Flood (dinosaurs) (see *ibid.* 53, 54, 60-64).[69] Views (3) and (4) do not seem to fit the commonly assumed connotations of the initial context as well as do views (1) and (2). However, views (3) and (4) are in harmony with White's later uses of "amalgamation." Referring to (5) the emergence of thorns and thistles (Gen. 3:18), she wrote: "Every noxious herb is of his [Satan's] sowing, and by his ingenious methods of amalgamation [malicious genetic engineering of plants] he has corrupted the earth with tares" (Ms 65, 1899, in 2SM 288; 1BC 1086; 16MR 247).[70] Finally, (6) she uses "amalgamation" in a moral sense to denote the moral declension of the righteous by association with the wicked. "By union with the world, the character of God's people becomes tarnished, and through amalgamation with the corrupt, the fine gold becomes dim" (RH, Aug. 23, 1892).

The most disturbing aspect of the amalgamation statements is their potentially racial implications. Two years after the first publication of the amalgamation statements, Adventist defectors B. F. Snook and W. H. Brinkerhoff published a pamphlet alleging that "these visions teach that the Negro race is *not human*" (italics in original) and not created by God.[71] In responding to Snook and Brinkerhoff, *Review* editor Uriah Smith denied the inference, pointing out that whatever race the amalgamation statements might refer to, they were still called "men," and thus human, not subhuman.[72] Smith seemed to concede that some "races of men now living" might actually be chimeras of humans and animals, citing unnamed naturalists as affirming that "the line of demarcation between the human and animal races is lost in confusion." Smith also gave the disclaimer that "in preparing these answers [to Snook and Brinkerhoff] we have had no consultation whatever with Sister White, nor received any suggestion or explanation from her on any point. We take the visions as they are published," he wrote, "and base our interpretation of any apparent discrepancy, on the language as it stands."[73]

Whatever she may have meant by the "amalgamation" passages, the interpretation that she viewed Blacks as less than fully human directly contradicts the entire tenor of her writings on race from 1851 to 1909. Over and over she reaffirmed both the full humanity (1SG 191; 1T 358) and the creation origin (7T 223) of the Black race. What follows is but a tiny sample of the hundreds of pages she wrote against racism, and in support of the full humanity of Blacks (see SW).[74]

In 1851, 13 years *before* she penned the amalgamation statements, she contrasted the "pious slave" who would "rise in triumph and victory and shake off the chains that bound him" with the "wicked master" who stood under the judgment of God (ExV 18; reprinted in EW 35). In 1858 she passionately defended the *humanity* of Africans in bondage: "The tears of the pious bond-men and bond-women, of fathers, mothers and children, brothers and sisters, are all bottled up in heaven. Agony, *human agony*, is carried from place to place, and bought and sold." With hot indignation she denounced "professed Christians" who "hold their *fellow-men* in slavery" and "cruelly oppress from day to day their *fellow-men*" (1SG 191; italics supplied; cf. EW 275, 276). In 1859 she charged Adventists to disregard the Fugitive Slave Law "whatever the consequences." "The slave is not the property of any man. God is his rightful master, and man has no right to take God's workmanship into his hands, and claim him as his own" (1T 201, 202).

In 1861 she concluded that the American Civil War was God's punishment on "this nation for the high crime of slavery" (*ibid.* 264). In 1863, still a year before the amalgamation statements, she declared: "Christ died for the whole human family, whether white or black. God has made man a free moral agent, whether white or black. The institution of slavery . . . permits man to exercise over his fellow man a power which God has never granted him, and which belongs alone to God" (*ibid.* 358). Two pages later she solemnly charged Adventists to disfellowship any of their number who clung to pro-slavery views (*ibid.* 360). On the contrary, she specifically declared Blacks to be equal with Whites "by creation and by redemption" (7T 223). "The black man's name is written in the book of life beside the white man's. All are one in Christ. Birth, station, nationality, or color cannot elevate or degrade men" (Ms 6, 1891, in 2SM 342).

Her hundreds of pages of passionate, pro-Black, anti-slavery writing certainly give strong evidence that, whatever she meant by the two brief enigmatic amalgamation statements, her belief in the full spiritual, moral, and intellectual equality of the Black race with all other humans is beyond question. According to Delbert Baker, one of the foremost scholars of Black Adventist history, "Ellen White can rightfully be called the initiator of the Black work. No person had a greater impact on the inclusion and status of Black people in the Adventist Church; it is impossible to talk about Black Adventist history without constantly referring to her contributions. . . . There would have been little hope for the Black work had Ellen White not championed the cause."[75]

Because one common denotation of the word "amalgamation" in nineteenth-century America was interracial marriage,[76] some have wondered if she viewed racial intermarriage as the sin so grievous that it brought on the Flood.[77] This interpretation is insupportable. She counseled against interracial marriage, not on the basis that it was inherently sinful, but on the grounds of the social difficulties it faced in a hostile, segregated, postslavery society—especially for the children, who, in that culture, often felt they were not fully accepted by either race (2SM 343, 344). But she did not criticize interracial marriage on moral or theological grounds (PP 383).

Because of the brevity and inherent ambiguity of the amalgamation statements, and the fact that Ellen White never publicly clarified her meaning, several of the interpretations given could be viable. From the perspective of current science, none of them is unreasonable. Human-animal genetic chimeras are routinely made today in molecular biology labs.[78] More controversial are chimeras made of cells from human and animal embryos.[79] Ironically, the problem with Ellen White's amalgamation statements from a scientific perspective is not that they may not be true, but that there are so many ways they could be true that it is difficult to figure out exactly what she may have meant.

Statement 12, masturbation: Ellen White repeatedly warned against this practice, describing its potential consequences to physical, mental, and moral health (see 2T 347, 361, 391, 392, 402-410, 469, 470, 481; 4T 97; 5T 78, 91; CG 444, 445, 457, 458).[80] An important issue is the exact meaning of Ellen White's language. She did not use the word "masturbation," which has a precise definition. In using the Victorian euphemisms "secret vice," "solitary vice," and "self-abuse," did she mean occasional masturbation, or primarily habitual, compulsive masturbation? Some of her language indicates a repetitive, habitual "practice" (ApM 18). If she meant compulsive masturbation, then some of her descriptions regarding its physical effects resonate with what contemporary specialists say about sexual addiction.

According to therapist Robert Weiss, for example, frequent masturbation stimulates various chemical reactions in the body, "resulting in the overproduction of sex hormones and neurotransmitters." This situation creates a "big change of body chemistry." [81] Psychologist William M. Struthers, author of *Wired for Intimacy: How Pornography Hijacks the Male Brain*, states that "masturbation is playing with neurochemical fire" because it "affects one emotionally and neurologically." Citing several scientific studies, Struthers states that men who masturbate compulsively "suffer from depression, memory problems, lack of focus, concentration problems, fatigue, back pain, decreased erections, premature ejaculation, and pelvic or testicular pain." [82] Perhaps science is only beginning to discover the impact of compulsive masturbation on the physical being.

A noteworthy feature in Ellen White's counsel on masturbation is the number of times she used the word "mind," as though "more were involved in the mind than in the purely physical." [83] For example, she wrote that "impure thoughts seize and control the imagination and fascinate the mind" and the "mind takes pleasure in contemplating scenes which awaken the lower and baser passions." This results in a "corrupt imagination." Thus, "the first work of reform is to purify the imagination." The "mind" should "be stimulated in favor of the right" (see *ibid.* 1-32; SG 434-468; and 2T 346-411, 468-471). This emphasis on the thought processes finds particular relevance for twenty-first-century Christians living in a culture "saturated with porn." [84]

Other factors by which masturbation could affect mental health range from excessive expenditure of nervous energy to nutritional deficiencies. An authority on zinc in nutrition, C. C. Pfeifer, Ph.D., M.D., wrote, "We hate to say it, but in a zinc-deficient adolescent, sexual excitement and excessive masturbation might precipitate insanity." [85] Another researcher, D. F. Harrobin, M.D., Ph.D., agreed: "It is even possible, given the importance of zinc for the brain, that nineteenth-century moralists were correct when they said that repeated masturbation could make one mad [insane]!" [86]

Regarding the effect of masturbation on *moral and spiritual development*, the teaching of Christ that lustful thoughts constitute a violation of the seventh commandment (Matt. 5:28), surely has implications for the habitual practice of masturbation.

The point White is most ridiculed for is her statements about the potential effects of masturbation on *physical health*. In her first discussion on the subject—*Appeal to Mothers* (1864)—she wrote, for example, that its continued practice can affect "the liver and lungs" and cause "neuralgia, rheumatism, affection of the spine, diseased kidneys, and cancerous humors" (ApM 18). [87] Elsewhere she wrote that it can damage the eyes and muscles, causing fatigue, headache, and diseases of almost every description (2T 402, 404, 481; CG 444). "Solitary vice," she wrote in 1876, "is killing thousands and tens of thousands" (4T 97). Critics argue that modern science has not confirmed any of these claims and that Ellen White was thus a child of her time, mirroring the physicians and moralists of her day who believed incorrectly that "solitary vice" was responsible for most physical and mental ailments. [88]

Although it is true that there are many similarities between Ellen White's teaching on masturbation and the physicians of her day, there are significant differences. [89] For example, nowhere in her counsel on secret vice did she ever advocate the extreme forms of cure used by physicians, such as circumcision, chastity belts, strong medications, and clitoridectomies.

Neither did she ever recommend the wearing of bandages on the sexual organs at night or tying the hands to the bedpost.[90] Her remedies were simple: a healthy diet, exercise, repentance, proper parental supervision, and avoidance of sexually stimulating literature.[91]

To date, however, no scientific research has connected masturbation to diseased organs, cancer, or deaths. In the absence of clear scientific evidence supporting Ellen White's statements on the physical results of masturbation, there are at least two interpretive options among students of Ellen White. One option is to consider both Ellen White's counsel and her explanation to be essentially correct, in the expectation that advancing science will eventually confirm that she was right. On several major health issues—including tobacco as a cause of cancer, the advantages of a vegetarian diet, and the dangers of older men conceiving children—her counsel initially appeared to be wrong but eventually was found to be true.

A second interpretive option would be to distinguish between the instruction and the explanation, considering the instruction true, but that she supported it from contemporary sources that overstated its consequences. This opinion would argue that just as she eventually revised certain historical details in *The Great Controversy* to conform to better historical data, so she might have updated some of her statements on the physical results of masturbation had she still been writing when better information was available. Some would cite, in support of this perspective, that her later works introduce subtle advances in her thought. For example, although *The Ministry of Healing* (1905) mentions "vice" in contexts parallel to those of her earlier statements (MH 227), the explicit reference to masturbation and the lists of resulting diseases are both absent. This interpretive option would see her counsel on masturbation as an example of her adopting commonly accepted ideas to reinforce sound counsel. Even if Ellen White's *explanation* of the physical effects of masturbation could be shown to be overdrawn, the basic *instruction* remains valid: for Christians who are striving for holiness, masturbation represents a self-centered indulgence that falls short of God's ideal, and as such is morally and spiritually detrimental.[92] Further, if spiritual and mental health directly influence physical health, then it follows that the addictive practice of self-stimulated sex would also be detrimental to physical health.

Conclusion

The three interpretive premises offered at the beginning of this article can account for the 12 statements that are the focus of this article: First, Scripture portrays an infallible God communicating eternal truths in imperfect human language, through prophets who were neither infallible nor inerrant. The result is "treasure in earthen vessels," eternal, immutable truths contained in imperfect, transient human language and thought forms. Second, because human knowledge in all fields is continually changing, statements of *human knowledge* in any historical context will eventually be seen as incomplete and imperfect, despite their *inspired adaptation* to the needs of the original audience. Third, the *inspired instruction*, because it is based on eternal principles, has enduring value, even if supported by *human explanations* adapted to the original audience—*human explanations* that because of time and change will eventually be less convincing to later generations.

Thus Adventists believe that Ellen White's basic *instruction* to her readers was good advice for the circumstances in which it was given. Even in cases in which the *explanation* might retrospectively seem dated, the *instruction* was valid, and readers who followed it in a commonsense manner would have benefited from so doing. G. E. Fraser, medical researcher at Loma Linda University, has documented more than 300 peer-reviewed publications in scientific literature, showing that individuals who follow White's health teachings—whether or not they fully understand all the reasons behind those teachings—have significantly longer life expectancy and less chronic disease than the general population. [93]

---

[1] William G. Rothstein, *American Physicians in the Nineteenth Century: From Sects to Science* (Baltimore: Johns Hopkins University Press, 1972), pp. 45-55, 194, 261-266.

[2] On the distinction between canonical and noncanonical prophetic authority, see Jud Lake, *Ellen White Under Fire* (PPPA, 2010), chap. 8.

[3] J. Moon, *W. C. White and Ellen G. White, the Relationship Between the Prophet and the Son* (AUP, 1993), pp. 427-436.

[4] "What human power can do divine power is not summond to do" (DA 535).

[5] See Lake, chapters 5 and 6, on the vertical and horizontal aspects of revelation-inspiration. For a biblical illustration of the combination of revealed and common knowledge, see 1 Corinthians 1:10-17. Believers accept the whole passage as inspired and theologically authoritative (see especially verse 17). But verses 11, 12 include common information gained from Chloe's family, and verses 14 and 16 are based on Paul's personal memory. Interestingly, Paul's lapse of memory between verses 14 and 16 actually strengthens his argument: the fact that he couldn't remember whom he had baptized adds credibility to his claim that "baptizing" was not his primary mission (verse 17).

[6] W. C. White to Our General Missionary Agents, July 24, 1911; W. C. White to Members of the Publication Committee, July 25, 1911, EGWE-GC; WCW, "The Great Controversy—1911 Edition: A Statement Made by W. C. White before the General Conference Council, October 30, 1911," Appendix A, in 3SM 433-444.

[7] "Flashlight pictures" denotes an early type of flash photography; i.e., the "pictures" were analogous to photographs.

[8] WCW to Our General Missionary Agents, July 24, 1911.

[9] WCW, "The Visions of Ellen G. White," Dec. 17, 1905, p. 5, SDoc.

[10] WCW to S. N. Haskell, Oct. 31, Nov. 4, 1912; W. C. White to W. W. Eastman, Nov. 4, 1912.

[11] WCW to S. N. Haskell, Oct. 31, 1912; for background on this letter, see George R. Knight, "The Case of the Overlooked Postscript: A Footnote on Inspiration," *Ministry,* August 1997.

[12] WCW to S. N. Haskell, Oct, 31, 1912.

[13] WCW to S. N. Haskell, Nov. 4, 1912. (Italics supplied.) W. C. White to W. W. Eastman, Nov. 4, 1912.

[14] WCW to W. W. Eastman, Nov. 4, 1912. (Italics supplied.)

[15] *Ibid.* (Italics supplied.)

[16] See Lake, chapter 11, on the "big picture" in Ellen White's writings.

[17] Moon, pp. 429-436.

[18] See Lake, chapter 11, on the "big picture" in Ellen White's writings.

[19] David Neff, "Ellen White's Theological and Literary Indebtedness to Calvin Stowe" (research paper, 1979, CAR); quoted in Robert W. Olson, *101 Questions on the Sanctuary and on Ellen White* (EGWE, 1981), pp. 104, 105. For examples in the field of health, Don S. McMahon noted that Ellen White changed incorrect contemporary statements about health into correct statements by changes in wording. Don S. McMahon, *Acquired or Inspired? Exploring the Origins of the Adventist Lifestyle* (Victoria, Australia: Signs Pub. Co., 2005), p. 141; cf. p. 116.

[20] For example, the book of Revelation was written as as revealed truth about the conflict between God and Satan; it was not written as a textbook on Greek grammar.

[21] Prophetic messages were given for success in real life (Deut. 6:6-9; 2 Chron. 20:20), for "practical purposes" (1SM 20). Accordingly, Ellen White makes frequent appeals to "common sense" in matters of health, religion, and all of life (CT 257; Ed 220; Ev 540). "The Bible with its precious gems of truth was not written for the scholar alone. On the contrary, it was designed for the common people; and *the interpretation given by the common people, when aided by the Holy Spirit, accords best with the truth as it is in Jesus*" (5T 331; italics supplied). To assume a technical meaning where none was intended may lead to a misunderstanding of the prophetic message.

[22] She adamantly disclaimed both infallibility and inerrancy. "In regard to infallibility, I never claimed it; God alone is infallible. His word is true, and in Him is no variableness, or shadow of turning" (Lt 10, 1895,

quoted in 1SM 37). "I wish that self should be hid in Jesus. I wish self to be crucified. I do not claim infallibility, or even perfection of Christian character. I am not free from mistakes and errors in my life. Had I followed my Savior more closely, I should not have to mourn so much my unlikeness to His dear image" (Lt 27, 1876, in DG 272). One example of fallibility would be mistakes in child training that were afterward pointed out to her through visions (EGW, "Testimony for James and Ellen White's Family," no date, Ms 8, 1862; EGW, "Testimony Regarding James and Ellen White," June 6, 1863, Ms 1, 1863). Another example of fallibility would be an incident on October 19, 1902. In council with General Conference president A. G. Daniells and other church officers, Ellen White approved their plan to close the Southern Publishing Association in Nashville because of its indebtedness and continuing financial losses. The following night she had a vision reproving her for giving erroneous counsel based on incomplete information. She immediately wrote Daniells a letter reporting her vision and retracting the counsel she had given. He was perplexed, but recalled the experience of Nathan and David in 1 Chronicles 17:1-4. For three nights in succession she had visions instructing her about that mistake and explaining why she had made it (see 5Bio 191-197; Moon, pp. 381-389).

[23] Don S. McMahon, "Probability," in *Acquired or Inspired? Exploring the Origins of the Adventist Lifestyle* (Warburton, Australia: Signs, 2005), pp. 122-138.

[24] See G. E. Fraser, *Diet, Life Expectancy, and Chronic Disease: Studies of Seventh-day Adventists and Other Vegetarians* (Oxford: Oxford University Press, 2003), pp. viii, 47, 58.

[25] "That which was truth in the beginning is truth now. Although new and important truths appropriate for succeeding generations have been opened to the understanding, the present revealings do not contradict those of the past. Every new truth understood only makes more significant the old" (RH, Mar. 2, 1886; cf. GC 297).

[26] For example, since 1930, when Pluto was discovered, there had been nine known planets in earth's solar system. That number changed with the discovery of Xena, a planetlike object slightly larger than Pluto. Rather than recognize 12 or more planets of diminishing size, the International Astronomical Union wrote a formal definition of "planet" that leaves only eight. Pluto and several similar-sized objects are now called dwarf planets (J. Adler, in *Newsweek*, Sept. 4, 2006).

[27] Leonard R. Brand ("Do Rabbits Chew the Cud?" *Origins* 4, no. 2 [1977]: 102-104) argues convincingly that rabbits' reingestion of feces to complete the process of digestion is biologically analogous to the cud-chewing of cattle, sheep, and deer. Nevertheless, he admits that when rabbits reingest feces "they apparently swallow [them] whole, without chewing." He is correct that Leviticus 11:6 should not be regarded as an error. It still stands, however, as an example of inspired instruction that was presented not in modern scientific terms, but in simple language adapted to the common knowledge of those to whom it was given.

[28] Roger W. Coon, Andrews University lecture outline, "Ellen G. White, Science, and Faith: Part I, the 'Problem' Statements," rev. May 9, 1995, pp. 13, 14, in CAR.

[29] See Leonard Brand and Don S. McMahon, *The Prophet and Her Critics* (PPPA, 2005).

[30] In order to protect human freedom of choice, God does not overwhelm humans with irrefutable proof of the reasonableness of His instructions. Instead, He promises that those who freely choose to do His will will have sufficient information to act on (John 7:17). He provides sufficient evidence on which to believe, but not so much as to make belief coercive or doubt impossible. Thus Ellen White advocated an intelligent faith, based not on unquestionable proof, but on the "weight of evidence" (DA 458).

[31] See Elisabeth McClellan, *History of American Costume 1607-1870* (New York: Tudor Pub. Co., 1969), pp. 486, 487, for a detailed description of the "chignon," also called a "waterfall."

[32] "The False Hair Industry," *The Watchman*, August 1910.

[33] In January of that same year the *Health Reformer* reported an incident of a woman who wore a jute switch and experienced burrowing parasites in her scalp. Quoting the Marshall *Statesman* and the Springfield (Mass.) *Republican*, the article stated: "The lady has consulted several physicians, but without help; and has used every application which seemed to promise relief, but entirely in vain. She is represented as nearly crazy from the terrible suffering, and from the prospect of the horrible death which physicians do not seem able to avert" (HR, January 1871). In her work with the HR, Ellen White was no doubt familiar with this story and most likely had it in mind when she wrote of "many" who had "lost their reason" and "become hopelessly insane" (HR, October 1871).

[34] Because of certain terminology Ellen White used in this article, such as "animal organs" and "unnatural heat" in relationship to the brain, some have conjectured that she believed in phrenology (see *Phrenology). Although she may have shared some vocabulary with phrenologists, there is no indication in her writings that she ever believed in phrenology. For discussion on this issue, see "A Critique of the Book Prophetess of Health," prepared by the staff of the Ellen G. White Estate, pp. 69, 70, online at www.whiteestate.org/issues/prophetess-of-health.pdf.

[35] Note a contemporary description of acute lead poisoning: "Neurological signs of acute poisoning typically are: paraesthesiae, pain, muscle weakness, encephalopathy (rare) with headache, convulsions, delirium, and coma" (J.M.S. Pearce, "Burton's Line in Lead Poisoning," *European Neurology* 57, no. 2: [2007]: 119). See also L. L. Brunton, D. Blumenthal, I. Buxton, K. L. Parker, eds., "Principles of Toxicology," in *Goodman and Gilman's Manual of Pharmacology and Therapeutics* (McGraw-Hill, 2008), p. 1131.

[36] See J. J. Du Mortier, "Lead Poisoning," *Yale Journal of Biology and Medicine* 2, no. 2 (December 1929): 149, for a similar description of palsy resulting from lead poisoning.

[37] "Brief History of Beauty and Hygiene Products," Duke University, online at http://library.duke.edu/digital collections/adaccess/cosmetics.html; Thomas Oliver, *Lead Poisoning: From the Industrial, Medical, and Social Points of View* (New York: Paul B. Hoeber, 1914), pp. 113, 114. In 1925 lead poisoning still resulted from using cosmetics, according to Joseph C. Aub, Lawrence T. Fairhall, A. S. Minot, and Paul Reznikoff, "Lead Poisoning," *Medicine* 4, nos. 1-2 (1925): 4-8. See also http://en.wikipedia.org/wiki/Lead poisoning, "History," accessed Jan. 15, 2012.

[38] See Du Mortier, "Lead Poisoning," and Rebeca C. Gracia and Wayne R. Snodgrass, "Lead Toxicity and Chelation Therapy," *The American Journal of Health-System Pharmacy* 64 (Jan. 1, 2007): 49.

[39] Erica E. Goode, "Putting the Lid on Dangerous Dinnerware," *U.S. News and World Report*, Aug. 10, 1987; see also note 37.

[40] Transcript of "News From Medicine" feature broadcast on Cable Network News Television, Sunday, Sept. 18, 1988, 8:30 p.m. EDT; see also "News From Congressman Ron Wyden," opening statement of chairman Ron Wyden (D-Oreg.) at a hearing on cosmetics health and safety issues before the small business subcommittee on regulation and business opportunities, Sept. 15, 1988; and "Cosmetic Safety: The Law Provides Little Protection," *Consumer Reports*, February 1991, p. 93; all cited in Coon.

[41] See, for example, Ruth Winter, *A Consumer's Dictionary of Cosmetic Ingredients, Seventh Edition: Complete Information About the Harmful and Desirable Ingredients Found in Cosmetics and Cosmeceuticals* (New York: Three Rivers Press, 2009); and Siobhan O'Connor and Alexandra Spunt, *No More Dirty Looks: The Truth About Your Beauty Products—and the Ultimate Guide to Safe and Clean Cosmetics* (Cambridge, Mass.: Da Capo Lifelong Books, 2010).

[42] "Lamarckism," in http://en.wikipedia.org/wiki/Lamarckism, accessed Dec. 29, 2011. "In biology, and specifically genetics, epigenetics is the study of heritable changes in gene expression or cellular phenotype, caused by mechanisms other than changes in the underlying DNA sequence—hence the name epi (Greek: επί, over, above, outer) genetics. . . . It refers to functionally relevant modifications to the genome that do not involve a change in the nucleotide sequence" (http://en.wikipedia.org/wiki/Epigenetics, accessed Dec. 29, 2011).

[43] Curt Wohleber, "From Cheese to Cheese Food," *Invention and Technology*, Summer 2001.

[44] Stanley Scheindlin, "The Food and Drug Legislation of 1906," *Molecular Interventions*, 8, no. 1 (February 2008): 5, 6; Otto L. Bettman, *The Good Old Days—They Were Terrible!* (New York: Random House, 1974), chaps. 7, 8.

[45] Carol White, "How Pasteurization Works," online at http://science.howstuffworks.com/environmental/life/cellular-microscopic/pasteurization.htm/printable; Wohleber.

[46] Grace Jacques with Patricia B. Mutch, "Dinner at Elmshaven," ed. Sylvia Fagal (2002), pp. 3, 13, 14, 17, 19, CAR.

[47] Arthur White to Brother ——, Nov. 11, 1940, in White Estate Q-A 22-C-1, quoting E. G. White and W. C. White. We are indebted to Denis Kaiser for the actual German translation of *The Ministry of Healing*: "*Strenger, scharfer Käse sollte nicht genossen werden*" (Strong, sharp cheese should not be eaten [lit., enjoyed, indulged]). *In den Fußspuren des großen Arztes* (Hamburg: Internationale Traktatgesellschaft, 1907), p. 306.

[48] Neal Nedley, M.D., *Proof Positive* (Ardmore, Okla.: Nedley, 1999), pp. 275, 276, 295.

[49] Neal Barnard, "Trends in Food Availability, 1909-2007," *American Journal of Clinical Nutrition* 91, suppl. (2010): 1530S-1536S; cited by Sylvia M. Fagal in review of *The Full Plate Diet*, in *Adventist Review*, Dec. 9, 2010.

[50] Reprinted from *How to Live*, no. 1, p. 58 (1865).

[51] For discussion, see Roy Gane, "Leviticus, Numbers," in *The NIV Application Commentary: From Biblical Text to Contemporary Life*, ed. Terry Muck (Grand Rapids: Zondervan, 2004), pp. 234-237.

[52] Roland K. Harrison, "Leper; Leprosy," *International Standard Bible Encyclopedia*, ed. Geoffery W. Bromiley (Grand Rapids: Eerdmans, 1986), vol. 3, pp. 104, 105; see also Coon, pp. 10, 11.

[53] Herbert William Morris, *Testimony of the Ages: or, Confirmations of the Scriptures* (1883), pp. 185, 186, quotes several sources, including Kitto, Michaelis, Plutarch, Pliny, and Smith's *Dictionary of the Bible*, pp. 3345, 3346.

[54] Robert Jamieson, A. R. Fausset, and David Brown, *Commentary, Critical and Explanatory, on the Whole Bible* (1871); online at www.biblestudytools.com/commentaries/jamieson-fausset-brown.

[55] R. L. Foster et al.,"Effect of Diet on Growth of *M. Lepre* in Mouse Footpads" (Leprosy Research Foundation, Loma Linda, Calif.), in *Indian Journal of Leprosy* 61, no. 3 (July 1989); see also R. L. Foster, et al., "Nutrition in Leprosy: A Review," in *International Journal of Leprosy* 56, no. 1 (1988): 66-68.

[56] See B. M. Clark, C. K. Murray, L. L. Horvath, et al., "Case-control Study of Armadillo Contact and Hansen's Disease," *American Journal of Tropical Medicine and Hygiene* 78, no. 6 (June 2008): 962-967; Richard Truman, "Armadillos as a Source of Infection for Leprosy," *Southern Medical Journal* 101, no. 6 (June 2008): 581, 582; S. Bruce, T. M. Schroeder, K. Ellner, et al., "Armadillo Exposure and Hansen's Disease: an Epidemiologic Survey in Southern Texas," *Journal of the American Academy of Dermatology* 43, no. 1 (2000): 223-228; Coon, pp. 11, 32-34.

[57] For a discussion on pork as one of the foods highest in saturated fat, see David Mendosa, "What's Wrong With Saturated Fat," www.healthcentral.com/diabetes/c/17/7868/whats-wrong-fat; see also "Cholesterol: List of Foods High in Cholesterol Content," online at www.dietaryfiberfood.com/cholesterol-high-avoid.php.

[58] See, for example, Ruth Feldman, Charles W. Greenbaum, and Nurit Yirmiya, "Mother-Infant Affect Synchrony as an Antecedent of the Emergence of Self-Control," in *Developmental Psychology* 35, no. 5 (1999): 223-231.

[59] Reprinted from *How to Live*, no. 2, p. 29 (1865).

[60] Lisa A. Croen, Daniel V. Najjar, Bruce Fireman, and Judith K. Grether, "Maternal and Paternal Age Risk of Autism Spectrum Disorders," *Archives of Pediatrics and Adolescent Medicine* 161, no. 4 (2007): 334-340.

[61] Thacker, "Biological Clock Ticks for Men, Too: Genetic Defects Linked to Sperm of Older Father," *Journal of the American Medical Association* 291 (2004): 1683-1685; cf. *New England Journal of Medicine* 347, no. 18 (Oct. 31, 2002): 1449-1451.

[62] J. Hope, "Birth Defect Risk 'Rises With Age of the Father,'" London *Daily Mail*, July 21, 2005, online at www.ndss.org/content.cfm?fuseaction=NwsEvt.Article&art.

[63] M. Lauritsen, C. Pedersen, and P. Mortensen, "Effects of Familial Risk Factors and Place of Birth on the Risk of Autism: a Nationwide Register-based Study," *Journal of Child Psychology and Psychiatry* 46, no. 9 (2005): 967.

[64] Francis White, born Sept. 29, 1913.

[65] O. Stutzer, *Geology of Coal* (Chicago: University of Chicago Press, 1940), pp. 309, 310; cf. E. E. Thurlow, "Western Coal," *Mining Engineering* 26 (1974): 30-33; and G. S. Rogers, "Baked Shale and Slag Formed by the Burning of Coal Beds," *U.S. Geological Survey Professional Paper*, 108-A (1918); all cited in Johns, "Ellen G. White and Subterranean Fires, Part 2," *Ministry*, October 1977.

[66] Glenn Stracher, *Geology of Coal Fires: Case Studies From Around the World* (Boulder, Colo.: Geological Society of America, 2007).

[67] See, e.g., "Giant Humans and Dinosaurs, online at www.biblebelievers.org.au/giants.htm; cf. www.aska biologist.org.uk/answers/viewtopic.php?id=1220.

[68] We are indebted to Michael W. Campbell and Timothy G. Standish for some of the material in this section; see also the entry Amalgamation in the topical section of this encyclopedia.

[69] Cf. F. D. Nichol, *Ellen G. White and Her Critics* (RHPA, 1951), pp. 306-322; *idem*, "Amalgamation: Ellen G. White Statements Regarding Conditions at the Time of the Flood," www.egwestate.org/issues/amalg.html.

[70] Nichol, *Ellen G. White and Her Critics*, pp. 306-322.

[71] B. F. Snook and W. H. Brinkerhoff, *The Visions of Mrs. E. G. White Not of God* (Cedar Rapids, Iowa: Cedar Valley Times Book and Job Print, 1866), p. 9. This pamphlet must have been released early in 1866 because Uriah Smith began responding to it in the *Advent Review and Sabbath Herald*, June 12, 1866. In 7T 223 E. G. White explicitly affirmed the creation origin of Blacks.

[72] Uriah Smith, "The Visions—Objections Answered: Obj. 37," RH, July 31, 1866.

[73] Uriah Smith, "Objections to the Visions," RH, June 12, 1866.

[74] Cf. Ronald D. Graybill, *E. G. White and Church Race Relations* (1970).

[75] Delbert W. Baker, "In Search of Roots: Adventist African-Americans, Part 1, Exploring the History," in *Adventist Review*, Feb. 4, 1993. Baker's statement here is based on the conclusions of his doctoral dissertation, *The Dynamics of Communication and African-American Progress in the Seventh-day Adventist Organization: A Historical Descriptive Analysis* (Ph.D. thesis, Howard University, 1993; Ann Arbor, Mich.: University Microfilms International, 1993).

[76] See, for example, Elizabeth Cary Agassiz, ed., letters from Dr. S. G. Howe to Louis Agassiz, Portsmouth, Aug. 3 and 10, 1863, in *Louis Agassiz: His Life and Correspondence* (chap. 20), online at www.gutenberg.org/dirs/etext04/agass10.txt; see also John Campbell, *Negro-Mania: Being an Examination of the Falsely Assumed Equality of the Various Races of Men* (Philadelphia: Campbell and Power, 1851), p. 11.

[77] There is a rich literature espousing this view around the time Ellen White wrote. See, for example, Ariel [Buckner H. Payne], *The Negro: What Is His Ethnological Status?* 2nd ed. (Cincinnati: The Proprietor, 1867), p. 31.

[78] For a spectacular example, see Aideen O'Doherty, Sandra Ruf, Claire Mulligan, Victoria Hildreth, Mick L. Errington, Sam Cooke, Abdul Sesay, Sonie Modino, Lesley Vanes, Diana Hernandez, Jacqueline M. Linehan, Paul T. Sharpe, Sebastian Brandner, Timothy V. P. Bliss, Deborah J. Henderson, Dean Nizetic, Victor L. J. Tybulewicz, and Elizabeth M. C. Fisher, "An Aneuploid Mouse Strain Carrying Human Chromosome 21 With Down Syndrome Phenotypes," *Science* 309 (Sept. 23, 2005): 2033-2037.

[79] *Kennedy Institute of Ethics Journal* 15, no. 2: 107-134, *Nature* 431: 885. The Human Fertilisation and Embryology Authority statement on its decision regarding hybrid embryos. Sept. 5, 2007, online at For a www.hfea.gov.uk/en/1581.html.

[80] For a complete listing of EGW statements on this issue, see "Ellen G. White Statements Concerning Secret Vice in Chronological Sequence" (1951; 65 pp.).

[81] Robert Weiss, "Understanding Compulsive Masturbation," on line at www.sexualrecovery.com/resources/articles/understanding-compulsive-masturbation.php.

[82] William M. Struthers, *Wired for Intimacy: How Pornography Hijacks the Male Brain* (Downers Grove,

Ill.: IVP Books, 2009), pp. 169, 172; see also Patrick J. Carnes, "Cybersex, Courtship, and Escalating Arousal: Factors in Addictive Sexual Desire," *Sexual Addiction and Compulsivity* 8, no. 1 (2001): 45-78; Al Cooper, David L. Delmonico, Eric Griffin-Shelley and Robin M. Mathy, "Online Sexual Activity: An Examaination of Potentially Problematic Behaviors," *Sexual Addiction and Compulsivity* 11, no. 3 (2004): 129-143; and G. Holstege, J. R. Georgiadis, A. M. Paans, L. C. Meiners, F. H. van der Graaf and A. A. Reinders, "Brain Activation During Human Male Ejaculation," *Journal of Neuroscience* 23, no. 27 (Oct. 8, 2003); 9185-9193.

[83] Alberta Mazat, *That Friday in Eden: Sharing and Enhancing Sexuality in Marriage* (PPPA, 1981), pp. 146, 147.

[84] See Struthers, "Saturated With Porn," pp. 19-39; and Michael Leahy, *Porn Nation* (Chicago: Northfield Publishing, 2008).

[85] C. C. Pfeifer, Ph.D., M.D., *Zinc and Other Micro-nutrients* (New Canaan, Conn.: Keats, 1978), p. 45.

[86] D. F. Horrobin, M.D., Ph.D., ed., *Zinc* (St. Albans, Vt.: Vitabooks, 1981), p. 8.

[87] According to the publishers, Ellen White did not read from "other works on the subject" until after the completion of this book (APM 4). Nevertheless, her thoughts mirror the medical authorities of the day.

[88] Some of the influential physicians of the day who discussed masturbation were Sylvester A. Graham, *A Lecture to Young Men on Chasity* (Providence: Weeden and Cory, 1834); Edward H. Dixon, *A Treatise on Diseases of the Sexual Organs* (New York: Burgess, Stringer, and Co., 1845); and John H. Kellogg, *Plain Facts for Old and Young* (Burlington, Iowa: I. F. Signer, 1882).

[89] For a comparison of the similarities and dissimilarities between the teaching of Ellen White and her contemporaries on masturbation, see Eric Bahme, "Ellen G. White and the History of Self-Abuse" (term paper, Seventh-day Adventist Theological Seminary, AU, Berrien Springs, Mich., 1987), pp. 22, 23, CAR.

[90] For discussion of the nineteenth-century concern over masturbation and the type of medical treatments used, see Frederick M. Hodges, "The Antimasturbation Crusade in Antebellum American Medicine," in *Journal of Sexual Medicine* 2 (2005): 722-731; Phillip A. Gibbs, "Self-control and Male Sexuality in the Advice Literature of Nineteenth-Century America, 1830-1860," *Journal of American Culture* 9 (1986): 37-41; James Whorton, "The Solitary Vice: The Superstition that Masturbation Could Cause Mental Illness," *Western Journal of Medicine* 175 (July 2001): 66-68; Brian Strong, "Sex, Character, and Reform in America, 1830-1920" (unpublished Ph.D. dissertation, Stanford University, 1972), pp. 36, 37; and Bahme, pp. 8-13, 23.

[91] Bahme, pp. 22, 23.

[92] Several popular Christian works resonate with Ellen White's general counsel against masturbation. See, for example, D. R. Heimbach, *True Sexual Morality* (Wheaton, Ill.: Crossway, 2004), pp. 222, 223; Stephen Arterburn and Fred Stoeker, *Every Man's Battle: Winning the War on Sexual Temptation One Victory at a Time* (Colorado Springs, Colo.: Waterbrook Press, 2000), pp. 112-114; and Shannon Ethridge, *Every Woman's Battle: Discovering God's Plan for Sexual and Emotional Fulfillment* (Colorado Springs, Colo.: Waterbrook Press, 2003), pp. 39-43.

[93] G. E. Fraser, *Diet, Life Expectancy, and Chronic Disease: Studies of Seventh-day Adventists and Other Vegetarians* (Oxford: Oxford university Press, 2003), pp. viii, 47, 58.

The Theology of Ellen G. White

Denis Fortin

Summarizing Ellen White's lifetime contributions at her funeral in 1915, A. G. Daniells, then president of the General Conference of Seventh-day Adventists, said, "No Christian teacher in this generation, no religious reformer in any preceding age, has placed a higher value upon the Bible. In all her writings it is represented as the book of all books, the supreme and all-sufficient guide for the whole human family. . . . Those who still believe that the Bible is the inspired, infallible word of the living God will value most highly the positive, uncompromising support given this view in the writings of Mrs. White" (LS 471, 472).

Daniells went on to list a number of highlights in her writings: "Christ is recognized and exalted as the only Savior of sinners," the gospel is the only means of salvation, the Holy Spirit is exalted as the heavenly teacher and guide sent to this world by Christ "to make *real* in the hearts and lives of men all that He had made *possible* by His death on the cross," the church instituted by Christ in the first century is the divine model of church order; through her writings Adventists received light and counsel "regarding vital questions that affect the betterment and [uplifting] of the human family," and "her writings present most comprehensive views regarding temperance reform, the laws of life and health" (*ibid.* 472, 473).

In conclusion he stated, "Perhaps we are not wise enough to say definitely just what part of Mrs. White's life work has been of the greatest value to the world, but it would seem that the large volume of biblical literature she has left would prove to be of the greatest service to mankind. . . . The many volumes she has left, dealing with every phase of human life, . . . will continue to mold public sentiment and individual character. Their messages will be cherished more than they have been in the past" (*ibid.* 475). Daniells' perspective on Ellen White's lifetime contribution and her writings reflects what many of her contemporaries expressed.

Ellen White did not receive any formal training in theological studies, and admittedly her numerous books did not form nor were they intended to be a complete systematic theology in which she expounded the meaning of various doctrines within a particular system of thought. Rather, her writings took basically two forms: an exposition and commentary on biblical narratives as found, for example, in her Conflict of the Ages Series,[1] and letters of counsels to church members or institutions as published in her *Testimonies for the Church* and other counsel books.

Many important figures in the history of the Christian church have had a ministry similar to Ellen White's. Though John Wesley never wrote a systematic theology, there is a sustained core to his theology around which revolve a number of key themes that he elaborated in his sermons, commentaries on Scripture, published journals, occasional pamphlets, and letters. The same can be said of Martin Luther, who as a prolific writer never wrote a systematic theology but nonetheless expressed his beliefs within a system of thought.

But admitting Ellen White's lack of theological training does not presuppose the absence of theological thinking on her part, for she readily expressed her thought within some definite theological categories. She employed theological themes to articulate her ideas, and she argued, at times forcefully, in favor of or against various doctrinal or theological concepts. For one thing, she did understand the importance of having a theological focus. For example, writing to pastors in 1901, she said, "The sacrifice of Christ as an atonement for sin is the great truth around which all other truths cluster. In order to be rightly understood and appreciated, every truth in the word of God, from Genesis to Revelation, must be studied in the light that streams from the cross of Calvary. I present before you the great, grand monument of mercy and regeneration, salvation and redemption—the Son of God uplifted on the cross. This is to be the foundation of every discourse given by our ministers" (Ms 70, 1901, in 20MR 336; cf. GW 315; Ed 125). Beyond the homiletical application of this reference to the importance of the sacrifice of Christ on Calvary, it is obvious that Ellen White understood that biblical doctrines are part of a broad system of interrelated beliefs, each doctrine having an impact upon other doctrines. Her corpus of writings bears the mark of a system of well-coordinated, biblically supported beliefs.

During her 70 years of ministry in the Seventh-day Adventist movement, Ellen White repeatedly engaged in doctrinal and theological discussions and controversies and took definite stands against some heresies or aberrant doctrines advocated by ministers or church leaders. She understood well the theological implications of J. H. Kellogg's pantheistic views in the early 1900s when she affirmed the personhood of God and that although "things of nature are an expression of God's character; . . . we are not to regard nature as God" (8T 263). "These [pantheistic] theories," she further explained, "followed to their logical conclusion, sweep away the whole Christian economy. They do away with the necessity for the atonement and make man his own savior. These theories regarding God make His Word of no effect, and those who accept them are in great danger of being led finally to look upon the whole Bible as a fiction" (*ibid.* 291).

As Seventh-day Adventist doctrines developed during the nineteenth century, people began to use the expressions "landmark doctrines" or "pillars" to refer to the core distinctive Adventist beliefs. During the heated debates of the General Conference session of 1888, delegates disputed the correct identification of one of the 10 horns of Daniel 7:7 and the identity of the "schoolmaster" law in Galatians 3:24. While strongly urging a broader study of the Bible, Ellen White deeply deplored the lack of Christian courtesy exemplified in these discussions. She became particularly troubled when some of the older ministers, as a means of closing the discussion, used the argument that all delegates should "stand by the old landmarks" and not accept any new views. In a manuscript written shortly after the session she reflected on what had happened and on her understanding of the meaning of the old landmarks. Her thoughts indicate that she had a theological understanding of these doctrines and that she was able to differentiate between core doctrines and secondary teachings. George Knight notes that these " 'landmark' doctrines were the nonnegotiables in Adventist theology. Adventists had carefully studied each of them in the Bible, and collectively they had provided the Sabbatarian Adventists and later the Seventh-day Adventists with an identity."[2]

"In Minneapolis God gave precious gems of truth to His people in new settings," she wrote. "This light from heaven by some was rejected with all the stubbornness the Jews manifested in rejecting Christ, and there was much talk about standing by the old landmarks. But there was evidence they knew not what the old landmarks were. There was evidence and there was reasoning from the word that commended itself to the conscience; but the minds of men were fixed, sealed against the entrance of light, because they had decided it was a dangerous error removing the 'old landmarks' when it was not moving a peg of the old landmarks, but they had perverted ideas of what constituted the old landmarks." (Ms 13, 1889, in CW 30).

Then she listed what she regarded as the "old landmarks": "The passing of the time in 1844 was a period of great events, opening to our astonished eyes the cleansing of the sanctuary transpiring in heaven, and having decided relation to God's people upon the earth, [also] the first and second angel's messages and the third, unfurling the banner on which was inscribed, 'The commandments of God and the faith of Jesus.' One of the landmarks under this message was the temple of God, seen by His truth-loving people in heaven, and the ark containing the law of God. The light of the Sabbath of the fourth commandment flashed its strong rays in the pathway of the transgressors of God's law. The nonimmortality of the wicked is an old landmark. I can call to mind nothing more that can come under the head of the old landmarks" (*ibid.*).

Five landmark doctrines emerge from this list. The first is the cleansing of the sanctuary in heaven and the distinctive Adventist emphasis on Christ's intercessory ministry. The efficacy of the work of Christ on the cross, His complete sacrifice of atonement, prepared the way for His work of intercession since His ascension and His additional work of cleansing starting in 1844. In Ellen White's thought: "The intercession of Christ in man's behalf in the sanctuary above is as essential to the plan of salvation as was His death upon the cross" (GC 489).

A second landmark doctrine is the prophetic proclamation of the three angels' messages of Revelation 14:6-12. These messages constitute God's last appeal to the world to accept salvation in Christ and to prepare humanity for His soon return. Part of these messages is the invitation to worship God, the Creator, and to reject all forms of Babylon and idolatrous worship. Ellen White understood these messages as a distinguishing mark of "the church of Christ at the time of His appearing" (*ibid.* 453).

The immutability and the perpetuity of the commandments of God is the third distinctive doctrine she highlights. Based on the fact that in the Old Testament the ark of the covenant contained the tables of stone on which God had written the Ten Commandments (Ex. 40:20), Ellen White understood that the vision of the ark of the covenant seen in the heavenly temple in Revelation 11:19 is an indication that the law of God (the Ten Commandments) is still valid and binding today and that faith in Christ cannot do away with obedience to it (*ibid.* 433-435). "The law of God, being a revelation of His will, a transcript of His character, must forever endure, 'as a faithful witness in heaven.' Not one command has been annulled; not a jot or tittle has been changed" (*ibid.* 434).

The fourth doctrine is closely related to the preceding ones and teaches the observance of the seventh-day Sabbath. Here, in Ellen White's thought, many doctrinal points find their interconnectedness. "In Revelation 14 [verse 7], men are called upon to worship the Creator; and the prophecy brings to view a class [of people] that, as the result of the threefold message, are keeping the commandments of God [verse 12]. One of these commandments points directly to God as the Creator. The fourth precept declares: 'The seventh day is the Sabbath of the Lord thy God: . . . for in six days the Lord made heaven and earth, the sea, and all that in them is, and rested the seventh day: wherefore the Lord blessed the Sabbath day, and hallowed it.' Exodus 20:10, 11" (*ibid.* 437).

The fifth landmark doctrine is the nonimmortality of the soul (conditionalism) and the eternal destruction of the wicked (annihilationism). Ellen White argued that Satan's first lie to Eve was in regard to the natural immortality of the soul. She also regarded the doctrine of eternal punishment as one of the most appalling doctrines to misrepresent the character of God (*ibid.* 531-536). Hence, she argued that only the doctrine of conditional immortality is consistent with the doctrine of the resurrection (*ibid.* 546, 547).

Although not included in this list, a sixth landmark doctrine included among the non-negotiable doctrines is the literal, premillenial second coming of Christ. Somehow Ellen White left it out of the list quoted above, likely because no one even thought of questioning something so central to being an Adventist.

This list of landmark doctrines and Ellen White's numerous attempts at clarifying theological issues indicate that she perceived her ministry as having a theological impact upon the growing denomination, and her writings bear the marks of theological learning and of a clear system of thought. To better understand Ellen White's theology, the rest of this article will first look at the theological and ideological currents of thought that are perceived in her writings, then will discuss several prominent theological themes of her writings. The reader will find more detailed discussion of particular doctrinal topics in the topical section of this encyclopedia.

I. Theological and Ideological Currents in the Writings of Ellen G. White

The Adventist system of belief did not arise in a theological or ideological vacuum.[3] Nineteenth-century American Protestantism was shaped by theological and religious currents and ideas that impacted the formation of Adventist identity and doctrines. Six such currents of thought can be seen in Ellen White's theology and system of beliefs: Protestant Reformation, Radical Reformation and restorationism, Wesleyan Methodism, deism, Puritanism, and millennialism.

Protestant Reformation

Perhaps it is stating the obvious that Ellen White's thought is Protestant. Early Adventists were conscious that the Protestant Reformation of the sixteenth century had brought a renewal and rediscovery of many neglected and forgotten truths. They readily saw themselves as heirs of Martin Luther, John Calvin, Ulrich Zwingli, and others. Along with these Reformers, Adventists accepted the two "distinctive doctrines of Protestantism—salvation through faith in Christ, and the sole infallibility of the Scriptures" (*ibid.* 89). Of these two doctrines, the supreme authority of the Bible as the rule of faith and practice is seen as the most fundamental Protestant principle, and it held a prominent place in Ellen White's doctrinal system, as we will see in more detail in the following section on her theological themes. Many times in her book *The Great Controversy* she reiterates the importance of this principle (cf. *ibid.* 204, 205). "The grand principle maintained by these Reformers . . . was the infallible authority of the Holy Scriptures as a rule of faith and practice. They denied the right of popes, councils, Fathers, and kings, to control the conscience in matters of religion. The Bible was their authority, and by its teachings they tested all doctrines and all claims. Faith in God and His Word sustained these holy men as they yielded up their lives at the stake" (*ibid.* 249).

White understood that during the Middle Ages, church councils and ecclesiastical leaders repeatedly compromised biblical truths, as pagan beliefs and practices were incorporated into the Christian faith. This compromise between Christianity and paganism and the ignorance of the Scriptures gave rise to widespread apostasy. "When the Scriptures are suppressed," she commented, "and man comes to regard himself as supreme, we need look only for fraud, deception, and debasing iniquity" (*ibid.* 55). Prominent among nonbiblical doctrines that arose during the Middle Ages, and that would be later challenged and rejected by the Protestant Reformers, were the doctrines of the natural immortality of the soul, the invocation of the saints and the adoration of the virgin Mary, the eternal torment of sinners, papal supremacy and infallibility, indulgences, purgatory, and the sacrifice of the Mass (*ibid.* 49-60). Crucial biblical doctrines were thus eclipsed by errors, only to be restored after a faithful return to the Bible as the only rule of faith and practice.

It is in this context that Ellen White speaks of the importance of the doctrines of the Sabbath and conditional immortality, two key doctrines in her system of beliefs. The traditional counterparts of both doctrines, the observance of Sunday and the natural immortality of the soul, are seen as the most flagrant examples of the inroads of paganism and nonbiblical tradition in early Christianity (*ibid.* 52, 53, 545, 549). She even foresaw that at the end of time, "through the two great errors, the immortality of the soul and Sunday sacredness, Satan will bring the people [i.e., the world] under his deceptions" (*ibid.* 588). She understood that unbiblical worship practices (e.g., the keeping of Sunday as the day of worship) and unbiblical philosophical presuppositions (e.g., a platonic dualistic view of human nature leading to belief in the natural immortality of the soul and its consequent belief in an eternally burning hell as a place of punishment) contain the basic elements of many more deceptions. It is only by clinging to the Bible that errors will be found and corrected. Although White believed that God has always had a faithful group of people who believed the truths of Scripture, she upheld the historical and prophetic importance of the Protestant Reformation as the divinely led movement to restore many forgotten biblical doctrines, including the observance of the Sabbath.

Her description of John Wycliffe's role in the Reformation illustrates how she perceived the crucial part played by other Reformers in the restoration of the Bible as the only infallible authority in the church. Seen as the "morning star of the Reformation," Wycliffe was God's agent to prepare "the way for the Great Reformation" (*ibid.* 80, 96).

Wycliffe's devotion to truth and study of the Scriptures prepared him to serve in a role similar to John the Baptist as the herald of a new era (*ibid.* 93). White claimed that he inaugurated a "great movement" that was to "liberate the conscience and the intellect" (*ibid.*).

The source of that movement was the Bible, which he accepted "with implicit faith as the inspired revelation of God's will, a sufficient rule of faith and practice" (*ibid.*). He taught that not only is the Bible "a perfect revelation of God's will, but that the Holy Spirit is its only interpreter, and that every man is, by the study of its teachings, to learn his duty for himself" (*ibid.*). In opposition to common belief, he declared that the Bible is the only true authority to be accepted as the voice of God (*ibid.*). Wycliffe's major contribution to the Reformation was his translation of the Bible into English, "so that every man in England might read, in the language in which he was born, the wonderful works of God" (*ibid.* 87). His translation provided his countrymen with "the most powerful of all weapons against Rome" (*ibid.* 88). Thus, according to White, Wycliffe "had done more to break the fetters of ignorance and vice, more to liberate and elevate his country, than was ever achieved by the most brilliant victories on fields of battle" (*ibid.*). As "one of the greatest of the Reformers," Wycliffe's life "is a testimony to the educating, transforming power of the Holy Scriptures" (*ibid.* 94). From England, Wycliffe's influence spread to other parts of Europe where the Bible also became a liberating force.

White ascribes to Martin Luther the greatest role in restoring the second distinctive doctrine of Protestantism: salvation through faith in Christ. Luther's study of Scripture led him to doubt the doctrine and sale of indulgences and a works-oriented salvation. His visit to Rome and his confrontations with Tetzel made him see "more clearly than ever before the fallacy of trusting to human works for salvation, and the necessity of constant faith in the merits of Christ" (*ibid.* 125). "He set before the people the offensive character of sin, and taught them that it is impossible for man, by his own works, to lessen its guilt or evade its punishment. Nothing but repentance toward God and faith in Christ can save the sinner. The grace of Christ cannot be purchased; it is a free gift" (*ibid.* 129).

Another Protestant principle that Ellen White readily endorsed is the priesthood of all believers, and she argued for the involvement of all Christians in the mission of the church. "Every soul whom Christ has rescued is called to work in His name for the saving of the lost" (COL 191). Although Christian men and women may have different roles to play within the church, some working as pastors while others serve as lay persons, nonetheless she believed that "God expects personal service from every one to whom He has intrusted a knowledge of the truth for this time. Not all can go as missionaries to foreign lands, but all can be home missionaries in their families and neighborhoods" (9T 30).

In spite of celebrating the historical and theological significance of the Reformation, White noted its limitations. "The Reformation did not, as many suppose, end with Luther. It is to be continued to the close of this world's history. Luther had a great work to do in reflecting to others the light which God had permitted to shine upon him; yet he did not receive all the light which was to be given to the world. From that time to this, new light has been continually shining upon the Scriptures, and new truths have been constantly unfolding" (GC 148, 149). This assessment of the Reformation underlies the foundation of Ellen White's next dominant current of thought in her teaching.

Radical Reformation and Restorationism

The deeper Protestant theological roots and orientation of early Adventism lie with the branch of the Reformation that is called the Radical Reformation or Anabaptism. While the mainline Reformers advocated the concept of *sola scriptura* (the Scriptures only are the basis of doctrines), the Anabaptists realized that an element of tradition was still part of the Protestant theological system of beliefs and decided to seek a complete return to the teachings of the Bible. They rejected many forms of church tradition and doctrinal developments since the time of the apostles and sought to return to the ideals and forms of the New Testament church. Hence they advocated believer's baptism, instead of infant baptism, and a strict separation of church and state, leading to "free" churches as contrasted with "established" (government-supported) churches.

In nineteenth-century American Protestantism the free-church branch of the Reformation was expressed in what church historians refer to as restorationism, or sometimes called primitivism. Restorationists believed that the Reformation begun in the sixteenth century had not been completed yet and that a firm return to the teachings and practices of the New Testament church was essential. They espoused a radical view of *sola scriptura* and held to no other creed than the Bible itself. Two of the Seventh-day Adventist founders, James White and Joseph Bates, were members of a restorationist denomination, the Christian Connexion.

It is easy to see in her writings that many of Ellen White's beliefs and theological themes fall within the Anabaptist and restorationist theological heritage. One of her most widely read books, *The Great Controversy*, depicts the history of the Christian church from the destruction of the city of Jerusalem in A.D. 70 to the earth restored after the final judgment. The first half of this classic is her historical narrative of the conflict between good and evil as it played out in the lives of God's faithful people from the time of the early church to about the middle of the nineteenth century. She describes significant events in the lives of the Waldenses in southern France and northern Italy, Jan Huss and Jerome in Prague, John Wycliffe in England, Martin Luther in Germany, Ulrich Zwingli in Switzerland, and John Calvin in France and Geneva. In continuity with these Reformers, she highlights the accomplishments of Menno Simons in the Netherlands, and the revivals of John and Charles Wesley in England.[4]

In her tracing of this history of the Reformation and of the contributions of various theologians and religious movements, White's basic line of thought is Anabaptist and restorationist. As I have already alluded to, her aim is to show that through the centuries God has always had a people faithful to Scripture and unyieldingly committed to following its teachings. Hence Ellen White perceives the history of the conflict between good and evil during the Christian Era as God's action to restore biblical truths lost through human traditions and the inroads of paganism into Christianity. One of the last truths to be "rediscovered," she mentions, is the belief in the premillennial, personal, and soon return of Christ. The nineteenth-century Baptist preacher who popularized this doctrine, William Miller, is called "an American reformer" by Ellen White (GC 317). Clearly in her thought the Adventist Church, born out of the Millerite movement, forms an important segment of God's intended purpose for Christianity at the end of time. In fact, she sees Adventism as the prophetic culmination of the Protestant Reformation and of the restoration of God's New Testament people. In its preaching of the soon return of Christ and of the fulfillment of Bible prophecies, Adventism is God's instrument to warn the world of impending destruction.

Also highlighting her Anabaptist and restorationist heritage is Ellen White's high view of Scripture and rejection of tradition. One common denominator appears in her descriptions of the events in the lives of the historical figures she presents in the first half of *The Great Controversy*: Satan sought to destroy them because they loved God and wished to remain faithful to the teachings of the Bible. She further points out that it has been Satan's aim to eclipse the Word of God and to reduce its appeal since those who do not know the Bible can be more easily deceived (*ibid.* 593). Hence, people who cling to the Scripture are the subjects of Satan's wrath and attacks. She also points out that at the end of time this conflict will be repeated in the lives of God's people who wish to follow unyieldingly biblical teachings above human opinions and traditions (*ibid.* 594, 595). "But God will have a people upon the earth to maintain the Bible, and the Bible only, as the standard of all doctrines and the basis of all reforms. The opinions of learned men, the deductions of science, the creeds or decisions of ecclesiastical councils, as numerous and discordant as are the churches which they represent, the voice of the majority—not one nor all of these should be regarded as evidence for or against any point of religious faith. Before accepting any doctrine or precept, we should demand a plain 'Thus saith the Lord' in its support" (*ibid.* 595). For Ellen White the Bible is the inspired, written Word of God and "contains all the principles that men need to understand in order to be fitted either for this life or for the life to come" (Ed 123). The Scripture can be understood by all (*ibid.*), and its language explained according to its obvious meaning, unless a symbol or figure is employed (GC 599).

Wesleyan Methodism

A third current of thought evident in Ellen White's theology is Wesleyan Methodism. Ellen White grew up in a devout Methodist home and for a period of time her family were members of the Chestnut Street Methodist Church in Portland, Maine. In Ellen White's biography she recalls a few events of her Methodist upbringing that had a crucial impact on her later life: her conversion to Christ, her baptism by immersion, and her early steps in spiritual growth (1Bio 32-42). White's spiritual development took a new direction after she attended two of William Miller's lecture series in Portland about the second coming of Christ. The first of these series was in March 1840 when she was 12 years old, the second in the summer of 1842. As a young girl, she was deeply impressed by these lectures and determined to prepare herself for Christ's second advent. In the months that followed, as her Christian commitment deepened, she received spiritual guidance from a Methodist pastor, Levi Stockman, who encouraged her to trust in Jesus. "During the few minutes in which I received instruction from Elder Stockman," she recalled, "I had obtained more knowledge on the subject of God's love and pitying tenderness than from all the sermons and exhortations to which I had ever listened" (*ibid.* 39).

However, as Ellen White family's commitment to William Miller's teaching on the second advent of Christ deepened, their relationship with their Methodist church was strained, reaching a point of crisis in September 1843, when officers of the Chestnut Street Methodist Church took steps to separate the Harmon family from membership. The family was disfellowshiped not for reasons of immoral conduct, but for believing a doctrine of Scripture "that Christ himself had preached" (*ibid.* 43). For White, this was a traumatic experience and likely strengthened her determination to follow the teachings of Scripture regardless of what creeds and church councils teach.

Although no longer a Methodist Church member, White nonetheless retained many Methodist concepts in her doctrines and lifestyle. Similarities with Methodism are also apparent in the title and content of her most translated book, *Steps to Christ* (published in 1892), which echo some of John Wesley's famous sermons on the *ordo salutis*, the way of salvation.[5] But the similarities are deeper than just in title. Like Wesley, White's teachings on the doctrine of salvation show evidence of following the Arminian system of thought when it comes to God's prevenient grace, the place of human free will in conversion, and the distinction between justification and sanctification.[6] *Steps to Christ* is among Ellen White's clearest publications in which she explains the experience of salvation within this Arminian Methodist frame of thought.

White begins *Steps to Christ* by first introducing the concept of God's revelation. Any knowledge humanity has about God comes to us because God chooses to reveal Himself. This divine revelation comes through both nature and special revelation (SC 9; cf. *ibid.* 85-91). In things of nature, " 'God is love' is written upon every opening bud, upon every spire of springing grass" (*ibid.* 10; cf. *ibid.* 85-87). Yet, although "God has bound our hearts to him by unnumbered tokens" of his love in the natural world, nature only imperfectly represents God's love to us, because the enemy of good has blinded the minds of human beings (*ibid.* 10). The better revelation of God is therefore to be found in the Word of God—in Jesus, who came to live among human beings to reveal to the world the infinite love of God (*ibid.* 10, 11).

Ellen White notes that at Creation humanity "was originally endowed with noble powers and a well-balanced mind" (*ibid.* 17). "But through disobedience, his powers were perverted," "his nature became so weakened through transgression that it was impossible for him, in his own strength, to resist the power of evil" (*ibid.*). One should note that she refers to the weakening of human nature, not to a total depravity. Her view of human nature is more optimistic than the Augustinian doctrine of the Magisterial Reformers. However, White rejects any thought of Pelagianism when she states that "it is impossible for us, of ourselves, to escape from the pit of sin in which we are sunken. Our hearts are evil, and we cannot change them" (*ibid.* 18). In contrast to the ideals of the Enlightenment, she then affirms that "education, culture, the exercise of the will, human effort, all have their proper sphere, but here they are powerless" (*ibid.*). These human efforts "cannot purify the springs of life" (*ibid.*). The only power that can operate a change in human hearts must come from Christ. "His grace alone can quicken the lifeless faculties of the soul, and attract it to God" (*ibid.*). Many years before publishing *Steps to Christ*, in a sermon given at the General Conference session in November 1883, Ellen White emphasized that "we must not think that our own grace and merits will save us; the grace of Christ is our only hope of salvation" (FW 36).[7]

If human nature is "weakened through transgression" and so deep in "the pit of sin in which we are sunken" that "it is impossible for us, of ourselves, to escape" from it, then how is one to be saved? Only by the grace of God. White refers to God's intervention in human life in ways similar to Wesley's concept of prevenient grace.[8] Prevenient grace is God's universal work of grace upon all humankind to draw them to Him. It is God, who taking the first step in humankind's salvation, yearns over lost humanity and desires to bring them back to Him (SC 21). God's "grace alone can quicken the lifeless faculties of the soul, and attract it to God, to holiness" (*ibid.* 18).

God's work of grace upon all human beings prepares them to receive His offer of salvation. This work of the Holy Spirit is universal, but it does not dictate or determine any particular response of the newly graced sinner. God's prevenient grace is possible only because Christ's sacrifice is for all humankind. Ellen White explains that the sinner does not need to do any work of repentance of his own before coming to Christ. In fact, it is Christ who is the source of every right impulse and who draws sinners to Him (*ibid.* 26, 27). Therefore: "An influence of which they are unconscious works upon the soul, and the conscience is quickened, and the outward life is amended" (*ibid.* 27). "The heart of God yearns over His earthly children with a love stronger than death," White explains. "In giving up His Son, He has poured out to us all heaven in one gift. The Savior's life and death and intercession, the ministry of angels, the pleading of the Spirit, the Father working above and through all, the unceasing interest of heavenly beings—all are enlisted in behalf of man's redemption" (*ibid.* 21; cf. FW 64).

Ellen White understood the fine theological distinctions between election and salvation, between God's call to repentance and one's salvation. While Reformed theology teaches that a person who is predestined by God to be saved cannot be lost, as the work of God's saving grace is irresistible, White understood that the universal work of prevenient grace upon a human heart is to prepare this heart to receive the offer of salvation. Salvation follows the work of prevenient grace only if a person accepts by faith this invitation of God. Clearly Arminian in thought, White believed that the work of God's grace can be spurned by humans. "Calling and justification are not one and the same thing," she stated in 1893, the year following the publication of *Steps to Christ*. "Calling is the drawing of the sinner to Christ, and it is a work wrought by the Holy Spirit upon the heart, convicting of sin, and inviting to repentance" (1SM 390).

As it is in Wesley's writings,[9] humankind's response to God's offer of salvation and to the influence of the Holy Spirit is a crucial step in one's journey with Christ in Ellen White's theology. In order to be saved, humankind must respond by faith to God's offer. "Christ is ready to set us free from sin," she states, "but He does not force the will; and if by persistent transgression the will itself is wholly bent on evil, and we do not *desire* to be set free, if we *will* not accept His grace, what more can He do?" (SC 34). "The very first step to Christ is taken through the drawing of the Spirit of God; as man responds to this drawing, he advances toward Christ in order that he may repent" (1SM 390).

For Ellen White repentance and confession are the appropriate human responses to God's offer of salvation. Once the conscience is awakened by the wooing of the Holy Spirit, drawn to the cross of Christ by God's love, a person can then respond with repentance and confession. Repentance, hence, is not a prerequisite in order to be loved by God. In fact, "repentance is no less the gift of God than are pardon and justification, and it cannot be experienced except as it is given to the soul by Christ" (*ibid.* 391). It is the work of God's prevenient grace, an outflow of His love, that leads one to repent. It is not a work that we initiate or do. "No man of himself can repent, and make himself worthy of the blessing of justification" (*ibid.* 390; cf. SC 28). Her classic definition of repentance highlights two important aspects of human response. "Repentance includes sorrow for sin and a turning away from it. We shall not renounce sin unless we see its sinfulness; until we turn away from it in heart, there will be no real change in the life" (SC 23).

Confession of sins, as a result of genuine repentance, is another step to Christ. God's promise in Proverbs 28:13 is for all people. It is also a condition of salvation. "The conditions of obtaining mercy of God are simple and just and reasonable. The Lord does not require us to do some grievous thing in order that we may have the forgiveness of sin. We need not make long and wearisome pilgrimages, or perform painful penances, to commend our souls to the God of heaven or to expiate our transgression; but he that confesseth and forsaketh his sin shall have mercy" (*ibid.*). Hence, confession is part of the human response to God's offer of salvation. Without confession of sins and one's faith response there is no salvation. To be clear, she wrote in 1890: "Salvation is through faith in Jesus Christ alone" (FW 19). "When the sinner believes that Christ is his personal Savior, then according to His unfailing promises, God pardons his sin and justifies him freely" (*ibid.* 101).

Faith is therefore a crucial element of salvation. In his sermon "Salvation by Faith," Wesley defined faith as "not only an assent to the whole gospel of Christ, but also a full reliance on the blood of Christ; a trust in the merits of his life, death, and resurrection." In a similar fashion, for White "faith is trusting God—believing that He loves us and knows best what is for our good" (Ed 253). Faith is also "an assent of the understanding to God's words which binds the heart in willing consecration and service to God, Who gave the understanding, Who moved on the heart, Who first drew the mind to view Christ on the cross of Calvary. Faith is rendering to God the intellectual powers, abandonment of the mind and will to God, and making Christ the only door to enter into the kingdom of heaven" (FW 25).

"Let the subject be made distinct and plain that it is not possible to effect anything in our standing before God or in the gift of God to us through creature merit," she wrote to pastors in 1890. "Should faith and works purchase the gift of salvation for anyone, then the Creator is under obligation to the creature. Here is an opportunity for falsehood to be accepted as truth. If any man can merit salvation by anything he may do, then he is in the same position as the Catholic to do penance for his sins. Salvation, then, is partly of debt, that may be earned as wages. If man cannot, by any of his good works, merit salvation, then it must be wholly of grace, received by man as a sinner because he receives and believes in Jesus. It is wholly a free gift. Justification by faith is placed beyond controversy. And all this controversy is ended, as soon as the matter is settled that the merits of fallen man in his good works can never procure eternal life for him" (*ibid.* 19, 20; cf. *ibid.* 70).

White's understanding of God's work of prevenient grace on all human beings, His offer of salvation to all, and the need of humankind's response to God's offer is an integrated synergism. She believes God created human beings with free will, that prevenient grace restores the power of choice, and that God will not force anyone to serve Him. This is an essential aspect of her understanding of the great controversy theme, as we will see below. Her understanding of the synergism between God's prevenient grace and human response is Arminian Wesleyan. "In the work of redemption there is no compulsion," she states in

The Desire of Ages. "No external force is employed. Under the influence of the Spirit of God, man is left free to choose whom he will serve" (DA 466). Repeatedly, and in different settings, she affirmed the prevenient work of God's grace on the heart. "We can no more repent without the Spirit of Christ to awaken the conscience than we can be pardoned without Christ. Christ is the source of every right impulse. He is the only one that can implant in the heart enmity against sin. Every desire for truth and purity, every conviction of our own sinfulness, is an evidence that His Spirit is moving upon our hearts" (SC 26; cf. 1SM 391). But at the same time she valued the importance of a free will, human response to God's gracious offer of salvation—keeping in mind that this response is possible only because of God's work of prevenient grace. "In the work of redemption there is no compulsion. No external force is employed. Under the influence of the Spirit of God, man is left free to choose whom he will serve. In the change that takes place when the soul surrenders to Christ, there is the highest sense of freedom. The expulsion of sin is the act of the soul itself. True, we have no power to free ourselves from Satan's control; but when we desire to be set free from sin, and in our great need cry out for a power out of and above ourselves, the powers of the soul are imbued with the divine energy of the Holy Spirit, and they obey the dictates of the will in fulfilling the will of God" (DA 466; cf. SC 43, 44, 47).

Ellen White's thought on salvation is also Arminian Wesleyan when it comes to justification and sanctification. Categorically she affirms that "justification is wholly of grace and not procured by any works that fallen man can do" (FW 20). "As the penitent sinner, contrite before God, discerns Christ's atonement in his behalf and accepts this atonement as his only hope in this life and the future life, his sins are pardoned. This is justification by faith" (*ibid.* 103).

In words reminiscent of Wesley's sermon "The Scripture Way of Salvation,"[10] White also stated that "pardon and justification are one and the same thing. Through faith, the believer passes from the position of a rebel, a child of sin and Satan, to the position of a loyal subject of Christ Jesus, not because of an inherent goodness, but because Christ receives him as His child by adoption. The sinner receives the forgiveness of his sins, because these sins are borne by his Substitute and Surety. . . . Thus man, pardoned, and clothed with the beautiful garments of Christ's righteousness, stands faultless before God" (*ibid.* 103). For White, "justification is the opposite of condemnation" (*ibid.* 104), and "however sinful has been his life, if he [the sinner] believes in Jesus as his personal Savior, he stands before God in the spotless robes of Christ's imputed righteousness" (*ibid.* 106; cf. 1SM 389). She also highlights the forensic nature of justification by faith: "Christ's character stands in place of your character, and you are accepted before God just as if you had not sinned" (SC 62).

Justification is wholly the work of God's grace and consists of the transferral of the sinner's sins to Christ and of Christ's righteousness to the believer. "The great work that is wrought for the sinner who is spotted and stained by evil is the work of justification. By Him who speaketh truth he is declared righteous. The Lord imputes unto the believer the righteousness of Christ and pronounces him righteous before the universe. He transfers his sins to Jesus, the sinner's representative, substitute, and surety. Upon Christ He lays the iniquity of every soul that believeth" (1SM 392).

While for Ellen White, justification is a divine declaration of forgiveness graciously given to repentant sinners, sanctification is the work of God's grace upon sinners to restore in them the image of God (MB 114). This work of sanctification is not instantaneous, but is "the work of a lifetime" (COL 65). This distinction between justification and sanctification is also found in Wesley's works.[11] In the chapter "Growing Up Into Christ" in *Steps to Christ*, she presents her understanding of sanctification and how one grows in Christ after justification.

Christian growth and sanctification are comparable to the life of a plant. As God first gives life to a plant when the seed germinates, it is also God who continues to give life to the plant as it grows. Never is the plant capable of making itself grow. "So it is only through the life from God that spiritual life is begotten in the hearts of men.... As with life, so it is with growth" (SC 67). "The plants and flowers grow not by their own care or anxiety or effort, but by receiving that which God has furnished to minister to their life. The child cannot, by any anxiety or power of its own, add to its stature. No more can you, by anxiety or effort of yourself, secure spiritual growth" (*ibid.* 68). In order to grow, we are invited to "abide in Christ." "You are just as dependent upon Christ, in order to live a holy life, as is the branch upon the parent stock for growth and fruitfulness. Apart from Him you have no life. You have no power to resist temptation or to grow in grace and holiness. Abiding in Him, you may flourish. Drawing your life from Him, you will not wither nor be fruitless. You will be like a tree planted by the rivers of water" (*ibid.* 69).

To those who misconstrue justification by faith and sanctification by human efforts and works, she states: "Many have an idea that they must do some part of the work alone. They have trusted in Christ for the forgiveness of sin, but now they seek by their own efforts to live aright. But every such effort must fail. Jesus says, 'Without Me ye can do nothing.' Our growth in grace, our joy, our usefulness—all depend upon our union with Christ. It is by communion with Him, daily, hourly—by abiding in Him—that we are to grow in grace. He is not only the Author, but the Finisher of our faith. It is Christ first and last and always. He is to be with us, not only at the beginning and the end of our course, but at every step of the way" (*ibid.*).

Another crucial step in growth is to daily surrender to Christ's will (*ibid.* 70) and to keep our eyes fixed upon Christ (*ibid.* 72). In other words, we are to live daily in the presence of Christ, by the power of His Holy Spirit. Such a life brings about transformation of character and obedience. White is careful to keep in balance the work of God's grace in justification and sanctification and the role of humankind in the process of growth. As a result of the work of God's grace on a sinner's life, characters are transformed into the likeness of Christ's character, and obedience to God's law and to the gospel become part of one's inner nature. "While the work of the Spirit is silent and imperceptible, its effects are manifest. If the heart has been renewed by the Spirit of God, the life will bear witness to the fact" (*ibid.* 57). One's character reflects this transformation: "The character is revealed, not by occasional good deeds and occasional misdeeds, but by the tendency of the habitual words and acts" (*ibid.* 57, 58).

As one's character is developed in likeness to Christ's character, obedience becomes a natural part of growth and of one's faithful response to the gift of the grace of God. "Instead of releasing man from obedience, it is faith, and faith only, that makes us partakers of the grace of Christ, which enables us to render obedience. We do not earn salvation by our obedience; for salvation is the free gift of God, to be received by faith. But obedience is the fruit of faith" (*ibid.* 60, 61; cf. 1SM 398; FW 85-87). White stated to believers in Sweden in 1886 that "true sanctification will be evidenced by a conscientious regard for all the commandments of God" and "a careful improvement of every talent, by a circumspect conversation, by revealing in every act the meekness of Christ" (FW 53). "While we are to be in harmony with God's law," she wrote a few years later, "we are not saved by the works of the law, yet we cannot be saved without obedience. The law is the standard by which character is measured. But we cannot possibly keep the commandments of God without the regenerating grace of Christ" (*ibid.* 95; cf. SC 62).

This process of sanctification is often invisible and imperceptible in one's life; it is therefore misguided to speak of perfectionism or of the possibility to attain a self-exalted, sinless life on this earth. In fact, White gave a veiled caution to those who preach perfectionism: "The closer you come to Jesus, the more faulty you will appear in your own eyes" (*ibid.* 64). "So we have nothing in ourselves of which to boast. We have no ground for self-exaltation. Our only ground of hope is in the righteousness of Christ imputed to us, and in that wrought by His Spirit working in and through us" (*ibid.* 63). She clearly stated that "we cannot say, 'I am sinless,' till this vile body is changed and fashioned like unto His glorious body" (ST, Mar. 23, 1888).

Yet, again in ways reminiscent of Wesley's thought,[12] Ellen White spoke of the possibility of character perfection in one's life.[13] Commenting on the parable of the talents in Matthew 25, she wrote: "A character formed according to the divine likeness is the only treasure that we can take from this world to the next. . . . The heavenly intelligences will work with the human agent who seeks with determined faith that perfection of character which will reach out to perfection in action" (COL 332). In fact, that perfection of character is a reflection of the loving character of God. As servants of God become more and more like Christ, they receive "the Spirit of Christ—the Spirit of unselfish love and labor for others." As a result, she states, "your love [will] be made perfect. More and more you will reflect the likeness of Christ in all that is pure, noble, and lovely" (*ibid.* 68). Ellen White thus "ties her discussion of Christian perfection to the internalization of God's loving character in daily life."[14]

For Ellen White, this perfection extends also to overcoming sin in one's life. While recognizing that the human nature will remain affected by sinful inclinations until the moment of glorification, she nonetheless affirmed the possibility of victory over sin. "We can overcome. Yes; fully, entirely. Jesus died to make a way of escape for us, that we might overcome every evil temper, every sin, every temptation" (1T 144). As mentioned above, no one can claim freedom from temptations in this life, yet the goal of the Christian life remains the same: to reflect Christ's character. This becomes all the more important for White when discussing last-day events. "Now, while our great High Priest is making the atonement for us, we should seek to become perfect in Christ. Not even by a thought could our Savior be brought to yield to the power of temptation. . . . He had kept His Father's commandments, and there was no sin in Him that Satan could use to his advantage. This is the condition in which those must be found who shall stand in the time of trouble" (GC 623).

Woodrow Whidden summarizes Ellen White's thoughts on the relationship between justification, sanctification, and perfection. "For Ellen White, perfection was just about synonymous with sanctification. But we must always remember that perfection (no matter what it meant in any given passage) was the goal of sanctification. In her thought justification and sanctification need to be *distinguished*, but not *separated*. The same goes for sanctification and perfection. Justification often defined perfection and always formed the foundation of the experience of sanctification. Sanctification often defined perfection, but at the same time perfection was always the goal of sanctification."[15]

Deism

A fourth current of thought that had an indirect impact on Ellen White's theology is deism, a philosophical and religious movement in the seventeenth and eighteenth centuries, born of the Enlightenment. The Enlightenment largely changed the Western culture's understanding of the human person and how we attain knowledge. It did this first by replacing God with humanity as the focus of its worldview. While for Medieval and Reformation worldviews human beings were important insofar as they fit into the story of God's activity in history, Enlightenment thinkers tended to reverse the equation and gauge the importance of God according to His value for the human story.

Enlightenment philosophers placed a high emphasis on human reason and appealed to reason rather than external revelation as the final arbiter of truth. In fact, they appealed to reason in order to determine what constitutes revelation. Anselm of Canterbury's maxim "I believe in order that I may understand" was replaced with the Enlightenment motto "I believe what I can understand." The assumption was clear: people should no longer blindly accept external authorities, such as the Bible and the church; rather the truth is to be found in human reason alone.

Deism, as a religious philosophy and movement, sought to reduce religion to its most basic elements. Deists typically rejected supernatural events, such as prophecy and miracles, and divine revelation through the Bible. Many dogmas of the church were dismissed to retain the existence of God and some kind of judgment after death. Organized religion was rejected in favor of natural religion that was conceived, not as a system of beliefs, but as a system for structuring ethical behavior.

Of course, deism drew numerous attacks from those who saw it as a threat to the Christian faith. By the time of the Second Advent movement that gave rise to the Adventist Church, deism was a dying movement and was being replaced with forms of ethical romanticism and Protestant liberalism. But its appeal to human reason as an approach to acquiring new knowledge never vanished. For Christians, though, the challenge was to find a way to balance the use of human reason, and belief in the reliability and infallibility of the Bible as a revelation from God and a source of knowledge.

William Miller, one of the spiritual founders of Adventism, was raised in a devout Baptist home but became a deist in his early-adult years. As a deist, Miller accepted the assumption that God is so transcendent that He cannot intervene in human affairs. He also rejected the concept that God reveals Himself through the Bible and that the supernatural activities of God as described in Scripture ever occurred.

In March 1841 the Millerite journal *Signs of the Times* reprinted a short article on Miller that a Massachusetts newspaper, the Lynn *Record*, had published. What is interesting about this article is that it gives an interesting reason for Miller becoming a deist. "Mr. Miller wishing to understand thoroughly everything he read, often asked the ministers to explain dark passages of Scripture, but seldom received satisfactory answers. He was told that such passages were incapable of explanation. In consequence of which, at the age of 22, he became a deist or disbeliever in the truth of Revelation. He thought an all-wise and just God would never make a revelation of his will which nobody could understand, and then punish his creatures for disbelieving it."[16]

As a deist Miller did not believe in the objectivity and perspicuity of God's revelation in Scripture. Not only was God so far removed from humanity that He could not intervene in human affairs, but neither could He reveal Himself through human language and certainly not through the Bible, as it was a book filled with unintelligible stories and symbols. The only revelation of God that was acceptable to a deist was through nature.

But Miller's deist worldview was destroyed when, during the War of 1812 between the United States and Great Britain, he survived the battle of Plattsburgh in September 1814. In spite of being surpassed in numbers, the American forces won this battle. Deist logic and reasoning could not account for the unexpected American victory and the defeat of the superior British army and navy. This battle became a turning point in Miller's religious life. Within a couple years he became convinced that only the grace and mercy of God could have intervened to allow the American side to win this battle. And consequently he began to question his deist worldview and to return to a biblical worldview in which God can intervene in human affairs. Further reflections also led him to revisit his assumption that God does not reveal Himself through Scripture. Within a few years of intense Bible study, which in good deist fashion he described as "a feast of reason,"[17] Miller became convinced that God indeed reveals Himself through the Bible since history proves the fulfillment of biblical prophecies. God can predict the future of humanity.

From then on, Miller deliberately rejected deism and its assumptions and became "the instrument of more conversions to Christianity, especially from deism, than any other man now living in these parts," recounted the Lynn *Record* article. "He has read Voltaire, [David] Hume, [Thomas] Paine, Ethan Allen, and made himself familiar with the arguments of deists and knows how to refute them."[18]

Although Millerism built on the American evangelical, pietist, and revivalist ethos of the first half of the nineteenth century, for all practical purposes Millerism became a counter-deism movement, openly rejecting the key philosophical assumptions of the Enlightenment that God does not reveal Himself through history and in Scripture and that the Bible is unreliable as a historical and authentic account of God's work of salvation. Though Ellen White never was a deist, her worldview, approach to Scripture and the natural world, and use of reason in attaining a personal knowledge of God's will are clearly framed in the context of and reaction to deism. William Miller's experience with deism and the subsequent birth of the Advent movement undergirded the experience of many Seventh-day Adventist pioneers, including Ellen White.

Even though Miller and his colleagues understood the limitations of the use of reason alone to attain objective truth and knowledge, they nonetheless continued to appreciate a logical and rational approach to the study of Scripture. Miller popularized a list of rules of biblical interpretation aimed at countering deist assumptions, yet his rules are highly rational and logical.[19] He believed in the objectivity of God's revelation in Scripture, that the text of the Scripture is inspired by God and thus a trustworthy revelation of His will, that Scripture can be understood by simply being attentive to the literal and obvious meaning of the words, and that through prophecies God predicts the future of humanity as it relates to the plan of salvation.

Miller's rules of interpretation had a strong impact on Adventist hermeneutics and were endorsed by early Seventh-day Adventist pioneers.[20] White's endorsement of Miller's rules of interpretation appeared in an article in the *Review and Herald* in 1884.

"Those who are engaged in proclaiming the third angel's message are searching the Scriptures upon the same plan that Father Miller adopted. In the little book entitled 'Views of the Prophecies and Prophetic Chronology,' Father Miller gives the following simple but intelligent and important rules for Bible study and interpretation: '1. Every word must have its proper bearing on the subject presented in the Bible; 2. All Scripture is necessary, and may be understood by diligent application and study; 3. Nothing revealed in Scripture can or will be hid from those who ask in faith, not wavering; 4. To understand doctrine, bring all the scriptures together on the subject you wish to know, then let every word have its proper influence; and if you can form your theory without a contradiction, you cannot be in error; 5. Scripture must be its own expositor, since it is a rule of itself. If I depend on a teacher to expound to me, and he should guess at its meaning, or desire to have it so on account of his sectarian creed, or to be thought wise, then his guessing, desire, creed, or wisdom is my rule, and not the Bible.'

"The above is a portion of these rules," she concluded, "and in our study of the Bible we shall all do well to heed the principles set forth" (RH, Nov. 25, 1884).

Ellen White also emphasized the "need of a return to the great Protestant principle—the Bible, and the Bible only, as the rule of faith and duty" (GC 204, 205). She believed in accepting all of Scripture as a source of beliefs and refused to seek a canon within a canon or to consider some portions of the Bible as less inspired, and therefore less authoritative, than others (Ed 190). For White, human reason cannot alone find its way to God, but can understand God's revelation in Scripture and must submit to its teaching.

Understandably, like Miller and other early Adventist pioneers, White held a high view of reason and gave it an important role in the Christian life. The capacity to reason, she wrote, is one of the "great masterly talents" entrusted to humanity by God (3MR 353). As part of the gift of God at the Creation, the mind, along with other human faculties, reflects the image of God and is capable of "comprehending divine things" (PP 45). She believed that God desires us to exercise our reasoning powers to their fullest extent and that a faithful study of the Bible "will strengthen and elevate the mind as no other study can do" (5T 703; cf. SC 109, 110). Human reason, guided by the influence of the Holy Spirit, can understand God's will as it is revealed in Scripture.

But in addition to her call for the highest development and use of the human mind, Ellen White also pointed to its limitations. She argued that human reason should not be deified by thinking that it can attain to all knowledge. It is also subject to the weaknesses and infirmities of humanity and, therefore, incapable of comprehending all mysteries (5T 703). Sin has brought degeneration to all parts of human nature, and the practice of sin has also perverted the mind. Because of the weakness of the human mind, reason alone cannot understand many things about God. "There are many things that can never be reasoned out by the strongest intellect or discerned by the most penetrating mind," she wrote in 1896. "Philosophy cannot determine the ways and works of God; the human mind cannot measure infinity" (RH, Dec. 29, 1896). Hence, all human faculties, including reason, are to be brought under the influence of the Spirit of God (ST, Nov. 5, 1894; ST, May 28, 1896).

For White, then, reason is not the absolute foundation of truth and knowledge, as it is with deism and rationalism, nor can it find truth about God on its own. Scripture is the only safeguard Christians have "against the influence of false teachers and the delusive power of spirits of darkness" (GC 593), and Scripture must be "the standard of all doctrines and the basis of all reforms" (*ibid.* 595).

In both Miller and White we see examples of what scholars have called the Scottish "commonsense" realism approach to religion, first introduced in the United States in the eighteenth century by professors at Princeton College (now University), in New Jersey. This school of thought, very prominent in nineteenth-century religious life, although critical of the conclusions arrived at by deism, nonetheless embraced a "commonsense" view of knowledge arrived at by assuming the objective reality of external objects and truth, and by following an inductive, logical approach to reasoning.[21]

Miller's logical and "commonsense" rules of interpretation and White's belief that human reason, aided by the influence of the Holy Spirit, could understand God's will as revealed in Scripture and nature reflect the predominant approach to Scripture found in the nineteenth century. This logical approach to the study of the Bible led them to affirm without ambiguity that they could "know the truth." Coupled with this religious and intellectual trend during the beginning of the Adventist movement was the general "confidence in the ability of the 'common person' to do almost anything, including theology."[22] Whereas doing theology had once been the prerogative of trained scholars, the nineteenth century opened up the possibility for laypersons to take the initiatives in searching for biblical knowledge and proclaiming the truths thus discovered. People understood that they could gather all the relevant facts (or texts) in the Bible and arrive at the proper interpretation of a text or doctrine.[23] In a real sense, this intellectual and religious trend allowed the growth of revivalism in the nineteenth century, another important factor that led to the birth of the Adventist movement and so was strongly supported by Ellen White.

Puritanism

A fifth current of thought in Ellen White's writings is Puritanism. In the mid-nineteenth century New England was still the home of descendants of the first Puritan colonists to Massachusetts, and many Congregationalist churches and denominations had roots going back to the early years of the colony.

Puritanism is a Protestant religious movement that originated in England during the reign of Elizabeth I (1559-1603) when more radical Protestants disapproved of Elizabeth's Religious Settlement, which was felt to be accommodating too much to Roman Catholic practices. Puritans were not all united in their opinions, but shared a belief that all existing churches had become corrupt through the influence of pagan worship practices (particularly those of the Church of Rome) and, therefore, were in need of "purifying." The central belief of Puritanism is God's supreme authority over human affairs, particularly in the church, and especially as expressed in the Bible. Puritans argued for the supremacy of the Bible in shaping and influencing all church practices and beliefs. Hence, this view led them to seek both individual and church conformity to the teachings of the Bible, whether in the smallest details of one's life or at the highest levels of ecclesial and social organizations.

Ellen White's writings reflect many religious ideas and concepts shared by Puritans. Like the Puritans, and as we have already seen, White emphasized the authority of the Bible in all matters of faith and practice. This emphasis was not only for the church in general but also for one's private life, and she recommended regular private study of the Bible. Statements such as this one illustrate how she emphasized the authority of Scripture: "In His Word, God has committed to men the knowledge necessary for salvation. The Holy Scriptures are to be accepted as an authoritative, infallible revelation of His will. They are the standard of character, the revealer of doctrines, and the test of experience" (GC vii). In her diary in 1902 she further commented on the authority of the Bible: "We must take our stand to acknowledge fully the power and authority of God's Word, whether or not it agrees with our preconceived opinions. We have a perfect Guidebook. The Lord has spoken to us; and whatever may be the consequences, we are to receive His Word and practice it in daily life, else we shall be choosing our own version of duty and shall be doing exactly the opposite of that which our heavenly Father has appointed us to do" (MM 255, 256).

Concurrent with the practice of personal Bible study, Puritans also believed in education for all people in society. In a world in which formal education was often perceived as the privilege of the rich, Puritans believed that both men and women should be educated inasmuch as this practice would also allow people to read the Bible for themselves. White also believed in education for both genders. During her lifetime she championed the establishment of schools and colleges where the curriculum would be faithful to the teachings of Scripture and would promote a healthy Christian lifestyle.

White's first major statement on education appeared in 1872 (3T 131-160). In this statement she highlighted the role of parents in the education of children and favored the centrality of the Bible in the school curriculum. She also discussed the importance of a balanced development of the student's mental, physical, and spiritual faculties. For White, true education "is the harmonious development of the physical, the mental, and the spiritual powers. It prepares the student for the joy of service in this world and for the higher joy of wider service in the world to come" (Ed 13). Thus the goals of education and redemption are one: to restore God's image in his creation and to bring the world and humankind back to its original perfection (*ibid.* 15, 16). Whoever cooperates with God in giving to the youth a knowledge of God and in molding the character into harmony with His accomplishes a noble work (*ibid.* 19). Today, as a result of White's emphasis on education, the Seventh-day Adventist educational system is the largest Protestant church-owned system in the world.

It is well known that Puritans advocated high standards of strict Christian living and behavior and restricted or disapproved of various forms of recreation. In fact, the word "puritan" has become synonymous with very conservative forms of Christianity. White's thought on the propriety of some personal habits and lifestyle also reflect a Puritan influence. For example, when in 1886 D. M. Canright, a successful and popular Adventist evangelist, recommended a list of good books for young people to the readers of the *Review and Herald* ("A List of Good Books for Young Folks," Sept. 7, 1886) in which he listed such "good" and "best" books as Daniel Defoe's *Robinson Crusoe* and Harriet Beecher Stowe's *Uncle Tom's Cabin*, White rebuked him for making "a mistake in writing that article" (5T 519).[24] What made her react so strongly to the reading of fiction, even as helpful as these two books may have been to effect changes in nineteenth-century American society, was her deeply felt conviction that reading such books is Satan's work to present stories "that fascinate the senses and thus destroy their [the youth's] relish for the Word of God" (*ibid.* 517). In the context of the antitypical day of atonement and the need of preparing oneself for heaven, "the great work is before us of leading the people away from worldly customs and practices, up higher and higher, to spirituality, piety, and earnest work for God" (*ibid.* 520). For Ellen White there is to be no compromise between worldly forms of entertainment and preparation for the second coming of Christ. Much of her writings on matters of entertainment, dress, and lifestyle reflect the Puritan principles of strict and uncompromising adherence to God's Word. Also of Puritan influence is her heartfelt desire to see others follow carefully what she said in these matters.

The proper way of doing church was also at the core of Puritan concerns. Puritans frowned upon what they considered as extravagant and nonbiblical forms of worship. Instead, they promoted a simplicity of worship, including extemporaneous prayers, congregational singing of hymns, and the preaching of God's Word. Their worship was nonliturgical and did not follow a prescribed calendar. Their pastors did not wear special vestments; their churches were unadorned with images, candles, or incense. That same simplicity of worship is reflected in Ellen White's writings when she affirms the simple worship of the Puritans as they struggled to follow their understanding of the gospel (cf. GC 252, 289, 290). Cognizant of the fact that it is easy for humans to depart from this simplicity, she encouraged Adventists to maintain simplicity in worship. "In our devotional meetings, our voices should express by prayer and praise our adoration of the heavenly Father, that all may know that we worship God in simplicity and truth, and in the beauty of holiness" (CT 245). "When professing Christians reach the high standard which it is their privilege to reach, the simplicity of Christ will be maintained in all their worship," she wrote to the Battle Creek church in 1899. "Forms and ceremonies and musical accomplishments are not the strength of the church," she went on to say. "Yet these things have taken the place that God should have" (Ev 512).

Puritans believed that the obligation to obey the law of God, i.e., the Ten Commandments, was still a requirement of the Christian life. In contrast to some Christian groups who traditionally have had a rather negative view of the law, Puritans, like other Reformed Christians, viewed the law of God from a positive perspective. While keeping in mind the dangers of legalism and attempting to keep a proper balance between law and grace, Puritans emphasized the obligation for Christians to obey the commandments of God. These commandments were not done away at the cross but were still binding on Christians, and were to be strictly enforced on others.

Hence, the use of images and statues was forbidden in worship and one's speech about God needed to be circumspect and clean. When it came to Sabbath observance, Puritans believed the Sabbath was still a Christian obligation and ought to be strictly observed, although they believed the Sabbath had been changed to Sunday. Family ties were to be honored, adultery and sexual promiscuity outside of marriage were forbidden, and acceptable business practices required one not to steal or bear false witness against one's neighbor. Puritan society was marked by faithful obedience to God and His institutions, proper decorum between the sexes, and a strong Protestant business ethic. The social enforcement of these behaviors ensured the blessings of God upon the land and its people.

To a large extent, Ellen White's thought on these religious and social matters is Puritan. Her belief in the immutability of the Ten Commandments is a basic foundation of her great controversy theme. She firmly believed that the eternal principles found in the Decalogue are the reflection of God's character and the very foundation of heaven's government. This thought she affirms at the beginning of *Patriarchs and Prophets:* "The law of love being the foundation of the government of God, the happiness of all intelligent beings depends upon their perfect accord with its great principles of righteousness. God desires from all His creatures the service of love—service that springs from an appreciation of His character" (PP 34). While Satan's enmity against the law of God sought to overthrow God's government (*ibid.* 338), God put in place the plan of redemption in order to "[make] it possible for man again to be brought into harmony with God, and to render obedience to His law" (PP 331). Obedience to the commandments of God is therefore not an option for the Christian. However exacting the commandments may be, God asks His people to obey them.

While the first four commandments of the Decalogue address our relationship with God, the last six refer to human relationships. Obedience to these commandments sustains the social fabric of all societies and groups of human beings. It is because Israel, time and time again, did not fully embrace God's will for them in faithful obedience to the commandments that it found itself ravaged by moral degradation, wars, and famines (cf. *ibid.* 335; AH 64, 65; PK 297-300). In a similar way, Ellen White believes that modern countries incur the same consequences by disregarding God's commandments (e.g., the United States during the Civil War [1T 264-268]; France during the French Revolution [GC 265-288]).

However, where White diverges from Puritan thought is in regard to the social enforcement of religious conformity. In contrast to Puritan practice, White was a strong advocate of the separation of church and state. In her book *The Great Controversy* she dedicates one chapter to the Pilgrim Fathers and their contributions to the founding of the American colonies. She upholds the early Puritans' determination to worship God only according to the regulations found in the Bible and their trust in God. "In the midst of exile and hardship their love and faith waxed strong. They trusted the Lord's promises, and He did not fail them in time of need. His angels were by their side, to encourage and support them" (*ibid.* 291). Their desire to worship God according to the dictates of their own conscience led them to the shore of America and to establish a new nation. Among Puritans, "the Bible was held as the foundation of faith, the source of wisdom, and the charter of liberty. Its principles were diligently taught in the home, in the school, and in the church, and its fruits were manifest in thrift, intelligence, purity, and temperance" (*ibid.* 296).

"Yet honest and God-fearing" as Puritans were, she comments, "the freedom which they sacrificed so much to secure for themselves, they were not equally ready to grant to others" (*ibid.* 292, 293). For her, "the doctrine that God has committed to the church the right to control the conscience, and to define and punish heresy, is one of the most deeply rooted of papal errors" (*ibid.* 293). This firmly established practice in Puritan colonies "led to the inevitable results" of intolerance and persecution (*ibid.*). "The union of the church with the state, be the degree never so slight, while it may appear to bring the world nearer to the church, does in reality but bring the church nearer to the world" (*ibid.* 297).

In this context the foundation of the Rhode Island colony by Roger Williams, who fled persecutions from Puritan Massachusetts, "laid the foundation of the first state of modern times that in the fullest sense recognized the right of religious freedom" (*ibid.* 295). For White, Rhode Island's twin principles of civil and religious liberty "became the corner-stones of the American Republic" and were engraved in the First Amendment of the American Constitution: " 'Congress shall make no law respecting an establishment of religion, or prohibiting the free exercise thereof' " (*ibid.*).

Although White's thought clearly reflects many principles of Puritanism, in her final analysis religious and moral uprightness cannot be enforced upon an individual's conscience. In this matter her Anabaptist theological roots take precedence over her Puritan affinities. In spite of all the good upheld by American Puritanism, it lacked one essential religious principle—that of religious liberty, which as we shall see later is a cornerstone of White's thought in her great controversy theme.

Millennialism

One last nineteenth-century theological and religious current evident in the writings of Ellen White is millennialism, the belief that humanity is now living in the last days of its history and that soon the world will be changed to herald the establishment of the kingdom of God.

Christian views on the order of last-day events have varied greatly since the Protestant Reformation. The passage in Revelation that speaks of Satan being locked away in the bottomless pit for 1,000 years and then released for one final battle against God and the New Jerusalem (Rev. 20:1-10) has captured the imagination of many people through the centuries. In the time of Ellen White two major millennialist views conflicted with each other: postmillennialism and premillennialism. The first, the dominant view among mainline denominations, held that Christ's second coming is *subsequent* to the millennium and happens at the same time as the final judgment. In this view Christ will reign spiritually during the millennium in and through the church. During this period the church will prepare the earth to receive the eternal kingdom of Christ after the final judgment. Through social actions and spiritual renewal the church is now preparing the kingdom of God on earth. In contrast to this view, premillennialism sees Christ's second advent as *preceding* the millennium, thereby separating the Second Coming from the final judgment by 1,000 years. In this view the earth as it stands cannot be redeemed by social and religious actions; therefore only the eradication of sin at Christ's second coming can provide the solution to the sin problem. Christ's reign during the millennium will be a physical reign—either on earth or in heaven, depending on the view adopted—and will be without the presence of evil and sin.[25]

During his study of the books of Daniel and Revelation, William Miller came to the premillennialist conclusion that Christ's second coming would be soon, in his time, and that it would occur before the millennium. To arrive at this conclusion, Miller did some detailed calculations of the prophetic time periods in the book of Daniel and concluded that Christ would return about the year 1843. Although many people scoffed at Miller's intricate chronologies, his calculations were very similar to those of his contemporaries, and many of these calculations appeared in the margins of their Bibles. What set Miller's computations apart from those of others, according to Whitney Cross, was that his were more accurate, which rendered them more dramatic and the predicted event more surprising. "On two points only was he dogmatically insistent: that Christ would come, and that He would come about 1843."[26]

But Miller's premillennial teachings clashed with the postmillennialism taught in most established churches of his time. These churches were expecting the dawning of a new millennium of peace and abundance brought about through social reforms and education. Charles Finney, an American revivalist of the 1820s and 1830s, summarized the state of expectancy the churches were in when he proclaimed in 1835: "If the church will do her duty, the millennium may come in this country in three years."[27] Historian Ernest Sandeen seized the mood of that time when he wrote, "America in the early nineteenth century was drunk on the millennium."[28]

In contrast, however, Miller predicted that the event would instead be the cataclysmic destruction of all the kingdoms of this earth and of all the unrepentant sinners. In other words, Miller implied that all the churches' good works were not good enough to establish God's kingdom on earth. Only the second advent of Christ and the end-time conflagration that would accompany his return would enable the establishment of God's eternal kingdom. Miller's radical teachings caused a major shift in the religious consciousness of his listeners by awakening a fear, or a hope, that he might in the end be right. Apart from his strong eschatological emphasis, Miller's teachings and views were faithful to the prevailing evangelical doctrines.[29]

Ellen White's eschatological scenario basically followed in the footsteps of Miller's premillennialism and is best described in her book *The Great Controversy*. She believed the world is living in the last days and that soon we will see the second coming of Christ. Like Miller she rejected the possibility of redeeming the earth through social reforms and accepted the view that at Christ's second coming sin will be eradicated from the earth. Prior to that moment the world will hear the three angels' messages of Revelation 14 (more will be said about these messages later), and all people on earth will make a final decision in regard to the gospel message and faithful obedience to God's commandments. The preaching of these messages will galvanize public opinion in favor or against the teachings of Scripture and lead to the persecution and tribulation of those who wish to follow God's Word (GC 603-612). In this time of trouble, however, God's people are protected from evil and finally rescued at the moment of Christ's coming (*ibid.* 613-634).

White further explained that on the day of Christ's second advent, the world as we know it will end. The redeemed who have died in the hope of eternal life will be resurrected, and the people of God who are alive will be granted immortality. Both groups will ascend to heaven, where they will live with Christ for 1,000 years (*ibid.* 635-652). During that time the earth is left desolate and uninhabited; it becomes the prison of Satan and his evil hordes (*ibid.* 653-661).

According to White, at the end of the millennium Christ and all the redeemed return to the earth with the New Jerusalem. At that point, all sinners are judged in the final judgment and along with Satan and his angels are destroyed for eternity. White espouses the view that sin and evil, sinners, and rebellious angels are destroyed in a complete annihilation at the end of the millennium (*ibid.* 662-673). For her, annihilationism is also intertwined with her view of human nature and conditional immortality. She disavows the Platonic concept of the immortality of the soul, which, she believes, is propagated by paganism and much of Christianity (*ibid.* 551-562). Instead, she sees conditional immortality as the biblical principle that corrects the popular interest in various forms of spiritualism—a delusion introduced into the world by Satan in Eden (*ibid.* 531-534; cf. Gen. 3:4, 5). One's natural death is seen as a sleeplike condition with no consciousness that only the resurrection interrupts (*ibid.* 550, 557, 558). Her belief in the conditional immortality of human life precludes the eternal existence of sinners and evil angels. For her, immortality is a gift of God, a reward granted only to the faithful redeemed children of God, and to no one else. This view led her to believe that eternal death, i.e., eternal nonexistence, is the ultimate consequence of sin.

Ellen White's eschatology is firmly premillennialist and dependent on her views about human nature, conditional immortality, and annihilationism. Her premillennialism, however, is not dispensationalist. She rejects the belief that Christ's second advent is divided into two events, first a secret rapture and then a glorious appearing, separated by a gap of seven years during which sinners on earth receive a second chance at salvation. Christ's second advent will be a single, visible, and personal event. She also rejects universalism and believes sinners have only this life to make a decision in regard to the gospel message and the offer of salvation. These views, therefore, influence her strong affirmation of the church's mission to spread the gospel to all peoples and nations on earth.

Paradoxical, however, is White's commitment to health reform, education, and social and personal welfare. Given her emphasis on premillennialism and the utter destruction of this earth and its treasures at the second advent of Christ, it is somewhat puzzling that she devoted so much of her writings and ministry to the promotion of a healthy and wholistic lifestyle (see her books *The Ministry of Healing* and *Counsels on Health*)—and today Seventh-day Adventists live on the average five to 10 years longer than the general population.[30] She also encouraged the development of a vast and extensive educational system (see her books *Education* and *Counsels to Parents, Teachers, and Students*), she promoted local welfare activities and reforms (see her books *Welfare Ministry* and *Temperance*), and helped in the development of a fairly large and well-structured church organization (see many of her testimonies in *Testimonies for the Church*). If White believed in the cataclysmic soon coming of Christ, she also certainly helped in establishing a significant Adventist "kingdom" on earth. Her emphasis on all these social activities and reforms, however, should be understood within the context of her missiological thought. White believed that the mission of the church is an extension of the work of Christ who went about teaching and healing. This mission to spread the gospel and the three angels' messages to all the world would be more effective and successful if all aspects of human life are touched. Hence, health and temperance reforms, education, and social welfare are integral aspects and functions of the mission of the church to proclaim a loving and saving message to a dying world in dire need of hope. Her eschatology influences her missiological views, which in turn drives her social thought.

II. Theological Themes in the Writings of Ellen G. White

Following a discussion of currents of thought that have had an impact on Ellen White's writings, it is appropriate now to highlight the major themes to be found in her writings. Although through the years people had identified various themes in her writings, George Knight in 1996 was the first to publish a list of seven theological themes, found in the last chapter of his book *Meeting Ellen White: A Fresh Look at Her Life, Writings, and Major Themes*. In the introduction to this chapter Knight comments: "[These themes] represent ideas that help us understand her theology and her burden for individuals and the church. Also they integrate the various strands of her thinking into a unified network of concepts that provide an interpretive framework for not only single documents but for entire sectors of her writings (such as health, education, and family living)."[31]

I concur with Knight in affirming that although Ellen White was not a trained theologian, in her writings she nonetheless used a number of theological themes to articulate her ideas, organize her counsels to individuals and the church, and write or comment on biblical subjects. Early in her ministry she did not set out to use these themes as her interpretive framework for her writings, but as her writings became more voluminous, these themes received more emphasis and slowly emerged and integrated the various strands of her thinking. These themes are so interrelated in her writings that it is hard to treat them separately without repeating what has already been said.

Love of God

The themes of the love of God and the great controversy between Christ and Satan are the foundational themes of Ellen White's theology. Of these two, Knight points out that "perhaps the central and most comprehensive theme" in her writings is that of "the love of God."[32] This is a theme that White repeatedly mentions and discusses in her books. It is this theme that provides the context for her telling of the great controversy story and serves as a theological principle of hermeneutics to understand her writings. The love of God existed prior to creation of any other beings and prior to the rise of Satan's rebellion.

As mentioned earlier, White's best-known series of books is the five-volume Conflict of the Ages Series. This series emerged through the years as she unfolded to her readers her understanding of the great controversy between good and evil from the fall of Lucifer in heaven to the new earth at the end of time. The first and last volumes of this series, *Patriarchs and Prophets* (1890) and *The Great Controversy* (1888), were written in the 1880s and highlight the integration of these two dominant themes. The phrase "God is love" appears as the first three words of *Patriarchs and Prophets* (p. 33) and the last three words of *The Great Controversy* (p. 678). Obviously White had a purpose in mind when she referred to the love of God as the beginning and end of her metanarrative. God's love emerges as the central focus of the cosmic struggle between good and evil and appears as a hermeneutical principle to understand her thought. It also provides the context for her telling of the great controversy story.

But this hermeneutical principle became apparent in her writings on the great controversy only later in her life. Her first book on the great controversy—the first volume of *Spiritual Gifts*—does not even once mention that "God is love." And the two-page description of the "law of love" which opens the Conflict of the Ages Series in *Patriarchs and Prophets* (pp. 34, 35) finds no parallel in either of her earlier writings in *Spiritual Gifts* (vol. 1) or *The Spirit of Prophecy* (vol. 1). It seems obvious then that as she amplified her narrative of the great controversy, she came to see the character of God as the major principle of articulation of this cosmic conflict. What may not have been apparent at first became more prominent in her later writings.

Other books also highlight this emphasis on the love of God. The first chapter of *Steps to Christ* begins with these words: "Nature and revelation alike testify of God's love" (p. 9). "The world, though fallen," she continues, "is not all sorrow and misery. In nature itself are messages of hope and comfort. There are flowers upon the thistles, and the thorns are covered with roses. 'God is love' is written upon every opening bud, upon every spire of springing grass" (*ibid.* 9, 10). Yet White points out that the things of nature in a world of sin "but imperfectly represent His love" (*ibid.* 10). Hence, the supreme and clearest illustration of God's love is Jesus, who came to this world to save us from our sins (*ibid.* 10-13).

In the first chapter of *The Desire of Ages* she points out that Jesus "came to reveal the light of God's love" (p. 19). "Both the redeemed and the unfallen beings will find in the cross of Christ their science and their song. It will be seen that the glory shining in the face of Jesus is the glory of self-sacrificing love. In the light from Calvary it will be seen that the law of self-renouncing love is the law of life for earth and heaven; that the love which 'seeketh not her own' has its source in the heart of God; and that in the meek and lowly One is manifested the character of Him who dwelleth in the light which no man can approach unto" (*ibid.* 19, 20). On the last page of *The Desire of Ages* her conclusion is that through Christ's sacrifice "love has conquered" (*ibid.* 835).

And at the end of *The Great Controversy* her concluding thoughts also point to the future and the promise of everlasting reconciliation between nature and God. "The great controversy is ended. Sin and sinners are no more. The entire universe is clean. One pulse of harmony and gladness beats through the vast creation. From Him who created all, flow life and light and gladness, throughout the realms of illimitable space. From the minutest atom to the greatest world, all things, animate and inanimate, in their unshadowed beauty and perfect joy, declare that God is love" (p. 678).

Great Controversy

Closely connected to this first theme of the love of God is the theme of the great controversy, that the universe is caught in a cosmic conflict between God and the forces of evil, and that this conflict is played out on earth for the allegiance of humanity. Ellen White emphasizes repeatedly that the focal point of the great controversy is Satan's aim to misrepresent the loving character of God. "The history of the great conflict between good and evil," she wrote at the beginning of *Patriarchs and Prophets*, "from the time it first began in heaven to the final overthrow of rebellion and the total eradication of sin, is also a demonstration of God's unchanging love" (p. 33). "Satan led men to conceive of God as a being whose chief attribute is stern justice—one who is a severe judge, a harsh, exacting creditor," she argued in *Steps to Christ*. "He pictured the Creator as a being who is watching with jealous eye to discern the errors and mistakes of men, that He may visit judgments upon them" (p. 11; cf. Ed 190).

In light of these thoughts in *Steps to Christ* and elsewhere, Herbert Douglass views White's great controversy theme as the "conceptual key" to understanding humanity's greatest questions regarding the origin of life, and the reasons for the existence of good and evil, suffering and death. This theme, he argues, allows Ellen White to provide the background for the development of evil in the story of Lucifer's rebellion against God's government. "Satan's argument is that God cannot be trusted, that His law is severe and unfair, and thus the Lawgiver is unfair, severe, and arbitrary." In contrast to Lucifer, God's purpose in this conflict is twofold: (1) to demonstrate before all the universe the nature of Satan's rebellion and, in doing so, to vindicate His character, and (2) to restore in men and women the image of God.[33] "The vindication of God's fairness and trustworthiness," concludes Douglass, "coupled with the concept of restoration as being the purpose of the gospel brought a biblical freshness to Ellen White's theological system and provided coherence to all other aspects of her teachings."[34]

Ellen White's writing of the story of the great controversy between Christ and Satan occupied a sizable portion of her time between 1858 and her death in 1915. In March 1858 she had a vision in which she was instructed to write the events she had seen. Amid personal afflictions she wrote that year the first volume of *Spiritual Gifts,* in which she summed up important periods of human history from the fall of Lucifer in heaven to the earth made new. For the first time in her writings, she revealed that a conflict of cosmic proportion is happening in the universe, an invisible struggle between the forces of good and evil for the control of humanity and the ultimate fate of the universe.[35]

For Ellen White, the misrepresentation of God's character by Satan is the core issue of the great controversy, but also part of Satan's challenge to God's character of love and justice is a challenge to His law that is a true representation of His character. White understands that Satan's aim is also to misrepresent and distort God's law. In her thought the character of God and the law of God are not two separate elements of this controversy; God's law is a reflection of His character. Hence, "Satan represents God's law of love as a law of selfishness. He declares that it is impossible for us to obey its precepts" (DA 24). "From the very beginning of the great controversy in heaven it has been Satan's purpose to overthrow the law of God. It was to accomplish this that he entered upon his rebellion against the Creator, and though he was cast out of heaven he has continued the same warfare upon the earth. To deceive men, and thus lead them to transgress God's law, is the object which he has steadfastly pursued. Whether this be accomplished by casting aside the law altogether, or by rejecting one of its precepts, the result will be ultimately the same" (GC 582).[36]

Key to understanding White's concept of the great controversy is also the emphasis she places on the freedom of choice God gave to all created intelligent beings. When the rebellion began in heaven, God could have easily destroyed all opposition but in doing so, she believes, He would have cast a shadow on His government and given some credibility to Satan's accusations.

"The inhabitants of heaven and of the worlds, being unprepared to comprehend the nature or consequences of sin, could not then have seen the justice of God in the destruction of Satan. Had he been immediately blotted out of existence, some would have served God from fear rather than from love. The influence of the deceiver would not have been fully destroyed, nor would the spirit of rebellion have been utterly eradicated. For the good of the entire universe through ceaseless ages, he must more fully develop his principles, that his charges against the divine government might be seen in their true light by all created beings, and that the justice and mercy of God and the immutability of His law might be forever placed beyond all question" (PP 42).

This freedom of choice given to angelic beings was also given to humanity at the Creation. Although created holy and innocent, Adam and Eve were not beyond the possibility of wrongdoing. "God made them free moral agents, capable of appreciating the wisdom and benevolence of His character and the justice of His requirements, and with full liberty to yield or to withhold obedience" (*ibid.* 48). It is in this context that White makes a most valuable theological contribution to understanding the character of God. While Satan uses lies and deception to fulfill his purpose against God and His government, God on the other hand uses only loving persuasion. He never forces someone to serve Him. As alluded to earlier, this concept is the basis of her understanding of religious liberty.

It was to reveal the true character of God and to answer the accusations of Satan against God's law that Christ came to this earth to redeem humanity (SC 11). "The act of Christ in dying for the salvation of man would not only make heaven accessible to men, but before all the universe it would justify God and His Son in their dealing with the rebellion of Satan. It would establish the perpetuity of the law of God and would reveal the nature and the results of sin. From the first the great controversy had been upon the law of God. Satan had sought to prove that God was unjust, that His law was faulty, and that the good of the universe required it to be changed. In attacking the law he aimed to overthrow the authority of its Author. In the controversy it was to be shown whether the divine statutes were defective and subject to change, or perfect and immutable" (PP 69; cf. DA 24-26).

Along with the theme of the love of God, this theme provides the theological framework that gives direction and context to the rest of White's writings.[37] According to George Knight, "the concepts of God's love and the great controversy lead to a third theme that permeates Ellen White's writings and links all the various themes together. That third theme focuses on Jesus, His death on the cross, and salvation through His grace."[38]

Jesus, His Death, and Heavenly Ministry

For Ellen White, Jesus was not only the victorious Redeemer over the forces of evil but also a very personal friend to her, and the Savior who died on the cross for each individual human being. Her intimate knowledge of Jesus as her personal Savior extends to all aspects of her discussion of His death and the salvation He brings to humanity.

For White, God's foremost demonstration of His love in the great controversy was His sending Jesus to redeem humanity. "It was to remove this dark shadow, by revealing to the world the infinite love of God, that Jesus came to live among men" (SC 11). Following the fall of Adam and Eve, Christ committed Himself to redeem humanity from the transgression of God's command. The plan of redemption was conceived in divine love for humanity. "The broken law of God demanded the life of the sinner," argued White. "In all the universe there was but one who could, in behalf of man, satisfy its claims. Since the divine law is as sacred as God Himself, only one equal with God could make atonement for its transgression. None but Christ could redeem fallen man from the curse of the law and bring him again into harmony with Heaven. Christ would take upon Himself the guilt and shame of sin" (PP 63).

In 1901 White described the theological significance of the death of Christ in a statement that reflects the Christological depth and focus of her thought: "The sacrifice of Christ as an atonement for sin is the great truth around which all other truths cluster. In order to be rightly understood and appreciated, every truth in the Word of God, from Genesis to Revelation, must be studied in the light that streams from the cross of Calvary. I present before you the great, grand monument of mercy and regeneration, salvation and redemption—the Son of God uplifted on the cross. This is to be the foundation of every discourse given by our ministers" (GW 315).

Clearly and consistently in her writings Ellen White viewed the sufferings and death of Christ as the core events of the plan of salvation. For centuries theologians have attempted to explain the purpose and meaning of Christ's death. Multiple theories, from the subjective Socinian exemplarist model to the objective Anselmic satisfaction theory, have been proposed, and a multitude of arguments have been discussed to support or reject various aspects of these theories. However, many scholars have argued along with Leon Morris that the reasons for Christ's death are so multifaceted that not one single theory embraces the totality of what God intended to do or accomplish at the cross.[39] What is perhaps most fascinating is to discover that White embraced all the major theories of atonement and therefore supported a broad understanding of the reasons for Calvary.

The most basic aspect of Ellen White's theology of atonement centers on the death of Christ as a demonstration of the love of God for lost humanity. "Who can comprehend the love here displayed," she wrote in 1869. "All this in consequence of sin! Nothing could have induced Christ to leave His honor and majesty in heaven, and come to a sinful world, to be neglected, despised, and rejected by those He came to save, and finally to suffer upon the cross, but eternal, redeeming love, which will ever remain a mystery" (2T 207). Moreover, she also affirmed that such a demonstration of the love of God exerts a powerful moral influence on humanity and transforms people's hearts who let themselves be touched by Christ's life and death. "Eternal interests are here involved. Upon this theme it is sin to be calm and unimpassioned. The scenes of Calvary call for the deepest emotion. Upon this subject you will be excusable if you manifest enthusiasm. . . . The contemplation of the matchless depths of a Savior's love should fill the mind, touch and melt the soul, refine and elevate the affections, and completely transform the whole character" (*ibid.* 213). She also wrote that reflecting on the events of Calvary will "awaken tender, sacred, and lively emotions in the Christian's heart" and remove "pride and self-esteem" (*ibid.* 212).

Years later Ellen White offered this same theme as the starting point of her book *The Desire of Ages:* "It was to manifest this glory [of God] that He came to our world. To this sin-darkened earth He came to reveal the light of God's love—to be 'God with us.' . . . In the light from Calvary it will be seen that the law of self-renouncing love is the law of life for earth and heaven; that the love which 'seeketh not her own' has its source in the heart of God" (pp. 19, 20). The same sentiments are echoed in *Patriarchs and Prophets.* With a quote from 1 John 4:16, she begins the Conflict of the Ages Series with the statement that "God is love," and then she affirms that "the history of the great conflict between good and evil, from the time it first began in heaven to the final overthrow of rebellion and the total eradication of sin, is also a demonstration of God's unchanging love" (p. 33).

White also affirmed that Calvary was a vindication of God's character, law, and just government. "His death did not make the law of none effect; it did not slay the law, lessen its holy claims, nor detract from its sacred dignity. The death of Christ proclaimed the justice of His Father's law in punishing the transgressor, in that He consented to suffer the penalty of the law Himself in order to save fallen man from its curse. The death of God's beloved Son on the cross shows the immutability of the law of God. . . . The death of Christ justified the claims of the law" (2T 201). In *The Desire of Ages* White asserted that Christ's death vindicated the character, law, and government of God against all Satan's accusations. "In the opening of the great controversy," she wrote, "Satan had declared that the law of God could not be obeyed" (p. 761). But, "by His life and His death, Christ proved that God's justice did not destroy His mercy, but that sin could be forgiven, and that the law is righteous, and can be perfectly obeyed. Satan's charges were refuted. God had given man unmistakable evidence of His love" (*ibid.* 762).

Since the time of the early church, the classical theory of atonement maintains that Calvary was the sign of Christ's ultimate victory over the powers of evil and Satan. This view was also held by Ellen White. At the cross, "Satan was then defeated. He knew that his kingdom was lost" (2T 211). White devoted an entire chapter to this theme in *The Desire of Ages.* In this chapter she affirmed unequivocally that Christ's death on the cross was God's appointed means to gain the victory over the forces of evil and Satan. "Christ did not yield up His life till He had accomplished the work which He came to do, and with His parting breath He exclaimed, 'It is finished.' . . . The battle had been won. . . . All heaven triumphed in the Savior's victory. Satan was defeated" (p. 758).

For White, Christ's death was also a substitutionary sacrificial death, Christ suffered our penalty for sins, died our death, and bore our sins. "Christ consented to die in the sinner's stead, that man, by a life of obedience, might escape the penalty of the law of God" (2T 200, 201). At Calvary, "the glorious Redeemer of a lost world was suffering the penalty of man's transgression of the Father's law" (*ibid.* 209). "The sins of the world were upon Him. He was suffering in man's stead as a transgressor of His Father's law" (*ibid.* 203). Commenting on Abel's sacrifice, she wrote in *Patriarchs and Prophets,* "Through the shed blood he [Abel] looked to the future sacrifice, Christ dying on the cross of Calvary; and trusting in the atonement that was there to be made, he had the witness that he was righteous, and his offering accepted" (p. 72). But perhaps White's clearest such statements is the following from 1901: "He [the Father] planted the cross between heaven and earth, and when the Father beheld the sacrifice of His son, He bowed before it in recognition of its perfection. 'It is enough,' He said. 'The atonement is complete'" (RH, Sept. 24, 1901). White believed that Christ was both sacrifice and priest on the cross, and thus could minister a sacrifice of atonement on Calvary's altar. "As the high priest laid aside his gorgeous, pontifical robes, and officiated in the white linen dress of a common priest, so Christ emptied Himself, and took the form of a servant, and offered the sacrifice, Himself the priest, Himself the victim" (RH, Sept. 7, 1897).

White argued as well that Christ's substitutionary sacrificial death is the means by which sinners can be justified by faith. Her classic statement in *The Desire of Ages* is clear: "Christ was treated as we deserve, that we might be treated as He deserves. He was condemned for our sins, in which He had no share, that we might be justified by His righteousness, in which we had no share. He suffered the death which was ours, that we might receive the life which was His. 'With His stripes we are healed'" (p. 25; see 8T 208, 209 for a variant of this important passage).

One final aspect of atonement, and perhaps one of the first ones to be rejected in our modern world, is the understanding that Christ died in order to propitiate the just wrath of God toward sin and sinners. Our modern sensibilities are uncomfortable with the idea of God requiring someone, His Son, to die in our place in order to assuage His wrath. Yet the apostle Paul wrote about Christ's sacrifice as a propitiation for our sins in view of God's wrath and judgment toward sinners (Rom. 1:18; 3:24, 25; 5:9). That Christ bore on our behalf and in our stead the wrathful judgment of God toward sinners is clearly supported by Ellen White. "Could mortals have viewed the amazement and the sorrow of the angelic host as they watched in silent grief the Father separating His beams of light, love, and glory from the beloved Son of His bosom, they would better understand how offensive sin is in His sight. The sword of justice was now to awake against His dear Son" (2T 207). In *The Desire of Ages* Ellen White further clarified her understanding of how Jesus bore the wrath of God on the cross. "Through Jesus, God's mercy was manifested to men; but mercy does not set aside justice. The law reveals the attributes of God's character, and not a jot or tittle of it could be changed to meet man in his fallen condition. God did not change His law, but He sacrificed Himself, in Christ, for man's redemption. 'God was in Christ, reconciling the world unto Himself'" (p. 762). In White's understanding of this concept of propitiation, there is no dichotomy or unreconcilable chasm between God's love and His justice. She does not believe that on the cross Jesus was attempting to influence God to love humanity. Rather, He was a self-renouncing God sacrificing Himself to redeem a lost humanity. "But this great sacrifice was not made in order to create in the Father's heart a love for man, not to make Him willing to save. No, no! 'God so loved the world, that He gave His only begotten Son.' John 3:16. The Father loves us, not because of the great propitiation, but He provided the propitiation because He loves us" (SC 13).

By these statements spanning her many years of ministry, Ellen White affirmed the importance and centrality of Calvary in her theology of atonement. Unequivocally she stated that atonement was accomplished at the cross. The death of Christ on the cross demonstrated the love of God for humanity and influenced humanity's moral behavior; it vindicated God's character, law, and government, triumphed over the powers of evil and Satan, was the appointed sacrificial substitute to redeem humankind from sin and to grant justification by faith, and propitiated the wrath of God against sin.

Like many of her contemporaries, White feared that a deficient view of atonement would lead to antinomianism and immorality. Yet she emphasized the impact upon one's life of the sufferings of Christ from His incarnation to Golgotha as the antidote to these problems. A true understanding of the cross and the character of God will lead one to realize that God's law could not be abrogated or abolished at the cross; in fact, it was because the law of God could not be changed that Christ had to die. She believed that an accurate picture of Christ's sufferings and death on behalf of sinners will also influence one to turn to God in repentance and transform the life of a repentant sinner.

We must be guarded, however, from giving the impression that Ellen White's views on atonement included only references to the cross. Her understanding of atonement was certainly cross-centered, but it also included the biblical understanding of Christ's intercessory ministry in heaven. A few examples will illustrate her thought. "The intercession of Christ in man's behalf in the sanctuary above is as essential to the plan of salvation as was His death upon the cross. By His death He began that work which after His resurrection He ascended to complete in heaven" (GC 489). Along the same thought, she wrote in 1893: "Jesus is our great High Priest in heaven. And what is He doing?—He is making intercession and atonement for His people who believe in Him" (RH, Aug. 22, 1893). Statements such as these indicate that her understanding of atonement also includes Christ's ministry in heaven.

A survey of White's writings reveals that she used the word "atonement" in three different ways, from a specific, focused meaning to a broad meaning. In a fair number of instances the word is used to describe Calvary as a complete atonement (cf. PP 72; ST, Aug. 25, 1887; ST, Dec. 30, 1889; ST, June 28, 1899; RH, Sept. 24, 1901). In these cases the meaning of atonement is specific and focused on a single event, the cross. In other places, atonement takes on a broader meaning and includes the work of atonement of the high priestly ministry of Christ in the heavenly sanctuary. In these instances, she refers to Christ ministering the benefits of His atoning sacrifice on behalf of repentant sinners (cf. Ms 29, 1906, in 7a BC 477; EW 260) or, in a few instances, refers to this work of Christ as atonement also (cf. FE 370; Ms 69, 1912, in 11MR 54). Christ's heavenly ministry is thus seen as an integral part of His work of atonement and redemption. A 1901 statement supports this second understanding of "atonement" when she described the two phases of Christ's priesthood: "He [Christ] fulfilled one phase of His priesthood by dying on the cross for the fallen race. He is now fulfilling another phase by pleading before the Father the case of the repenting, believing sinner, presenting to God the offerings of His people" (Ms 42, 1901, in 7BC 929).

Her third use of the word "atonement" is broader still and employs the word "atonement" in reference to the entire life of the sufferings of Christ. "We should take *broader and deeper* views of the life, sufferings, and death of God's dear Son. When the atonement is viewed correctly, the salvation of souls will be felt to be of infinite value" (2T 215; italics supplied). In this and other instances, her understanding of Christ's work of atonement becomes almost synonymous with Christ's entire work of redemption and thus embraces not only the cross as the central event of atonement but also all that Christ has done to save humankind, from the moment the plan of redemption was devised before the foundation of the world to the final eradication of sin at the end of time (cf. DA 494, 495, 565, 566; GC 503; 5BC 1101; Ms 21, 1895, in 2SAT 110-114). Here atonement is a process in time whose parts cannot be divorced.

Often Ellen White's view of atonement has been criticized for its lack of focus on the singularity of the cross event or for including other aspects of Christ's work. But to help us grasp her understanding of atonement, one should keep in mind that early Adventism did not conceive its theological system within the Aristotelian presuppositions of the Augustinian and Calvinist systems in which an immovable and impassible God exists only in timelessness. From these perspectives, crucial events of the plan of redemption are consequently the results of decrees God has proclaimed of all eternity, nothing new as such can be done by God and the entire plan of redemption is predetermined in God's eternal foreknowledge. Biblical references to heaven, the heavenly sanctuary, and Christ's intercessory ministry are ultimately considered as metaphors of God's eternal decrees of salvation.

Adventism adopted a different system of thought in which God actually interacts with humanity within time and space in various events of salvation history. In this system God's foreknowledge of future events is only descriptive of human responses and not prescriptive. This important difference in philosophical and theological presuppositions allowed Ellen White and other Adventist writers to see all the events of the plan of redemption, including atonement, as a linear process in which God is genuinely engaged rather than only a series of preordained punctiliar events shaped in the mind of God in eternity past. Thus, for White, heaven and its sanctuary are real places where Christ officiates a genuine intercessory ministry. This distinction in theological and philosophical presuppositions is crucial to understand Ellen White's theology of atonement.[40]

The Centrality of the Bible

Another important theme in Ellen White's writings is the Bible, the written Word of God. Through the years many criticisms have been directed at her writings regarding her views on various biblical doctrines and the level of authority we should give them; nonetheless, one cannot come away from reading her writings without the honest conclusion that she knew her Bible, and knew it well. A recurrent theme in her writings is the prominence she repeatedly gave to the Bible. At the end of her first book, *A Sketch of the Christian Experience and Views of Ellen G. White* (1851), she wrote: "I recommend to you, dear reader, the Word of God as the rule of your faith and practice" (EW 78). As one reads her books, particularly the Conflict of the Ages Series, it is obvious that White loved the Bible and made it the subject of her meditation. There is seldom a page in her writings that does not include either a text of Scripture or at least an allusion. Often her writings effuse with biblical wording or analogies. Those who knew of her devotional habits claim that she read her Bible every day. Hence it is understandable that she would make the following declarations about the importance of the Bible in Christian life and thought, and that the Bible should hold such a prominent place in the determination of faith and practice. Ellen White's views on the Bible fall within the Radical Reformation and restorationist context we observed earlier.

Her high view of Scripture is evident in her belief that the Bible is the Word of God, albeit given through human authors and in a language that is not heaven's language (1SM 21). With this assumption, respect for the Word of God is required of all those who read or hear it. "In the Bible the will of God is revealed to His children. Wherever it is read, in the family circle, the school, or the church, all should give quiet and devout attention as if God were really present and speaking to them" (5T 84).

In the introduction to *The Great Controversy* she wrote this crucial statement of her faith in Scripture: "In His Word, God has committed to men the knowledge necessary for salvation. The Holy Scriptures are to be accepted as an authoritative, infallible revelation of His will. They are the standard of character, the revealer of doctrines, and the test of experience. 'Every scripture inspired of God is also profitable for teaching, for reproof, for correction, for instruction which is in righteousness; that the man of God may be complete, furnished completely unto every good work'" (p. vii).

And to the ministers who were getting ready to assemble in Minneapolis for the General Conference session of 1888, during a period of time that ministers were hotly debating some issues of biblical interpretation, she clearly stated, "Search the Scriptures carefully to see what is truth. The truth can lose nothing by close investigation. Let the Word of God speak for itself; let it be its own interpreter. . . . Our people individually must understand Bible truth more thoroughly, for they certainly will be called before councils; they will be criticized by keen and critical minds. It is one thing to give assent to the truth, and another thing, through close examination as Bible students, to know what is truth. . . . Many, many will be lost because they have not studied their Bibles upon their knees, with earnest prayer to God that the entrance of the Word of God might give light to their understanding. . . . The Word of God is the great detector of error; to it we believe everything must be brought. The Bible must be our standard for every doctrine and practice. . . . We are to receive no one's opinion without comparing it with the Scriptures. Here is divine authority which is supreme in matters of faith. It is the Word of the living God that is to decide all controversies" (1888 Materials 38-45).

Also fundamental to Ellen White's view of Scripture is its perspecuity—the concept that the simple truths of the Bible can be understood by anyone, regardless of education or background. "I take the Bible just as it is, as the Inspired Word. I believe its utterances in an entire Bible. . . . Men of humble acquirements, possessing but limited capabilities and opportunities to become conversant in the Scriptures, find in the living oracles comfort, guidance, counsel, and the plan of salvation as clear as a sunbeam. No one need be lost for want of knowledge, unless he is willfully blind. We thank God that the Bible is prepared for the poor man as well as for the learned man. It is fitted for all ages and all classes" (Ms 16, 1888, in 1SM 17, 18).

Through the years many people have argued that because Ellen White was not trained as a biblical scholar or theologian her writings should be taken primarily as devotional materials and as such were not intended for doctrinal and theological guidance for Adventists.

Although nothing can be done about White's lack of theological training, nonetheless her writings do show evidence that she did have theological intentions when she wrote. Her use of the Bible in her writings is informed by her dedication to the Bible and her emphasis on its importance for our lives. I have found that she used the Bible in six different ways.

Typology. In her writings, but primarily in her Conflict of the Ages Series, Ellen White commented on the biblical story from the origin of sin in heaven to its final eradication from the universe after the millennium. She also applied the meaning of Scripture to people's lives or to the church. To do this she often used typologies when she understood or perceived a person or event in the Old Testament as a figure or illustration, i.e., a type of something or someone in the New Testament or in the church. In this fashion she perceived Elijah and Moses as types of the saints living on earth or resurrected at the second coming of Christ (PK 227). She also perceived Moses as a type of the incarnated Christ during his years of ministry (PP 330).

Moral lessons. Ellen White also used Scripture to weave moral lessons for Christians in her day. She drew moral lessons from events that happen to biblical people and applied these lessons to the church. Her account of the stories of Israel's failures in the wilderness are filled with such moral applications. Israel's lapse into idolatry at the foot of Mount Sinai, while Moses is on the mountain receiving God's instructions, is fraught with moral lessons for today. "How often, in our own day, is the love of pleasure disguised by a "form of godliness"! A religion that permits men, while observing the rites of worship, to devote themselves to selfish or sensual gratification is as pleasing to the multitudes now as in the days of Israel. And there are still pliant Aarons, who, while holding positions of authority in the church, will yield to the desires of the unconsecrated, and thus encourage them in sin" (*ibid.* 317). The sad story of the priests Nadab and Abihu is also filled with moral lessons to deter Christians from sin (*ibid.* 359-362).

Character sketches. Given the overarching theme of the great controversy in her writings, White perceived that the way biblical people related to God in this controversy between good and evil illustrates how one's life today should be lived in order to be victorious over the same powers of evil. Hence, she often illustrated her narratives of the biblical stories with insightful character sketches. In the chapter "Lives of Great Men" in *Education* White presented short character sketches of Joseph, Daniel, Moses, Elijah, and Paul. From this chapter is this often-quoted passage: "The greatest want of the world is the want of men—men who will not be bought or sold, men who in their inmost souls are true and honest, men who do not fear to call sin by its right name, men whose conscience is as true to duty as the needle to the pole, men who will stand for the right though the heavens fall" (p. 57).

Biblical analogies and parallelisms. Biblical analogies and parallelisms represent a fourth approach to Scripture used by White. She often drew parallels between various Bible stories, events, people, or texts and explained the meaning of a story by drawing on many texts in other parts of the Bible. In thus connecting together many stories and texts, she saw a basic harmony between all of the books of the Bible. One of the most obvious differences between her narratives of the great controversy story in her early books (*Spiritual Gifts* and *The Spirit of Prophecy*) and her later books in the Conflict of the Ages Series is her use of Scripture.

To the brief and concise narratives of the earlier books numerous Scripture passages have been added in the later books. Over time Ellen White became more conscious of the need to show how all of Scripture speaks about the various subjects she is addressing. In the first chapter of *The Desire of Ages,* in which she explains the meaning of Jesus' first advent, she refers to more than 20 different texts of Scripture.

Spiritual warfare. Spiritual warfare is another approach to Scripture in White's writings. In many of her chapters in the Conflict of the Ages Series she presents to her readers the "behind the scenes" events, conversations between Christ and Satan, or between evil angels, or how God interprets and reacts to events. This approach is again closely connected with her understanding of the great controversy. One of the best chapters illustrating this approach is "Satan's Enmity Against the Law" in *Patriarchs and Prophets* (pp. 331-342), in which she describes how Satan led the newly freed people of Israel to apostatize at Mount Sinai while Moses was receiving further instructions from God. This chapter is an interlude in her narrative; for a moment she stops her commentary on the biblical story to give this spiritual warfare insight into the story. She does the same in the book *The Desire of Ages* when discussing the birth of Jesus in Bethlehem (pp. 43-49) and the death of Christ on Calvary (pp. 758-764).

Exegesis. One last approach to Scripture Ellen White uses is simple exegesis. Although Ellen White was not academically trained in biblical scholarship, this did not prevent her from providing some exegesis or theology in her interpretation of Scripture. At times she explained the meaning of words, talked about the context and circumstances of the passages, and referred to other texts to shed light on a passage. Books such as *Thoughts From the Mount of Blessing* and *Christ's Object Lessons* are Bible commentaries in their own rights, in which she expounded the meaning of texts, stories, and narratives of Scripture. In fact, her use of typologies, moral applications, character sketches, and biblical analogies and parallelisms are all forms of biblical commentary used by many trained scholars. However, one must note carefully that, whether done consciously or not, at times her explanations of the biblical text omit other nuances or meanings of the text and tend to be more pastoral in their applications. Furthermore, in her commentaries on the Bible, White did not believe she was the last word on the interpretation of a Bible passage. Well-known theological discussions in Adventist history—such as the meaning of the law in Galatians, or the identity of the 10 horns of Daniel 7, or of the daily in Daniel 8, when she was urged to provide the definitive interpretation of these biblical symbols—show that she refused to be the final arbiter of biblical interpretation.

Herbert Douglass has said it well in regard to Ellen White's use of Scripture: "The space she devotes to Biblical events and persons is not always proportional to the space given in the Bible. Her emphasis on certain events or persons depends on how she believes those events and persons contribute to the unfolding of the Great Controversy Theme."[41]

Ellen White's emphasis on the Bible is based upon her belief that the Bible, as the Word of God, is a transforming power in the lives of those who accept it. "The study of the Bible will ennoble every thought, feeling, and aspiration as no other study can. It gives stability of purpose, patience, courage, and fortitude; it refines the character and sanctifies the soul. An earnest, reverent study of the Scriptures, bringing the mind of the student in direct contact with the infinite mind, would give to the world men of stronger and more active intellect, as well as of nobler principle, than has ever resulted from the ablest training that human philosophy affords" (GC 94).[42]

The Second Coming of Christ

Three other themes are evident in Ellen White's writings, and all three are closely interconnected. George Knight comments that for White, "the Second Coming is a focal point of truth in the Bible, it is the climax of salvation in Christ, it signals the beginning of the end of the great controversy between good and evil, it is a supreme expression of God's love, it is the point of the three angels' messages, and it provides an incentive for Christian living. The Second Coming left no part of Ellen White's thinking unaffected."[43] Some of White's most beautiful and inspiring prose was written in connection with the events surrounding the second coming of Christ and the life of the redeemed on the new earth (EW 285-289; GC 635-652).

The second coming of Christ became of central importance to Ellen White from the time of her conversion in the Millerite experience in the 1840s, and the reality of the nearness of the Advent dominated her life and shaped her writing career. "The truths of prophecy are bound up together," White wrote to Pastor C. W. Irwin in 1902, "and as we study them, they form a beautiful cluster of practical Christian truth. All the discourses that we give are plainly to reveal that we are waiting, working, and praying for the coming of the Son of God. His coming is our hope. This hope is to be bound up with all our words and works, with all our associations and relationships" (Lt 150, 1902, in Ev 220).

Ellen White's thought on the Second Advent certainly falls within the predominant millennialist mood of the nineteenth century. As already discussed previously, millennialism fashioned much of American social thought in her era, and this effervescent context certainly affected her theological thought. But, like William Miller's understanding of the Second Advent, White's premillennialism contrasted sharply with the hopeful mood of the postmillennialism taught in most Christian denominations at the time. She categorically rejected the belief that the earth and all human societies as they stood in her day would be improved and ultimately find themselves ready for Christ's advent. To the contrary, she believed the biblical prophecies regarding the second advent of Christ indicate that the earth and all its wicked ways would be utterly destroyed at the Parousia. The earth would be cleansed by a destructive fire and wait 1,000 years before being re-created by God to become the everlasting abode of the New Jerusalem and all the redeemed of humanity.

White's scenario of events preceding the second coming of Christ unfolds a series of steps closely related to the proclamation of the three angels' messages of Revelation 14. Whether recognized or not, for Ellen White all of humanity has a role to play in the great controversy between Christ and Satan, and thus much of her writings on the second advent also deal with how God's people are to prepare themselves for this momentous event.[44]

White believed that the signs of Christ's coming herald the soon return of the Savior. "Jesus declares: 'There shall be signs in the sun, and in the moon, and in the stars; and upon the earth distress of nations.' . . . Those who behold these harbingers of His coming are to 'know that it is near, even at the doors'" (GC 37, 38), and that great events of salvation history are approaching their fulfillment. Although she never provided a detailed timetable and chronology of events, she understood that the final events of earth's history would revolve around the issue of God's people's complete and full allegiance to God's law, as manifested in faithful obedience to the Sabbath, and that the final events would start unfolding once Christian nations legislate and start enforcing a Sunday observance law. Such a human law will ultimately force all human beings to make a decision regarding God's law and His Sabbath commandment. Those who profess to be Christians will be required to take a stand, and only those who acknowledge God's Sabbath day will be given a special outpouring and sealing of the Holy Spirit and be preserved through the time of trouble. While the nations suffer from the last seven plagues, God's people are protected and by faith are victorious to witness the second coming of Christ. Those who have been asleep in Christ are resurrected, and those who are alive are translated into immortal bodies. Christ's return is both a moment of celebration and victory for God's people, and a judgment on the nations who have refused to acknowledge God's will for their lives (see *ibid.* 582-652).[45]

The Three Angels' Messages and Adventist Mission

Within this eschatological context the three angels' messages of Revelation 14 form the foundation of Adventist identity and mission focus. "In a special sense Seventh-day Adventists have been set in the world as watchmen and light bearers," Ellen White wrote in the early 1900s. "To them has been entrusted the last warning for a perishing world. On them is shining wonderful light from the Word of God. They have been given a work of the most solemn import—the proclamation of the first, second, and third angels' messages. There is no other work of so great importance. They are to allow nothing else to absorb their attention. The most solemn truths ever entrusted to mortals have been given us to proclaim to the world. The proclamation of these truths is to be our work. The world is to be warned, and God's people are to be true to the trust committed to them" (9T 19).

As White explains so forthrightly in this passage, the message of the three angels of Revelation 14:6-13 is the central core of Seventh-day Adventist identity. This is where they receive their sense of divine calling to be a worldwide prophetic voice in the end time. Their theology interprets these conflicts between good and evil, between the faithful people of God and the powers of evil in the world, as the results of Satan's hatred for God's law and truth as found in the Scriptures. The messages of the three angels are meant to call the attention of all inhabitants of the earth, both Christians and non-Christians, to what God considers important in preparation for the second coming of Christ. White's detailed account of the purpose and fulfillment of each message is found in *The Great Controversy*.

Depicted by an angel flying in midair, the first messenger proclaims the everlasting gospel to every nation, tribe, language, and people on earth. This angel represents a group of people whom God calls to proclaim to the whole world His everlasting gospel. This is the eschatological fulfillment of Jesus' great commission (Matt. 28:19, 20). This first message contains three parts: a call to fear God, the hour of God's judgment has come, and to worship the Creator God.

Ellen White understood the first angel's message as referring to the Millerite movement in the 1830s and1840s and continuing thereafter in the proclamation of the soon return of Christ. William Miller and his associates set in motion the end-time proclamation of the three angels' messages with their study of the prophecies of the book of Daniel and prediction that Christ's second advent would occur about 1843. The proclamation of these prophecies and the anticipated soon return of Christ raised people's awareness of the time of the end and of God's judgment upon the world, and caused "a great religious awakening" "foretold in the prophecy of the first angel's message of Revelation 14" (GC 355). This awakening was not only in North America but was also felt in other parts of the world (*ibid.* 357-370).

While the first angel proclaims a message of good news that is to go to every inhabitant of the earth, the second and third angels send messages of warning. The second angel follows with a critical message: "Babylon is fallen" (Rev. 14:8). In its etymological meaning Babylon is a reference to confusion, and, in its wider interpretation, this concept refers to religious confusion and apostasy. Its proclamation is a call to reject or renounce false beliefs—particularly those unbiblical beliefs that have infiltrated churches since the early years of Christianity (*ibid.* 49-60). For White the angel's warning contrasts God's everlasting gospel message with the spurious, false, and apostate in religious beliefs at the time of the Second Advent. The day will come when false religions will be seen to be the vanity they really are, leading to destruction rather than to life. According to White, this message was first preached in the summer of 1843 during the Millerite movement and continues since. She concludes that as Christian Protestant denominations refused "the warning of the first angel [during the Millerite movement], they rejected the means which Heaven had provided for their restoration" (*ibid.* 380).

For White, the Babylon of the book of Revelation is a symbolic representation of Roman Catholicism and of all Protestant churches and religious organizations "that cling to her doctrines and traditions, and follow her example of sacrificing the truth and the approval of God, in order to form an unlawful alliance with the world" (*ibid.* 382, 383). However, the fall of Babylon, although started in 1843 when churches refused to accept the first angel's message, is not yet complete, and a "perfect fulfillment of Revelation 14:8 is yet future" (*ibid.* 390). The fall of Babylon is progressive as Christian churches, refusing to correct their erroneous beliefs and practices, unite more and more with the sinful principles of the world. In the meantime, however, White admits that "the great body of Christ's true followers are still to be found in their communion" (*ibid.*).[46]

The first two messages climaxed into the third. According to George Knight, "It is in the third message that Seventh-day Adventism found its commission and unique identity."[47] The third angel's message points to the ultimate showdown between good and evil at the time of the Second Advent. White understood this message as indicating the final end of those who have rejected truth and allowed themselves to be deceived by the beast and its image and who have received its mark. This is a dire message, the strongest warning, but its intent is also to lead people to experience the everlasting gospel described in the first message.

In the third angel's message all three messages find their consummation. The warning to avoid the mark of the beast is heeded when Christians "fear God" in the sense of respecting His will and commandments that were given to all humanity, when they also prepare their hearts and lives for God's judgment, when they willingly worship God as Creator, and when they reject Babylon and its teachings.

At the end of the third angel's message, in contrast to those who receive the mark of the beast, the people of God are identified in clear terms: "Here is the patience of the saints: here are they that keep the commandments of God, and the faith of Jesus" (Rev. 14:12). These two identifying marks of God's end-time people are crucial indicators for Ellen White.

Far from being a means to attain salvation, for this is only received by grace through faith in Christ, obedience to God's commandments is our response to His love and redemption. Thus a true fear of God involves total dedication on the part of His children to willingly obey the commandments. "In order to be prepared for the judgment, it is necessary that men should keep the law of God. That law will be the standard of character in the judgment" (*ibid.* 436).

Ellen White saw a close connection between the call of the first angel to worship God the Creator and the identity of God's last people as commandment keepers. The first angel's message warns that all people on earth should worship God, the Creator: "Worship him that made heaven, and earth, and the sea, and the fountains of waters" (Rev. 14:7). Significantly, this call quotes from the Decalogue's fourth commandment in Exodus 20:11, the only commandment in which God describes who He is. White understood this first angel's message as a call to all humanity to worship the only true God on His day of worship, the Sabbath of Creation, given to humanity (and not only to the Jewish people) as a memorial of God's creatorship and love. The Sabbath is the good news that tells us of creation and re-creation, of our roots and destiny. The overall link between loving God, obeying his commandments, and the announcement of his judgment depicts an all-inclusive message of total dedication to God on the part of earth's inhabitants. This message is thus an urgent call to all humanity to know God as the God of the everlasting gospel and to worship Him on His day, the Sabbath. "Had the Sabbath been universally kept, man's thoughts and affections would have been led to the Creator as the object of reverence and worship, and there would never have been an idolater, an atheist, or an infidel. The keeping of the Sabbath is a sign of loyalty to the true God. . . . It follows that the message which commands men to worship God and keep His commandments will especially call upon them to keep the fourth commandment" (*ibid.* 438).

The people of God at the end of time are also identified as those who have the faith of Jesus. For White this identifying mark refers to trusting in Jesus as the sin-pardoning Savior (Ms 24, 1888, in 1888 Materials 217) and believing in the teachings of Jesus as found in the Bible (1Bio 404). Since the proclamation of the third angel's message coincides with the beginning of God's judgment, this judgment, already started in heaven before the second coming of Christ, is intending to identify God's true and sincere people. Christ's ministry in the heavenly sanctuary is crucial in this time of the end as God's people are identified and made ready by receiving the seal of God, in contrast to those who receive the mark of the beast.

For White the three angels' messages are at the heart of Seventh-day Adventist identity and mission. She viewed the Seventh-day Adventist Church as much more than simply another denomination within Christianity. Rather, Adventism is an end-time movement that proclaims God's last-day message. Its sense of mission is taken from these prophecies of Scripture. It is this strong sense of prophetic identity that is motivating this relatively small group of Christians to reach out with the everlasting gospel to a world dying and lost without the knowledge of salvation in Jesus and of His will. Ellen White repeatedly taught that "this [the message of the third angel] is the last message" for a world soon to be destroyed. "There are no more [messages] to follow, no more invitations of mercy to be given after this message shall have done its work" (5T 206, 207). "When Christ entered the most holy place of the heavenly sanctuary to perform the closing work of the atonement, He committed to His servants the last message of mercy to be given to the world. Such is the warning of the third angel of Revelation 14. Immediately following its proclamation, the Son of man is seen by the prophet coming in glory to reap the harvest of the earth" (SR 379).

It is easy to see how Ellen White's extensive writings on salvation, the law of God, the Sabbath, the great controversy, and other topics are related to the third angel's message. But what is often overlooked is that her writings on education, health, publishing, and gospel ministry are also connected to the third angel's message. The purpose of Adventist education is to train young people to spread the third angel's message. The Adventist health message is to provide people with better health so that they can more adequately preach this message. Health institutions are witnesses to the truth of the three angels' messages. The publishing and gospel ministries are to spread this last message to a dying world.[48]

Practical Christianity and the Development of Christian Character

Another crucial theme in Ellen White's writings, and in the context of her understanding of the second coming of Christ and of the three angels' messages, is her emphasis on living a practical Christianity and the development of Christian character. In *Testimonies for the Church*, volume 9, published in 1909, she devoted a chapter to the role Christians must play in the last hours of earth's history. "It is not only by preaching the truth . . . that we are to witness for God," she argued. "Let us remember that a Christlike life is the most powerful argument that can be advanced in favor of Christianity, and that a cheap Christian character works more harm in the world than the character of a worldling. . . . It is the purpose of God to glorify Himself in His people before the world. He expects those who bear the name of Christ to represent Him in thought, word, and deed" (p. 21). In the other sections of this chapter she emphasized how important is the example of one's life as a reflection of Christ's life. "Those who have been buried with Christ in baptism are to rise to newness of life, giving a living representation of the life of Christ. Upon us is laid a sacred charge" (p. 20). "The life that Christ lived in this world, men and women can live through His power and under His instruction" (p. 22). "Those who love Jesus will bring all in their lives into harmony with His will" (p. 23).

White's standards of Christian living were high, and seemed exacting at times, but were always set in the context of God's grace and power for living. "God requires at this time just what He required of the holy pair in Eden—perfect obedience to His requirements," she said to Adventists in Sweden during a visit in 1886. "His law remains the same in all ages. The great standard of righteousness presented in the Old Testament is not lowered in the New. It is not the work of the gospel to weaken the claims of God's holy law but to bring men up where they can keep its precepts" (FW 52).

But this standard of righteousness and perfection can only be attained by faith in God's grace. "By faith we may conform our lives to the standard of righteousness," she wrote in 1890, "because we can appropriate to ourselves the righteousness of Christ" (*ibid.* 97). "Faith and works go hand in hand," she said in Switzerland in 1885. "They act harmoniously in the work of overcoming. Works without faith are dead, and faith without works is dead. Works will never save us; it is the merit of Christ that will avail in our behalf. Through faith in Him, Christ will make all our imperfect efforts acceptable to God. The faith we are required to have is not a do-nothing faith; saving faith is that which works by love and purifies the soul" (*ibid.* 48, 49).

For Ellen White the daily life of the Christian is one that is surrendered to the will of God and committed to faithful obedience to His commandments. "Pure, living religion is found in obedience to every word that proceeds out of the mouth of God" (*ibid.* 89). Thus, Christianity affects every part of a person's life. True Christianity is not something that touches people only when they are in church—it transforms people from the inside out.

To Ellen White, everything matters in the Christian life. Every decision the Christian makes may have an impact upon one's spiritual life or that of someone else. One small decision may make a big difference in the scheme of eternity. Hence, White discussed many difficult subjects, and sometimes her counsels seem stringent and demanding. She advocated abandoning harmful habits and destructive ways of relating to others; she counseled about discarding activities and attitudes that do not uplift one's spiritual life. She recommended a lifestyle of daily Bible study and prayer, and the benefits of good health habits. For her, Christianity changes the heart, and that inner change, if it is genuine, carries over into every aspect of life: family relationships, school, work, and recreation.

What matters most in White's writings on practical Christianity is that harmful, sinful, needless habits and ways of life be replaced with a life lived like Jesus did. Jesus is the Christian's example to follow. She believed that what Jesus wants to do most is to reproduce Himself in the hearts of Christians, and that those who have faith in Him will put away the self-centered life of Satan's kingdom for the loving service of God and others. Jesus came to earth not only to die for us, but "to give an example of obedience." "Christ revealed a character the opposite of the character of Satan" (DA 24, 25).

In the context of end-time preparation, White advocated a positive and genuine spirituality in which Christlikeness becomes the character of God's children. "Christ is waiting with longing desire for the manifestation of Himself in His church. When the character of Christ shall be perfectly reproduced in His people, then He will come to claim them as His own" (COL 69). This exhortation is set in her discussion of one of the parables of the sower (Mark 4:26-29) and how seeds grow into mature plants. White relates how God desires to see our lives be sanctified. "Sanctification is the work of a lifetime," she commented (*ibid.* 65). This work of growth is slow, silent and imperceptible yet continuous and progressive. By cooperating with divine agencies, by keeping "our minds stayed on Christ," "by constantly relying upon Christ as our personal Savior, we shall grow up into Him in all things" (*ibid.* 67). "Christ is seeking to reproduce Himself in the hearts of men." "The object of the Christian life is fruit bearing—the reproduction of Christ's character in the believer, that it may be reproduced in others" (*ibid.*). As the Savior forgot Himself and helped others; as He carried the burdens of others and worked for others with "unselfish love," so are we to reflect

His likeness (*ibid.* 68). "Thus to reproduce the character of Christ perfectly is to let Him live out His love in our daily lives," comments Knight.[49]

"Just as love is the central characteristic of God and the core issue in the great controversy," explains Knight, "so it is also at the heart of what it means to develop a Christlike character that finds expression in the practical affairs of daily life."[50] "Wherever there is union with Christ there is love. Whatever other fruits we may bear, if love be missing, they profit nothing. Love to God and our neighbor is the very essence of our religion. No one can love Christ and not love His children. When we are united to Christ, we have the mind of Christ. Purity and love shine forth in the character, meekness and truth control the life. The very expression of the countenance is changed. Christ abiding in the soul exerts a transforming power, and the outward aspect bears witness to the peace and joy that reign within" (1SM 337).

Conclusion

With these thoughts we have come full circle in our discussion of theological themes in the writings of Ellen White. The core issue of the great controversy between good and evil is the character of God: how Jesus came to demonstrate this character of love in His life and how it can be showcased in each believer today. The purpose for a practical Christianity and the development of Christian character is to reflect the love of God to others. "The last rays of merciful light, the last message of mercy to be given to the world, is a revelation of His character of love. The children of God are to manifest His glory. In their own life and character they are to reveal what the grace of God has done for them. The light of the Sun of Righteousness is to shine forth in good works—in words of truth and deeds of holiness" (COL 415, 416).

These themes in Ellen White's writings integrate her thought into a logical, theological system of beliefs. The love of God; the great controversy between good and evil; the reasons for Jesus' incarnation, death, and ministry; the centrality of the Bible; the second coming of Christ; the three angels' messages and their impact on Adventist identity and mission; and the development of a Christlike character are all themes that integrate her writings into a cohesive whole. Whatever critiques may be made against her writings and her ministry, Ellen White succeeded in her lifetime in presenting and articulating a system of beliefs that is just as comprehensive and phenomenal as those of John Calvin or John Wesley. Yet she has received little attention outside Adventism.

Much more could be said about the writings of Ellen White in Seventh-day Adventism. But I'll conclude with a statement from A. G. Daniells that I referred to at the beginning of this article.

"Perhaps we are not wise enough to say definitely just what part of Mrs. White's life work has been of the greatest value to the world, but it would seem that the large volume of Biblical literature she has left would prove to be of the greatest service to mankind. Her books number upwards of twenty volumes [at the time of her death, in 1915—today more than 100 titles are available in English]. Some of these have been translated into many languages in different parts of the world. They have now reached a circulation of more than two million copies, and are still going to the public by thousands.

"As we survey the whole field of gospel truth—of man's relation to his Lord and his fellow men—it must be seen that Mrs. White, in all her teaching, has given these great fundamentals positive, constructive support. She has touched humanity at every vital point of need, and lifted it to a higher level" (in LS 475).

---

[1] Ellen White's Conflict of the Ages Series is made up of five books in which she comments on the biblical story and historical events in regard to the cosmic conflict between good and evil, between Christ and Satan, from the time of Lucifer's fall in heaven to the re-creation of the earth at the end of time. The series includes these books: *Patriarchs and Prophets* (published in 1890), which covers the time period of the fall of Lucifer in heaven to the end of King David's reign; *Prophets and Kings* (published posthumously in 1917), covering the rest of the Old Testament period from the reign of King Solomon to the time of Malachi; *The Desire of Ages* (1898), about the life of Christ; *The Acts of the Apostles* (1911), about the story of the early church; and the *The Great Controversy* (1884, 1888, 1911), which covers the period of church history from the destruction of Jerusalem to the re-creation of the earth after the millennium. Although not technically part of the series, two other books could be included since they were prepared in connection with the publication of *The Desire of Ages*. These are: *Thoughts From the Mount of Blessing* (1896), on Jesus' teaching in the Sermon on the Mount (Matt. 5-7); and *Christ's Object Lessons* (1900), on the parables of Jesus. Two other well-known books on the gospel and Jesus' ministry also deserve mentioning: *Steps to Christ* (1892) and *The Ministry of Healing* (1905). The reader will find more detailed information about each of these books and their historical and literary development in the topical section of this encyclopedia and in the general article on the writings of Ellen White.

[2] George R. Knight, *A Search for Identity: The Development of Seventh-day Adventist Beliefs* (RHPA, 2000), p. 27.

[3] See Knight, pp. 29-37.

[4] Ellen White's book *The Great Controversy* (1888 edition) was published just four years after the fourth volume of *The Spirit of Prophecy* (1884), which also covered the period of Christian history from the destruction of Jerusalem to the new earth. In between the two books she spent two years in Europe and decided to add as much material as possible to the content of the 1884 book so that it would be more appealing to people outside of the church (Lt 57, 1911). Many chapters on the Protestant Reformation and other movements were added.

[5] Ellen White's books that most reflect her Wesleyan Methodist understanding of the plan of salvation are her classics *Steps to Christ* and *The Desire of Ages*. *Christ's Object Lessons* is another good example of her Arminian theology along with the compilation of sermons in *Faith and Works*. Woodrow W. Whidden includes an introductory chapter on Ellen White's early Methodist experience in his book *Ellen White on Salvation* (RHPA, 1995), pp. 15-22.

[6] For a succinct summary of the theological parallels between Adventism and Wesleyan Methodism, see Russell L. Staples' article "Adventism," in *The Variety of American Evangelicalism*, ed. Donald W. Dayton and Robert K. Johnston (Downers Grove, Ill.: InterVarsity Press, 1991), pp. 57-71.

[7] The book *Faith and Works* is a compilation of sermons and articles of Ellen White in which one finds some of the best comments she made on the plan of salvation, God's grace, and faith and works. These statements were made for the most part between 1881 and 1895, crucial years in Adventist theology during which much of the time was consumed in debating the concepts of righteousness by faith and the role of obedience and works in salvation. I will refer to many of these sermons and articles in this section on Wesleyan Methodism.

[8] John Wesley's sermon "The Scripture Way of Salvation" includes a section on prevenient grace and the universal work of God on human hearts.

[9] Wesley emphasized that salvation is received in a person's life through faith. The blessing of salvation is first of all a gift of God's grace. At the beginning of his sermon "Salvation by Faith" Wesley states, "Grace is the source, faith the condition, of salvation." One is saved by a disposition of the heart, inclined toward Christ. To be saved, one must acknowledge "the necessity and merit of his death, and the power of his resurrection."

[10] In his sermon "The Scripture Way of Salvation" John Wesley states that "justification is another word for pardon. It is the forgiveness of all our sins; and, what is necessarily implied therein, our acceptance with God."

[11] Also in his sermon "The Scripture Way of Salvation" Wesley explains that "justification is another word for pardon" and our "acceptance with God." At the time a person is justified, "in that very moment, sanctification begins." "From the time of our being born again, the gradual work of sanctification takes place."

[12] In his sermon "The Scripture Way of Salvation" Wesley defines perfection as "perfect love." "It is love excluding sin, love filling the heart, taking up the whole capacity of the soul."

[13] For a summary of Ellen White's thought on perfection, see Whidden, pp. 119-156.

[14] George R. Knight, *Meeting Ellen White: A Fresh Look at Her Life, Writings, and Major Themes* (RHPA, 1996), p. 126.

[15] Whidden, p. 119.

[16] *Signs of the Times*, Mar. 15, 1841.

[17] William Miller, *William Miller's Apology and Defense* (Boston: J. V. Himes, 1845), p. 12.

[18] *Signs of the Times*, Mar. 15, 1841.

[19] Miller's rules of interpretation can be found in Sylvester Bliss, *Memoirs of William Miller* (Boston: Joshua V. Himes, 1853), pp. 70-72, and in P. Gerard Damsteegt, *Foundations of the Seventh-day Adventist Message and Mission* (Berrien Springs, Mich.: Andrews University Press, 1977), pp. 299, 300.

[20] Even to this day Adventists prefer a highly intellectual study of the Bible, rather than an emotional or experiential knowledge. Knight, *A Search for Identity*, p. 34.

[21] This school of thought was also influenced by Francis Bacon's early scientific method. See James C. Livingston, *Modern Christian Thought: The Enlightenment and the Nineteenth Century*, 2nd ed. (Upper Saddle River, N.J.: Prentice-Hall, 1997), vol. 1, pp. 303, 304; and D. F. Kelly, "Scottish Realism," in Walter A. Elwell, ed., *Evangelical Dictionary of Theology* (Grand Rapids: Baker Book House, 1984), pp. 990, 991.

[22] Knight, *A Search for Identity*, p. 36.

[23] *Ibid*. It is interesting to note that the decline of deism in American life and the rise of Adventism also occurred at a period of time in American history when the earlier founders of the nation, who were all well-educated deists, were being replaced with a new generation of self-made men, such as Andrew Jackson (president between 1829 and 1837). The mind-set of the Jacksonian era encouraged people to study on their own and to reach their own conclusions in matters of doctrines and religious life.

[24] Later that year she also rebuked John Harvey Kellogg, superintendent of the Battle Creek Sanitarium and influential medical doctor, who recommended the same two books to his readers (Lt 6, 1886, in 6MR 256-260). In an article in the *Review and Herald* also published that same year to counter Canright's influence, she stated unequivocally, "Our youth and children, and even those of mature age, should firmly pledge themselves to abstain from indulgence in reading the fascinating novels and sensational literature of the day. They delude the imagination, and fill the mind with such an amount of trash that there is no room for storing the sacred utterances of the prophets and apostles, who wrote as they were moved upon by the Holy Spirit" (RH, Nov. 9, 1886). Interestingly, later in her life White recommended John Bunyan's *Pilgrim's Progress* to her readers (RH, May 30, 1912).

[25] For more information on the historical context of millennialism in Ellen White's time, see George R. Knight, *Ellen White's World* (RHPA, 1998), pp. 13-18, 85-90.

[26] Whitney R. Cross, *The Burned-over District: The Social and Intellectual History of Enthusiastic Religion in Western New York, 1800-1850* (Ithica, N.Y.: Cornell University Press, 1950), p. 291.

[27] Quoted in Edwin S. Gaustad, *A Religious History of America* (New York: Harper and Row, 1966), p. 151.

[28] Ernest R. Sandeen, *The Roots of Fundamentalism: British and American Millenarianism, 1800-1930* (Chicago: University of Chicago Press, 1970), p. 42.

[29] Cross, p. 320. Cross also explains that "all Protestants expected some grand event about 1843, and no critic from the orthodox side took any serious issue on basic principles with Miller's calculations" (p. 321). Ruth Doan has also commented that "Millerites were, in their origins, good evangelical Protestant Americans," (Ruth Doan, *The Miller Heresy, Millennialism, and American Culture* [Philadelphia: Temple University Press, 1987], p. 215). Many studies in the past four decades have demonstrated that it was Millerism's resemblance to other denominations that was a cause of tensions with them. These studies highlight how Millerism was certainly a movement within the popular trend to millennial fever, revivalism, and evangelical ethos found on both sides of the Atlantic in the first part of the nineteenth century. Cross's *Burned-over District* and David L. Rowe's *Thunder and Trumpets: Millerites and Dissenting Religion in Upstate New York, 1800-1850* (Chico, Calif.: Scholars Press, 1985) describe the social and religious conditions of western New York that assisted the emergence of Millerism. Other studies such as Sandeen's *The Roots of Fundamentalism*; J.F.C. Harrison's *The Second Coming: Popular Millenarianism, 1780-1850* (London: Routledge and Kegan Paul, 1979); and Richard Cawardine's *Transatlantic Revivalism: Popular Evangelicalism in Britain and America, 1790-1865* (Westport, Conn.: Greenwood Press, 1978) describe the religious and social similarities among English-speaking countries during Millerism's inception.

[30] One recent report on the relationship between Seventh-day Adventist lifestyle and longevity is Dan Buettner's Article "The Secrets of Long Life," *National Geographic* 208, no. 5 (November 2005): 2-27.

[31] Knight, *Meeting Ellen White*, p. 109.

[32] *Ibid.*, pp. 109, 110.

[33] Herbert E. Douglass, *Messenger of the Lord* (PPPA, 1998), pp. 256, 257. See also Joseph Battistone, *The Great Controversy Theme in E. G. White Writings* (Berrien Springs, Mich.: Andrews University, 1978).

[34] Douglass, p. 257.

[35] In subsequent visions during the following years she received further details of various phases of this supernatural conflict, and in 1864 volumes 3 and 4 of *Spiritual Gifts* were published, dealing more comprehensively with the fall of Lucifer, the creation of the world, the fall of Adam and Eve, the lives of the patriarchs, and

the experience of Israel. (Volume 2, published in 1860, was an autobiographical work.) In the late 1860s White decided to expand what she had written in *Spiritual Gifts,* and a new series of four volumes of about 400 pages each called *The Spirit of Prophecy* was thus conceived (2Bio 297). This series covered the biblical and historical events from the fall of Lucifer in heaven to the end of the reign of Solomon (vol. 1), the life of Christ from His birth to the triumphal entry into Jerusalem (vol. 2), and the sufferings, death, and resurrection of Christ and the early church (vol. 3). Volume four, published in 1884, was subtitled *The Great Controversy Between Christ and Satan From the Destruction of Jerusalem to the End of the Controversy.* The last steps in the development of her exposition of the great controversy theme began with a new revision of volume 4 of *The Spirit of Prophecy.* This new volume was published in 1888 and bore the title *The Great Controversy Between Christ and Satan.* Thereafter, Ellen White expanded the other volumes of *The Spirit of Prophecy* series into what became known as the Conflict of the Ages Series. See note above.

[36] For a brief analysis of how Ellen White understood all of Satan's accusations, see Herbert E. Douglass, *God at Risk: The Cost of Freedom in the Great Controversy* (Roseville, Calif.: Amazing Facts, 2004), pp. 37-41.

[37] For more information on the great controversy theme, see Frank B. Holbrook, "The Great Controversy," in R. Dederen, ed., *Handbook of Seventh-day Adventist Theology* (RHPA, 2000), pp. 980-1009.

[38] Knight, *Meeting Ellen White,* p. 113.

[39] Leon Morris, *Glory in the Cross: A Study in Atonement* (Grand Rapids: Baker Book House, 1966), p. 80. Morris states: "It is difficult, as we have said, for Christians to give a complete account of the atonement, and it is not really surprising that so many theories have been evolved. The reality is vast and deep, and all our understandings of it are but partial. Harm is done when it is insisted—as it often has been in the past, and still is in some quarters in the present—that any one theory covers all the facts. The great fact on which the New Testament insists is that the atonement is many-sided and therefore completely adequate for every need" (*ibid.*).

[40] For more information, see Raoul Dederen, "Christ: His Person and Work," in *Handbook of Seventh-day Adventist Theology,* pp. 160-204.

[41] Douglass, *Messenger of the Lord,* p. 419.

[42] For more information on the Adventist understanding of the role of Scripture and its interpretation see Peter M. van Bemmelen, "Revelation and Inspiration," in *Handbook of Seventh-day Adventist Theology,* pp. 22-57, and Richard M. Davidson, "Biblical Interpretation," in *Handbook of Seventh-day Adventist Theology,* pp. 58-104. A recent publication on Adventist hermeneutics and inspiration is George W. Reid, ed., *Understanding Scripture: An Adventist Approach* (Silver Spring, Md.: Biblical Research Institute, 2005). An important, although controversial book published on the Adventist understanding of the inspiration of Scripture and of Ellen White is Alden Thompson's *Inspiration: Hard Questions, Honest Answers* (Hagerstown, Md.: Review and Herald, 1991). Much of what Adventists have written on the inspiration of the Bible and of Ellen White since 1991 has been in response to or in dialogue with Thompson's book.

[43] Knight, *Meeting Ellen White,* pp. 117, 118.

[44] The compilation *Last Day Events* includes a few chapters on some citations of Ellen White regarding the needed preparation for the second coming of Christ (pp. 63-93).

[45] For more information on the Adventist understanding of the second coming of Christ, see Richard P. Lehmann, "The Second Coming of Christ," in *Handbook of Seventh-day Adventist Theology,* pp. 893-926.

[46] Much of Adventist evangelistic practice has been focused on the meaning of the second and third angels' messages. While confrontational and in condemning the wrong doctrines of other Christian churches, this message should be seen in its large context of an end-time movement to proclaim the soon return of Christ. Ellen White sought to temper this confrontational approach to evangelism that has too readily identified Adventism. "The Lord wants His people to follow other methods than that of condemning wrong, even though the condemnation be just. He wants us to do something more than to hurl at our adversaries charges that only drive them further from the truth. The work which Christ came to do in our world was not to erect barriers and constantly thrust upon the people the fact that they were wrong" (6T 121, 122).

[47] Knight, *Meeting Ellen White,* p. 121.

[48] For more information on the three angels' messages, see Hans K. LaRondelle, "The Remnant and the Three Angels' Messages," in *Handbook of Seventh-day Adventist Theology,* pp. 857-892.

[49] Knight, *Meeting Ellen White,* p. 126.

[50] *Ibid.,* p. 125.

Biographical Section

BIOGRAPHICAL SECTION

ABBEY, IRA (1815-1894) and **RHODA BICKFORD (RHODES)** (1813-1895). Adventists from Brookfield, New York, who were friends of James and Ellen White. In 1843 the Abbeys became Millerites, and in 1845 accepted the doctrine of the Sabbath. The Whites first met the Abbeys in 1848 (LS 114, 115) and thereafter frequently stayed at their home.

IRA ABBEY

RHODA ABBEY

The Abbeys had eight children, and James White complimented the Abbeys for raising themselves from "limited circumstances to a liberal competency," adding, "Your children are an honor to you" (JW to Brother and Sister Abbey, June 27, 1873). As early as 1865 James White wrote to the Abbeys urging them to move to Battle Creek (JW to Brother and Sister Abbey, May 8, 1865). Records indicate that the Abbeys likely came to Battle Creek in the late 1860s. In 1871 Ira became the superintendent of the *Health Reform Institute until November 1874. In 1876 they returned to Brookfield, New York. The Abbeys were known for their liberal giving to both the Health Reform Institute and the publishing association.

The Abbeys received a number of testimonies from Ellen White through the years. In 1867 she urged them to not overwork, and to embrace the principles of healthful living (Ms 9, 1867). A few years later, in 1872, she commended Ira Abbey for his influence and dedication: "In the providence of God, Bro. Abbey has given his interest and energies to the Health Institute. Bro. Abbey has had an unselfish interest, and has not spared or favored himself, to advance the interests of the Institute. If Bro. Abbey depends on God, and makes Him his strength and counselor, he can be a blessing to physicians, helpers, and patients. He has linked his interest to everything connected with the Institute. Bro. Abbey has been a blessing to others, in cheerfully bearing the burdens which were not few nor light. He has blessed others, and these blessings will reflect back upon him again" (PH138 33, 34). Ellen White also wrote him a number of letters of counsel on the importance of cleanliness and that patients should "strictly comply with the rules of the Health Institute" (Lt 45, 1874).

Yet, in spite of having this positive influence on the work of the church in Battle Creek, Ira Abbey also had his own shortcomings that Ellen White reproved. She repeatedly counseled him regarding his harsh demeanor toward his children. Of particular embarrassment to the Abbeys was their youngest daughter, Lillie, breaking the rules of the Institute (Lt 65, 1874), and their son-in-law, *Arthur Perry, engaging in reprehensible behavior with a patient at the Institute. Ellen White reproved Abbey for overreacting to Perry's behavior and his dismissal from the Institute (cf. Lt 39, 1875). These problems were particularly difficult for Ellen White to confront because of her close friendship with Abbey's daughter, *Lucinda Hall, one of Ellen White's closest friends (Lt 65, 1874). James and Ellen White spent many hours in prayer for Abbey, that God would pluck him "as a brand from the burning" (Lt 11, 1878).

In 1890 Ellen White reprehended Ira

Abbey for having an affair with *Annie Satterlee, a niece of his daughter Eleanor. White sent Abbey and Satterlee strong letters of rebuke and urged them to break their sinful relationship. Falling into despair and hopelessness, Abbey became so discouraged that he contemplated suicide, but White refused to give him up to be lost, and invited him to look to Jesus in faith (Lt 1d, 1890; cf. TSB 133-145). In the end he repented and confessed his wrongs.

See also: Carruth, Lillie (Abbey); Abbey, Samuel and Mary; Rhodes, Samuel.

Further reading: 2Bio 153, 154; obit. RH, Dec. 11, 1894; obit. RH, Sept. 10, 1895.

ABBEY, SAMUEL IRA (1846-1920) and **MARY LETTECE (SMITH)** (1848-1921). Samuel was born in Brookfield, New York, the oldest son of *Ira and Rhoda Abbey; Mary was born in Jackson, Michigan, the daughter of *Cyrenius and Louisa Smith. Mary was a charter member of the first Adventist congregation in Battle Creek organized in 1855. On Sunday evening, March 19, 1871, Ellen White spoke on the subject of dress reform. After she closed, James White performed a double wedding ceremony for Samuel and Mary, and for Samuel's younger sister Rosetta, who wedded Joseph Arthur Perry. "The brides stood up," according to James White, "both dressed in the approved style, a fine illustration of the evening's lecture" (HR, April 1871). In 1878 Mary went with Ellen White for two months as her traveling companion and literary assistant during a tour of the eastern United States (LS 236; 4T 298-301; 3Bio 95; Lt 47, 1878).

Further reading: obit. LUH, Aug. 3, 1921.

ALCHIN, STEPHEN (c. 1835-1908). Pioneer settler in Bushnell, Michigan, who converted to Adventism in 1862. In July 1867 James and Ellen White stayed at the Alchin home, where they held revival meetings. Also in 1867 Ellen White admonished the Alchins regarding their commitment to obey and "live out the truth." Among other things, she also admonished them to be faithful in their systematic benevolence, in their duty as parents, and in the example they gave (Lt 22, 1867, in 1T 543-549).

Further reading: 2Bio 189-191; obit. RH, Apr. 30, 1908.

ALDRICH, JOTHAM M. (1826-1870) and **JERUSHA B. (MANDIVILLE)** (1830-1915). Minister and administrator. The Aldriches first heard the Adventist message during tent meetings held in Somerset, New York, in 1860. Aldrich helped organize the New York Conference in 1862, and the following year chaired the session that organized the General Conference. In 1866 the Aldriches relocated to Battle Creek to assist James White with the publishing ministry of the church and were also instrumental in starting the Health Reform Institute. In 1867, after James White's resignation as head of the publishing work, Aldrich took his place and raised salaries without raising the prices of publications. In later years Ellen White reflected about her interactions with Aldrich. One of her greatest concerns was the increasing amount of secular publications printed at the Review and Herald and the justification Aldrich had given arguing that "religion is religion, business is business" (Lt 34, 1886). According to Ellen White, he had also begun to exhibit a "selfish grasping disposition . . . in [his] business transactions" (Lt 69, 1890). The publishing association was thrown into a financial crisis. When James White consulted with Aldrich over the mismanagement of the publishing house, Aldrich resigned, and a power struggled ensued. Ellen White warned that "Aldrich was idolized by some in Battle

Creek," particularly by Cornelia Cornell and Harriet and Uriah Smith (Lt 13, 1869). Unfortunately, Aldrich died the next year, but eventually Jerusha and the others resolved their differences.

Further reading: 1T 553-558; PH015; PH097; obit. RH, Sept. 27, 1870; G. Wheeler, *James White: Innovator and Overcomer* (RHPA, 2003), pp. 167, 175-177.

Michael W. Campbell

AMADON, GEORGE W. (1832-1913) and **MARTHA (BYINGTON)** (1834-1937). George

was a printer, typesetter, writer, and editor; Martha, the daughter of *John Byington, taught in the first Adventist school, held in the home of *Aaron Hilliard in Buck's Bridge, New York (1853). Introduced to the Ad–ventist message by *J. N. Loughborough (1853),

GEORGE W. AND MARTHA AMADON

George set type for the *Review and Herald* in *Rochester, New York. He was a foreman at the publishing house in *Battle Creek (1855-1902), and served as elder, *Sabbath school superintendent, vice president of the publishing association, conference treasurer, and editor of the *Youth's Instructor* (1858-1864). He learned Hebrew, Greek, German, Danish, Swedish, and French to set type for publications, and wrote on church organization, health reform, and Sabbath-Sunday issues. Martha also worked at the Review and Herald press, marrying George in 1860. She later sold health almanacs and Kellogg's medical books. Her prayer group formed the Dorcas and Benevolent Association (1874) to make garments, supply food, and care for orphans and widows.

Close friends with the Whites, George

witnessed Ellen's 1863 health reform vision and helped clear James of false charges regarding accumulating private wealth. Ellen White counseled George about his lack of good judgment and his "long prosy speeches." In 1869 she rebuked Martha for nosiness and faultfinding, urging her to "put the bridle upon yourself" (Lt 9, 1869). In 1893 she encouraged her to "talk faith; . . . talk hope; talk courage" (Lt 103, 1893). After the Review and Herald building burned in 1902, George went to Tennessee to assist *Edson White in printing the book *Gospel Primer* and the periodical *Southern Watchman*, but returned to Battle Creek as visiting pastor in 1904. Ellen White encouraged his ministry of reconciliation with *J. H. Kellogg, *A. T. Jones, and *A. R. Henry, challenging him to "fight decidedly on the Lord's side" (Lt 210, 1907).

In 1909 Ellen White and George Amadon attended their last General Conference session; in 1911 she sent him a copy of *The Acts of the Apostles*. The following year Ellen White assured him that "the Lord Jesus is your Friend and keeper. . . . His everlasting arms are underneath you" (Lt 44, 1912). He died in 1913 and was buried in Oak Hill Cemetery in Battle Creek. After his death Martha helped to establish the St. Joseph, Michigan, church (1913) and told pioneer stories to students who sang and prayed with her. She died at 103, saying, "I love Him; I want to see Him."

Further reading: obit. RH, Mar. 20, 1913; obit. RH, Jan. 21, 1937; M. R. Hook, *Flames Over Battle Creek* (RHPA, 1977).

Brian E. Strayer

ANDERSON, CHARLES J. (1860-1928) and **EDITH** (1867-1959). Adventist missionaries to Norfolk Island in the South Pacific. The Andersons became Adventists after meeting *J. O. Corliss in 1890. Ellen White wrote to Charles while he was a missionary on Norfolk

Island, telling him that he had mistaken his calling "as a teacher of the truth" (Lt 2, 1896). In another letter she counseled him and his coworker, *Stephen Belden, not to preach for more than 30 minutes and that Anderson should not feel that because he was the elder of the church, he must do all the speaking, "for a change of gifts is positively to the advantage of the audience" (Lt 1a, 1896, in 10MR 129-134). Later, during a period of marital difficulty, Edith wrote to Ellen White, seeking her counsel. White urged her to "watch unto prayer" and not to "retaliate" for her husband's provocations (Lt 51, 1905). She counseled Charles to humble his heart, bridle his tongue, and make the life of his wife less difficult (Lt 49, 1905).

Further reading: obit. *Australasian Record*, Nov. 12, 1928; obit. *Australasian Record*, Aug. 31, 1959; M. Hook, *Church in a Convict Gaol: Early Adventism on Norfolk Island* (Wahroonga, Australia: Department of Education, South Pacific Division, [c. 1985]), pp. 4-7.

ANDERSON, MRS. R. Adventist in Victoria, Australia, who met Ellen White during the Melbourne camp meeting in November 1895. Afterward White sent *O. A. Olsen a diary account of the meetings, which he published in the *Review and Herald* (Jan. 7, 1896). When the *Review* reached Anderson, she complained about a veiled reference to herself in the article. Her name was not given, but she was one of several anonymous individuals described who had attended the camp meeting and had made a decision to accept the truth they had heard. White responded to Anderson, "I wish to express to you my surprise and regret at the publication in the 'Review' of my letter containing a reference to yourself. . . . I assure you that the publication of this matter was without my knowledge and consent. I have given my friends permission to publish

extracts from my letters concerning our work and travels, but have directed that personalities should be omitted. I was as much surprised as you to see this matter in print" (Lt 1, 1896).

ANDRÉ, HATTIE (1865-1952). Bible instructor, teacher, and dean of women. André served as a Bible instructor in Ohio (1885-1889), graduated from Battle Creek College (1890), and founded and taught at the first Seventh-day Adventist school on Pitcairn Island (1893-1896). She also worked as Bible instructor in Kentucky (1897), and served on the faculty of *Oakwood Industrial School (1898-1899). André joined the staff at the Australasian Missionary College as a result of the direct intervention of *W. C. White and Ellen White (Lt 197, 1899; cf. Lt 217, 1899). From 1900 to 1908 she taught at the Australasian Missionary College (now *Avondale College); was dean of women and teacher at Pacific Union College (1909-1920), and taught at *Hinsdale Sanitarium and Hinsdale Academy (1920-1929). In a letter written from Avondale College in November 1903 André reported to Ellen White that the school was being blessed: "So often I find myself wishing that Sr. White might be privileged to behold with her own eyes the marked improvement and progress that is being made in every way." Ellen White was deeply concerned for the success of Avondale College and took interest in finding the right people to serve there. André's comment that "our faculty is a unit, and the work passes off so harmoniously" is a testimony of God's blessing on the school.

Further reading: obit. RH, Mar. 19, 1953; *SDA Encyclopedia* (1996), vol. 10, pp. 67, 68.

Teofilo Ferreira

ANDRÉ, ROSA (1867-1935). Housekeeper at the *Battle Creek Sanitarium for 17 years, and *Hinsdale Sanitarium for 29 years; younger sister of *Hattie André. In 1906, near the peak of the controversy around *J. H. Kellogg, Ellen White wrote to André urging her to leave *Battle Creek as part of a larger effort to help reduce the number of Adventists still congregated there (Lt 132, 1906). André soon thereafter transferred to the Hinsdale Sanitarium, where she worked in the same capacity for the remainder of her life.

Further reading: obit. RH, Mar. 14, 1935.

ANDREWS, EDITH (1863-1885). Missionary worker in the publishing house in Switzerland,

EDITH ANDREWS

daughter of William Andrews (1838-1878), granddaughter of *Edward Andrews. After the death of her cousin *Mary Andrews (1878), Edith returned to Europe to assist her uncle, *J. N. Andrews, and worked at the publishing house in Basel until her final illness. In a series of letters Ellen White admonished Andrews to amend the course of her life and to repent of her "careless indifference with regard to our relation to God" (Lt 6, 1885, in 10MR 53-58; cf. Lts 16, 17, 28, 1885). Ellen White also met with Andrews personally and continued to write to her after Andrews contracted tuberculosis (Lt 4, 1885). On Dec. 22 of that year White visited Andrews on her deathbed. Andrews told her that she had read her letters and had done everything possible to amend her life, yet she was still concerned whether God would indeed forgive her sins. White reassured her that God had indeed forgiven her. With tears in her eyes Edith responded, "I believe He accepts me" (Lt 25, 1885). Andrews then asked White to pray for her. "While praying," wrote Ellen White, "I felt that Jesus came very near to us. I felt the

assurance that Jesus did pardon her transgressions. All present were melted into tears. Our hearts were filled with peace and love to Jesus. Edith had no more trouble of mind, for she knew the Lord blessed her then in answer to prayer" (*ibid.*). That Sunday (December 24) Ellen White was by her side when she died. Edith Andrews is buried next to her uncle, J. N. Andrews, in Basel, Switzerland.

See also: Assurance of Salvation.

Further reading: obit. RH, Jan. 26, 1886; EGWEur 87-90.

Michael W. Campbell

ANDREWS, EDWARD (1798-1865) and **SARAH (POTTLE)** (1803-1899). Farmers in Paris,

EDWARD AND SARAH ANDREWS

Maine; and parents of *J. N. Andrews. Edward was a Millerite believer who after the *disappointment of 1844 became one of the earliest Sabbatarian Adventists in Maine. Following the 1844 disappointment Edward Andrews and many others in Maine indulged in fanatical behavior and advocated a "no work" doctrine. Repeatedly in the early years of her ministry Ellen White confronted this kind of fanaticism. In September 1849 James and Ellen White and other early Adventist colleagues visited Paris, Maine, and during a meeting with many estranged believers Andrews began to see his errors. Yet, although Andrews and others admitted their mistakes, his family and *Cyprian Stevens' family harbored ill feelings toward James and Ellen White for many years, apparently because of the forcefulness of the reproofs they received from the Whites. In 1855 the Andrews family relocated to Waukon, Iowa, where Edward farmed until his death in 1865. But the ill feelings and simmering resentment followed Andrews to Iowa. For many years Edward's relationship to James White was strained. As late as 1861 he accused James of cheating him out of $8 in 1850. This led to skepticism on the part of Andrews regarding the genuineness of Ellen White's testimonies. Two years before his death he showed a change of heart and wrote to the Whites "to confess all the ways my cruel unbelief has ever heaped on you" (E. Andrews to "Brother and Sister White," Jan. 25, 1863, EGWE-GC).

Further reading: obit. RH, May 2, 1865; G. Wheeler, *James White: Innovator and Overcomer* (RHPA, 2003), pp. 57-63, 101-108; R. Graybill, "The Family Man," in *J. N. Andrews: The Man and the Mission*, ed. H. Leonard (AUP, 1985), pp. 15-19, 26-28.

ANDREWS, JOHN NEVINS (1829-1883) and **ANGELINE (STEVENS)** (1824-1872). Minister,

JOHN AND ANGELINE ANDREWS AND CHILDREN, MARY AND CHARLES

missionary, writer, editor, and scholar; close friend of James and Ellen White. Born in Poland, Maine, Andrews "found the Savior" in February 1843 and began to observe the seventh-day Sabbath several years later. He met the Whites when they visited in Paris, Maine, in September 1849. During this visit the Whites staunchly rebuked the *fanaticism then prevalent among some Adventists. It was in this context that young Andrews exclaimed, "I would exchange a thousand errors for one truth" (LS 127). Later the Whites boarded with John's parents (November 1850-June 1851). In 1850 Andrews began itinerant preaching ministry in New England. In 1855 Ellen White urged that he marry Angeline Stevens, daughter of Cyprian Stevens, and not to disappoint her

as he had done to Annie (thought to be *Annie Smith) (Lt 1, 1855, in 9MR 313, 314). John and Angeline were married October 29, 1856, in Waukon, Iowa, where the Andrews and Stevens families had recently moved. Worn out by his ministerial labors, John spent his time farming while trying to regain his health. In June 1859 a conference in Battle Creek voted that Andrews should assist *J. N. Loughborough in tent evangelism in Michigan. Andrews returned to Waukon in the fall of 1860. During the Waukon years two children were born: Charles (1857) and *Mary (1861). It was also during this period that he wrote the first edition of his best-known literary work, *The History of the Sabbath and the First Day of the Week* (1859).

In the fall of 1861 Ellen White sent several testimonies to church members in Waukon who had doubted the genuineness of her ministry (cf. Lt 7, 1860, in PH016). These were received favorably, and John sent his own confession to the *Review and Herald* (Dec. 17, 1861). Additional messages from Ellen White prompted another confession—this time signed jointly by John and Angeline (Andrews Correspondence, Feb. 2, 1862, CAR). Other members of the Andrews and Stevens families wrote similar confessions.

In June 1862 Andrews left Waukon to work with the evangelistic tent in New York and assisted in the founding of the New York Conference. In November of that year Ellen White wrote to him that "God has accepted your efforts" in ministry, and that Angeline "has been learning to submit her will and way to God" (Lt 11, 1862, in 9MR 315). In February 1863 Angeline and the children moved from Waukon to join John in New York. Two more daughters were born to the Andrewses while in New York, both of whom died in infancy. In 1864, during the American Civil War, Andrews was chosen as the denominational representative to the provost marshal general in Washington, D.C., to secure recognition for Adventists as noncombatants. Andrews served as the third president of the General Conference (1867-1869) and editor of the *Review and Herald* (1869-1870).

Andrews also served as a theologian for the young denomination and made significant contributions to the development of various doctrines. His research on the time to begin the observance of the Sabbath (Friday at sunset) became the accepted position of the church ("Time for Commencing the Sabbath," RH, Dec. 4, 1855, pp. 76-78). He also wrote extensively on the history of the seventh-day Sabbath, and his book *History of the Sabbath and the First Day of the Week* (1859) went through several editions. Andrews also led in a study of what the Bible teaches regarding the support of the ministry, and as a result a plan known as Systematic Benevolence was adopted. In 1878 he served on the committee that recommended the tithing system.

After Angeline died from a stroke in 1872, John moved to South Lancaster, Massachusetts, where the children could stay with the Harris family. Two years later, John and his children, Charles and Mary, were sent as the first official missionaries to Europe. Ellen White noted the church had sent the "ablest man in all our ranks" (Lt 2a, 1878). As Andrews started a publishing house in Switzerland and an Adventist periodical in French, *Les Signes des Temps* (1876), Ellen White cautioned him against overwork and exhaustion. In 1878 Mary contracted tuberculosis and died soon after arriving for treatment at the *Battle Creek Sanitarium. Ellen White wrote a letter to Andrews to comfort him in his sorrow and told him that she had seen his wife and daughter "answering the call of the Life-giver" on the day of the resurrection, one of very few such statements she ever wrote (Lt 71, 1878).

Ellen White's severest rebuke to Andrews came in 1883. She deplored the fact that he had not followed her counsel to remarry before going to Europe in 1874. In this, she believed he had made a mistake. "If you had, before starting, selected you a godly woman who could have been a mother to your children, you would have done a wise thing, and your usefulness would have been tenfold to what it has been" (Lt 1, 1883, in TSB 35). The presence and support of a companion would have helped him to preserve strength and resist disease (Lt 9, 1883, in TSB 34). He responded to this message about a month before his death and asked her that if she still had other reproofs, to "not withhold them, I pray you. I beg you to believe me as ever one who sincerely desires to follow the right" (JNA to EGW, Sept. 17, 1883). Andrews died on October 21, 1883, and was buried in Basel, Switzerland. At his request, there was no eulogy for him, but a death notice appeared in the *Review and Herald* (JNA to Uriah Smith, Apr. 24, 1883, CAR).

Further reading: obit. RH, Oct. 23, 1883; J. N. Andrews, "Life Sketches," HR, April 1877, pp. 97-99; May 1877, pp. 129-131; June 1877, pp. 161-164; G. Balharrie, "A Study of the Contribution Made to the Seventh-day Adventist Church by John Nevins Andrews" (M.A. thesis, SDA Theological Seminary, 1949); P. G. Damsteegt, *Foundations of the Seventh-day Adventist Message and Mission* (Eerdmans, 1977), pp. 164-184, 195-208, 215-217, 289-293; *J. N. Andrews: The Man and the Mission*, ed. H. Leonard (AUP, 1985); *SDA Encyclopedia* (1996), vol. 10, pp. 68, 69.

Michael W. Campbell

ANDREWS, MARY FRANCIS (1861-1878). Editor and missionary; daughter of *J. N. Andrews. Born in Waukon, Iowa, she grew up knowing James and Ellen White from periodic visits they made to the Andrews home (cf. Lt 5, 1865). In 1872, Mary's mother, Angeline, died from a stroke. Two years later Mary and her older brother Charles accompanied their father to Switzerland. Wanting to learn the French language quickly, J. N. Andrews convinced Mary and Charles to avoid the use of English except for an hour in the evening. On December 24, 1876, they signed a mutual pledge to each other to only use the French language in their home (see original in CAR). Before long Mary was proofreading French publications, even finding mistakes that the French copy editors had missed. One French worker remarked: "Mary speaks French as though she were a French girl." In 1878 Mary contracted tuberculosis. When her father returned to Battle Creek for the 1878 General Conference session, Mary went along to receive treatment at the *Battle Creek Sanitarium, but died two months after arriving. "Mary, dear precious child, is at rest," Ellen White wrote to her father. "Through faith's discerning eye you may anticipate . . . your Mary with her mother and other members of your family answering the call of the Life-giver and coming forth from their prison house triumphing over death" (Lt 71, 1878). She is buried in Mount Hope Cemetery in Rochester, New York, next to her mother and sister, Carrie.

Further reading: obit. RH, Dec. 5, 1878; C. Byers, *Mary Andrews: Companion of Sorrows* (RHPA, 1983); *Legacy of Light* CD-ROM, art., "Mary Andrews."

Michael W. Campbell

ANDREWS, ROBERT FREDERICK (1834-1922) and **MARY (MITCHELL)** (1844-1930). Minister, missionary, and administrator. Soon after emigrating from Scotland to the United States, Andrews accepted the Adventist faith during meetings held by J. N. Loughborough in 1851.

He became Loughborough's tentmaster in 1855, began preaching in 1856, and in 1862 wedded Mary Mitchell. He served as president of the Illinois-Wisconsin Conference (1867-1870) and of the Illinois Conference (1870-1875, 1879-1885). In 1885, leaving his family behind, Andrews joined *S. H. Lane to pioneer the Adventist work in Ireland. When he returned discouraged, Ellen White encouraged him to reenter the ministry (Lt 17, 1887). He heeded the counsel, serving in Indiana and Illinois until 1901 when he and his family relocated to Nebraska.

Further reading: obit. RH, Feb. 1, 1923.

ANDROSS, ELMER ELLSWORTH (1868-1950). Evangelist, pastor, teacher, and administrator (United States, Britain, and Central America) for more than 50 years (1888-1942). Andross also authored scores of devotional and doctrinal articles for denominational periodicals, covering the whole gamut of biblical subjects and including numerous reports of Adventist world mission work. While serving as president of the Southern California Conference (1908-1912) and Pacific Union Conference (1912-1918), Andross had many conversations with Ellen White, some of which dealt with the accreditation of the medical program at the College of Medical Evangelists (cf. LLM 18) and the training of physicians (cf. LLM 486, 487; 1MR 86-88).

Probably Andross' greatest legacy is his 215-page book entitled *A More Excellent Ministry* (1912), a biblical response to *Albion Ballenger's attack on the Adventist understanding of the sanctuary. Already in 1905 Ellen White had clearly indicated both to Ballenger himself and to General Conference leaders that Ballenger was introducing heresy regarding the doctrine of the sanctuary (Mss 59, 62, 1905); however it remained for Andross, former associate with Ballenger while in

Britain, to provide a detailed reply to these aberrant views once they were published.

In *A More Excellent Ministry* Andross rebuts a dozen propositions advocated in Ballenger's *Cast Out for the Cross of Christ* (1909), giving particular attention to Ballenger's fundamental premise (based upon Hebrews 6:19, 20) that Christ at His ascension in A.D. 31 entered the Most Holy Place of the heavenly sanctuary to begin His antitypical day of atonement work. Andross concedes that according to Hebrews 6:19, 20, Christ indeed entered "within the veil" into the Most Holy Place upon His ascension, but then adduces a number of lines of biblical evidence (especially Ex. 40:2, 3, 9; Lev. 8:33, 35; 9:22-24; Dan. 9:24; John 20:17, 27; Acts 2:32-36; Heb. 9:19-21; 10:19-23; cf. AA 38, 39) to show that the purpose of this entrance was to dedicate the heavenly sanctuary and begin its services, in parallel with the Old Testament dedication of the earthly sanctuary, and not to commence the antitypical day of atonement, as Ballenger had mistakenly claimed. Andross also defends other crucial features of the Adventist understanding of the sanctuary doctrine called into question by Ballenger.

While Andross' unique interpretation of Hebrews 6:19, 20—that Christ entered the Most Holy Place at His ascension in order to dedicate the heavenly sanctuary—apparently did not become widely accepted in his lifetime, several recent Adventist studies have presented further biblical corroboration of (at least major elements of) his basic thesis. Andross must be credited with decisively meeting a major doctrinal challenge to Adventism at a critical juncture of denominational history, in harmony with Ellen White's warning of the impending crisis, honestly facing the issues raised and setting forth a carefully reasoned and credible biblical response to these issues.

Further reading: E. E. Andross, "Bible Study No. II," July 13, 1911; "Studies in the Sanctuary No. III," July 16, 1911 (DF 178; DF 197-d, CAR); R. Adams, *The Sanctuary Doctrine: Three Approaches in the Seventh-day Adventist Church* (AUP, 1981); A. V. Wallenkampf, "Challengers to the Doctrine of the Sanctuary," in *Doctrine of the Sanctuary: A Historical Survey*, ed. F. B. Holbrook, Daniel and Revelation Committee Series, (BRI, 1989), vol. 5, pp. 197-216; *SDA Encyclopedia* (1996), vol. 10, p. 82.

Richard M. Davidson

ARMITAGE, MARY CAROLINE (MORTENSON), see **MORTENSON, MARY CAROLINE**.

ARNOLD, DAVID (1805-1889). Early Adventist writer and administrator, and first president of the New York Conference. The Volney, New York, conference in 1848 was held in his "carriage house."

David Arnold became a Methodist at the age of 16. He later accepted the Millerite Adventist message and after the disappointment of 1844 became an observer of the seventh-day Sabbath. In the 1848 conference meeting where about 35 were present and hardly two of them agreed, Arnold had some ideas of his own. He believed that "the thousand years of Revelation 20 were in the past," "that the 144,000 were those raised at Christ's resurrection," and that the Lord's Supper should be observed only once a year, as "a continuation of the Passover." Ellen White, grieved by these "strange differences of opinion," fainted (2SG 98). As others prayed for her, she received a vision that pointed out the biblical references that refuted these views. After studying the scriptures revealed to her, Arnold put away his own theories and spent the rest of his life promoting the Adventist message.

In *Present Truth* in 1849 and 1850 Arnold wrote about the shut door, the 2300 days ending in 1844, and Christ's heavenly sanctuary high-priestly ministry. When the *Advent Review* began publication in 1850, Arnold was listed on the publication committee. Throughout the 1850s he wrote extensively on Adventist theology. In 1852 he advocated a weekly *Review*. In an 1853 article on spiritualism he sharply contrasted Ellen White's ministry with the influence of the Fox sisters. Arnold argued that in Scripture and in the ministry of Ellen White is found "a more sure word of prophecy" (2 Peter 1:19) (RH, July 21, 1853).

Arnold traveled widely in New York and also visited Michigan in support of church work. He helped construct the Roosevelt, New York, church in 1859 and in 1862 was elected the first president of the New York Conference.

We know of no extant letters from Ellen White to David Arnold, but he was present during several of her visions.

Further reading: 1Bio 140-142; D. Arnold, "The Shut Door Explained," PT, December 1849; L. E. Froom, *The Prophetic Faith of Our Fathers* (RHPA, 1954), vol. 4, pp. 1023, 1086-1088; G. R. Knight, *A Brief History of Seventh-day Adventists* (RHPA, 1999), pp. 52, 53.

Howard Krug

ARTHUR, JESSE (1845-1919) and **FLORENCE** (d. 1935). Attorney and judge from the southern United States who became the first legal counsel of the Seventh-day Adventist Church. Arthur served as a Confederate soldier during the American *Civil War and afterward completed a law degree at the Cincinnati Law School. He served as city attorney and mayor in Dayton, Kentucky, before being appointed circuit judge of his district. In 1889 the Arthurs moved to Washington Territory. He practiced

law in Spokane until 1897, part of which time he was one of three superior court judges. When failing health forced him to resign, he traveled to the *Battle Creek Sanitarium for treatment. There he became an Adventist and afterward served as legal counsel for the Seventh-day Adventist Church as well as the Battle Creek Sanitarium. In 1899 he chaired the building committee for the *Chicago building that was intended to house the American Medical Missionary College, but was never built because of Ellen White's opposition. Ellen White visited in his Battle Creek home in April 1901, and he and Florence were her guests at Elmshaven in the summer of 1902. They exchanged a series of cordial letters in 1902 and 1903. From 1904 to 1907, however, the alienation of J. H. Kellogg gradually drew in many of his close associates, one of whom was Judge Arthur. When the Battle Creek Tabernacle expelled Kellogg in 1907, Arthur was among a large group of others expelled at the same time.

See also: Chicago Building Vision.

Further reading: 5Bio 111, 173; 20MR 351; Coller Collection (WL), vol. 3, pp. 222, 223.

ATKINSON, FRANCES ELLEN (FOSS) (b. 1844). Niece of Ellen White (daughter of her sister, Mary [Harmon] Foss). In 1909 Ellen Atkinson contracted tuberculosis. To her niece's inquiry, Ellen White replied that the Loma Linda Sanitarium was unable to accept patients with the disease. In a postscript, one of Ellen White's unidentified literary assistants recommended that she find a dry climate to live outdoors—advice typical of the period (Lt 90, 1909).

ATWOOD, ASA B. (1832-1903). Adventist philanthropist and local church elder. Atwood assisted in helping found the Rural Health Retreat, forerunner of the *St. Helena Sanitarium (ST, Jan. 26, 1882). In 1890 Ellen White wrote to him and William Pratt appealing for harmony and humility in relation to a conflict with a certain Brother Rogers at the sanitarium (Lt 1c, 1890, in 15MR 153-157).

Further reading: obit. RH, Nov. 12, 1903.

AUSTIN, CAROLINE R. (CUMMINGS) (1821-1915). Early Sabbatarian Adventist originally from Cornish, New Hampshire. She and her husband, H. N. Austin (1818-1889), whom she married in 1840, became Sabbatarian Adventists in 1854. After the death of her husband, Austin relocated to Battle Creek, where she heard *J. V. Himes speak in 1895 (Lt 1a, 1895). Ellen White thanked her for her "thoughtful kindness and love . . . expressed toward me many times" (Lt 1, 1898).

Further reading: obit. RH, Mar. 25, 1915; obit. RH, Jan. 21, 1890.

BABCOCK, DAVID CALDWELL (1854-1932) and **ANN (DAVIS)** (d. 1901). Educated at Battle Creek College in the 1870s, Babcock served as a pastor in Delaware, Ohio, and Maryland in the 1880s before becoming president of the West Virginia (1892-1895) and Virginia (1817-1899) conferences. He served as a missionary to British Guiana (1900-1905, 1925-1927), British West Africa (1905-1914), Nigeria (1914-1917), Virgin Islands (1919-1925), and Curaçao, Dutch West Indies (1927). In 1901, while serving in British Guiana, Ann died. David remarried the following year, but was soon widowed again. He married Mina Bradshaw in 1903. After many years of illness, Babcock returned to America in 1927. Ellen White warned him in 1886 to curb his temper and control his appetite by giving up coffee, tea, and wine lest he become "a physical wreck" and even forfeit eternal life (Lt 53, 1886).

Further reading: obit. RH, May 5, 1932;

SDA Encyclopedia (1996), vol. 10, p. 147.

Brian Strayer

BAHLER, JOHN F. (1840-1918). Adventist in Texas with whom James and Ellen White stayed during their stay in Texas (1878-1879). At age 4 John emigrated with his family from Switzerland to Rochester, New York. Orphaned, he was apprenticed to a confectioner. At 18 he lost his eyesight as the result of an infection and subsequent eye surgery. After joining the Methodist Episcopal Church, he attended a school for the blind and in 1865 married Emma Smith in Wisconsin.

About 1870, after the birth of their son, Robert, they returned to Rochester. A natural salesman, John peddled brooms, books, and other items. After the death of Emma, John accepted the Adventist message through a series of lectures by *J. N. Andrews. Later he married Mary J. Cottrell, a niece of *R. F. Cottrell.

Bahler made sacrificial pledges to assist the Adventist work. In the mid-1870s, when James White made appeals for Tract and Missionary Societies, the Bahlers sold their home and donated a portion of the proceeds.

Living in Dallas, Texas, in 1876, Bahler became entangled in controversy with E. G. Rust, and by the time *Robert M. Kilgore arrived the following year, the Dallas church had been split. Kilgore met with the members of the church, conducted a church trial, and sided with Rust. Ellen White, then in Oregon, saw in vision on two separate occasions the state of the work in Texas. Two lengthy testimonies followed reprimanding Kilgore, Rust, J. S. Clark, and others for their verbal abuse of Bahler (4T 321-340).

In November 1878, when James and Ellen White visited Texas for the winter, Bahler offered the use of half of his home on Morgan

Street in southwest Denison. In appreciation James White worked with the publishing house in Battle Creek to bring out a new edition of Bahler's autobiography, including doctrinal information on the Sabbath and second advent of Christ. It was during the Whites' stay in the Bahler home that *Arthur G. and Mary Daniells became closely associated with the Whites. Arthur helped James with his business enterprises, and Mary cooked. It was also at the Bahlers' that *Marian Davis first began working for Ellen White as a *literary assistant. The enterprising group at Bahlers' raised $1,000 to assist with the new Dime Tabernacle (*Battle Creek Tabernacle) and to help retire the debt on the Oakland, California church. The Whites stayed with the Bahlers until their departure by *wagon train in late April 1879.

Bahler served for a time as a licensed minister in the Texas Conference, and helped to found an orphanage. Following Mary's death he married Pauline Paulson (d. 1911). During his later years Bahler traveled through the south living in Florida, and finally with his daughter Grace in Texas. In his later years he became discouraged, but before his death he was reconciled to the Dallas church. He is buried in Dallas, Texas.

Further reading: obit. RH, June 20, 1918; J. F. Bahler, *Thrilling Incidents in the Life and Experience of John F. Bahler* (Battle Creek, Mich.: SDA Pub. Assn., 1897).

Mary Ann Hadley

BAIRD, ALFRED SHERMAN (1864-1918) and **HELEN L. (LEBERT)** (1872-1956). Architect and builder. Alfred as a teenager worked on the Western Pacific Railroad, and by the age of 17 was supporting his widowed mother. He later studied drafting and architecture at Lafayette College in Iowa, and married Helen L. Lebert in 1889. In 1901 Baird was called to

Berrien Springs, Michigan, to design and superintend construction of the buildings at *Emmanuel Missionary College. In 1904 he was asked to design and build the new *Washington Training College, *Washington Sanitarium, and General Conference offices, in Takoma Park, Maryland. In 1907 Ellen White wrote to him recommending her grandson-in-law *W. D. Workman, who desired experience in construction (Lt 236, 1907). Evidently Baird was able to hire Workman, because later that year Ellen White thanked him for the interest he had taken in Workman, and expressed appreciation for the contribution he made to the church through the erection of buildings (Lt 362, 1907). Ellen White also wrote a letter of encouragement to his wife, Helen (Lt 238, 1907).

Further reading: obit. RH, May 30, 1918.

BAKER, DORINDA, see **DAMMAN** (also **DAMON, DAMMON**), **ISRAEL**.

BAKER, WILLIAM LEMUEL HENRY (1858-1933) and **JOSEPHINE LAURA** (1860-1941). William was an evangelist, conference administrator, and Bible teacher in the United States and Australia; William and Josephine were married in 1885. Ellen White worked closely with the Bakers while they were in Australia. She took an interest in William's spiritual life and encouraged him to practice faithfully the truth he believed in and to "look steadfastly to Jesus" (Lt 81, 1900).

While Baker served as a pastor in Australia in 1895, Ellen White wrote him and his wife a long letter (Lt 8, 1895). While most of the letter consists of her personal appeal for more efficiency in his evangelistic and pastoral work and invites him to be totally committed to Christ, one section in the middle of the letter has drawn much attention. In this section, which seems to be a response to a letter he had written to Ellen White, she discusses the theological meaning of the humanity of Christ and warns Baker, "Be careful, exceedingly careful as to how you dwell upon the human nature of Christ." She then continues with a statement in which she contrasts Christ's human nature with that of Adam's and his posterity. "Do not set Him before the people as a man with the propensities of sin. He is the second Adam. The first Adam was created a pure, sinless being, without a taint of sin upon him; he was in the image of God. He could fall, and he did fall through transgressing. Because of sin, his posterity was born with inherent propensities of disobedience. But Jesus Christ was the only begotten Son of God. He took upon Himself human nature, and was tempted in all points as human nature is tempted. He could have sinned; He could have fallen, but not for one moment was there in Him an evil propensity. He was assailed with temptations in the wilderness, as Adam was assailed with temptations in Eden." Since its publication in *Seventh-day Adventists Answer Questions on Doctrine* (RHPA, 1957; annotated ed. AUP, 2003), this section of the letter has been at the core of the Adventist debate on whether Christ had a postlapsarian or prelapsarian human nature. Many people leaning toward the prelapsarian position have understood this letter to indicate that Christ's humanity was not entirely identical to ours in that Christ was not born with an inner disposition to sin.

Further reading: Lt 8, 1895, is published in 13MR 13-30; obit. RH, Mar. 30, 1933; obit. RH, Sept. 4, 1941; R. Larson, *The Word Made Flesh: One Hundred Years of Seventh-day Adventist Christology, 1852-1952* (Brushton, N.Y.: Teach Services, 1986), pp. 66-154; A. L. Moore, *Theology in Crisis* (Corpus Christi, Tex.: Life Seminars, 1980), pp. 258-271; A. L. Moore, *Adventism in Conflict* (RHPA, 1995), pp. 145-157; W. W. Whidden, *Ellen White on the Humanity of Christ* (RHPA, 1997), pp. 59-66; J. Zurcher, *Touched With Our Feelings: A Historical Survey of Adventist Thought on the Human Nature of Christ* (RHPA, 1999), pp. 163-165; D. Fortin, review of J. R. Zurcher's *Touched With Our Feelings,* in AUSS 38, no. 2 (Fall 2000): 342-344; *SDA Encyclopedia* (1996), vol. 10, p. 155.

Denis Fortin

BALL, WILLIAM H. WORCESTER (1822-c. 1874). Adventist in Washington, New Hampshire, who opposed Ellen White in person and published articles against her in *The Hope of Israel* and the Advent Christian *World's Crisis.* As early as 1862 he challenged Ellen White on her 1849 statement that "the time for their salvation is past," referring to those who rejected the Adventist message in 1844 (EW 45 and Uriah Smith's response in RH, Jan. 21, 1862). His bitter spirit contributed to spiritual blight in his local church and the discontinuance of their Sabbath school. In 1867 James and Ellen White and *J. N. Andrews held revival meetings in Washington, New Hampshire, and appealed to Ball and others to change the course of their lives. In one of these meetings, Ball confessed his wrongs after Ellen White related what she "had seen in vision" about him (Ms 2, 1868; Ball is Brother V in 2T 103-111; cf. 1T 655-661). In 1872 Ball resumed his attacks upon Ellen White. She wrote to him to no avail (Lt 28, 1872) and two years later responded to false charges made against her from some who claimed that she had predicted a specific time for the *second coming of Christ (Lt 53, 1874). After this latest disaffection, Ball became a supporter of B. F. Snook and W. H. Brinkerhoff (see *Marion Party).

See also: William Farnsworth.

Michael W. Campbell

BALLENGER, ALBION FOX (1861-1921). Minister, critic of Adventism, son of John Fox Ballenger and brother of Edward S. Ballenger. Born in Illinois, Ballenger began working in the Seventh-day Adventist ministry in 1885 and was ordained in 1893. Between 1889 and 1897 he functioned primarily as a religious liberty advocate, serving as an officer of the International Religious Liberty Association and, for a short time, as an assistant editor of the *American Sentinel*. From late 1897 through 1899, he traveled on behalf of the General Conference to camp meetings and churches throughout the United States, promoting the Holiness theme, "Receive Ye the Holy Ghost." He based his book *Power for Witnessing* (1900) on the sermons he preached during this time. In 1901 the General Conference sent him to Great Britain, where he served as an evangelist and administrator until 1905. He returned home after announcing that he no longer accepted the sanctuary doctrine, the Adventist teaching that Christ had entered the Most Holy Place of the heavenly sanctuary in 1844, arguing instead that this event had taken place at Christ's ascension. After losing his ministerial credential in 1905, Ballenger worked as a farmer and at various odd jobs, first in Virginia and after 1908 in southern California. Following the publication of *Cast Out for the Cross of Christ* (c. 1909), he gradually entered into a preaching and writing career. Between 1911 and 1919 he made six cross-country trips, each lasting about a half year, speaking primarily to disaffected Adventists. In 1915 he took over the editing and publishing of *The Gathering Call*, a small magazine started by

ALBION F. BALLENGER

a Church of God (Seventh Day) minister. Also, he published two more books, *Forty Fatal Errors Regarding the Atonement* (c. 1913) and *The Proclamation of Liberty and the Unpardonable Sin* (1915).

Ballenger's first recorded interaction with Ellen White took place in 1891. The day after he had taken part in a meeting that debated the issue of how much prominence the *American Sentinel* should give to the Sabbath, Ellen White spoke to a ministers' meeting in which she described a vision (known as the Salamanca vision), experienced several months previously, that had portrayed the *Sentinel* discussion. After her account in which she urged that the magazine emphasize the Sabbath, Ballenger affirmed that she had reported the meeting accurately and confessed that he had taken the wrong side on the issue.

During his "Receive Ye the Holy Ghost" campaign, Ballenger conceived the idea of starting a new school for African-Americans. After being rebuffed by the General Conference, in 1899 he wrote to Ellen White, who was in *Australia, seeking her support for the project. She replied saying that he should remain in evangelism. At that point Ballenger seems to have dropped the idea.

After learning of Ballenger's new views on the sanctuary doctrine, Ellen White traveled to the 1905 General Conference session in Washington, D.C. She spoke to him at one point and, in addition to making several public addresses opposing errors that were creeping into the church, sent a testimony entitled "A Warning Against False Theories" (Ms 62, 1905) to the General Conference officials who were deciding Ballenger's case. She did not participate, however, in the hearings held on Ballenger's case during the conference.

Ballenger gradually became more critical of Ellen White. At his hearing in 1905 he urged his critics to use the Bible only and not her writings to evaluate his interpretation. In *Cast Out* he published a letter he had written to White, which he claimed had never been answered. He did not make a significant issue of her writings, however, until he published a series of articles in *The Gathering Call* in 1914. He later combined these articles into a tract entitled *The Spirit of Prophecy and the Gift to Prophesy* (1916), which criticized Adventism of elevating the writings of Ellen White over the Bible. He further rejected her as a religious authority in another series of articles gathered into a tract entitled *What About the Testimonies* (c. 1919).

See also: E. E. Andross.

Further reading: 5Bio 404-413; C. W. Edwards and G. Land, *Seeker After Light: A. F. Ballenger, Adventism, and American Christianity* (AUP, 2000); R. W. Olson, "The Salamanca Vision and the 1890 Diary" (EGWE, 1983, SDoc); A. L. White, "The Story of the Salamanca Vision" (EGWE, 1954, SDoc).

Gary Land

BALLENGER, EDWARD STROUD (1864-1955). Minister, critic of Adventism, editor of *The Gathering Call*, son of *John Fox Ballenger and brother of *Albion Fox Ballenger. The *Seventh-day Adventist Yearbook* listed E. S. Ballenger as a licentiate minister in the Southern California Conference between 1904 and 1908 and as a minister in 1910 and 1911. Between 1905 and 1909 he served on the educational committee of the conference, usually identified as the secretary. After his brother Albion moved to southern California, probably in 1908, Edward seems to have become critical of the church. The *Yearbook* listed him as holding "honorary ministerial credentials" in 1910 and 1911, after which his name disappears. In 1905 Ellen White asked Ballenger to look for a suitable site for a

sanitarium in Redlands, California, but there is no extant written response. Becoming concerned about Ballenger's views, *E. E. Andross, president of the Southern California Conference, took him to see Ellen White in 1909, but apparently with little effect, for a short time later Andross reported that Ballenger had resigned his official positions. Ballenger is the Brother A mentioned in 1SM 38, 39 (Ms 107, 1909). After Albion's death in 1921, Edward became the editor of *The Gathering Call*, in which he subsequently published highly critical views of both Adventists and Ellen White.

Gary Land

BALLENGER, JOHN FOX (1834-1921). Minister, father of *Albion F. and *Edward S. Ballenger. Son of a Methodist circuit rider, Ballenger was a farmer in Illinois when he converted to Adventism, probably in 1859, through the preaching of W. S. Ingraham. According to family tradition, he joined Ingraham in evangelism. The Illinois Conference licensed Ballenger as a minister in 1876 (at a camp meeting at which Ellen White spoke) and ordained him in 1878. He later served as a minister in Michigan and California. His son Albion, who had separated from the church in 1905 over his views on the sanctuary doctrine, moved about three years later to southern California, where John was living. Soon thereafter John accepted Albion's interpretations and subsequently was asked to surrender his ministerial credentials. The 1909 *Seventh-day Adventist Yearbook* was the last to list him as a minister.

Further reading: RH, Sept. 19, 1878.

Gary Land

BALLOU, GEORGE (1849-1925) and **SOPHIA** (**BAUER** or **BOWERS**) (1851-1923). Adventists in California. Ellen White employed George in 1882 to help plant her garden and to build a carriage house at her home in Healdsburg (Lts 5, 6, 1882). When Ballou entered the ministry, Ellen White reproved him for recurring moral failures and said his behavior disqualified him for this work. She also warned him not to become a physician for similar reasons (cf. Lt 27, 1887; Lt 51, 1888). He eventually became an optometrist.

Further reading: obit. RH, Feb. 18, 1926; obit. RH, Feb. 21, 1924.

BALLOU, JAMES MADISON (1816-1888) and **HULDA AMELIA (HART)** (1820-1903). Millerites in Mannsville, New York, who later became Sabbatarian Adventists. In October 1858, while James and Ellen White were spending a week in the Ballou home, Ellen became gravely ill, but was miraculously healed in response to prayer (J. N. Loughborough, *Great Second Advent Movement*, p. 336). The following Sabbath, October 21, she had a vision showing the dangers of the *Messenger Party and the need for church unity (Ms 2, 1858). Later the Ballous helped build a church in Mannsville, one of the earliest by Sabbatarian Adventists.

Further reading: 1T 204-209; 1Bio 381-383; Lt 7, 1856; obit. RH, June 12, 1888.

BANGS, ELIZABETH (HARMON) (1827-1891). Fraternal twin of Ellen White, and with her the last of Robert and Eunice Harmon's eight

children. Elizabeth was nicknamed "Lizzie" by her twin sister and family. It seems that Ellen was the dominant of the two twins, and remembered that as a child her sister was rather chubby and found it more difficult to climb.

ELLEN G. WHITE AND HER TWIN
SISTER, ELIZABETH BANGS

The records of the Chestnut Street Methodist Church in Portland, Maine, show that Lizzie was accepted as a member on probation on October 31, 1842, a few months after her twin was baptized. But there is no record of Lizzie being baptized or becoming a regular member. Robert and Eunice Harmon, together with their younger children (including Ellen), were removed from membership in September 1843. Presumably Lizzie's family connection prevented her from becoming a member. In 1849 she married Reuben M. Bangs, who had a Quaker background but was not religiously inclined. By 1857 they had settled in Gorham, Maine, where they had three children, Eva, Clarence, and Bertha.

In 1874 Ellen White observed that there were "no prayers" in her sister's home (Lt 51, 1874). Throughout her life Ellen White sought to influence her sister spiritually and bring her to conversion. Two examples illustrate the intensity of her efforts. In 1858 the Bangses lost their infant child Eva. A poem was composed and published in the *Youth's Instructor*, and Ellen White wrote a touching appeal to her twin sister describing how little infants will be reunited with their mothers at the resurrection but that some infants had no mothers there. She then wrote: "God grant that the dear mother of 'Eva' may be there, that her little wings may be folded upon the glad bosom of her mother" (YI, April 1858; 2SM 259, 260). How Lizzie responded to this appeal is not known, but during the last year of her life she received another urgent appeal from her twin sister. Ellen wrote to Lizzie: "I long to take you in my arms and lay you on the bosom of Jesus Christ. . . . My heart longs to see you trusting in Jesus. . . . He loves you. He wants to save you" (Lt 61, 1891). It is not known how Lizzie responded to this and other appeals. Reuben and Elizabeth Bangs and one daughter, Eva, are buried in the North Street

Cemetery not far from where they lived in Gorham, Maine.

Merlin D. Burt

BANKS, JACKSON (1819-1882). Early Adventist in Greenville, Michigan. Originally from England, Jackson immigrated to the United States in 1849 and became an Adventist in 1860 after attending meetings held in Greenville by J. B. Frisbie and R. J. Lawrence. In 1862 Banks wrote to Ellen White regarding a certain Brother Merril who had been drawn away by "unruly fanatics." She urged that Merril not be given a position of church leadership unless he confesses "his past course and comes out clean from it" (Lt 5, 1862).

Further reading: obit. RH, Nov. 21, 1882.

BATES, JOSEPH (1792-1872). The founder and developer of that branch of Adventism

COURTESY OF THE CENTER FOR ADVENTIST RESEARCH, ANDREWS UNIVERSITY.

JOSEPH BATES

that became known as Sabbatarian Adventism and later still as Seventh-day Adventism. Bates was the person who convinced James and Ellen White of the perpetuity of the seventh-day Sabbath.

Bates was born in Rochester, Massachusetts, on July 8, 1792, but the next year his family moved to New Bedford, which became the whaling capital of the United States by the middle of the nineteenth century. Just before his fifteenth birthday young Bates signed on as a cabin boy on a merchant ship. In 1810 he was shanghaied into the British navy and later spent a few years as a British prisoner during the War of 1812.

After the war he returned to his merchant marine calling, eventually becoming the captain and part owner of a small ship. The

early 1820s saw him take his first step in health reform when he gave up tobacco and alcohol in all their forms. Those reforms would be followed in the 1840s by a thoroughgoing vegetarianism. He became a baptized member of the Christian Connexion in 1827. During the 1830s he was a leading member of his congregation and an all around social reformer. He accepted the teachings of William Miller in 1839, soon becoming quite prominent in the movement.

After the October 1844 disappointment Bates struggled to make biblical sense of his Millerite experience. The spring of 1845 saw him accept the seventh-day Sabbath through the writings of T. M. Preble. In August 1846 Bates met James White and Ellen Harmon for the first time, the same month they were married. He shared the Sabbath doctrine with them but they rejected it. Ellen later wrote that she "thought that Bro. B. erred in dwelling upon the fourth commandment more than the other nine" (2SG 82). That same month Bates wrote a book titled *The Seventh Day Sabbath, a Perpetual Sign*. The newly married Whites read that book that autumn and thus received the Sabbath through the ministry of Bates.

About that same time Bates accepted the idea that Ellen White truly had the gift of prophecy. Up to that time he claims to have been a "doubting Thomas" on the topic. But in the autumn of 1846 he witnessed her in a vision that incidentally dealt with astronomy. Bates, being up-to-date in that field, concluded that she had received information on the topic that was beyond her own knowledge. From that time forward he accepted her as a prophet of God.

In January 1847 Bates published a new edition of *The Seventh Day Sabbath*, in which he highlighted the connection between the heavenly sanctuary and the Sabbath, saw both of them in the eschatological context of

Revelation, and worked out what would come to be known as great controversy theology from Revelation 12:17 up through the end of chapter 14. In April 1847 Ellen White had a vision confirming his understanding of great controversy theology and its importance at the end of time.

May 1847 witnessed James White publish a 24-page tract titled *A Word to the "Little Flock."* That publication would be the first that contained exclusively the writings of Bates and James and Ellen White. From the spring of 1847 they worked closely together in preaching among the ex-Millerites what they called the third angel's message.

Bates had published his understanding of the message of the third angel in his 1847 edition of *The Seventh Day Sabbath.* The Whites accepted his basic understanding of the third angel's message, even though James made some variations on Bates' presentation. But even though Bates and the Whites might have differed in detail, they were agreed that the Sabbath was reflected in Revelation 14:12 and that it would be a prophetic issue at the end of time.

In 1848 Bates and the Whites joined forces in a series of meetings (*Sabbatarian Bible Conferences) that extended at least until 1850 and functioned as an evangelistic means by which to gather in a body of Sabbatarian Adventists. The 1850s saw the Sabbatarian movement begin to develop toward a more formal denomination. At first Bates had been adamant against any formal organization, saying that all such was Babylon and that the next organization of God's people would be in heaven. But after James and Ellen began to write about "gospel order" in 1853 and 1854 Bates joined them, noting that true gospel order would be one of those things that would be restored by God's commandment-keeping people before Christ's second advent.

By the early 1860s Bates was chairing the meetings that eventually brought about the formation of the Seventh-day Adventist Church.

Soon after the formation of the General Conference of Seventh-day Adventists, Ellen White had her June 1863 health reform vision. Bates, of course, was quite in harmony with the content of her vision. Previously he had been largely quiet on the topic since he didn't want to be divisive. But after Ellen White's 1863 and December 1865 visions, Bates joined the Whites in proclaiming that health reform was an important aspect of the third angel's message and that it would be instrumental in preparing God's people for their translation at the Second Advent.

The last extant letter from Bates is one that he wrote to Ellen White on February 14, 1872. She had written him 12 days earlier, suggesting that he eat less abstemiously and that he retire and let the younger men carry the burden of the church work. His letter was a spirited response, indicating that his old fire had not gone out. But the next month, somewhat short of his eightieth birthday, Joseph Bates passed to his rest on March 19, 1872, and is buried in Monterey, Michigan.

Further Reading: obit. RH, Apr. 16, 1872; G. T. Anderson, *Outrider of the Apocalypse: Life and Times of Joseph Bates* (PPPA, 1972); Joseph Bates, *Autobiography* (1868; reprint AUP, 2004); G. R. Knight, *Joseph Bates: The Real Founder of Seventh-day Adventism* (RHPA, 2004).

George R. Knight

BATES, PRUDENCE M. (NYE) (1793-1870). Wife of *Joseph Bates. Along with her husband, Prudence Bates took part in the Millerite movement but did not accept his views on the seventh-day Sabbath until 1850. For years she voluntarily associated with Sabbatarian

Adventists but did not formally join them until 1864, a year after the organization of the General Conference, and only six years before her death. Ellen White corresponded with her a few times. On one occasion White shared with Bates a dream she had had about angels rescuing Bates from Satan's power on the day of the second coming of Christ (Lt 14, 1850). In another letter Ellen White reproved the Bateses, in particular Prudence, for being too lenient with their daughter, Mary, and also too apt to complain about church members (Lt 1, 1864).

Further reading: obit. RH, Sept. 6, 1870; G. R. Knight, *Joseph Bates: The Real Founder of Seventh-day Adventism* (RHPA, 2004).

BEAN, LEWIS (1823-1888). Early Sabbatarian Adventist from Vermont. Bean accepted the *three angels' messages in 1852. In 1858 he began to work as an itinerant preacher sharing his faith in Massachusetts (July) and in Canada East (November). Ellen White wrote to him in 1859 that the Lord had not called him to be an itinerant preacher, and believed he was not qualified for this work. Instead she admonished him to be ready to share his convictions whenever he could (Lt 20, 1859; cf. Ms 1, 1859). He is apparently the "Brother C" mentioned in 1T 448, 449. Twelve years later, in 1871, Ellen White wrote again of Bean, "God has not called him especially to minister in word and doctrine" (2T 639). In following years Bean continued to serve the church in various administrative positions. For many years in the 1860s and 1870s he served on the executive committee of the Vermont Conference, and for five years, from 1870 to 1875, was conference president. Although he held ministerial credentials during most of the 1870s, after becoming conference president there is little evidence in the *Review and Herald* that he engaged in

public evangelism. In 1880 his credentials were not renewed, and he left for Michigan, where he died eight years later.

Further reading: obit. RH, Apr. 24, 1888.

BEERMAN, MARIE SCHULTZ (1860-1938). Immigrant from Hamburg, Germany, who participated in the International Congress of Women of 1899, representing the needs of German women. Ellen White expressed appreciation for her "beautiful letter" and Beerman's gratitude to God for Ellen White's restoration from sickness (Lt 392, 1906).

Further reading: 6Bio 117; obit. NPUG, Jan. 3, 1939.

BELDEN, ALBERT (1800-1893) and **HANNAH** (1800-1886). Parents of *Stephen T. Belden; Albert was a farmer in Rocky Hill and Berlin, Connecticut. In April 1848 James and Ellen White attended a Sabbath Conference that "was held at Rocky Hill, Connecticut, in the large, unfinished chamber of Bro. Belden's house." E.L.H. Chamberlain of nearby Middletown had organized the conference and urged the Whites to attend (2SG 91, 93). Later Ellen referred to it as "the first conference that was ever held among Seventh-day Adventists" (Ms 76, 1886, in 1Bio 137). It was during this visit that James White mowed hay for 87½ cents an acre so that he and Ellen would have funds to travel to New York to attend a similar conference at Hiram Edson's home (JW to "Dear Brother," July 2, 1848, EGWE-GC). During their frequent travels, the Whites intermittently stopped to visit Rocky Hill, and it was also while here that Ellen White was given two visions. The first took place on December 16, 1848, and another on January 5, 1849, while "engaged in prayer with Brother Belden's family" (1Bio 154, 155; EW 36). In April 1849 the Beldens invited the Whites to live in their home, and enclosed funds to defray their moving expenses (Lt 5, 1849). They accepted the offer and, along with *Clarissa Bonfoey, set up housekeeping in "a part of Brother Belden's house at Rocky Hill" (LS 123). It was during this stay with the Beldens that James White prepared the first four issues of *The Present Truth*, the first Sabbatarian Adventist periodical. By January 1853, the Beldens were living in the nearby township of Berlin, Connecticut, in the village of Kensington (RH, Jan. 6, 1853). At "a conference in Kensington, Ct." in 1854 E.L.H. Chamberlain and Albert Belden were set apart as deacons by Joseph Bates (RH, May 30, 1854). The Beldens remained in Berlin the rest of their lives, where Albert is buried in the Christian Lane Cemetery (Berlin *Weekly News*, Oct. 26, 1893).

Further reading: obit. RH, Aug. 24, 1886; obit. RH, Nov. 14, 1893.

Michael W. Campbell

BELDEN, BYRON (1861-1895). Son of *Stephen and Sarah (Harmon) Belden, brother of F. E. Belden, and nephew of Ellen White. Byron and his wife, Sarah, went to Australia in 1886 for him to serve as pressman in the *Bible Echo* office. When Australia was hit with economic depression, Byron and other expatriates lost their jobs at the press. He then sought further training so that he could serve as a Bible worker and colporteur. Ellen White commended him for his hard work and thoughtfulness toward his father and stepmother. He died at the age of 34 of lung disease.

Further Reading: obit. RH, Jan. 14, 1896.

Jerry Chase

BELDEN, FRANKLIN EDSON (1858-1945) and **HARRIET (McDEARMON).** Hymn writer, trainer of literature evangelists, editor, author, Sabbath School pioneer, superintendent at the *Review and Herald publishing house, and

nephew of Ellen White. Born in *Battle Creek to *Stephen T. and *Sarah (Harmon) Belden, Frank grew up surrounded with the printing trade and curiosity seekers who came to his mother to get facts about her sister, Ellen. In 1862 the family left Battle Creek, partly because of the undue attention drawn to them as a result of their familial relationship to Ellen White. They would later return to Battle Creek in 1871, after Sarah's death in 1868.

Frank moved to Oakland, California, in 1875 to work in the *Signs of the Times* office.

FRANKLIN BELDEN

While there, he first lived with James and Ellen White, and then later with their son and Frank's cousin *Edson White and his wife, *Emma. (Frank later married Emma's sister, Harriet McDearmon.) Ellen White was concerned for Frank's spiritual life and counseled him on his headstrong, unteachable spirit, his manner of Sabbath observance, and his lack of financial management (Lt 41, 1877). Furthermore, in addition to being cousins, Frank and Edson were close friends, an association that Ellen viewed as detrimental to both young men (Lt 42, 1879). Both Edson and Frank would develop hard feelings toward Edson's younger brother *William C. White—in part stemming from James White's removal of Edson from the management of the *Pacific Press publishing house and giving the job to Willie. Ellen would later write Willie that he and James were too severe toward both Edson and Frank (J. Moon, *W. C. White and Ellen G. White*, p. 52).

In 1880 Frank traveled to Colorado, apparently for relief from bronchial problems, where he ended up in Harriet (Hattie) McDearmon's parents' home. The following year Frank and Hattie were married. The newlyweds joined an evangelistic team for a year during which time Frank composed many songs. Frank's genius in music and poetry was demonstrated by his ability to write a song to fit a sermon while it was being preached. He would reportedly "take the Scripture text of the sermon as his theme and, using the preacher's exposition, write the hymn text. Then he would compose the music for the newly written words." Finally, he and Harriet would sing the new hymn to conclude the service (W. Hooper, *Companion to the Seventh-day Adventist Hymnal*, p. 628).

Returning to Battle Creek, Frank began to prepare a book with his own music. But those plans changed as he became connected with the planning of a new denominational hymnal. Late in 1885 the committee listened to selections of Belden's music, and negotiations were made to incorporate his material into the new hymnal. He was retained as music editor along with Edwin Barnes, and Belden's previous work was incorporated in *The Seventh-day Adventist Hymn and Tune Book, for Use in Divine Worship* (1886). Belden was by far the most prolific Seventh-day Adventist contributor, with 80 texts and 87 tunes. In an agreement between Belden and the General Conference, Belden's share of royalties from *Hymns and Tunes* would go toward missions.

Belden continued to be active in music even as he rose in prominence at the Review and Herald publishing house. His next project was preparing *Bible Readings for the Home Circle* for publication. The next two years were largely spent promoting Adventist publications and training *colporteurs, first as the Michigan State book agent and then as general book agent for the denomination.

At the *General Conference session of 1888 Frank Belden was a principal force, along with *R. A. Underwood, in questioning Ellen White's claim to the prophetic gift, and

charging that she was being "influenced" by her son, W. C. White, as well as by *A. T. Jones and *E. J. Waggoner. This spirit of resistance showed itself in an action passed by the assembly in spite of her direct objections. Belden introduced a seemingly harmless resolution that colporteur experience be required for all ministers. Ellen White strongly favored colporteur experience as a valuable preparation for ministry, but objected to making it an absolute prerequisite for *all* ministers. Evidently, as an expression of their anger with her for supporting Jones and Waggoner, a majority of the committee voted the resolution despite her objections.

Following the 1888 session Belden and *Clement Eldridge continued working against Ellen White. They adopted a policy of promoting only one large book at a time for sale by colporteurs. By designating *Bible Readings* as the one book to be promoted, they effectively hindered the circulation of *The Great Controversy* and *Patriarchs and Prophets* (R. W. Coon, *Sourcebook of Documents and Study Outlines of Selected Issues in Prophetic Guidance* [1992, C-2, CAR]).

From 1888 to 1897 Frank's business and commercial concerns seem to have gradually eclipsed his spiritual priorities. Despite a brief period of revival around the turn of the century, he had a falling out with the Review and Herald and in 1905 sued them over his grievances. By December of that year they reached an agreement, though amended many times, that served as a basis of settling the lawsuit out of court. The Review agreed that it would no longer profit from royalties from *Hymns and Tunes*. That work was to be transferred back to General Conference ownership, with the profits being applied again toward missions, as according to the original agreement. Furthermore, Belden would enjoy specified income from ongoing sales of *Christ in Song* and *Bible Object Lessons and Songs for Little Ones* (RHPA, "Recommendation Agreed to Between F. E. Belden and the RHPA," Dec. 11, 1905, CAR).

While completing revisions for the 1908 edition of *Christ in Song*, Belden became embroiled in controversies at Battle Creek. After he brought a lawsuit in 1907 attempting to block the transfer of the Battle Creek Tabernacle to the West Michigan Conference, his church membership was dropped, and the Review and Herald moved to consolidate its interests in *Christ in Song* by distancing Belden publicly from the project. In a one-time payment of $6,000 (approximately six years' wages at the time) the plates and worldwide denominational rights for publishing and circulating were secured by the Review (RHPA Minutes, Sept. 24, 1907). Ads for the forthcoming edition touted that no private individual would receive any profit from the sale of the book.

Christ in Song climaxed Belden's musical output. First published in 1900, it was revised and enlarged by Belden to nearly 1,000 hymns by the 1908 edition. One of the most popular songbooks ever used by Seventh-day Adventists, it became the unofficial hymnal of the church, even continuing in active use after the appearance of the new *Church Hymnal* in 1941.

It is difficult to reconcile the Belden of gospel hymns with the later Belden at odds with the denomination and Ellen White. As with many, Belden's spiritual life had highs and lows. He fondly remembered the evangelistic experiences in the early 1880s when he wrote many of his early hymns. In 1887, writing to Hattie Belden, Ellen White commended Frank's work (Lt 86, 1887), but during the turbulent 1888 General Conference session, Frank joined those actively opposing Ellen White. Unfortunately, he would continue to work at

cross-purposes with Ellen White, even after many of her former antagonists had publicly confessed their wrongs and made peace. In 1897 Ellen White wrote to Belden, "I know you have a prayerless home" (Lt 29, 1897).

During the time Frank was preparing the 1900 edition of *Christ in Song* he seems to have experienced a spiritual revival to the extent that Ellen White invited him to join her staff as one of her literary assistants. At this point the rift between Frank and Ellen appears to have healed, but disdain and animosity toward W. C. White remained. Ellen commented: "I was willing to try you [Frank] in my work, but I can never, never place my work entirely in your control. Your criticism of W. C. [White], whose work bears the test of years, is cruel and unjust" (Lt 94, 1901). This proved to be a pivotal time in Belden's life. Frank mentioned his dissatisfaction with W. C. White as his reason for not working for Ellen White. Instead, he signed a contract to prepare and help circulate *J. H. Kellogg's book *Plain Facts* (Frank Belden to EGW, July 1, 1901, CAR).

Belden's choice to connect with Kellogg intensified his strong feelings not only against his cousin W. C. White, but against his aunt Ellen as well. In Belden's later years he bitterly denounced Ellen White and the denomination even as his hymns continued to bless the church. Kenneth H. Wood relates the story of a visit he and Carlyle B. Haynes had with Frank Belden several weeks before Frank's death in 1945. Before leaving, they asked if they might pray with him. Belden asked if they still believed in Ellen White. When they affirmed that they did, he declined the prayer, saying: "Not so long as you believe in that old woman." Several have drawn a tragic correlation between Belden's eventual experience and a warning Ellen White made to him a half century earlier: "Men may labor in connection with the work of God as did Noah's carpenters, and yet resist the divine influences" (Lt 15, 1895).

Further reading: J. Bingham, "Franklin Belden and Captain Eldridge: Their Reactions to the General Conference of 1888, and Their Work at the Review and Herald Publishing Association" (research paper, AU, 1982, CAR); J. Chase, "Spiritual Waymarks in the Life of Franklin E. Belden" (research paper, AU, 1997, CAR); S. Geraci, "The Enigma of Franklin E. Belden" (research paper, AU, 1977, CAR).

Jerry Chase

BELDEN, LILLIAN "LILLIE" A. (later **LILLIAN "LILLIE" A. [BELDEN] GILBERT**) (1862-1945). The youngest of *Sarah (Harmon) and *Stephen Belden's children. Following the death of her mother in 1868, Lillian and her siblings received from their aunt Ellen White special attention in both practical and spiritual matters. Sarah's dying request to her sister Ellen White had been that Ellen "keep . . . before Frank and Ella and Lillie and Charlie and Byron that I want them to love the Lord Jesus and at last meet me in heaven" (Lt 301, 1905). Ellen White sought to fulfill this wish by keeping in touch with her sister's children by visits and letters. An entry in her diary relates, "Made arrangements for Lillie Belden to come to my house every day to be instructed in sewing and kept in useful employment" (Ms 5, 1873). In 1879 Lillie married Henry J. Gilbert, and they had five daughters. Presumably, Ellen White wrote her a letter in 1880 (Lt 54, 1880) in which she pleaded with Lillie, after marrying an unbeliever, to be converted. Seven years later White noted with joy that "Lilly [sic] Belden Gilbert" "holds the faith firmly" despite threats and opposition from her husband (Lt 66, 1887, in 21MR 320). Ellen's

only other extant letter to Lillie came almost 20 years later (Lt 328, 1906).

Further reading: obit. PUR, Sept. 26, 1945.

Jerry Chase

BELDEN, SARAH B. (HARMON) (1822-1868). Fourth daughter of Robert and Eunice Harmon, five years older than the twins, Ellen and Elizabeth Harmon. For several years after Ellen's first vision in December 1844, Sarah often accompanied her sister Ellen to various towns and villages to relate her visions. On August 5, 1851, Sarah Harmon and Stephen Belden were married by James White in Saratoga Springs, New York. They worked with James and Ellen in the publishing work until at least 1860. For many of those years Stephen was superintendent of the type room at the publishing house (1Bio 321). When Ellen and Sarah heard that their brother Robert was losing his battle with consumption, Sarah went to Gorham, Maine, and cared for him until his death in 1853 (*ibid.* 215, 234). In 1868 Ellen received word that Sarah herself was dying of "quick consumption" (tuberculosis). Hoping to help her sister as she faced the prospect of leaving her five children motherless, Ellen immediately went to her. They spent a week together, and Sarah died a short time later at the age of 45 (2Bio 252). Sarah and Stephen had five children: *Byron, Charlie, *Lillian, Ella, and *Frank, a well-known hymn writer. Ella died at 16, and Byron and his wife, Sarah, went to Australia as missionaries during the time that Ellen White was there.

Norma Collins

BELDEN, STEPHEN T. (1829-1906) and **MELVINA MIGHELLS (DEVEREAUX).** Early foreman and business manager of the Review and Herald, brother-in-law to Ellen White, who assisted her in Australia and then went as a missionary to Norfolk Island, Australia. Belden was 19 when the first of the Sabbatarian conferences of 1848 was held in an unfinished chamber of the home of his father, Albert Belden, in Rocky Hill, Connecticut. The next year at Albert's invitation *James and *Ellen White came to live in the Belden home. In 1851 Stephen married Sarah Harmon, Ellen's older sister, and they became part of the team that in 1852 started the publishing work in Rochester, New York, and in 1855 relocated it to Battle Creek.

Because of Sarah Belden's connection to Ellen White, the Adventist women of Battle Creek frequently visited the Belden home to get the "facts" from Sarah on her sister Ellen. In 1862 the family moved away to a rugged rural location in Illinois and then on to Berlin, Connecticut, in 1864. James White repeatedly urged Stephen Belden to return to the *Review and Herald* office, but even though the $12-per-week wages that the *Review* offered were better by far than the "Illinois and Conn. privations" (F. E. Belden to WCW, Mar. 14, 1937, CAR), Sarah firmly resisted the move. This was the only issue on which their son *Frank remembered his parents arguing openly. Even Frank weighed in on the discussion. He remembered asking, "Mother, don't you want to go to heaven?" and her reply, "Frank, Battle Creek is not the gate" (F. E. Belden to WCW, Apr. 15, 1937, CAR). Sarah stood firm, and not until the winter of 1871, after Sarah's death from tuberculosis in 1868, did the Beldens move back to Battle Creek.

Sarah's untimely death left Stephen with children ages 6 to 11, and for their sake he married Charlotte Alley, who had been a faithful servant in the household. Unfortunately, shortly after this, Charlotte contracted a severe form of measles. The measles went to her brain, and she was eventually admitted to the Hospital for the Insane in Middletown, Connecticut, where she died in 1897.

The time of Stephen's marriage to Melvina ("Vina") Mighells Devereaux is uncertain. When the Beldens sold their home in Battle Creek in 1879, Charlotte was listed on the bill of sale. In the 1880 census S. T. Belden is listed in Minnesota as head of household, along with his wife, C. A., and children Frank, Charles, and Byron. (A second 1880 census indicates that the Beldens were living in the same home with another family, but had a "servant," Lavina Devereaux, keeping house.) There is no record of Ellen White counseling Stephen in regard to marrying Vina. The church and societal sentiments of the time, however, would certainly have opposed divorce on the ground of insanity, based upon the view that divorces should be granted because of fault and not misfortune (W. T. Nelson, *Nelson on Divorce & Annulment* [Chicago: Callaghan, 1895, 1945], p. 336). "At various times, individuals where Brother Belden lived undertook to secure his exclusion from the church because he had married without separation from his [second] wife on the charge of adultery. When appealed to in regard to this matter, Sister White said, 'Let them alone'" (TSB 225).

Stephen and Vina joined Ellen White in Australia in 1891. Eventually they went as missionaries to Norfolk Island. Regardless of how Ellen White may have regarded their original grounds for marriage, she was supportive and thoughtful of the couple in their later years. She helped them financially during hard times in Australia and saw to it that they had a house and regular support on Norfolk Island. She sought to relieve their loneliness by writing them personally and by sending copies of letters she had sent or received from others. Her letters ranged from personal news tidbits to counsels and encouragement to the believers. More than once she counseled Stephen to preach shorter sermons.

In 1899, feeling their work on Norfolk was done, the Beldens moved to Sydney, Australia, where for several months Stephen took training in dental work. But they received such constant and pressing appeals from the Norfolk Islanders to return that they decided to make a permanent return to Norfolk. Following Stephen's death in 1906, Ellen White continued to keep in touch with Vina, who chose to stay with the believers on Norfolk Island and eventually be buried next to her husband rather than come back to the United States.

See also: Sarah (Harmon) Belden.

Further reading: TSB 223-225; obit. AUCR, Dec. 3, 1906; obit. RH, Dec. 13, 1928; see also "Personal," UCR, Sept. 1, 1899.

Jerry Chase

BELL, GOODLOE HARPER (1832-1899). Founding teacher of the first denomination-

COURTESY OF THE CENTER FOR ADVENTIST RESEARCH, ANDREWS UNIVERSITY.

GOODLOE H. BELL

ally sponsored school, principal, tutor, editor, organizer and promoter of the *Sabbath school, administrator, and author. Bell was born near Watertown, New York, but later moved west with his family, settling finally in Ottawa County, Michigan. Here he farmed and worked as a teacher and inspector of schools in the counties around Grand Rapids from 1854 to the mid-1860s.

Declining health and the death of his wife brought him to the recently opened *Health Reform Institute in *Battle Creek, Michigan, in 1866. On a second visit in 1867 he embraced Seventh-day Adventist teachings and was soon invited to open a private school in Battle Creek with the encouragement of James and Ellen White. In 1869 he also accepted the responsibility of superintendent of the Battle Creek Sabbath school, and editor of the *Youth's

Instructor. He also served for one year as treasurer of the General Conference (1870-1871). On December 10, 1871, Ellen White was shown in vision "the case of Bro. Bell in connection with the cause and work of God in Battle Creek." She described his excellent qualifications as a teacher and recognized that his aim was to "accomplish permanent good" in the characters of his students, as he cared for their "physical, moral, and spiritual" interests. Nevertheless, she also drew attention to his unbalanced proclivity for order, perfection, and organization to the neglect of "the laws of health and life." She was concerned that he was becoming "exacting," intolerant of the views of others, and "extremely sensitive." This was making him dissatisfied unless people and programs were moving like "well-regulated machinery" (*Testimony to the Church at Battle Creek* [1872], PH123 1-15).

In March 1872 Ellen White encouraged him to become the teacher in the first church school to be officially sponsored by the Seventh-day Adventist Church. The school opened on June 3, and in 1874 it became *Battle Creek College, where Bell continued to teach until 1882.

In 1869 Bell was appointed superintendent of the Battle Creek Sabbath school. During the next 18 years he had a profound and lasting influence on the development of the church's Sabbath school program. He refined its organization, and introduced many lasting innovations.

Bell's many responsibilities both at the college and in the Sabbath school brought him considerable stress, which, added to his exacting nature, caused a deterioration in his relationships with both his students and his peers. In 1881 Ellen White noted that he had embarrassed mature students by his sarcastic remarks. She said that he was "naturally severe, critical, and exacting" (Ms 2, 1881).

Changes in leadership at the college also contributed to a deepening crisis there during 1881. In December Ellen White sent a manuscript entitled "Our College," to be read to the leaders of the church (5T 21-36). The final four paragraphs concerned Bell and the other teachers' attitudes toward him. She acknowledged that he had not always moved wisely. "Let him be dealt with tenderly," she appealed, for he deserved "respect for the good which he has done." He had "performed the labor which three men should have shared." She sympathetically counseled, "He is worn; God would have him lay off some of these extra burdens for a while" (*ibid.* 35, 36).

However, her counsel was ignored. The crisis exploded during the next three months, leading to Bell's resignation from the college February 20, 1882. In a letter she wrote to *Uriah Smith, chair of the college board, on March 28, 1882 (*ibid.* 45-62), she made it clear that she had "no sympathy" with the course that had been pursued toward Bell. In vision she had been shown the meetings called against him and had heard the testimonies of students who had received so much benefit from his instruction, yet who were now testifying against him. In his defense she said that there was no man in the church who had "devoted more time and thought to his work" than had Bell (*ibid.* 59; see also pp. 90-92).

To Bell's credit, he did not permit the events of 1882 to embitter him. Shortly after his resignation from Battle Creek College he was invited to be the founding principal of the *South Lancaster school (later Atlantic Union College). Highly committed to Ellen White's philosophy of Christian *education, he made great efforts to implement it in this school during the next two years. However, ill health and his weaknesses of character eventually led to his resignation from the

school and from denominational employment in mid-1884.

Bell returned to Battle Creek and continued to serve the church's youth for the last 15 years of his life until his tragic death on January 16, 1899. Many of his students later testified to the positive influence of his life and teaching. In Ellen White's words: "He was represented to me as a candle from which many others have been lighted" (*Testimony for the Church at Battle Creek* [1882], PH117 31).

Further reading: J. C. Bartholf, "Goodloe Harper Bell," YI, Feb. 9, 1899, pp. 101-106; A. G. Lindsay, "Goodloe Harper Bell: Teacher," in G. R. Knight, ed., *Early Adventist Educators* (AUP, 1982); A. G. Lindsay, *Goodloe Harper Bell: Pioneer Seventh-day Adventist Educator* (Ed.D. diss., AU, 1982).

Allan G. Lindsay

BELOW, ELSIE PHILOMELA (FLOWER) GREGG (1811-1889). Early Adventist from Mill Grove, New York. In 1825 she married John Gregg (d. 1839), and in 1835 both joined the Disciples of Christ Church. In 1842 a Seventh Day Baptist influenced her to observe the Sabbath, and in 1851 she accepted the "Adventist faith" from Joseph Bates. A few years after the death of her first husband, she married John C. Below (1785-1855), who also became a Sabbatarian Adventist in 1852. After his death Elsie Below moved to *Battle Creek at the invitation of James White, who offered to sell her the house recently vacated by Ellen's parents (JW to E. P. Below, Nov. 4, 1856, and Mar. 23, 1857). Ellen White described Sister Below as "very near our hearts" (Lt 9, 1856). Many years later Ellen White preached at her funeral.

Further reading: obit. RH, May 29, 1855; obit. RH, Dec. 10, 1889.

BICKNELL (or **BICKNALL**), **PRESTON F.** (1853-1939) and **HELEN** (1871-1934). Adventist workers at the *Claremont Sanitarium in South Africa. In a conflict at the sanitarium, Bicknell defended his employment there on the basis of a purported testimony by Ellen White that she did not remember writing. "My brother," Ellen White commented, "when you know that you are not wanted in the position you now occupy, it is certainly your duty to leave that position, and not follow your own independent judgment." She recommended that he listen to the counsels of others and advised him to "not at any time or in any place imperil the cause of God by your firm, determined will" (Lt 161, 1899; cf. Lt 158, 1899).

BLISS, CHARLES HENRY (1847-1925). Teacher, evangelist, and minister. Bliss began ministry in the Wisconsin-Illinois Conference at the age of 20, and was ordained by James White in 1871. In 1891 he wrote to Ellen White asking for advice with regard to a couple in his church whom some in his church were pressuring toward marital separation. In her reply Ellen White advised that although this couple did not follow biblical advice when they got married, the matter of their separation should not be pressed. "I advise that these unfortunate ones be left to God and their own consciences" (Lt 5, 1891, in TSB 218, 219).

Further reading: obit. RH, Jan. 28, 1926.

BOEKER, A. Manager of the St. Helena Sanitarium Health Food Factory in the early 1900s. Boeker first began selling health foods on his own, but Ellen White counseled him to consult with Dr. J. H. Kellogg, who had already put out "a large outlay of means" in preparing these foods (Lt 151, 1901). By the fall of 1901 Boeker had opened a health food factory at the St. Helena Sanitarium. Ellen White urged him not to overtax himself, to be cautious in his words, and to respect his fellow workers (Lt 196, 1901). She noted later that he had made a "full confession," which "has cleared away much fog" (Lt 114, 1902).

BOLLMAN, CALVIN P. (1853-1943). Editor connected with several periodicals, including *American Sentinel, Gospel Herald, Liberty, Review and Herald,* and *Southern Watchman.* Ellen White's counsel to Bollman on making the use of his capabilities more effective in the cause of God contained far-reaching principles for the work of the church in the public arena.

In 1895, when Bollman was associated with *A. T. Jones in publishing the *American Sentinel,* Ellen White sought to impress upon the two editors the destructive consequences of both their sharp, combative rhetoric against opponents in public battles over religious liberty, and their hard-line legalism on matters involving the Adventist Church's own relationship to civil government. To Bollman she wrote that a harsh, condemning style undermines the presentation of truth, leading the nonbeliever to reject it in view of its unchristlike source. Militant rhetoric further damages the cause because it tends to "unnecessarily stir up angry feelings and arouse the enmity of those who do not believe as we do."

Moreover, such combativeness alienates Adventists from worthwhile cooperation with others through whom God continues to work. While we are in the world, wrote Ellen White, "the Lord has given us a special work to do to save the world." In doing that work, "we are not to withdraw" in a pharisaical manner from "association with others." God remains present and active in the world and would not have His people imitate the narrow exclusivity that developed in the ancient Jewish nation, for that would prevent them from being "a wholesome, saving element in the world" (Lt 7, 1895, in 19MR 101-107).

Bollman received another testimony of multifaceted importance from Ellen White in 1902 when he was in the editorial office of the Southern Publishing Association in Nashville, Tennessee. She pointed out that his capabilities were hindered by an inclination to regard himself as "a complete whole," closed off from the expertise and judgment of other minds. She called him to greater kindness and humility: "Less of self and more of Christ would make you much more useful." In fact, she wrote, the entire office in Nashville needed more of the gentle spirit of Christ and less "irritability," "sourness of disposition," and censuring of little mistakes. In sum: "Brethren and sisters, sweeten up."

In this letter Ellen White also addressed the contentious spirit seen in quibbling over and exaggerating minor doctrinal disagreements, thus destroying unity and love among the believers. She recalled the "terrible experience" of bitter conflict over the law in *Galatians at the Minneapolis session and stated in emphatic terms that it should not be repeated: "Never should that which God has not given as a test be carried as was the subject of the law in Galatians" (Lt 179, 1902, in 1888 Materials 1787-1798).

That Bollman remained active in denominational editorial work for another 35 years—in fact, until he was in his mid-80s—suggests that Ellen White's counsel had a positive impact on him.

Further reading: obit. RH, Jan. 20, 1944.

Douglas Morgan

BOLTON, FRANCES "FANNIE" (1859-1926). Gifted but unstable literary assistant to Ellen White. Daughter of a Methodist minister, Bolton attended a women's seminary in Evanston, Illinois, and then worked as a correspondent for the *Daily Inter-Ocean*, a Chicago newspaper. She was drawn to Adventism

through the ministry of G. B. Starr in Chicago, where she spent a year in his Bible training course before working in Washington, D.C., as a Bible instructor. In 1887 she met Ellen White at a Springfield, Illinois, camp meeting, where she reported Ellen White's sermons for the *Daily Inter-Ocean*. Impressed with Fannie's talent, Ellen White employed her as a literary assistant. Fannie's work included the editing of some of Ellen White's letters as well as the fashioning of periodical articles from her sermons and writings. Bolton's work appears

COURTESY OF THE ELLEN G. WHITE ESTATE, INC.

FANNIE BOLTON

to have gone smoothly at first, for on February 13, 1888, Ellen White wrote S. N. Haskell, "Fannie Bolton is a treasure to me" (Lt 25, 1888).

There are no records of why it happened, but Fannie was soon separated from Ellen White's employment—the first of three such experiences in her lifetime. She then enrolled as a full-time student at the University of Michigan for the 1890-1891 school year. In the autumn of 1891, when Ellen White was preparing to leave for Australia, one of her helpers, Sarah McEnterfer, became sick and could not make the trip. A substitute was needed. For the second time Ellen White employed Fannie.

Yet all was not well. On November 23, 1892, less than a year after their arrival at Sydney, Ellen White wrote Elder Haskell, "There has been, especially with Fannie, but little harmony with me in my work since coming to Australia" (Lt 151, 1892). Fannie's tongue was getting her into trouble. In October 1892 she wrote Ellen White, "I have already asked your forgiveness for the unbecoming words I spoke to you. Do forgive, and try to forget. I am astonished when I think of speaking to you in so rude a way" ("The Fannie Bolton Story: A Collection of Source Documents" [1982, SDoc], p. 7). In spite of her regrets, Fannie continued to offer Ellen White her criticisms. She did not like the cutting words sometimes found in Ellen White's testimonies and told her so. On November 16, 1892, she wrote Ellen White, "I have often wondered if your words were not unnecessarily sharp" (*ibid.*, p. 9). In her editorial work Fannie chose at times to soften Ellen White's pointed language and substitute her own more mild expressions instead. This clearly disturbed Ellen White, who wrote to her son W. C. White, "Several have written me that when they could have the matter direct from my hand, it was far more forcible than after it had been prepared. . . . Fanny [*sic*] feels that many of my expressions can be bettered, and she takes the life and point out of them" (Lt 77, 1892). Fannie had a high regard for the work she was doing, and she desired public recognition for it. She asked G. B. Starr "if he thought it was right to give all the credit to Sister White, and make no mention of the workers, Marian and herself" (Lt 59, 1894). She may also have complained at this juncture about Ellen White's habit of using the works of other authors without credit, a practice not uncommon among religious writers in the nineteenth century (extract from *The Gathering Call*, in "The Fannie Bolton Story," p. 115). She seemingly complained to everyone who would listen. Ellen White wrote her son Willie that Fannie had brought her grievances to all the other workers on her staff, to several ministers, and to "how many others remains to be developed" (Lt 88, 1894).

For the second time Bolton was dropped from Ellen White's staff. Yet within a few weeks Ellen White decided to give Fannie "another trial" (Lt 137, 1894). Then, late in 1895, Ellen White learned that Fannie was still criticizing her behind her back. On October 29, 1895, she wrote Marian Davis, "I had a presentation of Fannie talking to different ones, exactly in the same strain as that we had to deal with two years ago" (Lt 102, 1895). Ellen White wrote her son Edson that Fannie "goes not only to those who believe and know me to tell her story but she goes to those newly come to the faith and tells her imaginative story" (Lt 123a, 1895).

There were also other problems with Fannie. She had become romantically involved with a man who had no biblical right to remarry (*W. F. Caldwell; Lt 14, 1895), and she was at times "as verily possessed by demons as were human beings in the days of Christ" (Lt 102, 1895). Not surprisingly, Ellen White for the third time decided to end her relationship with Fannie. She wrote her on November 7, 1895, "I now reluctantly and with grief in my heart say to Fannie Bolton: You are no longer in the employment of the General Conference in my behalf" (Lt 9, 1895).

The separation seemed to be final. Yet, unbelievably, only three months later Ellen White decided to take Fannie back again. It was "the only course" she could take conscientiously "and be a co-worker with Jesus Christ" ("Diary," Ms 12d, 1896). Fannie returned, but this time she did not stay long. She decided on her own to return to Battle Creek (WCW to O. A. Olsen, May 10, 1896), where Dr. J. H. Kellogg employed her briefly. On January 10, 1897, Kellogg wrote to Ellen White, "She has done some writing for me but I have not been able to make use of it. What she writes seems to exhibit the hysterical, nervous character which she shows in her manner. I think she is sick" ("The Fannie Bolton Story," p. 73). On March 16, 1900, G. A. Irwin, president of the General Conference, informed Ellen White that "Fannie Bolton is creating something of a sensation here in the church at Battle Creek. . . . She claims to have received the Holy Ghost, and is having a very wonderful experience and revelations from the Lord" (*ibid.*, p. 90).

In 1901 Bolton wrote her lengthy "Confession Concerning the Testimony of Jesus Christ" (*ibid.*, pp. 102-106), which strongly supported the ministry of Ellen White. But in 1914 she took an opposite view and was very critical of Ellen White (*ibid.*, pp. 108, 109). She spent a total of 16 months in the Kalamazoo State Hospital—from February 20, 1911, to March 18, 1912, and from October 9, 1924, to January 21, 1925 (R. A. Morter, M.D., to H. H. Cobban, July 25, 1959 ["The Fannie Bolton Story," p. 122]). She died June 28, 1926, at Battle Creek, and was buried at Eureka, Michigan.

Bolton was a diligent worker. W. C. White once stated that Fannie "handles mother's matters very intelligently and rapidly, turning off more than twice as much work in a given time as any other editor mother has ever employed" (WCW to J. E. White, Oct. 25, 1895, EGWE-GC). She was a gifted writer and was widely known for her poems. She adapted the hymn "Not I, but Christ," which, after more than 100 years, is still a favorite.

Further reading: "The Fannie Bolton Story: A Collection of Source Documents" (EGWE, SDoc).

Robert W. Olson

BONFOEY, CLARISSA "CLARA" (1821-1856). Close friend and housekeeper of James and Ellen White. In 1849 Bonfoey and the Whites moved into part of Albert Belden's home in Rocky Hill, Connecticut. Offering to live with them, she "cheerfully gave" them the use of the household furnishings she had inherited from her parents' estate (2SG 113). The Whites

considered her as part of their family (RH, June 12, 1856). Bonfoey assisted in the housework and often took care of the children, especially Henry and Edson, while James and Ellen White were traveling. She suffered from poor health, yet "she was a woman of remarkable faith" (Ms 147, 1907). It was often that ministers would pray for her physical and emotional healing. The Whites moved frequently during this time until they eventually settled in Battle Creek in 1855. On May 27, 1856, Ellen White had a vision in which she was "shown" by the angel that some present during a conference would be "food for worms" (1T 127-137). As she left the meetinghouse, Bonfoey remarked, "I feel impressed that I am one that will soon be food for worms" (2SG 208, 209). According to White's record she suffered from a disease of the lungs and later from a tumor, which was the apparent cause of her sudden death three days later. Her loss was a severe blow to the White family: "Poor Clara, yet not poor, sleeps in the cold grave; her loss we deeply feel; it can never be made up; it was so sudden" (Lt 1, 1856). Bonfoey was buried in the White family plot in Oak Hill Cemetery, Battle Creek, Michigan.

Further reading: obit. RH, June 12, 1856.

Theodore N. Levterov

BOURDEAU, AUGUSTIN CORNELIUS (1834-1916). French Canadian pioneer pastor in New England and Quebec, *Canada. Bourdeau accepted the Sabbatarian Adventist message in 1856 and thereafter began preaching in northern Vermont and Quebec and, with his brother, Daniel, and *Alfred Hutchins, was instrumental in organizing many churches in these areas in the 1860s and

AUGUSTIN C. BOURDEAU

1870s. At the request of the General Conference he and his brother spent a few months in Iowa in 1866 to help reorganize the church after the defections of the *Marion Party. In 1875 he began working with his son-in-law, Rodney S. Owen, in the eastern townships of Quebec. In 1877 he organized the South Stukely church, currently the oldest Seventh-day Adventist church in Canada. In 1880 he became president of the Quebec Conference, the first conference organized in Canada. In 1884, after the death of his first wife, *Charlotte, he worked four years in Europe and helped establish the work of Seventh-day Adventists in France, Italy, Romania, and Switzerland. While in Europe, Bourdeau remarried to *Martha Andrews, widow of William Andrews (who was a brother of J. N. Andrews) and stepsister of George I. Butler. Ellen White appreciated his many sacrifices for the work of the church in areas in which he labored. She also appreciated the fact that he and his brother were among the few experienced pastors who could speak French (Lt 25, 1870). For these reasons, while in Europe, she wrote him some candid letters regarding his character defects, and what she perceived as indolence and lack of consecration in his work. She felt strongly that he was not making good use of his time, and spending too much time at home taking care of little family matters (Lt 20, 1886). Feeling his sermons were dull and lifeless, she appealed to him to become a better preacher by diligently studying the Scriptures and not relying on the opinions and writings of others (Lt 33, 1886).

Further reading: obit. RH, Aug. 17, 1916; D. Fortin, *Adventism in Quebec: The Dynamics of Rural Church Growth, 1830-1910* (AUP, 2004); *SDA Encyclopedia* (1996), vol. 10, p. 224.

Denis Fortin

BOURDEAU, CHARLOTTE (SAXBY) (c. 1836-1883). First wife of *Augustin C. Bourdeau,

COURTESY OF THE CENTER FOR ADVENTIST RESEARCH, ANDREWS UNIVERSITY.

CHARLOTTE BOURDEAU

born in Bakersfield, Vermont. She accepted the message of Sabbatarian Adventists with her husband in 1856. The Bourdeaus pioneered much of the work of Seventh-day Adventists in northern Vermont and Quebec. Ellen White esteemed their work and personal sacrifices. Just before Bourdeau died of tuberculosis, White wrote her a touching letter, encouraging her to put her trust in Jesus, who loved her and her family very much. Ellen White mentioned that she also did not expect to live until Christ's second coming and would meet again with Bourdeau on the day of resurrection (Lt 28, 1883).

Further reading: obit. RH, Dec. 18, 1883.

BOURDEAU, DANIEL T. (1835-1905) and **MARION E. (SAXBY)** (1842-1929). Pioneer pastor and evangelist in northern Vermont and Quebec, and among French-speaking communities in Canada, the American Midwest, and Europe. Raised in a French Canadian Baptist family in Vermont, Bourdeau became a Sabbatarian Adventist in 1856 shortly after his brother, *Augustin. In succeeding years Bourdeau devoted his life to working for the Seventh-day Adventist Church. In 1861 he was married to Marion E. Saxby. With his brother, Augustin, and *Alfred Hutchins, he helped raise churches in Canada, Vermont, and New York. In 1868 he joined John Loughborough to work in California. He also devoted many years working in the Midwestern states, particularly

COURTESY OF THE CENTER FOR ADVENTIST RESEARCH, ANDREWS UNIVERSITY.

DANIEL T. BOURDEAU

among the French-speaking communities of Illinois and Wisconsin for which he felt a special burden. He was successful in raising a church among the French Canadian community of Ste-Anne-de-Kankakee, in Illinois, a community of former Roman Catholics who had immigrated to Illinois from Quebec with former priest Charles Chiniquy. Bourdeau also wrote a number of tracts in French. In 1876, and from 1883 to 1887, he worked in Europe. Bourdeau was an energetic person with a powerful mind. Ellen White readily recognized the gifts that Daniel and his wife, Marion, demonstrated in their work among French people in the Midwest. "I wish there were more Frenchmen who could labor where the Americans can do nothing," she commented (Lt 25, 1870). In fact, she felt both Bourdeau brothers had missed opportunities to work among the French population in Canada, and that they should have been more aggressive in this work (*ibid.*). Her genuine interest in the few experienced pastors who spoke French led her to take an active role in attempting to shape their ministry, in particular that of Daniel Bourdeau. She felt his first year in Europe in 1876 had been a disaster for the work there. Bourdeau's impulsive temperament, his constant interest in himself and his accomplishments, and his independent spirit and mind-set brought intolerable burdens on *J. N. Andrews. She felt strongly that Bourdeau should not go back to Europe unless other church administrators invited him to do so (Lt 21, 1879; Lt 4, 1881). In fact, Andrews wrote to Ellen White asking her to intervene when he heard that Bourdeau was planning to go back to Europe (Lt 5, 1881). When Bourdeau finally went back to Europe in 1883, White continued to send him letters encouraging him to be more patient and self-controlled. She felt he worked too hard at times and did not take enough time to relax, a lifestyle that also burdened his wife.

She also counseled him to be gentle in preaching against Catholics and other denominations, and not to arouse antagonism from other ministers unnecessarily (Lt 39, 1887).

Further reading: obit. RH, July 13, 1905; R. W. Coon, "Counsel to a Nervous Bridegroom," *Adventist Heritage* 13, no. 2 (Summer 1990): 17-23; D. Fortin, *Adventism in Quebec: The Dynamics of Rural Church Growth, 1830-1910* (AUP, 2004); *SDA Encyclopedia* (1996), vol. 10, pp. 224, 225.

Denis Fortin

BOURDEAU, MARTHA (PITT) ANDREWS

COURTESY OF THE CENTER FOR ADVENTIST RESEARCH, ANDREWS UNIVERSITY.

MARTHA BOURDEAU

(1842-1901). Second wife of *Augustin C. Bourdeau; stepsister of *George I. Butler; and granddaughter of Ezra Butler, the second governor of Vermont (1826-1828). Sometime after the death of her first husband, William Andrews, in 1878, Martha went with her daughters *Edith and Sarah Andrews to Switzerland to assist her brother-in-law, *J. N. Andrews, in the work of the Seventh-day Adventist Church in Europe. There she met and married *Augustin C. Bourdeau. While in Europe Ellen White wrote a number of letters to the Bourdeaus. She described Martha as "fine gold" and a great support to her husband and his children, greater than he was to her (Lt 37, 1886). Augustin's self-centeredness and overbearing personality seemed to have discouraged Martha, who received encouragements from Ellen White to look to Jesus (Lts 31, 35, 1887; cf. 3MR 209, excerpted in SC 116, 117). Martha died in 1901 after contracting tuberculosis in unfavorable living conditions while working in Montreal the year before.

Further reading: obit. RH, Sept 10, 1901.

BOURDEAU, PATIENCE, see **SISCO, PATIENCE S. (BOURDEAU).**

BOWLES, JAMES A. (c. 1827-1904). Adventist from Redlands, California, who asked Ellen White whether he should sell his orange orchards and devote himself to gospel ministry (Lt 167, 1904). She responded that he could witness of his faith with those he came in contact with, but that he should continue his ministry where he was. Ellen White cautioned him not to let church leaders depend upon him too much to relieve the debt of the Fernando Adventist School. Instead, they could raise the needed funds by selling her book *Christ's Object Lessons*, which she had devoted to help relieve school debts. She told him that funds would soon be needed for establishing a sanitarium "near Los Angeles in some rural district" (Lt 147, 1904). Later that year Bowles died and left half of his estate to the church (Lt 351, 1905).

Further reading: obit. PUR, Dec. 22, 1904.

BOYD, CHARLES L. (c. 1850-1898) and **MAUDE (SISLEY)** (1851-1937). Charles was a minister, administrator, and missionary from Vermont; Maude was a Bible in-structor, colporteur, and missionary, who was born in England and emigrated to Michigan in 1863. At the invitation of Ellen White, Maude moved to Battle Creek in 1867 to work as a compositor at the Review and Herald.

Maude participated in a number of denominational "firsts." She attended the first official Adventist camp meeting in Wright, Michigan, in 1868. She was one of the first tithers in Battle Creek when the tithing plan replaced Systematic Benevolence (*tithe) in the 1870s, and she was a charter member of the local *Tract and Missionary Society. She and Elsie Gates began a self-supporting ministry in Ohio, lending books, distributing tracts, and giving

Bible studies. In 1877 Maude joined J. N. Andrews in Switzerland, the first Seventh-day Adventist single female called to foreign service. She set type for the first tracts in Italian, learning on the job. In 1879 she left for England to assist J. N. Loughborough as a Bible instructor, colporteur, and tent evangelist.

Returning to the United States, she met Charles, and by 1884 they were married.

CHARLES BOYD

MAUD (SISLEY) BOYD

Together the Boyds pioneered the Adventist message in the American Northwest. At the 1886 General Conference session they were asked to be in the first group of missionaries to South Africa. The Boyds stopped at the 1887 European Adventist Council in Moss, Norway, on their way to the mission field. Ellen White wrote them a letter that is considered to be one of her most important missiological statements, outlining a strategy for establishing the Adventist Church in unentered territories. She urged them to abandon preconceived ideas about approaching people, but to "give dignity and character to the work." They should not feel "that the only way they can do [evangelism] is to go at the people pointedly, with all subjects of truth and doctrine as held by Seventh-day Advent-ists, for this would close their ears at the very onset." Instead, she urged them to study "the best method, that [they] may not raise prejudice nor stir up combativeness." This could be done by speaking upon points of agreement, giving evidence that one is a Christian, and expressing care for them.

In addition, Ellen White admonished Charles that "real common sense in health reform" was essential (Lt 12, 1887).

Returning to the United States in 1887, the Boyds conducted evangelistic meetings in the southern United States, where Charles died in 1898. The following year Ellen White, who was caring for Maude's sister, Nellie Starr, at Sunnyside, urged her to come to Australia and work with G. B. and Nellie Starr "in faith and hope and courage in the Lord" (Lt 30, 1899). Ellen assured the new widow that "your husband sleeps in Jesus," and that God "will give you much of His Holy Spirit, that you may have perfect assurance and peace" (*ibid.*). For nine years (1899-1908) Maude Boyd served as cafeteria director, women's dean, and teacher at Avondale College, followed by three years (1908-1910) as a Bible instructor in New South Wales and Victoria. Returning to the United States in 1910, she became a Bible instructor at Loma Linda Sanitarium and at Glendale Sanitarium, finally retiring at the age of 76. She died in 1937 and was buried beside her grandmother Sisley in the Avondale Cemetery.

Further reading: Ms 34, 1885; Ms 34a, 1885; obit. RH, July 12, 1898; obit. RH, Aug. 19, 1937; R. T. Banks, *A Woman's Place* (RHPA, 1992); J. G. Beach, *Notable Women of Spirit* (SPA, 1976); *SDA Encyclopedia* (1996), vol. 10, pp. 225, 226.

Brian E. Strayer and Michael W. Campbell

BRACKETT, LOUISA (FOSS) (1824-1861). Sister of *Hazen Foss; related to Ellen White through the marriage of Louisa's brother Samuel Foss to Ellen's sister *Mary (Harmon) Foss. Louisa accompanied Ellen Harmon on several of her journeys in 1845 (LS 77). She married Benjamin Brackett in 1852 and died after giving birth to their third child.

BRADFORD, JOEL PACKARD (1873-1949) and **ELIZA B. (BURLEIGH)** (1870-1950). Adventist believers from New Bedford, Massachusetts. Joel attended South Lancaster Academy and in 1900 received a medical degree from the University of Colorado. In 1905 the Bradfords returned to their hometown of New Bedford to start a sanitarium, but had difficulty securing funds from Gilbert Collins. Ellen White assured them that she was interested in the medical missionary work they were trying to do, but counseled them not to pressure Collins if he did not feel free to give to this cause (Lt 29, 1905). By 1907 their labors had led to the establishment of the Acushnet Sanitarium.

Further reading: obit. RH, Aug. 31, 1950; obit. RH, May 31, 1951; F. Howland, *A History of the Town of Acushnet* (New Bedford, Mass.: by the author, 1907), p. 270.

BRANDSTATER, CHARLES ALBERT (1873-1940). Adventist nurse born in Tasmania. Brandstater took nursing at Battle Creek Sanitarium (1894-1898) and married Margaret M. Kessler in 1899. Ellen White encouraged him to work with Dr. *F. E. Braucht in medical missionary work in New Zealand (Lt 107b, 1900). He served as nurse and medical administrator in several facilities in Australia and New Zealand. Later he became a dentist and practiced in California.

Further reading: obit. RH, May 30, 1940.

BRAUCHT, FREDERICK E. (b. 1868). Adventist physician. In 1895 Braucht and his wife, Mina A. (Owen), sailed on the ship *Pitcairn* as missionaries for Samoa (RH, May 14, 1895; RH, Dec. 17, 1895). In Samoa, Braucht first worked in a medical institution in Matautu, then at a new institution they started at Apia. In early 1903, as he was getting ready to leave Samoa to return to the United States, Ellen White urged him to "pull together" in unity with his fellow missionaries (Lt 40, 1903, in MM 44-46). She also asked him to critically examine his own religious experience (Lt 41, 1903, in MM 47, 48). Upon his return to the United States, he worked at the Kansas Sanitarium, of which he became superintendent in 1906.

Bree, Maggie (Hare). Literary assistant to Ellen White and daughter of William Hare, whose family greeted Ellen White upon her arrival in New Zealand in 1891. Hare later spent time at Avondale College, where she began working for Ellen White as one of her secretaries. When Ellen White returned to the United States in 1900, Maggie stayed in Australia with her husband, Harold Bree. Ellen White wrote to her several times expressing appreciation for her faithful work, extending an open invitation for her if she ever wanted to come to America to work for her (Lt 282, 1907; Lt 146, 1908). Finally, in 1910, Ellen White wrote to her that she missed her very much and asked her to come work for her, and that her husband would have no problem finding employment (Lt 144, 1910). Shortly after this, Maggie rejoined Ellen White's staff. During this time Maggie was in charge of compiling articles from Ellen White's writings for such church periodicals as the *Review and Herald* (6Bio 340).

Breed, Almon Jacob (1847-1938) and **Asenath Lois (Davis)** (d. 1908). Almon Breed was a minister and administrator originally from New York. He began his ministry in Wisconsin, married Asenath Davis in 1871, and continued in a variety of positions at the conference, union, and general conference levels. In 1900 Breed and S. N. Haskell were sent by the General Conference to investigate the *holy flesh heresy in Muncie, Indiana (5Bio 101, 102). Later Breed, as chair

of the *Walla Walla College executive committee, wrote to Ellen White reporting a public rumor that the college was to be sold and might be purchased by the *Mormons. Ellen White urged that he "contradict . . . such reports . . . promptly," and instead, when able, do the exact opposite of the rumors—purchase more land for Walla Walla. She encouraged both him and his wife not to let discouragements make them give up (Lts 61, 57, 1905).
Further reading: obit. RH, Oct. 6, 1938.

Brinkerhoff, William H., see **Marion Party**.

Brisbin, W. L. Adventist who, after the death of his wife, confessed to Ellen White (in a letter no longer extant) his cruel treatment of his wife. Ellen White replied that his prior course had indeed been wrong. In fact, his "wicked," "satanic" treatment had caused his wife's death of a broken heart. She added, "Every pang of anguish [she] endured by the blasting hail of your tongue was as if you had done this to Jesus Christ." Then she expressed sympathy and hope: "You cannot undo the past. You cannot make restitution to the dead." But "Jesus will pardon to the full the blackest crimes if repented of and forever forsaken" (Lt 28, 1884).
Further reading: obit. RH, Nov. 11, 1884.

Brown, Martha A. (c. 1865-1951). Young adult in *New Zealand who in 1893 invited Ellen White to rest at her mother's home in Long Point, New Zealand. During that visit Martha, then in her late 20s, decided to become an Adventist and was soon joined in that decision by her mother. Martha had 12 siblings, and during Ellen White's visit several of them were converted to Adventism (Lt 138, 1893; Ms 59, 1893; 4Bio 100). In 1895, when Martha traveled to Australia with her friend Ethel

May Lacey, Ellen White assisted both of them with clothing (Lt 107, 1895). Ellen White was so impressed with Martha that she lent her funds with which to obtain an education.

See also: Ethyl May (Lacey) White.

Further reading: Lt 1, 1893; Lt 74, 1893; Lt 121, 1893; Ms 81, 1893; obit. *Australasian Record,* Aug. 13, 1951.

BROWN, MARVIN HERRICK (1844-1931). Pastor and administrator. Son of Millerite parents, Brown became a Seventh-day Adventist in 1871. Subsequent to his ordination to ministry by James White in 1879, he worked in New York for 12 years. After being injured in a railroad accident in 1892, which prevented him from extensive traveling, he moved to Oakland, California, where he served as editor of the *Sabbath School Worker.* In 1901 he was elected secretary of the California Conference and later worked in North Carolina and Arkansas. In his later years of ministry Brown frequently corresponded with Ellen White and her son, W. C., and asked counsel regarding a number of administrative and personnel issues. In 1887 Ellen White heard a rumor that he and *M. C. Wilcox were teaching the flat earth theory and urged them not to teach such "hobbies" but to "stick to the message" (Lt 43, 1887). However, Brown responded that he neither believed nor taught this theory (M. H. Brown to EGW, Apr. 26, 1887).

Further reading: obit. RH, Apr. 23, 1931.

BROWNSBERGER, EDITH (DONALDSON) (1862-1948). Adventist from Oregon; daughter of John and Hannah Donaldson, early Adventist pioneers on the West Coast. Ellen White encouraged Edith to attend Battle Creek College, which she did (1878-1881), staying in the White home for much of that time. In 1879 Ellen White wrote to Edith asking her to stay in Battle Creek until the Whites returned

from Texas, and that when summer came they could spend it together in the mountains of Colorado. She also urged Edith to "lighten up on [her] studies" and to "be of good courage" (Lt 45, 1879). In 1887 she married *Sidney Brownsberger and accompanied him in his educational and evangelistic work.

Further reading: obit. *Southern Tidings,* Aug. 18, 1948.

BROWNSBERGER, SIDNEY (1845-1930). Educator and administrator. Born at Perrysburg, Ohio, Brownsberger grew up on the farm that his family had worked since 1822. He completed college preparatory studies at Baldwin University, now Baldwin-Wallace College, Berea, Ohio, in 1865. He enrolled in the University of Michigan in the autumn of 1865 and pursued a classical course of study that culminated in the A.B. degree in 1869. During his first year at the university he became a Seventh-day Adventist, but later ceased his observance of the Sabbath because he managed a boardinghouse for his brother in Ann Arbor and therefore could not keep it properly. Upon graduation from the University of Michigan he became superintendent of a public school in Maumee, Ohio. The school building there became the model that was adapted by *O. B. Jones for the first administration building at Battle Creek College. In 1872 Brownsberger became superintendent of the public schools of Delta, Ohio. There he resumed his observance of the Sabbath. In 1873 church leaders invited Brownsberger to head the school that *G. H. Bell had established in 1872 in Battle Creek, Michigan, and also to serve for a year as secretary of the General Conference.

SIDNEY BROWNSBERGER

Brownsberger became the first principal of Battle Creek College in 1874. Later that year he married Florinda Camp and the following year received an M.A. from the University of Michigan.

In addition to a classical curriculum culminating in the A.B. degree, Battle Creek College also offered the less-esteemed B.S. degree. Brownsberger organized departments of instruction at the college, established courses of study in business, teaching, and ministry, and developed the college library. A School of Hygiene organized in 1877, in affiliation with the Battle Creek Sanitarium, foreshadowed the extensive course offerings in the health sciences in later Seventh-day Adventist colleges and universities. The Dime Tabernacle became the Battle Creek College church during his administration. Brownsberger left Battle Creek at the end of the 1880-1881 academic year, citing health as the reason, and moved to Cheboygan, Michigan, where he and his wife taught public school. In 1882 he began a four-year term as first president of *Healdsburg College in California. During that time Ellen White wrote him a letter admonishing him and his wife to discipline their children (Lt 12, 1884). In 1886 she wrote to encourage him, warning that "the enemy will seek in every way to hurt you and to discourage you through your wife" (Lt 29a, 1886). In the spring of 1886 he resigned and moved back to Cheboygan, where he was self-employed for a year, and offered no opposition to his wife's seeking a divorce. In October 1887 he became reacquainted with Edith Donaldson, and they married in November. About nine years later Ellen White invited the Brownsbergers to come at their own expense to find work in Australia, but they did not go (TSB 219-223).

Brownsberger and *A. W. Spalding founded the Asheville Agricultural School and Mountain Sanitarium in North Carolina in 1909. Ellen White commended him for this endeavor "to be of still greater service to the cause of God" (Lt 56, 1910). He lived there until his death, August 13, 1930. Sidney Brownsberger was well educated for his day and made significant contributions to the Seventh-day Adventist Church as first president of two colleges, cofounder of a medical institution and school, and initiator of the first business and health curricula in an Adventist college.

See also: Edith (Donaldson Brownsberger.

Further reading: obit. RH, Oct. 2, 1930; J. G. Smoot, "Sidney Brownsberger: Traditionalist," in G. R. Knight, ed., *Early Adventist Educators* (AUP, 1983), pp. 72-94; *SDA Encyclopedia* (1996), vol. 10, p. 253.

Joseph Grady Smoot

BRUNSON, JOHN A. (1862-1943). Baptist minister living in Asheville, North Carolina, who became a Seventh-day Adventist during a series of evangelistic lectures *G. I. Butler held in that city in 1894 (RH, July 31, 1894). He was ordained to the Adventist ministry the following year (RH, Oct. 15, 1895). Brunson held a variety of pastoral positions that led to his prominence as a much-desired camp meeting speaker. He taught Bible at *Union College (1897-1898) and *Graysville Academy (1900), and then assisted *S. N. Haskell's evangelistic team in New York City (Lt 197, 1901). In 1903 he began to teach "the doctrine of once in grace always in grace" to the exclusion of keeping the seventh-day Sabbath (Lt 17, 1904). Ellen White called his attention to passages of Scripture, which she wrote out for G. I. Butler to give to him (Lt 267, 1903). She urged Butler to "save him [Brunson] if you can," but not to allow "his misleading theories to be printed in our papers" (Lt 17, 1904). Several weeks later she appealed to Brunson to come to the *St.

Helena Sanitarium (Lt 75, 1904). His name does not appear in denominational records after 1904.

Buchanan, Robert Ambrose (1866-1943). Adventist physician. Buchanan first attended Battle Creek College and then the California Medical College, from which he graduated in 1896. Buchanan was active in medical missionary work in San Francisco and founded the Buchanan Sanitarium in Lodi, California. In 1906 Ellen White wrote him two brief letters recommending that he employ *Herbert Kellogg at the Paradise Sanitarium (Lts 228, 246, 1906).

Further reading: obit. RH, Dec. 30, 1943.

Buck, Harry G. (1822-1902). Minister from Vermont. Buck was a minister for the Wesleyan Methodist Church until about 1853, when he joined the ranks of Sabbatarian Adventists. His early ministerial labors bore no fruit. Ellen White warned that he needed to remove self and make a "thorough reform" if he were to become successful (Lt 18, 1861). Until then, his labors were a hindrance to the cause (Lt 31, 1861). Buck relocated to Wright and later Monterey, Michigan, where he farmed and supported the church with his means (Ms 12, 1868).

Burden, John Allen (1862-1942) and **Eleanor A. (Baxter)** (1865-1933). Close friends and confidants of Ellen White, medical missionaries who founded sanitariums, restaurants, and health food factories. John was a minister and administrator, Eleanor a bookkeeper. At the age of 9 John attended Adventist meetings for the first

JOHN A. BURDEN

time and was introduced to the writings of Ellen White, which left a lifelong impression upon him. Five years later he was baptized, and at the age of 18 (1881) moved with his family to Oregon. Eleanor had previously moved with her family from Pennsylvania to California (1877). John and Eleanor met as students at Healdsburg College. They were married in 1888 while working for the Rural Health Retreat (later St. Helena Sanitarium), of which John became manager in 1891.

Ellen White felt that the Burdens were not adequately appreciated at the St. Helena Sanitarium and urged that they relocate to Australia (Lts 5, 12, 48, 1901). They accepted her invitation, uniting with M. G. Kellogg, who was developing the Wahroonga Sanitarium in Sydney (Lt 13, 1901). John, a talented administrator, was instrumental in developing a hygienic restaurant in Sydney (Lt 145, 1902) and a health food factory in Cooranbong (Lt 114, 1902). He was furthermore someone whom Ellen White could depend on to make sure that her brother-in-law, Stephen Belden, a missionary on Norfolk Island, received a small stipend and provisions (Lt 181, 1901). Ellen White frequently asked the Burdens to write her, stating that their letters were "like a drink of cold water to a thirsty soul" (Lt 69, 1902). She was continually concerned that they would overburden themselves (Lt 16, 1902; Lt 201, 1902), and she finally urged him to concentrate solely on sanitarium work (Lt 158, 1902; Lt 62, 1903). Further, "speaking as a mother," she counseled them regarding their diet (Lt 79, 1903) and encouraged them and Daniel and Lauretta *Kress to be flexible about the diet of sanitarium patients (Lt 44, 1903). Eventually, the Kresses were put in charge of the medical interests of the sanitarium, while John was left in charge of its business aspects (Lts 164, 171, 1903). In November 1903 Ellen White suggested that if they felt that their work in Australia was done, their help was needed in developing sanitariums in California (Lt 252, 1903).

By March 1904 the Burdens had returned to the United States (Lt 123, 1904). Following Ellen White's urging that the Burdens "not connect in any way with Battle Creek or with Dr. [J. H.] Kellogg" (Lt 199, 1904), John sought to establish a sanitarium near Los Angeles. Eight miles (13 kilometers) from the city he discovered the Glendale Hotel that had cost $60,000 to build in 1886. But by 1905, because of local business failures, property values had so declined that he was able to purchase it for $12,500 (Lt 109, 1905). When it opened in 1905, Burden was the manager of the sanitarium, and Eleanor the bookkeeper. Ellen White confirmed that "the location of the Glendale Sanitarium meets the representation given me of places God has reserved for us" (Lt 97, 1905). Such success prompted E. S. Ballenger, manager of the Paradise Valley Sanitarium, to push him to become conference president, but Ellen White discouraged such a move, insisting that the Burdens had a special work to do in building sanitariums (Lts 105, 106, 1905). Under the Burdens' capable management, the Glendale Sanitarium began to thrive, and facilities were soon filled to capacity (Lt 111, 1905).

In 1904 Ellen White urged the establishment of another sanitarium in southern California. On May 4, 1905, on her way to the General Conference session in Washington, D.C., she met with the Burdens and others at the Los Angeles railroad station. Burden told her that the Loma Linda Hotel near Riverside was for sale for $110,000, a price he considered too high. She expressed definite interest in it, asking him to write her about it after his next visit to the property. When Burden's letter arrived in Washington (Burden to EGW, May 7, 1905, EGWE-GC), she urged him by tele-

gram to "secure the property by all means. . . . This is the very property that we ought to have. Do not delay; for it is just what is needed" (Lt 139, 1905). Borrowing the down payment, Burden succeeded in purchasing the property for $40,000 and was put in charge of the new *Loma Linda Sanitarium (Lt 169, 1905). The final price, with discounts for early payment, came to $38,900. After Ellen White found out that the property was secured she wrote in her diary: "I am surprised more and more that the Lord has in His abundant mercy wrought in our behalf" (Ms 176, 1905).

It was not long until the Burdens and Ellen White conceptualized the idea of establishing a school at Loma Linda (Lt 244, 1905). She directed Burden to secure physicians, such as Dr. Julia White and Dr. *C. C. Nicola, to work in the sanitarium (Lt 272, 1905; Lt 312, 1907) in order to make such a medical missionary school "all you possibly can in the education of nurses and physicians" (Lt 325, 1905). As Burden began to gather teachers and students to begin a medical missionary school, she challenged him to build a health food factory as well (Lt 329, 1905), but cautioned against carrying too heavy of a personal workload (Lt 140, 1906). She wrote repeated letters of encouragement to the Burdens, stating that the Lord had placed upon them "responsibilities of no ordinary nature" (Lt 349, 1906).

The Burdens frequently sought counsel from Ellen White, and under her guidance the small school blossomed in 1909 into the College of Medical Evangelists (Lt 360, 1907; Lt 100, 1909). This school, she instructed, was to be of the highest order in the "blending of the evangelistic and medical work" (Lt 36, 1910). Graduates from this school, "fully qualified and legally recognized physicians," would play an important role in the finishing of God's work (Lt 61, 1910). Ellen White furthermore urged that "it is just as essential that women receive such training, and obtain their diplomas certifying their right to act as physicians" (Lt 22, 1911).

As late as 1913 a move was made to remove Burden from leadership, but Ellen White insisted that Burden's godly and intelligent leadership was just what Loma Linda needed (Ms 22, 1913). Burden continued to manage the facilities at Loma Linda until 1915, when he became manager, and Eleanor the matron, of Paradise Valley Sanitarium (1916-1924; 1925-1934). After Eleanor's death in 1933, John retired, but in 1939 returned to Loma Linda to serve as chaplain, counseling young medical missionaries and the staff of the College of Medical Evangelists. After his death Burden's personal collection of some 650 pages of Ellen White's letters (half of them addressed to him) was published as *Loma Linda Messages.

Further reading: 6Bio 22-32; obit. RH, Sept. 7, 1933; obit. RH, Aug. 27, 1942; SHM 354-361; *Legacy of Light* CD-ROM, article John Allen Burden (1862-1942); J. A. Burden, "The Story of Loma Linda: A Divine Providence in the Founding of the College of Medical Evangelists" (Loma Linda, Calif.: by the author, n.d.); *SDA Encyclopedia* (1996), vol. 10, p. 261.

Michael W. Campbell

BURDICK, LUCINDA S. A non-Sabbatarian critic who stated in writing that she saw the young Ellen Harmon engage in fanaticism during 1845. *Miles Grant published Burdick's statement in *The World's Crisis*, July 1, 1874, and in his tract, *True Sabbath: Which Day Shall We Keep? An Examination of Mrs. Ellen White's Visions* (pp. 71-74).

Burdick claimed that during 1845 Ellen Harmon was "in a wild fanaticism," predicted several dates for the Second Coming, and

taught an extreme version of the *shut door. As such, Burdick followed a course similar to *John Howell, Burdick's first husband. Within two months after the publication of the July 1, 1874, *World's Crisis*, Ellen White responded in a letter to *J. N. Loughborough: "I hereby testify in the fear of God that the charges of Miles Grant, of Mrs. Burdick and others published in the *Crisis* are not true" (Lt 2, 1874, in 8MR 228). She added: "Now the very ones who were deepest in fanaticism cruelly charge upon me that delusion which I had not the slightest sympathy with, but from which my soul recoiled. And I bore a straightforward testimony to condemn these fanatical movements from first to last. Mrs. Burdick has made statements which are glaring falsehoods. There is not a shade of truth in her statements. Can it be that she has repeated these false statements till she sincerely believes them to be truth?" (Lt 2, 1874, in 8MR 238).

About a year later Marion C. (Stowell) Truesdail (later *Crawford), who was acquainted with the young Ellen Harmon in 1845, responded to Burdick's charges in a public statement signed by herself and five others corroborating Ellen White's private letter to Loughborough ("A Statement Regarding the Charges of Mrs. L. S. Burdick," by Marion C. S. Truesdail). Fifteen years earlier, in 1860, Marion's maiden name, Marion C. Stowell, had already appeared in a public statement with 28 other names testifying that James and Ellen White were never "the least infected with the spirit or works of fanaticism" (2SG 301).

Further reading: Lt 2, 1874, in 8MR 228-243; M. Grant, *The True Sabbath: Which Day Shall We Keep? An Examination of Mrs. Ellen White's Visions* (Boston: Advent Christian Publication Society, 1874), pp. 71-74; Marion C. S. Truesdail, "A Statement Regarding the

Charges of Mrs. L. S. Burdick, by Marion C. S. Truesdail" (Warren, Ill.: Aug. 17, 1875, DF 266, EGWE-GC).

Jud Lake

BURKE, WILLARD P. (1850-1941). Adventist physician. In 1886 Burke joined the medical staff of the Rural Health Retreat (later the *St. Helena Sanitarium). Ellen White asked him and *J. S. Gibbs to work together in unity (Lt 10, 1886), not striving for supremacy (Lt 11, 1887); but when Burke did not become head of the institution, he resigned (Lt 9, 1887) and set up a rival institution in Fresno. She continued to appeal to him to be converted (Lts 14, 28, 56, 1888; Ms 12, 1888). After *M. G. Kellogg's resignation from the Rural Health Retreat in October 1890, Burke went back to the institution, managing it as well as continuing his employment at the Fresno sanitarium (GCB, Mar. 22, 1891; Lt 77, 1889). The following year, when he wasn't granted more control of the institution, he left again (Lt 91, 1890). Ellen White continued to admonish him (Lts 5b, 35, 40, 41, 47, 48, 55, 1891), but he refused to heed her warnings, resigned, and focused his energies on developing "Burke's Sanitarium," located in Santa Rosa (Lt 14, 1891). Ellen White, reflecting upon the experience, wrote that placing Burke in charge of the Rural Health Retreat was a serious mistake (Ms 183, 1897). Burke openly opposed her ministry after this second departure from denominational employment and was involved with *E. P. Daniels in a character defamation lawsuit against Ellen White. Burke objected to Ellen White's *testimonies "being thrown before the public" (W. P. Burke to EGW, Nov. 3, 1891, EGWE-GC). She in turn warned church members against him (Lt 15, 1892). In 1912 Burke was convicted of attempting to murder a nurse who claimed to have had an illegitimate child with him. He spent 10 years in the San Quentin prison, during which time his sanitarium closed ("Appellate Division Refuses to Reverse Superior Court in Dynamite Case," newspaper clipping, DF 218, EGWE-GC).

Michael W. Campbell

BURNHAM, ELIZA J. (c. 1847-1909). Editor and literary assistant to Ellen White. Burnham first worked for Ellen White in the 1880s (WCW to Mary K. White, Jan. 23, 27, 1885) preparing *Testimonies for the Church*, volumes 1-4 for publication (J. Moon, *W. C. White and E. G. White*, pp. 120-123). Later she served as the editor of the *Bible Echo* in Australia for about 10 years before rejoining Ellen White's staff in 1896 (Lt 13a, 1896). Sometime after Ellen White returned to the United States in 1900, Burnham connected with the Southern Publishing Association in Nashville, Tennessee, where she edited the *Gospel Sentinel* and was assistant editor of the *Southern Watchman* until her death.

BURWELL, ANTHONY L. (1806-1873) and **ACHSAH** (1810-1886). Early Adventists originally from Vermont. Both became ardent Millerites after hearing William Miller in 1837 and accepted the Sabbatarian Adventist message about 1850 in Vermont. In 1856 the Burwells moved to Parma, Michigan, where that same year two of their three children died, leaving only Anna Lucretia. At the same time the value of their property dramatically increased. In 1857 Ellen White appealed to the bereaved parents to avoid materialism and set an example for their only remaining child (Lt 1, 1857; Lt 2, 1857; 1Bio 362).

Further reading: obit. RH, Jan. 28, 1873; obit. RH, June 8, 1886.

BUSTER, JAMES R. (1858-1907). Colporteur and minister. In 1883 Buster became a Seventh-day Adventist and began colporteuring. For a time he held a ministerial license and planned to work for his African-American people in the South. Unfortunately, his inability to "obtain means to sustain his family" caused him to incur debts. Unable to pay these debts, he was told he should remain a colporteur until these debts were liquidated. Buster wrote to Ellen White appealing for help and light (J. R. Buster to EGW, May 29, 1894). Ellen White encouraged him to trust in God and He would open the way (Lt 4, 1894). She also sent a testimony to church leaders urging them to relieve his debts (Ms 34, 1894, in 1888 Materials 1268-1279). When denominational leaders turned a deaf ear to both her appeals and his, Buster became discouraged and ceased his ministerial work. In August 1906 he attended tent meetings held by Luther Warren and dedicated his life anew to God. He was again issued a ministerial license and began a mission for Blacks in Chicago.

Further reading: obit. RH, June 20, 1907.

BUTCHER, WILLIAM S. (1821-1908) and **MARILLA (BRAND)** (1830-1916). Adventist farmers from Vacaville, California. The Butchers were married in Marion, Iowa, in 1855 and moved to California, where they became Adventists in 1877. William was afraid to share his faith for fear of stammering, but in 1880, according to Ellen White, his speech impediment was miraculously "loosed" and he was given the gift of "clear speech." This event heightened local interest in the Adventist message (Ms 6, 1880; ST, May 13, 1880; Lt 378, 1906). In 1882 Marilla became very ill, but was healed in answer to prayer (Lt 31, 1882). Later White wrote the Butchers several letters (Lts 30, 31, 1888) to "revive their faith and their courage and life in the Lord" (Ms 23, 1888) and to correct some serious faults (Lt 378, 1906).

BUTLER, EZRA PITT (1796-1875) and **SARAH** (1799-1866). Farmers from Waterbury, Vermont; parents of *G. I. Butler. Ezra's father was governor of Vermont (1826-1828). Ezra

was a "zealous" Millerite who in 1848 accepted the doctrine of the Sabbath from Joseph Bates. He was ordained to the ministry in 1853, although his subsequent participation in ministry was limited. Ellen White noted that Butler par-

EZRA PITT BUTLER

ticipated in several conferences in New Hampshire and Vermont in October and November 1851. It appears that he belonged to a small group who, despite Ellen White's visions to the contrary, believed that the Second Coming would occur in October 1851. During the conferences, however, Butler radically revised his position, declaring: "I believe them [the visions] to be of God, [and I] am a full believer in the visions" (Lt 8, 1851).

In 1856 with several other New England families the Butler family migrated westward to Waukon, Iowa. Butler's move to Iowa appears to have coincided with a decline in his religious experience. In 1863 he wrote of "the stupidity and indifference that has rested upon me for six years" (RH, Apr. 7, 1863, p. 151). By 1868 *J. N. Andrews despaired that the Waukon church was suffering from some of the theological notions that Butler was pressing upon the members "to a ridiculous extent," "disfellowshipping all who did not make [these notions] a test of fellowship" (JNA to "Brother and Sister White," July 3, 1868, EGWE-GC). Nevertheless, by 1869 things had improved. "I think I can say something encouraging of Father," wrote his son, G. I. Butler, to James White. "He acts very different towards us all—attends meetings regularly, takes part, confesses he has been led by Satan in the course he has pursued" (GIB to JW, Feb. 3, 1869, EGWE-GC). Butler's last years were spent with his daughter in Battle Creek, Michigan.

Further reading: G. I. Butler, "Death of Another Pioneer in Reform," RH, Dec. 9, 1875; obit. RH, Sept. 18, 1866; E. K. Vande Vere, *Rugged Heart: The Story of George I. Butler* (SPA, 1979), pp. 9-13.

Michael Campbell

BUTLER, GEORGE IDE (1834-1918) and **LENTHA (LOCKWOOD)** (1826-1901). Minister,

GEORGE I. BUTLER

administrator, and author; son of *Ezra Pitt Butler. Originally from Vermont, Butler's parents were closely involved in the beginnings of Adventism, but George expressed leanings to infidelity. In 1853 his family moved to Iowa, where he was converted at age 22 and baptized by *J. N. Andrews. His decision prompted affirmation from Ellen White that "the Lord had . . . opened unto him [Butler] His Word, that he could see its beauty and harmony, and be led to love and worship its Author" (Lt 5, 1857). Butler settled on a farm and taught school during the winter months. On March 10, 1859, he married Lentha Lockwood (1826-1901) and settled near Waukon, Iowa, where he resumed teaching. He became a deacon and later replaced his father as elder of their local church. It was here that Butler listened to *M. E. Cornell speak about Ellen White's testimonies, convincing him of their genuineness (GIB to EGW, July 18, 1904, EGWE-GC).

In 1865, after the defection of B. F. Snook and W. H. Brinkerhoff (see *Marion Party), Butler was elected president of the Iowa

Conference. In June 1867 he was given a ministerial license, and in October was ordained. He worked indefatigably as an evangelist, bringing unity to the previously fragmented conference. As a result of his rebuttals to the Marion Party (who had focused their dissent upon the ministry of Ellen White), Butler became one of her foremost defenders during the 1860s and 1870s.

In 1872, when James White resigned because of failing health, Butler was elected president of the *General Conference. He was active in raising funds to start *Battle Creek College and to establish the *Pacific Press in Oakland, California. During this time Butler functioned as president but deferred most decisions to James White. When conflict arose in Battle Creek in late 1872, Butler chose to justify James White's conduct as a divinely appointed leader similar to Moses, Joshua, and Gideon. It was therefore James White's prerogative, argued Butler, to act with more authority. *Uriah Smith, *J. H. Waggoner, and others agreed with Butler and adopted his argumentation as a church policy statement, but Ellen White vigorously opposed this position (GIB to F. E. Belden, Mar. 14, 1907, EGWE-GC). "You greatly err in giving to one man's mind and judgment that authority and influence which God has invested in His church in the judgment and *voice of the General Conference," she wrote (3T 493). In August 1874 Butler resigned as president, and James White, now sufficiently recovered, took back the reins of leadership.

Butler returned to Iowa, where at the next session of the Iowa-Nebraska Conference he was elected president (1876-1877). He started a vigorous evangelistic program, but when James White's health began to falter a second time, Butler was once again elected General Conference president. This time he pleaded with Ellen White to veto the nomination, but instead she asked him to accept it (RH, Oct. 23, 1879). By October 1880 he had returned as General Conference president, frequently counseling with Ellen White. In 1882 he also became president of the Seventh-day Adventist Publishing Association.

In 1886 Butler perceived E. J. Waggoner to be challenging his authority by writing that the law in the book in Galatians was the moral and not the ceremonial law, as taught by most Adventist leaders up to that time. Butler countered with a pamphlet, *The Law in the Book of Galatians* (RHPA, 1886). Ellen White urged caution and theological unity, noting that since Butler had put his views in print, E. J. Waggoner should be given the same opportunity. Butler, Uriah Smith, and others began to wonder if Ellen White had been influenced by the youthful Waggoner and his associate *A. T. Jones. Although Butler was ill and unable to attend the *General Conference session of 1888 in Minneapolis, he sent a telegram urging those present to "stand by the old landmarks," i.e., to not give up traditional theological positions. This called forth a stern rebuke from Ellen White to Butler and others who were on the "wrong side" at Minneapolis.

After the 1888 session Butler's health further deteriorated until he could no longer continue in active ministry. The Butlers purchased a citrus farm in Florida, "Twin Magnolias," where they could recuperate. However, the following year Lentha suffered a debilitating stroke. During this time Ellen White continued to plead with him to repent for his wrong influence on the 1888 General Conference session. Her efforts culminated in Butler's public confession of his wrong course.

In 1901 Lentha died, and George was elected the first president of the Florida Conference. In January 1902 Butler visited Ellen White while she accompanied *P. T. Magan and *E. A. Sutherland during their search for

a site for a self-supporting school near Nashville, Tennessee. Later that year Butler became the first president of the Southern Union Conference and the *Southern Publishing Association. During these years Butler wrote frequently to Ellen White asking for advice on the development of the Adventist work in the southern United States (cf. Lts 27, 83, 93, 176, 177, 1902). During the summer of 1902 he contemplated marriage to Lorena Waite, a woman much younger than he. Ellen White encouraged the match despite their age difference, but Butler's children and Waite's sister and brother-in-law, *Delia and Irving Keck, pressured them to break off the relationship (Lts 77, 78, 117, 118, 1902; RY 115-120). In the end Waite "withdrew her promise" (GIB to WCW, Feb. 6, 1903; GIB to EGW, Dec. 7, 1903, EGWE-GC).

As Butler returned to active ministerial labor Ellen White noted that he was "one who has humbled his soul before God" and "has another spirit than the Elder Butler of younger years" (Lt 77, 1902). She urged him not to feel resentment for the "years [the Lord] has kept you out of the work." It was "because you chose your own way," she said, that he had been "brought into trial" (Lt 169, 1902). Ellen White appealed to him to be of good courage, and when others sought to replace him, she rebuked them (Lt 39a, 1903). She counseled him not to wear himself out (Lt 134, 1903; RY 123, 124), "to bear a plain testimony before the people," and to preach shorter sermons that would not weary him (Lt 219, 1903). In 1907 Butler married Elizabeth Work Grainger (1845-1927), whose husband had died in the mission field, and the next year they retired a second time.

Once Butler regained his confidence in the validity of the gift of prophecy as manifested in the life and ministry of Ellen White, he remained a supporter of her work throughout his life. Although he received many strong testimonies, his repentance led to spiritual renewal and new opportunities for service within the church. Excluding Ellen White's own family, Butler received the fourth-most letters from her (84 extant letters), after S. N. Haskell (first), J. H. Kellogg, and O. A. Olsen.

Further reading: obit. RH, Aug. 29, 1918; E. K. Vande Vere, *Rugged Heart* (SPA, 1979); *SDA Encyclopedia* (1996), vol. 10, pp. 265, 266.

Michael W. Campbell

BUTLER, HILAND GEORGE (1864-1929). Administrator in the preparation and sale of health foods; youngest son of *George I. Butler. In 1881 Ellen White noted Hiland's decision to be a Christian (Lt 6, 1881). He married Clara Kellogg in 1887, and soon thereafter moved to a ranch in Montana. In 1902 Ellen White urged Butler to assist his father in evangelistic work in the South (Lt 82, 1902; Lt 152, 1902). She also counseled him after his mother's death to "not regard it as a monstrous thing that his father should want a wife" (Lt 118, 1902; cf. Lt 117, 1902). *J. H. Kellogg's conflict with church leaders, pantheistic teachings, and eventual apostasy in the early 1900s exerted a "baleful influence" over Hiland's mind, causing him to become spiritually "confused" (Lt 244, 1906). As a result, Hiland left the church and about the same time was divorced by his wife. During *World War I he sought to serve in the military, but being too old, he enrolled in the Red Cross. On the battlefield he was handed a letter from his dying father pleading with him to return to God, but he tore it up lest someone else should read it. Upon his return to the United States he was befriended by *George A. Hare, who bought property adjacent to him. Butler returned to the church, remarried, and became active in working for the youth of the church.

Further reading: obit. RH, Nov. 28, 1929; W. Gardner, *Calhoun County, Michigan: A Narrative of Its Historical Progress, Its People, and Its Principal Interests* (Chicago: Lewis Pub. Co., 1913), pp. 676-680.

Michael W. Campbell

BYINGTON, JOHN (1798-1887) and **CATHERINE** (1803-1885). Farmer, circuit pastor and evangelist, administrator, first General Conference president, neighbor and close friend of James and Ellen White. Born in Vermont, Byington took over the religious duties in the family at age 12 because his father, a circuit-riding Methodist minister, was often absent. Upon turning 21, Byington followed his father's footsteps and became a preacher. After the death of his first wife, he moved to Buck's Bridge, in northern New York, where he pastored and, at nearby Morley, helped to build one of the first churches in the area.

COURTESY OF THE CENTER FOR ADVENTIST RESEARCH, ANDREWS UNIVERSITY.

JOHN BYINGTON

Like his father, he was active in the antislavery movement. He and his family were militant abolitionists, allowing no segregation in the church and never turning away a fugitive slave. He denounced slavery from the pulpit: "Slavery is an outrage. It is a sin." He advocated using all legal measures and even civil disobedience to destroy the immoral slave trade (Ochs and Ochs, p. 10). His homestead was reportedly a stop on the Underground Railroad to Canada, but no verifiable proof has been given for this tradition (Adams, p. 11, and Waller, pp. 9, 10).

While in Cleveland in 1843-1844 he heard the Millerite message, but was not convicted. In 1851 he gave up tobacco and tea drinking after his lifelong friend, *Aaron Hilliard, confronted him on those issues. In 1852, at age 54 he received an issue of the *Review and Herald*. After reading it, he opened his Bible to counter its heretical claims. Apparently he found none, for he not only began keeping the Sabbath, but for the next three years held meetings to teach others to do so also. He not only evangelized the countryside with his newfound faith, but also helped his daughter Martha start the first Seventh-day Adventist elementary school (a home school). In 1853 he allowed his son, John Fletcher Byington, to work with the Whites at the Review and Herald office on Mount Hope Avenue in *Rochester, New York. In the spring of 1855 he built one of the first Sabbatarian Adventist churches.

In the fall of 1855 James and Ellen White and others came to Buck's Bridge to hold a conference on the Byington farm. This was the beginning of a lifelong friendship and working relationship between the families. In 1857, when the Whites visited Buck's Bridge for a weekend meeting, Ellen White received a vision about the coming Civil War. According to Byington's daughter, Martha, Ellen White repeated several times, "This country is to be deluged with blood" (Amadon, p. 7). Byington was active in visiting and ministering to the people of New York and Vermont.

In 1858, at the request of James and Ellen White, the Byingtons moved from Buck's Bridge to Battle Creek, Michigan. Writing him about the urgency of doing the Lord's work, Ellen White wrote, "Your commission has not run out. Your time is not yours. God does not wait in His work for you to study your convenience or wait your time" (Lt 2, 1859, in 5MR 290). For the next 15 years "Father Byington," as he became known, traveled extensively, ministering to believers all across Michigan. His responsibilities grew, in both scope and roles, during his years in Michigan. When James White declined to become the first president of the General Conference, Byington was elected because he typified the "servant leadership" the people looked for. It was during his presidency that the Seventh-day Adventist Church gained official government recognition for its non-combatancy status in the American Civil War.

Further reading: obit. RH, Jan. 25, 1887; obit. RH, Mar. 17, 1885; L. Adams, "Behold the Stone," *The Quarterly* 15, no. 4 (October 1970): 11-15; R. Allen and H. Krug, *Rochester's Adventist Heritage: Tour Guide and Biographical Overview* (Rochester, N.Y.: Advent History Project New York, 2002); G. Amadon, "The First President of the General Conference," RH, June 22, 1944; J. R. Nix, "The Little-known General Conference President," AR, Apr. 5, 2001; D. A. Ochs and G. L. Ochs, *The Past and the Presidents* (SPA, 1974); J. O. Waller, "John Byington of Bucks Bridge: The Pre-Adventist Years" (unpublished paper, 1974, CAR); J. O. Waller, "John Byington: Our First General Conference President," AR, Dec. 6, 1979; Dec. 13, 1979; *SDA Encyclopedia* (1996), vol. 10, pp. 266, 267.

Howard Krug

CADY, MARION ERNEST (1866-1948). Educator and writer. Cady entered *Battle Creek College

MARION E. CADY

in 1886, taught at the Minnesota Conference Academy, then resumed his studies at Battle Creek College where he graduated in 1893. He married Minnie G. Case in 1894 and taught science at *Union College (1894-1898). He wrote a textbook on science, *Bible Nature Studies* (c. 1899) and a compilation of Ellen White's writings, **Principles of True Science* (Healdsburg College

Press, 1900, 1929). After teaching science for a brief period at Battle Creek College, Cady moved in 1900 to California, where he served as president of *Healdsburg College and educational secretary of the Pacific Union. There he had more frequent interaction with Ellen White. She advised him regarding the management of the college and its finances, cautioning the college board not to jump to conclusions in making decisions (Lts 194, 197, 1903). Cady served as president of *Walla Walla College (1905-1911) and of Washington Missionary College (1921-1922) and then served as field secretary of the General Conference Department of Education until his retirement in 1926. He wrote several books on pedagogy and compiled some of Ellen White's writings on education into the book *Fundamentals of Christian Education (SPA, 1923).

Further reading: obit. RH, Sept. 30, 1948; *SDA Encyclopedia* (1996), vol. 10, p. 267.

CALDWELL, WALTER F. (1861-1938). Adventist from the United States who became an ardent disciple of *A. W. Stanton, and traveled to Australia in the 1890s to proclaim that the Seventh-day Adventist Church had become part of eschatological Babylon. In 1893 he sent a telegram to Ellen White asking for advice. In response, she urged him to counsel with *G. B. Starr, and that a letter was on the way (Lt 92, 1893). That letter confirmed that Caldwell's supposed "new light" was "not of God" and urged him to enter the Avondale School to "more perfectly learn the way . . . of the Lord" (Lt 15, 1893). A follow-up letter commended him on his sincerity but urged him that the Lord had not given him "a message to call the Seventh-day Adventist church Babylon" (Lt 16, 1893). Caldwell heeded the testimony and remained a faithful member of the church. In 1895 Caldwell became romantically involved with *Fannie Bolton, and since

he had no biblical ground to remarry after leaving his wife, Ellen White strongly discouraged this relationship (TSB 206-217).

Further reading: obit. NPUG, Jan. 24, 1939.

CAMP, MAUD, see **SKINNER, THOMAS WILLIAM FARRINGTON** and **MAUD ELIZABETH LUCY (CAMP).**

CAMPBELL, EMILY CLARA (later **EMILY CLARA [CAMPBELL] FAY**) (1864-1963). Traveling companion, bookkeeper, housekeeper, nurse, and *literary assistant to Ellen White (1891-1895). Born in Ontario, Canada, Emily taught school in Michigan, where Ellen White first met her. She had an energetic, outgoing, yet gentle temperament, which appealed to Ellen White. Emily took secretarial training and soon thereafter joined White's staff—in time to leave in 1891 for Australia with her other assistants, *Marian Davis, *May Walling, and *Fannie Bolton (LS 331). During the trip Ellen White chose Emily to be her cabinmate (4Bio 18). Over the next four years Emily and Ellen White became close friends. Emily assisted Marian Davis in the preparation of the book *The Desire of Ages*. Later Ellen White spoke of her as "true as steel to her post" (Lt 117, 1893). In 1895, due to poor health, Emily returned to the United States to teach. Ellen White wrote several letters expressing her desire to see her, but unable to do so, gave updates on her health and the progress of missionary endeavors in Australia (Lt 19a, 1895; Lt 105, 1895). Ellen White wished Emily could return, but her health appears to have prevented her from doing so (Lt 6, 1898). In 1904 Emily married William Fay (d. 1929), a German immigrant.

Further reading: obit. RH, Mar. 5, 1964.

CAMPBELL, MALCOLM N. (1874-1958).

Minister and church administrator, born in Prince Edward Island, Canada. Campbell served in various pastoral positions from 1895 to 1907. After serving as a church administrator in Iowa, Canada, and England, he later became an officer of the General Conference.

In late 1906, at the age of 32, he was appointed pastor of the Battle Creek Tabernacle. Fearing that *J. H. Kellogg and *A. T. Jones would try to take possession of the tabernacle, Ellen White had said in 1906 that every effort should be made to secure the property of the tabernacle. Under Michigan law at the time, all corporations expired after 30 years of operation. The tabernacle incorporation had expired in 1892 and nothing had been done since to reincorporate the property. Following his appointment as pastor of the church, and knowing of the doctrinal tensions and personality conflicts within Adventism at the time, Campbell sought to proceed with the legal reincorporation of the tabernacle in spite of strong opposition from trustees and members who preferred to remain legally independent from the church. After hearing that the tabernacle trustees had asked the sanitarium trustees to do whatever they could to take over the tabernacle, Campbell sought the support of the congregation and succeeded after a number of business meetings to get the new charter of incorporation adopted. Just before the last meeting, Campbell received a short telegram from Ellen White that read only "Philippians 1:27, 28." This message from Ellen White gave courage to Campbell and others to go ahead with the reincorporation of the church edifice. Following this new incorporation, the new trustees and church

COURTESY OF THE CENTER FOR ADVENTIST RESEARCH, ANDREWS UNIVERSITY.

MALCOLM N. CAMPBELL

members deeded the property to the Michigan Conference. Among the people opposed to this reincorporation was *Frank Belden, Ellen White's nephew. She deplored his actions and believed that he had removed himself from under the influence of the Holy Spirit (Lt 116, 1907). In April 1914 Campbell, accompanied by two other ministers, visited Ellen White at her home in Elmshaven, California. During this visit he asked if she knew whether she would live until Christ returned. She replied that she had no light on the matter. He then asked her whether God would raise another prophet to take her place if she were to be laid to rest before Christ's coming. In reply she laid her hand on some of her books lying on a nearby table and answered, "The Lord has in these books given definite counsels for His people right down to the end of time." She chose to say nothing more regarding a possible successor.

Further reading: 6Bio 120-129, 403, 404; obit. RH, Mar. 27, 1958; *SDA Encyclopedia* (1996), vol. 10, p. 284; M. N. Campbell, "Experiences With Ellen G. White," (DF 421-c, CAR).

Denis Fortin

Canright, Dudley M. (1840-1919). A foremost Adventist preacher during the 1870s and early 1880s, but one who turned against the church and would become its, and Ellen White's, most well-known detractor after 1889. His *Seventh-day Adventism Renounced* (1889), *The Lord's Day From Neither Catholics Nor Pagans* (1915), and *Life of Mrs. E. G. White* (1919) became central in arguments against Adventism and Ellen White from the time of their publication.

Canright made a decision to become a Seventh-day Adventist through the preaching of James White in New York State in 1859. Almost immediately he began to convert others to his newfound faith. About two years after his conversion he traveled to Battle Creek, Michigan, to talk to James White about entering the ministry. White counseled him a little, then gave Canright a Bible and a couple of prophetic charts and told him to go out and try preaching. White's final word was that, if he believed he had made a mistake, he could return the Bible and charts. A few months later the two men met again, and Canright announced that White would not get them back.

COURTESY OF THE CENTER FOR ADVENTIST RESEARCH, ANDREWS UNIVERSITY

DUDLEY AND LUCRETIA CANRIGHT

Within a short time Canright became one of the most forceful and successful preachers of the Adventist message. He would also greatly influence the denomination through his writings on such topics as unclean foods and the distinction between the ceremonial and moral laws. One of his most momentous contributions would be the working out in the late 1870s of Adventism's understanding of tithing.

James White was deeply impressed with Canright, and he and the Whites often worked together. They also vacationed together in the Whites' summer cabin in Colorado. One of those occasions witnessed a falling out between the two families. In 1873 when both men were recovering from serious illnesses, White lost his temper at Canright, who responded in kind. Later the Whites sought to work things out with the Canrights, but Ellen wrote in her diary, "They both rose up and resisted everything we said." She went on to note that Canright poured out his complaints "upon us" and "we said some plain things to them" (Ms 10, 1873). The Canrights soon moved out, but after a few months the two couples were reconciled. A crisis had been successfully weathered, but seeds of discord had been sown, especially in the mind of Canright, who had never accepted reproof well.

Canright was a hard worker, a prolific writer, and perhaps the denomination's most successful evangelist during the height of his Adventist ministry. But he lacked emotional stability. At least four or five times during the 1870s and 1880s he left the Adventist ministry and at times stopped keeping the Sabbath, with James White and *G. I. Butler helping restore him to Adventism and its ministry.

Canright's experience in 1882-1884 is illustrative of this pattern. In 1882, after he had been back in the Adventist ministry for about two years, he gave up preaching and once again took up farming. In December 1883 he wrote to Uriah Smith that he disliked Ellen White very much and had been thinking of joining another church. But in September 1884 he was again convinced by Butler to return to his work for the church. He publicly confessed that he had held a grudge against Ellen White because of the testimonies that she had sent him. His problem, he claimed, went back to the 1873 experience in Colorado when he had received a testimony that he and his wife believed to be too severe. In his public confession he acknowledged that he tended to dwell on and magnify his doubts and prejudices. He was soon back laboring full-time in the ministry. Ellen White noted that her heart was "filled with joy" to see Canright back in the work (RH, Dec. 2, 1884).

Things went relatively smoothly for the restored preacher until the December 1886 General Conference session. By that time the law in *Galatians issue that would disrupt the 1888 session had become so problematic that Butler felt the need to bring the matter to a solution. As a result, he organized a theological committee to settle the issue without having to take it to the floor of the session.

But his plan backfired. The nine-person committee, which contained Canright, split five to four after several hours of argument.

The most visible casualty of the 1886 meetings was Canright, who, like Butler and many of his Adventist colleagues, had linked salvation to lawkeeping. In the heat of the debate over the law and the covenants he finally grasped the fact that Waggoner's gospel-oriented position destroyed Butler's position on the law and salvation. And, he later pointed out, if Adventism was wrong on the law, it was a lost cause. But instead of adopting Waggoner's view of the Ten Commandments as leading individuals to Christ, Canright dropped both the perpetuity of the law and Adventism. He would point back to the debate in 1886 as a major turning point, after which he rejected the Adventist position on the law, resigned from all official positions, and asked that his church membership be dropped. That request was granted on February 17, 1887.

Butler reported in the *Review* that Canright thought that the denomination was exalting the law above Christ. And to a large extent Canright was correct. Butler could no longer help Canright because Canright had seen the inadequacy of Butler's theology. Unfortunately, not being able to see the correct relationship between law and gospel, Canright went from one extreme to the other, espoused antinomianism, and became a Baptist.

By the time of the *General Conference session of 1888 Canright was authoring his *Seventh-day Adventism Renounced*, which presented Ellen White as a false prophet. He would fight against her the rest of his life.

Interestingly enough, however, he attended her funeral. His brother reported that as Dudley "stood at Sr. White's casket with one hand in my arm and the other on her coffin with tears streaming down his cheeks, he said: 'There's a noble Christian woman gone'"

(B. J. Canright to Elder Wight, Feb. 24, 1931).

Further reading: W. H. Branson, *Reply to Canright* (RHPA, 1933; also titled *In Defense of the Faith*, 1949); C. Johnson, *I Was Canright's Secretary* (RHPA, 1971); *SDA Encyclopedia* (1996), vol. 10, pp. 289, 290.

George R. Knight

CANRIGHT, LUCRETIA (CRANSTON) (1847-1879). Born in Lansing, Michigan, she was baptized by James White at age 11, and married *Dudley Canright in 1867. She traveled widely with her husband up until her final illness. The Canrights were close friends to Ellen and James White, with the Whites often staying in their home and vice versa. Lucretia sided with her husband in the falling out they had with the Whites in the latter's Colorado mountain retreat in 1873. She also shared with her husband in the heartfelt reconciliation of the two families in November of that year. She contracted "pulmonary consumption" (tuberculosis), and so her last year was one of declining health. Ellen White wrote to her a month before her death, and Lucretia's last-known letter was dictated in return to Ellen White on February 25, 1879. She died a few weeks later and was buried in Battle Creek, Michigan, in Oak Hill Cemetery.

Further reading: obit. RH, Apr. 3, 1879.

George R. Knight

CARO, EDGAR ROBERT (1872-1959). Medical doctor, son of *Margaret Caro, of New Zealand, and family friend of Ellen White; Edgar Caro was baptized by *A. G. Daniells in 1888. He studied at *Battle Creek College and later completed his medical degree at Ann Arbor in Michigan. Toward the end of his studies he married a young woman from Maine, a fellow Battle Creek student. After a brief time of postgraduate study in Germany and England, he went to Australia.

In the last years of the nineteenth century, Caro was instrumental in helping to establish the Adventist medical work in several Australian states and in Strathfield, Sydney, prior to the building of the present *Sydney Sanitarium and Hospital. During this period he received a number of letters of counsel from Ellen White. Some of the counsel, however, he found difficult to understand and accept. On one occasion, for example, he felt he had been misrepresented to Ellen White in regard to misappropriation of some donations from America. He replied that the allegation was not true. *W. C. White endorsed his letter of explanation to Ellen White, stating that he had read the letter and that the facts were as Caro had stated them. But Caro's manner of working, about which Ellen White counseled him, eventually lost him the confidence of his colleagues.

In 1902 Caro withdrew to New Zealand for personal and health reasons and for a time conducted a successful private practice in Napier. Difficulties in his marriage over alleged

COURTESY OF THE ELLEN G. WHITE ESTATE, INC.

DR. EDGAR R. CARO

infidelities on the part of his wife led to separation and eventually a divorce, which created difficulties and tensions in his relationship to the church and with Ellen White. He felt he had been misunderstood and misrepresented in a number of things and eventually suffered a nervous breakdown. Ellen White was greatly distressed over the situation and responded with compassion, but was unable to effect reconciliation between the parties.

Later he remarried and operated his own successful private practice and a private hospital in Strathfield, Sydney, remaining a supportive member of the church in spite of misunderstandings. He maintained

correspondence with the White family until 1907.

Further reading: The letter files in the White Estate contain 45 letters from E. R. Caro to Ellen White and/or her family and numerous letters from Ellen White to Caro.

Gilbert M. Valentine

CARO, MARGARET (1848-1938). Born in Wellington, *New Zealand, Caro, a dentist, was baptized by *A. G. Daniells during an evangelistic program in Napier, New Zealand,

COURTESY OF THE ELLEN G. WHITE ESTATE, INC.

DR. MARGARET CARO

in 1888. Her husband was a medical doctor who never joined the church but became a believer shortly before his death in 1902.

In 1893 Margaret Caro became personally acquainted with Ellen White during the first New Zealand camp meeting in Napier. Ellen White was a guest in the Caro home on several occasions, and she and Margaret became lifelong friends. Ellen White described Margaret as "a precious friend and helper" (Lt 117, 1903). Later, at Ellen White's request, Margaret Caro traveled to Wellington to extract several infected teeth (without "drugs" or anesthetic) and arranged for the fitting of dentures for Ellen White.

In the early 1890s Margaret Caro, at considerable expense, sent all three of her sons to *Battle Creek College. Their letters home in 1893 describing the enthusiasm for football on the college campus distressed their mother, who confided in Ellen White about the problem. The letters provided the occasion for several testimonies to college president *W. W. Prescott about the danger of such sports (Lts 47, 49, 1893). Prescott replied positively, but also observed that the Caro boys were not the easiest to handle and that perhaps Margaret Caro had not been given "the best view of matters here" (W. W. Prescott to EGW, Oct. 5, 1893). Two of the sons, Edgar and Eric, later completed medical training at Ann Arbor, Michigan.

In 1906 during a crisis in the Caro family, Ellen White provided refuge for a year or so for Margaret Caro; her daughter-in-law, Ethel Caro; and three small children in a little cottage on the Elmshaven estate. Ellen White became involved in trying unsuccessfully to reconcile Ethel's broken marriage to *Edgar Caro. Members of the two families kept up an occasional personal correspondence.

On her return to New Zealand, Margaret Caro worked for a time as matron and dean of women at the new Pukekura Training College near Hamilton. In 1921, at age 74, Margaret Caro went to *Avondale to train as a Bible worker. She spent a number of years in evangelistic work in New South Wales before failing health obliged her again to return to New Zealand. She died at age 90, remembered for her strong and striking personality and earnest Christian life.

See also: Homes of James and Ellen G. White.

Further reading: S. R. Goldstone, *Veneered Infidelity: The Story of the Seventh-day Adventist Church in Hawkes Bay, 1888-1932* (Napier, N.Z.: Daily Telegraph Co., 1979); *SDA Encyclopedia* (1996), vol. 10, p. 295.

Gilbert M. Valentine

CARPENTER, ALEXANDER (1826-1915) and **AMANDA (HARGER)** (1830-1902). Adventists in Otsego, Michigan. Formerly Baptists, they accepted Adventist teachings in 1862. In 1888, after the apostasy of *D. M. Canright, Ellen White warned them that although this recent apostasy had done little to affect the Otsego

church, the devil would try other means to discourage them. She included admonition on raising their children and on Alexander Carpenter's leadership in the local church (Lt 43, 1888).

Further reading: obit. LUH, Apr. 14, 1915; obit. RH, Mar. 17, 1903.

CARRUTH, LILLIE D. (ABBEY) (1855-1922). Youngest daughter of *Ira and Rhoda Abbey. Lillie was baptized at the age of 12, in 1867, and studied at *Battle Creek College. She suffered from poor health (Lt 46a, 1874) and worked as a bookkeeper at the *Health Reform Institute, where her father was superintendent. Ellen White expressed a great interest in Lillie, but warned her parents not to let her flirt with the patients. Such behavior, according to Ellen White, was unacceptable. Instead, she encouraged her parents not to spoil her, and to have her perform "useful labor" (Lt 41a, 1874). When Lillie's behavior did not change, Ellen White recommended her dismissal (Lt 65, 1874). In 1878 Lillie went with her sister, *Lucinda Hall, to California, where she worked at the *Pacific Press Publishing Association until 1881, when problems arose again and Ellen White urged her dismissal from the press (Lt 4a, 1881). She married C. W. Carruth in 1879.

Further reading: obit. PUR, Sept. 21, 1922.

CASE, HIRAM S., see *MESSENGER PARTY.*

CHAMBERLAIN, EZRA L. H. (1798-1855). Painter, the first person among former Millerites in Connecticut to accept the seventh-day Sabbath. Chamberlain and his wife invited the Whites to board at their home in Middletown, Connecticut, while they attended the first Sabbath Conference in the *Albert Belden home at Rocky Hill, Connecticut, in April 1848. In August, at the Volney, New York, Sabbatarian conference, Chamberlain joined

*Joseph Bates, *Heman Gurney, *Hiram Edson, and James White in praying for Ellen White's healing. In July 1849 he helped James White launch the *Present Truth*, and in September exposed the errors of half a dozen fanatics at Paris, Maine. During the late 1840s Chamberlain played a prominent role in the Sabbatarian movement as a delegate to conferences, a lay preacher, and an agent for the *Advent Review* in Connecticut. A few sources indicate that he may have spoken in tongues, a rare phenomenon among Sabbathkeeping Adventists. Despite his enthusiasm for the cause, however, he apparently was not very effective as a public speaker. Two of Ellen White's visions reveal that "it was not his duty to travel" and that "he was not one of the messengers [traveling ministers]" (Lt 10, 1850; see also Lt 4, 1852). During the 1850s he seldom ventured beyond the Middletown, Connecticut, area.

Further reading: Lt 18, 1859; LS 111, 127; 2SG 91-98, 116; 1T 84, 85; obit. RH, Jan. 24, 1856; James White to "My Dear Brother," July 2, 1848; S. Howland, Frances Howland Lunt, Rebecka [*sic*] Howland Winslow, and N. N. Lunt, "Gift of Tongues" (DF 311, EGWE-GC; DF 311-a, CAR); *SDA Encyclopedia* (1996), vol. 10, p. 319.

Brian E. Strayer

CHASE, MARY S. (1810-1889). James White's sister, a former member of the Christian Connexion Church and a Millerite of Palmyra, Maine. Mary accepted the Sabbath in 1866 and moved to Battle Creek in 1869. She loved to attend Adventist meetings to hear her brother preach. She and Ellen White occasionally swapped recipes. Rebuked by Ellen White in 1870 for her gossiping and fretfulness (Lt 2, 1870), Mary repented and later "[enjoyed] the presence of Jesus" in her life (Lt 28, 1877). After James White's death, Ellen White provided care for Mary and later urged

Mary's daughter, *Adeline Savage, to take responsibility for the care of her aging mother (Lt 30, 1884, in DG 198-200). Mary lived "a quiet, consistent Christian life" until her death in August 1889.

Further reading: 1T 661, 662; obit. RH, Sept. 10, 1889.

CHITTENDEN, CHARLES (1844-1934) and **LOTTIE** (d. 1896). Church members in San Francisco, California. Ellen White met the Chittendens for the first time during her first visit to San Francisco in late 1872. James and Ellen White stayed at their home and enjoyed cruising on the San Francisco Bay in Charles' boat. His spiritual life, however, soon gave way to unconsecration and loose behavior. In 1877 Ellen White wrote Charles a long letter regarding his lack of godliness and consecration to God (Lt 5, 1877). She pointed out his many lapses, likely caused by indulgence of his own strong inclinations to pleasure-seeking, and stimulated by association with worldly people. A few years later, however, Ellen White's concern shifted to Lottie's indiscreet behavior and adultery with an older married pastor, *J. H. Waggoner. Some of these letters are in TSB 182-193.

Further reading: obit. RH, Nov. 15, 1934; obit. RH, Dec. 15, 1896.

CHRISTENSEN, EUPHEMIA (1855-1948). Adventist philanthropist. In 1903 she wrote to Ellen White expressing an interest in lending $1,000 for the work in the southern United States (Lt 74a, 1903). Ellen White suggested that she lend the money to the *Southern Publishing Association, or that, if she preferred, to lend the money to herself and she would be responsible for it. "I am trying," wrote Ellen White, "in every way possible to help my son [J. Edson White] to get out the books that are needed in the Southern field" (Lt 155, 1903).

CHRISTIAN, LEWIS HARRISON (1871-1949). Evangelist and administrator; successor of Louis R. *Conradi as president of the European Division in 1922. Christian was instrumental in reorganizing the European Adventist mis-

LEWIS H. CHRISTIAN

sion in 1928, leading to the establishment of four separate European divisions. After the reorganization he was elected as president of the North European Division, with headquarters in London. Christian was one of the strongest supporters in

*Europe of Ellen White's prophetic ministry. His parents came from *Denmark and settled in Owatonna, Minnesota, where he was born. After Christian graduated from *Union College, Nebraska, in 1896, Danish-born *John G. Matteson, whom he considered his spiritual advisor, encouraged him to enter the ministry. Christian worked successfully for many years as an evangelist among the Scandinavian population of the midwestern United States. To improve his ministry among Scandinavian immigrants in the United States, he labored in Denmark from 1902 to 1904. As one of the secretaries of the General Conference Foreign Department, responsible for "Home Missions," he helped establish the Danish-Norwegian Seminary in Hutchinson, Minnesota. In 1914 Christian became president of the Lake Union Conference. Six years later he was sent to Europe as associate vice president of the General Conference. Christian faced a daunting task in post-*World War I Europe. He organized relief work for the poor, opposed the schismatic efforts of the so-called Reform Adventists, and strongly defended Ellen White's prophetic gift against increasing attack, especially after *L. R. Conradi left the Adventist Church (1932). Christian's most

important book, *The Fruitage of Spiritual Gifts* (1947), describes, according to the subtitle, the "influence and guidance of Ellen G. White in the Advent movement" and is considered a landmark in the history of Adventist apologetics. Christian wrote: "In Europe the genuineness of the spiritual gift of Ellen White was put to an entirely new test. . . . She was in strange lands, and among people whose mentality, customs, and language she did not understand. . . . Yet . . . she had as clear light as she had had in the testimony she bore in America. . . . The Advent movement in Europe would never have been the same if it had not been for her visit" (*Fruitage of Spiritual Gifts*, pp. 161, 163f.). In 1936 Christian returned to America, serving the General Conference in several capacities. He died in Sacramento, California.

Further reading: L. H. Christian, *Pioneers and Builders of the Advent Cause in Europe* (PPPA, 1937); L. H. Christian, *The Fruitage of Spiritual Gifts* (RHPA, 1947); *SDA Encyclopedia* (1996), vol. 10, p. 346.

Daniel Heinz

CHRISTIE, LOUIS. Young colporteur in New Zealand. In 1893 Ellen White wrote to Christie, cautioning him that his financial mismanagement leading to personal debt had also brought indebtedness on the Tract and Missionary Society that supplied him with books to sell. Furthermore, she told him that his personal life needed a complete conversion and a transformation of character (Lts 13, 14, 1893). Ellen White had hoped he might acknowledge his weaknesses during a camp meeting, but when this did not occur she wrote him a testimony of reproof to be read to him by *G. T. Wilson (Lt 14a, 1893). Christie denied everything and insisted that she had been influenced by gossip (Lts 28a, 137, 1893; Ms 81, 1893). Ellen White saw in this case an example of the need for a better understanding of "what constitutes a religious devotion to God" (Lt 12b, 1893).

MOSES J. CHURCH

CHURCH, MOSES JAMES (1813-c. 1890). Adventist philanthropist from the San Joaquin Valley, California. Church immigrated with his family to California in 1852, and in 1868 he constructed the first irrigation ditches where he later founded the city of Fresno (Bancroft, pp. 217, 218). Church was converted to Adventism at the 1873 Yountville camp meeting and because of his conviction about the seventh-day Sabbath, he stopped his employees from working on the Sabbath.

Known as the "Father of Fresno," he was also a friend of Ellen White's, and she encouraged him to donate funds to the European mission (Lt 61, 1886). As he became influential in the health retreat in Healdsburg (later the *St. Helena Sanitarium), she cautioned that he not be allowed to manage the retreat (Lt 10, 1886). About this time, influenced, she said, by disaffected employees, and in particular *W. H. Maxson, who had left the St. Helena Sanitarium, Church lost confidence in the institution (Lt 34a, 1887; Lt 55, 1888) and planned to build a health retreat in Fresno (Lt 32, 1888). Ellen White warned him that the Adventist Church was not yet ready for such plans (Lts 33, 33a, 1888). Part of her concern stemmed from the fact that in order to build a health retreat, Church would have to withdraw his stock from *Pacific Press (Lt 54, 1888). She furthermore urged that he consult with church leaders in such enterprises (Lt 33a, 1888). In the end no such sanitarium was built. As the church in Fresno grew he

built a beautiful church facility that was described by H. H. Bancroft as "the handsomest and most becoming house of worship in Southern California [in 1892]" (p. 218). Later Ellen White warned Church not to make too much of his own theories. "You have searched the Scriptures," she wrote, "but you have placed precious gems of truth in a false setting to substantiate errors" (Lt 8a, 1890). She later warned Church and others in Fresno against putting too much confidence in *E. P. Daniels (Lt 38, 1890). Some street names in Fresno still reflect Church's temperance views.

See also: W. P. Burke; J. D. Rice.

Further reading: H. H. Bancroft, *Chronicles of the Builders of the Commonwealth* (San Francisco: History Company, 1892), vol. 3, pp. 217, 218; H. A. McCumber, *The Advent Message in the Golden West* (PPPA, 1968), pp. 83-85.

Michael W. Campbell

CLOUGH, CAROLINE TRUE (HARMON) (1812-1883). Oldest daughter of Robert and Eunice Harmon; older sister of Ellen White. In 1835 Caroline married Mace R. Clough (pronounced "clow") (d. 1875), a minister in the Methodist Episcopal Church. In 1855 they moved to

ELLEN G. WHITE AND HER SISTER
CAROLINE CLOUGH

Kansas. In May 1872 James and Ellen White visited the Cloughs for two weeks in their "comfortable little painted frame house" on the prairie near Ottawa, Kansas. Writing to her children, Ellen White described their aunt: "She is an understanding, intelligent woman, living, I think, up to the best light she has. She is a powerful singer. . . . I think I never heard a voice that would thrill the soul like hers" (Lt 10, 1872). Five years later Ellen White wrote a few letters to her sister (Lts 35, 35a, 35b, 1877). Their daughter *Mary Clough worked for a time as one of Ellen White's *literary assistants. Ellen White hoped that through Mary she might be able to influence her mother in favor of the Adventist message. Caroline and Mace Clough are buried in Paola, Kansas.

Michael W. Campbell

CLOUGH, MARY L. (later **MARY [CLOUGH] WANLESS, MARY [CLOUGH] WATSON**). Ellen White's niece, daughter of her sister *Caroline (Harmon) Clough (pronounced "clow"). James and Ellen White first met Mary Clough on a trip to *Colorado in 1872, where Mary was homesteading 160 acres (65 hectares), on which she had built a little cabin. James White later bought Mary's Colorado homestead, and the little cabin became the Whites' mountain retreat for many years.

MARY L. (CLOUGH) WATSON, NIECE OF ELLEN G. WHITE

The Whites were favorably impressed with Mary and had every hope that she would accept the message of the seventh-day Sabbath and influence her mother to do likewise (Ms 4, 1872). To this end they invited Mary in 1875 to join them in California to work as a *literary assistant to Ellen White. In 1876, at the Michigan camp meeting, Clough reported for 32 newspapers, besides her work for Ellen White. When reporters realized what a facile pen she had, she was besieged with requests to furnish reports for various papers.

In 1877, after Mary showed open disrespect of the Sabbath and engaged in secret and deceptive actions, Ellen White told her that she felt forbidden by God to continue to employ her (cf. Lt 35b, 1877). Mary confessed

frankly that she had no interest in the Adventist faith, and had come to work for her aunt only as a matter of business. However, for a short time in 1878 she once again did a little work for Ellen White.

Mary married Col. John Wanless in 1877, and they lived in Colorado Springs, Colorado (Lt 37, 1877). He died about 1882, and in 1887 Mary married George W. Watson, of Hot Springs, Arkansas (Mary C. Watson to Addie Walling, Oct. 14, 1891).

In 1896 Mary again offered her services to Ellen White, who apparently considered giving her another chance. In the end, though, she did not employ Mary again.

Further reading: R. W. Coon, "Ellen White: The Person—I: The Human-Interest Story" (lecture outline, AU, Mar. 30, 1995, CAR); A. L. White, *Messenger to the Remnant* (RHPA, 1965), p. 119.

Norma J. Collins

COBB, STEPHEN MONTGOMERY (1852-1936). Minister and administrator. Originally from upstate New York, he was converted during evangelistic meetings held by C. O. Taylor in 1874. From 1890 to 1900 he pastored in New York. He then served as conference president in West Virginia (1900-1903), New South Wales in Australia (1903-1906), New Zealand (1906-1909), and Victoria (1909-1910); and as home missionary secretary in Queensland (1916-1924). Ellen White wrote him four letters of advice as a church leader (Lts 270, 330, 331, 395, 1906).

Further reading: obit. RH, Dec. 24, 1936.

COLCORD, WILLARD A. (1860-1935). Minister, administrator, editor. Born in Illinois, Colcord was baptized into the Adventist Church about 1884. He studied at Battle Creek College for a short time and began his work as a minister in 1886. He served as secretary of the General

Conference from 1891 to 1893, when he went as a missionary to Australia. While in Australia he performed editorial work for the Bible Echo Publishing House. In 1898 he was invited to join Ellen White's literary staff. Colcord returned to the United States in 1902, teaching at Union College for two years, then joining the General Conference Religious Liberty Department as an associate secretary. He later became a book editor at the Review and Herald publishing house. Ellen White corresponded with Colcord periodically during the 1890s and up into the early 1900s.

WILLARD A. COLCORD

About the time of her death, Colcord left the church for about 20 years. But in the early 1930s he published a confession and was rebaptized.

In 1896, while in Australia, Ellen White wrote to Willard's son, Charlie, appealing for him to surrender to God and to exert a good influence on others (Lt 135, 1896).

Further reading: obit. RH, Jan. 2, 1936.

George R. Knight

COLLIE, JOSEPH W. (1864-1904) and **ROSELLA B. (RUPP)** (1863-1951). Pastor and administrator. Joseph was born in Nova Scotia, but while still a boy moved with his parents to Minnesota, where in 1872 the family became Seventh-day Adventists. He attended Battle Creek College and for a time drifted away from the church, but returned and married Rosella at the Cleveland, Ohio, camp meeting in 1887. The next year Ellen White wrote to the young couple appealing for them to be fully converted (Lt 64, 1888). Apparently the letter made a positive impact, for they soon dedicated themselves to the ministry. Joseph was ordained in 1889 and labored in Florida and Ohio. In 1901 he became

president of the Ontario, Canada, Conference, but shortly thereafter contracted tuberculosis. In search of a milder climate they moved in 1903 to Colorado, where Joseph died a few months later.

Further reading: obit. RH, Jan. 28, 1904; obit. RH, Sept. 27, 1951.

COLLINS, GILBERT N. (1836-1905) and **DEBORAH L.** (1839-1852). Early Sabbatarian Adventists in Dartmouth, Massachusetts; children of *Philip and Nancy Collins. In 1849 Gilbert became deathly ill with whooping cough. At the request of his parents, the Whites visited them, and he was miraculously healed (2SG 108, 109). In September 1849 Ellen White wrote a brief letter to Gilbert and Deborah, encouraging them to be faithful to God and to obey His commandments (Lt 7, 1849). When the nearby New Bedford, Massachusetts, church was organized, Gilbert became a charter member and lifelong elder of the congregation (RH, June 29, 1905). Ellen White wrote to Gilbert several times asking for financial assistance, particularly for the work in Australia (Lt 33, 1897) and later for the Melrose Sanitarium (Lt 341, 1904). In 1902 Gilbert became very sick and was concerned he might not live long. Ellen White wanted to visit him, but unable to do so, wrote him a series of encouraging letters (Lt 6, 1902; Lt 305, 1904; Lt 341, 1904; Lt 149, 1905; Lt 157, 1905). She also suggested he consider making out a will so that "after your life ends, it is your privilege to carry forward His work" (Lt 6, 1902). She later encouraged him to give the use of his property to C. C. Nicola in exchange for long-term care at the *New England Sanitarium (Lt 305, 1904).

Further reading: obit. RH, Dec. 23, 1852; obit. RH, June 29, 1905.

COLLINS, PHILIP (c. 1809-1859) and **NANCY**

345

(1809-1882). Former Millerite believers and early Sabbatarian Adventists in Dartmouth, Massachusetts, and close friends of James and Ellen White. A few letters of the correspondence from James and Ellen White to the Collinses have been preserved. In 1849 Ellen White wrote a brief letter to their children, *Gilbert and Deborah, encouraging them to obey the commandments of God (Lt 7, 1849). When in 1849, their son, Gilbert, became very ill with whooping cough, they sent an urgent call to the Whites to come, and the child was miraculously healed in answer to prayer (2SG 108, 109; Ms 7, 1859). After the death of Philip in June 1859, Ellen White visited Nancy and Gilbert that September and described their home as "a good home for weary pilgrims" (Lt 8, 1859).

Further reading: obit. RH, June 23, 1859; obit. RH, June 13, 1882.

CONRADI, LOUIS (LUDWIG) RICHARD (1856-1939). Pioneer evangelist, administrator, and

LOUIS R. CONRADI

coworker of Ellen G. White during her stay in Europe (1885-1887). Conradi played a decisive role in shaping the course of European Adventism. Under his leadership Adventist congregations all over the continent witnessed a growth of membership never experienced before or since. In view of his missionary genius Ellen White publicly stated at the General Conference session in 1901: "Brother Conradi has carried a very heavy burden of work in Europe. . . . God has greatly blessed [his] labors. . . . He has opened doors for the angels, and they have entered" (GCB, Apr. 22, 1901). At the end of his life, personal alienation and doctrinal differences led to his break with Adventism

(1932). He joined the Seventh Day Baptist denomination and became an outspoken critic of Ellen G. White's prophetic ministry.

Conradi was born in Karlsruhe, Germany, and was raised as a Roman Catholic. Without a father to care for him, he experienced poverty and rejection. Yet as a child in school Conradi was unusually gifted and studious, even learning Greek and Latin in his early teens. His mother may have wanted him to become a Catholic priest. At the age of 16 he emigrated, without the consent of his mother, to America (1872), living the life of a drifter for the next six years. Finally, in 1878, through the loving Christian influence of a farmer's family in Iowa, Conradi became a devoted Seventh-day Adventist. After his graduation from Battle Creek College (1880), "the hardy Teuton," as he was nicknamed by his associates, worked as James White's personal secretary in the publishing house. During that time he edited the newly founded German Adventist church paper, *Stimme der Wahrheit*. Conradi's evangelistic career began in 1881 when he started to work as an itinerant preacher among German and Russian-German settlements in the Midwest and later in Pennsylvania. Within four years approximately 700 people joined the Adventist Church as a result of his labor.

In 1886 Conradi was sent to Europe as an evangelist and administrator to achieve the breakthrough in Adventist mission work that *M. B. Czechowski and *J. N. Andrews had not accomplished. During 1886 and 1887 he worked closely with Ellen White as her translator in Switzerland and Germany. In the following years Conradi opened the Adventist work in Germany, Holland, Russia, Austria-Hungary, Serbia, in today's Poland, Bulgaria, Romania, and the Baltic lands. While preaching in Russia, he was kept in prison for 40 days and barely escaped banishment to Siberia. By 1891 he was the superintendent of the Adventist work in Germany and Russia, which were then the fastest growing mission fields for Adventists in the world. Conradi also led out in mission work in North Africa, East Africa, and the Middle East, calling for increased training of native workers in those fields. He was convinced that "the chief burden of spreading the truth must be carried by the natives themselves" (RH, Dec. 17, 1903), arguing against any form of ethnocentricity in mission work.

As for Europe, Conradi developed a special mission strategy. By pointing out that the Advent movement is not merely a North American phenomenon but has roots that go back to the Reformation, he succeeded, at first, in strengthening the European Adventist identity. Then, instead of using aggressive modes of campaigning, such as revivalistic preaching, popular persuasion, or public religious debate, Conradi adopted in his evangelization efforts the lecture format ("Vortraege"), which proved to fit better the more conservative European clerical image. He regarded the main purpose of public evangelism in Europe as the reduction of prejudice; the actual recruitment of members took place through a well-organized colporteur network and regular Bible study groups ("Bibelstunden"). The city of Hamburg, Germany, became not only the center of Conradi's activity but also the place where the headquarters of the "European General Conference" was established in 1901. The organization of a separate General Conference in Europe through Conradi constituted a unique experiment in the history of Adventism. The growing autonomy of the European organization, however, led to its termination in 1907. Conradi, nevertheless, remained the president of the "European Division," as it was now called, until 1922. The extension and size of the European Adventist work reached its peak

under Conradi's leadership in 1914. The area of the European Division included not only one third of the world population but also one third of the populated surface of the earth. Since 1903 Conradi had also served as vice president of the General Conference. Circulation of his books and tracts is estimated from 12 to 15 million. His works include a revision and enlargement of J. N. Andrews' *History of the Sabbath* (1912). His book *Das Goldene Zeitalter* ("The Golden Age") (1923) was the first attempt by an Adventist scholar to demonstrate the place of Seventh-day Adventist apocalypticism in church history. The book strongly influenced L. E. Froom, who later published his four-volume set *The Prophetic Faith of Our Fathers* (1946-1954).

In the midst of his stunning success, however, signs of a growing tension between Conradi and American church leaders were becoming evident in power struggle and competition. Conradi's authoritarian personality made it difficult for his coworkers to get along with him. His relationship to Ellen White was also ambiguous. In a preface to the German edition of *Testimonies for the Church* (E. G. White, *Zeugnisse fuer die Gemeinde* [Hamburg: Internationale Traktatgesellschaft, 1904], vol. 1, p. vi) he stated: "We are thankful to God that the Spirit of Prophecy, being under scrutiny for fifty years, has revealed itself as a divine power." It is true that Conradi propagated, translated, and published Ellen White's works vigorously in Europe; at the same time, however, he asserted that "her writings are not a safe guide to us" (Heinz, *Conradi*, p. 97). Statements such as this may be understood as a reaction to some Adventists at the time who wrongly claimed verbal inspiration or infallibility for her writings, which Ellen White herself denied. He was also right when he rejected the elevation of her writings to the level of biblical authority.

Nevertheless, it remains questionable whether Conradi from the very outset ever fully accepted Ellen White as a prophet. It seems that he searched for a hermeneutical key to determine which of her writings were divinely inspired over against those that he thought to be of merely human origin. It was only after Conradi's break with the Adventist Church (1932) that he openly attacked her prophetic gift, sometimes in a rather severe and unfair manner.

The outbreak of World War I was the beginning of Conradi's final estrangement from the church leadership. Faced with the specter of the possible destruction of his life's work, he yielded to government pressure for compulsory conscription, rejecting the denomination's historic stand on conscientious objection. Conradi's compromise, which allowed Adventist draftees to bear arms and to perform duties on Sabbath, provoked a split within the Adventist Church that exists to this day. A. G. Daniells, president of the General Conference, spoke warmly about Conradi's efforts during the war, saying that he "has carried a tremendous load . . . (facing) the gravest problems and difficulties that have ever come to any of us" (RH, Jan. 22, 1920). However, this did not prevent his replacement as president of the European Division in 1922. This was a deep personal affront to him. In addition, he began criticizing the traditional Adventist doctrine of the heavenly *sanctuary. Eventually he came to believe that political events in the Middle East in 1844 fulfilled the prophecy of Daniel 8:14. In 1932, after serving the Seventh-day Adventist Church for nearly 50 years, Conradi voluntarily surrendered his ministerial credentials and became a Seventh Day Baptist pastor. He died seven years later in Hamburg, Germany. His legacy continues to be debated as Adventist historians balance the impact of his overall influence against the position he assumed near the end of his life. Nevertheless, the "Adventist" Conradi will always be remembered as a formidable champion and a courageous trailblazer for his church in Europe and in other parts of the world.

Further reading: L. R. Conradi, *Der Seher von Patmos* (Hamburg: Internationale Traktatgesellschaft, 1913); L. R. Conradi, *Weissagung und Weltgeschichte* (Hamburg: Internationale Traktatgesellschaft, 1919); EGWEur 286-296; D. Heinz, "Ludwig Richard Conradi: Patriarch of European Adventism," *Adventist Heritage* 12, no. 1 (Winter 1987): 17-24; D. Heinz, *Ludwig Richard Conradi: Missionar, Evangelist und Organisator der Siebenten-Tags-Adventisten in Europa* (Frankfurt/M.: Peter Lang, 1998 [English translation forthcoming]); *SDA Encyclopedia* (1996), vol. 10, pp. 406, 407

Daniel Heinz

COOK, JOSEPH (1826-1891). Born in England, Cook (a carpenter), his wife, and five children immigrated to America, becoming Adventists in the 1860s. In an 1878 letter Ellen White criticized him for his miserly business practices (Lt 51, 1878). While his wife earned $10-$12 a week for "brain wearing and soul burdening work," Cook paid himself $21 a week while cutting his employees' wages. His business ethics in Healdsburg, California, also caused James White "hard feelings and disappointment" (*ibid.*).

Further reading: obit. RH, Feb. 23, 1892.

Brian E. Strayer

COON, J. FRANKLIN (1854-1932). Adventist physician who compiled a 40-page booklet *The Searchlight* (Walla Walla, Wash.: by the author, c. 1911) on the church's medical work, using Ellen White's writings. "I was instructed to say," she wrote, "to the brother who has used my name and my writings so freely in that document, that he has no right to interpret my writings as he has done, and that it is wrong to place me and my teachings before the public in the light that his booklet represents them. I forbid the use of my writings in any such way" (Lt 108, 1911).

Further reading: obit. RH, Sept. 29, 1932.

CORKHAM, DAVID ANDREW (1854-1914). Adventist in Nova Scotia who struggled with *assurance of salvation. Ellen White encouraged Corkham to place his faith in God and not to let his emotional state affect his relationship with God (Lt 41, 1893). In a follow-up letter she noted that although there are circumstances in life that may bring depression and sadness, feelings should "not be made the test of the spiritual state," and she invited Corkham to depend upon the "Word of God" as the evidence of his "true standing before Him" (Lt 10, 1893).

Further reading: obit. RH, May 28, 1914.

CORLISS, JOHN ORR (1845-1923) and **JULIA A. (BURGESS)** (1843-1912). Pioneer evangelist

COURTESY OF THE ELLEN G. WHITE ESTATE, INC.

JOHN AND JULIA CORLISS

who became a Seventh-day Adventist in 1868 as a consequence of living in the home of *James and Ellen White, and studying the Bible with *Joseph Bates. He married Julia Burgess in 1868. That year he became superintendent of the Western Health Reform Institute in Battle Creek. He later worked as an evangelist in Michigan, Maine, Virginia, Colorado, and California. Corliss was a member of the group who, in 1885, under the leadership of *S. N. Haskell, first brought Adventism to *Australia. In spite of opposition, his preaching resulted

in more than 200 converts, particularly from the professional community. Notable was the significant number of entire families that made a decision to join the church as a consequence of the early ministry of Corliss in Australia.

After regaining his health in California, where he engaged in religious liberty and editorial work, Corliss returned to Australia, remaining there until 1896. He also worked in England as an evangelist between 1902 and 1904. Corliss was prominent in Adventist religious liberty work and taught Bible at *Battle Creek College (1897-1898). An advocate of Christian education, Corliss used inherited funds to educate 25 young people in addition to those in his own family.

Active to the end of his life, Corliss became ill after preaching at Pasadena, California, and died two days later, on September 10, 1923. Corliss was remembered in Australia as a "logical reasoner, and his keen, perceptive mind enabled him to write with a wonderful clearness. He very readily detected the weakness in the arguments of opponents and showed great facility in overthrowing false teaching" (*Australasian Record*, Nov. 5, 1923). In that context it is of interest that Ellen White, also living in Australia during the time Corliss was there in the mid-1890s, engaged in a considerable correspondence with him. Her counsel to him repeatedly focused on the need for a Christ-centered public presentation of Seventh-day Adventist doctrines. She warned against using sharp language that would antagonize others and against self-confidence. She encouraged him to be patient and suggested the need to guard against overwork and carrying the burdens of others.

Further reading: obit. RH, Oct. 4, 1923; obit. RH, Sept. 19, 1912; *Seventh-day Adventists in the South Pacific 1885-1985*, pp. 10, 13, 36, 37, 114; *SDA Encyclopedia* (1996), vol. 10, p. 410.

Lester D. Devine

CORLISS, WILLIAM BURR (1882-1969). Adventist young person, son of *J. O. Corliss. Corliss was the focus of high expectations. When he was 14, Ellen White wrote to him about his wayward ways and urged him to give his heart to the Lord (Lt 15a, 1896). He later became a medical doctor and worked for the Loma Linda Sanitarium.

Further reading: obit. RH, June 5, 1969.

CORNELL, JAMES (c. 1832-1897) and **ROXANNA (BACHELLER)** (1837-1895). James was the younger brother of *Merritt and Myron Cornell. In 1857 he married Roxanna Bacheller, an early worker in the Review and Herald office in *Rochester, New York. The Cornells moved to Boulder, Colorado, by 1870, and to Texas by 1876. Ellen White celebrated Christmas with the family in 1878 and gave each of their two daughters a dress as gifts (Lt 63, 1878). The next year they joined the Whites on their *wagon train trek across Texas and Oklahoma. She cautioned Cornell about a conflict between him and *J. O. Corliss, and counseled him not to be egocentric (Lts 37, 38, 1879).

Further reading: obit. RH, Mar. 8, 1898.

CORNELL, MERRITT EATON (1827-1893) and **ANGELINE M. A. (LYON)** (1828-1901). Early Millerite and Sabbatarian Adventist minister. In 1849 Merritt married Angeline Lyon, daughter of *Henry Lyon, and both became Sabbatarian Adventists through the efforts of *Joseph Bates in 1852. The Cornells met James and Ellen White during their first trip to Michigan (May 1853) when the Whites visited the home of Henry Lyon (Lt 2, 1853). Later that year Cornell joined *J. N. Loughborough on a preaching tour through Wisconsin. In 1854 Cornell and Loughborough held the first Adventist tent meetings in Battle Creek, Michigan. Cornell, Bates, and *J. H. Waggoner

formed a committee of three who prepared an address on spiritual gifts for the 1855 conference at Battle Creek, a conference that marked a turning point in the church's confidence in the prophetic gift of Ellen White.

In 1863 Ellen White wrote to Cornell cautioning him regarding fanaticism in Waukon, Iowa, and urging that *J. N. Andrews break away from its evil influence (Lt 2, 1863). She admonished the Cornells regarding Merritt's extravagant use of money and his jealousy of Loughborough, and appealed for Angeline Cornell to bear more of life's burdens as a minister's wife (Ms 8, 1863, in 21MR 260-264; Lt 10, 1863). Later Ellen White wrote to Angeline that she had several times seen her

COURTESY OF THE REVIEW AND HERALD PUBLISHING ASSOCIATION

M. E. CORNELL

case in vision, that she was not assisting her husband as she should (Lt 11, 1865). By 1871 Angeline had become a spiritualist (RH, June 13, 1871).

In 1871 and 1872 Cornell and Loughborough held the first Adventist tent meetings in San Francisco. During the meetings Cornell became careless in his association with a woman in the congregation. Although he claimed that he had done nothing wrong, a meeting was held to consider his behavior. Upon receiving a letter from Ellen White, Cornell handed Loughborough a written confession of his wrong. In that letter Ellen White warned him: "I was shown that you were not standing in the clear light and you are in danger of bringing a reproach upon the cause of God by moving as you happen to feel. It is Satan's intent to destroy you" (Lt 23, 1871, in TSB 166-168). Loughborough found that this letter came from a vision given to Ellen White while at Bordoville, Vermont, on December 10, 1871.

She did not mail her letter until January 12, 1872, and it arrived just when it was needed.

Cornell was allowed to resume his ministerial work later that year. Ellen White was shown in vision that his defects of character were crippling his labor (Lt 22, 1872). She was particularly concerned that "unbelievers" would judge other Adventists to have "the same stamp of character," noting how Cornell was causing "great injury to the cause of God" (Lt 27, 1872). Ellen White called Cornell to change the course of his life and urged his need of accountability (Lt 29, 1872, in 3T 227-243).

In 1874 Cornell held evangelistic meetings with *D. M. Canright in Oakland, California. Previous moral problems occurred again. Ellen White told him that in his present position he was "wholly unfit" to be a minister (Lt 52, 1876; cf. TSB 166-172). In the following years she continued to write the Cornells, expressing a deep interest for their souls (Lt 27, 1879; Lt 6, 1880, in TSB 172-182).

The Cornells remained in isolation for some years living in Maryland, where Ellen White visited them in January 1889 (Ms 17, 1889). Later that year they returned to Battle Creek, where they became reconciled to the church, and where Merritt resumed active ministry until his death in November 1893.

Further reading: obit. RH, Jan. 23, 1894; obit. RH, Jan. 7, 1902; *Legacy of Light* CD-ROM, article, Merritt E. Cornell; *SDA Encyclopedia* (1996), vol. 10, pp. 410, 411.

Michael W. Campbell

CORNELL, MYRON J. (1829-1920) and **CORNELIA A.** (**LYON**) (1836-1922). Early Sabbatarian Adventists; Myron was the younger brother of *M. E. Cornell, and Cornelia A. Lyon was the daughter of *Henry Lyon. They were married in 1853, became Sabbatarian Adventists in 1856, and were close friends of James and Ellen White. In 1902 Ellen White wrote to

Myron inquiring if he could collect outstanding debts for her house in Battle Creek (Lt 165, 1902). Four years later when *J. H. Kellogg was leaving the church she appealed for Myron to take a "stand decidedly on the side of truth and righteousness" (Lt 346, 1906).

Further reading: obit. RH, Jan. 27, 1921; obit. Feb. 17, 1921; obit. RH, Aug. 10, 1922.

COTTRELL, HAMPTON WATSON (1852-1940). Adventist minister and administrator. Cottrell and his family became Adventists in 1865. He later attended *Battle Creek College, where he married Margaret M. Grant (1849-1935) in 1877. In 1885 Hampton served as evangelist in Cleveland, Ohio, and in 1890 headed the Adventist work in the Canadian Maritime provinces and Newfoundland. Three years later Cottrell transferred to Massachusetts, where he served as conference evangelist (1893-1895), conference president (1895-1900), and Atlantic Union president (1900-1905), and was involved in the relocation of denominational headquarters from *Battle Creek to Washington, D.C., in 1903. While president of *Pacific Press (1906-1912) he worked closely with Ellen White, who had a high regard for his administrative skills and frequently wrote him letters of counsel (cf. Lts 107, 224, 1907; Lts 70, 88, 262, 1908; Lts 80, 160, 1909). Cottrell served in a variety of administrative posts for the church in the western United States until 1925, when he and his wife retired near *Paradise Valley Sanitarium.

Further reading: obit. RH, Jan. 30, 1941; *SDA Encyclopedia* (1996), vol. 10, pp. 413, 414.

Michael W. Campbell

COTTRELL, ROSWELL FENNER (1814-1892). Adventist minister, writer, and poet. Raised a Seventh Day Baptist, he became a Sabbatarian Adventist in 1851 through reading the *Review*

and Herald. He was ordained to the ministry in 1854 by James White, and the next year became a corresponding editor of the *Review* as well as a member of the editorial committee. After a conference in Battle Creek affirmed the prophetic ministry of Ellen White, he wrote an article in support of her work (RH, Dec. 18, 1855). This article impressed Ellen White (Lt 9, 1856), who in 1858 asked him to write a 12-page biblical presentation of the prophetic gift as the introduction to her book *Spiritual Gifts*, volume 1—the first book outlining what she had seen in her *great controversy vision. Cottrell was among those who opposed formal *church organization from the late 1850s. His reservations brought heated rejoinders from James White. Out of this came corrective counsel from Ellen White (see 1T 211, where Cottrell is referred to as Brother B). He later apologized for his opposition to denominational organization. Cottrell represented the Seventh-day Adventist Church to Seventh Day Baptists and served as secretary and president of the New York Conference. Toward the end of his life he served as chaplain of the *Battle Creek Sanitarium. Several of his poems have been set to music as hymns in *The Seventh-day Adventist Hymnal.*

COURTESY OF THE CENTER FOR ADVENTIST RESEARCH, ANDREWS UNIVERSITY

ROSWELL F. COTTRELL

Further reading: Legacy of Light CD-ROM, article, Roswell F. Cottrell; *SDA Encyclopedia* (1996), vol. 10, p. 414.

Michael W. Campbell

COVELL, WILLIAM HAMMOND (1863-1943). Adventist businessman in California and associate of *Stonewall Jackson Harris. In 1911, when Harris sought Ellen White's counsel regarding his method of finding God's will for his business investments, she disapproved of coin tossing and called upon Harris and Covell not to use her name in connection with their business (Lt 36, 1911). In a letter to W. C. White, Covell responded that he did not approve of Harris' method and felt sorry that he had lent his influence "to an enterprise somewhat uncertain as to its final outcome" (W. H. Covell to WCW, June 21, 1911, DF 150a, CAR).

Further reading: obit. PUR, July 28, 1943.

COVERT, WILLIAM (1842-1917). Conference administrator in Indiana to whom Ellen White appealed for deeper consecration in his life and his relationships with coworkers (Lt 26d, 1887). Covert authored a number of books on various themes of the plan of salvation.

Further reading: obit. RH, Dec. 6, 1917.

CRAIG, JOHN M. Adventist physician at the Chicago Mission who in the 1890s was secretary of the *International Medical Missionary and Benevolent Association and in 1900 was associated with the Nebraska Sanitarium at College View. In 1889 Ellen White wrote a letter of marital advice and admonition to Mrs. Craig for being too controlling of her husband (Lt 10, 1889). Mrs. Craig later confessed her wrong, but her change of heart was not lasting, prompting further admonition from Ellen White (Lt 34, 1890). A year later White wrote to John Craig warning of his wife's need to be converted and that until then she would undermine his work (Lt 8, 1891).

CRAW, HIRAM A. (1829-1911). Early Sabbatarian Adventist from Bowling Green, Ohio. Ellen White wrote him several times requesting funds for missionary use in Australia (Lt 53, 1899), for the preparation of her books (Lt 103, 1904), and finally, for new buildings being erected in Washington, D.C. (Lt 125, 1904). She encouraged him to share her letters and to encourage others to contribute. Additionally she noted that part of the work the Lord had presented before her was "to present before our church members their obligations to God. When a new field is to be opened, I am to present to those who have means the needs of this field, asking them to help" (*ibid.*).

Further reading: obit. RH, Oct. 5, 1911; Hiram A. Craw, *Diaries* (CAR).

CRAWFORD, MARION C. (STOWELL) (1829-1913). Early Sabbatarian Adventist from Paris, Maine, daughter of Lewis B. Stowell and sister of *Lewis O. Stowell. At the age of 15 Marion read the tract on the Sabbath by Thomas Preble and, convinced of its arguments, shared it with other people in Paris. This led to the conversion of many early Sabbatarian Adventist pioneers, including the *Edward Andrews and *Cyprian Stevens families. James and Ellen White became more closely acquainted with her while she was living with the *David Arnold family (1850-1852). The Whites found Marion "much worn" from her caregiving to the family, and urged on her the need of a change. She agreed to travel with them when they returned to their home in Saratoga Springs, New York. As they rode along, Crawford remembered Ellen saying, "James, everything that was shown me [in vision] about this trip has transpired but one. [I saw that] we had a little meeting with a private family. You spoke" on "the near coming of Christ." James objected that this could not happen on this trip, for no Adventists lived between where they were and Saratoga Springs. Ellen insisted the vision concerned "this trip," yet conceded, "I cannot see how it can come to pass." Hours later James remembered an Adventist family on their route. They stopped and were warmly

welcomed. After supper the family called in all the neighbors, and James White preached to them on the soon return of Christ. Marion later stated, "Not once from that time to this has Satan ever tempted me to doubt your visions" (Crawford to EGW, Oct. 9, 1908 [DF 349, EGWE-GC]; 1Bio 224-226).

Marion and her brother, Lewis, spent two years as press workers while the *Review and Herald* was being published in *Rochester, New York. In 1854 she moved with her family to Illinois, where in 1860 she married Delos Truesdaill. After his death she moved to Battle Creek, where in 1892 she married Franklin Crawford. In her later years Ellen White wrote several letters appealing for loans to help her prepare and translate her books (Lt 231, 1904; Lt 349, 1904; Lt 328, 1908; Lt 356, 1908) and to encourage Marion (Lt 122, 1907; Lt 126, 1907).

Further reading: obit. RH, Dec. 18, 1913.

CRISLER, CLARENCE CREAGER (1877-1936). *Literary assistant to Ellen G. White, and

COURTESY OF THE ELLEN G. WHITE ESTATE, INC.

CLARENCE C. AND
MINNIE CRISLER

missionary. Born in Brooklyn, Iowa, Crisler was 5 years old when his parents became Seventh-day Adventists. He graduated from high school in Florida (1892), was baptized the following year, and attended *Battle Creek College (1895-1897). He served as private secretary to General Conference presidents *O. A. Olsen, *G. A. Irwin, and *A. G. Daniells, and in 1901 became Ellen White's private secretary at her Elmshaven home in northern California. Four years later he married Carolyn Hathaway (1873-1911).

One of Crisler's most demanding assignments while working for Ellen White involved verification of more than 400 historical citations in her book *The Great Controversy.* When she decided in 1910 to prepare a new edition, she instructed her workers to find and credit the sources she had used in preparing the earlier 1888 edition. In this task Crisler traveled to several libraries in California and directed the efforts of other researchers in various parts of the world. His research work gratified Ellen White, who desired to give authoritative references for the historical events she used to illustrate the *great controversy theme. Later he assisted in the preparation of *Prophets and Kings. A dedicated bibliophile, Crisler developed a significant personal library, and in 1913 sold more than 500 volumes to Ellen White for her *library.

In her *will Ellen White named Crisler as one of five members of a board of trustees to manage her estate, and he served as first secretary of this board (1915-1917). In 1916, while traveling with *A. G. Daniells on a trip to the Orient, he was asked by the General Conference to serve as secretary of the Far Eastern Division, with headquarters in Shanghai, China. The next year he married Minnie Hawkins (1874-1963), who joined him in his new assignment. He was ordained by *I. H. Evans in 1922. While overseas Crisler retained membership on the White Estate board of trustees, but in 1926 specified *J. E. Fulton to serve "in my stead at such times as I am not in the States" (Crisler to Trustees of the Ellen G. White Estate, Nov. 3, 1926).

In 1925 Crisler completed work on a manuscript entitled *Organization, Its Character, Purpose, Place, and Development in the Seventh-day Adventist Church.* The manuscript was considered of such value that it was published posthumously by the Review and Herald in 1938, with a foreword by then General Conference president J. L. McElhany. Another book published posthumously, *China's Borderlands and Beyond* (RHPA, 1937), was autobiographical, giving an account of mission work in Tibet, Mongolia, and other remote areas. Crisler died of pneumonia while on a trip to Tibet in 1936 and is buried in Lanchow, China.

See also: Homes of James and Ellen G. White.

Further reading: 6Bio 302-321, 324-337; obit. RH, Apr. 9, May 21, 1936; obit. *The China Division Reporter* 6 (May 1936):5; *Legacy of Light* CD-ROM, article, Clarence C. Crisler; A. W. Spalding, "The Christian: Clarence Creager Crisler" (unpublished manuscript, DF 471, EGWE-GC); *SDA Encyclopedia* (1996), vol. 10, p. 419.

Kenneth H. Wood

CROSIER (or CROZIER), OWEN RUSSELL LOOMIS (1820-1912). Millerite preacher and early expositor of the *sanctuary doctrine. Born in Ontario County, New York, Crosier received ministerial training at the Wesleyan Seminary at Lima, Livingston County, in the late 1830s and early 1840s. In 1843 he joined the Millerite movement and began to lecture on the second coming of Christ. On the morning of the *disappointment, October 23, 1844, *Hiram Edson of Port Gibson, New York, invited a friend (identified by J. N. Loughborough as Crosier) to go with him to encourage a few Millerite families. While walking through a cornfield, Edson received a pivotal insight (perhaps a short vision) that on October 22 Christ had moved from the holy place into the Most Holy Place of the heavenly sanctuary to receive the kingdom from His Father (see Dan. 7:9-14; 8:14). Hence, the Millerite expectation that Christ would return to earth on that day was mistaken. This insight led Edson, Crosier, and Franklin B. Hahn to an in-depth Bible study of the cleansing of the sanctuary (Dan. 8:14).

Some of the group's preliminary views

appeared in the first issue of the *Day-Dawn, edited by Crosier and published by Hahn in Canandaigua, New York, in March 1845. But the first issue of the Day-Dawn had a limited circulation and its content did not go much beyond the notion that the eschatological marriage mentioned in Matthew 25:1-13 was the heavenly antitype of the Day of Atonement described in Leviticus 16. Crosier's view on the two-phase atonement in the heavenly sanctuary became more evident in a few of his letters published in 1845 in the Hope of Israel (Apr. 17), the Day-Star (Oct. 11, Nov. 15), and the Voice of Truth (Oct. 29). His most extensive and mature treatment of the subject is his article "The Law of Moses," published in the Day-Star "Extra" of February 7, 1846, with an endorsing note by Edson and Hahn.

The Day-Star "Extra" led Joseph Bates, James White, Ellen G. Harmon (White), and several others to a deeper understanding of Christ's two-phase priestly ministry in the heavenly sanctuary, and set the stage for the development of the Sabbatarian Adventist doctrine of the sanctuary. Ellen White wrote in 1847, "The Lord shew me in vision, more than one year ago, that Brother Crosier had the true light, on the cleansing of the Sanctuary, &c; and that it was his will, that Brother C. should write out the view which he gave us in the Day-Star, Extra, February 7, 1846. I feel fully authorized by the Lord, to recommend that Extra, to every saint" (WLF 12). This statement confirms the general tenor of Crosier's article without necessarily endorsing all its details.

In 1846, through the influence of Joseph Bates, Crosier reluctantly accepted the seventh-day Sabbath, and kept it for about a year. His decision in 1847 to join Joseph Marsh in editing the Advent Harbinger, in Rochester, New York, marked a major theological turning point. From then on Crosier opposed the seventh-day Sabbath and even his own earlier sanctuary doctrine, and began to advocate the "age-to-come" theory. Soon he also changed the spelling of his name to Crozier (with a "z"). In 1854 he moved to Grand Rapids, Michigan, where he worked as an evangelist for the Michigan Conference of the *Advent Christian Church. He died in Grand Rapids on September 15, 1912.

See also: Adventist Denominations.

Further reading: O.R.L. Crozier, "Early History of Ontario County Revealed in Story of Late Owen R. L. Crozier," The Daily Messenger (Canandaigua, N.Y.: Nov. 22, 1923), pp. 17, 22, 23; A. R. Timm, "O.R.L. Crosier: A Biographical Introduction" (research paper, AU, 1991); M. D. Burt, "The Day-Dawn of Canandaigua, New York: Reprint of a Significant Millerite Adventist Journal," AUSS 44, no. 2 (Autumn 2006): 317-330; M. D. Burt, "The Extended Atonement View in the Day-Dawn and the Emergence of Sabbatarian Adventism," AUSS 44, no. 2 (Autumn 2006): 331-339; SDA Encyclopedia (1996), vol. 10, p. 420.

Alberto R. Timm

CURROW, ETHEL MAY (LACEY), see **WHITE, ETHEL MAY (LACEY).**

CURTIS, ELI. Millerite who wrote articles for the *Day-Dawn (Canandaigua, New York) and *Day-Star (Cincinnati, Ohio). In a letter to Curtis (Apr. 21, 1847), reprinted in WLF 11, 12, Ellen White responded to several of his theological ideas. Between 1848 and 1850, as editor of the journal Girdle of Truth, Curtis reprinted excerpts from her visions contrary to her wishes (PT, May 1850; RH, Apr. 7, 1851). By 1851 he had become a spiritist. "I am not responsible," wrote Ellen White in 1883, "for all that has been printed as coming from me. About the time that my earliest visions were first published, several articles did appear purporting to have been written by me, and to relate what the Lord had shown me, but sanctioning doctrines which I did not believe. These were published in a paper edited by a Mr. Curtis" (Ms 4, 1883; 1SM 60, 61).

Further reading: SDA Encyclopedia (1996), vol. 10, pp. 424, 425.

CZECHOWSKI, MICHAEL BELINA (1818-1876). Former Roman Catholic priest, political

COURTESY OF THE REVIEW AND HERALD PUBLISHING ASSOCIATION

MICHAEL B. CZECHOWSKI

reformer in Poland and *Europe, who after his conversion to Adventism in America became the pioneer missionary of Adventism to Europe. Born in Poland, Czechowski attended school in Cracow, became a Bernardine monk, and was later ordained as a Franciscan reformer father. As a priest he opted in favor of the revolutionary fever sweeping Europe and aimed at social and political changes in the Old World. Friend and contemporary of many notable Polish intellectuals, he had a disappointing audience with Pope Gregory XVI in mid-October 1844, and slowly became disenchanted with Catholicism. Yet he continued as a priest-reformer first among Polish emigrants in Paris, and then fostering temperance activities in his homeland until 1850. After resigning from the priesthood, he married and sailed to New York in 1851.

Shortly after his arrival Czechowski became a Baptist minister and, in 1856, heard *James White and others preach about Christ's second coming. In 1857 he embraced Adventism at a camp meeting in Findley, Ohio. James White referred to him as "our good Brother Czechowski." James and Ellen White often gave money to support Czechowski's missionary activities

among immigrants in New York and Vermont. He wrote and published an autobiography entitled *Thrilling and Instructive Developments: An Experience of Fifteen Years as Roman Catholic Clergyman and Priest* (1862). Initially the church supported his work, but its leaders were not yet ready to support a foreign mission, because of a lack of funds. Experiencing continued difficulties to support himself and his family of six, and eager to return to Poland, Czechowski set his sights on moving back to Europe and becoming an Adventist missionary there. This he did on May 14, 1864, financing his travel from the sale of his book and with private donations from first-day Evangelical Adventists in Boston, who became his main supporters. He sailed for Europe with his family and with Annie Butler, the sister of later General Conference president *George I. Butler.

Ellen White mentioned Czechowski as the subject of a vision she received August 3, 1861, in Roosevelt, New York. From that vision she counseled him as to what would, and did, happen if he went his own way—"discouragement," "blame of the brethren," and "[exhausting] of their patience." But she also stated: "Your zeal is good. You are ambitious to see the work moving forward. You are conscientious and perfectly honest before God" (Lt 3, 1864).

Ten years before *J. N. Andrews became the first official foreign missionary of the denomination, Czechowski established himself among the *Waldenses in the Italian Piedmont valleys, where he baptized his first convert, Catherine Revel, and his first European coworker, Jean P. Geymet. Within four years some 50 people were baptized and Switzerland's Lake Neuchatel became the center of his mission. He established a printing press, published *L'Évangile Éternel*, a weekly missionary magazine, and in 1867 organized the first Adventist congregation in Tramelan, where 19 years later in 1886 Ellen White would preach a dedication sermon and visit on several occasions. Unable to sustain the operation of a diversified mission, abandoned by his supporters from Boston, and at odds with the leadership of the Seventh-day Adventist Church in Battle Creek, Czechowski moved on to France, Hungary, and finally to Romania, where he preached Adventist beliefs and established a foundation for what is now the largest national Seventh-day Adventist church in Europe.

On December 29, 1871, the church confirmed the missionary accomplishments of Czechowski in Europe when it stated, "We deem it duty to acknowledge the hand of God in planting the truth in Switzerland" ("Business Proceedings of the Tenth Annual Session of Seventh-day Adventists," RH, Jan. 2, 1872). In 1869 Adventist leaders had already reported on Czechowski's activities in Europe when J. N. Andrews, who was later to sail for Europe, stated that "we cannot take any credit to ourselves for being instrumental in raising up this company of commandment-keepers [in Europe]. . . . We should have taken greater pains to explain things that were misunderstood by him, and should have had greater interest in this noble hearted man" (J. N. Andrews, "The Seventh-day Adventists in Europe," RH, Nov. 30, 1869). Prior to his departure for Europe, Andrews wrote that Czechowski was not a "prudent manager, especially in financial matters," and was not supported in his mission to Europe by his church, but he admitted that Adventist leaders "regarded Eld. C. as an upright man, and one that feared God" (JNA, "The case of Eld. M. B. Czechowski," RH, July 8, 1873).

Czechowski died in Vienna, Austria, in 1876 and was buried in a common grave in the Central Friedhof Cemetery.

See also: Roman Catholic Church.

Further reading: M. B. Czechowski, *Thrilling and Instructive Developments: An Experience of Fifteen Years as Roman Catholic Clergyman and Priest* (Boston: by the author, 1862); R. L. Dabrowski and B. B. Beach, eds., *Michael Belina Czechowski, 1818-1876, Results of the Historical Symposium About His Life and Work Held in Warsaw, Poland, May 17-23, 1976, Commemorating the Hundredth Anniversary of His Death* (Warsaw, Poland: Znaki Czasu Pub. House, 1979); *SDA Encyclopedia* (1996), vol. 10, pp. 428, 429.

Rajmund L. Dabrowski

DAIGNEAU, JOHN M. (1832-1922) and **VITALINE M. (DION)** (1834-1908). French Canadian

COURTESY OF THE CENTER FOR ADVENTIST RESEARCH, ANDREWS UNIVERSITY.

JOHN DAIGNEAU

emigrants to Brandon, Vermont, who married in 1851. About 1854 the Daigneaus relocated to Battle Creek, Michigan, where John worked as a stonemason. In 1856 the Daigneaus bought property near to the lot on Champion Street, where Deacon *John White's home was later built, and the Wood Street home of James and Ellen White. (All three homes are now a part of Historic Adventist Village.) About that time, possibly through the influence of the Whites, the Daigneaus became Sabbatarian Adventists. In 1861 Ellen White wrote a letter of admonition to John (Lt 10, 1861). On November 5, 1862, John witnessed Ellen White in vision at the home of his next-door neighbor, J. N. Loughborough. Having never before seen her in vision, Daigneau proceeded to apply "many tests" until he was convinced that "she did not breathe" and "admitted that there was superhuman strength connected with [this] vision" (JNL, *Rise and Progress*, pp. 247, 248).

In 1863 John translated from French to English the letters from *Jean Vuilleumier, a Sabbathkeeping Adventist in Europe, to the General Conference in Battle Creek. In 1872 Ellen White wrote another testimony mentioning the Daigneau family (*Special Testimony for the Battle Creek Church*, pp. 19-25). Shortly thereafter they returned to Quebec, where they lived for 30 years before moving about 1902 to Benton Harbor, Michigan, to be near their children; they are both buried in Benton Harbor.

Further reading: obit. Benton Harbor *News Palladium,* May 29, 1922; obit. Benton Harbor *News Palladium,* Sept. 17, 1908; JNL, *Rise and Progress of the Seventh-day Adventists* (Battle Creek, Mich.: General Conference of SDA, 1892).

Michael W. Campbell

DAMMAN (also **DAMON, DAMMON**), **ISRAEL** (1811-1886). A Freewill Baptist-turned-Millerite preacher, associated briefly after 1844 with Ellen Harmon and James White in Maine. Later Damman became an Advent Christian minister (see *Adventist Denominations). He was remembered as "one of the most noisy and unaccountable of men," whose preaching was "especially conspicuous by shouting and jumping" (I. Wellcome, *History of the Second Advent Message and Mission* [Yarmouth, Maine: by the author, 1874], p. 350). In 1838 he married Lydia Rich; they had at least three children.

Damman's first recorded contact with Ellen Harmon and James White was at Exeter, Maine, in early February 1845. Apparently, based upon Ellen's vision of the "Bridegroom" given her there, Damman accepted the unfolding *shut door understanding.

From Exeter, James and Ellen traveled with Damman to Atkinson, Maine. There on Saturday night, February 15, 1845, at a meeting held in the home of James Ayer, Jr., Damman was arrested. Newspaper accounts of the subsequent trial reported on the activities of various ones that evening, including James and Ellen, though Damman was the only person actually being tried.

Despite attempts to locate the original court transcripts, the only account found to date is from the March 7, 1845, Piscataquis *Farmer*. In the reporter's introduction, he says he "abridged . . . [the] testimony," having "omitted . . . the most unimportant part, . . . but endeavored in no case to misrepresent" any witness ("Trial of Elder I. Dammon: Reported for the Piscataquis *Farmer,*" Piscataquis *Farmer* [Dover, Maine], Mar. 7, 1845).

Damman was charged with being "a vagrant and idle person, . . . going about . . . town . . . begging: . . . a common railer, or brawler, neglecting his calling, or employment, misspending his earnings, and . . . not [providing] for the support of himself [or] family." By all accounts the Saturday night meeting was noisy. The stated purpose for the gathering was so that Ellen Harmon and Dorinda Baker, another visionary, could share their visions.

Despite not being on trial, the activities of Ellen, James, and Dorinda all engendered considerable discussion by both prosecution and defense witnesses. Damman, during his own self-defense, as summarized in the newspaper, did not mention any of the three. But both prosecution and defense witnesses did. Dorinda was known to several defense witnesses, though none previously knew Ellen. Despite that, several testified to their belief in both women's visions. One prosecution witness appeared particularly hostile to Ellen, stating that she was called "Imitation of Christ," something denied by all defense witnesses who spoke to the issue.

Differences also occurred regarding descriptions of Dorinda Baker's activities that evening. Part of the time she was in a back room of the house making a "noise." Some claimed that men were in the room with her, including James White, though such charges were strongly denied by the defense witnesses. It was later confirmed that others besides James went into the bedroom to assist Dorinda during her "exercise." The one agreement among the witnesses pertained to what Ellen did that night. All stated that she was lying quietly on the floor, except when she sat up to relate a vision.

Dorinda's main message was to a man she claimed thought badly of her. In contrast, Ellen's comments all had a sense of urgency to them. Because of the group's belief that Jesus would return within days, it was reported that Ellen urged several to be baptized that night rather than risk going to "hell," a word possibly used by the reporter to summarize Ellen's comments, since nowhere else in her writings does she use such strong language.

Interestingly, despite being in the midst of all the fanatical activities that evening, not once was either Ellen or James shown to be involved. A point of interest is the contrasting accounts given by the newspaper reporter and Ellen White regarding Israel Damman's arrest that evening. The newspaper account reported that twice the sheriff had to send for reinforcements in order to extricate Damman from the meeting (Lt 2, 1874). In contrast, Ellen White later recalled that despite 12 reinforcements, the sheriff could not free Damman until God's power released him (2SG 40, 41; "Notes From a Talk With Mrs. E. G. White, Dec. 12, 1906" [DF 733-c, EGWE-GC]). Despite these unresolved differences, in *Spiritual Gifts*, volume 2, five witnesses attested to the accuracy of Ellen White's account regarding Damman's arrest (2SG 302). At court, apparently his conviction was eventually overturned.

The April 3, 1845, issue of *The Morning Watch* warned Adventists against "Israel Dammon, and John Moody, two married men, and Miss Dorinda Baker," who were traveling together to different places "teaching disgusting extravagances." Reference was made to the fact that "[Dammon's] . . . trial in Maine has been reported in all the papers."

About the same time Damman was again arrested regarding two other noisy meetings held in Garland, Maine. Apparently neither Ellen nor James were present, though Dorinda Baker was mentioned in one warrant. However, she was not listed as appearing before the justice of the peace the following day.

Later that year Ellen and James met Damman in Garland. Ellen would recall that there she had to oppose Damman's fanaticism. As a result, he rejected her testimonies and became her "enemy." Among other things, Damman believed that Christ had returned and that the dead had already been raised spiritually.

The last time Ellen and James apparently traveled with Damman, Joseph Bates was also present. Miraculously, the borrowed "partly broken colt" James was driving stood completely still the entire time Ellen was in vision, despite James' several attempts to make it proceed. The precise date of this story is unknown, though apparently it was after the Whites were married. That seems late, however, given Ellen's own comments regarding her interactions with Damman.

In the mid-1870s Sundaykeeping Adventists launched several attacks against Ellen White. In one Damman claimed that in vision years earlier she had seen him "crowned in the kingdom of God," but later she saw him "lost" (Miles Grant, *The True Sabbath: Which Day Shall We Keep? An Explanation of Mrs. Ellen G. White's Visions* [Boston: Advent Christian

Publication Society, 1874], p. 70). Although she acknowledged having seen him and others, she also recalled having cautioned them "not to become exalted, lest they lose [their] crowns" (Ms 7, 1876).

Further reading: Lt 3, 1847; Lt 2, 1874; G. H. Wallace, "Memories of Israel Dammon," *The World's Crisis*, Jan. 24, 1904; I. Dammon, "Letter From Bro. Dammon," *Jubilee Standard*, June 4, 1844; "State vs. Damon," *Penobscot County Court Records*, Apr. 8, 1845, Apr. 25, 1845, and Apr. 26, 1845; M. D. Burt, "The Historical Background, Interconnected Development, and Integration of the Doctrines of the Sanctuary, the Sabbath, and Ellen G. White's Role in Sabbatarian Adventism from 1844 to 1849" (Ph.D. diss., AU, 2002), p. 131.

James R. Nix

DANIELLS, ARTHUR GROSVENOR (1858-1935).

Minister and administrator. Born in Iowa, the son of a Union Army surgeon who died in the Civil War, Daniells accepted Seventh-day Adventism at the age of 10. Determined to make something of his life, he enrolled at Battle Creek College, but ill-health forced him to give up after only one year, and he began teaching public school. In 1877 he came under conviction to enter the gospel ministry. But when he offered his services to the denomination, the Iowa Conference committee rejected him. The next year, though, he joined *Robert M. Kilgore in Texas and became secretary to James and Ellen White for about six months. In later years he looked back fondly on the experience and came to consider her as a sort of second mother (Robertson, p. 99). He and Ellen White remained close for the rest of her life. Also

COURTESY OF THE CENTER FOR ADVENTIST RESEARCH, ANDREWS UNIVERSITY

ARTHUR G. DANIELLS

he worked closely with her son *William C. White. Daniells would consult him about Ellen White's thinking and thus not burden her directly with the many crises troubling the church, especially after 1901.

*George I. Butler invited Daniells in 1880 to preach back in Iowa. During his stay in the state he was ordained and successfully did what was then known as city mission evangelism. In 1886 he received a call to New Zealand, becoming only the third Adventist minister south of the equator. From 1889 to 1891 he served as president of the New Zealand Conference and from 1892 to 1895 as president of the Australian Conference. When Ellen White arrived in Australia, Daniells began to work closely with her. He became the first president of the Central Australian Conference in 1895 and then president of the Australasian Union Conference.

In Australia the denomination experimented with a number of new administrative structures. Tradition credits Daniells with helping to develop them, but some of them were first tried in South Africa and elsewhere. Historical evidence reveals that Daniells initially opposed such concepts as the departmental organization of local conferences and the creation of division conferences (Robertson, pp. 81, 82). But when he saw their merits in operation, he quickly began to support them.

By the end of the nineteenth century the denomination's limited organization was no longer adequate to serve the needs of a growing worldwide membership. It needed a new administrative structure that was more responsive to both local and global challenges. The church was all but bankrupt financially. When the *General Conference session of 1901 decided to grapple with some of the problems the church faced, it drafted Daniells as president because of his involvement in the various successful administrative experiments in Australia. Tradition often assumes that he was Ellen White's personal choice for president, but her correspondence indicates otherwise (Lts 121, 139, 1900). Daniells did constantly counsel with her, however, either directly or through her son, as the new administrative structures evolved.

The first decades of the twentieth century were traumatic ones for the Adventist Church. The *Kellogg controversy, along with problems associated with *A. T. Jones, *A. F. Ballenger, and others, threatened the very existence of the denomination. But Daniells' strong leadership was a major factor in holding the church together. He directed the transfer of the General Conference headquarters and the Review and Herald Publishing Association from Battle Creek to Washington, D.C. In addition, he championed the growth of missions around the world, city evangelism, and the teaching of righteousness by faith.

Daniells' single-minded and sometimes aggressive administrative style frequently created opposition. He could be harsh and impatient with incompetence or consume valuable time and effort dealing with details that he should have left to others. Although Ellen White strongly supported him, she would confront his flaws and mistakes when necessary. Once she refused to see him after he had traveled all the way to Elmshaven. His cautiousness toward using her unpublished material after her death contributed to an estrangement for several years between him and W. C. White (Robertson, pp. 106-108).

Resistance to Daniells' administrative style, along with his candid discussions of how the prophetic role operated in the life of Ellen White, especially at the 1919 Bible and history teachers conferences, eventually cost him the presidency. The 1922 General Conference session nominating committee deadlocked until Daniells withdrew his name from consideration. He served as secretary of the General Conference (1922-1926) and then as head of the denomination's ministerial association until his death.

His close association with Ellen White had taught him that her prophetic role did not always conform to the popular understanding of a prophet (see his discussion at the *Bible conference of 1919, *Spectrum* 10, no. 1 [Spring 1979]: 27-57). Unlike many of his contemporaries, though, Daniells was able to hold in balance both his firm conviction of the authenticity of her gift and role and the fact that he did not always understand how they functioned. Taking neither a rigid verbal inspiration approach (as many did), nor rejecting her (as some others did), Daniells acknowledged that there was a mystery to the working of the Holy Spirit in her life that human beings could not fully explain. He acknowledged the existence of rumors that he did not believe in her (*Spectrum* 10, no. 1 [Spring 1979]: 37, 43, 56), but he spent the rest of his life supporting her work and writings. His book *Christ Our Righteousness* (1926) expounded that topic from Scripture and the writings of Ellen White, in the context of Adventist history. The final revisions of his last book, *The Abiding Gift of Prophecy,* he completed in the hospital the day before his death.

In her last will and testament Ellen White named Daniells as one of the five original trustees of her estate. He was chair of the Ellen G. White Estate from 1915 to 1935.

Further reading: A. G. Daniells, *The Abiding Gift of Prophecy* (PPPA, 1936); G. R. Knight, *Organizing to Beat the Devil: The Development of Adventist Church Structure* (RHPA, 2001), pp. 103-140; M. C. Kuhn, *Leader of Men: The Life of Arthur G. Daniells* (RHPA, 1946); J. Moon, *W. C. White and Ellen G. White* (AUP, 1993), pp. 239, 240, see also pp. 155-210, 268-413; J. J. Robertson, *A. G. Daniells:*

The Making of a General Conference President, 1901 (PPPA, 1977); *SDA Encyclopedia* (1996), vol. 10, pp. 439, 440.

Gerald Wheeler

DANIELS, E. P. Adventist pastor and evangelist, no relation to *A. G. Daniells (note difference in spelling). The case of E. P. Daniels shows Ellen White's method of dealing with erring believers. To colleagues who criticized him, she emphasized his strengths and potential (5MR 243-245). To Daniels himself, she reproved his failings, but continually encouraged him that through the grace of God he could add real spiritual maturity to his natural talents (21MR 333). Daniels had at least three children, a daughter Zua (PH096 15, 45-48), a son Paul (3MR 212, 213; 4MR 164, 165), and a younger daughter (DG 204). When Paul was about 7 years old, Ellen White invited him to give his heart to the Lord. "I gave myself to Jesus," wrote Ellen White, "when I was not as old as you now are" (Lt 12, 1889, in 4MR 164).

COURTESY OF THE CENTER FOR ADVENTIST RESEARCH, ANDREWS UNIVERSITY.

E. P. DANIELS

Ellen White heard Daniels in Michigan and recognized him as an effective preacher (RH, Dec. 2, 1884). In 1885, in Healdsburg, California, his preaching led to revival, but was followed by fanaticism (5MR 243; 21MR 333). Ellen White affirmed that the revival was "genuine" and its "fruits were good," but that "the enemy always works" when God's cause is advancing (5MR 243-245; 21MR 147, 332-335).

Daniels' evangelism in Fresno, California, in 1887 produced some spectacular conversions (6MR 150, 151; see also *Will Smith). Ellen White publicly commended his ministry (ST, Apr. 20, 1888), but privately urged his

need of thorough conversion (PH096 23, 41, 42, 63). That September he "sought the Lord," became "entirely changed in spirit," and confessed his wrongs. Spiritually renewed, he became an instrument of revival to the Fresno church (1888 Materials 51, 53, 57-64). Unfortunately, both he and the congregation seemed to credit the revival to his personal talents as a preacher. Within a few months he reneged on his confession and became impervious to reproof (PH096 64, 65, 71-73), and had left the denomination by 1893 (Lt 40, 1893, in 1888 Materials 1209).

"Elder Daniels' peculiar talent is to move the feelings of the people," Ellen White observed. "But the examination of his own heart, his acts and motives, to see whether they are in accordance with the perfect standard of righteousness, is not pleasing to him. He has no desire to meditate and pray" (PH028 6, 8).

Jerry Moon

DAVIS, MARY ANN "MARIAN" (1847-1904). Ellen White's longtime companion, *literary assistant, editor, and compiler. She was born in North Berwick, Maine, August 21, 1847. At an early age she followed her parents in becoming Sabbathkeeping Adventists. In 1868 Marian's family moved to Battle Creek, Michigan, where they first became acquainted with James and Ellen White. A year of teaching in a country schoolhouse resulted in a complete breakdown of Marian's health. After being healed in answer to prayer, she worked for several years as a proofreader at the Review and Herald.

COURTESY OF THE CENTER FOR ADVENTIST RESEARCH, ANDREWS UNIVERSITY.

MARIAN DAVIS

On New Year's Day, 1879, Marian joined the Whites in Denison, Texas, as their literary helper. Ellen White was delighted. On January 6 she wrote her son Willie, "Marian is just what we need. She is splendid help" (Lt 4, 1879). For the next 25 years Marian was a permanent fixture in the White household. During this period a strong personal relationship developed between Ellen White and Marian. According to Marian's coworker, *Nellie Druillard, "Miss Davis loved her [Ellen White] dearly and Sister White thought that Marian was an angel" (Nellie Druillard to D. E. Robinson, Sept. 22, 1933).

In late April 1879 Marian, with the Whites and 28 others, embarked on an overland trek through Indian Territory (Oklahoma) to Kansas and Colorado. Later that year she returned to Battle Creek with the Whites. In 1882, a few months after James White died, Marian moved with Ellen White to Healdsburg, California. When Ellen White went to Europe in August 1885, Marian remained for six months near the publishing house in Battle Creek, caring for Ellen White's interests. Then, in February 1886, she joined Ellen White in Basel. When they returned to Battle Creek in 1887, Marian continued to live with Ellen White—in Michigan; at Healdsburg, California; in Australia; and finally at Elmshaven, near St. Helena, California.

Marian's primary responsibility was the fashioning of books from Ellen White's writings. Ellen White explained, "She is my bookmaker. . . . In preparing a chapter for a book, Marian remembers that I have written something on that special point, which may make the matter more forcible. She begins to search for this, and if when she finds it, she sees that it will make the chapter more clear, she adds it" (3SM 91). Marian did not depend on her memory alone to locate the desired materials. She made dozens of scrapbooks on various subjects from Ellen White's writings and drew from these as needed.

Among the books Marian prepared were *The Spirit of Prophecy*, volume 4 (1884), *The Great Controversy* (1888), *Testimonies for the Church*, volume 5 (1889), *Patriarchs and Prophets* (1890), *Steps to Christ* (1892), *Thoughts From the Mount of Blessing* (1896), *The Desire of Ages* (1898), *Christ's Object Lessons* (1900), *Testimonies for the Church*, volume 6 (1900), and *The Ministry of Healing* (1905) (D. E. Robinson to W. K. Kellogg, May 12, 1942, EGWE-LLU). Marian died of tuberculosis at St. Helena, California, on October 25, 1904. Her sister Ella (Mrs. W. K. Kellogg) and her niece Beth Kellogg cared for her during her final illness.

Further reading: obit. RH, Dec. 1, 1904; E. Lantry, *Miss Marian's Gold* (PPPA, 1981); R. W. Olson, "How *The Desire of Ages* Was Written" (EGWE, 1979, SDoc); *SDA Encyclopedia* (1996), vol. 10, p. 444.

Robert Olson

DAVIS, NATHANIEL "NATTIE" A. (1866-1945). *Colporteur and staff member of the Bible Echo Publishing House in *Australia. Converted to Adventism in the mid-1890s, Davis was described by Ellen White as a talented person, but financial debts soon brought discouragement and despair. Davis wrote to Ellen White asking for a message from the Lord, even if it was one of rebuke. In August 1897 he met with Ellen White several times and thereafter reentered the colporteur work. On August 15 his case was opened to Ellen White in vision, revealing the dual problems of debt and demonic influence (Lt 36, 1897, in 13MR 1-5).

Ellen White was concerned for Davis and asked *A. G. Daniells to visit him (Lt 39, 1897, in 15MR 338-344). With this letter she sent a personal *testimony for Daniells to read to Davis (Ms 176, 1897). Sensing the urgency, Daniells went immediately to visit his home. During this meeting Davis became very upset and even wielded a knife. Daniells reported that those present dropped to their knees in prayer. "The first thing I said," wrote Daniells, "was 'O Lord, we come to Thee in the all-prevailing name of Jesus.' . . . At the mention of the all-powerful name of Jesus he broke into sobs and the violence disappeared" (AGD to EGW, Sept. 12, 1897, EGWE-GC). After prayer, Daniells asked if the message was true, and Davis acknowledged that it was. Davis later wrote, "It affords me the most sincere pleasure to have the privilege of putting on record my appreciation of Sister E. G. White's work and my gratitude to my heavenly Father for the messages sent through her to His people. The faithful witness, thus bourne [sic], revealed to me the means whereby the bondage of Satan was broken when, owing to the influence of spiritualism, I had well nigh become a spiritual wreck. I have every reason to be positive in my confidence in Sister E. G. White as a true prophet" (Ellen White Autograph Album, dated Aug. 6, 1900, at Geelong, Victoria, Australia, EGWE-GC).

Further reading: R. W. Coon, *The Great Visions of Ellen G. White* (RHPA, 1992), pp. 108-121; H. M. Blunden to "Members of the North Fitzroy Church" (Aug. 8, 1957, EGWE-LLU).

Michael W. Campbell

DAVISON, LURA ELLEN (HUTCHINS) (1861-1960). Temperance worker. In 1888 she married Thomas Davison, held temperance meetings, and became a state secretary of the Women's Christian Temperance Union. After her husband's death in 1901 she returned to school, graduating from Washington Foreign Mission Seminary in 1909. During her student years Davison wrote a letter (no longer extant) to Ellen White, who encouraged her to study the Word of God as the "great need" for "calling the attention of the minds of men to Christ" (Lt 384, 1907). The letter contains several references concerning the qualifications and work of Christian teachers and the need of "self denial" to support "mission schools." Davison later taught school in 16 states, and served five years as a self-supporting missionary in Honduras and Panama.

Further reading: obit. PUR, Mar. 28, 1960.

DECKER, HENRY W. (1837-1926). Son of a pioneer Baptist minister in Wisconsin, Decker accepted Adventism in 1859. He and three others successfully appealed to the governor of Wisconsin to permit Adventist men to be noncombatants during the Civil War. Decker served as conference president in Wisconsin, Texas, and the Pacific Northwest, where he helped establish Walla Walla College and the Portland Sanitarium. He was probably the "Elder Decker" addressed in Lt 82, 1886.

Further reading: SDA Encyclopedia (1996), vol. 10, p. 452.

Brian E. Strayer

DIGGINS (or **DIGGINGS**), **WESLEY** (1806-1876) and **ELIZA.** Wesley Diggins was an Adventist in San Francisco, California, who accepted the Sabbath in 1872 (Lt 18, 1872). Ellen White wrote him a letter warning against the "dangerous" influence of a Mrs. S. E. Harris, who was disrupting the San Francisco Church (Lt 22, 1872). James and Ellen White had dinner in their residence on at least two occasions (Ms 5, 1872; Lt 2a, 1873), and they developed a close friendship. Eliza made "no profession of being a follower of Christ," which prompted a letter from Ellen White appealing for her to accept Christ (Lt 8, 1873). Wesley was one of three individuals (with James White and a "Brother" Morrison) chiefly responsible for the building of the first San Francisco church. He died soon after the house of worship was built (Ms 2, 1901; Lt 164, 1906).

DODGE, ABRAM A. (1817-1892) and **CAROLINE (SMITH)** (1830-1915). Early Sabbatarian Adventists from Jackson, Michigan. Abram was a traveling clock repairer, *Review and Herald* agent, music dealer, and beekeeper who shared his faith door to door. In 1851 he married Caroline, the oldest daughter of *Cyrenius and Louisa Smith. The Dodges were friends of James and Ellen White. Ellen White wrote several letters to them describing her desire to see Jesus return (Lts 4, 9, 1851), soliciting their prayers and offering advice (Lts 5, 6, 1853). On May 23, 1854, the Whites left Jackson on their way to Wisconsin. As they boarded the train, Ellen White felt impressed to move back to the last car on the train. Three miles (five kilometers) out of Jackson, the train crashed. Their car was separated from the wreck by about 100 feet (30 meters). Ellen White claimed that God had sent an angel to separate their car, which spared their lives. James White hiked back to the Cyrenius Smith home, from which James White and Abram Dodge took a carriage to return and pick up Ellen White.

Further reading: 1Bio 294-297; LS 153, 154; RH, Jan. 27, 1885; JNL, *Rise and Progress of the Seventh-day Adventists* (Battle Creek, Mich.: General Conference of SDA, 1892), pp. 200, 201.

DONALDSON, EDITH, see **BROWNSBERGER, EDITH (DONALDSON)**.

DONNELL, R. S., see **HOLY FLESH MOVEMENT**.

DRUILLARD, NELLIE HELEN (RANKIN) (1844-1937) and **ALMA** (1835-1903). Adventist church workers and missionaries. Alma was a businessman; Nellie, a school superintendent. Soon after they joined the Adventist Church in 1879, Alma entered the colporteur work. In 1889 they went as missionaries to South

COURTESY OF THE CENTER FOR ADVENTIST RESEARCH, ANDREWS UNIVERSITY.

NELLIE DRUILLARD

Africa, where they remained until 1895. While in South Africa, Nellie served as treasurer of the conference, secretary of the tract society, and secretary of the South African Women's Christian Temperance Union. Upon their return they spent several years at the Boulder Sanitarium where she served as matron and accountant, and Alma as treasurer. In December 1900 Ellen White invited the Druillards to join her staff at Elmshaven (Lt 161, 1900). The Druillards stayed for less than a year, Nellie serving as *literary assistant and Alma as a bookkeeper (Lt 167, 1901; 5Bio 46). Alma also supervised the construction of an office building behind Ellen White's Elmshaven home (5Bio 121). When it came time for them to leave, Ellen White urged them to stay, but respected their conviction that the Lord was calling them to join the staff of Emmanuel Missionary College (Lt 167, 1901). Even after they left, Ellen White continued to send them literary materials to critique (Lt 116, 1902). When Alma died at EMC in December 1903, Ellen White wrote Nellie a letter of sympathy (Lt 3, 1904).

In the summer of 1904 Ellen White accompanied *E. A. Sutherland, Nellie's nephew, and *Percy T. Magan in the selection of land for a self-supporting school in the South. In response to Ellen White's request (Lt 193, 1904), Nellie lent money for the purchase of the land, and soon moved to the Nashville Agricultural and Normal Institute (later *Madison College) to serve as the institution's treasurer and financial advisor. During this time Ellen White remained in close contact with Nellie, frequently offering advice and consenting to serve on the institutional board—the only managing board Ellen White was ever a member of. In 1927 Nellie founded (using mostly her own funds), near Nashville, Tennessee, the Riverside Sanitarium, a medical institution for African-Americans, and administered it until 1935, when she deeded it to the General Conference.

Further reading: obit. ST, Aug. 19, 1937; obit. RH, Jan. 28, 1904; *SDA Encyclopedia* (1996), vol. 10, p. 478; vol. 11, p. 461; *Legacy of Light* CD-ROM, article, Nellie Druillard (1844-1937).

Michael W. Campbell

DUCE, WILLIAM. Adventist who was concerned about Ellen White's counsel on Sunday labor. Duce wrote to Ellen White regarding *Testimonies for the Church*, volume 9, pages 232-238, in which she urges Adventists not to defy *Sunday laws but to instead devote the day to missionary work (originally written to G. A. Irwin as Lt 132, 1902). Duce questioned whether she had actually read the pages prior to publication, and furthermore, if she had, whether she was giving credence to Sundaykeeping. Ellen White replied that she had indeed "read this matter before it went to the printer" and that there is "nothing in it to give one reason to say that Sundaykeeping is there taught. Neither does the counsel there given contradict the Bible, nor former testimonies" (Lt 94, 1910).

DURLAND, JOHN A. and **FLORA** (1851-1915). Adventists from Iowa and missionaries to England (1885-1888). While in England Ellen White stayed in their home (Ms 16a, 1885) and later wrote John a letter of encouragement (Lt 57, 1887). In 1888 they returned to North America and worked in Ontario (1888-1891), California (1891-1895), and Michigan, where John edited the *Youth's Instructor* (1895-1896) and was conference president (1897-1898).

Further reading: obit. RH, Jan. 13, 1916.

EDSON, HIRAM (1806-1882). A Methodist layman turned-Millerite, best known for his cornfield experience near Port Gibson, New York, on the morning of October 23, 1844, which contributed to the development of the Seventh-day Adventist *sanctuary doctrine. Although sorely disappointed that Christ did not return as expected, Edson supported the fledgling Sabbathkeeping Adventist movement with both his time and money. Later he was ordained to the ministry.

The first connection between Edson in western New York State, and James and Ellen White and *Joseph Bates in New England, apparently followed the publication of O.R.L. Crosier's article on the heavenly sanctuary, published in the *Day-Star* Extra of February 7, 1846. A note at the end of the article signed by Hiram Edson and F. B. Hahn appealed for funds to help defray printing costs. In the fall of 1846 Bates traveled to Port Gibson. Originally James White was scheduled to accompany him, but circumstances prevented it. That was the first time Edson and Bates met, and it was when Edson started keeping the Sabbath. In 1847 Ellen White in *A Word to the "Little Flock"* recommended Crosier's 1846 *Day-Star* article, stating that she had been shown in vision more than a year earlier "that Brother Crosier had the true light, on the cleansing of the sanctuary," and that she felt "fully authorized by the Lord, to recommend that Extra, to every saint" (WLF 12). Thus, Ellen White was at least aware of Crosier, Edson, and Hahn's views in early 1846.

Edson apparently first met the Whites in mid-August 1848, when they, Bates, and others attended the second *Sabbatarian

HIRAM EDSON

COURTESY OF THE ELLEN G. WHITE ESTATE, INC.

conference held in *David Arnold's barn at Volney, New York. While there, Ellen White was given a vision during which she held up a Bible with her left hand, using the other hand to turn from text to text, placing her finger on each one before quoting it. Several present verified that she was quoting the texts correctly. Presumably Edson was present during this vision. From that conference the group, including Edson and his wife, the Whites, and Bateses, traveled to Edson's farm near Port Gibson, where the third conference was held August 27 and 28, 1848. On their way from Volney to Port Gibson, they stopped overnight in Hannibal, New York, where Ellen White was again given a vision at which Edson was likely present (1Bio 139, 143).

In July 1849 James and Ellen White named their second son, James Edson, in honor of Hiram Edson. In November of that year Hiram Edson again met the Whites at a conference at Centerport, New York. While there, Edson expressed strong concern for Elder *Samuel Rhodes, who had become discouraged and stopped preaching after the October 22, 1844, disappointment. During earnest seasons of prayer for Rhodes, a Brother [T.] Ralph from Connecticut (cf. 2SG 91) spoke twice in tongues, after the second of which Ellen White in vision confirmed that Edson and Ralph should try to recover Elder Rhodes. They did so, Brother Rhodes' faith was revived, and he returned to preaching. On August 24, 1850, Ellen White was shown in vision that Edson should be prepared to travel in search of souls. Shortly thereafter he and Joseph Bates did leave on such a journey (1Bio 167, 196-198).

Edson was listed as a member of the publishing committee for the *Advent Review,* printed in Auburn, New York, in 1850. He was also on the publishing committee for the second volume of the *Advent Review and Sabbath Herald,* printed in Saratoga Springs, New York, from 1851 to 1852. Both papers were edited by James White. When White needed funds to purchase a Washington hand press in 1852, Edson sold his farm in Port Byron, New York, and lent White enough to buy it.

In December 1852 a conference was held in Rochester, New York. On Sabbath morning Ellen White was shown in vision that young *J. N. Loughborough was correct in deciding to start preaching full-time. Edson, who lived about 40 miles (64 kilometers) east of Rochester, had not come to the meeting. However, his wife, impressed that he would soon need to travel, had prepared all his clothes. That same morning, while praying, Edson felt impressed to go to *Rochester. Taking the train after sundown, upon his arrival he asked James White if anything was needed of him. A day or two later Edson and Loughborough left on a six-week preaching tour. There is an Ellen White testimony to the churches of central New York State, the only extant copy of which is in Hiram Edson's handwriting. In it Edson is urged to "take his place" in the church rather than remaining "back for fear of getting out of his place" (quoted in Nix, p. 75).

Although suffering ill health, Edson appears to have attended the conference at Roosevelt, New York, held August 3 and 4, 1861. It was there that Ellen White had one of her Civil War visions. On October 22, 1861, a letter from Edson to James and Ellen White was published in the *Review and Herald.* In it he commented on their recent "friendly visit," the prayers offered for him, as well as the public meetings and encouragement he had received from her vision. He concluded by commenting favorably on the recent conference in Battle Creek pertaining to the organization of churches.

An appeal in the July 26, 1864, *Review* for

donations to help send Edson for a few months of treatments at Dr. *James C. Jackson's sanatorium in Dansville, New York, found James and Ellen White contributing $10 to the fund. Later that year the Whites spent three weeks at Dansville, where they met Hiram Edson and others. The following year, when James White's health failed and he needed to go to Dansville, Hiram Edson's $10 donation was the first to be listed. By early 1866 Edson felt strong enough to write and thank James White and the others for the $243.04 that had been contributed for his stay at Dansville. Edson was still well enough to attend the conference that opened October 26, 1867, at Roosevelt, at which the Whites were present. Ellen White spoke at least twice, delivering "pointed testimonies." Heartfelt confessions resulted. In 1875 Edson attended the New York Conference session, at which James White was present. Edson died in 1882.

In 1894, more than 10 years after Edson's death, Ellen White expressed relief that Edson's widow had not published a now-nonextant manuscript by Edson with funds he had left for that purpose (CW 155). Exactly which manuscript it was is not known for certain. However, J. N. Loughborough recalled that it included some "unsafe applications of Scripture that the publishing committee, and Brother [James] White, did not endorse."

Further reading: 1Bio 53, 78, 107, 108, 143, 144, 167, 181; obit. RH, Feb. 21, 1882; J. R. Nix, "The Life and Work of Hiram Edson" (unpublished manuscript, 1971, CAR); *SDA Encyclopedia* (1996), vol. 10, pp. 493, 494.

James R. Nix

EDWARDS, SANFORD PALMER STILLMAN (1873-1965). Physician who knew James and Ellen White from boyhood. Born in Westerly, Rhode Island, he graduated from South Lancaster Academy, Massachusetts, in 1892. He studied medicine at Battle Creek and received his medical degree from the American Medical Missionary College in 1899. He taught general science for two years at Battle Creek College (1899-1901) and during the first school year of Emanuel Missionary College. In 1902 he became the first medical secretary of the General Conference. After several years as medical superintendent of the Tri-City Sanitarium in Moline, Illinois, he served the St. Helena Sanitarium between 1909 and 1911. During a health crisis from overwork he was led to a deeper study of the writings of Ellen White. Later he taught at the College of Medical Evangelists in Loma Linda, California, and was connected with CME in other ways until 1950.

Of Ellen White, Dr. Edwards wrote, "Do you wonder that I loved Sister White? She was like a mother to me. She sang me to sleep in childhood days in old Connecticut. She counseled me in my early manhood. She wrote me letters of advice and reproof, and also just newsy, motherly letters. She stood by me when I was in need; she told me the truth when it did the most good; and so when she went to sleep, I, as well as her relations, lost a mother" (quoted by Ernest Lloyd).

Further reading: Ernest Lloyd, "Dr. S.P.S. Edwards, Noted Adventist Educator, Dies," PUR, Jan. 25, 1965; obit. RH, Mar. 4, 1965; S.P.S. Edwards to E. K. Vande Vere, 61 typewritten pages of reminiscent correspondence (Mar. 20, 1956, through Nov. 3, 1957, DF 967j, CAR).

EDWARDS, WILLIAM HERBERT (1854-1938). Church administrator for 52 years, Edwards graduated from a prestigious Boston business college. He and his parents were baptized by *D. M. Canright in 1877. In 1878 he moved to Battle Creek, married college student Mary Bierce (1856-1936), and joined the Review and Herald staff, first as manager of the book department (1878-1888) and then as secretary-treasurer (1888-1891). From 1891 to 1901 he served as General Conference treasurer, secretary-treasurer of the General Conference Association, and treasurer of the Foreign Mission Board. From 1901 to 1918 he was successively treasurer of the Michigan Conference, secretary-treasurer of the Lake Union Conference, and secretary-treasurer of the Northern Union Conference. After World War I he ran a printshop at the General Conference until his death in 1938. Ellen White wrote Edwards several friendly letters in 1882 requesting that he send her news and other items (Lts 27, 28, 29, 1882). But when in 1894 he misappropriated funds intended for Edson White's Southern work, she wrote from Australia, "I am moved . . . with indignation against those who have not the love of the true Shepherd," accusing Edwards of being found "wanting in justice, equity and the love of God" (Lt 23, 1894).

Further reading: obit. CUV, Oct. 6, 1938; *SDA Encyclopedia* (1996), vol. 10, p. 499.

Brian E. Strayer

ELDRIDGE, CLEMENT (1845-c.1907). Mariner; publishing and religious liberty leader. Originally from South Chatham, Massachusetts, "Captain" Eldridge was born to a mariner family and went to sea at the age of 24. In 1870 he married Susan Maria (Eldridge) (same surname but not related). During the American Civil War he served in the Navy for a year, and then joined the merchant marine and became a sea captain. Afterward he worked as a civil engineer in constructing a railroad, and then managed a cattle company in Texas. About 1884 he became an Adventist and in February 1885 became connected with the subscription book department at the *Review and Herald. Two years later he became associate manager, and then manager, of the Review. In the late 1880s Eldridge supported the founding of the National Religious Liberty Association, of which he became president.

In the 1890s he became the first general canvassing agent for the International Tract and Missionary Society, a forerunner of the General Conference Publishing Department directors.

Ellen White was deeply concerned that Eldridge was stifling the circulation of her books. As early as 1888 Eldridge promised Ellen White that her books would be widely circulated, but by the next year she had to write that she was "not pleased" that her books had continued to be neglected (Lt 25a, 1889; cf. Lt 124, 1896). This neglect continued till she claimed in 1895 that *The Great Controversy* (1888) and *Patriarchs and Prophets* (1891) had fallen "nearly dead from the press" (Lt 15, 1895, in 17MR 108). Another major concern of Ellen White's was Eldridge's exorbitant wages (he was making $30 a week while other employees were making $6) and that he seemed to have forgotten the spirit of self-sacrifice by which the publishing work was founded (Lt 42, 1893). These concerns continued to intensify until Ellen White claimed she could no "longer hold" her "peace" over the situation. She pleaded earnestly for self-denial to "characterize all the workers" (Lt 5, 1892, in 2SM 196). Furthermore, the fact that some were paid "higher wages" threatened to make "the spirit of self-sacrifice . . . extinct at the great heart of the work" (Lt 20a, 1893, in 2SM 210-218). She was worried lest Eldridge and her impressionable nephew *F. E. Belden make "shipwreck of faith" (Lt 9, 1893, in 1888 Materials 1187). The next year Eldridge threatened to leave, but she responded: "If you have no more heart interest in the work than is indicated by the fact that you can drop it so easily, I have nothing to say" (Lt 20a, 1893). Ellen White continued to write Eldridge about his spiritual condition, which she traced to his opposition to *A. T. Jones and *E. J. Waggoner at the *General Conference session of 1888 (Lt 20, 1894; see also Lts 57, 65, 1895). By 1894 the same spirit had begun to characterize other employees at the Review office (Lt 20, 1894). White was similarly concerned for Susan Eldridge, who carried a love "for extravagant display" (Lt 21, 1894). In early 1894 Clement Eldridge terminated his employment with the Review and Herald and joined a publishing firm in Chicago (Lt 22, 1894). Two years later Ellen White wrote her last known letter to him, expressing deep disappointment over the thought of what he might have become. "The Lord cannot save," she wrote, "the man who has a greater desire to win the crown than he has to bear the cross." She pleaded with him to "obtain a genuine experience in the things of God" (Lt 28, 1896; see also PM 247).

Further reading: *Portrait and Biographical Album of Calhoun County, Michigan* (Chicago: Chapman, 1891), pp. 332, 333; Captain Nautilus [Clement Eldridge], *The Boy Captain* (n.p., 1894).

Michael W. Campbell

ERZBERGER (or **ERZENBERGER** or **ERTZBERGER**), **JAMES "JAKOB"** (1843-1920). Pioneer Adventist evangelist in Europe, converted to Adventism under the influence of *M. B. Czechowski's missionary work. Erzberger was born in Seltisberg near Liestal, in the canton of Basel, *Switzerland. The town's birth records show him registered at birth as "Erzenberger." The town's records in the "family book" spell it "Erzberger"—the name by which he was known in later years among Adventist members in Europe. Coming from a very poor family, he felt that it was God's providence that he received work at the local hospital, although he was not the only applicant. This experience moved him to enter the evangelical Protestant Seminary of St. Chrischona in 1864. After one year of

ministerial training he was sent to the Jura Mountains as an itinerant evangelist and colporteur. In Tramelan he met a group of Advent believers organized by M. B. Czechowski, and was baptized by its leader, *Albert Vuilleumier, late in 1868, six years prior to the arrival of *J. N. Andrews in Europe. Czechowski had not revealed that there were Seventh-day Adventist believers in North America, and when the group in Tramelan discovered this, they decided to send Erzberger to the *General Conference session, convening in *Battle Creek, *Michigan, in May 1869. Staying at the *home of James and Ellen White, Erzberger familiarized himself with Adventist beliefs and practices. In 1870 he returned to Switzerland as the first ordained Seventh-day Adventist minister in Europe. From 1874 on, he worked closely with J. N. Andrews in Switzerland and *Germany. In 1876 Erzberger organized the first German Seventh-day Adventist congregation in Vohwinkel-Wuppertal, which emerged from the Sabbathkeeping Lindermann group. Between 1876 and 1878 Erzberger wrote several pamphlets and tracts to be used for the Adventist missionary work in Germany, but none of them have survived. These were the first Seventh-day Adventist writings to be published in Germany. After the death of Andrews (1883), Erzberger became a close associate of *L. R. Conradi, but he himself never occupied a leading position in the European church organization. He was an untiring "soul winner" until the end of his life, often working beyond his physical strength. His own records show, for example, that he gave 28 Bible readings and 49 sermons and lectures, and organized 17 church meetings, all in one month (April 1906). Erzberger died in Sissach, Switzerland.

Further reading: EGWEur; K. Waber, *Streiflichter aus der Geschichte der*

Siebenten-Tags-Adventisten in der Schweiz, 1865-1901 (Zurich: Advent-Verlag, 1995), pp. 36-48, 54-137.

Daniel Heinz

EVANS, D. T. Early Sabbatarian Adventist from Vermont. Ellen White was "shown in vision" that he "could do errands for the Lord," but because he was not a "thorough laborer" should not travel extensively (Lt 21, 1859; Ms 1, 1859). Evans worked as a lay preacher in Melbourne, Canada East, in the summer of 1860, and was subsequently ordained as a minister (RH, Nov. 13, 1860), the first Seventh-day Adventist minister to be ordained in Canada. To what extent Evans followed the advice in this letter is not clear, because Ellen White pointed out the same problems a few years later in 1T 448, 449 (Brother C). After the publication of this later testimony the Vermont Conference voted "that Bro. Evans be left under the watchcare of the Executive Committee for them to encourage him to preach in his sphere, only as fast as he complies with the requirements of the last testimony given for his benefit" (RH, June 28, 1864). Evans received ministerial credentials from 1868 to 1874 and subsequently was listed as a farmer in Nebraska in the 1880 census.

EVANS, IRWIN HENRY (1862-1945). Minister and administrator. Converted to Adventism in 1874, he began work as a minister in 1882. In 1886 he married Emma Ferry (1862-1903). In 1891 he became president of the Michigan Conference, during which time Ellen White rebuked him for misusing denominational resources when funds were desperately needed for missionary work overseas (Lt 23b, 1894, in 8T 48-53; see also Lt 23c, 1894). In 1897 he became a member of the General Conference Committee (a position he held until his death) and was elected presi-

dent of the General Conference Association.

Ellen White wrote him several strong testimonies warning against overcentralization in *Battle Creek (Lt 7a, 1897), and gave him guidance during a leadership crisis brought on by a lawsuit from *A. R. Henry (Lt 51, 1897; Lt 137a, 1898). In 1899 Evans became

IRWIN AND ADELAIDE EVANS

president of the *Foreign Mission Board, and in 1901 president and manager of the *Review and Herald. Ellen White rebuked him for diverting funds that were needed for the Adventist work in the southern United States, and asked him to make restitution for this "past neglect" (Lt 74, 1901). She also warned him against constructing new buildings in Battle Creek (Lt 205, 1901). Furthermore, she warned that spiritually impure commercial work at the press was "defiling the institution that God declared should be kept free from all moral and spiritual defilement" (written in June 1901, but filed as Lt 46, 1903). In 1903 Evans was also elected treasurer of the General Conference for a year. After the relocation of denominational headquarters to Takoma Park that same year, Evans was responsible for taking care of remaining business affairs in Battle Creek. Also in 1903 he married Adelaide Bee Cooper (1870-1958). Ellen White warned that Evans was in spiritual trouble, that he needed to give up self and to make sure he did not oppose God's plans (Lt 197, 1904, in 21MR 425-428). From 1905 to 1909 he was again treasurer of the General Conference. At one point Ellen White asked him to be ready to make a payment for the *Loma Linda property just in case funds fell through (Lt 200, 1905), and also asked him to send surplus funds to workers in the southern United States

(Lt 205, 1905; Lt 314, 1907). He later served in several additional administrative posts: president of Asiatic Division [mission] Field (1909-1913), president of the North American Division (1913-1918), vice president of the General Conference (1918-1936), and field secretary of the General Conference (1936-1941). Evans played a prominent role in the development of the Seventh-day Adventist Theological Seminary.

Further reading: obit. RH, Dec. 20, 1945; obit. RH, May 26, 1903; obit. Oct. 30, 1958; *SDA Encyclopedia* (1996), vol. 10, p. 525.

Michael W. Campbell

EVANS, THOMAS JEFFERSON (1871-1937). Physician. Born in Nebraska, Evans received a medical degree from the Hahneman Hospital College in San Francisco in 1900. He briefly headed the Halsted Street Dispensary in Chicago before becoming medical superintendent of the *St. Helena Sanitarium in 1903, where his wife, Margaret, was also a physician. There, in 1905, Ellen White pleaded with T. J. Evans to break off an affair with Mildred Groves, a nurse at the sanitarium (Lt 27, 1905; cf. Lt 33, 1905). White observed that he and Margaret had been "very happy together," but that "certain sentiments" in *J. H. Kellogg's *Living Temple* had led Evans into a spiritual delusion, unbalancing his discernment so that emotionally and spiritually he was no longer a "sane man." She pleaded with him to "come back" to the faith, to his wife, and to his work at the sanitarium (Lt 27, 1905). Evidently in response to those letters, Evans and Groves terminated their relationship.

A year later, however, Evans married Florence Mabel Lloyd and was expelled by the St. Helena church. In 1907 he and Florence began attending church near Boulder, Colorado, and were accepted into membership there. The *Boulder Sanitarium was just then looking for another physician, and when *F. M. Wilcox, administrator of the Boulder Sanitarium, met Evans, he recognized in him many qualities that would make him an asset to the sanitarium. Cautious, however, because of Evans' divorce and remarriage, Wilcox wrote letters to General Conference president *A. G. Daniells in Washington, D.C., and to Ellen and W. C. White in St. Helena, California, for counsel regarding the advisability of giving Evans another chance. Daniells advised against it, arguing that Evans' second marriage constituted a "living or continuous wrong" that disqualified him for church employment (A. G. Daniells to F. M. Wilcox, Mar. 8, 1907). Ellen White and W. C. White, however, were open to giving Evans another chance. In the ensuing correspondence Daniells' view prevailed until March 13, when Ellen White said to W. C. White, "I had a strange dream last night. I dreamed that I was in a room where the Managing Board of the Boulder Sanitarium were having a meeting and Dr. Evans was present and there seemed to be the most friendly feeling between him and the Board as they discussed the various matters pertaining to the work of the institution[,] and as I saw Dr. Evans and the Sanitarium people working together in friendly confidence, I said, This is as it ought to be." Ellen White instructed W. C. White to tell Wilcox that she did not regard the dream as "clear and positive" instruction for Wilcox to hire Evans, but she did regard it "as a suggestion" that Wilcox "not slam the door against Dr. Evans in a way that would injure him and cut off the opportunity for you to become intelligently satisfied for yourselves regarding his sincerity and acceptance by the Lord" (WCW to F. M. Wilcox, Mar. 17, 1907, GCAr).

Thus Ellen White did not accept Daniells' reasoning that the unbiblical marriage constituted a "continuous wrong" that precluded all further consideration. For her the decisive issue was not the details of the adultery and remarriage, but whether there was "intelligently [satisfying]" evidence of the repentant wrongdoer's "sincerity and acceptance by the Lord." In other cases of this kind, she repeatedly refused to make a rule based only on the external facts. What she wanted was evidence of the *Lord's* approval or disapproval, which might at times be communicated to her through a vision or dream, but which could be sought by every believer through prayer and fasting (TSB 234).

The Boulder Sanitarium did hire Evans, and he headed the eye, ear, nose, and throat department there from 1907 to 1909, then became medical superintendent of the Loma Linda Sanitarium. Evans held that position until 1917, except for two short stints in the same position at the Glendale and Paradise Valley sanitariums. During this period he helped establish the College of Medical Evangelists (now Loma Linda University) and served seven years as dean of surgery there. In 1917 he moved to Colorado Springs, Colorado, where he established the Crestone Heights Sanitarium and led it until his death.

See also: Marriage and Divorce.

Further reading: 5Bio 383-385; Lt 33, 1905; obit. CUR, Aug. 31, 1937; obit. RH, Sept. 16, 1937; F. M. Wilcox to WCW, Feb. 20, Mar. 2, Mar. 25, 1907; AGD to F. M. Wilcox, Feb. 25, Mar. 8, 1907; F. M. Wilcox to AGD, Mar. 2, 1907; WCW to F. M. Wilcox, Mar. 17, 1907, Aug. 18, 1908; WCW to AGD, Aug. 18, 1908.

Michael W. Campbell and Jerry Moon

EVERTS, ELON (1807-1858) and **ANNA MARIA (RIDER)** (d. 1856). Early Adventists from Vermont. Elon accepted the Sabbath in 1851 and traveled throughout New England as an agent of the *Review and Herald*. Several conferences were held near their home, and in

1853 Elon was ordained to ministry (RH, Nov. 15, 1853). In 1855 the Evertses moved to Round Grove, Illinois. The next year Elon accompanied the Whites on a trip from their home to Waukon, Iowa (1Bio 345-349). In July 1857 Ellen White counseled Everts that he should "cut loose" from his many possessions and large farms in order to contribute to the work of evangelism (Lt 14, 1857). A follow-up letter repeated this same message to the believers in Round Grove (Lt 5, 1857). In the development of Adventist theology, Elon Everts is noted as the first writer to use the expression "investigative judgment." In an expository letter to the editor of the *Review and Herald* Everts says it appears to him that since 1844 "the righteous dead have been under investigative judgment" (RH, Jan. 1, 1857). The editor, James White, evidently liked the term, because four weeks later he used it four times in an exposition of his own (JW, "The Judgment," RH, Jan. 29, 1857).

Further reading: 1Bio 353, 354; obit. RH, Nov. 6, 1856; obit. RH, Mar. 11, 1858.

Michael W. Campbell

FAIRFIELD, WILLIAM "WILLIE" JOSIAH (1853-1933). Medical doctor. Fairfield and his friend, W. B. Sprague were trained under Dr. *J. H. Kellogg at the *Health Reform Institute. Seeing their potential, James White paid for their medical education (RH, May 24, 1877; Ms 4, 1881). Both men graduated from the Bellevue Hospital College in 1878 and joined the sanitarium staff. Ellen White wrote Drs. Fairfield and Sprague a letter urging them to be reliable so that Kellogg could depend upon them, and thus ease Kellogg's heavy workload (Lt 4a, 1879). The next year Ellen White affirmed that "the Lord in His providence brought . . . [Sprague and Fairfield] in connection with His work." She furthermore encouraged Fairfield that God had not forsaken him during temptations, and that "angels of God are guarding you." Yet she warned that "serious dangers threaten you should you yield to Satan's suggestions" (Lt 1a, 1880). Many years later Ellen White reflected that Fairfield made the mistake of elevating science over faith (Lt 18, 1892). In 1882 Fairfield and Sprague, influenced by Kellogg's early interest in *pantheism, left the church (*Special Testimony to the Battle Creek Church* [1882], PH155 19, 20; see also 5Bio 303; Ms 7, 1882; Lt 271a, 1903). In July 1882 Fairfield opened a competing medical facility called "Health Home" only a few blocks from the Battle Creek Sanitarium, and in April 1883 he was appointed health officer by the city of Battle Creek. About 1910 Fairfield was thought to have drowned in Colorado, and was declared dead, but turned up two years later in Alaska. Fairfield later attributed Ellen White's visions to "hysterical trances," although it is believed he never had the opportunity to examine her while in vision (D. M. Canright, *Life of Mrs. E. G. White, Seventh-day Adventist Prophet: Her False Claims Exposed* [Cincinnati: Standard Pub. Co., 1919], p. 180; T. H. Jemison, *A Prophet Among You,* p. 414).

Further reading: Coller Collection (WL), vol. 24, pp. 39-42; vol. 32, pp. 291-297.

Michael W. Campbell

FARGO, JEROME (1824-1899) and **RACHEL C. (KING)** (1834-1889). Early Adventists from northern Michigan, converted to Adventism in 1860; Jerome was a minister. The Fargos were close friends of James and Ellen White, often dining at each other's homes and on occasion traveling together. In 1867 the Fargos, with A. W. Maynard and S. H. King, bought the Whites a light traveling carriage (1T 600). Two years later Ellen White encouraged the Fargos to adopt an orphan whose Adventist

parents had died, and followed this up with practical instruction on caring for the boy (Lt 15, 1869, in 2T 327-334; cf. 307-314). Another letter, after the *General Conference session of 1888, reproved Jerome for failing to discern *G. I. Butler's misguided opposition and then reinforcing Butler's misguided thinking, thus endangering both his and Butler's souls (Lt 50, 1889, in 1888 Materials 294-301).

Further reading: obit. RH, Nov. 5, 1889; obit. RH, Nov. 14, 1899.

FARNSWORTH, EUGENE WILLIAM (1847-1935). Evangelist and administrator, son of *William

COURTESY OF THE CENTER FOR ADVENTIST RESEARCH, ANDREWS UNIVERSITY.

EUGENE W. FARNSWORTH

Farnsworth. Born in Washington, New Hampshire, Eugene Farnsworth became a minister in his early 20s and served in the American Midwest. He presided over the Iowa-Nebraska Conference (1883-1884), served as Bible teacher at Union College (1892-1896), and worked as a pioneer evangelist in Australia, New Zealand, and England (1896-1904). Later in his career he served as president of the Atlantic Union Conference (1906-1909), head of the Bible Department at Washington Foreign Mission Seminary (1910), and president of the California Conference (1911-1915). Farnsworth married Carrie Eggleston (d. 1882) in 1879 and after her death married Lizzie Hornby (1845-1891). While teaching at Union College in the mid-1890s, Farnsworth married Vesta J. Cady Olsen (1855-1932). Between 1897 and 1906 Ellen White and Eugene and Vesta Farnsworth exchanged many letters in which Ellen White provided them with numerous administrative and personal counsels regarding their work overseas and in the United States. Speaking at Ellen White's funeral service at Elmshaven, Farnsworth declared that he knew of no other person who "has ever held up more insistently the grace of God for the salvation of men than [she] has" (LS 453-455).

Further reading: obit. RH, Jan. 30, 1936; obit. RH, Aug. 22, 1882; obit. RH, Oct. 6, 1932; *SDA Encyclopedia* (1996), vol. 10, pp. 540, 541.

FARNSWORTH, JOHN P. (1834-1918). Adventist minister, oldest son of *William Farnsworth. After the death of his first wife, Frances Jennette (Stevens) (1833-1868), Ellen White wrote to him about overcoming certain traits in his character. She furthermore urged him not to marry a certain Anna Hale, because "such temperaments as hers and yours should [not] unite" (Lt 21, 1868, in TSB 23, 24). Instead, he married Laura L. (1846-1870). A third wife outlived him.

Further reading: obit. RH, Jan. 16, 1919.

FARNSWORTH, WILLIAM (1807-1888). Believed to be the first Sabbatarian Adventist; resident of Washington, New Hampshire, and father of 22 children, many of whom worked for the Adventist Church, among them *Eugene W. Farnsworth. In December 1867, during a visit to Washington, New Hampshire, James and Ellen White and J. N. Andrews met with the congregation in Farnsworth's home. During the meeting Ellen White expressed words of comfort or encouragement to everyone in the room. When she came to Farnsworth, she revealed to all present that "this brother is a slave to tobacco. But the worst of the matter is that

COURTESY OF THE CENTER FOR ADVENTIST RESEARCH, ANDREWS UNIVERSITY.

WILLIAM FARNSWORTH

he is acting the part of a hypocrite, trying to deceive his brethren into thinking that he has discarded it, as he promised to do when he united with the church" (2Bio 218). Farnsworth acknowledged that he had not given up his secret habit. She attributed much of the spiritual lethargy of the Washington church to Farnsworth's lack of consecration to the light received on the health reform (Ms 2, 1868, in 2T 93-111; Farnsworth is Brother O in 2T 93-97).

Further reading: obit. RH, Feb. 19, 1889.

FARRINGTON, WILLIAM F. (b. 1800). Pastor of the *Chestnut Street Methodist Church in Portland, Maine, who visited the Harmon family in 1843 to inform them that the Harmons' belief in the near second advent of Christ was not in harmony with Methodism. Ellen White described him, but not by name, when he came to visit her family. She recalled that during this visit her father quoted several texts of Scripture to support his faith, but that the minister "did not attempt to refer to a single text that would prove us in error" (LS 51). Although the minister suggested that the Harmon family withdraw quietly from the church to avoid a church trial, the Harmon family refused to change their views, underwent a trial, and were discontinued from membership in September 1843 (LS 50-53; 1Bio 43, 44).

FAULKHEAD, NATHANIEL D. (1860-1923). Treasurer of the Echo Publishing House in Australia and a high-ranking member of a Masonic Lodge, and member of four other societies. Gifted, Faulkhead served the church well, but gave priority to his lodge responsibilities. Some who worked with him expressed their concern about this, but he was not amenable to their advice. Days after her arrival in Australia in December 1891, Ellen White learned of the conditions at the press in Melbourne and wrote to a number of the people there, including Nathaniel Faulkhead and his wife. However, the lengthy Faulkhead letter was not mailed, as Ellen White was under conviction that its contents would not be accepted (4Bio 50). A year passed, during which it seemed increasingly likely that Faulkhead's attitude would lead to the termination of his denominational employment.

NATHANIEL D. FAULKHEAD

COURTESY OF THE REVIEW AND HERALD PUBLISHING ASSOCIATION

On December 10, 1892, Faulkhead dreamed that Ellen White had a message for him. Deeply impressed, he sought her out when she returned to Melbourne a few days later and asked if she had something to say to him. She did have a message she had wanted to deliver for many months, but had been impressed not to do so, as it would have been unwelcome. She then discussed the 50-page document with Faulkhead, focusing mainly on his blunted spiritual perception as a consequence of his heavy commitment to Masonry and several other societies. She described what happened in the lodge meetings he attended, and twice made hand movements that startled Faulkhead, as they were secret signs known only to the highest ranking members of the Masonic Lodge movement—signs no ordinary lodge member and certainly no woman could possibly have known. When he pointed out what she had done, he learned that Ellen White was not aware she had provided these signals. This experience convinced Faulkhead that Ellen White's testimony to him was from God (Lt 46, 1892; cf. Lt 186, 1906). Although he resigned from all his lodge positions the next day, the resignations were not accepted. The Masons required him to complete the final nine months

of his elected term, hoping by so doing to change his mind. This was a time of trial for Faulkhead, but in September 1893 he was able to write to Ellen and Willie White that all his relationships with Masonry were ended. He also expressed his gratitude to God and His messenger for the direction his life had taken.

Faulkhead remained in contact with Ellen White after her return to the United States. In his February 20, 1908, statement he recalls the events that led to his resignation from Masonry, and the tone is supportive and appreciative of Ellen White. That document indicates he had "been a great help to many of them [Masons] and many have withdrawn themselves from the associations as a result of what I had told them took place between us."

While Faulkhead subsequently spent many years speaking against Masonry and was an elder in the Seventh-day Adventist Church right up to his sudden death in 1923, Masonic records document periodic membership in various lodges during the remainder of his life and that he was a member at the time of his death on March 13, 1923. The Masons conducted a funeral service for him according to their rites following the denominational committal at the cemetery.

Further reading: obit. *Australasian Record*, May 7, 1923; G. W. Jackson, grand secretary of the United Grand Lodge of the Antient, Free and Accepted Masons of Victoria, Australia, to K. Moxon (Apr. 2, 1968, DF 522a, EGWRC-AV); N. D. Faulkhead, statement (Feb. 20, 1908, EGWRC-AV); "Confident in the Gift," *Adventist World-NAD*, February 2006.

Les Devine

FAY, EMILY CLARA (CAMPBELL), see **CAMPBELL, EMILY CLARA.**

FIFIELD, GEORGE E. (1859-1926). Adventist

minister and writer. Born in New Hampshire, Fifield attended *Battle Creek College (1877-1879), afterward conducting evangelistic meetings with *L. T. Nicola. He married Mary A. Flood in 1888, and they had four children. In December 1890 Fifield accompanied Ellen White on a visit to Massachusetts, during which she noted his spiritual growth and success as an evangelist (Lt 109, 1890). During the 1890s he became a widely recognized expert on religious liberty and rose to prominence as a popular camp meeting speaker. In 1902 he was relocated to California because of his critical attitude and marital indiscretions (GCCMin, Feb. 15, 1902). He afterward became a Seventh Day Baptist minister in Battle Creek. In 1906 an article written by Fifield in 1895 was mistakenly attributed to Ellen White ("Religious Liberty," SW, May 1, 1906; first published in the *American Sentinel*, Jan. 17, 1895). He is buried in Oak Hill Cemetery in Battle Creek, Michigan.

FITCH, CHARLES (1805-1844). A Congregational clergyman who first accepted Adventism in 1838 after he had read William Miller's book *Evidence From Scripture* six times. In sincerity he preached his new belief to his ministerial colleagues, who intimidated him into silence.

COURTESY OF THE CENTER FOR ADVENTIST RESEARCH, ANDREWS UNIVERSITY

CHARLES FITCH

He was reconverted to Millerism in 1841 and remained one of its foremost preachers until his death in early October 1844. Fitch was well known in the larger Christian community and was intimate with such nineteenth-century greats as Charles Finney, Phoebe Palmer, and William Lloyd Garrison. He initiated the preaching of the second angel's message, which invited Millerite believers to withdraw from their churches; developed the famous "1843 chart"; and accepted conditionalism and annihilationism in January 1844. His death came about as a result of baptizing people in frigid Lake Erie just a few weeks before the disappointment of October 1844. Ellen White had a vision from which she inferred that Fitch would be in the kingdom (2SG 35; EW 17).

Further reading: G. R. Knight, *Millennial Fever and the End of the World* (PPPA, 1993), pp. 105-113.

George R. Knight

FITZGERALD, W. J. President of the East Pennsylvania Conference (1904-1907). In 1905 Fitzgerald asked Ellen White for her support in asking the General Conference to pay the debts of the Philadelphia Sanitarium. She declined his request and instead suggested that he "lay the whole matter before our own people in the Conference or section that is to be benefited, and let them share the burden." She additionally noted that *The Ministry of Healing* would soon be available, and urged that "every one be prepared to do his part in selling it, and thus lessen the debts on our sanitariums" (Lt 175, 1905), because she had dedicated the royalties of that book toward debt reduction for health institutions. Eight years later, at the 1913 Autumn Council of the General Conference, this letter was the focus of a heated argument over the subsequent financial failure of the Philadelphia Sanitarium.

Further reading: J. Moon, *W. C. White and Ellen G. White* (AUP, 1993), pp. 395-401.

FOLSOM (or **FOLSOME**), **PAUL** (b. c. 1817) and **MARGARET** (b. 1820). Adventists from Massachusetts who converted to Adventism about 1851. James and Ellen White visited their home in Massachusetts several times. In a letter to the Whites' 5-year-old son Willie, Ellen White reminded him that the Folsoms' was the place where they made candy, and described Margaret's two cats (Lt 9, 1859). In 1863 the Boston Seventh-day Adventist Church was organized in their home (RH, July 7, 1863). In 1859 Ellen White wrote a testimony of reproof to Paul and Margaret Folsom that is no longer extant (see Ms 5, 1859). Ellen White followed this up with two additional letters of warning. Not accepting Ellen White's reproof, the Folsoms went on to criticize the "brethren and [church] organization" (Lt 7, 1864). Ellen White was pained by their rejection of her testimony and urged them to reconsider their decision. She felt that Paul's life was devoid of "the fruits of the Christian religion" and that he had failed to learn of Jesus (Lt 56, 1876).

FORD, IRVING A. (1869-1944). Publishing director at the *Southern Publishing Association in Nashville, Tennessee. In 1905 Ellen White wrote two letters of counsel to Ford and others at the Southern Publishing office (Lts 269, 295, 1905). When Ford later wrote to Ellen White that a revival was taking place in the Nashville office, she responded that she had been shown that he needed a reformation in his own life (Lt 315, 1907).

Further reading: obit. RH, June 22, 1944.

FOSS, HAZEN LITTLE (1819-1893). Millerite visionary just before and after the *disappointment of 1844, but before Ellen Harmon's first vision in December of that year. Foss had visions pertaining to the experience of Advent believers. Knowing that anyone who claimed to have a vision from God would be ridiculed and scorned, he refused to communicate what he had seen. He was given another vision and instructed not to refuse to bear the message of the Lord, for if he did, it would be taken from him and revealed to the weakest of the weak (1Bio 66). Continuing to dread the

burden and reproach of publicly presenting a vision from God, he told the Lord that he would not do it. Then strange feelings came over him, and "a voice said, 'You have grieved away the Spirit of the Lord'" (Lt 37, 1890). "Horrified," Foss called a meeting to relate the vision. He told the group his experience, but when he attempted to tell the vision, he could not recall it. "He tried and tried to relate it, but he said, 'It is gone from me; I can say nothing, and the Spirit of the Lord has left me.' Those who gave a description of that meeting said it was the most terrible meeting they were ever in" (*ibid.*). Soon after this Ellen Harmon received her first vision.

Early in 1845 (probably in January) Ellen Harmon was invited to visit *Mary Foss, her older sister, in Poland, Maine. Despite illness, Ellen accepted her sister's invitation. Samuel, Mary's husband, brought 17-year-old Ellen in his sleigh the 30 miles (48 kilometers) from Portland to Poland. After arriving, Ellen traveled the three miles (five kilometers) from her sister's home to Megquier Hill, an Adventist meeting site, and gave her testimony. Hazen Foss was evidently present in the house, but not in the meeting. From a nearby room he heard Ellen speak. The next day Foss, perhaps at the home of his brother, Samuel, talked with Ellen Harmon. Foss stated that he had received a dream similar to hers, but that he had refused to relate it. Foss then said, "I shall be henceforth as one dead to spiritual things. . . . I believe the visions are taken from me, and given to you. Do not refuse to obey God, for it will be at the peril of your soul. I am a lost man. You are chosen of God; be faithful in doing your work, and the crown I might have had, you will receive" (1Bio 67). According to Mary, Hazen never again expressed an interest in religion (Mary P. Foss to EGW, Apr. 1, 1894, EGWE-GC).

See also: William E. Foy.

Further reading: 1Bio 65-69; D. Baker, *The Unknown Prophet* (RHPA, 1987), pp. 135-141; T. H. Jemison, *A Prophet Among You* (PPPA, 1955), pp. 486-489; *SDA Encyclopedia* (1996), vol. 10, pp. 562, 563.

Michael W. Campbell

FOSS, MARY PLUMMER (HARMON) (1821-1912). Third daughter of *Robert and *Eunice Harmon, six years older than her twin sisters, Ellen and Elizabeth. Mary married Samuel H. Foss in Portland, Maine, on July 5, 1842. In 1845 she invited her sister Ellen to visit their home in Poland, Maine, about 30 miles (48 kilometers)

MARY PLUMMER FOSS

north of Portland. Soon after she arrived, a little group of Advent believers was meeting at the chapel on Megquier Hill, and Mary invited Ellen to go with them. It was on this occasion that Ellen first told of her vision outside of Portland. The next morning at the Fosses' home she met *Hazen Foss, brother of Samuel. Hazen told Ellen that the same vision had been given to him by the Lord, with the instruction to tell others what had been revealed to him. He felt he could not bear such a burden, and refused to present it to others (1Bio 65-67).

Mary and Samuel had five children. Two of them, John H. and Ellen Frances, lived in Maine. John and his wife, Mattie, who lived with his parents, had two children, and Mattie died in childbirth with the third. This left Mary Foss to care for the two older girls, while Mattie's mother took the baby to live with her. John later brought a new wife into the home, and eventually more children. He and his family apparently lived with Mary and Samuel

until Samuel's death, after which Mary Foss went to live with her daughter, Ellen Frances, and later with her granddaughters, the two girls she had reared after the death of their mother, Mattie.

Mary and her sister, Ellen White, had a good relationship. Although they seldom saw each other, they often corresponded. Mary enjoyed gardening and sometimes asked her sister to send her cuttings of flowers from California and Australia. Ellen would share news of her home and family and give details of the progress and development of the Adventist Church in various areas (cf. Lt 143, 1902, in 16MR 20-25; Lt 112, 1906, in 14MR 258-262). Their last known visit came in 1904. Mary died in 1912 at the age of 91.

Norma J. Collins

FOSS, SAMUEL, see **FOSS, MARY PLUMMER (HARMON)**.

FOX SISTERS, see **SPIRITUALISM**.

FOY, WILLIAM ELLIS (1818-1893). Black pastor, preacher, and prophet who was part of the Millerite Adventist movement and received at least four visions prior to 1844. Tested and tried by the divine charge laid on him, Foy faithfully fulfilled his commission to share with others the messages of his visions. Until the end of his life he continued preaching the message of a soon-coming Savior.

Foy was born in 1818 in Kennebec County, near Augusta, Maine, to Joseph and Elizabeth "Betsy" Foy. William was the eldest of three boys and one girl in a family of free Blacks in a community of Black professionals, landowners, farmers, and skilled laborers. Foy was baptized in the Freewill Baptist Church during his teen years and early showed a proclivity toward spiritual interests.

Foy lived and ministered during the

mid-1800s, at the height of the Advent awakening. In 1842, while in his early 20s, he was given several dramatic visions. These consisted of lofty revelations of heaven and the judgment, events that were to take place before Christ's second coming, including God's care over the Advent believers. The visions were similar to those later given to *Hazen Foss and Ellen White.

Foy's experience has for years been presented erroneously. Although he was of light complexion, he is often incorrectly referred to as a mulatto. He has been accused of failing, like Hazen Foss, to tell the visions to others for fear of being ridiculed or persecuted. To the contrary, Foy, a minister of exceptional talent, demonstrated his complete cooperation to be used by God. He did pause in his preaching for a three-month period because of persecution, economics, and hardship, but after that time he continued sharing what he had seen in vision as long as there were invitations.

In 1845 Foy wrote a pamphlet entitled *The Christian Experience of William E. Foy Together With the Two Visions He Received in the Months of January and February 1842.* In this book Foy passionately portrayed his conversion, trials, the receiving of two visions and their content, and his deep longing for the soon coming of Christ. After the writing of this publication, his ministerial role evidently continued for almost 50 years.

Ellen White and *John Loughborough attested to the legitimacy of William Foy's revelatory experience, as did John and Charles Pearson, a medical doctor, eight local witnesses, and his wife. Said Ellen White: "[Foy] had . . . four visions: . . . It was remarkable testimonies that he bore" (EGW, "William Foy," DF 231). The visions were designed to warn, to prepare, and to prevent disappointment among those who would understand and heed them. Furthermore, these visions contain admonition, instruction, and exhortation for us today.

Ellen White said that she had printed copies of Foy's visions and, with her father, had heard Foy speak on a number of different occasions, hence was acquainted with him and his message. Some of the scenes they each saw in vision were similar. Certain terms and phrases used by Ellen White resemble those employed by Foy, although their emphases and styles were different. In no way competing, they both recognized the genuineness and authenticity of each other's work.

The manner in which William Foy and Ellen White received their visions was alike in many respects, but not in every particular. They both appeared to come under supernatural influence. Both had witnesses and a medical examination when in vision, which attested that the experience fell outside the realm of natural or self-induced phenomena. Ellen White's longest vision lasted approximately four hours, while Foy's longest was more than 12 hours.

William Foy's role was not that later filled by Ellen White. They stood at different moments in history, confronted with contrasting circumstances and challenges. Foy served as a spokesman for God to the Advent movement in the predisappointment period, whereas Ellen White was called to minister to the postdisappointment Adventist believers. Foy spoke to the early Advent movement; he received a limited number of visions with a set objective. He never suggested that his prophetic role would extend past 1844, or that he would receive more visions.

Foy was involved in the Millerite movement, though we have no indication that he expected Christ to come on October 22, 1844. Some Millerites didn't accept a specific date, although they didn't oppose it. They simply heralded the soon coming of Christ. In a pamphlet he wrote, Foy made no reference to the 1844 disappointment, but simply says he waited for Jesus' soon coming.

Foy's writings are profitable as inspirational and instructional reading. He fulfilled his task as a prophet to the Advent movement in the predisappointment time and continued to minister and serve God. William Foy died November 9, 1893, at age 75 and was buried in Ellsworth, Maine.

Further reading: D. W. Baker, *The Unknown Prophet* (RHPA, 1987); W. E. Foy, *Christian Experience* (Portland, Maine: J. and C. H. Pearson, 1845; reprint, intro. D. W. Baker, ed. M. D. Burt, AUP, 2005); T. Poirier, "Black Forerunner to Ellen White: William E. Foy," *Spectrum* 28, no. 5 (August 1987): 23-28; J. R. Nix and P. A. Gordon, *In the Footsteps of the Pioneers* (EGWE, 1990), pp. 18-20.

Delbert W. Baker

FRANKE, E. E. Evangelist in New York City in the late 1890s and early 1900s. An excellent preacher and teacher, Franke had considerable success. From the content and number of letters between Ellen White and Franke it is clear that she showed great interest in him as an individual and a worker in the cause (6MR 237, 377). She recognized Franke as one "especially fitted to labor for unbelievers in our large cities," and who "could stir the ungodly as but few" could (*ibid.* 244).

In the fall of 1900 *Stephen N. Haskell and his wife were also asked to do evangelistic work in New York City. The two evangelists differed sharply in personality and temperament. Franke was a younger man who "advertised rather lavishly, and sometimes spectacularly," while the *Haskells were older, self-effacing, "extremely economical" (5Bio 133), and preferred to arouse interest through

extensive personal work by colporteurs and nurses, along with some modest advertising. Before the end of 1900, "rather bitter conflicts" erupted between them (*ibid.*). When the Haskells left the city to regain their health, Franke also left, for Trenton, New Jersey. In January 1901 Ellen White told Franke that she had been shown that he was "making shipwreck" of faith and "becoming a religious dyspeptic" (21MR 269). She promised him that God would use him if he would avoid schism by uniting with his brethren, and be "willing to be used" in God's "appointed way" (11MR 275).

By midsummer 1901 the Haskells, who had a burden for the great city (16MR 195), had returned to New York. "Then, quite unexpected to them all" (5Bio 134) Franke returned as well, and rented a hall only a few blocks from where the Haskells were holding their meetings. Given the size of the city, this move caused perplexity to the Haskells, who expressed their frustration to Ellen White. She urged the conference president "not to encourage Elder Franke to return to labor in New York City" (5Bio 134; see also 4MR 313; Lt 149, 1901). But Franke objected that he could not retreat, for he had already advertised, distributed 10,000 leaflets, and made final arrangements (E. E. Franke to EGW, Oct. 25, 1901). Ellen White wrote back attempting for a compromise. In New York City "there is abundant room for you both," she urged, recommending that Franke labor in another part of the city (Lt 157, 1901, in 6MR 232).

While Ellen White endorsed Franke's abilities as an evangelist, she also pointed out significant flaws, which she pleaded for him to remedy. He had a "theatrical style of preaching" in which "truth is mingled with common, worldly methods" (9MR 387). She told him that he had exchanged "extravagance and display" for "right methods"(6MR 229), and that such "worldly plans" are sure to "make a failure" (1MR 17), because they are "entirely contrary to Christ's example" (Lt 150, 1901, in 6MR 232), and Christ "will not tolerate self-exaltation" (UL 85). "Elder Franke is impulsive, and he often treats church members as if they were school children," she wrote. "Then when his authority is questioned, he loses control of himself, and a tornado of angry words fall from his lips. Afterward he is sorry for this explosion of feeling." An implied cause of his impatience was that he was "not a thorough health-reformer" (6MR 244).

Ellen White sent a stream of letters to both Franke and Haskell, pleading for unity. Haskell she rebuked for failing to do what he could have done to reconcile and unite with Franke (6MR 231, 237; 3MR 279; Lt 171, 1902), while at the same time she pointed out Franke's pride and unrefined character (3MR 277, 279; 6MR 230, 244; Lt 21, 1901). After times of encouragement things went worse. Eventually Franke turned schismatic, leading a New Jersey church away from the denomination (6Bio 120; AGD to WCW, Apr. 4, 1909, DF 505, CAR).

Kenneth Jorgensen

FRASER, JANE "JENNY," or "JENNIE" later **JANE "JENNY" or "JENNIE" [FRASER] ROGERS)** (1821-1896), and **SANFORD ROGERS** (1830-1917). Early Sabbatarian Adventists. At the age of 25 Fraser immigrated to the United States from Scotland, after which she was employed and lived for a time with the family of Joseph Marsh, an early opponent of Sabbatarian Adventism. In 1852 she accepted the Sabbath and shortly thereafter lived with James and Ellen White in their home in *Rochester, New York, and later moved with them to *Battle Creek, Michigan.

JENNIE FRASER

Jennie was nanny to Henry, Edson, and Willie until 1862, when she married a recent widower from Wright, Michigan, Sanford Rogers. The Whites once asked the Rogerses to stay in and care for their home while they traveled (Lt 3, 1866). They later exchanged several letters (Lt 30, 1868, in 2T 50-55; Lt 23, 1870).

Further reading: obit. RH, June 30, 1896; obit. RH, June 21, 1917; 1Bio 230, 333, 337, 395; 2SG 208; J. Moon, *W. C. White and E. G. White* (AUP, 1993), pp. 2, 4, 6, 39.

FREY, HENRI. Young worker from Germany at the publishing house in Basel, Switzerland. As a young man Frey sought to prove himself a "man" through intemperate habits such as drinking beer and smoking tobacco. Ellen White was concerned for this young person and wrote to him of his need for a thorough conversion. She urged that he avoid the influence of other young people who held a detrimental sway over him (Lt 36, 1887). He eventually confessed his wrong course (Ms 29, 1887), but continued to struggle spiritually, which led to additional letters of counsel from Ellen White (Lt 47, 48, 49, 1887).

FRISBIE, JOSEPH BIRCHARD (1816-1882). Adventist minister. Licensed to preach for the Methodists in 1843, Frisbie was ordained in 1846. For years he bitterly opposed Seventh-day Adventist teachings. In 1853, being assigned by his bishop to debate the Sabbath with *Joseph Bates, Frisbie reversed his position and, with his wife, Delphia Jane, began to observe the Sabbath and to preach Adventist doctrines. Soon after, Frisbie first met James and Ellen White in Jackson, Michigan, where Ellen White was given a vision, after which she told him that "God had arrested a soul [i.e., Frisbie] by the light and power of the truth, and through him would get glory to Himself."

In 1855, when the Whites moved the *Review and Herald* to Battle Creek, Frisbie helped build the first *Battle Creek church on his property. He served as a minister for 29 years. Early in his ministry Ellen White advised

him not to spend his time writing books but to be more dedicated in his pastoral ministry (Lt 9, 1860; Lt 10, 1864). In the 1860s, when Ellen White warned against gathering in large numbers at Battle Creek, Frisbie was among the first to leave, and

JOSEPH B. FRISBIE

moved his family back to their old home in Chelsea, Michigan.

In 1882, *O.R.L. Crosier, who introduced the Adventist doctrine of the sanctuary and accepted the Sabbath in earlier days but eventually turned against both, visited Frisbie in Chelsea. Soon the conversation turned to Ellen White and her visions. Frisbie told Crosier how one time, discouraged by poor health, he had decided to give up the ministry in favor of farming in Kansas. Before moving he attended a conference in Battle Creek. Ellen White told him that in vision she was shown the discouragements he had been through and revealed things that no other person besides him knew about. She said it was God's will for him, not to move, but to continue in the ministry. Frisbie was not "disobedient to the heavenly vision," but threw his whole heart into the work again. Crosier, pacing across the room, finally sat down, leaned forward, and asked earnestly, "Elder,

do you really think there is anything in the visions?" Weighing every word thoughtfully, Frisbie answered, "There is no doubt whatsoever in my mind that Ellen White is the inspired prophet of God."

Further reading: obit. RH, Nov. 21, 1882; obit. RH, Feb. 6, 1908; W. E. Frisbie, "Regarding the Experience of Elder J. B. Frisbie" (unpublished paper, n.d., DF 592, CAR); *SDA Encyclopedia* (1996), vol. 10, p. 574.

Leo Van Dolson

FULLER, NATHAN (1825-1895). New York-Pennsylvania Conference evangelist (1862-1866) and president (1866-1868). Fuller experienced triumphs and tragedies during his association with Adventism. He and his wife, Artamyssia, were converted to Adventism in 1857 at Ulysses, Pennsylvania. Ordained to the ministry in 1858, he eventually baptized 300 converts. With James and Ellen White he urged church organization in the 1850s and drafted constitutions for the New York-Pennsylvania Conference (1862) and the General Conference (1863). Extremely charismatic, he rejoiced when listeners wept at his meetings. He represented the Seventh-day Adventists at the 1869 Seventh Day Baptist conference.

Yet tragedies destroyed him in the end. Lung fever, measles, and typhoid fever prostrated his family. James White urged Adventists to send $400 for their expenses. But Fuller's afflictions went deeper than physical illness. Lengthy absences from home led to temptations. Fuller allegedly accepted Ellen White's testimony (1867) about ministers who failed to live the truth they preached (1T 466-485). To encourage his repentance, the *Review and Herald* featured articles on adultery, theft, and immorality. Although *Testimony* No. 17 (1869) focused on moral pollution in the church

(2T 346-353), Fuller refused to confess. Finally, *Review* editor J. N. Andrews revealed that Fuller was guilty of adultery and stealing church funds. After being disfellowshipped, Fuller drifted west to Michigan, Iowa, and Minnesota. He died in Michigan in 1895. After one mention of his case Ellen White added, "my confidence in humanity has been terribly shaken" (PH011 46).

Further reading: G. I Butler to J. White, Sept. 12, 1872 (EGWE-GC); B. E. Strayer, "Nathan Fuller: The Man Who Shook Ellen White's Confidence in Humanity" (unpublished manuscript, 1998, CAR); B. E. Strayer, "The Triumph and Tragedy of Nathan Fuller," *Adventist Heritage* 4, no. 2 (Summer 1977): 3-12.

Brian E. Strayer

FULTON, JOHN EDWIN (1869-1945) and **SUSIE VIRGINIA (NEWLON)** (1871-1950). Adventist missionaries to Fiji (1896-1906). The Fultons faced many challenges including lack of wages and the death of their son, George (1897-

JOHN E. FULTON

1904). Their efforts, however, led to the establishment of the first church school in Fiji, and the construction of the first mission ship for Fiji the *Thina* ("Lamp"). Although the Fultons left Fiji after less than 10 years of service, their influence spread far beyond the shores of this small country and across Polynesia. John served as president of the New South Wales Conference (1906-1909), the Australasian Union Conference (1909-1916), the Asiatic Division (1916-1918), the Southern Asia Division (1918-1921), and the Pacific Union Conference (1921-1922). In 1922 he became president of the North American Division, then served as president of the Australasian Division (1922-1926), the Pacific Union Conference (1926-1932), and the Northern California (1933-1936) and Southern California (1936) conferences.

As the Fultons were about to sail from San Francisco in 1894 to begin their mission service in the South Pacific, John was given a copy of a letter Ellen White had written several years earlier to his uncle *Samuel Fulton (Lt 31, 1890), a message that had greatly lifted Samuel's spirits before his death a few days later. It was suggested that this letter could encourage another Fulton in the inevitable difficult moments in mission service. John promised to "keep it forever"—and apparently he did so.

Further reading: obit. *Australasian Record*, June 4, 1945; obit. PUR, May 9, 1945; obit. RH, June 1, 1950; E. B. Hare, *Fulton's Footprints in Fiji* (RHPA, 1969); A. G. Stewart, "In Memory of John Edwin Fulton," *Australasian Record*, Oct. 6, 1969; *Union Conference Record*, Dec. 13, 1909; *SDA Encyclopedia* (1996), vol. 10, p. 577.

Lester D. Devine

FULTON, SAMUEL (1847-1890). Adventist minister. Born in Nova Scotia, Fulton converted to Adventism in 1876 and entered pastoral ministry two years later, serving in Minnesota, Tennessee, and Florida. After he contracted tuberculosis, he traveled to the western United States in search of a drier climate to recover. A week before his death Ellen White sent him a letter of sympathy and reassured him: "I have evidence—the very best—that God loves you" (Lt 31, 1890, in 16MR 242-244).

Further reading: obit. RH, May 20, 1890.

GAGE, FRANK HERMAN (1868-1934). Adventist worker at Pacific Press; son of *W. C. Gage. Gage married Jessie A. Crandall in 1889. Although he initially worked in his father's printing establishment, he was invited to connect with Pacific Press—at first for about six months (Dec. 28, 1893, to July 6, 1894), and then from 1901 until his death. In 1904 Ellen White wrote to him against seeking worldly pleasure and the negative influence it had on his wife (Lt 317a, 1904).

GAGE, FRED W. (1866-1945). Printer and civic leader in Battle Creek; son of *W. C. Gage. As a young man Gage worked at the *Review and Herald, where he met Katherine M. Amadon (1866-1909), the head proofreader and the daughter of *George and Martha Amadon, whom he married in 1887. Gage later became a junior partner in his father's printing firm. In 1893 Ellen White appealed to him to no longer follow the direction he had set for his life, but to repent so that his soul might be saved (Lt 24, 1893). Soon after this Gage left the Adventist Church to join the Congregational Church; his wife, however, remained a Seventh-day Adventist. After his parents died, he opened his father's printing establishment on Saturdays, but allowed Adventist employees not to work on Saturdays.

Further reading: obit. RH, Sept. 23, 1909; Coller Collection (WL), vol. 27, pp. 36-45.

GAGE, WILLIAM CLAGGETT (1842-1907). Printer, minister, writer, and mayor of Battle Creek. Born in Massachusetts, he later relocated to New Hampshire, where in 1860 he married Nellie Lydia Jones (1844-1924), sister of *Charles H. Jones. William was converted to the Adventist faith in 1864 through tent meetings held by *M. E. Cornell in Manchester, New Hampshire. Gage left his work at a printshop to become tentmaster and song leader for Cornell (RH, July 19, 1864). The family moved to Battle Creek in 1867, where William worked as a foreman at the Review and Herald and served on the editorial

committee (1868-1870). Gage became an ardent health reformer, frequently writing for the *Health Reformer* and later editing the first Adventist cookbook, *The Health Reformer's Progressive Cook Book and Kitchen Guide* (Battle Creek, Mich.: Health Reform Institute, 1870).

On a holiday jaunt to Chicago Gage became ill from overexposure to the weather. Soon thereafter the Gages returned to New Hampshire so that William could recuperate. Once he had recovered he became press foreman for the Manchester *Daily Mirror and American*. Ellen White counseled him that he needed to focus more upon his duty to God and less on seeking pleasure (PH159 22). "I was shown," wrote Ellen White, "that Bro. Gage has serious deficiencies in his character, which disqualify him for being closely connected with the work of God where important responsibilities are involved" (PH159 23). Because Gage did not see his failings, Ellen White believed he could not truly reform. Gage soon drifted from Adventism, but his faith was rekindled in 1876 when as a news reporter covering the U.S. centennial exposition in Philadelphia, Gage met an Adventist minister. In 1878 Gage returned to Battle Creek, where he resumed employment at the Review and Herald. Ordained to the gospel ministry in 1881, that same year he collaborated with *Uriah Smith and *J. H. Kellogg in publishing a memorial tract after the death of *James White.

The following year Ellen White admonished him to be careful not to exert a worldly influence in Battle Creek (Lt 3, 1882). He took on many responsibilities, including secretary of the Michigan Conference (1882) and member of the Battle Creek College board, the Battle

COURTESY OF THE REVIEW AND HERALD PUBLISHING ASSOCIATION

WILLIAM C. GAGE

Creek local public school board, and the Battle Creek Board of Public Works. On April 3, 1882, Gage was elected mayor of Battle Creek, winning the election because of his *prohibition views (RH, Apr. 11, 1882). Afterward a crowd assembled in front of his home, where Gage gave a short speech indicating that people would not know during his administration whether he were an Adventist or Methodist.

During this time Ellen White rebuked Gage, *Uriah Smith, and *Alexander McLearn for their part in bringing "the church into difficulty"—specifically, for causing G. H. Bell to leave Battle Creek (Lt 21, 1882; Ms 7, 1882). Ellen White was gravely concerned that Smith was trusting in Gage as a "blind counselor" (Lt 24, 1882). In 1883 Gage lost his ministerial credentials and resigned his position at the Review and Herald to set up his own printing business. As late as 1890 Ellen White continued to urge Gage and Smith to confess the wrong they had done to Bell (Lt 40, 1890). In 1893 Ellen White wrote the Gages regarding their "spiritual decay" and especially the evil influence this had had upon their son, *Fred (Lt 22, 1893).

Further reading: obit. RH, Sept. 19, 1907; Coller Collection (WL), vol. 27, pp. 62-69.

Michael W. Campbell

GARMIRE, JAMES MONROE (1848-1931). Bible worker in Colorado who claimed that his family, and in particular his daughter Anna (b. 1870), received supernatural revelations. After Garmire printed 20,000 copies of a tract teaching that the close of probation would occur in 1884—40 years after the great *disappointment, Ellen White responded with a pamphlet *An Exposure of Fanaticism and Wickedness* (PH030), which denounced his theories as delusions of Satan. When the time passed, Garmire wrote to Ellen White seeking her advice on whether they were in error, and if so, to point out their mistake.

Ellen White's response to the Garmires (Lt 12, 1890, partly in 2SM 73-79, 82-84) is one of the most significant accounts of her interaction with other visionaries. She wrote that Garmire himself had "been deceived" and had "deceived others." His ideas were misinterpretations of Scripture and of her writings, and which he had "misapplied" to support "erroneous theories, borrowing . . . the light of Heaven to teach that which the testimonies have no harmony with, and have ever condemned." Furthermore, he had worked himself into "a high state of fanaticism," loved his own opinions more than God's Word, and cultivated enmity toward God's people. One "decided evidence," wrote Ellen White, "that these *exercises* are not of God is that they concur with your *views*" and "contradict the Word of God" (*ibid.*; italics supplied). Garmire was also encouraging his daughter to believe she was having visions.

After meeting with the Garmires in their home on August 23, 1890, Ellen White reaffirmed that Anna's visions "are not of God" (Lt 11, 1890, in 15MR 12-16; 1888 Materials 697-702). Again the Garmires pleaded with Ellen White to show them their error. "But how can I," she wrote, "prove your error by Scripture when you misinterpret and misapply it as you do? . . . You misinterpret my testimony, wrench it from its true meaning, and ring in my name whenever you think it will enforce whatever you have to say. But when the testimonies do not harmonize with your theories, I am excused, because I am the false prophet!" (*ibid.*). After Ellen White's visit, Anna Garmire ran away from home and became pregnant. Ellen White felt sorry for the girl and how she was deceived by her father (Lt 4, 1893).

Further reading: 10MR 310-312; 12MR 117, 118; 14MR 189, 190; 2SM 64, 65, 72-84, 89, 96.

Michael W. Campbell

EDWARD AND IDA GATES AND THEIR DAUGHTERS

GATES, EDWARD HARMON (1855-1940) and **IDA ELLEN (SHARP)** (1860-1946). Pioneer missionaries to the South Pacific; friends of Ellen White. The Gateses stayed with Ellen White in Australia after their journey on the first voyage of the ship *Pitcairn* (Ms 29, 1892). She afterward cautioned them regarding their diet (Lt 49a, 1892) and to "do all you possibly can to become strong" again in health (Lt 49, 1892). Later Ellen White wrote a news-filled letter about the progress of the Adventist work in Australia (Lt 23a, 1893). After the death of fellow missionary *J. R. McCoy's wife and daughter, she affirmed their need to "comfort one another" (Lt 1a, 1894).

Further reading: obit. RH, June 27, 1940; obit. RH, May 30, 1946.

GATES, ELSIE MAY (1852-1899). Bible worker at Crystal Springs Health Retreat (later the *St. Helena Sanitarium); sister of *E. H. Gates. After an anonymous complaint, Dr. *W. P. Burke planned to replace the current matron of the sanitarium with Elsie Gates. When Burke and Gates sought Ellen White's support, she told them that this was insufficient grounds for dismissal (Lt 44, 1891). Ellen White defended the current matron and counseled Gates to "close every door possible to the murmurers and complainers." This was

followed by an appeal for Gates to change her life (Lts 42, 46, 1891).

GIBBS, JUDSON STANLEY (1849-1912). Adventist physician at the Rural Health Retreat (later *St. Helena Sanitarium) in St. Helena, California. When the Rural Health Retreat did not have a physician in 1885, some feared the institution might have to be closed until *W. P. Burke could obtain medical training. Ellen White met Gibbs, a recent convert to Adventism, at a camp meeting in New York that summer. She felt he would provide the leadership necessary for the institution, and although

DR. JUDSON S. GIBBS

he had been trained in the use of drugs, he could learn how to use *natural remedies. She wrote frequently to Gibbs (cf. Lts 10, 11, 22, 1886). When Burke completed his medical training, she counseled both doctors to work together (Lt 16, 1886). She later cautioned Gibbs not to overwork (Lt 7, 1887). When others criticized that he was not learning natural remedies quickly enough, she asked them to be patient (Lt 10, 1887) and wrote in support of Gibbs's talent as a physician (Lt 30, 1887). After 1889 he left the health retreat to obtain further training in natural remedies (Ms 22, 1888; Lt 8, 1892). She later encouraged him to join the staff of the *Loma Linda Sanitarium, but her suggestion did not materialize.

Further reading: obit. RH, Oct. 24, 1912.

GILBERT, FREDERICK CARNES (1867-1946). Jewish Adventist minister and author. Gilbert grew up in London, England, where he was converted to Adventism in 1889. He attended *South Lancaster Academy (1890-1894). In 1896 he married Ella Graham (1865-1944) and worked in the Atlantic Union Conference, where he was ordained in 1898. Ellen White affirmed his work for his own people (Lt 47, 1903; see also Ms 1, 1908, in 5MR 211-213). He later worked for the North American Division, heading the "Jewish Department" (1911-1922), and served as a field secretary of the General Conference (1922-1943). He is best remembered for several books, including one about Ellen White's predictions.

Further reading: obit. RH, Feb. 17, 1944; obit. RH, Feb. 26, 1946; F. C. Gilbert, *Practical Lessons From the Experience of Israel* (South Lancaster, Mass.: by the author, 1902, 1914); F. C. Gilbert, *From Judaism to Christianity and Gospel Work Among the Hebrews* (South Lancaster, Mass.: Good Tidings Press, 1920); F. C. Gilbert, *Divine Predictions of Mrs. Ellen G. White Fulfilled* (South Lancaster, Mass.: Good Tidings Press, c. 1922); F. C. Gilbert, *Messiah in His Sanctuary* (RHPA, 1937).

GILBERT, LILLIAN "LILLIE" A. (BELDEN), see **BELDEN, LILLIAN "LILLIE" A.**

GILES, CHARLES EDISON (d. 1934). Adventist who wrote to Ellen White questioning whether he could have *assurance of salvation. In her first response she appealed to him to come to Jesus just as he was and not to rely on his emotions as an evidence of salvation (Lt 82, 1889). Two days later she wrote a second letter in which she encouraged him to believe in the promise of forgiveness and not to think that he had committed the unpardonable sin (Lt 20, 1889, in 5T 628-634).

Further reading: obit. *Southern Tidings*, Mar. 14, 1934.

GLEASON, ALEXANDER STRAHAN (1844-1909). Adventist proponent of the "flat-earth theory." In 1890 Gleason published his views on the flat earth in *Is the Bible From Heaven? Is the Earth a Globe?* (Buffalo: Buffalo Electrotype and Engraving, 1890), in which he stated that he is acquainted with a people who "claim to be giving that everlasting Gospel, styled the 'Third Angel's Message' of Rev. 14:6-12" (p. 382). A major portion of the book was devoted to Adventist doctrines. Ellen White twice mentioned meeting Adventists who advocated the flat-earth theory. She did not seek to enter debate over the shape of the earth, but sought to show that in light of the Adventist message certain questions fade into insignificance (GW 314; 21MR 412).

Further reading: obit. RH, Apr. 15, 1909; L. G. Seibold, "Is the Bible From Heaven? Is the Earth a Globe?" *Adventist Heritage* 15, no. 1 (Spring 1992): 26-29.

GLENN, WILLIAM NEWTON (1837-1906). After managing a general store and then a printshop in Kansas, Nebraska, and Nevada, Glenn joined the Union army and was stationed at the Presidio in San Francisco during the Civil War. After the war, he, his wife, Victoria Tripp, and their nine children edited two newspapers before converting to Adventism in 1875. From 1876 to 1906 Glenn was a Pacific Press proofreader, foreman, manager, and editor responsible for *Our Little Friend* (1893-1901), *Signs of the Times* (1900-1906), and the Apples of Gold, Bible Students', and Sentinel Library series. He wrote *Things Foretold*, a book on Bible prophecy. In 1879 Ellen White admonished him to hire fewer workers, put a cap on employees' wages, and get more sleep lest physical and mental labor take their toll on his health (Lt 44, 1879).

Further reading: obit. RH, Dec. 20, 1906; *SDA Encyclopedia* (1996), vol. 10, p. 615.

Brian E. Strayer

GLOVER, CHARLES S. C. (1814-1898) and

JANE (SHELDON) (1815-1873). Glover and his father, William (1790-1855), converted to Adventism in 1852 following meetings held by Joseph Bates. The following year Charles was ordained in Sylvan, Michigan, as one of the first two deacons among Sabbatarian Adventists in that state. Glover saw Ellen White in vision several times and in 1857, after one such vision, recorded the testimonial of a doctor who described the visions as "beyond his knowledge" and that "there is something supernatural about that" (JNL, *Rise and Progress*, p. 96). In 1860 Ellen White and her children spent a week at the Glovers' home (Lt 14, 1860). Glover received a testimony in which Ellen White admonished him to raise his children in the fear of the Lord (Lt 9, 1861). After the Glovers relocated to Kansas, the Whites visited them in May 1873. After Jane's death later in 1873, Glover married Clarissa E. (1826-1905) (cf. Mss 7, 11, 1873; Lt 13, 1873; Ms 4, 1879).

Further reading: obit. RH, May 24, 1898; obit. RH, July 1, 1873; obit. RH, Dec. 7, 1905.

GORDON, PAUL A. (1930-2009). Director of the Ellen G. White Estate (1990-1995). In 1952 Gordon graduated from Walla Walla College and married Donna Bresee. Gordon worked in Oregon doing evangelism, pastoral ministry, and academy Bible teaching. He was ordained in 1956 and joined the White Estate in 1967, where he remained for 31 years. While working for the White Estate, he helped develop the "Testimony Countdown" program, the Ellen G. White CD-ROM, and many compilations, including four devotional books. He also prepared study guides for several Ellen White books, led Adventist heritage tours, authored numerous periodical articles and four books, including *The Sanctuary, 1844, and the Pioneers* and *My Dear Brother M*, and visited more than 100 countries

promoting Ellen White's writings. After retiring to Oregon, Gordon condensed several Ellen White books for publication.

James R. Nix

GOTZIAN, JOSEPHINE (1855-1935). Adventist philanthropist. Originally from St. Paul, Minnesota, Gotzian and her husband made considerable money in the shoe industry. In the 1880s her husband was killed in a train wreck in Missouri, during which she also sustained a broken back and went to the *Battle Creek Sanitarium for treatment. The following summer she had a young *colporteur, *E. A. Sutherland, stay in her home. These relationships with Adventists led her to become a Seventh-day Adventist. After Gotzian sold her home in Minnesota, she went to Portland, Oregon, where she gave generously to build the Portland Sanitarium. She later spent some time as a patient at the *St. Helena Sanitarium, where she became a confidant and close friend of Ellen White's. Frequently Gotzian provided students with loans, particularly at the recommendation of Ellen White. She also helped to purchase the properties for the *Avondale Health Retreat, *Paradise Valley Sanitarium, and *Loma Linda Sanitarium (Lt 139, 1899; Lt 97, 1900; Lt 16, 1908), and led in the fundraising for the Ellen G. White Memorial Hospital in Los Angeles (H. O. McCumber, *Pioneering the Message in the Golden West* [PPPA, 1946], p. 215). In 1907 she moved to *Madison College, where she served on the board until her death.

GRAHAM, SYLVESTER (1794-1851). Minister and temperance advocate. In a time when the diet of most Americans contained mostly meat, Graham believed that dyspepsia (any illness related to the stomach) was directly connected to the removing of bran from flour. There was an "intimate relation," according to Graham, between whole flour and moral character. This temperance reform grew into a health movement that swept through America during the 1830s. In addition to unbolted flour, his regimen expanded to also include a natural (vegetarian) diet, sunshine, fresh air, rest, temperance, cleanliness, sensible dress, and much more. Graham published his teachings in *The Graham Journal*, a weekly paper published in Boston and edited by David Campbell, and in a two-volume treatise entitled *Lectures on the Science of Human Life* (London, 1849) that the Seventh-day Adventist Publishing Association republished in 1872. Ellen White heartily recommended graham flour, and at one point James White boasted that they had a 100-pound sack of it in their pantry (CTBH 256). In the 1860s most Adventist recipes for gems (small unleavened biscuits), gruel, and pudding called for graham flour (cf. Martha Amadon, "How to Use Graham Flour," RH, Nov. 1, 1864).

Further reading: R. H. Shryock, "Sylvester Graham and the Popular Health Movement, 1830-1870," in his *Medicine in America: Historical Essays* (Baltimore: Johns Hopkins Press, 1966), pp. 112-114; M. V. Naylor, "Sylvester Graham, 1794-1851," *Annals of Medical History*, 3rd series (May 1942), vol. 4, pp. 236-240; S. W. Nissenbaum, *Sex, Diet, and Debility in Jacksonian America: Sylvester Graham and Health Reform* (Westport, Conn.: Greenwood Press, 1980); R. L. Numbers, *Prophetess of Health: A Study of Ellen White*, 3rd ed. (Grand Rapids: Eerdmans, 2008), pp. 97-103.

Michael W. Campbell

GRAHAM, WILLIAM HENRY (1831-1925), **BRUCE** (b. c. 1834), and **ANDREW** (b. c. 1836). Early Adventist members and brothers in Kensington, Connecticut. William served as a deacon in the Berlin, Connecticut, church for 20 years and was the father-in-law of

*F. C. Gilbert. After a visit to Connecticut in 1859, Ellen White reproved the Graham brothers for "a fanatical spirit" and carrying things "to great lengths." In her letter she related the case of a number of believers in Connecticut that she had seen in a vision, including Mrs. Graham, their mother. She encouraged some and rebuked others for their excesses (Lt 7, 1859; cf. Ms 7, 1859; Lt 9, 1859).

Further reading: obit. RH, July 2, 1925.

GRAINGER, WILLIAM CALHOUN (1844-1899) and **ELIZABETH** (1845-1927). Teacher and second president of *Healdsburg College; first American Seventh-day Adventist missionary to Japan. After Abram LaRue converted him to Adventism, Grainger, an experienced public school teacher, began conducting evangelistic meetings. Ellen White told him at a camp meeting that he and his wife would be needed as teachers at the soon-opening Healdsburg school. After teaching at Healdsburg for four years, he became its president, serving from 1888 to 1894. Because his administrative style was not rigid enough for General Conference educational secretary *W. W. Prescott, he was replaced in 1894. This led to his decision to accompany one of his former students, T. H. Okohira, who was returning to his homeland to introduce Adventism in Japan. Grainger started an English language school in Tokyo, organized a church there, and launched a periodical before succumbing on October 31, 1899, to a four-week illness. After his death, his wife, Elizabeth, returned to the United States, where she married *G. I. Butler in 1907.

Further reading: obit. RH, Dec. 5, 1899; obit. RH, Jan. 16, 1900; obit. PUR, Feb. 2, 1928; A. W. Spalding, *Origin and History of Seventh-day Adventists* (RHPA, 1962), vol. 2, pp. 53, 55, 319, 326; W. Utt, *A Mountain, a Pickax, a College*, 3rd ed. (Angwin, Calif.: Pacific Union College, 1996), pp. 3, 11-17;

SDA Encyclopedia (1996), vol. 10, p. 623.

Dennis Pettibone

GRANT, MILES (1819-1911). Advent Christian leader and editor of *The World's Crisis*. While

COURTESY OF THE CENTER FOR ADVENTIST RESEARCH, ANDREWS UNIVERSITY

MILES GRANT

sharing with Seventh-day Adventists a common spiritual heritage in the Millerite movement, Advent Christians rejected the obligation of keeping the Sabbath and the validity of Ellen White's ministry. In the 1870s Miles Grant became a fierce opponent of Ellen White's ministry and used every opportunity to disparage her work and influence. In 1874 he published an article in which he claimed Ellen White had been involved in some forms of fanaticism in 1844 and had believed the whole world was condemned to eternal punishment. In her reply Ellen White contended that no such claims could be verified, and denied the charges against her (Lt 2, 1874, in 1SM 74). In succeeding years she felt his slanderous attacks were manufactured to discredit her ministry. "During all these years one of the principal burdens of his work seems to have been to follow on my track," she wrote in 1885, "and spread these statements which have been manufactured by false witnesses. . . . It has been shown again and again, both by pen and voice and by the testimony of many witnesses, that these reports have no foundation in truth; but what cares he for this? He loves his falsehoods too well to give them up" (HS 236).

In December 1885, when Ellen White and other pastors were holding evangelistic meetings near Torre Pellice, in northern Italy, Miles Grant followed them to also hold meetings in the same town and, in fact, in the same building. His main purpose was to expose the fallacies of Ellen White's visions. Ellen White, however, went right on with her meetings, making no reference to Grant, hoping to reach the hearts of the few who came to hear her (3Bio 335). "It has ever been against my principle to enter into controversy with anyone, or to spend my time in vindicating myself," she later reflected (HS 237).

In early April 1889, while conducting meetings in Chicago, Ellen White received a surprising visit of Mrs. Grant. "I had an introduction to her in my room, and we had a pleasant visit," she wrote to her son. "She said that she did not know that I would care to meet the wife of Miles Grant, as he and I were sharp antagonists, but I said to her that I had made no raid upon her husband, it was he that had followed me and made a raid upon me. She talked very pleasantly, and commended the manner in which we are doing our work in such cities as Chicago. She said that she had told her husband that as a people we were showing a commendable zeal in live missionary work, while they, as a people, were doing very little, and were really dying out for want of just such methods of labor as Seventh-day Adventists were employing" (Lt 1, 1889, in 7MR 245, 246).

Further reading: 3Bio 334-336; EGWEur 143-145; HS 235-239; J. N. Andrews, *Injustice of Eld. Miles Grant, Editor of the "World's Crisis," Toward Seventh-day Adventists* (Battle Creek, Mich., 1874); A. C. Johnson, *Advent Christian History* (Mendota, Ill.: Western Advent Christian Publishing Society, 1918), pp. 392-395; F. L. Piper, *Life and Labors of Miles Grant* (Boston: Advent Christian Publication Society, 1915).

Denis Fortin

GRAVELLE, MRS. J. J. Adventist from North Dakota who sent Ellen White *tithe money and an offering to use where she felt it would be most needed. "I will say," replied Ellen White, "that I shall not refuse to do this, but at the same time I will tell you that there is a better way.

"It is better," she continued, "to put confidence in the ministers of the conference where you live, and in the officers of the church where you worship. Draw nigh to your brethren. Love them with a true heart fervently, and encourage them to bear their responsibilities faithfully in the fear of God" (Lt 96, 1911, in 12MR 271-273). Ellen White also encouraged her not to allow her mind "to dwell upon the imperfections of others" lest her own soul "become filled with the leaven of evil," and not "to hoard . . . means for future years." If she had money that needed investing, she should invest the means "to create new interests in places where the need of truth is felt" (*ibid.*).

GRAY (or **GREY**), **HARVEY P.** (1841-1896) and **EMMA CAROLINE (HURD)** (1853-1926). Adventists from California; Harvey was a judge. The Grays were converted to Adventism in 1880 at a camp meeting at which Ellen White was one of the speakers (Lt 26, 1880). Emma was the older sister of *Hetty Haskell. The Grays were philanthropists who gave generously to help establish *Pacific Press, *Healdsburg College, and *St. Helena Sanitarium. Ellen White wrote a letter of counsel to Harvey (Lt 36, 1890). She later sent them a glowing account about the discovery of water at *Paradise Valley Sanitarium (Lt 317, 1904, in 14MR 218-220). Emma was part of the fund-raising committee to help establish the *White Memorial Medical Center.

Further reading: obit. RH, July 21, 1896; obit. PUR, Aug. 12, 1926.

GRIGGS, FREDERICK (1867-1952). Academy principal, college president, educational administrator, division president, and General Conference field secretary. In 1890 Griggs

COURTESY OF THE CENTER FOR ADVENTIST RESEARCH, ANDREWS UNIVERSITY.

FREDERICK GRIGGS

became principal of the Preparatory Department of Battle Creek College. During 1897-1898 he wrote a series of articles for *The Christian Educator* that were read by Ellen White. Concerned that Griggs was espousing humanistic philosophy, she counseled him against doing so (Lt 65, 1898, in 20MR 194-203). Distressed at the reproof, Griggs wrote a reply (F. Griggs to EGW, Oct. 20, 1898, Griggs Papers, CAR) and received a gentle, supportive and encouraging letter in response (Lt 117, 1898). Griggs came to value Ellen White's insights, and until her death he frequently sought her counsel. This was evident in 1903. Newly appointed secretary of the General Conference Department of Education, Griggs was confronted with *John H. Kellogg's initiative to reactivate Battle Creek College. Griggs understood Kellogg's motivation, but was also aware of the reasons the college closed in 1901. He sought Ellen White's counsel and accepted her advice that Battle Creek remained unsuitable for Adventist youth (Lt 189, 1903). He therefore took a strong stand against Kellogg's initiative (RH, Sept. 17, 1903).

A consensus seeker and educational moderate, Griggs played a pivotal role in the development of the Seventh-day Adventist system of education, including the establishment of the Home Study Institute (now Griggs University). He served two terms as secretary of the Department of Education (1903-1910, 1914-1918). He also served as president of Union College (1910-1914) and Emmanuel Missionary College (1918-1925), and later as president of the Far Eastern Division (1930-1935) and the China Division (1936-1938).

From 1939 until his death Griggs was a field secretary of the General Conference.

Further reading: A. C. Reye and G. R. Knight, "Frederick Griggs: Moderate," in G. R. Knight, ed., *Early Adventist Educators* (AUP, 1983), pp. 184-204; A. C. Reye, "Frederick Griggs: Seventh-day Adventist Educator and Administrator" (Ph.D. diss., AU, 1984).

Arnold C. Reye

GURNEY, HEEMAN S. (c. 1818-1896). Millerite Adventist who accepted the seventh-day Sabbath in the spring of 1845. Though a blacksmith by trade, Gurney was an excellent singer and associated with *Joseph Bates in Millerite evangelistic activity during the winter of 1843-1844. After hearing Ellen Harmon in the "Advent hall in New Bedford," in late 1845 or early 1846, Gurney traveled to Portland, Maine, to investigate the circumstances surrounding Harmon's visions. Convinced that the "fountain was good," he arranged for the publication of the first broadside of her visions, *"To the Little Remnant Scattered Abroad" (Apr. 6, 1846, Portland, Maine). Printed on one side of a large sheet, it contained the same information she had presented in her two *Day-Star* letters to *Enoch Jacobs (E. G. Harmon, "Letter From Sister Harmon," *Day-Star*, Jan. 24, 1846, and Mar. 14, 1846). Gurney covered half the printing cost of 250 copies. The first printing of this three-column broadside apparently left most of the third column empty. Gurney remembered: "The last page of the sheet was left partly blank so that those receiving this document could have a place to write out their opinion of the same whether favorable or unfavorable, and return it to the publisher"

COURTESY OF THE REVIEW AND HERALD PUBLISHING ASSOCIATION

HERMAN S. GURNEY

(H. S. Gurney, "Recollections of Early Advent Experience," RH, Jan. 3, 1888; H. S. Gurney, signed manuscript, May 15, 1891, EGWE-GC). In a subsequent printing the material concerning the Bridegroom vision and *time of trouble was added. This publication gave added visibility to Ellen Harmon's visions and placed her in a new position of leadership.

Gurney was a participant in the development of Sabbatarian Adventism and remained a faithful member of the Seventh-day Adventist Church. In 1853 he married the widow Anne E. Randall, daughter of William Gifford, who was also among the first group of Sabbathkeepers in Fairhaven, Massachusetts, during the spring of 1845 (RH, June 12, 1894). They had three children and moved first to Jackson, Michigan, in 1856 and then to Memphis, Michigan, about 1865. Gurney remained active as a blacksmith and as an evangelist throughout the remainder of his life. He served as president of the Michigan Conference for one year (1869-1870).

Further reading: obit. RH, Sept. 8, 1896.

Merlin D. Burt

HAINES, ELIZABETH. Millerite of Portland, Maine, who opened her home to teenage Ellen Harmon during her times of illness. Haines is listed as a delegate with Orinda Haines at the third Millerite General Conference held in Portland, Maine, during October 1841 ("Report of the Proceedings," *Signs of the Times*, Nov. 1, 1841). About the time of the 1844 disappointment, physicians had diagnosed Ellen Harmon as having tuberculosis. Because her chronic illness was exhausting her mother, *Eunice Harmon, Haines agreed to care for the young girl for a few days. It was thus that Ellen came to be at Haines' home when she had her first vision in December 1844 (JNL, "Some Individual Experience" [Companion to *The Great Second Advent*

Movement], unpublished manuscript [Oct. 27, 1918], p. 43). Several significant visions occurred in the Haines home during 1845. It was in this home that Ellen received a vision that rebuked *Joseph Turner for using mesmerism. In the spring of 1845, it was also in Haines' home that Ellen had her "new earth" vision that inspired *William Hyde to write a poem that has appeared in Adventist hymnals down to the present (*The Seventh-day Adventist Hymnal,* no. 453). After this vision Haines cared for Ellen in her home for two weeks during a bout with illness. During her illness Ellen experienced mental confusion. Joseph Turner and those associated with him extracted a signed statement by Haines concerning comments made by Ellen during her delirium in an attempt to discredit her. Haines later tearfully confessed to Ellen her regret that her name was ever attached to the document (2SG 69, 302). *J. N. Loughborough in company with James and Ellen White visited Haines in Portland, Maine, during 1858, and Haines, though not a Sabbathkeeper, willingly gave her name as a reference that Ellen White had not been a part of the fanaticism after 1844. Unfortunately, little is known about Elizabeth Haines. For many years Adventist tours visited the traditional site where it was believed that Haines lived, but research has shown that the location is incorrect.

See also: *Hypnotism and Mesmerism.*

Merlin D. Burt

HALL, D. P., see *MESSENGER PARTY.*

HALL, LUCINDA (ABBEY) (1839-1929). Literary assistant and close friend and confidant of Ellen White; daughter of *Ira and Rhoda Abbey. Born in Brookfield, New York, she moved to Battle Creek at the age of 21 (March 1860) to assist Ellen White with household chores and child care. About 1861 she married

COURTESY OF THE REVIEW AND HERALD PUBLISHING ASSOCIATION

LUCINDA HALL

William Hall, a pressman at the *Review and Herald who died a few years later from tuberculosis. During this time Ellen White wrote frequently to Lucinda (cf. Lts 27, 28, 29, 1861), and Lucinda continued to help the Whites intermittently (1861-1863). Her parents joined her in Battle Creek in 1871.

During the 1870s Hall began to work primarily as Ellen White's "copyist" (Lt 21, 1871) and served as "matron" of the White home during the Whites' travels (Lt 28, 1871). The Whites wrote frequently to the family, often addressing their letters to Lucinda, giving news reports of their journeys (cf. Lt 29, 1871). In 1872 Hall accompanied James and Ellen White on their first trip to California. They stopped briefly at their home in Washington, Iowa; took a short vacation in the mountains of Colorado; and finally went on to California, where Lucinda helped them set up their first home in Healdsburg (Lts 5, 13a, 1872). When James returned east to visit Battle Creek, Hall stayed behind with Ellen White (Lt 6, 1873). Later that year when Ellen White also returned east, Hall remained to manage their California home, and Ellen White had to write to her not to overwork (Lt 27, 1873). When James White established the *Signs of the Times* in Oakland, California, in 1874, she worked for a time as secretary-treasurer, proofreader, and assistant editor of the *Signs*. In 1881 she was invited by *Dr. J. H. Kellogg to be the matron (female supervisor) of the *Battle Creek Sanitarium, where she worked for more than 20 years.

A collection of 2,000 letters once owned by Hall was discovered in 1973, including correspondence from church leaders such as *George Amadon, J. H. Kellogg, *J. N. Loughborough, *Stephen Haskell, and James White. Of special significance were 48 handwritten letters to Hall by Ellen White. These letters had been stored in a family trunk for more than 100 years. Sometime around 1970 the trunk had been sold at auction as an antique. The letters, when discovered, were given to the buyer's 16-year-old niece, Susan Jaquette, who was interested in historical materials. As Jaquette began to read the letters, she noticed that several carried the Battle Creek Sanitarium imprint. She contacted chaplain Harold Flynt at the sanitarium, and he called the *Ellen G. White Estate office in Washington, D.C. *Arthur White, secretary of the White Estate, traveled to Jaquette's home and purchased the letters for the White Estate.

Among other things, these letters provided additional insights into the personal relationships between Ellen White and Lucinda Hall, and between Ellen White and her husband, James. In a series of four letters, written over a period of eight days in May 1876, Ellen White confided in Lucinda regarding stresses in her relationship with James because of personality changes that had resulted from his several strokes (Lts 64, 65, 66, 1876). In the fourth letter Ellen White apologized for troubling Hall with her perplexities, and requested that she destroy the letters she had received (Lt 67, 1876).

But Lucinda did not destroy them, and the White Estate, sensitive to Ellen White's request for privacy, laid them aside and did not place them in the regular archival file. However, in 1987, with an increased public awareness of the situation that Ellen White was wrestling with at the time (owing, in part, to unauthorized publication of excerpts from the letters), the White Estate made the letters available to its research centers. Eventually they were published in full, with historical setting, in *Daughters of God* (pp. 260-275).

In a letter to her husband, James, Ellen White described her close relationship with Lucinda: "I prize her society, and no other one can fill her place to us. . . . Her worth cannot be estimated by its weight in gold. She is my twin sister indeed in Christ" (Lt 44, 1874, in 5MR 427). Hall is buried in Brookfield, New York.

Further reading: obit. RH, Apr. 18, 1865; obit. RH, Sept. 19, 1929; 2Bio 424-445; DG 260-275; A. L. White, "Ellen White Letters Discovered in Historical Collection," RH, Aug. 16, 23, 1973.

Tim Poirier

HALL, WILLIAM H. (1841-1932). Administrator at the Battle Creek Sanitarium (1883 to at least 1894) whom Ellen White advised regarding the medical training of young European Adventists. She was concerned that these students were not receiving a training to equip them adequately for their work in their own countries and that mistakes made by the managers of the sanitarium did not leave them with a good impression and would hinder other European young people from coming to Battle Creek to receive their medical training (Lt 56, 1889).

Further reading: obit. RH, Nov. 17, 1932; *SDA Yearbook* (1883), pp. 7, 49; (1894), p. 9.

HANNAFORD, MARY BELLE (1869-1958). Housekeeper for Ellen White. Hannaford became an Adventist about 1900, briefly attended *Union College, and afterward worked in city mission work in Nebraska and New York City (1901-1904). From 1907 to 1909 she served as "the woman of my choice" to care for Ellen White's home (Lt 152, 1909). She later assisted *Eleanor Burden at the *Loma Linda Sanitarium, and in 1916 became assistant and later matron of the *Paradise Valley Sanitarium.

Further reading: obit. RH, May 29, 1958.

HANSEN, LARS, see **HAYWARD, OTIS MADISON.**

HARDY, WILLIAM J. (b. c. 1823). Black Adventist layperson near Grand Rapids, Michigan. In the summer of 1858 Hardy and his family, who had been Freewill Baptists, became Sabbathkeepers after *J. B. Frisbie held a series of meetings in his town (RH, Apr. 29, 1858). In January 1859, during a snowstorm, James and Ellen White stopped at the Hardy home on their way to a meeting in a nearby town. In her diary Ellen White commented, "This is a colored family. Although the house is poor and old, everything is arranged with neatness and exact order. The children are well behaved, intelligent, and interesting" (Ms 5, 1859). The story of the Hardy family is represented in a "Hardy home" at the Historic Adventist Village in Battle Creek, Michigan.

HARE, EDWARD (1847-1948) and **ELIZABETH** (1852-1941). Adventists in New Zealand; Edward was the son of Joseph Hare, Sr., who emigrated from Ireland with his family in 1865. When a group of missionaries first went to the South Pacific in 1885 to establish the Seventh-day Adventist Church in that part of the world, *S. N. Haskell met Edward and Elizabeth Hare in Auckland, New Zealand. After the Hares accepted Adventism, Edward invited Haskell to visit his father and other family members in Kaeo, New Zealand. This encounter led to most of the large Hare family becoming Adventists. In 1893 Ellen White wrote to Edward regarding *Louis Christie and suggested he be cautious about believing what Christie would tell him and others (Lt 28a, 1893).

Further reading: obit. *South Pacific Union Record*, Feb. 10, 1941; obit. *South Pacific Union Record*, Aug. 9, 1948.

HARE, ELSIE (or **ELIZABETH**) (**BROWN**) (1852-1920) and **WILLIAM JOHN** (1846-1890). Adventists in New Zealand, among the first to be baptized by *S. N. Haskell in 1886. John and Elsie were married in 1873. William John, the oldest son of *Joseph Hare, Sr., died trying to save a child from a falling tree in 1890. Their daughter, *Maggie (Hare) Bree, served as a literary assistant to Ellen White. In 1893 Ellen White wrote Elsie a letter of encouragement thanking her for a gift of a silk hairnet (Lt 94, 1893). Elsie later married Ralf William Weber.

Further reading: obit. BE, May 15, 1890.

HARE, GEORGE A. (1857-1936) and **JESSIE BLANCHE** (**DANIELLS**). Adventist physicians; George was born in Mount Pleasant, Iowa, and Jessie was the sister of A. G. Daniells. Both graduated from the University of Michigan School of Medicine in 1887 and served on the medical staff at the Battle Creek and Mount Vernon sanitariums. In 1903 George was asked to organize the new *Washington Sanitarium, a decision that Ellen White wholeheartedly agreed with (Lt 260, 1903). In connection with the erection of the Washington Sanitarium, Ellen White advised that the buildings not be for the "sake of display" or for "show" (Lt 83, 1904) and approved of the location for the sanitarium in Takoma Park, Maryland (Lt 335, 1904). She also encouraged the Hares to be faithful in their practice of the health reform and hence be examples for others to follow (Lt 214, 1904; Lt 208, 1905).

Further reading: obit. RH, May 21, 1936.

HARE, JOSEPH, SR. (1821-1919). Early settler

of New Zealand, among the first Adventists in that country. Originally a Methodist schoolteacher in Ireland, he married Maggie Metcalfe (1826-1866) in 1845. When a national school system was set up in Ireland forbidding instruction from the Bible, they immigrated to New Zealand with their 10 children in 1865. After their arrival Joseph chose not to accept land confiscated from the Maoris, but settled in the remote wilderness of Kaeo, where they worked the land. Eleven months after their arrival Maggie died in childbirth. Two years later Hare married a recent widow, Hannah Skinner (d. 1898). She had eight children from her previous marriage, and to their union were born an additional five children. After *S. N. Haskell met Joseph's son, *Edward, who lived in Auckland, Edward sent Haskell to Kaeo to visit his parents, who also became Seventh-day Adventists, along with many others of the Hare family. Ellen White wrote to Joseph expressing her joy that his children had given themselves to Jesus (Lt 32, 1893). After Hannah's death, Joseph married Caroline Dore (c. 1844-1928).

Further reading: obit. *Australasian Record*, May 26, 1919; E. B. Hare, *An Irish Boy and God* (RHPA, 1965).

HARE, JOSEPH (1851-1935) and **HARRIET.** Adventists in New Zealand; Joseph was a son of *Joseph Hare, Sr. Ellen White wrote him several letters of counsel on topics ranging from *perfection (Lt 109, 1893) to marital advice (Lt 8, 1893) and appealed to him to give himself unreservedly to the Lord (Lt 105, 1893).

Further reading: obit. *Australasian Record*, Jan. 6, 1936.

HARE, METCALFE (1855-1938) and **MARIA (DIXON)** (1861-1937). Adventists from New Zealand; Metcalfe was a son of *Joseph Hare, Sr., who emigrated from Ireland in 1865.

Metcalfe assisted *A. G. Daniells during the first tent meetings in New Zealand and in the 1890s helped establish the school at *Avondale. In 1908 the Hares immigrated to the United States, where Metcalfe worked in Tennessee and at the *Washington and *Loma Linda sanitariums. While working at Avondale, Ellen White reproved Metcalfe for his attitude and prejudice toward *S. N. Haskell (Lts 11, 12, 13, 1898). In 1908, when the Hares moved to the United States, Ellen White encouraged Metcalfe in his work at the food factory in Nashville, Tennessee (Lts 160, 156, 1908).

Further reading: obit. PUR, Sept. 28, 1938; obit. PUR, Dec 29, 1937.

HARE, ROBERT (1858-1953) and **HENRIETTA (JOHNSON)** (1865-1955). Evangelist, poet, and editor. Born in northern Ireland to *Joseph Hare, Sr., Robert immigrated with his family to New Zealand in 1865. In 1885 *S. N. Haskell met Hare while he was engaged in boatbuilding. He accepted the seventh-day Sabbath, sold his business, and traveled to America to attend *Healdsburg College. He graduated in 1888, was ordained to the ministry, married Henrietta, and returned to New Zealand to assist *A. G. Daniells in evangelism. In 1890 the Hares moved to Australia, where they worked in evangelism until 1928. He edited the *Bible Echo (1899-1902) and taught Bible at *Avondale College (1908-1911, 1914-1920). Hare was a gifted poet, and some of his poems were published in the *Review and Herald*. His sons, Reuben and Eric B., were Adventist missionaries. While living in Australia, Ellen White encouraged the Hares to "reach a higher standard" in their personal lives and pastoral ministry (Lt 9, 1892; cf. Lt 29, 1895).

Further reading: obit. RH, Oct. 15, 1953; obit. *Australasian Record,* Sept. 21, 1953; R. Hare, *Along Life's Journey* (RHPA, 1948);

E. B. Hare, *An Irish Boy and God* (RHPA, 1965); *SDA Encyclopedia* (1996), vol. 10, p. 665.

HARE, SAMUEL (d. 1928) and **GERTRUDE CONSTANCE** (1865-1901). Farmers in Kaeo, New Zealand. Samuel was a son of *Joseph Hare, Sr. Ellen White wrote two letters to the Hares encouraging them to stand fast in faith and to resist temptation (Lts 27, 30, 1893).

Further reading: obit. BE, Mar. 18, 1901.

HARE, WESLEY (1858-1933). Adventist in New Zealand and Australia. Son of *Joseph Hare, Sr.; emigrated from Ireland to New Zealand with his family in 1865. In 1897 Ellen White encouraged Hare's wife during a period of sickness (Lt 58, 1897), and she later thanked them for a donation (Lt 23, 1900).

Further reading: obit. *Australasian Record*, Sept. 18, 1933.

HARMON, CAROLINE, see **CLOUGH, CAROLINE TRUE (HARMON)**.

HARMON, ELIZABETH, see **BANGS, ELIZABETH (HARMON)**.

HARMON, ELLEN GOULD (1827-1915). Cofounder of the Seventh-day Adventist Church, writer, lecturer, who possessed what Seventh-day Adventists have accepted as the prophetic gift. Born November 26, 1827, to Robert and Eunice (Gould) Harmon, in Gorham, Maine, Ellen was married to James White, August 30, 1846, in Portland, Maine. She died at her Elmshaven home in St. Helena, California, July 16, 1915, and was buried in Oak Hill Cemetery, Battle Creek, Michigan.

See also: general article: For Jesus and Scripture: The Life of Ellen G. White.

HARMON, HARRIET, see **MCCANN, HARRIET (HARMON)**.

HARMON, JOHN B. (1815-1883). Oldest brother of Ellen G. White and third child of *Robert and Eunice Harmon. Harmon had three successive wives—Dorcas N. Gould (married August 11, 1836), Abigail Bagby, and Lucy J. Bagby—and a total of six children. By 1850 he had moved to Illinois, where, according to the Harmon genealogy, he "became wealthy." The United States federal census of that year listed his property value at $10,000 and his personal estate at $2,000.

Ellen White mentioned writing to John twice in 1859 and also in 1873. A letter written from Santa Rosa, California, on January 21, 1873, begins, "I have written you several letters but have not heard one word from you. We concluded you must be dead, but then again we thought if this was the case, your children would write us. Brother Stephen Belden has just sent your address. I am so glad. And now, dear brother, I am hungry to hear from my only brother. I am anxious to see him" (Lt 2a, 1873). In that letter she also wrote of meeting her sister Caroline and Caroline's children in Colorado in May 1872. Perhaps in an attempt to say something about herself that he would appreciate she described speaking at Caroline's request in Methodist churches and in a park. She also told that she had "dined with Governor Holden" of California and of visiting a banker that had a beautiful garden with roses and carnations. It is not known whether her brother ever responded to her letters.

John Harmon died on March 6, 1883, and is buried in the Hardin, Illinois, cemetery.

Further reading: A. C. Harmon, *The Harmon Genealogy Comprising All Branches in New England* (Washington, D.C.: Gibson Bros., 1920), p. 79.

Merlin D. Burt

HARMON, MARY, see FOSS, MARY PLUMMER (HARMON).

HARMON, ROBERT (1786-1866) and EUNICE (GOULD) (b. c.1787-c. 1863). Parents of Ellen G. (Harmon) White.

COURTESY OF THE ELLEN G. WHITE ESTATE, INC.

ROBERT HARMON, FATHER OF ELLEN G. WHITE

Robert Harmon was the seventh of 10 children born to Daniel and Sarah Harmon, a Congregationalist family in Durham, Maine. He married Eunice Gould in Portland on July 11, 1810, and served in the Massachusetts Militia in 1814. He was an active lay leader in the Methodist Church until he became a Millerite and was subsequently expelled in 1843 from the *Chestnut Street Methodist Church in Portland. Descended from English immigrants, Eunice Gould was one of 11 children born to Joseph and Lydia Gould, probably in Portland, Maine. Robert and Eunice had eight children, Caroline, Harriet, John B., Mary Plummer, Sarah B., Robert, Jr., Ellen Gould (later White), and Elizabeth M. The three older children were born between 1812 and 1816 and were married adults by the time Ellen Harmon reached adolescence.

Robert and Eunice lived successively in Portland (until 1826), Gorham (1826-1827), Poland (1829-1833), Portland (1834-1846), and Gorham (1846-1853). Throughout his life Robert was a hatter and sometimes farmer.

After their marriage in 1846, James and Ellen White lived for a time with the Harmons in Gorham. The Harmons accepted the Sabbath by 1848 (JW to "Dear Brother and Sister," Aug. 26, 1848 [EGWE-GC]). After moving from Maine, the Harmons lived for a time in Battle Creek, Michigan, in an addition built on James and Ellen White's Wood Street home. They also lived for some time with their daughter, Sarah Belden, in Battle Creek. At some point after 1860 they lived with their son, John B. Harmon, in Greene County, Illinois. After Eunice's death Robert Harmon spent his last years living with Sarah Belden in Connecticut.

Ellen White wrote that her "venerable parents" would awake at the "trump of God." "These who have toiled side by side in their Master's vineyard will meet in immortal vigor, to see in many of those who shall be saved by the influence of the third message the fruits of their labors and their prayers" (RH, Apr. 21, 1868).

George O. States was blessed by the ministry of Robert Harmon and recollected: "In 1860 we moved near Battle Creek, where we lived a number of years. Grandpa Harmon [Sister White's father] lived in Battle Creek, and used to visit us, sometimes staying a few days. Although he was quite an old man, yet he seemed to enjoy getting out in the field with us boys and helping hoe and rake. Although I was quite young, yet his earnest talks about the first angel's message and the power attending it are still fresh in my memory. At night he used to take charge, at mother's request, of the family worship. I shall always remember as we sat around the family circle his interesting talks explaining the truth, especially to father, and of the mighty power accompanying his daughter's visions. We used to enjoy his visits very much, and his talks had much to do in establishing father on points of truth that had been troubling him, especially in regard to the Testimonies; and he soon took his stand again for the whole truth and was baptized by Elder Loughborough uniting with the Battle Creek Church."

Eunice Harmon died of typhoid fever after a four-week illness. Robert Harmon died on November 6, 1866, in Kensington,

Connecticut, with all his daughters but Caroline around him.

Further reading: obit. RH, Jan. 26, 1864; W. G. Davis, *The Ancestry of Lydia Harmon: 1755-1856* (Boston: Stanhope Press, 1924); A. C. Harmon, *The Harmon Genealogy Comprising All Branches in New England* (Washington, D.C.: Gibson Bros., 1920), pp. 18, 41; G. O. States, "Lessons From Past Experiences," UCR, Mar. 4, 1907.

Merlin D. Burt

HARMON, ROBERT F., JR. (1825-1853). Older brother of Ellen White, born July 13, 1825, in Gorham, Maine. Converted in March 1840 through William Miller's first course of lectures on the Second Coming at the *Casco Street Christian Church in Portland, Maine (RH, Apr. 14, 1853), he was baptized by immersion and became a member of the *Chestnut Street Methodist Church. Ellen White remembered attending Methodist classes during which her brother, with a "heavenly light" "upon his usually pale countenance," testified of the soon coming of Jesus (CET 35). It seems that Robert, like Ellen, had an introverted nature. Ellen White spoke of him as having a "meek way" (*ibid.* 38) and more timid than herself (*ibid.* 66). Among her siblings, besides her twin sister, Elizabeth, Ellen White probably had the closest emotional bond to her brother Robert. He was expelled from the Methodist Church in 1843 along with most of the family for their Millerite views.

After 1844 Robert was affected by the confusion within the ranks of Adventism. He saw only two choices regarding the Advent message: give up his past experience or accept that Christ had come spiritually. Unable to believe that the Second Advent was only a spiritual event, he gradually lost faith in the soon coming of Jesus. In 1852 he rejoined the Methodist Church. He contracted tuberculosis

and passed away after an eight-month illness in February 1853 at the age of 27.

During the last months of his life he came to understand the *three angels' messages in connection with the 1844 *Midnight Cry and accepted the seventh-day Sabbath. In response to his renewed faith in the soon coming of Jesus he asked that his name be removed from membership in the Methodist Church. The Methodist minister who visited him remarked to Eunice Harmon, "That is a triumphant soul" (2SG 164). Robert died in his parents' home on Fort Hill Road in Gorham, Maine, and was buried in the nearby Fort Hill Cemetery. *Frederick Wheeler conducted the funeral.

Further reading: LS88 288-290; Sarah B. Belden, "He Sleeps in Jesus," RH, Apr. 14, 1853.

Merlin D. Burt

HARMON, SARAH B., see **BELDEN, SARAH B. (HARMON).**

HARPER, FLORENCE S. (KETRING), see **HARPER, WALTER** and **LAURA**.

HARPER, WALTER (1854-1937) and **LAURA**. Pioneer colporteur; became a Seventh-day Adventist in 1879 and began selling Adventist publications in 1881. Ellen White recognized his successful colporteur work and encouraged him to provide financial assistance to various church projects (Lt 307, 1905).

When he was still a young man, Walter Harper carried out the action he felt was suggested in Matthew 19:12 and made himself a eunuch. Although he made known his physical condition to his first wife, Laura, before getting married, his disability rendered his marriage to Laura most difficult. After Walter sought advice from Ellen White, she encouraged them to remain faithful to each other and to their marriage vows in spite of their difficult circumstances. She also felt very concerned at the contempt shown to Harper by church members in Oakland and strongly urged them to "keep still" and not meddle in Walter and Laura's relationship (cf. Lt 6, 1888). Her repeated pleadings with Laura (Lt 57, 1888; Lts 47, 51, 1889; and Lt 14a, 1891, in TSB 54-67), however, did not succeed in keeping the couple together, and Laura eventually divorced Walter and married someone else. Following Laura's remarriage, Ellen White felt Walter could remarry and receive the "affection of a woman who, knowing his physical defect, shall choose to give him her love" (Lt 50, 1895, in TSB 68). Walter married Florence S. Ketring, a 25-year-old young woman from Pennsylvania, in 1895 (Walter Harper to EGW, Apr. 23, 1895). Her mother, Sister Ketring, soon felt concerned about the circumstances in which her daughter found herself and asked Ellen White for counsel. In her reply (Lt 50, 1895, in TSB 67-74) Ellen White highlighted that both mother and daughter knew about Walter's defect before the marriage and that it would be wrong to seek the annulment of the marriage now. Furthermore, she believed that as a childless couple Walter and Florence would be able to dedicate more time and energy to the Lord's work. Unfortunately, Walter's second marriage also faltered, this time because of his strong desire to keep his second wife away from her mother and his refusal to support Florence with adequate financial assistance, a situation that was deplored by Ellen White (Lt 157, 1903, in 12MR 242-245). In 1907, after a period of estrangement from Walter, Florence asked Ellen White whether she should return to live with Walter. Ellen White candidly responded that this would not be the best thing to do if Walter's disposition toward Florence and her mother had not changed (Lt 148, 1907, in TSB 74, 75).

The section "A Mutilated Spouse" in TSB 54-75 contains many of the letters Ellen White wrote to Walter, Laura, Florence, and Sister Ketring concerning the difficult circumstances in which they found themselves. One important thought that comes through Ellen White's counsels regarding this situation is her emphasis on the sacredness of marriage vows and that no personal circumstances, however trying they may be, with the exception of adultery, should lead a couple to consider divorce as a solution to their problems.

Further reading: Lt 6, 1888; obit. RH, Aug. 5, 1937; *SDA Encyclopedia* (1996), vol. 10, p. 666.

Denis Fortin

HARRIS, CHAPIN HENRY (1852-1937). Young Adventist in South Lancaster, Massachusetts, son of Mary Elizabeth (Williams) Harris, a former Seventh Day Baptist and sister-in-law of Rachel Oakes Preston. When visiting South Lancaster, Ellen White often stayed at the home of Mary Harris (4T 301; cf. 9MR 384, 385; 21MR 317, 318). In 1879 and 1880 Ellen White rebuked Chapin Harris for his infatuated conduct toward Mattie Stratton, a young woman he later married. "Your influence has been demoralizing" to other young people, she wrote (Lt 3, 1879, in 9MR 384). Years later Harris thanked Ellen White for "your kind interest in me and for the way in which you brought to me the message of reproof and warning" (Harris to EGW, Nov. 23, 1902). He worked for many years at the *New England Sanitarium, in Melrose, Massachusetts.

Further reading: obit. AUG, Nov. 24, 1937; obit. CUV, Dec. 23, 1937; R. E. Harris, "Roots and Fruits" (manuscript, Aug. 11, 1979, DF 3260, CAR).

HARRIS, STONEWALL JACKSON. Adventist land surveyor and businessman in Mariposa County, California, who appealed to church members to invest in his real estate and mining company. When Ellen White first heard of his conversion, she was delighted and called it "a manifestation of the wonderful working of the power of God" (Lt 192, 1905). But when asked by Harris whether she would ask God in which business deals he should invest in, she replied that it was not her work to do this (Lt 192, 1905; cf. Harris to EGW, June 11, 1905). A few years later Harris again sought Ellen White's counsels regarding his business ventures. Of particular interest was his method of determining what opportunities to invest in or not. His wife, Ada Harris, related to Ellen White that Harris would toss a coin to find out the Lord's will, a procedure objected to by his wife and many friends. Since the advice of his friends had no influence on him, it was felt that perhaps a testimony from Ellen White would help. Her counsel was clear: "It is a haphazard method, which God does not approve. To men who have suggested such tests, I have said, 'No, no.' The sacred things which concern the cause of God must not be dealt with by such methods. God does not instruct us that we are to learn His will by any such way" (Ms 3, 1911; cf. 6Bio 350-354; 2SM 325-328). Ellen White also felt compelled to tell him "that God is not leading you in your large plans and speculations" and that "our conference presidents and those who hold responsible positions in the work should be careful to give no encouragement to speculative plans for the securing of means" (Lt 28, 1911). When she heard that Harris, and his associate, *W. H. Covell, had published a booklet about his business ventures that he intended to distribute to Seventh-day Adventists ("Joyful News" [DF 150a, CAR]), and had referred to her in it, she pointedly said, "I do not approve of your plans or methods, and protest against the use of my name or my writings in any connection with your work." She also implied that his method of tossing a coin to find the will of God was a "delusion" similar to those she encountered in the early years of Adventism (Lt 36, 1911). Soon afterward, Harris dropped from prominence in the Adventist Church.

Denis Fortin

HART, JOSIAH (1817-1858). Early Sabbatarian Adventist in Northfield, Vermont. Converted to Adventism through the influence of *Joseph Bates in 1850, Hart initially opposed the visions of Ellen White, but after he met her in person in November 1851 became "convinced that the visions were of God" (Lt 8, 1851, in 3MR 243). After a vision given to Ellen White in 1855, Hart was part of a group that called for their publication as *testimonies for the church (*Testimony for the Church*, no. 1 [Battle Creek, 1855], p. 8; cf. 1Bio 332, 333). By 1856 Hart and his family had relocated to Round Grove, Illinois. Later that year James and Ellen White visited Hart and other believers in Round Grove, Illinois, and then were accompanied by Hart and *Elon Everts to Waukon, Iowa (1Bio 345-349).

Further reading: 1Bio 216-222; obit. RH, Sept. 2, 1858.

HART, RUSSELL A. (1845-1936). Pastor and publishing house administrator, Hart worked for most of his career as manager of the Review and Herald publishing house in Battle Creek, Michigan. In 1903, after a fire destroyed the Review and Herald building in Battle Creek, Ellen White wrote to Hart, "Do not, I entreat of you, regard the destruction of the printing office as a matter with which the Lord had nothing to do" (Lt 160, 1903), even though some sneered at the suggestion that "God's judgments have been seen" "in the calamities which have befallen our institutions in Battle Creek" (Lt 253, 1904). Ellen. White invited Hart to be genuine in his walk with God and to not let himself be seduced by evil (Lt 38, 1907). She also urged him to counteract the influence of *A. T. Jones and *J. H. Kellogg, who wanted to get possession of the *Battle Creek Tabernacle in order to preach their deceptive theories (*ibid.*).

Further reading: obit. RH, May 21, 1936; G. Washington, *History of Calhoun County, Michigan* (Chicago and New York: Lewis Pub. Co., 1913), p. 1200.

HASKELL, HETTY (HURD) (1857-1919).

Trainer of Bible instructors, tireless worker

in evangelism, second wife of *S. N. Haskell, and sister of *Emma C. Grey. She served as a Bible instructor and taught Bible instructors in California and London, England, before accepting a call to Cape Town, South Africa, where she

HETTY HASKELL

met the recently widowed S. N. Haskell in the spring of 1895. In 1896 she followed him to Australia, where they were married in 1897. For two years they taught at Avondale College, then spent the rest of their lives in *city evangelism, notably in New York City, Nashville, New England, and California.

Further reading: L. F. Swanepoel, *The Origin and Early History of the Seventh-day Adventist Church in South Africa* (M.A. thesis, University of South Africa, 1972), pp. 18, 50, 55, 203.

HASKELL, MARY (HOW) (c.1812-1894).

Teacher, cofounder of the first Tract and Missionary Society (1870); first wife of *S. N. Haskell. At the time of their marriage,

Mary Haskell was 38 and "thought to be a hopeless invalid," but two or three years later

she was miraculously healed (S. N. Haskell to EGW, Dec. 29, 1909). Her teaching experience and her library became important sources of her husband's education. Two published testimonies are known to have been addressed to Stephen

MARY HASKELL

and Mary Haskell: "Errors in Diet" (1T 204-209) and "Experience Not Reliable" (3T 67-79; see S. N. Haskell to EGW, Nov. 5, 1893).

Further reading: obit. RH, Feb. 20, 1894.

HASKELL, STEPHEN NELSON (1833-1922).

Public and personal evangelist, administrator,

founder of institutions, missionary, staunch supporter of Ellen White, and pioneer in city evangelism. Born in Massachusetts, Haskell was 17 and a farmhand when he promised his dying employer Mr. How

STEPHEN N. HASKELL

that he would "take care of" How's invalid daughter, *Mary, who was about 38 (Robinson, *Man of Action*, p. 13). After some soul-searching he proposed to her, and they were married before he was 18. At 19 he became a self-supporting preacher. In 1853 he and Mary accepted the Sabbath. Ordained in 1868, S. N. Haskell became the first president of the New England Conference in 1870.

He and Mary founded the first Tract and Missionary Society (forerunner of the General Conference Personal Ministries Department), and from 1870 to 1889 Stephen promoted and organized that work from local societies to the General Conference. During this time he also served as president of the California, Maine, and New England conferences, and founded *South Lancaster Academy, forerunner of Atlantic Union College. He made a round-the-world fact-finding tour, the first by a Seventh-day Adventist, investigating openings for future mission work (1889-1891).

Haskell was not the originator of the Bible reading method of religious discourse, but discovering its effectiveness, he popularized it among Seventh-day Adventists. At a California camp meeting in 1883 Haskell asked his good friend W. C. White to pray with him for an understanding of recent counsel from Ellen White that Haskell "should do less preaching and more teaching" (Robinson, p. 66; cf. 6T 87, 88). Soon after, while Haskell was preaching, a rainstorm created such a drumming on the tent roof that Haskell could not make himself heard. Leaving the pulpit, he stood by the center pole, "asking questions and giving out Scripture texts to be read in answer." A few minutes later Ellen White asked some people passing her tent what was going on in the big tent. When they told her, she said, "That's what Elder Haskell should do; this is the way our people should be instructed." She later told Haskell that "what he had done was in harmony with the light she had received" (Robinson, p. 66). In November 1883 the General Conference session endorsed this question-and-answer method and authorized a monthly magazine, *Bible Reading Gazette*, forerunner of the book *Bible Readings for the Home Circle*. For Haskell, the Bible reading method became his favorite mode of presentation, which he taught to others through the *Bible Training School* and later *Bible Handbook*.

After the death of *Mary Haskell in 1894, Stephen spent the years 1894-1899 as a missionary in Africa and Australia. Intensely lonely and often depressed after Mary's death, he drew much encouragement from the letters of Ellen White. He received more letters from her than any other person outside her immediate family. Eventually he proposed marriage to her (Moon, "S. N. Haskell: A Three-Fold Cord," pp. 6, 7). She declined, but suggested that Hetty Hurd would make a good companion for him. Ellen White had seen an angel placing one hand on Stephen's shoulder and the other on Hetty's, saying, "Have I not raised up two [S. N. and *Hetty (Hurd)] Haskell] to stand by you [EGW]?" (S. N. Haskell to EGW, Dec. 10, 1906, EGWE-GC). Stephen and Hetty were married in 1897. As charter members of the *Avondale faculty they sought to fulfill Ellen White's vision for that school. They used holiday periods between school terms to raise up two new churches before returning to the United States in 1899.

From 1901 to 1912 they did city evangelism in New York; Nashville; San Bernardino and Oakland, California; and Portland, Maine. In New York City they rented a sixth-floor suite of rooms and began giving Bible readings to their neighbors in the same apartment house. Their working group eventually numbered 20, including nurses, Bible instructors, cooking school instructors, and young people who sold books and magazines on the streets. The publication and sale of books (*Daniel the Prophet* [1901] and *Seer of Patmos* [1905]) and a periodical (*Bible Training School*) became both an evangelistic method and a means of support. The income from the canvassers and nurses, plus the Haskells' two salaries ($10 and $8 per week), paid all the expenses of the evangelistic team. During these years Stephen also produced *The Cross and Its Shadow* and *Bible Handbook*. One of the Haskells' last major projects together was raising $60,000 to build the *White Memorial Medical Center in Los Angeles.

Further reading: obit. RH, Dec. 14, 1922; E. E. Lantry, *He Chose to Listen* (PPPA, 1983); J. Moon, "S. N. Haskell: A Three-Fold Cord" and "Seventh-day Adventist Medical Evangelism: Three Models, 1892-1922" (unpublished paper, 1989, CAR); E. M. Robinson, *S. N. Haskell, Man of Action* (RHPA, 1967); L. F. Swanepoel, *The Origin and Early History of the Seventh-day Adventist Church in South Africa* (M.A. thesis, University of South Africa, 1972), pp. 18, 19, 53, 65.

Jerry Moon

HASTINGS, LEONARD WOOD (1803-1883) and **ELVIRA** (c. 1808-1850). Adventist farmer.

LEONARD HASTINGS

Born in Massachusetts, Leonard moved at age 17 to New Ipswich, New Hampshire, where he and Elvira met and in 1832 were married. In 1843, because of their belief in the soon return of Christ, they withdrew from the local Congregational church. Hastings is best remembered for leaving his potatoes in the ground prior to the 1844 disappointment as a testimony of his faith (JNL, *Great Second Advent Movement*, pp. 166, 167). In 1847 their 8-week-old baby, Frederick, became sick. James and Ellen White traveled to pray and anoint the baby, who was miraculously healed (LS 122, 123). Tragically, on February 28, 1850, Elvira died of "colic." In a vision Ellen White saw Elvira among the *144,000 (Lt 10, 1850). Soon after her death Leonard sold his farm to help raise funds to assist in the *publishing work, and relocated nearby. In 1862 a small group of Adventists who had met in the Hastings home since 1843 were organized into a church. That same year Leonard married Martha Colburn

(1827-1888) from nearby Temple, New Hampshire. In his later years Leonard helped organize the New England Conference (1870) and became vice president of the New England Tract and Missionary Society (1875). The Hastingses were key supporters of *Joseph Bates and James and Ellen White in the early years of the Sabbatarian Adventist movement. Letters to them have survived and provide vital information on Adventist beginnings.

Further reading: obit. RH, June 5, 1883; *SDA Encyclopedia* (1996), vol. 10, p. 670.

HAUGHEY, JOSEPH HARVEY (1857-1935). Teacher for 38 years at Battle Creek College,

JOSEPH H. HAUGHEY

South Lancaster Academy, and Emmanuel Missionary College. Haughey graduated from Battle Creek College in 1882, earned a master's degree in mathematics from the University of Michigan, and taught primarily mathematics, astronomy, and biblical languages.

Haughey accepted Ellen White's gift of prophecy and inculcated in his students respect for the Adventist pioneers. Some said he could quote Ellen White's *Testimonies* as confidently as he did the Bible. Haughey corresponded many times with Ellen White and W. C. White, seeking their counsel. On one occasion she wrote him a long letter about modesty in women's apparel in response to Haughey's query on behalf of his wife, Sarah Elizabeth *née* Green, about the reform dress (Lt 19, 1897, in 3SM 252-255).

Haughey embraced wholeheartedly Ellen White's philosophy of education, particularly regarding the balance of academic study and manual labor. He modeled his belief throughout his career. At Emmanuel Missionary

College he supervised the orchards, berry patches, and vineyards and came to be known as an expert beekeeper, working outdoors alongside the students he taught in the classroom. Believing that teachers should be self-supporting, Haughey also ran his own farm and returned every penny he could to the church.

Further reading: obit. RH, Jan. 30, 1936; "Battle Creek College Faculty Minutes" (CAR); "Emmanuel Missionary College Faculty Minutes" (CAR); *Founders' Golden Anniversary Bulletin of Battle Creek College and Emmanuel Missionary College: 1874-1924* (Berrien Springs, Mich.: College Press, 1924); H. M. Tippett, "A Memorial Tribute to Joseph H. Haughey," LUH, Dec. 17, 1935, pp. 1, 2; E. K. Vande Vere, "Joseph Harvey Haughey," in *The Wisdom Seekers* (SPA, 1972), pp. 276-280; O. H. Young, "Remembering the Way We Were," *Focus* 14 (Winter 1978): 13-15.

Meredith Jones Gray

HAWKINS, CHARLES F. Adventist minister in Adelaide, South Australia, closely associated with *Stephen McCullagh. Both men were ordained in 1896 by *S. N. Haskell (RH, Dec. 29, 1896). In 1897 Ellen White wrote Hawkins warning him "not to make light of [the] third angel's message" (see *three angels' messages) and the Adventist experience (Lt 65, 1897), but he soon afterward left the church (RH, Aug. 24, 1897).

HAWKINS, HARRY. Adventist young adult; brother of Minnie (Hawkins) Crisler (see *Clarence C. Crisler). In 1896 Ellen White wrote Hawkins asking if he would let her be his friend. She appealed for him to make his decision "for time and for eternity" to come to Jesus (Lt 33, 1896). Harry later worked briefly for Ellen White as one of her *literary assistants.

HAWKINS, MINNIE, see **CRISLER, CLARENCE CREAGER.**

HAYES, ELMER G. (1869-1959). Pastor, Bible teacher, and conference president. In June 1880 Elmer's father took him to hear Ellen White speak on temperance at the first camp meeting held in the Dakota Territory. Soon thereafter Elmer joined the Adventist Church. He later attended Battle Creek College (1885-1890) and in 1896 became a pastor in the South Dakota Conference. While there, Ellen White wrote to him appealing "to our brethren in South Dakota to help . . . make a liberal gift to the *Madison School, that they may erect a chapel and school building" (Lt 40, 1907).

Further reading: obit. RH, Oct. 29, 1959; "E. G. Hayes," RH, Apr. 16, 1959.

HAYSMER, JAMES (1833-1908) and **ANNA M. (STAINES)** (1837-1923). Born in England, James immigrated to the United States at 19, married Anna in New York in 1856, and moved to Michigan the same year. Anna joined the Seventh-day Adventist Church in Bushnell, Montcalm County, Michigan, while James was serving in the army in the Civil War. When James returned, he too joined the church, and they remained lifelong members. After James White's first stroke, he and Ellen moved to Greenville in Montcalm County and began a lifelong friendship with the Haysmers. Their daughter and son-in-law, *G. T. and Jennie Wilson, became traveling companions of Ellen White in Australia. When G. T. died in 1900, Ellen White wrote several letters of comfort to the Haysmers (Lt 14, 1900; Lt 78, 1900).

HAYWARD, OTIS MADISON (1873-1961). Medical missionary doctor in the southern United States. In 1904 Hayward cofounded with Lars Hansen (1846-1934) the *Nashville

Sanitarium. As they planned for the school they sought Ellen White's counsel. She replied that the sanitarium should be located "out of the cities, but not so far out that the work can not be carried forward advantageously" (Lt 291, 1904; cf. Lts 267, 303, 1904). She also advised them that the sanitarium should be located in proximity to the Nashville Agricultural and Normal Institute so that both institutions might bless each other (Lt 369, 1904).

See also: Graysville, Tennessee; Madison College.

Further reading: obit. RH, Nov. 30, 1961; obit. RH, Feb. 7, 1935; O. M. Hayward, *Live* (Cleveland, Ga.: Hayward, 1952).

HEALEY, WILLIAM MAYHEW (1847-1932). Adventist minister and administrator. Originally from New Hampshire, Healey's parents were early Sabbatarian Adventists. In 1874 Healey moved with his family to California, where he became an evangelist. Ellen White respected his speaking skills and spoke at least once during his meetings (Lts 10, 11, 1878). For some reason Ellen White was unable to finish her topic during that visit and planned to return later to do so, but when she was not invited back, this prompted a letter of query (Lt 25, 1878). A decade later, just before the *General Conference session of 1888, Healey wrote to *G. I. Butler to warn him that Ellen White was being influenced by *A. T. Jones and *E. J. Waggoner (see Lt 7, 1888, in 1888 Materials 186-189; Lt 116, 1901, in 1888 Materials 1757-1761).

Further reading: obit. RH, Sept. 29, 1932.

HENRY, ARCHIBALD R. (1839-1909). Administrator and banker. Born in Iowa, Henry taught school until the Civil War, when he served as a private and then lieutenant in the 34th Regiment of the Iowa Volunteer

Infantry. After the war he resumed teaching and married Elizabeth Cottle (1841-1934) in 1865. Nine years later (1874) they relocated to Indianola, Iowa, where Henry owned a bank. About 1877 Henry converted to Adventism and, at the encouragement of James and Ellen White, sold his bank (1882) and moved to Battle Creek to replace *Henry Webster Kellogg as financial manager of the Seventh-day Adventist Publishing Association (Lt 39, 1886). Henry held this position until 1897, except for brief interludes as vice president (1885-1887) and as treasurer/manager (1893-1895). From 1883 to 1888 he served as treasurer of the General Conference and oversaw the finances of many other Adventist institutions. In 1889 he was president of the General Conference Association, in 1890-1891 its vice president, in 1892 its auditor, and in 1893 its treasurer. At the same time he was a board member of nearly all early Adventist medical and educational institutions in the western United States.

ARCHIBALD R. HENRY

COURTESY OF THE CENTER FOR ADVENTIST RESEARCH, ANDREWS UNIVERSITY

Ellen White was impressed with Henry's business acumen, but was at times gravely concerned over his secular and unspiritual business practices. Following his opposition to *A. T. Jones and *E. J. Waggoner's message on *righteousness by faith at the *General Conference session of 1888, Ellen White claimed that Henry no longer believed in her testimonies (Lt 86, 1891). As the spiritual decline in Battle Creek reached crisis proportions, she wrote a series of testimonies to *O. A. Olsen, then General Conference president, and the "men who occupy responsible positions," reproving A. R. Henry and *Harmon Lindsay for their lack of spirituality in business practices (Lt 4, 54, 55, 1895; Lt 4, 1896). It was during this time that Ellen White expressed her lack of confidence in the General Conference as the *"voice of God" (Ms 33, 1895; Lt 4, 1896; cf. 9T 260, 261). On March 10, 1897, Henry was dismissed from the Review and Herald. In May of that year, unable to sue Ellen White, who was in Australia, he blamed O. A. Olsen for distributing her testimonies and laid suit against the Seventh-day Adventist Publishing Association, of which Olsen was chair (*Henry v. SDA Publishing Association and Ellen White,* May 19, 1897 [QA 13-F-1]). "In the suit that you have instigated," wrote Ellen White, "you have revealed the spirit that for many years has prompted you to action." Henry was furthermore "in danger of making shipwreck of the faith" (Lt 66, 1897; Lt 67, 1897). Despite the lawsuit Ellen White continued to write strong admonitions warning that he was "deciding" his "eternal destiny" (Lt 15, 1898; Lt 41, 1898). It appears that in the end Henry repented, dismissed the suit, and remained in the church.

Further reading: obit. RH, Aug. 5, 1909; H. E. Douglass, *Messenger of the Lord* (PPPA, 1998), pp. 228, 229; R. W. Schwarz and F. L. Greenleaf, *Light Bearers* (PPPA, 2000), p. 262; Coller Collection (WL), vol. 32, pp. 597-599; *SDA Encyclopedia* (1996), vol. 10, pp. 690, 691.

Michael W. Campbell

HENRY, SAREPTA MYRENDA IRISH (1839-1900). A prominent figure in the national leadership of the Woman's Christian Temperance Union (WCTU) who joined the Seventh-day Adventist Church in 1896. Like Ellen White, then residing in Australia, S.M.I. Henry was a strong Christian leader, an

MRS. S.M.I. HENRY

eloquent and prolific writer, and a reform activist. The two women never met in person, but through extensive correspondence they reached across the Pacific Ocean to "clasp hands in faith and sweet fellowship" (4Bio 347).

The relationship between the two gifted women was of critical significance because Henry's conversion epitomized the rich rewards possible for Adventism through the cooperative action with the Woman's Christian Temperance Union (WCTU) that Ellen White had long advocated. The WCTU emerged out of a renewal of women's activism in the early 1870s, rapidly becoming one of the nation's leading organizations advocating prohibition and a wide range of related social reforms. Incapacitated by a heart ailment after nearly 20 hectic years of labor and travel as "national evangelist" for the organization, Henry entered Battle Creek Sanitarium in 1896. Gradually drawn to Adventism during her stay there, she was restored to health and to her role as a reformer after an anointing service led by A. T. Jones and W. W. Prescott.

Primarily because the WCTU in 1887 formally included on their agenda Sunday rest laws as a labor reform measure, Ellen White's efforts to get Adventists involved with the reform organization met with some reluctance. The enormous mutual benefit of working with the WCTU on shared causes, without compromising Adventist principles could now be glimpsed in Henry's work. Those involved with the WCTU now benefited, through Henry's witness, from greater exposure to the light of the Adventist message, which some of them embraced. The Adventist cause also benefited from her efforts in getting the WCTU to moderate its position on Sunday laws. Though the outcome was a compromise well short of the Adventist ideal, it constituted a meaningful advance in the direction of tolerance.

Moreover, S.M.I. Henry put the expertise and experience of the WCTU in action to mobilize Adventist women for "the work of the gospel ministry" ("Woman's Gospel Work," RH, Dec. 27, 1898). She began building a network for action and mutual support, linked by a Woman's Gospel Work department in the *Review and Herald*, before her work was suddenly cut short by death from pneumonia in January 1900. Her plan received fervent endorsement and timely encouragement from Ellen White, who was eager to see "a larger number of women engaged in the work of ministering to suffering humanity, uplifting, educating them how to believe—simply believe—in Jesus Christ our Saviour" (in "A Special Call to Our Women," RH, supplement, Dec. 6, 1898). This multifaceted woman's ministry was based in interpersonal and domestic relationships and prioritized heartfelt devotion to Christ and humanitarian service over doctrinal argumentation. Yet it also encompassed public speaking and in general encouraged women to exercise their gifts unconstrained by the sentiment "diligently cultivated" by the devil that a "woman must live in retirement; that much activity, even in the church, is unwomanly; and that when she does do anything, it must be as different from a man's way as possible" (*ibid.*).

Finally, S.M.I. Henry deployed her own rhetorical abilities to affirm the prophetic gift of Ellen White. She put forward a memorable image—the telescope—to describe the resolution she had reached after struggling with the question of whether the Testimonies constituted an extrabiblical authority in her new community of faith. When not misdirected or mistaken for itself being the field of vision, she wrote, the Testimonies "lead the eye and give it power to penetrate into the glories of the mysterious living word of God" ("My Telescope," *The Gospel of Health*, January 1898).

In 1921 Henry's granddaughter Margaret Rossiter married Ellen White's grandson *James Henry White.

Further reading: M. H. Rossiter, *My Mother's Life: The Evolution of a Recluse* (Chicago: Fleming H. Revell, 1900); T. R. Pegram, *Battling Demon Rum: The Struggle for a Dry America, 1800-1933* (Chicago: Ivan R. Dee, 1998); E. D. Syme, *A History of SDA Church-State Relations in the United States* (PPPA, 1973); M. Rossiter White Thiele, *Whirlwind of the Lord* (RHPA, 1953, 1998).

Douglas Morgan

HEWITT, DAVID (1805-1878) and **OLIVE** (1809-1876). First Seventh-day Adventists in

COURTESY OF THE ELLEN G. WHITE ESTATE, INC.

DAVID HEWITT

Battle Creek, Michigan. The Hewitts were married in 1831, probably in western New York, and moved to Battle Creek in the 1830s. There David Hewitt supported his family by door-to-door sales work and built a solid reputation for absolute honesty. In 1852 Joseph Bates, an evangelist and church planter traveling across Michigan by train, dreamed he was on a sailing ship that anchored at a port called Battle Creek. Taking the dream as divine leading, Bates got off the train at the village of Battle Creek, inquired for "the most honest man in town," and was referred to David Hewitt, a Presbyterian on Van Buren Street. Bates knocked on the Hewitt door and told them he had "important truth" for them. They invited him to share breakfast, then to conduct family worship, and then they were ready to hear his message. Hanging up his prophetic chart, he presented the hope of the Second Advent and, in the afternoon, the seventh-day Sabbath. The Hewitts kept the next Sabbath, and their home became the meeting place for Battle Creek Adventists until they erected their first little church in 1855. In the same year James and Ellen White moved to Battle Creek and built a cottage not far from the Hewitts.

In 1860, when the young denomination faced the necessity of choosing a legal name, David Hewitt moved that they take the name Seventh-day Adventists, a descriptive phrase already used informally to distinguish them from Sundaykeeping or first-day Adventists. Ellen White was not present at that meeting, but warmly approved the action taken. "The name Seventh-day Adventist carries the true features of our faith in front, and will convict the inquiring mind," she wrote in 1861. "Like an arrow from the Lord's quiver, it will wound the transgressors of God's law, and will lead to repentence toward God and faith in our Lord Jesus Christ" (1T 224).

Further reading: obit. RH, Nov. 30, 1876; G. R. Knight, *Joseph Bates: The Real Founder of Seventh-day Adventism* (RHPA, 2004), pp. 132, 177, 193; R. W. Schwarz and Floyd Greenleaf, *Light Bearers: A History of the Seventh-day Adventist Church* (PPPA, 2000), p. 77.

Jerry Moon

HIBBARD, EMMET J. (1860-1924). Minister and educator. Hibbard began his ministry in the Pennsylvania Conference in 1888. He afterward taught at *Battle Creek College (1894-1898), *Walla Walla College (1898-1899), the *American Medical Missionary College (1899-1901), and *Healdsburg College (1901-1905). In 1906 Ellen White publicly praised the evangelistic labors of Hibbard and *S. N. Haskell in southern California (RH, Nov. 29, 1906), but privately admonished Hibbard to avoid "exhibitions of a theatrical nature" and to avoid offending listeners (Lt

366, 1906). She later warned him against the apostasy of *A. T. Jones (Lt 210, 1908).

Further reading: obit. RH, July 31, 1924.

HICKOX, ARTHUR SWAIN (1861-1930). Colporteur and pastor. In the 1890s Hickox served for about eight years as a pastor in Australia and colporteur in New Zealand. During this time Ellen White often wrote to him to encourage him in his work and to not be disappointed by life circumstances. Hickox first began to work in the Sydney area, but somehow church leaders did not appreciate his work and he decided to go to New Zealand to do colporteur work. This situation displeased Ellen White, and she remarked to *A. G. Daniells that "the management of the case of Brother Hickox is after human methods, not after the methods which the Lord has ordained. . . . The Lord is not pleased with your management of this case" (Lt 40, 1897; cf. Ms 49, 1899). Although she admitted to Hickox that "the brethren have made a mistake" regarding his work (Lt 61, 1897), she encouraged him to be "prepared to take hold of the work anywhere" (Lt 30, 1896). When *S. N. Haskell began to work in Newcastle and Maitland, she invited Hickox to join him (Lt 87, 1899). Even though she felt encouraged by his work (Lt 30, 1900), she was concerned that he did not give it his undivided interest. "If you do not purpose doing the work faithfully, wholeheartedly, putting your very best powers to task, then in order to be true and honest you must give up the work," she told him candidly (Lt 126, 1900). Perhaps as a result of this counsel, Hickox and his family returned to the United States, where he studied medicine and later became a physician in California.

Further reading: obit. RH, Aug. 14, 1930.

HILLIARD, AARON HENDERSON (d. 1875). Early Sabbatarian Adventist from Buck's

Bridge, New York. In 1852 Hilliard shared the *Review and Herald* with his neighbor *John Byington, leading to Byington's conversion. The following year *Martha Byington (later Amadon) taught the first Adventist elementary school in the Hilliard home. In 1859 the Hilliards moved west to Otsego, Michigan. On the journey they visited *Battle Creek, Michigan, and stayed in the White home (Ms 6, 1859). The Hilliards settled on a farm about 25 miles (40 km) northwest of Battle Creek. Their home was a frequent stopping point for the Whites when they visited churches in their area. It was in this home that Ellen White received the *health reform vision of 1863.

Further reading: obit. RH, Sept. 2, 1875.

HIMES, JOSHUA VAUGHAN (1805-1895). Millerite leader and publisher. Himes' work

COURTESY OF THE CENTER FOR ADVENTIST RESEARCH, ANDREWS UNIVERSITY

JOSHUA V. HIMES

in promoting the teachings of *William Miller led E. N. Dick to title him the "Napoleon of the Press." Born in Wickford, Rhode Island, his parents intended for him to become an Episcopal priest, but when a business deal went sour, he was unable to complete his education and was apprenticed to a cabinetmaker in New Bedford, Massachusetts (1821-1825). At 18 he joined the *Christian Connexion church in New Bedford, where he was licensed as an exhorter. While living in New Bedford, he became acquainted with Joseph Bates, who then lived in nearby Farnham, Massachusetts. In November 1825 Himes married Mary Thompson Handy, and the following year was ordained to the ministry. Over the next few years he pastored several districts in Massachusetts before becoming pastor of the First Christian

Church in Boston (1830). There he rose to prominence, reviving a church that was near death, and becoming active in the educational, temperance, peace, and abolitionist reform movements of the day. He was an especially active abolitionist on whose head Southern slaveholders placed a $5,000 bounty. His reform activities led to a split in his church, from which emerged the famous Chardon Street Chapel.

Himes met William Miller in 1839 at Exeter, New Hampshire. Impressed, he invited Miller to speak at the Chardon Street Chapel. From these lectures Himes became convinced of the soon return of Christ, and sought opportunities for Miller to preach. In 1840 he published and edited the first Millerite newspaper, *The Signs of the Times*, in Boston. He led in organizing general conferences and camp meetings, and published hundreds of pamphlets as well as the second and third editions of Miller's lectures. He organized extensive lecture tours for Miller and himself as far west as Cincinnati, brought about the manufacture of the "great tent," at that time the largest tent in the United States, for use on these tours, and established a network of agents, book depots, and reading rooms from Boston to St. Louis. He also published the Thayer lithograph of the first Millerite prophetic chart, designed by *Charles Fitch and Apollos Hale. In 1842 he started a second newspaper, the *Midnight Cry*, in New York City. Himes' promotional work brought Millerism to the attention of the world.

Like Miller, Himes at first opposed the setting of October 22, 1844, as the exact date for the return of Christ, but accepted it shortly before the date arrived. After the 1844 *disappointment, he played a leading role in trying to reorganize the disappointed Adventists around the "original advent faith" at the Albany Conference in April 1845. When this failed, he became a leader of the Evangelical Advent-ists and their American Millennial Association (1858), opposing Sabbatarian Adventism and their understanding of the sanctuary as well as those who believed in conditional immor-tality and the reestablishment of Israel before Christ's second advent.

In 1863 Himes accepted the doctrine of conditional immortality, joined the Advent Christian Church, and moved his family west to Buchanan, Michigan, assuming a prominent leadership role among Advent Christians in "the west" and starting a news-paper, *The Voice of the West* (later *Advent Christian Times*). In 1865 he was the founding president of the American Advent Mission Society, and was further planning to start a college in Illinois. For the most part, Himes had a warm relationship with Seventh-day Adventists. His differences lay in their obser-vance of the seventh-day Sabbath, but he did not attack the ministry of Ellen White (cf. RH, Aug. 30, 1864). On occasion Himes preached in the Battle Creek Church (RH, Jan. 17, 1865). James White also recom-mended Himes' new periodical in the *Review and Herald* (cf. RH, Jan. 11, 1870). Himes' large vision and dynamic leadership proved too much for some Advent Christian leaders, most especially *Miles Grant, who used the excuse of a morals charge brought against Himes (at age 65 the first and only such charge ever made against him) to drive him from the Advent Christian ranks. (Grant was subsequently disciplined by leaders of the Advent Christian Church.)

After the death of his wife, Mary, in 1876, Himes at the age of 73 followed his son Wil-liam into the Episcopal Church, was ordained a deacon in 1878, and began mission work on the Dakota frontier. He married Hannah Combs Harley in 1879, and took charge of the Episcopal missions in Elk Point and Vermilion in present-day South Dakota. Here Himes, ever the reformer, introduced temper-ance reforms into the Dakotas, assisted in organizing the Dakotas' Episcopalian diocese, built church buildings with his own hands, trained young ministers, and in 1881 was ordained to the priesthood.

In 1894 Himes went to the *Battle Creek Sanitarium to receive treatment for cancer. Here he became reacquainted with old friends and spoke at the *Battle Creek Tabernacle. He heard some of Ellen White's *testimonies being read in the church one evening, which prompted him to write her, expressing appre-ciation for her ministry and including an offering to assist the Adventist work in Australia (Himes to EGW, Sept. 12, 1894, EGWE-GC). She responded with a letter of gratitude affirming him in his work (Lt 31a, 1895). He died in 1895 at the age of 90, active in his church to the end and greatly beloved in his community. He is buried in Sioux Falls, South Dakota.

Further reading: obit. *Union County Courier* [Elk Point, S.Dak.], Aug. 1, 1895; obit. *The Church News* [Sioux Falls, S.Dak.], August 1895; D. T. Arthur, "Joshua V. Himes and the Cause of Adventism, 1839-1845" (M.A. thesis, University of Chicago, 1961); *SDA Encyclopedia* (1996), vol. 10, pp. 694, 695.

Michael W. Campbell and David T. Arthur

HINDSON, JAMES and **ANNA L. (INGELS)** (1862-1933). Anna Ingels joined the Pacific Press in 1883, served as secretary of the California Tract Society (1883-1892), then of the Australia Tract Society (1893), and finally of the Australasian Union (1893-1898). In 1898 she married James Hindson, and together they organized tract societies in Western Australia and New South Wales. James pio-neered the health food work while Anna edited the *Australasian Record* and the

Missionary Leader for two decades while directing the young peoples', home missions, and Sabbath school departments for the Australasian Division. In 1901 Ellen White asked them to care for her brother-in-law, *Stephen Belden, who had a serious heart condition (Lt 103, 1901).

Further reading: obit. RH, Jan. 25, 1934; *SDA Encyclopedia* (1996), vol. 10, p. 695.

Brian E. Strayer

HIRSCHMILLER, CHARLES I. Adventist worker in South Lancaster, Massachussetts. In letters to Ellen White in 1907 and 1908, Hirschmiller expressed his lack of *assurance of salvation and feelings of sinfulness. In reply, Ellen White encouraged him to commit his life to Christ. "Your faith must rely not on feeling, but on the promises of God," (Lt 388, 1907, in 6L 337), she emphasized. "Do not depend on the state of your feelings for assurance that you are a child of God" (Lt 206, 1908, in 17MR 84).

HOBART, JOHN. Minister of the *Chestnut Street Methodist Church in Portland, Maine (1840-1841). He was sympathetic to the Millerite movement. According to church records, Ellen Harmon was recommended on September 20, 1841, for the customary six-month probationary period before baptism and eight months later, on May 23, 1842, was recommended for baptism. On June 26, 1842, Harmon was baptized by Hobart in Casco Bay, Portland, Maine.

HOLDEN, WILLIAM BURROUGHS (1873-1955). Trained as a physician at Battle Creek College (1879), Rush Medical College, and the University of Michigan, Holden joined the medical staff of Portland Sanitarium and Hospital in Portland, Oregon. Married to Worthie Harris (1871-1921) and Faye Beggs

(1890-1969), he served for 29 years (1910-1920, 1924-1943) as medical superintendent at the hospital. In 1905 Ellen White praised Dr. Holden as a man of "earnest, determined faith and unshaken courage in the Lord." She urged him to reconsider his refusal to come to Loma Linda Sanitarium as a teacher and surgeon, promising him that evangelistic and medical work there "will bring you lasting joy and satisfaction" (Lt 245, 1905).

Further reading: obit. RH, Dec. 29, 1955; obit. RH, Apr. 14, 1921; obit. PUR, Aug. 21, 1969; *SDA Encyclopedia* (1996), vol. 10, p. 700.

Brian E. Strayer

HOLMES, CLAUDE E. (1881-1953). Review and Herald linotype operator who believed that Ellen White's writings were infallible. When queried as to what he meant by this, he would reply, "They are scripture to me." He became concerned when he saw editorial changes being made by *W. W. Prescott in Ellen White's articles for the *Review and Herald*. Concerns escalated when Holmes learned of additional changes that were to be made for the 1911 edition of *The Great Controversy. Holmes saw this as undermining the inspiration of her writings. In 1919, because of a miscommunication with *A. G. Daniells, Holmes was granted access to private testimonies by Ellen White in the Review and Herald Publishing Association vault. Holmes made unauthorized copies. When asked to return them, he chose rather to resign from church employment. Holmes continued as a part-time linotype operator using his expertise to print hundreds of tracts of Ellen White quotes. At the 1922 General Conference session he and *J. S. Washburn circulated a tract attacking A. G. Daniells for his role in what they saw as undermining the writings of Ellen White.

Further reading: M. W. Campbell, "How Goes the Battle? Claude E. Holmes and Inspiration" (unpublished paper, AU, 2002, CAR).

HOOVER, W. L. Administrator at the Boulder Sanitarium, Colorado. In 1901 Ellen White counseled Hoover that he "should not be superintendent or manager in any of our institutions" (Lt 156, 1901) because he was self-conceited, self-deceived and "cherishing a confused science" (Lt 191, 1901). She was also concerned with his influence over and familiarity with young women and his spoiling "the purity of their thoughts" (Lt 87, 1901; cf. Lt 129, 1901). She admonished him to "abstain from every appearance of evil" (Lt 173, 1901).

Further reading: TDG 135; 5Bio 114, 115.

HOWARD, LUTHER L. (1825-1903). Adventist minister and first president of the Maine Conference (1867-1869). While attending the camp meeting in Skowhegan, Maine, in September 1870, Ellen White wrote a long testimony to Howard highlighting his lack of cooperation with other ministers and his "jealous, suspicious, and rebellious" spirit (Lt 11, 1870). In her estimation, he "has done more harm to the cause of God by his wrong course, his lack of energy, his envy, his jealousy, and suspicion than all the good he has done in this cause and work" (*ibid.*). Although Howard made a public confession of his wrongs during the camp meeting ("Maine State Conference," RH, Sept. 13, 1870), Ellen White felt he "had a strong desire to control matters in the State of Maine" (Lt 11, 1870).

Further reading: obit. RH, Aug. 4, 1903.

HOWE, FRANK. President of Healdsburg College (1894-1897). In 1895 Howe asked Ellen White, then in Australia, for her advice on the type of recreational activities that should be allowed at the college. In response, she urged that "disgraceful *games" not be permitted but replaced with "useful trades" and "manual training" (Lt 27, 1895). In her letter to Howe she gives some of her strongest arguments against the playing of sports in Adventist educational institutions.

Further reading: 4Bio 441-447; *SDA Encyclopedia* (1996), vol. 11, pp. 281, 284.

HOWELL, JOHN (1820-1861). Associate of *Joseph Turner and antagonist of Ellen Harmon during 1845, Howell married *Lucinda Burdick (8MR 239; Grant, p. 71) and later became a minister of the Advent Christian denomination. Howell is most noted for circulating a document seeking to discredit Ellen Harmon during her first visit to Massachusetts late in the summer of 1845. This document contained the recollections of *Elizabeth Haines, who had cared for Ellen Harmon during an illness involving delirium. Both Turner and Howell used this document to prove that Harmon was under the influence of mesmerism and that James White controlled her visions (Nichols, pp. 3, 4; Burt, p. 216).

While Ellen White was preparing her autobiographical sketch, first published in 1860 (2SG), she spoke with Elizabeth Haines concerning Howell's document and later explained the circumstances surrounding it: "Soon [Howell], who had opposed me in Maine, came in great haste to Massachusetts with a document to destroy my influence. I have never had the privilege of reading it, or hearing it read, and have not been able to obtain a copy of it to this day. This document was read in my absence, when I could not answer for myself. As near as I can learn, [Howell] got up the document, then urged a sister [Haines], who was occasionally with me during the two weeks of my extreme sickness, when my mind wandered, as stated on page 51, to sign it. She [Haines] was then [at the time Haines signed Howell's document] on a sick bed, suffering great confusion of mind, and to get rid of [Howell], consented to have him sign her name to the document. At a later period this sister confessed to me in tears her regret that her name was ever attached to the document. She is not a Sabbath-keeper, yet has since cheerfully given her name to a certificate on another page which kills the slanderous document" (2SG 69). This "certificate" appears in 2SG 301, 302, where Elizabeth Haines' name is found with seven other names testifying that "unfavorable reports" about James and Ellen White were false.

See also: Hypnotism and Mesmerism.

Further Reading: obit. *The World's Crisis*, Jan. 8, 1862; M. Burt, "The Historical Background, Interconnected Development, and Integration of the Doctrines of the Sanctuary, the Sabbath, and Ellen G. White's Role in Sabbatarian Adventism From 1844 to 1849," (Ph.D. diss., AU, 2002), pp. 215-217; "Statement by Otis Nichols" (DF 105, EGWE-GC), pp. 1-4; M. Grant, *The True Sabbath: Which Day Shall We Keep? An Examination of Mrs. Ellen White's Visions* (Boston: Advent Christian Publication Society, 1874), p. 71.

Jud Lake

HOWLAND, FRANCES (later **FRANCES [HOWLAND] LUNT**) (1829-1906). Eldest daughter of *Stockbridge and Louisa Howland, of Topsham, Maine; Frances was a dear friend of Ellen Harmon's. About the time she accepted the Sabbath in the spring of 1845, Frances contracted rheumatic fever. As her fever rose and her hands swelled, the local physician could do nothing to help her. But in response to prayers of faith by Ellen Harmon, James White, and others she was immediately restored. Days later, she was baptized outdoors in cold water with no ill effects (LS 74, 75; 2SG 42-44, 302). This miracle, an example of

faith healing among early Sabbathkeepers, strengthened conviction in the prophetic ministry of Ellen White. It was also the beginning of a friendship between Harmon and Frances that would span more than 60 years. In 1847, when the Whites' eldest son, Henry, was desperately ill, Frances offered to hold him for an hour so that Ellen could get some sleep. Frances bonded with the infant Henry and cared for him in her parents' home for five years. In 1869 she was married to Noah N. Lunt (1821-1902) in Battle Creek. In 1886 they moved to California. In 1906, after Noah's death, Ellen White wrote to his widow, Frances, and her sister Rebekah (Howland) Winslow, reminiscing of their early days in Maine (Lt 130, 1906; cf. 14MR 259).

HOWLAND, STOCKBRIDGE (1801-1883) and **LOUISA (MORSE)** (1806-1897). A civil engineer and Adventist lay leader in Topsham,

STOCKBRIDGE HOWLAND

LOUISA HOWLAND

Maine. Stockbridge and Louisa Howland opened their three-story home ("Fort Howland") to Adventist preachers and especially to the Whites. Stockbridge was a deacon in the Congregational Church (1821-1841) until he accepted William Miller's teachings. Deeming his conversion to Millerism as evidence that he was mentally unstable, his associates appointed a legal guardian over him. But when Topsham needed a bridge over the Kennebec River, they could find no engineer more qualified than he. Eventually people realized that Howland was a stable person, and his guardianship ended. The Howlands accepted the Sabbath in the spring of 1845, about the same time as Joseph Bates.

In the 1840s the Howlands' home in Topsham was a center for Adventist conferences and healings. *Frances Howland was healed of rheumatic fever after fervent prayer by the Whites in 1845; in 1846, following Ellen White's vision about the opening heavens that she received in their home, Joseph Bates became convinced of her prophetic gift. For a few years early in their married life James and Ellen White set up housekeeping in the Howland home (1847-1852), where Ellen's vision concerning the Sabbath commandment enshrouded in glory occurred in 1847. Also in Topsham the Whites laid plans in 1848 to publish the first Sabbatarian Adventist journal, *The Present Truth*. Their son *Henry was reared by the Howlands, who refused the $1.00 a week the Whites offered. James stated that the Howlands returned their son in 1853 "a well-trained, praying boy." A zealous lay leader, Stockbridge Howland quelled fanaticism in Paris, Maine, and strengthened *J. N. Andrews' conviction to become a Sabbathkeeper. In 1872 the Howlands moved to Battle Creek, Michigan. "Father Howland" died of pneumonia in 1883. Uriah Smith officiated at his funeral, and he was buried in Oak Hill Cemetery.

In 1906, writing to her sister Mary Foss, Ellen White described Howland's daughters, Rebekah (Howland) Winslow and Frances (Howland) Lunt, as among her "best friends." "They took care of Henry when he was a little child, and our family and their family were one" (Lt 112, 1906, in 14MR 259).

Further reading: LS 74, 75, 100, 105, 120, 141, 158; 2SG 116, 117; 1T 90, 98; WM 322; Lt 9, 1864; obit. RH, Apr. 17, 1883; obit. RH, Mar. 9, 1897; *SDA Encyclopedia* (1996), vol. 10, p. 716.

Brian E. Strayer

HUBBARD, G. Superintendent of the Helping Hand and Medical Mission in Melbourne, Australia, a self-supporting Adventist institution. Hubbard asked Ellen White whether the mission should accommodate patients who wished to eat meat and smoke on the premises. Hubbard, who was personally a vegetarian and a nonsmoker, felt the institution was losing patients because of its strict dietary and health standards (G. Hubbard to EGW, Nov. 7, 1898). In reply, Ellen White counseled him to "in no case provide a smoke room, where smoking shall be encouraged, or provide a meat diet. . . . The work in which you are engaged is an important one, and a non-meat diet is to be maintained. Leave the results with God" (Lt 95, 1898).

HUGHES, CASSIUS BOONE (1859-1921). Minister, Bible teacher, and founding principal of five industrial-type Adventist schools. Impressed by Ellen White's 1872 article "Proper Education" (FE 15-46) and her subsequent writings on industrial education, in 1894 Hughes determined to implement her educational ideals when he was appointed to lead the newly established Keene Industrial School (now Southwestern Adventist University). In particular he developed a curriculum that combined work and study. His enthusiasm for practical education was evident in a paper he presented to the 1897 General Conference session.

Ellen White meanwhile, disappointed at the failure of Battle Creek College to provide authentic Adventist education, worked with W. W. Prescott to develop the conceptual bases and curriculum for a "pattern school" in Australia. Hughes's presentation to the 1897 General Conference session revealed both a grasp of industrial education and a commitment to the educational ideals of Ellen White. Within months Cassius and his wife,

Ella (Smith), were en route to Australia to establish his second industrial school.

The Avondale School provided Hughes with an opportunity to implement Ellen White's ideas on Bible study, essential formal studies, development of a missionary spirit, industrial education, and the work-study program. The model school placed emphasis on short courses preparatory for missionary service. For the first three years Ellen White lived nearby and provided ongoing support, guidance, and counsel. She frequently addressed the students. Hughes was both encouraged and guided by Ellen White's 1898 testimony "The Avondale School Farm" (6T 181-192).

In April 1900, to celebrate the anniversary of the school's opening, faculty and students took a holiday and, after a morning chapel service, devoted the rest of the day to cricket, tennis, and other amusements, "some of which" were later described by Ellen White as "frivolous, rude, and grotesque." That night in vision Ellen White saw in the events of the afternoon the working of Satan to subvert "God's plan" for the "pattern school" (CT 348, 349). The next day she confronted Hughes, the faculty, and the students, calling the amusements a pathbreaking "departure from the instruction that God has given concerning our schools," a departure that would lead to "desire for further pleasure and less regard for the instruction of God's Word" (*ibid.* 352). Initially indignant and confused, Hughes, teachers, and students accepted Ellen White's counsel, and the amusements ceased. Between 1907 and 1920 Hughes established three other industrial schools: West Indian Training School at Riversdale, Jamaica (1908-1913); Battleford Academy, Saskatchewan, Canada (1916-1918); and another West Indian Training School (1919-1920), renamed West Indies College in 1959 and now Northern Carribean University, in Mandeville, Jamaica.

Further reading: 4Bio 306-308; obit. RH, Sept. 22, 1921; M. Hook, *Avondale: Experiment on the Dora* (Cooranbong, Australia: Avondale Academic Press, 1998); A. C. Reye, "'Home Thoughts From Abroad': The Avondale Letters of Cassius and Ella Hughes, 1897-1898," *Adventist Heritage* 18, no. 2 (Summer 1998): 11-24; *SDA Encyclopedia* (1996), vol. 10, p. 717.

Arnold C. Reye

HULL, MOSES (1836-1907) and **ELVIRA**. A Sundaykeeping Adventist for about six years (c. 1851 to 1857), Hull was ordained to the ministry by first-day Adventists when he was 18. Earlier he had been a Methodist. After learning about the Sabbath in 1857, he joined the Sabbathkeeping Adventists. In the fall of 1863 he left Seventh-day Adventism to become a spiritualist.

MOSES HULL

COURTESY OF THE CENTER FOR ADVENTIST RESEARCH, ANDREWS UNIVERSITY

While living in West Plum River, Illinois, Hull first heard from Solomon Myers, a layman, about Ellen White and her visions. It was Myers who also convinced Hull of the seventh-day Sabbath. Almost immediately following his conversion, Hull began preaching his newfound faith. He apparently first met James and Ellen White when they came to Iowa City, Iowa, in late July, 1858, where Hull and *J. H. Waggoner were doing tent evangelism. The Whites continued on to Crane's Grove, Illinois, where Hull next took his evangelistic efforts. While the Whites were at Crane's Grove, sometime between August 20 and 28, Hull was ordained by James White (RH, Sept. 23, 1858).

Several times during the following five years, Hull and his wife, Elvira, came in contact with James and Ellen White. The next occasion appears to have been from March 31 to April 1, 1860, in Knoxville, Iowa, where the Hulls then lived. In the August 14, 1860, issue of the *Review and Herald* James White made an open appeal for funds to buy a home in Fairfield, Iowa, for Elder Hull and his family. White gave a $10 donation to start the fund. Apparently, sufficient funds were not immediately forthcoming.

Moses Hull attended the important conference that opened in Battle Creek, Michigan, on September 28, 1860. It was at this conference that the publishing work was organized and the name Seventh-day Adventist chosen. Hull participated actively in the proceedings, and preached twice. It was he who made the motion that the subject of organization be discussed. After the name Seventh-day Adventist was eventually adopted, it was Moses Hull who moved that the new name be recommended to the churches. Immediately after the conference closed, he returned to Knoxville, Iowa, to conduct evangelistic meetings; the Whites soon followed. The following year, 1861, Hull and his family moved to Battle Creek. But soon he was gone again doing evangelism.

From time to time Ellen White counseled both Moses and Elvira. In one letter she warned Elvira against her habit of exaggerating and talking too much (Lt 20, 1862). In another testimony Ellen White warned Elvira about her "false tongue." She also pointed out to both Moses and his wife that wherever they go they "have trouble, for they carry it with them." Of Moses, Ellen wrote that though he could "do well to labor to bring souls into the truth . . . , he cannot build up a church. His judgment is not good." Furthermore, she said sadly of Moses, "He throws his soul into the work of preaching, labors with all his might, loves it, and would be the strongest man we

have among us as a laborer but for the lack of essential qualifications, which makes him weak" (Ms 6, 1862).

In 1862 Hull began debating spiritualists. In late October 1862, in Paw Paw, Michigan, he debated a spiritualist medium named William F. Jamieson. The debate lasted for six two-hour sessions. Hull returned from the debate confused, and reportedly ready to become a spiritualist (RH, Jan. 27, 1863; cf. 2Bio 55, 56). A season of prayer on November 5, 1862, at the home of J. N. Loughborough in Battle Creek seemed temporarily to bring Hull back to his former beliefs. During the prayer session Ellen White was given in vision a message for Hull. She warned him that he was presented to her "as standing upon the brink of an awful gulf, ready to leap. If he takes the leap, it will be final; his eternal destiny will be fixed" (1T 427). She also warned the wavering Hull that if he chose to follow Satan and his evil spirits, "you will find in the end that you will have a heavy and fearful toll to pay" (*ibid.*). Further in the testimony she predicted, "If you go down, you will not go alone; for Satan will employ you as his agent to lead souls to death" (*ibid.* 430). Not only did his wife and children follow Hull into spiritualism, but about six years later after repeatedly trying to retrieve him from spiritualism, his brother, Daniel W. Hull, ended up following Moses' lead in renouncing Adventism. One spiritualist source said about Moses Hull's evangelistic fervor for spiritualism, "More than . . . any other speaker, this man had the active missionary spirit. He taught Spiritualism constantly" (*Centennial Book of Modern Spiritualism in America* [1948], p. 128).

Less than a week after the prayer meeting held in the Loughborough home, Hull was in Monterey, Michigan, holding a weekend meeting with James and Ellen White (2Bio

56-58). They were determined, if at all possible, to save Hull for Adventism. A few weeks later, in early February 1863, after successfully treating two of her own boys for diphtheria by using water treatments, Ellen had the same success treating Elvira Hull's oldest daughter. At the time of the child's illness the two parents were back in Monterey, where Moses was holding evangelistic meetings. When a short time later request was made of those who had done business with Elder James White to describe the results of those dealings, Moses Hull's response was one of those printed in the pamphlet defending James White's business career. Hull was quite generous in his praise of White, describing him as "strictly honest in every particular," and "the most liberal man with whom I was ever acquainted" (*Vindication of the Business Career of Elder James White* [1863], p. 10).

One part of the vision given Ellen White on Friday evening, June 5, 1863, in Otsego, Michigan, was for Moses Hull. She counseled him against undue familiarity with women (1T 437). She also warned him against accepting flattery (*ibid.* 436, 437) and told him, "If you were a devotional, godly man, in the pulpit and out, a mighty influence would attend your preaching" (*ibid.* 433).

The last time that apparently Moses Hull was with James and Ellen White was September 5 and 6, 1863, when they came to where he and Elder J. N. Loughborough were holding tent meetings in Manchester, New Hampshire. Ellen White spoke for about 15 minutes that Sunday evening, having been introduced to the congregation by Moses Hull. The following Sunday evening, after his sermon, Hull told Loughborough that it was his last one; he was returning to his family. Hull then joined the spiritualists. A few weeks later he signed a statement regarding how he felt about Seventh-day Adventists. While not having "a word of

fault to find with them as to my temporal and spiritual good," he added, "Brother and sister White have been honest and kind, and not designed to abuse me. I think they are rather sharper than need be" (RH, Jan. 5, 1864).

In the early 1870s as a spiritualist, Hull not only practiced, but taught, free love so extensively that he embarrassed even some spiritualists. About the same time he and his first wife, Elvira, separated, and the remainder of his life Moses lived common-law with Mattie E. Sawyer, a spirit medium.

During the remainder of his life Hull continued to make occasional references to Adventism in his books and pamphlets, including a passing reference in 1896 to Ellen White. When he died in 1907 in San Jose, California, his obituary printed in the local newspaper included a reference to his having been an Adventist minister. Interestingly, after having been buried in a San Jose cemetery for a year, Hull's body was exhumed and transferred to a cemetery in Colma (near Daly City), California, where it was cremated.

Members of Hull's extended family who remained loyal Seventh-day Adventists reported on his remorse over having become a spiritualist. Hull's grandnephew quoted his uncle Moses as saying "that he would be willing to crawl on his hands and knees" from one large city to another "if by doing so he could be back where he once was in the church and in favor with God" (L. R. Ogden, "My Uncle Moses," RH, July 5, 1973). A niece of Moses Hull recalled it being "rumored that he said he would give his right arm if he could only get back with the Seventh-day Adventists just as he used to be." She also recalled him visiting "Grandma Seaward," who had refused to go hear Moses lecture against Adventist beliefs. When later Moses stopped in to see her, the elderly woman inquired, "Moses, you know I am growing old. You brought us the truth.

Now you have left it. Would you advise me to deny the faith and follow yours?" Hull answered, "No, you dear old Grandma. You stay just like you are" (Alice T. Edwards, "My Memories of Moses Hull").

In 1860, while still an Adventist minister, Moses Hull had written in the *Review and Herald*, "I may fall by the way; but if I do, I shall ever be thankful that the city is cheap enough for those who obtain it" (RH, Mar. 29, 1860).

Further reading: D. Hull, *Moses Hull* (Wellesley, Mass.: Maugus Printing Co., 1907); J. R. Nix, "Moses Hull" (unpublished manuscript, CAR); *SDA Encyclopedia* (1996), vol. 10, p. 718.

James R. Nix

HUNGERFORD, CARRIE (1866-1958). Nurse at the *St. Helena Sanitarium. Hungerford was with Ellen White for the final five months of her life, and on March 3, 1915, Ellen White related to Carrie her last known vision about the need of young people to build Christian character (6Bio 425; MYP 287-289).

Further reading: obit. RH, Nov. 27, 1958.

HUTCHINS, ALFRED S. (1823-1894). Pioneer pastor in Vermont and Canada East (Quebec).

COURTESY OF THE REVIEW AND HERALD PUBLISHING ASSOCIATION

ALFRED S. HUTCHINS

Before joining Adventism in 1852, Hutchins was a Freewill Baptist pastor in Vermont. He and his wife were in poor health most of their lives, a condition that hindered him from working more fully for the church. He worked mostly in Vermont and at times in Canada, where he helped *Augustin and *Daniel Bourdeau establish Adventist congregations. Hutchins assisted in the formation of the Vermont

Conference in 1862. In her counsels to Hutchins, Ellen White wished he would be more patient and less faultfinding in his ministry (Lt 5, 1864). In 1867, when many accusations were raised against James and Ellen White's leadership and ministry, Hutchins was one of the ministers who apologized in behalf of the Battle Creek church for their wrongful criticisms and favorably responded to reproofs given to the church.

Further reading: 1T 609-612; Brother I in 2T 646, 647; P. I. Tähti, "The Father of the Vermont Conference" (research paper, DF 5039, CAR); *SDA Encyclopedia* (1996), vol. 10, p. 730.

HYATT, WILLIAM SPENCER (1857-1936) and **SADIE (ARMITAGE)** (1860-1938). Adventist missionaries to South Africa. William and Sadie attended *Battle Creek College and afterward married in 1882. William began his ministerial labors in New York and was ordained in 1885. He found his faith renewed at the *General Conference session of 1888, and became conference president in Texas (1888-1892) and then pastor of the *Battle Creek Tabernacle. In 1898 the Hyatts and their three children went as missionaries to South Africa. Ellen White sent them several letters of counsel regarding the work in South Africa (Lts 79, 183, 184, 1899). She urged him that "nothing would be gained by making a decided distinction" in matters "of caste and colour" (Lt 26, 1900, in TSA 85). Hyatt became the first president of the South African Union Conference in 1902.

HYDE, WILLIAM H. (b. 1828). Millerite who witnessed Ellen Harmon's 1845 vision of the new earth (cf. EW 17-20). Hyde had earlier been miraculously healed from dysentery (2SG 44; LS80 200, 201; 1Bio 82). Soon after Ellen White's vision he wrote the earliest known hymn based on an Ellen White vision (cf. James White, in *Present Truth*, November 1850). The hymn, originally titled "The Better Land," now called "We Have Heard From the Bright, the Holy Land," was included in *J. V. Himes' Advent Harp* (1849) and James White's first hymnal, *Hymns for God's Peculiar People Who Keep the Commandments of God and the Faith of Jesus* (1849). It is also found in the current *Seventh-day Adventist Hymnal*. Advent Christian hymnals are known to have included it as late as 1888. The hymn was one of Ellen White's favorites, and in her old age she was heard humming it (Ella M. Robinson, "Hymns Loved and Sung by Ellen White" [DF 245g]; 6Bio 418).

Further reading: E. E. White, *Singing With Understanding* (Warburton, Australia: Signs Publishing, 1981), pp. 220, 221; *SDA Encyclopedia* (1996), vol. 10, p. 732.

INGRAHAM, WILLIAM S. (1821-1874) and **MELISSA** (1824-1897). Early Sabbatarian

COURTESY OF THE ELLEN G. WHITE ESTATE, INC.

WILLIAM S. INGRAHAM

Adventist minister and administrator who accepted the Adventist doctrine in 1839 from the preaching of *William Miller, and by 1851 was listed among the "preaching brethren" (RH, Nov. 25, 1851). Ingraham was a forceful evangelist who

held meetings in New England and Pennsylvania (1850s), Wisconsin and Illinois (1850s and 1860s), and Minnesota (1860s and 1870s). He was the first president of the Wisconsin and Illinois Conference (1862-1863). Ellen White received a vision at Crane's Grove, Illinois, in August 1858 in which she was shown Ingraham's negative attitude toward James White. A continuing failure to heed her warning led to a series of reproofs that

extended to include his failure in "family government" (Lt 17, 1861; see also Lt 32, 1861). While she affirmed Ingraham as a fine preacher, he needed not merely to preach, but also to solve "church difficulties" (Lt 15, 1862). This led to a published confession in the *Review and Herald* (Mar. 19, 1861).

Further reading: obit. RH, May 26, 1874; obit. RH, Aug. 3, 1897.

INGS, JENNIS (also "**JENNIE**," "**JENNY**," or "**JANE**") **L.** (**HUSSMAN**) (1841-1921) and

COURTESY OF THE REVIEW AND HERALD PUBLISHING ASSOCIATION

WILLIAM AND JENNY INGS

WILLIAM (1835-1897). Missionary and *literary assistant to Ellen White. An immigrant from Germany in the early 1860s, she migrated to Iowa, where she married William Ings. The Ingses were introduced to Adventism by *G. I.

Butler, and afterward William became an ordained minister. In 1866 James White invited them to work for the Seventh-day Adventist Publishing Association in Battle Creek. William became a shipping clerk, and Jenny set type for German and Danish publications. In 1876 William went to Switzerland to assist *J. N. Andrews in starting an Adventist publishing house while Jenny stayed behind to help Ellen White—she joined him in 1878. Together in 1879 they went as the first Adventist missionaries to *England. In 1882 at the invitation of Ellen White the Ingses returned to the United States; they stayed with Ellen White at her *home in Healdsburg, and Jenny served as Ellen White's nurse and literary assistant (Lts 11a, 20a, 1882). Jenny and Ellen White became very close, writing to each other in one another's absence, and Ellen White signing her letters "mother" (cf. Lt 23, 1884). The Ingses were particularly helpful to Ellen White when traveling with her during her stay in *Europe from 1885 to 1887. After their return to the United States in 1888, Jenny became matron of the Rural Health Retreat (later the *St. Helena Sanitarium), where they remained the rest of their lives.

Further reading: obit. RH, June 23, 1921; obit. RH, June 15, 1897; *SDA Encyclopedia* (1996), vol. 10, p. 769.

Michael W. Campbell

IRWIN, CHARLES WALTER (1868-1934). Educator; son of *G. A. Irwin. Irwin gradu-

CHARLES W. IRWIN

ated from *Battle Creek College in 1891, and became a teacher at *Union College where, in 1895, he wedded Minnie V. Hennig (1868-1927). In 1898 he became principal of the Graysville School (see *Graysville, Tennessee) and in 1901 principal of *Avondale College. While he was in Australia, Ellen White wrote several letters of encouragement to him (Lt 150, 1902; Lt 36, 1907). In 1908, realizing that she might never return to Australia, she asked him to sell her property at Avondale (Lt 124, 1908). In 1909 the Irwins returned to the United States, and he became president of Pacific Union College (1909-1921), then associate secretary of the General Conference Education Department, becoming head of that department in 1930.

Further reading: obit. RH, Sept. 6, 1934; *SDA Encyclopedia* (1996), vol. 10, p. 801.

IRWIN, GEORGE ALEXANDER (1844-1913) and **NETTIE (JOHNSON)** (1849-1919). Farmer, minister, missionary, administrator, and General Conference president (1897-1901). During the *Civil War he fought with the Ohio Volunteer Infantry, and was held by Confederates in the Andersonville prison camp. While detained, he read *Richard Baxter's *Saints' Everlasting Rest*, which led to his conversion and subsequent membership in the Congregational and Methodist churches. In 1867 he married Nettie Johnson and settled on a farm near Mount Vernon, Ohio. In 1885 the Irwins became Seventh-day Adventists through a series of Bible lectures held in a nearby schoolhouse. He soon entered denominational employment, first as district director, then as treasurer, and, during a period of crisis, as president of the Ohio Conference (1889-1895). While there the Irwins first became acquainted with Ellen White when she wrote them a series of letters (Lt 15, 1890; Lt 16a, 1891; Lt 17, 1891; Lt 18, 1891).

In 1895 Irwin was appointed superintendent of General Conference District no. 2 (the southern United States). In that position he assisted in selecting the site for Oakwood College (see *Oakwood Industrial School). Two years later he was elected president of the General Conference. During his presidency he often sought Ellen White's counsel, and she frequently urged him to use his influence as president to gather funds for missions (Lt 88, 1898; Lt 3, 1900). Another major concern of hers was that Adventist ministers "be true yoke fellows of Dr. [*J. H.] Kellogg" (Lt 36, 1899; Lt 42, 1898) and "seek to save Dr. Kellogg" (Lt 3, 1900), who was "in great peril of making shipwreck of faith" (Lt 170, 1900).

GEORGE AND NETTIE IRWIN

Ellen White saw those in Battle Creek in grave danger spiritually (Lt 145, 1899) and needing revival (Lt 51a, 1898; Lt 42,

1898; Lt 157, 1899). Altogether she wrote the Irwins more than 70 letters. During this time Nettie was active in what was then termed the Woman's Gospel Work, heading that department after the death of *S.M.I. Henry in 1900.

Irwin later chaired the *General Conference session of 1901, which led to a major administrative reorganization and the election of *A. G. Daniells as chair of the General Conference Executive Committee (de facto president). In turn, Irwin replaced Daniells as president of the Australasian Union Conference (1901-1905). Upon his return to the United States Irwin helped in planning for the *Washington Sanitarium (Lt 48, 1906; Lt 114, 1907; Ms 83, 1906), and used his influence in the Southern California Conference to help purchase the *Loma Linda property. Ellen White stayed with the Irwins at their home in Takoma Park for the 1909 General Conference session. He later served as president of the Pacific Union Conference (1910-1912), as president of the board of directors of the *College of Medical Evangelists (now Loma Linda University), and as vice president of the Pacific Union Conference. After George's death in 1913, Nettie served as preceptor and later as general matron of the Loma Linda Sanitarium.

Further reading: obit. RH, June 5, 1913; obit. RH, July 10, 1919; D. A. Ochs and G. L. Ochs, *The Past and the Presidents* (SPA, 1974), pp. 88-103; *SDA Encyclopedia* (1996), vol. 10, p. 801; *Legacy of Light* CD-ROM, art., "George A. Irwin."

Michael W. Campbell

ISRAEL, MENDEL CROCKER (1834-1921) and **LIZZIE (REDFORD)** (1836-1916). Carpenter, minister, and evangelist. Mendel was born in Nova Scotia, immigrated to Maine, and in 1858 moved to Oregon, where

MENDEL C. ISRAEL

LIZZIE ISRAEL

he married Lizzie Redford in 1867. Lizzie had moved with her family to Oregon from Missouri in 1864 after the death of her father in the *Civil War. In 1874 Mendel made a commitment to the Adventist message, and the following year at a camp meeting the Israels were baptized by *S. N. Haskell. The Israels relocated to California, where Mendel attended a Bible Institute held by *James White, *Uriah Smith, and *J. H. Waggoner. Convinced he should enter the ministry, Mendel conducted Bible readings and later did public *evangelism. He continued his ministry in the California Conference, and in 1878 was ordained by James White and *J. N. Loughborough. At the 1884 General Conference session, 10 years after Ellen White first called for missionaries to *Australia, the Israels, S. N. Haskell, *J. O. Corliss, and others became the first Adventist missionaries to Australia and *New Zealand. They arrived in 1885 and held evangelistic meetings in Melbourne and Adelaide. The Israels pioneered the work in Tasmania, and among those converted to Adventism were the Lacey family. One of the daughters in that family, May, became Ellen White's daughter-in-law when she married W. C. White in 1895, following the death of his first wife in 1890. Mendel also served as president of the New Zealand Conference (1890-1892). While in Australia, Ellen White became a close friend and confidant of Lizzie's. They exchanged a lengthy correspondence in which Ellen White told Lizzie that Jesus cared about her as the wife of an evangelist (cf. Lt 33, 1895). The Israels returned to California in 1896 and retired in 1905.

Further reading: obit. RH, Feb. 9, 1922; obit. *Australian Record*, Apr. 3, 1922; obit. PUR, May 11, 1916; N. P. Clapham, ed., *Seventh-day Adventists in the South Pacific 1885-1985* (Warburton, Australia: Signs Pub. Co., 1985); *SDA Encyclopedia* (1996), vol. 10, pp. 805, 806.

Lester D. Devine

JACKSON, JAMES CALEB (1811-1895). Early American health reformer. Jackson graduated from the Eclectic Medical College, Syracuse, New York. In 1847 while a patient at Dr. S. O. Gleason's water cure institution in Greenwood Springs, New York, Jackson proposed the establishment of a new "water cure" in collaboration with Gleason at Glen Haven, New York. The Glen Haven institution was the scene of a hygienic festival that drew 150 reformers, including Amelia Bloomer and Elizabeth Cady Stanton. In 1858 Jackson in association with Dr. Harriet Austin purchased a defunct water cure at Dansville, New

J. C. JACKSON'S WATER CURE HEALTH INSTITUTE "OUR HOME ON THE HILLSIDE"

York, and renamed it "Our Home on the Hillside." The regimen was heavily influenced by *Sylvester Graham and consisted among other things of two vegetarian meals a day interspersed with health lectures, treatments, simple exercises, and amusements. A patient

could be examined for a charge of $5, and treatments were "limited chiefly to half-baths, packs, sitz baths, plunges and dripping sheets." Drugs were never prescribed. In fact, Jackson based his beliefs on 10 health principles: "First, air; second, food; third, water; fourth, sunlight; fifth, dress; sixth, exercise; seventh, sleep; eighth, rest; ninth, social influence; tenth, mental and moral forces." Although a number of water cures quickly faded into obscurity in America, Jackson's "Our Home" prospered. From 1850 to 1862 an estimated 4,000 patients were treated at "Our Home."

James and Ellen White first became introduced to the healing methods of Jackson through an article by Jackson in the *Yates County Chronicle*. In this article Jackson talked about how to cure diphtheria through water treatments. Two of the Whites' boys had contracted the then-incurable disease, but survived as their parents applied water treatments to them. When the boys recovered, James White was exuberant and reprinted the article in the *Review and Herald* so that other Sabbatarian Adventists might benefit from such knowledge (2Bio 14, 15).

After this initial contact by the Whites, there were two other sources of information to Sabbatarian Adventists about the physicians and staff at "Our Home on the Hillside": visits by *J. N. Andrews, and visits by Sundaykeeping Adventists. The first Sabbatarian Adventist to visit "Our Home" was J. N. Andrews, who took his family there for medical treatment. It can be presumed that he shared with other church members the benefits that his family gained from those visits. Advent Christians Daniel T. Taylor and *Joshua V. Himes also benefited from treatments at "Our Home" and advertised health reform literature in their own publications. According to Ellen White, it was such an advertisement published in Himes' *Voices of the Prophets* in September

1863 that alerted James White to available health reform literature (RH, Oct. 8, 1867). It appears that Ellen White was incorrect in her recollection of exactly *when* James White requested literature, because Dr. Jackson had already responded to him during the previous month, but it seems entirely probable that it could have been an earlier announcement in the same paper or another Advent Christian publication that stimulated his request. In response, Jackson invited them to visit his water cure, offering board and treatments at the clergy rate of two dollars and fifty cents a week (J. C. Jackson to James White, Aug. 13, 1863 [EGWE-GC]). Ellen White wrote that she was determined to write out her views on *health reform, from her comprehensive *health reform vision of June 5, 1863, without being influenced by the writings of other health reformers. Accordingly, she said that after receiving the health reform literature they laid it aside until she could first write out her own views about health reform. By September 1864, after writing *Appeal to Mothers and *Spiritual Gifts, volume 4 (which contained a section on health), the Whites spent a few weeks at "Our Home" in Dansville, New York (RH, Sept. 6, 1864). During this first visit they received treatments and were impressed by the work Jackson was doing. Despite this, Ellen White did not agree with all of Jackson's views of health reform. Their differences would become more apparent during their second visit in the fall of 1865, following James's first stroke on August 16. Despite these differences, James White's health began to improve, and they were grateful for what they had learned.

At the end of the *Civil War the poor health of church leaders was crippling the leadership of the fledgling Seventh-day Adventist Church. As a result, a group of sick church leaders, which Uriah Smith dubbed the "Adventist invalid party," left Battle Creek to travel to "Our Home" for treatment. The Whites stayed as part of this group from September through December 1865. During this second stay the Whites and Jackson grew better acquainted with each other, and discovered that there were significant philosophical differences between them. To avoid conflict (as well as to save money), the Whites rented a cottage on the grounds near the facility. First and foremost, Ellen White disagreed with Jackson's philosophy of entertainment and religion. "In regard to a religious experience," reflecting back upon the experience, she wrote later, "Dr. [Jackson] presents dancing and playing cards a class of amusements as healthful, but presents religion as deleterious and dangerous to health" (Lt 8, 1867). She also disagreed with Jackson's philosophy of the intermingling of the sexes. He encouraged dancing and promiscuous behavior, which she could not condone. Third, she did not care for his self-exalted perception of himself and his views of health reform. She described him as someone who "would have his patients believe that his judgment is perfect. . . . Yet he often fails" (Ms 5, 1866, in 1T 616). For example, Jackson advocated the avoidance of all salt, but Ellen White wrote that she had been shown that a modest amount of salt was necessary for a balanced diet. These differences led Ellen White to summarize that she "saw that many of Dr. Jackson's ideas are valuable, while others are worthless and injurious" (Ms 21, 1902). While Jackson had initially invited the Whites to interact with patients, disagreements led Jackson to ask the Whites to be discrete about their differences.

By December 1865, James and Ellen White felt that they had gained all they could from Dr. Jackson and that James's health was improved enough for them to return home. For Ellen White, what was most startling of all was Jackson's prognosis that any physical or mental exertion on the part of James White would prove dangerous or even fatal to his health. Contrary to this, Ellen White believed that physical exertion was just what he needed to stimulate the body to overcome disease (RH, Oct. 8, 1867). Over the next 18 months Ellen White encouraged her husband to visit friends as his strength permitted, and in the spring of 1865 they purchased a small farm in Greenville, Michigan, where he could labor outdoors (see *homes of James and Ellen White). As James worked, his health began to improve.

On Christmas Day 1865, in Rochester, New York, Ellen White was shown in vision that Adventists should develop a health institution of their own where they could treat patients in harmony with their convictions. As a direct result of this vision, the denomination opened the *Health Reform Institute in Battle Creek in September 1866. At a time when many hydropathic health institutions were failing, White cautioned Adventists to make sure and steady steps so as not to jeopardize any progress they might make in starting a new health facility. While initially the institution was influenced largely by the principles and methods of Jackson's institution (the first superintendent, Dr. *H. S. Lay, had been on the staff of "Our Home"), Ellen White cautioned against unduly patterning the Health Reform Institute after the one in Dansville, New York, especially in matters of religion and amusement (see Lt 8, 1867). Thus the Health Reform Institute was placed on a spiritual foundation free from frivolous amusements, but at the same time utilizing the very best hydropathic treatments they had learned at "Our Home." The first few years for the Adventist facility were shaky, but after its reorganization in 1870 it began to thrive. The management of the institution was turned over in 1876 to the youthful and dynamic Dr.

*J. H. Kellogg, under whose management the institution grew into the world-famous *Battle Creek Sanitarium. While critics of Ellen White have suggested that she received her views on *health reform from Jackson, her time spent at "Our Home" showed instead that while she appreciated and respected Jackson, the basic tenets of her philosophy of health had already been formulated by the time she visited "Our Home." This is evidenced in the fact that she utilized what she saw as the best that she might glean in health reform teachings while at the same time distinguishing from what she saw as false. Despite these differences, during the 1860s the Whites continued to publish articles by Jackson in the *Review and Herald and *Health Reformer, and even included an article by him along with a glowing endorsement for "Our Home" in their compilation *Health: or How to Live (1865). Health reformers such as Jackson, *R. T. Trall, and *Sylvester Graham were regarded by early Seventh-day Adventists as pioneers in health reform, but as a new generation of Adventist physicians rose to prominence during the 1870s, and as medical science advanced, these earlier authors disappeared from the pages of Adventist health literature. In 1895 the Review and Herald carried news of Jackson's death (RH, July 30, 1895).

When Jackson retired in 1871, he turned over management of "Our Home on the Hillside" to his son and daughter-in-law, Drs. James H. and Kate J. Jackson. In June 1882 a fire completely destroyed the main building of "Our Home," but in October 1883 the Jacksons rebuilt a much larger brick facility and renamed it the "Jackson Sanatorium." The water cure thrived for several more decades, and management was turned over to their son Dr. J. Arthur Jackson. Advances in medical science spelled the doom of the water cure, and the then-called "Jackson Health Resort" was forced into bankruptcy (1914). The facility was purchased by health faddist Bernard Macfadden, and later by hotelier William Fromcheck, who closed the facility in 1971.

Further reading: RH, Feb. 20, 1866; 2Bio 76-89, 119-127; SHM 160-162; W. D. Conklin, *The Jackson Health Resort: Pioneer in Its Field, as Seen by Those Who Knew It Well; Being an Account of the Institution's Fiftieth Anniversary, With Records of the Seventieth and the One Hundredth, and a Supplement* (Dansville, N.Y.: the author, 1971); R. L. Numbers, *Prophetess of Health,* rev. ed. (Knoxville: University of Tennessee Press, 1992); J. C. Jackson, *How to Treat the Sick Without Medicine,* 11th ed. (Dansville, N.Y.: Our Home Pub. Dept., 1881); *idem, Our Home on the Hillside: What We Are Trying to Do and How We Are Trying to Do It* (Dansville, N.Y.: [Austin, Jackson & Co., c. 1870]).

Michael W. Campbell

JACOBS, ENOCH (1809-c. 1890). Best known in Adventist studies as the editor of Millerite periodicals published in Cincinnati, Ohio. Jacobs was born in Marlborough, Vermont, and married Electa Whitney in 1831. They had five children. After living for a time in Brooklyn, New York, the family moved in 1843 to Cincinnati, Ohio, where Jacobs replaced George Storrs as editor of the *Western Midnight Cry,* published by *Joshua V. Himes. Although Himes remained listed as publisher until the title of the paper was changed to the *Day-Star* on February 18, 1845, it was Jacobs who largely bore responsibility for the publication. Owing to this, and to Jacobs' and Himes' differing opinions concerning the relevance of the October 1844 experience, Jacobs declared himself both publisher and editor of the renamed paper.

After the 1844 disappointment Jacobs became a key stabilizing element for Bridegroom or Shut-Door Adventists, who continued to believe in the prophetic significance of the 1844 *Midnight Cry. His paper the *Day-Star* contained correspondence and articles from many who became Sabbatarian Adventists and later the key founders of the Seventh-day Adventist Church. Early in 1846, however, he became sympathetic to the Shaker view of a spiritual second coming of Christ. By the summer of 1846 he had helped influence perhaps 200 Millerites to embrace Shakerism. He left Shakerism in 1847 after refusing to abandon his marriage to Electa.

Later in life he embraced *spiritualism and was known for his military and civic activities. Until the *Civil War Jacobs engaged in the manufacture of ironworks as a junior partner in the firm of Vallean and Jacobs. He and his four sons all served with distinction in the Union army, and two of his sons were killed in the conflict. During the early 1870s Jacobs was in government service in Uruguay, South America. At other times he served as a school trustee, newspaper correspondent, justice of the peace, and local mayor.

See also: Adventist Denominations.

Further reading: H. A. Ford and K. B. Ford, *History of Hamilton County* (Cleveland: L. A. Williams, 1881), pp. 307, 308; M. D. Burt, "The Historical Background, Interconnected Development and Integration of the Doctrines of the Sanctuary, the Sabbath, and Ellen G. White's Role in Sabbatarian Adventism From 1844 to 1849" (Ph.D. diss., AU, 2002), pp. 72-74, 98-103, 232-242.

Merlin D. Burt

JACQUES, EVELYN GRACE (WHITE), see WHITE, EVELYN GRACE.

JAMES, GEORGE. Missionary in Maitland and Ballarat, Australia. In the 1890s James and his wife raised funds for the new hospital at Cooranbong. Because they faced much criticism and many trials in their work, Ellen White wrote encouraging letters motivating them to "be of good courage in the Lord" (Lt 15, 1901). "I feel a deep interest in your soul," she stated, asking him in 1899 to "give your heart to God as a New Year's gift" (Lt 44, 1899).

Brian E. Strayer

JAMES, IRAM (1863-1939). Farm manager for Ellen White. Ellen White first met James, his wife, Christina (1866-1934), and their children in *Australia in 1894. Shortly after they accepted the Sabbath in 1894, an economic downturn forced them into bankruptcy, and they lost their farm (Lt 146, 1894; 4Bio 141). Not long afterward Ellen White invited James to become her farm manager—and things prospered under his hand. When Ellen White returned to the United States in 1900, she invited the James family to join her at her new Elmshaven home, where a cottage was erected for them (5Bio 36). "I would not be willing," wrote Ellen White, "to exchange my farmer for any other person that I know of" (6Bio 136). After Ellen White's death, James bought her Elmshaven home from her estate.

Further reading: D. E. Galusha, "Iram James" (research paper, SDA Theological Seminary, 1985, EGWE-LLU).

JAYNE, JULIUS EDWARD (1864-1933). Minister and administrator. Jayne was converted in 1885, received a license to preach the following year, and served in a variety of administrative posts in the United States and Great Britain. From 1899 to 1903 he was secretary of the *Foreign Mission Board, during which time Ellen White wrote to him regarding concerns over *E. E. Franke's work in New York City, and encouraging Jayne to do all he could to assist *S. N. Haskell there (Lt 149,

1901). In his later years he assisted Dr. J. P. and Mrs. Bradford at their Acushnet Sanitarium (RH, July 6, 1933).

JEMISON, HEDWIG (NAGELE) (1912-2005). Secretary to Arthur L. White at the Ellen G. White Estate in Washington, D.C., 1950-1955. When the Seventh-day Adventist Theological Seminary moved from Washington, D. C., to Andrews University, the White Estate requested that a duplicate set of the Ellen White materials be put on file there. Administrators at the university and the seminary agreed that this would be most beneficial to the students. A fireproof vault was built to house the documents. Jemison helped to set up the vault, working part-time for W.G.C. Murdoch, dean of the seminary, and part-time for the White Estate. In 1963, after the death of her husband, she was appointed director of the White Estate Branch Office at Andrews University. Beginning in 1974, she set up Ellen G. White Research Centers in England, Australia, Mexico, Argentina, the Philippines, and India, as well as White Estate Study Centers in Singapore, Hong Kong, Japan, Korea, Indonesia, Peru, Chile, Trinidad, and the Inter-America Division office. She compiled four morning watch devotional books from the writings of Ellen White: *My Life Today, *Sons and Daughters of God, *Reflecting Christ, and *Lift Him Up (Hedy Jemison to Norma Collins, Apr. 12, 2002). Jemison retired in 1984.

Norma Collins

JOHNSON, LEWIS (1851-1940). Born in Denmark, Johnson immigrated to the United States in 1869 and became a Methodist preacher in Iowa. After he and his wife, Christine Henriksen, became Adventists in 1875, he was licensed in 1876 and ordained by *G. I. Butler in 1878. He preached among the Scandinavians in Iowa, Illinois, Minnesota,

North Dakota, and South Dakota from 1876 to 1889 before leaving for Norway. He replaced O. A. Olsen as Nordic Union president (1889-1899) and presided over the doubling of the church membership in Norway, Sweden, and Denmark before returning to North America as director of the Danish-Norwegian work (1899-1907) and president of the Washington Conference (1912-1916). From Australia in 1895 Ellen White urged him to be faithful in tithes and offerings despite his poverty, promising that if he would bring in his "limited offerings" from his "meager store," God would "make these willing contributions bountiful" (Lt 37, 1895).

Further reading: obit. NPUG, Feb. 20, 1940; obit. RH, Apr. 11, 1940; *SDA Encyclopedia* (1996), vol. 10, p. 831.

Brian E. Strayer

JONES, ALONZO TREVIER (1850-1923). Born in Ohio, A. T. Jones would become

ALONZO T. JONES

Adventism's most influential preacher in the 1890s, only to apostatize early in the twentieth century. Jones was baptized into the Seventh-day Adventist Church in 1874 while serving as an Army sergeant at Fort Walla Walla in Washington State. Being of an energetic nature, he soon began to raise up churches in the Pacific Northwest. By 1885 he was doing editorial work for the *Signs of the Times* and the *Sabbath Sentinel* (a religious liberty periodical). That position put him into close association with *Ellet J. Waggoner.

During his years working on the *Signs*, he and Waggoner began to develop progressive ideas on the place of Christ in Adventism and the plan of salvation. In addition, Jones began

developing into one of the denomination's foremost experts in the area of religious liberty, a topic of crucial importance to the denomination since the *Sunday legislation controversy had gained strength throughout the 1880s and would come to a climax in May 1888 when Senator H. W. Blair placed a national Sunday bill before the United States Senate.

Jones' interest in prophetic interpretation would eventually lead him into conflict with *Uriah Smith, the denomination's acknowledged expert on the topic. Their initial point of difference had to do with Jones' view on the identity of the 10 horns of Daniel 7. The conflict came to a head at the *General Conference session of 1888. That momentous session found Jones linked up with E. J. Waggoner in an unequal struggle with the General Conference leadership. While Jones made a contribution to the session on religious liberty, his and Waggoner's main contribution was the uplifting of the righteousness of Christ in salvation.

Ellen White, sensing that the young men from the West had a salvational message that the denomination desperately needed to hear, had been supporting their right to be publicly heard from at least 1887. She stood with them during the 1888 session, as she did also in 1889 and the early nineties in taking the message of Christ's righteousness to Adventism across North America. The resistance of some church leaders in the years following 1888, however, led Ellen White to alert the Adventist constituency repeatedly that the Lord had given Brother Jones a "most precious message" (TM 91). On the other hand, she didn't want people to think that his and Waggoner's teachings were "infallible" or that she agreed with everything they said (Ms 56, 1890; cf. Ms 15, 1888).

The late 1880s and early 1890s would also witness Jones taking on stature in Adventist eyes as he led out in the attack on the annual crop of national Sunday legislation put before the United States Congress. His first of many appearances representing the denomination before various committees of Congress took place on December 13, 1888.

Jones and Waggoner rapidly became the featured speakers at the General Conference sessions, a dominance they would hold throughout the 1890s. Jones, for example, preached 24 and 26 sermons at the 1893 and 1895 sessions, respectively. By early 1894 Ellen White would repeatedly lament that many put Jones and his ideas in the place where God should be (Lt 27, 1894; Lt 6a, 1894). One symbol of his stature is that by 1894 the denominational leaders wanted him to replace the venerable Uriah Smith as editor of the *Review and Herald*, one of the denomination's most influential positions. Unfortunately, however, Jones had tarnished himself in supporting the false prophetic claims of *Anna Rice (even going so far as to seek to bring about the latter rain through her writings at the 1893 General Conference session). But in 1897 he received the appointment, with Smith as his associate editor—truly a humbling position for the older man.

Jones' theology went through a metamorphosis during the early 1890s. By 1893 to some extent and by 1895 even more so, he and Waggoner had come to place at the center of their understanding of salvation the concept that Christ's humanity was just like that of every other human being, without a particle of difference. That teaching had not been absent in their theology in the late eighties and early nineties, but it had not been prominent. But by 1895 it had become central to Jones. That year he spent most of six of his General Conference sermons on the topic, proclaiming that Christ was exactly like every other human being, including the possession of sinful tendencies. But Jones had to deal with an audience-generated quotation from Ellen White that Christ "is a brother in our infirmities, but not in possessing like passions" (2T 202). In his answer to that challenge, Jones claimed that Christ's flesh was like ours, but not His mind (see 1895 GCB 231, 233, 327). In that answer Jones proved just the opposite of what he was arguing, but never seemed to notice. Meanwhile he and Waggoner had developed a teaching that would eventually lead to denomination-wide controversy in the 1950s.

The 1890s saw Jones take extreme views on religious liberty, prophetic interpretation, church organization, faith healing, and other topics. Several of his interpretations were met by straightforward rebuke and more moderate counsel from Ellen White.

For most of the 1890s Ellen White was in Australia. During those years her foremost spokesperson in the United States was Jones. Time after time she sent the fearless Jones testimonies for him to present to wayward denominational leaders because she knew that he had the courage to face even the most difficult situations. Unfortunately, she also had to rebuke him firmly for mixing in his own words with hers, expanding her intended meanings.

The 1890s would also see Jones set the stage for the problematic use of Ellen White's writings in the twentieth century. Especially serious were his making her writings a divine, infallible commentary on the Bible, his belief that her writings were verbally inspired and inerrant, and a verbalist hermeneutic that used Ellen White's words without considering their historical and literary contexts. By that latter strategy he could make Ellen White and others "say" just the opposite of what they meant. Ellen White took the opposite position in each of those four areas. In all of those areas, however, Jones set himself up for his eventual rejection of Ellen White's ministry. He also guided the denomination into a misuse and misunderstanding of her writings in the twentieth century.

By 1900 Jones had developed an extreme understanding of church organization based upon his holiness ecclesiology. Like the earliest Pentecostals, Jones believed that all church organization was wrong and that the Holy Spirit was the only organization needed. That is, if every person had the Spirit, all would move in harmony without external, human organization. He and Waggoner would fight vigorously for that position in the 1901 and 1903 *General Conference sessions. And having lost in a power struggle second to none in the denomination's history, both of them would join *J. H. Kellogg in leaving the church between 1904 and 1909. Subsequently, Jones would become a catalyst for attacks on Ellen White and on the Adventist Church in general, espousing a radical congregationalism that has continued to crop up in Adventism from time to time ever since.

Jones continued to keep the seventh-day Sabbath until his death in 1923. His last fellowship was with a congregation of Sabbath-keeping Pentecostals, until they committed the ultimate evil by developing an organization. Jones went to his grave warring against Adventism, *A. G. Daniells, and all organization. To be free from organization had for Jones become the essence of religious liberty.

See also: Rice, Anna C. (Phillips).

Further reading: obit. RH, June 28, 1923; G. R. Knight, "Adventist Faith Healing in the 1890s," *Adventist Heritage* 13 (Summer 1990): 3-15; idem, *From 1888 to Apostasy: The Case of A. T. Jones* (RHPA, 1987); A. L. White, "What Became of A. T. Jones and E. J. Waggoner" (EGWE, SDoc).

George R. Knight

JONES, CHARLES HARRIMAN (1850-1936). Adventist publishing house manager. After

CHARLES H. JONES

Seventh-day Adventists established their first publishing house, the *Review and Herald, at Battle Creek, Michigan, Jones left his employment as the printer for the state of New Hampshire and moved to Battle Creek. In 1879 he took a position in the Oakland, California, printing plant of the church's Pacific Publishing Association (later renamed *Pacific Press Publishing Association). This was the beginning of a career at Pacific Press that, with a few brief interruptions, was to span more than 50 years. During this time Jones served as manager, vice president, and president of Pacific Press.

Jones oversaw the relocation of Pacific Press from Oakland to Mountain View, California, in 1904. The move was initiated in response to continuing counsel from Ellen White regarding the need to remove the publishing house and its workers from the crowded conditions in Oakland and to reduce the amount of commercial work in which the press was engaged. Following the relocation of the institution to the more rural Mountain View, Jones briefly retired from Pacific Press.

Two years later the new brick facility in Mountain View was severely damaged by the *San Francisco earthquake on April 18, 1906. A wooden building was soon constructed in its place. But this building was completely destroyed by fire only a few months later on July 20. The cause of the fire was never determined. The board voted to rebuild yet again, but to cease all commercial work and confine the press to printing only materials for the church. Following the disasters of 1906, press leaders and Ellen White called for Jones to return as manager of Pacific Press. He did, and continued to serve the press until 1933. Mindful of Ellen White's advice regarding commercial work, Jones declared shortly after the disasters that befell Pacific Press in 1906: "We have been admonished by the earthquake and the fire. Let us not need the wind, but listen to the still small voice pleading, 'Do My work only.'"

In addition to his administrative responsibilities at Pacific Press, Jones helped to develop the church's Sabbath school work. From 1887 to 1898 he was president of the International Sabbath School Association—in addition to his role at Pacific Press. Jones also took an interest in organizing the funding and construction of a mission ship, the *Pitcairn, which was to serve the church's far-flung mission interests, primarily in the South Pacific.

In Ellen White's *will she named Jones as one of the original five trustees of the *Ellen G. White Estate (6Bio 455); Jones, with W. C. White, served as executor of her estate.

Further reading: SDA Encyclopedia (1996), vol. 10, p. 833; *Legacy of Light* CD-ROM, art., "C. H. Jones."

B. Russell Holt

JONES, DAN T. (1855-1901). Pastor and administrator. Jones accepted the Adventist faith in 1876 and became a minister in 1881. The following year he became president of the Missouri Conference (1882-1888) and then secretary of the General Conference (1888-1891). He later served as a church leader on the Pacific West Coast and in Mexico. Being secretary of the General Conference during the years immediately after the *General Conference session of 1888 put Jones in the forefront of Ellen White's counsels to church leaders. Although she addressed only

one letter to him specifically—about doing more evangelism in the Petoskey, Michigan, area (Lt 65, 1890)—Ellen White had repeated conversations with Jones and urged him to use his influence to help pastors understand the meaning of the doctrine of *righteousness by faith presented in Minneapolis in 1888 (cf. Lts 73, 83, 1890). During a ministerial institute in Battle Creek in the early months of 1890 Jones appeared prejudiced against Ellen White's ministry until he realized this was a temptation he should resist and, weighing the evidences, accepted that her gift of prophecy is an integral part of the Seventh-day Adventist message (cf. 3Bio 454-462).

Further reading: obit. RH, Oct. 29, 1901; *SDA Encyclopedia* (1996), vol. 10, p. 833; J. Moon, *W. C. White and Ellen G. White* (AUP, 1993), pp. 108-112.

JONES, EDWIN R. (1845-1892). Converted to Adventism at the age of 16 and ordained to the ministry in 1874, Jones worked in Michigan, Colorado, and California. In 1890, while he was working in California, Ellen White counseled him to refrain from a tendency to use exaggerated language in his sermons. Instead, she recommended that he should "be a calm, levelheaded thinker" (Lt 64, 1890; cf. Lt 15a, 1890; 1SM 176-184; 6MR 222; 1888 Materials 646).

Further reading: obit. RH, Feb. 23, 1892.

JONES, ORRIN B. (1825-1883). Carpenter and architect. Jones converted to Adventism in Monterey, Michigan, in 1857. Although there is no record that Ellen White ever addressed a letter to Jones, she mentioned him in letters to others. He supervised the construction of the third Battle Creek meetinghouse (1857), assisted in the erection of the first brick office building for the Review and Herald Publishing Association (1861), Battle Creek College

(1874), the Pacific Press Publishing Association on Casco Street in Oakland, California (1875), and the Battle Creek Sanitarium (1877).

JONES, VICTOR (b. c. 1826). Adventist from Monterey, Michigan, whom Ellen White admonished to follow "the only true unerring Pattern," Jesus, and to be "purified by obeying the truth." She urged him to abstain from alcohol and tobacco "that you may prove worthy of your name" (Lt 1, 1861). A couple years earlier Jones' poverty was the subject of a letter Ellen White addressed to his neighbor, *Sylsbre Rumery (Lt 9, 1857). Poverty and lack of support from church members had led Jones to drinking (see James White, "Report of Meetings!" RH, Oct. 22, 1857). In 1861 Victor and his wife, Elizabeth, divorced. Ellen White discouraged the divorce as having no merit, for there was no adultery involved, and urged that even though Victor "has dreadfully fallen, . . . if even now he humbly repents he may return to God" (Ms 2, 1863). They both later remarried: Victor to Emily Donalson and Elizabeth to *George T. Lay.

Further reading: 1Bio 465.

JORDAN, WILLIAM and **SARAH.** Young single Adventists, brother and sister, in Portland, Maine; mutual friends of Ellen G. Harmon and James White who played a part in bringing James and Ellen together. The Jordans invited Ellen Harmon to accompany them during a business trip to the eastern part of the state of Maine in the early months of 1845. One purpose for this trip was to return a horse William had borrowed from James White. During this second trip away from her home in Portland since receiving her visions, Harmon visited the towns of Orrington, Garland, and Exeter, where she told her early visions and spoke against fanatical experiences some Adventists were having. In Orrington Harmon

felt "the Spirit of God attended the message I bore at this place; hearts were made glad in the truth, and the desponding ones were cheered and encouraged to renew their faith" (LS 73). It is also during this visit to Orrington that she remembers meeting James White for the first time.

In 1845 Sarah Jordan came under the influence of *Joseph Turner, who mesmerized her and claimed he could do the same with Ellen Harmon. Harmon was shown in a vision the dangers of mesmerism (see *hypnotism and mesmerism) and particularly the dangerous influence of Turner's fanatical activities. He became a strong opponent of Ellen Harmon's ministry in 1845 and 1846 (cf. 1Bio 94-99).

Further reading: 1Bio 69, 70; 2SG 38-42.

KECK, IRVING A. (1846-1925) and **DELIA A. (WAITE)** (1853-1930). Adventists in Florida. Originally a bookkeeper from Washington, Iowa, in 1874 Irving moved to Bowling Green, Florida. In 1888 *G. I. and Lentha Butler retired near their home. After Lentha's death in November 1901, Butler considered marrying Delia's sister, Lorena Waite. Because of their age difference (Lorena was about 35; Butler, 68), the Kecks opposed the marriage, but despite her own initial hesitancy, Ellen White asked them to reconsider. A younger woman, she thought, might better be able to keep up with Butler and that perhaps "the hand of the Lord is in this attachment" (Lt 77, 1902, in RY 115-118). She wrote two additional letters asking the Kecks to pray about this and see if they might be able to give up their objections (Lts 78, 118, 1902). Because of continued opposition from the Kecks, Lorena "withdrew her promise" (GIB to WCW, Feb. 6, 1903; GIB to EGW, Dec. 7, 1903 [EGWE-GC]). In 1907 Butler married *Elizabeth Grainger.

Further reading: RY 115-120; obit. RH,

Sept. 24, 1925; obit. *Field Tidings*, Aug. 6, 1930.

KELLAR, PETER MARTIN (1873-1931) and **FLORENCE (ARMSTRONG)** (1875-1974). Adventist physicians and missionaries. Both attended *Battle Creek College in the 1890s. In 1899 Peter graduated from Jefferson Medical University in Philadelphia, and the following year Florence graduated from the *American Medical Missionary College in Battle Creek and Chicago. Soon after graduation both went separately as missionaries to New Zealand, where they met again and were married in 1901. In 1902 Ellen White appealed to them to become medical missionaries in Australia and asked them not to look "for some service that will distinguish them as workers of marked talent," but to instead "take up the work waiting to be done near" them (Lt 15, 1902). They later taught for many years at the *College of Medical Evangelists in Loma Linda, California, and Peter served briefly as medical superintendent of the *Glendale Sanitarium (1928-1931).

Further reading: obit. *South Pacific Union Record*, Oct. 19, 1931; "Life Sketch of Pioneer Doctor," *Australasian Record*, Jan. 4, 1974.

KELLOGG, HENRY WEBSTER (1840-1918). Farmer, mechanic, manager of the *Review and Herald Publishing Association (1873-1882), and longtime friend of James and Ellen White. During his tenure as manager the Review saw rapid growth, necessitating the addition of a large pressroom in 1881. In 1879 Ellen White wrote that his unselfish interest and "business tact" was a blessing to the office. She also noted that he carried "heavy responsibilities," and should receive more than a mechanic's wages (Ms 1, 1879). During this period Henry and his wife, Ella Annett (1841-1930), became close friends of

the Whites and were impressed by seeing Ellen in vision. When James White died in 1881, both Henry and Ella were present at his deathbed. They allowed his body to lie in state in their house until the *Battle Creek until the funeral services a week later (RH, Nov. 13, 1930).

Years later Ellen White wrote that in all her connection with "Brother Kellogg, I have ever found him kind, sympathetic, and tenderhearted. . . . I have the fullest confidence in him as being a wise counselor and adviser" (Lt 233, 1904). Having acquired significant financial resources in later life, Henry was generous with his means in supporting the work of the church. On several occasions he lent Ellen White money for various expenses (Lt 11, 1902; Lt 176, 1903; Lt 209, 1903). She later referred to him as her "old friend" (Lt 16, 1911).

Further reading: obit. RH, June 27, 1918; obit. RH, Nov. 13, 1930.

Jud Lake

KELLOGG, JOHN HARVEY (1852-1943). Physician, surgeon, inventor of flaked cereals and surgical instruments, pioneer in physiotherapy and nutrition, and prolific author. Born into a large family of 16 children, by age 10 Kellogg had begun working in his father's broom shop. When John was a youth, James and Ellen White took a particular interest in him. He was a schoolmate of their sons Edson and Willie (see *James Edson White and *William C. White), and in 1873 James and Ellen encouraged all three young men to attend R. T. Trall's Hygieo-Therapeutic College in New Jersey. Kellogg fell in love with medicine and continued his

DR. JOHN HARVEY KELLOGG

COURTESY OF THE CENTER FOR ADVENTIST RESEARCH, ANDREWS UNIVERSITY.

education at the University of Michigan and in New York City at Bellevue Hospital Medical College. He had a voracious appetite for learning and supplemented his classes by hiring additional tutoring during his spare time. Upon completion of his studies he returned to work at the *Health Reform Institute, where he was appointed superintendent at the age of 24. The fledgling institution founded only 10 years earlier thrived under his management, achieving worldwide recognition as the *Battle Creek Sanitarium.

Ellen White took a personal interest in Kellogg by mentoring him, and he made her one of his closest confidants. She took a motherly interest in him and sought for him to reach his highest potential both spiritually and professionally. Her high regard for Kellogg is evidenced in the fact that she frequently came to his defense when he was criticized by church leaders. Outside of White's own family, only *S. N. Haskell received more letters from her than did Kellogg. They had a deep mutual respect, and later in life she wrote that Kellogg had been a "true friend" (Lt 3, 1899). With the exception of one extant letter written in 1878, her extensive correspondence with Kellogg began in 1886 while Kellogg was superintendent of the Battle Creek Sanitarium.

From 1886 through 1890 Ellen White's counsels to Kellogg generally encompassed three major themes. First, she cautioned him against overwork. "You are living two years in one, and I utter my protest against this," she wrote (Lt 10, 1887). After the significant investment of resources in his education, not to mention his sheer raw talent, she knew what a setback it would be for the denomination if he worked himself into an early grave. Ellen White counseled him to save his own life so that he might save the lives of others (Lt 64, 1886; Lt 10, 1887). Second, she

counseled him about his spiritual life. "I want you to have heaven," she wrote. "I know of no one who would appreciate heaven more than yourself, who have been engaged here in working to relieve suffering humanity.... Live for Jesus. You can better work as a physician in the sanitarium if you make Christ your physician-in-chief. And still I say you must seek earnestly for the crown of life" (Lt 8, 1886). Part of her concern for Kellogg included cautions that he not exalt science above the Scriptures. And third, she warned him against his tendency to strive for supremacy over others (Lt 64, 1886), and advised him to surround himself with competent physicians who would help guide him and to whom he could delegate work. In his early years Kellogg took her counsels seriously and attributed his success to having heeded them.

Ellen White's correspondence with Kellogg increased during the 1890s while she was in Australia (1891-1900). During the early portion of the 1890s she counseled him about developments in Battle Creek, including the building of the Haskell Home, an Adventist orphanage, and a new chapel for the Battle Creek Sanitarium (Lt 18, 1890). At the same time she wrote guardedly against centralizing too much of the church work in one place while missionary work was struggling to survive in other parts of the world. White advised him about the need of adequate wages for sanitarium workers while physicians exacted "exorbitant prices" for their services (Lt 41, 1890). She emphatically warned Kellogg that he was in danger of placing human ideas of science above those of eternal importance (Lt 18, 1892). In addition, she counseled him to work with ministers who could play a role in lifestyle education (Lt 19, 1892). The medical profession was a high calling, and White discouraged physicians from leaving their practices to join the ministry (providing they were competent where they were) (Lt 34, 1892; Lt 86a, 1893). She furthermore trusted Kellogg to look out on her behalf for the welfare of several students whose education she had helped provide for in Battle Creek (Lt 36a, 1893; see *Maui Pomare). White also sought Kellogg's expert medical advice and tried to follow his prescriptions for her own benefit (cf. Lt 85, 1893; Lt 67, 1899).

As the 1890s progressed White became increasingly concerned about hard feelings between Kellogg and church leaders (Lt 86a, 1893). She also became very concerned for the spiritual well-being of Kellogg's younger brother, *Will Keith, and the importance of John's example to save his brother from skepticism (Lt 8a, 1899). She became particularly burdened with the desperate need of establishing the mission work in *Australia and other parts of the world instead of simply enlarging institutions in already-established areas (Lt 138, 1898). She warned Kellogg not to spend so much on nondenominational humanitarian work in Chicago as to eclipse the Adventist mission to carry its message to other parts of the world (see *Chicago Medical Mission). She especially did not like Kellogg's idea of the "Gospel Wagon," a clever marketing ploy to draw attention to health principles. "Some good will result from equipping Gospel Wagons in America, and thousands of dollars will be consumed in this way. When the season is ended, some sheaves may be gathered, but not many. The money could be used in lines that would have a more lasting influence" (Lt 124, 1898; see also Lt 114, 1898). Instead, she counseled him to send badly needed funds to Australia.

Even more important, by this time Ellen White saw Kellogg in great spiritual danger. "Satan is making masterly efforts to cause your feet to slide," she wrote (Lt 132, 1898; cf. Lt 126, 1898). She warned Kellogg that he was in danger of exalting himself like the biblical Nebuchadnezzar, and of "making shipwreck of your faith" (Lt 123, 1898; see also Lt 92, 1900). The lack of financial resources in Australia also led her to write to Kellogg and his associates a very direct appeal to develop denominational institutions around the world (Lt 4, 1899). Kellogg responded immediately by sending tubs and other furnishings to supply the Australian sanitarium. During the following year, until she left Australia, White sought Kellogg's advice about building this sanitarium and was thankful for Kellogg's pledge of $5,000 (Lts 28, 40, 1899).

During 1899 Ellen White issued repeated calls for unity between church leaders and those in the medical field (cf. Lt 55, 1899). A power struggle arose between Kellogg and denominational leaders, particularly General Conference president *G. A. Irwin. In response, Kellogg intimated that he might leave the Seventh-day Adventist denomination. But White assured Kellogg that the Lord had given him his position of influence, and counseled him against separating from the denomination (Lt 73, 1899). "You speak as though you had no friends," she later added. "But God is your friend, and Sister White is your friend" (Lt 215, 1899). Her counsels appear to have relieved tensions, at least for the time being. Yet she continued to counsel him against making himself his own authority and keeping in Battle Creek funds that were desperately needed for establishing other medical centers in the United States (Lts 135, 257, 1899). As the year progressed her warnings to Kellogg became increasingly more acute. She warned Kellogg of his great spiritual peril and urged him to "receive the messages of warning given you, [for] it will save you from great trial and mortification, and will be to the saving of your soul" (Lt 215b, 1899; see also Lt 232, 1899).

By early 1900 the relationship between White and Kellogg had become strained. During this time she wrote some of her strongest letters of warning to Kellogg, who upon receiving them expressed sorrow and frustration. She pointed out that she had been sending him counsels of caution and warnings for many years, and that she had *not* changed her attitude toward him. White again reiterated her plea that he not leave the Seventh-day Adventist Church (Lts 33, 45, 74, 1900). Furthermore, she continued to counsel him about his lack of judgment in his use of funds to help the poor in Chicago when funds should have been sent to Australia. While helping the depraved was good, she felt it was more important to enlighten the world with the third angel's message (see *three angels' messages) (Lts 41, 45, 1900). She believed Kellogg was in great peril of embracing "perverted ideas" that would "imperil the cause of God" (Lt 73, 1900).

During the year following the *General Conference session of 1901, they continued to exchange copious letters about church matters—particularly regarding the leadership of the Rural Health Retreat (see *St. Helena Sanitarium) in California (cf. Lt 5, 1901). While she continued to affirm his divine calling in the development of the Adventist medical work (Lt 180, 1901), these affirmations came with warnings to temper his ambitions and to seek spiritual renewal (cf. Lt 188, 1901). Soon after a devastating fire consumed the Battle Creek Sanitarium on February 18, 1902, White stated that this event was a judgment from the Lord specifically for Kellogg's not heeding the light given to him (Lts 123, 269, 1902) and urged him to rebuild a smaller facility and to spread out the medical work to other cities instead of concentrating so much in Battle Creek (Lts 124, 125, 1902). Kellogg instead rebuilt a larger sanitarium.

Just prior to the fire he had completed writing the manuscript for the book *The Living Temple* (Battle Creek, Mich.: Good Health Pub. Co., 1903), on the complete physiology of the human person. After the fire Kellogg donated the profits from the sale of this book to be used to help rebuild the sanitarium. When the book first appeared, some church leaders, including *A. G. Daniells and *W. W. Prescott, were alarmed by a *pantheistic section at the beginning of the book. These pantheistic teachings called forth some of the strongest warnings Ellen White ever wrote, stating that it was "the alpha of a train of heresies" that would face the church before the *second coming of Christ (Lt 265, 1903; see also Lts 232, 253, 1903). She continued to write many pathos-filled letters urging Kellogg to change the course of his life (Lts 55, 65, 80, 97, 107, 180, 181, 232, 245, 300, 301, 303, 1903). She repeated her much earlier warnings that Kellogg's greatest danger had been in exalting science above the God of science (Lt 239, 1903). For a time his future in the church hung in the balance, and White made every effort to save him. Perhaps Kellogg briefly acknowledged his perilous condition (Lt 257, 1903), but by this time the die appears to have been cast and his permanent separation from the church was the result. White appealed to him, stating that it was not too late for him to change the course of his life (Lt 360, 1905), but by 1906 it was clear to both Ellen White and church leaders that Kellogg had departed from the faith (Lt 225b, 1906). It therefore came as no surprise when after a final lengthy interview, Kellogg's name was removed from the membership list of the Battle Creek Tabernacle on November 10, 1907. He furthermore ceased corresponding with Ellen White, although she continued to appeal for him to come back (cf. Lt 100,

1911). Kellogg remained active in managing the Battle Creek Sanitarium until his death in 1943.

Further reading: The most extensive biography of Kellogg is by R. W. Schwarz: *John Harvey Kellogg, M.D.: Pioneering Health Reformer* (RHPA, 2006 [published by AUP, 1970, 1981]) based on his doctoral dissertation "John Harvey Kellogg: American Health Reformer" (Ph.D. diss., University of Michigan, 1964). See also J. Butler, "Ellen G. White and the Chicago Mission" (Berrien Springs, Mich.: Spectrum Reprints, 1970); R. G. Cooper, "A Comprehensive Bibliography of Dr. John Harvey Kellogg, 1852-1943" (Keene, Tex.: by the author, 1984); Michael Cascio and Susan E. Leventhal, exec. prod., *The Kellogg Brothers: Cornflake Kings*, 50 min. (New York: A&E Home Video, 1995); D. F. Lemons, "John Harvey Kellogg and the Chicago Medical Mission" (research paper, AU, 1977); *SDA Encyclopedia* (1996), vol. 10, pp. 851-853.

Michael W. Campbell

KELLOGG, JOHN PRESTON (1807-1881) and **ANN J. (STANLEY)** (1824-1893). Early Sabbatarian

JOHN P. KELLOGG

Adventists in Michigan. John, a young widower with five children (one of whom was *Merritt G. Kellogg), married Ann Stanley in 1842. To this marriage were added eight more children, including *J. H. Kellogg and *W. K. Kellogg. The Kelloggs became Sabbatarian Adventists in 1852 and quickly involved themselves in the development of the fledgling cause. J. P. Kellogg was one of the original group who pledged to build a publishing house in Battle Creek if James and Ellen White would relocate from

ANN J. KELLOGG

*Rochester, New York. After the Whites' arrival in *Battle Creek, they became close friends of the Kelloggs, who continued to be actively involved in the growth of the church. At a conference held in Battle Creek on May 20, 1856, Kellogg was appointed to a committee of five, of which he was treasurer, to manage Adventist tent operations for the state of Michigan. At the same meeting he was elected one of a publishing committee of three on the *Review and Herald*, and in this capacity participated in the formation of the Seventh-day Adventist Publishing Association in 1861. In 1867 he led the list with the largest personal contribution to the stock of the *Health Reform Institute, and was elected to the board of directors. There is one extant testimony from Ellen White to the Kellogg family about their home life (Lt 17a, 1864).

Further reading: obit. RH, May 31, 1881; obit. RH, May 30, 1893; M. G. Kellogg, *Notes Concerning the Kellogg's (sic)* (Battle Creek: by the author, 1927), WL; *SDA Encyclopedia* (1996), vol. 10, p. 853.

Michael W. Campbell

KELLOGG, MERRITT GARDNER (1832-1921). Minister, physician, and missionary. The oldest son of John P. Kellogg, he began medical school at the age of 16, and at age 20 accepted the Adventist faith. The following spring Kellogg became an Adventist preacher, and saw Ellen White in vision at his parents' home during the Whites' first visit to Michigan. He also became active in organizing the Sabbath school work in Battle Creek, being elected its first superintendent. In 1854 he married Louisa Rawson (1822-1894), and in 1859 they traveled by wagon to California with their son Charles (1856-1889) to become the first Adventists in that state (M. G. Kellogg, *Notes Concerning the Kellogg's* [*sic*] [Battle Creek, Mich.: by the author, 1927]).

Upon their arrival in San Francisco, Kellogg worked as a carpenter to support himself while sharing his faith. In 1861 he held a series of lectures in San Francisco and baptized 14 people. In 1867 Kellogg returned east to continue his medical education at R. T. Trall's Hygieo-Therapeutic College in New Jersey. During April 1868 the Kelloggs spent a month visiting James and Ellen White in their Greenville home, giving James treatments as he recovered from his stroke (Ms 15, 1868). The next month during the General Conference session Merritt made an impassioned plea for a minister to go to California, and as a result *J. N. Loughborough and *D. T. Bourdeau continued the work he had begun. Merritt Kellogg remained in Michigan as a health lecturer at the Health Reform Institute.

By 1870 Merritt had returned to California, where he teamed up with Loughborough in medical and evangelistic work. Two years later, at the recommendation of James and Ellen White, he was ordained as a minister, and returned to work at the Health Reform Institute. During this period Kellogg published *The Way of Life* engraving with an accompanying *Key of Explanation* (Battle Creek, Mich.: Steam Press, 1873), and four health tracts, which, combined together, formed the book *The Hygienic Family Physician* (Battle Creek, Mich.: Health Reformer, 1874), the first Adventist medical work by an Adventist physician. In 1878 Kellogg, once more in California, went with James and Ellen White to select the site for the Rural Health Retreat (later the *St. Helena Sanitarium), where he served as manager (1878-1879) until better trained persons could head the institution. It was while he was here that Ellen White wrote him about the need of doctors who discourage the use of drugs without discrediting all medical practices (Lt 88, 1889). Until 1893 Kellogg was able to support himself financially without having to draw funds from the growing denomination.

About 1892 Kellogg confessed that he had not heeded testimonies (no longer extant) that Ellen White had sent him, and as a result he had caused "many trials" at the Rural Health Retreat (M. G. Kellogg to EGW, n.d., EGWE-GC). As a result, Kellogg was ready for a change, and in 1893 the Foreign Mission Board asked him to be the physician on board the *Pitcairn* missionary ship. While journeying in the South Pacific in 1894, Louisa died, and the next year he married Eleanor Nolan (b. 1874). Several years later Kellogg helped build the Sydney Sanitarium in Australia (1902-1903). During these years in the South Pacific Ellen White felt concerned that he heed the cautions she had given him (Lt 11, 1901), not be discouraged in his work (Lt 49, 1901), and as he superintended the construction of the sanitarium that he remember the evangelistic purpose for *sanitariums (Lt 159, 1902). Returning to the United States in 1903, he spent the rest of his life in Healdsburg, California. In 1906 Meritt expressed doubts concerning the genuineness of Ellen White's visions, influenced in part by his brother J. H. Kellogg's departure from the denomination (M. G. Kellogg to J. H. Kellogg, Aug. 1, 1906, UM). But, unlike his younger brother, Merritt stayed within the denomination.

Further reading: obit. RH, Feb. 9, 1922; *SDA Encyclopedia* (1996), vol. 10, pp. 853, 854.

Michael W. Campbell

KELLOGG, WILL KEITH (1860-1951) and **ELLA (DAVIS)** (1858-1912). Cornflake manufacturer, son of *John P. Kellogg, brother of

*John Harvey Kellogg, half-brother of *Merritt G. Kellogg. Although in his youth Will was a practicing Seventh-day Adventist, he stopped attending worship services in his early 20s, though he remained loyal to Adventist health and temperance principles. Closely associated with his brother John in the early years of the *Battle Creek Sanitarium, by the early 1900s Will and John had frequent misunderstandings and parted company. In 1906 Will incorporated the Battle Creek Toasted Corn Flake Company, and began to manufacture and sell the now-famous cornflakes.

W. K. Kellogg's association with James and Ellen White began in his youth. At the age of 19 he was asked by James White to go to Texas to manage a broom factory that White and *George King had set up in Dallas. The following year, James performed Will's marriage to Ella Davis, sister of *Marian Davis, who served as a literary assistant to Ellen White for many years. Although informal interactions between Ellen White and W. K. Kellogg occurred through the years, it was only when doctrinal and administrative conflicts between John Kellogg and the denomination arose that Ellen White wrote to Will to ask for his help. Despite the fact that he was not an active church member, she still addressed him as a "brother" and a Seventh-day Adventist. Perceiving from Australia that John was attempting to remove the Battle Creek Sanitarium from the influence of the church, she sent Will copies of some letters she had sent to John and invited his assistance in reclaiming his brother before his strong personality alienated him any further from the church (Lt 7, 1900). Two years later she also expressed to Will her concern for his and John's spiritual condition in response to a promise she had made to his mother. "You both need to feel the deep working of the Spirit of God, that you may know that you are building upon the sure foundation"

she wrote. "Willie Kellogg, I earnestly entreat you to give yourself without reserve to Jesus. Whatever course your Brother John may choose to take, his choice will not excuse your noncommittal position" (Lt 180, 1902). Will was dropped from church membership about 1907. Though he never rejoined the Adventist Church, he remained a Christian and cordial to the church. Ella remained a Seventh-day Adventist all her life. Both are buried in *Oak Hill Cemetery, Battle Creek, Michigan. After Ella's death, Will married Carrie Staines, a teacher and physician (Powell, pp. 249, 250).

Further reading: obit. RH, Sept. 26, 1912; H. B. Powell, *The Original Has This Signature— W. K. Kellogg* (Englewood Cliffs, N.J.: Prentice-Hall, 1956); *SDA Encyclopedia* (1996), vol. 10, pp. 854, 855.

Denis Fortin

KELSEY, MARY, see **WHITE, MARY (KELSEY)**.

KERR, MATILDA (ELDERKIN) (1853-1929). Adventist believer from Honolulu, Hawaii. Originally from England, she married Lawrence Bingham Kerr in New Zealand, and four years later they moved to Hawaii, where they lived until his death in 1927. In 1886 through the acquaintance of Abram LaRue she became interested in Adventism and two years later became an Adventist. Ellen White stayed at her home briefly on her way to Australia in 1891. She recalled that Mr. Kerr, although not a believer, generously gave her an "upholstered rocking chair from his parlor set as a birthday present, because I happened to mention that it was an easy [comfortable] chair. It has been a great comfort to me on the voyage, when sitting on deck" (Lt 32a, 1891, in 4MR 43; cf. LS 332; 4Bio 19, 20). White and Matilda Kerr corresponded with each other (Lt 85, 1897; Lts 145, 148, 1900), and on Ellen White's return trip from Australia to the United States, she stayed at their home again (5Bio 22). In 1908 Ellen White wrote a friendly letter expressing her gratitude to God (Lt 278, 1908).

Further reading: obit. PUR, Aug. 1, 1929.

KETRING, "SISTER," see **HARPER, WALTER AND LAURA**.

KILGORE, ROBERT M. (1839-1912). Adventist evangelist and administrator. Texas had only 35 Adventists in 1877 when Ohio-born Civil War veteran R. M. Kilgore arrived as a self-supporting evangelist. In 1878 Texas Adventists held a camp meeting attended by James and Ellen White, who were delighted to see their "old friends" the Kilgores (LS 240). A year later, when the Texas Conference was organized, Kilgore was elected president. When he left this position in 1885 to become Illinois Conference president, there were 800 Adventists in Texas.

COURTESY OF THE ELLEN G. WHITE ESTATE, INC.

ROBERT M. KILGORE

Kilgore resisted the emphasis on *righteousness by faith at the *General Conference session of 1888, but later repented of his opposition and in 1889 urged attendance at meetings on the subject presented in Chicago by Ellen White and *Alonzo T. Jones. "I wish you could see and hear Elder Kilgore," Ellen White reported. "He says he has had a new conversion," and "sees clearly that it is Christ's righteousness that he must rely upon" (1888 Materials 287).

From 1888 to 1891 Kilgore served as president of the Illinois Conference and superintendent of District Two (southeastern United States). From 1891 until 1895 he devoted full time to District Two. When he accepted this position, this region had no denominational institutions and only one conference. He facilitated the launching of a publishing house, sanitariums, and schools, including Graysville Academy (see *Graysville, Tennessee), the forerunner of Southern Adventist University. After five years as superintendent of District Five (Texas and neighboring states) he returned to the Southeast as president and then vice president (1902-1907) of the newly-organized Southern Union Conference as well as president of the Georgia Conference.

Further reading: 3Bio 98, 106, 428-429; 4T 305; LS 240; VSS 287; D. Pettibone, "An Adventist Apostle to Dixie," *Adventist Heritage* 14, no. 3 (Fall 1991): 4-11, 33.

Dennis Pettibone

KING, GEORGE A. (1847-1906). Pioneer *colporteur, born in Toronto, who became a Seventh-day Adventist in his early 20s. By 1879 King was working in Texas, where he associated himself with James White in the starting of a broom factory. That year Ellen White gave him several counsels on how to manage his business endeavors. She advised him to "act upon regular and well-matured plans," to keep accurate financial records of his transactions, and not to be impulsive in his dealings with others. "Industry, faithfulness, a firm adherence to right, and trust in God will ensure success" (Lt 5, 1879). Within two years he was pioneering the Adventist colporteur work by selling a subscription edition of Uriah Smith's *Thoughts on Daniel and the Revelation*. King's dedication and example led hundreds of church members to take up the colporteur work and sell Adventist literature. After working for

COURTESY OF THE CENTER FOR ADVENTIST RESEARCH, ANDREWS UNIVERSITY

GEORGE A. KING

more than 20 years selling books in many states and in the West Indies, he died in New York City in 1906.

Further reading: obit. RH, Dec. 6, 1906; *SDA Encyclopedia* (1996), vol. 10, pp. 866, 867.

KING, MARTHA L. (SMITH) BYINGTON (1837-1920). Adventist in Massachusetts, first married to Dr. J. Fletcher Byington (1832-1872). Upon the death of her second husband, Mr. King, Martha moved in with her daughter, Dr. Mary Byington Nicola, at the Melrose Sanitarium (see *New England Sanitarium) in Massachusetts. Shortly after the *San Francisco earthquake in April 1906, Ellen White wrote a short letter to Martha and Mary and *C. C. Nicola and described the devastation in the city. She reminisced also about the construction of the Seventh-day Adventist church in San Francisco and felt thankful that it had not been damaged by the earthquake (Lt 164, 1906).

Further reading: obit. RH, Feb. 14, 1920.

KING, SENECA H. (1812-1893). Early Adventist in Michigan. In the 1860s Ellen White wrote several letters to King and his family regarding their home atmosphere and family dynamics. According to Ellen White, Seneca's second wife lacked parental skills and did not show sufficient concern toward her stepchildren. Her selfishness, impatience, and lack of compassion alienated the affection of her husband's children, particularly his daughter Lucia, and ultimately drove them away from the Christian faith. Ellen White counseled Seneca to not be swayed by his wife's selfish ambitions and to be more involved in his children's needs (Lt 23, 1862; Lt 3, 1863; Lt 18, 1868). When the Kings later decided to care for a foster child, Ellen White again highlighted that Mrs. King was not fit to be a mother and that her influence in the home would not be helpful

to this child's salvation (Lt 1, 1870). Although forthright and at times appearing even harsh, Ellen White's letters to the Kings nonetheless present many valuable counsels to stepparents and the inner interpersonal dynamics of reconstituted families. In March 1868 Seneca suffered a massive head injury when he was thrown from his carriage. James and Ellen White cared for him at their home in Greenville, Michigan, until he recovered sufficiently to return home (2Bio 223-225). In the following years King served many times as a delegate from Michigan to the General Conference sessions in Battle Creek.

Further reading: obit. RH, Mar. 21, 1893.

KNOX, WALTER TINGLEY (1858-1931). Pastor and church administrator. Born in Pittsburgh, Pennsylvania, Knox married Barbara Bell Childs (1864-1950) in 1885, and both became Seventh-day Adventists in 1889. Soon thereafter he became a pastor in California. He served as president of the California Conference (1897-1900; 1906-1908), president of the Pacific Union Conference (1901-1904), and treasurer of the General Conference (1909-1922). While Knox served in his various administrative responsibilities, Ellen White wrote to him regarding the purchase of land for the *Paradise Valley Sanitarium (Lt 13, 1903) and *Healdsburg College (Lt 368, 1908). During his second term as president of the California Conference (1906-1908) Ellen White became very concerned about Knox's style of leadership and ultimately called for his replacement. She felt he was too domineering and controlling of other pastors' functions and work, and that the conference had not grown spiritually under his leadership. "You are not in a condition spiritually to help the churches. . . . I am instructed to say to you that a different administration must now come into the California Conference" (Lt 56, 1908;

cf. Lt 54, 1908). The following year Knox was replaced by *S. N. Haskell and became treasurer of the General Conference. During his years of service at the General Conference he had an extensive correspondence with W. C. White and often sought counsel from Ellen White through her son.

Further reading: obit. RH, Dec. 17, 1931; *SDA Encyclopedia* (1996), vol. 10, p. 874.

KRESS, DANIEL H. (1862-1956) and **LAURETTA (EBY)** (1863-1955). Pioneer missionary physicians and health educators. At the time of their marriage in 1884, Daniel was a Baptist minister. When the Kresses became Adventists, he joined the Seventh-day Adventist ministry. From 1891 to 1894 they both studied medicine at the University of Michigan and then began Adventist medical work in England. Following their return to the United States, they were called to Australia as the physicians for the new hospital then planned for Wahroonga, near Sydney. Following their service in Australia, Daniel became the first medical superintendent of the new *Washington Sanitarium and Hospital, and Lauretta was employed as a staff physician. Daniel specialized in internal medicine and was a noted health educator, particularly on tobacco issues. Lauretta specialized in obstetrics. Intending to retire to Florida in 1939, the Kresses found themselves pressed into further service as physicians at the Florida Sanitarium and Hospital. When they did eventually retire, the Kresses wrote their autobiography, *Under the Guiding Hand.*

DANIEL H. KRESS

When the Kresses received their call to Australia in 1900, they were in no hurry to go. Building the Sydney Sanitarium would take several years, and they were quite busy in the United States. However, Ellen White repeatedly urged them to go quickly, finally being quite insistent that they should be on the next boat. This they did, and by omitting a planned stopover in Hawaii arrived in Australia a month earlier than expected. They immediately filed for registration to practice medicine, and their applications were approved by the New South Wales Medical Board. A few days later the New South Wales state government announced that American-trained physicians would no longer be registered, and soon this action was followed by the other states in Australia. Thus the Kresses' obtaining medical registration in New South Wales was a direct consequence of Ellen White's persistence in encouraging them not to delay taking up their Australian appointments.

Daniel Kress had not been well for some time, and once he was in Australia his condition worsened to the point where his death was considered imminent, and Lauretta arranged for him to be buried in the Avondale College cemetery. Daniel had pernicious anemia, which was considered incurable at the time. He was expected to die within hours when a letter arrived from Ellen White in which she advised he be given eggs, cooked or raw, and that he be given fresh-beaten eggs in grape juice, as "this will supply that which is necessary to your system" (Lt 37, 1901, in 12MR 168-178; MM 286-289). At first it was difficult for Daniel even to take a sip of water, but as he followed the counsel given, he slowly began to recover. Although mail from America brought letters of condolence to Lauretta, Kress fully recovered and lived another 55 years. Interestingly, their autobiography does not mention this story, but attributes Daniel's recovery to a nationwide day of prayer and his anointing by the ministers and board members of the Cooranbong Health Retreat.

Although Ellen White's letter urged that special prayer of faith be offered on behalf of Daniel, "I beseech you to call for the elders of the church without delay," it also reprimanded Daniel for being too radical and extreme in his health and diet practices. He had discarded from his diet both eggs and dairy products in an era when necessary substitutes were yet unknown. Possibly in their later years the Kresses were embarrassed by the fact that Daniel's earlier extreme health views almost led to an early death. Today it is known that pernicious anemia is the consequence of vitamin deficiency. Eggs supplied an essential need in Daniel's unbalanced vegan diet.

Further reading: obit. *Australasian Record*, Aug. 15, 1955; D. H. Kress (DF 13, 396, 2045); *Under the Guiding Hand* (Washington, D.C.: College Press, 1941); M. M. Freeman, "The Doctors Kress and the Establishment of Our Medical Work," *Australasian Record*, July 13, 1970.

Lester D. Devine

KYNETT, WILLIAM HENRY (1842-1909) and **EUNICE H. (TREMBLY)** (1843-1919). Adventists in Allegan, Michigan. William served during the *Civil War and married Eunice in 1865. Two years later they became Adventists. In 1885 William graduated as a physician from the Chicago College of Physicians. In 1891 Ellen White rebuked them for their lack of "home religion" in one of her most extensive letters on the subject. She urged both of them to subdue self so that their home might become a miniature of heaven on earth. The "home atmosphere" needed to be cultivated by "thoughtful courtesy." She also admonished them for the "crime" of casting Eunice's mother out of their home, who, in her old age, needed their care (Lt 18b, 1891, in 13MR 74-91). In a follow-up letter, written two months

afterward, Ellen White counseled them not to alienate one another, but instead, to cherish each other. She also rebuked Eunice for her stubborn will and threatening attitude (Lt 18a, 1891).

Further reading: obit. RH, Dec. 16, 1909; obit. RH, Aug. 7, 1919.

LACEY, ETHEL MAY, see **WHITE, ETHEL MAY (LACEY)**.

LACEY, HERBERT CAMDEN (1871-1950) and **LILLIAN (YARNALL)** (1873-1965). Religion teacher and pastor, brother-in-law to William C. White, and family friend of Ellen White. Herbert was born in England but spent his early childhood in India, where his father served in the Indian civil service.

COURTESY OF THE ELLEN G. WHITE ESTATE, INC.

HERBERT C. LACEY

At the age of 11 Herbert moved to Tasmania, Australia, with his family, where they joined the Adventist Church in 1887. With financial assistance from Ellen White he studied at *Healdsburg College in California, completing the ministerial course in 1892. Then he pastored in California (1890-1892) and Michigan (1893) before going to *Battle Creek College to complete a degree in the classics. Following graduation in 1895 he married Lillian Yarnall of California and returned to Australia to assist in the establishment of *Avondale College.

Lacey's younger sister, May, was married to *William C. White in April 1895. Later the Lacey parents also moved from Tasmania to Cooranbong, and the two families enjoyed a degree of social intimacy. According to Lacey, who occasionally took Ellen White out for drives during this period, Ellen White confided in him at one time that she had recently received a proposal of marriage from longtime associate *Stephen Haskell but had decided to decline the offer (H. C. Lacey to L. E. Froom, Aug. 30, 1945, CAR). A bout with typhoid fever nearly took Herbert's life in 1897 but for the timely intervention of Ellen White, who advised a course of treatment in opposition to that prescribed by the doctor (Lts 181, 189, 1897).

In 1897 the Avondale College board appointed Lacey as president of the fledgling college, but Ellen White, who had not been consulted, had the decision reversed because she thought him too young and inexperienced for the task and was not much impressed by his classical education at Battle Creek (Lt 140, 1897). The curriculum at Avondale was to be a Bible-based curriculum. She recalled that she had to "speak plainly" to "keep out the breezes coming from Battle Creek" (Lt 140, 1897). Lacey accepted the change gracefully.

During this period at Avondale, Lacey was called upon occasionally by *Marian Davis to provide editorial advice on the preparation of *The Desire of Ages* (H. C. Lacey to L. E. Froom, Aug. 30, 1945; H. C. Lacey to A. W. Spalding, June 5, 1947, CAR). He later developed a reputation as a strong advocate of Trinitarian doctrine.

Lacey taught Bible at the college until 1900 and spent summers in colporteuring and conducting evangelistic meetings. From 1900 to 1902 he was a pastor and evangelist in New Zealand. Returning to the United States, he taught Bible at Healdsburg College (1902-1904); then at Stanborough Park College in England (1904-1913); and then Union College (1914-1919) and Washington Missionary College (1919-1920). Then over the next five years he spent 15 months traveling throughout the world assisting *I. H. Evans in holding church conventions.

At the *Bible Conference of 1919, Lacey,

along with *W. W. Prescott, and *A. G. Daniells, was an outspoken advocate that the church adopt a more accurate and adequate view of the process of inspiration and the processes involved in the preparation of Ellen White's publications. Following the conference Lacey was heavily criticized by ultraconservative pastors, and a "preposterous rumour" circulated in parts of the church alleging he had claimed to have written *The Desire of Ages*. He vehemently rejected the charge as "ridiculous and malicious" (H. C. Lacey to "Dear Brother," July 24, 1936, DF 508, CAR) and affirmed "wholeheartedly" his conviction that the writings were the "genuine product" of the "Spirit of Prophecy." Because of a reactionary theological climate and a hypercritical atmosphere that subsequently developed in the church during the late 1920s and early 1930s Lacey declined to accept further teaching positions at Adventist colleges and chose to spend his remaining years of service in pastoral work first in New York City and later in southern California, where for a time he taught biblical languages at the *College of Medical Evangelists (L. H. Wood to C. W. Irwin, May 25, 1931; L. H. Wood to L. E. Froom, June 3, 1931, Pres. Corr., AU Admin. Vault, CAR).

Further reading: 4Bio 304-309; obit. RH, Jan. 25, 1951; obit. PUR, Apr. 18, 1966; White Estate files (1893-1915) contain numerous items of correspondence between H. C. Lacey and the White family.

Gilbert M. Valentine

LAMSON, DAVID HENRY (1835-1897) and **ELIZABETH LOUISA (CHAPPEL)** (1838-1926). Early Adventist workers in Michigan; David was a cousin of Joseph Bradley Lamson. David was introduced to Adventism in 1853 during some meetings held by *J. N. Loughborough in Clarkson, New York (RH, Sept. 27, 1853), and two years later moved to Michigan, where he married Elizabeth in 1857. Ellen White encouraged the Lamsons to keep up their courage in the "present truth" (Lt 10, 1856). David was ordained as a minister in 1870. He later received a letter full of practical advice from Ellen White (Lt 48, 1888). Having witnessed Ellen White's conditions while receiving visions, he was asked to give his testimony at the General Conference session of 1893 (GCDB, Jan. 31, 1893).

Further reading: obit. RH, Oct. 26, 1897; obit. RH, Aug. 19, 1926.

LAMSON, DRUSILLA ORTON (1831-1919). Daughter of *Jonathan and Caroline Orton, of Dansville, New York. After moving to *Rochester, New York, Lamson accepted the Millerite message and looked for Jesus to come in 1844. In 1852 she, her parents, the *Loughboroughs, and others in the Rochester area were convinced to keep the Sabbath. They formed a part of the nucleus of believers who supported James and Ellen White while they lived in Rochester.

In 1856 Drusilla married Joseph Bradley Lamson. James and Ellen White stayed with the Lamsons during most of December 1865. The Whites were returning to Battle Creek, Michigan, after James White had received treatment for nearly three months at *James Jackson's hydropathic health institution, "Our Home on the Hillside," in Dansville, New York. It was in the Lamson home on the evening of December 25, 1865, while the Lamsons, Ortons, Loughboroughs, and others were gathered to pray for James White, that Ellen White had her fourth major health reform vision. In this vision she was shown that Seventh-day Adventists should establish their own health institution.

J. B. Lamson died suddenly from illness in 1870. By 1876 Drusilla had moved to Battle

Creek and had become matron for the sanitarium. She remained in this capacity until 1883, when she returned to Clifton Springs, just south of Port Gibson, New York, and worked in a similar position until her retirement in 1896. Drusilla received a testimony from Ellen White regarding lifestyle issues, particularly concerning the "display of fashionable dress on the occasion of Dr. Kellogg's marriage" (*Testimony for the Physicians and Helpers of the Sanitarium* [1879], PH100 77). She also received counsel to move out of the Rochester, New York, area to protect her children from worldly influences (*Testimony to the Church* [1872], PH159 180).

Further reading "Drusilla Orton Lamson," Clifton Springs *Press*, Jan. 19, 1919.

Merlin D. Burt

LAMSON, PHOEBE M. (1824-1883). Physician. Lamson decided in 1855 to study medicine

DR. PHOEBE LAMSON

SANDS H. LANE

and afterward joined the medical staff of *James C. Jackson's "Our Home on the Hillside" in Dansville, New York. She became a Sabbatarian Adventist in 1859 and strongly supported the prophetic ministry of Ellen White (RH, Aug. 11, 1859; RH, Nov. 15, 1864). In January 1867 she became the second physician to join the staff of the fledgling *Health Reform Institute in Battle Creek. She worked closely with Ellen White in educating church members about *health reform and *dress reform.

Further reading: obit. *Good Health*, September 1883.

LANE, SANDS H. (1844-1906). Evangelist, conference president, and missionary, Lane was born near Battle Creek, Michigan, and worked at the Review and Herald press. He was an evangelist and president of the Indiana Conference (1877-1884), then missionary to England (1885-1889). At his tent meetings in Risely, near London (1886), Ellen White assured him that "God's eye is upon His conscientious, faithful children in England" (Ev 418, 419). During his career Lane was also conference president in New York (1889-1895, 1903-1906), Illinois (1895-1899), and Southern Illinois (1902-1903), and president of the publishing association board and a trustee of the General Conference Association. Ellen White urged Lane to be more earnest in his sermons (Lt 61, 1896); to show more tenderness (Lt 185, 1902); and to manifest a "sanctified intellect and living faith" (Lt 162, 1903). But after Lane's death, she assured his widow "that he was a true child of God, . . . striving to follow in the right course" (Lt 362, 1906). Lane was buried near his sister, Arvilla M. Bacheller, in the Bacheller family plot in Battle Creek's *Oak Hill Cemetery.

Further reading: obit. RH, Sept. 6, 1906; B. E. Strayer, *Where the Pine Trees Softly Whisper: The History of Union Springs Academy* (Union Springs, N.Y.: Alumni Association, 1993); *SDA Encyclopedia* (1996), vol. 10, p. 897.

Brian E. Strayer

LARSON, MATTHEW. Adventist pastor from Iowa. Offended by remarks Ellen White made in a meeting of the ministerial institute held in Battle Creek in March 1890, Larson openly rebuked her. In response she explained to him that she had not intended anything personal but that she was still attempting to clarify what had transpired at the Minneapolis *General Conference session of 1888. Yet Larson's attitude led her to believe that he did not know what spirit was controlling him. "You will never come to a knowledge of the truth as it is in Jesus, until you put away the spirit which has controlled you at this meeting" (Lt 18d, 1890, in 1888 Materials 586; cf. Ms 4, 1890; Lt 80, 1890). "You are not fitted to teach the truth to your brethren, until you have the transforming grace of Christ upon your own heart" (*ibid.*). As the meetings progressed, Ellen White used her influence to break a strong opposition held by many pastors, including Larson, to the teaching of *righteousness by faith. On March 11, in a letter to her son Willie, she wrote that earlier that day "the backbone of the rebellion" had been "broken in those who have come in from other places" and that "Brother Larson then spoke and confessed that his feeling had not been right. I responded and he took his position on [in favor of] the testimonies" (Lt 30, 1890, in 1888 Materials 625). Larson continued to work in the Iowa Conference until 1895 and later served in Arizona and New Mexico. In the 1920s Larson joined *Margaret Rowen's Seventh-day Adventist Reform Church.

LAWRENCE, L. N. Adventist from Michigan who brought his family to Australia at his own expense in response to an appeal by Ellen White for self-supporting missionaries (4Bio 148). Lawrence assisted the early beginnings of the *Avondale school (*ibid.* 146-161). His family initially set up a tent at Dora Creek to be caretakers of the school property and to transport church leaders. Lawrence was later placed in charge of the industrial department and the orchards. His daughter Mattie worked for a time as one of Ellen White's *literary assistants (Lt 3, 1894). Lawrence later became disaffected over his low wages, and joined J. G. Shannon in bitter complaining that resulted in their removal from church employment (cf. Lts 86, 214, 1897).

Lay, George Talbot (1822-1901). Prosperous farmer in Monterey, Michigan; brother of *Horatio S. Lay. In 1851 Lay married Mary E. Barber (1825-1862). About 1858 they embraced the seventh-day Sabbath from *Joseph Bates and joined the Monterey church in Michigan. In 1864 Ellen White admonished the Monterey church for their lack of a Christian spirit toward him (Lt 2, 1864). That same year George married Elizabeth L. Jones (1833-1908). In 1874 Ellen White sent Lay a no longer extant testimony stating he was warring against the Spirit of God (cf. Lts 58, 61, 1874). He soon afterward left the Adventist Church. Lay prospered financially during the 1870s and in 1883 helped organize the Michigan Buggy Company in Kalamazoo. In 1900 Ellen White affirmed Lay's renewed commitment to the church. In her letter she also described the progress of the Adventist work in Australia and the need of funds to build the *Sydney Sanitarium (Lt 15, 1900).

Further reading: obit. RH, Dec. 16, 1862; obit. RH, Apr. 16, 1901; obit. RH, Sept. 10, 1908.

Lay, Horatio S. (1828-1900) and **Julia M. (Barber)** (1831-1893). Medical doctor and founding director of the *Health Reform Institute. Lay attended Western Reserve College in Cleveland, Ohio, obtained a medical degree from the Detroit Medical College, and afterward settled in Allegan, Michigan, to practice medicine. In 1852 he married Julia M. Barber (1831-1893), and four years later embraced

DR. HORATIO S. LAY

COURTESY OF THE ELLEN G. WHITE ESTATE, INC.

Sabbatarian Adventism as a result of meetings held by *M. E. Cornell.

In 1862, as a result of his wife's poor health, he took her to *James C. Jackson's "Our Home on the Hillside" to receive *natural remedy treatments. Lay joined the staff of the institution until 1866, when he returned to Allegan. Soon afterward he was asked to open and superintend the first Adventist medical institution, the *Health Reform Institute in *Battle Creek, Michigan. He also became the founding editor of the first Adventist health periodical, the *Health Reformer*. In 1867 Ellen White rebuked Julia for her "diseased imagination," and exhorted her to be supportive of her husband (Lt 6, 1867, in 5MR 388). She admonished them for erring in the management of their children (Lt 30, 1870), and later, for laying up their treasures on earth instead of in heaven (Lt 1a, 1872). In 1870 Horatio resumed his medical practice in Allegan, and in 1880 moved north to Petoskey, Michigan. In 1884 he retired from his medical practice and became a minister for the Michigan Conference. He is buried in the Poplar Cemetery in Monterey, Michigan.

Further reading: obit. RH, Sept. 12, 1893; obit. RH, Mar. 13, 1900.

Leadsworth, John Russell (1865-1944). Physician. In 1901 Ellen White wrote Leadsworth a letter of encouragement and urged him to continue as superintendent of the Mountain View Sanitarium in Spokane, Washington (Lt 35a, 1901). On at least one occasion he invited Ellen White to rest for a few days at his medical facility (J. R. Leadsworth to WCW, Apr. 28, 1901). In 1904 Ellen White received treatments at the Glendale Sanitarium, then operated by Leadsworth (5Bio 375).

Further reading: obit. RH, July 20, 1944.

Lewis, Dio (1823-1886). Physician; prominent nineteenth-century temperance reformer.

Lewis studied at the Harvard Medical School and afterward discarded the use of *drugs in his medical practice in Buffalo, New York. In 1852 he began lecturing on hygiene and physiology, and in 1863 he founded the Boston Normal Physician Training School. James and Ellen White respected Lewis as a medical authority and cited his writings in their first *health reform compilation, *Health: or How to Live (1865). Articles by Lewis appeared frequently in the *Review and Herald and the *Health Reformer. In 1871 Ellen White visited Dr. Lewis in Boston, Massachusetts, to understand better the effects of overwork and to learn how to help her debilitated husband (cf. Lt 15a, 1871). When Lewis indicated his own need of change and his plan to seek rest on the Pacific Coast, Ellen White invited him to visit the *Health Reform Institute in Battle Creek on his journey west (Lt 17, 1871). In 1873 Dr. Lewis helped found the *Woman's Christian Temperance Union. In 1878, while giving a public discourse on temperance in Oakland, California, Ellen White recognized Lewis in the audience, and invited him to address the crowd. He commended her presentation and appealed for those present to sign temperance pledges (Lt 15, 1878).

LICHTENSTEIN, MARCUS. First Jewish Seventh-day Adventist. As a youth Lichtenstein became an Adventist and came to work at the Seventh-day Adventist Publishing Association. This unusual convert to Adventism caught the attention of Ellen White, who saw a unique opportunity for Adventists to reach out to Jews (see *Israel and the Jewish people) and produce publications in Hebrew. The "lack of conscientiousness" on the part of other Review workers, according to Ellen White, caused Lichtenstein to "stumble" (3T 192, 193, 205, 206). As a result, the church lost a "gift which God had given to it" (*ibid.* 206). Ellen White

visited with Lichtenstein and appealed to him in a no longer extant letter (Mss 4, 13, 1873). His eventual departure from the church prompted strong admonitions to Adventist believers in Battle Creek (3T 192, 193).

See also: Hannah More.

LINCOLN, ABRAHAM (1809-1865). Sixteenth president of the United States of America. Born in poverty in Kentucky and largely self-educated, Lincoln became a successful lawyer. He entered politics in 1834, serving in the Illinois state legislature (1834-1842) and the United States House of Representatives (1846-1848). His 1858 debates with Stephen Douglas on the issue of slavery brought national attention and led to Lincoln's presidential campaign in 1860. Lincoln won the deeply divided election with about 40 percent of the national vote, mostly from the Northern states. As a result, the pro-slavery Southern states seceded from the Union, forming the Confederate States of America, and Lincoln was faced with civil war.

Though opposed to slavery, Lincoln considered his primary political duty to be the preservation of the Union, and directed his efforts toward that goal. Slavery, however, came to be more and more important. Following the Union victory at Antietam in 1862, Lincoln issued his Emancipation Proclamation on January 1, 1863, declaring that slaves in Confederate territory were "then, thenceforward, and forever" free. The Emancipation Proclamation was confirmed by the passage of the Thirteenth Amendment to the U.S. constitution in 1865, which abolished slavery in the United States. Lincoln worked ceaselessly to bring the Southern states back into the Union. His attitude was summed up in his second inaugural address in 1865: "with malice toward none, with charity for all." Lincoln's search for successful generals led eventually to William T. Sherman and Ulysses S. Grant, whose attacks in 1864 and 1865 defeated the Confederacy. Lincoln himself did not live to see the final victory; on April 14, 1865, he was assassinated by the actor John Wilkes Booth, a Southern sympathizer.

Lincoln's own religious views are almost completely unknown. He was never a member of any Christian denomination, though he attended Presbyterian churches in Illinois and Washington, D.C. He never spoke about religion even with close friends, though his interest in it appears to have grown after the death of his son Willie in 1862, and the growing pressure of the Civil War. His wife, Mary Todd Lincoln, had some interest in spiritualism and attended a number of séances.

According to James White, Seventh-day Adventists voted for Lincoln in 1860 if they voted at all, but there was little discussion of the president in Adventist literature at the time, as Adventists were more concerned with slavery and the draft (2Bio 41-43). Ellen White mentioned Lincoln approvingly as one who had learned "the lesson of self-denial in the school of poverty" (Lt 47, 1893, in 2MR 220).

Further reading: R. Branson, "Ellen G. White—Racist or Champion of Equality?" RH, Apr. 9, 1970; R. Branson, "Slavery and Prophecy," RH, Apr. 16, 1970; J. G. Nicolay and John Hay, *Abraham Lincoln: A History* (New York: Century Co., 1890); Carl Sandburg, *Abraham Lincoln* (New York: Scribner's, 1940); J. G. Randall, *Lincoln, the President* (New York: Dodd, Mead, 1945-1955); S. B. Oates, *With Malice Toward None: The Life of Abraham Lincoln* (New York: Harper & Row, 1977).

Tony Zbaraschuk

LINDSAY, CHARLES W. (1840-1915) and ELIZABETH O. (d. 1915). Early Adventists from Olcott, New York; Charles was the brother of *Harmon Lindsay. In December 1865 the Lindsays were asked to pray for the healing of James White after he suffered his first stroke (LS 171; RH, Feb. 27, 1866). Later, in *A Testimony for the Church at Olcott, N. Y.* (1868), Ellen White admonished Elizabeth to be more careful in her use of words (pp. 6, 7) and urged Charles "to seek for more spirituality" (p. 10).

Further reading: obit. RH, May 20, 1915; obit. RH, Oct. 7, 1915.

LINDSAY, HARMON (1835-1919). Financial administrator, brother of *Charles W. Lindsay, elder of the Battle Creek church and member of the General Conference Executive Committee (RH, Dec. 2, 1873). In 1874 he was elected to a one-year term as General Conference treasurer. About that time Ellen White cautioned him regarding his deficiencies of character (Lt 24, 1875, in 2Bio 476). During much of the 1890s he was treasurer of the General Conference (1888-1899). He participated in the development of Battle Creek College and Oakwood College. He was the treasurer and secretary of the Review and Herald Publishing Association and the Board of Foreign Missions. While in Australia, Ellen White entrusted her business affairs to Lindsay and, through him, arranged for a settlement out of court in her litigation with W. B. Walling, father of her niece's daughters, *May and Addie Walling (see *Addie [Walling] MacPherson) (cf. 4Bio 17).

Through the 1890s Lindsay became increasingly secular in his business dealings. "Since the [1888] meeting at Minneapolis," wrote Ellen White, "you have followed in the tread of the scribes and Pharisees" (1888 Materials 1344). His persistent rejection of her warnings, stemming initially from his rejection of *A. T. Jones' and *E. J. Waggoner's message on *righteousness by faith, was causing him to stumble (Lt 51a, 1895). When *O. A. Olsen was reelected General Conference president in 1895, Olsen leaned heavily upon Lindsay and *A. R. Henry for counsel on church management. Ellen White had misgivings about both of these advisors and their inclination to do business in a secular, unspiritual way. It was during this time, the late 1890s, when decisions of the General Conference were in the hands of a few men of this character, that Ellen White expressed her lack of confidence in the General Conference as the *voice of God (9T 260, 261). Lindsay later left the Adventist Church and joined the Church of Christ, Scientist.

She also wrote a number of letters to his son "Charley" (Lts 18e and 18f, and Ms 22, 1890).

See also: General Conference Session of 1888.

Further reading: H. E. Douglass, *Messenger of the Lord* (PPPA, 1998), pp. 228, 229; R. W. Schwarz and F. L. Greenleaf, *Light Bearers* (PPPA, 2000), p. 262; *Legacy of Light*, s.v. "Harmon Lindsay"; *SDA Encyclopedia* (1996), vol. 10, p. 928.

Michael W. Campbell

LINDSAY, HARMON WILLIAM (1869-1923) and **ANNIE (WESSELS).** Adventist missionaries;

COURTESY OF THE ELLEN G. WHITE ESTATE, INC.

HARMON W. LINDSAY

Harmon was the son of *Charles W. Lindsay. Soon after graduation from Battle Creek College in 1892, Lindsay went to South Africa as a missionary, where he married Annie Wessels. From 1894 to 1895 the Lindsays, with Annie's mother, *Anna Wessels, made a world tour during which they were guests of Ellen White at Avondale College and gave $5,000 to the work in Australia (Lt 124, 1894; 4Bio 180, 181). In 1898 Ellen White wrote to Lindsay urging him to improve his use of talents (Lt 78, 1898). For two years (1899-1901) he was president of the Claremont Union College at Cape Town and also served as treasurer of the conference and manager of the sanitarium in Cape Town. At the same time, Ellen White wrote to him that he might better improve his talents by relocating to Australia instead of taking leadership roles he was unprepared for in South Africa (Lt 78, 1899). His close connection to the Wessels family placed him, according to Ellen White, in a position of influence to be "a great blessing to that family," but she was concerned about his failure to grow in grace (Lt 111, 1899). She continued to urge him to improve his "talents for the Master" (Lt 112, 1899; Lt 159, 1899). Ellen White also wrote several letters of counsel and encouragement to Annie (Lt 235, 1903). In 1905 the Lindsays moved to the United States, where they taught at *South Lancaster Academy. Harmon then worked as business manager of *Paradise Valley Sanitarium for a few years, a decision that pleased Ellen White (Lt 192, 1908; Lt 32, 1909). Later he served as manager of the *Glendale Sanitarium (c. 1910-1912) and helped the nursing school obtain accreditation in 1911.

Further reading: obit. RH, Apr. 26, 1923.

Michael W. Campbell

LINDSAY, KATHERINE "KATE" (1842-1923). Founder of the first Adventist nurses' training

COURTESY OF THE CENTER FOR ADVENTIST RESEARCH, ANDREWS UNIVERSITY

DR. KATHERINE LINDSAY

school at the Battle Creek Sanitarium, Lindsay was educated in Wisconsin log schoolhouses, where she read about Florence Nightingale and decided to become a nurse. She worked at the Western Health Reform Institute before attending Dr. R. T. Trall's Bellevue Institute (1867-1869). She enrolled in the second medical class at the University of Michigan to accept women (10 of them, 1871), graduating first in her class (1875). She then became J. H. Kellogg's staff physician at the sanitarium. Using Trall's and Florence Nightingale's programs as models, Lindsay developed a three-year curriculum for the Sanitarium Medical Missionary Training School in 1883. The dean of Michigan's medical society called her "the best-informed physician" in the society.

In South Africa (1897-1900) she established the Claremont School of Nursing. When the Boer War broke out in 1899, Ellen White urged her to come to Avondale. "I know of no one whom I would be more pleased to have tarry with us awhile than yourself," she wrote. "We need your assistance" (Lts 113, 158, 1899, in 19MR 144, 145). But Lindsay went instead to Boulder Sanitarium in Colorado, where she trained nurses and wrote articles for journals. Her code of nursing principles is known as the "Kate Lindsay Pledge." In 1960 Loma Linda University erected the Kate Lindsay Women's Residence Hall in her honor.

Further reading: obit. RH, May 10, 1923; R. T. Banks, *A Woman's Place* (RHPA, 1992), pp. 56, 57; J. G. Beach, *Notable Women of Spirit* (SPA, 1976), pp. 77-85; K. Nelson, *Kate Lindsay, M.D.* (SPA, 1963); *SDA Encyclopedia* (1996), vol. 10, p. 928.

Brian E. Strayer

LITCH, JOSIAH (1809-1886). Methodist minister, prophetic expositor, theologian, and third most influential Millerite after *William Miller and *J. V. Himes. Born in Higham, Massachusetts, and converted at 17, Litch became a minister of the Methodist Episcopal Church in Rhode Island and was active in the

JOSIAH LITCH

temperance and anti-slavery movements. In 1838 he became the first well-known minister to adopt Miller's views, and the first to join Miller as a full-time ministerial associate.

When Litch was first handed a copy of Miller's lectures, the idea of attempting to discover the time of the Second Coming seemed so strange that Litch could hardly bring himself to read it. But as he read, he found Miller's case so clear, simple, and scriptural that he couldn't refute it. That conviction sparked a fierce internal struggle between his pastoral duty to proclaim truth and his dread of public criticism. The struggle continued, he wrote later, "until the Lord, *in a night dream,* showed me my own vileness, and made me willing to bear reproach for Christ, when I resolved, at any cost, to present the truth on this subject" (in *Advent Shield,* p. 55; italics supplied). Thus Litch, like Miller, was called to the Advent cause by such forceful evidence that to resist, they both believed, would be tantamount to turning from the Lord. Having made this decision, Litch began immediately to write, publish, and preach about the Second Advent.

In 1841 Litch became the first among the Millerites to argue for a pre-Advent judgment, the starting point for the concept Sabbatarian Adventists later termed *investigative judgment. Litch argued that if the elect are rewarded at the Second Advent (Matt. 24:30), then the judgment according to works (Rev. 20:12, 13; cf. Rev. 22:11, 12) must occur before that, for both the living and the dead (Acts 10:42). Therefore the judgment must include at least two phases, a pre-Advent "trial" phase, and a "penal," or executive, phase (Litch, *An Address to the Public and Especially the Clergy* [1841], pp. 37-39; see also Litch, *Prophetic Expositions* [1842], vol. 1, pp. 49-54).

What aroused much more attention was Litch's prediction in 1838, on the basis of Revelation 9:5, 15 that the Ottoman Empire's power to dominate its European neighbors would be broken in the month of August 1840 (*The Probability of the Second Coming of Christ About A.D. 1843*, p. 157). In common with other expositors of the time, Litch held that the fifth and sixth trumpets of Revelation 9 referred to the spread of Islam, particularly the Ottoman Empire. Litch also interpreted Revelation 9:5, 15 by the year-day method of prophetic interpretation that understood the symbolic "days" of certain prophecies as representing literal years. By this reasoning, the "five months" of Revelation 9:5 represented 150 years (5 x 30 days), in which the Ottomans could harass but not "kill" what was left of the Eastern Roman Empire with its (now Greek) capital at Constantinople. Later, according to verse 15, the Ottomans would be "released to kill," i.e., conquer and dominate Eastern Europe for a second period symbolized as an "hour and day and month and year." Interpreted by the year-day method, the "year," or 360 days, symbolized 360 actual years, the "month," or 30 days, represented 30 years, the "day" represented one year, and the hour represented a twenty-fourth of a 360-day prophetic year, or 15 days. Combining these yielded a total of 391 years and 15 days for the domination period of Revelation 9:15, which followed the 150-year harassment period of verse 5.

For the beginning point of the first period, Litch turned to the best authority available to him, Edward Gibbon's *Decline and Fall of the Roman Empire*. He was impressed to discover that Gibbon specially noted the "singular accuracy," based on two Latin sources, of the date July 27, 1299, for the beginning

of the Ottoman invasion of the Byzantine Empire (vol. 7, p. 24). Beginning with July 27, 1299, and adding the 150 years and the 391 years and 15 days, pointed to a terminus of August 11, 1840 (Litch, "Fall of the Ottoman Empire in Constantinople," *Signs of the Times*, Aug. 1, 1840; *Prophetic Expositions*, vol. 2, pp. 180-200).

On the basis of this reasoning, Litch predicted in 1838 that the Ottoman Empire would lose its power in August 1840. He later honed his prediction to the specific date, August 11, 1840 (in *Signs*, Aug. 1, 1840). This was widely regarded as a test case for the year-day method, and both Millerites and their opponents anxiously awaited news from the Middle East.

The immediate political situation was an ongoing war between Egypt and the Ottoman Empire, in which Egypt, formerly subservient to Constantinople, had risen under the brilliant leadership of its Pasha, Mehemet Ali, and defeated the Ottomans (Karsh and Karsh, pp. 36-41; Palmer, pp. 103-109). Ali's economic policies and his political ambitions so alarmed the Four Powers of Europe (England, Austria, Prussia, and Russia) that on July 15, 1840, they signed the Treaty of London, overturning the outcome of the war between Egypt and the Ottomans and pledging their protection of the Ottoman Empire ("From the [London] *Times*: Determined Hostility of Mehemet Ali to the Quadruple Treaty, *Museum of Foreign Literature*, pp. 231-236).

In Litch's view, this treaty of European support for the Ottoman Empire made official the already de facto situation—that the Ottoman Empire had grown too weak to defend itself. Thus Litch viewed the implementation of the Treaty of London as the terminus of Revelation 9:15, ending the consecutive periods of Ottoman harassment and then dominance that had begun in 1299. The only detail remaining to be seen was when the treaty would become effective. Since it was essentially an ultimatum to Mehemet Ali, Litch considered that the treaty would become effective upon its delivery to Ali, which took place in Alexandria on August 11, 1840 (London *Morning Chronicle*, Sept. 18, 1840, quoted in Litch, *Prophetic Expositions*, vol. 2, p. 196; cf. "The Quadruple Treaty," p. 233).

The news that the treaty had been delivered to Ali in Egypt on the very day Litch had specified created great excitement in North America about the Millerite cause. Litch reported that within a few months he received letters from more than 1,000 prominent infidels, testifying that they now accepted the Bible as divinely inspired.

In the years since 1840, various explanations have been offered about Litch's prediction. Historically, its fulfillment was widely viewed in late 1840 and early 1841 as confirming the Millerite methods of prophetic interpretation. Thus it greatly increased the popular momentum of the movement. Ellen White clearly believed that Litch's prediction was used by God to advance the Millerite movement (GC 334, 335). Litch's initial expositions included one unrecognized assumption—that the end of the 391-year period of Ottoman *dominance* would also mark the end of the Ottoman's *existence* as a nation, i.e., the "fall of the Ottoman Empire." Litch eventually (1842) recognized and clarified this blurring of two distinct ideas, but his earlier rhetoric of "fall," raised an expectation not warranted by the text of Revelation 9:15. This unfulfilled expectation eventually exposed Litch to severe criticism (Anderson), not unlike the criticism received by those who revised their understanding of the event that closed the 2300 years (in 1844) from a visible coming of Christ to earth to a heavenly coming of Christ to judgment (Dan. 7:9, 10, 13). In both cases the event did fulfill the prophecy, though it did not fulfill the expectations of those who proclaimed the prophecy. Many still hold that Litch's interpretation of Revelation was correct, or introduce minor modifications (C. M. Maxwell), while others argue for substantially different interpretations.

After the *disappointment of October 1844, Litch held to his earlier position for a time, but in April 1845 he and Himes led the Albany Conference in formally rejecting the view that the 2300 days closed in 1844. "I believe we erred, and ran off our track about one year ago," Litch wrote in May 1845. He no longer saw any prophetic significance in the year 1844 (in *Advent Herald,* May 21, 1845).

Thus Litch likely became one of those Ellen White identified as influencing the aging Miller to turn away from the message that would have "explained his disappointment," "cast a light and glory on the past," "revived his exhausted energies, brightened his hope, and led him to glorify God." Miller "leaned to human wisdom instead of divine," she wrote, "but being broken with arduous labor in his Master's cause and by age, he was not as accountable as those who kept him from the truth" (EW 257, 258).

Litch later became a physician, but for some 30 years he remained on the publication committee of the *Advent Herald* and continued writing on prophecy. In 1878 he was an observer at an interdenominational prophetic conference in New York City. In 1880 he was invited to Quebec to oppose *D. T. Bourdeau, who was conducting evangelistic meetings and advocating the biblical Sabbath. In rebuttal, Bourdeau poignantly reminded Litch of his illustrious past, when he had courageously advocated unpopular truth.

Further reading: E. Anderson, "The Millerite Use of Prophecy," in R. L. Numbers and J. M. Butler, eds., *The Disappointed* (Bloomington, Ind.: Indiana University Press, 1987;

reprint Knoxville: University of Tennessee Press, 1993), pp. 78-91; E. Gibbon, *Decline and Fall of the Roman Empire*, ed. J. B. Bury (New York: Macmillan, 1900), vol. 7, p. 24; E. Karsh and I. Karsh, *Empires of the Sand: The Struggle for Mastery in the Middle East, 1789-1923* (Cambridge: Harvard University Press, 1999), pp. 36-41; [J. Litch], "The Rise and Progress of Adventism," in J. V. Himes, S. Bliss, and A. Hale, eds., *The Advent Shield and Review* (Boston: J. V. Himes, 1844), p. 55; J. Litch, *The Probability of the Second Coming of Christ About A.D. 1843* (Boston: David H. Ela, 1838); J. Litch, *An Address to the Public and Especially the Clergy* (Boston: J. V. Himes, 1841), pp. 37-39; J. Litch, *Prophetic Expositions*, 2 vols. (Boston: J. V. Himes, 1842), vol. 1, pp. 49-54; vol. 2, pp. 180-200; J. Litch, in *Signs of the Times*, Aug. 1, 1840; J. Moon, "Josiah Litch: Herald of 'The Advent Near' " (1973), CAR; C. M. Maxwell, *God Cares*, vol. 2, *The Message of Revelation* (PPPA, 1985), pp. 262-267; A. W. Palmer, *The Decline and Fall of the Ottoman Empire* (Barnes and Noble, 1995), pp. 103-109; "The Quadruple Treaty," *Museum of Foreign Literature, Science, and Art* (Philadelphia: E. Littell, 1929), pp. 231-236; U. Smith, *Daniel and the Revelation* (SPA, 1944), pp. 493-517.

Jerry Moon

LITTLEJOHN, WOLCOTT HACKLEY (1834-1916).

COURTESY OF THE ELLEN G. WHITE ESTATE, INC.

WOLCOTT H. LITTLEJOHN

Minister, teacher, administrator, and author. Although he preferred to become a lawyer, Littlejohn was unable to finish his college degree because of an eye infection that ultimately caused complete blindness. After studying the Bible for 15 years, he became a Seventh-day Adventist in 1866. Soon thereafter he became a minister and held camp meetings and tent revivals throughout the United States. He brought about a spiritual revival in Battle Creek while he served as principal of Battle Creek College (1883-1885). In 1883 he married Adeline P. Harvey. In close collaboration with James White, he was a member of key committees on education and mission. He authored many pamphlets, tracts, and books on the role of America in prophecy and current political trends, Sunday legislation, and the Sabbath. As a regular contributor to the *Review and Herald*, Littlejohn defended Ellen White's role as a prophet. He was also outspoken about G. I. Butler's leadership style as General Conference president. Though Ellen White rebuked his approach and some of his ideas, she encouraged constructive conversations. Several letters and diary entries reflect the close relationship Ellen White and he enjoyed (cf. Lts 44, 79, 1886; Lts 48, 49, 1894).

Further reading: obit. Nov. 30, 1916; *SDA Encyclopedia* (1996), vol. 10, pp. 934, 935.

Eike Mueller

LOCKWOOD, RANSOM G. (1824-1897) and AURORA (BUTLER) (1827-1902).

Early Adventists from Vermont; close friends of James and Ellen White. Aurora was a Millerite believer and the younger sister of *G. I. Butler. She accepted the Sabbatarian Adventist message about 1850 and the next year married Ransom G. Lockwood. Soon after the Whites moved to Battle Creek in 1855 the Lockwoods relocated there and Aurora served as head of the bindery for the Review and Herald. They later moved with the Whites to California and took care of the Whites' home on the West Coast when the Whites were traveling (cf. Lt 9, 1886). Aurora occasionally helped as one of Ellen White's *literary assistants.

Further reading: obit. RH, Sept. 21, 1897; obit. RH, Jan. 28, 1902.

LOUGHBOROUGH, ANNA MARIAH (DRISCOLL), see **LOUGHBOROUGH, JOHN NORTON** and **MARY J. (WALKER).**

LOUGHBOROUGH, JOHN NORTON (1832-1924) and **MARY J. (WALKER)** (1832-1867). Pioneer evangelist and administrator, Loughborough was the first Seventh-day Adventist to publish a denominational history, *The Rise and Progress of Seventh-day Adventists* (1892), revised and enlarged as *The Great Second Advent Movement, Its Rise and Progress* (RHPA, 1905). In 1868 with *D. T. Bourdeau he pioneered the Adventist work in California and in 1878 went to England for five years. Upon his return to the United States, Loughborough served many years in various administrative roles for the church.

Loughborough married Mary Walker in 1851, and both became Sabbatarian Adventists the following year. Loughborough first met

JOHN AND MARY LOUGHBOROUGH

James and Ellen White in Rochester, New York, in the fall of 1852. During this first meeting Ellen White had a vision. While the physical phenomena he observed provided him with interesting and convincing evidence, it was what Ellen White said about a man not known to all present, someone she had never met nor known of, that soon provided indisputable proof to the questioning Lough-

borough. This man was a traveling preacher and while away from home was having an affair with another woman. A few weeks later Ellen White recognized him in a group of people and pointed out to others that he was the man she had seen in vision. Once confronted, this man confessed his errors, thus giving confirmation to Loughborough that Ellen White's gift was authentic (1Bio 237-239).

John and Mary Loughborough were closely associated with James and Ellen White in the early years of their respective ministry. While their husbands were holding meetings and visiting churches in Michigan, Ellen and Mary often visited each other, the two women being "close in spirit" (1Bio 411, 468). Trials also drew them in close fellowship, as each family lost a child in 1860 (*ibid.* 431). James White's opinion of John Loughborough's labor was ever gracious. To the readers of the *Review and Herald* in 1863 he declared: "His [Loughborough's] firm and persevering efforts on organization, systematic benevolence, et cetera, added to his preaching talent, and the qualifications before mentioned, make him, with the blessing of God, the man to build up churches, and have the especial oversight of the work in the East" (RH, Oct. 6, 1863, in 2Bio 65).

Several of Ellen's testimonies were directed to Mary and John, and in each case they were thoughtfully and gratefully received. In a few letters to Mary, Ellen pleaded with her to be more submissive to God and to her husband. She reminded Mary that her influence upon others mattered very much and also cautioned her about the way she talked to John in public, "as though he were a little boy." Others had noticed that Mary's tone of voice sounded impatient. This "hurts your influence," warned Ellen White. She also reminded Mary that women are to be subject to the husband. "He is the head, and our judgment and views and reasonings must agree with his if possible" (Lt 5, 1861, in 1Bio 469).

When early Adventists joined in the *dress reform movement and discarded the heavy hoop skirts, Mary hesitated, preferring to keep wearing them. Ellen White again pleaded with Mary that her influence was important and that as a minister's spouse she was to set the example other women are to follow. "God would have us utterly discard" the hoops, Ellen White concluded, and "this I believe is one of the abominations which causes God's people to sigh and cry . . . the people of God should not have the least to do with it" (Lt 6, 1861).

After Mary died in 1867, Loughborough married Maggie (1840-1875). In the late 1860s, when many church members and close friends in Battle Creek began to oppose the Whites' ministry, Ellen was troubled with John Loughborough's lack of support for James White. "I felt that you were distant, and we knew that the Lord was with us, and why you did not see and make reports to this effect when you returned, has always troubled me" (Lt 10, 1869). This detachment, however, did not last very long, and the two families soon regained their earlier sense of fellowship.

While helping to establish the Seventh-day Adventist work in England and other parts of Europe in 1878-1883, Loughborough and his third wife, Anna Mariah (née Driscoll) (1839-1907), received a long letter from Ellen White, to the effect that his weaknesses were hampering the progress of the Adventist work in Europe. She warned him against devoting "much time to little particulars," while neglecting "the work that you can do which others cannot do." She urged him to be less critical of others and to spend more time with God in devotional "soul culture." She advised that more time in the study of Scripture would make his sermons less dry. She also invited

him to trust other workers and bring them into his confidence. "If you have success in your mission, you must put 'I' out of sight and live with an eye single to the glory of God" (Lt 40, 1879).

Upon his return to the United States, Loughborough served as California Conference president (1873-1878; 1887-1890), superintendent of various General Conference districts (1890-1896), and president of the Nevada Association (1876), the Upper Columbia Conference (1884-1885), and the Illinois Conference (1891-1895). During these administrative assignments Ellen White often confided in him in regard to special situations she felt called by God to address or counsel. She had faith and confidence in Loughborough's abilities and skills.

At Ellen White's funeral at Elmshaven in July 1915, Loughborough was one of the speakers. In his tribute he emphasized the fact that her writings tended to the purest morality, to lead others to Christ and to the Bible, and to bring rest and comfort to weary and searching hearts (LS 451).

Further reading: obit. RH, June 19, 1924; obit. RH, July 2, 1867; obit. RH, Apr. 29, 1875; obit. RH, June 20, 1907; JNL, *Miracles in My Life*, ed. Adriel Chilson (Angwin, Calif.: Heritage Publications, n.d.); *SDA Encyclopedia* (1996), vol. 10, pp. 960, 961.

Denis Fortin

LOVELAND, REUBEN (1807-1898) and **BELINDA (BOUTWELL)** (1812-1906). Farmers and friends of James and Ellen White in Johnson, Vermont. Originally Methodists, the Lovelands accepted the message of the *Second Coming from *William Miller, and in 1850 accepted the seventh-day Sabbath from *Joseph Bates. The Lovelands gave some money to assist James White in starting the *Review and Herald*. Ellen White wrote them thanking them for their financial gift and sympathizing with them in their trials (Lt 26, 1850; cf. Lt 30, 1850). Ellen White cautioned them regarding the baleful influence of a "Brother" [Nelson A.] Hollis who was traveling about trying to defame James White's character (Lt 6, 1851). Later she wrote to them about the Whites' home in Battle Creek and exhorted them in *practical godliness (Lt 13, 1857).

Further reading: obit. RH, Mar. 22, 1906.

Lucas, "Brother" and "Sister." Adventists living near Battle Creek, Michigan. Ellen White reproved Lucas for not making his "past wrongs right" (Lt 63, 1888). Later that year, after a talk Ellen White gave on the subject of robbing God, he confessed that he had not paid his tithes (Ms 25, 1888). The next day Ellen White called upon them at home, where he pledged to "make restitution to the Lord" (Lt 83, 1889). A few days later after another visit, Lucas wrote a note pledging to pay "the snug little sum of $571.50." The next day Ellen White saw him again in passing across town. She noted that he had just returned from paying his note. "He was," said Ellen White, "as happy a man as I have seen in a long time" (*ibid.*).

Lunt, Frances (Howland), see **Howland, Frances.**

Lunt, Noah Norton (1821-1902). Early Sabbatarian Adventist in Portland, Maine.

NOAH N. LUNT

Lunt accepted the Second Advent message (see *Second Coming) during *William Miller's first visit to Portland in 1839. He was also present during some of Ellen Harmon's earliest visions, including the time in January 1845 when she related her first vision. He accepted the Sabbath doctrine from *Joseph Bates in 1846, about the same time that the Whites did. During these early years Ellen White corresponded with Lunt, although none of these letters are extant (Ms 5, 1859). After the death of Lunt's first wife, Rebecca E. Chamberlain, he married her sister Sarah H. Chamberlain (1833-1868). In 1864 Lunt was ordained an elder when *J. N. Loughborough organized a church in Portland, Maine. Two years later he and his wife Sarah relocated to *Battle Creek, Michigan, where Sarah died in 1867. In 1869 Lunt married *Frances "Fannie" Howland, the daughter of *Stockbridge Howland. After 1886 the Lunts moved to Oakland, California, to live with his oldest daughter and her husband, *C. H. Jones.

Further reading: obit. RH, Jan. 28, 1902; obit. RH, June 2, 1868.

Lyon, Henry M. (1796-1872) and **Deborah** (1796-1874). Early Adventist believers from Plymouth, Michigan. The Lyons were converted through *Joseph Bates in 1852 (RH, Sept. 16, 1852). The next year James and Ellen White stayed with them during the Whites' first tour of Michigan (1Bio 274, 275). In the early 1850s the Lyons sold their farm to help raise funds to assist the Whites in moving from *Rochester, New York, to Battle Creek. Henry worked with *Cyrenius Smith to build an office for the Review and Herald. Henry also served on the committee overseeing the finances of the journal (RH, Oct. 2, 1855).

Further reading: 1Bio 321; obit. RH, May 28, 1872.

Lyon, Mary H. (1825-1864). Early Adventist in Battle Creek, Michigan; apparently the daughter of *Henry Lyon's brother, Samuel Lyon, a Methodist Episcopal clergyman. In

1861, Ellen White warned Lyon that her love for fellow believers was growing cold and to exert her influence for God (Lt 19, 1861). A follow-up letter warned that she was under a dark cloud and about "to make shipwreck of your faith." The danger came partly from "trials at home" with her parents and partly from a "Brother Phillips" who had broken "the seventh commandment" (Lt 14, 1862). According to 1860 census records, it is possible that the "Brother Phillips" referred to was a neighbor by the name of James Phillips. About 1863 Lyon married Enoch Cummings and died in childbirth the following year. She and her deceased infant were buried beside her father in Oak Hill Cemetery.

MACKIN, RALPH (c.1875-1931). Adventist from Ohio who, with his wife, sought Ellen White's counsel regarding their experience of speaking in foreign tongues and casting out demons. In November 1908 the Mackins traveled to Ellen White's residence in California to ask her whether their unusual experiences were endorsed by God or a delusion. A verbatim transcript of the interview was kept (see 3SM 362-378).

Although Ellen White did not have an immediate response to their query, she highlighted how in her early years of ministry she had opposed various forms of fanaticism. "There is constant danger of allowing something to come into our midst that we may regard as the working of the Holy Spirit, but that in reality is the fruit of a spirit of fanaticism," she told them. "We are to be sanctified through obedience to the truth. I am afraid of anything that would have a tendency to turn the mind away from the solid evidences of the truth as revealed in God's Word. I am afraid of it; I am afraid of it. We must bring our minds within the bounds of reason, lest the enemy so come in as to set everything in

a disorderly way" (*ibid.* 373). Always mindful of the reputation of the church she added that "we cannot allow excitable elements among us to display themselves in a way that would destroy our influence with those whom we wish to reach with the truth. It took us years to outlive the unfavorable impression that unbelievers gained of Adventists through their knowledge of the strange and wicked workings of fanatical elements among us during the early years of our existence as a separate people" (*ibid.* 374).

When Mackin asked Ellen White whether this history of her past experience applied directly to the Mackins' case, she replied that she "could not say," but that she was "afraid" of the type of experience they were having because it appeared to be "along that line that I have met again and again" (*ibid.* 375). She emphasized that emotions and feelings were not the proper foundations on which to establish one's faith in the Seventh-day Adventist message and that the only safe course was to turn to the Bible for evidence (*ibid.* 375). A month later, after receiving a vision regarding the Mackins' experience, Ellen White wrote to the Mackins that they were "making some sad mistakes" and that their situation was similar to those she encountered in her early years of ministry. "Your wife, in speech, in song, and in strange exhibitions that are not in accordance with the genuine work of the Holy Spirit, is helping to bring in a phase of fanaticism that would do great injury to the cause of God, if allowed any place in our churches" (*ibid.* 376). She urged them to stop these experiences, because they "not only endanger your own souls, but [also] the souls of many others" (*ibid.* 377).

Further reading: A. L. White, "The Ralph Mackin Story," RH, Aug. 10, 17, 24, 1972.

Denis Fortin

MacPherson, Addie (Walling) (1868-1956).

COURTESY OF THE CENTER FOR ADVENTIST RESEARCH, ANDREWS UNIVERSITY.

ADDIE WALLING MACPHERSON

Granddaughter of Ellen White's sister *Caroline (Harmon) Clough. Addie and her younger sister, *May, became acquainted with James and Ellen White in 1872 when the Whites, on vacation, visited the Wallings' home in *Colorado. Because of turmoil in the family, their father, *William B. Walling, asked the Whites to care for the two girls. The Whites consented to this as a temporary arrangement, and the girls went on to *California to live with the Whites (2Bio 405).

This arrangement, however, continued indefinitely, and the Whites raised the girls as their own children and paid for their education (Lt 92, 1886). By 1877 Addie and May were living with *William C. White in Battle Creek, where they attended school. The following year James White baptized Addie (3Bio 92). By 1882 they were living with Ellen White in California (3Bio 195). In 1891, 18 years after they went to live with the Whites, their father asked the girls to return home to keep house for him. When they refused, Walling sued Ellen White for alienating his daughters' affections. She eventually arranged to settle out of court so that the girls would not be forced to testify against their father (4Bio 17, 268, 269). In 1906 Addie married Donald MacPherson (1864-1926), who had recently converted to Adventism and who was serving as a tentmaster for *A. G. Daniells (R. W. Olson interview with Kenneth MacPherson, June 1, 1977 [DF 511, EGWE-GC]).

Further reading: obit. RH, Aug. 30, 1956.

Magan, Percy Tilson (1867-1947) and Ida May (Bauer) (1869-1904).

Physician and administrator. Born in Ireland, Magan immigrated to Red Cloud, Nebraska, in 1886, where he became an Adventist through the influence of L. A. Hoopes. After doing *colporteur work, he received a license to preach in 1887. Magan first met Ellen White at the *General Conference session of 1888, and lived in her home while he attended *Battle Creek College.

COURTESY OF THE ELLEN G. WHITE ESTATE, INC.

PERCY T. MAGAN

In 1889 Magan served as secretary to *S. N. Haskell, traveling with him in an around-the-world tour assessing potential mission fields. He was associate secretary of the *Foreign Mission Board (1890-1891), and head of the Department of Bible and History at Battle Creek College (1891-1901). There he met and married Ida May Bauer (1892) and was ordained to the ministry (1899). About 1899 Magan and *E. A. Sutherland began planning to move Battle Creek College to a rural location, in harmony with earlier counsels of Ellen White. She advised them to first remove the debt on the school lest they give an impression that the school was forced to close (Lt 163, 1899; Lt 129, 1900). Then she counseled them to wait and watch for the opportune moment to relocate (Lt 141, 1900).

In 1901 the opportunity came to relocate the college to a 256-acre farm in Berrien Springs, Michigan. Magan served as dean and Sutherland as president of the new school, renamed *Emmanuel Missionary College. This move enabled them to carry out some of Ellen White's educational reforms, specifically, moving away from a classical education to one with a greater emphasis upon biblical, practical, and vocational training. Their work was made harder by criticism, even from church leaders, but Ellen White kept up a stream of encouragement. "I cannot but feel assured that you have found the very place in which to begin your school work" (Lt 89, 1901, in 8MR 28; see also Lts 161, 172, 184, 1901). She cautioned Magan in particular against overwork and suggested he take a vacation to regain his health (Lt 184, 1901). She suggested that students and faculty sell her new book *Christ's Object Lessons, whose royalties she donated to raise money for the fledgling institution (Lt 56, 1902). Magan was a close friend of Ellen White's and several times secured loans to assist her with publication and translation of her books (Lt 71, 1902). When Magan and Sutherland's leadership at the new school was resisted by some students and faculty, Ellen White stood by them and encouraged them to "not be easily disturbed by what others may say" (Lt 96, 1902). In 1902, when Ida became sick, Ellen White wrote a letter expressing her concern for Ida and reaffirming her support, contradicting false rumors "that Sister White is working or will work against Brother Magan." She also counseled them to again take a vacation so that they both could recover their health (Lt 111, 1903). She also warned them against the *pantheism in J. H. Kellogg's new book, The Living Temple (Lt 214, 1903).

During the 1904 *Berrien Springs meeting Ellen White stayed in the Magan home. She commended Sutherland and Magan on their work and encouraged their plan of founding a *self-supporting school in the American South. *W. K. Kellogg offered Magan $10,000 of stock in the cornflake business if he would join his new company. Magan reflected later that he would "stick to this message and give whatever time and talent I had to the making of Adventists rather than to the making of cornflakes" (For God and C.M.E., p. 104). Following the Berrien Springs meeting, Sutherland and Magan rode with Ellen White and her son *Edson White in Edson's boat, the *Morning Star, on the Cumberland River near Nashville, Tennessee. On this trip they located a farm on which to establish *Madison College. Its board was the only institutional board Ellen White ever served on. While she strongly supported their work, she also counseled them to harmonize with church leaders (Lt 273, 1904; Lt 168, 1907), and advised them about school matters (Lt 172, 1907; Lt 102, 1909; Lt 148, 1910).

Magan earned the M.D. degree from the University of Tennessee (1910-1914) and helped to start the Madison Sanitarium, then became dean (1915-1928) and president (1928-1940) of the *College of Medical Evangelists. For many of those years he served simultaneously as superintendent of *White Memorial Medical Center (1920-1927; 1929-1930). Under his leadership the medical school was able to obtain *accreditation during a period when many medical schools were being closed. After Ida's death in 1904, Magan married Lillian Eshleman (1870-1965).

Further reading: obit. RH, Jan. 29, 1948; obit. RH, June 9, 1904; obit. RH, June 3, 1965; M. L. Neff, *For God and C.M.E.: A Biography of Percy Tilson Magan Upon the Historical Background of the Educational and Medical Work of Seventh-day Adventists* (PPPA, 1964).

Michael W. Campbell

MARTIN, "BROTHER," "SISTER," and CHRISSIE. Adventists from Auckland, New Zealand. When Ellen White visited their home in 1893, Brother Martin had recently been converted, and Ellen White was instrumental in the conversion of his wife and their daughter, Chrissie (Lt 26, 1893; Mss 5, 64, 1893). Ellen White later wrote a letter of encouragement to Chrissie (Lt 51, 1894) and invited her to spend a weekend at her Norfolk Villa *home (Lt 108, 1894). Later she invited Chrissie to work and live at her Sunnyside home to help Chrissie pay her way at the *Avondale school (Lts 97, 98, 1897).

MASON, PAUL CLINTON (1878-1956). Bookkeeper for Ellen White (1907-1915). Previously an employee at *Pacific Press, Mason replaced *Sarah Peck on Ellen White's staff (6Bio 130). White occasionally corresponded with him about financial matters (cf. Lt 106, 1911; Lt 46, 1912).

Further reading: obit. RH, Nov. 29, 1956.

MATTESON, JOHN GOTTLIEB (1835-1896). Evangelist, pioneer missionary, author and editor, hymn writer, administrator, and Bible teacher. Born in Langeland, Denmark, Matteson moved to the United States, and after his conversion to Adventism worked among the Scandinavian immigrants, growing the Danish-Norwegian church in the American Midwest to nearly 200, and over his lifetime leading nearly 2,000 people into the Advent movement. Matteson and his Norwegian wife, Anna Sieverson, were the first Seventh-day Adventist missionaries sent to Scandinavia, where they served from 1877 to 1888.

JOHN G. MATTESON

Matteson helped raise the first Seventh-day Adventist church in Chicago; founded the first non-English Adventist magazine, the *Advent Tidende;* was the first to translate one of Ellen White's books (*A Sketch of the Christian Experience and Views of Ellen G. White* [1851]) into another language; founded a publishing house in Norway as well as a health magazine called *Sunhedsbladet*—the oldest health magazine in Norway; established the Danish and Norwegian conferences, and, along with J. P.

Rosquist, cofounded the Swedish Conference.

Matteson had a lifelong relationship with the White family. In 1874 he received a dream concerning the struggles of James and Ellen White, which proved encouraging to Ellen White, whom he had not yet formally met (1T 597-599). While serving the church in Scandinavia, she and Matteson had two "confrontations," both in Stockholm, Sweden. The first concerned a future speaking engagement by Ellen White, in which Matteson suggested that she "speak less about duty and more in regard to the love of Jesus." She declined his advice, resolving to "speak as the Spirit of the Lord shall impress me," and "did not round the corners at all" (Ms 26, 1885, in EGWEur 105 and 3SM 64). The second instance concerned the possibility of Matteson having to step down from his leadership position and make room for *O. A. Olsen (Ms 25, 1886; EGWEur 196, 197). Neither instance was ever spoken ill of by either party.

Further reading: 3Bio 237; EGWEur 91-126; 1T 597-599; obit. RH, Apr. 14, 1896; G. D. Asholm, "John Gottlieb Matteson: How He Became a Missionary" (unpublished paper, 1966, CAR); A. D. Chilson, *Gospel Viking* (RHPA, 1981); L. H. Christian, *Sons of the North* (PPPA, 1942); Magne Fuglheim, "Infidel Turns Missionary—1," AR, Feb. 22, 1979; M. Fuglheim, "Infidel Turns Missionary—2," AR, Mar. 1, 1979; H. Dunton et al., eds., *Heirs of the Reformation* (Grantham, Eng.: Stanborough Press, 1997), pp. 70-73, 161, 162, 216-218; HS; J. G. Matteson, *Mattesons Liv* [autobiography] (College View, Nebr.: International Pub. Assn., 1908); J. G. Matteson, "A Few Items Relative to the Cause," RH, May 29, 1866.

Erik C. Carter

MAXSON, W. H. and **HARRIET (SANDERSON)** (1860-1920). Adventist medical doctors. After the Maxsons finished their medical training at the Battle Creek Sanitarium, Ellen White sought to have them join the staff of the St. Helena Rural Health Retreat (see *St. Helena Sanitarium and Hospital) in California although they preferred to go to Ohio. "I am quite anxious that you should connect with the St. Helena Health Retreat, because we have not a lady physician there, and this is our great need now. We also need another gentleman physician" (Lt 5, 1887). After reluctantly going to St. Helena and working there for a short time, the Maxsons left the sanitarium disgruntled over Dr. *J. S. Gibbs' use of drugs instead of more natural remedies. Ellen White regretted their leaving St. Helena, given the state of things there, but especially faulted them for leaving at such a time and following their own selfish interests (Lts 87, 55, 1888). She faulted them even more when she learned they were planning to open another sanitarium in Fresno, California, as she felt it would weaken the work done at St. Helena (Lt 55, 1888; Lt 26a, 1889). While in Australia, Ellen White continued to encourage them to work faithfully for the church and to return to the St. Helena Health Retreat. She felt pleased when she learned that they had returned to St. Helena and "were determined to do [their] utmost to make it a success" (Lt 21a, 1892). Although she had confidence in their abilities as physicians, she did not believe in W. H. Maxson's administrative skills and urged him not to take the management of the institution. "The managing and controlling of the Health Retreat is not your work" (Lt 69a, 1896). She also warned Maxson that he had too much "unsanctified independence and self-confidence" (Lt 21c, 1892) and that both he and his wife needed a "decided reformation in the texture of your character" (Lt 71, 1896). She pleaded with them not to consider sanitariums as hotels in attempting to provide for all the wishes of their patients. She felt sanitariums should be teaching true principles of health reform and offer only a vegetarian diet to their patients (Lt 72, 1896; cf. Lt 73a, 1896, in SpM 38-45; Lt 73, 1896, in 20MR 104-118).

Further reading: Obit RH, Feb. 10, 1921; "History of the Inception and Early Development of the St. Helena Sanitarium" (EGWE, DF 14).

Denis Fortin

MAYNARD, AUGUSTUS W. (1822-1906) and **PHIDELIA** (1830-1873). Residents of Greenville, Michigan, who became Adventists in 1860 through the influence of *J. B. Frisbie. When the Greenville Adventist Church was organized (1862), Augustus was chosen elder of the church, a position he held for most of his life. Beginning in January 1867, the Whites lived for six weeks in the Maynard home,

COURTESY OF THE ELLEN G. WHITE ESTATE, INC.

AUGUSTUS MAYNARD

making it their headquarters while they labored with the churches in Greenville and Orleans (LS 174; cf. 2Bio 166-175). That same year the Whites built their own home in Greenville and became friends of the Maynards. They entrusted them with the care of their teenage son, *Willie, during their travels. She wrote: "I should feel very anxious were he [Willie] in any other family. You seem to understand him so well" (Lt 17, 1867). In other letters she inquired about their home in Greenville and expressed appreciation for their friendship (Lt 1, 1868; Lt 1, 1872).

Further reading: obit. RH, Apr. 15, 1873; obit. RH, May 17, 1906.

MCCANN, HARRIET (HARMON) (1814-c. 1875). Older sister of Ellen White, second daughter of *Robert F. and Eunice Harmon, married to Rev. Samuel McCann; together they raised six children in Poland Springs, Maine (Lt 95, 1886, in DG 190). In 1875, while visiting the state of Maine, Ellen White visited her sister one last time as she was dying of tuberculosis (2Bio 479). Fifteen years later Ellen visited Harriet's daughter Emma and her family in Danvers, Massachusetts (Ms 51, 1890).

MCCLURE, NATHANIEL C. (1837-1919). Pastor in Healdsburg, California; president of California Conference (1890-1891, 1894-1896). Born in Indiana, he accepted the Advent message when he was in the prime of life. Ellen White described him as "not a speaker, but a good counsellor, a good worker" (Lt 46, 1890, in 1888 Materials 647). In 1888 when Ellen White was seriously ill she attended the camp meeting in Oakland, California, where McClure and his wife, Frances (1844-1909), "were attentive to my every want" (1888 Materials 48). Later McClure assisted Ellen White with the sale of her Healdsburg home (Lt 245, 1904). Portions of a letter (Lt 166, 1901) from Ellen White to the McClures appear in CG 249, 250. The letter gives strong counsel concerning discipline problems involving the McClures' adopted son, Rodney, a student at the Healdsburg school. McClure spent his final years in Los Angeles and was buried beside his companion at St. Helena, California.

Further reading: obit. RH, Jan. 29, 1920; obit. RH, Jan. 20, 1910.

Alfred C. McClure

MCCOY, JAMES RUSSELL (1845-1924). Chief magistrate (1870-1872, 1878-1879, 1883, 1886-1889, 1904-1906) and president of the council (1893-1896, 1898-1904) of Pitcairn Island. McCoy was converted by Adventist missionaries on the schooner *Pitcairn* in 1890 and joined the crew for part of its first voyage. While visiting in Australia, McCoy received a telegram from Pitcairn that his wife, Eliza, daughter Ella May, and his wife's father, "Brother Young," had all died of typhoid fever (cf. Ms 89, 1893). Ellen White talked with him for an hour, and, upon his departure to return to Pitcairn, wrote him a letter of comfort reminding him of the hope of the *resurrection (Lt 52, 1894, in 15MR 265-268).

Further reading: A. H. Christensen, *Heirs of Exile* (RHPA, 1955), p. 258.

MCCULLAGH, STEPHEN (c. 1865-1951). Pioneer Australian evangelist who worked closely with Ellen White and whose miraculous healing was considered by her as special evidence of God's leading in the 1894 purchase of the Brettville Estate, upon which *Avondale College was later established. However, by 1897 McCullagh had resigned after nine years as a committed and successful Adventist evangelist. Not only did he leave the church—he destabilized other members and made a deliberate attempt to split the church in Adelaide, South Australia (A. G. Daniells to EGW, Apr. 15, 1897). McCullagh objected to Ellen White's claims of inspiration, as well as the Adventist views on *atonement, the *sanctuary, 1844, and the *health reform message. His apostasy was not sudden; Ellen White had been concerned for the family for some years.

Having apparently made a complete turnaround in his life and confessed that his wrong attitude toward Ellen White stemmed from his resistance to "very searching reproof" (UCR, May 20, 1899), McCullagh returned to the ministry, following rebaptism and reordination (UCR, Sept. 1, 1899). This was not to last, however, as in 1902 he made a final break with the church. After some time with the Zion City Movement in America he returned to Australia and entered the theater business in Sydney. While generous in making theater facilities available to Adventist evangelists, he continued to disparage the work of Ellen White and is thought by some to have been the first to accuse her of plagiarism (see *literary borrowing) in the preparation of *The Desire of Ages.

Late in life (c. 1947-1948) McCullagh, then a Pentecostal minister, was visited by K. E. Williamson while canvassing (see *colporteurs) door to door. McCullagh gave Williamson his copy of The Desire of Ages, with the pencilled annotations recording his conclusions of plagiarism. R. H. Abbott also visited the McCullaghs (1948-1951), and they attended his tent mission in Northam, Western Australia. On at least six occasions (1948-1951) Abbott had long talks with McCullagh, who reminisced, though not critically, of his working with Ellen White. According to Abbott, McCullough several times remarked, "She was a marvelous woman."

Further reading: Lt 40, 1893; 4Bio 78, 151, 152, 275-286, 453; "R. H. Abbott Affidavit" (DF 28-C-I-b); A. G. Daniells to EGW, Apr. 15, 1897 (DF 28-C-I-b); "Personal," UCR, May 20, 1899; UCR, Sept. 1, 1899; K. E. Williamson, "Comment on S. McCullough" (DF 28-C-I-b, EGWRC-AV); EGW, "Autograph Album 1900" (DF 504b, EGWRC-AV).

Lester D. Devine

McDEARMON, EMMA, see **WHITE, EMMA L. (McDEARMON)**.

McENTERFER, SARA (1855-1936). Nurse, traveling companion, household manager, *literary assistant, and private secretary to Ellen White. Converted at the age of 19, she attended *Battle Creek College, where she earned a degree in nursing. Upon graduation (1878) Sara worked as a book binder at the *Review and Herald. After the death of

SARA McENTERFER

James White (1881) she was recruited by *W. C. White to be Ellen White's personal secretary.

For a few months her work for Ellen White was interspersed with work at *Pacific Press. In 1883 she accompanied Ellen White on a tour back to the eastern United States. Later she was Ellen White's traveling companion to Europe (1885-1887), after which she served as her personal assistant until Ellen White left for Australia in 1891. At that time Sara became sick in Battle Creek and spent most of 1892-1893 recuperating and earning money to return to California. In 1894 she worked as a stenographer in the California Conference. In 1895 she went to Australia to work for Ellen White (RH, Dec. 3, 1895). One of her tasks included preparing mail to be sent to the United States. When the *Avondale school opened, Sara solicited funds to buy a school bell. Frequently the sick were brought to Ellen White's home for Sara to care for, or to have Sara deliver a baby. She functioned, with Ellen White's blessing, as a "community nurse." After 1900 Sara wrote letters (always signing her own name) in response to many inquiries sent to Ellen White and was with Ellen White at the time of her death. In Ellen White's later years Sara gained the reputation of being her "watchdog," because Sara guarded her from unnecessary visitors and intrusions. Sara was essentially in charge of Ellen White's household and was the "head" secretary among her office staff. When Ellen White died, Sara was the one who closed her eyes, and she (with W. C. White) accompanied the body across the plains to Battle Creek for the final funeral service and interment in *Oak Hill Cemetery.

After Ellen White's death she returned to working as a book binder at Pacific Press, and as a private-duty nurse.

Further reading: obit. RH, Feb. 20, 1936; "The Funeral of Sister Sara E. McEnterfer Held in the S.D. Adventist Church in Mountain View, Thursday, at 2:30 p.m., January 9, 1936" (DF 525, EGWE-LLU; this document contains life sketches by W. C. White and I. M. Burke).

Michael W. Campbell

McKIBBIN, ALMA E. (BAKER) (1871-1974). Educator and writer, church school teacher in California, and author of Adventist Bible textbooks. Alma graduated from *Healdsburg College and was married to Edwin McKibbin in 1892 (Baker, pp. 27, 33). After Edwin died in 1896, she started the first Seventh-day Adventist elementary school in California at Centralia in 1897 (*ibid.*, pp. 45, 47), and later taught in several other church schools. After Ellen White returned from Australia and settled at Elmshaven, she rented her Healdsburg home to Alma McKibbin. Ellen White's periodic visits to Healdsburg evoked many memories, which she related to McKibbin (5Bio 121-123). McKibbin later taught at Pacific Union College (c. 1912-1922) and at Mountain View Academy (1922-1925). She is buried in Healdsburg next to her mother.

COURTESY OF THE ELLEN G. WHITE ESTATE, INC.

ALMA MCKIBBIN

Further reading: obit. RH, Nov. 28, 1974; A. Baker, *My Sister Alma and I* (PPPA, 1980); A. McKibbin, "My Memories of Sister White," Feb. 15, 1956 (DF 967, EGWE-LLU); M. L. Myers, "Historical/Analytical Study of the Contributions of Alma E. McKibbin to the Seventh-day Adventist Church School System" (Ph.D. diss., AU, 1992); L. C. Thomas, "Biography of Alma McKibbin and Hedwig Jemison" (research paper, AU, 1977).

McLEARN, ALEXANDER. Educator. A Baptist minister with a Doctor of Divinity degree, he accepted Adventism—but apparently never officially became a church member—only a few days before he became president of *Battle Creek College during a tumultuous period (1881-1882). McLearn clashed with *G. H. Bell over the operation of the school, and when matters intensified, McLearn resigned. Subsequently, Battle Creek College was closed for a year (1882-1883). Concerned about the state of affairs at the college, Ellen White wrote a long testimony to the Battle Creek church (PH155). McLearn later joined the *Marion Party and eventually became a *Seventh Day Baptist.

Further reading: R. W. Schwarz and F. Greenleaf, *Light Bearers: A History of the Seventh-day Adventist Church* (PPPA, 2000), pp. 126, 127; E. K. Vande Vere, *The Wisdom Seekers* (SPA, 1972), pp. 42-47.

McPHERSON, SAMUEL A. (1823-1898). Adventist businessman in Michigan whom Ellen White urged to prepare himself for heaven. She pointed out that his political views were not in harmony with God's Word and that his overbearing spirit needed to be converted (Lt 1a, 1867). Evidently his response was positive, because four years later he was one of the businessmen invited by name to move to Battle Creek to help manage Adventist institutions (RH, July 18, 1871).

Further reading: obit. RH, Feb. 28, 1899.

McREYNOLDS, CHESTER C. (1853-1937) and **MARY CORNELL (COOK)** (1880-1955). Educator, minister, and administrator. As secretary of the Kansas Conference (1888-1891) McReynolds admitted to Ellen White to having been on the wrong side at the

*General Conference session of 1888 (Lt 50, 1889). He served as the president of conferences in the midwestern and southern United States, and became the first president of the Southwestern Union Conference (1901-1902). In 1908 McReynolds married Mary Cornell Cook, who later became a physician. After the McReynoldses settled at Pacific Union College in 1922, Mary McReynolds became the first teacher in the denomination to teach a course on prophetic guidance and the ministry of Ellen White. As president of the Wisconsin Conference (1905-1910) Chester McReynolds sought Ellen White's advice about a piece of property that was being considered for an industrial school in Doswell, Virginia (near Richmond), and she encouraged him to proceed, as God would open the way (Lt 8, 1909). In 1910 he shared with her the decision of some teachers at Walderly, Wisconsin, who refused to allow young people living near the school to attend unless they lived with the teachers in the school home (McReynolds to WCW, July 17, 1910). To Ellen White this idea was "a new and strange idea." "Let it not be urged," she declared, "that children must in all cases be separated from their parents" in order to attend an Adventist school. "Whenever possible, let the family be held together" (Lt 60, 1910, in 15MR 43-46).

Further reading: obit. RH, Apr. 15, 1937; obit. RH, Aug. 25, 1955; M. C. McReynolds, *Prophetic Guidance Textook* (DF 107-I, CAR); *SDA Encyclopedia* (1996), vol. 11, pp. 601, 906, 907.

MEARS, OLIVER (1820-1913). Converted to Adventism in 1858, Mears became the leader of the Lovett's Grove, Ohio, church (where Ellen White had her great controversy vision in 1858). He continued farming while serving three terms as Ohio Conference president

(1863-1866, 1869-1870, 1873-1875). In 1864 Ellen White warned him that he had been overly indulgent with his daughters and counseled him to curb their "frivolity," "coquetry," and "flippant behavior" with men. In the same letter she rebuked Mears for being "too sharp" with other believers and for dwelling on his "discouragement and distress." He needed to have more "compassionate tenderness" and "brotherly love" and focus on Christ (Lt 11, 1864).

Further reading: *SDA Encyclopedia* (1996), vol. 11, p. 46.

Brian E. Strayer

MEYRAT, ADOLPHE L. Adventist who lent money to *Albert and Luke Vuilleumier, demanded repayment, and used Ellen White's writings in support of his actions. In response Ellen White cited her experiences with her own *finances, in forgiving the debts of persons who were unable to repay her. At that moment of writing she said she was carrying a debt of $10,000 at 8 percent interest, "and yet I am glad I have not required the payment of these notes which were my just due." In addition, Ellen White cautioned Meyrat not to expect repayment when banks fail (presumably the reason the Vuilleumiers were unable to repay the money) (Lt 111, 1886).

MICHAELS, CHARLES P. Employee at the *Echo Publishing House and church administrator. From 1896 to 1898 Michaels was on the publishing house board and a member of the Australasian Union Conference executive committee. He later became vice president of the Central Australian Conference (1899), and served on the executive committee of the Victoria Conference (1900) and on the board of directors of the Australasian Publishing House (1900-1901). Ellen White counseled Michaels that in order to bring a more spiritual atmosphere into both the Echo office and the North Fitzroy church, they should study "the science of true godliness" (Lt 5, 1898, in 3MR 320).

MILLER, HOWARD W. (1848-1931) and **MADISON BOTTENFIELD** (1844-1917). Ministers (brothers) from Michigan who opposed Ellen White's ministry at the *General Conference session of 1888. In the months that followed the session Ellen White pointed out to Howard Miller that "for years you have been in great need of spirituality, and have not discerned the necessity of weaving Christ into all your labors. . . . You have been filled to a great degree with Pharisaism" (Lt 5, 1889, in 1888 Materials 330, 331). Her appraisal of Madison Miller's experience was no better. "He does not know what it is to walk by faith. . . . He does not possess a personal interest in the truth as it is in Jesus" (Lt 4, 1889, in 1888 Materials 388). Although by March 1890 Madison seemed to have understood his situation and repented from his ways, a year later things were no different, in her opinion. "Both are unfit to be trusted with responsibilities, because they have chosen a set, determined will of their own, to yield to no one, to be independent" (Ms 40, 1891, in 1888 Materials 888). By 1893, however, both Millers, along with other ministers, had admitted their mistakes and accepted what Ellen White was attempting to tell them (cf. Lt 79, 1893; Ms 80, 1893).

Further reading: obit. RH, Oct. 15, 1931; obit. RH, Feb. 8, 1917.

MILLER, MADISON BOTTENFIELD, see **MILLER, HOWARD W. and MADISON BOTTENFIELD**.

MILLER, WALTER H. B. (1864-1930). Printer and businessman, one of the first converts to Adventism in Australia. In 1886 Miller and

*J. H. Woods learned about Seventh-day Adventist doctrine after they incidentally found a tract left in a fence in Melbourne. The two of them later worked at the *Echo Publishing House. In the early 1890s Miller was sent to work for a while at Pacific Press in order to learn the methods of Adventist publishing work. Upon his return to Australia in 1895, however, Miller and Woods started their own printing business, a decision that upset church leaders, including Ellen White (Lts 129, 65, 1896). "Your action was not in the order of God," she wrote them (Lt 39, 1898). Miller later worked again at Pacific Press (1899-1903). In 1897, while Miller's wife was sick, Ellen White encouraged them to place their faith and hope in God (Lts 95, 94, 93, 1897).

Further reading: obit. *Australasian Record*, Aug. 11, 1930.

MILLER, WILLIAM (1782-1849). Baptist preacher, born at Pittsfield, Massachusetts,

COURTESY OF THE CENTER FOR ADVENTIST RESEARCH, ANDREWS UNIVERSITY

WILLIAM MILLER

in 1782, the oldest of 16 brothers and sisters. William's father was a captain in the Revolutionary War, and his mother was a Baptist preacher's daughter. He had only 18 months of formal schooling, but was an avid reader, and gained a more than average education in this way.

From an early age Miller was known for his writing skills, and was a poet. At age 15 he began a personal diary. The following entry appeared in 1803: "Be it remembered that on this day, it being a Sunday in the afternoon of the aforesaid day, I did bind myself and was bound to be, the partner of Miss Lucy Smith, of Poultney. And by these presents do agree to be hers and only hers till death shall part us (provided she is of the same mind)" (in F. D. Nichol, *The Midnight Cry*, p. 20). They were married that year, and their marriage lasted until Miller's death, nearly 50 years later.

Through reading infidel writers such as Voltaire and Thomas Paine, Miller became a deist, believing that God made the world but had no interest in human events. Neither did he believe in an afterlife. Although he made fun of religion, mimicking his grandfather and uncle, both Baptist ministers, he was not happy. The year of his marriage he wrote: "Come, blest religion, with thy angel's face, dispel this gloom, and brighten all the place; drive this destructive passion from my breast; compose my sorrows, and restore my rest" (in S. Bliss, *Memoirs of William Miller*, p. 27).

Miller entered public life in 1809, eventually becoming a justice of the peace. He was a respected member of his local community, and when the War of 1812 began, 47 men enlisted to serve under his command as a lieutenant in the U.S. Army. Later, as a captain, he wrote: "I began to feel very distrustful of all men. In this state of mind, I entered the service of my country. I fondly cherished the idea, that I should find one bright spot at least in the human character, as a star of hope: *a love of country*—Patriotism" (in Bliss, pp. 23, 24).

Much of the War of 1812 took place within 100 miles (161 kilometers) of Miller's home at Low Hampton, New York. He participated in the Battle of Plattsburgh, at which the American forces, outnumbered nearly three to one, defeated the British. Miller commented: "So surprising a result against such odds did seem to me like the work of a mightier power than man" (W. Miller, *Apology and Defense*, p. 4).

After the war Miller attended church regularly, though he was not a member. In 1816 the Low Hampton community planned a celebration of the Battle of Plattsburgh. On the following Sunday Miller was called upon to read the sermon. He began to read, but could not finish, as his emotions overcame him. It was the beginning of his conversion. Within a few weeks "the Scriptures" "became my delight; and in Jesus I found a friend" (in Bliss, p. 67). In 1818 he came to the conclusion from Daniel 8:14 and other texts that Jesus would return "about 1843."

At first Miller shared his findings only with personal friends. But he was impressed that he should preach. But who would listen to a farmer? Finally, on a Saturday morning in August 1831, he made a covenant with God that if someone asked him to preach, he would do so. Thirty minutes later his nephew was at the door with a request to come to nearby Dresden to preach. The boy had traveled 16 miles (26 kilometers) by foot, boat, and horseback. He had started on his way *before* Miller had promised to preach. After much wrestling with God, Miller agreed to go. Upon his return from Dresden after a week of revival, there was another invitation to preach at Poultney, Vermont. Over the next 13 years he preached more than 3,200 times.

At first he preached in small towns. But after he met *Joshua V. Himes, promoter and editor, in 1839, Miller's audiences in the larger cities began to number in the thousands. Though he met opposition from many sides, it is estimated that from 50,000 to 100,000 became "Adventists," or Millerites.

Miller's preaching impressed even secular editors. One wrote: "We have overcome our prejudices against him by attending his lectures, and learning more of the excellent character of the man, and of the great good he had done and is doing. . . . No one can hear him five minutes without being convinced of his sincerity, and instructed by his reasoning and information" (in Bliss, p. 137). In Portland, Maine, where young Ellen Harmon likely heard him twice in 1840 and 1842, one writer said he was "self-possessed and ready, distinct in his utterance. . . . He succeeds in chaining the attention of his auditory from an hour and a half to two hours" (in Bliss, p. 149).

After two disappointments when Christ did not appear, he wrote: "Although I have been twice disappointed, I am not yet cast down or discouraged. Although surrounded with enemies and scoffers, yet my mind is perfectly calm, and my hope in the coming of Christ is as strong as ever" (letter, Nov. 10, 1844 [in *Herald of the Midnight Cry*, p. 107]).

Ellen White devoted five chapters in *The Great Controversy* to William Miller and the Second Advent movement (GC 317-408). She had fond memories of Miller's 1842 visit to Portland, Maine, and recalled how he was "rightly called 'Father Miller,' for he had a watchful care over those who came under his ministrations, was affectionate in his manner, of a genial disposition and tender heart" (LS 27). She viewed his ministry and influence in a continuum with the Protestant Reformation and called him an "American reformer" (GC 317). She believed "angels of heaven were guiding his mind and opening the Scriptures to his understanding" (*ibid.* 321) and protected him in times of danger (*ibid.* 337). In April 1846 *Otis Nichols sent to Miller a copy of a broadside relating Ellen White's first vision. On the back of this broadside Nichols introduced White's experience and encouraged Miller to accept the genuineness of her gift. There is no record of a response from Miller (1Bio 74-77).

Miller went blind in 1848, and died in December 1849 still looking for the return of Christ. Ellen White wrote, of his grave in Low Hampton: "Angels watch the precious dust of this servant of God, and he will come forth at the sound of the last trump" (EW 258).

Further reading: S. Bliss, *Memoirs of William Miller* (Boston: J. V. Himes, 1853); E. N. Dick, *William Miller and the Advent Crisis*, with a foreword and historiographical essay by Gary Land (AUP, 1994); G. R. Knight, *Millennial Fever and the End of the World: A Study of Millerite Adventism* (PPPA, 1993); W. Miller, *Apology and Defense* (Boston: J. V. Himes, 1847); F. D. Nichol, *The Midnight Cry* (RHPA, 1944).

Paul A. Gordon

MILLS, GEORGE WASHINGTON (1842-1918) and **SARAH MARGARET (HATFIELD)** (1850-1910). Adventists from Healdsburg, California, converted through the influence of *J. N. Loughborough in 1868. The Millses became founding members of the Healdsburg Seventh-day Adventist Church, and George served for many years as head elder of that congregation. In 1894 Ellen White wrote to Mills asking him to sell her carriage in Healdsburg to raise funds for the developing mission work in *Australia (Lt 51a, 1894). Later Ellen White urged him to "make every effort possible to be in harmony with your brethren." Gossiping members had created disharmony in the church, and she appealed to the Millses to forgive those who had wronged them (Lt 23, 1901; cf. Lt 100, 1901).

Further reading: obit. RH, Mar. 31, 1910; obit. RH, June 20, 1918.

MOON, ALLEN (1845-1923). Educated in Quaker schools, Moon first joined the Methodists before converting to Adventism in 1871 in Minnesota. Ordained in 1880, he served as a pastor, Foreign Mission Board president (1890s), and conference president in Minnesota (1889-1890), Illinois (1901-1902), Northern Illinois (1902-1904), the Lake Union (1904-1914), and Massachusetts (1914-1915). Moon also directed the General

Conference Religious Liberty Department and pastored the Takoma Park, Maryland, church. Although widely known as "a man of sterling integrity," Moon received a letter from Ellen White in 1898 urging him to spend less on buildings in Battle Creek and send more money to "destitute fields," such as India and Australia (Lt 109, 1898).

Further reading: obit. NPUG, Dec. 20, 1923; obit. RH, Dec. 20, 1923; *SDA Encyclopedia* (1996), vol. 11, p. 120.

MORAN, FRANK B. (1866-1954). Physician. Converted to Adventism during the early 1890s while receiving treatments at the *Battle Creek Sanitarium. In 1894 he completed his medical education at the University of Michigan and married Adelaide Adams (1867-1954). The Morans relocated to Healdsburg, California, where they taught at *Healdsburg College, and soon afterward Dr. Moran became superintendent of the *St. Helena Sanitarium. In 1897 the Morans went as *medical missionaries on behalf of the St. Helena Sanitarium to open vegetarian restaurants and treatment rooms (small sanitariums) in San Francisco and later Los Angeles, California. In March 1901 while in Los Angeles Ellen White became ill and was treated by Moran (5Bio 58). In 1902 Moran planned to enlarge his small Los Angeles Sanitarium into a fully fledged medical facility, partly financed by non-Adventist companies, but Ellen White counseled against that idea (Lt 70, 1902; Ms 173, 1902), and the expansion never materialized. After a brief term of service on the staff of the *Battle Creek Sanitarium, Moran opened a medical practice in Dallas, Texas, where he practiced for nearly 50 years.

Further reading: obit. RH, Oct. 28, 1954; Frank B. Moran collection, CAR.

MORE (or MOORE), HANNAH (1808-1868). Early convert to Seventh-day Adventism

(1866). She was a much experienced missionary, teacher, and prodigious Bible student whose shabby treatment at Battle Creek and isolated death in northern Michigan occasioned some of Ellen White's most impassioned prose (1T 666-679; 2T 140-144). Born in Union, Connecticut, to a large farming family, More received an excellent education at Nichols Academy (now Nichols College) and Monson Academy. Known as a deep Bible student who had committed the entire New Testament to memory, she found employment in young adulthood as a schoolteacher in her native region. At age 31, moved by the plight of the Cherokee and Choctaw tribes, who had been forced by the U.S. government to relocate to present-day Oklahoma, Hannah applied to the American Board of Commissioners of Foreign Missions (ABCFM) for service among them, and arrived at Dwight Mission (near Vian, in present-day Oklahoma) in early 1841. As a teacher and preceptor for six years, she achieved fluency in both Native American languages, and formed deep bonds with her Native American pupils.

Following a two-year stint (1848-1850) as a schoolteacher in Connecticut and upstate New York, More sailed for West Africa in late 1850 under the sponsorship of the abolitionist American Missionary Association (AMA). Her six years in Sierra Leone as a teacher, preceptor, and preacher among the *Amistad* survivors brought her into close contact with native religions, Islam, and intense tribal warfare.

Returning to the United States in 1857, she again taught school, attended a course of lectures at Oberlin College, and eventually found employment as the principal of a female seminary in Maxville, Kentucky. Her profound abolitionism, however, required her to move north as the Civil War loomed. In 1862 she met Elder Stephen Haskell in her home region and received Adventist books and literature from him. Returning to West Africa as a missionary, she worked a variety of mission postings for four years, eventually reading herself into belief in Adventist doctrines and sending reports of her conversion and subsequent dismissal by her mission agency to the *Review and Herald.* When her health faltered in 1866, she returned to Boston, and was baptized in South Lancaster, Massachusetts.

In the spring of 1867 she traveled to Battle Creek, expecting to find employment and a place to live in the growing Adventist community. Arriving when Ellen and James White were away on a travel itinerary, she was unable to find either a job or a place to live among church members, some of whom apparently thought her "out of fashion." Denied a place in Battle Creek, she finally accepted the invitation of a mission colleague from Africa to live with his family in northwestern Michigan.

Her correspondence with the Whites through late 1867 and early 1868 was marked by pledges from the Whites to help her relocate in Battle Creek after the winter. In February 1868 More grew ill, probably from congestive heart failure and associated respiratory difficulties, and died on March 2, 1868. Notice of her death was sent to the *Review and Herald* by her former mission colleague, with the expectation that she would be reinterred at Battle Creek (RH, Mar. 24, 1868). She remains in her resting place in Leland, Michigan, to this day.

Ellen White's sharply worded condemnation of More's treatment by the church members at Battle Creek contains some of her most confrontational language. Hannah More "died a martyr to the selfishness of a people who profess to be seeking for glory, honor, immortality, and eternal life," she wrote (2T 332). Years later, as the young denomination was

sending its first official foreign missionary, Ellen White lamented, "Oh, how much we need our Hannah More to aid us at this time in reaching other nations" (3T 407).

Further reading: Bill Knott, "A Winter's Tale," AR, Jan. 22, 1998; W. M. ("Bill") Knott, "Foot Soldier of the Empire: Hannah More and the Politics of Service" (Ph.D. diss., George Washington University, 2006).

Bill Knott

MORRISON, CHARLIE and **EMMA (McCANN)** Emma was Ellen White's niece, the daughter of her sister Harriet (Harmon) McCann. Emma became Charlie Morrison's second wife after the death of his first wife, Emma's sister, Mary McCann. In 1879 Ellen White appealed to Charlie and Emma to give their hearts to Christ (Lt 26, 1879) and in 1890 visited them in their home in Danvers, Massachusetts (Ms 51, 1890).

MORRISON, JAMES H. (1841-1918). Adventist minister and administrator. Born in Pennsylvania, Morrison was raised in Iowa and attended the Baptist college at Pella, Iowa. In 1862 he became a Seventh-day Adventist and then a minister. He was ordained in 1872. From 1886 to 1892 he served as president of the Iowa Conference. At the *General Conference session of 1888 Morrison opposed the message of *righteousness by faith as presented by *A. T. Jones and *E. J. Waggoner. In 1889 Ellen White pleaded with him to "let go [of] your prejudice and . . . come to the light" (Lt 49, 1889, in 1888 Materials 274). Because of Morrison's continuing opposition, she declined his invitation to attend the Iowa Conference camp meeting, explaining, "I do not think we would labor in harmony" (*ibid.*). Three years later she again appealed to him to "come to the light," "fully acknowledge the light, rejoice in the light, and not make half way work with the matter in order to preserve your dignity" (Lt 47, 1892, in 1888 Materials 1085).

Further reading: R. A. Underwood, "Another Pioneer Fallen," RH, Dec. 26, 1918; G. R. Knight, *Angry Saints* (RHPA, 1989), pp. 34, 107, 108.

MORSE, GEORGE WARREN (1847-1929). Publishing worker; son of *Washington and Olive Morse. Born in Vermont, Morse moved with his family to Minnesota in 1855. In 1868 he married Eliza Jane Baker (1849-1946) and became involved in the newspaper business. From 1885 to 1889 he worked at the *Review and Herald in Battle Creek, then moved to Toronto, Canada, to head its branch office. In 1898 the Morses went to Australia to assist with the health work and the *Echo Publishing Company. While in Australia, Ellen White counseled him against self-confidence and not to "suppose" that he had "qualifications for a certain position and work" (Lt 152, 1899). In 1901 Morse returned to Battle Creek, where he became head elder of the *Battle Creek Tabernacle. In 1907 Morse and his wife retired to Florida.

Further reading: obit. RH, Oct. 31, 1929.

MORSE, JOHN F. (1872-1935). Physician and surgeon, son of Washington Morse and brother of George Warren Morse. In 1889 Morse began the nurses' training course at the *Battle Creek Sanitarium. He later studied medicine, received the M.D. degree in 1899, and became an assistant surgeon at the Battle Creek Sanitarium. Ellen White twice urged him to connect with the recently opened *Loma Linda Sanitarium and get away from the *pantheism that was being taught in Battle Creek (Lts 247, 277, 1905; Lt 194, 1906). Morse married Jean H. Whitney in 1906 and left the Battle Creek Sanitarium in 1910 to go

to Scotland to receive further medical training.

Further reading: obit. RH, Sept. 12, 1935.

MORSE, WASHINGTON (1816-1909) and **OLIVE** (1818-1901). Adventist ministerial couple from Vermont; parents of George Warren Morse and John F. Morse. Raised a Methodist, W. Morse embraced the Millerite (see *disappointments, Millerite) message only to become profoundly "bewildered" when Christ did not come. Through the encouragement of Ellen Harmon in the spring of 1845, this modern-day Jonah, as she described Morse, shed his disappointment and "gathered up the rays of precious light that God had given His people" (LS 77, 78). In 1849, in Corinth, Vermont, the Morses began observing the seventh-day Sabbath. In 1852, at the urging of James White, Morse began to preach the Sabbatarian Adventist message, and was ordained. However, some misconduct led to his leaving Vermont in 1855 and then being dropped from membership (RH, July 24, 1856). He moved to Illinois and then to Minnesota, where in 1859 he wrote a letter to the *Review and Herald*, asking forgiveness and requesting that his membership be reinstated (RH, Jan. 27, 1859). At the organization of the Minnesota Conference in 1863 he was elected its first president. Elder Morse retired from ministry in 1865, although he continued to *colporteur and do other evangelistic work until his death. About 1896 the Morses moved to Canada to be near their children. After Olive's death in 1901, he moved to Florida, where he died.

Further reading: "Decease of a Pioneer," RH, May 7, 1901; 1Bio 84-86; *SDA Encyclopedia* (1996), vol. 11, p. 123.

MORTENSON, MARY CAROLINE (later **MARY CAROLINE [MORTENSON] TRIPP, MARY CAROLINE [MORTENSON] ARMITAGE)**

(1859-1950). Missionary to Africa. Born in Denmark, Mary emigrated with her parents to Minnesota in 1865. She worked as a Bible instructor before attending *Battle Creek College. In 1891 the widowed *W. C. White employed her as a guardian to his two daughters, Ella and Mabel, while he and his mother accepted an appointment to Australia. Not sure how long he would stay, he thought best for the girls to remain in Battle Creek until he could either return or establish a home in Australia.

In 1895, when W. C. White became engaged to May Lacey (see *Ethel May [Lacey] White), he began arranging to bring Ella and Mabel to Australia. The initial plan, suggested by Ellen White, was to bring Mary Mortenson also, to continue as the girls' custodian so that May Lacey White would be free to accompany her husband in his frequent travels (Lt 145, 1895). However, when the Whites learned from Ella through *O. A. Olsen that Mary Mortenson, whom the girls loved very much, had entertained the hope of becoming their stepmother, Ellen concluded that to bring Mary Mortenson to Australia would not be wise.

Shortly after Ella and Mabel White left Battle Creek for Australia, Olsen, then General Conference president, received a visit from George Byron Tripp, seeking counsel. Tripp, former president of the West Virginia Conference, was a widower under appointment to mission service in Africa. Perplexed about caring for his 9-year-old son, he became acutely conscious of his need of a wife to go with him. He had known Mary Mortenson in a casual way for many years (they were both from Minnesota), and wondered if Olsen thought it would be wise for him to talk to her about marriage. Olsen gave Mary a high recommendation, Tripp proposed, and in a few days they were married and left for Africa,

where Tripp became the founding director of Solusi Mission.

Three years later, in the winter of 1898, overwork and a malaria epidemic took the lives of four of the missionaries, including G. B. Tripp, his son George M. Tripp, and the wife of F. B. Armitage (V. Robinson, *Solusi Story* [RHPA, 1979], pp. 64-66). In 1899 the widow Mary Mortenson-Tripp and the widower F. B. Armitage were married. They worked in Africa for 26 more years, founding the Lower Gwelo Mission and serving at the Maranatha Mission until Mary's health failed in 1925. After recuperation, they did ministerial work in California for another eight years.

Further reading: obit. RH, June 1, 1950; obit. RH, Apr. 24, 1952; W. H. Anderson, *On the Trail of Livingstone* (PPPA, 1919), pp. 8 (portrait), 125-136.

Jerry Moon

MORTON, ELIZA HAPPY (1852-1916). Educator, author, and friend of Ellen White. Morton began her career as a public school teacher in Maine. From 1880 to 1883 she served as head of the normal and commercial departments at *Battle Creek College. From 1893 to 1910 she was secretary and treasurer of the Maine Conference and Missionary Tract Society. She authored many books of poetry. Morton kept in close contact with Ellen White during her lifetime exchanging frequent letters with *W. C. White. Ellen White wrote several letters to her. She expressed sympathy for the death of Morton's mother (Lt 98, 1903) and later invited Morton to meet her at the General Conference session of 1909 in Washington, D.C. (Lt 70, 1909).

Further reading: W. O. Howe and Jennie R. Bates, "Life Sketch of Eliza H. Morton," RH, Oct. 5, 1916; *SDA Encyclopedia* (1996), vol. 11, p. 124.

NELSON, HELGE T. Adventist from Michigan who claimed the prophetic gift and to be the successor to Ellen White. After meeting *Fannie Bolton in 1900, Nelson believed himself to be the man she had seen in a vision and who would bring up some supposed inconsistencies in Ellen White's life. In March 1901 Nelson traveled to see Ellen White at her home in California. While visiting with Ellen White, he informed her that she "had been appointed by God to occupy the position occupied by Moses, and that he, Nelson, was to occupy the position of Joshua" (Ms 21, 1901, in 1SM 43, 44). Then he told her that he had a message for her, that she had mistreated her workers. Ellen White replied that he had misinterpreted the Scriptures and that anyone in her family would know that the testimony he gave concerning the treatment of her workers was entirely false (Ms 30, 1901). "I feel very sorry for this poor brother," she wrote in her diary, "for he is certainly not in his right mind" (Ms 21, 1901).

Later that year, during the General Conference session in Battle Creek, Nelson insisted that he be given a hearing by the General Conference. When this was denied, he met with Ellen White and the General Conference leaders. During this interview Ellen White met the false claims squarely and stated, "God has not given Brother Nelson the work of acting as Joshua in connection with His people. . . . I know that God never gave mortal man such a message as that which Brother Nelson has borne concerning his brethren" (RH, July 30, 1901; cf. 5Bio 99). However, things did not end there, and Ellen White met Nelson again at the General Conference session of 1903 in a rather dramatic way. As she was stepping down from the platform after speaking to the conference, Nelson rushed to the front and attempted to assault her. People in the audience rescued her, and Nelson was hustled to the police station (cf. 5Bio 254, 255). Nine years later Nelson wrote an open letter calling for Ellen White to repent of her "spiritual blood-poisoning" ("An Open Letter to Mrs. Ellen G. White From Helge T. Nelson" [n.p., 1912], p. 5). He later republished all of his pamphlets attacking Ellen White in the book *Answer to President Wilson's Speech Before the Manhatten Club in New York on the Evening of November 4, 1915, With Two Letters to Mrs. Ellen G. White* (Chicago: [by the author], 1917).

NELSON, MARY J. Cook and housekeeper for Ellen White from 1901 to 1905 (5Bio 132). White described Nelson as "an excellent cook" who "takes careful charge of everything in the house and is very neat and orderly" (Lt 133, 1902). In March 1905 Nelson left Ellen White's employment to complete her nurses' training (Lt 109, 1905). Many years later, in 1939, Nelson reported to *Arthur White her thoughts on beginning employment with Ellen White in 1901. Nelson was then in her 20s and White was in her mid-70s. As Nelson "crossed the continent to enter Mrs. White's employ, she contemplated, 'I am going to the home of the prophet. How will it be?' The evening of the first day Mrs. White and the new housekeeper were thrown together for a time, and after quite a silence, Mrs. White spoke, pausing between each sentence: 'Sister Nelson, you have come into my home. You are to be a member of my family. You may see some things in me that you do not approve of. You may see things in my son Willie you do not approve of. I may make mistakes, and my son Willie may make mistakes. I may be lost at last, and my son Willie may be lost. But the dear Lord has a remnant people that will be saved and go through to the Kingdom, and it remains with each of us as individuals whether or not we will be one of that number' "

(A. L. White, *Ellen G. White: Messenger to the Remnant,* rev. ed. [EGWE, 1965], p. 127).

NICHOL, FRANCIS DAVID (1897-1966). Editor, author, and arguably the leading twentieth-century apologist for Adventism and the prophetic ministry of Ellen White. An Australian by birth, Nichol's parents became Seventh-day Adventists after reading, in a discarded copy of the *Review and Herald,* an article written by Ellen White. In 1905 the Nichols emigrated to Loma Linda, California, and in 1920 Nichol graduated from *Pacific Union College. The following year he joined the editorial staff of *Signs of the Times,* and in 1927 became associate editor of the *Review and Herald.* He remained at the *Review* for 39 years, as associate editor and then editor, until his death in 1966. Concurrent with his years as an associate editor of the *Review and Herald,* he also edited *Life and Health* magazine, the church's health evangelism journal. Nichol was also a prolific author of important apologetic works, including *Answers to Objections* (1932/1952), and *The Midnight Cry* (1944). His most lasting editorial achievement came with his service as general editor of the monumental *Seventh-day Adventist Bible Commentary* (1953-1957). Nichol was a lifelong defender of the continuing, prophetic, authoritative ministry of Ellen White for the Seventh-day Adventist Church. For 15 years he was member of the *Ellen G. White Estate Board of Trustees, the last three years of his life serving as board chair. In 1951 he authored an exhaustive and often trenchant defense entitled *Ellen G. White and Her Critics: An Answer to the Major Charges That Critics Have Brought Against Mrs. Ellen G. White* (RHPA, 1951). Later, he wrote *Why I Believe in Mrs. E. G. White* (RHPA, 1964). He concluded that more inspirational work by printing a personal oral testimony he had prepared at the time

of writing *Ellen G. White and Her Critics* more than a dozen years before. It read, in part: "I end this work fully and irrevocably persuaded in my mind and heart that Mrs. White was what she claimed to be, a humble handmaiden of God, to whom He gave revelations, authoritative and unique, to guide and direct the Advent people in these last days" (*Why I Believe in Mrs. E. G. White,* p. 128).

Further reading: obit. RH, June 10, 1966; K. H. Wood, "A Tribute to Francis David Nichol," RH, June 10, 1966; M. G. Wood and K. H. Wood, *His Initials Were F.D.N.: A Life Story of Elder F. D. Nichol, for Twenty-one Years Editor of the* Review and Herald (RHPA, 1967).

Ronald A. Knott

NICHOLS, HENRY. Early Sabbatarian Adventist from Massachusetts; son of *Otis and Mary Nichols. As a youth Nichols sometimes traveled with James and Ellen White and assisted with the publication of *Present Truth* in Paris, Maine. Their appreciation for him was such that they gave his name to their eldest son, *Henry Nichols White. By 1860, however, Nichols had moved to Waukon, Iowa, where he fell under the influence of some disaffected members who expressed doubts in the visions of Ellen White. As a result he lost his faith in the Adventist message (Lts 7, 8, 1860). In 1903 Nichols again accepted the Sabbath. In response to a letter he wrote to Ellen White, she expressed her excitement and reminisced about some of the good times she and her husband, James, had had at his parents' home (Lt 99, 1903).

HENRY NICHOLS

NICHOLS, OTIS (1798-1876) and **MARY** (1799-1868). Sabbatarian Adventist pioneers from Dorchester, Massachusetts, who accepted the Millerite message in 1843. They were among the earliest Adventists to accept the seventh-day Sabbath from Joseph Bates, as well as the genuineness of Ellen White's visions. Otis Nichols' acceptance of Ellen White's gift led him to write a letter to William Miller in April 1846 encouraging him also to consider her gift (1Bio 74-77). During White's first years of ministry (1845-1850) she frequently stayed at the Nichols home (2SG 75). "They [the Nicholses] were ever ready with words of encouragement to comfort me when in trial," wrote Ellen White, "and often their prayers ascended to heaven in my behalf" (LS 68).

OTIS NICHOLS

The Nicholses' generosity also provided for many of the Whites' expenses and financial support in the first years of their marriage (cf. CET 116; 2SG 91, 108; RH, Apr. 21, 1868). Otis was a lithographer and produced (1850) the earliest prophetic charts used by Sabbatarian Adventist preachers after the disappointment. Ellen White later re-marked that "God was in the publishment [sic]

MARY NICHOLS

of the chart by Brother Nichols" (Ms 1, 1853, in 13MR 359). Ellen White had some of her earliest visions in the Nichols home. His account of her longest recorded vision—nearly four hours—can be found in 2SG 77-79. It was also in his home in 1848 that she received the vision that led to the beginning of the denomination's publishing work (Ms 5, 1850).

In 1859 Ellen White wrote to the Nicholses in preparation for her autobiographical account of her ministry (2SG) and asked them to "write out the particular events that occurred under his observation" (Lt 1a, 1859). Her last visit to the Nicholses was in 1874, when she noted that although Otis had aged he still talked "intelligently" (Lt 51, 1874).

Further reading: obit. RH, Feb. 11, 1868; *SDA Encyclopedia* (1996), vol. 11, p. 179.

NICOLA, BEN EUGENE (1865-1943). Adventist minister, educator, and physician; son of Zalmon and Mary Nicola, born in Washington County, Iowa. In 1894 Nicola married Hattie M. Case (1868-1927) and soon afterward began pastoral ministry in Iowa. In 1899 he was ordained to the ministry and served briefly on the faculty of *Union College. He was then invited to serve as president of Oakwood Junior College (see *Oakwood Industrial School) (1899-1904). Ellen White warned that his qualifications were not what they should be to continue in that capacity and advised him to leave Oakwood immediately (Lt 337, 1904). Nicola left that position and worked as principal of Battle Creek Academy. He soon afterward began studying medicine and graduated in 1910. He eventually served on the medical staffs of a number of Adventist sanitariums.

Further reading: obit. RH, Mar. 23, 1944.

NICOLA, C. C. (d. 1911) and **MARY (BYINGTON)** (1869-1935). Adventist physicians; Mary was the granddaughter of *John Byington. The Nicolas were married in July 1899 and soon afterward founded the *New England Sanitarium. On January 1, 1905, after part of the New England Sanitarium burned down (see RH, Jan. 12, 1905), Ellen White encouraged them to look upon this calamity as a blessing in disguise and counseled them to rebuild the sanitarium as soon as possible (Lt 23, 1905). She later wrote a series of letters urging them to sever their ties with Dr. *J. H. Kellogg and others in Battle Creek who were at the time breaking away from the church (Lts 150, 164, 174, 1906). In 1907 C. C. Nicola resigned his position as superintendent of the New England Sanitarium for health reasons (RH, Apr. 18, 1907). After expressing her concern for C. C.'s health in a letter to Mary (Lt 124, 1907), Ellen White invited them to join the medical staff of the *Loma Linda Sanitarium (Lts 220, 221, 242, 1907). Instead, the Nicolas worked briefly at the *Hinsdale Sanitarium in Chicago, where Kellogg exercised much influence. "I want you to understand that you are both in positive danger," she wrote (LLM 277). Ellen White repeated her counsels to them not to go to Battle Creek, but to instead come to Loma Linda. "You do not understand how the enemy is working to place you in opposition to the truth and the work of God" (*ibid.* 276). After C. C.'s health returned, the Nicolas returned to New England, where they worked at a private sanitarium in Attleboro, Massachusetts. In 1911 C. C. Nicola was lost overboard from a steamship while returning from the Bermuda Islands (RH, Mar. 9, 1911). When Ellen White heard the news, she wrote to Mary expressing her condolences (Lt 110, 1911).

Michael W. Campbell

NICOLA, LEROY THOMAS (1856-1940). Colporteur, minister, and secretary of the *General Conference. Born in Pilotsburg, Iowa, he attended *Battle Creek College during its inaugural year (1874). He interrupted his studies because of an urgent need of pastors in Iowa and graduated in 1880. He subsequently resumed ministry, married Sylvia Hillis (1858-1918) in 1881, and was ordained five years

later. At the *General Conference session of 1888 he was "urgently requested" by his conference president, *J. H. Morrison, to assist him in a public rebuttal against *E. J. Waggoner and *A. T. Jones. Nicola later apologized to Ellen White for the position he had taken: "I permitted my sympathies to control my actions, and I did not get the good from the meeting that I should have received" (L. T. Nicola to EGW, Mar. 24, 1893). Ellen White responded, "I freely forgive you" (Lt 69, 1893, in 1888 Materials 1192), and acknowledged that Nicola had written "a most thorough confession of the part he acted in Minneapolis" (Ms 80, 1893, in 4Bio 86). From 1893 to 1897 he served as secretary of the General Conference. He was later placed in charge of the International Tract Society in New York City (1898-1901) and served as a pastor in New York, Massachusetts, and Michigan. In 1920 he returned to Battle Creek to care for his aging parents. While there, he preserved a number of Adventist historical items of ongoing value to the church. He is buried in *Oak Hill Cemetery.

Further reading: obit. RH, Feb. 8, 1940; *SDA Encyclopedia* (1996), vol. 11, p. 180.

Michael Campbell

NIX, JAMES R. (1947-   ). Director of the Ellen G. White Estate since 2000. Nix graduated from Loma Linda University, Riverside, California (now La Sierra University) in 1969. While a college student he took a particular interest in collecting early Adventist books and interviewing people who remembered Ellen White. Following graduation from the Theological Seminary at Andrews University, Loma Linda University (LLU) hired Nix in 1972 to develop a Heritage Room, of which he became director in 1974. Two years later he helped open a White Estate Research Center there, which was granted branch office status in 1985. In 1981 Nix cofounded Adventist Historic Properties, Inc., now known as Adventist Heritage Ministry. He served four years as its president, and since 1997 has been its board chair. He wrote the *Master Plan* for Historic Adventist Village in Battle Creek, Michigan, and was directly involved with the purchase of the William Miller and Hiram Edson farms in New York State, plus the Joseph Bates boyhood home in Massachusetts. Earlier he served nine years on the Elmshaven Advisory Committee. Nix also has served as program chair for several heritage-related church weekends, the largest of which was the one held at the William Miller farm over the weekend of October 22, 1994. For many years he has led Adventist heritage tours in New England and elsewhere. Nix transferred to the main office of the Ellen G. White Estate in 1993 as an associate director, became vice director in 1995, and director in 2000. Ordained in 1994, Nix has master's degrees in divinity and library science.

During his career Nix served 10 years as managing editor of *Adventist Heritage* magazine and five years as managing editor of the *Seventh-day Adventist Periodical Index*. Between 1984 and 1990 he wrote 52 articles for the Adventist Scrapbook column in the *Adventist Review*. In 1994 he wrote a weekly column for the *Adventist Review* entitled The Way It Was. Nix founded *Research Center News Notes* for Ellen White Research Center directors and division Spirit of Prophecy coordinators in 1979; he served as its editor from 1979 to 1993. In 1985 he founded *AHM Bulletin* for Adventist Heritage Ministry, serving as its editor from 1985 to 1993. From 1993 to 2002 Nix edited the annual *Spirit of Prophecy Day Sermon*. Additionally, he has written a number of articles that have appeared in various Adventist periodicals and has authored or contributed to several books, including *Early*

Advent Singing, Laughter and Tears of the Pioneers, and *In the Footsteps of the Pioneers.*

As director of the White Estate, Nix has fostered the development of materials to make Ellen White better known, especially to young people and for those worldwide where Ellen White's books are not readily available. At his encouragement, an associate director was hired by the White Estate specifically to work with young people. Likewise, Nix also was a strong supporter of the publication of *Messiah*, an adaptation of *The Desire of Ages*. In an effort to provide Ellen White materials in English to more Adventist pastors and teachers worldwide, Nix arranged for White Estate CD-ROM products to be made available to those church employees at greatly reduced prices adjusted to their local wages. He also strongly supported the General Conference's Connecting With Jesus project for the global distribution of 10 Ellen White books to church members who otherwise do not have ready access to them. Nix has also fostered more active involvement of the White Estate Board of Trustees in the selection of Ellen White Research Center directors worldwide, plus formalized guidelines for those who prepare future Ellen White book compilations. He has also helped set up Ellen White-SDA Research Centers in France, Jamaica, Kenya, Russia, Peru, and at Southwestern Adventist University in Texas.

NOBBS, ALFRED (1847-1906). Adventist minister on Norfolk Island, South Pacific, of whom Ellen White inquired about her nephew and his wife, *Stephen and Vina Belden, who also worked on Norfolk Island (Lt 75, 1896; cf. Lts 103, 181, 1901). Nobbs and his wife, Emily, were among the first converts to Adventism on Norfolk Island and served as pastor of the church there from 1895 to 1906.

Both Nobbs and Belden died in 1906 and were buried on Norfolk Island.

Further reading: obit. UCR, Dec. 3, 1906.

NORMAN, HENRY. Purported sea captain who became an Adventist after meeting Adventist missionary F. H. Westphal on his way to the 1899 General Conference session. At that session an appeal was made for mission funds for the Adventist work in Australia, to which "Captain" Norman responded with a pledge of a large sum of money (GCDB Mar. 7, 1899). Ellen White wrote him a letter thanking him for his donation (Lt 83, 1899; 4Bio 417). Shortly thereafter Norman began courting a church employee. She became his fiancé and lent him $300, which he promised to repay upon his return. But he defaulted, never to be seen or heard from again (4Bio 418). "It is a strange thing that occurred in reference to Captain Norman," wrote Ellen White. "I understand all that business of his liberal donations is a fraud. . . . We did hope for donations to help us out of our difficulties, but if we cannot obtain the means in that way, the Lord can open up some other way to help us" (Lt 243, 1899, in 4Bio 417; see also Lt 88, 1899).

Further reading: 4Bio 417-419.

OAKS-PRESTON, RACHEL (HARRIS) (1809-1868). Best known for bringing the Sabbath to Adventists in Washington, New Hampshire, and particularly to *Frederick Wheeler, who is believed to be the first Sabbathkeeping Adventist minister in North America.

Rachel was born to Sylvanus and Nancy Harris on February 22, 1809, in Vernon Township, Windham County, Vermont. She joined the Methodist Church at the age of 17 (First Verona Seventh Day Baptist Church records, Jan. 20, 1838; Seventh Day Baptist Church Historical Records, Janesville,

Wisconsin). In 1824 she married Amory Oaks in Vernon, Vermont. Rachel gave birth to their only child, Rachel Delight, on August 9, 1825 (town records for Vernon, Vermont, vol. 4, pp. 485, 507). Amory died April 8, 1835, after bringing his wife and daughter to Verona, New York (Surrogate Court Minutes and Orders, 1830-1836, pp. 362, 363, Oneida County, New York). Rachel joined the Seventh Day Baptist Church in the same year her husband died. Verona Seventh Day Baptist Church records refer to her as a widow, and the church took care to protect her from unscrupulous individuals. She was remembered in Verona as a schoolteacher with some property.

During the early 1840s Rachel's daughter, Delight, was offered a teaching job in Washington, New Hampshire. Both mother and daughter moved there and attended the Christian church, which had adopted the Millerite Adventist view of the Second Coming. Faithful to share her Seventh Day Baptist beliefs, Rachel distributed Sabbath tracts and sought opportunities to speak about the Sabbath to the Advent believers in Washington, New Hampshire. Most showed little interest. She was, though, successful in convincing Wheeler, the Adventist minister, who lived in Hillsborough, just south of Washington. Later in life, when he lived in New York State, Wheeler told a neighbor, F. W. Bartle, how it happened. Bartle recalled: "He [Wheeler] told me that they had held a quarterly meeting in the church, celebrating the Lord's supper. In his sermon about the service he made the remark that all persons confessing communion with Christ in such a service should be ready to follow Him, and obey God and keep His commandments in all things. Later, he said, he met Mrs. Preston [Rachel Oaks Preston], who reminded him of his remarks about the meaning of communion with Christ. 'I came near getting up in the meeting at that point,' she told him, 'and saying something.' 'What was it you had in mind to say?' he asked her. 'I wanted to tell you that you would better set that communion table back and put the cloth over it, until you begin to keep the commandments of God.' Elder Wheeler told me that these words cut him deeper than anything that he had ever had spoken to him. He thought it over, and soon he began to keep the Sabbath" (Spicer).

It is presumed that Rachel became an Advent believer in 1845. During that year she sent a letter to the Seventh Day Baptist church in Verona, New York, requesting that she be removed from membership. Also in Washington, New Hampshire, Rachael married Nathan T. Preston. They were living there as late as 1856.

It seems that the critical spirit against James and Ellen White that was particularly inspired by *Worcester Ball influenced Rachel. She and her second husband moved to her native town of Vernon, Vermont, where they both lived for the remainder of their lives.

Rachel Oaks Preston did not actually become a Seventh-day Adventist until the last year of her life. Her obituary notice explained: "Hearing much said against Bro. and Sr. White, at different times, by individuals who were disaffected in consequence of reproof which they needed, and who sought to relieve their minds by poisoning others [possibly a reference to *Stephen Smith and/or Worcester Ball], she became cold in religion, and prejudiced to some extent against the Testimonies, having never seen Bro. and Sr. White" (Haskell). Toward the end of October 1867 Ellen White published her *Testimony* No. 13 (now in 1T 569-629). This tract dealt largely with the hard spirit that had been manifested against James White during his illness (*ibid.* 572). It also included

a testimony of reproof by Ellen White for her husband on the subject (*ibid.* 612-614). James White's sorrow for his failings was clearly evident (*ibid.* 583, 606, 614). After reading *Testimony* No. 13, which an unknown friend sent her, Rachel Preston changed her mind about James and Ellen White. Shortly before her death she also heard of the 1867 Christmastime revival in Washington, New Hampshire, and rejoiced. She died on February 1, 1868.

Further reading: Merlin D. Burt, *Adventist Pioneer Places: New York and New England* (RHPA, 2011); W. A. Spicer, "Our First Minister," RH, Feb. 15, 1940; S. N. Haskell, "Obituary Notices," RH, Mar. 3, 1868.

Merlin D. Burt

O'KAVANAGH, M.M.J. Woman in Australia who inquired of Ellen White regarding the Adventist stand on the use of alcohol and tobacco. In her reply Ellen White invited O'Kavanagh to attend her lectures on temperance at the Brighton camp meeting (Lts 99, 99a, 1894). Of interest in this letter is Ellen White's definition of vegetarianism: "All [Adventists] are vegetarians, many abstaining wholly from the use of flesh food, while others use it in only the most moderate degree" (Lt 99, 1894, in 4Bio 119). Mrs. O'Kavanagh is likely the Catholic woman who pleaded with Ellen White during the Brighton camp meeting not to allow "the selfishness of taking the lives of animals to gratify a perverted taste." This plea had a great impact on Ellen White, who determined to "no longer patronize the butchers" and to "not have the flesh of corpses on my table" (Lt 73a, 1896, in Nichol, p. 389). From that moment on, Ellen White abstained completely from eating meat.

Further reading: 4Bio 113-124; R. W. Coon, *Ellen White and Vegetarianism* (PPPA, 1986); F. D. Nichol, *Ellen G. White and Her Critics* (RHPA, 1951), pp. 388, 389.

OLSEN, OLE ANDRES (1845-1915). Minister and administrator. Born in Skogan, Norway,

OLE A. OLSEN

Olsen immigrated with his parents to Wisconsin in 1850, where four years later the family became Sabbatarian Adventists. Olsen was baptized in 1858. His education included two winter sessions at Milton Academy (a school founded by *Seventh Day Baptists in Milton, Wisconsin) and a year at Battle Creek College. In 1869 the Wisconsin Conference issued him a ministerial license, and he began working among the growing Scandinavian immigrant population. He was ordained in 1873. He served as president of the Wisconsin (1874-1876; 1880-1881), Dakota (1882-1883), Minnesota (1883-1885), and Iowa (1884-1885) conferences. When the Adventist message entered the Scandinavian countries, the General Conference sent him in 1886 to lead the church there.

When in 1888 *George I. Butler was not reelected as General Conference president, Ellen White suggested Olsen's name for the position. She had spent time with him during her visit to Europe (1885-1887) and was favorably impressed with his spirituality and leadership skills. Also, having not been present at the *General Conference session of 1888 in Minneapolis, he was not identified with either side of the controversy. In addition, Butler was acquainted with Olsen's service as conference president, and thus Olsen was acceptable to Butler's supporters. When Olsen returned to the United States five months later to assume the presidency, he sought to mollify the divisions caused by the controversy in Minneapolis. Nominally supportive of the message of *righteousness by faith, he did not make it his first priority. He supported the growth of schools and other institutions, and presided over the organization of the Australasian Union Conference during his visit to that country in 1894.

Early in Olsen's presidency Ellen White reproved him for working "on the high pressure plan," carrying too many responsibilities, neglecting rest, and "presumptuously" imperiling his health (1888 Materials 677). But her severest criticism was directed at Olsen's willingness to sacrifice principle in order to get along with diverse elements in the church. She said Olsen acted as did the biblical Aaron in yielding to the influence of two men who were particularly averse to Ellen White's counsel: *A. R. Henry and *Harmon Lindsay (1888 Materials 1608). Henry, a former cattle dealer and bank president, joined the Review and Herald in 1882. He turned the publishing house around financially, but sometimes through questionable business practices. Developing a banking system at the Review for both individuals and denominational institutions, he was accused of borrowing church funds to finance personal projects, including a livery stable, lumber and coal yards, and rental properties. His personality was abrasive and domineering. Ellen White told her son Edson that "Brother Olsen has made him [A. R. Henry] his right-hand man" (Lt 152, 1896, in 4Bio 255). To Olsen himself she said he was "being bound hand and foot" and "tamely submitting to it" (Lt 87a, 1896, in 4Bio 255). Lindsay had been a part of the General Conference since 1874, serving as its treasurer as well as treasurer of the Review and Herald and as president of the General Conference Association, the legal entity that held title to denominational property.

As members deposited money with the church to earn interest, the denomination used the lent funds to expand its institutions more rapidly than it should have. An economic downturn in the United States in the 1890s put financial pressure on the growing church, and offerings declined. At the same time Dr. J. H. Kellogg, head of the Adventist health institutions, began numerous expensive projects that further strained the church's resources. By the end of 1898 the General Conference had only $61.20 in cash and owed thousands of dollars.

Insecure about his own financial judgment, Olsen relied upon both Henry and Lindsay, though he was aware of their often shady practices. Ellen White strongly urged him to replace them (18MR 274; 1888 Materials 1421, 1578), but he did not do so until near the end of 1895. Even then he praised the two men as they departed. Olsen also found himself unable to object to Kellogg's proposals for expansion and other projects.

As did many early denominational leaders, Olsen worked himself into exhaustion, which led to bouts of depression. Ellen White wrote to him about his danger (1888 Materials 677), but he was too busy to pay much attention at first. When he did not immediately respond to her advice, some began to spread a rumor that Olsen did not believe in her as a prophet. Eventually he wrote an article assuring the church membership that he did believe in and accept her authority (RH, Jan. 26, 1897).

After leaving the General Conference presidency in 1897, he worked in South Africa, Europe, and Australia (1905-1909). In 1909 the church elected him secretary of the North American Foreign Department and added the position of North American Division vice president in 1913.

Further reading: obit. RH, Feb. 4, 1915; D. A. Ochs and G. L. Ochs, *The Past and the Presidents: Biographies of the General Conference Presidents* (SPA, 1974), pp. 75-87; R. W. Schwarz and F. Greenleaf, *Light Bearers: A*

History of the Seventh-day Adventist Church, rev. ed. (PPPA, 2000), pp. 246-249; *SDA Encyclopedia* (1996), vol. 11, pp. 243, 244.

Gerald Wheeler

OLSON, ROBERT WESLEY (1920-   ). Director of the Ellen G. White Estate from 1978 to 1990. Born the son of two Adventist educators, Olson attributed his desire to work for the Adventist denomination and his love for Ellen White to their influence upon his life. He later attended Adventist schools and graduated from Pacific Union College in 1943. Although he had trained to become a Bible teacher, he was soon persuaded that he could be a more effective educator after some experience as a minister. For this reason he pastored in several districts in central California. In 1946 he became youth pastor at the Loma Linda University church, where he also was an adjunct member of the religion faculty. In 1954 he become associate religion professor at Washington Missionary College, where he taught the Spirit of Prophecy course. As part of the school's affiliation with Newbold College, Olson taught at Newbold briefly, and also served as president of the college (1956-1960). In 1961 he accepted a call to chair the Division of Religion at Pacific Union College. While there he pursued a Ph.D. degree at Baylor University, and graduated in 1972 from their affiliated campus at Southwestern Baptist Theological Seminary with a dissertation entitled "Southern Baptists' Reactions to Millerism."

In 1974 he became associate secretary of the Ellen G. White Estate. *Arthur L. White utilized Olson's writing expertise to compile and write many position papers for the White Estate. Olson was elected secretary of the White Estate in 1978 upon the resignation and semiretirement of his predecessor, Arthur L. White, who wished to give his full time to the writing of the Ellen White biography volumes. Olson's appointment marked the first time since the appointment of *C. C. Crisler more than 60 years earlier that the secretary was not a member of the White family. Olson's biblical and theological training proved to be a valuable asset to the White Estate and the church. During the first decade of his term, critics mounted major challenges against the doctrine of the pre-Advent judgment and against Ellen White for literary borrowing. By means of public forums, articles, and numerous publications, Olson sought to bring the church to a better understanding of inspiration and revelation. He began holding annual consultations between board members of the Ellen G. White Estate and General Conference leaders, during which they invited scholars to discuss major historical and theological issues. Under his keen administrative eye the White Estate staff grew larger and more diverse. New research centers opened up around the world during his tenure. Some of his significant publications include *The Crisis Ahead* (1970, 2000), *How* The Desire of Ages *Was Written* (1979), *One Hundred and One Questions on the Sanctuary and on Ellen White* (1981), *The "Shut Door" Documents* (1982), an anthology, *Periodical Articles Concerning Inspiration, Ellen G. White, and Adventist History* (1986), *Righteousness by Faith* (1988), and *The Humanity of Christ* (1989).

Further reading: M. W. Campbell, *An Interview With Robert W. Olson*, Adventist Oral History Series, LLU, 2005.

Tim Poirier

ORTON, JONATHAN T. (1811-1866). Adventist neighbor of James and Ellen White in Rochester, New York, later murdered after a financial dispute. In 1852 Orton offered the use of his home as a place of meeting for Sabbath services and conferences for the fledgling Sabbatarian

Adventist group. Some of the publishing staff worked and lived there, including *Uriah Smith, *Annie Smith, and *J. N. Loughborough. The Whites made their second Rochester home next to the Ortons on Monroe Avenue. The Ortons and others were not always supportive of the Whites and their work (PH 123, 72, 73), and in 1855 the Whites relocated to *Battle Creek, Michigan. Afterward the Ortons relocated to Waukon, Iowa, with many other early Sabbatarian Adventists, but later moved back to Rochester.

In 1865, following his first stroke, James White spent almost 11 weeks at "Our Home on the Hillside," in Dansville, New York, south of Rochester. When, on December 4, the Whites traveled from Dansville to Rochester, Orton was waiting at the depot to take the Whites from the train to the house of his son-in-law J. B. Lamson, about three miles (five kilometers) distant (RH, Feb. 27, 1866).

The Whites invited J. N. Andrews and others "who had faith in God, and felt it their duty" (2Bio 126) to come to Rochester and pray for James White's healing. For three weeks they held lengthy seasons of prayer twice a day. On December 25, in the late afternoon, Ellen White was shown in vision that Satan had tried to destroy her husband, but the prayers of the believers had thwarted his efforts (*ibid.* 127). She then warned the group that Satan would seek revenge for this victory, and cautioned them to "live very near to God that you may be prepared for what comes upon you" (*ibid.*). Three months later Orton was murdered. It was initially thought that the unsolved murder was because of his Adventist beliefs, but later research showed that it probably stemmed from a business dispute in which Orton unwisely contended too adamantly for his legal rights. According to Ron Graybill's research, Orton gave a neighbor a loan, for which he received a chest as collateral. Orton apparently expected the neighbor to be grateful for his help, but this expectation was not realized. When the neighbor did not repay the loan, Orton sold the chest, which enraged the man. After the case had twice been taken to court, and both times the judge ruled in Orton's favor, the irate neighbor reportedly vowed revenge, and hired a third party to commit the murder. No one was ever convicted of Orton's murder.

Further reading: R. H. Allen and H. Krug, *Rochester's Adventist Heritage: Tour Guide and Biographical Overview* (Rochester, N.Y.: Advent History Project, 2002), pp. 13, 14, 31-33; R. Graybill, "The Murder of Jonathan Orton," *Insight*, Dec. 5, 1978; JNL, *The Great Second Advent Movement, Its Rise and Progress* (PPPA, 1905).

Howard Krug

OTTOSEN, CARL JACOB (1864-1942). Adventist physician, founder of *Skodsborg Sanitarium. As a youth in Denmark, Ottosen attracted Ellen White's attention during her travels in 1887 through that country (EGWEur 303, 305). By 1889 Ottosen was studying at the Battle Creek Sanitarium. Ellen White wrote to friends entreating them to care for him (Lt 56, 1889). Upon his return to Denmark, Ottosen established the Fredrikshavn School in 1893 and the Skodsborg Sanitarium in 1898. Ellen White later wrote to him supporting his medical missionary work in Denmark (Lt 154, 1900).

Further reading: SDA Encyclopedia (1996), vol. 11, p. 272.

OYEN, A. B. (b. 1856). Adventist minister and missionary sent to Scandinavia in 1884 to supervise the publishing work in Norway; secretary of the General Conference (1881-1883). Oyen was born in Norway, became an Adventist in the United States, where he married his wife, Jennie (b. 1850). From October 30 through November 2, 1885, Ellen White stayed in his home while she visited Adventists in Christiana (Oslo). She appreciated being able to converse with him in English (Ms 27, 1885, in 2MR 116-121) and he served as her interpreter. Ellen White later counseled him against an unwise attachment with a young woman (Lt 81, 1886).

PACKHAM, WILLIAM JAMES (1877-1916). Adventist from Australia who was converted by reading * *The Great Controversy* in 1897. In 1903 he moved near the *St. Helena Sanitarium, where he assisted Ellen White in her orchard (Lt 201, 1903). Ellen White counseled him not to isolate himself and to "impart to others the light and knowledge He has given you" (Lt 101, 1905).

Further reading: obit. RH, Nov. 16, 1916.

PALMER, DAN R. (1817-1897). One of the earliest Sabbatarian Adventists in Michigan. In 1849 blacksmith Dan Palmer and his wife, Abigail, became *Joseph Bates' first converts in Jackson, Michigan. Soon 15 people were worshipping in their home (1Bio 273). The Palmers often boarded traveling ministers, giving each a $5 gold piece, a generous practice that Ellen White thought could make ne'er-do-wells impose on them. From Palmer's home in 1854 the Whites boarded a train for Wisconsin, which was wrecked near Jackson with lives lost (*ibid.* 294-296). In 1858, before beginning to write her vision on the *great controversy in *Spiritual Gifts*, Ellen was paralyzed; in response to the Palmers' prayers, she revived (*ibid.* 371, 372). The Palmers donated property for the Jackson congregation's first meetinghouse (1854) and throughout their lives gave more than $8,000 for evangelism, publishing, the Dime Tabernacle, and other projects. Palmer served on the Michigan

PALMER, EDWIN R.

Conference and General Conference executive committees. The Palmers were instrumental in the conversion of *Merritt and Angeline Cornell (1852) and the Spalding family (1877), parents of historian Arthur W. Spalding.

Further reading: B. E. Strayer, "Advent Waymarks in Jackson (Mich.), 1849-1999" (unpublished manuscript, 1999, CAR); B. E. Strayer, "Blacksmith on the Battleground" (unpublished manuscript, 1999, CAR); A. W. Spalding, *Footprints of the Pioneers* (RHPA, 1947); A. W. Spalding, *Origin and History of Seventh-day Adventists* (RHPA, 1961), 4 vols.

PALMER, EDWIN R. (1869-1931). *Colporteur and publishing house manager. For most of

COURTESY OF THE CENTER FOR ADVENTIST RESEARCH, ANDREWS UNIVERSITY

EDWIN R. PALMER

his ministry Palmer worked in the publishing area of the Seventh-day Adventist Church. Born in Vermont, he attended *South Lancaster Academy in Massachusetts. After his graduation and marriage to Eva Maynard in 1893, he served first as a colporteur in Vermont (1893-1894), agent of literature sales in Oklahoma (1894-1895) and Australia (1895-1899), general agent of literature work for the world field (1901-1902), secretary of the Publishing Department of the General Conference (1907-1912), and general manager of the Review and Herald (1912-1931). He also served as principal of Avondale College (1899-1901) and manager of Paradise Valley Sanitarium (1904-1905).

While serving in Australia, Ellen White advised Palmer, along with *A. G. Daniells and other church leaders, regarding a number of issues related to church workers (Lt 50, 1897) and the work being done at Avondale (Lt 46,

1897; Lt 141, 1899) and in other parts of Australia (Lt 47, 1897). When Ellen White heard that Palmer would become general canvassing agent for the world field in 1901, she commended him for his decision and stated that "canvassing is an important work, a work equal in importance to the ministry of the word" (Lt 10, 1901, in PM 298, 299). She also counseled him on the work of canvassing and the publication of books in publishing houses (Lt 155, 1901; Lt 21, 1902; Lt 10, 1903). In 1902, however, she became concerned that Palmer's attempt at centralizing the publication of books in Battle Creek to the detriment of smaller publishing houses elsewhere was "a work that God had not appointed him to do" (Lt 212, 1902, in PM 122). After the destruction of the Review and Herald Publishing House in December 1902, Ellen White invited Palmer to consider working somewhere else. "Place yourself, if possible, where you will have little cause to worry over the work of others. As a teacher of canvassers you have talents that will make you very useful in the cause of God" (Lt 92, 1903, in 21MR 18).

Upon hearing of Eva's death, Ellen White sent Palmer words of encouragement (Lt 143, 1903), but he suffered a breakdown. While seeking rest at the Phoenix Sanitarium, he met his second wife, Cora E. Hutchins (1867-1939). After their marriage in 1903, he managed the Paradise Valley Sanitarium and again received words of affirmation from Ellen White for his work at that institution (Lt 323, 1904; Lts 53, 75, 1905). But Palmer's greatest strengths were in the publishing work, and he soon returned to denominational headquarters to direct the Publishing Department. Ellen White encouraged him in this work, urging him to "secure as canvassers men and women of ability" and to dedicate as much effort to the sale of doctrinal books as was being done for medical books (Lt 72, 1907, in CM 141).

Further reading: obit. RH, Mar. 5, 1931; obit. RH, Feb. 8, 1940; D. R. McAdams, "Edwin R. Palmer, Publishing Secretary Extraordinary," *Adventist Heritage* 2, no. 1 (Summer 1975): 51-62; *SDA Encyclopedia* (1996), vol. 11, pp. 290, 291.

Denis Fortin

PALMER, WILL OTIS (c. 1876-1930). Pastor and associate of *J. Edson White in pioneering

COURTESY OF THE CENTER FOR ADVENTIST RESEARCH, ANDREWS UNIVERSITY

WILL O. PALMER

the Adventist work among the *African-American population in the southern United States in the 1890s and early 1900s. Will grew up in Battle Creek, where he was known as "the wildest son of old Brother Palmer" (Graybill, pp. 14, 15). In 1893 and 1894 Palmer and Edson White both found spiritual renewal, gained a new sense of purpose, and began to collaborate on the construction of the steamboat *Morning Star*, from which they launched a mission of literacy education and evangelism among former slaves in the American South.

"When you and Edson were companions in labor," wrote Ellen White, "I felt that it was in the order of God" (Lt 90, 1896). After Palmer and Edson White established the *Southern Publishing Association in Nashville, Tennessee, Palmer became its first manager and received encouragement from Ellen White, who felt confident this new publishing house was established in the right place. She also opposed any plans by the managers of the Review and Herald to control the work done in other publishing houses (Lt 67, 1901). When she heard that Palmer and Edson White were thinking of establishing a health food factory in the South, she did not encourage them (Lt 23, 1902), because she felt Palmer had "fallen

into loose, careless habits of business management" learned from his association with worldly businessmen (Lt 163, 1902, in 14MR 212; cf. Lts 94, 120, 1902). This situation also led her to send him fervent appeals regarding his spiritual life (Lts 178, 192, 1902; Lt 62, 1906).

Further reading: obit. RH, July 24, 1930; R. D. Graybill, *Mission to Black America* (PPPA, 1971).

PARMELE, RUFUS WELLS (1869-1945). Joining Adventism in 1886, Parmele became a colporteur in Kansas and Illinois, then a stenographer at the General Conference. After marrying Viola Kirk in 1891, he served as secretary-treasurer in Oklahoma, Kansas, and the Southwestern Union Conference (1890s), and taught business courses at Union College (1904-1906). When Viola died, he married Dr. Lydia Kynett (1865-1935) in 1902, and together they taught at Union College (1904-1906) before he became circulation manager at the Southern Publishing Association (1906-1907) and conference president in Florida (1907-1912), Louisiana (1912-1915), and Cumberland (1915-1916). After retiring as the superintendent of the North Latin American Missions (1916-1922), he served as pastor of the Glendale, White Memorial, and Pomona churches in California (1922-1935). When Lydia died, he married Dona Burnett in 1936. In 1908 Parmele wrote to W. C. White to enquire whether land should be purchased near Orlando, Florida, in order to establish a sanitarium. Ellen White responded that indeed "the time has come for Florida to have a sanitarium" and encouraged him to proceed with this plan (Lt 220, 1908, in 12MR 310). This sanitarium is now Florida Hospital.

Further reading: obit. PUR, Jan. 31, 1945; obit. RH, Feb. 15, 1945; *SDA Encyclopedia* (1996), vol. 11, p. 305.

PARSONS, DANIEL ALONZO (1879-1954). Pastor and church administrator. Parsons served as a missionary in England and Ireland (1901-1907), and then as a pastor in various conferences before becoming president of the Utah Conference (1910-1912). In 1906 he married Annie Howell (1884-1949). In 1909 and 1910 Ellen White encouraged Parsons in his work in North Carolina (Lt 62, 1909) and urged him to work for the spiritual revival of church members, pastors, and physicians (Lt 42, 1910). In 1986 an unfounded rumor about Ellen White predicting a massive earthquake in California erroneously cited Parsons as a witness. The article debunking the rumor also contains biographical details about Parsons (Nix).

Further reading: obit. RH, Dec. 30, 1954; J. R. Nix, "The Unrecorded Earthquake Vision," AR, June 19, 1986.

PATTEN, ADELIA, see **VAN HORN, ISAAC DOREN** and **ADELIA P. (PATTEN)**.

PAULSON, DAVID (1868-1916), and **MAUDE "MARY" ANN (WILD)** (later **MAUDE "MARY" ANN [WILD] NEALL**) (1872-1956). Physicians

COURTESY OF THE REVIEW AND HERALD PUBLISHING ASSOCIATION

DRS. MARY AND DAVID PAULSON

who cofounded *Hinsdale Sanitarium. Born to Danish immigrants in Wisconsin, David studied medicine at *Battle Creek College, the University of Michigan, and Bellevue Medical College in New York, receiving the M.D. in 1894. Mary Wild completed her M.D. from the Northwestern University Medical School in Evanston, Illinois, in 1896 and married David the same year. Closely associated with *J. H. Kellogg, David taught in the *American Medical Missionary College (AMMC) and in 1899 became head of the *Chicago Medical Mission (including the Chicago Branch Sanitarium and the Chicago division of the AMMC), and editor of its magazine, the *Life Boat*. As Paulson sought and prayed for a new sanitarium near Chicago yet out of the city, one of his wealthy patients learned of the need and gave financial assistance, leading to the purchase of property in 1904 for the Hinsdale Sanitarium.

As Kellogg's conflict with church leaders moved toward schism, Paulson never wavered in his friendship with Kellogg, or in his loyalty to the church and Ellen White. Attempting to mediate, he wrote Ellen White for clarification of some issues, and her replies were later published in the *Review and Herald* ("Correct Views Concerning the Testimonies," Aug. 30 and Sept. 6, 1906). Paulson was a physician of great integrity and great faith, who regularly prayed with his patients and saw remarkable recoveries. But his own health was never robust, and he died at 48.

Dr. Mary Paulson, "considered one of the best woman diagnosticians in Chicago" (Clough, p. 150), had earlier led the Department of Gynecology at *Battle Creek Sanitarium. She also taught at AMMC and in 1905 organized the Hinsdale Sanitarium School of Nursing. In 1921 she married John Howard Neall, also a physician at Hinsdale. In 1934 they started a small sanitarium in Quincy, Illinois. After John's death in 1936, Mary continued managing the Quincy Sanitarium until 1939, when she retired to Azusa, California.

Further reading: obit. RH, Nov. 2, 1916; obit. PUR, Oct. 26, 1916; obit. RH, Apr. 26, 1956; obit. PUR, May 7, 1956; *Century: Hinsdale Hospital 1904-2004* (Hinsdale, Ill.: Hinsdale Hospital, 2004); C. L. Clough, *His Name Was David* (RHPA, 1955); H. G. Dugan, *Hinsdale Sanitarium and Hospital* (Hinsdale, Ill.: 1957); D. Paulson, *Footprints of Faith* (autobiography) (Hinsdale, Ill.: *Life Boat,* 1921; PPPA, 1978);

SDA Encyclopedia (1996), vol. 10, p. 696; vol. 11, pp. 308, 309.

Jerry Moon

PEARSALL, A. B. (1822-1895) and **ADALINE** (1823-1906). Former Millerites who accepted the Sabbatarian Adventist message in 1853 while living in Grand Rapids, Michigan. He was one of the persons who financed the move of the *Review and Herald* to Battle Creek from Rochester, New York, in 1855. They moved to Battle Creek in 1858. In 1854 Ellen White urged Pearsall to be more circumspect in his behavior with women and not to dwell on nonessential things in other people's lives (cf. Lt 3, 1854, in 7MR 208).

Further reading: obit. *RH*, Mar. 19, 1895; obit. *RH*, July 12, 1906.

PEARSON, JOHN, SR. Millerite from Portland, Maine, who at one time opposed Ellen Harmon's "manifestations" (visions). During a prayer meeting in her home Harmon received a vision during which, according to Pearson, something like a "ball of fire" struck "Sister Ellen" "right on the heart." When she awoke from her vision, Pearson declared he would never again doubt the genuineness of her visions (CET 66, 67; 1Bio 64). Pearson was the father of John Pearson, Jr., who, with *Joseph Turner, edited the Millerite paper *The Hope of Israel*. John Pearson, Jr., is believed to have been the person to first introduce James White to Ellen Harmon in Portland, Maine, in the summer 1843.

PECK, SARAH ELIZABETH (1868-1968). Educator, writer, missionary, and *literary assistant to Ellen White. Originally from Wisconsin, Peck trained at Battle Creek College, after which she served in South Africa as one of the denomination's first women missionaries.

COURTESY OF THE CENTER FOR ADVENTIST RESEARCH, ANDREWS UNIVERSITY.

SARAH E. PECK

In 1898, after several prior invitations (Ms 8, 1894; Lt 76, 1897), Ellen White finally convinced Peck to join her staff in Australia. She was to design a new filing system for Ellen White's unpublished writings (PaM 51; 4Bio 451) and assist as her bookkeeper (Lt 133, 1902). She assisted in compiling White's writings on education that eventually appeared in *Testimonies,* volume 6 (1900), and *Education* (1903). In 1900 Sarah Peck returned with Ellen White to the United States, where Peck and her mother shared a cottage on the Elmshaven property (Lt 70, 1903). In 1903 Peck became a teacher at a nearby church school started with Ellen White's hearty approval (Lt 70, 1903; Lt 112, 1903). Although Peck's teaching responsibilities lessened the time she could work for Ellen White, she continued to handle Ellen White's *finances. When Sarah Peck was appointed educational secretary for the West Coast, Ellen White reluctantly agreed to let her go in order to be of greater service to the church (Lt 265, 1905). Peck edited the series *True Education Readers* and wrote other school textbooks. She also taught at Union College (1907-1914) and served as educational superintendent in the California Conference (1915-1917) before joining the General Conference Education Department in 1918, where she served until her retirement in 1923.

Further reading: Ms 7, 1904; obit. *RH*, Aug. 8, 1968; S. E. Peck, "Personal Reminiscences of Ellen G. White," *RH*, Mar. 19, 1964; E. N. Dick, *Union: College of the Golden Cords* (Lincoln, Nebr.: Union College Press, 1967), p. 310; S. A. Welch, "The Life and Writings of Sarah Elizabeth Peck" (research paper,

1977, CAR); *SDA Encyclopedia* (1996), vol. 11, p. 309.

Shirley Mulkern

PERRY, JOSEPH ARTHUR (d. 1908) and **ROSETTA RHODA (ABBEY)** (1848-1943). Rosetta was the daughter of *Ira Abbey and served for a while as a *literary assistant to Ellen White. Arthur and Rosetta were married in 1871 and raised four children. In 1875, while employed at the *Health Reform Institute, in Battle Creek, Arthur engaged in homosexual behavior with patients, for which he was dismissed. When his father-in-law heard of the matter, he got upset and talked to many people about it. Ellen White told Abbey forthrightly to calm down and said the case had already been managed with the greatest discretion. "The very least you have to say about [it] either in condemnation or vindication of Arthur's case, the better. Had you let it entirely alone, it would have been better for you, better for Arthur, and better for the reputation of the Institute" (Lt 39, 1875).

Further reading: obit. RH, Nov. 25, 1943.

PHILLIPS, ANNA, see **RICE, ANNA C. (PHILLIPS)**.

PHILLIPS, DANIEL C. (1813-1882). Adventist itinerant preacher from Roxbury, Vermont, whom Ellen White described as having "the gift of exhortation" but "lets feeling govern him too much" (Ms 1, 1859). She told him that he was not called to give his entire time to preaching but only as needed, and exhorted him to give more support to the cause of God (Lt 22, 1859; cf. Lt 15, 1857). In the early 1860s Phillips became involved in some compromising situations that curtailed his possibilities for service and ministry (cf. Lt 2, 1862; Lt 9, 1863; Lt 4, 1864; Lt 4a, 1864).

Further reading: obit. RH, July 11, 1882.

PIERCE, STEPHEN (1804-1883). Pioneer Adventist minister and conference administrator. Pierce was born in Cavendish, Vermont, where he lived for most of his life before moving to Stewartsville, Minnesota, and later Mount Pleasant, Iowa. Known for his commitment to the church, he served as conference president in Vermont (1863-1865) and Minnesota (1866-1870), and was a corresponding editor of the *Review and Herald*. He was specifically noted as a leading participant in the *Sabbatarian Bible conferences (TM 24; Ms 135, 1903).

STEPHEN PIERCE

In 1903 Ellen White remarked that "my husband, Elder Joseph Bates, Father Pierce, Elder Edson, and many others . . . were among those who, after the passing of time in 1844, searched for truth" "as for hidden treasure" (Lt 135, 1903, in 3MR 412, 413). While studying the Bible at these meetings, Pierce and others witnessed Ellen White in vision and believed this to be a manifestation of God's leading in their movement. These visions were said to take place whenever those studying came to a place where they could go no further. Believing that God had invested Ellen White with the gift of prophecy, Pierce became a staunch supporter of Ellen White. In the early years of his ministry with Sabbatarian Adventists, Ellen White advised him not to rely so much on feelings and emotions, but instead to depend entirely on Jesus (Lt 2, 1851, in 18MR 248-253). James White thought that with "his experience, sound judgment, and ability," Pierce was worth more than "ten young, inexperienced preachers" (2Bio 67). He was characterized as a man of deep genuine piety who loved God, loved Bible study, and was an able expositor of the Scripture. Pierce spent his last days in Madison, Dakota Territory, and died of typhomalarial fever.

Further reading: obit. RH, Oct. 9, 1883; *SDA Encyclopedia* (1996), vol. 11, p. 351.

Lloyd Wilson

PIPER, ALBERT H. (1875-1956). Minister, missionary, and administrator. Born in Wellington, New Zealand, Piper left a promising position in the New Zealand government to attend school at *Avondale, where he lived in Ellen White's home for a year. Upon completion of his education, Piper had an unpaid debt to a fellow student, *Martha Brown, which Ellen White encouraged him to pay off before leaving for the mission field (Lt 112, 1900). Piper was the first missionary sent to the Pacific Islands by the Australasian Division and later held several administrative posts within the Australasian Union.

Further reading: obit. UCR, Feb. 20, 1956; obit. RH, Mar. 29, 1956; *SDA Encyclopedia* (1996), vol. 11, p. 354.

PIPER, JESSE FRANCIS (1874-1945). Pastor and church administrator. Piper became a Seventh-day Adventist about 1892 through the influence of his sister, Dora, and attending Battle Creek College. In 1895 he married Anna B. Stillwell (1871-1972). Piper worked as a pastor in Iowa (1904-1906); Baltimore, Maryland (1906-1909); Rochester, New York (1909-1911); and Seattle, Washington (1913-1914). He also served as conference president in Maine (1911-1913), Washington State (1914-1919), West Michigan (1919-1926), East Michigan (1926-1930), and Colorado (1930-1931). In 1931 he became president of the Central Union Conference, a position he held for 10 years. While Piper worked in Portland, Maine, Ellen White expressed her "deep interest" in the work he was doing there (Lt 26, 1911).

Further reading: obit. RH, June 21, 1945; obit. RH, July 6, 1972.

PIPER, WENSLEY (c. 1855-1900), and **"MRS." PIPER.** Adventists in Petone, New Zealand, parents of *Albert H. Piper. Their son Albert had lived in Ellen White's home for a year while he was a student at *Avondale. However, when the Pipers asked if their daughter, Nina, could accompany Ellen White in her travels, she wrote a letter explaining that she could not take Nina with her because of Nina's health difficulties (Lt 96, 1893).

PLACE, ALBERT E. (1856-1950). Pastor and conference president. Place was ordained to ministry in 1884 and worked in the New York Conference for 15 years. He served as president of the New York (1895-1898) and Central New England (1903-1906) conferences. For some years he was associated with his brother, Dr. *O. G. Place, at the Boulder Sanitarium. He then worked in California before retiring to Rome, New York. Ellen White wrote four letters to Place. The first was written while he was president of the Central New England Conference, to enlist his support in rebuilding the Melrose Sanitarium (see *New England Sanitarium) after a fire (Lt 25, 1905). The other three letters were more controversial. In 1906 Ellen White advised Place against his apparent plan to join his brother, O. G. Place, in Boulder, Colorado. His brother had started a private sanitarium in close proximity to the original Colorado Sanitarium, an initiative she did not favor. Instead of his going to Colorado, she encouraged Place to begin "tent meetings" near Boston to build up the church there and to promote interest in the Melrose Sanitarium (Lts 198, 202, 1906). Her efforts, however, did not succeed, and Place joined his brother. In her last letter to him she stated clearly, "You are not in the place that the Lord

491

has appointed you to be." She also deplored the influence his brother was having on him and encouraged him to return to pastoral ministry (Lt 38, 1908; cf. Lt 286, 1907). Perhaps this advice was not totally unheeded, for Place left Boulder in 1913 and worked in California until his retirement.

Further reading: obit. RH, June 1, 1950.

Tyler Bower

PLACE, OLNEY GALEN (1860-1926). Adventist physician, brother of *Albert E. Place. O. G. Place was born in Oswego, New York, and graduated from the University of Michigan School of Medicine in 1885. He was an assistant surgeon at the *Battle Creek Sanitarium for seven years. He married Julia Chapman (1858-1905) in 1887. He also did postgraduate studies in surgery in New York City (1889-1890), Chicago (1893-1894), and London, England. He was medical superintendent of the Mount Vernon [Ohio] Sanitarium (c. 1890-1892). While in Mount Vernon, Place received several letters from Ellen White calling him to be converted anew (Lt 22c, 1890; Lt 50, 1891). In 1895 he became the first medical superintendent of the Colorado Sanitarium (later renamed *Boulder Sanitarium), and spent five years (1896-1901) launching Adventist medical work in Calcutta, India, but because of Julia's ill health, they returned to the United States. After Julia died, he married Ida Louise Moench.

On returning to Boulder in 1901, he founded the privately owned Place Sanitarium, in direct competition with the church-operated Colorado Sanitarium, an initiative that Ellen White did not favor (Lts 217, 221, 1905; Lt 196, 1906). Her final extant letter to him, in August 1907, was also addressed to the Colorado Conference committee. She said Place had been "weighed in the balance . . . [and had] been found wanting," and urged the

conference not to support his institution (Lt 252, 1907; cf. Lt 286, 1907).

Further reading: obit. RH, May 13, 1926; *Semi-Centennial History of the State of Colorado* (Chicago: Lewis, 1913), pp. 309, 310; *SDA Encyclopedia* (1996), vol. 11, p. 355.

Tyler Bower

POMARE, MAUI (1876-1930). The first New Zealand Maori to train as a physician. Introduced to Adventism while at high school, the young son of a Maori chief was baptized in 1893 in Napier, New Zealand (Ms 85, 1893). He was befriended by Ellen White, who, together with her dentist friend, *Margaret Caro, offered to sponsor him to the United States for medical studies (Lt 36a, 1893). Conflicting counsel from church leaders in America discouraged him and occasioned a vigorous exchange of correspondence among Ellen White's associates in 1894-1895. Pomare finally went to the United States in 1896 to study at Battle Creek College and at the *American Medical Missionary College in Chicago under *John Harvey Kellogg. Returning home after his graduation but no longer as a practicing Adventist, Pomare was appointed government health officer. Elected to parliament in 1912, he rose rapidly to cabinet rank and served continuously as a minister of the crown in a variety of senior portfolios. Knighted by King George V in 1922 for his services to New Zealand, Sir Maui Pomare attributed his success to Adventist principles of the "gospel of health" he had learned from Kellogg. His untimely death in 1930 from tuberculosis occurred at St. Helena Sanitarium among old Adventist friends. He was buried in New Zealand.

Further reading: G. M. Valentine, "Maui Pomare and the Adventist Connection," in P. H. Ballis, ed., *In and Out of the World* (Palmerston North, New Zealand: Dunmore Press, 1985), pp. 82-108; J. F. Cody, *Man of*

Two Worlds: Sir Maui Pomare (Wellington and Reed, 1953).

Gilbert M. Valentine

PORTER, CHARLES WHITMAN (1843-1926). Adventist minister from Iowa. At the *General Conference session of 1888 Porter opposed the message of *righteousness by faith. This reaction drew a stern rebuke from Ellen White. The following year she counseled with Porter, who then "yielded" his "opposition and surrendered to God" (Lt 14, 1889, 1888 Materials 324; cf. Lt 83, 1890, in 13MR 49-58; Lt 50, 1889).

Further reading: obit. RH, Apr. 15, 1926.

PRATT, WILLIAM (1827-1896). Adventist in St. Helena, California. After attending meetings held by *J. N. Loughborough and *Isaac Van Horn in St. Helena, California, in 1873, Pratt and his wife became charter members of the St. Helena church. Three years later Pratt gave a piece of land on the side of the mountain near Crystal Springs for a medical institution (5Bio 30), which became the Rural Health Retreat (now the *St. Helena Sanitarium). In 1885 Pratt's brother Robert, a railroad executive, built the house that Ellen White bought in 1900 and named "Elmshaven."

Further reading: obit. RH, Mar. 17, 1896; 5Bio 30.

PRESCOTT, AMOS L. (b. c. 1852), and **EMMA ELIZABETH (STURGES)** (c. 1850-1921). Adventists in New York; Amos was a brother of *W. W. Prescott; Emma served as a *literary assistant to Ellen White in the late 1860s. Amos and Emma were married in 1872. After being active in the Adventist Church for many years, Amos abandoned his religious convictions sometime in the 1890s (cf. Ms 42, 1890). In 1899 Ellen White urged him to "believe in Christ as your personal Savior" and to use his talents for God's glory (Lt 52, 1899).

Although Emma remained a faithful Adventist, there is no indication that Amos responded to Ellen White's appeal.

Further reading: obit. RH, Apr. 21, 1921.

PRESCOTT, WILLIAM WARREN (1855-1944). Writer, scholar, and administrator. Between

WILLIAM W. PRESCOTT

1885 and 1944 Prescott occupied many senior positions in educational leadership, publishing, and at the General Conference and was a member of the General Conference Executive Committee for 42 years. The son of a Millerite (see Millerite *disappointments and *William Miller) lay preacher, Prescott graduated from Dartmouth College in 1882 and was for many years one of the few church members to hold a master's degree. He was a confidant and close friend of Ellen White's until the relationship became strained in the last years before her death. Ellen White also related warmly to the professor's wife, Sarah, and their son, Lewis. During his career he maintained an extensive personal correspondence with Ellen White and her son, *W. C. White. According to *A. G. Daniells, Prescott possessed "some of the rarest gifts of any man in our ranks" (AGD to I. H. Evans, May 13, 1910, GCAr), and *I. H. Evans considered that there were "few men of his ability anywhere" (I. H. Evans to AGD, Apr. 29, 1910, GCAr).

As president of *Battle Creek College (1885-1894) and as education secretary for the General Conference (1887-1897), he worked closely with Ellen White in developing a distinctively Adventist curriculum. Ellen White provided the prophetic reform impetus and the visionary ideals, while Prescott attempted to work out the curricular details.

He organized the landmark *Harbor Springs teachers' conference in 1891 and persuaded Ellen White to attend. At this conference the expression "Christian education" first began to be used in Adventist educational discourse. Following the conference he attempted over a number of years to implement Ellen White's counsel to discard the study of the classical languages in favor of required Bible and religion classes, but encountered vigorous opposition and faculty resistance. At both *Union College and *Walla Walla College, where he served as founding president, he also attempted to implement the new curricular ideals. During this period he edited and published without supervision the Ellen White manuscripts for *Christian Education (1893) and *Special Testimonies on Education (1897), many of which had been sent personally to him for guidance in the leadership of Battle Creek College.

Requested by W. C. White to visit Australia in 1895-1896, Prescott again spent many occasions in personal visits with Ellen White discussing educational reform issues. In consultation with Ellen White, Prescott set out the curricular pattern for the *Avondale school, which was intended to serve as a model of an Adventist college, with the Bible at the center of the curriculum instead of the classics. A large part of Ellen White's vision for Adventist education became a reality through the work of W. W. Prescott.

During his Australian visit Prescott also spent time at Ellen White's request assisting *Marian Davis through some difficulties in the preparation of the manuscript for *The Desire of Ages. It was substantially reworked, and publication was delayed until 1898. His theological presentations and his Christocentric preaching in Melbourne and on the Avondale campus made a deep impression

on Ellen White, her son W. C. White, and Marian Davis. One consequence was the clarification of Ellen White's teaching in her publications at this time on the doctrine of the Trinity (see *Godhead) and the person of the *Holy Spirit (H. C. Lacey to L. E. Froom, Aug. 30, 1945, CAR).

Prescott was also closely associated with Ellen White in her post-1888 struggles to bring the church to an acceptance of the *righteousness by faith emphasis. During this period they consulted together on how to bring reconciliation to the divided church. In 1891 he was the agent of reconciliation in the estrangement that had occurred between *Uriah Smith and Ellen White and the church over the law in *Galatians issue (D. T. Jones to R. A. Underwood, Jan. 10, 1891, GCAr).

In 1897 Ellen White hoped that Prescott, as a crusader for reform, would be elected as the next president of the General Conference, sharing many things with him about the troubles at headquarters that she could not share with her son, and counseling him on how to respond should he be elected (W. W. Prescott to EGW, July 16, Aug. 9, 1896; Lt 89, 1896). Instead he was assigned by the General Conference to England, but continued to keep up a close personal correspondence with Ellen White.

Prescott was again brought back to church headquarters in 1901, where he worked closely with A. G. Daniells and Ellen White in helping to implement the reorganization plans for the General Conference. He was appointed editor of the *Review and Herald, as well as the first vice president of the General Conference, and helped shape the direction of the church for the new century. As editor of the Review and president of the publishing house he led in relocating the publishing house to the new church headquarters in Washington, D.C. During this period he was the denomination's primary theological spokesperson in the struggle against *J. H. Kellogg and his pantheistic writings and again kept up a close correspondence with Ellen White on these issues during the period.

During Ellen White's later years at Elmshaven (see *homes of James and Ellen G. White), Prescott as editor of the *Review and Herald* wrote the foreword for *Steps to Christ* and assisted Ellen White's literary assistants in clarifying historical details for the book *Prophets and Kings*. In 1909 at the request of W. C. White he provided an extensive list of suggestions for revisions and corrections for *The Great Controversy*. Rumors of his work on this troubled Ellen White's older ministerial colleagues. At the same time his advocacy of the new theological understanding of the expression the *daily in Daniel 8:11-13 put him even further at odds with the more conservative friends of Ellen White. She began to worry about him and advised that he not make "a mountain out of a molehill" in his emphasis of the new view (Lt 224, 1908, but not sent until late 1910; in 6Bio 248).

In 1909, during a crisis over the neglect of *city evangelism, she urged A. G. Daniells to personally lead the advance. She also counseled that Prescott move from the editorship of the *Review and Herald* to city evangelism. This pained Prescott badly and strained his relationship with Ellen White. In the years following her death, Daniells brought the professor back into General Conference leadership.

The professor never wavered from his deep conviction that Ellen White exhibited the genuine gift of prophecy, but on the basis of his own intimate acquaintance with the editorial process involved in preparing her publications, he advocated the need for more openness on the part of the White Estate and the church about the dynamics of the editorial process (cf. W. W. Prescott to *WCW, Apr. 6, 1915, GCAr). He felt strongly that this was needed to enable the church to develop a healthier and more adequate view of the nature of her inspiration and writings.

See also: Bible Conference of 1919; *The Great Controversy*; Anna C. (Phillips) Rice; W. C. White.

Further reading: obit. RH, Feb. 17, 1944; "The 1911 Edition of *Great Controversy*" (EGWE, SDoc, 13 pp.); "W. W. Prescott and the 1911 Edition of *Great Controversy*" (EGWE, SDoc, 39 pp.); "Letter of April 1915 of W. W. Prescott to W. C. White" (EGWE, SDoc); G. M. Valentine, *W. W. Prescott: Forgotten Giant of Adventism's Second Generation* (RHPA, 2005); G. M. Valentine, *The Shaping of Adventism* (AUP, 1992); G. M. Valentine, "W. W. Prescott: Giant Among Leaders," AR, Nov. 28, 1985; G. M. Valentine, "W. W. Prescott: Editor Extraordinaire," AR, Dec. 5, 1985; G. M. Valentine, "Controversy: A Stimulus for Theological Education," AR, Nov. 3, 1988; G. M. Valentine, "A Response to Two Explanations of W. W. Prescott's 1915 Letter" (unpublished paper, 1981, CAR).

Gilbert M. Valentine

PRESTON, CHANDLER B. and **ELIZA ANN.** Millerites from Camden, New York, who became early Sabbatarian Adventists. In 1850 and 1851 Ellen White visited the Prestons and attended a conference in their home, where she received visions (2SG 124-127, 150, 151; RH, May 19, 1851; see *Camden Vision). The Prestons testified to the authenticity of the events that occurred during the first visit (2SG 303). In a letter five months later Ellen White expressed her hope to see them (Lt 1, 1851, in 8MR 223).

RADLEY, "BROTHER" AND "SISTER." Fruit growers from Castle Hill, New South Wales,

Australia, who attended Adventist meetings in 1894. Mrs. Radley became an Adventist, but Mr. Radley, not having made a decision, lost interest. Ellen White later described him as a "reading man" and said that she was instructed by an angel to place her books before him and that this would save his soul. On her next visit to their home she appealed for him to improve his talents and to read her books *The Great Controversy and *Patriarchs and Prophets. In a vision she saw that he and his neighbor, Brother Whiteman, were specifically called by the Lord to accept truth. Mr. Radley became a Seventh-day Adventist and soon shared his newfound faith with his friends. When he died, Ellen White wrote a letter of comfort to his wife (Lt 167, 1905) and her children (Lt 165, 1905).

Further reading: GCB, Apr. 5, 1901; 4Bio 142, 143.

RAMSAY (or **RAMSEY**), **CHARLES CORNELL** (1857-1942). School principal and lawyer. In 1885 *S. N. Haskell invited Ramsay, who was then teaching at *Healdsburg College, to become the third principal of *South Lancaster Academy, where he remained until 1888. He then studied at Harvard University and later served as principal and superintendent of public schools in Massachusetts and New York. He became a lawyer in 1914. Although not working for the denomination after 1888, Ramsay kept an interest in the progress of Atlantic Union College and helped it secure the privilege of granting the A.B. degree in 1933. In 1886 Ellen White stated that "if you make God your trust you will be the right man in the right place" and gave him a few counsels regarding his functions at South Lancaster Academy, for which he felt appreciative (Lt 42, 1886; C. C. Ramsay to EGW, Apr. 22, 1886).

Further reading: obit. AUG, Sept. 2, 1942;

M. F. Wehtje, *And There Was Light: A History of South Lancaster Academy, Lancaster Junior College and Atlantic Union College* (South Lancaster, Mass.: Atlantic Press, 1982); R. E. Purdon, *The Story of a School: A History of Atlantic Union College* (South Lancaster, Mass.: College Press, c. 1940), pp. 25-31.

RAND, HOWARD FREDRICK (1859-1937). Adventist physician. Rand became an Adventist in 1884, attended Battle Creek College, and in 1894 graduated from the University of Michigan Medical School. From then to 1903 Rand worked for the *Battle Creek Sanitarium. He served as medical superintendent of *Boulder Sanitarium (1903-1906), head physician at *St. Helena Sanitarium (1906-1912), and at *Glendale Sanitarium (1912-1917). Ellen White admired his medical expertise and as early as 1901 appealed to Rand to join the St. Helena Sanitarium (Lt 42, 1901). In 1905 she counseled him not to be influenced by *J. H. Kellogg (Lt 189, 1905). The following year, when he decided to become chief physician at the St. Helena Sanitarium, she affirmed his decision, stating he was the Lord's chosen physician for that institution (Lt 64, 1906; Lt 86, 1911).

Further reading: obit. RH, Mar. 18, 1937.

RASMUSSEN, ANNA M. (1840-1931). Born in Denmark, she came with her husband to America in 1863. By 1875, probably widowed, she was working with Lucinda Hall in Oakland, California (Lt 44, 1875). In 1885 Anna traveled with Ellen White to Europe (EGWEur 23, 48) and in 1902 lived in White's home in California (5Bio 171). In later years Rasmussen lent money to White for her publishing and other ministries (Lts 28, 78, 1909; Lt 58b, 1910).

Further reading: obit. RH, Aug. 27, 1931; Lt 44, 1875, in 13MR 400; Lt 64, 1889, in 1888 Materials 382, 383.

READ, A. J. Adventist physician and missionary to the South Pacific Islands. In 1891 Read and his second wife, Ella V. (Butler) (1856-1910), sailed on the maiden voyage of the *Pitcairn* as the first permanent Adventist missionaries to Tahiti. Two years later he was elected the first secretary of the Seventh-day Adventist Medical Missionary and Benevolent Association while he continued his missionary service in the South Pacific. In 1904 Ellen White warned him about *J. H. Kellogg's book *The Living Temple* and urged him to break loose of Kellogg's influence on him (Lt 277, 1904; cf. Lt 212, 1906). In 1909 Ellen White invited him to visit with her at his next opportunity (Lt 116, 1909).

Further reading: obit. RH, Sept. 8, 1910; *SDA Encyclopedia* (1996), vol. 10, p. 677.

REASER, GEORGE W. (1859-1945). Missionary and administrator who joined Adventism in 1884 through the efforts of *G. I. Butler. Later that year Reaser began a 10-year term of work at *Pacific Press. He served in a variety of administrative positions in the northwestern part of the United States, including president of the Upper Columbia Conference (1898-1901). In 1885 Reaser married Bertha E. Unger (1863-1958) and in 1902 went as a pioneer missionary to South Africa, where he organized the first Seventh-day Adventist church in that country. After his return to the United States he served as president of the Southern California Conference (1905-1908) and the Arizona Conference (1912-1914), and helped to establish the Mexico Mission. While he served as president of the California Conference, Reaser counseled frequently with Ellen White, particularly during the founding of the *Glendale, *Paradise Valley, and *Loma Linda sanitariums (cf. Lt 274, 1906), and other administrative matters in southern California (cf. Lt 193, 1905).

Further reading: obit. RH, Oct. 25, 1945; obit. RH, Nov. 27, 1958.

REBOK, DENTON E. (1897-1983). Educator and administrator. In 1919, with his wife, Florence (1895-1976), Rebok sailed for China, where he spent more than half of his 44 years of denominational service. When World War II forced his return to the United States, Rebok joined the faculty of Washington Missionary College and later served as president of Southern Missionary College (1942-1943). He was president of the Seventh-day Adventist Theological Seminary (1943-1951) and then general field secretary of the General Conference, during which time he chaired the *Ellen G. White Estate Board of Trustees (1952).

DENTON E. REBOK

At a Bible conference in Washington, D.C., in 1952, Rebok presented three major studies entitled "The Spirit of Prophecy in the Remnant Church" (these appear in *Our Firm Foundation* [RHPA, 1953], vol.1). The following year he presented 12 studies on the subject to church leaders in Poona, India. The Southern Asia Division printed these studies in a booklet titled *Divine Guidance*. An expanded version, *Believe His Prophets*, was published by the Review and Herald in 1956. In the preface Rebok expressed his deep confidence in Ellen White as God's inspired messenger to the remnant church, then added: "God has spoken to His remnant church, and His people must hearken to that voice and walk in the light of that counsel." Rebok's last four years before retirement were spent at La Sierra College as a professor of sociology and religion.

Further reading: obit. AR Mar. 8, 1984.

Herb Ford

RHODES, SAMUEL W. (c. 1813-1883). Early Sabbatarian Adventist minister from Oswego,

New York. After the *disappointment of 1844 Rhodes became discouraged and retired for three years to a remote region of New York State. Twice *Hiram Edson visited Rhodes, trying to persuade him to rejoin the Adventists. At the close of a *Sabbatarian Bible Conference in Centerport, New York, November 17, 18, 1849, Edson enlisted a Brother [T.] Ralph (cf. 2SG 91) to go with him on a third visit to Rhodes. Ralph prayed silently for a sign that they should go see Rhodes, and as Edson prayed aloud, Ralph suddenly broke out in an unknown tongue, followed by an interpretation that Ralph should go with Edson to reclaim Rhodes. They did so, and Rhodes responded, accepting the *Sabbath and returning to active ministry.

Rhodes was a member of the *Advent Review* committee and designer of the first Sabbatarian Adventist prophetic chart (lithographed by *Otis Nichols in 1850). Ellen White cautioned him to beware his strong personality and harsh spirit, and to exert a more positive influence upon church members (Lt 16, 1859; Lt 4, 1870).

Further reading: 1Bio 196-199; *Present Truth*, December 1849; *SDA Encyclopedia* (1996), vol. 11, p. 450.

RICE, ANNA C. (PHILLIPS) (1865-1926). Anna Rice for a brief time claimed to be another

COURTESY OF THE CENTER FOR ADVENTIST RESEARCH, ANDREWS UNIVERSITY.

ANNA C. RICE

Adventist prophet. Born Anna Phillips, she was, in 1892, legally adopted in her mid-20s into the family of Elder *Jesse D. Rice. Never having had a home of her own during her younger years, Anna was more than happy to be their obedient child.

Unlike some aspiring after the prophetic gift down through history, Anna Rice was far from a charlatan. She appears to have been a sincere young woman with a simple faith in God and a great deal of personal insecurity. Sometime in 1892 she began to have what she thought might be prophetic experiences. Her first thought was to seek advice from Ellen White, but White was in Australia. The next-best thing, Anna reasoned, was to validate her gift through *A. T. Jones. After all, hadn't Ellen White said that Jones had advanced light? If he approved her gift, she concluded, then her gift was genuine.

Jones not only approved of her gift but encouraged her repeatedly up through February 1894. Beyond encouragement, Jones used Rice's "testimonies" in public meetings to demonstrate that the latter rain had begun and that her testimonies were evidence of that fact. At the 1893 General Conference session Jones and *W. W. Prescott wanted to use Anna Rice's testimonies to bring about the outpouring of the Holy Spirit, but the General Conference president *O. A. Olsen refused to let them read them publicly. But 10 months later, with President Olsen in Australia, Jones and Prescott brought about a great charismatic excitement in Battle Creek through Rice's testimonies. At that point the denomination witnessed various charismatic excesses.

The Anna Rice episode was brought to a sudden halt early in 1894 by several letters from Ellen White indicating that the visions had been endorsed "without sufficient evidence of their genuine character" (2SM 92). The whole business, Ellen White claimed, was not Anna's fault, but the fault of those who had encouraged her in her visions. Jones and Prescott apologized for their part and promised to be more careful in the future. Anna Rice, realizing that she had been misled, gave up her claims. She would later faithfully serve the denomination as a Bible worker.

Further reading: G. Baker, "Anna Phillips," AR, Feb. 6, 1986; G. R. Knight, *From 1888 to Apostasy: The Case of A. T. Jones* (RHPA, 1987), pp. 92-116.

George R. Knight

RICE, JESSE DAN (1857-1952). Rice is significant in Adventist history mainly because in 1892 he legally adopted the 27-year-old Anna Phillips (see *Anna C. Rice), who was only eight years younger than he was. Anna claimed to have had a vision that he was to adopt her. Ellen White wrote several letters to J. D. Rice regarding Anna's claims. On November 1, 1893, for example, Ellen White wrote to him rebuking him for encouraging Anna in the idea that she had a prophetic ministry. Such a course, she wrote, would only do injury to Anna (Lt 54, 1893). After the passing of the Anna Rice crisis in early 1894, J. D. Rice sailed on the *Pitcairn as a missionary to the Raratonga Islands, where he served until 1903. Most of his work after that was in the San Francisco Bay area in northern California.

Further reading: obit. RH, Mar. 19, 1953.

George R. Knight

RILEY, WILLIAM HENRY (1849-1929). Physician and superintendent of *Boulder Sanitarium (1896-1902). Before going to Colorado, Riley worked at the Battle Creek Sanitarium and taught at the American Medical Missionary College. Ellen White wrote Riley two letters of encouragement (Lt 281, 1904, in BCL 111-114; Lt 148, 1901).

Further reading: obit. *Southwestern Union Record*, Aug. 20, 1929.

ROBBINS, "MR.," see **SARGENT, G.**

ROBINSON, ASA THERON (1850-1949). Pastor and administrator; brother of *Dores A. Robinson, and father of *Dores E. Robinson. Born in a

Baptist family in New Brunswick, Canada, Robinson went to live with his brother Dores

ASA T. ROBINSON

in New Hampshire in 1870 and through the influence of his brother became a Seventh-day Adventist. In 1876 he married Loretta Farnsworth (1857-1933), daughter of William Farnsworth.

In 1882 the Robinsons became colporteurs, selling Uriah Smith's *Thoughts on Daniel and the Revelation*. At *S. N. Haskell's invitation, Asa entered pastoral ministry in 1884 and was ordained two years later. In 1891 the Robinsons went to South Africa, where he organized the first conference there, and established a number of institutions, including a college and a sanitarium. In 1894 Robinson and *Pieter Wessels secured from Prime Minister Cecil J. Rhodes a 12,000-acre tract of land on which they established the first permanent Seventh-day Adventist mission in Africa, *Solusi Mission. Robinson then served as a church administrator in Australia (1898-1903) before returning to the United States. During the next 18 years he served as conference president in Nebraska (1903-1910), Colorado (1913-1917), and Southern New England (1917-1920). During his years of service in South Africa and Australia Robinson was instrumental in developing the system of union conferences that was adopted at the General Conference session of 1901. While in South Africa and Australia Robinson exchanged numerous letters with Ellen White. "I feel deeply in regard to the missionary work in South Africa," she wrote in 1896. "I do hope you will not look to men, nor trust in men, but look to God and trust in God" (Lt 92, 1896, in TSA 67). While he worked in Australia she counseled him regarding the work of a conference president and other administrative responsibilities (Lts 87, 94, 1898).

Further reading: obit. RH, Dec. 29, 1949; A. T. Robinson, "Autobiographical Sketch—The Life of Asa Theron Robinson" (1947, DF 3125, CAR); *SDA Encyclopedia* (1996), vol. 11, pp. 462, 463.

Denis Fortin

ROBINSON, DORES A. (1848-1899). Minister and missionary, brother of *Asa T. Robinson.

DORES A. ROBINSON

Born in New Brunswick, Canada, Robinson moved to Maine and accepted Adventism in his youth. After attending Battle Creek College (1872-1874), he was ordained in 1876 and worked in the New England Conference (1874-1887).

Dores and his wife, Edna, then joined C. L. Boyd, Carrie Mace, and two colporteurs as the first missionaries to Cape Town, South Africa (1887-1888). They later served in England (1888-1895) and India (1895-1899), where he died of smallpox at the Karmatar Mission in 1899. Edna returned to America with their adopted English and Indian daughters; she died in 1905 in South Lancaster, Massachusetts, near the academy she had helped establish. In 1887, as they were beginning their work in South Africa, Ellen White urged both Robinson and Boyd to preach "practical godliness," take risks by faith, and to "keep up the elevated character" of their missionary work (Lt 14, 1887, in TSA 9-12). Eleven years later Ellen White encouraged the Robinsons in their work in India and that although they were separated by a long distance they had a common friend (Jesus), "who is ever near us" (Lt 28, 1898).

Further reading: obit. RH, Jan. 16, 1900; obit. RH, Feb. 13, 1900; Mar. 27, 1900; obit. Nov. 30, 1905; *SDA Encyclopedia* (1996), vol. 11, pp. 463, 464.

Brian E. Strayer

ROBINSON, DORES EUGENE (1879-1957).

DORES E. ROBINSON

Secretary, compiler, and editor for Ellen White. Robinson was born in Washington, New Hampshire, the second son of *Asa T. and Loretta Robinson, his mother being the twelfth of 22 children fathered by *William Farnsworth. In 1891 the Robinsons went to South Africa as missionaries, leaving 12-year-old Dores in the United States. Two years later, when Claremont Union College (now Helderberg College) was established near Cape Town, he rejoined the family and spent the next four years in South Africa. In 1897, while his parents sailed for *Australia, he went to Scotland to begin the medical course. The next year he followed them, continuing his medical training in Melbourne. When poor health caused him to drop out, Ellen White invited him to serve as one of her secretaries, which he did for several months. It was here that he first became acquainted with Ella (see *Ella May White), the oldest of Ellen White's seven grandchildren.

After returning to the United States, Robinson worked briefly in *Battle Creek and taught for a year in Montana, then was employed again by Ellen White. In 1905 he married Ella White. He continued as secretary and compiler for Ellen White until her death in 1915, working on such books as the 1911 edition of *The Great Controversy* and *Life Sketches*. Robinson spent the next two years in Colorado as a pastor and teacher, then served on the editorial staff of the Southern Publishing Association in Nashville until called to South Africa in 1920 as editor at the Sentinel Publishing Company. Later he served for three years at the Rusangu Mission in Northern Rhodesia (now Zambia). Robinson returned to the United States in 1928. With the exception of teaching one year at Humboldt Academy in northern California, from 1928 until retirement 25 years later he served on the staff of the Ellen G. White Estate, first at "Elmshaven," in California, and then in Washington, D.C. He wrote numerous books and pamphlets about Ellen White's ministry and her writings, one of the best known being *The Story of Our Health Message: The Origin, Character, and Development of Health Education in the Seventh-day Adventist Church* (SPA, 1943, 1955, 1965).

Further reading: obit. RH, Aug. 29, 1957; *SDA Encyclopedia* (1996), vol. 11, p. 464.

Kenneth H. Wood

ROBINSON, ELLA MAY (WHITE), see **WHITE, ELLA MAY.**

ROGERS, FRED R. (1869-1920). Pioneer educator for *African-Americans in the American South. In 1898 Rogers joined *J. Edson White in founding the *Southern Missionary Society and opened a school for Blacks in Yazoo City, Mississippi. When the Caucasian teachers were forced to leave Yazoo City because of local opposition, Rogers became the first superintendent of instruction for the Southern Missionary Society in the state of Mississippi. In 1904, at Ellen White's suggestion, he became principal and business manager of the *Oakwood Industrial School in Huntsville, Alabama (ST, Nov. 30, 1904). She encouraged him not to doubt God's goodness and to be of good courage in his work, because "heavenly angels are watching that farm" (the Oakwood school) (Lt 345, 1904, in SpTB 12).

Further reading: obit. LUH, May 5, 1920; obit. RH, May 27, 1920; R. D. Graybill, *Mission to Black America* (PPPA, 1971).

ROGERS, JANE "JENNY" or "JENNIE" (FRASER) and **SANFORD,** see **FRASER, JANE "JENNY"** or **"JENNIE,"** and **SANFORD ROGERS.**

ROOSEVELT, THEODORE (1858-1919). President of the United States (1901-1909). Ellen White, accompanied by Sarah McEnterfer, met President Roosevelt while driving their horse carriage in Rock Creek Park, in the District of Columbia, in July 1904. Roosevelt greeted the women by tipping his hat to them (5Bio 348). In 1905, when church leaders were considering the purchase of the Loma Linda property in southeastern California, Roosevelt's comments two years earlier regarding the beauty of the scenery of that area encouraged Adventists in establishing a sanitarium there (LLM 124, 159). Also in 1905, during the General Conference session held in Washington, D.C., a delegation of ministers met with Roosevelt and expressed to him the denomination's views and attitude toward civil government (5Bio 403, 404).

ROSS, ALEXANDER (1810-1888) and **CAROLINE** (1810-1866). Adventists from Roosevelt, New York. Saying they were a "burden" and a "hindrance" to their local church, Ellen White reproved them for their lack of self-denial and urged them to draw nearer to God and to receive "the powerful influence of divine love" (PH159 78-94; 3T 57-64). Alexander was the "Brother A" sternly denounced for his pro-slavery sentiments (Lt 24, 1862, in 1T 358-360). He accepted the rebuke, but almost two years passed before he fully and heartily confessed and renounced his previous views.

He is buried in the cemetery across from the Roosevelt, New York, church.

Further reading: obit. RH, June 12, 1888.

ROSSITER, FREDERICK M. (1870-1967). Adventist physician. Rossiter attended Battle Creek College (1889-1893), where he organized the first Foreign Mission Band, and compiled the first scriptural *index to Ellen White's writings, and married Mary Henry, daughter of *S.M.I. Henry. Rossiter continued his medical training at Rush Medical College and then at the University of Pennsylvania Medical College, where he graduated in 1897. He taught at the *American Medical Missionary College and practiced at the *Battle Creek Sanitarium. He later established the Yakima Valley Sanitarium and served on the faculty of the *College of Medical Evangelists. Ellen White wrote him a letter of encouragement (Lt 20, 1912). His daughter, Margaret, was married to *James Henry White.

Further reading: obit. RH, Dec. 7, 1967.

ROTH, MARY AMBERG (1861-1928). Adventist in Switzerland who served as Ellen White's translator (EGWEur 190). Her family helped build the first Adventist church in Europe at Tramelan, Switzerland (Ms 49, 1886). At Ellen White's own expense, Roth went to the *Battle Creek Sanitarium in 1887 to receive treatments (Lt 9, 1887). The following year Ellen White admonished Mary for her "finding fault" with the college and sanitarium. "I cannot longer be responsible for any of your expenses," she wrote. "For one year I have stood prepared to help you, and it is not right for me to do this while you in any way injure the institutions of God's appointment" (Lt 62, 1888). She later also rebuked Mary for her selfish spirit while living with the *W. C. Gage family and appealed to her to repent (Lt 53, 1893).

Further reading: obit. RH, Apr. 25, 1929.

ROUSSEAU, LEMUEL JOSEPH (1857-1898) and **EMMA LOUISE (ESHELMAN)** (1858-1936). Born in Iowa and raised in Kansas, Joseph became a licensed minister in 1884 and was ordained two years later. He studied at Battle Creek College in 1885 and 1890. He and his wife, Emma, were appointed to establish the first Seventh-day Adventist training school in Australia. In Australia the Rousseaus became associated with Ellen White and her family, especially in relation to school affairs. Leaving America in 1891, Rousseau opened the school in rented quarters during August 1892 in the Melbourne suburb of St. Kilda. The school functioned until September 1894, when it was moved to the permanent site, where it eventually became *Avondale College. Ellen White first wrote to Rousseau at the Melbourne school, asking him to take a special interest in a Maori student named William Makeiro. She asked that Rousseau procure any new clothes Makeiro needed and charge them to her account (Lt 100, 1893). At the new school site Rousseau assisted as an overseer for the early land-clearing operations. Mr. Worsnop, a Seventh-day Adventist from Melbourne with a rough colonial exterior, came to the estate asking for work. Rousseau refused him. White then wrote to Rousseau on Worsnop's behalf. She pleaded with Rousseau not to treat Worsnop as the priest and Levite (of Luke 15) would a neighbor in trouble. "Give him a chance to show what he is," she continued. Rousseau complied (Lt 69, 1895). In 1896 Rousseau enrolled at the Battle Creek Sanitarium, hoping to return to Australia as a medical missionary. However, in 1898, just prior to his final examinations, he tragically died of pleurisy (E. L. Rousseau to W. C. and M. White, Sept. 30, 1898). His wife, Emma, served with him in Australia and received many letters of encouragement from Ellen White. After Joseph died, she worked as a matron at the New England Sanitarium and afterward lived with her sister, Dr. Lillian Magan, in California.

Further reading: obit. RH, Sept. 6, 1898; obit. PUR, Feb. 17, 1937; M. Hook, *A Temporary Training School* (Wahroonga: South Pacific Division Department of Education [1987]).

Milton Hook

ROWEN, MARGARET MATILDA (WRIGHT) (1881-1955). Adventist, converted from Methodism about 1912, who claimed to receive visions beginning on June 22, 1916, and to be Ellen White's prophetic successor. A number of witnesses began to attest to her physical condition while in vision. One such report stated that Rowen held her "hands folded  across her breast and wide-open, unwinking eyes looking upward. . . . There was no breathing, as far as we could tell, and the body was rigid." Such reports led some to believe that her visions were genuine. These earliest visions were furthermore compiled into a 28-page booklet entitled *A Stirring Message for This Time* (n.p., c. 1916) and drew the attention of church leaders, who advised that they exercise caution "before expressing judgment in the matter." In February 1917 the Pacific Union Conference appointed a subcommittee to look into this matter more closely, and a group of church leaders (I. H. Evans, W. C. White, E. E. Andross, and M. M. Hare) visited Rowen and her assistant, Mrs. McCausland, to obtain more information. After their visit the Southern California Conference issued a formal statement that they had failed to find any evidence that "these manifestations" were

MARGARET ROWEN

COURTESY OF THE ELLEN G. WHITE ESTATE, INC.

of "divine origin" (*Claims Disproved* [n.p., 1917]).

In the autumn of 1919 Rowen claimed to have seen in vision a document in the manuscript files of the *Ellen G. White Estate, dated August 10, 1911, in which Ellen White stated that Mrs. Rowen would be a future messenger sent of God. The document, however, bore immediate evidence of forgery: the sheets were not perforated like other documents in the file; the typeface was different; there was no document file number; Ellen White was not in St. Helena when the document was dated; and the signature was a demonstrable forgery.

Rowen attracted a small but active following of those who accepted her as a divinely sent messenger. On November 15, 1919, Rowen was disfellowshipped from the South Side Seventh-day Adventist Church in Los Angeles. Her followers organized a new church, taking the name "Los Angeles, California, Seventh-day Adventist Reform Church," published a journal, *The Reform Advocate*, and were pejoratively referred to as "Rowenites." In November 1923 Rowen announced that the close of probation would occur on February 6, 1924, and that Christ would come in glory on February 6, 1925. Her sensational announcement received widespread coverage by news agencies around the world and was falsely attributed to the Seventh-day Adventist Church. When Rowen's time prediction failed, her loose band of followers started to disintegrate.

Dr. Burt E. Fullmer, a physician and zealous follower of Rowen, became disillusioned with Rowen after his discovery that she had embezzled $17,000 from her own organization. Disenchanted, on March 12, 1926, he confessed that he had inserted the spurious Ellen White manuscript on November 11, 1919, into an open drawer of manuscripts in the White Estate vault. On February 27, 1927,

Dr. Fullmer was summoned to render medical assistance to an alleged tourist at a nearby motel. Upon entering, Fullmer was struck on the head with a piece of pipe by Dr. Jacob Balzer, while Balzer's nurse, Mary Wade, attempted to inject morphine and strychnine into Fullmer's arm. A struggle ensued, and nearby hotel guests summoned the police. Upon discovery of a shovel, burlap, and rope in the room, apparently for disposing of the body, the police immediately arrested Balzer and Wade. Rowen subsequently turned herself in to police. The three were sentenced on a plea-bargain confession of guilt to "assault with a deadly weapon, with intent to do great bodily harm." All three were incarcerated at the San Quentin Prison in August 1927. Released on good behavior after serving only one year, Rowen fled from parole, and disappeared from public life. She sought refuge in Florida for a while before returning to California, where she went by her maiden name and continued to attract a small following.

Further reading: Larry White, "Margaret W. Rowen: Prophetess of Reform and Doom," *Adventist Heritage* 6, no. 1 (Summer 1979): 28-40; A. L. White, "False Prophets I Have Known" (unpublished manuscript); R. W. Schwarz and F. Greenleaf, *Light Bearers* (PPPA, 2000), pp. 618, 619; C. Shaw, Jr., "The Rowen Deception" (research paper, 1977, CAR); DF 364; DF 364-b; *SDA Encyclopedia* (1996), vol. 11, p. 428.

Michael W. Campbell

RUBLE, WELLS ALLEN (1868-1961). Converted to Adventism in 1893 and trained at Battle Creek College, Ruble married Edith Davies in 1897 and together they became missionaries to South Africa. Physician and administrator, he became president of Claremont Union College, South Africa, during the 1890s, while Edith taught at the college. Returning to the United States, Ruble earned his medical degree at the American Medical Missionary College in Battle Creek in 1906, then helped establish the *College of Medical Evangelists (CME) in Loma Linda, California, in 1910. He became the first president of CME (1910), then director of the General Conference Medical Department, and later superintendent of Stanborough Park Sanitarium, England (1918-1927) and the *New England Sanitarium (1927-1943). In 1911, in a letter to Ruble, *J. A. Burden, *I. H. Evans, and other workers at Loma Linda, Ellen White highlighted the importance of "faithfulness and consecration" in their work and urged them to train more women in the medical profession and especially as midwives. She also uplifted the life of the prophet Elijah as an example of consecration and spiritual reform among workers (Lt 22, 1911). After World War I Ruble served as a missionary in England (1921-1929).

Further reading: obit. RH, Aug. 3, 1961; *SDA Encyclopedia* (1996), vol. 11, p. 473.

Brian E. Strayer

RUMERY, SYLSBRE (1820-1884). Adventist from Monterey, Michigan. In 1857 Ellen White was shown in vision that Rumery's love of money hindered his and his family's spiritual growth, and she urged him also to provide some help to *Victor Jones (Lt 9, 1857). Although Rumery appeared to mend his ways (cf. Ms 5, 1859), Ellen White later cautioned him again for the same weakness (Ms 16, 1868) and for bringing "our faith . . . into disrepute" by his "selfish dealing" with local merchants (PH099 34; Lt 46a, 1874).

Further reading: obit. RH, Dec. 2, 1884.

RUSSELL, C. P., see *MESSENGER PARTY*.

RUSSELL, SUSAN G. (1825-1864). Adventist from Dartmouth, Massachussetts. In 1862, as Russell was battling with tuberculosis, Ellen White wrote to her about the *assurance of salvation. "A soul whom God had forsaken would never feel as you have felt and would never love the truth and salvation as you have loved it. . . . You must not gratify the enemy in the least by doubting and casting away your confidence. Said the angel, 'God leaves not His people, even if they err. He turns not from them in wrath for any light thing. If they sin they have an advocate with the Father, Jesus Christ the righteous.' . . . He who so loved you as to give His own life for you will not turn you off and forsake you unless you willfully, determinedly forsake Him to serve the world and Satan. Jesus loves to have you come to Him just as you are, hopeless and helpless, and cast yourself upon His all-abundant mercy and believe that He will receive you just as you are" (Lt 17, 1862, in HP 119).

Further reading: obit. RH, Jan. 31, 1865.

RUSSELL, WILLIAM (1832-c. 1910). Minister, homeopathic physician. Born in Hancock County, Ohio, Russell became an Adventist after Joseph Bates visited there in 1854. In 1855 Russell moved to the country near Mauston, Wisconsin, where he became a frequent correspondent in the *Review and Herald* during the late 1850s and early 1860s. He became a licensed minister in 1864.

In the fall of 1867 Russell joined the medical staff of the Western Health Reform Institute in Battle Creek. There is no record that he had any formal medical training, but the 1870 census gave his occupation as homeopathic physician. In the fall of 1868 he developed a plan to establish his own health institute in Mauston, Wisconsin. Aware of this plan, Ellen White pointed out that he lacked the "wise calculation and good judgment" to start his own institute. She advised him to accept the work for which he was actually qualified. "You

are naturally a kind-spirited man," she wrote, "but you lack energy and wisdom to manage business." She urged him to "counsel with men who have made life a success, and be guided by their counsel" (Lt 17, 1869, in PH107 3, 4, 6, 7). Russell reacted by writing to the *Marion Party, a group who did not believe in Ellen White's inspiration, expressing his doubts about her visions and asking for the evidence they had on the subject. On July 12, 1869, Dr. Russell told them he thought that "Mrs. White's visions were the result of diseased organization or condition of the brain or nervous system."

During 1869 and 1870 Russell wavered between supporting the Seventh-day Adventists or the Marion Party. At one point he became a corresponding editor of the *Hope of Israel*, published by the Marion Party. In 1870 Henry E. Carter wrote *Mrs. E. G. White's Claims to Divine Inspiration Examined* and included the above quote by Russell.

Meanwhile, in 1869, *J. N. Andrews, *Uriah Smith, and E. S. Walker published a pamphlet warning people not to invest in Russell's Wisconsin institute and included the testimony of Ellen White. In March 1870 a two-page supplement to the *Review and Herald* detailed Russell's contacts with the Marion Party and the attempts by the Whites to make things right with Russell (RH, Supplement, Mar. 15, 1870). In 1871 Russell apologized to the Whites and J. N. Andrews and returned to his post at the Health Reform Institute in Battle Creek.

The institute continued to have operating difficulties. In 1876 the institute board invited *John Harvey Kellogg to reorganize the institute. When Kellogg took charge on October 1, 1876, only 20 patients were being treated. Dr. Russell left with six of the patients and set up a water cure in Ann Arbor, Michigan (R.W. Schwarz, "John Harvey Kellogg: American Health Reformer" [Ph.D. diss., UM, 1964], p. 175).

Dr. Russell and his family appear in the 1880 census for Ann Arbor, Michigan. From 1885 to 1909 or 1910, Russell operated a private sanitarium in Minneapolis, Minnesota. The 1910 census lists Mrs. Russell as a widow operating a sanitarium, indicating that he died in 1909 or early 1910.

Further reading: RH, Apr. 25, 1871; RH, May 2, 1871; RH, May 9, 1871.

Lawrence W. Onsager

SADLER, WILLIAM SAMUEL (1875-1969) and LENA CELESTIA (KELLOGG) (1875-1939). Physicians. Lena was the daughter of *J. H. Kellogg's half brother, Smith Moses Kellogg. Both attended Battle Creek College, where William became a minister and Lena a nurse. After William's graduation in 1894, he was employed in J. H. Kellogg's *Chicago Medical Mission. He and Lena married in 1897 and moved to California, where William was ordained to the ministry and became youth director for the California Conference. At the same time he was president of the San Francisco Medical Missionary and Benevolent Society, and apparently both of them were attending Cooper Medical College. About 1904 they returned to the medical mission in Chicago, where William became the founding editor of *The Life Boat* magazine. Both Sadlers completed their medical degrees from the *American Medical Missionary College in 1906. That same year Ellen White wrote to Sadler warning him of the *pantheism in Battle Creek and inquiring what he purposed to do (Lt 118, 1906). In reply Sadler expressed his perplexities concerning the inspiration of her writings (W. S. Sadler to EGW, Apr. 26, 1906). She answered some of his questions from statements already published, assuring him that "the character of my work and my messages has not changed" (Lt 224, 1906). After several more exchanges he chose to leave the denomination (Lts 224a, 225c, 225d, 234, 1906). He later pursued a career in psychiatry, studied under Freud, Adler, and Jung in Europe, and for 27 years taught pastoral psychiatry at McCormick Theological Seminary in Chicago.

Further reading: obit. Chicago *Tribune*, Apr. 27, 1969; *Who Is Important in Medicine* (New York: Institute for Research in Biography, 1945, DF 247, EGWE-LLU).

Michael W. Campbell

ST. JOHN, HIRAM ALLEN (1840-1917). Minister to whom Ellen White responded about a physician coming to work at the St. Helena Sanitarium in 1884 (Lt 16, 1884). Converted to Adventism in 1857, St. John was married 10 years later and ordained to ministry in 1872. He held evangelistic meetings in Ohio and during the early 1880s moved to California, where he spent the remainder of his ministry. His responsibilities included being Bible and history teacher at Healdsburg College and chaplain of the St. Helena Sanitarium.

Further reading: obit. PUR, Nov. 1, 1917; *SDA Encyclopedia* (1996), vol. 11, p. 524.

SALISBURY, HOMER RUSSELL (1870-1915). Educator, administrator, and editor; brother of *Wilbur D. Salisbury. In 1893 he accepted an invitation to teach at Claremont Union College in South Africa, and later studied Hebrew in London, England. From 1897 to 1901 he taught Hebrew and church history at *Battle Creek College. During that time Ellen White wrote a series of letters of counsel to him and other church leaders (cf. Lt 48, 1897). In 1901, at the request of the General Conference, Salisbury established a training school for workers in England. After he returned to the United States, Ellen White expressed her pleasure that he was located in

Washington, D.C., where he served as president of the Foreign Mission Seminary from 1907 to 1910 (Lt 368, 1907). He later served as secretary of the General Conference Department of Education. In 1913 he was elected president of the India Union Mission. In 1915, during World War I, while Salisbury was returning to India from denominational meetings in the United States, his ship was torpedoed, and he was lost at sea.

Further reading: obit. *Eastern Tidings*, April 1915.

SALISBURY, WILBUR D. (1861-1946). Publishing house manager; brother of *Homer R. Salisbury. Raised in an Adventist family in Battle Creek, at the age of 17 Salisbury was enlisted by Uriah Smith to work at the *Review and Herald publishing house, a decision that became a life career. In 1885 he moved to *Pacific Press, in Oakland, California, and in 1890 became factory superintendent of the Stanborough Press in England. Three years later Salisbury was sent to Australia, where for 17 years he worked at the *Echo Publishing House and the Signs Publishing Company in Melbourne. In 1910 he returned to the United States and for a time was business manager of the *Washington and *Loma Linda sanitariums. Along with other church leaders in Australia, Ellen White wrote to Salisbury and counseled him on various matters related to the management of the Echo Publishing House (Lt 27, 1896) and the starting of new publishing houses in Melbourne (Lt 87, 1898; Lt 123, 1899) and Warburton (Lt 310, 1906; Lt 26, 1907).

Further reading: obit. PUR, Jan. 8, 1947; *SDA Encyclopedia* (1996), vol. 11, p. 527.

SANBORN, ISAAC (1822-1913). Evangelist and church administrator. Born in Pennsylvania, Sanborn moved with his family to Indiana and later to Wisconsin. He became a Sabbatarian

Adventist in 1855 and was ordained by James White a year later. He worked in 19 states and Ontario, with most of his ministry in Wisconsin. He served as president of the Illinois-Wisconsin Conference (1863-1867) and Wisconsin Conference (1870-1873). He also participated in the organization of the General Conference in 1863. Ellen White addressed two letters to Sanborn: one regarding his family life (Lt 10, 1867) and the other about his work and his relationship with other ministers (Lt 46, 1880).

Further reading: obit. RH, June 19, 1913; E. K. Vande Vere, "The Heart of the Lake Union," LUH, Apr. 27, 1976; *SDA Encyclopedia* (1996), vol. 11, p. 532.

SANDERSON, ARTHUR JAMES (1865-1927). Physician and pastor. Sanderson earned his medical degree from Cooper Medical College, where before his graduation he married Alice Smith. After Alice's death in 1892, he married Emma Griggs. After the loss of his second wife, he married Neva Huenergardt. Sanderson worked at the *St. Helena Sanitarium for about 10 years, during eight of which he served as the medical superintendent. He also operated a private El Reposo Sanitarium in Berkeley for about 21 years (1906-1927), at the same time serving as pastor of the Berkeley church. In 1901, during the St. Helena years, Ellen White warned Sanderson repeatedly concerning the dangers of "mind control" and "mind-cure"—"speculative theories" that he seemed to be fascinated with. She pleaded with him not to resist the influence of God on his life. She also counseled him that his wife was not a good influence on the sanitarium nurses and called her to shun the "worldly, frivolous entertainments," by which she was "slighting God" (Lt 133, 1901, in 18MR 265).

Further reading: 18MR 79-82, 263-273; obit. RH, July 14, 1927; "Letters to a Physician-in-Chief of a Large Sanitarium," *The Sanderson Collection* (DF 160, CAR); G. A. Roberts, "Dr. A. J. Sanderson," AR, Aug. 25, 1927.

Eriks Galenieks

SANTEE, CLARENCE (1856-1930). Adventist minister and administrator. Originally from New York, he was raised in Missouri, and in 1879 began to preach in Kansas. Santee was ordained in 1891 and in 1894 began to teach a small Bible school in Minneapolis. He afterward served as president of the Iowa (1896-1900), California (1900-1901), Southern California (1901-1905), Texas (1905-1908), and Southwestern Union (1906-1907, 1908-1910) conferences. These administrative posts placed him in close contact with Ellen White, whose advice he frequently sought. Ellen White cautioned him against starting a sanitarium in Long Beach (Lt 143, 1901) and counseled him on the founding of San Fernando Academy (Lts 88, 90, 1903). Santee also worked closely with Ellen White in the founding of the *Glendale and *Loma Linda sanitariums. He later taught at the *College of Medical Evangelists and afterward served as president of the Northern California Conference (1915-1924).

Further reading: obit. RH, Oct. 16, 1930; *SDA Encyclopedia* (1996), vol. 11, p. 542.

SARGENT, G. Adventist in the vicinity of Boston, Massachusetts, who with a Brother Robbins and others opposed Ellen Harmon's gift of prophecy. Accompanied by *Otis Nichols and by her sister *Sarah (Harmon) Belden, Harmon visited various groups of early Adventists near Boston in the fall of 1845. Some of these Adventists held the fanatical belief that Christ had already come "spiritually" and that the seventh millennium of rest had begun, and therefore concluded that to work was a sin, a denial of their faith.

In her early ministry Ellen Harmon often rebuked such fanatical beliefs, calling people to a more balanced religious life. Sargent and Robbins openly declared that her visions were of the devil. Yet, after meeting her during her visit to Boston, they agreed to listen to her testimony the following Sunday at a prearranged location in Boston. However, the night before the appointed meeting, Harmon received a vision showing Sargent and Robbins' hypocrisy and that there would be no meeting in Boston. The following morning Harmon and her friends went to the town of Randolph, about 13 miles (21 kilometers) south of Boston, where they found Sargent and Robbins with a large group of Adventists meeting in a private home. While meeting with this group that afternoon Ellen Harmon had a vision during which she held a large Bible and pointed out passages about the judgment of the wicked. While some people present were convinced of her gift, others, including Sargent and Robbins, were not (cf. 1Bio 99-105).

SATTERLEE, ANNIE (b. c. 1866). Young woman who had an affair with *Ira Abbey; niece of his daughter Eleanor (Abbey) Satterlee. In the 1880s Satterlee and her younger brother, Willard, lived with Ira and Rhoda Abbey in Brookfield, New York, in whose home she worked as a servant. In January 1890 Ellen White, who had been aware for some time of an adulterous relationship between Satterlee and Ira Abbey, wrote Satterlee two strong letters of rebuke asking that her relationship with Abbey be ended (Lts 23a, 24a, 1890, in TSB 137-142; cf. TSB 133-145). "I hope you will now confess your sins before it shall be forever too late," implored Ellen White (Lt 23a, 1890, in TSB 137, 138). "Your deliverance is to be found in Christ, and Him alone," she added in her second letter (Lt 24a, 1890, in

TSB 141). It appears that Abbey confessed his sin and ended the relationship.

Further reading: obit. RH, Dec. 11, 1894.

SAVAGE, ADELINE. Niece of James and Ellen White; daughter of James White's sister *Mary Chase, who lived with James and Ellen until James White's death in 1881. After that, Ellen White felt she could no longer bear the responsibility for Mary Chase, so in 1884 she wrote to Mary Chase's daughter, Adeline Savage, urging her to fulfill her duty to care for her aging mother, Mary Chase (Lt 30, 1884, in DG 198-200).

SAWYER, ROBERT (1830-1910). Adventist from Auburn, New York, who was converted through reading a tract published by James White (c. 1849). In 1855 Sawyer married Mary Ann Mapes (c. 1834-1859), and they moved to *Battle Creek, Michigan, where he worked at the *Review and Herald office. In 1863, after the death of his first wife, he married Mary J. Mead (1834-1890) and relocated to Potterville, Michigan. While they lived there Ellen White counseled them about their family and Sabbath school (Lt 8, 1863, in 3MR 261, 262). Later, when Sawyer was 78, she counseled him to attend to his personal appearance in order to better influence others (Lt 336, 1908).

Further reading: obit. RH, Dec. 1, 1910.

SEMMENS, ALFRED WILLIAM (1867-1940). An Australian physician converted after reading *The Great Controversy* (1888), Semmens went to America to receive training in nursing at Battle Creek Sanitarium. There he married Emma Pallant, and together they returned to Australia to teach in the Adventist school in Melbourne and, at Ellen White's urging, to open the first Adventist hydrotherapy clinics in Sydney and Adelaide. Later they managed the Sydney Sanitarium and engaged in private medical practice. In 1911 they returned to the United States, where Alfred earned a medical degree in 1915 at the College of Medical Evangelists in Loma Linda. The Semmenses then returned to Australia in 1916 and maintained a private medical practice until their retirement in 1940. In 1896 Ellen White sent them funds, encouragement, and guidance on training their son (Lt 98a, 1896). In another letter she gave him advice on how to use hydrotherapy treatments for fevers (Lt 112a, 1897).

Further reading: obit. RH, Oct. 31, 1940; *SDA Encyclopedia* (1996), vol. 11, p. 569.

SHARP, SMITH (1847-1931). Born at Mount Pleasant, Iowa, Sharp accepted the Adventist message from *Moses Hull in 1860. In 1865 he married Nettie Kilgore, sister of *R. M. Kilgore, and was ordained by James White in 1876. He served as president of the Kansas Conference (1878-1881), did missionary work in New Mexico and Colorado, and for a while, at the urging of Ellen White, was a missionary to the United Kingdom (Lt 41, 1886). After his return to the United States, he worked closely with *G. I. Butler in the American South. He was the first president of the Cumberland Conference (1900-1903) and also served as financial agent for the Southern Union. When he was tempted by negative thoughts, Ellen White encouraged him to look upon the bright side of life and to place himself "in right relation with God" (Lt 93, 1901).

Further reading: obit. RH, June 25, 1931.

SHIREMAN, DAN T. (1834-1920). Brickmason, carpenter, general mechanic, and *self-supporting evangelist and colporteur. Born in Shiremanstown, Pennsylvania, he married Amelia McDowell (1839-1905) in 1857 and a year later accepted the Adventist teaching on the seventh-day Sabbath. Without a formal education, Shireman responded to Ellen White's call to work in areas where there were no Seventh-day Adventists, and moved from place to place, establishing Adventist communities. In 1890 he went to North Carolina, where he raised up churches and schools, and founded an orphanage at Hildebran. He also worked as a self-supporting evangelist and colporteur in Iowa and Kansas. Sherman was ordained in 1892; his lifework resulted in more than 45 church-related buildings erected in different locations. Ellen White repeatedly commended Shireman's ministry for planting church after church: "Many more should work as Brother Shireman has been working" (Ms 16, 1902) and "God has given us Brother Shireman's work as an object lesson" (2SAT 157; cf. Ms 35, 1901).

Further reading: obit. RH, June 17, 1920; obit. RH, Apr. 6, 1905; Ms 37, 1901; Lt 122, 1902; GCDB, Apr. 8, 1901; GCDB, Apr. 25, 1901; B. Haloviak, "The Orphan, the Angel, and the Long Way," AR, May 31, 1990; *SDA Encyclopedia* (1996), vol. 11, p. 604.

Eriks Galenieks

SHORTRIDGE, ELIAS WILLETS (1826-1890). Disciples of Christ minister who accepted the Adventist teaching on the *Sabbath after listening to a debate by *Moses Hull in 1860 (cf. RH, Dec. 4, 1860; RH, Dec. 11, 1860). Shortridge soon afterward began preaching for the Adventists in Iowa. In 1861 Ellen White counseled him that reforms were needed in his personal life before he could be an effective minister of the gospel (Lt 30, 1861). In the summer of 1862 Shortridge joined the *Marion Party and left the denomination (RH, Nov. 18, 1862). Following his departure, Ellen White published her earlier testimony to him (RH Supplement, August 1862; see also RH, Oct. 28, 1862; RH, Nov. 18, 1862).

SIMPSON, ABBIE WINEGAR (1865-1949) and **W. RAY** (1862-1940). Physician and business manager, respectively. Abbie Winegar became a Seventh-day Adventist at the age of 24 and later studied medicine at Northwestern Medical College in Chicago. Upon finishing her degree in 1894, she worked at the Battle Creek Sanitarium. She married W. Ray Simpson in 1903 and after moving to California the next year helped in founding the *Glendale Sanitarium. In 1904 Ellen White encouraged the Simpsons in their work at the sanitarium (Lts 251, 343, 1904) and gave Abbie a few counsels regarding her role as the stepmother of her husband's children (Lt 329, 1904). In succeeding years Ellen White encouraged them in their work at the Glendale and Long Beach sanitariums (Lt 418, 1907; Lts 126, 190, 1908; Lt 34, 1910).

Further reading: obit. RH, Feb. 24, 1949; obit. RH, Dec. 12, 1940.

SIMPSON, WILLIAM WARD (1872-1907). Adventist evangelist. Born in the United States but raised in England, at age 11 Simpson moved to Florida with his family. After his mother became a Seventh-day Adventist, the family moved to Battle Creek,

WILLIAM AND NELLIE SIMPSON

Michigan. In 1890 he decided to become a colporteur, and shortly thereafter the Michigan Conference granted him a license to preach. Working first in Michigan and then among indigenous people in Ontario, Simpson soon became a talented evangelist. In 1899 he married Nellie F. Ballenger (1869-1952), daughter of *John F. Ballenger, and was ordained to the ministry the same year.

Because of a persistent lung disease, in 1902 he and his family moved to southern California, where he won large numbers of converts to Adventism.

Part of Simpson's success came as a result of his use of visual aids and charts to depict the prophecies of the books of Daniel and Revelation. In 1906, before the age of moving pictures, videos, and computer animation, he commissioned the construction of seven papier-mâché beasts representing various powers and kingdoms in Daniel 7 and 8 and Revelation 13. At the appropriate moment during his sermons these beasts would be rolled onto the stage to invariably captivate his audience. Ellen White commended his evangelistic methods—his "ingenuity and tact to provide suitable illustrations" (i.e., the papier-mâché beasts) in his sermons—and expressed her gladness "that you exalt the Word, allowing the Bible to speak for itself" (Lt 376, 1906; cf. Lts 326, 350, 1906; Ev 204, 205; RH, Nov. 29, 1906).

Deeply interested in his work in Los Angeles, San Diego, and Oakland, and aware of his lung disease, Ellen White counseled him to "not break down under the strain of long, continuous effort" and to share his burdens with his colleagues (Lt 367, 1904, in 9MR 15). She was particularly worried about Simpson's overtaxing his throat, lungs, and digestive system during his extended series of evangelistic meetings (Lt 310, 1904), and earnestly encouraged him to get some rest at a nearby sanitarium (Lt 344, 1906). Yet another of Ellen White's concerns was the influence of his brother-in-law, *A. F. Ballenger, on Simpson's interpretation of Bible prophecies. While Ballenger was rejecting the traditional Adventist interpretation of the beginning of the cleansing of the heavenly sanctuary in 1844, Ellen White reminded Simpson that "the truths given us after the passing of the

time in 1844 are just as certain and unchangeable [now] as when the Lord gave them to us in answer to our urgent prayers" (Lt 50, 1906). Simpson remained faithful to Adventist teachings and to Ellen White's gift of prophecy until his death at age 35. Simpson's papier-mâché beasts are on display at the Center for Adventist Research at Andrews University.

Further reading: obit. RH, May 23, 1907; F. M. Ramsey, "A Study of William Ward Simpson's Evangelistic Personality" (research paper, AU, 1971, DF 3128, CAR).

Denis Fortin

SISCO, PATIENCE S. (BOURDEAU) (1869-1970). Physician, wife of Dr. Henry N. Sisco (1870-1943), and daughter of *Daniel and Marion Bourdeau. While Ellen White was in Europe in 1885-1887, Patience, then a teenager, served as an interpreter for White on her shopping trips. Patience received her medical degree in 1902, and in 1905 accepted Ellen White's encouragement to join the medical staff and "manage" the *Washington Sanitarium (Lt 177, 1905; DG 98, 99).

Further reading: obit. RH, Apr. 2, 1970.

SISLEY, WILLIAM CONQUEROR (1850-1932). Architect. At various times Sisley worked as  a builder, president of the Michigan Tract and Missionary Society, carpenter and secretary of Battle Creek College (1886), manager of the Review and Herald Publishing Association (1894-1899), and a person whom Ellen White and other pioneers relied upon for his business acumen.

WILLIAM C. SISLEY

Ellen White saw the Sisley family—William, his parents and siblings—in vision prior to their migration to America from England. She identified the Sisleys six years later (1863) as they entered a meeting in Battle Creek. There she correctly predicted that family members would become workers for God. The Sisleys settled in Convis, Michigan, but Ellen White persuaded them to move to Battle Creek. In 1874 Sisley began studies at Battle Creek College. The next year he married Frederika House (1852-1934), Uriah Smith officiating. It was about this time that he presumably became acquainted with Adventist architect William K. Loughborough and building superintendent *Orrin B. Jones. In 1877 he was elected to the Battle Creek College board. Sisley worked closely with denominational educators, and in the late spring of 1889 became architect and building supervisor for Union College. Campus planning and architectural work for Walla Walla College, Keene Industrial Academy, and Avondale College followed. During the 1890s he was the architect for the Haskell Home for 150 orphans, Dr. J. H. Kellogg's residence, the Sanitarium Company Helper's Home, and the northern addition to the college, all in Battle Creek. From 1896 to 1900 Sisley was manager of the Review and Herald Publishing Association in Battle Creek. In February 1899, after consulting with church leaders in Australia, Ellen White invited him and his family to join them in Australia (Lt 31, 1899). Sisley, however, decided to remain in Battle Creek, and from 1901 to 1918 he continued in architectural and publishing work for the denomination in Europe.

Further reading: obit. RH, October 1932; "The Sisley Family Seen in Vision" (Ms WDF 1116, Item 2, 1938, EGWE-LLU); E. L. Coombs and D. Minchin-Comm, "The Sisleys: Lives of Sacrifice and Service," *Adventist Heritage* 16, no. 1 (Spring 1993): 70-77; E. Dick, *Union College of the Golden Cords* (Lincoln, Nebr.:

Union College Press, 1967), pp. 27-31, 43, 44, 103, 104; *Lest We Forget* (Keene, Tex.: Southwestern Adventist College, 1985), pp. 16, 21; *Walla Walla College: 60 Years of Progress* (Walla Walla, Wash.: College Press, 1952), pp. 94, 105.

David J. Stafford

SKINNER, THOMAS WILLIAM FARRINGTON and **MAUD ELIZABETH LUCY (CAMP)** (1873-1936). Adventists from New Zealand. For about two years Maud Camp served as Ellen White's cook and traveling assistant. When Thomas asked to work at the Avondale school (later *Avondale College), White replied that they needed such help, and as she understood he was soon to be married to Maud (which took place about a month later), she invited both of them to Australia to receive an education, and thus prepare to educate others (Lt 105, 1897).

SMITH, ANNIE REBEKAH (1828-1855). Writer, teacher, editor, and poet from West Wilton,

SELF-PORTRAIT OF ANNIE R. SMITH

New Hampshire. She, along with her younger brother, *Uriah, waited for Christ to return in 1844, but after the *disappointment her interest in Adventism waned, and she took up teaching. Through a remarkable set of circumstances Smith met *Joseph Bates in 1851. Smith had a dream of entering a room in which a stranger was preaching; Bates also had a dream that while he was preaching, a young woman entered the meeting. When Smith walked into Bates' evangelistic meeting, both persons recognized the exact fulfillment of what they had dreamed. Smith continued to attend Bates' meetings, three weeks later accepted the *Sabbath, and soon wrote her first poem for the *Review and Herald (Sept. 16, 1851), entitled "Fear Not, Little Flock." *James White, impressed by her talent, invited her to join the *Review staff in Saratoga Springs, New York. At first Smith declined because of eye trouble, but eventually accepted. After an anointing and prayer for healing, her eyesight improved. When the *Review moved to Rochester, New York, in 1852, she went along and continued to work as proofreader and copy editor. At times when the Whites were away she was given full responsibility of the *Review*. During the three years she worked for the *Review*, 45 of her poems appeared in that journal and the *Youth's Instructor. Annie had a strong bond of affection with the Whites, and her mother testified during Annie's last illness that "Annie loved them." Smith returned home with tuberculosis in November 1854 and died a few months later at age 27.

Further reading: obit. RH, Aug. 21, 1855; R. Graybill, "The Life and Love of Annie Smith," *Adventist Heritage* 2, no. 1 (Summer 1975): 14-23; R. Smith, *Poems: With a Sketch of the Life and Experience of Annie R. Smith* (Manchester, N.H.: John B. Clarke, 1871); Annie Smith, *Home Here; Home in Heaven* (Rochester, N.Y.: Advent Review Press, 1855); *SDA Encyclopedia* (1996), vol. 11, pp. 617, 618.

Michael W. Campbell

SMITH, CYRENIUS (1804-1874) and **LOUISA (SAWYER)** (1806-1881). Farmer, carpenter, and dealer in stationery. Originally from New England, the Smiths moved to New York, and in 1833 settled in Jackson County, Michigan. They became Millerites and accepted the Sabbath from *Joseph Bates in August 1849.

The Smiths quickly became friends of James and Ellen White—the Whites frequently staying with them and the Smiths sending clothes to them while they were in desperate need in

CYRENIUS SMITH

LOUISA SMITH

Rochester, New York (Lt 7, 1853; JW to Cyrenius Smith, Aug. 29, 1854, EGWE-GC). Ellen had at least one vision in their home (JNL, *Rise and Progress*, p. 189). One of the first Adventist church schools in Michigan was conducted in the Smith home, and Cyrenius was one of the first deacons ordained among Sabbatarian Adventists (RH, Jan. 24, 1854). The next year the Smiths sold their farm to contribute to the Advent cause and relocated to *Battle Creek. They joined *Dan Palmer, *J. P. Kellogg, and *Henry Lyon in raising funds to build a publishing office, and encouraged the Whites to relocate from *Rochester to Battle Creek. Cyrenius helped build many of the early buildings in Battle Creek, including the White home on Wood Street. He also served on the financial committee that oversaw the publication of the *Review and Herald until the Seventh-day Adventist Publishing Association was organized in 1861.

Further reading: 1Bio 282; 2SG 181-182, 304; Lt 13, 1864; obit. RH, June 30, 1874; JW, *Life Incidents*, pp. 297, 298; RH, Oct. 2, 1855; R. Conrad, "Growing Up With the Third Angel's Message—No. 4," RH, May 2, 1935; W. C. White, "The Frisbie House a Center" (DF 451a, CAR).

Michael W. Campbell

SMITH, HARRIET NEWALL (STEVENS) (1831-1911). Wife of *Uriah Smith, daughter of Cyprian Stevens and sister of *J. N. Andrews' wife, Angeline, Harriet was known for her hospitality and charitable deeds. Harriet and Uriah were married in June

HARRIET N. SMITH

1857. Ellen White counseled Harriet regarding a lack of faith that tended to discourage her husband and other church members. Although Harriet publicly confessed this fault, others considered her insincere, which nearly caused her to lose faith in God and humanity. Ellen White sympathized with Harriet, and her faith revived after a group prayer session. Also of concern to White was Uriah's mild disposition and Harriet's "undue affection" that made it difficult to discipline their five children. They were advised to be more firm with the four boys and to take special care not to spoil their only girl, Annie (*Testimony to the Church at Battle Creek*, pp. 34-50). The admonitions evidently had the desired effect, since all five became respected citizens and church members.

Further reading: obit. RH, Mar. 30, 1911.

Eugene F. Durand

SMITH, LEON A. (1863-1958). Editor, son of *Uriah and *Harriet Smith. Like his father, Smith worked as an editor for the Review and Herald Publishing Association in Battle Creek and later at the Stanborough Press in England, and at the Southern Publishing Association in Nashville, Tennessee. In early 1890, sensing that Smith's critical attitude was detrimental to his spiritual life, Ellen White encouraged him to have a "much deeper experience . . . with God" (Lt 53, 1890, in 1888 Materials 528-532). The following year he inquired of Ellen White what counsels she could give him while he studied at the University of Michigan in Ann Arbor. Ellen White expressed her concerns that Adventist students who attend secular schools, when they have the privilege of an Adventist education, "are in danger of not preserving [their] connection with God." She encouraged him to be like Daniel and to seek wisdom from above. She also emphasized that "the youth who go to Ann Arbor must receive Jesus as their personal Savior or they will build upon the sand, and their foundation will be swept away" (Lt 26, 1891, in 3SM 231-233).

Further reading: obit. RH, June 19, 1958.

SMITH, STEPHEN (1806-1889). Early Sabbatarian Adventist in New Hampshire. From the early 1850s Smith was openly critical of the prophetic ministry of Ellen White.

STEPHEN SMITH

At a conference in Washington, New Hampshire, in November 1851, attended by James and Ellen White, Smith persisted in opposing Ellen White's ministry. Consequently, the members attending the conference decided to disfellowship him until such time as he would lay aside his erroneous views. This decision was one of the first disciplinary actions taken by Sabbatarian Adventists (Lt 8, 1851; RH, Nov. 25, 1851). Smith was welcomed back into the church a short time later, only to be disfellowshipped again. This scenario was repeated a few times in the 1850s. After one of his lapses around 1857, Ellen White wrote him a testimony in which she depicted what his life would be if he persisted in his wrongful views and attitudes. Instead of reading her letter, Smith placed it in a chest and forgot about it until the summer of 1885. After three decades of estrangement from the church, Smith began to realize that those who had opposed the church and its message had not prospered, while those who had supported it had been blessed. While attending revival meetings conducted by *E. W. Farnsworth at the Washington, New Hampshire, church in 1885, Smith remembered the forgotten testimony he had received from Ellen White and read it. After the worship service the following Sabbath, he confessed being wrong all those years and that he should have read and listened to the spiritual counsels sent to him. He admitted that Ellen White's depiction 28 years earlier of what his life would be were he to keep the same attitude and views had proved accurate. Finally convinced of the genuineness of her gift, Smith laid aside his resentment, reunited with the church, and remained faithful until his death.

Further reading: Lt 8, 1851, in 3MR 242-244; Ms 2, 1858, in 21MR 373-377; 1Bio 217-219, 490-492; obit. RH, Jan 28, 1890; *Notes and Papers Concerning Ellen G. White and the Spirit of Prophecy* (EGWE, 1971), pp. 351-354; H. E. Douglass, *They Were There* (PPPA, 2006), pp. 35-38.

Denis Fortin

SMITH, URIAH (1832-1903). Editor, administrator, preacher, prophetic expositor, profes-

URIAH SMITH

sor, poet, inventor, and artist-engraver, he was the most versatile of the Adventist pioneers. By serving as an editor of the *Review and Herald* for 50 years, authoring 20 books, and writing some 4,000 editorials, Smith exerted a steadying influence on the young church exceeded only by that of cofounders *James and Ellen White and *Joseph Bates. Throughout the denomination's history only its presidents have carried

more weight with the members than the *Review* editor-in-chief, a position Smith held for 34 years, longer than anyone else.

Born in New Hampshire, Smith met James and Ellen White in 1852 at a conference in the town of Washington, New Hampshire, where the Whites were speaking on Adventist beliefs. Soon afterward Smith was baptized and joined not only the church but the *Review and Herald* staff at the invitation of editor James White, who was impressed by the young convert's writing ability. The press and its staff, for a time, shared the Whites' rented *home in *Rochester, New York. This close association marked the beginning of a 50-year relationship between Smith and Ellen White, he being only five years her junior. In 1855, 23-year-old Smith became the *Review* editor, and the publication moved to Battle Creek, Michigan, where it remained till the year of his death. Smith and James White alternated as chief editor (with the exception of *J. N. Andrews for one year) until White's death in 1881, whereupon Smith took over for most of the next 16 years. When James White began publication of *Signs of the Times* in California in 1874, Uriah Smith served with him as an editor for 13 years, though he remained in Michigan.

Smith is best known for his books *Thoughts on Daniel* and *Thoughts on the Revelation*, which have remained in print for more than 120 years. The first Seventh-day Adventist *colporteur, *George King, asked for Smith's two books to be published as one volume. That combined volume was released in 1882 and has since gone through five editions. With some exceptions, it has remained representative of the Adventists' basic prophetic interpretation. That *Daniel and Revelation* continues to be published owes much to its endorsement by Ellen White, who wrote, "the interest in *Daniel and the Revelation* is to continue as

515

long as probationary time shall last. God used the author of this book [Smith] as a channel through which to communicate light to direct minds to the truth" (Ms 174, 1899, in 1MR 63). She urged its study by students in Adventist schools as well as by the church's ministers, and its sale by colporteurs. This and similar recommendations (see 1MR 60-65) fostered a rumor that Ellen White claimed an angel stood by Smith's side as he wrote the book. But nowhere in her writings can such a statement be found. Nor did she consider the book inspired or without error. Yet she knew of no other book that could take its place, calling it "the very book for this time" (Ms 174, 1899, in 1MR 60). White urged that it be translated into many languages, as indeed it has been.

During the last 30 years of his life Smith held many seminars for ministers featuring lectures on biblical topics, grammar, penmanship, writing for publication, and parliamentary procedure. Ellen White heartily endorsed these biblical institutes in different states and believed more time should be given to them. In 1894 Smith held institutes in five European cities. The lectures were published, thereby expanding their influence.

Smith became the first Bible teacher at the church's first college, *Battle Creek College. As chair of the board of trustees he came into conflict with Ellen White over educational policy. He favored a theoretical, classical curriculum, while she argued for a practical manual-type education and preparation for gospel work, with emphasis on the Bible. White urged a country location, while Smith defended the small Battle Creek campus. When Smith became critical of English professor *Goodloe Harper Bell (who seconded White's ideas), resulting in the teacher's resignation (February 1882), Ellen White rebuked Smith sharply (cf. 5T 45-62). She was surprised that one who had been too tenderhearted to

reprove wrongs at the publishing house, in the church, or in his own family had now become an unjust accuser. Smith defended his actions, feeling she had been misinformed. But nine years later he admitted that Ellen White knew him better than he knew himself and sought Bell's forgiveness. She held no animosity toward Uriah and asked him to write the introduction to her book *Patriarchs and Prophets*, in which he defended her divine inspiration.

At the *General Conference session of 1888 in Minneapolis *Signs of the Times* editor *E. J. Waggoner presented lectures emphasizing *righteousness by faith, as did associate editor *A. T. Jones and Ellen White. Uriah Smith feared that this new emphasis would weaken the Adventist position on the importance of the *law and the Sabbath. Ellen White responded, "He doesn't know what he is talking about." He is acting "as though we were discarding the claims of God's law, when it is no such thing" (Ms 5, 1889, in 1888 Materials 348). When Smith continued emphasizing the law in his *Review* editorials, she warned him against blindness and deception, declaring, "We have preached the law until we are as dry as the hills of Gilboa" (RH, Mar. 11, 1890). Again she wrote, "You have been working at cross purposes with God." She reproved him for being self-deceived, influencing others against the light God had given her, by suggesting she had been influenced by others. She had wept and prayed for him to cast off his blindness (Lt 40, 1890, in 1888 Materials 790-801). This appeal touched his heart, and he responded with tears of repentance and a public confession of his wrong attitude. Her confidence in him was restored. Yet in subsequent years Ellen White was pained to read *Review* articles by Smith presenting the same old emphasis on the law. Church leadership felt the same way. As a result, in 1897 Smith was replaced by A. T. Jones as *Review* editor.

Throughout his life Smith's writings strongly championed the work of Ellen White as God's special messenger endowed with the gift of prophecy. His 1868 book *The Visions of Mrs. E. G. White* presented the reasons for his confidence in her divine calling. Yet when she had occasion to reprove his own course of action, he found it difficult to accept that such messages came from God, and sank under discouragement. He would claim that her letters were not the result of heavenly visions and hence not inspired as her other writings were. Then, after talking with her, he would see things in a different light and admit that she had been right about him.

Uriah Smith was closely connected with Ellen White. Together they traveled and spoke at Adventist gatherings on many occasions and places. In spite of their occasional differences, she expressed confidence in him after his confessions and declared that he should remain the *Review* editor as long as he could write.

For the last 35 years of Smith's life Ellen White pleaded with him to take care of his health. He was too inclined to work at his desk both at the office and at home, day and night. She told him to get away to church gatherings, watch his diet, and engage in light labor or recreation outdoors. No one could benefit more from Adventist health reform than Uriah Smith, she declared. His love of writing and his artificial leg limited his physical activities, but he sought to follow this counsel, and to the extent that he did, he extended his life. But by age 70 he had become old before his time, and in early 1903 he died of the long-feared stroke while walking to the publishing plant to deliver what became his last article.

Further reading: E. F. Durand, *Yours in the Blessed Hope, Uriah Smith* (RHPA, 1980); R. J. Hammond, "The Life and Work of Uriah Smith" (M.A. thesis, AU, 1944); *SDA Encyclopedia* (1996), vol. 11, pp. 618, 619.

Eugene F. Durand

SMITH, WILL. Criminal, radically reconverted under the preaching of *E. P. Daniels in Fresno, California, in 1887. Ellen White met him at camp meeting a year later (1888 Materials 81-83; Lt 47, 1888, in 6MR 150, 151). Smith, "a tall, . . . powerfully built man," had been an Adventist, but "for some reason gave it up, and the devil took possession of him, and he became a desperado." His wife was a Sabbathkeeper and he loved her, "but not enough to stop his evil course. He did not care for the spoil of his robberies," but did it for the excitement. He had burned houses and barns, and even planned a murder, but his victim did not appear when expected.

When Smith entered a meeting at which E. P. Daniels was preaching on confession, Smith turned pale and fled, but returned. After the meeting he demanded, "Is there any hope for me? I am a lost man. . . . Will you pray for me? I dare not leave this place to go home for fear the Lord will cut me down in my sins" (1888 Materials 82). The ministers prayed, Smith was converted, and he set out immediately to confess to a man he had stolen 31 sheep from. The startled response was "Where did you get this? . . . I did not know that there was any such religion as this." Smith and an accomplice said to the authorities, "We deliver ourselves up. Do with us as you see fit" (*ibid.*). But when the case came to court, the judge refused to sentence one so obviously transformed. "The influence of these confessions," Ellen White concluded, "is as far reaching as eternity. This man in his wickedness had nothing, but since his conversion the Lord has blessed him greatly with means, and he is using it in making restitution and in advancing the cause of truth. . . . He has done more missionary work alone the past year than the whole Fresno church together" (6MR 151, 152).

Jerry Moon

SMOUSE, CHARLES W. (1853-1932) and **LEILA** (1861-1943). Adventists from Mount Pleasant, Iowa, whom Ellen White considered some of her "old friends." The Smouses financially supported Adventist missionary work and promoted various fund-raising activities (cf. *Gospel Herald*, August 1898, p. 23). Several times they either donated or lent funds to Ellen White. In 1898 she thanked them for a donation they made for the Adventist work in Australia (Lt 131, 1898).

SNOOK, B. F., see **MARION PARTY**.

SPERRY, CHARLES W. (c. 1820-1861) and **RACHEL ANN (GARDNER)** (1831-1863). Millerites and early Sabbatarian Adventist minister in Vermont. Both Charles and Rachel united with a Baptist church in Vermont at an early age and joined the Millerite movement in 1843. In 1851 they accepted the doctrines of Sabbatarian Adventists and thereafter contributed their talents and efforts to their new cause. In the early years of their association with Sabbatarian Adventists, Sperry was closely connected with other Adventist ministers and at first objected to the group selecting the official name of Seventh-day Adventist in 1860 (1Bio 423). In 1861 Ellen White addressed a letter to the Sperrys about a dream she had had regarding Rachel's father, Henry Gardner. Ellen White felt the Gardners "[clung] to money closely," keeping them from sharing of their means with others, and this attitude had a negative influence upon Charles and Rachel (Lt 4b,

1861; cf. Lt 8, 1861). Charles appears to have suffered from lung disease (likely tuberculosis) for many years, and his persistent illness drew cautions from Ellen White, who urged him to rest from his labor, a caution he did not follow (2T 117). "When he was dying," Ellen White recalled, "he sent for my husband and me to come and pray for him. While we were with him, he said, 'Oh, Sister White, I need not now be dying had I heeded the warnings that you gave me'" (Lt 367, 1904, in 9MR 15). Yet she was confident that Sperry now rested from his labors "till the voice of Jesus shall call the righteous from their graves to a glorious, immortal life" (ST, Aug. 12, 1875; cf. Lt 8, 1861). Rachel died of the same disease two years later.

Further reading: obit. RH, Oct. 1, 1861; obit. RH, Nov. 24, 1863.

Denis Fortin

SPERRY, JAMES BYRON (1854-1928). Son of *C. W. Sperry, James lost both his parents as a young boy. In 1875 Ellen White remembered how Sperry, then about 4 years old, was a playmate to her son Willie (Lt 19a, 1875, in 3MR 177). Later, as a youth, Sperry received a letter from Ellen White about his association with other boys who were a corrupting influence upon him (*Special Testimony for the Battle Creek Church* [1869], PH085 27). Years later, after he had lost both his wife and infant daughter, she pleaded with him not to make a shipwreck of his faith (Lt 207, 1904).

Further reading: obit. RH, Sept. 20, 1928.

SPRAGUE, W. B., see **FAIRFIELD, WILLIAM "WILLIE" JOSIAH**.

STANTON, A. W. Secretary for the Montana Tract Society in 1892. To further the work of the Seventh-day Adventist Church, Stanton offered to donate about $40,000 to the church.

But becoming dissatisfied with certain decisions made, he developed a critical attitude toward the church and its ministry. This led him to propagate a message of judgment against the church. The "new light" of his judgment message spread rapidly. After Stanton resigned from his position, *Dan T. Jones, district superintendent for Montana, conversed with him, and for a short while Stanton gave up his critical attitude. Early in 1893, however, Stanton published a 64-page booklet called *The Loud Cry! Babylon Fallen! Weighed in the Balances—Found Wanting*. The first part of the tract consisted of questions answered by short quotations from Scripture and Ellen White's writings. The second part contained longer Ellen White quotations on the need of reform in the church. The book's main thrust was that the Seventh-day Adventist Church is spiritually bankrupt, has become a part of Babylon and is fallen (Rev. 18). According to Ellen White, Stanton misused her writings by printing only her messages of rebuke, separated from the promises of grace and mercy. Thus he concluded that the Adventist Church had been rejected by God and that believers must separate from it. The pamphlet was widely distributed, sent overseas, and translated into Danish and German. One of Stanton's followers, *W. F. Caldwell, abandoned his wife and family and went to Australia to promulgate Stanton's views there. Through the intervention of *G. B. Starr and Ellen White, Caldwell found his way back to the church. Ellen White was in Australia when Stanton published his book. On March 22, 1893, she wrote him a letter (Lt 57, 1893), later published as a four-part article in the *Review and Herald* (Aug. 22 to Sept. 12, 1893; see TM 32-62). She told Stanton that he had been deceived by the devil and that the Seventh-day Adventist Church was not Babylon. She acknowledged that the church is still the "church militant," not yet "triumphant," and contained tares and wheat. But the Babylon described in the Bible fosters "poisonous doctrines . . . such as the natural immortality of the soul, the eternal torment of the wicked, the denial of the pre-existence of Christ prior to His birth in Bethlehem, and advocating and exalting the first day of the week above God's holy and sanctified day" (TM 61; see also 2SM 63-71 and TM 15-62). She further rebuked Stanton for withholding tithe in contradiction to Malachi 3, and setting a date for Christ's second coming (TM 60, 61). This decided response ended the "Stanton movement" (2SM 96).

Further reading: 4Bio 80-85; TSB 206-217 for letters addressed to W. F. Caldwell; *Issues: The Seventh-day Adventist Church and Certain Private Ministries* (Silver Spring, Md.: North American Division of Seventh-day Adventists, 1992), pp. 56-60.

Ekkehardt Mueller

STARR, GEORGE BURT (1854-1944) and **NELLIE (SISLEY)** (1854-1934). Evangelist, pastor, and church administrator. Converted to Christianity in 1874, G. B. Starr joined the Congregationalist Church and worked as an evangelist with Dwight L. Moody in Chicago in 1875. The following year he embraced the Seventh-day Adventist message, began to preach, and was ordained in 1879. He married Nellie Sisley, sister of *Maud (Sisley) Boyd, in Battle Creek in 1883. The Starrs' first field of labor was in Nebraska, and in 1884 they were asked to help establish a city mission in Chicago. There they remained until they accompanied Ellen White to Australia in 1891, where George held various functions for the next 18 years. From the time they first associated with Ellen White on her voyage to Australia until her death in 1915, the Starrs exchanged numerous letters with Ellen White and her son W. C. White. Most of Ellen White's letters to them were about personal matters and sharing information about her work. In a few cases, however, she counseled them regarding George's methods of work, his style of preaching and personal visitation in homes (Lts 94, 95, 1896), and about the conflicts they were facing in Adelaide (Lts 212, 106, 1897). Indicative of her confidence in the Starrs are her words of affirmation in a 1903 letter: "Sometimes I wish you were in America, and then again, when I think of the work that there is to be done in Australia, I am glad that you are there. You are the Lord's evangelist, and He will surely be your comfort, and your helper, and your guide, and your exceeding great reward" (Lt 22, 1903). Upon their return to the United States, the Starrs worked at the Melrose Sanitarium, a decision that pleased Ellen White (Lt 170, 1909; cf. Lt 138, 1910). Closely associated with Ellen White for many years, the Starrs had firsthand experience with her guidance and leadership while they lived in Australia. In 1931 he wrote a large manuscript of his personal recollections of events and anecdotes he had witnessed.

Further reading: obit. RH, Apr. 20, 1944; G. B. Starr, "Personal Experiences and Observations With the Prophetic Gift in the Remnant Church" (unpublished manuscript, 1931, DF 496); *SDA Encyclopedia* (1996), vol. 11, p. 702.

Denis Fortin

STARR, JOHN ANKEY (1868-1938) and **LILLIS (WOOD)** (1865-1938). John was an accountant and business manager, and the brother of *George B. Starr; Lillis was a physicianwho obtained her medical degree from the University of Michigan in 1891, and two years later began a medical clinic in Mexico as the first woman physician in that country. Ill health caused Lillis to return to the United States in

1895, at which time she met and married John.

Ellen White first became acquainted with John when they met at the Colorado camp meeting in September 1891. Starr's doubts regarding *assurance of salvation prompted Ellen White to follow up their meeting by a letter counseling him not to despair and that Jesus loved him (Lt 85, 1891; cf. Lt 88, 1894). Later Lillis and John worked for *Paradise Valley Sanitarium in southern California. Lillis helped train medical missionaries, and at the urging of Ellen White became active in the *Woman's Christian Temperance Union (Lt 278, 1907; Lt 302, 1907). Both were "greatly tried," according to Ellen White, but God's "angels have preserved you" (Lt 160, 1907). John seemed to continue to have doubts regarding his assurance of salvation, and according to Ellen White entertained suicidal thoughts. She urged him again that he was not worthless in God's sight, that Jesus loved him, and that his life had been graciously spared and that God would heal him (Lt 136, 1908). Her last letter to him expressed special interest in his case (Lt 350, 1908).

Further reading: obit. PUR, Apr. 13, 1938; obit. PUR, July 27, 1938.

Michael W. Campbell

STEED, DAVID. Adventist pastor in *Australia. Steed worked with several congregations in the Sydney area (Kellyville, Parramatta, Stanmore), and was under appointment to work in *New Zealand when in early 1900 he received five letters from Ellen White. She counseled him about deficiencies in his character generally, and in particular his overvalued opinion of himself. She asserted his need of conversion (Lt 40, 1900) and indicated it was inappropriate for the New Zealand Conference to provide him with ministerial credentials (Lt 48, 1900). She insisted that he was not in a "fit state to go into Dunedin," New Zealand, alone (Lt 48a, 1900). On page 198 of an autograph book given to Ellen White August 26, 1900, on her departure from Australia (see 4Bio 458) Steed provided a pleasant and appreciative message about her work. Yet within three years or less Steed had left the church. The *Union Conference Record* (Jan. 1, 1904) reports his speaking in opposition to an evangelistic program, and there being publicly challenged by one of his earlier Adventist converts—at which point Steed left the meeting.

Lester D. Devine

STEPHENSON, J. M., see *MESSENGER PARTY*.

STEVENS, ANGELINE, see **ANDREWS, JOHN NEVINS** and **ANGELINE (STEVENS)**.

STEVENS, CYPRIAN (1795-1858). Former Millerite and early Adventist pioneer in Paris, Maine; father-in-law of *Uriah Smith, who married Harriet Stevens, and *John N. Andrews, who married Angeline Stevens. With the *Edward Andrews family, the Stevens family were among former Millerites who following the 1844 disappointment indulged in strange fanatical behavior (see *fanaticism). In fact, Stevens' strange fanatical behavior alarmed the local community to the point where he was placed under guardianship in 1845 and declared insane. This was lifted later, but not before the family suffered great hardship.

Repeatedly in the early years of her ministry Ellen White confronted fanaticism. In September 1849 James and Ellen White and other early Adventist colleagues visited Paris, Maine, and met with estranged believers, many of whom began to see their errors. Yet although Stevens and others admitted their mistakes, the Stevens and Andrews families harbored for many years some ill feelings toward James and Ellen White, apparently because of the

forcefulness of the reproofs they received from the Whites. The ill feelings and simmering resentment followed Stevens to Waukon, Iowa, after his family and Andrews' family moved there in 1855. The resentment between the Whites and the Stevens and Andrews families was finally resolved only after Stevens died from a rattlesnake bite in 1858.

Further reading: 1Bio 95; G. Wheeler, *James White: Innovator and Overcomer* (RHPA, 2003), pp. 56-59; 63, 101-108.

STEVENS, HARRIET NEWALL, see **SMITH, HARRIET NEWALL (STEVENS)**.

STEWARD, MARY ALICIA (1858-1947). Born in Wisconsin, educated at Battle Creek College, Steward joined the *Review and Herald staff as a proofreader (1880-1892). It was during this period that in 1891 Ellen White urged Steward to learn "meekness and lowliness of heart" so that she could acquire "good home religion" and "achieve a destiny on earth worthy of heaven" (Lt 26a, 1891). For several years Steward was *J. H. Kellogg's personal secretary. In the late 1890s she taught music and English at the academy in *Graysville, Tennessee, and then worked at the *Southern Publishing Association (1900-1906). In 1906 she joined Ellen White's editorial staff at Elmshaven, beginning an index to her writings that was completed and published in 1926. From 1915 to 1937 she was a copy editor at the Review and Herald Publishing Association, retiring at age 79.

Further reading: obit. *Southern Tidings*, Feb. 12, 1947; *SDA Encyclopedia* (1996), vol. 11, p. 705.

COURTESY OF THE CENTER FOR ADVENTIST RESEARCH, ANDREWS UNIVERSITY.

MARY STEWARD

STEWARD, THADDEUS M. (1827-1907) and **MYRTA E. (WELLS)** (1832-1928). Early Seventh-day Adventists. Converted in the Baptist Church in 1843, Thaddeus became a Sabbatarian Adventist in 1852 and soon became a traveling preacher, joining his efforts to other Adventist pioneer preachers. Myrta was raised in a Seventh Day Baptist home in New York. Her family moved to Milton, Wisconsin, in 1852, where she heard and accepted the Seventh-day Adventist message. In 1854 Thaddeus and Myrta were married and later had two children: *Mary Alicia, who served as a literary assistant to Ellen White, and John William.

COURTESY OF THE CENTER FOR ADVENTIST RESEARCH, ANDREWS UNIVERSITY.

THADDEUS M. STEWARD

In 1852 T. M. Steward was among the first Sabbatarian Adventists to preach in the state of Wisconsin. In 1862 Ellen White rebuked the Stewards for their criticisms of James White's leadership (1Bio 478, 479; 2Bio 26-31). Because of his jealousy and suspicion toward James and Ellen White, Steward opposed attempts at church organization in northern Wisconsin and allowed spurious visions and other fanatical experiences to be practiced among the believers. Ellen White felt strongly that Thaddeus and Myrta's participation in these experiences—Myrta claimed to have visions (1Bio 428)—and his lack of resolve to correct the spiritual experiences of his church members had damaged the Adventist cause in that region. All this because he had refused to receive guidance from other church leaders (Lt 18, 1862, in 1T 311-325). He evidently accepted the rebuke, because he continued to work in the Illinois-Wisconsin Conference until 1874, when he moved to Battle Creek. In 1902, seeking a warmer climate, the family moved to Graysville, Tennessee.

Further reading: obit. RH, May 23, 1907; obit. RH, June 6, 1907; obit. RH, Nov. 1, 1928.

Denis Fortin

STEWART, CHARLES E. Physician who served as vice president to *J. H. Kellogg at the Battle Creek Sanitarium. In the early 1900s Stewart, *David Paulson, and *W. S. Sadler were Kellogg's most visible associates. Paulson and Sadler led the *Chicago Medical Mission, and Stewart was Kellogg's associate in Battle Creek. As the conflict between Kellogg and denominational leadership approached its climax, Stewart compiled the *Blue Book, alleging contradictions, inconsistencies, and other errors in the writings of Ellen White, and citing the *Chicago Building vision as supporting evidence. Like Kellogg, he was never fully reconciled to Ellen White and eventually broke ties with the denomination. By 1927 Kellogg was 75, spending his winters in Florida, and leaving the administration of the *Battle Creek Sanitarium to younger colleagues. It was Stewart, as chair of the board of directors, who promoted the plan of adding an opulent 14-story "towers addition" to the sanitarium, which required borrowing some $3 million. The aging Kellogg opposed the financial risk, but was no longer in control. The "towers" were completed in 1928, but one year later the stock market crashed, destroying the wealth of many who not only had been regular patients, but had paid in proportion to their income, providing the bulk of the sanitarium's cash flow. Immediately the patient census dropped from 1,300 to 300, and in 1933 the sanitarium went into bankruptcy.

Further reading: *A Tour Through the Past and Present of the Battle Creek Federal Center* (Battle Creek, Mich.: Battle Creek Federal Center, 1987), p. 13; *The Government Years at the Battle Creek Federal Center* (Battle

Creek, Mich.: Battle Creek Federal Center, 1990), pp. 6, 7.

Jerry Moon

STOCKMAN, LEVI S. (1814-1844). Methodist minister from East Poland, Maine, who became a Millerite preacher and gave spiritual counsel to young Ellen Harmon. He was converted at the age of 15 and joined the Methodist Episcopal Church at 22. From 1836 to 1843 he served as an itinerant preacher. He contracted pulmonary tuberculosis and passed away June 25, 1844, leaving a wife and three children. He is buried in an unmarked grave in the Western Cemetery, Portland, Maine. Though he was expelled from the Maine Methodist Conference for his Millerite views, he was described as "one of the best and most acceptable preachers" (B. F. Tefft, "Rev. L. S. Stockman," *Zion's Herald*, July 24, 1844), and "a man of deep piety" (LS88 180). In her teen years Ellen Harmon confided to Stockman her sorrows and perplexities and he encouraged her to have faith and trust in the love of God. "During the few minutes in which I received instruction from Elder Stockman," wrote Ellen White, "I had obtained more knowledge on the subject of God's love and pitying tenderness, than from all the sermons and exhortations to which I had ever listened" (LS 37). In her first vision, received a few weeks following Stockman's death, Ellen White saw him with the redeemed in heaven (EW 17).

Further reading: 1Bio 39; EW 12, 298; M. D. Burt, "Ellen G. Harmon's Three Step Conversion Between 1836 and 1843 and the Harmon Family Methodist Experience" (lecture outline, AU, 1998, CAR).

Merlin D. Burt

STONE, CHARLES WESLEY (d. 1883). A Vermont delegate to the General Conference session of 1876, Stone was elected General Conference secretary. He later served as an auditor of the Review and Herald Publishing Association and secretary of the Vermont Conference (1870s). Ordained in 1879, he returned to Battle Creek (1880s) to teach business and music both at Battle Creek College and in public schools in the city. Stone helped compile the songbook *Better Than Pearls* (RHPA, 1881). He lost his life in a railroad accident in 1883. General Conference president *G. I. Butler considered him the most musically gifted of Adventist ministers. In 1882, in a letter addressed to Butler, *A. B. Oyen, *J. H. Kellogg, and Stone, Ellen White regretted the actions of many in condemning *G. H. Bell, principal of Battle Creek College. Although she admitted Bell had made mistakes and had shown a weakness of character, she felt that those who were zealous in condemning him should have been confessing their own sins to God (Lt 11, 1882).

Further reading: 2SM 166; obit. RH, July 31, 1883; *SDA Encyclopedia* (1996), vol. 11, pp. 706, 707.

STONE, WILLIAM JAMES (1851-1930). Pastor and church administrator. Born in Ohio, Stone became a Seventh-day Adventist in 1876 after attending meetings held by *H. A. St. John. He became a pastor in 1881 and for six years worked in Ohio. Then he served as conference president in West Virginia (1887-1893), Tennessee (1899-1903), Indiana (1903-1909), and Virginia (1911-1914). While serving in Indiana, Stone received encouragement from Ellen White in regard to the establishment of a sanitarium in Lafayette (Lt 249, 1905; Lt 218, 1908). She felt that "the people in Indiana are in need of the instruction that can be given by those who should be connected with such an institution" (Lt 249, 1905).

Further reading: obit. RH, Apr. 24, 1930.

STOWELL, LEWIS OSWALD (1828-1918). Adventist pioneer originally from Paris, Maine; former Millerite who with his family was among the first to join the ranks of Sabbatarian Adventists; son of Lewis B. Stowell (1793-1886). In March 1849 Ellen White visited the Stowell family and helped to establish them in the "present truth" (Lt 5, 1849, in 5MR 93, 94). Lewis O. Stowell worked for many years at the Review and Herald publishing house. He married Melissa Bostwick (1839-1899) and had six daughters. In 1905 Ellen White wrote a short letter to Stowell, sharing with him news of her current activities in California and expressing her hope to see him at an upcoming meeting in San Diego (Lt 243a, 1905).

Further reading: obit. RH, Jan. 4, 1887; obit. RH, Oct. 17, 1918.

STOWELL, MARION, see **CRAWFORD, MARION C. (STOWELL)**.

STURGESS, EMMA, see **PRESCOTT, AMOS L.** and **EMMA ELIZABETH (STURGESS)**.

SUTHERLAND, EDWARD ALEXANDER (1865-1955). Educational reformer, college founder, and physician. Raised on a farm in Iowa, Sutherland, upon graduation from high school in 1884, went to Battle Creek intending to become a physician. When *J. H. Kellogg's one-year premedical program was canceled, he returned to Iowa and taught public school for three years. In 1887 he returned to Battle Creek to study for the ministry and teaching. While attending the educational convention at Harbor Springs, Michigan, in 1891, he made four life-changing

EDWARD A. SUTHERLAND

decisions: to trust wholly in Christ's righteousness for salvation, to accept the counsels of Ellen White as applicable to him personally, to become a vegetarian, and to teach Bible and be dean of men at Battle Creek College. Upon completing his studies at Battle Creek College in 1890, he married Sally V. Brailliard (1871-1953). In 1954 he married M. Bessie DeGraw (1871-1965).

In 1892 he founded and became acting principal (*W. W. Prescott was officially president) of *Walla Walla College. Based on his reform successes there (he implemented what was almost certainly the first successful Adventist program of free community education), he was called in 1897 to become president of *Battle Creek College, where he sought to implement three reforms: initiating an agriculture-based work-study program, establishing more than 150 Adventist elementary schools (prompting A. W. Spalding to call him the "originator and builder of the elementary and secondary school system"), and giving every branch of education at Battle Creek College a decidedly missionary emphasis. (He did not ever, as some have asserted, advocate the Bible as the only textbook.)

In 1901, at Ellen White's urging, Sutherland and his colleague, *Percy T. Magan, moved the college to Berrien Springs, Michigan, and named it *Emmanuel Missionary College. For three years they continued the reforms begun earlier, and also implemented the Cooperative Plan, in which faculty, staff, and students together administered every aspect of the institution. But in the face of growing resistance and criticism by some in church leadership who also resented their initial support of the reopening of Battle Creek College by Kellogg in 1903, the two men resigned in 1904.

Near Nashville, Tennessee, in 1904, Sutherland and Magan, at Ellen White's urging, established the Nashville Agricultural and Normal Institute, a self-supporting school. She also served on the school board—the only school board she ever served on. The school established a sanitarium (Sutherland and Magan obtained their M.D. degrees to lend stability because few doctors would serve at such meager wages), a food factory, and a treatment room and vegetarian cafeteria in nearby Nashville. In 1937 the school's name was changed to *Madison College and in 1938 the *Reader's Digest* featured an article about it, titled "Self-supporting College," which praised Madison as the only college in the United States at which a destitute young person could acquire an education during the Great Depression.

After 41 years as president of Madison College, Sutherland became, in 1946, the General Conference secretary of the newly organized Commission on Rural Living, the forerunner of ASI, now Adventist-laymen's Services and Industries. In 1950 he retired, and a few years later, as an 89-year-old widower, married Bessie DeGraw. He presided over his last committee meeting one week before he died at age 90. As a lifelong educational reformer, he left an impressive legacy for his church and Adventist education.

Further reading: obit. RH, July 28, 1955; W. S. Ashworth, "Edward Alexander Sutherland and the Seventh-day Adventist Education System: The Denominational Years" (Ph.D. diss., AU, 1986); J. Moon, ed., *E. A. Sutherland and Madison College, 1904-1964: A Symposium* (Berrien Springs, Mich.: by the editor, 1989); *SDA Encyclopedia* (1996), vol. 11, pp. 722, 723.

Warren S. Ashworth

TAIT, ASA OSCAR (1858-1941). Pastor and editor. Converted to Adventism at the age of 19, Tait became a pastor in 1881 and was ordained three years later. He worked in Illinois until he was asked to become the secretary of the Religious Liberty Association in Battle Creek in 1891. In 1895 he began his career in publishing as the circulation manager of the *Review and Herald, and in 1898 went to Pacific Press, where he remained for most of the next 43 years. In 1913 he became the editor-in-chief of *Signs of the Times*. Ellen White believed in Tait's abilities and confided to her son Edson that "Brother Tait is another who has been greatly blessed and will give the trumpet a certain sound" (Lt 14a, 1889, in 1888 Materials 292). While Tait worked at the Review and Herald in Battle Creek, she wrote him a few letters from Australia. In these letters she counseled him against the tendency of some church leaders to centralize all denominational activities in Battle Creek, to the detriment of smaller institutions or publishing houses elsewhere in the country (Lt 76, 1895; Lt 100, 1896); she advised him also on the matter of royalties given to authors (Lt 75, 1895) and regarding the work in the South (Lt 73, 1895).

Further reading: obit. RH, May 22, 1941; *SDA Encyclopedia* (1996), vol. 11, p. 740.

TAY, JOHN I. (1832-1892). Pioneer missionary to Tahiti, Pitcairn, and Fiji (1886-1892). Tay  joined the Adventist Church in 1873. By working as a carpenter, he paid his passage on six ships to reach Pitcairn in 1886, and soon converted the entire island to Seventh-day Adventism. As a result, in 1887 the General Conference purchased a sailing ship and renamed it *Pitcairn* for work in the South Pacific. From 1890 to 1892 Tay and his wife, with other missionaries, worked

JOHN TAY

COURTESY OF THE REVIEW AND HERALD PUBLISHING ASSOCIATION

in Tahiti, Fiji, and other South Pacific islands. Though zealous for his faith, he needed counsel about his headstrong, dictatorial spirit and unyielding manner toward relatives and acquaintances (Lt 17, 1879). Tay died at his post of duty in Suva, Fiji.

Further reading: obit. BE, Feb. 15, 1892; H. Ford, *Island of Tears: The Story of John Tay* (PPPA, 1990); S. O. Engen, *John Tay, Messenger to Pitcairn* (PPPA, 1981); *SDA Encyclopedia* (1996), vol. 11, p. 750.

Brian E. Strayer

TAYLOR, CHARLES LINDSAY (1867-1918). Pastor and teacher. Born in an Adventist family in western New York, Taylor entered the ministry in 1890. The following year he married Lucy E. Brown. After teaching for a few years at Mount Vernon Academy and *Walla Walla and *Healdsburg colleges, he became the chaplain at *St. Helena Sanitarium in 1901, a position he held for nine years with intervals given to evangelistic work in California. He later taught in Adventist schools in California, Georgia, Minnesota, and Michigan, and authored the book *The Marked Bible* (PPPA, 1919). In 1901 Taylor asked counsel of Ellen White whether he should go to India. In her response Ellen White told him she could not give any advice in that matter, but also said "there is work which you can do in California" (Lt 88, 1901). A few years later Taylor was one of the people Ellen White met with to discuss the age of school entrance for children (cf. 6MR 348-373). In 1906, while he worked as a chaplain at St. Helena Sanitarium, she invited him to consider joining *S. N. Haskell in an evangelistic effort in Loma Linda (Lt 190, 1906).

Further reading: obit. RH, Feb. 6, 1919; *SDA Encyclopedia* (1996), vol. 11, pp. 750, 751.

TAYLOR, CHARLES O. (1817-1905). Pastor in New York. First a Millerite believer, Taylor accepted Sabbatarian Adventist beliefs and began to work as a pastor in 1854. From 1867 to 1868 he wrote many reports for the *Review and Herald*, three of which refer to a Brother Goodwin in Oswego, New York (RH, Aug. 6, 1867; RH, Mar. 3, 1868; RH, June 9, 1868). Shortly after the publication of the latter, Ellen White exhorted Taylor not to give too much attention to Goodwin, but to give better wages to his own hired servants (Lt 16, 1868; cf. 2T 156-161).

Further reading: RY 16, 18; 2SM 223, 224; *SDA Encyclopedia* (1996), vol. 11, p. 751.

TENNEY, GEORGE CIDUS (1847-1921). Editor, minister, teacher, and administrator. Following his ordination in the mid-1870s, Tenney worked in his home state of Wisconsin and the Dakota Territory.

GEORGE AND ELSIE TENNEY AND THEIR CHILDREN, IVERS AND RUTH

In 1887 Tenney went to *Australia, where he edited the *Bible Echo* and the following year became the first president of the Australian conference. In 1892 Ellen White complained of his lack of managerial skills and financial acumen (Ms 13, 1891; Lt 19b, 1892; Lt 40, 1892). She described Tenney as a "kindhearted, well-disposed man anxious to do something, but is not able to do the very things which will need to be done," which resulted in Ellen White's urging his return to America (Lt 95, 1892). The following year he accepted a call to teach and serve as chaplain at the *Battle Creek Sanitarium, and edit the *Medical Missionary Magazine*. From 1895 to 1897 he served as coeditor with *Uriah Smith of the *Review and Herald*. In 1903 Ellen White warned Tenney of the dangerous *pantheistic sentiments in *The Living Temple* (Lt 217, 1903). She urged him and *A. T. Jones to help *J. H. Kellogg back onto the platform of truth (Lt 266, 1903), but he fell under the influence of Kellogg and "out of harmony with the people of God" (Lt 33, 1906). She later said Tenney had "departed from the faith" so that he was no help to Dr. Kellogg (see Lts 121, 208, 242, 1906; Ms 20, 1906).

Further reading: obit. RH, Dec. 22, 1921; *SDA Encyclopedia* (1996), vol. 11, p. 758; N. Clapham, ed., *Seventh-day Adventists in the South Pacific, 1885-1985* (Warburton, Australia: Signs Pub. Co., 1985), p. 116; G. C. Tenney, *Travels by Land and Sea; A Visit to Five Continents* (Battle Creek, Mich.: International Tract Society, 1895).

Lester D. Devine

THOMASON, GEORGE W. (1872-1947). Physician. Thomason began medical training at *Battle Creek Sanitarium and the *American Medical Missionary College, but took his final year from the Jefferson Medical College in Philadelphia, graduating in 1899, after which he was appointed assistant surgeon at the Battle Creek Sanitarium. He married Ananora Aldrich in 1900. Four years later they moved to South Africa, where Thomason was medical director of the *Claremont Sanitarium near Cape Town. In 1911 he became director of the General Conference Medical Department. While medical superintendent of the *St. Helena Sanitarium, he had an interview with Ellen White about his work and the wages of physicians (Ms 10, 1914). The same year, he

became professor of surgery at the *College of Medical Evangelists, where he served for the rest of his life.

Further reading: obit. RH, Apr. 24, 1947.

THORPE, MARY (CHINNOCK) (1837-1925). Employee and friend of Ellen White. After the death of James White in 1881, Chinnock watched over Ellen White as she recuperated from an illness at the Battle Creek Sanitarium (Lt 9, 1881). They remained friends for life, and Ellen White often referred to Mary in letters to her family. In 1915, during Ellen White's last illness, Mary was at her bedside when she died (6Bio 431).

Further reading: obit. LUH, Jan. 20, 1926.

TRALL, RUSSELL T. (1812-1877). Hydropathic physician in America who had some contact with and influence on Adventist health reform in the 1860s. Hydropathy became well known in Europe through the work of Vincent Priessnitz, a layman who opened a water-cure center in Silesia, Prussia, in 1826, where he treated some 7,000 patients in the 1830s. Priessnitz's theory of health was simple. He held that the natural tendency of the body was to be healthy and that the body would cure itself of most diseases if it were only freed from the external causes that produced those diseases. Injuries might require surgery, but even in treating injuries such as broken bones he placed highest faith in the body's own healing processes. His regimen included frequent bathing, no beverage except water, a simple diet, fresh air, exercise, and total avoidance of medication. His patients recovered, apparently because they replaced the way of life that was killing them with some basic good health habits, and got away from the ordinary pressures of life long enough for the body to renew itself (Cayleff, pp. 20-24).

Joel Shew, Russell T. Trall, and Mary Gove

Nichols helped introduce Preissnitz-style hydropathy to America in the 1840s. Dr. Joel Shew opened the first water-cure establishment in New York City in 1843, and was closely associated with David Campbell, the originator of the *Water-Cure Journal*. Dr. Trall also opened a water-cure institution in New York City in 1843 or 1844, and by 1849 was in partnership with Shew. The most prolific contributor to the *Water-Cure Journal*, he served as its editor for many years. Mary Gove Nichols began practicing the Preissnitz water-cure methods on her daughter as early as 1832, learned more from one of Preissnitz's patients in 1840, and in 1845 became a resident physician at one of Shew's water-cure establishments. A fourth figure, *James Caleb Jackson, learned hydropathic methods from a student of Trall's in 1847 and by 1858 had purchased a water cure on a hillside near Dansville, New York, which he renamed "Our Home on the Hillside." Of the four, Trall and Jackson would exert the most direct influence on Adventist health reform in general and on John Harvey Kellogg in particular (Weiss and Kimble, pp. 19, 20, 69-89, 155, 156, 176; Cayleff, pp. 21-25, 30, 36, 94, 115).

James and Ellen White spent three weeks at Jackson's institution in Dansville, New York, in 1864, and three months in 1865, and from those experiences, and a vision of December 25, 1865, recommended that Adventists found a *Health Reform Institute of their own (SHM 127-142).

Forty years later, during a 1906 sermon to Adventist restaurant and health-care workers in Los Angeles, California, Ellen White recounted a conversation with Dr. Trall during his heyday. Trall had heard White speak and admonished her, "you put forth too much strength when you stand before the people. If you continue to do as you are doing you cannot live over three years," and maybe only three months. White had with her a copy of her book *Health, or How to Live*, and asked Trall if he would read it. He said he would, and she lent it to him. When they met again, Trall asked her, "Mrs. White, where did you get your instruction in medical science?" She replied that she had "received it by revelation from God." As he handed the book back to her, he said, "That book is filled with truth. I hope it may have a wide circulation." "He is now dead," she concluded, "and I, whom he thought could live only a short time, have been preserved all these years. I shall soon be seventy-eight years old. I have placed myself in the hands of God, and He has sustained me, enabling me to bear my testimony in many parts of the world" (1SAT 354).

Further reading: S. E. Cayleff, *Wash and Be Healed: The Water-Cure Movement and Women's Health* (Philadelphia: Temple University Press, 1987); H. B. Weiss and Howard R. Kemble, *The Great American Water-Cure Craze: A History of Hydropathy in the United States* (Trenton, N.J.: Past Times Press, 1967); D. E. Robinson, *The Story of Our Health Message: The Origin, Character, and Development of Health Education in the Seventh-day Adventist Church* (Nashville: SPA, 1943; 3rd ed., 1965).

Jerry Moon

TRIPP, MARY CAROLINE (MORTENSON), see **MORTENSON, MARY CAROLINE.**

TRUTH, SOJOURNER (c. 1797-1883). Born into slavery as Isabella Baumfree in Ulster County, New York; sold at auction three times by 1810; in 1826 she escaped to freedom in Canada with her infant daughter. After New York State emancipated slaves in 1827, she returned to Ulster County, New York, to work for Isaac Van Wagenen, a Christian who refused to let her call him master, because, he said, "Your Master is mine." There she converted to Christianity, took her employer's surname, Van Wagenen, and, asserting her rights as a free person, won a landmark lawsuit to recover her son, Peter, who had been illegally sold into slavery in Alabama. In 1843 she adopted the name Sojourner Truth and in 1844 joined the utopian Northhampton Association in Northhampton, Massachusetts, where she met abolitionists Frederick Douglass, William Lloyd Garrison, Wendell Phillips, and Giles Stebbins, the health reformer *Sylvester Graham, and feminist abolitionist Olive Gilbert, who coauthored the first edition of Truth's biography, *Narrative of Sojourner Truth* (1850).

At the 1851 women's rights convention in Akron, Ohio, she delivered her famous speech "Ain't I a Woman?" arguing that Black women deserved the same respect as White women. A year later at an abolitionist meeting in Salem, Ohio, she shared the platform with Frederick Douglass. At the close of an impassioned oration in which Douglass expressed deep pessimism about the success of the abolitionist cause, Truth stood up with a courageous, one-sentence rebuttal: "Frederick, is God dead?"

Truth first visited Battle Creek, Michigan, in 1856 to address a Friends of Human Progress convention organized by local Quakers. The next year she sold her property in Northhampton, Massachusetts, and bought a house in Harmonia, a spiritualist community, then six miles (10 kilometers) west of Battle Creek. In 1867 she purchased a lot on College Street in Battle Creek, remodeling a small barn into a home that was her main residence for the rest of her life.

After the Emancipation Proclamation in 1863, thousands of ex-slaves fled to Washington, D.C., expecting to find freedom and safety. Instead, the encampment called Freedman's Village offered terrible housing, little food, and

SOJOURNER TRUTH

no employment. In 1864 Truth moved to Freedman's Village, where she protested and stopped the kidnapping of Black children, forced the desegregation of Washington streetcars, investigated why clothing donated for free distribution was being sold to the destitute, worked as a counselor instructing women in home nursing, and sought tirelessly to relocate her fellow Blacks to less-populated areas, such as Battle Creek, Michigan, where Quakers led the way in providing for the former slaves until they could find jobs and housing. The first 36 freed people came to Battle Creek in 1866, and as word got back to Washington, D.C., that Battle Creek was a safe haven, many more followed.

As a 26-year resident of Battle Creek, Truth met many Seventh-day Adventists, who then had their world headquarters and major institutions in Battle Creek. She is said to have addressed the Sabbath School Association and given temperance lectures at the Battle Creek Tabernacle. A later edition of her biography, *The Life of Sojourner Truth* (1875, 1878), was published by the Review and Herald in 1884. In 1883 Truth developed ulcers on her legs and was treated at the Battle Creek Sanitarium by *J. H. Kellogg, who gave her a graft of his own skin. The original painting of Truth's 1864 meeting with Abraham Lincoln at the White House hung in the sanitarium from 1894 till the fire of 1902. There is no documentary support, however, for rumors that she became an Adventist. Although initially announced to be held in the Dime Tabernacle, her funeral was held in the Congregational church, with Reed Stuart presiding (*Heritage Battle Creek*, p. 42); "Death of

Sojourner Truth," *Good Health,* December 1883). The Sojourner Truth Institute in Battle Creek opened in 1997, the 200th anniversary of her birth.

Further reading: O. Gilbert, *Narrative of Sojourner Truth* (1850) (reprints: New York: Arno Press, 1968; Baltimore: Penquin, 1998 [with introduction and notes by N. I. Painter]); *Heritage Battle Creek* 8 (Fall 1997): 18, 26, 27, 30, 36, 37, 39, 42, 43, DF 574, CAR; C. Mabee with S. Mabee Newhouse, *Sojourner Truth: Slave, Prophet, Legend* (New York: New York Univ. Press, 1993); N. I. Painter, *Sojourner Truth: A Life, A Symbol* (New York: Norton, 1996); E. Stetson and L. David, *Glorying in Tribulation: The Lifework of Sojourner Truth* (East Lansing, Mich.: Michigan State University Press, 1994); S. Truth, *The Life of Sojourner Truth* (RHPA, 1884).

Jerry Moon

TURNER, JOSEPH (1807-1862). Millerite editor, minister, and writer who became the most significant antagonist of Ellen Harmon during 1845 and 1846. Turner was editor with John Pearson, Jr., of the Portland, Maine, paper *Hope of Israel* during 1844. Turner moved to Poland, Maine, in the spring of 1845, where he remained until moving to Hartford, Connecticut, in March 1850. He remained in Hartford for the rest of his life and became an active minister and editor with the Second Advent Union Missionary Association. He authored at least six monographs and two published debates. Additionally he served as editor of the *Bible Advocate* during 1848, the *Advent Watchman* from 1851 to 1854, and the *Christian Reformer* during 1855 and 1856. Turner is credited by J. V. Himes and I. C. Wellcome as the principal *shut door advocate during the first months of 1845. Turner and Apollos Hale jointly published the one-issue (January 1845) *Advent Mirror*, which promoted

a Matthew 25 Bridegroom explanation for the October 1844 disappointment. Turner successfully convinced Samuel Snow to accept the Bridegroom view that Snow and B. Matthias then promoted through their New York publication, the *Jubilee Standard.*

Turner had numerous interactions with Ellen Harmon during 1844 and 1845. Ellen White's first extant letter to Joseph Bates includes an account of her reluctance to share her first vision, fearing that Turner would reject it. Her fears were not realized, and Turner accepted her vision. But by early 1845 Harmon again feared to trust Turner when he offered to convey her to Portsmouth, New Hampshire (Ms 131, 1906). During 1845 Turner was involved in mesmerism (see *hypnotism and mesmerism) and attributed Ellen Harmon's visions to mesmeric influence. He was active in mesmerizing various young girls, one being *Sarah Jordan, and believed he could control Ellen Harmon as well. The showdown between Harmon and Turner came after Harmon returned from her first trip to Vermont and New Hampshire. In Grantham, New Hampshire, she was shown in vision the danger of fanaticism and particularly the mesmeric activity of Turner. Upon returning to Portland, she attended a meeting in the home of *Elizabeth Haines, where Turner was present. During the meeting she received a vision, and as she spoke, Turner gave his support. But then Ellen Harmon indicated that Turner was transgressing the commandments of God by his attention to various women. After coming out of vision, Harmon counseled two girls to have nothing to do with Turner, and then she went to visit Turner's wife to assure her that she was not lost. It seems from Harmon's recollection that Turner had convinced his wife that she was lost because she opposed his staying up late in the parlor with different young women (*ibid.*). Shortly thereafter Harmon went to Poland, Maine, to stay with her sister *Mary Foss. Turner also came to Poland and told a group of Adventists that he could cause Ellen Harmon to have a vision and that he could keep her from having one. Perhaps affected by her previous encounter with Turner, Harmon became ill. Following prayer by her family, she received a vision that directed her to confront Turner. She was given the assurance that God would send as many angels as she needed to protect her. With this assurance she attended a meeting at which Turner was present. It seems he attempted to mesmerize her. She recollected: "He had his eyes looking right out through his fingers, and his eyes looked like snake's eyes, evil. I turned and looked right around, I raised both hands, and [cried out,] 'Another angel, Lord; another angel.' The Spirit and power of God came upon me, and I was taken off in vision right there" (*ibid.*). After the meeting, when asked why he had not prevented her from having a vision, Turner remarked "Oh, some of you would have her talk." Ellen White wrote, "With strong confidence, rejoicing in God, we returned to my sister's" (2SG 62, 63, 69).

After these confrontations Turner became a dedicated antagonist of Ellen White. During the late summer and fall of 1845 Harmon traveled south to Massachusetts. Turner with John Howell had convinced Elizabeth Haines to sign a statement against Ellen Harmon. (Haines later recanted that statement.) This they circulated with some effect (Otis Nichols, "Statement by Otis Nichols," n.d., EGWE-GC). Nevertheless Harmon was able to gain some friends and supporters in the state. Later Turner attempted to cover up his involvement in mesmerism (Joseph Bates, *A Vindication of the Seventh-day Sabbath, and the Commandments of God: With a Further History*

of *God's Peculiar People, From 1847 to 1848* [New Bedford, Mass.: Benjamin Lindsey, 1848], pp. 15-17).

Merlin D. Burt

UNDERWOOD, RUFUS ANSEL (1850-1932). Adventist minister and administrator. Born

RUFUS A. UNDERWOOD

in Ohio to parents who converted to Adventism through the influence of *J. H. Waggoner in 1864, Underwood followed their example five years later after reading a series of articles by *Uriah Smith in the *Review and Herald*. In 1877 he entered full-time ministry and later served as Ohio Conference president (1883-1889). At the *General Conference session of 1888, Underwood was one of the ministers who opposed the view of *A. T. Jones and *E. J. Waggoner. Ellen White rebuked him for his role in opposing these men, and for helping to prejudice the mind of *G. I. Butler (1888 Materials 230-256). She also counseled Underwood against building a sanitarium at that time in Mount Vernon, Ohio, when the need was so much greater in Cleveland (1888 Materials 264). Underwood later held a variety of administrative posts and served on the General Conference Executive Committee (1885-1920). While he was president of the Northern Union Conference (1904-1912), Ellen White affirmed his choice in securing property for a school in Chamberlain, South Dakota (Lts 252, 318, 320, 1908).

Further reading: obit. RH, May 5, 1932; R.J.A. Cooper, "R. A. Underwood: A Biographical Sketch" (research paper, AU, 1979, DF 3258 CAR); *SDA Encyclopedia* (1996), vol. 11, pp. 809, 810.

Van Horn, Amanda M. (Patten) (1844-1911). Adventist from Michigan; younger sister of *Adelia (Patten) Van Horn. When Amanda left her husband, Cornelius C., and children in order to devote her efforts to evangelistic work, Ellen White counseled her not to "suppose that God has given you a work that will necessitate a separation from your precious little flock" (Lt 28, 1890, in TSB 42).

Further reading: obit. RH, May 4, 1911.

Van Horn, Isaac Doren (1834-1910) and **Adelia P. (Patten)** (1839-1922). Isaac was a schoolteacher, preacher, evangelist, and

COURTESY OF THE ELLEN G. WHITE ESTATE, INC.

ISAAC AND ADELIA VAN HORN

administrator; as a young woman, Adelia lived with James and Ellen White, served as a *literary assistant to Ellen White, and edited the *Youth's Instructor* from 1864 to 1867. Isaac was converted to Adventism through the efforts of Joseph Bates in 1859. In 1865 they were married by James White at the Battle Creek church.

From 1874 to 1882 the Van Horns labored in California, Oregon, and Washington. In April 1874 the Van Horns began to do evangelistic work in Walla Walla, Washington, where their efforts led to the conversion of *Alonzo T. Jones. In 1877 Isaac Van Horn became president of the newly formed North Pacific Conference.

In 1876 Ellen White criticized Adelia's priorities in her life and the adverse impact they had on their evangelistic ministry. "You could not have rest or peace of mind separated from your children; and the worrying disposition you have closes up the way for your work," commented Ellen White (Lt 48, 1876). This situation persisted for the next couple years

and led to Ellen White writing another letter about the Van Horns' lack of commitment to their work (Lt 51a, 1878). In August 1880 Isaac Van Horn wrote to Ellen White, accepting the testimony she had delivered to the couple (I. D. Van Horn to EGW, Aug. 4, 1880).

In 1888 Isaac Van Horn became president of the Michigan Conference and was among the group of pastors and church leaders who opposed the new emphasis on righteousness by faith presented by E. J. Waggoner and A. T. Jones at the *General Conference session of 1888. After receiving reproof from Ellen White for his attitude and not walking in the light of God's Word (Lt 61, 1893), Van Horn accepted the new doctrine (I. D. Van Horn to EGW, Mar. 9, 1893; Lt 60, 1893). During his later years Van Horn traveled extensively for the denomination, and he continued to be an effective evangelist. In 1907 a sunstroke left him incapacitated until he died three years later. Adelia died in 1922.

In 1903 Ellen White wrote a letter to their youngest son, Charles W. (1880-1908), who at the age of 4 had suffered an accident that caused him lifelong pain and an early death at age 28. Ellen White assured him of God's love and urged him to "look on the bright side," for you are "precious in His sight" (Lt 69, 1903, in TDG 122).

Further reading: obit. RH, Sept. 24, 1908; obit. RH, Oct. 6, 1910; obit. LUH, July 26, 1922; D. Johnson, *Adventism on the Northwestern Frontier* (Berrien Springs, Mich.: Oronoko Books, 1996), pp. 13-52; C. Thurston, *Sixty Years of Progress: Walla Walla College* (College Place, Wash.: College Press, 1952); *SDA Encyclopedia* (1996), vol. 11, p. 828.

Terrie Aamodt

Vaucher, Jules-Alfred (1859-1914). Young Adventist in Switzerland who sought Ellen White's counsel regarding his desire to marry a young woman, Élise, whose father, *Albert Vuilleumier, objected to the relationship. In

COURTESY OF THE ELLEN G. WHITE ESTATE, INC.

JULES-ALFRED VAUCHER

her response, Ellen White emphasized that Vaucher should be mindful of the father's feelings and should not pursue the relationship against the parents' wishes. She also mentioned that Vaucher's persistent determination to carry out his own interest was an evidence the Spirit of God was not a controlling power in his life (Lt 25, 1886, in 8MR 429, 430). In a second letter written a few days later Ellen White reemphasized Vaucher's headstrong and willful disposition and lack of willingness to follow counsel (Lt 3, 1886, in 18MR 303-320). Vaucher decided not to pursue his relationship with Élise Vuilleumier. He later married Méry Revel, daughter of Catherine Revel, in Torre-Pellice, Italy. Their son, Alfred-Félix Vaucher, served for many years as a professor of theology at the Adventist seminary at Collonges-sous-Salève, France.

VIERA ROSSANO, JUAN CARLOS (1938-   ). Born in Uruguay, Viera served as pastor, evangelist, and union president in South America before joining the Ellen G. White Estate as an associate director in 1988. Between 1995 and 2000 he was the White Estate director—the first foreign-born person elected to that position. During his term Viera organized the White Estate into several departments for which specific associate directors were responsible. As a researcher and a lecturer, he stressed a biblical approach to the gift of prophecy. Viera holds an M.A. in religion from Andrews University (1976) and an M.A. and a doctorate in missiology from Fuller Theological Seminary (1990, 1992). Books published include *Listos para el encuentro con Cristo* (PPPA, 1996),

The Voice of the Spirit (PPPA, 1998), and *Año 2000: ¿Será éste el fin?* (PPPA, 1999).

Humberto M. Rasi

VUILLEUMIER, ALBERT FREDERIC (1835-1923). Pastor, evangelist, and one of the first Seventh-day Adventists in Europe. Vuilleumier accepted Adventist beliefs in 1867 through the influence of *M. B. Czechowski and was ordained to the Seventh-day Adventist ministry in 1885. During Ellen White's years in Europe (1885-1887) she met with Vuilleumier on a number of occasions and encouraged him in his work in Switzerland (Lts 28, 45, 1886).

Further reading: obit. RH, Apr. 19, 1923; *SDA Encyclopedia* (1996), vol. 11, pp. 847, 848.

WADE, PITT ABRAHAM (1869-1947). Born in Wisconsin the son of a physician who was also a Baptist preacher, Wade converted to Adventism around 1886. In 1897 he graduated from Barnes Medical College in St. Louis, Missouri, and took an internship at the *Battle Creek Sanitarium and worked for a time at the Chicago Lying-in [maternity] Hospital. In 1899 he moved to Cañon City, Colorado, where he practiced medicine for the next 44 years. Wade married Alice Zener on December 31, 1900.

By a series of creative publicity strategies, he quickly built up a large practice in Cañon City and sought to establish a sanitarium. Meanwhile the Adventist sanitarium in *Boulder, Colorado, had been struggling financially since its establishment in 1895. Its situation was made even more difficult when Dr. *O. G. Place, a former employee of the Boulder Sanitarium, opened a competing institution only a short distance away and sought to buy out the institution whose financial problems he had exacerbated. Given this development, church leaders did not encourage Wade's project in Cañon City.

Early in September 1905 Wade traveled to California to meet with Ellen White, hoping to get her endorsement of the project. After expressing some concerns with the project, she pointed out that Wade was not the best person to head this institution because of his tendency to cherish feelings of anger and bitterness and lash out against anyone who did not agree with him and support his plans. She predicted a life path of bitter headache and sorrows if he did not submit to the Lord and accept the needed changes in his life (Lts 283, 285, 1905; cf. SpTB05 32, 36, 44-52; 6Bio 37-43).

The Cañon City sanitarium never became a reality, and Wade did have, in many respects, a difficult life. He was involved in bitter church conflicts and unsuccessful business ventures. But according to family oral tradition, the setbacks and hurts he experienced eventually accomplished the transformation he needed, and before he died he testified that he was at peace and free of bitterness.

Further reading: obit. RH, May 29, 1947; L. Wade, "Pitt A. Wade and the Cañon City Sanitarium" (2005, CAR).

Loron Wade

WAGGONER, ELLET JOSEPH (1855-1916). Seventh-day Adventist physician, minister, teacher, editor, writer and revivalist; son of *J. H. Waggoner (1820-1889). E. J. Waggoner rose to great prominence as one of the "messengers" of the "righteousness by faith" revival that unfolded in the aftermath of the *General Conference session of 1888 in Minneapolis. His name has often been associated with his fellow minister

DR. ELLET J. WAGGONER

and editorial coworker A. T. Jones, and this dynamic duet has become legendary in Seventh-day Adventist history as "Jones and Waggoner."

Receiving a "classical" education at Battle Creek College (1874-1875, 1876-1877), Waggoner took medical training at the University of Michigan at Ann Arbor for one year (1875-1876). He received his medical degree from Long Island College Hospital of Brooklyn, New York, in 1878 and began his career on the staff of the Battle Creek Sanitarium. In March of 1879 he married Jessie Fremont Moser. After a brief period of ministry in Iowa they moved to northern California in the spring of 1880, where he served on the staff of the Rural Health Retreat (St. Helena Sanitarium). Sometime before 1883 he switched to full-time ministerial work.

The "turning point" in his life was a remarkable spiritual experience that occurred during a dismal, rainy afternoon meeting at the Healdsburg camp meeting in October of 1882. "Suddenly a light shone about me, and the tent seemed illumined, as though the sun were shining; I saw Christ crucified for me, and to me was revealed for the first time in my life the fact that God loved *me*, and that Christ gave Himself for me personally" (McMahon, p. 20). Waggoner was convinced then and there to dedicate his life to "making known to others the biblical message of God's love for individual sinners" (Webster, p. 160).

In 1883 he was called to the Pacific Press to assist his father, who was then editor-in-chief of the *Signs of the Times*. In 1884 he met A. T. Jones, and in mid-1886 he and Jones became coeditors. Waggoner remained at this post until 1891.

His public career can be conveniently divided up into the following periods: rise to prominence (1882-1888); the 1888 Minneapolis General Conference session and its immediate aftermath (late 1888 through early 1892); the English/European years (mid-1892-1903); the years of decline (1903-1916).

The key development during his rise to prominence was the unfolding of his controversial interpretation of the "law in Galatians" and his growing emphasis on Christ as the one who justifies the penitent believer by faith, not by works of the law. Stoutly opposed by the entrenched establishment figures in Battle Creek, most notably G. I. Butler (General Conference president) and Uriah Smith (longtime editor of the *Review and Herald*), the flash point came at the Minneapolis General Conference session of 1888. While Waggoner's position on the identity of the "law in Galatians" (he understood it to have primary reference to the moral, not the ceremonial, requirements) provided the major part of the background for the controversy with older church leaders, the major emphasis of Waggoner's presentations at the 1888 session was to uplift Christ and His justifying grace.

In the face of the stiff opposition to Waggoner's emphases, Ellen White gave strong personal support to his (and Jones's) basic theological thrust. Her outspoken affirmations of Jones and Waggoner's Christ- and grace-centered emphasis would be sustained until at least 1896. And in the immediate aftermath of the 1888 General Conference session she would unite her efforts with those of the two young editors/revivalists in extensive travels to camp meetings, church and college revivals, and ministerial institutes to proclaim more fully the "glad tidings" of Christ and His righteousness. The Christ-centered focus of Jones and Waggoner was the inspiration for the most concerted emphasis that Ellen White would ever make on "justification by faith" in the "imputed merits of Christ." When all that she ever wrote on justification by faith

from 1844 to 1902 is surveyed, roughly forty-five percent of the entire mass was written between late 1888 and late 1892.

Soon after Ellen White left for Australia (late 1891), Waggoner was called by the General Conference to minister in England and Europe (where he labored from 1892 to 1903). His major work during this period was editing the British missionary journal *Present Truth*. While Waggoner's personal influence centered more in Europe, he did return to North America for the General Conference convocations of 1895, 1896, 1897, 1898, 1899, 1901, and 1903. He was the principal speaker for the Bible study sessions at each of these conferences except the last.

The most contentious issue of Waggoner's legacy involves the extent of Ellen White's affirmation of his theology. There is no doubt that Ellen White gave both Jones and Waggoner strong, sustained support. But claims that she ascribed to them a certain "canonical" authority to define the message of righteousness by faith and its attendant doctrines have proved problematic. The doctrinal issues that have been most contentious are justification, perfection, the covenants, the deity and humanity of Christ, and the final generation vindication of God's fairness in dealing with sin and sinners. What then was it in their message and ministry that generated her strong support?

There are numerous themes that she highlighted in her most comprehensive statement on the significance of his message preached at Minneapolis in 1888 and afterward. Among the most prominent were (1) the uplifting of Christ as Savior (not just lawgiver); (2) the justification by faith in Jesus; (3) the connection between the righteousness of Christ and obedience to God's commandments; (4) the need for Adventists to focus on Jesus; (5) that Christ's righteousness or "righteousness by faith" has an intimate relationship to the third angel's message of Revelation 14:9-12; (6) that Jesus has special "covenant blessings" for His children; (7) that Adventists had been emphasizing the law but neglecting Jesus and the importance of faith in His sacrifice; and (8) that God had raised up Jones and Waggoner to redirect the gaze of Adventists to Jesus, to faith in His sacrifice and merits (TM 91-93; see also Knight, *A User-friendly Guide*, pp. 21, 22) .

The interpreters of Ellen White have continued to debate the extent of her convergence with Waggoner (and Jones) on justification by faith alone, perfection, the human nature of Christ, the covenants, and the role of the final generation of saints in the vindication of God. While there is little doubt about his influence on Ellen White and subsequent theological developments in Adventism, most certainly the efforts to understand her agreements and differences with Waggoner's more distinct ideas (and whether they should be embraced by the church at large) will continue.

What clearly stands out in Waggoner's writings is his great emphasis on obedience to the law of God through faith in the indwelling Christ. Some have suggested that this subjective emphasis was what led him into his excessive emphasis on the immanence of God (verging on pantheism); others have suggested that the clearly evident pantheistic sentiments only exerted a mildly parasitic effect on his legitimate emphasis regarding the power of the Christ who effectually works in the believer by faith. Hopefully, a more comprehensive and sustained study of Waggoner's life and writings will bring greater clarity to these controverted issues.

It was during the European years that the seeds of both theological irregularity and marital failure were sown. Even Waggoner's most ardent admirers acknowledge that by 1896 his stress on the immanence of God was manifesting pantheistic (or panentheistic) tendencies. Furthermore, by the time of the 1901 General Conference session he was enthusing over "new light" regarding "spiritual affinities." The gist of the latter idea was that a person could have such an "affinity" with a person who was not his/her spouse in this world and then be married to that person in heaven. The emergence of these trends would result in theological decline, separation from denominational employment (1904), loss of church membership (1905), being divorced by his first wife (1905), and his subsequent marriage to Edith Adams. Thus the period from 1903 until his death in 1916 represents an era of decline with no further path-breaking theological influence on the Adventist Church. Thus, the years from 1901 to 1908 were the most painful in the relationship between Waggoner and Ellen White.

Until 1901 she had been positive in her assessments of Waggoner and his work (Lt 77, 1898; Lt 28, 1900; Ms 81a, 1901). After the 1901 General Conference session in Battle Creek, however, she became quite apprehensive of his views. She plainly warned him about his pantheistic tendencies, calling them "fanciful views of God" that were similar to a "misrepresentation of God" that she was called upon to oppose at the "beginning" of her work when she was 17 years old. On October 3, 1903, she not so subtly suggested that such "fanciful views" would result in "apostasy, spiritualism, [and] free-loveism" (Lt 230, 1903, in 21MR 172). Three days later she directly confronted Waggoner's subtle but adulterous "free-loveism": Satan "hopes to lead you into the maze of spiritualism. He hopes to wean your affections from your wife, and to fix them upon another woman" (Lt 231, 1903, in TSB 200). In 1908 she would reiterate that Waggoner's ideas were "similar in character to those we had met and rebuked in several places where we met fanatical movements after the passing of time in 1844"; she then plainly stated that "Dr. Waggoner was then [in 1901] departing from the faith in the doctrine he held regarding spiritual affinities" (Lt 224, 1908, in 10MR 358).

Along with these dire warnings in 1901 and 1903, Ellen White still continued to work for Waggoner's recovery. Writing to P. T. Magan and E. A Sutherland, she advised them to "take him into the school at Berrien Springs" as a teacher and "help him to place his feet on solid ground, even the Rock of Ages." She optimistically expressed the hope "that he will recover his former clearness and power" (Lt 214, 1903, in SpM 338). Sadly, all such efforts were to no avail. Waggoner's speculative "views" ultimately led not only to divorce and remarriage but also to separation from denominational employment (1904). The last 10 years of his life were lived in relative obscurity. The once-forceful "messenger" of "righteousness by faith" in the "matchless charms of Christ" had been shorn of his power and influence.

Further reading: obit. RH, June 29, 1916; W. W. Whidden, *E. J. Waggoner: From the Physician of Good News to Agent of Division* (RHPA, 2008); G. R. Knight, *A User-friendly Guide to the 1888 Message* (RHPA, 1998); G. R. Knight, *From 1888 to Apostasy: The Case of A. T. Jones* (RHPA, 1987); D. P. McMahon. *Ellet Joseph Waggoner: The Myth and the Man* (Fallbrook, Calif.: Verdict Publications, 1979); C. L. Wahlen, "Selected Aspects of Ellet J. Waggoner's Eschatology and Their Relation to His Understanding of Righteousness by Faith, 1882-1895" (M.Div thesis, AU, 1988); E. C. Webster, *Crosscurrents in Adventist Christology* (New York: Peter Lang, 1984/

Berrien Springs, Mich.: AUP, 1992); W. W. Whidden, "The Soteriology of Ellen G. White: The Persistent Path to Perfection, 1836-1902" (Ph.D. diss., Drew University, 1989); W. W. Whidden, *Ellen White on Salvation* (RHPA, 1995); R. J. Wieland, *The 1888 Message: An Introduction*, rev. and enl. (Paris, Ohio: Glad Tidings Publishers, 1997); R. J. Wieland and D. K Short, *1888 Re-Examined: Revised and Updated by the Original Authors* (Leominster, Mass.: Eusey Press, The 1888 Message Study Committee, 1987); *SDA Encyclopedia* (1996), vol. 11, pp. 848, 849; A. L. White, "What Became of A. T. Jones and E. J. Waggoner" (EGWE, SDoc).

Woodrow W. Whidden

WAGGONER, JOSEPH HARVEY (1820-1889). Evangelist and editor; father of *E. J. Waggoner.

In his youth Waggoner joined the Baptist Church. When Sabbatarian Adventist preachers came to Wisconsin in 1851 and convinced him of the binding obligation to keep the Sabbath, he joined their ranks and began to preach their doctrines. Although, like other Adventist pioneers, he continued to work at his trade (printing), he intermittently held meetings in nearby towns. In 1878 he moved to California to become the manager and later editor of *Signs of the Times*. Self-taught, Waggoner was an indefatigable student and wrote many influential books in early Adventism, such as *The Kingdom of God* (1859), *The Atonement: An Examination of a Remedial System in the Light of Nature and Revelation* (1868), and *From Eden to Eden* (1888).

Over a period of 25 years Ellen White wrote many letters to Waggoner, all dealing

JOSEPH H. WAGGONER

COURTESY OF THE REVIEW AND HERALD PUBLISHING ASSOCIATION

with either his relationship with his wife, Mariette (1823-1908), or his harsh, overbearing, and critical temperament. Because it seems that Waggoner's wife refused to be transformed by the gospel message, Ellen White considered her influence on him to be detrimental to his work and, hence, recommended that he not bring her along when he held evangelistic meetings in other towns (Lt 4, 1860; Lt 6, 1870). Ellen White also warned him that, at the instigation of his wife and because of her unsanctified influence, he tended to be too harsh and judgmental of others (Lt 3, 1872).

Ellen White's strongest rebuke came while Waggoner worked at the Pacific Press office in Oakland, California, when he got involved in an adulterous relationship with a married woman, *Lottie Chittenden, a situation that Ellen White bluntly chastised him for (Lt 10, 1885, in TSB 182-184; cf. Lts 73, 74, 51, 1886; TSB 184-193; 21MR 378-387). Given the situation in which he had placed himself, she pleaded with him: "There are but few who know to what extent this intimacy has gone, and God forbid it shall be known and your influence lost to God's cause and your soul lost. I beg of you to not take it upon you to pronounce judgment against anyone but yourself" (Lt 10, 1885, in TSB 183, 184). In response to her counsel, Waggoner left California for Battle Creek, but Ellen White continued to labor with him for deeper repentance (Lt 51, 1886, in 21MR 380). She wanted to invite him to Europe, but not until she was sure his heart had been changed and not only his outward behavior (21MR 378). Evidently she was convinced of his thorough reformation, for in 1886 he went to Europe, where he became editor-in-chief of Adventist periodicals in German and French until his death in 1889. He was buried beside *J. N. Andrews.

Further reading: obit. RH, Sept. 3, 1889; *SDA Encyclopedia* (1996), vol. 11, p. 849.

Denis Fortin

WALES, WILLIAM CHARLES (1856-1934). Colporteur, teacher, and minister born in Melbourne, Quebec. In 1880 he graduated from *Battle Creek College, entered the ministry, and wedded Emma Rebecca Miller (1859-1906). Marital difficulties led to divorce (see *marriage and divorce) in 1892 and estrangement from the church. That same year he married Myrtle May Stebbins (1870-1967). In 1901 Wales rejoined Adventism. When his family urged him to leave his second wife (J. Edson White to EGW, Oct. 30, 1901), Ellen White advised against this and encouraged him to "stand forth in the strength of the Lord as an overcomer" (Lt 41, 1902, in 7MR 341). Wales began work in the Cumberland Conference with reinstated ministerial credentials, but in 1906, after another affair, he left the ministry for colporteur work (GIB to EGW, July 3, 1906). William and Myrtle eventually settled in Alabama, whereupon Wales wished to reenter ministry once more. Conference officials sought Ellen White for advice. She recommended that those who had dealt with his case in the past should make a decision. Furthermore, she stated that those who have "thoroughly repented" should be allowed to work for Christ, but not in positions of responsibility (WCW to C. F. McVagh, Sept. 15, 1911). Wales traveled to Elmshaven to plead his case, to no avail. In the meantime, conference officials heard from Wales' former colleagues, all of whom advised against reinstating him (E. B. Hayes to WCW, Jan. 31, 1913).

Further reading: obit. RH, Sept. 27, 1934; TSB 225-235.

WALLING, ADDIE, see **MACPHERSON, ADDIE (WALLING)**.

WALLING, FREDERICK (b. 1859). Son of *William and Louisa (Clough) Walling and brother of *Addie (Walling) MacPherson and *May Walling. In 1887 Addie had returned from Ellen White's home in California to her father's home in Nevada and for various reasons had been detained there longer than expected. A few months later, in 1888, Ellen White corresponded with Fred Walling expressing her caring feelings for both Addie and her younger sister, May, and explaining that she wished to have Addie return to her home as soon as possible because she appreciated the assistance Addie gave her (Lt 2, 1888; 8MR 109, 110). In one of her letters to Fred, Ellen White recounted how she came to care for Addie and May, and that their father did not support her financially for doing so (Lt 1, 1888).

WALLING, MAY (1869-1953). Granddaughter of Ellen White's sister *Caroline Harmon

COURTESY OF THE ELLEN G. WHITE ESTATE, INC.

MAY WALLING

Clough. May and her older sister, *Addie (Walling) MacPherson, were raised by Ellen White at the request of their father, *William B. Walling. "Mother White," as May referred to her, served as a surrogate mother throughout her life. During Ellen White's last few years (1913-1915) May lived with her, serving as her nurse and personal aide. She was present on February 13, 1915, when Ellen White broke her hip, and when she died on July 16, 1915.

WALLING, WILLIAM B. (b. 1836). Father of *Addie (Walling) MacPherson and *May Walling, granddaughters of Ellen White's sister, *Caroline (Harmon) Clough; William was married to Louisa Clough and together

had five children: *Frederick, Bertie (Hurbert), Edward, Addie, and May. In 1872, during a vacation in Colorado, James and Ellen White first visited Walling and his family near Denver and enjoyed the scenery of the mountains for a few weeks before continuing on to California (2Bio 342-355). In the summer of 1873 the Whites again visited the Walling family and spent many weeks in the mountains nearby. Before the Whites left Colorado in November, Walling urged them to take along his two daughters because he and his wife were having marital difficulties and he did not want the girls exposed to their conflicts (2Bio 392, 393). The Whites agreed, thinking the arrangement would last for only a few months. After William and Louisa divorced (cf. Lt 40, 1875) and neither took any steps to change the temporary arrangement, the Whites reared and educated the two girls as if they were their own (Lt 80, 1874).

Eighteen years later, in 1891, when the girls were young women, Walling, who was living alone, sought their return so that they could look after his home. They refused, choosing to stay with Ellen White. Walling then brought a $25,000 suit against Ellen White, claiming that she had alienated the affections of his daughters. On September 12, 1891, while at the Colorado camp meeting, Ellen White was served with the papers (Ms 34, 1891, in 4Bio 17).

Litigation continued over a period of four years, until finally Ellen White, through Harmon Lindsay, an officer of the General Conference to whom she had entrusted her business affairs while in Australia, arranged for a settlement out of court. Ellen White gave Walling a cash payment of $1,500 to remove the lawsuit, and paid $2,000 for attorney's fees (4Bio 17, 268, 269).

Those familiar with the matter felt certain that if the case had been brought to court,

Walling would have lost. Ellen White, however, explained why it was not handled that way: "I could have decided to go into court, but this would have brought the children where they would have been obliged to testify on oath against their father, and would have led to endless trouble. The mother would have been brought into court, and you [her niece, Mary (Clough) Watson (see *Mary L. Clough)] would probably [have] had to act a part. There is no knowing what lies might have been sworn to, or how much disgrace might have been brought upon us all" (Lt 128, 1896, in 4Bio 269).

Denis Fortin

WANLESS, MARY L. (CLOUGH), see CLOUGH, MARY L.

WARREN, LUTHER WILLIS (1864-1940). Youth

leader. At Hazelton, Michigan, in 1879, Luther

LUTHER AND BELLE WARREN

Warren (age 14) and Harry Fenner (age 17) formed one of the first Adventist youth societies. An evangelist and youth leader, Luther and his wife, Jessie Belle (Proctor) Warren, established two churches (Frankfort and Bear Lake, Michigan), started Sunshine Bands (1894), founded orphanages, formed 186 Missionary Volunteer societies, and baptized thousands. Called "the cyclone preacher," he was counseled by Ellen White to seek God's help for his depression, to leave New York City for his health, and to be gentler in speech (Lt 104, 1902). She promised that angels would cooperate with him in revival efforts, which took him across America and to three foreign countries. This "Pied Piper of Adventism" wrote thousands of letters and memorized the names of children who followed him around campgrounds and on nature hikes, thrilled with the songs and games he taught them. Taking Ellen White's words to heart, he spread "the fragrance of Christlikeness" (Lt 260, 1908) around him until his death.

Further reading: obit. RH, June 27, 1940; obit. RH, Aug. 25, 1960; J. Bertoluci, "Luther Warren, the Preacher and Man of Projects" (research paper, 1974, CAR); S. Boucher, *Luther Warren: Man of Prayer and Power* (RHPA, 1959); P. Edsell, "The Contribution of Luther Warren to the Guidance and Development of the SDA Youth Program" (research paper, 1982, CAR); B. E. Strayer, "Frankfort: The Church That Nearly Missed the Boat!" (unpublished manuscript, CAR); Luther Willis Warren, Letters (1898-1924) (CAR).

Brian E. Strayer

WASHBURN, JUDSON SYLVANUS (1863-1955).

Minister, evangelist, and missionary born in Waukon, Iowa. In 1890 he married Orra Ellen Riddle (1866-1932). As a young minister Washburn was "severely shaken" by the *General Conference session of 1888 (Washburn, "Half a Century" [GCAr], p. 1). He suspected that Ellen White was influenced by Jones and Waggoner on their way to the meetings, and, as a result, began to question the genuineness of Ellen White's inspiration. Afterward, Washburn arranged for a personal interview with Ellen White in which "all doubts were settled and forever set at rest" (*ibid.*). Washburn received further clarification in an article she wrote for the *Review and Herald*, August 19, 1890, in answer to his queries (Lt 36a, 1890).

Renewed by this experience, Washburn became an evangelist in Washington, D.C., and, in 1891 went to England, where Ellen White supported his innovative evangelistic techniques such as speaking from in front of the pulpit, and preaching without notes.

Washburn returned to Washington, D.C., in 1902 and with the support of Ellen White helped raise the funds to secure the Sligo property on which Washington Missionary College (see *Washington Training College) and *Washington Sanitarium were later built. He later spent time as an evangelist in Tennessee (1906-1913), and in the Columbia Union (1913-1932). After Ellen White's death in 1915, he allied with *Claude Holmes in a battle for an inerrant view of *inspiration.

Further reading: obit. RH, Aug. 25, 1955; J. S. Washburn, "An Open Letter to Elder A. G. Daniells and an Appeal to the General Conference" (GCAr); B. P. Phillips, "A Century of Adventism in Wales 1885-1985: A History of Seventh-day Adventism in Wales and the Border Counties" (Ph.D. diss., University of Glamorgan, Pontypridd, 1993).

Michael W. Campbell

WATERMAN, CORA B. Colporteur from Wisconsin whom Ellen White rebuked for sexual immorality (see *sexuality). Ellen White stated that she had a decided message from the Lord that although Waterman's sin was "heinous," her case was not without hope. White acknowledged that Waterman had confessed her sin to God and that God would pardon according to His promise [1 John 1:9], but urged that repentance is to uplift the sinner to a "high and holy standard." White called Waterman to seek for deeper repentance by meditating on Jonah 3:8-10. "Now, please take your case to the Lord, and if you are in communion with Him, He will hear your prayers, and will guide you in judgment." In an unusual conclusion, White advised Waterman to forsake her sin, but not to mention it to anyone, lest by giving it publicity she close the door to further service. "I have no disposition to expose you," White wrote, "but leave you to develop character. I pity you and hope

that you will move in discretion, and become altogether that which God would have you" (Lt 95, 1893, in TSB 163-166).

WATSON, G. F. (1857-1949). Adventist pastor and president of the Colorado Conference (1900-1908). In late 1904 Watson and other officers of the Colorado Conference became perplexed when they heard that church members were sending their *tithe funds directly to the *Southern Missionary Society (the recognized organization fostering work among the Black population in the southern United States), an action considered not only irregular but wrong and censurable, as it did not follow the proper channels of giving in the church. When the matter became known to Ellen White, she wrote to Watson and said that at times church members had given her tithe money to dispense to needy pastors or to the Adventist work in the South, but that she did not wish to encourage this publicly. She urged Watson to "keep cool and not become stirred up and give publicity to this matter, lest many more shall follow their example" (Lt 267, 1905, in 5Bio 394-396).

Further reading: obit. RH, Sept. 29, 1949; J. Moon, *W. C. White and E. G. White* (AUP, 1993), 401-415.

WATSON, MARY (CLOUGH), see **CLOUGH, MARY L.**

WEBBER, EMMA (1856-1912). Young worker from Union City, Michigan, who heard *Joseph Bates preach in 1865. The following winter Webber obtained a job as a housekeeper for the *Abram Dodge family in *Battle Creek. In 1867 she began working at the *Health Reform Institute. During this time she was in close contact with the White family, although she did not decide to become a Christian until *J. N. Andrews and *A. S. Hutchins pleaded with her. On June 12, 1868, Emma went to hear Ellen White address the young people (2Bio 232-238). That evening Ellen White had a vision for about 20 minutes. It made such an impact on Emma that the next day she was baptized by *James White. Sometime in late 1873 it appears that Webber received a testimony from Ellen White. Webber noted in her diary, "Yesterday I was rereading the letter from EGW for the hundredth time. How thankful I ought to be. May I even be glad for reproof. But so sorry I need it" (E. M. Webber Diary, Feb. 15, 1874). Although this letter is no longer extant, Ellen White did write another letter admonishing her for her pride, worldliness, and danger of backsliding (Lt 37, 1891)—traits Emma faults herself for in her diaries. Webber later held several positions in the *Battle Creek Sanitarium (1884-1904).

Further reading: Lt 76a, 1898; obit. RH, Feb. 20, 1913; L. E. Foll, "Emma Webber's Diary: Window Into Early Battle Creek, 1865-1874" *Adventist Heritage* 7, no. 2 (Fall 1982): 53-61.

Michael W. Campbell

WELLMAN, GEORGE O. (1858-1945) and **ADA (DE YARMOND)** (1860-1926). Adventists in Oakland, California; George was a builder; Ada served in the *Review and Herald and *Pacific Press as a proofreader. They went on the third voyage of *Pitcairn to the South Pacific islands (RH, June 12, 1894). After their return from mission service Ellen White thanked them for their liberal donation for the mission work in Australasia (Lt 260, 1899; Lt 212, 1900).

Further reading: obit. RH, May 24, 1945; obit. RH, July 15, 1926.

WESSELS, ANDREW E., see **WESSELS, DANIEL** and **ANDREW E.**

WESSELS, DANIEL (b. 1878), and **ANDREW E.** (b. 1880). Sixth and seventh sons, respectively, of *Johannes Wessels, Sr., and Anna Wessels of South Africa. In December 1894, when Ellen White was living in Granville, near Sydney, Australia, she was visited by "Mother" Wessels, with her sons Daniel and Andrew, ages 16 and 14; her daughter Annie and Annie's husband, *Harmon Lindsay; and the Lindsays' 4-month-old child. The Wessels family were on a yearlong world tour, which would include the 1895 General Conference session in Battle Creek (7WCW 105, 106, cited in 4Bio 180-181). Letters to Daniel include Lts 15, 16, 1899. Letters to Andrew include Lts 218, 226, 236, 1903; Lt 248, 1905; Lt 398, 1907.

Jerry Moon

WESSELS, FRANCIS (or **FRANÇOIS**) **H.** Fifth son of *Johannes Wessels, Sr., and Anna Wessels of South Africa. Francis and his brother Henry gave *J. H. Kellogg $40,000 in 1893 to found the Chicago Sanitarium (see *Chicago Medical Mission) and *American Medical Missionary College. Ellen White wrote at least one letter specifically to him (Lt 65, 1893; cf. Lt 107, 1896), as well as including him in several letters addressed to the family as a group (e.g., Lt 94, 1895; Lt 112, 1896; Lts 17, 151, 1899).

Further reading: SHM 276; L. F. Swanepoel, *The Origin and Early History of the Seventh-day Adventist Church in South Africa* (M.A. thesis, University of South Africa, 1972), p. 196; *SDA Encyclopedia* (1996), vol. 10, p. 324.

WESSELS, HENRY (or **HENDRIK**) **S. P.** Fourth son of *Johannes Wessels, Sr., and Anna Wessels of South Africa, who, with his brother, Francis H. Wessels, gave *J. H. Kellogg $40,000 in 1893 to found the Chicago Sanitarium.

Henry married Johanna Sophia (van Jaarsveld) (1872-1956). Their wedding was reputedly the first in the old Beaconsfield church. In 1895 Henry was elected to the Publishing Committee and the Medical Missionary Board of the South African Conference. During a time of spiritual searching in 1895, he wrote to Ellen White inquiring about the way of salvation. She responded with a winsome, hope-filled letter containing many of the principles found in her book *Steps to Christ* (Lt 97, 1895, in 4MR 158-164). She wrote him at least three other extant letters (Lts 91, 95, 1895; Lt 66, 1899).

Further reading: obit. *South African Union Lantern*, Mar. 1, 1957; L. F. Swanepoel, *The Origin and Early History of the Seventh-day Adventist Church in South Africa* (M.A. thesis, University of South Africa, 1972), pp. 48, 196, 203, 204; *SDA Encyclopedia* (1996), vol. 10, p. 324; SHM 276.

WESSELS, JOHANNES JACOBUS, SR. (1818-1892), and **ANNA ELIZABETH (BOTHA)** (1840-1918). Dutch farmers in the Orange Free State, South Africa, near the large diamond mine at Kimberley in Northern Cape; among the earliest converts to Adventism in South Africa. They reportedly sold a diamond

DANIEL, ANDREW, ANNA, AND FRANCIS WESSELS

field to the De Beers diamond company in 1891 for £350,000 (then about $1.7 million). After becoming Adventists, the family invested much of their wealth to advance the mission

of the church in South Africa, Australia, and America. The matriarch, "Mother" Wessels, traveled widely and was an influential advisor to her sons on their business enterprises (Lt 109, 1899). She visited Ellen White in Australia in December 1894. Two years later, when building on the Avondale school came to a standstill for lack of funds, Mother Wessels made a loan of £1,000 (then $5,000), which enabled the building program to get under way again (4Bio 269). In 1907, after Ellen White's return to the United States, Mother Wessels and several other members of the Wessels family again visited Ellen White at her home in northern California (6Bio 120).

The Wessels family included 10 children, seven sons—*Pieter ("Petrus" or "Peter") Johannes Daniel, who was the first Adventist in the family and influenced his parents and siblings to follow his example; * Philip (Philipus) Wouter B.; *Johannes (John) Jacobus, Jr.; *Henry (Hendrik) S. P. (or D.); Francis (François) H.; *Daniel; and *Andrew E.—and three daughters—Jacoba Johanna (married Roussouw); Johanna (married Marcus); and Anna (Annie) Elizabeth, who married *Harmon W. Lindsay, an Adventist missionary to South Africa.

From 1890 through 1908 Ellen White addressed some 115 extant letters to the various members of the Wessels family, many of them to Mrs. A. E. Wessels. In 1899, after Mother Wessels had influenced her son John to decline Ellen White's call to Australia, White admonished the family that their wealth, their attitudes toward that wealth, and their family and social connections all involved temptations they did not always recognize. She advised that as Abraham was called to leave his kindred in order to follow God, so for their spiritual prosperity some of them would be benefited by moving away from their family and familiar surroundings (Lt 109, 1899).

A major theme of Ellen White's letters to the Wessels family members was that the work in South Africa not replicate the mistakes made in Battle Creek. She repeatedly chastised leadership in Battle Creek during the 1890s for building large new buildings in Battle Creek, when rapidly expanding mission fields had such desperate needs. Leaders justified the lavish buildings as "[giving] character to the work," but their real motives, according to White, were "pride, selfishness, avarice, and covetousness" (17MR 189). "Money was misappropriated" to serve "ambition and outward display." One result of this corruption was its effect on the minds of visitors to Battle Creek, such as the Wessels family. Ellen White said they were "confused and led astray by the pride and outlay of means" they witnessed. Consequently, "the errors of Battle Creek would be seen in all they undertook in South Africa. Their experience might have been of an entirely different character had the work in Battle Creek been carried forward in simplicity" (1888 Materials 1693, 1694). The history of the work in South Africa supports this assessment. Claremont Union College near Cape Town was built in 1893 at a cost of £67,000 (then $335,000), and the Claremont Sanitarium in 1897 for about £50,000 ($250,000). But church membership was under 250 members, and when the Wesselses' money began to run out, the conference was left in difficult straits for many years (*SDA Encyclopedia* [1996], vol. 11, p. 632). Further, while the Wesselses gave generously to initiate mission work among African tribes, funds for long-term mission work were scarce because the conference had a disproportionate amount of capital tied up in institutions. These outcomes, however, Ellen White did not blame on the Wesselses primarily, but on the misguided example they received from Battle Creek.

The Wesselses story has given rise to a considerable mythology. A public presentation in 1974, still widely distributed, contains many statements contrary to fact, though sincerely reported as tradition (see Durand, "The Story of a Story").

Further reading: R. W. Schwarz, *Light Bearers* (PPPA, 1979), pp. 223-225, 232; L. F. Swanepoel, *The Origin and Early History of the Seventh-day Adventist Church in South Africa* (M.A. thesis, University of South Africa, 1972), pp. 25, 87, 196, 197; E. F. Durand, "The Story of a Story," RH, Feb. 14, 1985; Feb. 21, 1985; and Feb. 28, 1985 (DF 506, CAR); *SDA Encyclopedia* (1996), vol. 10, p. 324; 11:630-632, 865.

Jerry Moon

WESSELS, JOHANNES (or **JOHN**) **JACOBUS** (or **JAMES**), **JR.** (1867-1951), and **RUBY ELECTA** (**ANTHONY**) (1869-1956). Minister, administrator, third son of Johannes Wessels, Sr., of South Africa. He was closely connected with the founding of the first Adventist institutions in that country, including the Claremont Union College (1892) in Cape Town (forerunner of Helderberg College), *Claremont Sanitarium, and an orphanage in Plumstead. Some 28 letters he and his wife received from Ellen White are still extant.

In 1897 Ellen White invited John to Australia. "I have not been given the message, Send for Brother [Wessels] to come to Australia," she explained, "therefore I do not say, I know that this is the place for you. But it is my privilege to express my wishes, even though I say I speak not by commandment. But I do not want you to come because of any persuasion of mine. I want you to seek the Lord most earnestly and then follow where He shall lead you. . . . Nevertheless, it is my privilege to present the wants of the work of God in Australia" (Lt 129, 1897, in 2MR 151, 152). At first he declined, apparently under pressure from family members, especially his mother. In reply, Ellen.White cautioned the family that their wealth, family, and social connections involved temptations they did not always recognize. She advised that as Abraham was called to leave his kindred in order to follow God, so for their spiritual prosperity some of them would be benefited by moving away from their family and familiar surroundings (Lt 109, 1899). At this, John and his wife, Ruby, accepted the call to Australia, where he became chair of the board of *Sydney Sanitarium (UCR, Sept. 1, 1899). Moving to the United States in 1902, he managed the *Paradise Valley (1907), *Glendale (1907-1909), and *St. Helena sanitariums (1911-1914).

Two uncertainties exist about John Wessels, Jr. One source, "Early Experiences of Mr. P.J.D. Wessels," calls him Johannes *M.* Wessels. The "M" could be a typewriter error for the nearby "J" key, or it could be a third initial, which would be consistent with the names of most of his siblings. Another source calls him a "stepbrother" of Pieter Wessels—without elaborating (Swanepoel, p. 5). If John was Pieter's stepbrother, it would imply that one or both of their parents had been married before, and some of the children would be stepsiblings. This could account for the seeming duplication of names.

Further reading: obit. RH, Nov. 29, 1951; obit. RH, Aug. 30, 1956; L. F. Swanepoel, *The Origin and Early History of the Seventh-day Adventist Church in South Africa* (M.A. thesis, University of South Africa, 1972), pp. 5, 28, 39, 40, 66, 121, 203, 204; Pieter Wessels, "Early Experiences of Mr. P.J.D. Wessels" (DF 506, CAR); *SDA Encyclopedia* (1996), vol. 11, pp. 629-634, 732, 733, 865.

Jerry Moon

WESSELS, PHILIP (or **PHILIPUS**) **WOUTER B.** and **HELENA ELIZABETH** (**GROENEWALD**)

(1868-1927). Philip was a businessman of South Africa, second son of *Johannes Wessels, Sr., and Anna E. Wessels. Philip and Helena received at least 20 letters from Ellen White, not including letters addressed to multiple members of the family. With his brother *Pieter, Philip attended the 1893 General Conference session in Battle Creek, where they met *A. R. Henry and *Harmon Lindsay. According to Ellen White, these men "leavened and corrupted" his mind by "false representations" that resulted in Philip's "separation from God, and His work" (17MR 188). In 1897 and 1898 Ellen White wrote to Helena, seeking to bolster her faith (DG 183-186). Evidently her efforts succeeded, because by early 1899 Philip had returned to the church. "You will be tempted, you will be tried," she counseled him, but "put your entire trust in the Lord. Serve Him with heart and soul, and believe that He pardons your transgressions and forgives your sins" (17MR 133). Later that year she again appealed to Philip to "be true to your profession of faith," warning that he did not understand himself. He had made large investments in a "worldly business" in which he was "transgressing the fourth commandment." White pleaded with him to invest his wealth where it would bring him "rich returns, great satisfaction, and heavenly blessings in this life," so that he could grow "strong spiritually" instead of "losing his faith." Specifically she challenged Philip to lead out in publishing Adventist literature "translated into Dutch and in other languages" (Lt 109, 1899). In a letter about Philip to *W. S. Hyatt, conference president in South Africa, she faulted the conference for accepting the Wesselses' money, but neglecting to involve the Wesselses personally in church work. "Lines of work could have been entered into that would have called the young men of the Wessels family to act a part in God's cause.

Then they would not have drifted away into the world to invest their money in worldly enterprises" (Lt 183, 1899, in 1888 Materials 1695). Helena's obituary gives her husband's initials as "P.J.B." (See last paragraph of previous entry.)

Further reading: obit. RH, Feb. 9, 1928; L. F. Swanepoel, *The Origin and Early History of the Seventh-day Adventist Church in South Africa* (M.A. thesis, University of South Africa, 1972), pp. 4, 27, 28, 47, 76, 81.

Jerry Moon

WESSELS, PIETER (also **PETRUS** or **PETER**) **JOHANNES DANIEL** (1856-1933) and **MARIA ELIZABETH (VAN ZYL)** (1860-1942). Born in the Orange Free State, the eldest son of *Johannes Wessels, Sr., and Anna Wessels, Pieter was a South African farmer (Boer) and entrepreneur. Converted to Adventism by the American miner William Hunt in 1885 and miraculously healed of tuberculosis through prayer, Wessels and some friends paid the fare for the families of *D. A. Robinson and *C. L. Boyd and two colporteurs to come to South Africa as missionaries in 1887. A self-supporting preacher and diamond millionaire, Wessels' generosity funded the Union College in Claremont, *Claremont Sanitarium in Cape Town, *Solusi Mission, and other institutions in Africa, and Avondale College in Australia. In 1895 he was elected vice president of the South Africa Conference (Swanepoel, p. 42). During the 1890s Ellen White wrote him and his brother Philip frequently, appealing for funds to help the work in Australia and America (cf. Lt 107, 1896), yet warning the family of the danger their wealth posed for their spiritual lives (Lt 115, 1899; Lt 173, 1899). She encouraged Pieter and Maria "to stand firmly for the truth" and to "think much of the tender compassion of Christ" (Lt 119, 1897).

Further reading: LS 362-364; obit. RH, May 18, 1933; *SDA Encyclopedia* (1996), vol. 11, p. 865; L. F. Swanepoel, *The Origin and Early History of the Seventh-day Adventist Church in South Africa* (M.A. thesis, University of South Africa, 1972); DF 506, CAR.

Brian E. Strayer

WHEELER, FREDERICK (1811-1910) and **LYDIA (PROCTOR)** (1814-1886). Circuit-riding minister and farmer from Hillsboro, New Hampshire, who was ordained in the Methodist Episcopal Church in 1840. Two years later he was invited to help build the *Christian church in the nearby village of Washington, and added this congregation to his pastoral circuit. He became a Millerite the same year after reading the writings of *William Miller. In the spring 1844 he accepted the seventh-day *Sabbath from Rachel Oakes (later Preston), becoming the first Sabbatarian Adventist minister. In 1845 Wheeler was influential in *Joseph Bates' acceptance of the Sabbath doctrine. He remained in the vicinity of Washington, New Hampshire, until 1851, when James White encouraged him to travel more widely. In 1857 Wheeler moved to Brookfield, New York, where Ellen White was shown his case in vision on August 3, 1861. This vision resulted in two letters in which she admonished the Wheelers for their unbelief in her visions and their judgmental attitude toward *Ira and Rhoda Abbey (Lt 20, 1861; Lt 13, 1862). In the fall of 1861 Wheeler retired to a farm in West Monroe, New York, where he remained a supporter of the ministry of Ellen White. He later stated that he knew what a "great blessing" the testimonies had been in his own life (RH, Oct. 4, 1906).

Further reading: obit. RH, Nov. 24, 1910; W. A. Spicer, "Our First Minister," RH, Feb. 15, 1940; *SDA Encyclopedia* (1996), vol. 11, p. 871.

Michael W. Campbell

WHITE, ANNA (1822-1854). Younger sister of *James White, editor of the *Youth's Instructor*, and proofreader of the *Review and Herald*. Very little is known about Anna's life, except that in 1853 she and her brother *Nathaniel came to live with James and Ellen White at 124 Mount Hope Avenue in *Rochester, New York, when both were nonbelievers and Nathaniel was already in an advanced stage of tuberculosis. During the months they lived in Rochester, Anna and Nathaniel "weighed the evidences of our position, and conscientiously decided for the truth," wrote Ellen White (LS 147). Among Anna's contributions before her death was the compilation of *Hymns for Youth and Children*, the first Adventist youth hymnal (1853). In January 1854 Anna became editor of the *Youth's Instructor*, making her the first woman to edit a Sabbatarian Adventist publication. That same year she also contracted tuberculosis, from which she did not recover. Her last days were not spent in self-pity, but in organizing her belongings and writing her parents, *John and Betsey White, pleading with them to accept the Sabbath. A few years later they accepted the Sabbatarian Adventist message after moving to Battle Creek and living across the street from Ellen and James.

Further reading: LS80, 146-148, 155, 156, 296, 297, 309-311; obit. RH, Dec. 12, 1854; R. H. Allen and H. Krug, *Rochester's Adventist Heritage: Tour Guide and Biographical Overview* (Rochester, N.Y.: Advent History Project, 2002), pp. 7, 35, 36.

Howard Krug

WHITE, ARTHUR LACEY (1907-1991). Grandson of Ellen White, third son of *William Clarence and *Ethel May (Lacey) White. Arthur was not quite 8 years old when his grandmother died, so his memories of her were mostly as a kind and loving grandmother. His father,

ARTHUR L. WHITE

COURTESY OF THE CENTER FOR ADVENTIST RESEARCH, ANDREWS UNIVERSITY

W. C. White, taught his children the practical skills of life, and Arthur early learned to be a responsible person.

Arthur White and Frieda Belle Swingle were married on June 26, 1928, and became the parents of three sons, James A., William E., and Arthur H. Soon after the wedding they drove to *Madison College, in Tennessee, where Arthur was an assistant accountant. A year later he was called back to California to become secretary to his father and to serve as treasurer/business manager of the *Ellen G. White Estate at Elmshaven.

After the death of W. C. White in 1937, a preplanned move was put in motion to transfer the Ellen G. White Estate to the General Conference in Washington, D.C. At that time the board of trustees appointed Arthur White to take his father's place on the board. He was 30 years old. From that time until his retirement in 1978 he served as secretary (director) of the board of trustees.

Arthur White was ordained to the ministry in Takoma Park, Maryland, in 1940. He conducted seminars and workshops around the world, many of them in conjunction with Andrews University. In 1973, in recognition of his contribution to Seventh-day Adventist education, Andrews University awarded him an honorary Doctor of Divinity degree. During the more than 40 years he served as secretary of the White Estate, many compilations were produced from the writings of Ellen White. White himself wrote more than 150 articles in various journals of the church, as well as authoring several books. He also helped in developing the concept of Ellen G. White/Seventh-day Adventist Research Centers in each division of the church in order to bring the writings of Ellen White to church members around the world. Several of these were opened while he was still secretary of the White Estate.

For a number of years the White Estate board had seen the need for a comprehensive biography of Ellen White, and Arthur White was asked to write it. But a heart disease, bacterial endocarditis, affected his health, and it soon became evident that he couldn't oversee the office work *and* write the biography. A new director, *Robert Olson, was appointed. White formally retired in 1978 and had open-heart surgery in 1979. After recuperating from the surgery, he set himself a taxing schedule of writing one chapter of the biography each week. He began his writing with the later years of her life, as more research had already been done on those years and the writing would go more quickly. Also he still had several sisters living who could add anecdotal information that would be lost with their passing. It took six years to complete the six-volume biography of Ellen G. White, with the last volume completed in 1985. At the General Conference session in New Orleans in 1985, White was presented with the church's Distinguished Achievement Award. The following year he received the Charles E. Weniger Award of Merit from Pacific Union College.

Arthur White died in St. Helena, California, January 12, 1991.

Further Reading: obit. PUR, Nov. 4, 1991; J. R. Nix, "Arthur L. White," AR, Feb. 28, 1991; DF 795-b; *SDA Encyclopedia* (1996), vol. 11, pp. 871-873.

Norma J. Collins

WHITE, BETSEY, see **WHITE, "DEACON" JOHN** and **ELIZABETH "BETSEY" (JEWETT)**.

WHITE, ELLA MAY (later **ELLA MAY [WHITE] ROBINSON**) (1882-1977). Oldest grandchild

of James and Ellen White, daughter of William C. and Mary (Kelsey) White, born in Oakland, California. Ella recalled that although James White knew he was to become a grandfather, he did not live to see his first grandchild. Her earliest recollections of her grandmother were while the family lived in Basel, Switzerland from 1885 to 1887. One time grandmother

ELLA (WHITE) ROBINSON

and granddaughter got lost while on a walk. Not meeting anyone who spoke English, they were an hour getting home. Like any proud grandmother, Ellen White enjoyed talking about her grandchildren. In a sermon given November 25, 1888, in Pottersville, Michigan, Ellen White recounted a recent story about little Ella's determination to fully surrender her will to Christ (Ms 20, 1888).

Ella's mother died of tuberculosis in 1890. Ellen White promised her dying daughter-in-law that she would take special care of Ella and her younger sister, *Mabel (Lt 9, 1904; Lt 82, 1911). When Ella's father and grandmother went to Australia in 1891, the sisters remained in Battle Creek, Michigan, in the care of *Mary Mortenson. After their father's remarriage in 1895, both girls traveled to Australia. Ella recalled living in a tent with her grandmother while Sunnyside was being built near Avondale College. She also recalled that her dresses were sometimes made from her grandmother's old ones. Although the backs of the skirts had become worn, there was still plenty of cloth from the fronts for making into dresses for Ella and her sister. Since Ellen White was a widow, she wore, as was then the custom, black or dark-maroon dresses the last years of her life. Knowing that her granddaughters would not like all dark dresses, Ellen White instructed her seamstress to add some bright trim on them for the girls.

Once while living in Australia, Ella, her sister, and two other small girls found some old clothes in the rag bag. Dressing up as beggars, they went around the place begging for pennies, food, anything. Ellen White was very amused by the girls as she looked around her room for some little things to give them.

Ella recalled that her grandmother had no use for "sour piety," as she called it. Ellen White did not think that long faces properly represent the Christian religion. One day when Ella was feeling kind of glum, her grandmother said to her, "If you could think of a person who . . . had nothing to be thankful for, no friends, no money, was suffering from an incurable disease . . . yet [had] the plan of salvation and the promises of a glorious future, aren't they sufficient to keep that person singing from morning to night?" Ella's favorite recollection of her grandmother was from one Sabbath when Ellen White was preaching about Jesus' matchless love. Pausing in the middle of her sermon, she seemed momentarily to forget the audience that was seated in front of her. Looking up as if into the face of Jesus, Ellen White exclaimed, "O Jesus, how I love You! How I love You!"

Ella returned to the United States in 1900 with her family. She attended Healdsburg College for two years and then taught church school in Reno, Nevada. On May 1, 1905, she married *Dores Eugene Robinson, one of her grandmother's secretaries. Ella had first met Dores in Australia in 1899. Ellen White spoke and offered a prayer during the wedding ceremony (Ms 170, 1905). Ella and Dores had three children: Virgil, Mabel, and Gladys. Besides several teaching assignments in California, Colorado, Tennessee, and Washington, D.C., the Robinsons worked in Africa for eight years (1920-1928). Returning to the United States in 1928, Ella's husband, Dores, would work for a total of 20 years for the Ellen G. White Estate, first at the Elmshaven office in California, and later after it relocated at the General Conference in Washington, D.C. He retired in 1953 and died in 1957. During her retirement years Ella authored several books, including biographies of J. N. Loughborough (*Lighter of Gospel Fires* [RHPA, 1954]) and S. N. Haskell (*S. N. Haskell, Man of Action* [RHPA, 1967]), as well as stories about Ellen G. White (*Stories of My Grandmother* [SPA, 1967] and *Over My Shoulder* [RHPA, 1982]). She also authored two hymns that were published in *Choir and Solo Melodies:* "The Lamb of God" (p. 32); and "Benediction Prayer-Song" (p. 68). Ella died in Loveland, Colorado; she is buried next to her husband in Monticeto Memorial Park in Loma Linda, California.

Further reading: E. M. Robinson, "Early Recollections of My Grandmother," YI, Mar. 16, 23, 30, 1948; interview with Ella May Robinson by James R. Nix (typed transcripts, June 11 and July 25, 1967, Oral History Collection, EGWE-LLU).

James R. Nix

WHITE, ELLEN GOULD (1827-1915). Cofounder of the Seventh-day Adventist Church, writer, lecturer, who possessed what Seventh-day Adventists have accepted as the prophetic gift. Born November 26, 1827, to Robert and Eunice Gould Harmon, in Gorham, Maine, Ellen was married to James White, August 30, 1846, in Portland, Maine, and together had four boys: Henry Nichols, James Edson, William Clarence, and John Herbert. She died at her Elmshaven home in St. Helena, California, July 16, 1915, and was buried in Oak Hill Cemetery, Battle Creek, Michigan.

See: general article: For Jesus and Scripture: The Life of Ellen G. White.

WHITE, EMMA L. (McDEARMON) (1848-1917). Daughter-in-law of Ellen White; she married *James Edson White on his twenty-first birthday, July 28, 1870. The couple likely came to know each other during the 1860s when the Whites built a rural *home in Greenville, Michigan, about 30 miles (48 kilometers) from Wright, where the McDearmon family lived. The Whites made frequent trips to the church in Wright, and by 1867 it appears that Emma and Edson had taken an interest in each other (Lt 21, 1867). The following year Edson's mother appears to have dropped a hint to him when she wrote that she thought Emma was "the best girl in Wright" (Lt 2, 1868).

EMMA WHITE

COURTESY OF THE CENTER FOR ADVENTIST RESEARCH, ANDREWS UNIVERSITY.

During their engagement Ellen White cautioned them not to enter too hastily into marriage and that marriage required careful preparation (Lt 7, 1869). Emma's parents expressed reservations about Edson's ability to be financially responsible, and would not allow the marriage to proceed until Edson learned how to both "keep money" and to "economize as well as to gain by industry" (Lt 16, 1869). Edson worked on McDearmon's farm, and following a successful season her parents agreed to the marriage.

Edson was the first of Ellen White's two sons who survived to adulthood and marriage (Willie was five years younger). Having had only boys, Ellen White found in Emma the daughter she never was fortunate enough to have had (Lt 18, 1872). They appear to have developed a deep mutual respect for each other and frequently exchanged letters. Ellen White's large correspondence to her daughter-in-law contains everything from spiritual counsel to practical marital advice (cf. Lts 16a, 22, 1870). She frequently wrote how much she appreciated hearing from Emma (Lt 18, 1872). Upon occasion Emma became a traveling companion to Ellen White, who expressed gratefulness for the special care Emma gave her (Ms 3, 1878). In return, Ellen White often took care of Emma, who was often sick, sometimes giving her *hydrotherapy treatments (Ms 15, 1868; Ms 15, 1884; Ms 38, 1890).

During the 1880s Edson and Emma gradually drifted away from the church through a series of financial setbacks that brought them embarrassment and strained their relations with church leaders. Disappointed by this situation, Ellen White nonetheless continued to offer her counsels and stayed in touch with her son and daughter-in-law even after she left for Australia in 1891.

When she heard about the rekindling of their faith, Ellen White rejoiced with Edson and Emma and encouraged them in their decision to do missionary work for *African-Americans in the American South. Emma played a central role in her husband's work on their boat, the *Morning Star. She felt a special burden for women and taught them how to read. After Ellen White's return to the United States in 1900, she wrote how thankful she was to see her daughter-in-law for the first time in more than a decade (Ms 223, 1902). Two years later she stayed with them again on the Morning Star in a special guest room they had prepared for her (Ms 143, 1904).

By 1913 Emma's severe rheumatism forced her and Edson to retire from their missionary work in the South. They relocated to Marshall, Michigan, where four years later Emma died. She is buried by the side of her husband in *Oak Hill Cemetery in Battle Creek.

Further reading: obit. RH, Aug. 30, 1917.

Michael W. Campbell

WHITE, ETHEL MAY (LACEY) (later **ETHEL MAY [LACEY] CURROW**) (1873-1969). Second wife of *William Clarence White. Born in Cuttack, India, where her father was a colonial police officer, May, as she was known in her family, was sent to a boarding school in England at the age of 5. When she was 9, the Lacey family moved to Australia and settled near Hobart, Tasmania, where they later became Seventh-day Adventists. In 1894 May enrolled in the Melbourne Training School. While there she met Ellen White. When W. C. White, son of Ellen White, asked if May would like to work after school hours for his mother, the young woman agreed. Willie,

W. C. WHITE AND HIS SECOND WIFE, ETHEL MAY. THE TWO OLDER GIRLS ARE MABEL (LEFT) AND ELLA (RIGHT), DAUGHTERS OF W. C. AND HIS FIRST WIFE, MARY (KELSEY) WHITE. THE TWIN BABY BOYS ARE JAMES HENRY AND HERBERT CLARENCE.

himself a widower, eventually proposed marriage. Although at first not interested in marrying either a widower or minister, May was strongly encouraged to change her mind by none other than her future mother-in-law. After praying and thinking about it, May decided to accept Willie's proposal. Ellen White offered the prayer in the wedding ceremony that was conducted at May's father's place near Hobart on May 9, 1895 (4Bio 195).

A year later May and Willie had twin boys. In naming her grandsons, Ellen White included the names of her four boys, her husband's name, plus the name of May's brother. She named one twin *James Henry. James was for her husband and for her second son, James

Edson; Henry was for her oldest son. The other baby she named *Herbert Clarence. Herbert was for Ellen White's youngest child, as well as for May's brother, Professor *Herbert C. Lacey; and Clarence was for the baby's father, Ellen White's third son.

When in 1900 a daughter was born to Willie and May, Ellen White wanted her to have her grandmother's initials. May suggested the name Evelyn, and Ellen White suggested the baby's middle name, Grace. May eventually had two additional sons, *Arthur (1907) and *Francis (1913). Ellen White was especially pleased to have lived long enough to see "Frankie" born.

May lived in close proximity to her mother-in-law, both in Australia, and after the family returned to the United States in 1900. During the 20 years that May knew Ellen White, she recalled her as being a kind and gentle mother-in-law, a loving grandmother, as well as a warm and generous Christian. On occasion May traveled with her mother-in-law, though by nature May was not a public person. She attended the first two of the three funerals held for Ellen White.

W. C. White died in 1937. In 1955 May married a widower, Arthur L. Currow (1872-1964), who had been a friend from her youth in Melbourne. May's death came one day short of her ninety-sixth birthday. She is buried next to W. C. White in the White family plot in *Oak Hill Cemetery in Battle Creek, Michigan.

Further reading: obit. PUR, Oct. 23, 1969; "Life Sketch of May Lacey White Currow" (DF 791a); "Life With My Mother-in-law, Ellen G. White" (undated oral history interview conducted by Ed Christian, DF 791a); Interview with May White Currow conducted by James R. Nix (typed transcript, June 11, 1967, Oral History Collection, EGWE-LLU).

James R. Nix

WHITE, EVELYN GRACE (later **EVELYN GRACE** [**WHITE**] **JACQUES** (1900-1995). Fifth grand-child of James and Ellen White, the oldest daughter of William C. and Ethel May (Lacey) White. Born in Cooranbong, Australia, Grace was given the same initials as her grandmother,

EVELYN GRACE (WHITE) JACQUES

Ellen G. White. About three and one-half months after Grace's birth, her parents and family, along with Ellen White, returned to the United States from Australia. Growing up as the only girl among four boys (her older twin brothers, Herbert and Henry, plus her two younger brothers, Arthur and Francis), Grace was loved by them all. When Ellen White bought the house that she named Elmshaven, she gave seven acres (three hectares) of the property to her son W. C. White on which to build his own home. Nearby, a small playhouse was built that was Grace's private domain.

Grace grew up with many fond memories of her grandmother. She assisted in her grandmother's kitchen, as well as earned a little money helping to pick prunes from the orchard for drying in her grandmother's fruit business. Among Grace's favorite memories were the family worships at Elmshaven that opened and closed the Sabbath. Other high-lights included the picnic lunches on the way back home from nearby churches after her grandmother had been the morning speaker, preparing bouquets of flowers with which to decorate Elmshaven for Sabbath, and observing Christmases at their home, including the exchange of simple gifts, with which her grandmother participated. Grace was among the family members who were present when Ellen White died on July 16, 1915.

On June 26, 1919, Grace married John Godfrey Jacques, an immigrant from Russia who later became a medical doctor. Grace's wedding, held at Elmshaven, was a double ceremony with her older brother, Henry White. Their father, William C. White, offered a blessing afterward. Grace and John had four children: Oliver, Sylvan, Viola, and Lenora. For many years Grace taught elementary school in Loma Linda and Inglewood, Cali-fornia. She wrote her recollections of her grandmother in an article published in the December 5, 1961, issue of the *Youth's Instruc-tor*. After she and John retired, they moved in 1965 to Elmshaven, where they became resident caretakers. Grace's memories proved invaluable during the 1979 and 1981 extensive restoration of Elmshaven. Because of her detailed recollections, the home today looks much like it did when Ellen White lived there from 1900 to 1915. Through the years thou-sands of visitors to Elmshaven enjoyed listening to Grace recall her many fond memories of her grandmother. Grace's husband died in 1980. She continued welcoming visitors to Elmshaven until 1986, at which time she moved to the Adventist-owned retirement center in Yountville, California. Later she moved back to her family home where she had grown up, now a retirement home known as Rosehaven, where she died. Grace is buried in the St. Helena Cemetery in St. Helena, California.

Further reading: "Dinner at Elmshaven: An Interview With Mrs. Grace Jacques, Granddaughter of Ellen G. White" (EGWE, SDoc).

James R. Nix

WHITE, FRANCIS EDWARD FORGA (1913-1992). Youngest son of *William C. and *Ethel May (Lacey) White, he was born and raised in the vicinity of Deer Park, California, attend-ing Adventist schools there through twelfth grade. In 1936 he married Rachel Rub and worked for a while for an alcohol-rehabilitation program in Oakland, California. In 1938 they moved to Mountain View, California, where Francis worked for *Pacific Press as an electroplater in the foundry until his retirement in 1974.

Further reading: obit. St. Helena *Star*, July 2, 1992 (DF 306, CAR).

WHITE, HENRY NICHOLS (1847-1863). Firstborn son of James and Ellen White, named after a family friend, *Henry Otis Nichols; Henry was born at Ellen's parents' home in Gorham, Maine. The baby's arrival, four days before his parents' first anniversary, found the family homeless, relying on the hospitality of friends. *Stockbridge and Frances Howland invited the Whites to share their large farmhouse in Topsham, Maine. Nineteen-year-old Ellen hoped that with Henry's birth she could now stay at home and not do so much traveling. A vision, however, and an illness that brought Henry near death, convinced Ellen that this was not to be. As the Whites agonized in prayer for their baby's healing, Ellen committed herself to go wherever God led.

HENRY NICHOLS WHITE

Henry's recovery led Ellen to a heartwrenching decision. Unable to give her son stability and discipline while traveling, she entrusted him to the Howlands. In so doing, she likened herself to Hannah, who had given up her firstborn, Samuel, to the Lord's work. For five years Henry remained with the Howlands, where he was loved, disciplined, and well cared for. During that time Ellen was often plagued by feelings of deep anxiety and grief because of their separation.

When Henry was 6, the Whites settled into a rented house in *Rochester, New York. Near the banks of the Erie Canal, Henry and his brother *Edson became reacquainted, and another brother, *Willie, was born. When Henry was 8, the family moved to *Battle Creek, Michigan, where Henry frequented the new printing office, running errands and folding papers. In time, he began setting type for the *Review and Herald* after school. He also had a gift and love for music and a clear, full, tenor voice. During the summer of 1862, by selling vegetable seeds he and Edson earned $100, which they used to purchase a melodeon, a small reed organ operated by foot pedals.

In January 1863 a time of spiritual revival drew 13 youth, including Henry and Edson, into the icy waters of the Kalamazoo River to be baptized by James White. Despite this hopeful sign, James and Ellen were deeply concerned about their sons' fascination with the American *Civil War. Henry was even dreaming of entering the army as a drummer—an appalling prospect to his noncombatant parents (2Bio 60). Determined to take their boys away from these influences, the Whites decided to take them east for a few months. Invited to stay with the Howlands, the entire family returned to Topsham, Maine. While his parents traveled, Henry remained at the Howlands, employed at mounting prophetic charts on cloth backing for sale to Adventist evangelists. One day after swimming in the river, he flopped down by a window, fell asleep in a cool draft, and caught cold, which turned to pneumonia. His parents called a doctor, who employed the customary *drugs of the day, and Henry rapidly declined.

Sensing that he might die, Henry drew near to God. There was a time of confession, forgiveness, weeping, and embracing in the family circle. Henry encouraged his father by noting that if he died, at least he wouldn't be drafted into the army. Henry promised his mother he would meet her in heaven, and asked to be buried alongside his baby brother, *John Herbert, so they could come up together on the resurrection morning. December 8, 1863, after kissing his family goodbye, Henry pointed upward and whispered his last words, "Heaven is sweet." Fifty years later Ellen White's granddaughter *Grace, recalled her grandmother once remarked about her firstborn son, "If we had only known then what we know now, we could have saved Henry."

Further reading: An Appeal to the Youth: Funeral Address of Henry N. White, at Battle Creek, Mich., Dec. 21, 1863 (Battle Creek, Mich.: Steam Press, 1864); 2 Bio 59-63, 70-72.

Kathy Lewis

WHITE, HERBERT C. (1896-1962). Printer and publisher, oldest son of William C. and

COURTESY OF THE CENTER FOR ADVENTIST RESEARCH, ANDREWS UNIVERSITY.

HERBERT C. WHITE

Ethel May (Lacey) White, twin brother of *James Henry White. Born in Australia, Herbert grew up in St. Helena, next to Ellen White's Elmshaven home, and just down Howell Mountain from *Pacific Union College. With equipment provided

by their grandmother Ellen White, he and his twin operated a printshop that they called the Elmshaven Press (6Bio 357, 358, 396, 432). When they entered college, they moved their printshop to Angwin, where it eventually became the Pacific Union College Press. From 1923 to 1929 Herbert managed the Signs of the Times Publishing House in Shanghai, China. In later years he learned professional photography, did public lecturing, and operated H. C. White Publications in Riverside, California. Herbert was married

to Anna Louise (1892-1984) and had two daughters.

Further reading: obit. RH, Jan. 3, 1963.

WHITE, JAMES EDSON (1849-1928). Early leader of Adventist work among *African-Americans; second son of James and Ellen White. At the age of 15 White was employed at the *Review and Herald publishing office, of which his father was founder and president, and mastered the printer trade. On July 28,

COURTESY OF THE CENTER FOR ADVENTIST RESEARCH, ANDREWS UNIVERSITY.

JAMES EDSON WHITE

1870, he married Emma McDearmon (her sister Harriet later married *F. E. Belden, White's cousin). In April 1877 Edson was asked to care for the business interests of the newly established Pacific Seventh-day Adventist (later *Pacific

Press) Publishing Association in Oakland, California, where as secretary of the association, he was business manager of the printing plant. He held this position about three years, during which he led in the publication of the first Adventist Sabbath school songbook, *Song Anchor*, a work in which F. E. Belden and D. S. Hakes collaborated and to which they contributed largely. *Song Anchor* was the first hymnbook issued by Seventh-day Adventists in which all the songs were set to music.

While residing in Battle Creek, Michigan, in the fall of 1880, and being deeply interested in the rapidly developing Sabbath school work, White attended the third annual session of the General Sabbath School Association, held on the nearby campground. In the absence of the president, White was chosen chair pro tem, and then elected vice president for the ensuing year. For six years he was closely linked with the interests of the Sabbath school work, serving on the executive committee, the publishing committee, and as chair of the Sabbath school lesson committee. He led in launching the *Sabbath School Worker* in 1885. In 1886 he helped to bring out a second Sabbath school songbook, *Joyful Greetings for the Sabbath-School.*

During the 1880s White operated the J. E. White Publishing Company in Battle Creek and published, for subscription sale by agents, books on etiquette, cookery, and business forms. For a number of years he had been especially interested in music publishing, and acquired considerable skill in setting music in type. Both he and F. E. Belden were musicians and showed talent as composers. It was natural, then, that when the General Conference developed a hymnbook with music appearing on each page, *Hymns and Tunes* (1886), edited by F. E. Belden and Edwin Barnes, they should turn to the J. E. White Publishing Company to set the type for both music and words.

In 1893, at a time of personal religious awakening, Edson read a copy of Ellen White's *Our Duty to the Colored People* (1891), an appeal for Adventists to engage in active missionary work for Blacks in the southern United States. He immediately determined to engage personally in educational and evangelistic work among the Black people in the South. Having had some experience in steamboat navigation on the Mississippi River, he built a missionary steamboat, the *Morning Star*, at Allegan, Michigan, in 1894 at a cost of $3,700. The vessel provided a residence for the owner, staterooms for other workers, chapel, library, printshop, photographic darkroom, kitchen, and storerooms.

White recruited a small company of like-minded men and women who supported themselves and the enterprise by selling small books written and published by J. E. White, principally the *Gospel Primer*, a simple Bible-based textbook for classes in basic literacy. The work began along the Yazoo River in Mississippi. Meetings held in the ship's cabin were followed by schoolwork offered to both children and adults in the same quarters, with Emma White teaching the older women to read. As the work developed, inexpensive church and school structures were erected in towns near which the *Morning Star* had moored for a time. Within a few years 50 such schools were operating. Many Black Adventist ministers and teachers traced their first contacts with Seventh-day Adventists to the *Morning Star* and the schools that its crew founded. In 1895 the self-supporting workers engaged in this enterprise organized themselves into the *Southern Missionary Society, with headquarters at Yazoo City, Mississippi.

Through frequent letters Ellen White, then in Australia, encouraged her son and his wife in their unique type of service. Early in 1897, while engaged in this work, J. E. White was ordained to the ministry. In 1898 he published on the *Morning Star* a 115-page booklet titled *The Southern Work. It consisted of (1) his mother's initial appeal that encouraged him to enter this work, (2) nine of her articles published in the *Review and Herald* in 1895 and 1896, presenting to the church its duty to work in the South, and (3) some portions of her communications regarding the conduct of missionary work among African-Americans. The *Gospel Herald*, a monthly journal, was launched at Yazoo City, Mississippi, in 1898 to inform Adventists of the developing work among Black people.

Ever sensing the need of funds for missionary work, White pushed forward with the writing and publishing of books, 12 in all. Among them were *The Coming King* (1898), *Best Stories From the Best Book* (1900), and *Past, Present, and Future* (1909), all of which have sold in the hundreds of thousands, with the latter for many years the leading subscription book produced by Adventists on the Second Advent.

In 1900 White and the Southern Missionary Society started a small printing office at 1025 Jefferson Street, in Nashville, Tennessee, which eventually became the *Southern Publishing Association. When the Southern Union Conference was organized in 1901, it gradually assumed responsibility for the various interests of the Southern Missionary Society. As White was thus step-by-step freed from the burdens of administering a far-flung work, he continued to make his headquarters near Nashville and devoted his time primarily to writing and publishing books, some of which were translated into several languages.

In 1912, because of Emma White's failing health, the Whites moved back north and settled in Marshall, Michigan. After her death in 1917, Edson took up residence in Battle Creek, where for five years he engaged in the making of stereopticon slides used by Adventist ministers. In 1922 he married Rebecca Burrill, and they moved to Otsego, Michigan, where he continued his business in stereopticon slides as long as his health permitted.

Edson White's funeral was held in the *Battle Creek Tabernacle, and he was buried in the White family lot in *Oak Hill Cemetery, Battle Creek, Michigan. He had no children.

Further reading: obit. RH, July 5, 1928; R. D. Graybill, *Mission to Black America* (PPPA, 1971); A. Robinson, "James Edson White: Innovator," in G. R. Knight, ed., *Early Adventist Educators* (AUP, 1983), pp. 137-158; *SDA Encyclopedia* (1996), vol. 11, pp. 889, 890.

Michael W. Campbell

WHITE, JAMES HENRY (1896-1954). Printer, missionary, professional photographer,

grandson of Ellen White. Born in Cooranbong, New South Wales, Australia, to William C. White and Ethel May (Lacey) White, he was associated with his grandmother the first 19 years of his life. After their return to the United States, Ellen White purchased a printing press and a set of type for Henry and his twin brother *Herbert, by which they learned the printing trade and earned their way through academy and college. After their graduation in 1921, their Elmshaven Press became the College Press at *Pacific Union College (6Bio 357, 358, 396, 432). On November 15, 1921, Henry was married to Margaret Rossiter, daughter of *Frederick Rossiter, and they spent eight years in mission service in northern China (1921-1929). After Henry White's death (1954), Margaret married biblical scholar Edwin R. Thiele. She wrote several books, including a biography of her grandmother, S.M.I. Henry (*The Whirlwind of the Lord* [RHPA, 1953, 1998]), and condensed A. L. White's six-volume biography, *Ellen G. White*, into a single volume for translation (*Ellen White: Woman of Vision* [RHPA, 2000]).

Further reading: obit. RH, May 20, 1954; obit. PUR, June 28, 1954.

WHITE, JAMES SPRINGER (1821-1881). Husband of Ellen White and cofounder and

JAMES SPRINGER WHITE

leader of the Seventh-day Adventist Church. White spearheaded the development of the church's organizational structure and participated in the formation of most of its major institutions. He was born August 4, 1821, in the township of Palmyra, Somerset County, Maine. A sickly child, he suffered severe fits or seizures at age 2 or 3. Eye problems and perhaps dyslexia kept him from learning to read until he was in his teens. Forced to drop out of school, White worked on the family farm. At age 19 he enrolled as a beginning student in a local academy. His formal education would consist of 12 weeks of elementary school and 29 weeks of high school (*Life Incidents*, p. 14). After earning a teaching certificate, he taught elementary school for a couple of terms.

In the early 1840s James' father, *John White, began to read William Miller's lectures on the second coming of Christ. At first James regarded Miller's ideas as fanatical. But when his mother decided to support Millerism, James had to take it more seriously. Coming under a growing conviction that Miller might be right, he felt impressed that he should present the teaching of Christ's return about 1843 or 1844 to his former students. Eventually he became a Millerite preacher. Contemporary reports suggest that during the winter months of 1842-1843 more than 1,000 people responded to his preaching.

White's family were members of the *Christian Connexion (or Christian Church), where his father served as a deacon for nearly 40 years. The Christian Connexion was the first indigenous American religious movement and an example of the Restorationist tradition that sought to return Christianity to a New Testament pattern of belief and organization. James was baptized into the Connexion at age 16 and ordained to the ministry in 1843. Many members of the Christian Connexion accepted Millerism. From the Christian Connexion James White, Joseph Bates, and other future members of the Seventh-day Adventist Church would receive an emphasis on the Bible as the only rule of faith and the concept that truth is always growing. But James White would lead the Seventh-day Adventist Church away from other Christian Connexion themes, such as a resistance to organization.

The failure of the Millerite expectation that Christ would return on October 22, 1844, devastated James White. Later he reported that he wept like a child (*Life Incidents*, p. 182). But although he struggled with doubt, he did not give up his belief in Christ's return. For a time he speculated on additional dates for the Second Advent (JW to Brother Jacobs, Sept. 20, 1845).

During the summer of 1843 White, with John Pearson, Jr. (see *John Pearson, Sr.), worked in evangelism in Portland, Maine. While there he first noticed a young woman named Ellen Harmon. Later describing her as "a Christian of the most devoted type," he said that although she was only 16, "she was a laborer in the cause of Christ" (LS80 126). Sometime during the winter of 1844-1845 he heard that she had had a vision confirming that God had been leading in the Millerite movement.

Introduced again to Ellen by *William Jordan, White began to accompany her and another female companion as Ellen journeyed about relating her visions and dealing with the fanaticism that sprang up among some of the former Millerites. His travels with her began to raise criticism that he feared might destroy the credibility of her prophetic message. Eventually James decided that it was God's will that they should marry, even though he himself had recently thought, and many former Millerites still believed, that marriage was a denial of faith in an imminent return of Christ.

On Sunday, August 30, 1846, Charles Harding, a Portland, Maine, justice of the peace, married them in a civil ceremony. James was 25 and Ellen was 18. As he observed years later, they entered married life "penniless, with few friends, and broken in health" (*ibid.* 126). For many years they had no home of their own and lived with family or friends, surviving on the financial help of others and what James could earn through hard manual labor. But they kept on traveling, encouraging fellow Adventist believers, building friendships, presenting the messages Ellen received in her visions, and dealing with the fanaticism that had crept into the isolated little groups of believers.

Early in 1846 Joseph Bates introduced the Whites to the doctrine of the seventh-day Sabbath. At first James and Ellen questioned the necessity of observing it, but after reading Bates' 48-page tract on the topic, they began to keep the Sabbath by that autumn. That same year James printed the first account of Ellen's visions (*To the Remnant Scattered Abroad*) as a broadside (a large single-page publication), which was expanded into a 64-page pamphlet (*A Sketch of the Christian Experience and Views of Ellen G. White*) in 1851. James served as her chief literary assistant until his death and was a tireless supporter of her spiritual gift. In later years he proclaimed that one of the clearest evidences of the validity of her prophetic calling was all that she had accomplished despite her limited education. In fact, he suggested, God had chosen her because of that fact. No one could then claim that her writings were of her own doing.

From 1848 to 1850 James used a series of weekend conferences (see *Sabbatarian Bible Conferences) to forge a stronger doctrinal consensus among the scattered Sabbatarian Adventists. At one of them in Dorchester, Massachusetts, Ellen received a vision urging James to begin regular publishing as a way to communicate with the isolated believers. Finances prevented him from doing anything until July 1849, when he printed the first issue of *Present Truth. His publishing was sporadic until a general meeting of believers voted in 1852 to purchase a printing press and establish it in *Rochester, New York. The fledgling

publishing house would remain there until October 1855. Publishing would be the major emphasis of James' life. Through it he shaped the emerging Seventh-day Adventist Church. He wrote several books and countless articles and editorials.

The *Review and Herald,* which was first published in 1850, following the earlier short-lived *Present Truth*, became the forum for Sabbatarian Adventists to work out their beliefs further in the areas of doctrine, spirituality, and worship. The periodical also helped develop a sense of community among its isolated and lonely readers, as we see in its letters to the editor. For many years the publishing office was also the headquarters of the Sabbatarian Adventist movement.

Poverty, illness, and discouragement almost destroyed the little publishing office in Rochester, but it survived because of the sacrifice and dedication of those who worked there and because of James White's business skills. Besides his preaching tours and extensive writing, he sold Bibles, concordances, tracts, and other religious publications. Later he would be active in paper jobbing and real estate, plowing the money he made back into the publishing work and other church projects. During his lifetime he invested tens of thousands of dollars in the denominational cause at a time when the average laborer earned only $300-$500 a year. While his financial skill greatly blessed the church, it also aroused some resentment. At least three times denominational leadership had to convene official investigations to deal with the criticism.

In 1855 believers in Michigan and Vermont each requested that White move the publishing office to their state. White accepted the Michigan offer, and the transfer to Battle Creek, Michigan, put the institution on a stronger financial basis. But it brought a major problem into focus. Because the Sabbatarian

Adventists had no formal organizational structure, the publishing work was owned in James White's name. If anything happened to him, the believers could lose the institution. White then began to advocate formal church organization. His efforts led to the formation of the Seventh-day Adventist Publishing Association (see *Review and Herald Publishing Association) on October 1, 1860 (incorporated May 3, 1861), the Michigan Conference of Seventh-day Adventists in October 1861, and the General Conference of Seventh-day Adventists in May 1863. The delegates to the organizing session elected James White president of the new denomination, but he declined the position lest it appear that he had urged organization just to gain power for himself. He later served several terms as president, for a total of 10 years.

Throughout his life James White would overwork until he collapsed from exhaustion and illness. On August 16, 1865, he suffered the first of a series of strokes, the effects of which he would struggle with for the rest of his life. They intensified personality traits that had often made him difficult to work with. At times the stroke damage not only troubled his relationships with fellow church leaders but also strained family ties. Yet despite his health and personality problems he continued to advance the denomination he so loved. He and Ellen had to work through some problems together, but his love for her never failed, nor did his confidence in her prophetic gift.

During the 1870s he established the Pacific Press publishing house in California and was active in the development of a denominational college. The man who had only a few months of formal education served as titular president of Battle Creek College. His vision was often far ahead of the rest of the denomination as he challenged it to develop new programs in publishing and evangelism. He saw the mission of the church as extending to the whole world.

Not only did White establish many of the church's institutions—he also was called on to save them when they fell into financial difficulties. He helped to restore the denomination's publishing association, its health journal, and the Health Reform Institute to stronger economic health.

One of White's lesser-known but highly significant contributions to the Seventh-day Adventist Church was his emphasis on the centrality of Christ in the plan of salvation. It would help set the stage for the emphasis on *righteousness by faith during the 1880s and 1890s. In 1850 he declared that the Millerite message had "weaned us from this world, and led us to the feet of Jesus, to seek forgiveness of all our sins, and a free and full salvation through the blood of Christ" (in *Present Truth,* April 1850). "The hope of eternal salvation hangs upon Christ," he wrote in his 1868 *Life Incidents.* "Adam hung his hope there. Abel, Enoch, Noah, Abraham, and the believing Jews hung theirs there. We can do no more. The hope of the next life depends upon Christ. Faith in His blood alone can free us from our transgressions" (*Life Incidents,* p. 359; cf. pp. 344, 345, 254). This became a litany throughout his writings, especially his articles in *Signs of the Times* and the tracts he published through Pacific Press. One tract proclaimed that "the Scriptures reveal but one plan by which fallen men may be saved," and that was that "Jesus Christ is the Redeemer of sinners in all ages of probation" (*Christ in the Old Testament,* p. 3). "When sin had separated man from God, the plan of salvation made Christ the connecting link between God and the offending sinner" (*ibid.,* p. 11).

Shortly before his death, James wrote in his letters about his dreams of publishing a colporteur book on "the subject of

Redemption through Christ" that could be translated into various languages (JW to WCW, Sept. 16, 1880; JW to WCW, Sept. 18, 1880). The book would center on a revised version of his allegorical engraving on the plan of salvation, *The Way of Life* (JW to EGW, Feb. 11, 1881). He would call it *Behold the Lamb of God* and would have a larger Christ on the cross at the center of the engraving. Unfortunately, although he had done much work with the engraver, James died before he could bring the new engraving out or write the book. Ellen White would bring out the engraving two years after his death. James' death cut short his and Ellen's plan to prepare together a series of studies on "the glorious subject of Redemption [that] should long ago have been more fully presented to the people" (*In Memorium*, p. 54).

Although Ellen kept urging her husband to lighten his load before he totally destroyed his health, he found it difficult to turn over church leadership to others. "Where are the men to do this work?" he would ask her (LS88 248). In late July 1881 the Whites accepted a speaking appointment in Charlotte, Michigan. On the way back James told Ellen that he did not feel well. Although J. H. Kellogg treated him, James apparently experienced an additional stroke and died from complications of malaria on Sabbath, August 6, 1881. Business friends and townspeople joined the 2,500 people who attended the funeral in the Dime Tabernacle on August 13. He was buried in the White family plot in Oak Hill Cemetery. Ellen would miss him the rest of her life, later referring to him as "the best man that ever trod shoe leather" (Ms 131, 1906, in 1Bio 84).

Further reading: 1Bio; 2Bio; 3Bio; *In Memorium. A Sketch of the Last Sickness and Death of Elder James White, Who Died at Battle Creek, Michigan, Aug. 6, 1881, Together With the Discourse Preached at His Funeral*

(Battle Creek, Mich.: SDA Pub., 1881); V. Robinson, *James White* (RHPA, 1976); G. Wheeler, *James White: Innovator and Overcomer* (RHPA, 2003); James White, *Christ in the Old Testament* (PPPA, 1877). Much of James White's correspondence is available on microfilms (CAR; EGWE-GC).

Gerald Wheeler

WHITE, "DEACON" JOHN (1785-1871) and **ELIZABETH "BETSEY" (JEWETT)** (1788-1871).

COURTESY OF THE CENTER FOR ADVENTIST RESEARCH, ANDREWS UNIVERSITY

"DEACON" JOHN WHITE

COURTESY OF THE CENTER FOR ADVENTIST RESEARCH, ANDREWS UNIVERSITY

ELIZABETH "BETSEY" WHITE

Parents of *James White. John was born in Skowhegan, Maine, the son of Salmon and Nancy (Springer) White. In his early 20s he moved to Palmyra, Maine, where he married Betsey Jewett, a native of Exeter, New Hampshire, who had moved to Palmyra with her parents, David and Mary "Polly" (Shepard) Jewett. John and Betsey, both deeply religious, set before their nine children high standards of Christian and moral behavior that profoundly affected them all of their lives. John was baptized by sprinkling in 1806 and joined the Congregational Church. However, not satisfied that sprinkling was a proper form of baptism, he joined the Baptist Church about 1810 and was baptized by immersion. He served as a deacon in the Baptist Church for about 10 years until he joined the *Christian Connexion, where he was also a deacon for nearly 40 years. At Palmyra, in 1828, John organized a Sunday school that he thought to have been the first in the state of Maine and took his children with him to church.

This made such an impression on his son James that 25 years later when he recalled the impact Sunday school had made on his life, he organized the first Adventist Sabbath school in Rochester, New York.

In the early 1840s both John and Betsey became convinced that the lectures of *William Miller were sound and scriptural, and they accepted the leading points of the Advent doctrine. Betsey earnestly discussed the Millerite beliefs with her son James, who reluctantly agreed that they were founded on Scripture. In 1842 James attended an Advent camp meeting, where he committed his life to telling the world that Jesus is coming. In the late 1850s John and Betsey left the hard life of farming Maine's rocky soil and moved to Battle Creek, Michigan. At first they lived in the home of their son James and his wife, Ellen, but in 1859 they moved across the street to a little home of their own. While living in the west Battle Creek community known locally as "Advent Town," they embraced the seventh-day Sabbath and observed it for the remainder of their lives. Betsey White died on January 9, 1871, and John White, having requested that his gravestone carry the inscription "Deacon John White," died just six months later on July 5. They are buried in the White family plot in *Oak Hill Cemetery. In the *Review and Herald*, July 18, 1871, James White described his mother as "one of the sweetest and best women that lived," and his father as "a man of sterling integrity and godly life." Their home, restored to the period in which they lived in it, can be visited in Historic Adventist Village in Battle Creek, Michigan.

Further reading: G. Wheeler, *James White: Innovator and Overcomer* (RHPA, 2003), pp. 18-23; J. R. Nix, "John and Betsey (Jewett) White" (unpublished manuscript [2006]).

Alice R. Voorheis

WHITE, JOHN HERBERT (Sept. 20-Dec. 14, 1860). Fourth son of James and Ellen White. Perhaps they were expecting a girl (1Bio 419), for they had no boy's name prepared when he was born, and at 6 weeks old he was still the "nameless one" (Lt 18, 1860, in 8MR 15). His mother exulted that he was "fat and rugged, and very quiet," a "hearty fellow" who "takes so much nurse, I am very hungry most of the time" (1Bio 426). But on November 19 the child's head and face became swollen and inflamed with erysipelas, an acute infectious disease especially dangerous to infants. Erysipelas is caused by a type of streptococcus bacteria and characterized by fever and widespread deep-red inflammation of the skin. "Twenty-four days and nights we anxiously watched over him," wrote his mother, "using all the remedies we could for his recovery, and earnestly presenting his case to the Lord. At times I could not control my feelings as I witnessed his sufferings. Much of my time was spent in tears, and humble supplication to God. But our heavenly Father saw fit to remove my lovely babe" (2SG 296). James White preached the funeral from Jeremiah 31:15-17. By then little "nameless" had become John Herbert.

Further reading: 1Bio 419, 426-431; 2SG 294-296; 1T 244-246; 10MR 22; obit. RH, Dec. 18, 1860.

WHITE, JULIA ANN (1870-1957). Adventist physician from Wisconsin unrelated to Ellen White. Julia White received her medical degree from the *American Medical Missionary College (AMMC) in 1900. For the next six years she practiced at the *Battle Creek Sanitarium while jointly serving on the faculty of AMMC. At the request of Ellen White she served as the first woman physician at *Loma Linda Sanitarium, where she practiced obstetrics and gynecology (Lt 291, 1905). Julia White founded the School of Nursing at Loma Linda in 1906, and five years later founded the *Glendale Sanitarium School of Nursing. She served as secretary for the "woman's movement" that raised funds to build the White Memorial Hospital (see *White Memorial Medical Center), and devoted her life to building up the Adventist medical work in southern California.

Further reading: obit. RH, Aug. 29, 1957.

WHITE, MABEL EUNICE (later **MABEL EUNICE [WHITE] WORKMAN**) (1886-1981). Second grandchild of James and Ellen White, the daughter of William C. and Mary (Kelsey) White. Mabel was born in Basel, Switzerland, where her parents and grandmother worked from 1885 to 1887. As Mabel's mother was dying of tuberculosis

ELLA AND MABEL WHITE

in 1890, Ellen White promised her dying daughter-in-law that she would take special care of Mabel and her older sister, Ella (Lt 9, 1904; Lt 82, 1911). When Mabel's father and grandmother went to Australia in 1891, the sisters remained in Battle Creek, Michigan, under the care of *Mary Mortenson. After their father's remarriage in 1895, both girls traveled to Australia. Mabel recalled their grandmother taking her and her sister out into the neighborhood and telling them stories. Other children would soon gather around, followed by their parents. Often Ellen White would bring clothes to the children who came to listen to the stories. In this way, Ellen White reached out to her neighbors who lived near the new Avondale College.

Mabel returned to the United States in 1900 with her family. Because of health problems she was unable to attend Healdsburg College for very long. Although Mabel loved the outdoors, for many years she suffered from poor health, particularly poor eyesight. In 1906 she married Wilfred D. Workman (1880-1947). Their first child, a boy, lived three days; later they had Wilfred, Jr., and adopted Clifford.

As Ellen White lay dying in her Elmshaven home on July 16, 1915, Mabel sat by the bedside of her unconscious grandmother, gently rubbing her hand just in case her grandmother would momentarily regain consciousness. Mabel served as matron (director of food service) at several institutions: Paradise Valley Sanitarium and Healdsburg College in California; Washington Missionary Seminary in Maryland; and Loma Linda Sanitarium, also in California. From 1919 until Wilfred's death in 1947, Wilfred and Mabel farmed in southern California. Afterward, Mabel lived in Loma Linda, where she did so much for others she was called a "second Dorcas." She later lived for a time at Elmshaven. Mabel died in National City, California, and is buried next to her husband in Montecito Memorial Park in Loma Linda, California.

Further reading: obit. AR, Aug. 13, 1981; obit. RH, Oct. 30, 1947; Interview with Mabel Workman conducted by James R. Nix (typed transcript, Aug. 6, 1967, Oral History Collection, EGWE-LLU).

James R. Nix

WHITE, MARY (KELSEY) (1857-1890). Editor, treasurer, missionary, first wife of William C.

MARY (KELSEY) WHITE

White. The Kelsey and White families became acquainted after the Whites moved to Battle Creek in 1855. The Kelseys evidently lived some distance out in the country from Battle Creek. Mary's father died before her second birthday in 1859.

In the fall of 1874 Mary lived with the Whites while attending the opening term of Battle Creek College. She was majoring in French and working as a typesetter at the publishing house. In 1875 she went with the Whites to Oakland, California, where she and Willie White both worked at the Pacific Press. On February 9, 1876, Willie and Mary were married, and in April, just before Mary's nineteenth birthday, she was elected treasurer of the Pacific Press and managing editor of the *Signs of the Times.*

In 1877 Willie and Mary returned to Battle Creek College to study French and German in preparation to assist *J. N. Andrews and the Adventist publishing work in Europe. For the next nine years they filled various positions at the Review and Herald, the General Conference, the Pacific Press again, and Healdsburg College, and added a daughter, *Ella (b. 1882), to their family before sailing for Europe with Ellen White in 1885.

In Europe Mary served as literary assistant to Ellen White. A second daughter, Mabel, was born in Basel, Switzerland, in 1886. About the same time it became evident that during the two winters spent in the inadequately heated new publishing house in Basel (which was both home and workplace) Mary had contracted tuberculosis. Despite therapy at the *Battle Creek Sanitarium, Mary continued to decline. Ellen White bought a small house in Burrough Valley, California, hoping the desert climate would aid her recovery, but despite all efforts to save her life, Mary died at age 33.

Further reading: Mary Kelsey White: Remarks by Eld. U. Smith, at the Funeral, June 25, 1890 (RHPA, 1890); J. Moon, *W. C. White and Ellen G. White* (AUP, 1993), pp. 22-27, 32, 33, 67, 69-82, 85, 89.

Jerry Moon

WHITE, NATHANIEL (1831-1853). Youngest brother of James White and supporter of James and Ellen White's work in *Rochester, New York. In 1852 the Whites invited James' brother Nathaniel and sister Anna to live with them. Both were sick when they accepted the invitation to join the Review and Herald publishing office (housed at 124 Mount Hope Avenue) in Rochester. Ellen White said, "I loved him when he first came because he was brother to my husband, . . . but soon he seemed as near to me as a natural brother" because of his soft spirit and for being a caring and godly man (LS80 297, 298). Nathaniel made no great contribution to the early Sabbatarian years, except for the story of his faith as he faced death on a windy May morning in 1853. His death came as a shock to every one of the young people at the Review office, except Ellen White. Many times when the group of believers gathered to pray for each other, healings came as a result. With Nathaniel, it was different. It seemed the prayers for Nathaniel were the first ones that God chose not to answer, or did He? Nathaniel admitted to Ellen White that he might never have been saved had not God allowed him to be brought so low. "I regret," confessed the dying Nathaniel, "that I have been unreconciled to my sickness. I have felt that I could not have it so, and that the Lord dealt hard with me. But I am now satisfied it is just; for nothing but this sickness could bring me where I am. God has blessed me much of late, and has forgiven me all my sins" (in 2SG 176; LS80 297).

Further reading: R. H. Allen and H. Krug, *Rochester's Adventist Heritage: Tour Guide and Biographical Overview* (Rochester, N.Y.: Advent History Project, 2002), pp. 7, 38, 39; V. Robinson, *James White* (RHPA, 1976); James White, *A Brief Account of the Last Sickness and Death of Nathaniel White, Who Died*

May 6th, 1853 (Rochester, N.Y.: Advent Review Office, 1853).

Howard Krug

WHITE, WILLIAM CLARENCE (1854-1937). Organizer, administrator, editor, counselor, third son of James and

WILLIAM CLARENCE WHITE

Ellen White, and second secretary (now called director) of the *Ellen G. White Estate; known officially as W. C. White, but widely referred to as "Willie" because that was what his mother called him, even to the end of her life; he also was referred to sometimes as Will White.

W. C. White was born in *Rochester, New York, just a year before the center of Sabbatarian Adventist leadership and publishing moved from Rochester to *Battle Creek, Michigan. He grew up in Battle Creek and followed his father's footsteps in the publishing work. At age 20 he followed his parents to California, was appointed acting business manager of the *Pacific Press in Oakland, California, and was promoted to business manager a year later. At 21 he married Mary Kelsey. A year later, in 1877, the two of them returned to Battle Creek to study French and German in preparation for service in Europe. Willie was soon pressed into a range of administrative responsibilities: membership on the *Battle Creek College board, one of the directors of the *Health Reform Institute, a member of the executive committee of the Sabbath School Association, and vice president of the Seventh-day Adventist Publishing Association (see *Review and Herald Publishing Association) under his father as its president. At 24 he became acting foreign missions secretary of the General Conference, and at 25, vice

president of Pacific Press. Shortly after James White's death in 1881, the California Conference voted to establish a school, and elected W. C. White as president of the board of *Healdsburg College. In 1883 he was elected to the five-member General Conference Executive Committee and ordained to the ministry. Except for a brief resignation for health reasons, he remained on that committee for the rest of his life, a 50-year tenure (1883-1897, 1901-1937).

When the 1888 General Conference session elected *O. A. Olsen as president, Olsen was in *Europe. Olsen would need almost six months to close up his work in Scandinavia and voyage to Battle Creek, so the executive committee appointed W. C. White, then 34, as acting president of the General Conference. Thus he continued the work of his father.

But W. C. White also worked closely with his mother. By the time he was 20 years old she had begun mentoring him to help prepare her manuscripts for publication (Moon, pp. 21, 63-65). When James White died in 1881, the 27-year-old Willie became his mother's closest confidant, escort in travel, spokesman, and business manager.

Willie and *Mary (Kelsey) White accompanied Ellen White to *Europe in 1885, where Willie's experience at *Pacific Press and *Review and Herald enabled him to be an effective consultant to Adventist publishing houses in Europe. He also led out in conference meetings, kept up an extensive correspondence as a General Conference officer, did editorial work (compiling and editing *Historical Sketches of the Foreign Missions of the Seventh-day Adventists* [Basel: 1886]), and looked after the needs of his mother.

Living through two Swiss winters in the newly constructed but not well heated publishing house in Basel, Mary White contracted tuberculosis. The Whites' return to Battle

Creek in 1887 came too late to turn the course of Mary's disease, and she died in 1890 at age 33, leaving two daughters, *Ella, 8, and *Mabel, 4. When Willie and Ellen White sailed for Australia in 1891, Ella and Mabel remained in Battle Creek in the care of *Mary Mortenson until their father could again provide a home for them.

Willie went to Australia as "district superintendent" (representing the General Conference Committee) for Australasia, which in Adventist usage of the time designated the two British colonies of Australia and New Zealand, with mission responsibility for the islands of the South Pacific (Moon, pp. 154, 155). Three years later, at age 40, White helped organize the Australasian Union Conference and became its first president. He presided over the formation of local conferences in Australia and helped to establish Avondale College, chairing its board, 1894-1900. He also served on the boards of the Avondale Health Retreat, the Sydney Sanitarium, the Summer Hill Sanitarium, and the Bible Echo Publishing House, and on the committee that initiated Adventist health food manufacturing in Australia (*ibid.*, pp. 179, 218).

The turning point of W. C. White's career arose from a longstanding vocational dilemma between helping with his mother's work, which he saw as most important, and his conference responsibilities, which he particularly loved. Trying to do both brought him by 1896 to physical and mental exhaustion. Consequently he resigned from the union presidency and GC Committee, in favor of rest and giving more time to his mother's work. He was promptly returned to office as vice president, but the change was enough to improve his health (*ibid.*, pp. 172-174). With his career accent now on his relationship to his mother, White became a conduit for her counsel to the new president, *A. G. Daniells.

That communicative relationship between Daniells and Ellen White, through Willie, expanded in 1901 when Daniells became General Conference president.

Amid all these responsibilities, W. C. White had not forgotten his daughters back in Battle Creek, nor his own loneliness since the death of Mary. In 1894 in Tasmania he met a young woman, May Lacey, who reminded him of Mary. That fall she enrolled in the Australasian Bible School in Melbourne, Victoria. When in December Ellen White had an opening for a household employee, Willie urged his mother to hire May so that Ellen could become better acquainted with her (Lt 117, 1895). With her approval, Willie and May were married May 9, 1895, at her father's home in Tasmania. His daughters, Ella and Mabel, arrived from America the same month. They lived in Granville, near Sydney, until settling in Cooranbong later in the year. In April 1896 were born twin sons, Herbert and Henry, and a fifth child, Evelyn Grace, in 1900 (Moon, pp. 167, 168).

After the return from Australia in 1900, W. C. White settled his family at St. Helena, California, near his mother's home, Elmshaven. Here his children grew up under May's supervision, while their father traveled widely in the service of the General Conference. Here also, two more sons were born, *Arthur in 1907 and *Francis in 1913.

During the *Kellogg crisis of 1902 to 1907, W. C. White was the liaison between his aging mother and General Conference president A. G. Daniells, as well as between her and the head of the medical work, Dr. *J. H. Kellogg. The recognition that Ellen White was approaching 80, while Willie was about 50 and obviously in a position of great influence with his mother, gave rise to speculations that the counsels she was writing to Daniells and especially to Kellogg reflected not her views but Willie's. This was a central theme of the famous *Kellogg interview of 1907.

A thorough reconstruction, however, of her relationship with Willie during the 61 years of their association from his birth to her death shows that their relationship was a reciprocal partnership in which her influence was prior and predominant. They had an open relationship, in which she encouraged Willie to think for himself, speak his mind, and follow his own convictions of "duty"; nevertheless, the deciding current of influence was consistently from her to him, not vice versa. Almost everything she received from him in later years was an extension and development of the ideals and values she had carefully built into him. The predominant motive for behavior and decision-making that she began to inculcate in him as early as age 5 was that of his personal accountability to God. She early taught him to pray, and by the time he was 13 she urged on him his personal responsibility for his discipleship to Christ. Only when she saw that habits of piety were becoming well established did she begin training him specifically for leadership (*ibid.*, pp. 439, 440).

From his infancy her rapport with him was closer than with either of her older sons. The other two sons were independent, but Willie was compliant and loved to please his mother. As he matured he emulated her frugality and work ethic so completely that they easily became kindred spirits. Thus by the time of his marriage at age 21 he had fully accepted her worldview, religious beliefs, and social and ethical values. When he accompanied her to Europe and to Australia, their relative isolation from other associates deepened their reliance on each other. She, however, relied on him for supporting roles, while he sought and followed her guidance on the full range of issues he faced as a church administrator. It appears that W. C. White's lifelong willingness to be molded by her counsels was a major reason she leaned so heavily on his counsel in her later years. Their mental and spiritual compatibility resulted from her intentional training and his receptive spirit since his earliest days. Thus most of the counsel that Ellen White drew out from her son's mind in later years was the direct or indirect product of what she herself had so carefully instilled during his earlier years (*ibid.*, pp. 440, 441).

Her influence on him had an important limit, however: the principle of his personal accountability to God. That principle is seen in her consistent refusal to coerce or override his conscience. During the Australian years her acute sense of advancing age burdened her with urgency to hasten the publication of her writings, and she repeatedly begged and pleaded for more of Willie's time. Yet with her strongest appeals are found the counterbalancing acknowledgments that he must ultimately do what he himself believed to be God's will. When her acute sense of need for his help conflicted with his load of conference responsibilities, she finally gave him an ultimatum: either help her, or she would get others to do so. Yet she left him free to make that choice. She refused to set herself in any degree as conscience for him. Thus the defining elements in their relationship were her leadership and the recognition that his followership must ultimately be directed not to her, but to God. The balance between these two elements was an indispensable prerequisite for his role as her advisor. It was essential that he freely express his personal convictions, and she expected him to do that (*ibid.*, p. 441).

In his role as her advisor he eventually developed the confidence to respectfully disagree with her and to attempt to persuade her to a change of viewpoint. He was neither rebelling or testing the limits of her authority. He was simply bringing up additional perspectives for her consideration. She greatly valued this, because insights came to her in many ways. Besides unmistakable visions, she also had impressions, convictions based on past experience, and information that came through ordinary human channels. Like others, she had to think and pray over decisions. As a sympathetic partner who not only accepted the divine origin and authority of her visions but also shared her entire belief system, the mature W. C. White was well equipped to help her think through the evidence surrounding any given decision. Because he believed that her inspiration affected everything she did, he accepted as a given that her counsels consistently embodied wisdom superior to his own. He also believed God expected him to use his own abilities to think and pray about an issue, considering all the factors that might affect the interpretation of a particular statement or the probable outcome of a proposed action. In most cases this broader study reinforced his confidence in her counsel. But if his study suggested some potentially negative outcomes, he would share with her the problems and options that he had thought of. Meanwhile she might also have acquired additional information or revelation. The ensuing discussion would usually lead to a fuller understanding of the situation and the complete harmonizing of their views. If, however, she remained unconvinced of his alternatives and confident of her own view, he would accept her perspective as expressing higher wisdom than his own and would act on it accordingly, whether or not he could explain or defend it to others (*ibid.*, pp. 442-444).

The same basic principles and dynamics governed his relationship to her as editor, as spokesman for her, and as interpreter of her writings. Ellen White's own stated goal for the editorial process was "to improve everything, as far as possible bringing it to perfection, that it might be accepted by intelligent minds. As far as possible every defect should be removed from all our publications" (Lt 11, 1884, in 3MR 258; 3SM 97). Because of the early interruption of her formal education, Ellen White was not strong in the editorial skills of spelling, punctuation, and the fine points of written grammar and syntax. Therefore she enlisted trusted *literary assistants to do this technical work for her. While her most experienced workers were authorized to rearrange the sequence of words and sentences and even incorporate clarifying passages from other Ellen White manuscripts, two restrictions were placed on all her editorial assistants: (1) they were never to change her thought, but only to clarify it; and (2) as far as grammatically possible, they were to preserve even her characteristic style and vocabulary. W. C. White's role included supervising other members of Ellen White's editorial staff, editing letters and periodical articles, planning books, and compiling books from existing manuscripts. In her later years she gave him broader authority and discretion than she had earlier, but the evidence is persuasive that his work as editor had her consistent approval (Moon, pp. 126, 445, 446).

His role as her spokesman included receiving incoming information and correspondence, communicating his mother's views through his own correspondence, representing her as her personal delegate, and expounding and interpreting her writings. First, from 1882 to 1891 his position as a General Conference administrator gave him opportunities to communicate her views to his colleagues and their views to her. Second, from 1886, and even more so in the 1890s, he developed a significant correspondence on her behalf. Church leaders such as A. G. Daniells, aware of the load of her correspondence, often addressed their concerns to Willie, asking him to consult his mother for them and relay back to them her counsel. Such letters would report the gist of her oral counsel, but the signature on the letter was W. C. White's (*ibid.*, pp. 232-239, 447, 448).

White's role as his mother's personal representative developed later in life, because through the end of the 1880s she was usually her own spokesperson at scores of camp meetings, conferences, and councils every year. After 1900, as her vigor declined, she attended fewer such convocations, often sending W. C. White to read manuscripts on her behalf. Thus his role as her representative during her life prepared him to be an expositor of her writings and principles to a broader audience after her death. Likewise, his role as a trustee of her estate after her death was not an entirely new role, but largely an extension of responsibilities he had already carried for many years (*ibid.*, pp. 448-450).

W. C. White held, with his mother (cf. 1SM 21), and with the General Conference resolution of 1883, that prophetic inspiration works "by the enlightenment of the mind, thus imparting the thoughts, and not (except in rare cases) the very words in which the ideas should be expressed," and therefore it was entirely consistent to make "such verbal changes" as were needed "to remove the above-mentioned imperfections, as far as possible, without in any measure changing the thought" ("General Conference Proceedings [Concluded]," RH, Nov. 27, 1883; also in 3SM 96).

In this W. C. White differed with *W. W. Prescott, who held to a type of verbal inspiration (see WCW to L. E. Froom, Jan. 8, 1928, in 3SM 454). When in 1910 W. C. White invited Prescott to suggest improvements for the 1911 edition of *The Great Controversy*, this was deeply unsettling to Prescott.

Believing that inspired writings should not need improvement, Prescott struggled, evidently for years, to reconcile the fact of Ellen White's editorial process with his own view of inspiration.

This is the background of Prescott's letter to W. C. White (Apr. 6, 1915) calling for more openness regarding Ellen White's editorial process, and the background of Prescott's comments at the *Bible Conference of 1919 (*Spectrum* 10 [May 1979]: 55, 56). To W. C. White, Ellen White's editorial process was entirely consistent with a view of inspired ideas conveyed in human words (see Moon, pp. 410-415, 427-436). To Prescott, the same editorial process was evidence that Ellen White was not inspired in the same way as the biblical prophets. The two men were colleagues who worked harmoniously in virtually every other area for many years, but because they held different concepts of inspiration, it is not surprising that they could not agree on how to educate the church about the relationship between inspiration and the editorial process.

W. C. White's responsibility as the leading trustee of the *Ellen G. White Estate had been specified in her will in 1912, but legally took effect upon her death July 16, 1915. Most of her staff soon found employment elsewhere. Of her literary assistants, only *Clarence and Minnie Crisler remained in the autumn of 1915. Ellen White's death also brought a drastic decline in W. C. White's influence in denominational affairs. He remained on the General Conference Committee and the boards of *Pacific Union College and the *St. Helena Sanitarium, but was not reelected to many other boards he had previously belonged to. After the Crislers left for China in 1916, the Elmshaven staff was reduced to W. C. White working alone, mostly in preparing his mother's books for translation and foreign-language publication. That was the situation that led to his absence from the 1919 Bible Conference (*ibid.*, pp. 451-453).

Ellen White's will and other statements included clear directives mandating the trustees to complete several specific book projects, as well as authorizing them to release her unpublished writings in general, at their discretion. But the trustees were divided on these issues, and not till 1925 did the General Conference Committee " 'come across' and declare (without record) that the question of printing testimony MSS. *[sic]* belonged to the Trustees." According to White, the letter "that set free the trustees" was given on Friday, November 20, 1925 (see WCW to Ella May Robinson, Dec. 8, 1925, WCW Correspondence File, EGWE-GC, quoted in Moon, p. 454). That authorization was eventually followed by funding for some secretarial and editorial help. In 1929 Arthur L. White, then 22, joined the office as secretary to his father. Despite the difficulties, W. C. White succeeded in preparing for publication 10 posthumous compilations between 1920 and 1933 (*Colporteur Evangelist, Christian Experience and Teachings of Ellen G. White, Fundamentals of Christian Education, Counsels on Health, Testimonies to Ministers and Gospel Workers, Christian Service, Principles of True Science, Messages to Young People, Medical Ministry, Life and Teachings of Ellen G. White*), and most notably the first 865-page *Scriptural and Subject Index to the Writings of Ellen G. White*, in 1926 (Moon, pp. 451-454).

By the early 1930s denominational leaders apparently realized anew the value of White's knowledge and experience, and he began to receive some of the respect and consideration that had been withheld in the years immediately following his mother's death. In 1935 and 1936 he was invited to address the students at the Seventh-day Adventist Advanced Bible School (forerunner of the Theological Seminary) while it remained at Pacific Union College. White's final written legacy was a series of 64 articles in the *Review and Herald.* Under the general title "Sketches and Memories of James and Ellen G. White," the series ran about twice a month from February 1935 through February 1938.

On August 31, 1937, two days after White's eighty-third birthday, he retired early following a full day's work. He awoke before midnight complaining of shortness of breath and died two hours later, apparently of an embolism of the heart. He was buried in the White family plot in *Oak Hill Cemetery, Battle Creek, Michigan.

Further reading: obit. RH, Oct. 21, 1937; "Letter of April 1915 of W. W. Prescott to W. C. White" (EGWE, SDoc); J. Moon, *W. C. White and Ellen G. White: The Relationship Between the Prophet and Her Son*, AU Seminary Dissertation Series (AUP, 1993), vol. 19.

Jerry Moon

WHITELOCK, THOMAS SYDNEY (1863-1938). Adventist physician. Whitelock was converted in 1891 and after attending the Bible Institute in *Battle Creek, entered ministerial work with W. A. Sweaney. In 1895, in response to an appeal by *David Paulson to enter medical missionary work, he attended the medical training program at Battle Creek. In 1898 he entered the University of Colorado Medical School; after securing his medical degree there, he began to practice medicine in San Diego, California, in 1900. At the encouragement of Ellen White, Whitelock helped secure for $20,000 the property that became *Paradise Valley Sanitarium. The price was reduced until it was eventually purchased in January 1904 for $4,000. Whitelock became the first medical superintendent of the Paradise Valley Sanitarium

(1904-1906), after which he returned to his practice in San Diego.

Further reading: obit. RH, June 30, 1938; T. S. Whitelock, "History of the Paradise Valley Sanitarium" (DF 2a, EGWE-GC).

WHITNEY, BUEL LANDON (1845-1888). Adventist pioneer missionary to *Europe. Born in Vermont, he moved, at age 12, with his family to New York, and soon afterward accepted Sabbatarian Adventism with his mother and brother. He began pastoral ministry in 1874 and the next year was elected president of the New York and Pennsylvania Conference. He continued in this capacity until 1883, when he went to Europe to replace *J. N. Andrews. Before he left, Ellen White counseled him about the state of the leadership there (Lt 2, 1883). Whitney was placed in charge of the Swiss Conference and supervised the establishment of the Basel Publishing House. In 1887 he returned to the United States because of poor health.

Further reading: SDA Encyclopedia (1996), vol. 11, p. 899.

WICKS, ELI (1822-1900) and **MARY E.** Adventist believers from Clyde, Illinois, converted to Adventism in 1857 through the work of *J. N. Loughborough and *William S. Ingraham. *James White visited the Wickses on a preaching tour in November 1860. A few nights earlier James had had a dream that his son *John Herbert would become gravely sick. Upon his arrival, James received a telegram from Ellen White "stating that the child was at the point of death, and requesting us to return home immediately" (LS80, p. 352; cf. 1Bio 429-431). Later Ellen White wrote *testimonies to the Wickses (Ms 7, 1866; Lt 29, 1868).

Further reference: obit. RH, June 19, 1900; JNL, *Miracles in My Life*, p. 55.

WILCOX, FRANCIS MCLELLAN (1865-1951). Minister, author, administrator, editor of the *Review and Herald*, and a charter trustee of the *Ellen G. White Estate. Wilcox entered *South Lancaster Academy (now Atlantic Union College) in 1882, the year it opened. He spent four years in evangelism and *city

COURTESY OF THE CENTER FOR ADVENTIST RESEARCH, ANDREWS UNIVERSITY.

FRANCIS M. WILCOX

mission work in New York (1886-1890) and was ordained in 1889. After editing the *Sabbath School Worker* (1891-1893) and the *Home Missionary* (1893-1897), he became chaplain at the *Boulder Sanitarium (1897-1909), serving part of that time as its business manager. In 1909 he became associate editor of the *Review and Herald*, and was its editor from 1911 to his retirement in 1944. During his career Wilcox exchanged many letters with Ellen White and W. C. White, seeking Ellen White's counsel regarding his work (see, e.g., *T. J. Evans). He was the main author of the 1931 statement of Adventist fundamental beliefs, which was officially endorsed by the 1946 General Conference session. Ellen White's last will and testament appointed him one of the five original trustees of her estate, a position he held for 36 years (1915-1951). Among his many books is one on the gift of prophecy, *The Testimony of Jesus* (1934).

Further reading: obit. RH, Sept. 27, 1951; SDA Encyclopedia (1996), vol. 11, p. 900.

WILCOX, MILTON CHARLES (1853-1935). Pastor and editor. Wilcox became a Seventh-day Adventist at age 25 and was ordained to ministry in 1880. He served as a missionary in England (1884-1887) until his wife's illness necessitated their return to the United States. While in England he started the journal

Present Truth. He went on to work as assistant editor (1887-1891) and then editor (1891-1913) of the *Signs of the Times* in Oakland, California. His last reponsibility was book editor at Pacific Press (1913-1933). After his wife's health improved in 1887, Ellen White wrote from Europe counseling Wilcox to seek the will of God regarding his return to England. She assured him that the leadership in England would be glad to see him, even though she felt his temperament did not make him a "safe missionary" (Lt 41, 1887). She also affirmed his work for the *Present Truth.* While he served as a pastor in California, Wilcox received a few letters from Ellen White regarding various administrative responsibilities (Lt 62, 1900; Lt 35b, 1901; Lt 27, 1903).

Further reading: obit. RH, Nov. 14, 1935; *SDA Encyclopedia* (1996), vol. 11, p. 901.

WILLIAMS, ISAAC N. (1841-1934). Adventist minister and administrator. Williams joined the Adventist Church in 1878 and soon became a pastor. He was president of the Pennsylvania (1892-1895, 1897-1899, 1908 acting, 1910-1911) and Quebec conferences (1899-1901). In 1896 Ellen White asked him to help *W. F. Caldwell, whom she had employed while in Australia but who had returned to the United States after he had carried on a clandestine affair with *Fannie Bolton, following which he divorced his wife (Lts 18, 104, 1896).

Further reading: obit. RH, Mar. 8, 1934; *SDA Encyclopedia* (1996), vol. 11, pp. 312-316.

WILSON, GILBERT T. (1858-1899) and **JENNIE.** Early Adventist workers in *Australia and *New Zealand. In 1893 Ellen White assisted G. T. and Jennie Wilson in evangelistic meetings in New Zealand. During these meetings Ellen White daily addressed those attending

the meetings (4Bio 104-111). Later, in 1897, the Wilsons helped start the *Avondale school (4Bio 303). In 1898 Ellen White cited Jennie Wilson's work as an example of a minister's spouse who should also receive denominational wages for the soul-winning work she did (12MR 160).

WOOD, KENNETH H., JR. (1917-2008). Minister, author, editor. Born of missionary parents in Shanghai, China, Wood lived in Asia until he was 15, and became bilingual in Chinese and English. He was educated at the Far Eastern Academy, La Sierra Academy, Pacific Union College, and Potomac University (now Andrews University). In the late 1930s he conducted evangelistic tent meetings in California's San Joaquin Valley, then was a pastor in West Virginia and Ohio. For nine years he served as a departmental director in the New Jersey and Columbia Union conferences. In 1955 he became associate editor of the *Review and Herald* (now *Adventist Review*), serving on the staff for 27 years, the last 16 as editor. In that capacity he began several editions in languages other than English. He also reinstated an old feature: Letters to the Editor. In 1975, during the Vienna, Austria, General Conference session, he arranged to publish the daily *Bulletin* in Vienna for the delegates, and in Washington, D.C., for regular subscribers. In 1980, while still editor of the *Review*, he was elected chair of the Board of Trustees of the *Ellen G. White Estate, a post he held for 27 years. During that time he also edited books for the White Estate, among which were the condensed editions of the *Conflict of the Ages five-volume series; adaptations of *Steps to Christ* for people whose birth language is not English; *The Story of Redemption* for those who are blind or hearing-impaired; and *Messenger of the Lord*, a college/seminary textbook by Herbert E. Douglass. Advocating a policy of giving wide access to Ellen White materials, he encouraged production of a CD (compact disc) containing all of her published works, and later a CD with her unpublished writings. He also urged the creation of Web sites to make available Ellen White's writings and information about her ministry. *The Christ of the Narrow Way,* an 8' x 30' mural at the General Conference office in Silver Spring, Maryland, is a tribute to his vision and energetic support. It features young Ellen's first vision set against a background of church historical places, events, and leaders. Wood's books include *Meditations for Moderns* (1964) and *Short Essays on Relevant Religion* (1972).

Further reading: K. H. Wood, "What Ellen White's Inspired Writings Have Meant to Me," *Ellen White and Current Issues Symposium* 1 (2005): 88-95, CAR; [Sandra Blackmer], "The Life and Times of Kenneth H. Wood," AR, Jan. 24, 2008.

Herbert E. Douglass

WOODRUFF, AZMON (1802-c.1889). Early Adventist believer in Oswego, New York, who was converted in 1851 through reading the **Review and Herald.* Ellen White in 1858 was shown in vision while in Ohio that evil angels were causing church members to "make the truth disgusting" and an "abhorrence." She added that "the cause of God in Oswego County had been cursed by wrangling and strife" among Sabbatarian Adventists. She sent a copy of the description of her vision to Woodruff, cautioning that each believer in Oswego should be converted and develop "a religious character for themselves" (Lt 2, 1858, in 21MR 258, 259).

Further reading: "Dear Bro. White," *Advent Review*, March 1851; "Dear Bro. White," RH, May 12, 1853; "Extract of Letters," RH, Sept. 26, 1854.

WOODS, J. H. (1863-1925). One of the earliest converts to Adventism in Australia, Woods operated a printing business with **W.H.B. Miller. Soon after Woods became an Adventist in 1886, he and Miller sold their business to join the Bible Echo Publishing House in North Fitzroy, near Melbourne. In 1896 Ellen White wrote to Woods and his wife expressing her regrets that they had not attended the camp meeting. She also felt that "there was a great need of a revival effort in the church at North Fitzroy" (Lt 117, 1896). When Woods and other workers decided to leave the publishing house in 1896, Ellen White wrote them a long letter expressing her disappointment over their decision. She said that able and talented workers were needed at the publishing house and that sacrifices were needed in order to see success and growth. "The brethren who have separated themselves from the Echo office have opened a door to temptation to themselves and to the church. Their movement was not in the order of God" (Lt 39, 1898; cf. Lt 65, 1896). After receiving this counsel, Woods became a pastor and was ordained in 1898. Until his death in 1925, he served in various positions, including president of the New South Wales Conference.

Further reading: obit. *Australasian Record*, Feb. 23, 1925.

WORKMAN, MABEL EUNICE (WHITE), see **WHITE, MABEL EUNICE.**

WORKMAN, WILFRED D., see **WHITE, MABEL EUNICE.**

WORTH, WILLIAM O. Adventist car manufacturer who in the 1890s started the Chicago Motor Vehicle Company. In January 1902 Ellen White made a brief stop in Chicago to inspect the branch sanitarium that *J. H. Kellogg had begun. After a long train ride, when she arrived she was pleased to find *H. W. Kellogg had one of Worth's "automobiles waiting to take us to the sanitarium. It was a covered carriage, shaped like a streetcar, and I lay down on one of the seats running along each side. It was a great relief to me to be able to lie down" (Lt 11, 1902, in 6MR 255; 5Bio 144).

Further reading: G. S. May, "William O. Worth: Adventist Auto Pioneer," *Adventist Heritage* 1, no. 2 (July 1974): 43-53.

ZELINSKY, FRANK H. (b. 1870) and **CLARA B.** (1881-1965). Young Adventist physician in whom Ellen White saw so much potential that she asked her friend *Josephine Gotzian to sponsor him through his medical training. Upon his graduation Zelinsky practiced medicine at the *St. Helena Sanitarium (1902-1905), during which time Ellen White counseled him regarding his career and married life. She warned him against yielding to worldly ambition and that in himself he lacked the wisdom necessary to direct a sanitarium. She furthermore counseled him and his wife as newlyweds not to spoil the life God had given them (Lt 31, 1902). She particularly noted their need of conversion and to gain victory over their stubborn wills (Lts 55, 57, 1902). In 1906 Zelinsky joined the Glendale Sanitarium.

Topical
Section

TOPICAL SECTION

ABOLITION, see **SLAVERY;** *SOUTHERN WORK, THE*; **RACE RELATIONS; AFRICAN-AMERICANS, ADVENTISM AMONG.**

ABRIDGMENTS OF ELLEN G. WHITE'S BOOKS, see **BOOKS, PREPARATION OF ELLEN G. WHITE'S.**

ACCREDITATION. Although the regional accreditation of colleges in the United States did not begin until 1913, Ellen White's counsel guided the Seventh-day Adventist Church and its colleges through a difficult 30-year period ending in the late 1930s. Curricular changes, absence of effective governmental control, and increasing institutional diversity produced chaos in American colleges in the last third of the nineteenth century. The solution was the creation of regional, voluntary-membership educational associations that brought together secondary schools and colleges to discuss problems and improve articulation between them. The associations established membership criteria that eventually became accreditation standards. The North Central Association of Colleges and Secondary Schools was the first to accredit institutions: secondary schools in 1905 and colleges in 1913.

During the 1860s and 1870s Adventists developed methods and institutions to fulfill their enlarging concept of mission. In 1866 they established the Health Reform Institute, which evolved into the Battle Creek Sanitarium under the direction of Dr. John Harvey Kellogg. Operating medical institutions profoundly impacted the nature of the church, as did entry into higher education in 1874 with the establishment of Battle Creek College. These ventures—especially medical education—brought Adventists into contact with the broader American society.

In 1895 Kellogg established the *American Medical Missionary College (AMMC), which was eventually admitted to membership in the Association of American Medical Colleges and recognized by the London Medical Council. When Kellogg was dropped from church membership in 1907, the church lost control of the AMMC and withdrew its endorsement. Most Adventist students chose to attend other medical schools. With 60 sanitariums, the church needed a dependable supply of physicians.

In 1905 the Southern California Conference established a sanitarium in Loma Linda. Ellen White urged that Loma Linda be not only a sanitarium but also an educational center for the training of nurses and *gospel medical missionary evangelists,* a term that left church administrators and faculty and staff of the new Loma Linda College of Evangelists, established in 1906, uncertain as to what she meant. During the next four years her explanation of her vision for the college increasingly sounded like a regular medical curriculum with a distinctive Seventh-day Adventist perspective. Fearful of the cost of operating a medical school, church leaders proposed that the college offer only the first two years of medicine and that students transfer to other medical schools to finish their programs. Ellen White rejected the idea, advising that the church should operate its own state-chartered medical school that taught the courses required by state medical authorities so that its graduates would be qualified for medical licensure (MM 62).

In October 1909 the General Conference authorized the college to secure a state charter as a medical school, but leaders felt the need for further counsel from Ellen White. Her response in January 1910 was clear: the college must provide the education to prepare medical missionary workers who were professionally recognized, fully qualified physicians (*ibid.* 57, 58). In December 1909 the college secured a charter authorizing the newly named *College of Medical Evangelists (CME)to offer courses and grant degrees in the liberal arts, the sciences, dentistry, and medicine.

It was the most inopportune time to establish a medical school. The range in quality of American medical education was dramatic. The American Medical Association was endeavoring to effect major improvements in medical education and had begun to rate or accredit medical schools as class A (acceptable), B (needs improvements), or C (needs complete reorganization). At its request, Abraham Flexner of the Carnegie Foundation for the Advancement of Teaching conducted a major study of American medical schools. Published in 1910, his report of tragic deficiencies in many schools resulted in the closure of nearly half of them by 1930 and stimulated public demand for medical reforms, including higher admission requirements and tougher state licensing laws.

Especially critical of low entrance requirements, Flexner advocated admitting only academically qualified applicants with a minimum of two years of college study featuring biology, chemistry, and physics. At the time, fewer than half of the country's medical schools required even one year of collegiate study with an emphasis on sciences. By 1915, 53 percent of them required one year of college, and 42 percent required two or more years.

Every state adopted new medical licensure laws or strengthened existing ones. State medical boards relied on the AMA's ratings of medical schools in determining whether to accept their degrees. As early as 1914, graduates of class C schools—such as CME—were denied the right to practice in 31 states, and the National Board of Medical Examiners would examine only graduates of class A schools. State boards soon began to dictate medical school entrance standards by stipulating premedical requirements prerequisite to licensure. By 1918 a minimum of two years of collegiate premedicine was required by all state boards.

Born at the time when the AMA and the public were working to raise medical education standards and close poor-quality medical schools, CME was subjected to critical examination by the AMA and the state medical board. Recognizing that admission standards played a significant part in the rating a school received from the AMA, CME steadily increased its requirements. In 1909 students were admitted to the first medical class with only a high school diploma, the minimum required by the AMA. As AMA premedicine requirements steadily increased, CME followed those requirements. In 1910 the college required a bachelor's degree or a secondary school diploma plus a few collegiate preprofessional courses. In 1915 the admission requirement was two years of collegiate premedicine, including a specified number of credits in physics, chemistry, and biology. The next major change took effect in January 1922: the AMA ordered that class A medical schools—the rating that CME was on the verge of earning—admit only applicants who had completed premedicine in accredited liberal arts colleges, a requirement that precipitated a major crisis in the Adventist Church and its educational system.

Ellen White foresaw these issues and had provided straightforward counsel on how the church should respond. As early as 1903 she had written, "If there are legal requirements . . . that medical students shall take a certain preparatory course of study, let our colleges teach the required additional studies" "to carry their students to the point of literary and scientific training that is necessary" (FE 490).

In her definitive statement in January 1910 Ellen White clearly reiterated her belief that the church's liberal arts colleges "should be placed in the most favorable position for qualifying our youth to meet the entrance requirements specified by state laws regarding medical students" and that CME must provide medical education that would "enable them to pass the examinations required by law of all who practice as regularly qualified physicians" (CT 479, 481).

In the summer of 1914 Ellen White had several conversations regarding CME with Dr. *E. A. Sutherland. Her counsel remained consistent: CME would have to meet the legal requirements to train physicians.

In Ellen White's counsel, said Arthur L. White, "is found the justification for accrediting Seventh-day Adventist educational institutions" (6Bio 280). Within a few years the issues confronting CME directly impacted Adventist liberal arts colleges. Ellen White's advice reassured most church leaders, educators, and laypersons during the debate over accrediting Adventist colleges, which lasted from 1922 until 1936, that the colleges must be accredited.

Further reading: L. W. Otto, "An Historical Analysis of the Origin and Development of the College of Medical Evangelists" (Ed.D. diss., University of Southern California, 1962); R. Utt, *From Vision to Reality, 1905-80: Loma Linda University* (Loma Linda, Calif.: Loma Linda University Press, 1980); E. C. Walter, "A History of Seventh-day Adventist Higher Education in the United States" (Ed.D. diss., University of California, Berkeley, 1966); W. G. White, Jr., "Accreditation of Seventh-day Adventist Liberal Arts Colleges in the North Central Association Region of the United States, 1922-1939" (Ph.D. diss., University of Reading, 2002); W. G. White, Jr., "Flirting With the World: How Adventist Colleges in North America Got Accredited," *Adventist Heritage: A Journal of Adventist History* 8 (Spring 1983): 40-51.

William G. White, Jr.

ACTS OF THE APOSTLES, THE (PPPA, 1911, 630 pp.). The fourth book of the Conflict of the Ages Series; its full title being *The Acts of the Apostles in the Proclamation of the Gospel of Jesus Christ.* One of the last books published while the author was alive. No sooner had the 1911 edition of *The Great Controversy* been sent to the press than Ellen White and her assistants undertook the long-deferred task of preparing an updated and expanded "book on the work of the apostles" (Lt 30, 1911, in 6Bio 341). From her perspective, *The Acts of the Apostles* is not merely a meditation on the corresponding biblical book and on some writings of Paul, Peter, and John, but a reflection on the life, experiences, writings and the raison d'être of the Christian church. Like many of her works, this book is a meticulous rewriting, amplification, and adaptation of two previous books, *The Spirit of Prophecy*, volume 3 (1878), and *Sketches From the Life of Paul* (1883), with additional materials selected from sermons, manuscripts, and articles. Ellen White was much involved in this editorial process. In some historical descriptions she used the phraseology of *The Life and Epistles of St. Paul*, a book coauthored by British clergymen W. J. Conybeare and J. S. Howson. (The percentage of known and documented literary borrowing in *The Acts of the Apostles* is about 3 percent, though the percentage was considerably higher in the earlier work *Sketches From the Life of Paul.*) The essence of Ellen White's message in *The Acts of the Apostles* reflects a balanced approach between the free gift of salvation and Christian ethics. "John did not teach that salvation was to be earned by obedience; but that obedience was the fruit of faith and love" (AA 563). Love actually is the main emphasis of this book. It is demonstrated through God's infinite generosity to His imperfect church, the omnipresent centrality of the cross (pp. 201-210), and the life of the early church (pp. 318, 319). In this book Ellen White gives the clearest explanation of her theology of Christian perfection, not as a pharisaic concept and a religion of avoidance, but as a gift of God and a humble desire to reflect grace in one's daily Christian existence (pp. 557-567). With its gospel orientation, *The Acts of the Apostles* reflects Ellen White's vision for what the church should be in the world until the second coming of Christ.

Further reading: 6Bio 338-349.

Jean-Luc Rolland

ADORNMENT, see **DRESS AND ADORNMENT.**

ADULTERY, see **MARRIAGE AND DIVORCE.**

ADVENT REVIEW, see **REVIEW AND HERALD ARTICLES, ELLEN G. WHITE PRESENT TRUTH AND.**

ADVENTIST CHURCH, see **SEVENTH-DAY ADVENTIST CHURCH.**

ADVENTIST DENOMINATIONS. While the Millerite movement demonstrated a unique ecumenical spirit in rallying people of many denominations to belief in the imminent second advent of Christ, the movement splintered after 1844, eventually resulting in six different Adventist denominations. Some tensions had already begun to appear before the October 22, 1844, *disappointment, but believing that Christ would soon return, most Millerites chose to avoid debating issues they believed would soon be settled by Christ Himself. After the disappointment, however,

the unity of the movement was replaced by sectarianism and division. During this period of consternation and confusion three interpretations of the Millerite movement were offered. A first interpretation advocated that the calculations for a precise date for the second coming of Christ had been wrong or at least misguided. By far, the majority of Millerite believers favored this interpretation. The second interpretation advocated by a small group expanded on ideas previously presented by William Miller and others and explained the delay of the Second Coming through the bridegroom concept as expressed in the parable of the ten virgins of Matthew 25:1-13. These Bridegroom Adventists held that the great prophecies had been fulfilled and identified Jesus as the bridegroom, the heavenly New Jerusalem as the bride, the marriage as the act of Christ receiving His kingdom in heaven, and the Advent believers as the virgins. Thus Jesus would soon return to take the virgins to heaven for the marriage supper.

A third interpretation of the Millerite movement appeared among Bridegroom Adventists: the advocation of a "spiritual" second coming of Christ. This was another attempt to reconcile the conviction that prophecy had been fulfilled on October 22 with the obvious nonappearance of Jesus on that day. The spiritualizers claimed that Jesus *had* come on that date—not literally, but "spiritually" to those who believed it. While William Miller had held to the literal interpretation of the Bible and of the Second Advent, spiritualizers taught that Christ had already come, that the millennium had begun, and that true faith in this teaching was evidenced by refusal to work, thus keeping a perpetual Sabbath rest. Some held that true Christians were henceforth perfect, sinless, and even immortal. These perfectionistic beliefs led to some aberrant behaviors, such as crawling in streets, spiritual marriage and other improper behaviors between men and women (holy kissing and promiscuous foot washing), practices that were frowned upon by non-Millerite Christians and condemned by society in general. The main redeeming factor among the spiritualizers was that they did believe that a prophecy had been fulfilled on October 22, 1844. Some of these spiritualizing groups were objects of Ellen White's earliest prophetic ministry, as she denounced their false humility, unsanctified lives, and unbiblical doctrines and practices (LS 77-94). A few of these people were reclaimed from fanaticism and joined the nucleus of the non-spiritualizing Bridegroom Adventists who became the pioneers of the Seventh-day Adventist Church; many of the others followed their leader, *Enoch Jacobs, into Shakerism.

To combat the spread of what they considered to be fanatical aberrations, Millerite leaders convened a conference in Albany, New York, in April 1845 that became a turning point in Adventist history. The call for the conference invited only those Adventists "who still [adhered] to the original Advent faith" (*Advent Herald*, Mar. 26, 1845). Excluded were the fringe groups, including Bridegroom Adventists and all who had developed new doctrines and practices since the disappointment. After three days of discussion, the Albany Conference adopted a 10-point doctrinal platform emphasizing the Second Advent and salvation in Christ. The conference laid plans for continuing evangelism, and voted a series of resolutions rejecting the religious practices of the non-Albany Adventists. Thus the Albany Conference lumped together the no-work and spiritual-marriage spiritualizers with the nonspiritualizing group who also held to a form of the shut door. As a result, while the Albany Conference helped to define

and unify the "moderate" Adventists by rejecting all new doctrinal developments (*Advent Herald*, May 14, 1845), it polarized and helped to make permanent the divisions among Adventists.

Following the conference, Albany Adventism centered on the leadership of William Miller, Joshua V. Himes, and their colleagues, and their primary journal, the *Advent Herald*, published in Boston. By the time of Miller's death in December 1849, the focus of discussion among Albany Adventists was no longer the doctrines and practices of the fringe Adventists. The in-group struggle was now over organization and what ecclesiastical shape Adventism was to take. Many early Adventists believed that any form of ecclesiastical organization would be a step toward the creation of a new Babylon. By the end of the 1850s, however, Albany Adventists had adopted the rudiments of a congregationalist organization. This struggle regarding *church organization was overshadowed, however, by a more divisive one, over the doctrine of the immortality of the soul.

George Storrs had promoted the doctrine of conditional immortality (conditionalism) and the eternal destruction of the wicked at the end of time (annihilationism) among the Millerites beginning in 1841. But after 1845 Joshua Himes, as editor of the *Advent Herald*, refused to allow the journal to become a public platform for conditionalism, which he considered to be a minor issue, and encouraged individuals to go elsewhere to publish their views on this topic. Himes' refusal set the stage for a schism in the Albany Adventist ranks. In 1854 a new journal, the *World's Crisis*, became the rallying point of conditionalist Adventists. The tension between the two major groups of Adventists came to a head in 1858, when the *Herald* Adventists formed the American Evangelical Adventist

Conference to disseminate "original" Adventism as defined in Albany in 1845. By adopting a constitution and electing officers, they de facto formed a denomination. While this action horrified many conditionalist Adventists, the organization of the Evangelical Adventists, however, forced the *Crisis* Adventists to reexamine the organizational issue, and by the fall of 1860 they also had formed their own organization, the Advent Christian Association.

Conditionalist Adventists were not all united in their doctrinal ideas, however, and divisions among them continued to occur. In 1863 a group of believers under the leadership of George Storrs formed the Life and Advent Union. This group distinguished itself from other conditionalists in believing that sinners will not be resurrected at the final judgment and that only believers in Christ receive life.

A fourth group related to Albany Adventists was the "age-to-come" Adventists. This group taught a variant of British premillennialism—that the Jews would return to Israel and that individuals would have a second chance to be saved during the millennium (the "age to come"). The anti-organizational feelings among them were perhaps the strongest of all post-Millerite Adventists, and an extreme individualism hindered even the organization of local congregations. Lasting attempts at church organization failed until 1921, when the Church of God of the Abrahamic Faith was organized with headquarters in Oregon, Illinois (moved to Morrow, Georgia, in 1991).

Because these four Adventist denominations arising from the Albany Conference adopted congregationalist forms of church government, none of them developed a strong centralized church government. This is perhaps one reason that contributed to their demise or lack of growth. In the 1860s Evangelical Adventists comprised the largest Adventist denomination. Their only distinctive belief, compared to the general Protestant Evangelical denominations, was their belief in the premillennial advent of Christ. When a large segment of conservative Protestantism adopted forms of this belief in the latter part of the nineteenth century, Evangelical Adventists lost their uniqueness and, by the early twentieth century, ceased to exist as a separate denomination. Advent Christians, the largest continuing group of Adventists from the Albany Conference, now number about 28,000 in the United States. In 1964 the Life and Advent Union merged with the Advent Christians. The Church of God of the Abrahamic Faith numbers about 6,000 (Knight, *Millennial Fever*, p. 329).

Two Sabbatarian Adventist churches originated from the nonspiritualizing Bridegroom Adventists after the Millerite movement. Under the leadership of Joseph Bates and James and Ellen White, a group of Sabbathkeeping Adventists emerged in the eastern United States in the late 1840s. With the publication of their journal, the *Advent Review and Sabbath Herald*, and a series of conferences on their particular beliefs, they succeeded in attracting an ever-increasing number of believers, drawn at first from the ranks of former Millerites and Albany Adventists. The largest group of Sabbatarian Adventists took the name Seventh-day Adventist in 1860 and began the organization of local churches and conferences the following year. Their *General Conference was organized in 1863. They numbered about 1 million members in the United States in 2009, 17 million worldwide, and today form the largest of the Adventist denominations.

In the 1850s, as the Seventh-day Adventist group developed in the American midwest, dissatisfaction among ministers in Michigan and Wisconsin led to a schism and the formation of a group called the *Messenger* Party.

The belief that marked them, in contrast to the other Sabbatarian Adventists, was their "age-to-come" doctrine, also held by a group of Albany Adventists. The *Messenger* Party lasted for about four years, during which time Ellen White labored actively to convince people of their doctrinal errors (1T 116, 117, 714; 1Bio 310-315). Many defectors returned to the main group of Sabbatarian Adventists, while others united with other "age-to-come" Adventists to form the group that later became the Church of God of the Abrahamic Faith.

A second schism among Sabbatarian Adventists occurred in the mid-1860s when two ministers in Iowa, B. F. Snook and W. H. Brinkerhoff, led a group opposed to church organization and to the Seventh-day Adventist leadership in Battle Creek, Michigan. This group attracted other dissatisfied or unaffiliated Sabbatarian Adventists and came to be known as the *Marion Party, from their location in Marion, Iowa (2Bio 146-151). Although the group failed to enlist many Seventh-day Adventists, it grew and later formed the Church of God (Adventist) in Stanberry, Missouri. Today this group is named Church of God (Seventh Day) (Denver, Colorado) and numbers about 10,000 in the United States. Thus of the six Adventist denominations that emerged from the Millerite movement, four still exist today.

During her lifetime Ellen White had numerous interactions with Adventists of other denominations. It was to former Millerites and Albany Adventists that she and her husband ministered most in their early years. Under the generic name of "first-day Adventists," or sometimes "nominal Adventists," she referred to all Adventists who kept Sunday as a day of worship. By the 1880s, however, this term applied mainly to Advent Christians. Ellen White's relationship with Advent Christians remained ambivalent for most of her life. Although she always wished to entertain good relations with them, the abrasive and assertive personality of their longtime leader, *Miles Grant, did not facilitate communication and discouraged good will (3Bio 334-336).

But things were different with another Adventist leader, *Joshua V. Himes, Millerite leader and longtime editor of the *Advent Herald*. As a teenager in Portland, Maine, Ellen White had heard Himes preach on the second advent of Christ. While receiving care at the Battle Creek Sanitarium during his last illness in 1894-1895, Himes sent $40 to Ellen White for the work of evangelism in Australia. Ellen White was delighted by his letter and responded warmly to his gift (Lt 31a, 1895, in 4Bio 180). Himes said he believed the work done by Seventh-day Adventists was the continuation of the work he and William Miller had begun. Had he been 25 years younger, he said, he would have joined the work of Seventh-day Adventists (4Bio 180).

Further reading: G. R. Knight, *Millennial Fever and the End of the World* (PPPA, 1993), pp. 245-293; C. E. Hewitt, *Midnight and Morning* (Charlotte, N.C.: Venture Books, 1983), pp. 203-284; D. L. Rowe, *Thunder and Trumpets: Millerites and Dissenting Religion in Upstate New York, 1800-1850* (Chico, Calif.: Scholars Press, 1985), pp. 141-160; M. Burt, "The Historical Background, Interconnected Development, and Integration of the Doctrines of the Sanctuary, the Sabbath, and Ellen G. White's Role in Sabbatarian Adventism From 1844 to 1849" (Ph.D. diss., AU, 2002).

Denis Fortin

ADVENTIST HOME, THE (SPA, 1952, 583 pp.). Compilation of Ellen White's writings on the home and family. Ellen White wrote upon every phase of home life. Hundreds of her personal letters were addressed to people and families living in difficult situations, and offer specific instructions on the problems that concern thoughtful parents today. The 87 chapters are subdivided into 18 topical sections. The book begins with sections on the biblical foundations of the home and the family's influence in the community. Counsels on choosing a life partner and establishing a successful marriage are followed by admonitions on raising children, home discipline, and the roles of father and mother. Counsels on the use of family finances and on social and recreational activities are also provided. A study guide was prepared in 1965. *The Adventist Home* was abridged in a paperback edition in 1971 under the title of *Happiness Homemade.*

ADVENTIST REVIEW, see **REVIEW AND HERALD ARTICLES, ELLEN G. WHITE PRESENT TRUTH AND.**

AESTHETICS, see **BEAUTY.**

AFRICA. Ellen White was deeply interested in the many peoples of the African continent. In the mid-1880s the *Wessels family of Kimberly, South Africa, after discovering the biblical Sabbath, began a small Sabbathkeeping community without any knowledge that there were others who shared their newly discovered beliefs. In 1886 they discovered and contacted the Seventh-day Adventist Church and requested the General Conference to send them help. The following year *D. A. Robinson with *C. L. Boyd, their families; two colporteurs, George Burleigh and R. S. Anthony; and a Bible instructor, Carrie Mace, were sent to Cape Town, South Africa.

Robinson and Boyd crossed paths with Ellen White while en route, and she wrote them letters of advice showing her deep interest in the success of their missionary labors.

She wrote similarly to S. N. Haskell in 1889, and again to A. T. Robinson when he went to Africa as an administrator in 1891.

Although Ellen White never was able to visit Africa herself, she had a deep concern for mission work there (Lt 64, 1893)and considered traveling there. However, pressing needs elsewhere, combined with her poor health, prevented her from going. At one point she fully expected to go, but her plans did not materialize (Lt 57, 1894).

At the time of Haskell's trip, she began writing letters to local leaders in Africa. Very prominent in her correspondence was a wealthy Afrikaans family named Wessels. The entire family evoked her deepest interest, including their spiritual welfare, personal problems, and the correct stewardship of their wealth for the establishment of Adventism. The Wessels family members became benevolent benefactors not only in South Africa but also in Australia and the United States. Other letters to Adventists in Africa addressed issues surrounding the *Claremont Sanitarium, personal counsel, mistakes in method, exhortations, statements of principles applying to church work, and spiritual instruction (Lt 112, 1901; Lt 39, 1903; Lt 248, 1905). She urged believers in South Africa to reflect the love and character of Christ in dealing with each other (Lt 112, 1901; Lt 39, 1903; Lt 248, 1905), and to refrain from faultfinding (especially of those in leadership). She admonished that faultfinders are answerable to God for their own character and the fruit of the Spirit in their own lives. She invited people to imitate Christ in all their relationships, as a means of developing Christian character (Lt 63, 1893, in TSA 45-47).

While Ellen White does not seem to have extensively addressed racial issues in a specifically African context, she did write in 1899 that "had the work in Africa been carried forward as it should have been, the present [Anglo-Boer] war would not have been as it now is." Her rationale was that "the presentation of Bible truth, accompanied by the medical missionary work, would have found favor with the people who if properly treated are not treacherous and cruel" (Ms 178, 1899, in TSA 56). Adherence to her counsels to Africa would have resulted in healthy race relations. Major themes that would have impacted on race matters included how Christians were to relate to each other in character development and the fruit of the Spirit. She strongly urged all who labor in Africa to have characters that could be identified as Christlike (Lt 23c, 1892, in TSA 63-66).

See also: Solusi Mission.

Further reading: *Testimonies to Southern Africa*.

Michael D. Pearson

AFRICAN-AMERICANS, ADVENTISM AMONG. Adventist work among African-Americans had its origin in the Millerite movement, long before the end of slavery in the United States. Prominent Black ministers such as William Still, Charles Bowles, *William Foy, and John Lewis played a significant role in the preaching of the imminent second coming of Christ. These men were coworkers with William Miller and fully accepted his reckoning that the Second Coming was to take place in 1844.

Many prominent Black persons, including Frederick Douglass and *Sojourner Truth, were acquainted with and deeply interested in William Miller's Advent teachings, which provided a bright hope that slavery's deadly reign was soon to end. The Millerite movement essentially collapsed in the wake of the 1844 Disappointment. However, seeds of interest in the Second Advent had been sown and remained among free Blacks in the North and Blacks in slavery in the South.

William Ellis Foy, a Black minister, received visions pertaining to the Second Coming and events pertaining to the glorious entry into heaven of the redeemed saints. He shared what he had seen via the spoken and written word and continued to preach the second advent of Christ until his death in 1893. As a girl, Ellen White, along with her father, heard Foy speak in Portland, Maine, and later talked with him after receiving her first visions. She kept a copy of Foy's four visions and remarked, concerning his experience: "It was remarkable testimonies that he bore" (17MR 96). Foy's prophetic ministry lasted approximately two years (1842-1844) in the context of Millerite Adventism. He has often been confused with *Hazen Foss.

Ellen White was the most prominent Adventist promoter of work for African-Americans. Along with the heavy obligation of leading out in the organization of the Seventh-day Adventist Church, she had a special burden for the Black people of the South. She knew that Black people, because of the evils of slavery, were struggling in neglect and poverty.

After years of prodding the recalcitrant church, Ellen White delivered in 1891 a historic presentation entitled "Our Duty to the Colored People." This watershed message to the General Conference session in Battle Creek, Michigan, was an emphatic appeal to the leaders of the Seventh-day Adventist Church on behalf of developing a systematic work for Black people in the South. Her words were instrumental in motivating the church to become more active in the Southern work. Further, her message influenced her son *Edson White to dedicate his efforts to the work among Black people in the Southern states.

In 1893 Edson White and *W. O. Palmer attended meetings in Battle Creek, where they read Ellen White's 1891 appeal, noted above, in which she called for workers to "consecrate themselves" (SW 16) to the education of Blacks in the South. In response, Palmer and White, for mobility and safety purposes, innovatively constructed a steamboat on the banks of the Kalamazoo River at Allegan, Michigan. Launched in 1894, the *Morning Star* steamed up and down the Mississippi waterways for close to a decade. Initially the *Morning Star* served as the headquarters of the Southern Missionary Society, organized about 1895 by Edson White for the development of church work among Blacks in the South.

The *Gospel Herald,* predecessor to the *Message* magazine, the church's outreach magazine to people of color, was first printed aboard the *Morning Star.* Edited by Edson White, the *Gospel Herald* (1898-1923) chose as its objective the "reporting and promoting [of] the work among the Colored people in the South." Archived copies of this magazine provide one of the most complete and reliable resources available on the early Adventist work among Blacks in the southern United States.

*Oakwood Industrial School was established in 1896 in response to the appeals of Ellen White to develop a training center in the South for Black leaders. It became Oakwood College in 1943 and then Oakwood University in 2008. General Conference leadership purchased a 360-acre (145-hectare) farm (the property later included 1,200 acres [486 hectares]) about five miles (eight kilometers) north of Huntsville, Alabama. It was named Oakwood because of its 65 oak trees.

Ellen White was a strong believer and supporter of Oakwood because she saw that this institution was to be a major force in the development and building of the Black work through its teaching ministry and influence. She became the dominant voice that motivated

the General Conference to establish the school. Further, not only did Ellen White visit the school several times—she also wrote valuable counsel to its students and administrators on how it should be operated. Through the decades Oakwood has trained more than 80 percent of the workers who have staffed the regional conferences.

Charles Kinney, sometimes referred to as the father of Black Adventism, is believed to have been the first Black ordained Seventh-day Adventist minister. In Reno, Nevada, Kinney accepted the Adventist truth as a result of the preaching of John Loughborough and Ellen White. First a colporteur, then a preacher and evangelist, Kinney was ordained in 1889. He had a deep burden for his people. In an 1885 issue of the *Review and Herald,* he wrote: "I earnestly ask the prayers of all who wish to see the truth brought 'before many peoples . . . ,' that I may have strength, physical, mental, and spiritual, to do what I can for the colored people."

The concept of Black conferences was first suggested by Kinney when confronted by efforts to segregate Black and White members at a camp meeting on the day of his ordination. He advocated Black conferences as a way to work more effectively among Blacks and to help ease the racial tensions in the church. By the time of his death in 1951, after the creation of regional conferences, he saw the Black membership in North America increase to more than 26,000.

Ellen White's writings on the Black work have exerted far-reaching effects on church policy. The most prominent of these writings are *The Southern Work,* first published by Edson White aboard the *Morning Star* (1898, reissued in 1966), and *Testimonies for the Church,* volumes 7 (1902) and 9 (1909). While by no means exhaustive, these books contain messages that helped shape the Black work.

Though these publications contain statements that may appear problematic when read out of context, they clearly indicate that work among Blacks was a priority with Ellen White.

Prior to the early 1870s Adventists confined their efforts primarily to the northern part of North America. However, as a result of the personal efforts of M. B. Czechowski, the Adventist message was carried to Central and Eastern Europe in the late 1860s. Appeals from Czechowski's converts led the church to send J. N. Andrews to Switzerland as the church's first official missionary in 1874. In 1895 Ellen White highlighted an important inconsistency: "We should take into consideration the fact that efforts are being made at great expense to send the gospel to the darkened regions of the world, . . . to bring instruction to the ignorant and idolatrous; yet here in the very midst of us are millions of people . . . who have souls to save or to lose, and yet they are set aside and passed by as was the wounded man by the priest and the Levite" (SW 20). Ellen White left the church little room to excuse its lack of effort in this area.

The work in the South among Blacks resulted from the combined efforts of the entire church. The *Morning Star* initiative received financial support from the General Conference at a time when funds were scarce. Because of the racial climate at the time, the White and Black Adventists who went South to work did so at great sacrifice and personal risk. Records indicate that in 1890 there were only 50 Black members. However, the work among Blacks began to pick up momentum. By 1910 there were more than 3,500 Black members. Similar increases were realized in tithe, mission schools, workers, and churches. In spite of the challenges faced by the Black work, God blessed with success.

The North American Negro Department was established in 1910. This development signaled a significant structural recognition of the importance of the Black work at the highest levels of the organization. The Black work became—and remains—an integral part of the administrative structure of the church. The first Black General Conference departmental director was William H. Green, who headed the department from 1918 to 1928. Meanwhile, the Southern Missionary Society continued the work among Blacks in the South that Edson White had initiated with the *Morning Star.*

In spite of obstacles and problems, extraordinary progress was made, and the Black work increasingly came to be recognized as a viable and significant part of the Adventist organization. Incorporated in 1898, by 1901 the Southern Missionary Society reported churches and schools in nine states, with all buildings held free of debt. In 1901 the organized work among Blacks in the South was finally legitimatized by its merger into the newly formed Southern Union Conference. The society, its property, and assets became a branch of the new union conference. Eventually assets of the society served as the framework for the newly organized regional or Black conferences in that union.

Ellen White's influence on behalf of the Adventist work among African-Americans was felt long after her death and even today. Black church institutions that arose in the early decades of the twentieth century included Oakwood University (founded in 1896, became a university in 2008); Harlem (later Northeastern) Academy (1920); Riverside Hospital (1927); *Message* magazine (1934); and Pine Forge Academy (1946). Near the end of the century Breath of Life telecast was created in 1981 with African-American and people of color in North America as a primary target audience.

Further reading: The Southern Work; D. W. Baker, *The Dynamics of Communication* and *African-American Progress in the Seventh-day Adventist Organization: A Historical Descriptive Analysis* (Ph.D. diss., Howard University, 1993); D. W. Baker, "Regional Conferences: 50 Years of Progress," AR, November 1995; D. W. Baker, compiler, with the Caucus of Black SDA Administrators, *Telling the Story: An Anthology on the Development of the Black SDA Work* (Loma Linda, Calif.: Loma Linda University Printing Services, 1996); D. W. Baker, ed., *Make Us One: Celebrating Spiritual Unity in the Midst of Cultural Diversity: Removing Barriers, Building Bridges* (PPPA, 1991); R. Graybill, *Ellen G. White and Church Race Relations* (RHPA, 1970); L. B. Reynolds, *We Have Tomorrow: The Story of American Seventh-day Adventists With an African Heritage* (RHPA, 1984); C. B. Rock, ed., *Perspectives: Black Seventh-day Adventists Face the Twenty-first Century* (RHPA, 1996); R. Branson, "Ellen G. White—Racist or Champion of Equality?" RH, Apr. 9, 1970; R. Branson, "Slavery and Prophecy," RH, Apr. 16, 1970; R. Branson, "The Crisis of the Nineties," RH, Apr. 23, 1970.

Delbert W. Baker

AGE OF SCHOOL ENTRANCE, see **SCHOOLS, CHURCH**.

"AGE-TO-COME" ADVENTISTS, see **ADVENTIST DENOMINATIONS**.

AGRICULTURE IN SCHOOLS. In addition to other trades, Ellen White believed that agriculture should have an important role in Adventist schools, first of all as a means of character-building (AH 142-146), but also as vocational training (CG 355, 356), as a source of outdoor exercise and wage income for students (CT 311), and as a source of fresh produce for the school kitchen (6T 179). "No line of manual training is of more value than agriculture," she wrote, and deserves more attention than it has received so far (CG 356, 357). Teachers should draw students' attention to biblical principles concerning agriculture (Ed 214), and the parables of Jesus drawn from agriculture (SpTEd 67). For all these reasons Ellen White believed that "study in agricultural lines should be the A, B, and C of the education given in our schools. This is the very first work that should be entered upon" (6T 179). "Working the soil is one of the best kinds of employment, calling the muscles into action," "resting the mind" (*ibid.*), teaching young people the true dignity of labor, and "creating a new moral taste in love of work, which will transform mind and character" (SpTEd 100). Therefore, she urged that every school have cultivable land (*ibid.*), and that teachers "take their students with them into the gardens and fields" (FE 325).

The balanced mental development of young people should be of great concern to educators (CT 317). Blessings that accompany physical exercise bring to young peoples' lives a well balanced and stable character. Furthermore, spending time in practical activities such as agriculture is "an important aid to the youth in resisting temptation" (FE 322).

The cultivation of gardens and fields in Adventist schools is of utmost importance not only for the reasons mentioned above but also for the financial support of those who are in need. Students need a place where they will earn tuition money to cover expenses. In this respect, if for nothing else, agriculture should be available to needy students as an important resource for their self-support (CT 311). Finally, agriculture should be taught in such a way as to produce experts in the field who in turn will be able to teach others (*Bible Advocate*, Mar. 1, 1901).

In North America many Adventist academies and colleges no longer have agriculture programs because agriculture was often seen primarily as an industry to provide students with work opportunities and to produce financial profit to support other aspects of education. When the school farm made a profit, the profit was used for other purposes than to enhance the farm's productivity. Thus the farm declined, and when it no longer made a profit, it was closed. In parts of the world in which agriculture is valued as an end in itself, and not just as a means to other ends, agriculture is still a significant part of Adventist education.

Further reading: G. R. Knight, *Myths in Adventism* (RHPA, 1985), pp. 239-241.

Paul Z. Gregor

ALBANY ADVENTISTS, see **ADVENTIST DENOMINATIONS**.

ALCOHOL, see **TEMPERANCE**.

ALPHA AND OMEGA. The first *(alpha)* and last *(omega)* letters of the Greek alphabet (see Rev. 1:11; 22:13), terms used by Ellen White to describe a progression of heretical teachings emanating from the Kellogg *pantheism controversy of the early twentieth century. "In the book *Living Temple* there is presented the alpha of deadly heresies," she warned. "The omega will follow, and will be received by those who are not willing to heed the warning God has given" (1SM 200). In 1904 she wrote, "We have now before us the alpha of this danger. The omega will be of a most startling nature" (*ibid.* 197).

By directly associating the "alpha" with heresies presented in Kellogg's *Living Temple*, there is little doubt that Ellen White was referring to his unorthodox views regarding the "presence and personality of God" (*ibid.* 203). In contrast, Ellen White's prediction of a future "omega" heresy has spawned a variety

of speculative interpretations ever since the warning was first issued. W. C. White stated that "not less than 12 different things have been urged as the omega by good-hearted brethren" by the time of the 1930s (Question and Answer File 31-13-7).

While the true meaning of Ellen White's "omega" statements will likely continue to be debated, a contextual clue may be found in her repeated association of the "alpha" with sentiments that led to the post-1844 fanaticism she confronted in New England. Referring to her reading of *The Living Temple*, she wrote, "I recognized the very sentiments against which I had been bidden to speak in warning during the early days of my public labors. When I first left the State of Maine, it was to go through Vermont and Massachusetts, to bear a testimony against these sentiments. *Living Temple* contains the alpha of these theories. I knew that the omega would follow in a little while; and I trembled for our people" (1SM 203).

"Some of the sentiments now expressed are the alpha of some of the most fanatical ideas that could be presented. Teachings similar to those we had to meet soon after 1844 are being taught by some who occupy important positions in the work of God" (2SM 26). "One, and another, and still another are presented to me as having been led to accept the pleasing fables that mean the sanctification of sin. *Living Temple* contains the alpha of a train of heresies. These heresies are similar to those that I met in my first labors in connection with the cause in Maine, New Hampshire, Vermont, then in Boston, Roxbury, New Bedford, and other parts of Massachusetts" (11MR 247).

If the *Living Temple* contained the "alpha [or beginning] *of these theories*," the "omega of the statements contained in *Living Temple*" (Ms 168, 1907; cf. 1SM 201-208) may refer to a revived form of those same post-1844 fanatical theories—a species of "false sanctification" whereby one was believed to be so possessed by the Holy Spirit that all one's feelings, impressions, and actions were considered holy (the "cannot-sin" theory) (see LS 83).

Accordingly, Kellogg's heretical theories of God's immanence within each person's physical mind and body may be seen as containing the seeds (alpha) for the logical conclusion (omega) that all one's impressions, thoughts, and actions are holy and free from sin—making of none effect the objective and normative authority of the teachings of the Word of God, as well as a proper recognition of church organization and authority. Ellen White warned that such sentiments would be revived at the very close of time.

Further reading: R. Coon, "How Near Is the Omega?" *Ministry*, April 1980.

Tim Poirier

AMALGAMATION. Term used by Ellen White to describe how Satan corrupted the world (3SG 64, 75; 1SP 69, 78). Examples in which she uses the term in a moral sense include the corruption of monotheism by "being amalgamated with the worship of graven images" (2SP 144), and the corruption of "God's people" through union with "worldly agencies" (RH, Aug. 23, 1892). Similarly, she speaks of biblical truth being "amalgamated with human devising" and "worldly opinions," leading to "apostasy" and to spiritual "light" becoming "darkness" (UL 310, 318). She warns of the "obedient and the disobedient" becoming "so amalgamated" (mingled) that the distinction between those who serve God and those who do not serve Him "will become confused and indistinct" (18MR 26). She also uses "amalgamation" to refer to the physical realm. Satan's work in altering plants produced thorns and thistles (Gen. 3:18), a metaphor

for his work of "amalgamation" in the spiritual realm (Matt. 13:27, 28). "All tares are sown by the evil one. Every noxious herb is of his sowing, and by his ingenious methods of amalgamation he has corrupted the earth with tares" (2SM 288).

These other uses of "amalgamation" may provide clues to its meaning in 3SG and 1SP when describing reasons God sent the Flood. In a chapter titled "Crime Before the Flood," White states: "But if there was one sin above another which called for the destruction of the race by the flood, it was the base crime of amalgamation of man and beast which defaced the image of God, and caused confusion everywhere" (3SG 64; 1SP 69). Further, "the confused species which God did not create, which were the result of amalgamation, were destroyed by the flood. Since the flood there has been amalgamation of man and beast, as may be seen in the almost endless varieties of species of animals, and in certain races of men" (3SG 75; 1SP 78).

The grammatical construction of these statements, their context, and Ellen White's general use of the term "amalgamation" allow four possible interpretations: (1) the practice of bestiality, (2) genetic combination of human and animal genomes to create chimeras, (3) corruption of both humans and animals by sin, thus marring God's original creation, and (4) intermarriage and/or other kinds of union between righteous and unrighteous people, so that the distinction between righteous and wicked is lost. Note that these interpretations are not necessarily logically exclusive; for example, the practice of bestiality (1) might well be expected to mar the image of God in humans (3) as much as any other "base" practice. Much discussion of these statements has its basis either in perceived racism on the part of Ellen White, or in the racial views of those using her writings. Positions incorporating race with one or more of the interpretations given above are common.

Two years after the first publication of the amalgamation statements, Adventist defectors B. F. Snook and W. H. Brinkerhoff (see *Marion Party) published a pamphlet accusing Ellen White of racism on the basis that her expression "certain races of men" was a reference to Africans. In responding to Snook and Brinkerhoff, Uriah Smith took the position that some "races of men now living" are actually chimeras of humans and animals. He invoked then-current science, citing unnamed naturalists as affirming that "the line of demarcation between the human and animal races is lost in confusion" (RH, July 31, 1866). Smith's views were later republished in a book *The Visions of Mrs. E. G. White* (objection 39, pp. 102-105), which was endorsed by James White. Smith's line of reasoning was accepted and expanded over the course of time by Ellen White's secretary *D. E. Robinson, her son *W. C. White, and scientist Harold Clark, among others.

The mechanism of amalgamation commonly given by advocates of the "man with beast" interpretation was "cohabitation" of men with animals (bestiality), which was biblically condemned as a crime requiring the death of both the human and the animal participants (Lev. 20:15, 16), and which was, according to the King James Version, "confusion" (Lev. 18:23). To explain the apparent barriers to reproductive unions between humans and animals today, greater "vital force" in antediluvian animals and humans may be invoked. More recent advocates of this interpretation have suggested some kind of genetic engineering.

A different line of argument can be traced back at least to George McCready Price, who strongly opposed Darwinian evolution. Price embraced the idea that "created kinds" could not possibly interbreed. His thinking was further developed by Frank L. Marsh and ultimately by F. D. Nichol. This alternative interpretation hinges on the ambiguity of the critical phrase "of man and beast" which could refer to one process, man *with* beast, or to two separate processes, "amalgamation of man and [of] beast." Price argued strongly for the implied insertion of the second "of." He and subsequent writers argued that of the two possible interpretations, the first conflicts with its own context and with then-known science (Nichol, *Ellen G. White and Her Critics*, p. 308). The results Ellen White attributes to "amalgamation" were "species of animals" and "races of men," "but not any kind of amalgam of animals with human beings" ("Comments Regarding Unusual Statements in Ellen White's Writings," SDoc, CAR). The second grammatical option, "amalgamation of man and [of] beast," also fits the rest of the sentence. The "amalgamation of man" "defaced the image of God" and the amalgamation of "beast" "caused confusion everywhere" (3SG 64, 75; 1SP 69, 78). The claim that science supports this interpretation may be weakened somewhat by the creation in recent years of various organisms with specific human genes, and chimeras of human and animal embryos (*Kennedy Institute of Ethics Journal* 15, no. 2 [2005]: 107-134; *Nature* 431, no. 7011 [2004]: 885). In addition hybridization has been observed in nature to produce both new plant and animal species from apparently different species.

Proponents of the theory that "amalgamation of man" denotes a separate phenomenon from "amalgamation of beast" cite statements by Ellen White identifying marriage between the righteous and the unrighteous as the "base sin" that led to the Flood. In this view, when the antediluvian Sethite "sons of God" intermarried with the "idolatrous race of Cain," they not only lost their "holy character," but also became debased physically (1SP 66; 3SG 60, 61; cf. PP 81, 82, 338) both of which "defaced the image of God." The most common objection to this interpretation is the intuitive assumption that intermarriage between believer and unbelievers could not be identified as the "base crime" that "called for the destruction of the race by the flood" (3SG 64; 1SP 69). But White elsewhere reminds that "every act, however small, has its place in the great drama of life. Consider that the desire for a single gratification of appetite introduced sin into our world, with its terrible consequences. Unhallowed marriages of the sons of God with the daughters of men resulted in apostasy which ended in the destruction of the world by a flood" (5T 93). White's point is that intermarriage between the righteous and the wicked nearly brought the line of the righteous to extinction. The last eight of the righteous boarded the ark. Thus intermarriage threatened the entire plan of salvation. The New Testament forbids being "unequally yoked together with unbelievers" (2 Cor. 6:14-18) because the goal of the plan of salvation is the restoration of the image of God in humans, through humans participating in the divine nature (2 Peter 1:4; John 17:3, 20-23). This requires a life wholly surrendered to God. In the experience of Jesus Himself, White noted that among the 12 disciples, Judas became a "channel" through which Satan could "influence the other disciples" (DA 720). The warfare to overcome *self is made more difficult when believers form intimate unions with unbelievers. Thus it is seen that the question of intermarriage is not a trivial variation from the ideal, but a basic compromise that threatens the integrity of one's union with Christ.

While the theory that amalgamation referred to human-animal chimeras was present in early Adventist literature, the imputation of racism to Ellen White is not supported. First, Smith acknowledged that "in preparing these answers [to Snook and Brinkerhoff] we have had no consultation whatever with sister White, nor received any suggestion or explanation from her on any point" (U. Smith, "Objections to the Visions," RH, June 12, 1866). Second, regarding the inferred reference to Africans, Smith pointed out that if she had had them in mind, she still called them "men," and thus members of the human race, not subhuman (U. Smith, "The Visions—Objections Answered: Obj. 37," RH, July 31, 1866). Third, the interpretation that she viewed Blacks as less than fully human directly contradicts the entire tenor of her writings on race from 1851 to 1909. Over and over she reaffirmed both the full humanity (e.g., 1SG 191; 1T 358) and the creation origin (7T 223) of the Black race. What follows is but a tiny sample of the hundreds of pages she wrote against racism, and in support of the full humanity of Blacks (see also E. G. White, *The *Southern Work*; Graybill, *E. G. White and Church Race Relations*).

In 1851, thirteen years *before* she penned the amalgamation statements, she contrasted the "pious slave" who would "rise in triumph and victory and shake off the chains that bound him" with the "wicked master" who stood under the judgment of God (ExV 17 [1851], reprinted EW 35 [1882]). In 1858 she passionately defended the *humanity* of Africans in bondage: "The tears of the pious bond-men and bond-women, of fathers, mothers and children, brothers and sisters, are all bottled up in heaven. Agony, *human* agony, is carried from place to place, and bought and sold." With hot indignation she denounced "professed christians" who "hold their *fellow-men* in slavery" and "cruelly oppress from day to day their *fellow-men*" (1SG 191, 192; italics supplied [EW 275, 276]).

In 1859 she charged Adventists to disregard

the Fugitive Slave Law "whatever the consequences." "The slave is not the property of any man. God is his rightful master, and man has no right to take God's workmanship into his hands, and claim him as his own" (1T 201, 202). In 1862 she declared that the American Civil War was God's punishment on "this nation for the high crime of slavery" (*ibid.* 264). In 1863, still a year before the amalgamation statements, she declared, "Christ died for the whole human family, whether white or black. God has made man a free moral agent, whether white or black. The institution of slavery . . . permits man to exercise over his fellow man a power which God has never granted him, and which belongs alone to God" (*ibid.* 358). Two pages later she solemnly charged Adventists to excommunicate any of their number who clung to pro-slavery views (*ibid.* 360). On the contrary, she specifically declared Blacks to be equal with Whites "by creation and by redemption" (7T 223). "The black man's name is written in the book of life beside the white man's. All are one in Christ. Birth, station, nationality, or color cannot elevate or degrade men" (Ms 6, 1891, in 2SM 342).

If she ever held racist views, it must have been before she began writing. She certainly gave no indication of it later in life. The hundreds of pages of her passionate, pro-Black, anti-slavery writing certainly give strong evidence that, whatever she meant by the two brief enigmatic amalgamation statements, her belief in the full spiritual, moral, and intellectual equality of the Black race with all other humans is beyond question (Graybill, pp. 117, 118).

As Delbert Baker, former president of historically Black Oakwood University and one of the foremost scholars of Black Adventist history, put it: "Ellen White can rightfully be called the initiator of the Black work. No person had a greater impact on the inclusion and status of Black people in the Adventist Church; it is impossible to talk about Black Adventist history without constantly referring to her contributions. . . . There would have been little hope for the Black work had Ellen White not championed the cause" ("In Search of Roots," pp. 12-14).

One final question can now receive an unequivocal answer. Because one common usage of "amalgamation" in nineteenth-century America was in reference to interracial marriage, some have wondered if she viewed racial intermarriage as the sin so grievous that it brought on the Flood. This speculation is completely unsupportable on several grounds. First of all, as noted above, the premise that by "amalgamation" she meant to say anything at all about the Black race is not supported by the evidence. Second, she never denounced interracial marriage as immoral or sinful in itself. She generally counseled against interracial marriage, not on the basis that it was inherently sinful, but on the grounds of the social difficulties it caused in a nineteenth-century postslavery society, especially for the children, who often felt they were not fully accepted by either race (2SM 343, 344 [1896]). But she never opposed interracial marriage on moral or theological grounds (cf. PP 383).

Although Ellen White still used the word "amalgamation" in other contexts, references to antediluvian amalgamation were omitted from treatments of the Flood narrative after 1871 (cf. PP 81, 82 [1890], 3SM 452). W. C. White attributes this to the hostile use made of these quotations by "Southern authors," and the change in Ellen White's target audience from those personally familiar with her life and special gift to a more general audience (W. C. White, "Some Early Statements—Why Not Reprinted?" DF 316, EGWE-LLU).

Further reading: D. W. Baker, "In Search

of Roots: Adventist African-Americans Part 1, Exploring the History," AR, Feb. 4, 1993; H. E. Douglass, *Messenger of the Lord* (PPPA, 1998), pp. 491, 492; R. D. Graybill, *E. G. White and Church Race Relations* (RHPA, 1970); F. D. Nichol, *Ellen G. White and Her Critics* (RHPA, 1941), pp. 306-322 [http://www.egwestate.org]; G. Shigley, "Amalgamation of Man and Beast: What Did Ellen White Mean?" *Spectrum* 12, no. 4 (June 1982): 10-19; U. Smith, "Obj. 39" in "The Visions—Objections Answered," RH, July 31, 1866; U. Smith, "Objections to the Visions," RH, June 12, 1866; U. Smith, *The Visions of Mrs. E. G. White* (Battle Creek: Steam Press, 1868), pp. 102-105; E. G. White, *The Southern Work* [First ed. 1898] (RHPA, 1966); P. Karpowicz, C. B. Cohen, D. van der Kooy, "Developing Human-Nonhuman Chimeras in Human Stem Cell Research: Ethical Issues and Boundaries," *Kennedy Institute of Ethics Journal* 15, no. 2 (2005): 107-134; E. Check, "Biologists Seek Consensus on Guidelines for Stem-Cell Research," *Nature* 431, no. 7011 (2004): 885.

Michael W. Campbell and Timothy G. Standish

AMERICAN MEDICAL MISSIONARY COLLEGE. Adventist medical school in Chicago (1895-1910), closely associated with the *Battle Creek Sanitarium. Funded initially through a $40,000 donation from *Francis (François) H. Wessels and *Henry (Hendrik) S. P. Wessels, Adventist diamond miners in South Africa, AMMC received continuing support from the Battle Creek Sanitarium, other donations, and proceeds from Dr. J. H. Kellogg's cereal enterprises.

Ellen White's influence on the development of AMMC began at least by 1872, when she wrote of the need for "consecrated" physicians who would "keep prominent the health reform from a religious standpoint"

(3T 168). Subsequent testimonies combined forceful calls for Christian physicians to reach a "high standard of excellence" with warnings about the spiritual pitfalls of the popular medical colleges (5T 446-448). From the fall of 1891 to at least the summer of 1893 the church rented a house near the University of Michigan in Ann Arbor to provide an Adventist home environment for 18 Adventist medical students (Robinson, pp. 266-269). Despite this improvement, Ellen White wrote again in 1893 about her continuing burden that Adventist young people not attend the state university "unless it is a positive necessity" (Lt 50, 1893, in 5MR 404). She observed that "by attending such schools," "many have become unfitted to do missionary work" (Ms 9, 1894, in CT 374). These concerns, plus the growth of the Battle Creek Sanitarium, the *Chicago Medical Mission, and other health-care institutions convinced the denomination in 1895 that the time had come to open a medical college.

In 1898, only three years after the opening of the AMMC, White mourned that its students heard "insinuations from time to time that disparage the church and the ministry." She pleaded with the medical leaders not to "instill into the minds of the students ideas that will cause them to lose confidence in God's appointed ministers. But this you are most certainly doing, whether you are aware of it or not" (LLM 250, 251).

After 1901, when the former Battle Creek College was moved to Berrien Springs, Michigan, and renamed Emmanuel Missionary College, the college campus in Battle Creek was sold to the Battle Creek Sanitarium with the understanding "that the buildings and grounds would be used for the American Medical Missionary College," a plan that Ellen White supported (RH, Dec. 3, 1903).

Although "the Sanitarium and the American Medical Missionary College" "occupied" the former Battle Creek College campus (A. T. Jones, in RH, Aug. 25, 1903), the Chicago site of the AMMC remained its main campus. The AMMC offered in Battle Creek some introductory medical courses for the benefit of students working at the Battle Creek Sanitarium. The sanitarium, with 400-700 patients, employed some 160 medical and nursing students as staff. But the students would not stay long without courses of study. And to pay their expenses, the students needed the wage work provided by the sanitarium. This interdependence between the sanitarium and the school, plus the rising requirements of *accreditation, led the sanitarium leadership in 1903 to reopen the still-accredited Battle Creek College to support the Sanitarium Training School for Nurses, and to supply accredited graduates for the AMMC in Chicago (*ibid.*).

During its 15 years of existence the AMMC graduated some 190 doctors of medicine. At the peak of the AMMC's prosperity, Kellogg's "regular weekly surgical clinic" was rated by the Judicial Council of the Association of American Medical Colleges as "not surpassed by any similar clinic in the country" (Schwarz, p. 105). By 1910 Kellogg's break with the church, and the opening of another Adventist medical school in Loma Linda, California, attracted the majority of Adventist medical students away from the AMMC; to cope with the declining enrollment, the AMMC merged with the medical school of the University of Illinois.

Further reading: LLM 247-255; SHM 249-283; R. W. Schwarz, *John Harvey Kellogg, M.D.* (SPA, 1970; AUP, 1981), pp. 104-107, 171; *SDA Encyclopedia* (1996), vol. 10, p. 63.

Jerry Moon

AMERICAN SENTINEL, THE. Predecessor to *Liberty* as the church's periodical devoted to advocacy of religious liberty, the *American Sentinel* was launched in 1886 by Pacific Press Publishing Association, and edited by *A. T. Jones, *E. J. Waggoner, and *J. H. Waggoner. Ellen White's counsel in connection with the *Sentinel* during the subsequent decade set lasting markers for the Adventist Church's stance toward civil government, though debate over the application of that counsel has persisted.

In December 1888 Ellen White sought to rouse the church from "stupor and death-like slumber" (RH, Dec. 18, 1888) to support the *Sentinel* with much greater zeal in defending religious liberty against the movement for a constitutional amendment declaring the United States to be a "Christian nation." This movement, led by the National Reform Association since the 1860s, was gaining new momentum and national prominence, leading to the introduction of various measures in Congress during 1888-1889, including a national Sunday rest bill. Ellen White, aligned with Jones and E. J. Waggoner in the gospel emphasis debated at the recently completed General Conference session in Minneapolis, wrote that influences were at work in the church to undermine indirectly both the *Sentinel* and her own testimonies.

These influences had become more apparent by the General Conference session of March 1891, at which a plan was presented to consolidate control of the church's publishing and medical missionary work in Battle Creek. This overall strategy included widening the popular appeal of the *Sentinel* by muting its Adventist identity and no longer including articles that connected religious liberty with Adventism's distinctive theological principles.

Between the time of her vision in *Salamanca, New York, on November 3, 1890, and the General Conference session the following March, Ellen White described in her diary having seen councils during which these plans were under discussion. She commented that the misguided plan to take the *Sentinel* in a nonsectarian direction would backfire, for "the world . . . will look upon us as dishonest, as hiding our real sentiments and principles out of policy" (Ms 16, 1890, in CW 95; cf. LS 328-330; TM 467-471). Another concern recorded in her diary in March 1891 was the un-Christlike spirit of strife and sarcasm that pervaded the councils she saw.

When Ellen White later bore her testimony based on the Salamanca experience in a meeting of ministers at the General Conference session on March 11, some present declared, to her astonishment, that the council she described had just taken place the previous night. *Albion F. Ballenger and others confessed to having been on the "wrong side of the question" and repented of their course (Ms 190, 1891, in 3Bio 480).

While Adventist identity and principles were not to be obscured in the *Sentinel*, Ellen White also affirmed that the publication should have its own distinct editorial mission and approach. The *Sentinel* had in fact never given prominence to doctrinal expositions as such. Rather, it addressed current issues of church and state on the basis of an Adventist theological perspective in a way that made plain the church's basic teachings about the Sabbath and eschatology. While in Australia in 1895 she objected to a proposal to combine the *Sentinel* with *Signs of the Times* and thus have one "missionary paper." Each of the church's periodicals had been established to do a "specific work," she declared, and the needs addressed by each still remained (GCB, Feb. 27, 1895).

From Australia Ellen White also once again addressed the problem of sharp, ridiculing invective in the *Sentinel*, directed both at opponents outside of and within the Adventist Church. Adventists should "speak the truth in love," she wrote, and she pleaded in particular for cessation of "sharp thrusts" against Catholics (Lt 11, 1895, in 16MR 157). In Ellen White's view the prevalence of "scathing remarks" created two problems in connection with those outside the church. First, it was not winsome: it "cannot reach hearts" (1888 Materials 1485). Second, it risked antagonizing authorities unnecessarily and prematurely, stirring retribution that would hinder the Adventist work. It would "bring on the time of trouble before the time" (Lt 11, 1895, in 16 MR 169).

The *Sentinel* editors, now *Calvin Bollman along with A. T. Jones, also had taken it as their duty to monitor the Adventist Church's own actions for deviations from a rigorous standard of separation of church and state. They decried the hypocrisy of churches, including Adventist, accepting tax-exempt status. They also denounced the church's plan to accept a gift of land in southern Africa from Cecil Rhodes' British South Africa Company as both an unholy link between church and state and an imperialist land grab. In meeting these criticisms, Ellen White took the position that considerable scope should be given as to how general principles are worked out in specific locales and situations. As in the time of Cyrus of Persia, she wrote, the Lord still prompts kings and rulers to take action that aids the advancement of the cause of God, and reception of that benefit should not be cut off by denouncing, from a great distance away and on the basis of abstract theories, those "on the ground where the work is being done" (D. E. Robinson, in RH, Mar. 23, 1911).

Further reading: "The Salamanca Vision and the 1890 Diary," MR 1033, SDoc; H. E. Douglass, *Messenger of the Lord: The Prophetic Ministry of Ellen G. White* (PPPA, 1998), pp. 188, 189; G. R. Knight, *From 1888 to Apostasy: The Case of A. T. Jones* (RHPA, 1987); D. Morgan, *Adventism and the American Republic: The Public Involvement of a Major Apocalyptic Movement* (Knoxville: University of Tennessee Press, 2001); E. Syme, *A History of SDA Church-State Relations in the United States* (PPPA, 1973); D. E. Robinson, "A Study of Principles," RH, Mar. 9, 16, 23, 1911.

Douglas Morgan

AMUSEMENTS, see **GAMES AND SPORTS; COMPETITION.**

ANCESTRY OF ELLEN GOULD (HARMON) WHITE. The Ellen G. White Estate holds that Ellen Gould (Harmon) White was of Anglo-Saxon origin; that her ancestors came directly from England to New England.

The first two documented inquiries about the ancestry of Ellen White came from relatives. On February 13, 1913, Mrs. Hattie E. Potts wrote to W. C. White, Ellen's son, asking for information regarding her family: the McCanns, the Harmons, and the Goulds. Mrs. Potts was a granddaughter of Harriet (Harmon) McCann (one of Ellen's older sisters). W. C. White responded on April 16, 1913, expressing his regrets that he was unable to provide the information that Mrs. Potts had requested. On August 3, 1916, W. C. White answered a letter from W. C. Foss, a son of Ellen White's sister, Mary Plummer (Harmon) Foss. Foss had written asking about various members of Ellen White's family. W. C. White's responses to Mrs. Potts and Mr.

VIEW THE FULL-SIZE CHART ON PAGE 1298

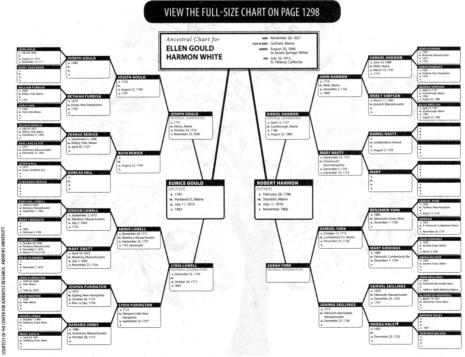

ANCESTRAL CHART OF ELLEN G. WHITE

Foss indicate that his knowledge of his mother's family was limited (WCW to H. E. Potts; A. C. Harmon, *The Harmon Genealogy*, pp. 41, 79, 80; WCW to W. C. Foss).

In 1920 the White Estate was an unintended beneficiary of genealogical research that was done on the Harmon family when Artemas C. Harmon published *The Harmon Genealogy*, which provided valuable information about Ellen White's paternal ancestry.

The first White Estate-sponsored genealogical inquiries about Ellen White were a by-product of an action taken by the White Estate Board of Trustees on July 20, 1950, authorizing the preparation of a definitive biography of Ellen White (EGWE board minutes). F. D. Nichol was selected to write it.

For 12 years (1954-1966) the White Estate staff assembled pertinent materials for Nichol to use in his writing. After Nichol's sudden death June 10, 1966, the Board of Trustees asked Arthur White to prepare the biography (EGWE board minutes). In the course of that project, the White Estate began researching Ellen White's genealogy.

Ron Graybill initiated that process on January 23, 1973, by writing to Elder Theodore Burton, director of the Genealogical Society of the Church of Jesus Christ of Latter-Day Saints. Graybill, then assistant to the secretary of the White Estate, explained that the White Estate was preparing an official biography of Ellen White; that he was doing background research and organizing the material, but that Arthur White would do the actual writing (Graybill to Burton). Graybill mentioned that Harmon's *Genealogy* had provided some information on the family of Ellen's father, Robert Harmon; that Ellen appeared on page 41 of that book; and that the White Estate had traced her ancestry back from there in this particular volume (*ibid.*).

Graybill's response suggested that the

White Estate was content with the thoroughness of the material on Ellen's paternal genealogy provided in Harmon's book. He noted that the White Estate knew almost nothing about the family of Eunice (Gould) Harmon, Ellen's mother, and his letter addressed that deficiency. The White Estate wanted to know more about Ellen's maternal heritage for the biography and for the White Estate's vault records. Graybill asked Burton about the nature of the services rendered by the Genealogical Society and about the cost of having a trained person do genealogical research work (*ibid.*).

Burton's February 21, 1973, response was quite helpful. Following leads provided by Burton, Graybill did research and also engaged, on behalf of the White Estate, the services of certified genealogists to help prepare a genealogical pedigree of Ellen Gould (Harmon) White.

The information that seems to have given shape and direction to the genealogical research on Ellen White's maternal family came in a document dated November 30, 1975, from C. L. Gould, of Wellton, Arizona. He affirmed that the Eunice Gould, who had married Robert Harmon in July 1810 and mothered Ellen, was from a branch of the Gould family whose immigrant ancestor was Jarvice Gold (Gould).

The need for further detail became apparent in April 1977 when E. E. Cleveland, associate secretary of the General Conference Ministerial Association, received a telephone call from a layman, Darryl L. Brown, who asked: "Was Mrs. Ellen G. White a Black woman?" Cleveland said he did not know and encouraged Brown to write a letter detailing his questions and concerns about the ethnicity of Ellen White (Cleveland, *Let the Church Roll On* [PPPA, 1997], p. 88).

The ethnic origins of Ellen White had long

been an item of discussion among African-American Seventh-day Adventists. Many African-American church members had often mused: "Since Sister White looks Black, wouldn't it be great if someone could prove that she was Black?" Darryl Brown's letter gave voice to such musings. Cleveland forwarded Brown's letter of April 13, 1977, to Arthur L. White, secretary of the White Estate, with a cover letter stressing that Brown's letter reflected the thinking of a wide audience and questions that were assuming increasing importance among Black believers (Cleveland to White).

Arthur White's April 25, 1977, response noted: (1) his personal surprise to learn that many Black Adventists had questions regarding Ellen White's ancestry; (2) his willingness to discuss the matter freely and frankly; (3) his desire to dispel any notion that the White Estate, the White family, or the General Conference were intentionally covering up certain points relating to Ellen White's ancestry; (4) his conviction that Ellen's Gould family was a White New England family; (5) the White Estate's position that any burden of proof that Ellen White had a Black heritage rested with those who were raising the question; (6) the White Estate's willingness to help if such an investigation was undertaken; and (7) the White Estate's heavy reliance on *The Harmon Genealogy*.

At that time the White Estate had nothing more definitive to share than *The Harmon Genealogy*, which did not address Ellen White's maternal heritage. The value of the genealogical research project launched by Graybill's letter to Elder Burton in early 1973 was now apparent. Unfortunately, that genealogical research had not yet yielded substantive and definitive results regarding Ellen White's maternal lineage. A Ron Graybill letter dated August 8, 1977, reveals: (1) that Graybill

himself had been doing genealogical research that he characterized as preliminary; (2) that his research did not support the contention that Ellen White had Black ancestry; (3) the White Estate's inability, but not unwillingness, to provide a definitive answer based on genealogical research; (4) Graybill's conviction that this matter could not "be finally settled without a very thorough genealogical study and perhaps not even then"; and (5) that on this matter the White Estate could not answer with clarity, partly because its staff did not have the time to do the research (R. Graybill to W. L. Johns). The Ellen White biography was the project consuming the time of Arthur White and the White Estate staff. Thus, in 1978, Arthur White asked the White Estate board to replace him as secretary so that he might give full time to working on the biography, and so that a successor could give more time to other pressing concerns. That request was granted (5Bio 12).

Following a May 20, 1982, action of the board, the White Estate hired professional genealogist Alice Soule to trace Ellen White's lineage on her mother's side. The following points fueled the White Estate's commitment to the genealogy project in early 1983: (1) the desire to develop Ellen White's genealogical chart back to her great-great-great-grandparents; (2) the resolve to maximize the degree of certainty for each name on the chart; (3) the belief that the larger family connections had been made and that the genealogical task now involved filling in the missing pieces; (4) the fact that the Gould family tree had not been fully developed back to five generations before Ellen (it had stopped with Eunice (Gould) Harmon's grandmother, Lydia Purrington; hence, there was need for information on at least two more generations of the Purrington family); (5) the fact that, after all, the White Estate

599

was not content with the information in hand about Ellen's paternal pedigree and wanted more information about Ellen's paternal grandmother, Sarah York, as well as more information about the Skillings and Hasty family connections; and (6) the White Estate's hope that this genealogical research project would be completed during 1983 (Graybill to Soule; Soule to Graybill; Graybill to Soule).

In 1983 the White Estate completed this research project contracted with the professional genealogists. The desire to have Ellen White's family tree developed to five generations before her was almost achieved. The exception comes on her father's side. An ancestral chart was printed in 1983 that reached "back five generations on Ellen's maternal side to John Gold, son of Jarvis and Mary Gold," who had come to Hingham, Massachusetts, from Kent County, England, in 1635 on "the ship *Elizabeth* with Clement Bates" (White Estate "Statement of Present Knowledge"; Gould, "The Family").

The matter rested there until March 2000, when the White Estate engaged the services of board-certified genealogist Roger D. Joslyn, president of the American Society of Genealogists. And what prompted the hiring of another genealogist? Several items that we have noted before come back into play here: 1. Ron Graybill's conviction that this matter could not be finally settled without a very thorough genealogical study and "perhaps not even then" (Graybill to Johns). 2. The 1997 publication of E. E. Cleveland's autobiography, *Let the Church Roll On*, in which he asserts his conviction that Ellen White was a Black woman; that she had Black roots. Cleveland reports that C. E. Dudley was profoundly impacted by his book and its position on Ellen White's ethnicity (Newborn/Cleveland interview). 3. Arthur White's letter of April 25,

1977, in which he maintained that "any burden of proof in this line would have to rest with those who are raising the question."

Charles E. Dudley, Sr., a retired church administrator, took on that burden of proof and launched an inquiry into Ellen White's pedigree. Dudley maintains that this line of inquiry was prompted, in part, by what he considered to be a denial of Ellen White's Negro/Indian heritage (Dudley, p. 23). In light of such dramatic assertions, the White Estate and Dudley corresponded throughout 1999. White Estate representatives met with the Dudleys on October 28, 1999. Dudley stated at that meeting that while there was no question in his mind that Ellen White was of mixed blood, additional research was needed to document his conviction. It was agreed that at that time genealogical research had not established that Ellen White had mixed-blood heritage, but that research would continue. Even so, Dudley published his convictions in November 1999 in his book: *The Genealogy of Ellen Gould Harmon White: The Prophetess of the Seventh-day Adventist Church, and the Story of the Growth and Development of the Seventh-day Adventist Denomination as It Relates to African-Americans.*

Dudley wrote that the ethnic background of Ellen Gould (Harmon) White had been discussed for years and that many had considered Sister White a *soul sister* (Dudley p. 18). Dudley took seriously the idea of confirming and circulating the notions that: (1) Ellen White was Black; (2) Eunice *Gould* Harmon, Ellen's mother, was a mulatto whose roots can be traced to New Jersey and the Caribbean; and (3) Ellen's father, Robert Harmon, had roots from the African/Moor/Nanticoke Indian and English *Colored people* living on the eastern shores of Delaware (Dudley, p. 33).

In December 1999 the White Estate released *A Statement of Present Knowledge* entitled: "Was Ellen White of Mixed-Blood Ancestry?" The statement summarized the White Estate's understanding of Ellen White's genealogy and the White Estate's interaction with Dudley.

During its January 7-9, 2000, meetings, the White Estate Board of Trustees was apprized of Dudley's new book and of the White Estate staff's interaction with him. In response to the significant claims of Dudley's book, and in keeping with the White Estate staff promise to assist Dudley in his research into Ellen White's genealogy, the board voted to commission another research project into the genealogical background of Ellen White (EGWE board minutes).

The task of finding and engaging the services of a professional genealogist fell to Tim Poirier, associate director and archivist of the Ellen G. White Estate, Inc. Poirier spent several weeks searching and enquiring before his March 15, 2000, contact with Roger D. Joslyn. As a genealogist, Joslyn specializes in New Jersey and New England. His official report was received by the White Estate May 8, 2002 (and updated April 9, 2003). The following excerpts summarize Mr. Joslyn's findings: "Basically, the Gould ancestry of Ellen Gould (Harmon)White remains as established in the past—that her mother, Eunice (Gould) Harmon, traces back through her father, Joseph Goold/Gould, an American Revolutionary soldier who after the war moved from Kittery to Portland, Maine; to his father, Joseph Gould of Kittery [, Maine]; to his father, yet another Joseph Gould, who settled in Kittery in the first decade of the eighteenth century and was likely from Taunton, Massachusetts; to his father, John Gould of Taunton and probably the one born in Hingham, Massachusetts Bay Colony, to Jarvis Gold, a 1635 immigrant from England. . . . ["That the John born to

Jarvis and Mary Gould was the one who went to Taunton is established through land records."]

"The focus of the research was on finding primary evidence, preferably in primary documents, linking Ellen Gould (Harmon) White to her parents, her mother to *her* parents, and so on back through the Gould ancestral line. . . . The results are somewhat mixed, so that there is not a clear, unbroken chain of Ellen's ancestry based on solid evidence. On the other hand, the information that is presented in this report . . . is fairly consistent with respect to Ellen's Gould ancestry, with no obvious contrary evidence suggesting her Gould line could be traced in another direction. . . .

"All in all, I have concluded that there is no, or even a hint of, evidence among the material I sought independently or that was provided me from either the Ellen G. White Estate records or Dr. Dudley's research that there is a connection between the Gould family ancestral to Ellen Gould (Harmon) White and those of the name Gould who settled in Gouldtown, New Jersey, from the West Indies.

"Dr. Dudley is correct on one point, however, and that is it makes no difference what Ellen's racial heritage was with respect to the person she was. For historical accuracy, however, it cannot be claimed she had any known ancestry that could be classified as non-white, at least not through her Gould line ancestry based on the research conducted for this report."

Dudley has challenged Joslyn's conclusions and continues his line of inquiry. The White Estate maintains that since no documented evidence to the contrary has been found and until such time as genealogical evidence to the contrary is found, it can arrive at no other conclusion than that Ellen Gould (Harmon) White was of Anglo-Saxon origin, that her ancestors came directly from England to New England in 1635.

Further reading: 1Bio 17, 18, 487; C. E. Dudley, Sr., *The Genealogy of Ellen Gould Harmon White* (Nashville: Dudley Publishing, 1999); J. R. Nix, "Ellen White's Racial Background," "Ellen White and Current Issues" Symposium, CAR (2005), vol. 1, pp. 26-40; White Estate, "A Statement of Present Knowledge" (December 1999, SDoc); J. Nix, "Report of Meeting Between Elder Charles Dudley, Sr., and Representatives From the Ellen G. White Estate" (Oct. 28, 1999, EGWE-GC); R. D. Graybill, "Leaves From Ellen White's Family Album," *Adventist Heritage* (Spring 1982): 18; A. C. Harmon, *The Harmon Genealogy: Comprising All Branches in New England* (Washington, D.C.: Gibson Bros., 1920); Roger D. Joslyn, "The Genealogy of Ellen G. White: A Report Based Upon Currently Available Records," www.whiteestate.org/issues/genealogy.html.

Craig H. Newborn

ANDREWS UNIVERSITY, see **BATTLE CREEK COLLEGE**; **EMMANUEL MISSIONARY COLLEGE**.

ANGELS. Supernatural beings who have played a crucial role in the great controversy between Christ and Satan. Ellen White subscribes to the biblical teaching regarding the existence of angels. They are superior to human beings (Ps. 8:5) and were created by God (Ps. 148:2, 5). But not all of these beings are angels of God; some are the devil's angels (Matt. 25:41), who became evil when they "sinned" (2 Peter 2:4) and left "their first estate" (Jude 6). There are various orders of angels (4SP 331), such as "the archangel" (Jude 9), "cherubims" (Gen. 3:24), and "seraphims" (Isa. 6:2). Angels were a living reality to Ellen White. Her descriptions of their appearance, activity, and visitations have the ring of an eyewitness account.

Ellen White's writings trace the origin, history, and destiny of angels in connection with the cosmic history of sin (GC xi, 511). Her most significant statements regarding this largely unseen struggle may be divided into three main sections: (1) the events relating to the origin of evil and the early history of this earth up to Israel's entrance into Canaan; (2) the events surrounding Christ's earthly ministry and the period of the early Christian church; and (3) the events related to the Second Coming, the close of the millennium, and the hereafter. The activity of angels in the intervening centuries she describes in much less detail.

"Lucifer . . . [the] first of the covering cherubs" (GC 493, 494), was "the highest of all created beings" (DA 758). "Not content with his position, . . . he ventured to covet the homage due alone to the Creator" (PP 35), who was Christ (5T 421). Evil originated with him when he indulged this presumptuous aspiration (16MR 180). "One third of the angels" joined him in his rebellion (5T 291). As a consequence "Satan and all his sympathizers were cast out of heaven" (RH, May 30, 1899). After his expulsion, Gabriel took "the position from which Satan fell" (ST, June 3, 1897; DA 693). After he was cast out, Satan introduced sin into our world by seducing Adam and Eve into eating the fruit of the forbidden tree (Gen. 3:1-7).

Even before the Fall, angels could be visible or invisible to humans, at will. Satan possessed this power, for when he tempted Eve, she did not see him as he really was, but saw instead a serpent, which he used "as a medium" (1SP 36). Satan can even transform himself "into an angel of light" (2 Cor. 11:14), and so can his angels (RH, Apr. 1, 1875). Ever since Satan uttered his original lie (Gen. 3:4-6) that when one dies, one really doesn't die, but rather one's soul or spirit survives as a conscious entity, he and his angels have perpetuated this falsehood by personating the dead. When God's angels appear as human beings, they are often described as taking male form (e.g., Gen. 18:1-8). Ellen White described as a "young man" (LS 208) the angel whom she frequently saw in her visions.

Good and evil angels contend for control of the eternal destiny of human beings. "Could our eyes be opened," wrote Ellen White, ". . . we should see evil angels all around us, urging their presence upon us, and watching for an opportunity to tempt and overthrow us; we should also see holy angels guarding us, and with their light and power pressing back the evil angels" (HS 156). "The battles waging between . . . [good and evil angels] are as real as those fought by the armies of this world" (PK 176), but let us ever remember that "a word of prayer to the Lord Jesus goes like an arrow to the throne of God, and angels of God are sent to the field of battle. The tide is turned" (HP 297).

Since evil angels can observe us, while we cannot observe them, they possess enormous powers to deceive. Humans cannot hope to cope with angelic deceptions in merely human strength. Furthermore, since evil angels can also appear as "angels of light" (ST, Apr. 12, 1883), it behooves us to be cautious about accepting every preternatural manifestation as from God. Humans can thwart demonic devices only the way that Christ met Satan in the wilderness of temptation—with the Word of God. They must compare Scripture with what the supernatural being teaches, or even implies by its presence (RH, July 2, 1889). "The people of God must be prepared to withstand these [evil] spirits with the Bible truth that the dead know not anything, and that they who appear to them are the spirits of devils" (EW 87). Ellen White says that near the end of time both good and evil angels will appear with increasing frequency on the stage of earthly affairs (RH, Aug. 5, 1909).

Further reading: The Truth About Angels; PP 33-43, 65; DA 143, 700-715, 779-781, 788-790; AA 145-154, 434, 435; GC 511-517, 630-632; D. E. Mansell, *The Truth About Angels* (PPPA, 1996); D. E. Mansell and V. W. Mansell, *Angels and the Unseen Conflict* (PPPA, 2000).

Donald E. Mansell

ANIMAL ETHICS. In view of Ellen White's well-known advocacy of vegetarianism it is of interest to discover her understanding of the moral relationship between humans and animals. It is clear that for Ellen White humans are in a special moral and existential category above the animals. God is said to have made the animals "to minister to man's comfort and happiness, to serve him, and to be controlled by him. But this power was not to be used to cause pain by harsh punishment or cruel exaction" (ST, Nov. 25, 1880; cf. PP 442). "The beast is trained to be submissive to his master. The master is mind, judgment, and will for his beast" (CE 6). Furthermore, she contrasts humans with beasts in that the former have a "soul" to save, which the beast does not (AH 168; MH 203; GCB, Oct. 1, 1899). She views human lives as more valuable than animal lives (2SM 427).

Ellen White urges the duty of relieving the suffering of both humans and animals (2MCP 514; PP 443), but voices opposition to lavishing care and affection on animals while ignoring human suffering (AH 168; MH 203, 204; RH, Nov. 6, 1888; RH, Oct. 27, 1885). She declares that showing greater care for animals than for humans illustrates the working of all false religions. "Every religion that wars against the sovereignty of God defrauds man of the glory which was his at the creation, and which is to be restored to him in Christ. Every false religion teaches its adherents to be careless of human needs, sufferings, and rights" (DA 287).

Ellen White did not, however, see human superiority over the animals as justification for cruel treatment. Commenting on Balaam's beating of his donkey, she states that humans who are cruel to animals face God's judgment, and unless they overcome the disposition to cruelty they will never enter heaven. "Harsh treatment, even to the brutes, is offensive to God," she declares. "Abuse to animals, or suffering brought on them by neglect, is a sin" (ST, Nov. 25, 1880). "He who will abuse animals because he has them in his power is both a coward and a tyrant. A disposition to cause pain, whether to our fellow men or to the brute creation, is satanic" (PP 443; 2MCP 514).

Part of the reason for treating animals with compassion is that "animals have a kind of dignity and self-respect, akin to that possessed by human beings. If abused, . . . their spirits will be crushed, and they will become nervous, irritable, and ungovernable" (ST, Nov. 25, 1880). "The intelligence displayed by many dumb animals approaches so closely to human intelligence that it is a mystery. The animals see and hear and love and fear and suffer. . . . They form attachments for man which are not broken without great suffering to them" (MH 315, 316). Thus animals are said to have affections and to be capable of grief.

While generally promoting vegetarianism on physical and spiritual grounds, after 1894 Ellen White cites the extreme suffering caused in the slaughter process as a moral argument against eating meat (TSDF 72; 7MR 422, 423). She also says, "The moral evils of a flesh diet are not less marked than are the physical ills. . . . Think of the cruelty to animals that meat eating involves, and its effect on those who inflict and those who behold it. How it destroys the tenderness with which we should regard these creatures of God!" (MH 315). She *never*, however, argues that eating meat is wrong because animals have equal rights with or are kin to humans.

In sum, Ellen White sees humans as superior to animals, and human interests as taking precedence over animal interests. It would appear that her understanding of our moral obligations to animals is rooted ultimately in God's ownership of and care for the animals. "Will you go out and begin to kick and scold your cattle, and beat them, and bruise them? They are God's dumb animals and cannot retaliate. He made them. You must respect your cattle" (1SAT 198). Thus she appears to take an "indirect duty" moral model for the treatment of animals, "indirect" in the sense that, by fulfilling direct duties to God's animals, humans indirectly fulfill duties to God.

Stephen Bauer

ANIMALS, ELLEN WHITE'S. Though Ellen White had a watchdog named Tiglath-pileser at her Sunnyside home in Australia (4Bio 213; 5Bio 19), there is no known written record of indoor pets in the White home. Yet she took a genuine interest in the welfare of her farm animals. Ellen White felt that God directed in her selection of Charlie, a faithful horse given to the White family to draw a donated carriage (1Bio 178). Ellen White bought milk cows in Australia, did not use the customary confinements for milking, treated them gently, and wrote that her cows were "docile" (4Bio 225, 226). Through the years she named several of her farm animals. Grace Jacques, Ellen White's granddaughter, remembered a canary kept in the kitchen of Ellen White's Elmshaven home. Alma McKibbin recalled seeing Ellen White sitting in her Elmshaven garden with newly hatched chicks in her lap. She owned livestock at her northern

California home, and enjoyed going out to see the new calves (cf. Lt 91, 1904). Ellen White wrote several times of her discomfort in seeing animals mistreated (1T 25). One of her objections to a flesh diet was the "cruelty to animals" that such a diet involves (MH 315). "A disposition to cause pain," she wrote, "whether to our fellow men or to the brute creation, is satanic" (PP 443).

Cindy Tutsch

ANNIHILATION, see **WICKED, FATE OF THE.**

APOCRYPHA, ELLEN G. WHITE'S USE OF THE. Eight references to the Apocrypha appear in Ellen White's earliest writings, raising the question whether she considered the Apocrypha to be inspired Scripture. Many of the English Bibles used by Millerites and early Adventists included the Apocrypha. The large family Bible in Ellen White's childhood home, printed in Boston in 1822, was one of these Bibles. Until 1827, Bibles printed by the British and Foreign Bible Society included the Apocrypha in a separate section between the Old and New Testaments. Consequently the apocryphal books were familiar to most English-speaking Christians in the 1840s. Although many Christians did not consider them as inspired, allusions to the Apocrypha were not uncommon because even Protestants believed that much wisdom and even truth could be found in these writings. Early Adventists also acknowledged that relevant information and historical facts could be found in the Apocrypha. This was particularly true of the book of 2 Esdras, which contains visions filled with symbols and apocalyptic prophecies.

In May 1847 James White published a booklet titled *A Word to the "Little Flock,"* which included references to 2 Esdras in his own article on the seven last plagues (pp. 2, 3), and in his footnotes to two letters from

Ellen White (pp. 15-20). These references suggest that James White and his early Adventist readers viewed the book of 2 Esdras as a source of information on last-day events.

Ellen White's first published writing was a letter addressed to *Enoch Jacobs regarding her first vision. That letter in the *Day-Star* of January 24, 1846, contained two allusions to the Apocrypha. For many Millerites who were struggling to understand the meaning of the 1844 *disappointment, her vision seemed to be a confirmation of what other Millerites were discovering through prayerful Bible study. The original letter in the *Day-Star* did not contain many direct references to Scripture, but when James White republished this letter in *A Word to the "Little Flock"* under the title "To the Remnant Scattered Abroad" (pp. 14-18), he added, in footnotes, more than 40 references supporting biblical allusions made by Ellen White, including two taken from 2 Esdras 2 (notes V and LL). Her second published document alluding to apocryphal sources was a letter to Joseph Bates of April 7, 1847, also published in *A Word to the "Little Flock"* (pp. 18-20). To this letter James White also added footnotes with references to Scripture, among which were four references to 2 Esdras and one to the Wisdom of Solomon (notes M, N, T, U, and BB). Should these references lead us to believe that Ellen White considered the Apocrypha as inspired Scripture?

A comparison between Ellen White's letters and their corresponding apocryphal references shows obvious similarities in wording in some cases, while other references are more elusive. While this indicates that Ellen White was conscious of the content and wording of 2 Esdras and Wisdom of Solomon, we have no way of knowing whether she intended to quote from them directly. Clearly these allusions reflect her familiarity with apocryphal texts but do not necessarily indicate that she considered them as inspired. James White's insertion of biblical references in his wife's writings gave credibility to her gift of prophecy and to her visions. What perhaps enlightens us most about these footnote references inserted by her husband is that although Ellen White did not include any of those references in subsequent publications of her visions, she nevertheless left all the textual allusions intact (see EW 13-20, 32-35). Since many Bibles included the Apocrypha, early Adventists likely read these books and were familiar with them, especially those with an apocalyptic motif such as 2 Esdras. It is therefore understandable that among his references to Scripture, James White would also give references to the Apocrypha where Ellen White's letters contained allusions to them.

On January 26, 1850, Ellen White had a vision concerning the end-time preparation of God's people awaiting the return of Christ. Toward the end of the manuscript that she wrote to describe this vision, she discusses the importance of the Word of God and makes an obscure reference to the Apocrypha as "the hidden book" and remarks that "the wise of these last days should understand it" (Ms 4, 1850, in 16MR 34). This statement has no parallel elsewhere in her writings, and it is difficult to know with certainty what she really intended to say by this reference to the Apocrypha. The immediate context refers to the Bible as the Word of God, pure and unadulterated, the "standard Book" that will judge all people at the last day. It seems logical to understand her comment on the Apocrypha in the context of these references to the Bible. Yet the passage does not make clear whether she views the Apocrypha as a part of the Bible or whether she is contrasting the Apocrypha with the standard as found in the Bible. What is it in

the "hidden book" that should be understood by "the wise of these last days"? Does she have in mind a particular book of the Apocrypha, such as 2 Esdras, or all the books of the Apocrypha? These questions remain unanswered.

This unique reference to the Apocrypha becomes even more perplexing when one realizes that it was not reproduced in her first publication of this manuscript a few months later in *The Christian Experience and Views of Ellen G. White* (1851)(also in EW 48-52). In fact, in her subsequent 65 years of writing, Ellen White never again referred to the Apocrypha. A possible explanation to Ellen White's overall use of the Apocrypha in her early writings is that perhaps she did not at first know the difference between the apocryphal books and the rest of the canon of Scripture. Once she understood this difference, she never referred to them again.

Further reading: A. L. White, "Ellen G. White and the Apocrypha," 15MR 65-67; R. Graybill, "Under the Triple Eagle: Early Adventist Use of the Apocrypha," *Adventist Heritage* 12, no. 1 (Winter 1987): 25-32; D. Fortin, "Sixty-six Books or Eighty-one? Did Ellen White Recommend the Apocrypha?" AR, Mar. 28, 2002; DF 31-C-2, CAR.

Denis Fortin

APOCRYPHAL VISIONS AND STATEMENTS MISTAKENLY ATTRIBUTED TO ELLEN G. WHITE. The word "apocryphal" has been used to describe statements and visions that have been credited to Ellen White but that are not believed to be of her authorship or authentic. Even in her own day Ellen White met unfounded reports, garbled testimonies, and misstatements regarding what she had actually said or written, as evidenced by her comments published in 5T 692-696 and TM 57. This article will look first at a number of "apocryphal" visions, and then consider specific statements that have been incorrectly attributed to Ellen White.

Over the years the Ellen G. White Estate has identified nine questionable documents purporting to be accounts of visions Ellen White received between the dates of March 1850 and September 1852. In addition, two "unrecorded" visions, supposed to have been received between 1906 and 1909, have received wide circulation.

In 1931 the nine early "apocryphal" visions were transferred to Document File 103 to distinguish them from the regular manuscript file for one or more of the following reasons: (1) they were of uncertain origin, meaning that no Ellen White handwritten original was known to exist, the copies derived from second- or third-hand sources, and/or supportive records were lacking; (2) their dating conflicted with known itineraries or is otherwise unverifiable; and/or (3) they contained unusual or questionable content when compared with authenticated documents.

In 1956, when asked about the veracity of one of these visions, Arthur L. White replied, "We can neither attest to its accuracy, nor can we say positively that certain elements were not based on something Ellen White wrote" (A. L. White to M. D. Lewis, Oct. 23, 1956). This more or less described the official status of these documents until 1987, when the White Estate staff restudied the collection, evaluated the evidence for and against each record, and compared the content and language of the disputed visions against a computer database of Ellen White's authentic writings.

While it was recognized that the absence of an Ellen White original should not necessarily discredit the authenticity of a vision, it was concluded that because only copies existed (and often with numerous variants), any acceptance of their *content* should be qualified

by a disclaimer as to their accuracy of *expression* or *wording*.

The nine visions are listed below, with brief summaries of their content, and current White Estate evaluations:

March 11, 1850 (New Ipswich, New Hampshire)—"Affliction of Sr. Hastings." An account of Satan's efforts to afflict Elvira Hastings with sickness. *Evaluation*: Internal and external evidence supports the authenticity of this vision, if the date of March 11, 1850, is corrected to March 11, 1849. See 2SG 112 for context. The document is currently filed as Ms 7, 1849.

August 24, 1850—Concerning the need for baptism of believers since 1844. *Evaluation*: Ten variants are known. All but half a sentence of the text is found in other authenticated Ellen White writings, under the dates of July 28 and August 3 or 24, 1850. The text is most likely a hybrid, suggesting that the texts of Ms 5, 1850, and EW 59, 60 (ExV 47, 48) should be preferred.

October 23, 1850 (Dorchester, Massachusetts)—On the "gathering time," the 1843 chart, and the future Sabbath conflict. *Evaluation*: Fifteen variants are known. Ellen White was in Dorchester on this date. Nearly all of one paragraph appears in *Present Truth*, November 1850, under the date of September 23, 1850. All but three sentences are found in Ms 15, 1850, which should be relied upon as a more dependable record of the vision.

April 27, 1851 (Paris, Maine)—A series of phrases spoken in vision. *Evaluation*: There is no supporting evidence for a vision on this date; however, it is probable that the unauthenticated account represents notes taken by one witnessing the vision.

June 29, 1851 (Camden, New York)— Concerning the relationship between God's people and the ungodly. *Evaluation*: A vision that has long been disputed because of its strong "shut door" sentiments. Two variants are known. The date conflicts with Ellen White's itinerary, as records indicate that the Whites were in Camden only from June 18 to June 23 (see RH, June 9, 1851). The only source for the *Camden vision is a copy provided by R. R. Chapin, one of Ellen White's opposers. Uriah Smith responded to controversial phrases cited from the "Camden vision" in *The Visions: Objections Answered* (1868), suggesting that he might have accepted the authenticity of the vision, but that suggestion is tempered by his comment that he has referenced all "shut door" expressions "that are *claimed* to have been given through any vision, either published or unpublished" (p. 28; italics supplied). By this time (June 1851) the shut door was understood to apply only to those who had willfully rejected the Second Advent message (see Lt 4, 1850; 5MR 91). The White Estate views the evidence currently available as insufficient to determine whether the report of the purported vision is genuine.

March 14, 1852 (Ballston, New York)— Extracts of a vision urging the need to be prepared for the time of trouble. *Evaluation*: No other record of this vision exists, although the Whites were in Ballston attending a conference on this date. The last half of the account duplicates the first portion of the March 18, 1852, vision, described below. The document is currently filed as Ms 2, 1852.

March 18, 1852 ("The Nations")—A mix of expressions apparently spoken in vision and summary statements concerning the time of trouble, the latter rain, and obtaining victory. *Evaluation*: Seven variants are known. The first half is identical to the last half of the March 14, 1852, vision, noted above. One typewritten copy (dated not earlier than 1903) contains Ellen White's handwritten interlineations, indicating her acceptance of its

content. It is currently filed as Ms 1, 1852.

September 1852 (Washington, New Hampshire)—The record of this vision consists of only two sentences: "You are getting the coming of the Lord too far off. I saw the latter rain was coming as suddenly as the midnight cry, and with ten times the power" (found in SpM 4). *Evaluation*: Three variants are known, one with two extra paragraphs that duplicate material from the October 23, 1850, vision, noted above. Records show that the Whites were in Washington, New Hampshire, September 10-12, 1852, and James White reported that some were "putting the coming of the Lord too far off" (RH, Oct. 14, 1852), indicating that the statements are probably authentic. The document is currently filed as Ms 4, 1852.

Undated (April 15, Dartmouth, Massachusetts)—A description of "the state of the churches" and a call to "come out of her, my people." *Evaluation*: No supporting evidence found. The account remains unauthenticated.

In addition to the nine visions of questionable documentation, two additional reports of purported visions have been termed "unrecorded" because they have no written primary documentation, but rest solely on oral accounts of questionable veracity. A purported vision (c. 1906-1909) concerning the destruction of the entire Los Angeles basin area of California, including Loma Linda, was reported by an Adventist minister who heard the account around 1950 from two elderly people who claimed to have been present when Ellen White recounted it. *Evaluation*: The White Estate has no record of the alleged vision, nor is there any record of the meeting between Ellen White and the persons named in the story as hearing her report the vision. Additionally, *after* the time she is said to have received this vision, Ellen White continued to take the lead in securing and expanding the properties in Loma Linda, initiatives that would be inexplicable if she had had a vision about an impending earthquake or some other devastating destruction. In one report of this "unrecorded vision," as related in 1982, Arthur L. White is quoted by the speaker as saying that the vision was true and documented by some who were there. In response to an inquirer about his alleged confirmation of the vision, Arthur White wrote, "I have replied that I was aware of reports of such [a vision], but could not attest to the truthfulness of the reports, for we had no records of sound witness which would support the report" (A. L. White to C. Webb, Mar. 14, 1985).

Another vision was allegedly told (c. 1908) by Ellen White in the presence of Will Ross, Sara McEnterfer, and Dores Robinson, concerning a coming storm of persecution in which the church's leaders abandon their posts and after which Adventists would arise "like a great flock of sheep . . . without shepherds." *Evaluation*: The vision, apparently not cited before the 1940s, is not found in any of Ellen White's published or unpublished writings, and, contrary to the account, D. E. Robinson wrote to an inquirer, "I can say unqualifiedly not only that I do not remember any such statement ever having been made in my presence, or found in the manuscripts which as one of Mrs. White's secretaries it was my privilege to copy on the typewriter or to edit, or to index. . . . Not only do I feel certain that she did not make such a prediction, but I know that it is not in harmony with her own attitude toward the work, nor in her confidence in the leaders of the church up until the time of her death" (D. E. Robinson to Mrs. L. Parker, Oct. 26, 1955).

A number of statements mistakenly credited to Ellen White are listed in Appendix C of the *Comprehensive Index to the Writings of Ellen G. White*, 3189-3192. These are reproduced below, rearranged according to alphabetical order, and updated to include additional statements that have circulated since the publication of the *Comprehensive Index* in 1963.

Angels Rearranging Environments and Changing Circumstances. These words and the statement that follows that the prayers for "disinterested souls" lodged on heaven's altar will be answered before the censer is thrown down are not from the pen of Ellen G. White, but are the expressions of S. N. Haskell, *Story of the Seer of Patmos*, p. 147.

Apostasy of Seventh-day Adventist Churches or Conferences. The report that Ellen White predicted the apostasy of entire Seventh-day Adventist churches and conferences is without support. She did write, "Company after company from the Lord's army joined the foe and tribe after tribe from the ranks of the enemy united with the commandment-keeping people of God" (EW 269-273; 8T 41).

Attitudes Toward Elders Jones and Waggoner. The statement attributed to Ellen G. White comparing the asserted rejection of the teachings of Elders Jones and Waggoner in and following 1888 to the rejection of Caleb and Joshua on the part of Israel is not a part of the Ellen G. White writings. Various impressive but incorrect credit lines have been used in connection with the statement in circulation.

Counsel on Planning and Living. Interestingly enough, the counsel to plan and live "as though you had 1,000 years to live, and as you would if you knew you must die tomorrow," originated in the writings of Mother Ann Lee of the Shakers, not in Ellen White sources (*Time*, July 28, 1961). Ellen White wrote, "We should watch and work and pray as though this were the last day that would be granted us" (5T 200).

Daniel and the Revelation, by Uriah Smith. The report of an early minister that Ellen

White declared in his presence that she had seen an angel standing by the side of Elder Uriah Smith, inspiring him as he wrote *Thoughts on Daniel and the Revelation,* is seriously undercut by the historical facts. It is contrary to authentic Ellen White statements that would remove Smith's book from the category of "inspired." However, Ellen White esteemed this volume highly and freely recommended it (CM 123).

France and Religious Liberty. Reports that Ellen White named France as the last haven of religious liberty cannot be supported.

Last Mediatorial Work of Christ. A statement attributed to Ellen White and bearing various source references such as *Review and Herald,* 1890, 1898, or 1912, to the effect that Christ's last mediatorial work will be in behalf of youth who have wandered from the fold has not been traced to any Ellen White source. She did write: "When the storm of persecution really breaks upon us, . . . many who have strayed from the fold will come back to follow the great Shepherd" (6T 401; cf. GC 608, 609).

Legalized Liquor and Sunday Laws. Reports directly linking the repeal of the prohibition amendment of the United States Constitution with the passage of a national Sunday law are without foundation. These must be associated with a general statement (PK 186) that points out the "daring impiety" of legislators anywhere and at any time who would enact "laws to safeguard the supposed sanctity of the first day of the week" but who "at the same time are making laws legalizing the liquor traffic."

Loud Cry Message Rejected. A statement credited to "Taking Up a Reproach" predicts that the message of the angel of Revelation 18:1 will be "spoken against, ridiculed, and rejected by the majority." No Ellen White source has been found for this statement; some of its expressions parallel TM 468, 469.

Melchizedek, Identity of. Ellen White reportedly identified Melchizedek as the Holy Spirit, according to the memory of one man. There is no support in her writings for this teaching, and the memory statement is offset by denials of others who were present when Ellen G. White was supposed to have made this statement. While she did not identify Melchizedek, she did say that Melchizedek was not Christ (1BC 1093).

Midnight, Events at. Some mistakenly think that Ellen White indicated that Christ will come literally at midnight. A careful reading reveals that God's people are "at midnight" delivered from the death sentence (EW 285; GC 635, 636), and events from that hour happen rapidly until "soon there appears in the east a small black cloud, about half the size of a man's hand" (GC 640).

Mountain Hideouts for Time of Trouble. Reports that Ellen White designated some particular mountain spots as safe hideouts in the time of trouble have no known support in any of her writings, published or unpublished.

144,000 and Ellen G. White. Nowhere in the Ellen White writings is there an explicit or unambiguous statement to the effect that she would be *one of* the *144,000. An angel did tell her, when she was in vision and seemed to be visiting another planet and desired to remain there, that "if you are faithful, you, with the 144,000, shall have the privilege of visiting all the worlds" (EW 40; cf. 2SM 263).

144,000, Study on. A paragraph selected from a letter of one of Ellen White's secretaries, expressing his opinion as to the importance of studying the question of the 144,000, has been presented in certain printed works as of Ellen G. White origin. She denied that the question of the precise identity of the 144,000 was of saving importance (see 1SM 174, 175).

Political Party or Family Name of Last President of the United States. Reports that Ellen White indicated directly or indirectly the family name or political party of the president of the United States at the time of earth's closing scenes are pure fiction.

Prayer From Ellen G. White's Bible. A description of true prayer as one that "modulates our wishes" has been credited to Ellen White and said to have been found in the flyleaf of her Bible. The quotation is not from Ellen White but from a sermon by British preacher F. W. Robertson (1816-1853).

Prayer Is the Answer to Every Problem in Life. A paragraph regarding the power of prayer that begins "Prayer is the answer to every problem in life" is not from Ellen White, but from an unknown author quoted in an article that appeared in the *Review and Herald*, October 7, 1965. The statement, as usually circulated, carries the incorrect date of October 7, *1865*. She did write: "Keep your wants, your joys, your sorrows, your cares, and your fears before God. . . . There is no chapter in our experience too dark for Him to read; there is no perplexity too difficult for Him to unravel. No calamity can befall the least of His children, no anxiety harass the soul, no joy cheer, no sincere prayer escape the lips, of which our heavenly Father is unobservant, or in which He takes no immediate interest" (SC 100).

Public Schools. There is no statement from Ellen White that "the worst Adventist (or church) school is better than the best public school." She did, however, warn of the dangers of public schools, and strongly emphasized the many advantages of Christian education over the false theories, influences, and associations connected with the public school system. See, for example, 6T 193-196.

Religious Liberty. The title of an article appearing in *The Southern Watchman* (May 1, 1906) mistakenly attributed by the editor to Ellen White. The article was written by *George E. Fifield and first printed in *The American Sentinel* (Jan. 17, 1895).

Sabbath Meal at Another Planet. The report, based on the memory of one person, that Ellen White stated in a dinner-table conversation that the inhabitants of other worlds are gathering fruit for the Sabbath-day entertainment of the translated saints en route to heaven is without support. The assertion that the words were stenographically reported also is without foundation. Ellen White makes only the simple statement in *Early Writings,* page 16, that "we . . . were seven days ascending to the sea of glass." No mention is made by Ellen White of the Sabbath spent en route.

Seventh-day Adventists Urged to Leave the United States. A statement that "the day is coming, and is not far off, when every Seventh-day Adventist will wish . . . that he were out of the United States" has been incorrectly attributed to Ellen White. It is part of a sermon by A. T. Jones (GCB, Apr. 16, 1901).

Sign Indicating the Close of Probation. A published statement that appeared in the *Review and Herald* Supplement of June 21, 1898, to the effect that a literal darkness will cover the earth as a sign to God's people that probation has closed has been attributed wrongly to Ellen White. It was actually written by a Seventh-day Adventist minister. Such teaching is contrary to her statement: "When the irrevocable decision of the sanctuary has been pronounced and the destiny of the world has been forever fixed, the inhabitants of the earth will know it not" (GC 615).

Specific Targets of Impending Disaster. Reports that Ellen White has identified specific catastrophes (earthquakes, fires, floods, tidal waves, submersions beneath the sea, or enemy invasions) to hit particular cities or areas in the future are without foundation, and likely stem from an association of ideas found in more general statements dealing with coming disasters. She did describe seeing destructive "scenes that would soon take place in Chicago and other large cities," and she predicted fires destroying "lofty buildings" (LDE 113; 9T 12, 13). On the basis of such coming destruction of cities, Ellen White counseled Seventh-day Adventists not to locate large institutions in the heart of Los Angeles (LDE 113, 114). For her statement regarding the linking of specific areas with predictions of disaster, see LS 411-414. Contrary to unsubstantiated reports, Ellen White made no prediction concerning the destruction of a *twin-towered building* in New York City or any other place in the world. She described scenes involving the ruin of "magnificent," "lofty buildings" (see references above), but nowhere does she mention any currently identifiable buildings.

Status of Students in School Preparing for the Lord's Work. Many believe Ellen White taught that should the Lord come while our young people are in school, they would be accounted as if laboring in the harvest field. There is no known written authentication of this. This concept, probably correct, may find its support in an association of ideas: "He [Jesus] was doing God's service just as much when laboring at the carpenter's bench as when working miracles for the multitude. And every youth who follows Christ's example of faithfulness and obedience in His lowly home may claim those words spoken of Him by the Father through the Holy Spirit, 'Behold my servant, whom I uphold; mine elect, in whom my soul delighteth.' Isaiah 42:1" (DA 74).

Using Testimonies in the Pulpit. A purported Ellen White statement credited to "Proper Use of the Testimonies," pages 4, 5, to the effect that her writings should never be read from the pulpit, is unauthenticated.

World Could Have Been Warned Within

Two Years After 1888. A statement reportedly found in the *General Conference Bulletin* of 1892. S. N. Haskell provided that reference from memory in a talk published in 1899. No *Bulletin* was published in 1892, nor has the statement been found in any other published or unpublished source.

Work to Close Up First in the South. Ellen White is reported to have said that the work of the church would close up first in the southern United States. If the statement was made, apparently it was made only in oral form, as there is no known support for the report in Ellen White's writings, published or unpublished.

Further reading: *Comprehensive Index to the Writings of Ellen G. White*, vol. 3, pp. 3189-3192; J. R. Nix, "The Unrecorded Earthquake Vision," AR, June 19, 1986.

Tim Poirier

APPEAL TO MOTHERS RELATIVE TO THE GREAT CAUSE OF THE PHYSICAL, MENTAL, AND MORAL RUIN OF MANY OF THE CHILDREN OF OUR TIME (SDA Pub. Assn., 1864, 64 pp.). Treatise on the evil effects of *masturbation. A brief advertisement in the *Review and Herald* described this work "as a warning against one of the greatest and most insidious evils of this age" (RH, Apr. 12, 1864). The pamphlet is divided into three sections: introduction (pp. 3, 4), the Appeal to Mothers, by Ellen White (pp. 5-34), and a final section containing extracts "from men of high standing and authority in the medical world" corroborating "what she has written" (pp. 35-63). Ellen White argued in this booklet that "solitary vice," or "secret vice," was the cause of "physical, mental, and moral evils," that it "inflames the passions, fevers the imagination, and leads to licentiousness" (p. 9). Her key concern was that masturbation lessens spirituality and a desire for heavenly things. Hence, she appealed to mothers to earnestly intervene in the lives of their children and youth, to teach them self-control, virtue, and purity (p. 10), to keep them busy and avoid indolence (p. 18). The mother should "faithfully present this subject to them in its true light, showing its degrading, downward tendency. Try to convince them that indulgence in this sin will destroy self-respect, and nobleness of character" (p. 14). Many critics of Ellen White have insisted that she was strongly influenced by her Puritan and Victorian age in her writings on the evils of masturbation and that many claims she makes regarding the dangerous effects of this practice, in particular its dire and debilitating physical effects on the body (p. 18), have never been supported by science. Others, however, have concluded that masturbation, especially when excessive or addictive, may lead to some of the effects she mentions (see TSB 268-270).

See also: general article: Current Science and Ellen White: Twelve Controversial Statements.

APPEAL TO THE YOUTH, AN. FUNERAL ADDRESS OF HENRY N. WHITE AT BATTLE CREEK, MICH., DEC. 21, 1863, WHO DIED AT TOPSHAM, MAINE, DEC. 8TH. ALSO A BRIEF NARRATIVE OF HIS LIFE, EXPERIENCE, AND LAST SICKNESS. HIS MOTHER'S LETTERS, ETC. (Battle Creek Steam Press, 1864, 64 pp.; 2nd ed., 95 pp.). This booklet, commonly referred to as *Appeal to the Youth*, was published to commemorate the life of *Henry N. White, oldest son of James and Ellen White. While on a tour of churches in New York State in 1863, James and Ellen White left their three sons, Henry, Edson, and Willie, with the *Stockbridge Howland family in Topsham, Maine. One day, after a walk, Henry received a chill while taking a nap near an open window. While visiting in the home of Ira Abbey in

Brookfield, New York (RH, Dec. 8, 1863), James White had a premonition that all was not well with their children (AY 23). James and Ellen returned early from their itinerary to be with their children. When they first arrived, all were apparently in good health, except Henry. Soon afterward Henry's cold turned to pneumonia, and he died 12 days later (December 8). A funeral was held in a nearby Baptist church, with *M. E. Cornell officiating, and on December 21, a much larger funeral was held in the meetinghouse in *Battle Creek. One of Henry's dying wishes was that he be buried by the side of his infant brother, *John Herbert, in *Oak Hill Cemetery (2Bio 70-72).

Appeal to the Youth was prepared by *Adelia I. Patten (later Van Horn) at the request of James and Ellen White. A second edition, published the same year, expanded the publication to 95 pages. As noted in the subtitle, its first section is the funeral address given in Battle Creek by *Uriah Smith (pp. 5-15). Next is a "Brief Narrative" of his life by Adelia Patten (pp. 16-33), who notes that on Henry's deathbed he appealed to "all my young friends" to "give up the world and be Christians" (p. 28). After this follow several of Henry's favorite hymns (pp. 34-39), and a collection of letters from Ellen White to her sons (pp. 40-80). Among the letters is one to Willie, including the words "wicked children God does not love. He will not take them to the beautiful City, for He only admits the good, obedient, and patient children there" (p. 62; cf. Lt 3, 1860). Later she would warn parents not to speak to their children as she had to hers. "Do not teach your children that God does not love them when they do wrong," she admonished. "Teach them that He loves them so [much] that it grieves His tender Spirit to see them in transgression, because He knows they are doing injury to their souls" (ST, Feb. 15, 1892). She assured them that Christ's "heart is drawn out, not only to the best-behaved children, but to those who have by inheritance objectionable traits of character. Many parents do not understand how much they are responsible for these traits in their children," she said. "But Jesus looks upon these children with pity. He traces from cause to effect" (DA 517). At the end of the booklet are a number of condolences from friends (pp. 81-94) and a poem by Uriah Smith (p. 95). A lithograph "likeness" of Henry is included at the front of the booklet.

Michael W. Campbell

ARIANISM. The beliefs of Arius, a fourth-century presbyter from Alexandria, Egypt. Arius is credited with teaching that Christ was a created being who became the Son of God on the basis of God's foreknowledge of His obedience. His teaching on Christ was rejected at the Council of Nicea in A.D. 325. That council used the term *homoousios* to define that the Father and Son were of the same nature. However, shortly afterward most of the bishops who had agreed to the term backed away from it as allowing modalism, which made no distinction between Father and Son, viewing them as the same person in different modes. After more than 50 years of argument and various attempts at terminology, the formula of the Father, Son, and Holy Spirit being *homoousios* (of the same nature) but three in terms of *hypostasis* (personhood) was adopted at the Council of Constantinople in A.D. 381.

The label has returned throughout Christian history to denote any group or doctrine that tends to put too much separation between the Father and the Son or tends to subordinate the Son to the Father. Unfortunately, it has also been used to denote groups who tended to disagree with Trinitarian terminology, regardless of their conception of Christ,

whether or not they would have agreed with Arius.

Another label, "semi-Arian," became popular in the eighteenth and nineteenth centuries to describe those who hold that the Son is subordinate to the Father, but did not hold the Son to be a created being. This development reserved the term "Arian" for those who held the Son to be emphatically subordinate and a creature by nature. Church historians have also attempted to use "semi-Arian" to describe a fourth-century group who proposed the term *homoiousios* to describe the Son as having a similar nature to the Father. The labels "Arian" and "semi-Arian"—as well as the common label "extreme Arian"—are often used to describe relative degrees of separation between Father and Son (in terms of overindividuation), and subordination of the Son to the Father.

Many of the earliest Seventh-day Adventists held that the Son was inferior to the Father, and a few believed that the Son had been created by the Father. Ellen White eventually rejected both these views, asserting that the Father, Son, and Holy Spirit were a perfect unity of three coeternal divine persons (Ev 613-617). Of the Son she wrote, "In Christ is life, original, unborrowed, underived" (DA 530).

See also: Godhead.

Further reading: W. Whidden, J. Moon, and J. W. Reeve, *The Trinity: Understanding God's Love, His Plan of Salvation, and Christian Relationships* (RHPA, 2002), pp. 190-231; J. Moon, "The Adventist Trinity Debate, Part 1: Historical Overview," AUSS 41, no. 1 (Spring 2003): 11-129; *idem*, "The Adventist Trinity Debate, Part 2: The Role of Ellen G. White," AUSS 41, no. 2 (Autumn 2003): 275-292.

John W. Reeve

ARMADALE CAMP MEETING. The third Adventist camp meeting held in Australia

(October 17 to November 11, 1895), in Armadale, a suburb of Melbourne, Victoria, about three miles (five kilometers) southeast from the city center. Ellen White and her son William C. White attended the meeting. She spoke 20 times at length and also many times from 20 to 30 minutes (Lt 105, 1895). She was much impressed by the large attendance and the warm response of the people. She noted that they did not come out of curiosity, as they had at the first camp meeting held in *Brighton two years before, but went "straight to the large meeting tent, where they listened intently to the word." Hardly a discourse was given that she thought could be called "a doctrinal sermon," but "in every sermon Christ was preached." Reporting on the evening meetings presented by *William W. Prescott, *John Corliss, and *Arthur G. Daniells, she wrote, "All presented the truth as it is in Jesus Christ." Twenty people were baptized on the day before the meeting concluded (RH, Jan. 7, 1896).

Further reading: 4Bio 229-234.

Allan Lindsay

ARMAGEDDON. The climactic battle between "the kings of the earth" and "the kings of the east" at the end of the world. The word "Armageddon" appears only once in the Bible (Rev. 16:16). Ellen White's clearest statement on this subject is found in Ms 175, 1899 (quoted in 7BC 983): "We need to study the pouring out of the seventh vial. The powers of evil will not yield up the conflict without a struggle. But Providence has a part to act in the battle of Armageddon. When the earth is lighted with the glory of the angel of Revelation eighteen, the religious elements, good and evil, will awake from slumber, and the armies of the living God will take the field." Clearly, for Ellen White, "the battle of Armageddon" is a "struggle" between "religious

elements, good and evil," and hence, a spiritual battle. It begins "when the earth is lighted with the glory of the angel of Revelation eighteen," and ends when Providence acts its part at "the pouring out of the seventh vial."

Since the lighting of the earth with the glory of the angel of Revelation 18 takes place *before* the close of probation, and "the pouring out of the seventh vial" takes place *after* the close of probation, "the battle of Armageddon" is fought during this interval. Although Ellen White's writings speak of war in the last days, they know nothing of a great military conflict in the Middle East that fulfills the description of "the battle of that great day of God Almighty" of Revelation.

The sixth vial of the seven last plagues is *not* Armageddon. Rather, it is the drying up of the symbolic Euphrates—the "waters" upon which the Babylonian harlot sits that represent "peoples, and multitudes, and nations, and tongues" (Rev. 17:1-5, 15). Just as ancient Babylon fell when Cyrus and Darius, the ancient kings of the East, dried up the waters of the literal Euphrates, so figurative Babylon will fall when the Son of man comes sitting at the right hand of the Father (Matt. 26:64). Thus Christ and the Father constitute the Kings of the East of Revelation 16:12. At their appearance the waters of the symbolic Euphrates—the "peoples, and multitudes, and nations, and tongues"—withdraw their support from symbolic Babylon, and when the "seventh" vial is poured out, Babylon is shattered into its "three [component] parts" (Rev. 16:17-19).

Further reading: L. F. Were, *The Certainty of the Third Angel's Message* (Adelaide: Modern, 1945); L. F. Were, *What Is Armageddon?* (Adelaide: Modern, 1942); L. F. Were, *The Trials and Triumph of Truth: My Reply to Misrepresentations* (East Malvern, Victoria, Australia: A. F. Blackman, 1956); H. K.

LaRondelle, *Chariots of Salvation* (RHPA, 1987); D. E. Mansell, *Adventists and Armageddon* (PPPA, 1999); D. E. Mansell, *The Shape of the Coming Crisis* (PPPA, 1998).

Donald E. Mansell

ASSURANCE OF SALVATION. The inward witness of the Holy Spirit (Rom. 8:16; Gal. 4:6) that one has present *salvation in Christ. Ellen White held that it is possible to have salvation without assurance (DA 638; cf. Rom. 2:11-16), or false assurance without salvation (1T 133, 134, 158, 163, 242, 243), but that genuine biblical assurance of salvation is essential to the normal Christian life (1T 242, 243; 1SM 373). Her teaching on assurance is based on scriptures too numerous to list here, but among them are John 3:16; John 6:37; 1 John 1:9; 2:1; 5:11-13 (4MR 356); Luke 15:20; 1 Timothy 1:15; 2:4; Isaiah 1:18-20; 55:6, 7; 64:6; Jeremiah 31:3; and Ezekiel 36:26, 27. She read these texts not from a predestinarian perspective, but from an Arminian conviction that salvation and assurance are grounded in God's unwavering purpose and persistent initiative (DA 175; 5T 632) to save all who will accept the salvation provided through the life, death, resurrection, and high-priestly intercession of Jesus Christ (SC 26, 27, 68).

Ellen White's concept of assurance includes three essential elements: "[1] justification through faith in the atoning blood of Christ, and [2] the renewing power of the Holy Spirit upon the heart, [3] bringing forth fruit in a life conformed to the example of Christ" (GC 256). Most of the misconceptions about her view of assurance arise from misunderstandings of these three elements and their relations to each other.

First, Ellen White insisted that the "root" and "ground" of *justification is always and only the work of Christ, received by faith (*ibid.*). (In justification she included both forgiveness and change of heart [MB 114; SC 49], but change of outward behavior she classed as a "fruit" of justification [GC 256]). "The blessings of the new covenant are grounded purely on mercy in forgiving unrighteousness and sins," and "all who humble their hearts, confessing their sins, will find mercy and grace and assurance" (Lt 276, 1904, in 7BC 931). She declares emphatically that those who come to Jesus must "believe that He saves them *solely through His grace.* . . . Through faith we receive the grace of God; but *faith is not our Savior. It earns nothing.* It is the hand by which we lay hold upon Christ, and appropriate *His merits,* the remedy for sin. And *we cannot even repent without the aid of the Spirit of God.* . . . [Acts 5:31 quoted.] Repentance comes from Christ as truly as does pardon" (DA 175; italics supplied).

The second essential in her view of assurance is that when Christ is received by faith, "the Spirit of God . . . produces a new life in the soul" (*ibid.* 176). Her insistence on the absolute necessity of this ongoing "life in the soul" constitutes the major distinction between her understanding of assurance and the popular conception that a one-time act of believing is enough to ensure eternal security. "We must not base our salvation upon supposition; we must know of a surety that Christ is formed within, the hope of glory. We must know for ourselves that the Spirit of God is abiding in our hearts, and that we can hold communion with God. Then if He should come to us quickly, if by any chance our life should suddenly be ended, we should be ready to meet our God" (Ms 21, 1903, in 6MR 32). "Sinful man can find hope and righteousness only in God, and no human being is righteous any longer than he has faith in God *and maintains a vital connection with Him.*" As the "flower of the field must have its root in the soil; it must have air, dew, showers, and sunshine," so the believer must "receive from God that which ministers to the life of the soul" (TM 367; italics supplied). This ongoing "life of the soul" is the difference between those who merely profess faith in Christ and those who truly know Him and walk by faith in Him. It is both the believer's highest privilege (MH 99; 6MR 31; RH, Apr. 15, 1884) and the most basic essential. "We may have the assurance today that Jesus lives, and is making intercession for us. We cannot do good to those around us while our own souls are destitute of spiritual life" (RH, Apr. 22, 1884).

Third, because "those who are in connection with God are channels for the power of the Holy Spirit," the "inner life of the soul will reveal itself in the outward conduct" (HP 22). The human response of grateful love to God, bearing fruit in obedience and service, is in no sense the root or ground of salvation, but it does constitute visible evidence that there is life in the soul. "As the mother watches for the smile of recognition from her little child, which tells of the dawning of intelligence, so does Christ watch for the expression of grateful love, which shows that spiritual life is begun in the soul" (DA 191). "If Christ is dwelling in the heart, it is impossible to conceal the light of His presence" (MB 41). This impossibility of concealing the divine life in the soul is the consideration that explains Ellen White's frequent emphasis on the external evidences of salvation. The lack of visible change in the life of a professed Christian she regards as clear evidence that there is no divine life within, hence that the new birth has not yet occurred. If the new birth has not yet occurred, the person does not have salvation, and any claim to assurance would be self-deception.

Summarizing so far, Ellen White held that the *ground* of assurance is justification by grace alone through faith alone; the *experience* of assurance is the ongoing life of the Holy Spirit in the soul, and the *outward evidence* of assurance is fruit bearing in obedience and loving service. Where any of these is absent, assurance must be called in question. Where these are present, believers should rejoice and not let Satan steal away their sense of security.

Her concept of security is expressed in an Arminian framework that recognizes that believers retain forever the freedom to turn away from God, hence the privilege and necessity of a daily renewal of *conversion (MB 150). But for those who yield to the Lordship of Christ through the Holy Spirit, daily seeking a deeper experience in His love and a more complete surrender to His will, there is abundant and solid security. It is not the security of an irreversible guarantee, but the security of serving a God whose persistence in seeking the sinner goes far beyond the weakness of the believer's faith. The one who keeps on coming to Him will *never* be cast out (John 6:37). Thus she writes, "All who have put on the robe of Christ's righteousness will stand before Him as chosen and faithful and true. Satan has no power to pluck them out of the hand of the Savior. Not one soul who in penitence and faith has claimed His protection will Christ permit to pass under the enemy's power" (PK 587; cf. MB 71).

One of Ellen White's favorite texts on security was 1 John 2:1. To a woman in need of assurance, she reported hearing this text in vision, quoted by an angel. "Said the angel, 'God leaves not His people, even if they err. He turns not from them in wrath for any light thing. If they sin they have an advocate with the Father, Jesus Christ the righteous.'" She continued, "He who so loved you as to give His own life for you will not turn you off and forsake you unless you willfully, determinedly forsake Him to serve the world and Satan"

(Lt 17, 1862, to *Susan G. Russell, excerpted in HP 119). Again she wrote, "if any man sin, he is not to give himself up to despair, and talk like a man who is lost to Christ. 'If any man sin, we have an Advocate with the Father, Jesus Christ the righteous'" (ST, Jan. 3, 1895).

Confronting some who were anxious and worried, "talking fears and doubts" as to whether they would be saved, she challenged, "Brethren, you have expressed many doubts; but have you followed your Guide? You must dispense with Him before you can lose your way; for the Lord has hedged you in on every side" (RH, Apr. 15, 1884). Climaxing one of her most powerful appeals to trust in Christ, she declared, "Faith comes by the word of God. Then grasp His promise, 'Him that cometh to me I will in no wise cast out.' John 6:37. Cast yourself at His feet with the cry, 'Lord, I believe; help *Thou* mine unbelief.' *You can never perish while you do this—never*" (DA 429; italics supplied).

To a mature Christian who, because of depression due to illness, found it hard to believe, Ellen White wrote, "The message from God to me for you is 'Him that cometh unto me I will in no wise cast out' (John 6:37). If you have nothing else to plead before God but this one promise from your Lord and Savior, you have the assurance that you will never, never be turned away. It may seem to you that you are hanging upon a single promise, but appropriate that one promise, and it will open to you the whole treasure house of the riches of the grace of Christ. Cling to that promise and you are safe. 'Him that cometh unto me I will in no wise cast out.' Present this assurance to Jesus, and *you are as safe as though inside the city of God*" (10MR 175; italics supplied). Despite the possibility of backsliding, she believed in present assurance and security. "If you are right with God today, you are ready if Christ should come today" (HP 227).

Her counsels on how to find true assurance underscore the truth that the ground of salvation is in the merit of Christ alone. To those seeking to merit salvation, she writes, "It makes all the difference in the world with us spiritually whether we rely upon God without doubt, as upon a sure foundation, or whether we are seeking to find some righteousness in ourselves before we come to Him. Look away from self to the Lamb of God, that taketh away the sin of the world." To others who "seem to feel that they must be on probation, and must prove to the Lord that they are reformed before they can claim His blessing," she reassures that "these dear souls may claim the blessing of God even now. They *must have His grace, the spirit of Christ, to help their infirmities, or they cannot form Christian characters*. Jesus loves to have us come to Him just as we are—sinful, helpless, dependent" (RH, Apr. 22, 1884; italics supplied).

To those who doubt the availability of *present* assurance, she cautions, "You are not to look to the future, thinking that at some distant day you are to be made holy; it is *now* that you are to be sanctified through the truth. . . . No one can make himself better, but we are to come to Jesus as we are, earnestly desiring to be cleansed from every spot and stain of sin, and receive the gift of the Holy Spirit. *We are not to doubt his mercy, and say, 'I do not know whether I shall be saved or not.'* By living faith we must lay hold of his promise, for he has said, 'Though your sins be as scarlet, they shall be as white as snow'" (ST, Apr. 4, 1892; italics supplied). "Each one of you may know for yourself that you have a living Savior, that He is your helper and your God. *You need not stand where you say, 'I do not know whether I am saved.'* Do you believe in Christ as your personal Savior? If you do, then rejoice" (GCB, Apr. 10, 1901; italics supplied). "It is God that circumcises the heart. The whole work is the Lord's from the beginning to the end. The perishing sinner may say: 'I am a lost sinner; but Christ came to seek and to save that which was lost. He says, "I came not to call the righteous, but sinners to repentance" (Mark 2:17). I am a sinner, and He died upon Calvary's cross to save me. *I need not remain a moment longer unsaved.* He died and rose again for my justification, and *He will save me now.* I accept the forgiveness He has promised' " (1SM 392; italics supplied).

On maintaining the experience of assurance, she declared that "nothing is apparently more helpless, yet really more invincible, than the soul that feels its nothingness and relies wholly on the merits of the Savior. By prayer, by the study of His Word, by faith in His abiding presence, the weakest of human beings may live in contact with the living Christ, and He will hold them by a hand that will never let go" (MH 182).

Her frequent concentration on the external evidences of salvation is an expression of her concern that many who think they are saved will find out too late that they are lost (Matt. 7:21-23; 8:11, 12). In view of this danger she often quotes Paul: "Examine yourselves, whether ye be in the faith" (2 Cor. 13:5; FE 214). "Deal truly with your own soul," she warns. "Be as earnest, as persistent, as you would be if your mortal life were at stake. This is a matter to be settled between God and your own soul, settled for eternity. A supposed hope, and nothing more, will prove your ruin" (SC 35). Again: "Desires for goodness and holiness are right as far as they go; but if you stop here, they will avail nothing. Many will be lost while hoping and desiring to be Christians. They do not come to the point of yielding the will to God" (*ibid.* 47, 48).

Most of the misconceptions about her concept of assurance spring from a few passages that are clearly warnings against false assurance, particularly antinomianism, but are not denials of true assurance. She warns that "we are never to *rest in a satisfied condition,* and *cease to make advancement,* saying, 'I am saved.' " Her opposition here is not against the words "I am saved," but against an attitude sometimes expressed by those words, that ongoing spiritual life and growth are unnecessary. "When this idea is entertained, the motives for watchfulness, for prayer, for earnest endeavor to press onward to higher attainments, cease to exist. . . . As long as *man is full of weakness—for of himself he cannot save his soul*—he should never dare to say, 'I am [eternally, irrevocably] saved' " (1SM 314; italics supplied). Notice that the ground of her warning against a presumptuous claim of assurance is the fundamental gospel fact that "man" "cannot save his soul." The one who knows he or she has no basis for salvation except the atonement of Christ will be the most careful not to sin against such love presumptuously.

A similar admonition against false assurance cautions that "never can we safely *put confidence in self or feel, this side of heaven, that we are secure against temptation. . . .* Those who accept Christ, and in their first confidence say, I am saved, are in danger of trusting to themselves. They lose sight of their own weakness and their constant need of divine strength. They are unprepared for Satan's devices, and under temptation many, like Peter, fall into the very depths of sin. . . . 'Let him that thinketh he standeth take heed lest he fall.' 1 Cor. 10:12. Our only safety is in constant distrust of self, and dependence on Christ" (COL 155; italics supplied). "Saved" is here equated with putting "confidence in self" and feeling that one is "secure against temptation." But right in the midst of these cautions occurs the balancing assertion that "when we give ourselves to Christ" we may "know that He accepts us," showing that her polemic is not against true biblical assurance, but against presumption leading to false assurance.

But the few instances of warning against false assurance do not by any means negate her strong teaching on true assurance. On the contrary, she insisted that "it is *essential* to have faith in Jesus, and to believe you are saved through Him" (RH, Nov. 1, 1892; italics supplied). Of herself she wrote, *"Jesus has saved me,* though I had nothing to present to Him" (RH, July 14, 1891; italics supplied). "The perishing sinner" "need not remain a moment longer unsaved" (1SM 392). Repentant sinners may "claim the blessing of God even now" (3SM 150). The believer "need not stand where you say, 'I do not know whether I am saved'" (GCB, Apr. 10, 1901). And the one who clings to Christ with present active faith can be "as safe as though inside the city of God" (10MR 175).

In summary, those who come to God in the way that Scripture has prescribed have every right to claim His salvation, and He will keep them to the end. Ellen White's warnings against the misuse of the claim "I am saved" were directed, not at a true biblical concept of present assurance in Christ, but against the idea of an irreversible guarantee leading to self-confidence, presumption, and casual disobedience. She was just as forceful about the necessity of true present assurance, understood in the context of justification by faith, daily connection with Christ, and obedience to the known will of God.

See also: Righteousness by Faith.

Further reading: 5T 629-635; 19MR 338-355; 2SAT 193-203; H. E. Douglass, *Should We Ever Say, "I Am Saved"? What It Means to Be Assured of Salvation* (PPPA, 2003); J. Moon, "Are You Saved? Should You Say So? What Ellen White Taught About Assurance," CAR.

Jerry Moon

ATLANTIC UNION COLLEGE, see **SOUTH LANCASTER ACADEMY.**

ATONEMENT. Ellen White's writings on atonement reflect a broad understanding of the plan of salvation that includes all aspects of the work of Christ for the redemption of humankind, His death on the cross as the central and pivotal event to reconcile humanity to God, and Christ's intercessory ministry in the heavenly sanctuary. In some instances her thoughts on atonement are synonymous with her understanding of the plan of salvation. While some of her most trusted colleagues (e.g., J. H. Waggoner and Uriah Smith) limited the atonement of Christ to His intercessory work in the heavenly sanctuary, Ellen White distinguished herself by focusing more broadly on all aspects of the work of Christ and particularly on the effects and accomplishments of His sufferings in Gethsemane and death on Calvary.

For centuries theologians have attempted to explain the purpose and meaning of Christ's death. Multiple theories, from the subjective Socinian exemplarist model to the objective Anselmian satisfaction theory, have been proposed and a multitude of arguments have been discussed to support or reject various aspects of these theories. However, many theologians have argued that the reasons for Christ's death are multifaceted and that not one single theory embraces the totality of what God intended to do at the cross. What is perhaps most fascinating is that early in her ministry Ellen White embraced all the major theories or models of atonement and supported a broad understanding of the reasons for Calvary.

In 1869 Ellen White published a small pamphlet titled "The Sufferings of Christ" (PH169) and the same year published it a second time in *Testimony for the Church*, number 17 (now in 2T 200-215). This pamphlet was republished a few more times: in 1879 as a series of articles in *Signs of the Times*, as an expanded version in 1885-1886 in *Present Truth*, and in *Bible Echo* in 1892. In 1889 Pacific Press published it under the title "The Sufferings of Christ: A Vivid Portrayal of the Humiliation, Suffering, and Death of the Son of God."

In "The Sufferings of Christ" Ellen White described the sufferings Christ experienced during His life, ministry, and events surrounding His death on the cross and, in this context, used the word "atonement" three times. In her first reference to atonement she highlighted a broad understanding of the subject. "In order to fully realize the value of salvation, it is necessary to understand what it cost. In consequence of limited ideas of the sufferings of Christ, many place a low estimate upon the great work of the atonement. The glorious plan of man's salvation was brought about through the infinite love of God the Father. In this divine plan is seen the most marvelous manifestation of the love of God to the fallen race" (2T 200). Her other two references occur at the end of the pamphlet (*ibid.* 213, 215) and also highlight the limited views of atonement that have led some people to a depreciation of Christ's sufferings and death, and of the salvation provided for sinners.

Conceivably the most basic aspect of Ellen White's theology of atonement centers on the death of Christ as a demonstration of the love of God for lost humanity. "Who can comprehend the love here displayed!" she wrote. "All this in consequence of sin! Nothing could have induced Christ to leave His honor and majesty in heaven, and come to a sinful world,

to be neglected, despised, and rejected by those He came to save, and finally to suffer upon the cross, but eternal, redeeming love, which will ever remain a mystery" (*ibid.* 207). Moreover, she also affirmed that such a demonstration of the love of God morally influences humanity to do right. "Eternal interests are here involved. Upon this theme it is sin to be calm and unimpassioned. The scenes of Calvary call for the deepest emotion. . . . The contemplation of the matchless depths of a Savior's love should fill the mind, touch and melt the soul, refine and elevate the affections, and completely transform the whole character" (*ibid.* 213). She also wrote that reflecting on the events of Calvary will awaken sacred emotions in the Christian's heart and remove pride and self-esteem (*ibid.* 212). The manifestation of such divine love at the cross was the means of reconciliation between the Father and humankind (*ibid.* 211, 212). Here we see that she agreed with the subjective aspects of the theory of atonement espoused by medieval theologian Peter Abelard.

But in the same pamphlet she supported aspects of many objective theories. In ways reminiscent of Hugo Grotius' governmental theory, she affirmed that Calvary was a vindication of God's character, law, and just government. "His death did not make the law of none effect; it did not slay the law, lessen its holy claims, nor detract from its sacred dignity. The death of Christ proclaimed the justice of His Father's law in punishing the transgressor, in that He consented to suffer the penalty of the law Himself in order to save fallen man from its curse. The death of God's beloved Son on the cross shows the immutability of the law of God. . . . The death of Christ justified the claims of the law" (*ibid.* 201).

Since the time of the early church the classical theory of atonement has affirmed that Calvary was the sign of Christ's ultimate victory over the powers of evil and Satan. This view was also held by Ellen White. "He was about to ransom His people with His own blood. . . . This was the means through which an end was to be finally made of sin and Satan, and his host to be vanquished" (*ibid.* 209). At the cross "Satan was then defeated. He knew that his kingdom was lost" (*ibid.* 211).

For Ellen White, Christ's death was also a substitutionary death; Christ died our death and bore our sins. "Christ consented to die in the sinner's stead, that man, by a life of obedience, might escape the penalty of the law of God" (*ibid.* 200, 201). At Calvary "the glorious Redeemer of a lost world was suffering the penalty of man's transgression of the Father's law" (*ibid.* 209). "The sins of the world were upon Him. He was suffering in man's stead as a transgressor of His Father's law" (*ibid.* 203). In 1898 she argued as well that Christ's substitutionary death is the means by which sinners can be justified by faith. "Christ was treated as we deserve, that we might be treated as He deserves. He was condemned for our sins, in which He had no share, that we might be justified by His righteousness, in which we had no share. He suffered the death which was ours, that we might receive the life which was His. 'With his stripes we are healed'" (DA 25).

One final aspect of atonement, and perhaps one of the first ones to be rejected in our modern world, is the understanding that Christ died in order to bear or propitiate the just wrath of God toward sin and sinners. This Anselmian (and Pauline) aspect of atonement was clearly affirmed by Ellen White. "Could mortals have viewed the amazement and the sorrow of the angelic host as they watched in silent grief the Father separating His beams of light, love, and glory from the beloved Son of His bosom, they would better understand how offensive sin is in His sight.

The sword of justice was now to awake against His dear Son" (2T 207). "But bodily pain was but a small part of the agony of God's dear Son. The sins of the world were upon Him, also the sense of His Father's wrath as He suffered the penalty of the law transgressed. It was these that crushed His divine soul" (*ibid.* 214).

This pamphlet was not a unique publication of Ellen White on the subject of atonement. In 1870, in the chapter titled "The Plan of Salvation" in the first volume of *The Spirit of Prophecy* (pp. 45-54), she makes similar uses of the word "atonement" in regard to the death of Christ as the appointed means to redeem humanity after the Fall of Adam and Eve. The same applications of the word "atonement" are also found in an expansion of this chapter under the title "The Plan of Redemption" in *Patriarchs and Prophets* (pp. 63-70 [1890]). Clearly and consistently Ellen White viewed the sufferings and death of Christ as the core events of the plan of salvation and used the word "atonement" to describe their effect in favor of lost sinners.

From statements in her other writings, we find other significant affirmations of the importance and centrality of Calvary in her theology of atonement. Unequivocally she stated that atonement was accomplished at the cross. Commenting on Abel's sacrifice, she wrote, "Through the shed blood he [Abel] looked to the future sacrifice, Christ dying on the cross of Calvary; and trusting in the atonement that was there to be made, he had the witness that he was righteous, and his offering accepted" (PP 72). "Our great High Priest completed the sacrificial offering of Himself when He suffered without the gate. Then a perfect atonement was made for the sins of the people" (Ms 128, 1897, in 7BC 913). Perhaps Ellen White's clearest such statement is the following from 1901: "He [the Father] planted the cross between heaven and earth, and when the Father beheld the sacrifice of His Son, He bowed before it in recognition of its perfection. 'It is enough,' He said. 'The atonement is complete'" (RH, Sept. 24, 1901).

Ellen White believed that a deficient view of the atonement could lead to antinomianism and immorality and emphasized the impact upon one's life of the sufferings of Christ from His incarnation to Golgotha as the antidote to these problems. A true understanding of the cross and the character of God will lead one to realize that God's law could not be abrogated or abolished at the cross—in fact, it was because the law of God could not be changed that Christ had to die. She affirmed that an accurate picture of Christ's sufferings and death on behalf of sinners will also influence one to turn to God in repentance, and will transform the life of a repentant sinner.

We must not, however, give the impression that Ellen White's views on atonement included only references to the cross. Her understanding of atonement was certainly cross-centered, but it also included the biblical understanding of Christ's intercessory ministry in heaven. A few examples will illustrate her thought. In 1911 she wrote, "The intercession of Christ in man's behalf in the sanctuary above is as essential to the plan of salvation as was His death upon the cross. By His death He began that work which after His resurrection He ascended to complete in heaven" (GC 489; see also GC 421, 428, 623). Along the same thought she wrote in 1893, "Jesus is our great High Priest in heaven. And what is He doing? He is making intercession and atonement for His people who believe in Him" (RH, Aug. 22, 1893). Statements such as these indicate that her understanding of atonement also included Christ's ministry in heaven. In fact, already in 1869 her pamphlet "The Sufferings of Christ"

pointed to Christ's entire life of sufferings as part of her concept of atonement.

Ellen White's use of the word "atonement" may seem confusing, but a survey of her writings reveals that she used the word in three different ways, from a specific, focused meaning to a broad meaning. In a fair number of instances the word is used to describe Calvary as a complete atonement (cf. PP 72; ST, Aug. 25, 1887; ST, Dec. 30, 1889; ST, June 28, 1899; RH, Sept. 24, 1901). In these cases the meaning of atonement is specific and focused on a single event, the cross. In other places atonement takes on a broader meaning and includes the work of atonement of the high-priestly ministry of Christ in the heavenly sanctuary. In these instances she refers to Christ ministering the benefits of His atoning sacrifice on behalf of repentant sinners (cf. Ms 29, 1906, in 7ABC 477, 478; EW 260) or, in a few instances, refers to this work of Christ as atonement also (cf. FE 370; Ms 69, 1912, in 11MR 54). Christ's heavenly ministry is thus seen as an integral part of His work of atonement and redemption. A 1901 statement supports this second understanding of atonement when she described the two phases of Christ's priesthood: "He [Christ] fulfilled one phase of His priesthood by dying on the cross for the fallen race. He is now fulfilling another phase by pleading before the Father the case of the repenting, believing sinner, presenting to God the offerings of His people" (Ms 42, 1901, in 7BC 929).

Her third use of the word "atonement" is broader still and, as we saw in the pamphlet "The Sufferings of Christ," employs the word in reference to the entire life of the sufferings of Christ. "We should take *broader and deeper* views of the life, sufferings, and death of God's dear Son. When the atonement is viewed correctly, the salvation of souls will be felt to be of infinite value" (2T 215; italics supplied).

In this and other instances her understanding of Christ's work of atonement becomes almost synonymous with Christ's entire work of redemption and thus embraces not only the cross as the central event of atonement but also all that Christ has done to save humankind, from the moment the plan of redemption was devised before the foundation of the world to the final eradication of sin at the end of time (cf. DA 494, 495, 565, 566; GC 503; 5BC 1101; Ms 21, 1895, in 2SAT 110-114). Here atonement is a process in time whose parts cannot be separated.

To help us grasp this understanding of atonement, one should keep in mind that early Adventism did not conceive its theological system within the Aristotelian presuppositions of the Augustinian and Calvinist systems in which an immovable and impassible God exists only in timelessness. From these perspectives, crucial events of the plan of redemption are consequently the results of decrees God has proclaimed of all eternity, nothing new as such can be done by God, and the entire plan of redemption is predetermined in God's eternal foreknowledge. Adventism adopted a different system of thought in which God actually interacts with humanity within time and space in various events of salvation history. In this system God's foreknowledge of future events is only descriptive of human responses, not prescriptive. This important difference in philosophical and theological presuppositions allowed Ellen White and other Adventist writers to see all the events of the plan of redemption, including atonement, as a linear process in which God is genuinely engaged rather than only a series of preordained punctiliar events shaped in the mind of God in eternity past.

In 1901 Ellen White described the theological significance of the death of Christ in a statement that reflects the Christological depth and focus of her thought: "The sacrifice of Christ as an atonement for sin is the great truth around which all other truths cluster. In order to be rightly understood and appreciated, every truth in the Word of God, from Genesis to Revelation, must be studied in the light that streams from the cross of Calvary. I present before you the great, grand monument of mercy and regeneration, salvation and redemption—the Son of God uplifted on the cross" (GW 315).

See also: Redemption; Wrath of God.

Further reading: R. Dederen, "Christ: His Person and Work," in R. Dederen, ed., *Handbook of Seventh-day Adventist Theology* (RHPA, 2000), pp. 160-204; D. Fortin, "The Cross of Christ: Theological Differences Between Joseph H. Waggoner and Ellen G. White," JATS, Fall 2003, pp. 131-140; G. R. Knight, *The Cross of Christ* (RHPA, 2008); A. M. Rodríguez, *Spanning the Abyss: How the Atonement Brings God and Humanity Together* (RHPA, 2008); *Seventh-day Adventists Answer Questions on Doctrine*, annotated edition by G. R. Knight (AUP, 2003), pp. 271-311, 549-574; J. W. Wood, "The Mighty Opposites: The Atonement of Christ in the Writings of Ellen G. White," in A. V. Wallenkampf and W. R. Lesher, eds., *The Sanctuary and the Atonement: Biblical, Historical, and Theological Studies* (RHPA, 1981), pp. 694-730.

Denis Fortin

AUSTRALIA. Ellen White spent nearly nine years in Australia from December 1891 to late August 1900. Her stay had a profound and lasting impression on the young and growing Seventh-day Adventist Church in the South Pacific.

Her attention had been directed to Australia in visions of April 1, 1874, and January 3, 1875 (cf. 4Bio 12). However, it was not until 1885 that the first party of Seventh-day Adventists arrived in the country. By 1891 there were 492 members in seven churches. At the General Conference session of March 1891 a request from the Australian church was presented to open a school (GCDB, Mar. 9, 1891). Church leaders, including *Stephen N. Haskell, believed that a visit by Ellen White would provide inspiration and practical guidance for this project and for the church at large.

She did not, at first, respond warmly to the invitation. At the age of 64 she longed "for rest, for quietude" and to complete her book on the life of Christ (Ms 29, 1891, in 1SAT 156). There seemed to be no clear indication from the Lord for such a visit and she dreaded the long journey, but in vision she had seen the needs and spiritual condition of the church in Australia. On the other hand, during the same 1891 General Conference session at which she was invited to go, she was shown in vision that certain members of the General Conference Committee wanted "to separate all who have connection with me and my work, from the great whole," in order to have "Sister White" "out of the way" (Lt 86, 1891). As she weighed the needs of the church, her sense of duty, in spite of her personal preferences, eventually sealed her decision to go for a period initially planned for two years.

Ellen White, with her son *William C. White and three assistants, *May Walling, *Fannie Bolton, and *Emily C. Campbell, sailed from San Francisco on November 12, 1891, reaching Sydney on December 8. Her first major responsibility in Australia was to attend the fourth annual session of the Australian Conference that opened in Melbourne on December 24. The principal item of business was to plan for a school. During the session, however, she fell seriously ill with malarial fever and inflammatory rheumatism. For the next 11 months she "experienced the most terrible suffering" of her "whole life,"

yet they were "the happiest months of my life, because of the companionship of my Savior" (Ms 75, 1893, in 4Bio 31-33).

In spite of her pain she rejoiced, early in 1892, to receive her first copy of her book *Steps to Christ, published by Fleming H. Revell in Chicago. The publisher described it as "a remarkable book" that had received a phenomenal reception in the United States. The Bible Echo Publishing Company located in Melbourne soon published the first edition of the book to be released outside of North America.

By September 1892 her health had improved sufficiently to enable her to make an 11-week visit to the churches in Adelaide, South Australia, and Ballarat, Victoria. She returned to Melbourne in time to attend the closing exercises of the first term of the school on December 13, and the fifth session of the Australian Conference, January 6-15, 1893. A month later she left Australia for the North Island of *New Zealand, where she remained until December 16 (4Bio 69-112).

History was made in the Australian church when the first camp meeting to be held in Australia began in *Brighton, a suburb of Melbourne, on January 5, 1894. Ellen White's sermons both at the camp meeting and in the evangelistic meetings that followed were greatly appreciated. With her encouragement a resolution was passed to find a permanent site for a school where young people could be trained to be "laborers for Christ."

In March 1894 Ellen White, her son, and her helpers moved from Melbourne to Sydney, where she followed a busy schedule of letter writing, speaking in churches, giving liberally to the erection of new church buildings, and helping church members who had lost their farms, homes, and furniture because of the severe depression affecting Australia during the 1890s.

Responding to an invitation from the committee searching for land for the new school, she visited the Brettville Estate in *Cooranbong on May 23, 1894. Favorably impressed by her visit, she later wrote to *Marian Davis stating that having had the matter of the land and its cultivation presented to her "at different times," she was "more than ever convinced that this is the right location for the school" (Lt 14, 1894, in 4Bio 154). However, it was not until November 20, 1894, that the conference voted to establish the school on the Cooranbong land.

In October the second Australian camp meeting was held in Ashfield, a suburb of Sydney. Ellen White's preaching on her favorite subject—the paternal love of God—brought encouragement to many (WCW, "The Ashfield Camp Meeting," BE, Nov. 5, 1894).

In April 1895 she traveled to Tasmania, where she spoke at the first SDA convention to be held there. After the convention closed on Sunday, May 5, she remained in Hobart until the following Thursday to attend the wedding of her son William to Ethel May Lacey (see *Ethel May [Lacey] White).

Two months later she purchased a small acreage of the Cooranbong estate, on which she built her home Sunnyside (see *homes of James and Ellen G. White). While the building was proceeding, she attended the *Armadale camp meeting in Melbourne in October and then returned to Tasmania for a camp meeting there in November.

Soon after her return to Sydney on December 19, 1895, she moved into her new home, where she lived until her departure from Australia in August 1900. Her proximity to the school enabled her to outline principles concerning its planning and operation. The school opened April 28, 1897 (see *Avondale College). She wrote more on the subject of Christian education during her years in Australia than in any

other decade of her life, for she hoped the school in Australia would be a "pattern school" to guide the operation of Adventist schools around the world (CT 349).

In 1899 she urged that the newly formed health food business be connected with the school. Her counsel had initiated the establishment of this work two years earlier and would play a major role in the future outreach of the church in Australia and the South Pacific region.

In her Cooranbong home the relentless demands of her literary work continued. Many visions provided the content for letters of counsel, articles for church journals, and the preparation of book manuscripts. Her ministry to the sick and poor and her evangelistic preaching in the surrounding districts touched many lives. Between 1897 and 1900 she spoke at camp meetings in Stanmore, New South Wales (1897), Brisbane, Queensland (1898), Newcastle, New South Wales (1898), Toowoomba, Queensland (1899), Maitland, New South Wales (1899), and in Geelong, Victoria (1900).

After many years of writing on the life of Christ, she was "very well pleased" to receive the first copy of her book *The Desire of Ages on December 10, 1898. She had written so much on this crowning theme of her career that two other books on the teachings of Jesus were published during her Australian years, *Thoughts From the Mount of Blessing (1896) and *Christ's Object Lessons (1900).

Ellen White's final major contribution to the work in Australia was her involvement in the selection of the site in 1899 for the church's sanitarium in Sydney and in the counsel she gave that laid a firm Christian foundation for what would later become New South Wales' largest private hospital (see *Sydney Sanitarium).

Ellen White was as reluctant to leave Australia as she was to come. But she felt led to return to the United States. She had stimulated the expansion of the Adventist work in Australia and consolidated its mission. Her Christ-centered Bible-based writings and preaching had presented a fresh and relevant picture of God and challenged her church to practical Christian living. She left to the church in Australia a legacy worthy of her prophetic role.

Further reading: LS 331-378; 4Bio; S. R. Goldstone, *The Angel Said Australia* (Signs Pub. Co., 1980); A. G. Lindsay, "The Influence of Ellen White Upon the Development of the Seventh-day Adventist School System in Australia, 1891-1900" (M.Ed. thesis, University of Newcastle, 1980); A. Patrick, "Ellen White: Mother of the Church in the South Pacific," *Adventist Heritage* 16, no. 1 (Spring 1993): 30-40.

Allan G. Lindsay

AUTHORITY OF ELLEN G. WHITE AND HER WRITINGS. The Bible makes it clear that God is the ultimate source of all authority (Gen. 17:1; Ps. 83:18). As Creator and Lord of all nature and history, God has the right to exercise authority over humanity (Ps. 96:2-6; Isa. 45:22, 23). In Old Testament times God delegated His authority to certain people called prophets (1 Sam. 3:20; 9:9; 2 Sam. 7:2), with whom He communicated through visions and dreams (Num. 12:6). They were God's spokespersons to the people (Jer. 13:12; Eze. 24:21), just as Aaron was the spokesperson for Moses (Ex. 4:16).

In the New Testament Jesus delegated His authority to His disciples and the New Testament prophets. Paul, therefore, could say in 1 Thessalonians 2:13: "You received the word of God which you heard from us . . . not as the word of men, but as it is in truth, the word of God" (NKJV). The prophetic word has authority because God gives it His authority. Moses knew that he was authorized to speak on God's behalf, Isaiah knew it, Paul

and Peter knew it (2 Cor. 10:8; 2 Peter 3:1, 2, 15, 16), and the people of God accepted them as His messengers.

Scripture mentions canonical prophets, such as Moses and Jeremiah, whose writings became part of the biblical canon, and noncanonical prophets, such as Nathan (1 Chron. 29:29), Ahijah, and Iddo (2 Chron. 9:29), whose writings, though inspired, did not become part of the biblical canon. Why God selected some books and not others we do not know. Obviously He knew what humanity would need to understand the plan of salvation. However, what the noncanonical prophets said or wrote was just as authoritative and binding for the people of their time as were the books of Moses and Isaiah (2 Sam. 12:7-15). The authority of a prophetic book lies in its inspiration, not in the book's place in the canon. But since John the revelator's time the canon has been closed—that is, no other inspired books can be added to it.

If archaeologists would find the book of Nathan today, it would not be added to the canon, but would remain an inspired book outside of the canon. And whatever theological statements were to be found in it, it would remain inspired and authoritative statements outside of the canon. The canon is simply the collection of books that under God's guidance was put together as the rule of faith and practice for God's people by which everything else has to be measured. It contains everything a person needs to know to be saved.

Scripture is God's message for all time and all people. It is the standard, the measuring stick, against which everything else is to be measured. It is the supreme guideline for every Christian. The writings of Ellen White, on the other hand, are viewed by Seventh-day Adventists as God's messages for a particular people—His *remnant church, at a particular time in history: the end time. Her writings are not a new or additional standard of doctrine, but a help for the church in the time of the end. Hence her writings have a different purpose from Scripture; they are the "lesser light to lead . . . to the greater light" (CM 125).

In 1982 the Biblical Research Institute of the General Conference of Seventh-day Adventists issued a statement of affirmations and denials in regard to Ellen White's writings (*Ministry*, August 1982). One of the affirmations said, "We believe that Ellen White was inspired by the Holy Spirit and that her writings, the product of that inspiration, are applicable and authoritative especially to Seventh-day Adventists." The denials made clear that while the quality or degree of *inspiration in the writings of Ellen White is no different from that of Scripture, Seventh-day Adventists "do not believe that the writings of Ellen White are an addition to the canon of Sacred Scripture."

It was concluded, therefore, that "a correct understanding of the inspiration and authority of the writings of Ellen White will avoid two extremes: (1) regarding these writings as functioning on a canonical level identical with Scripture, or (2) considering them as [merely] ordinary Christian literature."

Seventh-day Adventists reject the idea that there are degrees of inspiration. They believe that Ellen White was a messenger of God and that she was inspired in the same manner that the Old and New Testament prophets were. If Ellen White was inspired the same as the Old and New Testament prophets, what authority do her writings have? The answer can only be: They have the same authority that the writings of the noncanonical prophets had for their time.

Ellen White left her readers in no doubt about the source of her writings. There were only two possibilities, "God is either teaching His church, reproving their wrongs and strengthening their faith, or He is not. This work is of God, or it is not. God does nothing in partnership with Satan. My work . . . bears the stamp of God or the stamp of the enemy. There is no halfway work in the matter. The Testimonies are of the Spirit of God, or of the devil" (4T 230; cf. 5T 671). In a letter to the church in Battle Creek she wrote, "I do not write one article in the paper expressing merely my own ideas. They are what God has opened before me in vision—the precious rays of light shining from the throne" (5T 67; cf. 1SM 27).

For those who accept her claim that the source of what she wrote was divine, her words have authority. To some who refused to accept her writings as having divine authority she wrote, "When I send you a testimony of warning and reproof, many of you declare it to be merely the opinion of Sister White. You have thereby insulted the Spirit of God. You know how the Lord has manifested Himself through the *spirit of prophecy [i.e., the Holy Spirit working through the prophetic gift in her ministry]" (5T 64; cf. 1SM 27).

At the same time she emphasized her submission to the Bible, which she called "the greater light" (CM 125). "We are to receive God's Word as supreme authority," she wrote (6T 402). "The Holy Scriptures are to be accepted as an authoritative, infallible revelation of His will. They are the standard of character, the revealer of doctrines, and the test of experience" (GC vii). Therefore, she said, "the testimonies of Sister White should not be carried to the front. God's Word is the unerring standard. . . . Let all prove their positions from the Scriptures and substantiate every point they claim as truth from the revealed Word of God" (Ev 256). At a meeting held in the Battle Creek College library on the eve of the General Conference of 1901 she told the leaders, "Lay Sister White right to one side. . . . Don't . . . [ever] quote my words again as long as you live, until you can obey the Bible" (SpM 167).

Yet for her this did not negate the manifestation of the prophetic gift in her ministry. "The fact that God has revealed His will to men through His Word has not rendered needless the continued presence and guiding of the Holy Spirit. On the contrary, the Spirit was promised by our Savior, to open the Word to His servants, to illuminate and apply its teachings" (GC vii).

From the beginning the Seventh-day Adventist Church recognized the tremendous value and the authority of the writings of Ellen White. As early as 1855, Sabbatarian Adventists in conference issued a formal statement that "while we regard them [the writings of Ellen G. White] as coming from God, and entirely harmonizing with His Written Word, we must acknowledge ourselves under obligation to abide by their teachings, and be corrected by their admonitions. To say that they are of God, and yet we will not be tested by them, is to say that God's will is not a test or rule for Christians, which is inconsistent and absurd" (RH, Dec. 4, 1855). Ever since then, sessions of the General Conference have from time to time issued statements expressing confidence in the writings of Ellen White "as the teaching of the Spirit of God" (RH, Feb. 14, 1871).

In 1980 the General Conference session voted the adoption of a statement of 27 fundamental beliefs (expanded to 28 in 2005). Belief 18 deals with the gift of prophecy as manifested in the ministry of Ellen White. It reads in part as follows: "As the Lord's messenger, her writings are a continuing and authoritative source of truth which provide for the church comfort, guidance, instruction, and correction." Though nearly a century has elapsed since Ellen White laid down her pen, her inspired and therefore authoritative

writings continue to be a guiding and unifying factor in the Seventh-day Adventist Church.

Further reading: H. E. Douglass, *Messenger of the Lord* (PPPA, 1998), pp. 416-425; G. Pfandl, *The Gift of Prophecy: The Role of Ellen White in God's Remnant Church* (PPPA, 2008), pp. 73-80.

Gerhard Pfandl

AVONDALE COLLEGE. A four-year college with some graduate programs in Cooranbong, New South Wales, Australia. Land was purchased in 1894, some classes began in 1895 for students helping with building construction, and the official opening was in 1897.

AVONDALE COLLEGE IN COORANBONG, N.S.W., AUSTRALIA, c. 1897.

Ellen White played a vital role during the institution's earliest years. A temporary Seventh-day Adventist training school had been established in suburban Melbourne (1892-1894), but it did not match Ellen White's educational philosophy. She preferred a rural setting for the school in order to provide manual labor for students as a balance to their academic pursuits. During the temporary school's life span church leaders busily searched for a suitable site where White's work-study ethic could be implemented. Extensive investigations led them in May 1894 to favor a 1,500-acre (600-hectare) property at Cooranbong, New South Wales.

A remarkable answer to prayer occurred

while Ellen White was visiting the site with the search group. Their company included Pastor *Stephen McCullagh, who was suffering from a persistent bronchial malady that hindered his public preaching. He was made the focus of their morning prayers, and his recovery allowed him to preach normally again. The healing of McCullagh was seen as a token of divine favor on the decision to buy the property. From that point Ellen White pressed ahead with plans for the school, overcoming legal setbacks and financial difficulties.

White's letters and diary entries of the time make it clear she was captivated by Cooranbong's rural surroundings. The tranquil waters of Dora Creek, the tall eucalyptus trees, and the nearby blue-green Wattagan hills composed an idyllic picture for her eyes. She envisioned school fields yielding abundant crops, predicting that the future school farm would be a model for the entire district. She showed her faith in the success of the college by purchasing a small subdivision of the estate, on which she built a two-story home, "Sunnyside." She and her helpers moved in on Christmas Day 1895.

Living in close proximity to the fledgling institution, Ellen White worked tirelessly in its favor. She raised cash and loans for the purchase of the estate and the erection of buildings. In recognition of her leading role, she was invited to lay the foundation stone in a simple ceremony on October 1, 1896. Not being a trained teacher, she did not usually involve herself in the daily administration of the school. However, she strongly advocated a faculty committed to an Adventist philosophy of *education. For this reason she happily accepted *Cassius Hughes as the first principal and insisted that evangelists and church planters *Stephen and Hetty Haskell also be given leading parts. Neither Haskell nor his wife, however, were formally trained schoolteachers, a fact that contributed to a rift that developed between them and other staff members. White interceded, and her efforts dampened the crisis, allowing the Haskells to remain for another 12 months.

White was one of the speakers at the official opening of the school on April 28, 1897, using the opportunity to press for an elementary school as an adjunct to the senior division. Her immense satisfaction with the Avondale school was evident later that year in her observation that Avondale was "the best school in every respect that we have ever seen, outside our people, or among Seventh-day Adventists" (4Bio 322). "It was to be a pattern school," she wrote, that others could safely emulate (CT 349). White returned to America in August 1900, her educational philosophy continuing on as the school developed into a college.

See also: Memorials and Monuments of Ellen G. White.

Further reading: 4Bio 42-49, 146-161, 176-182, 215-227, 260-271, 287-322; M. Hook, "The Avondale School and Adventist Educational Goals, 1894-1900" (Ed.D. diss., AU, 1978); *idem*, "The Avondale School: A Holy Experiment," *Adventist Heritage* 7, no. 1 (Spring 1982): 34-45; *idem*, "Avondale College," in *Seventh-day Adventists in the South Pacific, 1885-1985*, ed. Noel Clapham (Warburton, Victoria, Australia: Signs Pub. Co., [1985]), pp. 144-165; *idem*, *Avondale: Experiment on the Dora* (Cooranbong: Avondale Academic Press, 1998); A. G. Lindsay, "The Influence of Ellen White Upon the Development of the Seventh-day Adventist School System in Australia, 1891-1900" (M.A. thesis, University of Newcastle, New South Wales, 1978).

Milton Hook

AVONDALE HEALTH RETREAT. A health-care institution located adjacent to the Avondale school in Cooranbong, New South Wales, Australia. To meet the medical needs of the isolated Avondale community in the late 1890s, Ellen White urged the building of a small hospital. She provided guidance and counsel on the building's appearance and size, and its location on 20 acres (eight hectares) near the school's entrance. A two-story wooden building with 15 rooms was dedicated December 27, 1899. Late in 1900 Drs. *Daniel H. and Lauretta Kress arrived from the United States. In 1901 they commenced a nurses' training school that provided a sound practical training in institutional and district nursing. With the opening of the Sydney Sanitarium in 1903, the nursing school moved to Sydney, but the retreat continued for some years. The building later became an overflow dormitory for college students, then a block of flats that was eventually demolished in 1935.

Further reading: 4Bio 437-441.

Allan G. Lindsay

BABYLON IN ESCHATOLOGY. In Ellen White's writings the word "Babel" refers primarily to the Tower of Babel in Genesis 11 (PP 117-124), and "Babylonia" is mentioned just once (PK 556), but "Babylon" is found frequently referring to the Neo-Babylonian Empire (*ibid.* 344), the ancient city Babylon (*ibid.* 523), and the province of Babylon (SL 37). Furthermore, the term is used in a figurative sense (3SM 257; 1T 270; Te 24), and it also points to end-time Babylon.

In discussing eschatological Babylon, Ellen White deals with four different aspects: (1) its interpretation in church and early Adventist history, (2) its character, identity, condition, and fate, (3) the position of some critics that the Seventh-day Adventist Church is Babylon, and (4) the responsibility to proclaim the messages of Revelation 14:7-12 and 18:2-4.

Ellen White agreed with many of the Reformers in declaring that the "Church of Rome" is "the apostate Babylon" (4SP 70; GC 65). This interpretation was further expanded in 1843-1844 when Adventists left those Protestant churches that had rejected the first angel's message and regarded them also as Babylon (EW 237, 238; SR 364-366; 1T 53, 54). While wrestling with the issue of organization in the 1850s, Sabbatarian Adventists even debated whether or not any ecclesiastical organizational structure would represent a form of Babylon (1T 270).

As a figurative harlot, Babylon is characterized by corruption and apostasy (PP 167), as manifested in: its opposition to God's law (4T 13), especially its disregard of the Sabbath and the coercion of Sunday observance (8T 94; PK 188); its refusal to accept God's "sign or seal" (RH, Nov. 5, 1889), and its propagation of the doctrines of "the natural immortality of the soul" (2SM 118; 3SM 405), "the theory of eternal torment," and other "false doctrines" (4SP 357). Babylon attempts to control the consciences of individuals and to suppress religious liberty. It seeks to form a universal confederacy of apostate powers and satanic forces (3SM 392, 393; 19MR 242) and "a union of Church and State" (4SP 424) and persecutes God's remnant (14MR 152; 18MR 29), using "the best modes of deception and battle" (8MR 347).

Ellen White discusses Babylon in the context of the sea beast and its image (see Rev. 13:1; 3SM 406), as well as the "man of sin" (see 2 Thess. 2; 14MR 152, 153). Babylon is the symbol of the apostate and world-loving church of the last days (COL 179; PP 124), which will undergo judgment and destruction (4SP 470). She reasons that since the messages of Revelation 14 and 18, proclaiming Babylon's fall, are given "in the last days; therefore it [Babylon] cannot refer to the Roman Church alone, for that church has been in a fallen condition for many centuries" (GC 383). Thus she included in Babylon both the Church of Rome (*ibid.* 59, 60, 383, 384; 4SP 233; 3SM 406) and lamblike Protestantism, which "speaks with the voice of a dragon" (7BC 983; cf. Rev. 13:11), churches that have "fallen from their spiritual state" to become persecuting powers (TM 117). In this connection she also mentions spiritualism as a part of Babylon (GC 603, 604).

For Ellen White the word "fallen" points primarily to apostasy and increasing corruption (EW 273, 274). Since the fall of Babylon is progressive, she says, "the perfect fulfillment of Revelation 14:8 is yet future." It will be complete when the churches are completely united with the world (GC 390). Nevertheless, "there are God-fearing men and women in the fallen churches" who are called to come out of Babylon (9T 110). At the end of world history "there will be only two classes in the world" (RH, July 28, 1904). Whereas "Babylon is a symbol of the world at large" (ST, Dec. 29, 1890), the other group is God's remnant.

Ellen White maintained that the Seventh-day Adventist Church is not Babylon. It does not exhibit its essential characteristics (1MR 296-304; TM 32-62), but rather is keeping the commandments of God. This church is called "to be a peculiar treasure" unto God (1MR 155; 2SM 397).

For Ellen White, Adventists are challenged to proclaim the fall of Babylon (Rev. 14:8; 18:1-4) "with boldness and power" (14MR 160; SR 399). The churches and the world must be warned (10MR 315; SW, Oct. 8, 1907), and in this work the publishing houses will have a crucial role (7T 140).

Further reading: GC 375-390, 603-612; 6Bio 326-328.

Ekkehardt Mueller

BABYLON NOT THE SEVENTH-DAY ADVENTIST CHURCH, see **STANTON, A. W.**

BALL GAMES, see **GAMES AND SPORTS; COMPETITION.**

BAPTISM. Ellen White recognized baptism as a religious rite of prime importance and a ceremony of initiation into God's spiritual kingdom. Christ has made it a positive condition with which every believer must comply (Mark 16:16; cf. Jesus' own example in Matthew 3:13-17; Mark 1:9-11; Luke 3:21, 22). When people are baptized in the threefold name of God the Father, the Son, and the Holy Spirit (Matt. 28:19), they thereby publicly declare that they make all worldly considerations secondary to their new relation in Christ (6BC 1075; 6T 91). Baptism is the public confession of receiving Christ into one's life and a pledge to live a new life of loyalty to God (6BC 1075). Thus, baptism is the visible dividing line between the past life of sin and the future life of obedience. It is to mark true repentance and signal the new birth (Ev 306, 309).

According to Ellen White the ordinance of baptism is a symbol of a covenant relationship (6T 98, 99) and as such signals a mutual pledge between God and the believer before the whole universe (6BC 1074, 1075). In this mutual pledge the law of God determines the conduct and sets the guidelines for the covenant relationship that one consciously enters into through baptism (6T 91, 92). It is God's grace that enables the believer to keep God's law. Thus, baptism cannot be separated from *faith. Rather, faith is a prerequisite for biblical baptism, hence she supports the view of a believer's baptism (cf. Mark 16:16; cf. Ev 306). Baptism does not make children Christians, nor does it convert them (CG 499). Rather, baptism must be preceded by faith, repentance, and genuine conversion (SR 289; 2T 540; 5T

412; 6T 94). Baptism is an important outward sign, but it is not a sacrament that is effective in and of itself.

For Ellen White the meaning of baptism is intimately related to its mode. The act of symbolically crucifying the old life with Christ and the public confession of receiving Christ into one's life is symbolized in the burial through baptism in the watery grave and the resurrection from death to new life in the fellowship with Jesus Christ the Lord and Savior (cf. Rom. 6:3-7; 6BC 1074). Ellen White accepted baptism by immersion as the only biblical mode of baptism (1T 19). Any other mode of baptism (i.e., baptism by sprinkling or by pouring water on the baptismal candidate) does not qualify as biblically valid, because there is no Scripture warrant for such a practice. She herself was baptized by immersion at her own request, while she was still a Methodist believer, most likely on June 26, 1842, when she was 14 years old (cf. 1Bio 37).

Since baptism is understood as a covenant sign, rather than a sacrament, Ellen White also allowed for the possibility of rebaptism or baptismal renewal. She particularly called for rebaptism in the case of apostasy from faith and genuine reconversion (Ev 375) or in the case of those who habitually and constantly demonstrated an unchristian character and who for years had cherished and displayed a wrong spirit (Lt 63, 1903, in 7MR 262-266; Lt 60, 1906, in 7MR 266, 267). Another situation in which she saw rebaptism as appropriate was the case of a person who gained a significantly new understanding of the claims of God's law (LP 132, 133; AA 285), leading to a renewal of his or her covenant with Christ.

Ellen White herself was rebaptized by her husband, James White, when they accepted the Sabbath truth shortly after their marriage in 1846 (JW, *Life Incidents*, p. 273). Nevertheless, she does not support a hasty or superficial

reenactment of this sacred ordinance. What is true for baptism in general also applies to the question of rebaptism: there is the need for a thorough preparation on the part of the candidate before baptism should take place (cf. 6T 91, 92, 95, 96; Ev 308, 309). Nor did she believe anyone should be pressured toward rebaptism. "The subject of rebaptism should be handled with the greatest care.... No one should become the conscience for another or urge and press rebaptism. This is a subject which each individual must conscientiously take his position upon in the fear of God" (Ev 372, 373).

Since baptism is a most sacred and important ordinance, "there should be no undue haste to receive the ordinance" of baptism (6T 93). Thorough Bible study leading to an evident change of heart, thoughts, and purposes should always precede baptism (*ibid.* 95). It is God who should do the work of convincing the heart and mind with regard to baptism and rebaptism. No one should be pressured. Baptism is the sign of a free decision of those who desire to follow the example of Jesus.

Further reading: D. E. Robinson, "Rebaptism: A Statement in Reply to the Question of Mrs. White's Advocacy of Rebaptism" (1932, CAR); M. Markkinen, "A Study of the Teaching of Ellen G. White About Baptism and the Methods of Clinching Decisions" (project report, AU, 1982); F. M. Hasel, "Taufe und Tauferneuerung in der Adventgemeinde—Theologische und Historische Aspekte," in *Die Taufe in Theologie und Praxis*, ed. Roberto Badenas (Lüneburg: Advent-Verlag, 2002), pp. 118-158; *idem*, "Le renouvellement du baptême dans l'Église Adventiste du 7ę Jour: aspects historiques et théologiques," in *La théologie et la pratique du baptême,* ed. Richard Lehmann (Dammarie-les-Lys, France: Éditions Vie et Santé, 2002), pp. 157-201; H. Kiesler, "The Ordinances:

Baptism, Foot Washing, and Lord's Supper," in R. Dederen, ed., *Handbook of Seventh-day Adventist Theology* (RHPA, 2000), pp. 582-609.

Frank M. Hasel

BATTLE CREEK, MICHIGAN. Located in Calhoun County, in south-central *Michigan, Battle Creek was the headquarters of Sabbatarian Adventists from 1855 through 1902. In 1826 the United States government authorized the construction of territorial roads from Detroit to Chicago. The one going through what is now Battle Creek was laid out in 1832. Calhoun County, organized in 1829, was named after John C. Calhoun, vice president of the United States under both John Quincy Adams and Andrew Jackson. In 1831 Sands McCamley, George Redfield, and John J. and Daniel G. Gurnsey purchased what is now Battle Creek, and settlers began to move in. Polydore Hudson opened the town's first store in 1832. Then followed a schoolhouse, a sawmill, and a gristmill. By 1837, the year Michigan became a state, Battle Creek boasted six stores, two taverns, two sawmills, two flour mills, two machine shops, one cabinet factory, and two Blacksmith shops. By 1840 there were 29 sawmills in Calhoun County. In 1845 the Michigan Central Railroad brought to the city a new level of civilization and many additional settlers. The Village of Battle Creek was chartered in 1850 with a population of 1,050; by 1860, the population was 3,508. The city was incorporated in 1859.

Battle Creek seemed to welcome various reforms and movements, making it a comfortable place to grow a new religious movement. Battle Creek citizens, led by Erastus Hussey, a staunch Quaker abolitionist, made the town a frequent stop on the Underground Railroad. In 1848, Hussey represented the citizens at the Buffalo Convention, which organized the Free-Soil Party, committed to restrict the extension of slavery and eventually destroy it. Elected to the Michigan State House in 1849, he with other abolitionists united the anti-slavery parties in the state to form the Michigan Republican Party in 1854. As a state senator in 1855, Hussey introduced a law protecting fugitive slaves, charging the prosecuting attorney at state expense to protect persons charged with being fugitive slaves, to give such fugitives the right of trial by jury, the right of habeas corpus, and the right of appeal; and prohibited the use of any jail or any prison in the state for detaining fugitives. Earlier he had edited the *Liberty Press*, the state organ for abolitionists. The temperance movement came to Battle Creek during the winter of 1841-1842, beginning with a meeting at the Methodist church. The movement soon gained momentum and spread to the surrounding areas.

All the above factors helped make Battle Creek a fertile field for the growth of the Seventh-day Adventist Church. Beginning in 1852 with Joseph Bates' visit and the conversion of David and Olive Hewitt, the company of believers steadily grew to about 24. In the autumn of 1855 the Whites and several other workers connected with the *Review and Herald* arrived in town, swelling the numbers by about 14. Soon Battle Creek developed into the "great center" of the denomination. By 1900 the congregation numbered more than 1,000 members, many of whom were employed at the printing office (*Review and Herald Publishing Association), the sanitarium (*Battle Creek Sanitarium), the college (*Battle Creek College), the General Conference, the Tract Society, and other branches of the church work.

The health reform movement has played a major role in Battle Creek for more than a century. The presence of the *Battle Creek Sanitarium, other rival health institutions, and dozens of "health food" and breakfast cereal manufacturers led C. W. Post, marketer of Grape-Nuts and Postum, to dub the city "Wellville." Only three cereal companies still remain in Battle Creek—Kellogg's, Post, and Ralston—but the city is still widely known as "Cereal City."

Though a place she experienced many trials, Battle Creek was still special to Ellen White. She wrote, "From the time we moved to Battle Creek, the Lord began to turn our captivity. We found sympathizing friends in Michigan, who were ready to share our burdens and supply our wants" (1T 100).

Major fires in 1902 destroyed the Battle Creek Sanitarium and the Review and Herald publishing plant. Ellen White favored relocating the publishing house and the denominational headquarters, and they were moved to the outskirts of Washington, D.C. Thus began an exodus from Battle Creek that over the next 20 years sharply reduced the Adventist population there. In 1922 the 3,000-seat Dime Tabernacle (see *Battle Creek Tabernacle) burned to the ground and was replaced by a building less than half its seating capacity.

Further reading: W. Gardner, *History of Calhoun County, Michigan: A Narrative Account of Its Historical Progress, Its People, and Its Principal Interests* (Chicago: Lewis, 1913), 2 vols.; *Biographical Review of Calhoun County, Michigan, Containing Historical, Biographical, and Genealogical Sketches of Many of the Prominent Citizens of To-day and Also of the Past* (Chicago: Hobart & Mather, 1904); B. B. Lowe, *Tales of Battle Creek* (Miller Foundation, 1976); L. B. Massie and P. J. Schmitt, *Battle Creek—The Place Behind the Products: An Illustrated History* (Woodland Hills, Calif.: Windsor, 1984).

Stanley D. Hickerson

BATTLE CREEK COLLEGE (1872-1901). The first official Seventh-day Adventist school. It began as a one-room school in 1872 and met in various temporary quarters until a college building was erected in 1874 and dedicated in January 1875 (Vande Vere, pp. 18-26). Ellen White envisaged this school as unique and a model for subsequent Adventist schools. Prior to its opening in 1872, she penned her first major testimony on education (FE 15-46). This testimony established Ellen White's reform agenda based on the physical, mental, moral, and religious needs of the whole person. The curriculum was to reflect this balanced approach to learning through its redemptive focus, the elevation of biblical studies, the inclusion of industrial education, and implementation of a work-study program. This school was to nurture a missionary spirit and regulate student interaction with its external environment.

From one perspective Battle Creek College proved a success story. Elementary, secondary, and college-level courses were offered on the one campus. There was strong growth in student numbers, from an initial enrollment of 12 in 1872 to a peak of 768 students in 1893. Over a 17-year period (1875-1892) substantial buildings were constructed, and an imposing campus developed. The college contributed to a strong Seventh-day Adventist presence in Michigan. Furthermore, it provided the denomination with workers.

Battle Creek College failed, however, to become the educational model intended by Ellen White. In an effort to shape the college as a worthy model, Ellen White directed hundreds of pages of general and specific counsel to college trustees, faculty, and students (see FE; CE). Ellen and James White had urged the college trustees to acquire a large rural estate. Contrary to this advice, in 1874 the trustees purchased a 12-acre (five-hectare) property in Battle Creek's West End. This locality offered little scope for agriculture and industrial education. Campus land use was further compromised by the sale of several acres to raise finances and by the incremental construction of buildings. Despite her disappointment over the site chosen, she supported the new school.

Locating the college in Battle Creek also diminished the school's influence over its external environment. Ellen White lamented: "How much more favorable it would be if the school buildings that are now in Battle Creek were far off from the city, and separated from so large a colony of professed Sabbathkeepers!" (TM 86). She was concerned about student exposure to a variety of worldly amusements, to the adoption of worldly fads, and to the pernicious influence of a large number of "backslidden" Adventists.

Ellen White was also concerned about educational purposes. Key administrators, such as George I. Butler, supported the use of the pagan classics and urged education as an end in itself (RH, July 21, 1874). Butler envied the scholarship of the Protestant Reformers, declaring the mind to be "the noblest part of man" (RH, Jan. 11, 1877). Sidney Brownsberger had ambitions for a graduate program and aimed to grow Battle Creek into one of "the best of American colleges" (RH, Sept. 9, 1880). Ellen White, however, perceived the great end of education as personal piety and missionary zeal.

Another concern was the college's curriculum. By their selection of Sidney Brownsberger as president (1873-1881), the trustees embedded the classics in the curriculum. Brownsberger's expertise lay in classical languages, and when challenged by Ellen White to introduce farming and industrial education, he confessed an inability to implement such a curriculum. Although over

time the classics gradually waned, they remained a cornerstone of the curriculum until the arrival of president Edward A. Sutherland (1897-1901).

If the classics were hard to remove, it was equally hard to incorporate elements Ellen White saw as essential. Bible subjects were initially offered only as electives. In 1881 Ellen White urged: "The study of the Scriptures should have the first place in our system of education" (5T 21). Several years later she lamented that "the Bible was for a time excluded from our schools," and she observed that "the Bible is not exalted to its [rightful] place" (FE 130, 131). As late as 1897 Ellen White counseled that the Bible not "be sandwiched in between infidelity. The Bible must be made the groundwork and subject matter of education" (*ibid.* 474).

While biblical studies eventually became foundational, this was not the case with industrial studies. Two presidents, Wolcott H. Littlejohn (1883-1885)and William W. Prescott (1886-1894), introduced practical subjects, but their efforts were resisted by students, parents, and faculty. Practical education was a key element of the reform agenda and, pointing to the Avondale school as a successful model (6T 181-192), Ellen White urged that "because difficulties arise, we are not to drop the industries that have been taken hold of as branches of education" (*ibid.* 176). But a genuine work-study program was never implemented at Battle Creek College.

Initially, courses were academic and long. Ellen White believed that this blunted missionary zeal and subverted the college from its role in preparing ministers (5T 22). Prescott made an effort to reduce the length of courses, but Sutherland moved the school further in that direction, adopting the name "Training School for Christian Workers" and introducing short missionary-type courses. Sutherland, more than any of his predecessors, grasped the reform nature of Ellen White's educational ideals. He endeavored to implement those ideals, but found that the size of the campus, its urban location, and proximity to a large Adventist population presented insuperable hurdles to genuine educational reform. The solution was closure and relocation to a more favorable environment. This was agreed to. The college closed at the end of the spring term 1901 and relocated to Berrien Springs, Michigan, where it was renamed Emmanuel Missionary College and in 1960 became Andrews University.

Further reading: G. R. Knight, ed., *Early Adventist Educators* (AUP, 1983); E. K. Vande Vere, *The Wisdom Seekers* (SPA, 1972).

Arnold C. Reye

BATTLE CREEK CONGREGATION. The *Battle Creek, *Michigan, congregation began in 1852 when *Joseph Bates first visited the city. The earliest converts were David and Olive Hewitt. The *Review and Herald* records David being baptized in August 1852. Soon other names began to be mentioned in the *Review*. In October 1853 *J. B. Frisbie, once an ardent opponent of the Sabbath, converted only a few months earlier, moved from Chelsea, Michigan, and began to lead the group of 15 members in Battle Creek. Under his spiritual guidance the group continued to grow. In November or December of 1853 *Henry and Deborah Lyon moved to town from Plymouth, Michigan, and strengthened the ranks of the growing congregation. Later *Cyrenius Smith and his family moved from Jackson, Michigan, and further increased the congregation. By the late summer of 1855 the regular worshippers included: David and Olive Hewitt; Joseph B. Frisbie and his wife, Delphia; Henry and Deborah Lyon; Mr. and Mrs. Samuel B. Warren; Cyrenius and Louisa Smith and their children

William M., Martha, Asahel, Asenath, Hannah, and Mary; Walter and Nancy Grant; Jarvis P. and Matilda Munsell; Mrs. Mary E. Tozer; Mr. and Mrs. Zerah Brooks; Mr. and Mrs. Jonah Lewis and children; *Abraham and Caroline Dodge; Willard Holden; and Martin Phillips. Asa P. H. Kelsey, his wife, Eunice, and children Oliver, Hannah, and George came up regularly from Leroy to worship with the group. Some lists add Lorinda Smith, a grown daughter of Cyrenius and Louisa's.

Then something happened that would forever change the church at Battle Creek. At a conference held in the city April 28-29, 1855, the believers voted to invite James White to move the *Review* office from *Rochester, New York, to Battle Creek. That autumn the invitation was acted on. When the Whites moved the printing press and office staff from Rochester, New York, the little Battle Creek congregation suddenly gained 14 new members: James and Ellen White, *Henry, *Edson, and *Willie; house-helpers *Clarissa Bonfoey and *Jennie Fraser; Ellen's sister and brother-in-law, *Sarah B. and *Stephen Belden; and additional printing office workers, *Uriah Smith, *George Amadon, and J. Warren Batchellor, who also brought his mother, Cynthia, and sister, Roxanna.

At first they met for worship in private homes, such as that of Henry and Deborah Lyon or of David and Olive Hewitt, but by November 16, 1855, they were worshipping together in a just-completed little board-and-batten "house of prayer" 18′ x 24′ (5.5 meters x 7.5 meters) on the north end of Elder Frisbie's lot on Cass Street between Van Buren and Champion.

In the next few months J. Fletcher Byington, *Merritt E. and Angeline Cornell; *Myron J. and Cornelia Cornell; *John Preston and Ann J. Kellogg and their children *Merritt G., Smith, Albert, Julia, Mary, Laura, Emma, and

*John Harvey, joined the little band of believers.

In just over a year they outgrew their "house of prayer," and began planning a larger one. On the weekend of November 6-8, 1857, the new meetinghouse, around the corner on Van Buren Street, was dedicated. This building was 28′ x 44′ (8.5 meters x 13.5 meters). The above-mentioned members, along with several others, made up a group of 72 who on October 24, 1861, signed the covenant to "keep the commandments of God, and the faith of Jesus," thus comprising the charter members of the Battle Creek congregation. Soon outgrowing their second meetinghouse, in 1866 the congregation purchased the land now occupied by the present Battle Creek Tabernacle and built a third meetinghouse measuring 40′ x 65′ (12 meters x 20 meters) and containing a gallery. The third meeting house was replaced by the Dime Tabernacle (see *Battle Creek Tabernacle) (105′ x 130′ [32 meters x 40 meters]), which stood on the same location from 1878 to 1922. The present Battle Creek Tabernacle was dedicated in 1926.

The special needs of the Battle Creek congregation called forth several special *testimonies from Ellen White, including a dozen different booklets of 14 to 84 pages each that were sent to the church between 1860 and 1900. Some of these dealt very specifically with individual sins and problems, and others with broader philosophical issues. Besides these pamphlets, many letters and at least one telegram were sent by Ellen White to this congregation. Although these testimonies were often difficult for members to accept, over and over the messages were proved correct, and ultimately increased the church's confidence in God's special messages and Ellen White's ministry. The Battle Creek congregation was Ellen White's church home for many years. And though often away from home, and often misunderstood, she considered these members her brothers and sisters in the faith.

Stanley D. Hickerson

BATTLE CREEK SANITARIUM. The premier Adventist health-care institution from 1877 to 1906, when it was separated from church ownership. The "San," as it was commonly called, was the direct result of instruction to Ellen White in a vision of December 25, 1865. "Our people should have an institution of their own, under their own control, for the benefit of the diseased and suffering among us," she wrote (1T 492). In response to this instruction, Adventists opened in 1866 the *Health Reform Institute in Battle Creek, Michigan. In 1876 *J. H. Kellogg became medical superintendent, and in 1877 changed the name to Battle Creek Medical and Surgical Sanitarium, hence the short form Battle Creek Sanitarium. The name "Medical and Surgical Sanitarium, Battle Creek, Michigan," was the official name of the institution at least until its reorganization in 1898 (GCB, Third Quarter, 1897; cf. Schwarz, *John Harvey Kellogg, M.D.,* pp. 66, 67).

By *sanitarium Kellogg meant a place where people learn to stay well. It was to be more a university than a hotel. He later coined the phrase "biologic living" to sum up the system of healthful living he spent his life promoting—a system that, generally speaking, reflected the influence of the health counsels of Ellen White and others of the era's most sensible health reformers. Both to cure disease and to help people stay well, Kellogg taught obedience to natural law as a moral duty, necessary to physical and mental health. Biologic living required total abstinence from alcohol, tea, coffee, tobacco, and animal flesh. It included proper diet, adequate rest and exercise, fresh air, healthful dress, and (in case of illness) simple, natural remedies (Schwarz, *John Harvey Kellogg, M.D.*, p. 37).

Many of these concepts Kellogg had received directly from Ellen White. He was 14 when he read her first general health book, *Health: or How to Live*. Almost 40 years later he recalled that it was "the sweetest thing I ever heard, and I got hold of it and have tried to stick to it the best I could ever since" (*Medical Missionary* 14 [March 1905]).

For many years Kellogg continued to hold the counsels of Ellen White in high esteem. Around 1895 he explained to *David Paulson how "the Battle Creek Sanitarium is able to keep five years ahead of the medical profession." When a new idea came out in the medical world, claimed Kellogg, "I know" immediately from Ellen White's writings whether the new idea "belongs in our system or not. If it does, I instantly adopt it and advertise it while the rest of the doctors are slowly feeling their way, and when they finally adopt it, I have a five-year start on them." On the other hand, Kellogg continued, if a medical innovation did not "fit the light we have received," he simply ignored it. When other doctors discovered their mistake, they wondered how Kellogg had avoided it (T. H. Jemison, *A Prophet Among You* [PPPA, 1955], pp. 491, 492). Another testimonial of Kellogg's confidence in Ellen White's health principles is his preface to *Christian Temperance and Bible Hygiene*, by James and Ellen White (1890), pp. iii, iv. Thus he gave major credit to Ellen White's counsels for the pathbreaking leadership of the Battle Creek Sanitarium.

As the sanitarium prospered, Kellogg kept enlarging it, until by 1900 it was the largest institution of its kind in the world. People came from all over the world to become well and to learn how to stay well. But Kellogg resented the fact that ministers, some of them not themselves practicing health reformers,

held major influence on the board of the sanitarium, and he laid plans to separate the sanitarium from the denomination (SHM65 293-300; Schwarz, *John Harvey Kellogg, M.D.*, pp. 66-72). This set him on a collision course with Ellen White, though she continued to support him publicly even while she saw him drifting from his earlier commitments.

In 1897, when the sanitarium's 30-year charter expired, Kellogg wrote into the new charter the word "undenominational," explaining that it meant the sanitarium would accept anyone as a patient regardless of their religious convictions. He later would argue that the word made the sanitarium legally independent from church control. Ellen White's response to this development was unequivocal: "It has been stated that the Battle Creek Sanitarium is not denominational," she wrote. "But if ever an institution was established to be denominational, in every sense of the word, this Sanitarium was" (BCL 51).

The fire that burned the Battle Creek Sanitarium to the ground, February 18, 1902, brought the issue of ownership and control to the front. Ellen White had told Kellogg a few months earlier that the sanitarium "should be moved into the country and not be so large. Unless there is a change, God's hand will be laid heavily upon you." After the fire, she recommended a modest rebuilding in the country near Battle Creek, but she opposed erecting a "mammoth institution." She believed that the "purpose of God" would be better carried out "by making plants in many places" (see Jerry Moon, *W. C. White and Ellen G. White* [AUP, 1993], pp. 276, 277). Kellogg, however, chose to rebuild on the same site, on an even larger scale. When the new building was completed in 1903, Ellen White made it clear that even though some aspects of her counsel had been disregarded, the sanitarium was still to be regarded as the Lord's institution. "Now that the building has been put up," she instructed, God "wants this institution to be placed on vantage ground," built up "in the name of the Lord" (GCB, Apr. 2, 1903, in 5Bio 163). To help pay for rebuilding the sanitarium, Kellogg authored a health book, *The Living Temple* (see *Pantheism), but its theology proved controversial. Furthermore, his opposition to the no-debt policy of General Conference president A. G. Daniells deepened the division between the medical and ministerial leaders.

COURTESY OF THE REVIEW AND HERALD PUBLISHING ASSOCIATION

BATTLE CREEK SANITARIUM BUILDING AFTER ITS RECONSTRUCTION IN 1903 AND THE ADDITION OF THE TWIN TOWERS IN 1928

By 1906 these and other conflicts led to the complete separation of the Battle Creek Sanitarium from the denomination—a loss that seemed then "a severe blow" to the *medical missionary work. "Yet the fate of the 'undenominational' institution, on the one hand, and the continued growth of the denominational health-care service on the other were both a continued witness to their respective philosophies" (Schaefer, p. 154). For some years the accustomed prosperity continued, but as Kellogg aged and administrative control passed to younger colleagues, the board of directors, headed by *Charles Stewart, plunged the sanitarium into a $4 million indebtedness for an opulent fourteen-story "towers addition" completed in 1928. When the stock market crashed in 1929, the

patient census dropped from 1,300 to about 300, and in 1933 the sanitarium went bankrupt. It emerged from bankruptcy in 1938—but with new management said to have little interest in Kellogg's health philosophy. In 1942 the building was sold to the United States Army, becoming the Percy Jones Army Hospital. In 1954 the huge building was remodeled again as a government office building. Now known as the Hart-Dole-Inouye Federal Center, the former sanitarium is still a prominent landmark on the Battle Creek skyline (Stewart, pp. 6-8).

Further reading: SHM65 293-300; R. Schaefer, *Legacy: The Heritage of a Unique International Medical Outreach* (PPPA, 1990); R. W. Schwarz, *John Harvey Kellogg, M.D.* (SPA, 1970; reprint AUP, 1981), pp. 66-72, 174-192; idem, *John Harvey Kellogg, M.D.: Pioneer Health Reformer* (RHPA, 2006); P. Stewart [, ed.], *The Government Years at the Battle Creek Federal Center* (Battle Creek, Mich.: BC Federal Center, 1999).

Duff Stoltz

BATTLE CREEK SEVENTH-DAY ADVENTIST CHURCHES, see **BATTLE CREEK TABERNACLE.**

BATTLE CREEK TABERNACLE. The fourth Adventist meetinghouse in Battle Creek. It was built in 1878 and 1879 and placed on the same location as the third meetinghouse on the west side of Washington Street between Van Buren and Main, directly across from the town square. It was to seat at least 3,000 persons, be built in an inexpensive manner, and be paid for by members from the world church donating 10 cents per month, or a dollar per year in advance. The name voted was "Dime Tabernacle," indicating not only the means of fund-raising but also the motivation behind it. In view of the soon return of Christ, the building was not intended to last hundreds of years or to require an extravagant expenditure of means.

*Henry W. Kellogg, a manager at the publishing house (see *Review and Herald Publishing Association), was chosen as building committee chair. Work began in August 1878. The third meetinghouse was moved from its foundations to the publishing house property, and the new foundations were added in September. All had hoped to complete the structure by the end of the year, but three additional months were required to finish the project. Just seven months from the commencement of the project, the Dime Tabernacle was completed. The building was 105′ x 130′ (32 meters x 40 meters) with a 108-foot (33-meter) clock tower over the main entrance on the southeast corner of the building. Inside, a large audience room 65′ x 85′ (20 meters x 26 meters) and seating 900, was surrounded on three sides with spacious vestries, also used for children's Sabbath schools, seating 250, 350, and 250, respectively, and separated by vertically sliding, counterweighted panels, each containing two large ground-glass windows. With these panels up, the vestries all became a part of the main auditorium, thus swelling the main floor seating capacity to 1,750. Galleries surrounded the main audience room on three sides, adding an additional 800 seating. Wall seats and chairs in the aisles, etc., added 650 more seats, bringing the total capacity to 3,200. At the dedication service 3,649 persons were present by actual count as they left the building.

Above the two rear vestibules were committee rooms, accessible from the passages leading from the platform to the rear entries. In addition to the two large curving stairs on either side of the platform going up to the gallery, stairs also led from the gallery to the two front vestibules. Above and inside the circle of the galleries was a 45-foot (14-meter) diameter dome, terminating in a 20-foot

(six-meter) diameter skylight. Triple windows behind the pulpit contained quotations from the Scriptures: the left window, Romans 3:24; the center, Exodus 20:3-17; and the right, Revelation 14:12.

The local non-Adventist citizens of Battle Creek, at the invitation of Elder James White, donated moneys for a $600 Seth Thomas clock that served as the town clock, chiming each hour. Also in the tower, the bell that had previously hung in the third church rang out at the beginning and close of each Sabbath. The Dime Tabernacle was, for many years, the largest auditorium in the city, and was used not only for regular church services, prayer meetings, Missionary Volunteer meetings, and General Conference sessions, but also for graduation services for Battle Creek College, the Battle Creek Sanitarium School of Nursing, as well as Central High School.

BATTLE CREEK TABERNACLE

Funerals of prominent citizens also were held in the building, including those of James and Ellen White.

After the removal of the college to Berrien Springs in 1901, and the publishing house and General Conference offices to Washington, D.C., in 1903, an attempt was made by some leaders at the sanitarium to take control of the tabernacle. Letters and a telegram from Ellen White helped to avert the crisis, leaving the property in the control of the Michigan Conference. Fifteen years later, on a Sabbath evening in 1922, the building caught fire, and in spite of the best efforts of the firefighters, it was totally destroyed. The congregation dedicated a smaller tabernacle on the same site in 1926 and still worships in it today.

Further reading: J. G. Smoot, "Building the 'Dime' Tabernacle," LUH, April 10, 1979; *idem*, "Dedicating the 'Dime' Tabernacle," LUH, Apr. 17, 1979.

Stanley D. Hickerson

BAXTER, RICHARD (1615-1691). English Puritan preacher, scholar, and writer; prominent representative of moderate, centrist Puritanism. Among Baxter's nearly 200 works are the devotional classic *The Saints' Everlasting Rest* (1650), *The Reformed Pastor* (1656), and *The Christian Directory* (1673), a massive compendium on Christian ethics and lifestyle. His writings influenced English and American Puritanism and Methodism, and through them the development of American Protestantism.

Ellen White mentions Baxter's conversion experience (2MCP 809) and approves him for testing all doctrines by the Bible and renouncing whatever the Bible condemns (GC 609). She quotes his exclamation that "the thoughts of the coming of the Lord are most sweet and joyful to me," and his exhortation that all "believers should long and pray for the second coming of Christ" (GC 303). She recommends his *Reformed Pastor* and *Saints' Everlasting Rest* (*ibid.* 253) and had his *Call to the Unconverted to Turn and Live* in her private library. Twenty-two lines of a poem by Baxter appear in a letter to Ellen White from *Hannah More (quoted in 1T 671-674).

BEAUTY. In the nineteenth century, a period when Western philosophical thinking was being nudged by David Hume and Immanuel Kant to regard sense perception as unreliable, Ellen White insisted on a different perspective. Very often her writings point to the importance of beauty, especially in nature, and also the beauty of truth and its effective results in the human being. She instructs that God is the author of all beauty, and is Himself a lover of the beautiful (AH 455). For her, there was no division between the human senses and the human mind. Her wholistic epistemological approach closely aligns the two in a person's experience of the world and the perception of truth. In fact, beauty itself has a convicting power in the human life. For example, nature, though affected by sin, is still "rich and beautiful in the tokens of life-giving power" (Ed 27). White urges the study of the natural world, a "treasure house of knowledge," for consideration of the beauty therein will bring new perceptions of truth (LHU 112). This study will continue in heaven, where Christ Himself will "unfold to us the beauty and glory of nature. . . . Truth we cannot know now, because of finite limitations, we shall know hereafter" (Mar 364).

White's link of beauty and truth is especially emphatic. She many times insists on the convicting power of the "beauty of truth." When discussing biblical truth, she describes the truth of God being understood as the Holy Spirit reveals "its beauty to the mind" with the striking result of its transforming power on the character (RH, Mar. 29, 1906). She constantly extols the grand beauty of Scripture. The converted heart will love the truth of God's Word and see "new charms in the living oracles; for divine beauty and celestial light seem to shine in every passage" (FE 182). "The greatness of its themes, the dignified simplicity of its utterances, the beauty of its imagery, quicken and uplift the thoughts as nothing else can. No other study can impart such mental power as does the effort to grasp the stupendous truths of revelation" (Ed 124). To the converted heart, even the divine requirements will be beautiful (ST, Sept. 8, 1909). The three angels' messages of Revelation 14 are depicted as "unblemished pure beauty" (1888 Materials 940).

Ellen White extensively underscores the truth of Scripture, which she regularly links with the beauty of biblical doctrines as having inspired "the most sublime and impassioned utterances of the sacred writers" (GC 300). A diligent student of Scripture will discover a system of truth with "a beauty and harmony which will captivate their attention, elevate their thoughts, and give them an inspiration and an energy of argument that will be powerful to convict and convert souls" (4T 526). White waxes lyrical with her own testimony: "As I have read the Holy Scriptures, the gems of truth have shone with such lustre, and the beauty and harmony of truth has so impressed me, that I could not forbear praising God" (RH, Apr. 29, 1884).

Thus it is not surprising to find White describing Jesus' method of teaching the Old Testament Scriptures as "expounding their truths, . . . clothing them with freshness and richness and beauty the people had never beheld before" (TMK 195). "The work of Christ was to give again to the world the truth in its original freshness and beauty" (FE 237). Each Christian should also develop skills in presenting biblical truth so that "the truth will lose none of its force and beauty by being bunglingly presented" (SpM 200). This God-given task White describes as having "beauty . . . symmetry and harmony" (RH, Apr. 4, 1907). In fact, Christians have "been made the depositories of sacred truth to be given to the world in all its beauty and glory" (GCDB, Jan. 29, 1893). "God calls upon all who claim to believe present truth, to work diligently in

gathering up the precious jewels of truth, and placing them in their position in the framework of the gospel. Let them shine in all their divine beauty and loveliness, that the light may flash forth amid the moral darkness" (RH, Nov. 15, 1892).

Ellen White's concept of beauty is noteworthy. Her link of truth and beauty is profound. She follows in the ancient tradition of the psalmist (34:8), who does not reduce the experience of God to mere mental assent, but bids one "taste and see that the Lord is good."

Jo Ann Davidson

BERRIEN SPRINGS MEETING, 1904. The 1904 session of the Lake Union Conference, which met on the campus of Emmanuel Missionary College, Berrien Springs, Michigan, from May 18 to 25. On this occasion Ellen White made a supreme effort to draw together three diverging groups within the denomination—medical workers, led by J. H. Kellogg; educational reformers, led by E. A. Sutherland and P. T. Magan; and church administrators, led by A. G. Daniells and W. W. Prescott. Specific issues of conflict included Kellogg's theology, Daniells' no-debt policy, and Sutherland and Magan's administration of the college.

Virtually every notable event of the conference related to one of these issues. The session opened Wednesday evening, May 18, with an address by Ellen White against the pantheistic theology in Kellogg's book *The Living Temple*. On Thursday P. T. Magan's wife, Ida, died after an illness aggravated by vicious gossip against her husband. Ellen White intimated that she had died a martyr to the strife within (5Bio 336, 337). Friday night Prescott delivered a blistering attack against pantheism, a choice of topic that Ellen White had first advised, then sought to prevent through a note that W. C. White, with her permission, had not delivered to Prescott (Moon, pp. 371-375). At the 5:45 a.m. meeting on Monday, A. T. Jones gave a two-hour-long, fiery rebuttal of Prescott's Friday night sermon. After Jones' sermon, Sutherland and Magan resigned from the leadership of the college.

That afternoon Kellogg had just begun to address the delegates when Ellen White entered the chapel. Offered the pulpit, she made an eloquent appeal for reconciliation, directed to all present, but especially to J. H. and W. K. Kellogg. The conference is considered to have been a tipping point for the Kelloggs, who were separated from church membership in 1907.

Further reading: 5Bio 329-339; G. R. Knight, *From 1888 to Apostasy* (RHPA, 1987), pp. 212-214; C. M. Maxwell, *Tell It to the World* (PPPA, 1982), pp. 260, 261; J. Moon, *W. C. White and Ellen G. White: The Relationship Between the Prophet and Her Son* (AUP, 1993), pp. 140-144, 304-306, 371-375; R. W. Schwarz, *Light Bearers to the Remnant* (PPPA, 1979), p. 294; G. M. Valentine, *The Shaping of Adventism: The Case of W. W. Prescott* (AUP, 1992), pp. 156-159; E. K. Vande Vere, *The Wisdom Seekers* (SPA, 1972), pp. 115-117.

Jerry Moon

BEVERAGES. Ellen White promoted the use of pure water as a health-promoting beverage to quench the thirst (MH 237). She advised that water should be drunk between meals rather than with the meals. Taken with the meal, water diminishes the flow of salivary juices and hinders digestion (CD 420). She especially wrote against the use of ice water with the meal, since this arrests digestion until the stomach contents warm up to body temperature (*ibid.*). She recommended that those who were thirsty during a meal should eat some fruit rather than drink water with the meal. When used freely, water was a great

blessing, since it helped the body to resist disease, alleviate fever in sickness, and cleanse the body tissues (*ibid.* 419, 420).

While Ellen White spoke in favor of sweet cider and pure, unfermented grape juice, she certainly spoke strongly against the fermented forms of these beverages (*ibid.* 432-436). She was even cautious to endorse sweet apple cider fully, because of the high possibility of wormy and decayed apples being used in its preparation (MH 332).

Moderate amounts of tomato juice, carrot juice, and grape and other fruit juices often appeared on Ellen White's table (6Bio 395). Orange and lemon juice were prepared in her household for drinks (6MR 135). She also used lemon juice to flavor her cooked greens (CD 324), and recommended it for rheumatism and malaria (2MR 48).

Tea and coffee are described by Ellen White with various terms. She describes these hot beverages as unnatural nerve stimulants that poison the blood and produce a form of intoxication (MH 325, 326; CD 421, 426). She described their action as that of arousing the mind, stimulating the heart, and energizing the system for a short period of time. She warned that the nervous excitement produced by tea and coffee was always followed by languor and debility (MH 326), exhaustion and nervous prostration (CTBH 34, 35), and feelings of depression (CD 425). Furthermore, she described their continued use as producing headaches, wakefulness, palpitations, indigestion, and trembling (MH 326). Clearly Ellen White was referring to the many physiological effects of caffeine upon different systems of the human body.

She described coffee as being worse than tea (CD 421) and that the use of tea and coffee could be habit-forming (*ibid.* 422). She warned that the continued use of tea and coffee may lead to the need for stronger stimulants (MH

327), a warning that these other beverages may become a gateway to the use of alcohol and other more dangerous substances. Tea and coffee were often grouped in her writings with tobacco and alcoholic drinks. She considered that the effect of tea and coffee, while lesser in the degree of their influence, tended to be in the same direction as alcohol and tobacco (CTBH 34; CD 425, 426). Ellen White advised that the only safe rule for a Christian regarding tea and coffee was not to touch it or taste it (3T 488). On numerous occasions she suggested that tea and coffee drinking was a danger to the spiritual life. She described the use of such beverages as being ruinous to the mental and moral powers (CD 421), causing paralysis of mental and moral powers (*ibid.*), injuring the soul, blunting the ability to discern sin, and making it difficult to appreciate truth and spiritual things (*ibid.* 425; 1T 549).

She discouraged the use of all hot drinks, which she described as debilitating (CD 420) and injurious to both the stomach and other digestive organs (*ibid.* 432). She did recommend the use of a cereal coffee as a substitute for using either tea or coffee. Ellen White herself used a simple homemade cereal coffee on occasions (*ibid.*).

See also: Milk.

Further reading: W. J. Craig, *Nutrition and Wellness: A Vegetarian Way to Better Health* (Berrien Springs, Mich.: Golden Harvest Books, 1999), pp. 324-355.

Winston J. Craig

BIBLE, AUTHORITY OF THE. Ellen White considered the Bible to be the very Word of God, the supreme revelation of His will, the infallible, unerring standard of Christian faith and practice, and the highest authority for human beings. For her, the supreme authority of the Bible is rooted in its claim that God is its author (GC v). "The Bible is God's voice speaking to us, just as surely as though we could hear it with our ears" (6T 393). The Bible reveals the will of God. "The Holy Scriptures are to be accepted as an authoritative, infallible revelation of His will" (GC vii). "Man is fallible, but God's Word is infallible" and "the unerring standard" (1SM 416; MH 462). Therefore we are "to receive God's Word as supreme authority" (6T 402). She fully agreed with the English Reformer *Wycliffe, who taught that the Bible is an "inspired" and "perfect revelation of God's will" (GC 93). Finally, she accepted the authority of the Bible without any support of extrabiblical arguments. For her "the evidence of the truth of God's Word is in the Word itself" (8T 157).

The Bible is "the revealer of doctrines," "the standard by which all teaching . . . must be tested" (GC vii). "True Christianity receives the Word of God as the great treasure house of inspired truth and the test of all inspiration" (*ibid.* 193). "The Bible, and the Bible alone," she emphasized, "is our rule of faith" (CSW 84). There is a need for Christians to return "to the great Protestant principle—the Bible, and the Bible only, as the rule of faith and duty" (GC 204, 205). Although Ellen White was not in favor of creeds, she urged believers to adopt one creed for their lives: "The Bible, and the Bible alone, is to be our creed" (1SM 416). Expressing her passionate faith in the self-authenticating authority of Scripture for faith and doctrine, she says: "I would have both my arms taken off at my shoulders before I would ever make the statement or set my judgment upon the Word of God as to what is inspired and what is not inspired. . . . Never let mortal man sit in judgment upon the Word of God" (7BC 919).

Ellen White placed the authority of Scripture above that of any other book and taught that the Bible is the only source of truly objective history. Nevertheless, she recognized that "an understanding of the customs of those who lived in Bible times" is "practical knowledge" that "aids" Bible study (CT 518). Regarding its accuracy and objectivity Ellen White said, "Here only can we find a history of our race unsullied by human prejudice or human pride" (PP 596). The Bible lights up "the far distant past, where human research seeks vainly to penetrate. In God's Word alone we find an authentic account of creation" (5T 25). "Here only do we find an authentic account of the origin of nations" (Ed 173).

Ellen White recommended the study of sacred history as studied in Israel's schools of the prophets as a model for the modern study of history. "In the record of His [God's] dealings with the nations were traced the footsteps of Jehovah. So today we are to consider the dealings of God with the nations of the earth. We are to see in history the fulfillment of prophecy, to study the workings of Providence in the great reformatory movements, and to understand the progress of events in the marshaling of the nations for the final conflict of the great controversy" (MH 441, 442).

"Such study will give broad, comprehensive views of life. It will help us to understand something of its relations and dependencies, how wonderfully we are bound together in the great brotherhood of society and nations, and to how great an extent the oppression and degradation of one member means loss to all" (*ibid.* 442).

She suggested that a knowledge of the Bible is basic to the study of science because Scripture contains "the foundation of all true science" (COL 107). This knowledge is not simply an intellectual understanding, but must be of a personal experiential nature. One "who has gained a knowledge of God and His Word through personal experience is prepared to engage in the study of natural science" (MH 461). It is "in the light shining from the cross," that "we can rightly interpret nature's teaching" (*ibid.* 462). "Apart from Christ we are still incapable of interpreting rightly the language of nature" (8T 257).

Through the experiential knowledge of God and the Bible one obtains "a settled faith in the divinity of the Holy Scriptures" (MH 462) and a conviction about its "divine authority" (CE 193). One who has such a faith "does not test the Bible by man's ideas of science. He brings these ideas to the test of the unerring standard" (8T 325). "The Bible is not to be tested by men's ideas of science" because "human knowledge is an unreliable guide" (PP 114).

In "God's Word alone we find an authentic account of creation," she wrote (5T 25). "Apart from Bible history, geology can prove nothing" (PP 112). "Moses wrote under the guidance of the Spirit of God, and a correct theory of geology will never claim discoveries that cannot be reconciled with his statements" (*ibid.* 114). Those who have been so confident in the discoveries of geology have "no adequate conception" of the size of people, animals, and vegetation of the antediluvian world or "the great changes which then took place. Relics found in the earth do give evidence of conditions differing in many respects from the present, but the time when these conditions existed can be learned only from the Inspired Record" (*ibid.* 112). She concluded, "In the history of the flood, inspiration has explained that which geology alone could never fathom" (*ibid.*).

She commented on efforts to judge the Bible by science: "Again and again men have attempted to put the Bible and the writings of men [scientists] upon a common basis; but the attempt has proved a failure; for we cannot serve God and mammon" (FE 181). It is "only in the light of revelation" that nature's teaching can be "read aright" (Ed 134).

Ellen White exalted the authority of Scripture over human wisdom, character, and experience. "The ingenuity of man has been exercised for ages to measure the Word of God by their finite minds and limited comprehension," she wrote (1SM 18). "But the Word of the Lord is not to be judged by a human standard" (5T 301), and "philosophy cannot determine the ways and works of God; the human mind cannot measure infinity" (6BC 1079). "Man's measurement of God will never be correct" (3SM 308). She warns, "The Scriptures need not be read by the dim light of tradition or human speculation. As well might we try to give light to the sun with a torch as to explain the Scriptures by human tradition or imagination" (COL 111). "God's Holy Word needs not the torchlight glimmer of earth to make its glories distinguishable" because "it is light in itself—the glory of God revealed, and beside it every other light is dim" (*ibid.*).

The Holy Scriptures "are the standard of character" and "the standard by which all . . . experience must be tested" (GC vii). The Bible is the "test of experience" and "the sole bond of union" among believers (*ibid.*; 1SM 416).

See also: Revelation and Inspiration.

Further reading: GC v-xii; 1SM 15-23; P. G. Damsteegt, "Ellen White on Theology, Its Methods, and the Use of Scripture," JATS 4, no. 2 (1993): 115-136; *idem*, "The Inspiration of Scripture in the Writings of Ellen White," JATS 5, no. 1 (1994): 155-179; *idem*, "Ellen White, Lifestyle and Scripture Interpretation," JATS 6, no. 2 (1996): 34-50; P. M. van Bemmelen, "The Authority of Scripture," in G. W. Reid, ed., *Understanding Scripture: An Adventist Approach* (BRI, 2005).

P. Gerard Damsteegt

BIBLE, BIG, see **VISIONS OF ELLEN G. WHITE.**

BIBLE, ELLEN G. WHITE'S RELATIONSHIP TO THE. A correct understanding of Ellen White's relationship to the Bible is essential for understanding all of her other counsel. To Ellen White the Bible was absolutely central, it was to be "the only rule of faith and doctrine" (RH, July 17, 1888). "Our position and faith is in the Bible," she wrote in 1894. "And never do we want any soul to bring in the *Testimonies ahead of the Bible" (Ev 256).

Her husband took the same position on the place of her writings in relation to the Bible as did the other early Seventh-day Adventist leaders. In his earliest published position on the topic of Ellen's gift (1847) James wrote that "the Bible is a perfect, and complete revelation. It is our only rule of faith and practice." But that did not mean, noted James, that God couldn't use a last-day prophet (see Joel 2:28-31) to aid His people. "True visions," he wrote, "are given to lead us to God, and His Written Word; but those that are given for a new rule of faith and practice [such as in Mormonism], separate from the Bible, cannot be from God, and should be rejected" (JW, WLF, p. 13).

Ellen White never tired of uplifting the Bible. In her first book (1851) she wrote: "I recommend to you, dear reader, the Word of God as the rule of your faith and practice" (EW 78). And 58 years later (1909) she stood for the last time before a General Conference session with a Bible in her hands, saying, "Brethren and sisters, I commend unto you this Book."

For her the centrality of the Bible was based upon the fact that it contained everything men and women needed to know for salvation. She consistently held that all Christian teaching, including her own, needed to be tested by the teachings of the Bible itself (GC vii).

Ellen White saw her purpose as bringing people "back to the word that they have neglected to follow" (5T 663). "The written testimonies," she asserted, "are not to give new light, but to impress vividly upon the heart the truths of inspiration already revealed" in the Bible (*ibid.* 665). Perhaps her most graphic illustration of her function was that she saw her writings as "a *lesser light to lead men and women to the greater light [the Bible]," since they had given so little heed to the Bible (CM 125).

Another point to note is that Ellen White believed that her mission was to help people understand the principles of the Bible for their lives. In a dream in 1871 she saw herself surrounding the Bible with several of her *Testimonies for the Church.* "You are not familiar with the Scriptures," she heard herself saying to the people. "If you had made God's Word your study, with a desire to reach the Bible standard and attain to Christian perfection, you would not have needed the *Testimonies.* It is because you have neglected to acquaint yourselves with God's inspired Book that He has sought to reach you by simple, direct testimonies, calling your attention to the words of inspiration which you had neglected to obey, and urging you to fashion your lives in accordance with its pure and elevated teachings" (2T 605).

Her testimonies, she noted in the same dream, "are not to give new light, but to impress vividly upon the heart the truths of inspiration already revealed" in the Bible. She went on to say that the *Testimonies* were not given to give new truth but to simplify the truths already given in the Bible and impress those truths on the minds of His people, "that all may be left without excuse" (*ibid.*). She consistently expressed the idea that "the Testimonies are not by any means to take the place of the Word. They are to bring

you to that neglected Word" (GCB, Apr. 3, 1901).

James White was equally as clear on his wife's role in relationship to the Bible. "Every Christian," he wrote, "is therefore duty-bound to take the Bible as a perfect rule of faith and duty. He should pray fervently to be aided by the Holy Spirit in searching the Scriptures for the whole truth, and for his whole duty. He is not at liberty to turn from them to learn his duty through any of the gifts. We say that the very moment he does, he places the gifts in a wrong place, and takes an extremely dangerous position. The Word should be in front, and the eye of the church should be placed upon it, as the rule to walk by, and the fountain of wisdom, from which to learn duty in 'all good works.' But if a portion of the church err from the truths of the Bible, and become weak, and sickly, and the flock become scattered, so that it seems necessary for God to employ the gifts of the Spirit to correct, revive and heal the erring, we should let him work" (RH, Apr. 21, 1851; cf. RH, Feb. 25, 1868).

In summary, from the perspective of James and Ellen White and other early Adventist leaders, the Bible contained everything Christians needed for salvation and Christian living. The primary role of Ellen White's writings was not to give new light, but to lead people back to the Bible and to help them apply Bible principles to their specific context. "The written testimonies are not to give new light, but to impress vividly upon the heart the truths of inspiration already revealed. Man's duty to God and to his fellow man has been distinctly specified in God's Word; yet but few of you are obedient to the light given. Additional truth is not brought out; but God has through the *Testimonies* simplified the great truths already given and in His own chosen way brought them before the people to awaken and impress the mind with them, that all may be left without excuse" (2T 605).

Thus Ellen White's role was always seen in relationship to the Bible (and never independent of it). Whereas she claimed equal inspiration with the Bible writers, she did not claim equal authority. Rather than having canonical authority, her prophetic authority was derived from the authority of the Bible. The early Adventists believed that the authority of all spiritual gifts, including the prophetic ministry of Ellen White, was derived from the Bible and must always be tested by it.

See also: Daily; Galatians, Law in.

Further reading: H. E. Douglass, *Messenger of the Lord* (RHPA, 1998), pp. 416-425; G. R. Knight, *Reading Ellen White* (RHPA, 1997), pp. 16-29; D. E. Rebok, *Believe His Prophets* (RHPA, 1956), pp. 160-182; R. W. Olson, *One Hundred and One Questions on the Sanctuary and on Ellen White* (EGWE, 1981, SDoc), pp. 41, 42; A. L. White, "The Position and Relationship of the Writings of Ellen G. White to the Bible, and the Bible Only" (EGWE SDoc).

George R. Knight

BIBLE, ELLEN WHITE'S USE OF. Ellen White used Scripture extensively and in various ways. She was steeped in the language of the Bible, and when she spoke or wrote on a topic, she would frequently use biblical language and biblical texts to convey the message she had received in vision. She had the highest regard for the Bible, considering it to be "God's voice speaking to us, just as surely as though we could hear it with our ears" (6T 393). The Scriptures were for her the "authoritative, infallible revelation of His will" (GC vii). She used them constantly in her personal and family devotions as well as in her preaching. She counseled that devoting "one hour or even half an hour each day . . . to the Word of God" (CSW 42), particularly in the "contemplation of the life of Christ" (DA 83), would be of great benefit to all. Her life and work testify to the truth of these statements.

As a means to understanding Scripture, she recognized the importance of the historical and cultural background of a passage. Such knowledge, she said, "aids in making clear the figures of the Bible and in bringing out the force of Christ's lessons" (CT 518). She also recognized that "understanding what the words of Jesus meant to those who heard them" is a prerequisite to understanding the "deeper lessons" of the text today (MB 1). In dealing with difficult passages she would compare scripture with scripture, believing that "the Bible is its own expositor" (Ed 190). "One passage will prove to be a key that will unlock other passages, and in this way light will be shed upon the hidden meaning of the Word" (FE 187).

Many times she explains the deeper meaning of a particular text. For example, she applied Jesus' words in John 6:53, "Unless ye eat the flesh of the Son of man, and drink his blood, ye have no life in you," to the Lord's Supper (DA 661). But beyond that she explained in practical terms that "by receiving His word, by doing those things which He has commanded" we become one with Him, i.e., we eat Jesus' flesh and drink His blood (*ibid*. 660).

At other times she simply used the language of Scripture to express what God had instructed her to say to the church. In using texts in this way, she did not claim to be explaining what the author originally meant. The meaning the original author intended the text to have may be quite different from the message Ellen White was conveying through its use of its language. For example, Ellen White frequently used the phrase "search the scriptures," found in John 5:39, as an admonition to study the Bible (CSW 17). In the context of John 5, however, Jesus is not admonishing His hearers to study the Bible, as a look into any modern translation will show. Many of them believed that knowledge of the law would assure them of eternal life. But Jesus reminded them that the scriptures in which they thought to find eternal life were the very writings that testified of Him. However, when Ellen White discussed this passage in the context of the dialogue in John 5, she used the Revised Version of John 5:39, "Ye search the scriptures, because ye think that in them ye have eternal life; and these are they which bear witness of me," thereby pointing to the text's original meaning (DA 211).

Often she drew practical lessons from a passage of Scripture. Referring to Israel's crossing of the Red Sea after the Exodus from Egypt, she wrote: "The great lesson here taught is for all time. Often the Christian life is beset by dangers, and duty seems hard to perform. The imagination pictures impending ruin before and bondage or death behind. Yet the voice of God speaks clearly, 'Go forward.' We should obey this command, even though our eyes cannot penetrate the darkness, and we feel the cold waves about our feet" (PP 290).

In recounting the history of the *great controversy between Christ and Satan she often added to the biblical text details that provide deeper insights into the events recorded in Scripture. In her description of the flood she wrote, "Satan himself, who was compelled to remain in the midst of the warring elements, feared for his own existence" (*ibid.* 99). When she recounted the visit of the Magi to Bethlehem, she wrote, "Through the gifts of the magi from a heathen country, the Lord supplied the means for the journey into Egypt and the sojourn in a land of strangers" (DA 65).

As an interpreter of the Bible, Ellen White

was more of an evangelist than an academic theologian. She was more of a prophet than an exegete of the Bible, because she was more interested in the people to whom she was writing than the people the Bible writers were addressing.

Gerhard Pfandl

BIBLE, INSPIRATION OF, see **REVELATION AND INSPIRATION**.

BIBLE, INTERPRETATION OF. The principles of interpretation employed by William Miller and others in the Advent awakening of the early nineteenth century were generally within the Protestant hermeneutical tradition, and Ellen White espoused these same basic hermeneutical principles. William Miller summarized 13 "Rules of Bible Interpretation," including five general ones and eight dealing specifically with apocalyptic eschatology (prophecy, figures/symbols, and parables). In 1884 White quoted verbatim Miller's five general rules, giving them her full endorsement: "Those who are engaged in proclaiming the third angel's message are searching the Scriptures upon the same plan that Father Miller adopted. . . . '1. Every word must have its proper bearing on the subject presented in the Bible; 2. All Scripture is necessary, and may be understood by diligent application and study; 3. Nothing revealed in Scripture can or will be hid from those who ask in faith, not wavering; 4. To understand doctrine, bring all the scriptures together on the subject you wish to know, then let every word have its proper influence; and if you can form your theory without a contradiction, you cannot be in error; 5. Scripture must be its own expositor, since it is a rule of itself. If I depend on a teacher to expound to me, and he should guess at its meaning, or desire to have it so on account of his sectarian creed, or to be thought wise, then his guessing, desire, creed, or wisdom is my rule, and not the Bible.' . . . In our study of the Bible we shall all do well to heed the [five general] principles set forth" (RH, Nov. 25, 1884). Throughout her written works Ellen White often elaborated, and built upon, these basic principles, and substantiated the principles from Scripture itself; but she never provided a systematic treatment of biblical hermeneutics (the most extensive sustained treatment is a 20-part series [ST, Mar. 21-Oct. 17, 1906] entitled "Our Great Treasure-House").

Foundational to White's whole hermeneutical approach to Scripture is "the great Protestant principle" of *sola scriptura*, "the Bible, and the Bible only, as the rule of faith and duty" (GC 204, 205; cf. EW 78; RH, Dec. 15, 1885, in 1SM 416). The Bible alone is to be the "standard by which all teaching and experience must be tested," (GC vii), and its authority is to take precedence over the deductions of science, human reason, philosophy, tradition, or extrabiblical revelation (EW 78; GC 595; Ev 256; COL 39; 5T 700; MH 462; COL 110, 111; ST, Mar. 21, 1906; 2SM 85-100). The Bible alone is all-sufficient to provide knowledge of every truth essential for salvation (ST, Oct. 18, 1883; Apr. 18, 1906; GC 93, 173; RH, June 1, 1886; Dec. 15, 1896).

Many references in Ellen White's writings warn against the use of higher criticism—with its techniques of "dissecting, conjecturing, reconstructing"—which places human reason above Scripture and passes judgment upon the Word and thereby "is destroying faith in the Bible as a divine revelation" and "robbing God's Word of power to control, uplift, and inspire human lives" (AA 474; cf. BE, Feb. 1, 1897; BE, June 1, 1893; MH 142; UL 35; RC 344; 1SAT 255).

Many chapters of *The Great Controversy* are devoted to tracing the Protestant Reformers'

recapturing of the *sola scriptura* principle of the Bible (see Isa. 8:20), which White sees as the essential foundation for recovering other precious biblical truths (such as the gospel of righteousness by faith) lost during the church's apostasy from primitive Christianity (see especially GC 68, 89, 93, 120, 126, 132, 173, 174, 193, 203, 243, 249).

Accompanying *sola scriptura* is the principle of *tota scriptura*: the whole Bible, as an inseparable union of the divine and human (GC vi; 5T 709), is equivalent to the Word of God (6T 393; 5T 533; COL 39; 7BC 919). Since the whole Bible is ultimately the product of one divine Author, there is a fundamental unity and consistency among all the various parts of Scripture, even as there is a progressive unfolding of truth (EW 221; PP 114; Ed 123, 124; 1SM 19, 20; GC v, 344). Because of this analogy (or harmony) of Scripture, the Bible is its own expositor (i.e., the Protestant principle of *scriptura sui ipsius interpres*): all that the Bible says on a given subject is to be taken into account, one scripture being allowed to interpret another (EW 221; Ed 190; TM 106; 2MR 89-92; Ms 40, 1895, in 2MR 96; RH, Nov. 25, 1884; FE 187; ST, Mar. 21, 1906; OHC 210; GC 173; CT 437). There is clarity in Scripture, so that it may be understood by all, both scholar and common people alike (SC 89; ST, July 11, 1906). The language of Scripture "should be explained according to its obvious meaning, unless a symbol or figure is employed" (GC 599).

As a final general hermeneutical principle, Ellen White endorses the Protestant principle of "spiritual things are spiritually discerned" (*spiritalia spiritaliter examinatur*). This means, on one hand, the need for the Holy Spirit's assistance in interpreting the Scriptures. "A true knowledge of the Bible can be gained only through the aid of that Spirit by whom the Word was given" (Ed 189; cf. 8T 157; TM

108; GC vii), and without the Holy Spirit's guidance, men and women "shall be continually liable to wrest the Scriptures or to misinterpret them" (5T 704; cf. COL 410, 411). On the other hand, this principle implies the need for a Spirit-filled life on the part of the interpreter: approaching the Bible under the influence of the Holy Spirit (2SM 114) with "a prayerful, humble, teachable spirit" (GC 521; cf. 5T 704; ST, Mar. 28, 1906); eagerly and earnestly searching for truth as for hidden treasure (ST, Sept. 5, 1906; Oct. 3, 1906; Ed 189); pleading with God for wisdom to understand and sense the importance of scriptural truths (GC 530, 599, 600; ST, Oct. 3, 1906); emptying oneself of every prejudice (CT 463; ST, Oct. 3, 1906) and sinful practice (OHC 207); and being willing to obey God's will as revealed in His Word (5T 705) and to yield personal judgment to the counsel of godly brethren of experience (5T 293).

Along with these general hermeneutical principles, Ellen White sets forth, both by precept and example, specific guidelines for biblical interpretation, most (if not all) of which are subsumed under what today is known as the grammatical-historical method. While underscoring the miraculous divine preservation of the Hebrew and Greek manuscripts of the Sacred Scriptures, Ellen White acknowledges the possibility of minor and inconsequential copyist and translation errors (EW 220, 221; 1SM 16). Accordingly, White quotes from a variety of modern *Bible translations.

The thousands of pages of inspired exposition of Scripture in the Conflict of the Ages Series (and its predecessors) reveal White's careful attention to historical context. She was convinced that the Bible presents "authentic histories of actual individuals," "a plain, unvarnished account of what actually occurred and the genuine experience of real characters"

(4T 9; cf. Ed 173). This includes a reliable account of earth's origins and the early history of our world (PP 113; MM 89). White emphasizes the importance of understanding the ancient customs, culture, geography, and chronology of Bible times, calling this information "practical knowledge" (CT 518)! She also stresses the value of appreciating the literary beauty of Scripture (Ed 159-161, 188), and recognizes the various literary styles and forms and structures of the different human writers of Scripture (GC vi; 1SM 22, 23; 2MR 89-92; Ed 125; ST, Apr. 11, 1906).

White urges the need for careful verse-by-verse analysis of Scripture, allowing each word to have its bearing, and interpreting the meaning of words and phrases in light of their immediate context instead of taking isolated passages out of context or overstraining the meaning of sentences in an attempt at originality (Ed 189; GC 521; DA 719; 2MR 89-92; 1SM 20). At the same time, she points out how each passage of Scripture must be viewed in light of the Bible's multifaceted "grand central theme, of God's original purpose for the world, of the rise of the great controversy, and of the work of redemption" (Ed 190; cf. Ed 125, 126), and how the various truths of Scripture must be searched out and brought together to grasp the Bible's "great system of truth" (ST, Sept. 19, 1906). White also suggests the value of topical study, bringing together all that the Bible says about a given subject and allowing the contours of that subject to emerge naturally, without selectively fitting texts into a predetermined (or even false) structure (FE 187; CG 511; SC 90, 91; 2SM 82).

Regarding so-called scriptural difficulties, White insists that these cannot be solved by human scientific or philosophical methods, but require a prayerful, humble, teachable dependence upon God to see the underlying harmony beneath apparent surface contradictions, and a recognition that some mysteries are given by the infinite God to provide strong evidence of the Bible's divine inspiration and will never be fully grasped until in the future life (GW 312; 1SM 20; GC vi, 599; 8T 261; 5T 533; ST, Apr. 25, 1906; Ed 169-172). She points out the need of special care and specific principles in the interpretation of scriptures pointing beyond themselves: the Old Testament covenant promises to Israel (PK 713, 714), the prophecies of Daniel and Revelation (TM 112, 113; 2SM 101, 102; ST, July 4, 1906), the system of types and symbols in Scripture (AA 14; COL 105, 133; 7BC 933; 6BC 1095; Ed 124; GC 420, 352; PP 365, 594), and the parables of Jesus (CT 140; COL 17, 18, 21).

Finally, Ellen White places strong emphasis upon the practical, contemporary personal application of the Bible to one's own life (Lt 13, 1888, in 2MR 92; Ms 22, 1890, in 2MR 97; Lt 69, 1901, in 2MR 95; MM 37), personalizing Scripture as God's word to us individually (DA 390, 391; 6T 393; 7BC 920; ST, Apr. 4, 1906). In sum, Ellen White presents solid principles of biblical interpretation, in harmony with the hermeneutical stance of the Protestant Reformers, and ultimately rooted in the interpretative principles inherent within Scripture itself.

See also: Revelation and Inspiration.

Further reading: GC v-xii; 1SM 15-23; R. F. Cottrell, "Ellen G. White's Evaluation and Use of the Bible," in *A Symposium on Biblical Hermeneutics*, ed. G. M. Hyde (RHPA, 1974), pp. 143-161; P. G. Damsteegt, "Ellen White on Theology, Its Methods, and the Use of Scripture," JATS 4, no. 2 (Autumn 1993): 115-136; idem, *Foundations of the Seventh-day Adventist Message and Mission* (Grand Rapids: Eerdmans, 1977); R. M. Davidson, "Biblical Interpretation," in R. Dederen, ed., *Handbook of Seventh-day Adventist Theology* (RHPA, 2000), pp. 58-104; A. Hale, "[William] Miller's

Rules of Bible Interpretation," in *The Second Advent Manual: In Which the Objections to Calculating the Prophetic Times Are Considered; the Difficulties Connected With the Calculation Explained; and the Facts and Arguments on Which Mr. Miller's Calculations Rest Are Briefly Stated and Sustained* (Boston: J. V. Himes, 1843), pp. 103-106, in Damsteegt, *Foundations of the Seventh-day Adventist Message and Mission* (Eerdmans, 1977), pp. 299, 300; C. M. Maxwell, "A Brief History of Adventist Hermeneutics," JATS 4, no. 2 (Autumn 1993): 209-226; G. W. Reid, ed., *Understanding Scripture: An Adventist Approach* (BRI, 2005).

Richard M. Davidson

BIBLE, NECESSITY OF STUDYING. To study the Word of God, the Bible, Ellen White says, is to eat from the tree of life (Ev 138). God's Word is spirit and life, and as the physical body is sustained by food, so spiritual life must be sustained by the Word of God in order to have spiritual strength (7BC 941). We are not to receive it merely through someone else's mind (DA 390).

The study of Scripture is necessary as the ground of *faith. Commenting on Christ's post-Resurrection response to the questions by the two disciples on the road to Emmaus, she says, "Had He first made Himself known to them, their hearts would have been satisfied. . . . But it was necessary for them to understand the [Scriptures]. . . . Upon these their faith must be established" (DA 796-799).

Believers should study the Bible daily (5T 573-580), but never without requesting to be changed (GC 598-601). It is one thing, she says, to treat the Bible as a book of morals, but another to accept it as it really is, the word of the living God to mold the reader's actions, words, and thoughts (Ed 260). To purify the thoughts, soften the disposition, and direct minds and hearts God-ward, the heart must be exposed to the Word of God. It is only by the power of the Holy Spirit speaking through Scripture that believers can daily partake of the divine nature (COL 100-102).

Finally, it is necessary to study Scripture in order to understand that two great principles are contending for supremacy of people's lives, to trace their workings in history and prophecy, and to see how this controversy enters into every phase of one's experience (Ed 190). As Ellen White says: "In the word of God the curtain is drawn aside, and we behold, behind, above, and through all the play and counterplay of human interests and power and passions, the agencies of the all-merciful One, silently, patiently working out the counsels of His own will" (ibid. 173).

Throughout her writings Ellen White directs people's attention to the necessity of studying the Bible. "But those who bring to the investigation of the Word a spirit which it does not approve will take away from the search a spirit which it has not imparted" (RH, Aug. 22, 1907). A certain pride can be mingled with studying the Bible, and when God's Word is studied without prayer, humility, and the guidance of the Holy Spirit, the Scriptures can be misunderstood and misinterpreted (SC 108-110).

"An intensity such as never before was seen is taking possession of the world. In amusement, in moneymaking, in the contest for power, in the very struggle for existence, there is a terrible force that engrosses body and mind and soul. In the midst of this maddening rush, God is speaking. He bids us come apart and commune with Him. 'Be still, and know that I am God'" (Ed 260).

Further reading: CT 438-447; DA 383-394; Ed 185-192, 253-261; FE 129-137; GC 593-602; SD 105-113; 1SM 15-23; 5T 573-580.

Jack Blanco

BIBLE AND EARTH SCIENCES. Ellen White held up Scripture as the model for the discovery of truth and considered the Bible to be the test of faith and practice, including the study of earth science and geology. Her belief that nature and revelation share the same author and that true science and religion share an intrinsic harmony shaped her cosmological worldview. When contemporary science contradicted Scripture, she decidedly maintained submission to the Word of God. Biblical truth was the lens through which she viewed chronological, historic, and scientific claims.

White's educational model is based upon the *imago Dei*, the restoration in humanity of the wholistic image of God. The challenge to the accomplishment of that anthropological restoration is found in her larger framework: the theme of the *great controversy between Christ and Satan. Central to this framework is the authority of Scripture, which declares (1) Christ as Creator of all things, (2) the creation event in six literal days, (3) the seventh-day Sabbath as the memorial of creation, (4) the complete restoration of Eden at the second advent of Christ, including the restoration of direct communication between God and humanity, and the absence of death and predation, and (5) the continuance of the observance of the seventh-day Sabbath as the memorial to God's creation initiative. In White's great controversy framework Satan continues, until the end of time, to increase the intensity of his diabolical efforts to thwart those purposes.

Because this model is central to all of Ellen White's writings, it is impossible to remove one segment of the structure without seriously compromising the integrity of all her writings. Her theological authority hinges on maintaining the framework of her primary purpose. Though White is not considered to be either a historian or a scientist, her definition of the nature of the Creator and her account of the creation event are pivotal concepts in establishing her theology and understanding of the relationship between the Bible and science.

This great controversy model, then, is authoritative in determining the continuing veracity of such pivotal doctrines as *salvation, the *Sabbath, the mystery of death, the *second coming of Christ, and the *sanctuary. Questions regarding the origin and primary purpose of the Sabbath become more significant in Ellen White's discussion of science than do discussions of areas of less significance, such as two creation accounts, the precise age of the earth, or the source of volcanoes. She claimed that the great themes of redemption and creation were shown to her in vision; geographical and chronological details were often supplied by standard works and occasionally subjected to later revision for increased accuracy. Thus, her statements relating to some aspects of geology and earth chronology could be interpreted in the context of a larger, more primary purpose than establishing the precise age of the earth. Her larger purpose was to establish the veracity of a literal seven-day creation week and a global flood, concepts that are affirmed by Scripture and that were an integral part of her worldview.

Although Ellen White did not use the phrase "unity in diversity" (see 8MR 67) in the context of theological or doctrinal discussions, she did state that "instructors in our schools should never be bound about by being told that they are to teach only what has been taught hitherto" (Ms 8a, 1888, in 1888 Materials 133). At the same time, she maintained that the landmarks and pillar doctrines of the Adventist message were to remain (CET 203; CC 210; GC 583). In a similar way, she "was

shown" that some concepts that impact the science of geology are also to be considered as permanent. These include (1) six literal, empirical, historical 24-hour days of creation, culminating with a literal 24-hour Sabbath day of rest (EW 217; 1SP 85), and that (2) human life on earth did not exist before the literal creation week described in Genesis (1SP 87, 88; Ed 128-134). Recognizing that all truth in a fallen world is vulnerable to distortion, Ellen White continually repeated her clarion call to elevate Scripture over humanity's ideas of science. True science, in her view, always needed to be brought to the test of the unerring standard of Scripture (3SG 90-93).

In her day White was aware of ideas similar to the uniformitarianism of James Hutton. She was also aware of the scholarly scorn leveled against the notion of a recent historical creation week, similar to the scorn offered by Schleiermacher's caricature in 1829 that only "gloomy creatures" believe in ancient literalism. In this milieu of Genesis reconstruction with its converging concept of "deep time," she could state that "the work of creation cannot be explained by science" (MH 414) and that "true science and Bible religion are in perfect harmony" (Lt 57, 1896, in 4BC 1167).

Not only did Ellen White reject popular scientific notions of her day relating to geology—she recognized that higher criticism could undermine the Genesis account of creation by proposing hierarchical concepts of polygenesis, thus providing a religious rationale for the preservation of racial hierarchy. In an era in which notions regarding the biological, social, and civilizational inferiority of Blacks were commonly accepted as scientific, she challenged science by such statements as "the black man's name is written in the book of life beside the white man's. All are one in Christ. Birth, station, nationality, or color cannot elevate or degrade men" (2SM 342; cf. AA 474).

Thus Ellen White demonstrated both inclusiveness in her ministry and a Spirit-driven ability to filter through conflicting scientific claims to define truth. Her unique voice contrasts with the increasing solidarity in biblical reconstruction and revisionism of her time and today.

Adventist interpretation of Ellen White's comments on science and religion is predicated on the affirmation of the source of her information. In at least three places regarding earth history we find White making the following claims: "I was then carried back to the creation, and was shown that the first week, in which God performed the work of creation in six days and rested on the seventh day, was just like every other week" (1SP 85). Regarding the size of pre-flood animals she writes: "I was shown that very large, powerful animals existed before the flood, which do not now exist" (*ibid.* 87). Finally, concerning geology White says: "I have been shown that, without Bible history, geology can prove nothing" (*ibid.* 88). She claimed that her information on the history of the creation and flood came from divine visions regarding these historical events.

The above statements help to explain her strong conviction regarding the authority and reliability of God's Word concerning earth history: "There should be a settled belief in the divine authority of God's Holy Word. . . . Moses wrote under the guidance of the Spirit of God, and a correct theory of geology will never claim discoveries that cannot be reconciled with his statements" (PP 114). This statement also shows that the relationship between field evidence and the biblical account of the flood is a crucial issue. Commenting upon this point, Ellen White wrote, "relics found in the earth do give evidence of

conditions differing in many respects from the present, but the time when these conditions existed can be learned only from the Inspired Record" (*ibid.* 112). She indicated that the implications that human research draws from field data must be informed and guided by biblical claims, i.e., by a worldview constructed by the Bible. Thus White rejected methodological naturalism in favor of creationist catastrophism. Her application of the catastrophism model is implied in her discussion of fossils when, in regard to antediluvian life, she stated that "men, animals, and trees, many times larger than now" existed then (*ibid.*), implying by this that different biosphere conditions existed in the past than exist now. Conversely, she denied the claim that these same fossils show that life forms existed millions of years ago, which she believed to be an unwarranted deduction from the field data. She believed that "in the history of the Flood, inspiration has explained that which geology alone could never fathom" (*ibid.*).

Explaining some implications of the historical event of the flood, White notes that during the flood humans, animals, and trees were "buried, and thus preserved as an evidence to later generations that the antediluvians perished by a flood. God designed that the discovery of these things should establish faith in inspired history; but . . . the things which God gave them [i.e., to humans] as a benefit, they turn into a curse by making a wrong use of them" (*ibid.*). In these words she implied that God intended paleontology and the biblical record to shed light upon each other. According to Ellen White, God encourages the search for and study of fossils, and actually intends that their discovery should help to ground personal belief in the historical reliability of the Genesis account of the creation and the flood.

Ellen White believed that the accounts of

Genesis 1-11 are divinely intended to be interpreted historically, and not only theologically. According to her worldview, the only true biblical understanding of the creation and the flood stories is to interpret them as referring to empirical, historical events that are of interest to the natural sciences. These insights can help to formulate sound, scientifically responsible field research projects.

In the light of her statements on creation and the flood, Ellen White affirmed a recent historical creation week and a global flood even in the face of challenges presented by scientific theories and evidences in her day. Her views on science and the Bible encouraged perseverance and faith in the historical reliability of Genesis 1-11, and the pursuit of scientific research informed accordingly.

Further reading: Ed 128-134; PP 44-51, 105-116; 3SM 232, 446-448; MH 439, 440; 9T 257-261; P. Gordon, "The Testimony of Ellen G. White on the Bible, Science, and the Age of the Earth" (EGWE, SDoc); "E. G. White Statements Relating to Geology and Earth Science" (EGWE, SDoc).

Cindy Tutsch

BIBLE CONFERENCE OF 1919. The first meeting of Seventh-day Adventists that extensively discussed the nature and authority of Ellen White's writings after her death (1915). The conference was convened by the General Conference Executive Committee to study issues related to the historical fulfillment and interpretation of biblical prophecies. Although the conference was delayed for several years, primarily because of World War I (1914-1918), church leaders intended to bring together leading educators, writers, and administrators to discuss issues, obtain a consensus, and thereby achieve a higher degree of harmony within the denomination.

At the very outset of the meeting General

Conference president *A. G. Daniells cast a broad vision for the work that the Seventh-day Adventist Church should be doing in calling the attention of the world to the *second coming of Christ. He compared their meeting to other prophecy conferences that were being

TEACHERS AND CHURCH ADMINISTRATORS AT THE 1919 BIBLE CONFERENCE

held with great fanfare by conservative Christians across the United States. Daniells and other church leaders such as *W. W. Prescott believed that by candidly exploring biblical and historical issues, the denomination could become more united and then hold similar conferences for the public.

The conference opened with 65 attendees representing the most highly educated group of Adventist thinkers officially convened to that time. It was actually two conferences: a Bible conference held during the daytime, July 1-19, and a teachers' council that was held during the evenings, July 1-19, and then continued through August 9. Controversial topics generally had two sessions, during which leading proponents from each side of a topic presented their most persuasive case, followed by a discussion period. Scheduled topics were frequently postponed to allow conferees more time for discussion.

The nature and authority of Ellen White's writings was not on the initial list of topics. Instead her writings came up as a necessary step to resolving conflicts over other issues.

It became obvious as conferees discussed these issues that there were two schools of thought on the interpretation of both the Bible and Ellen White's writings: the self-styled "progressives". versus the "traditionalists." Both groups held Ellen White's writings in high esteem—the question was the nature of these inspired writings and their relationship to the Bible. Thus the writings of Ellen White came to the forefront of discussion at four major points during the 1919 Bible Conference.

The first discussion about Ellen White's writings occurred on July 10, 1919, in the context of studying Adventist positions on prophetic interpretation. After this initial discussion, A. G. Daniells, also serving as conference chair, recognized the importance of this discussion and shared (July 16) with the conferees a personal, informal account of his own experiences with Ellen G. White. Unfortunately this talk by Daniells was only partially recorded. Apparently Daniells' statement of his own experience was sufficient to resolve the issues for most of the pastors and administrators. But when Daniells returned (July 30) to talk with the educators about the importance of ministerial education, it became evident that in the minds of this smaller group of 18 people, the previous topic had not yet been resolved. Over the next several days Daniells participated in a "round-table talk" about how to apply his previous presentation on Ellen White (July 16) to the teaching of Bible and history. In so doing, he gave this smaller group a more detailed glimpse into his thinking about the nature and authority of Ellen White's writings, four years after her death.

Daniells began with the recognition that there were some things in Ellen White's writings that were difficult to understand. He had personally received testimonies from Ellen White. Although such rebukes were difficult

to take, he claimed that he had consistently benefited by following her counsel. As Daniells viewed it, the current controversy over *revelation and inspiration began when individuals such as *A. T. Jones and *J. H. Kellogg advocated a very literal and rigid view for interpreting Ellen White's writings. During the ensuing power struggle, especially with Jones, Daniells was criticized for not adhering to Jones and Kellogg's view of inspiration. "It is of no . . . use," Daniells stated, "for anybody to stand up and talk about the verbal inspiration of the Testimonies, because everybody who has ever seen the work done knows better, and we might as well dismiss it" (*Report of Bible Conference, Held in Takoma Park, D.C., July 1-19, 1919* [hereafter RBC], Aug. 1, 1919, p. 1234). Daniells was similarly concerned about how the church presented the gift of prophecy. As he saw it, there was danger in focusing on the miraculous instead of on Ellen White's overall life contribution to the church. This was especially apparent in the areas of missions, education, and the spirit of service (RBC, July 30, 1919, pp. 1190-1193).

During the next few days the discussion shifted to the relationship of Ellen White's writings to the *Bible. Two contrasting positions were presented: the "progressives" claimed to know from personal experience that Ellen White's writings were not infallible. Although the "progressives" agreed on the inspiration of her writings, they held varying views among themselves about what "verbal inspiration" meant for the Bible. Some suggested that the difference between Ellen White's writings and the Bible was that her writings were not infallible, while the Bible is inerrant (infallible). Another group of conferees, the "traditionalists," regarded the writings of Ellen White as both infallible and equal to Scripture. These two schools of thought about the relationship of Ellen White's writings to the Bible epitomized the hermeneutical rift that divided the conferees in 1919. Little did they realize the significance their discussions would have for the later development of Adventist theology.

In the end, no consensus was reached about Ellen White's writings. J. N. Anderson, a professor of biblical languages from Union College, suggested that to avoid a serious crisis in the future, church leaders needed to begin educating members regarding inspiration. Others feared that church members would become "terribly upset" if they should discover that Ellen White was fallible (RBC, Aug. 1, 1919, pp. 1231, 1238, 1239, 1241). The failure to reach consensus led to the approximately 1,200 pages of conference proceedings being tucked away in the General Conference basement and all but forgotten, until F. Donald Yost, while setting up the newly formed General Conference Archives, discovered them in 1974.

Further reading: M. W. Campbell, "The 1919 Bible Conference and Its Significance for Seventh-day Adventist History and Theology" (Ph.D. diss., AU, 2008); B. Haloviak, "In the Shadow of the 'Daily': Background and Aftermath of the 1919 Bible and History Teachers' Conference" (unpublished paper, GCAr, 1979); H. E. Douglass, *Messenger of the Lord* (PPPA, 1998), pp. 434-443; B. Haloviak and G. Land, "Ellen White and Doctrinal Conflict: Context of the 1919 Bible Conference," *Spectrum* 12, no. 4 (June 1982): 19-34; "Report of Bible Conference, Held in Takoma Park, D.C., July 1-19, 1919," Aug. 1, 1919, GCAr [www.adventistarchives.org]; G. W. Shearer, "The 1919 Bible Conference: A Bibliographical Guide" (unpublished paper, PUC, 2001, CAR).

Michael W. Campbell

BIBLE ECHO AND SIGNS OF THE TIMES. The first periodical published by the Seventh-day Adventist Church in Australia. Within six months of the arrival of the first Adventist missionaries in Melbourne on June 16, 1885, three of them, *J. O. Corliss, *M. C. Israel, and printer Henry L. Scott, published the first number of the *Bible Echo and Signs of the Times*, dated January 1886. Eight thousand copies of this first 16-page issue were printed. Its lead article, by Ellen White, was titled "Science and the Bible in Education." During her stay in Australia (1891-1900) she contributed an article in practically every issue of the paper. The periodical was printed monthly until 1889, when it became semimonthly. From 1894 it was released weekly. The issue of August 1, 1892 (7, no. 15) was the last with the title *Bible Echo and Signs of the Times*. The new title *The Bible Echo* was kept until January 19, 1903 (18, no. 3), after which it was changed to *Australasian Signs of the Times*.

Allan G. Lindsay

BIBLE IN SEVENTH-DAY ADVENTIST SCHOOLS. Ellen White, who was the most influential individual in the founding and development of the Seventh-day Adventist system of education, envisioned schools in which the study of the Bible would "have the first place" in the curricula (CT 86). In response, Battle Creek College, the first SDA educational institution, was founded in 1874 to be a reform institution that would uplift the Bible. Battle Creek College, however, rapidly devolved into a liberal arts college that almost totally neglected the curricular primacy of the Bible.

Following her first major statement on education ("Proper Education") in 1872 (3T 131-160; FE 15-46), Ellen White produced a stream of additional articles exalting the role of the Bible as the "foundation," "groundwork," and "subject matter" of Christian education (FE 393, 451, 474). An 1881 statement, "Our

College" (5T 21-36), maintained it was "God's purpose" that students "should have an opportunity to study the sciences, and at the same time to learn the requirements of His Word" (CT 86). While she thus endorsed the study of sciences, she insisted that the Bible should not be merely "sandwiched in between" other subjects to give a religious flavor to the curricula (FE 474). On the contrary, she pressed the importance of the Bible as the foundation for understanding all knowledge, and the need for other fields of study to be integrated with the Bible and the biblical worldview.

Ellen White's counsels on education, particularly those concerning the centrality of the Bible in the curricula and the importance of a balanced development of the student's mental, physical, and spiritual faculties, have been a continual stimulus to improvement for Adventist schools. From 1872 to the present, her goals of achieving and maintaining the proper relationship between the Bible and other curricular subjects, of integrating biblical principles into all other subjects, and teaching all subjects from the biblical worldview still remain a challenge for Adventist education. For Ellen White the Bible was not to comprise the entire curricula, but instead, to be the foundation and context of all areas of study within the curricula.

Further reading: M. E. Marroquin, "The Historical Development of the Religion Curriculum at Battle Creek College, 1874-1901" (Ph.D. diss., AU, 2001).

Medardo Marroquin

BIBLE SANCTIFICATION (PPPA, 1882, 82 pp.). Reprint of a series of articles titled "Sanctification" that Ellen White wrote for the *Review and Herald* between January 18 and May 3, 1881. *Bible Sanctification* was first published in 1882 by Pacific Press. Two more printings came in 1884 and 1886, both from the press in Battle Creek, Michigan; and in 1889 it became the first book in the Bible Students' Library series. In 1937 *Bible Sanctification*, with the addition of one paragraph from *Prophets and Kings*, was reissued and renamed *The Sanctified Life*. It is this title that is listed in indexes to the writings of Ellen White. The theme of the book is based on 1 Thessalonians 5:23—"And the very God of peace sanctify you wholly; and I pray God your whole spirit and soul and body be preserved blameless unto the coming of our Lord Jesus Christ." This is the biblical definition of true sanctification: sanctification of the whole person, the goal of which is "entire conformity to the will of God" (SL 9). Such sanctification is a daily, lifelong work (*ibid.* 10); in fact, the more sanctified Christians become, "the more deeply will they feel their own defects" (*ibid.* 7). Thus, only those who are disconnected from Christ and far from holiness will make claims to (completed) sanctification (*ibid.* 7, 8). Trials will reveal those who possess true sanctification (the meritorious robe of Christ's righteousness) and those who cling to false sanctification (their worthless self-righteousness). The majority of the book is dedicated to showing, through the lives of Daniel and John, true models of Bible sanctification.

Marla Samaan Nedelcu

BIBLE TRANSLATIONS, ELLEN G. WHITE'S USE OF. During her writing career (1845-1915) Ellen White quoted Scripture profusely, using several Bible translations. Though she never published on the topic, her use of the Bible and her stories of the Reformers who translated Scripture into the languages of the people are instructive.

Ellen White says nothing about the intense nineteenth-century interest in early Bible manuscripts, yet she was quick to reap the practical benefits. She immediately began using the two significant English translations that were published in her lifetime. The Revised Version (RV), the first serious revision of the King James Version in nearly 300 years, appeared in Britain in 1881 (New Testament) and 1885 (Old Testament), followed by its American counterpart, the American Standard Version (ASV), in 1901. The Scripture index in volume 1 of the *Comprehensive Index to the Writings of Ellen G. White* (1962) documents her use of these translations.

Arthur L. White, Ellen White's grandson, lists eight *Review and Herald* articles from the 1880s (mostly reprints from other publications) informing Adventists about the revision. Otherwise, A. L. White declares, the revisions went largely unnoticed in the *Review* ("The E. G. White Counsel on Versions of the Bible," EGWE, Dec. 9, 1953; revised May 1991). His statistics, however, show that Ellen White quickly began using the new versions: *The Great Controversy* (1888) cites some 850 texts, including a handful from the RV. In the 1911 edition one RV text is replaced by one from the ASV. In *The Ministry of Healing* (1905) she used more than 50 texts from the RV and ASV, plus a small number from Leeser (1853) and Noyes (1869).

Some books use RV texts "frequently": PP, SC, MB, DA, Ed, and 8T; others contain only "a few": COL, 7T, 9T, AA, CT, GW, and PK. *Patriarchs and Prophets* also contains two renderings from Bernard (1842) and at least one from Boothroyd (1833). *Education* cites one from Rotherham (1868-1902).

As for the history of Bible translations, Ellen White is mostly silent. She refers to the Greek Old Testament once (DA 33), but does not use the word "Septuagint." Also unmentioned are the Masoretes, the careful Jewish copyists of the Hebrew Old Testament (500-1000); Origen (d. 254), producer of the massive Hexapla, a six-column parallel Old Testament; and Jerome (d. 420), the first Christian scholar to master Hebrew (and the last until the Renaissance), and the translator of the Latin Vulgate.

But the Reformers who gave the Bible back to the people do receive more of her attention: John Wycliffe (d. 1384), translator of the first English Bible (GC 79-96); William Tyndale (d. 1536), translator of the first printed English New Testament (1525)(GC 245-247); and Martin Luther (d. 1546), translator of the Bible into German (New Testament in 1522) (GC 193) all earn high praise. Even Erasmus merits mention for printing the Word of God in the "original tongue" (Greek) for the first time (GC 245).

Reacting to the classical language curriculum at Battle Creek College, White observed that "a knowledge of [classical] Greek and Latin is not needed by many." In those days of almost universal ignorance of the laws of health, White rightly recognized that teaching students basic principles of physical, mental, and spiritual health was a higher priority than Latin (CT 382). Further, she regarded classical Greek and Latin literature as teaching to foster infidelity. But she never denigrated the study of modern languages or of the original biblical languages. "Nearly every minister in the field," she wrote, "had he exerted his God-given energies, might not only be proficient in reading, writing, and grammar, but even in languages" (TM 194).

That practical bent matches Ellen White's commonsense approach to Bible translations. Her son W. C. White said that his mother "occasionally" referred to her copy of the Revised Version, but did not use it in preaching, lest she cause "perplexity" to older members. Yet she readily recommended its use in publications. W. C. White could recall no instance, either oral or written, that his mother condemned modern translations (see A. L. White, "Mrs. White and Revised Versions," *Ministry*, April 1947, citing DF 579 [1931]). Indeed, given her passion for an understandable Bible, she could never have supported any kind of "KJV-only" movement of the kind that became prominent after her death (cf. B. G. Wilkinson, *Our Authorized Version Vindicated* [1930]). Her support would go to the KJV translators themselves, who wrote that the *translation* of the king's speech, even when roughly done, "is still the king's speech." Likewise with the Bible: "Even the very worst translation of the Bible in English," wrote the translators, "is the word of God" (Erroll F. Rhodes and Liana Lupas, eds., *The Translators to the Reader: The Original Preface of the King James Version of 1611 Revisited* [American Bible Society, 1997], p. 78).

Alden Thompson

BICYCLE. In 1894, while in Australia, Ellen White received a vision about some events in Battle Creek. In this vision she saw that "there seemed to be a bicycle craze. . . . A bewitching influence seemed to be passing as a wave over our people there. . . . Satan works with intensity of purpose to induce our people to invest their time and money in gratifying supposed wants. This is a species of idolatry. . . . There were some who were striving for the mastery, each trying to excel the other in the swift running of their bicycles" (8T 51, 52). The context of this testimony to church members in Battle Creek reveals that Ellen White was addressing the spirit of competition and rivalry, the desire for supremacy, and specially the lack of proper stewardship of time and money. "Money was spent to gratify an enthusiasm" and to "encourage selfishness," she stated (*ibid.*). All of these, she saw, violated clear biblical principles of Christian behavior.

The historical context supports her conclusions. "Toward the end of the . . . [nineteenth] century the American people were swept with a consuming passion which left them with little time or money for anything else. . . . What was this big new distraction? For an answer the merchants had only to look out the window

EARLY BICYCLE MODEL

and watch their erstwhile customers go whizzing by. America had discovered the bicycle, and everybody was making the most of the new freedom it brought. . . . The bicycle began as a rich man's toy. Society and celebrity went awheel. . . . The best early bicycle cost $150, an investment comparable to the cost of an automobile today. . . . Every member of the family wanted a 'wheel,' and entire family savings often were used up on supplying the demand" (Frank Tripp, "When All the World Went Wheeling," *Reader's Digest,* December 1951). Within a few years, however, the rapid strides in technology and manufacturing made the bicycle one of the most economical means of transportation.

See also: Games and Sports; Competition.

Denis Fortin

BIG BIBLE, see **VISIONS OF ELLEN G. WHITE.**

BIRTHDAYS, see **HOLIDAYS.**

BLACKS, WORK FOR, see **AFRICAN-AMERICANS, ADVENTISM AMONG.**

BLESSINGS, see THOUGHTS FROM THE MOUNT OF BLESSING.

BLUE BOOK. An 89-page booklet by *Charles E. Stewart, M.D., so-called because the first edition had a blue cover and the actual title was too cumbersome for easy use (*A Response to an Urgent Testimony From Mrs. Ellen G. White Concerning Contradictions, Inconsistencies and Other Errors in Her Writings* [Battle Creek, Mich.: Liberty Missionary Society, October 1907]). The book placed quotations from Ellen White in parallel columns to highlight apparent contradictions and to demonstrate literary dependence. It reiterated some well-known issues and placed in writing some charges that had previously been circulated only as rumors.

Seven months earlier, in March 1907, Ellen White had written an open letter ("To Those Who Are Perplexed Regarding the Testimonies Relating to the Medical Missionary Work"), promising that if those who had questions about her work would write to her, she would try to explain the difficulties. This letter elicited responses from many individuals, including physicians *David Paulson, *W. S. Sadler, and Charles E. Stewart. Ellen White personally wrote more than 30 letters and four *Review and Herald* articles (see *Further reading*) in answer to their questions. Some of the questions she referred to members of her staff, particularly *W. C. White and *C. C. Crisler, and a few questions she declined to answer yes or no, because, she said, "I must not make statements that can be misconstrued" by those who "try to vindicate their personal unbelief" (Lt 206, 1906, in 1SM 29, 30). Paulson found her replies convincing, and Sadler seemed to be satisfied for a time, but Stewart was not. He felt that Ellen White's decision not to attempt a definitive answer for some questions amounted to "dodging the issue" (C. E. Stewart

to WCW, Oct. 22, 1906). Consequently, in May 1907 Stewart wrote Ellen White a letter, which in October 1907, with help from A. R. Henry, was published as the "Blue Book."

W. C. White, W. W. Prescott, and General Conference president *A. G. Daniells discussed Stewart's letter by mail and in a council meeting at Elmshaven (see Homes of James and Ellen G. White) in January 1908. Ellen White compared Stewart to earlier dissidents Snook and Brinkerhoff (see *Marion Party) and advised against attempting any comprehensive reply. The committee subsequently noted that some of the questions were so trivial that a formal response was unnecessary, and that others had been answered in an earlier publication (*A Statement Refuting Charges Made by A. T. Jones Against the Spirit of Prophecy* [May 1906]). A few topics—such as the use of milk, eggs, and butter; drug medications; the rebuilding of the Battle Creek Sanitarium; the charge of plagiarism; and the proper use of tithe—were considered important enough to be addressed individually in small pamphlets or other brief writings. *E. S. Ballenger reprinted the Blue Book in the 1930s.

Further reading: 1SM 24-39; 6Bio 89-103; RH, July 26, Aug. 9, Aug. 30, Sept. 6, 1906; J. Moon, *W. C. White and Ellen G. White: The Relationship Between the Prophet and Her Son* (AUP, 1993), pp. 317-324; Tim Poirier, "To Those Who Are Perplexed . . . " (EGWE-GC, n.d.); [WCW], "Memorandum of Plans Agreed Upon in Dealing With 'The Blue Book'" ([Feb. 1908], RG 261, F. M. Wilcox Reference Files, Folder: E. G. White Testimonies of Special Interest, GCAr).

Jerry Moon

BOOKS, PREPARATION OF ELLEN G. WHITE'S. The preparation of her books for publication, the selection and arrangement of materials from her writings, the editing, and the approval of illustrations, if any, were Ellen White's responsibility. However, the publishing house generally chose the titles for her books, with the possible exceptions of *The Great Controversy* and *Testimonies for the Church*. For her book on the life of Christ the publisher (Pacific Press) suggested two titles—*The Desire of All Nations* and *The Desire of Ages*—and allowed her to make the final choice (4Bio 390).

Ellen White's first booklet, a 64-page work entitled *A Sketch of the Christian Experience and Views of Ellen G. White*, was published in 1851. While Ellen had natural literary talent, she lacked a formal education, so never became proficient in the technicalities of grammar. Consequently, it was necessary from the very first for her to have assistance in preparing her books for publication. James White must be credited with editing and arranging his wife's first three pamphlets, *A Sketch of the Christian Experience and Views of Ellen G. White* (1851), *Supplement to Experience and Views* (1854), and *Spiritual Gifts* (1858), all of which were republished in 1882 under the title *Early Writings*. He probably also assisted his wife editorially in the preparation of *The Spirit of Prophecy*, volume 1, the predecessor of *Patriarchs and Prophets*. During the years 1874-1876 Ellen White's niece, *Mary Clough, assisted her in preparing for publication *The Spirit of Prophecy*, volumes 2 and 3, two books on the life of Christ (3SM 456). Others who assisted her editorially over the years included *Sarah Peck, on the book *Education* (4Bio 450); *C. C. Crisler, *Maggie (Hare) Bree, and Minnie Hawkins, on *The Acts of the Apostles* (6Bio 342, 343); and *Mary Steward, *D. E. Robinson, *W. W. Prescott, C. C. Crisler, *A. G. Daniells, and *Homer Salisbury, on the 1911 edition of *The Great Controversy* (ibid. 307; 3SM 457). The literary assistant who gave Ellen White the greatest help during the years 1879-1904 was *Mary

Ann Davis (3SM 91), nicknamed Marian by Ellen White and usually referred to by this name in her correspondence. Marian's appreciation of literary beauty as well as her skillful organizing ability resulted in the preparation for publication of the 1888 edition of *The Great Controversy* (ibid. 111), *Patriarchs and Prophets* (3Bio 435, 443), *The Desire of Ages* (4Bio 382, 383), *Christ's Object Lessons* (ibid. 448), *The Ministry of Healing* (5Bio 378), and others.

Actually, Ellen White needed two kinds of literary help. She needed assistants who would check grammar, spelling, and phraseology for her letters and periodical articles. She also needed those who could select, from her voluminous writings on given topics, passages that would then be arranged and organized for publication as books. In a letter to George Irwin, General Conference president, Ellen White explained the exact nature of this kind of help: "How are my books made? Marian does not put in her claim for recognition. She does her work in this way: She takes my articles which are published in the papers, and pastes them in blank books. She also has a copy of all the letters I write. In preparing a chapter for a book, Marian remembers that I have written something on that special point, which may make the matter more forcible. She begins to search for this, and if when she finds it, she sees that it will make the chapter more clear, she adds it. The books are not Marian's productions, but my own, gathered from all my writings. Marian has a large field from which to draw, and her ability to arrange the matter is of great value to me. It saves my poring over a mass of matter, which I have no time to do" (Lt 61a, 1900, in 3SM 91).

This type of work required some changes in wording at times. The working papers for *The Desire of Ages* used in Ellen White's office in Cooranbong, Australia, in 1897 and 1898 reveal that two of her assistants did suggest changes in wording that Ellen White accepted. Marian's caution in this regard is evident from Ellen White's comment to her daughter-in-law Mary White: "Every little change of a word she [Marian Davis] wants us to see" (Lt 64a, 1889, in 3SM 92, 93). It appears that some changes in wording were made for purely aesthetic reasons.

To another General Conference president Ellen White explained why she had no time for work that could safely be trusted to someone else: "I have so many interruptions that I cannot write as I should. It is not much use for me to try to do this, and yet have the care of the churches, the responsibility of a household, and the work of a hotel-keeper; for comers and goers are continually creating an excitement at my home" (Lt 59, 1895, in 19MR 271). In spite of the pressures she lived under she nevertheless found time to write so much on the life of Christ that three books resulted— *The Desire of Ages*, *Thoughts From the Mount of Blessing*, and *Christ's Object Lessons*.

Although it was essential for Ellen White to hire literary helpers, she followed their work closely. According to W. C. White, manuscripts that her helpers had arranged were submitted to his mother early in the morning for her approval. She would go over them, carefully adding words, phrases, sentences, or otherwise making improvements, after which the manuscripts were returned to the secretary for another copying (6Bio 342, 343). At the same time she welcomed criticism from those she trusted. She once requested her husband to submit one of her manuscripts to J. H. Waggoner and J. N. Loughborough for their appraisal. She especially valued Elder Waggoner's abilities as a theologian (3SM 104). To another theologian, W. H. Littlejohn, she declared, "I have all my publications closely examined. I desire that

nothing shall appear in print without careful investigation. . . . I laid out all my manuscript on *Patriarchs and Prophets* and on Vol. IV [*The Great Controversy*] before the book committee for examination and criticism. I also placed these manuscripts in the hands of some of our ministers for examination. The more criticism of them the better for the work" (Lt 49, 1894, in 10MR 12, 13). In the end Ellen White took full responsibility for what was published under her name. To her sister Mary she wrote, "I read over all that is copied, to see that everything is as it should be. I read all the book manuscript before it is sent to the printer" (Lt 133, 1902, in 3SM 90).

Of all the books that came from Ellen White's pen, *The Great Controversy* appears to have been her favorite. She was "more anxious to see a wide circulation for this book than for any other" she had written (CM 127). She valued it "above silver or gold" (*ibid.* 128). *The Great Controversy* had its beginning in a vision given Ellen White at a funeral at Lovett's Grove, Ohio, on March 14, 1858, when, for the second time, the Lord revealed to her the history of the great conflict between Christ and Satan. She was instructed that she must "write it out" (3SM 99). By September of that year announcement was made that *Spiritual Gifts—The Great Controversy Between Christ and His Angels and Satan and His Angels* was ready for distribution. This early work later became known as *Spiritual Gifts*, volume 1. Its 219 pages touched only briefly the high points of the conflict between Christ and Satan. It was later enlarged to four volumes of about 400 pages each. Volume 1, issued in 1870, covered the period from the fall of Satan to the time of Solomon. Volumes 2 and 3, issued in 1877 and 1878, dealt with the life and work of Jesus and the apostles. The last volume in the series, published in 1884, dealt with the postbiblical period. It was called *The*

Spirit of Prophecy, volume 4, in its black cloth binding, and *The Great Controversy* in its less-common olive-colored binding (3Bio 243, 249). Within three years 50,000 copies of "volume 4" had been sold at a time when the Seventh-day Adventist Church had only 20,000 members. It became immediately clear that this was a book that had an appeal to non-Adventists as well as to Adventists. From 1885 to 1887 Ellen White visited Europe. When *C. H. Jones, manager of the Pacific Press, informed W. C. White that the 1884 printing plates were worn out and the type would have to be reset, Ellen White decided to use this as her opportunity to add some materials on the Reformation and subtract certain pages that could be offensive to many non-Adventist readers. The result was the 678-page 1888 edition. (The deleted pages may be found in TM 472-475.)

Again, in 1910, when the printing plates of the 1888 edition were so badly worn that they needed to be replaced, Ellen White recognized this as yet another opportunity to improve the book. She gave orders for references to be inserted for all the historical quotations used, as had been requested by the colporteurs. She also asked church leaders for any suggestions they might have for bettering the book. On July 25, 1911, she wrote F. M. Wilcox, editor of the *Review and Herald*, "As a result of the thorough examination by our most experienced workers, some changing in the wording has been proposed. These changes I have carefully examined, and approved" (Lt 56, 1911, in 3SM 124). The changes dealt largely with historical details. For example, on page 65, "The Waldenses were the first" in the 1888 edition was changed to "The Waldenses were among the first" in the 1911 edition; on page 272 "The great bell of the palace" in the 1888 edition became "a bell" in the 1911 edition; on page 273 "The

Word of God was prohibited" in the 1888 edition became "The worship of the Deity was abolished" in the 1911 edition, etc.

Ellen White stoutly maintained that she was "not the originator of these books" (the Conflict of the Ages Series). She declared, "They contain the instruction that during her lifework God has been giving her" (CM 125). Yet she found it helpful at times to use the works of other authors for insights and details that the Lord did not see fit to supply, such as the chronological sequence of events in the life of Christ. From Basel she wrote her sons Willie and Edson, who were in attendance at the General Conference session in Battle Creek, "Tell Mary [Marian Davis] to find me some histories of the Bible that would give me the order of events. I have nothing and can find nothing in the library here" (Lt 38, 1885, in 3SM 122). When working on *Patriarchs and Prophets* in Basel, Ellen White wrote A. C. Bourdeau, "I would be very much pleased if you would look among your books and find me *Jewish Antiquities*. It is there, for I saw it and I would so much like to have the use of it for a while" (Lt 37, 1886). A few weeks later she wrote Albert Vuilleumier, "I am anxious to obtain the loan of a book entitled *The Giant Cities of Bashan*. Will you please send it to me? I will take good care of it and return it to you again soon" (Lt 45, 1886).

W. C. White explained how these and other books helped her: "In some of the historical matters such as are brought out in *Patriarchs and Prophets* and in *Acts of the Apostles*, and in *Great Controversy*, the main outlines were made very clear and plain to her, and when she came to write up these topics, she was left to study the Bible and history to get dates and geographical relations and to perfect her description of details" (3SM 462). In fact, as she penned her manuscripts she felt free to use the language found in the books she examined. W. C. White speaks of "her habit of using parts of sentences found in the writings of others and filling in a part of her own composition" (*ibid.* 460). This evidently was also her practice when she was writing on the life of Christ in Australia.

The books commonly referred to as the *Testimonies* were prepared for publication in a somewhat different manner from those referred to above. They were not prepared so that each volume presents a full treatment of one particular subject or theme. Rather, each of the first five volumes, in particular, provide counsels given at a specific period in the church's history. The *Testimony* series began in 1855 at a conference at Battle Creek in which Ellen White was given a vision describing the spiritual state of the infant church. Shortly afterward six church leaders formally requested that the vision be published (*ibid.* 94). In response to this request a small pamphlet bearing the title *Testimony for the Church* (now 1T 113-126) was published. This was followed a year later by a second pamphlet (now 1T 127-140). There continued a steady stream of testimony pamphlets, many written under unfavorable circumstances, and so containing grammatical imperfections.

In 1883 it was decided to republish numbers 1-30 in four volumes, but not until these imperfections had been corrected. The General Conference session of that year voted "that in the republication of these volumes, such verbal changes be made as to remove the above-named imperfections, as far as possible, without in any measure changing the thought" (3SM 96). A committee of five was appointed to do the work required. All changes of importance were laid before Ellen White for her approval (*ibid.* 96-98; cf. Moon, pp. 121-128). The new edition, which now appears as *Testimonies for the Church*, volumes 1 to 4, was published in 1885, with volume 5

following in 1889. The material in the last four volumes, unlike the earlier ones, was presented in topical form. Volume 6 carried a large section on education, volume 7 spoke especially to the publishing interests, while volume 8 met the pantheistic heresy. The *Testimony* series was brought to a close with the publication of volume 9 in 1909.

When Ellen White died in 1915, the majority of the trustees of her estate were at first reluctant to publish anything from her writings that had not already appeared in print before her death. Eventually, however, they decided to follow the instruction left in her will, which included the printing of compilations from her manuscripts (F. D. Nichol, *Ellen G. White and Her Critics* [RHPA, 1951], p. 677). It was determined that to be useful, compilations on a given subject should cover the full range of Ellen White's teachings on that topic, including not only previously published materials, but previously unpublished letters and manuscripts as well. Such compilations would not have the advantage of a final approval by Ellen White, so special care that nothing be quoted out of context would be required.

Most compilations have been prepared by staff members or former staff members of the White Estate. At times others have assisted staff members. A case in point is the book *Evangelism*. Initially request was made by the Ministerial Association of the General Conference for a book giving Ellen White's counsels on public and personal evangelism. After Arthur White determined that there was adequate material on the subject, Louise Kleuser of the Ministerial Association was appointed to assist White in organizing the passages selected into book form. A 5,000-card index was especially useful in locating these materials. Today the CD-ROM is an indispensable aid to anyone who wishes to gain a balanced understanding of Ellen White's teachings on any given subject.

Other Ellen White titles include several that have been simplified or adapted for special audiences. *Christ Our Saviour* is the life of Christ reduced to childlike language. *Steps to Jesus* is *Steps to Christ* intended for children or for persons whose first language is not English. *The Story of Redemption in Easy English* was prepared especially for those who are deaf. "Contemporary adaptations," by Jerry D. Thomas, include *Messiah* (adapted from *The Desire of Ages*), and *Blessings* (from *Thoughts From the Mount of Blessing*). These carry the adapter's name as author because they go beyond paraphrase in adapting the language to twenty-first-century readers.

Further reading: N. J. Collins, "What Compilations Are and What They Are Not" (EGWE, SDoc); J. Moon, *W. C. White and Ellen G. White: The Relationship Between the Prophet and Her Son* (AUP, 1993), pp. 60-64, 112-129, 146-149, 221-225, 349-361, 427-436, 445, 446; R. W. Olson and R. Graybill, "How *The Desire of Ages* Was Written" (EGWE, 1979, SDoc); J. D. Thomas, *Blessings* (PPPA, 2008); J. D. Thomas, *Messiah* (PPPA, 2003); WCW, "How Ellen White's Books Were Written" (EGWE, 1935, SDoc); WCW and D. E. Robinson, "Brief Statements Regarding the Writings of Ellen G. White" (EGWE, 1933, SDoc).

Robert W. Olson

BOULDER SANITARIUM. The Boulder Sanitarium, about 30 miles north of Denver, opened as a health boarding home on University Hill on December 4, 1893. On June 10, 1895, ground was broken for three buildings on a 90-acre (35-hectare) site on upper Mapleton Hill. The largest was six stories high. The construction costs were estimated to be $30,000, but were actually $75,000. The General

Conference Association lent money to complete construction, and the building was dedicated on July 1, 1896. Dr. *O. G. Place was the medical superintendent. Ownership was transferred in the 1890s to the International Medical Missionary Association for $45,000.

In May 1901 Ellen White visited the Boulder Sanitarium for two days. Based on her observations, she advised that nursing and all other students include more variety in their studies, so that their minds would not be required to focus on a single topic for hours (Ms 170, 1901, in 10MR 302-305).

In 1904, under the management of *F. M. Wilcox, the sanitarium was finally able to pay one year's interest and $4,000 on the note. The next year Dr. Place offered $50,000 to purchase the Boulder Sanitarium. He had left the sanitarium's employment and established a competing sanitarium about a half mile away that served meat, in contrast to the vegetarian policy at the Boulder Sanitarium. Ellen White vigorously opposed the sale (6Bio 35-37).

At the same time another Adventist physician, *Pitt A. Wade, with support from Colorado Conference president *G. F. Watson, was planning to start another sanitarium in Cañon City, about 100 miles (160 kilometers) south of Denver. Ellen White also opposed the formation of that sanitarium, stating, "The Lord forbids, at this time, any movement that would tend to draw to other enterprises the sympathy and support that are needed just now by the Boulder-Colorado Sanitarium. This is a critical time for that institution" (SpTB05 32). G. A. Irwin, General Conference vice president, personally delivered her testimonies to Watson, who accepted her counsel.

Ellen White spoke three times at the Colorado camp meeting held at the Chautauqua grounds near Boulder August 26-September

5, 1909. A thousand people, including a teenager named H.M.S. Richards, who in 1929 would start the first regular Adventist radio broadcast, heard her speak. During the Sabbath morning service two inches of rain falling on a metal roof threatened to drown the various speakers' words, but the audience crowded to the front, and Richards testified that Ellen White's voice rang out above the storm. During the camp meeting she visited the Boulder Sanitarium and addressed the staff. Her addresses were recorded in the *Review and Herald*, January 13, 1910, with introductory words from W. C. White.

In 1910 ownership was transferred to the Central Union Conference. The Boulder Sanitarium was renamed the Boulder-Colorado Sanitarium and Hospital in 1956, and Boulder Memorial Hospital in 1962. In the late 1980s the hospital was struggling for market share and could not expand, because of zoning restrictions. The building was sold to Boulder Community Hospital and is currently known as its Mapleton Center. Avista Adventist Hospital, in nearby Louisville, Colorado, took its place, opening in 1990.

Del L. Johnson

BOWLING, see **GAMES AND SPORTS; COMPETITION**.

BOXING, see **GAMES AND SPORTS; COMPETITION**.

BRIDEGROOM ADVENTISTS, see **ADVENTIST DENOMINATIONS**.

BRIGHTON CAMP MEETING. The first camp meeting held in Australia, January 5-28, 1894, on a 10-acre (four-hectare) tract of land in the Melbourne suburb of Middle Brighton, nine miles (14 kilometers) south from the city center. In the *Bible Echo* (Dec. 8, 1893) Ellen White appealed for an outstanding attendance, believing the meeting would "mark a new era in the history of the work of God" in Australia (BE, Dec. 8, 1893; cf. LS 344-348).

By Friday, January 12, there were 108 family tents erected, with 445 people occupying them. Ellen White reported that the meeting was a marvel of wonder to the people. She observed that she had never seen such decided interest to hear the truth among those not of our faith (Lt 37, 1894, in 4Bio 119). About 1,000 people attended the afternoon and evening meetings during the week.

Important actions voted in the business session included the establishment of a new organizational unit between the local conference and the General Conference (a plan later adopted by the SDA Church around the world), and the appointment of a committee to secure a permanent site for a school in Australia (see *Avondale College). Ellen White spoke 16 times during the meeting and observed that it had been in every way a success (Ms 4, 1894, in 4Bio 124). About 100 people were baptized as its immediate fruitage (Lt 40b, 1894, in 4Bio 124).

During this camp meeting Ellen White came to a strong personal conviction that she should completely abandon the use of flesh foods in her diet. Although she had been a committed vegetarian since she received the light on this subject in the 1860s, she occasionally departed from a vegetarian diet during her travels or when circumstances made it difficult. At one point during the camp meeting Ellen White was approached by a Catholic woman (likely Mrs. *M.M.J. O'Kavanagh) who appealed to her not to allow "the selfishness of taking the lives of animals to gratify a perverted appetite" (TSDF 67). This plea had a great impact on Ellen White, who determined to "no longer patronize the butchers" and to "not have the flesh of slain animals on my table" (Lt 73a, 1896, in Nichol, pp. 388, 389). From that moment on, Ellen White abstained completely from eating meat.

Further reading: 4Bio 113-124; R. W. Coon, *Ellen White and Vegetarianism* (PPPA, 1986); F. D. Nichol, *Ellen G. White and Her Critics* (RHPA, 1951), pp. 388, 389.

Allan G. Lindsay

BUNYAN, JOHN (1628-1688). Prolific English Puritan writer best known for his allegorical work on the Christian journey, *The Pilgrim's Progress* (1678). "John Bunyan breathed the very atmosphere of Heaven," wrote Ellen White, "and there [in a dungeon] he wrote his wonderful allegory of the pilgrim's journey from the land of destruction to the celestial city. For two hundred years that voice from Bedford jail has spoken with thrilling power to the hearts of men. Bunyan's *Pilgrim's Progress* and *Grace Abounding to the Chief of Sinners* have guided many feet into the path of life" (4SP 174; GC 252). Ellen White added that the book *Pilgrim's Progress* "portrays the Christian life so accurately, and presents the love of God so attractively, that through its instrumentality hundreds and thousands have been converted" (RH, May 30, 1912). Occasionally she made allusions to particulars of Bunyan's allegory, such as the slough of despond (Lt 1, 1873, in 15MR 239; Ms 37, 1902) and the man with the muckrake (9T 217; Ms 77, 1903; Ms 107, 1908). Ellen White, furthermore, upheld John Bunyan's life as an illustration of the power of Christ to transform a life of profanity and use it for his own purpose (Ms 87, 1898; Ms 90, 1900).

Further reading: J. Brown, *John Bunyan,*

PHOTO CREDIT: UNKNOWN

JOHN BUNYAN, ENGLISH PURITAN, AUTHOR OF *THE PILGRIM'S PROGRESS*

1628-1688, His Life, Times, and Work (Hamden, Conn.: Archon Books, 1969); F. M. Harrison, *John Bunyan, a Story of His Life* (London: Banner of Truth, 1964).

Heidi Olson Campbell

BUSINESS ETHICS. Scripture teaches that "God, as the Giver of all our benefits, has a claim upon them all; that His claim should be our first consideration; and that a special blessing will attend all who honor this claim" (CS 65). "We are stewards, entrusted by our absent Lord with the care of His household and His interests, which He came to this world to serve. He has returned to heaven, leaving us in charge, and He expects us to watch and wait" for His return (8T 37). Ellen White reminds Christians that property (4T 480, 481; CS 80), learning (6BC 1081), talents (4T 619), and strength (2T 432) belong to God. These words encapsulate well her teachings on business ethics. From this premise can be derived several biblically based principles from her writings.

First, she points to the Scriptures as the textbook. "There is no branch of legitimate business for which the Bible does not afford an essential preparation. Its principles of diligence, honesty, thrift, temperance, and purity are the secret of true success" (AH 391).

Christians are not to disconnect their religious convictions from their business (CD 267), because the business world is not outside the limits of God's government and because Christianity is not meant only for church one day a week (4T 494). It is at the place of business that a follower of Christ will impact on his or her associates the most, as they observe "the manner in which our Lord would conduct business enterprises" (DA 556). But the contrary is equally true. The lack of thoroughness, diligence, and orderliness brings reproach to our faith. Lack of faithfulness in business is associated with lack of faithfulness in religious life (2T 83).

Wisdom and foresight (3T 116, 117) and even "shrewdness and close calculation are needed," as long as these do not become "a ruling power. Under proper control, they are essential elements in the character; and if you keep the fear of God before you, and His love in the heart, you will be safe" (4T 540).

Ellen White cautions against speculation (CS 237, 238) and risk investment (4T 596) for fear of gambling-like obsession (CS 234; GW 341). Temperance in the time spent at work (6T 256; 4T 412; FE 154) will protect the marriage and family relations (1T 695; AH 214; FE 154). The danger of defrauding the poor (1T 224, 225) or of exploiting those with disabilities (3T 514; 2SM 181) or "any worker" will meet God's justice. "He requires that integrity be cherished in the soul and revealed in the life" (MM 172). She reminds all of the great day when God will right all wrongs. "Any injustice done to saint or sinner will then be rewarded accordingly. Christ identifies His interest in all the afflictions of His people. God will avenge those who shall treat the widow or the fatherless with oppression, or who shall rob them in any way" (WM 218, 219). But He will bless those who follow the golden rule in their business transactions (MH 187-189), who are fair and honest (MM 127), and who deal with equity (CS 145, 146).

Miroslav Kiš

CALENDAR, KARAITE, see **KARAITE CALENDAR.**

CALIFORNIA. Adventist work in California began when *M. G. Kellogg located there in 1859, and upon his return to Michigan appealed to the 1868 General Conference session to send a missionary to California. In response

to this appeal, the session appointed *J. N. Loughborough and *D. T. Bourdeau to establish Adventist ministerial work in California (PUR, July 3, 1913).

The Whites first visited California in September 1872 and stayed through the following spring, doing evangelism and organizing the California Conference (Feb. 14-18, 1873). Ellen White appreciated the warm climate, and also found that she was able to accomplish more writing when away from the administrative center in *Battle Creek. During this first visit she wrote most of *The Spirit of Prophecy, volume 2. Over the next decade the Whites first rented and later bought *homes in which they lived while visiting the western United States. For much of the next decade they spent the first half of each year in California, and then returned east to manage administrative duties in Michigan and travel to various speaking appointments.

During their second visit (December 1873-June 1874) James White started a new journal, the *Signs of the Times, and Ellen White called for Adventists to build a publishing house and health institution in California (Lt 29, 1874, in 2Bio 418). The Whites left California in June 1874 to raise funds for these new institutions. Returning from their fund-raising tour in January 1875, they established the *Pacific Press over the next three months (2Bio 467-470). The Whites returned to California again in September 1875 for much of the rest of the year (ibid. 482). On November 11, 1875, James White announced that he would return east and leave Ellen behind to write. She remained in California until May 1876, when she rejoined her husband for speaking appointments in the east. In November 1876 the Whites returned to California, leaving in the summer of 1877 to attend camp meetings.

In December 1877 they visited Healdsburg

and St. Helena in northern California for the first time. Ellen White remembered what a blessing their country home in Greenville, Michigan, had been to help James recover his health, and she hoped that a home in the mountains near Healdsburg would accomplish the same purpose while allowing her to be more productive in her writing (Lt 42, 1877, in 3Bio 79). With this in mind they purchased a home two miles (three kilometers) outside of Healdsburg. By Christmas 1877 they had moved in, and the next spring they began to make periodic forays to Oakland to monitor the progress of the Pacific Press (March-May 1878). In May 1878 James left California to be treated at the *Battle Creek Sanitarium. While he was there, his wife began a speaking itinerary that ended up with both of them attending the 1878 General Conference session in Battle Creek that October. By February 1880 Ellen had returned to California while James remained in *Battle Creek to carry on his many administrative duties (3Bio 132-139). She left California in August 1880 to rejoin her husband on a camp meeting tour, but clearly preferred her California home as a place where she accomplished more writing.

After James White died in August 1881, Ellen White spent some time in *Colorado before attending the California camp meeting in October (3Bio 185). At this camp meeting, delegates voted to establish *Healdsburg College (now Pacific Union College)(3Bio 191). Ellen White returned to Oakland (near Pacific Press), but in early 1882, sensing a need to be closer to the new school, she purchased a cottage near Healdsburg College. This was her residence whenever she was in the western United States until she left for *Australia in 1891 (3Bio 202, 203). She continued her previous pattern of staying on the West Coast to write during the first half of the year and then traveling the remainder of the year.

In July 1885 Ellen White left California to visit Europe (through October 1887). After her return from Europe, the 1887 General Conference session was held in Oakland, California, so that she could spend the remainder of the winter in California and complete the 1888 edition of *The Great Controversy. In 1888 Ellen White purchased a 50-acre (20-hectare) ranch in Burroughs Valley, Fresno County, California, hoping that the mild, dry climate would help her daughter-in-law *Mary (Kelsey) White recover from her tuberculosis. (However, Mary died in 1890, and Ellen White sold the ranch in 1891.) Ellen White remained in California until October 1888, when she left to attend the next General Conference session in Minneapolis. From that session she traveled almost constantly, returning only briefly to her home in Healdsburg (October 1889; April-May 1890; September-November 1891) until she left for Australia in 1891.

When Ellen White returned from Australia, landing in San Francisco, California, in September 1900, she hoped to find a new home quickly. Considering her age, she felt that the warm climate of California would be best for her (5Bio 27). While resting at the *St. Helena Sanitarium, she learned of the *William Pratt home, which she purchased and named "Elmshaven" (5Bio 34). Here she spent most of her later years until her death in 1915. During these years Ellen White felt an intense burden for the development of Adventist health institutions in southern California, and was instrumental in founding Paradise Valley Sanitarium (1904), Glendale Sanitarium (1905), and Loma Linda Sanitarium (1905).

Further reading: J. C. Haussler, "The History of the Seventh-day Adventist Church in

California" (Ph.D. diss., University of Southern California, 1945); H. O. McCumber, *The Advent Message in the Golden West* (PPPA, 1968); *SDA Encyclopedia* (1996), vol. 10, pp. 274-277.

Michael W. Campbell

CALL TO STAND APART, A (RHPA, 2003, 120 pp.). A paraphrased compilation from Ellen White's writings on issues faced by youth and young adults in the twenty-first century. Themes include salvation and spiritual disciplines, relationships, health, social justice, careers, and the authority of Scripture. The language is modernized and sentences and paragraphs have been condensed while retaining Ellen White's original content, ideas, and principles. The book is an effort by the trustees of the Ellen G. White Estate to communicate prophetic principles to youthful readers. Each thematic section is prefaced by the actual scriptural citations from which the commentary is drawn, and by testimonies of young adults who have found in Ellen White's books the inspiration that he or she would like to have other young persons share.

Cindy Tutsch

CALVIN, JOHN (1509-1564). Sixteenth-century French Reformer who spent his most productive years in Geneva, Switzerland, helping to lead the reform movement there. He was best known for systematizing Reformed theology. In *The Great Controversy* Ellen White devotes about 10 pages (219-224, 233-236) to his life and thought and is generally positive about his influence in both leadership and theological influence.

Raised a Roman Catholic in France, John Calvin was educated in medieval scholastic theology at the University of Paris and in law at the University of Orleans. About a generation younger than Martin Luther and Ulrich

Zwingli, he was 8 years old when Luther nailed his 95 theses to the door of the Castle church in Wittenberg in 1517, and was still in school when Zwingli died in battle in Switzerland in 1531. It is not clear when Calvin's sympathies for the Protestant cause began, but in 1534, when Francis I changed his policy toward French Protestants from toleration to persecu-

JOHN CALVIN, FRENCH REFORMER IN GENEVA, SWITZERLAND

tion, Calvin as a Protestant went into hiding. By the following year he was teaching in exile in Basel, Switzerland, where in 1536 he published the first edition of his *Institutes of the Christian Religion*. This work, originally a single book covering Protestant beliefs, was expanded in four later editions through 1560 to become the first major Protestant systematic theology.

Late in 1536 Calvin left Basel intending to go to Strasbourg, where Protestantism had been firmly established and where there was a library in which he could continue his scholastic life. Forced to travel by way of Geneva since the more direct route was blocked by military operations, Calvin planned to stop in Geneva only one night. Guillaume Farel, who was struggling to organize and pastor the newly Reformed town, upon hearing that the author of the recently published *Institutes* was passing through, immediately went to meet Calvin. After intense persuasion Farel convinced Calvin to stay in Geneva. Calvin was to divide his time between pastor and scholar for the rest of his life. He spent more than 25 years as a pastor in Geneva, interrupted by three years under the pastoral tutelage of Martin Bucer in Strasbourg when Calvin and Farel were driven out of Geneva by the town government in 1538. Calvin returned to Geneva in 1541 and remained a pastor there until his death in 1564.

Three different chapters of the 1888 and 1911 editions of *The Great Controversy* address John Calvin. All other references to Calvin in Ellen White's extant writings are excerpts from these passages. Calvin is not mentioned in *The Spirit of Prophecy*, volume 4, the 1884 predecessor to the expanded 1888 edition of *The Great Controversy*. This strongly suggests that she wrote the passages on Calvin when she was in Europe in 1885-1887, during the same time she wrote much of the other Reformation material in *The Great Controversy*. Two of the three chapters mentioning Calvin contain only a brief reference. One refers to Farel and Calvin, who "had spread the truth of the Reformation" in Geneva and in so doing prepared the way for the later presentation of the Second Advent by Gaussen (GC 364). Another reference is a brief paragraph of quotations from John Calvin showing that he urged Christians to anticipate the second coming of Christ (*ibid*. 303). The quotations were apparently collected from a secondary work by Daniel T. Taylor, *The Reign of Christ on Earth: or, The Voice of the Church in All Ages* (pp. 134, 158).

In the middle of the chapter entitled "The French Reformation" White narrates the events surrounding Calvin's conversion to the Reformation cause and briefly mentions his schooling and work up to that time (GC 219-224). Later in the chapter she writes of the interaction with Farel that convinced Calvin to remain and work in Geneva (*ibid*. 233, 234). The final page of the chapter includes a summary paragraph on the labors and influence of John Calvin (*ibid*. 236). As with most of the Reformation material Ellen White wrote, these passages include quotes both from and about Calvin from three prominent Protestant historians: J. H. Merle D'Aubigné,

History of the Reformation of Europe in the Time of Calvin (1866); W. Carlos Martyn, *The Great Reformation* (1866-1868); and J. A. Wylie, *The History of Protestantism* (c. 1877).

Ellen White's summary statement of the work and influence of John Calvin expresses her assessment of his value to the work of God both in Geneva and across Europe. "His course as a public leader was not faultless, nor were his doctrines free from error. But he was instrumental in promulgating truths that were of special importance in his time" (GC 236). These final words include both a disclaimer and an affirmation. White would no doubt have regarded Calvin's acceptance of the religious intolerance in Geneva and his role in the condemnation and execution of Michael Servetus among Calvin's faults. Also, Calvin's strong views on predestination directly contrasted with her own Arminian position on human free will. In spite of these and other differences between Ellen White and John Calvin, she presents him as of positive value to God in holding fast to the present truth of his time, which included "the principles of Protestantism," such as justification by faith and the authority of Scripture over tradition. These Calvin faithfully advanced in the face of the rising Counter-Reformation during the second generation of the Reformation movement.

Further reading: D. Fortin, "The French Reformation and John Calvin in Ellen White's *Great Controversy*," in *Ellen White and Current Issues Symposium* 5 (2009); "John Calvin," *Christian History* 5, no. 4 (1986): 1-36; J. L. González, *The Story of Christianity*, vol. 2, *The Reformation to the Present Day* (San Francisco: Harper, 1985), pp. 61-69; J. Pelikan, *The Christian Tradition: A History of the Development of Doctrine*, vol. 4, *Reformation of the Church and Dogma (1300-1700)* (Chicago: University of Chicago Press, 1984), pp. 183-244, 322-331;

J. A. Wylie, *The History of Protestantism* (New York: Cassell, Petter and Galpin, c. 1877), vol. 2, pp. 146-173, 219-237, 280-376.

John W. Reeve

CAMDEN VISION. A disputed vision allegedly received by Ellen White in Camden, New York, in 1851, in the home of *Chandler B. Preston (2SG 150, 151). In June 1851 James and Ellen White attended conferences in Camden, New York (June 20-22), and in West Milton, New York (June 27-30). While in Camden, Ellen White had one or perhaps two visions, of which there are four different accounts, none of them original to Ellen White. While it is recognized that the absence of an original manuscript should not necessarily discredit the authenticity of a vision of Ellen White's, caution has nonetheless been used in accepting the content and wording of a copied account.

The first account of a Camden vision (Ms 1, 1851, in 1SM 188, 189) is dated June 21, 1851, and originally written out by "A. A. D."—presumed to be Abraham Dodge—in Milton, New York, a few days later (June 29). (The initials were mistakenly given as "A. A. G." when first printed in the *Review and Herald*, March 22, 1892, and reprinted in 1SM.) In this account Ellen White saw that, contrary to the beliefs of some Sundaykeeping Adventists, the second coming of Christ would not occur in 1851, and that Sabbatarian Adventists were not to set any further dates for that event. "The Lord showed me," she stated, "that the message must go, and that it must not be hung on time; for time never will be a test again" (Ms 1, 1851, in 1SM 188). Two other accounts of a vision at Camden are dated June 23, 1851, and relate Ellen White's counsels to the Camden group regarding a Sister Almira Preston and a Brother and Sister Edward and Georgianna Prior. In these two

accounts nothing is said about time setting. The first of these two accounts (Ms 2, 1851) was copied by Elmor W. Waters and refers only to Preston's situation; the second account, written by E.L.H. Chamberlain (Ms 2a, 1851), refers to both Preston and the Priors.

The most controversial account of a vision at Camden is one copied by R. R. Chapin and dated June 29, 1851 (Ms 1a, 1851; a variant account bears the date of June 24). The content of this account is entirely different from the other three. In this account Ellen White promotes an extreme view of the shut door and is stating that God's Spirit and sympathy are so withdrawn from the world that Christians should not have any sympathy for the ungodly and "that the wicked could not be benefitted by our prayers now." What is problematic with this account is that it was first circulated by Chapin some years after 1851 and after he left the early Sabbatarian Adventist group to join an opposing group called the *Messenger Party*. What also makes this account problematic is a statement by Russell F. Barton, of Waterbury, Vermont, added at the end of the account stating that "in a letter to me a few years before his death, Eld. J. N. Loughborough, who knew all about this 'vision,' stated that it is authentic." In spite of this apparent statement of authenticity, Loughborough did not have any firsthand knowledge of this vision because he became an Adventist in 1852 and first met Ellen White later that year. Furthermore, writing in 1905 and after visiting people in Camden, Loughborough stated briefly that Ellen White had a vision in Camden in *early 1850* and that this "vision applied definitely and especially" to the case of a "certain hypocritical woman" and not to the "condition of sinners generally" (*The Great Second Advent Movement*, p. 233; cf. LS 129, 130). Hence it is reasonable to assume that the Barton statement at the end of the Chapin account may have been intended for a vision received in Camden during an earlier visit in 1850 and mistakenly applied to Chapin's account. (Ellen White recounts this first visit to Camden in 2SG 124-127, and both Chandler and E. A. Preston acknowledge the veracity of this account in 2SG 303.)

Uriah Smith also referred indirectly to Chapin's account in his 1868 response to some shut-door expressions used by Ellen White. Although Smith cited some phrases from Chapin's account, he did not necessarily accept their authenticity, since his purpose was also to discuss statements that are "*claimed* to have been given through any vision, either published or unpublished" (*The Visions of Mrs. E. G. White* [1868], p. 28; italics supplied). Although this view of the shut door presented in Chapin's account appears to be anachronistic—Sabbatarian Adventists had moved away from various shut-door theories by 1850 (see Lt 4, 1850, in 5MR 91), the shut-door expressions used in this account need not be understood any differently than how Ellen White interpreted her use of the same language in her first visions, that is, "the wicked of the world who, having rejected the light, had been rejected of God" (1SM 64).

Given the lack of clear evidences regarding what Ellen White saw at Camden, only the first of these accounts (Ms 1, 1851) is considered unquestionably genuine and authentic, since she quotes it herself. Mss 2 and 2a, 1851, also appear to be credible accounts, but neither was ever endorsed by Ellen White. The Chapin account (Ms 1a, 1851), on the other hand, is likely spurious.

See also: Apocryphal Visions and Statements.

Further reading: F. D. Nichol, *Ellen G. White and Her Critics* (RHPA, 1951), pp. 229, 230, 615-619; W. H. Johns, "1851 Camden Vision: Genuine or Counterfeit?" (unpublished paper), DF 103-b, CAR; D. E. Robinson, "That Alleged 'Camden Vision,'" *Ministry*, March 1943; see other documents in DF 103-b, CAR.

Denis Fortin and Gilbert Valentine

CAMP MEETINGS. Revival and evangelistic meetings held outdoors over an extended period of time, during which most participants lived in tents. Millerite Adventists organized their first camp meeting in Hatley, Quebec, in 1842 and another a few days later in East Kingston, New Hampshire. Twenty-nine other such meetings took place that year, 40 in 1843, and 55 in the climactic year of 1844. These meetings generally followed the pattern developed by the Methodists, including three open-air preaching services each day interspersed by social and prayer meetings. Tents were pitched in a semicircle around a main assembly area. Although generally well ordered, these meetings sometimes exhibited emotionalism, as participants shouted "Hallelujah" and "Glory" and some fell prostrate.

As the Sabbatarian Adventist movement developed in subsequent years, organizing as the Seventh-day Adventist Church between 1861 and 1863, it at first avoided using camp meetings because of concern over potential disciplinary problems. But local churches soon began to meet with other churches in their region for four-day quarterly meetings, a practice that led the Illinois-Wisconsin Conference to organize a conference-wide "convocation" meeting at Johnstown Center, Wisconsin, in September 1867. A camp meeting in all but name, this gathering drew some 300 campers, including Ellen and James White. When Ellen spoke on Sunday, nearly 1,200 attended the service. Shortly after the Wisconsin meeting, a similar meeting took place at Pilot Grove, Iowa, which the Whites also attended.

The success of these meetings encouraged

the General Conference to sponsor the first official Seventh-day Adventist camp meeting at Wright, Michigan, September 1-7, 1868. Ellen White spoke five times, with attendance sometimes reaching 2,000. Afterward she spoke at meetings in Clyde, Illinois (Sept. 23-30), and Pilot Grove, Iowa (Oct. 2-7). The following year the General Conference recommended that state conferences organize all future camp meetings, stating that the Whites would attend as many "as the providence of God may direct" (2Bio 270). Of the six camp meetings held that year, the Whites attended five.

As the number of Adventist camp meetings increased during the 1870s, the Whites attended as many as possible, traveling by wagon, riverboat, and train. In 1876 they urged that the meetings be held near train stations so that they could more easily move from one appointment to another. Some of the meetings acquired significance because of visions Ellen experienced while attending or themes that she pursued in her public speaking. During the 1875 New York camp meeting, she had a vision urging wider distribution of Adventist literature; afterward she encouraged development of the *colporteur ministry. In 1879 she began emphasizing *temperance, a focus that continued for the next two years. Her presentations on this subject frequently attracted many listeners from nearby communities and sometimes led to invitations to speak in other venues, as when she spoke in the Methodist church in Milton, Oregon, in 1880. At the Des Moines, Iowa, camp meeting in 1881 she strongly recommended that Adventists, who up to that point had been reluctant to participate in elections, vote in favor of prohibition. That same year, during the Sacramento, California, camp meeting, she urged that the local conference establish a school, which led

to the development of *Healdsburg College.

Until James White's death in 1881, Ellen normally traveled to camp meetings with him. Sometimes, however, she traveled with another woman, including daughter-in-law *Mary White in 1877 and a Mrs. McOmber in 1884. In 1883 and frequently thereafter she was accompanied by *Sara McEnterfer, her editorial assistant.

As Adventism spread beyond North America, Ellen participated in its activities. She spoke at the first European camp meeting, held at Moss, Norway, in 1887. Moving to Australia in 1891, she participated in its camp meetings throughout the decade. During camp meetings in Brisbane and Newcastle in 1898, she experienced "night visions." That same year she stated that camp meetings constituted one of the best means of evangelism.

After returning to the United States in 1900 and settling in northern California, Ellen White attended several New England camp meetings in 1904, but for the most part she attended only meetings in her new home state. At the 1905 Southern California Conference camp meeting she successfully urged financial support for the new sanitarium at *Loma Linda; two years later, unable to attend and with Loma Linda still an issue, she sent a message to be read publicly at the camp meeting, calling on conference leaders to stand behind the sanitarium and developing medical school. In 1909 she traveled across the nation, frequently visiting camp meetings in route. On the way home she spoke at the Colorado camp meeting, held near Boulder from August 26 to September 6. This appears to have been the last such event she attended.

See also: Groveland Camp Meeting.

Further reading: E. N. Dick, "Adventist Camp Meetings of the 1840s," *Adventist Heritage* 4, no. 2 (Winter 1977): 3-10; Gary

Land, "Adventism and the Camp Meeting Tradition," LUH, May 23, 1978.

Gary Land

CANADA. Ellen White, accompanied by her husband, James, visited Canada three times, all three times in the Eastern Townships region of the province of Quebec. In July 1850 she visited believers in the town of Melbourne, where on an earlier visit Joseph Bates had established a group of Sabbatarian Adventists. She recalled that during this visit she was healed from a sore throat so that she could respond to former Millerites who opposed the observance of the Sabbath (LS 132, 133). This visit was one of many *Sabbatarian Bible conferences James and Ellen White attended to share the doctrinal foundation of Seventh-day Adventism among former Millerites in the 1848-1850 period. Canada East, as Quebec was called at the time, was a region in which Millerism had been a strong religious movement in the early 1840s. On their way back to Vermont the Whites also held meetings in Eaton and Hatley, where they met with other former Millerite believers. Their second visit was in August 1861 to North Sutton, where Augustin and Daniel Bourdeau had been holding meetings since January of that year. During this visit the Whites emphasized the need of proper organization among Seventh-day Adventist believers in northern Vermont and Canada, and encouraged local believers to organize themselves into congregations. Yet it took about a year before the first Adventist congregation was organized in that area in Troy and Potton in June 1862. Another one followed in December in Richford and Sutton. Both congregations were made of church members from Canada and Vermont. Their third visit occurred at the Quebec camp meeting held in Magog in August 1880. On Sunday afternoon, August 15, Ellen White spoke on the subject of temperance to a crowd of about 2,500 people. The next day James White organized the Quebec Conference of Seventh-day Adventists, the first conference in Canada. Ellen White felt that had they not attended this camp meeting, "it would have been a fearful discouragement upon the cause and work in Canada. I never saw a people so grateful for our labors as in this place" (Lt 39, 1880, in 5MR 57, 58; see also Lt 42, 1880, in 5MR 58-60). Ellen White received an invitation to attend the dedication of the South Stukely church in 1883 (Lt 26, 1883), but was not able to, as she had another speaking appointment in Maine.

Further reading: D. Fortin, *Adventism in Quebec: The Dynamics of Rural Church Growth, 1830-1910* (AUP, 2004), pp. 61, 62, 78, 79,118-120, 125, 126.

Denis Fortin

CAÑON CITY SANITARIUM, see **WADE, PITT A.**

CANVASSERS, see **COLPORTEURS.**

CASCO STREET CHRISTIAN CHURCH. A Christian Connexion or Freewill Baptist church once located on the corner of Casco and Cumberland in Portland, Maine. It was in this church that William Miller presented two courses of lectures on the second coming of Christ, first in March 1840 and again in June 1842. During Miller's meetings in 1840, a great revival swept through Portland, resulting in hundreds of conversions. Lorenzo Dow Fleming, the pastor of the Casco Street church and an ardent Millerite preacher, baptized 185 people in the four months following Miller's lectures. Ellen Harmon attended the meetings and sought salvation at the "anxious seat," but did not at that time find assurance. The 1842 meetings were less successful, as popular sentiment had begun to turn against Miller. The Harmon family remained ardent Millerites and were eventually expelled from the *Chestnut Street Methodist Church, where they were active members. The Casco Street Christian Church hosted one other major Millerite event —the third Millerite General Conference in October 1841.

Merlin D. Burt

CATHOLIC CHURCH, see **ROMAN CATHOLIC CHURCH.**

CD-ROM AND THE INTERNET, ELLEN G. WHITE WRITINGS ON (Ellen G. White Estate, 1990, 1994, 1998, 2005, 2007, 2009+). The idea of providing computer access to all of Ellen White's published writings arose along with the growing popularity of personal computers in the 1980s. The first Ellen G. White CD-ROM for PCs was introduced in 1990, followed by a Macintosh version two years later. In 1994 a second edition of these CDs updated the collection and enhanced compatibility for evolving operating systems. As software search capabilities expanded, a third edition of the CD-ROM was produced in 1998 using Folio Views. This software provided more sophisticated search capabilities, easier browsing, and additional options for printing and exporting text. The third edition added the *Comprehensive Index to the Writings of Ellen G. White.* It also made the electronic text available for the first time in two versions: a Research Edition (all her published writings), and the Standard Edition (77 of her most popular books). A new optional multimedia CD-ROM, *Legacy of Light,* featuring Adventist history within the world of Ellen White, was made available with either of the regular versions. Besides the English editions, CDs of translated Ellen White writings have been produced in Spanish (1997), Korean (1999), Portuguese (2000), and other languages. Updates to both software and text were incorporated in the 2005 and 2007 English releases, along with additional White Estate research documents and reference volumes. In 2009 the Comprehensive Research Edition was issued, adding the extensive resources of the Adventist Pioneer Library. Having the Ellen G. White database in electronic form for the CD-ROM also enabled the White Estate to put a searchable version of it on its Web site, www.WhiteEstate.org, beginning in 1995. Advances in Internet and Web-based technology are enabling the White Estate to continue its commitment to make Ellen White's writings available on CD-ROM, as well as on the Internet, in a growing number of languages.

Larry Crews

CHAIN GANGS, see **SUNDAY LEGISLATION.**

CHARACTER DEVELOPMENT. "Character building is the most important work ever entrusted to human beings; and never before was its diligent study so important as now" (Ed 225). Ellen White believed and taught that God's people could be neither effective witnesses for God (COL 340) nor fit citizens for His kingdom (CH 44) without a Christlike character. Believing in Christ's soon return, she wrote profusely on the topic, repeatedly exhorting her readers to cooperate with the transforming power of the Holy Spirit in the development of a Christlike character (SD 337).

A key to Ellen White's concept of character development is her understanding that in Exodus 33:18, 19; 34:5-7; John 17:22, 24; and 2 Corinthians 3:18, "glory" primarily denotes moral character. "It is his righteous character that constitutes the glory of God; and it is this same glory that Christ prays may be given to

His followers upon the earth" (RH, Nov. 3, 1896; cf. SD 337).

As to the ability of fallen humans to make themselves Christlike in character, Ellen White is clear: "We cannot change ourselves. We cannot be good, or do good to others, of ourselves. Christ has said: 'Without me ye can do nothing' [John 15:5]" (RH, May 31, 1892). Therefore, if humans are to experience this transformation of character, they must be changed by a power outside of themselves. However, though humans must "be changed"— a passive verb—Ellen White emphasizes that humans are *not* passive in the process, for "in order to reflect this glory, we must cooperate with God" (RC 37). In clarifying what she means by "cooperate," she cites another of her favorite texts. "Our daily and hourly work is set forth in the words of the apostle: 'Looking unto Jesus the author and finisher of our faith' [Heb. 12:2]" (5T 744). For this reason Ellen White throughout her ministry urged people to spend quality daily time in studying, meditating on, and talking about the life of Christ (ST, July 30, 1896; 6BC 1098, 1099; DA 83).

A further insight is provided by her definition: "The thoughts and feelings combined make up the moral character" (5T 310). This implies that developing a Christlike character involves learning to think and feel as Jesus does, gaining the "mind of Christ" (see Phil. 2:5) in our attitudes and reactions to all the issues of daily life. "When we have the mind of Christ, we shall love and work as Christ has loved and worked. When the love of Christ is in the heart, it exerts a controlling influence over the thoughts and affections" (ST, Feb. 24, 1890). "Having the mind of Christ, His followers reveal the graces of His character" (LHU 301).

Also crucial to Ellen White's understanding of character development is her concept that "the law of God is the standard of character; it is the expression of the character of

God Himself" (BE, July 29, 1895). As both the "standard" of human character and the "expression" of the character—the "thoughts and feelings"—of God, the law is far more than a code of outward conduct—it has jurisdiction over the inner conduct of the mind. "God's law is spiritual. It takes cognizance of our most secret thoughts, purposes, and motives. The judgment, the will, and the affections must be controlled by its precepts. Its principles require love to God and to man; without this love, external compliance will not be accepted" (ST, June 9, 1881).

Thus if Christians are to be more than "whited sepulchres" which only appear beautiful outwardly (Matt. 23:27), if they are to develop an inner beauty of character that radiates genuine love, their thoughts and feelings, even their motives and desires, must be in harmony with the spirit of the law which is love. "Supreme love for God and unselfish love for one another" is the fulfilling of the law (TDG 287). Seen in its spiritual nature and requirement, the law is not only "a transcript of God's character" (RH, Feb. 4, 1890) but also a gracious God-given "standard" for Christian character building.

But before the law can be a guide for character building (Ps. 19:7) it must "bring us unto Christ, that we might be justified by faith" (Gal. 3:24, in 1SM 234). Ellen White is very clear in this matter. Nowhere has she ever said that it is by becoming Christlike in character that we are *justified*. For a correct understanding of this topic, it is imperative to recognize that to her, character development is the means by which we are *sanctified*, not *justified*. It has to do with gaining a fitness for heaven, *not* an entitlement to heaven (RH, June 4, 1895). Thus character development is entirely removed from the realm of the meritorious (AG 331).

Ellen White's understanding of the original

Fall categorically precludes humans from ever becoming righteous before God by virtue of their character development. Unequivocally she states: "It was possible for Adam, before the fall, to form a righteous character by obedience to God's law. But he failed to do this, and because of his sin our natures are fallen and we cannot make ourselves righteous. Since we are sinful, unholy, we cannot perfectly obey the holy law. We have no righteousness of our own with which to meet the claims of the law of God" (SC 62). "Selfishness is the great law of our degenerate nature" (ST, June 2, 1887) and "the spirit of selfishness is the spirit of Satan" (AA 339). Precisely for this reason, "the carnal [or natural] mind is enmity against God; for it is not subject to the law of God, neither indeed can be" (Rom. 8:7, in ST, May 30, 1895). "The natural, selfish mind, as it exists in its carnal state, acts without reference to God, and is evil, and only evil, continually" (ST, June 22, 1888).

But there is hope. "Christ came to this world to live a life of perfect obedience to the laws of God's kingdom. He came to uplift and ennoble human beings, to work out an enduring righteousness for them. He came as a medium through which truth was to be imparted. In Him are found all the excellencies necessary to absolute *perfection of character" (RH, July 4, 1912). "He came to this earth, and stood at the head of humanity, to work out for you and for me a faultless character by obedience to God's law" (AUG, Aug. 26, 1903). Having culminated that life of perfect obedience by dying for our sins, Christ now "offers to take our sins and give us His righteousness. If you give yourself to Him, and accept Him as your Savior, then, sinful as your life may have been, for His sake you are accounted righteous. Christ's character stands in place of your character, and you are accepted before God just as if you had not sinned" (SC 62). Through faith in Him the believer is credited with Christ's character, which is "an infinitely perfect character" (6T 60; cf. COL 315). To lose sight of this point is to fall into a subtle but deadly form of legalism—*justification by character development.

It is true that sinners are justified by a perfect character, but not by their own; the character that justifies them is the infinitely perfect character of Jesus Christ, graciously credited to their account when they surrender themselves to Him. Any attempt to build a Christlike character that does not have its foundation on justification by faith in the imputed righteousness of Christ alone is doomed to be a miserable exercise in futility. "There are those who profess to serve God, while they rely upon their own efforts to obey His law, to form a right character, and secure salvation. Their hearts are not moved by any deep sense of the love of Christ, but they seek to perform the duties of the Christian life as that which God requires of them in order to gain heaven. Such religion is worth nothing" (SC 44).

Ellen White's understanding of the Gospel avoids both legalism (trying to merit heaven by our obedience) and cheap grace (trying to enter heaven without our obedience). She explains succinctly and unequivocally: "The righteousness by which we are justified is imputed; the righteousness by which we are sanctified is imparted. The first is our title to heaven, the second is our fitness for heaven" (MYP 35). Thus God's *grace is twofold in its function. Justifying grace credits Christ's character perfection *to* us thereby giving us a legal right to live forever in heaven. Sanctifying grace restores Christ's character perfection *in* us, thereby giving us a moral suitability to enjoy living in the company of holy beings through the ceaseless ages of eternity (AA

273). We may praise God that "by the sacrifice of Christ, every provision has been made for believers to receive *all things* that pertain to life and godliness. The perfection of His character makes it possible for us to gain perfection" (PUR, Feb. 9, 1905). Thus Ellen White could make the remarkable statement that "*through the measure of His grace* furnished to the human agent, not one need miss heaven. Perfection of character is attainable by every one who strives for it" (RH, Apr. 5, 1898; italics supplied).

Only in depending exclusively upon what we are in Christ rather than what we are in ourselves can believers be kept from despair, for "the closer you come to Jesus, the more faulty you will appear in your own eyes; for your vision will be clearer, and your imperfections will be seen in broad and distinct contrast to His perfect nature. . . . The less we see to esteem in ourselves, the more we shall see to esteem in the infinite purity and loveliness of our Savior" (SC 64, 65). This experience keeps believers from self-exaltation (NPUG, Jan. 29, 1908), while Christ's promise "My grace is sufficient for thee: for my strength is made perfect in weakness" (2 Cor. 12:9) keeps them from giving up. Precious is the *assurance that "the Father beholds not your faulty character, but . . . sees you as clothed in [Christ's] perfection" (DA 357).

For those who truly love Christ, growing into His character likeness can become their greatest joy in this life and in eternity. "It is our lifework to be reaching forward to the perfection of Christian character, striving continually for conformity to the will of God" (4T 520), but it is also our greatest honor and privilege. So with rejoicing let us "press toward the mark for the prize of the high calling of God in Christ Jesus" (Phil. 3:14), fully confident that "the efforts begun upon earth will continue through eternity" (4T 520).

See also: Conversion; Sanctification.

Stephen Wallace

CHARISMATIC EXPERIENCES, see **ECSTATIC EXPERIENCES**.

CHECKERS, see **GAMES AND SPORTS**; **COMPETITION**.

CHEESE. Most of Ellen White's few references to cheese were written between 1870 and 1890. Nineteenth-century health reformers commonly regarded cheese as unhealthful. Ellen White's writings often list cheese together with flesh meats, butter, rich pastries, and spicy foods as tending to derange the stomach, excite the nerves, enfeeble the intellect, and produce a poor quality of blood (3T 136; CH 114; CTBH 46, 47; 7MR 347). She did not, however, consider the use of cheese as a sinful indulgence in the same category as the use of tobacco, beverage alcohol, tea, and coffee (3SM 287; 2MR 107).

Ellen White never considered making cheese an article of diet, and wished that others in her household would abstain from eating cheese (15MR 246). Some in her extended family wanted cheese placed on the table, but she opposed this (TSDF 14). She reproved church leaders for allowing cheese to be sold at camp meetings (CD 329). Although the cheese was new, she considered it "too strong for the stomach." She commented that while cheese was commonly considered a wholesome food, it was actually very injurious to health (*ibid.* 369).

She reiterated on numerous occasions that eating cheese was deleterious to one's health, and that people needed to be educated to abstain from cheese as well as meat and butter (TSDF 14; 3SM 287; CH 114). Cheese was considered more objectionable than butter, wholly unfit for food (MH 302), and an item that should never be introduced into the stomach (2T 68).

Since cheese was a common household item in Germany and other parts of Europe, the German translators of *The Ministry of Healing* were concerned about her statement that cheese was wholly unfit for food (MH 302). When asked for clarification about this, Ellen White approved the use of the phrase "strong, sharp cheese" to indicate what she disapproved (CD 368). Some have suggested that by using the phrase "strong, sharp cheese," she was referring to ripened cheese rather than the mild, unripened cheeses such as Mozzarella, Ricotta, and cottage cheese.

Why she wrote so strongly against eating cheese is a matter of speculation. The saturated fat and cholesterol content of all cheeses is noted, but this would hardly merit a total ban on cheese. The unhygienic methods of milk production in her day could be another concern, although pasteurization became commercially available in 1882. By 1900, standards had been established in the United States to ensure a reasonably safe milk supply. The process involved heating the milk to 145°F (63°C) for 30 minutes.

Cheese was considered by other health reformers of her day, such as William Alcott, to be quite indigestible because it was too concentrated a substance. Alcott, a physician from Boston and a popular health writer of the mid-nineteenth century, reported several incidents in which large numbers of people were poisoned from eating cheese. While the cause of the poisoning was undeclared, it was observed that women added a small piece of arsenic in cheesemaking, especially when the milk was old.

See also: general article: Current Science

and Ellen White: Twelve Controversial Statements.

Winston J. Craig

CHESS, see **GAMES AND SPORTS; COMPETITION.**

CHESTNUT STREET METHODIST CHURCH. The church in Portland, Maine, where *Robert and *Eunice Harmon and several of their children, including Ellen Harmon were members from 1840 to 1843. The Chestnut Street church was dedicated on February 17, 1811. In 1836, when the church was enlarged, a pipe organ was installed—the first in an American Methodist Church. The original church where the Harmons attended was destroyed by fire on April 26, 1860. (The congregation, however, had moved next door into another church building in 1859. This building is still standing.) Within months of joining the church on February 26, 1840, Robert Harmon was made a class leader and became involved in establishing a "preaching place" at the Brackett Street School near the Harmon home.

Typically a six-month probation was required for new members before they were baptized, and on September 20, 1841, 13-year-old Ellen Harmon was recommended for probation. On May 23, 1842, Ellen was among 18 who were passed for full membership. Accordingly, Pastor John Hobart baptized Ellen by immersion in Casco Bay on June 26, 1842. Shortly after Ellen's baptism, the Maine Conference transferred Hobart, because of his support of the Millerite movement (see *William Miller; *Disappointments, Millerite). When William F. Farrington, the new preacher, arrived, he began to address the Millerite "problem" in the church. The class leaders' minutes of the church suggest that Robert Harmon and his family were the first to be examined. Because of Harmon's leadership positions in the church and the high esteem in which he was held by other class leaders, the discipline process was difficult and protracted.

On February 6, 1843, a committee of two was formed to "wait on [Brother] R. Harmon in reference to his anti-Methodistical conduct." There is no record of any report from this committee. A succession of four committees followed, with varying results. On March 27 Gideon Foster was made a committee of one to "visit [Brother] Harmon in reference to his irregularities." When he returned an apparently positive report on April 23, it was "not accepted or laid on the table," and another committee of three was formed before whom Harmon was "cited to appear and answer for himself." This committee also did not bring a report, and on May 29 another three-person committee was formed "on [Brother] R. Harmon's irregularities." Finally on August 14 a "committee of trial" was formed "on the cases of Robert Harmon & those of his family" who had "violated the rules," been "long" absent from the church, and supported anti-Methodist doctrine and "Millerism." One week later the committee's report was accepted, and Robert and Eunice Harmon together with their children *Sarah, *Robert, and Ellen, were removed from membership for "breach of discipline." The expulsion did not include *Mary Harmon (see *Mary Foss), presumably because she had married *Samuel Foss on July 5, 1842, nor did it include Ellen's twin sister, Elizabeth, who had been admitted on probation but not yet baptized.

After their exclusion from the church, the Harmons appealed the ruling to the quarterly meeting, as was allowed under Methodist discipline. On September 2, 1842, with Charles Baker, the presiding elder in the chair, Robert Harmon personally defended himself and his family. The effort was to no avail, and the conference unanimously sustained their expulsion from membership. After making the Harmon family an example, many others were also excluded for their Millerite views.

Merlin D. Burt

CHICAGO BUILDING VISION. A major point of disagreement between Ellen White and *J. H. Kellogg, which became for him conclusive evidence that Ellen White's testimonies were unreliable and derived only from human sources of information.

In 1899 the *American Medical Missionary College (AMMC), operated in Chicago by the *Battle Creek Sanitarium, sought accreditation from the Association of American Medical Colleges. The main obstacle to accreditation was the lack of an adequate building in Chicago. So the AMMC board appointed a building committee, of which Jesse Arthur, a Battle Creek Adventist attorney, was chair. The committee drew plans for a building and opened negotiations for the purchase of a site on Thirteenth Street in Chicago, estimating the total cost at $100,000 or more. On June 26, 1899, the committee voted to approve the plans, but postponed further action until they could consult with Kellogg, who was traveling in Europe.

Meanwhile, in Basel, Switzerland, Kellogg received a letter from Ellen White in Australia, reproving him for erecting a large elaborate building in Chicago (J. H. Kellogg to EGW, Apr. 17, 1899). The letter's contents are inferred from his response and her later recollection in 1903 (Lt 135, 1903), for the original letter was lost; but all parties concerned seemed to agree it had been written in 1899, and to accept her 1903 statements as a fair summary of the original letter's contents (Chas. E. Stewart to WCW, Mar. 19, 1906; WCW to AGD, Mar. 30, 1906). On receiving the letter, Kellogg was indignant: "It is evident that many statements have been made to you that are utterly false," he protested, "and I feel inclined to write you the truth about some of these matters, but I shall not trouble you. The Lord knows all about the matter, and I leave it with him" (J. H. Kellogg to EGW, Apr. 17, 1899; cf. Lt 135, 1903, in 6Bio 96, 97). On Kellogg's return to Battle Creek he learned about the building plans and canceled them (cf. Schwarz, pp. 178, 179).

In February 1900 Ellen White, still in Australia, came across an article in an old New York *Observer* reporting that Kellogg was spending "over $1,000 per month" in his Chicago projects. Seizing on it as support for what she had seen in vision the previous year, she cited the article in another letter to Kellogg. Far from convinced, Kellogg received this as fresh evidence that all her letters on the subject had been based on hearsay, not on visions, and it reinforced his conviction that not all of her testimonies were inspired.

Ellen White remained puzzled. She had no doubt about having seen a particular building in vision. Not until after her return to the United States did she learn the rest of the story. When Jesse Arthur visited Elmshaven in June 1902, she described to him the building she had seen in vision. Arthur said, "I can tell you something in regard to that building. A plan was drawn up for the erection of just such a building in Chicago. . . . Various locations were considered. One of the plans discussed was very similar to what you have described" (Ms 33, 1906, in PC 50).

Arthur's subsequent written account makes it clear that in April 1899, when Kellogg wrote to Ellen White from Basel, no plans for the new building in Chicago had yet been laid. On June 25, 1899, while Kellogg was still in Europe, three of his colleagues in Battle Creek (A. B. Olsen, W. K. Kellogg, and Judge Jesse Arthur) suggested the idea and voted to purchase property and draw up architectural plans (Jesse Arthur to WCW, Aug. 27, 1902). When Kellogg learned of the plans, he vetoed them, but apparently did not mention the letter he had received from Ellen White. Later, however, as Kellogg became frustrated at her for opposing other projects of his, he began to cite the 1899 letter as proof that her testimonies were derived only from human sources.

Ellen White protested this misrepresentation of the incident. "Repeatedly it has been shown me," she declared to Kellogg, "that in many cases you have worked upon minds to undermine confidence in the Testimonies. . . . Over and over again you have told others how I once sent you a testimony reproving you for erecting a large building in Chicago, before any such building had been erected there. In the visions of the night a view of a large building was presented to me. I thought that it had been erected, and wrote you immediately in regard to the matter. I learned afterward that the building which I saw had not been put up.

"When you received my letter, you were perplexed, and you said, 'some one has misinformed Sister White regarding our work.' But no mortal man had ever written to me or told me that this building had been put up. It was presented to me in vision. If this view had not been given me, and if I had not written to you about the matter, an effort would have been made to erect such a building in Chicago. . . . At the time when the vision was given, influences were working for the erection of such a building. The message was received in time to prevent the development of the plans and the carrying out of the project.

"You should have had discernment to see that the Lord worked in this matter. The very feature of the message that perplexed you [its timing] should have been received as an evidence that my information came from a higher source than human lips. But instead, you have over and over again related your version of the matter, saying some one must have told me a falsehood" (Lt 239, 1903, in PC 50, 51).

Kellogg responded with a faint apology. "I am exceedingly sorry," he said, "that I have ever allowed myself to mention to anybody anything in relation to the buildings which you wrote me about. It had never occurred to me that the medical college building which Dr. Olsen and some others made plans about when I was in Europe was what you referred to. Certainly it was not best for us to erect any building at that time and I am very glad we didn't. I have never felt free to put up any building in Chicago.... There has been strong pressure brought to bear upon me for years to do this, but I have steadily opposed it. After receiving this message from you in reference to such a building I never would have dared erect it" (J. H. Kellogg to EGW, Nov. 12, 1903).

In spite of this admission by Kellogg, he continued to cite the Chicago building letter as an example of Ellen White's giving erroneous counsel. Ellen White, however, reasoned that the rebuke would have been worthless had it come after the building had already been erected. In her view, the timing of the 1899 letter tested Kellogg's sincerity by giving him an excuse for doubt, but came in time to prevent the action it reproved.

Further reading: 5Bio 173; 6Bio 96, 97; J. Moon, "The 'Chicago Building' and Related Visions of Ellen G. White" (unpublished paper, 2003, CAR); R. W. Schwarz, *John Harvey Kellogg, M.D.* (AUP, 1981), pp. 178, 179.

Jerry Moon

CHICAGO MEDICAL MISSION. Medical and philanthropic mission opened in Chicago by J. H. Kellogg in 1893 and closely linked with the Chicago Sanitarium, also begun in 1893

as a branch of the Battle Creek Sanitarium. The Chicago Medical Mission began as a medical dispensary operated at the Pacific Garden Mission and expanded into a network of major institutions, including the *American Medical Missionary College, an important partner to both the mission and the sanitarium; a Settlement House, to help immigrants become settled in a new country; a Workingmen's Home, which provided inexpensive meals, lodging, and clothing for poor and homeless men; the Life Boat Mission, continuing the work of the original dispensary; the Life Boat Maternity Home, for unwed and destitute mothers; the Life Boat Rescue Service, an intervention-reclamation program for prostitutes; and the Life Boat Rescue Home, a combined maternity home and halfway house for former prostitutes. In addition there were several smaller clinics, a health and recreation center for mothers and children in the stockyards district of the city, an employment agency for ex-prisoners, a store whose profits helped to support the mission, and a monthly magazine, the *Life Boat*. By 1898 the expenses of the mission had grown to twice the profits of the Chicago Sanitarium, creating a financial crisis.

Ellen White commended the good work being done in Chicago (Lt 43, 1895, in 4MR 131), and after her return to the United States she personally visited "Life Boat Mission and the Workingmen's Home" (RH, Feb. 9, 1905). In 1909 she spoke at the dedication service of the Life Boat Rescue Home in Hinsdale. However, she also cautioned Kellogg about several aspects of the work: (1) the massive expenditures concentrated in Chicago would be better invested in smaller missions in several cities; (2) the Chicago Mission was "overspecialized" in focusing on the poor to the neglect of other classes; (3) medical ministry should neither be exalted over evangelistic ministry or separated from evangelistic ministry; (4) for a work that was more philanthropic than evangelistic, the mission absorbed too great a proportion of denominational funds and personnel; and (5) the Chicago Mission tended to deemphasize the distinctive and entire Adventist message in favor of a nondenominational philanthropic message (Butler; 4MR 131-134). Because of financial crises and Kellogg's alienation from the church, the Chicago Medical Mission went into decline, leading to closure in 1913.

See also: City Evangelism; S. N. Haskell.

Further reading: J. Butler, "Ellen White and the Chicago Mission," *Spectrum* 2, no. 1 (Winter 1970): 41-51; R. Rice, "Adventists and Welfare Work: A Comparative Study," *Spectrum* 2, no. 1 (Winter 1970): 52-63; R. W. Schwarz, "Adventism's Social Gospel Advocate: John Harvey Kellogg," *Spectrum* 1, no. 2 (Spring 1969): 15-28; R. W. Schwarz, *Light Bearers* (RHPA, 1979), pp. 210, 317, 318; *SDA Encyclopedia* (1996), vol. 10, pp. 324, 376, 377.

Jerry Moon

CHILD GUIDANCE (RHPA, 1954, 616 pp.). Compilation of counsels to parents concerning the raising of children. *Child Guidance* follows basically the same format as the companion book *The Adventist Home* (1952). Its 83 chapters are subdivided into 19 sections and are drawn from Ellen White's published and unpublished works. In her several books, numerous periodical articles, and hundreds of personal letters to various individuals and families, Ellen White wrote a wealth of counsels to parents and dealt specifically with problems families face. She provided detailed counsels on discipline, character building, and physical, spiritual, and moral education. *Child Guidance* sets forth many of the principles which she believed should guide parents in the raising of their children. It was her firm belief that parents

have a solemn duty to guide their children to learn to do the will of God and to actively take up this responsibility in preparation for eternal life (p. 13). "Upon all parents there rests the obligation of giving physical, mental, and spiritual instruction. It should be the object of every parent to secure to his child a well-balanced, symmetrical character. This is a work of no small magnitude and importance—a work requiring earnest thought and prayer no less than patient, persevering effort" (p. 17).

CHILDREN, TRAINING OF. In the most fundamental sense, the biblical mandate to train children is a directive for religious instruction in the home (Deut. 6:4, 7); a command to every parent and teacher to "train up a child in the way he should go" (Prov. 22:6; cf. Deut. 11:19; Gen. 18:19). Ellen White viewed parents, teachers, church, and school, as responsible agents for training children, and gave instruction regarding what to teach, methods of training, and what results to expect.

For Ellen White, children are the property and heritage of the Lord. Their training is the highest service parents can render to God. Each family needs to consecrate their household to God, and become a training center in which pupils prepare for the higher school in the heavenly mansions (ST, Sept. 10, 1894). In her thought, both the firm, restraining influence of the father, and the gentle, sympathetic love of the mother are essential to the development of balanced characters in children (HR, Feb. 1, 1878). A mother should realize that she is entrusted with the greatest mission ever given to humans, and, as a result, should not accept burdens at the expense of her children (AH 246). The father must prioritize the training of children in the way of the Lord (*ibid.* 221). Together they should share the responsibility of raising children.

The responsibility of parents is primary,

and when they do their work well, the work of the teacher is made easier. Still, many children are lost because of the ignorance of teachers (FE 20). Educators need to improve their ability to instill "a sound mind in a sound body" (*ibid.* 59). The local church also plays a role in providing shelter from harmful influences (CG 312).

Child training should include, from the child's earliest days, familiarity with the life of Jesus. Children should be encouraged to worship God and obey His commandments (ML 285). They should learn self-restraint and be taught how to maintain physical, mental, and moral health. Practical skills and duties, such as hygiene, diet, exercise, cooking, and housekeeping, should be taught and encouraged. Steady progress is made through repetition and discipline.

Ellen White believed that the importance of *early* training of children could not be overemphasized. The lessons learned and habits formed during infancy and childhood have more to do with the formation of character and direction of life than all the instruction of later years (CG 193). Even prenatal influences have much to do with children's later character (SA 113).

Thus, it is impossible for parents to give correct training unless they have first given themselves to God, surrendering their own will and inclination and seeking in all things the will of the Lord. By understanding the principles, learning right methods, seeking the highest culture of their own mind and soul, they can be an example to their children. As parents learn in the school of Christ lessons of self-control, meekness, and lowliness of heart, and cultivate habits of self-denial and love, they will be enabled to guide their children by words and actions (AH 421).

Children require different methods of training (CT 115). Parents need to recognize the particular temperaments of their children, and study both their strengths and their weaknesses, in order to instruct, polish, refine, and guide them toward heaven. Parents who understand the influence of the world upon minds will guard their children from exciting amusements. Children should be trained in such a way that when they are older they will have pleasant memories of well-spent childhood years.

In a sermon given during that General Conference session of 1901 in Battle Creek, Ellen White gave a few hints of her own practice of child raising. "Let us do all we can to show our children that there is a heaven to win and a hell to shun. Let us teach them to strive for everlasting life. And remember that you will not help them by scolding. This stirs up the worst passions of the human heart. Make home pleasant. Be kind and gentle, but at the same time, be firm, requiring obedience. I have brought up children who by others were pronounced incorrigible. I never struck them a blow. I won their love and their confidence. They knew that I would ask them to do nothing but what was for their happiness. I did not whip them, knowing that this would not make them righteous. Prayer was my strength. Bring your children up in the admonition of the Lord, and you have fitted them to work in the church, you have fitted them to go forth into missionary fields, you have fitted them to shine in the courts of the Lord" (1SAT 328).

Further reading: CG 17-287; FE 15-46, 139-161; AH 159-296.

Helena R. Gregor

CHRIST, CENTRALITY OF. Christ became central in the life of Ellen White in her childhood and continued on through her ministry to the end of her life. Ellen grew up in a Christian home and was exposed to the love of Christ through the Methodist Episcopal

Church. The school she attended required each student to have a New Testament and assignments included reading religious biographies.

At the age of 9, Ellen had a facial injury that required several weeks of bed rest. Not prepared to die, she earnestly prayed for the forgiveness of her sins, and the peace of Jesus filled her heart. As she regained her strength and attempted unsuccessfully to continue her education, she was shunned by friends and made Jesus even more the center of her life.

In 1840, while listening to sermons on the second coming of Christ, she was convinced that Christ would soon come back, but she was filled with terror. This, she tells us, continued for months. The following summer, at a Methodist camp meeting, Ellen learned that only by connecting with Jesus through faith can a sinner become a child of God. As she knelt with others to pray, her burden lifted, and she repeated softly to herself, "I am a child of God, His loving care is around me. I will be obedient and in no way displease Him, but will praise His dear name and love Him always" (1T 19).

But with a strong Methodist emphasis on sanctification, Ellen began to despair. She believed she had experienced justification, but thought sanctification was an entirely separate experience that she did not have. This concept, together with the strong preaching on hell, made her heart sink. She could not get it out of her mind. She confided in Elder *Levi Stockman, who told her that God was a God of love who loved her very much. Ellen felt blessed. She saw more clearly that the Father was a kind and tender parent, not a tyrant compelling obedience, and the assurance of Christ filled her heart.

At the age of 17 she was called to the prophetic ministry and told to share with the people what she saw in vision. Prior to this her thought of Jesus' love and what He had done for her would fill her with a confidence that surprised even her. But when she was shown the difficulties she would face in carrying out her ministry, it seemed too much. She felt she would rather die. A pastor by the name of *John Pearson, who earlier had not acknowledged her call, urged her to surrender her will to God and obey Jesus, which she did. This surrender also carried over into her marriage and her relationships with others. She taught that when people give themselves to Christ and accept him as Savior, they are accepted by God as if they had never sinned (SC 62).

Over the years she frequently reminded ministers that preaching the law (i.e., a legalistic religion) without Christ was as dry as fields without rain. At the General Conference sessions, especially those of 1883 and 1888, she firmly insisted that the *righteousness of Christ was the sinner's only hope. At the turn of the century her published works *Steps to Christ, *Thoughts From the Mount of Blessing, *The Desire of Ages, and *Christ's Object Lessons speak highly of the centrality of Christ in her faith and life. To her Christ was the "Rose of Sharon" (RH, Aug. 14, 1894), the "chiefest among ten thousand," and "the One altogether lovely" (AA 275).

She believed that Christ existed from all eternity. There never was a time when He was not. He was one with the Father. In Him was life, original, unborrowed, and underived (DA 530). She also believed that in agreement with the Father, Christ created the heavens and the earth. It was His hand that hung the worlds in space, fashioned the flowers, and filled the air with song.

Regarding the Incarnation, she believed and taught that Christ became part of the human family. He came down to our level and became one with us. He lived a sinless life, and when crucified, He could have come down from the cross, but because He chose not to save Himself, we have the hope of pardon and being reconciled to God. She never doubted the resurrection. To her the tomb was empty and the Savior alive.

Though education and human effort have their place, it is the power of Christ through the Holy Spirit that alone can quicken the lifeless faculties of the soul and bring about a new birth. Christ is the source of the believer's life and strength. He is the author and finisher of their faith. To make self the center turns one away from Christ, but by loving Him, copying Him, depending wholly on Him, humans are transformed into His likeness. This was the goal of White's life and the goal that she set before others.

Christ was the center of Ellen White's life from childhood to the end of her 70 years of ministry, and at the core of her teachings. A few days before she died she confidently whispered, "I know in whom I have believed" (LS 449).

See also: *Christ, the Way of Life* Prints.

Jack J. Blanco

CHRIST, DIVINITY OF. Most of Ellen White's colleagues among the early Adventist pioneers (her own husband, James; Joseph Bates; Uriah Smith; and others) were Arian or semi-Arian in their understanding of Christ, a belief inherited from their former religious affiliation. They saw Christ as having a derived existence, subordinate to the Father. And though we have no evidence that Ellen White ever consciously joined them in that view, one gets the sense from reading her earliest descriptions of Christ that she might have been affected somewhat by the atmosphere all around her.

This is much in evidence as one reads the opening pages of *Patriarchs and Prophets*, published in 1890, but with its first chapters based on material written much earlier. It is difficult not to see in many of her descriptions of the preincarnate Christ what church historians would call subordinationism (or *Arianism). There is, for example, a reference to Christ as "an associate" of God, "a co-worker" (PP 34). She reports on an assembly called by God to make clear before the host of heaven "the true position of His Son and show the relation He sustained to all created beings" (*ibid.* 36). The need for such a clarification is a puzzlement to us. Nor is the situation helped by White intimating that Christ "shared the Father's throne" (*ibid.*). Is the throne the Father's—and not also, by inherent right, Christ's? And where is the Holy Spirit in this configuration?

"Sin originated," White said, "with him who, next to Christ, had been most honored of God" (*ibid.* 35). When one considers the infinite gulf between Creator and creature, how could a created being be described as "next to Christ"? And why did Christ need to be "honored of God"? Why did Lucifer "envy" Christ (*ibid.* 37)? Did Christ give Lucifer the idea that His own stature was somehow on par with his? Why was "the exaltation of the Son of God as equal with the Father" considered by other angels an "injustice to Lucifer"? (*ibid.* 37). Why would Christ need to be *exalted* by God in the first place? And why was there even the faintest notion that that could be an "injustice" to Lucifer?

Peter spoke about the Old Testament prophets struggling to understand what the Spirit was saying to them, searching for greater clarity (1 Peter 1:10, 11). And what we have in Ellen White, apparently, is a similar search— but one that looks in the opposite direction. In that first chapter of *Patriarchs and Prophets*, in which she deals with the emergence of sin in the universe, White is grappling with dateless prehistory, and with issues of enormous complexity. Inevitably influenced by her postincarnation location in time, she seems unconsciously to read back into that prehistory understandings about the incarnate Christ that, technically, do not belong there.

To what degree White herself reflected on these difficulties we will never know precisely. But in an 1892 letter to O. A. Olsen, then president of the General Conference, we get a glimpse of her struggles as she prepared copy for *The Desire of Ages*: "I walk with trembling before God," she said. "I know not how to present subjects in the living power in which they stand before me. I tremble for fear lest I shall belittle the great plan of salvation by cheap words. I bow my soul in awe and reverence before God and say, 'Who is sufficient for these things?'" (Lt 40, 1892, in 3SM 115).

What the full evidence shows is that White, very early—and notwithstanding the strong Arian atmosphere around her—came out with the strongest statements on Christ's deity. In 1869, for example, she spoke of Christ as "the express image of His [Father's] person," and as "equal with God" (2T 200). She expressed similar sentiments in 1875 (3T 566) and 1880 (4T 458).

But it was beginning in the early 1890s and reaching to the end of her life that she wrote the most unequivocal affirmations of Christ's divinity. In an 1893 article, as if borrowing a term from church history, she spoke of Christ as being "of one substance [with the Father], possessing the same attributes" (ST, Nov. 27, 1893). The healing of the paralytic (Mark 2) called for "nothing less than creative power," and came from the same voice that spoke life into existence in the beginning (DA 269, 270). Christ, she said in 1905, is "the fullness of the Godhead manifested" (Ev 614). Repudiating the anti-Trinitarianism held by

some of her fellow pioneers, she spoke of the Father, Christ, and the Holy Spirit as the "three living persons of the heavenly trio" (*ibid.* 615). She counseled Adventist evangelists not to bring forward the controversial points of faith until people "have [had] opportunity to know that we are believers in Christ . . . in His divinity and in His pre-existence" (*ibid.* 231).

Other statements left no doubt where she stood. Christ "came forth from the grave by the life that was in Himself" (DA 785). He is "the self-existent, eternal, unchangeable One" (7BC 955). A lowly Galilean rabbi, Jesus took "the name of God, given to Moses to express the idea of the eternal presence" and "claimed [it] as His own," announcing Himself to be "the self-existent One . . . 'whose goings forth have been from of old . . .' (Micah 5:2, margin)" (DA 469, 470; cf. John 8:58). To deny Christ's divinity, as some in the first century had done (AA 553), was a "dangerous error" (GC 524).

When He arose from the grave, Christ did so by His own power (YI, Aug. 4, 1898). He had power over His own life (YI, June 21, 1900; 5BC 1136). "Christ was God essentially, and in the highest sense," she said. "He was with God from all eternity" (RH, Apr. 5, 1906; 5BC 1126).

When her teachings on Christ's divinity are considered as a whole, one finds it astonishing that the least educated among the early Adventist pioneers could have developed a position that synchronizes so perfectly with the New Testament and with the historic position of the Christian church. What is perhaps her strongest statement on the subject came in her magnum opus on the life of Christ, *The Desire of Ages*: "In Christ is life, original, unborrowed, underived." That, she says, "is the believer's assurance of eternal life" (DA 530).

See also: Godhead.

Further reading: R. Dederen, "Christ: His

Person and Work," in R. Dederen, ed., *Handbook of Seventh-day Adventist Theology* (RHPA, 2000), pp. 160-204; E. F. Harrison, ed., *Baker's Dictionary of Theology* (Grand Rapids: Baker, 1973); J. Moon, "The Adventist Trinity Debate, Part 1: Historical Overview," AUSS 41, no. 1 (Spring 2003): 113-129; J. Moon, "The Adventist Trinity Debate, Part 2: The Role of Ellen G. White," AUSS 41, no. 2 (Autumn 2003): 275-292; A. Richardson, *A Dictionary of Christian Theology* (Philadelphia: Westminster, 1976); A. L. White, *Ellen G. White: Messenger to the Remnant* (Washington, D.C.: Ellen G. White Estate, 1959); *SDA Encyclopedia* (1996), vol. 10, pp. 352-354.

Roy Adams

CHRIST, HUMANITY OF. Ellen White clearly taught the reality of the humanity of Christ and described His humanity in the following unmistakable language: a humanity "perfectly identical with our own nature" (16MR 182); the "same nature as man" (RH, Feb. 18, 1890; 1SM 408); that which He "really took upon Himself" (17MR 336); "not a make-believe humanity" (5BC 1124); a "complete humanity," "fully human" (ST, June 17, 1897); Christ "was a real man" (1SM 244) who "consented to an actual union with man" (17MR 26), and "He possessed all the human organism" (5BC 1130).

While she also very forthrightly declared His full deity, she made it abundantly clear that His deity did not qualify in any way His full humanity: His divine nature "was not humanized; neither was humanity deified by the blending or union of the two natures" (16MR 182).

Ellen White's comments on the humanity of Christ are permeated with biblical terms. While her comments on the following verses can be characterized as biblical, it mainly takes the form of running exposition rather

than detailed historical/grammatical (exegesis) interpretation. Though much of her key terminology is biblical ("took on him" [see Heb. 2:14] "likeness of sinful flesh" [Rom. 8:3]), she was quite willing to use terms not specifically used by Bible writers ("propensity," "inclination," "tendency") to elaborate what she considered the biblical teaching on Christ's humanity.

Besides key terms from Hebrews 2:14 and Romans 8:3, she often employed phraseology from numerous other passages: Hebrews 4:15 ("in all points tempted"); Hebrews 2:16 ("he took not on him the nature of angels; but he took on him the seed of Abraham"); Hebrews 2:17 ("In all things . . . made like unto his brethren"); Hebrews 2:18 ("suffered, being tempted, he is able to succour them that are tempted"); Hebrews 4:15 ("touched with the feelings of our infirmities"); Hebrews 5:2 ("compassed with infirmity"); 1 Peter 2:21 ("Christ also suffered for us, leaving us an example"); John 14:30 ("the prince of this world cometh, and hath nothing in me"); Isaiah 53:4 ("borne our griefs"); Matthew 4:1-11, Luke 4:1-13, and Mark 1:12, 13 (the temptation of Christ by Satan); John 1:51 (she likens His humanity to the lower rungs of Jacob's ladder); and Luke 1:31-35 (the annunciation to Mary, especially Christ being called "that holy thing").

Based on both explicit biblical terminology and the expressions and concepts that she felt fully reflected the biblical teaching, Ellen White not only strongly affirmed the reality of Christ's humanity, but also taught that it carried implications that were absolutely essential to the saving efficacy of His perfect life of obedience, death, and intercession and the dynamic application of personal salvation to responsive sinners.

The following are some of the key salvational implications that she understood to flow from the humanity of the Son of man:

1. Christ "clothed His divine nature with the garb of humanity, and demonstrated before the heavenly universe, before the unfallen worlds, and before the fallen world how much God loves the human race" (5MR 114).

2. The humanity that Christ "took" was genuinely real, and it was in this human nature that He experienced genuine and real temptations, with the very real possibility that He could have fallen (DA 49, 117; 16MR 182; 3SM 129; RH, Feb. 18, 1890).

3. His full identity with humanity in temptation enabled Christ to be humanity's sympathetic example in victoriously resisting temptation. Repeatedly Ellen White makes the point that through Christ's example of dependence on the impartation of divine power, humans may be fully victorious over every temptation (2T 201, 202; RH, Apr. 19, 1870).

4. His sinlessness of human nature and perfect obedience (His character) were essential to the efficacy of His atoning sacrifice (RH, Dec. 17, 1872; RH, Dec. 20, 1892; ST, June 17, 1897; ST, Nov. 24, 1887).

5. The basis of all of Christ's temptations was to use His inherent divine power to fend off the force of any temptation (RH, Apr. 1, 1875); even "His character," which was "superior to that of fallen man," made His temptations more difficult to resist (2SP 88; 5T 422).

6. His humanity, along with His full deity, fitted Christ to be an effectual mediator between God and man (1SM 344; ST, Aug. 24, 1891).

7. Christ's perfect obedience testified "to all the unfallen worlds and to fallen humanity that man could keep the commandments of God through the divine power granted to him of heaven" (3SM 136); thus He "proved to us by actual facts that man can keep the commandments of God, giving contradiction

to Satan's falsehood that man cannot keep them" (*ibid.* 139).

There appear to be no significant developmental factors in her understanding of the subject. Her major contributions were evident right from the beginning (her first recorded comments coming in 1858) of her treatment of this subject. Her three key contributions were: (1) the reality of His humanity; (2) the fact that Christ could have fallen to temptation (but did not); and (3) the very delicate manner in which she negotiated the mysteriously balanced relationship between Christ's "likeness" to "sinful flesh" (she even used the expressions "fallen human nature" [3SM 134; cf. 4BC 1147] and "sinful nature" [MM 181]) and the sinlessness of His nature.

It is the latter issue that has been the source of the most significant and persistent controversy. The debate began in earnest in the mid-1950s with the publication of *Questions on Doctrine* (1957) and still does not give any evidence of a satisfactory resolution. While all the participants in this protracted controversy agree that Christ really and truly took human nature and that He did not sin in any manner (either in thought or action), there has been no agreement on how to interpret the meaning of the phrase "sinful nature."

Before we review some of the major interpretive positions, it needs to be pointed out that Ellen White never raised this issue (how to interpret "sinful nature") to the level of a "pillar" or "landmark" of "present truth." She provided a welter of intriguing, insightful comments, but none of the various "schools" of thought within Seventh-day Adventism have been able to convincingly carry the day to a strong interpretive consensus. This should come as no surprise, since the broader Christian tradition has experienced a similar impasse. While consensus Christian orthodoxy has clearly affirmed the reality of Christ's full humanity and deity, there has been no agreement on the meaning of "likeness of sinful flesh" (Rom. 8:3).

Two major "schools" of the interpretation have developed: the "pre-Fall" and "post-Fall."

While these descriptive expressions do reflect clearly differing interpretive positions, they are somewhat misleading: neither "school" has wanted to say that Christ's humanity was *totally* "pre" or "post" Fall. It would be more helpful and instructive if both "schools" would use the terminology of "identity" (the "post-Fall" elements) and "uniqueness" (the "pre-Fall" elements) to describe Ellen White's position: when she spoke of Christ as humanity's great example in providing help in meeting and resisting temptation, she employed the language of strong "identity." When she wrote on the issue of His work as a sinless, sacrifice of atonement and Intercessor (who provides the assurance of justifying grace), she used language that highlighted the "uniqueness" of His human nature. Both elements are present in a broadly blended way in her understanding of Christ's real humanity.

Thus the key question is this: how much like human "sinful flesh," or "fallen human nature," did Christ need to become to be able to identify sufficiently with sinful humanity as an effectual example and yet be totally sinless in His human nature to provide a fully effectual, atoning sacrifice and intercession for sinners?

The issue that seems to function as the backdrop for the entire debate is expressed in Ellen White's comments regarding "erroneous views of the human nature of our Lord." She warned that "when we give to His human nature a power that is not possible for man to have in his conflicts with Satan, we destroy the completeness of His humanity" (7BC 929). And both the "pre-Fall" and "post-Fall"

interpreters have struggled to develop a position that would not leave them guilty of the charge that they had destroyed "the completeness of His humanity."

The two positions can be summarized as follows. The "post-Fall" interpreters understand "sinful nature" to mean that Christ took or assumed human nature that involved some sort of inherent, natural tendencies or inclinations to sin. They claim that if He did not experience such inclinations to sin, He did not feel the full force of temptation; thus such a lack of inclination would destroy His role as an effectual human example.

The "pre-Fall" interpreters admit that Christ was subject to human weaknesses (Ellen White described Christ's humanity as "weak," "frail," "infirm," "degraded," "degenerate," "deteriorated," "wretched," and "defiled" [with DA 49 and 117 providing the main sources for these strong expressions of "identity"]) and He took all the normal appetites of the human organism. However, they deny that Christ took or had sinful inclinations, propensities, or tendencies. They claim that such sinful inclinations would have spoiled the efficacy of His atoning sacrifice. Furthermore, they claim that the basis of Christ's identity and sympathy with "sinful flesh" was based not on the sinful inclinations of corrupt flesh or human nature (either "inherited" or "cultivated"), but on the central common issue involved in every occasion of temptation— human self-dependence as opposed to trustful God-dependence for power to resist.

The key arguments of the various "post-Fall" advocates go this way: using Ellen White's practical distinctions between the "higher" (mental) and "lower" (physical) natures of humanity, one group of "post-Fall" interpreters claim that sinful inclinations resided only in Christ's "lower" nature, but did not infect His "higher" powers. They then usually go on to claim that His "higher" powers were purified through a special converting work of the Holy Spirit that was operative sometime during the time of His conception and birth. When challenged that such a prenatal purifying or converting work would have given Christ an advantage, they normally respond that all humanity can gain the same advantage through their own experience of conversion. The "pre-Fall" interpreters' response to this interpretation is first to argue that there is no explicit Ellen White statement that says that Christ was corrupted with sinful propensities, inclinations, or tendencies in either His "higher" or "lower" natures. Second, they claim that there is no clear testimony from either the Bible or Ellen White to suggest that Christ needed to experience the new birth or conversion.

Another group of "post-Fall" thinkers interpret the expressions "sinful propensities" or "evil propensities" to refer to actual participation in sin, not to sinful, evil proclivities or bents that naturally tend to thoughts and acts of sin. In other words, "propensities of sin," an "evil propensity," or an "inclination to corruption" are used in her letter to *W.L.H. Baker (5BC 1128: one of the strongest pieces of "pre-Fall" evidence) only to deny that Christ actually "yielded to corruption." Thus they understand Ellen White as having denied that Christ committed acts of sin, but that she still taught that He took or assumed normal, human, sinful passion with inclinations, bents, or proclivities to sin. The "pre-Fall" response to this latter interpretation is to point out that contextually this interpretation will not stand up and that the more natural way to interpret these expressions is to understand them as evil proclivities or natural bents to do the wrong thing, not the actual doing of them. Thus the "pre-Fall" interpreters understand "propensities of sin," "inherent

propensities of disobedience," "a taint of sin," "an evil propensity," and "inclinations to corruption" as expressions to be used primarily to describe the same phenomenon: what Adam's children are "born" with, not their subsequent actions and character development. And the obvious implication is that Christ was not born with such natural "inclinations to corruption" or sin. In other words, Christ not only did not commit acts of sin, but He also did not take sinful inclinations (understood as leanings, bents, proclivities, and tendencies).

While there are other intricacies to both the "pre" and "post" Fall interpretive positions, the above are the main thrusts of the respective positions. Can there be any satisfying resolution?

The best possible answer seems to be: while Christ was "affected" by sin, He was not "infected" with sin in either His "inherited" human nature or in any "cultivated tendencies" and acts of sin in His human character.

As to the persistent charges of the "post-Fall" advocates that if Christ did not possess the same "sinful tendencies" as all other humans, the completeness of His humanity is destroyed (7BC 929), the following points seem helpful:

1. The very fact that Christ never sinned (which both "schools" agree to) from His very conception gave Him an inherent advantage. In other words, the very fact of His sinlessness of nature and character places Him in a "unique" category from the very beginning of His incarnate experience.

2. Far from destroying the completeness of His human identity, His sinless human nature, along with His inherent divine nature, provide the key to the issue of identity with sinful humanity in any and every temptation: self-dependence versus God-dependence is the key issue in every occasion of temptation.

And One who is sinless and inherently divine would seem to have a far greater temptation to self-dependence than would come to one who is imperfect and human. So much for any advantage that the sinlessness of Christ's human nature might have afforded Him.

3. Finally, the effectiveness of Christ's intercessory work requires the sinlessness not only of His character but also of His human nature. This is another issue that Ellen White addressed in numerous statements: even the best things that "true believers" do, through the imparted grace of Christ, need the purifying work "of the righteousness of Christ" ministered through His heavenly intercession. And why is this so? "The religious services, the prayers, the praise" and even "obedience" of "true believers" are so "defiled" by "passing through the corrupt channels of humanity" that they must be "purified by blood" or "they can never be of value with God" (1SM 344). If "true believers," with their "defiled" and "corrupt channels of humanity," are in constant need of the intercessions of Jesus, *could Jesus intercede for them if His incarnate human nature had also been "defiled" and "corrupt"* with the same "sinful propensities"? It seems obvious that He could not, and this seems to be the reason that Ellen White so persistently denied that Christ took or assumed sinful passions, inclinations, bents, propensities, and so forth.

With all due respect to the mystery inherent in the sinlessness of the humanity of Christ, it seems best to sum up the issue this way: according to Ellen White, Christ's humanity was *affected* enough by sin to identify sufficiently with sinful humans in their struggles with temptation, but was without the *infection* of sin to the degree that His sinlessness of nature enabled Him to offer a fully effectual sacrifice of atonement for penitent "true believers" and thus function as a fully effectual divine/human intercessor.

Further reading: R. Adams, *The Nature of Christ* (RHPA, 1994); R. Dederen, "Christ: His Person and Work," in R. Dederen, ed., *Handbook of Seventh-day Adventist Theology* (RHPA, 2000), pp. 160-204; E. E. Heppenstall, *The Man Who Is God* (RHPA, 1977); "What Human Nature Did Jesus Take?" *Ministry*, June 1985; R. Larson, *The Word Was Made Flesh: One Hundred Years of Seventh-day Adventist Christology, 1852-1952* (Cherry Valley, Calif.: Cherrystone Press, 1986); J. Sequeira, *Saviour of the World* (PPPA, 1996); E. C. Webster, *Crosscurrents in Adventist Christology* (AUP, 1992); *Seventh-day Adventists Answer Questions on Doctrine*, annotated edition, ed. G. R. Knight (AUP, 2003); W. W. Whidden, *Ellen White on the Humanity of Christ* (RHPA, 1997); W. W. Whidden, "The Humanity of Christ Debate—What Did Ellen White Teach?" *"Ellen White and Current Issues," Symposium* 2 (2006): 41-74; R. J. Wieland, *"The Golden Chain": Is There a Broken Link?* (Paris, Ohio: 1888 Message Study Committee, 1995); R. J. Wieland and D. K. Short, *How Could Jesus Be Sinless as a Baby . . . if He Took Our Fallen, Sinful Nature? An Exploratory Essay on an Intriguing Subject* (Berrien Springs, Mich.: Glad Tidings Publishers, 1997); Jean Zurcher, *Touched With Our Feelings: A Historical Survey of Adventist Thought on the Human Nature of Christ* (RHPA, 1999).

Woodrow W. Whidden

CHRIST, TEMPTATIONS OF. In order to understand Christ's temptations, one must first comprehend the purpose of His mission. Ellen White speaks about two dimensions of that mission: (1) to save humankind (DA 31), and (2) to impact the universe (*ibid.* 19). Fallen humanity and unfallen beings of heaven and "innumerable worlds" (PP 51) needed a revelation of God through Christ in order to understand better the rebellion of Satan against God. This theme is unfolded in Ellen White's *Conflict of the Ages Series (PP, PK, DA, AA, GC). Satan disputed the supremacy of Christ, called into question God's wisdom and love (PP 36), opposed the law of God, and promised a new and better government (*ibid.* 40). Satan led angels and humans to doubt God's word and to distrust Him (DA 22). He claimed that God was not self-denying, that He made no sacrifice (GC 502). To answer these charges, God allowed time for Satan to reveal what he and his plans are like (PP 41; GC 497), and sent Jesus to the world to reveal what God and His plans are like. The contrast between Satan and God must be revealed (DA 22). Satan must be unmasked (GC 498), and God must show that His government is just and His law is perfect (*ibid.*). God's government is founded on His law of love (*ibid.* 493), which Satan calls a law of selfishness, and claims it cannot be obeyed (DA 24). Christ became a human in order to show that the law can be kept (*ibid.*). Power to obey comes from a relationship with Him (*ibid.* 668).

Christ came as the second Adam, to succeed where Adam failed. Both Adams were sinless when tempted in Eden and the wilderness. Unlike Adam, Christ bore the sins of humanity; unlike Adam in full power of life, Christ was emaciated and about to die. Eden was paradise; the wilderness, desolate and repulsive (1SM 272, 275, 288). Christ overcame where Adam failed and stood the test on appetite, the love of the world, and the love of display leading to presumption (DA 116, 117). Christ had a disadvantage compared to Adam, for in clothing His divinity with humanity (4BC 1163), He took fallen human heredity to share human sorrows and temptations at the risk of failure and eternal loss (DA 49). As such, He "bore the sins and infirmities"

of humanity (RH, July 28, 1874). He took "the nature but not the sinfulness of man" and was "born without a taint of sin" (7BC 925). He came to the world to show that man as God created him, if connected with God, can obey God (*ibid.* 926). He came to become personally acquainted with the "temptations and frailties" of humans in order to help them (ST, Feb. 21, 1878). To understand His temptations one must hold together both His uniqueness and His identity with Adam. In His human nature, He was both like and unlike Adam.

As eternal God, Christ exercised "absolute power" throughout the universe, but in becoming a man it was as difficult for Him to keep to the human level as it is for humans to rise above their depraved natures and partake of the divine nature (7BC 930). This means His greatest temptation was to use His own divinity (1SM 276-278). This is a temptation not shared by other created beings. It was because He was divine, and could use His own divinity, that the temptation to turn stones into bread was so real. The thrust of temptation is to break a dependent relationship upon God. Sin separates a person from God. Sinners have such a separation from birth. Christ did not have this separation. He was the God-man, coming to do the will of His Father. But, and here is the key, He did not use His own divinity to resist temptations; He came to obey as a man (7BC 929). He was tempted in all points as we are (6BC 1074). It was as a victorious man that He demonstrated to the universe that the law can be kept.

Christ was both like and unlike other humans. He was like them in suffering temptations. Yet His temptations were far greater than those of other humans (ST, Apr. 10, 1893). What other humans live with the realization that with one sin their mission is over? What other humans carry the heavy burden of overcoming every temptation in order to save a race? What other humans experience the personal envy and jealousy of Satan heaped on them constantly? What other humans carry the weight of all human sins upon them, as Jesus did in the wilderness, in Gethsemane, and at Calvary?

Yet Christ had no power that humans do not have to overcome temptations (7BC 930), and He earnestly sought help from God with strong crying and tears (ST, May 10, 1899). In so doing, Christ as the Son of man gave humans an example of obedience, whereas as the Son of God He gives humans the power to obey (DA 24).

The wondrous good news is this: Christ did not have to come to live a human life and suffer constant temptations in which Satan and the whole confederacy of evil besieged Him (ST, Feb. 20, 1893) and every weapon of hell was used against Him (DA 116). He came voluntarily because of His great love for every human being (*ibid.* 22, 23). He came to give humans an example of how to be victorious and keep the law, and so exposed as false Satan's charge to the contrary.

But Christ did more. Christ overcame for us (ST, Oct. 17, 1900). His victory over Satan puts humanity on vantage ground (6BC 1074). Christ saved humans from their sins (RH, Mar. 16, 1886); restored in humans the moral image of God (RH, Mar. 1, 1898); clothed humans with His perfect lawkeeping life as a robe of righteousness (ST, July 26,1899); and united humans more closely to God than before the Fall, for Christ is also human (DA 25). Humans, in partaking of the divine nature, can overcome temptations as He overcame them, through an utter reliance upon the power of God and His Word (*ibid.* 123).

Gethsemane and Calvary reveal the depths of God's love and the unchangeable nature of His law. Christ became sin for humanity in His last hours. He took the place of all sinners, carried their guilt, and suffered to the depths a separation from His Father (DA 686-690, 753). Satan tempted Christ, saying that bearing the guilt of the world would bring an eternal separation from His Father (*ibid.* 686, 687). That is why Christ's life was being crushed out in Gethsemane and why it was a terrible temptation to let the human race bear its own guilt (*ibid.* 687, 688). "The fate of humanity trembled in the balance," as three times Christ's humanity shrank from the ordeal, but Christ commited Himself to save humans whatever the cost to Himself (*ibid.* 690-693).

The Father suffered with His Son (*ibid.* 693). On the cross Satan "wrung the heart of Jesus" with "fierce temptations." In His humanity Christ could not see beyond the tomb. He thought His death would be eternal, and this broke His heart. He plunged into eternal death so humans could have eternal life—in His place (*ibid.* 753). Yet beyond this gloom, in utter reliance on the evidence of His Father's prior acceptance, His faith clung to the Father—"into thy hands I commend my spirit"—and the humanity of Christ died a dependent victor (*ibid.* 756).

Norman R. Gulley

CHRIST, THE WAY OF LIFE PRINTS. The *Way of Life* prints were originally developed by Merritt G. Kellogg in 1873. The first print, by an unknown artist, was a "vivid portrayal of the plan of salvation" that came with an accompanying explanatory tract (*A Key of Explanation of the Allegorical Picture Entitled "The Way of Life"* [Battle Creek, Mich.: Steam Press, 1873]). James White advertised it as an "Allegorical Picture Showing the Way of Life and Salvation Through Jesus Christ From Paradise Lost to Paradise Restored" (RH, Feb. 17, 1874). In October 1876, 1,000 copies of a new improved edition were published by

James White. The most striking feature of the 1876 lithograph was the centrality of the Ten Commandments. Though the cross was evident, it was not prominent.

THE WAY OF LIFE, FROM PARADISE LOST TO PARADISE RESTORED

CHRIST, THE WAY OF LIFE

Four years later James White produced a new sketch, which he called "Behold the Lamb of God." Christ on the cross is made larger and placed in the center. White worked on the new edition throughout 1880 and 1881 and planned to entitle it *Christ, the Way of Life, From Paradise Lost to Paradise Restored*. His death, on August 6, 1881, prevented his completion of the project. His project, however, was fulfilled by Ellen White and her sons in 1883 when a new steel plate engraving pictured Christ on the cross as the dominating center of the plan of salvation. Soon a new tract, *A Key to the Allegorical Engraving Entitled the Way of Life, From Paradise Lost to Paradise Restored*, was published to accompany the chart (RHPA, PPPA, 1884).

The main significance of the changes in these prints was not artistic but theological. The marked change from the centrality of the law to that of the cross reflected a deep concern of both James and Ellen White that the Adventist message be refocused in a more Christ-centered manner. Ellen White seemed to sense that there was widespread, unwitting legalism and lack of Christian assurance. Speaking to the students at the General Conference Bible school in early 1890, she told of vows taken at her husband's deathbed to bring "an element [into] this work that we have not had yet" (Ms 9, 1890, in 1888 Materials 540). And most certainly that "element" was the primacy of justification.

It was during the period following James' death (1881) that Ellen White commenced a strong emphasis on the primacy of the understanding and experience of justification by faith alone. Beginning with her presentations at the 1883 Battle Creek General Conference session, there would be an expanding accent on justifying grace that was to climax with her presentations that followed the Minneapolis General Conference session of 1888 (especially the years 1889-1893).

Further reading: "History of the *Way of Life* Pictures" (EGWE, SDoc); L. E. Froom, *Movement of Destiny* (RHPA, 1971), pp. 184, 185 (pictures); W. W. Whidden, "The *Way of Life* Engravings: Harbingers of Minneapolis?" *Ministry*, October 1992.

Woodrow W. Whidden

CHRIST AS HIGH PRIEST. In Ellen G. White's understanding of salvation, Christ's role as high priest is as essential to salvation as His death on the cross. Following New Testament descriptions (e.g., 1 Cor. 3:16; Heb. 4:14-16; 7-10; Rev. 1:12-20), she portrays Christ as compassionately interceding for His people and ministering for His church on earth through the Holy Spirit from His headquarters in God's heavenly sanctuary. Like the Aaronic priests, whose role foreshadowed His, Christ makes *atonement by officiating His sacrifice. However, as both deity and sacrificial victim, He is superior to them.

While some aspects of Christ's intercessory function began during His life on earth, His inauguration as high priest and king came after His ascension, as signified by the outpouring of the Holy Spirit at Pentecost (cf. Acts 2). Since then He has served as the only true mediator between God and humanity, presenting to His Father the praises, prayers, and confessions of His people and representing in His person the efficacy of His sacrifice as the basis for mercy toward those who truly repent.

In harmony with biblical teaching that atonement is a process of divine-human reconciliation that requires priestly application/distribution of atoning blood following sacrificial death (e.g., Lev. 4-7; 17; Heb. 9:11-14), White maintained that continuation of Christ's priestly work of atonement is necessary because His people continue to commit sins. From early in her career she recognized Old Testament ritual (Leviticus) and prophetic (Daniel) backgrounds to the books of Hebrews and Revelation as bases for teaching that Christ's priestly ministry follows a two-phased trajectory prefigured by the division of ancient Israelite priestly officiation into daily mediatorial (primarily in the holy place) and yearly Day of Atonement (uniquely involving the Most Holy Place) phases.

She held that the final stage of Christ's ministry, typified by the Day of Atonement services, purges the heavenly sanctuary by removing the record/residue of sins that has accumulated there (cf. Lev. 16) through the earlier phase of atonement by which God's people were forgiven (compare Lev. 4; 5; 6:27, 28; 10:17). This cleansing of the heavenly sanctuary is accomplished through an investigative judgment of all professed believers that takes place in heaven not long before Christ's second advent (cf. Dan. 7:9, 10, 13, 14; 8:14; Heb. 10:25-30; Rev. 14:7). Only those who persevere in their loyalty to God receive the benefit of its cleansing/vindication (cf. Lev. 16:16, 29-31; 23:27-32).

Ellen White continued to accept the Millerite interpretation of the prophetic chronology of Daniel 8:14, according to which the heavenly sanctuary was to be justified/cleansed in 1844 after 2300 prophetic days/years. However, with the other ex-Millerites who eventually became Seventh-day Adventists, she came to believe soon after the disappointment in 1844 that the cleansing of the sanctuary in Daniel 8:14 is an end-time judgment in heaven (see above), through which Christ's church is married to Him (cf. Matt. 25; Rev. 19:7, 8), rather than the cleansing of earth by fire at Christ's second advent, as William Miller and his associates taught (GC 426-432).

Ellen White emphasized a definitive change in Christ's ministry from closure of the first phase to commencement of the second phase. She recorded an early vision in which God the Father and then Christ moved in 1844 from the holy place into the inner sanctum of the heavenly temple to commence the judgment (EW 55). Many Seventh-day Adventists have taken this scenario to imply that Christ did not even enter the Holy of Holies at all from His ascension to 1844, just as Leviticus 16 teaches that the Israelite high priest was not permitted to enter the inner apartment until the Day of Atonement. Others have objected that following His ascension, Christ entered "within the [inner] veil" (Heb. 6:19, 20). Rather than pitting Leviticus and White against Hebrews, a mediating position finds it preferable to view the inspired sources as complementary: As sinless deity, Christ enjoyed full *access* within the heavenly temple following His ascension, but He moved into an additional "Day of Atonement cleansing" *role* in 1844.

White understood that during the pre-Advent judgment Christ continues to intercede for His people so that they can be forgiven, as He did from His ascension to 1844 (cf. Num. 28:1-8, which shows that there was a regular sacrifice every day, including the Day of Atonement). However, following the end of the pre-Advent judgment, when all destinies are fixed, He will no longer need to atone for the sins of His people. Through Christ's ministry His people will be morally victorious and prepared to live through an unprecedented time of trouble (cf. Dan. 12:1). Thus she viewed spiritual commitment, growth, and purification as crucial priorities for the modern people of God, who should be focused on what Christ is doing for them now (cf. Lev. 16:29-31; 23:27-32; Rev. 14:6-12). Her approach is disturbing to those who mistakenly regard a high level of obedience to God through the sanctifying empowerment of His Spirit as legalism and/or who do not accept the biblical teaching that God is able to mature the lives of His people in harmony with His character of love (Rom. 5:5; Eph. 5:25-27; 1 Thess. 3:12, 13; Titus 3:4-7; Rev. 19:7, 8).

Also after the close of the pre-Advent judgment, Christ will place the sins of the righteous upon Satan as the tempter and originator of sin, just as the Israelite high priest loaded all moral faults of the Israelites upon a live goat for Azazel (cf. Lev. 16:20-22; Rev. 20:1-3). White's statement that Satan bears punishment of those who are saved (EW 178) can be understood in light of the biblical principle that a malicious false witness, which is what Satan is when he accuses

redeemed people of being lost (Zech. 3:1-5; Rev. 12:10), suffers the same punishment that the defendant would have borne had he/she not been vindicated (Deut. 19:16-21). So the punishment rightfully belongs to Satan; in no sense does he bear sins vicariously as Christ does.

In White's writings Christ's antitypical priestly ministry parallels the overall contours of the typical services at the Israelite sanctuary. However, within the framework of this continuity, her portrayal shows some discontinuities that are the result of the uniqueness and superiority of Christ's priesthood. While a number of these differences are explicitly stated in the Bible (especially Heb. 7-10), others, most notably relating to heavenly geography, are not. For example: whereas the Aaronic high priest cleansed the Israelite sanctuary by applying blood in the inner sanctum, in the outer sanctum, and at the outer altar (Lev. 16), Christ's cleansing of the heavenly sanctuary is concentrated in the inner sanctum. For White it is of utmost importance that the people of God understand what their heavenly High Priest is presently doing there for them so they can be in touch with Him "within the veil" by faith (GC 488, 489).

See also: Investigative Judgment.

Further reading: Christ in His Sanctuary; AA 33, 39; 6BC 1078; 7BC 913, 929-933, 989; DA 166, 734, 752; Ed 78; Ev 223, 224; EW 36, 42, 43, 48, 55, 58, 71, 85, 86, 178, 243, 244, 251-256, 260, 279-281; FE 275, 370; GC 352, 399, 400, 409-430, 480-490, 613, 614, 658; GW 34; PK 586-589, 685; PP 351-358, 365, 366; SC 37; 1SM 66-69, 74, 125, 343, 344; SR 376-378, 387, 402, 403; 2T 190-192; 4T 122, 393; TM 37; 15MR 104; R. Dederen, "Christ: His Person and Work," in R. Dederen, ed., *Handbook of Seventh-day Adventist Theology* (RHPA, 2000), pp. 160-204; E. E. Heppenstall,

Our High Priest (RHPA, 1972); F. B. Holbrook, ed., *Doctrine of the Sanctuary: A Historical Survey (1845-1863),* (Silver Spring, Md.: BRI, 1989); A. M. Rodriguez, *Future Glory* (RHPA, 2002), pp. 69-80.

Roy Gane

CHRIST IN HIS SANCTUARY (PPPA, 1969, 128 pp.). Compilation from Ellen White sources consisting primarily of chapters from *Patriarchs and Prophets* and *The Great Controversy,* with some other materials. The book affirms the doctrine of the *sanctuary, based on many passages of Scripture, especially Daniel 8:14 and the 2300 day/year prophecy of the cleansing of the sanctuary. The sanctuary doctrine was pivotal to the early Sabbatarian Adventist faith and was first published in 1845 by *O.R.L. Crosier in the *Day-Dawn* as a result of study by *Hiram Edson, Dr. F. B. Hahn, and Crosier. The following year the article was expanded and published in the *Day-Star* Extra of February 7, 1846. In April 1847 Ellen White wrote, "The Lord showed me in vision, more than one year ago, that Brother Crosier had the true light, on the cleansing of the sanctuary" (p. 5; WLF 12). In 1906 she wrote, "I know that the sanctuary question stands in righteousness and truth, just as we have held it for so many years" (p. 16; GW 303). *Christ in His Sanctuary* has nine chapters, each with study questions, covering such topics as "The Heavenly Sanctuary in Miniature," "Daniel 8:14 and Steps in God's Mysterious Leadings," and "The Glorious Temple in Heaven."

Further reading: P. G. Damsteegt, "Ellen White's Use of Scripture to Explain the Sanctuary Doctrine," in *Doctrine of the Sanctuary: A Historical Survey*, ed. F. B. Holbrook (Silver Spring, Md.: BRI, 1989), pp. 171-196.

Jack Blanco

CHRIST OUR SAVIOUR, see **STORY OF JESUS**.

CHRIST TRIUMPHANT (RHPA, 1999, 384 pp.). Eighteenth daily devotional book published by the Ellen G. White Estate. Its general theme is the *great controversy between Christ and Satan, good and evil, from the fall of Lucifer in heaven through the end of time and the restoration of the new earth. Many pivotal events in salvation history, such as the wandering of Israel in the wilderness and the life and death of Christ, are presented, shedding light on this controversy and including practical applications for today's Christians in preparation for Christ's return. Although this theme is already well covered in the five books of the *Conflict of the Ages Series, this devotional book complements other books by including heretofore-unpublished materials from Ellen White's letters and manuscripts. One new feature in this book is the editing of Ellen White's writings to use gender-inclusive language.

CHRISTIAN BEHAVIOR, STANDARDS OF, see **STANDARDS OF CHRISTIAN BEHAVIOR**.

CHRISTIAN CONNEXION. Beginning independently in several sections of the United States around 1800, a movement known as restorationism or primitivism arose. Its goal was to reform the churches by restoring all of the teachings of the New Testament. *Restorationism held the view that the Reformation began in the sixteenth century but would not be completed until the last vestiges of tradition were gone and the teachings of the Bible were firmly in place in the church. The task of the restorationist movement was to complete the unfinished Reformation.

The Christian Connexion was one branch of restorationism. Like the movement in general, the Connexionists espoused a radical view of *sola scriptura*. They wanted Bible evidence for every position they set forth. The Bible was to be their only guidebook in faith and practice. They claimed they had no creed but the Bible itself.

The Christian Connexion way of thinking became extremely important in early Seventh-day Adventism because two of its three founders had belonged to the Connexion—James White and Joseph Bates. Ellen White had never belonged to the Christian Connexion, but her family came into Millerite Adventism through attending meetings in the *Casco Street Christian (Connexion) Church in Portland, Maine. The historical framework of *The Great Controversy* is restorationist, and her family probably was influenced toward conditionalism and annihilationism through their contacts with the Christian Connexion. Beyond that, the Connexionist belief that spiritual gifts, including the gift of prophecy, would be in the church until the Second Advent undoubtedly led many early Sabbatarian Adventists to entertain an openness to Ellen White's gift.

Further reading: D. A. Foster et al., eds., *The Encyclopedia of the Stone-Campbell Movement* (Grand Rapids: Eerdmans, 2004), pp. 190, 191; R. T. Hughes and C. L. Allen, *Illusions of Innocence: Protestant Primitivism in America, 1630-1875* (Chicago: University of Chicago Press, 1988), pp. 102-132.

George R. Knight

CHRISTIAN EDUCATION (International Tract Society, 1893, 255 pp.). Ellen White's second book on education, comprising 24 chapters and a group of "fragments," compiled by *W. W. Prescott from published manuscript sources. A publication notice appeared in the *Review and Herald* of October 24, 1893. The book was a reprint and enlargement of an earlier publication titled *Selections From the Testimonies Concerning the Subject of Education* (1886). A *Supplement to Christian Education* was also issued (1894). All these were superseded in 1903 by her new book, *Education*, designed and organized to serve a broader reading audience. *Christian Education* was prepared not only for teachers but also for parents. Ellen White addresses a variety of topics in this book, presenting principles and suggestions applicable to every stage of child development.

Ivan Leigh Warden

CHRISTIAN EXPERIENCE AND TEACHINGS OF ELLEN G. WHITE (PPPA, 1922, 268 pp.). Selections from the writings of Ellen White regarding her life, early ministry, and major teachings. The first biographical work on the life and ministry of Ellen White appeared in 1860 as *Spiritual Gifts*, volume 2, with the subtitle *My Christian Experience, Views, and Labors, in Connection With the Rise and Progress of the Third Angel's Message*. This narrative of her life and labors to 1860 was amplified twice by her and published in 1880 and in 1888 as part of a larger work, *Life Sketches of James White and Ellen G. White*. Her biography was further extended to include her life and labor from 1888 to her death in 1915 and published in 1915 as *Life Sketches of Ellen G. White. Christian Experience and Teachings of Ellen G. White* is a shorter version of this later book and includes many illustrations and photos of Ellen White and other pioneers. Appendices include two articles on the prophetic gift in Scripture and the biblical tests of a genuine prophet, written by R. W. Munson and D. E. Robinson. Another abridged biographical sketch appeared in 1933 under the title *Life and Teachings of Ellen G. White*.

CHRISTIAN EXPERIENCE AND VIEWS OF ELLEN G. WHITE, see **SKETCH OF THE CHRISTIAN EXPERIENCE AND VIEWS OF ELLEN G. WHITE**.

CHRISTIAN LEADERSHIP (EGWE, 1973, 1985, 77 pp.). A compilation of Ellen White's writings prepared by Arthur White for a series of Christian Leadership seminars. Topics presented in this book include a variety of subjects relevant for church leadership, such as teamwork and influence, selection of personnel, management, decision-making, authority, and delegating. Emphasis is placed upon effectiveness and efficiency in leadership and in training lay members for leadership roles. Personal qualities of a leader are also discussed and include honesty, spirituality, and self-sacrifice. After the original printing sold out, continuing demand led to its reissue in a revised edition.

Adelino Libato

CHRISTIAN SERVICE (RHPA, 1925, 283 pp.). A compilation of Ellen White's counsels to help individuals and churches be more effective in Christian service and attracting individuals to Christ. It was initially compiled by the General Conference Stewardship Department from published material. The book presents effective methods of witnessing drawn from the examples of Jesus and the early church. The book's essence is summarized by an early statement: "A distinct work is assigned to every Christian." "Every true disciple is born into the kingdom of God as a missionary. He who drinks of the living water becomes a fountain of life. The receiver becomes a giver" (p. 9). The rest of the book is devoted specifically to the importance, methods, examples, and rewards of authentic, dedicated, evangelistic, and missionary endeavor. Nothing tends more to sustain deep religious experience than Christian service. All whose hearts are touched by the Spirit of the Great Evangelist will want to learn how to be effective in His service. Ellen White wrote as one who enjoyed a rich experience in sharing her faith under many and varied circumstances.

This volume covers a wide array of subjects, including the call of God to young and old to be engaged in service to Him and their fellow man, turning the home and the church into training centers, the importance of medical missionary work, and techniques and methods to be used in outreach to various groups of people.

Ellen White dealt also with personal qualifications for successful service, such as Christian dignity, genuineness, determination, zeal, patience, and consecration. Ultimately the most important qualifications are love and faith. "The worker for God needs strong faith. . . . The strength of those who, in faith, love and serve God, will be renewed day by day" (p. 234). The work of God can be accomplished only by the Spirit of God (cf. pp. 250-256). God is eager and willing to give the Holy Spirit to those who serve Him. "At all times and in all places, in all sorrows and in all afflictions, when the outlook seems dark and the future perplexing, and we feel helpless and alone, the Comforter will be sent in answer to the prayer of faith" (p. 251).

S. Joseph Kidder

CHRISTIAN TEMPERANCE AND BIBLE HYGIENE (Battle Creek: Good Health Pub. Co., 1890, 268 pp.). Two-part volume consisting of a compilation of Ellen White's writings on various aspects of Christian temperance (pp. 7-162) with the addition of several articles by James White on Bible hygiene (pp. 163-236). The final chapter, "Personal Experience," is a sketch of the life and experience of two Adventist pioneers, Joseph Bates (pp. 237-258) and J. N. Andrews (pp. 258-268). This book was compiled under the supervision of Ellen White, by a committee appointed by her for this purpose. The preface, written by J. H.

Kellogg, indicates that the book is in some sense an abstract of her writings on the subject of health (p. iv). Prior to the publication of *Christian Temperance and Bible Hygiene*, similar counsels had appeared in *Spiritual Gifts*, volume 4, in *Health: or How to Live*, and in *Testimonies for the Church*.

For Ellen White, "the relation which exists between the mind and the body is very intimate" and "the condition of the mind affects the health of the physical system" and vice versa (p. 13). Hence, she argues that those who belong to God should abstain from practices that "fill them with corruption and disease" (p. 12). She presents the benefits of a proper, balanced vegetarian diet and the avoidance of such practices as alcohol consumption and smoking. She emphasizes the importance of health education in the home, proper dress, hygiene, and mental purity. Amid all her counsels, Ellen White assures her readers that with God's blessing and power it is possible to overcome harmful habits and live a better life (pp. 146-149).

CHRISTMAS, see **HOLIDAYS.**

CHRIST'S OBJECT LESSONS (RHPA, 1900, 436 pp.). Commentary on the parables of Christ that applies Christian spiritual practices to life circumstances. Ellen White wrote the book during her years in Australia at the same time as she worked on *The Desire of Ages* and *Thoughts From the Mount of Blessing*. She donated all royalties from *Christ's Object Lessons* to the Seventh-day Adventist educational work and urged conference presidents and other administrators to encourage both the study and sale of the book by teachers and students. The proceeds from the sales were to provide debt relief for Adventist educational institutions. "It was [God's] plan that the book, *Christ's Object Lessons,* should be given for the relief of our schools, and He calls upon His people to do their part in placing this book before the world" (6T 469). In the sale of *Christ's Object Lessons* by student literature evangelists, she anticipated a fourfold blessing—to the schools, to the world, to the church, and to the colporteurs themselves. She specifically recommended that *Christ's Object Lessons* also be translated and circulated in Europe and other lands, and that church members make it available at tourist centers.

In response to Ellen White's desire that *Christ's Object Lessons* help with the cost of Christian education, in 1987 the Michigan Conference and the Review and Herald Publishing Association created the first "magabook" (book in magazine paper size), a special edition of *Christ's Object Lessons* designed for student literature evangelists. Today hundreds of students devote their summers to distributing this book (retitled *He Taught Love*), as well as other magabooks, to defray their tuition expenses at Seventh-day Adventist academies and colleges.

Further reading: 9T 83-86; 6T 468-478; CM 124; CT 525, 529, 530, 547; FE 523.

Cindy Tutsch

CHRONOLOGY, BIBLICAL. Ellen White's statements on chronology may be divided into three major categories: creation chronology, historical chronology, and prophetic chronology, of which the first will require the longest discussion because of Seventh-day Adventist interest in origins and earth history.

Similarly, her statements on creation chronology may be subdivided into three categories: the time *before* creation week, the time *during* creation week, and the time *after* creation week. Concerning the time *before* creation week, we find that Ellen White clearly allows for a lengthy history of the universe and even of created beings prior to the creation of this planet in six days. According to her, "all the hosts of heaven" were brought into existence prior to "the creation of the earth and its inhabitants" (PP 36; cf. 4BC 1143). In her thought many other worlds with their inhabitants were created prior to the creation of our own earth: "God's government included not only the inhabitants of heaven, but of all" created worlds during the time of Satan's rebellion in heaven prior to the creation of this earth (PP 41; cf. PP 331, 332). Nothing in the writings of Ellen White excludes the idea that the universe with its extraterrestrial inhabitants may have existed for ages prior to the creation of Planet Earth. Nothing would prevent those who value her writings today from accepting the conventional age for the universe determined by scientists.

Regarding the time *during* creation week, Ellen White clearly sides with the plain reading of the biblical text. Speaking of creation week, she unequivocally writes: "Like every other [week], it consisted of seven literal days" (*ibid.* 111). The seven literal days are seen as the historical origin of the seven-day week: "When the Lord declares [Ex. 20:11] that He made the world in six days and rested on the seventh day, He means the day of twenty-four hours, which He has marked off by the rising and setting of the sun" (TM 136; cf. 3SG 90). Ellen White opposed two speculative theories, popular in her day, which had been developed to harmonize Genesis 1 with geology: the day-age theory, which describes each day of creation as a geological age of millions of years; and the gap theory, which views a literal creation week as a "re-creation" of a prior creation that had taken place millions of years earlier (PP 111; cf. Ed 128, 129). Speaking of creation week, she affirms: "It was then that the foundation of the Sabbath was laid" (1SG 113). She saw a creation week of seven literal days as foundational to the doctrine of the Sabbath.

Regarding the time *since* creation week, Ellen White's writings are chronologically less precise. She allows for conjecture based upon extrabiblical findings and facts, as long as such conjecture does not contradict the direct statements of Scripture: "It may be innocent to speculate beyond what God's Word has revealed, if our theories do not contradict facts found in the Scriptures" (PP 113). The context of this statement refers to scientific research and specifically geological research. Concerning a possible age for the earth, that is, a date for creation, Ellen White endorsed "the view that creation week was only seven literal days, and that *the world is now only about six thousand years old*" (3SG 92; italics supplied). However, when this statement was incorporated into *Patriarchs and Prophets*, the reference to the 6,000 years for earth history was omitted, possibly suggesting that the main issue was not the age of the earth but the time allowed for creation itself (see PP 111-116). Some believe that Ellen White's references to about 6,000 years of earth history and about 4,000 years from creation to the Incarnation cannot rightfully be used to provide a complete chronology, because Ellen White relied upon Archbishop James Ussher for these and other dates that were found in the margins of most Bibles in the mid-nineteenth century (W. H. Johns, "Ellen G. White and Biblical Chronology," *Ministry*, April 1984).

Regarding Ellen White's historical chronology, she made more than 2,500 statements regarding the chronology of certain biblical events subsequent to creation (*ibid.*). With rare exceptions these statements harmonize closely with Ussher's dates in the margins of the King James Version Bible. On the length of the sojourn in Egypt, if the 400/430 years extend from Abraham to the Exodus, they would support only a "short sojourn" of about 200 years in Egypt. If, however, the 400/430 years began with Jacob's migration into Egypt, that would support a "long sojourn" of about 400 years, much of which was in slavery. Interestingly Ellen White published some six statements between 1864 and 1891 that seem to favor the "short sojourn," about 12 statements between 1894 and 1905 that can be interpreted as supporting the "long sojourn" view, and a third group of statements that are debatable, reflecting the same ambiguities as the biblical texts (Gen. 15:13, Ex. 12:40, Acts 7:6, and Gal. 3:17) (see W. H. Johns, "Ellen G. White and the Age of the Earth" [unpublished paper, 1995, CAR], pp. 3-6, and Appendix A).

Regarding prophetic chronology, Ellen White has fewer statements than those on either historical or creation chronology. Her office library contained several books on chronology—authored by S. Bliss, W. Hales, R. C. Shimeall, T. Tegg, and J. Ussher. Some of these and other works she possessed had extensive discussions on biblical chronology in relation to prophetic fulfillment. In explaining the prophecies of Daniel and Revelation, Ellen White's chronology is similar to that used by such Adventist contemporaries as James White, J. N. Andrews, and Uriah Smith. Her date for the crucifixion (A.D. 31), for example, is not original with her, but is derived from the Millerite/Adventist interpretation of the 70-weeks prophecy of Daniel 9 (4BC 851-855). Just as we should caution against using Ellen White's writings to settle the date for creation, so we must caution against using her writings to settle the date for the Incarnation or the Crucifixion. For her, chronology is never an end in itself, but a means to an end. The goal of all her writings is to uplift Christ as Savior and coming Redeemer. None of her chronological statements can be rightfully used to predict either an approximate or an exact date for the end of the world and the coming of Christ, for she herself warned against such *time setting (1SM 185-192; cf. GC 456, 457).

Warren H. Johns

CHRONOLOGY, HISTORICAL, see **HISTORIANS, ELLEN G. WHITE'S USE OF.**

CHURCH. The role of the church in God's plan for the redemption of the human race is a major theme throughout Ellen White's writings. Because from beginning to end her prophetic ministry was intimately connected with the rise and growth of the *Seventh-day Adventist Church, much of what she writes about the church is addressed primarily to Seventh-day Adventists. Yet her concept of the church is broad, including the entire sweep of its history from the time of Christ and His apostles until the consummation at Christ's second coming. "From the beginning, faithful souls have constituted the church on earth. In every age the Lord has had His watchmen, who have borne a faithful testimony to the generation in which they lived" (AA 11). In a broader sense, she includes God's people in Old Testament times in God's universal church. Of the people of Israel, she states that God by His mighty power "delivered them out of the hand of Pharaoh, and made them His church which was a representation of His church in all ages" (16MR 329).

The origin of the Christian church Ellen White attributes emphatically to Jesus Christ. Referring to the events described in the first chapter of the Gospel of John, she writes, "With the calling of John and Andrew and Simon, of Philip and Nathanael, began the foundation of the Christian church" (DA 141). The experience described in Mark 3:13, 14, when Jesus chose 12 apostles from among

His disciples "that they should be with him, and that he might send them forth to preach," she designates as "the first step . . . to be taken in the organization of the church that after Christ's departure was to be His representative on earth" (DA 291). The office of the twelve apostles "was the most important to which human beings had ever been called, and was second only to that of Christ Himself. They were to be workers together with God for the saving of the world," and just as "in the Old Testament the twelve patriarchs stand as representatives of Israel, so the twelve apostles were to stand as representatives of the gospel church" (*ibid.*). However, Ellen White rejects the idea that Jesus created an ecclesiastical hierarchy to be perpetuated by so-called apostolic succession. She wrote, "Apostolic succession rests not upon the transmission of ecclesiastical authority, but upon spiritual relationship. A life actuated by the apostles' spirit, the belief and teaching of the truth they taught, this is the true evidence of apostolic succession" (*ibid.* 467).

While Ellen White highlights the significance of the unique calling and ministry of the apostles, she strongly affirms the New Testament teaching that Christ alone is the true foundation and the head of the church. Commenting on the words of Matthew 16:18, "Upon this rock I will build my church," she explains, "Christ founded His church upon the living Rock. That Rock is Himself—His own body, for us broken and bruised" (DA 413). After quoting from Ephesians 1:22, 23 the words that God "gave him to be the head over all things to the church, which is his body," she states, "The church is built upon Christ as its foundation; it is to obey Christ as its head. It is not to depend upon man, or to be controlled by man" (*ibid.* 414). She rejects the teaching that the bishop of Rome "is the visible head of the universal church of Christ" and considers the doctrine of papal supremacy to be "directly opposed to the teachings of the Scriptures" (GC 50, 51).

The idea that Christ is the head of the church is in the Epistles of Paul closely connected with the idea that the church is the body of Christ. Ellen White frequently takes up this image and elaborates on its implications. This imagery implies that "connection with Christ . . . involves connection with His church" (Ed 268), and illustrates "the close and harmonious relationship that should exist among all members of the church of Christ" (AA 317). Referring to Paul's description of the body and its members in 1 Corinthians 12, she stresses that in the body of Christ "there are various members, and one member cannot perform exactly the same office as another," but "all are united to the body to do their specific work and should be alike respected, as they conduce [contribute] to the comfort and usefulness of the perfect whole" (4T 128). Repeatedly Ellen White warned individuals not to maintain a stubborn independence "contrary to the decision of the general body" (9T 260; cf. 3T 414; 8T 161). Rather, there should be a spirit of mutual submission, for in his wisdom the Lord "has arranged that by means of the close relationship that should be maintained by all believers, Christian shall be united to Christian and church to church" (AA 164).

Frequently Ellen White focuses on God's purpose for His church, sometimes in a single paragraph, sometimes in an entire article or chapter (see *Further reading*). Her book *The Acts of the Apostles*, which traces the development of the apostolic church, begins its first chapter, "God's Purpose for His Church," with these words: "The church is God's appointed agency for the salvation of men. It was organized for service, and its mission is to carry the gospel to the world. From the beginning it has been God's plan that through His church shall be reflected to the world His fullness and His sufficiency" (*ibid.* 9). "The purpose which God seeks to accomplish through His people today is the same that He desired to accomplish through Israel," namely that "by beholding the goodness, the mercy, the justice, and the love of God revealed in the church, the world is to have a representation of His character" (6T 12). This purpose she finds expressed in such biblical passages as Deuteronomy 7:6; 4:5-8; and Ephesians 3:8-10.

In order to realize God's purpose, the church must, of necessity, be distinct from the world and yet aggressively active in the world. According to Ellen White, "believers are to shine as lights in the world. A city set on a hill cannot be hid. A church, separate and distinct from the world, is in the estimation of heaven the greatest object in all the earth" (3SM 17). While separate "from the customs, habits, and practices of the world" (6T 9), it has always been God's intention "through His people to bring blessing to the world" (AA 13). "To the ancient Egyptian nation God made Joseph a fountain of life. . . . Through Daniel God saved the life of all the wise men of Babylon. . . . Everyone in whose heart Christ abides . . . is a worker together with God for the blessing of humanity" (*ibid.*).

Following Christ's inauguration as high priest at the right hand of the Father, the Holy Spirit was poured out upon the disciples. Ellen White refers to the Holy Spirit as "Christ's representative," sent "to be His successor on earth," but "divested of the personality of humanity, and independent thereof" (DA 669). Christ "is still by His Spirit the minister of the church on earth" (*ibid.* 166). God's purpose for the church cannot be realized without the Holy Spirit. The Spirit is "to animate and pervade the whole church, purifying and cementing hearts" (9T 20), "to give power and efficiency to our work" (6T 51). For "without the presence and aid of the Holy Spirit," the preaching of the Word is of no avail (GW 284; cf. DA 671). The presence of the Holy Spirit is as essential to the church now as it was in the days of the apostles. "To the end of time the presence of the Spirit is to abide with the true church" (AA 55).

Ellen White's emphasis on the great controversy between Christ and Satan is reflected in her doctrine of the church. She distinguishes between the true church and an apostate church, symbolized by the women of Revelation 12 and 17, "a virtuous woman representing a pure church, a vile woman an apostate church" (GC 381). By adopting pagan customs and traditions, "the Christian religion became corrupted and the church lost its purity and power," and then the fallen church persecuted "the true church of Christ" (EW 211). Two prominent marks of the latter are "the commandments of God, and the faith of Jesus" (Rev. 14:12) and especially the Sabbath of the fourth commandment is a mark or sign "by which the people of the world are to know God's true followers" (ST, Nov. 22, 1899). "Upon all who through Christ become a part of the true Israel, the observance of the Sabbath is enjoined" (*ibid.*).

Another important distinction for Ellen White is that between the church militant and the church triumphant. Against any triumphalistic concepts of the church she warns that "the church militant is not the church triumphant, and earth is not heaven. The church is composed of erring, imperfect men and women, who are but learners in the school of Christ" (ST, Jan. 4, 1883, in LDE 61). Similar counsel was frequently repeated (see 9MR 154; RH, Sept. 12, 1893; GCB, Apr. 22, 1901). More than once she refers to the parable of the wheat and the tares in Matthew 13:24-30 to stress the fact that even in God's true church not all are genuine believers (TM 45, 47, 61). This, however, is no reason for discouragement. While "the church militant must wrestle and toil" (GCB, Apr. 22, 1901), she will be victorious. "The work is soon to close. The members of the church militant who have proved faithful will become the church triumphant" (Ev 707).

Not only does Ellen White contrast the church militant and the church triumphant, but also the church below and the church above or the church on earth and the church in heaven. However, she stresses the close connection between the two. "The church of God upon the earth are one with the church of God above. Believers on earth, and those who have never fallen in heaven, are one church" (ST, June 6, 1895). "The church above, united with the church below, is warring the good warfare upon the earth" (1888 Materials 27). Only in this close connection can God's purpose of salvation be realized. "A working church on earth is connected with the working church above. God works, angels work, and men should work for the conversion of souls" (TM 204). The church below also functions as a preparatory school for eternal life. Church members "are to regard themselves as pupils in a school, learning how to form characters worthy of their high calling. In the church here below, God's children are to be prepared for the great reunion in the church above. Those who here live in harmony with Christ may look forward to an endless life in the family of the redeemed" (7T 264).

Many other aspects of Ellen White's doctrine of the church are discussed elsewhere in this encyclopedia (see below). Although deeply convinced of the imperfection of the church and its individual members, she could confidently say: "The church of Christ,

enfeebled, defective as she may appear, is the one object on earth upon which He bestows in a special sense His love and His regard. The church is the theatre of His grace, in which He delights in making experiments of His mercy on human hearts. . . . The church is God's fortress, His city of refuge, which He holds in a revolted world" (1888 Materials 1554). Against the church built upon the foundation of Christ, the Rock, she was sure "the gates of hell could not prevail" (DA 413).

See also: Baptism; Church Organization; Evangelism; Kingdom of God; Laodicean Message; Lord's Supper; Ministry; Mission; Ordinances; Ordination; Remnant Church; Social Meeting; Women, Ministry of; Worship.

Further reading: AA 593-601; 3SM 14-26; TM 15-62; 4T 16-20; 6T 9-13; 8T 14-18; RH, Aug. 4, 1891; Dec. 4, 1900; ST, Nov. 22, 1899; R. Dederen, "The Church," in R. Dederen, ed., *Handbook of Seventh-day Adventist Theology* (RHPA, 2000), pp. 538-581.

Peter M. van Bemmelen

CHURCH, REMNANT, see **REMNANT CHURCH**.

CHURCH AND STATE. Ellen White believed that close ties and relationships between church and state facilitated religious persecution and caused numerous outbreaks of intolerance in the past and the present, and would do so again in the future.

During the latter part of the nineteenth century scores of Seventh-day Adventists were arrested for violations of *Sunday legislation. In self-defense, the denomination began to aggressively agitate on behalf of *religious liberty. Perceiving the free exercise of religion and the separation of church and state to be intimately related, denominational leaders proclaimed Sunday laws to be a form of religious establishment. They were equally outspoken in their opposition to anything tending toward establishment as they were in opposing overt threats to religious liberty.

To publicize these views, Seventh-day Adventists launched *The American Sentinel* in 1886. Committed to defending "the religious rights of all, whether Catholic, or Protestant, ... Jew or Christian, religious or nonreligious" (*American Sentinel*, Jan. 30, 1889), its editors opposed a wide range of governmental activity that they believed violated church-state separation: subsidizing church-operated schools on Indian reservations, reading the Bible and teaching Protestant principles in public school, exempting churches from taxation, and outlawing blasphemy on the basis of its alleged sinfulness. Adventism's most outspoken advocate of church-state separation in the late nineteenth century was *Alonzo T. Jones, one of the editors of the *Sentinel*.

Jones and other Adventist separationists found themselves in basic opposition to the work of the National Reform Association, an interdenominational organization dominated by members of the Reformed Presbyterian Church. The mission of the NRA was to secure official constitutional recognition of Jesus Christ as the nation's sovereign and to promote legislative enforcement of His commandments. They were especially interested in the passage of national Sunday legislation, which they declared would be tantamount to a national recognition of Jesus' lordship.

Ellen White clearly supported the separation of church and state. Predicting that a church-state alliance would precipitate the final eschatological crisis and recalling the intolerance of the Middle Ages, she said the "inevitable result" of "the employment of secular power on the part of the church" was "intolerance and persecution" (GC 442). She believed such an alliance also had a detrimental effect on religious groups seeking political influence. "The mingling of churchcraft and statecraft," she said, "is weakening all the power of the churches" (Ms 63, 1899, in 4BC 1168, 1169). Citing the words of Jesus "My kingdom is not of this world" (John 18:36), she declared, "The union of the church with the state, be the degree never so slight, while it may appear to bring the world nearer to the church, does in reality but bring the church nearer to the world" (GC 297).

Yet Ellen White opposed the extreme lengths to which Jones and his colleagues sometimes took the concept of church-state separation. In a letter to Jones about the reading of the Bible in public schools, she agreed with him in principle, saying the church had no "right to enforce anything of a religious character upon the world," yet suggested that it was unwise for Seventh-day Adventists to be speaking out against the practice, and pointed out that some good might come from the reading of God's Word even under improper circumstances (Lt 44, 1893, in 1888 Materials 1164).

Her reaction was similar regarding actions taken by the denomination's governing body that would have required Seventh-day Adventist churches to subject themselves to taxation and would have forced missionaries in Rhodesia (now Zimbabwe) to pay for the land they had been given. In this regard she said, "I am often greatly distressed when I see our leading men taking extreme positions" (TM 201). Because of her influence, the implementation of these actions was aborted. This suggests that her strong support for church-state separation was tempered with moderation.

See also: Politics and Voting; Sunday Legislation; Religious Liberty.

Further reading: GC 442-444, 579-581, 591, 592; 5T 449-454; 9T 16, 17; Ev 227, 234, 235; TM 200-203; ChS 167-172; 4Bio 183-186; "Spirit of Prophecy Counsels Relating to

Church-State Relationships" (EGWE, SDoc); G. R. Knight, *From 1888 to Apostasy: The Case of A. T. Jones* (RHPA, 1987), pp. 77-79, 122-130; D. L. Pettibone, "Caesar's Sabbath: The Sunday-law Controversy in the United States, 1879-1892" (Ph.D. diss., University of California, Riverside, 1979), pp. 19-21, 90-93, 340, 341; *idem*, "The Christian Voice," *Liberty*, January-February 1981; March-April 1981; May-June 1981; A. L. White, *The Spirit of Prophecy and Government Favors*, RH, Jan. 16, 1969; RH, Jan. 23, 1969; RH, Jan. 30, 1969; R. W. Coon, *Ellen White and the Issues of State Aid: The Solusi Experience*, in *Public Funds and Private Education: Issues of Church and State*, ed. D. S. Penner (Silver Spring, Md.: Office of Education, North American Division of SDA, 1991); E. D. Syme, *SDA Concepts on Church and State* (Ph.D. diss., American University, 1969), pp. 136-143; *American Sentinel*, 1886-1893 (see especially Oct. 23, 1889; Jan. 2, 1890; Sept. 18, 1890; Apr. 16, 1891; July 16, 1891; Jan. 14, 1892); U.S. Senate, Fiftieth Congress, second session, misc. doc. no. 43, p. 78; ST, Sept. 22, 1890.

Dennis Pettibone

CHURCH ORGANIZATION. The earliest Sabbatarian Adventists were anti-organizational. Many of them, including Ellen White, had been expelled from their denominations during the peak of the Millerite experience in the early 1840s. As a result, many early Sabbatarians saw any form of church organization as a form of Babylon in the sense that Babylon had oppressed the Jews in the time of Daniel and the church had oppressed sincere believers in the Middle Ages.

But "*Babylon" would take on new meanings in the 1850s as the Sabbatarians began to see themselves more as a church and less as a "scattered flock." By late 1853 James White would emphasize another biblical meaning

for the word when he defined "Babylon" as confusion. By the late 1850s he was quite certain that the Sabbatarian movement was really too confused and disorganized to carry out its mission effectively. The movement needed "gospel order," or church organization.

Ellen White stood firmly with her husband in this matter. As early as December 1850 she had written that "I saw that everything in heaven was in perfect order" (Ms 11, 1850, in 5MR 227).

The Sabbatarian movement had grown rapidly in the early 1850s and had found itself an easy prey to unauthorized preachers. As a result, by 1853 the leaders had taken steps to protect their congregations through the certification of ministers. December of that year also saw James and Ellen White begin to make a strenuous call for "gospel order." James led out with a series of articles in the *Review and Herald*.

Joining her husband, Ellen wrote in late December 1853 that "the Lord has shown that gospel order has been too much feared and neglected. Formality should be shunned; but, in so doing, order should not be neglected. There is order in heaven. There was order in the church when Christ was upon the earth, and after His departure order was strictly observed among His apostles. And now in these last days, while God is bringing His children into the unity of the faith, there is more real need of order than ever before" (EW 97; see also EW 99, 101).

The 1850s witnessed an ongoing public debate in the *Review and Herald* on the topic of organization, with such things as the appointment of local elders and deacons and a plan for remunerating ministers (Systematic Benevolence [see *Tithe]) gradually being accepted.

Meanwhile, the issues of holding property

and carrying out an effective mission were still problematic. By the middle of 1859 James White was ready to begin his final drive for formal church organization. Once again Ellen stood solidly with him in his call for church order. The next three years would see victory in the struggle, with the choosing of a name and arrangements made for holding church property in 1860, the formation of local conferences in 1861, and the establishment of the General Conference in 1863.

Ellen White approved of the new organization, but disagreed with those General Conference presidents who abused their authority. The issue came to a head with the high-handed *G. I. Butler in the early 1870s. His abuse of power offered Ellen White an opportunity to discuss the authority of the *General Conference as an institution. "You," she penned to Butler, "did not seem to have a true sense of the power that God has given to His church in the voice of the General Conference." Her understanding was that the General Conference "is the highest authority that God has upon the earth," but, she noted that that authority resides in the church as a body rather than in one person (3T 492).

She held that position for the rest of her life, even though some of her statements seemed to indicate otherwise. In 1891, for example, she wrote that "I was obliged to take the position that there was not the *voice of God in the General Conference management and decisions. Methods and plans would be devised that God did not sanction, and yet Elder *[O. A.] Olsen [the president] made it appear that the decisions of the General Conference were as the voice of God." But many of the positions taken had been only "the voice of one, two, or three men who were misleading the Conference" (Ms 33, 1891, in 17MR 167). Five years later she indicated that the General Conference "is no longer the

voice of God" (Lt 4, 1896, in 17MR 186).

Barry Oliver, in his analysis of such statements, concluded that they refer to occasions when the General Conference did not act as a representative body, when its decision-making authority was centralized in a person or a few people, or when the General Conference had not been following sound principles (SDA Organizational Structure, p. 99).

That conclusion lines up with Ellen White's statements across time. She specifically spoke to the point in a manuscript read before the delegates of the 1909 General Conference session in which she responded to the schismatic/congregational activities of *A. T. Jones and others. "At times," she told the delegates, "when a small group of men entrusted with the general management of the work have, in the name of the General Conference, sought to carry out unwise plans and to restrict God's work, I have said that I could no longer regard the voice of the General Conference, represented by these few men, as the voice of God. But this is not saying that the decisions of a General Conference composed of an assembly of duly appointed, representative men from all parts of the field should not be respected. God has ordained that the representatives of His church from all parts of the earth, when assembled in a General Conference, shall have authority" (9T 260, 261).

The 1890s saw extensive worldwide growth of the church and its institutions. During that decade Ellen White repeatedly called for the decentralization of authority. The decade witnessed several initiatives toward reorganization. One would be led by A. T. Jones and E. J. Waggoner, who set forth a congregational approach. Ellen White argued against that position, noting that "Satan would rejoice to get in among this people, and disorganize the work at a time when thorough organization is essential" (Lt 37, 1894, in 14MR 202).

Meanwhile, a helpful approach to church organization that utilized union conferences and a departmental structure for the institutional sectors of the denomination was being experimented with in South Africa and Australia by *A. T. Robinson and *A. G. Daniells. Ellen White found their approach to be much more in harmony with the needs of the mission of the church.

The 1901 General Conference session witnessed the restructuring of the church for its international mission. Daniells and Ellen White took the initiative. On April 1 she made a powerful statement before selected leaders that called for an "entire new organization" that broadened the governing base. She left no doubt that "kingly ruling power" and any administrator who had a "little throne" would have to go. She called for "renovation without . . . delay" (Ms 43a, 1901; SpM 163-165). The next day she and Daniells pushed for reforms on the floor of the session itself. The session accomplished a reorganization that aimed at both diversity through the union conference system and unity through the creation of the departmental system, all under the leadership of the General Conference. The 1903 session saw modification to the system, even though it remained essentially the same.

Several points should be kept in mind when one thinks of Ellen White's perspective on church organization: (1) she advocated *unity in diversity; (2) even though she consistently argued for church organization, she never initiated any specific form of organization; (3) she believed organization should be flexible, able to change with the needs of the church and its mission.

See also: Kingly Power; Voice of God, General Conference as the.

Further reading: C. C. Crisler, Organization: Its Character, Purpose, Place, and Development in the Seventh-day Adventist Church (RHPA,

1938); G. R. Knight, Organizing for Mission and Growth: The Development of Adventist Church Structure (RHPA, 2006); A. G. Mustard, James White and SDA Organization: Historical Development, 1844-1881 (AUP, 1987); B. D. Oliver, SDA Organizational Structure: Past, Present, and Future (AUP, 1989).

George R. Knight

CITIES, LIVING IN. The world's great cities provided Ellen White an ambivalent situation. On the one hand, there is not the slightest doubt that she saw the ideal for Christian families to be rural living, where they could avoid the corruption, wickedness, and health-related problems of the cities while at the same time nourishing their spirituality in the atmosphere of nature. On the other hand, she had a burden that Adventism had neglected gospel work in the cities. Correcting that neglect would be a focal point of her ministry between 1901 and 1910.

For Ellen White the issue was not the need to work the cities but how best to do it. Her leading role in advocating city work has given her and her counsel on the topic a central place in Adventist discussions on how best to spread the gospel in the city.

Those who have studied city mission through Ellen White's writings have generally arrived at an understanding called "outpost evangelism." The outpost concept is found in several places in her writings. "It is God's design," she wrote in 1903, "that our people should locate outside the cities, and from these outposts warn the cities, and raise in them memorials for God" (Ev 76). "The cities," she had written a year earlier, "are to be worked from outposts. Said the messenger of God, 'Shall not the cities be warned? Yes; not by God's people living in them, but by their visiting them, to warn them of what is coming upon the earth'" (2SM 358).

Those two quotations are similar to many others that she wrote over the years. As a result, some have held that Ellen White's perspective is that it is wrong to locate Adventist evangelistic workers inside the cities. That position, however, takes only part of her counsel into consideration. It is all too easy not to examine everything she wrote on the topic or even to read carefully the context of her quotations.

Her counsel on education provides us with an interesting example of her breadth on the topic of city work. The earliest Adventist schools had been in small towns, but by 1894 Ellen White had become quite convinced that that had been a mistake. As a result, in relation to the founding of the Avondale school in Australia she wrote that "*never* can the proper education be given to the youth in *this country, or any other country*, unless they are *separated a wide distance* from the cities. The customs and practices in the cities unfit the minds of the youth for the entrance of truth" (FE 312; italics supplied). Following that counsel and the fact that Ellen White claimed that Avondale was to be a pattern school for other Adventist schools, the next 15 years saw Adventist schools around the world establish rural campuses.

But then in the early twentieth century the church began to make inroads among the poorer classes in some of the larger cities. What was her counsel in the face of that development? "*So far as possible*," she wrote in 1909, "these schools should be established outside the cities. *But* in the cities there are many children who could not attend schools away from the cities; and for the benefit of these, schools should be opened in the cities as well as in the country" (9T 201; italics supplied).

"Never" is worlds away from "so far as possible," but those terms represent the breadth of Ellen White's counsel—a breadth often overlooked. She wrote on the topic in terms of both the ideal and the real. Her ideal was always rural schools, but the reality of mission dictated that there would be Adventist schools in the city.

Ellen White also expressed a distinction between the ideal and the real in other areas of city mission. In one of her more forceful statements on outpost evangelism, for example, she noted (in the context of establishing a sanitarium in the New York area) that "it will be a great advantage to have our buildings in retired locations *so far as possible*" (MM 309; italics supplied), indicating as she did in the educational field that it wouldn't always be possible. When it came to a conflict between the denomination accomplishing its mission and rural living, the need to complete the mission successfully always won out in Ellen White's counsel.

Both of the above illustrations had to do with Adventist institutions. That was no accident, because each of the 22 quotations on outpost evangelism found in *Medical Ministry*, *Selected Messages*, *Country Living*, and *Evangelism* is written in the context of establishing Adventist medical, educational, and publishing institutions. It should be noted, however, that Ellen White's perspective can be misunderstood if her outpost statements are not read in the light of their full context.

It is true that she was opposed to institutions being established in cities *if* it was at all possible to avoid it. It is also correct to say that she sought to avoid large numbers of families being unnecessarily settled in the cities in relation to institutional work. *But she did not emphasize the outpost approach in relation to local churches.* To the contrary, she penned in 1907: "Repeatedly the Lord has instructed us that we are to work the cities

715

from outpost centers. In these cities we are to have houses of worship, as memorials for God; *but* institutions for the publication of our literature, for the healing of the sick, and for the training of workers are to be established outside the cities" (2SM 358; italics supplied).

Ellen White not only advocated churches in the city, but she repeatedly spoke to the point of how the evangelistic work of those churches should be carried out. In *The Acts of the Apostles*, for example, she noted that "while it is in the order of God that chosen workers of consecration and talent should be stationed in important centers of population to lead out in public efforts, it is also His purpose that the *church members living in these cities* shall use their God-given talents in working for souls" (AA 158; italics supplied).

Along that same line, she wrote in 1909 that "the Lord has presented before me the work that is to be done in our cities. The believers in these cities are to work for God *in the neighborhood of their homes*" (9T 128; italics supplied). A year later she counseled: "Especially are the church members living in the cities to exercise, in all humility, their God-given talents in laboring with those who are willing to hear the message that should come to the world at this time" (MM 332).

Some years earlier she had been quite explicit that some Adventists needed to *move to the cities* to raise up churches. "We see," she wrote, "the great need of missionary work to carry the truth not only to foreign countries, but to those who are near us. Close around us are cities and towns in which no efforts are made to save souls. *Why should not families who know the present truth settle in these cities and villages, to set up there the standard of Christ*, working in humility, not in their own way, but in God's way, to bring the light before

those who have no knowledge of it? . . . There will be laymen who will move into towns and cities, and into apparently out-of-the-way places, that they may let the light which God has given them shine forth to others" (ChS 180; italics supplied).

Thus we find in Ellen White's writings two sets of parallel counsel—one related to institutions, advocating outpost ministry; and a second dealing with local church work, advocating missionary work from within the city. Unfortunately, only one set of counsel has received much publicity. The reason for that imbalance is that statements from the one perspective have been collected and repeatedly published in compilations, while the other, even though equally valid and important, has been neglected. Thus Adventists traditionally have highlighted only one half of Ellen White's perspective on city mission.

Further reading: G. R. Knight, "Another Look at City Mission," AR, December 2001; N. C. (Ted) Wilson, "A Study of Ellen G. White's Theory of Urban Religious Work as It Relates to Seventh-day Adventist Work in New York City" (Ph.D. diss., New York University, 1981).

George R. Knight

CITY EVANGELISM. How Christians should relate to the cities of the world is an issue with which Ellen G. White wrestled for most of her public ministry. White had strong feelings on the issue, a complex one that triggered seemingly contradictory statements from her. In her day many Christians were ambivalent about the city, viewing it with a mixture of enchantment and aversion, simultaneously being drawn to and repulsed by it. Within Adventism there remains an anti-urban bias, based in part on an incomplete reading or, in some cases, a misreading of Ellen White's statements about the urban community.

Admittedly, Ellen White promoted life in the country as the ideal for the Christian (7T 87). In the vast expanses of the countryside, with its pristine environment and unhurried lifestyle, Christians would not be contaminated by the crime, chaos, and corruption so characteristic of cities. As a consequence, Christians would live healthier, less-stressful, and longer lives.

Yet White's desire to see the cities of the world won for Christ bordered on an obsession. She was profoundly disturbed by the benign neglect with which the denomination was treating the cities of her day, and came down hard on church leaders she thought were tardy in launching a strategic urban ministry initiative (6Bio 223-228).

That Ellen G. White was averse to the denomination establishing institutions in the city is beyond question. Wherever and whenever possible, it would be "a great advantage to have our buildings in retired locations," she counseled (MM 309). The city was not the most ideal place to locate the denomination's medical and publishing facilities, and because she believed that city conditions could not facilitate the ideal development of the minds of the young, she advocated that Adventist schools should not be situated in them. White's thinking gave rise to what became known as the outpost concept of evangelism, the belief that Adventists should penetrate the city from the safety and sobriety of the suburbs and country (Ev 76; 2SM 358).

Yet Ellen White was a pragmatist whose passion to see lost souls find the love of Jesus allowed her to advocate that some schools may need to be located in cities, especially among the poor who could ill afford the commute to country schools (9T 201). Additionally, although institutions were to be located outside cities, churches were to be planted in them as "memorials for God" (2SM 358). Further,

Adventists whose life situation made it advisable were to move into cities intentionally, taking up residence there to maximize their witness. Their incarnational presence would be a potent force for good and transformation. Asked White: "Why should not families who know the present truth settle in these cities and villages, to set up there the standard of Christ, working in humility, not in their own way, but in God's way, to bring the light before those who have no knowledge of it?" (ChS 180). She personally encouraged individuals to relocate to the city, writing to one couple that their move to and experience in New York City could serve as a model of how the cities of the world were to be won for Christ (Ev 385, 386).

A cursory reading of her writings may lead to the conclusion that White always advocated leaving the city, and those seeking support for life in the suburbs and country will find it in her writings. Yet a complete and unbiased reading of all that Ellen White had to say about cities reveals that she did not issue simple, unmitigated statements about them. She never unequivocally stated that Christians are not to worship or live in cities. Perhaps reflecting the complexity of the city itself, White's statements about the city are complex, though not completely ambivalent. For Ellen White the ideal was the country. Reality mandated, however, that Christians not only could live and work in the city, but whenever and wherever they had clear evidence of God's leading, should move into them with vision and purpose. After all, the earth is the Lord's, including its cities with their teeming millions.

See also: Cities, Living in; *Country Living.*

Further reading: FE 312; LS 396, 397; MM 305, 308, 309; 2SM 357, 358; AA 158; 7T 34-36, 54, 55, 80-88; 9T 89-152; Ev 25-44; GW 345-366; W. A. Westerhout, comp., *Science*

of Metropolitan Medical Missionary Evangelism; Gathered From the Messages of Ellen G. White (Loma Linda, Calif.: School of Public Health, 1969); N. C. (Ted) Wilson, "A Study of Ellen G. White's Theory of Urban Religious Work as It Relates to Seventh-day Adventist Work in New York City" (Ph.D. diss., New York University, 1981).

R. Clifford Jones

CIVIL WAR. Regarding the primary cause of the Civil War, much disputed to the present day, Ellen White was unambiguous: "It is this [the system of *slavery], and this alone, which lies at the foundation of the war" (1T 254). The societal sin of slavery, along with the Adventist ethical dilemma over participation in military combat—both interpreted in the light of apocalyptic judgment and redemption—dominated her perspective on the war. While these two concerns came into tension at certain points, the unifying imperative that Ellen White brought to bear on them was the Adventist calling to be a nonconformist prophetic minority bearing witness to "the commandments of God, and the faith of Jesus" in the midst of apostasy from the shining Protestant and republican ideals that the nation still claimed.

As the sectional crisis that led to the Civil War deepened in the 1850s, Ellen White wrote with vivid moral passion against the "enormous and grievous sin" of slavery. She envisioned Christ's second coming as bringing judgment on the slaveholding nation and the "jubilee" that would free the slaves (1SG 191, 192; 206). In 1859 she defiantly expressed her outrage toward the Fugitive Slave Act and asked her fellow believers not to obey this unjust law. "The law of our land requiring us to deliver a slave to his master, we are not to obey; and we must abide the consequences of violating this law. The slave is not the property of any man. God is his rightful master, and man has no right to take God's workmanship into his hands, and claim him as his own" (1T 202).

On January 12, 1861, in the midst of the first wave of secession by seven Southern states, but three months before the beginning of the war and the secession of four more states in April, Ellen White, according to later accounts by John N. Loughborough, experienced a vision lasting 20 minutes in Parkville, Michigan. After the vision she told the congregation that it had been revealed to her that other states would join the secession and that a war far more terrible and deadly than widely expected would result (1Bio 462, 463).

The Union's humiliating defeat in the war's first major battle—in Manassas, Virginia, seven months later—indeed smashed widespread optimism about a "ninety-days" war (referring to the enlistment period of the first wave of Union volunteers). Soon after, on August 3, a vision in Roosevelt, New York, prompted commentary by Ellen White on the war, published early the following year in *Testimony* No. 7, in which she introduced apocalyptic realities overarching the military struggle.

The war, she affirmed, is in the hands of a God who through it is judging the nation for the "high crime of slavery"—not only the South for its aggressive defense of the institution but also "the North for so long suffering its overreaching and overbearing influence" (1T 264). The bewildering reversal of fortunes at the battle at Manassas was thus revealed to have unfolded within the divine purpose that the war not serve to sustain and fortify slavery. The somewhat chaotic early advances of the Union forces were thwarted by an angel, Ellen White saw in vision, for two reasons: (1) to prevent a great Union triumph that would short-circuit God's punishment on the North for complicity with slavery; and also

(2) to prevent the even greater triumph that the Confederate cause would eventually have realized if the Northern army had "pushed the battle still further in their fainting, exhausted condition" (*ibid.* 267).

Ellen White's conviction that God would not allow the "slave power" to be victorious appears definite. On the other hand, she appears far less confident that military victory by the North would be the instrumentality for ending slavery. She lamented the moral and strategic failures of the Northern government as a means for liberation, a theme she would further develop in subsequent testimonies. Her message on the Roosevelt, New York vision concludes with a scene of pervasive "war, bloodshed, privation, want, famine, and pestilence," followed by a brief time of apparent peace, and then a return to "utmost confusion" throughout the earth, with other nations now engaged in war bringing famine and pestilence (*ibid.* 268).

Ellen White's analysis of the nation's peril was part of a widespread abolitionist outcry that began after the Union defeat at Bull Run stirred greater recognition of the dimensions of Southern resistance. Antislavery advocates demanded that extermination of slavery be made the purpose of the war, against President Lincoln's reiterated policy that the war's purpose was to preserve the slaveholding Union (James M. McPherson, *Battle Cry of Freedom: The Civil War Era* [New York: Oxford University Press, 1988], pp. 348-358).

A message entitled "The North and the South," dated January 4, 1862, and placed at the beginning of *Testimony* No. 7, amplified the woeful inadequacy of the North's response to the Southern rebellion, and the disaster it signaled for a divided nation. Ellen White could find little cause for optimism in the government's conduct of the war. First, she concurred with abolitionist Frederick Douglass'

view that the morally deficient purpose of preserving a slaveholding Union was self-defeating and demoralizing for the thousands who had put life and limb on the line thinking they were volunteering for a fight to abolish slavery (1T 254, 255; cf. McPherson, p. 354). The mistreatment and even return of escaped slaves to their masters by Northern officers constituted the glaring and graphic evidence of the North's utter lack of abolitionist resolve (1T 257).

Second, "strong antislavery men" in the Northern ranks had been "placed under censure, or removed from responsible stations" by an administration fearful of alienating proslavery unionists (*ibid.* 258; on John C. Fremont as a prominent example, see McPherson, pp. 352-358). With proslavery commanding officers, under whom "our armies have been repulsed and unmercifully slaughtered," and deep disunity in the Northern ranks over the purpose of the war, it looked "impossible to have the war conducted successfully" (1T 256).

Third, Ellen White pointed out that denial of an abolitionist purpose to the war worked against England coming to the aid of the North. With other abolitionists she cited the weakness of the government in dealing with the slave system as giving other nations reason to conclude that the ineffectiveness was the result of the United States government not being monarchial. Such monarchies now "admire their own government, and look down, some with pity, others with contempt, upon our nation, which they had regarded as the most powerful upon the globe" (*ibid.* 259, 260).

The government compounded its hypocrisy about slavery by proclaiming national fasts to accompany prayer for a "speedy and favorable termination" (*ibid.* 256) of the war. Ellen White characterized such fasts as "an insult to Jehovah" (*ibid.* 257). Citing the biblical prophet Isaiah's declaration that the "fast" of the Lord's choosing is "to let the oppressed go free, and . . . break every yoke" (Isa. 58:6), she wrote: "When our nation observes the fast which God has chosen, then will He accept their prayers as far as the war is concerned; but now they enter not into His ear" (*ibid.* 258).

At that point Ellen White appeared to have little hope for such national repentance. "This nation will yet be humbled into the dust," she warned; divided, "it must fall" (*ibid.* 259, 260). Again here, she feared international war emerging in connection with America's internal war (*ibid.* 259; cf. Nichol, pp. 122, 123).

Regarding the issue of Adventists' own participation in the war, James White contended, in an editorial titled "The Nation" that appeared in the *Review and Herald* in August 1862, that if military law were to coerce citizens to fight, the government would assume the responsibility for the violation of the Ten Commandments. Resistance would be suicidal. The editorial sparked vigorous debate, much of it published in the *Review*. Several voices urged that Adventists must take a decisive stand against military combat based on loyalty to Christ and His commandments, while others raised the question of whether Adventists actually had a moral duty to join the war to combat slavery.

Like the Adventist community in general, Ellen White was not "fully settled" on the matter of taking up arms, as she put it in a letter to a Sister Seward in Wisconsin dated a week after "The Nation" appeared. However, she saw wisdom in her husband's position that Adventists should not court martyrdom through draft resistance. Such action would only mark them as disloyal to the Union cause, and would not serve as a witness to the religious convictions of the Adventist cause. It would be a victory for Satan, she wrote, if Adventists were "shot down so cheaply" (2Bio 43, 44).

In *Testimony* No. 9, which appeared in January 1863, Ellen White defended her husband, saying that in "The Nation" he had given "the best light that he then had," and then went on to bring into focus further light, formulating a nuanced yet principled stand for noncombatancy (1T 356). She rebuked the rash action of the Adventists in Iowa who had unsuccessfully petitioned the state legislature for recognition as pacifists. Their zeal for martyrdom had unnecessarily attracted unfavorable attention to a movement that was in a very vulnerable state as new and marginal in society, yet energetically proclaiming radical apocalyptic teachings in public tent meetings. At the same time, she viewed the Iowans' attempt to find protection through a governmental measure as betraying, behind their bravado, a lack of true faith in God.

If she viewed the actions in Iowa as imprudent and premature, Ellen White nonetheless felt that Adventists now needed to be ready to take a clear stand as noncombatant yet pro-Union and anti-slavery. Reminding readers of their identity as subjects of God's everlasting kingdom, and of their loyalty to divine law over human precepts, she declared: "I was shown that God's people, who are His peculiar treasure, cannot engage in this perplexing war, for it is opposed to every principle of their faith. In the army they cannot obey the truth and at the same time obey the requirements of their officers" (*ibid.* 361).

Those committed to such a course of unswerving obedience to the divine commandments, she counseled, should not seek confrontation with boastful pronouncements. Rather, if questioned by authorities, they should "simply state what they are obliged to say in order to answer the inquirer, and then let it be understood that they have no sympathy with the Rebellion" (*ibid.* 357).

Despite the Emancipation Proclamation issued January 1, 1863, Ellen White, again in this testimony, presented a litany of the failures of the Northern war effort as an instrument of moral purpose. Collusion with the rebels, racial bigotry, reliance on spiritualism for guidance, and the treachery of pro-slavery generals combined to sabotage the Union cause. While convinced that God would not allow the Northern army to be "utterly destroyed" (*ibid.* 365), she remained despairing of full victory. "How can God go forth with such a corrupt army?" she concluded (*ibid.* 367).

Ellen White made little further direct comment on the Civil War, but the guidance she gave had lasting significance for the Adventist community. When Congress, in July 1864, restricted the option of paying a commutation fee in lieu of military service to conscientious objectors, Adventists sought and won government recognition as "a people unanimously loyal and anti-slavery" but unable to shed blood because of their views of the Ten Commandments and the teachings of the New Testament (J. N. Andrews, "Seventh-day Adventists Recognized as Non-combatants," RH, Sept. 13, 1864).

The decision to seek governmental recognition was not made lightly or without a deep ambivalence that Ellen White still felt more than 20 years later when Adventists began stepping up activism for religious liberty in the political arena. In 1886 she commented that the question of whether such an approach would indicate a lack of full trust in God had "been a burden of my soul for some time." However, recollection of what God had shown her in regard to the draft helped bring her to firm affirmation that "we should use every power we can to avert the pressure that is being brought to bear upon our people" (Lt 55, 1886, in 2SM 334, 335).

Adventists, she wrote soon after, should speak out for liberty, not only for themselves, but to "arouse the spirit of true Protestantism, awaking the world to a sense of the value of the privileges of religious liberty so long enjoyed" (5T 716). Thus, Ellen White's guidance in the tensions with government caused by the Civil War helped shape the character of Adventism's public witness. As a faithful, nonconformist minority, they were to include, in their work, action in the public arena to uphold the American republic's highest political ideals, as well as relativizing the republic through proclamation of God's kingdom as the only genuine and lasting guarantor of liberty.

See also: Military Service.

Further reading: R. Branson, "Ellen G. White: Racist or Champion of Equality?" RH, Apr. 9, 1970; P. Brock, *Freedom From Violence: Sectarian Resistance From the Middle Ages to the Great War* (Toronto: University of Toronto Press, 1991), pp. 230-245; H. E. Douglass, *Messenger of the Lord* (PPPA, 1998), pp. 486, 487, 572, 573; H. Mayer, *All on Fire: William Lloyd Garrison and the Abolition of Slavery* (New York: St. Martin's, 1998), pp. 333-585; J. M. McPherson, *Ordeal By Fire: The Civil War and Reconstruction*, 3rd ed. (Boston: McGraw-Hill, 2001), pp. 283-302; D. Morgan, *Adventism and the American Republic: The Public Involvement of a Major Apocalyptic Movement* (Knoxville: University of Tennessee Press, 2001), pp. 11-44; F. D. Nichol, *Ellen G. White and Her Critics* (RHPA, 1951), pp. 112-130; R. Schwarz and F. Greenleaf, *Light Bearers: A History of the Seventh-day Adventist Church* (PPPA, 2000), pp. 83-99; A. W. Spalding, *Origin and History of Seventh-day Adventists* (RHPA, 1961), vol. 1, pp. 11-44.

Douglas Morgan

CLAREMONT SANITARIUM. Medical facility in Claremont, South Africa. The idea for the sanitarium came from a letter Ellen White wrote to Anna Wessels, a resident of Claremont, South Africa, in 1893 in which she outlined the importance of medical missionary work (Lt 64, 1893). Within four years the Claremont Sanitarium, a 51-bed medical institution, was established in Claremont, Cape Town, South Africa, operated under the auspices of the *International Medical Missionary and Benevolent Association. It was in its time the best-equipped medical institution in the Southern Hemisphere, costing £50,000, of which the Wessels family provided £30,000. Dr. R. S. Anthony became the first medical director of the institution and was soon joined by Dr. *Katherine Lindsay from the Battle Creek Sanitarium.

The institution met with immediate success, with every bed filled within the first week after opening. Soon adjacent buildings were rented to cope with demand. By 1899 Ellen White expressed concerns to the Wessels family regarding their administration of the medical missionary work and its resulting influence (TSA 57). In 1900, during the height of the Anglo-Boer War, British forces requisitioned much of the main building of the sanitarium as a convalescent home for military personnel. The high standards with which the sanitarium had begun were ignored, as regular barracks, including a bar, were established.

In July 1901 Ellen White told J. H. Kellogg to stay clear of the Claremont Sanitarium, because trouble would come to it. She then told him that trouble would also come to the Battle Creek Sanitarium (Lt 112, 1901). In the economic depression that followed the Anglo-Boer war, the Claremont Sanitarium had all but lost its evangelistic purpose and was experiencing heavy losses. Contrary to Ellen White's advice at the sanitarium's founding (Lt 64, 1893), the Wessels family took control of the institution, but patronage continued to decline, until a final attempt was made to keep the doors open by turning the sanitarium into a hotel. Bankruptcy followed, and in 1905 the building burned to the ground, an event that many have compared to the Battle Creek Sanitarium fire of 1902.

See also: Africa.

Further reading: TSA; L. F. Swanepoel, *The Origin and Early History of the Seventh-day Adventist Church in South Africa* (M.A. thesis, University of South Africa, 1972), pp. 168-180; *SDA Encyclopedia* (1996), vol. 10, p. 377.

Michael D. Pearson

CLEAN AND UNCLEAN FOOD, see **UNCLEAN FOOD**.

CLOTHING, see **DRESS AND ADORNMENT**.

COFFEE, see **BEVERAGES**.

COLLEGE OF MEDICAL EVANGELISTS. Founded in 1906, forerunner of Loma Linda University, Loma Linda, California. In 1906 Ellen White emphasized that Loma Linda was to be "not only a *sanitarium, but also an educational center. With the possession of this place comes the weighty responsibility of making the work of the institution educational in character" (RH, June 21, 1906, in MM 56).

The 1906 calendar for the new school offered four courses: collegiate, nurses, gospel workers, and a three-year evangelistic-medical course that included standard medical school classwork plus Bible classes. Ellen White had counseled, "The healing of the sick and the ministry of the Word are to go hand in hand" (LLM 182). On September 20, 1906, a portion of the faculty met for morning devotions and declared school in session. But there were no lesson assignments because there were no students. However, by October 4, the remainder of the faculty and approximately 35 students had arrived, and instruction began (Schaefer, *Legacy*, p. 89).

On October 23 *John Burden, the institution's business manager, wrote to Ellen White, asking her counsel regarding the future curriculum of the college. Should administration seek legal recognition as a school of medicine? Or should they seek legal recognition for a class of healer, such as the homeopath, the chiropractor, the osteopath, or some eclectic blend of healing methodologies? Or should they simply provide instruction for "medical evangelists," even though they would have no legal recognition and could not legally practice medicine? (*ibid.*, p. 90).

At the time, Ellen White had received no divine counsel to answer these perplexing questions. A year later, when Burden again asked whether the school was "simply to qualify nurses" or whether it should "embrace also the qualification for physicians," she replied, "Physicians are to receive their education here" (MM 76).

In February 1908, 17 months after the College of Evangelists opened, a local committee met in Loma Linda to study relationships between the Adventist educational institutions in southern California. It seemed obvious that some young people should be educated as fully accredited physicians. But the committee estimated that laboratories and other needed facilities for a medical school would cost $40,000 to $50,000—more than the original cost of the sanitarium. When asked whether the needed facilities should be provided, Ellen White cautioned against premature action: "The plans you suggest seem to be essential; but you need to assure yourselves that they can be safely carried.

. . . If you had the talent and means to carry such responsibilities, we should be glad to see your plans carry" (Lt 82, 1908, in LLM 9; see also LLM 354).

A month later she cautioned: "We should not at this time seek to compete with worldly medical schools. Should we do this, our chances of success would be small. We are not now prepared to carry out successfully the work of establishing large medical institutions of learning" (Lt 90, 1908, in LLM 10; see also LLM 316).

By 1909 the College of Evangelists was offering a three-year course. The faculty could only encourage those who wanted to become physicians to hope that their education would be accepted as equivalent to the first two years at public schools of medicine, or that it would count toward graduation at Loma Linda, should it become an accredited school of medicine.

In September Burden sent a letter to Ellen White outlining the questions in the minds of faculty and students. She replied that the church should "have a school of [its] own" to educate physicians, and that it would not be a violation of principle to obtain a charter (Ms 71, 1909, in LLM 426).

Despite seemingly immovable obstacles, the administration decided to follow Ellen White's counsel. Church leaders then changed the school's name from College of Evangelists to College of Medical Evangelists (CME)and incorporated under the laws of the State of California on Thursday, December 9, 1909. The Articles of Incorporation authorized CME to grant degrees in the liberal arts and sciences, dentistry, and medicine.

Shortly after CME's incorporation, the Pacific Union Conference, meeting at Mountain View, California, for its fifth biennial session, decided that in order to support such an ambitious enterprise, church officers must be sure that they correctly understood the counsel from Ellen White. In a letter placed in Ellen White's hands on January 26, 1910, they asked, "Are we to understand that, according to the light you have received from the Lord, we are to establish a thoroughly equipped medical school, the graduates from which will be able to take state board examinations and become registered, qualified physicians?" (RH, May 19, 1910).

Ellen White's reply the next day declared: "The light given me is, We must provide that which is essential to qualify our youth who desire to be physicians, so that they may intelligently fit themselves to be able to stand the examinations required to prove their efficiency as physicians.... The medical school at Loma Linda is to be of the highest order, because those who are in that school have the privilege of maintaining a living connection with the wisest of all physicians [Christ], from whom there is communicated knowledge of a superior order. And for the special preparation of those of our youth who have clear convictions of their duty to obtain a medical education that will enable them to pass the examinations required by law of all who practice as regularly qualified physicians, we are to supply whatever may be required, so that these youth need not be compelled to go to medical schools conducted by men not of our faith. Thus ... our young men and young women, whose spiritual interests the Lord desires us to safeguard, will not feel compelled to connect with unbelievers in order to obtain a thorough training along medical lines" (PUR, Feb. 3, 1910, in MM 57, 58).

To establish such a school would require the broad-based financial support of the entire denomination. *I. H. Evans, a vice president of the General Conference, spoke enthusiastically of advancing by faith. "We have before us ... a plain, straightforward statement from Sister White, in regard to the establishment of a medical school. There is no guess-work about it; there is no equivocation; there is no false construction that need be put upon these words. The question is, Will we follow the counsel given?" (*Medical Evangelistic Library*, no. 1, pp. 5, 15).

Church members responded with a heartfelt enthusiasm that ensured united action on behalf of the new medical college. Even though none believed their financial resources or talents were sufficient for the enterprise, many believed that God had shown them that the time was right.

Incorporated December 9, 1909, as part of the College of Medical Evangelists, the infant medical school, with its faculty of five family doctors, could not have been born into a colder legal climate. In 1910 the *Abraham Flexner Report*, financed by the Carnegie Foundation for the Advancement of Teaching, supported what the Council on Medical Education had started in 1906 in closing inadequate medical schools in the United States. New strict accreditation procedures graded each surviving school, and closed those that did not soon measure up. By 1932 authorities had closed 84 schools of medicine in the United States (S. Jonas, *Medical Mystery: The Training of Doctors in the United States* [New York: Norton, 1978], p. 223). New stricter accreditation procedures graded each surviving school, and those that did not soon measure up were closed also. Accreditation authorities told CME administrators that it would be impossible for a new, poorly equipped, church-related school of medicine to measure up to these strict standards.

On May 11, 1910, the CME board of trustees created a new corporation, consolidating the sanitarium and the college and their respective boards of trustees. The first AMA accreditation inspection in 1915 resulted in a "C" rating; a "B" grade was achieved in 1917; and the "A" rating was received in 1922. In 1961 the College of Medical Evangelists became Loma Linda University. As of 2008 the School of Medicine had graduated 9,646 physicians.

Further reading: M. L. Neff, *For God and C.M.E.* (PPPA, 1964); R. A. Schaefer, *Legacy: Daring to Care, the Heritage of Loma Linda University Medical Center* (Loma Linda, Calif.: Legacy, 1990); *Medical Evangelistic Library* (Loma Linda, Calif.: College Press [c. 1910]); *SDA Encyclopedia* (1996), vol. 10, pp. 940-954.

Richard A. Schaefer

COLORADO. James and Ellen White first visited Colorado in 1872, seeking a reprieve from their labors. Much of the state was then still a frontier wilderness, largely untouched by the conveniences of modern civilization. En route from Battle Creek to California, they stopped to visit Ellen's sister, Caroline (Harmon) Clough, and her family near Ottawa, Kansas. Caroline urged them to visit her daughter Louisa (Clough) Walling and son-in-law William B. Walling, who were in Colorado.

The Whites reached Colorado July 18 and spent the next two months in the mountains, staying at William Walling's sawmill south of Rollinsville, about 45 miles (75 kilometers) northeast of Denver. James' health improved, owing in no small part to a strenuous trip across Boulder Pass (now Rollins Pass) to Hot Sulphur Springs. As the trip began, Ellen was thrown from her pony when a bedroll came loose and spooked the animal. She was in pain for much of the trip, and her injury sometimes troubled her in later life. At Hot Sulphur Springs James presided at the first Caucasian funeral in Middle Park, according to Ellen's niece, Mary Clough (another of Caroline's daughters), who later became Ellen's

secretary. Seventeen-year-old Willie enjoyed hunting, picking berries, and bathing in the hot springs.

The family returned to Colorado in June 1873, this time staying at Walling's older mill, about two miles (three kilometers) farther south, which was no longer in use. James and Ellen both spent much of their time writing, she working on *Testimony* no. 23 (now 3T 252-338). James invited *Dudley M. and Lucretia Canright to join them in the mountains. Unfortunately, the cabin where they stayed was crowded, with five adults (including *Lucinda Hall), a teenager (Willie), and the Canrights' 14-month-old daughter, Genevieve. After three weeks James and Dudley got into an argument, which prompted the Canrights' departure. Dudley traced his doubt of Ellen's inspiration to those events and her siding with James in the argument between James and Dudley. Canright went down the hill to Golden, where he conducted the first Adventist evangelistic series in Colorado, then left the ministry for several months.

In mid-September the Whites crossed Boulder Pass again, headed to Grand Lake. When their wagon broke down, they spent a week camped at the timberline, braving snow and freezing temperatures while Walling went to repair their broken axletree. Charles Glover, an old Adventist acquaintance, returned with the fixed axletree to enable them to continue their trip. At Grand Lake Glover and Willie spent some time hunting and fishing. One day Willie shot two gray squirrels "to make broth for Brother Glover." (The current Adventist position on *unclean food had not developed yet.) In order to help his father meet a deadline for revising a pamphlet about the Sabbath, Willie scraped the fat from a prairie wolf carcass to make a candle.

Earlier in 1873 William and Louisa Walling had separated. As winter approached, William asked the Whites to continue caring for his two daughters, Addie and May (5 and 3 years old), who had stayed with the Whites for several weeks that summer. The Whites reluctantly agreed, taking them to California and later Battle Creek. Addie and May spent the next 16 years living with their great-aunt and great-uncle.

About the same time, James lent Walling some money. In 1876 Walling signed his Nederland sawmill over to James, perhaps in partial payment of the debt. In August 1878 James purchased the older sawmill, where they stayed in 1873, at a reduced price, planning to make it the Whites' summer headquarters. It came to be referred to as "White's Ranch."

In July 1878 the Whites again visited Colorado with Dudley Canright and Mary K. White, Ellen joining them for two and a half weeks, preaching twice at a Boulder evangelistic series conducted by M. E. Cornell. Halfway through her stay Dudley Canright left on good terms. A week after Ellen left, their son Edson arrived and assisted his father in a Georgetown tent meeting during September.

The Whites returned to Colorado in the summer of 1879 following a mule drive by *wagon train from Dallas, Texas. They were in Boulder when the Seventh-day Adventist church was organized on August 2. The next Monday James was summoned to Boulder County Court in connection with debts incurred by the Nederland sawmill operations. He promptly sold the sawmill to the Gilpin County district attorney at a substantial loss. As August drew to a close the couple assisted with Denver's first evangelistic series.

In 1881 Ellen spent a month at their mountain cabin with Mary White, mourning James' death. Three years later she sold the property. In 1909 she returned to Colorado one last time and spoke at the camp meeting in Boulder (6Bio 215, 216).

See also: Boulder Sanitarium; P. H. Abraham Wade.

Further reading: 2Bio 341-355, 385-393; 3Bio 92, 93, 181-185; D. Johnson, *Colorado Vacations of James and Ellen White, 1872-1879* (EGWE-LLU); E. D. Dick, "For Health and Wealth: The Birth of Seventh-day Adventism in Colorado," *Adventist Heritage* 7, no. 2 (Fall 1982): 18-27; J. Moon, *W. C. White and E. G. White* (AUP, 1993), pp. 13-19.

Del L. Johnson

COLUMBIA UNION COLLEGE, see **WASHINGTON TRAINING COLLEGE**.

COLPORTEUR EVANGELIST, THE, see **COLPORTEUR MINISTRY**.

COLPORTEUR MINISTRY (PPPA, 1953, 176 pp.). Compilation of Ellen White's counsels on the ministry of literature evangelists, or *colporteurs. Since the beginning of the publication of Seventh-day Adventist literature in the late 1840s, millions of copies of books and periodicals have been distributed by literature evangelists and missionary-minded laypersons. Throughout her ministry Ellen White provided guidance regarding the publication and circulation of such literature. "The canvassing work," she wrote in 1900, "properly conducted, is missionary work of the highest order, and it is as good and successful a method as can be employed for placing before the people the important truths for this time" (p. 6).

In 1902 a number of statements from Ellen White's *Testimonies for the Church* and other sources relating to colporteur ministry were assembled and published in *Manual for Canvassers* (PPPA). Subsequent counsels from Ellen White led to the enlargement of this 73-page booklet and the publication in 1920 of *The Colporteur Evangelist* (PPPA). This second compilation was further enlarged with additional statements from Ellen White found in her books, periodical articles, and unpublished letters and manuscripts, and published in 1953 as *Colporteur Ministry*. The statements are topically arranged and present such subjects as the purpose and mission of colporteur evangelism, the qualifications of a colporteur, and the types of literature to sell. In 1973 Pacific Press published selections from *Colporteur Ministry* under the title *That Other Angel* (64 pp.).

COLPORTEURS. Also known as canvassers and/or literature evangelists, colporteurs are self-supporting missionaries who utilize a variety of methods to sell and distribute literature for the purpose of evangelizing. Responsible for the beginning and the expansion of Adventism in many parts of the world, they are considered God's messengers to spread the good news of the gospel through the printed page. According to Ellen White, "there is no higher work than evangelistic canvassing, for it involves the performance of the highest moral duties" (6T 331). In her opinion, "the intelligent, God-fearing, truth-loving canvasser should be respected; for he occupies a position equal to that of the gospel minister" (*ibid.* 321).

Adventist literature was first printed in the 1840s, and was initially distributed by church members and sent out by mail. In 1880 Ellen White urged those in responsible positions to work up plans so that books would be broadly circulated and not "lie on the shelves, falling dead from the press" (4T 388). She advocated that "in all parts of the field canvassers should be selected, not from the floating element in society, not from among men and women who are good for nothing else and have made a success of nothing, but from among those who have

good address, tact, keen foresight, and ability" (*ibid.* 389).

In 1881 *George King, a Canadian who had the desire to be a preacher and had started selling books and subscriptions to *Good Health* and *Signs of the Times*, proposed that the Review and Herald Publishing Association put into operation Ellen White's plan of evangelistic bookselling. The plan was based on an existing commercial practice of selling books door-to-door by subscription. King suggested combining and publishing Uriah Smith's two small books *Thoughts on Daniel* and *Thoughts on the Revelation* in one volume. With the sale of this book King officially started the canvassing program in the denomination. Later he began to recruit and train others to do this work and was so successful that in less than two decades virtually every conference had literature evangelists and colporteur leaders in its territory.

The proven success of the canvassing enterprise, as well as the statements of Ellen White about the importance of literature evangelism, led several church administrators to introduce, during the Minneapolis *General Conference session of 1888, a resolution recommending that all persons wishing to enter Bible work or pastoral ministry be trained in the canvassing work first (RH, Nov. 13, 1888). In spite of Ellen White's opposition to that idea, the resolution was approved. Shortly after the session she wrote to *R. A. Underwood, who was among those who had supported the resolution, to reaffirm her disappointment. "This was to be an absolute rule, and notwithstanding all I had to say against this resolution, it was carried. It was not right for the conference to pass it. It was not in God's order, and this resolution will fall powerless to the ground. I shall not sustain it, for I would not be found working against God. This is not God's way of working, and

I will not give it countenance for a moment" (Lt 22, 1889, in 2MR 62).

Ellen White stressed that it was incorrect to think that everyone could be a canvasser (i.e., colporteur, someone who sells religious books from door to door), for "some have no special adaptability for this work" (6T 333). However, she recognized that "those who are fitting for the ministry can engage in no other occupation that will give them so large an experience as will the canvassing work" (ibid. 334) and that "in evangelistic canvassing, young men may become better prepared for ministerial labor than by spending many years in school" (CM 34). Canvassing was recommended not only as a means of education for those who wanted to enter the ministry, but also as an invaluable experience for students in general. "Let those who have been in school go out into the field and put to a practical use the knowledge they have gained. If canvassers will do this, . . . their talents will increase by exercise, and they will learn many practical lessons which they could not possibly learn in school. The education obtained in this practical way may properly be termed higher education" (6T 331).

Ellen White wrote extensively about the selection, role, duties, and many other aspects related to the work of colporteurs. She advised, for example, that absolute honesty was to characterize the colporteurs' business transactions (CM 50, 94) and that they should practice economy and not incur debt (ibid. 92-99). In her view, the spirit of gain and selfishness should not control their motives (ibid. 97). Energy, enthusiasm, and hard work were also required from them (ibid. 62). They were to cultivate Christian virtues, such as gentleness, patience, meekness, tact, courtesy, helpfulness, and temperance (PM 307). In addition, they were counseled to constantly improve their manners, habits, spirit, and methods, so as

to do their activities in a more successful way (CM 55-60). She called canvassing a "work of great responsibility" (ibid. 14) and a "sacred" work (ibid. 29). Literature evangelists are "the Lord's helping hand" (ibid. 20) to reach all classes of people and "sow beside all waters" (ibid. 10). "As long as probation continues, there will be opportunity for the canvasser to work" (6T 478).

Further reading: CM; 6T 313-340; R. Coon, "Minneapolis/1888: The 'Forgotten' Issue," Nov. 18, 1987 (DF 189-r, CAR); B. Strayer, "125 Years of Literature Ministry," AR, Aug. 19, 1993; *SDA Encyclopedia* (1996), vol. 10, pp. 931-933.

Mario Martinelli

COMMUNION, see **LORD'S SUPPER**.

COMPETITION. Competition was not a word used much by Ellen White, but the principles undergirding it are found throughout her writings, often expressed through the word "rivalry." Her views on the topic need to be seen in two contexts. First, the macrocosmic level features the competitive rivalry of Lucifer, who fell because he wanted to be equal to if not greater than God. Selfishness, self-centeredness, and desire for supremacy fueled his fall and became the genesis of sin. Opposed to Satan's principles were those of Christ, who not only modeled service and love but was self-effacing and humble as He cooperated with the Father in the plan of salvation.

The second context is the microcosmic level, in which each individual person is faced with the issue of character development. The choice faced by all is whose principles to form a character upon—those of Satan or those of Christ. Ellen White's most significant statements on competition are nearly always in the immediate context of character development.

In *Education*, for example, she writes that "character building is the most important work ever entrusted to human beings" (p. 225). The next paragraph goes on to note that much education "is a perversion of the name" because it is based on "self-seeking." But "in true education the selfish ambition, the greed for power, the disregard for the rights and needs of humanity, that are the curse of our world, find a counterinfluence. God's plan of life has a place for every human being. Each is to improve his talents to the utmost; and faithfulness in doing this, be the gifts few or many, entitles one to honor. *In God's plan there is no place for selfish rivalry.* Those who measure themselves by themselves, and compare themselves among themselves, are not wise. 2 Corinthians 10:12" (pp. 225, 226; italics supplied). By way of contrast, "much of the education now given" appeals to "emulation and rivalry; it fosters selfishness, the root of all evil" (p. 226).

Again, in the context of the ongoing struggle among the disciples about who was the greatest, Ellen White noted that in God's kingdom "there will be no rivalry, no self-seeking, no desire for the highest place. You will have that love which seeks not her own, but another's wealth" (DA 439). In another context she writes that "the leaven of truth will not produce the spirit of rivalry, the love of ambition, the desire to be first. True, heaven-born love is not selfish and changeable. It is not dependent on human praise. . . . Self is not struggling for recognition" (COL 101, 102).

That principle is applicable in all realms, including education, business, and even recreation. Regarding ball playing, for example, Ellen White notes that it is not the playing but the overdoing of it that is the problem, along with the temptation to "self-glorifying," which is not favorable toward the development of Christian character. "The Lord God of heaven protests against the burning passion cultivated for supremacy in the games that are so engrossing" (AH 500). On the other hand are the principles of heaven, which uplift each person in developing their talents, be they few or many, to the fullest extent of their God-given ability, for service to God and other humans (Ed 226; COL 102), principles that feature cooperation as the ideal of God's kingdom (see, e.g., Ed 285; 7T 174).

See also: Games and Sports.

Further reading: *Guidelines for Activities With Elements of Competition* (General Conference Department of Education, c. 1976); G. R. Knight, *Myths in Adventism* (RHPA, 1985), pp. 225-229.

George R. Knight

COMPILATIONS OF ELLEN G. WHITE'S WRITINGS, see **BOOKS, PREPARATION OF ELLEN G. WHITE'S**.

CONDENSATIONS, see **BOOKS, PREPARATION OF ELLEN G. WHITE'S**.

CONFERENCES, 1848, see **SABBATARIAN BIBLE CONFERENCES**.

CONFLICT AND COURAGE (RHPA, 1970, 381 pp.). Ninth daily devotional book published by the Ellen G. White Estate. Selections from Ellen White's writings were taken mostly from her published writings, especially the *Conflict of the Ages Series. The book presents brief biographical sketches of biblical men and women depicted in roughly chronological order. These readings draw lessons of courage from those who triumphed in the midst of conflicts, and teach wisdom and trust in God's will from the experiences of those who made unwise choices.

CONFLICT OF THE AGES SERIES. Five-volume series depicting the cosmic conflict between Christ and Satan, from the fall of Lucifer in heaven down through history to the end of the millennium. These five volumes provide the theological framework for everything else Ellen White has to say.

The Conflict of the Ages Series went through three progressive stages of development. The first stage was the four volumes entitled *Spiritual Gifts*. Volume 1 (1858) carried the subtitle of *The Great Controversy Between Christ and His Angels, and Satan and His Angels* and set the tone for her lifelong expansion on the Conflict of the Ages theme. That first volume treated the fall of Satan in heaven, the fall of Adam and Eve, the work of Christ, the apostolic church, the great apostasy, the Reformation, and the period running from the rise of Millerism up through the end of the millennium. (Volume 2 in this series was Ellen White's autobiography.)

The material covered in volumes 3 (1864) and 4 (1864) was much more restricted, with volume 3 recounting Bible history from creation to the giving of the Mosaic law. The first part of volume 4 continues that history from the building of the wilderness tabernacle up to the time of Christ. Thus in essence volumes 1, 3, and 4 covered the entire time of the conflict. The treatment, however, was not even in coverage, nor did it have the depth of her later contributions to the Conflict of the Ages theme.

The second stage in the development of the Conflict series was the four volumes entitled *The Spirit of Prophecy*. Volume 1 (1870) opened with the fall of Lucifer and dealt with biblical history to the time of Solomon. It was largely an amplification of the material presented in *Spiritual Gifts*, volumes 3 and 4. The second volume (1877) covered the life of Christ from His birth to the triumphal entry into Jerusalem. It was largely an expanded version of the material found in the first half of *Spiritual Gifts*, volume 1. Twenty chapters of the third volume (1878) dealt with the last days of the ministry of Christ, and 11 chapters covered the life and work of the apostles. As with volume 2, this one was also an amplification of materials found in the first volume of *Spiritual Gifts*. Volume 4 (1884) covered the period from the destruction of Jerusalem to the end of the millennium and was an expansion of the materials found in the second half of the first volume of *Spiritual Gifts*. In 1885 this volume was formatted for colporteur sale to the non-Adventist public, and its subtitle became its title: *The Great Controversy Between Christ and Satan During the Christian Dispensation*. Under that title the book would be revised in 1888 and again in 1911 to become volume 5 in the Conflict of the Ages Series.

The third and final stage in the development of the Conflict of the Ages Series had five volumes, building upon but greatly amplifying the materials previously developed in the *Spiritual Gifts* and *Spirit of Prophecy* volumes. The first volume was *Patriarchs and Prophets* (1890). It carried the story of the struggle between God and Satan from the rebellion in heaven up through the reign of David. *Prophets and Kings* (1917) picked up the story with Solomon and continued through to the end of the Old Testament period.

Many people consider the third volume, *The Desire of Ages* (1898), to be Ellen White's finest work. It covered the life, death, and resurrection of Jesus. The preparation of *The Desire of Ages* was a labor of love that took the better part of a decade. Ellen White wrote that "God would be pleased to see *The Desire of Ages* in every home" (CM 126).

The Acts of the Apostles (1911) was the fourth volume of the Conflict of the Ages

Series. It traced the struggle between good and evil from the book of Acts up through John's Revelation. The years between the publication of *The Spirit of Prophecy*, volume 3, in 1878 and the publication of *The Acts of the Apostles* saw Ellen White publish *Sketches From the Life of Paul* (1883). That 32-chapter work provided the basis for the later development of *The Acts of the Apostles*.

The fifth volume in the Conflict of the Ages Series was *The Great Controversy*. That volume, as we noted above, was first published as volume 4 of *The Spirit of Prophecy* in 1884. But since it became a book sold to the general non-Adventist public in 1885, Ellen White and the publishers thought it best to modify it for that larger audience in 1888. Another revision at Ellen White's request was published in 1911. That final edition corrected certain factual material of a historical nature and supplied credits to the authorities cited. *The Great Controversy* developed the struggle between Christ and Satan during the post-biblical period. It began with the destruction of Jerusalem in A.D. 70, ran through the course of church history, and climaxed with the events predicted in Scripture to be connected with the second coming of Christ. The final chapters of *The Great Controversy* also placed Millerism and Seventh-day Adventism in the flow of prophetic history.

The Great Controversy rivaled *The Desire of Ages* as being Ellen White's most important work. Ellen White said that she appreciated it "above silver or gold" (CM 128). She also wrote that she was "more anxious to see a wide circulation for this book than for any others I have written; for in *The Great Controversy*, the last message of warning to the world is given more distinctly than in any of my other books" (*ibid.* 127).

Ellen White developed the five-volume Conflict of the Ages Series with both Adventist and non-Adventist readers in mind. She desired these books to be sold widely so that she could get her message before the public. Used in conjunction with Bible study, the volumes have led many to a closer walk with God and a better understanding of His Word. There is no better place to become acquainted with Ellen White's writings than with a reading of the Conflict series. A condensed version of this series was published by Pacific Press in the 1980s and is currently being reissued in a modern English format.

All three sets of books in the great controversy sequence are still in print. They all set forth a theme Ellen White claims was first revealed to her in vision about 1848 and reinforced through an expanded vision at Lovett's Grove, Ohio, in the spring of 1858. Beyond the visions, Ellen White studied both the Bible and church history in order to fill in the outline of the history of the conflict between good and evil provided by the visions (see GC xi, xii).

See also: *Life of Christ, The.*

George R. Knight

CONFRONTATION (RHPA, 1971, 93 pp.). At various times Ellen White wrote about the *temptation and fall of humanity, the plan of *redemption, and the victory of Christ in the wilderness. In 1874 and 1875 she wrote a series of 13 articles in the *Review and Herald* focusing on lessons drawn from the experiences of Adam and Eve and Jesus Christ in meeting temptation. Two biblical narratives are drawn upon: the story of Adam and Eve in the Garden of Eden, their temptation and fall, and the account of Christ in the wilderness and His victory over temptation. These are then applied to Christian living. The *Review* articles were later republished in a 96-page pamphlet, the second of eight pamphlets to make up the *Redemption* series (1878). Twenty years after the *Redemption* series, Ellen White again treated the temptation of Christ in two chapters of *The Desire of Ages* (pp. 114-131). There are, of course, some basic parallels between *The Desire of Ages* (pp. 114-131), and the central part of *Confrontation* (pp. 27-57). While they expound the same Scriptures, they do so in different ways. *The Desire of Ages* is more polished, but *Confrontation* contains some vivid descriptions and spiritual insights not found in *The Desire of Ages*. *Confrontation* provides the reader with practical encouragement for Christian living as it relates to issues of temptation and spiritual conflict.

Michael D. Pearson

CONSCIENCE. A function of the mind that identifies what is right and wrong and commends or condemns what is done (RH, Jan. 1, 1875). Ellen White understood that the conscience can be well informed, misinformed, or ignorant about right and wrong and God's revealed will (1MCP 323; RH, Jan. 24, 1899; DA 638; 7T 196; Ed 231). Rather than an infallible inner compass received at birth to guide one's decisions, the conscience is better understood as a repository of values that are acquired through the learning process (7T 196; Ed 231; 1MCP 323, 324). The mind has the inherent capacity to discriminate among alternatives, but the knowledge of what is right and wrong is imparted to the intellect, and implanted within the conscience under the influence of the Holy Spirit (RH, July 25, 1899). Though affirmed by reason and approved by conscience, truth may not affect behavior until it is embraced by the heart (1MCP 324; RH, Sept. 25, 1883; Ev 291).

Ministers are to make direct and arresting appeals to conscience as they present God's truth in ways that are well suited to the hearers (RH, Apr. 20, 1897; RH, Feb. 13, 1894; RH, May 24, 1892). Overzealous efforts to move people toward compliance with principles of truth at a pace that is too rapid for them may result in their discouragement and a turning away from truth (CD 468; HL 35). Equally sincere Christians may have consciences that do not harmonize on certain issues (1MCP 322). While conscientiously differing among themselves, they have no right to assume responsibility over, or to attempt to regulate, the consciences of others (2MCP 707). God never forces the conscience, but Satan and his human agents seek to coerce people to compromise conscience (RH, Feb. 7, 1893; RH, Jan. 10, 1893; RH, Sept. 7, 1897). No one should allow a spouse, a teacher, a minister, or anyone else to dictate a course of action that is contrary to conscience (PC 403; ChL 29; RH, July 14, 1885; RH, Apr. 20, 1911; 2T 118).

As has happened in past history, individuals in positions of authority will seek to bind and control people's consciences through the enactment of laws (7BC 977; ST, May 13, 1897; ChS 155). But political and ecclesiastical authorities sin against God when they attempt to compel people to go against conscience (ChL 30; RH, Mar. 26, 1895).

Repeated sinning hardens or sears the conscience so that wrong actions appear benign (3T 257; RH, June 12, 1894). Persistent disobedience makes it increasingly difficult to hear, and respond to, the promptings of the Holy Spirit (ST, July 22, 1886; PH167 8). The functioning of conscience is impaired by the use of alcohol and other mind-altering substances (PCP 26; 2MCP 407). The use of unhealthy food or overindulgence in good food can becloud the mind (CTBH 134; YI, Jan. 1, 1903). An excess of social excitement and merrymaking, and efforts to attract attention to one's appearance and personal charm, have a desensitizing effect on the conscience (ST, Aug. 18, 1881; MYP 387). Indulging romantic infatuations and engaging in impure practices interfere with the correct functioning of conscience (AH 51; RH, Sept. 26, 1899; PH085 24). Oversensitive consciences can torment people with feelings of guilt even when their sins have been forgiven (AG 109; ST, Feb. 10, 1876; DA 223; LLM 180). Overactive consciences can drive people to extremes and fanaticism (1NL 38). Healthy consciences instantly recognize the distinction between right and wrong, warn against error, and champion the course of action that is pleasing to God (3T 22; Ed 57; PH167 40). The correctly functioning conscience approves what is right and good in the life and this knowledge of rightdoing produces enduring joy and contentment in the heart (4T 44-47; RH, Mar. 4, 1875; ST, Jan. 1, 1885; 2T 327).

Further reading: 1MCP 319-328.

H. Peter Swanson

CONSCIENTIOUS OBJECTORS, see **MILITARY SERVICE**.

CONTROVERSIAL STATEMENTS, see general article: **CURRENT SCIENCE AND ELLEN WHITE: TWELVE CONTROVERSIAL STATEMENTS**.

CONVERSION. For Ellen White, true conversion is a "change of heart, a turning from unrighteousness to righteousness" (HP 20); "a change from selfishness to sanctified affection for God and for one another" (1SM 115). It involves the whole person "heart and mind and soul" in a change from "self-indulgence" to "self-denial and self-sacrifice" (1MCP 334; cf. MM 264).

Being originally created in the image of God, and therefore in perfect harmony with the law of God, humanity was meant for fellowship with God. But sin alienated mankind from his Maker, for "the carnal mind is enmity against God: for it is not subject to the law of God, neither indeed can be" (Rom. 8:7). Thus

God gave His Son so that "through the merits of Christ he [humanity] can be restored to harmony with his Maker" (GC 467). "Genuine conversion brings us daily into communion with God" (TDG 277).

The Christian life begins when "in conversion the sinner finds peace with God through the blood of the atonement" (GC 470). The steps in conversion are commemorated in *baptism. The repentant believer "goes down into the water in the likeness of Christ's death and burial, and he is raised out of the water in the likeness of His resurrection—not to take up the old life of sin, but to live a new life in Christ Jesus" (3SP 204; cf. LHU 79; FLB 147), a life of "repentance, faith, and willing obedience" (LHU 79).

"In true conversion, the sinner is first convicted of his real condition. He realizes that he is a transgressor of God's law. . . . He sees that the connection between himself and God has been broken, but that if he repents of his transgression, confesses his sin, and takes hold by faith upon the grace of Christ, the connection that has been broken will be restored" (1888 Materials 130). Thus "the law of God is an agent in every genuine conversion," for it brings conviction of sin and demonstrates the need for dependence upon the atoning sacrifice of Christ for salvation. The law provides no remedy. Repentance and faith are the gift of Christ alone (4SP 297; cf. FW 19-26; FLB 127-129, 131; MM 264).

"Genuine conversion is [a] transformation of character. New purposes, new moral tastes are created. Defects of character are overcome" (TSA 30). It "is a decided change of feelings and motives" (1MCP 349), a transformation, a renewing of mind and character (TMK 62, 134; 5BC 1144). The power of divine grace sanctifies the heart (4T 534). "True conversion is a radical change" (4T 17). We partake of resurrection power, and become new again in Christ (5BC 1113). Thus we receive the mind of Christ (RC 35; TDG 277).

Biblical truth plays a major role in conversion. "The Scriptures are the great agency in the transformation of character" (COL 100; cf. RH, Aug. 26, 1909; FW 63; FLB 123). The vital influence of biblical truth is to have a role in every aspect of life (2SAT 120), and we are to manifest "a daily conversion to the principles of truth" (HP 67; cf. 3T 329). However, truth must not be understood merely as a theory. The truth must be understood in its Christ-centeredness so that it may be experienced and lead to the practice of truth in obedience (5T 218, 619; TSB 196; 16MR 236; HP 162). The preaching of the Word must be attended by the Spirit of God, who brings conviction of sin, conversion of the soul, and the creation of new life in the heart (3SM 189; FLB 141).

Conversion brings about the transformation of "an earthly, sin-loving mind" into one that understands "the unspeakable love of Christ" (FLB 82). "True conversion is a change from selfishness to sanctified affection for God and for one another" (1SM 115; cf. SD 334; 3SM 200).

"A genuine conversion changes hereditary and cultivated tendencies to wrong" (6BC 1101). "Conversion is a work that most do not appreciate. It is not a small matter to transform an earthly, sin-loving mind and bring it to understand the unspeakable love of Christ, the charms of His grace, and the excellency of God, so that the soul shall be imbued with divine love and captivated with the heavenly mysteries. When he understands these things, his former life appears disgusting and hateful. He hates sin, and, breaking his heart before God, he embraces Christ as the life and joy of the soul. He renounces his former pleasures. He has a new mind, new affections, new interest, new will; his sorrows, and desires, and love are all new. The lust of the flesh, the lust of the eye, and the pride of life, which have heretofore been preferred before Christ, are now turned from, and Christ is the charm of his life, the crown of his rejoicing. Heaven, which once possessed no charms, is now viewed in its riches and glory; and he contemplates it as his future home, where he shall see, love, and praise the One who hath redeemed him by His precious blood" (2T 294).

Conversion is not a one-time event; it does not place an individual beyond the reach of temptation (Mar 236; FLB 157; 2T 505). But the struggle for conquest over self, for holiness and heaven, is lifelong (5T 412). We "need a fresh conversion every day" (1T 699; cf. 4MR 46).

Conversion takes place in the context of the great controversy and is a matter of life and death. We are either on the side of Christ or Satan (FW 65). We are to witness to the power of God's grace by our lives (RC 185, 287). "From the moment of conversion those who receive Christ are to become the light of the world" (HP 339). Comprehending the value of eternal life with God, "for the conversion of one soul we should tax our resources to the utmost" (Mar 29). Those who preach and teach must first of all be converted themselves (TSS 49; AG 67). In the process of conversion, the work of the human agent is to preach the Word, and the work of the Lord Jesus through the agency of "His Holy Spirit is to make the Word efficacious and powerful" (2SM 18; cf. KC 126; RH, July 7, 1904).

Further reading: HP 20; RH, July 7, 1904.

Ed Zinke

CONVERSION, ELLEN G. WHITE'S. Though not able to define the exact date of her conversion, Ellen Harmon experienced a protracted period of intense spiritual awakening during her childhood. This period extended for almost seven years from 1836 to 1843 and can be divided into three distinct phases—a deathbed conversion, finding forgiveness for her sins, and coming to grips with issues regarding sanctification.

In the fall of 1836 Ellen Harmon was injured when an older school classmate threw a stone that broke her nose and did other serious injury. After a period of delirium, she overheard conversations that caused her to believe that her death was imminent. With the simple faith of a child she gave her life to Jesus and as a result "felt peace of mind" (2SG 9). Her peace was demonstrated when she clapped her hands for joy while watching a dramatic aurora borealis, probably in January 1837, for she believed that Jesus was about to come.

As her health improved, she began to hope that she might return to school, and she attempted at various times to continue her education. Finally in 1839, after she briefly attended a girls' school, her health collapsed. She was forced to acknowledge that her fragile health would not allow her to study. Coming to grips with her disability brought resentment, which in turn caused her to feel guilt. This, together with an ignorance about what constituted Christian experience, her belief that God was a "stern tyrant," the doctrine of eternal torment, and her introverted personality, caused Ellen to sink into chronic depression. When William Miller came to Portland, Maine, March 11-23, 1840, Ellen was convinced that Jesus was coming soon, and made her way to the anxious seat at the conclusion of a meeting. Yet she did not find peace. Her discouragement and depression continued until about September 1841, when she and her family attended a Methodist camp meeting in Buxton, Maine. At this camp meeting Ellen heard a sermon on Queen Esther that gave her courage to seek the Lord. While at

the altar she prayed "Help, Jesus; save me, or I perish!" She described what happened: "I felt my needy, helpless condition as never before. As I knelt and prayed, suddenly my burden left me, and my heart was light. . . . I felt that the Savior had blessed me and pardoned my sins" (1T 17, 18). Finding assurance and justification by faith was a great relief.

Soon after the Buxton camp meeting Ellen Harmon sought membership in the Methodist Church. She was granted the customary six-month probationary membership, and on June 26, 1842, was baptized by immersion in Casco Bay.

Soon after her baptism, she began to struggle with sanctification issues. She wrote, "I felt a constant dissatisfaction with myself and my Christian attainments" (LS 26). "I could claim only what they called justification. In the Word of God I read that without holiness no man should see God. Then there was some higher attainment that I must reach before I could be sure of eternal life" (*ibid.* 29). Wrestling with a sense of personal sinfulness resulted in a second period of extended depression. Finally two dreams gave her courage to speak with her mother about her doubts and fears. Eunice Harmon then arranged for Ellen to meet with *Levi Stockman, a devout Methodist minister who was also a believer in the Advent message. Stockman helped Ellen Harmon to understand that God was a "kind and tender parent, rather than a stern tyrant compelling men to a blind obedience" (*ibid.* 39). Her "heart went out toward Him in a deep and fervent love" (*ibid.*).

Shortly after receiving this pastoral counsel, Ellen attended a meeting at her uncle's home in Portland, where she found courage to pray aloud. It was during this prayer that she experienced what Methodists called the "second blessing" of sanctification. Thus in the months leading up to 1844, Ellen Harmon became an active Christian worker, including occasional public testimony.

See also: Chestnut Street Methodist Church.

Further reading: M. D. Burt, "My Burden Left Me: The Conversion of Ellen G. White," AR, Oct. 25, 2001.

Merlin D. Burt

COORANBONG, AUSTRALIA. A village in which Ellen White established her home Sunnyside from 1895 to 1900 and located *Avondale College. It is situated about 75 miles north of Sydney in New South Wales.

In 1894 church leaders visited the 1,500-acre (600-hectare) Brettville Estate in Cooranbong, searching for a site for a new Australian school. Much of the land was judged to be poor, sour, and sandy, and some opposed its purchase. Ellen White, however, convinced by light given her by God, strongly endorsed the purchase of the land, and it became the location for Avondale College (4Bio 146-161).

In July 1895 Ellen White bought a small acreage from the property to demonstrate that the soil, if well worked, would produce its treasures for the benefit of all (16 MR 152-156). On Christmas Day 1895 she with her helpers moved into the newly constructed 11-room cottage, which she named Sunnyside (see *homes of James and Ellen G. White).

Before Ellen White left Cooranbong in late August 1900, three other institutions that received her support and encouragement were established on the former Brettville Estate: the Cooranbong church (1897); a health food factory (1898) (later called the Sanitarium Health Food Company); and the *Avondale Health Retreat, for the care of the sick (1899).

Further reading: 4Bio 215-222, 315-322, 357-362, 437-441.

Allan G. Lindsay

CORRESPONDENCE, ELLEN G. WHITE'S. The letter and manuscript files in the Ellen G. White Estate contain approximately 50,000 pages of typewritten material. The letter file includes mostly letters to individuals or families, with some addressed to conference or institutional groups (such as "Brethren in the Iowa Conference," "Managers of Pacific Press," etc.). The manuscript file includes her personal diaries and journals, sermons and similar public presentations, and other manuscripts, such as prepublications drafts of periodical articles.

Ellen White wrote under a wide variety of conditions and circumstances—at home, while traveling, during the day, in the middle of the night, when she was rested, and when she was exhausted. Sometimes at *camp meetings or *General Conference sessions she had a small table set up in the main auditorium so that whenever she was not directly involved in the meeting she could write. For nearly 70 years letters, articles, and manuscripts flowed from her pen.

Some of her letters were sent by postal mail, arriving in distant places just in time to meet a special need (1SM 27; 5T 67). Other letters she read personally, aloud, to the addressee, either privately or with family or associates present. Some she handed to people she was in regular contact with; and some she laid aside and prayed over for months, waiting for just the right time that the individual would be open to receive her message.

She penned letters of condolence to the grieving, letters of assurance to the discouraged, and letters of counsel and warning to those in danger of making major mistakes in their lives or their work. She poured her heart into her letters. In one letter to the Battle Creek church she wrote, "I seldom weep, but now I find my eyes blinded with tears; they are falling upon my paper as I write" (PH117 60; 5T 77).

She wrote to family members; she wrote to children—her own and those of others; she wrote to General Conference presidents and others in leadership; and she wrote to hundreds of church members in a wide variety of occupations. According to counts by Michael Campbell, the most letters she addressed to one person were to her second son, *J. Edson White (570 extant letters), and the second most were to her third son, W. C. White (544). The next 14 to whom she wrote many letters are: *S. N. Haskell (277), *J. H. Kellogg (178), *A. G. Daniells (121), *James White (117), *O. A. Olsen (103), "Children," i.e., circular letters addressed to her sons and their spouses (99), *G. I. Butler (84), *J. A. Burden (80), *D. H. Kress (70), *Lucinda Hall (69), *G. A. Irwin (62), *Mary (Kelsey) White (58), *Uriah Smith (47), and *Frank Belden (47).

The thousands of letters still extant were because she made copies for her files. In the early years she often mailed handwritten letters to individuals she knew, asking them to make a copy for themselves (handwritten, of course; there were no photocopiers, computers, or even typewriters) and then return the original to her. Those who appreciated her letters were often happy to do this, but those who chafed at her counsel sometimes neglected or refused to return them. So she gradually began the practice of making file copies of the most important letters before mailing them. After 1885 her secretaries used typewriters to make copies of her letters and other manuscripts.

During some periods of her ministry the volume of her correspondence alone would have been a full-time job had she done her own typing; but in addition to correspondence, she also did much preaching, traveling, and consulting, as well as producing books, articles, and sermons. The simple need to make the most efficient use of her time was perhaps

the first reason for her use of *literary assistants. A second reason was that with a limited formal education, Ellen White freely admitted that she was neither a scholar nor a grammarian (Diary, Jan. 11, 1873, in 3SM 90). Her husband, James, was her first literary assistant. Later she employed other secretaries, typists, and editors to assist in her work.

The perennial task of Ellen White's staff was the preparation of letters, which could involve much more than merely typing the handwritten manuscript. Many of her letters were brief and involved not much more than merely typing, and making carbon copies for the files. Others were a greater challenge. W. C. White mentioned to his mother how the staff handled the preparation of one long letter. "Yesterday we received your letter accompanied by a long one for Bro. A. C. [Bourdeau]. Mary [White] will try to fix it as she has strength. I had not the heart to give it to Marian [Davis]. She is worn out with this sort of work and it is a great burden to her to take these very long manuscripts, and decide how to fix them" (WCW to EGW, Nov. 22, 1886). The letter referred to (EGW to A. C. Bourdeau, Nov. 20, 1886) was some 4,000 words long, making 11 typewritten pages.

W. C. White explained why there was such a variation in the amount of work required to type his mother's letters. "As many matters are revealed to her in a very short space of time, and as these matters are sometimes similar, and sometimes different; so she writes them out, sometimes many pages on one subject, and sometimes dealing with many subjects in a few pages. In her eager haste to transfer to the written page the thoughts that have been pictured to her mind, she does not stop to study grammatical or rhetorical forms, but writes out the facts as clearly as she can, and as fully as possible" (WCW to G. A. Irwin,

May 7, 1900, 15WCW 587-589, EGWRC-GC; excerpted in Moon, pp. 222-225).

"Sometimes when Mother's mind is rested and free, the thoughts are presented in language that is not only clear and strong, but beautiful and correct; and at times when she is weary and oppressed with heavy burdens of anxiety, or when the subject is difficult to portray, there are repetitions and ungrammatical sentences" (*ibid.*). "When corrected and plainly copied with the typewriter or the pen, the manuscripts are all carefully examined by Mother, and corrected, wherever correction is required, and then copied again, if the corrections are numerous. This is done with many manuscripts, not only because corrections are made in the work of the copyist, but because Mother sees a way to express the thought a little more clearly, or more fully." Finally, "none of Mother's workers are authorized to add to the manuscripts by introducing thoughts of their own. They are instructed that it is the words and thoughts that Mother has written or spoken that are to be used" (*ibid.*).

Obviously there was a high degree of trust between Ellen White and her assistants. In many cases they lived in her home, ate at her table, and traveled with her. She knew them very well. She sometimes had visions about their spiritual life, and often gave them personal counsel. Of their personal loyalty to her, W. C. White wrote: "I have been very familiar with Mother's work for many years, and with the work that is required of her copyists, and editors," and "I do not know of any one who has ever been connected with her work [except Fannie Bolton], but would as quickly put their hand into the fire and hold it there, as to attempt to add any thoughts to what Mother had written in any testimony to any individual" (*ibid.*).

What motivated these helpers who did such exacting work for small wages? It was

the sense of the privilege of working in close partnership with what God was doing through Ellen White. As W. C. White put it: "Those who have been entrusted with the preparation of these manuscripts have been persons who feared the Lord, and who sought Him daily for wisdom and guidance, and they have shared much of His blessing, and the guidance of His Holy Spirit in understanding the precious truths that they were handling. I, myself, have felt the same blessing, and heavenly enlightenment in answer to prayer for wisdom to understand the spiritual truths in these writings, that I have in studying the Bible. This was a sweet fulfillment of the promise of the Holy Spirit as a teacher and guide, in understanding the Word. And in answer to prayer, my memory has been refreshed as to where to find very precious statements amongst Mother's writings that, brought in connection with the manuscript at hand, would make a useful article" (*ibid.*). But he was quick to clarify: "However thankful the copyist may be for *this quickening of the mind and memory*, it would seem to me to be wholly out of place for us to call this 'inspiration,' for *it is not in any sense the same gift as that by which the truths are revealed to Mother*" (*ibid.*; italics supplied).

Further reading: N. Collins, "Compilations—What They Are and What They Are Not" (EGWE, SDoc); J. Moon, *W. C. White and Ellen G. White* (AUP, 1993), pp. 63, 64, 114-116, 221-224, 349-353, 397-410, 445, 446.

Norma Collins and Jerry Moon

COSMETICS, see **DRESS AND ADORNMENT.**

COSMIC CONFLICT (PPPA, 1971, 640 pp.). Reprint in paperback of *The Great Controversy* under a title designed to catch the attention of non-Adventist readers. The text is identical except for a different pagination.

COUNSELING, see PSYCHOLOGY AND COUNSELING.

Counsels for the Church (PPPA, 1991, 462 pp.). Compilation based on the nine-volume *Testimonies for the Church* and other works of Ellen White, providing a representative selection of these counsels for economical publication and translation purposes. For each of the 66 chapters references to the original sources are given. Topics covered include counsel to individuals and church institutions, and general themes. The last chapter, "'Behold, I Come Quickly,'" appropriately ends with one of her best-known statements: "We have nothing to fear for the future, except as we shall forget the way the Lord has led us, and His teaching in our past history" (p. 359). In addition to the foreword, there is a lengthy chapter titled "The Prophetic Gift and Ellen G. White," by the Trustees of the Ellen G. White Estate; an 80-page subject index; and a 20-page scripture index.

Nikolaus Satelmajer

COUNSELS ON DIET AND FOODS (RHPA, 1938, 1976, 511 pp.). Compilation of Ellen White's writings on diet and nutrition. Topically organized, this reference tool provides the source and date with each entry, showing the reader where to find the entire statement in its full context. It is unique among the Ellen G. White books in that it arranges the entries under topical headings with no attempt to provide continuity in reading.

Starting as early as 1848, Ellen White received information in visions regarding the close connection between food and one's physical and spiritual welfare. By 1926 *Testimony Studies on Diet and Foods,* a compilation of her dietary counsels from letters, articles, pamphlets, and book sources, was made available primarily for the students of dietetics at the College of Medical Evangelists (now Loma Linda University) at Loma Linda, California. This compilation was originally done by Dr. Harold M. Walton. When this printing soon sold out, it was realized that the information had broad appeal. In 1938 the Ellen G. White Estate published an enlarged edition of the 1926 compilation, entitled *Counsels on Diet and Foods.* In 1946 a third edition came out with the type reset, but no change in the text. The fourth edition in 1976 again involved no changes in text or pagination. A footnote about cheese was added to page 368 in editions published after August 4, 1988. The fifth edition (2001) featured a new cover design and introduction and a larger page and print size, but no modification of the text.

White was given dietary information at a time when ignorance and misinformation on this topic were rampant. The conflicting, often erroneous dietary information available could be harmful. Her counsel set a safe course through this minefield, giving information that has stood the test of increased knowledge. Dr. Clive McCay, a Unitarian, read *Counsels on Diet and Foods* in the 1950s while teaching nutrition at Cornell University. A specialist in the history of nutrition, he knew what nutrition authors and lecturers of the nineteenth and early twentieth centuries were saying. His amazement at White's ability to avoid the untrue and ludicrous, writing only what proved to be sound advice, led to his publishing a three-part review of her dietary counsel in the *Review and Herald* in 1959.

In the introduction to the 2001 edition, the trustees of the White Estate offered counsel about using the book. They warned against taking a part of Ellen White's instruction on a topic for the whole of it. They urged reading the entire statement on a topic of interest and studying with an open mind. They cautioned against taking matters to extremes. And they encouraged readers also to take advantage of the growing knowledge available from others on diet and health, provided the conclusions "harmonize with the counsels given through inspiration."

Further reading: C. M. McCay, "A Nutrition Authority Discusses Ellen G. White," RH, Feb. 12, 1959, reprinted in AR, Jan. 8, 1981; *idem.*, "Science Confirms Our Health Teachings," RH, Feb. 19, 1959, reprinted in AR, Jan. 15, 1981; *idem.*, "Our Health Teachings Further Confirmed," RH, Feb. 26, 1959; "Dr. Clive McCay: A Nutrition Authority Discusses Mrs. White" (EGWE, SDoc); D. S. McMahon, *Acquired or Inspired? Exploring the Origins of the Adventist Lifestyle* (Victoria, Australia: Signs Pub. Co., 2005).

Sylvia M. Fagal

COUNSELS ON EDUCATION (PPPA, 1968, 312 pp.). Facsimile reproduction of chapters on education from the nine volumes of the *Testimonies for the Church*, released at the 1968 Quadrennial Council for Higher Education, sponsored by the General Conference Department of Education. Each chapter retains its original facsimile *Testimony* format, with page content, volume number, and pagination; a continuous pagination appears in brackets at the bottom of each page. A useful historical introduction to Ellen White's writings on education, written by Arthur L. White, precedes the text and provides an informative resource in establishing the relationship between this and her other books on education.

Ellen White wrote her first treatise on the subject of education in 1872, titled "Proper Education" (found in 3T 131-160). Eventually seven of the nine volumes of *Testimonies for the Church* contained chapters on education. The basis of her educational philosophy is

that the Bible is "the root and branch of all wisdom and intellectual attainments" (6T 157). Education is more than the training of the intellect; it is the harmonious development of mind, body, and spirit. Such education begins in the home, where parents teach their children from God's second book, "properly directing them to think and act for themselves" (CE 3). Children should not begin formal schooling when they are too young (*ibid.* 7), and teachers should have a gentle spirit and a concern for their students' salvation (*ibid.* 5, 33, 219). Students should not enfeeble their bodies and minds by so much study that they are unable to exercise the body or perform the practical duties of life. The goal of Adventist education is to fit students for a lifetime of service and witness in whatever career they choose. With the Bible as their guide, they will lead many to a saving knowledge of Jesus, the greatest teacher of all.

Marla Samaan Nedelcu

COUNSELS ON HEALTH (PPPA, 1923, 1957, 687 pp.). Compilation of Ellen White's writings on health principles and the management of health-care institutions. The second edition of this book differs from the first in that each article includes the date of writing or of first publication. It has valuable information for health educators, including physicians, nurses, schoolteachers, health food workers, and medical missionaries. The book clearly explains the foundation for a healthy life and how it is interrelated closely to the spiritual, intellectual, social, and emotional aspects of life. The prescriptions outlined in this book aim at preserving one's health.

Counsels on Health also provides guidelines on how to design successful health-care institutions and emphasizes the importance of having physicians and health-care workers who have a close connection with the Source of all wisdom so as to provide compassionate care to all patients. This book was published with the hope of contributing to the purest and most unselfish practice of healing and medicine, expecting each health-care worker to be molded after the likeness of the Mighty Healer.

Kathleen H. Liwidjaja-Kuntaraf

COUNSELS ON SABBATH SCHOOL WORK (RHPA, 1938, 192 pp.). Compilation of Ellen White's counsels on the work of *Sabbath schools. Materials selected for this book were drawn from *Testimonies on Sabbath School Work* (1900) and other published books and periodical articles. The book is subdivided into six sections that address the importance and purpose of Sabbath schools as a soul-winning agency of the church, the study of the Bible, the role and spiritual qualifications of the teacher, mission offerings, and guiding principles in the administration of Sabbath schools. *Counsels on Sabbath School Work* was also intended to serve as resource material for Sabbath school teacher training classes.

COUNSELS ON SPEECH AND SONG (PPPA, 1988, 2007, 480 pp.). Originally titled *The Voice in Speech and Song*, compilation of Ellen White's counsels on the use of one's voice and gift of speech in public speaking, singing, and evangelism. The book highlights the importance of speech education, presents Christ as the ideal speaker, and offers guidelines in Christian attitudes and effective methods in public speaking. In an era when public-address systems did not yet exist, Ellen White often emphasized the need for voice culture—to train the voice to speak clearly and to express words distinctly and forcibly whether one is reading, singing, or preaching (pp. 173-180). She recommended that voice culture be given as prominent a place in the elementary school curriculum as reading, writing, and spelling (p. 175) and that ministers be well trained in public speaking (p. 177). "No man or woman can be that which they might be as laborers together with God in propagating the seed of truth without making earnest, painstaking effort in voice and word culture" (p. 190). Her purpose in giving such counsels was pragmatic: not only the sermon but everything pertaining to one's person should be helping to preach the truth (p. 178). "Let all make the most of the talent of speech" (p. 176).

COUNSELS ON STEWARDSHIP (RHPA, 1940, 372 pp.). Compilation of Ellen White's writings prepared by the General Conference Stewardship Department in response to a widespread request for material on *stewardship. The book takes much of its content from *Review and Herald* articles and other material that was not readily available to church members in 1940. Topics include benevolence, God's ownership, man's stewardship, support of God's work, the tithe, individual faithfulness, wealth, liberality, nonmember contributions, motives in giving, speculation and investment, borrowing and debt, savings, vows and pledges, estate planning, and the rewards of faithfulness. At the end of each of the 15 sections of the book there is a list of related materials for further study that was previously published in the *Testimonies for the Church,* the *Conflict of the Ages Series, and other volumes.

G. Edward Reid

COUNSELS TO EDITORS, see **COUNSELS TO WRITERS AND EDITORS**.

COUNSELS TO STUDENTS, see **STUDENTS, COUNSELS TO**.

COUNSELS TO TEACHERS, PARENTS, AND STUDENTS REGARDING CHRISTIAN EDUCATION (PPPA, 1913); retitled **COUNSELS TO PARENTS, TEACHERS, AND STUDENTS REGARDING CHRISTIAN EDUCATION** (PPPA, 1943, 575 pp.). From 1872 to 1897 Ellen White wrote much on education to guide the development of Adventist schools. Her 1903 masterpiece, *Education*, largely replaced her previous works on this subject. But *Education* was intended to reach an audience that was wider than the Adventist Church; thus, counsels that were denominationally specific were not included in it. The publication of *Counsels to Teachers, Parents, and Students* (1913) and *Fundamentals of Christian Education* (1923) helped to preserve these counsels for Adventist educators from going out of print. The former book received a larger preface and its current title in 1943.

The opening words are a precis of the book: "Higher education is an experimental knowledge of the plan of salvation, and this knowledge is secured by earnest and diligent study of the Scriptures" (p. 11). Education has failed if it merely equips the student for this world and not the next. True higher education prepares the student to be a citizen of heaven by seeking to restore the image of God in people (p. 49). To be like Jesus is indeed the highest education (p. 36). This is accomplished through the guidance of the Spirit of God and by making the Bible the most honored and most foundational of all textbooks. Teachers also must have a living connection with Christ so that they may learn from the Master Teacher and draw their students to themselves and to God with "strong cords of love." Adventist schools should be as the biblical schools of the prophets, educating the whole person by balancing spiritual, intellectual, and physical development. They should train ministers and other professionals to

enter their God-ordained field of labor as missionaries eager to bring the good news to a dying world.

Marla Samaan Nedelcu

COUNSELS TO WRITERS AND EDITORS (SPA, 1946, 192 pp.). Compilation of Ellen White's counsels to writers and editors of Seventh-day Adventist publications and periodicals. The Ellen G. White Estate issued in 1939 a small compilation of Ellen White's instructions to editors in the form of a paperbound book entitled *Counsels to Editors*. This compilation was distributed to editors who attended an editorial council in August of that year, and it rapidly went out of print. Soon after the stock was exhausted, the White Estate decided to publish an expanded edition of this work for the general public. *Counsels to Writers and Editors* includes all the chapters of the first book and the addition of a few chapters to broaden its scope in order to better fit the needs of the larger group to which the volume is addressed. Throughout her ministry Ellen White wrote many letters and articles concerning the publication of the Adventist message. Her numerous counsels dealt with the character and mission of Adventist periodicals and publishing houses, and the publication and sale of Adventist books. Her own experience, good and bad, as the author of numerous books and hundreds of periodical articles and pamphlets gave her many insights into such a ministry, insights included in this volume.

COUNTRY LIVING (RHPA, 1946, 32 pp.). Short compilation of Ellen White's counsels and appeals regarding living in a rural setting, collected by E. A. Sutherland while he was director of the Adventist Commission on Rural Living. As the subtitle points out, country living is described as "an aid to moral and social security." Although this booklet presents us with an idyllic picture of the moral and social benefits of living in a rural environment, it is foremost a compilation aimed at discouraging Adventists from living in *cities. Cities are described as "hotbeds of iniquity" (p. 12) and "vice" (p. 5), where life "is false and artificial" (p. 6) and "increasing in wickedness" (p. 9). Ellen White's counsels, most of them written between 1890 and 1910, make earnest appeals to Adventists not to live in cities, nor to colonize around those institutions which had already been established in urban settings. " 'Out of the cities; out of the cities!'—this is the message the Lord has been giving me" (p. 31), she wrote emphatically.

Ellen White's appeals in favor of country living center around three main arguments. First, living in a rural setting is more conducive to producing a life of simplicity, self-sacrifice, and economy in young people (p. 15), as opposed to the love of pleasure and idleness found in cities (p. 6). Second, it brings better health to body, mind, and soul (p. 16). The third reason is typological. Ellen White argued that modern cities are no better than cities in the time of Noah (p. 14) or Lot (p. 31) and thus should be warned of impending judgments (p. 7). Adventists should establish restaurants in cities (p. 11) and have houses of worship (p. 31) to serve as memorials for God, but should not unnecessarily live in cities and be subjected to their immoral influence.

Country Living has been one of the smallest yet most influential compilations of Ellen White's writings. It had a profound impact upon many aspects of Adventist ethos, including its philosophy of education, home life, and methods of evangelism. The counsels brought together in this booklet were largely responsible for Adventism's intrinsic fear of the cities, which is still strong today, and may

have contributed to the years of slow progress of its work in urban centers. Unfortunately, her equally strong and numerous calls to evangelize the cities did not receive such wide circulation as did the contrasting counsels compiled in *Country Living*. The two sets of counsels may be reconciled by the observation that those directly involved in evangelizing the cities may be called to live in them, but that those who choose to live in the cities without any strong conviction of evangelistic vocation may be sacrificing eternal values for temporal ones. Both sets of counsels (for country living and *city evangelism) were written at a time when North America was going through an intense period of demographic changes, with the rapid urbanization of large cities. Many feel that these appeals are difficult to follow today, given the scarcity of rural land in many areas. Yet the intent of her counsels regarding the benefits of outdoor activities and communion with nature are still relevant today and widely advocated in the general public.

See also: Cities, Living in; City Evangelism.

Further reading: Ted N. C. Wilson, "A Study of Ellen G. White's Theory of Urban Religious Work as It Relates to Seventh-day Adventist Work in New York City" (Ph.D. diss., New York University, 1981).

Denis Fortin

COVENANTS. Ellen White's major exposition of the covenants occurs in *Patriarchs and Prophets* (pp. 363-373). She recognized that "as the Bible presents two laws, one changeless and eternal, the other provisional and temporary, so there are two covenants" (PP 370). The first covenant made in Eden (Gen. 3:15) was the "covenant of grace" which "offered pardon and the assisting grace of God for future obedience through faith in Christ" (*ibid.*). "This same covenant was renewed to

Abraham [Gen. 22:18]" (*ibid.*), whose faith in God's promises (Gen. 26:5; 17:7) was accounted to him for righteousness (Gen. 15:6; Gal. 3:6). This Edenic-Abrahamic covenant is also the everlasting covenant and was called the *new* covenant in the NT because "it could not be ratified until the death of Christ" (*ibid.*).

The second covenant was established at Sinai. In answer to the question "Why was another [*old*] covenant formed at Sinai?" Ellen White noted that the Israelites, after their Egyptian bondage, "had to a great extent lost the knowledge of God and of the principles of the Abrahamic covenant" (*ibid.* 371). They "had no true conception of the holiness of God, of the exceeding sinfulness of their own hearts, their utter inability, in themselves, to render obedience to God's law, and their need of a Savior. All this they must be taught" (*ibid.*).

Before giving the Ten Commandments (see *law of God) at Sinai, God had promised Moses and Israel: "Now therefore, if ye will obey [literally, "listen carefully to"] my voice indeed, and keep my covenant, then you shall be a peculiar treasure unto me above all people: for all the earth is mine" (Ex. 19:5). But "the people did not realize the sinfulness of their own hearts, and that without Christ it was impossible for them to keep God's law" (*ibid.* 371, 372). Not realizing their inability to keep God's law, "they readily entered into covenant with God," declaring, 'All that the Lord hath said we will do, and be obedient' [Ex. 24:7]" (*ibid.* 372). This covenant, characterized by self-confident human promises, is now known as the "old" covenant.

Ellen White clearly contrasted both covenants: "The terms of the 'old covenant' were, Obey and live. . . . The 'new covenant' was established upon 'better promises'—the promise of forgiveness of sins and of the grace of God to renew the heart and bring it into harmony with the principles of God's law. 'This shall be the covenant that I will make with the house of Israel; After those days, saith the Lord, *I will put my law* in their inward parts, *and write it in their hearts*. . . . I will forgive their iniquity, and I will remember their sin no more' [Jer. 31:33, 34]" (*ibid.*).

Thus, for Ellen White, the difference between the two covenants is not so much historical as experiential. The so-called *new* covenant and the Edenic and Abrahamic covenants are the same; they describe God's promises of pardon and power to those who trust Him in faith to perform His promises. The *everlasting* covenant is "an arrangement for bringing men again into harmony with the divine will, placing them where they could obey God's laws" (*ibid.* 371). In contrast, the "old" covenant does not describe a time period, from Sinai to the cross, but an attitude that reflects reliance on external obedience to law without the heart's transformation that produces "the fruits of the Spirit" (*ibid.* 372).

The law given at Sinai is the same law written by the Holy Spirit "in their hearts" (Jer. 31:33). The same provisions of the Edenic and Abrahamic covenants—the "new" or "everlasting" covenant—apply today: the gospel precedes obedience. Jesus as our Savior atones for our sins, and our hearts are renewed by the Holy Spirit. "Through the grace of Christ we shall live in obedience to the law of God written upon our hearts" (*ibid.*).

See also: Salvation, Plan of.

Further reading: S. MacCarthy, *In Granite or Ingrained?* (AUP, 2007).

Herbert E. Douglass

CREATION AND EVOLUTION. Unlike many participants in the debate about science and the Bible, Ellen White built her argument on an entirely biblical, rather than philosophical, foundation. At the same time, she recognized the value of science and advocated that it be taught in Adventist schools. "A knowledge of science of all kinds is power," she declared, "and it is in the purpose of God that advanced science shall be taught in our schools as a preparation for the work that is to precede the closing scenes of earth's history" (FE 186). She proposed that a high view of Scripture and the keeping of the seventh-day *Sabbath would act as qualifying limiters in the science and religion discussion (SR 382, 383), and that the *Flood (see *Bible and Earth Sciences) provided the only true explanation for major portions of the geologic column (Ed 129).

Ellen White believed that Scripture and nature were God's two books, that Scripture provided the key to a correct understanding of nature (*ibid.* 128), and that rightly understood, science and Scripture are in harmony. "All truth," she stated, "whether in nature or revelation, agrees" (ST, Mar. 13, 1884), because, for instance, the laws governing the "human machinery" are as "truly divine in origin, in character, and in importance as the Word of God" (MM 221). Further, she asserted that "God does not annul His laws or work contrary to them, but He is continually using them as His instruments" (PP 114).

White advocated her view of Scripture as the voice of God speaking "to us individually" (FLB 9) in spite of the modernistic scientific approach to Scripture and nature that was already in her day becoming prominent. She noted that "evolution and its kindred errors are taught in schools of every grade, from the kindergarten to the college. Thus the study of science, which should impart a knowledge of God, is so mingled with the speculations and theories of men that it tends to infidelity," even in the children of kindergarten age (Ed 227). She warned that "as in the days of the apostles men tried by tradition and philosophy to destroy faith in the Scriptures, so today, by

the pleasing sentiments of higher criticism, evolution, *spiritualism, theosophy [i.e., a term used to refer to certain systems of thought coming from the Orient, which stressed clairvoyance and telepathy, and were introduced into Western thought through the philosophy of religion], and pantheism, the enemy of righteousness is seeking to lead souls into forbidden paths" (RC 344). Thus such individuals, when unable to explain the Creator and His works by natural law, come to "regard Bible history as unreliable" and, eventually, to "doubt the existence of God" (CE 193).

White held that the creation was completed at the end of the first literal week (Ed 130) and was global in extent. Thus the "entire landscape" was decorated more beautifully than the "grounds of the proudest palace" (PP 44), filled with things "useful to man" (*ibid.* 47), and "the earth was not one extensive plain, but the monotony of the scenery was broken by hills and mountains" (LHU 47). Further, God created humanity with the capability to recognize His signature in the created works (1SP 27).

God created the earth in perfection (SR 20). Originally "there were no loathsome swamps or barren deserts.... The air, untainted by foul miasma, was clear and healthful," and the entire landscape was exceedingly beautiful (PP 44). Every created thing, whether plant, animal, or human, whether animate or inanimate, God "ordained" to have "the wonderful adaptation of means to end, of supply to need" (Ed 133). Thus nothing, especially in regard to humanity, was an afterthought, but had been a part of God's purpose, "designed before the fall of Satan" (LHU 47).

Humanity was to bear God's image in "outward resemblance and in character.... His nature was in harmony with the will of God. His mind was capable of comprehending divine things" (PP 45). Thus "Adam could reflect that he was created in the image of God" (TMK 13), and the longer humanity lived, the more they were to reveal God's image and reflect His glory (FLB 29). God made humanity "with no bias toward evil," endowed man with "high intellectual powers, and presented before him the strongest possible inducements to be true to his allegiance," which "was the condition of eternal happiness" (PP 49). White asked, "Shall we reject that genealogical record—prouder than any treasured in the courts of kings—'which was the son of Adam, which was the son of God'? Luke 3:38" (Ed 130). Humanity did not evolve "by slow degrees of development, from the lower forms of animal or vegetable life. . . . The genealogy of our race, as given by inspiration, traces back its origin, not to a line of developing germs, mollusks, and quadrupeds, but to the great Creator" (FLB 29). Therefore, humanity's degeneration and the devastation of the earth are not a result of God's design or causation, but "the work of man," through the indulgence of "wrong habits and abuses, by violating the laws that God had made to govern man's existence" (LHU 64).

The Sabbath as the memorial of creation played an important role in White's discussion of creation and evolution. Contrary to the popular opinion of the day, she asserted that while God created the earth in six days and rested on the seventh, "He could have spoken it into existence in one" (Lt 7a, 1878, in 8MR 412). She strongly rebuked "the infidel supposition that the events of the first week required seven vast, indefinite periods for their accomplishment" because it "strikes directly at the foundation of the Sabbath of the fourth commandment. . . . It is the worst kind of infidelity. . . . It charges God with commanding men to observe the week of seven literal days in commemoration of seven

indefinite periods, which is unlike His dealings with mortals and is an impeachment of His wisdom" (1SP 86, 87).

White warned against the theories of evolution and interpretations of geology that "dispute the Mosaic record" (ibid. 90). She pointed out that "infidel geologists claim that the world is very much older than the Bible record makes it. They reject the Bible record because of those things which are to them evidences from the earth itself that the world has existed tens of thousands of years" (ibid. 87). Even ministers, she lamented, preferred the "suppositions of geologists" above that of the biblical record (ibid. 90).

Contemplating the results of such interpretations, White warned that "in the last days, the earth will be almost destitute of true faith. Upon the merest pretense, the Word of God will be considered unreliable, while human reasoning will be received, though it be in opposition to plain Scripture facts" (ibid. 89). God designed that the evidences of the flood found in the geologic column "should establish the faith of men in inspired history" and lead them to exalt God (ibid. 90). Thus White believed that the book of Genesis was a historically accurate record. She affirmed, "I take the Bible just as it is, as the Inspired Word. I believe its utterances in an entire Bible" (FLB 13). Thus Genesis 1:27 presents the origin of humanity in such a plain fashion "that there is no occasion for erroneous conclusions" (ibid. 29). Further, the "wonderful things which are found in the earth," such as the fossils in the geologic column, help to confirm "that the world is now only about six thousand years old" (1SP 87). The "conclusion" that it had taken millions of years for the earth to evolve from chaos "is wholly uncalled for," she wrote. "The Bible record is in harmony with itself and with the teaching of nature" (Ed 129). Thus the mysteries of the geologic column were to be understood in light of the Genesis account, and apart from the inspired Word would never be understood (3SG 94).

In attributing the fossil record of the geologic column to a global flood rather than to evolutionary development, White took an interpretative position that was in opposition to that of the scientific method, which proposed that nature was "the key" to the interpretation of Scripture. The scientific method further asserted that nature opened the understanding "to conceive the true sense of the Scripture by the general notions of reason and the rules of speech" (Francis Bacon, *Advancement of Learning* [1902], p. 71). On the contrary, White noted that "in the history of the flood, inspiration has explained that which geology alone could never fathom" (PP 112). Relics found in the earth do give evidence of a state of things differing in many respects from the present. But the time of their existence, and how long a period these things have been in the earth, are to be understood only by Bible history (1SP 87).

Finally, God preserved in the ark every species He had created. Those types that had been produced by *amalgamation were destroyed by the Flood. She attributes the "almost endless varieties of species of animals" now evident on earth to continuing "amalgamation," i.e., hybridization through interbreeding, genetic engineering, etc. (*ibid.* 78).

White's view of creation stands in marked contrast to evolutionary theory. Evolutionary cosmology presents a world that improves by the process of chance through long periods of suffering, privation, and death. In stark contrast, White, in concert with Scripture, points to a beneficent Creator God, who created the world in perfection and who designed humanity in His own image. She concluded that even though "sin has marred God's perfect work, yet that handwriting remains" (LHU

46). In the end God will restore the earth and humanity to their original state of perfection (3SG 89).

Further reading: J. T. Baldwin, ed., *Creation, Catastrophe, and Calvary: Why a Global Flood Is Vital to the Doctrine of Atonement* (RHPA, 2000); P. Gordon, "The Bible, Science, and the Age of the Earth" (EGWE, SDoc); "E. G. White Statements Relating to Geology and Earth Sciences" (EGWE, SDoc); W. H. Shea, "Creation," in R. Dederen, ed., *Handbook of Seventh-day Adventist Theology* (RHPA, 2000), pp. 418-456.

Karen K. Abrahamson and John T. Baldwin

THE CRISIS AHEAD, ELLEN WHITE COMMENTS ON (RHPA, 2000, 202 pp.). Compilation of Ellen White's statements relating to prophecies that remain to be fulfilled prior to the return of Christ, prepared by *Robert W. Olson for a course on Ellen White taught at Pacific Union College, Angwin, California. Materials found in this book were selected from her published and unpublished writings. Although the book is not an attempt to finalize dogmatically the sequence of future events, it includes a wide range of topics, such as the union of churches, *Sunday legislation, the *latter rain, the *loud cry, the *seal of God, and the *mark of the beast. The book was later expanded and republished under the title *Last Day Events*.

CRITICISM, ELLEN G. WHITE'S HANDLING OF. Ellen White's responses to critics of her prophetic gift depended on different circumstances. To those who had an aversion to spiritual gifts in modern times, she was most sympathetic and patient, counseling that "if persons are not settled in regard to the visions, they should not be crowded off.... Some have been required to endorse the visions when they could not conscientiously do so, and in this way some honest souls have been driven to take positions against the visions and against the body [the church] which they never would have taken had their cases been managed with discretion and mercy" (1T 382).

In the summer of 1861 she counseled that those who were "God's children" and yet "doubted the visions" "should not be deprived of the benefits and privileges of the church. ... Long patience and brotherly love should be exercised toward them until they find their position and become established for or against." However, if such people reject the validity of her prophetic gift and "if they carry their opposition so far as to oppose that in which they have no experience, and feel annoyed when those who believe that the visions are of God speak of them in meeting, ... the church may know that they are not right. ... When professed believers in the truth oppose these gifts, and fight against the visions, souls are in danger through their influence, and it is time to labor with them, that the weak may not be led astray by their influence" (ibid. 328, 329).

Ellen White advised two approaches toward "opponents who deal in slander and misrepresentations." First, believers should not spend much "time and strength" providing long answers to those who "manufacture quibbles" against the truth. "We are not wise to take them [quibbles] from their hands, and pass them out to thousands who would never have thought of them had we not published them to the world. ... They will die out more speedily to be left unnoticed, to have their errors and falsehoods treated with silent contempt" (3T 36, 37). Her second approach was to follow Christ's example in meeting opposition. In His answers to criticisms, Christ "was plain and simple, striking directly at the root of the matter, and the minds of all were met." In answering criticisms, it is not necessary to be

very explicit "and say all upon a point that can be said, when a few arguments will cover the ground and be sufficient for all practical purposes to convince or silence opponents" (ibid. 37).

One of the few times Ellen White extensively defended herself was during the *Kellogg crisis of 1906-1907. In response to a range of questions (later epitomized in the *Blue Book), she wrote some 30 personal letters. But on some questions she was "instructed" to give no reply because people would misconstrue her statements. She said that some were "endangering their souls" by "listening to deceptive representations" regarding her message. "Through many twistings and turnings and false reasonings on what I have written, they try to vindicate their personal unbelief. ... They do not see clearly. Therefore I dare not communicate with them" (Lt 206, 1906, in 1SM 29, 30). One notable example of Ellen White speaking in response to criticism is the following: "The angels of God in their messages to men represent time as very short. Thus it has always been presented to me. It is true that time has continued longer than we expected in the early days of this message. Our Savior did not appear as soon as we hoped. But has the word of the Lord failed? Never! It should be remembered that the promises and threatenings of God are alike conditional" (Ms 4, 1883, in 1SM 67).

Further reading: 1SM 406-416; H. E. Douglass, *Messenger of the Lord* (PPPA, 1998), pp. 478-485.

Herbert E. Douglass

CROSS OF CHRIST, THE. Ellen White's writings are permeated with paragraphs, chapters, and articles focusing on the cross of Christ. The cross of Calvary "is the great, central theme of all wisdom" (ST, Apr. 8, 1889). "The crucified Messiah is the central point of all

Christianity" (CT 23, 24). Christ crucified is the "one great central truth to be kept ever before the mind in the searching of the Scriptures" (6BC 1084). Similar statements abound throughout her letters, books, and articles.

To White the cross of Christ is the supreme revelation of God's love. "The revelation of God's love to man centers in the cross. Its full significance tongue cannot utter, pen cannot portray, the mind of man cannot comprehend" (MH 423; 8T 287). "With our finite comprehension we may consider most earnestly the shame and the glory, the life and the death, the justice and the mercy, that meet in the cross," yet even "with the utmost stretch of our mental powers we fail to grasp its full significance" (GC 651). Not only should we meditate on the life and death of Christ every day of our present life, but the cross of Christ "will be the science and the song of the redeemed through all eternity. In Christ glorified they will behold Christ crucified" (ibid.). The theme of the cross, of redemption through Christ, "is an inexhaustible theme, worthy of our closest contemplation" (1SM 403).

In order for us to grasp the true meaning of Christ's sufferings and death on the cross, it is essential to understand the nature of that death. Ellen White raises the question of how different was the death of God's Son from that of martyrs, who also suffered death by crucifixion or by slow tortures. Her answer is unambiguous: "The death of the martyrs can bear no comparison with the agony endured by the Son of God" (2T 215). In fact, "bodily pain was but a small part of the agony of God's dear Son"; rather it was the crushing burden of the sins of the world and the sense that His Father had forsaken Him that caused to Christ unspeakable anguish and broke His heart. "The separation that sin makes between God and man was fully realized and keenly felt by the innocent, suffering Man of Calvary" (ibid. 214; see also SC 13). The Father suffered with the Son, "for the heart of God yearned with greatest sorrow when His Son, the guiltless, was suffering the penalty of sin" (7BC 924).

For a clear comprehension of the cross it is also important to realize that it was a voluntary sacrifice on the part of the eternal Son of God. Ellen White repeatedly stresses the fact that Christ's incarnation, sufferings, and death were completely voluntary. "He voluntarily assumed human nature. It was His own act, and by His own consent. He clothed His divinity with humanity" (RH, July 5, 1887); "He voluntarily laid down his life. . . . He yielded up his life a sacrifice, that man should not eternally die. He died, not through being compelled to die, but by his own free will" (ibid.).

Ellen White repeatedly emphasizes that Christ's death on the cross is the outworking of God's eternal plan for the human race and for the universe. "The purpose and plan of grace existed from all eternity. . . . Redemption was not an afterthought—a plan formulated after the fall of Adam—but an eternal purpose to be wrought out for the blessing not only of this atom of a world but for the good of all the worlds which God has created" (ST, Apr. 25, 1892). "The covenant of grace is not a new truth, for it existed in the mind of God from all eternity. This is why it is called the everlasting covenant" (ST, Aug. 24, 1891).

The death of Christ on the cross won the decisive victory in the great controversy between Christ and Satan. Ellen White eloquently describes Christ's final agony and His ultimate victory over Satan and all the powers of darkness in *The Desire of Ages*, especially in the chapters entitled "Calvary" and " 'It Is Finished' " (DA 741-764). "Upon Christ as our substitute and surety was laid the iniquity of us all. . . . The guilt of every descendant of

Adam was pressing upon His heart." "Satan with his fierce temptations wrung the heart of Jesus." But "it was the sense of sin, bringing the Father's wrath upon Him as man's substitute, that made the cup He drank so bitter, and broke the heart of the Son of God" (*ibid.* 753). Yet the apparent defeat of Christ was in reality His ultimate victory over sin and Satan.

The deep significance of Christ's final exclamation, "It is finished" (John 19:30), is thoroughly developed by Ellen White in the chapter by that title. She shows how Christ's perfect life and sacrificial death refuted Satan's charges against God's government and character. "In the opening of the great controversy, Satan had declared that the law of God could not be obeyed, that justice was inconsistent with mercy, and that, should the law be broken, it would be impossible for the sinner to be pardoned" (*ibid.* 761). After the first humans broke the law of God, "Satan claimed that the human race must be forever shut out from God's favor. God could not be just, he urged, and yet show mercy to the sinner" (*ibid.*). The cross of Christ was God's decisive response to Satan's accusations. "By His life and His death, Christ proved that God's justice did not destroy His mercy, but that sin could be forgiven, and that the law is righteous, and can be perfectly obeyed. Satan's charges were refuted" (*ibid.* 762).

There is no question in Ellen White's mind that all blessings in this life and in the future life "come through a Mediator. . . . Every gift is stamped with the cross and bears the image and superscription of Jesus Christ" (FW 22; cf. COL 362). "From the smallest benefits up to the largest blessing, all flow through the one Channel—a superhuman mediation sprinkled with the blood that is of value beyond estimate because it was the life of God in His Son" (FW 22). Through his death on the cross Christ made *atonement for sin, satisfied the justice of God, showed the

immutability of the law of God, revealed God's love for sinners as well as His hatred for sin, gained the victory over sin and death, unmasked Satan as a liar and murderer, and provided pardon and eternal life for all who believe in Christ as their Savior (see, e.g., 1SM 226-228, 308-310, 340-344, 383-388).

Ellen White sees a close connection between the cross of Christ and His mediation in heaven at the right hand of the Father. "The intercession of Christ in man's behalf in the sanctuary above is as essential to the plan of salvation as was His death upon the cross" (GC 488). "Christ as high priest within the veil so immortalized Calvary that though He liveth unto God, He dies continually to sin, and thus if any man sin, he has an advocate with the Father" (1SM 343). The typical sacrifices presented to God in the earthly sanctuary need no longer be made, but, stresses Ellen White, "the atoning sacrifice through a mediator is essential because of the constant commission of sin. Jesus is officiating in the presence of God, offering up His shed blood, as it had been a lamb slain" (*ibid.* 344).

One thing is stressed and repeated by Ellen White many times: Christ's death on the cross did not abolish the moral law of God, the Ten Commandments, but rather confirmed and established the law. "It was not His [Christ's] purpose to abolish by His death the law of God, but rather to show the immutability of its sacred claims" (RH, Aug. 6, 1895; cf. FW 30, 89; 1SM 312, 323). Satan has foisted on the Christian world the deception that Christ's cross abrogated the law of God. Ellen White refutes this idea emphatically. To abrogate the law "would be to immortalize transgression, and place the world under Satan's control. It was because the law was changeless, because man could be saved only through obedience to its precepts, that Jesus was lifted up on the cross" (DA 762, 763). Over this issue "will come the last conflict of the great controversy between Christ and Satan" (*ibid.* 763).

Ellen White holds the cross to be central to every aspect of Christian life and witness. She frequently quotes from Luke 9:23: "If any man will come after me, let him deny himself, and take up his cross daily, and follow me." In these words Jesus "explained to His disciples that His own life of self-abnegation was an example of what theirs should be," pointing to "complete self-surrender," following Christ "in the path He trod" (*ibid.* 416, 417). In response to the question "What is the cross of Christ?" she responds, "It is not an ornament to the neck, but something that cuts right across our pathway"; it means that "however unpleasant it may be, we should take up the humble duties of life" (3MR 109).

All who minister in teaching and preaching, must exalt the cross: "We are to let the cross of Christ stand in prominence in all our teaching" (ST, Dec. 25, 1893). The Son of God uplifted on the cross "is to be the foundation of every discourse given by our ministers" (Ev 190; GW 315). In the concluding paragraphs of a chapter entitled "Exalting the Cross" she writes: "To remove the cross from the Christian would be like blotting the sun from the sky. . . . Without the cross, man could have no union with the Father. On it depends our every hope. From it shines the light of the Savior's love, and when at the foot of the cross the sinner looks up to the One who died to save him, he may rejoice with fulness of joy, for his sins are pardoned. Kneeling in faith at the cross, he has reached the highest place to which man can attain" (AA 209, 210).

Further reading: G. R. Knight, *The Cross of Christ* (RHPA, 2008).

Peter M. van Bemmelen

Crystal Springs Health Retreat, see **St. Helena Sanitarium and Hospital.**

Daily, The. The term "daily" is the English word used to translate the Hebrew *tamid* in Daniel 8:11-13; 11:31; and 12:11. *Tamid* is elsewhere in the Old Testament translated "continual(ly)," "perpetual(ly)," and "regular(ly)." The King James Version consistently renders *tamid* in Daniel as "daily *sacrifice*," while the Revised Standard Version uses the phrase "continual burnt offering"—the words "sacrifice" and "burnt offering" being supplied by the respective translators.

The consensus view of Seventh-day Adventists during the nineteenth century originated with William Miller and came to be known among Adventist expositors as the "old view." The old view taught that the substantive adjective *tamid* should be understood as modifying the word "abomination." Thus the "daily [abomination]" represented the ancient pagan religion of the Roman Empire, which was "taken away" by the rising Papacy, a transition that Miller also saw referred to in 2 Thessalonians 2:3-6.

The "new view" was first hinted at by O.R.L. Crosier in the *Day-Dawn*, but went virtually unnoticed among Seventh-day Adventists until about 1900, when L. R. Conradi arrived independently at similar conclusions. The new view held that the "daily," or "continual," referred to the heavenly highpriestly ministry of Christ, which was "taken away" in the sense of being supplanted by the usurpations of a human priesthood, auricular confession, human priestly absolution, etc.

Expositors of both views held that the Papacy had been the active agent in "[taking] away" the "daily." Furthermore, both views held that the "[taking] away" of the daily occurred in the sixth century, linking the rise of the Papacy with the rise of Clovis the Frank, who in 508 was named the "first Catholic majesty." The honors given to Clovis could be seen from either view as marking the beginning of a 1290-year alliance between France and the Papacy, a relationship that would endure until 1798. Major expositors of both views saw 538 as the beginning of the 1260-year prophetic period that would also terminate in 1798. The 1335 day-years of Daniel 12:12 were believed to extend from 508 to 1843.

Ignoring some minor differences between individual expositors, the new view offered two basic changes from the old one. First, the new view simplified the exposition of Daniel 8 by identifying the three occurrences of the English word "sanctuary" in verses 11, 13, and 14 as the same sanctuary, the heavenly (although two different Hebrew terms stand behind the English word "sanctuary" in these verses). Second, the new view changed the focus of attention to the ministry of Christ, thus highlighting "the true sanctuary service" as the context of Daniel 8:14. The new view also claimed to correct some of the historical *argumentation* set forth by supporters of the old view, although the historical *conclusions* of the two sides were virtually identical.

Thus the two views had a great deal in common. In fact, both sides agreed on the historical and theological conclusions. Both sides believed that the capital of Imperial Rome had become the seat of papal Rome, and both sides believed that the Papacy had obscured from many people a true under-standing of the heavenly priesthood of Christ. The disagreement was largely a debate over which view represented the best exegesis of the passages in Daniel. Haskell said he believed the issue would not have amounted to "a hill of beans" had not Ellen White made a state-ment about it (S. N. Haskell to WCW, Dec. 6, 1909). But the crux of the debate concerned how to interpret Ellen White's single reference to the "daily" in *Early Writings*.

"I saw," she had reported of an 1850 vision,

"in relation to the 'daily' (Dan. 8:12) that the word 'sacrifice' was supplied by man's wisdom, and does not belong to the text, and that the Lord gave the correct view of it to those who gave the judgment hour cry. When union existed, before 1844, nearly all were united on the correct view of the 'daily'; but in the confusion since 1844, other views have been embraced, and darkness and confusion have followed. Time has not been a test since 1844, and it will never again be a test" (EW 74, 75).

The supporters of the old view believed that the *Early Writings* statement forever settled the issue of the "daily." The new-view proponents argued that the context and focus of the 1850 statement was a then-current attempt to reinterpret the "daily" *as a basis for recalculating the 2300 days* in order to predict the time of the Second Coming. They believed that since their view led neither to time setting nor to unsettling faith in the 2300-day prophecy, it did not contradict *Early Writings*.

In May 1910 Ellen White and W. C. White issued a joint call to "a meeting for prayer and Bible study" between the two sides. However, the adherents of the old view declined to participate. In declining Ellen White's invitation, Haskell opined that further dialogue would be fruitless. "There is no hope of these old people [adherents of the old view] who lived back in the early days of the Message being converted to this new light," he assured Ellen White, "even if they [the new-view proponents] bring volumes of histories to prove it. Because they [the old-view supporters] give more for one expression in your testimony than for all the histories you could stack between here and Calcutta" (S. N. Haskell to EGW, May 30, 1910).

When the old-view adherents declined to participate in any further conference, Ellen White issued a statement designed to squelch the controversy. "It has been presented to me," she declared in words often used to denote revelation, "that this is not a subject of vital importance." "I cannot consent that any of my writings shall be taken as settling this matter. The true meaning of 'the daily' is not to be made a test question. I now ask that my ministering brethren shall not make use of my writings in their arguments regarding this question; for I have had no instruction on the point under discussion" (Ms 11, 1910, in 1SM 164).

Four times in this manuscript she asked that her writings not be used to settle the debate over the "daily." Twice she said the "daily" was not a "test question." Regarding the concern of the new-view men to make corrections in older Adventist publications, she advised care and restraint, but did not oppose changes. "In some of our important books," she said, ". . . there may be matters of minor importance that call for careful study and correction. Let such matters be considered by those regularly appointed to have oversight of our publications." She cautioned, however, that no one should "magnify these matters in such a way as to lessen the influence of these good, soul-saving books" (Ms 11, 1910, in 1SM 165). Finally, she called for all on both sides of the controversy to "follow out the light given us at the last General Conference," namely her pointed insistence on prioritizing evangelism in the great cities (Ms 11, 1910). "While the present condition of difference of opinion regarding this subject exists," she reiterated four days later, "let it not be made prominent. Let all contention cease. . . . The duty of God's servants at this time is to preach the Word in the cities" (Lt 62, 1910, in 1SM 168).

Ellen White repeatedly disclaimed having any specific light on the "daily" as a doctrinal or exegetical issue. In an interview with A. G. Daniells, W. C. White, and C. C. Crisler (date unknown, but interview independently attested by Daniells and W. C. White), she elaborated that her intent in the *Early Writings* passage was to endorse the October 22, 1844, date for the close of the 2300 days, and to warn Adventist expositors against all further time setting. When Daniells asked her "to tell what had been revealed to her about the rest of the 'daily'—the Prince, the host, the taking away of the daily and the casting down of the sanctuary"—she told the group that "these features were not placed before her in vision as the time part was." Her statement convinced them that in her understanding, the *Early Writings* statement pertained to the time period connected with the "daily," not to the historical identity of the "daily" (Moon, pp. 415-427).

In summary, Ellen White's main opposition was directed toward the disunity, the rancor, the time spent in debate, and the distraction from evangelism. She disclaimed having any light on the specific interpretations involved except that the issue was not of salvational importance, not a test of orthodoxy, and not worth the division it was causing. Further, she insisted that the matter should be settled by biblical exegesis and historical research, rather than by appeal to her writings. In this respect the conflict over the "daily" paralleled the 1888 debate over the meaning of "law" in the book of *Galatians. In both cases, defenders of the established view appealed largely to a single Ellen White reference as proving their position. The conflict over the "daily" contrasts sharply, however, with her approach toward *J. H. Kellogg's *pantheism and *A. F. Ballenger's sanctuary doctrine. In both of those cases she unequivocally declared that the new views advocated were unbiblical and incompatible with established doctrines.

See also: General Conference Session of 1888.

Further reading: 6Bio 246-261; G. F. Hasel, "The 'Little Horn,' the Heavenly Sanctuary and the Time of the End: A Study of Daniel 8:9-14," in *Symposium on Daniel: Introductory and Exegetical Studies,* ed. Frank B. Holbrook, DARCOM 2 (BRI, 1986), pp. 399, 400, 408-425, 439-457; D. Kaiser, "The History of the Adventist Interpretation of the 'Daily' in the Book of Daniel From 1831 to 2008" (M.A. thesis, AU, 2009); C. M. Maxwell, *God Cares,* vol. 1, *Message of Daniel* (PPPA, 1981), pp. 153-173; J. Moon, *W. C. White and Ellen G. White* (AUP, 1993), pp. 321, 322, 413-424, includes extensive documentation and references to most of the extant primary and secondary sources; G. M. Valentine, *W. W. Prescott: Forgotten Giant of Adventism's Second Generation* (RHPA, 2005), pp. 214-235; *SDA Encyclopedia* (1996), vol. 10, pp. 429-433.

Jerry Moon

DAIRY PRODUCTS, see **CHEESE; EGGS; MILK.**

DANIEL, BOOK OF. The book of Daniel is one of the Old Testament books most often referred to by Ellen White. She made major statements on the study of Daniel (TM 112-119), the stories of Daniel 1-6 (PK 479-548), the life of Daniel and his friends (SL 18-24, 34-52), and the prophecies of Daniel (GC 325-328, 409, 410; DA 233-235; PK 698, 699).

Ellen White was convinced that the book of Daniel carried a divine message for the last days. Daniel's prophecies "were not fully understood even by the prophet himself," for the book has been sealed until the time of the end, which began in 1798 (PK 547; GC 356). Only then was it to be fully understood (DA 234). She believed that much could still be learned from Daniel: "As we near the close of this world's history, the prophecies recorded by Daniel demand our special attention, as they relate to the very time in which we are living" (PK 547) and "present most important instruction" concerning the final events before Christ's return (GC 341).

Ellen White strongly encouraged a study of the books Daniel and Revelation together. These books should "have attention as never before in the history of our work" (TM 112). Believers need to be acquainted thoroughly with their texts (Ev 363). Describing the relationship between them she wrote: "one is a prophecy, the other a revelation; one a book sealed, the other a book opened" (7BC 971; cf. AA 585). Their prophecies "interpret each other" (7BC 949, 971). She advised also the study of Daniel in connection with the minor prophets, particularly Malachi, to understand the events "in the last days of earth's history" (RH, Nov. 10, 1896).

Ellen White was convinced that a "special blessing" will accompany the study of the prophecies (PK 547). She especially recommended contemplation of the sanctuary theme in Daniel's visions (RH, Nov. 27, 1883). A better understanding of the book of Daniel will deepen spiritual life and provide "an entirely different religious experience" (TM 114). Ministers (GW 148) and teachers (6T 131) especially, should grasp the theological and spiritual meaning of the prophecies.

The book of Daniel consists of two halves: the stories in Daniel 1-6 and the prophetic visions in Daniel 7-12. It is easy to concentrate on one half of the book and neglect the other. Ellen White kept both parts in focus: the prophecies as well as the exemplary behavior of Daniel and his friends, who "walked with God as did Enoch" (PK 486). Next to Christ, she upheld Daniel as the biblical life most worthy of emulation (RH, Nov. 7, 1882). She held that his prophecies center on Christ and constitute the basis of Seventh-day Adventist faith (GW 148). Hence, the entire book is capable of uplifting "Jesus as the center of all hope" (TM 118).

The book of Daniel is also one of the best illustrations of the "philosophy of history." Above, behind and through all history God is in control. His sovereign purpose will overrule and prevail (Ed 175-177; PK 500). Ellen White holds the traditional opinion that the author of the book of Daniel was the prophet Daniel in the sixth century B.C. Brought to Babylon when about 18 years of age (4T 570), he served in high positions under the Babylonian and Persian empires (Ed 56; PK 545, 546) and received his visions around 500 years before Christ's first coming (SL 49-51; PK 553-556; DA 98).

Ellen White advocates the historicist model of interpretation: the major lines of prophecy span the entire historical period from Daniel's day to the opening of judgment and the second coming of Christ (GC 356). For example, Nebuchadnezzar's dream in Daniel 2 disclosed "the events of the future, reaching down to the end of time" (PK 498; cf. *ibid.* 503). The dreams and visions, symbolic in nature (*ibid.* 485), foretell a succession of world kingdoms that she identified as Babylon, Medo-Persia, Greece, and Rome (*ibid.* 535, 548; cf. RH, Feb. 6, 1900). She explained the prophecies of Daniel 2, 7, and 8 as basically in parallel.

Although parts of Daniel's prophecies concern the first century (GC 341; DA 234), she believed that the end-time is their special focus. The revelations were "given especially for these last days," and the visions reported in Daniel 8 and 10-12 "are now in process of fulfillment, and all the events foretold will soon have come to pass" (TM 112, 113). In fact, Ellen White held that the prophecy of Daniel 11 "has nearly reached its complete fulfillment" (9T 14) and that her generation lived in the unstable time of division

represented by the toes of the image of Daniel 2 (1T 361).

Selected noteworthy points of Ellen White's interpretation may be summarized as follows: The test of food in Daniel 1 was not only a question of paying homage to the Babylonian gods, but also one of temperance, of keeping mentally and physically fit (PK 481, 482), and of divine dietary laws, for the royal food included unclean meat (SL 19; Ms 122, 1897, in 4MR 126, 127).

The fact that Nebuchadnezzar could not remember the particulars of his dream (PK 491) ensured that the Babylonian wise men "should not place upon it a false interpretation" (FE 412); thus their pretensions were exposed (SL 34). The succession of world empires in Nebuchadnezzar's dream represented an ever-increasing deterioration of religion and morality, reaching the end of time (RH, Feb. 6, 1900; PK 501, 502).

Ellen White compares the setting up of the golden image in Daniel 3 with the eschatological establishment of a false Sabbath (ST, May 6, 1897). Through Nebuchadnezzar's seven-year loss of reason, judgment, and wisdom (PK 520), he "was finally thoroughly converted" (RH, Jan. 11, 1906). She identifies the hand that wrote the judgment message on the wall of Belshazzar's palace (Dan. 5:5) as the hand of God, the Holy Watcher, which is the same hand that rent the Temple veil at the moment of Christ's death (Ms 101, 1897, in 5BC 1109; 4T 14). Concerning the enigmatic figure of Darius the Mede, she stated that he reigned over Medo-Persia until his death, about two years after the fall of Babylon, while his nephew Cyrus served as general (RH, Mar. 21, 1907; PK 523, 556, 557); thus sharing a popular opinion of her time that identified Darius with Cyaxares II, son of Astyages, according to Xenophon.

Ellen White locates the throne room scene

of Daniel 7:9, 10 in the heavenly temple (GC 414, 424). The coming of the Son of man before the Ancient of Days represents Christ's coming to the Father at the end of the time period prophesied in Daniel 8:14, that is, A.D. 1844. This marks the beginning of the heavenly pre-Advent judgment when the books of the deeds of all humans are opened and the cases of the professed people of God are reviewed (GC 426, 479, 480). She identifies the little horn of Daniel 7 as the Papacy (GC 446). The time prophecy in Daniel 7:25 covers 1260 years, representing the time of the medieval papal power oppressing God's people, the "holy ones of the Most High," from A.D. 538 to 1798 (GC 439). The changing of "times and laws" by this power involved, in particular, the day of worship (GC 51-54, 446). The transference of the kingdom to God's people prophesied in Daniel 7:27 will occur at the Second Coming (MB 108).

For Ellen White's position on the meaning of "the *daily" in the book of Daniel, see that entry and 1SM 164-168.

Ellen White regarded Daniel 8:14 as "the scripture which above all others had been both the foundation and the central pillar of the advent faith" (GC 409). It was decisive for her that this prophecy concerned a heavenly sanctuary, not an earthly one (ibid. 417). In A.D. 1844 Christ started the "closing work of His priestly office" in the inner sanctum (RH, Nov. 27, 1883), cleansing the heavenly sanctuary and finishing the atonement for God's people, preparing them for His second coming (EW 251; 1T 58). She confirms the connection between the 2300 "evening-mornings" in Daniel 8:14 and the 70-weeks prophecy in Daniel 9. The latter period is said to be "cut off" from the one in Daniel 8 so that both prophetic time periods have the same starting point, the autumn of 457 B.C. Daniel 9 thus becomes pivotal to understanding when the

cleansing of the heavenly sanctuary begins (GC 325-328, 410).

She understood the 70-weeks prophecy as denoting 70 weeks of years (GC 326-328, 410; DA 233, 234; PK 698, 699), starting with the decree of Artaxerxes in 457 B.C. and pointing specifically to "the time of Christ's [first] coming, His anointing by the Holy Spirit, His death, and the giving of the gospel to the Gentiles" (DA 234). Part of Daniel 9:24, if not the entire verse, is a prophetic description of the work of Christ (1SM 396). The last week of years began with Christ's baptism and anointing in A.D. 27, reached its midpoint when Christ died in A.D. 31, and concluded with the stoning of Stephen and the conversion of Saul in A.D. 34 (GC 327, 328; PK 699).

Ellen White perceived the cosmic battle between good and evil supernatural beings most clearly in Daniel 10 (Lt 201, 1899, in 4BC 1173; RH, Dec. 5, 1907; PK 571, 572), but also in Daniel 6, where the praying Daniel takes a powerful part in it (1T 295). She wrote almost nothing explicitly on Daniel 11 except that the prophecy has "nearly reached its complete fulfillment" (9T 14; cf. RH, Nov. 24, 1904). She remained silent about the king of the north and the king of the south. The standing up of Michael in Daniel 12:1 signifies the end of Christ's high-priestly ministry and the beginning of the "time of trouble" when the wrath of God in the form of "the seven last plagues will be poured out" (EW 36). At this time "every case is decided; there is no longer probation, no longer mercy for the impenitent" (5T 213). The rising of those who sleep (Dan. 12:2; cf. Rev. 1:6) she perceived as a special resurrection just before the Second Coming (GC 637).

In 1850 Ellen White mentioned the 1335 days of Daniel 12:12 in connection with a certain Brother Hewit who had made "errors in the past." However, it is unclear whether the passage "that the 1335 days were ended" was his error or her correction (16MR 208). Historical context suggests the latter, but the statement remains ambiguous.

Christ is central to Ellen White's understanding of the book of Daniel. Not only is His ministry the center and climax of the prophecies in Daniel 7-12; she also identified several figures in Daniel with the preincarnate Christ: the fourth individual in the fiery furnace (SL 40, 41; PK 509), the "Son of man" (GC 424), Michael (PP 761; PK 572), the man dressed in linen in Daniel 10:5-9 and 12:6, 7 (RH, Feb. 8, 1881; SL 49-51), and possibly the prince of the heavenly host in Daniel 8:11 (PC 317).

Further reading: J. B. Doukhan, *Secrets of Daniel* (RHPA, 2000); *The SDA Bible Commentary,* vol. 4, pp. 39-78; Z. Stefanovic, *Daniel: Wisdom for the Wise* (PPPA, 2007).

Martin Pröbstle

DANIEL AND REVELATION, STUDY OF. Key elements of Ellen White's views on the study of Daniel and Revelation are compiled in *Testimonies to Ministers,* pages 112-119. She taught that Daniel is "complemented" by the Revelation to John, for in the book of Revelation Christ unsealed the book of Daniel. These books show that "the connection between God and His people is close and decided. A wonderful connection is seen between the universe of heaven and this world" (TM 114, 115). Thus the study of these books should be marked by a Christ-centered focus and personal humility before God and His people, a faithfulness to God's Word and to world history, and a desire to search the Scripture with a clear mind.

First, "the giving of the prophecy" and "the events portrayed" "teach that the human agent is to be kept out of sight, hid in Christ" (*ibid.* 112). "Be not too ready to take a controversial attitude. There will be times when we must stand still and see the salvation of God. Let Daniel speak, let the Revelation speak, and tell what is truth. But whatever phase of the subject is presented, uplift Jesus as the center of all hope" (*ibid.* 118). Students should pray "with contrite hearts" for "knowledge which He alone can give" (*ibid.* 116), for Christ "will bless all who will seek humbly and meekly to understand" Daniel and Revelation (*ibid.* 114).

Second, the study of Daniel and Revelation is to be faithful to God's Word and to world history. White writes: "It was my idea to have the two books bound together, Revelation following Daniel, as giving fuller light on the subjects dealt with in Daniel" (*ibid.* 117). "A few explanations of certain portions might be added, but I am not sure that these would be needed" (*ibid.*). The "other prophecies of the Old and New Testaments" should also be studied (*ibid.* 112). Because "past history will be repeated" (*ibid.* 116), it is essential to study "the history of the kingdoms" identified in Daniel and Revelation (*ibid.* 112), including the one that "made the Sunday law a distinctive power" and oppressed the people of God (*ibid.* 118). However, "we may have less to say in some lines, in regard to the Roman power and the papacy" (*ibid.* 112). This prophecy of Revelation will be fulfilled when "the churches, represented by Babylon," and the beast having "horns like a lamb" (Rev. 13:11) engage in the persecution of faithful believers (*ibid.* 117; Mar 166, 172).

Third, we should have a desire to search the Scripture with a clear mind. Students of Daniel and Revelation "should keep the mind clear. Never should they indulge perverted appetite in *eating or drinking*" (TM 114; italics supplied). "If they do this, the brain will be confused; they will be unable to bear the strain of digging deep to find out the meaning" (*ibid.*). In contrast, "those who *eat the flesh and drink the blood* of the Son of God" will bring from these books "truth that is inspired by the Holy Spirit. They will start into action forces that cannot be repressed" (*ibid.* 116; italics supplied). "Believers will have an entirely different religious experience" (*ibid.* 114), and there will be a reformation in our churches (*ibid.* 118). "One thing will certainly be understood from the study of Revelation—that the connection between God and His people is close and decided" (*ibid.* 114).

Further reading: 4BC 1166-1174; 7BC 958-990; *The SDA Bible Commentary,* vol. 4, pp. 39-78; vol. 7, pp. 103-132.

Martin Hanna

DANIEL AND REVELATION, THOUGHTS ON, see **SMITH, URIAH.**

DANSVILLE, NEW YORK, see **JACKSON, JAMES CALEB.**

DAUGHTERS OF GOD (RHPA, 1998, 275 pp.). Compilation of Ellen White's counsels to women taken from her published books and periodical articles and unpublished letters. Included are chapters on women in the Old and New Testaments, on women as teachers, physicians, and soul winners, on self-respect, and on balance in all aspects of life. In the publication of *Daughters of God* the Ellen G. White Estate emphasized the importance and value of women in God's sight. The book "is designed to be an encouragement, inspiration, and affirmation to women around the world. It includes counsels that lead women to strive for the highest ideals in whatever walk of life they find themselves, be it personal or professional" (DG 12). In the appendix are found examples of types of public ministry Ellen White engaged in (*ibid.* 241-247), exhibits relating to the ordination of women (*ibid.*

248-255), and the publication of her letters to *Lucinda Hall in 1876 in which she discusses the strains in her relationship with James White (*ibid.* 260-275).

DAY-DAWN. An irregularly published periodical edited by *O.R.L. Crosier between 1845 and 1847, the launching of the paper being reported in the *Morning Watch* of April 3, 1845, and in the *Day-Star* of April 15, 1845. First published with Dr. Franklin B. Hahn in Canandaigua, New York, during March 1845, the paper expanded on the Bridegroom ideas presented in the *Advent Mirror* (O.R.L. Crosier and F. B. Hahn, *Day-Dawn* published on last page of *Ontario Messenger,* Mar. 26, 1845). It suggested that in October 1844 Jesus had begun a new and unique extended Most Holy Place atonement ministry in the heavenly sanctuary. Over time this idea was expanded by Crosier and published in the seminal February 7, 1846, *Day-Star* Extra.

Crosier's second issue of the *Day-Dawn,* on July 18, 1846, sought to counter Enoch Jacobs' Shaker influence on Bridegroom or shut-door Adventists. With more than a year between the first two editions of the *Day-Dawn* (March 1845 and July 1846), the paper was initially issue-oriented. But beginning at least by August 1846 and continuing into April 1847, the paper appeared more regularly. During this active period, more than a dozen issues were published. Only the first two issues mentioned above, and three numbers from volume 2, are extant. The three numbers from volume 2 provide an enlightening view of O.R.L. Crosier and Sabbatarian Adventists during the early spring of 1847. During the first months of 1847 the *Day-Dawn* became the vehicle of communication for the emerging Sabbatarian Adventist movement.

From at least 1845 Crosier focused his

hopes for the second coming of Jesus on the spring of 1847. When the time passed, he ceased publication of the *Day-Dawn*, abandoned his shut door and seventh-day Sabbath view, and set an 1877 date for the Second Coming (JW to Leonard and Elvira Hastings, Aug. 26, 1848, EGWE-GC). Sabbatarian Adventists keenly felt the loss of the *Day-Dawn*. James White noted in his introduction to *A Word to the "Little Flock"* that his material had originally been gathered for publication in the *Day-Dawn* (WLF 1).

See also: Joseph Turner.

Further reading: M. D. Burt, "The *Day-Dawn* of Canandaigue, New York: Reprint of a Significant Millerite Adventist Journal," AUSS 44, no. 2 (Autumn 2006): 317-330; M. D. Burt, "The Extended Atonement View in the *Day-Dawn* and the Emergence of Sabbatarian Adventism," AUSS 44, no. 2 (Autumn 2006): 331-339.

Merlin D. Burt

DAY-STAR. A Millerite periodical previously titled the *Western Midnight Cry*, first published during 1843 in Cincinnati, Ohio, by J. V. Himes. By December 1843 Enoch Jacobs had replaced George Storrs as editor. On February 18, 1845, Jacobs became publisher as well as editor and named the paper the *Day-Star*. During 1845 and early 1846 the *Day-Star* was an important means of communication for those who would later become Sabbatarian Adventists. The *Day-Star* interacted with other short-lived or irregularly published papers such as *Hope of Israel, Hope Within the Veil, Jubilee Standard*, and *Voice of the Shepherd*.

Ellen Harmon's visions are first mentioned by James White in the *Day-Star* in an August 19, 1845, letter. Altogether, five letters from James White were published between September 1845 and January 1846 in the *Day-Star*. The first published material from

the pen of Ellen Harmon (later White) appeared in the *Day-Star* on January 24 and March 14, 1846. In these letters she gave an account of her first major visions. During 1845 and the first months of 1846 others who later became important to Sabbatarian Adventism were also published in the *Day-Star*. O.R.L. Crosier wrote eight articles and letters including his important February 7, 1846, *Day-Star* Extra article titled "The Law of Moses," which provided a heavenly-sanctuary explanation for the 1844 disappointment. Ellen White endorsed Crosier with the words "The Lord shew me in vision, more than one year ago, that Brother Crosier had the true light, on the cleansing of the Sanctuary. . . . I feel fully authorized by the Lord, to recommend that Extra, to every saint" (WLF 12). The names of other *Day-Star* correspondents include E.L.H. Chamberlain, J. B. Cook, Hiram Edson, H. S. Gurney, F. B. Hahn, and Otis Nichols.

Jacobs made his paper more notable by allowing a diversity of opinions to be expressed. Of particular interest are letters and articles on the Sabbath, coverage of Emily Clemons and her paper *Hope Within the Veil*, dialogue on the time expectation of the fall of 1845, and the energetic discussion of what constituted the second coming of Christ. As 1845 progressed, an increasing number of Bridegroom Adventists embraced the idea that Jesus had come spiritually, that the dead had been resurrected, and that the saints were living in the New Jerusalem. This idea, championed by a New York paper titled the *Voice of the Shepherd*, was repeatedly countered in print by James White, Ellen Harmon, and others. After Jacobs succumbed to the spiritualizing view and joined the Shakers, future Sabbatarian Adventists transferred their focus to O.R.L. Crosier's reactivated paper, the *Day-Dawn*.

See also: Adventist Denominations.
Merlin D. Burt

DEBT. Ellen White mentions debt more than 1,000 times, usually opposing it, in three primary contexts—church, institutional, and personal. She also gave a number of guidelines for situations in which debt may be "necessary."

Regarding church buildings, she saw being "crippled with debt" as "almost like a denial of . . . faith" and "dishonoring to God" (CS 260, 261). She insisted that church buildings be free from debt before being formally dedicated to God (*ibid.* 259). She urged that members should not spend "even sixpence" (Australian coinage then equivalent to 12 cents U.S.) for their "own gratification while the house of God is under mortgage" (*ibid.* 260). Instead, there should be in the church a "self-denial box" as a means of paying off debt (6T 103). She decried the annual loss of money "swallowed up by the interest paid on debts" (CS 259; cf. 7T 284).

Institutions should be governed by the same financial principles as the local church, though with some modifications (for an extensive treatment, see 7T 206-209). Debt is unwise, a yoke of bondage (CS 274, 275, 281; 6T 464), an embarrassment (7T 206), and should be shunned as leprosy (CS 272). If there is debt, prayer and effort should be invested to lift it. One method of liquidating debt is for members to sell, to friends and neighbors, books published for that purpose (9T 71, 79, 88; 1SM 104; PM 364). Institutional expansion should be gradual, in keeping with actual growth of patronage. "Let the best possible use be made of fewer facilities, rather than to increase debt" (MM 166). Church elementary schools should raise tuition, or even be closed temporarily, rather than run into debt (6T 217).

Similar principles apply to personal debt. Debt has a demoralizing effect on the believer (CS 255), bringing discouragement (AH 374) and weakening faith (*ibid.* 393), and is "one of Satan's nets, which he sets for souls" (*ibid.* 392; CS 254). Church members indifferent to debt she viewed as bringing reproach on the whole body (5T 179), and failure to pay debts because of indolence, she regarded as fraud (*ibid.*). She advised those in debt to deny themselves and cut their expenses, even if you must "live on porridge and bread" to get free from debt (CS 257). To those with strength to work, she advised, it is better to "deny yourself food and sleep" than fail to pay just debts (5T 180). Debt, however, should not be paid with funds due God (1T 220, 225; CS 92, 93). Indeed, Malachi 3:8-11 specifies that "the condition of prosperity depends upon bringing to God's treasury that which is His own" (TM 305). Nevertheless, Ellen White also taught that for those unable to free themselves from debt, other believers have a duty to help them get free of debt (AH 394; WM 181).

While Ellen White abhorred the slavery of long-term indebtedness (6Bio 158), she also addressed the opposite extreme, "a caution that savors of unbelief" (AH 394). She personally borrowed money to produce new books for sale (21MR 439), and to cover short-term emergencies in cash flow (1888 Materials 656, 1266). Among the situations in which she viewed borrowing as "necessary" were to obtain valuable land (14MR 45), to extend evangelistic or mission work into new fields (1888 Materials 1233), and to seize clearly providential opportunities for acquiring new institutions or facilities essential to the advancement of the church's mission (LLM 124, 488; cf. 6Bio 145, 146). What all these have in common is that they represent an acceptance of short-term debt in emergencies, investments such as buying a home or church building, and especially for advancing the mission of the church.

The gospel mission was her life's passion, and to advance that purpose she was willing even to assume debt. She insisted that when the church encounters genuinely providential opportunities to "secure valuable facilities" for "rapid advancement" of its mission, "the idea that we are not to purchase any such properties, unless first the money is in hand, is not in accordance with the mind of God." Many times, she recalled, God made facilities available "at a cost far below their real value," but "at a time when we had no money." She and her associates "met the situation by borrowing money on interest" because, had they "hesitated, the precious cause would have been retarded rather than advanced" (LLM 488; PC 305, 306).

This is the main reason that at the turn of the twentieth century Ellen White found herself in debt "more than ten thousand dollars" (Lt 128, 1899), yet still needing "means for the publication" of her books (Lt 102, 1908). Yet—and this may be pertinent to her definition of debt—her indebtedness did not exceed her net worth. Because her last *will and testament endowed her estate as a self-perpetuating legal entity with full authority to continue publishing her manuscripts, she knew that in the long term her assets would be more than sufficient to cover her liabilities. What no one foresaw was that the court-appointed appraiser would evaluate her unpublished manuscripts only for what they would bring at immediate sale. Consequently, at the time of her death, her debts exceeded her court-appraised assets. The General Conference, however, knowing the real value of her assets, purchased them for an amount sufficient to pay the debts.

See also: Finances, Ellen White's; Will and Testament, Ellen G. White's Last, and Settlement of Her Estate.

Kenneth Jorgensen

DECEPTION, SATAN'S LAST. Satan's final deception is presented under two categories: within the Seventh-day Adventist Church, and in the world. The latter predominates in Ellen White's writings. Within the Seventh-day Adventist Church, "the very last deception of Satan will be to make of none effect the testimony of the Spirit of God," "to unsettle the confidence of God's remnant people in the true testimony," a reference to Ellen White's own counsels (1SM 48; LDE 177, 178; 10MR 311). Satan cannot effectively deceive men and women where the counsels of the Spirit of God are heeded (1SM 48). Those Adventists who eventually change sides "will first give up their faith in the warnings and reproofs contained in the Testimonies of God's Spirit" (3SM 84; LDE 177). In support, Ellen White cites Proverbs 29:18: "Where there is no vision, the people perish." Having lost confidence in God's guidance through the last-day manifestation of the gift of prophecy, they are prepared to distrust also the testimony of Scripture itself, causing them to be deceived by the final deception that Satan brings on the world.

The final deception that Satan will bring on the world will be to impersonate Christ and bring a message that conflicts with the testimony of God's Word. It entails convincing people to trust their own judgment above the Word of God. Since the first lie in Eden, Satan has been preparing for his final effort to deceive the world (GC 561). All who are not grounded by faith in the Word of God will be swept away by the final delusion. "The last great delusion is soon to open before us. . . . So closely will the counterfeit resemble the true that it will be impossible to distinguish between them except by the Holy Scriptures" (*ibid.* 593). Spiritualism, miracles, and false revivals will be primary means of deceiving minds to receive falsehoods and to prepare the way for the final, grand delusion (Ev 604; EW 87; GC 464, 528, 624; 1T 412).

"As the crowning act in the great drama of deception, Satan himself will personate Christ.... In different parts of the earth, Satan will manifest himself among men as a majestic being of dazzling brightness, resembling the description of the Son of God given by John in the Revelation" (GC 624). The people believe that Christ has come, and they prostrate themselves before him, while he lifts his hands and pronounces a blessing upon them. He teaches some of the same gracious, heavenly truths that Jesus uttered during His earthly ministry; he heals the sick; and "he will cause fire to come down from heaven in the sight of men to prove that he is God" (MM 88). "Then, in his assumed character of Christ, he claims to have changed the Sabbath to Sunday, and commands all to hallow the day which he has blessed. . . . This is the strong, almost overmastering delusion" (GC 624; cf. 5T 698; 6BC 1106).

It is Satan's plan "to lead astray, if possible, even the elect" (Matt. 24:24, RSV). The saints have been crying unceasingly for Christ to come, and Satan hopes by this deception to "make them think their prayers are answered" (LDE 165). But the people of God are not misled. His teachings are not in accordance with the Scriptures, and he is not permitted to counterfeit the universal manner of Christ's return, which will be witnessed by the whole world (Matt. 24:24-27, 31; 25:31; 1 Thess. 4:16, 17; Rev. 1:7). "Only those who have been diligent students of the Scriptures and who have received the love of the truth will be shielded from the powerful delusion that takes the world captive. By the Bible testimony

these will detect the deceiver in his disguise. To all the testing time will come" (GC 625).

Further reading: LDE 155-171, 177, 178.
Edwin Reynolds

DEFENSE OF ELD. JAMES WHITE AND WIFE: VINDICATION OF THEIR MORAL AND CHRISTIAN CHARACTER (Battle Creek, Steam Press, 1870, 112 pp.). Booklet published by a committee of three, *J. N. Andrews, *G. H. Bell, and *Uriah Smith, in response to accusations that James White was becoming rich by manipulating church organizations, specifically the publishing house, or through mishandling funds. The booklet includes a historical background of James White's involvement in the publishing work (pp. 1-23), followed by 32 testimonials testifying to his good character (pp. 23-42) and a challenge by James White that he would restore fourfold to any who could provide proofs of his mishandling of funds (pp. 42, 43). A second committee, consisting of Uriah Smith, *George Amadon, and E. S. Walker, interviewed those with whom James White had transacted business. This committee also cleared his name (pp. 43-48), presenting an additional 37 character testimonials and a list of 59 other individuals whose full testimonials could not be included for lack of space, all testifying to White's financial integrity (pp. 50-75). This second committee declared they could "heartily commend Bro. White to the confidence and sympathy of Christians everywhere" (p. 76). Also included are an article entitled "Ellen G. White and Her Visions," by J. N. Andrews and *J. H. Waggoner (pp. 78-98), which countered articles by T. M. Preble attacking Ellen White, a character testimonial of Ellen White by Mrs. J. H. Waggoner (pp. 98, 99), and responses to additional miscellaneous accusations (pp. 99-112). In the end the editorial committee concluded that these accusations were nothing more than "shameful slanders" intended "to destroy the reputation of Sr. White" (p. 112). A second, longer edition (155 pp.) of this booklet was published the same year under the title *Defense of Eld. James White and Wife: The Battle Creek Church to the Churches and Brethren Scattered Abroad.*

See also: *Vindication of the Business Career of Elder James White*; Finances of Ellen G. White.

Michael W. Campbell

DENMARK. Country located in northern Europe consisting of the Jutland peninsula and 500 islands, of which 100 are inhabited. During Ellen White's stay in *Europe (1885-1887) she visited Denmark three times. Her first visit occurred October 8-14, 1885, when she stayed in Copenhagen at the home of *John G. Matteson. About 35 people attended the Friday night and Sabbath services. After this visit she went on to visit *Norway and *Sweden.

Her second visit took place the next year, July 17-26, 1886. She again preached several sermons and encouraged the developing work of a group of colporteurs. Matteson, an experienced colporteur, joined her in visiting several interesting places, including the Round Tower, 118 feet (36 meters) high, built in 1642 by King Christian IV. As she stood on the top of the tower and looked down on the great city she thought about what would become of Copenhagen and other great European cities on the day of the second coming of Christ (RH, Oct. 26, 1886; cf. EGWEur 209).

During Ellen White's third and final visit to Denmark, June 1-8, 1887, she rejoiced in the progress of the Adventist work in Copenhagen since her prior two visits. She commented that "in this great city the [Adventist] work may still progress if the workers will not get above the simplicity of the work, but will keep humble and holy and dependent upon God" (Ms 33, 1887, in EGWEur 299).

Altogether Ellen White spent 25 days in Copenhagen and preached 21 sermons. She met with several individuals and expressed her burden for their souls and well-being. One such person was a young student, *Carl Ottosen (1862-1942), who became the founder and chief physician of Skodsborg Sanitarium (1898-1992).

The Tract and Missionary Society, the Colporteur and Mission School, and the Sabbath School Department were organized during her visits to Denmark. To date, 27 of Ellen White's books and hundreds of her articles have been translated into Danish.

Further reading: EGWEur 93-101, 208-210, 297-299.

Hans Jorgen Schantz

DENOMINATIONS, RELATIONS TO OTHER. Since its origins the Seventh-day Adventist Church has been concerned with the lack of unity within Christianity and has advocated a unity based upon the teachings of the Bible, and the beliefs and practices of the early church. Seventh-day Adventists view unity at a level transcending mere visible church organization and understand their mission of spreading the everlasting gospel to be universal in character. Although they have endeavored at times to foster good relations with other denominations, their church has not become a member of the World Council of Churches or other regional ecumenical bodies. They believe that membership in ecumenical organizations would compromise or put at risk their missionary activities and freedom to communicate their message to all. Given their firm belief in the separation of church and state, they have also been reluctant to be associated with the political involvements of some ecumenical activities and organizations. Furthermore, the relationship of the Seventh-day Adventist Church with other denominations has been based traditionally on a prophetic understanding that in the end-time most Christian churches will reject crucial Bible teachings such as the observance of the biblical day of rest (Sabbath) and the conditional immortality of the soul, and will unite in their rejection of such teachings to impose their own views on the consciences of others (GC 444, 445, 588).

Yet in spite of such reluctance in associating with other denominations, Ellen White has written forthrightly that until the end of time Christ will have true followers in all churches and that the rejection of biblical truth by denominations will be a progressive movement until the second coming of Christ (*ibid*. 389, 390). Prior to the return of Christ all true followers of God will be invited to come out of the religious confusion in traditional churches to follow wholeheartedly the teachings of Scripture (*ibid*. 603-612). Out of respect for all people, she cautioned Adventist ministers not to arouse the antagonism of other denominations by "making denunciatory speeches" or harsh comments (Ev 564), nor to get into controversy with other clergy (*ibid*. 562). Such behavior will inevitably shut doors of influence and close the minds of honest people. Instead she invited Adventist ministers to meet with clergy of other denominations, to pray for them and with them (6T 77, 78). She counseled ministers who preached for the first time in new areas not to give the impression to ministers of other denominations "that they are wolves stealing in to get the sheep," but rather to seek a common ground and "to call the attention of the people to the truths of God's Word" that are dear to all Christians before attempting to present the distinctive beliefs of Seventh-day Adventists (Ev 143, 144). Writing to a minister and his wife who were going to South Africa to serve as missionaries, she said, "In laboring in a new field, do not think it your duty to say at once to the people, We are Seventh-day Adventists; we believe that the seventh day is the Sabbath; we believe in the non-immortality of the soul. This would often erect a formidable barrier between you and those you wish to reach. Speak to them, as you have opportunity, upon points of doctrine on which you can agree. Dwell on the necessity of practical godliness. Give them evidence that you are a Christian, desiring peace, and that you love their souls. Let them see that you are conscientious. Thus you will gain their confidence; and there will be time enough for doctrines. Let the heart be won, the soil prepared, and then sow the seed, presenting in love the truth as it is in Jesus" (GW 119, 120; cf. Lt 12, 1887, in TSA 14-20).

Denis Fortin

DEPRESSION, see **PSYCHOLOGY AND COUNSELING.**

DESIRE OF AGES, THE (PPPA, 1898, 835 pp.). An exposition of the life and teachings of Christ; the middle volume in the *Conflict of the Ages Series. *The Desire of Ages* had its beginnings in visions received in 1848 and especially the *great controversy vision of March 14, 1858 (LS 162; 3SM 99). These and subsequent visions, together with careful Bible study, became the baseline criteria for Ellen White's subsequent use of other sources, such as harmonies of the Gospels, Bible histories and dictionaries, other accounts of the life of Christ, and Christian devotional literature.

Ellen White early received assurance that "in the reading of religious books and journals, she would find precious gems of truth" that she would be enabled to "recognize" and "separate" from contexts of error (WCW and

D. E. Robinson, *Brief Statements*, p. 6, quoted in R. W. Olson, *101 Questions*, p. 72). She eventually accumulated office and personal libraries of some 1,300 works, including at least 30 books known to have been used in writing *The Desire of Ages* (E. M. Anderson, pp. 4, 7).

*Marian Davis played a significant role as Ellen White's "bookmaker" in the preparation of *The Desire of Ages* (3SM 91). Davis assembled some 30 "scrapbooks" of Ellen White's previous writings on the subject, gathered from White's earlier books, unpublished manuscripts, letters, sermon transcripts, and diaries. Davis used harmonies of the Gospels and other sources to work out an approximate chronology of events and to suggest the scope and content of chapters. Many of her suggestions Ellen White accepted, and some she did not accept (MR728 25). But Marian was intensely conscientious about her work, and Ellen White valued her most highly (MR728 22; 2SM 252; 3SM 93).

Ellen White's first 51-page book section on the life of Christ came out in 1858 (1SG 28-79). That section she enlarged in 1876 to form a separate volume, *The Spirit of Prophecy*, volume 2, subtitled *Life, Teachings and Miracles of Our Lord Jesus Christ* (1877, 400 pp.). That she did not view her writings as dictationally inspired is shown by her plan to quickly get out a first edition (of 2SP), even if it were not "so very, very exact," and then publish "a more perfect edition" later (Lt 45, 1876, in 3SM 108; cf. 9MR 35, 36). She followed a similar aggressive plan with volume 3, *The Death, Resurrection and Ascension of Our Lord Jesus Christ*, and extending through the martyrdoms of Peter and Paul. The first printing (1878) contained 392 pages; the second printing added five more chapters, for a total of 442 pages.

The General Conference voted in 1883 to translate and publish *The Spirit of Prophecy*, volumes 2 and 3, in several European languages. The result was a one-volume *Life of Christ*, eventually published in Danish-Norwegian (*Jesu Kristi liv*), Swedish (*Kristi lefnad*), German (*Das Leben Jesu*), French (*La vie de Christ*), and Finnish (*Kristuksen Elämä*). For this purpose, Ellen White and her staff provided a manuscript based on *The Spirit of Prophecy*, volumes 2 and 3. The first four chapters of volume 2 were expanded into eight chapters for the new manuscript. Several other changes and insertions were made as well, in harmony with White's plan seven years earlier to publish "a more perfect edition" later (Lt 45, 1876, in 3SM 108). According to research by Denis Kaiser, all the chapters dealing with the life of Christ in *The Spirit of Prophecy*, volume 3, were used without any changes. This enlarged manuscript was never actually published in English. Before it was ready, White had begun again to improve it.

Between 1885 and 1891 White worked sporadically at enlarging her book on the life of Christ between other pressing responsibilities and the enlarging of her other book, *The Great Controversy*. Not until 1892 in Australia was she able to again make a sustained effort on the life of Christ, leading to the publication of *The Desire of Ages* in 1898 (3SM 115-120). Before it was finished, her "life of Christ" had become too large for one volume, so two parts were published separately. Her exposition of the Sermon on the Mount became *Thoughts From the Mount of Blessing* (1896), and that of the parables became *Christ's Object Lessons* (1900).

In her later years White often mentioned *The Desire of Ages* with *The Great Controversy* and *Patriarchs and Prophets* as books that she felt most urgent about circulating (CM 124). Many Adventists trace the beginnings of their personal discipleship to Christ to the reading of *The Desire of Ages*. Its treatment of the events from Gethsemane to the Resurrection occupies more than 100 pages, reflecting a pervasive theme of the book: "It would be well for us to spend a thoughtful hour each day in contemplation of the life of Christ. We should take it point by point, and let the imagination grasp each scene, especially the closing ones. As we thus dwell upon His great sacrifice for us, our confidence in Him will be more constant, our love will be quickened, and we shall be more deeply imbued with His spirit. If we would be saved at last, we must learn the lesson of penitence and humiliation at the foot of the cross" (DA 83).

A contemporary adaptation of *The Desire of Ages* under the title *Messiah,* prepared by Jerry D. Thomas, was published in 2002 (PPPA, 446 pp.).

See also: The Desire of Ages Sources, Study of.

Further reading: 4Bio 375-393; E. M. Anderson, "Learning From the *Desire of Ages* Project" (1999, DF 51-B-1, CAR); R. W. Coon, "Ellen White's Use of Literary Assistants: The Prophet as Writer" (lecture outline, Apr. 13, 1995, pp. 8, 9, CAR); R. W. Olson and R. Graybill, "How *The Desire of Ages* Was Written" (EGWE, 1979, SDoc); W. C. White, "How Ellen White's Books Were Written" (EGWE, 1935, SDoc).

Jerry Moon

THE DESIRE OF AGES SOURCES, STUDY OF (1988). Research commissioned by the General Conference of Seventh-day Adventists to investigate Ellen G. White's use of literary sources in writing *The Desire of Ages*, her major work on the life of Christ. Fred Veltman, professor of New Testament literature at Pacific Union College, Angwin, California, directed the investigation.

Throughout her long life as a religious leader and prophetic voice in the Adventist Church, Ellen White was a prolific writer and popular speaker. Her limited formal education, however, contributed to her lack of confidence in her abilities as a writer. To meet the demands of the developing church on her prophetic ministry and to fulfill her self-understood mission as a "messenger of the Lord," she leaned heavily upon the literary skills of others. In addition, she utilized the writings of others in the composition of her works, a fact that was known but not generally recognized for more than a century. The nature and scope of her *literary borrowing for any book other than *The Great Controversy* was, until 1980, a matter of speculation.

In January of 1980 Walter Rea, an Adventist pastor in southern California, presented evidence to an ad hoc committee of the General Conference that Ellen White's literary dependency was greater than had been previously known. The questions about her inspiration and the charges of plagiarism that followed from this new information made it both timely and appropriate that the Adventist Church undertake a serious analysis of Ellen White's literary dependency. *The Desire of Ages* (DA), one of the best loved of all her books, was chosen as the focus of the investigation. This book was the obvious choice for anyone concerned over her inspiration. Nearly every one of the 87 chapters is based upon verses of Scripture and includes both narrative and theological commentary. An in-depth study of her writing methods would hopefully answer the questions being raised over her literary dependency. How much verbatim material was there in her writings relating to Scripture? To what degree was she dependent upon literary sources? From what writers did she borrow and from what kinds of books? Did Ellen White do the copying herself, or was it done by her literary assistants? Could she have unconsciously used the literary expressions of other authors—did she have a "photographic" memory? These and similar issues had to be addressed before one could treat the charge of plagiarism leveled against Ellen White and the questions being raised over the nature of her inspiration.

The original plan of the research project called for a study of the entire text (835 pages) of *The Desire of Ages*. Early in the development of the research methodology it became obvious that the resources allotted for research and writing were not nearly adequate considering the magnitude and complexity of the task. Ellen White's motivation to write the book stemmed from her desire to prepare a more complete and accurate portrayal of the life of Christ than was contained in *The Spirit of Prophecy*, volumes 2 and 3. She wanted a new book with gospel appeal that Adventist colporteurs could sell to the public. Marian Davis, whom Ellen White referred to as her "bookmaker," was given the task of collecting the earlier writings on the life of Christ, published and unpublished, and arranging them in "scrapbooks." When it was found that certain events in the life of Christ had not been covered, or needed enlargement or revision, Ellen White would write on those areas. She became so caught up in the subject that she produced enough material to fill two additional books, *Thoughts From the Mount of Blessing* (1896) and *Christ's Object Lessons* (1900). Much of what she wrote on the life of Christ first saw publication as articles in various Adventist journals.

When Ellen White's method of composing her books was understood, the focus of the research moved from *The Desire of Ages* to the earlier stages of the text, to her diaries, "scratch books," and manuscripts. The dependency of Ellen White on other writers would be most clearly recognized in her handwritten or typescript materials. These findings made

it necessary to decrease the breadth of the *The Desire of Ages* text to be reviewed and to increase the depth of the research.

To reduce the textual base to manageable size, two statisticians selected 15 chapters that would serve as a random sample of the 87 chapters of *The Desire of Ages*. Five chapters were chosen from the 29 shortest of the 87 chapters, five were chosen from the 29 longest chapters, and five were chosen from the middle-length 29 chapters. Using the subject matter of the 15 chapters as the content control, all the earlier writings of Ellen White were searched, to locate the letters, manuscripts, and articles in which she had written on these same subjects. The lack of an apparent order in the writing or a topical index to her scratch books made it difficult and time-consuming to locate specific content. The variation in the subject matter of the diary material has been described as a "flow of consciousness." As a result, there is often no boundary to the specific content comparable to the specific chapter divisions of *The Desire of Ages* text. These earlier texts were designated as pre-*Desire of Ages* to distinguish them from the text of *The Desire of Ages*.

The major research tool applied to the Ellen White text was source analysis (commonly called source criticism), with the independent sentence being used as the unit of comparison between the major text and the possible source text carrying an earlier date of publication. A scale of seven levels of dependency was applied to each sentence. The criteria differentiating between these levels of dependency were the amount of verbatim words and the order of word elements in the parallel sentences. If a sentence from an Ellen White text was in every respect identical to a sentence in a source text, the sentence was classified as *strict verbatim* and given a dependency value of seven. In cases in which the sentences were identical except for an obvious synonym being substituted for a word or a slightly different form of punctuation, the sentence was identified as *verbatim* and given a value of six—indicating that it had a lesser degree of dependency than *strict verbatim,* with its value of seven.

As the verbatim words became fewer and the order of similar elements in the parallel texts followed separate arrangement, the dependency ratings were lowered to *strict paraphrase, simple paraphrase,* or *loose paraphrase,* with accompanying lesser values on the scale of dependency. When the Ellen White text and the source were identical because both writers were depending directly on an obvious text of Scripture for the story being told, the sentence was labeled *Bible quotation* and given a value of zero. If the text of Scripture was identical but not one usually associated with the story, the sentence received the label *source Bible* and given a value of two. In those instances when part of the sentence exhibited strong parallelism and yet a significant part of the sentence was clearly not dependent in the wording, it was given a value of one and designated as *partial independence.* When there was no clear indication of literary dependency, the sentence was classified as "independent" and given a dependency value of zero—even when the content of *The Desire of Ages* text was very similar to that of the source text. Because of the temptation of "parallelomania" (an obsession to find parallels), and the likelihood at times that two writers will use identical words by reason of the commonality of human expression for describing similar events or telling well-known stories, the researchers took a conservative approach to the identification of source parallels.

Literary dependency, however, is not limited to parallel sentence structure and verbal similarities. Authors may also consult sources for the arrangements of the sentences and the thematic development of a significant portion of the text of a chapter. Therefore, the analysis of *The Desire of Ages* text included a limited study of possible editorial or redactional dependency.

More than 500 works were reviewed as possible sources for *The Desire of Ages* text, mostly nineteenth-century works on the life of Christ. The list of works was developed from the authors mentioned in Ellen White's writings and from the lists of books in her personal and office libraries at the time of her death. Many of these works would today be classified as historical novels. Ellen White, of course, was not limited to this type of literature, as her library records clearly reveal. She also had access to sermons, devotional books, Bible society tracts, Bible commentaries, and general Christian literature, and could have borrowed materials from any of these sources. Her associates in the leadership of the Adventist Church were preachers, teachers, and administrators who also wrote books as well as articles for the Adventist readership. In view of the fact that not all of the possible life-of-Christ sources available to Ellen White were included in the study, much less the literature from other genres she is known to have read and from which she borrowed, it is recognized that this probe cannot be considered exhaustive.

The conclusions of the *Desire of Ages* project were set forth in chapter 18, the last chapter (100 pages) of the more-than-1,000-page research report, with its 1,600 additional pages of supporting documentation and bibliographies. First and foremost among the findings was the established fact that Ellen White, not her literary assistants, composed the basic content of the *Desire of Ages* text. She was the one who took literary expressions from the works of other authors without giving them credit. She used the literary sources consciously and intentionally. The literary parallels were not the result of accident or "photographic" memory. It should also be noted that no *Desire of Ages* chapter was found entire in either handwritten or copy form. Several sentences from three chapters were found in Ellen White's diaries, and significant portions of three additional chapters were developed from manuscripts dating from 1897. Handwritten and copied texts do exist for portions of the pre-*Desire of Ages* text that treat content found in 10 of the 15 *Desire of Ages* chapters.

In respect to the degree of literary dependency, no instances of strict verbatim were found. Of the 2,624 sentence units of the *Desire of Ages* text studied, 29 (1.1 percent) were labeled as verbatim, and 183 (6.9 percent) were classified as strict paraphrase. A total of 823 of the 2,624 sentence units of the *Desire of Ages* text (31 percent) clearly exhibited some degree of dependency consisting of one parallel word or more. When the 1,612 independent sentences are factored in, the average level of dependency was 3.3, or just a little higher dependency than loose paraphrase.

Though not every sentence in the scattered pre-*Desire of Ages* texts covering the same general content of the 15 *Desire of Ages* chapters was evaluated, out of the 1,180 sentences reviewed, six (0.5 percent) were labeled strict verbatim, 80 (6.8 percent) were labeled verbatim, and 232 (19.6 percent) were classified as strict paraphrase. The average rate of dependency for the pre-*Desire of Ages* text was 3.57, slightly higher than the *Desire of Ages* text. The *Desire of Ages* text, however, being largely an edited and conflated compilation of earlier writings, generally represented a much lesser degree of literary dependency than did the pre-*Desire of Ages* text, as may

be clearly seen by the significantly higher number of verbatim sentences in the earlier writings. When the independent sentences were factored in, the average rate of dependency was statistically distorted, because of the often different content of the independent sentences. Ellen White often introduced commentary on topics not usually found in writings on the life of Christ, and for that reason those sentences were not examined for their literary dependency.

The 15 chapters of *The Desire of Ages* contained literary parallels from a minimum of 23 sources. Among those authors whom Ellen White used often were William Hanna, Daniel March, John Harris, Frederic Farrar, Henry Melvill, and Octavius Winslow. The longer chapters of *The Desire of Ages* revealed no greater use of sources than did the shorter ones. And though content analysis was not an integral part of the research, no significant differences in content were noted between the dependent and the independent sentences. Both categories of sentences included descriptive, devotional, spiritual, and theological commentary, as well as moral exhortation.

Even though the *Desire of Ages* chapters often reflected the use of multiple sources, they usually contained parallels from one dominant source. Because of her own special emphases, the final structure of each chapter exhibited its own arrangement of content rather than that of any given source. Within the chapter, however, those sections that contained several parallel sentences from a given source would often follow the thematic development of the major source. In most instances Ellen White's diary entries floated freely from topic to topic, not offering extensive comment on any given subject. But where the later dependent pre-*Desire of Ages* manuscripts treated a topic, they usually followed the thematic development of the source.

Evidently Ellen White used one source at a time as she worked on a given topic. When writing on the same subject on another occasion, she tended to use a different source. The fact that the *Desire of Ages* chapters contained literary parallels from multiple sources more likely represented the editorial work of Marian Davis in conflating several separate manuscripts or journal entries rather than Ellen White's use of several sources to compose a chapter.

While the investigation followed through on its initial method of research, in the final analysis it was not able to ascertain the full extent of Ellen White's literary dependence, given the amount and variety of her writings and the limitations of time and research personnel. Nevertheless there can no longer be any doubt that she used sources regardless of the subject content. And though there are many facets of her dependency yet to explore, and questions about her borrowing that beg for answers, there is also something to be said about her independence and originality. The research clearly shows that the sources were her slaves, never her master. She readily recognized what expressions in her sources would enhance her writing and serve her purposes. Ellen White, with the aid of her literary assistants, built out of the common quarry of stones not a replica of another's work but rather a customized literary composition that reflected the particular faith and Christian hope she felt called to share with her fellow Adventists and the Christian community at large.

Further reading: Copies of the *Full Report of the Life of Christ Research Project* (1988) were distributed to all Ellen G. White research centers and to every Seventh-day Adventist college and university throughout the world. The report is available online at the General Conference Office of Archives and Statistics Web site: www.adventistarchives.org/doc archives.asp. A synopsis of the investigation, from which much of the content of this article has been drawn, appeared in a two-part series: F. Veltman, "The *Desire of Ages* Project: The Data," and "The *Desire of Ages* Project: The Conclusions," *Ministry*, October 1990, and December 1990. The secretary of the Ellen G. White Estate at the time the investigation was completed also offered his evaluation of the study: R. W. Olson, "Olson Discusses the Veltman Study," *Ministry*, December 1990. M. A. King and K. L. Morgan, *More Than Words: A Study of Inspiration and Ellen White's Use of Sources in* The Desire of Ages (Berrien Springs, Mich.; Honor Him Pub., 2009); R. W. Olson and R. Graybill, "How the *Desire of Ages* Was Written" (EGWE, SDoc).

Fred Veltman

DEVIL, see **SATAN**.

DEVOTIONAL BOOKS. In the early 1900s the Seventh-day Adventist Church initiated a program of daily personal devotions called the Morning Watch, consisting of the reading and/or memorizing of a Bible text along with personal prayer. The first Morning Watch calendar was published in 1908. In the mid-1940s the denomination published its first Morning Watch devotional books. These consisted of 365 daily readings, each including a Bible text and a page of devotional reading. The first devotional book drawn from Ellen White's writings was published in 1946 and has been followed by a new one about every three or four years since. The first of these were compiled from her published books, but later ones included materials from her unpublished letters and manuscripts as well. Yearly themes have also guided the selection of materials. Twenty devotional books have been published as of 2010. The reader will find brief descriptions of each one of these in this encyclopedia. They are: *Radiant Religion (1946), *With God at Dawn (1949), *My Life Today (1952, 1980), *Sons and Daughters of God (1955, 1983), *The Faith I Live By (1958, 1973, 2000), *Our High Calling (1961, 1989, 2000), *That I May Know Him (1964, 1992), *In Heavenly Places (1967, 1995), *Conflict and Courage (1970, 2005), *God's Amazing Grace (1973, 2001), *Maranatha, the Lord Is Coming (1976), *This Day With God (1979), *The Upward Look (1982, 2008), *Reflecting Christ (1985, 2008), *Lift Him Up (1988), *Our Father Cares (1991), *Ye Shall Receive Power (1995),*Christ Triumphant (1999), *To Be Like Jesus (2004), and *From the Heart (2010).

Further reading: SDA Encyclopedia (1996), vol. 11, p. 122.

Denis Fortin

DEVOTIONAL LIFE OF ELLEN G. WHITE, see **SPIRITUALITY OF ELLEN G. WHITE**.

DIARIES AND JOURNALS OF ELLEN G. WHITE.
The term *diary/journal* has been used to describe the handwritten volumes in which Ellen White not only chronicled her day-to-day activities but also wrote drafts of general articles and occasionally letters. There are 63 extant diary/journals in the archives of the *Ellen G. White Estate, the earliest dating to 1859 and continuing intermittently up to the closing years of her life. They vary from commercial calendar-type diaries and blank pages bound together, to large ruled journals (8½ " x 14" [21.6 centimeters x 35.6 centimeters]) that she seemed to favor after her return from *Australia in 1900.

Most of the diaries/journals contain entries or articles spanning several years, apparently written without regard to chronological order. But this phenomenon is explained by the knowledge that it was Ellen White's practice, upon completion of an article, to pass the journal to a secretary to be transcribed, necessitating that she use a different blank volume when resuming her writing. Thus several volumes might be in use at any given time.

Much of the content of these diaries/journals was transcribed, placed on file, and used in publications under Ellen White's direct supervision. Some matter, however, remained uncopied at the time of her death in 1915. When the White trustees decided to publish a comprehensive biography of Ellen White in the 1950s, all of these volumes were compared with the file, and any autobiographical materials not previously copied were transcribed and added to the manuscript file. In addition, nonbiographical entries that were not found on file were noted. In the 1980s and 1990s, with the aid of computer text searching, the White Estate once again surveyed these handwritten volumes in an effort to ensure complete transcription of the volumes.

Tim Poirier

DIET. Ellen White attributed her counsel on diet to the instruction she received in vision. She saw diet as an integral part of the Christian's responsibility to God and that "a close sympathy exists between the physical and the moral nature" (CD 43). This makes study into healthful living all the more imperative. "We need to learn that indulged appetite is the greatest hindrance to mental improvement and soul sanctification" (*ibid.* 45). "It is just as much sin to violate the laws of our being as to break one of the ten commandments, for we cannot do either without breaking God's law" (*ibid.*).

Early in White's 70-year prophetic career (1848), coffee and tea were named as injurious (*ibid.* 495). She subsequently made strong statements about these stimulants: "Tea and coffee drinking is a sin . . . which, like other evils, injures the soul" (*ibid.* 425). She suggested that "caramel cereal [beverages], made as nicely as possible, should be served in the place of these health-destroying beverages" (*ibid.* 431).

In 1863 White was given a comprehensive health reform vision that formed the basis for her six articles in *Health: or How to Live* (1865). She was shown that a diet without meat was best, reflecting the original diet that God gave to Adam and Eve. White strongly recommended a meatless diet as best where a variety of foods are available: "We do not mark out any precise line to be followed in diet; but we do say that in countries where there are fruits, grains, and nuts in abundance, flesh food is not the right food for God's people" (9T 159). But the *type* of vegetarian diet she recommended is open to discussion. While some statements mention only plant sources, other statements include milk and eggs: "Fruits, grains, and vegetables, prepared in a simple way, free from spice and grease of all kinds, make, with milk and cream, the most healthful diet" (CD 321). Eggs, in moderation and from healthy hens, "contain properties that are remedial agencies in counteracting certain poisons" (*ibid.* 352). She did not teach the vegan or total vegetarian diet, and in one comment associated the vegan diet with the time of trouble (*ibid.* 206). But at the same time, she said to be ready to do without animal products. Because disease in animals will increase, "the use of milk and eggs will become more and more unsafe" (*ibid.* 365).

Ellen White made a conscious effort not to prejudice people against health reform. James White reported her as "forcible, yet prudent, so that she carried the feelings of the entire congregation with her" (*ibid.* 495). She was aware that diet reform was slow work, requiring patience and advancement step by step "in a manner not calculated to disgust and prejudice those whom we would teach and help" (*ibid.* 328). White urged extremists to slow down and those slow to accept the counsels to speed up. She was distressed when these two types of warnings were twisted in the opposite direction: "When we seek to pull people out of the fire on the one hand, the very words which then have to be spoken to correct evils are used to justify indulgence on the other hand" (*ibid.* 210).

She herself wanted to be exemplary: "I want to be a pattern of temperance and of good works to others" (*ibid.* 490). However, she did not want her own dietary practices to be the criterion for another. When addressing General Conference attendees, she made it clear that a person's convictions on health reform had to be their own, not mimicking her dietary selections as the authority. She added, "Now I want you to think of these things, and do not make any human being your criterion" (8MR 350).

White recognized that one diet plan would not work for all. Rather, "the demands of the systems differ greatly in different persons. What would be food for one, might be poison for another; so precise rules cannot be laid down to fit every case. I cannot eat beans, for they are poison to me" (CD 494). Efforts to apply her every statement on health reform to every individual are therefore contrary to her own instructions. Ellen White further warned of those who "select from the testimonies the strongest expressions and, without bringing in or making any account of the circumstances under which the cautions and warnings are given, make them of force in every case" (3SM 285, 286).

Ellen White counseled about the strength of appetite, and how to work with people. "We must go no faster than we can take those with us whose consciences and intellects are convinced of the truths we advocate. We must meet the people where they are. . . . It is slow work to obtain a reform in diet. . . . In reforms we would better come one step short of the mark than go one step beyond it. And if there is error at all, let it be on the side next to the people" (3T 20, 21). "The diet reform should be progressive" (MH 320).

White advocated holding cooking schools to involve people in the diet reform progression. Every church should conduct cooking schools (*ibid.* 149). "Good service can be done by teaching the people how to prepare healthful food. This line of work is as essential as any that can be taken up. More cooking schools should be established, and some should labor from house to house, giving instruction in the art of cooking wholesome foods" (CD 472). We are to teach and to practice an appetizing diet: "Food should be prepared with simplicity, yet with a nicety which will invite the appetite" (*ibid.* 200). Ellen White said of her own home, "I tell our family, 'Whatever you do, do not get a poverty-stricken diet. Place enough on the table to nourish the system'" (*ibid.* 489; cf. 2T 383, 384).

Neither should one become obsessed over diet reform. "Some are continually anxious lest their food, however simple and healthful, may hurt them. To these let me say, Do not think that your food will injure you; do not think about it at all. Eat according to your best judgment; and when you have asked the Lord to bless the food for the strengthening of your body, believe that He hears your prayer, and be at rest" (MH 321).

See also: *Counsels on Diet and Foods.*

Sylvia Fagal

DIME TABERNACLE, see **BATTLE CREEK TABERNACLE.**

DISAPPOINTMENTS, MILLERITE. Historians of Millerism generally identify two definite disappointments during the final months of the movement. The word "disappointment" refers to the Millerites' unrealized expectation that the second coming of Christ would occur either *by*, or specifically *on*, a publicly anticipated date. The first disappointment for Millerite believers occurred on March 21, 1844. Miller and his associates for more than 10 years had been preaching that Christ would return "about the year 1843." As a general rule, they refused to be more specific in their predictions. Later adjustments in their calculations suggested that the terminal year would fall between March 21, 1843, and March 21, 1844. Thus, Christ could come at any time during that period, but not later than March 21, 1844. When that day passed uneventfully, the Millerites widely acknowledged their disappointment and endured widespread ridicule in the popular press.

The second, or so-called great, disappointment of the Millerties occurred when Christ did not return on October 22, 1844. This latter date had been introduced in August of that year and was based on a detailed argument regarding the typology of the Hebrew Day of Atonement, which occurred on the tenth day of the seventh Jewish month and, under the *Karaite Jewish calendar, corresponded to October 22, 1844. With renewed vigor the Millerites revived their preaching of the "midnight cry" message (cf. Matt. 25:1-13).

When Christ did not return on October 22, the thousands of Millerite believers were devastated to a degree that can barely be imagined. One of their number, Hiram Edson, described his feelings thus: "Our fondest hopes and expectations were blasted, and such a spirit of weeping came over us as I never experienced before. It seemed that the loss of all earthly friends could have been no comparison. We wept, and wept, till the day dawn. I mused in my own heart, saying, My advent experience has been the richest and brightest of all my Christian experience. If this had proved a failure, what was the rest of my Christian experience worth? Has the Bible proved a failure? Is there no God, no heaven, no golden home city, no Paradise? Is all this but a cunningly devised fable? Is there no reality to our fondest hope and expectation of these things? And thus we had something to grieve and weep over, if all our fondest hopes were lost. And as I said, we wept till the day dawn" (Hiram Edson manuscript, DF 588, CAR).

The disappointment of October 22 effectively ended Millerism as a mass movement phenomena on the American religious landscape. Ellen White was within a month of turning 17 years old when she experienced the Millerite disappointment. For a brief time, like thousands of others in the movement, she lost her confidence in the "midnight cry" message and the accuracy of the time calculations that pointed to 1844. Sometime in December, just a few weeks after October 22, she experienced her first vision, the import of which confirmed her faith, and that of a few other Millerites, in the validity of the "midnight cry" message that had been focused on October 22. While her vision did not explain why the Millerites had been disappointed, the burden of its meaning was that they should hold on confidently to the message, including the accuracy of the time element (cf. EW 13-20).

The disappointment played two vital roles in the work and thought of Ellen White. First, it was the initial event that prepared the way for her unique, lifelong ministry. Her reports of her earliest visions were specifically intended to lead the Advent believers out of the disappointment. Those reports, and the standing they gave her among

early believers, marked the cornerstone of her prophetic role among the Advent people in perpetuity. Second, the disappointment—or the "passing of the time," as she more often referred to it—became in her major writings an important metaphor, analogous of two other epic crises of God's people in sacred history: the crossing of the Red Sea by the Israelites, and the Crucifixion (GC 404, 405, 457). In the same way that the ancient Hebrews and Christ's disciples saw their devastating disappointment turned into deliverance, so too would Advent believers who kept their faith in the message of 1844.

See also: Shut Door.

Further reading: G. R. Knight, *Millennial Fever and the End of the World* (PPPA, 1993), pp. 159-166, 217-236; F. D. Nichol, *The Midnight Cry* (RHPA, 1944), pp. 158-173, 247-260.

Ronald A. Knott

DISEASE AND ITS CAUSES, see **HEALTH: OR HOW TO LIVE**.

DIVORCE, see **MARRIAGE AND DIVORCE**.

DOCTRINES, ELLEN G. WHITE'S ROLE IN THE DEVELOPMENT OF SEVENTH-DAY ADVENTIST. Perhaps one of the most disputed issues concerning Ellen White's ministry has been in regard to her involvement and influence in the development of Seventh-day Adventist doctrines. Many believe that her visions were the origin of the distinctive doctrines of Adventism. However, a brief look at the historical development of these doctrines within Adventism reveals a different picture. Adventist pioneers accepted a set of distinctive doctrines based on their study of the Bible, and Ellen White's influence in these early years was limited to confirmation and clarification of these doctrines. Never was she the initiator of these doctrinal beliefs.

Second advent of Christ. Adventists take their name from their belief in the near, visible, and literal second advent of Christ, which will then be followed by the millennium (John 14:1-3; 1 Thess. 4:13-18; Rev. 19:11-20:6). They are not the only Christians to believe in a premillennialist eschatology, and many believed in this understanding of the second coming of Christ long before the time of Ellen White. She herself learned of this doctrine as a young girl, along with other members of her family, as she listened to lectures of *William Miller and other early Adventist preachers. In succeeding years her influence was largely one of reasserting this doctrine among Adventists and to invite Adventists to be ready for Christ's advent.

Observance of the seventh-day Sabbath. A knowledge of the doctrine of the Sabbath was brought to Adventists in Washington, New Hampshire, in early 1844 by Rachel Oakes [later Preston], a Seventh Day Baptist. Far from being an innovation of the nineteenth century, this doctrine has been observed by Christians since the beginning of Christianity and by Seventh Day Baptists since the seventeenth century. In early 1845 two ministers in the Washington, New Hampshire, area, Thomas Preble and Frederick Wheeler, accepted this doctrine and began to propagate their views. Thus it came to the attention of *Joseph Bates, who would later—with James and Ellen White—become one of the three cofounders of the Seventh-day Adventist Church. When Bates first approached Ellen White on the doctrine of the Sabbath in 1846, her initial reaction was negative. "I did not feel its importance," she later wrote, "and thought that he erred in dwelling upon the fourth commandment more than upon the other nine" (LS 95). In August 1846 Bates published his first tract, *The Seventh-day Sabbath, a Perpetual Sign*, and gave a copy of it to James

and Ellen White. From the biblical evidence presented in the book, and not because Ellen had received a vision, they decided to accept this doctrine (1T 75). In 1874 she recalled in a letter to John Loughborough, "I believed the truth upon the Sabbath question before I had seen anything in vision in reference to the Sabbath. It was months after I had commenced keeping the Sabbath before I was shown [in vision] its importance" (Lt 2, 1874, in 8MR 238).

A similar scenario occurred also regarding the time to begin the observance of the Sabbath, an issue that was not settled among Sabbatarian Adventists until November 1855. Four views of when the Sabbath begins coexisted among them during the late 1840s and early 1850s: (1) sunrise Saturday morning; (2) midnight Friday night ("legal time"); (3) 6:00 p.m. Friday ("equatorial time"), the position favored by Bates, who knew that the sun rises at 6:00 a.m., and sets at 6:00 p.m., at the equator; and (4) sunset on Friday, the Jewish and Seventh Day Baptist position. *J. N. Andrews was commissioned to study out the matter from Scripture, and write a report for a conference in Battle Creek in November 1855. On the basis of biblical evidence, Andrews concluded that the proper time to begin the Sabbath was sunset on Friday (RH, Dec. 4, 1855). While the attendees at this conference accepted Andrews' biblical study and conclusions, Bates initially held out for "equatorial time," and so did Ellen White, who sided with Bates. Three days later, however, during a season of prayer "at the close of the conference," Ellen White received a vision correcting her position, which she immediately shared with the other believers (A. L. White, *Messenger to the Remnant*, pp. 35, 36; 1T 116; 1Bio 323, 324). In subsequent years Ellen White continued to give her strong support to the doctrine of the Sabbath and its theological and spiritual meaning. She also provided numerous counsels regarding Sabbathkeeping.

Christ's ministry in the heavenly sanctuary. Following the Millerite *disappointment in October 1844, Millerites sought to understand their spiritual experience and the meaning of the prophecies of Daniel that had led them to believe that Christ would return that year. A few of them came to understand that the prophetic calculations they had done were accurate but that the event predicted was mistaken. A study of the Bible, extending over a period of months, first done by *Hiram Edson, *O.R.L. Crosier, and Frederick Hahn, led a small group of Millerite Adventists to conclude that the two phases of ministry in the Old Testament *sanctuary services were a type of Christ's ministry in the heavenly sanctuary since His ascension, and that Christ had begun a new phase of His ministry in October 1844. Edson, Crosier, and Hahn published their findings in the *Day-Dawn* (Canandaigua, New York) during the winter of 1845-1846 and again as an Extra in the *Day-Star* (Cincinnati, Ohio) of February 7, 1846. Ellen White's first written statement upon this subject came about a year after the conclusions of Edson, Crosier, and Hahn had been published. In a letter to Eli Curtis, April 24, 1847, she wrote, "The Lord shew me in vision, more than one year ago, that Brother Crosier had the true light, on the cleansing of the Sanctuary, etc., and that it was His will, that Brother C. should write out the view which he gave us in the *Day-Star*, Extra, February 7, 1846. I feel fully authorized by the Lord, to recommend that Extra, to every saint" (WLF 12). Here also her role was largely to confirm the conclusions of these brethren, not to initiate them. In later years, when this doctrine seemed not to be as well understood by some Adventist pastors, she repeatedly urged church members to read articles upon

this subject written by the pioneers of the Advent movement (Lt 99, 1905, in CW 26). In 1983 Paul A. Gordon, then associate secretary of the White Estate, collected more than 400 articles on the sanctuary doctrine and related topics published between 1846 and 1905. The anthology he produced, *Pioneer Articles on the Sanctuary, Daniel 8:14, the Judgment, 2300 Days, Year-Day Principle, [and the] Atonement, 1846-1905*, contained 1,009 pages. Although Ellen White received 11 visions on the subject of the heavenly sanctuary between 1845 and 1851, she consistently referred church members to articles written by the pioneers explaining from Scripture the doctrine of the sanctuary. In these articles her visions and writings were never used to back up their views.

Three angels' messages of Revelation 14. The messages proclaimed symbolically by three angels in Revelation 14 form the basis of the Adventist self-understanding and mission. In the first message an angel proclaims the everlasting gospel and the hour of God's judgment to all nations (verses 6, 7). The second message proclaims the fall of Babylon (verse 8), while the third message warns against the mark of the beast (verses 9-11). References to these messages began during the Millerite movement. William Miller and his associates used the imagery of the first angel's message to preach that the time of God's judgment had arrived and that Christ would soon return.

Charles Fitch seems to have been the first to preach on the second angel's message on July 26, 1843. This message referring to the fall of Babylon never really "caught on" among Millerite preachers, although many believers accepted it. Previously Protestants had tended to identify Roman Catholicism with spiritual Babylon. Fitch broadened the category to include contemporary Protestants who refused to accept the doctrine of an imminent Second Advent. As long as the predicted time for the Second Advent was still some years distant, the Millerite movement had been fairly well received by most Protestant denominations. But as the time grew nearer, its radical implications could no longer be ignored, and many churches began harassing and expelling their Millerite members. Fitch's sermon came in reaction to this growing antagonism. Joseph Bates was the first Sabbatarian Adventist minister to articulate and integrate all three messages with the doctrines of the Sabbath and the sanctuary. In his pamphlets published between 1846 and 1848, he argued that the observance of the Sabbath was the *seal of God and that the keeping of Sunday was a *mark of the beast. Similar conclusions were later published by James White in the *Present Truth* (April 1850). During this period of time Ellen White wrote little on the three angels' messages, and her role was limited to endorsing the presentations done by other speakers and writers, with the exception of one vision on the seal of God she received in December 1848 that significantly enhanced Bates' understanding of the subject at that time.

Conditional immortality and annihilation of the wicked. George Storrs (1796-1879), a Methodist minister who became a Millerite preacher in 1842, was the first in the Millerite movement to advocate the unconscious state of human beings in death. It was probably Storrs' ideas that influenced Eunice Harmon, who then shared them with her daughter Ellen, who was about 15 at the time. Ellen's initial reaction was one of strong disapproval; but after a careful study of the biblical evidence, she accepted it (1T 39, 40). Later she became a strong advocate of Storrs' "soul-sleep" doctrine of conditional immortality, and she considered it to be one of the half-dozen "pillar" doctrines of the Seventh-day Adventist

Church (Ms 13, 1889, in CW 30, 31). Her role in promoting it, however, was largely in the nature of endorsing Storrs' views; she did not break any major "new ground."

*The doctrine of *spiritual gifts.* Seventh-day Adventists believe that the gifts of the Holy Spirit mentioned in 1 Corinthians 12 and Ephesians 4:11-13 are to function for the perfecting of the saints and for the edification of the body of Christ until His return. Just as they were needed in the early church to confirm the work of the apostles and to provide guidance in the young congregations, Adventists believe these gifts are also needed today. On the basis of Revelation 12:17 and 19:10 they hold that the gift of prophecy is an identifying mark of the last-day remnant people of God. This gift they believe was manifested in the life and ministry of Ellen G. White. Naturally the point may be raised as to whether this doctrine was adopted in order to validate Ellen White's ministry. In a foreword to volume 1 of her book *Spiritual Gifts* (1858), R. F. Cottrell stated the substance of what has since been the denomination's position in regard to the gift of prophecy as manifested in Ellen White. He recognized the unique position of the Bible as the sole criterion by which all claims to the prophetic gift must be evaluated. With the support of numerous Bible texts, he argued that the Bible itself points to a continuing manifestation of spiritual gifts in the Christian church until the return of Christ and particularly at the end of time. Hence Adventists have argued that while Ellen White's ministry and writings are valued as a genuine gift of the Spirit, her authority is considered secondary to the Bible. One of the earliest and clearest statements regarding what Ellen White believed to be her relationship to the Bible is the following: "I recommend to you, dear reader, the Word of God as the rule of your faith and practise. By that Word we are to be judged. God has, in that Word, promised to give visions [here a reference to her own ministry] in the "*last days*"; not for a new rule of faith, but for the comfort of His people, and to correct those who err from Bible truth" (EW 78).

Between November 1846 and the fall of 1847 Joseph Bates, James and Ellen White, Hiram Edson, and a few other pioneers of Sabbatarian Adventism met at irregular times to articulate the distinctive doctrines of what would become Seventh-day Adventism. During these meetings they studied the Bible, prayed, and sometimes fasted. The pioneers who led out in these meetings were mainly James White and Joseph Bates. Although Ellen White attended, her participation and influence in the discussions were limited. In 1904 she recalled her experience during these conferences: "During this whole time I could not understand the reasoning of the brethren. My mind was locked, as it were, and I could not comprehend the meaning of the scriptures we were studying. This was one of the greatest sorrows of my life" (1SM 207). She went on to explain that sometimes when the brethren were at a standstill in their study, she would have a vision to confirm the understanding of some texts they had arrived at or to point out a mistake in an interpretation. It was only after the participants at these meetings had reached a dead end, so to speak, that her visions played an influential role. That role was limited to guidance and confirmation and did not include the initiation or generation of new doctrines.

See also: Sabbatarian Bible Conferences.

Further reading: M. Burt, "The Historical Background, Interconnected Development, and Integration of the Doctrines of the Sanctuary, the Sabbath, and Ellen G. White's Role in Sabbatarian Adventism From 1844 to 1849" (Ph.D. diss., AU, 2002); P. Gordon,

"Doctrinal Development, Authority, and Ellen White" (EGWE, SDoc); G. Knight, *Joseph Bates: The Real Founder of Seventh-day Adventism* (RHPA, 2004), pp. 101-103, 116, 153, 161, 162; J. Moon, "Wrestling Till Dawn: Close Bible Study and Fervent Prayer Launched This Movement," AR, July 9, 1998; A. L. White, *Ellen G. White, Messenger to the Remnant* (RHPA, 1969), pp. 34-40.

Denis Fortin

DOCTRINES, IMPORTANCE OF. While most of Ellen White's writings dealt with practical counsels and concerns for the well-being of Christians, her understanding of the importance of doctrine encompassed more than abstract ideas and theoretical constructs. On many occasions she alluded to the practical aspects of doctrines and frequently referred to ministers as those who "labor in word and doctrine" (cf. GW 13).

An emphasis on the Bible as the foundation of all doctrine permeates her writings. She did not equate doctrine and Bible but stated that "the Bible is the only rule of faith and doctrine" (FE 126). "God will have a people upon the earth to maintain the Bible, and the Bible only, as the standard of all doctrines and the basis of all reforms. The opinions of learned men, the deductions of science, the creeds or decisions of ecclesiastical councils, as numerous and discordant as are the churches which they represent, the voice of the majority—not one nor all of these should be regarded as evidence for or against any point of religious faith. Before accepting any doctrine or precept, we should demand a plain 'Thus saith the Lord' in its support" (GC 595).

Jesus is presented as the "center of all true doctrine" (CT 453), and the Word of God is the "standard by which all doctrines and theories must be tested" (4SP 214). God's revelation in the Bible and the life of Christ are the only basis for doctrine. In contrast, she warned against using any other foundations for doctrines, including her writings (1SM 41), and urged church members "to unify upon a true, scriptural basis" (1SM 175). Emphasizing the rational aspects of doctrine, she stressed: "The Lord desires that every soul who claims to believe the truth shall have an intelligent knowledge of what is truth" (2SM 392).

In contrast to biblical doctrines, Ellen White warned against false doctrines. She traced to Satan the origin of such false doctrines as the "doctrine of eternal torment as a punishment for sin" (FE 176), as well as the doctrine of the immortality of the soul (Ev 247). She condemned the doctrine of papal supremacy and other false teachings that spread during the Middle Ages (GC 51). Many times she also censured incorrect presentations of justification and sanctification. To withstand the influence and deceptiveness of false doctrines she counseled that "we cannot depend upon the doctrine which comes to our ears, unless we see that it harmonizes with the Word of God" (RH, May 3, 1887, in Ev 590).

Ellen White alluded to the distinctive doctrines of Adventism as the "pillars of our faith, the reasons why we are Seventh-day Adventists" (CG 495). She described these doctrines as the "old landmarks" (CW 30) and "Bible landmarks" (CSW 35). She stressed that doctrine is at the center of the great controversy (PK 625), in which she gives prominence to the doctrine of the Second Coming. Other central doctrines are the Sabbath and the "solid pillar" of the sanctuary doctrine (RH, May 25, 1905). Other biblical doctrines that she emphasized include: conversion, the resurrection, righteousness by faith, and sanctification. In her last years she spent much time describing how doctrines relate to salvation. She stressed that "justification by faith in Christ will be made manifest in transformation of character. This is the sign to the world of the truth of the doctrines we profess. The daily evidence that we are a living church is seen in the fact that we are practicing the Word. A living testimony goes forth to the world in consistent Christian action" (6BC 1071).

Efrain Velazquez

DOCUMENT FILE (DF). Materials not authored by Ellen White but that contribute to an understanding of her ministry, her teachings, and the history of the Seventh-day Adventist Church are referred to as documents and are located in the document file of the Ellen G. White Estate. While original documents, such as Ellen White's ministerial credentials, are kept in the vault at the White Estate office in Silver Spring, Maryland, photocopies of the most significant documents have been made for all the research centers around the world and may be accessed online on the White Estate Web site: http://drc.whiteestate.org. The document file includes biographical files; historical materials; and materials on theological matters, church and state relationships, diet, the Scriptures, education, the gospel ministry, eschatology, and other topics that relate to Christian experience and Christian conduct.

Robert Olson

DOOR, OPEN AND SHUT, see **SHUT DOOR.**

DOUBT. In a letter to A. T. Jones in 1905 Ellen White warned: "Let not your lips utter a sentence of doubt. Do not come before the people with an uncertain sound. Know what is truth and proclaim truth. Christ's teaching was always positive in its nature. Never, never utter sentiments of doubt. Bear with a certain voice an affirmative message" (Lt 65, 1905, in UL 58). While for Ellen White Christianity is a revealed and reasonable religion, she also understood that at times *faith must precede reason and that not all occasions for doubts can be removed from one's religious experience (PP 432). "Those who wish to doubt will have opportunity; while those who really desire to know the truth will find plenty of evidence on which to rest their faith" (SC 105; cf. 1SM 28; GC 527; 3T 258). She assumed doubt to be destructive to one's faith in God and in the church. For her, doubt is a spiritual issue in the great controversy between good and evil; it is "the special work of Satan to lead fallen man to rebel against God's government" (3SG 94). To illustrate the ultimate consequences of doubt, Ellen White used the metaphor of shipwreck. "Those who love to dwell in the atmosphere of doubt and questioning unbelief can have the unenviable privilege. God gives sufficient evidence for the candid mind to believe; but he who turns from the weight of evidence because there are a few things which he cannot make plain to his finite understanding will be left in the cold, chilling atmosphere of unbelief and questioning doubts, and will make *shipwreck of faith*. . . . Jesus never praised unbelief; He never commended doubts" (4T 232, 233; italics supplied).

In contrast to negative doubt, however, Ellen White saw the benefit of having an inquiring mind, searching for truth, and being able to discern errors as found in the experience of the Berean Jews (cf. Acts 17:11; AA 231, 232). The antidote to doubt is faith and receiving the light God shines upon the believer. "There is but one course for those to pursue who honestly desire to be freed from doubts. Instead of questioning and caviling concerning that which they do not

understand, let them give heed to the light which already shines upon them, and they will receive greater light. Let them do every duty which has been made plain to their understanding, and they will be enabled to understand and perform those of which they are now in doubt" (GC 528).

A related issue is the emotional sense of God-forsakenness, closely related to depression, and to the spiritual expression "dark night of the soul," something similar to the kind of experience Elijah lived through after he received threats from Jezabel (1 Kings 19). Ellen White knew this subject by personal experience. Chapter 3 of an early autobiography is tellingly titled "Feelings of Despair" (2SG 15-21; later in *Life Sketches* the same chapter is titled "Strivings Against Doubt"). The chapter shows what can happen to devout, serious-minded believers who are seeking to please God. She confessed that during her teen years, "many times the wish arose that I had never been born" (1T 25). Much of her difficulty she traced to the doctrine of an ever-burning hell. But even after she became convinced of the nonimmortality of the soul, she was still vulnerable to depression and despair.

When she was called to her prophetic ministry at age 17 to tell others her visions, the burden became so heavy that, in her words, "I coveted death as a release from the responsibilities that were crowding upon me. At length the sweet peace I had so long enjoyed left me, and despair again pressed upon my soul. My prayers all seemed vain, and my faith was gone. Words of comfort, reproof, or encouragement were alike to me; for it seemed that no one could understand me but God, and He had forsaken me. The company of believers in Portland were ignorant concerning the exercises of my mind that had brought me into this state of despondency; but they knew that for some reason my mind had become depressed, and they felt that this was sinful on my part, considering the gracious manner in which the Lord had manifested Himself to me" (*ibid.* 63, 64). "I feared that God had taken His favor from me forever. As I thought of the light that had formerly blessed my soul, it seemed doubly precious in contrast with the darkness that now enveloped me. Meetings were held at my father's house, but my distress of mind was so great that I did not attend them for some time. My burden grew heavier until the agony of my spirit seemed more than I could bear" (*ibid.* 64).

In another example (from 1862) White described how "the powers of darkness gather about the soul and shut Jesus from our sight, and at times we can only wait in sorrow and amazement until the cloud passes over. These seasons are sometimes terrible. Hope seems to fail, and despair seizes upon us. In these dreadful hours we must learn to trust, to depend solely upon the merits of the atonement, and in all our helpless unworthiness cast ourselves upon the merits of the crucified and risen Savior. We shall never perish while we do this—*never!* When light shines on our pathway, it is no great thing to be strong in the strength of grace. But to wait patiently in hope when clouds envelop us and all is dark requires faith and submission which causes our will to be swallowed up in the will of God. We are too quickly discouraged, and earnestly cry for the trial to be removed from us, when we should plead for patience to endure and grace to overcome" (*ibid.* 309, 310).

Concerning the experience of Elijah, she wrote, "Into the experience of all there come times of keen disappointment and utter discouragement—days when sorrow is the portion, and it is hard to believe that God is still the kind benefactor of His earthborn children; days when troubles harass the soul, till death seems preferable to life. It is then that many lose their hold on God and are brought into the slavery of doubt, the bondage of unbelief. Could we at such times discern with spiritual insight the meaning of God's providences we should see angels seeking to save us from ourselves, striving to plant our feet upon a foundation more firm than the everlasting hills, and new faith, new life, would spring into being" (PK 162).

Emotional depression, spiritual despair, and doctrinal doubts are all experiences that can affect true believers. Some personalities are more vulnerable to one kind of experience and some to another. In some cases these experiences are also attacks of the enemy, who seeks the destruction and ruin of lives committed to God. The important thing is to recognize these phenomena for what they are and to rely totally on God for grace and strength to endure.

Further reading: SC 105-113; R. W. Coon, "The Danger of Doubt and the Nature of Faith" (lecture outline, 1996, DF 331-e, CAR); P. C. Jarnes, "The Problem of Doubt" (research paper, SDA Theological Seminary, 1940, DF 331-e, CAR).

Denis Fortin

DRAMA AND THEATER. Ellen White used the terms *drama* and *theater* in different contexts. In a figurative way, she used the term *drama* in the context of parental education of children, especially daughters: children must be prepared to "take their place upon the stage of action . . . [and] act their part in the drama of life" (HR, May 1, 1873). Overfond mothers are warned to guard themselves from spoiling the character of their daughters, and encouraged to train them in self-denial, physical and domestic labor, orderliness, economy, and responsibility, rather than solely in the arts and humanities. Such training will prepare young women appropriately for the challenges of everyday life and help them to become efficient wives and mothers.

Also in a figurative sense, Ellen White believed our world is the "theater" of the last great "drama" of humankind. The focus of the last scene in this "drama" is deception, as Satan will try to impersonate the coming Christ (cf. 2 Thess. 2:8, 9). In this sense the church is the "theater" of God's grace. She applies the term *theater* to groups of people who play a role in this last conflict: the faithful people of God become a "theater unto the world" as witnesses of God's goodness unto men and the angels (cf. 1 Cor. 4:9); the church becomes the theater of God's grace in the great controversy (AG 338); and the fallen world is appointed as "a theater on which would be fought out the grand struggle between good and evil" (*ibid.* 36).

Yet White's predominant use of *drama* is in the context of theater as a mode of amusement. Although in her time, evangelistic meetings were often held in theaters as the only places available for larger public meetings, she expresses many concerns with the theater as a center of amusement. She deals with the threefold issue of the influence of its setting, the indecent content of the programs, and the delusive character of the experience. Her references to theater are often given in association with gambling, liquor drinking, dancing, card playing, horse racing, reveling, dissipation, and idolatry and, therefore, imply a demoralizing and debasing effect. She points to theater's tendency to and appearance of evil, as it glorifies immorality and educates the mind to "familiarity with sin" (AH 406). The theater numbs sensitivities, breaks down the barriers of principle, and opens the door to sensual indulgence (4T 578; AH 516). The addictive character of theater fascinates the imagination (2MCP 590), stimulates passions

(COL 54), and intoxicates the mind with unnatural excitement (RH, Feb. 20, 1866). It creates a "fever of unrest" that undermines the desire and capacity for a life of usefulness (4T 578). The theater experience leads people to forget God and lose sight of eternal interests. Health, intellect, and spirituality are squandered, and the individual is turned away from righteousness and holiness, from the noble and pure (RH, Mar. 31, 1896).

A study of theater and drama in the United States from the 1860s on confirms White's descriptions and provides a helpful context. In speaking about theater, she refers first of all to a distinctively American form of popular theatrical entertainment at that time. Her early descriptions fit especially the western United States situation, where theaters developed during the 1850s California gold rush alongside saloons, gambling rooms, and bordellos; often all three events were housed under the same roof, with the theatergoer subjected to the peripheral activities surrounding the theater. Theater programs were typically a mixture of drama and variety shows thrown together in a same evening program: scenes from high tragedy (e.g., Shakespeare) alternated with farce, burlesque, blackface minstrelsy, circus, etc.; often the latter consisted in satirizing the former. Numbers included medleys of songs, drama recitation, pantomimes, dance, comic imitations, tableaux with scenes of nudity, and acrobatics. Many songs and imitations were of a very coarse nature, and scenes of indecency became favorites. Only in later years were there efforts to "clean up" this type of theater to change it to a traditional family entertainment. Attempts to separate serious and burlesque elements in theater, as it was practiced in the eastern United States, were interpreted as elitism in conflict with the egalitarian ideals of the nation. The "variety show" character of theater was purposefully cultivated in contrast to the "European" opera and classical theater.

While the general environment of theater in the United States may have changed today, Ellen White's opposition to theater as entertainment was not based primarily on the theater as location or even as genre, but on the moral content of the entertainment presented. Therefore, the moral principles of her critique of theater and drama still apply to dramatic entertainment today, whether acted live on stage or in the many productions of the movie industry, television, video, DVD, etc. Whenever such presentations lead viewers into vicarious enjoyment of or participation in sexual immorality, violence, greed, deception, intemperance, disrespect for parents and other legitimate authorities, or the trivializing of sacred things, the moral principles of Scripture are violated (Phil. 4:8; Matt. 5:28; 1 Cor. 10:6; Ps. 101:3; Col. 3:5-10; 2 Cor. 10:5; Isa. 5:20). The increasing sophistication of modern technology does not lessen, but rather increases, the impact of the content presented, so that it becomes more harmful rather than less so.

Beyond White's concerns for the many negative influences of the theater and its environment, another point in her speaking out against it lies in her disappointment with the failed aspirations of multitudes. She saw people seeking in theater entertainment, freedom, joy, and peace, trying to "satisfy the restless craving" of their hearts, a longing that can be satisfied only by God (ST, Mar. 23, 1904). She condemned this pervasive phenomenon of delusion and deception.

Another of Ellen White's concerns has to do with theatrical behavior in religious contexts. Most often she predominantly uses the word "theatrical" to refer to a set of attitudes and behavior in the context of public meetings, such as the pulpit, temperance meetings,

evangelistic meetings, Sabbath school, and fund-raiser meetings. Many of her references to theatrical attitudes deal with the preacher's behavior in the pulpit. White especially denounces "assuming attitudes and expressions calculated for effect," "undignified, boisterous actions," and "coarseness" during which preachers "storm, halloo, [and] jump up and down" (Ev 640; GW 172; RH, Aug. 8, 1878). Such behavior was typical of nineteenth-century camp meeting preaching that was characterized by a highly pragmatic and individualistic approach favoring spontaneity and excitement in order to "arouse" the congregation. With the sermon as the climax of the service came the temptation for exhibitionism and the spectacular. In further comments about theatrical attitudes in preaching, White also condemns a "spirit of frivolity" that she contrasts with genuine cheerfulness; or the "exhibition of self" by mixing the comical with the religious through a careless, clownish, and irreverent manner that misrepresents Christ, instead of preaching the Word in a way to create a solemn impression (GW 18, 132; FE 462; ST, Oct. 13, 1890). Rather than using anecdotes to amuse the congregation, the preacher should strive for qualities such as dignity, simplicity, goodness, and loveliness. She furthermore speaks out against the use of "smartness upon the stage" in order to show off, or the desire to gain success through the cultivation of sensationalism and outward display, and using cheap nonsense to make meetings attractive and interesting (5T 127).

What is condemned in all these theatrical attitudes is a "surface" approach that confuses the senses and eclipses truth. White encourages the use of sensible and rational methods characterized by vital experience, true piety, and humble godliness. Through the cultivation of expressions that elevate and ennoble, the intellect will be strengthened and the morals will be confirmed. Simplicity, humility, graceful dignity, and wisdom should be the qualities that govern the presentation of truth so that the hearers might be impressed favorably.

Further reading: D. I. Davis, "Hotbed of Immorality: Seventh-day Adventists and the Battle Creek Theater in the 1880s," *Adventist Heritage* 7, no. 1 (Spring 1982): 20-33; F. H. Londré and D. J. Watermeier, *The History of North American Theater* (New York: Continuum, 1999); B. McArthur, "Amusing the Masses," in *The World of Ellen G. White*, ed. Gary Land (RHPA 1987), pp. 176-191; R. Nye, *The Unembarrassed Muse: The Popular Arts in America* (New York: The Dial Press, 1970); R. Sanjek, *American Popular Music and Its Business: The First Four Hundred Years* (New York: Oxford University Press, 1988); C. Scriven and M. Scriven, "Another Look at Ellen White on Music," *Spectrum* 10, no. 2 (August 1979): 42-52; "Dramatic Productions in SDA Institutions" (EGWE, SDoc).

Lilianne Doukhan

DREAMS, see **VISIONS OF ELLEN G. WHITE.**

DRESS AND ADORNMENT. Ellen White devoted much attention, in extent and detail, to the issues of dress and adornment, partly because of her theological understanding of human nature as wholistic. This essential unity of all human dimensions creates a reciprocal influence and interdependence between our *being* and our *doing.* In other words, who we are (being) and what we do (doing) are closely and reciprocally related, and affect each other for good or for evil. That is, Christianity is not only confessed or even professed—it is a lived and practiced lifestyle (James 1:22).

Ellen White believed that invisible Christian virtues will become obvious in the visible image we portray. "We judge of a person's character by the style of dress worn. A modest, godly woman will dress modestly. A refined taste, a cultivated mind, will be revealed in the choice of a simple, appropriate attire. The young women who break away from the slavery of fashion will be ornaments to society. The one who is simple and unpretending in her dress and in her manners shows that she understands that a true woman is characterized by moral worth" (MYP 353; also 7BC 941).

The line of demarcation between society and its lifestyle dress and the church and its lifestyle and dress must be obvious (MYP 349), yet the difference must not be intended to shock for the sake of effect. "Christians should not take pains to make themselves gazing-stocks by dressing differently from the world. But if, in accordance with their faith and duty in respect to their dressing modestly and healthfully, they find themselves out of fashion, they should not change their dress in order to be like the world." But difference from the world is not to be maintained for the sake of difference. "If the world introduces a modest, convenient, and healthful mode of dress, which is in accordance with the Bible, it will not change our relation to God to adopt such a style of dress" (*ibid.* 350).

Christian balance between slovenliness and following daring models of fashion is the secret of a positive influence (*ibid.* 349; 1T 464). But how can we achieve this balance?

For Ellen White, self-examination, paying attention to our wishes and evaluating them, is of paramount importance. Intentions of the heart are involved in the process of choosing our wardrobe, and people perceive these intentions through our appearance. She comments: "Dear youth, a disposition in you to dress according to the fashion, and to wear lace and gold and artificials for display, will not recommend to others your religion or the truth that you profess. People of discernment will look upon your attempts to beautify the external as proof of weak minds and proud hearts. . . . In no better way can you let your light shine to others than in your simplicity of dress and deportment. You may show to all that, in comparison with eternal things, you place a proper estimate upon the things of this life" (3T 376; see also 4T 645). "The influence of believers would be tenfold greater if men and women who accept the truth, who have been formerly careless and slack in their habits, would be so elevated and sanctified through the truth as to observe habits of neatness, order, and good taste in their dress" (MYP 349, 350).

A number of basic principles in regard to dress and adornment are present in Ellen White's writings. Modesty appears as one of the most important principles to guide Christian taste in dress (ibid. 350; MH 287; CSW 20, 21; 1T 464); it will "guard virtue" (2T 458) and show humility of mind (CG 144). Health is another crucial guide for appearance. In an era when articles of clothing were used to reshape a woman's profile in conformity with culture-imposed ideals, Ellen White advocated a reform in dress. Thousands of women "are dissatisfied with nature's arrangements," she wrote, "and in their earnest efforts to correct nature, and bring her to their ideas of gentility, they break down her work, and leave her a mere wreck" (2SM 473). In Ellen White's time even children were subjected to heavy hoops in dress, tight clothing preventing the free circulation of blood, and boots with thin soles incapable of providing the necessary warmth (ibid. 470). "The skirt that sweeps the ground" is labeled by Ellen White as "uncleanly, uncomfortable, inconvenient, unhealthful" (MH 291). It uses superfluous material, it hangs heavy on the hips, it constrains freedom of breathing, and it causes a number of ailments (ibid. 291-293; see also Ed 199).

Economy in the selection of clothes must show a healthy common sense. Clothing made with materials of inferior quality may not show good business sense. Durability (ChS 28) and good material are to be preferred (CG 414).

In their dress Christians must also fit within the age in which they live. There is no virtue in looking outdated: "Let our sisters dress plainly, as many do, having dress of good, durable material, appropriate for this age, and let not the dress question fill the mind" (ibid.). But clothing must also be appropriate for the kind of work we engage in, be of good taste, and be adapted for the season of the year and the kind of work or activity (1T 425, 464; 2T 532). Other principles found in her writings include comfort (MH 382; ML 138), neatness (CG 424, 425, 461; ChS 28, 29; 4T 72), plainness (CG 107, 462; 2SM 438), simplicity (CG 107, 424, 425; ChS 28, 29), and tidiness (FE 156).

In addressing the question of adornment Ellen White rarely isolated jewelry from all other forms of self-display. To her, the fundamental principles on adornment found in the Bible present the proper stand on true beauty. Often quoting 1 Peter 3:3-5, Ellen White urged her readers to comply "with the injunctions of God's Word" (4T 644) and not follow the customs of the world (Ev 270, 271). Instead of giving the message to onlookers, "Look at me, admire me," the Christian should choose simplicity in appearance (4T 645). In 1 Peter 3 "the apostle presents the inward adorning, in contrast with the outward, and tells us what the great God values. The outward is corruptible. But the meek and quiet spirit, the development of a beautifully symmetrical character, will never decay. It is an adornment which is not perishable. In the sight of the Creator of everything that is valuable, lovely, and beautiful, it is declared to be of great price" (ML 123).

For Ellen White, dress and adornment also have a moral influence. "The love of dress endangers the morals and makes woman the opposite of the Christian lady characterized by modesty and sobriety. Showy, extravagant dress too often encourages lust in the heart of the wearer and awakens base passions in the heart of the beholder. God sees that the ruin of the character is frequently preceded by the indulgence of pride and vanity in dress. He sees that the costly apparel stifles the desire to do good" (4T 645).

One of Ellen White's most basic principles in regard to simplicity in dress and adornment urged Christian believers to invest their resources in human needs and mission activities instead of costly dress and apparels. "The more means persons expend in dress, the less they can have to feed the hungry and clothe the naked; and the streams of beneficence, which should be constantly flowing, are dried up" (*ibid.*). "There are many whose hearts have been so hardened by prosperity that they forget God, and forget the wants of their fellow man. Professed Christians adorn themselves with jewelry, laces, costly apparel, while the Lord's poor suffer for the necessaries of life" (2BC 1012). "Every dollar of our accumulation is stamped with the image and superscription of God. As long as there are hungry ones in God's world to be fed, naked ones to be clothed, souls perishing for the bread and water of salvation, every unnecessary indulgence, every overplus of capital, pleads for the poor and the naked" (WM 269).

Further reading: M. M. Kiš, "Christian Lifestyle and Behavior," in R. Dederen, ed., *Handbook of Seventh-day Adventist Theology* (RHPA, 2000), pp. 675-723; D. E. Rebok,

Believe His Prophets (RHPA, 1956), pp. 249-276; SHM65 112-130, 165-169, 441-445.

Miroslav M. Kiš

DRESS REFORM. The nineteenth century was an age of reforms in the United States, and Adventists advocated many of them. Ellen White brought the question of dress reform to the attention of Seventh-day Adventists in the early 1860s (and more specifically in 1865) in the last of a series of six articles in *Health: or How to Live* (2SM 410, 473-479). "My sisters, there is need of a dress reform among us" she urged (*ibid.* 473).

The typical dress worn by American women during this period was characterized by long, trailing skirts that literally swept the streets, tightly fitting corsets, and multiple layers of petticoats under the skirt and on top of a large hoop. Such a tight, heavy, cumbersome, and unsanitary dress style seriously affected the health of women. In the 1850s an alternative style of dress was suggested by some reformers as an attempt to better women's conditions. The "reform dress," or American costume, as it was called, first advocated by Elizabeth Miller, Elizabeth Cady Stanton, and Amelia Bloomer, consisted of a short skirt and long, loose trousers worn under the skirt. Sometimes the trousers, also called "bloomers," were buttoned at the ankles. Praise and commendation on the one hand, and opposition and sarcasm on the other, were the polarized responses to the dress reformers. Although the popular agitation over dress reform and the peculiar styles of dress advocated lasted only two or three decades, the principles for which these reformers contended ultimately prevailed.

Ellen White began to speak about dress reform 13 years after the "reform dress" was suggested. The first stage in Seventh-day Adventist dress reform consisted simply of a rejection of the hoop. "Hoops," wrote Ellen White, "were an abomination, and every Sabbathkeeper's influence should be a rebuke to this ridiculous fashion" (RH, Aug. 27, 1861). The fact that spiritualists were among the advocates of the dress reform inhibited Adventists from readily accepting the suggested American costume. Ellen White found it an "immodest apparel, wholly unfitted for the modest, humble followers of Christ" (1T 421).

The next stage was the development of an Adventist style of reform dress. Following her visit to Dr. James Jackson's "Our Home on the Hillside" in Dansville, New York, in 1864, Ellen White wrote to Ransom and Aurora Lockwood regarding dress reform: "They have all styles of dress here. Some are very becoming, if not so short. We shall get patterns from this place and I think we can get out a style of dress more healthful than we now wear and yet not be bloomer or the American costume. Our dresses according to my idea should be from four to six inches shorter than now worn and should in no case reach lower than the top of the heel of the shoe and could be a little shorter even than this with all modesty. I am going to get up a style of dress on my own hook which will accord perfectly with that which has been shown me. Health demands it. Our feeble women must dispense with heavy skirts and tight waists if they value health" (Lt 6, 1864, in 5MR 380). Her objections to the conventional dress were based largely on health principles. She felt strongly that the unnecessarily heavy weight of conventional dresses were injurious to a woman's abdominal organs, the tight-fitting corsets interfered with proper breathing, and the trailing of long skirts in the dirt of streets gathered its filth into homes and spread diseases (1T 459). On the other hand, she felt the American costume was unbecoming for a woman and too short.

As she advocated such a reform among Adventist women, Ellen White encountered many unpleasant experiences that eventually led her to lay aside the promotion of this entire issue. First came the question of how long, or how short, the dress should be. Many intimated from her estimate that a dress "should be from four to six inches [10 to 15 centimeters] shorter than now worn" (i.e., about nine inches [23 centimeters] from the floor) to be a direct revelation from God and, therefore, the divinely revealed length of a woman's dress. Any departure from this length was considered a transgression of God's will. However, Ellen White explained that the exact length of the skirt had not been revealed to her in vision and that she had estimated the approximate length. The type of dress she saw "as proper, modest, and healthful" had a skirt that "cleared the filth of the street and sidewalk a few inches under all circumstances, such as ascending and descending steps" (3SM 278). Furthermore, she explained that "some have supposed that the very pattern given was the pattern that all were to adopt. This is not so. But something as simple as this would be the best we could adopt under the circumstances. No one precise style has been given me as the exact rule to guide all in their dress" (ibid. 254).

But the experience that led her to put aside the promotion of this issue was the very attitude of church members. "While many of our sisters accepted this reform from principle," she explained, "others opposed the simple, healthful style of dress which it advocated. It required much labor to introduce this reform among our people. It was not enough to present before our sisters the advantages of such a dress and to convince them that it would meet the approval of God. Fashion had so strong a hold upon them that they were slow to break away from its control, even to obey the dictates of reason and conscience. And many who professed to accept the reform made no change in their wrong habits of dress, except in shortening the skirts and clothing the limbs. Nor was this all. Some who adopted the reform were not content to show by example the advantages of the dress, giving, when asked, their reasons for adopting it, and letting the matter rest there. They sought to control others' conscience by their own. If they wore it, others must put it on. They forgot that none were to be compelled to wear the reform dress. It was not my duty to urge the subject upon my sisters" (4T 635, 636).

As time passed, the prevailing styles of women's dress changed for the better. In 1897 Ellen White advised that "the dress question is not to be our present truth. . . . Follow the customs of dress so far as they conform to health principles. Let our sisters dress plainly, as many do, having the dress of good, durable material, appropriate for this age, and let not the dress question fill the mind" (Ms 167, 1897, in 4Bio 333).

Further reading: 1T 456-466; M. W. Campbell, "The Development of the 'Reform Dress' Among Seventh-day Adventists, 1864-1876" (unpublished paper, CAR); R. W. Coon, "The 'Dress' Message" (lecture outline, Feb. 27, 1996, CAR); SHM65 112-130, 166-169; F. D. Nichol, *Ellen G. White and Her Critics* (RHPA, 1951), pp. 136-160; D. E. Rebok, *Believe His Prophets* (RHPA, 1956), pp. 249-276; "Seventh-day Adventists and the Reform Dress" (EGWE, SDoc).

Denis Fortin

DRUGS. Drugs are chemicals obtained from plants (digitalis from foxglove, quinine from cinchona bark), animals (insulin, thyroid hormone), and the earth (iron, copper), or are synthesized in a laboratory (sulfanilamide, antihistamine). The words "medicine" and "drug" are used interchangeably and are used for any substance or chemical used therapeutically for the treatment and prevention of disease, and for the relief of pain and suffering. Whether an anticancer agent or an antibiotic, a medicinal herb or a synthetic chemical, a hormone or an antimalarial—all are classed as medicines or drugs.

Ellen White wrote extensively on drug medication, and with few exceptions her comments were condemnatory. But was she speaking of all drug medications, or was she referring to some specific group or class of therapeutic agents? How did she herself identify the word "drug"? The answer is to be found in her reply to a letter from *Edgar Caro, a third-year medical student. Caro wrote, "Several of the students are in doubt as to the meaning of the word 'drug' as mentioned in [*Health: or] How to Live. Does it refer only to the stronger medicines as mercury, strychnine, arsenic, and such poisons, the things we medical students call 'drugs,' or does it also include the simpler remedies, as potassium, iodine, squills, etc.? We know that our success will be proportionate to our adherence to God's methods. For this reason I have asked the above question" (Edgar Caro to EGW, Aug. 15, 1893, in 2SM 278). Caro inquires about two classes of medicinals: stronger medicines or drugs, as he and the medical students called them, and simpler remedies. Which did she have in mind in her comments in *How to Live*? Obviously Caro was trying to be very specific in his inquiry, and Ellen White's reply is equally precise.

"Your questions, I will say, are answered largely, if not definitely, in *How to Live*" (2SM 279). Notice, she refers him back to *How to Live*. In her section in this book she describes seeing three sick individuals. In each case they were administered one or more "drug poisons." The patients all died. The drugs prescribed were opium (which contains morphine and codeine), calomel (a mercury compound), and nux vomica (strychnine). Clearly the three medicines she refers to represented the type of agent she considered "drugs" and was condemning. She then reinforces her answer by accepting Caro's grouping of remedies: "Drug poisons mean the articles which you have mentioned" (*ibid.*). The medical student had called them "stronger medicines" or "drugs." Ellen White referred to them as "drug poisons." She clearly agreed with Caro as to what he and others called "drugs." There was some overlapping between the examples each gave, but four different drugs are named: opium, strychnine, arsenic, and mercury. Elsewhere she names quinine (4aSG [1864] 139). It seems quite clear that between Caro and Ellen White five drugs are specifically named.

In a final question, Caro's inquiry used the adjective *only*: "Does it refer *only* to the stronger medicines ... or does it also include the simpler remedies?" She answers, "Drug poisons mean the articles which you have mentioned" (italics supplied). Her reply excludes the simpler, less-harmful remedies.

Ellen White was among the drug/health reformers of the latter half of the nineteenth century who, along with others, attacked the unbelievably harsh and severe procedures then commonly employed by physicians. To bleed the patient was the first step in a deadly routine. The blood was drained from the sick in large and repeated quantities, often removing from half to three fourths of all the blood in the body. At the same time, the patient was vomited, purged, expectorated, sweated, urinated, and often blistered. The agents used were strong, harsh, and noxious. Those commonly used for catharsis were called "drastics" because of the severity of their actions—

severe cramping and the stools a bloody flux.

Perhaps the mercury compound calomel was the most commonly used agent of that era. "One physician reminisced that in the early decades of the century, 'when a practitioner was puzzled about the administration of any medicine in a disease, it was deemed perfectly proper for him to prescribe a dose of calomel; which he did conscientiously, with well satisfied assurance, that if he did not give the exact medicine adapted to the case, he could not be far wrong!' Many physicians believed that omission of calomel in desperate cases was tantamount to abandoning the patient without a final saving effort" (Nathaniel Chapman, *Elements of Therapeutics and Materia Medica*, 6th ed. [Philadelphia: Casey and Lea, 1831], p. 50).

Unfortunately calomel (mercurous chloride) was often administered in large and prolonged doses, so that chronic mercury poisoning was all too common. "The mouth feels unusually hot, and is sometimes sensible of a coppery or metallic taste; the gums are swollen, red, and tender; ulcers make their appearance and spread in all directions, the saliva is thick and stringy, one has that peculiar, offensive odor characteristic of mercurial disease; the tongue is swollen and stiff, and there is some fever, with derangement of the secretions. The disease progressing, it destroys every part that it touches, until the lips, the cheeks, and even the bones have been eaten away before death comes to the sufferer's relief. . . . This happens when mercury performs *a cure*" (W. G. Rothstein, *American Physicians in the Nineteenth Century* [Baltimore: Johns Hopkins University Press, 1985], pp. 50, 51).

Notice the following comment from Ellen White: "Preparations of mercury and calomel taken into the system *ever retain their poisonous strength as long as there is a particle of it left in the system. . . .* All are better off without these dangerous mixtures. Miserable sufferers, with disease in almost every form, misshapen by suffering, with dreadful ulcers, and pains in the bones, loss of teeth, loss of memory, and impaired sight, are to be seen almost everywhere. They are victims of poisonous preparations" (4aSG 139; italics supplied).

Ellen White's condemnation of "drugs" was directed to this class of agents: strong, harsh, and poisonous. Today they are no longer used.

See also: Herbal Remedies; Natural Remedies; Simple Remedies.

Further reading: M. G. Hardinge, *A Physician Explains Ellen White's Counsel on Drugs, Herbs, and Natural Remedies* (RHPA, 2001).

Mervyn G. Hardinge

EARLY WRITINGS OF ELLEN G. WHITE (PPPA, RHPA, 1882, 1906, 1945, 1963, 2000). A republication of Ellen White's first three books: *A Sketch of the Christian Experience and Views of Ellen G. White* (1851); * *Supplement to the Experience and Views of Ellen G. White* (1854); and *Spiritual Gifts*, volume 1 (1858). The first reprinting of these books was made in 1882 in two small volumes and included some editorial changes and the additions of footnotes and two dreams (one of Ellen White and one of William Miller). These two small volumes were reissued as a single volume the same year under the title *Early Writings*. In 1906 the type was reset to print the third edition, which had a wide distribution. The paging for this edition became the standard for all reference work. The fourth edition of *Early Writings* was published in 1945. Modern spelling and current forms of punctuation were employed, and a new preface reviewed briefly the history of the book. The fifth edition (1963) added a historical prologue (pp. vii-xxxii) to furnish the reader with a

knowledge of the times and circumstances of the various parts of the book and added several appendix notes (pp. 297-304) to explain expressions and situations not so well understood now as at the time of the writing. The preface was updated in the 2000 edition, but no changes were made to the text of the book.

Experience and Views presents Ellen White's first autobiographical sketch, briefly tracing her experience through the Advent movement of 1840-1844. Then follow a number of early visions, many of which first appeared in print in broadside or periodical article form. The *Supplement* explains certain expressions of the earlier work that had been misunderstood or misconstrued, and gives additional counsel to the church. *Spiritual Gifts*, volume 1, is the first published account of the cosmic conflict between Christ and Satan. This book is cherished for its vivid descriptions and its compactness, touching only on the more salient points. In succeeding years this brief account of the conflict was greatly amplified in the four volumes of *The Spirit of Prophecy* (1870-1884) and in the *Conflict of the Ages Series* (1888-1917).

Denis Fortin

EASTER, see **HOLIDAYS.**

ECHO PUBLISHING COMPANY. First denominational publishing house in Australia. Within a few weeks of the first Adventist missionaries' arrival in Australia in 1885 the publication of a paper began in the rented "Burnham House" in North Fitzroy, Melbourne. By 1889 this arrangement was no longer adequate, and land was purchased in Best Street, North Fitzroy. The Echo Publishing Company Limited was established in April of that year in a new three-story building. The economy was depressed in the early 1890s, but the press remained busy and developed a reputation for quality work—to the point where it became the official publisher for His Excellency Lord Brassey, K.C.B., the governor of the State of Victoria. By 1889 the Echo Publishing Company employed 83 people and had become the third-largest Adventist publishing house in the world. Even though the company prospered it had periods of difficulty, and Ellen White, who took a great interest in its activities, was forthright in upholding the mission of the institution.

In 1903 the board of the Echo Publishing Company proposed moving to a rural location in support of the views of Ellen White, who consistently advocated country living. While it was acknowledged that such a move would cost the company its commercial printing—about two thirds of its production—the board believed the time had come to devote the full energy of the press to denominational work. In early 1906 the press equipment was moved to Warburton, 50 miles (80 kilometers) north of Melbourne. Many employees bought large lots of land in the new community in order to grow food, for they were convinced that with the loss of commercial work there would be periods of only part-time employment. However, in spite of the financial challenges and the difficulty of obtaining materials during World War I, the publishing house prospered, and the early fears of its workforce were never realized. With the move to Warburton came a new name—Signs of the Times Publishing Association. Later the name was changed again to the current Signs Publishing Company.

Further reading: Ms 13, 1891; Ms 60, 1898; N. P. Clapham, ed., *Seventh-day Adventists in the South Pacific 1885-1985* (Warburton: Signs Pub. Co., 1985), pp. 60-65; documents in DF 57a; *SDA Encyclopedia* (1996), vol. 11, pp. 610, 611.

Lester D. Devine

ECSTATIC EXPERIENCES. Religious enthusiasm found plentiful expression during the American Second Great Awakening that began before 1800 and peaked during the 1820s. The last wave of these revivals, expressed in the Millerite movement of the 1840s, drew upon such enthusiasm. Sabbatarian Adventists, inheritors of these traditions, sought meaning from such practices both in religious worship (i.e., prostration, swooning, and shouting) and in supernatural manifestations (i.e., visions, speaking in tongues, dreams, and miraculous healings). Some were considered genuine expressions of the Holy Spirit by early Sabbatarian Adventists, while others were denounced as the self-induced frenzy of fanatics.

There was nothing more troubling for postdisappointment Millerites than supernatural manifestations. These phenomena were commonplace in New England and were personified by people such as *William Foy, Emily Clemons, *Hazen Foss, and eventually Ellen Harmon (later White), to name only a few. Many such claims by visionaries led William Miller and those at the 1845 Albany, New York, Conference to dismiss wholesale such persons as "enthusiasts" or "fanatics." This led to initial hesitation on the part of Ellen Harmon to share the visionary messages she received, and when she did, to distinguish herself from other visionaries.

Quite often Harmon described how she was so "overpowered by the Spirit of God as to lose all strength" in conjunction with her early visionary experiences (1T 44). References to religious worship often included descriptions of people who were slain in the Spirit, "prostrated as one dead" while those around "stood weeping" (*ibid.* 45; cf. 2SG 221). She described some experiences in which "the power of God came upon us like a mighty rushing wind. All [present] arose upon their feet and praised God with a loud voice. . . . The voice of weeping could not be told from the voice of shouting. It was a triumphant time. . . . I never witnessed such a powerful time before" (Lt 28, 1850, in 16MR 206, 207). James White described such religious experiences as "Holy Ghost times" when God made Himself near. Similar experiences are recorded by other early Adventist leaders, such as *Hiram Edson, *E.L.H. Chamberlain, and *Joseph Bates, to name a few. The worldview of these early Sabbatarian Adventists included a conscious awareness of supernatural forces. Believers were "attacked" by Satan, but often left meetings "victorious" or "triumphant" over the powers of evil. Even disease was brought upon them by the power of Satan or evil spirits, and could be removed through prayer and the rebuke of these evil spirits (2SG 139).

A pivotal change in the expression of such charismatic experiences occurred after a vision Ellen White had in December 1850, when she stated that "we should strive at all times to be free from unhealthy and unnecessary excitement." She discouraged these practices, stating that "implicit confidence" should "not be placed in these exercises" because the burden of the Adventist message depended upon the "Word of God" (Ms 11, 1850, in 13MR 299, 300). While it is clear that early Sabbatarian Adventists, and in particular White, prior to 1850, expressed their beliefs in enthusiastic ways, after 1850 such occurrences became less frequent and more guarded. If for no other reason, this was to distinguish them from other more fanatical groups of Adventists who had brought disrepute upon themselves through their promiscuity.

While ecstatic experiences became less frequent after 1850, it did not necessarily dampen religious enthusiasm or fervor. Religious services during the 1850s continued

to have frequent descriptions of those who had become "prostrated" by the power of God—in one case a woman fell off her chair during a meeting (2SG 220, 221). Early Sabbatarian Adventist leaders continued to pray for supernatural healings, which continued to occur (*ibid.* 117, 118, 136, 137, 139).

There are four recorded incidents of speaking in tongues among early Sabbatarian Adventists. Some of these incidents were considered genuine and others spurious (for a detailed analysis of these four incidents, see: A. L. White, "Tongues in Early SDA History," RH, Mar. 15 and 22, 1973).

Although Ellen White participated in ecstatic religious experiences during and following the Millerite movement, for her the Bible was always paramount over religious experience. She often quoted: "To the law and to the testimony: if they speak not according to this word, it is because there is no light in them" (Isa. 8:20). She insisted that "even the work of the Holy Spirit upon the heart is to be tested by the Word of God. The Spirit which inspired the Scriptures always leads to the Scriptures" (GCDB, Apr. 13, 1891, in 1SM 43). In the face of rampant fanaticism it is significant to note that as the early Sabbatarian Adventist believers formulated a system of doctrines, they chose to rely on the primacy of the Bible over religious experience.

Further reading: M. D. Burt, "Ellen G. White and Religious Enthusiasm in Early Adventist Experience" (White Estate Consultation, June 1998); A. Taves, *Fits, Trances, and Visions: Experiencing Religion and Explaining Experience From Wesley to James* (Princeton, 1999), pp. 128-130, 153-165, 169, 174, 225; A. L. White, "Charismatic Experiences in Early Seventh-day Adventist History" (EGWE, SDoc); J. M. Wilson, "Enthusiasm and Charismatic Manifestations in Sabbatarian Adventism With Applications for the Seventh-day Adventist

Church of the Late Twentieth Century" (D.Min. project, AU, 1995).

Michael W. Campbell

ECUMENISM, see **DENOMINATIONS, RELATIONS TO OTHER.**

EDUCATION. (PPPA, 1903, 324 pp.). An enlarged presentation of an earlier book, *Christian Education* (1893), written for both Seventh-day Adventists and the general public, setting forth Ellen White's philosophy of education. For White, true education "is the harmonious development of the physical, the mental, and the spiritual powers. It prepares the student for the joy of service in this world and for the higher joy of wider service in the world to come" (p. 13). Thus the goals of education and redemption are one: to restore God's image in His creation and to bring the world and humankind back to its original perfection (pp. 15, 16). Whoever cooperates with God in giving to the youth a knowledge of God and in molding the character into harmony with His accomplishes a noble work (p. 19).

To illustrate what true education is, Ellen White first relates how God sought to accomplish the principles of education by giving to Israel the sanctuary services and their accompanying festivals as object lessons of holiness, consecration, and reverence (pp. 33-44). Another illustration is found in the schools of the prophets, which combined the development of the mental, spiritual, and physical aspects of the human being (pp. 45-50). A well-balanced approach to education helped biblical characters such as Joseph, Daniel, and Elisha become leaders in Israel and thus bring God's people closer to Him (pp. 51-70). But the best illustration of these principles of education is the life, ministry, and methods of Jesus (pp. 73-96).

In the central sections of the book, making up more than half of its content, White addresses four essential aspects of education. First, true education includes an emphasis on the natural world, learning of God through nature. As people understand how God works in nature, they will be better able to see how He can also work in their lives (p. 99). A second essential aspect of education is the use of the Bible. The Word of God is a treasure of infinite resources, and no merely human book can equal its usefulness (pp. 123-127). Searching, reading, and meditating on the Bible fosters a mental and spiritual culture not found in any other book. In the lives and experiences of its various characters, the Bible offers principles of right living and teaches how to avoid dangers and pitfalls.

A third aspect of true education is physical culture. Understanding the functioning of the human body and the laws of health is important to arrive at a balanced lifestyle. Ellen White emphasizes that far from being a detriment, manual training is an asset to life and that "the youth should be led to see the true dignity of labor" (p. 214). One last important aspect of education is that of character building. "True education does not ignore the value of scientific knowledge or literary acquirements; but above information it values power; above power, goodness; above intellectual acquirements, character. The world does not so much need men of great intellect as of noble character. It needs men in whom ability is controlled by steadfast principle" (p. 225).

For Ellen White these principles of education are crucial concepts by which educators train and lead young people to develop a closer relationship with God in preparation for eternal life. Education on earth is never completed and only prepares the way for the school of the hereafter (p. 301).

In 2000 an adaptation of *Education* was published under the title *True Education* (PPPA, 192 pp.).

Denis Fortin

EDUCATION, ELLEN G. WHITE'S ROLE IN ADVENTIST. Ellen White's vision for the development of Adventist education was fully grasped by but few in her lifetime. Her written contribution to the purpose and philosophy of Adventist education began in 1872 (3T 131-160; FE 15-46). In these seminal pages White developed her principal themes, which included: "the physical, mental, moral, and religious education of children" (FE 15); "the habits and principles of a teacher should be considered of even greater importance than his literary qualifications" (*ibid.* 19); "daily, systematic labor should constitute a part of the education of the youth" (*ibid.* 44); students "may reach to the highest point of intellectual greatness; and if balanced by religious principle they can carry forward the work which Christ came . . . to accomplish" (*ibid.* 48).

But these principles and more were not understood by her contemporaries. In the establishment of Battle Creek College in 1874 the trustees opted for a small acreage while James and Ellen White urged a much larger piece of land for industries and farming. Even more disappointing, the leaders organized the school along the classical lines of conventional collegiate education. The founders could not grasp, for example, the principles of combining study with a daily work program. Even biblical studies were offered only as electives.

In 1881 Ellen White responded with the warning that "there is danger that our college will be turned away from its original design" (5T 21). Earlier that year *Alexander McLearn had replaced *Sidney Brownsberger as college president. Neither man, both classical

educators, understood White's educational philosophy. In the chapter "Our College" (*ibid.* 21-36), she strongly emphasized that "the Bible shall have its proper place in the education of the youth" (*ibid.* 26).

On August 10, 1882, Battle Creek College closed for a year because of internal conflict. But as a result church leaders and college administrators decided to reorder its priorities to include manual labor and greater emphasis on the Bible in all departments of study.

The next pivotal moment in Adventist education occurred at the *Harbor Springs, Michigan, educational convention in 1891. Encouraged by the fresh understanding of *"righteousness by faith" that was generated by the 1888 General Conference session, new educational emphases stressed making Adventist schools more focused on the Adventist mission and message. Along with White's main principles emphasized in earlier writings, at Harbor Springs she advocated "the elimination of pagan and infidel authors from our schools, the dropping of long courses in the Latin and Greek classes, and the substitution of the teaching of the Bible and the teaching of history from the standpoint of the prophecies" (P. T. Magan, "The Educational Conference and Educational Reform," RH, Aug. 6, 1901, p. 508).

This well-rounded conference became the high-water mark for new standards for classic Adventist education. Ellen White wrote six powerful, unambiguous articles in the *Review and Herald* (RH, Nov. 10-Dec. 15, 1891) recapping the issues that had weakened Adventist curricula in the formative years (cf. FE 167-200). Here again she emphasized the central role of the Bible in rescuing truth from obscurity and placing it in its proper framework. Her educational philosophy revealed the principles of the *great controversy, including "the two agencies in the salvation of man"—"the divine influence" and "the strong, living faith of those who follow Christ." The union of these two agencies is achieved when the divine initiative meets the "cooperation of His church" (FE 189).

In the 10 years following the Harbor Springs convention Ellen White had an unexpected opportunity to oversee personally the implementation of her educational principles. Responding to the invitation to move to Australia in 1891, it was not long before she saw the need to establish a college to train workers for that area of the world's mission field.

But while the few Adventists in Australia were organizing themselves in the midst of a financial depression, Ellen White continued to counsel collegiate leadership in Battle Creek. She wrote to Battle Creek College president *W. W. Prescott in 1893 that the original purpose of the College was to establish "a school at Battle Creek that should not pattern after any school in existence. . . . Teachers were to educate in spiritual things, to prepare people to stand in the trying crisis before us; but there has been a departure from God's plan in many ways" (*ibid.* 221). In other words, the college had built on the wrong pattern—the conventional pattern of secular schools. Her counsel always advocated "quality education," but from a Christian standpoint, not that of classical education.

Ellen White's writings during this Australian period unfolded in even greater detail her broad visionary principles. She now had the opportunity to watch these principles be embedded from the ground up in Avondale. She knew that Avondale must be a new kind of Adventist college: "No breezes from Battle Creek are to be wafted in. I see I must watch before and behind and on every side to permit nothing to find entrance that has been presented before me as injuring our schools

in America" (Lt 138, 1897, in 20MR 215).

From time to time, White emphasized that the Avondale school "must not pattern after any schools that had been established in the past. This was to be a sample school. It was organized on the plan that God had given us, and He prospered its work" (CT 533).

The living experiment at Avondale and Ellen White's constant stream of fresh insights invigorated young educators in North America in the late 1890s. *E. A. Sutherland and *P. T. Magan reorganized Battle Creek College along these living principles—a task that succeeded only when the college was moved to a rural location near Berrien Springs, Michigan (see *Emmanuel Missionary College).

These two men later established a new school near Madison, Tennessee (see *Madison College), where they could more fully develop the reformed educational principles that White advocated. The board of trustees of the Madison school was the only board that Ellen White ever served on.

Another aspect of Adventist education to which White gave aggressive advocacy was the development of elementary schools. From nine Adventist elementary schools in 1895, to 220 in 1900, to 417 in 1905, the elementary school movement was largely spurred by her position that in countries where "parents are compelled by law to send their children to school," every Adventist church should establish a school, even "if there are no more than six children to attend" (Lt 141, 1897, in 6T 199; cf. Knight, p. 43).

Loma Linda University (see *College of Medical Evangelists), with its international leadership in medicine, dentistry, public health, and related fields, was launched because in 1905 Ellen White forged ahead with borrowed money to purchase the campus of a failed resort hotel. The new medical institution would not have survived its early years without the profound impetus of her leadership and ability to attract needed funds. Similar stories of her personal and financial advocacy can be told about most of the Adventist colleges and many of the smaller institutions established during her lifetime.

See also: Education, Philosophy of; Teachers and Teaching.

Further reading: H. E. Douglass, *Messenger of the Lord* (PPPA, 1998), pp. 354-361; G. R. Knight, *Early Adventist Educators* (AUP, 1983), pp. 26-49.

Herbert E. Douglass

EDUCATION, PHILOSOPHY OF. Ellen G. White's philosophy of education outlines the foundations upon which the Seventh-day Adventist Church organization has been educating youth since its beginnings.

Her definition of education goes clearly beyond the scholastic realm. For Ellen White education is more than pursuing studies. It covers the preparation for this life and for the life to come. It encompasses not only cognitive development but also physical, moral, and spiritual growth (Ed 13). The purpose of education is not to secure a merely intellectual culture in order to obtain recognition or wealth, but rather to "gain knowledge and wisdom that we may become better Christians, and be prepared for greater usefulness, rendering more faithful service to our Creator" (CT 49).

The three most salient pillars of White's educational philosophy seem to be redemption, wholeness, and permanence. These are emphasized in most of her educational writings, whether theoretical or practical. Redemption is the first and most important aim in education. She says, in fact, that "in the highest sense the work of education and the work of redemption are one" (Ed 30). Redemption is the greatest need of humankind,

and education must serve as a channel to bring salvation to students. This understanding implies that educational institutions should: (a) aim to restore in pupils the lost image of God (*ibid.* 15); (b) hire teachers who "possess the attributes of Christ's character" and "give evidence of what grace can do through human agents who make God their trust"(CT 151); (c) include the Bible as an integral part of the academic program (COL 42); (d) utilize methodology that directs the students' minds toward their Creator (Ed 14); and (e) be located if possible in a nonurban environment "where the eye will rest upon the things of nature instead of clusters of houses" (FE 322). Conventional goals having to do with learning, training, thinking, etc., are considered powerless unless the redemptive power of Christ becomes a reality across the entire educational program (SC 18). In fact, education without this component may be "more harmful than beneficial" (CT 412). Therefore, all components of the curriculum, whether personal or material, are to be geared to bringing to students the opportunity of redemption and salvation through the Lord Jesus Christ.

The second pillar of White's educational philosophy is wholeness. On hundreds of occasions Ellen White writes about the need for the physical, mental, moral, and spiritual faculties to be developed in a balanced way. "True education is the preparation of the physical, mental, and moral powers for the performance of every duty; it is the training of body, mind, and soul for divine service. This is the education that will endure unto eternal life" (COL 330). In contrast, she criticizes schools and systems that place heavy emphasis on the intellectual domain, while leaving the physical and the moral-spiritual areas virtually unattended (CT 295).

As a result, one of the most distinctive

traditions of SDA schools is physical exercise through practical work that brings balance as well as additional income. This finds different applications in different parts of the world, depending on social and economic contexts. Yet, care for the physical side of existence is consistently upheld. Likewise, the moral-spiritual component has resulted in the inclusion of a number of relevant activities, such as Bible study, prayer, devotionals, sacred music, various outreach activities, and service activities.

Wholeness is applied to a variety of educational areas. Early childhood education already offers the opportunity to provide balanced training (Ed 276). Curricula are to avoid one-sided education, and plan for "moral philosophy, the study of the Scriptures, and physical training. . . . For unless all are equally developed, one faculty cannot do its work thoroughly without overtaxing some part of the human machinery" (5T 522). Teacher training is to be imbued with the concept of wholeness, and the Christian teacher is expected to have "an equal interest in the physical, mental, moral, and spiritual education of his scholars" (3T 135). The ever-present idea of wholeness is inextricably linked to the development of right character (RH, June 24, 1890), which is the only treasure we can take from this world to the next (CG 161).

Ellen White's third educational pillar characterizes the concept and purpose of education as permanent. Unlike conventional academic programs, "true education" includes the "whole period of existence possible to man. . . . It prepares the student for the joy of service in this world and for the higher joy of wider service in the world to come" (Ed 13).

In a sense, education is to begin during the prenatal stage (AH 255-259) and is to follow throughout childhood, adolescence, and adulthood (CG 26). Even in the hereafter,

students in the school of Christ will continue to learn (FE 544). "There every power will be developed, every capability increased. The grandest enterprises will be carried forward, the loftiest aspirations will be reached, the highest ambitions realized. And still there will arise new heights to surmount, new wonders to admire, new truths to comprehend, fresh objects to call forth the powers of body and mind and soul" (Ed 307).

The basic texts containing Ellen G. White's philosophy of education are: "Proper Education" (3T 131-160); "First Principles" (Ed 13-30); and "The Higher Education" and "The Aim of Our Schools" (CT 11-70).

See also: Teachers and Teaching.

Further reading: E. M. Cadwallader, *Principles of Education in the Writings of Ellen G. White* (Ph.D. diss., University of Nebraska, 1951); G. R. Knight, *Philosophy and Education: An Introduction in Christian Perspective,* 4th ed. (AUP, 2006); G. R. Knight, *Myths in Adventism* (RHPA, 1985).

Julian Melgosa

EGGS. As with other animal products, Ellen White cautioned against the use of eggs because of the fear that such products may transmit animal diseases to humans (MH 320), and to some people she went as far as to say that "eggs should not be placed upon your table" (2T 400). While she advocated vegetarianism and discouraged the use of red meat and poultry, she did not classify eggs and dairy products in the same category (7T 134, 135). "In some cases the use of eggs is beneficial" (*ibid.* 135), she advised, and "eggs contain properties that are remedial agencies in counteracting certain poisons" and may "supply the system with proper nourishment" (9T 162). To people who discarded eggs and dairy products without providing balanced and wholesome replacements, she counseled to avoid extremes and to "not deprive yourself of that class of food which makes good blood" (CD 366). One such example of extremism happened in the life of Dr. Daniel Kress, who became anemic from his abstinence of all animal products without a proper wholesome diet in replacement. Ellen White recommended that he change his eating habits and eat a raw egg in a glass of grape juice two or three times a day in order to receive "the nourishment that he greatly needed" (Lt 37, 1904, in CD 367; cf. Knight, pp. 74-76). Vitamin B_{12} is now known to be a critical nutrient for treating anemia, and is recommended for all who do not or cannot use eggs and dairy products. Although Ellen White did recommend the use of eggs, she highlighted that only eggs and dairy products from healthy animals should be consumed (MH 320) and that a time will come when such animal products may need to be discarded because of the increase in animal diseases (CD 367; 9T 162).

Further reading: H. E. Douglass, *They Were There: Stories of Those Who Witnessed Ellen White's Prophetic Gift—and Believed* (PPPA, 2006), pp. 11, 12; G. R. Knight, *Reading Ellen White* (RHPA, 1997), pp. 74-76.

Denis Fortin

1844, ELLEN G. WHITE'S COMMENTS ON, see **DISAPPOINTMENTS, MILLERITE.**

1888 MATERIALS, ELLEN G. WHITE. (Ellen G. White Estate, 1987; 4 vols., 1,821 pp.). In connection with the centenary of the General Conference session of 1888 held in Minneapolis, Minnesota, the White Estate endeavored to bring together in one chronological collection every known Ellen White manuscript, letter, article, and sermon in which reference is made to the Minneapolis conference. The collection is not a compendium on the topic of righteousness by faith per se, nor is it a reference

work on the principal personalities associated with the session, except as Ellen White makes direct reference to the Minneapolis meetings. Unlike any previous collection, nearly all the manuscripts and letters were photocopied directly from the original files, foregoing the grammatical editing generally done for published works. Ellen White's handwritten interlineations may also be observed on many of the documents. A companion volume consisting of non-Ellen White resources from the White Estate archives was also issued under the title *Manuscripts and Memories of Minneapolis* (PPPA, 1988, 591 pp.).

Tim Poirier

1888, MESSAGE OF, see **GENERAL CONFERENCE SESSION OF 1888.**

ELECTRIC PHYSICIAN. A nineteenth-century synonym for practitioners of magnetic healing, animal magnetism, mesmerism (hypnotism), "sympathetic remedies," and similar forms of spiritualistic psychology (5T 193, 198). In this context, the word "electric" has no connection with the development of commercial *electricity, but refers to practitioners who claimed to "cure the diseased" (RH, Jan. 15, 1914) using "the sorcery of Satan" (3SP 426). Ellen White denounced them as "agents of Satan" (RH, June 27, 1882) and "channels for Satan's electric currents" (Ev 609). She warned that to consult such is to "deliberately venture upon Satan's ground" and come under his "spell" (CTBH 115, 116), and will lead to an outcome that is the "reverse" of the benefits hoped for (5MR 230). At the same time, Ellen White declared that "the electric power of the brain, promoted by mental activity, vitalizes the whole system, and is thus an invaluable aid in resisting disease" (Ed 197). As with many issues in life, Satan uses that which is not necessarily evil in itself, to forward his cause. The spiritualistic healer tells those who come under his spell that "they need love and sympathy." "Pretending great interest in their welfare," he charms them until they are "completely in his power; sin, disgrace, and ruin are the terrible sequel" (5T 198).

Further reading: For a representative list of nineteenth-century sources, see 2MCP 721.

Kenneth Jorgensen

ELECTRICITY. A term with a wide range of meanings in Ellen White's era. She used the term to refer to commercial electric power, to legitimate methods of medical therapy, to natural forces in plants and humans, to supernatural divine healing, and to spiritualistic counterfeit healers (*electric physicians).

Commercial electric power in the form of 60-cycle alternating current (AC) was introduced in the United States in 1891. Battle Creek had electric lights at least by 1902 (5Bio 223). By 1903 J. H. Kellogg was using electric-light baths to give therapeutic dry heat at the Battle Creek Sanitarium (2SAT 233). Electric lights were installed at the Paradise Valley Sanitarium in 1904 (RH, Mar. 16, 1905), and were mentioned in 1904 as one of the "advantages" of Mountain View, California, then the site of Pacific Press (LDE 106).

Before the coming of commercial electricity, related terms were widely used both literally and metaphorically. Ellen White used the word "electric" and related words to describe a force in plants, animals, and humans. The "electricity that gives life to the seed" of plants was created by and proceeded from God (3MR 322). Likewise, human beings were endowed with "electrical energy" from the day they were created (3T 138). She declared that "the electric power of the brain, promoted by mental activity, vitalizes the whole system, and is thus an invaluable aid in resisting

disease" (Ed 197). This "electric power" of the nervous system to resist disease becomes a link from the natural to the supernatural, because White not only speaks of "electric currents in the nervous system" that strengthen the "vital powers," but affirms that "the brain nerves which communicate with the entire system are the only medium through which Heaven can communicate to man and affect his inmost life" (2T 347). Furthermore, the natural "electric power" of the nervous system can be recharged by the infusion of supernatural power. "The mighty energies of the Holy Spirit" can "fall like an electric shock on the palsy-stricken soul, causing every nerve to thrill with new life" (5T 267).

This connection between the natural and the supernatural introduces another of White's uses of electricity, to describe the means of healing from spiritual, mental, and physical disease, not only in ancient biblical times, but in her own era and her own family (2T 428; 7MR 118; 2MCP 539; 4Bio 152; RH, Feb. 20, 1866; 4T 280, 281; and HR, July 1, 1872). To fully set in motion this "electrifying influence" (1T 517) requires faith and obedience to the laws of health, especially outdoor exercise, pure air, water, sunlight, rest, and temperance in working, eating, and drinking (*ibid.* 515-517; 2T 67, 68; MH 127).

White also uses the concept of electricity to describe the spiritual connection of the believer with God: "Reach up and grasp His hand, that the touch may electrify you and charge you with the sweet properties of His own matchless character" (4T 63; cf. 5T 267; 2MCP 801; RH, July 19, 1898).

Kenneth Jorgensen

ELLEN G. WHITE ESTATE, INCORPORATED. The last *will and testament of Ellen G. White dated February 9, 1912, provided for an organization that would serve as her agent in the custody of her writings, handling her properties, including "conducting the business thereof." Ellen White's will (printed in its entirety in H. E. Douglass, *Messenger of the Lord,* pp. 569-572) named five church leaders to serve as a board of trustees: *Arthur G. Daniells, president of the General Conference; *Charles H. Jones, manager of the Pacific Press; *Francis M. Wilcox, editor of the *Review and Herald*; *William C. White, her son; and *Clarence C. Crisler, one of her secretaries. Four of the five were also members of the Executive Committee of the General Conference.

Trustees were appointed for life. Ellen White stipulated that "if a vacancy shall occur for any reason among said trustees, or their successors, a majority of the surviving trustees" were "empowered and directed to fill such vacancy"; or if for any reason that were to fail, the General Conference Executive Committee should appoint someone to fill the vacancy. The will gave the major portion of the existing and potential royalty incomes from her books to the work of the trustees. (For additional information, see "The Settlement of Ellen G. White's Estate" in 6Bio 453-459).

At the death of Ellen White, July 16, 1915, this self-perpetuating board began to function. It soon sold her real estate, consisting mainly of Elmshaven, her home property near St. Helena, California. Then began the ongoing care of her literary properties. As described in her will, these included: (1) possession of the copyrights to her writings and the care and promotion of her books in the English language; (2) preparation of manuscripts for and promotion of the translation and publication of her writings in other languages; and (3) custody of the files and original manuscripts and other holdings of the estate, and the selection of matter from the manuscript files for publication in new compilations.

The board now carries several other responsibilities that have been added through the years: (4) acquainting Seventh-day Adventists and others regarding the life and ministry of Ellen G. White; (5) serving as the official promoter of the history of the Seventh-day Adventist Church on behalf of the General Conference; and (6) the members of the White board of trustees serving as the constituency for Adventist Heritage Ministry.

When the organization of the original board took place in 1915, A. G. Daniells served briefly as president, followed by F. M. Wilcox, and then once again Elder Daniells. The secretaryship, after being held for a couple of years by Clarence Crisler, went to W. C. White, the only member of the board devoting full time to the work of the trustees. He filled this office until his death in 1937. From 1915 to 1937 the work was carried on at Elmshaven in Ellen White's former office building, rented from the new owners. Originally it contained one vault, built during Ellen White's lifetime, that housed the E. G. White materials. Eventually a second vault was added.

During the 19 years the original board members worked together, in addition to routine tasks they (1) published 10 posthumous compilations; (2) produced an 865-page *Comprehensive Index to the Writings of Ellen G. White,* published in 1926; (3) continued indexing Ellen White's manuscript files; and (4) at the request of, and in counsel with, the leading officers of the General Conference in 1933 and 1934, laid the legal foundation for continuing the trusteeship in perpetuity. The steps taken to ensure the perpetuation of the trusteeship were: (a) in 1933 the trustees, as the constituency, formed a corporation under the laws of the State of California "to carry out and perform the provisions of the charitable trust created by the last will and testament of Ellen G. White, deceased"; (b) the General Conference agreed to provide adequate financial support for the work of the trustees in the form of an annual budget; the trustees, in turn, assigned to the General Conference all royalty incomes produced by the Ellen G. White books; (c) it was agreed to move the property and work of the trustees at some appropriate future time to the offices of the General Conference, then located in Washington, D.C. The Ellen G. White Estate was first listed in the 1935 edition of the *Seventh-day Adventist Yearbook*.

When three of the original trustees died— one in 1935 and two in 1936—the vacancies were filled in harmony with the provisions of Ellen White's will and the bylaws of the 1933 corporation. The full-time secretary, W. C. White, died September 1, 1937. He was replaced by his son, *Arthur L. White, who for nine years had worked as his father's secretary and for four years as assistant secretary of the White Estate. The work of the White Estate was moved to the General Conference in January 1938.

With steadily increasing demands being placed upon the trustees because of the growth of the church worldwide and numerous constituencies to be represented, in 1950 the trustees increased the board's membership from five to seven. That number was increased to nine in 1958, of which seven were life members and the other two were elected to terms corresponding to those of the General Conference elected personnel (originally four years, but now five). In 1970 the board was increased to 11; in 1980, to 13; and in 1985, to 15. In 1998 the number of life trustees was again reduced to five. In 2000 the bylaws were modified to stipulate that a life trustee who has attained the age of 75 during a quinquennium will be granted emeritus trustee status at the next regular quinquennial meeting of the board, and a new life trustee will be chosen to fill the vacancy thus created. In 2009 this

provision was extended to cover term trustees. At quinquennial meetings the board also elects the director and associate directors, as well as the officers of the corporation, as provided for in the bylaws.

Through the years a close working relationship has been maintained between the White trustees and the General Conference. Several of the trustees are members of the General Conference Executive Committee. Various matters, such as promoting the overseas publication of the Ellen G. White material, appropriation of funds to assist in the foreign language publication of the Ellen G. White books, and overall planning of Spirit of Prophecy promotion, including preparation of materials for the annual Spirit of Prophecy Sabbath, although intimately related to the work of the White trustees, are beyond the sphere of their direct responsibility. These are handled through a General Conference subcommittee known as the Spirit of Prophecy Committee. This committee includes a minimum of one White Estate trustee. The duties of this subcommittee and the working relationship between the General Conference Committee and the White Estate are currently set forth in a joint agreement adopted by the General Conference Committee and the White Estate trustees on October 10, 1957.

Subsequent to the agreement, on June 12, 1958, the General Conference corporation took an action disclaiming any "rights, title, or interest in and to manuscripts, diaries, books, library volumes or magazines, document files, correspondence files, card indices, and copyrights in or derived from the estate of Ellen G. White, deceased," in favor of the Ellen G. White Estate, Incorporated. Two weeks later new bylaws for the White Estate were adopted, which revision still serves as the basis of the current bylaws governing the work of the White Estate. Between the General

Conference and the White Estate there is an interlocking and at times overlapping of responsibilities. Nevertheless, a smooth and efficient working relationship between the two organizations is maintained—one that is mutually interdependent while at the same time recognizing the total legal independence of the White Estate from the General Conference, as Ellen White originally envisioned.

The work of the White Estate includes routine work. The paid staff members: (1) safeguard and maintain the original materials in the custody of the trustees, and the indexes thereto, in such a manner as to serve the church; (2) handle the copyrights to the Ellen G. White works; (3) conduct such research in these works and the related historical materials as may be called for; (4) respond to questions that may be directed to the White Estate in personal interviews and in a world-wide correspondence; (5) assemble, when authorized by the trustees, materials for compilations from Ellen G. White's writings; (6) foster, in conjunction with the Spirit of Prophecy Committee, the ever-widening publication of these writings in various languages and at times make selections or abridgments as called for and authorized; (7) fill assignments in church, institutional, and field visitation as the needs and best interests of the expanding work of the church require; (8) conduct tours of historical sites of denominational interest, especially in the New England states; and (9) prepare articles, correspondence lessons, and text materials.

Productions of special value to the church include the four-volume Comprehensive *Index to the Writings of Ellen G. White* (1962, 1992); the six-volume facsimile reprints of the Ellen G. White *Present Truth* and *Review and Herald* articles; the four-volume Ellen G. White *Signs of the Times* articles; the Ellen G. White *Youth's Instructor* articles; the

Periodical Resource Collection volumes; the six-volume biography of Ellen G. White, by Arthur L. White; *Messenger of the Lord,* by Herbert E. Douglass; and *The Complete Published Writings of Ellen G. White on Compact Disc* (*CD-ROM) and the Comprehensive Research Edition CD-ROM, including the multimedia disc, *Legacy of Light.*

The White Estate currently maintains branch offices in three locations: Andrews University, Berrien Springs, Michigan; Loma Linda University, Loma Linda, California; and Oakwood University, Huntsville, Alabama. These offices contain duplicates of the Ellen White documents and other historical materials housed in the main office at the General Conference headquarters. Beginning in 1974 the White Estate, in cooperation with the various world divisions of the church, also set up Ellen G. White Seventh-day Adventist Research Centers on the campuses of 15 Adventist colleges and universities outside North America in the countries of Argentina, Australia, Brazil, England, France, Jamaica, India, Kenya, Korea, Mexico, Nigeria, Peru, the Philippines, Russia, and South Africa. The General Conference assists with the operation of one research center per division; in the case of the Inter-American and South American divisions, the second center is operated under the same rules as all other centers, but solely at the expense of the host division. In 2004 the first research center operated under the same rules governing all other centers but totally at the expense of an academic institution was opened at Southwestern Adventist University in Keene, Texas. In 2009 the Peruvian Adventist University in cooperation with the Peruvian Union Conference opened a research center.

During the later years of her life Ellen White often used her unique 50,000-page manuscript file in the preparation of published works. The White Estate trustees have continued to utilize this for the compilations made since her death. These manuscripts constitute an invaluable basic file of historical records and of counsel to the church. The copyright of these manuscripts resides solely with the board of trustees.

While all of Ellen White's writings are available for research, the unpublished letters, manuscripts, and other materials in the Ellen G. White files do not constitute a public archive. The sacred nature of the files generally and the confidential nature of many of the communications in the files require that they be cared for and used responsibly. Even the manuscripts whose primary value is historical in nature must not be used in a solely secular manner. "Spiritual things are spiritually discerned" (DA 55; cf. 1 Cor. 2:14). Because of this, during the first few decades following Ellen White's death, careful policies governing the use and release of unpublished materials were set up, ultimately resulting in the publication of 21 volumes known as *Manuscript Releases*. In recent years, because of the passage of time so that those mentioned in the unpublished materials are no longer living, nor are their children, the earlier restrictive policies have been adapted to accommodate the increased research requests received by the White Estate.

The two chief officers of the board are the chair and the secretary. The secretary is also the president of the corporation, and serves as director of the organization, being responsible for the day-to-day operations of the office and staff. Beginning in 1915, when the terms of Ellen White's will went into effect, the White Estate has had 11 chairs and seven secretaries/directors (the title having been changed in 1995).

Board chairs: Arthur G. Daniells, 1915, 1922-1935; Francis M. Wilcox, 1915-1922, 1938-1944; J. E. Fulton, 1935-1936; J. L. Shaw, 1936-1937; Milton E. Kern, 1944-1951; Denton E. Rebok, 1952; A. V. Olson, 1952-1963; Francis D. Nichol, 1963-1966; W. Paul Bradley, 1966-1980; Kenneth H. Wood, 1980-2008; Don Schneider, 2008- .

Secretaries/Directors: Clarence C. Crisler, 1915-1917; William C. White, 1917-1937; Arthur L. White, 1937-1978; Robert W. Olson, 1978-1990; Paul A. Gordon, 1990-1995; Juan Carlos Viera, 1995-2000; James R. Nix, 2000- .

James R. Nix

ELLEN G. WHITE MEMORIAL HOSPITAL, see **WHITE MEMORIAL MEDICAL CENTER**.

ELLEN G. WHITE PERIODICAL RESOURCE COLLECTION (PPPA, 1990). Multivolume set of Ellen White's articles published in various Adventist periodicals. This resource collection was intended to complete the facsimile reproduction of all of Ellen White's articles that appeared in English-language Adventist periodicals. (Articles from the *Present Truth*, the *Review and Herald*, the *Signs of the Times*, and the *Youth's Instructor* had already been published separately.) Currently only two volumes of the *Periodical Resource Collection* have been published; the publication of volumes 3 and 4 is anticipated in the future. Volume 1 (662 pp.) includes articles published in *Advance, Advocate of Christian Education (Training School Advocate), Apples of Gold Library, Atlantic Canvasser, Atlantic Union Gleaner, [Australasian] Union Conference Record, [Battle Creek] College Record*, and *The Bible Echo and [Australasian] Signs of the Times*. Volume 2 (642 pp.) includes articles from *Bible Students' Library, Bible Training School, Central Advance, Central Union Outlook, Christian Education, Christian Educator, Church and Sabbath School Bulletin, Church Officers' Gazette, Day-Star, East Michigan*

Banner, *Echoes From the Field*, *Educational Messenger*, *Field Tidings*, and the *General Conference [Daily] Bulletin*. While each volume reprints only articles not already republished in books or collections still in print, a complete index in the back of each volume lists *all* of Ellen White's articles published in the periodicals featured in that volume, with the republication references for articles not included in this collection.

ELLEN G. WHITE PRESENT TRUTH AND REVIEW AND HERALD ARTICLES, see **REVIEW AND HERALD ARTICLES, ELLEN G. WHITE PRESENT TRUTH AND.**

ELLEN G. WHITE PUBLICATIONS, see **ELLEN G. WHITE ESTATE, INC.**, and general article: **ELLEN G. WHITE'S WRITINGS.**

ELLEN G. WHITE SIGNS OF THE TIMES ARTICLES, see **SIGNS OF THE TIMES ARTICLES, ELLEN G. WHITE.**

ELLEN G. WHITE THE YOUTH'S INSTRUCTOR ARTICLES, see **YOUTH'S INSTRUCTOR ARTICLES, THE, ELLEN G. WHITE.**

ELLEN G. WHITE'S LAST WILL AND TESTAMENT, see **WILL AND TESTAMENT, ELLEN G. WHITE'S LAST, AND SETTLEMENT OF HER ESTATE.**

ELMSHAVEN, see **HOMES OF JAMES AND ELLEN G. WHITE.**

ELMSHAVEN PRESS, see **HERBERT C. WHITE; JAMES HENRY WHITE.**

EMMANUEL MISSIONARY COLLEGE (1901-1960). Located in Berrien Springs, Michigan; successor to Battle Creek College, first SDA institution of higher learning (1874-1901);

now Andrews University. Ellen White, one of the founders of Battle Creek College, also participated in the establishment of Emmanuel Missionary College at Berrien Springs in 1901 through her counsels to *Edward A. Sutherland, founder and first president of Emmanuel Missionary College. Sutherland, as president of Battle Creek College from 1897, wanted to move the school out of the city to a more rural location. He sought and waited for the approval of Ellen White, who urged him to move slowly in selling and leaving the Battle Creek campus. In the meantime, Sutherland and his academic dean, *Percy T. Magan, explored much of southwestern Michigan on bicycle, looking for land on which to relocate the college.

Having returned to Battle Creek for the General Conference session of 1901, Ellen White made public her counsel concerning the college on April 12. Her long testimony on education culminated in the direct advice: "God wants the school to be taken out of Battle Creek." She added, "This move is in accordance with God's design for the school before the institution was established" (GCB, Apr. 14, 1901).

Sutherland was already prepared to suggest Berrien Springs as the best location for the college. Although Ellen White never visited the new location before the school moved, she received glowing reports from Sutherland and Magan. She wrote that she was very pleased with the descriptions of the Berrien Springs property and added, "The good hand of the Lord appears to be in this opening" (Lt 80, 1901, in 6MR 407).

Ellen White visited Emmanuel Missionary College once, at the *Berrien Springs Meeting of the Lake Union Conference session in May of 1904. She and her party traveled to Berrien Center by train and from there to the campus in two hacks. Magan offered his home for her stay on campus. The session, held in the newly finished study hall, was a stormy one, dominated by acrimonious discussions over John Harvey Kellogg's pantheistic leanings and his book *The Living Temple*.

During her time on the Emmanuel Missionary College campus, Ellen White presented devotional talks for the conference, spoke to the student body, and spoke at Ida Magan's untimely funeral. When discussions in the main session reached a dramatic height, she took the floor and attempted to restore harmony by her balanced criticism and encouragement of both sides. Finally, she counseled once more with Sutherland and Magan, approving their plans to resign from Emmanuel Missionary College and go south to establish what would become *Madison College.

Although subsequent presidents at Emmanuel Missionary College did not enjoy the close personal relationship with Ellen White that its founders did, they continued to value highly her written counsel and attempted to follow it in their administration of the college.

Further reading: Lt 163, 1904; GCB, Apr. 16, 1901; *Founders' Golden Anniversary Bulletin of Battle Creek College and Emmanuel Missionary College: 1874-1924* (Berrien Springs, Mich.: College Press, 1924); M. Jones Gray, *As We Set Forth* (AUP, 2002); P. T. Magan, "Diary," May 22, 1904 (EGWE-LLU and CAR); "SDA Educational Society Minutes" (CAR); Emmett K. Vande Vere, *The Wisdom Seekers* (SPA, 1972).

Meredith Jones Gray

EMMANUEL MOVEMENT. A religious movement founded in 1906 by Elwood Worcester, priest at Emmanuel Episcopal Church in Boston, Massachusetts. Worcester advocated a synthesis of religious and medical practices and sought to heal various forms of "nervousness," alcoholism, and addictions. The basic tenets of the Emmanuel movement included elements of Asian and modern pantheism, spiritualism, and evolution. Its psychotherapeutic methods placed patients in a hypnotic or semihypnotic state.

Ellen White described the Emmanuel movement as one of the "more pleasing forms of spiritism" (Ev 606) and noted that many were attracted to it. Classing it with Christian Science, she warned against consulting healers who "attribute their power to electricity, magnetism, the so-called 'sympathetic remedies,' or to latent forces within the mind of man" (*ibid.*).

Further reading: Ev 606, 607; RH, Jan. 15, 1914; *The Emmanuel Movement: Its Theology, Its Psychology, and Its Methods of Treatment* (RHPA, c. 1921); K. McCarthey, "Psychotherapy and Religion: The Emmanuel Movement," *Journal of Religion and Health* 23 (Summer 1984): 92-105; *idem*, "Early Alcoholism Treatment: The Emmanuel Movement and Richard Peabody," *Journal of Studies on Alcohol* 45, no. 1 (1984): 59-74; E. Worcester, *The Christian Religion as a Healing Power: A Defense and Exposition of the Emmanuel Movement* (New York: Moffat, Yard and Company, 1909).

Eriks Galenieks

ENGLAND. The British Mission began in Southampton, England, in 1878 under the supervision of *J. N. Loughborough. The progress was slow, however, and when Ellen White arrived in Liverpool, England, on her way to Europe in 1885, there were only three organized churches and 60 baptized believers.

This was the first of her three visits to England; it lasted for two weeks. Beginning August 18, 1885, she gave five addresses in public halls, besides speaking in the three churches. The first weekend was spent in Grimsby, a small town on the east coast where the headquarters and publishing work had just been established. She gave an address in the town hall there and also spoke at the nearby church in Ulceby. She then traveled to the south coast, via London, where she spent the second weekend in Southampton before leaving for *Switzerland. While in London, W. M. Jones, a Seventh Day Baptist pastor, took Ellen White and her party on a two-hour tour of the famous British Museum (EGWEur 44).

Ellen White returned to England the next year for about four weeks, beginning on September 16, 1886. She spent most of her time in Grimsby, attending workers' meetings and the fourth annual session of the European Mission Council. Her third visit lasted nearly five weeks, beginning on June 30, 1887, before she returned to America. This time she went to Kettering, near Birmingham, where a fourth church had been organized, as well as again visiting London and Southampton.

Ellen White's visits to England were an encouragement to the workers and believers. She was concerned, however, about the slow progress, which was partly the result of a lack of financial resources and workers. She believed that a promising beginning had been made, but that better halls should have been hired and the big cities entered, particularly London, where the headquarters should have been.

This advice was soon acted upon by the new superintendent, *Stephen Haskell, who moved the printing press and headquarters to London, employed more workers, and soon organized a new church. By the time the British Union was organized in 1902, the membership had reached 844.

Further reading: HS 161-166, 173; EGWEur 35-46, 307-312.

Nigel Barham

ENVIRONMENT. Ellen White appears to say little directly addressing issues related to the environment and its care. However, certain statements in regard to universal and natural law, the dominion over nature given to human beings prior to the fall, and the necessity to become "conversant" with nature in order to derive moral lessons from it provide some foundation for deriving an orientation toward environmental issues.

Ellen White argues that there is an all-embracing cosmic order, governed by universal, unchanging laws given by God. "The same great laws that guide alike the star and the atom control human life. . . . To transgress His law, physical, mental, or moral, is to place one's self out of harmony with the universe, to introduce discord, anarchy, ruin" (Ed 99, 100). Thus, she clearly sees that which introduces "discord, anarchy, ruin" to the universe, including Planet Earth, as an evil to be avoided. She sees humans and nature closely knit together under one law. "The unity of man with nature and with God, the universal dominion of law, the results of transgression, cannot fail of impressing the mind and molding the character" (CG 55, 56). Note especially that there is a "unity of man with nature." The two are not to be antithetically opposed.

Ellen White notes that prior to the entrance of sin humanity's dominion over the earth was conditional, derived. Humans were not free to do whatever their whims called for, but rather their rule was an extension of God's loving, nurturing, sustaining care for the world. "Satan's dominion was that wrested from Adam, but Adam was the vicegerent of the Creator. His was not an independent rule. . . . Adam was to reign subject to Christ" (DA 129). In the context of financial stewardship, she reiterates this principle: "We are stewards of God's possessions. . . . [They are] not ours to use for the gratification of corrupt desires, for selfish indulgences" (ST, Dec. 1, 1887). And when Jesus fully reclaims Adam's lost dominion, "the groanings and lamentations of the creation shall cease" (GC 359). Thus the original rule of humanity was clearly perceived by Ellen White to be a nondestructive, nurturing, godly dominion. Humans were to care for the Garden of Eden as part of this nurturing rulership in cooperation with God (RH, Feb. 24, 1874).

For Ellen White, to resist this orientation of cooperation with the laws of nature and selfless nurture of the natural world by humanity is to resist God and thus lose the moral lessons God intended people to find in nature. "When men and women cease trying to counter-work the purposes of Divinity; when they place themselves under the discipline of grace, they will see that they have a work to do in becoming conversant with plant and animal life." If "more time" were "spent in the contemplation of God's works in nature, men and women would be better fitted to serve their Creator" (BE, Aug. 7, 1899).

Ellen White thus seems to advocate a stewardship model of relating to the earth, where duties to the environment are actually indirect duties to God, who owns the earth. She never treats the earth as a sacred object to be treated with care because it is holy. The strongest evidence that she did not have a "sacred" view of earth is her rejection of the pantheism that invaded Adventism in the early 1900s. Current "sacred earth" models of environmentalism are usually associated with a pantheistic or panentheistic view of God, which Ellen White categorically rejected (see 8T 255-318; MH 427-438). (Panentheism has God literally present in the materials comprising the universe [just as pantheism does], but it also recognizes a transcendent dimension of God that standard pantheism rejects.) Thus it would seem safe to conclude

that Ellen White would advocate environmental responsibility and care, but clearly not at the expense of human welfare (HS 165). In her view, humankind is to care for nature, but nature is not to be elevated above human beings. It seems unlikely that she would advocate radical environmentalism, but more likely that she would advocate responsible care and use of earth's environment.

See also: Animal Ethics.

Stephen Bauer

ESCHATOLOGY. Doctrine and study of last-day events. Ellen White presents her understanding of last-day events within the context of the cosmic controversy between good and evil. Her thoughts on this controversy are best unfolded in her Conflict of the Ages Series (PP, PK, DA, AA, GC). Her last book in this series, *The Great Controversy,* depicting the unfolding of this conflict from the destruction of the old Jerusalem to the coming of the New Jerusalem, is the best presentation of her thought on last-day events. The book, *Last Day Events,* a compilation published in 1992, is also a good source of information on her eschatology.

Ellen White's great controversy paradigm impacts her eschatology. She follows a historicist interpretation of prophetic data, rather than a preterist or futurist hermeneutic. This is documented throughout her Conflict of the Ages Series. Within this historicist understanding of biblical prophecy she presents a premillennial eschatology, in which she articulates her belief in the resurrection of the saints at the second coming of Christ. The resurrection of the wicked occurs after the millennium and is followed by the final judgment and the annihilation of the wicked.

At the beginning of the great controversy Satan pretended to promote the good of heaven's government while seeking its over-throw (PP 38). He does the same in the end-time (GC 591). He questioned the necessity of God's laws for angels (PP 37), and ever since has attempted to overthrow God's law (GC 582). Throughout human history he has worked through deception. In Eden he employed the medium of a serpent (*ibid.* 531), and in the end-time he will pretend to be Christ (*ibid.* 624). In heaven he railed against an alleged absolute Ruler (PP 37), and in the end-time he will have absolute control of his followers (EW 280). He promised angels freedom in heaven (PP 41), and offers the world liberty compared to the allegedly stern decrees of God (GC 534, 535).

Ellen White's eschatology rejects setting a date for Christ's return (FE 335) and points to His unexpected coming (8T 28). Time prophecies ended in 1844, and there is no prophetic time after that date (2SM 73). Biblical prophecies are conditional (DA 633, 634). Christ would have come before now if the conditions had been met (Ev 695, 696), but He waits for His people to reflect His character (COL 69), for the wicked to reach a level of rebellion that brings His judgment (5T 524), and for the gospel to be communicated to all the world (Matt. 24:14; Ev 697).

Character preparation for Christ's return is an important theme in Ellen White's escha-tology. God's people must be fitted for heaven (AA 273). This includes being firmly rooted in Christ (Ev 361, 362), every moment under the control of the Holy Spirit (PP 421), dili-gently studying Scripture and becoming conformed to its precepts, and committing biblical texts to memory (4T 459; 6T 81). Only those who have a love of the truth will be shielded from the final delusion that cap-tivates the world (GC 625).

As Pentecost launched the gospel under the power of the Holy Spirit, a second Pentecost,

referred to as the *latter rain, empowers the last gospel invitation (EW 86) and prepares God's people to stand through final events (7BC 984). Only persons yielded to Christ can be fitted by Him for the coming latter rain (1SM 191). The latter rain will seal God's people intellectually and spiritually so that they are immovable (4BC 1161). This involves a quality of revival not witnessed since apos-tolic times. Satan schemes to counteract this latter rain with a preemptive counterfeit revival. He sends excitement, a mingling of truth with error, so that members believe God is blessing them, and thus makes them unin-terested in the coming genuine revival (GC 464). The final pentecostal message includes a manifestation of Christ's glory in the lives of its presenters (COL 415, 416). Although God is not dependent upon the abilities of humans, only those qualified by the Holy Spirit will be used, including the uneducated and children (5T 80-82; Ev 700).

According to Ellen White the Sabbath is the final issue that agitates the whole world (Ev 236). In America, Protestants, Catholics, and spiritualist movements will join hands to restrict religious liberty (GC 588). The immortality of the soul and Sunday sacredness are the doctrines held in common by these three entities. Through these two errors Satan brings people under his control (*ibid.*). Fallen angels will impersonate dead loved ones and declare that the Sabbath has been changed to Sunday (EW 87). Fallen angels impersonate the apostles, who contradict what they wrote and deny the divine origin of the Bible (GC 557). Satan himself personates Christ and performs miracles (2SM 394). He appears in different parts of the world. He looks like the description of Christ in Revelation 1:13-15, claims to have changed the Sabbath to Sunday, and commands all to keep the day he has blessed (GC 624). He causes fire to fall from heaven to prove that he is God (MM 87, 88) and commands believers to worship him (6BC 1106). Judges will favor the law of the land rather than the law of God (ST, May 26, 1898), and Sabbathkeepers will be treated as traitors (6T 394). Sundaybreaking will be blamed as the cause of moral disarray and judgments of God (GC 591, 592). Persecutors will have the same spirit as those who betrayed Jesus (3SM 416). During these last events the image to the beast, imaging the Papacy, is a union of church and state, in which the church uses the state to enforce its dogmas (GC 445).

For Ellen White, faithfulness to the teachings of the Bible is a crucial element in end-time events. Although miracles can never supersede Scripture (2SM 48), Satan presents spiritual manifestations in place of Scripture. Spiritualism as a revival of ancient witchcraft and other false religions takes on a Christian guise in the end-time (GC 556-558). Thus Satan's lying wonders take the world captive (2SM 51). Only through the Bible can the difference between the genuine and the counterfeit be discerned (GC 593). When God's law is made void, a great number of Christians are seduced by fallen angels and their doctrines (2SM 368) and renounce their faith (5T 463). Even those who once had great light reject the truth (6T 400, 401). A large number of Christians are deceived and join the opposition (GC 608), so the church appears to fall (2SM 380), but it does not fall, for large numbers join the Sabbathkeepers (8T 41). Those who join Sabbathkeepers respond to the *loud cry final invitation (GC 603, 604, 606). It is clear for Ellen White that all whose faith is not anchored in Scripture will be deceived (*ibid.* 560). Only those whose minds are fortified with biblical truths will remain committed in the final conflict (*ibid.* 593, 594).

In these last events humans will receive either the *seal of God or the *mark of the beast. The seal of God as a confirmation of faithfulness to God's Word is seen outwardly in Sabbathkeeping (8T 117); on the other hand, the mark of the beast is seen outwardly in Sundaykeeping, although no one receives this mark until the end-time light on the Sabbath is rejected (Ev 234, 235). The close of probation comes suddenly (2T 191), a short time before the second coming of Christ (GC 490). The period between probation's close and the Second Advent is called the great time of trouble (GC 614). This begins when angels no longer hold back winds of strife (Ed 179, 180) and Satan begins his cruel work of destruction (Ms 134, 1898, in LDE 242; GC 614). The seven last plagues enrage the wicked to pass a death decree against Sabbathkeepers (EW 36, 37). This decree is an attempt to force Sabbathkeepers to renounce the biblical Sabbath and observe Sunday (EW 282, 283). These seven plagues will be the worst scourges ever known to humans, but Sabbathkeepers will be shielded by angels, who also provide for their needs. No child of God is harmed during this great time of tribulation (GC 628, 629).

As evil angels urge the wicked to implement the death decree, and as they rush upon Sabbathkeepers, a rainbow from God's throne encircles each praying group. This begins *Armageddon, the final battle of the great controversy. Armageddon climaxes with the second coming of Christ, in which He destroys the enemies of His people and brings final deliverance of the saints (7BC 982, 983).

The beginning of that deliverance is when God manifests His presence, and halts the implementation of the death decree. Sabbathkeepers are given a view of the throne room of heaven with God and the Son. God says, "It is done" (GC 635, 636). When Christ descends, the resurrection of the righteous dead and the translation of the righteous living bring immortality to both groups (*ibid.* 644, 645).

There are three phases to God's judgments in Ellen White's writings. The pre-Advent judgment (*ibid.* 479-491), the millennial judgment (*ibid.* 660, 661), and the postmillennial judgment (*ibid.* 666-673). God doesn't need these judgments, for He knows all things. They are for the benefit of all intelligent beings to see the justice of God. These include (1) unfallen beings, (2) redeemed humans, and (3) lost humans. The final judgment involves all created beings because it is the time for the resolution of the great controversy. Prior to the postmillennial judgment the wicked are raised by God, and Satan deceives them by saying that he brought them to life. He tells them that he has come to rescue them from a great tyranny (*ibid.* 663). They make instruments of war, and surround the New Jerusalem city (*ibid.* 664). The coronation of Christ takes place, and then the books of judgment are opened. As Christ looks on the wicked, each one is reminded of every sin they committed (*ibid.* 666). Above the throne a panoramic view of Calvary replays the last scenes of Christ's death. All are transfixed by the scene. Christ also holds the tables of the law in His hands. All see that their exclusion from heaven is just, all exclaim how great and just are God's ways, and everyone bows before Him. Satan sees that heaven would be extreme torture to him, and he bows, confessing that his sentence is just. All know that Satan's works have condemned him. He then rushes with a frenzy to stir up his followers to go and take the city, but they turn on him. No longer is Satan able to deceive. Fire falls from heaven and destroys the wicked (*ibid.* 667-673). There is no eternal hell for them (*ibid.* 545), for that would disallow a resolution to the great controversy. A new heaven and a new earth are free from sin and sinners, and controversy will never arise again, for all have seen the justice of God revealed and the injustice of Satan exposed.

Further reading: 4BC 25-38.

Norman R. Gulley

ETHICS, ANIMAL, see **ANIMAL ETHICS**.

EUROPE. Europe was the first continent after North America on which Seventh-day Adventists began mission work. Adventists had always been attracted by the Old World because of their interest in *Reformation history and the fulfillment of biblical prophecy (4SP 66-187; GC 89, 61-264). Adventism first gained a foothold in Europe in 1864 upon the private initiative of *M. B. Czechowski, a former Roman Catholic priest from Poland who had been converted to Adventism in America. He was followed by *J. N. Andrews in 1874. Andrews began work in the area of Neuchâtel, *Switzerland, and in 1876 moved to Basel, which became the center of European Adventist work in the years to come. Basel was also the home of Ellen White during her stay in Europe (1885-1887).

Adventist missionaries faced a number of problems in Europe that were unknown in their work in North America. Apart from language barriers and cultural diversities, the greatest problem was the close alliance between the established churches and the state, an alliance that left hardly any room for the development of new religious movements. After several years of missionary work in Europe, Andrews stated resignedly: "I have never at any time in America seen so great an accumulation of difficulties as we have had to meet in Europe" (RH, Jan. 1, 1880). Nevertheless, at the time of Ellen White's arrival in Europe, the European Adventist membership numbered approximately 1,000, in more than 30 local congregations.

The trip to Europe was Ellen White's first overseas itinerary. European Adventists of the time considered her visit a spiritual highlight that brought revival, unity, and strength to the dispersed and isolated members, living in an often hostile environment. Initially she thought that her stay would be only for a few months, possibly until May 1886. However, realizing the "great work before us" in Europe, she devoted two full years of her life, visiting *Switzerland, *Denmark, *Sweden, *Norway, *England, *Germany, *Italy, and *France, where she assisted Seventh-day Adventist leaders in pastoral and evangelistic work.

Ellen White constantly pleaded for a stronger Adventist identity among the various national groups, more love and acceptance among church members, and higher moral standards. During her stay in Europe she also received a number of visions concerning the needs and the future of European Adventism. However, the most important work she accomplished for Europe is found in her writings. Her books have been translated into almost every European language and have been, to the present day, an even greater spiritual blessing for Adventist believers in Europe than was her visit—important as it was, historically, for Adventist beginnings in Europe.

Ellen White's invitation to Europe came as a petition from the delegates at the second session of the European Missionary Council held in Basel from May 28 to June 1, 1884. The services of her son *W. C. White, an expert in the publishing work, were also urgently requested. At first Ellen White was hesitant to accept the invitation, as she had not received any instruction by vision from God for this venture. Moreover, her health was weakened from a heavy load of labors during the summer of 1884. However, obedient to what seemed duty, she embarked on the journey and reached Liverpool, England, on August 18, 1885. She was accompanied by her son William, his wife, *Mary (Kelsey) White, and their first child, *Ella. Also in the party were *Sara McEnterfer, *Anna Rasmussen, Bertha Stein, and two of *A. C. Bourdeau's children, Arthur and Jesse.

The following two weeks were spent in England, visiting places such as Grimsby, Ulceby, Riseley, London, and Southampton. The total Adventist membership in Great Britain amounted to slightly more than 100 at the time. At Grimsby, a seaport town on the east coast where the British headquarters of the Adventist mission had been established, Ellen White lectured in the temperance hall. She spoke to more than 1,200 in the town hall about God in nature, making Jesus "the first, the last, the best in everything" (EGWEur 42). After visiting London, she felt burdened with the tremendous challenge of Adventist mission work in Europe's large cities: "There are five million people in London. . . . Who will come up to the help of the Lord against the mighty?" (Lt 22, 1885, in EGWEur 45).

From England, Ellen White went on to Basel, Switzerland, where the largest Adventist institution in Europe at that time, the Imprimerie Polyglotte publishing house, had just been completed. She recognized the pressroom of the publishing house as one of the places she had seen 10 years before. In a remarkable vision on January 3, 1875, she had been shown presses running in different countries and many lights symbolic of companies of believers in Europe who would be enlightened by literature from these presses (3Bio 293, 294). The publishing house was the scene of two important meetings, which Ellen White attended in September of 1885. At the Swiss Conference she encouraged the workers and spoke about proper methods of labor: the need to visit people in their homes, the importance of lay evangelism, and the usefulness of social meetings, in which believers may regularly be trained to be witnesses for Christ. The third European Missionary Council followed, at which Ellen White emphasized the need for unity. She was opposed in this way by D. T. Bourdeau, who favored separate European conferences because of traditional national differences. At one point Bourdeau felt so offended that he planned to leave the council, but with untiring efforts for reconciliation Ellen White was able to win Bourdeau over while remaining true to her position. Bourdeau, on his part, became convinced that her prophetic gift was genuine and confessed that it not only reproves without "partiality" but also inspires "hope, faith, and courage" (RH, Nov. 10, 1885). As a result, the council became a turning point for the Adventist work in Central Europe, and can be rightly characterized as a "miniature general conference" (3Bio 299; EGWEur 66).

The rest of the year 1885 was filled with travels to Denmark, Sweden, Norway, and Italy. In the Scandinavian countries, she was accompanied by *J. G. Matteson, who served as her translator. On her trip to northern Italy she was especially impressed by the Waldensian valleys, which she visited two more times in 1886. "Here, for a thousand years," she wrote, "witnesses for the truth maintained the ancient faith" (GC 66). Near Torre Pellice, Ellen White unexpectedly crossed paths with *Miles Grant, a prominent Advent Christian minister and active opposer of Seventh-day Adventism. Despite his strong criticisms of her, Ellen White refrained from replying to his charges. Her goal was to strengthen the few Italian believers. Among them were the first Seventh-day Adventist converts in Europe, won by M. B. Czechowski as early as 1865.

After returning to her headquarters in Basel, Ellen White set out during the spring of 1886 to visit the Adventist believers in Switzerland. In Tramelan, she met the *Roth family, who had built the first Adventist chapel in Europe. She would return at the end of the year to speak at its dedication service.

Meanwhile, in the summer of 1886, she embarked on a second Scandinavian tour to attend conferences in Sweden and Denmark. Conference president J. G. Matteson had placed an emphasis on training for colporteurs in that field. Recently a new publishing house had also been established in Christiania (Oslo), Norway, to provide the colporteurs with literature. Ellen White was eager to introduce a new worker from America, Norwegian-born *O. A. Olsen, to bring breadth and strength to the growing work in Northern Europe. Once again a local leader, Matteson, was fearful of being pushed aside. Ellen White saw clearly that different minds and talents would be needed to give balance to the work. She realized that a common temptation for church leaders is to dominate the work they are engaged in. While recognizing the benefit of strong leadership, Ellen White stressed that more work can be done when it is carried on more than one shoulder. With her caring personality she was able to gain the full confidence of Matteson, who accepted her advice—the same advice that would later be rejected by *L. R. Conradi.

After she returned from Scandinavia to Basel, her next trip took her to the fourth European Council in Grimsby, England (September/October 1886). The council reaffirmed previous resolutions to hold regular training schools for Bible workers and colporteurs. Meetings with Adventist believers in France and Germany were the next challenges that she took upon herself. She visited France in October 1886, where her Bible-centered public lectures helped to establish a congregation in Nîmes, in the southern part of the country. In the neighboring city of Valence, she experienced the impressiveness of a *Roman Catholic worship service in the Cathedral of St. Apollinaire. This proved helpful as she described Roman liturgy in *The Great Controversy (pp. 566, 567), which she was expanding while in Europe. The lasting impressions that the environment of Reformation history made on her led to plans for the enlargement of this volume. Then, in May 1887, already on her homeward journey, Ellen White succeeded in reviving and reconciling the members of the Vohwinkel congregation in present-day Wuppertal, Germany. There she had a vision that prompted her to organize a *"social meeting" with a testimony service—virtually unknown among the German members. This experience and her calls for unity helped to restore harmony, which proved to be the basis for the successful missionary work of the Adventist Church in Germany under L. R. Conradi's direction in the years to come. En route from Germany, Ellen White paid a last visit to Denmark, Norway, Sweden, and England. At Moss, Norway, she participated in the first Adventist camp meeting held in Europe. Then, on August 3, 1887, she boarded a ship in Liverpool for the eight-day journey to New York City. She brought a good report with her: "After a two years' stay in Europe we see no more reason for discouragement in the state of the cause there than at its rise in the different fields in America. . . . The word has gone forth to Europe, 'Go forward.' . . . The greater the difficulties to be overcome, the greater will be the victory gained" (RH, Dec. 6, 1887).

Further reading: 3Bio 287-373; HS 159-249; EGWEur; *Ellen G. White and Europe. Symposium*

Papers 1987 (Bracknell, Eng.: Ellen G. White Research Center, 1987).

Daniel Heinz

EVANGELISM. No area of practical theology consumed more of Ellen White's time than did her emphasis on evangelism. It permeates nearly everything she wrote. She perceived Adventism as a mission movement and, therefore, assessed all the activities of the church by their ability to help the church fulfill its mission. One cannot understand Ellen White's counsels in practical theology without comprehending the backdrop of evangelism.

The formative years of the Adventist Church were a period of strong evangelistic advance. Ellen White expanded the limited vision of the early Adventists (reaching only those involved in the Millerite movement) to include North America and ultimately the entire globe. Her counsel included both vision casting and a multitude of practical counsels on every form of evangelism: preaching, personal Bible studies, small groups, church planting, need-meeting events (medical missionary work), etc. Whatever the evangelistic topic, new or old, Ellen White has given counsel in that area.

While providing considerable counsel regarding traditional evangelistic methodology, Ellen White also consistently pushed the denomination to explore new methods of evangelizing. She urged: "make use of every means" (9T 109); "different methods of labor" (TM 251); "new methods" (Ev 70); "untried methods" (*ibid.* 125); "something out of the common course of things" (*ibid.* 123); "no fixed rules" (*ibid.* 105). She further nudged the church organization not to prescribe the "exact way in which we should work" (6T 116). Because of the tendency of people to criticize new methodology she reminded

Adventists that there is to be "no unkind criticism, no pulling to pieces of another's work" (Ev 106).

Since evangelism is the heartbeat of the church, Ellen White constantly chided the church to refocus and reignite evangelism. Her advocacy of the pastoral role as primarily church planting stemmed partially from her desire to see those who worked for the church spend most of their time evangelizing. Members were to be discipled not to depend on a pastor for spiritual nourishment.

Ellen White's view of evangelism was wholistic. Evangelism was not just reaching people; it also included fully discipling them into people ready for Jesus to come. Thus evangelism was never considered "short-term." The evangelistic process needed to be long enough to facilitate the discipleship of the new believers (TM 128).

Upon Ellen White's return to North America from Australia in 1900, she discovered that the North American church had degenerated into a nonevangelistic agency. Evangelism had become "baptizing the children," with no major outreach to unreached people. Clergy were beginning to "hover over the churches" rather than plant churches and evangelize (2SM 156). The urbanization of North America was beginning, and Adventism was largely a rural church with no major work in the large cities.

Ellen White spent the last 15 years of her life attempting to recover in the North American Adventist Church the passion for evangelism. In spite of all her efforts for reform in this area, little happened for more than 10 years. In desperation, after the 1909 General Conference session, she toured several Eastern cities, holding evangelistic meetings herself at 82. She led by precept and by example.

In the spring of 1910 she wrote a scathing letter to General Conference president A. G. Daniells, in which she placed the responsibility for evangelism squarely on his shoulders. A few months later, while visiting California, Daniells stopped by to see Ellen White. She refused to see him until he obeyed the counsel he had already received and led the church forward in evangelistic advance. It was enough. Daniells went home and wrote her that he was committed. The next decade under Daniells' leadership witnessed the Adventist Church in North America experiencing its highest growth rate of the twentieth century (6Bio 219-230).

In Ellen White's personal lifework evangelism played a major role from start to finish. The global vision of the Adventist Church is directly attributable to her counsels. There was to be no part of the work of Seventh-day Adventists that was not evangelistic in nature. All Adventist institutions were originally founded to facilitate the church's evangelistic advance.

The publishing work began with a vision directing James White to begin publishing a paper (LS 125). The medical work was begun to facilitate "health reform," but even that was to be done in such a way as to win people to Jesus (FE 488; MM 26). When J. H. Kellogg attempted to make the Battle Creek Sanitarium an interdenominational humanitarian work, not serving the evangelistic arm of the church, he ran into a direct confrontation with Ellen White (5Bio 159, 160).

Adventist educational work was also designed to train men and women for evangelistic ministry (RH, Apr. 14, 1910). Even camp meetings were held, not to benefit believers only, but to train church members for evangelism while also attracting a sizable number of other people to the evangelistic component of the meetings. That is why she advocated moving camp meetings from place to place annually (Ev 20-21). Clearly there was no single ministry of the church that did not have evangelistic potential. Ellen White believed that any ministry that did not serve the evangelistic advance of the church had no reason to exist and draw financial support from the church. She consistently urged Adventists to sacrifice personal comforts for the sake of reaching people for Jesus. This was one of the main motivations for the early Adventist emphasis on simplicity of lifestyle.

Ellen White's role was formative and crucial for the growth of the Adventist Church. Without her counsel and leadership in evangelism, Adventism might well have become only a small North American denomination. In contrast, her influence led to the development of one of the world's most international Christian denominations.

Russell Burrill

EVANGELISM (RHPA, 1946, 747 pp.). Compilation of Ellen White's statements on public evangelism, published by the White Estate in 1946 in response to a 1944 request from R. A. Anderson and L. E. Froom, representing the Ministerial Association of the General Conference. The book deals primarily with evangelism as conducted by ministers and trained instructors, mostly excluding the topics of lay evangelism and medical missionary work, which have only a chapter each. *The Ministry of Healing* (1905), *Counsels on Health* (1923), and *Medical Ministry* (1933) had previously covered medical missionary work. Lay evangelism is addressed especially in *Christian Service* (1925), but also in *Gospel Workers* (1892, 1915) and *Welfare Ministry* (1952) (pp. 71-113).

Evangelism is organized thematically. It deals first with the different geographic audiences for evangelistic campaigns (cities, towns, and rural areas) and then proceeds through the course of a typical campaign, beginning with organization and planning for evangelistic efforts, presenting doctrines, and then advice on making and keeping converts. More chapters on city work and work outside North America follow, and then a selection of special topics (personal evangelism, music, medical evangelism, special target audiences, and dealing with false doctrines). There are two chapters on the qualifications and need for both men and women in evangelism, and a final chapter on the nearness of Christ's return as a reason for evangelism. According to Arthur White, the book's plan of organization arose naturally from the major themes of Ellen White's statements on the subject, once brought together in one place.

About one quarter of the material was drawn from then-available Ellen White books, another quarter from various periodical articles, and the remaining half from unpublished manuscripts. The actual work of compilation was performed by Louise Kleuser, of the Ministerial Association, and Arthur White.

Further reading: A. L. White, "In Defense of Compilations," *Spectrum* 16, no. 3 (August 1985): 14-20; idem, *Messenger to the Remnant* (EGWE, 1959 revision), pp. 95, 96.

Tony Zbaraschuk

EVANGELISM, OUTPOST, see **CITIES, LIVING IN**.

EVIL, ORIGIN AND NATURE OF, see **SATAN; SIN**.

EVOLUTION, see **CREATION AND EVOLUTION**.

FAITH. For Ellen White, genuine faith is the Christian's response to God's grace, and its quality depends on a correct view of the character of God. Error does not become truth merely because a person has faith in it

815

(1SM 346). The apostle Paul had faith in his Jewish heritage, which prompted his zeal for legal obedience in forms and ceremonies, but his "faith [was] out of Christ." When Paul saw the truth "as it is in Jesus," his "mind and character" were transformed and nothing ever after "could shake his faith" (*ibid.*). Faith is a characteristic of Christians who acknowledge God's will, trust His judgment, and claim His grace of pardon and power in their desire to reflect their Lord (GC 469).

Genuine faith, in contrast to nominal faith, joins the "enlightened intellect" with "a heart that can discern and appreciate the heavenly treasure," leading to "repentance and transformation of character" as it accepts "the gospel treasure, with all the obligations which it imposes" (COL 112). A "nominal faith in Christ . . . accepts Him merely as the Savior of the world" but does not embrace Him as a personal Savior. Faith is more than "mere intellectual assent to the truth," more than "an opinion." "Saving faith is a transaction by which those who receive Christ join themselves in covenant relation with God. Genuine faith is life. A living faith means an increase of vigor, a confiding trust, by which the soul becomes a conquering power" (DA 347).

More than "a casual faith," or a "mere consent of the intellect," Ellen White asserted that "faith that is unto salvation . . . is . . . rooted in the heart, . . . [embracing] Christ as a personal Savior. . . . This faith leads its possessor to place all the affections of the soul upon Christ; his understanding is under the control of the Holy Spirit, and his character is molded after the divine likeness. His faith is not a dead faith" (1SM 391). Such faith has "an appreciation of the cost of salvation," for "when you feel that Jesus died for you on the cruel cross of Calvary" "you have an intelligent, understanding faith that His death makes it possible for you to cease from

sin, and to perfect a righteous character through the grace of God, bestowed upon you as the purchase of Christ's blood" (RH, July 24, 1888).

A mere "profession of faith" and the "possession of truth" are "two different things" (COL 97). "A legal religion is insufficient to bring the soul into harmony with God. The hard, rigid orthodoxy of the Pharisees, destitute of contrition, tenderness, or love, was only a stumbling block to sinners. . . . The only true faith is that which 'worketh by love' (Gal. 5:6) to purify the soul. It is as leaven that transforms the character" (MB 53).

Genuine faith is a process and attitude by which we "come to know God by an experimental knowledge," proving for ourselves "the reality of His Word, the truth of His promises." Through this "knowledge of God and His Word through personal experience," the Christian "has a settled faith in the divinity of the Holy Scriptures. He has proved that God's Word is truth, and he knows that truth can never contradict itself" (MH 461, 462).

Because faith is the key element in *righteousness by faith, a limited or false understanding of faith leads to erroneous doctrines regarding how men and women are saved. "The only way in which . . . [they] can attain to righteousness is through faith. By faith" the believer "can bring to God the merits of Christ, and the Lord places the obedience of His Son to the sinner's account. . . . This is how faith is accounted righteousness" (1SM 367).

Further, a correct understanding of genuine faith also understands that "while God can be just, and yet justify the sinner through the merits of Christ, no . . . [persons] can cover . . . [their souls] with the garments of Christ's righteousness while practicing known sins, or neglecting known duties. God requires the entire surrender of the heart, before justification can take place; and in order for man to retain justification, there must be continual obedience, through active, living faith that works by love and purifies the soul" (*ibid.* 366).

The Christian's life of continual obedience is possible only because "genuine faith appropriates the righteousness of Christ, and the sinner is made an overcomer with Christ; for he is made a partaker of the divine nature, and thus divinity and humanity are combined" (*ibid.* 363, 364). Genuine faith becomes the attitude of mind and heart whereby we abide in Christ (*ibid.* 335).

Presumption is Satan's counterfeit of faith. "Faith claims God's promises, and brings forth fruit in obedience. Presumption also claims the promises, but uses them as Satan did, to excuse transgression. . . . It is not faith that claims the favor of Heaven without complying with the conditions on which mercy is to be granted. Genuine faith has its foundation in the promises and provisions of the Scriptures" (DA 126).

Faith is not a blind leap when all else fails, because "God never asks us to believe, without giving sufficient evidence upon which to base our faith. His existence, His character, the truthfulness of His Word, are all established by testimony that appeals to our reason; and this testimony is abundant. Yet God has never removed the possibility of doubt. Our faith must rest upon evidence, not demonstration. Those who wish to doubt will have opportunity; while those who really desire to know the truth will find plenty of evidence on which to rest their faith" (SC 105). Knowing the truth about God motivates faith to trust God, "believing that He loves us and knows best what is for our good. . . . Truth, uprightness, purity . . . [are] secrets of life's success. It is faith that puts us in possession of these principles" (Ed 253).

Further reading: COL 95-114; SC 49-55, 105-113; H. E. Douglass, *Faith, Saying Yes to God* (SPA, 1978).

Herbert E. Douglass

FAITH AND WORKS (SPA, 1979, 122 pp.). Compilation of 19 presentations on the subjects of righteousness by faith, and the role of faith and works in the Christian life, written by Ellen White between 1881 and 1902. These presentations, published in chronological sequence, were taken from sermons and articles published in the *Review and Herald* and *Signs of the Times*. Although no attempt was made to be exhaustive, the basic themes highlighted in this book permeate many of her other books, and so the sermons and articles selected here provide a good sample of Ellen White's thoughts on these doctrines.

In her presentations of the subject, Ellen White attempted to keep a balance between the biblical teachings that salvation is a gift of God's grace accepted in the Christian's life through faith and that at the same time true faith "will lead to perfect conformity to the law of God. Faith is manifested by works" (p. 52). Hence she saw a close harmony between the law of God and the gospel of salvation in Jesus Christ and avoided any denigration of the importance of either in the plan of redemption.

FAITH HEALING, see **PRAYER FOR THE SICK.**

FAITH I LIVE BY, THE (RHPA, 1958, 384 pp.). Fifth daily *devotional book published by the Ellen G. White Estate. Materials selected for these daily meditations were drawn from Ellen White's published writings, with references for each citation given at the end of the book. Each month follows a different theme and presents selections intended to provide both inspiration and information on the principal doctrines of the Christian faith. Monthly topics include God's Word, the Godhead, Satan and the great rebellion, God's remedy for sin, conversion and the new life in Christ, the sanctuary of God, the Christ-centered home, the last church of Christ, and end-time events. The book also includes an index to daily readings and a subject index.

FAMILY, see **HOME AND FAMILY.**

FANATICISM. Ellen White labeled several categories of behavior as fanaticism. This variety is exemplified in an interview which she had with a Mr. and Mrs. Ralph Mackin, who claimed to have special gifts of the "Spirit." In a conversation recorded by a stenographer, Ellen White recalled early encounters with "some who had strange exercisings of the body" and "others who were governed largely by their own impressions. Some thought it wrong to work. Still others believed that the righteous dead had been raised to eternal life. A few sought to cultivate a spirit of humility by creeping on the floor, like little children. Some would dance, and sing 'Glory, glory, glory, glory, glory, glory,' over and over again. Sometimes a person would jump up and down on the floor, with hands uplifted, praising God; and this would be kept up for as long as half an hour at a time" (3SM 370, 371). She later wrote regarding the Mackins, who claimed the power to cast out demons, "The work of declaring persons possessed of the devil, and then praying with them and pretending to cast out the evil spirits, is fanaticism which will bring into disrepute any church which sanctions such work" (*ibid.* 378). In the first years of her prophetic ministry Ellen White encountered many instances of fanaticism and strange behavior. Many of these experiences happened while she still lived in Maine

before her marriage to James White (1Bio 70-72, 79-87; cf. *Israel Damman).

Fanaticism did not only refer to strange behavior, though. White also used the term in referring to "new light" urged on the church by some. "After the passing of the time in 1844," she wrote, "we had fanaticism of every kind to meet. Testimonies of reproof were given me to bear to some holding spiritualistic theories" (8T 292). In the early 1900s *pantheism was another of those "spiritualistic theories" that White had to combat (*ibid.* 291, 292).

There were several reasons White seemed quite opposed to anything that hinted at fanaticism. "Any manifestation of fanaticism takes the mind away from the evidence of truth—the Word itself" (3SM 372). "There is constant danger of allowing something to come into our midst that we may regard as the working of the Holy Spirit, but that in reality is the fruit of a spirit of fanaticism" (*ibid.* 373). The clear teachings of the Bible were the sure guide for the faithful.

Often White had to counsel others who were convinced they had a special outpouring of the Holy Spirit. While not denying the gifts of the Spirit, of which she was most keenly aware, she was most protective of them. She wrote, "We must go to the people with the solid Word of God; and when they receive that Word, the Holy Spirit may come, but it always comes, as I have stated before, in a way that commends itself to the judgment of the people" (*ibid.*).

The appearance of fanaticism to outsiders was also of high importance. "There are persons of an excitable temperament who are easily led into fanaticism; and should we allow anything to come into our churches that would lead such persons into error we would soon see these errors carried to extreme lengths; and then because of the course of these disorderly elements a stigma would rest upon the whole body of Seventh-day Adventists" (*ibid.*).

In addition to the Mackins mentioned above, the case of Anna Phillips (see *Anna [Phillips] Rice) also had a close tie with fanaticism. White wrote regarding church leaders who encouraged Phillips' visions, "I am more sorry than I can express to you that the matter has been handled unwisely. We shall have scores of just such developments, and if our leading brethren shall catch up things of this character and endorse them as they have done in this case, we shall have one of the most sweeping tidal waves of fanaticism that has been seen in our experience" (2SM 92).

The *Holy Flesh doctrine that emerged in 1900 at a camp meeting in Indiana was another example of wrong beliefs leading to fanatical, extreme religious behavior. In response White wrote, "The manner in which the meetings in Indiana have been carried on, with noise and confusion, does not commend them to thoughtful, intelligent minds. There is nothing in these demonstrations which will convince the world that we have the truth" (*ibid.* 35). The impact of fanaticism on the onlooking public was another important factor behind White's firm commitment to hold fanatical movements in check.

Further reading: 2SM 13-60; 3SM 361-378; 1MCP 38-47.

Thomas Toews

FICTION, see **LITERATURE AND READING**.

FINANCES, ELLEN G. WHITE'S. From the perspective of dollar value, the story of Ellen White's personal finances moved through three distinct stages: (1) poverty (1846-1855), gradually improving from near pennilessness (at the time of her marriage to James White) to a more comfortable middle-class status

and the first home of James' and Ellen's own (when they moved to Battle Creek in 1855), the fruit of James' entrepreneurial efforts; (2) asset development (1855-1881), interrupted by two years of austerity as a result of James' stroke (1865), but otherwise continuing up to his death in 1881, and sparked by James' business acumen and his energetic but frequently criticized business pursuits; (3) asset development (1881-1915), primarily in literary works, continuing until her death in 1915, with income being generated primarily by book and article royalties.

Because of Ellen White's remarkable generosity to worthy people and causes, her estate was technically bankrupt when she died. The declared deficit was $21,528.13, though the estimated value of her literary assets more than covered all obligations. The court's puzzlement over how to assess the value of her literary assets led to the deficit declaration. To resolve the issue, the General Conference purchased the entire estate, an arrangement that made it possible to cover the deficit through future royalties.

In significant ways her husband, James, helped to shape Ellen White's attitudes toward money. Both of them were deeply imprinted with the sturdy New England virtues of "thrift and economy." And regardless of their own financial state, both of them were unstintingly generous to the Advent cause and to people in need, in some cases even giving away money or extending no-interest loans with funds they themselves had borrowed at 10 percent interest.

Both of them recognized that stinginess was a major hazard of a life of thrift. Repeatedly Ellen White warned against the danger of a "close, penurious spirit": "Some . . . have wasted much precious time for the sake of saving a little, when their time was worth a great deal more than that which they gained.

This displeases God. It is right that economy should be used, but it has by some been stretched into meanness with no other object than to add to their treasures" (1T 153).

In 1870, writing in his own defense (while confessing his sins!), James White noted a similar danger (though motivated by altruism rather than by greed)—namely, that thrift and hard work, even in the interest of good, can diminish one's effectiveness: "We now regret that we have robbed ourselves and family to help others, and have robbed the cause of God of more efficient service, by wearing out too soon, in the exercise of too rigid industry and economy" (RH, Jan. 11, 1870).

It was probably the influence of James, however, that enabled Ellen White to make peace with the need to buy quality goods in the interest of efficiency and comfort rather than settling for lesser goods at a lower price. An incident when James was recovering from his stroke (1866) illustrates Ellen White's impulse in this direction, though one that probably needed James' constant reinforcement. As reported in the *Testimonies for the Church*, she had set out to buy a more comfortable chair so that James could sit up instead of having to lie down all the time. The dealers had none at her preferred price of $15, but offered her a fine $30 chair for $17. Yielding to the arguments of the brother who was with her, however, Ellen special-ordered a chair for $14 and had it delivered.

Rumors of the Whites' "extravagance" spread everywhere. Though the purchase was made in New York, Ellen White herself heard about it in Wisconsin and Iowa. Her response was pointed: "Had I the same to do over again, I would do as I did, with this exception: I would rely upon my own judgment, and purchase a chair costing a few dollars more, and worth double the one I got" (1T 594).

James' health crisis also led to the purchase of a new carriage. Ellen White's description of the event illustrates the Whites' increasing concern for quality and comfort: "Our old, hard-riding carriage had been well-nigh killing us and our team," she wrote. Brothers King, Fargo, and Maynard saw the need and "decided that in mercy to ourselves and team we should have a light, comfortable carriage." So they took James out and bought one. "This was just what we needed and would have saved me much weariness in traveling in the heat of summer" (*ibid.* 599, 600).

James' preference for good horses and a comfortable carriage was sometimes a cause of grumbling among the believers, perhaps not without some justification. In 1880 he wrote to Ellen: "I now have the best team and carriage as a whole, that I ever owned and mean to enjoy them" (JW to EGW, Apr. 7, 1880). A few days earlier he had written that the cushions in his new carriage were "the softest I ever saw" (JW to EGW, Apr. 4, 1880). But both of them knew they would need all the help they could get if they were to survive their many travels. In their later years, whether traveling by ship, rail, or carriage, they often opted for comfort and convenience, with its enhanced health benefit, even though it cost more. After James was gone, Ellen White continued the practice of making travel as comfortable and healthful as possible.

That preference for comfort may seem surprising in the light of this more austere view of traveling, also reported in the *Testimonies* (1879): "Young men who engage in tent labor should be careful not to indulge in unnecessary expense. . . . The wants of the cause are many, and, without stinginess, the most rigid economy should be used in this matter. It is easier to run up a bill than to settle it. There are many things that would be convenient and enjoyable that are not needful, and that can be dispensed with without actual suffering. It is very easy to multiply hotel bills and railroad fares, expenses that might be avoided or very much lessened. We have passed over the road to and from California twelve times, and have not expended one dollar for meals at the restaurants or in the attached dining car. We eat our meals from our lunch baskets. After being three days out, the food becomes quite stale, but a little milk or warm gruel supplies our lack" (4T 299).

While the Whites were not tempted to indulge in commercially prepared food when they traveled, space, (smoke-free) fresh air, and peace and quiet were priorities for which they were willing to pay. Nevertheless, it appears that Ellen was more austere than James. In 1874 James wrote to their son Willie: "Do not consent to her [Ellen's] economical ideas, leading you to pinch along. See that everything like her dresses, shawls, saques, shoes, bonnet, etc., are good. And be sure to dress yourself in a respectable manner." In the same letter he exclaims: "I am done with that economy that tends to [cheapness] of dress and equipage. . . . I am done [with] this pinching and saving, so much" (JW to WCW, July 5, 1874).

In comparing their differences over the quality versus thrift issue, one might characterize Ellen's view as that of "save and give," a view shaped by two Gospel stories: the rich young ruler (Luke 18:22: "Sell all that you own and distribute the money to the poor") and the widow's mite (Luke 21:4: "She out of her poverty has put in all she had to live on"). By contrast, James' view was "invest and share," a view shaped by the parable of the talents, in which the master commends those who doubled their money by wise investment (Matt. 25:14-30) and by the story of Zacchaeus, whom Jesus pronounced a saved man even though he had volunteered to give only half his goods to the poor (Luke 19:1-10).

Perhaps a factor in Ellen White's outlook was the realization that her mission and the work of the church would have been severely hampered without the aggressive enterprising work of her husband. Instead of shunning the world as wicked, James harnessed "worldly" potential for the sake of the kingdom of God.

It is clear that Ellen White would never have been able to do all that she did if James hadn't been a natural-born entrepreneur. In Rochester, before the move to Battle Creek in 1855, he became an agent for a variety of products to help keep himself and the press afloat: charts, stationery, Bibles, Bible dictionaries and concordances, atlases and medical books. During the Civil War he once bought a dealer's full supply of stationery for $1,200; then, taking advantage of the inflationary effects of the war, he sold what he had not used for $2,400. At a time when a good working wage was a dollar a day, it would have been startling to see a church leader invest the equivalent of three years' income and doubling his investment shortly thereafter.

James especially liked to work with real estate. Beginning with the first home of their own, which they built in Battle Creek in 1856, by the time of James' death in 1881 the Whites had built or purchased at least 11 homes in four states: Michigan, Iowa, Colorado, and California (see *homes of James and Ellen G. White).

The funds from James' various projects were used to help others with food, housing, transportation, and clothing. In the White household in *Rochester, for example, more than 16 family members and workers—along with the press itself—lived together in the same house. The Whites cared for them all. After the press moved to Battle Creek in 1855, the pressure on the Whites was reduced, but the giving continued. Indeed, James was not at all hesitant to give away the clothes off his own back. J. O. Corliss, a young preacher whom the Whites had helped by taking him into their own home for two years, noted that he had seen James "give no less than three overcoats in a single winter to poor preachers needing such garments" (RH, Aug. 23, 1923).

Interestingly enough, in 1865, even while James was busily augmenting his regular work through various entrepreneurial projects, Ellen White wrote a testimony to the workers at the press cautioning them about that very thing: "If trafficking which has no connection with the work of God engages the mind and occupies time, the work will not be done thoroughly and well. At the best, those engaged in the work have no physical or mental energy to spare" (1T 586). At one point James seems to have agreed with those sentiments: "I should have been supported in my calling," he wrote in the *Review*, "and had nothing to do with selling books" (RH, Mar. 26, 1867).

But old temptations die hard. In 1878-1879, for example, when James was in Texas, the entrepreneurial fever struck with intensity. Not only did he develop a scheme for buying mules in Texas and selling them for a profit in Colorado—he also embarked on a host of other ventures: buying buffalo and wildcat skins to sell in the Northeast, purchasing Michigan butter, nuts, and beans to sell in Texas. Once he sold $4 worth of brooms in a single day.

Ellen did not approve of all James' business exploits; those in Texas she found particularly troubling (Lt 32, 1879). Still, she and the church profited from James' endeavors. Three years after James' death she wrote to James' brother John that the loss of the "wisdom and ability" of her husband in helping her plan and bring in means meant that her resources were "steadily decreasing" (Lt 61, 1884, in 6MR 307).

But perhaps the most hurtful result of James' business ventures was the criticism

that it engendered against both James and Ellen. As early as 1851 rumors circulated that the Whites had a better horse than necessary and were living off donated money. Ironically, a key instigator turned out to be a brother known only as N.A.H., an impoverished man to whom James had given his own overcoat and $20 of donated money and for whom the believers had purchased a horse and carriage at James' urging.

The criticisms were fully addressed, but not banished. Indeed, they became so acute that the believers initiated formal investigations in 1854, 1863, and 1869. In each instance the Whites were exonerated. The 1863 investigation yielded a 39-page booklet: *Vindication of the Business Career of Elder James White;* after the 1869 investigation a 155-page book was published: *Defense of Eld. James White and Wife: The Battle Creek Church to the Churches and Brethren Scattered Abroad.* The latter publication moved beyond finance to address wider issues, including doctrine and the ministry of Ellen White. The book even went so far as to denounce slanderous reports that Ellen White had borne children out of wedlock and that she had visions advocating that James White and another church member swap wives (*Defense*, pp. 143-146).

A number of factors had complicated the issues. In the early years believers often simply handed cash to James and other church leaders for them to use as they saw fit. Typically there was no accounting. People simply trusted their leaders.

James' stroke in 1865 significantly complicated matters. Suddenly James no longer had the ability to generate funds. Initially he told his fellow believers that they had adequate resources and would ask for help if the need arose. They first sold off some of their possessions and then did ask for help. When their cow died, for example, they let it be known that it would be helpful if the believers could replace it. To help cover James' cost at Jackson's Dansville water-cure establishment, the church in Monterey, Michigan, led by Joseph Bates, sent them $60; a Sister Gates sent them $10. A few months later when James had to have most of his teeth pulled and needed dentures, J. N. Andrews and Uriah Smith sent $10 each and Mrs. M. J. Cornell sent $5. The cumulative effect of all these incidents, however, somehow made it easy to believe that James White was "crazy for money."

The rumors were swirling so wildly that James called for a "council of brethren" in Battle Creek to assess the situation and put the rumors to rest. After the investigation everyone present was astonished to learn that the real value of the White property was only $1,500, besides their horses and carriage. The rumor that the Whites were "wealthy, worldly, and grasping for more"—Ellen White's words (1T 607)—simply were not true. She summarized the situation as follows: "In looking over my husband's business matters for ten years, and his liberal manner of handing out means to help the work in all its branches, the best and most charitable conclusion is that our property has been used in the cause of present truth. My husband has kept no accounts, and what he has given can be traced only from memory and from what has been receipted in the *Review*. The fact that we are worth so little, appearing at this time when my husband has been represented as wealthy and still grasping for more, has been a matter of rejoicing to us, as it is the best refutation of the false charges which threatened our influence and Christian character" (*ibid.*).

Perhaps the most astonishing development of all is what happened at James White's funeral in 1881. Breaking all the rules of funeral etiquette, Uriah Smith, in the funeral homily itself, tackled head-on the criticisms against

James: "No individual has been wronged, and not a dollar has been taken unjustly from the treasury of any branch of this work; while he has himself, within the last eight years, put into the different branches of the cause, the sum of twenty thousand dollars of his own means" (Uriah Smith, *In Memoriam*, pp. 34-36). The $20,000 amount becomes even more significant in light of the fact that for nearly two years James had accepted no money at all from the Review, an observation he made in a letter to Willie (JW to WCW and Mary White, Feb. 17, 1881). Based on the average figures of an annual wage of $500 then and $50,000 today, that would mean that the Whites gave to the work of the church the equivalent of $2 million over an eight-year period.

Turning to the later ministry of Ellen White, especially the years following the death of James in 1881, a crucial incident may easily be overlooked because it happened during the chaotic events surrounding James' stroke and recovery and the turmoil over his integrity. The incident involved the aged missionary *Hannah More, who had accepted the Sabbath and consequently lost her job at an orphanage run by evangelical Protestants in Africa. She came to Battle Creek in search of work and friends, but found neither. The Whites were gone at the time. Sister More ended up going to northern Michigan to live with former colleagues of hers who were still Sundaykeepers. When the Whites found out about her, they did everything they could to bring her back to the Adventist community. But winter came, transportation closed down, and Hannah More passed to her rest.

In addition to the passionate story found in 1T 666-680, Ellen White refers to Hannah More in several later *Testimonies* volumes (2T 140-145, 332; 3T 407, 408). The fact that a dedicated but aged servant of Christ could move through Battle Creek without anyone paying particular attention was very troubling to the Whites. But the significance of the event for our purposes here is to show how it galvanized Ellen White's attitude toward the use of money. Here are key excerpts: "When we learned our real circumstances, as set forth in *Testimony* No. 13 [1T 606, 607], we both took the matter joyfully and said we did not want the responsibility of means. This was wrong. God wants that we should have means that we may, as in time past, help where help is needed" (1T 678). "We see outcasts, widows, orphans, worthy poor, and ministers in want, and many chances to use means to the glory of God, the advancement of His cause, and the relief of suffering saints, and I . . . [lack] means to use for God. The experience of nearly a quarter of a century in extensive traveling, feeling the condition of those who need help, qualifies us to make a judicious use of our Lord's money. I have bought my own stationery, paid my own postage, and spent much of my life writing for the good of others, and all I have received for this work, which has wearied and worn me terribly, would not pay a tithe of my postage. When means has been pressed upon me, I have refused it, or appropriated it to such charitable objects as the Publishing Association. I shall do so no more. I shall do my duty in labor as ever, but my fears of receiving means to use for the Lord are gone. This case of Sister More has fully aroused me to see the work of Satan in depriving us of means" (*ibid.* 678, 679).

The die was cast. From now on Ellen White would take money and use it. Furthermore, the "pinching and saving" that had irritated James virtually vanished from sight. After James had died, Ellen White became the enterprising one, reaching out, helping, motivating, challenging. Her home was often a grand central station; guests were welcomed and fed well. If necessary she would move to larger quarters to accommodate the flow, as she did in Australia: "We shall keep a free hotel as long as we are living in Granville; for there is no other way to do," she wrote to S. N. Haskell. "We shall have to have council meetings and committee meetings at our home, and those who come to these meetings must be entertained at our house, and sit at our table. We like to have them here, but it is almost a constant draft upon us" (Lt 11, 1895, in 7MR 83).

One feature of Ellen White's use of money reflected James' aggressive example while he was alive, namely, putting one's name at the head of a list of contributors for significant projects. Even before James' death, she did not hesitate to carry this method to audacious extremes when by herself. When she visited the newly formed North Pacific Mission in Oregon, for example, she confronted some of the wealthy brothers who had responded to J. N. Loughborough's appeal in 1877 by pledging to buy $5,000 worth of stock in support of the Pacific Press—but then reneged. Telling the story at the Michigan camp meeting in 1891, Ellen White described what happened: "There were all these men of wealth. Those who had the most were complaining the most," she said. Confronting one of the delinquents by name [Aaron Miller, from Milton], she pressed him on his unpaid pledge. Then she turned to Brother Isaac Van Horn, and told him to put her name down in place of Brother Miller's. " 'I will stand where he stands. I will be responsible for him.' I called for another in the same way, and when I called for a third, they got ashamed and began to feel that they would not allow Sister White to pay their money" (1SAT 167; cf. Doug Johnson, *Adventism on the Western Frontier* [1996], p. 43).

To sum up, the finances of Ellen White are best understood through a double focus on her life and her writings. And in both cases consideration of time and place are crucial. Two twentieth-century events, however, have made that more difficult for Adventism. First, the Fundamentalist movement in the 1910s and 1920s reinforced the natural tendencies of devout believers to grant "inspired" messengers absolute authority. Approaching Ellen White's experience with the assumptions of verbal inspiration makes it almost impossible to deal adequately with the dynamism evident in her life and writings. Second, the Great Depression of the 1930s led the church to emphasize the more austere "thrift and economy" elements in Ellen White's writings, obscuring the way in which Scripture, the Spirit, and the energetic tutelage of her husband, James, all worked together to enable Ellen White to become an enterprising, buoyant, and generous Christian, one who eagerly used her financial resources to bless the church and those in need. The generosity was always there; but the "pinching and saving" impulses exhibited in her early experience were conquered by the gifts God gave her in increasing measure as she continued to serve him.

See also: Debt.

Further reading: V. Robinson, *James White* (RHPA, 1976); G. Wheeler, *James White: Innovator and Overcomer* (RHPA, 2003).

Alden Thompson

FLOOD, see **BIBLE AND EARTH SCIENCES**.

FOOD, UNCLEAN, see **UNCLEAN FOOD**.

FOOT WASHING, see **LORD'S SUPPER**.

FOREIGN MISSION BOARD. From 1889 to 1903 the Foreign Mission Board (FMB) operated as one of the many semi-independent associations that directed various functions of the Seventh-day Adventist Church. The FMB was established by the General Conference

session of 1889, with the General Conference president directing its work. The FMB enjoyed far-reaching authority in guiding and supervising Adventist mission work, setting priorities, raising funds, and selecting and training missionaries. The *General Conference session of 1903 transferred the responsibilities of the FMB to the General Conference Committee.

Ellen White's references to the FMB deal with several issues. She supported the FMB in its focus on mission and appealed to conference leadership and Adventist members to likewise support its work. She rebuked *J. H. Kellogg for expecting the FMB to take financial responsibility for his medical work in America. She reminded church members in Australia that the FMB had contributed much to the work in Australasia; she counseled concerning the choice of people to serve on the FMB, that they not be conceited or self-important, but have a living connection with God and an understanding of the harvest fields around the world.

Further reading: B. L. Bauer, "Congregational and Mission Structures and How the Seventh-day Adventist Church Has Related to Them" (D.Miss. diss., Fuller Theological Seminary, School of World Mission, 1982); B. D. Oliver, *SDA Organizational Structure: Past, Present, and Future* (AUP, 1989), pp. 82-85, 155-162, 175.

Bruce L. Bauer

FORGIVENESS. For Ellen White forgiveness is not only a judicial act of God that frees the sinner from condemnation and commutes the ultimate death penalty, but also an "outflow" of divine love that "transforms the heart" (MB 114; cf. YI, Nov. 29, 1894). This pardon equates with justification and rests on the substitutionary death of Christ on the cross (FW 103).

A divine influence draws the sinner toward

forgiveness by convicting the mind of the malignity of the sinful act, and by convincing the heart of God's graciousness (1SM 390; ST, Mar. 18, 1903). Confession of specific sins to God and the exercise of faith in His promises are necessary to repentance; and repentance precedes forgiveness (SC 38; ST, Mar. 18, 1903). Enabled by Christ to repent, and readied to receive unmerited forgiveness, the sinner demonstrates gratitude by inviting the indwelling Spirit to transform the life (UL 38).

Forgiveness bestowed can be retained only by maintaining a saving relationship with the Forgiver (10MR 289), and rebellion against God nullifies past forgiveness (COL 251). Though sins are fully forgiven, and not remembered against the individual by God, the record of sins is not expunged from heaven's record books until the final atonement is consummated (PP 357). Thereafter, the remembrance of sin will not be brought to mind (*ibid.* 358). Forgiveness granted does not cancel temporal consequences, though sometimes they may be averted through the mercy of God (19MR 265; 1SP 378, 379).

Some sins are primarily offenses against God, and of these, only one is unforgivable (RH, June 29, 1897). The sin against the Holy Spirit is not beyond God's capacity to forgive. It is unpardonable because the sinner has, through deliberate and repeated rebellion, so hardened his or her heart against God that he or she has become unimpressible, and completely unresponsive to the drawing influence of the Holy Spirit (5BC 1092, 1093).

The most reprehensible sins against fellow beings can be forgiven by God (7MR 341), but pardon for these sins is contingent upon earnest efforts to right the wrongs committed against His children (5T 646). Generous grace received prompts unstinting and gracious forgiveness of those who offend the forgiven sinner (MB 22). Forgiveness does not excuse the offense nor preclude just reparation; the offending debtor is admonished to repent and repay (COL 247; RH, Jan. 3, 1899). No excuse is too persuasive, no pattern of offenses is too frequent, no evil deed is too loathsome, to prevent the forgiven and sanctified child of God from extending forgiveness to friends and foes (RH, Nov. 30, 1886).

Further reading: COL 243-251; MB 113-116.

H. Peter Swanson

FRANCE. Visited by Ellen White between October 13 and November 3, 1886. From 1885 to 1887 Ellen White lived in Europe and visited Adventist families and some sympathizers to strengthen their young faith in the second coming of Jesus and the Advent message. Before her visit, the work of *M. B. Czechowski (1864-1876)and *J. N. Andrews (1874-1883) among French-speaking Europeans gave birth to the future Seventh-day Adventist Church in France. While in Europe Ellen White made her home at the church's headquarters in Basel, Switzerland. She arrived in France after having already visited England, Italy, Denmark, Sweden, and Norway. To a great extent, her ministry in France was aimed at strengthening a young church with her Christ-centered messages and writings.

At the time France had approximately 50 Adventist Sabbathkeepers residing in Valence, Branges, Bastia (Corsica Island), Lacaze, and Alsace (which belonged to the second German Reich between 1871 and 1918). During her 20-day visit Ellen White spent most of her time in Nîmes, where Daniel T. Bourdeau had been working for four months with the help of Jean-Pierre Badaut, Albert Vuilleumier, and Jacques Erzeberger. Nîmes was an old Roman city whose antique ruins she contemplated with admiration: "There are many things here that make it worthwhile to see.

There are the most ancient buildings I have ever looked upon" (Lt 108, 1886, in 17MR 75). In this "very wicked city" she noted seeing "the finest work of art" (Lt 109, 1886). She appreciated her visit to the Versailles palace and other monuments in Paris (EGWEur 229, 230) and the work done to care for the poor people in this country.

Ellen White's numerous references to France in her published writings indicate her deep interest in the culture, history, and spirituality of this old European country. Her chapter on the *French Revolution (GC 265-288) reveals many relevant and remarkable insights into the causes of the secularism of present-day France. Today an Ellen G. White Research Center is located at the Salève Adventist University in Collonges, France, near Geneva, Switzerland.

Further reading: GC 211-236, 265-288, 585; *Centennial Symposium: Ellen G. White and Europe 1885/1887* (Bracknell, Eng.: Ellen G. White Research Centre, 1987), pp. 360-412; D. A. Delafield, *Ellen G. White in Europe* (RHPA, 1975), pp. 226-246; *Seventh-day Adventist Encyclopedia* (1996), vol. 10, pp. 564-567; Gérard Poublan, *Ellen G. White en France: d'après son journal et sa correspondance* (Castres: unpublished paper, 1987); *idem*, *Ellen G. White en France: sermons et lettres* (Castres: unpublished paper, second edition, 1991).

Jean-Luc Rolland

FREEMASONRY, see **SECRET SOCIETIES**.

FRENCH REVOLUTION. Ellen White's portrayal of the French Revolution shows a clear developmental progression. *Spiritual Gifts*, volume 1 (1858), a panoramic view of history from Adam to the Second Advent, never mentioned the French Revolution. The expanded *Spirit of Prophecy*, volume 4 (1884) (chapter "The Two Witnesses"), devoted six pages to it (4SP

188-193). *The Great Controversy* (1888), however, included a 24-page chapter, "The Bible and the French Revolution," with quotes from unnamed sources; in the revised 1911 edition these nine sources were identified by C. C. Crisler and W. W. Prescott.

The introduction to the 1888 edition explained Ellen White's purpose and methodology. She wanted to trace the history of the controversy between Christ and Satan, truth and error, and to shed light on future struggles. She transcribed "flashlight scenes" of events received in vision, selecting highpoints in church history that revealed "the unfolding of the great testing truths," and quoting from authors whose descriptions offered a "forcible presentation of the subject" (GC88 g, h). Yet she never claimed to be a historian. Her son W. C. White acknowledged that "Mother has never claimed to be authority on history" and did not wish readers to "take it [*The Great Controversy*] as authority on historical dates or use it to settle controversy regarding details of history." Instead, he said, she "made use of good and clear historical statements" to clarify for the reader the "flashlight pictures" seen in vision (WCW, "*The Great Controversy*, 1911 edition" and "W. C. White Statement Made to W. W. Eastman," in 3SM 433-450).

Arthur G. Daniells told the 1919 Bible Conference delegates that Ellen White in her chapter on the French Revolution was weaving "the interpretation of Bible prophecy" (Rev. 11) through selected events in French history (AGD to Bible Conference delegates, July 30, 1919, in *Spectrum* 10, no. 1 [May 1979]: 34; see also GC 265, 266). Both she and Uriah Smith (whose 1873 *Thoughts on Daniel and the Revelation* was her model for the organization, citations, and deletions in *The Great Controversy*) had been shaped by their cultural milieu and their religious convictions in the selection of sources to quote. Both preferred authors (such as Scott, Wylie, Thiers, D'Aubigné, de Felice, and Alison) whose point of view reflected their own: conservative, anti-papal, anti-Catholic, anti-revolutionary, and pro-democracy.

Scholarly archival research was impossible in France during the time Ellen White wrote *The Great Controversy*. She did not know French and was not a research scholar, and the relevant archives were not professionally organized until the 1890s. Relying on popularly written histories for certain facts about French history, however, meant that she and Smith also accepted some information disputed by later scholars (e.g., Albigensian beliefs, which bell signaled the start of the St. Bartholomew's Day Massacre, Jesuit presence in France in 1789, etc.).

Although she touches on social, political, and economic events during the revolution, her purpose is to show that the end result of the Gallican Church's centuries-old persecution of Bible truth was the French revolutionaries' destruction of Christianity during the Reign of Terror (1792-1793). Like ancient Egypt and Sodom, France had made "war against the Bible"; rejecting spiritual light had brought the atheism of Voltaire and the moral debasement of the "Goddess of Reason." The same intolerant spirit that had killed the Waldensians and the Huguenots brought the Reign of Terror, with its rejection of Christian worship. On the Place de Grève the guillotine replaced the stake. For Ellen White, the French bishops in the sixteenth and seventeenth centuries "had begun the work" that the Jacobins completed in the eighteenth century.

Recent scholarship supports this interpretation. Dale Van Kley's *The Religious Origins of the French Revolution: From Calvin to the Civil Constitution, 1560-1791* (New Haven, Conn.: Yale University Press, 1996) and Brian Strayer's *Huguenots and Camisards as Aliens in France, 1598-1789: The Struggle for Religious Toleration* (Lewiston, N.Y.: E. Mellen Press, 2001) highlight the long-term results of persecution in France. For more than 250 years Gallican bishops, the General Assembly of the Clergy, the Jesuits, the Society of the Most Holy Sacrament, and the Society for the Propagation of the Faith had adamantly opposed religious toleration. Their lobbying efforts led kings and church leaders to strip the Huguenots of their rights. But when their descendants gained power during the revolution, they led a violent backlash against the church. As Ellen White wrote a century ago, "all too well the people had learned the lessons of cruelty and torture which Rome had so diligently taught" (GC 283).

See also: Historians, Ellen G. White's Use of.

Further reading: 3SM 433-465; E. Anderson, "Ellen White and Reformation Historians," *Spectrum* 9, no. 3 (July 1978): 23-26; "Bible Conference of 1919," *Spectrum* 10, no. 1 (May 1979): 23-57; R. D. Graybill, "How Did Ellen White Choose and Use Historical Sources?" *Spectrum* 4, no. 3 (Summer 1972): 49-53; D. Hackleman, "General Conference Committee Studies Ellen White's Sources," *Spectrum* 10, no. 4 (March 1980): 9-15; D. McAdams, "Shifting Views of Inspiration," *Spectrum* 10, no. 4 (March 1980): 27-41; B. McArthur, "Where Are Historians Taking the Church?" *Spectrum* 10, no. 3 (November 1979): 9-14; J. Moon, *W. C. White and Ellen G. White* (AUP, 1993), pp. 427-435; W. Peterson, "Ellen White's Literary Indebtedness," *Spectrum* 3, no. 4 (Autumn 1971): 74-84; J. Voerman, "Ellen White and the French Revolution," AUSS 45, no. 2 (2007): 247-259; J. Wood, "The Bible and the French Revolution: An Answer," *Spectrum* 3, no. 4 (Autumn 1971): 55-72.

Brian E. Strayer

FROM THE HEART (RHPA, 2010, 377 pp.). Twentieth book of daily *devotional readings published by the Ellen G. White Estate. The daily readings are selected from Ellen White's more than 5,000 articles published during her lifetime in the various church journals. These articles became her regular contact with church members, and for many years her articles appeared on the covers of these journals. Many of them were written specifically for publication. Some were transcriptions of sermons she preached; others were notes of travel, accounts of her writing (especially of the *great controversy story), or personal letters. This devotional book is evidence of the diversity of her counsels to church leaders, pastors, and church members. Always uplifting the Bible as her source of guidance, she wrote about Bible characters, the use of talents, time, and money, and doctrinal beliefs.

FUNDAMENTALS OF CHRISTIAN EDUCATION (SPA, 1923, 576 pp.). Compilation of Ellen White's thoughts on Christian education. Materials found in this book were selected from previously printed sources that were long out of print, including periodical articles and chapters from *Christian Education, *Special Testimonies on Education, and *Christian Temperance and Bible Hygiene. Two previously unpublished manuscripts were also included. All articles are printed without abridgment and are arranged chronologically. Most chapters end with a list of supplementary readings that provide additional references on the subject of Christian education. The publication of Fundamentals of Christian Education was the culmination of many works on the subject published by Ellen White during her life. The first collection of articles from her pen on this subject was published in 1886 under the title of Selections From the Testimonies Concerning the Subject of Education (see *Testimony Treasures). A reprint and enlargement of this booklet came out in 1893 entitled Christian Education. In 1897 Special Testimonies on Education was published, containing entirely new material that constituted the major part of Ellen White's writings on education during the years 1893-1896. *Testimonies for the Church, volume 6, published in 1900, included a large section on education (pp. 126-218) and stressed the need of educational reform. In 1903 the book *Education was published dealing with larger principles of education, while the publication in 1913 of *Counsels to Teachers, Parents, and Students Regarding Christian Education dealt with detailed aspects of educational practice.

GALATIANS, LAW IN. Adventist teachings on the law in Galatians (Gal. 3:24, 25) became a controversial issue in the 1880s when the editors of the Signs of the Times and American Sentinel, *Alonzo T. Jones and *Ellet J. Waggoner, began to teach that the law Paul referred to in his epistle was the Ten Commandments rather than the Old Testament ceremonial law, as traditionally held by Adventist pioneers. Before 1854, many Adventists, including James White, J. N. Andrews, and Joseph Bates, had held that the law in Galatians was the Ten Commandments. But after *Joseph H. Waggoner had published The Law of God: An Examination of the Testimony of Both Testaments (Rochester, N.Y.: Advent Review Office, 1854), which took the Ten Commandments view on the law in Galatians, Stephen Pierce publicly challenged Waggoner and argued that the law in Galatians referred to the entire "law system" of the Old Testament dispensation, and not only the Ten Commandments (RH, Oct. 8, 1857, pp. 180, 181). Pierce's argument came to be associated with the ceremonial law because he opposed Waggoner's moral law view. But it wasn't one or the other for Pierce. In a limited way, Pierce's view won the argument, and for the next three decades Adventists taught that the law in Galatians was the ceremonial law.

In the 1880s, when E. J. Waggoner began to teach views similar to what his father, J. H. Waggoner, had taught 30 years earlier, *G. I. Butler, president of the General Conference, and *Uriah Smith, editor of the *Review and Herald*, were quick to point out that Ellen White had had a vision on the subject in 1854 and had written to J. H. Waggoner that the law in Galatians was the ceremonial law rather than the moral law. However, when asked to produce this document, Ellen White was unable to find it. In a letter to Jones and E. J. Waggoner in February 1887 she recalled that she had written to J. H. Waggoner "that I had been shown that his position in regard to the law was incorrect," but that she could not recall exactly what was incorrect about it. One thing was clear to her, however: the various positions on the law in Galatians were not vital points, and they should not be made an issue (Lt 37, 1887, in 15MR 18-20). Two months later, in a letter to Butler and Smith, she again referred to the lost letter to J. H. Waggoner and pointed out that the counsel may not have been on doctrine at all. "It may be that it was a caution not to make his ideas prominent at that time, for there was great danger of disunion" (Lt 13, 1887, in 16MR 281).

Butler and Smith, however, disagreed with that recollection, holding that Ellen White had seen in vision that J. H. Waggoner had been wrong theologically. Hence, in their view, not only was this issue posing a threat to the traditional Adventist teaching on the perpetuity and immutability of the Ten Commandments, and the cherished doctrine of the Sabbath, but it also threatened Ellen White's own prophetic ministry and reliability if she changed her mind on theological issues.

The intense discussion reached its climax at the *General Conference session of 1888 in Minneapolis, Minnesota. There Ellen White insisted that she had not been shown the answer to the question about the law in Galatians, and that the issue needed to be settled by Bible study. She claimed that "truth will lose nothing by investigation" (Ms 15, 1888, in 1888 Materials 163). She acknowledged that "some interpretations of Scripture given by Dr. Waggoner I do not regard as correct." But "the fact that he honestly holds some views of Scripture differing from yours or mine is no reason why we should treat him as an offender, or as a dangerous man, and make him the subject of unjust criticism" (*ibid.* 164). She recognized that Waggoner's major contribution in this discussion was in building a bridge between the law and the gospel. "I see the beauty of truth in the presentation of the righteousness of Christ in relation to the law as the doctor [E. J. Waggoner] has placed it before us," she told the assembly in Minneapolis (*ibid.*).

In the months following the session, Ellen White joined Waggoner and Jones in presenting to the Adventist membership their new perspectives on the law and the gospel. Ellen White eventually understood the law in Galatians to refer to both the ceremonial and moral law; the former as a "schoolmaster to bring sinful human agents to a consideration of Christ the Foundation of the whole Jewish economy" (Ms 87, 1900, in 1SM 233), and the latter as the law that "reveals sin to us, and causes us to feel our need of Christ and to flee unto Him for pardon and peace" (Lt 96, 1896, in 1SM 234; cf. 1SM 233-235). Although the struggle did not end quickly, Waggoner's point of view on the law in Galatians eventually prevailed in Adventism and facilitated a better understanding of *righteousness by faith.

Further reading: G. I. Butler, *The Law in the Book of Galatians: Is It the Moral Law, or Does It Refer to That System of Laws Peculiarly Jewish?* (RHPA, 1886); E. J. Waggoner, *The Gospel in the Book of Galatians* (Oakland, Calif.: n.p., 1888); G. R. Knight, *From 1888 to Apostasy: The Case of A. T. Jones* (RHPA, 1987), pp. 23-27, 37-41; R. W. Schwarz, *Light Bearers to the Remnant* (PPPA, 1979), pp. 394, 395.

Denis Fortin

GAMBLING. Among addictive games, Ellen White considered gambling as one of the worst. In some instances she refers to public gambling places as "gambling hells" (15MR 70, 73). She mentions other amusements such as card playing, chess, and checkers, which contribute to the development of an addiction to gambling (CT 346). There are, however, many other contributing factors and circumstances. While some, who desire to have a higher standard of living, "are drawn into the gambling hells to gain money fast enough to meet expenses" (15MR 70), others gamble as a last resort to solve their economic problems and desperate situations (Lt 30a, 1894, in 12MR 94). Even churches' supposedly harmless fund-raising activities may influence "the youth to make them lovers of pleasures more than lovers of God," leading them to think they are "safe in taking an interest in lotteries, and engaging in gambling to win money for special objects" (ST, Apr. 19, 1883). Not only young people but even church leaders are tempted by unlawful means of getting rich (15MR 72; ST, Feb. 23, 1882). According to Ellen White, money is given for the sustenance of life and to help those in need, but never for gambling (12MR 91). Gambling she considered to be

Satan's invention (RH, Mar. 31, 1896) and a sign of the end of time (Mar 35).

Paul Z. Gregor

GAMES AND SPORTS. Ellen White shunned competitive sports in virtually all their forms. In fact, her writings make clear that she held little enthusiasm for sporting activities of any kind. The root of her opposition lay in the combative spirit inherent in most sports and more generally in their distraction from the more serious tasks of life.

Ellen White's statements on sports largely came during the last half of her life, when athletics were becoming a prominent part of the American scene. These included amateur sports on college campuses and professional sports, such as baseball and boxing. In either case, the American passion for spectator sports seemed boundless. As Americans left farms for cities, traditional recreations such as hunting, fishing, ice skating, and various informal competitions (sometimes organized by particular immigrant groups as a way to retain ethnic identity) gave way to highly structured, commercial athletic competitions. An urban population demanded periodic release from the constraints of city life. Sports offered a ritualized outlet for these energies. Identification with a local sports team provided a new source of social identity, helping to blend immigrant groups together in the proverbial American melting pot.

Baseball became the first great professionalized spectator sport. The formation of the National League in 1876 marked the beginning of a shifting constellation of professional leagues in the following decades. Baseball quickly proclaimed itself the "American sport," and indeed it won the hearts of both spectators and players who participated at various amateur and professional levels. Yet the national sport was besmirched by the taint of gambling, a problem that long refused to go away despite the efforts of owners. Further, ballparks were male venues, marked by drinking, profanity, and tobacco; the wholesome family atmosphere that baseball now cultivates came considerably later.

Football, incongruously enough, originally assumed the air of a more gentlemanly sport. This is because it was nurtured on the campuses of America's elite colleges in the late nineteenth century. Walter Camp, of Yale University, who deserves the title of "Father of American Football," dignified the game with an elaborate code of sportsmanship and social etiquette. But no amount of patrician rule-setting could disguise the fact that football had become a violent exercise. With little protective gear and a strategy that stressed brute force, the game had by the turn of the century witnessed a number of deaths each year. President Theodore Roosevelt publicly threatened to ban the sport unless reform was effected.

Given the characteristics of the two major team sports of the age, Ellen White's skepticism about them is unsurprising. She went so far as to attribute competitive sports to Satan. "He has invented sports and games, into which men enter with such intensity that one would suppose a crown of life was to reward the winner. At the horse races and football matches, which are attended by thousands and thousands of people, lives for which Christ shed His blood are thrown away. What will become of the souls of the men and boys whose lives are thus extinguished?" (RH, Sept. 10, 1901). However, her counsel generally addressed less the issue of attending baseball or football contests than the matter of athletics on the nascent Adventist college campuses. The question arose on campuses from Australia to America. Her views were

consistent in every case: Organized sports had no place in a Christian institution.

The matter first arose at Battle Creek College, where in 1893 students got up a school football team that began playing other college teams from Michigan. The sport became a focus of campus attention. When word of this reached White (then in Australia), she sent a message to W. W. Prescott decrying the competition. Students "act as if the school were a place where they were to perfect themselves in sports, as if this were an important branch of their education. . . . This is all wrong, from beginning to end" (4MR 255). A faculty-student convocation discussed her counsel and canceled further matches.

Few of the early Adventist colleges escaped controversy over athletics. Healdsburg College in the mid-1890s had been "demoralized by disgraceful games" (Lt 27, 1895, in 11MR 160). White asked where were the watchmen when these "unseemly games and athletic sports" were occurring? (ibid. 161). From Union College came a letter to White complaining of the nonsensical cheers set up by spectators at the sports contests. At the Keene Institute in Texas, the broomshop manager complained to White that he could not keep workers on the job, so strong was the lure of football and baseball. Moreover, there had been a rash of playing injuries.

The sharpest conflict White ever experienced on the issue came at the young Avondale school in Australia in 1900. Adventist students in the sports-mad country were not exempt from their countrymen's predilections. Thus, for a founder's day afternoon picnic the faculty purchased equipment and organized games of cricket and tennis. White (who had spoken for chapel that very morning), on hearing of the games, rebuked school leaders for encouraging a "species of idolatry" in which the "forces of the enemy gained a decided victory, and God was dishonored" (CT 350). School leaders were distraught and defensive over what they viewed as innocent recreation. C. B. Hughes, school principal, felt White had acted "rashly," but he and the students ultimately bowed to her admonition.

What common thread runs through White's reactions to these situations? First, what she did not urge was a disregard for recreation. The need for regular breaks from study recurs in her counsels on education. Nor did she oppose all games or ball playing. "I do not condemn the simple exercise of playing ball," she once wrote (2SM 322). But these games were to be kept within careful bounds, more in the spirit of spontaneous play than as structured competition. Moreover, she often urged that necessary physical exercise could better be obtained through "manual training and by letting useful employment take the place of selfish pleasure" (CT 354). One might be tempted to think White confused the quite different imperatives of exercise as play and exercise as productive manual labor. Yet in the context of her various admonitory letters it seems that her real concern was that organized athletics were interfering with systematic manual labor. "Do not substitute play, pugilistic boxing, football, matched games, and animal exercises, for manual training," she wrote the president of Healdsburg, "All of this stripe and type should be vigilantly prohibited from the school grounds" (Lt 27, 1895, in 11MR 161).

Ellen White's implacable stand against organized sports on Adventist campuses was rooted in her understanding of how all-encompassing athletics could become on college campuses. They compromised the earnestness with which schools were to prepare their students for life. Her sense of high purpose for Adventist higher education was particularly acute in the case of Avondale, which was to be a "pattern school." As such, every aspect of student life took on great significance, and distractions such as athletics needed to be excised. Additionally, certain kinds of sports were inherently corrupting. "Some of the most popular amusements, such as football and boxing, have become schools of brutality. . . . The love of domination, the pride in mere brute force, the reckless disregard of life, are exerting upon the youth a power to demoralize that is appalling" (Ed 210).

White occasionally alluded to the games of ancient Greece and Rome in her discussion of sports (aptly so, since no parallel to contemporary spectator sports had been seen since the days of Imperial Rome). She typically made two points here. First, the degradations of ancient Roman games were insinuating themselves in modern times and needed to be shunned. Second, and more positively, she cited Paul's analogy of the rigorous marathon training of Greek athletes to the discipline necessary for the Christian life. But if the prizes for foot races are ephemeral, those for the Christian life are eternal.

The debate over the place of sports on Adventist college campuses reoccurred throughout the twentieth century. The White Estate office received numerous inquiries on the issue—so much so that Ellen White's grandson Arthur L. White finally prepared a seven-page document on the topic in 1959, drawing upon many of the statements referenced above. In general, Ellen White's counsel against competitive, intercollegiate athletic programs defined educational policy through most of the past century. Only in the last two decades of the twentieth century did many Adventist academies and colleges begin promoting interscholastic sports teams. Even then, however, some Adventist institutions held back, a testimony to White's enduring influence on this issue.

Further reading: Ed 207-222; 2T 288-291; AA 310, 311; AH 498-520; 4Bio 441-447; D. C. Matacio, "A Study of the Historical Context of Selected Counsels by Ellen G. White on the Subject of Sports" (research paper, AU, 1973); E. K. Vande Vere, *The Wisdom Seekers* (SPA, 1972), pp. 63, 138, 152, 169, 170, 210, 231; A. L. White, "Sports in Seventh-day Adventist Academies and Colleges" (EGWE, SDoc, CAR).

Benjamin McArthur

"GATHERING" TIME, see **"SCATTERING" AND "GATHERING" TIMES**.

GENEALOGY OF ELLEN G. WHITE, see **ANCESTRY OF ELLEN GOULD (HARMON) WHITE**.

GENERAL CONFERENCE AS THE VOICE OF GOD, see **VOICE OF GOD, GENERAL CONFERENCE AS THE**.

GENERAL CONFERENCE BULLETIN. Medium of communication from the General Conference to the church containing reports of meetings, records of proceedings, and general information and statistics concerning the work of the church, published from 1895 to 1922; including Ellen White's addresses, sermons, and remarks made or read at meetings of the General Conference, from 1895 to 1913. From 1895 to 1903 the *General Conference Bulletin* was published quarterly, with extras during the General Conference sessions of 1895 and 1901; during that period it also filled the place of the *Yearbook*. Between 1903 and 1922 it served as the published record of the proceedings of the General Conference. The record of the proceedings of other sessions of the General Conference appeared in the *Review and Herald* until 1887; in the *General Conference Daily Bulletin* for sessions from 1888 to 1893,

and 1901, 1903, 1909, 1913, 1918, and 1922; and in the *Review and Herald* since 1926. Many of Ellen White's addresses published in the *General Conference Bulletin* and *General Conference Daily Bulletin*, including those between 1891 and 1900, when she was in Australia, were sent to the sessions by Ellen White and read by someone present. All her messages in GCB and GCDB are reproduced in volume 2 of the *Ellen G. White Periodical Resource Collection*.

Further reading: SDA Encyclopedia (1996), vol. 10, pp. 586, 590.

GENERAL CONFERENCE COMMITTEE, see **GENERAL CONFERENCE OF SEVENTH-DAY ADVENTISTS**.

GENERAL CONFERENCE DAILY BULLETIN, see *GENERAL CONFERENCE BULLETIN*.

GENERAL CONFERENCE OF SEVENTH-DAY ADVENTISTS. (1) Initially, a general meeting (conference) of Adventists, as distinguished from local or regional meetings; (2) the highest governing body of Seventh-day Adventist church organization, formed in 1863; (3) the offices where the General Conference is located, i.e., the world headquarters of Seventh-day Adventists; (4) official sessions of the General Conference, at which representatives of the church in all the world meet to elect officers and conduct other official business.

According to James White, the *Sabbatarian Conference held in Rocky Hill, Connecticut, April 20-24, 1848, was "the first general meeting" of Sabbatarian Adventists (JW, *Life Incidents*, p. 271). A "general" conference in 1855 settled the question that the biblical Sabbath begins at sunset (rather than midnight, sunrise, or 6:00 p.m.). A "general" conference held in 1860 was the occasion for the choice of the name Seventh-day Adventist and the legal incorporation of the SDA Publishing Association. A similar general meeting in 1861 laid the groundwork for the formation of state conferences.

In 1863, 20 delegates from six of the seven state conferences (Iowa, Michigan, Minnesota, New York, Ohio, and Wisconsin; Vermont sent no delegate) met in Battle Creek to organize a General Conference as a central governing body to unify and coordinate the state conferences and their work. That General Conference had its headquarters in Battle Creek, Michigan, from 1863 to 1903, when it was moved to Washington, D.C. In 1989 the world headquarters was moved again, to Silver Spring, Maryland, just north of Washington, D.C.

From 1863 to 1889, official sessions of the General Conference were held more or less annually. From 1889 to 1905, sessions were held every two years. From 1905 to 1970, sessions were held every four years (with some irregularities because of the World Wars); and since 1970, sessions have been held every five years.

Ellen White exercised major influence in the initial organization of the General Conference. A vision in 1852 called for "gospel order" (EW 97-104, cf. 1Bio 286), and she worked closely with her husband, who became the chief promoter and organizer through his personal influence and his persuasive writings in the *Review and Herald*.

By 1901 the rapidly growing denomination had outgrown the organization formed in 1863. At the *General Conference session of 1901 Ellen White again exercised major influence, publicly calling for a complete reorganization. As in 1863, she did not specify in detail how the reorganized structure should be designed, but set forth the goals of reorganization and the principles that should characterize it, hence the criteria by which the planned reorganization should be evaluated. She called for decentralizing authority from the General Conference toward the local conference level; for authority at every level to be vested in many persons rather than few; for integral linking of the different levels of denominational structure to maintain doctrinal and spiritual unity; and for the election of officers who were persons of genuine faith, integrity, and humility.

A basic structural change voted by the 1901 session was the institution of union conferences throughout the world field, as an intermediate level of organization between the local conferences and the General Conference. (In the 1890s Adventists had conducted successful experiments with a union conference in Australasia and departments within the conference in South Africa.) "Divisions" of the General Conference were added in 1913, not as an additional constituency-based level of organization, but rather as subdivisions of the General Conference, representing that body in the various parts of the world.

See also: General Conference Session of 1888; Voice of God, General Conference as the.

Further reading: C. C. Crisler, *Organization: Its Character, Purpose, Place, and Development in the Seventh-day Adventist Church* (RHPA, 1938); G. R. Knight, *Organizing for Mission and Growth: The Development of Adventist Church Structure* (RHPA, 2001); A. G. Mustard, *James White and SDA Organization: Historical Development, 1844-1881* (AUP, 1988); B. D. Oliver, *SDA Organizational Structure: Past, Present, and Future* (AUP, 1989).

Jerry Moon

GENERAL CONFERENCE SESSION OF 1888. One of the most significant sessions in Adventist history, it was also a major waymark in Ellen White's long ministry.

By the 1880s the Seventh-day Adventist Church had been doing for 40 years an excellent job at preaching such distinctive doctrines as the Sabbath, the Second Advent, the state of the dead, and the sanctuary message. But in the process of uplifting that which was distinctively Adventist, it had largely neglected the great truths of Christ and salvation that it shared with other denominations. For many Adventists, the law had come to be more central than Christ, and a strong emphasis on salvation by lawkeeping (legalism) was evident.

In that context, two relatively young preachers, *Ellet J. Waggoner and *Alonzo T. Jones (both editors of *Signs of the Times in Oakland, California), had begun in about 1884 to preach a message that was more Christ- and faith-oriented. Their new emphasis was challenged by *George I. Butler (*General Conference president) and *Uriah Smith (General Conference secretary and Review and Herald editor), who feared that the importance of the *Sabbath might be lost in the wake of the new emphases.

The context of the times especially made the situation explosive. State Sunday laws were being enforced, and a bill for a national Sunday law was placed before the United States Senate in May 1888. In short, it was a time of prophetic excitement. It was in that explosive context that Waggoner began to set forth a new understanding of the law in *Galatians that Butler feared would play into the hands of those who would do away with the *Ten Commandments (see *law of God) and Jones began to reinterpret the 10 horns of Daniel 7, a move that Smith believed would bring all of the denomination's apocalyptic interpretation into question.

Here was a situation that the denominational leaders took seriously. Beginning in June 1886 Butler opened a letter-writing campaign aimed at getting Ellen White to side openly with him on the Galatians issue, a request that she refused to respond to. Butler's second move took place in December at the 1886 General Conference session, where he organized a theological committee to settle the issue of the 10 horns and the law in Galatians. Butler's final strategy was to silence the younger men. Along that line, the 1886 session passed a resolution aimed at Jones and Waggoner that stipulated that no new teachings could be set forth in Adventist papers or taught in denominational schools until they had been examined and approved by the leading ministers (RH, Dec. 14, 1886). Another goal, as might be expected, was to keep the two men and their concerns off the agenda of the 1888 session.

Ellen White was of a different mind. She saw that Jones and Waggoner were being unfairly treated in an unequal struggle and that they had a message that the church needed to hear. As a result, throughout 1887 and 1888 she urged the denomination's leadership and ministry to keep their minds open to Bible truths. The climax to her campaign came in an August 8, 1888, circular letter. She was adamant that the ministers needed to search the Bible for themselves to discover truth rather than merely receiving their theological views from "others' lips" (i.e., Smith and Butler). The letter also cautioned the ministers to have a Christlike spirit as they dealt with one another (Lt 20, 1888, in 1888 Materials 40).

The 1888 General Conference session was held in Minneapolis, Minnesota, from October 17 to November 4. A ministerial institute lasting from October 10 through October 19 preceded the formal session. Tensions ran high because of the division among the ministry and because both Waggoner and Jones had a major place on the speaking agenda. But the emotional pressure had been too much for Butler, who had suffered a breakdown and did not attend the meetings.

Both the meetings themselves and the events leading up to them had been marred by rumors of conspiracy as the leaders of the church gave credence to unfounded reports that the California contingent (especially Jones, Waggoner, and W. C. and Ellen White) hoped to change the denomination's theology. The acceptance of the rumors had generated what Ellen White called the "spirit of the Pharisees" or the "spirit of Minneapolis" among the Smith/Butler faction. As a result, the unchristlike spirit that Ellen White had feared marred the meetings.

The sharpness was directed not only at Jones and Waggoner but also at Ellen White, who had strongly supported both their Christ-centered message and their right to be heard. "Never in my life experience," she would write, "was I treated as at that conference" (Lt 7, 1888, in 1888 Materials 187). The conference had been a crisis point in Ellen White's ministry.

The crisis had to do with the heart of Adventist theology and the methods by which theological issues were to be decided. The General Conference leadership had sought to solve the theological issues troubling the denomination by such means as expert opinion, authoritative position, creedlike legislation, and Adventist tradition. But Ellen White and the reforming element had argued for Bible answers at every point.

Having failed in their bid to use human authority in the struggle, Butler and his colleagues sought to solve the issue of biblical interpretation by relying on Ellen White's authority. But she refused that approach and repeatedly directed the denomination back to the Bible as the only valid authority by which to solve issues of biblical interpretation. She refused to let her writings settle the law in Galatians issue (see G. R. Knight, *Angry Saints*, pp. 104-109).

Ellen White utilized the events surrounding the Minneapolis General Conference session to repeatedly uphold the place of the Bible. "The Bible," she wrote, "is the only rule of faith and doctrine" (RH, July 17, 1888).

Ellen White not only stood against the General Conference leadership regarding the authority issue—she also came out against their legalism. During the 1888 session and extending into the 1890s she argued for a central place in Adventist theology for Christ and saving faith in Him. On October 24 she cried out to the delegates, "I have seen that precious souls who would have embraced the truth [of Adventism] have been turned away . . . because Jesus was not in it. And this is what I have been pleading with you for all the time—we want Jesus" (1888 Materials 153). Again, in discussing the place of the law in Adventism, she told an audience of Adventist leaders in 1890: "Let the law take care of itself. We have been at work on the law until we get as dry as the hills of Gilboa. . . . Let us trust in the merits of Jesus" (1888 Materials 557).

Perhaps her major contribution to Adventist understanding in the events surrounding the Minneapolis meetings was her position on the place of righteousness by faith in the third angel's message (see *three angels' messages). "The third angel's message," she penned in late 1888, "is the proclamation of the commandments of God and the faith of Jesus Christ. The commandments of God have been proclaimed, but the faith of Jesus Christ has not been proclaimed by Seventh-day Adventists as of equal importance, the law and the gospel going hand in hand." She went on to discuss the meaning of "the faith of Jesus" in Revelation 14:12, which "is talked of, but not understood." The faith of Jesus, she wrote, means "Jesus becoming our sin-bearer that He might become our sin-pardoning Savior. . . . He came to our world and took our sins that we might take His righteousness. Faith in the ability of Christ to save us amply and fully and entirely is the faith of Jesus." Adventists needed by faith to lay hold of the righteousness of Christ (1888 Materials 217).

Looking back from the perspective of 1895, Ellen White summed up her evaluation of the significance of the 1888 General Conference session. "The Lord," she penned, "in His great mercy sent a most precious message to His people through Elders Waggoner and Jones. This message was to bring more prominently before the world the uplifted Savior, the sacrifice for the sins of the whole world. It presented justification through faith in the Surety; it invited the people to receive the righteousness of Christ, which is made manifest in obedience to all the commandments of God. Many had lost sight of Jesus. They needed to have their eyes directed to His divine person, His merits, and His changeless love for the human family.... This is the message that God commanded to be given to the world. It is the third angel's message....

"The message of the gospel of His grace was to be given to the church in clear and distinct lines, that the world should no longer say that Seventh-day Adventists talk the law, the law, but do not teach or believe Christ" (TM 91, 92).

Ellen White was deeply appreciative of the gospel-centered message given by Jones and Waggoner, but that did not mean that she agreed with all they taught, even in 1888. A comparative analysis of their writings with hers will discover several significant theological differences (see Knight, *A User-friendly Guide*, pp. 73-77). On the other hand, she never tired of upholding them in their emphasis on Christ and salvation in Him through faith.

The aftermath of the 1888 session witnessed a power shift in Adventism. Butler and Smith

lost their leadership positions, with Smith eventually being replaced by Jones as editor of the *Review*. Meanwhile Jones and Waggoner became the most influential theologians in the church during the 1890s, virtually dominating the Bible study sessions at all General Conference sessions for the next decade.

The 1888 session also was a turning point in Ellen White's ministry. During the early 1890s she would team up with Jones and Waggoner in taking the message of Christ and His righteousness to the church. Her writing ministry also saw a radical shift as it focused more on Christ. After 1888 she would publish such great Christ-centered works as *Steps to Christ* (1892), *Thoughts From the Mount of Blessing* (1896), *The Desire of Ages* (1898), *Christ's Object Lessons* (1900), and the opening chapters of *The Ministry of Healing* (1905). She would to the end of her days continue to uplift the Christ highlighted in 1888.

Unfortunately, the 1950s and beyond would see several teachings related to the 1888 General Conference session arise that were based upon the assumption that Ellen White approved of almost everything taught by Waggoner and Jones. The new views generally took Waggoner's and Jones' ideas as the source of their theology, even when those views were on shaky ground in the light of the teachings of the Bible and Ellen White. To see what Ellen White upheld in Jones and Waggoner, it is safer to go to her books on salvation and Christ written after 1888 and her summary statement of Jones' and Waggoner's contribution in *Testimonies to Ministers* (pp. 91-94) rather than to adopt an uncritical acceptance of the two men, both of whom developed serious theological aberrations in the 1890s.

Further reading: *The Ellen G. White 1888 Materials* (1987), 4 vols.; *Manuscripts and*

Memories of Minneapolis 1888 (1988); "Minneapolis/1888: The 'Forgotten Issue'" (EGWE, SDoc); G. R. Knight, *Angry Saints* (1989); *idem, A User-friendly Guide to the 1888 Message* (1998); J. A. Moon, *W. C. White and E. G. White* (AUP, 1993), pp. 82-86, 95-108; A. V. Olson, *Thirteen Crisis Years, 1888-1901* (RHPA, 1981); A. V. Wallenkampf, *What Every Adventist Should Know About 1888* (RHPA, 1988); W. W. Whidden, *E. J. Waggoner: From the Physician of Good News to Agent of Division* (RHPA, 2008), pp. 88-213.

George R. Knight

GENERAL CONFERENCE SESSIONS OF 1901 AND 1903. At its General Conference session of 1901, the Seventh-day Adventist Church began a major reorganization of its administrative structures. The impetus for change continued two years later at the 1903 session. The changes that were made at those sessions were based on the principles of organization established at the denomination's founding in 1861-1863. By 1901 it was recognized that those principles needed to be updated and applied in the contemporary context. Four major changes were made in 1901 and 1903: the formation of union conferences as the constituent bodies of the General Conference; the decentralization of much decision-making from the General Conference administration to union conference executive committees; the consolidation of departments of the General Conference and the dissolution of independent incorporated entities that had been operating departments and some institutions; and the title of the chief officer of the General Conference, from "president" to "chairman of the board." At the 1903 General Conference session the title "president" was reinstated.

At the forefront of the impetus for change was Ellen G. White. As with her initial call for organization in the 1850s, she did not attempt to prescribe the exact nature of organizational reform. However, she did call for urgent and innovative change. The day before the commencement of the session in 1901, she called the leaders together and in no uncertain terms told them that "God wants a change . . . right here. . . . We want to know what can be done right now" (SpM 164).

The church had grown and diversified since 1863. The organizational structures that had been set in place in 1863 needed revision in order to cope with numerical and geographical growth. The increase in departments and institutions established to care for the publishing, educational, health, and missionary interests of the church had not been anticipated in 1863. By 1901 each had become a separate entity in itself outside the existing organizational structure of the church. They had been legally incorporated as independent bodies that had their own officers and executive boards or committees. Although they were all part of the Seventh-day Adventist Church—officers being appointed by and reporting to the General Conference session—they were not administered directly by the General Conference. Because of their independent status, coordination and integration were perennial problems during the 1890s. Not until the 1901 General Conference session were the auxiliary organizations integrated into the conference structure as departments of the General Conference.

One of the reasons Ellen White became so adamant that change must take place had been her observation that the emerging global missionary consciousness of the church was accompanied by increased centralization of administrative control. Centralization of authority was most evident in the tendency of the General Conference to deprive the constituent bodies of the organization of their decision-making authority.

As a corrective to the tendency to leave the prerogative for decision-making in the hands of one or two, Ellen White advocated decentralization through the proper use of the committee system that had been established when the General Conference had been organized in 1863. Union conferences were also established in order to give greater decision-making prerogative to those who were "on the ground." She made it clear that in the operation of institutions, one person's mind was not to control the decision-making process. She emphasized that "God would not have many minds the shadow of one man's mind," but that in "a multitude of counselors there is safety" (Lt 7, 1886, in ChL 45).

The financial predicament was also a major impetus in reorganization. When G. A. Irwin had assumed the presidency of the General Conference in 1897, he wrote to N. W. Allee that the General Conference was "living from hand to mouth" (G. A. Irwin to N. W. Allee, May 5, 1897, GCAr). The situation remained desperate until the session of 1901. At the beginning of 1901 the General Conference was $41,589.11 in deficit. In August the deficit was still $39,600 (AGD to Members of the General Conference Committee, Aug. 2, 1901, GCAr; see also AGD to J. E. Jayne, Aug. 3, 1901, GCAr). The inability of the denomination to support its growth financially was having an effect on its whole missionary enterprise. In the last five years of the nineteenth century there had been a considerable slackening of missionary activity.

The financial and administrative crises at home were having an effect on the church's ability to commence work in new areas and were preventing the placement of new missionaries in the field. Between 1895 and 1900

the number of missionaries being sent from the shores of North America decreased markedly in comparison to the increasing number during the first half of the decade. The failure to commence any new work between 1897 and 1899 and the decrease in the number of missionaries being sent abroad between 1895 and 1900 does not appear to have been the result of any marked decline in the church's commitment to its end-time beliefs and mission, although there was a marked declension in spirituality among some administrators in Battle Creek. In addition to the lack of spiritual power, the centralized organization as it had existed was simply not able to cope financially and administratively with its missionary enterprise.

In 1901 and 1903 changes in the administrative structure of the church were made both to accommodate the growth of the past and to facilitate growth in the future. The fulfillment of its mission was the focus of the church and its leadership.

See also: Kingly Power; Voice of God, General Conference as the; A. R. Henry; Harmon Lindsay.

Further reading: B. D. Oliver, *Seventh-day Adventist Organization: Past, Present and Future* (AUP, 1989); G. R. Knight, *Organizing for Mission and Growth: The Development of Adventist Church Structure* (RHPA, 2001), pp. 103-131; R. W. Schwarz and F. Greenleaf, *Light Bearers: A History of the Seventh-day Adventist Church* (PPPA, 2000), pp. 241-264; Andrew Bates [A. Thompson], "The Use and Abuse of Authority: What We Can Learn From the Struggles of the Seventh-day Adventist Church of 1901," *Ministry*, June 2002; A. L. White, "The Story of the General Conference Session of 1901 and the E. G. White Appeal for Reorganization of the General Conference" (EGWE, SDoc).

Barry D. Oliver

GERMANY. Ellen White crossed Germany several times on her way to Scandinavia and England. Her longest stay in Germany was from May 26 to May 31, 1887, when she paid a visit to the Adventist congregation in Vohwinkel-Wuppertal. L. R. Conradi, who served as her translator, accompanied her. The Vohwinkel congregation represented the first Adventist church in Germany, organized in 1876 by J. Erzberger. At the time of Ellen White's visit this church was also the only Adventist congregation in the country. Here Erzberger and J. N. Andrews had found a group of autonomous Christians of the Pietist tradition, led by Johann H. Lindermann, a weaver and Reformed lay minister, who had discovered the Sabbath commandment independently of Seventh-day Adventists in North America. The group, called Getaufte Christen-Gemeinde, also practiced adult baptism and was strongly convicted that Christ would soon return. The nucleus of the Vohwinkel Adventist congregation was formed from among Lindermann's followers, although Lindermann himself did not become an Adventist. When Ellen White arrived, she found the Vohwinkel believers in difficulty. Unkind criticism had separated the church into factions. During her first night she had a dream, which obviously applied to the situation of the company in Vohwinkel. In the dream she saw Jesus, unrecognized at first, address the group, admonishing to keep unity and peace, and to love in spite of mistakes. When the hearers recognized Jesus, they wept and confessed their sins to one another. This vision prompted Ellen White to organize a *"social meeting" with a testimony service, virtually unknown among the members in Vohwinkel. Her healing ministry at Vohwinkel proved to be a turning point in establishing harmony and in strengthening the evangelistic outreach of the early German Adventists. Later, under Conradi's leadership, many of Ellen White's published writings were translated into various European languages and printed at the Adventist publishing house (Internationale Traktatgesellschaft) in Hamburg for the European colporteur ministry.

Further reading: Historical Sketches of the Foreign Missions of Seventh-day Adventists (Basel: Imprimerie Polyglotte, 1886; AUP, 2005); D. A. Delafield, *Ellen G. White in Europe, 1885-1887* (RHPA, 1975), pp. 275-285; B. E. Pfeiffer, "Ellen G. White in Germany," *Ellen G. White and Europe. Symposium Papers 1987* (Bracknell, Eng.: Ellen G. White Centre, Europe, 1987), pp. 414-426; D. Heinz, "Johann Heinrich Lindermann und die pietistisch-freikirchlichen Wurzeln der deutschen Adventisten," *Adventecho* 99, No. 4 (April 2000): I-IV.

Daniel Heinz

GETHSEMANE. Ellen White saw Christ's sufferings in mental anguish in the Garden of Gethsemane as determining the destiny of the world and the fate of sinful humanity, "the last fearful struggle" of the forces of evil attempting to prevent Christ from going to the cross (DA 686, 687). Everything was at stake in this hour. Had Christ refused to drink the cup presented to Him, humanity would have been lost forever. Beyond the events described in the Gospel accounts, she understood that in Gethsemane all the powers of evil were tempting Christ to abandon humanity to its fate. Christ knew He was sinless, but when in Gethsemane all the sins of humanity were laid upon Him as the divine sin-bearer, His Father's presence was withdrawn from Him. Another aspect of His temptation was the fear that His coming death would be eternal. He could have abandoned humanity and returned to heaven; but not willing to forsake the people He had come to redeem,

He confirmed in Gethsemane His resolve to become humanity's substitute and to taste "the sufferings of death for every man" (*ibid.* 694). During these hours of agony Christ sought comfort from His disciples but found them asleep three times. Seeing them praying and keeping watch with Him would have encouraged Him and given relief. In the end, His own humanity faltered and would have died under the horror of the sense of sin had not an angel from God strengthened Him to bear the agony. While the Father suffered and all of heaven looked on in silence, the angel gave Christ courage through the assurance of the Father's love and ultimate power over death. Moments later, as Judas led a mob to arrest Jesus, the same angel moved between Christ and the mob, momentarily illuminating Christ's face with a supernatural brilliance. At the theophany, the mob fell to the ground, prostrate at Jesus' feet. In spite of the fearful events to follow, Christ appeared as the master of His own destiny. After the angel withdrew, the mob arrested Jesus and led Him to be tried, but the fate of evil had been decided.

Further reading: DA 685-697; 2T 203-207.

Denis Fortin

GLENDALE SANITARIUM. Adventist sanitarium established in 1905, located eight miles (13 kilometers) north of Los Angeles, California. The property was located under the direction of Ellen White, who had been instructed by the Lord that a medical institution should be established near Los Angeles (Ms 152, 1901, in 1MR 246, 247; Lt 147, 1904, in 1MR 255, 256; Lt 211, 1904, in 5Bio 372). In 1904 *John Burden led a group of Adventist leaders in a search for suitable property. One such property was the Glendale Hotel, with 75 rooms. The building had originally cost $60,000 during the California land boom of 1880, but in the

depression that followed, it was closed before it could open. For four years it was used as an Episcopal school for girls, and then during 1901-1902 as a public high school. By 1904 ownership had passed to Leslie C. Brand, a real estate developer who was asking $26,000 for it. The conference, already deeply in debt, was unable to raise the money. Burden decided that if the price could be lowered to $15,000

GLENDALE SANITARIUM, IN LOS ANGELES, CALIFORNIA, ESTABLISHED IN 1905

he would see it as a sign of the Lord's leading. When Brand lowered the price to $12,500, the California conference constituency still hesitated, until conference president *Clarence Santee joined Burden in pledging to pay the $1,000 down payment out of their own pockets if necessary. At that crucial moment Ellen White urged the delegates not to delay. She even persuaded two church members to contribute $1,000 each, to reach the amount of $4,500 for the initial payment in September 1904. After her first visit to the grounds in December 1904, White wrote, "We feel very grateful to God that our brethren and sisters in southern California have secured a property . . . well adapted for sanitarium purposes" (LLM 29). Later she wrote that "the location of the Glendale Sanitarium meets the representation given me of places God has reserved for us" (Lt 97, 1905, in LLM 86). The sanitarium opened in August 1905 with Burden as the business manager, Dr. Abbi Winegar-Simpson as the first medical superintendent, and Lenora

Lacey as head nurse. The institution is now known as the Glendale Adventist Medical Center.

Further reading: 5Bio 371-376; W. L. Johns and R. H. Utt, eds., *The Vision Bold* (RHPA, 1977), pp. 160-169; *SDA Encyclopedia* (1996), vol. 10, pp. 613-615.

Michael W. Campbell

GOD THE FATHER. Ellen White built her understanding of God the Father directly on Scripture. She saw the Father as an eternal (GC88 493), unchangeable (RH, July 9, 1895), infinite (AA 333), invisible (Ev 614), personal being (HL 287) whose reality cannot be described by earthly or spiritualistic representations (Ev 614). We should understand her statements about God the Father within the context of the doctrine of the Trinity (see *Godhead). She considered that the Father is one of the three persons in "the heavenly trio" (Ev 615) or one of "the three dignitaries and powers of heaven" (6BC 1075). He dwells in unapproachable light (AA 333). God the Father is "the source of all being, and the fountain of all law" (GC 479).

Ellen White emphasized the love of the Father for fallen humanity. According to her, the formulation of the plan of salvation in eternity resulted directly from the Father's love (ST, Dec. 23, 1897). She identified the central piece of the plan Christ's covenant with the Father to represent the love of God by taking human form (16MR 192). Thus, the view that the Father is a stern being devoid of sympathy and love is wrong and brings discouragement to the believers. The truth is that "our gracious heavenly Father loves, pities and wants to save" sinners (RH, May 4, 1876).

The Father is also involved in the execution of the plan of salvation throughout human history. Thus, for instance, He was with the Son at Sinai (PP 339) and at Calvary (DA 754,

755). Ellen White affirmed not only that the Father was a witness to Christ's trial and crucifixion but also that He gave Himself in His Son (BE, May 29, 1899; 17MR 214). Not surprisingly, then, she wrote that Christ's incarnation reveals the Father (LHU 75) so precisely that, had the Father—and not the Son—been incarnated, the life of Christ would not have changed at all (TMK 338).

Sinners are called to come to the Father and the Son because it is the law of the Father that has been transgressed, and Christ is their advocate pleading in their behalf (RH, May 4, 1876). By faith, believers come into communion with Christ and, through Him, with the Father also (ST, Jan. 5, 1891). In the end, when the execution of the plan of salvation will reach its climax, every tongue shall confess that Jesus Christ is Lord, to the glory of God the Father (HP 358).

Fernando Canale

GODHEAD. Word used in Colossians 2:9 for the essence of Deity; commonly used as a collective expression for the Father, Son, and Holy Spirit. Many of the earliest Sabbatarian Adventists held *Arian or semi-Arian views of the Godhead. That is, they believed in one God, the Father; in the Son of God (whom they saw as not eternally preexistent, but derived from the Father at some point before the creation of the world); and in the Holy Spirit (whom they viewed as an aspect of God, a manifestation of the power and presence or influence of God, but not a divine person with intellect, will, and emotions).

These anti-Trinitarian views were gradually modified toward a Trinitarian concept over many years. The Bible study that led Adventists to eventually espouse a Trinitarian view of God was stimulated partly by internal debate and awareness of the shortcomings of the Arian view, partly by new converts from

Trinitarian backgrounds, but largely by the writings of Ellen G. White. Her theology of God developed over half a century through clearly discernible stages.

As early as 1850 she reported visions that confirmed the individual personhood of Christ and the Father, and opposed views that tended to blur their real personality. "I have often seen the lovely Jesus, that He is a *person*," she wrote. "I asked Him if His Father was a person and had a form like Himself. Said Jesus, 'I am in the express *image* of My Father's *person*'" (EW 77; cf. 51, 54). By 1869, contrary to her anti-Trinitarian colleagues, she affirmed the eternal preexistence of Christ and His complete equality with the Father (2T 200). From 1872 and onward, as she gained a deeper understanding of salvation through substitutionary atonement, she saw clearly that only a Savior who had life in Himself, and who was fully equal with the Father in every way, could be a sacrifice "of sufficient value" to make atonement (RH, Dec. 17, 1872; cf. GC88 493; RH, Dec. 22, 1891).

The continental divide for her and the church on this issue came in 1897-1898. In a small pamphlet addressed to ministers she for the first time set forth the Holy Spirit as "the third person of the Godhead" (SpTA10 25, 37). In 1898 her landmark work on the life and work of Christ, *The Desire of Ages*, contained two statements that made her position unmistakable. Commenting on John 11:25, she wrote, "In Christ is life, original, unborrowed, underived," and a few pages later she identified the Holy Spirit as "the Third Person of the Godhead" (DA 530, 671).

Her capstone statements about the "three highest powers in heaven," the "heavenly trio" (SpTB07 [1905] 51, 63, in Ev 615, 617), and the "eternal heavenly dignitaries" (Ms 145, 1901, in Ev 616) are clearly Trinitarian in concept. She avoided the word "Trinity,"

probably because traditional Trinitarianism is associated with philosophical concepts that she adamantly rejected, such as soul-body dualism, divine impassibility, and divine timelessness (see Canale, pp. 148-157; and Whidden, Moon, and Reeve, pp. 166-181). But she was fully in harmony with the clear biblical assertions that *God is one* (Deut. 6:4; John 10:30; 17:10, 11) in nature, character, purpose, and love, and yet *God is three* (Matt. 28:19; John 14:16-20; 15:26; 16:12-15). She explained, "The unity that exists between Christ and His disciples does not destroy the personality of either. They are one in purpose, in mind, in character, but not in person. It is thus that God and Christ are one" (MH 422). The biblical concept that God is one unity of three persons is the simple essence of Trinitarian faith, and Ellen White's mature writings fully support that concept.

Further reading: F. Canale, "Doctrine of God," in R. Dederen, ed., *Handbook of Seventh-day Adventist Theology* (RHPA, 2000), pp. 105-159; J. Moon, "The Adventist Trinity Debate, Part 1: Historical Overview," AUSS 41 (Spring 2003): 113-129; *idem*, "The Adventist Trinity Debate, Part 2: The Role of Ellen G. White," AUSS 41 (Autumn 2003): 275-292; T. Poirier, "Ellen White's Trinitarian Statements: What Did She Actually Write?" *"Ellen White and Current Issues" Symposium* 2 (2006): 18-40, CAR; W. Whidden, J. Moon, and J. Reeve, *The Trinity: Understanding God's Love, His Plan of Salvation, and Christian Relationships* (RHPA, 2002).

Jerry Moon

GODLINESS, PRACTICAL. Expression commonly used by Ellen White to identify demonstrable, practical Christianity. The term is often used to contrast a theoretical or nominal Christian life: "What is needed today is practical Christianity, not merely for a day or a year, but for a lifetime. The man who professes to be a Christian, and yet reveals in his life no practical godliness, is denying Christ" (RH, Jan. 28, 1904).

"Practical godliness" appears more than 200 times in her original writings and in a variety of contexts. She gives a number of scriptural references that exemplify and amplify the expression, such as 2 Peter 1, James 1:27, and Micah 6:8 (1888 Materials 779; 6T 263; PK 326; see ST, Jan. 11, 1899; Ev 171; DA 607; AA 470, 471). Her use of the expression is found in relationship to preaching, to children and the home, to evangelism, and to Christ and His love as the motivation for practical godliness.

Adventist ministers were admonished to preach messages that dwelt "more upon practical godliness" and less on the mere theory of the truth (GW92 13), showing "evidence that you are a Christian" (GW 120). The ministers' lack was that Christ Himself was not abiding in their own hearts, for "practical godliness" meant a "great deal less of self, and more of Jesus" (ST, Feb. 3, 1890). She linked the preaching of "practical godliness" with that of "Christ and Him crucified" (GW 158, 159).

She understood the practice of godliness in direct relation to the level of intimacy with which Christians know God's love and grace toward them. "If you yield to the claims of God, and become permeated with His love, and filled with His fullness, children, youth, and young disciples will look to you for their impressions of what constitutes practical godliness; and you may thus be the means of leading them in the path of obedience to God" (SD 262). She considered critical the need for parents to "bring practical godliness into the home" (CG 147; cf. CT 132, 362; FE 114), saying that "all that God expects of you and all other Christians is that you live out your profession" (TSB 52).

She herself lived out her Christian profession of faith daily. Ellen White regularly gave clothes to the needy, helped neighbors, bought food and other items for the destitute. "Oh, that all knew the sweetness of giving to the poor, of helping do others good, and making others happy," she exclaimed (WM 324). With her husband, she visited the sick and administered to them natural remedies. Those sent home to die were brought to the Whites' own home, where, after earnest prayer and loving care, they saw a number of them recover. She took in students or colporteurs, sometimes for months, until their financial situation improved.

Such practical godliness opens minds and hearts to the gospel. The love of Christ, yielding the fruit of the Spirit, attracts others to God (Ev 400). "Dwell on the necessity of practical godliness. Give them evidence that you are a Christian, desiring peace, and that you love their souls. Let them see that you are conscientious. Thus you will gain their confidence; and there will be time enough for doctrines. Let the heart be won, the soil prepared, and then sow the seed, presenting in love the truth as it is in Jesus" (GW 120).

Further reading: 5T 532-541; VSS 344-348; BTS, Nov. 1, 1916; H. E. Douglass, *Messenger of the Lord* (PPPA, 1998), pp. 80-92.

Ron E. M. Clouzet

GOD'S AMAZING GRACE (RHPA, 1973, 2001, 383 pp.). Tenth daily devotional book published by the Ellen G. White Estate. Materials selected for these meditations were drawn from Ellen White's published books and periodical articles. References to each citation are given at the end of the book. As the title indicates, the theme of this devotional book is God's grace, a theme that permeates Ellen White's writings. She understood grace to be "an attribute of God shown to undeserving human beings. We did not seek after it, but it was sent in search of us" (p. 10). The daily readings are arranged by monthly topics such as the kingdom of grace, the purpose of grace, the cost of grace, and the power of grace. The book was republished in 2001.

GORHAM, MAINE. Birthplace of Ellen G. Harmon. During Ellen's childhood, her father, *Robert Harmon, alternated between farming in Gorham and Poland and operating a hat shop in Portland. Shortly after the birth of Ellen and her twin, Elizabeth, in 1827, the family moved to Portland. In 1829 they relocated to Poland, Maine, and about 1833 returned to Portland, where they lived during the remainder of Ellen's childhood. Shortly after James and Ellen White's marriage, Robert and Eunice Harmon purchased a farm on Fort Hill Road in Gorham. The newlyweds lived there with their parents for a little more than a year, where their first son, Henry Nichols White, was born on August 26, 1847. Though Ellen's parents shared many aspects of faith with their daughter and son-in-law, they did not at first accept the Sabbath. This produced tension during the time the two families lived together. Other Harmon family connections to Gorham include Robert, Jr., who lived with his parents and died at the home on Fort Hill Road. Ellen's twin sister, *Elizabeth Bangs, married a native of Gorham and settled there for the remainder of her life.

Merlin D. Burt

GOSPEL, see **RIGHTEOUSNESS BY FAITH; SALVATION, PLAN OF.**

GOSPEL ORDER, see **CHURCH ORGANIZATION.**

GOSPEL PRIMER (SPA, 1895, 128 pp.). Teaching aid prepared by *J. Edson White and *W. O. Palmer, first conceived to help in their educational efforts for *African-Americans in the southern United States and sold by colporteurs as a means to raise funds for advancing the Seventh-day Adventist work among Blacks. But soon after its publication, managers of Adventist publishing houses decided on a marketing plan to promote only one major book at a time, and *Gospel Primer* was not part of this program. Upon hearing from her son W. C. White what was being done to delay the sale of this book, Ellen White dispatched a stern letter to then General Conference president O. A. Olsen. "Did your devising in regard to the *Gospel Primer* meet the approval of God?" she asked. "No; the principle upon which you acted was wrong" (Lt 65, 1895, in ChL 29; cf. 6MR 173, 174). "The Lord has been opening some matters before me," she also wrote to C. H. Jones, president of Pacific Press. "I have been instructed to say that some of the actions of men in important positions of trust are not approved by God. . . . Pressure was brought to bear, first to hinder, and then to get control of *The Gospel Primer*, and in place of the work in the South being aided by the sale of this book, as it might have been, the income was reduced and diverted to other uses. What a blind selfishness!" (21MR 143). By 1901 Ellen White still felt that many church leaders had hindered the advancement of the work in the Southern fields, and claimed that they had been dishonest and underhanded in their marketing of the book and financially benefitting themselves from its sale instead of providing more financial support for the work in the South (Ms 37, 1901). Yet in spite of this difficult beginning, the sale of *Gospel Primer* was a success and ultimately reached more than 1 million copies. J. E. White published another *Gospel Primer* (no. 2) in 1910 (RHPA, 96 pp.).

Further reading: 5Bio 189, 190; C. R.

Upshaw, "An Historical Survey of SDA Religious Literature for Blacks" (research paper, AU, 1971; DF 43-b, CAR), pp. 3-8.

Denis Fortin

GOSPEL WORKERS (RHPA, 1915, 534 pp.). A compilation of Ellen White's counsels to those engaged in gospel ministry. One of the last books produced under Ellen White's direct supervision before her death in 1915, it was revised and enlarged from the original edition of 1892. Designed to guide, enrich, and make more effective and fruitful the work of pastors, this handbook of practical counsels on gospel ministry and Christian service is also helpful for every Christian. Consisting of 12 sections of varying length and emphasis, the book covers a wide variety of biblical subjects related to the calling, character, and work of gospel ministers—those who in every age and place have been committed to serve God and speak to the people the Word of God. "In every period of this earth's history, God has had His men . . . to whom He has said, 'Ye are my witnesses'" (p. 13). *Gospel Workers* also discusses the needed preparation and qualifications of the minister. Effective ministers of righteousness are always learning from Jesus Christ and working in the power of the Holy Spirit. Their ultimate reward is to fulfill the will of the heavenly Father. A statement from the chapter "Power for Service" epitomizes the book: "Nothing is more needed in our work than the practical results of communion with God. We should show by our daily lives that we have peace and rest in the Savior. His peace in the heart will shine forth in the countenance. It will give to the voice a persuasive power. Communion with God will ennoble the character and the life. Men will take knowledge of us, as of the first disciples, that we have been with Jesus. This will impart to the worker a power that nothing else can give. Of this power he must not allow himself to be deprived" (p. 510).

S. Joseph Kidder

GRACE, see **SALVATION, PLAN OF.**

GRAYSVILLE, TENNESSEE. Adventist headquarters for the southeastern United States from about 1892 to 1901; location of a boarding school and sanitarium visited by Ellen G. White in June 1904. The Graysville church, organized in 1888 with nine members, grew rapidly after 1892 when George W. Colcord founded Graysville Academy. In 1895, 19 Graysville Adventists, including Colcord and two other members of the academy faculty, were arrested for working on Sunday. Eight of them were required to work on a chain gang. In 1902 Ellen White said the Lord had led in the establishment of the academy, and she urged that a sanitarium also be established at Graysville (7T 231, 232). That year Adventists began building a four-story sanitarium on Lone Mountain, a short distance from the school. The denomination operated the sanitarium until 1914, after which it was managed by Adventist laypersons for several years. In 1916 Graysville Academy was relocated to a site near Chattanooga, where it grew into the present Southern Adventist University.

Further reading: 5Bio 346, 347; LDE 101; RY 205; 7T 231, 232; M. R. Reiber, *Graysville: Battle Creek of the South, 1888-1988* (Collegedale, Tenn.: College Press [1989]); L. A. Hansen, *From So Small a Dream* (SPA, 1968), pp. 121-123, 155, 216, 244; D. Pettibone, *A Century of Challenge: The Story of Southern College* (Collegedale, Tenn.: Southern College of Seventh-day Adventists, 1992), pp. 9-50.

Dennis Pettibone

GREAT CONTROVERSY BETWEEN CHRIST AND SATAN, THE (RHPA, 1888, 1911, 719 pp.). Fifth volume of the *Conflict of the Ages Series, covering the history of the Christian church from the destruction of Jerusalem to the restoration of earth at the end of time, one of the most widely read and translated books of Ellen White. Concerning it she wrote, "The book *Great Controversy* I appreciate above silver or gold, and I greatly desire that it shall come before the people" (Lt 56, 1911, in 3SM 123).

Ellen White's writing of the story of the *great controversy between Christ and Satan occupied a sizable portion of her time between 1858 and her death in 1915. In March 1858 she had a vision in which she was instructed to write the events she had seen. Amid personal afflictions she wrote that year the first volume of *Spiritual Gifts, in which she summed up important periods of human history from the fall of Lucifer in heaven to the earth made new. Here, for the first time in her writings, she revealed the invisible struggle between the forces of good and evil for the control of humanity. In subsequent visions during the following years she received further details of various phases of this supernatural conflict, and in 1864 volumes 3 and 4 of *Spiritual Gifts* appeared, dealing more comprehensively with the fall of Lucifer, the creation of the world, the fall of Adam and Eve, the lives of the patriarchs, and the experience of Israel. (Volume 2, published in 1860, was an autobiographical work.) When the demand came in the late 1860s for a new printing of *Spiritual Gifts,* Ellen White decided that it would be better to expand the work. Plans were laid for a series of four volumes of about 400 pages each called *The Spirit of Prophecy.* Volume 4 of this series, published in 1884, was subtitled *The Great Controversy Between Christ and Satan From the Destruction of Jerusalem to the End of the Controversy.* At the time of writing this volume Ellen White regarded it,

as she did all her other writings, as primarily a message to the church, and in it she used some material and many phrases and expressions especially adapted to Seventh-day Adventists.

From 1885 to 1887 she visited Europe. While there, her contact with people and visits to some of the historic sites brought to her mind many scenes she claimed to have seen in her visions. And as plans were discussed to translate *The Spirit of Prophecy,* volume 4, into many European languages, she decided to make additions to the book and to write more graphically and fully the events. She also decided to adapt this new edition to the general public and remove from it segments and expressions understood by Adventists but not appropriate for others. This edition came out in 1888 and was prepared while she was in Europe.

By the end of the first decade of the twentieth century the electrotype plates for the publication of the 1888 edition were so badly worn that it became necessary to reset the type for *The Great Controversy.* Again Ellen White decided to make revisions. New illustrations were chosen, references to historical works were inserted, and in a few instances clearer historical citations were substituted for older out-of-print or difficult-to-find ones. She also decided to modify some expressions potentially offensive to people of other churches. All this work was done by her *literary assistants and approved by Ellen White. This final edition was published in 1911 and is the current edition still in print.

Different Spanish editions of *The Great Controversy* have been published, the most widely known being the translation done by Eduardo Francisco Forga, published in 1913 and reflecting the changes effected by Ellen White in the 1911 English edition. Of interest in the Spanish translation is the addition of a chapter (13) on the Reformation in Spain. This chapter was written by Clarence C. Crisler (one of Ellen White's secretaries) and H. H. Hall and was inserted with Ellen White's approval. (A footnote on the first page of that chapter notes that it was approved, but not written, by Ellen White.)

Ellen White's use of *historians in *The Great Controversy* has raised a number of issues in relationship to her inspiration, particularly when she referred to historical facts now thought to be inaccurate. Some believe *The Great Controversy* contains more borrowed material than in any other of her books. F. D. Nichol estimated that direct quotes compose 12 percent of the book (*Ellen G. White and Her Critics*, p. 420). However, in addition to the material in quotation marks, there are also sentences and paragraphs paraphrased from other sources, such as J. A. Wylie's *The History of Protestantism*, D'Aubigné's *History of the Reformation*, and from Adventist authors Uriah Smith, John N. Andrews, and her husband, James White. Two main reasons appear to have motivated Ellen White to borrow from other authors. First, she felt her own deficiencies in vocabulary and literary composition, and was always seeking to improve her writing. A second reason for relying on other authors was her own limited knowledge of history and geography. In her introduction to *The Great Controversy* she stated: "In some cases where a historian has so grouped together events as to afford, in brief, a comprehensive view of the subject, or has summarized details in a convenient manner, his words have been quoted; but in some instances no specific credit has been given, since the quotations are not given for the purpose of citing that writer as authority, but because his statement affords a ready and forcible presentation of the subject" (p. xii).

In *The Great Controversy* Ellen White presents how the cosmic conflict between God and Satan has unfolded in the postbiblical period and through the course of church history in such a way as to prepare the mind of the reader to understand clearly how the controversy is going on in our day. These events were predicted in Scripture and culminate with the second advent of Christ. In the final chapters of the book she places Adventism within the flow of prophetic history. Two major theological themes, among several, emerge from this book. The first is the love of God. Many of her books, such as *Steps to Christ* and *The Desire of Ages*, highlight God's love for humanity and His willingness to do all He can to redeem it from sin. This theme is also present in *The Great Controversy*. The phrase "God is love," found at the beginning of *Patriarchs and Prophets* (p. 33), the first book in the Conflict of the Ages Series, is also the very last phrase of *The Great Controversy* (p. 678). Clearly the foremost intent of this cosmic conflict is to demonstrate that God is love. While it has been Satan's endeavor to present Him as a god of vengeance and terror (p. 500), clothing "with his own attributes the Creator and Benefactor of mankind" (p. 534), God has sought to reveal His character of love and mercy (p. 498).

A second major theme is faithfulness to Scripture. The first half of *The Great Controversy* tells the history of the Christian church from the destruction of Jerusalem to the time of *William Miller (1782-1849). Ellen White is careful to describe how the cosmic conflict played in the lives of the early Christians, the Waldenses, John Wycliffe, Huss and Jerome, Martin Luther, and many others. In her description of the events in the lives of these historical figures, she presents one common denominator: "The grand principle maintained by these Reformers . . . was the infallible authority of the Holy Scriptures as a rule of faith and practice. They denied the right of popes, councils, Fathers, and kings, to control the conscience in matters of religion. The Bible was their authority, and by its teaching they tested all doctrines and all claims. Faith in God and His Word sustained these holy men as they yielded up their lives at the stake" (p. 249). In this great controversy she explains that Satan sought to destroy them because they loved God and wished to remain faithful to the teachings of the Bible as they understood them. She points out that it has been Satan's aim to eclipse the Word of God and to reduce its appeal, since those who don't know the Scriptures can be more easily deceived (p. 593). Hence, people who cling to the Bible are the subjects of his wrath and attacks. Ellen White also points out that at the end of time this conflict will be repeated in the lives of God's people, who wish to follow unyieldingly the teachings of Scripture above human opinions and traditions (pp. 594, 595). Then, as always, following the teachings of Scripture is the only safeguard (pp. 593-602).

There are other important themes in *The Great Controversy* that should be mentioned. Ellen White describes the rise and importance of the Advent movement in the 1840s in relation to the development of the *prophetic interpretation of the books of Daniel and Revelation (pp. 299, 390). She understands the three angels' messages of Revelation 14 as foundational to a proper understanding of the work of *Christ as high priest in the heavenly *sanctuary (pp. 391-491). She devotes the last third of her book to the snares of Satan and his attempts at deceiving humanity (pp. 492-562) and of the final events of earth's history in the great controversy between good and evil, Christ and Satan (pp. 563-678). Her last chapters on the *second coming of Christ and the re-creation of the earth are among the best known of her writings and have

encouraged countless readers (pp. 635-678). *See also*: general article: The Theology of Ellen G. White.

Further reading: 6Bio 302-337; 3SM 433-465; F. D. Nichol, *Ellen G. White and Her Critics* (RHPA, 1951), p. 637; R. W. Olson, "Ellen G. White's Use of Uninspired Sources" (EGWE, SDoc); A. L. White, *The Ellen G. White Writings* (RHPA, 1973), pp. 25-38, 107-136; "The 1911 Edition of *Great Controversy* (EGWE, SDoc); "W. W. Prescott and the 1911 Edition of *Great Controversy* (EGWE, SDoc).

Denis Fortin

GREAT CONTROVERSY THEME. One overarching theme in the writings of Ellen White is the great controversy theme. She understood that a controversy of cosmic proportion exists between God and *Satan over whose plan is better for the universe—God's will, as expressed in His commandments, or Satan's notion of individual self-determination. The heart of this conflict has been Satan's charges that God is unfair, severe, unforgiving, arbitrary, revengeful, supremely selfish—"a being whose chief attribute is stern justice" (SC 11; ST, Jan. 20, 1890; Ed 154; PK 311; 5T 738; GC 569). God's defense has been both passive and active—passive in that God has allowed time to proceed so that Satan's principles could be seen in all their suicidal destructiveness; active in that He has revealed His character of love and trustworthiness so that all inhabitants throughout the universe as well as on earth could make up their minds as to who has been right and wrong in the controversy (PP 39-43; 68-70). In the life and death of Jesus, God's wisdom and trustworthiness has been vindicated, and will be further vindicated in the redeemed, who shall be "the praise of the glory of His grace" (Eph. 1:6, NKJV). The great controversy theme became for Ellen White her organizing principle. All areas of her thought unfolded out of this internally consistent principle, making all of her varied concerns coherent and interactive.

The Godhead, being essentially love (1 John 4:8), created responsible beings also capable of love, both angels and intelligent beings on worlds throughout the universe (PP 42). Love entails choice and thus risk; love by these created beings, in response to God's love, "springs from an appreciation of his character" (*ibid*. 34), a voluntary act. "Without freedom of choice . . . obedience would not have been voluntary, but forced. . . . Such a course would have been contrary to God's plan in dealing with the inhabitants of other worlds. It would have been unworthy of man as an intelligent being, and would have sustained Satan's charge of God's arbitrary rule" (*ibid*. 49). But this freedom was "perverted" when Lucifer, the "prince of angels," indulged in "self-exaltation" and "aspired to power" and "supremacy," leading to "misconstruing and distorting" the truths about God (PP 35-38; GC 492-497). Here *sin entered the universe, the rebellion of a created being, one who allowed himself to "become a contradiction" to God's will (5MR 348).

Thus, "from the opening of the great controversy it has been Satan's purpose to misrepresent God's character and to excite rebellion against His law, and this work appears to be crowned with success" (PP 338). And at the end of time, "the last great conflict between truth and error is but the final struggle of the long-standing controversy concerning the law of God," "a battle between the laws of men and the precepts of Jehovah, between the religion of the Bible and the religion of fable and tradition" (GC 582).

The whole intelligent universe is involved in the controversy. It was God's purpose, "not merely to put down the rebellion, but to demonstrate to all the universe the nature of the rebellion. . . . God's plan was unfolding, showing both His justice and His mercy, and fully vindicating His wisdom and righteousness in His dealings with evil" (PP 78). Even the unfallen angels needed to observe God's plan worked out, because "without the cross they would be no more secure against evil than were the angels before the fall of Satan" (ST, Dec. 30, 1889). In short, "the plan of redemption had a yet broader and deeper purpose than the salvation of man" because it was "to vindicate the character of God before the universe" (PP 68).

God's response to Satan's accusations is the central theme of the Bible. "The student should learn to view the Word [the Bible] as a whole, and to see the relation of its parts. He should gain a knowledge of its grand central theme, God's original purpose for the world, of the rise of the great controversy, and of the work of redemption. He should understand the nature of the two principles that are contending for supremacy, and should learn to trace their working. . . . He should see how this controversy enters into every phase of human experience; how in every act of life he himself reveals the one or the other of the two antagonistic motives; and how, whether he will or not, he is even now deciding upon which side of the controversy he will be found" (Ed 190).

That "grand central theme" unfolds how God has responded to Satan's challenge: "The central theme of the Bible, the theme about which every other in the whole book clusters, is the redemption plan, the restoration in the human soul of the image of God" (*ibid*. 125). Here we have the purpose of the gospel—the goal of God's plan is to rescue men and women from their rebellion. More than forgiveness, the goal of redemption is to restore in men and women the image of their Maker (COL 419, 420). The living evidence that God is not unfair and unforgiving, that He does not make laws that cannot be kept, that He is not supremely selfish and unmoved by the plight of sinners, was first demonstrated in the life of Jesus (ST, Jan. 20, 1890; DA 24). By His example, Christ proved that sinful men and women may also resist Satan's temptations, be overcomers, and thus provide additional evidence that Satan's accusations are false (*ibid.* 763, 828; PP 88, 89; SC 62, 63).

Grace is the word the Bible uses to express the "attribute of God exercised toward undeserving human beings" (MH 161). It includes whatever sinners need, not only that whisper of the Holy Spirit that works upon every human soul (COL 206), not only repentance (AG 138); but also the "renewing of the heart that the grace of God works to transform the life" so that the sinner "can be fitted for the kingdom of glory" (COL 97, 96). Amazing as the thought may be, "through the grace of Christ we may accomplish everything that God requires" (*ibid.* 301). But "God's free grace" is not something that "must be earned" (*ibid.* 390). Christ alone gives the grace of pardon and power (*ibid.* 402).

Central in the work of grace is the role of the Holy Spirit, whose primary task is to imbue "the receiver with the attributes of Christ" (DA 805). In fact, "the Spirit was to be given as a regenerating agent, and without this the sacrifice of Christ would have been of no avail. . . . It is the Spirit that makes effectual what has been wrought out by the world's Redeemer. . . . Christ has given His Spirit as a divine power to overcome all hereditary and cultivated tendencies to evil, and to impress His own character upon His church" (*ibid.* 671). All of which is proving Satan wrong when he said that sinners would not and could not freely and fully obey the will of God (*ibid.* 24, 664).

Ellen White saw the direct connection between the great controversy theme, focusing on restoration, and her philosophy of education, noting their mutual purpose and goal: "To restore in man the image of his Maker, to bring him back to the perfection in which he was created, . . . this was to be the work of redemption. This is the object of education, the great object of life" (Ed 15, 16).

On many occasions she emphasized the close relationship among the physical, mental, emotional, and spiritual powers. "The relation" of physical health "to the spiritual life is one of the most important branches of education" (COL 348), and "anything that lessens physical strength enfeebles the mind and makes it less capable of discriminating between right and wrong" (*ibid.* 346).

Because God is fair and respectful of the freedom He gave His created intelligent beings, "it is no part of Christ's mission to compel men to receive Him. It is Satan, and men actuated by his spirit, that seek to compel the conscience" (DA 487). Further, God does not predestine all events that happen, nor the destiny of any created being—He is willing to abide by the choices made by uncoerced intelligences. In contrast to Calvinist predestination, "[God's] power awaits the demand of those who would overcome. . . . The Lord designs that His human agents shall act as rational, accountable beings in every respect" (1SM 380; SC 47). In fact, "God has made provision that we may become like unto Him, and He will accomplish this for all who do not interpose a perverse will and thus frustrate His grace" (MB 76).

But freedom involves risk and contingency—when Jesus became man, and when God purposed to work out His plan through people, first Israel, and then the Christian church. When Jesus became man, "like every child of Adam He accepted the results of the working of the great law of heredity. . . . He came with such a heredity to share our sorrows and temptations, and to give us the example of a sinless life. . . . [God] permitted Him to meet life's peril in common with every human soul, to fight the battle as every child of humanity must fight it, at the risk of failure and eternal loss" (DA 49).

Through Israel in Old Testament times, God "designed that the principles revealed through His people should be the means of restoring the moral image of God in man" (COL 286). According to their faithfulness Israel would "embrace the world" (*ibid.* 290); but "all their advantages were appropriated for their own glorification": "misrepresenting God's character, dishonoring His name, and polluting His sanctuary" (*ibid.* 291, 292).

But God was not defeated. Jesus gave to His church the same assignment that had been given to Israel: "Through His people Christ is to manifest His character and the principles of His kingdom. . . . the Lord desires through His people to answer Satan's charges by showing the results of obedience to right principles" (*ibid.* 296). But the church has also caused Jesus to wait for the end of the great controversy: "It is true that time has continued longer than we expected. . . . It was not the will of God that the coming of Christ should be thus delayed. God did not design that His people, Israel, should wander forty years in the wilderness. . . . The same sins have delayed the entrance of modern Israel into the heavenly Canaan" (1SM 67-69).

Thus, in order to place the future of the universe "on an eternal basis of security, . . . time must be given for Satan to develop the principles which were the foundation of his system of government" (DA 759), and for God's people to "be a sanctified, purified, holy people," "exemplifying the truth in their lives . . . [to] be a praise in the earth" (8T 14). But in the end, "there will be but two classes. Every

character will be fully developed; and all will show whether they have chosen the side of loyalty or that of rebellion." All will "receive the results of their own choice" (DA 763, 764). In the final judgment, "profession is as nothing in the scale. It is character that decides destiny" (COL 74).

The great controversy ends when "every question of truth and error in the longstanding controversy has now been made plain. . . . The working out of Satan's rule in contrast with the government of God has been presented to the whole universe. . . . With all the facts of the great controversy in view, the whole universe, both loyal and rebellious, with one accord declare, 'Just and true are Thy ways, Thou King of saints' " (GC 670, 671).

See also: Christ, Humanity of; Will, Human; Perfection.

Further reading: J. Battistone, *The Great Controversy Theme in the E. G. White Writings* (AUP, 1978); H. E. Douglass, comp., *The Heartbeat of Adventism: The Great Controversy Theme in the Writings of Ellen G. White* (PPPA, 2010); *idem, Messenger of the Lord* (PPPA, 1998), pp. 256-277; *idem, God at Risk: The Cost of Freedom in the Great Controversy Between God and Satan* (Amazing Facts, 2004); F. B. Holbrook, "The Great Controversy," in R. Dederen, ed., *Handbook of Seventh-day Adventist Theology* (RHPA, 2000), pp. 980-1009; G. R. Knight, *The Cross of Christ* (RHPA, 2008); *idem, Sin and Salvation* (RHPA, 2008); R. Rice, "The Great Controversy and the Problem of Evil," *Spectrum* 32, no. 1 (Winter 2004): 46-55; A. M. Rodríguez, *Spanning the Abyss: How the Atonement Brings God and Humanity Together* (RHPA, 2008).

Herbert E. Douglass

GREAT CONTROVERSY VISION. Vision Ellen White had on March 14, 1858, in Lovett's

Grove, Ohio, outlining the *great controversy theme. The *Review and Herald* announced a trip by James and Ellen White to visit Adventists in Ohio (RH, Feb. 18, 1858), which included a final stop at Lovett's Grove near Bowling Green. Here James and Ellen White found a company of 40 Sabbathkeepers, recently converted through the labors of George W. Holt. On Sunday afternoon, March 14, James White preached a funeral discourse during which—he noted afterward—"God manifested His power in a wonderful manner," adding that "several [had] decided to keep the Lord's Sabbath and go with the people of God" (RH, Mar. 25, 1858).

During that same service Ellen White received a two-hour-long vision in which was outlined practical counsel to meet problems among area church members (2SG 266), and, more significantly, a cosmic sweep of the ages-long conflict "between Christ and His angels, and Satan and his angels" (see 1SG title). While a limited view of the great controversy theme had been given 10 years earlier, the 1858 vision gave a greatly expanded view of its issues and events, and this time she was instructed to write it out. She was also warned that she would "have to contend with the powers of darkness, for Satan would make strong efforts to hinder" her in sharing that message (2SG 270). As the extended vision concluded, Ellen White observed that a "great solemnity rested upon those who remained" (*ibid.* 271).

The next day the Whites began their return journey to *Battle Creek, stopping en route, on March 16, to visit *Daniel and Abigail Palmer in Jackson, Michigan. While there, Ellen White (at age 30) was stricken with her "third shock . . . of paralysis," but as her husband and friends prayed for her she began to recover, giving God the glory that "the power of Satan was broken" (*ibid.* 271, 272).

The next day she felt sufficiently strong to complete the remaining 40 miles (65 kilometers) back to Battle Creek. Over the next several weeks, in a crippled condition, Ellen White began to write out the details of that which she had been bidden to relate. As she wrote, her strength increased, so that within five months she composed the manuscript for the 219-page book *Spiritual Gifts,* volume 1 (RH, Sept. 9, 1858). This small book would be expanded through several editions, eventually becoming part of the *Conflict of the Ages Series.

See also: Visions of Ellen G. White.

Further reading: 2SG 266-272; 1Bio 374; W. C. White, "A View of the Age-Long Conflict," RH, Feb. 20, 1936; R. Coon, *The Great Visions of Ellen White* (RHPA, 1992), pp. 62-75; A. W. Spalding, *Origin and History of Seventh-day Adventists* (RHPA, 1961), vol. 1, p. 223; A. L. White, "Vision in a Schoolhouse," RH, Feb. 5, 1959, pp. 12-14.

Michael W. Campbell

GREENVILLE, MICHIGAN, see **HOMES OF JAMES AND ELLEN G. WHITE.**

GROVELAND CAMP MEETING. On August 27, 1876, Ellen White addressed a crowd of some 20,000 people, the largest in her entire life (Lt 42, 1876, in 7MR 288). The campgrounds for this *camp meeting, four miles (6.5 kilometers) from Haverhill, Massachusetts, and about 30 miles (50 kilometers) north of Boston, could be reached by train and river excursion boats from both Boston and Haverhill. Fifty-five tents, including three large pavilions—45, 55, and 65 feet (13.7 meters, 16.8 meters, and 19.8 meters) in diameter—were pitched in a beautiful grove. "Five hundred camped on the grounds. . . . River steamers ran twice a day from Haverhill . . . and every hour on Sunday. Eighteen trains ran each day, all stopping at the campground" (3Bio 45, 46).

On Sunday, August 27, special excursion trains from Lawrence, Newburyport, and Haverhill brought record-breaking crowds that by 9:00 a.m. filled the auditorium, where James White preached about an hour. "Still the people poured in from the towns about," reported *Mary Clough, "and the trains came loaded with their living freight. After an intermission of thirty minutes, Mrs. White ascended the platform, amid the profound stillness of that vast multitude, and addressed the people on the subject of Christian temperance. The morning trains were crowded, but the noon trains flooded the grove, and the two-thirty trains from Lawrence brought fifteen cars literally packed with people, the platform and steps were full also." The grove was so crowded that some climbed trees to get a better view of the speaker (ST, Sept. 14, 1876). Ellen White spoke at the Groveland camp meeting the following year, again to huge crowds (3Bio 67-69).

Further reading: LS 225-227; 4T 278-281; RH, Sept. 6, 1877.

GUIDELINES TO MENTAL HEALTH (EGWE, 1966, 491 pp.). Preliminary working compilation of Ellen White's writings that formed the basis for *Mind, Character, and Personality*, published in 1977.

HABITS. Ellen White wrote extensively on habits, emphasizing not only the importance of correct and good habits but also the demoralizing effect of wrong and evil habits. Habits, formed by repeated thoughts and actions, "form character, and by the character our destiny for time and eternity is decided" (COL 356).

Habits of "right thinking" are the foundation of right actions, she taught. "The power of self-restraint strengthens by exercise. That which at first seems difficult, by constant repetition grows easy, until right thoughts and actions become habitual" (MH 491).

Ellen White often explained that "right and correct habits, intelligently and perseveringly practiced, will be removing the cause of disease, and the strong drugs need not be resorted to" (MM 222). But even more important was Ellen White's concern for moral disease caused by wrong habits: "We should never be slow in breaking up a sinful habit. Unless evil habits are conquered, they will conquer us, and destroy our happiness" (4T 654).

Long before the discovery of how brain nerves form habit patterns, Ellen White cautioned that habits are not reversed easily: "Let none flatter themselves that sins cherished for a time can easily be given up by and by. This is not so. Every sin cherished weakens the character and strengthens habit; and physical, mental, and moral depravity is the result. You may repent of the wrong you have done, and set your feet in right paths; but the mold of your mind and your familiarity with evil will make it difficult for you to distinguish between right and wrong. Through the wrong habits formed, Satan will assail you again and again" (COL 281).

One of the purposes of the gospel is to mature people so that they will have "habitual tenderness of feeling, Christlike love, and holy deeds" (AG 235) "until right thoughts and actions become habitual" (MH 491).

Herbert E. Douglass

HAPPINESS DIGEST (Better Living Publications, 1983, 64 pp.). Paperback edition of Ellen White's *Steps to Christ* published for free distribution to the public. The book has a different pagination than the standard edition and includes color drawings.

HAPPINESS HOMEMADE (SPA, 1971, 188

pp.). Abridged paperback edition of *The Adventist Home. Happiness Homemade* is comprised of selections from 61 chapters of the original 87 of *The Adventist Home,* with titles of chapters slightly reworded in some instances. Sections of the original work left out include counsels on choosing a life partner, factors that make for success or failure in a marriage, and counsels on types of recreational activities. *Happiness Homemade* sought to make available in a more attractive format Ellen White's counsels and insights on the Christian home and family.

HARBOR SPRINGS, MICHIGAN. A small town in the northern part of Michigan's lower peninsula, located across Little Traverse Bay from Petoskey, where Ellen White had a summer home. The convention held at Harbor Springs in July and August 1891 proved to be a turning point in Adventist education.

*W. W. Prescott, the denomination's educational leader, called the meeting in order to disseminate to the schools the fruits of the recent revival in the church's emphasis on "Christ our righteousness" and Bible study in education. About 100 of Adventism's foremost educators attended the nearly six-week convention. Ellen White would leave Harbor Springs with ideas of educational reform at the center of her thinking. Those ideas would soon bear fruit during her extended role as one of the founders of the *Avondale school in Australia, a school that provided, according to Ellen White, a pattern for the reform of Adventist education around the world.

Both Prescott and *P. T. Magan came to view the Harbor Springs convention as the most significant turning point in Adventist educational history. Before the convention, Adventist education had been largely an adaptation of that of other institutions. Afterward it became both more Christian and more Adventist. With *A. T. Jones, Ellen White, *J. H. Kellogg, and Prescott as the main speakers, the conference addressed such issues as the place of the Bible in Adventist education, the elimination of the "heathen" classics, and the importance of physiology and health. All topics were discussed within the context of the Christ-centered emphasis that had been uplifted in the church since the *General Conference session of 1888.

Ellen White made at least six presentations that are still extant. By 1891 she had come to realize that the biblical perspective would never find its proper place in Adventist education as long as the classics held the center. The reforms initiated at Harbor Springs did much to shape Adventist education as it spread around the world in the late 1890s.

Further reading: G. R. Knight, ed., *Early Adventist Educators* (PPPA, 1983), pp. 32-39; *idem*, "The Dynamics of Educational Expansion," *Journal of Adventist Education*, April/May 1990, pp. 13-19, 44, 45; G. M. Valentine, "William Warren Prescott" (Ph.D. diss., AU, 1982), pp. 174-182; C. S. Willis, "Harbor Springs Institute of 1891" (research paper, AU, 1979).

George R. Knight

HEALDSBURG COLLEGE. A coeducational boarding school operated in Healdsburg, California, from 1882 to 1908. At Ellen White's urging, the 1881 session of the California Conference voted to "establish a school by Seventh-day Adventists in California." *W. C. White was elected chair of the founding board. He traveled to Michigan in December to persuade Professor and Mrs. *Sidney Brownsberger to head the new school, and on April 11, 1882, they opened classes, eight days before *S. N. Haskell—in friendly rivalry with White—opened *South Lancaster Academy in Massachusetts. By summer, the

Healdsburg school had six teachers and 152 students. At the request of the town, the school took the name of Healdsburg College (rather than Academy), though it did not award its first collegiate diploma until 1889.

Despite the eventual acquisition of additional acres, the city location proved too restrictive, so in 1909 the campus was moved to a rural location and renamed *Pacific Union College. W. C. White served on the board of Healdsburg and its successor for 55 years, from the founding of Healdsburg in 1882 until his death in 1937.

Further reading: 1MR 317-323; 3Bio 191-193; W. C. Utt, *A Mountain, a Pickax, a College: A History of Pacific Union College* (Angwin, Calif.: Pacific Union College, 1968); *SDA Encyclopedia* (1996), vol. 11, pp. 280-284.

HEALING, FAITH, see **PRAYER FOR THE SICK.**

HEALTH FOOD MINISTRY, THE (Ellen G. White Publications, 1970, 95 pp.). Compilation of statements from Ellen White's writings relating to the commercial production and distribution of vegetarian foods as a part of the work of the church. In the late 1890s Ellen White wrote a number of messages regarding the importance of food ministry that were published in *Testimonies for the Church* (vol. 7, pp. 110-137). Acting on the request of Loma Linda Foods (a Seventh-day Adventist company producing health foods), the White Estate in 1934 prepared a 50-page pamphlet, *The Health Food Work,* to supplement earlier messages published in the *Testimonies.* The *Health Food Ministry* is a reprint of both documents, with a topical outline following the table of contents. Ellen White recommended the establishment of health food factories in connection with Adventist schools and sanitariums and the establishment of

vegetarian restaurants in large cities. She saw such institutions as a means of attracting the spiritual interest of people in secular environments, of teaching Adventist health principles, and of helping people live a better life (cf. CD 267-277). However, she felt concerned that such institutions would not become simply commercial enterprises but would reflect a genuine ministry to the lost. She emphasized that "this work must be carried forward as a means of gospel enlightenment to those who have not given themselves to the Lord" (HFM 89). "In every work to which the people of God put their hands, soul-saving is to be made of the first importance. Let not those engaged in the food work think that their efforts can bear the approval of God unless they do all they possibly can to reach with the truth those whom they supply with temporal food" (*ibid.* 69, 70).

Denis Fortin

HEALTH: OR HOW TO LIVE (1865). Series of six pamphlets, including six articles written by Ellen White and a large number of articles by several physicians and popular health reformers who were included to demonstrate that contemporary "authorities" supported the health reform concepts White was promoting. Following her major vision on *health reform in June 1863, Ellen White began to write extensively on the subjects of health, nutrition, and lifestyle. Her first presentation of the subject appeared in *Spiritual Gifts* in a chapter titled "Health" (vol. 4a, pp. 120-151). In 1865 she amplified this chapter into a series of six articles published as part of the pamphlets series *Health: or How to Live.* That same year James White published the six pamphlets in a booklet under the same title, in which he also included a number of articles by other health reformers of the time, not all of which espoused views adopted by the church or in harmony with Ellen White's teachings. The six Ellen White articles were later republished in shorter segments in the *Review and Herald* in 1899 and 1900, and again in 1958 in *Selected Messages* (book 2, pp. 409-479) under the title "Disease and Its Causes." Later, fuller presentations such as *The Ministry of Healing* (1905) replaced many earlier publications on health, including the *Health: or How to Live* series. These six Ellen White articles dealt with a wide variety of subjects: nutrition and vegetarianism; overeating versus self-control of appetite; various aspects of temperance, especially abstinence from alcohol; home environment and the responsibilities of parents toward their children, prenatal influences on the unborn; use of *drugs, causes of diseases and treatment of the sick, and slavery to fashion. In all these areas Ellen White urged faithful observance of God's natural laws of health and hygiene.

Denis Fortin

HEALTH REFORM. The purpose of the health message given to Ellen White was to equip believers for a spiritual mission. She saw the health message as closely linked with the gospel "as the hand is with the body" (3T 62; Rev. 14:6-12), and spoke of the health ministry as the "right arm" of Christ's body, the church (6T 288). This fundamental linkage is based on three principles:

1. The humanitarian principle. The "work of health reform is the Lord's means for lessening suffering in our world," she averred (9T 112, 113). Current scientific research provides massive evidence in support of her basic health concepts. Fraser (see *further reading* below) cites more than 300 scientific articles in peer-reviewed publications.

2. The evangelical principle. Ellen White saw health reform as a bridge by which the gospel can meet people where they are. She called the health message a "great entering wedge," a "door through which the truth for this time is to find entrance to many homes" and "do much toward removing prejudice against our evangelical work" (Ev 513, 514). "The great object of receiving unbelievers into the [health-care] institution," she wrote, "is to lead them to embrace the truth" (1T 560).

3. The salvation principle distinguished the Adventist health message from general health reform. Ellen White's *great controversy theme teaches that the goal of salvation is the "restoration" in believers of the image of God, physically, mentally, and spiritually (Ed 125). Whatever subject she focuses on, this goal integrates all of its aspects. Thus the great controversy theme informs the basis and purpose of health reform. The Adventist emphasis on health was to help "prepare a people for the coming of the Lord" (3T 161). "He who cherishes the light which God has given him upon health reform has an important aid in the work of becoming sanctified through the truth, and fitted for immortality" (CTBH 10). She did not hesitate to point out the direct relationship between daily habits and character development: "A diseased body and disordered intellect, because of continual indulgence in hurtful lust, make sanctification of the body and spirit impossible" (CD 44).

"We believe without a doubt that Christ is soon coming," she declared often. "When He comes He is not to cleanse us of our sins, to remove from us the defects in our characters, or to cure us of the infirmities of our tempers and dispositions. If wrought for us at all, this work will all be accomplished before that time. When the Lord comes, those who are holy will be holy still [Rev. 22:11]. Those who have preserved their bodies and spirits in holiness, in sanctification and honor, will then receive the finishing touch of immortality" (2T 355).

The threefold linkage of the principles

mentioned above has not always been understood. Some have seen the health message as an end in itself, to be fulfilled in merely developing a worldwide network of hospitals and clinics; others have made health a compelling public relations strategy. Both of these are worthy uses of the health message, but both fall short of its distinctive primary purpose: to bring spiritual, mental, and physical wholeness to the daily life of the average person. Placing health matters within the intent of the gospel raised the health issue from personal opinion to the level of spiritual commitment and character development.

Early Adventist leaders such as *J. H. Waggoner perceived the distinct difference between contemporary voices of health reform and Ellen White's "advanced principle." Waggoner wrote: "We do not profess to be pioneers in the general principles of the health reform. The facts on which this movement is based have been elaborated, in a great measure, by reformers, physicians, and writers on physiology and hygiene, and so may be found scattered through the land. But we do claim that by the method of God's choice it has been more clearly and powerfully unfolded, and is thereby producing an effect which we could not have looked for from any other means.

"As mere physiological and hygienic truths, they might be studied by some at their leisure, and by others laid aside as of little consequence; but when placed on a level with the great truths of the third angel's message by the sanction and authority of God's Spirit, and so declared to be the means whereby a weak people may be made strong to overcome, and our diseased bodies cleansed and fitted for translation, then it comes to us as an essential part of *present truth*, to be received with the blessing of God, or rejected at our peril" (RH, Aug. 7, 1866; quoted in SHM65 79, 80).

Thus the pursuit of optimum health became a spiritual obligation. "Our first duty toward God and our fellow beings is that of self-development," wrote White. "Hence that time is spent to good account which is used in the establishment and preservation of physical and mental health. We cannot afford to dwarf or cripple any function of body or mind" (CD 15; cf. COL 329).

Yet she kept her priorities straight, ever placing heart reform before health reform. "Men will never be truly temperate until the grace of Christ is an abiding principle in the heart," she observed. "No mere restriction of your diet will cure your diseased appetite," she reminded one person. "What Christ works within will be worked out under the dictation of a converted intellect. The plan of beginning outside and trying to work inward has always failed, and always will fail" (CD 35).

Another motive for the health message was preparation for the *latter rain and the *loud cry. "God's people are not prepared for the loud cry of the third angel. They have a work to do for themselves which they should not leave for God to do for them," she wrote in 1867. "Lustful appetite makes slaves of men and women, and beclouds their intellects and stupefies their moral sensibilities to such a degree that the sacred, elevated truths of God's Word are not appreciated" (*ibid*. 32). The cleansing of the appetite and the practice of self-denial are essential before God's people can "stand before Him a perfected people" (*ibid*. 381).

The effect of ill health on moral judgment has been one of the most compelling concepts in Ellen White's health message: "Anything that lessens physical strength enfeebles the mind and makes it less capable of discriminating between right and wrong. We become less capable of choosing the good and have less strength of will to do that which we know to be right" (COL 346). Not only discernment between right and wrong, but one's ability to plan and organize is affected by one's health: "Often, when the greatest self-denial should be exercised, the stomach is crowded with a mass of unhealthful food. . . . The affliction of the stomach affects the brain. The imprudent eater does not realize that he is disqualifying himself for . . . laying plans for the best advancement of the work of God" (CD 53; cf. 2T 357).

Among early Adventists the connection between diet and physical health was quickly grasped, but the connection between temperance (self-control) and spiritual discernment was not so easily recognized. Most, at first, saw no link between preaching the gospel (or their own spiritual growth) and what they ate. Against many who thought she was advocating extremes, Ellen White maintained her course and resolutely led her colleagues into thinking more clearly: "Some have sneered at this work of reform, and have said it was all unnecessary; that it was an excitement to divert minds from present truth. They have said that matters were being carried to extremes. Such do not know what they are talking about. While men and women professing godliness are diseased from the crown of their head to the soles of their feet, while their physical, mental, and moral energies are enfeebled through gratification of depraved appetite and excessive labor, how can they weigh the evidences of truth, and comprehend the requirements of God?" (CD 50, 51).

Another motive for guarding health was unselfish thoughtfulness toward family and associates. Ellen White was intensely practical. Her counsel was easy to understand. In those days before modern hospitals and the latest antibiotics, when the extended family often lived under one roof, sick ones became the burdens of whoever happened to be healthy at the moment. Ellen White, observing how heavy that burden fell on young, busy mothers and other family members, wrote: "Many by their actions have said, 'It is nobody's business whether I eat this or that. Whatever we do we are to bear the consequences ourselves.' Dear friends, you are greatly mistaken. You are not the only sufferers from a wrong course. . . . We that are around you . . . are also affected by your infirmities" and bear "the consequences of your wrongs." "If, instead of having a buoyancy of spirit, you are gloomy, you cast a shadow upon the spirits of all around you." Thus, she concluded, "It is impossible for you to pursue any wrong course without causing others to suffer" (2T 356, 357).

The highest motive for preserving health is the desire to glorify God by serving others. In the words of Paul, "whether you eat or drink, or whatever you do, do all to the glory of God" (1 Cor. 10:31, NKJV). Ellen White referred to this motivation as the "glory of self-sacrificing love," "the love which 'seeketh not her own' [1 Cor. 13:5]," which "has its source in the heart of God," and is the "law of life for earth and heaven" (DA 20). Side benefits of this highest motivation include longer life and less disease. But if the higher motivation is eclipsed, health reform can become self-centered and neglectful of the well-being of others. Caring for one's health is a spiritual matter, not merely a physical concern.

Consequently, the issue of uniting or separating the physical from the spiritual is not merely a philosophical issue or a matter of personal opinion. Ellen White saw it as a crucial battlefield in the war between good and evil. She believed that the unity of physical, mental, and spiritual in human nature, and the consequent need to integrate health with the gospel, demanded a corresponding unity between physicians and ministers in the work of the gospel. This was one purpose for having health, educational, and ministerial institutions close together in *Battle Creek. Physicians and ministers were to work like harnessed horses, pulling the Adventist carriage at the same speed with a mutual, common purpose: to encourage the willing in keen thinking and robust health in order to be better prepared for the return of their Lord.

The *Kellogg crisis of the 1890s and early 1900s climaxed in a power struggle, but it sprang from deeper issues. Underlying the power struggle was the belief of the medical leadership, based on considerable evidence, that the ministerial leadership accepted only a part of the health message. Some denominational leaders actually resented Kellogg's enthusiastic endorsement of Ellen White's larger view of healthful living—especially her condemnation of flesh foods. Kellogg found it difficult to accept criticism of his health book, *The Living Temple*, from meat-eating ministers.

However, administrative "surgery," which in the 1900s rightly subordinated the "right arm" (the medical work) to the body, did not heal the wound. Reducing the political power of the "right arm" in relation to denominational organization did not solve the deeper issues of how physical habits directly affect mental and spiritual health. The ensuing separation between the medical and evangelical work of the church was termed by Ellen White "the worst evil" that could be placed on the Adventist Church (MM 241).

The vocational isolation of physicians from ministers is not a mere theoretical disagreement. Not including the principles of the health message within the fullness of the "everlasting gospel," hinders growth in grace (RH, May 27, 1902) and directly affects the preparation of the church to fulfill its gospel commission.

For this reason, Ellen White boldly encouraged church members who sense "the dead level in which they have been" to reconnect the health message to the theological message: "Send into the churches" workers who "live the principles of health reform," who "see the necessity of self-denial in appetite" (6T 267), and who "will set the principles of health reform in their connection with the third angel's message before every family and individual. Encourage all to take a part in work for their fellowmen, and see if the breath of life will not quickly return to these churches" (TM 416).

Ellen White declared emphatically that the work of preparing a people for Christ's second coming "*must not be a divided work. . . .* There is to be *no division* between the ministry and the medical work. The physician should labor equally with the minister, and with as much earnestness and thoroughness [as the minister] for the salvation of the soul as well as for the restoration of the body" (MM 237; italics supplied).

See also: Battle Creek Sanitarium; Diet; General Conference Sessions of 1901, 1903; International Medical Missionary and Benevolent Association; Natural Remedies; Vegetarianism.

Further reading: T. C. Campbell, *The China Study: The Most Comprehensive Study of Nutrition Ever Conducted* (Dallas: BenBella, 2006); H. E. Douglass, *Messenger of the Lord* (PPPA, 1998), pp. 278-342; C. B. Esselstyn, *Prevent and Reverse Heart Disease* (New York: Penguin, 2007); G. E. Fraser, *Diet, Life Expectancy, and Chronic Disease: Studies of Seventh-day Adventists and Other Vegetarians* (Oxford: Oxford University Press, 2003); D. S. McMahon, *Acquired or Inspired? Exploring the Origins of the Adventist Lifestyle* (Warburton, Australia: Signs, 2005); G. W. Reid, "Health and Healing," in R. Dederen, ed., *Handbook of Seventh-day Adventist Theology* (RHPA, 2000), pp. 751-783; SHM65.

Herbert E. Douglass

HEALTH REFORM INSTITUTE (1866-1878). First Adventist health institution, located in *Battle Creek, Michigan. On December 25, 1865, Ellen White was given a vision in Rochester, New York, on health reform (1T 485). In this vision she was shown that the church needed to establish its own health-care institution (*ibid.* 489). She presented what she had seen at the General Conference session in May 1866. Church leaders received her instructions and called for the establishment of such an institution (*ibid.* 485-495; RH, May 22, 1866, pp. 196, 197). By July 10 a site of nearly six acres (2.4 hectares) had been purchased as well as the large and relatively new home of Judge B. F. Graves, which was remodeled for the institute (RH, July 10, 1866). An additional building was soon erected and the necessary plumbing and furniture installed to provide for a reservoir, bath, dressing and pack rooms (HR, August 1866, p. 16; RH, Sept. 11, 1866). On September 5, 1866, the Western Health Reform Institute opened under the charge of Dr. *H. S. Lay, and its name was very soon shortened to Health Reform Institute. The goal of the institute was to treat diseases using *natural remedies and to educate patients about *health reform. The institute was large enough to hold 40 to 50 patients, and met with initial success. Board and treatment were available for $8 to $14 a week, and a personal examination cost $5 (RH, Aug. 7, 1866). J. N. Loughborough, the first president of the institute, led in its development and organization. Dr. *Phoebe Lamson joined the medical staff in January 1867. The facilities soon became overcrowded. Lay made plans for a $25,000 expansion (RH, Jan. 8, 1867), but with financial pledges

lagging, he asked Ellen White to write out more fully what she had seen in her vision in order to strengthen financial support (2Bio 192-194). Soon afterward Ellen White was shown in vision that they should not yet enlarge the building (Lt 135, 1903). Later that year the Michigan legislature passed a bill for the incorporation of health institutions and incorporated the Health Reform Institute on April 9, 1867 (RH, May 28, 1867). Ellen White wrote extensive counsels for the leaders at the institute (cf. 1T 564-568, 633-643) and visited there herself as a patient (cf. Ms 6, 1873). In the early 1870s, as the institution faced a financial crisis, James White took over its management long enough to recover its financial stability (2Bio 314). In 1872 Ellen White wrote a pamphlet, *The Health Reform and the Health Institute* (Battle Creek Steam Press, 1872, in 3T 161-185), putting her earlier counsels into perspective because some had been misused. In August 1876 *J. H. Kellogg was placed in charge of the institute, and the directors invited James White and *O. B. Jones to return to Battle Creek to build a new building that in 1877 became the Battle Creek Medical and Surgical Sanitarium, commonly shortened to simply *Battle Creek Sanitarium (3Bio 19).

Further reading: SHM65 143-190.

Michael W. Campbell and Jean Davis

HEALTH REFORMER, THE. First Adventist journal devoted to health education. In 1879 its name was changed to *Good Health*. Ellen White published about 75 articles in this journal from its inception in August 1866 to 1887 and addressed a variety of practical subjects, such as dress reform and the evils of fashion, alcohol consumption and temperance, the influence of the mother in the home, the home environment, and hygiene. In 1871 and 1872 she addressed some then-current issues in ways inconsistent with twenty-first-century sciences. Several of these statements occur in a series of six articles titled "Words to Christian Mothers," in which she decried the evils of fashion and the unhealthy consequences of some behaviors. In these articles she often quoted from other journals and drew lessons from them to illustrate and support her thoughts. In their historical setting these statements were solid, practical advice, though using some nineteenth-century concepts not representative of science today.

See also: general article: Current Science and Ellen White: Twelve Controversial Statements.

HEALTH RETREAT, see **SANITARIUMS**.

HEALTHFUL LIVING (Battle Creek, Michigan, Medical Missionary Board, 1897, 284 pp.). Compilation from Ellen White's books and periodical articles prepared by Dr. David Paulson on the principles of health. Citations are numbered consecutively and arranged topically; the third edition (1898, 336 pp.) added a scriptural index. In order to present Ellen White's teachings on health reform and related matters in a concise and condensed form, the publishers made, in some instances, "slight verbal changes in connecting words or phrases" (p. 3). For this reason the White Estate does not consider this book a primary source. The entire publication was superseded by *The Ministry of Healing* in 1905.

HEAVEN AND NEW EARTH. Though Ellen White spoke often of heaven and the new earth, she recognized the limitations of human comprehension and language as she tried to represent eternal realities (EW 289). "No finite mind can comprehend the glory of the Paradise of God" (GC 675). On the one hand, she warned speculators against trying "to measure the conditions of the future life by the conditions of this life" (GW 314), such as expecting marriages and births in the new earth (1SM 172, 173).

On the other hand, Ellen White also warned that the "fear of making the future inheritance seem too material has led many to spiritualize away the very truths which lead us to look upon it as our home" (GC 674, 675), and she urged her readers to contemplate the future life as an extension of the best they enjoy on earth. For example, "that world of beauty" now only glimpsed through the telescope and microscope will then be clearly seen, apparently with the unaided eye, after the "blight of sin" (Ed 303) is removed. "With undimmed vision" the redeemed will "gaze upon the glory of creation" (GC 677) and all the "treasures of the universe" (Ed 307).

Among the awesome experiences the redeemed will share is tireless travel "from world to world" (7BC 990), sharing the "song of their experience" (Ed 308; cf. GC 677). There will be no boredom in the future life, for the redeemed will enjoy "occupations and pleasures that brought happiness to Adam and Eve" (PK 730). Full with questions, the redeemed will converse with their guardian angel, who "from [their] earliest moment . . . watched [their] steps . . . who was with [them] in the valley of the shadow of death, who marked [their] resting place, who was the first to greet [them] in the resurrection" (Ed 305).

Everyone will be fully recognized, though once "deformed, diseased, or disfigured in this mortal life." All will "rise in perfect health and symmetry; yet in the glorified body their identity will be perfectly preserved" (DA 804). The re-created bodies will bear "the same individuality of features, so that friend will recognize friend" (LDE 291). "Every saint connected in family relationship here will know each other there" (3SM 316).

Above all other blessings will be the privilege of holding "open communion with the Father and the Son" "without a dimming veil between" (GC 676, 677). Between Christ and the redeemed "there will be a close and tender relationship" (DA 606). In this "open communion" God will unfold "the course of the great conflict" from "the inception of sin." He will trace how "truth that, swerving not from its own straight lines, has met and conquered error" (Ed 304). The redeemed will be given "a distinct, intelligent knowledge of what their salvation has cost" (GC 651). "Our Redeemer will ever bear the marks of His crucifixion. Upon His wounded head, upon His side, His hands and feet, are the only traces of the cruel work that sin has wrought" (*ibid.* 674).

God will also make plain "the perplexities of life's experiences" (Ed 305). Jesus will explain the "dark providences through which on this earth He brought us in order to perfect our characters" (8T 254). God will remove any doubt that may exist as to why certain people are not in heaven (GC 666-671). The *characters of the redeemed will not be suddenly changed at the resurrection. For Ellen White, there is no mystery as to whom eternal life is entrusted: "If you would be a saint in heaven, you must first be a saint on earth. The traits of character you cherish in life will not be changed by death or by the resurrection. You will come up from the grave with the same disposition you manifested in your home and in society. Jesus does not change the character at His coming. The work of transformation must be done now. Our daily lives are determining our destiny. Defects of character must be repented of and overcome through the grace of Christ, and a symmetrical character must be formed while in this probationary

state, that we may be fitted for the mansions above" (13MR 82; cf. 2T 355; TM 430).

However far the redeemed "advance in the knowledge of God's wisdom and His power," there will always be "an infinity beyond" (LDE 305). "Every power will be developed, every capability increased. The grandest enterprises will be carried forward, the loftiest aspirations will be reached, the highest ambitions realized. And still there will arise new heights to surmount, new wonders to admire, new truths to comprehend, fresh objects to call forth the powers of body and mind and soul" (Ed 307).

More than self-development beyond human imagination, more than the endless surprises that God will continue to lay out in front of the most ambitious minds, will be the "richer and still more glorious revelations of God and of Christ." In fact, the more humans learn of God, "the greater will be [their] admiration of His character" (GC 678) and "the more intense will be [their] happiness" (DA 331).

Throughout eternity the redeemed of earth will live on a planet without decay, confusion, pain, or death. No created intelligence throughout the universe will ever wonder again as to the fairness and unselfish love of God—for the first time since the rebellion of Lucifer the entire universe is eternally secure (*ibid.* 759). "One pulse of harmony and gladness beats through the vast creation" (GC 678).

Herbert E. Douglass

HELL, see **WICKED, FATE OF THE.**

HERBAL REMEDIES. Ellen White recommended the use of herbs in cases of illness. "The Lord has given some simple herbs of the field that at times are beneficial. . . . These old-fashioned, simple herbs, used intelligently, would have recovered many sick who have died under drug medication" (2SM 294). "This is God's method. The herbs that grow for the benefit of man, and the little handful of herbs kept and steeped for sudden ailments, have served tenfold, yes, one hundred-fold better purpose, than all the *drugs hidden under mysterious names and dealt out to the sick" (Lt 69, 1898, in PC 31). "There are herbs that are harmless, the use of which will tide over many apparently serious difficulties" (2SM 291). "There are simple herbs that can be used for the recovery of the sick, whose effect on the system is very different from that of those drugs that poison the blood and endanger life" (*ibid.* 288).

Herbs or plants are made up of hundreds if not thousands of chemicals. In certain plants, among their many chemicals, occurs one (or more) that have therapeutic properties. These substances that distinguish a plant as medicinal may be either harmless or harmful to the human body. The class of harmful plants includes: strychnine (from nux vomica), colchicine (from colchicum seeds), belladonna or atropine (from root of deadly nightshade), aconite (from root of monkshood) and quinine (from cinchona bark). Such compounds, when isolated from the other chemicals present in the plant or herb, are considered drugs.

"Harmless" herbs used as medicine refer to food plants. At the time of Ellen White's writing vitamins and minerals needed by the human body had not as yet been identified. Pioneering research had shown that whole-grain rice and wheat cured beriberi and pellagra, and that lemon juice cured scurvy. Today we know that some 50 or more vitamins and minerals are needed by our bodies, and are readily obtained from grains, fruits, vegetables, and nuts (and from foods of animal origin). These, when used in appropriate amounts, preserve health and cure deficiency diseases when present. When obtained (preferably from foods) in appropriate quantities, they are

harmless. Another class of medicinal compounds recently discovered in foods is phytochemicals. Knowledge regarding their role is still fragmentary, but it is understood that their absence in the diet may result in such diseases as arteriosclerosis, coronary heart disease, and a variety of malignancies. Ellen White suggested the use of herbs to supplement one's diet and recommended "the leaves of the yellow dock, the young dandelion, and mustard" (CD 324) and thistle greens cooked "with sterilized cream and lemon juice" (*ibid.*).

The question arises as to which plants or herbs and roots Ellen White had in mind in her statements recommending the use of herbs as medicine. She herself used catnip, hop, eucalyptus, red clover, and ginger. She indicates there were many others: "There are many more simple remedies which will do much to restore healthful action of the body" (2SM 297). Ellen White recommended herbal remedies in common use among the medical profession and objected to the custom of concealing their identity by writing prescriptions in Latin (19MR 48, 49; PC 31; 2SM 290, 294). "The common words by which we know simple remedies are as useful as are the technical terms used by physicians for these same remedies. To request a nurse to prepare some catnip tea answers the purpose fully as well as would directions given to her [by a physician] in language understood only after long study" (Ms 169, 1902, in 19MR 48).

How does one distinguish the good herbs from the bad? How does one determine whether an herb preparation is harmless, less harmful, or harmful? This question was asked her by a junior medical student, Edgar Caro, who requested her to give him a list of what he should or should not use. She replied, "I do not think I can give you any definite line of medicines compounded and dealt out by doctors, that are perfectly harmless." And then she adds: "And yet it would not be wisdom to engage in controversy over this subject" (2SM 279).

The majority of medications prescribed during the latter part of the nineteenth and early years of the twentieth century were herbal preparations or derivatives from them. Of these she considered and used many as *simple remedies.

See also: Drugs, Natural Remedies, Simple Remedies.

Further reading: M. G. Hardinge, *A Physician Explains Ellen White's Counsel on Drugs, Herbs, and Natural Remedies* (RHPA, 2001).

Mervyn G. Hardinge

HERMENEUTICS, see **BIBLE, INTERPRETATION OF**; **INTERPRETATION OF ELLEN G. WHITE'S WRITINGS.**

HIGHWAYS TO HEAVEN (RHPA, 1952, 384 pp.). A reprint of Ellen White's book *Christ's Object Lessons* on the parables of Jesus. Although the text of this book is the same as the original edition published in 1900, the titles of chapters and pagination were changed and color pictures added to facilitate the sale of the book by literature evangelists.

HILLCREST SCHOOL. An Adventist school established in 1908 near Nashville, Tennessee, to educate African-American church workers to take the gospel to those of their own race. Ellen White had been deeply moved in the early 1890s for work among the Blacks of the South. She was supportive of her son *Edson's work with the *Morning Star*, but she also believed that something needed to be done in the Nashville area. In 1903 she wrote that "a school for colored people should be established outside the city of Nashville, on land that can be utilized for industrial purposes" (*Hillcrest School Farm*, p. 7).

In November 1907 a property of 93 acres (38 hectares) was purchased about six miles (10 kilometers) northwest of Nashville. The leaders were brethren Staines and Bralliar (PH037 33). The school was to be a practical school patterned after the *Madison school (also near Nashville) founded by *E. A. Sutherland and *P. T. Magan in 1904. Both schools were to teach manual labor and other practical skills to prepare self-supporting and other workers for the church. The institutions were separated, since they existed in a racially segregated South, yet Ellen White had called for the Black teachers and White teachers to "counsel together" so that "both" groups would "be strengthened" by learning from each other (Lt 215, 1904, in 14MR 43).

The school was chartered by the state of Tennessee in January 1908. As in other self-supporting units, the reconstruction of old buildings and the erection of new ones was done by the students and teachers. They also combined their efforts in running the school farm. Ellen White visited the farm in 1909.

Further reading: Hillcrest School Farm (PH037); R. C. Jones, "'Until the Lord Shows Us a Better Way': Ellen G. White and the Issue of Regional Conferences," in *Ellen G. White and Current Issues Symposium* 2 (CAR, 2006), 75-94; A. W. Spalding, "Lights and Shades in the Black Belt" (unpublished manuscript, c. 1910), pp. 304-333.

George R. Knight

HINSDALE SANITARIUM. Adventist medical facility, now known as Hinsdale Hospital, 17 miles (27 kilometers) west of the business center of Chicago, Illinois. It was founded in 1904 by Drs. *David and Mary Paulson, who left the *Battle Creek Sanitarium to pioneer Adventist *medical missionary work. Ellen White visited the Hinsdale Sanitarium on at least two different occasions. On the first visit

(May 26, 1904) she had a six-hour layover in which David Paulson gave her a tour of the facilities that had recently been secured for developing a *sanitarium. She admired the location where "sick people would find health in driving through the fine streets and looking at the lovely scenery" (Lt 181, 1904; cf. RH, Aug. 11, 1904), and later wrote that "this place answered to the representations that had been given me of places that would be obtained by our people for sanitarium work outside of the large cities" (Ms 33, 1906, in PC 51). The first patient arrived June 6, 1905, and the sanitarium was formally dedicated September 20, 1905. On a second visit to the Hinsdale Sanitarium in August 1909 Ellen White spoke several times to patients and workers, observing that "every opportunity seems favorable for the work being carried on here in a way that God would have it" (Mss 129, 132, 133, 1909).

Further reading: *Century: Hinsdale Hospital 1904-2004* (Hinsdale, Ill.: Hinsdale Hospital, 2004); H. G. Dugan, *Hinsdale Sanitarium and Hospital: 1904-1957* (Hinsdale, Ill.: s.n., 1957); D. Paulson, *Footprints of Faith* (Hinsdale, Ill.: Life Boat, 1921); *SDA Encyclopedia* (1996), vol. 10, pp. 695-697.

HISTORIANS, ELLEN G. WHITE'S USE OF. The extensive writings of Ellen White on matters as diverse as health to Reformation history have from time to time raised issues concerning her use of historical sources.

The accusation of *plagiarism by D. M. Canright in 1887 has been followed with similar charges more recently by Walter Rea, Donald McAdams, Ronald Numbers, and others questioning the honesty and integrity of Ellen White. Several important questions are involved. From an ethical perspective, did Ellen White intend to deceive readers regarding her use of historical sources? From a legal perspective, did Ellen White infringe

on copyright laws of her time? The ethical question has been answered in the negative. Ellen White openly informed readers that she used historical sources in the 1888 (GC88 g, h) and 1911 (GC xi, xii) prefaces of *The Great Controversy*. It has also been pointed out that the books from which Ellen White quoted or paraphrased were widely available in the libraries of other Adventists who would be referring to her work. In several cases she even endorsed and recommended these books to general readers before the publication of her books (ST, Feb. 22, 1883; RH, Dec. 26, 1882). Her monthly columns in the *Health Reformer* also regularly gave credit to other authors and recommended that readers secure referenced books (cf. HR, July 1873).

The legal charge of plagiarism has been evaluated by F. D. Nichol and others who have maintained that while plagiarism was a known issue during the late 1800s, the legal aspects of plagiarism have constituted a "changing viewpoint of different generations as to how extensively a writer may properly copy from others without acknowledgment" (Nichol, p. 410). The 1981 legal opinion of Attorney Vincent L. Ramik, of Diller, Ramik, and Wight, Washington, D.C., is significant. After an extensive study of 1,000 copyright cases in American law, Ellen White's works, and her critics, Ramik concludes: "Ellen White was not a plagiarist, and her works did not constitute copyright infringement/piracy" ("Memorandum of Law," p. 17). In fact, Ellen White's writings "stayed well within the legal boundaries of 'fair use'" (*ibid.* p. 14). Ellen White used the writings of others; but in the *way* she used them, she made them uniquely her own.

Two questions have also been raised concerning Ellen White's historical statements in view of recent historical research. Was the way Ellen White cited sources accurate? Does her description of historical events stand against modern historical scrutiny? On the one hand, she did not claim infallibility regarding details of history; her purpose was not to certify historical details but to present the great themes of salvation history. On the other hand, though some historians differ with her on some details, she is generally well within the range of scholarly consensus. For example, McAdams and others asserted that there were several apparent errors in historical detail regarding John Huss in *The Great Controversy*, including Ellen White's statements that (1) the pope put Prague under interdict (GC 100); (2) the interdict caused a "tumult" in Prague (*ibid.* 101); (3) Huss was the leader of the reform movement from the Bethlehem Chapel (modern historians make Stanislaw of Znojmo the actual leader) (*ibid.* 102, 103); and (4) the location of two contrasting pictures drawn by two artists from England (*ibid.* 99, 100). These and other assertions were reevaluated in two extensive papers prepared by Gerhard Hasel. Hasel showed that Ellen White's reference to the pope as the issuer of the interdict was not a contradiction, for "'only the Apostolic See may impose interdicts affecting larger areas or groups' (R. C. Clouse, 'Interdict,' *New International Dictionary of the Christian Church*, ed. J. D. Douglas [Grand Rapids: Zondervan, 1974], p. 513)." Prague was the intellectual center of central Europe, and the archbishop probably did not act on his own. Spinka states that in 1409 Pope Alexander V issued a bull to "uproot Wyclifism from the country and punish all who should be professing 'these damnable heresies'" (*John Hus' Concept*, p. 93). Could this bull also have authorized an interdict? Spinka implies such a connection (*Advocates of Reform*, p. 192). Regarding the effect of the interdict, Spinka states: "priests and prelates who defied his order" and were "deprived of

their positions. . . . This obviously hopeless struggle continued to be waged by the archbishop for two weeks" (*John Hus: A Biography*, p. 125). The "struggle" between the secular government and the church is confirmed by other modern historians including Walker (p. 272) and Friedenthal (p. 181). Again Spinka clearly states that when Huss was appointed "to the famous center of the Czech reform movement, the Bethlehem Chapel . . . he became the leader of the Czech populace supporting the reform" (*John Hus' Concept*, p. 42). In these cases a modern authority such as Spinka, whom McAdams consistently cites, actually *confirms* the historical accuracy of Ellen White. As to the location of the paintings, Wylie is said to have located the pictures in the corridor of the house in which the artists resided, while Spinka puts them in the Bethlehem Chapel. Ellen White does not identify the place where the pictures were located; she simply says, "In a place open to the public they drew two pictures" (GC 99). Not only are Ellen White's historical conclusions in this case confirmed by modern scholarship, but where there may have been difficulties she is cautiously less specific than contemporary historians.

The extent of her use of historical sources has brought up the issue of how they relate to her claims to inspiration. It has been pointed out that various biblical writers used and referred to historical sources as they were guided under inspiration to write God's messages to His people (Num. 21:14; Joshua 10:13; 2 Sam. 1:18; Luke 1:1-4). Ellen White states the process of her writing this way: "Although I am as dependent upon the Spirit of the Lord in writing my views as I am in receiving them, yet the words I employ in describing what I have seen are my own, unless they be those spoken to me by an angel, which I always enclose in marks of quotation" (RH, Oct. 8,

1867). In its original context this statement was a denial, not of her use of historical sources, but of a dictational view of inspiration. The words she used to describe what she saw in vision were words of her own choosing, but not necessarily of her own origination.

In the introduction to *The Great Controversy*, she acknowledged that some of her writings relied on historical works. "The great events which have marked the progress of reform in past ages are matters of history, well known and universally acknowledged by the Protestant world; they are facts which none can gainsay. This history I have presented briefly, in accordance with the scope of the book, and the brevity which must necessarily be observed, the facts having been condensed into as little space as seemed consistent with a proper understanding of their application. In some cases where a historian has so grouped together events as to afford, in brief, a comprehensive view of the subject, or has summarized details in a convenient manner, his words have been quoted; but in some instances no specific credit has been given, since the quotations are not given for the purpose of citing that writer as authority, but because his statement affords a ready and forcible presentation of the subject" (GC xi, xii). Historical sources referenced by Ellen White were used to "amplify or state more forcibly her own transcending themes; she was the master, not the slave, of her sources" (Douglass, p. 461) with the entire process "dependent upon the Spirit."

In 1912, in a letter to W. W. Eastman, at the time secretary of the Publishing Department of the Southwestern Union Conference, W. C. White made the following statement regarding his mother's use of historians: "Regarding Mother's writings, I have overwhelming evidence and conviction that they are the description and delineation of what God has revealed to her in vision, and where

she has followed the description of historians or the exposition of Adventist writers, I believe that God has given her discernment to use that which is correct and in harmony with truth regarding all matters essential to salvation. If it should be found by faithful study that she has followed some expositions of prophecy which in some detail regarding dates we cannot harmonize with our understanding of secular history, it does not influence my confidence in her writings as a whole any more than my confidence in the Bible is influenced by the fact that I cannot harmonize many of the statements regarding chronology" (3SM 449, 450).

See also: Plagiarism; *The Desire of Ages* Sources, Study of; Revelation and Inspiration.

Further reading: H. E. Douglass, *Messenger of the Lord* (PPPA, 1998), pp. 456-465; R. Friedenthal, *Ketzer und Rebell. Jan Hus und das Jahrhundert der Revolutionskriege*, 2nd ed. (Munich: Piper, 1972); R. Graybill, "Historical Difficulties in *The Great Controversy*," rev. ed., June 1982 DF; G. F. Hasel, "Hus' Letter About His Withdrawal From Prague and E. G. White's *Great Controversy*," rev., Jan. 31, 1978 (EGWE-GC); *idem*, "A Review of the White Estate Paper 'The Role of Visions and the Use of Historical Sources in the Writings of the *Great Controversy*,'" rev. ed., Oct. 24, 1977, EGWE-GC; D. R. McAdams, "Ellen G. White and the Protestant Historians: The Evidence From an Unpublished Manuscript of John Huss," rev. ed., October 1977; *idem*, "Shifting Views of Inspiration: Ellen G. White Studies in the 1970s," *Spectrum* 10, no. 4 (1980): 27-41; F. D. Nichol, *Ellen G. White and Her Critics* (RHPA, 1951), pp. 403-467; R. L. Numbers, *Prophetess of Health: Ellen G. White and the Origins of Seventh-day Adventists*, rev. ed. (Knoxville: University of Tennessee Press, 1992); R. W. Olson, "Ellen White's Use of Historical Sources in *The Great Controversy*,"

AR, Feb. 23, 1984; *idem*, "Ellen White's Denials," *Ministry*, February 1991; V. L. Ramik, "Memorandum of Law: Literary Property Rights 1790-1915," Aug. 14, 1981; *idem*, "There Simply Is No Case," AR, Sept. 17, 1981; W. T. Rea, *The White Lie* (Turlock, Calif.: M. and R. Pub., 1982); M. Spinka, *John Hus' Concept of the Church* (Princeton, N.J.: Princeton University Press, 1966); *idem*, *John Hus: A Biography* (Princeton, N.J.: Princeton University Press, 1968); *idem*, *Advocates of Reform* (Philadelphia: Westminster Press, 1953); W. Walker, *A History of the Christian Church*, rev. ed. (Edinburgh: Clark, 1963); *A Critique of* Prophetess of Health (EGWE, 1976, SDoc).

Michael G. Hasel

HISTORICAL SKETCHES OF THE FOREIGN MISSIONS OF THE SEVENTH-DAY ADVENTISTS (Basel, Switzerland: Imprimerie Polyglotte, 1886, 294 pp.). The volume contains descriptions and histories of different Adventist mission fields in *Europe and *Australia, as well as Ellen White's travel notes to various countries. B. L. Whitney introduces the Central European Mission and describes how the Adventist Sabbath message was first conveyed to people in *Switzerland, *Germany, *France, *Italy, and Romania through the work of *M. B. Czechowski and later by *J. N. Andrews. *J. G. Matteson, a former Baptist minister, describes the Scandinavian mission field and the establishment of a publishing house. *M. C. Wilcox introduces the British Mission, documenting the history of early Sabbathkeeping in sixteenth-century *England. The Australian Mission, as well as the work among the Maori, is presented by *S. N. Haskell. Haskell also reports on the European Missionary Councils of 1883, 1884, and 1885, and deals with issues encountered among new European Adventist congregations. Ellen White's notes of travel

in Europe include details of places visited, customs of people, and religious beliefs and practices. She makes frequent remarks about Europeans' attitude toward religious reform, and references to the religious history of this continent, especially the Reformation. *L. R. Conradi's account of his missionary visit to Russia closes the volume. The book is highly valuable as a historical record and for tracing the development of the understanding of mission among Seventh-day Adventists. Several maps and illustrations are included. Unfortunately, very few original copies exist, but the book has been reprinted by Leaves of Autumn Books (Payson, Ariz.: 1979, 1985) and by Andrews University Press (2005), with an introduction by George R. Knight.

Cristian Dumitrescu

HISTORY, PHILOSOPHY OF. Although she never wrote a formal statement of her philosophy of history, Ellen White nonetheless gave considerable attention to the meaning and processes of the human experience. The 1888 and 1911 editions of *The Great Controversy* contain her most extended statements on history, but *Patriarchs and Prophets*, *Prophets and Kings*, and *Education* also include important comments.

Ellen White understood that history is both meaningful and linear, shaped by what she called the "*great controversy between Christ and Satan." She explained history as a trial in which God has put Himself in the dock, charged by Satan that He is unfit to rule the universe. Fallen human beings, unfallen angels, and inhabitants of the unfallen worlds comprise the jury, which observes the unfolding conflict and ultimately judges the case as it sees the consequences of Satan's principles and rejection of divine authority work themselves out within the historical process. In this philosophy of history, therefore, both good and evil play major roles.

Because Satan has challenged His goodness and authority, God has initiated a plan that has a beginning (Creation), a central event (the incarnation, death, and resurrection of Jesus), and a climax (the Second Coming) as He seeks to save the human race from sin. This plan becomes effective because God is sovereign over all of history. Although the affairs of nations may seem to be under human control, White believed, God ultimately rules the course of events. The Bible reveals the working of God, she wrote, "through all the play and counterplay of human interests and power and passions" (Ed 173).

God's sovereignty, however, in White's view did not necessarily translate into His constant intervention in human affairs. He communicates with those who seek Him (MH 509; 4T 542), but in her understanding, God allows humans to exercise free choice in deciding whom to follow. History then reveals the natural consequences of these choices. The supreme example of the true nature of sin is the death of the sinless Jesus on the cross, an event that revealed to the entire universe the ultimate impact of evil. By allowing the sacrifice of His Son on behalf of humanity, God left no doubt regarding the moral superiority of His law; by the resurrection of Jesus God defeated His challenger. Subsequent history would reveal the meaning of that defeat.

Although Ellen White did not explicitly use the concept of "natural law," she believed that God's principles were built into the structures of human existence. If human beings follow God's law in their personal lives and social institutions, she believed, they will experience happiness and security. On the other hand, human failure to follow His principles will result in unhappiness and tragedy, not because God takes punitive action

but because of the outworking of natural effects.

According to White, human beings can find these principles in the Bible, which through both its historical accounts and prescriptive teachings reveals the source of true greatness and prosperity. In discussing the experience of Israel, she identified loyalty to God and His law (the Ten Commandments), stable families, moral education, respect for life, personal integrity, an effective justice system, and periodic redistribution of wealth as essential to national greatness. Nations prosper or decline to the degree that their members, both individually and collectively, follow these principles, as illustrated by Israel's experience.

Applying this philosophy to historical events, White emphasized great reformatory movements, particularly the Protestant Reformation and the establishment of the United States, a story she told in *The Great Controversy.* Although she extolled reform, she rejected the idea of human progress, recognizing that good and evil are ambiguously mixed in the historical process and that everyone is subject to God's judgment. When the course of history has vindicated divine authority by demonstrating the destructive nature of Satan's principles, White believed, God will bring the end by sending His Son to earth again, this time to receive the faithful of all ages and take them to heaven. After the millennium, the saints will return to a re-created earth, where Christ will reign and sin will arise no more.

Further reading: Ed 173-184; R. Graybill, "Ellen G. White's Understanding and Use of History" (EGWE, 1979, SDoc); Gary Land, *Teaching History: A Seventh-day Adventist Approach* (AUP, 2001); C. Ward, "Historical Interpretation in the Writings of Ellen White," *Journal of Adventist Education* 41 (April-May

1979): 5-7, 40, 41; J. Battistone, *The Great Controversy Theme in E. G. White Writings* (AUP, 1974).

Gary Land

HOLIDAYS. Besides comments on biblical holy days and feasts, Ellen White also addressed the issue of religious and civic holidays observed during her day. In repeated references to Christmas, Thanksgiving, New Year's, and birthdays, but only one to Easter (GC88 387), she did not promote an observance of these holidays, but instead, acknowledged their observance by the Christian world. She encouraged the best possible attitude toward them, suggesting that Christians align their observance of such holidays to Christian principles of life. Ellen White perceived them as opportunities for glorifying God, supporting mission work, and helping the needy. Within this context, she states that Adventists should not ignore Christmas and Thanksgiving, but celebrate them with a true Christian spirit (AH 482). It is also important to note that besides her emphasis on Christian service, she was not against the innocent joys related to the holiday season. She counsels: "When you have a holiday, make it a pleasant and happy day for your children, and make it also a pleasant day for the poor and the afflicted. Do not let the day pass without bringing thanksgiving and thank offerings to Jesus" (*ibid.* 476).

Ellen White recognized that the date of Christ's birth is unknown and, according to her, was providentially concealed in order to give glory to Christ and not to the day on which He was born (*ibid.* 477). However, since December 25 is commonly observed as the birth of Christ, she recommended that the day "should not be passed by unnoticed" (*ibid.* 472), but that every church should take the opportunity to organize "attractive and interesting" gatherings (RH, Dec. 15, 1885). These meetings commemorate the birth of Christ the Redeemer, contemplate the work of redemption, and provide opportunity for celebration and material support of missionary work. She also emphasizes that attention should be given to children at Christmas. Parents are encouraged to provide an interesting, happy atmosphere filled with pleasant activities so that children won't be exposed to destructive amusements. The children's interest in giving presents can be constructively channeled, and was something that she herself practiced with her own family (AH 478, 479).

Ellen White wrote that Thanksgiving is a holiday to give thanks to the Lord for His bounties. "Let not any more Thanksgiving days be observed to please and gratify the appetite and glorify self" (*ibid.* 475). In 1884 she challenged the members of the Battle Creek church to eat a simple Thanksgiving dinner and give the money saved on extras as an offering to God (*ibid.*).

Regarding birthdays, she noted that these should be opportunities to teach children that their lives, as well as every blessing, come from God. Upon each birthday, parents should take the opportunity to teach their children to reflect upon the past year in terms of their responsibility before God in everything they do. Birthdays should commemorate God's goodness, and God should be the recipient of praise (*ibid.* 473, 474).

With regard to giving gifts, Ellen White said that there is "no harm" in giving or receiving useful presents (RH, Jan. 4, 1881). She herself both received and gave presents. "It is right to bestow upon one another tokens of love and remembrance if we do not in this forget God, our best friend" (AH 479). Ellen White was concerned that gifts could be misused, too. She appealed for moderation in buying gifts, which should not be too costly, extravagant, or of a frivolous nature. The best gifts are useful ones. She reminded people to remember those who are needy (RH, Jan. 4, 1881).

She also cautioned lest worldly ways of celebrating even religious holidays "divert the mind from Christ." In a New Year's Day essay, she reported her personal resolution "to make Christ first and last and best in everything. . . . My heart has ached as I have seen men honored, while Jesus was neglected and almost forgotten" (ST, Jan. 4, 1883). Wrong motives and practices such as self-indulgence, pride, fashion, gluttony, prodigal expenditure, pleasure seeking, and frivolity she describes as "patterning after the world" (AH 472).

In her later years Ellen White noted her own preference regarding receiving gifts: "I have said to my family and my friends, I desire that no one shall make me a birthday or Christmas gift, unless it be with permission to pass it on into the Lord's treasury, to be appropriated in the establishment of missions" (*ibid.* 474).

Further reading: "Ellen G. White Statements Regarding Holiday Gifts and the Observance of Christmas" (EGWE, SDoc).

Arkadiusz Bojko

HOLINESS, see **SANCTIFICATION**.

HOLY FLESH MOVEMENT. The holy flesh movement was a radical Holiness-oriented revival that arose among Seventh-day Adventists in Indiana in 1899 and 1900. This movement had its roots in a Holiness thrust that began sweeping through North American Adventism in 1892. The first wave of this revival, led by A. T. Jones and W. W. Prescott, took place between 1892 and 1894, particularly in the area around Battle Creek, Michigan. Jones and Prescott preached that the Holy Spirit was about to descend in a "latter rain" that would produce the "loud cry" of the third angel of Revelation 14:9. They also promoted physical healing as a manifestation of the Holy Spirit's work. Controversy over the writings of Anna Rice, whom these men briefly promoted as an inspired prophet, largely brought this revival to an end in 1894.

But others continued to preach on Holiness themes, having a major impact on A. F. Ballenger, a young minister, at the 1897 Pennsylvania camp meeting. Shortly thereafter the General Conference sent Ballenger to Battle Creek, where he, along with Jones and others, in the fall of 1897 stirred a second revival by calling for the people to "receive ye the Holy Ghost." For the next two years Ballenger, under General Conference direction, traveled throughout the United States preaching that after receiving forgiveness of past sins the Christian must move to a second stage, a baptism of the Holy Spirit. Ballenger believed baptism of the Holy Spirit would bring not only victory over all sin but also "power for witnessing" and "salvation from sickness." Consequently, healing became a significant element of his preaching, as it had been in the 1892-1894 revival. As with other themes in Ballenger's preaching, this emphasis on healing paralleled the teaching of such Holiness preachers outside Adventism as A. J. Gordon and A. B. Simpson.

Although sources for understanding the development of holy flesh teaching are limited, it is apparent that R. S. Donnell and S. S. Davis, respectively president and evangelist of the Indiana Conference, radically interpreted the Holiness themes preached by Ballenger and others during the previous few years. They taught that true conversion replaces corruptible earthly flesh with incorruptible "translation" flesh, an experience through which Christ had passed in the Garden of Gethsemane and that now must take place among those believers expecting to be alive at Christ's return. In contrast to these "born" sons, Christians who did not have this experience were "adopted"; they would die and then be resurrected at the Second Coming. This understanding appears to have interpreted apocalyptically the stronger perfectionist statements of Ballenger, Jones, and S.M.I. Henry—another leader in the revival—regarding victory over sin and the healing of the body through appropriation of Christ's atonement.

This holy flesh preaching produced highly emotional revival meetings. S. N. Haskell, who attended the Indiana camp meeting in 1900, told Ellen White in September that the music at the meetings was similar to that used by the Salvation Army and included such instruments as tambourines, a bass drum, horns, and fiddles. He compared the singing to the shrieks of the near insane, saying that one could not hear the words. White, who reported that she had seen the holy flesh movement in a January 1900 vision while still in Australia, returned to the United States to attend the 1901 General Conference session, partly for the purpose of combating the influence of these teachings. On April 17 she addressed an early-morning workers' meeting, which included both Donnell and Davis, stating strongly that humans cannot obtain holy flesh. Describing the movement as confused and noisy, she argued that acceptance of holy flesh teachings would lead to the belief that the truly converted could not sin, out of which would then grow the concept that everything done by them was holy. Thus, in White's view, the movement was not only wrong theologically but held the potential for moral anarchy. The following day Donnell confessed his error, and thereafter the holy flesh movement was largely dead.

Further reading: 5Bio 97-113; 2SM 31-39;

C. W. Edwards and G. Land, *Seeker After Light: A. F. Ballenger, Adventism, and American Christianity* (AUP, 2000); G. Land, "At the Edges of Holiness: Seventh-day Adventism Receives the Holy Ghost, 1892-1900," *Fides et Historia: Journal of the Conference on Faith and History* 33 (Summer/Fall 2001): 13-30.

Gary Land

HOLY SPIRIT. Ellen White's writings demonstrate a rich and deepening understanding of the deity, person, and work of the Holy Spirit. Taking her cue for the importance of the Holy Spirit in the plan of salvation from Christ, she noted that although "Christ, the Great Teacher, had an infinite variety of subjects from which to choose, but the one upon which He dwelt most largely was the endowment of the Holy Spirit" (1SM 156). She spoke often of His relationship with and dependence upon the Holy Spirit during His earthly ministry (e.g., 5T 161; ML 17; DA 671; COL 139).

Contrary to the popular opinions of her day, White did not advocate the view of the Holy Spirit as an impersonal influence or power. Rather, she believed that the Spirit was "as much a person as God is a person" (Ev 616); that He "has a personality, else He could not bear witness to our spirits and with our spirits that we are the children of God" (*ibid.* 617). As Christ's representative, he was "divested of the personality of humanity, and independent thereof. Cumbered with humanity, Christ could not be in every place personally. . . . By the Spirit the Savior would be accessible to all. In this sense He would be nearer to them than if He had not ascended on high" (DA 669).

While the work of the Holy Spirit is complex and multifaceted, the effects are clearly seen. Recalling Christ's description of the Holy Spirit to Nicodemus (John 3), White noted that the work of the Holy Spirit upon the heart "can no more be explained than can the movements of the wind. . . . Little by little, perhaps unconsciously to the receiver, impressions are made that tend to draw the soul to Christ. . . . Suddenly, as the Spirit comes with more direct appeal, the soul gladly surrenders itself to Jesus. By many this is called sudden conversion; but it is the result of long wooing by the Spirit of God" (*ibid.* 172).

Ellen White portrayed the Holy Spirit as an educator (CT 37, 38). As part of the work of education, He inspired and illumined the Scriptures. The writing of the Scriptures was not a merely human invention. "It is not the words of the Bible that are inspired, but the men that were inspired. Inspiration acts not on the man's words or his expressions but on the man himself, who, under the influence of the Holy Ghost, is imbued with thoughts" (7BC 945, 946). The words of Scripture could be understood in their full sense only by the illumination of the Spirit upon the reader. (*ibid.* 945).

The Holy Spirit "convicts of sin," and "expels it from the soul by the consent of the human agent" (ML 43). This re-creation of the human being into the image of God is "the work of a lifetime" (2T 448), for "the Christian's life is not a modification or improvement of the old, but a transformation of nature," a change that can be "brought about only by the effectual working of the Holy Spirit" (DA 172). The result of the Spirit's working in the life is the development of the fruits of the Spirit (PP 372). These *imperishable* fruits are the evidence of the unseen moving of the Spirit upon the individual life (COL 68).

But lest any fail to appreciate fully the work of the Spirit in the life, White warns that it is a serious matter to ignore the Spirit of God, for to do so is to place oneself where

God has no power to reach the soul (5BC 1092). "The sin of blasphemy against the Holy Spirit does not lie in any sudden word or deed; it is the firm, determined resistance of truth and evidence" (5BC 1093). But for those who sincerely ask for His guidance, God will never turn away their requests (MB 132).

The Holy Spirit also plays a role in the completion of earthly history. White compares the Spirit's action to that of the latter rain, which comes just before the harvest. This manifestation of the Spirit "represents the spiritual grace that prepares the church for the coming of the Son of man" (TM 506; LDE 183). White notes that "it was by the confession and forsaking of sin, by earnest prayer and consecration of themselves to God, that the early disciples prepared for the outpouring of the Holy Spirit on the Day of Pentecost. The same work, only in greater degree, must be done now" (TM 507).

Ellen White distinguished between erroneous and true eschatological manifestations of the Spirit. She warned that "in the last days [Satan] the enemy of present truth will bring in manifestations that are not in harmony with the workings of the Spirit" (2SM 41). However, the influence of the Spirit will not degrade God's people before the world, but will bring His people into "sweet harmony with His will" (5T 647). Thus, the manifestation of the Spirit is characterized by "calm, sensible labor . . . to convince souls of their condition" (2SM 35). "Mere noise and shouting are no evidence of sanctification, or of the descent of the Holy Spirit. . . . Wild demonstrations create only disgust in the minds of unbelievers" (*ibid.*).

Thus, the gift of the Holy Spirit given to the believers at Pentecost and Ephesus was manifested in the ability "to go forth to proclaim the gospel in Asia Minor" (AA 283). Just as the Spirit gave the early church the tools that they would need to carry out their mission—the ability to speak in other languages and to prophesy (*ibid.*)—so He is willing to give the church of today the tools it needs to accomplish its mission (ChS 98; Ev 701; RH, Mar. 19, 1895).

The final work of the Holy Spirit in the plan of redemption is the sealing of the people of God. This sealing completes the judgment. Then Christ's ongoing intercession for the salvation of sinners ceases, and humans will live without Christ's mediation for sins (Rev. 22:11, 12). But during this time, the Holy Spirit does not leave God's people. Refreshed by the latter rain, they are sheltered by the Holy Spirit as they await the imminent return of Christ (Mar 41).

Karen K. Abrahamson and John T. Baldwin

HOME AND FAMILY. "The restoration and uplifting of humanity begins in the home. The work of parents underlies every other. Society is composed of families, and is what the heads of families make it. . . . The heart of the community, of the church, and of the nation is the household. The well-being of society, the success of the church, the prosperity of the nation, depend upon home influences" (MH 349). This statement highlights the importance that Ellen White placed on home and family. She gave it the highest priority. She followed up this emphasis by writing: "There is no more important field of effort than that committed to the founders and guardians of the home. No work entrusted to human beings involves greater or more far-reaching results than does the work of fathers and mothers" (*ibid.* 351).

White wrote widely on these issues, and much of her counsel has been preserved in two posthumous compilations—*The Adventist Home* and *Child Guidance*. However, her most comprehensive statement, published during her lifetime (1905), was a 58-page section in *The Ministry of Healing* (pp. 349-406). Given space limitations, this article will concentrate on that source.

Preparation for marriage must be taken seriously. It is a blessing whenever it is "entered into intelligently, in the fear of God, and with due consideration for its responsibilities" (pp. 356, 357). Choosing a life companion should be considered so as to best "secure physical, mental, and spiritual well-being for parents and for their children" (pp. 357, 358). Early marriages are to be discouraged, because to make wise choices mental and physical powers must be well developed (p. 358).

Samson is an example of rushing into marriage against the counsel of parents and God (PP 563). "It is only in Christ that a marriage alliance can be safely formed. Human love should draw its closest bonds from divine love. Only where Christ reigns can there be deep, true, unselfish affection" (MH 358).

A Christ-centered home will have warm, supportive relationships. "Determine to be all that it is possible to be to each other. Continue the early attentions. In every way encourage each other in fighting the battles of life. Study to advance the happiness of each other. Let there be mutual love, mutual forbearance. Then marriage, instead of being the end of love, will be as it were the very beginning of love. The warmth of true friendship, the love that binds heart to heart, is a foretaste of the joys of heaven" (p. 360).

Husbands and wives should not merge their individuality, but each have a personal relation to God. "Neither the husband nor the wife should attempt to exercise over the other an arbitrary control. Do not try to compel each other to yield to your wishes. You cannot do this and retain each other's love. Be kind, patient, and forbearing, considerate, and courteous" (p. 361).

White recommends rearing children away from the cities with their sinful influences and among the peace and simplicity of natural surroundings (pp. 363-370). "Better than any other inheritance of wealth you can give to your children will be the gift of a healthy body, a sound mind, and a noble character" (p. 366).

Preparation for children should begin before their birth. The mother must practice temperance and self-control and not overwork her strength. She needs to cultivate a cheerful, contented, and happy disposition (pp. 371-374). "No other work can equal hers in importance. . . . It is hers, with the help of God, to develop in a human soul the likeness of the divine" (p. 378). Parents are "to stand in the place of God to their children" (p. 375).

"Too much importance cannot be placed upon the early training of children. The lessons learned, the habits formed, during the years of infancy and childhood have more to do with the formation of the character and the direction of the life than have all the instruction and training of after years" (p. 380). Parents should understand the principles of child-rearing, including the physical and mental needs. "To assume the responsibilities of parenthood without such preparation is a sin" (p. 380).

White also held that children have rights and preferences and that when these are reasonable, they should be respected (p. 384). Children should be taught to reason from cause to effect in order to learn how to make wise choices in life (p. 386). "Above all things else, let parents surround their children with an atmosphere of cheerfulness, courtesy, and love. A home where love dwells, and where it is expressed in looks, in words, and in acts, is a place where angels delight to manifest their presence" (pp. 386, 387).

The atmosphere of the home is crucial in the development of children. The mother's

presence should be its greatest attraction. "An approving glance, a word of encouragement or commendation, will be like sunshine in their hearts, often making the whole day happy" (p. 388). While the youth should not be led to think that they are the center, and that everything must revolve around them, they should not be neglected. Parents must not be too busy to spend time with their children, or they will look to other sources for sympathy and companionship (p. 389).

The father is also crucial in the training of his children. He should enforce and model energy, honesty, patience, courage, diligence, and practical usefulness. He should not discourage the little ones, but combine "affection with authority, kindness and sympathy with firm restraint" and give some of his leisure hours to them (pp. 390, 391).

Daily family worship is of utmost importance. "The father is the priest of the household. . . . But the wife and children should unite in prayer and join in the song of praise" (p. 392). Father and mother should daily gather their children around the family altar and plead for "the guardianship of holy angels," that the members may resist the temptations threatening them (p. 393).

Parents are told to "let your children see that you love them and will do all in your power to make them happy. If you do so, your necessary restrictions will have far greater weight in their young minds" (p. 394). "They should be taught that they are a part of the home firm" and that "they should respond . . . by bearing their share of the home burdens and bringing all the happiness possible into the family" (p. 394).

The home should be a place for missionary training. Children "are to obtain an education that will help them to stand by the side of Christ in unselfish service" (p. 395). "To surround them with such influences as shall lead them to choose a life of service, and to give them the training needed, is" the parents' "first duty" (p. 396). "The home is the child's first school, and it is here that the foundation should be laid for a life of service" (p. 400).

"Very early the lesson of helpfulness should be taught," and the child should be given "duties to perform in the home." Children should be encouraged to "put others' happiness before [their] own" (p. 401). They should be taught the laws of physical health and be given training and practical experience in various lines of missionary effort (p. 402).

There are many temptations and dangers facing the youth in the world around them. In light of this, "parents who love and fear God are to keep their children under 'the bond of the covenant'—within the protection of those sacred influences made possible through Christ's redeeming blood" (pp. 403, 404).

Perhaps Ellen White's emphasis on the importance of family life could be best summed up by this statement: "One well-ordered, well-disciplined family tells more in behalf of Christianity than all the sermons that can be preached. Such a family gives evidence that the parents have been successful in following God's directions, and that their children will serve Him in the church" (AH 32).

Roger Dudley

HOMES OF JAMES AND ELLEN G. WHITE.

James and Ellen White considered themselves pilgrims and strangers on this earth, willing to move from place to place as the varied needs of the cause directed. Because of their itinerant lifestyle, it is not possible to list every place they lived. This article creates for the reader a synopsis of James and Ellen White's residences and provides a framework for understanding their lives and ministry (*buildings known to still exist are followed by the abbreviation "ss"—still standing*). The Whites

lived in many places in the United States, and after James' death in 1881, Ellen also lived in both Europe and Australia. However, if there is one place they could call home, it was *Battle Creek, Michigan, for no matter how far-flung their travels, from 1855 to 1891 they usually maintained a home there.

Both James and Ellen White grew up in Maine. James was born and raised in a farm house (ss) in Palmyra, Somerset County, Maine. At the age of 19 he enrolled in nearby St. Albans Academy. After returning from his second winter teaching, he learned from his mother the Adventist teachings, embraced them, and began traveling as an itinerant preacher. Ellen Harmon was born in Gorham, Cumberland County, Maine, at an unknown location, where she lived for a short time before her family moved to a home (ss) in Poland Springs, and then to Portland, Maine, where they lived on property now a part of the playground of a local school. It was in Portland (or Orrington, Maine, by another account) that James met Ellen, and they were later married in Portland by a justice of the peace on August 30, 1846.

For about a year the newlyweds set up housekeeping with Ellen's parents, who had returned to live in a farmhouse (ss) in Gorham, Maine. In October 1847 *Stockbridge and Louisa Howland invited James and Ellen with their newborn son, *Henry, to share their home (ss but relocated) in Topsham, Cumberland County, Maine. Determined to be financially independent, they set up housekeeping in the second story of the Howland home while James worked nearby chopping cordwood for 50 cents a day and hauling stone for a railroad (1Bio 134). From there James and Ellen traveled to meet appointments throughout New England.

For the next three and a half years the Whites moved throughout the northeast

United States as their ministry was needed. Their son, Henry, remained with the Howland family in Topsham. The first four numbers of *Present Truth* were printed while staying with the *Stephen Belden family in Rocky Hill, Hartford County, Connecticut. In the winter and spring of 1849-1850 they spent several months in Oswego, Oswego County, New York. The summer of 1850 found them in Auburn, Cayuga County, New York. From November 1850 till June 1851 they lived at Paris, Oxford County, Maine; from August 1851 till April 1852 they stayed in the vicinity of Saratoga Springs, Saratoga County, New York; and then settled in a rented house in *Rochester, Monroe County, New York, where Henry rejoined the White family.

Times were hard, as the Whites with a dozen young printers, preachers, and writers lived and worshipped together in the one house at 124 Mount Hope Avenue in Rochester. At first the home was also shared with the printing press and binding equipment, but by October 1852 the press was moved to a rented third-floor office on South St. Paul Street in downtown Rochester.

After turning down an invitation to move to Vermont, they accepted the invitation of believers in Jackson and Battle Creek, Michigan, to relocate to Battle Creek in the fall of 1855. They rented a small house on the south side of Van Buren Street across from David Hewitt's home for $1.50 a week. Ellen White describes the place as having "scarcely any conveniences." There was no good place to store firewood, and the family needed to "go a great distance for water" (Lt 9, 1856).

On January 8, 1856, the Whites bought a building lot in Ellen's name in anticipation of building a place of their own, but sold the lot on May 5 of the same year to John Preston Kellogg. On August 4, 1856, the Whites bought approximately an acre and a half (0.6 hectare)

of land on Wood Street. With the help of fellow believers they constructed a small one-and-two-thirds-story frame house (ss).

HOME OF JAMES AND ELLEN WHITE ON WOOD STREET IN BATTLE CREEK, MICHIGAN

Within a few months they added a room on the north side to accommodate extended family. Then in 1861 a larger addition was built on the back of the house, including a large kitchen, pantry, and bedroom. This is the first home the Whites ever owned.

Orchards, berries, and vegetable gardens were planted to supply the family's needs. Homes for each of their parents were provided across the street. James' parents lived in the little home at the corner of Wood and Champion streets (ss) for several years, but the home on the corner of Wood and Manchester was occupied by Ellen's parents for only a short time.

Wishing to be nearer to the publishing office, in 1863 they purchased a home on the northeast corner of Washington and Champion streets. This home was frequently referred to as the "corner house." It was here that James suffered his first debilitating stroke. In 1866, wanting to live a little farther from the noise and traffic of the busy corner, the Whites sold the corner house and purchased two parcels totaling 11 acres (4.5 hectares) a little north of the Health Reform Institute. They remodeled a home on the southernmost parcel (nearly five acres [two hectares]) fronting on

Washington Street and built a barn. But less than one year later, feeling the need to be even farther from the stress of work (because of James' poor health and troubles in Battle Creek), they sold the house along with both parcels to the Health Reform Institute, and purchased a home (ss) on nearly 46 acres (18.6 hectares) of farmland in Greenville, Montcalm County, Michigan. There they built a home, hoping that James would recover more rapidly in a country setting. Soon they added a barn, and James planted 100 apple trees and an assortment of other small fruits.

HOME OF JAMES AND ELLEN WHITE IN GREENVILLE, MICHIGAN

During these years they made periodic extended visits back to Battle Creek. In 1868 they reacquired the north six acres (2.4 hectares) of their recently sold property in Battle Creek, after the Health Reform Institute defaulted on their payments. Here they constructed a nice home with lumber given in payment for the remainder of the institute debt to them, and maintained an intermittent residence there until 1873, when it was again sold to the Health Reform Institute. Then they repurchased the "corner house" the same month. Although often away, they periodically stayed there when business brought them back to Battle Creek. While they were absent they sometimes rented out the place as a boardinghouse.

In 1869 the Whites purchased a small house in Washington, Washington County,

Iowa. They thought that the seclusion would be a blessing to them both. But they never lived there for extended periods of time, staying over only a few days at a time as they traveled back and forth to California or Midwestern camp meetings.

In 1872 the Whites began working in California, and over the years owned and rented several homes there. In 1874 they rented "Fountain Farm," an abandoned water-cure facility, about four miles from Oakland in Alameda County, and began to lay plans for the Pacific Press and the *Signs of the Times*. In April of the following year they began construction of a home (ss but relocated) in Oakland near the corner of Eleventh and Castro streets, near the press building which was also under construction (ST, Oct. 7, 1875). In the winter of 1877-1878, motivated again by James' declining health, they built a home (ss) on a 30-acre (12-hectare) farm on West Dry Creek Road near Healdsburg, Sonoma County, California.

Summers in the 1870s found the Whites often in the mountains of Colorado, visiting Ellen's niece Louisa Clough Walling and her family. The family was struggling financially and emotionally, and James purchased some property from William Walling to help him out. Later the Whites purchased additional land and fixed up a rustic cabin for summer camping. They referred to this retreat as "White's Ranch." Two of the Walling girls, Addie (see *Addie [Walling] MacPherson) and *May, later became part of the White household.

In November 1880, after returning from California, James White purchased the home of his dreams on a hill overlooking the city of Battle Creek. The property included 32 acres (13 hectares) and a three-story, 16-room brick house with a cupola. The Whites had the privilege of living there together for less than a year, however, for James died in 1881.

Following his death, his body lay in state in their old "corner house," close to the sanitarium and the Review office.

In early 1882 Ellen moved back to their Healdsburg farm on Dry Creek Road. Soon she purchased a small home on Powell Avenue in Healdsburg and had a second floor added (ss). While living in this home, Ellen White wrote the manuscript of the 1884 edition of *The Great Controversy*, also known as *Spirit of Prophecy*, volume 4.

In 1884 Ellen purchased 8.5 acres (3.4 hectares) adjacent to the *St. Helena Sanitarium and had a small cottage constructed on the site (3Bio 244). She named the home "Iliel" (ss) and from time to time stayed at her new little retreat. It was here that her daughter-in-law *Mary (Kelsey) White spent time during her last illness (3Bio 382). She purchased the property knowing that the sanitarium would one day need the room to expand. Ellen White also owned another cottage nearby that she rented to workers.

In 1885 Ellen White sailed for Europe. While there she maintained an apartment on the third floor of the Imprimerie Polyglotte, the European Adventist publishing house, located on the corner of Weiherweg and Rudophstrasse in Basel, Switzerland. Her travels, however, took her throughout Europe, including Great Britain.

In 1887, after spending two years in Europe, she returned to her Powell Street home in Healdsburg, where she completed *The Great Controversy* (1888) and *Patriarchs and Prophets* (1890). (She kept this home for many years, later leasing it to *Alma [Baker] McKibbin; her brother, Alonzo Baker; and their mother.) In 1888 Ellen White purchased a 50-acre (20-hectare) ranch in Burroughs Valley, Fresno County, California, hoping that the mild, dry climate would help her daughter-in-law Mary (Kelsey) White recover from tuberculosis.

They spent several summers there, away from the heat of the lowlands, but Mary died in 1890, and Ellen White sold the ranch in 1891.

During much of this time Ellen White also maintained a home in Battle Creek at 303 West Main Street (now Michigan Avenue), a little south and west of the Dime Tabernacle (see *Battle Creek Tabernacle). In this house Ellen lived with her son and daughter-in-law Edson and Emma and her office staff. In the summer of 1891 she lived for a few months in a cottage she had built in Petoskey, Michigan, overlooking the beautiful Little Traverse Bay of Lake Michigan.

Ellen White arrived in Sydney, *Australia, on December 8, 1891, and after visiting *A. G. Daniells for about a week, she traveled to Melbourne, the capital of the state of Victoria. At the time Melbourne had the largest group of Adventist believers on that continent and was the location of the *Echo Publishing House. On January 10, 1892, she moved into a rented place on St. Kilda's Road in Preston. Inexpensive public transportation allowed them to commute to the publishing house in about 20 minutes (Lt 92, 1892; 4Bio 43).

In September 1892 Ellen White relocated to Adelaide, about 500 miles (800 kilometers) from Melbourne, where she spent the next few months in a rented home. She wrote that she was "comfortably situated" there and that the climate was more healthful for her (Lt 36, 1892). By December 12 she had returned to Melbourne, where she rented a second-floor room (Lt 23a, 1892; 4Bio 47).

Ellen White continued her frequent travels with a 10-month sojourn to *New Zealand (February through December 1893). She set forth her intentions during this trip that upon her return she would relocate near Sydney, where the climate was more beneficial to her health (Lt 55, 1893).

From March 27 through July 8, 1894, Ellen

White lived on Williams Street, in Granville, a small town about 13 miles (21 kilometers) from Sydney. The rented one-story cottage, called "Per Ardua," cost her $27 a month. The house was too small for the "frequent visitors" who came by, so she purchased a tent for $35 to be "brought into use when company comes" (Lt 50, 1894). The home was located only about a mile and a half (2.5 kilometers) from the Parramatta meetinghouse—the first Seventh-day Adventist church built in Australia, and centrally located between three other Adventist congregations.

When an economic depression caused rental prices to decrease, Ellen White was able to rent a home nearly twice the size of Per Ardua for only $25 a month. On July 8, 1893, Ellen White moved into "a nice, large, two-

HOME OF ELLEN WHITE, "SUNNYSIDE," IN COORANBONG, AUSTRALIA

story house up on the hill" from the Per Ardua, named "Norfolk Villa" (ss). While Ellen White believed that Granville had the best climate of anywhere she had yet lived in Australia, the Per Ardua home she felt was "too low in its location," and this new property on the hill was better ventilated (Lt 54a, 1894). "Our dwelling," she wrote, "is one of the first order in every respect. . . . The scenery is rather attractive . . . [with] only one house close by us. The location is all that we could desire. The rooms are light and airy, and we have plenty of them. Willie has his office on the lower floor and his sleeping room on the second floor. He

is more conveniently situated than he has ever been in his life" (Lt 46a, 1894).

In August 1894 Ellen White wrote of her intent to purchase property from the land being acquired at the time for the *Avondale school in Cooranbong. During the spring and summer of 1895 Ellen White was involved with the construction of her new Cooranbong home on the school land—a move that would save her money, provide badly needed funds for the school, and visibly show her support of the new educational venture (Lt 25, 1894). During the summer of 1895 she alternated between the Avondale property and her Norfolk Villa home (where some of her *literary assistants continued to work). Now 68 years old, she described her temporary residence at Avondale as a "comfortable family tent" that she shared with her granddaughter Ella May White. Around her was a "village of tents" for her workers and the men constructing her house (headed by a Mr. Shannon) (Lt 42, 1895, in 8MR 92-94). On Christmas Day 1895 Ellen White moved into her new home, along with her belongings and remaining workers from Norfolk Villa. During the summer Ellen White had already dubbed her new home "Sunnyside" (Lts 111, 112, 1895; LS 358). W. C. White described the house as having 11 rooms. The main building was 32′ x 32′ (9.7 meters x 9.7 meters), with a veranda in the front and a hall running through the center. The house contained four rooms (12′ x 12′ [3.6 meters x 3.6 meters]) on the ground floor and four additional rooms nearly as large upstairs. The back of the house had a lean-to (14′ x 22′ [4.2 meters x 6.7 meters]) that was used as a kitchen. Soon afterward an addition (16′ x 22′ [4.9 meters x 6.7 meters]) was attached to one of the back rooms to be divided into a kitchen, bathroom, and storeroom. This home was the base of Ellen White's operations for the remainder of her stay in

Australia. Today the Sunnyside home is a museum.

When Ellen White returned to the United States in 1900, she purchased a home on 35 acres (14 hectares) of property in the Napa Valley, about 60 miles (96 kilometers) northeast of San Francisco (ss). This property, which she named "Elmshaven," is where she spent the last 15 years of her life (1900-1915) and wrote many Adventist classics, including *Education*, *The Ministry of Healing*, and *The Acts of the Apostles*. The property included three acres (1.2 hectares) of fruit orchards, 2,000 prune trees, olive trees, and five acres (two hectares) of grapes. The house contained seven rooms and was completely furnished, including a barn with two horses and four carriages. Ellen White was able

HOME OF ELLEN WHITE, "ELMSHAVEN," IN ST. HELENA, CALIFORNIA

to purchase the property for $8,000, immediately selling off a parcel for $3,000, reducing her cost to $5,000. The St. Helena Sanitarium was only a 12-minute walk away.

When the decision to move the General Conference headquarters to the vicinity of Washington, D.C., was made in 1903, Ellen White rented a nearby apartment in Takoma Park known as "Carroll House" so that she could be closely involved in this major relocation effort.

In 1915 Ellen White broke her hip at her Elmshaven home. Never recovering, she died in the second-floor writing room on Friday afternoon, July 16, 1915, at the age of 87. After

her death the property was sold, but the Ellen G. White Estate rented office space on the property until it moved to Washington, D.C., in 1938. Her last home was acquired by the Pacific Union Conference in 1956, subsequently restored, and is now open to the public as a museum.

The Whites owned, at least briefly, many other properties in the United States. Some they purchased to provide financial assistance to needy families, as was the ranch in Burroughs Valley, California; some for family or friends who needed a place to live, such as the home purchased for Mary Chase in Battle Creek, Michigan; some to secure land surrounding our institutions that the growing ministries would later need, as was "Iliel" near St. Helena Sanitarium; and some because of their potential value. While economic growth sometimes worked in their favor, on other occasions they sold the properties for less than they had invested in them.

Often the Whites owned four or five homes simultaneously. During the 1870s they owned homes in Battle Creek, Michigan; Oakland and Healdsburg, California; Washington, Iowa; and a cabin at Walling's Mills, Colorado. As their ministry took them back and forth across the United States, these homes provided offices in which to work, facilities in which to entertain travelers, and places to rest and recuperate. They also provided venues for safely investing moneys that would later be needed for God's work.

Further reading: For directions to sites in North America, see *In the Footsteps of the Pioneers* (RHPA, 1990); D. A. Johnson, "Mountain Trails and Retreats With the Whites" (unpublished manuscript, 1988); *idem*, "Colorado Vacations of James and Ellen White, 1872-1879" (unpublished manuscript, n.d.).

Stanley D. Hickerson and Michael W. Campbell

HUMAN NATURE. The set of qualities all human beings possess in common. "Nature" in this connection refers to the inborn character, innate disposition, or inherent tendencies. Ellen White used "human nature" and "nature of man" as synonymous expressions in most instances. However, "nature" may also mean the essence or constitutive characteristics of a being, and indeed she also used "nature of man," in line with this alternative sense, to denote the constitutive parts of the human being, which have implications, among other things, for the state of the dead. In the overwhelming majority of instances she used "human nature" in its theological sense. This article will focus on inborn disposition and tendencies found in humans in general.

In order to assess Ellen White's conception of human nature correctly, one should set it against the background of early-nineteenth-century New England thinking. The "transcendental philosophy" of Ralph W. Emerson and Henry D. Thoreau had semireligious feelings toward the physical universe and emphasized the natural goodness of human beings in a typically romantic way. This optimistic conception of human capabilities was correlated in America with individualism, social reformism, and a conception of Christ not far removed from ordinary human beings, which contributed to widespread *Arianism in America at the time. Among church bodies temporarily engulfed by this tendency was the Christian Connexion, in which James White and other prominent leaders of the early SDA movement received their baptism and ministerial ordination. In contrast, Ellen White, who had been brought up in the Methodist Church, rejected Arianism and consequently also the underlying "philosophies of human nature," which had led to "confusion and shame" by emphasizing the natural capabilities of man instead of his dependence on God (MH 465). She embraced instead the clear statements of Scripture about the depravity of fallen and unregenerate human nature, such as Romans 7:18-23; 8:7; Ephesians 4:18; 2 Timothy 3:2-4; and Titus 1:15.

Though she did not discuss human nature in any systematic or comprehensive way, her conception emerges very clearly from the hundreds of occurrences of "human nature" in her published writings. Her views may be arranged along the great controversy theme, so familiar to her readers.

The nature of man, in its original condition, bore the image and likeness of God, to whom it stands in an "unchangeable relation" (GC 262). The "governing power in the nature of man" is the will, which "is not the taste or the inclination, but it is the deciding power" for obedience or disobedience (5T 513). Man's original perfection was not static, for "all his faculties were capable of development. . . . Throughout eternal ages he would have continued to gain new treasures of knowledge, to discover fresh springs of happiness. . . . More and more fully would he . . . have reflected the Creator's glory" (Ed 15).

Satan's work, since the Garden of Eden, has been "to destroy the moral image of God in man, by making void the divine law" (RH, Jan. 26, 1897) and so "to mold human nature into his own image of moral deformity" (RH, Aug. 25, 1896). "Through the medium of influence, taking advantage of the action of mind on mind, he prevailed on Adam to sin. Thus at its very source human nature was corrupted" (RH, Apr. 16, 1901). The result is described in many terms, such as a "depraved," "perverted," "offending," "vile," "deformed," or "weak and wicked" human nature. By whatever name, it now could not keep the law, even if it wanted to, for it "was led captive at the will of Satan" (RH, Feb. 28, 1888). Transgression implies "separation from God. And to fallen human nature this means ruin" (MH 428).

Some people will never accept the message of the gospel, because "there is a depth of depravity in unbelieving human nature that will never be healed" (LLM 144). In addition, Satan's work goes on, and even today "he will, if possible, deprave human nature, and assimilate it to his own corrupt principles" (RH, Sept. 14, 1897). He promises honors, riches, and pleasures on condition that "integrity shall be yielded, conscience blunted," thereby degrading human faculties (RH, Aug. 25, 1896). He also employs "the indulgence of the passions, thus brutalizing the entire nature of man" (4SP 374).

The defects of fallen human nature are in evidence everywhere, for this fallen nature is "ever struggling for expression, ready for contest" (MB 15). It has a "continual opposition to God's will and ways" (RH, Oct. 24, 1912). It is "so ignorant, so liable to misconception," that it does not realize how its acts affect others (MH 483). Its basic selfishness, pride, and self-sufficiency are the source of its "disposition to envy, jealousy, and cruel distrust" (3T 343). It is prone to impatience, contentiousness, greed, vanity, and extremism (*ibid.* 515, 550; 4T 12, 644; 5T 305). Human nature finds it difficult to control appetite, bear reproof, find joy in the ways of the Lord, deal frankly with the erring, forgive them before seeing reform in their behavior, or judge mercifully, among other things (4T 293; 3T 323, 329; RH, Apr. 15, 1880; SW, Jan. 1, 1907; RH, Jan. 3, 1893). It tends to confuse God's love with weakness and so excuses sin (RH, Feb. 8, 1898). Even in believers, "there are in human nature elements of destruction, which, under certain conditions, break forth to consume" (RH, Jan. 14, 1904).

On the other hand, "human nature is worth working upon" and includes many God-given attributes, such as motherly love and other tender, fine feelings. Therefore it should not be spurned, but "elevated, refined, sanctified, and fitted with the inward adorning" (CT 236; ST, July 3, 1893). "Human nature may take hold of the strength of God, and be victorious" (YI, Dec. 28, 1899).

Hence there is need for a thorough knowledge of human nature. God used a perfect knowledge of this nature when designing the plan of salvation; Jesus uses His intimate knowledge of fallen human nature when interceding for His followers, while Satan assiduously studies it in order to gratify its tendency to evil (RH, Feb. 6, 1900; ST, Jan. 3, 1878; GC 555; 3SP 195; 4SP 374). Humans are quite ignorant of their own nature, and cannot reach this knowledge without diligent study (ST, Aug. 26, 1889). Pastors should mingle with people and study their minds in order to understand the different "phases" of human nature and avoid feeding it improper food from the pulpit (GW 191). Education, whether by mothers or teachers, also requires study of human nature (HR, Dec. 1, 1877; Ed 279), as do church administration and pastoral counseling (PH084 17).

True biblical religion, as revealed from Eden onward, aims to transform human nature. The elevation and restoration of human nature is the purpose of Christ's incarnation (MH 180), sacrifice (RH, July 15, 1909), and sending of His Spirit (RH, Apr. 5, 1906). This is a supernatural work bringing into human nature supernatural elements (DA 324); "Christ supplies the efficiency, and man becomes a power for good" (RH, Mar. 10, 1903). The effects of this renewal are manifest in the character as a new tenderness of sentiments (ST, Nov. 28, 1892), cheerfulness (HR, June 1, 1871), spiritual energy (RH, June 21, 1898), power to resist sin (MH 180), and change in cherished habits and practices (PC 418).

Even in a born-again servant of God, however, "the infirmities of human nature are upon him, and he is not infallible" (RH, Nov. 4, 1875), but since Christ is the ladder connecting heaven and earth, there is no excuse for His followers to become "more like human nature" (RH, Oct. 1, 1889), for "heaven is a ceaseless approaching to God through Christ" and so, for the believer, "heaven begins here. . . . All that human nature can bear, we may receive here" (DA 331, 332).

What emerges from Ellen White's views of human nature, then, is a very conservative conception of the biblical doctrine on the subject, in contrast to its optimistic assessment by transcendentalism and romanticism. In line with historical mainstream Christian thought, Ellen White emphasizes the fallenness of human nature, but also its potential for regeneration under the power of the Holy Spirit. Far less common is the marked duality of states in which she casts human nature, as the moral image either of Christ or Satan. This is also related to the great overarching theme of her writings, the great controversy between those two contenders for the allegiance of humankind.

Further reading: A. E. Cairus, "The Doctrine of Man," in R. Dederen, ed., *Handbook of Seventh-day Adventist Theology* (RHPA, 2000), pp. 205-232; "Transcendentalism," in D. D. Runes, ed., *Dictionary of Philosophy* (Savage, Md.: Littlefield, Adams & Co., 1983).

Aecio E. Cairus

HUMILITY, ORDINANCE OF, see **LORD'S SUPPER**.

HUMOR, ELLEN G. WHITE'S USE OF. Although Ellen White condemned needless levity or joking, she also opposed a smileless, joyless, humorless Christian lifestyle.

Many Christians consider it unthinkable that Christ ever laughed, grinned, chuckled, or smiled—partly because of a misguided piety that views humor as intrinsically profane, incompatible with the sacred Word of God. For Adventists this misconception has also influenced attitudes toward the counsels and person of Ellen White. This perception seems plausible because many *photographs of early Adventists, including Ellen White, portray individuals who appear somber, joyless, all business, and no pleasure. Unfortunately, the appearance of these photographs had nothing to do with whether a person was happy or not, but was the result of primitive photographic techniques that made it necessary for people not to move for a short time (and thus not to smile) while the camera properly exposed the photograph.

Throughout her life Ellen White said nothing directly about the use of humor in the life of the Christian. She did address related topics, such as fun, joking, laughter, and amusements, with her primary focus being on the "frivolous" aspects of such activities. She counseled against frivolous laughter and talking in church (5T 492), ministers using anecdotes or incidents to create a laugh in their sermons, thereby detracting from the message being presented (GW 166), and excessive and worldly amusements that draw people away from God (AH 512). In her view, frivolous levity and joking was to be avoided, since a Christian's first duty was to stay focused on the seriousness of their high calling by God.

Early in her ministry some of Ellen White's statements reflect a very serious approach to spirituality. These statements contribute to an image of a humorless and joyless Ellen White. In 1868 she wrote, "Christ is our example. . . . Christ often wept but never was known to laugh. I do not say it is a sin to laugh on any occasion. But we cannot go astray if we imitate the divine, unerring Pattern. . . .

As we view the world bound in darkness and trammeled by Satan, how can we engage in levity, glee, careless, reckless words, speaking at random, laughing, jesting, and joking? It is in keeping with our faith to be sober" (Ms 11, 1868, in 6MR 91).

However, Ellen White did not view the Christian life as joyless and devoid of happiness and laughter. She frequently talked about the true happiness and joy that comes from Christ, which should characterize the life of the Christian. "Let us never lose sight of the fact that Jesus is a wellspring of joy. He does not delight in the misery of human beings, but loves to see them happy" (AH 513). In fact, in her own personal life Ellen White found that "the more I know of Jesus' character the more cheerful I am" (Ms 1, 1867, in 6MR 90).

Much of Ellen White's counsel against frivolous laughter, amusements, and joking was directed toward young people who were being attracted by the pleasures of the world and getting caught up in "frivolity and fashion," as well as "empty, vain talking and laughing." Instead, she challenged Christian young people to be "sober-minded" (1T 499). According to her, the key for any Christian was to be balanced, to show "temperance in amusements, as in every other pursuit." To her there was a significant distinction between enjoyable recreation and frivolous, worldly amusements (AH 512).

In reality Ellen White's approach to laughter, humor, and fun was quite balanced. She spoke against individuals who approached religion as if it was a tyrant ruling over them with a rod of iron, who were devoid of love, who always had a frown on their face, who were offended by laughter, and who considered all recreation and amusement a sin. She called such people "extreme," as she did those at the other end of the spectrum who continually sought amusement, excitement, and diversion (1T 565).

In a letter to Elder *S. N. Haskell regarding how to work with young people, Ellen White counseled: "Do not be afraid to let them know you love them. . . . Do not make it a season of grave decorum as though they were standing about a coffin, but have it a social season where every countenance is full of joy and happiness, where naught but cheerful words are spoken. . . . Approve whenever you can; smile whenever you can; do not arrange your countenance as though a smile would bring the condemnation of heaven. Heaven is all smiles and gladness and gratitude. . . . I will work against this cold, cast-iron, unsympathizing religion as long as I have strength to wield my pen" (Lt 19, 1886, in 6MR 92, 93).

Substantial evidence as to Ellen White's view on the appropriate use of humor and the place of laughter in the Christian life can be seen in her own life as remembered by those who knew her at home. Her grandson Arthur White wrote that "life was not strained in the White home. There was no place for a long-faced, smileless religion. Instead, . . . it was a joyous religion in a joyous home. Ellen White would join in a hearty laugh at an amusing or awkward situation or a nice turn of words. . . . Once she wrote: '. . . A hearty, willing service to Jesus produces a sunny religion'" (A. L. White, "Ellen G. White the Person," *Spectrum* 4, no. 2 [Spring 1972]: 11; cf. Ms 1, 1867).

On one occasion Ellen White recounted a humorous incident in her house involving two sisters, Lillie and Rosette, and their mother, Mrs. Rhoda Abbey, who were staying with Ellen White. Rhoda Abbey was supposed to be resting, but was having difficulty refraining from doing things around the house. Ellen White reported that Abbey was "real smart and cheerful as a bird," and then she recounted an incident that had occurred. "I heard a great rumpus yesterday in the dining room—laughing and protesting," said Ellen White. "I found out your mother was washing dishes. Rosette had got her round the waist and called Lillie, who took her feet, and they tugged her and put her on the lounge, and she was so overcome with laughter—and they too—it was difficult for them to explain to me their mischief" (Lt 27, 1873, in 5MR 431). Another houseguest, Mrs. H. E. Rogers, who as a child had lived in the White home for a while, recalled Ellen White being interested in their childhood games and allowing the kids, once a week, to have a pillow fight (P. Ricciutti, *Ellen* [PPPA, 1977], p. 131).

Humor and laughter manifested itself, not only in Ellen White's home, but in her correspondence with family and friends, as well as her accounts of experiences when traveling. She told about crossing the English Channel, during which one of her party became seasick. She reported that "Brother Aufranc, we know, did not sleep scarcely any. He was sightseeing by moonlight" (Lt 84a, 1886). And following another boat trip, she wrote, "When I got off the boat, when I walked up through the streets, it seemed to me as though I was still on the boat, and I would step so high that people must have thought I was drunk" (Ms 4, 1878, in 5MR 178).

On another occasion, when she was preaching at St. Helena, California, her son W. C. White was sitting on the platform with her. Noticing that people in the congregation were beginning to titter, she turned around to find Willie taking a nap. Ellen White humorously apologized to the audience, saying, "When Willie was a baby, I used to take him into the pulpit and let him sleep in a basket beneath the pulpit, and he has never gotten over the habit." Then she simply continued on with her sermon (AR, Apr. 30, 1987;

see also Roger Coon, "Ellen G. White: The Person—II, The Wit and Wisdom of the Prophet" [lecture outline, 1995]).

Clearly Ellen White viewed the Christian life as one of joy and happiness, characterized by temperance in all areas, including humor, laughter, and recreation.

Further reading: 5Bio 139; 6Bio 395, 425; HS 222; Lt 2a, 1873; Lt 5, 1876; Lt 10, 1901; Lt 21, 1884; Lt 22, 56, 83, 1902; Lt 84, 84a, 1886; Lt 144, 1903; 6MR 90-95; Ms 24, 1901; Ms 29, 1885; Mss 22, 81, 1893; 1T 464; G. M. Baker, "The Humor of Ellen White," AR, Apr. 30, 1987; R. Graybill, "Tell Them There Is a Great Deal More to Sister White Than Most People Think," *Insight*, Aug. 14, 1973; G. R. Knight, *Walking With Ellen White* (RHPA, 1999), pp. 17-25; A. Thompson, "The Scary Lady of Adventism Learns to Have Fun," *Insight*, Oct. 2, 1993; E. Trueblood, *The Humor of Christ* (New York: Harper & Row, 1964), p. 15.

Glen M. Baker

HUNTSVILLE TRAINING SCHOOL, see **OAKWOOD INDUSTRIAL SCHOOL**.

HUSS, JOHN (c. 1372-1415). Early Protestant Reformer. John Huss (or Hus) was born in

PHOTO CREDIT: UNKNOWN

JOHN HUSS, EARLY PROTESTANT REFORMER IN BOHEMIA

the village of Husinec in southern Bohemia, c. 1372. After studying for the priesthood at the Prachatice school, Huss matriculated at the University of Prague, completing his Bachelor of Arts in 1393. After completing his master's degree and two subsequent years of teaching, he was named rector of the university and preacher at the Bethlehem Chapel. Although a papal bull had been issued forbidding public worship in the native

Bohemian tongue, the Bethlehem Chapel had been founded largely for the purpose of providing preaching in the Czech language, and it was here that Huss exerted a wide influence among the people. Through Jerome, who had studied at Oxford, Huss became acquainted with the works of John Wycliffe. Together Huss and Jerome became strong voices for the Reformation in Bohemia. The published 14 volumes of Huss's sermons testify to the depth and maturity of his theological views. The Council of Constance in 1415 condemned Huss to be burned at the stake for his beliefs. Ellen White refers to his reforming influence in an extensive chapter found in *The Great Controversy* (pp. 97-119). Here she relies on authoritative works on the subject while emphasizing new aspects of historical significance and personal character that shaped and gave rise to the Reformation in Bohemia. Several additional references emphasize: (1) the example of Huss as one who stood for truth in the midst of great difficulty and personal loss (SR 337-339; 9MR 275-277); and (2) the place of Huss in the line of Reformers in Europe (AA 598; CC 9; Ed 254; RH, Dec. 24, 1908; RH, Nov. 11, 1915). White wrote that his "martyr's constancy, his faith, his example, has been reflecting its light down along the times for centuries," "encouraging others to submit their souls and bodies to God alone" (9MR 276).

Further reading: G. F. Hasel, "Hus' Letter About His Withdrawal From Prague and E. G. White's *Great Controversy*," rev. Jan. 31, 1978 (EGWE-GC); J. Loserth, *Wiclif and Hus* (London: Hodder and Stoughton, 1884); D. S. Schaff, *John Huss: His Life, Teachings and Death* (New York: Scribner, 1915); M. Spinka, *John Hus and the Czech Reform* (Chicago: University of Chicago Press, 1941); idem, *John Hus: A Biography* (Princeton: Princeton University Press, 1968); idem, *The*

Letters of John Hus (Manchester: Manchester University Press, 1972); H. B. Workman and R. M. Pope, *The Letters of John Hus* (London: Hodder and Stoughton, 1904).

Michael G. Hasel

HYDROTHERAPY. The treatment of illness through the internal or external use of water. Hydropathy, the forerunner of hydrotherapy, was popularized in Europe by Vincent Priessnitz, a layman who opened a water-cure center in Prussia in 1826 and treated some 7,000 patients in the 1830s. His regimen included frequent bathing, no beverage except water, a simple diet, fresh air, exercise, and total avoidance of medication. In the 1840s hydropathy came to America, where two hydropathic physicians, *Russell Trall and *James C. Jackson, exerted significant influence on Adventist health reform (Cayleff, *Wash and Be Healed*, pp. 20-24).

Through a vision in 1863 Ellen White was directed to lead Adventists in a comprehensive package of health reform principles. "Drugs never cure disease," she wrote. "Nature alone is the only effective restorer, and how much better could she perform her task if left to herself." But if "sufferers . . . would resort to the simple means they have neglected—the use of water and proper diet, nature would have just the help she requires, and" "the patient [would] generally recover" (4aSG [1863] 134; *Health: or How to Live* [1865], no. 6, pp. 57-64).

In response to another vision, Adventists in 1866 launched a journal, the *Health Reformer*, and opened a small *Health Reform Institute in Battle Creek (2Bio 118-144). A shortage of qualified physicians led them to send to medical schools several of their young people, including *John H. Kellogg. In 1876, 10 years after the opening of the Health Reform Institute, Kellogg was appointed its medical director, and soon changed its name to Battle Creek Medical and Surgical Sanitarium. But while he learned much from the more progressive of the "regular" physicians, he never forsook his roots. The 1,193-page textbook of his health-care methodology he titled *Rational Hydrotherapy* (1st ed., 1900). Kellogg here echoes two basic principles of Ellen White (above) and other health reformers: that healing is the work of the body itself; and that water, used internally or externally, is an "agent" that "cooperates with the healing powers of the body." Kellogg used water, not as a panacea, but as the chief among a variety of therapeutic strategies, including "rational diet," exercise, healthful clothing, and abstinence from "tea, coffee, tobacco, and alcoholic beverages" (*Rational Hydrotherapy*, 2nd ed. [1902], pp. vii, viii). Kellogg particularly emphasized avoidance of the metallic and poisonous *drugs routinely prescribed in the nineteenth century. Regular physicians of the era used arsenic and strychnine to stimulate, compounds of mercury to induce bowel movements, and opium to control pain. Kellogg achieved the same ends through hydrotherapy—to stimulate blood circulation, induce bowel movements, and control pain.

Historians of medicine credit Kellogg's *Rational Hydrotherapy*, which went through several editions, with helping to "transform sectarian hydropathy into the hydrotherapy of scientific medicine" (see Cayleff, *Wash and Be Healed*, p. 209, note 39; R. L. Numbers and R. B. Schoepflin, "Ministries of Healing," in *Women and Health in America: Historical Readings*, pp. 387, 388).

Further reading: S. E. Cayleff, *Wash and Be Healed: The Water-Cure Movement and Women's Health* (Philadelphia: Temple University Press, 1987); J. H. Kellogg, *Rational Hydrotherapy*, 2nd ed. (Philadelphia: F. A. Davis, 1902), pp. vii, viii; R. L. Numbers and R. B. Schoepflin, "Ministries of Healing: Mary Baker Eddy, Ellen G. White, and the Religion of Health," in J. W. Leavitt and R. L. Numbers, eds., *Women and Health in America: Historical Readings* (Madison: University of Wisconsin Press, 1984); SHM65; R. H. Shryock, *Medicine in America: Historical Essays* (Baltimore: Johns Hopkins University Press, 1966).

Jerry Moon

HYMNS ELLEN WHITE LOVED. Hymns were an important part of Ellen White's Christian experience. "When the evil one begins to settle his gloom about you," she wrote in 1890, "sing praise to God. When things go crossways at your homes, strike up a song about the matchless charms of the Son of God. . . . You can drive out the enemy with his gloom" (HP 95).

Recollections of her family members indicate that in the White home hymns were an essential part of family worships and of Ellen White's personal life. Morning worships often started with "Lord, in the Morning," and evening worships often included "Sweet Hour of Prayer." When it was Ellen White's turn to choose a hymn during family worship, she often picked "There Is Sunlight on the Hilltop." One time several of her office staff wanted to attend an evening activity, and so planned to dispense with the singing during worship. Not aware of their plans, Ellen White was handed a Bible to read from; she immediately asked, "Do we not have time tonight to worship the Lord in song?" The hymnbooks were passed out!

One day someone came to Ellen White asking how to stop another person from gossiping with them so much. She responded, "You might start singing the doxology!" Another time, after singing "In the Glad Time of the Harvest," she remarked that a strain in that hymn reminded her of the angels she had heard sing in vision. Still again, when a congregation was listlessly singing the hymn she had chosen, she stopped them. "I have heard the angels sing in vision, and they sing with feeling. Can't we do better?" she asked. It is reported they did.

Ellen White told her grandchildren, "We must learn to sing the songs of Zion here if we would join the angel choir yonder." Often she was overheard singing to herself the doxology or some other hymn as she went about her work. She also enjoyed singing while walking or taking buggy rides. One of her granddaughters described the hymns her grandmother most enjoyed as "hymns of progress." Ellen White's favorite hymn was "Jesus, Lover of My Soul."

Ellen White occasionally quoted lines or stanzas from hymns in her published (e.g., 1SM 332, 333) and unpublished (e.g., Lt 11, 1892) writings, as well as in her personal diaries (e.g., Ms 126, 1906). The *Seventh-day Adventist Hymnal* and *Early Advent Singing* contain several hymns that she is known to have especially liked: "All Hail the Power of Jesus' Name"; "Angels Hovering Round"; "Holy, Holy, Holy"; "I'm a Pilgrim"; "I Heard the Voice of Jesus Say"; "I Saw One Weary"; "I Will Follow Thee, My Savior"; "In the Glad Time of the Harvest"; "Jesus, I My Cross Have Taken"; "Jesus, Lover of My Soul"; "Just as I Am"; "Lord, in the Morning Thou Shalt Hear"; "O Worship the Lord"; "Praise God From Whom All Blessings Flow"; "Resting By and By"; "Rock of Ages"; "Soldiers of Christ, Arise"; "Sweet Hour of Prayer"; "There Is Sunlight on the Hilltop"; "There's a Land That Is Fairer Than Day"; "We Have Heard"; "We Speak of the Realms"; "When I Survey the Wondrous Cross"; and "You Will See Your Lord a-Coming."

In 1845 William Hyde was present when young Ellen Harmon received a vision of heaven. After listening to her description of its glories, Hyde wrote "We Have Heard," the oldest distinctively Adventist hymn. Ellen White continued singing it the remainder of her life. A few weeks before her death, family and staff gathered around Ellen White's bed at her Elmshaven home to sing hymns to close the Sabbath. When someone started singing "Sweet By and By," Ellen White's lips whispered the words as she anticipated singing with the angelic choir in heaven.

Further reading: Ella M. (White) Robinson, "Hymns Ellen White Loved" (EGWE, SDoc).

James R. Nix

HYPNOTISM AND MESMERISM. The practice of inducing a sleeplike state characterized by heightened susceptibility to suggestion, popularized by F. A. Mesmer (1734-1815), an Austrian physician. "Mesmerism" was originally a general term for *all* of Mesmer's psychological theories. Later, as hypnosis became the most famous of his theories, "mesmerism" came to mean simply "hypnosis." Although opponents of early Sabbatarian Adventists (c. 1845-1852) sometimes attributed the Adventists' spiritual exercises, and Ellen White's visions, to mesmerism (EW 21, 108, 109; 2SG 57; 1T 71), Ellen White vigorously opposed all such practices of mind control, considering them to be forms of spiritualism (LS 83, 133; 2SG 46-48; 5BC 1081; 2SM 349, 350). She claimed that *phrenology and mesmerism were methods invented by Satan to possess minds (2SM 352), place them under his control (1T 297), deceive, and destroy faith in God and Scripture (*ibid.* 296).

One early statement in 1862 apparently reflects the changing meaning of "mesmerism" in popular usage. "Phrenology and mesmerism are very much exalted," she wrote. "They are good in their place, but they are seized upon by Satan as his most powerful agents to deceive and destroy souls" (*ibid.*). The phrase "good in their place" evidently refers to the early meaning of "mesmerism" as a forerunner of modern psychology. Twenty years later she repeated the thought, but in slightly different words: "The *sciences which treat of the human mind* are very much exalted. They are good in their place; but they are seized upon by Satan as his powerful agents to deceive and destroy souls. His arts are accepted as from heaven, and he thus receives the worship which suits him well. The world, which is supposed to be benefited so much by phrenology and animal magnetism, never was so corrupt as now. Through these sciences, virtue is destroyed, and the foundations of spiritualism are laid" (ST, Nov. 6, 1884, in 2SM 352; italics supplied). "The advantage he [Satan] takes of the sciences, sciences which pertain to the human mind, is tremendous. Here, serpentlike, he imperceptibly creeps in to corrupt the work of God" (ST, Nov. 6, 1884, in 2SM 351).

Ellen White believed that as the second coming of Christ drew nearer, the power of minds controlling other minds would become a dangerous method used by Satan to carry out his designs (1T 290; 8T 294). She wrote, "It is not God's purpose that any human being should yield his mind and will to the control of another, becoming a passive instrument in his hands. No one is to merge his individuality in that of another. . . . His dependence must be in God" (MH 242). She added, "The theory of mind controlling mind was originated by Satan, to introduce himself as the chief worker, to put human philosophy where divine philosophy should be. Of all the errors that are finding acceptance among professedly Christian people, none is a more dangerous deception, none more certain to separate man from God, than this. Innocent though it may appear, if exercised upon patients it will tend to their destruction, not to their restoration. It opens a door through which Satan will enter to take possession both of the mind that is given up to be controlled by another, and of the mind that controls" (*ibid.* 243). While temporary relief might be experienced, the mind would be forever weakened. As such, mesmerism and hypnotism should be rejected and regarded with fear. They should never be brought into any Adventist institution (MM 116), and should be resisted in all forms (*ibid.* 110).

Ellen White linked hypnotism and mesmerism with Christian Science, Theosophy, and Eastern religions (PK 210) as forms of spiritualism. Though their claimed power to heal is attributed to *electricity, magnetism, or "sympathetic remedies," they are actually channels through which Satan casts his spell over the bodies and souls of humanity (PK 211; 5T 193).

While White was deeply opposed to hypnotism and all related practices that claimed to awaken the imagined latent forces within humans, she was not opposed to all methods of mind cure. Instead, she called on physicians to educate patients to look from the human to the divine. Patients should look to God for true healing of the mind, recognizing that such healing cannot come from within (MM 112, 116). The true science of mind cure is to be found in the One who gives genuine rest through salvation, restoration, and a living faith in a divine Savior (*ibid.* 117; cf. ML 176).

See also: Mind and Body; Phrenology.

Further reading: Ev 606-609; MH 241-259; MYP 57, 58; 2SM 349-353; 1T 296-300.

Michael D. Pearson

ICEBERG VISION. Vision of early October 1903 that called Ellen White to confront the "pantheism" connected with J. H. Kellogg's book *The Living Temple*. Prompted by the vision, White wrote from Elmshaven two letters that had a pivotal effect on the General Conference autumn council of 1903. Fully occupied with issues related to establishing denominational headquarters, a publishing house, sanitarium, and college in Washington, D.C., the council agenda did not include *The Living Temple,* but near the midpoint of the two-week council the topic came up anyway.

After an intense but inconclusive discussion on October 13, David Paulson, a leading Adventist physician, accompanied General Conference president A. G. Daniells from the meeting, arguing for the correctness of the views in *The Living Temple.* "As we stood under a streetlamp," Daniells later recalled, "he said to me, 'You are making the mistake of your life. After all this turmoil, some of these days you will wake up to find yourself rolled in the dust, and another will be leading the forces.'" To this Daniells replied, "I do not believe your prophecy. At any rate, I would rather be rolled in the dust doing what I believe in my soul to be right than to walk with princes, doing what my conscience tells me is wrong" (Daniells, pp. 336, 337).

Arriving home that night, Daniells found two letters from E. G. White. When he read them to the council the next morning, the debate of the previous day turned into a season of thanksgiving that continued the rest of the morning. Paulson, who was present, later reported how those two letters impacted him. "In spite of the 'new light' that I had received [from Kellogg] regarding the testimonies, I had enough spiritual sense left to appreciate that there was something in that testimony that would have to be reckoned with either in time or eternity, so I stepped to a long-distance telephone and rang up Dr. Kellogg in Battle Creek and asked him to come down. After he arrived the following evening, he and I spent a good share of the night in the New Willard hotel earnestly seeking God for wisdom and for light, and it was during this experience that there came from Dr. Kellogg's lips one of those brilliant flashes of truth which I had so often heard him enunciate in other great crises and perplexities on other questions.

"He said, 'Doctor [Paulson], this talk of the "human side" of the Testimonies has been a snare to us. No doubt there is a human side to the Testimonies, but with all that there is so much more divinity in the Testimonies than there is in us, that God will never permit us feeble mortals to show up or point out this human side. A weaker thing can never destroy a stronger thing. We must treat whatever comes from that source with the highest respect and seek God for wisdom how to apply it to our lives and our course.'

"I saw in an instant that he had enunciated correct principles of how to relate ourselves to the Testimonies, and I told him gratefully, 'Doctor [Kellogg], you have given me light, light that I needed'" (Moon, p. 300, number 2).

Kellogg himself was moved to tell the council on October 18 that he would revise the book and "work in harmony with the General Conference." In circular letters to "all" his "medical missionary colleagues," he tactfully confessed he had made some fundamental mistakes in his career and now desired to work in the "capacity of a servant." His change of attitude was transient, however (*ibid.,* pp. 300, 301).

Following the close of the autumn council, Daniells and Prescott attended the session of the Atlantic Union Conference at South Lancaster, Massachusetts. While there Daniells received another letter from Ellen G. White revealing the basis of her previous two letters. This account of the "iceberg vision" became a major point of reference for Daniells and Prescott during the next four years.

"Shortly before I sent the testimonies that you said arrived just in time," Ellen White wrote to Daniells, "I had read an incident about a ship in a fog meeting an iceberg. For several nights I slept but little. I seemed to be bowed down as a cart beneath sheaves. One night a scene was clearly presented before me. A vessel was upon the waters, in a heavy fog. Suddenly the lookout cried, 'Iceberg just ahead!' There, towering high above the ship, was a gigantic iceberg. An authoritative voice cried out, 'Meet it!' There was not a moment's hesitation. It was a time for instant action. The engineer put on full steam, and the man at the wheel steered the ship straight into the iceberg. With a crash she struck the ice. There was a fearful shock, and the iceberg broke into many pieces, falling with a noise like thunder upon the deck. The passengers were violently shaken by the force of the collision, but no lives were lost. The vessel was injured, but not beyond repair. She rebounded from the contact, trembling from stem to stern, like a living creature. Then she moved forward on her way.

"Well I knew the meaning of this representation. I had my orders. I had heard the words, like a living voice from our Captain, 'Meet it!' I knew what my duty was, and that there was not a moment to lose. The time for decided action had come. I must without delay obey the command, 'Meet it!'

"This is why you received the testimonies when you did. That night I was up at one o'clock, writing as fast as my hand could pass over the paper.

"We have all stood at our posts like faithful sentinels, working early and late to send to the council instruction that we thought would help you" (Lt 238, 1903, in 5Bio 301; Moon, pp. 301, 302).

"I do not think you will ever be able to know," Daniells wrote to W. C. White, "what great relief these communications from your mother bring to us. We have been under a strain of anxiety and perplexity that cannot be described" (AGD to WCW, Nov. 20, 1903, in Moon, p. 302). The uncertainty among denominational leaders, including Ellen White, over how to "meet the iceberg" aggressively led to a further confrontation at the *Berrien Springs Meeting of 1904.

See also: Visions of Ellen G. White.

Further reading: 5Bio 294-302, 332; A. G. Daniells, *The Abiding Gift of Prophecy* (PPPA, 1936), pp. 336, 337; J. Moon, *W. C. White and Ellen G. White* (AUP, 1993), pp. 297-302, 304-306, 371-375.

Jerry Moon

IMAGE OF GOD, see **HUMAN NATURE**.

IMPENDING CONFLICT, THE (PPPA, 1960, 127 pp.). Booklet made up of a selection and abridgment of 10 of the last 14 chapters of Ellen White's *The Great Controversy* and used for distribution by Adventist media organizations.

IN HEAVENLY PLACES (RHPA, 1967, 382 pp.). Eighth daily devotional book published by the Ellen G. White Estate. Materials selected for this book were drawn largely from Ellen White's unpublished and out-of-print books at the time of publication. No monthly themes guided the selection of materials other than to provide admonition, encouragement, and instruction, enabling Christians on their journey to the kingdom of God to daily dwell by faith "in heavenly places" (Eph. 1:3).

INDEBTEDNESS, see **DEBT; FINANCES OF ELLEN G. WHITE**.

INDEPENDENT MINISTRIES, see **SELF-SUPPORTING WORK**.

INDEXES TO THE WRITINGS OF ELLEN G. WHITE. Reference works to the published writings of Ellen White. The first such works, *Index to the Scripture References and Quotations Contained in the Writings of Mrs. E. G. White,* was published in 1896. This 114-page index is limited to Scripture references found in Ellen White's writings in print in the mid-1890s. Clifton L. Taylor's *Outline Studies From the Testimonies,* published in 1911, also served as an early index to Ellen White's writings. The third edition, published in 1918, contained 221 pages of references to 127 topics and a Scripture index (cf. ST, Dec. 23, 1919). By the fifth edition in 1955, this index had grown to 480 pages. Another index, compiled by Mary Steward and H. A. Washburn, *Scriptural and Subject Index to the Writings of Ellen G. White,* was published in 1926. A 112-page supplement was added to the index in 1942. This 864-page volume covered the 28 books then available and consisted of a scriptural index, in which are given the references to all the Scripture texts quoted and to many commented on, and a subject index arranged alphabetically.

In 1954 the White Estate decided to work on a new comprehensive index, which would include close to 50 available books (as of 1958) and the supplement sections to the seven volumes of *The Seventh-day Adventist Bible Commentary.* This three-volume work, *Comprehensive Index to the Writings of Ellen G. White,* published in 1962-1963, totals 3,216 pages, and consists of a scriptural index (vol. 1, pp. 21-1760), a topical index (vol. 1, p. 177-vol. 3, p. 3104), and a quotation index (vol. 3, pp. 3105-3176). A few appendixes are also included. A fourth volume was added to this set in 1992 and covers previously unindexed portions of 27 books and booklets, most of which had been published since 1958. This fourth volume, consisting of a Scripture index and a topical index, brought the total number of pages to 4251.

Following the facsimile publication in the 1960s and 1970s of Ellen White's periodical articles, the White Estate decided to publish in 1977 a *Subject Index to the Ellen G. White Periodical Articles.* This index includes references to her articles in the *Review and Herald, *Signs of the Times, *Youth's Instructor, *General Conference Bulletin, *Health Reformer,* and a few other miscellaneous sources. A *Scripture Index to the Review and Herald Articles by Ellen G. White* was published in 1978. Other research aids and resources are available in most Ellen G. White research centers or branch offices. These resources include chronological and numerical lists of Ellen White's letters and manuscripts, correspondence sent to Ellen White, and a biography file of her daily activities. The most useful research tool is the *CD-ROM of *The Published Writings of Ellen G. White on Compact Disc,* including the multimedia disc *Legacy of Light.*

Denis Fortin

INERRANCY AND INFALLIBILITY, see **REVELATION AND INSPIRATION.**

INSPIRATION, see **REVELATION AND INSPIRATION.**

INSPIRATION, DEGREES OF. From their Millerite beginnings, Seventh-day Adventists have strongly defended the divine inspiration of Scripture against outside critical challenges. However, in the 1880s an internal crisis regarding the nature and authority of Ellen White's writings raised the issue of degrees of inspiration. Administrative problems and conflicts of personality at Battle Creek College led Ellen White to send testimonies of reproof to Uriah Smith, then editor of the *Review and Herald* and president of the college board.

Perhaps not unrelated was Smith's wrestling with what would now be called the relationship between *"revelation" and "inspiration." He questioned whether all of Ellen White's writings were equally inspired. In 1883 Smith became convinced that while her "visions" were truly inspired, her "testimonies" were not. It seems that in order to harmonize such a problematic position George I. Butler, then General Conference president, wrote a series of 10 articles for the *Review and Herald* in which he sought to provide a rationale for a theory of "degrees of inspiration" in the Bible. (These articles were published in 1884 on January 8, 15, 22, 29; February 5; April 15, 22; May 6, 27; and June 3.) If Butler could demonstrate that the Bible contained human elements, then the implication was that the *Testimonies* would contain many more and could not be regarded as absolutely trustworthy. Butler proposed that inspiration varies according to various forms of revelation. Since Scripture resulted from different forms of revelation, Butler also assumed different degrees of inspiration, of authority, and of imperfection in the Bible. The resulting hierarchy elevated the books of Moses and the words of Christ to the highest level, the writings of the prophets and apostles and some portions of the Psalms to the second level, the historical books to the third level, while Proverbs, Ecclesiastes, the Song of Songs, and the book of Job were relegated to the lowest level. Butler even pointed out some specific Bible passages that he felt could hardly be inspired at all. His ideas were so influential that they may have contributed to the distrust of Ellen White's testimony by some delegates to the *General Conference session of 1888 (1888 Materials 1564).

Ellen White waited five years to respond, hoping that Butler would correct his wrong position, but when others began to promote it at Battle Creek College, she wrote: "Both in the [Battle Creek] Tabernacle and in the college the subject of inspiration has been taught, and finite men have taken it upon themselves to say that some things in the Scriptures were inspired and some were not. I was shown that the Lord did not inspire the articles on inspiration published in the *Review,* neither did He approve their endorsement before our youth in the college. When men venture to criticize the Word of God, they venture on sacred, holy ground, and had better fear and tremble and hide their wisdom as foolishness. God sets no man to pronounce judgment on His Word, selecting some things as inspired and discrediting others as uninspired. The testimonies have been treated in the same way; but God is not in this" (1SM 23).

Ellen White believed that what the Bible writers wrote originated in God. Therefore "every part of the Bible is given by inspiration of God" (CT 462; cf. 2 Tim. 3:16; 2 Peter 1:21). "The Holy Ghost is the author of the Scriptures and of the Spirit of Prophecy" (3SM 30). Either those writings are the product of inspiration or they are not. Either prophets are genuine and have the spirit from above, or they are false prophets and have a spirit from beneath (5T 671, 64-67). Even prophets who wrote none of the Bible (Agabus, Deborah, Elijah, Elisha, Enoch, Huldah, Miriam), enjoyed the same authority as other canonical prophets of their time.

Ellen White rejected any grading of the biblical material that relegates some portions as less inspired. She warns those who "in measuring by their finite rule that which is inspired and that which is not inspired" "have stepped before Jesus to show Him a better way than He has led us" (1SM 17). She bemoans that "some sit in judgment on the Scriptures, declaring that this or that passage is not inspired. . . . Others for different reasons question portions of the Word of God. Thus many walk blindly where the enemy prepares the way. Now, it is not the province of any man to pronounce sentence upon the Scriptures, to judge or condemn any portion of God's Word.... When a man feels so very wise that he dares to dissect God's Word, his wisdom is . . . counted foolishness" (*ibid.* 42). She maintained the same position with regard to her own writings (3SM 68-70). "My work . . . bears the stamp of God or the stamp of the enemy. There is no halfway work in the matter. The *Testimonies* are of the Spirit of God, or of the devil" (5T 671).

In prophetic writing there are no degrees of inspiration, neither in the Bible nor with Ellen White. According to Ellen White, no one has the liberty to dissect her writings by claiming that "God has given you ability to discern what is light from heaven and what is the expression of mere human wisdom" (*ibid.* 691). At the same time, Ellen White was keenly aware of the distinction between the "sacred" and the "common," everyday topics in what she wrote (cf. 1SM 38, 39; 3SM 59, 60; 5T 658).

There is no indication in Scripture or in the writings of Ellen White that allows for any concept of partial inspiration or degrees of inspiration. To categorize prophetic writings by degrees of inspiration inevitably leads to a canon within the canon, which leaves some portions devoid of full divine authority. The idea of degrees of inspiration elevates the human interpreter above the inspired text, and obliterates the authority of God's Word as the final norm for faith and practice.

Further reading: J. H. Burry, "An investigation to Determine Ellen White's Concepts of Revelation, Inspiration, 'The Spirit of Prophecy,' and Her Claims About the Origin, Production and Authority of her Writings" (M.A. thesis, AU, 1991); H. E. Douglass, *Messenger of the*

Lord (PPPA, 1998), pp. 409, 410; A. R. Timm, "A History of SDA Views on Biblical and Prophetic Inspiration," JATS 10, no. 1-2 (1999): 486-542; P. M. van Bemmelen, "Revelation and Inspiration," in R. Dederen, ed., *Handbook of Seventh-day Adventist Theology*, (RHPA, 2000), pp. 22-57.

Frank M. Hasel

INSTITUTIONS, ELLEN WHITE'S ROLE IN ESTABLISHING. Most of the medical, educational, publishing, and other institutions of the Seventh-day Adventist Church are traceable directly or indirectly to the counsels of Ellen G. White. She influenced the founding of institutions in at least four ways. First, she repeatedly called for a specific institution to meet an immediate need, often on the basis of a *vision. Second, she made general calls for the church to develop additional institutions as needed to extend the work of the church. Third, she was willing to move forward on borrowed money when she believed the opportunity justified it. Fourth, when she had helped start an institution, she did everything humanly possible to ensure that it would succeed. She typically remained in contact with such institutions for years, giving counsel, public promotion, and financial support.

One of her earliest counsels leading to establishment of an institution was given at the *Sabbatarian conference in Dorchester, Massachusetts, in 1848. Coming out of vision, she said to her husband: "I have a message for you. You must begin to print a little paper and send it out to the people. Let it be small at first; but as the people read, they will send you means with which to print, and it will be a success from the first. From this small beginning it was shown to me to be like streams of light that went clear round the world" (LS 125). James White accepted that counsel and began a little paper titled *Present*

Truth, which later merged with a second paper, the *Advent Review*, to form the *Second Advent Review and Sabbath Herald*. The "little paper," which soon necessitated the first Adventist publishing house, is still published under the name *Adventist Review*. Other institutions established as the result of direct counsel include the *Health Reform Institute, which became the *Battle Creek Sanitarium (1T 485, 489); *Battle Creek College (FE 285); *Signs of the Times* and *Pacific Press; *St. Helena Sanitarium; *Avondale College; the *Glendale and Paradise Valley sanitariums; *Loma Linda Sanitarium and the *College of Medical Evangelists; and many others.

Second, based on these successful patterns, she made general calls for the church to establish similar ones adapted to the needs of new territories. For example, in 1874, just 14 years after the organization of the first publishing house, she wrote, "I have been shown that our publications should be printed in different languages and sent to every civilized country, at any cost. What is the value of money at this time, in comparison with the value of souls? Every dollar of our means should be considered as the Lord's, not ours; and as a precious trust from God to us; not to be wasted for needless indulgences, but carefully used in the cause of God, in the work of saving men and women from ruin" (*True Missionary*, Jan. 1, 1874, in LS 214). Many similar exhortations furnished the impetus for institutional development throughout the world.

One of the most striking examples of Ellen White's philosophy of institutional finance is the purchase of Loma Linda Sanitarium, now the Loma Linda University Medical Center. On reading *John Burden's description of the Loma Linda property, she delegated him to purchase it immediately. When church leaders, fearing debt, opposed the plan, she charged

Burden, "Secure the property by all means, . . . and then obtain all the money you can and make sufficient payments to hold the place." To calm his anxiety, she made this telling statement: "Be assured, my brother, that I never advise anything unless I have a decided impression that it should be carried out, and unless I am firmly resolved to assist" (LLM 2).

Ellen White was willing to start or purchase institutions on borrowed money when (1) the enterprise was essential to the church's mission (often verified through vision), (2) a unique opportunity needed to be grasped immediately, and (3) she believed that by aggressive promotion it could be paid for in due time. When these factors came together, she felt that the risk of indebtedness was preferable to the risk of delay. For example, the Loma Linda Hotel represented an investment of $155,000 offered for $40,000, and White wrote to Burden, "We will do our utmost to help you raise the money. I know that Redlands and Riverside are to be worked, and I pray that the Lord may be gracious, and not allow anyone else to get this property instead of us" (*ibid.*).

Fourth, when they had started a project, the Whites did everything humanly possible to ensure that the enterprise would succeed. They put all available resources—time, energy, personal funds, and influence—into every project they were involved with. For instance, in launching Avondale College, she called for the establishment of a school, participated in the choice of land and the campaign to pay for it, moved to the property and lived in a tent while school buildings and her own house were being built, and continued to give frequent counsels for the next five years until her return to the United States. Arthur White documents some 13 incidents during the Australian years in which Ellen White advanced the mission of the church by personal donations or by loans. She often served "as a bank to the cause" by borrowing from individuals (who trusted her more than they trusted the church as a creditor) so that she could in turn lend the same funds to the conference (4Bio 266, cf. 44, 45, 69, 105, 162, 183, 193, 235, 269, 305, 370, 408).

Ellen White never lost interest in the institutions she helped to bring into existence. When through mismanagement or misfortune they came into financial straits, she repeatedly lent her influence to rally support and restore financial viability. In 1900, more than 25 years after the founding of Battle Creek College, the school had sunk into debt. To remove that debt, and the debt of many other church schools, she donated the royalties on her new book, *Christ's Object Lessons, and enlisted students, *colporteurs, and church members to sell the book. In this way more than $300,000 was raised for Adventist schools (5Bio 92, 200). In 1905 she made a similar donation of *The Ministry of Healing* for reducing debts on Adventist health-care institutions. Thus as a mother she stood by her institutional children. In retrospect she recognized that her "life work" had been "closely intermingled" with the history of Adventist "enterprises" and "institutions," for which both she and her husband had "labored with pen and voice" (LS 196).

Further reading: J. Moon, *W. C. White and E. G. White* (AUP, 1993), pp. 211-213.

Jerry Moon

INSURANCE. Much discussion occurred earlier among Seventh-day Adventists concerning whether Christians should purchase insurance plans for protection against loss, particularly life insurance. Many felt that the purchase of life insurance was incompatible with a full trust in God's providence for one's life.

While much of the early discussion among Adventists dealt with a rejection of insurance of all kinds, slowly a change of attitude developed as the denomination began to acquire more properties and as the risks of losing property by fire or storm increased. Ellen White accepted to insure her properties in order to safeguard them against possible loss and instructed her son W. C. White to make sure her house was insured (Lt 17, 1880).

Life insurance, however, was seen in a different light, and her 1867 testimony on the subject influenced the denomination for many years. "Sabbathkeeping Adventists should not engage in life insurance," she wrote. "This is a commerce with the world which God does not approve" (1T 549). "Life insurance is a worldly policy which leads our brethren who engage in it to depart from the simplicity and purity of the gospel" (*ibid.* 550). She believed, the best life insurance policy is the assurance given to the Christian that eternal life is secure in Christ (RH, May 26, 1904). After counseling a worker in Australia to give up his life insurance policy, she wrote him that "the assurance of heaven is the best life insurance policy you can possibly have. The Lord has promised His guardianship in this world, and in the world to come, He has promised to give us immortal life" (Lt 21, 1893). A review of such statements from Ellen White indicates that life insurance, as it was practiced in her day, was a practice contrary to Christian principles. Her counsels, however, should be understood within the context of the fraudulent practices of insurance companies in her lifetime, which were largely unregulated by law, and of the popular practice of purchasing life insurance, like a lottery ticket, on persons thought to be near death, so as to profit when they died.

Although she rejected the need for life insurance, Ellen White repeatedly counseled people to make sure they could provide for themselves and their family members in case of emergencies. "Had you and your wife understood it to be a duty that God enjoined upon you," she wrote to a church member, "to deny your taste and your desires, and make provision for the future instead of living merely for the present, . . . your family [could] have had the comforts of life" (2T 432, 433). Providing for the future of one's family is an obligation Christians should always keep in mind (AH 395-398).

As the insurance industry became closely regulated by government, and many former practices prohibited, the purchase of life insurance became respected as a legitimate business. Consequently, many Adventists today believe that insurance policies, including life insurance, offer a reasonably priced provision for meeting life's emergencies.

Further reading: "Seventh-day Adventists and Life Insurance: Background of the Issue" (GC, 1985, EGWE, SDoc); F. M. Wilcox, "Life Insurance," DF 516.

Denis Fortin

INTERNATIONAL MEDICAL MISSIONARY AND BENEVOLENT ASSOCIATION (1893-1904). Legal corporation founded in 1893 under the name Medical Missionary and Benevolent Association, renamed International Medical Missionary and Benevolent Association in 1896. The aim of the association was to promote the medical activities of the denomination and to hold the properties of the church's medical and charitable enterprises. Although the association was intended to be a holding corporation for several Adventist sanitariums and other institutions, in practice it became a consultative body with a constituency composed of the General Conference committee, presidents of local conferences,

several individuals appointed to two-year terms by the General Conference in session, all donors of $1,000 or more to its treasury, and delegates from the various sanitariums and subsidiary organizations. On the administrative side, it became the employing agency for Adventist *medical missionaries. Dr. *J. H. Kellogg was the prime mover and president of the organization for many years. Ellen White wrote several letters to the leaders of the International Medical Missionary and Benevolent Association and on several occasions met with them (Lts 76, 157, 1902; Lts 54, 256, 1903). The organization was eventually replaced by the Medical Department of the General Conference in 1905 after the church restructured its organization (at the *General Conference sessions of 1901 and 1903) and Kellogg left the denomination.

Further reading: SDA Encyclopedia (1996), vol. 10, p. 787.

INTERPRETATION OF ELLEN G. WHITE'S WRITINGS. Reading Ellen White's counsels is one thing; understanding them is another. She herself was well aware of the fact that her writings needed to be interpreted. And over the years she gave some guiding principles of interpretation, often in connection with those who were misusing her works and doing injury to the church and its members.

Some might question the need for interpretation. But not Ellen White. She never, for example, urged people who had wayward thoughts to actually pluck out their right eye (see Matt. 5:29). All of us interpret such statements. We all utilize interpretive principles, whether we consciously recognize that fact or not. The following list of interpretative principles are some of the most important for an accurate understanding of Ellen White's writings.

1. *Focus on the central issues.* A person

can read Ellen White's writings in at least two ways. One is to look for her central themes; the other is to search for those things that are new and different. The first way leads toward an accurate understanding, while the second leads toward distortion of the author's meaning and often toward extremes that Ellen White detested. She herself advocated in Bible study that readers seek to "gain a knowledge" of the Bible's "grand central theme" (Ed 190). For her that theme was the plan of redemption and the great controversy between good and evil. "Viewed in the light" of the great central theme of the Bible "every topic has a new significance" (*ibid.* 125).

In short, her counsel was to read for an understanding of the big picture, which then provides the context for interpreting all other issues in terms of both meaning and importance. That principle applies equally to the Bible and Ellen White's writings.

2. *Emphasize the important.* Back in the early twentieth century when some church leaders were using her writings combatively to substantiate certain prophetic points that she believed were of minor importance, she wrote that "the enemy of our work is pleased when a subject of minor importance can be used to divert the minds of our brethren from the great questions that should be the burden of our message" (1SM 164, 165).

3. *Account for problems in communication.* Communication is not as simple as we might at first suspect. Part of the problem, Ellen White wrote in relation to Bible study, is that "human minds vary. The minds of different education and thought receive different impressions of the same words, and it is difficult for one mind to give to one of a different temperament, education, and habits of thought by language exactly the same idea as that which is clear and distinct in his own mind" (*ibid.* 19). It is human differences, she asserted,

that supply the necessity for four different Gospels and the writings of Paul and the other New Testament writers. "Not all comprehend things in exactly the same way" and God wanted to maximize His opportunity of reaching all (CT 432).

James White recognized the problems caused by communication in his wife's work. He wrote in 1868 that at times she makes strong appeals, "which a few feel deeply, and take strong positions, and go to extremes." As a result of those extremes "she is obliged to come out with reproofs for extremists in a public manner" (RH, Mar. 17, 1868; cf. 2Bio 301, 302). Such verbal maneuvering was a necessity, but it sometimes leaves readers with the impression that she is contradicting herself.

At the very least the facts presented in this section ought to make us cautious in our reading. We will want to make sure that we have read widely what Ellen White has presented on a topic, and study those statements that may seem extreme in the light of those that might moderate or balance them.

4. *Study all available information on a topic.* Arthur White pinpointed the issue when he wrote that "many have erred in interpreting the meaning of the testimonies by taking isolated statements or statements out of their context as a basis for belief. Some do this even though there are other passages, which, if carefully considered, would show the position taken on the basis of the isolated statement to be untenable" (*Ellen G. White: Messenger to the Remnant*, p. 88).

5. *Avoid extreme interpretations.* By not following the advice Ellen White gave during her lifetime, some individuals re-create her in their own extremist image. In her own life she tended toward a moderation that is sadly lacking in some who claim to be her faithful followers. For example, some utilize a

statement in which Ellen White frowned upon ball playing to condemn all such games, whereas she herself wrote that "I do not condemn the simple exercise of playing ball; but this, even in its simplicity, may be overdone" (AH 499). As in so many situations, Ellen White was a moderate rather than an extremist.

6. *Take time and place into consideration.* Because of change across time and space, it is important to understand the historical context of many of Ellen White's counsels. One only has to think of her counsel to mid-nineteenth-century women to shorten their dresses eight inches (20 centimeters). One could hardly use that quotation as if she had written it in the era of the miniskirt. "Regarding the testimonies," Ellen White wrote, "nothing is ignored; nothing is cast aside; but time and place must be considered" (1SM 57). She repeatedly offered that counsel throughout her ministry.

7. *Study each statement in its literary context.* People have too often based their understandings of Ellen White's teachings upon a fragment of a paragraph or an isolated statement entirely removed from its setting. Speaking of the misuse of her writings by some, she wrote that "they quote half a sentence," they leave "out the other half, which, if quoted, would show their reasoning to be false" (3SM 82). Again she comments about those who by "separating . . . statements from their connection and placing them beside human reasonings make it appear that my writings uphold that which they condemn" (Lt 208, 1906, in MR760 28).

8. *Recognize Ellen White's understandings of the ideal and the real.* Ellen White often provided counsel on the same topic on two levels. The first can be thought of as the ideal. At this level we find hard-and-fast utterances that allow of no exceptions. Examples of this first level are her counsel relating to the ideal that parents should be the "only teachers of their children until they have reached eight or ten years of age" (3T 137) and her counsel that schools in all locations and places must be "separated a wide distance from the cities" (FE 312). Such statements represent the ideal.

On the other hand, when she dealt with situations in the everyday world she often moderated her counsel to fit the needs of real people with real limitations. Thus she moderated her counsel on parents being the "only" teachers by claiming that that ideal could hold "if" parents were both able and willing to do the job. If not, young children should be sent to school (3SM 215-217). Likewise, she toned down her strong counsel on the location of schools when the church began to make converts among the urban poor. "In the cities there are many children who could not attend schools away from the cities; and for the benefit of these, schools should be opened in the cities as well as in the country" (9T 201).

Ellen White never lost her sense of the ideal, but she was ready to moderate her counsel to meet situations in the real world. One of the plagues of her life were those who collected only the ideal statements and then sought to "drive them upon every one, and disgust rather than win souls" (3SM 286).

9. *Use common sense.* Quotations from Ellen White do not solve every problem. Sometimes they just don't fit. When problems came up because some people pushed her statement (mentioned above in point 8) about parents being the only teachers of their children until 8 or 10 years of age, she responded by claiming that "God desires us to deal with these problems sensibly" (*ibid.* 215).

She went on to note that she was stirred up by those who took the attitude that "Sister White has said so and so, and Sister White has said so and so; and therefore we are going right up to it." Her response to such people was that "God wants us all to have common sense, and He wants us to reason from common sense. Circumstances alter conditions. Circumstances change the relation of things" (*ibid.* 217). Her advice was that her readers needed to use common sense even though they might have a quotation from her on the topic.

10. *Discover the underlying principles.* At the turn of the twentieth century Ellen White wrote that it would be well "if girls . . . could learn to harness and drive a horse" (Ed 216, 217). That was practiced in her day, but is of not much use today. However, the principle undergirding that counsel is very important today. That is, young women should be self-sufficient in transportation. Thus in our day they should be able to drive a car and change a tire. The exact specification of a counsel may change, but the underlying principles have lasting value.

11. *Avoid making the counsels prove things they were never intended to prove.* Some, for example, sought in her day to use her writings to prove historical facts. "Regarding Mother's writings," her son *W. C. White penned, "she has never wished our brethren to treat them as an authority on history. . . . When [*The Great Controversy*] was written, Mother never thought that the readers would take it as an authority on historical dates and use it to settle controversies, and she does not now feel that it ought to be used in that way" (WCW to S. N. Haskell, Oct. 31, 1912). At the end of that letter Ellen White appended a note saying, "I approve of the remarks made in this letter" and then signed her name. (See *historians, Ellen G. White's use of.)

Some readers of Ellen White have created endless difficulties for both themselves and the church by seeking to use her writings to prove things they were never intended to prove.

12. *Make sure Ellen White said it.* Many statements are attributed to Ellen White that she never made. The only safe course is to utilize those statements that can be found in her published works or statements from her unpublished writings that can be validated through one of the Ellen White research offices. Many have been led astray by statements attributed to her that she never made. (See *apocryphal visions and statements.)

Further reading: R. W. Coon, "Hermeneutics: Interpreting a Nineteenth-Century Prophet in the Space Age" (EGWE, SDoc); H. E. Douglass, *Messenger of the Lord* (PPPA, 1998), pp. 372-407; P. A. Gordon, "Hermeneutical Principles Bearing on the E. G. White Writings" (EGWE, SDoc); G. R. Knight, *Reading Ellen White: How to Understand and Apply Her Writings* (RHPA, 1997); "Helpful Points in the Interpretation and Use of the Ellen G. White Writings," *Comprehensive Index to the Writings of Ellen G. White,* vol. 3, pp. 3211-3216.

George R. Knight

INVESTIGATIVE JUDGMENT. A pre-Advent judgment of the professed people of God carried on by Christ in the heavenly sanctuary between 1844 and the final close of probation. The concept is derived from the integration of at least four basic teachings. First, in the context of the great cosmic controversy between good and evil, Satan accuses God of being biased in His relationship with humanity. For this reason God has to demonstrate before the universe His impartiality and justice in allowing some humans to be eternally destroyed and others to receive eternal life (Job 1:6-12; 2:1-6; Rev. 12:7-12). Second, human freedom of choice makes all human beings morally responsible before God and demands, therefore, a judgment even of the righteous (Matt. 22:11-14; 2 Cor. 5:10; Rev. 11:1). Third, the "resurrection of life" grants eternal life to all those who died in Christ, which implies that any judgment of the righteous has to take place prior to that resurrection reward (John 5:27-29; Rev. 22:11, 12). And, finally, the end-time cleansing of the sanctuary comprises a heavenly-court trial installed at the end of the 2300 symbolic evenings and mornings (Dan. 7:9-14; 8:9-14), which Adventists hold to have terminated on October 22, 1844.

The view of a pre-Advent judgment (cf. Rev. 14:7) was advocated within Millerism by Josiah Litch and George Storrs. Litch argued in 1842 that since the resurrection is the "separating process" of the judgment, a trial of the dead has to take place "in the invisible and spiritual world, before Jesus Christ comes in the clouds of heaven" (*Prophetic Expositions*, vol. 1, p. 51). Storrs added in early 1844 that a judgment has to occur "before the first resurrection" in order to make "known who should come up in that resurrection, and who [should] be left behind" (*Bible Examiner*, January 1844). Soon after the October 1844 disappointment a few other Millerite leaders (Enoch Jacobs, Apollos Hale, Joseph Turner, and even William Miller) suggested, at least for a short while, that a special judgment of God's people had begun in the heavenly courts (cf. Dan. 7:9-14) on October 22, 1844, preparing the way for the imminent second coming of Christ.

By 1845 the concept of an already-convened judgment of God's people vanished almost completely out of the former Millerite circles through an increasing denial that the 2300 evenings and mornings could have ended in 1844. Meanwhile, early Sabbatarian Adventists were strengthening their confidence that on October 22, 1844, Christ began a new phase of His priestly ministry in heaven. O.R.L. Crosier's article "The Law of Moses," published in the *Day-Star* Extra of February 7, 1846, convinced Joseph Bates, James White, Ellen G. Harmon, and several others of the biblical bases of Christ's two-phase priestly ministry in the heavenly sanctuary, setting the stage for the development of the Seventh-day Adventist doctrine of the sanctuary.

Thus the *concept* of a pre-Advent investigative judgment has been held by most Sabbatarian Adventists since the late 1840s. James White was an exception. At first he vigorously denied a pre-Advent judgment until at least the early 1850s (WLF 23, 24). But the *expression* "investigative judgment" appeared for the first time in a letter by Elon Everts (RH, Jan. 1, 1857). Four weeks later James White employed the same expression several times in his article "The Judgment" (RH, Jan. 29, 1857). Although Ellen White would begin to use that *expression* in her published writings only from the early 1880s (e.g., RH, Aug. 28, 1883), she espoused the *concept* much earlier.

Already her coming-of-the-Bridegroom vision (February 1845) endorsed the idea of a transition in Christ's heavenly ministry, in which He followed the Father into the Most Holy Place of the heavenly sanctuary to receive the "kingdom" (Dan. 7:9-14). This was theologically connected with His "wedding" (Matt. 25:1-13) and His ministry "before the Father" as "a great High Priest" in behalf of the saints (E. G. Harmon, "Letter From Sister Harmon," *Day-Star*, Mar. 14, 1846). This vision has been regarded as having "prepared people to accept the researches of Edson, Crosier, and Hahn" on the sanctuary (D. F. [Neufeld], "A Significant Early Vision," AR, Jan. 31, 1980). Ellen White's great controversy vision (March 1858) stated more explicitly that since 1844 the "judgment" was going on in the heavenly sanctuary, first "for the righteous dead, and then for the righteous living" (1SG 198).

Ellen White's most comprehensive treatments of the investigative judgment were published in the 1880s. In *The Spirit of Prophecy*, volume 4 (1884), she devoted a whole chapter to the topic (4SP 307-315). The content of that chapter was significantly revised and expanded for the 1888 edition of *The Great Controversy* (GC88 479-491) and retained with identical wording in the 1911 edition (GC 479-491). Another major exposition was published in *Testimonies for the Church*, volume 5, pages 467-476 (1885), and significantly revised in *Prophets and Kings*, pages 582-592 (1917). Several of her most significant statements on the subject were republished in the 1958 devotional book titled *The Faith I Live By* (FLB 206-212). Her last writing on the subject directly addressed the required condition for those whom Christ approves in the judgment. Christ says: "They may have imperfections of character; they may have failed in their endeavors; but they have repented, and I have forgiven and accepted them" (PK 589).

The pre-Advent investigative judgment is described in her writings as taking place in the Most Holy Place of the heavenly sanctuary and as being concerned only with the cases of "professed Christians." The standard of judgment is "the law of God" (cf. Eccl. 12:13, 14), and all cases are evaluated according to the records found in "the book of life" (Rev. 20:12), the "book of remembrance" (Mal. 3:16), and the record of human sin (cf. Dan. 7:10). Jesus is the "advocate" who pleads in behalf of His people. "When the investigative judgment closes, Christ will come, and His reward will be with Him to give to every man as his work shall be" (GC 485).

In 1884 Ellen White stated, in regard to the investigative judgment, that "soon—none

know how soon—it will pass to the cases of the living" (4SP 315; also GC 490). The emphasis of this statement is on the solemnity of the present eschatological time. It does not support the false assumption that once the name of someone living is considered in the heavenly courts, that person loses immediately his or her freedom of choice. The time of grace does not close for anyone while a chance remains to save them. God's decision in the judgment reflects the cumulative results of each individual's personal choices. "I saw," wrote Ellen White in 1849, "that Jesus would not [cease His intercession] until every case was decided" (EW 36). Thus probation will last for the living until it finally closes for the whole world shortly before Christ's second coming. But this should not lead anyone into procrastination (cf. Heb. 3:7-15; 4:6, 7). Ellen White points out that "while the investigative judgment is going forward in heaven, while the sins of penitent believers are being removed from the sanctuary, there is to be a special work of purification, of putting away of sin, among God's people upon earth" (GC 425).

Further reading: "The Integrity of the Sanctuary Truth" (MR 760, EGWE, SDoc); P. A. Gordon, *The Sanctuary, 1844, and the Pioneers* (RHPA, 1983); G. F. Hasel, "Divine Judgment," in R. Dederen, ed., *Handbook of Seventh-day Adventist Theology* (RHPA, 2000), pp. 815-856; F. B. Holbrook, ed., *Doctrine of the Sanctuary: A Historical Survey (1845-1863)* (BRI, 1989); G. R. Knight, *A Search for Identity* (RHPA, 2000), pp. 80, 81; W. H. Shea, *Selected Studies on Prophetic Interpretation* (BRI, 1982), pp. 1-24; R. W. Olson, "The Investigative Judgment in the Writings of E. G. White" (EGWE, SDoc); *idem, One Hundred and One Questions on the Sanctuary and on Ellen White* (EGWE, 1981, SDoc).

Alberto R. Timm

ISRAEL AND THE JEWISH PEOPLE. Ellen White's thinking about Israel and the Jews revolves around four main issues: (1) the rejection of God by Israel; (2) the rejection of Israel by God; (3) last-day prophecies about Israel and the Jews; and (4) the mission to the Jews.

To the first issue, whether Jews rejected God in crucifying Jesus, Ellen White gives a nuanced answer: It is especially the Jewish leaders (and not the Jewish people as a whole) who were first responsible for the Crucifixion (DA 618, 619; cf. COL 306), and who were therefore, as the husbandman of the parable of the vineyard, those who rejected "the Holy One of Israel" (COL 294). Ellen White infers, then, that the Jews of that time should be distinguished from their leaders. Although the people are bearing some responsibility in this iniquity, they are significantly characterized as misinformed and deceived by their leaders (*ibid.* 293). On the other hand, the Jewish leaders are blamed for having "made their choice" (*ibid.* 294), suggesting that the latter bore the primary guilt.

Second, for Ellen White, Israel has not been rejected: "Even though Israel rejected His Son, God did not reject them" (AA 375). And yet she also writes: "Through unbelief ... Israel as a nation [has] lost her connection with God" (*ibid.* 377).

The expression "as a nation" refers to the political entity with its theocratic claim, and not the Jews as individuals or as a corporate and a temporal entity (RH, Dec. 13, 1898).

This direction of interpretation is confirmed through an interesting semantic case concerning her negative use of the expression "race of the Jews" (1SG 106), which was changed 24 years later into "Jewish nation" (EW 212). Indeed, this correction suggests that the phrase "Jewish nation" refers to something other than the initial words "race of the Jews." For

the latter expression could be misunderstood, as it could point to the Jews as a corporate entity, that is, Jews of all times, in the past as well as in the future (we know indeed the confusion that the concept of "race" has generated).

Similarly, the cause of the divine curse is attributed essentially to the Jewish leaders. Thus Ellen White associates the doom of the "Jewish nation" with the wickedness of the Jewish leaders (COL 294, 295). She warns, however, that "the children were not condemned for the sins of the parents" (GC 28). For such a curse could not be effective as long as a "knowledge of all the light" is not presented to them (*ibid.*), a condition that is implied in the fact that for Ellen White the rejection of the law by Christians is as grave a sin as the rejection of Christ by the Jewish rulers (1SM 229).

She held that the crime of the Jewish leaders had consequences also in the past at the fall of Jerusalem as well as in the future on the day of judgment (DA 739). But for Ellen White, the historic suffering of the Jews was not instigated by God; it is instead the result of the wickedness of unconverted Christians and heathens (EW 212). She denounced "those professed Christians" who "thought that the more suffering they could bring upon them [the Jews], the better would God be pleased" (*ibid.* 212, 213).

Third, for Ellen White the Jewish people were not only "especially chosen of God as ... the keepers of His law, the depositaries of His sacred oracles" (Ms 91, 1894, in 7MR 333), but many from among the Jews will also play an active role in the future history of salvation. She predicts this on the basis of Hosea's prophecy that "many" Jews will be converted at the time of the end (PK 298; Ev 578, 579; RH, June 29, 1905). The fact that before this eschatological event the Jews are still called "His commandment-keeping people" (PK 299) suggests that for Ellen White the Jews as a people may have still a role to play in regard to the testimony of the Law.

Fourth, Ellen White found it "strange" that so few ministers feel the call to work for the Jews (6MR 326; AA 380, 381; Ev 578). She urges God's people to take a "particular interest in the Jewish people" (AA 381) and be more involved in this "special" ministry (6BC 1079; Ev 141).

In emphasizing the importance of the mission to the Jews, Ellen White proposed a set of recommendations on how to present the truth to them: (1) the need for "wisdom" (Ev 246); (2) a strategy of reconciliation and love, "not of rejection and contempt" (Ms 87, 1907); (3) an argumentation based on messianic prophecies (AA 221); (4) a progressive approach (Ev 246); (5) the need to involve "converted" Jews (Ev 579; Ms 66, 1905); (6) the distribution of literature (report by S. A. Kaplan, DF 35, CAR).

The texts of Ellen White on the Jews and Israel are to be handled with care, as she was approaching this issue mostly from a spiritual perspective, either homiletically to take lessons from past history, or prophetically within the framework of the time of the end. She addresses issues regarding specific Jewish individuals only incidentally, as she was exposed to converted Jews such as F. C. Gilbert or M. Lichtenstein. It is also important to realize how much her language reflected her historical situation: for instance when she used expressions such as "Old Jerusalem" (PT, Nov. 1, 1850) or "modern Israel" (2T 109) for spiritual and heavenly realities.

The way she confronted injustices against Jews and her frequent admonitions that the Jews should not be despised (6MR 323-330), in addition to her readiness to change her terminology to adjust to new meanings,

suggests that today, after the Holocaust, it is possible that she would likely express herself differently on some matters. Such an observation makes it imperative to interpret her writings in context, and should prevent a too literal and mechanical interpretation of her writings.

Further reading: J. B. Doukhan, *The Mystery of Israel* (RHPA, 2004); *idem, Israel and the Church: Two Voices for the Same God* (Peabody, Mass.: Hendrikson, 2002); R. Dederen, ed., *Handbook of Seventh-day Adventist Theology* (RHPA, 2000), pp. 543-545, 858-866.

Jacques B. Doukhan

ITALY. During her stay in Europe, Ellen White made three short visits to Italy. She first visited Torre Pellice on November 26, 1885, accompanied by her daughter-in-law Mary K. White, Augustine and Martha Bourdeau, and B. L. Whitney. She described Italy as a hard field with "honest people" living in poverty. The small company in Torre Pellice was struggling to obey God, being isolated and under pressure to abandon their Adventist beliefs. Ellen White encouraged them to walk "in the light, regardless of the opinions or course of the world" (EGWEur 141; MS 231), and preached 10 sermons on the "strait gate" and the Sabbath. Attacks from former Sabbathkeepers were another reason of discouragement among the Italian company. Even in the heart of these mountains Ellen White was followed by people who denigrated her work and calling. J. P. Malan interrupted her several times during her sermons demanding a yes-or-no answer on whether Sabbathkeeping was necessary for salvation. Miles Grant, an Advent Christian leader from the United States, held meetings in the same building, simultaneous with Ellen White's presentations, trying to convince people that her visions were not from God (EGWEur 141-144).

Ellen White also visited other places in the Piedmont valleys, climbing the mountains and exploring the caves where Waldensians lived and suffered for their faith during the Middle Ages. Impressed by the incredible sights from the tops of mountains, and feeling closer to God, she and her companions prayed that God would give them the same spirit of "true devotion and firm adherence to principle" that the Waldensians had manifested (HS 241).

Ellen White left the Italian valleys with mixed feelings—with appreciation for the history of those places and the honesty of their people, and with sorrow for their lack of desire to continue the heroic history of their predecessors. She made two more visits to the Waldensian valleys to speak to little Adventist congregations: April 15-29, 1886, with her son and his wife; and November 3-20, with William and Jenny Ings, on the way back to Basel after laboring two weeks at Nîmes, France. She also visited Milan and Turin on the way.

Further reading: Lt 28, 1885; 5MR 268-276; LS 281-290; HS 226-249; 3Bio 330-343; RH, June 1, 1886; *Ellen G. White in Europe* (RHPA, 1975), pp. 133-145, 175-180, 236-238.

Cristian Dumitrescu

JEROME OF PRAGUE (c. 1379-1416). Fifteenth-century Reformer in Bohemia, now the Czech Republic; disciple of *John Huss (Jan Hus). Jerome studied in Prague before going to Paris and Oxford, and returned from England with copies of several of *John Wycliffe's treatises. In Prague, Jerome was known more for his preaching than for writing. After Huss was condemned by the Council of Constance in

JEROME OF PRAGUE, EARLY PROTESTANT REFORMER AND FRIEND OF JOHN HUSS

1415, Jerome set out to Constance in an unsuccessful attempt to aid his master. He fled Constance, was tracked down, arrested, and imprisoned. Initially he recanted Huss' doctrines, but then repented of his recantation. He was accordingly condemned and burned to death on May 30, 1416.

Ellen White's initial writings on the early Reformation mentioned Jerome only briefly, in a single paragraph in volume 4 of *The Spirit of Prophecy* (p. 92), the 1884 edition of *The Great Controversy*. For the 1888 edition Ellen White expanded her account of Huss and Jerome considerably, spending 10 pages on Jerome alone (GC88 110-119). She drew a considerable portion of the historical details from Reformation historians J. A. Wylie (*The History of Protestantism*) and Émile de Bonnechose (*Reformers Before the Reformation*), as can be seen in the references in the 1911 edition (GC 110-119). Since space allowed only one chapter in the revised edition for Huss and Jerome, Ellen White had her literary assistant Marian Davis, in Basel, considerably shorten the original handwritten draft before forwarding it to Ellen White in England for final approval (3Bio 437, 439, 440). Ellen White's writing on Jerome concentrated on his spiritual experience during imprisonment, trial, recantation, repentance, and execution. She used him as an example of a Christian ultimately steadfast in the face of persecution.

Further reading: Paul P. Bernard, "Jerome of Prague, Austria, and the Hussites," *Church History* 27 (1958): 3-22.

Tony Zbaraschuk

JEWELRY, see **DRESS AND ADORNMENT**.

JEWS, see **ISRAEL AND THE JEWISH PEOPLE**.

JOHNSTOWN FLOOD. On June 1, 1889, the city of Johnstown, Pennsylvania, was destroyed after the South Fork Dam burst after many days of heavy rain. Twenty million tons (18 million metric tons) of water created a wall 60 feet (18.3 meters) high that crashed through the city of 30,000, killing thousands and devastating many homes and businesses.

Two days before, on Thursday, May 30, Ellen White had boarded a train at Battle Creek to keep a promise she had made to preach at the Williamsport, Pennsylvania, camp meeting. As she traveled she encountered much difficulty, but she resolved to stay aboard the train and go forward, trusting in God. In many places the rain had washed the tracks away, and the train had to stop while workers rebuilt the tracks. White and her secretary, Sara McEnterfer, who was accompanying her, had to wait at Canton, where the train could go no farther. The last 40 miles (65 kilometers) would be treacherous, but Ellen White was "determined to take no backward steps until we felt assured that it was all we could do" (RH, July 30, 1889). On Sunday morning, June 2, a man from Roaring Branch heard they were in Canton and came to meet them. He offered to take them in his horse-drawn carriage to Williamsport. Along the journey they met another man walking to Williamsport who joined their party. The two men, McEnterfer, and Ellen White (age 62 and a few weeks after a sprained ankle) traveled many miles by horse and carriage, by raft, and even on foot, reaching Williamsport on Wednesday, June 5, for the final days of the camp meeting. A journey that was to take two days by train ended up taking six days, including much walking and 17 miles (27 kilometers) of floating on a raft. She kept the promise she had made to "the brethren of Pennsylvania that if the Lord would give me strength, I would attend their camp meeting" (*ibid.*).

Further reading: 3Bio 429-431; E. Lantry, "Ellen White's Johnstown Flood Adventure," AR, Jan. 18, 1990; R. Peck, "Ellen G. White and the Johnstown Flood" (CAR).

Howard Krug

JOY. Ellen White understood joy to be a fruit of the Holy Spirit in a Christian's life (COL 68). Joy is central to the kingdom of God (TM 497) and is the norm for the unfallen universe (AH 548). It is the measure of character, both of Christ and of Christians (*ibid.* 535). It is therefore an evidence of conversion and will be reflected by those who are closest to Christ. She called on those suffering under difficult circumstances to trust God to use trial as a means of refining while holding on to their joy (CG 567), realizing that afflictions are often mercies in disguise (DG 223).

The joy that encourages pride and self-gratification is inappropriate (AH 514), but that which will not dissipate the mind or leave a sad afterinfluence to destroy self-respect or bar the way to usefulness is to be encouraged (*ibid.* 513). "Great rejoicing" is a characteristic of the redeemed (PK 558).

Joy originates with Christ (AH 513) and is learned through exposure to nature (CG 48) and home nurture (*ibid.* 525; AH 159). It is found when the Holy Spirit takes possession of the heart (DA 173; EW 55), in companionship with heavenly beings (DA 639), soul winning (COL 57, 58), service (MH 401), honest work (CTBH 98), obedience (CT 98), self-denial (*Confrontation*, p. 93), unselfish liberality (AA 342-344), and faithful stewardship (CS 136). Joy is also found in sharing in the sufferings of Christ (MB 30), wherever the love of God is cherished in the soul (AH 19) and the principles of the character of Christ are possessed (COL 298). Finally, it happens when true religion is practiced (CG 567), and departs when people attempt to keep the commandments from a sense of obligation

(COL 97). When fully experienced, joy brings healing and health (CH 587; AH 431).

Michael D. Pearson

JUDGMENT, INVESTIGATIVE, see **INVESTIGATIVE JUDGMENT**.

JUDGMENTS, GOD'S. God's judgments, the circumstances that prompt them, and their ultimate results comprise a major theme in the writings of Ellen White. For her, Satan's rebellion against God and His law is the foundational cause of all other rebellions against God, and hence, of all other acts of divine judgment (PP 40; DA 114). Thus God's judgments began with the expulsion of Satan and his followers from heaven (Rev. 12:7-9; Isa. 14:12-14; Eze. 28:14-16) and occur throughout biblical history to the last judgment. Such events as the expulsion of Adam and Eve from Eden to keep them from eating of the tree of life and becoming immortal sinners (PP 61), the Flood that destroyed a world of rebellion (*ibid.* 98-104), and the confusion of languages during the construction of the Tower of Babel (*ibid.* 119, 120) are examples of these acts of God. Before the destruction of the world at the time of the Flood and the dispersion of people at the Tower of Babel, Satan almost accomplished his aim as the world followed him in rebellion against God. The destruction of Sodom shows that one purpose of God's judgments is to put a check on sin (*ibid.* 160), to set a limit beyond which humans may not go (*ibid.* 164, 165). Even the judgment of Sodom came only after a long period of mercy and a final invitation to escape.

All these judgments not only destroyed evil but did so to preserve the existence of good for later generations. Had not God intervened, humans would have become captives of Satan, without hope of a faithful

people or the possibility of a future Savior. In Ellen White's writings God's past local judgments often become types of future global judgments. God's judgments of the antediluvians, of Sodom and Gomorrah, and of the golden calf worshippers at Sinai are types of what will take place in the end-time judgment when fire destroys the planet (*ibid.* 100, 324).

Throughout human history Satan has worked to establish systems of false worship and to defeat Christ's plan of salvation. He has sought to accomplish this through (1) major political powers, (2) the corruption of God's chosen people, and (3) counterfeit Christianity. In Egypt, Satan worked to prevent the release of God's people through Pharaoh (*ibid.* 257, 263). So God sent the plague judgments (*ibid.* 257-280), protected His people (*ibid.* 266-269), and won their release (*ibid.* 281, 282). At the Red Sea the Egyptian army was poised to destroy God's people, but God's judgment in drowning the army was the means of delivering and preserving His people (*ibid.* 283-290).

In *Prophets and Kings* Ellen White showed that Satan also worked through God's chosen people to achieve his purpose. Most of the kings were disloyal to God, and the prophetic messages of judgment given by the prophets were usually rejected (PK 297). God's judgments scattered His people to other countries (*ibid.* 569)—Israel to Assyria (*ibid.* 279-292), and Judah to Babylon (*ibid.* 452-463). During the last 50 years before its captivity in Assyria, the northern kingdom of Israel sank to the level of those who experienced the Flood (*ibid.* 281) and never recovered from the Assyrian captivity (*ibid.* 287). Likewise, Judah stubbornly resisted God until it received the consequences of its apostasy (*ibid.* 425).

In *The Desire of Ages* Ellen White showed how Satan used corrupt religious leaders to counteract the effects of Christ's ministry (DA

405, 406, 572, 580, 601, 602) and to crucify Him (*ibid.* 309). Later, as the disciples of Jesus were also treated with cruelty, God withdrew His presence, and Satan took full control (GC 28). God's judgment was manifested in the destruction of Jerusalem (*ibid.* 28-35), a city otherwise destined to stand forever (*ibid.* 19).

In *The Great Controversy* Ellen White showed that Satan has also worked through a counterfeit Christianity. The changing of the day of worship from Saturday to Sunday (*ibid.* 447, 448, 574) was part of Satan's plan to take control of Christianity. The final issue of loyalty to God in the end-time is over the Sabbath (*ibid.* 604, 605), and God's judgments fall on those who do not keep God's commandments (*ibid.* 626-633).

All these acts of judgment are preceded by various prejudgment steps. For Ellen White, God's final judgment comprises three distinctive phases: the pre-Advent judgment reveals why some will be saved and others lost at Christ's second advent; the millennial judgment allows the saved to see why others are lost; and the postmillennial judgment allows the lost to see that the verdict is fair. Angels keep books of record on every human being (*ibid.* 487), a book of life and a book of remembrance (*ibid.* 480, 481). God's process of judging involves testing the character, "secret purposes and motives" of the heart, by God's law to see whether the person loves God and his neighbors (*ibid.* 481, 482; cf. DA 763). While Satan accuses God's people (GC 484), Christ is their advocate (*ibid.* 482), and the Father is the judge (*ibid.* 479). So before God's end-time judgment to destroy the world there is not only an invitation to escape but a judging process, too. Christ's intercession during the judgment "is as essential to the plan of salvation" as was His death (*ibid.* 489; 15MR 104). Christ's death on Calvary as a substitute for repenting sinners also foretold

the destruction of Satan and his followers. In essence, the question in the judgment is "Has the person accepted or rejected Christ's judgment for them in their place at the cross?" Those appropriating and internalizing His death reveal His love in what they think and do; they minister to the needy as unto Christ (DA 637-641).

Hence, any discussion of God's judgments must include a look at Calvary. Ellen White presents the cross as the focal point of all the teachings of the Bible (GW 315). Christ is the substitute for humans, bearing their sin on the cross. On the cross He experienced God's judgment of wrath, the terrible separation from God that sinners will experience when Christ no longer pleads for sinners. "Christ was treated as we deserve, that we might be treated as He deserves. He was condemned for our sins, in which He had no share, that we might be justified by His righteousness, in which we had no share. He suffered the death which was ours, that we might receive the life which was His" (DA 25).

The final end-time judgment also involves Calvary. When Satan leads the wicked to surround the New Jerusalem, Christ is revealed far above the city in brilliant glory, seated on the throne with His Father's glory surrounding Him. Books of judgment are opened. As Christ looks at the wicked, each one is conscious of all their sins (GC 665, 666). Above the throne is replayed across the heavens the major events of the plan of salvation, climaxing in Christ's ministry and death upon the cross. Calvary reveals what Christ did for humanity on that judgment day, and exposes what Satan and his fiends did to judge and crucify Him (*ibid.* 666, 667). In the light of this revelation of God and the final unmasking of Satan, all will see that Satan's claim to give created beings a better government with a better law is groundless. The final judgment destroys sin and sinners, but comes only after all have gazed on the judgment of God at Calvary, so that those accepting or rejecting that gift see that in so doing they decided their own destinies, and therefore all admit that their destiny is just, and that God is just (*ibid.* 666-671).

See *also*: Investigative Judgment.

Norman R. Gulley

JUSTIFICATION. The sweetest melodies that come from God through human lips, Ellen White says, are justification by faith and the righteousness of Christ (6T 426). They are water to the thirsty traveler, a free gift from God (1SM 360). Justification is by *faith alone (*ibid.* 389), and the moment that sinners exercise true faith in the merits of the atoning sacrifice of Christ, claiming Christ as their personal Savior, they are justified (3SM 195). At that moment their sins are pardoned. This is justification by faith (FLB 116). "Justification is a full, complete pardon of sin" (*ibid.* 107), and sinners are justified because they have been pardoned (OHC 52).

However, Ellen White cautions that when speaking of justification there is danger of placing merit on faith (FW 25). "Faith is not our Savior. It earns nothing. It is the hand by which we lay hold upon Christ" (DA 175). Faith recognizes and accepts Christ as the only door by which to enter the kingdom of heaven (FW 25).

She also addresses the theological issue of legal or forensic justification. "The grace of Christ and the law of God are inseparable" (1SM 349). Justice is the foundation of God's throne and the fruit of His love (DA 762), and since His government has been violated and His law transgressed, the penalty for sin is death (3SM 193). Without Christ the sinner is under the condemnation of the law (1SM 330). "Justification is the opposite of condemnation" (FW 104), and the sinner is justified only when God pardons sins and remits punishment (3SM 194). "A full, complete ransom has been paid" by which humans are pardoned (1SM 363). "At the cross justice was satisfied" (*ibid.* 349). The sinner now "stands before God as a just person" (3SM 191). God imputes to the believer the righteousness of Christ and pronounces or declares them "righteous before the universe" (1SM 392).

Besides the forensic aspect of justification, there is also the subjective aspect. The atonement of Christ is not merely a legal means by which to satisfy God's justice and pardon the sinner, but also a divine remedy for healing and restoration. It is the means whereby the righteousness of Christ is "not only upon" them, but "in" their "hearts and characters" (6BC 1074). "Those who are justified by faith must have a heart to keep the way of the Lord" (1SM 397). It is by continual surrender of the will to Christ that the blessing of justification is maintained (*ibid.*; SC 62). The fact that Jesus paid humanity's indebtedness does not give individuals license to transgress the law of God (1SM 229, 230). "In order for man to retain justification, there must be . . . active, living faith that works by love and purifies the soul," leading to "continual obedience" (*ibid.* 366). While good works will not save a single soul, it is impossible even for one soul to be saved without good works (*ibid.* 377), because the faith that justifies always produces good works, as the fruit of that faith (3SM 195; SC 61).

There is danger, Ellen White cautions, of trying to define too minutely the distinction between justification and sanctification (6BC 1072). "Justification means the saving of a soul from perdition, that he may obtain sanctification, and through sanctification, the life of heaven" (7BC 908). The righteousness by which a sinner is justified by Christ is their title to heaven. The righteousness by which they are being sanctified and restored also comes from Christ; it is their fitness for heaven (MYP 35).

Ellen White did not teach justification apart from faith and repentance. While she says, "Christ made satisfaction for the guilt of the whole world, and all who will come to God in faith will receive the righteousness of Christ" (1SM 392); she also says, "He is a Savior who forgiveth transgression, iniquity, and sin, but will by no means clear the guilty and unrepentant soul" (*ibid.* 361). Sin is expiated and guilt is removed through the process of repentance and faith, not prior to it (*ibid.* 393).

Calling and justification are not one and the same thing (*ibid.* 390). "Calling is the drawing of the sinner to Christ . . . by the Holy Spirit." As one "responds to this drawing," he or she "advances toward Christ" in order to repent and be pardoned and justified (*ibid.*). The graces of repentance and contrition are gifts from Christ as truly as are pardon and justification (SC 26).

Ellen White urges Christians not to continue in ignorance of the wonderful gift of salvation that has been provided for them through justification. They are not to think that at some future time a great work will yet be done for them. That work has been done by Christ. It is complete (1SM 394, 395).

Further reading: SC 59-62; 1SM 377-382, 389-398; 3SM 190-204.

Jack J. Blanco

KARAITE CALENDAR. The Millerite teaching that the Day of Atonement (Yom Kippur) in 1844 occurred on October 22 was based on the calendar of Karaite Judaism, which conformed more closely to the biblical specifications than did the Rabbinical Jewish calendar. Some scholars have questioned this reasoning, claiming that the Karaite calendar had been abandoned long before 1844 and argue that Millerites, and subsequently Seventh-day Adventists, are wrong in regard to the date for the Day of Atonement in 1844. However, there is evidence that the Karaite calendar was still recognized in Israel at least as late as 1836, and that whether or not it was in use in 1844, it represented the most biblical form of reckoning the calendar, thus supporting the Millerite interpretation.

A brief look at the history of Karaism provides background for understanding the Karaite calendar. Toward the end of the eighth century a back-to-the-Bible movement called Karaism (or Caraism) arose in opposition to Rabbinic Judaism. The Rabbinate followed the traditions of the Talmud in addition to the Scriptures, but the Karaites abandoned such traditions to follow Scripture only. This resulted in a different method of reckoning the calendar, and the Karaites often kept their festivals in different months than other Jews.

The Julian and Gregorian calendars are solar calendars based on the number of days that the earth takes to revolve about the sun. Muslims, on the other hand, like the biblical Jews, follow a lunar calendar, based on the number of days that the moon takes to revolve around the earth. The Julian and Gregorian calendars keep in synchronization with the seasons through an intercalary day (February 29) every fourth year, commonly called leap year. The Gregorian calendar skips three of these intercalary days every 400 years, and is thus more accurate than the Julian calendar.

The Islamic calendar uses no intercalation. Thus it falls behind the seasons 11 additional days every year. After 33 years or so, their months have rotated through the seasons, until they are back to where they were before. The biblical Jewish calendar uses an intercalary month. In a leap year, which occurs about seven times every 19 years, the twelfth month, Adar, is followed by a Second Adar, which postpones for one month the beginning of the first month of Nisan. Both Muslims and Karaite Jews begin their months when the new crescent moon is first visible.

The Bible specifies that the Passover must be celebrated during the first month. It also specifies that on the morrow after the Sabbath after the Passover (differing interpretations identify this as either a Sunday or the sixteenth of Nisan), a sheaf of ripe barley was to be waved before the Lord (Lev. 23:10-12). Up until the second century, Rabbinic Judaism added intercalary months in such a way that there was always ripe barley for Passover. Later they relied on mathematical calculations based on the equinox, disregarding whether or not the barley was ripe. Thus their calendar no longer followed Scripture regarding setting the beginning of the year. Karaism restored the biblical way of calculating the beginning of the year.

Beginning in the summer of 1844 Millerites in general, though not William Miller himself, became convinced that Christ would return on October 22 of that year, on what was considered the Day of Atonement by Karaite reckoning. The specific date of October 22 was first advocated by Samuel S. Snow.

Without question, Karaites outside of Palestine were using Rabbinic reckoning long before 1844. And at some point, apparently prior to 1860, the Karaites in Palestine also began using Rabbinic reckoning. Concerning the exact date of this change, historical evidence is fragmentary. Yet regardless of what the Karaites were or were not doing in 1844, the biblical date for the Day of Atonement would be found using the Karaite lunar calendar. The precise date is difficult to specify without detailed crop reports from that year, but the relationship

between the date of the barley crop and the date of Yom Kippur is clearly shown by an example from recent years. According to Karaite leader Nehemia Gordon, in 1999 the barley crop was not ripe until mid-April, and therefore Yom Kippur (Day of Atonement) for the Karaites fell on October 20. But most Jews around the world observed Yom Kippur in 1999 on September 20, exactly a month earlier.

This was similar to the interval that the Millerites were aware of in 1844. More than a year before Snow set forth his interpretation in August 1844, Millerites were studying the Karaite calendar. In an April 1843 article on the Jewish year, Millerite writer Nathaniel Whiting explained: "The rabbinical calculation makes the first day of Nisan commence with the new moon *nearest* the day on which the sun enters Aries, on the vernal equinox. It ought, however, to be observed, that the Caraite Jews maintain that the rabbins have changed the calendar, so that, to present the firstfruits on the sixteenth of Nisan would be impossible if the time is reckoned according to the rabbinical calculations, since barley is not in the ear at Jerusalem till a month later. The accounts of many travelers confirm the position of the Caraites" (*Midnight Cry,* Apr. 27, 1843, reprinted in *Midnight Cry,* Oct. 11, 1844). Whiting claimed that "many travelers" to Palestine around 1843 had confirmed that when the beginning of the year was calculated by Rabbinate reckoning, the barley was not ripe for Passover.

Two months later another Millerite paper (*Signs of the Times,* June 21, 1843), continued the discussion of the Karaite calendar: "Now there is a dispute between the Rabinnical, and the Caraite Jews, as to the correct time of commencing the year. . . . The Caraite Jews, on the contrary, still adhere to the letter of the Mosaic, and commence with the new moon nearest the barley harvest in Judea; and which is one moon later than the Rabinnical year. The Jewish year of A.D. 1843, as the Caraites reckon it in accordance with the Mosaic law, therefore commenced this year with the new moon on the 29th of April, and the Jewish year 1844 will commence with the new moon in next April, when 1843 and the 2300 days, according to their computation, will expire."

At this point Millerites were simply seeking a basis for determining the close of the biblical year 1843. This was a full year before Snow raised the issue of the Day of Atonement. But if the Jewish year of 1844 began with the new moon of April 1844, then Yom Kippur, a little more than six months later, would fall on October 22, not September 23.

In December 1843 the same paper again discussed the Karaite calendar. Quoting "an 'Economical Calendar' of Palestine, which has been prepared with the greatest care," the *Signs* showed that "wheat, zea or spelt and *barley* ripen" in "the month commencing with the new moon of *April*" (*Signs of the Times,* Dec. 5, 1843). As the Karaite Jewish year 1843 entered its final month, and after the *Signs* was renamed the *Advent Herald and Signs of the Times Reporter,* much of this article was reprinted, with some additions, on March 20, 1844.

It is evident that in the years just preceding 1844 most Jews in Palestine started the year so early that the barley was not ripe for Passover. Records of Karaite practices in other localities are not necessarily helpful, since those outside of Palestine began using Rabbinic reckoning long before those in Palestine did. Whether or not Karaites in Palestine were still using the biblical reckoning in 1844, it is apparent that Rabbinic reckoning was almost without question a month too early that year. Further questions, therefore, about the validity

of October 22 for Yom Kippur in 1844 are mere speculation unless someone discovers an 1844 crop report for Palestine. If such a crop report did turn up, and if it showed that the barley had entered the Abib stage by March 20, then and only then would there be evidence that September 23 was the true Day of Atonement for that year.

See also: Investigative Judgment.

Further reading: B. Pickle, *A Response to the Video: Seventh-day Adventism: The Spirit Behind the Church* (Halstad, Minn.: Pickle Publishing, 2002), pp. 17-19, 23; http://www.karaite-korner.org; W. H. Shea, "Day of Atonement and October 22, 1844," in *Selected Studies in Prophetic Interpretation* (GC, 1982), pp. 132-137.

Bob Pickle

KELLOGG CRISIS (1902-1907). Also called the Battle Creek crisis, triggered by the fires of the *Battle Creek Sanitarium and the *Review and Herald publishing house, both in 1902. The sanitarium fire led to the publication of *J. H. Kellogg's book *The Living Temple,* intended as a denomination-wide fund-raising effort for rebuilding the sanitarium. Instead the book sparked a major theological controversy that contributed to Kellogg's leaving the church in 1907.

The publishing house fire led to the decision not to rebuild in Battle Creek, but to relocate both the publishing house and church headquarters on the outskirts of Washington, D.C. Eventually a college and a sanitarium were also established there, completing the removal of the administrative center of Adventism from Battle Creek, where it had been since 1855.

Kellogg was a major player in all the ramifications of the crisis. As head of the International Medical Missionary and Benevolent Association (IMMBA), he was the chief administrator for some 1,500 physi-cians, nurses, and other health-care workers, outnumbering the ministerial and evangelistic employees of the church at the time. Kellogg was an aggressive entrepreneur committed to expanding and multiplying Adventist health institutions, even by deficit spending. *A. G. Daniells, General Conference president, was equally committed to halting the rise in denominational debt. The collision between Daniells and Kellogg spanned the issues of church finance (debt versus frugality), doctrine (philosophical panentheism versus biblical theism), and church leadership. At the 1903 General Conference session Kellogg tried to remove Daniells from the presidency, and declined to accept the integration of the medical work as a department of the General Conference. An emotional tipping point came at the *Berrien Springs meeting of 1904, when Kellogg walked out during Ellen White's appeal for unity.

The organizational conflict between the General Conference and the International Medical Missionary and Benevolent Association virtually ended with Kellogg's dissolution of the IMMBA (a legal process begun in 1904 and completed in 1905) and the denomina-tion's creation of the General Conference Medical Department in 1905. All but two of the denomination's health institutions accepted the decision of the church to integrate the medical work as a department of the General Conference. Two sanitariums followed Kellogg out of church ownership—those in Battle Creek, Michigan, and Guadalajara, Mexico, along with the *American Medical Missionary College in Chicago, a subsidiary of the Battle Creek Sanitarium. Also in 1905 the denomi-nation acquired the property that became the Loma Linda Sanitarium and eventually Loma Linda University.

The one major dimension of the crisis still unresolved in 1906 was a rather widespread questioning of Ellen White's authority, the validity of her claims, and the integrity of W. C. White as her assistant and representa-tive. This aspect of the crisis involved the publication of several pamphlets critical of church leadership and Ellen White, written by persons close to Kellogg in 1906 and 1907.

The crisis cooled after the expulsion of Kellogg and others from the *Battle Creek Tabernacle in 1907, but reminders of the crisis persisted for many years. The changes in Battle Creek and the removal of church headquarters to Washington, D.C., were a wrenching transi-tion for many who had built their livelihood around the Adventist institutions and com-munity in Battle Creek.

Further reading: 5Bio 148-339; 6Bio 56-73, 89-103, 118-129; J. Moon, *W. C. White and Ellen G. White: The Relationship Between the Prophet and Her Son* (AUP, 1993), pp. 274-321; *SDA Encyclopedia* (1996), vol. 10, p. 787.

Jerry Moon

KELLOGG INTERVIEW OF OCTOBER 7, 1907. Stenographically reported interview with *J. H. Kellogg that represented the emotional and rhetorical climax of the developing schism between him and the denomination. On two grounds, doctrinal heresy in *The Living Temple* and many years of sporadic attendance, the Battle Creek congregation proposed to remove Kellogg from membership. The process required a visit from church officers to inquire about his relationship to the church and to notify him of the possibility of the action. This was the setting for Kellogg's famous "Last Interview as an Adventist." The original manuscript exceeds 100 pages, but has been skillfully condensed by R. W. Schwarz.

Interviewed by two veterans of the church, *G. W. Amadon and *A. C. Bourdeau, Kellogg reiterated many of the real or supposed grievances that he had rehearsed to others on earlier occasions. One of Kellogg's major themes was that Ellen White's testimonies could not be trusted because through misinformation she was vulnerable to manipulation. In support of this thesis he attacked several church leaders, particularly W. C. White. In the course of the conversation Kellogg gave colorful glimpses of early Adventist history, personalities, and issues. The challenge for the reader is to discern how much of the story is reliable. According to Kellogg's biographer, R. W. Schwarz, the account is far from objective. Schwarz quotes *W. K. Kellogg, who wrote to the doctor: "I notice that for some things you have a very unusual memory. Sometimes I think you have a memory for details of things that really never happen" (W. K. Kellogg to J. H. Kellogg, Sept. 23, 1915, in Schwarz, "Kellogg Versus the Brethren," *Spectrum* 20, no. 3 [April 1990]: 48). Despite demonstrable distortions and misrepresentations, the interview affords an extensive view of then-recent events from Kellogg's perspective.

Further reading: J. T. Case and R. V. Ashley, stenographers, "Interview at Dr. J. H. Kellogg's House, Oct. 7, 1907, Between George W. Amadon, Elder A. C. Bordeau, and Dr. J. H. Kellogg" (DF 45k, CAR); *The Kellogg File: Closed 1907, Reopened 1986* (Tempe, Ariz.: Omega Historical Research Society, 1986); Tim Poirier, "The 1907 Interview With John Harvey Kellogg" (EGWE, 1987, SDoc); R. W. Schwarz, ed., "Kellogg Versus the Brethren: His Last Interview as an Adventist—October 7, 1907," *Spectrum* 20, no. 3 (April 1990): 46-62; *idem*, "Kellogg Snaps, Crackles, and Pops; His Last Interview as an Adventist—Part 2," *Spectrum* 20, no. 4 (June 1990): 37-61.

Jerry Moon

KING OF THE NORTH. Daniel 11 portrays a long war between the king of the south and the king of the north, a war that impacts God's people. Early Adventist expositors of Daniel 11 generally agreed on the interpretation of verses 5-35, following the interpretation given by William Miller, who derived the historical aspects of his interpretation largely from Rollin's *Ancient History* (see Miller, *Works*, vol. 2, lecture 6). Thus verses 5-13 were understood to refer to the Ptolemies (south) and Seleucids (north) after the death of Alexander and the breakup of his empire. Verses 14-28 were applied to Imperial Rome, verses 29, 30 to the division of Rome, and verses 32-35 to the period of papal supremacy. Yet Adventists, however, were not agreed over the identity of the king of the north in verses 36-45.

James White was one of the main proponents of the original school of interpretation, which identified the king of the north in verses 36-45 as the Papacy. This agreed with William Miller's early interpretation of Daniel 11:45. From the mid-1850s to 1867 most Seventh-day Adventists agreed with this view, including Uriah Smith. James White arrived at his understanding by letting Daniel interpret itself. Starting from the premise that Daniel 2, 7, 8, and 11 are parallel prophecies, he reasoned that chapter 11 must end with the Papacy (a Roman power), because Daniel 2 also ends with Rome and not Turkey (RH, Oct. 3, 1878).

In 1867 Uriah Smith introduced another interpretation of the king of the north, which after James White's death in 1881 became the leading interpretation "for more than seventy years" (Mansell, p. 47). Smith saw a correlation between Daniel 11:45 and Revelation 16:12-21, taking both of these texts as references to the last war, Armageddon. Further, he read a literal interpretation of the Euphrates River back into Daniel 11:45 by identifying Turkey, the geographical origin of the Euphrates

River, with the king of the north (RH, June 18, 1857; RH, Dec. 2, 1862). A majority of William Miller's contemporaries and predecessors had also identified the Euphrates and the last power of Daniel 11 with the "Turco-Mohammedan" Empire (Mansell, p. 24). For many people the significance of Turkey in prophecy had already been established by Josiah Litch's 1838 prediction of the Ottoman Empire's loss of power in August 1840 (based upon his application of the year-day principle to the sixth trumpet of Revelation 9) (Schwarz and Greenleaf, p. 33). But Smith did not pursue his interpretation with confidence until after 1871, with the defeat of the French in the Franco-Prussian War. The French had been the supporters of the Papacy from the beginning, and their defeat in this war strengthened his expectation that the Papacy would become irrelevant (Mansell, p. 39; RH, Nov. 5, 1871).

Later events in the international scene helped to make his view popular among Adventists. The Italo-Turkish War (1911-1912), Turkey's entrance into World War I in 1914, and the Greco-Turkish War (1919-1922) all helped to fuel speculation. Not until the Turkish Parliament abolished the Caliphate on March 3, 1923, did this school of thought begin to receive more critical scrutiny (Mansell, pp. 57-69).

The two schools of thought were also divided on the nature of Armageddon. This debate was known among Adventists as the "Eastern Question." Smith believed Armageddon to be a literal war between earthly nations and armies. He expected the Turks to move their capital from Constantinople to Jerusalem, after which the Turkish power would come to its end (Dan. 11:45). Armageddon would be fought over Jerusalem, by powers from the "east" (Rev. 16:12). He expected the Eastern powers to be Islamic powers. Another Adventist interpreter, A. T. Jones, proposed a slightly

different view, that these Eastern powers would be Western militaries stationed in the Far East (A. T. Jones, *The Great Nations of To-day* [RHPA, 1901], p. 88). James White, on the other hand, believed that Armageddon would be a religious-spiritual war between the powers of heaven and earth (RH, Jan. 21, 1852; Mansell, p. 33).

Ellen White commented on Daniel 11 in only three places in all her writings (see RH, Nov. 24, 1904; 9T 14; Lt 103, 1904, in 13MR 394), all traced, no doubt, to the single statement found in Lt 103, 1904. In the statement she shared her conviction that nearly the entire chapter had been completely fulfilled. She clearly positioned the church of her day near the end of Daniel 11 and therefore near the end of history. But she never ventured into further detail, and was apparently silent in regard to the identity of the king of the north. She did not enter into the then-contemporary controversy surrounding this issue. Apparently the only time she came even close to the controversy was when she was shown in vision that her husband erred in confronting Uriah Smith publicly regarding his interpretation of the king of the north (Mansell, p. 44). It may be significant that all three of her comments on Daniel 11 appeared in print only after her husband was dead. The timing of these comments may show her resolve to avoid the appearance of partiality (*ibid.*, p. 45).

However reticent she may have been to take a clear public stand on the identity of the king of the north, one of her comments sheds light on how we should interpret the king of the north in verses 40-45. She wrote, "Much of the history that has taken place in fulfillment of this prophecy will be repeated. In the thirtieth verse a power is spoken of that 'shall be grieved, and return, and have indignation against the holy covenant: so shall he do; he shall even return, and have intelligence with them that forsake the holy covenant. [Verses 31-36 quoted.] Scenes similar to those described in these words will take place" (Lt 103, 1904, in 13MR 394). Her view that similar events as described in verses 30-36 will in principle be repeated in the future agrees with the literary structure of Daniel 11 (J. B. Doukhan, *Secrets of Daniel* [RHPA, 2000], pp. 170-179). According to a thematic analysis of Daniel 11 the attack against the "holy covenant" in verses 30-36 parallels or is repeated in the attack against the "holy mountain" in verse 45. First, both sections are preceded by fighting between the north and the south. Second, in both sections the king of the north turns against God and His people. Ellen White's comment that verses 30-36 will be repeated may suggest a method for identifying the king of the north in Daniel 11:45. If the historical events represented by verses 30-45 can be identified, then the identity of the king of the north could be uncovered at the same time. There was complete consensus among early Adventists that verses 31-35 were fulfilled in the history of the Papacy's warring against Protestants. If this view is sound, then it must also be granted that the Papacy is the king of the north in Daniel 11:40-45.

Further reading: D. E. Mansell, *Adventists and Armageddon* (PPPA, 1999); R. W. Schwarz and F. L. Greenleaf, *Light Bearers* (PPPA, 2000), p. 33.

André Scalfani

KINGDOM OF GOD. The kingdom of God, one of the key themes in Scripture, occupies a central place in the writings of Ellen White. The phrase "kingdom of God" is used almost interchangeably with the "kingdom of Christ," and sometimes with the expression the "kingdom of heaven," especially in its establishment at the first advent of Christ. Three key aspects

of the biblical concept of the kingdom of God receive attention in her writings: the nature of the kingdom, its establishment and development, and the church's relation to it.

In keeping with the biblical evidence, Ellen White emphasizes the fact that the kingdom of God is not a temporal kingdom. Yet she maintains with equal vigor the position that, historically, the kingdom was established at the first advent of Christ. Indeed, He came purposely to establish the kingdom, the timing of which is based on Daniel 2. The apparent tension between the two positions, which is reflective of the theological notion of "the already, and not yet," is resolved by her use of the concepts of "kingdom of grace" and "kingdom of glory." In her view, the kingdom of grace is brought to view in Hebrews 4:15, 16, while Matthew 25:31, 32 points to the future kingdom of glory. Primarily the kingdom is a spiritual kingdom, which is "established . . . by the implanting of Christ's nature in humanity through the work of the Holy Spirit" (Ev 531). In this sense, the kingdom of God (i.e., the kingdom of grace) has already been established. Yet there remains an eschatological manifestation of the kingdom (i.e., the kingdom of glory), which "is not to be set up until the second advent of Christ" (GC 347).

Although the kingdom of grace was established at the first advent of Christ, it was instituted immediately after the fall of humanity. Then it "existed in the purpose and by the promise of God; and through faith, men could become its subjects. Yet it was not actually established until the death of Christ" (*ibid.* 347, 348). Now the kingdom of grace is being established daily as hearts that have been full of sin and rebellion yield to the sovereignty of Christ's love. Such comprise the kingdom of God as taught by the parables of wheat and tares and the fishing net, for only those who, as a result of the influence of Christ in the soul, "do right will have an entrance into the kingdom of God" (5T 569). The nature of the development of the kingdom is equally taught in Christ's early parables. The parables of the sower, growth of the mustard seed, and the effect of leaven are noted to be indicative of the progress of the kingdom of grace.

Although the kingdom is established in peoples' hearts by the Spirit, "nothing will so build up the Redeemer's kingdom, as will the love of Christ manifested by the members of the church" (*ibid.* 168). In this sense humans have a hand in building up the kingdom of God, although its ultimate destiny is in God's hands. Without identifying the visible church with the kingdom of God, Ellen White none-theless maintains a crucial role for the church in the progress of the kingdom of grace. In her view the parable of the mustard seed represents not simply the growth of Christ's kingdom, but the experience of the growth of the church in every generation. Thus the "signal and triumphant fulfillment" (COL 79) in the last generation of the mustard seed parable is linked to the last message of warn-ing and mercy in Revelation 14:6-12, which goes to every nation, kindred, and tongue.

Further reading: COL 78, 79, 253, 397; FE 142; 3T 566; DA 333, 437, 820; AA 30; GC 345-349.

Kwabena Donkor

KINGLY POWER. During the 1890s Ellen White often used the expression "kingly power" to protest the controlling power of one man or a small group of people over the administration of the church. At times she referred to the General Conference president, but more often to the treasurer or to leaders of the medical or publishing work. At the 1901 session she declared, "God has not put any kingly power in our ranks to control this or that branch of the work. The work has been greatly restricted by the efforts to control it in every line" (GCB, Apr. 3, 1901).

Though exacerbated by inadequate orga-nization, the temptation to kingly power is rooted in human nature. Except for John Byington, every president during Ellen White's lifetime, from James White to A. G. Daniells, was reproved for wrong use of authority. O. A. Olsen was reproved for allowing kingly power in associates, while G. I. Butler's administrative style received repeated reproofs.

In the 1901 call for structural reorganiza-tion, Ellen White also called for leaders to humble their hearts and seek spiritual renewal. But structural reorganization was not matched by spiritual renewal. Thus the first decade of the twentieth century was again marked by reproofs to those using "kingly power" to consolidate control of the publishing work and to manipulate wages. Many warnings were given to J. H. Kellogg, Adventism's most powerful "king," who sought to control the entire medical work and its other leaders (8T 232).

At the 1903 session Kellogg and A. T. Jones attempted to remove Daniells from the church because he resisted their powerful moves. In October 1903 Ellen White declared that the experience at the 1901 session had been led by God, but held that Kellogg's failure in 1901 to do "thorough work" in personal spiritual renewal was responsible for "the terrible experience" of 1903 (Lt 242, 1903, in 6MR 217). Overcentralized organization that con-centrates authority in too few hands contributes to kingly power; but its cure requires that leaders continually humble themselves before God and their fellow workers (8T 231-238).

A. Leroy Moore

KNOWING HIM BETTER (RHPA, 1981, 125 pp.). Adaptation of *Steps to Christ*, also published under the title *Steps to Jesus*. The language of the original edition was simplified for people whose second language is English. With only a few exceptions, the Bible verses quoted in this book are from the *Good News Bible,* Today's English Version.

LABOR UNIONS. Ellen White's counsels on the development and activities of labor unions and Adventists' relation to them are limited in number. However, what she wrote was forceful and direct. She was opposed to unions that arose in her time and to those that would emerge after her time. She gave strong counsels regarding Adventist involvement in labor unions.

Following the Civil War in the United States the growth of manufacturing industries was extensive and rapid, especially in the Northern states. This rapid industrialization of society happened at the same time as millions of immigrants arrived from Europe in the latter part of the nineteenth and early twentieth centuries. In addition to this, extensive rural-to-urban migration occurred in the United States. Most of these migrants were desperately poor and needed work. The desire for accumulation of wealth on the part of industrialists was clearly seen by resentful workers as exploitation. The stage was set for extensive industrial conflict.

In unionization, anxious workers found a collective voice for representing their interests. A National Labor Union was formed in 1866, but was short-lived. The Knights of Labor followed in 1869, but grew slowly because of a policy of secrecy. Public opinion forced a reversal of this policy, and thereafter it began to disintegrate. In 1886 the American Federation of Labor followed, but attracted workers slowly. What these unions had in common was, first, a wide diversity of interest to attract members, and second, an interest by workers to mount action quickly in the

form of strikes to remedy perceived injustices. Thus strikes and violent confrontation became increasingly common. Major strikes included the one at the McCormick Reaper Company in Chicago, and the 1894 strike against the Pullman Palace Car Company, also near Chicago. Violence and bloodshed were commonplace in these and other strikes during this turbulent period.

Most of what Ellen White wrote was penned in the late nineteenth and early twentieth centuries. It should be noted that White was equally critical of corporate greed leading to exploitation of workers (9T 12-14) and of the coercion and violence by which unions defended their interests. There was no ambiguity about her warnings. She saw that the lives of those who refused to unite with these unions would be in peril. She counseled against uniting with *secret societies and trade unions (cf. 2SM 120-139). Unions, she affirmed, were one of the signs of the last days, and those who became involved in them could not keep the commandments of God. Because of union activities it would soon become very difficult to carry on Adventist work in the cities. "The trade unions," she wrote, "will be one of the agencies that will bring upon this earth a time of trouble such as has not been seen since the world began" (Lt 200, 1903, in 4MR 88). The predictive element and the future tense employed in her statement carry Ellen White's concern about Adventists and labor unions past her time and into the future.

In the years since her death (1915) the church has sought to keep the warnings of Ellen White before the membership through articles in church publications. Furthermore, such men as C. S. Longacre, H. H. Votaw, and E. D. Dick were asked to press the church's position on labor union leaders. When such efforts fell short, the General Conference of Seventh-day Adventists obtained legal counsel to secure the rights of Adventists.

Later Carlyle B. Haynes was named executive secretary of the Council on Industrial Relations, and a secretary for the Commission on Rural Living, to further the Adventist viewpoint to church members. Through the *Review and Herald* (now *Adventist Review*) he urged Adventists to follow the "better solution" by leaving cities, where unions were then strong, and moving to the country, where they were not yet a problem. In this he advocated what Ellen White had urged years before, suggesting that the time had come to follow her advice more fully (C. B. Haynes, "Out of the Cities," RH, Apr. 25, 1946).

In 1954 R. R. Figuhr, General Conference president, announced that responsibilities of the Council on Industrial Relations had been shifted to the Religious Liberty Department of the General Conference. Informed through church publications, members could take their stand personally and call on religious liberty leaders in the church to assist them with any difficulties encountered. This approach continues to the present.

Further reading: "Labor Unions and Confederacies: Counsels From the Spirit of Prophecy" (EGWE, SDoc); R. C. Kistler, *Adventists and Labor Unions in the United States* (RHPA, 1984).

Robert C. Kistler

LACE, see **DRESS AND ADORNMENT**.

LANDMARK DOCTRINES. Expression used by Ellen White to describe the distinctive and fundamental doctrines of Seventh-day Adventism. Similar expressions include "pillars" and "waymarks." The use of this expression among Adventists may have been derived from Proverbs 22:28, "Remove not the ancient landmark, which thy fathers have set." Early Adventists used the expression first to refer to the end of the prophetic period of the 2300 days in Daniel 8:14 (JW, in WLF 5). Ellen White's earliest use was also in connection with this prophecy. In reference to those who had abandoned Miller's chronology of the 2300 days and set a new date for the end of this period, she said that they had "removed the landmarks" (PT, March 1850).

As Seventh-day Adventist doctrines developed, the term came to include other distinctive Adventist teachings. During the heated debates of the *General Conference session of 1888, delegates disputed the correct identification of one of the 10 horns of Daniel 7:7 and the identity of the "schoolmaster" law in Galatians 3:24. While strongly urging a broader study of the Bible, Ellen White deeply deplored the lack of Christian courtesy exemplified in these discussions. She became particularly troubled when some of the older ministers, as a means of closing the discussion, used the argument that all delegates should "stand by the old landmarks" and not accept any new views. In a manuscript written shortly after the session she reflected on what had happened and on her understanding of the meaning of the old landmarks.

"In Minneapolis God gave precious gems of truth to His people in new settings. This light from heaven by some was rejected with all the stubbornness the Jews manifested in rejecting Christ, and there was much talk about standing by the old landmarks. But there was evidence they knew not what the old landmarks were. There was evidence and there was reasoning from the word that commended itself to the conscience; but the minds of men were fixed, sealed against the entrance of light, because they had decided it was a dangerous error removing the 'old landmarks' when it was not moving a peg of the old landmarks, but they had perverted ideas of what constituted the old landmarks." Then she listed what she regarded as the "old landmarks": "The passing of the time in 1844 was a period of great events, opening to our astonished eyes the cleansing of the sanctuary transpiring in heaven, and having decided relation to God's people upon the earth, [also] the first and second angels' messages and the third, unfurling the banner on which was inscribed, 'The commandments of God and the faith of Jesus.' One of the landmarks under this message was the temple of God, seen by His truth-loving people in heaven, and the ark containing the law of God. The light of the Sabbath of the fourth commandment flashed its strong rays in the pathway of the transgressors of God's law. The nonimmortality of the wicked is an old landmark. I can call to mind nothing more that can come under the head of the old landmarks" (Ms 13, 1889, in 1888 Materials 518; CW 30, 31).

Five landmark doctrines emerge from this list. The first is the cleansing of the sanctuary in heaven (see *investigative judgment) and the distinctive Adventist emphasis on Christ's intercessory ministry. The efficacy of the work of Christ on the *cross, His complete sacrificial *atonement, prepared the way for His work of intercession since His ascension and His additional work of cleansing starting in 1844. In Ellen White's thought: "The intercession of Christ in man's behalf in the sanctuary above is as essential to the plan of salvation as was His death upon the cross" (GC 489).

A second landmark doctrine is the prophetic proclamation of the *three angels' messages of Revelation 14:6-12. These messages constitute God's last appeal to the world to accept salvation in Christ and to prepare for His imminent return. Part of these messages is the invitation to worship God, the Creator, and to reject all forms of Babylon and idolatrous worship. Ellen White understood these messages as a distinguishing mark

of "the church of Christ at the time of His appearing" (ibid. 453).

The immutability and the perpetuity of the commandments of God is the third distinctive doctrine. Based on the fact that in the Old Testament the ark of the covenant contained the tables of stone on which God had written the Ten Commandments (Ex. 40:20), Ellen White understood that the vision of the ark of the covenant seen in the heavenly temple in Revelation 11:19 is an indication that the *law of God (the Ten Commandments) is still valid and binding today and that faith in Christ cannot do away with obedience to it (ibid. 433-435). "The law of God, being a revelation of His will, a transcript of His character, must forever endure, 'as a faithful witness in heaven.' Not one command has been annulled; not a jot or tittle has been changed" (ibid. 434).

The fourth doctrine is closely related to the preceding ones and teaches the observance of the seventh-day *Sabbath. Here, in Ellen White's thought, many doctrinal points find their interconnectedness. "In Revelation 14, men are called upon to worship the Creator [verse 7]; and the prophecy brings to view a class [of people] that, as the result of the threefold message, are keeping the commandments of God [verse 12]. One of these commandments points directly to God as the Creator. The fourth precept declares: 'The seventh day is the sabbath of the Lord thy God: . . . for in six days the Lord made heaven and earth, the sea, and all that in them is, and rested the seventh day: wherefore the Lord blessed the sabbath day, and hallowed it.' Exodus 20:10, 11" (ibid. 437).

The fifth landmark doctrine is the nonimmortality of the soul (conditionalism) and the eternal destruction of the wicked (annihilationism). Ellen White argued that Satan's first lie to Eve was in regard to the natural immortality of the soul. She also regarded the doctrine of eternal punishment as one of the most appalling doctrines to misrepresent the character of God (*ibid.* 531-536). Hence she argued that only the doctrine of conditional immortality is consistent with the doctrine of the resurrection (*ibid.* 546, 547).

On several occasions Ellen White warned that attempts would be made to remove the landmarks of the Seventh-day Adventist faith, particularly as the second advent of Christ draws closer (RH, Dec. 13, 1892; ST, Mar. 31, 1890). For this reason she insisted that these doctrines be strengthened in the minds of the people (2SM 390).

Further reading: *SDA Encyclopedia* (1996), vol. 10, pp. 895, 896; DF 464g (CAR).

Denis Fortin

LAODICEAN MESSAGE. A message of rebuke from Jesus Christ to the church in Laodicea, recorded in Revelation 3:14-22. In general, Adventists follow the historicist method of interpretation, which sees the great sequential prophecies of Daniel and Revelation as extending from the times of the respective prophets until the second coming of Christ. As Laodicea is the last in the series of seven churches in Revelation 2 and 3, Adventists since the 1840s have interpreted Laodicea as representing the final phase in the history of the Christian church, though the precise details of interpretation have changed over time.

Millerite Adventists (see *disappointments, Millerite) were initially a nondenominational movement, largely characterized by their lack of sectarian rivalry. Interpretation of biblical prophecy was central to their faith, and they identified themselves with the sixth of Revelation's seven churches, Philadelphia, which means "brotherly love." The implication was that Laodicea, the "lukewarm" church, symbolized the nominal Christians who,

despite their profession, did not accept the Millerite message of the soon return of Christ.

After the 1844 disappointment Millerism splintered into many parts, most of which soon gave up the idea that any biblical prophecy had been fulfilled in the 1844 experience. Dissenting from this consensus, one group maintained the original Millerite Adventist belief that a genuine fulfillment of prophecy had occurred in 1844, though not in the way they had expected. This group went on to accept the seventh-day (Saturday) Sabbath and became known as Seventh-day Adventists, in contrast to the rest of the Millerites, whom they called "first-day Adventists" or "nominal Adventists." As a series of *Sabbatarian conferences (1848-1850) resulted in a growing sense of unity, the Sabbatarian Adventists began to apply the label "Laodicea" to their first-day Adventist detractors (cf. RH, June 10, 1852).

The first hint of a change in viewpoint appeared on the last page of Ellen White's first *Testimony for the Church* (1855), where she applied the warning of Revelation 3:15, 16 to the spiritual decline among Sabbathkeeping Adventists. "We either gather with Christ or scatter abroad," she declared. "We are decided, wholehearted Christians, or none at all. Says Christ: 'I would thou wert cold or hot. So then because thou art lukewarm, and neither cold nor hot, I will spew thee out of my mouth'" (1T 126).

In October 1856 James White began a series of editorials in the *Review*, arguing, from Scripture and from observation, that the "state of the Laodiceans (lukewarm, and neither cold nor hot)" fitly illustrates the condition of Sabbathkeeping Adventists (RH, Oct. 9, 1856; in 1Bio 343). Ellen White was in full agreement, and many Adventists wrote letters to the *Review* acknowledging their acceptance of the message (LS88 329; cf. 1Bio 344, 345). *Testimony for the Church*, no. 3, published in April 1857, was largely devoted to the Laodicean message (1T 141-146, 153).

Two years later she wrote another major article reaffirming that "the testimony to the Laodiceans applies to God's people at the present time," and calling the church to persevere in it. "When it was first presented, it led to close examination of heart. Sins were confessed, and the people of God were stirred everywhere." However, "as they failed to see the powerful work accomplished in a short time, many lost the effect of the message. I saw that this message would not accomplish its work in a few short months" (*ibid.* 186 [1859]). The rest of the article is a practical exposition of the necessity and means of developing Christian character while waiting for the second coming of Christ.

A major dynamic of this message is that trials and temptations are permitted by God to reveal "*what is in the heart.* Some endure at one point, but fall off at the next. At every advanced point the heart is tested and tried a little closer. . . . Said the angel: 'God will bring His work closer and closer to test and prove every one of His people.' Some are willing to receive one point; but when God brings them to another testing point, they shrink from it and stand back, because they find that it strikes directly at some cherished idol. Here they have *opportunity to see what is in their hearts* that shuts out Jesus. They prize something higher than the truth, and their hearts are not prepared to receive Jesus. . . . Those who come up to every point, and stand every test, and overcome, be the price what it may, have heeded the counsel of the True Witness, and they will receive the *latter rain, and thus be fitted for translation" (*ibid.* 187; italics supplied).

Further reading: 2SG 222-230; 3T 252-272; 4T 83-93; JW, editorial, "The Seven Churches," RH, Oct. 16, 1856.

Jerry Moon

LAST DAY EVENTS (PPPA, 1992, 330 pp.). Compilation relating to the final events of this world's history; an expansion of *The Crisis Ahead* (1970) first compiled by Robert Olson at Pacific Union College. Topics covered include signs of Christ's return, God's last day church, *Sunday laws, Satan's last day deceptions, the *shaking, the *latter rain, the close of *probation, the seven last *plagues, Christ's return, and others. These topics have been presented in a logical arrangement, but the compilers do not claim that all future events have been listed in the exact order in which they will occur. While the books *The Great Controversy Between Christ and Satan* (1911) and *Maranatha* (1976) deal largely with final events, *Last Day Events* was published in response to Ellen White's appeal: "Great pains should be taken to keep this subject [Christ's second coming] before the people" (LDE 16).

Robert Olson

LATTER RAIN. In Palestine "latter rain" refers to the rain that falls at the end of the growing season to ripen the grain and prepare it for harvest, in contrast to the "early rain," which helps to germinate the seed (Joel 2:23; Jer. 5:24; James 5:7). Ellen White likens the literal "early rain" to the outpouring of the Spirit that began in the days of the apostles and continues to the present in the lives of believers. She likens the literal "latter rain" to the end-time outpouring of the Spirit that prepares the church for the second coming of Jesus (AA 54; GC 611, 612; TM 506).

In the experience of the individual Christian the early rain brings daily growth in character that prepares one for the spiritual latter rain, which brings to "completion" the "work of God's grace in the soul. By the power of the Holy Spirit the moral image of God is to be perfected in the character" (TM 506). As the initial germination and subsequent growth of the grain is an essential requisite for the ripening phase of development, so the initial reception of the Holy Spirit, resulting in the daily Christlike character development (Gal. 5:22, 23). Just as the late-season rains cannot ripen grain that was not previously germinated and matured, so the spiritual latter rain cannot compensate for the neglect of the early-rain experience (TM 507, 509-511; 1SM 191).

In the mid-1850s many Adventists were praying for the latter rain and a quick finish to the gospel commission. But Ellen White told them that the end-time Laodicean message (Rev. 3:14-22) could not be accomplished "in a few short months" because it was "designed to arouse the people of God . . . that they may be . . . fitted for the loud cry of the third angel." If this message "had been of as short duration as many of us supposed, there would have been no time for them to develop character" [and] "receive the latter rain, and thus be fitted for translation" (1T 186, 187).

Experiencing the latter rain reflects the divine-human cooperation that lies at the core of the plan of salvation. "Divine grace is needed at the beginning . . . [and] at every step of advance. . . . If we do not progress, if we do not place ourselves in an attitude to receive both the former and the latter rain, we shall lose our souls, and the responsibility will lie at our own door. . . . Man's cooperation is required" (TM 508).

The spiritual latter-rain phenomenon will replicate, but with greater global impact, the early rain at the opening of the gospel on the day of Pentecost. "By thousands of voices, all over the earth, the warning will be given. Miracles will be wrought, the sick will be healed, and signs and wonders will follow the believers. . . . Notwithstanding the agencies combined against the truth, a large number [will] take their stand upon the Lord's side" (GC 612).

See also: Loud Cry; Seal of God; Shaking.
Herbert E. Douglass

LAW IN GALATIANS, see **GALATIANS, LAW IN**.

LAW OF GOD. Ellen White's writings reflect three major aspects of the law of God: the moral, the ceremonial, and the natural (which includes the laws of health).

Basic to her thinking is God's moral law. For her, the moral law was not primarily the Ten Commandments. She is quite clear that there are eternal principles that are more basic than the Decalogue. Thus she writes that "the law of God existed before man was created. The angels were governed by it. Satan fell because he transgressed the principles of God's government. . . . After Adam's sin and fall nothing was taken from the law of God. The principles of the Ten Commandments existed before the Fall, and were of a character suited to the condition of a holy order of beings" (3SG 295; 1SM 220). In another connection she noted that after Adam's transgression the principles of the law "were definitely arranged and expressed to meet man in his fallen condition" (1SM 230).

To her, as for the New Testament (see Matt. 22:36-40; Rom. 13:8-10; Gal. 5:14), love was the principle that undergirded the Ten Commandments (ML 52; DA 329; Ed 76). It was the "law of love" that provided "the foundation of the government of God" (PP 34). Sin at the most basic level was, in her thinking, a transgression of the law of love: "It is the outworking of a principle at war with the great law of love which is the foundation of the divine government" (GC 493).

"When Satan rebelled against the law of Jehovah," Ellen White wrote, "the thought that there was a law came to the angels almost as an awakening to something unthought of"

(MB 109). In her thought, the angels were surprised because they had not been confronted with a list of "thou shalt nots." Rather, the principle of love was written in their hearts, and it was natural for them to act out the law of love. It was not until after the fall of Adam that the meaning of the principle of the law was made explicit for fallen beings as they related to God and one another. Thus the law proclaimed by Christ on Sinai was an explication of the eternal principle of the law of God (DA 329, 307).

Both the principle of the law and the Ten Commandments were given for the happiness and joy of humanity (Ed 76; 1SM 235). God's law was "ordained to life" (6BC 1094). It was God's plan that human happiness would result from being in harmony with His law.

But rebellion (sin) entered God's universe, and death and discord followed (PP 522). In the post-Fall world the law condemns lawbreakers, "but there is in it no power to pardon or to redeem. . . . It brings bondage and death to those who remain under its condemnation" (6BC 1094).

It is at the point of the condemning nature of the moral law that the importance of the ceremonial law comes into Ellen White's writings. In her thinking, the ceremonial law in its various aspects was an object lesson of the substitutionary sacrifice of Christ. The "sacrificial offerings" pointed "forward to the death of Christ as the great sin offering" (PP 363). "The whole arrangement of the typical system was founded on Christ. Adam saw Christ prefigured in the innocent beast suffering the penalty of his transgression of Jehovah's law" (6BC 1095).

Ellen White appreciated the ceremonial law as God-given, but she never lost sight of its limitation or purpose. It was not God's solution to the problems associated with the broken moral law, but it pointed toward the solution in the atoning blood of Christ (PP 372). For her the law and the gospel went hand in hand, with the gospel being necessary because of the broken law (1SM 240, 241).

Beyond the moral and the ceremonial laws, Ellen White had a great deal to say about law in the realm of nature, including laws related to health. Once again they were God's laws created for human good. As with the moral law, it is those who live in harmony with the laws of nature who are truly healthy and happy. Natural law is an expression of God's basic law of love.

The eternal law of love and its extension in the Decalogue is, for Ellen White, the law written upon the heart of the redeemed in the New Covenant relationship (DA 329; PP 372). A central function of the progressive sanctification of the saved is "to bring them into harmony with the principles of the law of heaven" (MB 50). Those same principles "will exist unchanged in Paradise restored. When Eden shall bloom on earth again, God's law of love will be obeyed by all beneath the sun" (*ibid.* 51).

Further reading: M. Veloso, "Law of God," in R. Dederen, ed., *Handbook of Seventh-day Adventist Theology* (RHPA, 2000), pp. 457-492.

George R. Knight

LAWSUITS. Ellen White's view of lawsuits was guided by Scripture, most notably two passages, Matthew 18:15-18 and 1 Corinthians 6:1-9. The former passage instructs believers to deal with erring fellow Christians within the framework of the church. The latter forbids believers from taking disputes with brethren to secular legal authorities. These two passages, along with the larger biblical context, provided the main principles for how Ellen White viewed lawsuits among believers, suits against church institutions, and the use of lawyers generally. Once these principles are understood, it is possible to see when the use of the legal system may be appropriate for believers and the church.

As a general rule, Ellen White was strongly opposed to civil lawsuits among believers. In the context of being wronged by a fellow believer, she wrote that "Christians need not contend for their rights. . . . In matters of difficulty between them and their brethren, they are not to appeal to Caesar or to Pilate" (RH, Jan. 3, 1899). If the Christian is abused, he or she is to "take it patiently; if defrauded of that which is his just due, he is not to appeal to unbelievers in courts of justice. Rather, let him suffer loss or wrong" (*ibid.*; cf. 1 Cor. 6:7). Ellen White believed that righting these matters was in the hands of God. "God will deal with the one who defrauds his brother and the cause of God. 'Vengeance is mine,' he says, 'I will repay' " (*ibid.*).

But to say justice was in the hands of God did not mean that she believed the wronged Christian had no earthly recourse. Rather, believers qualified by wisdom and experience should hear the dispute and correct the one in error. "Those who are lawful and obedient are the only ones who are empowered by Christ to deal with the cases of the erring" (RH, Mar. 26, 1895). Those that will "judge the world" can certainly judge the "things that pertain to this life" (1 Cor. 6:2, 3). To carry out this counsel, churches should have procedures in place to deal with disputes between believers in a just and impartial manner. Where such procedures are in place, the practical test of a "fellow believer" would be willingness to submit to the authority of a tribunal of fellow believers (Matt. 18:17, 18).

Ellen White applied the same rule about lawsuits between believers to those brought by believers against church institutions. If anything, she viewed such an act with even greater concern. To one member planning such a suit she counseled that "you will not only betray yourself; you will betray the cause of God into the hands of its enemies, and you will crucify the Son of God afresh and put Him to an open shame" (Lt 18, 1901, in 5MR 444).

Such actions open the church to reproach and ridicule by the world. "Matters connected with the church," she wrote, "are to be kept within its borders." To go to court on church-related matters was to place the "interests of the cause of God" in the hands of men who "have no connection with heaven," who have not "the wisdom which comes from above," and are not qualified to "pass judgment on matters connected with God's cause." Often such judges are intemperate and corrupt, and operate from principles of worldliness and selfishness. Decisions made by such judges would "retard the work of God" (5MR 410, 411).

There is no indication in Ellen White's writings that she would view any differently lawsuits brought by church institutions against believers, even when those believers are in error. Rather, in issues relating to the "kingdom of Christ no compulsion or forcing of conscience is permitted. No blood is to be shed, no force of arms employed, no prison is to be opened for the incarceration of one who does not choose the kingdom of God and His righteousness." Rather, "if one of Christ's followers offend, his faults are not to be opened up to unbelievers, not to be brought before earthly tribunals by his brethren" (RH, Mar. 26, 1895).

Further, while the church should have competent legal counsel in conducting its business, it should "not go for help to lawyers not of our faith" (5MR 410). The work of God is "not to be committed to men who have no connection with heaven" (*ibid.* 411). The worldly legal practices of obscuring true meanings and burying unfavorable elements beneath legal jargon and technicalities are to be rejected (Lt 53, 1903). In its legal and business dealings, the church should act carefully, directly, and clearly, and require the same from those with whom it is working (Lt 59, 1903).

The context of Ellen White's comments above had to do with civil disputes between church members. They should not be read as applying in the same way to intentional criminal misconduct. Crimes offend not merely the individual but the state. "There is no virtue," Ellen White wrote, "in advocating that theft or fraudulent behavior shall go unpunished" (RH, Jan. 3, 1899). Paul notes that the civil ruler is "the minister of God" to punish evildoers (Rom. 13:4). Christians may at times have not only a right but a moral duty to cooperate with civil rulers and report criminal misconduct involving church members. This is especially true when those crimes are against the weak, young, or otherwise unprotected (cf. ST, May 21, 1896; Matt. 18:6; Isa. 1:17).

Ellen White saw a proper role for Christian lawyers also in the civil context. "There may be Christian lawyers, Christian physicians, Christian merchants. Christ may be represented in all lawful callings" (WM 111). She understood that believers may need to protect their interests from fraud by those outside the fellowship of Christ. She indicated that forgiving our debtors does not mean we cannot require "our just dues from our debtors." But even here, unbelieving debtors are not to be "treated harshly, oppressed, nor placed in prison" (RH, Jan. 3, 1899). Lawsuits are costly and time-intensive, generate ill-will, often have unexpected outcomes, and are thus generally to be avoided, even against worldly defrauders. But Ellen White leaves open the

possibility that some circumstances may allow for recourse to civil courts.

Another situation in which her principles may allow for lawsuits is one in which the real party in interest is not actually the party named in the lawsuit. Here the injunction not to sue fellow believers may not apply, because the believer may not be the actual target of the suit. This can occur in recovering from insurance companies, which may require a lawsuit to be filed before they will reimburse a lawful claim. Thus, if church members have a car accident, it may be that to receive compensation from an insurance company, one member will have to sue the other in name, but the real defendant will be the insurance company, who will pay for the damages. A similar circumstance may occur when church entities are covered by insurance companies. But to remain consistent with Ellen White's principles, claimants in these cases should not seek to recover from individual defendants portions of an award in excess of the insurance policy limits. At times, the church itself may acknowledge that it lacks the expertise or authority to adjudicate certain matters, such as in child-custody cases or the administration of wills, and resort may of necessity be made to a court of law (see *Seventh-day Adventist Church Manual,* 17th ed. [2005], pp. 185-200).

Even when appropriate, civil suits should not be motivated by revenge or hostility. "Personal revenge is not becoming to a child of God" (RH, Jan. 3, 1899). The adversarial nature of court proceedings can quickly create a contentious relationship in which originally peace and friendship existed. Counsel and guidance from church leaders and qualified members should be sought in those rare instances in which suits seem justified, so that believers may continue to "stand shoulder to shoulder, heart to heart, with the truth, the present truth for this time, in possession of the heart" (3SM 303).

Ellen White showed both her desire for justice and her concern for harmony and goodwill in her own dealings with the law. She had helped raise her grandnieces May and Addie Walling at the request of their father during a time of family difficulty. The short-term request evolved into a lengthy commitment. The father made no effort to retrieve the girls, but allowed James and Ellen White to raise and educate them for nearly two decades. But sometime after the girls turned 18, their father desired them to return and keep house for him. They did not want to return, and he sued Ellen White for alienation of affection (4Bio 17). She litigated the case, with a lawyer, for a number of years. But when it came time for the trial, she was unwilling to have the girls "testify on oath against their father" in court, which would have "led to endless trouble" (Lt 128, 1896, in 14MR 330). To avoid this, and despite the fact that most thought she would have surely won the case, she settled it out of court for $1,500. She also had to pay $2,000 in attorneys' fees (4Bio 269). Neither was an insignificant sum in those days. This story shows Ellen White's use of the legal system to stand up for truth and justice, and also her willingness to forgo her own legal rights to minimize distress to people and relationships. It is a balance that all those led by the Spirit will seek in their legal dealings.

Nicholas P. Miller

LEADERSHIP. Ellen White would not have imagined herself to be a leadership theorist. However, within her writings, passionate spirituality, empowered calling, relational community, and mission priority are principles of leadership that provide timeless guidance for the church. The most important

contributions to understanding leadership are so universal, constant, or subtle in their foundational character that they are often overlooked. So it is with Ellen White's counsel. She saw leadership not as limited to specific positions, but as everyone's opportunity to serve in the mission of Christ (COL 330).

In contrast to individual qualities of selected men and women of position, the dominant theme of her counsel on leadership is in the context of community. She envisions relationships, empowered by the Holy Spirit, in which the influence is multidirectional. The influence flows among believers as they adapt to mission contexts, and is not coercive (6T 418, 419). In this type of relational leadership people exert influence in both the roles of leading and following, and those roles become fluid. Good leaders are good followers, and good followers are good leaders. "In His lessons of instruction to His disciples, Jesus taught them that His kingdom is not a worldly kingdom, where all are striving for the highest position; but He gave them lessons in humility and self-sacrifice for the good of others. . . . Worldlings are constantly striving to exalt themselves one above another; but Jesus, the Son of God, humbled Himself in order to uplift man. The true disciple of Christ will follow His example" (FE 142, 143).

Producing changes that reflect the revealed will of God is not the responsibility of a few in administrative positions, but rather the shared and mutual responsibility of a Spirit-led community, in Ellen White's view. "God has made His church on the earth a channel of light, and through it He communicates His purposes and His will. He does not give to one of His servants an experience independent of and contrary to the experience of the church itself. Neither does He give one man a knowledge of His will for the entire church while the church—Christ's body—is left in darkness" (AA 163).

Five aspects of this community-oriented relational process may be noted in Ellen White's counsel. First is her understanding that leadership happens as a church visions together. The influence of vision exists both within a disciple's experience with God and in the corporate nature of vision among the people of God. As a congregation or fellowship of congregations seeks divine guidance in prayer and surrenders to the moving of the Holy Spirit, God grants a shared vision that brings glory to His purpose (CET 231).

Second, the church leads together. Leadership roles are shared, people are empowered, and trust is evident. People are developed to accomplish the shared work of the church. "In matters of conscience the soul must be left untrammeled. No one is to control another's mind, to judge for another, or to prescribe his duty. God gives to every soul freedom to think, and to follow his own convictions. . . . In Christ's kingdom there is no lordly oppression" (DA 550, 551).

Third, the church learns together. The Holy Spirit guides as truth is sought and shared. Each is a learner, and biblical knowledge in particular equips each for their place in the leadership task (TSA 90).

Fourth, the church acts together. Christian disciples, ministering according to their spiritual gifts, join and organize for achieving a shared vision (7T 185).

And fifth, the church communicates together. Churches exercise leadership in a climate of mutual understanding produced by conversation, understanding, and prayer. "When this Spirit is appreciated, and those controlled by the Spirit communicate to others the energy with which they are imbued, an invisible chord is touched which electrifies the whole" (ST, Jan. 4, 1899).

Ellen White's vision for leadership finds its theological foundation in the biblical view of servant leadership expressed in the person of Jesus. "All who share this salvation, purchased for them at such an infinite sacrifice by the Son of God, will follow the example of the true Pattern. Christ was the chief Cornerstone, and we must build upon this Foundation. Each must have a spirit of self-denial and self-sacrifice. The life of Christ upon earth was unselfish; it was marked with humiliation and sacrifice. And shall men, partakers of the great salvation which Jesus came from heaven to bring them, refuse to follow their Lord and to share in His self-denial and sacrifice? . . . Is the servant greater than his Lord?" (FLB 151).

When speaking of the person of the leader, White's first developmental concern is transformational. Character formation is the first preparation for all Christian service. The journey of leadership development is the same (see AA 482, 483). Character formation yields disciples who contribute to the leadership culture of the church. Out of the regenerated life flow transformed leadership practices. As noted above, the first of these is vision.

The second of these transformed leadership practices is extraordinary hope provided by faith. "Discouragements will arise, but it is your privilege at all times to lay hold of the hope set before you in the gospel. Watch unto prayer. Believe that God will help you to speak words that will cheer and encourage and increase the faith of those with whom you associate" (MM 201).

Third is integrity. "Honor, integrity, and truth must be preserved at any cost to self" (GW 447). "God calls for men of heart, men of mind, men of moral integrity, whom He can make the depositaries of His truth" (3T 23).

Fourth is an unswerving belief in empowering people. White's counsel to her husband,

James, is typical: "I have been shown that it is my husband's duty to lay off responsibilities. . . . My husband's ready judgment and clear discernment . . . have led him to take on many burdens which others should have borne" (*ibid.* 497). She urged that "youth" be "educated" to "take the leadership" and thus "meet the approval of God" (CSW 70).

Fifth is courage. "God cannot use men who, in time of peril, when the strength, courage, and influence of all are needed, are afraid to take a firm stand for the right" (PK 142). Sixth is confidence and trust in the abundant provisions of God for the church (see OHC 192).

Ellen White recognized both the power of loving service rendered by a servant leader and the dangers of power in the hands of individuals. No aspect of her counsels to individuals in leadership is more striking than her warnings regarding abuse of authority, sometimes referred to as *kingly power. Authority is the ability or "authorization" to act, granted to persons to carry out certain functions. Ellen White frequently describes the dangers that accompany authority. To a conference president she wrote: "It is dangerous work to invest men with authority to judge and rule their fellow men. Not to you nor to any other man has been given power to control the actions of God's people" (ChL 33). "No man is ever to set himself up as a ruler, as a Lord over his fellow men, to act out his natural impulses. No one man's voice and influence should ever be allowed to become a controlling power" (*ibid.*).

Ellen White believed the church as a community guided by the Holy Spirit is be trusted, but not to be considered infallible. As the church seeks God's counsel in prayerful submission to the Spirit's leading, God may choose to reveal His will. In contrast to individual authority, she advocated the assembled judgment of the *General Conference of the church as the highest authority on earth. "At times, when a small group of men entrusted with the general management of the work have, in the name of the General Conference, sought to carry out unwise plans and to restrict God's work, I have said that I could no longer regard the voice of the General Conference, represented by these few men, as the *voice of God. But this is not saying that the decisions of a General Conference composed of an assembly of duly appointed, representative men from all parts of the field should not be respected. God has ordained that the representatives of His church from all parts of the earth, when assembled in a General Conference, shall have authority" (9T 260, 261).

Leadership is a relational process in which people empowered by the Holy Spirit freely associate in Christian service for the purpose of mission. The authority of the church is defined within the distribution of ministering gifts to each in the body. Thus the church becomes a ministering community empowered and organized by the Holy Spirit. Those who serve the body with distinct services of administration or leadership are not to rule over others. The mutual respect each has for another empowers all the gifts, including those that contribute to the organizational structures required to respond to changing mission contexts.

Further reading: *Christian Leadership*; 8T 236-238; C. Tutsch, *Ellen White on Leadership: Guidance for Those Who Influence Others* (PPPA, 2008).

Skip Bell

LEGACY OF LIGHT, see **CD-ROM AND THE INTERNET, ELLEN G. WHITE WRITINGS ON.**

LEGALISM. Ellen White describes several kinds of human attempts to please God. Some

Christians, like the Pharisees, devoid of faith, find their security in ritual and external correctness (DA 172, 280; 6T 417, 418); some thrive on constant repentance, thinking that sinning and repenting is all that is expected (COL 316; RH, Apr. 21, 1891); others sincerely try hard and harder, but feel only gloom and frustration (SC 116-118).

In the Sermon on the Mount Jesus said: "Unless your righteousness exceeds the righteousness of the scribes and Pharisees, you will by no means enter the kingdom of heaven" (Matt. 5:20, NKJV). Ellen White amplified this warning by explaining why the righteousness of the Pharisees "was worthless. . . . All their pretensions of piety, their human inventions and ceremonies, and even their boasted performance of the outward requirements of the law, could not avail to make them holy. They were not pure in heart or noble and Christlike in character" (MB 53).

She then adds her classic description of legalism: "A legal religion is insufficient to bring the soul into harmony with God. The hard, rigid orthodoxy of the Pharisees, destitute of contrition, tenderness, or love, was only a stumbling block to sinners. They were like the salt that had lost its savor; for their influence had no power to preserve the world from corruption. The only true faith is that which 'worketh by love' (Gal. 5:6) to purify the soul" (MB 53).

Ellen White frequently decried several kinds of legalism and their consequences. "Legalism" does not "have a proper estimate of sin" (ST, Apr. 9, 1894). Legalists, like the priests and rulers in Christ's day, were "fixed in a rut of ceremonialism" "satisfied with a legal religion" "made up of ceremonies and the injunctions of men" (AA 15). A legalist who "is trying to reach heaven by his own works in keeping the law is attempting an impossibility. There is no safety for one who

has merely a legal religion, a form of godliness" (DA 172). "A legal religion can never lead souls to Christ; for it is a loveless, Christless religion. . . . The round of religious ceremonies, the external humiliation, the imposing sacrifice, proclaim that the doer of these things regards himself as righteous, and as entitled to heaven; but it is all a deception" (ibid. 280). "Icy hearts . . . [have] only a legal religion" (3SM 177). Legalists "go crippling along, dwarfed in religious growth, because they have in their ministry a legal religion. The power of the grace of God is not felt to be a living, effectual necessity, an abiding principle" (ibid. 189). "The spirit of bondage is engendered by seeking to live in accordance with legal religion, through striving to fulfill the claims of the law in our own strength" (YI, Sept. 22, 1892).

When legalism prevails, either self-righteousness and pride, or discouragement and spiritual depression, soon follow. Intent on being Christians, legalists (often unknowingly) see only rigor, demand, and checklists. Jesus as their personal Savior, their personal enabler, their closest friend, as faithful high priest, becomes obscured. Though such Christians desire to please God, they feel the stress and see only the cloud, because "he who is trying to reach heaven by his own works in keeping the law is attempting an impossibility" (FW 94). For Ellen White, the answer to legalism is not to eliminate "commandment keeping" (antinomianism), but to focus on Christ as the atoning substitute and "all-powerful mediator" (GC 488); for "it is as necessary that He should keep us by His intercessions as that He should redeem us with His blood" (15MR 104). In the face of "the insufficiency of legal or natural religion," He offers "moral renovation" and "divine enlightenment" (RH, Apr. 30, 1895). An understanding of His righteousness brings the realization that even from "true believers," the most genuine worship, "prayers and penitence" are valueless apart from the continual intercession of Christ. Unless he "purifies all [this service] by His righteousness, it is not acceptable to God." But "perfumed with the merits" of Christ's atonement, the service of believer's "comes up before God wholly and entirely acceptable" (1SM 344).

See also: Justification; Righteousness by Faith; Sanctuary.

Herbert E. Douglass

LESSER LIGHT. A biblical allusion comparing the moon to the sun (Gen. 1:16, 1SAT 255), which Ellen White used in comparing her own message to that of Scripture. "Little heed is given to the Bible," she wrote, "and the Lord has given a lesser light to lead men and women to the greater light" (RH, Jan. 20, 1903; CM 125; cf. Ev 257). Three considerations clarify the meaning of this sentence: her varied uses of "lesser light," the grammar and context of the key sentence, and other statements about the relation of her writings to Scripture.

First, she uses "lesser light" in several different ways. When she compares the "glory of the Jewish age" to that of the Messiah, the "greater light" is Christ (ST, Aug. 25, 1887). "The wisest men the world has ever known" are "lesser lights" in comparison to "Christ, the Source of light" (TMK 97; YI, Sept.16, 1897). Likewise in personal experience, when believers "obtain clear views of Christ's true glory," all "minor things sink into insignificance, just as the lesser lights vanish when the sun appears" (RH, Feb. 25, 1896). Another biblical allusion is to John the Baptist. Christ Himself called John "*a* burning and a shining light," but then declared, "But I have *greater* witness [*light*] than that of John" (John 5:35, 36; cf. John 9:5). Thus in comparison to Christ, John was a lesser light, though in comparison

to other prophets, Christ said none was greater than John (Luke 7:28). Finally, the fact that she described her books as "great light" in contrast to other books of "lesser light" (PH079 7) shows that she could speak of them as either "greater" or "lesser" depending on what they were being compared to.

Second, the reference to her books as "a lesser light" (RH, Jan. 20, 1903) can imply either Scripture or Christ as the "greater light." Both interpretations are supported by her writings. For Christians, it goes without saying that all other sources are "lesser light" in comparison to Christ. In the original context of the statement referred to above, the preceding paragraph says Ellen White's "books" contain "light" that will lead men and women "to the Savior" (RH, Jan. 20, 1903). If the clause "the Lord has given a lesser light to lead men and women to the greater light" were exactly parallel to the use of the previous paragraph, then the "greater light" would refer to Christ. However, in the sentence "Little heed is given to the Bible, and the Lord has given a lesser light to lead men and women to the greater light," "lesser light" must mean lesser in comparison to the Bible; otherwise she would have written, "Little heed is given to the Bible, and the Lord has given [another] lesser light to lead men and women to the greater light."

In her view those in Christ will experience both Christ and the Scriptures as the "living word" of God (RH, Apr. 24, 1900; RH, Aug. 19, 1909). "The living Word is the sword of the Spirit" (RH, Oct. 13, 1904). Christ "was Himself the living Word," who said, " 'The words that I speak unto you, they are spirit, and they are life' " (ST, Sept. 5, 1895). She held Christ and Scripture in perfect union as supreme authorities for the Christian. Thus her writings are a "lesser light" to both Scripture and Christ.

Third, she wrote extensively on the relation of her writings to Scripture. Echoing the sixteenth-century Reformers' insistence on the unity of Word and Spirit, White declared, "The Spirit was not given—nor can it ever be bestowed—to supersede the Bible; for the Scriptures explicitly state that the Word of God is the standard by which all teaching and experience must be tested [1 John 4:1 and Isaiah 8:20 quoted]" (GC vii).

In her very first book, Ellen White recognized the subordinate relation of her writings to the Bible. "I recommend to you, dear reader, the Word of God as the rule of your faith and practice. By that Word we are to be judged. God has, in that Word, promised to give visions in the '*last days*'; not for a new rule of faith, but for the comfort of His people, and to correct those who err from Bible truth" (ExV 64; italics supplied; cf. EW 78; 3SM 29).

In 1870 she wrote, "The Word of God is sufficient to enlighten the most beclouded mind and may be understood by those who have any desire to understand it. But . . . some who profess to make the Word of God their study are found living in direct opposition to its plainest teachings. Then, to leave men and women without excuse, God gives plain and pointed testimonies, bringing them back to the word that they have neglected to follow" (2T 454, 455).

Another comparison between Scripture and her writings comes from 1871. "I took the precious Bible," she wrote, "and surrounded it with the several *Testimonies for the Church*, given for the people of God. Here, said I, the cases of nearly all are met. The sins they are to shun are pointed out. . . . But there are not many of you that really know what is contained in the *Testimonies*. You are not familiar with the Scriptures. If you had made God's Word your study, with a desire to reach the Bible standard and attain

to Christian perfection, you would not have needed the *Testimonies*. It is because you have neglected to acquaint yourselves with God's inspired Book that He has sought to reach you by simple, direct testimonies, calling your attention to the words of inspiration [Scripture] which you had neglected to obey, and urging you to fashion your lives in accordance with its [the Bible's] pure and elevated teachings" (*ibid.* 605).

Notice the running comparison between her writings and Scripture: "The Lord designs to warn you, to reprove, to counsel, through *the testimonies* given, and to impress your minds with the importance of the truth of *His Word [Scripture]*. The written *testimonies* are not to give new light, but to impress vividly upon the heart the *truths of inspiration already revealed [in Scripture]*. Man's duty to God and to his fellow man has been distinctly specified in *God's Word [Scripture]*; yet but few of you are obedient to the light given. *Additional truth is not brought out; but God has through the* Testimonies *simplified the great truths already given* and in His own chosen way brought them before the people to awaken and impress the mind with them, that all may be left without excuse. . . . The *Testimonies* are not to belittle the *Word of God* [Scripture], but to exalt it and attract minds to it, that the beautiful simplicity of truth may impress all" (*ibid.* 605, 606; italics supplied).

Repeatedly she affirmed the primacy of Scripture (3SM 30-33), and the function of her writings to explain and emphasize the teachings of Scripture. The testimonies are *not* an "addition" to the biblical canon, but are "to bring the minds of His [God's] people to His Word, to give them a clearer understanding of it" (4T 246). In 1889 she wrote, "The Word of God abounds in general principles for the formation of correct habits of living, and the testimonies, general and personal, have been calculated to call their attention more especially to these principles" (5T 663, 664). "God has been speaking to His people in the *Testimonies* of His Spirit, in the Spirit of Prophecy, to lead the minds of His people to the Bible teaching" (4MR 213). Again she called her message "light [that] is to bring confused minds to His Word," the Bible (3SM 29).

This was the common understanding of early Adventists. James White wrote: "Let the gifts have their proper place in the church. God has never set them in the very front, and commanded us to look to them to lead us in the path of truth, and the way to heaven. His Word He has magnified. The Scriptures of the Old and New Testament are man's lamp to light up his path to the kingdom. Follow that. But if you err from Bible truth, and are in danger of being lost, it may be that God will in the time of His choice correct you, and bring you back to the Bible, and save you" (RH, Feb. 25, 1868, quoted in 1Bio 325, 326).

Even though Ellen White understood her writings as a "lesser light" compared to the canonical authority of Scripture, she believed her inspiration was of the same kind and from the same Source as that of the Bible writers. "In ancient times God spoke to men by the mouth of prophets and apostles," she wrote in 1876. "In these days He speaks to them by the *Testimonies* of His Spirit. There was never a time when God instructed His people more earnestly than He instructs them now" (4T 147, 148; 5T 661). She believed that "the Holy Ghost is the author of the Scriptures and of the Spirit of Prophecy" (3SM 30; cf. 29-33, 48-51). In 1894 she wrote: "Let none be educated to look to Sister White, but to the mighty God, who gives instruction to Sister White" (5MR 140).

Yet, while holding that Scripture and the testimonies had the same divine source, White saw her writings as a secondary norm to the supreme norm of Scripture (3SM 30). Thus

her writings were to be tested by the Bible, not vice versa: "If the *Testimonies* speak not according to the Word of God, reject them. Christ and Belial cannot be united" (5T 691). "Even the work of the Holy Spirit upon the heart is to be tested by the Word of God. The Spirit which inspired the Scriptures always leads to the Scriptures" (1SM 43). "The *Testimonies* were not given to take the place of the Bible," she warned. "The *Testimonies* are not to belittle the Word of God, but to exalt it" (5T 663, 665).

She taught that her writings were not to displace the Bible in personal faith and life. "The Lord desires you to study your Bibles. He has not given any additional light to take the place of His Word. This light [her writings] is to bring confused minds to His Word, which, if eaten and digested, is as the lifeblood of the soul" (3SM 29). "The Bible must be your counselor," she wrote in 1907. "Study it and the testimonies God has given; for they never contradict His Word" (*ibid.* 32).

She reinforced such counsel with examples of how and when *not* to use her writings. "In public labor do not make prominent, and quote that which Sister White has written, as authority to sustain your positions. . . . Bring your evidences, clear and plain, from the Word of God" (*ibid.* 29; cf. 1888 Materials 165). Some Adventists in private conversations with persons of other faiths "had taken an unwise course" in citing White's writings "instead of going to the Bible for proof" of their beliefs. With persons unacquainted with their source, she insisted, "the *Testimonies* can have no weight" and "should not be referred to in such cases" (5T 669).

Among those who believed that her writings were from God, however, White clearly believed there were times for them to be read publicly. She often requested that her testimonies be read in church. To the "Brethren and Sisters in New York," she wrote, "Will you please to read this in your churches?" (PH039 13; cf. 5T 62). To George Amadon, one of the elders of the Battle Creek church, she wrote, "Please read to the church what I am sending you." A few sentences later she added, "please read . . . 'How to Receive Reproof' [5T 683]" (PC 93; SpM 466). Many other examples can be cited (PC 49; PaM 146; RH, May 19, 1903; 3MR 195; 10MR 128, 144; 15MR 202, 207). Because she regarded her messages as "the word of the Lord," she urged those who read them in meetings to "be sure not to mix in your filling of words, for this makes it impossible for the hearers to distinguish between the word of the Lord to them and your words" (6T 122, 123).

In the light of these many requests to read her writings in the churches, it is clear that her exhortation that "The Bible . . . alone should be heard from the pulpit" occurs in a different context. Here she is contrasting the Bible to fable and tradition, by which "the Bible has been robbed of its power," so that the "hearers cannot say, 'Did not our heart burn within us, while he talked with us by the way, and while he opened to us the scriptures?' Luke 24:32" (PK 626). Similarly, she warned ministers "not to accept the opinion of commentators as the voice of God," but to "make the Bible its own expositor" (TM 106).

Thus Scripture and the prophetic gift were to work in perfect harmony: Scripture as the ancient, unchanging, and sufficient source of doctrine, and the prophetic gift as explaining and applying Scripture to the present life of the church. She assured those who preserved this unity between her writings and Scripture that they would "be safe from the many delusions" of the "last days" (3SM 84; cf. 1SM 48).

In conclusion, the metaphor "lesser light," based on the moon's reflection of the sun, consistently denotes human reflectors of light (John, the Hebrew dispensation, great teachers), in contrast to the divine Source of light. Every prophet is thus a "lesser light" compared to Christ. Ellen White also called her books "lesser light" compared to the canonical Scripture, the cumulative light from Christ that is the test of all other light. Thus, while she always maintained that her "light" was of the *same kind* and from the *same Source* as that of the biblical prophets, the word "lesser" referred to the subordinate *function* of her writings in relation to Christ and Scripture.

A. Leroy Moore

LESSONS FROM THE LIFE OF NEHEMIAH (Ellen G. White Estate, n.d., 61 pp.). Series of 19 articles on the life and work of Nehemiah published by Ellen White in 1904 in *The Southern Watchman*. Although much of the material contained in these articles can be found throughout her other publications, this collection focuses on "the responsibility of church leadership in the context of a revival and reformation among God's people" (introduction). To Ellen White, Nehemiah was a man "true to principle," "who esteemed the service of God above every earthly advantage," and "who would honor God at the loss of all things" (p. 1). She sees his spirit of zeal and earnestness as an example to "those who occupy positions of influence and responsibility in the church" (p. 17). A series of study guides accompanies these articles.

LETTERS TO YOUNG LOVERS (PPPA, 1983, 94 pp.). Compilation composed primarily of letters written by Ellen White to young people to assist them in making right choices regarding courtship and marriage, in order to establish happy homes. While some names have been changed, the compilers have added helpful background information, including additional related counsels from Ellen White.

A range of topics is covered, from marriage as a foretaste of heaven, through sexual responsibility. Direct and practical advice is given, such as "What a Young Man Should Look for in a Wife" and "Questions a Girl Should Ask Before Marriage." Positive encouragement is given, such as how to nourish love within the family. Also, strong cautions are sounded, such as the corrupting influence of exciting love stories and impure pictures. Photo reproductions of actual letters with Ellen White's signature give this volume a personal touch.

Ron du Preez

LIBRARY OF ELLEN G. WHITE. The Ellen G. White library is composed of four sections: (1) her private library; (2) her office library; (3) a library of nearly 600 books sold to her in 1913 by Clarence C. Crisler; and (4) the books located today in the Ellen G. White Estate Office dating back to her time, but lacking her bookplates or signature. Not only books (monographs), but also many bound volumes of periodicals, are found in these libraries.

The three major portions of the Ellen G. White library (1-3) have been identified largely on the basis of an inventory made of the books in her possession at the time of her death in 1915. In addition to the inventory we know of a few titles not on the inventory that are now found in the Ellen G. White Estate, having a bookplate either with "The Private Library of Ellen G. White" or "The Office Library of Ellen G. White" (4, above). There are 66 books in this category, the majority of which are from non-Seventh-day Adventist authors. When these 66 titles are included in the first three portions of the Ellen White library—the private and office libraries, and the Crisler additions—we have a list of approximately 1,300 titles in her collection that we know of a certainty that she possessed at the time of her death, not including the ones she authored herself. Nearly all of these were published by authors who were not Seventh-day Adventists, but who wrote mostly upon biblical and spiritual topics. These are compiled in *A Bibliography of Ellen G. White's Private and Office Libraries* (EGW, 1993, SDoc). Other topics found in these works include health/temperance reform, church history, and advocacy of the cause of the American Blacks, for example. There are also a considerable number of reference works, including language dictionaries and grammars. Obviously Ellen White did not read all these books, but we know she read some of them by the marks she placed in the margins of a page adjacent to the part she wanted to be able to refer back to.

The purpose of the Ellen G. White library was to provide assistance both to Ellen White and to her literary assistants in the writing of her books. The fact that many of the books are reference and historical works indicates that she wished to have her writings as accurate as possible, both in content and in style. This is also borne out in her private correspondence that touches upon her literary works. There was no effort on her part to conceal the fact that she relied upon the great Christian literature of her day, and her use of those materials was both legal and ethical, as recent studies have demonstrated.

See also: Plagiarism.

Further reading: W. H. Johns, "Ellen White: Prophet or Plagiarist?" *Ministry*, June 1982.

Warren H. Johns

LIFE AND TEACHINGS OF ELLEN G. WHITE (PPPA, 1933, 128 pp.). Full title: *A Brief Sketch of the Life and Teachings of Ellen G. White: A Narrative of Early Experiences and Choice Selections From Her Writings.*

Compilation of Ellen White's writings on her life experiences and public ministry. Materials selected for this book were drawn from Ellen White's published works, in particular *Life Sketches of Ellen G. White* (1915 edition). The first part presents Ellen White's childhood life, her experience in the Advent movement in the 1840s, and her first visions. The second part includes materials describing the beginning of her public ministry, her marriage to James White, and their early efforts at publishing the *Review and Herald* and establishing the foundations of the Seventh-day Adventist Church up to about 1855. The third part sketches her public labors from 1855 to 1915. Finally, the editors give a brief presentation of Ellen White's gift of prophecy and how it fulfilled biblical tests of a genuine prophet.

LIFE AT ITS BEST (PPPA, 1964, 314 pp.). Abridged edition of Ellen White's book *The Ministry of Healing,* which was first published in 1905. A similar abridgment had already been published in 1943 under the title of *Your Home and Health.* Many chapters from the original edition have different titles and have been rearranged in a different order. The book is illustrated with contemporary photographs.

LIFE INCIDENTS (SDA, 1868, 373 pp.). Autobiography of James White's early life, beliefs, and career in Millerite and Sabbatarian Adventism to 1868. Since *Life Incidents* followed Ellen White's *Spiritual Gifts,* volume 2 (1860), it did not repeat Ellen's part of the story, but simply referred the reader to *Spiritual Gifts.* That is why *Life Incidents,* a book of more than 300 pages, contains only three pages of biographical material on Ellen (pp. 271-274).

Life Incidents is structured along three lines. The organizing thread is James White's own strong and often fascinating story, into which is woven the broader history of the Millerite and Sabbatarian Adventist movements, supported by a third component, the exposition of biblical passages and themes foundational to those movements.

James White's personal experience begins with his ancestry and early years to age 21, when he first heard William Miller in 1842 (pp. 9-25). At this point an almost 50-page parenthesis sketches Miller's life, labors, and message (pp. 25-72). The account of White's early preaching, 1842-1844, is intense, fast-paced, occasionally humorous, and sometimes hair-raising (pp. 72-120). This section is full of stories that show the courage, urgency, and assertiveness that would characterize his later leadership of the Seventh-day Adventist denomination (pp. 88-96).

White was present (p. 157) at the Exeter, New Hampshire, camp meeting of August 12-18, 1844, the meeting that launched the message that Jesus would come on October 22, less than nine weeks from then. The Adventists' expectation that Christ would return on the "tenth day of the seventh month of the Jewish year 1844," i.e., October 22, climaxed in disappointment. James White argues movingly, however, that "the impressions made and left upon the minds of believers" in that movement "were deep and lasting," never to be fully effaced. "Let [one who was there] hear the subject afresh; let the simple facts be again brought before his mind, and he will feel upon this subject as he can feel upon no other" (p. 181).

The last half of the book recounts the rise and progress of Seventh-day Adventism. In the section titled "Present Position and Work," White highlights four salient beliefs of Seventh-day Adventists: (1) that the Advent is near, but without setting a definite time; (2) that the Millerite time preaching was "the design of God" to herald to the world the 2300-day prophecy that reached to the beginning of "the investigative Judgment" (pp. 321, 322); (3) the perpetuity of spiritual gifts; and (4) that the seventh-day Sabbath is the truth by which God especially tests the people of this age (pp. 331-334). In sum, *Life Incidents* provides a snapshot, from James White's point of view, of the state of Adventism in 1868. The subhead "Volume One" on the title page suggests that the author originally planned to extend the narrative to a second volume. There was, however, no volume 2. When James White updated the work in 1880, it was renamed *Life Sketches* and incorporated Ellen White's story as well.

Further reading: J. White, *Life Incidents: In Connection With the Great Advent Movement as Illustrated by the Three Angels of Revelation XIV* (Battle Creek, Mich.: SDA Pub. Assn., 1868; reprinted, with historical introduction by J. Moon, AUP, 2004).

Jerry Moon

LIFE INSURANCE, see **INSURANCE**.

LIFE OF CHRIST, THE. An adapted, non-English one-volume edition of *The Spirit of Prophecy*, volumes 2 and 3; forerunner of *The Desire of Ages*. In 1883 the General Conference session voted to translate those two volumes into different European languages. Ellen White and her staff provided a manuscript based on *The Spirit of Prophecy*, volume 2, which expanded the first four chapters into eight new chapters. Several other changes and insertions were made as well. The chapters of volume 3 that deal with Christ's life were used without any changes. Between 1885 and 1893 a Danish-Norwegian edition was published under the title *Jesu Kristi liv* in Christiania, Norway, and in Battle Creek, Michigan. From 1886 and probably until 1888 the Swedish *Kristi lefnad* was published in Stockholm, Sweden, and Battle Creek, Michigan. In 1887 the German *Das Leben Jesu Christi* and the French *La vie de Christ* were published at Basel, Switzerland; Oakland, California; and Battle Creek, Michigan. The French edition went through several printings until 1891, and the German edition until 1893. In terms of sales to people of the respective language groups, these editions ranked among the most successful Adventist *colporteur books of their day, in the United States as well as in Europe. Planned editions in Dutch, Spanish, and English were not realized, because Ellen White wanted to revise the manuscript further and add new material before the book was republished. However, as late as 1897 a Finnish edition was published at Helsinki, Finland, under the title *Kristuksen Elämä*.

In preparing the manuscript for *The Desire of Ages* (1898), Ellen White and her literary assistant, Marian A. Davis, followed the French *Life of Christ* "as nearly as seemed feasible" in regard to the details and the arrangement of the content (M. A. Davis to J. E. White, Dec. 22, 1895, EGWE). Further, they used the basic material of *The Life of Christ*, amplified it, and added new material. In fact, some of the material used in *The Desire of Ages* can be traced back only to these European editions and not to any other existing sources. The suggestions made for the revision of *The Life of Christ* editions were also considered in preparing the new book. Thus, *The Life of Christ* forms a distinct stage in the preparation of *The Desire of Ages*, and a link between *The Spirit of Prophecy*, volumes 2 and 3, and *The Desire of Ages*.

See also: *The Desire of Ages* Sources, Study of.

Further reading: 3Bio 219, 237, 435, 443-445; D. Kaiser, "A Forgotten Chapter of European Adventist History: Ellen White's

Life of Christ" (research paper, AU, 2008, CAR); D. Kaiser, "Ellen White's *Life of Christ*: Forerunner of *Desire of Ages*," Seminary Scholarship Symposium Papers (AU, Feb. 6, 2009); F. Veltman, "Full Report of the *Life of Christ* Research Project" (Angwin, Calif., n.l., 1988), pp. 119-123.

Denis Kaiser

LIFE OF CHRIST RESEARCH PROJECT, see *THE DESIRE OF AGES SOURCES, STUDY OF.*

LIFE OF JESUS, see *STORY OF JESUS.*

LIFE SKETCHES OF ELLEN G. WHITE (PPPA, 1915, 480 pp.). Autobiography released shortly after Ellen White's death. It was the sixth in a series of autobiographical works that began with *A Sketch of the Christian Experience and Views of Ellen G. White* (Saratoga Springs, N.Y.: James White, 1851), followed by her *Spiritual Gifts,* volume 2 (1860) and James White's *Life Incidents* (1868).

The fourth in this series of autobiographies was the first to be called *Life Sketches.* Coauthored by James and Ellen White, it was titled *Life Sketches: Ancestry, Early Life, Christian Experience, and Extensive Labors of Elder James White and His Wife, Mrs. Ellen G. White* (Battle Creek, Mich.: SDA Pub. Assn., 1880). Pages 1-130 are James' story, updated from *Life Incidents* (1868). Pages 131-324 are Ellen's story, adapted from *Spiritual Gifts.* The third section (324-411) is again from James, giving him 218 pages to his wife's 212.

The fifth in the series was the 1888 edition of *Life Sketches,* which extended the autobiography only to 1881, to include an account of James White's death. For this reason, in the sixth volume, *Life Sketches of Ellen G. White* (1915), Ellen White's first-person account reaches only through 1881 (p. 254). The rest of the volume (pp. 255-480) was compiled by *C. C. Crisler, with assistance

from *W. C. White and *D. E. Robinson (LS 6). Also, as the change of title indicates, the 1915 volume omits the previously published sections by and about James White.

Jerry Moon

LIFT HIM UP (RHPA, 1988, 382 pp.). Fifteenth book of daily devotional readings published by the Ellen G. White Estate. This devotional focuses on Christ and the reasons to exalt Him as Savior and Redeemer. Each month features a different theme, such as lifting up Christ as the Son of God, the Bread of Life, the Crucified One, or the Coming King. These daily readings are selected from Ellen White's published works, diaries, and letters. The book also includes seven pages of biographical notes on Ellen White (pp. 7-13).

LIGHT, LESSER, see **LESSER LIGHT.**

LITERARY ASSISTANTS. Ellen White's first literary assistant was her husband, James White. He was her helper and counselor as she prepared the messages given to her by God. After she wrote instructions received in vision, he helped her correct grammatical errors and remove repetition for a smoother reading of the material. As her work grew, and especially after he died in 1881, she employed conscientious and God-fearing secretaries to correct the grammar in her writings.

Ellen White used the word "editing" with reference to the work of some of her most trusted assistants (see, e.g., Lt 128, 1896; Lt 131, 1893). However, there were two important differences from the common use of that word. First, Ellen White's helpers were to remove imperfections of grammar without changing her *thought*. They were absolutely forbidden to alter Ellen White's concepts or intrude any personal ideas of the assistant into the manuscript (WCW to G. A. Irwin, May 7, 1900, Letter Book 15, pp. 587-589, EGWRC-GC). Second, even Ellen White's characteristic *vocabulary* was not to be changed. *Fannie Bolton was discharged partly because she substituted her own style and vocabulary for that of Ellen White (Lt 78, 1892).

Ellen White did not use the typewriter, nor did she dictate her material. The many thousands of pages that appear in print were originally written by hand. The first commercially practical typewriter was marketed in 1874; 11 years later (in 1885, when EGW was 58), she purchased these machines for her office staff. She was a progressive person who wanted up-to-date equipment for her helpers. Her literary assistants were originally termed "copyists" because the bulk of their work was transcribing her handwritten copies with a typewriter, or using multiple layers of carbon paper to make duplicate copies. That Ellen White herself, however, never learned to type is fortunate for researchers today, because the first draft of all her manuscripts was written in longhand—indisputable evidence of her authorship. *Arthur L. White, who worked with her manuscripts for more than 60 years, was so familiar with her handwriting that he would often astound visitors to the vault by asking them to select one at random, then hold a hand over the date, and allow him to guess the date of origin. According to Roger W. Coon, Arthur White seldom missed by more than a year or two (Coon, p. 8).

A primary task of the literary assistants was to transcribe Ellen White's handwritten material on the typewriter, making such editorial corrections as were within the prescribed guidelines. The typewritten copy would then be handed to Ellen White, who would mark between the lines whatever changes or additions were necessary. These interlineations on many existing letters and manuscripts show how carefully she read every sentence.

If the changes were many, the assistant would retype the manuscript or letter, and Ellen White would review it again before it was put into the mail or sent to the printer. It was her habitual practice to read and approve every letter, manuscript, article, or book chapter. These documents were signed by her in her own handwriting. A signature stamp was used when several copies were made, but the original was hand signed. When she traveled, one of her secretaries usually went along to stenographically report her public addresses (Dores Robinson to R. F. Correa, Apr. 28, 1943, DF 51a).

The editorial process followed by Ellen White's literary assistants was a blend of putting the work into proper grammatical form and rearranging, assembling, and compiling the material into a new literary work. Many times the manuscripts and letters needed only slight editing; other times, as she wrote in haste or under pressure, they needed a good deal more work. As W. C. White put it, her "workers of experience . . . are authorized to take a sentence, paragraph, or section from one manuscript where the thought was clearly and fully expressed, and incorporate it with another manuscript where the same thought was expressed but not so clearly" (WCW to G. A. Irwin, May 7, 1900).

Over the years Ellen White employed some 20 literary assistants—of which the name of *Marian Davis is probably the most recognized. Some of the other well-known names are *C. C. Crisler, *Sarah Peck, Eliza Burnham, *Fannie Bolton, *Maggie (Hare) Bree, *Minnie Hawkins (see *C. C. Crisler), *Nellie Druillard, *Emily Campbell, *Dores E. Robinson, *Lucinda (Abbey) Hall, *Adelia (Patten) Van Horn, Anna Hale Royce, Emma Sturgis Prescott, *Mary Clough, and *Mrs.

J. I. Ings. There were others who served for only short periods of time. Most of them, at one time or another, lived in her home and were part of her family. She paid her workers from her own pocket, as well as housing and feeding those who lived in her home.

With rare exceptions (see Fannie Bolton) Ellen White's copyists and assistants were conscientious and faithful in following her instructions that no change of thought and no additional thought be brought into the work by them. So there would be no misunderstandings in their reading of the handwritten material, she habitually looked over the typescript, making any necessary adjustments before giving her approval. Only then was it sent to the printer, or put into the mail as letters to individuals or groups (DF 52a).

Nellie Druillard reported that Ellen White's "workers all felt that they should guard the copy signed and ready for the mail, that not a pen nor pencil should be used on it." "Not one of them would wish to make a change if they could; they were more anxious to have every word just as Mrs. White wanted it than to have it otherwise" (N. Druillard to Dores Robinson, Sept. 22, 1933, DF 393).

After Ellen White's death, when she was no longer available to give guidance to her helpers and to read materials in their final form, the editorial assistants were limited to correcting spelling and grammatical constructions. Their responsibility was understood not to include interpretation of her writings. If a passage was unclear, it was left that way rather than try to make it say clearly what the editor might understand it to mean. The *Ellen G. White Estate currently follows virtually the same editing guidelines as in 1915 and as prescribed in her last *will and testament.

See also: Correspondence, Ellen G. White's; *The Desire of Ages; The Desire of Ages* Sources,

Study of; *Testimonies for the Church;* White, W. C.

Further reading: "Guidelines for Editing Ellen G. White Material Released by the White Estate" (EGWE, SDoc); "Work of Editors on EGW Books" (DF 52a); N. Collins, "Compilations—What They Are and What They Are Not" (EGWE, SDoc); R. W. Coon, "EGW's Use of Literary Assistants: The Prophet as a Writer" (AU lecture outline, rev. Apr. 13, 1995); M. A. King and K. L. Morgan, *More Than Words: A Study of Inspiration and Ellen White's Use of Sources in* The Desire of Ages (Berrien Springs, Mich.: Honor Him Pub., 2009); J. Moon, *W. C. White and Ellen G. White* (AUP, 1993), pp. 63, 64, 114-116, 221-224, 349-353, 397-410, 445, 446; R. W. Olson, "Inspired Writers' Literary Assistants" (EGWE, SDoc); R. W. Olson, *One Hundred and One Questions on the Sanctuary and on Ellen White* (EGWE, 1981, SDoc); R. W. Olson, *The Fannie Bolton Story* (EGWE, SDoc); T. Poirier, "Work of Literary Assistants" (EGWE, SDoc); *idem*, "Exhibits Regarding the Work of Ellen White's Literary Assistants"; W. C. White, "How Ellen White's Books Were Written" (EGWE, SDoc); A. L. White, *Ellen G. White: Messenger to the Remnant* (RHPA, 1969).

Norma Collins

LITERARY BORROWING, see **PLAGIARISM**.

LITERATURE AND READING. Appropriate literature, particularly the reading of fiction and novels, has long been a concern within Adventism. Many of Ellen White's statements are categorical in their denunciation of fiction and novels. She writes, "The readers of fiction are indulging an evil that destroys spirituality" (MYP 272). More pointedly, she says, "Put away every novel" (*ibid.* 286), since "all [novels] are pernicious in their influence" (2T 236). "For the lover of fiction" "total abstinence is his only safety" (MH 446). With such statements it would seem that those who read novels or any form of fiction are putting their spirituality in danger. Such statements have led many Seventh-day Adventists to avoid all fictitious writing, especially novels. Is such an interpretation justified, or does the setting in which Ellen White wrote about fiction help us to understand her counsels on the topic?

What makes this an issue are the apparent contradictions between Ellen White's counsel and standard scholarly understandings of the terminology and purpose of literature, including the two controversial genres—fiction and the novel. Central to the issue are contradictory meanings implicit in the terms. Fiction is often used as an antonym to fact. In a literary sense, fiction refers to imagined or invented writing. While all writing, including factual reports, is imaginative, fiction emphasizes this element. Yet literary scholars emphasize the truth of fiction because it is typically expected to mirror reality. Scholars also expect well-written fiction to be universal and probable and to resemble reality closely by reflecting what is known to be true about human experience and character. The novel, often used synonymously with fiction, is easier to define. A novel is a lengthy prose work telling a story involving recognizably human characters. To literary scholars, genre is not an issue. As genres, fiction and novels are methods of inventive writing, not something inherently destructive of spirituality.

Complicating the issue are apparent contradictions between Ellen White's statements and her own writings and practice. Her statements also seem to conflict with the practice of the biblical writers. While the Bible does not have extensive fiction, there are clearly fictional passages. Although typically described in less pejorative terms, such as parable, fable, and allegory, nevertheless they are fiction.

Included are Jotham's fable of the trees in Judges 9 and Paul's allegory on the parts of the body in 1 Corinthians 12. The book of Esther uses many techniques associated with fiction—dialogues, hyperbole, a structured plot, and stylized characters. And one parable, the rich man and Lazarus, demands a fictional understanding if one wishes to avoid doctrinal misreading. From the example of the Bible itself, fiction is an accepted genre.

Ellen White's own practice also seems to conflict with her statements. At least once she recommends the reading of one novel, John Bunyan's *Pilgrim's Progress*, calling it a "wonderful allegory" (GC 252). Even some of her visions are written in a fictional manner. Her vision of travelers with loaded wagons, who switch to horseback as the road narrows, and who finally dismount and travel on foot before swinging across a chasm on slender cords, reads like a short story (2T 594-597). Readers do not treat the story as a literal occurrence. A fictional or allegorical format makes it more enjoyable to read and easier to understand.

In 1965 John Waller made a thorough study of Ellen White's writings on the subject of fiction. His study brought attention to scrapbooks of stories and articles collected by Ellen White, some of which were subsequently published in *Sabbath Readings for the Home Circle*. An avid reader of magazines of her time, she collected useful or interesting stories, making at least nine scrapbooks of stories and articles. While four have been lost, the five remaining scrapbooks are with the White Estate. Waller found that most of the stories were anonymous, many were fiction, and a few were by well-known fiction writers of her time, including Hans Christian Andersen, noted for his fairy tales, and Harriet Beecher Stowe, author of *Uncle Tom's Cabin*. Waller concluded: "On the evidence of the scrapbooks and *Sabbath Readings* . . . absence of sheer factuality was not Mrs. White's definition of fiction. At least between 1850 and 1880 she herself read and preserved for future reference many relatively short, . . . nonfactual stories that appeared in various magazines. . . . Thus, in practice, she established the principle of exercising moral discrimination in dealing with simple, clearly moralistic fiction" (Waller, p. 21).

An understanding of the historical context of novels and fiction in the nineteenth century, however, helps resolve these apparent contradictions between Ellen White's condemning statements and her own apparent practice. John Wood's study, "The Trashy Novel Revisited: Popular Fiction in the Age of Ellen White," provides information on popular fiction from 1850 to 1900, when Ellen White was making her most scathing statements. There were millions of copies of certain types of novels widely available. For instance, the now relatively unknown yet most prolific novelist of the time, Mrs. E.D.E.N. Southworth, wrote more than 60 novels, each selling more than 100,000 copies (pp. 17, 18).

The type of novel is also significant. Categorized as "domestic" or "sentimental" fiction, these melodramatic novels typically contained plots that involved the unpleasant experiences of a wife or young woman dealing with a husband or boss who drank liquor or chased women, or with an erring child, or with sickness and poverty. The heroine always triumphed over such trials by living a pure life. Another common type was the "sensational" novel involving Native American warpath or Civil War stories, rags-to-riches experiences, or stereotypical American Western accounts of ranchers versus outlaws—stories typically filled with incredible accounts of bloodshed and dire dangers. Religious magazines were filled with similar stories—but with obvious moral overtones. When Ellen

White criticizes stories with a semblance of religion, she probably has in mind such sentimental or sensational but morally correct domestic stories that were published primarily to raise revenue.

Publisher's attitudes and the labels they used were also significant. Most novels were first published as serialized stories in weekly or monthly magazines. When the public clamored for the entire novel at once, publishers issued inexpensive paperbacks at 10 cents a copy, thus the term "dime" novel. The only concern was quick publication and sales. Writers churned novels out as quickly as possible. One novelist, Wood notes, wrote a 40,000-word novel in 24 hours (p. 21).

However, if a work became popular with high enough sales, it was reissued in a more expensive format and its stature improved. If sales continued to increase, or, as Wood comments, "if a novel was successful enough . . . it was considered 'High Class Fiction.' Advertisements referred to it as such, fit for the shelf of the fine lady or gentleman. Thus popularity became an index of worth" (Wood, p. 18). What publishers called "classic fiction" in the last half of the nineteenth century would, by literary standards today, be categorized as "pulp" fiction—a genre still with little literary merit.

Ellen White was not alone in her condemnation of popular pulp fiction. Most mid-nineteenth century denominations were equally vehement in their denunciations. However, Ellen White continued to condemn trashy fiction even when other churches began to accept and even to publish it to increase magazine sales. Ellen White's comments against fiction clearly condemn this particular type of fiction prevalent in her day. A study of her comments highlights certain recurring adjectives and phrases—"sentimental," "sensational," "worthless," "love stories," "frivolous," "exciting tales," "trashy," or books published "as a money-making scheme" (CT 132-134, 137). These terms describe exactly the typical fiction read by a majority of American readers during this period. One other publication factor needs to be considered. Most "domestic" and "adventure" novels of this time were for children. Not coincidentally, Ellen White's comments are largely directed toward children's reading.

When viewed from this historical perspective, one recognizes that Ellen White is not categorically rejecting all fiction or all novels. She is condemning a particular manifestation of novels and fiction that appeared overwhelmingly in the last half of the nineteenth century, especially in North America. In fact, when one considers Ellen White's statements advocating literary study, we recognize how highly she admired literary skills. She comments, "It is no sin to appreciate literary talent, if it is not idolized" (FE 120, 121). More important, she writes of the "pressing need of men and women of literary qualifications" (*ibid.* 192). Ellen White, then, admired good writing, but deplored writing that had neither moral nor literary value.

It is important to recognize that Ellen White's comments on reading and literature were essentially calling for readers to develop the ability to discriminate between good and bad writing rather than calling for an absolute ban on fiction and novels. Her practice and her counsel, if understood within a historical context, suggest that reading matter should not be determined by genre, be it novel, fiction, poetry, or essay, but rather by intellectual and spiritual discrimination of content and purpose. In fact, Ellen White's positive counsel is for men and women to become as highly literate as possible.

She especially recommended the Bible as the world's greatest literature, including history, biography, poetry, drama, logic, rhetoric, and philosophy (CT 427-430). "The perusal of works upon our faith, the reading of arguments from the pen of others, while an excellent and important practice, is not that which will give the mind the greatest strength. The Bible is the best book in the world for intellectual culture" (CE 204; GW 99, 100).

Further reading: D. Davis, *Teaching Literature: A Seventh-day Adventist Approach* (AUP, 2002); R. Dunn, ed., *Seventh-day Adventists on Literature* (LLU, 1974); V. Wehtje, ed., *Language Matters: Notes Toward an English Program* (SPA, 1978); J. O. Waller, "A Contextual Study of Ellen G. White's Counsel Concerning Fiction" (unpublished manuscript, 1965, CAR); J. Wood, "The Trashy Novel Revisited: Popular Fiction in the Age of Ellen White," *Spectrum* 7, no. 4 (1976): 16-24.

Charles H. Tidwell, Jr.

LITERATURE EVANGELISTS, see **COLPORTEURS**.

LITTLE FLOCK, see *WORD TO THE "LITTLE FLOCK," A*.

LIVING IN THE SUNLIGHT (RHPA, 2004, 80 pp.). An abridgment of **Thoughts From the Mount of Blessing*, it incorporates a more modern translation of Bible texts, more gender inclusiveness, and some modification in language and reading level. Developed as an inexpensive sharing publication.

LIVING TEMPLE, THE, see **KELLOGG, JOHN HARVEY; PANTHEISM**.

LOMA LINDA MESSAGES (Payson, Arizona, Leaves-of-Autumn Books, 1981, 621 pp.). Typewritten reproduction of Ellen White's messages relating to the founding and development of the *College of Medical of Evangelists at Loma Linda, California. Only five copies of the original work were produced by *John

A. Burden. When later retyped in a different format, the later version included the original page numbers in brackets. The materials selected include, mostly in chronological order, letters and manuscripts that Ellen White wrote to individuals, groups of people, and church institutions in regard to the establishment of a medical college at Loma Linda. The first 38 pages give a brief historical account of how the decision was made to secure the Loma Linda property and establish a college there. This account includes minutes of conference meetings, a transcript of a conversation with Ellen White, and letters from John Burden to Ellen White.

LOMA LINDA SANITARIUM. The last of three sanitariums established by Seventh-day Adventists in southern California in 1904-1905, the forerunner of the Loma Linda University Medical Center, Loma Linda, California. In 1902, from her home near St. Helena, California, Ellen White predicted that properties on which buildings were already erected, in localities especially suited to sanitarium work, would "be offered to us at much less than their original cost" (SpTB03a 7). In 1904 church members purchased the Paradise Valley Sanitarium—an original investment of $25,000—for $4,000, and the Glendale Hotel (now Glendale Adventist Medical Center), representing an investment of $50,000, was purchased for only $12,000. Though at the time it seemed financially impossible, Ellen White urged the

LOMA LINDA SANITARIUM, ESTABLISHED IN 1905

COURTESY OF THE CENTER FOR ADVENTIST RESEARCH, ANDREWS UNIVERSITY

purchase of a *third* institution, because of a site she had seen in vision that was not matched by either of the first two purchases.

In a vision received in October 1901 Ellen White had seen a southern California property where patients were sitting in wheelchairs outdoors under shade trees that seemed to form tentlike canopies. But she knew of no property that matched this description. Later in 1904 she asked church members to look between Riverside, San Bernardino, and Redlands for the property. In May 1905 word came to church leaders that a 76-acre (31-hectare) property in Loma Linda, five miles (eight kilometers) from Redlands, worth $155,000 could be purchased for $110,000.

When Pastor John Burden reported his findings to Ellen White, she urged him to return several times, until he found the price eventually lowered to $40,000. Although the sum still seemed astronomical, under Ellen White's direction Burden decided to buy. The terms of sale agreed to included a $5,000 down payment and three payments of $5,000 each to be made in August, September, and December 1905. The remaining $20,000 was due in three years. On Friday afternoon, May 26, 1905, participants came to sign the contract of sale. Because the Sabbath was about to begin, Burden and the few church members with him postponed the sale until the following Monday. On the intervening Sunday, May 28, Burden received a telegram from G. W. Reaser, president of the Southern California Conference, telling him not to make a down payment on the Loma Linda property. As a Christian gentleman, he had already agreed to the terms of the deal. Now, because it seemed certain that there would be no funds available to make either the deposit or the subsequent payments, his immediate supervisor had told him to discontinue the purchase. However, because of Ellen White's assurance that the Lord would provide, on Monday, May 29, 1905, Burden paid $1,000 to secure an option to buy Loma Linda, taking personal responsibility for the payment.

Two weeks later Ellen White visited Loma Linda for the first time. As she arrived with her son, she gazed at the main building and stated that "I have been here before" (6Bio 18). As she inspected the facility, she said repeatedly that she recognized it as the very place she had been shown years before. In a letter to Stephen Haskell she predicted that someday this Loma Linda property would become not only a center of medical and spiritual healing but also "an important educational center" (Lt 277, 1905, in PC 203). However, in spite of clear evidence that God was leading, financial realities loomed ahead. Some church leaders argued that if the Loma Linda Association with all its resources had failed to operate a successful health-care institution, why should their small church group think they could succeed?

Nevertheless, encouraged by Burden's faith in Ellen White's counsel, local Adventists contributed the remaining $4,000 of the June 15 down payment. In order for the venture to succeed, greater support must be secured. On June 20, 1905, delegates of nearly all 22 churches in the Southern California Conference met to endorse the purchase. Finally, the Southern California Conference committee agreed to support the project. Funds to meet the agreed-to payments often arrived providentially, and the Loma Linda property was paid in full in less than six months, thus gaining additional discounts and bringing the final purchase price to $38,900—"much less than [its] original cost," just as Ellen White had predicted (SpTB03c 7). The sanitarium opened in November 1905.

Today Loma Linda University and Medical Center is a Seventh-day Adventist health science institution offering degrees in allied health professions, dentistry, medicine, nursing, and public health.

Further reading: 6Bio 11-32; R. A. Schaefer, *Legacy: Daring to Care, the Heritage of Loma Linda University Medical Center* (Loma Linda: Legacy Pub. Assn., 1990); *SDA Encyclopedia* (1996), vol. 10, pp. 940-954.

Richard A. Schaefer

LOMA LINDA UNIVERSITY, see **COLLEGE OF MEDICAL EVANGELISTS.**

LORD'S SUPPER. Ellen White's thoughts on the Lord's Supper are found in three main segments of her published writings: DA 642-661, Ev 273-278, and a series of articles in RH, May 31 to July 5, 1898. In her writings she expounds a Zwinglian understanding of the Lord's Supper and advocates for open Communion.

In her description of the Lord's Supper, Ellen White pictures the scene in the upper room as a genuine Passover celebration, laying particular emphasis on the meaning of the foot-washing service. During the ceremony Jesus performed foot washing as a "religious service" (DA 650) to demonstrate His humiliation and to end the quarrels among the disciples. With this act Jesus intended more than bodily cleanliness. He desired to wash the alienation, jealousy, and pride from the hearts of His disciples (*ibid.* 649). Judas was impressed and later received even the emblems of Jesus' broken body and spilled blood. Although being convinced of Jesus' divinity, he decided to carry out his betrayal, thereby committing the unpardonable sin. Ellen White stresses that Jesus used unleavened cakes and unfermented grape juice (*ibid.* 653) as special symbols. Before Jesus left the upper chamber with His disciples, His voice was heard "in the joyful notes of the Passover hallel" (*ibid.* 672). Theologically the Lord's Supper put an end to the sacrifices and festivals of the Jewish people (5BC 1139). Similar to the Passover's pointing back to past deliverance and forward to the promised Messiah, the Lord's Supper commemorates the expiatory sufferings of Christ and looks forward to His second coming (DA 659, 660).

According to Ellen White, Paul criticized the Corinthians' manner of celebrating the Lord's Supper because the church had departed from the simplicity of the faith and had patterned its understanding to a great degree after the idolatrous feasts of the Greeks, and the wealthy had turned it into a gluttonous banquet and selfish enjoyment (6BC 1090).

Because of their importance, "baptism and the Lord's supper are two monumental pillars" (Ev 273) and are to be administered by ordained ministers (EW 101). Contrary to the annual Passover, the Lord's Supper should be observed more frequently (LS 111; 6BC 1090). As the example of Judas demonstrates, Christ does not want exclusiveness at the Communion service. Applying 1 Corinthians 5:11 to the Lord's Supper, Ellen White relates that only "open sin" excludes someone from participation. She encourages self-examination and participation even if unworthy individuals take part in or administer the ordinance (DA 656). Ellen White clearly stated in the 1890s that those who still have a restricted knowledge of truth and holiness but accept Christ as their Savior are to be admitted to the service (Ev 276, 277).

The act of foot washing is to clear away the misunderstanding of self-exaltation (DA 650), to kindle a desire for a higher spiritual life (*ibid.* 651), to enable confession of sin and reconciliation (*ibid.* 659; Ev 274, 275), and to help and bless others (DA 651). Therefore, it is "something to test and prove the loyalty of the children of God" (Ev 275). The foot-washing service draws the believers closer to one another and "as we wash the feet of Christ's followers, it is as though we were indeed touching the Son of God" (5BC 1139), who is present on every occasion when foot washing is performed (RH, June 14, 1898). Under the influence of the Holy Spirit sins are confessed and forgiven (DA 651). In early Adventist history different opinions were held in regard to the procedure to follow in foot washing and whether men and women could wash each other's feet. Ellen White was uncomfortable with such a practice and counseled against a man washing a woman's feet (EW 117, 302; 5MR 192).

With the Lord's Supper Jesus wants His "followers [to] realize their continual dependence upon His blood for salvation" (ST, Mar. 25, 1880). The cup has for "those who drink in faith, peace-making, soul-cleansing efficacy" (5BC 1102). The service with bread and wine reminds Christians of "the solemn scenes of His betrayal and crucifixion for the sins of the world" (3SG 227). Although the Communion service is not a season of sorrowing and lament of shortcomings (DA 659), nor mere form (*ibid.* 660), or a tedious ceremony (EW 117), it has to convey proper solemnity (Ev 278). The Lord's Supper offers the possibility to receive spiritual strength (DA 661) and "to bring love and grace and peace into hearts" (Ev 278).

Further reading: R. Graybill, "Foot Washing Becomes an Established Practice," RH, May 29, 1975, pp. 6, 7; H. Kiesler, "The Ordinances: Baptism, Foot Washing, and Lord's Supper," in R. Dederen, ed., *Handbook of Seventh-day Adventist Theology* (RHPA, 2000), pp. 582-609; B. Ulrich, "Das Abendmahl—eine offene Feier? in *Abendmahl und Fußwaschung*, ed. Euro-Afrika Division (Hamburg: Saatkorn-Verlag, 1991), pp. 231-244.

Johannes Kovar

LOUD CRY. The proclamation of the message of the angel of Revelation 18:1-4, which joins and augments the third angel's message (see *three angels' messages) of Revelation 14:9-12 and is therefore often referred to as the "loud cry of the third angel" (CD 32; EW 261; 1SM 363; 1T 486). Adventists in 1843-1844 applied the second angel's message (Rev. 14:8), announcing the fall of *Babylon, to the churches that rejected the Second Advent message. According to Ellen White the future loud cry of the fourth angel announces the doctrinal and moral fall of churches that have rejected the Sabbath and persecute Sabbathkeepers (Rev. 18:1-4; GC 603). While genuine Christians, whom God recognizes as "my people," still remain in these churches, the loud cry announces impending judgment and gives the invitation "Come out of her, my people, lest you share in her sins, and lest you receive of her plagues" (Rev. 18:4, NKJV; GC 603, 604).

As God invited Lot to leave Sodom to escape its judgment by fire, the loud cry invites God's people to leave Babylon to escape the seven last *plagues (EW 279). The loud cry unites with the third angel's message of Revelation 14, with its judgment on those who receive the *mark of the beast (GC 604, 605).

In the loud cry, God speaks through human instruments qualified by the Holy Spirit (RH, July 23, 1895). The power of the latter rain impels them to expose the sins of Babylon, which has been overtaken by spiritualism and false doctrines. People visit families and intercede for them (9T 126). Ellen White saw this loud-cry message as exposing the unbiblical support of Sunday observance, to the amazement of many hearers who will then realize that the churches have rejected the truth about the Sabbath of the fourth commandment. Like the Pharisees in Christ's day, church leaders will soothe their followers' fears and denounce those who advocate

observing the Sabbath. Catholics and Protestants together will appeal to the state to enforce Sunday observance to oppose the message of the loud cry (GC 606, 607).

As a result, those who refuse to observe Sunday will be imprisoned, exiled, or treated as slaves, and their obedience to God's Word will be treated as rebellion. Under this pressure, some Sabbathkeepers will abandon the Sabbath, join the opposition, and become the worst enemies of their former brethren (*ibid.* 608). Leaders of church and state will bribe, persuade, or compel all to honor Sunday. Liberty of conscience will no longer be respected (*ibid.* 592). Like the great Reformers of the past, such as *Wycliffe, *Huss, and *Luther, Sabbathkeepers will insist on Scripture as the only, ultimate test for truth (*ibid.* 609).

Ellen White saw the loud cry of the third angel's message as God's last invitation of mercy to the world. The messengers proclaim it, not fearing the consequences (*ibid.* 609, 610; 9T 19, 20). The restraining influence of the Holy Spirit remains while Christ still intercedes in heaven. Conscientious states-persons will be used by God to hold evil in check, and some of these will respond to the loud cry and join Sabbathkeepers (*ibid.* 610, 611). This message prepares God's people to stand through the great time of trouble after Christ ceases His intercession in heaven (Dan. 12:1; EW 277).

The loud cry will involve divine miracles, signs, and wonders (*ibid.* 278). Satan will make counterfeit fire fall from the sky (Rev. 13:13; GC 612). According to Ellen White, this movement will be far greater than the midnight cry of 1844 (EW 278), even greater than Pentecost (Ev 701). It will result not so much from the presentation of arguments as from a fearless proclamation (EW 278) under the deep conviction of the Spirit of God (GC 612). The knowledge of salvation will be taken to "every city and town" around the world (RH, Oct. 13, 1904). The whole earth is enlightened with the glory of the Lord (6T 401), a large number of people respond to the loud-cry invitation (GC 612), and multitudes leave Babylon (Ev 700) to take their stand upon the Word of God.

Further reading: SDA Encyclopedia (1996), vol. 10, pp. 959, 960.

Norman R. Gulley

LOVE OF GOD. For Ellen White the Christian life begins as the believer realizes how he or she has been loved. It does not originate in our human efforts to have access to God, but above all is the initiative of God: "God has made the first advance. . . . Christ teaches that salvation does not come through our seeking after God but through God's seeking after us. . . . We do not repent in order that God may love us, but He reveals to us His love in order that we may repent" (COL 189). Following the apostle John (1 John 4:19), White declares that God's quest for humanity reorients human existence toward the experience of love, "the basis of godliness": "If we love God because He first loved us, we shall love all for whom Christ died. We cannot come in touch with divinity without coming in touch with humanity. . . . The pity and compassion of Christ will be manifest in our life" (COL 384, 385). Nevertheless humans "can never come into possession of this spirit by *trying* to love others" (*ibid.* 384). Rather, this "spirit" is the fruit of contemplation: "We shall contemplate the character of Him who first loved us. By contemplation of God's matchless love, we take upon us His nature" (TM 226).

In her writings White expresses a high concern for God's character and seeks to address false conceptions of His character. Unfortunately the human perception of God is often deeply influenced by evil, leading humans to project, on God, the nature of Satan himself: "The enemy of good blinded the minds of men, so that they looked upon God with fear; they thought of Him as severe and unforgiving. Satan led men to conceive of God as a being whose chief attribute is stern justice—one who is a severe judge, a harsh, exacting creditor. He pictured the Creator as a being who is watching with jealous eye to discern the errors and mistakes of men, that He may visit judgments upon them. It was to remove this dark shadow, by revealing to the world the infinite love of God, that Jesus came to live among men" (SC 10, 11). Ellen White says that God's generosity toward humanity is a delight: "So surely as there never was a time when God was not, so surely there never was a moment when it was not the delight of the eternal mind to manifest His grace to humanity" (ST, June 12, 1901).

Ellen White's writings are full of descriptions of God in which she describes Him as merciful, compassionate, tender, and loving. In her understanding of love God is essentially presented as a giving God who accompanies and saves humankind by His generosity. This is the gist and substance of Ellen White's thinking, especially evident in her *great controversy theology, in which she is highly preoccupied with an accurate understanding of God's identity. In her *Early Writings* she refers to "the tender love that God has for His people" and "the great love and condescension of God" (EW 39, 125). This preoccupation is especially evident in her later writings. Her *Conflict of the Ages Series begins and ends with references to the love of God. From the first sentence of *Patriarchs and Prophets* to the last phrase in *The Great Controversy*, White structured the Conflict of the Ages Series around the concept that "God is love." This is also noticeable in the last chapter of *Christ's Object Lessons* and the first chapters of *Prophets* *and Kings, The Desire of Ages,* and *The Ministry of Healing.* Each of these works either opens or ends with a portrait of God's love. In a similar way she added a first chapter to *Steps to Christ* in 1896 in which she established the love of God as the context for humanity's salvation, a chapter not included in the original 1892 edition. For Ellen White the history of the angelic rebellion in heaven and the fall of humankind is, in its essence, the history of a distortion of God's character. Since then, false worship has attempted to portray God as a vengeful God in need of appeasement.

Ellen White herself grew in her understanding of the love of God. She recalled that in her childhood she feared God. She saw that her mother "tenderly sympathized with and encouraged me, advising me to go for counsel to Elder Stockman. . . . During the few minutes in which I received instruction from Elder Stockman, I had obtained more knowledge on the subject of God's love and pitying tenderness, than from all the sermons and exhortations to which I had ever listened" (LS 36, 37). Only the knowledge of being loved by God is able to nourish a genuine Christian life that will lead to a lifestyle of loving obedience.

Methods of evangelism are affected by this understanding of the love of God. The first task of any personal or public evangelism is to proclaim, by our attitude and words, the love of God. "The very first and most important thing is to melt and subdue the soul by presenting our Lord Jesus Christ as the sin-pardoning Savior. Never should a sermon be preached, or Bible instruction in any line be given, without pointing the hearers to 'the Lamb of God, which taketh away the sin of the world' (John 1:29). We are to proclaim to the people Christ and His love, presenting all our doctrines in their relation to this important theme. Every true doctrine makes Christ the center, every precept receives force from His Word" (PH130 26). "The badge of Christianity is not an outward sign, not the wearing of a cross or a crown, but it is that which reveals the union of man with God. By the power of His grace manifested in the transformation of character the world is to be convinced that God has sent His Son as its Redeemer. No other influence that can surround the human soul has such power as the influence of an unselfish life. The strongest argument in favor of the gospel is a loving and lovable Christian" (MH 470).

Ellen White conceived her ministry as a means to help people realize God's ultimate dream of seeing His children, close to humanity in this painful time as He never saw it before, and imagining them resembling Jesus Christ, just before His second coming. Not merely specializing at transmitting biblical concepts, but also being compassionate, loving, generous, and tender as He is. Ellen White often speaks about this end-time mercy. In the framework of Matthew's parable of the ten virgins, she shows the same concern for incarnated love: "It is the darkness of misapprehension of God that is enshrouding the world. Men are losing their knowledge of His character. It has been misunderstood and misinterpreted. At this time a message from God is to be proclaimed, a message illuminating in its influence and saving in its power. His character is to be made known. Into the darkness of the world is to be shed the light of His glory, the light of His goodness, mercy, and truth. . . . The last rays of merciful light, the last message of mercy to be given to the world, is a revelation of His character of love. The children of God are to manifest His glory. In their own life and character they are to reveal what the grace of God has done for them. . . . It is the privilege of every soul to be a living channel through which God can communicate to the world the treasures of His grace, the unsearchable riches of Christ. There is nothing that Christ desires so much as agents who will represent to the world His Spirit and character. There is nothing that the world needs so much as the manifestation through humanity of the Savior's love" (COL 415-419).

As the world hungers for God in the twenty-first century, Ellen White's spiritual vision of God offers messages of great spiritual quality and depth. Her passionate emphasis on God's love is not merely a pious emphasis, but the core of her spiritual vision. Although some of her writings are sometimes perceived as exacting, emphasizing duty and proper behavior, Ellen White's message is above all a depiction of God's character. For her, love is not merely one attribute of God among many others. Love defines His very being. He is love. For God, to exist and to love are the same reality. White speaks of Christ's life and ministry as the most perfect and most concrete revelation of God's character. To contemplate Jesus and to imitate His life and character are the goal of the Christian life.

While many Christian authors share a message, an ethic, and a spirituality grounded in God's love, the writings of Ellen White reveal a deep desire to make this divine love the key principle that determines every dimension of piety and every aspect of private and community life. White's contribution consists in making this principle the foundation of a Christian life, which is perceived above all as a reflection of God's character. Her understanding of God's love encourages a hermeneutic of love that structures the believer's faith and existence. She invites Christians to associate with others out of genuine concern for their eternal salvation. She is aware that suffering and evil are the strongest objections to the idea of a fair and loving God. But she believes that God does not remain indifferent to the scandal of suffering. He takes evil and suffering upon Himself, and by doing so He gains the right to talk about it with humankind. Only the cross of Christ can measure up to speaking about evil.

In its essence White's understanding of the gospel is not an encyclopedia of cognitive information. It is the story of a presence, the good news of a loving encounter between the divine Jesus and the Palestinian people of the first century, between the Creator of the universe and humanity. This merciful and compassionate presence is the source of genuine human relationships. Full of hope in the nearness of the second coming of Christ, White extends humanity's admiration of God's character to all eternity: "And the years of eternity, as they roll, will bring richer and still more glorious revelations of God and of Christ. As knowledge is progressive, so will love, reverence, and happiness increase. The more men learn of God, the greater will be their admiration of His character. . . . The great controversy is ended. Sin and sinners are no more. The entire universe is clean. One pulse of harmony and gladness beats through the vast creation. From Him who created all flow life and light and gladness, throughout the realms of illimitable space. From the minutest atom to the greatest world, all things, animate and inanimate, in their unshadowed beauty and perfect joy, declare that God is love" (GC 678).

Further reading: H. E. Douglass, *Messenger of the Lord* (PPPA, 1998), pp. 403, 404, 457, 458; G. R. Knight, *Meeting Ellen White: A Fresh Look at Her Life, Writings, and Major Themes* (RHPA, 1996), pp. 109-113; R. Rice, "The Great Controversy and the Problem of Evil," *Spectrum* 32, no. 1 (Winter 2004): 46-55; Jean-Luc Rolland, *Le cadeau de Dieu: regard sur une parole rafraîchissante d'Ellen White sur la gratuité du salut* (Collonges-sous-Salève:

Faculté adventiste de théologie, 1999); *idem*, "Le prophétisme whitien (1844-1915): sa substance," in *Christianisme et prophétisme* (Collonges-sous-Salève: Faculté adventiste de théologie, 2005), pp. 153-180; *idem*, "The Generosity of God: Introduction to Ellen White's Hermeneutics of Mercy," *Spes Christiana* 18 (2008); J. Skrzypaszek, "Ellen White's Relevance in the 21st Century: Exploring the Pathway of the Spiritual Journey" (unpublished paper, EGWE World Advisory, Oct. 12-15, 2006); A. Thompson, *Escape From the Flames: How Ellen White Grew From Fear to Joy and Helped Me to Do It Too* (PPPA, 2005).

Jean-Luc Rolland

LOVE UNLIMITED (PPPA, 1958, 313 pp.). Republication in one volume of two of Ellen White's most influential books, *Steps to Christ and *Thoughts From the Mount of Blessing. When these two books were combined, the text of the standard editions remained unchanged and the original pagination and titles have been maintained. In the preface the editors remark that "*Love Unlimited* is the title selected for this work because the mind and character of Him who is love is here so fully revealed" (p. 4).

LOVETT'S GROVE, VISION AT, see **GREAT CONTROVERSY VISION; BOOKS, PREPARATION OF ELLEN G. WHITE'S.**

LUCIFER, see **SATAN; SIN.**

LUTHER, MARTIN (1483-1546). Adventists understand the Reformation of the sixteenth century to be not simply a historic turning point but an act of God on behalf of the Christian world for a renewal of the center of the gospel and for the adjustment of faith and life according to the Word of God and not according to human tradition. This event can be summed up in the person and work of Martin Luther, for "he *is* the Reformation" (J. Lortz). Going back more than 1,000 years and referring to the original Paul and his doctrine of justification by faith alone, he opened, by his theology, the way for a "return to the Gospel" (H. Küng).

Ellen White, in her writings, gives proper attention to this fact. First, by rediscovering, in his time, the teaching of justification by faith alone, the "mighty beacon to guide repentant sinners into the way of life" (AA 373), Luther established the material principle of the Reformation. Second, finding this, in clarity, only in the Scriptures—especially in Paul—he arrived also at the formal principle, *sola scriptura*, which had indeed been recognized already by the Waldenses and Wycliffe (GC 126, 249).

For this reason Ellen White considered Luther the greatest Reformer of the sixteenth century (SR 340). In her eyes he was the "herald of the Bible" (GC 126) and the "expounder of the truth" (*ibid.* 170), God's instrument in the struggle "against the errors and sins of the papal church" (EW 223). Therefore, in the final edition of *The Great Controversy* (1911) she dedicated to Luther and the Reformation in Germany four chapters totaling some 75 pages and gave to Zwingli and Calvin, in spite of deep respect for them, only one chapter each. She followed, however, Luther's development and career only as far as the Diet of Augsburg (1530), which she called "the triumph of the Reformation in Germany" (GC 211).

The fact that she made use of Protestant church historians of her time—especially J. H. Merle D'Aubigné, and J. A. Wylie—makes it inevitable that her presentation reflects the Luther research of her era. The account of Paul Luther, a son of the Reformer, who localized the father's salvation experience in Rome

(1510/1511) when Luther ascended the Lateran staircase and was suddenly struck by the word of the apostle Paul in Romans 1:17 ("The just shall live by faith") may serve as an example (GC 125; see D'Aubigné, *Geschichte der Reformation des 16ten Jahrhunderts* [Stuttgart: J. F. Steinkopf, 1861], vol. 1, p. 195). In the form related by D'Aubigné the story is regarded by present-day Luther scholars as a "mistake of memory" (Walter von Loewenich, *Martin Luther* [Munich: List, 1983], pp. 67, 68). On the contrary, the description of Luther's reformational breakthrough, the so-called *Turmerlebnis* (tower experience) between 1512 and 1518, is entirely missing in Ellen White's presentation, since this issue—brought up by the Catholic Luther researcher H. Denifle (1904)—has become vital only in recent times.

The story of the struggle against indulgences and the nailing of the 95 theses (1517), however, requires a rather broad space in her work (GC 127-131). Philip Melanchthon's account of the nailing of the theses, which today is sometimes doubted (see Erwin Iserloh, "M. Luther und der Aufbruch der Reformation," in Hubert Jedin [ed.], *Handbuch der Kirchengeschichte* [Freiburg: Herder, 1967], vol. 4, pp. 49, 50), is regarded, however, as authentic by a considerable number of modern Protestant church historians (cf. R. Bainton, H. Bornkamm, W. v. Loewenich). In accordance with modern research, White stresses also the fact that Luther, at that time, was still a "papist of the straitest sort" (GC 128) and his separation from Rome was the result of a rather long development (*ibid.* 139) whose effects, however, influenced nearly the whole European continent (*ibid.*).

The rich literary activity Luther manifested in the years from 1518 to 1530 is honorably mentioned by Ellen White in these words: "His pen was never idle" (*ibid.* 169) and his "pen was a power" (6T 403). She recognized

that the "new interest in the Holy Scriptures" which his writings "had kindled everywhere" (GC 139) "stirred the world" (6T 403).

Luther's publications—for example, the three great treatises of 1520 ("To the Christian Nobility of the German Nations," "The Babylonian Captivity," and "The Freedom of a Christian")—are only partially touched. On page 140 of *The Great Controversy* one comes across a quotation from "To the Christian Nobility" cited according to D'Aubigné (vol. 2, p. 91), while the rest is not mentioned, although D'Aubigné deals with it (vol. 2, pp. 115-118, 126, 127). The Diet of Worms (1521), however, is dealt with at some length (GC 145-170), and the translation of the New Testament at the Wartburg castle is referred to (*ibid.* 169).

The most important adversaries of Luther's early years also appear on the scene: The papal legate H. Aleander (*ibid.* 146-148, 150), the social revolutionary Thomas Münzer (*ibid.* 191), the Catholic polemicist J. Eck—though in connection with Zwingli (*ibid.* 182-184)— and the humanist Erasmus of Rotterdam in connection with the French Reformation (*ibid.* 216, 217). There is only a hint of the Peasants' War of 1525 (*ibid.* 191, 192), and the conflict with Erasmus (see Luther's *Bondage of the Will*) in the same year is not mentioned. There is an extensive account (GC 197-210) of the Diets of Spires (1526/1529) and Augsburg (1530), but Luther in his old age (1530-1546) does not come into focus. Overall, in choosing historical incidents to include in her description of Luther's life and role in the Protestant Reformation, White chose events that fit within the scope of *The Great Controversy* (p. xii) and did not seek to provide a complete history.

As to the doctrine of the Reformer, Ellen White gives credit to it by emphasizing in her own words the so-called *particulae exclusivae,* the famous "sole" formulas: human beings are saved by Jesus Christ alone—*solo Christo* (EW 222, 223; FW 19); the saving act of Christ is a manifestation exclusively of grace—*sola gratia* (GC 129; DA 175; FW 20); humans obtain salvation only through faith—*sola fide* (GC 125; ST, Mar. 24, 1890); and everything that pertains to salvation can be found in the Scriptures alone—*sola scriptura* (GC 132).

Luther's famous formula *simul justus et peccator*—believers being just and sinners at the same time—is viewed in modern Luther research under a double aspect: of totality and partiality (see Paul Althaus, *Die Theologie M. Luthers* [Gütersloh: G. Mohn, 1975], pp. 211-213). In themselves believers remain sinners, but through Christ's forgiveness they are totally justified. At the same time faith in Christ has to be renewed continually, and therefore the believers progress in sanctification. However, this process finds its termination only at the end of life (*Luther's Works,* Weimar Edition, vol. 7, p. 337), and therefore sanctification is never finished on this side of eternity. But faith fulfills the requirements of God's law (*ibid.,* vol. 45, p. 147). Similar thoughts can be found also in the writings of Ellen White: Justification is forgiveness of sins (ML 250). It is followed by the process of sanctification, which is a lifelong one (SL 10). Therefore, believers cannot claim to be sinless (*ibid.* 65); they have to fight continually with sin (COL 331; AA 560), but in Christ they can overcome every temptation (MYP 114). The standard of sanctification is God's law (GC 467).

Ellen White also stresses Luther's disdain for the Catholic dogma of the soul's immortality (1513, Fifth Lateran Council) and underlines the importance of his doctrine of the soul's sleep (GC 549), although the Reformer was, in this respect, not consistent in his teaching (see Althaus, pp. 343-349).

According to a quotation by D. T. Taylor, Luther is said to have expected the end of the world in 300 years (GC 303). But in Luther's own calculations (1541, "Supputatio annorum mundi") the end was to occur in his time or shortly afterward (see Ernst Staehelin, *Die Verkündigung des Reiches Gottes in der Kirche Jesu Christi* [Basel: F. Reinhardt, n.d.], vol. 4, pp. 65, 66).

Ellen White was deeply convinced that God had spoken through Luther (GW 34, 35), and thus he excelled other great men of history (4T 519). Although the message of justification by faith was "present truth in the days of Luther" (GC 143), the Reformer did not have the whole light (*ibid.* 148). Courageous (*ibid.* 141, 142), pious, and a man of prayer (*ibid.* 122), Luther also made great mistakes (1SM 402) and was often tempted to go to extremes (EW 224). According to the Reformer's self-understanding (see Letter to Melanchthon, June 29, 1530), he should not be used as final authority and criterion (1SM 402), for, in verity, the Reformation process has to go on (GC 148).

Johann (Hans) Heinz

MADISON COLLEGE. Founded in 1904 near Madison (now suburban Nashville), Tennessee, by *E. A. Sutherland, *P. T. Magan, *Nellie Druillard, and M. Bessie DeGraw, it set the pattern for much of the *self-supporting movement in Adventist education. Its legal name, Nashville Agricultural and Normal Institute, indicated its two original components: a farm and a teacher training (normal) school that became Madison College. Ellen White showed her support by volunteering to sit on the managing board—the only such position she ever held (Gish and Christman, pp. 103, 104).

During a visit to the school in 1906 Ellen White remarked, "This would be a good place for a *sanitarium." She urged them to break ground, even though they had no money. They did so, and waited for developments. When a worn-out businessman from Nashville came seeking treatment, they nursed him back to health. As he told others of his recovery, many came to Madison, providing means for the building of an 11-room cottage that grew into Madison Sanitarium. As early as 1907 Ellen White advised that a food factory would be advantageous and provide employment for the students. In 1918 Madison acquired a food factory, which it operated until 1964.

Madison was noted among Adventist colleges for its emphasis on vocational as well as academic skills, for the way that graduates could go out and replicate the Madison pattern in small self-supporting mission schools (of which more than 50 had been planted by 1946), and for the program that enabled students to earn their entire way without loans

MADISON COLLEGE, c. 1955

or outside support. By 1939 enrollment exceeded 450.

The school's infrastructure and financial policies, however, did not keep pace with its enrollment. Sanitarium fees and college tuition were extremely low in comparison to other institutions, but so were faculty wages. From 1904 to 1918 faculty received $13 per month. By 1925 they received $13 per month plus 15 cents per hour (Sandborn, pp. 168-172). W. C. White in 1920 reminded Sutherland of

his early promise to his faculty that when the school became financially prosperous, they would "share in the prosperity" by receiving better wages. White protested that "While Mother [Ellen White] lived, she often spoke of the danger you [Sutherland] were in of consenting to conditions which would be oppressive to some of your faculty" (W. C. White to E. A. Sutherland, Apr. 23, 1920, CAR). Twenty years later Sutherland's determination to maintain essentially the original wage scale was the final stumbling block in Madison's drive for accreditation (Sandborn, pp. 63-66). The subsequent decline led to closure in 1964. The Madison legacy continues in Adventist-laymen's Services and Industries (ASI, founded in 1947 as the Association of Adventist Self-supporting Institutions); Outpost Centers International (OCI); and hundreds of schools on the Madison pattern, all over the world.

Further reading: I. Gish and H. Christman, *Madison: God's Beautiful Farm* (PPPA, 1979); J. Moon, ed., *E. A. Sutherland and Madison College, 1904-1964: A Symposium* (1989, CAR); *idem*, "The Rise of the Self-supporting Movement in SDA Education" (1989, CAR), pp. 14-43; W. C. Sanborn, "History of Madison College" (Ed.D. thesis, Peabody College, 1953).

Jerry Moon

MAGNETIC HEALERS, see **HYPNOTISM AND MESMERISM**.

MAN, NATURE OF, see **HUMAN NATURE**.

MANASSAS, BATTLE OF, see **CIVIL WAR**.

MANUAL FOR CANVASSERS, see ***COLPORTEUR MINISTRY***.

MANUSCRIPT RELEASES. A "manuscript release" consists of previously unpublished

Ellen White material made available for public use by the trustees of the Ellen G. White Estate. The 21-volume *Manuscript Releases* was published by the Ellen G. White Estate between 1981 and 1993.

From statements made by Ellen White near the close of her life and from her last will and testament, it is clear that she envisioned the continued usefulness of the writings she left to her estate, many of which were not published during her lifetime. However, in the years following Ellen White's death in 1915, there were strong differences of opinion among church leaders as to what use should be made of her unpublished materials.

W. C. White, mindful of his mother's instruction, urged a middle-ground position whereby Ellen White's manuscripts—excluding those of a more private nature—might be used by the trustees when and where needed. Key General Conference officers were more hesitant, taking the position that if unpublished materials were to be circulated at all it should be done only with the approval of the General Conference.

In 1934 a "working policy" was agreed upon whereby the trustees would forward requested material they had reviewed and approved for release to the General Conference officers for their consideration and approval. Only those documents "mutually approved for circulation" would be released. This policy underwent several revisions before its first published appearance in the 1955 General Conference *Working Policy*. Later, the General Conference-appointed Spirit of Prophecy Committee, composed of White Estate trustees and church leaders, became the liaison committee giving final approval to release requests.

With consistent representation of General Conference leadership on the White Estate board, responsibility for the release of unpublished documents eventually shifted entirely to the trustees. In 1989 the General Conference *Working Policy* was revised to read: "The decision as to the suitability of unpublished materials for general release rests with the [White Estate] Board, which shall approve both the release and the manner of release."

Two years later the trustees voted to discontinue the manuscript release policy in view of their past action to publish all of Ellen White's letters and manuscripts chronologically with annotation. That effort is currently under way, and while the White Estate reserves publication rights for Ellen White's unpublished materials, action by the trustees is no longer required for researchers to make "fair use" of these documents.

Under the former release process, persons interested in making public use of an unpublished Ellen White document requested permission first from the White Estate board. If approved, the document was retyped (with misspellings and ungrammatical expressions corrected) and submitted to General Conference leadership for final approval. The document was made available to the person requesting it, with the expectation that it would also be further distributed through some sort of White Estate bulletin. At first the releases were generally only short sentences. Later, longer passages were approved for release. By the end of the period when the release policy was in effect, generally entire letters or at least several paragraphs were released.

Beginning in 1941, approved documents were assigned release numbers in the order that the request was considered. Thus the *release* numbers have no connection to the documents' *file* numbers. That is, Manuscript Release No. 171, processed in 1965, has no relation to Ms 171 or Lt 171 of any given year.

By 1981 more than 800 releases had been

processed by the White Estate, but their circulation was limited primarily to the EGW-SDA Research Centers. As the plan for a bulletin was never realized, it was decided to publish them in a series of volumes entitled *Manuscript Releases From the Files of the Letters and Manuscripts Written by Ellen G. White*. The series was completed when the last of the volumes, volume 21, was published in 1990 on *The Published Ellen G. White Writings* *CD-ROM, and in printed form in 1993.

Tim Poirier

MARANATHA, THE LORD IS COMING (RHPA, 1976, 383 pp.). Eleventh daily devotional book published by the Ellen G. White Estate. Materials were selected from Ellen White's published and unpublished writings. The theme of this book is the second coming of Jesus, a doctrine that Ellen White considered "the very keynote of the Sacred Scriptures" (p. 5). The daily readings follow a different theme each month and highlight various aspects of the doctrine, such as personal readiness for the Second Coming, signs of Christ's return, and events preceding and following the advent. Although a compilation, this book gives a fair and condensed presentation of her thought on eschatology, premillennialism, and the final judgment.

MARION PARTY. An offshoot movement based in Marion, Iowa, during the 1860s. The schismatic group began with B. F. Snook and W. H. Brinkerhoff, Adventist ministers in the Iowa Conference who had doubts and conflicts related to Ellen White's prophetic gift, *James White, and the *Battle Creek church. The

COURTESY OF THE REVIEW AND HERALD PUBLISHING ASSOCIATION

W. H. BRINKERHOFF

movement engaged the remnants of earlier defecting groups in *Michigan and eventually became the forerunner of the present Church of God (Seventh Day), with administrative offices in Denver, Colorado.

The Snook and Brinkerhoff rebellion began at the Iowa State Conference session in July 1865. Snook later admitted that he had had for some time "apparent difficulties in relation to sister White's visions," but kept those feelings to himself. In 1865, however, he "went to the Iowa Conference full of opposition and strongly fortified against sister White's visions" (B. F. Snook, "From Bro. Snook," RH, July 25, 1865). Brinkerhoff had similar difficulties, considering James and Ellen White to be "enemies" and having no "confidence in the testimonies of Sister White" (W. H. Brinkerhoff, "From Bro. Brinkerhoff," RH, July 25, 1865). During the Iowa Conference meeting the two ministers met the Whites, received answers to their objections, and experienced a change of attitude (U. Smith, G. W. Amadon, and J. M. Aldrich, "Remarks," RH, Jan. 23, 1866). Consequently they realized they had been in the wrong, and a few weeks later sent to the *Review letters of confession that were published in the July 25, 1865, issue. Despite their confessions, however, the Iowa Conference committee led by James White elected a new president, *George I. Butler, and a new secretary, H. E. Carver, and Snook and Brinkerhoff submitted their resignations.

After their confessions and the apparent reconciliation with the church, the controversy died down for a while. Toward the end of 1865, however, Snook and Brinkerhoff relapsed into a new stage of doubts and criticism (W. S. Ingraham, "Report From Bro. Ingraham," RH, Dec. 19, 1865; "Matters in Iowa," RH, Jan. 23, 1866). The two men now questioned major Seventh-day Adventist beliefs, such as the *three angels' messages, the application of the two-horned beast of Revelation 13:11 to the United States, and the 2300 days and their end in 1844 (J. Dorcas, "Meeting in Marion, Iowa," RH, Feb. 13, 1866; "From Bro. Dorcas," RH, Feb. 13, 1866). This brought quite a stir among the believers in Iowa. Butler wrote years later that the two ministers "went from church to church in that state, and did their utmost to destroy the confidence of our people in the work and in the visions [of Ellen White]. They had great advantages at the time, as they had been the only ministers of our people in the state, and the principal officers in the conference." As a result a number of churches were broken up and nearly "one third of the membership went with them for a time" (GIB, "A Brief History of the 'Marion' Movement," RH Supplement, Aug. 14, 1883). This disaffected group formed what came to be known as the Marion Party, named after Marion, Iowa, where the movement established its headquarters.

The next General Conference session, May 1866, recommended to the Iowa Conference to drop the names of Snook and Brinkerhoff "from their minutes," since the two "openly renounced the work of the third angel's message" (John Byington and Uriah Smith, "Fourth Annual Session of General Conference," RH, May 22, 1866). By that summer Snook and Brinkerhoff published the first book attacking Ellen White's claim to the prophetic gift. It was titled *The Visions of E. G. White, Not of God.* The 27-page book put forth numerous arguments in order to show the visions of Ellen White as "short of the divine standard" (p. 3). The Seventh-day Adventist response to Snook and Brinkerhoff's book came from the pen of Uriah Smith. Smith was asked to prepare a manuscript answering the objections of Snook and Brinkerhoff. Smith's manuscript appeared as a series of articles titled "The Visions—Objections Answered." The articles were published in the *Review* from June 12 to July 31, 1866, and two years later appeared in book form, titled *The Visions of Mrs. E. G. White, A Manifestation of Spiritual Gifts According to the Scriptures.*

The Marion Party later united with the remnants of the Gilbert Cranmer group (which called itself the Church of Jesus Christ; see also *Messenger* Party). They acquired the handpress used by *The Hope of Israel,* and started a paper called *The Advent and Sabbath Advocate*—clearly an imitation of the *Advent Review and Sabbath Herald,* published by Seventh-day Adventists (2Bio 149). The movement, however, did not have further success among Seventh-day Adventists. Snook soon abandoned the group and became a Universalist minister. Brinkerhoff also left and returned to his earlier profession of being a lawyer. In the 1870s the group adopted the name Church of God (later Church of God [Adventist]), with headquarters at Stanberry, Missouri, and still later took the name Church of God (Seventh Day), with present headquarters in Denver, Colorado.

Further reading: 2Bio 141-153; GIB, "A Brief History of the 'Marion' Movement," RH, Supplement, Aug. 14, 1883; F. S. Mead, *Handbook of Denominations in the United States,* 11th ed. (Nashville: Abingdon, 2001), pp. 33, 34; B. F. Snook and W. H. Brinkerhoff, *The Visions of E. G. White, Not of God* (Cedar Rapids, Iowa: Cedar Valley Times, 1866); J. Sabo, "The History of the Marion Party" (research paper, AU, 1977, CAR); R. W. Schwarz and F. Greenleaf, *Light Bearers: A History of the Seventh-day Adventist Church,* rev. ed. (PPPA, 2000), pp. 612, 613; L. Tarling, *The Edges of Seventh-day Adventism: A Study of Separatist Groups Emerging From the Seventh-day Adventist Church (1844-1980)*(Barragga Bay, Australia: Galilee, 1981), pp. 24-40.

Theodore N. Levterov

MARK OF THE BEAST. The mark of the beast, as an identifying sign of the worshippers of the first beast of *Revelation 13, has been variously interpreted through the centuries. In general, expositors of the Apocalypse before the fourteenth century saw it simply as a mark of the coming antichrist, without defining its precise meaning or how it would be applied in the future. A new way of looking at the mark of the beast came with the fourteenth-century pre-Reformation expositors, who identified the antichrist with the Papacy, and began to see the mark of the beast as a mark of subservience to the Papacy. This view was further elaborated by Protestant expositors who came to regard the mark of the beast as submission to the authority and regulations of the Roman Catholic Church. This was the prevailing interpretation of the Protestant historicist commentaries from the seventeenth to the beginning of the nineteenth century (see Froom, 127, 128).

The roots of the early Adventist interpretation of the mark of the beast are found in the above-described Protestant identification of the Papacy with the first beast of Revelation 13. From the very beginning Adventists applied the mark of the beast to the historic tampering with the *Law of God, and the change of the seventh-day *Sabbath to the first day of the week. *Joseph Bates was the first among the Sabbatarian Adventists to equate the "mark of the beast" with the observance of Sunday (*The Seventh-day Sabbath, a Perpetual Sign* [1847], p. 59). This view was soon endorsed by Ellen White. Writing to Bates in the same year—after she saw the vision of Christ by the ark of the covenant in the Most Holy Place of the *sanctuary in heaven, and a halo of light around the fourth commandment—she identified the receiving of the mark of the beast as the act of giving up "God's Sabbath" and keeping "the Pope's" sabbath (WLF 19).

This soon became the accepted position among Sabbatarian Adventists. *James White, *Roswell F. Cottrell, *J. N. Andrews, *J. N. Loughborough, and *Uriah Smith all held that the mark of the beast constituted the observance of Sunday as a papal institution, over against the observance of the biblical seventh-day Sabbath (Froom, pp. 128, 129).

Later the concept was more precisely defined. In 1850 James White denied that the mark of the beast would be a literal mark, visible on the forehead (PT, April 1850). Two years later he also denied that anyone then had the mark of the beast. "We do *not* teach that those who 'keep the first day as a Sabbath, and . . . believe the Sabbath is abolished, have the mark of the beast'" (RH, Mar. 2, 1852; italics supplied). He maintained that the reception of the mark of the beast was still future. Only after the Sabbath message has been preached and Sunday observance enforced by law, "*then* will be the danger of receiving the mark of the beast" (*ibid.*). Other leading Adventists believed similarly. The subject was more fully developed by Uriah Smith in *Thoughts on the Revelation* (1865), which eventually became standard Adventist teaching.

Ellen White's treatment of the mark of the beast may best be viewed as a confirmation and endorsement of the early Adventist understanding, in particular that held by James White, J. N. Andrews, and Uriah Smith. Her most extensive treatment of the matter is found in chapter 25 of *The Great Controversy* (1888, 1911), titled "God's Law Immutable." Other short statements provide additional insight into her interpretation of the mark of the beast, especially during the last period of her life and ministry. A comparison of her early statements with the comments she made during the last period of her life indicates a consistency in her identification of the mark of the beast.

The key to Ellen White's treatment of the mark of the beast is her identification of the mark as the counterfeit of the *seal of God. For her, the command to observe the seventh-day Sabbath lies at the very heart of the Decalogue. The seventh-day Sabbath is the seal of the law of God. The change from the biblical seventh-day Sabbath to Sunday—the first day of the week—is a result of the apostasy in the Christian church. "What then is the change of the Sabbath, but the sign, or mark, of the authority of the Roman Church—'the mark of the beast'?" (GC 448).

In 1899 she made a similar declaration: "The change of the Sabbath is the sign or mark of the authority of the . . . [Roman] church. . . . The mark of the beast is the papal sabbath, which has been accepted by the world in the place of the day of God's appointment" (Ev 234). Again she declared in 1904: "The sign, or seal, of God is revealed in the observance of the seventh-day Sabbath, the Lord's memorial of creation. . . . The mark of the beast is the opposite of this—the observance of the first day of the week" (8T 117). Similarly she held in 1910: "The Sabbath of the fourth commandment is the seal of the living God. It points to God as the Creator, and is the sign of His rightful authority over the beings He has made. Those who obey this law will bear the seal of God, for He has set apart this day as a sign of loyalty between Himself and His people. . . . The mark of the beast is the opposite of this—the observance of the first day of the week as the sabbath enforced by human law. This mark distinguishes those who acknowledge the supremacy of the papal authority from those who acknowledge the authority of God" (ST, Mar. 22, 1910).

The observance of Sunday as the first day of the week, however, does not in itself indicate that a person has the mark of the beast. The time for the reception of the mark, as she repeatedly emphasized, is yet future. The issue in the final conflict of this earth's history will be regarding the Decalogue, especially the Sabbath commandment. Those who knowingly, willingly reject the law of God will then receive the mark of the beast: "When Sunday observance shall be enforced by law, and the world shall be enlightened concerning the obligation of the true Sabbath, *then* whoever shall transgress the command of God, to obey a precept which has no higher authority than that of Rome, will thereby honor popery above God. . . . He is worshiping the beast and his image. . . . And it is *not until* the issue is thus plainly set before the people, and they are brought to choose between the commandments of God and the commandments of men, that those who continue in transgression will receive 'the mark of the beast' " (GC 449; italics supplied). In 1899 she emphasized: "No one has yet received the mark of the beast. The testing time has not yet come. There are true Christians in every church, not excepting the Roman Catholic communion. None are condemned until they have had the light and have seen the obligation of the fourth commandment. But when the decree shall go forth enforcing the counterfeit sabbath, and the loud cry of the third angel shall warn men against the worship of the beast and his image, the line will be clearly drawn between the false and the true. Then those who still continue in transgression will receive the mark of the beast" (Ev 234, 235). That same year she penned another emphatic statement: "Sundaykeeping is *not yet* the mark of the beast, and *will not be until* the decree goes forth causing men to worship this idol sabbath. The time will come when this day will be the test, but *that time has not come yet*" (Ms 118, 1899, in 7BC 977; italics supplied). She further insisted that the mark of the beast is not a visible, physical mark, just as the seal of God "is not any seal or mark that can be seen, but a settling into the truth, both intellectually and spiritually" (Ms 173, 1902, in 4BC 1161; cf. PH086 6, 7).

Although the identification of the mark of the beast was for Ellen White a matter of fact, in 1900 she cautioned that *how* it will take place has not yet been revealed. "The mark of the beast is exactly what it has been proclaimed to be. Not all in regard to this matter is yet understood, nor will it be understood until the unrolling of the scroll" (6T 17). Yet she held that the Sunday legislation that will bring on the mark of the beast will be initiated by the United States, whose example will then be followed by other nations of the world (GC 448, 449, 587, 588).

Further reading: L. E. Froom, *Movement of Destiny* (RHPA, 1971), pp. 122-129; *SDA Encyclopedia* (1996), vol. 11, pp. 35, 36.

Ranko Stefanovic

MARRIAGE AND DIVORCE. Ellen White wrote a great deal about marriage and ideal home life, as well as about situations that fall short of the ideal. Much of her *Testimonies*, volumes 1-9, deals with home life. Sizable compilations that distill the essence of her thoughts on related topics include *The Adventist Home, *Child Guidance, *Testimonies on Sexual Behavior, Adultery, and Divorce,* as well as seven chapters in *The Ministry of Healing.* The compilations derive their material from private letters, public testimonies, unpublished manuscripts, periodical articles, and public sermons. Many principles on marriage, divorce, and remarriage can be found in her writings.

To couples considering marriage she made broad appeals emphasizing that to avoid "miserable, unhappy reflections after marriage, they must make it a subject of serious, earnest reflection now." Taken unwisely, the decision to marry can make life "a burden, a curse." Nothing can more "effectually ruin a woman's happiness and usefulness, and make life a heartsickening burden, as her own husband; and no one can do one hundredth part as much to chill the hopes and aspirations of a man, to paralyze his energies and ruin his influence and prospects, as his own wife" (AH 43).

For young men she wrote: "Let a young man seek one to stand by his side who is fitted to bear her share of life's burdens, one whose influence will ennoble and refine him, and who will make him happy in her love. . . . In your choice of a wife study her character. Will she be one who will be patient and painstaking? Or will she cease to care for your mother and father at the very time when they need a strong son to lean upon? And will she withdraw him from their society to carry out her plans and to suit her own pleasure, and leave the father and mother who, instead of gaining an affectionate daughter, will have lost a son?" (*ibid.* 45, 46).

To young women, she advised: "Before giving her hand in marriage, every woman should inquire whether he with whom she is about to unite her destiny is worthy. What is his past record? Is his life pure? Is the love which he expresses of a noble, elevated character, or is it a mere emotional fondness? . . . Will she be allowed to preserve her individuality, or must her judgment and conscience be surrendered to the control of her husband? . . . Has my lover a mother? What is the stamp of her character? . . . Will he be patient with my mistakes, or will he be critical, overbearing, and dictatorial?" (*ibid.* 47).

Ellen White, though a Victorian woman, was no prude. She declared that Jesus "did not enforce celibacy" and that He did not come "to destroy the sacred relationship of marriage." Although she may not have used the common expressions we use today to describe marital intimacies, she chose words that everyone understood well, phrases such as "every privilege of the marriage relation" and "privacy and privileges of the family relation." But she did advise married couples to consider it "a religious duty to govern their passions," because "passion of just as base a quality may be found in the marriage relation as outside of it" (*ibid.* 121-124).

She also cautioned against enlarging the family until parents "know that their children can be well cared for and educated." In fact, to parents who were not able to instruct their children properly, she said: "It is a sin to increase your family." Further, she said that parents have "no right to bring children into the world to be a burden to others. . . . They commit a crime in bringing children into the world to suffer for want of proper care, food, and clothing" (*ibid.* 163-165).

On the question of divorce and remarriage, Ellen White often stated that adultery is the only biblical basis for divorce. In 1863 she wrote that "a woman may be legally divorced from her husband by the laws of the land and yet not divorced in the sight of God and according to the higher law. There is only one sin, which is adultery, which can place the husband or wife in a position where they can be free from the marriage vow in the sight of God" (*ibid.* 344). She often emphasized that marriage is a contract for life, linking "the destinies of the two individuals with bonds which naught but the hand of death should sever" (*ibid.* 340). She did not see divorce as an option except for sexual misbehavior (see Lt 168, 1901).

However, circumstances did arise in which husbands and wives were so incompatible that Ellen White counseled separation until the difficulties could be resolved. On one occasion she advised the husband to take his "child-wife, so overbearing, so unyielding, and so uncontrollable," back to her mother, "who has made her what she is. . . . If her husband consents to keep her by his side, to wear out his life, he will become discouraged and unfitted for the Lord's service. He is under no obligations to keep one by his side who will only torture his soul" (TSB 77).

In other cases Ellen White encouraged wives and mothers to stay by their homes. To one wife, whose husband was "a profane man, vulgar and abusive in his language to her," even teaching the children to "disregard" their mother's authority, Ellen White still advised her to persevere for the sake of her children. "Whatever trials you may be called to endure through poverty, through wounds and bruises of the soul, from the harsh, overbearing assumption of the husband and father, do not leave your children; do not give them up to the influence of a godless father" (AH 348).

The question of unscriptural marriages, particularly remarriage without a biblically sanctioned divorce, has long been a thorny issue (Matt.19:1-10; TSB 271). In 1891 an Adventist minister, C. H. Bliss, asked Ellen White's advice about a couple whom some were advising to separate. She objected to such meddling as causing "a most deplorable condition of things. . . . I hope to learn that this matter is not pressed, and that sympathy will not be withdrawn from the two whose interests have been united." She advised that they "be left to God and their own consciences, and that the church shall not treat them as sinners until they have evidence that they are such in the sight of the holy God" (*ibid.* 218, 219).

In another case Ellen White's sister Sarah died, leaving a husband and five children. After she died, her husband, *Stephen Belden, needing someone to care for the children, married again. Shortly after the marriage, the second wife succumbed to a severe case of measles that affected her brain, causing her to become insane and committed to an asylum for life. The struggling father, still with five growing children, then married a "very good, efficient woman," who remained with him the rest of his life. Following this third marriage, the local church considered expelling him for remarrying without a biblically sanctioned divorce. But when they asked Ellen White's counsel, she said, "Let them alone" (*ibid.* 224, 225).

In 1854 Ellen White observed, regarding one local church, that "the seventh commandment has been violated by some who are now held in fellowship by the church. This has brought God's frown upon them" and has had a "corrupting influence upon the young. They see how lightly the sin of breaking the seventh commandment is regarded, and the one who commits this horrid sin thinks that all he has to do is to confess that he was wrong and is sorry, and he is then to have all the privileges of the house of God." Like Paul (1 Cor. 5), she held that "those who break the seventh commandment should be suspended from the church" (*ibid.* 248). She also held, with Paul, that thorough repentance could lead to reacceptance, but that not all who were remorseful were truly repentant (2 Cor. 2:6-11; 8:9-11; *ibid.* 241, 242).

Concerning ministers who committed adultery, she wrote, "Cleanse the camp of this moral corruption, if it takes the highest men in the highest positions. . . . There is much we will never know; but that which is revealed makes the church responsible and guilty unless they show a determined effort to eradicate the evil" (TM 427, 428). She advised that those with a long record of moral impurity and unrepentance would have to be released from the ministry. Regarding ministers who humbled

themselves in deep repentance, she pleaded with General Conference president G. I. Butler to give one an opportunity to "prove himself," and to give another "a chance for his life" (TSB 240).

"I am compelled to deal plainly and rebuke sin," she continued, but also "I have it in my heart, placed there by the Spirit of Christ, to labor in faith, in tender sympathy and compassion for the erring. . . . I will not leave them to become the sport of Satan's temptations. . . . There are those who have fallen into great sin, but we have labored with and for them, and God has afterwards accepted their labors[;] when these have pleaded for me to let them go and not to burden myself for them, I have said, 'I will not give you up; you must gather strength to overcome.' These men are now in active service" (*ibid.* 241).

"I am more pained than I can express to see so little aptitude and skill to save souls that are ensnared by Satan. I see such a cold Phariseeism, holding off at arm's length the one who has been deluded by the adversary of souls, and then I think: What if Jesus treated us in this way? . . . If we err, let it be on the side of mercy rather than on the side of condemnation and harsh dealing" (*ibid.* 242).

See also: S. T. Belden, S. Brownsberger, M. E. Cornell, T. J. Evans, N. Fuller, W. Harper, V. Jones, J. D. Rice, J. H. Waggoner, W. C. Wales, C. B. Waterman, and *Testimonies on Sexual Behavior, Adultery, and Divorce.*

MARRIAGE OF JAMES AND ELLEN WHITE.
Took place August 30, 1846, following a courtship of about 18 months. James first noticed Ellen Harmon in Portland, Maine, when he briefly served there as an apprentice pastor sometime before the *disappointment (see JW, *Life Incidents*, pp. 157, 182). He recalled that "although but sixteen" (he was about six years older), she was "a Christian

of the most devoted type" and "a laborer in the cause of Christ in public and from house to house" (JW, LS80 126; cf. 1Bio 71). She apparently never noticed him until February 1845, when she accompanied two friends and her sister Sarah on a journey to eastern Maine, where she several times presented the substance of her first few visions for the encouragement of small groups of Millerite Adventists (LS 73). James White came to hear her, accepted her message as from God, and offered his horse and buggy for her transportation. He observed that she was frail and in poor health and needed a masculine escort to provide transportation and arrange meetings for her.

MARRIAGE CERTIFICATE OF JAMES AND ELLEN WHITE

It was revealed to her in vision that she could trust James White (1Bio 84), so for about three months in the winter and spring of 1845 they traveled together until they had visited all the scattered groups of Adventists in Maine and New Hampshire (*ibid.* 74, 75; 2SG 38). Though always accompanied by respected friends or family members, rumors began to spread, causing consternation at home. Ellen's mother begged her, for the sake of her reputation, to come home, and her brother (probably John) offered to support her financially if she would not disgrace the family by going about as a preacher. "Disgrace the family!" she retorted. "Can it disgrace the family for me to preach Christ and Him crucified! If you would give me all the gold

your house could hold, I would not cease giving my testimony for God" (ST, June 24, 1889). But she did come home for a while.

A year earlier James White had criticized other Millerites for marrying and thus denying their faith in a soon second coming of Christ. But the difficulties of traveling together convinced James that Ellen needed a legal protector who could accompany her without compromising her reputation. After both had individually obtained evidence of God's approval, they went ahead with plans for marriage. Because both of them had been expelled from their former churches for becoming Millerites, they were married in a civil ceremony in Portland, Maine.

Among the strengths of the Whites' marriage were: their supreme devotion to God (they were willing to accept any sacrifice to follow God's will); their firm belief that the Millerite Adventist movement had been specially raised up by God; other shared values (both were natives of Maine, accustomed to poverty and hard work); their certainty that God had chosen Ellen as a special messenger to the Adventist believers (while James occasionally chafed under a divine rebuke sent through his wife, his confidence in the validity of her gift never faltered); their commitment to team ministry; and a deep, consistent, unconditional love (J. Moon, "Interpersonal Relationships in the Family of James and Ellen G. White," pp. 16, 17, 21, 22). After 34 years of marriage James testified: "We were married August 30, 1846, and from that hour to the present she has been my crown of rejoicing" (LS80 126; 1Bio 112). For her part, Ellen called James "the best man that ever trod shoe leather" (1Bio 84).

Stresses on the Whites' marriage included: extreme poverty in the early years, no home of their own the first five years of their marriage, and disagreements over child training.

Of their four sons (*Henry Nichols, *James Edson, *William Clarence, and *John Herbert), two died young: Henry of pneumonia at age 16; and John Herbert of erysipelas at 3 months of age. The normal stresses of team ministry were heightened by the challenge of harmonizing his authority as General Conference president with that of her prophetic gift. James suffered at least four strokes, which increased his tendencies to be irritable, defensive, and domineering.

Consequently the Whites had their share of ordinary disagreements, as well as periodic conflicts of opinion concerning God's will for them, especially in James White's later years of depression and failing health. During one such period in May 1876 Ellen confided in her closest female friend, *Lucinda Hall, about a conflict Ellen was having with James (DG 260-274). But through prayer, mutual communication, and even traveling in different directions for a time, they worked through their differences and maintained a strong marriage characterized by mutual respect, close partnership, and lasting love.

Further reading: 1Bio 110-126; 2Bio 424-445; DG 260-274; "Testimony for James and Ellen White's Family," n.d., Ms 8, 1862; "Testimony Regarding James and Ellen White," June 6, 1863, Ms 1, 1863; J. Moon, "Interpersonal Relationships in the Family of James and Ellen White" (unpublished paper, 1998, CAR); J. Moon, *W. C. White and Ellen G. White* (AUP, 1993), pp. 1-68; H. E. Douglass, *Messenger of the Lord* (PPPA, 1998), pp. 48, 52-60, 543, 544; V. Robinson, *James White* (RHPA, 1976); G. Wheeler, *James White: Innovator and Overcomer* (RHPA, 2003); James White, *Life Incidents* (Battle Creek, Mich.: SDA Pub. Assn., 1868).

Jerry Moon

MASONIC LODGE, see **SECRET SOCIETIES**.

MASTURBATION. Ellen White did not employ the word "masturbation" in her writings, though it was not an unused word in her generation. Although the word is listed in the *Webster's Dictionary* of her day, she used only euphemisms, such as "solitary vice," "secret vice," and "self-abuse."

The concept of physical harm brought on by masturbation came to the fore in the United States in the eighteenth century. A European physician, Dr. S. Tissot, took up the cause against the practice, and brought to America his theories, which condemned not only masturbation but some sexual conduct between husbands and wives as well. The list of disorders following such sexual behaviors were said to cause problems all the way from "acne to suicide." Parents were alerted to this proclaimed evil to every system of the body. Much energy, time, and money were spent on "cures" to put an end to this activity. These consisted of preventive measures that included mechanical devices and surgical procedures, many of which would now be considered abusive.

Biblical scholars seem to agree, however, that though the Bible speaks very forthrightly against adultery, fornication, homosexuality, bestiality, and impure thinking, it does not explicitly prohibit masturbation. It has, however, been suggested that even if not an ontic evil, it is a practice that falls short of the potential for social and spiritual intimacy intended by the Creator in mutual sexual expression. Further, occasional masturbation can easily become habitual, compulsive, or addictive, or lead to other forms of sexual behavior that are clearly sinful. For this reason Christians cannot be entirely indifferent to its practice.

Many have understood that when Ellen White used such terms as "solitary vice," "secret vice," or "self-abuse" she referred to masturbation. She attributed to this practice a number of physical, intellectual, emotional, and spiritual conditions or results.

The physical effects attributed to "solitary vice" include headaches, dizziness, wakefulness, feverishness, exhaustion, nervousness, pain, loss of appetite, and disease. Among the intellectual consequences are forgetfulness, inattention, idiocy, and derangement of the fine nerves of the brain. Emotional outcomes include apathy, gloom, sadness, jealousy, rebellion against authority, and premature marriage. The spiritual consequences include death to spiritual matters, destruction of high resolve and earnest endeavor, and removal of oneself from holy influences.

One cannot help being impressed, when reading *An Appeal to Mothers*, *Child Guidance* (pp. 439-470), and *Testimonies for the Church* (2T 346-489), how many times Ellen White uses the word "mind," as though much more were involved than merely a physical act. In fact, she was more concerned with thought processes, attitudes, fantasies, etc., as indicated in the following quotes: "The effect of such debasing habits is not the same upon all minds" (CG 447); "Impure thoughts seize and control the imagination" (2MCP 592); "The mind takes pleasure in contemplating scenes which awaken the lower and baser passions" (CG 439). Ellen White's straightforward comments regarding the corrupting of one's mind and imagination also apply to the use and effects of pornography and immoral fantasizing (*ibid.* 439, 440).

While science has not verified that the medical conditions attributed to masturbation through the years have any validity, there is agreement that obsessive masturbation is harmful and may indicate physical, psychological, or other problems in the person involved. There is also little disagreement that the sexual proscriptions in Scripture mentioned above (adultery, fornication, prostitution, homosexuality, bestiality, incest, rape, and immoral thoughts) may have undesirable and dreaded effects and consequences. These sexual practices can also be classified as abusive and are usually undertaken in "secret." Could it be that in her writings about "secret vice," Ellen White may sometimes have referred to some of these practices and not necessarily or only to masturbation? Current terminology applies the term "sexual addiction" to obsessive, undesirable sexual behaviors. This term may cover such situations as described by Ellen White. But since one cannot with certainty claim to know her mind on this complex topic for which she does not employ current terminology, it seems unwise to unquestioningly ascribe to the practice of masturbation all of the many statements she makes about such practices as "secret vice" or "self-abuse."

See also: general article: Current Science and Ellen White: Twelve Controversial Statements.

Further reading: H. E. Douglass, *Messenger of the Lord* (PPPA, 1998), pp. 493, 494; A. Mazat, "Masturbation" (BRI, 1983).

Alberta Mazat

MEDICAL MINISTRY (PPPA, 1932, 1963, 355 pp.). Compilation of Ellen White's writings presenting the wide range of her counsels to medical personnel and the Seventh-day Adventist medical work. This book was the first posthumous compilation composed largely of unpublished materials. The preface to the second edition published in 1963 includes a historical background of her writings on health (pp. vii-xv). In her teaching, Ellen White placed a great emphasis on obedience to the laws of God as one of the primary conditions necessary for good health. Furthermore, in her wholistic approach to life, she claimed that the perfect remedy for the ills of humankind is the appreciation, observance, and combination of the spiritual, mental, and physical laws of our being. *Medical Ministry* is a practical book that includes counsels on the place of God and faith in healing, the Adventist philosophy of medical missionary work, and how to teach health principles. The book also includes instructions to physicians and the management of *sanitariums and hospitals. Ellen White understood the genuine medical profession as a form of ministry for God and argued that "there is to be no division between the [gospel] ministry and the medical work. The physician should labor equally with the minister, and with as much earnestness and thoroughness for the salvation of the soul as well as for the restoration of the body" (p. 237).

MEDICAL MISSIONARY AND BENEVOLENT ASSOCIATION, see **INTERNATIONAL MEDICAL MISSIONARY AND BENEVOLENT ASSOCIATION**.

MEDICAL MISSIONARY WORK. The work of ministering to human physical needs, as an expression of the love of Christ and a complement to the "ministry of the Word." The term includes a wide range of service, from the practice of medicine, nursing, and all branches of health education to feeding the hungry, clothing the naked, and disaster-relief work. "Medical missionary work," Ellen White taught, should be combined with "the ministry of the Word" in order to meet people "right where they are, whatever their position or condition, and help them in every way possible." "By these combined agencies opportunities are given to communicate light and to present the gospel to all classes and all grades of society" (WM 121). Ellen White's extensive writings on the topic describe its origin, its relation to the gospel, its function, its results, its practice, its workers, and their preparation and education.

Medical missionary work "is of divine origin, and has a most glorious mission to fulfill" (MM 24). Christ Himself is "the originator of medical missionary work" (CH 497; cf. MM 131). This work is portrayed in Isaiah 61:1-4 (CH 530). Christ is the Great Medical Missionary, and His ministry of teaching, preaching, and healing is a perfect example to His followers (Matt. 4:23; CH 317). Christ's disciples today have the same high calling and commission Christ gave to the twelve and the seventy (Matt. 10:1, 7, 8; Luke 10:8, 9; MM 253; CH 530, 531). This calling is also "outlined in the commission which Christ gave to His disciples just before His ascension" (Matt. 28:18-20; CH 509). Christ's Great Commission mandated His "chosen servants to take up medical missionary work after His ascension" (Mark 16:20; CH 553; cf. MH 139).

There is an intimate relation between the medical missionary work and the gospel. Ellen White sees from Isaiah 58 that "medical missionary work is to be bound up with the message, and sealed with the seal of God" (Ev 517). She describes medical missionary work as "the gospel in illustration" (CH 524), "the gospel practiced, the compassion of Christ revealed" (MM 239), and "the pioneer work of the gospel, the door through which the truth for this time is to find entrance to many homes" (CH 497). She warns that no one should separate medical missionary work from the gospel ministry. "These two must blend. They are not to stand apart as separate lines of work" (CME 44; MM 250). The reason for this close connection is that "the gospel ministry is needed to give permanence and stability to the medical missionary work; and the ministry needs the medical missionary work to demonstrate the practical working of the gospel. Neither part of the work is complete without the other" (CH 514). The relationship between the medical missionary work and "the gospel message for these last days" (*ibid.* 524), she compares with that of the arm to the body (6T 288).

The medical missionary work plays a vital role in preparing the world for the Second Advent but must be conducted in such a way that the "message" about the Advent "will not be eclipsed nor its progress hindered" (*ibid.* 293). The unique function of the medical work is to make human minds more receptive to receive Jesus Christ. She wrote that "the medical missionary work is to be a great entering wedge, whereby the diseased soul may be reached" (CH 535). This entering wedge is especially related to removing prejudice against the gospel message, for "this work will break down prejudice as nothing else can" (9T 211).

Medical missionary work practiced "in connection with the ministry" becomes the best way to reveal Christ to others (MM 319). It is effective in gospel planting as well as reaping: "When connected with other lines of gospel effort, medical missionary work is a most effective instrument by which the ground is prepared for the sowing of the seeds of truth, and the instrument also by which the harvest is reaped" (CME 42, 43). Finally, medical missionary work plays an important role in the closing work of the gospel. "The gospel minister should preach the health principles, for these have been given of God as among the means needed to prepare a people perfect in character. Therefore, health principles have been given to us that as a people we might be prepared in both mind and body to receive the fullness of God's blessing" (*ibid.* 43). Ellen White had a special burden that ministers be trained to administer simple remedies for the relief of suffering. They should be prepared by education and practice to combat disease of the body as well as the soul (MM 253). Ministers who

understand how to treat disease will be twice as successful as those who do not labor as medical missionaries (*ibid.* 245).

Because "medical missionary work is a sacred thing of God's own devising," Ellen White saw its results as divinely assured. Those who "cooperate with God," following Christ's example, "will be wholly successful" (*ibid.* 131). "In new fields no work is so successful as medical missionary work" (*ibid.* 239). Medical missionary workers are "welcome in any place, because there is suffering of every kind in every part of the world" (HL 139). In contrast, a church that neglects medical missionary work is crippled in its ministry, just as a "body which treats indifferently the right hand, refusing its aid, is able to accomplish nothing" (MM 238). Ellen White foresaw a time—evidently in the final crisis—when "there will be no work done in ministerial lines but medical missionary work" (CH 533).

To carry on the medical missionary work Christ began, Ellen White urged Adventists to establish institutions "where men and women suffering from disease may be placed under the care of God-fearing physicians and nurses" (*ibid.* 249), trained in "God's methods of treating disease" (7T 59). Said she, "It is the Lord's purpose that His method of healing without drugs shall be brought into prominence in every large city through our medical institutions" (MM 325). But this work should not be confined to a few medical institutions (*ibid.* 326). She encourages individual medical missionary workers to begin in a small way by using whatever there is on hand (*ibid.* 239). As the medical missionary uses "the simple remedies which God has provided for the cure of physical suffering, he is to speak of Christ's power to heal the maladies of the soul" (*ibid.* 39).

Medical missionary work is to emphasize

that prevention is better than cure. "Teach the people that it is better to know how to keep well than to know how to cure disease" (MYP 218). Medical missionaries are to teach not only principles of healthful living but also "the principles of truth" (Ev 519). Although this work can reach all classes of society, it is especially useful for reaching the higher classes (MM 241).

Ellen White called for a harmonious balance among the various branches of the work. God "uses the gospel ministry, medical missionary work, and the publications containing present truth to impress hearts. All are made effectual by means of faith. . . . One is not to supersede the other" (Ev 547). To be most effective, medical missionary physicians should work together with ministers of the gospel (MM 250).

Medical missionary work is of such importance that it "should be a part of the work of every church" (6T 289; cf. 7T 62). In order to meet this responsibility, church members need to be trained in medical missionary work. "They are to learn to minister to the needs of both soul and body" as "with the knowledge and experience gained by practical work, they go out to give treatments to the sick" (CH 497; cf. Ev 519).

White cautions that just because persons are health professionals does not mean that they are medical missionaries. Much more than scientific training is needed. Medical missionaries need an experiential knowledge of the power of the grace of Christ and of the truth (CH 213). Those who are prepared to do medical missionary work need a right concept of God, "based on a constant study of God's Word and of the character and life of Christ," and an awareness "that we are nearing the end of this earth's history" (MM 91). They also need to learn of Christ how to deal tactfully with minds (2MCP 438, 439)

and realize that "a solemn dignity is to characterize genuine medical missionaries" (CME 44). Finally, medical missionary workers need to be purified, sanctified, and ennobled, molded after the divine similitude and "transformed by the grace of Christ" (MM 259; cf. 8T 168).

Further reading: "Call to Medical Evangelism and Health Education" (EGWE, SDoc).

P. G. Damsteegt

MELROSE SANITARIUM, see **NEW ENGLAND SANITARIUM.**

MEMORIALS AND MONUMENTS OF ELLEN G. WHITE. Ellen White made no request to have monuments erected in her memory. She saw her major legacy in her writings (see 1SM 55) and in the *institutions she helped to found (LS 196). One such institution was the Loma Linda, California, Sanitarium, which grew into what is now the Loma Linda University and the LLU Medical Center. On April 4, 1912, she had endorsed the plan of giving the clinical training for Loma Linda medical students, as much as possible at Loma Linda, but also at a hospital in Los Angeles, where the medical students could gain experience in treating the wide range of diseases and injuries that occur in a great city. On May 9, 1915, she responded with joy to the news that seed money had been donated for a teaching hospital in Los Angeles (SHM65 398-400). On July 16 she died.

In November 1915 the denomination's Autumn Council met at Loma Linda. High on the agenda was the financial crisis at the fledgling medical school. The school was $400,000 in debt, and on November 18 the question before the committee was whether the church could afford to operate a four-year medical school. Accreditation would require building a teaching hospital for the clinical instruction. As the debate tended toward fiscal caution and giving up the dream of a full medical school, *A. G. Daniells stood up to speak. "My brethren," he said, "I am astounded and I must speak. . . . We all profess faith in the spirit of prophecy, but we forget that one of the last things the prophet ever wrote was that our young men and women should be given their full training in our own school and not be forced to go to worldly schools. And here we are, before the prophet is hardly cold in her grave, proposing that our young men and women shall only have half their education from us and then shall be turned loose in these worldly schools. Now, I protest against it. . . . We can build up this school. We can support it. We can do anything that God wants us to do" (in Neff, pp. 175, 176). Others joined in support of keeping the school. Four leading women, who were not part of the committee but knew about the crisis, proposed to lead a denomination-wide fund-raising campaign to finance the teaching hospital, which would then be named in memory of Ellen G. White. Their proposal was accepted, and in 1918 was dedicated the hospital now known as the *White Memorial Medical Center. Since then many other Adventist schools and institutions have been named in honor of James and/or Ellen White. A comprehensive list of memorials and monuments is beyond the scope of this article, but it will highlight a few of the most notable ones in the United States and Australia.

Battle Creek, Michigan, is the site of many historical reminders of Ellen G. White. Near the family grave site in Oak Hill Cemetery stands a state historical marker that briefly eulogizes both James and Ellen White for their contributions to the development of Battle Creek and Michigan. The grave site itself includes the graves of James and Ellen White; their four sons, Henry, Edson, William,

and Herbert; Edson's first wife, Emma; William's first wife, Mary, and second wife, Ethel May; James White's parents, John and Betsey White; James White's sister Mary Chase; and Clarissa Bonfoey, who for several years lived with the Whites and cared for Henry, Edson, and Willie.

A few blocks from the *Battle Creek Tabernacle and the former *Battle Creek Sanitarium is the Historic Adventist Village. The village includes the Wood Street home, still on its original site, where James and Ellen White lived from 1856 to 1863. The home was fully restored in 2001 under the direction of professional restoration architects. The village also includes the home of John and Betsey White, James White's parents; the home that *Willie and *Mary (Kelsey) White and their first two daughters occupied from about 1887 to 1894; a replica of the 1857 Battle Creek Adventist Meeting House, where the General Conference of Seventh-day Adventists was organized in 1863; the restored Parkville, Michigan, Adventist Church, where Ellen White received her first Civil War vision in 1861; a nineteenth-century Michigan log cabin, typical housing in frontier Michigan; an 1870s country schoolhouse, representing the historical context of White's writings on education; a replicated barn; and a carriage house. The welcome center, at the corner of Wood Street and Wesr Van Buren, features many exhibits from the Battle Creek Sanitarium and *John Harvey Kellogg, showing the influence of Ellen White's writings on health. Tours of the village are conducted daily, May through August, by appointment at other times, or as posted at the welcome center.

The *Birthplace Monument*, a historical marker in the general area where it is believed that Ellen Harmon was born, is located on Highway 114 about 1.5 miles (2.4 kilometers) north of Gorham, Maine. The inscription reads: "BIRTHPLACE OF ELLEN G. WHITE. BORN HERE NOV. 26, 1827. CO-FOUNDER SEVENTH-DAY ADVENTIST CHURCH. DEDICATED MAY 22, 1983, BY SEVENTH-DAY ADVENTIST CHURCH, GORHAM HISTORICAL SOCIETY."

Half a world away, on the campus of *Avondale College (Cooranbong, New South Wales, Australia), stands the *Furrow Monument* to the prophetic guidance that launched a college. The monument reads, "ABOUT 500 YARDS EAST OF THIS SPOT WAS FOUND THE FURROW SEEN IN A DREAM BY ELLEN G. WHITE WHICH LED TO THE ESTABLISHMENT OF THE AUSTRALASIAN MISSIONARY COLLEGE IN THIS DISTRICT IN 1894." Ellen White's account describes the discovery of a "neat-cut furrow that had been plowed one quarter of a yard deep and two yards in length" (Ms 62, 1898, in 4Bio 155) with no evidence of a plow or other equipment in sight. When two men in the party declared that the land was no good and would not raise a thing, Ellen White told them that is just what she dreamed they would say. "But One stood upon the upturned furrow, and said, 'False testimony has been borne concerning this soil' " (Lt 350, 1907, in 4Bio 156). Also at Avondale College is *Sunnyside*, Ellen White's home from 1894 to 1899.

Elmshaven, a large Victorian home at 125 Glass Mountain Road, St. Helena, California, was the last home of Ellen White. While en route from Australia to the United States in 1900, Ellen White had been assured that God had "a refuge prepared" for her. This well-constructed, pleasant, and comfortable seven-room, two-story frame house was then just 15 years old, having been built in 1885. It was completely furnished, including carpets, drapes, linens, and dishes. When she found that "the same price" she had received for her home in Cooranbong would "bring this

beautiful, healthful residence, in good order for us to possess," she was certain this was the place God had planned for her (Ms 96, 1900, in 5Bio 33). This "haven among the elms" is located 2.5 miles (four kilometers) northwest of St. Helena, within sight of the sanitarium, now called St. Helena Hospital. Fully restored, Elmshaven was designated a National Historic Landmark in 1995.

The Ellen G. White Memorial Chair in Religion at Southern Adventist University, Collegedale, Tennessee, was endowed in 1987 through an anonymous gift that supports one full professorship in religion more than the regular religion department budget could afford. Because the chair is a memorial to Ellen White's ministry and prophetic calling, a source of "crucial instruction and counsel in theological, pragmatic and administrative matters," the endowment is administered by trustees governed by written criteria to ensure that the occupant of the chair will foster a reverent approach to the inspiration of Ellen White. A commemorative plaque picturing Ellen White, with space for pictures of the first eight successive occupants of the memorial chair, is displayed in the Religion Center, So-Ju-Conian Hall, on the campus of Southern Adventist University (*Adventist Perspectives: A Journal of Topics in Religion* 1 [Southern College, 1987]: 41-52).

See also: Homes of James and Ellen G. White.

Further reading: 6Bio 368, 369, 429; M. Burt, *New England Adventist History Tour Book* (Berrien Springs, Mich.: Adventist Heritage Center, 2009), includes GPS coordinates, full-color pictures, and extensive documentation of the major sites of Adventist history in Maine, Massachusetts, New Hampshire, New York, and Vermont; *In the Footsteps of the Pioneers: A "Go-It-Yourself" Guide to Places of Interest in the Early History of Seventh-day Adventists in New England,*

New York, and Quebec (EGWE, 1990); M. L. Neff, *For God and C.M.E.: A Biography of Percy Tilson Magan* (PPPA, 1964); SHM65.

Alice R. Voorheis

MESMERISM, see **HYPNOTISM AND MESMERISM**.

MESSAGES TO YOUNG PEOPLE (SPA, 1930, 498 pp.). A book on practical spirituality and lifestyle for Adventist youth, compiled primarily by John F. Simon, associate director of the General Conference Missionary Volunteer (Youth) Department, and then submitted to *W. C. White for revisions. Major sources were Ellen White's articles from the *Youth's Instructor* and other writings especially for youth. The 157 chapters cover a wide range of subjects relevant to Christian young people. Among them are character development and spirituality, health, financial and cultural choices, recreation, social relationships, love, and marriage.

MESSENGER OF THE LORD. Ellen White frequently used the phrase "messenger of the Lord" (Mal. 2:7) in referring to biblical prophets who had specific messages from God for the people. She used this expression, rather than the term *prophet,* to describe her ministry. In her self-perception, she saw herself to be a "frail instrument," "a channel for the communication of light" (10MR 343). Before the Battle Creek church, on October 2, 1904, she said: "I am not, as I said yesterday, a prophet. I do not claim to be a leader; I claim to be simply a messenger of God, and that is all I have ever claimed" (5Bio 355). (She wanted to make clear that her work was more than was commonly understood to be that of a "prophet"—one who primarily made predictions.) In a letter to Dr. J. H. Kellogg in 1905 she said: "It is not right for you to suppose I am striving to be first, striving for leadership.

. . . I want it to be understood that I have no ambition to have the name of leader, or any other name that may be given me, except that of a messenger of God" (5MR 439). In 1906 she again emphasized: "I have had no claims to make, only that *I am instructed that I am the Lord's messenger;* that He called me in my youth to be His messenger, to receive His word, and to give a clear and decided message in the name of the Lord Jesus" (1SM 32). "To claim to be a prophetess is something that I have never done. If others call me by that name, I have no controversy with them. But my work has covered so many lines that I cannot call myself other than a messenger, sent to bear a message from the Lord to His people, and to take up work in any line that He points out" (*ibid.* 34).

See also: Prophet, Ellen G. White Not a.

Further reading: 1SM 31-36; H. E. Douglass, *Messenger of the Lord* (PPPA, 1998), pp. 170-179.

Herbert E. Douglass

MESSENGER PARTY. The first offshoot group among Sabbatarian Adventists in the early 1850s. It began in Jackson, Michigan, with two Adventist ministers, H. S. Case and C. P. Russell, as a result of controversy over the validity of Ellen White's prophetic gift.

In 1853 Case and Russell, from Jackson, Michigan, accused Mrs. Dan Palmer of losing her temper and using a "vile name" against an irritating neighbor. The accused sister denied using the word they specified. Meanwhile, the Whites came to visit the church in Jackson. While there, Ellen White had a vision concerning the disputed situation. It was revealed to her that the woman had not behaved as a true Christian and had lost her temper. At this point Case and Russell were pleased with the prophet's counsel and exulted over the woman they had accused. On the following day Ellen White had a second vision in which she was shown that Mrs. Palmer had not used the certain word she was accused of using, and that God was displeased with the unkind and uncompassionate spirit shown by the two ministers. At this point Mrs. Palmer admitted calling her neighbor a "witch," but not the cruder word a bystander had reported. While Palmer confessed and asked for forgiveness, Case and Russell turned against Ellen White and condemned her visions as false and unreliable. Consequently, in June 1853 the first offshoot appeared (1Bio 276; Maxwell, *Tell It to the World*, pp. 134, 135).

When Case and Russell began to publicize their ideas in a paper called the *Messenger of Truth*, their supporters became known as the *Messenger* Party. The *Messenger of Truth* paper seems to have lasted until about 1857, when it ceased publication for lack of financial support. The paper contained mainly allegations against Ellen White's visions and fraud charges against *James White and his work at the *Review and Herald Publishing Association. As more allegations followed, the Sabbatarian believers in Michigan held a conference, in February 1854, in which they examined and found Case not "qualified to travel and teach the third angel's message" ("H. S. Case," RH, Apr. 18, 1854). Russell was also disfellowshipped because of his "unchristian walk" and attempts to divide the believers ([JW], "The Advent Harbinger," RH, July 4, 1854).

Several Sabbatarian leaders made plans to respond to the accusations published in the *Messenger of Truth*. According to *J. N. Loughborough's memory, however, Ellen White had a vision after which she advised the Sabbatarian leaders to "let the *Messenger* people alone, and pay no attention to their work." She told them that in a short while the movement would disintegrate and their paper would cease to exist (PUR, June 30, 1910; cf.

1T 122, 123). The Sabbatarian group seemed to have accepted Ellen White's advice. In a general conference held in December 1855 in *Battle Creek, they decided not to fight against the accusations of the party, but to devote their energy to advocating the "present truth" (J. Bates and U. Smith, "Business Proceedings of the Conference at Battle Creek, Mich.," RH, Dec. 4, 1855).

The *Messenger* group was soon joined by J. M. Stephenson and D. P. Hall from Wisconsin. These two were former first-day Adventist ministers who had accepted the Sabbatarian belief but continued to hold their previously accepted *"age-to-come" theory, a belief that during the millennium humanity would receive a second chance for salvation. Since James White refused to give any publicity to the "age-to-come" doctrine in the *Review*, Stephenson and Hall eventually left the Sabbatarian group, aligned themselves with the *Messenger* Party, and started publishing their views in the *Messenger of Truth*.

Within a few years, however, the *Messenger* Party and the "age-to-come" advocates had a falling out. James White reported that they started "biting and devouring one another" until the movement "crumbled and disappeared" (JW, "A Sketch of the Rise and Progress of the Present Truth," RH, Jan. 14, 1858). Stephenson and Hall also left the movement.

Thus the first offshoot from the Sabbatarian group had virtually disappeared by 1858. The few who remained allied themselves later with Gilbert Cranmer, a Michigan Seventh-day Adventist, who was refused a license to preach because of his refusal to stop using tobacco. In 1865 the Cranmer group joined the *Marion Party, another disaffected group in Marion, Iowa. Eventually this group would establish the Church of God (Adventist) from which came the Church of God (Seventh Day).

Further reading: 1T 116-118, 122, 123; 1Bio 276, 277, 305-315; R. Coulter, *Story of the Church of God (Seventh Day)*(Denver: Bible Advocate Press, 1983); J. N. Loughborough, *Rise and Progress of the Seventh-day Adventists* (Battle Creek, Mich.: General Conference of the Seventh-day Adventists, 1892), pp. 196-209; C. M. Maxwell, *Tell It to the World* (PPPA, 1982), pp. 134-136; L. Tarling, *The Edges of Seventh-day Adventism: A Study of Separatist Groups Emerging From the Seventh-day Adventist Church (1844-1980)*(Barragga Bay, Australia: Galilee, 1981), pp. 24-40.

Theodore N. Levterov

MESSIAH, see **THE DESIRE OF AGES.**

METHODISM. Religious movement that originated from a small group at Oxford University gathered together by *John and Charles Wesley in the 1730s in quest of a devotional life of depth and discipline. The theological foundations of the Wesleys' understanding of the way of salvation was broadened during the ensuing years. On a trip to the new colony of Georgia in America he made the acquaintance of the Moravians and through them came to a fuller understanding of the Reformation doctrine of justification by faith. However, assuring as this doctrine was, he experienced difficulty in accepting it and its corollary, the imputation of Christ's righteousness, as a complete expression of the way of salvation. He was also studying the Early Eastern Fathers and discovered that their understanding of salvation went beyond forgiveness to include a healing of the wounds of sin and a growing up into Christ, to becoming "participants of the divine nature" (2 Peter 1:4, NRSV). John Wesley wrestled with these two understandings and ultimately joined them in a progressive unity. Upon returning to England, Wesley felt "his heart strangely warmed" in a profound religious experience on May 24, 1738. He was assured that God had forgiven his sins and fully accepted him. Charles had undergone a similar experience a few years earlier. The Methodist movement was born in this spiritual renewal of the Wesley brothers and their associates.

The special contribution of Methodism was set in the acceptance of a dual work of grace. The first, justification by faith alone— "what God does *for* us"—was derived from the Reformation. The second, sanctification, a second work of grace in which the believer is freed from sin and perfected in love—"what God does *in* us"—was derived from the Early Fathers. It was the joining of these two doctrines in the practical experience of the believer that constituted the theological basis and organizing principle of the Wesleyan revival. This was the message the Wesleys preached and sang.

Methodism grew into a large renewal movement within the Anglican Church in England and spread to the 13 American colonies by migrating Methodists. A relatively small Methodist Episcopal Church was established at the Christmas Conference in Baltimore in 1784 with the aim "to reform the nation and establish Christian holiness over these lands." Methodism soon emerged as the most powerful religious movement in the new nation. Its emphasis on God's free grace for all, the ability of people to accept that grace, the presence of the Divine in everyday life, and forms of popular, and at times emotional, religious expression appear to have been in tune with the optimistic spirit of the age. Its network of classes promoted stability, its traveling preachers, mobility, and its *camp meetings, vitality and renewal. It spread with dramatic rapidity along the seaboard and fairly exploded in the frontier areas to the

West. It had become the largest denomination in America by 1840, and by 1850, 34 percent of American Christians were Methodists. Some historians refer to the period from 1825 to 1914 as the "Methodist Age in America."

This became true because the greater part of the way of salvation preached during the Second Great Evangelical Awakening in America was Arminian, and Methodists were actively involved. In a broad sense the Millerite preaching might be regarded as both contributing to and benefiting from this revival. It is thus perhaps not surprising that almost half of the 174 Millerite preachers that can now be identified were Methodists even though Methodism, at the time, endorsed a postmillennial eschatology. So many Methodists became Millerites that the church in defense practically forced a sense of primary allegiance by disfellowshipping ardent Millerites. Among the latter was the *Robert Harmon family. This probably made it more likely that persons thus disfellowshipped would, after the *disappointment of 1844, remain with one of the Millerite groups rather than returning to a congregation that had alienated them.

In contradistinction to the followers of the Magisterial Reformation, for whom grace and the doctrine of election had all but pushed aside the doctrine of divine judgment, John Wesley held a high view of law as a guide to the Christian life, and concomitant to this a biblical doctrine of final judgment. It is not surprising, then, that it was a Methodist Millerite preacher, *Josiah Litch, who extended Miller's message to include a "judicial scene of judgment" preceding the resurrection and the final "execution of judgment."

The Harmon family became Methodists soon after the turn of the nineteenth century, and Ellen's early Christian consciousness was shaped in Methodist class meetings and Holiness camp meetings. Many Methodists became Seventh-day Adventists, and the general theological milieu in which Adventist understandings of law and judgment, gospel and the way of salvation, justification and sanctification, and the daily life of the Christian in the presence of the Lord subsequently took shape was that of Wesleyan Arminianism. Patterns of church organization and ministry adopted by the early Seventh-day Adventist Church were also, in some respects, similar to those of Methodism.

See also: Chestnut Street Methodist Church.

Russell Staples

MICHAEL. The transcendent being Michael is referred to by name in three books of the Bible: Daniel 10:13, 21; 12:1; Jude 9; and Revelation 12:7. Since Jude calls him "Michael the archangel," the mention of the archangel in 1 Thessalonians 4:16 may also be seen as a reference to Michael. Two interpretations of Michael have emerged in Christian history: (1) the dominant view that Michael is the highest of and leader of the angels; (2) the minority but persistent view that Michael is the divine Christ.

The angelic interpretation was likely influenced by his title "archangel" and by the Jewish pseudepigraphal book 1 Enoch, written around the second century B.C., where Michael appears as the most prominent of the seven archangels. The view that Michael is the highest angel has, through the centuries, consistently remained the Catholic interpretation.

The messianic interpretation gains support from the passages in which Michael's name appears. In these passages he is given an identity and prominence never elsewhere in Scripture accorded to an angel. In Daniel he is called, "Michael your [plural] prince," (10:21), that is, prince of Israel; and "the great prince who stands guard over the sons of your people" (12:1, NASB). Thus in Daniel, Michael is given the guardian function over Israel which Yahweh reserved to Himself in Deuteronomy 32:12: "the Lord alone guided him" (NASB).

It is Michael who leads the angelic armies against Satan and his angels (Rev. 12:7), who disputes with the devil and rebukes him at the resurrection of Moses (Jude 9), and who arises in prominence at the final resurrection to eternal life (Dan. 12:1). The fact that it is "the voice of the archangel" (1 Thess. 4:16) and "the voice of the Son of God" (John 5:25) that is heard at the resurrection suggests that the archangel *is* the Son of God.

The concern that Michael is called the arch*angel* may be resolved by the fact that the Old Testament heavenly Being called the "angel of the Lord" (Ex. 3:2 and elsewhere) is, at the burning bush, referred to as "God" (verse 6) and "Yahweh" (verse 15). The basic meaning of "angel" is "messenger." The "Angel of Yahweh" is God in messenger form, in self-manifestation. Michael appears to be another example of the Deity in transcendent self-manifestation.

The Christian work *Shepherd of Hermas*, and the Christian Ebionite sect (both second century A.D.), both seemed to have identified Michael with Christ. This appears true of third-century Hippolytus as well. In the Reformation, George Joye (1545) and John Calvin (1561) believed Michael to be Christ, a view echoed by the popular Bible commentator Matthew Henry (c. 1712). John Milton (d. 1674) stated, "It is generally thought that Michael is Christ." George Faber (1828) and the widely influential E. W. Hengstenberg (1839) argued forcefully that Michael must be Christ. More recently André LaCocque (1979) identified Michael with the Son of man (Dan. 7:13) and the Angel of Yahweh (Ex. 23:20ff.).

Ellen White did not set forth an argument that Michael was Christ, but rather—in harmony with widespread Protestant thinking in her time—assumed that identity. In reference to Daniel 12:1 she mentioned a series of events, "that Michael had not [yet] stood up," but that later, "when our High Priest has finished His work in the sanctuary, He will stand up" (EW 36).

In another passage based on Jude 9, where Michael said, "The Lord rebuke you" (NKJV), she described Christ confronting Satan at the resurrection of Moses: "Christ meekly referred him to His Father, saying, 'The Lord rebuke thee'" (SR 173, 206). Michael's activity was thus Christ's activity.

In reference to the burial of Moses, Ellen White wrote, "Michael, or Christ, with the angels that buried Moses, came down from heaven, after he [Moses] had remained in the grave a short time, and resurrected him" (4aSG 58). Similarly, quoting Daniel 10:21, she wrote, "'There is none that holdeth with me in these things, but Michael [Christ] your Prince'" (DA 99).

Enlarging on Daniel 10:13, she penned, "Christ Himself came to Gabriel's help." "Gabriel declared: '. . . but, lo, Michael, one of the chief princes, came to help me'" (RH, Dec. 5, 1907). Concerning other Old Testament prophets, she believed that "He [Christ] was revealed to them as the Angel of Jehovah, the Captain of the Lord's host, Michael the Archangel" (PP 761, note 7).

Further reading: L. O. Anderson, Jr., "The Michael Figure in the Book of Daniel" (Th.D. diss., AU, 1996); John Calvin, *Commentaries on the Book of the Prophet Daniel* (Grand Rapids: Eerdmans, 1950), vol. 2, p. 253; J. Doukhan, *Daniel: The Vision of the End* (AUP, 1987); E. W. Hengstenberg, *Christology of the Old Testament* (Grand Rapids: Kregel, 1956 [original 1839]), vol. 4, pp. 266-268; Matthew Henry, "Daniel," in *Matthew Henry's*

Commentary on the Whole Bible (Old Tappan, N.J.: Revell, n.d. [original 1712]), vol. 4, pp. 1100, 1101; A. LaCocque, *The Book of Daniel* (Atlanta: John Knox, 1979); C. M. Maxwell, *Daniel* (PPPA, 1981).

Lewis O. Anderson

MICHIGAN. Becoming the twenty-sixth state of the United States, in 1837, Michigan is centrally located in the northern tier of states bordering Canada. There was an early presence of Millerites in that state whose numbers swelled with westward expansion. *Joseph Bates made several early trips to Michigan, and as early as 1851 Ellen White wrote a letter expressing her Christian love for believers in that part of the country (Lt 9, 1851). In the spring of 1853 she and James White made their first trip to that state (1Bio 273-281; LS 149, 150; 1T 91, 92), followed by another trip the following year (CET 147). These early trips were made by wagon and characterized by ubiquitous "rough logways" and "mud sloughs" (1T 94; LS 361). In 1855, as debts mounted for the Whites, then in *Rochester, New York, relief came from a group of believers located around Battle Creek who invited them to relocate the Review and Herald "office" to Battle Creek, promising to build a publishing house. "From the time we moved to Battle Creek," she wrote, "the Lord began to turn our captivity" (LS 159).

With the relocation of the Whites to Battle Creek in 1855, Michigan became the central hub for Sabbatarian Adventists until 1903, after the sanitarium and Review and Herald publishing house burned in 1902, and the denominational headquarters was moved to Washington, D.C., and a suburb, Takoma Park, Maryland. During this period of approximately 50 years the church grew from a coalition of Sabbatarian Adventist believers to an organized denomination that had grown

around the world. It was also while they were in Michigan that many of the organizational structures of the church began to take shape. The press in Battle Creek (the initial impetus for relocating) was officially organized in 1861 as the Seventh-day Adventist Publishing Association. Two years later the *General Conference was officially organized. In three more years, in 1866, the *Health Reform Institute (which grew into the world-famous *Battle Creek Sanitarium) was founded. The first official denominational camp meeting was held in Wright, Michigan, about 100 miles (160 kilometers) north of Battle Creek. Ellen White was able to see the church in Michigan grow from a few small pockets of believers to more than 7,000 members by the time of her death in 1915. Before her death she wrote expressing joy at the progress of the Adventist Church in Michigan (LS 232).

Overall the Whites loved Michigan and spent the largest portion of their lives in that state. Despite this fact, their lives were not ones of ease. The climate in Michigan in the nineteenth century was much colder than it is today. Ellen White at times could write disparagingly of the cold, bone-chilling winters that contributed to an "unhealthful" climate (Lt 45, 1879). She was also concerned about the spread of malaria from mosquitoes, and outbreaks of tuberculosis—a leading cause of death among early Adventists. As she grew older she often spent the winter in *California, and came back to visit Michigan during the summer and fall. Both James and Ellen White, as well as all four of their sons, are buried in Battle Creek, Michigan.

Further reading: SDA Encyclopedia (1996), vol. 11, pp. 62-65.

Michael W. Campbell

MIDNIGHT CRY. The term was used by Millerite Adventists in three ways: (1) the message that

Christ would return "about 1843"; (2) the name of a prominent Millerite periodical; (3) the message that began in the summer of 1844 that Jesus would come on October 22, 1844 (the "true midnight cry"). The inspiration for this message was taken from the parable of the 10 virgins in Matthew 25:1-13: "While the bridegroom tarried, they all slumbered and slept. And at midnight there was a cry made, Behold, the bridegroom cometh; go ye out to meet him" (Matt. 25:5, 6). The proclamation of the midnight cry started in the summer of 1844 and continued till October 22 of the same year, when Daniel's prophetic period of 2300 years ended. Millerites understood that the end of Daniel's prophecy should coincide with the Jewish Day of Atonement, which symbolized a type of the purification of the earth on the day of judgment occurring at the second coming of Christ.

The midnight cry reinforced the preaching of the second angel's message of Revelation 14 and was proclaimed by thousands of believers. As the expected day drew closer, Millerites searched their hearts in full repentance before their Savior. The midnight cry reached believers of all kinds and united them in strong bonds of affection for each other and Jesus.

Within a month or two after the disappointment, Ellen Harmon, with most of the Millerite Adventists, had given up the belief that their preaching had represented any genuine fulfillment of prophecy. This is why her first vision created such excitement among them. In that vision she "saw a straight and narrow path, cast up high above the world. On this path the Advent people were traveling to the city, which was at the farther end of the path. They had a bright light set up behind them at the beginning of the path, which an angel told me was the midnight cry. This light shone all along the path and gave light for their feet so that they might not stumble. If they kept their eyes fixed on Jesus, who was just before them, leading them to the city, they were safe." But for those who "denied the light behind them and said that it was not God that had led them out so far," the "light behind them went out" and "they lost sight . . . of Jesus, and fell off the path" (EW 14, 15). By identifying the midnight cry as a light that shone all the way to the heavenly city, she asserted that the climax of the Millerite movement had been, not an aberration, but an integral part of God's purpose.

Further reading: 1T 58, 59; GC 396-408; EW 13-20, 238-243, 249, 250; P. G. Damsteegt, *Foundations of the Seventh-day Adventist Message and Mission* (AUP, 1977), pp. 40-44, 96-100; G. R. Knight, comp. and ed., *1844 and the Rise of Sabbatarian Adventism: Reproductions of Original Historical Documents* (RHPA, 1994), pp. 106-119; *idem, Millennial Fever and the End of the World* (PPPA, 1993), pp. 187-216; *SDA Encyclopedia* (1996), vol. 11, p. 68.

Anna Galeniece

MILITARY SERVICE. The Seventh-day Adventist position on military service is that the ideal is conscientious cooperation as expressed in noncombatant service.

The denomination was faced with this issue early in its history. The American Civil War (1861-1865) put the young denomination in a difficult situation. The leaders of the movement did not feel that Adventists should volunteer, since that would place them in a position of taking human life and working on the Sabbath. But, said James White in a very controversial *Review and Herald* editorial on August 12, 1862, if a draft were initiated and Adventists were drafted, then the government had assumed the responsibility of their violation of the law of God. White went on to note that it would be foolishness to resist or to be shot down for disobedience. Adventist young men, he added, needed to render both Caesar and God their due.

That article set off a veritable deluge of responses for the next few months in the *Review*, ranging all the way from total pacifism to the arming of a regiment of Sabbathkeepers whom God would use to win the war. Fortunately, there was no draft as yet, and the denominational leaders had time to think.

By the end of the war a draft had been instituted, but the government had opened up a noncombatant option for those draftees who belonged to a church that had conscientious convictions against the bearing of arms with the intent of taking human life. Church leaders took immediate steps to secure such a noncombatant accommodation for Seventh-day Adventist draftees. Conscientious objector status from the federal government was granted on September 1, 1864 (see appendix note in 1T 716, 717).

Ellen White had remarkably little to say on the issue. She did, however, remark on its complexity. "I saw," she wrote, "that it is our duty in every case to obey the laws of our land, unless they conflict with the higher law which God spoke . . . from Sinai. . . . The wisdom and authority of the divine law are supreme" (1T 361).

She went on to write that she was shown that God's people "cannot engage in this perplexing war, for it is opposed to every principle of their faith. In the army they cannot obey the truth and at the same time obey the requirements of their officers. There would be a continual violation of conscience" (*ibid.*).

In the same article she made reference to her husband's controversial article of August 1862, in which he had said that in case of drafting it would be madness to resist to the point of being shot down and that the government assumes the responsibility for draftees for breaking the law of God. The published comments in the *Testimonies* (1T 356, 357) don't help to resolve the issue, but a week after his article she refers to it in an unpublished letter in which she noted that "the piece my husband wrote in the *Review* . . . expresses my mind, although I am not fully settled in regard to taking up arms. . . . I think it would please the enemy for us to obstinately refuse to obey the law of our country . . . and sacrifice our lives" (Lt 7, 1862).

After the Civil War the denomination assigned J. N. Andrews the task of thoroughly studying the military issue from the Bible and presenting his findings before a General Conference session. Unfortunately, Andrews never finished the task, because of its complexity in both the biblical data and in the varying opinions of some Adventist leaders, including future General Conference president G. I. Butler, who argued a just war position from the Old Testament and certain New Testament passages.

The one point everyone seemed to be agreed on was that Adventist youth should not volunteer for military service. Being drafted, however, was beyond their control. During the 1880s Ellen White encouraged young men in their service to their country if conscripted, but she was also quite happy to see young Europeans immigrate to America to escape compulsory conscription (cf. Lt 55, 1886, in 12MR 322).

The issue of military service would come up for the last time in Ellen White's lifetime during World War I. Conscription during that war caused little problem for Adventists in the United States, since the denomination had been on record for 50 years as a noncombatant denomination. Most young Adventists served as medics, a position in which they could save lives. But that option was not open in Germany, a nation with a strong militaristic tradition. To make matters worse, the leaders in the German work, not having had adequate time to consult on the issues before the crisis, openly espoused a position of combatancy. That decision split German Adventism. Ellen White, because of her age, had little to say about World War I, but her few comments, at least as reported by her son, seem to be in harmony with those she made in relation to her husband's August 1862 article (A. L. White, "Ellen G. White and World War I" [EGWE, 1979, SDoc]).

Her basic position on military service supported the noncombatancy stand of the church, while at the same time leaving space for individuality for those who had alternative convictions. The church's position on noncombatancy remains the same today.

Further reading: R. G. Davis, "Conscientious Cooperators: The Seventh-day Adventists and Military Service, 1860-1945" (Ph.D. diss., George Washington University, 1970); G. R. Knight, "Adventism and Military Service: Individual Conscience in Ethical Tension," in T. F. Schlabach and R. T. Hughes, eds., *Proclaim Peace* (Urbana, Ill.: University of Illinois Press, 1997), pp. 157-171; W. C. White, D. E. Robinson, and A. L. White, "The Spirit of Prophecy and Military Service" (EGWE, SDoc); F. M. Wilcox, *Seventh-day Adventists in Time of War* (RHPA, 1936); *SDA Encyclopedia* (1996), vol. 11, pp. 184-186.

George R. Knight

MILK. The milk of domesticated animals (cows, sheep, and goats) has been utilized by humans since antiquity. Fermented (cultured) milk has been a favorite since early times, especially among peoples living in hot climates. Ellen White suggested that plant foods prepared simply with a little milk or cream, and free from spices and grease, provided the most

healthful diet (CH 115). Ellen White herself used, and recommended others using, a little milk or cream or something equivalent to make vegetable dishes more palatable (CD 355; 9T 162). She also used a little boiled milk in her homemade cereal coffee (CD 432). She urged that whenever milk is used, it should be thoroughly sterilized to reduce the danger of contracting disease from its use (MH 302). In addition, she warned against eating large quantities of milk and sugar together. This harmful combination was suggested to affect the brain, cause injury to the body, and impart impurities to the system (2T 369, 370).

Milk has been promoted in modern times as a valuable source of a number of important vitamins and minerals. Since the early to mid-1990s the use of milk has become a controversial issue among Adventists. Anti-dairy positions promoted by John Robbins and others have provided some church members with a basis for discarding dairy products from their diet. Church members have taken different statements from the writings of Ellen White to support their position for or against the use of dairy.

Ellen White warned in 1900 that milk was becoming more and more objectionable because of the diseases in cattle (CD 350). In 1902 she suggested that the time had not yet come but would soon come when there would be no safety in using milk and dairy products, as well as eggs. Her reason for this was that disease in animals was increasing in proportion to the increase in the wickedness among the human population (7T 135). She emphasized that the time was near (at the turn of the twentieth century) when the whole animal creation would be groaning under disease because of the sinfulness of humanity. This increased disease in cattle would lead many to discard milk from their diet (CD 356). Factory farming methods have certainly attempted to maximize profits at the expense of the animals' well-being, comfort, and health. Contagious diseases have spread rapidly among animals housed in the close quarters typical of factory farming.

In her writings Ellen White stated that God promised that He would give people the ability to prepare wholesome food without the use of milk and eggs, and that they should teach others how to prepare food without the use of milk and eggs (7T 135). Ellen White emphasized that God would make it clear to His people when it is no longer safe to be using dairy products (CD 353), and He would prepare the way for this position (9T 162). Dairy products contain a number of micronutrients that are difficult to obtain elsewhere in a vegetarian diet. Today, with the availability of milk substitutes made from soy or rice, or other plant materials, that are properly fortified with calcium, riboflavin, vitamin D, and vitamin B_{12}, there are products in the marketplace available that can adequately substitute for cow's milk.

While she cautioned against the danger of radical health reform and warned the church against taking extreme positions in health reform (ibid.), Ellen White admonished those who discarded dairy and eggs to replace these items with healthful substitutes in order to obtain proper nutrition (ibid. 161, 162). Ellen White suggested that the work of the church could be crippled by overzealous people promoting a very strict diet, and that we should not discard milk and eggs until such time as circumstances demand it (ibid. 162). In 1909 she warned about unnecessarily bringing upon ourselves perplexity by premature discarding of dairy products and eggs and following an extremely restrictive diet. She warned that we should not create our own time of trouble by running ahead of the Lord's timetable (CD 355, 356; MH 302). It was especially important that families who cannot afford the vegetarian substitutes for milk and eggs should continue to use these animal products, rather than adopt such a strict diet that would put them at nutritional risk (7T 135).

Winston Craig

MILLENNIUM. Ellen White presents her understanding of the millennium of Revelation 20 primarily in three main segments (EW 51-54, 289-295; GC 657-678). Continuing the line of thought already expressed in the Millerite awakening (see LS 21, 44), she opposes the idea of a temporal and triumphant reign of the Messiah on earth (PP 103; 2SP 21, 22) and argues in favor of premillennialism with the following sequence of events. First, the *second coming of Christ ushers the beginning of the millennium with the destruction of the wicked and the first *resurrection of the righteous. Second, the redeemed reign in heaven for 1,000 years while *Satan is bound on earth and the impious are dead. Third, the millennium is followed by a second resurrection and the final destruction of Satan and the unjust.

With the return of Christ the unrighteous die, while nature and earth are left in a state of desolation. As the scapegoat of Leviticus 16 was sent into the wilderness, so Satan will suffer his confinement to a devastated earth where he has to reflect upon the results of his rebellion. He and his angels are limited to earth without any access to other worlds. During this period of 1,000 years the saints inhabit the New Jerusalem still in heaven and, together with Christ, judge evil human beings and fallen angels according to their works (1 Cor. 6:2, 3). Jointly they determine the severity of punishment. At the close of this long period Christ returns in the fullness of His majesty to the Mount of Olives on earth, accompanied by the saints within the Holy City. The wicked come forth to life, but their bodies bear the traces of disease and death. Satan pretends to have resuscitated them from death and urges his huge army of men and angels to attack the New Jerusalem. Jesus and the saints with glittering crowns upon their heads ascend to the top of the city. Christ addresses His enemies, who realize what glory they have missed and acknowledge the justice of their sentence. Then Satan and the wicked are punished. Heavenly fire destroys some of them quickly; others suffer many days. Satan's torment, however, will exceed that of others because he bears not only the weight of his own sins but also the guilt of all the sins he instigated in others. In this sense he is said to bear the ultimate guilt for all the sins that were removed from the righteous by the atoning sacrifice of Christ. Finally, the fire of judgment destroys the whole earth, and God creates a new earth, where the saints inherit an everlasting kingdom (2 Peter 3:10-13).

Further reading: 7BC 883-887; E. C. Webster, "The Millennium," in R. Dederen, ed., *Handbook of Seventh-day Adventist Theology* (RHPA, 2000), pp. 927-946.

Johannes Kovar

MILLERISM, see **WILLIAM MILLER**; **DISAPPOINTMENTS, MILLERITE.**

MILTON, JOHN (1608-1674). Puritan writer, philosopher, and politician, best remembered for his epic poem *Paradise Lost* (1667). According to Perry Miller, the influence of Milton was extensive on American religious, social, and cultural life, and, more specifically, upon American theology (*Errand Into the Wilderness* [Harvard University Press, 1956]). The dawn of the Enlightenment and the process of democratization diversified American Christianity, but in particular,

these trends impacted Protestant Christians in New England, who continued to hold to Puritan ideals within American culture. Thus many Evangelical Christians in the nineteenth century continued to be influenced by Milton and Puritan thought.

COURTESY OF THE REVIEW AND HERALD PUBLISHING ASSOCIATION

JOHN MILTON, ENGLISH PURITAN AND AUTHOR OF *PARADISE LOST*

There are no obvious or direct links within Ellen White's writings about John Milton. She does not refer to him by name in either her published or unpublished writings. Furthermore, there is no record of her ever owning a copy of Milton's most famous work, *Paradise Lost*, although it seems likely that she read it. An early family account suggests that *J. N. Andrews gave her a copy of *Paradise Lost* soon after he heard her describe her *great controversy vision. Despite her having possibly received such a copy, Milton's name is conspicuously absent from the list of Puritan luminaries in her magnum opus on the history of Christianity, *The Great Controversy*. Yet such an omission in no way diminishes the impact of Milton upon either Ellen White or other early Sabbatarian Adventists. One of the best examples of this influence is the publication in 1854 by James White of a tract printed by the Advent Christian writer and printer Horace L. Hastings, in which Milton defended his position on the nonimmortality of the soul (RH, Nov. 14, 1854). Hastings (who was also affiliated with George Storrs) corresponded with the Whites (although this correspondence is no longer extant). Initially they each viewed the other with caution, but their mutual interest in the state of the dead and the *Second Coming kept them in communication with each other. James White carried for sale a wide array of Hastings' publications, including a tract published by Hastings that reprinted Milton's views on the immortality of the soul. White republished it several times in the *Review and Herald* and still later as a tract that went through numerous editions from the *Review* office.

Some critics of Ellen White have suggested that she borrowed her ideas from Milton through the work of Hastings. Up through the early 1860s James White carried an extensive supply of publications from Hastings, and printed excerpts of his books and articles in the *Review and Herald*. In 1858 James White advertised Hastings' book, *The Great Controversy Between God and Man* (Rochester, N.Y.: [the author], 1858), in the *Review and Herald* for Adventists to purchase (RH, Mar. 18, 1858). There does not appear to be any significant *literary borrowing beyond similar theological interests. The most noticeable difference lies in the very title itself: for Hastings, it was the *Great Controversy Between God and Man*, but for Ellen White, it was *Spiritual Gifts: The Great Controversy Between Christ and His Angels, and Satan and His Angels*. After Hastings, in 1862, attacked the validity of spiritual gifts, and in particular the modern manifestation of prophecy, the Review office ceased to carry his publications, and *M. E. Cornell responded to his criticism through a series of articles in the *Review* that were later published in pamphlet form as *Miraculous Powers: The Scripture Testimony on the Perpetuity of Spiritual Gifts* (Battle Creek, Mich.: Steam Press, 1862).

Yet did Ellen White borrow her ideas directly from Milton? Ruth Elizabeth Burgeson, in her master's thesis, contends that there are parallels between Ellen White's writings in *Patriarchs and Prophets* and Milton's *Paradise Lost*, but each author had a different purpose in writing, reflecting their contrasting views of theodicy. Their divergent purposes determined their form and length of writing, and, most noticeably, the emphasis each author placed upon narrative. Burgeson found "no disagreement between the two authors in stating significant facts," but did find "frequent differences in manner of statement, in amount of detail, in emphasis given, or even in the exact order of a series of events, but none in facts pertinent to the biblical story" (p. 73). What was most significant for Burgeson were seven extrabiblical scenes that two authors 200 years apart took the time to describe: (1) loyal angels in heaven trying to dissuade disaffected angels from rebelling against God; (2) warnings issued to Eve to stay by her husband's side; (3) the elaborate setting for the actual temptation, with Satan's arguments analyzed in detail; (4) a detailed description of the immediate results of sin on Adam and Eve, and especially upon the plant and animal kingdom; (5) explanation for the basic reason for Adam's fall; (6) angel's chronicling of future events to Adam; and (7) feelings of both Adam and Eve as they left the Garden of Eden. Unfortunately, Burgeson falls short of drawing any meaningful conclusions. She quotes *Arthur L. White, who wrote that according to his father, *W. C. White, *J. N. Andrews gave her a copy of *Paradise Lost* after he heard Ellen White present her views of the great controversy shortly after her vision in 1858. According to this memory statement she refrained from reading his work until after she had written out what she had seen in vision. This statement, if correct, is very similar to what she claimed about reading the writings of other health reformers after her 1863 *health reform vision. Ellen White's later work, *Patriarchs and Prophets*, was published in 1891, more than 30 years after her first published book on the *great controversy theme (1858). Thus, it seems consistent with her pattern of reading from other Christian authors that she may have gained insights from Milton as her understanding of the great controversy theme matured. Critics of Ellen White argue that such similarities are proof that Ellen White maliciously plagiarized from other authors, but it can also be argued that her literary borrowing was consistent with her view of the process of *revelation and inspiration.

See also: Interpretation of Ellen G. White's Writings.

Further reading: R. E. Burgeson, "A Comparative Study of the Fall of Man as Treated by John Milton and Ellen G. White" (M.A. thesis, Pacific Union College, 1957); A. L. White, "The Prophetic Gift of Action," *Ministry*, June, 1944.

Heidi Olson Campbell and Michael W. Campbell

MIND AND BODY. Ellen White wrote extensively regarding the mind and the interaction of the mind and the body, focusing primarily on the importance of the mind to spiritual life. In many cases White seems to use brain, mind, and head interchangeably. Occasionally character, will, heart, conscience, soul, morals, emotions, or passions appear to be used to describe mental functions or characteristics (e.g., 1MCP 51).

The relationship between the mind and the body White always describes as interdependent and reciprocal. In many instances the mind controls the body (3T 136; 1MCP 72; CH 586): "when the soul is sick, the body also is affected" (6T 301). Nine tenths of diseases have their foundation in the mind, she says (5T 444; 1MCP 59). The mind affects the physical system in powerful ways. For example, cheerfulness encourages freer circulation of the blood and tones up the entire body (CH 28; 1MCP 60). The will and self-control (mind)

can preserve and recover health (Ed 197). Cheerfulness, unselfishness, and gratitude have life-giving power, while anger, discontent, selfishness, and impurity have depressing and even ruinous effects (*ibid.*).

At other times, depending on the content and purpose of her writing, White can emphasize how the body can lead in the behavior and affect the mind. The words "body," "appetite," and "passions" seem in many instances to be used interchangeably. "The body is the only medium through which the mind and the soul are developed for the upbuilding of character" (MH 130). "The indulgence of appetite beclouds and fetters the mind, and blunts the holy emotions of the soul" (3T 310).

White also gives many examples of how the body affects the mind positively. Exercise and fresh air rest and relax the mind (4T 264, 265; 1MCP 116); lead to composure and serenity, and induce sound, sweet sleep (1T 702; 1MCP 116); relieve the wearied brain and prevent the mind from overwork (3T 152; 1MCP 117). Other physical conditions that invigorate the mind include manual labor (4T 264, 265; 2MCP 383), bathing (3T 70; 2MCP 383), other physical activity (1MCP 362, 364; CE 211; 5T 522; TM 241), sleep, and rest (7T 247).

White also identifies physical issues that impair the functioning of the brain/mind: loss of sleep and irregular hours for sleeping lessen mental and physical strength, blunting discernment (YI, May 31, 1894; CD 122, 176; 3T 242; Ed 205). Wrong habits of eating (1MCP 317), as well as the use of alcohol, tobacco, coffee, and tea also impair the mind (Te 79, 80; MH 329; 1MCP 321).

One of Ellen White's favorite topics was Christian temperance. Here she found a platform for teaching the effects of the body upon the mind, soul, and character. In this context she spoke of "artificial stimulants" (CD 421), which were often associated with appetite. White clearly stated that Satan gains control of the mind through appetite (Te 14).

Regarding "degrees in the scale" of artificial stimulation, White wrote: "Tea, coffee and tobacco, as well as alcoholic drinks, are different degrees in the scale of artificial stimulants" (CD 421). Flesh meats and tea and coffee prepare the way for stronger stimulants. Tobacco and liquor follow (Te 57). Condiments and spices also pave the way for stronger stimulants: tobacco and wine (ST, Oct. 27, 1887; Te 57). "[Tobacco] excites and then paralyzes the nerves. It weakens and clouds the brain" (MH 327, 328).

According to White, the effects of stimulants on the mind include: benumbing (Te 73, 74) and beclouding (4T 28) of the mind and intellect; weakening the intellect (*ibid.*) and mental power (CH 432); injuring the mind (Te 78) and character (MH 335); and unbalancing the mind (Te 78, 79). Narcotics, opium, and morphine are "hurtful" and "ruinous to the physical, mental, and moral powers" (CD 421). Such stimulants lessen the influence of the Holy Spirit (Te 80) and hinder worship of God (CD 426).

The list of damaging influences also included: overeating (CD 62; MH 306, 307); irregularity in eating and drinking (CD 62); bedtime snacks (MH 303); condiments such as mustard, pepper, spices (CD 339); self-abuse and masturbation (2T 361, 469, 470; 5T 91); and free use of flesh meats (CD 389; MH 311-317; CD 373-416). Diet also affects the mind and spirituality (2MCP 385-395; CD 43-65). Indulged appetite is the greatest hindrance to mental improvement and soul sanctification (CD 45). The reading of novels and frivolous stories is also a stimulant that negatively affects the mind and the spiritual life (AH 414, 415; CSW 21; 2MCP 591; OHC 275).

At times White described a reciprocal relationship and interdependence between the mind and the body. "The brain is the organ and instrument of the mind, and controls the whole body. . . . If by correct habits of eating and drinking the blood is kept pure, the brain will be properly nourished" (MM 291; 1MCP 60). "Between the mind and the body there is a mysterious and wonderful relationship. They react upon each other. . . . To neglect the body is to neglect the mind" (2MCP 373). Balance should exist between mental and physical activity (1MCP 3, 364; 2MCP 377; MH 128; Ed 197; 5T 322; YI, Apr. 7, 1898).

Most diseases originate in mind sickness, and their cure lies in the mind (5T 444; 1MCP 59-64; MH 241-259). "Depressing emotions . . . [hinder] the process of digestion . . . [and thus] interfere with nutrition. . . . Grief and anxiety . . . can do great harm" (1MCP 62, 63). "Peace of mind, which comes from pure and holy motives and actions, will give free and vigorous spring to all the organs of the body" (2T 327). Cheerfulness increases the circulation and body tone, and helping others benefits one's own heart and life (CH 28). Brain electric power vitalizes the whole system and is an invaluable aid in resisting disease (Ed 197; 2MCP 396).

In view of the close and sympathetic relationship between mind and body, White placed great emphasis on the development of the mind. Humans were created in the image of God, and, she averred, one of God's greatest gifts is the power of the mind, the aptitude to think and to reason. This unique endowment distinguishes humans from all other living things. "Every human being, created in the image of God, is endowed with a power akin to that of the Creator—individuality, power to think and to do. . . . It is the work of true education to develop this power, to train the youth to be thinkers" (Ed 17; 1MCP 361).

The main purpose of the development of the human mind is to worship its Creator, honoring him by sound moral decisions, and serving him guided by the principles of true love. Thus the mind's almost infinite potential for development can only be realized under the direction of God. The highest development of the mind can only occur under the influence of the Holy Spirit (DA 251; GW 285; CH 164; COL 24). Prayer, nature study, and useful work are also essential for mental development (CSW 40; CG 49, 50; CE 205; PP 642; Ed 21; AH 286).

The study of the Bible under the guidance of the Holy Spirit is the best means to reach the highest possibilities of mental development. Sincerely grasping the God-given truths will confer clear comprehension and sound judgment. The study of the Scriptures will elevate and ennoble the mind, develop a well-balanced mind, lead to greater mental efficiency, and build breadth of mind, nobility of character, and stability of purpose (CE 58; SC 90; FE 394; 1MCP 91; 5T 703).

Healthy mental development is assured through a continuous communion with the Source of all wisdom, knowledge, and power. The intellect is developed, strengthened, and surrounded with genuine peace (CH 163; MH 58; COL 146). God will give "understanding in temporal as well as in spiritual matters" (COL 146).

The individual has a large role to play in the development of the mind, through diligence, self-discipline, and practice (1MCP 289; CH 405; 4T 561; 3T 32; 2MCP 287, 588). "The most brilliant talents are of no value unless they are improved; industrious habits and force of character must be gained by cultivation. A high moral character and fine mental qualities are not the result of accident.

God gives opportunities; success depends upon the use made of them" (5T 321).

The development of the mind is affected by the subjects that occupy the thoughts (CE 65; CT 460), as well as the emotional atmosphere surrounding the individual (MH 257, 387). Physical factors play a large role in the development of the mind, both positively and negatively (see the first section above). Other negative influences mentioned by White include overloading the mind (CT 296), moral perversion (5T 682), and worthless or trivial reading material (FE 452).

The ability to memorize is very important, especially memorizing the Scriptures. The memory can be strengthened through discipline and exercise (CT 506; 4T 399; Ed 251, 252; 3T 12; GW 100). The use of music, object lessons, associations, and illustrations help store information in the memory (Ed 167, 168, 186; FE 95; CG 515; PP 592). A regular, orderly, disciplined life also aids memory (CG 111, 112; CD 137, 138; FE 227).

Memory is a gift from God enabling humans to store securely in their minds the truths of God's Word so that we may share them with the world. A knowledge of God's promises gives the believer comfort and courage to press onward in the Christian life, and provides the weapons necessary to meet Satan's temptations (CS 116; ML 28; GC 600). However, memory is not a substitute for other kinds of learning. In addition to memory, the mind must be trained to use the reasoning powers to think independently and make decisions. Dependence on rote memory leaves the conscience dormant and eventually renders it incapable of judging right from wrong (Ed 230).

In summary, White emphasizes the intimate association of mind and body. What affects one, affects the other. "If our physical habits are not right, our mental and moral powers cannot be strong; for great sympathy exists between the physical and the moral" (TE 13). "The brain nerves which communicate with the entire system are the only medium through which Heaven can communicate to man and affect his inmost life" (2T 347). Since the mind is God's communication channel with humans, the importance of maintaining a healthy body to support the mind, and of developing the mind to its greatest capacity in order to worship God, honor Him through sound moral decisions, and serve Him guided by the principles of true love, cannot be overemphasized. The relationship with God depends on the state of the mind.

Donna J. Habenicht and Herald A. Habenicht

MIND AND EDUCATION. The mind and how mental processes affect every facet of human existence is a frequently mentioned topic in the writings of Ellen G. White. One indication of the breadth and quantity of her writings in this area is the two-volume, 882-page compilation *Mind, Character, and Personality.* The human mind in relation to education and the training of youth also attracted her authorial attention.

Ellen White insisted that the task of educating the mind should begin in early childhood, because then is when the mind is most impressionable and efforts will obtain the best results. This responsibility lies with both father and mother. Parents are to encourage each other and provide an atmosphere of peace at home. Traits such as pleasantness, kindness, patience, and the like will contribute to healthy minds in their children.

Educating the mind is not limited to studying from books. For Ellen White, mental development, especially in the preschool years, begins with moral instruction. "Give your children intellectual culture and moral training. Fortify their young minds with firm, pure principles. While you have opportunity, lay

the foundation for a noble manhood and womanhood. Your labor will be rewarded a thousandfold" (CT 131). One repeatedly mentioned aid to a healthy mind is contact with nature. Lessons from the book of nature are unlimited and they bring to children much delight. Furthermore, God's name is written on "every leaf of the forest and stone of the mountains, in every shining star, in earth and sea and sky" (CG 45); and this provides an excellent way to introduce the love of God to small children.

By the time children attend school, teachers become a significant source of influence upon their minds. In order to be successful, teachers need not only scientific knowledge but also wisdom and tact to gain the respect and confidence of their pupils (Ed 278, 279). They also need to be truly converted and have the love of Jesus in their hearts. Lacking this will make the task of dealing with human minds more difficult and even detrimental to their pupils. "Their [teachers'] own insubordinate hearts are striving for control; and to subject the plastic minds and characters of the children to such discipline is to leave upon the mind scars and bruises that will never be removed" (CT 193). It is, therefore, imperative to observe the relationship between the teacher's own character and his or her ability to educate the minds of the youth (3T 131).

Because educating the mind involves the concept of personal freedom, children and adolescents should be taught to think for themselves. There are parents who, exerting a rigid discipline, bring up youth incapable of thinking. "These children have been so long under iron rule, not allowed to think and act for themselves in those things in which it was highly proper that they should, that they have no confidence in themselves to move out upon their own judgment, having an opinion of their own. And when they go out from their parents to act for themselves, they are easily led by others' judgment in the wrong direction. They have not stability of character. They have not been thrown upon their own judgment as fast and as far as practicable, and therefore their minds have not been properly developed and strengthened. They have so long been absolutely controlled by their parents that they rely wholly upon them; their parents are mind and judgment for them" (3T 132, 133). Distinction is made between training (as it is done with animals) and education—shaping the mind for individual decisions. Children trained with no will of their own will be "deficient in moral energy and individual responsibility. They have not been taught to move from reason and principle; their wills have been controlled by another, and the mind has not been called out, that it might expand and strengthen by exercise" (CT 74; 3T 132).

Specific advice is given on how to develop the mind, so that God's followers may reach the goal of thinking Christ's thoughts (FE 520) and discerning spiritual things (2T 265). As the physiological system must be sustained by healthful food, so the mental capabilities must also be nourished with wholesome thoughts. Thoughts of rivalry, jealousy, frustration, fear, and selfishness tend to produce undesirable acts, whereas thoughts of love, trust, acceptance, and sympathy bear fruit in acceptable deeds. Young people are, therefore, urged to feed their minds on pure and holy thoughts so that they may develop in the right direction (CE 109).

As a major source of knowledge, reading is also important for the development of the mind. There are books (the Bible especially) capable of elevating mind and spirit to bring it in close contact with God. Other books (such as many novels) have the potential of crippling mental strength and hindering

vigorous thought and research (MYP 280). Were Ellen White writing today, it seems likely that she would apply the same principles to the selection of radio, television, and other current information media.

Finally, manual labor is identified as a source of mental strength, especially as compensation to the erroneous emphasis on intellectual activity as the sole source of mental power. Ellen White indicates that physical work and useful exercise have a beneficial effect on mind and character: "Without physical exercise, no one can have a sound constitution and vigorous health; and the discipline of well-regulated labor is no less essential to the securing of a strong and active mind and a noble character (PP 601).

Further reading: L. B. Caviness, "Brain Research, Does It Support Ellen G. White's Counsels to Educators?" *Journal of Adventist Education* 63 (December 2000/January 2001): 16-22.

Julian Melgosa

MIND, CHARACTER, AND PERSONALITY (SPA, 1977, 882 pp.). Two-volume compilation of Ellen White's writings on the study of the mind (psychology) and "guidelines to mental and spiritual health" (subtitle), based upon an earlier publication, *Guidelines to Mental Health*. The set has continuous pagination, and includes scripture and subject indexes at the end of the second volume. A large portion of the work presents general guiding principles interspersed and supplemented with practical admonitions and counsels to teachers, ministers, physicians, and parents. Obviously Ellen White did not write on this subject as a psychologist and did not use scientific vocabulary familiar to this field. Nonetheless, her insights on the various aspects of the mind—its vital place in the human experience, its potential, and the factors that lead to its optimum functioning—enhance the understanding of human nature, especially in its psychospiritual dimensions. One of the greatest contributions of Ellen White's writings to Adventist thought on psychology and mental health is in regard to the psychosomatic unity of the human being. "The relation which exists between the mind and the body is very intimate. When one is affected, the other sympathizes. The condition of the mind affects the health of the physical system" (pp. 59, 60). Furthermore, she emphasizes that this unity also has an impact on one's spiritual life. "The brain nerves which communicate with the entire system are the only medium through which Heaven can communicate to man and affect his inmost life" (p. 73). Hence, her insistence that since body and mind are so closely interrelated, and affect one's spiritual life, one should keep "both in the very best condition" (p. 77).

MINISTRY. The ministry of the church was an area of deep concern to Ellen White. A multitude of articles proceeded from her pen detailing every aspect of ministry. These are elaborated in her published works, such as *Gospel Workers, Testimonies to Ministers, Pastoral Ministry,* and *Evangelism.* In these writings Ellen White details two main concerns about ministers. First, ministers were to be evangelists, and their primary work has to be soul winning. Second, she was concerned that the churches not depend on the ministers for their spiritual life. These two concerns, mission-centeredness and nondependency, are in evidence in much of her writings.

For the first 40 to 50 years after the Seventh-day Adventist Church was organized, almost no settled pastors were placed over churches. Instead Adventist clergy were free for evangelism and church planting while churches provided their own pastoral care. This format was no accident, nor was it solely on account of the embryonic stage of the church—it was a deliberate plan, endorsed by Ellen White, to facilitate both the mission and nurture of the church.

In the early 1900s some members began to request that ministers be placed over large churches. Ellen White resisted this idea with many counsels (AUG, Jan. 8, 1902). It is in this context that she declared that ministers should not be "hovering over the churches" (Ev 381), but instead should be doing evangelism. This was such a major issue with Ellen White that she even declared that anyone who needed to depend on a minister for nurture and spiritual growth needed to be reconverted and rebaptized (*ibid.*). To her, discipleship was a major issue. If people needed to depend constantly on the clergy, then obviously the minister had not functioned adequately in discipling new believers. A properly disciplined church member should be able to grow spiritually on his or her own without a preacher.

However, Ellen White did not envision the Adventist church member being neglected. Instead her divine guidance suggested that church members were best nourished and strengthened when there was no pastor to depend on. There were times when Adventist ministers would spend time with believers, but those times would be rare. When ministers labored among the members, she declared that they should be training and equipping the members for their ministries and not babysitting the saints (GW 196).

Her view, consistent with Paul's counsels on spiritual gifts in Ephesians 4:11-14, viewed the work of the minister as training and equipping church members. The Adventist pastor was to put the members to work, and failure to do so meant that the minister should be fired (*ibid.* 197, 198). She had no use for a minister who hovered over the churches, caring only for the saints. Such work would be counterproductive and would not produce good nurture. On the contrary, she believed the minister must be aggressively involved in sharing the faith. Ministers who did not follow this practice should not be part of the paid ministry (RH, May 7, 1889).

Again and again Ellen White urged ministers to spend their time training church members (GW 196). Every Adventist was to be involved in ministry. In her understanding of the minister's role, training was to occupy a higher priority than even preaching (7T 20). Ellen White was not negative to preaching; she advocated it strongly, especially evangelistic preaching. However, she was emphatic that Adventists should not depend on preaching for their spiritual life. Therefore they should not expect a sermon every Sabbath (LLM 179, 180). Sermon dependency in her view created weak Christians and immature churches.

Ellen White did not expect the minister to be continually settling church problems. Churches with such care usually produced religious weaklings (7T 18). In her view, nurture for the sake of nurture produced spiritual feebleness, and church members were best nourished while engaged in aggressive ministry. "Strength to resist evil is best gained by aggressive service" (AA 105). To be an overcomer, one must become "intensely interested in the salvation of others"—nothing else could enable one to prevail (FE 207).

This strong call for discipleship, for non-dependency, occupied much of her counsels to ministers. Her concern here is primarily the health and nurture of the church. Yet there was another major reason for this emphasis on a nondependent ministry: the evangelization of the lost. Ellen White was vitally concerned for the harvest that needed to be reaped and felt the resources of the church should be channeled into reaching people rather than performing ministry to church members. Her strong mission emphasis is the second reason undergirding her view of the ministry.

Even with no settled pastors, Ellen White was still concerned that the ministers were spending too much time with the churches. She even declared that "nine tenths" of their work for the churches could be eliminated and they would then be able to spend more time winning the lost (7T 18). Church members were to care for themselves while the minister sought the "lost sheep" (RH, May 7, 1889). Ellen White counseled pastors that spending time nurturing members not only made them weak, but also made the minister weak. She could not understand why ministers would be hovering over churches that have received great light while new fields desperately needed to be opened and churches planted (13MR 208). Her view envisioned Adventist pastors being primarily church planters and evangelists. This was important for the health of the church as well as for church planting and evangelism.

Further reading: R. Burrill, *Recovering an Adventist Approach to Life and Mission in the Local Church* (Hart, 1998); idem, *Revolution in the Church* (Hart, 1993); idem, *Radical Disciples for Revolutionary Churches* (Hart, 1996); idem, *The Revolutionized Church of the 21st Century* (Hart, 1997); idem, *Rekindling a Lost Passion: Recreating a Church Planting Movement* (Hart, 1999).

Russell Burrill

MINISTRY OF HEALING, THE (PPPA, 1905, 1909, 540 pp.). Ellen White's culminating work on healthful living, climaxing four decades of writing on the subject. In *The Ministry of Healing* Ellen White presents the sacrificial life of Christ, who "devoted more time to healing the sick than to preaching"

(p. 19) as the supreme example of compassion in caring for the sick and those in need, the ultimate source of healing, and the originator of the principles of health and wellness. The book is divided into eight sections, which may be summarized under four major themes.

The book's first theme is the healing ministry of Christ (pp. 17-107). Although the life of Christ was one of constant toil, it was also a "life of health" and "an example of what God designed all humanity to be through obedience to His laws" (p. 51). Fallen human beings begin the restorative process by recognizing their need (pp. 63-66), coming to Christ in faith, and receiving cleansing (pp. 67-71). Although a person may not receive an answer to prayer for temporal blessings, this is "not so when we ask for deliverance from sin" (p. 70). No person is so hopeless that Christ cannot save them. When Christ healed, He healed "both the soul and the body" (p. 77). Furthermore, the gospel of salvation appoints each disciple as a missionary for "revealing Christ to the world" (p. 100).

The next major theme of the book is the work of medical missionaries (pp. 111-268). "Christ," she wrote, "is the true head of the medical profession" (p. 111). Sin is the cause of disease, and medical workers are to point people to Jesus Christ—the source of all healing. Christian medical personnel have the responsibility of pointing people to the divine Physician for help and to educate their patients in the principles of healthful living (p. 147). All classes of society—the unemployed, the homeless, and the rich—should be reached by medical workers (pp. 183-216). A key component of Ellen White's thought on medical ministry is helping all patients understand the importance of the laws of health (pp. 219-224). *Prayer for the sick should not be neglected (pp. 225-233) and as far as possible physicians should try to use *natural remedies

(pp. 234-240). Complete health includes a healthy state of mind (pp. 241-259) facilitated by spending time in *nature (pp. 261-268).

The third major theme is principles of healthful living (pp. 271-346). This includes a knowledge of general hygiene (pp. 271-286), dress (pp. 287-294), diet (pp. 295-324), and the avoidance of stimulants and narcotics (pp. 325-335) such as tea, coffee, tobacco, and alcohol (pp. 337-346).

A fourth major theme is the psychosocial dimensions of health. These include *marriage and the setting up of a home (pp. 356-370), family relationships (pp. 371-387), and the goal of the home as a place for "the restoration and uplifting of humanity" (p. 349; cf. pp. 388-394). The "essential knowledge" for optimum mental and spiritual health is knowledge of God and His Word as the basis for "true" education (pp. 409-466). The final section deals with the spiritual needs of caregivers and all who are workers with Christ. Considered one of her finest writings on practical Christian living, this section (pp. 469-516) has been separately published under the title *Help in Daily Living* (PPPA 1964, 2001).

The Ministry of Healing is one of Ellen White's best illustrated and most widely distributed books published during her lifetime. Ellen White began preparation for this volume in late 1903 when she assigned her *literary assistant *Marian Davis to compile extracts from her writings for the various chapters of the book. The following year Ellen White wrote of her plans to donate the proceeds from the book to relieve the financial strain experienced by Adventist medical institutions (*sanitariums) (Lt 63, 1904). By that November the book was nearly ready for publication, but funds were needed for illustrations, to prepare printing plates, and to cover the cost of printing. In the *Review and Herald* of June 8, 1905 (p. 13), the General Conference expressed appreciation to Ellen White for the gift of the proceeds from the sale of the book for the relief of debts incurred by Adventist medical institutions, and urged its vigorous circulation. The General Conference also took over the financial responsibility for its publication. Later a relief bureau was organized by *E. R. Palmer to coordinate the sale of *The Ministry of Healing*. The bureau was also responsible for selling *Christ's Object Lessons* to raise funds for educational institutions and *Story of Jesus* to raise funds for Adventist work among *African-Americans in the American South (RH, Sept. 7, 1905). The first 10,000 copies of the book were released on September 12, 1905, and sold initially for $1.50 (RH, Sept. 14, 1905). *The Ministry of Healing* met with immediate success, and within two months the book was reprinted.

Further reading: R. Graybill, "The Making of *The Ministry of Healing*," *Insight*, July 10, 1979; J. R. Nix, "*The Ministry of Healing*: The History Behind Ellen G. White's Classic Work on Health," AR, Mar. 31, 2005.

Michael W. Campbell

MINNEAPOLIS GENERAL CONFERENCE SESSION, see **GENERAL CONFERENCE SESSION OF 1888.**

MISSION. Throughout her ministry Ellen White was at the forefront in shaping and changing the Adventist view of mission. After the disappointment of 1844 Ellen White, for a short time and like many of the early Millerites, believed that the door of probation was closed (see *shut door) for those who had not responded to the Millerite message (1SM 63). While some early Sabbatarian Adventists continued to hold this view until 1851, a vision she received in 1848 encouraged the printing of a little paper to disseminate their views. She saw that their small

publishing beginning would in time grow into a publishing enterprise that would be like streams of light encircling the world (LS 125).

Although Ellen White early envisioned a worldwide approach to mission, it took many years for Adventists to grasp the necessity of this formidable task. In the 1850s Uriah Smith and other Adventist leaders believed the gospel commission could be interpreted to mean that since all the nations of the world were located in the United States, mission could be accomplished in America merely by preaching to the immigrant population (RH, May 27, 1858; RH, Feb. 3, 1859). There is no evidence, however, that Ellen White ever shared that view. By 1874 Ellen White was urging Adventists to use literature to spread their beliefs to other nations, mentioning Australia by name (LS 208-210). Writing from Australia in 1892, she talked about the need to work in Africa, India, and China (FE 208, 209). As her view of mission expanded she was tireless in both urging and practicing widespread participation in the missionary task.

Much was written by Ellen White concerning each Christian's responsibility to engage in mission. She was concerned that many pastors and church members were not participating in the mission task because too many pastors were spending the majority of their time trying to fan the feeble spark of faith of those who were spiritually dead. Instead of seeking out the lost in the world, pastors had to work among longtime members (DA 825). Meanwhile millions upon millions who were still bound by chains of ignorance and sin were dying; millions who had never heard of Christ's love were perishing (HP 225).

Ellen White felt that most believers, if asked whether they believed the Word of God, would answer in the affirmative, yet by their actions showed that God's Word was not having much impact on their lives. If Christians took seriously the Word of God, then why was there so little self-denial and self-sacrifice for those who have never heard? How will so-called Christians, who are in good and regular standing, face the countless millions at the judgment bar of God who were allowed to pass, unwarned, to eternal separation from God? (*Notebook Leaflets*, vol. 1, p. 34). She characterizes Christians who show little concern for lost people as lacking in love, moving in a stupor, and having a paralysis that keeps them from engaging in the task that is needed. A suffering world living in misery elicits no response from many (6T 445).

Ellen White lived and worked in Europe from 1885 to 1887 and in Australia from 1891 to 1900. The 11 years spent outside the United States gave her firsthand knowledge of the challenges of cross-cultural work and contributed to her understanding of missionary principles. She believed that each area of the world and each group of people needed to be understood; cultures and languages needed to be studied in order that the biblical message could be presented in a way that allowed for no excuse or misunderstanding (RH, Dec. 21, 1891). The Holy Spirit guides missionaries to understand people and their culture, in order to adapt mission work to the particular ideas of the people and thus meet their needs (TM 213). She encouraged people to work intelligently in presenting the good news (GW92 297, 298), and to use a variety of methods, since what works in America should not necessarily be taken to other parts of the world (TSA 97). Christian witnesses are to meet people where they are and must adapt their methods to the conditions of the people to whom they are ministering (Ev 57).

In the presentation of various doctrinal subjects, she felt the sequence of topics should be carefully selected so as not to create barriers to the truths being presented, and that it is better to leave some things unsaid in initial presentations (GW 117). She also suggested that it is not necessary to identify oneself as a Seventh-day Adventist initially, if that would erect a barrier that would keep people from coming to understand biblical truths. This principle has many implications for ministering in the hostile environments in our present-day world (*ibid.* 119, 120). Another principle that Ellen White stressed was the necessity of introducing change slowly. Even those changes that would promote the good of the people should not be introduced too rapidly so that controversies surround the work (*ibid.* 468).

Several principles in her book *Evangelism* have implications for cross-cultural mission work. The gospel should be presented to people with whom good relationships have been developed. We should never tear down their religious systems; rather our mission is to build up (p. 227). Those aspects of the Adventist message that condemn local customs and practices and that are in direct opposition to the opinions of the people should be presented only after the basic principles of our faith are understood (p. 231). Unique beliefs should not be presented too quickly to new believers (p. 246). It is especially counterproductive for those who present the Christian message to place immediate and undo emphasis on difficult areas of belief, for this often only increases the people's prejudice and stirs up more opposition. When confronting methods are used, many people who could have been won to Christ become resistant. Instead of a combative, debating approach, a Christlike approach is needed in order to reach people where they are (pp. 248, 249).

Ellen White believed that foreign language acquisition is important for cross-cultural witness. She knew that middle-aged missionaries could have difficulty in learning a new language, but suggested that God could bless and bring people into His kingdom even when missionaries did their witness through an interpreter (FE 537). However, the best approach would be for people to witness in their own language and speak to people from their own cultural background. Therefore, she encouraged missionaries to seek out and train local leaders who could evangelize their own people more effectively (GW92 294).

Ellen White often talked about the positive influence of foreign missions upon a local field. As a congregation gives monetary support for missions in foreign lands the work in the local area will also be benefited (CET 222). Liberal giving and self-sacrifice for missions has a reflex action that blesses the work at home (GW 465, 466).

Many of the leaders in early Adventism, including Ellen White, had come out of churches in which there was an emphasis on plain dress and simplicity. Ellen White continued to promote that emphasis, tying the need for such a simple lifestyle directly to the need for funds in foreign fields. The appeal was for members to deny themselves fancy houses, adornment, and gratifications in appetite (CSW 135). Instead of spending for needless things, God's people should give the money saved for the support of missions (CS 290). If the money that Adventists had spent on their own self-gratification had been given in support of missions, God's work would have been established in all parts of the world. She appealed for self-denial, the putting aside of comfortable and desirable things, and the laying off of ornaments in order that mission work have the means needed to carry out its purposes in overseas areas (*ibid.* 290, 291).

In Ellen White's thought the work of evangelism and the work of relief, development, and health should not be carried out separately. Providing physical help must be coupled with the preaching of the Word of God (CH 557). There is a danger that as Adventists work to alleviate the temporal needs of poor and suffering people, the importance of sharing God's love with them could be forgotten (*ibid.* 515, 516).

Ellen White affirmed the centrality of salvation only in Christ, yet believed that even those who know little of theology, those who know nothing of the law of God (DA 638), and those among the heathen who have lived according to the light they received from God do have access to salvation too (*ibid.* 239; PK 253).

While Adventists still face challenges in cross-cultural missionary work, in contextualization, and in knowing how to present the gospel to peoples living in hostile cultural and religious environments, the principles and guidelines Ellen White shared with the Adventist Church during her lifetime still hold great relevance for today's mission.

Further reading: P. G. Damsteegt, *Foundations of the Seventh-day Adventist Message and Mission* (Grand Rapids: Eerdmans, 1977); B. Schantz, "The Development of Seventh-day Adventist Missionary Thought: Contemporary Appraisal" (Ph.D. diss., Fuller Theological Seminary, School of World Mission, 1983).

Bruce L. Bauer

MONEY, USE OF, see **STEWARDSHIP**.

MORMONISM. Adventism and Mormonism have been confused by some people because both arose in the 1830s and 1840s in the northeastern part of the United States and both claim to have a modern-day prophet. Ellen White noted in 1860 that the "cry of Mormonism is often raised, especially in the west, at the introduction of the Bible argument of the perpetuity of spiritual gifts" by Adventists.

In fact, one man reported that he had known Ellen and James White "twenty years ago, when we [the Whites] were leaders among the Mormans [*sic*] at Nauvoo!" She went on to point out the ridiculousness of his accusation by noting that she would have been only 12 years old at that time (2SG iv). Presumably it was because of such confusions that she never claimed the title of prophet. Why? "Because in these days many who boldly claim that they are prophets are a reproach to the cause of Christ; and because my work includes much more than the word 'prophet' signifies" (1SM 32).

Of course, Ellen White and Joseph Smith (the Mormon "prophet") did have some things in common. For one thing, the year 1844 was significant in both of their lives. For Ellen White 1844 was the year of her first vision; for Joseph Smith it was the year he met his death at the hands of a mob at the Carthage, Illinois, jail. Another similarity is that both leaders were concerned with the soon return of Jesus. That concern is reflected in the titles of the religious movements they helped to found—the Seventh-day Adventist Church and the Church of Jesus Christ of Latter Day Saints.

But at a deeper level Ellen White and Smith and their respective denominations were diametrically opposed. That is nowhere truer than in the area of prophetic authority. For Ellen White the Bible was the "only rule of faith and doctrine" (RH, July 17, 1888), and the 66 books of the Old and New Testaments were the sum total of Scripture. The biblical canon had closed with the book of Revelation. That same position is not held by Joseph Smith and his followers. Thus such Smith writings as those contained in the *Book of Mormon*, the *Pearl of Great Price*, and the *Doctrine and Covenants* are considered to be canonical. For Latter Day Saints the writings of Smith are

the foundation of doctrine. Beyond that, the continuing divine revelation from God from the time of Smith to the present leadership of the Mormon Church is the highest authority in religious matters (see D. H. Ludlow, ed., *Encyclopedia of Mormonism*, vol. 1, p. 401).

Further reading: D. V. Pond, *Pillars of Mormonism* (RHPA, 1978); R. J. Thomsen, *Latter-day Saints and the Sabbath* (PPPA, 1971).

George R. Knight

MORNING STAR. Steam-powered paddlewheel riverboat built by *J. Edson White and *William O. Palmer as a floating mission base for their work among *African-Americans. The hull was built in the Battle Creek shop of Captain A. T. Orton during the winter of 1893-1894. In the spring it was shipped to Allegan, Michigan, on the banks of the Kalamazoo

THE *MORNING STAR* WAS BUILT ON THE KALAMAZOO RIVER NEAR ALLEGAN, MICHIGAN, IN 1894. IT SERVED AS A FLOATING CHAPEL, MOBILE WELFARE CENTER, HOME FOR WORKERS, AND MEANS OF TRANSPORTATION IN MISSION WORK IN THE SOUTHERN PART OF THE UNITED STATES.

River, where from March to May 1894 White and Palmer completed the construction. The boiler they made themselves, and a church member built the steam engine for them at cost. The hull was 72 feet (22 meters) long and 12 feet (3.6 meters) wide. The cabin was 67 feet (20.4 meters) long and 16 feet (4.9 meters) wide, thus projecting two feet (0.6 meters) over the hull on each side. The boat had five staterooms, an office in the bow, a kitchen, and a 12′ x 16′ (3.6 meters x 4.9

meters) main cabin. Below deck was an ice chest that could carry a ton of ice. The hull was made of 7,000 feet (2,134 meters) of Michigan white oak, 2.5 inches (6 centemeters) thick, and held together by more than a ton of bolts and spikes. The flooring was of white oak, the partitions and paneling quarter-sawed sycamore, and window casings and trim of red oak—all in natural finish.

Before it was even launched, some were criticizing the boat as an extravagance, but White retorted that this boat was his and Emma's home. If other ministers owned homes in Battle Creek, didn't he also have a right to a home suited for his mission? In addition, the vessel had staterooms for other workers, and the hurricane deck had room for chairs to seat 200 people.

When construction was finished, White and his crew sailed the *Morning Star* down the Kalamazoo River to Lake Michigan, where a larger lake steamer towed it across to Chicago, almost losing it in a violent nighttime storm. From there the *Morning Star* steamed through the Illinois and Michigan Canal and the Illinois River to the Mississippi River. At various stops along the way south, new volunteers joined the crew, and to house them Edson obtained a 42' x 9' (12.8 meters x 2.7 meters) cabined barge to tow behind the steamer. Because it followed the *Morning Star*, they called it *Dawn*. The missionaries reached Vicksburg, Mississippi, in January 1895, where they immediately began evangelistic visits, meetings, and a night school where children of former slaves and some of their parents and grandparents learned reading and spelling and sang lively gospel music. Within a few months they purchased land and built a little church for $160, using it immediately for a school as well.

In 1896, having proved the practicality of the ship, Edson overhauled it with a new engine and boiler; lengthened the hull, allowing a

deck of 105 feet (32 meters); and added a new second deck as living quarters, with a 10' x 10' (3 meters x 3 meters) study, a 12-foot (3.6-meter) sitting room, an 8' x 12' (2.4 meters x 3.6 meters) bedroom, clothes closets, and bathroom. Behind these rooms he built a chapel and reading room. The remodeled lower deck now had room for a printing office, with two small presses powered by steam from the ship's boiler. From this small base he published *The Southern Work* (1898) and a monthly periodical, the *Gospel Herald*, which promoted the work of the *Southern Missionary Society.

Edson and Emma White made their home on the *Morning Star* until the summer of 1899. In 1900 they moved to Nashville, and the *Star* went into semiretirement at a nearby anchorage on the Cumberland River. The boat made one further noteworthy voyage. In June 1904 it carried *E. A. Sutherland, *P. T. Magan, and Ellen White up the Cumberland River in search of land on which to establish the school that became *Madison College. In 1905 Edson had the *Star* hauled onto the riverbank to be used for an office, but not long afterward it burned. Its bell and metal star can still be seen at Oakwood College.

Further reading: R. D. Graybill, *Mission to Black America* (PPPA, 1971), pp. 23-32, 76-78, 113, 116, 135; A. Robinson, "James Edson White: Innovator," in G. R. Knight, ed., *Early Adventist Educators* (AUP, 1983), pp. 137-158.

Jerry Moon

MORNING WATCH DEVOTIONAL BOOKS, see **DEVOTIONAL BOOKS**.

MOUNT OF BLESSING, see **THOUGHTS FROM THE MOUNT OF BLESSING**.

MUSIC. Music occupies an important place in the writings of Ellen White. Also, during the early years of the Advent movement, the White family was extensively involved in matters of music making: compiling, publishing, and composing hymns, and performing at evangelistic meetings. Ellen White's writings about music claim their own place within the general context of nineteenth-century concerns for better music making. This can be seen in the heritage of John Wesley's prompting for better and more spiritual hymn singing; the presence of singing schools to improve congregational singing; and the contributions of Lowell Mason in the field of formal music education.

Her remarks on music may be observed on three levels: statements of a general nature on the purpose of music; the proper use of music during worship; and a concern for misuses of music, with a special burden for youth.

Ellen White's comments on the purpose of music were much inspired by her observation of musical practices in the Bible. Statements abound in her writings about the purpose of music. Music is a divine gift that occupies a large part in the great cosmic events of human history: Creation, salvation, and the Second Coming (Ed 161; DA 20, 780, 830-833; EW 288; GC 645). "By divine direction," Moses set the law of God to music to be sung by the Israelites (Ed 39). Music thus becomes one of the favorite places of encounter of heaven and earth (*ibid.* 161). In this perspective, musical practice and enjoyment transcend the purpose of mere entertainment and enter the realm of responsibility. Indeed, those who have been given a talent for music are to devote it to the service of God so that it may acquire a power for good and become a great blessing (1T 497). The "holy" purpose of music is to lift thoughts to that which is "pure and noble and elevating," and to fill hearts with gratitude to God (RH, Oct. 30, 1900). The

very idea of gratitude runs like a leitmotif through Ellen White's writings about music: it is indeed praise that creates holy music and an atmosphere of heaven (YI, Apr. 16, 1903; YI, Mar. 29, 1904).

Another purpose of music is to impart spiritual, mental, and social benefits (Ed 167, 168). Jesus used song to ward off temptation (*ibid.* 166). The desired qualities of music, "beauty, pathos, and power" (4T 71), touch the spiritual realm: beauty implies wonder, transcendence, and excellence; pathos moves and stirs the soul, and impresses the heart with spiritual truth; the power of music inclines the heart toward transformation and change. Music sharpens mental capacities by quickening thought and fixing words into memory (Ed 167, 168, 42). Similarly, musical activities benefit the development of social skills: they soften rude and uncultivated natures, calm restless and turbulent spirits, awaken sympathy, teach order and unity, and bring people into closer touch with one another (*ibid.* 39, 168).

As we consider Ellen White's statements about music in worship, we need to keep in mind the general context of worship in her time. There was great need for improvement of congregational singing, generally a strong opposition toward the use of instruments in church, and isolated occurrences of charismatic meeting styles.

In speaking about worship music, Ellen White deplores that Christians do not "make the most of this branch of worship" (4T 71). She likens singing to prayer (PP 594) and encourages people to emulate as much as possible the harmony of the heavenly choirs (SC 104). She warns, however, that music in itself does not constitute worship: "the richest music" is not able to "meet the wants of the spirit" or to "satisfy the thirst of the soul" (ST, Sept. 23, 1897). Time and again Ellen White underlines the importance of how music making is conducted. When done in a light and trifling manner, without care and skill, or in such a way as to create excitement and confusion, music can quench "all desire for the Spirit of God" (RH, July 24, 1883), divert the attention from God (PP 594), or misrepresent and dishonor the truth (2SM 35, 36). While she strongly encourages the use of instrumental music in church, she is quick to add that it must be done skillfully and handled carefully (9T 144). Much emphasis is put on the need for organization, discipline, consultation, and leadership, as well as time for practice in the preparation of worship music (4T 71). There is repeated counsel given on the manner of singing, such as to give "credit to the truth" and "honor to God" (RH, July 24, 1883), and have a proper effect on the minds of the people (4T 71). The songs chosen should be cheerful yet solemn, a tension that characterizes true worship whenever the human encounters the divine. Good manner of singing reflects proper training of the voice, with clear intonation and distinct utterance of the words. Instead of loud singing, a natural tone and modulated, softened, subdued voice are desired (ST, June 22, 1882). Preference should be given at all times to congregational singing (9T 144); however, this should not be done from impulse, nor should the congregation be left to blunder along (4T 71); here again, proper preparation and leadership are needed to obtain correct and harmonious singing, to add to the glory of God (1T 146). At the core of authentic worship music lies the sanctified heart of the musician: "If the heart is right, the actions will be right" (RH, June 20, 1882; cf. Ev 512). The musician's source of inspiration is found in his/her daily intimate communion with God (PP 641; CE 204).

On repeated occasions Ellen White drew attention to the fact that music may detract the heart and minds, especially of the youth, from their true focus. Some of these observations belong to the context of singing schools where frivolous conversations and increased interest in amusement had taken the place and time of prayer and focus on Christ. Ellen White warns how Satan, in a charming and deceiving manner, uses music as a channel to gain access to the minds of the youth (1T 506). This can lead them into friendship with the world and unprofitable "pleasure gatherings" (PH117 71; PH036 10), push them toward ambition for display, and ultimately to dishonoring God (Lt 6a, 1890). As the attention is diverted from God and the contemplation of eternal things, Christ is no more desired (1T 497). Music is used instead as a means to excite and divert mind and senses; the strength and courage that can be found only in God are mistakenly understood as being imparted by the music (*ibid.*; Ev 512).

Ellen White encourages the reader to consider and heed, as an antidote to these challenges, the counsel of the Word of God and her testimonies. Keeping a close connection with Christ will help each individual, and particularly the musician, to resist Satan's devices (2SM 35, 36), to "take a higher stand" (1T 497) and to subordinate their music to the "principles of true religion" (JW, in RH, Mar. 3, 1869).

See also: Hymns Ellen White Loved.

Further reading: P. Hamel, *Ellen White and Music: Background and Principles* (RHPA, 1976).

Lilianne Doukhan

MY LIFE TODAY (RHPA, 1952, 377 pp.). Third daily devotional book published by the Ellen G. White Estate. Materials were selected largely from Ellen White's unpublished writings and periodical articles not available in print at the time. References are provided at the end of the book. The readings for each month follow a different theme and provide counsels and encouragement for daily living on such topics as a spirit-filled life, a healthful life, a life of service, and a victorious life.

NASHVILLE AGRICULTURAL AND NORMAL INSTITUTE, see **MADISON COLLEGE**.

NASHVILLE SANITARIUM. Operated from 1904 to 1913 in Nashville, Tennessee. The work had begun when Lars Hansen opened treatment rooms in Nashville in 1897. His practice was apparently one of the initiatives Ellen White had in mind when she wrote in 1902 that "sanitarium work also has been begun in Nashville" (7T 234). In 1904 the Southern Union Conference purchased Hansen's business and invited Dr. *O. M. Hayward from Graysville, Tennessee, to join him. Together Hansen and Hayward operated "treatment-rooms, a health food store, and physicians' offices in a large house in the city," while renting another house in the country for nurses and longer-term patients. Ellen White visited both of these places in 1904 and thereafter wrote repeatedly to stimulate donations to enlarge and improve the Nashville Sanitarium (SpTB18 11; cf. RH, Aug. 18, 1904). A year later she announced the purchase (for $8,750) of 33 acres (13.4 hectares) of land four miles (6.5 kilometers) south of Nashville, for a new sanitarium building (RH, Sept. 7, 1905). This new building was the subject of another exhortation: "Let not the work on the Nashville Sanitarium . . . be hindered for lack of means" (SW, Apr. 16, 1907).

In 1912 the Nashville Sanitarium was evidently attracting too few patients and too little money, because some were advocating that it be closed and its work transferred to the *Madison Sanitarium, also in the Nashville area. In response to this crisis White issued a pamphlet titled "The Nashville Sanitarium," compiling under one cover counsels written since 1902. She climaxed her appeal with a 1912 manuscript declaring, "The Nashville Sanitarium must not be closed. God forbid that this should be." She called for a thorough financial investigation and for strengthening the staff with some new people, but assured the conference that "when our conceptions of the work that is to be done in the Southern field are broadened, we shall see that there is an abundance of work for both institutions" (SpTB18 35). Because of "its failure from the very first to pay expenses," and its losing "from two to five thousand dollars each year," the sanitarium closed in 1913 (GCB, May 25, 1913).

See also: Rock City Sanitarium.

Further reading: 5MR 363; 7MR 411; SpM 387, 402-405; 6Bio 191; L. A. Hansen, *Interesting Experiences in Medical Missionary Work in Nashville, Tennessee: Address in the Tabernacle, Battle Creek, Michigan, May 28, 1904* (DF 10, CAR).

Jerry Moon

NATURAL REMEDIES. Ellen White used a number of terms to describe "natural remedies." They included "true remedies," "nature's remedies," "God's remedies," "heaven-sent remedies," "God's appointed remedies," and "God's medicines." She identified some of the main ones in the statement: "Pure air, sunlight, abstemiousness, rest, exercise, proper diet, the use of water, trust in divine power—these are the true remedies" (MH 127).

Analysis reveals that all of these are physiologically necessary for health and some are absolutely essential for life itself. We tend to take for granted air, water, and food as we breathe, drink, and eat. The remaining five are left to the circumstances of life—when and how much we sleep, our exposure to sunlight, whether or not we engage in exercise, avoid harmful indulgences, and allow divine power to influence our lives.

Pure air and water (free from chemical and particulate contamination), adequate exercise and rest, a nutritious diet, appropriate exposure to sunshine (but protecting the skin from overexposure), avoidance of excesses, deficiencies, and health-destroying habits (smoking, drinking, and illicit drugging), and freedom from emotional stress (by trusting in divine power)—are fundamental physiological principles on which health exists. They become "remedies" only when we omit them from our lifestyle or violate them by the way we live. Practiced within physiological limits—not too little or too much—they do no harm and have no toxic side effects. For example, there are certain countries in which constipation is epidemic. The free use of water to drink and the consumption of unrefined grains, such as wheat and rice, would provide for moist, generous stools. On the other hand, the complaint can be handled by the use of botanic drugs (senna, cascara, etc.) or regular drugs (laxatives, cathartics). Type 2 diabetes is rapidly increasing in developed areas of the world because of the excessive intake of refined carbohydrates—sugar, sugar-containing foods and drinks, refined grains, and foods of animal origin, all virtually free of fiber. A change to whole-grain products and increased consumption of fruits, vegetables, and nuts would reverse the condition in most cases and make the disease more easily controlled. The use of insulin and other agents would be eliminated or greatly reduced. These two examples illustrate how natural health-enhancing principles become therapeutic agents.

Ellen White mentions numerous features in the natural world and modifications in one's lifestyle that can become healing agencies. "In the efforts made for the restoration of the sick to health, use is to be made of the beautiful things of the Lord's creation. . . . The flowers, . . . the ripe fruit, . . . the happy songs of the birds, have a peculiarly exhilarating effect on the nervous system. . . . By the influence of the quickening, reviving, life-giving properties of nature's great medicinal resources, the functions of the body are strengthened, the intellect awakened, the imagination quickened, the spirit enlivened. The mind is prepared to appreciate the beauties of God's Word" (Lt 71, 1902, in MM 231).

She also refers to the "life-giving properties in the balsam of the pine, in the fragrance of the cedar and the fir," and asserts that "other trees also have properties that are health restoring" (MH 264). "Life in the open air is good for body and mind. It is God's medicine for the restoration of health. Pure air, good water, sunshine, beautiful surroundings—these are His means for restoring the sick to health in natural ways" (Ms 41, 1902, in MM 233).

Our behavior is also involved in our wellbeing. "Good deeds are twice a blessing, benefiting both the giver and the receiver of the kindness. The consciousness of right-doing is one of the best medicines for diseased bodies and minds" (MH 257). "If those who are suffering from ill-health would forget self in their interest of others; if they would fulfill the Lord's command to minister to those more needy than themselves, they would realize the truthfulness of the prophetic promise, 'Then shall thy light break forth as the morning, and thine health shall spring forth speedily'" (ibid. 258). Thus natural remedies, when applied to the sick and suffering, include the healing elements in the natural world and the physiological principles operating within the human body.

See also: Simple Remedies; Drugs; Sanitariums.

Further reading: M. G. Hardinge, A Physician

Explains Ellen White's Counsel on Drugs, Herbs, and Natural Remedies (RHPA, 2001).

Mervyn G. Hardinge

NATURE. Ellen White's perspective on nature or the natural world is best understood in terms of harmony between God's two books—Scripture and nature. "The book of nature and the written Word do not disagree" (7BC 916). "By different methods, and in different languages," nature and the Bible "witness to the same great truths" and "shed light upon each other" (Ed 128). "A correct understanding of both [nature and the Bible] will always prove them to be in harmony" (3SM 307, 308). However, "inferences erroneously drawn from facts observed in nature have . . . led to *supposed conflict* . . . ; and in the effort to restore harmony, interpretations of Scripture have been adopted that undermine and destroy the force of the Word of God" (Ed 128). "In order to account for His works [in nature], must we do violence to His word [in Scripture]?" (*ibid.* 129). For White the answer to this question is a resounding no!

"The book of nature is a great lesson book, which [we are to use] in connection with the Scriptures" (CH 164). On the one hand, it is "necessary that the study of the Bible should have a prominent place among the various branches of scientific education" (FE 285). "To man's unaided reason, nature's teaching cannot but be contradictory and disappointing. Only in the light of revelation [Scripture] can it be read aright" (Ed 134). "The greatest minds, if not guided by the Word of God in their research, become bewildered in their attempts to trace the relations of science and revelation" (PP 113).

On the other hand, Scripture is not a textbook for all the facts of nature. The study of nature itself leads to a knowledge of God (MH 462; COL 107). "As we observe the things

of the natural world, we shall be enabled, under the guiding of the Holy Spirit, more fully to understand the lessons of God's Word" (Ed 120). Contemplation of "the things of nature" provides "a new perception of truth" (MH 462). "All true science is but an interpretation of the handwriting of God in the material world" (PP 599). Therefore, we need to give ourselves "to greater diligence in the perusal of the Bible and to a diligent study of the sciences" (CT 510).

Further reading: Principles of True Science; Ed 99-101; COL 17-32; CG 45-52.

Martin Hanna

NEW EARTH, see **HEAVEN AND NEW EARTH.**

NEW ENGLAND SANITARIUM. Adventist *sanitarium located near Boston, Massachusetts, also known as Melrose Sanitarium. The institution was chartered on April 28, 1899, as the New England Sanitarium and Benevolent Association, located near *South Lancaster Academy. The hospital became the eastern branch of the *Battle Creek Sanitarium, but

NEW ENGLAND SANITARIUM, IN SOUTH LANCASTER, MASSACHUSETTS, ESTABLISHED IN 1899

its constitution was amended in 1907 to attach it directly to the New England Conference. By 1901 the sanitarium had served more than 600 patients.

In August 1902 *C. C. Nicola, superintendent of the sanitarium, wrote to Ellen White regarding local conditions that confirmed warnings she had given about locating sanitariums too close to wealthy homes, where it would be "unfavorably commented upon" because it receives "suffering humanity of all classes" (7T 89). He reported that the administrators had found a new location for the sanitarium that perfectly matched descriptions Ellen White had given of ideal locations for sanitariums. The Langwood Hotel property in Stoneham, a few miles north of Boston, and near the Melrose railroad station, was purchased for only $40,000 and converted into a sanitarium.

After Ellen White visited the institution in August 1904, she wrote that the transfer of the sanitarium to "a place much nearer Boston, and yet far enough removed from the busy city so that the patients may have the most favorable conditions for recovery of health," was in God's providence (SpTB13 3; cf. RH, Sept. 29, 1904; Lt 379, 1904).

An additional hospital wing was constructed in 1924, and a more modern, four-story brick building was completed in 1952. In 1967 the name of the hospital was changed to New England Memorial Hospital, and a major modernization and expansion program was begun. Renamed the Boston Regional Medical Center in 1995, the institution closed in 1999.

Further reading: SDA Encyclopedia (1996), vol. 10, pp. 219-221.

NEW ZEALAND. Ellen White visited New Zealand twice, both times on the North Island. The first time was a brief stopover on her way to Australia in December 1891. The Adventist message had been introduced to New Zealand several years earlier, through *S. N. Haskell and *A. G. Daniells, and several congregations had been established. One of Haskell's early converts, *Edward Hare, whose progeny was to become a prominent New Zealand Adventist family, welcomed Ellen White at ship's arrival, inviting her to stay at his home. After several days Ellen White sailed to Australia, intending to return to New Zealand later, which she did in February 1893.

The first few days of Ellen White's second visit were spent in preaching appointments in Auckland. Following this, she embarked on a three-week visit to Kaeo, at the northernmost tip of the North Island, the residence of the Hare family. While there, Ellen White visited members of the Hare family who had not yet embraced Adventism, as well as other interested families. She also spoke at community meetings. Her efforts resulted in increased local church membership, and an increased awareness and more positive image of the church within the community.

In March-April 1893 Ellen White attended the first Adventist camp meeting in the Southern Hemisphere, in Napier, New Zealand. Here Ellen White presented a variety of messages, ranging from doctrinal to health-related. She then traveled to Wellington, located on the southernmost tip of the North Island, where she engaged in visitation, evangelistic meetings, and other speaking appointments. She encouraged church leaders to try new methods of evangelism, and supported the work among the Maori population, the native inhabitants of New Zealand. While in Wellington, Ellen White resumed work on her masterpiece on the life of Christ, later published as *The Desire of Ages* (4Bio 93; cf. 3Bio 21-35).

In November-December 1893 Ellen White attended a second camp meeting, this time in Wellington. Her reputation as an eloquent speaker, as well as the wide circulation of her books, drew church members from all over New Zealand and also local guests. The most welcome result of the Wellington camp meeting was the breaking down of anti-Adventist bias in that city. Following the camp meeting, after a nine-month stay and a significant contribution to the Adventist work in New Zealand, Ellen White returned to Australia.

See also: Edgar R. Caro; Margaret Caro; Maui Pomare.

Further reading: 4Bio 21, 69-112; N. E. Clapham, *Seventh-day Adventists in the South Pacific, 1885-1985: Australia, New Zealand, South-Sea Islands* (Warburton: Signs Pub. Co., 1985); S. R. Goldstone, *Veneered Infidelity: The Story of the Seventh-day Adventist Church in Hawke's Bay, North New Zealand, 1888-1932* (Napier, N.Z.: Daily Telegraph, 1979).

Darius Jankiewicz

1919 Bible and History Teachers Conference, see **Bible Conference of 1919.**

Norway. Fifth European country visited by Ellen White during her stay in Europe (1885-1887). During her first visit in October and November 1885 she visited the capital city of Christiania (Oslo) and made a brief visit to Drammen, a short distance to the southwest. At the time of her visit Norway could claim the only Adventist institution in Scandinavia—a publishing house—and also the largest single congregation, with 120 members. When she visited the publishing house, she remarked that she had seen the place and the presses before in a vision. Ellen White spoke a few times to large audiences and met with the Christiania church members on a few occasions to strengthen their faith. One important challenge that she addressed was the required school attendance of children on Sabbath. She urged that some accommodation be worked out with school authorities, but if this were to fail, "then their duty is plain," she stated, "to

obey God's requirements at whatever cost" (EGWEur 121). Her second visit occurred in July 1886, during which she confronted a harsh spirit of criticism and faultfinding in the church and appealed to church members to put away the sins that shut out the "sweet spirit of Christ from the church" (Ms 58, 1886, in EGWEur 206). In the end a good spirit prevailed, and her testimony made a deep impression on the people (cf. 3Bio 346-352). Ellen White's last visit to Norway happened in June 1887, when she attended the first Adventist camp meeting in Europe held in connection with the fifth session of the European Council, in Moss, Norway. At this camp meeting the first Norwegian Conference was organized, with Norwegian *O. A. Olsen as president.

Further reading: EGWEur 115-126, 199-207, 300-304; Byörgvin Snorrason, "The Origin and Development of the Norwegian Seventh-day Adventist Church From the 1840s to 1887" (Ph.D. diss., AU, 2009); *SDA Encyclopedia* (1996), vol. 11, pp. 217-219.

Denis Fortin

Notebook Leaflets From the Elmshaven Library (RHPA, 1945, 218 pp.). Republication of a series of 54 loose-leaf pamphlets first published by W. C. White in the 1920s and 1930s. These leaflets were originally printed on colored paper and intended to serve as inserts in pastors' sermon booklets. They included some previously unpublished messages from Ellen White on Christian experience, the church, education, and methods of evangelism. Many of the articles have since been published in other books, such as *Selected Messages.

Notes and Papers Concerning Ellen G. White and the Spirit of Prophecy (EGWE, 1971, 1974, 404 pp.). Compilation of materials prepared by *Arthur L. White for the course "Prophetic Guidance" taught at the Seventh-day Adventist Theological Seminary at Andrews University. Most of the materials are documents written about Ellen White or her ministry; a few are selections from her own writings. The purpose of this compilation was to provide students with "a number of confidence-confirming stories which can be used in presenting the Spirit of Prophecy" (p. 2). Several editions of this document were produced, each adding new materials. In the 1974 edition the materials were divided and rearranged in topical groups. The subjects discuss inspiration and the prophetic gift, health reform, Ellen White's dealing with various problems, subversive movements and apostasy, and the preparation of her books. The book ends with stories from Ellen White's life and ministry.

NOVELS, see **LITERATURE AND READING.**

OAK HILL CEMETERY. Established in 1844, the cemetery is located on South Avenue, southeast of downtown Battle Creek. This cemetery is the resting place of many Seventh-day Adventist pioneers, including James and Ellen White, and their sons and daughters-in-law.

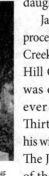

WHITE FAMILY MARKER IN THE OAK HILL CEMETERY, BATTLE CREEK, MICHIGAN

James White's funeral procession from the Battle Creek Tabernacle to Oak Hill Cemetery in 1881 was one of the largest ever in Battle Creek. Thirty-four years later his wife's was even larger. The July 25, 1915, issue of the local newspaper stated, "Thousands followed the hearse to the cemetery; for this purpose every carriage in the city was used, and there were a number of automobiles, and then besides this, there were nine streetcars. No fares were collected on these cars, as they were provided by the church."

The White family lot is also the resting place of James White's parents, John and Betsey White, one of James' sisters, Mary Chase, and a young woman who was their housekeeper when they first came to Battle Creek, Clarissa Bonfoey. Also buried in this cemetery are many Seventh-day Adventist pioneers and leaders; among them are *G. H. Bell, *John Byington, *F. E. Belden, *M. E. Cornell, David and Olive Hewitt, *J. H. Kellogg, *J. P. Kellogg, and *Uriah and *Harriett Smith, as well as other noted citizens of Battle Creek, such as *Sojourner Truth, a Black abolitionist reformer who was well acquainted with Adventists, though she was a Christian of another faith.

Duff Stoltz

OAKWOOD INDUSTRIAL SCHOOL. An institution started on November 16, 1896, by the General Conference of Seventh-day Adventists in the interests of African-Americans. Located in Huntsville, Alabama, its total physical plant at the time consisted of 360 acres (145 hectares), 65 oak trees, four buildings, and nine slave cabins that once had been the Peter Blow Plantation and a periodic stopover for Andrew Jackson, military leader and president of the United States. That Dred Scott, of the famed Dred Scott U. S. Supreme Court decision, had worked here as a slave adds historical drama to the locale.

Prophetic encouragement for supporting the Oakwood School came from Ellen White herself, who wrote: "In the night season I was taken from place to place, from city to city, in the Southern field. I saw the great work to be done—the work that ought to have been done years ago. We seemed to be looking at many places. . . . One of the places that I saw was . . . Huntsville. The Lord led in the establishment of [the school]" (Lt 25, 1902, in 2MR 64). Repeating the theme two years later, she declared that "I would call your special attention to the needs of the Huntsville School. . . . It was in the providence of God that the Huntsville School farm was purchased" (Lt 313, 1904). That same year Ellen White gave further guidance during a visit to Oakwood. "In regard to this school here at Huntsville, I wish to say that for the past two or three years I have been receiving instruction . . . [as to] what it should be, and what those who come here as students are to become. All that is done by those connected with this school . . . is to be done with the realization that this is the Lord's institution" (SpTB12x 9; cf. 6MR 211).

On the school's opening day in 1896 there were 16 students, a principal, and three teachers. The Oakwood Industrial School later became Oakwood Manual Training School (1904-1917), Oakwood Junior College (1917-1945), Oakwood College (1948-2007), and Oakwood University (2007-present). Today it is an accredited four-year liberal arts institution with approximately 1,800 students, more than 100 faculty, and 1,300 acres (526 hectares) of land—thus fulfilling the foresight and vision of Ellen White when she presaged that Oakwood "is to educate hundreds" (SpTB12x 10).

The idea of a Seventh-day Adventist Christian school for Blacks in the American South came from an array of sources. One of the most influential examples from outside the church during the 1890s was Booker T. Washington's Tuskegee Institute in Alabama. The idea whose time had come received a strong support within the church from Ellen White, who published a series of articles in the *Review and Herald* in 1895 and 1896. In these articles she wrote specifically of the needs of the "colored race"

in the South. Her immediate focus included also support for the missionary endeavors of her son Edson White, who skippered his *Morning Star* boat down the Mississippi River to the Vicksburg area in 1895, an endeavor that would help serve as a student feeder to Oakwood (RH, Nov. 12, 1895; Nov. 26, 1895; Dec. 3, 1895; Dec. 10, 1895).

Ellen White acknowledged that the type of educational enterprise for which she was campaigning was already being done by "various denominations, and God honored their work" (RH, Dec. 17, 1895). In the same article she gave specific guidelines for the school's curriculum in reference to reading, various trades, and business enterprises. George I. Butler, twice General Conference president, also supported Ellen White's ideas and published several articles of his own in which he specified the Tuskegee Institute and the Hampton Institute, operated in Virginia by Samuel C. Armstrong, as prime models for Oakwood (RH, Jan. 7, 1896; Feb. 25, 1896). The *Review and Herald* even published a complete speech of Booker T. Washington, "The Progress of the Negro" (RH, Feb. 25, 1896). Clearly the pattern was set: the Oakwood Industrial School was to stand alongside other Christian educational institutions in fostering a wholistic preparation for the present life as well as the life to come.

Further reading: B. J. Baker, comp., *A Place Called Oakwood* (Huntsville, Ala.: Oakwood College Press, 2007); C. Sepulveda and L. Harding, eds., *The Ladies of Oakwood* (Huntsville, Ala.: Oakwood College Press, 2003); M. A. Warren, *Oakwood! A Vision Splendid: 1896-1996* (Collegedale, Tenn.: Collegedale Press, 1995).

Mervyn A. Warren

OBEDIENCE. According to Ellen White, God created humans with the power of free will to choose obedience or disobedience. Unfortunately, they chose disobedience and thus "broke the golden chain of implicit obedience of the human will to the divine" (3SM 138). The charm of obedience faded away, and the sense of its importance and necessity was lost from the human mind. This loss "opened the floodgates of woe upon our world" (BE, Dec. 17, 1894). However, in Jesus Christ humanity has an example of perfect obedience to God. He took human nature and demonstrated that through intimate union with God obedience is possible and that this union is available to every human being (ST, Jan. 25, 1899). Not only by the words of His mouth but also by His everyday life of abiding in union with God (John 5:19, 24, 30; 15:1-8), He showed humans how to live in obedience to God. Therefore obedience is a fruit of faith (Rom. 1:5) and oneness with Christ (RC 274).

White makes it clear that any obedience that does not spring from faith (Rom. 14:23) is not genuine obedience, nor is it acceptable to God. "The man who attempts to keep the commandments of God from a sense of obligation merely—because he is required to do so—will never enter into the joy of obedience. He does not obey. When the requirements of God are accounted a burden because they cut across human inclination, we may know that the life is not a Christian life. True obedience is the outworking of a principle within. It springs from the love of righteousness, the love of the law of God" (COL 97).

With reference to *salvation, obedience earns no merit, but is the natural fruit of genuine conversion. With reference to the *law, White insists that apart from the grace of Christ obtained through faith, obedience is impossible for sinful human nature. The law convicts of sin and shows the need of a Savior. Then through the new birth and the union of the believer with Christ through the Holy Spirit, obedience becomes not only possible but joyful and habitual.

"All true obedience comes from the heart," she writes. "It was heart work with Christ. And if we consent, He will so identify Himself with our thoughts and aims, so blend our hearts and minds into conformity to His will, that when obeying Him we shall be but carrying out our own impulses.... When we know God as it is our privilege to know Him, our life will be a life of continual obedience. Through an appreciation of the character of Christ, through communion with God, sin will become hateful to us" (DA 668; cf. COL 312).

Just as in the beginning, so even today, the whole future of humanity is conditioned by obedience. The way of eternal life is marked by the obedience that springs from faith. Obedience to God's will should be practiced every day in such a manner as to radiate joy and happiness, and should start at home. Children should be taught at an early stage to love and obey God's Word. This ought to be the priority of every parent because "it is God's design that even the children and youth shall understand intelligently what God requires, that they may distinguish between righteousness and sin, between obedience and disobedience" (CG 81). Obedience is to be required in every home even during the early stages of childhood. It is not advisable for parents to delay their request for obedience to the later years of their children's lives. Children should be taught early to obey their parents and to respect their authority. As an infant, not yet old enough to reason, is the best time for a child to begin learning obedience (ibid. 82). In learning to trust and obey parents, children will learn to trust and obey God, and thus be better prepared to face the disobedient world in which they will live.

Paul Z. Gregor

OBERLIN COLLEGE. Founded in 1833 in Lorain County, Ohio, early Oberlin College was an outstanding example of an evangelical educational institution that saw its main aim as bringing in the *millennium through social reform. As such, Oberlin became the first American institution of higher learning to allow both men and women and Whites and Blacks to study together.

Many of the educational reforms pioneered by Oberlin in the 1830s would be quite similar to those espoused by Ellen White from the 1870s through the 1890s. One of the first announcements of the school, for example, noted that Oberlin would educate the whole person, including body, heart, and intellect. In order to facilitate that balanced education, Oberlin was from the beginning a literary institution dedicated to manual labor. The school's *First Annual Report* emphasized that the manual labor department was considered *indispensable* to a complete education. In order to preserve the students' health and enable them to earn funds for school expenses, students of both sexes were required to labor several hours daily. Oberlin was also an avid health reform institution in its early days, espousing vegetarianism, fresh air, plenty of water, and many other measures later emphasized by Ellen White. In the realm of intellectual studies the Oberlin reformers uplifted Bible study in place of the "heathen classics" and stood over against frivolous novels.

There were no direct contacts between Ellen White and the Oberlin reformers. In fact, by the 1850s their most radical educational reforms were past history, even though the institution would remain active in social reform throughout the century. Later Adventist tradition would hold that *Goodloe Harper Bell (Adventism's first "official" educator) and *George Amadon had gone to Oberlin,

but the institution's records indicate otherwise. There were, however, two students from a family that would later become Adventist who attended Oberlin during the 1852-1853 school year. They were Merritt G. and Albert J. Kellogg, older half brothers of *J. H. Kellogg.

Further reading: R. S. Fletcher, *A History of Oberlin From Its Foundation Through the Civil War* (Oberlin College, 1943); G. R. Knight, "Oberlin College and Adventist Educational Reforms," *Adventist Heritage* 8, no. 1 (Spring 1983): 3-9.

George R. Knight

OBJECTORS, CONSCIENTIOUS, see **MILITARY SERVICE.**

OMEGA, see **ALPHA AND OMEGA.**

144,000. The number of those who receive the *seal of God (Rev. 7:1-8; 14:1-5). According to Ellen White, the 144,000 are those who go victoriously through the great *time of trouble and the seven last *plagues just before Christ's *second coming. They refuse to worship the beast and its image, or receive the beast's *mark, or the number of its name. They do not defile themselves with the false teachings of *Babylon, but bear the seal and name of God. To them will be revealed the hour of Christ's return, and they will meet their Savior without seeing death (GC 648, 649; LS 65). The full identity of this group is disclosed neither in Scripture nor in the writings of Ellen G. White. Nor is there an explicit statement whether the number is figurative or literal, although she strongly denied an opinion circulating in 1885 "that the Lord would have a certain number, and when that number was made up, then probation would cease." Condemning this "speculation" that God had a set number of "elect," she asserted, "the Lord Jesus will receive all who come unto Him. He died for the ungodly and every man who will come, may come" (3SM 315).

It is clear, however, that the 144,000 do *not* compose the entire group of the saved, but because of their spiritual victory they "enjoy special honors in the Kingdom of God" (1SM 66). They will stand upon Mount Zion with Jesus and sing the song of their redemption. Only they will be privileged to enter the holy temple in heaven where Ellen White saw their names engraved in golden letters on tables of stone. She did not specify that she would be included in this number; she only mentioned the promise that "if faithful" she would be "with the 144,000" (EW 39, 40). There are others whom Ellen White also saw would be "with the 144,000" (2SM 263). She urged Christians to "strive with all the power that God has given us to be among the hundred and forty-four thousand" (7BC 970).

Further reading: 2SG 32-34; EW 15, 16; LS 65, 66; 1T 59-61, 69.

Anna Galeniece

OPEN DOOR, see **SHUT DOOR**.

ORDER, GOSPEL, see **CHURCH ORGANIZATION**.

ORDINANCES. The term *ordinance* is used in Ellen White's writings to refer to a variety of subjects. She frequently refers to the Old Testament ceremonial or ritual laws as ordinances. However, she emphasizes the fact that such ordinances pointed to Christ, that they were fulfilled by Christ as the great antitype, and that the Jewish leaders in Jesus' day failed to recognize their true meaning (DA 29; FE 397, 398). Although White does not use the expression "creation ordinances," she mentions marriage as "one of God's sacred ordinances" (AH 121), which together with the seventh-day Sabbath dates back to the Creation week and is to be held sacred through all time (MB 63, 64; PP 46). Also quotations from the King James Version referring to "the ordinances of the moon and of the stars for a light by night" (Jer. 31:35) occur several times in her writings (DA 106; 2SP 52; cf. her reference to God's ordinances in Ps. 119:91 in a paragraph dealing with the laws of nature in MH 416).

With Jesus' death and resurrection the purpose of the ceremonial sacrifices and ordinances was fulfilled, and Jesus instituted in their place the ordinances of the new covenant: *baptism, the *Lord's Supper, and the ordinance of foot washing. "The ordinances of baptism and the Lord's Supper" she calls "two monumental pillars," and upon "these ordinances Christ has inscribed the name of the true God" (6T 91; Ev 273). She does not hesitate to refer to the Lord's Supper as the "sacramental supper" or the "sacramental service." "In instituting the sacramental service to take the place of the Passover, Christ left His church a memorial of His great sacrifice for man. 'This do,' He said, 'in remembrance of Me' " (RH, June 22, 1897; Ev 273). The ordinance of foot washing and the sacramental supper were "to be observed through all time by His followers in every country" (ST, May 16, 1900; Ev 276). It is clear, however, that White does not imply by the use of expressions such as "sacrament," "sacramental supper," or "sacramental service" that these ordinances administer grace automatically (*ex opere operato*). Rather, she stresses the presence of Christ with His people in the celebration of these ordinances, which are memorials of his humility and self-sacrifice. She regrets that "these ordinances are regarded too much as a form, and not as a sacred thing to call to mind the Lord Jesus," when "He meets with and energizes His people by His personal presence" (RH, May 31, 1898).

Further reading: Ev 273-278; RH, June 22, 1897; E. G. White, "The Lord's Supper and the Ordinance of Feet-Washing," series of six articles in RH, May 31 to July 5, 1898; H. Kiesler, "The Ordinances: Baptism, Foot Washing, and Lord's Supper," in R. Dederen, ed., *Handbook of Seventh-day Adventist Theology* (RHPA, 2000), pp. 582-609.

Peter M. van Bemmelen

ORDINATION. Ellen White's thoughts on ordination are framed within her understanding of the church as the representative of God on earth (DA 290) and that all Christians are His instruments to witness to the universe of His love, mercy, and justice (6T 12). "God has made His church on the earth a channel of light, and through it He communicates His purposes and His will" (AA 163; see also AA 9-16). In this context her comments emphasize the pragmatic functions of the church, its role and purpose.

While in the Old Testament only selected men ordained to the priesthood could minister within the sanctuary (PP 398, 399), Ellen White believes that no one is restricted from serving God even if one is not an ordained minister; every Christian has a role to play in the great controversy between good and evil (RH, Nov. 24, 1904). Two passages of Scripture are foremost in her understanding of this concept, which is referred to as the priesthood of all believers. The first is 1 Peter 2:9: "But you are a chosen race, a royal priesthood, a holy nation, God's own people, that you may declare the wonderful deeds of him who called you out of darkness into his marvelous light" (RSV). The second is John 15:16: "Ye have not chosen me, but I have chosen you, and ordained you, that ye should go and bring forth fruit, and that your fruit should remain: that whatsoever ye shall ask of the Father in my name, he may give it you." Many times she referred to or quoted parts of these two texts in support of dedicated Christian service and to insist

that all Christians are called by God to serve him (TM 422, 212, 213).

This concept of the priesthood of all believers underlies her understanding of both Christian service and ordination. Throughout her ministry Ellen White made repeated appeals to church members to engage in wholehearted Christian service. For her it is a fatal mistake to believe that only ordained ministers are workers for God and to rely solely on them to accomplish the mission of the church (RH, Mar. 24, 1910). She stated that "all who are ordained unto the life of Christ are ordained to work for the salvation of their fellow-men" (ST, Aug. 25, 1898). "Those who stand as leaders in the church of God are to realize that the Savior's commission is given to all who believe in His name. God will send forth into His vineyard many who have not been dedicated to the ministry by the laying on of hands" (AA 110). Every Christian is a minister for God (RH, Nov. 24, 1904) and, consequently, every Christian is ordained by Christ to minister for Him. Emphatically she commented, "Although ministerial hands may not have been laid upon you in ordination, Christ has laid His hands upon you and has said: 'Ye are My witnesses'" (6T 444). Hence she could add, "Many souls will be saved through the labors of men who have looked to Jesus for their ordination and orders" (RH, Apr. 21, 1903). Church ordination, therefore, is not a prerequisite to serve God, because it is the Holy Spirit who gives fitness for service to Christians who in faith are willing to serve (AA 40). In fact, as in the case of Paul and Barnabas, ordination from above precedes ordination done by the church (*ibid.* 160, 161).

This is also how Ellen White understood her own call to ministry. Although she was never ordained as a minister by the Seventh-day Adventist Church, she believed that God

Himself had ordained her to her prophetic ministry. In her later years, while recalling her experience in the Millerite movement and her first vision, she wrote, "In the city of Portland, the Lord ordained me as His messenger" (Lt 138, 1909, in 6Bio 211).

If the concept of the priesthood of all believers is the fundamental qualification for Christian service—because every Christian is a priest of God and is in a spiritual sense ordained by God to this priesthood—then what does ordination mean and why does the church practice ordination? Ellen White saw ordination as closely related to church organization and to preserving harmony and order in the church. For her the ordination of elders and deacons in the New Testament and the ordination of ministers in the early Adventist movement were answers, provided under the guidance of the Holy Spirit, to meet the needs of the church at a time that disorganization was threatening the very survival of Christianity and Sabbatarian Adventism respectively (EW 100, 101). Building upon the experience of the early church in Acts 6, she counseled the brethren in the early Adventist movement that God desires His people to follow the New Testament model in the ordination of ministers. They were to select men "and set them apart to devote themselves entirely to His work. This act would show the sanction of the church to their going forth as messengers to carry the most solemn message ever given to men" (EW 101). Harmony and order could then be preserved in the Adventist movement through the ordination of ministers as it had been preserved in the early church with the ordination of elders and deacons (AA 95, 96).

The ordination of deacons, elders, and ministers has been God's chosen model to provide stability, guidance, and direction to local churches. Hence, the ordination of these leaders must be a matter of prayer (*ibid*. 161)

and done without hurry (4T 406, 407). Through ordination a minister receives the public recognition and the authority of the church to accomplish his functions (AA 161, 162). Ordination is also viewed by Ellen White as an *ordinance and not a sacrament, as the ceremony of ordination does not confer on the individual any new grace or virtue, but is rather an acknowledgment by the church of one's designation to an appointed office (*ibid.*).

Also building upon this biblical model, she articulates that the structure of the church should be adaptable to the service of the people. In the context of the ordination of the seven deacons in Acts 6, she mentions that the apostles took "an important step in the perfecting of gospel order in the church by laying upon others some of the burdens thus far borne by themselves" (*ibid*. 88, 89). This "perfecting of gospel order" was accomplished when "the apostles were led by the Holy Spirit to outline a plan for the better organization of all the working forces of the church" (*ibid*. 89). Commenting on the ordination of the seven deacons, Ellen White understands that the "organization of the church at Jerusalem was to serve as a model for the organization of churches in every other place. . . . Later in the history of the early church, . . . the organization of the church was further perfected, so that order and harmonious action might be maintained" (*ibid*. 91, 92).

Her description of these events indicates that changes to the organizational structure of the church, and the institution of a new ordained ministry, were made as the leadership realized that new needs required new actions. This, in some sense, meant the perfecting of the structure the apostles had inherited from Jesus; it also meant that this structure had not achieved a static rigidity. The organizational structure of the church could be modified, or perfected, if, under divine guidance, the membership and the leadership thought it should. This understanding of the adaptability, or the further perfecting, of church organization is an important element to understand how early Seventh-day Adventists viewed the development of their own model of church governance. Consequently, with this theological understanding that church structures must reflect harmony and order and be adaptable to new needs, Ellen White believed the church can determine, through study of Scripture and the guidance of the Holy Spirit, which new ministries are beneficial to its ministry and who is to function as an officer in the church.

While all Christians are ordained by God to represent Him and to serve in various ministries in the church, some church officers occupy specific functions for which they are ordained. For this reason Ellen White cautioned that individuals ordained to ministry in the church ought to be carefully selected (4T 406). Her description of the ordination of Paul and Barnabas before being sent on their first missionary journey (Acts 13:1-3) highlights the role the church plays in determining who will represent the church and speaks authoritatively for it. Their ordination meant that the church invested them with full authority to teach the truth, perform baptisms, and organize churches; it was a public recognition that they had already been chosen by the Holy Spirit for a special work to the Gentiles. Thus we see that Ellen White's definition of ordination is largely pragmatic: it is a public recognition of divine appointment and an "acknowledged form of designation to an appointed office" (AA 162).

Within this perspective Ellen White allowed for the church to decide whether some people, other than ministers, could be ordained or set apart by the laying on of hands in other ministries. She earnestly believed that the ordained pastoral ministry alone is not sufficient to fulfill God's commission, that God is calling Christians of all professions to dedicate their lives to His service (MM 248, 249). Since the church can branch out into different kinds of ministries to meet the needs of the people and to preach the gospel, she favored, for instance, the ordination by laying on of hands of *medical missionaries and *women gospel workers.

"The work of the true medical missionary is largely a spiritual work. It includes prayer and the laying on of hands; he therefore should be as sacredly set apart for his work as is the minister of the gospel. Those who are selected to act the part of missionary physicians are to be set apart as such. This will strengthen them against the temptation to withdraw from the sanitarium work to engage in private practice" (Ev 546). Here Ellen White drew a parallel between the setting apart of the medical missionary and the minister of the gospel. To sacredly set apart a medical missionary is viewed as a form of ordination in which the church acknowledges the blessings of God upon the chosen individual and serves as a means of strengthening the dedication of the worker in service for God.

Ellen White also favored women as gospel workers. In 1898, while in Australia, she recalled how God had impressed her with the injustice that had been done to some women, wives of ordained ministers. Some ministers' wives had been very active in gospel ministry, visiting families and giving Bible studies, yet without receiving any due recognition or financial compensation. She understood that these women "are recognized by God as being as necessary to the work of ministry as their husbands" (Ms 43a, 1898, in 5MR 30). In this context she favored that women in specific lines of service and gospel ministry be also set apart or ordained. "Women who are willing to consecrate some of their time to the service of the Lord should be appointed to visit the sick, look after the young, and minister to the necessities of the poor. They should be set apart to this work by prayer and laying on of hands. In some cases they will need to counsel with the church officers or the minister; but if they are devoted women, maintaining a vital connection with God, they will be a power for good in the church. This is another means of strengthening and building up the church. We need to branch out more in our methods of labor" (RH, July 9, 1895).

Ellen White's basic reason for supporting the setting apart of medical missionaries and women gospel workers concurs also with her views on the adaptability of church structures to meet new needs. Under divine guidance the church can and should branch out in its methods of labor by setting apart in ordination people serving in various ministries. But more important, she implied here that God is leading the church in this direction, that it is God's will for the church to branch out and be strengthened by ordaining people to their various kinds of ministry. Ordination is thus a means of publicly recognizing God's will and call for an individual.

See also: Women, Ministry of.

Further reading: DG 248-255; D. Fortin, "Ordination in the Writings of Ellen G. White," in Nancy Vyhmeister, ed., *Women in Ministry: Biblical and Historical Perspectives* (AUP, 1996), pp. 115-133; A. Mustard, *James White and SDA Organization: Historical Development, 1844-1881* (AUP, 1987).

Denis Fortin

OREGON. The state of Oregon and the territory of Washington (Washington gained statehood in 1889) remained an isolated frontier until the arrival of the northern transcontinental railroads in the early 1880s.

Though a few Adventists had moved to the region in the 1860s and early 1870s, it was not until Isaac Van Horn, a minister, located in Walla Walla, Washington Territory, in 1874 that the denomination made progress.

During the 1870s and early 1880s Ellen White made three visits to the camp meetings of the Pacific Northwest. Because of poor health, James was unable to accompany her on the first two trips. By the third, he had died. Ellen White's initial visit (1878) was to attend the Northwest's first camp meeting in Salem, Oregon, where she received several visions (4T 286-296). On her second trip (1880) she attended both Northwest camp meetings (Milton, Oregon, and Salem) and participated in the formation of the Upper Columbia Conference.

In 1884 Ellen White and a delegation from California attended two camp meetings in the Northwest (Walla Walla, Washington, and Portland, Oregon). They dealt with a number of serious problems in the Upper Columbia and North Pacific conferences. John Loughborough claimed that Ellen White had her last public vision at the Portland camp meeting (GCDB 5, no. 2 [Jan. 29, 30, 1893]: 19, 20).

Ellen White's final visit to the Pacific Northwest took place in 1901. On this trip she visited the Upper Columbia Conference camp meetings in Waitsburg and Walla Walla College, and the camp meeting in Portland. Several testimonies that pertain to the Northwest can be found in 5T 249-302.

Further reading: 3Bio 85-89, 139-142, 247-249; D. R. Johnson, *Adventism on the Northwestern Frontier* (AUP, 1996).

Doug R. Johnson

ORGANIZATION, see **CHURCH ORGANIZATION**.

ORPHAN CHILDREN. In her writings Ellen White pointed out that multitudes of children have been deprived of the guidance of parents and the subduing influence of a Christian home. Yet such children are younger members of God's family, and in His sight they are just as precious as are other children. She believed this to be a large field for missionary labor. She suggested that if childless couples would take in orphan children they would see their own happiness increase. But the choice of children should be first made from among those who have been left orphans by Sabbathkeeping parents (AH 169).

In 1890 Ellen White recommended that the church establish a home for orphan children and concluded that Adventists lag far behind other denominations in this respect (8T 133). She felt it should not be a large and expensive enterprise, but invited those who feel the burden of establishing an orphanage to raise funds among church members and neighbors. Her pleas led to the establishment of the Haskell Home for orphan children in Battle Creek (3SM 218).

In spite of a busy schedule of activities Ellen White took into her home orphan children, cared for them, educated them, and trained them for responsible positions. She took in children of 3 and 5 years old, as well as boys from 10 to 16 years of age. She also reared Addie and May Walling, children of her niece. The girls lived in the Whites' home, and she was like a mother to them (DG 196). While living in Australia, she also took into her home orphan children (1SM 34).

She admonished "those who claim to love God with all their heart, and their neighbors as themselves" not to neglect works of benevolence toward orphans or selfishly hoard the bounties God has given for the fatherless (MM, Nov. 1, 1894; 4T 627).

Further reading: AH 167-171; 3SM 218-220; DG 196-198; 12MR 264.

Helena Ruzica Gregor

OTTOMAN EMPIRE, see **LITCH, JOSIAH.**

OUR FATHER CARES (RHPA, 1991, 350 pp.). Sixteenth daily *devotional book published by the Ellen G. White Estate. Materials selected for these meditations were drawn from 12 of her previously published daily devotional books. Each calendar month in *Our Father Cares* was reproduced from the corresponding month in an earlier Ellen White devotional book. The list of selected books appears on page 14. The theme for the book, "Our Father Cares," reflects Ellen White's thought that "Christ's favorite theme was the paternal character and abundant love of God" (6T 55; OFC 6). This was also one of Ellen White's favorite themes. The publisher indicates that the readings not only were selected on the topic of God's great love and care for us, but also reflect the fact that God cares so much for us that He is interested in every aspect of our daily lives.

OUR HIGH CALLING (RHPA, 1961, 380 pp.). Sixth daily *devotional book published by the Ellen G. White Estate. Materials selected for this book were drawn from Ellen White's published and unpublished writings, periodical articles, manuscripts, and letters of counsel to individuals. References to each excerpt are given at the end of the book. No particular theme was chosen for the selection of the materials apart from providing counsels "to encourage, instruct, and inspire us in victorious practical everyday Christian living and witnessing . . . in view of the imminence" of Christ's second advent (p. 5).

"OUR HOME ON THE HILLSIDE," see **JACKSON, JAMES CALEB.**

OUTPOST EVANGELISM, see **CITIES, LIVING IN.**

OYSTERS, see **UNCLEAN FOOD.**

PACIFIC PRESS PUBLISHING ASSOCIATION.
Organized by *James White in Oakland,
California, on April 1, 1875, as the Pacific
Seventh-day Adventist Publishing Associ-
ation.

Adventist publishing on the West Coast
of the United States had actually begun a few
months earlier when James White began
publishing *Signs of the Times,* using a commercial printshop in Oakland. The first issue
of *Signs* was dated June 4, 1874, and succeeding
numbers appeared at irregular intervals for
several months. Ellen White contributed
articles for the new journal, a practice she
continued throughout her life, until by the
time of her death in 1915 some 2,000 articles
from her pen had appeared in its pages.

In October 1874, at a camp meeting held
in Yountville, California, G. I. Butler appealed
for funds to establish a West Coast publishing
house. The response was $19,414 in gold and
pledges. When James White managed to raise
an additional $10,000 in pledges from the
East, a building was constructed on Castro
Street in Oakland.

In addition to producing *Signs of the
Times,* the new publishing house busied itself
with printing books, tracts, and nonchurch
job printing. Two years later the work had
expanded, and a larger building was erected
on an adjoining lot. State-of-the-art printing
equipment made Pacific Press the largest and
best-equipped printing facility on the West
Coast at that time.

From 1875 until his death in 1881, James
White was closely connected with Pacific
Press, serving two terms as its president.
During these years his sons *James Edson
and *William Clarence (also known as W. C.
and among family members as "Willie") were
associated with their father in the affairs of

the publishing house. W. C. began his "publishing" work by transporting the paper, type
forms, and printed sheets of *Signs of the Times*
in a wheelbarrow. In 1876, at the age of 21,
he was elected president of the board and
business manager of the publishing house.
His brother Edson officially served as secretary
of the institution, but his duties actually
involved managing the business affairs of the
printing plant. In 1888 the institution's name
was changed to Pacific Press Publishing
Company and changed again in 1904 to the
present Pacific Press Publishing Association.

PACIFIC PRESS PUBLISHING HOUSE, IN OAKLAND, CALIFORNIA, C. 1885

By the turn of the twentieth century Ellen
White was calling for Pacific Press to move
away from the crowded conditions in Oakland
to a more rural environment. She also warned
against the excessive amount of commercial
work that was being done by the press and
urged that the workers keep in mind the
spiritual mission God intended for them and
Pacific Press. Typical of her counsel is this
warning written in 1896: "I was shown that
a work was to be done by this institution
[Pacific Press] which would be to the glory
of God if the workers would keep His honor
ever in view; but that an error was being
committed by taking in a class of work which
had a tendency to corrupt the institution"
(*Special Testimonies Concerning the Work and
Workers in the Pacific Press,* p. 50).

In 1902, in response to this ongoing

counsel from Ellen White regarding the dangers of relying too heavily on commercial work, the Pacific Press board voted to reduce the amount of such work being done at the institution and to look for a more rural location. Two years later, in 1904, Pacific Press moved some 40 miles (65 kilometers) south of San Francisco and built a two-story brick building on five acres (two hectares) in Mountain View, California. This building was severely damaged in the disastrous San Francisco earthquake of April 18, 1906. Its replacement, a wooden structure, was completely destroyed by fire on July 20 of the same year. The origin of the fire was never determined. Following this fiery destruction, the board agreed to rebuild the facility and also stop all further commercial work.

Pacific Press prospered in Mountain View following this decision. As the work grew, branch offices were opened in various locations. In 1915 Pacific Press took over the work of providing non-English language publications for the church in North America and absorbed the International Publishing Association located in College View, Nebraska. The international branch was relocated to Brookfield, Illinois, in 1916. In 1917 a branch factory was established in Cristobal, Canal Zone, to serve the Inter-American Division with Spanish-language publications. This facility was closed in 1955 and operations transferred to Brookfield, Illinois, which was itself closed in 1959 when the publishing house in Mountain View took over responsibility for producing non-English language publications.

In the 1980s the plant in Mountain View began to face mounting financial difficulties because of a variety of factors, including an increasingly inefficient plant and the high cost of living and doing business in the Bay Area of California. After much discussion the board made the decision to sell the Mountain View property and move to a location that would allow the press to continue operating under more favorable financial circumstances. Several locations throughout the western part of the United States were considered, and eventually the decision was made to move to Nampa, Idaho.

A new facility—smaller and designed for more efficient operation—was constructed in Idaho, and the process of moving began. Since the factory portion of the new building was completed first, the presses and binding equipment, along with the workers who operated them, were the first to move. Later that year the office workers moved into temporary rented quarters in Boise while the office portion of the new facility was completed. By spring 1985 all operations were again united in the new Nampa, Idaho, facility.

During the years since the relocation to Idaho, Pacific Press has continued to carry out the mission for which it was founded back in 1875—nurturing the church and spreading the gospel through books, magazines, music, and other media. Among the resources Pacific Press produces today are two missionary outreach magazines, *Signs of the Times* in English and *El Centinela* in Spanish; the children's periodicals *Our Little Friend* and *Primary Treasure;* various editions of the *Adult Sabbath School Bible Study Guide*, elementary- and secondary-level Bible textbooks for schools, as well as books for both the trade and subscription markets, and other evangelistic and church-related materials.

Further reading: H. O. McCumber, *Pioneering the Message in the Golden West* (PPPA, 1946), pp. 127-139.

B. Russell Holt

PACIFIC UNION COLLEGE. A coeducational college in Angwin, California, opened in

1909 after the closure of its forerunner, *Healdsburg College. Ellen White and W. C. White, who had helped to found Healdsburg College, continued to lead out in the relocation process. The search for land focused in 1908 on an estate near Sonoma, but a series of problems ended negotiations. Some were discouraged, but Ellen White was sure that God had something better for them. On September 1, 1909, the Pacific Union Conference purchased the Angwin resort on Howell Mountain, not far from the St. Helena Sanitarium and the Elmshaven home of Ellen White. Among the advantages of the Angwin location were 200 acres (81 hectares) of wooded land with adequate water, plus buildings, swimming pool, orchards, and livestock. At the dedication Ellen White said she was thankful the Sonoma property had not worked out. "God wanted us here, and He has placed us here" (Ms 65, 1909, in PUR, Oct. 7, 1909).

Even before she learned of the Angwin property, Ellen White had recommended C. W. Irwin to lead the future school, because of his prior experience at Avondale College in Australia. The same month the property was purchased, Pacific Union College opened with 42 students. After teaching classes in the mornings, faculty led students in logging, gardening, and building. Ellen White's Elmshaven home was just a few miles down Howell Mountain from PUC, and in her later years she spoke there several times.

In 1932 the college became the first Adventist college to receive both regional and denominational accreditation. During the summers of 1934-1936, the college hosted an Advanced Bible School that in 1937 moved to Washington, D.C., and became the Seventh-day Adventist Theological Seminary. In 2007 Pacific Union College had about 100 teaching faculty and 1,500 students.

Further reading: 6Bio 176-188; W. C. Utt, *A Mountain, a Pickax, a College: A History of Pacific Union College* (Angwin, Calif.: Pacific Union College, 1968); *SDA Encyclopedia* (1996), vol. 11, pp. 280-284.

PANTHEISM. Ellen White described pantheism as "the theory that God is an essence pervading all nature" (8T 291). To clarify this connection between God and nature and to emphasize the personhood of God she wrote, "God's handiwork in nature is not God Himself in nature. The things of nature are an expression of God's character; by them we may understand His love, His power, and His glory; but we are not to regard nature as God" (*ibid.* 263). She regarded pantheistic theories as "framed by Lucifer, the fallen angel" (UL 336). This "speculative" theory regarding the nature and personality of God caused a great stir in the Adventist Church, especially during the years 1902-1904.

*John Harvey Kellogg was closely connected with the "new light" of pantheism and its introduction into Adventism. Much of what White wrote regarding pantheism was in response to Kellogg's book *The Living Temple* (1903), though she wrote many letters in the years leading up to the book's publication urging Dr. Kellogg and those close to him at Battle Creek to be cautious in their attempts to lead the church in a new direction. It is important to note that White described Kellogg's teaching as the "alpha of deadly heresies" from which the "omega" would follow (1SM 200).

Concern existed in the minds of some that Ellen White's writings themselves supported pantheistic ideas. "In the controversy that arose among our brethren regarding the teachings of this book, those in favor of giving it a wide circulation declared: 'It contains the very sentiments that Sister White has been teaching.' This assertion struck right to my heart" (*ibid.* 203). To the 1903 Autumn Council she wrote, "I have some things to say to our teachers in reference to the new book *The Living Temple.* Be careful how you sustain the sentiments of this book regarding the personality of God. As the Lord presents matters to me, these sentiments do not bear the endorsement of God" (Lt 211, 1903, in 5Bio 297).

White drew a connection in her writings between philosophic, scientific, and speculative knowledge on the one hand and pantheism on the other. Pantheism, as speculative knowledge based upon so-called scientific principles, was against the pillars of Adventism. Were pantheistic views to be accepted, she wrote, "Our religion would be changed. The fundamental principles that have sustained the work for the last fifty years would be accounted as error. . . . A system of intellectual philosophy would be introduced" (1SM 204).

What White saw as the greatest danger from pantheism was what she described as a sweeping away of the whole Christian economy. "They do away with the necessity for the atonement and make man his own savior. These theories regarding God make His Word of no effect, and those who accept them are in great danger of being led finally to look upon the whole Bible as a fiction. They may regard virtue as better than vice; but, having shut out God from His rightful position of sovereignty, they place their dependence upon human power, which, without God, is worthless" (MH 428, 429). This "sweeping away" is explained by the following statement: "If God is an essence pervading all nature, then He dwells in all men; and in order to attain holiness, man has only to develop the power within him" (*ibid.* 428).

Further reading: SpTB02 49-58; 8T 5, 6, 255-297; 5Bio 280-306, 329-339.

Thomas Toews

PARABLES OF CHRIST, see ***CHRIST'S OBJECT LESSONS.***

PARADISE VALLEY SANITARIUM. Former Adventist sanitarium southeast of San Diego in National City, California. The property was originally owned by Dr. Anna Longshore Potts, who opened a sanitarium there in 1888, but had to close it for lack of water. An Adventist physician, *T. S. Whitelock, heard of the property and began to negotiate for it. When Ellen White visited the property in September 1902 (Lt 153, 1902), she was impressed with the facilities and convinced that they must secure it. Because the California Conference was in debt and unable to assist, the purchase was delayed. Even when the original price was reduced to $6,000, church leaders still hesitated to purchase the property. When Ellen White heard of the deal, she met with *Josephine Gotzian, and together they "clasped hands over my writing table that we would be responsible for the purchase of that grand building" (Lt 363, 1905). Ellen White borrowed $3,000 and telegraphed Dr. Whitelock to make an offer of $4,000. The offer was accepted, and the property was, for Ellen White, obtained in the providence of the Lord (SpTB14 4, 5).

Ellen White described the purchase as a "well-constructed, three-story building of about fifty rooms, with broad verandas, standing upon a pleasant rise of ground, and overlooking a beautiful valley" (*ibid.* 8). "I never saw a building offered for sale that was better adapted for sanitarium work," she added. "If this place were fixed up, it would look just like places that have been shown me by the Lord" (*ibid.* 9).

The next step was for the principal financial investors, Josephine Gotzian, Ellen White, and *E. S. Ballenger (whose family had covered some additional expenses), to find someone to manage the property. They found such an individual in *E. R. Palmer and his wife, Cora, who had just returned from Australia and that same month (April 1904) took charge of the sanitarium. As Palmer set to work it became obvious that the lack of water that had closed the facility originally still threatened the sanitarium. An already-existing drought that had plagued the sanitarium continued through the summer of 1904. "The poor, drying up, dying trees," wrote Ellen White, "are beseeching us by their appearance for refreshing streams of water" (Ms 147, 1904, in 14MR 221). According to later oral accounts Ellen White recommended that Palmer secure the services of an Adventist well digger, Salem Hamilton, to dig a well, which he began on the southwest corner of the property. Ellen White observed the progress with interest as they reached a depth of 80 feet (24 meters). At that point she asked him what he intended to do. Mr. Hamilton responded by asking if she was certain that the Lord had shown her this property. Ellen White replied that she was. "All right," he said. "The Lord would not give us an elephant without providing water for it to drink" (W. L. Johns and R. H. Utts, eds., *The Vision Bold* [RHPA, 1977], p. 146). Soon afterward Hamilton reached water, which filled the well so quickly that the diggers were forced to leave their tools behind. "I cannot express to you how glad we all are made," wrote Ellen White. "Water means life. . . . The Lord has answered all our expectations, and we shall have reason for thanksgiving" (*ibid.* p. 147).

On March 2, 1905, the articles of incorporation for the Paradise Valley Sanitarium were filed, and on April 24, 1906, the sanitarium was dedicated. The sanitarium was managed as a private entity until the Southern California Conference was able to take over responsibility in 1912. From 1962 until it was sold in 2007,

the facility was known as Paradise Valley Hospital. It closed in 2008.

Further reading: SpTB14 2-16; R. D. Graybill, "Paradise and Providence," in W. R. Judd and J. M. Butler, eds., *Thirsty Elephant: the Story of Paradise Valley Hospital* (Riverside, Calif.: La Sierra University Press, 1994), pp. 35-58; *SDA Encyclopedia* (1996), vol. 11, pp. 299, 300.

Michael W. Campbell

PARAPHRASES, see **BOOKS, PREPARATION OF ELLEN G. WHITE'S.**

PARENTAL RESPONSIBILITY, see **HOME AND FAMILY.**

PASTORAL MINISTRY, see **MINISTRY.**

PASTORAL MINISTRY (RHPA, 1995, 287 pp.). Compilation of Ellen White's writings on the work of ministers of the gospel, prepared by the General Conference Ministerial Association and the Ellen G. White Estate. For more than a half century Ellen White worked closely with pastors and shared with them many counsels. She held a high view of their calling and repeatedly encouraged them to live a life of commitment to God and to fully use their talents to serve His people. This book brings together a selection of her counsels that apply most directly to the life and work of the local church pastor. Topics include the pastor's personal spiritual life and family, church growth and evangelism, lay training, worship, pastoral care and nurture, and church organization. Along with *Gospel Workers* and *Testimonies to Ministers and Gospel Workers*, this volume forms a rich collection of her counsels to pastors.

Denis Fortin

PATRIARCHS AND PROPHETS (PPPA, RHPA, 1890, 805 pp.). First book in the five-volume

*Conflict of the Ages Series, titled: *The Story of Patriarchs and Prophets as Illustrated in the Lives of Holy Men of Old*. From the time Ellen White received her vision on the *great controversy in 1858, she wrote extensively on the cosmic conflict between Christ and Satan and continually amplified her accounts of this conflict in her writings. *Patriarchs and Prophets* is her final amplification of how the theme of the great controversy is depicted in the story of the world from the fall of Lucifer (see *Satan) in heaven to the end of King David's reign. Earlier accounts of this period of biblical history appeared in volumes 1, 3, and 4 of *Spiritual Gifts* and in volume 1 of *The Spirit of Prophecy*. An introduction (pp. 19-28) written by Uriah Smith sets forth the Adventist understanding of the doctrine of spiritual gifts and in particular the gift of prophecy.

Intended for both Seventh-day Adventists and the general public, *Patriarchs and Prophets* is a Christ-centered description and commentary of the events of biblical history it covers. Of particular interest are Ellen White's presentations of why sin was permitted (pp. 33-43), the fall of Adam and Eve and the plan of redemption (pp. 52-70), the giving and purpose of the law (pp. 303-342), and the institution of the ceremonial system and the old covenant (pp. 343-373). A significant addition, which does not appear in *Spiritual Gifts* and *The Spirit of Prophecy*, is the wonderful two-page description of God's "law of love," with which the book opens. Her theological reflections on theodicy, the plan of salvation and Christ's sacrifice of atonement, the purpose of the law, and the covenant with Israel are expressed in the context of the love of God (p. 33) and show how the gospel of grace was already present in the Old Testament and illustrated in the lives of its various biblical characters.

Denis Fortin

PERFECTION. The words "perfection," "sanctification," and "holiness" are used as virtually interchangeable terms by Ellen White to describe the process of the believer's character change into the likeness of Christ. In terms of the goal of the Christian life, perfection and holiness describe the objective of the process of sanctification. For Ellen White, justification and sanctification need to be *distinguished*, but not *separated*. The same goes for sanctification and perfection. Justification always formed the foundation for sanctification, and perfection was always the goal of sanctification.

Her understanding of the transformed life was, in the grace of Christ, more optimistic than the view espoused by some Reformers. In this she was directly influenced by her Wesleyan/Methodist background. While she used the words "sanctification" and "perfection" (and their verbal variations) in a very Wesleyan manner and shared a similar optimism of grace, she was very clear that sanctification was an open-ended process, the work not of a moment, but "of a lifetime." In other words, she did not share the classic Wesleyan and American Holiness teaching that sanctification would lead to a moment of instantaneous perfection before glorification—the "second work of grace."

Ellen White devoted large amounts of published space to the subject of salvation, and within her writings on salvation gave her most extended attention to the subjects of sanctification and perfection. She used many biblical passages as springboards for her expositions of the subject of character change. The passage that she employed the most was Matthew 5:48: "Be ye therefore perfect, even as your Father which is in heaven is perfect." Normally it was in the context of expositions on this passage that she expressed the greatest optimism for full and complete victory over "inherited" and "cultivated tendencies to evil." The second most often used passage to express her thought of the full victory over besetting sins was 2 Peter 1:4: "Whereby are given unto us exceeding great and precious promises: that by these ye might be partakers of the divine nature." One other passage was repeatedly used, especially to express the completeness of gracious deliverance from both the guilt and the power of sin—"Ye are complete in him" (Col. 2:10). Though not used quite as often, she would often employ Philippians 3:12-15 and John 15:1-10 (illustration of the vine and the branches) to express the dynamic and ongoing nature of the experience of being perfected in Christ.

Her normal use of Scripture was to take key biblical expressions as inspirations to topical expositions of perfection, not detailed interpretations of any particular passage (except Matthew 5:48). Such use of Scripture included not only the above-mentioned key texts (and many others) but also the citing of major biblical characters as exemplars of the experience of perfection. Of course, the great exemplar was Christ. She often repeats the theme that Christ came as a true human being to demonstrate that perfect obedience to God's law was possible, and that what He demonstrated can be replicated in the sanctification experience of His dedicated followers. Aside from Christ, other favorite exemplars are Enoch, Daniel, Joseph, Paul, John the Beloved, and Abraham. Jacob and Isaiah merit occasional citation.

To grasp Ellen White's teaching on perfection, the importance of the genuine experience of justification by faith alone is absolutely essential. Forgiveness and the knowledge that Christ stands as the penitent believer's constant advocate and intercessor form the foundation and the motivational springboard for all growth in grace. Repeatedly she will say that

the "imputed" "merits of Christ" are the means for a rich experience of perfection through the grace of Christ (5T 744). If, however, someone is claiming justification by faith and is not living a life of obedience, such faith is condemned as false. Throughout her writings she repeatedly employs the phrase that sinners are "saved *from* [their] sins, not *in* them" (RH, Sept. 27, 1881).

What she means by being saved *from,* not *in,* sin is quite clearly explained. Most certainly the sincere believer who is in Christ by faith is forgiven all past sins and Jesus makes up for their "unavoidable deficiencies" (3SM 196). Such an experience of justifying grace, however, cannot belong to one who is presuming on the grace of God in either of two distinct ways. First, there cannot be willful or premeditated acts of known sin (plainly going against the known will of God). Second, there should not be manifest attitudes of excuse for any character defect. Thus, to be saved from sin, not in sin, means to be receiving the grace of Jesus that leads to loving obedience to the whole will of God and manifesting a ready and hearty acknowledgment of penitence for any failure. In fact, one of the key marks of any Christian experience of perfection is repentance (ST, July 29, 1889).

So within the "in Christ" or "union with Christ" experience will be obedience through the power of God's grace and a profound manifestation of penitential Christian humility. Yet there are other key characteristics of perfection that round out Ellen White's understanding of the "higher life" in Christ.

Ellen White clearly expressed a very high *goal of perfection* and maintained that this goal is attainable (at least in important qualified senses) this side of glorification. "We can overcome. Yes; fully, entirely. Jesus died to make a way of escape for us, that we might overcome every evil temper, every sin, every temptation" (1T 144). Possibly the most explicit statement of this high goal is her claim that believers, after the Fall, must meet the same standard as required of Adam before the Fall: God's requirement of "Adam in paradise before he fell" is just the same "at this moment" for all who live "in grace" (RH, July 15, 1890). She further enforced this by declaring that it is "not the work of the gospel to weaken the claims of God's holy law, but to bring men up where they can keep its precepts" (RH, Oct. 5, 1886). The attainment (before the close of probation) was assured and the key evidence was to be found in the examples of numerous biblical characters, with Jesus Christ serving as the primary exhibit.

The vision of this attainment is clarified through her employment of numerous distinguishing qualities. Perfection arises out of *full surrender* and consecration to God's will. No halfhearted commitment could attain the high goal of entire victory. The attainment of perfection is not a passive affair, but requires the special, *active effort* of the believer. While there was to be conscious, cooperative effort by the believer, such effort would lead to a certain *natural and imperceptible spontaneity of obedience.* "And if we consent, He will so identify Himself with our thoughts and aims, so blend our hearts and minds into conformity to His will, that when obeying Him we shall be but carrying out our own impulses" (DA 668).

Perfection results from the *experience of sanctification,* which was conceived as the dynamic and progressive work of a lifetime. There is nothing static in Bible sanctification. Perfection in some qualified sense is attainable, but for the spiritually perceptive Christian it will always be a consciously receding horizon, and *no one is to claim perfection.* Sanctification involves *full obedience* to the law of God. Sinners are not saved by works of obedience,

but neither are they saved without them (ST, July 13, 1888).

Obedience in the life of a Christian is to be symmetrical, and there is to be a balance in carrying out God's will—not emphasizing one duty at the expense of another (3T 243-251). Perfect believers are still subject to temptation and will be beyond temptation's reach only after glorification (ST, June 9, 1881; ST, Mar. 23, 1888). Any claim to freedom from temptation smacks of perfectionism, not the true perfection experience. Feelings and impressions have their proper sphere, but are not the determining factors in Christian perfection. The perfect Christian does not cherish or excuse sin, but only Jesus is absolutely, sinlessly perfect. Those who claim to be "equal with Him in perfection of character" commit "blasphemy" (RH, Mar. 15, 1887). Ellen White also declared that "you cannot equal the Pattern, but you can resemble it" (2MR 126). Three particular expressions of Christian perfection stand out: (1) a deep desire for unity among believers (ST, Oct. 23, 1879), (2) humility (GC 470-472), and (3) patience (HS 134).

Perfecting grace is primarily ministered through the Word of God and the Spirit working together with the believer's responsive faith. The overall vision that Ellen White portrayed for the perfect believer can be summed up in six levels of maturity.

1. *Reckoned perfection*: the moment the penitent believer trusts the saving merits of Jesus is the moment he/she is reckoned or accounted as legally or forensically perfect in him (SC 62; HP 23; ST, July 4, 1892). This level of perfection pertains to justification, and the one who is "perfectly forgiven" is a child of God and should enjoy full assurance of salvation.

2. *Dynamic growth seen as a relative perfection*: those who are progressing in the Christian

life, growing in grace, are *relatively* perfect. Though still deficient in some areas, growing believers are nonetheless perfect in the sense of Philippians 3:13-15.

3. *Dynamic growth features loving obedience and the absence of willful sinning and attitudes of excuse for sin.* "The law demands perfect obedience. . . . Not one of those ten precepts can be broken without disloyalty to the God of heaven. The least deviation from its requirements, by neglect or willful transgression, is sin, and every sin exposes the sinner to the wrath of God" (ST, Apr. 15, 1886; 1 SM 218; cf. GC 472; OHC 177; ST, Dec. 15, 1887; 1888 Materials 144; 2T 400).

4. *Perfection in the "time of trouble"*: while this is one of the most controverted aspects of perfection, the key characteristics of the perfected saints in this end-time crisis are total lack of open, identifiable sinning and a loyalty to God that shows they would rather die than knowingly sin (GC 621, 623). Furthermore, the tried and tested saints will have no sins that they can recall that have not been repented of or forsaken (*ibid.* 620). Nevertheless, their "earthliness" must be removed during this trying time so that they may reflect the character of Christ more perfectly (*ibid.* 621). Thus in some sense, they are still sinners by nature, but not sinning (cf. PK 589).

5. *Sinless perfection at glorification*: perfection, sinlessness in the fullest sense of the word, comes about only at the second coming of Jesus. This is when the perfected believer will receive immortality and will no longer be subject to the passions of their sinful natures and Satan's temptations.

6. *Constant growth in perfection throughout eternity*: perfection will continue to manifest itself as the knowledge of God and love for Him increase (GC 678). Thus, there will be constant growth in Christ's likeness throughout eternity.

Further reading: H. E. Douglass, E. Heppenstall, H. K. LaRondelle, and C. M. Maxwell, *Perfection: The Impossible Possibility* (SPA, 1975); H. E. Douglass, *God at Risk* (Riverside, Calif.: Amazing Facts, 2004), pp. 178-184; J. Fowler, "The Concept of Character Development in the Writings of Ellen G. White" (Ed.D. diss., AU, 1977); G. R. Knight, *The Pharisee's Guide to Perfect Holiness* (PPPA, 1992); H. K. LaRondelle, *Perfection and Perfectionism* (AUP, 1971); W. R. Lesher, "Ellen G. White's Concept of Sanctification" (Ph.D. diss., New York University, 1970); A. L. Moore, *The Theology Crisis* (Corpus Christi, Tex.: Life Seminars, 1980); R. W. Olson, "Outline Studies on Christian Perfection and Original Sin," *Ministry* Supplement, October 1970; H. Ott, *Perfect in Christ* (RHPA, 1987); D. E. Priebe, *Face to Face With the Real Gospel* (PPPA, 1985); W. W. Whidden, *Ellen White on Salvation* (RHPA, 1995); J. R. Zurcher, *Christian Perfection: A Bible and Spirit of Prophecy Teaching* (RHPA, 1967).

Woodrow W. Whidden

PETER'S COUNSEL TO PARENTS (RHPA, 1981, 62 pp.). Booklet prepared by the Department of Education of the General Conference of Seventh-day Adventists. Ellen White was fascinated with the apostle Peter's Second Epistle (cf. AA 529-538). She loved its optimism and often used it as a touchstone for letters, sermons, and articles. Of special interest to her was the clear help 2 Peter provides in the area of child guidance and education (PCP 7). The booklet focuses on Ellen White's counsels on the value of practical Christian living and the development of a Christian character in preparation for Jesus' second coming.

PETS OF ELLEN WHITE, see **ANIMALS OF ELLEN WHITE**.

PHILANTHROPY, see SOCIAL ISSUES.

PHOTOGRAPHS. The time period of Ellen White's life and the formation of the Seventh-day Adventist Church closely parallel the early developments of photography (1850-1930). The first photographic process was called a daguerreotype, named after its inventor, a Frenchman, Louis Daguerre. His experiments with the use of a plated copper surface sensitized by chemicals allowed for the creation of the "fixed" image—the ability to take a moment in time and render it on a two-dimensional surface.

Taking a photograph during Ellen White's time was a more lengthy process than what transpires now. Exposure times that then ranged from minutes to a few seconds now take a fraction of a second. Speculations based on observations of portraits taken of her have centered on Ellen White's overall demeanor and how she must have been a stern, serious individual. The reality is that two factors existed in that period of photography that dictated the results. The existing technology compelled individuals to show a formal, frozen look because the necessity for long camera exposure times made it virtually impossible for the subjects to portray a smile. In addition, candid shots were impossible because of photographic apparatuses that included a head rest that kept the subjects' heads and bodies still. Another factor that contributes to Ellen White's stern appearance has to do with what society viewed as appropriate attitude, the social way one presents oneself. This time period dictated dark-colored clothing because that was considered "Sunday best" and the proper clothing for portraits, showing gentility.

The daguerreotype and subsequent tintype took the world by storm. The most popular size during the mid-1800s was roughly 2¾"

x 3¼" (7 centimeters x 8 centimeters). These cost around 50 cents at that time, a half day's wage for many people in the 1850s. It was not uncommon for homes to be filled with these pictures, and it was in response to this fad (which she described as a "species of idolatry") that Ellen White wrote about the dangers of misusing the Lord's money and that individuals should keep priorities straight (1T 500; MYP 316; CS 295; 2SM 317).

Don May

PHRENOLOGY. A nineteenth-century "science" founded on presuppositions that (1) the faculties of the human mind are localized in the human brain; and (2) the location and development of these faculties can be discovered by observing protrusions of the human skull. The practice of phrenology involved the study of face, manner, and temperament, but especially the shape of the head and "bumps" on the head. One positive aspect of phrenology was its wholistic view of education, embracing physical, mental, and moral aspects of the human being.

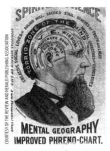

PHRENOLOGY CHART USED TO LOCATE "BUMPS" ON THE HEAD AND TO DETERMINE A PERSON'S TEMPERAMENT

Ellen White's writings on phrenology must be understood in the context of the history and changing character of phrenology. In the 1840s phrenology was viewed positively, as one of the precursors of modern *psychology (see Maxwell, pp. 24, 25). During the Whites' stay at Our Home on the Hillside, a hydropathic health center in Dansville, New York, Ellen White's sons Edson and Willie had phrenological examinations by Dr. *J. C. Jackson. Ellen White reported to friends that Jackson "pronounces Willie's head to be one of the best that has ever come under his observation" and also "gave a good description of Edson's character and peculiarities" (Lt 6, 1864, in 6MR 346).

But by the 1880s phrenology was widely associated with mesmerism, *hypnotism, and *spiritualism (2MCP 720, 721). In general her few positive references to phrenology reflect the earlier connotation of the term. Thus in 1862 she referred to "phrenology and mesmerism" as "good in their place," but "seized upon by Satan as his most powerful agents to deceive and destroy souls" (1T 296). When she republished this article in 1884, she reworded the sentence: "The *sciences which treat of the human mind*" "are good in their place; but they are seized upon by Satan as his powerful agents to deceive and destroy souls" (ST, Nov. 6, 1884, italics supplied; cf. 2MCP 720, 721).

Most of her references to phrenology emphasize its use by Satan as a "snare" to destroy faith in the Bible and counterfeit the work of character development that can be accomplished only through the power of God (1T 294-297; Ev 605). "The world, which is considered to be benefited so much by phrenology and animal magnetism, never was so corrupt. Satan uses these very things to destroy virtue and lay the foundation of Spiritualism. ... Thousands, I was shown, have been spoiled through the philosophy of phrenology and animal magnetism, and have been driven into infidelity" (RH, Feb. 18, 1862). Thus she rebuked some Adventist ministers for practicing phrenology (see 9MR 3-6; Lt 9, 1892; Lt 78, 1893; Mss 12, 29, 46, 76, 78, 1893).

Further reading: 1T 290-297, 551; 1MCP 18, 19; 2MCP 711-721; RH, Feb. 18, 1862; J. D. Davies, *Phrenology, Fad and Science: A 19th-Century American Crusade* (New Haven, Conn.: Yale University Press, 1955); C. M. Maxwell, *Tell It to the World* (PPPA, 1976),

pp. 24, 25; "Phrenology: A Science" (DF 160-c, CAR); A. L. White, "Paralleling Statements Regarding Mesmerism and Hypnotism" (DF 160-c, CAR).

Erik C. Carter

PHYSICIANS, see **MEDICAL MISSIONARY WORK**; **HEALTH REFORM**.

PHYSIOLOGY. As used by Ellen White, the science of human life; the study of the structure, normal functioning, and natural laws of the human body (CH 38). She argued that health is so closely related to happiness that, generally speaking, people without health are not happy. In order to be healthy, persons must have a "practical knowledge of the science of human life." "It is therefore of the highest importance that among the studies selected for childhood, physiology should occupy the first place" (CH 38). In addition, she pointed out that "ignorance of physiology, and a neglect to observe the laws of health, have brought many to the grave who might have lived to labor and study intelligently" (FE 321).

"A knowledge of physiology and hygiene should be the basis of all educational effort," she wrote (CG 361). She urged, therefore, that mothers should teach their preschool children, "in simple, easy lessons, the rudiments of physiology and hygiene" (*ibid.* 362). The same instruction initiated by parents (7T 65) should be continued in the school (CG 362), reinforced and amplified by schoolteachers, administrators (CT 125), and ministers (6T 302, 376; HL 16). "The youth should be taught to look upon physiology as one of the essentials" (*Advocate*, Oct. 1, 1899). She especially bemoaned that students devoted much time to arcane and theoretical subjects while "physiology and hygiene are barely touched upon" (HL 14).

Regarding the content of instruction, White

cautioned that in drilling students in the "technicalities" of physiology, teachers must not overlook two "matters of far greater value to the student" (CG 363). First, "as the foundation principle of all education in these lines, the youth should be taught that the laws of nature are the laws of God—as truly divine as are the precepts of the Decalogue. The laws that govern our physical organism, God has written upon every nerve, muscle, and fiber of the body. Every careless and willful violation of these laws is a sin against our Creator" (*ibid.*). As students become "impressed with the thought" that the body is God's temple, "they will be inspired with reverence. Instead of marring God's handiwork, they will have an ambition to make all that is possible of themselves, in order to fulfill the Creator's glorious plan. Thus they will come to regard obedience to the laws of health, not as a matter of sacrifice or self-denial, but as it really is, an inestimable privilege and blessing" (Ed 201).

Her second admonition to teachers of physiology is to especially emphasize its practical applications, namely, "how to preserve health, so that they might use their knowledge to the best account after they had obtained it" (CT 83). "Pupils should be led to see the value of physical energy and how it can be so preserved and developed as to contribute in the highest degree to success in life's great struggle" (CG 343).

Jerry Moon

PICTURES, see **PHOTOGRAPHS**.

PILLAR DOCTRINES, see **LANDMARK DOCTRINES**.

PITCAIRN. A Pacific island of approximately one by two miles (0.6 by 1.2 kilometers), located about midway between Panama and New Zealand, and the missionary ship named

after it. In 1890 it became the staging base for Seventh-day Adventist missionary work on many islands in the Pacific Ocean.

In 1790 nine sailors who had mutinied against Captain William Bligh on the H.M.S. *Bounty* made their way to Pitcairn along with a group of Polynesian women and men. There the group hid for 18 years before they were discovered.

In 1876 James White and J. N. Loughborough sent a box of literature to the island. Adventist layman John I. Tay went to Pitcairn some 10 years later. As a result of his Bible studies,

SEVENTH-DAY ADVENTIST MISSIONARY SHIP *PITCAIRN*

COURTESY OF THE ELLEN G. WHITE ESTATE, INC.

most of the Pitcairners requested baptism, so Tay returned to the United States and appealed for an ordained minister to answer the Pitcairners' request. After a tragic loss of the missionary ship *Phoebe Chapman*, the Adventist missionary schooner *Pitcairn* reached the island in 1890. Most of the Pitcairners were then baptized.

The *Pitcairn* made six Pacific voyages from San Francisco carrying missionaries and supplies, each time calling first at Pitcairn Island. On its departure from the island the ship carried Pitcairners to serve as lay missionaries on other islands. James Russell McCoy, for many years both a spiritual and governmental leader on Pitcairn, served for some years as coworker of Ellen White in Australia. During the course of her ministry Ellen White often referred to the island and the work of the *Pitcairn* ship. She wrote three letters of comfort and instruction to the believers on Pitcairn Island.

Further reading: A. H. Christensen, *Heirs of Exile: The Story of Pitcairn Island* (RHPA, 1955); R. W. Schwarz and F. Greenleaf, *Light*

Bearers (PPPA, 2000), pp. 215-217; *SDA Encyclopedia* (1996), vol. 11, pp. 354, 355.

Herb Ford

PLACE CALLED OAKWOOD, A: INSPIRED COUNSEL (Huntsville, Ala.: Oakwood College, 2007, 177 pp.). A comprehensive collection of Ellen G. White's counsel to the pressent Oakwood University from its inception in 1896 as "the Huntsville School," to the end of her life in 1915. All of her published and unpublished counsel to Oakwood is gathered here in one volume compiled by Benjamin J. Baker. The compilation sets forth Oakwood's divine purpose, its remarkable development, and its achievements in educating men and women for global service to God and humanity.

Following the foreword, to prepare the reader to grasp the historical nuances of the main text, the compiler has thoughtfully provided four reference sections. The first, called Oakwood Keys, consists of key terms (definitions in historical context), key individuals (biographical sketches), key places, and key references (explanations of allusions). The section titled Oakwood Names includes the official names of the school—Oakwood Industrial School (1896), Oakwood Manual Training School (1904), Oakwood Junior College (1917), and Oakwood College (1943), to which can now be added Oakwood University (2008). There is also a list of titles or phrases by which Ellen White referred to Oakwood. The third reference section, entitled Oakwood Timeline, lists key events in Ellen White's interaction with Oakwood, from 1891 to 1915. The fourth reference section is Oakwood Leaders, including its principals and presidents from 1896 through 2007.

The actual compilation is arranged in five chapters: Speeches, Letters, Articles, Manuscripts/ Testimonies, and Unpublished Documents.

These are followed a by five-part appendix: Oakwood Categories defines and illustrates seven categories of White's counsels about Oakwood; Oakwood Quotables lists 15 memorable quotations; Oakwood Principles distills 21 timeless lessons from Ellen White's counsel to Oakwood; "Our Duty to the Colored People" is Ellen White's landmark address on race and the gospel, delivered to the General Conference session, March 21, 1891, in Battle Creek, Michigan. Describing this speech as "pointed and direct," Benjamin Baker identifies it as "the catalyst to the Seventh-day Adventist Southern work." The appendix concludes with a Source Document Legent, and is followed by a bibliography and an index. *A Place Called Oakwood,* abbreviated PCO, is found on the *Ellen G. White Writings* CD, Comprehensive Research Edition, 2008 and later.

See also: African-Americans, Adventism Among; Oakwood College; *Southern Work.*

Further reading: B. J. Baker, *Crucial Moments: Twelve Defining Events in Black Adventist History* (RHPA, 2005).

PLAGIARISM. In recent years one of the most discussed issues regarding the writings of Ellen White is the use, in her own literary productions, of material she borrowed, or allegedly plagiarized, from other sources without giving explicit credit to the original author(s). Ellen White (cf. GC xi, xii) and people close to her (cf. 3SM 451-465) openly acknowledged that she borrowed from other authors. The real issue, however, is not whether she borrowed without giving proper credit, but whether she borrowed in such a way as to deceive the reader. There is both "good" and "bad" literary borrowing. "Good" literary borrowing is what every researcher does and is perfectly legitimate, provided it is done correctly and documented accurately. "Bad" literary borrowing (plagiarism) is wrong per se because an author extensively copies the thoughts of another and claims those thoughts as his or her own. The charge that Ellen White practiced plagiarism affects not only the credibility of her claim to a prophetic gift, but also the very integrity and genuineness of her personal life. She has been accused of being a thief, a liar, and an exploiter of church members who constituted a captive market for her books.

The allegation of plagiarism was first raised in 1887 by Dudley M. Canright, former Adventist minister and colleague of James and Ellen White, in his book *Seventh-day Adventism Renounced* (Kalamazoo, Mich.: Kalamazoo Pub. Co., 1887). Canright's personal knowledge of her life and ministry made his attacks even more cutting and persuasive to many. Among the many critiques he raised was that of plagiarism—the charge that she had copied her books from other authors.

The Seventh-day Adventist Church has repeatedly addressed these accusations. In 1951 Francis D. Nichol's *Ellen G. White and Her Critics* (RHPA) gave a synopsis of the charges and provided answers that satisfied the membership for many years (pp. 403-467). But renewed and intensified charges of plagiarism in the 1970s and early 1980s led the church to begin an extensive study into Ellen White's borrowing of external material in the production of her works. At the same time, a legal opinion was sought, and the charge that Ellen White plagiarized her books was reviewed by Attorney Vincent L. Ramik. In his August 14, 1981, report, after spending more than 300 hours researching about 1,000 relevant cases in American legal history, he concluded that "Ellen White was not a plagiarist, and her works did not constitute copyright infringement/piracy." Ramik explained that "nowhere have we found the

books of Ellen G. White to be virtually the 'same plan and character throughout' as those of her predecessors. Nor have we found, or have critics made reference to, any intention of Ellen White to supersede . . . [other authors] in the market with the same class of readers and purchasers." Instead he found that "she invariably introduced considerable new matter to that which she borrowed, going far beyond mere 'colorable deviations,' and, in effect, created an altogether new literary work" (AR, Sept. 17, 1981).

Another aspect of this issue is that the practice of borrowing from other authors without giving explicit or detailed credit was widespread among writers of the eighteenth and nineteenth centuries. Although by today's literary standards this practice is unacceptable, it forms the historical context of Ellen White's own practice. Such a practice was followed, for example, by John Wesley in writing his *Explanatory Notes Upon the New Testament*. "It was a doubt with me for some time," he wrote in the preface, "whether I should not subjoin to every note I received from them the name of the author from whom it was taken; especially considering I had transcribed some, and abridged many more, almost in the words of the author. But upon further consideration, I resolved to name none, that nothing might divert the mind of the reader from keeping close to the point of view, and receiving what was spoken only according to its own intrinsic value" (quoted in F. D. Nichol, *Ellen G. White and Her Critics*, p. 406).

Ellen White's reasons for not naming her sources were similar to Wesley's: she did not want to "divert the mind of the reader" from the context and purpose of what she was writing. In her introduction to *The Great Controversy* Ellen White openly acknowledged her practice of literary borrowing. "The great events which have marked the progress of reform in past ages are matters of history, well known and universally acknowledged by the Protestant world; they are facts which none can gainsay. This history I have presented briefly, in accordance with the scope of the book, and the brevity which must necessarily be observed, the facts having been condensed into as little space as seemed consistent with a proper understanding of their application. *In some cases where a historian has so grouped together events as to afford, in brief, a comprehensive view of the subject, or has summarized details in a convenient manner, his words have been quoted; but in some instances no specific credit has been given, since the quotations are not given for the purpose of citing that writer as authority, but because his statement affords a ready and forcible presentation of the subject. In narrating the experience and views of those carrying forward the work of reform in our own time, similar use has been made of their published works*" (pp. xi, xii; italics supplied).

In two letters to L. E. Froom (Jan. 8, 1928, and Dec. 13, 1934) W. C. White explained how his mother used some of the historical materials she found in other books. "The great events occurring in the life of our Lord were presented to her in panoramic scenes as also were the other portions of *The Great Controversy*. In a few of these scenes chronology and geography were clearly presented, but in the greater part of the revelation the flashlight scenes, which were exceedingly vivid, and the conversations and the controversies, which she heard and was able to narrate, were not marked geographically or chronologically, and she was left to study the Bible and history, and the writings of men who had presented the life of our Lord, to get the chronological and geographical connection. Another purpose served by the reading of history and the *Life of Our Lord* and the *Life of St. Paul* was that

in so doing there was brought vividly to her mind scenes presented clearly in vision, but which were, through the lapse of years and her strenuous ministry, dimmed in her memory. Many times in the reading of Hanna, Farrar, or Fleetwood, she would run on to a description of a scene which had been vividly presented to her, but forgotten, and which she was able to describe more in detail than that which she had read" (3SM 459, 460). "In some of the historical matters such as are brought out in *Patriarchs and Prophets* and in *Acts of the Apostles*, and in *Great Controversy*, the main outlines were made very clear and plain to her, and when she came to write up these topics, she was left to study the Bible and history to get dates and geographical relations and to perfect her description of details" (*ibid.* 462).

As she admitted, Ellen White did borrow from other authors without giving references. In *The Great Controversy* (in all three editions—1884, 1888, and 1911) materials are borrowed from Merle D'Aubigné's *History of the Reformation*, J. A. Wylie's *History of the Waldenses*, and from Adventist authors J. N. Andrews' *History of the Sabbath*, Uriah Smith's *The Sanctuary and Its Cleansing*, and her husband, James White's *Life of William Miller*, itself drawn from other sources as admitted on its title page. The five works referred to were well known to the Adventist membership. Less than two years before the publication of the 1884 edition of *The Great Controversy*, she specifically encouraged members to read D'Aubigné's book. In an article titled "Holiday Gifts" she recommended, "Provide something to be read during these long winter evenings. For those who can procure it, D'Aubigné's *History of the Reformation* will be both interesting and profitable. From this work we may gain some knowledge of what has been accomplished in the past in the great work of reform" (RH, Dec. 26, 1882). Wylie's book was also well known and sold through the Review and Herald office, as were the three books written by Adventist pioneers. Obviously Ellen White and her readers knew about these books, and many would have readily seen the literary parallels between her books and others sold by the Review. A study done by the Ellen G. White Estate to document passages in her writings known to be verbally dependent upon prior external material indicates that about 15 percent of *The Great Controversy* (1911 edition) is taken from sources for which she gave the proper references and about 5 percent is from uncredited sources.

Ellen White's *Sketches From the Life of Paul* (1883) has also been cited as an example of extensive literary borrowing. Her writings on the life of Paul expanded slowly through the years, with a few chapters appearing in *Spiritual Gifts*, volume 1 (1858), in *The Spirit of Prophecy*, volume 3 (1878), and in a pamphlet of the *Redemption* series the same year. The charge against *Sketches From the Life of Paul* states that she copied large sections from a work found in her library, W. J. Conybeare and

J. S. Howson's *The Life and Epistles of St. Paul* (New York: Crowell, n.d.). Covering similar themes and historical events as her own book, this book contains descriptions of the historical context and culture of the Middle East as it relates to the life and ministry of the apostle Paul. This was a well-known book among Adventists and was also recommended as good reading. An advertisement for Conybeare and Howson's book appeared in the *Signs of the Times* of February 22, 1883, with an endorsement from Ellen White: "*The Life of St. Paul,* by Conybeare and Howson, I regard as a book of great merit, and one of rare usefulness to the earnest student of the New Testament history." The fact that her own book on the life of Paul was about to be released in June of that year is strong evidence that Ellen White made no attempt to hide from church members the obvious parallels between her work and that of Conybeare and Howson.

To understand Ellen White's levels and types of literary borrowing better, consider two examples taken from passages her critics claim to be flagrant cases of plagiarism.

Conybeare and Howson *The Life and Epistles of St. Paul* (1858)	**Ellen White** *Sketches From the Life of Paul* (1883)
Eustathius says that the mysterious symbols called "Ephesian Letters" were engraved on the crown, the girdle, and the feet of the goddess. . . . When pronounced they were regarded as a charm, and were directed to be used especially by those who were in the power of evil spirits. When written, they were carried about as amulets. . . . The study of these symbols was an elaborate science, and books, both numerous and costly, were compiled by its professors. (p. 392)	Upon it [the statue of the goddess Diana] were inscribed mystic characters and symbols, which were believed to possess great power. When pronounced, they were said to accomplish wonders. When written, they were treasured as a potent charm to guard their possessor from robbers, from disease, and even from death. Numerous and costly books were written by the Ephesians to explain the meaning and use of these symbols. (pp. 134, 135)

Conybeare and Howson	Ellen G. White
This statement throws some light on the peculiar character of the miracles wrought by Paul at Ephesus. We are not to suppose that the apostles were always able to work miracles at will. An influx of supernatural power was given to them at the time and according to the circumstances that required it. And the character of the miracles was not always the same. They were accommodated to the peculiar forms of sin, superstition, and ignorance they were required to oppose. Here, at Ephesus, Paul was in the face of magicians, like Moses and Aaron before Pharaoh; and it is distinctly said that his miracles were "not ordinary wonders," from which we may infer that they were different from those which he usually performed. . . . A miracle which has a closer reference to our present subject is that in which the hem of Christ's garment was made effectual to the healing of a poor sufferer and the conviction of the bystanders. So on this occasion garments were made the means of communicating a healing power to those who were at a distance, whether they were possessed with evil spirits or afflicted with ordinary diseases. Yet was this no encouragement to blind superstition. When the suffering woman was healed by touching the hem of the garment, the Savior turned round and said, "Virtue is gone out of *me* [italics theirs]." And here at Ephesus we are reminded that it was God who "wrought miracles by the hands of Paul" (v. 11), and that "the name," not of Paul, but "of the Lord Jesus, was magnified" (v. 17). (pp. 392, 393)	As Paul was brought in direct contact with the idolatrous inhabitants of Ephesus, the power of God was strikingly displayed through him. The apostles were not always able to work miracles at will. The Lord granted his servants this special power as the progress of his cause or the honor of his name required. Like Moses and Aaron at the court of Pharaoh, the apostle had now to maintain the truth against the lying wonders of the magicians; hence the miracles he wrought were of a different character from those which he had heretofore performed. As the hem of Christ's garment had communicated healing power to her who sought relief by the touch of faith, so on this occasion, garments were made the means of cure to all that believed; "diseases departed from them, and evil spirits went out of them." Yet these miracles gave no encouragement to blind superstition. When Jesus felt the touch of the suffering woman, He exclaimed, "Virtue is gone out of *me* [italics hers]." So the scripture declares that the Lord wrought miracles by the hand of Paul, and that the name of the Lord Jesus was magnified, and not the name of Paul. (p. 135)

Comparison between the source documents and her writings shows how she used her sources and adapted them to fit her own thoughts and spiritual applications. The first example is taken from *Sketches From the Life of Paul* on the experiences of the apostle in

Calvin E. Stowe *Origins and History of the* *Books of the Bible* (1867)	Ellen G. White Manuscript 24, 1886
It is not the words of the Bible that were inspired, it is not the thoughts of the Bible that were inspired; it is the men who wrote the Bible that were inspired. Inspiration acts not on the man's words, not on the man's thoughts, but on the man himself; so that he, by his own spontaneity, under the impulse of the Holy Ghost, conceives certain thoughts and gives utterance to them in certain words, both the words and thoughts receiving the peculiar impress of the mind which conceived and uttered them, and being in fact just as really his own, as they could have been if there had been no inspiration at all in the case. . . . Inspiration generally is a purifying and an elevation, and an intensification of the human intellect subjectively, rather than an objective suggestion and communication; though suggestion and communication are not excluded. The Divine mind is, as it were, so suffused through the human, and the human mind is so interpenetrated with the Divine, that for the time being the utterances of the man are the word of God. (pp. 19, 20)	It is not the words of the Bible that are inspired, but the men that were inspired. Inspiration acts not on the man's words or his expressions but on the man himself, who, under the influence of the Holy Ghost, is imbued with thoughts. But the words receive the impress of the individual mind. The divine mind is diffused. The divine mind and will is combined with the human mind and will; thus the utterances of the man are the word of God. (1SM 21)

Ephesus. The similarities in thought and wording between Conybeare and Howson's book and White's parallel passages are obvious.

These two paragraphs show that in some instances Ellen White paraphrased key words and expressions from Conybeare and Howson. In other sentences she borrowed almost verbatim, changing only a few words. In *Sketches From the Life of Paul* the borrowed material, estimated at 12 percent, was often

limited to historical information and backgrounds, and was often rearranged by Ellen White to fit her own thought and chapter outline. Whereas Conybeare and Howson give little spiritual application of and commentary on the events Paul encountered, White emphasizes the spiritual lessons to be gained from these events. In these spiritual applications she borrows little from the earlier authors. When in 1911 Ellen White published an expanded edition of *Sketches From the Life of Paul* and included its content in *The Acts of the Apostles*, she used even less material from Conybeare and Howson and added more of her own theological and practical commentary.

A second example compares Ellen White's thought on the doctrine of inspiration in her Manuscript 24, 1886 (published in 1SM 19-21), a manuscript that Seventh-day Adventists have referred to extensively to understand her view of her inspiration, and pages 13-20 of Calvin E. Stowe's *Origin and History of the Books of the Bible, Both the Canonical and the Apocryphal, Designed to Show What the Bible Is Not, What It Is, and How to Use It* (Hartford, Conn.: Hartford Pub., 1867). In this case one critic has argued that she took, not simply fine language and historical information from other authors, but ideas as well (*Spectrum* 3, no. 4 [Autumn 1971]: 73-84). However, a careful comparison between White and Stowe reveals a different perspective. "We have evidence of her writing most of the ideas which are common to her and Dr. Stowe at a time prior to the writing of this manuscript. Indeed, some of these references antedate any possible awareness on her part of Dr. Stowe's book. In addition to the common theological material, there are several points at which the two authors diverge or have distinctively different emphases" (D. Neff, "Ellen White's Alleged Literary and Theological Indebtedness to Calvin Stowe" [unpublished paper, 1979, CAR], p. 25).

In this second example, much more than in the first one, which dealt mainly with historical information and background, Ellen White's thought and theology are clearly different from Stowe's on the concept of inspiration. Note that at the end of the passage Ellen White leaves out key words from Stowe's text that would have pointed her theology of inspiration in a different direction.

Had Ellen White simply copied Stowe's words without thinking carefully through their ramifications, she might have adopted a theology of inspiration similar to that later developed by theologians such as Karl Barth or Emil Brunner. Stowe advocated a theory of inspiration in which the subjective elements of the prophet are predominant and in which inspiration is an encounter between the divine and the human. There is no actual transmission of information between God and the prophet. Note that two key phrases on the inspiration of thoughts in Stowe's explanation of the process of inspiration at the beginning of his paragraph are not inserted by Ellen White in her own shorter text. While Stowe mentions that a prophet's thoughts are not inspired, Ellen White's explanation of inspiration gives a greater role to the Holy Spirit in imparting inspired thoughts to a prophet. In her explanation of the process of inspiration there is an actual objective transmission of information between God and the prophet. The two views are very different. It seems obvious from this example that she had Stowe's text nearby when she wrote her own. Yet she did not mindlessly copy from Stowe but carefully weighed the concepts and understood the difference she wished to emphasize in her own understanding of the process of inspiration.

Many other examples of literary borrowing could be given, but these representative examples suffice to illustrate that she did not attempt to deceive her readers, nor did she copy mindlessly the words and thoughts of other authors. She was fully engaged in the process and adapted the external material to fit her thought. There is evidence to support the conclusion that she used other sources, not as a mere compiler, but as an original author. She used external material not in lieu of her own thought, but to enhance her expression of her thought. Her minimal references to her borrowing no doubt reflect her concern not to blur the distinction between her own inspired message and those of other authors from which she received supporting information and useful terms of expression.

The repeated accusations of plagiarism have certainly raised serious questions about the writings of Ellen White and her prophetic ministry. In spite of this, the church has benefited from discussions regarding the role and ministry of Ellen White. The apologetic approach of earlier years (as in Nichol's *Ellen G. White and Her Critics*) has been replaced with a more open acknowledgment and discussion of Ellen White's use of borrowed sources. Far from eliminating the influence of her writings on Adventist thought, a clearer understanding of how she wrote her books has helped the church to better understand and explain how the process of revelation and inspiration operated in her ministry and how her literary assistants helped her in her work.

See also: *The Desire of Ages* Sources Project; Literary Assistants; Historians, Ellen G. White's Use of.

Further reading: R. W. Coon, "Ellen G. White and the So-called 'Plagiarism' Charge: An Examination of Five Issues" (Lecture, Apr. 30, 1999, CAR); R. W. Coon and K. H. Woods, "Was Ellen G. White a Plagiarist?" (EGWE, SDoc); H. E. Douglass, *Messenger of the Lord* (PPPA, 1998), pp. 456-465; P. Gordon, "Why Did Ellen White Borrow?" (EGWE, SDoc); F. D. Nichol, *Ellen G. White and Her Critics* (RHPA, 1951), pp. 403-467; AR, Sept. 17, 1981; J. Moon, "Who Owns the Truth? Another Look at the Plagiarism Debate," *Ellen White and Current Issues Symposium* (CAR, 2005), vol. 1, pp. 41-66; R. W. Olson, "Ellen White's Denials," *Ministry*, February 1991; R. W. Olson, *One Hundred and One Questions on the Sanctuary and on Ellen White* (EGWE, 1981,

SDoc), pp. 64-110; Fred Veltman, "*The Desire of Ages* Project: the Conclusions," *Ministry*, December 1990.

Denis Fortin

PLAGUES, SEVEN LAST. Final events of earth's history, beginning with the close of *probation and ending with the *second coming of Jesus Christ. Ellen White describes a sequence in which these events take place (EW 36, 37; LDE 256, 257). Preparatory to the pouring out of these plagues is the anger of the nations (Rev. 11:18), followed by a short *time of trouble that will be held in check as long as Christ remains in the heavenly *sanctuary (EW 85, 86). Events during this short time of trouble require all people to decide their spiritual loyalty, either to God and His *law, as found in His Word, or to human institutions and laws (7T 141; LDE 251). During this time the *latter rain of the *Holy Spirit will be poured out to give power to the *loud cry of the third angel (see *three angels' messages) and to prepare the saints to stand during the seven last plagues. When all have had opportunity to choose on which side of the conflict they will stand, God's people will receive the *seal of God (Rev. 7:2-4) and the rest will receive the *mark of the beast (Rev. 13:16, 17; 14:9-11; 16:2; 20:4). At that point Jesus will stand up (Dan. 12:1), declare the close of human probation (Rev. 22:11), end His work in the heavenly sanctuary (Rev. 8:5; 11:19; 15:5-8), put on the garments of vengeance (Isa. 63:1-4), and command that the seven last plagues be poured out on the impenitent (Rev. 11:18; 16; 19:15). This time of God's wrath coincides with the time of Jacob's trouble for the people of God (Jer. 30:5-7).

The four angels of Revelation 7:1-3 are holding back the winds of strife, which, when released, will bring the final time of trouble on the earth. No one has yet received the mark of the beast, since the issues are not yet clear and decisive before the world. Although God is already allowing some judgments to fall on the earth (9T 11; 5MR 15-17), these are not the seven last plagues, which are not poured out till after probation closes and the Spirit of God is withdrawn from the earth (CET 187, 188; LDE 253; PP 201).

The seven last plagues are especially reserved for those who have willfully violated God's holy law, especially the Sabbath (EW 65). The Sabbath will be the great question of importance in the end (*ibid.* 85). As the plagues begin to fall, ministers will declare from the pulpits that the world is being punished because Sunday is not honored as it should be (LDE 256; RH, Sept. 17, 1901). A decree will finally be issued against those who honor the Sabbath, giving the world permission, after a certain time, to put them to death (GC 615, 616; LDE 261, 262; cf. Rev. 13:15).

God's true people will not be allowed to suffer martyrdom at this time (EW 284; LDE 263; Mar 277; cf. Ps. 27:5; Isa. 26:20, 21; Mal. 3:17). Angels will shield the righteous and supply their needs (FLB 340; GC 629; cf. Isa. 33:16). The universal decree for the destruction of the righteous justifies God in pouring the plagues of His wrath upon their oppressors (Rev. 16:4-7). "By condemning the people of God to death, they have as truly incurred the guilt of their blood as if it had been shed by their hands" (GC 628).

While the seven last plagues are a manifestation of the *wrath of God against sin in the earth, God does not act directly to cause the pain, suffering, and death in these plagues. "I was shown that the judgments of God would not come directly out from the Lord upon them, but in this way: They place themselves beyond His protection. He warns, corrects, reproves, and points out the only path of safety; . . . if they choose their own way, then He does not commission His angels to prevent Satan's decided attacks upon them. It is Satan's power that is at work at sea and on land, bringing calamity and distress" (14MR 3; LDE 242).

The plagues are literal rather than spiritual in nature. They are similar to but more extensive and terrible than the plagues on Egypt (FLB 340; GC 627, 628). Not only is there physical suffering on the part of the recipients, but the earth also experiences cataclysmic effects. "The whole earth heaves and swells like the waves of the sea. Its surface is breaking up. . . . Mountain chains are sinking. Inhabited islands disappear. . . . Seaports . . . are swallowed up by the angry waters. . . . The proudest cities . . . are laid low" (GC 637).

The plagues are not universal, or the inhabitants of earth would be wholly cut off; but they will be the most awful scourges known to humanity. All previous judgments have been mingled with mercy, but in the final judgment, wrath is poured out without mercy (FLB 340; GC 628, 629). "To our merciful God the act of punishment is a strange act. . . . The severity of the retribution awaiting the transgressor may be judged by the Lord's reluctance to execute justice" (GC 627).

No length of time has been specified for the pouring out of the plagues, but the impression is left that these events take place in a short period of time. They follow one another in rapid succession, escalating rapidly to the final plague, in which the earth is destroyed by a massive earthquake and devastating hailstones (Rev. 16:17-21). This seventh plague involves a theophany (verses 17, 18) associated with the battle of the great day of God Almighty (verse 14), frequently called the battle of *Armageddon (verse 16). This is a spiritual battle, Satan's "last struggle against the government of heaven" (*ibid.* 624). But the victory belongs to the Lord. As the earth is shaken, the firmament appears to open and shut. The glory from the throne of God seems to be flashing through. Graves are opened in a special *resurrection, and all who have died in the faith of the third angel's message (see *three angels' messages) come forth glorified, to hear God declare the day and hour of Jesus' coming and deliver the everlasting *covenant to His people (*ibid.* 636, 637; EW 285, 286). Soon after this the great white cloud appears bearing the Son of man (1SM 76; LDE 273). The wicked in trembling agony behold the approach of Christ and call upon nature to hide them from the face of Him who sits on the throne, while the righteous rejoice at their deliverance (TMK 356; LDE 273; cf. Rev. 6:16).

Further reading: GC 613-644; LDE 238-280; Mar 262-290.

Edwin E. Reynolds

PLAN OF SALVATION, see **SALVATION, PLAN OF**.

POLITICS AND VOTING. A prevailing sentiment against voting and political involvement characterized the "come out of Babylon" stance seen in the formative decade (c. 1846-1856) of the Sabbatarian Adventist movement. Their course was driven, not by apathy or aversion to controversial public issues, but by intense dedication to an uncompromising moral witness against evil—including the evils of slavery, intemperance, and suppression of human rights. Political involvement threatened dilution of that witness through melding with evil forces and distraction from the Second Advent cause they had embraced as the great reform under which all others were subsumed.

However, during the tumultuous years of deepening sectional crisis and Civil War, the consensus shifted to the recognition, as expressed in an 1865 General Conference session resolution, that it could well be "highly proper" for a Second Advent believer to exercise the influence of his vote "in behalf

of justice, humanity, and right" (2Bio 115). Ellen White shared this consensus. Behind an effort in 1859 by "men of intemperance" to flatter the Battle Creek Adventists into continuing their avoidance of the polls, she had perceived a satanic agenda. Not voting in this context would be to abet evil by default (2SM 337).

Ellen White's subsequent career reflects a conviction that the possibility of exerting influence in a democratic society places Adventists under a moral imperative that at times requires voting and may lead to holding political office. In her work for temperance and prohibition in the 1870s and beyond, Ellen White became a fervent advocate of "movement politics"—discriminating involvement in the political process on behalf of benevolent reform in contrast to partisan politics centering on advancing the power of a political party.

In a *Review and Herald* article published on November 8, 1881, she depicted machine politics and the liquor interests in a corrupt and vicious nexus that kept society in "moral paralysis." The laws licensing the sale of liquor "sustain an evil which is sapping their very foundations," she wrote. The result was an alarming increase in domestic abuse, crime, poverty, immorality, and "the burdens of taxation." She further maintained that no one can escape responsibility for these conditions: "In our favored land, every voter has some voice in determining what laws shall control the nation." Thus, temperance advocates fail to fulfill their duty unless they include the vote for prohibition among their means for exerting influence.

In an address given at Battle Creek College in 1884, Ellen White affirmed the political arena as one in which Adventist young people might aspire to make their contribution for the cause of Christ. "Dear youth, what is the aim and purpose of your life? Are you ambitious for education that you may have a name and position in the world? Have you thoughts that you dare not express, that you may one day stand upon the summit of intellectual greatness; that you may sit in deliberative and legislative councils, and help to enact laws for the nation? There is nothing wrong in these aspirations. You may every one of you make your mark" (FE 82). She urged the students to dismiss any notion that it would be necessary to sacrifice principle in order to achieve such goals. Taking "firm hold on divine power," they were to "stand in society to mold and fashion, rather than to be fashioned after the world's model" (*ibid.* 89).

If the political realm presented opportunity, even obligation, for Christian service, it also presented dangerous influences that threatened to mold those involved, rather than vice versa. In view of this challenge, Ellen White impressed upon believers the principle that citizenship in Christ's kingdom must animate and control their interaction with the political powers of earth. For Adventists, that transcendent citizenship entailed the particular vocation of a climactic heralding of Christ's return to usher in the fullness of His everlasting kingdom. Partisan politicking destructive to that controlling identity and loyalty could not be countenanced, and its presence in the church became a major concern to Ellen White in the 1890s.

Apparently Adventist ministers and teachers had openly taken sides in the national political controversy as it was heated up by the Populist movement. That movement reached the peak of its influence in 1896 when it fused with the Democratic Party behind the presidential candidacy of William Jennings Bryan. The Democratic platform, while avoiding some of Populism's most idealistic reforms, made central a proposal for coinage of silver

currency as a panacea for the economic injustices suffered by the nation's rural and working classes.

Ellen White viewed "the changing of the circulating currency" as a plan deriving from the devil rather than God. Its danger lay, not in the envisioned economic justice for the poor, but in the fact that its result would be the very opposite of its promise. It would "cause a state of things that will bring oppression to the poor, and create great distress. (TM 321). The direction from the voice of the Son of God, she declared, is "ye will not give your voice or influence to any policy to enrich a few, to bring oppression and suffering to the poorer class of humanity" (*ibid.* 333).

Her main interest, however, was not in taking a side in the currency debate, but instead to stress the dangers posed by partisan politics to the identity, integrity, unity, and mission of the church. "There is fraud on both sides," she wrote in a "special testimony" sent from Australia to the General Conference session of 1897 (held in Bryan's home base— Lincoln, Nebraska). Thus she urged those for whom the Lord Jesus is "the Captain" to "file under His banner" and avoid "linking up with either party" (GCDB, Feb. 17, 1897). Adventists, she wrote two years later, have their "citizenship . . . in heaven. . . . They are to stand as subjects of Christ's kingdom, bearing the banner on which is inscribed, 'The commandments of God, and the faith of Jesus'" (FE 478, 479).

In addition to blurred identity and compromised integrity, linking with political parties threatened the unity of the church as an alternative, reconciling community. Ellen White was pained by the spectacle of "those who believe we are now under the third angel's message, the last message of mercy to the world, brothers in the same faith . . . wearing the badges of opposing political parties, proclaiming opposite sentiments and declaring their divided opinions" (GCDB, Feb. 17, 1897). Moreover, the church cannot side with political factions in a way that pits classes of humanity against each other, because it is to be a reconciling force. "There is to be no party strife in the family of God; for the well-being of each is the happiness of the whole. No partition walls are to be built up between man and man. Christ as the great center must unite all in one" (FE 479).

Ellen White was adamant, therefore, that the church and its funds should not be used to underwrite partisan political advocacy. "The tithe should not be used to pay anyone for speechifying on political questions," and any "teacher, minister, or leader in our ranks who is stirred with a desire to ventilate his opinions on political questions" must either "be converted" or give up working for the church, along with any credentials (*ibid.* 477).

The danger of crippling the church's mission by provoking a backlash from the powers that be with injudicious, even if accurate, criticisms also came to the forefront during the late 1890s. During these years (c. 1895-1910) the state governments of the American South were bringing the system of legal segregation and racial repression into full force, and resistance was met with brutal, often violent reprisal. Under these conditions Ellen White warned against the impulse to "mix up in politics" in the Southern states by speaking out against the injustices done to the African-Americans.

Her premise was not indifference to racial injustice, but that direct confrontation of such a thoroughly repressive political system would result in greater harm to the Black population, and would make it virtually impossible for the Adventist mission to thrive among both Black and White people in the South. Thus, the necessity of maintaining silence about

glaring injustice, even though "there cannot but be the burning indignation that longs to express itself" (*Gospel Herald*, Aug. 1, 1899). By thus prioritizing the Adventist message over political action for racial equality that appeared futile in this context, she hoped that the Adventist cause could thrive in the South. The ideal of that wholistic mission would be to bring education and economic empowerment as well as gospel truth to oppressed Blacks, and bring both races into a united fellowship under the "third angel's message," in which racial prejudice would be eradicated (9T 213-224; SW).

Ellen White's forceful warnings in response to the crises of the 1890s should not be mistaken for her full legacy with regard to politics and voting. The higher loyalty of citizenship in Christ's kingdom that she continually made central also had positive implications with regard to the political powers of earth. Christ's kingdom, she wrote in 1898, while not of this world, "imprints its influence on earthly governments," though "it cannot take the slightest imprint from them without marring the divine similitude" (IMCP 14).

Thus, when the terms are set by kingdom loyalty, informed and judicious political action may be required. Even in her lengthiest warning about the dangers associated with politics, Ellen White reminded readers "not to live reclusive lives" (FE 482) but, like Christ, to be involved in meeting human need. Specifically she exhorted Adventists to "take your position without wavering" (*ibid.*) on the temperance question, and in fact repeatedly prodded them to be more involved in working with the Women's Christian Temperance Union in mobilizing political influence for prohibition.

Finally, Ellen White saw that Adventists could, in a sense, make their most profound political impact by living up to their calling as a faithful remnant, a people true to Christ's kingdom of liberty and compassion in the midst of oppressive earthly kingdoms, as she had urged them to be in resisting the Fugitive Slave Act prior to the Civil War (1T 202). In so doing, they would join the "royal line" (Ed 255) of movements that have advanced the cause of liberty through history by witnessing "to the power of God's Word against human power and policy in support of evil" (*ibid.* 254).

The kingdom that Christ came to earth to establish, she wrote in 1896, was one that "would use no force" and whose "subjects would know no oppression." Christ in turn "required of His subjects that they give aid and protection to the oppressed." Those who would so respond could be assured that "there are triumphs yet to be accomplished through the blood shed for the world, that will bring glory to God and to the Lamb. His kingdom will extend, and embrace the whole world" (RH, Aug. 18, 1896).

Ellen White held out to Adventists the ideal of participation in the triumphs of Christ's kingdom. No other political entanglements should be permitted to turn them from the way of that kingdom. Yet she also tried to show them how kingdom faithfulness should lead them to discerning involvement in the political process so as to leave an imprint of the divine ideal of "a government that protects, restores, relieves, but never savors of oppression" (Ms 29, 1895, in 3MR 37, 38).

Further reading: Y. D. Anderson, "The Bible, the Bottle, and the Ballot: Seventh-day Adventist Political Activism, 1850-1900," *Adventist Heritage* 7, no. 2 (Fall 1982): 38-52; R. Branson, "Ellen G. White—Racist or Champion of Equality?" RH, Apr. 9, 1970; Apr. 16, 1970; Apr. 23, 1970; J. M. Butler, "Adventism and the American Experience," in E. S. Gaustad, ed., *The Rise of Adventism: Religion and Society in Mid-Nineteenth-Century* *America* (New York: Harper & Row, 1974), pp. 173-206; P. A. Gordon, "Shall I Exercise the Right to Vote?" (EGWE, SDoc); R. D. Graybill, *Ellen G. White and Church Race Relations* (RHPA, 1970); J. Kearnes, "Ethical Politics: Adventism and the Case of William Gage," *Adventist Heritage* 5, no. 1 (Summer 1978): 3-15; M. Kellner, "How Would Ellen White Vote?" AR, Sept. 11, 2008; D. Morgan, *Adventism and the American Republic: The Public Involvement of a Major Apocalyptic Movement* (Knoxville, Tenn.: University of Tennessee Press, 2001); Z. Plantak, *The Silent Church: Human Rights and Adventist Social Ethics* (New York: St. Martin's Press, 1998); E. D. Syme, *A History of SDA Church-State Relations in the United States* (PPPA, 1973).

Douglas Morgan

POLYGAMY. The practice of having multiple spouses at one time. The more technical word for having multiple wives is "polygyny," but in line with popular use, Ellen White used the generic "polygamy" or the phrase "plurality of wives" (SR 76).

Beginning in the book of Genesis, Ellen White observes that the marriage institution was established by God Himself in the Garden of Eden to be a blessing and benefit to humanity (2SM 421; AH 102). Noting that this first marriage, in which "God gave the man one wife," was to be "an example of what all marriages should be," she states that "wherever polygamy is practiced, it is against our heavenly Father's wise arrangement" (YI, Aug. 10, 1899).

Furthermore, Ellen White indicates that polygamy is "a violation of the law of God" (PP 145), "contrary to His will" (SR 76), and "directly opposed to the law of Jehovah" (7MR 74). More specifically, she considers polygamy a contravention of the seventh commandment, a satanic attempt "to pervert the marriage institution" (PP 338). Asserting that

"God has not sanctioned polygamy in a single instance" (SR 76), she says: "The gospel condemns the practice of polygamy" (ST, Oct. 26, 1888).

Ellen White comments on God's response to those who took a plurality of wives: Polygamy was "one of the great sins of the inhabitants of the old world, which brought the wrath of God upon them" (SR 76), in the form of the Flood. Similarly, regarding the actions of King David, she notes that "God shows His displeasure at David's having a plurality of wives by visiting him with judgments" (4aSG 87).

She maintains that besides direct punishments, additional problems result from polygamy. For the husband, marital peace is marred (3SG 126; SR 76), life is embittered (PP 190), and a long train of evil follows (ST, Feb. 5, 1880; Oct. 26, 1888). In fact, "the more men multiplied wives to themselves, the more they increased in wickedness and unhappiness" (3SG 63). The plural wives suffer from rivalry, envy, jealousy (PP 190), bitterness, and discontentment (ST, Dec. 18, 1879); and the children who experience such discord and rivalry may grow up revengeful, jealous, uncontrollable (*ibid.*), contentious, and impatient (PP 209).

The evil consequences of polygamy are not restricted to the immediate family. Ellen White notes that other contemporaries can be negatively affected (PK 59), as well as future generations (PP 145). Under the practice of polygamy "the race degenerates, and all that makes married life elevated and ennobling is blasted" (YI, Aug. 10, 1899). This is the surest way in which Satan can "deface the image of God in man and open the door to misery and vice" (PP 338).

Concerning the resolution of this issue, Ellen White indicates that God's purpose in directing Abraham to send away his second wife Hagar, was to "teach all a lesson in this,

that the rights and happiness of the marriage relation are to be ever respected and guarded, even at a great sacrifice" (SR 80). For Sarah was "the only true wife of Abraham," and "her rights as a wife and mother no other person was entitled to share" (PP 147).

From 1864, when the material currently in *Spiritual Gifts*, volumes 3 and 4, was first published, until her final major work, **Prophets and Kings*, Ellen White never vacillated in the consistent position she held against the practice of polygamy. These statements were not simply obsolete Victorian views or isolated personal pronouncements against the polygamous practices of nineteenth-century Mormons. Rather, her approach was a thoroughly biblical one in which she maintained that only faithfulness to the God-ordained, Edenic model of monogamous marriage would bring blessing, for "it elevates the physical, the intellectual, and the moral nature" (PP 46).

Further reading: R. M. Davidson, *The Flame of Yahweh: Sexuality in the Old Testament* (Peabody, Mass.: Hendrikson, 2007), pp. 177-212; R. du Preez, "Polygamy in the Bible With Implications for Seventh-day Adventist Missiology" (D.Min. project report, AU, 1993); *idem*, "Polygamy in the Writings of Ellen G. White, With Implications for Church Policy" (research paper, AU, 1988, CAR); R. L. Staples, "The Church and Polygamy in Sub-Saharan Africa" (typescript, 1981, CAR); *idem*, "Evangelism Among Resistant Peoples With Deeply Entrenched Polygamy," in Bruce L. Bauer, ed., *Adventist Responses to Cross-cultural Mission* (Berrien Springs, Mich.: Department of World Mission, AU, 2006), vol. 2, pp. 113-149.

Ron du Preez

POOR, see **WELFARE MINISTRY**.

PORK, see **UNCLEAN FOOD**.

PORTLAND, MAINE. Home of Ellen White during her childhood and adolescence and site of many of her early spiritual experiences. In the 1830s and 1840s Portland was a busy commercial seaport with a population of 15,218 in 1840; it was also home to American poet Henry Wadsworth Longfellow. Ellen White was born in the village of *Gorham, Maine, in 1827, about 12 miles (19 kilometers) west of Portland, and, with her family, moved to Portland when she was only a child. While the family lived on Clark Street her father, *Robert Harmon, engaged in a hatmaking business, and Ellen attended a nearby school on Brackett Street. At the age of 9, while returning home from school, she was injured by a stone thrown by a classmate. Ellen suffered a broken nose and severe concussion that left her in a coma for three weeks. This "misfortune" affected her for the rest of her life and prevented her from continuing her education (LS 19).

The Harmon family were members of the *Chestnut Street Methodist Church, where Robert served as an "exhorter," whose duties included those of a lay preacher as well as the opportunity to give a response to the Sunday sermon. This church was distinguished as one of the first Methodist churches in the United States to install a church organ, a controversial decision that took place during the Harmon family's membership there. In March 1840, and again in June 1842, Ellen and her family heard *William Miller preach in the *Casco Street Christian Connexion Church on the second advent of Christ and accepted his views that Christ would return about 1843. "These lectures produced a great sensation," she recalled about Miller's first visit, "and the Christian church on Casco Street, where the discourses were given, was crowded day and night. No wild excitement attended the meetings, but a deep solemnity pervaded the minds

of those who heard. Not only was a great interest manifested in the city, but the country people flocked in day after day, bringing their lunch baskets, and remaining from morning until the close of the evening meeting. In company with my friends, I attended these meetings. Mr. Miller traced down the prophecies with an exactness that struck conviction to the hearts of his hearers. He dwelt upon the prophetic periods, and brought many proofs to strengthen his position. Then his solemn and powerful appeals and admonitions to those who were unprepared held the crowds as if spellbound" (*ibid.* 20).

Later in the summer of 1840 (or possibly 1841) the family attended a camp meeting in the nearby village of Buxton, and Ellen made the decision to give her heart to God. Following a period of probation, she was baptized by immersion by Methodist pastor John Hobart in Casco Bay on June 26, 1842, and later that day was accepted into the Methodist Church. But the family's beliefs in the soon advent of Christ caused some tension with other church members, and in September 1843, after they refused to give up this belief, they were disfellowshipped from the church (*ibid.* 43-53).

A few weeks after the Millerite disappointment in October 1844, Ellen Harmon, now 17, had her first vision while staying with some friends at the home of *Elizabeth Haines. Haines was a close friend of Ellen's, one "whose heart was knit with mine." "In the morning we bowed at the family altar," she recalled. "It was not an exciting occasion. There were but five of us present, all females. While praying, the power of God came upon me as I never had felt it before." Then she described her first vision and the scenes she was shown (2SG 30, 35; cf. LS 64-68). Soon after this experience she shared her vision with the Adventist group in Portland and, from her home, went forth visiting other nearby towns to share with other Adventists the first visions she received. During one of these trips she recalled meeting James White for the first time in Orrington (LS 73)—although he remembered seeing her in Portland in 1843 or 1844 (JW, *Life Sketches* [1880], p. 126). On August 30, 1846, Ellen Harmon and James White were married by Justice Charles Harding in Portland. After making their home in her parents' house for a few weeks, James and Ellen White left Maine for good and began a life of ministry together for the next 35 years.

Ellen White returned to Portland many times during the early years of her ministry whenever she and James participated in meetings in the Eastern states. During a visit in September 1884, in connection with a camp meeting, she visited a number of places from her childhood. "I visited localities of special interest in connection with my early life, among them the spot where I met with the accident that has made me a lifelong invalid. . . . I passed the spot where the house once stood where Jesus revealed Himself to me in power, and I seemed to see His blessed face beaming upon me in divine love and gentleness. I also visited my early home, and the house where my first vision was given me; but railroad buildings have crowded out many dwellings that used to stand in this locality. In the chamber of the last-mentioned house, I once passed a night of anguish at the thought that I must go out and relate to others the things that God had presented before me. . . . I felt the deepest interest in the meeting in Portland, where my childhood and youth were passed. Some of my old schoolmates made themselves known to me on the ground. I also met a number of relatives who were my neighbors forty years ago. It afforded me great pleasure to meet and greet these old friends" (RH, Nov. 25, 1884; 3Bio 260, 261).

Ellen White's last visit to Portland occurred 25 years later, in July 1909, again to attend a camp meeting, and she stayed at the home of her nephew Clarence S. Bangs, son of her twin sister, *Elizabeth Bangs (6Bio 211-214). In connection with this visit she recalled that "in the city of Portland, the Lord ordained me as His messenger, and here my first labors were given to the cause of present truth" (Lt 138, 1909, in 6Bio 211).

See also: Conversion, Ellen G. White's.

Further reading: LS 17-64; 1Bio 22-63, 112; 3Bio 260, 261; 6Bio 211-214; *SDA Encyclopedia* (1996), vol. 11, pp. 873, 874; F. Hoyt, "Ellen White's Hometown: Portland, Maine, 1827-1846," in Gary Land, ed., *The World of Ellen G. White* (RHPA, 1987), pp. 13-31.

Denis Fortin

POWER, KINGLY, see **KINGLY POWER.**

PRAISE. For Ellen White all praise and thanksgiving are due God alone (YI, Nov. 24, 1903). All human beings have much to be thankful for, and praising God for His goodness and mercy should be a way of life. Whether in personal devotions or in public worship services, in times of affliction or in times of happiness, we should praise God (5T 315-319). "For life, health, food, and clothing, no less than for the hope of eternal life, we are indebted to the Giver of all mercies; and it is due to God to recognize His gifts, and to present our offerings of gratitude to our greatest benefactor" (RH, Dec. 9, 1890; AH 473). "A sense of the gratitude due to God will lead him [the Christian] to improve every opportunity for expressing thanksgiving, which will be accepted as a testimony of loyalty. Faithfulness toward God in the performance of good works will bring God's blessing. As we show ourselves faithful in fulfilling our trust, our influence leads others to do likewise. They are filled with thanksgiving and praise to God as the one to whom praise is due" (RH, Sept. 19, 1899).

While Ellen White invites parents to teach their children to be thankful and grateful for what they have (CG 148, 149) and to join with the heavenly angels in giving all praise to God (CT 246), she insists that praise toward human beings is contrary to God's will. To pastors she repeatedly counseled not to permit anyone to praise them (Ev 630), nor to strive for praise and applause (*ibid.* 181). Such praise, resembling flattery, is a weapon of the devil to ruin souls (COL 161). We are to express "appreciation, sympathy, and encouragement, but care should be taken not to foster . . . a love of praise" in people (Ed 237), as it tends to foster self-confidence and to corrupt rather than purify the soul (3T 474).

PRAYER. To Ellen White, prayer was simply talking to God as to a friend (SC 93). When she prayed, she was not engaged in a dry, ritualistic duty. Through praise and petition she was connecting her heart to the heart of her dearest Friend, Jesus, and tasting a bit of heaven on earth in His presence. She felt that no concern was too trivial to bring before the Lord in prayer. "We may bring Him our little cares and perplexities as well as our greater troubles" (5T 200, 201). Even a toothache was not too small an item for Ellen White to pray about. In 1893 many of Ellen White's teeth were abscessing and causing her a great deal of pain. By letter she invited *Margaret Caro, a dentist in whose home Ellen White had once stayed, to come to Wellington and extract her troublesome teeth. Because of bad reactions to medication, Ellen White endured having eight teeth extracted without anything to deaden the pain. She wrote about the experience in her diary: "I did not wince or groan. . . . I had asked the Lord to strengthen me and give me grace to endure the painful

process, and I know the Lord heard my prayer" (4Bio 98).

Ellen White believed that faith and prayer were closely linked, and that there was a "divine science" to prayer that needed to be mastered (Ed 257). That "science" consisted of (1) asking consistent with God's will, (2) asking for things that He has already promised (i.e., for the Holy Spirit, a Christlike attitude, for forgiveness of sin, power and wisdom to do His work, for any gift He says we can have), (3) believing that we actually receive the things we are requesting, and (4) giving thanks to God that we *have* received them (*ibid.* 258). A surrendered life in which there is a continual awareness of need and dependence on God was also a vital element in this science of prayer.

A childhood memory belonging to Edith Donaldson, who had traveled with the Whites on a trip from Oregon to Michigan, gives us a window into the private prayer life of Ellen White. As a young girl Edith had often slept in the same room with Ellen and was awakened early each morning by her prayers. Ellen White would kneel beside her bed, "her eyes open and looking upward, her hands clasped and moving one over the other, in the manner familiar to those who have seen her in prayer. She prayed aloud, and although Edith was but a child, these words, which she heard, have rung in her ears throughout all her life. 'He is the chiefest among ten thousand and altogether lovely.' 'He is high and lifted up, and the train of His glory fills the temple'" ("For a Purpose," YI, Sept. 4, 1945). It is apparent from this anecdote that praise as well as petition was a regular feature of Ellen White's communion with God. To her, prayer was more than asking for things (cf. 5T 317). It provided her with the opportunity to focus on the beauty of God's character, and to adore Him with words of affirmation, admiration, and praise.

From this anecdote we receive a picture of Ellen White praying "aloud" with "eyes open and looking upward." Not that she made herself a pattern for other Christians to follow, but from Scripture as well as from her example we can confidently engage in a variety of postures and expressions in prayer. Scripture shows God's people praying while standing (Neh. 9:4, 5; Luke 18:11, 13; 1 Kings 8:14, 22, 23, 55), kneeling (1 Kings 8:54), sitting (2 Sam. 7:18; Ex. 17:11, 12), and lying down (Joshua 7:6; Matt. 26:39; Ps. 6:6-9; 63:6). While Ellen White taught that kneeling is always appropriate, especially for the main prayer of the worship service (2SM 311), she also led in prayers while standing (3SM 267-270), or while the congregation remained seated (Diary, Feb. 20, Ms 29, 1887, in 1SM 147; 3SM 267, 268). She believed that reverence, humility, and dependence on God are expressed by kneeling, but "there is no time or place in which it is inappropriate to offer up a petition to God" (SC 99; cf. MH 310, 311; GW 258). On February 13, 1892, in Melbourne, Australia, because of severe rheumatism, she had to be carried up a long stairway to a meeting hall in the arms of her son and a layman. She lamented that "I was not able to bow my knees in the opening prayer or when I entered the desk [pulpit] as I usually do, *but the form is not the essential part.* My heart went up to God in earnest prayer, and He did help me and, I believe, gave me a decided message for the people assembled" (Ms 29, 1892; italics supplied).

It is also apparent from this story that praise as well as petition was a regular feature of Ellen White's communion with God. To her, prayer was more than asking for things (cf. 5T 317). It provided her with the opportunity to focus on the beauty of God's character, and to adore Him with words of affirmation, admiration, and praise.

In regard to prayers offered in public, Ellen White emphasized that they should be "short and to the point" (Ev 146); "long, prosy talks and prayers" are inappropriate anywhere in her opinion, and bring fatigue to angels and humans alike (RH, Oct. 10, 1882; 4T 70). She instructed that for the most part, family concerns should be dealt with at the "family altar," while a present blessing should be sought for in the public meeting (1T 145, 146).

Family worship was also important to Ellen White. "In every family," she wrote, "there should be a fixed time for morning and evening worship" (7T 43). In the White household these times of worship were not drawn-out and boring events that the children dreaded. Rather, they were times of thanksgiving that were filled with interest and involvement from everyone.

The daily worship program was fairly consistent in the White family. By 6:00 a.m. everyone was up. Many times Ellen White had already been writing for two or three hours before this. Breakfast was served by 6:30. At 7:00 everyone gathered for worship. James White would read from the Bible, share some devotional thoughts, and then lead the family in singing a song of praise. This time of singing was followed by prayer. This prayer, usually offered by James White, was not stiff and formal. "He *prayed* with earnestness and with solemn reverence. He pleaded for those blessings most needed by himself and his family, and for the prosperity of the cause of God" (1Bio 402). When James White was away from home, Ellen would lead the family worship. If both were gone, the appointed caretaker led out. "The worship hour was as regularly observed as the hours for breakfast and dinner" (*ibid.*). Between 7:00 and 8:00 in the evenings, this scene was repeated again, with the added feature of Ellen White reading an interesting article or story from a magazine or book. "There is no reason why this hour of worship should not be the most pleasant and enjoyable of the day," she wrote. "God is dishonored when the hour of worship is made dry and irksome, when it is so tedious, so lacking in interest, that the children dread it" (7T 43).

*Prayer for the sick formed a vital part of Ellen White's life and ministry. She believed that medical and natural treatments should be combined with "simple, fervent prayer . . . for the blessing of healing" (3SM 296). She made no distinction between the days of the disciples and modern times in terms of God's willingness and ability to heal the sick. "His disciples in this time are to pray for the sick as verily as the disciples of old prayed. And recoveries will follow; for 'the prayer of faith shall save the sick.' . . . The Lord's promise, 'They shall lay hands on the sick, and they shall recover' (Mark 16:18), is just as trustworthy now as in the days of the apostles" (MH 226).

Though believing and experiencing the power of God through prayer, Ellen White was a realist and knew that not all prayers are answered the way we expect or desire. Sin that is not repented of, selfishness in not returning to God a faithful tithe, claiming the promises without complying with the conditions (COL 144), praying halfheartedly without faith—these are some of the causes for failure in prayer.

Communion with God in prayer was always considered the highest of privileges by Ellen White. She believed that prayer was the key to revival (1SM 121-128), and the breath of the soul. She believed that while God doesn't answer every prayer the way we expect, in His infinite love and wisdom He always gives us "those things which we most need" (4T 531).

See also: Prayer for the Sick; Spirituality.

Further reading: *Prayer*; SC 93-104.
Randy Maxwell

PRAYER (PPPA, 2002, 320 pp.). A compilation of 32 relatively short chapters drawn from Ellen White's numerous references to prayer in her previously published writings. The book covers a wide range of topics; from God's willingness to hear prayer to demonic deceptions about prayer. It includes chapters on private prayer, prayer and soul winning, prayer and faith, counterfeit prayers, attitudes in prayer, prayer and revival, prayer for the sick, answered prayer, prayer in the last days, and Jesus' example in prayer. The book ends with four of Ellen White's most significant chapters on prayer published in their entirety.

Ron E. M. Clouzet

PRAYER FOR THE SICK. Ellen White was a strong supporter of prayer for the sick, stressing that God never turns away from the sincere seeker, that He is just as willing to restore the sick today as when the psalmist wrote (Ps. 107:20), that God heals (MH 225), and that Christ has the same compassion today for the sick as when He was on this earth (FLB 315).

Ellen's White's theology was very clear concerning the cause and remedy for sickness, suffering, and death. Satan and the sin that resulted from his rebellion are clearly identified as the cause for both physical and spiritual disease. It is God who restores (MM 11), not humans or anointing services, and not even God's chosen messenger (3SM 295). Healing is God's work.

Ellen White took part in anointing services even though she was not an ordained elder (5MR 239; 1Bio 404). She believed that the encouragement to call the elders for prayer and anointing in James 5:14 was primarily for those "among us." That is, the ceremony of anointing should ordinarily be reserved for those who are willing to "keep God's commandments" (PaM 234). Anointing services should not be employed for every little ailment, but should be for those who are sick upon their beds (MM 16). Prayer without anointing may be used for all people and all ailments (see below).

She recognized that not all sick persons whom church members pray for will be healed. Neither should a lack of healing be used as a basis for telling the sick person that they lack faith (GW 218, 219). Rather, the sick should be encouraged to trust in Jesus, to be cheerful, and to put aside discouragement. Anxiety and worry do nothing to encourage health and healing, but actually lead to weakness and disease (MH 229).

Two conditions that often hinder God from His work of healing are mentioned. First, when Christians are covetous and worldly, God cannot work through them, for unbelief and sin block the power of God. Those praying for the sick must live holy lives (2SM 347) and should not expect the promises for healing to be fulfilled if they are living in sin (MH 227). A second hindrance to healing occurs when God's people are unable to deal correctly with spiritual blessings and healings. Instead of giving God the glory and realizing that God heals because He is loving and compassionate, believers often take the credit for themselves, feeling that they are good and righteous (2T 149).

One statement seems to contradict the many other statements concerning God's willingness to heal when she says that God cannot now work through miraculous healings because Satan also performs such miracles (MM 14). The statement was made in the context of early Adventism, when many miraculous healings occurred as a direct answer to prayer but those healed continued to practice the same unhealthful lifestyle (5Bio

387). Ellen White suggested that what was needed was a health institution where the teaching of principles of healthful living could be combined with the teaching of the Word of God (MM 14).

Several general principles dealing with prayer for the sick are stressed. Perhaps that which is most often neglected in the Christian world is the importance of combining faith in God's healing power with a personal effort by the sick person to practice principles of healthful living (HL 238). The sick should use simple remedies and observe the laws of health and life (CD 26), and do everything within their power to encourage healing.

Prayers offered for the sick should take the form of petitions and not commands for healing (MH 230; GW 218), since only God knows what is right and best for each situation (2T 148). Early in Ellen White's ministry she and others had prayed insistent prayers for the sick, only to see them, after being healed, continue to live degraded and sinful lives, bringing shame upon their families, their church, and their God (2T 148, 149). Therefore, those praying for the sick should only pray for God's will to be done in each situation (GW 217).

Modern healing services where the pastor or evangelist shouts and commands the sick to be healed do not fall within the parameters of God's ideal. Healings do not happen because of shouting, excitement, or zeal, but because of God's compassion and will to heal (2T 147). Ellen White often refers to praying for the sick as a solemn task, not something to enter into lightly or presumptuously.

Prayers of presumption would include praying for those who have total disregard for healthful habits of eating, drinking, dressing, and working or praying for those living in open sin and rebellion (MH 227, 228). Before praying for healing, provision should be made for the sick person to make restitution, for sins to be confessed and for wrongs to be righted (HL 236). But that does not mean that we should not pray for those who break the laws of health, or for those who live outside of God's will; rather we should combine prayer with education concerning God's will and teach the principles of health (MH 227; GW 215, 216).

Christ still desires to show His presence in the sickroom, but when people neglect to pray, the sick are deprived of God's blessing (MM 195). The church today would see many more healings if more prayers were offered for the sick (3SM 295).

Bruce L. Bauer

PRAYER MEETING, see **SOCIAL MEETINGS**.

PREACHING. Ellen White believed that "preaching of the gospel is God's chosen agency for the salvation of souls," and that "no department of the work of God" is "as constantly under the eye of God as is the preaching of the Word" (5T 87; Lt 32, 1875). Preaching thus held a high place in her thought and writings. The majority of her experience and writing about preaching came after her husband's death in 1881, when she was 53 years of age. Her counsel on preaching can be organized under four categories: source, objective, function, and delivery (Turner, pp. 36-46, 91ff.).

First, she maintained that the *source* of the sermon should be the Bible. Her view of the Bible led her to the conviction that it was the written Word of God and thus "God's voice speaking to us" (6T 393). Accordingly, she exhorted ministers to thoroughly study the Scriptures and then "preach the Word." Three times she wrote articles for the *Review and Herald* titled "Preach the Word" (Apr. 24, 1888; Sept. 28, 1897; Nov. 3, 1904). Her book *Gospel Workers* (1915) included an

entire section entitled "The Minister in the Pulpit," with subsections headed "'Preach the Word'" and "Breaking the Bread of Life to Souls" (GW 147-155). By "preach the Word," she meant that ministers should proclaim the truths in the Old and New Testaments "as the word of the living God" (RH, Nov. 3, 1904). While discussing 2 Timothy 4:1, 2, where Paul charged Timothy to "preach the word," she admonished ministers to "speak in sincerity and deep earnestness, as a voice from God expounding the Sacred Scriptures" (GW 147). Such was her understanding of the source for preaching.

Second, Ellen White saw the *objective* of preaching to be the salvation of souls. This was a consistent theme in her counsel on preaching from the late 1870s to 1915 and agreed with the teaching in American homiletical textbooks of the time (Turner, pp. 38-41). Third, her early concept of the *function* of preaching centered on arousal, conviction, and persuasion (1T 645; 2T 336; 4T 413). In the 1880s she added the dimension of teaching (5T 298, 300). The minister, she admonished, must "teach the saving power of Jesus" and the "great practical truths that must be brought into the life" (GW 147). Thus, by the 1890s Ellen White viewed the sermon as a vehicle for arousal, conviction, persuasion, and instruction.

Fourth, her counsel on *delivery* reflected her Methodist background. As such, she urged preachers to preach with simplicity and calmness while relying on the deep movings of the Holy Spirit to bring conviction to the listeners (RH, Feb. 22, 1887). She was against using humor of a "joking" or "clownishness" kind (Turner, p. 95). Illustrations can be used but should be chosen with guidance from the Holy Spirit in order not to detract from the main objective of saving souls (*ibid.*, p. 93). Also, the length of sermons should not generally exceed 30 minutes (Lt 1a, 1896). Finally, less dependence on sermon notes and more dependence on the Holy Spirit should characterize sermon delivery (GW 165).

Ellen White's preaching covered a variety of subjects. According to Shaw and Turner (Turner, pp. 146-148), among the 471 sermons studied from the period 1865-1915, she covered the following range of topics: Christian faith and life (284), ministry (65), education (39), medical work (31), miscellaneous topics (28), health and temperance (20), and publishing (4). Her sermons reflected a conversational style in which one thought tended to suggest another. While Scripture was the major source of her sermons, she used a hybrid method of the topical and textual methods. Her sermons, therefore, were not expository in the sense of the biblical passage controlling the outline of the sermon. Nevertheless, she admonished ministers to preach biblical sermons (PaM 188-190). One notable characteristic in her preaching was the frequency of appeals. In every one of her sermons on Christian faith and living she made one or more appeals for listeners to make a life change (Shaw, p. 350; Turner, p. 102).

One area where her practice was inconsistent with her theory concerned the length of sermons. While she advocated short sermons in theory, her actual practice was to preach more than an hour. She considered herself an exception, and when questioned on this issue admitted that she may "have ventured too far even in the exception" (Ms 19b, 1890, in 2SAT 85). Concerning Ellen White's effectiveness in the pulpit, Turner noted that the prime force for her effectiveness in preaching "was not her ability as an orator," but "her personal ethos in and out of the pulpit" (Turner, p. 103).

While her counsel on preaching reflected the mainstream of American homiletical thought in the latter nineteenth century, she maintained a close affinity with Wesleyan thought. As such, in the 1890s she was found advocating a method of preaching similar to *John Wesley. First, present Jesus Christ as the sin-pardoning Savior; second, bring judgment and conviction by presenting the law; and third, point the listeners to the gospel as the only hope for salvation (6T 53, 54; Turner, p. 111). Accordingly, she repeatedly emphasized that Christ and His redemptive works should fill the mind of the minister and result in an attitude of "love and deep earnestness" during sermon delivery (4T 400; PaM 190-192). Ultimately, the preacher should "lift up Jesus" and present Him "as the hope of the penitent and the stronghold of every believer" (GW 160).

Further reading: Sermons and Talks; PaM 187-200; L. Hardinge, "An Examination of the Philosophy of Persuasion in Pulpit Oratory Advocated by Ellen Gould White" (M.A. thesis, SDA Theological Seminary, 1950); L. Hardinge, "A Survey and Evaluation of the Theory of Illustration of Ellen Gould White" (B.D. thesis, SDA Theological Seminary, 1953); J. H. Shaw, "A Rhetorical Analysis of the Speaking of Mrs. Ellen G. White, a Pioneer Leader and Spokeswoman of the Seventh-day Adventist Church" (Ph.D. diss., Michigan State University, 1959); R. E. Turner, *Proclaiming the Word: The Concept of Preaching in the Thought of Ellen G. White* (AUP, 1980).

Jud Lake

PREDICTIONS OF ELLEN G. WHITE. The word "prophet" may suggest to modern minds the ability to make predictions. Ellen White never claimed to be a "prophet," because her work included "much more than this name signifies. I regard myself as a messenger, entrusted by the Lord with messages for His people," she wrote (1SM 36). The test of a prophet/messenger lies in a direction other than to focus on the number of his or her predictions. Further, the principle of conditional prophecy as it applies to both the biblical prophets and to Ellen White must be taken into account. However, Ellen White did make some dramatic and far-reaching predictions that have stood the test of time, some of them becoming more relevant as the years pass.

Two visions about the American Civil War were especially notable. In early January 1861, even though South Carolina had voted, December 20, 1860, to secede from the Union, actual secession did not appear certain, and virtually no one believed there would be war. On January 12, 1861, exactly three months before the first shots of the Civil War were fired at Fort Sumter, White had a vision at a meeting in Parkville, Michigan, predicting civil war. At that early date she was shown the naïveté of the North, the rapid coalition of the Southern states, and the "terrible war" that would result—even the sober fact that families at that Parkville meeting in January 1861 would lose sons in that war (1T 253, 254, 260; 1Bio 462, 463; JNL, *The Great Second Advent Movement*, pp. 337, 338).

On August 3, 1861, at Roosevelt, New York, White had her second Civil War vision, again with depth and breadth not foreseen by others. It focused on the evil of slavery—the North was to blame for the continuing extension of slavery, and the South for the sin of slavery. For the next few years she penned a continuing analysis of the motives and intrigue that characterized both Southern and Northern leaders (1T 264-268, 355-368; PUR, Mar. 7, 1912).

In the middle of the nineteenth century White's preview of world conditions in the end-times may have seemed overdrawn. Her predictions of the rise of spiritualism were given when spiritualistic manifestations were local, isolated, and more of a curiosity than anything else. Distinct from mysticism or classical spirituality, or Eastern religions (which advocate direct contact with God through mystical means, such as contemplative prayer, mantras, etc.), occult spiritualism promotes contact with the unseen world by communication with the dead through séances, Ouija boards, rappings, etc., or through the mind of a medium.

In 1848 White was shown that the strange "rappings" involving the Fox sisters in Hydesville, New York, were the first indications of the revival of spiritualism in modern times: "I saw that the mysterious knocking in New York and other places was the power of Satan, and that such things would be more and more common, clothed in a religious garb so as to lull the deceived to greater security" (EW 43). Spiritualism has never been more prominent in the history of the world than it is today. Adherents include people at all levels of society and in every economic class.

Another prediction that seemed unlikely in the middle of the nineteenth century was the revival of the Papacy as a worldwide power that would influence the merger of spiritualism and Protestantism with itself. When under "this threefold union, our country shall repudiate every principle of its Constitution as a Protestant and republican government, and shall make provision for the propagation of papal falsehoods and delusions, then we may know that the time has come for the marvelous working of Satan and that the end is near" (5T 451). The end product will be coercive religious laws: "Let the principle once be established in the United States that the church may employ or control the power of the state; that religious observances may be enforced by secular laws; in short, that the authority of church and state is to dominate the conscience, and the triumph of Rome in this country is assured" (GC 581).

One of her most far-reaching predictions of the mid-nineteenth century was that the

United States, a comparatively insignificant young nation at that time, would become a global superpower before the end of time: "As America, the land of religious liberty, shall unite with the papacy in forcing the conscience and compelling men to honor the false sabbath, the people of every country on the globe will be led to follow her example" (6T 18).

Another startling aspect of her general predictions in the waning years of the nineteenth century was directly against the prevailing emphasis, especially between 1890 and 1914. In 1903, at the height of this period of optimism that some called the "golden age," she wrote: "Step by step, the world is reaching the conditions that existed in the days of Noah. Every conceivable crime is committed. The lust of the flesh, the pride of the eyes, the display of selfishness, the misuse of power, the cruelty, and the force used to cause men to unite with confederacies and unions—binding themselves up in bundles for the burning of the great fires of the last days—all these are the working of Satanic agencies. This round of crime and folly men call 'life.' . . . The whole world appears to be in the march to death" (Ev 26).

Regarding economic and social impasses, she wrote: "There are not many, even among educators and statesmen, who comprehend the causes that underlie the present state of society. Those who hold the reins of government are not able to solve the problem of moral corruption, poverty, pauperism, and increasing crime. They are struggling in vain to place business operations on a more secure basis. If men would give more heed to the teaching of God's Word, they would find a solution of the problems that perplex them" (9T 13).

Ellen White's practical comments on health, *diet, and the environment have stood the test of the years—something that probably cannot be said about any other writer in the

nineteenth century. Among her numerous comments we can refer to her profound emphasis on how the mind affects the body in producing sickness (1T 566; 3T 184; MH 241); her concern for prenatal influences, including drugs and alcohol (2SM 441, 442; PP 561); and her monumental interactive system of dietary principles that are increasingly supported by nutritional research, including the dangers of the free use of sugar and animal fats, the problems of obesity and irregularity in eating, the towering value of exercise, the challenge of childhood diet patterns, the dangers in flesh food, tea, and coffee (CD 15-51).

Ellen White also predicted denominational matters. In November 1848, at a time of great financial stress, and appealing to no more than 100 Sabbatarian Adventists, she predicted that the periodical her husband was starting would be "small at first," but eventually its "streams of light" would go "clear round the world" (LS 125). Adventist publications today are distributed in more than 230 languages by representatives in more than 204 countries.

In November 1901 White wrote a severe warning to the board of trustees of the Review and Herald Publishing Association. Problems included the fact that 90 percent of their work was commercial, some of it clearly inappropriate for a religious press. Ellen White sounded the warning—a prediction: "I have been almost afraid to open the *Review*, fearing to see that God has cleansed the publishing house by fire. . . . Unless there is a reformation, calamity will overtake the publishing house, and the world will know the reason" (8T 91-96). Thirteen months later, December 30, 1902, a fire of "unknown origin" destroyed the complex—nothing of value was saved.

On October 13, 1902, she wrote that properties with buildings "especially suited to sanitarium work" could be bought "at much less than their original cost" (Lt 157, 1902, in 4MR 280). Thus she pushed reluctant administrators to purchase land for several Adventist health-care institutions in southern California. Before church leaders could catch their breath after purchasing the Loma Linda property, Ellen White was painting the future of Loma Linda as the principal center for educating medical personnel. Without these insights, constantly encouraging the small denomination, the Glendale Adventist Medical Center and the Loma Linda University and Medical Center would not be the centers of humanitarian service that they are today. But far beyond any human aspiration, she was calmly adamant: "This will be" (in SHM 352).

See also: Apocryphal Visions and Statements; Prophet, Ellen G. White Not a.

Further reading: H. E. Douglass, *Messenger of the Lord* (PPPA, 1998), pp. 150-169; *idem, Dramatic Prophecies of Ellen White: Stories of World Events Divinely Foretold* (PPPA, 2007); JNL, *The Great Second Advent Movement: Its Rise and Progress* (RHPA, 1905).

Herbert E. Douglass

PRESENT TRUTH. Ellen White makes the explicit claim that ever since 1844 she had been proclaiming what she described as *present truth*. We may understand what this concept meant for Ellen White and the early Adventists from two angles. Formally, and primarily, the concept meant truth that was time-sensitive; truth that was chronologically destined to be proclaimed at that time. In at least two places she refers to "truth for this time" (1SM 161; 6T 291), although this was not to suggest that what she called present truth was significant for their time *only*. While elsewhere there seems to be the suggestion that each period has had its present truth, the present truth that she proclaimed was definitive: by it the world will be tested. Furthermore, this present truth

is to prepare God's people for the kingdom of glory, and no new light will contradict it.

In a material and general sense, however, the *present truth* was Bible-based, and embraces the whole gospel. This present truth had its particular expression in the truths that were developed and continue to be held by Seventh-day Adventists. In the context of 6T 290, 291, it is quite clear that by "present truth" Ellen White has in mind the cluster of truths that surround the three angels' messages of Revelation 14. The present truth, however, is a philosophy in the sense that it is not an abstract truth, but truth that influences the life. Its effect is to "work in man the very changes that will make evident the power of God's grace upon the heart" (6T 291). The message of present truth must be proclaimed everywhere, and the success of this effort will depend on the purity in heart and life of its messengers.

Further reading: EW 262; GW 27, 265; 1SM 160-163; 2SM 102; 2T 78, 355; 3T 205.

Kwabena Donkor

PRESENT TRUTH, THE. Ellen White published articles in two separate Adventist journals called *The Present Truth.* As the group of Sabbatarian Adventists began to take shape and unify around a set of key doctrines in 1848 and 1849, James White, upon the urging of Ellen White, began the publication of a "little paper," *The Present Truth,* devoted at first largely to the Sabbath doctrine. Eleven numbers were printed between July 1849 and November 1850. Soon this paper was accompanied by another one, *The Advent Review,* in an attempt to show how Sabbatarian Adventists were carrying forward the prophetic Advent message discovered during the Millerite movement. Five numbers were printed between August and November 1850. In December 1850 these two journals were merged to form the *Second Advent Review and Sabbath Herald,* today known as the *Adventist Review*. In *The Present Truth* Ellen White published five accounts of her visions (August 1849; September 1849; March 1850; April 1850; November 1850), most of which were republished in her *Sketch of the Christian Experience and Views of Ellen G. White* (1851) (see EW 36-52).

When Seventh-day Adventists began their work in England, church leaders felt it necessary to also start a journal for European English-speaking people. The British *Present Truth* began to be published in 1885, and between November 1885 and September 1893 carried 15 articles written by Ellen White—seven of which are a reprint and expansion of her pamphlet "The Sufferings of Christ," first published in 1869 (2T 200-215).

PRINCIPLES OF TRUE SCIENCE: OR, CREATION IN THE LIGHT OF REVELATION (Takoma Park, Md.: Washington Missionary College Press, 1929, 720 pp.). The combined and expanded contents of two earlier compilations: the first, compiled from Ellen G. White's writings, was also entitled *Principles of True Science* (Healdsburg College Press, 1900); the second, containing biblical references to the subject of science, was titled *Science in the Bible* (Healdsburg College Press, 1903). *Marion E. Cady, compiler of both earlier books, also edited this expanded compilation. Alphabetically arranged entries are thoroughly cross-referenced. Along with much about the life of Christ and biblical history, content ranges from health advice to condemnation of clairvoyants. Within this milieu—much of it tangential to modern ideas of science—the most familiar Ellen White statements on science are present and accessible through a brief index. A major theme of the book is that nature can be understood only in light of revelation.

Timothy G. Standish

PROBATION, CLOSE OF. Ellen White understood the close of probation to refer to that time prior to the second advent of Jesus when the eternal destiny of all people living on earth has been decided. The righteous have been sealed (endorsed by God as people He can trust), and the wicked deepen their resistance to the Holy Spirit's pleading. Both Daniel (12:1) and John the revelator (Rev. 22:11) refer to this end-time event, which includes a heavenly decree proclaiming that probation time has ended, followed by an unprecedented *time of trouble (seven last *plagues, Rev. 15; 16) and the deliverance of the redeemed at Christ's return. In sanctuary language Jesus, our high priest, has ended His mediatorial work—the cases of all, living or dead, have been decided, and thus there remains no need for time to linger. Those living in this end-time are either sealed (settled "into the truth, both intellectually and spiritually, so they cannot be moved" [LDE 220]) or "marked" as opposed to God's will (Rev. 13:16)—so settled in their resistance to truth that they can never be moved to repentance.

Solemn is the thought that probation closes when the last of the living have settled into their unmovable character patterns. No second probation follows this end-time closing of probation. When Jesus returns, "He is not to cleanse us of our sins, to remove from us the defects in our characters, or to cure us of the infirmities of our tempers and dispositions. If wrought for us at all, this work will all be accomplished before that time.... This is all to be done in these hours of probation" (2T 355).

See also: Investigative Judgment; Sanctuary; Seal of God.

Further reading: GC 613-634; TM 235, 236; 2T 355, 356; 1SM 66; LDE 227-237.

Herbert E. Douglass

PROBLEM STATEMENTS, see general article: **CURRENT SCIENCE AND ELLEN WHITE: TWELVE CONTROVERSIAL STATEMENTS.**

PROHIBITION. Ellen White's growth to young adulthood in Maine—the first state to enact a prohibition law (1851)—placed her in the geographical center of the first wave of nineteenth-century American *temperance reform. When the second reform wave hit in 1873, women, Ellen White among them, took the lead and remained the movement's dominant force for the subsequent quarter of a century. The *Woman's Christian Temperance Union (WCTU) organized women into a national network of activists under visionary leadership, addressing not only the liquor industry but also the poverty, domestic abuse, oppression of workers, and political corruption that they believed were fueled largely by alcohol. Ellen White persistently prodded Adventists to work with this progressive reform association, and modeled such involvement by becoming a well-regarded lecturer at temperance rallies led by the WCTU and other reform organizations. In the opening decades of the twentieth century, as a third wave led the movement closer to the victory represented by national prohibition, Ellen White remained an indefatigable and fervent advocate of Adventist involvement in the prohibition movement. She was still active in preparing articles for periodicals when the final one on that topic during her lifetime appeared in the *Review and Herald* of October 15, 1914.

During her 40-year stretch of public advocacy for prohibition, Ellen White charted a course that, in several ways, transcended typical labels and categories, holding together values often thought to be polar opposites.

1. Personal piety *and* public activism. By the time Ellen White began to speak out for temperance in the public arena in 1874, the church had already taken important steps toward resolving the tension between their radical Christian piety and the self-serving, morally-compromised realm of partisan *politics and voting. A consensus supported by Ellen White had emerged: use of the vote on behalf of a just and humane cause could be a Christian duty, particularly when doing nothing would aid and abet evil.

Thus, as a temperance reformer, Ellen White became adamant that any approach to the issue would be entirely inadequate if it did not include working through the political process for prohibition laws. A striking case in point came at the Iowa camp meeting in 1881. As she prepared for sleep on a Sunday evening, Ellen White was summoned back to the main tent to head off a move to delete, from a proposed resolution, the phrase "the ballot box" as a means for supporting temperance. She declared that Adventists should vote for prohibition "to a man, everywhere," adding, "perhaps I shall shock some of you if I say, If necessary, vote on the Sabbath day for prohibition if you cannot at any other time" (3Bio 160).

The following November she published an article in the *Review and Herald* illustrative of dozens that appeared with her byline in Adventist periodicals from 1878 to 1914, making the case for prohibition in prose burning with moral passion and emotion-stirring depictions of the liquor traffic's devastating impact on society. In addition to the abuse of women and children in the home resulting from drunkenness, she wrote, "Society is corrupted, workhouses and prisons are crowded with paupers and criminals, and the gallows is supplied with victims. . . . The burdens of taxation are increased, the morals of the young are imperiled, the property, and even the life, of every member of society is endangered" (RH, Oct. 15, 1914; GW 386, 387).

Commendable efforts to help individuals change would never bring success to the temperance cause, she argued, so long as the law supports the liquor traffic in creating a societal environment in which the allure of drink overwhelms human weakness. By licensing the sale of liquor "our laws sustain an evil which is sapping their very foundations" and is causing a "moral paralysis on society." Because in America "every voter has some voice" in those laws, she reasoned, all share responsibility for them. Thus: "The advocates of temperance fail to do their whole duty unless they exert their influence by precept and example—by voice and pen and vote—in favor of prohibition and total abstinence" (RH, Oct. 15, 1914; cf. Te 253, 254).

A broad conception of human interconnectedness emerged in Ellen White's writings as a foundation for caring about suffering and evil in the wider world beyond one's immediate sphere, and therefore exerting political influence on behalf of prohibition: "We are all woven together in the web of humanity. The evil that befalls any part of the great human brotherhood brings peril to all" (MH 345).

Corollary to holding together social reform and individual piety, Ellen White's advocacy for prohibition held together activism for social change in the present with hope for the future grounded fully in the return of Christ. When the city of San Francisco reopened the saloons after closing them briefly in the aftermath of the great earthquake in 1906, Ellen White warned of impending apocalyptic judgment and the soon return of Jesus. The action for which she called in light of that apocalyptic warning, however, was societal change in the present: "O that our cities might reform! In places where the judgments of heaven have fallen, God is now proving those whose lives He has spared, as to whether they will continue to allow health and reason to be destroyed by the sale of maddening drink" (RH, Oct. 25, 1906).

Ellen White did not view movements for societal change as bringing about the final realization of God's new world, but she did characterize such endeavors as being in continuity with that world to come. She assured *S.M.I. Henry, a WCTU leader who joined the Adventist Church in 1896, that "labor spent in advancing the kingdom of God in this world will carry its results into the future eternal kingdom of God" (RH, May 9, 1899).

2. Adventist distinctiveness and interchurch coalitions. Ellen White's career as a public temperance lecturer began in the summer of 1874 when temperance organizers in Battle Creek asked her to speak at a citywide rally in McCamly Park. Collaboration with the Battle Creek Reform Club and the WCTU led to an event on an even grander scale in the summer of 1877, at which Ellen White lectured before an audience of 5,000. Also in 1877 a report in the *Daily Bulletin* of Haverhill, Massachusetts, where she had spoken on temperance to huge Sunday afternoon throngs at camp meeting for two years running and in city hall at a meeting of the Haverhill Reform Club the previous year, described her as a "forcible and impressive speaker" who "holds the crowd with her clear utterances and convincing logic" (3Bio 67). Instances of Ellen White's eager collaboration with civic and reform organizations recurred frequently throughout her travels in the United States, Europe, and Australia over the next couple of decades (see LLM 238, 239).

In addition to her own involvement, Ellen White repeatedly impressed upon a seemingly reluctant church the enormous reciprocal benefits of cooperating with interchurch reform agencies "in benefiting and elevating humanity" (RH, Feb. 10, 1885; Te 221). She envisioned

Adventists "at the head in the temperance reform" (RH, Oct. 21, 1884; Te 233), indeed, "in the forefront of every true reform" (RH, Aug. 29, 1907; Te 234)—but recognized their need—of guidance from experienced activists in pursuing that goal. Thus, she recommended that WCTU women be invited to Adventist camp meetings to teach "our sisters how to work" (LLM 235; Te 224). The Adventist people had "lost much" as a consequence of "holding ourselves aloof from the workers of the W.C.T.U.," Ellen White lamented in 1907, adding that in some respects "they are far in advance of our leaders" (LLM 258-260; 1MR 128).

Conversely, the WCTU workers lost much in being deprived of the Adventists' witness concerning the "gospel Sabbath." In Ellen White's thinking, interchurch cooperation was never about Adventists gaining acceptance into the cultural mainstream by blending in and diluting their message. Adventists would bring their contribution to such alliances, and thereby advance their distinctive, wholistic mission.

The most prominent factor in the church's reluctance to become involved with the WCTU was that organization's support, formalized in 1887, for Sunday rest laws as a means for protecting the rights and welfare of industrial workers. This connected the WCTU with the very legislative movements Adventists believed were signaling the last days. However, in remarks at the annual meeting of the American Health and Temperance Association held in Oakland in 1887, Ellen White urged Adventists not to be put off by the situation but view it as an opportunity: "You say they are going to carry this [temperance] question right along with the Sunday movement. How are you going to help them on that point? . . . How are you going to let your light shine without uniting with them in this temperance question?" (RH, Feb. 14, 1888).

If WCTU women could derive from Adventists enlightenment concerning the law of God, Ellen White believed, "their educated ability will do much more than it is now doing to create working forces for the advancement of truth and righteousness" (LLM 235). The current of benefit from such witness would then feed into a better-equipped Adventist work and from there flow to a needy world (see LLM 258, 259).

A winsome witness amid those dedicated to reform could not be conducted in the argumentative and triumphalist mode that often characterized Adventist evangelism. Work with the women of the WCTU required a "discretion" and "Christlike tenderness" that honors the nobility of their work and their spiritual integrity, rather than a disputatious spirit that treats them as enemies of the truth, Ellen White wrote (LLM 236). Instead of aggressive assertion of controversial doctrine, she approved the course taken by S.M.I. Henry of genuine cooperation in shared causes combined with a Christlikeness of spirit. In such contexts, Ellen White observed, it may be wise not to "dwell publicly upon the prominent features of our faith." Rather, "the oil of grace revealed in your conscious and unconscious influence will make known that you have the light of life" (LLM 234).

3. Empowerment for women *and* gender-based role distinctions. The prominence of women, specifically, in working for prohibition does not appear to be incidental to Ellen White's warm enthusiasm for the cause. In general the WCTU sought to expand rather than defy the conventional sphere of feminine influence. Its goal was to apply the feminine role of fostering love, education, and moral discipline in the home to the larger society. Ellen White's commitment to prohibition reflects a generally similar outlook. While holding generally accepted assumptions about

the domestic responsibilities of women, she viewed temperance activism as a way for women to break free of dehumanizing subjugation and find individual dignity and meaning through service in the cause of Christ.

In writing to S.M.I. Henry in 1899 that she had felt an "intense interest in the W.C.T.U. workers," Ellen White described them as "heroic women" who "know what it means to have an individuality of their own" (*ibid.*). Earlier that year she commended Henry's work in organizing Adventist women for service because it gave them a similar sense of individual value and purpose before God. "Our sisters have generally a very hard time, with their increasing families and their unappreciated trials," she wrote. Taking an active role for temperance and other forms of gospel work, she believed, would not lead to a neglect of "the essential duties of the home" but rather their being done "much more intelligently" (RH, May 9, 1899).

In connection with prohibition and the WCTU, Ellen White envisioned a work of utmost importance that only Adventist women with their distinctive capabilities could do. She maintained that "some of our best talent should be set at work for the W.C.T.U., not as evangelists, but as those who fully appreciate the good that has been done by this body." This mission could not be accomplished "through the learned arguments of ministers, but through the wise efforts of women of influence and tact who can devote time and thought to this line of work" (LLM 235, 236).

Further reading: S. E. Alhstrom, *A Religious History of the American People* (New Haven, Conn.: Yale University Press, 1972); Y. D. Anderson, "The Bible, the Bottle, and the Ballot: Seventh-day Adventist Political Activism, 1850-1900," *Adventist Heritage* 7, no. 2 (Fall 1982): 38-52; J. M. Butler, "Adventism and the American Experience," in Edwin Scott Gaustad,

ed., *The Rise of Adventism: Religion and Society in Mid-Nineteenth-Century America* (New York: Harper & Row, 1974), pp. 173-206; J. Z. Giele, *Two Paths to Women's Equality: Temperance, Suffrage, and the Origins of Modern Feminism* (Twayne, 1995); G. R. Knight, *Ellen White's World: A Fascinating Look at the Times in Which She Lived* (RHPA, 1998); D. Morgan, *Adventism and the American Republic: The Public Involvement of a Major Apocalyptic Movement* (Knoxville, Tenn.: University of Tennessee Press, 2001); T. R. Pegram, *Battling Demon Rum: The Struggle for a Dry America, 1800-1933* (Chicago: Ivan R. Dee, 1998); E. D. Syme, *A History of SDA Church-State Relations in the United States* (PPPA, 1973); L. L. Vance, *Seventh-day Adventism in Crisis: Gender and Sectarian Change in an Emerging Religion* (Urbana, Ill.: University of Illinois Press, 1999); R. Whitaker, "Drying Up the Stream," AR, Jan. 22, 2004.

Douglas Morgan

PROPHET, ELLEN G. WHITE NOT A. In October 1904 Ellen White addressed 2,500 Battle Creek Tabernacle members and townspeople concerning her life and work. Speaking without notes, she was evidently responding to allegations that she regarded herself as the leader of Seventh-day Adventists. "They say she is a prophetess, they say she is this and that and the other thing—I claim to be no such thing. . . . Mrs. White does not call herself a prophetess or a leader of this people. She calls herself simply a messenger." The following day she reiterated, "I am not, as I said yesterday, a prophet. I do not claim to be a leader; I claim to be simply a messenger of God, and that is all I have ever claimed" (5Bio 354).

News agencies widely reported Ellen White's alleged self-admission that she did not, after all, consider herself to be inspired of God. In subsequent efforts at clarification (RH, Jan. 26, 1905; Ms 63, 1906, in UL 160), she drew a crucial distinction between the *title* of "prophet" (which she never claimed, calling herself simply a "messenger of God"), and the *role* of a prophet (which, however, she never disclaimed—nor corrected anyone who applied it to her). She simply distinguished between the biblical *denotation* of "prophet," and the popular *connotation* of the word. Ellen White had no quarrel with the biblical *definition* of a prophet's role. But she had at least four reasons for not claiming the *title*.

The immediate trigger for her surprising statement of October 1904 was apparently some news reports during the *Kellogg crisis, which referred to her as the prophet and head of the Seventh-day Adventist denomination, implying a power struggle between her and other leaders, such as *Dr. J. H. Kellogg. She had never held an office in the denomination and vehemently denied any pretensions to denominational leadership. "I have had no claims to make," she protested, "only that *I am instructed that I am the Lord's messenger; that He called me in my youth to be His messenger, to receive His word, and to give a clear and decided message in the name of the Lord Jesus. Early in my youth I was asked several times, Are you a prophet? I have ever responded, I am the Lord's messenger. I know that many have called me a prophet, but I have made no claim to this title"* (1SM 32).

A second reason Ellen White gave for not claiming the *title* of prophet was that "in these days many who boldly claim that they are prophets are a reproach to the cause of Christ" (1SM 32; cf. 3SM 74)—perhaps an allusion to Mormon founder Joseph Smith (cf. 2SG iv), who styled himself "Prophet, Revelator, and Seer," or to Mary Baker Eddy, founder of Christian Science. For various reasons she did not wish to be identified with some contemporaries who claimed the title of prophet.

A third reason was that most people in Ellen White's day (as today) thought of a "prophet" almost exclusively in terms of a predictor of future events. But while she did make *predictions, some quite far-ranging, Robert W. Olson estimated that of her lifetime output of writing, "probably not over two percent" dealt with "future events" ("Ellen White's Predictions," White Estate unpublished monograph, Nov. 6, 1989, p. 1).

Prophets mentioned in Scripture exercised their ministry in many different roles. While Moses wrote some predictive prophecies, his role was concerned primarily with the formation of a nation—legal, judicial, theological, spiritual, and organizational leadership. John the Baptist, identified by Christ as the "greatest" prophet (Matt. 11:11), made no known predictions, "did no miracle" (John 10:41), and wrote none of the Bible. Ellen White did not want her role to be narrowly circumscribed by the popular notion that a prophet's main function was merely predicting the future.

Her fourth reason for not claiming the title of prophet was that "my commission embraces the work of a prophet, but it does not end there" (3SM 74). "My work includes much more than the word 'prophet' signifies" (1SM 32). She described her "special work" as including at least seven dimensions: (1) delivering faithfully the messages given her in visions; (2) teaching and practicing "health reform," setting "an example to the church" by caring for the sick in her own home; (3) speaking to "large assemblies" on "the subject of Christian temperance"; (4) urging "upon those who profess to believe the truth, the necessity of practicing the truth," i.e., "sanctification"; (5) advocating for "justice and equity in all our institutions" and reproving oppression, especially "any arbitrary or overbearing action toward the ministers of the gospel by those having official authority"; (6) pleading the cause of "aged ministers" and those "feeble in health"; (7) caring for orphans, "taking some under my own charge for a time, and then finding homes for them" (*ibid.* 33, 34).

For all these reasons, she did not claim the title of prophet. *"If others call me by that name, I have no controversy with them,"* she said. "But my work has covered so many lines that I cannot call myself other than a messenger, sent to bear a message from the Lord to His people, and to take up work in any line that He points out" (1SM 34, italics supplied; SpM 482; RH, July 26, 1906).

Further reading: R. W. Coon, "Ellen White's Disturbing Disclaimer of 1904," AR, May 13, 1999.

Roger W. Coon

PROPHET, TESTS OF A. In her writings Ellen White insisted that the ministry of prophets should be evaluated by biblical tests. Several such tests have been given and applied to her own writings. The first test is agreement with the Bible. "All scripture is given by inspiration of God, and is profitable for doctrine, for reproof, for correction, for instruction in righteousness" (2 Tim. 3:16). "To the law and to the testimony: if they speak not according to this word, it is because there is no light in them" (Isa. 8:20; cf. Acts 17:11). Ellen White was emphatic that the extracanonical gift of prophecy "was not given—nor can it ever be bestowed—to supersede the Bible; for the Scriptures explicitly state that the Word of God is the standard by which all teaching and experience must be tested." "Since it was the Spirit of God that inspired the Bible, it is impossible that the teaching of the Spirit [through prophets] should ever be contrary to that of the Word" (GC vii).

The second biblical test of a prophet is "By their fruits you shall know them" (Matt. 7:20). Concerning her own ministry White declares: " 'Let the testimonies be judged by their fruits.' . . . 'What is the spirit of their teaching? What has been the result of their influence? . . . God is either teaching His church, reproving their wrongs, and strengthening their faith, or He is not. This work is of God, or it is not. God does nothing in partnership with Satan. My work . . . bears the stamp of God, or the stamp of the enemy. There is no halfway work in the matter' " (CET 245).

A third Bible test is given in Jeremiah 28:9. "When the word of the prophet shall come to pass, then shall the prophet be known, that the Lord hath truly sent him." Ellen White describes her own prophetic experience as follows: "Past, present, and future have passed before me. I have been shown faces that I had never seen, and years afterward I knew them when I saw them. I have been aroused from my sleep with a vivid sense of subjects previously presented to my mind; and I have written, at midnight, letters that have gone across the continent, and, arriving at a crisis, have saved great disaster to the cause of God. This has been my work for many years" (CET 245). (See *Predictions of Ellen G. White.)

The fourth Bible test is presented by the apostle John: "Beloved, do not believe every spirit, but test the spirits, whether they are of God; because many false prophets have gone out into the world. By this you know the Spirit of God: Every spirit that confesses that Jesus Christ has come in the flesh is of God" (1 John 4:1, 2, NKJV). Ellen White's prophetic ministry was centered in the truth about Jesus. She writes: "The great plan of the redemption of a fallen race was wrought out in the life of Christ in human flesh" (FE 408). "[Christ] was, in life and teaching, the gospel, the foundation of all pure doctrine" (TMK 97). "The gospel is glorious because it is made up of His righteousness. It is Christ unfolded, and Christ is the gospel embodied. Every page of the New Testament Scriptures shines with His light. Every text is a diamond, touched and irradiated by the divine rays [of Christ]" (7BC 907).

Further reading: CET 244-258; GC v-xii; G. Bradford, *Humans Are Prophets* (Victoria: Signs Pub. Co., 2004), pp. 71-91; H. E. Douglass, *Messenger of the Lord* (PPPA, 1998), pp. 26-40; T. H. Jemison, *A Prophet Among You* (PPPA, 1955), pp. 99-116; F. Holbrook, "The Biblical Basis for a Modern Prophet" (EGWE, SDoc).

Martin Hanna

PROPHETESS OF HEALTH, see general article: **BIBLIOGRAPHIC ESSAY ON PUBLICATIONS ABOUT ELLEN G. WHITE.**

PROPHETIC GUIDANCE IN THE ADVENT MOVEMENT: A SEVENTH-DAY ADVENTIST CORRESPONDENCE COURSE (Los Angeles: Prophetic Guidance School of the Voice of Prophecy, 1960). Series of 24 lessons on the gift of prophecy and the ministry of Ellen G. White. This correspondence course was prepared as a means of nurturing the faith of Seventh-day Adventists in God's leadership through the prophetic ministry of Ellen White and used generally during the midweek prayer meeting. Lessons dealt with a variety of subjects, such as: the biblical gift of prophecy, tests of a true prophet, Ellen White's call to ministry, her role in the Adventist movement, her relationship to church leaders and to Bible doctrines. *The Spirit of Prophecy Treasure Chest: An Advent Source Collection of Materials Relating to the Gift of Prophecy in the Remnant Church and the Life and Ministry of Ellen G. White* (Voice of Prophecy, 1960, 192 pp.) was used as supplemental materials and textbook for the correspondence lessons.

PROPHETIC INTERPRETATION. Biblical prophecies, particularly those of Daniel and the Revelation, were seen by Ellen White as "the foundation of the faith of Seventh-day Adventists" (Ev 196). She urged that the "prophecies of Daniel and the Revelation should be carefully studied, and in connection with them the words, 'Behold the Lamb of God, which taketh away the sin of the world'" (*ibid.*), because she believed that when Daniel and Revelation are understood in relation to each other (7BC 971), and in relation to Christ and His righteousness, "increased light will shine upon all the grand truths of prophecy" (Ev 198). She called upon parents to instruct their children in the prophecies (CG 512), and urged ministers and all believers to unite in a "strong effort to call the attention of the world to the fast-fulfilling prophecies of the Word of God" (Ev 193). Consequently she wrote a great deal about the nature and purpose of prophecy, prophetic history, principles of interpretation, progressive revelation, prophetic "landmarks," symbols, time periods, types, and parables.

Foundational to Ellen White's interpretation of prophecy is the historical or historicist view—that the prophecies of Daniel and Revelation reveal the history of the controversy between God and worldly powers within history, from the time of the prophet to the end of the world (see Dan. 2:36-45). This view, which closely correlates biblical prophecy with prophetic history, was the common view of the leading Protestant Reformers Luther and Calvin, as well as Wesley and Isaac Newton; early-American expositors Increase Mather, president of Harvard University; Jonathan Edwards, president of Princeton; Timothy Dwight, president of Yale; and scores of others (Froom, *Prophetic Faith*, vol. 4, p. 144).

There are various perspectives from which to write history, such as political, economic, sociological or cultural perspectives. Ellen White held that the Bible is concerned with important events in prophetic, not secular, history. This means that historians who are not aware of Bible prophecies may hardly mention or completely overlook crucial events in the history of divine Providence. Failure to recognize the variety of approaches to writing history has led many to doubt the validity of the historicist view of prophecy, because the most recent historians fail to mention these prophetic events.

Ellen White used the phrase "prophetic history" in connection with both Daniel (SpTEd 10) and the Revelation. She identified the scroll in Revelation 5 as "the roll of the history of God's providences, the prophetic history of nations and the church. . . . In symbolic language has . . . the influence of every nation, tongue, and people from the beginning of earth's history to its close" (9MR 7). Likewise the symbols of the great red dragon, the leopard-like beast, and the lamb-like horn beast in Revelation 12 and 13 reveal the "governments which are especially engaged in trampling upon God's law and persecuting His people. Their war is carried forward to the close of time" (4SP 276).

In order that people not be deceived in this battle called the *great controversy, Ellen White called on Adventists to proclaim "in the line of prophetic history the things that have been and the things that will be" (2SM 105).

A dominant motif in her interpretation of prophecy is that God is the sovereign ruler of nations, who tests "every nation" that has been permitted to occupy its place on the earth, that it might be seen whether it would fulfill His purposes. "Prophecy has traced the rise and fall of the world's great empires— Babylon, Medo-Persia, Greece, and Rome. With each of these, as with nations of less power, history repeated itself. Each had its

period of test, each failed, its glory faded, its power departed, and its place was occupied by another" (Ed 177).

Prophetic history "tells us where we are today in the procession of the ages, and what may be expected in the time to come." Seeing the fulfillment of past prophecies "traced on the pages of history" assures the believer that "all which is yet to come will be fulfilled in its order" (ibid. 178). Prophetic history teaches "how worthless is mere outward and worldly glory" (ibid. 183). It is through the study of "God's purpose in the history of nations and in the revelation of things to come, that we may estimate at their true value things seen and things unseen; that we may learn what is the true aim of life; that, viewing the things of time in the light of eternity, we may put them to their truest and noblest use" (ibid. 184).

Ellen White considered the prophetic heritage of the Second Advent movement of vital importance for correctly interpreting Bible prophecy: "The scripture which above all others had been both the foundation and the central pillar of the advent faith was the declaration: 'Unto two thousand and three hundred days; then shall the sanctuary be cleansed.' Daniel 8:14" (GC 409). She believed that "God directed the mind of *William Miller to the prophecies and gave him great light upon the book of Revelation" (EW 231). She saw that "angels of God repeatedly visited that chosen one, to guide his mind and open to his understanding prophecies which had ever been dark to God's people" (ibid. 229). While she did not hold Miller to be without error, she strongly recommended the use of his principles of interpretation (GC 320), "searching the Scriptures upon the same plan that Father Miller adopted" (RH, Nov. 25, 1884). Quoting from Miller's book Views of the Prophecies and Prophetic Chronology, she particularly endorsed five of Miller's principles as "simple but intelligent and important rules for Bible study and interpretation" (*ibid.*).

The first rule calls for the careful study of each word of the biblical text: "Every word must have its proper bearing on the subject presented in the Bible." The second focuses on the relevance and importance of the whole canon: "All Scripture is necessary, and may be understood by diligent application and study." The third asserts the power of prayer in connection with study: "Nothing revealed in Scripture can or will be hid from those who ask in faith, not wavering." The fourth rule brings out the vital function of the *analogy of Scripture* principle: "To understand doctrine, bring all the scriptures together on the subject you wish to know, then let every word have its proper influence; and if you can form your theory without a contradiction, you cannot be in error." The fifth rule is that "Scripture must be its own expositor, since it is a rule of itself. If I depend on a teacher to expound to me, and he should guess at its meaning, or desire to have it so on account of his sectarian creed, or to be thought wise, then his guessing, desire, creed, or wisdom is my rule, and not the Bible" (*ibid.*). "The above," she said, "is a portion of these rules; and in our study of the Bible we shall all do well to heed the principles set forth" (*ibid.*).

Regarding the relation of the prophets to their prophecies, Ellen White observed that in many cases, biblical prophets did not fully understand their own prophecies. Commenting on 1 Peter 1:10-12, she noted that the Old Testament prophets did not "understand fully" their revelations, but they were given for the benefit of later ages (GC 344). Regarding 1 Corinthians 10:11, she wrote that "the ancient prophets spoke less for their own time than for ours, so that their prophesying is in force for us" (3SM 338). Their "messages were given, not for those that uttered the prophecies, but

for us who are living amid the scenes of their fulfillment" (2SM 114).

She remarked that the "wonderful prophecies" of Daniel 7-12 "were not fully understood even by the prophet himself"; but "they relate to the very time in which we are living" (PK 547).

This is the meaning of Daniel's book being sealed until the time of the end (Dan. 8:17, 26; 12:4). "But at the time of the end, says the prophet, 'many shall run to and fro, and knowledge shall be increased'" (GC 356). Daniel 9, she explained, had special significance for the first advent of Christ, while the other prophecies of Daniel she associated with the Second Advent (DA 233, 234). She taught that the prophecies of Daniel 8 and 11 "are now in process of fulfillment, and all the events foretold will soon come to pass" (TM 113).

In defining what constitutes "present truth," or the truth for this time, Ellen White stressed the importance of certain fundamental *landmark doctrines that were discovered around 1844 and firmly established. Among these landmarks she listed the prophecies of "the cleansing of the *sanctuary transpiring in heaven" (Dan. 8:14), "the first and second angels' messages and the third, unfurling the banner on which was inscribed, 'the commandments of God and the faith of Jesus'" (Rev. 14:6-12), and "the temple of God . . . in heaven, and the ark containing the law of God" (Rev. 11:19) (CW 30, 31).

For interpreting prophetic symbols Ellen White insisted on the use of Scripture as its own interpreter. She objected to the practice of some who, with "an active imagination, seize upon the figures and symbols of Holy Writ, interpret them to suit their fancy, with little regard to the testimony of Scripture as its own interpreter, and then they present their vagaries as the teachings of the Bible" (GC 521).

Instead, she advocated that "the language of the Bible should be explained according to its obvious meaning, unless a symbol or figure is employed. Christ has given the promise: 'If any man will do his will, he shall know of the doctrine.' John 7:17. If men would but take the Bible as it reads, if there were no false teachers to mislead and confuse their minds, a work would be accomplished that would make angels glad and that would bring into the fold of Christ thousands upon thousands who are now wandering in error" (*ibid.* 599).

In interpreting prophetic time, Ellen White accepted the principle that "a day in symbolic prophecy represents a year" (GC 324; Num. 14:34; Eze. 4:6; cf. DA 233; PK 698), and in the 70-week prophecy of Daniel 9 she saw a confirmation of the accuracy of this principle. This prophecy was to start with the "going forth of the commandment to restore and to build Jerusalem" (Dan. 9:25), which she identified as the decree of the Persian king Artaxerxes (Ezra 7; GC 326, 327). The beginning of the 70 prophetic weeks, or 490 years, "is fixed beyond question at 457 B.C., and their expiration in A.D. 34" (*ibid.* 328). The prophecy predicted that the Messiah would begin His ministry after a period of seven weeks and 62 weeks, that is, after a total of 69 prophetic weeks, or 483 years. It was precisely at the end of this period, in A.D. 27, that Jesus was anointed as the Messiah at His baptism (Acts 10:38). Referring to the fulfillment of this prophecy, Jesus proclaimed, "The time is fulfilled, and the kingdom of God is at hand: repent ye, and believe the gospel" (Mark 1:15; cf. GC 327). In accordance with this prophecy, the Messiah's crucifixion was to occur in the midst of the seventieth week (Dan. 9:27). At the exact time, "in A.D. 31, three and a half years after His baptism, our Lord was crucified" (*ibid.*).

Another prophecy that Ellen White cited as proving the accuracy of the year-day principle occurred under the sixth trumpet of Revelation 9 and predicted the dominance of a powerful empire for the duration of "an hour, and a day, and a month, and a year" (Rev. 9:15). Ellen White considered the incident at the end of this period a "remarkable fulfillment of prophecy" (*ibid.* 334). She noted that when the "event exactly fulfilled the prediction" "multitudes were convinced of the correctness of the principles of prophetic interpretation adopted by Miller and his associates, and a wonderful impetus was given to the advent movement" (*ibid.* 335).

Other prophetic time periods to which she positively applied the year-day principle were the "time, times, and half a time," the 42 months, and the "1260 days" (Dan. 7:25; 12:7; Rev. 11:2; 12:6, 12; 13:5). These various expressions predicted a time period of severe persecution for God's people that was to last for 1260 prophetic days. This period she identified with the 1260 years of papal supremacy, during which the church of Christ hid in the "wilderness" (Rev. 12:6, 14-17). This prophetic period lasted from 538 till 1798, when, during the French Revolution, the French took the pope captive, dealing a severe blow to the Papacy (*ibid.* 54, 55, 266, 267, 356).

The last and longest prophetic time period to which she applied the year-day principle was the 2300 prophetic days of Daniel 8:14, after which the sanctuary was to be cleansed. This text, Ellen White believed, is the "foundation and central pillar of the advent faith" (*ibid.* 409). Based on the thematic connections between Daniel 8 and 9, the 2300 days and the 70 prophetic weeks are seen to have the same starting point. Thus the 2300 years covers a period from 457 B.C. to 1844. The principle of typology contributed toward the understanding that in 1844 Christ began His final atoning ministry in the Most Holy Place of the heavenly sanctuary during the antitypical day of *atonement, which involves a work of *investigative judgment (*ibid.* 328, 424, 457).

In accord with other Adventist expositors, such as *O.R.L. Crosier, *J. N. Andrews, and *Uriah Smith, Ellen White saw in the Old Testament sanctuary typology profound prophetic significance for understanding the final acts of Christ's ministry in the heavenly sanctuary. "The tabernacle, or temple, of God on earth was a pattern of the original in heaven," she wrote. "All the ceremonies of the Jewish law were prophetic, typical of mysteries in the plan of redemption" (6BC 1095). "The whole system of types and symbols was a compacted prophecy of the gospel, a presentation in which were bound up the promises of redemption" (AA 14). Believers today are "to lift up Jesus, to present Him to the world as revealed in types, as shadowed in symbols, as manifested in the revelations of the prophets" (1SM 363).

Several of Christ's parables also had prophetic significance according to Ellen White. For instance, she held that the parable of the mustard seed (Matt. 13:31, 32) has special relevance for earth's last generation (COL 79). In Christ's enigmatic remark about the destruction of the Temple (John 2:19) she saw a twofold prediction of the "destruction of the temple of His body" and its direct consequence, the destruction of the Temple in Jerusalem (DA 164). The parable of the ten virgins (Matt. 25:1-13) she interpreted as a prophecy illustrating the experience of the Second Advent movement in the 1840s (GC 393, 394, 398, 426-428) and the experience of God's people just before Christ's return (COL 405-421).

Finally Ellen White alerted believers to several factors that prevent a correct interpretation of prophecy. Studying prophecy with "prejudice," "unbelief," "pride," "selfish

desires," or without "spiritual insight," i.e., the illumination of the Holy Spirit will lead to a wrong understanding (AA 119; DA 30). Preconceived erroneous interpretations, influenced by "the customs and traditions of men," also confuse the mind and hinder the understanding of prophecy (RH, Oct. 14, 1890). Another source of prophetic misinterpretation is *time-setting, which largely results from a failure to give the *three angels' messages of Revelation 14 "their proper place in prophetic history" (Ev 613).

Progress or delay in the proclamation of these messages can hasten or delay the final fulfillment of prophecy, because God is "not willing that any should perish, but that all should come to repentance" (2 Peter 3:9). Nevertheless, the second coming "will not tarry past the time that the message is borne to all nations, tongues, and peoples" (Ev 697), for the gospel "shall be preached in all the world as a witness unto all the nations; and then shall the end come" (Matt. 24:14).

Further reading: P. G. Damsteegt, *Foundations of the Seventh-day Adventist Message and Mission* (Grand Rapids: Eerdmans, 1977; reprint AUP, 1988); L. E. Froom, *The Prophetic Faith of Our Fathers* (RHPA, 1946-1954); W. G. Johnsson, "*Biblical Apocalyptic*," in R. Dederen, ed., *Handbook of Seventh-day Adventist Theology* (RHPA, 2000), pp. 784-814.

P. Gerard Damsteegt

PROPHETS AND KINGS (PPPA, 1916, 1917, 752 pp.). The second of five volumes in the Conflict of the Ages Series, covering the history of Israel from the reign of Solomon to the end of the Old Testament; with the original title of *The Captivity and Restoration of Israel: The Conflict of the Ages Illustrated in the Lives of Prophets and Kings.* Though the last volume to appear in the Conflict series and published posthumously, *Prophets and Kings* actually completes the Old Testament, the companion volume to *Patriarchs and Prophets,* which covers through the reign of David. In the two antecedent series, **Spiritual Gifts* (1858-1864) and **The Spirit of Prophecy* (1870-1884), Ellen White wrote little about the biblical material covered in *Prophets and Kings.* Before moving to the New Testament, for example, *The Spirit of Prophecy,* volume 1 (1870), simply ends its Old Testament coverage with chapters entitled "Solomon" and "The Ark of God," both taken virtually unchanged from *Spiritual Gifts,* volume 4a (1864).

During the 1870s Ellen White wrote "quite fully" on the monarchy, exile, and restoration (LS 435). But until 1917 none of this material had appeared in any of her earlier biblical narrative commentary series (SG, SP). After returning from Australia (1900), she began working on the Old Testament material "intermittently for more than ten years" (LS 436). During her last two years, assisted by C. C. Crisler and others, all of *Prophets and Kings* was prepared for publication—all, that is, except "the last two chapters" (identified in 1916 by Crisler as chapters 58 and 59, not 59 and 60 [DF 51d]) which "had been sufficiently blocked out to admit of completion by the inclusion of additional matter from her manuscript file" (LS 436).

Theologically, chapter 47, "Joshua and the Angel," is especially important. An exposition based on Zechariah 3, the narrative unfolds as a *"righteousness by faith" commentary on the *investigative judgment, though that label is never used in the chapter. The history behind the chapter is suggestive. In 1880 Ellen White asked in vision: "Where is the security for the people of God in these days of peril?" (*ibid.* 324). The angel pointed her to Zechariah 3, a chapter previously unmentioned in her writings. The literary antecedent of this chapter

was published five years later, in 1885 (5T 467-476), three years before the "righteousness by faith" *General Conference session of 1888. In comparison with the 1885 version, the *Prophets and Kings* edition reveals two significant and "encouraging" revisions, one an omission, the other an addition. The omitted sentence is no doubt true, but potentially discouraging: "No sin can be tolerated in those who shall walk with Christ in white" (*ibid.* 472). The addition is part of Jesus' defense of His people over against the accuser, Satan: "They may have imperfections of character; they may have failed in their endeavors; but they have repented, and I have forgiven and accepted them" (PK 589).

Further reading: D. E. Robinson, "Authorship of Last Two Chapters in *Prophets and Kings*," Dec. 1, 1952, DF 51d; A. L. White, "The Story of *Prophets and Kings*," AR, June 25, 1981.

Alden Thompson

PROTESTANTISM, see REFORMATION, PROTESTANT.

PSYCHOLOGY AND COUNSELING. Though repeated in several places, there are only two statements using the word "psychology" in the writings of Ellen White. In one she asserts without elaboration that "the true principles of psychology are found in the Holy Scriptures" (1MCP 10). The second statement appears a number of times in different tenses. "The sciences of phrenology, *psychology*, and mesmerism have been the channel through which Satan has come more directly to this generation, and wrought with that power which was to characterize his work near the close of probation" (MYP 57, italics supplied; cf. 2MCP 698). The compilers of **Mind, Character, and Personality* provide contextual and historical perspective to White's use of the word "psychology" in her writings. "The reference to phrenology, psychology, and mesmerism, as here combined, describing the manner in which Satan takes advantage of the human mind, may seem a bit obscure to one not familiar with the literature of the time and its emphasis. Scientific works devoted to physiology and the care of the sick carried advertising lists at the back informing the public of literature available. One such work, *The Water Cure Manual* (284 pages), published in 1850 by Fowlers and Wells, carries a list of sixty-five different works on physical and mental health, and of these, twenty-three are devoted to phrenology, psychology, mesmerism, and clairvoyance" (1MCP 19). Sensational and exaggerated claims were apparently made about the pretended benefits of psychology.

Of greater significance are her statements about something much more sinister. She recognized that Satan, in true opportunistic fashion, operated through the practitioners of the so-called sciences of phrenology, psychology, and mesmerism to poison the thinking of their subjects, and to seductively lead them to believe the lies of the great deceiver (*ibid.* 18, 19). While "the sciences which treat of the human mind are" "good in their place," Satan and those under his influence can use them to corrupt the thinking of people, and to prepare them to embrace spiritualism (*ibid.* 20).

Given the paucity of references to psychology in her writings and the lack of linkage of her comments to contemporary psychological practice, care should be exercised to avoid attributing to her either support of or opposition to the modern field of psychology.

The word "counseling," which today is understood as a means of treating mental health problems, was not used in that way by Ellen White. She wrote of the need of younger ministers for counseling with more experienced workers (TM 501), and of Jesus sending the disciples out two by two so that in

counseling together they could strengthen each other (DA 350). Parents have a particular duty to counsel their children (OHC 304).

She repeatedly emphasized the imperative of receiving counsel from God through the Bible and applying it to the life (CH 371; FE 390; GW 253). She cautioned against preferring human over divine counsel (3BC 1138; RH, Nov. 24, 1910); however, she affirmed as trustworthy counselors who had a firm hold on God (RH, Oct. 26, 1905). She encouraged special respect for the counsel of those whose years of rich experience qualified them to impart wisdom (AA 573), and she valued the assistance of people with expertise in business matters (14MR 217). She urged great caution about the circumstances under which counsel should be given by ministers (2MCP 768), and specified topics that should be avoided (*ibid.* 766, 767). While strongly discouraging the disclosure of private sins (5T 645; CH 373), and stressing the folly of a person assuming the role of a confessor (GW 418; 2MCP 767; 2T 302; TSB 205), she indicates that some individuals may need a person with a compassionate heart to hear about their sinfulness and misery (SpM 144).

Mental illnesses were thought of, and described differently today than in White's time, but she wrote about some of these disorders with remarkable insight and recommended preventive and remedial steps consistent with recent advances in treatment modalities. For example, she recognized the link between negativity and depression (TDG 233; 1T 696), and counseled against ruminating about gloomy and discouraging matters (4T 103; 1MCP 62). She also decried the detrimental effects of association with depressed and critical people (RH, June 12, 1894; 21MR 8). She indicated that depression could be triggered by the use of unhealthful substances (2SM 447; CG 403), by satanic influences (MM 43;

RH, Jan. 2, 1908; 6MR 393), by the fear of hell (2MCP 454), and by guilt (CH 324). She also recognized the influence of family history upon mental health (2MCP 489, 809). She was aware of the distortion that depression can have on one's thinking, and though she was morally opposed to suicide (HR, Jan. 1, 1873; TSB 143), she intimated that on rare occasions (HP 52) when depressed, she herself experienced thoughts of death and dying (LS80 195; 1T 185; 2Bio 435). White noted that Elijah (PK 161), Paul (LP 175, 176), and Jesus (3SP 94) experienced depression, though what she describes sounds more like brief episodes of deeply depressed mood than major depression. Her counsel for those with depression includes attention to living conditions (1T 702, 703; HR, Apr. 1, 1871), modifying habits and practices (HR, Apr. 1, 1871; 1MR 255; PH096 54), avoiding social isolation (3MR 318; TSB 34), maintaining a positive focus (2MCP 537; AH 258, 259; 2MCP 490; Ed 197), and reliance on God (2MCP 538; CH 382; PK 164).

Further reading: Mind, Character, and Personality, 2 vols.

H. Peter Swanson

PUBLISHING HOUSES. Institutions responsible for the production of books, magazines, tracts, and other materials used for the spiritual nurture of church members and for the dissemination of the Seventh-day Adventist message. As a result of Ellen White's counsels on *publishing work and the dedicated efforts of the Adventist pioneers to circulate biblical truths, a publishing house, which became the *Review and Herald Publishing Association, was established early in the denomination's history. It became the first institution to be owned and operated by Adventists, even before the church had a name and a formal organizational structure. In 1875 what became the *Pacific Press Publishing Association was

also organized, and after that, other publishing facilities began to operate overseas, forming a chain that includes more than 60 publishing houses worldwide. They are vital to maintain the unity of faith; to affirm the core of Adventist teachings, principles, and doctrines; and to convey information to the worldwide church through the printed pages they generate. In addition, they play a crucial role in developing relevant materials for, and in providing support for, colporteurs in accomplishing their mission. Publishing houses are among the important institutions of the denomination; Ellen White referred to them as "special monuments of God's workings" among humanity that are "sacred to His service" (PM 58) in the proclamation of the gospel at the end of time (7T 140).

Ellen White recommended that Adventists should avoid centralization of power (*ibid.* 171), that publishing houses should work in cooperation with each other (*ibid.* 174), but never to the point that one would have power to dictate the management of another (PM 152, 153). They should be established in missionary lands (7T 145, 169), in rural districts, and near but outside large cities (PM 185-187). Although printing facilities "should show marked prosperity" (4T 392), she advocated that they should not be built to compete with worldly institutions in size or splendor (PM 189, 190). For the functioning of Adventist publishing houses, God requires "exactness, skill, tact, wisdom, and perfection" (*ibid.* 41). He expects them to be led with no kingly authority but with the spirit of Christ (*ibid.* 127-140). They are to be managed by leaders who are spiritually minded, who love and fear God, and who are prepared to do business (*ibid.* 64, 65). As part of God's plan for the publishing houses "every effort should be made to stand free from debt" (7T 206), to "economize in every possible way," "watch the little outgoes," and "stop every leak" (PM 105). At the same time, a portion of the revenue derived from the sale of literature is to be used to increase production facilities and in strengthening the work of the church (9T 62; PM 124).

Workers of publishing houses have an honorable and exalted position before God (PM 58). They should be trained to become proficient and to carry out the work with perfection and professionalism (*ibid.* 78-84). They also should be efficient, apt, and practical, and, as faithful sentinels, take care that nothing is wasted and none of the machinery damaged (*ibid.* 106-108). Workers should be characterized as tenderhearted, principled, and consecrated people (*ibid.* 139, 151). Beyond their regular daily business, they should exert a spiritual influence in the community in which they live, participate in the local church, study the Bible, and care for the spiritual welfare of others (*ibid.* 61-69). Special counsels were also given to writers and editors. They are called to be watchmen and "are held by God accountable for the souls of their fellow men" (CW 89). They are advised to "sit at the feet of Jesus, and learn from Him" (*ibid.* 122), and not to praise or exalt human beings (*ibid.* 98, 99). Editors should publish "nothing that savors of dissension" (*ibid.* 74), but should instead "attract the attention of their readers to the Book of books, and to those books and periodicals which present the Word of God in its true bearings" (*ibid.* 122).

After the Review and Herald and Pacific Press were established, both houses started soliciting commercial printing to keep the machinery used on a full-time basis and produce income that would help maintain operations. Such work, ranging from the printing of simple office forms to finished books, became detrimental over time, leading both houses to print products that contained doctrinal errors, that were not of an uplifting character, and that were even demoralizing to the workers (7T 164-168). Ellen White called upon the church leaders and the managers of these institutions several times to reform their business practices and restrict the facilities mainly to denominational work. "We have no permission from the Lord to engage either in the printing or in the sale of such publications; for they are the means of destroying many souls," she wrote (*ibid.* 166). "To allow matter of this character to pass through our institutions is to place in the hands of the employees and to present to the world the fruit of the forbidden tree of knowledge. It is to invite Satan to come in, with his bewitching science, to insinuate his principles in the very institutions that are set for the advancement of the sacred work of God" (*ibid.* 166, 167). These counsels were not accepted until both houses were destroyed by fires, the Review and Herald in 1902 and the Pacific Press in 1906. These fires were acknowledged as direct judgments from God for such practices (PM 165-175). In spite of strongly condemning publishing houses for printing certain categories of literature, White indicated that some types of commercial work could be acceptable. However, under no circumstances should it come first or interfere with the spirituality of Adventist institutions (*ibid.* 160-166). She advised that presses should be "constantly employed in publishing light and truth" (9T 65).

Publishing houses "are to stand as witnesses for God, teachers of righteousness to the people" (7T 138), and as "repairers of the breach, restorers of paths to dwell in" (*ibid.* 139). They "are to stand before the world as an embodiment of Christian principles" (*ibid.* 142), to be centers of influence to develop the talents of believers and to unify new churches (*ibid.* 145), and "to prepare a people to meet

God" (*ibid.* 139). Adventist publishing houses were to be models of how all denominational institutions should be run. They were to be living examples of Adventist beliefs put into practice. As God's institutions, publishing houses should be regarded by both workers and church members "as a holy trust, to be guarded as jealously as the ark was guarded by ancient Israel" (*ibid.* 193).

See also: Publishing Work.

Further reading: PM; CW; 7T 138-219; 9T 61-88; *SDA Encyclopedia* (1996), vol. 11, pp. 276-278, 402, 403, 445-450.

Mario Martinelli

PUBLISHING MINISTRY, THE (RHPA, 1983, 430 pp.). Compilation of Ellen White's counsels on the purpose, establishment, operation, and management of Seventh-day Adventist publishing houses. Before releasing this volume, the Ellen G. White Estate published two related books, *Colporteur Ministry* and *Counsels to Writers and Editors*. However, several areas of concern to the Adventist publishing ministry were not treated in either of these two specialized volumes. *The Publishing Ministry* includes 40 chapters arranged in seven sections, beginning with the early history and purpose of the Adventist publishing work. Section II treats the establishment and operation of publishing houses; Section III, challenges of management; and Section IV, products, prices, royalties, and wages. Section V deals with elements of successful leadership of literature evangelists, recruiting, training, and supervising. Section VI deals with marketing and sales through Adventist bookstores, and Section VII focuses on the place of Adventist publications in spreading the gospel.

PUBLISHING WORK. A vital ministry of the *Seventh-day Adventist Church that embraces the production and distribution of printed

and other media materials prepared for outreach purposes and to foster the spiritual growth of church members. Publications were first utilized by Adventist pioneers to spread early Sabbatarian Adventist doctrines. Later they became one of the entering wedges to penetrate new places with the Seventh-day Adventist message. Today they represent a worldwide enterprise that includes a large variety of books, magazines, pamphlets, textbooks, songbooks, and multimedia materials produced in more than 340 languages and dialects by more than 60 publishing houses, and distributed by *colporteurs, bookstores, Adventist institutions, and church members. They are an integral part of the "publishing work," so called by Ellen White, which "was established by the direction of God and under His special supervision" (PM 41).

In November 1848, following a vision, Ellen White said to her husband, "I have a message for you. You must begin to print a little paper and send it out to the people. Let it be small at first; but as the people read, they will send you means with which to print, and it will be a success from the first. From this small beginning it was shown to me to be like streams of light that went clear round the world" (CM 1). In response to this instruction James White began publishing a small journal in July 1849 titled *The Present Truth*, which marked the official starting point of the Adventist publishing ministry. Already early Sabbatarian Adventists had published a few pamphlets by *Joseph Bates and *Hiram Edson. James White had published *A Word to the "Little Flock"* in 1847 and three broadsides of Ellen White's visions. But the publication of *The Present Truth* was the beginning of a sustained publishing ministry. In 1850 another paper, the *The Advent Review*, was published for a few months until it was merged with *The Present Truth* to form the *Second Advent Review* and *Sabbath Herald*, commonly known as the *Review and Herald*. In 1978 it became the *Adventist Review*, and in 2005 the monthly *Adventist World* was added. In addition to other magazines and pamphlets, books began to be published. Hymnals and doctrinal books came off the press in the early 1850s, while books on health first appeared in 1865. In the 1870s Ellen White's counsels were also influential in beginning publishing work outside North America. Later on, in the 1880s, works to be sold to the general public by house-to-house colporteurs were introduced.

Ellen White strongly defended the concept that "the power and efficiency of our work depend largely on the character of the literature that comes from our presses" (7T 150). For this reason she advised that "our energies should be devoted to the publication of literature of the purest quality and the most elevating character" (PM 48), "to strengthen every pin and pillar of the faith that was established by the Word of God and by the revelations of His Spirit" (9T 69). She remarked that books, papers, and tracts should be produced on different subjects, according to the needs of the field (PM 193, 216), at a fair price (*ibid.* 334, 335), and that publications should be translated into every language (*ibid.* 47).

White also wrote extensively about the establishment and operations of Adventist *publishing houses (*ibid.* 57-249) and bookstores (*ibid.* 323-330), and the distribution of literature through the work of colporteurs, church members (*ibid.* 368-374), and church institutions (*ibid.* 344-348; CT 524-530). She advised that literature should not be distributed exclusively through a single channel (PM 323, 324), but scattered "like the leaves of autumn" (*ibid.* 325, 327; CM 5, 25). Church members are advised to spend their money on books, rather than on unnecessary ornaments for the home (PM 381). They should buy publications to be lent to neighbors and to be given away (*ibid.* 370-374), to be given as Christmas gifts (*ibid.* 345, 346), and to be sent through the mail (*ibid.* 371). In order to accomplish greater circulation of Adventist literature, she challenged every believer to "scatter broadcast tracts and leaflets and books containing the message for this time" (CM 21) "in all the cities and villages in the land" (PM 44).

According to her view, "the press is a powerful instrumentality which God has ordained to be combined with the energies of the living preacher to bring the truth before all nations, kindreds, tongues, and peoples" (CM 148). Because the printed page is so influential, "we should treat as a sacred treasure every line of printed matter containing present truth. Even the fragments of a pamphlet or of a periodical should be regarded as of value" (*ibid.* 151). She revealed that "our publications are now sowing the gospel seed, and are instrumental in bringing as many souls to Christ as the preached word. Whole churches have been raised up as a result of their circulation" (*ibid.* 150). In addition, she considered books to be "silent messengers" (*ibid.* 100), through which the Holy Spirit will impress the minds of many people and lead them to the truth: "More than one thousand will soon be converted in one day, most of whom will trace their first convictions to the reading of our publications" (*ibid.* 151).

"The publishing branch of our cause has much to do with our power," she wrote. "I do desire that it shall accomplish all that the Lord designs it should. If our bookmen do their part faithfully, I know, from the light God has given me, that the knowledge of present truth will be doubled and trebled" (PM 38).

See also: Publishing Houses.

Further reading: CM; PM; CT 524-530;

3T 202-211; 9T 61-88; *SDA Encyclopedia* (1996), vol. 11, pp. 403-407, 873-888.

Mario Martinelli

QUESTIONS ON DOCTRINE, SEVENTH-DAY ADVENTISTS ANSWER (RHPA, 1957, 720 pp.). Book intended to clarify Seventh-day Adventist beliefs in response to doctrinal questions from evangelicals. Among Adventists it became the most controversial book ever published by the denomination, particularly on two issues, the *atonement and the *humanity of Christ. In connection with these discussions, the book included a compilation of Ellen White statements that were later republished as appendices in *The Seventh-day Adventist Bible Commentary*, vol. 7-A ("Christ's Place in the Godhead," pp. 437-442; "Christ's Nature During the Incarnation," pp. 443-456; and "The Atonement," pp. 457-488).

Further reading: Seventh-day Adventists Answer Questions on Doctrine, annotated ed. by G. R. Knight (AUP, 2003); H. E. Douglass, *A Fork in the Road* (Coldwater, Mich.: Remnant Publications, 2008); W. R. Martin, *The Truth About Seventh-day Adventism* (Grand Rapids, Mich.: Zondervan, 1960); A. L. Moore, *Questions on Doctrine Revisited* (Truth or Consequences, N. Mex.: A. L. Moore, 2005); J. Nam, "Reactions to the Seventh-day Adventist Evangelical Conferences and Questions on Doctrine, 1955-1971" (Ph.D. diss., AU, 2005); T. E. Unruh, "The Seventh-day Adventist Evangelical Conferences of 1955-1956," *Adventist Heritage* 4, no. 2 (1977): 35-46.

RACE RELATIONS. Ellen White was a staunch supporter of the equal rights of all races at a time in American history when popular tradition and practices did not give equal rights to all races, and to Blacks in particular. She spoke out against slavery and asserted equal rights for Black people. She aggressively promoted and supported the work of Adventism among Blacks by writing, preaching, and counseling the church to provide means and resources for such work.

Most of her writings on racial issues were produced between 1891 and 1908. A major statement titled "Our Duty to the Colored People" was read to church leaders at the 1891 General Conference session, calling their attention to the urgent need for a much more aggressive work among American Blacks. The manuscript and 12 related articles and letters were compiled in the first edition of *The Southern Work*, published by her son Edson White. He printed it in his printshop on board the *Morning Star* in the summer of 1898 (SW 6) and distributed it as a way of raising funds to support his work among Blacks. Further counsels, cautions, and admonitions concerning the work for Blacks were added in a supplement to *The Southern Work* (c. 1901) and in *Testimonies for the Church*, volume 7 (pp. 220-245), volume 8 (pp. 34, 59-61, 91, 137, 150, 205), and volume 9 (pp. 199-226).

The historical context in which she wrote—the last decade of the nineteenth century—was one of the most turbulent periods of race relations in American history. It marked the high point in the lynching of Blacks, the consolidation of White supremacy, the disenfranchisement of Black political power, and the concoction of "scientific theories" to prove Negro inferiority. Alongside these developments was the rise of American international power and the rise of American and European missionary work to "civilize and Christianize" Blacks. The twentieth century, anticipated as a coming era of "progress," opened tragically in the U.S., with 214 lynchings in the first two years. Clashes between the races occurred almost daily, and the tension between races seemed to offer little hope of progress.

Several principles about race relations

emerge from her writings. Ellen White blames the ignorance of Black slaves not on some inherent racial defect (which was a popular idea of the time) but on the results of slavery and lack of educational opportunities (Lt 80a, 1895, in 4MR 5-7). She eloquently affirms the equality of Blacks by comparing them to the "best developed white man," and declares that Christians who concede to popular expressions of racial prejudice are "giving their influence to sanction" the long history of racial "neglect," "insult," and "oppression" (Ms 17, 1896, in 4MR 8, 9). She condemns racial prejudice as a moral evil and calls on Christians to follow the principle of equality in their relationships with Blacks (9T 213-232; Ms 107, 1908, in 4MR 33).

Ellen White's views on race were based on the doctrines of *creation and *redemption. "Christ came to this earth with a message of mercy and forgiveness. He laid the foundation for a religion by which Jew and Gentile, black and white, free and bond are linked together in one common brotherhood, recognized as equal in the sight of God" (7T 225). She affirms the common relationship of all races by creation and redemption and the rights of all to the blessings of freedom and declares that a believer cannot practice any form of oppression or injustice to the least child of humanity.

Ellen White's principles regarding race did not change, but she adapted her application of those principles to changing circumstances. In 1859 she advocated civil disobedience to the Fugitive Slave Law (1T 202). In 1863 she demanded that any pro-slavery sympathizers among Adventists be expelled from the church (ibid. 358-360). In "Our Duty to the Colored People" (1891) she urged White members to accept Blacks within their congregations and advocated integration. By 1902, in view of the sharp increase of racial violence noted above,

she reluctantly conceded to separate churches because of necessity, but still firmly asserted the principles of brotherhood and equality (7T 225), saying that this position would have been unnecessary if Christ's love dwelt in the human heart. As racial animosity increased in America (1905-1909), Ellen White urged a change of method. In order not to infuriate Southern White opposition and thus hinder the work (9T 206, 208) she advised caution and restraint. She recommended a temporary concession to the social custom of having separate houses of worship for Blacks as the wisest course of action "until the Lord God shows us a better way" (ibid. 206-208). But in the same context she made it clear that this course of action was not done "to exclude" Blacks "because they are black," but because in the immediate historical situation, integration could not be practiced "without imperiling lives" (ibid. 206).

In summary, it cannot be said of Ellen White that she either advocated broad principles of racial segregation or harbored racial prejudice. She constantly urged working toward the ideal, but she showed flexibility by adopting certain changes under adverse circumstances for the good of the work. Her later counsels on separation must be viewed as temporary measures, not lifelong principles in dealing with the race issue. She must be judged in light of her lifelong advocacy and practice of the principles of the equality and brotherhood of the human race.

See also: African-Americans, Adventism Among.

Further reading: D. W. Baker, "The Dynamics of Communication and African-American Progress in the Seventh-day Adventist Organziation: A Historical Descriptive Analysis" (Ph.D. diss., Howard University, 1993); D. W. Baker, ed., *Telling the Story: An Anthology on the Development of the Black SDA Work* (Loma

Linda, Calif.: Loma Linda University Printing Services, 1996); R. D. Graybill, *E. G. White and Church Race Relations* (RHPA, 1970); C. B. Rock, "Institutional Loyalty Versus Racial Freedom: the Dilemma of Black Seventh-day Adventist Leadership" (Ph.D. diss., Vanderbilt University, 1984); "Ellen G. White's Use of the Term 'Race War' and Related Insights" (EGWE, SDoc).

Trevor O'Reggio

RADIANT RELIGION (RHPA, 1946, 271 pp.). First daily devotional book published by the Ellen G. White Estate. Materials were selected from Ellen White's published books and follow the overall theme of joy and rejoicing in God. Each meditation is less than a page in length and amplifies a parallel Bible text. Because all the selections are from Ellen White's previously published books, this book is not indexed separately. Nearly 20 such daily meditation books have been published since this one. The simplicity of this first book easily contrasts with later books, with their themes of emphasis, tables of contents, and Scripture indexes.

REASON, HUMAN. The debate regarding the role of human reason in life and in the acquisition of knowledge goes back at least as far as the Greek philosophers. For rationalist philosophers, complete certainty and direct knowledge of the nature of things was infallible and gained only by the exercise of reason. Sense experience was an unreliable means to understand the structure of reality. The scholastic theologians of the Middle Ages were heavily indebted to the rationalism of Aristotle. The era of the enlightenment shifted the emphasis toward empiricism, when sense experience provided the foundation for knowledge. Reason was employed not as a foundation, but as a tool for understanding and applying the knowledge gained from the senses. Other philosophies look to other foundations for knowledge, i.e., structure of human existence (existentialism), what works in practice (pragmatism), etc.

Ellen White held a high view of reason and gave it an important role in life and knowledge. Reason, she wrote, is one of the "great masterly talents entrusted to the human agent" by God (3MR 353; cf. SD 238). As the creation and gift of God, reason, along with other human faculties, reflects the image of God. The human mind is therefore capable of "comprehending divine things" (YI, Aug.10, 1899). Since reason is the gift of God, it belongs to God. It is to be consecrated to Him and used for His glory by serving others (RH, Sept. 25, 1894; LUH, Dec. 23, 1908; AH 280, 509).

Ellen White decries those who act as though they were "bereft of reason" (CS 150; CD 399; cf. GC88 234) and who allow their reason to be "dethroned" by Satan or intemperance (Te 25; CT 27). God desires us to exercise our reasoning powers to their fullest extent (5T 703; COL 358) in order "that with all the mind we may know and love our Creator" (COL 333; cf. 19MR 277). Since we are intelligent human beings, we are to use our common sense when it comes to health and fashion, reasoning from cause to effect to choose food and dress that will promote physical, mental, and spiritual health (2SM 427, 442; ST, Apr. 4, 1895; YI, Sept. 14, 1893; KC 144; Lt 103, 1897, in 1MCP 197).

Reason is not to be left untrained or uncultivated (BE, Nov. 1, 1893). "The faculties need to be strengthened by exercise, the mind is to be trained and expanded by taxing study" (CT 425). Time should be used wisely for this purpose (COL 343; SpTEd 40). Each one's eternal welfare depends upon the use made of entrusted talents, intellect, and reason (SW, Oct. 24, 1899).

"The study of the Bible will strengthen

and elevate the mind as no other study can" (1MCP 91). Philosophy and science cannot do for the mind what the Bible can do (CE 66, 107). The Bible disciplines, ennobles, purifies, refines, enriches, uplifts, strengthens, and energizes the mind (CE 66, 103, 107, 189; CG 507; Ed 171). In addition, "inward peace and a conscience void of offense toward God will quicken and invigorate the intellect" (CG 353). And God Himself can "sharpen the intellect" (ChS 262; cf. COL 146) and give it vigor (COL 288).

The exercise of the faculty of the mind should be held in balance with the rest of the God-given faculties. The mind will reach its highest achievement when the moral and physical powers are also strengthened for the development of the whole human being (CE 17, 211; 1MPC 197). When "appetites are perverted, the mental powers are weakened" (CTBH 19; cf. CG 187, 188, 392, 380, 403). Christ was an example of keeping appetite under the control of reason (CTBH 19; Con 50; cf. 1SM 275-279; CD 145). Anything that beclouds the intellect—such as tobacco (ST, Apr. 17, 1901), lust (COL 200), alcohol (Te 30; GCB, Apr. 1, 1899; RH, May 8, 1894), or amusements (AH 499, 521)—is sin (CTBH 8); for anything that lessens mental powers diminishes one's ability to "appreciate the plan of salvation" and to have "exalted views of God" (Con 62).

"It is God's purpose that the kingly power of sanctified reason, controlled by divine grace, shall bear sway in the lives of human beings. He who rules his spirit is in possession of this power" (AG 256). Such self-discipline places sanctified reason and conscience in control of passion and appetite (8T 49; ML 70; 1MCP 326; Con 58), impulse (TDG 269), human feelings (18MR 307), emotion (5T 177), and every word and deed (AG 256; Ev 668). She strongly warned against the yielding of one's will or reason to the control of another person (CE 6).

In addition to her call for the highest development and use of human reason, Ellen White also points to its limitations. Sin has brought degeneration, and the practice of sin has perverted the mind. The love of sin causes many to turn away from God and the Bible because they are a sting to the conscience (SpTEd 56; ST, Nov. 5, 1894). "Human intellect is not omnipotent" (5T 24). Because of the weakness, ignorance, and narrowness of the human mind, reason alone cannot understand or form a correct idea of God. "Philosophy cannot determine the ways and works of God; the human mind cannot measure infinity." This knowledge comes from the Bible and Jesus Christ alone (6BC 1079). "To human reason the whole plan of salvation is a waste of mercy" (YI, July 19, 1900; cf. FW 65; COL 104; 1SM 402; SC 107). "Truths are to be received not within the reach of our reason, and not for us to explain." Such truths given by Revelation are to be "implicitly received" by faith, (rather than by human reason) "as the words of an infinite God" (13MR 20; 1SM 163).

For Ellen White, then, reason is not the absolute foundation of truth and knowledge, as it is with rationalism. Christians must not give trust and pride to human wisdom, nor fall into the sin of exalting, idolizing, or deifying human reason. To place human reason above the Word of God is arrogance and conceit (RH, Jan. 19, 1886; 5T 79, 703), leading to infidelity and apostasy (SW, Mar. 1, 1909; GC 600, 601).

Ellen White decried those who publicly exalt human reason "above the teachings of the Word" (PK 170), and "boast of the sufficiency of human reason" (PP 124). Reason and science should not be placed above Scripture, the unerring standard (PK 170, 171; 4BC 1142; CT 425). Not the rationalism of the school men but the Bible is to be the foundational authority (GC88 193; cf. 8T 298). Human reason must bow before "the majesty of divine revelation" (Ed 170).

All human faculties, including reason, are to be brought under the influence of the Spirit of God (ST, Nov. 5, 1894; May 28, 1896). The Holy Spirit convicts (RH, Nov. 5, 1895), enlightens, and reveals to the mind the things of God (TMK 206), and opens the human mind to truth (COL 59). The possibilities of the human mind are not limited even by eternity. Since God is infinite, "we may to all eternity be ever searching, ever learning, yet never exhaust the riches of His wisdom, His goodness, or His power" (Ed 172).

Ed Zinke

REBAPTISM, see **BAPTISM**.

RECREATION, see **STANDARDS OF CHRISTIAN BEHAVIOR; GAMES AND SPORTS; COMPETITION**.

REDEMPTION. The basic ideas of the biblical concept of redemption (a costly reclaiming or deliverance from oppression, especially reclaiming from sin and restoration to holiness through the blood of Christ [1 Cor. 1:30; Eph. 1:17]) are all evident in Ellen White's writings. In the Bible, God is the Redeemer and humanity the redeemed. From this perspective Ellen White expounds on the breadth and depth of redemption. For her it is the central theme of the Bible, an inexhaustible theme that passes the comprehension of the deepest thought, a theme that angels desire to look into, and that will be the science and song of the redeemed throughout eternity (ML 360). She often emphasizes the aspect of restoration: "Redemption is that process by which the soul is trained for heaven. This training means a knowledge of Christ. It means emancipation from ideas, habits, and

practices that have been gained in the school of the prince of darkness. The soul must be delivered from all that is opposed to loyalty to God" (DA 330). "It is the purpose of redemption, not only to blot out sin, but to give back to man those spiritual gifts lost because of sin's dwarfing power" (COL 266). This purpose was achieved at a tremendous cost: heaven was imperiled by it, Christ gave all for it, yet the cost of it will not be realized until the redeemed stand before God's throne. The basis of redemption is love; redemption accomplished more than humanity's salvation, and because of it all things belong to God.

See also: Atonement; Cross of Christ; Gethsemane; Salvation, Plan of; *Redemption*; *The Story of Redemption*.

Further reading: COL 196, 362; CT 32, 462; DA 19, 20, 131, 626; 1SM 403; SC 45, 88.

Kwabena Donkor

REDEMPTION (RHPA, 1877-1878). Series of eight pamphlets written by Ellen White on the life and ministry of Christ and the early church. Pamphlet 1 is entitled *Redemption, or the First Advent of Christ, With His Life and Ministry*; number 2 is *Redemption, or the Temptation of Christ in the Wilderness*; number 3, *Redemption, or the Miracles of Christ, the Mighty One*; number 4, *Redemption, or the Teachings of Christ, the Anointed One*; number 5, *Redemption, or the Sufferings of Christ, His Trial and Crucifixion*; number 6, *Redemption, or the Resurrection of Christ, and His Ascension*; number 7, *Redemption, or the Ministry of Peter and the Conversion of Saul*; and number 8, *Redemption, or the Teachings of Paul, and His Mission to the Gentiles*. With the exception of number 2, *The Temptation of Christ in the Wilderness*, which was written earlier and in more detail, the *Redemption* series was a rearrangement of the chapters of *The Spirit of Prophecy*, volumes 2 and 3, published simultaneously. Pamphlet 2 was republished in 1971 as the booklet *Confrontation. Although the original series was printed as individual pamphlets, they were also printed two pamphlets together and came as a box set.

REFLECTING CHRIST (RHPA, 1985, 382 pp.). Fourteenth daily devotional book published from selections of the writings of Ellen White drawn mainly from periodicals such as *Youth's Instructor, Review and Herald, Signs of the Times,* her books, and unpublished writings. Many of the passages were abridged in order to fit into the desired length for each daily reading. The title reflects the theme of the book as well as the desire of her own life. In each reading the writer points to the example of Jesus Christ and holds Him up as the model for every Christian to emulate.

Michael D. Pearson

REFORMATION, PROTESTANT. In Ellen White's writings the significance and essence of the Protestant Reformation, which began in the sixteenth century, is captured by the following depiction of Martin Luther and his work: "Zealous, ardent, and devoted, knowing no fear but the fear of God, and acknowledging no foundation for religious faith but the Holy Scriptures, Luther was the man for his time; through him God accomplished a great work for the reformation of the church and the enlightenment of the world" (GC 120). The breadth of the Reformation, however, is understood by Ellen White to go beyond Luther's work in Germany to include similar developments in other parts of Europe, all of which she describes in considerable detail. These areas include Bohemia, Switzerland, France, the Netherlands, Denmark, Sweden, and England. Although Ellen White sees some variations in the local manifestations of the Reformation, she perceives the vital principle

of the Reformation to be consistent throughout: the Sacred Scriptures contained the vital principle of the Reformation. "It was the work of the Reformation to restore to men the Word of God" (*ibid.* 388).

Flowing from the vital principle of the Reformation, namely, the Scriptures as the only foundation for religious belief, Ellen White mentions several collateral benefits of the Reformation. Not only did the Reformers base their work on Scripture, but as a result of their work, the Scriptures were given to all people, although the interpretive authority of the church somewhat hindered the testimony of the Scriptures. Similarly, she notes that in the face of persecution and death, the Reformers carried the truth of God's Word to all classes of people, high and low, rich and poor, learned and ignorant. Since the Reformation presented an open Bible to the world, it had the net effect of "unsealing the precepts of the law of God and urging its claims upon the consciences of the people" (*ibid.* 230), leading to a better understanding of the Sabbath. "When the Reformation swept back the darkness that had rested down on all Christendom, Sabbathkeepers were brought to light in many lands" (SR 354). Implied in the foregoing statement is the idea that the Reformation had the overall effect of lifting the darkness that had been resting on Christendom during the Middle Ages.

What made the Reformation possible? It is customary to observe that the social and educational conditions of the age were important precursors to the Reformation. Without discounting these factors, Ellen White gives a special place to divine providence and superintendence with regard to the personalities and timing of the Reformation. From Wycliffe, through Huss and others to Luther, she discerns the divine hand, for through them "The minds of men were directed to the long-forgotten Word of God. A divine hand was preparing the way for the Great Reformation" (GC 96). The spiritual origin of the Reformation is further acknowledged when Ellen White writes: "From the secret place of prayer came the power that shook the world in the Great Reformation" (*ibid.* 210).

In spite of the noted significance of the Reformation of the sixteenth century, Ellen White has the following assessment of it: "The Reformation did not, as many suppose, end with Luther. It is to be continued to the close of this world's history. Luther had a great work to do in reflecting to others the light which God had permitted to shine upon him; yet he did not receive all the light which was to be given to the world. From that time to this, new light has been continually shining upon the Scriptures, and new truths have been constantly unfolding" (SR 353).

Further reading: GC 96, 171-245, 596; 4T 403.

Kwabena Donkor

RELIGIOUS LIBERTY. Propelled into the fight for religious liberty by opposition to Sunday legislation, Seventh-day Adventists quickly developed a broader agenda, declaring that they would "violate the golden rule" if they acquiesced in religious legislation that wasn't directed at themselves (*American Sentinel*, Oct. 23, 1889). Through the *American Sentinel* (forerunner of *Liberty*) and the National Religious Liberty Association, they agitated against all forms of governmental restrictions on liberty of conscience.

Although Sunday laws were the primary focus of most *American Sentinel* articles, the magazine also dealt with such issues as a proposal to outlaw parochial schools, the requirement that public school students— including Roman Catholics—listen to the King James Version of the Bible, and an attempt

to keep a Universalist from preaching at a retirement home of soldiers because his views were not considered orthodox. The *Sentinel* saw each of these as infringements or attempted infringements on religious freedom. In time, Seventh-day Adventists would be recognized as some of America's most prominent advocates of religious freedom and the separation of church and state.

The denomination's entry into the religious liberty arena was enthusiastically supported by Ellen G. White. Viewing the issue historically and prophetically as well as reacting to contemporary conditions, she described such early religious dissidents as John Wycliffe, the Protestant Reformers, and the Puritans as fighting for freedom of conscience, even though they were "not entirely free" from a "spirit of intolerance" and didn't all fully "comprehend the great principle of religious liberty" (GC 292, 293). She especially praised Roger Williams for realizing, unlike many others, that religious "freedom was the inalienable right of all, whatever . . . their creed" (*ibid.* 293). "The banner of truth and religious liberty held aloft . . . during the centuries that have passed," she said, "has, in this last conflict, been committed to our hands" (AA 68, 69).

Declaring that Satan "works to restrict religious liberty" (7T 180), and that government officials who pass such restrictive laws "assume the right that is God's alone" (DA 630), she predicted the eventual demise of religious freedom, even in the United States (Ev 236). Urging Seventh-day Adventists to resist vigorously developments in that direction, she said, "It is our duty, as we see the signs of approaching peril, to arouse to action." She also added, "We are not doing the will of God if we sit in quietude, doing nothing to preserve liberty of conscience" (5T 713, 714).

See also: Church and State; Sunday Legislation; United States in Prophecy.

Further reading: 5T 711-720; 9T 227-231; TM 206, 219; SR 338, 339; GC 80, 201, 251, 252, 289-298, 363; *American Sentinel*, 1886-1893 (see especially Jan. 30, June 26, and Oct. 23, 1889, and Mar. 6, 1890); D. Morgan, *Adventism and the American Republic: The Public Involvement of a Major Apocalyptic Movement* (Knoxville, Tenn.: University of Tennessee Press, 2001); A. Phelps Stokes and L. Pfeffer, *Church and State in the United States*, rev. one-vol. ed. (New York: Harper & Row, 1964), pp. 344, 345; L. Pfeffer, *Church, State, and Freedom*, rev. ed. (Boston: Beacon Press, 1967), p. 340.

Dennis Pettibone

REMEDIES, see **NATURAL REMEDIES; HERBAL REMEDIES; SIMPLE REMEDIES; DRUGS.**

REMNANT CHURCH. The use of the term *remnant* in Ellen White's writings has, with a few exceptions, a fundamental theological content. Even in cases in which she makes reference to the remnant of Judah, e.g., those who returned from exile (PK 376, 426), those who remained in the land (*ibid.* 333), or the remnant of the Jews who accepted Jesus as the Messiah (AA 376, 377), the emphasis is always on their relationship with God. Most of the uses are found in the context of events related to the nature, mission, and experience of the end-time people of God. Her use of the term is predominantly eschatological.

White's view of the identity of the end-time remnant is determined by her understanding of Revelation 12:17. The passage describes what will take place during the last days, when, after the experience of the church during the Christian Era, the dragon gets ready to launch his last attack against the remnant of the seed of the woman (DA 398). That end-time remnant is described as those who have the patience of the saints, keep the commandments of God, and have the testimony and the faith of Jesus (Rev. 12:17; 14:12; TM 58; ST, Nov. 1, 1899; RH, July 28, 1904). Although the Adventist movement is recognized by her as the only one meeting that particular description (LDE 43), she does not conclude that the people of God are found exclusively in the Adventist Church. On the contrary, "the greater part of the followers of Christ" is found "in the various churches professing the Protestant faith" (GC 383). Many individuals who "have not bowed the knee to Baal" (PK 188) are found throughout the world (e.g., in Catholic countries, in Europe, South America, China, and India [*ibid.* 188, 189]). Even "among unbelievers" (RH, Nov. 10, 1904) there is a remnant characterized by willingness to serve the Lord according to the light they have received and by openness to new biblical light (ST, Nov. 23, 1904).

Ellen White believed, however, that the end-time remnant is embodied in the Adventist movement for a particular divine purpose. The remnant is a reform movement within Christianity responsible for the spiritual restoration of truths rejected or ignored by professed believers (CC 269; cf. CD 36). They are particularly responsible for restoring the breach made in the law when the Sabbath was substituted by Sunday (PK 678). In the past God had always preserved a remnant to serve Him in a world of apostasy and idolatry (PP 125). The presence of the remnant meant that God had not completely forsaken His people but that He was calling them, through the remnant, to return to complete loyalty to Him. Through them He was preserving His truth, plans, and revealed will (PP 545; PK 22). It is that commitment to biblical truth that characterizes the end-time remnant (PC 57, 58). They are to proclaim to the world the truth as it is in Jesus (9T 274), the unity of law and gospel (2SM 385), and the present truth of the three angels' messages of Revelation 14:6-12 (10MR 314; 2SM 224, 225).

According to Revelation 12:17 the dragon is angered against and at war with the eschatological remnant (2T 105). It is opposed to their mission, the proclamation of the messages of the three angels (2SM 117), and hates them for obeying God's commandments (7BC 974). In its attack against them, the dragon, who is disconcerted by their oneness and unity, tries to divide them (1T 327), to make them doubt the leading of God in their existence (1MCP 95). Through the use of human instrumentalities, the dragon attempts to overthrow the remnant through false teachings (5T 295, 296; 1SM 204) and by making of none effect the testimony of the Spirit of God in their experience (FLB 296). The confrontation between the two will reach its climax when the dragon threatens the remnant by death, if they do not worship the beast and receive the mark of the beast (CET 188). Its intention is to exterminate them from the face of the earth in order to rule over the world without opposition (9T 231). But the remnant finds their defense in God (CET 188).

The conflict between the dragon and the remnant will result in the final polarization of the human race. At the close of the great controversy every individual will have to take a stand for or against God's last message to the human race (CH 208; EW 261). At that time the law of God will be almost universally rejected, except by the remnant people of God (ST, Apr. 22, 1889). Consequently, iniquity will reach a height never before witnessed on the planet, opposed only by a remnant that will remain true to God (RH, July 24, 1913; ST, June 9, 1881). At that time a large number of professed believers will deny their faith (AA 535; GC 608) and the result will be apostasy in the Protestant world and the formation of an end-time coalition of evil

powers against the remnant people of God (5T 449). But the remnant will not be overcome by this coalition.

The end-time remnant will be triumphant over the dragon (AA 590). God is gathering them (EW 69); they rely only on God's mercy, find in prayer their defense (5T 473), and overcome through the blood of the Lamb and the word of their testimony (EW 114). At the second coming of Christ, He will gather them from among the nations of the earth (PK 728). But before that happens, the remnant will pass through a cleansing process (1888 Materials 878). Among the end-time remnant are those who profess to be members of it, but when the final test comes and they face the deceptions of the dragon they will be sifted out and the chaff will be separated from the wheat (Mar 203). Then, during the final polarization of the human race, the true people of God will be clearly identified (Ev 592) and many others from every nation and people will take their stand for the Lord against the forces of evil (GC 607). That faithful eschatological remnant will endure to the end.

The important role of the remnant in the closing of the great controversy explains the many exhortations that Ellen White addresses to them. She advises against internal conflicts in the remnant church (3SM 19, 23), fanaticism (*ibid.* 378), indifference against the needs of a perishing world (8T 24) and against the peril of deemphasizing their unique message (2SM 385). She calls them to wake up from their lethargy and prepare for the coming of the Lord (1T 263; EW 119). They are exhorted to experience true conversion (CD 36), to be obedient to the truth (2SM 380), to live lives characterized by genuine love to God and to others (1SM 387), and to pray for the gift of the grace of love (BTS, June 1, 1903). They are invited to seek the childlike simplicity that characterized their Savior (18MR 11).

Further reading: G. F. Hasel, *The Remnant: The History and Theology of the Remnant Idea From Genesis to Isaiah* (AUP, 1972, 1980); H. K. LaRondelle, "The Remnant and the Three Angels' Messages," in R. Dederen, ed., *Handbook of Seventh-day Adventist Theology* (RHPA, 2000), pp. 857-892; R. W. Olson, "God's True Church" (EGWE, SDoc); G. Pfandl, "The Remnant Church and the Spirit of Prophecy," in *Symposium in Revelation—Book II*, ed. Frank Holbrook (BRI, 1992), pp. 295-333; G. Pfandl, *The Gift of Prophecy* (PPPA, 2008), pp. 39-47; Ángel M. Rodríguez, ed., *Toward a Theology of the Remnant* (BRI, 2009).

Ángel Manuel Rodríguez

REMNANT CHURCH, THE (PPPA, 1952, 72 pp.). A compilation of statements taken from Ellen White's articles and letters. The book's purpose is to counter the assertions of some who had left the denomination, claiming God had forsaken it, and to assure those who remain that God is still guiding the church as in earlier years. The 72-page booklet has three sections, which contain Ellen White's thoughts on support for church organization, warnings against disorganization, a reaffirmation of God's love for the church, the importance of the denominational name, and confidence in a globally representative General Conference. Retitled in 1994 as *God's Remnant Church*.

Jack Blanco

REPENTANCE. In the experience of salvation, repentance is the sinner's response to God's saving activity on his or her behalf. It is a reversal of a wrong attitude toward God, a change of life's direction. Opposite to a life in sin, it is a "turning from self to Christ" (MB 87). It is a growing experience (AA 561), a new orientation of the believer that affects

the whole human existence in all its spheres.

Ellen White's thoughts on repentance build on the biblical material (Joel 2:12, 13; Amos 5:6; Jer. 15:19; Eze. 18:30-32; Matt. 3:2; 4:17; Acts 2:38; 5:31; Rom. 2:4; 2 Cor. 7:10; Rev. 2:5; 3:19). Repentance "includes sorrow for sin and a turning away from it" (SC 23). It leads to "forsaking of sin" (AA 324). She seriously calls to repentance God's people of today, the Laodicean church, which needs to experience a wholehearted return to God (Rev. 3:19; 1SM 126).

According to Ellen White, repentance is not a human achievement, but "the gift of God, and whom He pardons He first makes penitent" (1SM 324). It is true that repentance does precede the forgiveness of sins. "But must the sinner wait till he has repented before he can come to Jesus? Is repentance to be made an obstacle between the sinner and the Savior?" No. The unrepentant may come to Christ as they are and receive from Christ the gift of repentance (SC 26; Acts 5:31; John 6:37). Thus repentance is God's work accomplished through the Holy Spirit (ML 49) and the Word of God (1SM 393). It comes from Christ (SC 25; 1SM 343). Only in this way can new life be born. The knowledge of God's kindness and goodness leads people to repentance (COL 202; Rom. 2:4). Christ's love and death evoke repentance (1SM 341). A knowledge of God's plan of salvation (PP 630) and his judgment can lead people to repentance (PK 309). The Spirit of God transforms a sinner by the power of God's grace (ML 49).

Repentance is a new orientation and direction in life. It is a radical change of mind (1SM 393), a new thinking about God, life, sin, the law of God, ourselves, the world, and service. God never turns away one who repents (CTBH 13). There is no salvation without repentance (1SM 365), because forgiveness of sin can be obtained only if preceded by sincere repentance.

Artificial or superficial repentance regrets the consequences of sin but does not have remorse over sin itself (DA 300; PP 392). Repentance must be thorough (MM 96) and sincere (MYP 108). Repenting persons accept responsibility for their sin (SC 41). True repentance brings joy (MYP 108). David is taken as a model of a genuine repentance (SC 24, 25).

Further reading: SC 23-26; RH, Apr. 1, 1890.

Jiří Moskala

RESEARCH CENTERS, see **ELLEN G. WHITE ESTATE, INC.**

RESTAURANTS. In the late 1890s and early 1900s Ellen White wrote a number of messages regarding the importance of food ministry (see 7T 110-137; HFM). She recommended the establishment of health food factories in connection with Adventist schools and sanitariums and the establishment of vegetarian restaurants in large cities. She saw vegetarian restaurants as a means of attracting the spiritual interest of people in secular environments, of teaching health principles, and of helping people live a better life (cf. CD 274-277; CH 481-488). She felt concerned that these institutions would not become simply commercial enterprises but would reflect a genuine spiritual ministry to the lost. Thus, she suggested that Adventist literature on temperance and dietetic reform be available for patrons to read and that restaurant workers be instructed on how to minister to people (CH 482). "This work must be carried forward as a means of gospel enlightenment to those who have not given themselves to the Lord," she emphasized (HFM 89).

RESTORATIONISM. The impulse in church history to perfect the church through bypassing historical tradition (with its failures and apostasy) in order to restore the primitive purity of the apostolic age. Also called "primitivism" or "restitutionism," this phenomenon flourished in nineteenth-century North American Protestantism. The main American manifestations arose out of the revivalism of Barton W. Stone (1772-1844) and the Campbells (Thomas [1763-1854], but mostly his son Alexander [1788-1866]) in the Ohio River valley and the mid-South. They were mainly referred to as "Christians" or "Disciples of Christ."

However, the wing of the Christianite movement that most directly influenced developments in Adventism was the Christian Connexion. Strongly anti-Calvinistic and closely associated with the Freewill Baptists, its geographic strongholds were in Vermont, New Hampshire, and Maine. The main theological features of the Connexion movement (besides its decisively Arminian views) were its congregational polity (suspicious of hierarchy), practice of open Communion, emphasis on freedom of opinion (hence an anti-creedal, "no creed but the Bible" mentality), a decidedly rationalistic bent (if it was not reasonable and simple, it was probably wrong), and anti-Trinitarian or unitarian tendencies. A number of their ministers and lay preachers were active in the Millerite movement, including two leading pioneers of Seventh-day Adventism—James White and Joseph Bates.

Richard Hughes has distinguished between three major types of primitivistic or restorationist tendencies in church history: (1) *ecclesiastical*, (2) *ethical*, and (3) *experiential*. In these restorationist terms Ellen White seems closest to the categories of *ethical* and *experiential* restorationism. For her, the *experiential* category could be characterized as the recovery of a "premillennial" eschatological experience of the early church and its attendant *ethical* experiences (through saving grace) that would prepare a people to meet their God at the literal, visible, and imminent return of Christ. While most of the pre-Civil War restorationists in America were deeply concerned with matters of polity and tended to downgrade the Old Testament and the Law, Ellen White called for the restoration of the authority of the whole Bible, not just the New Testament, including the ethical authority of the Ten Commandments. Furthermore, she ultimately saw the Bible as the key source of not only *ethical* and *experiential* eschatology, but as the catalyst for a dynamic experience of Jesus as Savior and Lord. Beyond these adaptations of the restorationist heritage of American Protestantism, she embraced almost none of its other major emphases.

There is, however, one other type of restorationism in the thought of Ellen White: her *Great Controversy* (and in a broader sense the whole *Conflict of the Ages Series) was written from a restorationist perspective of the Reformation. A major theme of these volumes is the "restoration" of all the Bible doctrines lost in church history. Thus Ellen White embraced what could be called *doctrinal* restorationism, which may have some points in common with Hughes' *ecclesiastical* type of restorationism. But though Hughes' *ecclesiastical* restorationism had theological overtones, it was concerned mainly with practical church governance, not with restoration of doctrine.

By contrast, in developing church structures for Seventh-day Adventism the Whites even opposed a certain type of *ecclesiastical* restorationism. The restorationist or primitivist model called for every feature of church organization to have some sort of explicit New Testament precedent. The Whites saw

no need for such a rationale. James White argued that the lack of a New Testament precedent for a publishing house showed that such precedent was unnecessary. Thus the Whites moved beyond biblical literalism in church polity, justifying organizational innovation on the basis of recovering the New Testament doctrine and mission. Certainly Ellen White's work of *doctrinal* restorationism is in a different category than the classic restorationism of nineteenth-century-Protestant New Testament primitivism.

Further reading: S. E. Ahlstrom, *A Religious History of the American People* (Garden City, N.Y.: Image Books, 1975), vol. 1, pp. 540-548; D. E. Harrell, Jr., "Restorationism and the Stone-Campbell Tradition," in C. H. Lippy and P. W. Williams, eds., *Encyclopedia of the American Religious Experience* (New York: Scribner's, 1988), vol. 2, pp. 845-858; R. T. Hughes, "Christian Primitivism as Perfectionism: From Anabaptists to Pentecostals," in S. M. Burgess, ed., *Reaching Beyond: Chapters in the History of Perfectionism* (Peabody, Mass.: Hendrickson Publishers, 1986), pp. 213-255.

Woodrow W. Whidden

RESURRECTION. Ellen White speaks of three eschatological resurrections: a "special" resurrection, followed by the first and second general resurrections. She locates the special resurrection during the seventh plague preceding the *second coming of Christ. When God declares, "It is done," a mighty earthquake (Rev. 16:17, 18) opens graves, "and 'many of them that sleep in the dust of the earth . . . awake, some to everlasting life, and some to shame and everlasting contempt' (Dan. 12:2). All who have died in the faith of the third angel's message come forth from the tomb glorified, to hear God's covenant of peace with those who have kept His law. 'They also which pierced him' (Rev. 1:7), those that mocked and derided Christ's dying agonies, and the most violent opposers of His truth and His people, are raised to behold Him in His glory and to see the honor placed upon the loyal and obedient" (GC 637). The purpose of the special resurrection is to permit certain groups of both righteous and wicked to be raised to witness the final events and the return of Christ in glory. Jesus promised Caiaphas that he would witness this event (Matt. 26:64). Also, Revelation 14:13 promises a special blessing on those who would die in faith after the giving of the third angel's message. Ellen White saw in this verse a promise that those "keeping the Sabbath" (FLB 182) would be "blessed" by coming forth in the special resurrection.

Soon after the special resurrection, the righteous hear the voice of God declaring the day and hour of Jesus' coming (GC 640). As the earth experiences the fury of the seventh plague, "the voice of the Son of God calls forth the sleeping saints" (*ibid.* 644) in the first general resurrection. Though they come from the grave the same in physical size as they entered the tomb (*ibid.*), their bodies are changed from corruptible to incorruptible (1 Cor. 15:52), and they rise in immortal health and vigor to meet their Lord in the air (EW 287).

Regarding the resurrection of believers' children who died before they were capable of personal faith and accountability, Ellen White wrote that "the faith of the believing parents covers the children, as when God sent His judgments upon the firstborn of the Egyptians" (3SM 314). "As the little infants come forth immortal from their dusty beds, they immediately wing their way to their mother's arms. They meet again nevermore to part" (2SM 260). "Whether all the children of unbelieving parents will be saved we cannot

tell," she wrote, "because God has not made known His purpose in regard to this matter" (3SM 315). Some, however, will be raised: "Many of the little ones have no mother there. . . . The angels receive the motherless infants and conduct them to the tree of life" (2SM 260; LDE 293). She noted the case of a mentally impaired man who unfortunately had only the reasoning capacity of a child, but who also had the "submission and obedience of a child," and would "have an inheritance among the saints in light" (LDE 293, 294).

The second general resurrection takes place after the *millennium. Jesus, the angels, and the saved precede the New Jerusalem to the earth (GC 663). "Then in terrible, fearful majesty, Jesus called forth the wicked dead; and they came up with the same feeble, sickly bodies that went into the grave" (EW 292). "Those who lived before the flood, come forth with their giant-like stature, more than twice as tall as men now living upon the earth, and well proportioned"—but bearing the marks of disease and death (3SG 84; cf. GC 662). As they behold the glory of Christ, the wicked exclaim with one voice, " 'Blessed is He that cometh in the name of the Lord!' It is not love to Jesus that inspires this utterance. The force of truth urges the words from unwilling lips" (GC 662). They have the same spirit of rebellion with which they died, but they have "no new probation in which to remedy the defects of their past lives"(*ibid.*) A second probation would gain them nothing, because their characters are unchanged. The purpose of the second resurrection is to arraign all before God in judgment. All are sentenced according to their works, as recorded in the books of heaven. Then all the wicked are thrown into the "lake of fire" (Rev. 20:14, 15; 21:8), where they are consumed until they cease to exist (WLF 12).

Many question why the wicked are raised

again only to be destroyed by God. It is because the first death, which each has suffered, is not the wages of sin (Rom. 6:23) and is not in accordance with works (Matt. 16:27; 2 Cor. 5:10; Rev. 20:12, 13; 22:12). The righteous also have suffered the first death. The wicked must be judged and sentenced according to the record of their own works (GC 544). This judgment takes place during the 1,000 years between the first and second resurrections (1 Cor. 6:2, 3; *ibid.* 660, 661).

Further reading: FLB 182-184; GC 636, 637, 644, 662, 663; LDE 271-278; Mar 281, 282; J. C. Brunt, "Resurrection and Glorification," in R. Dederen, ed., *Handbook of Seventh-day Adventist Theology* (RHPA, 2000), pp. 347-374.

Edwin E. Reynolds

RESURRECTION OF CHRIST. Ellen White's clearest descriptions of the resurrection of Christ are found in *The Desire of Ages* (pp. 779-794) and *Early Writings* (pp. 181-190). Sunday morning before daybreak the angel Gabriel descended from heaven to roll away the stone of the tomb. After another angel unwrapped the linen from the head of Jesus, when Gabriel gave the command "Son of God, Thy Father calls Thee! Come forth" (EW 182; cf. DA 780) Jesus rose from the tomb by His own power, "by the life that was in Himself" (DA 785; cf. COL 358).

Many people witnessed His resurrection. The Roman soldiers saw the glorified Savior and fell as if dead (1SM 303). Then, trembling with fear, they spread the news in Jerusalem, alarming the priests and Pilate (Matt. 28:2-4, 11-15). Many others came forth from their graves and gave their testimony in the city (Matt. 27:52, 53). The women and disciples who came early that day at different times represent further witnesses of what happened (Matt. 28:5-7). When Mary met Jesus, He

said, "Detain Me not." He "refused" to accept her worship until He had ascended to the Father and received "the assurance that His sacrifice was accepted" (DA 790; John 20:11-18).

According to Ellen White, the theological meaning of the resurrection of Jesus includes victory over sin and death, and ultimately the destruction of Satan and his kingdom (EW 182). Christ's words "I am the resurrection, and the life" could be spoken "only by the Deity" (DA 785). Because He "has life in Himself," He has "the right to give immortality" (*ibid.* 786, 787). The memorial of Christ's resurrection, baptism by immersion (Rom. 6:4), points Christians to the day when "the same power that raised Christ from the dead will raise His church" (*ibid.* 787; Rom. 8:11). As the risen Christ was recognized by His disciples in the upper room, so also at the *second coming of Christ the new bodies of the saints will preserve their former identity (*ibid.* 804; 6BC 1092).

Johannes Kovar

RETIREMENT YEARS, THE (RHPA, 1990, 240 pp.). Compilation from the published and unpublished writings of Ellen White on the subjects of retirement, seniors, and old age. Ellen White, who died at the age of 87 in 1915, continued a very active life in her later years. During the last 20 years of her life, part of which she lived in Australia (1891-1900), she served as a counselor to the work of Seventh-day Adventists, attended hundreds of meetings with church administrators and local churches, and wrote some of her most important books and hundreds of letters and periodical articles. Her life, to some extent, is an example to others that seniors can live a meaningful and active life.

The Retirement Years includes many of Ellen White's thoughts and counsels on the usefulness of older workers for the church, the care of seniors, the obligation of children to aged parents, and the importance of wills. A few chapters also give examples of her words of assurance and comfort to those who were afflicted with illnesses, who faced death, and who were bereaved. The book's four appendices include a detailed and fascinating sketch of Ellen White's activities after age 65 (pp. 191-215) and a transcript of G. B. Starr's comments at Ellen White's Elmshaven funeral service (July 18, 1915) describing his last visit with her before she died (pp. 216-222).

Denis Fortin

REVELATION, BOOK OF. Ellen White's view of the book of Revelation is most clearly discerned in the two major treatments in which she directly addresses her understanding of the context and purpose of the book. The first and most comprehensive treatment was published in *Testimonies to Ministers* (pp. 112-119). The second treatment consists of two chapters in *The Acts of the Apostles* (pp. 568-592).

Ellen White's approach to Revelation was informed by the basic conviction that an end-time explosion in the understanding of Daniel and Revelation was the key factor behind the rise of the Advent movement. She felt, in other words, that in her time God had lifted a veil from off these books, enabling them to be fully understood (TM 113). The book of Revelation, therefore, was addressed to those living in the last days and the time of fulfillment was near (*ibid.* 113, 115, 116; 6T 61, 62).

Although the Adventist pioneers had invested much in the study of Revelation, Ellen White was convinced that the book had not yet been fully understood (TM 113). Those wishing a deeper understanding would need to approach the book "humbly and meekly" (*ibid.* 114). The deeper understanding of

Revelation that they gained would be a great boon to character development (*ibid.*). There would be a "great revival" (*ibid.* 113) marked by "an entirely different religious experience" (*ibid.* 114). So a primary goal of Revelation, in her thinking, was not merely to impart knowledge, but to develop character.

In terms of method, this deeper study would need to take two somewhat contrasting forms. On the one hand, Ellen White advocated studying Revelation in the context of Daniel, as a follow-up to the visions given in the latter book (*ibid.*; EW 231). The two books were to be treated as close companions (TM 115; AA 585). On the other hand, she urged people to study Revelation in the context of all the other prophecies in the Bible (TM 112). She even went so far as to suggest that in the book of Revelation "all the books of the Bible meet and end" (AA 585). So a whole-Bible approach, with special attention to Daniel, was the basic method she thought should be applied to Revelation. But while Daniel and Revelation are complementary, the two books are not the same. Daniel contains much that was sealed up (Dan. 12:4), but Revelation was never sealed—its mysteries have always been "open to the study of all" (*ibid.* 584; RH, Aug. 31, 1897).

Ellen White articulated a high spiritual purpose for the book of Revelation. First, the book was designed to keep the human agent out of sight and to exalt God and His law (TM 112). When readers view the glory of God portrayed there, human pride is laid in the dust. Second, the close connection between heaven and earth in the visions was designed to teach that the connection between God and His people is "close and decided" (*ibid.* 114; cf. AA 586). Third, rightly understood, Revelation enables presenters to "uplift Jesus as the center of all hope" (TM 118). Revelation was not designed to satisfy curiosity about the future but to fix human eyes on Jesus and encourage a closer walk with God.

Ellen White's view of Revelation's authorship and time of writing was in harmony with the traditions of the Early Church Fathers, as well as the conservative consensus around the turn of the twentieth century. She affirmed that the author of Revelation was the last survivor of the disciples, presumably John the son of Zebedee (AA 569). The Apocalypse was written in the time of Emperor Domitian, who summoned John to Rome to be tried for his faith, had him cast into a cauldron of boiling oil, and then exiled him to the Isle of Patmos, a place of banishment for criminals (*ibid.* 569, 570).

Where her statements are clear, Ellen White seems to consistently apply the *historicist* method to the text of Revelation (EW 230). "Some of the scenes depicted in this prophecy are in the past, some are now taking place; some bring to view the close of the great conflict between the powers of darkness and the Prince of heaven, and some reveal the triumphs and joys of the redeemed in the earth made new" (AA 584). At the same time, she also acknowledged that the book of Revelation was given "for the guidance and comfort of the church throughout the Christian dispensation" (*ibid.* 583), something more akin to the "idealist" approach. The promises to the overcomer at the end of each of the seven letters (e.g., Rev. 2:7; 3:5; and 3:21) belong to all the faithful ones striving against evil throughout the centuries of darkness and superstition (*ibid.* 588). The message to Ephesus offers ministers today an example of how to reprove sin (Ms 136, 1902, in 7BC 956). The message to Laodicea applies to all who profess to keep the law of God but are not doers of it (RH, Oct. 17, 1899; DA 489, 490).

Whichever way one studies Revelation, however, Ellen White saw the book of

Revelation fulfilling a special role in the final era of earth's history (TM 113, 115, 116; GC 341, 342). The truths of the book are "addressed to those living in these last days" (TM 113; cf. 8T 301). Many parts of Revelation she cites in this context (Rev. 15:2, 3; 21:2-22; 22:1-5, 14; and 14:2-5) are directly concerned with the ultimate triumph of God's remnant church (AA 590-592). She believed that her generation was nearing the time that those prophecies would be fulfilled (TM 113). So while historicism was her primary approach to Revelation, she understood that the entire book would have special significance for the very last days (*ibid.* 116; 9T 267). Even the chains of history portrayed in Revelation would help God's people correctly estimate the value of things and discern "the true aim of life" (PK 548).

Ellen White's interpretation of events or passages of the book of Revelation are scattered throughout her writings, particularly in *The Great Controversy*. The examples that follow are covered in the order of the texts in Revelation to which they apply, beginning with chapter 1 and ending with chapter 22. White understood the "Lord's day," when the Spirit came upon John (Rev. 1:9, 10), to be the Sabbath day (AA 581; YI, Apr. 5, 1900). She associated the heavenly scene of Revelation 4 and 5 with the ascension of Christ to heaven after His resurrection (DA 834, 835). The lion and the lamb (Rev. 5:5, 6) are both symbols of Christ, representing the union of omnipotent power with self-sacrificing love (AA 589). The heavenly signs of the sixth seal (Rev. 6:12-14) are usually associated with events leading up to the Advent movement in the mid-nineteenth century (GC 333, 334).

While her language falls short of an endorsement, White approvingly reported the predictions of Josiah Litch related to the fifth and sixth trumpets (*ibid.* 334, 335). The scene of Revelation 10 describes a point in history during which the time periods of Daniel have reached their conclusion and the final proclamation of the gospel has begun (Ms 59, 1900, in 7BC 971). The two witnesses of Revelation 11 represent the Old and New Testaments, and the descriptions of the chapter portray how the Bible was treated in the course of the French Revolution (GC 265-288).

Ellen White described the war in heaven of Revelation 12:7-12 in two different but complementary ways. On the one hand, the scene describes a threat to the government of heaven that occurred even before the creation of the world. Satan, and all the angels who followed him, were physically cast out of heaven at that time (RH, Jan. 28, 1909; Lt 114, 1903, in 7BC 973). On the other hand, the casting out of the dragon also reflects the impact of the cross on the affections of the universe (Ms 50, 1900, in 7BC 974). At the cross, Satan lost any spiritual credibility he may have retained in heavenly places (3SP 194, 195).

Ellen White understood the sea beast of Revelation 13:1-10 to represent the Papacy of the Middle Ages (GC 49-60), which is to have an end-time role in opposition to the true people of God (ibid. 445-450). While many of her statements against the leadership of the Roman Catholic Church are strong by today's standards (ibid. 563-581), other statements caution against personalizing one's opposition to the Papacy (Ev 576). She also recognized that time and place need to be considered when expressing that opposition (TM 112; Ev 573-577).

Ellen White identified the land beast of Revelation 13:11-14 as the United States of America in its end-time collaboration with the Roman hierarchy (GC 439-445). The mark of the beast is received when one rejects God's final call to true Sabbathkeeping and instead submits to the end-time enforcement of Sunday worship (ibid. 445-450). The three angels of Revelation 14:6-12 represent believers in God's end-time message who spread the last gospel message throughout the world (ibid. 311, 312).

Ellen White did not consider the battle of Armageddon (Rev. 16:16) a military affair in the Middle East or elsewhere. Rather, she understood Armageddon to be a last-day spiritual conflict between the people of God and the forces of evil (note several comments in 7BC 982, 983). During that last conflict fundamental spiritual principles will be clarified and people will be brought to decision concerning them. It will be a time that faith, rather than physical power or skill, is tested (Ms 1a, 1890, in 7BC 983).

Regarding Revelation 20, Ellen White affirmed a premillenialist position, that the millennium will be a 1,000-year period after the second coming of Jesus. During that period the earth will be desolate, without the presence of human beings (although Satan and his angels are confined there). The people of God are taken up to heaven at the Second Coming to spend the 1,000 years with God (GC 653-661). At the close of the millennium the wicked of all time are resurrected, and God's people return to earth with the New Jerusalem to witness the final destruction of sin, sinners, and Satan (ibid. 662-673). The earth is then destroyed by fire, and God creates a new heaven and a new earth in which God's faithful people will dwell forever in joy and perfect harmony (ibid. 673-678). In White's view, however, the best definition of heaven is not riches and glory, but the presence of Christ (undated Ms 58, in 7BC 989).

Jon Paulien

REVELATION AND INSPIRATION. The concept of the divine revelation and inspiration of

Holy Scripture plays an important role in Ellen White's writings and thinking. She believed that God has specially revealed Himself to chosen individuals and through them continues to reveal Himself to humanity (cf. 1 Sam. 3:21; Isa. 22:14; Joel 2:28, 29; Matt. 11:27; Eph. 3:3; 2 Peter 1:19-21). This process of divine self-disclosure encompasses a wide variety of revelatory experiences, such as visions and dreams, verbal communication, and panoramic views presenting "past, present, and future" (5T 64, 65; cf. GC xi). In addition to those aspects of special revelation, she also speaks about a general revelation of God in nature.

For Ellen White general revelation is distinctly different from God's supernatural revelation, as given in Scripture. Nature testifies of God's intelligence (PP 114), power (1SM 294), love (MH 411), and existence (Ed 99; HL 287), but nature does not share the quality of inspiration as does Scripture. In fact, she clearly distinguishes the "book of nature" from the "pages of inspiration" (AA 571). The Bible is God's inspired book. Nature is not. While "the book of nature is a great lesson book," it should be used "in connection with the Scriptures" (COL 24), for "the Bible is second to no other book; it is without a rival" (OHC 35).

Because of the Fall, "to man's unaided reason, nature's teaching cannot but be contradictory and disappointing. Only in the light of revelation can it be read aright" (Ed 134). Thus, God's special revelation (Scripture) has precedence over general revelation (nature) because nature, as it exists today, is distorted by sin (PP 112-114). We cannot interpret nature correctly on our own, but need the guidance of divine revelation (MH 461, 462; 8T 255-258). Scripture provides the spectacles that help to gain a reliable and correct understanding of the book of nature. "Those who question the reliability of the Scripture records

have let go their anchor and are left to beat about upon the rocks of infidelity" (8T 258). When both are rightly understood, however, there will be perfect harmony between the revealed Word of God and the natural world, for "all truth, whether in nature or in revelation, is consistent with itself in all its manifestations" (PP 114; cf. 8T 258; MH 462).

In contrast to general revelation in nature, special revelation includes the communication of knowledge that otherwise would not be available to fallen human beings (GCDB, Feb. 18, 1897). Therefore the Bible is called "the revealed word of God" (PP 124). At the same time she states that the Bible is "the inspired word of God. Holy men of old wrote this Word as they were moved by the Spirit. God did not leave His Word to be preserved in the memories of men and handed down from generation to generation by oral transmission and traditional unfolding. Had He done this, the Word would gradually have been added to by men. We would have been asked to receive that which is not inspired. Let us thank God for His written word" (UL 52).

For Ellen White the process of revelation and inspiration is closely intertwined. Both concepts are interrelated and cannot be separated from each other. She believed the Bible to be "divine revelation" (Ed 170), "God's revelation" (8T 325), and a "complete revelation" (UL 187; BE, July 20, 1896).

At the same time she refers to Scripture as the "inspired" Word of God (OHC 207). She equates the Bible with the "word of inspiration" (RH, Mar. 11, 1902; 1MR 52), the "volume of inspiration" (PP 596), and the "great treasure house of inspired truth" (GC 193). For her, *all* Scripture is given by inspiration of God (2 Tim. 3:16; AA 502; Ed 171; FLB 12; SW 46; SpTEd 148; BE, Oct. 1, 1892). Scripture is "the inspired word of God" (ST, Mar. 21, 1906). She calls the biblical record an "inspired history," written by "inspired writers" (4T 9), recorded by "the pen of inspiration" (*ibid.* 12), God's "written word" (YI, July 24, 1902).

In other words, Ellen White did not sharply distinguish between the concepts "revelation" and "inspiration," as is customary today (cf. Burry, pp. 41ff.). Thus she writes that "the preparation of the written word began in the time of Moses. *Inspired revelations* were then embodied in an inspired book" (GC v; italics supplied). Elsewhere she states that David gave Solomon minute directions for building the Temple with patterns of every part, "as had been *revealed* to him by *divine inspiration*" (PP 751; italics supplied).

Apparently revelation and inspiration are so closely intertwined in her thought that it is difficult and fruitless to separate them. Her concern was rather to stress unambiguously the reality of the supernatural origin and nature of Scripture (Ed 170). Since God is the ultimate author of Holy Scripture, the Bible is called the "sure Word of God" (FW 47; 7BC 918; RH, Sept. 21, 1886).

The result of this divine revelation-inspiration process is that the Bible can be fully trusted. It is the "one trustworthy book" (RH, Apr. 20, 1897) in which God has given "definite, unmistakable instructions" and therefore we should heed "these inspired injunctions" (5T 248; cf. 8T 299). It is "the guidebook to the inhabitants of a fallen world" (1SM 16), "an unerring guide" (AA 506; 5T 389) and an "unerring standard" (Ev 256; CT 425; cf. 4T 312), by which even man's ideas of science have to be tested (8T 325). It is "the Book of books, which God has given to man to be an infallible guide" (FE 394; cf. 4T 312; LS 472). "The Bible is God's voice speaking to us, just as surely as though we could hear it with our ears" (6T 393). Hence "the Holy Scriptures are to be accepted as an authoritative,

infallible revelation of His will" (GC vii; FLB 13). As such the Bible is "the standard of character, the revealer of doctrines, and the test of experience" (GC vii; LHU 118). It "is plain on every point essential to the salvation of the soul" (5T 706).

Ellen White did not question the divine revelation of Scripture; neither did she doubt its divine inspiration and trustworthiness. In fact, she strongly warned all those who with their finite minds think themselves to be competent to pass judgment upon what is divine and what is human in Scripture. This is contrary to God's will and has disastrous effects (*ibid.* 709). Instead she encouraged all to "let the word of God stand just as it is" (*ibid.* 711), "as the Inspired Word" (1SM 17). She deplored that infidelity "is undermining faith in the Bible as a revelation from God" (PP 166) and that "higher criticism, in dissecting, conjecturing, [and] reconstructing, is destroying faith in the Bible as a divine revelation" (AA 474; Ed 227). It is Satan who is making the world believe that the Bible is uninspired, no better than a storybook (EW 91, 265). Therefore no "living man ... [should] dissect God's Word, telling what is revelation, what is inspiration and what is not, without a rebuke" (7BC 919).

The foundation for the divine authority of Scripture is the supernatural process of revelation and inspiration. This is the basis for its internal unity and accounts for a proper biblical hermeneutic where the whole Bible can function as its own interpreter (*sola scriptura*). Scripture is to be compared with scripture (1SM 413; RH, Apr. 3, 1888), for "scripture can be correctly interpreted only by scripture" (ST, Jan. 11, 1899). Hence in our time "there is need of a return to the great Protestant principle—the Bible, and the Bible only, as the rule of faith and duty" (GC 204, 205; cf. GC 595).

For Ellen White the primary focus of the inspiration process is the prophet or the apostle. "The Bible is written by inspired men. . . . It is not the words of the Bible that are inspired, but the men that were inspired. Inspiration acts not on the man's words or his expressions but on the man himself, who, under the influence of the Holy Ghost, is imbued with thoughts. But the words receive the impress of the individual mind. The divine mind is diffused. The divine mind and will is combined with the human mind and will; thus the utterances of the man are the word of God" (1SM 21).

This important passage indicates that while inspiration begins to function at the level of the thoughts of the inspired writer, the process of inspiration also extends to some degree to the written result of inspiration, whereby "the utterances of the man are the Word of God" (*ibid.*). In the words of the apostle Paul: "All *scripture* is given by inspiration of God" (2 Tim. 3:16). Likewise, Ellen White repeatedly affirms that the product of the inspired writers is inspired by God: "I take the Bible just as it is, as the Inspired Word" (*ibid.* 17).

Thus, the biblical process of inspiration involves "thoughts as well as words" (van Bemmelen, p. 40). For her, inspiration is not limited merely to the thoughts of the prophet, who is then left completely alone in writing down what God has shown; but neither did she believe that the written words are mechanically dictated by God.

Ellen White rejected the concept of inspiration that God mechanically dictated every word to the prophet, which would make everything in Scripture "as inspired as the Ten Commandments" (*ibid.* 24), i.e., written word by word by God's own finger. She never employed the phrase "verbal inspiration," so often associated with a mechanical mode of inspiration. Instead she spoke of the "truth

of Scripture" (PP 238) and of the "reliability of the records of the Old and New Testaments" (GC 522; CE 193; cf. 8T 258).

Even though she never called attention to any specific error in Scripture, she admitted that in some instances words of Scripture were changed by learned men (EW 220, 221), in the process of translation and copying (1SM 16), in order to support their established views, governed by tradition. Yet she was convinced that in spite of this "true seekers for truth need not err" (1SG 117), because those "mistakes will not cause trouble to one soul, or cause any feet to stumble, that would not manufacture difficulties from the plainest revealed truth" (1SM 16).

Occasionally Ellen White used the phrase that "the scribes of God wrote as they were dictated by the Holy Spirit" (4T 9; RH, Jan. 22, 1880; cf. 1SG 176). This expression, however, should not be interpreted to mean an endorsement of a mechanical understanding of a verbal dictation model of inspiration (cf. Burry, pp. 48-50). A careful investigation of the use of the word "dictated" in her own writings makes clear that she employed this expression not to describe a mechanical dictation of written material but to emphasize the divine origin and motivation of various actions (cf. 17MR 221; SpM 435; 5T 101; 3T 507; YI, May 4, 1893). Just as humanity's purpose is "dictated by the wisdom of Satan" (RH, July 26, 1898), Ellen White wants to emphasize that the biblical writers were not guided by Satan but prompted and motivated by God. They wrote under the impulse and influence of the Holy Spirit so that "the inspired writers did not testify to falsehoods" but have given "a plain, unvarnished account of what actually occurred" (4T 9).

Ellen White was convinced that God is able to use human language effectively to communicate His truth to humanity in a reliable manner. Although "the Bible is not given to us in grand superhuman language" (1SM 20), she affirms that "God speaks to the human family in language they can comprehend" (TM 136). The expressions of the Bible are not exaggerated (1SM 22). Rather the Spirit of God guides in choosing "appropriate words with which to express the truth" (3SM 51).

Ellen White acknowledges that "different meanings are expressed by the same word" (1SM 20), thereby giving everything human an imperfect touch. Yet she claims that the Bible is nevertheless characterized by a "simple beauty of language" and an "unerring truthfulness" (YI, May 7, 1884; LHU 127).

Ellen White did not deify Scripture: to her "God alone is infallible" (Lt 10, 1895, in 1SM 37). But she also firmly believed that Scripture shares in the infallibility of God. "Man is fallible, but God's Word is infallible" (1SM 416; cf. RH, Feb. 6, 1900). "His word is true" (Lt 10, 1895, in 1SM 37) and "reliable" (ST, Oct. 1, 1894). The Bible "is infallible; for God cannot err" (ML 27). She left no doubt that the Bible is "an unerring counselor, and infallible guide" (FE 100). Even though written by human hands, God is acknowledged as the ultimate author (GC v; 1SM 25), who "gives the message and then takes especial care that it is not corrupted" (Lt 8, 1860, in 6MR 333; 1MR 307). Ellen White affirmed God's supervision in the revelation-inspiration process, where the prophet, "under the guidance of the Holy Spirit, presents what is most forcibly impressed upon his own mind" (1SM 26). She was convinced that God "by His Holy Spirit, qualified men and enabled them to do His work. He guided the mind in the selection of what to speak and what to write" (1SM 26; see GC vi).

Of her own prophetic ministry she wrote: "I am just as dependent upon the Spirit of the Lord in relating or writing a vision, as in having the vision. It is impossible for me to call up things which have been shown me unless the Lord brings them before me at the time that He is pleased to have me relate or write them" (1SM 36, 37; cf. 8T 231).

Yet God's supervision did not eliminate the freedom of the prophet. The words used are not a heavenly Esperanto that is verbally dictated. The words are freely chosen by God's messengers. Their personalities and modes of conveying the truth presented by the Holy Spirit were still their own. The Holy Spirit did not cramp the mind of the biblical writer, "as if forced into a certain mold" (1SM 22). Speaking of her own ministry, she states: "Although I am as dependent upon the Spirit of the Lord in writing my views as I am in receiving them, yet the words I employ in describing what I have seen are my own, unless they be those spoken to me by an angel, which I always enclose in marks of quotation" (RH, Oct. 8, 1867; 1SM 37).

The divine-human character of Scripture is compared by Ellen White with the divine-human nature of Jesus Christ. "The Bible, with its God-given truths expressed in the language of men, presents a union of the divine and the human. Such a union existed in the nature of Christ, who was the Son of God and the Son of man. Thus it is true of the Bible, as it was of Christ, that 'the Word was made flesh, and dwelt among us' (John 1:14)" (GC vi; cf. 5T 747).

Jesus veiled the glory of His divinity with the limitations of His humanity. However, Jesus wants to be accepted for who He really is: not merely a human being but the divine Son of God who became man in the fullest sense. Similarly, in the inspiration of Scripture the divine truth is placed within the compass of limited human language to express divine ideas in human speech (GC vi, vii; 1SM 22,

25). Yet the Bible is to be accepted for what it really is: God's Word, written by human agents.

Jesus became a man in time and space. However, this fact neither eliminated His divinity nor made His message and salvation historically relative. In a similar way God's written Word was given in time and space. But rather than being historically conditioned by immanent cause-and-effect relations, thereby rendering it relative, God's Word "is divinely conditioned and historically constituted" (F. M. Hasel, pp. 208, 209), thereby remaining binding for all men, revealing God's will to humanity. Just as Jesus is our only true "unerring Pattern" (LHU 41; 1T 241), the Bible is called the "unerring word of God" (ST, May 16, 1895; cf. 2SM 88), where "the unerring pen of inspiration" traces with "exact fidelity" the events before the Flood and the history of Israel (4T 370; RH, Jan. 11, 1906), even though parallel accounts may vary in some details. This does not, of course, remove the need for sound methods of *interpretation of Ellen White's writings (1SM 57; 3SM 217).

The Bible owes its origin to the process of God's revelation and inspiration. In like manner her own writings have the same Holy Spirit as the author (5T 661; Lt 92, 1900, in 3SM 30). Thus, her writings share the same quality of inspiration as do the biblical writings. Yet Ellen White does not claim to be an addition to the biblical canon (4T 246). The canon is closed. Her writings are not to take the place of Scripture (5T 691). The Bible explicitly declares that the Word of God is the norm for every doctrine and teaching (*ibid.* 665; Isa. 8:20; Acts 17:11).

Her writings are but "a *lesser light to lead men and women to the greater light" of Holy Scripture (RH, Jan. 20, 1903; 3SM 30). If the *Testimonies* do not speak according to the Word of God, we should reject them (5T 691),

for either they are "of the Spirit of God, or of the devil" (4T 230). She did not make a distinction between inspired and less-inspired sections in the Bible or in her own writings.

From early in life to the end of her ministry, Ellen White continually emphasized the importance of the divine revelation-inspiration process for the origin of Scripture, as well as for her own writings. She consistently accepted all of Scripture as divinely inspired and as a complete revelation. As such, she always upheld the complete trustworthiness and veracity of all the Bible, not just those statements dealing with salvation but the rest of the biblical record as well, including the historicity of the biblical accounts. Thus the process of divine revelation and inspiration forms the basis for the assuring promise that "all your words are true" (Ps. 119:160, NIV) and that the Word of God is given as a lamp unto our feet, and a light unto our path (Ps. 119:105). As such, the Bible accurately reveals God's character and provides an infallible and sufficient rule of faith and practice, for perfecting character and pointing the way to salvation (GC vii).

Further reading: G. S. Bradford, *More Than a Prophet* (Berrien Springs, Mich.: Biblical Perspectives, 2006); J. H. Burry, "An Investigation to Determine Ellen White's Concepts of Revelation, Inspiration, 'The Spirit of Prophecy,' and Her Claims About the Origin, Production and Authority of Her Writings" (M.A. thesis, AU, 1991); R. W. Coon, "Inspiration/Revelation: What It Is and How It Works" (EGWE, SDoc); P. G. Damsteegt, "The Inspiration of Scripture in the Writings of Ellen G. White," *Journal of the Adventist Theological Society* 5, no. 1 (Spring 1991): 155-179; R. Dederen, "The Revelation-Inspiration Phenomenon According to the Bible Writers," in F. Holbrook and L. Van Dolson, eds., *Issues in Revelation and Inspiration* (Berrien Springs, Mich.: Adventist

Theological Society, 1992), pp. 9-29; H. E. Douglass, *Messenger of the Lord: The Prophetic Ministry of Ellen G. White* (PPPA, 1998); P. A. Gordon, "Revelation-Inspiration: Ellen White's Witness and Experience" (EGWE, SDoc); L. Hardinge, "An Exploration of the Philosophy of Inspiration in the Writings of Mrs. Ellen G. White" (unpublished manuscript, CAR); F. M. Hasel, "Reflections on the Authority and Trustworthiness of Scripture," in F. Holbrook and L. Van Dolson, eds., *Issues in Revelation and Inspiration* (Berrien Springs, Mich.: Adventist Theological Society, 1992), pp. 201-220; G. F. Hasel, *Understanding the Living Word of God* (PPPA, 1980); G. R. Knight, *Myths in Adventism* (RHPA, 1985); G. R. Knight, *Reading Ellen White* (RHPA, 1997); S. Koranteng-Pipim, *Receiving the Word* (Berrien Springs, Mich.: Berean Books, 1996); G. W. Reid, ed., *Understanding Scripture: An Adventist Approach* (BRI, 2005); U. Smith, "Which Are Revealed, Words or Ideas?" RH, Mar. 13, 1888 (also EGWE, SDoc); A. Thompson, *Inspiration: Hard Questions, Honest Answers* (RHPA, 1991); A. Thompson, "Adventists and Inspiration," series of four articles published in AR, Sept. 5, 12, 19, 26, 1985; A. Thompson, *Escape From the Flames* (PPPA, 2005); A. R. Timm, "A History of Seventh-day Adventist Views on Biblical and Prophetic Inspiration (1844-2000)," *Journal of the Adventist Theological Society* 10, nos. 1, 2 (1999): 486-542; P. M. van Bemmelen, "Revelation and Inspiration," in R. Dederen, ed., *Handbook of Seventh-day Adventist Theology* (RHPA, 2000), pp. 22-57; A. L. White, *The Ellen G. White Writings* (RHPA, 1973); A. L. White, *Inspiration and the Ellen G. White Writings* (RHPA, 1979).

Frank M. Hasel

Ellen White's Statements on Revelation and Inspiration. Two statements have come to be regarded as Ellen White's most significant ones regarding the inspiration of the Bible and of her own writings.

The Great Controversy, Introduction, pp. v-xii:

Before the entrance of sin, Adam enjoyed open communion with his Maker; but since man separated himself from God by transgression, the human race has been cut off from this high privilege. By the plan of redemption, however, a way has been opened whereby the inhabitants of the earth may still have connection with heaven. God has communicated with men by His Spirit, and divine light has been imparted to the world by revelations to His chosen servants. "Holy men of God spake as they were moved by the Holy Ghost." 2 Peter 1:21.

During the first twenty-five hundred years of human history, there was no written revelation. Those who had been taught of God communicated their knowledge to others, and it was handed down from father to son, through successive generations. The preparation of the written word began in the time of Moses. Inspired revelations were then embodied in an inspired book. This work continued during the long period of sixteen hundred years—from Moses, the historian of creation and the law, to John, the recorder of the most sublime truths of the gospel.

The Bible points to God as its author; yet it was written by human hands; and in the varied style of its different books it presents the characteristics of the several writers. The truths revealed are all "given by inspiration of God" (2 Timothy 3:16); yet they are expressed in the words of men. The Infinite One by His Holy Spirit has shed light into the minds and hearts of His servants. He has given dreams and visions, symbols and figures; and those to whom the truth was thus revealed have themselves embodied the thought in human language.

The Ten Commandments were spoken by God Himself, and were written by His own hand. They are of divine, and not of human composition. But the Bible, with its God-given truths expressed in the language of men, presents a union of the divine and the human. Such a union existed in the nature of Christ, who was the Son of God and the Son of man. Thus it is true of the Bible, as it was of Christ, that "the Word was made flesh, and dwelt among us." John 1:14.

Written in different ages, by men who differed widely in rank and occupation, and in mental and spiritual endowments, the books of the Bible present a wide contrast in style, as well as a diversity in the nature of the subjects unfolded. Different forms of expression are employed by different writers; often the same truth is more strikingly presented by one than by another. And as several writers present a subject under varied aspects and relations, there may appear, to the superficial, careless, or prejudiced reader, to be discrepancy or contradiction, where the thoughtful, reverent student, with clearer insight, discerns the underlying harmony.

As presented through different individuals, the truth is brought out in its varied aspects. One writer is more strongly impressed with one phase of the subject; he grasps those points that harmonize with his experience or with his power of perception and appreciation; another seizes upon a different phase; and each, under the guidance of the Holy Spirit, presents what is most forcibly impressed upon his own mind—a different aspect of the truth in each, but a perfect harmony through all. And the truths thus revealed unite to form a perfect whole, adapted to meet the wants of men in all the circumstances and experiences of life.

God has been pleased to communicate His truth to the world by human agencies, and He Himself, by His Holy Spirit, qualified men and enabled them to do this work. He guided the mind in the selection of what to speak and what to write. The treasure was entrusted to earthen vessels, yet it is, nonetheless, from Heaven. The testimony is conveyed through the imperfect expression of human language, yet it is the testimony of God; and the obedient, believing child of God beholds in it the glory of a divine power, full of grace and truth.

In His word, God has committed to men the knowledge necessary for salvation. The Holy Scriptures are to be accepted as an authoritative, infallible revelation of His will. They are the standard of character, the revealer of doctrines, and the test of experience. "Every scripture inspired of God is also profitable for teaching, for reproof, for correction, for instruction which is in righteousness; that the man of God may be complete, furnished completely unto every good work." 2 Timothy 3:16, 17, RV.

Yet the fact that God has revealed His will to men through His Word has not rendered needless the continued presence and guiding of the Holy Spirit. On the contrary, the Spirit was promised by our Savior, to open the word to His servants, to illuminate and apply its teachings. And since it was the Spirit of God that inspired the Bible, it is impossible that the teaching of the Spirit should ever be contrary to that of the Word.

The Spirit was not given—nor can it ever be bestowed—to supersede the Bible; for the Scriptures explicitly state that the Word of God is the standard by which all teaching and experience must be tested. Says the apostle John, "Believe not every spirit, but try the spirits whether they are of God: because many false prophets are gone out into the world." 1 John 4:1. And Isaiah declares, "To the law and to the testimony: if they speak not according to this word, it is because there is no light in them." Isaiah 8:20.

Great reproach has been cast upon the work

of the Holy Spirit by the errors of a class that, claiming its enlightenment, profess to have no further need of guidance from the Word of God. They are governed by impressions which they regard as the voice of God in the soul. But the spirit that controls them is not the Spirit of God. This following of impressions, to the neglect of the Scriptures, can lead only to confusion, to deception and ruin. It serves only to further the designs of the evil one. Since the ministry of the Holy Spirit is of vital importance to the church of Christ, it is one of the devices of Satan, through the errors of extremists and fanatics, to cast contempt upon the work of the Spirit and cause the people of God to neglect this source of strength which our Lord Himself has provided.

In harmony with the Word of God, His Spirit was to continue its work throughout the period of the gospel dispensation. During the ages while the Scriptures of both the Old and the New Testament were being given, the Holy Spirit did not cease to communicate light to individual minds, apart from the revelations to be embodied in the Sacred Canon. The Bible itself relates how, through the Holy Spirit, men received warning, reproof, counsel, and instruction, in matters in no way relating to the giving of the Scriptures. And mention is made of prophets in different ages, of whose utterances nothing is recorded. In like manner, after the close of the canon of the Scripture, the Holy Spirit was still to continue its work, to enlighten, warn, and comfort the children of God.

Jesus promised His disciples, "The Comforter, which is the Holy Ghost, whom the Father will send in my name, he shall teach you all things, and bring all things to your remembrance, whatsoever I have said unto you." "When he, the Spirit of truth, is come, he will guide you into all truth: . . . and he will shew you things to come." John 14:26; 16:13. Scripture plainly teaches that these promises, so far from being

limited to apostolic days, extend to the church of Christ in all ages. The Savior assures His followers, "I am with you alway, even unto the end of the world." Matthew 28:20. And Paul declares that the gifts and manifestations of the Spirit were set in the church "for the perfecting of the saints, for the work of the ministry, for the edifying of the body of Christ: till we all come in the unity of the faith, and of the knowledge of the Son of God, unto a perfect man, unto the measure of the stature of the fullness of Christ." Ephesians 4:12, 13.

For the believers at Ephesus the apostle prayed, "That the God of our Lord Jesus Christ, the Father of glory, may give unto you the *Spirit of wisdom and revelation* in the knowledge of him: *the eyes of your understanding being enlightened;* that ye may know what is the hope of his calling, and . . . what is the *exceeding greatness* of his power to usward who believe." Ephesians 1:17-19. The ministry of the divine Spirit in enlightening the understanding and opening to the mind the deep things of God's holy Word was the blessing which Paul thus besought for the Ephesian church.

After the wonderful manifestation of the Holy Spirit on the Day of Pentecost, Peter exhorted the people to repentance and baptism in the name of Christ, for the remission of their sins; and he said: "Ye shall receive the gift of the Holy Ghost. For the promise is unto you, and to your children, and to all that are afar off, even as many as the Lord our God shall call." Acts 2:38, 39.

In immediate connection with the scenes of the great day of God, the Lord by the prophet Joel has promised a special manifestation of His Spirit. Joel 2:28. This prophecy received a partial fulfillment in the outpouring of the Spirit on the Day of Pentecost; but it will reach its full accomplishment in the manifestation of divine grace which will attend the closing work of the gospel.

The great controversy between good and evil will increase in intensity to the very close of time. In all ages the wrath of Satan has been manifested against the church of Christ; and God has bestowed His grace and Spirit upon His people to strengthen them to stand against the power of the evil one. When the apostles of Christ were to bear His gospel to the world and to record it for all future ages, they were especially endowed with the enlightenment of the Spirit. But as the church approaches her final deliverance, Satan is to work with greater power. He comes down "having great wrath, because he knoweth that he hath but a short time." Revelation 12:12. He will work "with all power and signs and lying wonders." 2 Thessalonians 2:9. For six thousand years that mastermind that once was highest among the angels of God has been wholly bent to the work of deception and ruin. And all the depths of satanic skill and subtlety acquired, all the cruelty developed, during these struggles of the ages, will be brought to bear against God's people in the final conflict. And in this time of peril the followers of Christ are to bear to the world the warning of the Lord's second advent; and a people are to be prepared to stand before Him at His coming, "without spot, and blameless." 2 Peter 3:14. At this time the special endowment of divine grace and power is not less needful to the church than in apostolic days.

Through the illumination of the Holy Spirit, the scenes of the long-continued conflict between good and evil have been opened to the writer of these pages. From time to time I have been permitted to behold the working, in different ages, of the great controversy between Christ, the Prince of life, the Author of our salvation, and Satan, the prince of evil, the author of sin, the first transgressor of God's holy law. Satan's enmity against Christ has been manifested against His followers. The same hatred of the principles of God's law, the same policy of deception, by which error is made to appear as truth, by which human laws are substituted for the law of God, and men are led to worship the creature rather than the Creator, may be traced in all the history of the past. Satan's efforts to misrepresent the character of God, to cause men to cherish a false conception of the Creator, and thus to regard Him with fear and hate rather than with love; his endeavors to set aside the divine law, leading the people to think themselves free from its requirements; and his persecution of those who dare to resist his deceptions, have been steadfastly pursued in all ages. They may be traced in the history of patriarchs, prophets, and apostles, of martyrs and reformers.

In the great final conflict, Satan will employ the same policy, manifest the same spirit, and work for the same end as in all preceding ages. That which has been will be, except that the coming struggle will be marked with a terrible intensity such as the world has never witnessed. Satan's deceptions will be more subtle, his assaults more determined. If it were possible, he would lead astray the elect. Mark 13:22, RV.

As the Spirit of God has opened to my mind the great truths of His Word, and the scenes of the past and the future, I have been bidden to make known to others that which has thus been revealed—to trace the history of the controversy in past ages, and especially so to present it as to shed a light on the fast-approaching struggle of the future. In pursuance of this purpose, I have endeavored to select and group together events in the history of the church in such a manner as to trace the unfolding of the great testing truths that at different periods have been given to the world, that have excited the wrath of Satan, and the enmity of a world-loving church, and that have been maintained by the witness of those who "loved not their lives unto the death."

In these records we may see a foreshadowing

of the conflict before us. Regarding them in the light of God's Word, and by the illumination of His Spirit, we may see unveiled the devices of the wicked one, and the dangers which they must shun who would be found "without fault" before the Lord at His coming.

The great events which have marked the progress of reform in past ages are matters of history, well known and universally acknowledged by the Protestant world; they are facts which none can gainsay. This history I have presented briefly, in accordance with the scope of the book, and the brevity which must necessarily be observed, the facts having been condensed into as little space as seemed consistent with a proper understanding of their application. In some cases where a historian has so grouped together events as to afford, in brief, a comprehensive view of the subject, or has summarized details in a convenient manner, his words have been quoted; but in some instances no specific credit has been given, since the quotations are not given for the purpose of citing that writer as authority, but because his statement affords a ready and forcible presentation of the subject. In narrating the experience and views of those carrying forward the work of reform in our own time, similar use has been made of their published works.

It is not so much the object of this book to present new truths concerning the struggles of former times, as to bring out facts and principles which have a bearing on coming events. Yet viewed as a part of the controversy between the forces of light and darkness, all these records of the past are seen to have a new significance; and through them a light is cast upon the future, illumining the pathway of those who, like the reformers of past ages, will be called, even at the peril of all earthly good, to witness "for the word of God, and for the testimony of Jesus Christ."

To unfold the scenes of the great controversy

between truth and error; to reveal the wiles of Satan, and the means by which he may be successfully resisted; to present a satisfactory solution of the great problem of evil, shedding such a light upon the origin and the final disposition of sin as to make fully manifest the justice and benevolence of God in all His dealings with His creatures; and to show the holy, unchanging nature of His law, is the object of this book. That through its influence souls may be delivered from the power of darkness, and become "partakers of the inheritance of the saints in light," to the praise of Him who loved us, and gave Himself for us, is the earnest prayer of the writer.

Selected Messages, book 1, pp. 15-22:

This is a time when the question with all propriety may be asked, "When the Son of man cometh, shall he find faith on the earth?" (Luke 18:8).

Spiritual darkness has covered the earth and gross darkness the people. There are in many churches skepticism and infidelity in the interpretation of the Scriptures. Many, very many, are questioning the verity and truth of the Scriptures. Human reasoning and the imaginings of the human heart are undermining the inspiration of the Word of God, and that which should be received as granted is surrounded with a cloud of mysticism. Nothing stands out in clear and distinct lines, upon rock bottom. This is one of the marked signs of the last days.

This Holy Book has withstood the assaults of Satan, who has united with evil men to make everything of divine character shrouded in clouds and darkness. But the Lord has preserved this Holy Book by His own miraculous power in its present shape—a chart or guidebook to the human family to show them the way to heaven.

But the oracles of God have been so

manifestly neglected that there are but few in our world, even of those who profess to explain it to others, who have the divine knowledge of the Scriptures. There are learned men who have a college education, but these shepherds do not feed the flock of God. They do not consider that the excellencies of the Scriptures will be continually unfolding their hidden treasures as precious jewels are discovered by digging for them.

There are men who strive to be original, who are wise above what is written; therefore, their wisdom is foolishness. They discover wonderful things in advance, ideas which reveal that they are far behind in the comprehension of the divine will and purposes of God. In seeking to make plain or to unravel mysteries hid from ages from mortal man, they are like a man floundering about in the mud, unable to extricate himself and yet telling others how to get out of the muddy sea they themselves are in. This is a fit representation of the men who set themselves to correct the errors of the Bible. No man can improve the Bible by suggesting what the Lord meant to say or ought to have said.

Some look to us gravely and say, "Don't you think there might have been some mistake in the copyist or in the translators?" This is all probable, and the mind that is so narrow that it will hesitate and stumble over this possibility or probability would be just as ready to stumble over the mysteries of the Inspired Word, because their feeble minds cannot see through the purposes of God. Yes, they would just as easily stumble over plain facts that the common mind will accept, and discern the Divine, and to which God's utterance is plain and beautiful, full of marrow and fatness. All the mistakes will not cause trouble to one soul, or cause any feet to stumble, that would not manufacture difficulties from the plainest revealed truth.

God committed the preparation of His divinely inspired Word to finite man. This Word, arranged into books, the Old and New Testaments, is the guidebook to the inhabitants of a fallen world, bequeathed to them that, by studying and obeying the directions, not one soul would lose its way to heaven.

Those who think to make the supposed difficulties of Scripture plain, in measuring by their finite rule that which is inspired and that which is not inspired, had better cover their faces, as Elijah when the still small voice spoke to him; for they are in the presence of God and holy angels, who for ages have communicated to men light and knowledge, telling them what to do and what not to do, unfolding before them scenes of thrilling interest, waymark by waymark in symbols and signs and illustrations.

And He [God] has not, while presenting the perils clustering about the last days, qualified any finite man to unravel hidden mysteries or inspired one man or any class of men to pronounce judgment as to that which is inspired or is not. When men, in their finite judgment, find it necessary to go into an examination of scriptures to define that which is inspired and that which is not, they have stepped before Jesus to show Him a better way than He has led us.

I take the Bible just as it is, as the Inspired Word. I believe its utterances in an entire Bible. Men arise who think they find something to criticize in God's Word. They lay it bare before others as evidence of superior wisdom. These men are, many of them, smart men, learned men, they have eloquence and talent, the whole lifework [of whom] is to unsettle minds in regard to the inspiration of the Scriptures. They influence many to see as they do. And the same work is passed on from one to another, just as Satan designed it should be, until we may see the full meaning of the words of Christ, "When the Son of man cometh, shall he find faith on the earth?" (Luke 18:8).

Brethren, let not a mind or hand be engaged in criticizing the Bible. It is a work that Satan delights to have any of you do, but it is not a work the Lord has pointed out for you to do.

Men should let God take care of His own Book, His living oracles, as He has done for ages. They begin to question some parts of revelation, and pick flaws in the apparent inconsistencies of this statement and that statement. Beginning at Genesis, they give up that which they deem questionable, and their minds lead on, for Satan will lead to any length they may follow in their criticism, and they see something to doubt in the whole Scriptures. Their faculties of criticism become sharpened by exercise, and they can rest on nothing with a certainty. You try to reason with these men, but your time is lost. They will exercise their power of ridicule even upon the Bible. They even become mockers, and they would be astonished if you put it to them in that light.

Brethren, cling to your Bible, as it reads, and stop your criticisms in regard to its validity, and obey the Word, and not one of you will be lost. The ingenuity of men has been exercised for ages to measure the Word of God by their finite minds and limited comprehension. If the Lord, the Author of the living oracles, would throw back the curtain and reveal His wisdom and His glory before them, they would shrink into nothingness and exclaim as did Isaiah, "I am a man of unclean lips, and I dwell in the midst of people of unclean lips" (Isaiah 6:5).

Simplicity and plain utterance are comprehended by the illiterate, by the peasant, and the child as well as by the full-grown man or the giant in intellect. If the individual is possessed of large talents of mental powers, he will find in the oracles of God treasures of truth, beautiful and valuable, which he can appropriate. He will also find difficulties, and secrets and wonders which will give him the highest satisfaction to study during a long lifetime, and yet there is an infinity beyond.

Men of humble acquirements, possessing but limited capabilities and opportunities to become conversant in the Scriptures, find in the living oracles comfort, guidance, counsel, and the plan of salvation as clear as a sunbeam. No one need be lost for want of knowledge, unless he is willfully blind.

We thank God that the Bible is prepared for the poor man as well as for the learned man. It is fitted for all ages and all classes.—Manuscript 16, 1888 (written at Minneapolis, autumn 1888).

Human minds vary. The minds of different education and thought receive different impressions of the same words, and it is difficult for one mind to give to one of a different temperament, education, and habits of thought by language exactly the same idea as that which is clear and distinct in his own mind. Yet to honest men, right-minded men, he can be so simple and plain as to convey his meaning for all practical purposes. If the man he communicates with is not honest and will not want to see and understand the truth, he will turn his words and language in everything to suit his own purposes. He will misconstrue his words, play upon his imagination, wrest them from their true meaning, and then entrench himself in unbelief, claiming that the sentiments are all wrong.

This is the way my writings are treated by those who wish to misunderstand and pervert them. They turn the truth of God into a lie. In the very same way that they treat the writings in my published articles and in my books, so do skeptics and infidels treat the Bible. They read it according to their desire to pervert, to misapply, to willfully wrest the utterances from their true meaning. They declare that the Bible can prove anything and everything, that every sect proves their doctrines right, and that the most diverse doctrines are proved from the Bible.

The writers of the Bible had to express their ideas in human language. It was written by human men. These men were inspired of the Holy Spirit. Because of the imperfections of human understanding of language, or the perversity of the human mind, ingenious in evading truth, many read and understand the Bible to please themselves. It is not that the difficulty is in the Bible. Opposing politicians argue points of law in the statute book, and take opposite views in their application and in these laws.

The Scriptures were given to men, not in a continuous chain of unbroken utterances, but piece by piece through successive generations, as God in His providence saw a fitting opportunity to impress man at sundry times and divers places. Men wrote as they were moved upon by the Holy Ghost. There is "first the bud, then the blossom, and next the fruit," "first the blade, then the ear, after that the full corn in the ear." This is exactly what the Bible utterances are to us.

There is not always perfect order or apparent unity in the Scriptures. The miracles of Christ are not given in exact order, but are given just as the circumstances occurred, which called for this divine revealing of the power of Christ. The truths of the Bible are as pearls hidden. They must be searched, dug out by painstaking effort. Those who take only a surface view of the Scriptures will, with their superficial knowledge, which they think is very deep, talk of the contradictions of the Bible, and question the authority of the Scriptures. But those whose hearts are in harmony with truth and duty will search the Scriptures with a heart prepared to receive divine impressions. The illuminated soul sees a spiritual unity, one grand golden thread running through the whole, but it requires patience, thought, and prayer to trace out the precious golden thread. Sharp contentions over the Bible have led to investigation and revealed the precious jewels of truth. Many tears have been shed, many prayers offered, that the Lord would open the understanding to His Word.

The Bible is not given to us in grand super-human language. Jesus, in order to reach man where he is, took humanity. The Bible must be given in the language of men. Everything that is human is imperfect. Different meanings are expressed by the same word; there is not one word for each distinct idea. The Bible was given for practical purposes.

The stamps of minds are different. All do not understand expressions and statements alike. Some understand the statements of the Scriptures to suit their own particular minds and cases. Prepossessions, prejudices, and passions have a strong influence to darken the understanding and confuse the mind even in reading the words of Holy Writ.

The disciples traveling to Emmaus needed to be disentangled in their interpretation of the Scriptures. Jesus walked with them disguised, and as a man He talked with them. Beginning at Moses and the prophets He taught them in all things concerning Himself, that His life, His mission, His sufferings, His death were just as the Word of God had foretold. He opened their understanding that they might understand the Scriptures. How quickly He straightened out the tangled ends and showed the unity and divine verity of the Scriptures. How much men in these times need their understanding opened.

The Bible is written by inspired men, but it is not God's mode of thought and expression. It is that of humanity. God, as a writer, is not represented. Men will often say such an expression is not like God. But God has not put Himself in words, in logic, in rhetoric, on trial in the Bible. The writers of the Bible were God's penmen, not His pen. Look at the different writers.

It is not the words of the Bible that are inspired, but the men that were inspired.

Inspiration acts not on the man's words or his expressions but on the man himself, who, under the influence of the Holy Ghost, is imbued with thoughts. But the words receive the impress of the individual mind. The divine mind is diffused. The divine mind and will is combined with the human mind and will; thus the utterances of the man are the Word of God.—Manuscript 24, 1886 (written in Europe, 1886).

There is variety in a tree, there are scarcely two leaves just alike. Yet this variety adds to the perfection of the tree as a whole.

In our Bible, we might ask, Why need Matthew, Mark, Luke, and John in the Gospels, why need the Acts of the Apostles, and the variety of writers in the Epistles, go over the same thing?

The Lord gave His word in just the way He wanted it to come. He gave it through different writers, each having his own individuality, though going over the same history. Their testimonies are brought together in one Book, and are like the testimonies in a social meeting. They do not represent things in just the same style. Each has an experience of his own, and this diversity broadens and deepens the knowledge that is brought out to meet the necessities of varied minds. The thoughts expressed have not a set uniformity, as if cast in an iron mold, making the very hearing monotonous. In such uniformity there would be a loss of grace and distinctive beauty. . . .

The Creator of all ideas may impress different minds with the same thought, but each may express it in a different way, yet without contradiction. The fact that this difference exists should not perplex or confuse us. It is seldom that two persons will view and express truth in the very same way. Each dwells on particular points which his constitution and education have fitted him to appreciate. The sunlight falling upon the different objects gives those objects a different hue.

Through the inspiration of His Spirit the Lord gave His apostles truth, to be expressed according to the development of their minds by the Holy Spirit. But the mind is not cramped, as if forced into a certain mold.—Letter 53, 1900.

The Lord speaks to human beings in imperfect speech, in order that the degenerate senses, the dull, earthly perception, of earthly beings may comprehend His words. Thus is shown God's condescension. He meets fallen human beings where they are. The Bible, perfect as it is in its simplicity, does not answer to the great ideas of God; for infinite ideas cannot be perfectly embodied in finite vehicles of thought. Instead of the expressions of the Bible being exaggerated, as many people suppose, the strong expressions break down before the magnificence of the thought, though the penman selected the most expressive language through which to convey the truths of higher education. Sinful beings can only bear to look upon a shadow of the brightness of heaven's glory.—Letter 121, 1901.

REVIEW AND HERALD ARTICLES, ELLEN G. WHITE PRESENT TRUTH AND (RHPA, 1962). Six-volume facsimile reproduction of Ellen White's articles published in *The Present Truth* in 1849 and 1850, and in the *Review and Herald* from 1851 to her death in 1915. Volume 1 contains all her articles in *The Present Truth*, and in the *Review and Herald* from 1851 to 1885. Volume 2 includes the articles published in the *Review and Herald* from 1886 to 1892; volume 3, from 1893 to 1898; volume 4, from 1899 to 1903; volume 5, from 1904 to 1909; and volume 6, from 1910 to 1915. The last volume also includes letters from W. C. White to the editor of the *Review* about his mother's situation from the time of her accident in February 1915 until her death in July of that year. Also included is the issue of the *Review and Herald* that covers Ellen White's funeral.

The Present Truth was the first periodical published by Sabbatarian Adventists from July 1849 to November 1850 and placed a major emphasis on the seventh-day Sabbath and the doctrine of the sanctuary. Ellen White published some of her earliest messages and letters in six of its 11 issues. From August to November 1850 Sabbatarian Adventists also published six issues of a second journal, *The Advent Review*, a publication so named because it reprinted and reviewed certain teachings advocated during the Millerite movement in 1844. (Ellen White did not publish any article in this journal.) In November 1850 *The Present Truth* and *The Advent Review* were merged to form the *Second Advent Review and Sabbath Herald* (commonly called the *Review and Herald*). The *Review and Herald* became the leading paper of the Sabbatarian Adventists, and a major means of unity during the decade before the legal organization of the new denomination. It is now called the *Adventist Review*.

The publication of Ellen White's articles in the *Review and Herald* was irregular from 1851 to the early 1880s. In fact, only one article from her pen appeared in the years 1852, 1855, 1858, 1859, and 1864, and none in 1860 and 1865. One main reason for the scarcity of her articles in those early years was a decision on the part of James White and Uriah Smith, the first two editors, to avoid giving the impression that Ellen White's writings were the basis or foundation of Seventh-day Adventist doctrines and teachings. Her articles appeared a little more frequently in the 1870s and early 1880s, and were published almost on a weekly basis starting in 1884. These articles became her weekly messages to the church until her death. About 2,000 articles were published in the *Review and Herald* and touched on a variety of subjects.

Scores of her sermons were first written down by assistants and then sent to Adventist periodicals (including also *The Signs of the Times* and *The Youth's Instructor*). These sermons touch on practical counsels and doctrinal expositions and are filled with instructions and words of encouragement. At times Ellen White published chapters or sections of chapters of books she had been working on or gave biographical accounts of her travels for the church, which has contributed much to the present knowledge of denominational history. Ellen White's weekly articles in the *Review and Herald* had a profound influence upon the Seventh-day Adventist Church during her lifetime and have been an ongoing influence on subsequent generations.

Denis Fortin

REVIEW AND HERALD PUBLISHING BUILDING, BATTLE CREEK, MICHIGAN

REVIEW AND HERALD PUBLISHING ASSOCIATION. The oldest Seventh-day Adventist institution, it predates the organization of the church itself. Ellen White's relationship with the Review and Herald involved three main facets. She was a major stimulus that led to its founding, she supplied a wealth of material for it to publish, and she acted as its spiritual and ethical conscience.

As James White began preparing material for the emerging Sabbatarian Adventist movement, Ellen White received visions that supported his publishing efforts. At first James used commercial printers, but it bothered him that his articles and tracts about the sacredness of the Sabbath were being printed on the Sabbath. He urged that Adventists do their own printing. An 1852 meeting at Saratoga Springs, New York, voted to buy a printing press. White then set up primitive printing facilities in Rochester, New York. In 1855 Adventists in Battle Creek, Michigan, invited him to move the fledgling publishing house there.

The Advent Review Publishing Association was organized September 28, 1860, and incorporated as the Seventh-day Adventist Publishing Association on May 3, 1861. The association elected James White as its president. The need to deal with the ownership of the publishing house was a major stimulus to denominational organization. (The General Conference of Seventh-day Adventists did not come into being until May 1863.)

The publishing house grew under the leadership of James White, then declined financially when a stroke forced him to give up direct administration of the press (1865-1868). When he regained his health, he had to remedy the financial problems that had arisen during his absence. But after his death in 1881 a number of problems that greatly worried Ellen White began to emerge.

One of the major causes of those problems was commercial printing for non-Adventist clients. The Review solicited it to keep its equipment busy. Ellen White did not consider it inherently wrong. Actually, she saw it as an opportunity to witness to the world around them (PM 160). But the publishing house went after so much commercial work that it had to buy more machinery, and it then had to get even more commercial business to pay for the equipment. When the Review grew into at least the second-largest printer in the state of Michigan, becoming so busy it had little time to print church material, Ellen White pointed

out that commercial printing had become all-absorbing (*ibid.* 161). G. A. Irwin estimated that by 1899, 80 percent of the work of the Review consisted of commercial printing. (Many Adventist colporteurs even began selling such commercial work instead of denominational publications.) In addition, the topics of such books disturbed her (*ibid.* 162-165).

This commercial printing explosion led to other problems. Management began to think of the publishing house as a commercial business instead of a church ministry, and a new attitude pervaded it, one mirroring the aggressive capitalism of the time. Ellen White expressed concern about "loud, boisterous talking and unsanctified zeal in [the Review's] council meetings" (Ms 23, 1891, in 5Bio 227). She saw secular mind-sets, selfishness, and an entangling web of political alliances permeating the leadership (*ibid.* 227, 228). Many of the employees were non-Adventists, and administrators had little interest in evangelizing them. The publishing house was losing its spiritual identity. In a letter to *A. R. Henry, the general manager, she wrote that "there has been need of self-examination on the part of the workers. Every man who has to do with sacred things should perform his work in a Christlike manner. There must be no sharp practice" (Lt 20a, 1893, in 1888 Materials 1100). Furthermore, the Review leadership engaged in financial speculation while oppressing the employees (Lt 4, 1896, in 17MR 186; Lt 28, 1896, in 5Bio 230, 231).

The Review managers were not content to have charge of the press in Battle Creek; they sought to gain control of all Adventist publishing. Opposed to this monopoly, Ellen White was particularly concerned to preserve the independence of the Pacific Press (Lt 81, 1896, in PM 141) and felt personally the hostility of some toward herself. "The men in leading positions in the office of publication do not respect either the messenger or the messages graciously given them of God" (Ms 23, 1891, in 5Bio 228).

Tension between Ellen White and Review management focused on several issues. One involved the large salaries the managers received while holding down wages for the rest of the employees. When Henry claimed that he needed more money to support his family, she replied, "Other families, much larger than yours, sustain themselves without one word of complaint on half the wages you have" (Lt 20a, 1893, in PM 113). The publishing house had lost the spirit of sacrifice with which James White had begun it.

To pay for those large salaries, Review management sought to cut every expense possible, including royalties to authors. They wanted royalties to remain with the publishers, and considered anything written by publishing house employees as belonging to the house. But royalties were especially important to Ellen White. She paid all initial publishing expenses out of her own pocket, then would recoup them through her royalties. In addition, she used her royalties to support countless mission and other projects in the church (2SAT 254).

When she was ready to publish *The Great Controversy,* she let the Review management talk her into accepting a reduced royalty in exchange for the promise that the publishing house would get the book out as quickly as possible. But after it came off the press, managers consigned it to the warehouse and instead promoted *Bible Readings for the Home Circle.* Pacific Press followed the lead of the Review, also promising to promote *The Great Controversy* in exchange for a minimum royalty and then ignoring it. Because she had borrowed against her expected royalties to support numerous causes, she found herself in financial difficulty for the rest of her life (PM 206-208, 237, 354, 355; Arthur L. White, oral presentation at North American Division Editorial Council, New York, May 25-29, 1968).

Although the Review leadership ignored her, Ellen White continued to protest conditions there. "The publishing house," she charged, "has been turned into desecrated shrines, into places of unholy merchandise and traffic. It has become a place where injustice and fraud have been carried on, where selfishness, malice, envy, and passion have borne sway. Yet the men who have led into this working upon wrong principles are seemingly unconscious of their wrong course of action. When warnings and entreaties come to them, they say, Doth He not speak in parables? Words of warning and reproof have been treated as idle tales" (Lt 31, 1898, in PM 167).

She became so frustrated with these conditions that she urged nonadministrative employees to refuse to go along with management policies and to refuse to work on some commercial material printed by the Review (7T 167, 168).

Some church leaders did join her call to reform the Review. In 1897 A. T. Jones headed a small task force to examine every facet of the work of the Review. After its investigation its report chastised the management's tight-fisted policies and described a general lack of Christian principles. Ellen White wrote to Jones that he had not done enough in dealing with the situation (Lt 80, 1897, in PH146 8-15). W. W. Prescott also attempted to reform the publishing house.

Eventually A. R. Henry and *Harmon Lindsay, two individuals especially responsible for the problematic climate at the Review, left church employment. But the mind-set remained for many years.

Ellen White continued to focus on the issue of commercial printing as symbolic of the many problems plaguing the publishing house. Since some of the material published contradicted

Seventh-day Adventist teachings, she urged the publishing house to stop accepting such publications, commenting in a letter to its board, "I have been almost afraid to open the *Review*, fearing to see that God has cleansed the publishing house by fire" (8T 91). Morale at the Review plummeted, and vandalism and deliberate carelessness plagued the institution.

On the evening of December 30, 1902, fire did destroy the publishing house. Afterward Ellen White wrote to her son Edson, "Oh, I am feeling so sad, because . . . the Lord has permitted this, because His people would not hear His warnings and repent, and be converted. . . . Many have despised the words of warning" (Lt 214, 1902, in 5Bio 225).

In response to the destruction the board voted to discontinue commercial printing and, also at her suggestion, to move the publishing house to Washington, D.C. After 80 years in suburban Washington, D.C., the Review moved in 1983 to its present location in Hagerstown, Maryland.

Further reading: PM 127-182; 5Bio 223-235; *Testimonies on Fair Dealing and Book Royalties* (PH102); G. R. Knight, *From 1888 to Apostasy: The Case of A. T. Jones* (RHPA, 1987), pp. 172-175; *SDA Encyclopedia* (1996), vol. 11, pp. 445-450; G. M. Valentine, *W. W. Prescott: Forgotten Giant of Adventism's Second Generation* (RHPA, 2005), pp. 192, 193, 200-210.

Gerald Wheeler

RIGHTEOUSNESS BY FAITH. Ellen White wrote and preached extensively on "righteousness by faith." For her, this subject became the umbrella for all other aspects of the plan of salvation. Her understanding of this topic determined her definitions of such core concepts as grace, *faith, *justification, and *sanctification.

Her theological understanding of this subject is close to that of John Wesley. They both acknowledge the New Testament emphasis on righteousness by faith as God's dual gift of pardon and power, expressed theologically as justification and sanctification. They both assert the truth that "the righteousness by which we are justified is imputed; the righteousness by which we are sanctified is imparted. The first is our title to heaven, the second is our fitness for heaven" (RH, June 4, 1895; see John Wesley, "Sermon on the Wedding Garment," *Wesley's Sermons*, vol. 2, CXXIV, pp. 457, 458).

Ellen White clearly distinguishes justification by faith from sanctification by faith, but never separates them in the sense that they have different sources or represent different kinds of faith. Probably her clearest statement of this inseparable union is found in her classic *Steps to Christ*: "Our only ground of hope is in the righteousness of Christ imputed to us, and in that wrought by His Spirit working in and through us" (SC 63).

But receiving "the righteousness of Christ imputed to us" and "wrought . . . in and through us" (*ibid.*) requires faith. Faith is not a passive experience but "is rendering to God the intellectual powers, abandonment of the mind and will to God, and making Christ the only door to enter into the kingdom of heaven" (FW 25). Thus, faith is our response to grace but faith is not, in itself, human merit by which we can earn forgiveness (*ibid.* 23-25). Further, "faith that is unto salvation is not a casual faith . . . not the mere consent of the intellect, it is belief rooted in the heart, that embraces Christ as a personal Savior. . . . This faith leads its possessor to place all the affections of the soul upon Christ; his understanding is under the control of the Holy Spirit, and his character is molded after the divine likeness. His faith is not a dead faith, but a faith that works by love, and leads him . . . to become assimilated to the divine character" (1SM 391, 392).

Ellen White strongly emphasizes the dynamics of God and man cooperating in the plan of salvation, forming "a copartnership in which all the power is of God and all the glory belongs to God. The responsibility rests with us. . . . Divine power and the human agency combined will be a complete success, for Christ's righteousness accomplishes everything" (FW 26, 27).

This amazing cooperation makes both justification and sanctification happen. "As the penitent sinner, contrite before God, discerns Christ's atonement in his behalf and accepts this atonement as his only hope in this life and the future life, his sins are pardoned. This is justification by faith. . . . Pardon and justification are one and the same thing. Through faith, the believer passes from the position of a rebel, a child of sin and Satan, to the position of a loyal subject of Christ Jesus, not because of an inherent goodness, but because Christ receives him as His child by adoption. . . . Justification is the opposite of condemnation" (*ibid*. 103, 104). Penitent sinners are no longer rebels because they choose to be loyal to God. God honors this choice, this faith, which includes trust and willingness to be God's obedient children.

Christianity has long been divided regarding whether the experience of justification has any conditions, either prior to being justified or in maintaining the justified state (*ibid*. 111-113). Ellen White clearly states that "Christ pardons none but the penitent, but whom He pardons He first makes penitent" (1SM 393, 394). Change has happened in the lives of the penitent. They sense that "in order to obtain the righteousness of Christ, it is necessary for the sinner to know what that repentance is which works a radical change of mind and spirit and action. The work of transformation must begin in the heart, and manifest its power through every faculty of the being. . . . He who would become a child of God must receive the truth that repentance and forgiveness are to be obtained through nothing less than the atonement of Christ. Assured of this the sinner must put forth an effort in harmony with the work done for him, and with unwearied entreaty he must supplicate the throne of grace, that the renovating power of God may come into his soul" (*ibid*. 393).

The faith that accepts God's forgiveness and the new experience of being justified by Christ's atonement is the same faith that maintains the justified experience. Justification is not a once-in-a-lifetime experience leading to the error of believing in "once saved, always saved." The experience of justification by faith is not "legal fiction." Although God is eager to bring the peace of justification (Rom. 5:1), White makes clear that "no man can cover his soul with the garments of Christ's righteousness while practicing known sins, or neglecting known duties. God requires the entire surrender of the heart, before justification can take place; and in order for man to retain justification, there must be continual obedience, through active, living faith that works by love and purifies the soul" (1SM 366).

The experience of justification is the basis of assurance as the Christian advances "daily in the divine life" and "experiences a conversion to God every day" (2T 505). This daily experience, as the Christian continues to walk with Jesus, keeps the maturing Christian grateful for the mercies of a forgiving Lord and describes the experience of sanctification by faith—the Holy Spirit's "working in and through us" (SC 63).

On many occasions White differentiated the dual aspects of righteousness by faith (justification by faith and sanctification by faith). Regarding the experience of justification she wrote in *Steps to Christ*: "We have no righteousness of our own with which to meet the claims of the law of God. But Christ has made a way of escape for us. . . . If you give yourself to Him, and accept Him as your Savior, then, sinful as your life may have been, for His sake you are accounted righteous. Christ's character stands in place of your character, and you are accepted before God just as if you had not sinned" (*ibid.* 62).

She then continues her thought with a description of the experience of sanctification, undergirded by the daily experience of justification: "More than this, Christ changes the heart. He abides in your heart by faith. You are to maintain this connection with Christ by faith and the continual surrender of your will to Him; and so long as you do this, He will work in you to will and to do according to His good pleasure. So you may say, 'The life which I now live in the flesh I live by the faith of the Son of God, who loved me, and gave himself for me.' Galatians 2:20. . . . Then with Christ working in you, you will manifest the same spirit and do the same good works—works of righteousness, obedience. So we have nothing in ourselves of which to boast. We have no ground for self-exaltation. Our only ground of hope is in the righteousness of Christ imputed to us, and in that wrought by His Spirit working in and through us" (*ibid.* 62, 63).

Unfortunately, many trust their future on God's part of the justified experience, thinking that their responsibility rests only on "believing" that Jesus died for them. They do not see the indissoluble union between the faith of justification and the faith of sanctification: "All these expect to be saved by Christ's death, while they refuse to live His self-sacrificing life. They extol the riches of free grace, and attempt to cover themselves with an appearance of righteousness, hoping to screen their defects of character; but their efforts will be of no avail in the day of God. . . . Those who reject the gift of Christ's righteousness are

rejecting the attributes of character which would constitute them the sons and daughters of God. They are rejecting that which alone could give them a fitness for a place at the marriage feast" (COL 316, 317).

Because both justification and sanctification (dual gifts of righteousness by faith) are possible only through sincere faith, and because both justification and sanctification contribute to the same goal, we can better understand why Ellen White said: "Many commit the error of trying to define minutely the fine points of distinction between justification and sanctification. Into the definitions of these two terms they often bring their own ideas and speculations. Why try to be more minute than is Inspiration on the vital question of righteousness by faith? Why try to work out every minute point, as if the salvation of the soul depended upon all having exactly your understanding of this matter? All cannot see in the same line of vision" (6BC 1072).

White consistently depicts the goal of righteousness by faith (justification and sanctification) as the "wedding garment" portrayed in the parable of Matthew 22:1-14 and in Revelation 19:8: "By the wedding garment in the parable is represented the pure, spotless character which Christ's true followers will possess. . . . The fine linen, says the Scripture, 'is the righteousness of saints.' Rev. 19:8. It is the righteousness of Christ, His own unblemished character, that through faith is imparted to all who receive Him as their personal Savior" (COL 310).

In summary, "righteousness by faith" for Ellen White describes what happens to a person who, by the grace of God, has been set right by what Jesus has done *for us* and is kept right by what Jesus is doing *in* and *through* us (SC 63). It depicts a person in harmony with God, beginning with repentance, contrition, and a desire to grow in grace in maturing this right relationship with God. Making clear how sinners are redeemed when God gives them righteousness by faith is one of the chief reasons Jesus became human (ST, Jan. 20, 1890).

Herbert E. Douglass

RINGS, see **DRESS AND ADORNMENT; WEDDING RING.**

RIVERSIDE SANITARIUM, see **ROCK CITY SANITARIUM.**

ROCHESTER, NEW YORK. *Home of James and Ellen White from 1852 to 1855; birthplace of the *Review and Herald publishing office; and location of Mount Hope Cemetery, burial place of early Sabbatarian Adventists. In 1843 *Joshua Himes preached a series of meetings in the New Public Market in Rochester, where an estimated 7,000 people attended. In preparation for the meeting Joseph Marsh started a Millerite paper, the *Glad Tidings* (Rochester *Democrat*, June 8, 1843). In 1852 Sabbatarian leaders meeting in Balston Spa, New York, decided they should own their own printing press. Among other reasons, they wanted to be sure their publications about resting on the Sabbath would not be the cause of a printer working on the Sabbath. The publishing office began with a newly purchased Washington hand press in a rented home off Mount Hope Avenue in Rochester. The widespread interest in the Millerite message, the close proximity of the Erie Canal, a loan for the press by *Hiram Edson, and the rapid growth of the city of Rochester were factors in the Whites' decision to establish their work in Rochester, New York.

Under discouraging circumstances, James and Ellen White set up housekeeping with little money and with the press office located on the first floor of their home. Lacking all worldly luxuries, Ellen White described her furniture: "Two old bedsteads for twenty-five cents each. My husband brought me home six old chairs, no two of them alike. . . . The frames are strong, and I have been seating them with drilling. . . . Our first meals were taken on a fireboard placed upon two empty flour barrels. We are willing to endure privations if the work of God can be advanced" (LS 142).

The same year the Whites moved to Rochester, the city was hit with a cholera epidemic, and Ellen White remembered the wagons filled with the dead going by throughout the night on their way to the newly commissioned cemetery. Their son Edson fell ill with cholera, but was healed in answer to prayer (*ibid.* 143, 144). In the fall of 1852 James White's sister and brother, *Anna and *Nathaniel White, moved to Mount Hope to work with him and to learn the *three angels' messages. Ellen and James White were deeply afflicted when Nathaniel died of tuberculosis in the spring of 1853 and Anna fell to the same disease in the fall of 1854 (*ibid.* 147; "Obituary [Anna White]," RH, Dec. 12, 1854).

Within a year of arriving in Rochester, the Whites moved the press to St. Paul Street while they themselves moved into a home on Monroe Avenue, next to *Jonathan Orton's house. The ages of workers in the *Review* office in 1853 testify to the youthfulness of the movement, with the oldest workers being James White and *Clarissa Bonfoey, both 32, and the youngest being Warren Bacheller at 14. In 1852 James White began the publication of *The Youth's Instructor*, and started the first Adventist Sabbath schools.

Although many residents of Rochester had accepted the Millerite message before the 1844 disappointment, they were not very accepting of the early Sabbatarian Adventists. This nonacceptance, combined with infighting among Rochester Adventists, prompted the discouraged Whites to move further west. In 1855, after three challenging years in Rochester, the Whites moved to Battle Creek, Michigan. One notable later visit to Rochester came in 1865, where on Christmas Day Ellen White had a vision at the home of Joseph and *Drusilla Lamson. In this vision she was shown that Seventh-day Adventists should establish their own *health reform institution. Ellen White, in a sermon in Battle Creek in 1875, averred that if "the brethren and sisters in Rochester and vicinity had been less selfish and less jealous of those whom God had selected to bear the heaviest burdens, . . . if they had shown their faith by their works; if they had been consecrated to God, and really loved the truth, and shown fruits of the same by manifesting a personal interest in the success and advancement of the work of God, the office of publication would not have been removed from Rochester" (PH159 175).

Other Adventist pioneers had roots in Rochester. *J. N. Andrews, who worked at the *Review* office, later held many meetings in Rochester. *J. N. Loughborough, who was born in nearby Victor, worked in Rochester for many years.

Further reading: LS 142-156; 1Bio 227-239, 271-274, 281-283, 301-306, 319; R. H. Allen and H. Krug, *Rochester's Adventist Heritage: Tour Guide and Biographical Overview* (Rochester, N.Y.: Advent History Project New York, 2002).

Howard P. Krug

ROCK CITY SANITARIUM. Health-care institution in Nashville, Tennessee, which Ellen White visited in April 1909 shortly after it opened (6Bio 191). The forerunner of the Rock City Sanitarium was the first Adventist health-care institution established especially to serve African-Americans, a set of treatment rooms

opened in Nashville by Fred and Fannie Young in 1901. The Youngs envisioned that this small beginning would become a sanitarium with a school of nursing. About the same time, another group of treatment rooms across town was becoming the forerunner of the *Nashville Sanitarium. Context suggests that Ellen White was referring to both of these initiatives when she wrote in 1901-1902 that "sanitarium work also has been begun in Nashville" (7T 234). She urged the need of strong support for the fledgling institutions and warned church leaders not to "rush into" any further projects until the present ones could be "strengthened" (*ibid.*). The Youngs were joined in 1902 by Lottie C. Isabel, M.D., a graduate of the *American Medical Missionary College.

In 1904 Ellen White visited the sanitarium, spoke highly of the work being done there, and appealed to Adventists to support it with "liberal gifts" (ST, Nov. 30, 1904; cf. SW, Oct. 25, 1904; RH, Aug. 18, 1904). Unfortunately, the hoped-for support was not forthcoming; the enterprise soon failed, and Dr. Isabel moved to Birmingham, Alabama.

In 1908, however, the Southern Union Conference purchased a building for the Rock City Sanitarium, the equipment from the earlier treatment rooms was transferred to it, and Dr. Lottie Isabel Blake, now married, returned as the medical superintendent, assisted by her husband, D. E. Blake, a minister who later became a physician. Again, however, the sanitarium failed to thrive.

In 1927 *Nellie Druillard opened the Riverside Sanitarium in Nashville to serve African-Americans. She founded it with her own funds and managed it until 1935, when she deeded it to the General Conference. It was sold in 1983.

Further reading: SDA Encyclopedia (1996), vol. 11, pp. 461, 462.

Jerry Moon

ROMAN CATHOLIC CHURCH. Ellen White's comments regarding the Roman Catholic Church fall into two basic categories: while the first category deals with historical and theological arguments against many claims made by the Catholic Church, the second category of statements offers counsels on how to reach Roman Catholics.

The first category of statements occurs in the context of her expounding of the *great controversy theme and most of her historical and theological analyses of Roman Catholicism appear in her book *The Great Controversy. Key to her understanding of Catholicism is that many Catholic teachings arose during a time of apostasy that saw the gradual increase of nonbiblical teachings and practices in the church, the suppression of the Bible as the only standard of teaching, the disregard of the second commandment, the substitution of the observance of Sunday for the Sabbath, and the establishment of the Papacy and its claims to infallibility and supremacy over temporal rulers (GC 49-60). She understood Catholicism as a static institution and further explained how, in spite of showing good will toward Protestants, it will never change (*ibid.* 564, 581). She also expressed concern that Roman Catholicism in America will ultimately attempt to control governments and people's consciences, as it once did by deceiving Protestants into believing that it has changed. Hence both Roman Catholicism and an apostatized Protestantism will "clasp hands" "in trampling on the rights of conscience" and impose upon all people beliefs and practices that are not supported by Scripture (*ibid.* 588).

While much anti-Catholic rhetoric and sentiments published in Protestant publications in the United States in the second half of the nineteenth century tended to spread harsh remarks, and dispense rumors and evil surmising toward Roman Catholics, Ellen White did not espouse such attitudes and kept her comments about Roman Catholicism to historical and theological arguments against the system of thought and practices it represented. She substantiated her thoughts with available support from known historians and within a historicist and eschatological interpretation of the prophecies of *Daniel and *Revelation. Central to her arguments is also the belief that Scripture has primacy over any human institution and that tradition, decisions of councils or creeds cannot "be regarded as evidence for or against any point of religious faith" (*ibid.* 595).

But her comments concerning Roman Catholicism are not limited to denunciations of its doctrinal errors. She also makes a distinction between the Catholic Church as a system and individual Roman Catholic believers, and writes about reaching Roman Catholics with the Adventist message. Repeatedly she emphasizes that there are many conscientious Christians in the Roman Catholic Church (9T 243), that "a great number will be saved" (Ev 574), and that Adventists should avoid antagonizing Catholics by making harsh comments in publications and public meetings (*ibid.* 573-577; 9T 241-244). In that context, she made several changes to the wording of her 1911 edition of *The Great Controversy* in order "to avoid giving unnecessary offense" (3SM 435; "The 1911 Edition of *The Great Controversy*" [SDoc]).

See also: M.M.J. O'Kavanagh.

Further reading: R. Bruinsma, *Seventh-day Adventist Attitudes Toward Roman Catholicism, 1844-1965* (AUP, 1994).

Denis Fortin

RURAL HEALTH RETREAT, see **ST. HELENA SANITARIUM AND HOSPITAL.**

SABBATARIAN BIBLE CONFERENCES. A series of meetings held during 1848-1850 to communicate to former Millerites foundational doctrines that a core group of leaders had already agreed on (2SG 97, 98). Also called "Sabbath Conferences" or "Sabbath and Sanctuary Conferences," the word "Sabbatarian" recognizes that the doctrinal scope was wider than only Sabbath and the sanctuary, and also that the name Seventh-day Adventist was not formally adopted until 1860.

Contrary to common assumptions, the conferences of 1848-1850 did not *initiate* the process of doctrinal formation among Sabbatarian Adventists. A close reading of the primary sources shows that several features often associated with the conferences of 1848-1850 were actually more characteristic of earlier meetings in 1846-1847. The picture that emerges includes two kinds of meetings termed "conferences"—smaller formative meetings, sometimes called conferences, during 1846-1847, and the larger evangelistic conferences of 1848-1850.

The formative conferences involved a small group of leaders—Joseph Bates, James and Ellen White, Hiram Edson, and others—who combined intense study and discussion with prayer, and sometimes fasting. Ellen recalled that they often studied late into the night, and sometimes all night. Repeatedly when the group reached an impasse, Ellen White "would be taken off in vision" and given a "clear explanation of the passages we had been studying" (1SM 206, 207; cf. TM 24, 25). This close collaboration between Bates and the Whites apparently began in 1846, when the Whites accepted the Sabbath from Bates, and Bates became convinced that Ellen's visions were from God (Burt, p. 277).

Among these "formative" conferences, four are well known. At a meeting in Topsham, Maine, November 1846, Ellen's vision on the "opening heavens" convinced Bates that her visions were of more than human origin, leading Bates and the Whites to begin united labors. Another took place in Fairhaven, Massachusetts, Bates' home, March 6, 1847. Hiram Edson hosted a conference at his home in Port Gibson, New York, where Edson and O.R.L. Crosier convinced Bates of their new insights into Christ's ministry in the heavenly sanctuary, and Bates convinced them to keep the seventh-day Sabbath. At a conference April 3, 1847, in Topsham, Maine, a vision confirmed the permanency of the Sabbath; "the Sabbath commandment was not nailed to the cross" (LS 100, 101). Thus by early 1847 Bates, the Whites, and a few others had become settled on the doctrines that would become the foundations of Sabbatarian Adventism. These included belief in (1) a premillennial Second Advent, (2) Christ's two-phase ministry in the heavenly sanctuary, (3) the seventh-day Sabbath, and (4) the nonimmortality of the wicked, all in the context of the three angels' messages of Revelation 14:6-12 (Knight, *Joseph Bates*, pp. 102, 103).

Bates had already integrated these beliefs into an Adventist theology by January 1847 when he published his revised edition of *Seventh Day Sabbath: A Perpetual Sign* (Knight, *Joseph Bates*, pp. 110-117). James White's *A Word to the "Little Flock"* (May 1847), which also included sections by Bates and by Ellen White, represented another early summary of the "landmark" doctrines of Sabbatarian Adventism (cf. CW 30, 31). These publications provoked, in late 1847, a six-month publishing war among former Millerites over the Sabbath, culminating in complete schism between Sabbatarian and Sunday-observant Adventists. The Sabbatarian response to this general rejection was to launch a series of evangelistic conferences designed to gather in as many as possible of those still undecided on the Sabbath (Burt, pp. 324-326, 346, 352).

The evangelistic conferences (1848-1850) involved larger groups of up to 50. The focus was on teaching to other former Millerites the doctrines that Bates and the Whites had already come to a consensus on. The precise number of these conferences is uncertain, because some (often called "general") were publicized in advance and drew attendees from a wider area, while others were more localized, held on shorter notice, and left few records. Some 22 major or "general" conferences are known, including six in 1848, six in 1849, and 10 in 1850, plus many minor ones.

Thus the Sabbatarian Conferences represent an advance step in the development of Adventist theology, from the initial acceptance and systematic integration of four foundational beliefs to the promulgation of that integrated core to a larger audience of former Millerites. The conferences also signal the transition from the *"scattering" time or disintegration of Millerism (1844-1848), to the "gathering" time or rising of Sabbatarian Adventism, from 1848 onward (see LS 115).

A brief survey of the 1848 conferences will illustrate their format and content. The "first general meeting held by Seventh-day Adventists" (JW, *Life Incidents*, p. 270), convened April 20-24, 1848, at Rocky Hill, near Hartford, Connecticut, in a large unfinished room of a new house owned by *Albert Belden. Total attendance was about 50. Joseph Bates spoke on the Ten Commandments, and Ellen White related what she had seen in vision about the Sabbath. Two minor conferences met in nearby Bristol and Berlin, Connecticut, in June and July (see J. White to "Dear Brother [Stockbridge Howland]," July 2, 1848).

The second major conference met August 18-19, 1848, at Volney, northwest of Syracuse, New York. Ellen White recalled that of some 35 present, hardly two agreed, and all "were anxious for an opportunity to advance their sentiments, or to preach to us. They were told that we had not come so great a distance to hear them, but had come to teach them the truth" (2SG 98). This statement clearly shows the evangelistic emphasis on the already-established doctrinal foundations.

A third major conference of 1848 would be held a week later, August 27-28, at *Hiram Edson's barn near Port Gibson, southeast of Rochester, New York (1Bio 139, 141-144). On the way from Volney to Port Gibson, Joseph Bates, the Whites, Brother and Sister Edson, and a Brother Simmons stayed overnight with the Snow family in Hannibal, New York, where there were eight or 10 believers. This brief stopover took on the character of another minor conference (Burt, pp. 356-358). James reported that the morning of August 26, "Ellen was taken off in vision, and while she was in vision, all the [brethren and sisters] came in. It was a powerful time. One of the number was not on the Sabbath but was humble and good. Ellen rose up in vision and took the large Bible, held it up before the Lord, talked from it, then carried it to this humble brother who was not on the Sabbath and put it in his arms. He took it while tears were rolling down. . . . Then Ellen came and sat down by me. She was in vision 1½ hours, in which time she did not breathe at all. It was an affecting time. All wept much for joy" (James White to Brother and Sister Hastings, Aug. 26, 1848).

The fourth major conference returned to Albert Belden's home in Rocky Hill, Connecticut, September 8-9. A fifth was held October 20-22 at Topsham, Maine, in the home of *Stockbridge Howland, a civil engineer. The sixth major conference of 1848 was held November 17-19 in Dorchester, now part of Boston, Massachusetts, in the home of *Otis Nichols, a printer. Bates presented a Bible study on the seal of God, further light came through a vision to Ellen White, and the group then tested the new concepts by further Bible study.

In neither the formative nor the evangelistic conferences did the visions initiate major doctrines. Each of the four foundational doctrines had already been established from Scripture by people who never became Seventh-day Adventists (Second Advent, by William Miller and others; Sabbath, by Seventh Day Baptists; sanctuary, by O.R.L. Crosier; and nonimmortality of the wicked, by George Storrs). Bates took these biblical doctrines essentially worked out by others and united them, using the three angels' messages of Revelation 14 as the integrating framework (Knight, *Bates*, p. 153; cf. Knight, *Search for Identity*, pp. 55-89). The visions of Ellen White served to confirm or refine concepts that had already been discovered in Scripture. An example from the Volney conference illustrates how Ellen White's visions confirmed, and thus promoted the acceptance of, the doctrines that had already been published following the formative conferences.

*David Arnold, whose new carriage house was the meeting place, held some unusual opinions—that the 144,000 were those raised at Christ's resurrection; that the Lord's Supper should be held only once a year, at Passover time; and that the millennium of Revelation 20 was already past (a published contemporary anti-Millerite view). As Arnold "spoke of the 1,000 years being in the past," Ellen White was sure he was wrong, but did not know how to convince him of it. "Great grief pressed my spirits," she recalled, "for it seemed to me that God was dishonored" (2SG 98). Under this anxiety she fainted. Immediately others present formed a prayer circle and interceded for her. She revived—but not to normal consciousness. In a visionary state, unaware of what was going on around her, she took up a Bible

and began to turn the pages, pointing out texts relevant to the issues under discussion. At the same time her eyes were turned "upward and in an opposite direction from the Bible," as if looking at something distant (JNL, in *Review and Herald*, Mar. 3, 1885; cited in 1Bio 142). While those around her were curiously documenting her outward behavior, she herself was "lost to earthly things." When the vision was over and she again became aware of her surroundings, she told the group that her "accompanying angel" had explained "some of the errors of those present, and also the truth in contrast with their errors" (2SG 98).

It is noteworthy that the method by which the vision resolved disagreement was by calling attention to specific Scripture passages on the points at issue. As John Loughborough noted later, "the reason these persons gave up their differences was not simply because Sister White said they must give them up, but because in the same vision they were pointed to plain statements of Scripture that refuted their false theories, and had presented before them in contrast a straight and harmonious track of Bible truth" (1Bio 142).

In addition to the biblical evidence that Ellen's auditors found so compelling, there was another reason her visions had such dramatic impact. The reason she became so anxious about Arnold's view of the millennium was not that she was unacquainted with the biblical evidence. She had already summarized in *A Word to the "Little Flock"* her understanding of the biblical millennium. There was a reason she didn't just reiterate what she had already written. "During this whole time" (1846-1849), she remembered, "I could not understand the reasoning of the brethren. My mind was locked, as it were, and I could not comprehend the meaning of the scriptures we were studying. This was one of the greatest sorrows of my life. I was in this condition of mind until all the principal points of our faith were made clear to our minds, in harmony with the Word of God. The brethren knew that when not in vision, I could not understand these matters, and they accepted as light direct from heaven the revelations given" (SpTB02, in 1SM 207). The combination of her inability to understand theological arguments when not in vision, plus the cogency of her reasoning and the clear biblical evidence she presented when in vision, reinforced observers' convictions that her visions were not of her own devising.

The time period of this mental disability apparently extended from sometime in 1846 to September 1849. "For two or three years," Ellen recalled, "my mind continued to be locked to the Scriptures. In 1846 I was married to Elder James White. It was some time after my second son was born that we were in great perplexity regarding certain points of doctrine. I was asking the Lord to unlock my mind that I might understand His Word. Suddenly I seemed to be enshrouded in clear, beautiful light, and ever since, the Scriptures have been an open book to me" (Ms 135, 1903, in 3MR 413, 414).

Parallel sources confirm that some six weeks after the birth of her second son (J. Edson White, July 28, 1849), the Whites attended a meeting in Paris, Maine on September 14, 1849 (LS80 260, 261). Ellen wrote that "in the course of our labors, my husband and I visited Father [Edward] Andrews," the elderly father of J. N. Andrews (1SM 207). During that visit Father Andrews was healed of inflammatory rheumatism. After the healing of Father Andrews, Ellen reported that "an angel's hand was laid upon my head. From that time to this I have been able to understand the Word of God" (*ibid.*). The verb "visited" points to September 1849, when they briefly passed through Paris, Maine, not to December

1850, when they were making that same Andrews home their place of residence. This termination is solid, resting on two dates—Edson's birth July 28, 1849, and the conference in Paris, Maine, September 14, 1849.

If this mental disability of "two or three years" ended in September 1849, it may have begun as early as the fall of 1846, which would account for Ellen's mention of her marriage in this context (see two paragraphs above). It was just after their marriage on August 30, 1846, that the Whites read Bates' tract *The Seventh Day Sabbath: A Perpetual Sign*, began to keep the Sabbath, and formed a collaborative relationship with Bates.

Both the formative and the evangelistic conferences were constructed around the union of prayer and study. The participants deliberately chose to minimize minor points of disagreement. In addition to biblical presentations, there was discussion in which "each one expressed his opinion freely." Their response to deadlocked disagreement was to separate for individual prayer and study (TM 25). Recalling the intensity of their search, Ellen White wrote: "Often we remained together until late at night, and sometimes through the entire night, praying for light and studying the Word" (1SM 206). "Often we fasted, that we might be better fitted to understand the truth" (TM 24).

They remembered that a single unbiblical idea had led to the disappointment of 1844. (Erroneously believing that the *sanctuary of Daniel 8:14 was the earth, the Millerite Adventists thought the "cleansing of the sanctuary" meant the cleansing of the earth by fire at Christ's second coming.)With this painful lesson still fresh in their memory, they "sought most earnestly that the Scriptures should not be wrested to suit any man's opinions" (*ibid.* 25).

The order of their study was to first search

the Scriptures until they reached the limits of their ability to understand the available evidence. Revelation through visions was not given to take the place of thorough Bible study. But at the point where they could humanly do nothing more, Ellen White would often be taken in vision and given insights that resolved the immediate difficulty and enabled the Bible study to continue (1SM 206, 207). The combination of biblical basis and prophetic confirmation gave the believers a sense of certainty. On December 13, 1850, Ellen White wrote to friends, "How plain our position is: We know that we have the truth" (Lt 30, 1850).

The Sabbatarian Bible Conferences remain significant for several reasons. First, the conferences brought into working harmony a group of hardheaded New England individualists that prior to the conference had been characterized as "hardly two agreed" on biblical topics other than the Millerite theme of Christ's second coming (2SG 97).

Second, they came to that degree of harmony by maintaining both the unity of, and the clear distinction between, Scripture and the visions. Adventists hold that the visions of Ellen White have the same *origin*—the inspiration of the Holy Spirit—as the visions of the biblical prophets, but Adventists do not hold that the visions have all of the same *functions* as the scriptural canon ("The Inspiration and Authority of the Ellen G. White Writings," *Ministry*, February 1983).

Third, the fact that the visions brought harmony, not by asserting superior authority, but by pointing the participants to further Bible study, established a distinctive theological approach that has characterized Seventh-day Adventism. The centrality of Scripture was enhanced, not diminished, by the visions given. The visions directed the believers' attention to Scripture passages that corrected their mistakes. Thus, to the degree that their

consciences were captive to the Word of God, there was both freedom of conscience and doctrinal unity: freedom of conscience because ultimate authority was vested in God and His Word, not in human authority; and doctrinal unity because of their conviction that the Word does not contradict itself. That freedom of individual conscience and corresponding unity in the Word are the enduring legacy of the Sabbatarian Conferences.

See also: general article: For Jesus and Scripture: The Life of Ellen G. White.

Further reading: 2SG 93-104; 1SM 206, 207; TM 24, 25; 1Bio 322-326; M. Burt, "The Historical Background, Interconnected Development, and Integration of the Doctrines of the Sanctuary, the Sabbath, and Ellen G. White's Role in Sabbatarian Adventism From 1844 to 1849" (Ph.D. diss., AU, 2002), pp. 352-364; G. R. Knight, *Joseph Bates: The Real Founder of Seventh-day Adventist* (RHPA, 2004), pp. 92-134; idem, *A Search for Identity: The Development of Seventh-day Adventist Beliefs* (RHPA, 2000), pp. 55-89; JW, *Life Incidents: In Connection With the Great Advent Movement* (Battle Creek, Mich.: SDA Pub. Assn., 1868; reprint AUP, 2003, with historical introduction by J. Moon), pp. 270-290.

Jerry Moon

SABBATH, DOCTRINE OF THE. The meaning of the Sabbath in the writings of Ellen White derives from what it *is*, what it is *made of*, who made it, and the *purpose* for which it was made. First, the "doctrine of the Sabbath" speaks to what the Sabbath *is*. Several statements in Ellen White's writings clearly define and identify the nature of the Sabbath. Fundamentally, the Sabbath is a day; hence its essence is time. Yet it is not any time or any day, but the seventh day; it is literal time, not metaphoric time. The particularity of the Sabbath time is understood in its connection to God's creative work.

On the basis of Genesis 2:1-3 Ellen White describes the seventh day as a *memorial* of God's creative work. The Sabbath was instituted to commemorate the completion of the Creation. Furthermore, when the foundations of the earth were laid, then was also laid the foundation of the Sabbath. In this way, the day, the seventh day, is inextricably linked to God's creative work, thus giving it theological significance. The Sabbath is not simply a day, or the seventh day, but a memorial of Creation. As a memorial the seventh-day Sabbath serves as a sign to help people remember the creative event. This sign (the Sabbath) cannot be thought of apart from the thing signified (Creation). Furthermore, the memorial takes on the nature of an *institution* in Ellen White's writings. It is quite evident that the characterization of the Sabbath as a *memorial* and *institution* is to highlight not only its enduring nature but also its public character.

Following the nature of the Sabbath as a memorial and institution, we are logically led to another theological insight into what the Sabbath *is* in Ellen White's writings. As a celebrative event the Sabbath is a memorial of everlasting value that is enjoined on all humanity in the form of an enduring commandment. The interconnection of the Sabbath, Creation, and its juridical demands on humanity is a consistent theme in Ellen White. One final theological insight into the Sabbath as a memorial may be pointed out. Noting God's satisfaction at the Creation (Gen. 1:31), and the fact of the "morning stars" and "sons of God" shouting for joy at the Creation (Job 38:7), Ellen White describes the Sabbath not just as a day of rest, but as a day of rejoicing (DA 769; 6T 349). The Sabbath is a gift from God that He deliberately set apart to a holy use and gave to Adam as a day of rest (DA 281). To summarize, the Sabbath *is* specifically the literal seventh day of the week by virtue of its biblical connection to Creation, of which it is a memorial. Consequently, all people are commanded to observe its enduring demands and join in its celebration.

Second, if the seventh-day Sabbath is a memorial of God's creative work, and all are commanded to observe it as a day of rejoicing and rest, it is so because of what the Sabbath entails in itself. Ellen White writes that "God set up the memorial of His work of creation, in placing His blessing upon the seventh day" (PP 48). In other words, the seventh day acquired the status of a memorial by virtue of God's blessing it. She summarizes that "great blessings are enfolded in the observance of the Sabbath" (6T 349). Elsewhere this statement appears to be explained when she quotes Exodus 31:16 and remarks that the reason Israel was required to observe the Sabbath was that God "sanctified and blessed the seventh day and made it His sacred memorial" (MM 215). The blessings of the Sabbath (in this context, divine comfort and consolation), however, are not limited to Israel but await all who refrain from labor on the Sabbath. Evidently the invitation in the writings of Ellen White to observe the seventh-day Sabbath of Creation does not depend simply on what the Sabbath *is* formally: a memorial of everlasting value that is enjoined on all not only in the nature of an enduring commandment, but also on the basis of what the Sabbath *is made of* materially: God's blessings, sanctification, and presence.

Third, in Ellen White the meaning of the Sabbath is also reflective of its origin, related as it is to *who made it*. Connecting Mark 2:28, "therefore the Son of man is Lord also of the sabbath," with John 1:3, "all things were made by him," she draws the conclusion that Christ made the Sabbath and it belongs to Him. It points to Him as both Creator and Sanctifier.

Furthermore, it was Christ who called Moses into the mount and made known the law of Jehovah, including the charge to remember the Sabbath day to keep it holy. Further, the Sabbath declares that Christ, the head of the church, by whom all things hold together, has the power to reconcile humanity to God. To see Christ in the Sabbath is to call to mind the lost peace of Eden and the peace restored through the Savior (DA 288, 289).

Finally, in view of what the Sabbath *is*, what it is *made of*, and *who* made and gave it to humanity, it is shown to have great purposes and significance for humanity. First, the Sabbath has significant didactic value in salvation history. Ellen White states quite explicitly that the value of the Sabbath as a means of education is beyond estimate. On the basis of Exodus 31:13 and 20:11 she notes that the Sabbath is a sign of creative and redemptive power. Pointing to God as the source of life and knowledge, the Sabbath, she observes, "recalls man's primeval glory, and thus witnesses to God's purpose to re-create us in His own image" (Ed 250). The power that created all things is the power that re-creates the soul in God's own likeness. Hence the Sabbath is a sign of sanctification. The Sabbath commandment has pedagogic value in its relation to the rest of the commandments. Indeed, she remarks that if the Sabbath had always been universally observed, there could never have been an atheist or idolater. Furthermore, because the Sabbath commandment is the only one in the Decalogue that names and defines the Lawgiver (Ex. 20:1), it contains in a spiritual sense the seal of God that distinguishes the living Creator from every false god (GC 437, 438).

The Sabbath, however, is not only about God. For humankind the Sabbath has a critical purpose. One's response to the Sabbath has significant existential implications. Keeping the seventh-day Creation Sabbath signifies that one worships the true God. The Sabbath's critical function gains intensity toward the end of time. As the point of truth that is especially controverted, the Sabbath will be the great test of loyalty to God. By it a "line of distinction will be drawn between those who serve God and those who serve Him not" (*ibid.* 605).

Furthermore, the Sabbath has practical value for humanity. The object of the Sabbath after humanity's creation, White observes, was to benefit humanity and "meet [human beings'] necessities" (2T 582). She mentions at least two basic necessities for which the Sabbath was essential to humanity, even in Paradise. First, humanity needed and still needs to lay aside their own interests and pursuits for rest on the seventh day so that the works of God may be contemplated and His power and goodness meditated upon. Second, humanity needed and still needs the Sabbath to be reminded of God and awaken gratitude, because all that is enjoyed and possessed comes from the hand of the Creator. All the blessings of the Sabbath to humanity are realized as the mind is called from secular labor to contemplate the goodness and glory of God. Hence, both God's command to Israel to do all His statutes "that he might preserve us alive" (Deut. 6:24), and the blessings of Sabbath observance enunciated in Isaiah 56:6, 7 are claimed by Ellen White for contemporary Sabbath observers. This shows her conviction that what the Sabbath *is*, what it is *made of*, *who* made it, and the *purpose* for which it was made have not been altered since the day God first gave the Sabbath to humankind.

Finally, she believed that the Sabbath would become progressively more significant as the world draws nearer the Second Coming. In an early vision she saw that "at the commencement of the time of trouble, we were filled with the Holy Ghost as we went forth and proclaimed the Sabbath more fully" (EW 33). In her eschatology, the Sabbath, one of the Ten Commandments, is an identifying mark of the *remnant church (Rev. 12:17; 14:12), the special focus of the *seal of God (Rev. 7:1-3; 14:1-5), and the antithesis of the *mark of the beast (Rev. 14:9-12). In the temple of God, the *sanctuary in heaven, the *law of God, including the Sabbath commandment, is enshrined in the ark of the covenant as the basis of the divine government (Rev. 11:19). Many have recognized that these eschatological connections give the Sabbath an urgency and power that is not otherwise so apparent. White observed in 1862, "Separate the Sabbath from the [three angels'] messages [of Revelation 14], and it loses its power; but when connected with the message of the third angel, a power attends it which convicts unbelievers and infidels, and brings them out with strength to stand, to live, grow, and flourish in the Lord" (1T 337).

Further reading: PP 48, 111, 307, 336; PK 178-183; DA 206, 207, 281-289, 769; Ed 250-252; 6T 349, 350; EW 217; GC 53, 54, 437, 438; A. J. Heschel, *The Sabbath: Its Meaning for Modern Man* (New York: Farrar, Straus, and Young, 1951); K. J. Holland, *The Magnificent Seventh* (PPPA, 1970); K. A. Strand, "The Sabbath" in R. Dederen, ed., *Handbook of Seventh-day Adventist Theology* (RHPA, 2000), pp. 529-535.

Kwabena Donkor

SABBATH, OBSERVANCE OF. Ellen White's theological reflections on the biblical Sabbath are both rich and extensive. She discusses how God saw that the Sabbath was essential for humankind, even before sin. By laying aside personal interests and pursuits on the seventh day, His human children might more fully contemplate creation and meditate upon

His power and goodness. The Sabbath was necessary to recall the goodness of the Creator and thus to awaken gratitude for the beneficent hand of God (PP 48).

White never suggests that there is some magical quality about the Sabbath that automatically transmits holiness or sanctification. Rather, the Sabbath is the day God has set aside for special fellowship with His people on earth. God makes the day holy or sacred by gracing it with His presence. By communing with God, we actually partake of His holiness. Because Sabbath hours are filled with intimate fellowship between human beings and their Creator, the Sabbath becomes the sign of the entire life of sanctification and the high point of each week. Thus, Ellen White instructs that "all through the week we are to have the Sabbath in mind and be making preparation to keep it according to the commandment. We are not merely to observe the Sabbath as a legal matter. We are to understand its spiritual bearing upon all the transactions of life" (LDE 77, 78). And "when the Sabbath is thus remembered, the temporal will not be allowed to encroach upon the spiritual. No duty pertaining to the six working days will be left for the Sabbath" (6T 354). "Before the Sabbath begins, the mind as well as the body should be withdrawn from worldly business. God has set His Sabbath at the end of the six working days, that men may stop and consider what they have gained during the week in preparation for the pure kingdom which admits no transgressor. We should each Sabbath reckon with our souls to see whether the week that has ended has brought spiritual gain or loss" (*ibid.* 356).

In seeking to unfold the true meaning of Sabbath, White is ever balanced in her counsel: "The necessities of life must be attended to, the sick must be cared for, the wants of the needy must be supplied. He will not be held guiltless who neglects to relieve suffering on the Sabbath. God's holy rest day was made for man, and acts of mercy are in perfect harmony with its intent. God does not desire His creatures to suffer an hour's pain that may be relieved upon the Sabbath or any other day" (DA 207).

However, Ellen White's broad understanding of the Sabbath is not limited to cognitive reflection. She also encourages the experiential aspect of the Sabbath. Biblical faith is always wholistic, involving much more than just the thinking mind. For example, the psalmist urges a person to "taste and see that the Lord is good" (Ps. 34:8). Just so, Ellen White also embraces the experience of the Sabbath of the Lord, reflecting the invitation to "call the sabbath a delight" at the bidding of God Himself in Isaiah 58:14. Her suggestions are warm and inviting.

She regularly draws attention to the glories of the created world and their connection with the Sabbath. In fact, White regularly links Sabbath hours with the resplendence of nature: "Since the Sabbath is the memorial of creative power, it is the day above all others when we should acquaint ourselves with God through His works. In the minds of the children the very thought of the Sabbath should be bound up with the beauty of natural things" (Ed 251). The Sabbath bids each person to "open the great book of nature and trace therein the wisdom, the power, and the love of the Creator" (PP 48). She suggests that especially on the Sabbath the glory of the Lord can be seen through His created works by studying "the messages that God has written for us in nature. . . . As we come close to the heart of nature, Christ makes His presence real to us, and speaks to our hearts of His peace and love" (COL 26).

White encourages Christian households to revel in the glories of the Sabbath: "All who love God should do what they can to make the Sabbath a delight, holy and honorable. . . . They can do much to exalt the Sabbath in their families and make it the most interesting day of the week. . . . The Sabbath should be made so interesting to our families that its weekly return will be hailed with joy" (2T 584, 585). "The Sabbath school and the meeting for worship occupy only a part of the Sabbath. The portion remaining to the family may be made the most sacred and precious season of all the Sabbath hours. Much of this time parents should spend with their children" (6T 358).

White's Sabbath instruction focuses attention on the grace of the Creator: "God's love has set a limit to the demands of toil. Over the Sabbath He places His merciful hand. In His own day He preserves for the family opportunity for communion with Him, with nature, and with one another." And then Ellen White makes this warm promise: "By such associations parents may bind their children to their hearts, and thus to God, by ties that can never be broken" (SD 181).

In fact, White tightly entwines the family unit with Sabbath joys: "The Sabbath and the family were alike instituted in Eden, and in God's purpose they are indissolubly linked together. On this day more than on any other, it is possible for us to live the life of Eden. It was God's plan for the members of the family to be associated in work and study, in worship and recreation" (FLB 36). She encourages families to spend part of the Sabbath outdoors so that children with their parents can "receive a more correct knowledge of God," letting "their young minds be associated with God in the beautiful scenery of nature. . . . As they view the beautiful things which He has created for the happiness of man, they will be led to regard Him as a tender, loving Father. . . . As the character of God puts on the aspect of love, benevolence, beauty, and attraction, they are drawn to love Him. The Sabbath—oh!—make it the sweetest, the most blessed day of the whole week" (*ibid.*).

Further reading: 6T 349-368; Ed 250-252; 2T 582-585; K. A. Strand, "The Sabbath," in R. Dederen, ed., *Handbook of Seventh-day Adventist Theology* (RHPA, 2000), pp. 529-535.

Jo Ann Davidson

Sabbath Readings: Moral and Religious Lessons for Youth and Children (Battle Creek, Mich.: SDA Publishing Assn., 1863). Series of 25 sixteen-page tracts of moral and religious stories compiled by Ellen White; totaling 400 pages and containing 129 short stories and 25 poems. The series was republished in 1873 without any changes. Between 1877 and 1881 Ellen White expanded the original series to make a new series of four volumes titled *Sabbath Readings for the Home Circle*, published by Pacific Press. This second series contained about 200 stories and 86 poems in 1,551 pages. In 1905 the four volumes were condensed into one illustrated volume of 58 stories and about 30 poems (South Lancaster, Mass.: M. A. Vrooman, 1905, 400 pp.) to be sold by colporteurs. This one-volume edition was republished by the Review and Herald in 1960.

A short advertisement in the *Review and Herald* in June 1863 announced that "Mrs. White, assisted by Sister *A. P. Patten [later Van Horn], is publishing a series of tracts . . . for youth and children. She has a vast amount of moral and religious reading which she has been collecting during the past fifteen years, from which she is selecting and compiling these tracts" (2Bio 94). The same goals were indicated in the preface to the first volume of *Sabbath Readings for the Home Circle* (1877), where Ellen White explained that for more

than 20 years she had been collecting—in large scrapbooks—numerous stories filled with moral and religious instruction for the entire family that she had found in various journals. These readings contained lessons for the family and inculcated such principles as obedience to parents, kindness and affection to other members of the family, and benevolence to the poor (1:3), and sought to "defend a sound morality, and breathe a spirit of devotion, tenderness and true piety" (3:3).

Through the years many people have wondered about Ellen White's selection of many of the stories found in *Sabbath Readings for the Home Circle* and whether all the details and facts of these stories were accurate. Although the scrapbooks from which the stories selected for publication are no longer extant, her other scrapbooks stored at the Ellen G. White Estate office in Silver Spring, Maryland, contain clippings of many stories written by known popular fictional authors of her day. Since the stories she collected were gleaned from religious and secular journals and magazines she read, it is argued that she likely did not verify the veracity and the accuracy of these stories before publishing them. Hence factual details may not have been a concern for her as long as the stories seemed credible and true-to-life, and upheld biblical and moral ideals.

See also: Literature and Reading.

Further reading: 3Bio 52-55; 5T 516-520; J. O. Waller, "The Question of 'Fiction' in Five Scrapbooks of Mrs. Ellen G. White" (unpublished manuscript, 1965, DF 51-z, CAR); J. O. Waller, "A Contextual Study of Ellen G. White's Counsel Concerning Fiction" (unpublished paper, 1965, DF 51-z, CAR); D. L. Vanterpool, "The Literature Controversy" (research paper, 1977, DF 436-a, CAR).

Denis Fortin

SABBATH SCHOOL. Historical documentation is unclear as to Ellen White's direct role in the initiation of Sabbath school among Seventh-day Adventists. Though she likely influenced its inception, James White authored and published the first Sabbath school lessons beginning in 1852 in the inaugural issue of the *Youth's Instructor* and organized the first Sabbath school in Rochester, New York, in 1852. The first lessons were a set of four articles intended for "children," an all-encompassing term for anyone younger than adults.

At first Sabbath school targeted youth exclusively. This is reflected implicitly in many places in Ellen White's writings. As late as 1900 she expressed "a deep interest in our Sabbath schools. . . . Constant efforts should be made by both parents and teachers to interest the youth in matters of eternal importance" (TSS 35).

In the same publication she outlined the timeless twofold objective for Sabbath school: Bible study and Christian discipleship: "The Sabbath school is an important branch of the missionary work, not only because it gives to young and old a knowledge of God's Word, but because it awakens in them a love for its sacred truths, and a desire to study them for themselves; above all, it teaches them to regulate their lives by its holy teachings" (*ibid.* 109, 110).

The *Sabbath School Worker* began publication in 1885, at first as a means of improving teaching methods, but later adding lesson helps for teachers and program helps for leaders. Excerpts from Ellen White's frequent articles in the early years of the *Sabbath School Worker* were compiled into booklet form in *Testimonies on Sabbath School Work* in 1900 and in *Counsels on Sabbath School Work* in 1938. These sources make up the best representation of her vision for the Sabbath school.

Ellen White considered Sabbath school to be the place for diligent, prayerful investigation of God's Word, in which scripture would be compared with scripture and new meanings would be gleaned from familiar passages. Parents were to be considered as educators, and teachers to be learners, in an atmosphere that would fortify all against temptation and heresy.

"The object of Sabbath-school work," Ellen White wrote, "should be the ingathering of souls" (*ibid.* 47). This effort was to be focused both inwardly toward the faith community and outwardly toward society in general. She frequently described Sabbath school as a soul-winning agency in which Christian workers were to be trained for outreach work. Pointing to scriptural promises of strength and wisdom, she counseled tenderness and respect as Sabbath school efforts focus on the development of such witnessing programs as home visitation and children's ministries.

She also advocated the importance of celebrating God's care and love through systematic giving toward mission work, both far and near. Citing higher motives for giving than mere sympathy, she endorsed such approaches as thanksgiving and birthday offerings as means of overcoming selfishness and teaching benevolence.

Gary B. Swanson

SACRAMENTS, see **ORDINANCES.**

ST. HELENA SANITARIUM AND HOSPITAL. Located in the Napa Valley about 70 miles (113 kilometers) north of San Francisco and 3.5 miles (5.7 kilometers) northeast of St. Helena, California, it is the oldest continuously operated Adventist health-care facility in the world. The site was selected in 1877, and the first two-story frame building erected in early 1878. The visions of Ellen White played a significant part in its founding.

*J. N. Loughborough told W. A. Pratt that Ellen White had foreseen a health-care institution in the west, and after personally conferring with her, Pratt gave $3,000 and 10.5 acres (4.3 hectares) of land for the institution. A neighbor, A. B. Atwood, gave $1,000, and physician Merritt G. Kellogg, older half brother of J. H. Kellogg, gave $1,000 and became the first medical superintendent.

Initially called the Rural Health Retreat, by 1882 it was called Crystal Springs Health Retreat (ST, Jan. 26, 1882), and in the 1890s took the name St. Helena Sanitarium. The surrounding community continued for many years to be known as Crystal Springs (now Sanitarium), California (3SM 206, 212).

In 1884 Ellen White purchased land and built a small cottage, which she named Iliel, next door to the sanitarium (3Bio 244). On her return from Australia in 1900 she purchased another home, which she named Elmshaven, near the sanitarium. When the institution added a four-story hospital in 1907, Ellen White gave the dedicatory address. During her last illness in 1915 she was attended by physicians from the St. Helena Sanitarium.

Further reading: J. R. Ferren, "St. Helena Sanitarium Celebrates Fiftieth Anniversary," RH, July 26, 1928; *SDA Encyclopedia* (1996), vol. 11, pp. 522-524.

SALAMANCA VISION. Suffering from headache and a cold, Ellen White preached three times in Salamanca, New York, in early November 1890. While resting for the night at the Hicks home on November 3, she received a vision on matters relating to the *publishing work. In vision she saw men in Battle Creek discussing whether they should drop articles about the Sabbath and the Second Advent from the *American Sentinel* in order to increase its circulation. The next day she tried twice to recall this vision for W. C. White and A. T.

Robinson, but could not. In the weeks that followed she traveled to Virginia, Connecticut, Massachusetts, and Washington, D.C., before returning to Battle Creek at the end of December. Repeatedly during her travels she received further visions about the same matter and noted some of these details in her diary. On Sabbath, March 7, 1891, she tried again to relate this vision to delegates at the General Conference session in Battle Creek, but she could not remember it. However, on Sunday morning, March 8, she awoke "with a decided impression that I should go into the ministers' meeting, and bear the message which the Lord had given me at Salamanca, New York, in our three months' tour" (Ms 19a, 1891, in 3Bio 479). After writing an account of this vision for about two hours, she went to the early-morning ministers' meeting in the Tabernacle, where she described the words and actions of men who wished to drop references to Adventist doctrines in the *Sentinel*.

When she sat down, *A. F. Ballenger arose. "I was in that council meeting . . . last night. . . . I was on the wrong side of the question, and now take my position on the right side" (3Bio 480). *A. T. Robinson, *Dan. Jones, and 30 others in attendance at the secret Saturday-night meeting also testified that Ellen White's description of the meeting was accurate and confessed that they had been wrong.

Stunned, Ellen White exclaimed, "Last night!" She thought that the meeting had taken place months ago, when it was shown to her in vision. She then realized why she had not been permitted to recall the vision prior to March 8: the meeting described therein had not yet taken place. Needless to say, the relating of this vision made a profound impression on the people who were present that morning.

See also: Visions of Ellen G. White.

Further reading: 3Bio 464-482; LS 309-318;

2SG 292, 293; R. W. Olson, "The Salamanca Vision and the 1890 Diary" (EGWE, SDoc); A. L. White, "The Story of the Salamanca Vision" (DF 107-b, CAR); H. E. Douglass, *Messenger of the Lord* (PPPA, 1998), p. 151 note 24; pp. 188, 189.

Brian E. Strayer

SALVATION, ASSURANCE OF, see **ASSURANCE OF SALVATION**.

SALVATION, PLAN OF. This expression is often employed by Ellen White to refer to the overall sweep of the plan that the Godhead conceived of and instituted to meet the intrusion of sin into the universe. The expression is employed hundreds of times throughout her writings in narrative, practical, and theological settings. The most concise expositions of this theme, however, are found in the books *Patriarchs and Prophets*, chapter 4 ("The Plan of Redemption," pp. 63-70), and *The Desire of Ages*, chapter 1 ("'God With Us,'" pp. 19-26).

Closely associated with the "plan of salvation" theme is the "*great controversy" motif (introduced and articulated in *Patriarchs and Prophets*, chapter 1 ("Why Was Sin Permitted?" pp. 33-43), and *The Great Controversy*, chapter 29 ("The Origin of Evil," pp. 492-504). It is within the context of these two major themes that Ellen White portrays the narrative of salvation from sin. Embedded in the exposition of these two key themes lies an articulation of a comprehensive theodicy that she claims will vindicate God's right and fitness to be the moral governor or ruler of His created universe. All of this plays out over against the challenges that Satan has made to God's nature of love.

The plan of redemption demonstrates not only how God can redeem fallen sinners, but also how God can bring a satisfying solution to the problem of evil and the seemingly inexplicable suffering that evil has inflicted on the universe, which was created to reflect and enjoy divine love.

The most condensed development of the salvation/redemption theme, especially with reference to the great controversy motif, is found in *The Desire of Ages*, pages 761-763 (the very heart of her explanation of the meaning and purposes of the death of Christ). It is in the setting of Calvary that Ellen White exhibits a most profound eloquence on the question of God's love: it is at this key moment of the incarnate work of Christ that the redemption of fallen sinners and the vindication of God's governance of the universe is effectively, though provisionally, decided. What follows is a narration of the key stages in the plan of redemption.

The drama centered on the jealousy that arose in the heart of Lucifer and the creation of Planet Earth. Lucifer attempted to usurp the position of Christ as Creator, and his rebellion spilled over into the host of the heavenly angels. After lengthy, failed attempts at reconciliation, Lucifer was cast out of heaven.

Lucifer and his sympathizers were not immediately destroyed. To do so, without a full demonstration of his principles and those of God's governing love, would have caused the intelligent beings of the universe to serve God out of fear. Thus Satan was allowed access to unfallen worlds, including the newly created earth. The only world that succumbed to his deceptions was the newly created Planet Earth.

Ellen White makes much of the fact that while the fall of the human race was a terrible tragedy, it was not an unforeseen emergency. The plan of salvation had been carefully conceived in a "council of peace." It was in this great pre-Fall conference that the Godhead had decided that Christ would become the "point man" of the Trinity to provide a way of redemption for the fallen race.

The initial intimations of this great plan were first given in Genesis 3:15 and the sacrifices that Adam and Eve offered at the very gates of the Garden of Eden. The plan would be further unfolded to the patriarchs and prophets of the Old Testament in types and ceremonial sacrifices. The most notable of these types were portrayed in the Jewish sanctuary services. All of these types were but shadowy anticipations of the coming of Christ to be both the Son of God and the Son of man.

The key elements of the work of Christ were to provide both active and passive obedience to God's commandments. In the active obedience of Christ to the law, Jesus not only provided an example of obedience for the fallen race, but put the lie to Satan's charge that obedience to the law was impossible for human beings. Furthermore, it was through Christ's submissive obedience, manifested in the death on Calvary, that the basis of a just forgiveness was provided for sinful humans. This was all in response to Satan's charges (1) that self-sacrifice was impossible with God, and (2) that He could not forgive sinners and remain a God of justice. But God "sacrificed Himself, in Christ, for man's redemption" and in so doing He clearly demonstrated His self-sacrificing nature and the justice of His forgiving mercy (DA 762). It was in the life and death of Christ that the mercy and justice of divine love was demonstrated. Finally, Christ's active and passive righteousness were vindicated in His resurrection from the dead. Thus full provision for salvation was completed.

Though Satan was effectively cast down in the affections of the unfallen beings, the issue was not yet fully settled. Though full provision for the salvation of the lost world and the vindication of God had been effectively made, there were still three more key issues to be settled.

The first issue had to do with the installation of Christ as the high-priestly advocate or intercessor in the heavenly sanctuary. Ellen White repeatedly affirms that this heavenly work of intercessory atonement is just as necessary to the success of the plan of salvation as Christ's death on the cross. And this great work played out in two phases, corresponding to the daily and yearly rituals of the Old Testament sanctuary. The "antitype" (the heavenly reality) corresponds to the "type" of the daily and the yearly priestly ministry of the earthly sanctuary, with the daily commencing at the Ascension and antitype of the yearly in 1844 with the work of the "final atonement" and the pre-Advent "investigative judgment." In Christ's ministry in the heavenly sanctuary, the life, death, and resurrection of Christ were immortalized and made available to every penitent soul.

It is in the setting of the final atonement of the Most Holy Place that Satan's final two charges against God are refuted. After the death of Christ to vindicate the justice of God's law and His merciful forgiveness of sinners, Satan then went on to claim that Christ's death does away with the just demands of the law and that some specifications of it have been set aside. Here is the issue of the last great conflict.

In the setting of Christ's heavenly ministry, the law of God is fully sustained by showing that mercy does not do away with the justice of God and His law in the forgiveness of penitent believers; furthermore, the disposition of each case will demonstrate that God has been completely consistent in His application of justice and mercy. The trial, or "investigative," phase of the judgment precedes the Second Advent as a demonstration that God does not judge arbitrarily, but on the basis of the objective evidence from each life.

During the investigative phase of the

judgment, God leads every believer through a testing process that reveals to each individual his or her sinful defects of character. The tests, trials, and temptations of life, as well as biblical and prophetic rebukes, bring self-knowledge, which leads to repentance, forgiveness, and transformation, which result in joy. Thus, through an interactive, cooperative process, God develops in each believer a character that He can approve at the close of the judgment process (see 1T 186, 187; 3T 252-272; 4T 83-94).

Following the completion of the pre-Advent judgment, rewards are given at the second advent of Christ (Rev. 22:11, 12). The righteous, living and dead, are given eternal life, and the living wicked are destroyed by the "brightness of his coming" (2 Thess. 2:8). But the Second Coming is not the ultimate climax of the plan of salvation.

The Second Coming ushers in a millennial rule of Christ in heaven, where God fully vindicates the decisions of the pre-Advent judgment in the minds of the redeemed and paves the way for the final "great white throne" judgment at the end of the *millennium. It is at this juncture that the New Jerusalem descends to the earth and the wicked dead are raised in the second *resurrection. In one final, desperate attempt to usurp God's rule, Satan leads the wicked in an attack on the Holy City.

It is then that the ultimate climax, or finale, of the "great controversy" transpires: Satan and his minions are arrested, and before the "great white throne" all of the fallen rebels will finally admit that God has been just in all of His dealings with sin and sinners. A vast panorama of the history of sin and salvation is followed by the destruction of the wicked in the "lake of fire," and the new heaven and earth arise out of the ashes of this last great conflagration.

The "plan of salvation" comes to its fruition with two great purposes having been settled by the outflowing of divine love. First, the "salvation of man" was finally accomplished. Still, there was a "broader and deeper purpose." "It was not merely that the inhabitants of this little world might regard the law of God as it should be regarded," but also to "vindicate the character of God before the universe" (PP 68). Such is the sweeping vision of the plan of salvation in the writings of Ellen G. White. With the comprehensive solution to the sin problem and the salvation of believing sinners, God is fully vindicated. The plan of redemption is finally complete. From "the minutest atom to the greatest world, all things, animate and inanimate, in their unshadowed beauty and perfect joy, declare that God is love" (GC 678).

Further reading: SR; I. T. Blazen, "Salvation," in R. Dederen, ed., *Handbook of Seventh-day Adventist Theology* (RHPA, 2000), pp. 271-313; A. V. Wallenkampf and W. R. Lesher, eds., *The Sanctuary and the Atonement: Biblical, Historical, and Theological Studies* (RHPA, 1981), pp. 639-730; W. W. Whidden, *Ellen White on Salvation* (RHPA, 1995).

Woodrow W. Whidden

SAN FRANCISCO CENTRAL CHURCH. One of the earliest Seventh-day Adventist churches in California. On June 16, 1871, *J. N. Loughborough erected a tent on the south side of Market Street between Fifth and Sixth streets. The next day *M. E. Cornell arrived, and meetings continued until November 21, when the church was organized. Very soon the new congregation faced division over improprieties between M. E. Cornell and a recent convert, Mrs. Sarah E. Harris. Both refused to acknowledge that their interactions were too familiar. On Sunday, January 28, 1872, a trial was scheduled by Loughborough and the church to address this problem. Cornell received a letter from Ellen White on the evening preceding the meeting. She reproved his course of action and included details that Cornell was certain she could have known only through vision. Deeply impressed, he confessed his guilt in the matter, and the trial was canceled. A part of Ellen White's correspondence included: "Be careful how you are enticed to make women your confidants or to allow them to make you their confidant. Keep aloof from the society of women as much as you can. You will be in danger" (Lt 23, 1871, in TSB 167).

The background to this experience is significant. Ellen White had first been shown Cornell's situation at a December 10, 1871, vision in Bordoville, Vermont. She began to write Cornell on December 27, but, pressed by other matters, left the letter unfinished. Early in the morning on January 18, 1872, she was awakened and urgently impressed to finish the testimony. After quickly completing the letter, she sent her son Willie to hand-deliver the letter directly to the postmaster. This made it possible for the letter to arrive just in time to prevent a serious division among the leading ministers in California.

Though Cornell acknowledged responsibility in January 1872, he did not change his ways. When James and Ellen White arrived in California later in the year, the problem was finally dealt with directly. At a December 3, 1872, meeting Ellen White read a long testimony to Elder Cornell, part of which was published in *Testimonies for the Church* (vol. 3, pp. 227-243). "Your conduct, Brother Cornell and Mrs. Harris, has been highly censurable. You have taken liberties with each other which should never be between even natural brothers and sisters. You have sinned against God; but this is not all; you have brought a deep wound upon His precious cause and greatly burdened

the work of God in San Francisco and in Woodland." Ellen White also wrote of God's mercy: "Brother Cornell, God is very pitiful, for He understands our weaknesses and our temptations; and when we come to Him with broken hearts and a contrite spirit, He accepts our repentance, and as we take hold of His strength to make peace with Him He promises we shall have peace with Him" (Lt 29a, 1872).

Cornell repented with tears, but Sarah Harris refused to acknowledge any guilt or responsibility. The minutes of the meeting quote Harris as saying that she "admitted some things in Mrs. White's testimony" but "denied it in the main, and that if she had committed an error it was of the head and not the heart" (San Francisco Church Minutes, Dec. 3, 1872). Her long denial ended with a refusal to make confession. The church endorsed Ellen White's testimony, and on December 15, 1872, Sarah Harris was removed from membership (Church Minutes, Dec. 4, 1872). A group of sympathizers defended Sarah Harris, and for many years the local congregation remained divided over the Cornell/Harris incident. The church minutes reveal a longstanding undercurrent of doubt toward Ellen White's prophetic ministry.

The San Francisco Central church continues today as a viable congregation in an urban setting with a distinctive historic building. The difficulties caused by Cornell's indiscretions are now a matter of history, and the local congregation is faithful to the Seventh-day Adventist message.

Further reading: JNL, *Rise and Progress of the Seventh-day Adventists With Tokens of God's Hand in the Movement and a Brief Sketch of the Advent Cause From 1831 to 1844* (Battle Creek, Mich.: General Conference Association, 1892), pp. 281-286; "San Francisco Church Minutes, 1871-1890" (Archives and Special Collections, LLU); "J. N. Loughborough Diary"

(Advent Source Collection, CAR); H. E. Douglass, *They Were There* (PPPA, 2006), pp. 56-59.

Merlin D. Burt

SAN FRANCISCO EARTHQUAKE. In the early-morning hours of Wednesday, April 18, 1906, the city of San Francisco was devastated by a powerful earthquake that took hundreds of lives and completely destroyed the city. At the time, Ellen White was in southern California visiting the newly established Loma Linda Sanitarium. On her way back home in early May, she traveled through San Jose, then went to Mountain View, where she visited the Pacific Press, which had been greatly damaged in the earthquake. From there she went to San Francisco and saw firsthand the devastation that the city had experienced in the earthquake. She later remarked, "Buildings that were sup-

VIEW OF SAN FRANCISCO AFTER THE EARTHQUAKE OF APRIL 18, 1906

COURTESY OF THE REVIEW AND HERALD PUBLISHING ASSOCIATION

posed to be proof against disaster are lying in ruins. In some instances buildings were partially sunken into the ground. The city presents a most dreadful picture of the inefficiency of human ingenuity to frame fire-proof and earthquake-proof structures" (RH, May 24, 1906).

Remarkably, two days before the earthquake she had a vision in which she saw "houses shaken like a reed in the wind. Buildings, great and small, were falling to the ground.

Pleasure resorts, theaters, hotels, and the homes of the wealthy were shaken and shattered. Many lives were blotted out of existence, and the air was filled with the shrieks of the injured and the terrified. The destroying angels of God were at work. One touch, and buildings so thoroughly constructed that men regarded them as secure against every danger quickly became heaps of rubbish. There was no assurance of safety in any place. I did not feel in any special peril, but the awfulness of the scenes that passed before me I cannot find words to describe. It seemed that the forbearance of God was exhausted, and that the judgment day had come" (*ibid.*).

What impressed her most in that vision was the instruction she received from the angel regarding the wickedness existing in large cities and that God's judgment was impending. "Terrible as was the representation that passed before me, that which impressed itself most vividly upon my mind was the instruction given in connection with it. The angel that stood by my side declared that God's supreme rulership and the sacredness of His law must be revealed to those who persistently refused to render obedience to the King of kings. Those who choose to remain disloyal must be visited in mercy with judgments, in order that, if possible, they may be aroused to a realization of the sinfulness of their course" (9T 93).

Some people have claimed that Ellen White predicted the San Francisco earthquake. Although her description of what she saw in that vision before the earthquake did fit what happened in San Francisco, she did not predict it. In the vision she received at Loma Linda no city was named. She also denied seeing in vision that the next cities to be destroyed with such intensity would be Los Angeles and New York (LS 411). But the scene of destruction she saw in vision and particularly the instruction given by the angel in connection with it prepared her to write forcefully on the subject of natural disasters in the context of God's end-time judgments (RH, May 24, 1906; July 5, 1906).

See also: Daniel Alonzo Parsons.

Further reading: LS 407-415; 6Bio 79-88; 9T 92-96; J. R. Nix, "The Unrecorded Earthquake Vision," AR, June 19, 1986. The Center for Adventist Research at Andrews University has a full-circle panoramic photo of San Francisco taken shortly after the earthquake.

Denis Fortin

SANCTIFICATION. For one to understand Ellen White's doctrine of sanctification it is important to understand the place of sanctification in the life of the Christian. She wrote, "When in conversion the sinner finds peace with God through the blood of the atonement, the Christian life has but just begun. Now he is . . . to grow up 'unto the measure of the stature of the fullness of Christ'" (GC 470). This "growing up" of the new believer is sanctification. It begins after the sinner has become a believer and has received *justification from Christ.

In defining sanctification, White wrote, "The sanctification of the soul by the operation of the Holy Spirit is the implanting of Christ's nature in humanity. It is the grace of our Lord Jesus Christ revealed in character, and the grace of Christ brought into active exercise in good works" (3SM 198). This highlights the general tenor of her teaching on sanctification. It is a work that is carried out by the Holy Spirit on the believer's character. The end result is that the nature of Christ is revealed both internally by means of a Christlike character and externally through good works. "To love God supremely and our neighbor as ourselves is genuine sanctification. Pride will be expelled from the sanctified

heart, and with all lowliness of mind we shall esteem others better than ourselves" (ST, Feb. 24, 1890).

Although the power of God is essential for sanctification, God does not work alone in this process. Another key aspect of sanctification she pointed out is the work required of the individual believer. Sanctification begins because of God's initiative but only continues with the believer's cooperation. "Let no man present the idea that man has little or nothing to do in the great work of overcoming; for God does nothing for man without his cooperation. Neither say that after you have done all you can on your part, Jesus will help you. Christ has said, 'Without me ye can do nothing' (John 15:5). . . . Man's efforts alone are nothing but worthlessness; but cooperation with Christ means a victory" (1SM 381). Though White asserted that the human agent can do nothing alone, yet she also insisted on never diminishing the work that the individual played in his or her own sanctification. So strong was this conviction that she could write, "The expulsion of sin is the act of the soul itself" (DA 466). By itself this truly seems beyond what anyone could hope to achieve. White elucidates, however, what she means in this assertion by immediately stating, "True, we have no power to free ourselves from Satan's control; but when we desire to be set free from sin, and in our great need cry out for a power out of and above ourselves, the powers of the soul are imbued with the divine energy of the Holy Spirit, and they obey the dictates of the will in fulfilling the will of God" (*ibid.*). She further added, "The work of transformation from unholiness to holiness is a continuous one. Day by day God labors for man's sanctification, and man is to cooperate with Him, putting forth persevering efforts in the cultivation of right habits. He is to add grace to grace; and as he thus works on the plan of addition, God works for him on the plan of multiplication" (AA 532).

The preceding statement draws to the fore another key aspect of White's understanding of sanctification. The cooperative effort between God and the believer is a continual work. It is to have no end, until the death of the believer or the second advent of Christ. This idea is expressed by an oft-quoted saying in her writings. "Sanctification is the work of a lifetime" (COL 65). Elsewhere she wrote, "There is no such thing as instantaneous sanctification. True sanctification is a daily work, continuing as long as life shall last" (RH, Jan. 18, 1881).

When asserting that the believer has a cooperative work to do in the process of sanctification, the danger close at hand is that of falling into the practice of seeking righteousness by works and human efforts. In countering the charge which was made by some to this effect, she wrote, "We do not believe that the law sanctifies anyone. We believe that we must keep that law or we will not be saved in the kingdom of heaven.... It is not the law that sanctifies anyone, nor saves us; that law stands and cries out, repent, that your sins may be blotted out" (4MR 343). This distinction is important. *Obedience to the *law does not save anyone, but a person who lives in willful disobedience has not yet received God's salvation.

The emphasis upon a cooperative effort in the sanctification process also explains why White closely linked sanctification with the concept of truth. Quoting from John 17:17, she wrote, "The Redeemer of men prayed to His Father, 'Sanctify them through thy truth: thy word is truth'" (4MR 340), and also that "truth, precious truth, is sanctifying in its influence" (3SM 198). Based upon this connection with biblical truth, she then linked sanctification directly with the law of God.

"This is true Bible sanctification, to love God and to keep His commandments" (4MR 340).

This further illustrates White's concept of a cooperative effort. God gives sanctification to the believer, but He does so only to those who choose to obey His commands. As noted previously, in White's view this did not give room for a righteousness obtained by human efforts. Salvation is only through faith. "The soul is to be sanctified through the truth. And this also is accomplished through faith. For it is only by the grace of Christ, which we receive through faith, that the character can be transformed" (3SM 191).

Ellen White cautioned against some misunderstandings of sanctification. In response to certain elements of *fanaticism she wrote, "Mere noise and shouting are no evidence of sanctification, or of the descent of the Holy Spirit" (2SM 35). She further counseled, "I have often been warned against overstrained ideas of sanctification. They lead to an objectionable feature of experience that will swamp us unless we are wide awake. Extreme views of sanctification which lead men to criticize and condemn their brethren are to be feared and shunned" (10MR 87). In a further word of caution she wrote, "Sanctification does not consist in strong emotional feelings. Here is where many are led into error. They make feelings their criterion. When they feel elated or happy, they claim that they are sanctified. Happy feelings or the absence of joy is no evidence that a person is or is not sanctified" (RH, Jan. 18, 1881).

In the context of Christ's parable of "first the blade, then the ear" (Mark 4:26-29), White wrote, "The germination of the seed represents the beginning of spiritual life, and the development of the plant is a beautiful figure of Christian growth. As in nature, so in grace; there can be no life without growth. The plant must either grow or die. As its growth is silent and imperceptible, but continuous, so is the development of the Christian life. At every stage of development our life may be perfect; yet if God's purpose for us is fulfilled, there will be continual advancement" (COL 65). Here is highlighted an important concept in her thought in regard to sanctification and Christian *perfection. In each stage of the believer's life he or she may be perfect. And yet in White's view this perfection gives no license for complacency. Rather, it is a call to continued growth throughout the believer's Christian experience. Furthermore, this understanding emphasizes the high standard to which sanctification elevates the believer. "Here is the standard which all must reach who enter the heavenly city. The end of our faith is the perfection of human character, the sanctification of the entire being" (RH, Oct. 1, 1901).

Further reading: SL; 3SM 190-204; COL 62-69; 4MR 339-357; ML 248-277; W. R. Lesher, "Ellen White's Concept of Sanctification" (Ph.D. diss., New York University, 1970).

Thomas Toews

SANCTIFIED LIFE, THE (RHPA, 1937, 69 pp.; 1956, 110 pp.). Reprint of a series of 10 articles published by Ellen White in the *Review and Herald* between January 18 and May 3, 1881. Under the general title of "Sanctification" she examined the elements of biblical sanctification and contrasted these with popular theories on the subject. She viewed sanctification as "a grace wrought by the Holy Spirit" (p. 15), "a daily work" (p. 92), and "a progressive work" (p. 94) in the life of a Christian. In her presentation of the subject, she used the examples of the prophet Daniel and the apostle John as illustrations of good moral characters. Of Daniel, she said, "He was a bright example of what men may become when united with the God of wisdom" (p.

18). Concerning John, she wrote that he "desired to become like Jesus, and under the transforming influence of the love of Christ, he became meek and lowly of heart. Self was hid in Jesus. He was closely united to the Living Vine, and thus became a partaker of the divine nature. Such will ever be the result of communion with Christ. This is true sanctification" (pp. 54, 55). These articles were republished in 1889 as a booklet titled *Bible Sanctification*. In 1937 the booklet was reissued in its entirety, with the addition of one paragraph from *Prophets and Kings*, under the current title of *The Sanctified Life*. Also added in 1956 were Scripture and subject indexes.

SANCTUARY, CLEANSING OF, see **INVESTIGATIVE JUDGMENT.**

SANCTUARY, DOCTRINE OF THE. The biblical doctrine of the sanctuary lies at the heart of Adventism and is intimately and inextricably related to the life and teachings of Ellen White. As a teenager Ellen Harmon actively participated in the Advent awakening of the late 1830s and early 1840s. She shared the common Millerite understanding, based upon the historicist year-day principle, that the 2300-day prophecy of Daniel 8:14 ("Unto two thousand and three hundred days; then shall the sanctuary be cleansed") began in 457 B.C. (as indicated by Daniel 9:24-27) and would terminate on the Day of Atonement in the fall of A.D. 1844, when the sanctuary (widely interpreted as the earth) would be cleansed by fire at the *second coming of Christ. Along with other Millerite Adventists, she experienced the *disappointment of October 22, 1844, when Christ did not return to this earth as anticipated. Whereas the great majority of Millerites denounced their former position that the 2300 days/years ended in 1844, a few

Adventists, including *Hiram Edson, F. B. Hahn, and *O.R.L. Crosier, through further reflection and Bible study became convinced that the 1844 fulfillment date was correct but that the sanctuary to be cleansed was the heavenly sanctuary, and not the earth, as they had formerly believed. Arguing from the typology of the Old Testament sanctuary services, they came to the conclusion that Christ had been serving in the holy place of the heavenly sanctuary since His ascension in A.D. 31, but at the end of the 2300-day prophecy on the Day of Atonement in 1844 (October 22 according to the Karaite reckoning), Jesus began His Most Holy Place ministry in the heavenly sanctuary (Crosier, in *Day-Star*, Feb. 7, 1846).

In December of 1844 Ellen Harmon received her first vision, which confirmed that God had given guiding light in the Midnight Cry message regarding the 2300-day prophecy (*Day-Star*, January 1846; cf. EW 13-20), and in February of 1845, she was shown in another vision that at the end of the 2300 days, the Father and Son had moved to the Holy of Holies of the heavenly sanctuary, where Jesus was presently engaged in His high-priestly ministry (*Day-Star*, March 1846; cf. EW 54-56). On April 21, 1847, the newly wedded Ellen White wrote that more than a year before she had been shown in vision that the overall view of Crosier (in his *Day-Star* article on the cleansing of the sanctuary) was correct (WLF 12).

Forty years after the Great Disappointment, in 1884, Ellen White reflected on how "the subject of the sanctuary was the key which unlocked the mystery of the disappointment of 1844" and how "it opened to view a complete system of truth, connected and harmonious, showing that God's hand had directed the great advent movement and revealing present duty as it brought to light the position

and work of His people" (GC 423). Twenty years later, in 1904, White reminisced about the divinely guided process in which the doctrine of the sanctuary was hammered out from Scripture in the period of several years following 1844 by many sessions of intense, prayerful (and often all-night) Bible study among the Adventist pioneers (including her husband, *James White; *Joseph Bates; *Stephen Pierce; *Hiram Edson; and others), during which time her mind was "locked" from understanding the Scriptures unless (when the study group could go no further) she was given light on the passages under study while in vision (1SM 206, 207).

On April 3, 1847, White received a vision in which she visited the heavenly temple and saw the holy place and Most Holy Place; in the latter she was shown the ark of the covenant, which Jesus opened (cf. Rev. 11:19), revealing the Ten Commandments, with the fourth commandment shining brighter than the rest, surrounded by a halo of glory. She saw that this *Sabbath commandment was still in force and would be the great question to unite and test the hearts of God's saints in the last days. Thus the biblical seventh-day Sabbath was inextricably linked with the sanctuary message.

In 1858 White summarized what she was shown in her earlier visions (and largely repeated in the *great controversy vision of March 14, 1858) concerning the sanctuary (1SG 157-162; cf. LS 162; EW 250-253). These rudimentary contours of the sanctuary doctrine were expanded (in 1SP [1870] and 4SP [1884]) and most fully developed as White set forth her mature understanding of this biblical teaching in various later writings, but concentrated in several carefully arranged chapters of her Conflict of the Ages volumes *The Great Controversy* (1888, 1911) and *Patriarchs and Prophets* (1890).

In *The Great Controversy* Ellen White traces the history of the Advent awakening throughout the world as predicted in the *three angels' messages of Revelation 14, focusing in particular upon the experience of Millerite Adventism in the "Seventh-month Movement," culminating in the *Midnight Cry and the disappointment of October 22, 1844 (GC, chaps. 18-22). In a central chapter entitled "What Is the Sanctuary?" (chap. 23), White summarizes the study of the Advent believers after the Great Disappointment regarding the sanctuary of Daniel 8:14, pointing to the Scriptural evidence that the prophetic calculations regarding the timing of the 2300-day prophecy (457 B.C. to A.D. 1844) were solid, but that the sanctuary referred to was not the earth (as they had mistakenly held), nor the earthly sanctuary/Temple of the Israelites (which was destroyed for the last time in A.D. 70 and did not exist in 1844), but rather the heavenly sanctuary. Biblical evidence uncovered by Adventist pioneers for the reality of the heavenly sanctuary is surveyed (see Ex. 25:9, 40; Dan. 7:10; Zech. 6:12, 13; Heb. 8:1-5; 9:23, 24; Rev. 4:5; 11:19), and it is argued that since the earthly sanctuary was constructed as a copy of the heavenly it is appropriate to see the basic contours of the earthly sanctuary and its services as typologically representing the realities of the heavenly sanctuary and Christ's work therein.

At the death of Christ the system of types and shadows connected with the earthly sanctuary ended, and the antitypical dispensation of Christ's ministry in the new covenant heavenly sanctuary began. White provides an overview of the two divisions of ministration in the earthly sanctuary: the daily in the holy place throughout the year, in which confessed sins of the repentant sinner are in figure transferred by means of the blood of the sacrifice (or the eating of the sacrifice by the priest) into the sanctuary; and the yearly service on the Day of Atonement, at the end of the religious year, in which the high priest entered the Most Holy Place (with the blood of the Lord's goat) for the cleansing of the sanctuary, and upon exiting the sanctuary placed the sins upon the scapegoat, who bore these sins into the wilderness, thus rendering the whole camp clean. She then shows how what transpired each year in the Old Testament typical services occurred in reality in the heavenly sanctuary. Upon His ascension Christ formally began His intercessory work in the heavenly holy place, in which the confessed sins of the repentant are by faith placed upon Christ and transferred to the heavenly sanctuary. During the antitypical day of atonement, beginning in 1844, Christ is engaged in the additional work of final atonement, cleansing (i.e., blotting out) the sins there recorded (which involves an investigative judgment to reveal who are entitled to the benefits of the atonement). Ultimately these sins will be placed upon Satan, the author and instigator of all sin, thus cleansing the entire universe from the presence of sin and sinners.

In succeeding chapters of *The Great Controversy* White examines many other biblical passages connected to the end-time cleansing of the sanctuary and the investigative judgment (GC, chaps. 24, 28). Emphasis is placed upon the individual work of penitence and affliction of soul (cleansing the soul temple) on the part of persons living during the time of the antitypical day of atonement; but at the same time White makes clear that the only basis of assurance and acceptance in the judgment is the imputed righteousness of Christ (GC 484, 485; cf. 1SM 344). Later chapters of *The Great Controversy* are also pregnant with sanctuary themes: the origin of evil in the setting of the heavenly sanctuary (chap. 29), the close of probation as Christ ceases His heavenly sanctuary mediatorial work (chap. 39), Satan's banishment during the millennium, fulfilling the scapegoat ritual at the end of the Day of Atonement (chap. 41), and the windup of the great controversy, when Satan and sinners are destroyed and the tabernacle of God is finally "with men" (chap. 42).

The book *Patriarchs and Prophets* broadens the coverage of sanctuary theology, delineating the institution of the sacrificial system in Eden after the Fall (chap. 5), discussing the typology of the Passover (chap. 24) and the other annual festivals (chap. 52), and detailing the typological significance of the sanctuary precincts, furniture, priesthood, and the daily and yearly services (chap. 30, which partially overlaps the treatment in GC, chap. 23). The remainder of Ellen White's vast corpus is suffused with sanctuary references and allusions (too far-reaching to encompass in this article), revealing that the entire sanctuary message centers in Jesus, and also has a practical spiritual application for the church as a whole and for individual believers.

In countering those who from within Adventism challenged the church's understanding of the sanctuary doctrine in the early 1900s (in particular J. H. Kellogg and A. F. Ballenger), White reaffirmed the reality of the sanctuary in heaven and underscored that "the correct understanding of the ministration in the heavenly sanctuary is the foundation of our faith" (Ev 221). White also points to the existence of rich insights yet to be uncovered in the study of the sanctuary: "The significance of the Jewish economy is not yet fully comprehended. Truths vast and profound are shadowed forth in its rites and symbols. . . . Far more than we do, it is our privilege to understand these wonderful themes. We are to comprehend the deep things of God" (COL 133). Thus White teaches that the doctrine

of the sanctuary as understood by Seventh-day Adventists is solidly rooted in Scripture, lies at the foundation of Adventist faith, and affords a fruitful field for further study.

See also: Investigative Judgment; Sabbatarian Bible Conferences.

Further reading: "The Integrity of the Sanctuary Truth" (MR 760, EGWE, SDoc); P. G. Damsteegt, *Foundations of the Seventh-day Adventist Message and Mission* (Grand Rapids: Eerdmans, 1977); P. A. Gordon, *The Sanctuary, 1844, and the Pioneers* (RHPA, 1983; reprint, Silver Spring, Md.: Ministerial Association, General Conference of Seventh-day Adventists, 2000); G. F. Hasel, "Divine Judgment," in R. Dederen, ed., *Handbook of Seventh-day Adventist Theology* (RHPA, 2000), pp. 815-856; F. B. Holbrook, ed., *Doctrine of the Sanctuary: A Historical Survey*, Daniel and Revelation Committee Series (BRI, 1989), vol. 5; R. W. Olson, "The Investigative Judgment in the Writings of E. G. White" (EGWE, SDoc); *idem, One Hundred and One Questions on the Sanctuary and on Ellen White* (EGWE, 1981, SDoc); Á. M. Rodríguez, "The Sanctuary," in R. Dederen, ed., *Handbook of Seventh-day Adventist Theology* (RHPA, 2000), pp. 375-417; A. R. Timm, *The Sanctuary and the Three Angels' Messages: Integrating Factors in the Development of Seventh-day Adventist Doctrines* (Berrien Springs, Mich.: ATS Publications, 1995).

Richard M. Davidson

SANITARIUMS. Adventist health-care institutions that minimized or completely avoided drug therapy. They used some surgery, but relied largely on *hydrotherapy, physical therapy, diet and exercise therapies, and other *natural remedies. Not to be confused with sanitoriums, which were long-term care facilities dedicated to treating chronic diseases such as tuberculosis or mental illness, sanitariums emphasized health education and intentional lifestyle change to help patients regain and maintain health. To augment this distinction was probably one of the reasons *J. H. Kellogg coined the phrase "Medical and Surgical Sanitarium," a phrase that other Adventist sanitariums used as well (e.g., *Claremont Medical and Surgical Sanitarium, Cape Town, South Africa).

The development of Adventist health-care institutions, later called sanitariums, was the direct result of a vision received by Ellen White in Rochester, New York, December 25, 1865 (1T 485), identifying the "water cure establishment" at Dansville, New York, as "the best institution" of its kind "in the United States," except for its faulty "religious principles" (*ibid.* 490). She then set forth the twofold purpose of Adventist health-care institutions, calling Adventists to establish a similar "institution of their own, under their own control," (1) "for the benefit of the diseased and suffering among us." She predicted (2) that "such an institution, rightly conducted, would be the means of bringing our views before many whom it would be impossible for us to reach" in other ways. "By thus being placed under the influence of truth, some will not only obtain relief from bodily infirmities, but will find a healing balm for their sin-sick souls" (*ibid.* 492, 493). In response to this call, Adventists established the *Health Reform Institute in Battle Creek in 1866.

The word "sanitarium" was introduced to Adventists by *J. H. Kellogg in 1877 when he renamed the Health Reform Institute the Battle Creek Medical and Surgical Sanitarium, which became a prototype of similar institutions all over the world. Adventist sanitariums flourished in North America until the Great Depression of 1929-1939. The larger ones, such as Battle Creek (which separated from church control in 1907), became popular "spas" for the wealthy, who paid according to their ability, enabling the sanitarium to treat the poor for small fees or for free. During the Depression the wealthy class in America was largely ruined financially, and fewer people could afford lengthy stays at a sanitarium. After the Depression, the coming of health insurance led to standardized fees for all, accompanied by strict guidelines mandating the shortest possible stays for patients. Extended stays of two or three weeks or longer for natural remedies and lifestyle change were not covered by health insurance, and most Adventist sanitariums in North America became acute-care hospitals.

Further reading: F. D. Nichol, "The Genius and Scope of Our Medical Work—Nos. 1-3," *Ministry,* August-October 1949; SHM.

Jerry Moon

SATAN. A real being, not a mythical figure or a mere symbol of evil. Before his fall into sin, Satan was beautiful and intelligent. Ellen White's views about Satan are built on biblical passages such as Genesis 3; Job 1 and 2; Isaiah 14:12-15; Ezekiel 28:11-19; Matthew 4:1-11; Luke 10:18; Jude 6-9; Revelation 12:7-17; and Revelation 20.

God created not Satan but Lucifer, an anointed cherub, who by rebellion against God became Satan, the adversary (PP 40). From the time of his creation Lucifer was blameless, a perfect being. He had the highest position among all created beings (DA 758), next in honor to Jesus Christ (1SG 17; SR 13). However, he craved to be equal to God Himself. "Little by little Lucifer came to indulge the desire for self-exaltation" (PP 35), and "gradually assumed command which devolved on Christ alone" (SR 13). Ellen White gives a specific time when an evil attitude toward God burst out in the life of

Lucifer. It happened before the actual creation of humans: "When God said to His Son, 'Let us make man in our image,' Satan was jealous of Jesus. He wished to be consulted concerning the formation of man, and because he was not, he was filled with envy, jealousy, and hatred. He desired to receive the highest honors in heaven next to God" (EW 145; cf. 3SG 33, 34).

Why this perfect being became evil and originated rebellion in heaven is a mystery (SC 106; GC 493). There was no reason for this development. If a reason for it could be given, sin would be justified. Lucifer's fall is described in terms of pride, envy, hatred, ambition, jealousy, and selfishness (SR 14; EW 145, 146; DA 762). To achieve his ambitions, he accused God of instituting an unjust government and law (DA 761). "God in His great mercy bore long with Lucifer. . . . Again and again he was offered pardon on condition of repentance and submission. Such efforts as only infinite love and wisdom could devise were made to convince him of his error. . . . But pride forbade him to submit" (GC 495, 496).

As a result of his rebellion, Satan and the angels who associated with him were expelled from heaven. He also incited the sin of Adam and Eve in the Garden of Eden. However, God did not immediately destroy him, because it was necessary that all created beings clearly understand the corrupt nature of sin and the true nature of God's character of love (PP 42, 43). God's treatment of Satan's rebellion will be an eternal "safeguard to all holy beings, to prevent them from being deceived as to the nature of transgression" (PP 43).

Satan performs miraculous signs, heals diseases, and appears as an angel of light in order to mislead. "As the crowning act in the great drama of deception, Satan himself will personate Christ." His last powerful act of seduction will be to claim to have changed the Sabbath to Sunday (GC 624).

Satan's defeat was assured on the cross (DA 758), but he will be annihilated only at the end of the millennium in the last judgment (DA 764; GC 671-674), when the great controversy between good and evil will ultimately be settled.

Further reading: PP 33-43; GC 492-562; SR 13-31; EW 145-147.

Jiří Moskala

"SCATTERING" AND "GATHERING" TIMES. In post-Millerite understanding, the scattering time began soon after the October 22, 1844, disappointment. On October 23 Josiah Litch wrote to William Miller that "the sheep are scattered—and the Lord has not come yet" (J. Litch to W. Miller and J. Himes, Oct. 24, 1844).

The Sabbatarian Adventists would use the scattering metaphor in referring to the period of time between October 1844 and 1848, by which time they had developed their key doctrines and had integrated them into the prophetic package of the three angels' messages of Revelation 14:6-12. Beginning in 1848 the Sabbatarian leaders began to gather in a people who would eventually become the Seventh-day Adventist Church through the publication of periodicals and the holding of conferences to disseminate their message. Thus, by 1849 James White could write: "The scattering time we have had; it is in the past, and now the time for the saints to be gathered into the unity of the faith . . . has come" (JW to Bro. Bowles, Nov. 8, 1849; cf. EW 74-76).

See also: Sabbatarian Bible Conferences.

Further reading: 1Bio 187-196, 211, 220, 237.

George R. Knight

SCHOOLS, CHURCH. As early as 1853, Sabbatarian Adventists began to establish some private schools. The first denomination-ally sponsored school was opened in Battle Creek, Michigan, in 1872. In 2007 there were more than 7,000 Seventh-day Adventist elementary and secondary schools, with close to 1.5 million students worldwide. The inception and growth of this unique system of education is the result of, to a great extent, the counsels of Ellen White.

For Ellen White the purpose of church schools is to offer "true education," the "harmonious development of the physical, the mental, and the spiritual powers," preparing students for "the joy of service in this world and for the higher joy of wider service in the world to come" (Ed 13; cf. FE 328). This includes preparing workers to share the good news of salvation (cf. CT 493) and to aid parents in the difficult task of training their children (Ed 46).

Among the most distinctive features that Ellen White calls for in Adventist church schools are the following: First, they are to be centered on the Bible as an integral part of the school life (6T 109), not only as a subject of study but also as a source of counsel and inspiration. Second, church schools are to be an agent of salvation. They are to provide an environment conducive to the spiritual conversion of pupils (CG 310). Third, they aim for high academic standards. Teachers are not only to be consecrated but also to possess a "thorough knowledge of the sciences" (CT 199). Fourth, church school curricula should include practical components that allow students to develop skills in useful trades (Ed 218). Historically, school programs have included agriculture, construction, food preparation, etc. Currently the same principle supports the teaching of computer technology. Fifth, wherever possible, schools are to be in rural areas, although the needs of children in urban environments are not to be neglected

(CG 306). The ideal location is a natural environment with plenty of land and access to nature (FE 312, 314). Sixth, church schools are to be ubiquitous—available wherever there are Seventh-day Adventists. There should be a school to serve the needs of every church (CT 168), and it is better to have schools established in many localities than large schools in only a few places (6T 199). Seventh, schools should be operated on sound financial principles and frequently audited. If a school cannot be operated without debt, she advises closing it until resources are available (*ibid.* 217).

The proper age for school entrance was a debated idea among Adventists. In 1872 Ellen White had written that "parents should be the only teachers of their children until they have reached eight or ten years of age" (3T 137). The same statement reappeared in *Education* in 1903. Many Adventists took this statement as an unvarying rule for the age of entrance into Seventh-day Adventist schools. When Ellen White was asked about this, however, she explained that when this counsel was given (1872), there were no Adventist schools yet and her counsel had specific reference to the "common" [public] schools (Ms 7, 1904, in 3SM 216, 217). Children younger than 8 or 10 were not prepared to discern and resist the temptations they would meet in the public schools. As the Adventist school system became more extensive, she advised students of all ages to attend Adventist schools wherever they were available (MM 57, 58). In connection with the establishment of a kindergarten program near the St. Helena Sanitarium, she stated that no one would oppose the idea of mothers keeping their younger children at home if they were competent to provide adequate discipline and education for these children. But she would rather have young children in a school than to leave them without adequate supervision and education. She advised using "common sense" (3SM 217) in this regard and not to make her comments on entrance age an unbending rule and thus miss the underlying principle.

Further reading: 3SM 214-226; 5Bio 312-317.

Julian Melgosa

SCIENCE AND THEOLOGY, RELATIONSHIP BETWEEN. Ellen White proposes that the progressive recognition of the true harmony between science and theology involves: (1) a Christ-centered, biblical focus, (2) a correct understanding, (3) mutual interaction between science and theology, (4) the use of faith and reason, and (5) spiritual conversion.

First, there is a Christ-centered connection between science and theology, because God "is revealed in His word, in Christ, [and] in nature" (5T 174). On the one hand, the Bible "unfolds a . . . complete system of theology" (CE 106), "Christ is the complete system of truth" (3SM 198), and the Bible "is the mine of the unsearchable riches of Christ" (COL 107). Therefore, "theology is valueless unless it is saturated with the love of Christ" (LHU 134). On the other hand, Christ "calls on nature to reflect [to] human minds the light that floods the threshold of heaven. . . . And nature does the bidding of the Creator" (SpM 186). "The veil that sin has cast over the face of nature, He came to draw aside, bringing to view the spiritual glory that all things were created to reflect. His words placed the teachings of nature as well as of the Bible in a new aspect, and made them a new revelation" (COL 18, 19). The disciples of Jesus learned from "the central source of all the world's light . . . that which worldly-wise men, with all their boasted science [and] theology . . . did not comprehend" (RH, Apr. 23, 1895). "We

cannot afford to separate ourselves from Jesus. . . . The world is flooded with error; it meets us on every hand. It . . . lurks in theology . . . [and] in science" (ST, Mar. 6, 1884).

Second, "rightly understood . . . the revelations of science . . . are in harmony with the testimony of Scripture" (Ed 130). "The book of nature and the Written Word do not disagree; each sheds light on the other. Rightly understood, they make us acquainted with God and His character by teaching us something of the wise and beneficent laws through which He works. We are thus led to adore His holy name, and to have an intelligent trust in His Word" (ST, Mar. 20, 1884). "When the Bible makes statements of facts in nature, science may be compared with the Written Word, and a correct understanding of both will always prove them to be in harmony. One does not contradict the other" (ST, Mar. 13, 1884). "By different methods, and in different languages, they witness to the same great truths. Science is ever discovering new wonders; but she brings from her research nothing that, rightly understood, conflicts with divine revelation [in Scripture]" (Ed 128). Nevertheless, not just any harmony will do. "Inferences erroneously drawn from facts observed in nature have, however, led to supposed conflict between science and revelation; and in the effort to restore harmony, interpretations of Scripture have been adopted that undermine and destroy the force of the Word of God" (*ibid.*). "In order to account for His works [in nature], must we do violence to His Word?" (*ibid.* 129). White's answer is a resounding "No!"

Third, the study of theology should encourage the study of science. "Above all other people on earth, the man whose mind is enlightened by the Word of God [in Christ— see CT 509, 510] will feel that he must give himself to greater diligence in the perusal of the Bible and to a diligent study of the sciences" (CT 510). It is "necessary that the study of the Bible should have a prominent place among the various branches of scientific education" (FE 285). "The deepest students of science are constrained to recognize in nature the working of infinite power. But to man's unaided reason, nature's teaching cannot but be contradictory and disappointing. Only in the light of revelation [in Scripture] can it be read aright" (Ed 134). "The greatest minds, if not guided by the Word of God in their research, become bewildered in their attempts to trace the relations of science and revelation" (PP 113). "By those who make the Scriptures their constant study, true natural science is far better understood than it is by many so-called learned men" (3MR 434).

Similarly, the study of science should encourage the study of theology. "Science . . . flashes light upon many hidden things in God's Word" (ibid.). Scripture is not to be regarded as a textbook for all facts about nature or God, because study of nature itself is indispensable and leads to a knowledge of God (MH 462). "In the study of the sciences . . . we are to obtain a knowledge of the Creator. . . . Science brings from her research only fresh evidences of the wisdom and power of God" (PP 599). "As we observe the things of the natural world, we shall be enabled, under the guiding of the Holy Spirit, more fully to understand the lessons of God's Word" (Ed 120). "Scientific research will open vast fields of [theological] thought and information." Contemplation of "the things of nature" provides "a new perception of truth" (MH 462). In contrast, as the next two paragraphs will show, false science and theology irrationally misinterpret the light of God in Scripture and in nature (MM 97).

Fourth, the study of science involves the use of reason and faith. God wants individuals

to use their brains in scientific investigations. He does not desire them to be less acute, less inquiring, less intelligent. However, it is a sin of the mind to extol and deify reason to the neglect of Scripture. To exalt reason unduly is to debase it; to place the human in rivalry with the divine is to make it contemptible. Scientific reason alone can never explain creation. Reason is limited and in need of faith because God is supreme (1MCP 3-9; 2MCP 742-744; GC 522, 600, 601; MH 427). But when false science manifests a "show of plausibility" by placing satanic "ideas of science and nature" (ST, Mar. 27, 1884) above the Word of God, it becomes idolatry, or what White terms "false science" (Ev 600). This is a disguised infidelity that does not recognize the rational limits of science and misinterprets the facts of nature which actually provide reasons for faith in Scripture. The attempt to explain nature by natural law alone leads false science to deify nature by attributing infinite power to nature. Such science does not distinguish as it should philosophy, theory, speculation, and fact (3SG 90-96; ST, Mar. 20, 1879; Mar. 13, 20, 27, 1884; 2BC 1011).

Similarly, the study of theology involves the use of reason and faith. False theology irrationally ignores the "connected chain of truth" in the Bible and manifests "a disjointed medley of ideas" supported by isolated passages of Scripture "woven together in a tissue of falsehood" (ST, Mar. 27, 1884). The ignorance and folly of these "disconnected theories [are] arrayed in new and fantastic dress—theories that it will be all the more difficult to meet because there is no reason in them" (ibid.). Reason is one of the "great masterly talents" that "will be taken to heaven" (3MR 353). God desires that we be "intellectual Christians" (RH, Mar. 8, 1887). He does not promise to remove every doubt, but He gives sufficient evidence as a reason for faith in Christ. The

Bible strengthens the intellect (RH, Jan. 24, 1899; 5T 703, 704; 1MCP 91). "There are many who believe without a reason on which to base their faith, without sufficient evidence. . . . They do not reason from cause to effect. Their faith has no genuine foundation, and in the time of trial they will find that they have built upon the sand" (2MCP 535, 536; cf. 4SP 349). "Many . . . will be found wanting. They have neglected the weightier matters. Their conversion is superficial, not deep, earnest, and thorough. They do not know why they believe the truth. . . . They can give no intelligent reason why they believe" (ChS 45, 46).

Fifth, spiritual conversion is necessary in order to perceive the harmony between science and theology. "Through the creation we are to become acquainted with the Creator. The book of nature is a great lesson book, which in connection with the Scriptures we are to use in teaching others of His character, and guiding lost sheep back to the fold of God. As the works of God are studied, the Holy Spirit flashes conviction into the mind. It is not the conviction that logical reasoning produces; but unless the mind has become too dark to know God, the eye too dim to see Him, the ear too dull to hear His voice, a deeper meaning is grasped, and the sublime, spiritual truths of the Written Word are impressed on the heart" (COL 24). "In itself the beauty of nature leads the soul away from sin and worldly attractions, and toward purity, peace, and God. Too often the minds of students are occupied with men's theories and speculations, falsely called science. . . . They need to be brought into close contact with nature. Let them learn that creation and Christianity have one God. Let them be taught to see the harmony of the natural with the spiritual" (*ibid.* 24, 25).

Further reading: Ed 128-134; ST, Mar. 13, 20, 27, 1884; COL 17-27; "Ellen G. White Statements Relating to Geology and Earth Sciences" (EGWE, 1982, SDoc).

Martin F. Hanna

SEAL OF GOD. A sign of God's ownership and approval of His people brought to view especially in Revelation 7:1-4 (cf. Eze. 9:1-6). This passage portrays a seal being placed on the foreheads of faithful believers before probation closes and the seven last plagues are poured out on the unfaithful. To the question of Revelation 6:17, "Who shall . . . stand?" in the "day of [God's] wrath," Revelation 7:1-4 answers: the 144,000 who are "sealed . . . in their foreheads." Thus the seal signifies a fitness or preparation to "stand" during that trying time.

The linkage between the sealing and the *144,000 was made in Ellen White's first vision in which she saw the 144,000, "sealed and perfectly united. On their foreheads was written, God, New Jerusalem, and a glorious star containing Jesus' new name" (EW 15). She later described the seal of God as an invisible mark that can, however, be seen by the destroying angel (GH, June 11, 1902). "It is not any seal or mark that can be seen, but a settling into the truth, both intellectually and spiritually, so they cannot be moved" (Ms 173, 1902, in 1MR 249, 250). Thus the forehead symbolizes the seat of character and the seal represents God's approval of that character.

The divine approval of human character involves two dimensions that absorb Ellen White's attention in most of her references to the seal of God. The more general dimension is the internal transformation to reflect the Father's character: "Not one of us will ever receive the seal of God while our characters have one spot or stain upon them" she wrote. "It is left with us to remedy the defects in our characters, to cleanse the soul temple of every defilement. Then the latter rain will fall upon us" (5T 214). "It is now that we must wash our robes of character and make them white in the blood of the Lamb" (*ibid.* 215, 216). Continuing, she warns, "Those who are uniting with the world are receiving the worldly mold and preparing for the mark of the beast. Those who are distrustful of self, who are humbling themselves before God and purifying their souls by obeying the truth—these are receiving the heavenly mold and preparing for the seal of God in their foreheads. . . . Their character will remain pure and spotless for eternity" (*ibid.* 216).

The more specific dimension of the seal is the seventh-day Sabbath as a test of loyalty to God and a sign of character transformation (Ex. 31:13-17; Eze. 20:12, 20). "The fourth commandment [Ex. 20:8-11] is the only one of all the ten in which are found both the name and the title of the Lawgiver. It is the only one that shows by whose authority the law is given. Thus it contains the seal of God" (PP 307). She predicted that in the end-time "the Sabbath will be the great test of loyalty. . . . While one class, by accepting the sign of submission to earthly powers, receive the mark of the beast, the other, choosing the token of allegiance to divine authority, receive the seal of God" (GC 605; RH, Apr. 27, 1911).

The experiential issue that links both Sabbathkeeping and character development is faith and supreme love for God, bearing fruit in obedience. "Love is expressed in obedience. . . . Those who love God have the seal of God in their foreheads, and work the works of God" (SD 51; cf. John 14:15; 1 John 5:3). On the contrary, "many will not receive the seal of God because they do not keep His commandments or bear the fruits of righteousness" (Lt 76, 1900, in 7BC 970).

Further reading: Chang-Soo Kim, "A Study of the Teaching of Ellen G. White About the Seal of God" (unpublished paper, 1981, CAR); Trofino L. Atiga, "A Study of Some Aspects of the Seal of God" (unpublished paper, 1963, CAR); *SDA Encyclopedia* (1996), vol. 11, pp. 563, 564.

A. Leroy Moore

SECOND COMING OF CHRIST. The blessed hope (Titus 2:13; 6T 406) of the premillennial return of Christ is a pervasive theme throughout the writings of Ellen G. White. Christ comes at the darkest hour of human history (COL 414), and like a thief in the night (DA 635). His coming has been delayed (8T 115, 116), but can be hastened (2 Peter 3:12; MB 109). Even though the exact time is not yet known (DA 633), we can know when it is near (*ibid.* 235), and it will not tarry beyond the preaching of the gospel to the whole world (Matt. 24:14; Ev 697). Only after this work is completed and probation closes will Christ announce the day and the hour of His return to His waiting people on earth (EW 15). In the meantime Ellen White consistently says it is very near (*ibid.* 58; 2T 355; 9T 62).

Just before the Second Advent, mountains sink, islands disappear, great hailstones pound the planet, and a mighty earthquake shakes the world to its foundations (Rev. 16:18-21). Prison walls are rent asunder, releasing saints, and all who died with faith "in the third angel's message" come forth in a special resurrection. A hand holds the Ten Commandments in the sky (GC 636-639). Those who crucified Christ also come forth to see Him in glory (Rev. 1:7; LDE 275).

Christ's coming is literal and personal (AA 33) and not merely spiritual (2SG 72-74). He comes with angels and great glory (DA 632), even the glory of His Father (PP 339) that outshines the noonday sun (GC 641). The wicked flee from His presence while saints rejoice (COL 421). Angels gather the saints from all over the world and reunite family and friends (GC 645), who rise to meet Christ in the air (*ibid.* 302). Satan cannot counterfeit this manner of Christ's coming (*ibid.* 625). While physical changes take place at the Second Coming (2T 355), individuals' characters are not changed (GC 322, 323). Entrance to heaven is on the basis of fitness to live there, which comes from believing on and following Christ (COL 405-421), one evidence of which is help given to the poor and needy (Matt. 25:31-46; DA 637-641).

Further reading: N. R. Gulley, *Christ Is Coming: A Christ-centered Approach to Last-Day Events* (RHPA, 1998); R. P. Lehmann, "The Second Coming of Jesus," in R. Dederen, ed., *Handbook of Seventh-day Adventist Theology* (RHPA, 2000), pp. 893-926.

Norman R. Gulley

Second Coming of Christ, Delay of. Ellen White was consistent in her analysis of what would hasten and what continues to delay the second coming of Christ. The delay of the Second Advent involves the interdependent issues of character development and carrying the gospel to the world. On the one hand, the reproducing of Christ's character in His followers is the essential preparation for being maximally used by the Holy Spirit to share the gospel. One cannot give what one does not have. On the other hand, it is also clear that before Christ can return, the gospel and Revelation's three angels' messages must be proclaimed to all the world by a people totally consecrated to God.

Ellen White linked Matthew 24:14 (the final preaching of the gospel) with the emphasis that the coming of the Lord "will not tarry past the time that the message is borne to all nations," because "God's forbearance to the wicked is a part of the vast and merciful plan by which He is seeking to compass the salvation of souls" (RH, June 18, 1901). The limit of God's forbearance is reached only when "the final test has been brought upon the world, and all who have proved themselves loyal to the divine precepts have received 'the seal of the living God.'" Then "the restraint which has been upon the wicked is removed, and Satan has entire control of the finally impenitent" (GC 613, 614). Until then, angels are appointed to restrain the forces of human strife until God's people are *sealed for the crisis (see Rev. 7:1-3). Embedded in God's justice is His concern for fair play: He "will not send upon the world His judgments for disobedience and transgression until He has sent His watchmen to give the warning. He will not close up the period of probation until the message shall be more distinctly proclaimed" (6T 19).

This message that must be "more distinctly proclaimed"—the church's "appointed work"—became one of Ellen White's major emphases: "By giving the gospel to the world it is in our power to hasten our Lord's return. We are not only to look for but to hasten the coming of the day of God. . . . Had the church of Christ done her appointed work as the Lord ordained, the whole world would before this have been warned, and the Lord Jesus would have come to our earth in power and great glory" (DA 633, 634).

Many times Ellen White emphasized the connection between the character of God's professed people, their appointed work, and a delayed advent. In the 1850s she wrote: "I saw that this message would not accomplish its work in a few short months. It is designed to arouse the people of God, to discover to them their backslidings, and to lead to zealous repentance, that they may be favored with the presence of Jesus, and be fitted for the loud cry of the third angel. . . . If the message had been of as short duration as many of us supposed, there would have been no time for them to develop character. Many moved from feeling, not from principle and faith, and this solemn, fearful message stirred them. . . . Those who come up to every point, and stand every test, and overcome, be the price what it may, have heeded the counsel of the True Witness, and they will receive the latter rain, and thus be fitted for translation" (1T 186, 187).

With a similar emphasis she wrote in 1883, "It was not the will of God that the coming of Christ should be so long delayed and His people should remain so many years in this world of sin and sorrow. But unbelief separated them from God. As they refused to do the work which He had appointed them, others were raised up to proclaim the message. In mercy to the world, Jesus delays His coming, that sinners may have an opportunity to hear the warning and find in Him a shelter before the wrath of God shall be poured out" (GC 458). "It is the unbelief, the worldliness, unconsecration, and strife among the Lord's professed people that have kept us in this world of sin and sorrow so many years" (1SM 69).

One of her clearest statements was written in 1888 in her discussion of the events following the disappointment of 1844: "But the people were not yet ready to meet their Lord. There was still a work of preparation to be accomplished for them. Light was to be given, directing their minds to the temple of God in heaven; and as they should by faith follow their High Priest in His ministration there, new duties would be revealed. . . . Through the grace of God and their own diligent effort they must be conquerors in the battle with evil. While the *investigative judgment is going forward in heaven, while the sins of penitent believers are being removed from the sanctuary, there is to be a special work of

purification, of putting away of sin, among God's people upon earth. This work is more clearly presented" in the *three angels' messages of Revelation 14 (GC 424, 425).

A few years later in 1901 she admonished church members not to blame God or seek other excuses for the delay: "We may have to remain here in this world because of insubordination many more years . . . but for Christ's sake, His people should not add sin to sin by charging God with the consequence of their own wrong course of action" (Ev 696). Thus the "unbelief," "unconsecration," and "insubordination" of God's people are directly linked with their failure to "proclaim the message."

Ellen White devoted a chapter in *Christ's Object Lessons* to unfolding the parallels between the timing of the Advent and the character of God's end-time followers: "So the divine Husbandman looks for a harvest as the reward of His labor and sacrifice. Christ is seeking to reproduce Himself in the hearts of men; and He does this through those who believe in Him. The object of the Christian life is fruit bearing—the reproduction of Christ's character in the believer, that it may be reproduced in others. . . . As you receive the Spirit of Christ—the Spirit of unselfish love and labor for others—you will grow and bring forth fruit. . . . Your faith will increase, your convictions deepen, your love made perfect. More and more you will reflect the likeness of Christ in all that is pure, noble, and lovely" (COL 67, 68). "Christ is waiting with longing desire for the manifestation of Himself in His church. When the character of Christ shall be perfectly reproduced in His people, then He will come to claim them as His own" (*ibid.* 69). This "perfectly reproduced" character refers to motives of love (*ibid.* 68, 69), not to flawless behavior (cf. PK 589). "It is the privilege of every Christian not only to look for but to hasten the coming of our Lord Jesus Christ. . . . Were all who profess His name bearing fruit to His glory, how quickly the whole world would be sown with the seed of the gospel. Quickly the last great harvest would be ripened, and Christ would come to gather the precious grain" (COL 69).

Further reading: R. E. Neall, *How Long, O Lord?* (RHPA, 1988); R. E. Neall, "The Nearness and the Delay of the *Parousia* in the Writings of Ellen G. White" (Ph.D. diss., AU, 1982).

Herbert E. Douglass

SECRET SOCIETIES. Early in her ministry in Australia Ellen White wrote a 50-page letter to a prominent worker in the publishing house, *Nathaniel D. Faulkhead, who was a member of five Free Mason lodges (4Bio 49-56). "Those who stand under the blood-stained banner of Prince Immanuel cannot be united with the Free Masons or with any secret organization," she wrote to Faulkhead. "The seal of the living God will not be placed upon anyone who maintains such a connection after the light of truth has shone upon his pathway" (Lt 21, 1893, in 2SM 140). Her straightforward counsels to Faulkhead (Lt 21, 1893; Lt 21a, 1893, in 14MR 9-16; Lt 113, 1893, in 20MR 282-290) led him to sever his relationship with such organizations.

It is in this context that in 1893 she wrote a pamphlet titled "Should Christians Be Members of Secret Societies?" (2SM 120-139). This pamphlet highlights several reasons Christians should not be members of secret societies. The first reason she gives is based upon Paul's injunction in 2 Corinthians 6:14, "Be ye not unequally yoked together with unbelievers." To Ellen White this counsel "refers not only to the marriage of Christians with the ungodly, but to all alliances in which the parties are brought into intimate association, and in which there is need of harmony in spirit and action" (2SM 121). "There are those who question whether it is right for Christians to belong to the Free Masons and other secret societies. . . . If we are Christians at all, we must be Christians everywhere, and must consider and heed the counsel given to make us Christians according to the standard of God's Word" (*ibid.* 122).

A second reason highlights the need for Christians to constantly do the will of God and to be faithful to their covenantal relationship with Him. "While there may be in these societies much that appears to be good, there is, mingled with this, very much that makes the good of no effect, and renders these associations detrimental to the interests of the soul" (*ibid.* 124). A third reason reminds Christians that within secret societies, actions and motives are often contrary to God's law, and such memberships create divided loyalties and injure spiritual lives. "Christ will never lead His followers to take upon themselves vows that will unite them with men who have no connection with God, who are not under the controlling influence of His Holy Spirit. The only correct standard of character is the holy law of God, and it is impossible for those who make that law the rule of life to unite in confidence and cordial brotherhood with those who turn the truth of God into a lie, and regard the authority of God as a thing of nought" (*ibid.* 127).

Fourth, Ellen White insisted that investing time, energy, and money in secret societies is contrary to the stewardship principles of Scripture. "Many are laying up their treasure in these secret societies, and can we not see that their heart is there? However powerful may be the evidences of truth, little by little it loses its brightness, loses its force, heaven fades from the mind, the eternal weight of glory, the gift of God for a life of obedience, appears a matter unworthy of notice in comparison with the supposed benefits to be realized in laying up earthly treasure" (*ibid.* 135).

Further reading: "Secret Societies—Mr. Faulkhead and the Secret Signs" (EGWE, SDoc); D. K. Stevens, "Ellen G. White Deals With Free Masonry" (research paper, 1972, Q/A 13-A, CAR); J. R. Rice, *Lodges Examined by the Bible* (Wheaton, Ill.: Sword of the Lord Publishers, 1943).

Denis Fortin

SECRET VICE, see **MASTURBATION**.

SELECTED MESSAGES, books 1, 2, 3 (1958, 1958, 1980). Compilations issued to meet developing needs and interests in the life of the church. The contents were drawn from out-of-print pamphlets and periodical articles, as well as from previously unpublished manuscripts and letters. Book 1 contains major sections on prophetic inspiration of the biblical writers as well as of Ellen White, the law and the gospel, the nature and work of Christ, and justification by faith, among others. Book 2 contains sections on meeting fanaticism and erroneous teaching, membership in secret societies and labor unions, remuneration of church employees, the use of medicinal drugs, last-day events, and a variety of counsels on other issues. An appendix reprints six pamphlet articles that originally appeared in *Health: or How to Live* (1865). Book 3, prepared 22 years later, presents further material on some of the same issues: inspiration, the preparation of Ellen White's books, the incarnation of Christ, salvation, education, Christian behavior, health, last-day events, and other miscellaneous issues. The manuscripts for the three volumes were compiled by Ellen G. White Estate staff under the authorization of the board of trustees.

Further reading: 1SM 9-12; 2SM 9, 10; 3SM 9-11.

Norma Collins

SELECTIONS FROM THE TESTIMONIES, see **TESTIMONY TREASURES**.

SELF, CONCEPT OF. The word "self" is prominent in Ellen G. White's writings. It occurs thousands of times, predominantly in hyphenated words such as self-love, self-denial, self-exaltation, self-sacrifice, etc., but also as a single word. The concept is used in positive and negative connotations and, in Ellen White's understanding, highlights basic issues of the *great controversy and the plan of *salvation.

As a single word, "self" is used negatively to refer to the unsanctified, sinful self, which is "the enemy we most need to fear" (MH 485). On Isaiah 57:20, 21 Ellen White comments, "Sin has destroyed our peace. While self is unsubdued, we can find no rest" (DA 336). Although love for the Lord should be supreme, "self interposes its desire to be first" (6T 103). The basic problem is that human beings are "naturally inclined . . . to live for self" (5T 382). To live for self leads to death, while to live for others leads to life. The first is the spirit of Satan; the latter is the spirit of Christ (COL 259).

Ellen White uses many composites of the word "self" to express the negative characteristics and consequences of the natural inclination to live for self, such as self-abuse, self-aggrandizement, self-conceit, self-deception, self-exaltation, self-glorification, self-gratification, self-importance, self-indulgence, self-justification, self-love, self-righteousness, self-seeking, self-will, and self-worship, among many others. All these are manifestations of making self rather than the Creator the center of one's existence. "Satan's aim has been to lead men to self first"; and the result is that "nations, families, and individuals are filled with a desire to make self a center" (RH, June 25, 1908).

Egotism and selfishness are seen as the essence of depravity, which has filled the world with oppression, misery, and strife; for "egotism always works against Christ" (LHU 229).

The origin of sin is attributed by Ellen White to the desire for self-exaltation on the part of Lucifer. "God entrusted him with power and wisdom; but he became filled with self-exaltation and thought that he should be first in heaven. Through this self-seeking, this striving for supremacy, sin entered into the world" (RH, Sept. 7, 1897). In order to justify his rebellion against God and to draw others into sympathy with himself, Lucifer, who became Satan the adversary, "misrepresented God, attributing to Him the desire for self-exaltation" (DA 21). He accused God of requiring self-denial of His creatures, while God Himself knew nothing of what self-denial meant. This accusation against God is at the heart of the great controversy.

Composites of the word "self" with a spiritually positive connotation, such as self-abnegation, self-denial, self-forgetfulness, self-renunciation, self-sacrifice, self-surrender, and others, are perhaps used by Ellen White even more often than those with a spiritually negative meaning. Especially does she use the former in reference to Jesus Christ. While through self-exaltation "our first parents lost the dominion over this fair earth," it is "through self-abnegation that Christ redeems what was lost" (MB 17). "Christ, in His life and His death, has forever settled the deep and comprehensive question whether there is self-denial with God" (RH, Oct. 21, 1902).

Christ demonstrated that self-denial is a basic law of God's universe. This law applies to all beings created in the image of God,

whether angels or human beings. Ellen White often quotes Christ's words, "If any man will come after me, let him deny himself, and take up his cross, and follow me" (Matt. 16:24), or parallel statements. This self-denial is essential to a true Christian life. "All who desire to share His glory hereafter must share His self-denial and self-sacrifice at every step heavenward" (BE, July 20, 1896). This can be realized only in a lifelong struggle against the sinful self. "Our great conflict is with unconsecrated self" (CS 21). But victory is possible. Through Christ's grace we "can gain the victory over self and selfishness" (7T 49).

The word "self" is also used by Ellen White in a positive sense to refer to a person's God-given individuality. She wrote to a denominational leader, "We need to be self-reliant; it is the duty of all to respect self" (1888 Materials 1626). God bought us with the price of His blood, and in view of that fact, "we need not exalt self, neither need we take special words to God, to depreciate self. We are the Lord's property" (15MR 4).

In other words, Christ takes away both sinful self-superiority and self-inferiority. This positive concept of self Ellen White gives expression in composites of self, such as self-appreciation, self-command, self-control, self-culture, self-development, self-discipline, self-education, self-reliance, self-respect, and others. The following statements illustrate her understanding of the self. "Our first duty toward God and our fellow beings is that of self-development" (CH 107; cf. COL 329). "The object of discipline is the training of the child for self-government. He should be taught self-reliance and self-control" (Ed 287). "You should cultivate self-respect by living so that you will be approved by your own conscience and before men and angels" (1MCP 260).

The self, redeemed by the blood of Christ

and transformed by the Holy Spirit, is to be freely given in service to God and humanity. "Those who for Christ's sake sacrifice their life in this world will keep it unto life eternal" (DA 623, 624). "Self-renunciation is the great law of self-preservation, and self-preservation is the law of self-destruction" (ST, July 1, 1897).

Peter M. van Bemmelen

SELF, OVERCOMING. The "grand work of overcoming and conquering self," as Ellen White describes it (3BC 1164), involves "death" to the "works of the flesh" (i.e., the sinful "self"), in order that the "fruit of the Spirit" may be revealed in the life (Gal. 5:19-23). "The greatest conquest" for every Christian is "to bring self into obedience to the law of God" (RH, Aug. 18, 1885), but "the Lord will help every one of us where we need help the most" (3BC 1164).

The two key elements in the process of overcoming self are spoken of under many terms, such as detachment from sin and attachment to Christ (5T 231), emptying of self and filling with the Holy Spirit (GW 287), dying to self and rising to life in Christ (3T 543), exchanging the old life for new life in Christ (GC 468; SC 70; Ev 598, 599), or self-will for God's will (5T 513, 514). White saw this process as essential to "genuine sanctification, which is nothing less than a daily dying to self, and daily conformity to the will of God" (ST, Sept. 12, 1878).

The theme is pervasive in Scripture; Ellen White supports it with more than 30 biblical texts, including Psalms 34:18; 51:17; Matthew 16:24; Luke 14:27-33; John 3:7; 5:30; 12:24; 15:4, 5; Romans 5:1-6; 6:3, 4, 11-13; 12:1, 2; 1 Corinthians 15:31; 2 Corinthians 4:10; 5:17; Galatians 2:20; 5:24; 6:14; Philippians 1:21; Col. 1:29; 3:1-5; 1 Peter 5:6; and Revelation 3:21.

White's first written mention of "dying to self" came in 1850. By then, Adventists had become settled on the perpetuity of God's law, the seventh-day Sabbath, and several other core beliefs. But this doctrinal clarity involved a danger few of them recognized—that adherence to doctrinal truth could become a substitute for deep heart affection for Christ. In this context Ellen White received a vision, during which her "accompanying angel said, 'Time is almost finished. Do you reflect the lovely image of Jesus as you should?' . . . Said the angel, 'Get ready, get ready, get ready. Ye will have to die a greater death to the world than ye have ever yet died'" (EW 64). Reporting the vision, White commented, "Heaven will be cheap enough, if we obtain it through suffering. We must deny self all along the way, die to self daily, let Jesus alone appear, and keep His glory continually in view" (*ibid.* 67).

Denying self and dying to self appear to be two different processes that go on simultaneously. Dying to self necessarily includes denying self. Because we die to self, we are willing to deny self. Because self is denied, self is gradually, over time, emasculated, so that we are less vulnerable to temptation. However, the potential to fall under temptation remains, and is controlled only through the victory-rendering power of God (AA 560, 561).

The emphasis on dying to self appears designed to counteract certain temptations that accompanied the doctrinal certainty of the young movement. During the 1860s and 1870s some Adventist evangelists (e.g., *Moses Hull and *D. M. Canright) became formidable debaters because of the biblical clarity of their doctrines. But the emphasis on correct doctrine and behavior, to the neglect of love to Christ, fostered a dynamic of spiritual pride and self-confidence that by 1888 brought the movement to the brink of disaster. The 1850 vision introduced a spiritual dynamic to counter the natural human bent toward denominational pride, self-sufficiency, and legalism.

The power of this concept was that it went deeper than merely opposing open sin. It addressed the hidden sins of the heart, such as pride, self-will, and lack of love. It taught that all trials permitted by a loving Creator would ultimately prove beneficial to His trusting children (Rom. 8:28; MB 71). "In the wise providence of God, obstacles are permitted, yes, ordered, as a means of discipline, and to nerve us with determination not to be conquered by circumstances" (ST, Oct. 22, 1885). "The very trials that test our faith most severely, and make it seem that God has forsaken us, are designed to lead us nearer to Christ, that we may lay all our burdens at His feet, and receive the peace He will give us in exchange" (GW92 372).

Prominent in the early references are the themes of dying to self and cheerfully enduring suffering for Christ's sake (RH, Feb. 17, 1853). Walking the "narrow way" meant enduring trials through the "courage and strength" supplied by Jesus (RH, Feb. 21, 1856). In 1860 she urged, "Those who are saved must yield their will, their way, and be controlled by the Spirit of God. They must die daily all the way along, die, die to self and be purified by the truth" (15MR 330). "Can we persevere in such a warfare as this?" she asked. "The whole strength of self is opposed to the victory. Can we take up the cross and bear it after Jesus?" (RH, Nov. 26, 1861).

Under the theme of "bearing the cross" she included both the overcoming of wrongdoing and the willingness to serve: "To bear the cross of Christ is to control our sinful passions, to practice Christian courtesy even when it is inconvenient to do so, to see the wants of the needy and distressed and deny ourselves in order to relieve them, and to open our hearts and our doors to the homeless orphan, although to do this may tax our means and our patience" (4T 627).

From the deep root of an entire surrender that can accept, as from the hand of Jesus, life or death, comfort or hardship, she drew applications to overcoming specific habits of sin. To one with an unsubdued temper, she quoted Colossians 3:3 ("For ye are dead, and your life is hid with Christ in God"), then added, "Those who are dead to self will not feel so readily and will not be prepared to resist everything which may irritate. Dead men cannot feel. You are not dead. If you were, and your life were hid in Christ, a thousand things which you now notice, and which afflict you, would be passed by as unworthy of notice" (2T 425; cf. MB 16). "Why is it so hard to lead a self-denying, humble life?" she asked. "Because professed Christians are not dead to the world. It is easier living for Christ after dying to the world" (ST, Apr. 1, 1880).

In "The Necessity of Dying to Self," she wrote: "That which hinders your progress in a large degree is your self-esteem, the high opinion that you entertain of your own ability. If there was ever a place where self needed to die, it is here. Let us see the death struggle. Let us hear the dying groans. Self-exaltation ever separates the soul from God, no matter in whom it is found" (RH, June 18, 1889).

She identified the root cause of defeat in the Christian life as the failure to die to self, that is, attempting to surrender specific sins to God, without surrendering the whole self—heart, will, plans, ambitions, and desires—to God. "The new birth is a rare experience in this age of the world," she wrote. "This is the reason why there are so many perplexities in the churches. Many, so many, who assume the name of Christ are unsanctified and unholy. They have been baptized, but they were buried alive. Self did not die, and therefore they did not rise to newness of life in Christ" (Ms 148, 1897, in 12MR 51; 6BC 1075). "When you took your baptismal vows," she asked, "were you dead to sin and to the world, or were you buried in baptism while you were still alive? It is an awful thing to be buried alive" (BE, Mar. 23, 1903).

"Human nature is ever struggling for expression," she wrote. "He who is made complete in Christ must first be emptied of pride, of self-sufficiency. Then there is silence in the soul, and God's voice can be heard. Then the Spirit can find unobstructed entrance. Let God work in and through you. Then with Paul you can say, 'I live; yet not I, but Christ liveth in me' [Gal. 2:20]" (ST, Apr. 9, 1902).

While she upheld the importance of "entire renunciation of self," she insisted that "no man can empty himself of self. We can only consent for Christ to accomplish the work" (COL 159). What she meant by "only consent" she explained by the potter motif. "The Potter cannot mold and fashion unto honor that which has never been placed in His hands. The Christian life is one of daily surrender, submission and continual overcoming. Every day fresh victories will be gained. Self must be lost sight of, and the love of God must be constantly cultivated. Thus we grow up into Christ" (4BC 1154). "As the clay is in the hands of the potter, so we are to be in His hands. We are not to try to do the work of the potter. Our work is to yield ourselves to the molding of the Master Worker" (8T 187).

She taught that crucifixion of self is ultimately God's work, but that it requires human consent. "God sees these sins to which you may be blinded, and He works with His pruning knife [cf. John 15:2] to strike deep and separate these cherished sins from you. *You all want to choose for yourselves the process of purification*. How hard it is for you to *submit* to the crucifixion of self; but *when the work is all submitted to God*, to Him who knows our weakness and our sinfulness, *He takes the very best way to bring about the desired results*" (3T 543; italics supplied).

The "greatest battle" ever fought "is the surrender of self to the will of God, the yielding of the heart to the sovereignty of love. ... You are not able, of yourself, to bring your purposes and desires and inclinations into submission to the will of God; but if you are 'willing to be made willing,' God will accomplish the work for you" (ST, May 18, 1904). God "hews and polishes the rough stones He has quarried out of the world," she wrote. "He works through men who realize that they must submit to the ax, the chisel, and the hammer, lying passive under the divine hand. Through those who voluntarily submit themselves to Him in all matters, who seek Him in faith and hope, He works out His plans" (ST, Aug. 14, 1901). But in the absence of full surrender, "the religion of self makes easy conversions. Scripture is perverted, God dethroned, and self deified. The operation of the Holy Spirit on hearts is denied. This is the new, broad way, substituted as an improvement on the strait gate and the narrow way" (18MR 271).

Perhaps the capstone of her teaching on the conquest of self is the paradox that those who have made the most progress in dying to self are least aware of it, and indeed, experience a continually deepening repentance. "The nearer we come to Jesus," she wrote, "and the more clearly we discern the purity of His character, the more clearly shall we see the exceeding sinfulness of sin, and the less shall we feel like exalting ourselves. There will be a continual reaching out of the soul after God, a continual, earnest, heartbreaking confession of sin and humbling of the heart before Him. At every advance step in our Christian experience our repentance will deepen. We shall know that our sufficiency is in Christ alone and shall make the apostle's confession our own: 'I know that in me (that is, in my flesh,) dwelleth no good thing' [Rom. 7:18]" (AA 561). Then she quoted Paul's triumphant shout: "God forbid that I should glory, save in the cross of our Lord Jesus Christ, by whom the world is crucified unto me, and I unto the world" (Gal. 6:14).

"No one can serve two masters" (Matt. 6:24). Every believer daily chooses which master he will serve: self or Christ. Every temptation offers a choice: to exalt the Savior and "crucify self," or to exalt self and crucify the Savior (RH, May 25, 1876). "Will you not be faithful in overcoming self, that you may have the peace of Christ and an indwelling Savior?" (4T 365).

Further reading: AA 557-567; DA 172, 280, 324; GW92 227, 228; RH, Apr. 10, 17, 1894; 4T 83-94.

Daniel E. Augsburger

SELF-ABUSE, see **MASTURBATION**.

SELF-DENIAL BOX. A box or other container used as a bank in which to accumulate money saved by self-denial; also called missionary box (21MR 433; CD 329; CS 291), charity box (WM 270), contribution box (RH, Nov. 11, 1902), or "box for the church [building] fund" (1MR 191). One of the projects for which Ellen White specifically promoted and use of self-denial boxes was to support educational work among Blacks in the southern United States (Lt 304, 1904, in 2MR 70; PCO 30). In White's thought, the self-denial box was a simple but effective way to educate Christians in habits of thrift and economy.

In a New Year's message in 1881 she explained the basic idea. "I advise my brethren and sisters to supply themselves the coming year with a home missionary box, wherein to deposit small bits of money for offerings to God, besides the regular tithe. Whenever there is an extra outlay for the gratification of the appetite, let an equal amount also be dropped into this savings-bank." For every "needless expenditure . . . drop the same amount into this receptacle. Let parents prepare a box for each of their children, and after explaining the principle, leave them with their conscience and their God" (RH, Jan. 4, 1881). She saw, in this practice, at least four benefits. First, the process of deciding which expenses called for a matching deposit in the "home missionary box" would sensitize believers to recognize unnecessary expenditures. Second, since the amount in the "home missionary box" would equal the money spent on self-indulgence, they could see how much these trivial items amounted to in a year. Third, they would save up a considerable offering for the Lord's work. Fourth, they could see that if instead of putting into the box an amount just equal to the self-indulgence, they had actually denied themselves the indulgence and put that money into the box as well, they would have twice the offering to give at the end of the year. She concluded, "Do not neglect to provide yourselves and your children with the little banks. The very fact that for every penny needlessly expended another must be deposited here will prevent many an unnecessary outlay" (*ibid.*).

Thus she saw the "self-denial box" as a practical tool for developing habits of thrift for the purpose of generosity. "Let everyone have a self-denial box in his home," she wrote in 1898, "and when he would spend pennies and shillings in self-gratification let him remember the needy and starving in Africa and India and those close by his own door."

"Practice economy." "Turn from the worship of self" to "relieve suffering humanity" (WM 273). She challenged children to voluntarily restrict their spending for candies, gum, ice cream, and snack foods (CD 329). She called youth to "deny themselves of needless ornaments and articles of dress" (WM 270). She urged all to "dress plainly but neatly. Spend as little as possible upon yourselves" (9T 131).

She saw discarding the unneeded items as merely the first step in the process of learning thrift economy. The next step was to actually imitate the self-denial, self-sacrificing life of Jesus. "Let the members of the church now put away their pride and lay off their ornaments. Each should keep a missionary box at hand, and drop into it every penny he is tempted to waste in self-indulgence. But something more must be done than merely to dispense with superfluities. Self-denial must be practiced. Some of our comfortable and desirable things must be sacrificed. The preachers must sharpen up their message, not merely assailing self-indulgence, and pride in dress, but presenting Jesus, His life of self-denial and sacrifice. Let love, piety, and faith be cherished in the heart, and the precious fruits will appear in the life" (CS 291; HS 293).

She urged "those of mature age" to "stop when they are examining a gold watch or chain, or some expensive article of furniture, and ask themselves the question: Would it be right to expend so large an amount for that which we could do without or when a cheaper article would serve our purpose just as well? By denying yourselves and lifting the cross for Jesus, who for your sakes became poor, you can do much toward relieving the suffering of the poor among us; and by thus imitating the example of your Lord and Master, you will receive His approval and blessing" (4T 511). "Practice economy in your homes," she urged. "Give up your selfish pleasure. Do not,

I beg of you, absorb means in embellishing your houses; for it is God's money, and it will be required of you again. Parents, for Christ's sake do not use the Lord's money to please the fancies of your children" (CG 134, 135). Give useful but not unnecessary gifts (RH, Nov. 13, 1894).

"Let those that have work bringing the highest wages come forward and act a part proportionate to the wages they receive. Let the men who have limited wages have an interest in this matter also. Do what you can, and lay aside something besides your tithe money. Have you a box for this purpose? Explain to your children that it is the self-denial box, in which you lay aside every penny, every shilling, that you can obtain and do not need to spend for actual necessities. It is for the Lord's house. It is sacred self-denial money. It is a gift to the Lord, to lift the God-dishonoring debt from the meeting house. Doing this, every member of the family will be blessed" (10MR 126).

Further reading: CG 132; 2MR 70; PCO 30; PH126 8-11; RH, Aug. 18, 1904; AUG, Oct. 5, 1904; YI, Nov. 1, 1904; ST, Nov. 30, 1904; RH, June 22, 1905; GH, July 1, 1905; GH, Nov. 1, 1906; GH, June 1, 1908; GH, May 1, 1910.

Jerry Moon

SELF-SUPPORTING WORK. Missionary vocations carried on by persons not dependent on denominational pay. The biblical archetype was the apostle Paul, who supported himself by tentmaking (Acts 18:3; 20:34; 1 Thess. 2:6, 9; AA 347, 355; MH 154). The earliest Sabbatarian Adventist ministers were all self-supporting because there was as yet no *church organization to provide regular support.

Ellen White used the term first with reference to individual financial independence. "It is a noble, generous ambition that dictates the wish to be self-supporting. Industrious habits and frugality are necessary" (AH 374; cf. CT 275). She particularly applied this to students, urging the "self-supporting" plan of working at colporteuring or other jobs to pay school expenses, rather than going to school on borrowed money and graduating with large debt (CT 527). She often promoted the *colporteur work to church members in general as a means of self-supporting missionary work (LS 285, 286).

At least by 1901 she had begun to urge the need for Adventist laypeople to go forth as missionaries even to foreign lands, on a self-supporting basis (*ibid.* 384). Rather than depending on denominational support, men and women should go out "depending on their own abilities and on the help of the Lord," to create "an interest in the truth in places in which nothing has been done to give the warning message. . . . Work with your hands, that you may be self-supporting, and as you have opportunity proclaim the message of warning" (Lt 60, 1901, in MM 321, 322).

It was partially in response to such calls that *E. A. Sutherland and *P. T. Magan, at the *Berrien Springs meeting in 1904, resigned from the leadership of Emmanuel Missionary College, vowing to find an obscure place in the rural South where they could establish a small school that would be self-supporting and thus independent of denominational control. Ellen White did not condemn their intentions, but said their plans were too small. She went with them in their search for land and urged them to buy a farm near Nashville where they could have an influence on that great city. The resulting institutions—*Madison College, Madison Sanitarium, and Madison Foods—became prototypes for more than 50 "daughter" institutions in the southern United States during the first half of the twentieth century. During the second half of that century

newer institutions benefiting from the Madison example spread all over the world.

The issues of finance, fund-raising, and administrative control were points of friction that continually tested the oft-repeated promises of love, respect, and cooperation between the self-supporting institutions and the "regular channels" of denominational administration and finance. To facilitate better understanding and closer cooperation, the denomination in 1946 invited E. A. Sutherland, founder and longtime president of Madison College, to head a Rural Living Department of the General Conference, to regularize the relationship between the General Conference and the self-supporting institutions. In the late 1940s the department was renamed the Association of Self-supporting Institutions (ASI). Since then the acronym has remained, though the name has gone through several modifications. Currently the ASI includes not only educational and medical institutions but also hundreds of individually owned businesses and industries dedicated to spreading the Adventist message through excellent service and adventurous witness in the work and marketplaces.

Further reading: "Spirit of Prophecy Counsels on Self-supporting Work" (EGWE, SDoc); W. D. Frazee, *Another Ark to Build* (Harrisville, N.H.: Mountain Missionary Press, 1979); J. Moon, "A Brief History of Seventh-day Adventist Self-supporting Work" (unpublished paper, 1989, CAR); R. Pierson, *Miracles Happen Every Day* (PPPA, 1983).

Jerry Moon

SERMONS AND TALKS (Ellen G. White Estate, 1990, 1994). Two-volume set of public discourses by Ellen White selected from her unpublished manuscripts. It is estimated that during the 70 years of her public ministry (1844-1915) she delivered at least 10,000 sermons and addresses on three continents. She spoke at worship services on Sabbath, camp meetings, ministerial councils, General Conference sessions, temperance rallies, church dedications, and wherever else she was invited to speak. The range of her interests, both in writing and speaking, was very broad. She addressed such topics as health and temperance; issues affecting the ministerial, medical, educational, and publishing work of the church; and, especially, subjects encouraging Christian faith and living. In her public messages, as in her articles and books, Ellen White uplifted Jesus Christ with conviction and skill. Christ was the center of her life and the focus of her preaching. The messages reproduced in these two volumes were delivered in public and stenographically reported. Many others of her sermons may be found in the *Review and Herald* and the *Signs of the Times*. Nearly all the sermons selected for these volumes had not been published before.

SERMON ON THE MOUNT, see *THOUGHTS FROM THE MOUNT OF BLESSING*.

SEVEN LAST PLAGUES, see **PLAGUES, SEVEN LAST**.

SEVENTH DAY BAPTISTS. Denomination founded in England about 1650 and introduced into North America in 1671, where it played a prominent role in the history of the state of Rhode Island. When the Seventh Day Baptist General Conference was organized in 1802, membership in North America stood at 1,130. Their periodical, *Sabbath Recorder*, was read by many Millerites. In 1843 SDBs observed November 1 "as a day of fasting and prayer that Almighty God would arise and plead for His holy Sabbath." A few months later SDB *Rachel Oakes witnessed her faith to a Millerite Adventist minister, *Frederick Wheeler,

leading to the formation of the first Sabbathkeeping Adventist church, in Washington, New Hampshire. Seventh Day Baptist tracts about the Sabbath played a major role in communicating that truth to Adventists. Among early converts from SDB to SDA were the Roswell Cottrell family in 1853 (1Bio 274).

There was a close friendship between SDB Abram H. Lewis (1836-1908) and SDA *J. N. Andrews (1829-1883), each of whom was considered within his own denomination as the "foremost Sabbath theologian of his time" (Roeske, p. 10). Lewis studied Adventist doctrines in 1859 (*ibid.*, p. 37), and stood with Adventist *A. T. Jones in 1888 and in 1893 against Sunday legislation (*ibid.*, p. 294; Edwards, p. 16).

J. H. Kellogg's wife, Ella, was a Seventh Day Baptist and a graduate of Alfred University, of which Lewis was the president. Lewis was also Ella Kellogg's former pastor. He and his wife became personal friends of the Kelloggs and visited them several times in Battle Creek. S.P.S. Edwards, who was a medical student under Kellogg in the 1890s, became acquainted with the Lewises at the same time. In 1902, when Edwards was teaching physiology at Emmanuel Missionary College, Lewis visited Edwards' class. After class Lewis took issue with Edwards' views of a personal God, asserting that "God is a presence, an essence; He is everywhere, in the trees, in the flowers, [in] the food we eat." Edwards disagreed: "To me He has hands; He holds my hand. He has feet; I walk in His footsteps. He has ears; He hears my prayers. He has eyes; He sees my sins and forgives them, my weakness and gives me strength, my heart yearning and gives me grace. God is a person to me." This conversation convinced Edwards that Lewis was the main source of the pantheistic sentiments that influenced J. H. Kellogg and other leading Adventists in the early 1900s (Edwards, pp. 9-12, 15, 16).

Ellen White held Seventh Day Baptists in high respect. She wrote approvingly of the Seventh Day Baptists as reformers who "have stood for two hundred years in defense of the ancient Sabbath" (4SP 184). Passing through London in 1885, she was led on a two-hour tour of the British Museum by W. M. Jones, pastor of the SDB church there and editor of the *Sabbath Memorial* (EGWEur 44). In 1890 she spoke in Adams Center, New York, a Seventh Day Baptist community (MR1033 26), where in 1863 "nearly a whole Seventh Day Baptist church" had become Seventh-day Adventists (2Bio 67).

For many years after the formation of the SDA General Conference in 1863, SDAs and SDBs exchanged representatives at their respective General Conference sessions. J. N. Andrews was the SDA representative to the SDB General Conference sessions in 1868, 1871, and 1873. At the 1872 SDA session, SDB Nathan Wardner was seated as a delegate, and James White was appointed a delegate from SDAs to the next SDB session (*ibid.* 335). In 1866, 1869, and 1878, representatives of both denominations expressed the desire for a close working relationship between the two groups.

Ellen White applauded these efforts. "Why should not the Seventh-day Adventist and Seventh-day Baptist harmonize?" she wrote. "Why not cooperate? Why not unite in the work and become one without compromising any principle of truth, and without damage to any interest worth preserving? Both are in defense of the law of God. The Bible and the Bible alone is to be the rule of our faith, the sole bond of our union, and they who evade the truth of the Bible will not desire more intimate relationship. But if these two bodies would unite . . . in the effort to open the Word of God to the people, a work would be done

that would not please the artful foe at all" (SSW, Oct. 1, 1886).

Despite hopeful beginnings, the cooperative relationship between Seventh Day Baptists and Seventh-day Adventists cooled somewhat after the 1880s, as both denominations faced up to the fact that while they held a common belief regarding the Sabbath, they differed rather sharply on other significant issues, such as the role of the Sabbath in eschatology, the human condition in death, and the ministry of Ellen White. Regarding the importance of the Sabbath for eschatology, White commented, "Separate the Sabbath from the [three angels'] messages [of Rev. 14], and it loses its power; but when connected with the message of the third angel, a power attends it which convicts unbelievers and infidels, and brings them out with strength to stand, to live, grow, and flourish in the Lord" (1T 337). Others also have recognized that the Adventist combination of Sabbath, sanctuary, and three angels' messages in a last-day setting gives an urgency and power to the Sabbath that is not so apparent when it is viewed in isolation from these broader connections.

Further reading: S.P.S. Edwards, "Letters," to E. K. Vande Vere (1956, DF 967j, CAR); C. M. Maxwell, *Tell It to the World*, rev. ed. (PPPA, 1982), pp. 67-73, 90-94, 275; S. Roeske, "A Comparative Study of the Sabbath Theologies of A. H. Lewis and J. N. Andrews" (Ph.D. diss., AU, 1997); D. A. Sanford, *A Choosing People: The History of Seventh Day Baptists* (Nashville: Broadman, 1992).

Jerry Moon

Seventh-day Adventist Bible Commentary, Supplement: Ellen G. White Comments, The (RHPA, 1953-1957). Selections from Ellen White's periodical articles and unpublished letters and manuscripts included as supplementary materials at the end of each of the seven volumes of *The Seventh-day Adventist Bible Commentary*. The comments were selected for their relevance to specific texts of Scripture. No attempt was made, in these supplementary materials, to reproduce comments already generally available in her books; but references to her books were given at the end of the general commentary on each Bible chapter. Hence, the material found in the supplements is somewhat fragmentary and does not attempt to cover all that she said on a particular Bible passage. In 1970 all seven supplementary sections were combined in a single volume 7-A of 692 pages. Each supplementary section is reproduced as it appeared in the original volume with the same pagination. (A continuous pagination appears at the bottom of each page in brackets.) Volume 7-A also includes the three appendices of Ellen White's comments published in the 1957 volume *Seventh-day Adventists Answer *Questions on Doctrine*. These three appendices deal with Christ's place in the Trinity, His nature during His incarnation, and His work of atonement.

SEVENTH-DAY ADVENTIST CHURCH. A Protestant denomination whose name highlights two distinctive beliefs: expectation of a literal, premillennial second coming ("advent") of Christ; and observance of the Sabbath on the seventh day of the week (Saturday). Adventists are evangelical in holding that eternal life cannot be merited, but is received only as a free gift through faith in Christ. They rest from ordinary work on the Sabbath as an outward expression of the believer's inward spiritual rest in Christ's gift of salvation (Heb. 4:1-3, 9, 10) and in obedience to the Ten Commandments (Ex. 20:8-11).

Adventist origins go back to the Second Advent (Millerite) movement that looked for the Second Coming in 1843/1844. Following the disappointment of the Millerite expectations, most of the Millerites concluded that the time calculations had been wrong. One group, however, located the Millerite error, not in the time calculations, but in the expected event. (See *Doctrines, Ellen G. White's Role in the Development of Seventh-day Adventist.) By 1847 they came to a consensus regarding basic points of faith that became the foundation of the Seventh-day Adventist Church. The *General Conference of Seventh-day Adventists was organized in 1863.

From 1844 the visions of Ellen White exerted a major influence on the development of the Seventh-day Adventist denomination. Her role in doctrinal development was seldom, if ever, to initiate major doctrinal concepts, but rather to confirm or clarify conclusions reached through Bible study. A large part of her work was in forming Adventist spirituality and lifestyle through her testimonies, applying biblical standards of conduct in practical ways to church leaders, individuals, and churches. Virtually every major organizational advance was influenced by her visions, including the first Adventist periodicals *Present Truth* (1849) and the *Advent Review* (1850), church organization (1850-1863), the health message (1863), the first health-care institution (1865-1866), denominational schools (1872), foreign missions advances, and the founding of *institutions. Her life and work were so closely intertwined with the Seventh-day Adventist Church that A. L. White's six-volume biography, *Ellen G. White,* is also a resource on virtually every major development in Adventist history to 1915.

An obsession with evangelistic success to the neglect of personal piety and genuine conversion led some evangelists in the 1860s and 1870s to emphasize distinctive Adventist beliefs, such as the Sabbath and the law of God, apart from their proper relation to the gospel and the cross of Christ. This emphasis inevitably produced converts who were characterized more by self-reliant rule-keeping than by a deep, heart-changing love for Jesus Christ. By the 1880s this wrong emphasis had given the denomination a pervasive tendency toward legalism. Seeking to counteract this trend, Ellen White urged the need for authentic revival. In this effort she was joined by two young preachers and editors, *E. J. Waggoner and *A. T. Jones, who called on Adventists to repent of their self-righteous dependence on rule keeping and instead depend on the righteousness of Christ alone, received as a gift and lived out by faith. Jones and Waggoner still upheld the law of God, but gave supremacy to the cross of Christ. Despite significant resistance at the 1888 General Conference session, the new emphasis continues to influence Adventist experience.

The General Conference, denominational headquarters, was organized in Battle Creek, Michigan, in 1863, moved to Washington, D.C., in 1903, and to Silver Spring, Maryland, in 1989. Statistics at the end of 2007: baptized members, 15,660,000; churches and companies, 125,378; health-care institutions, 601; publishing houses, 62; universities and colleges, 107; secondary schools, 1,577.

See also: General Conference Sessions of 1901 and 1903.

Further reading: G. R. Knight, *A Search for Identity: The Development of Seventh-day Adventist Beliefs* (RHPA, 2000); R. W. Schwarz and F. Greenleaf, *Light Bearers: A History of the Seventh-day Adventist Church,* rev. ed. (PPPA, 2000); H. E. Douglass, *Messenger of the Lord* (PPPA, 1998), pp. 198-200, 234, 235, 374, 417, 423, 482; N. J. Vyhmeister, "Who Are Seventh-day Adventists?" in R. Dederen, ed., *Handbook of Seventh-day Adventist Theology* (RHPA, 2000), pp. 1-21; *SDA Encyclopedia* (RHPA, 1996).

Jerry Moon

SEVENTH-DAY ADVENTIST PUBLISHING ASSOCIATION, see **REVIEW AND HERALD PUBLISHING ASSOCIATION**.

SEXUALITY. Sexuality is an authentic dimension of any healthy human being created in the image of God, and sexual intercourse is a normal expression of sexuality (Gen. 1:26-29). Ellen White reinforces this positive biblical view (AH 121), and one will look in vain in her writings for even a hint that sex, by its nature, is sinful or evil. Christians are called to consider sexual relations in the light of Creation: exclusively in the context of heterosexual marriage. The current phrases such as "sexual relations" or "sexual orientation," used so frequently today and referring to any and all types of sexual activity, are not found in the White corpus. In this she shadows the biblical worldview faithfully. When she speaks positively about sexual relations, she uses such phrases as "marriage relations" (*ibid.* 121-128), "real, genuine, devoted, pure love" (2T 381), a God-given blessing (AH 124); and when she refers to perversions, or abuses, she speaks of "animal passions," "gross sensuality" (2SM 423), "loathsome practices" (AH 124), and the like.

According to Ellen White, nurturing a healthy sexual identity begins early in childhood. Parents are charged with teaching their children the first healthy concepts of maleness and femaleness. Basic anatomy and physiology of the human body, including the "mysteries of life," must not be left to secular influences (7T 65; CT 126). As childhood develops, the contact between boys and girls can blossom into a healthy self-esteem, and mutual respect when "mingling" happens in the context of some useful project or healthy recreation (2T 482, 483). In this way the youth will learn to know each other in the company of friends, become friends, and have the benefit of a safe fellowship. It is the task at hand that unites them. But when associations between young men and young women aim only at fun and entertainment, the youth are placed on dangerous ground. "The corrupting doctrine which has prevailed, that, as viewed from a health standpoint, the sexes must mingle together, has done its mischievous work" (2T 482). "Thus a door of temptation is opened before them, passion rouses like a lion within their hearts, every consideration is overborne, and everything elevated and noble is sacrificed to lust" (4T 95).

Ellen White strongly affirms the biblical stand on chastity before marriage (AH 58, 59). As a precaution she urges avoidance of time spent alone with the other gender. It is impossible to watch over all the feelings and urges of the body and mind in such encounters. Intentions and promises are no match for sexual drive. When petting and other expressions of intimacy, which belong to marriage, are indulged outside of the marriage union, they erode and weaken moral powers and threaten the chances for future happiness (TSB 116-119).

In professional and adult relationships she calls for "refinement and delicacy." She advises that patients should be seen by physicians of the same sex whenever possible (CH 363-365). Even the appearance of evil must be carefully avoided (2T 458, 459). Any special considerations or undue familiarity must be shunned (MM 145, 146). Those in leading and administrative positions must insist on purity of relationships among personnel, modesty in dress, and decency in language. Speaking to married women, she wrote, "If you have tender, loving words and kindly attentions to bestow, let them be given to him whom you have promised before God and angels to love, respect, and honor while you both shall live" (2T 462).

Sexual abuses were of great concern to Ellen White. She counseled married couples who passionately love each other to watch lest their passion gives way to excesses that can easily injure or outrage the "fine and tender sensibilities" of the spouse (*ibid.* 381). "The marriage relation is holy, but in this degenerate age it covers vileness of every description. It is abused and has become a crime which now constitutes one of the signs of the last days. . . . When the sacred nature and claims of marriage are understood, it will even now be approved of Heaven; and the result will be happiness to both parties, and God will be glorified" (AH 121, 122).

In this context she addresses husbands in particular. Lust for self-gratification, unbridled desires for pleasure, and loose rein to the lower passions debases what is holy. "The bedchamber, where angels of God should preside, is made unholy by unholy practices. And because shameful animalism rules, bodies are corrupted; loathsome practices lead to loathsome diseases. That which God has given as a blessing is made a curse. Sexual excess will effectually destroy a love for devotional exercises, will take from the brain the substance needed to nourish the system, and will most effectively exhaust the vitality" (*ibid.* 124). Careful, attentive, constant, faithful and compassionate husbands will manifest true love. When he "has the nobility of character, purity of the heart, elevation of mind that every true Christian must possess, it will be made manifest in the marriage relation. If he has the mind of Christ, he will not be a destroyer of the body, but will be full of tender love, seeking to reach the highest standard in Christ" (*ibid.* 125).

In her counsels to wives she cautions against extravagant apparel that "too often encourages lust in the heart of the wearer and awakens base passions in the heart of the beholder" (4T 645). She insists that the wife's first allegiance is to God (2T 475), and when her best and the highest love is sent to God first, it will return to her abundantly (7T 46). She has no obligation to satisfy the inordinate and wild sexual fancies of her husband (AH 126). "Let the wife decide that it is the husband's prerogative to have full control of her body, and to mold her mind to suit his in every respect, to run in the same channel as his own, and she yields her individuality; her identity is lost, merged in that of her husband. She is a mere machine for his will to move and control, a creature of his pleasure. He thinks for her, decides for her, and acts for her. She dishonors God in occupying this passive position. She has a responsibility before God which it is her duty to preserve. When the wife yields her body and mind to the control of her husband, being passive to his will in all things, sacrificing her conscience, her dignity, and even her identity, she loses the opportunity of exerting that mighty influence for good which she should possess to elevate her husband" (2T 476). But when women become mere instruments to minister "to the gratification of low, lustful propensities" of their husband, they run into the arms of tragedy. They must know that no man "can truly love his wife when she will patiently submit to become his slave" (*ibid.* 474).

On the subject of pornography, homosexuality, and "unnatural" practices Ellen White stands firm on the side of Scripture. She deplored the appearance of handbills "on which indecent pictures are printed [and] are posted up along our streets to allure the eyes and deprave the morals. These presentations are of such a character as to stir up the basest passions of the human heart through corrupt imaginings. These corrupt imaginings are followed by defiling practices like those in which the Sodomites indulged. But the most

terrible part of the evil is that it is practiced under the garb of sanctity" (TSB 120). The cities of Sodom and Gomorrah were destroyed "through the gratification of unnatural appetite" that enslaved them, and "they became so ferocious and bold in their detestable abominations that God would not tolerate them upon the earth" (3T 162; cf. PP 90, 91).

These strong words depicting sexual deviances are matched by equally straight and stirring calls for reform, repentance, and purity. "Those who put their trust in Christ are not to be enslaved by any hereditary [genetic] or cultivated [environmental] habit or tendency. Instead of being held in bondage to the lower nature, they are to rule every appetite and passion. God has not left us to battle with evil in our own finite strength. Whatever may be our inherited or cultivated tendencies to wrong, we can overcome through the power that He is ready to impart" (MH 175, 176).

Miroslav M. Kiš

SHAKING. A process of spiritual destabilization leading to apostasy, and especially to the final apostasy within the end-time church. The shaking is prefigured in one of Christ's parables as an event taking place in "the time of the harvest" before the harvest is completed. The "wheat" (loyal Christians within the church [COL 70, 71]) is "first" separated from the tares (disloyal Christians within the church [*ibid.* 71]), after which the tares are bound in bundles to be burned (Matt. 13:24-30). Paul doubtless had this separation in mind when he wrote of a major "falling away" within the church as a "first" act in the final end-time drama, and prayed that his readers might not be soon "shaken" out (2 Thess. 2:2, 3).

Apostasy, the ultimate personal tragedy of the Christian, is as old as the Christian church itself; and Ellen White herself recognized that "there always has been, and till the conflict is ended, there will always be a departing from God" (Ms 135, 1902, in UL 318). But as early as 1850 she reported that a "mighty" shaking had already begun within Adventism (EW 50, 51); and 12 years later she ruefully recognized that "we are now in the shaking time" (1T 429).

Ellen White's basic understanding may be summarized as follows: 1. The shaking was a process already operating within the Seventh-day Adventist Church of her day. 2. It would continue—and accelerate—until the close of *probation. 3. This shaking would have multiple causes and produce various baleful effects. 4. Eventually the shaking would lead a large number—possibly even a "majority" (5T 136)—to leave the church. Those leaving would include many in leadership roles (GC 608; PK 188), some of whom would become its bitterest opponents (DA 630; 5T 463). 5. The shaking, however, would not be terminal for the movement; for while a large number would leave the church, as many, or even more, would take their places under the *loud cry, which follows the outpouring of the *latter rain of the Holy Spirit (EW 271; LDE 182; 3SM 422). 6. Although the church at this time "may appear" as about to fall, in the end it does not. Instead, "the sinners in Zion are sifted out"—a "terrible ordeal" (2SM 380), while the faithful are "settled" into the truth, both intellectually and spiritually, so firmly that they cannot be moved (4BC 1161), and are thus prepared for the *time of trouble and the second coming of Christ.

Ellen White saw at least four causes of the shaking: (1) unremitting persecution from outside the church (4T 89; 5T 81); (2) false theories from within the church (TM 112; UL 135, 352)—including an unidentified omega (see *Alpha and Omega) of apostasy (1SM 197, 200, 203); (3) an eroding worldliness, caused both by a failure to receive the love of the truth (6T 400, 401; GC 625) and a consequent failure to be "sanctified through obedience to the truth" (GC 608; cf. UL 318); and (4) resistance to the "straight testimony ... of the True Witness"—a virtual rejection of the writings of all of the prophets, including herself (1T 181; 3T 272; 4T 211; 5T 719, 720; EW 270). She often speaks of a "sifting" in close association with the shaking. A few see the sifting as a separate though related phenomenon, in contradistinction to the shaking, in which the shaking first separates church members into two groups. Then the "sifting" removes one of those groups from the church (e.g., Joseph W. Sharp, *The Shaking and the Sifting* [privately published by the author, undated]). Others, however, see Ellen White simply employing these two terms synonymously.

Roger W. Coon

SHUT DOOR. A biblical expression drawn from Matthew 25:10 and Revelation 3:7 that Millerite Adventists first applied to the close of human probation just before the *second coming of Jesus (William Miller, *Evidence From Scripture and History of the Second Coming of Christ About the Year 1843: Exhibited in a Course of Lectures* [Troy, N.Y.: Kemble & Hooper, 1836], pp. 97, 98).

After the October 1844 *midnight cry proclamation, Millerite Adventism divided into two branches. The larger group abandoned faith in both the shut door as the close of probation and the significance of the 1844 date. They looked to a future date for Jesus to come. A minority of Millerites continued to believe the prophetic importance of the fall 1844 date. This second group has been called shut-door or Bridegroom Adventists and, later, Sabbatarian Adventists. For them the concept of the shut door represented faith in the 1844 midnight cry. Beginning at the time of the *disappointment and continuing until about 1852, the meaning of the shut door progressively changed from the simple belief that Jesus had closed *probation for the world to a dramatically different idea that Jesus had opened a new door into the Most Holy Place of the heavenly *sanctuary that required a proclamation of the *Sabbath to the world. An outline of this transition is helpful in examining Ellen White's view and her role in the progression.

Joseph Turner and Apollos Hale established the baseline view for the Bridegroom or shut-door Adventists in their January 1845 single-issue publication, the *Advent Mirror*. By connecting Matthew 25:1-13 and Daniel 7:9, 10, 13, 14, Turner and Hale argued that in October of 1844 Jesus had gone into a heavenly marriage and that soon He would return for the wedding supper at the literal Second Coming. In their understanding, Christ had changed His role from intercessor to king. The controversial aspect of this argument was that the October 1844 midnight cry had been the final proclamation of the gospel to the world and that "sinners," or the "great mass of the world," could no longer be saved. They defined "sinners" as particularly those who had "rejected the truth" of the Advent message; but they also applied the term to all those who had not made a personal commitment to Christ.

Though they believed the world had been warned, they were very careful to explain that probation had not closed for everyone. Some individuals could still be saved, even those who were outside of the Millerite movement, as long as they had not spurned light and were still "subjects of [God's] mercy" (A. Hale and J. Turner, "Has Not the Savior Come as the Bridegroom?" *Advent Mirror*, January 1845). While Turner and Hale represented the mainline bridegroom view, there was a

great deal of diversity of opinion and confusion among bridegroom or shut-door Adventists during the first years following 1844. Nevertheless, the *Advent Mirror* view remained dominant until 1847 and the emergence of Sabbatarian Adventism and a new heavenly-sanctuary-oriented perspective on the shut door.

Bridegroom Adventism divided over whether the Second Coming, resurrection, New Jerusalem, heaven, etc., were literal or spiritual events and places. The majority eventually adopted the spiritualizing view. By the first half of 1846 the spiritualizers had drifted off to Shakerism or abandoned the Bridegroom view. The "little flock" that became Sabbatarian Adventists, while believing in the shut door, utterly rejected the spiritualizing approach and held to a literal view. Ellen White was at the forefront in opposing the Bridegroom spiritualizers.

Between 1847 and 1849 Sabbatarian Adventists redefined the shut door by applying it to the partition between the two apartments of the heavenly sanctuary—the holy place and Most Holy. They came to understand that Jesus had closed the door to the first apartment and opened a door to the Second Apartment in October 1844, and had begun a new work there. Using Revelation 11:19, *Joseph Bates first suggested this view in print in a tract of January 1847, and James White continued the theme in his tract of May 1847 (J. Bates, *The Seventh Day Sabbath: A Perpetual Sign From the Beginning to the Entering Into the Gates of the Holy City, According to the Commandment*, 2nd ed. [New Bedford, Mass.: Benjamin Lindsey, 1847]; JW, *A Word to the "Little Flock"* [1847]).

Bates, together with James and Ellen White, linked the new heavenly sanctuary ministry of Jesus in the Most Holy Place to the Sabbath and the law of God contained in the ark of the covenant (Rev. 11:19). This linkage gave the Sabbath new eschatological significance. In 1848 and 1849 Bates further proposed that the Sabbath was the seal of God and thus was to be proclaimed throughout the world to gather the 144,000 (Joseph Bates to Leonard and Elvira Hastings, Aug. 7, 1848; *idem, A Seal of the Living God: A Hundred Forty-four Thousand of the Servants of God Being Sealed in 1849* [New Bedford, Mass.: Benjamin Lindsey, 1849], pp. 34, 61, 62).

The rapidly developing doctrines of the Sabbath and sanctuary led to a discontinuity between the earlier idea of a shut door for "sinners" and the newer need for evangelistic proclamation. Sabbatarian Adventists resolved this discontinuity between 1849 and 1852. During this time the evangelistic focus of Sabbatarian Adventists gradually shifted from former Millerites to include other Christians and the world in general.

The meaning of "sinners" had been applied most specifically to those who had rejected the midnight cry message. Because they had proclaimed the Advent message so widely and none seemed interested in it for several years after 1844, most Sabbatarian Adventists concluded that their work of warning the world was finished. In practical (if not theological) terms they extended the word "sinners" to include the world at large. By 1850 Sabbatarian Adventists were more specific in redefining the original *Advent Mirror* view of "sinners" to be only those who personally had rejected the Advent, but not necessarily referring to the world at large. James White wrote that "sinners," or those who had "rejected the offers of salvation," were "left without an advocate, when Jesus passed from the Holy Place" ([JW], "The Sanctuary, 2300 Days, and the Shut Door," *Present Truth*, May 1850; JW, *The Sanctuary, the 2300 Days, and the Shut Door* [Oswego, N.Y.: n.p., May 1850], p. 14). He and others used Hosea 5:6, 7 to express this sentiment (*ibid.*; David Arnold, "The Shut Door Explained," *Present Truth*, December 1849). J. White suggested that "the reason why they do not find the Lord" was "simply" that "they seek him where he is not; 'he hath withdrawn himself' to the Most Holy Place" (*ibid.*). A few months earlier James White had noted the conversion of "one brother, who had not been in the advent, and had made no public profession of religion until 1845, [but] came out clear and strong on the whole truth." "He had never," White continued, "opposed the advent, and it is evident that the Lord had been leading him" (JW, "Our Tour East," *Advent Review*, August 1850). By 1851 James White was explicit regarding three categories of people that might be converted— erring brethren, children, and "hidden souls." He wrote: "Conversion, in the strictest sense, signifies a change from sin to holiness. In this sense we readily answer that it does not 'exclude *all* conversions,' but we believe that those who heard the 'everlasting gospel' message and rejected it, or refused to hear it, are excluded by it. We have no message to such. They have no ears to hear us" ([JW], "Conversions . . . ," RH, Apr. 7, 1851).

He continued, "God has reserved to Himself a multitude of precious souls, some even in the churches. . . . They were living up to what light they had when Jesus closed His mediation for the world, and when they hear the . . . third angel they will gladly receive the whole truth." For a short time James White believed that Sabbatarian Adventists were not to work for these "hidden souls" as a group (*ibid.*). Soon this reservation fell away as an increasing number accepted "present truth." "The open door we teach," he wrote, "and invite those who have an ear to hear to come to it and find salvation through Jesus Christ" ([JW], "Call at the Harbinger Office," RH, Feb. 17, 1852). He observed: "A large portion of those who are sharing the blessings attending the present truth were not connected with the advent cause in 1844" ([JW], "The Work of the Lord," RH, May 6, 1852). The growth increased until the number of "advent brethren" in the state of New York had grown from "about a score" to "near one thousand" ("A Brief Sketch of the Past," AR, May 6, 1852).

James White had previously believed that Jesus had finished His mediation for the world, but he would write in May 1852 that Jesus was mediating for the world from the Most Holy Place of the heavenly sanctuary. "With great delight," he exclaimed, "we make mention of the ark of God as well as of the mercy seat, and believe that both exist in this dispensation. We love the mercy seat, before which our merciful High Priest now stands ready to plead the case of those who come to Him in sincerity and truth" ([JW], "The Ark and the Mercy Seat," RH, May 27, 1852). In fact, for James White and the other Sabbatarian Adventists in 1852, the new conversions were occurring because Jesus was before the mercy seat of the Most Holy Place.

The transition of the shut-door view was thus complete. Sabbatarian Adventists were settled that sinners in general should hear the gospel message in the context of present truth and that only those who had "wickedly rejected the light of truth" in the midnight cry were excluded from salvation. This would remain as the permanent position of Sabbatarian Adventists.

Ellen White's view on the shut door seems to have been generally in harmony with the above-described progression with some exceptions. Early statements suggest that she had a view similar to the *Advent Mirror*. Her description in her first vision of "all the wicked world which God had rejected" (WLF 14) suggests that she believed that God had closed probation at least for sinners who had rejected

the Millerite message. The fact that even Turner and Hale were willing to allow that sincere individuals could still be saved suggests that Ellen White was not saying that probation for all humans was closed. Additionally, Millerite believers who were interacting with her in Atkinson, Maine, during February 1845 believed that individuals could be converted or saved (Burt, "Historical Background," pp. 136, 137).

There were, though, significant differences between Ellen White's view and those of some prominent shut-door advocates. Joseph Turner and Samuel Snow argued that Jesus had closed the door of probation and ended His work as high priest. In contrast, Ellen White's second major vision affirmed that Jesus was still ministering in the sanctuary as a high priest. In this February 1845 vision, sometimes called the Bridegroom vision, she saw first the Father and then Jesus go from the holy to the Most Holy Place of the heavenly sanctuary. Those who had their eyes on Jesus moved with Him into the Most Holy Place while Satan took up a counterfeit role, posing as from the holy place. She wrote: "Satan's object was to keep them deceived and to draw back and deceive God's children" (EW 56). The fact that Satan was working so hard suggested that there was still hope for those who were deceived, though she does not specifically define who the "deceived" ones were. Thus very early Ellen White presented a heavenly-sanctuary-oriented perspective on the shut door, and though not yet named, an open door for those who would follow Jesus to the Most Holy Place.

Ellen White joined her husband in arguing that conversions were possible for those who had not been a part of the Millerite movement. In a February 1850 letter she wrote: "Souls are coming out upon the truth all around here. They are those who have not heard the Advent doctrine and some of them are those who went forth to meet the Bridegroom in 1844, but since that time have been deceived by false shepherds until they did not know where they were or what they believed" (Lt 4, 1850, in 5MR 91). At the same time she described counterfeit Christian revivals among those who had rejected the midnight cry and believed that the "time for their salvation is past" (ExV 27; ExV54 4). Throughout the remainder of her life Ellen White believed that probation had closed for those who had rejected the 1844 message. In 1883 she wrote: "I was shown in vision, and I still believe, that there was a shut door in 1844. All who saw the light of the first and second angels' messages and rejected that light were left in darkness" (Ms 4, 1883, in 1SM 63). Through the years critics have challenged Ellen White on the shut door. The first major published retrospective criticism was by B. F. Snook and William H. Brinkerhoff (see *Marion Party) in 1866. Down to the present, various arguments concerning the shut door have been used to discredit her prophetic gift. But in light of the progression of shut-door understanding, several points need to be emphasized. While Ellen White's visions steadfastly affirmed the continued significance of the October 1844 prophetic message, they also affirmed that probation had not yet closed and that Jesus was still functioning as a high priest. She never stated that individuals could not be saved or wrote that the "door of mercy" was closed. The tenor of her statements suggests that for a time she may have believed that evangelistic work for the world at large was finished. Nevertheless her visions theologically implied a more open view. This discontinuity was resolved within a few years and the terms shut door and open door embodied the new theological understanding that integrated the Sabbath and the sanctuary, explained the 1844 experience, and gave a reason for new evangelistic outreach to the world.

James White reflected in later years on the benefit they had received by moving more slowly in abandoning some of their misunderstandings concerning the shut door. "Some of this people did believe in the shut door, in common with the Adventists generally, soon after the passing of time. Some of us held fast this position longer than those did who gave up their Advent experience, and drew back in the direction of perdition. And God be thanked that we did hold fast to that position till the matter was explained by light from the heavenly sanctuary" (*Life Incidents*, p. 207).

Further reading: 1SM 59-64; M. D. Burt, "The Historical Background, Interconnected Development, and Integration of the Doctrines of the Sanctuary, the Sabbath, and Ellen G. White's Role in Sabbatarian Adventism From 1844 to 1849" (Ph.D. diss., AU, 2002); *idem*, "Ellen White and the Shut Door," *Ellen White and Current Issues Symposium* 1 (CAR, 2005): 67-87; P. G. Damsteegt, *Foundations of the Seventh-day Adventist Message and Mission* (Grand Rapids: Eerdmans, 1977; reprint: AUP, 1995), pp. 104-124; H. E. Douglass, *Messenger of the Lord* (PPPA, 1998), pp. 500-512, 560-569; F. D. Nichol, *Ellen G. White and Her Critics: An Answer to the Major Charges That Critics Have Brought Against Mrs. Ellen G. White* (RHPA, 1951), pp. 161-252; R. W. Olson, "The Shut Door Documents: Statements Relating to the 'Shut Door,' the Door of Mercy, and the Salvation of Souls by Ellen G. White and Other Early Adventists Arranged in a Chronological Setting from 1844 to 1851" (EGWE, 1982, SDoc); R. J. Poehler, "'... And the Door Was Shut': Seventh-day Adventists and the Shut-Door Doctrine in the Decade after the Great Disappointment" (research paper, AU, 1978, CAR); A. L. White, "Ellen G. White and the Shut Door" (EGWE, SDoc).

Merlin D. Burt

Sifting, see **Shaking.**

Signs of the Times Articles, Ellen G. White (PPPA, 1974). Four-volume facsimile reproduction of Ellen White's articles published in *Signs of the Times* from its inception in Oakland, California, in 1874 to her death in 1915. The editors of the periodical, in their search for materials to print, often drew materials from Ellen White's current books or reprinted articles that had appeared in the *Review and Herald* or earlier issues of *Signs of the Times*. Such reprints account for close to one third of her 2,000 articles that were published in *Signs*. After 1906 Ellen White wrote little new material for this journal, but articles continued to appear, drawn largely from other of her published sources. In planning for the facsimile republication of these articles, the compilers decided to reprint only those not duplicated in her other publications. While all the articles are listed in the table of contents, only the new materials were reproduced in facsimile. The table of contents in each volume gives a list in chronological order of all articles published within the period of time covered by that volume and includes for each article its title, date of publication in the *Signs,* and place of publication if published elsewhere first. At the back of volume 4 is found an alphabetical list of all reproduced articles in the four volumes. Volume 1 includes articles from 1874 to 1885; volume 2, 1886 to 1892; volume 3, 1893 to 1898; and volume 4, 1899 to 1915.

In contrast to the *Review and Herald,* which was the official paper of the church, *Signs of the Times* became a missionary journal and sought to reach the general population with the Seventh-day Adventist message. Ellen White considered a wide range of subjects in her *Signs of the Times* articles. Many of her sermons were published and present practical counsels on the Christian life. There are many articles of doctrinal exposition, while others are biographical in nature, relating her travels and giving glimpses of the developing work of the church.

Simple Remedies. In Ellen White's day the phrase "simple remedy/ies" was used to designate a medicinal herb, its extract, or the active ingredient obtained from the herb. According to the *Oxford English Dictionary,* "simple remedy" was, from the fifteenth through the eighteenth centuries, the primary term for a medicinal herb. Interestingly, the word "simple" was itself defined as "a medicinal herb [as *country simples*] or medicine obtained from an herb: so called because each vegetable was supposed to possess its particular virtue and, therefore, to constitute a simple remedy." When "simples"—medicinal herbs—were used to make "remedies," the result was simple remedies. In the nineteenth century, however, the old term for medicinal herbs ("simples"), and their medicinal extracts ("simple remedies") was gradually replaced by the word "drug." Of course, "simple" was also to be used as an adjective to mean "not complex" and therefore easy to understand and/or apply.

Ellen White used the phrase "simple remedies" in at least three ways. In line with "simple" as a medicinal herb or medicine obtained from an herb are the following: "A cup of tea made from catnip herb will quiet the nerves. Hop tea will induce sleep. Hop poultices over the stomach will relieve pain" (2SM 297).

Second, she used simple in the sense of "not complex" or "easy to apply," referring to hydrotherapy or to common herbs or foods. "If the eyes are weak, if there is pain in the eyes, or inflammation, soft flannel cloths wet in hot water and salt will bring relief quickly. When the head is congested, if the feet and limbs are put in a bath with a little mustard, relief will be obtained. There are *many more simple remedies* which will do much to restore healthful action to the body. All these *simple preparations* the Lord expects us to use for ourselves" (*ibid.;* italics supplied). In a parallel use she wrote to Mrs. *Metcalfe Hare in 1909: "Take warm footbaths into which have been put the leaves from the eucalyptus tree." Try "this remedy which is so simple, and which costs you nothing" (*ibid.* 301). "I have already told you the remedy I use when suffering from difficulties with my throat. I take a glass of boiled honey, and into this I put a few drops of eucalyptus oil, stirring it in well. . . . I take a teaspoonful of this mixture, and relief comes almost immediately. . . . This prescription may seem so simple that you feel no confidence in it, but I have tried it for a number of years and can highly recommend it" (*ibid.*).

A third way she used "simple remedy" could refer to the extract or active ingredient from a medicinal herb. In 1893 Edgar Caro, a medical student (*ibid.* 278, 279), asked White to clarify "the meaning of the word 'drug' as mentioned in *[Health: or] How to Live. Does it ["drug"] refer only to the stronger medicines as mercury, strychnine, arsenic, and such poisons, the things we medical students call 'drugs,' or does it also include the simpler remedies, as potassium, iodine, squills, etc.?" Her reply described the second group, the "simpler remedies," as "less harmful in proportion to their simplicity." Such "simpler remedies" were not completely harmless, however, for she added that they were often used "when not at all necessary." A related statement illustrates what she included under the heading "simple remedies": "The common words by which we know simple remedies are as useful as the technical terms used by physicians for these same remedies. To request a nurse to prepare some catnip tea answers

the purpose fully as well as would directions given her [by a physician] in language [Latin] understood only after long study" (Ms 169, 1902, in 19MR 48). Simple remedies commonly employed by physicians included the common foxglove (*Digitalis purpurea,* or squills) for the treatment of heart failure, tea and coffee for the treatment of seasickness and asthma, and ephedra (Mormon tea) for bronchial asthma.

In summary, Ellen White used the phrase "simple remedies" to designate (1) a therapy that was not complex, hence easy to use; (2) a remedial substance (food or herb) that was harmless; or (3) a botanic drug (medicinal herb, its extract, or active ingredient) that was less harmful than the traditional drugs used at the time.

See also: Drugs, Herbal Remedies, Natural Remedies.

Further reading: M. G. Hardinge, *A Physician Explains Ellen White's Counsel on Drugs, Herbs, and Natural Remedies* (RHPA, 2001).

Mervyn G. Hardinge

SIN. In Ellen White's thought, sin involves all the ways in which the evil of the present world deviates from the original perfect Creation; but she defines sin particularly in opposition to the *law of God and a breaking of relationship with God as the law of God is a reflection of His character. "What is sin? It is the result of Satan's administration. It is his work to make of no effect the law of God" (RH, Aug. 9, 1898). An understanding of her concept of sin involves its origins, its definitions, its effects, its implications for Christian life, and its end.

According to Ellen White, "Nothing is more plainly taught in Scripture than that God was in no wise responsible for the entrance of sin" (GC 492, 493). Satan is "the author of sin and all its results" (DA 471). Satan's rebellion started a process that had wide-ranging consequences. The origin of sin in heaven is a mystery "too deep for the human mind to explain, or even fully to comprehend" (SC 106). Sin cannot be explained, because to explain it would mean to give a reason for its existence (GC 492), and such a reason does not exist. "No cause for sin exists" (GC 503). To attribute it to a cause would be to justify, excuse, and defend its existence; and this is impossible.

On Planet Earth sin began with the disobedience of Adam and Eve in the Garden of Eden. Satan led humans to sin by "the same misrepresentation of the character of God as he had practiced in heaven," causing God to be "regarded as severe and tyrannical" (*ibid.* 500). As a consequence, human minds have been perverted by sin (MH 451; PK 233).

Ellen White defines the sin of Adam and Eve as "distrust of God's goodness, disbelief of His word, and rejection of His authority, . . . that brought into the world a knowledge of evil" (Ed 25). The nature of sin is thus described as unbelief leading to a broken relationship with God, the attempt to live independently of Him, and a rebellious or hostile state of mind toward Him. Sin is an autonomous life without God.

This is supported, not contradicted, by her well-known statement that "our only definition of sin is that given in the Word of God; it is 'the transgression of the law;' it is the outworking of a principle at war with the great law of love which is the foundation of the divine government" (GC 493). The last half of the sentence gives her understanding of the first half. The essence of sin is whatever is "at war with the great law of love which is the foundation of the divine government" (*ibid.*).

In another place where she calls 1 John 3:4 "the only definition of sin," she goes on to talk about the "natural heart" as "deceitful

above all things, and desperately wicked" (1SM 320). Elsewhere she links 1 John 3:4 with 1 John 5:17, "all unrighteousness is sin" (RH, July 24, 1888), and describes sin as simply "the opposite of holiness" (TM 145). All these are elaborations of her basic definition that sin is anything contrary to the character of God as expressed in His law.

She therefore does not confine sin only to willful "transgression"; rather, she broadens the connotation of transgression to include all opposition to or variance from God's holy law. The intention of her statement is to stress that all sin is characterized by disharmony with the law of God, which is a transcript of the divine character. This is the united witness of the Word of God. She emphasizes that in the matter of sin, one's attitude to the clear will of God is the key issue and a very serious matter, because the law is the expression of God's character, and disobedience is a visible sign of that broken relationship with God and thus with the law of God. Thus for her the "transgression of the law" stands not for mere outward disobedience, but for everything that is hostile to God's law in the sinful, "deceitful" heart. Under this main heading of conflict with God's law her writings present a very complex picture of sin, with a wide spectrum of subdefinitions.

Sin is not only an act, a wrongdoing, but also a principle in the selfish *nature* of humanity, an *inclination* to sin. Humans all have the *propensity* to sin, being born with a sinful nature. Sin begins with evil thoughts (5T 177); it starts in the mind before the committing of a sinful act (2T 561; MYP 76). Because sin is a condition in which we are born, "everything that we of ourselves can do is defiled by sin" (COL 311). Selfishness is the basis from which all other sins come out (LS 241; 4T 384), and the most common sin is covetousness (PP 496). Thus sin is an intruder (GC 493), a parasite that lives only because good exists. Evil cannot originate life (PP 264).

Ellen White underlines: "There is no sin greater than unbelief" (ML 14). Acts of sin spring from a lack of faith (Rom. 14:23; GC 436), "distrust of God's goodness, disbelief of His Word, and rejection of His authority" (Gen. 3; Ed 25), and in its relational results, sin separates humans from God (SC 13). Thus every sin is ultimately a sin against God Himself (PP 722), not only against the integrity of a human person, or even the law of God. This recognition is based on numerous biblical texts, such as Genesis 39:9 and Psalm 51:4.

Ellen White echoes James 1:14, 15 that specific acts of human sin begin in the individual mind (5T 177). "If you indulge in *vain imaginations*, permitting your mind to dwell upon impure subjects, you are, in a degree, as guilty before God as if your thoughts were carried into action. All that prevents the action is the lack of opportunity" (2T 561; italics supplied). Sin is also the *intention* to do wrong even though we had no possibility to actually realize it. "Every act is judged by the motives that prompt it" (COL 316). Matthew 5:28 reveals that our *sinful intentions* are taken seriously by God, because they indicate what is in the heart. The mental choice to commit sin, even though never acted outwardly, brings guilt, because the law of God demands perfect purity of thoughts, feelings, motives, and actions (2MCP 477, 478). "The books of heaven record the sins that would have been committed had there been opportunity" (ST, July 31, 1901). Sinful thoughts produce visible results, actual wrongdoing, and disobedience (6MR 336, 338; 1BC 1083). Sin is thus not only an outward reality, a deed, an act, but also an inward reality.

Sins of the mind include indifference (RH, Sept. 30, 1873), selfishness, love of pleasure (TM 129), and negligent forgetfulness (3T 12). Pride, selfishness, and covetousness "are sins that are especially offensive to God" (5T 337). The most hopeless and incurable sin is pride and self-sufficiency (COL 154).

"God does not regard all sins as of equal magnitude; there are degrees of guilt in His estimation as well as in that of finite man" (5T 337; SC 30). However, "no sin is small in the sight of God" (5T 337), for "sin crucified the Son of God" (TM 145). White believed that "only in the light of the cross" can the "terrible enormity" of sin be discerned (SC 31, 32).

Regarding the effects of sin, White remarks that "sin can bring only shame and loss." It is an antagonistic power that separates from God, alienates humans, brings blaming, sickness, violence, abuse, and death (Ed 150, 151). Because of sin, humans lost the capacity to discern between good and evil, and appreciate the good (Ed 25). For all these reasons God can never justify sin (4T 370). His "hatred of sin is strong as death" (DA 57). Those who continue in sin will bear its consequences, and the consequences are like an avalanche that destroys everything that is good, valuable, and worthwhile.

The problem of sin is such a horrible reality that it has no solution apart from supernatural power (PP 717, 718). "In freeing our souls from the bondage of sin," she writes, "God has wrought for us a deliverance greater than that of the Hebrews at the Red Sea" (PP 289). Because only Christ can cleanse from sin, White never speaks about sin without pointing to the Savior, who died for the sins of the world. "God cannot forgive sins at the expense of His justice, His holiness, and His truth" (7BC 912, 913); but Christ's victory God offers to humans as a free gift. "As soon as there was sin, there was a Savior" (DA 210). In her thought, salvation is inseparable from deliverance from sin. Christ is the only remedy for sin (COL 254), and He alone can cleanse humans from sin (1SM 317), but He forgives sins, He does "that fully. There are no sins He will not forgive in and through the Lord Jesus Christ. This is the sinner's only hope, and if he rests here in sincere faith, he is sure of pardon and that full and free" (Lt 12, 1892, in 7BC 913). She assures her readers that "every sin acknowledged before God with a contrite heart, He will remove" (TM 93). Christ came to save humankind from sin, not in sin (DA 668). He did not die that human beings might continue in sin (TM 161, 162). Jesus Christ "died for us, and now He offers to take our sins and give us His righteousness. If you give yourself to Him, and accept Him as your Savior, then, sinful as your life may have been, for His sake you are accounted righteous. Christ's character stands in place of your character, and you are accepted before God just as if you had not sinned" (SC 62). Confessed sin is blotted out by Christ's atoning blood (PP 202), but cherished sin (3T 543) can only destroy a person.

Habits of sin can be overcome only by long and persevering effort (AA 560) in daily dying to self. Through God's grace and strength (3T 115), a person in Christ may overcome sin (SD 154). The Spirit of Christ brings hatred of sin (5T 171). Not temptation itself, but the yielding to it, is sin (4T 358; 5T 426). Ellen White shows pastoral concern when she advised that all should confess and forsake their own sin before trying to correct others (MB 127). God is longing for people who are so totally dedicated to Him that they would rather die than commit sin (4T 495; 5T 53).

Finally, nothing is clearer in her thought than that one day sin will be fully and eternally eradicated (Nahum 1:9; GC 503, 504, 678).

See also: Temptation.

Further reading: GC 492-504; PP 33-43,

52-62; Ed 23-27; J. M. Fowler, "Sin," in R. Dederen, ed., *Handbook of Seventh-day Adventist Theology* (RHPA, 2000), pp. 233-270; E. Heppenstall, *The Man Who Is God* (RHPA, 1977), pp. 107-128; G. R. Knight, *Sin and Salvation* (RHPA, 2008), pp. 28-51; W. W. Whidden, *Ellen White on Salvation* (RHPA, 1995), pp. 41-46; *idem, Ellen White on the Humanity of Christ* (RHPA, 1997), pp. 18-24, 99-104.

Jiří Moskala

SINLESSNESS, see **PERFECTION**; **SIN**.

SIX THOUSAND YEARS, see **CHRONOLOGY, BIBLICAL**.

SKETCH OF THE CHRISTIAN EXPERIENCE AND VIEWS OF ELLEN G. WHITE, A (James White, 1851, 64 pp.). Generally referred to as *Experience and Views*, this pamphlet, the first book by Ellen White, was published in Saratoga Springs, New York, to place Ellen White's first visions in permanent form (1Bio 214). It was later republished and remains in print as the first section of **Early Writings* (pp. 11-83). James White's preface gives two purposes of the book: to remove "prejudice" against Ellen White's visions, and to counter suggestions that her visions derived from **mesmerism or **fanaticism (p. 2). The book consists of two sections. The autobiographical section (pp. 3-9) details Ellen White's conversion and first vision and explains her initial reluctance to share the vision. The second section (pp. 9-64) includes short summaries of at least 19 other visions, some of which had been published previously as broadsides or as articles in the **Present Truth* or the **Review and Herald* Extra of July 21, 1851. A **Supplement was issued in 1854.

Further reading: "Ellen White's First Book" in *Legacy of Light CD-ROM*.

SKETCHES FROM THE LIFE OF PAUL (PPPA, RIIPA, 1883, reprint 1974, 334 pp.). This book on the life of Paul, from conversion to martyrdom, was written to assist in the study of the Sabbath school lessons for the second quarter 1883. Some of the content had already appeared in the last two small books of the *Redemption* series on the life of Paul published in 1878. Printed by both the Review and Herald and the Pacific Press (RH, Dec. 26, 1882), it was sold to the public by literature evangelists. A subsequent study has shown that about 12 percent of the content was taken from W. J. Conybeare and J. S. Howson's *The Life and Epistles of St. Paul* (1852), a book recommended to church members by Ellen White (ST, Feb. 22, 1883). In selecting materials from Conybeare and Howson, Ellen White avoided theological concepts not in harmony with what was conveyed to her by revelation. One example of this is Paul's understanding of Christ's second coming in 1 and 2 Thessalonians. Conybeare and Howson held the view that "the early church, and even the apostles themselves, expected their Lord to come again in that very generation. St. Paul himself shared in that expectation" (*The Life and Epistles of St. Paul*, p. 314). In contrast Ellen White wrote, "Paul, however, did not give them [the Thessalonians] the impression that Christ would come in their day.... Paul foresaw that there was danger of his words being misinterpreted" (LP 83, 84). This book was revised and expanded in 1911 to become *The Acts of the Apostles.*

See also: Literary Borrowing.

Further reading: 3Bio 211, 215-217; F. D. Nichol, *Ellen G. White and Her Critics* (RHPA, 1951), pp. 403-467; H. E. Douglass, *Messenger of the Lord* (PPPA, 1998), p. 463, note 9.

Jack Blanco

SKODSBORG SANITARIUM. First European Seventh-day Adventist medical institution established in 1898 in Skodsborg, a suburb of Copenhagen, Denmark, by Dr. *Carl Ottosen (1862-1942). It was sold in 1992. In 1901 Ellen White pleaded with church leaders and laypeople to give adequate financial support to the Skodsborg Sanitarium and the Christiana [Oslo] publishing house in Norway. She felt these Scandinavian institutions were "established for the illustration and promulgation of the principles of reform and Christian living" (6T 464).

Further reading: 6T 463-467; *SDA Encyclopedia* (1996), vol. 11, p. 616.

SLAVERY. Slavery has been called the "peculiar institution" in American history. In 1861 the *Review and Herald*, quoting from the Civil Code of the State of Louisiana, defined it as follows: "A slave is one who is in the power of his master, to whom he belongs. The master may sell him, dispose of his person, his industry, his labor; he can do nothing, possess nothing, acquire nothing, but what must belong to his master" (Law of Louisiana, Civil Code, art. 35, in RH, Oct. 1, 1861). The same writer also quoted from a South Carolina law: "Slaves shall be deemed, sold, taken, reputed, and adjudged in law, to be chattels personal in the hands of their owners and possessors, and their executors, administrators, and assigns, to all intents, purposes, and constructions whatsoever" (*Prince's Digest*, p. 446, in RH, Oct. 1, 1861).

American slaves were legally defined as property. Slaves were not deemed to be persons but property to be bought and sold at the wishes of their masters. Their humanity was disregarded, as they were treated as nonpersons. Their rights were defined in terms of their value as property.

The long and painful saga of Black slavery in America began in 1619 when a Dutch slave trader exchanged a group of Africans for food at Jamestown, Virginia. These first Africans were classified as indentured servants ("A Brief History of Jamestown"). By the 1680s, however, African-American slaves had become essential to the economy of Virginia. Because of the success of tobacco planting, African slavery was legalized in Virginia and Maryland and became the foundation of Southern agrarian economy. In later years African slavery would spread throughout all of the English colonies in North America.

Initially slavery in America was not limited to Blacks. Tens of thousands of Native Americans were also enslaved, but they proved to be unsuitable for the task. Africans eventually came to be the only group enslaved, and they became so intimately identified with slavery that Blackness was directly associated with bondage. American slavery became racial slavery.

As the slave system spread throughout American society, laws proliferated in the various states concerning the conduct of slavery. Americans adopted the harsh and inhuman Roman laws on the treatment of slaves: defined as chattel or movable property, a slave could be branded for trying to escape. A child born of a slave mother was defined as a slave. Slaves could not testify in courts. They were severely punished for minor offenses, and they were treated as nonpersons, having few rights if any at all. All the slave codes made slavery a permanent condition. Many of the state laws made freedom impossible for slaves and even if they were to obtain that freedom the taint of inferiority clung to them as White Americans asserted their superiority over people of African ancestry.

During most of the colonial period slavery received little opposition from White Americans. White America had come to accept a social structure that resorted to harsh and repressive measures to keep the slave system intact.

While Whites fought for freedom for themselves, and proclaimed liberty, freedom, and justice for all men, they used their own freedom to deny the same freedom rights to Blacks.

As the plantation economy developed, there was a continuing demand for more labor. African slaves were the labor of choice because of the Africans' tremendous resiliency and stamina in tropical agriculture. More and more slaves were imported, until in some Southern states they constituted more than 50 percent of the population.

Just when antislavery organizations were on the rise, the invention of the cotton gin in 1793 increased the commercial profitability of cotton. Because cotton growing required intensive labor, slavery was further perceived as a necessity for Southern prosperity. Slave uprisings led by Denmark Vesey and Nat Turner in 1822 and 1831, respectively, created a climate of fear in the South that resulted in the elimination of most antislavery societies from the South, and the imposition of harsh and repressive measures against slaves and free Blacks.

From this milieu emerged political sectionalism in regard to the spread of free or slave states. From the 1830s through the 1860s this debate dominated American politics until it flared up into actual warfare. Through the Underground Railroad many slaves escaped to freedom in the nonslave states or in Canada. In order to appease Southern interests, the federal government sought to close this avenue of escape. The Fugitive Slave Law of 1850 required citizens to assist in the recovery of fugitive slaves, punished those who aided slaves to escape, and denied fugitives the right to a jury trial.

Advocating civil disobedience to this law, Ellen White urged fellow believers to help runaway slaves. "The law of our land requiring us to deliver a slave to his master, we are not to obey; and we must abide the consequences of violating this law," she wrote. "The slave is not the property of any man. God is his rightful master, and man has no right to take God's workmanship into his hands, and claim him as his own" (1T 202).

Ellen White's views on slavery stood in sharp contrast to those of many Americans in the mid-nineteenth century. Her rhetoric against slavery was strong and unequivocal. She repudiated the belief that slaves are the property of their masters (*ibid.* 358), and she affirmed the equality of all regardless of status or birth. "The religion of the Bible recognizes no caste or color. It ignores rank, wealth, worldly honor. God estimates men as men. With Him, character decides their worth. And we are to recognize the Spirit of Christ in whomsoever it is revealed. No one need be ashamed to speak with an honest black man in any place or to shake him by the hand. He who is living in the atmosphere in which Christ lives will be taught of God and will learn to put His estimate on men" (9T 223).

She described pro-slavery sentiments as proceeding from the devil and slavery as an accursed sin in the sight of heaven, even counseling the church to disfellowship members who hold and promote pro-slavery views (1T 358-360). She called slavery a blot upon the nation's history (RH, Dec. 17, 1895) and advocated restitution (RH, Jan. 21, 1896). She indicted those Americans who made no effort to fight against slavery, arguing that even people who took no active part in slavery are responsible to help improve the conditions of Blacks. "Those who have taken no active part in enforcing slavery upon the colored people are not relieved from the responsibility of making special efforts to remove, as far as possible, the sure result of their enslavement" (RH, Jan. 21, 1896).

In proclaiming that Christ died for all people, Ellen White noted that "the Lord has looked with sadness upon that most pitiful of all sights, the colored race in slavery. He desires us, in our work for them, to remember their providential deliverance from slavery, their common relationship to us by creation and by redemption, and their right to the blessings of freedom" (7T 223). Hence, she charged her church to work especially for the oppressed. God "loves them all, and makes no difference between white and black, except that He has a special, tender pity for those who are called to bear a greater burden than others" (2SM 487, 488).

White identified slavery itself, not inferior genetic makeup, as the cause of the deplorable conditions in which Blacks found themselves after the Civil War. "Those who labor in the Southern field will meet with deplorable ignorance. The colored people are *suffering the results of the bondage in which they were held*. When they were slaves, they were taught to do the will of those who called them their property. They were kept in ignorance, and today [1896] there are thousands among them that cannot read.... *The whole system of slavery was originated by Satan, who delights in tyrannizing over human beings*. Though he has been successful in degrading and corrupting the black race, many are possessed of decided ability, and if they were blessed with opportunities, they would show more intelligence than do many of their more favored brethren among the white people. Thousands may now be uplifted, and may become agents by which to help those of their own race. There are many who feel the necessity of becoming elevated, and when faithful teachers open the Scriptures, presenting the truth in its native purity to the colored people, the darkness will be dispelled under the bright beams of the Sun of righteousness. Directed in their search for truth by those who have had advantages enabling them to know the truth, they will become intelligent in the Scriptures" (RH, Jan. 28, 1896; italics supplied).

Questions have arisen concerning Ellen White's predictions concerning a revival of slavery. Careful reading of these statements does not suggest a revival of the institution of slavery as it was in nineteenth-century America. One statement predicts that in the final crisis, "some will be treated as slaves" (GC 608). Here she speaks of the final persecution of the righteous, when their captors will subject them to slavelike conditions, restriction of freedom, oppression, loss of all rights, etc. Without the restraining Spirit of God, evildoers will revert to barbarism and savagery in their treatment of God's people. Her later statement that "many of all nations and of all classes, high and low, rich and poor, black and white, will be cast into the most unjust and cruel bondage" (*ibid.* 626) is analogous with her previous statement. Within the context of persecution against God's people, this "cruel bondage" involves both Blacks and Whites.

Her statement in *Early Writings*, "The last call was carried even to the poor slaves" (EW 278), may be an example of conditional prophecy, describing final events as they would have occurred had the Second Advent occurred before the Emancipation (see *Second Coming of Christ, Delay of). This statement has also been interpreted to indicate the presence of slaves during the last days, suggesting a revival of slavery. Chillingly, despite the end of legally sanctioned slavery in North America, reliable scholars have documented that global slavery is on the rise. An estimated 27 million people worldwide are currently forced to work, under threat of violence, for no pay (Bales, pp. 8, 9). "There are more slaves today [2008] than at any [previous] point in human history" (Skinner, p. xv).

It is abundantly clear that Ellen White hated slavery as a crime against humanity. She repeatedly denounced it and persistently urged her church to reach out in ministry to help ameliorate the condition of the slaves. She indicted the nation for permitting this terrible evil to exist, and held it accountable for reparations to the slaves. She decisively repudiated the prevailing theories on race and affirmed the common humanity of all people.

See also: Race Relations; Civil War.

Further reading: 2Bio 34-53; RH, Dec. 17, 1895; RH, Jan. 21 and 28, 1896; *Southern Work*; 1T 355-368; 7T 220-230; 9T 199-226; "Slavery: Will It Be Revived?" (EGWE, SDoc); K. Bales, *Disposable People: New Slavery in the Global Economy* (Berkeley: University of California Press, 1999); R. Branson, "Ellen G. White—Racist or Champion of Equality?" RH, Apr. 9, 1970, pp. 2, 3; *idem*, "Slavery and Prophecy," RH, Apr. 16, 1970, pp. 7-9; *idem*, "The Crisis of the Nineties," RH, Apr. 23, 1970, pp. 4-6; "A Brief History of Jamestown" (Richmond, Va.: Association for the Preservation of Virginia Antiquities, 2000); N. Coombs, *The Immigrant Heritage of America* (Boston: Twayne Press, 1972); S. DeFord, "How the Cradle of Liberty Became a Slave-owning Nation," Washington *Post*, Dec. 10, 1997, p. 101; E. B. Skinner, *A Crime So Monstrous: Face to Face with Modern-Day Slavery* (New York: Free Press, 2008); T. M. Whitefield, *Slavery Agitation in Virginia, 1829-1932* (New York: Negro Universities Press, 1930).

Trevor O'Reggio

SLAVES, FATE OF LOST. Ellen White regarded the institution of *slavery as an "enormous and grievous sin," a "crime and iniquity" that morally degraded both its victims and its perpetrators (EW 275). Just before the American *Civil War she wrote (1858): "All heaven beholds with indignation human beings, the workmanship of God, reduced by their fellow men to the lowest depths of degradation and placed on a level with the brute creation. Professed followers of that dear Savior whose compassion was ever moved at the sight of human woe, heartily engage in this enormous and grievous sin, and deal in slaves and souls of men. Human agony is carried from place to place and bought and sold. Angels have recorded it all" (*ibid.*).

The passage goes on to mention three groups who were directly involved in the wretched system of slavery. The first group are "pious bondmen and bondwomen" whose "tears" are "all bottled up in heaven," an allusion to their salvation (Ps. 56:8). She describes seeing, at the second coming of Christ, "the pious slave rise in victory and triumph," clearly indicating possession of eternal life (EW 275, 286; cf. EW 278).

The second group mentioned are the perpetrators. "I saw that the slave master will have to answer for the soul of his slave whom he has kept in ignorance; and the sins of the slave will be visited upon the master" (*ibid.* 276). The passage is vivid with expressions of wrath toward the slave masters: "Said the angel, 'The names of the oppressors are written in blood, crossed with stripes, and flooded with agonizing, burning tears of suffering. God's anger will not cease until He has caused this land of light to drink the dregs of the cup of His fury,'" an apparent reference to the coming Civil War (EW 276; cf. RH, Dec. 17, 1895).

The third group mentioned are slaves who had been "kept in ignorance and degradation, knowing nothing of God or the Bible, fearing nothing but [their] master's lash" (EW 276). These "God cannot take to heaven," because in "ignorance" of God and the Bible, with virtually every tie of human

love broken by force, and their moral freedom brutally suppressed, they had become so spiritually and morally disabled that, in terms of their ability to make moral choices, they were in "a lower position than the brutes," i.e., incapable of making a faith response to God (*ibid.*). White did *not* see this spiritual disability being a result of their racial heritage, but only a result of the treatment they had received, for she wrote elsewhere that "many among this race have noble traits of character and keen perception of mind" (RH, Dec. 17, 1895). Their degradation she blamed solely on the fact that "white people" with the "slave master's spirit" viewed Blacks as "no more than beasts," and treated them "worse than the dumb animals because they are in the form of man, having the marks of the black— Negro-race." That is, the oppressors hated the very humanity of the slaves and sought to destroy it (4MR 11, 12). White repeatedly denounced this satanic system and its "horrible" effects, involving physical, mental, moral, and spiritual bondage, as the sole reason for Blacks' lack of advancement (4MR 1-7).

For many of the slaves, this set of circumstances was spiritually fatal, not because of their own choices, but because of a lifetime of demonic treatment imposed on them against their will. In view of the fact that their moral ruin had unfitted them for heaven, what could a just God do? "He does the best thing for [them] that a compassionate God can do. He permits [them] to be as if [they] had not been, while the master must endure the seven last plagues and then come up in the second resurrection and suffer the second, most awful death. Then the justice of God will be satisfied" (EW 276).

Some find it difficult to believe that humans can lose eternal life primarily through the misdeeds of others. But White clearly held that many—of all races—will be eternally lost who might have been saved had those who knew the way of salvation put forth appropriate effort at the right time (ChS 91-93; Ev 63, 656, FW 46). Further, she insisted that the basic set of a person's character, either in submission to God or in rebellion against God, is fixed during this present life (RH, Aug. 25, 1885 [7BC 990]; 3SP 40; ST, May 4, 1888; ST, Aug. 29, 1892). Every action of life contributes to the formation of character (CG 165). Even well-meaning Christian parents may provoke rebellion in their children by unwise exercise of authority (CG 285; ST, May 14, 1894). Actions repeated become habits, habits form character, and character determines destiny (CG 162-164; DA 101; Ed 108, 109). Thus, under a comprehensive system of evil coercion (whether slavery or some other tyranny), many develop characters unfit for heaven, not only by their own choices, but through acts habitually repeated under coercion.

But how can it be fair for one person to lose eternal life because of another's actions? Sin has never been fair. Sins of omission or commission are regularly the cause of people rejecting the gospel. If such persons continue to travel the wrong road, resist opportunities for conversion, and ultimately form characters of settled rebellion against God, the fact that someone else's sin triggered their initial straying will not change the tragic reality that their characters remain out of harmony with God. If they were admitted to heaven, they would not be happy there. "It is no arbitrary decree on the part of God that excludes the wicked from heaven; they are shut out by their own unfitness for its companionship" (SC 18). Her mention of "pious bondmen and bondwomen" who will be saved makes it clear that by no means all who were subjected to the dehumanizing institution of slavery became

demoralized by it. What White seems to be saying in the paragraph under discussion (EW 275, 276) is that those morally and spiritually destroyed by a demonic institution are still objects of God's pity and mercy, and He will not inflict on them additional suffering to no purpose.

Some have objected to the basic idea of "exemption" from the second resurrection. But from White's conditional-immortality, annihilationist perspective, the eventual fate of *all* the lost is to "be as if they had not been" (Obadiah 1:16; cf. Mal. 4:1; Ps. 37:20; Rev. 20:14; 21:8; see also *human nature; *judgments, God's; *wicked, fate of the). In effect, White suggests that for some people, God mercifully allows their first death to be their final one.

While the passage under discussion occurs in the context of White's outrage over slavery, she elsewhere applies the same principles of divine justice and mercy to other cases of doubtful accountability, such as children who die in infancy, and some persons of severe mental disability. Regarding children who die in infancy, she held that many will be saved and some will not be, according to God's love and wisdom, though He has not revealed to humans the precise basis on which He will make those decisions (LDE 293, 294; 8MR 209, 210; 2SM 260). Regarding cases of mental disability, she wrote that "all accountable beings" can understand God's law if they will, but "idiots will not be [held] responsible" (3T 161). In other words, God will not hold "accountable" those who through no fault of their own lack the capacity for accountability. Those who are "not accountable" will not be punished with the accountable wicked in the lake of fire, but if their character—their moral identity—is evil, neither could they be happy in heaven, the reward of the righteous. "It is no arbitrary decree on the part of God that excludes the wicked from heaven; they are shut out by their own unfitness for its companionship" (SC 17, 18).

Further reading: 1SG 191-193, 195, 206; EW 275, 276, 278, 286; RH, Dec. 17, 1895; H. E. Douglass, *Messenger of the Lord* (PPPA, 1998), pp. 489, 490; R. D. Graybill, *Ellen G. White and Race Relations* (RHPA, 1970), pp. 108-114.

Jerry Moon

SOCIAL ISSUES. The century during which Ellen White lived most of her life was one in which American society wrestled with several thorny social issues. With the still-young nation experiencing growing pains, and the world transitioning from an agrarian, rural society to an industrial, urban one, White and the Adventist Church found themselves confronting such social issues as poverty, urbanization (producing congestion, pollution, and overcrowding in cities), the environment, civil rights (of women and other minorities), temperance, and race relations. Ellen White was anything but mute when it came to social issues. In fact, the evidence is clear: she had a "social conscience," and she often spoke out against the injustices and inequities that plagued nineteenth-century American society. She was not afraid to challenge the status quo, even when doing so was unpopular within and without the church. Her perspectives on three daunting social issues of her era are illustrative of those she held on others.

The passion that characterized Ellen White's statements about the Christian's responsibility to the poor approximates that of several Old Testament prophets who were deeply sensitive to the plight of the poor. To warrant her public positions concerning the poor and disadvantaged, White often referenced Amos and Isaiah as well as other prophets. The result is that her book *Welfare Ministry*, alone, contains more than 120 Scripture quotations from 13 Old Testament and 19 New Testament books.

Ellen White refused to accept a simplistic explanation of poverty, holding that it resulted from a myriad of factors. She believed poverty was triggered by disasters, physical illness, misfortune, social injustice, and negligence, and was sometimes in the will of God. She referred to those caught in the throes of poverty as "the Lord's afflicted ones" (6T 277). Yet, whatever the cause of poverty, the poor were to receive ongoing assistance from Christians.

White held that the closest needs should receive the first help: "It is the duty of each church to make careful, judicious arrangements for the care of its poor and sick" (WM 181). Next in priority are the needs of the broader community: "Wherever a church is established its members are to do a faithful work for the needy believers. But they are not to stop there. They are also to aid others, irrespective of their faith" (*ibid.* 180). Finally, Ellen White pointed Christians to the entire world, saying that "any human being who needs our sympathy and our kind offices is our neighbor. The suffering and destitute of all classes are our neighbors. . . . Our neighbors are the whole human family" (*ibid.* 45, 46).

For Ellen White the Christian's responsibility to the poor and needy was not a peripheral matter that might be ignored, or a secondary priority to be preempted by other pressing concerns. When she stated that God's cause is to "take precedence. . . . Then the poor and needy are to be cared for," she was arguing for an accurate understanding of the use of the tithe (*ibid.* 277). Ellen White did not drive a wedge between working on behalf of the poor and the work of the gospel, as though the two are mutually exclusive. She saw the two as complementary, if not synonymous

(6T 276). White identified with the poor, and often extended material assistance to those in need.

Adventists distrustful of the government and the political process have been known to cite Ellen White as one reason for their non-involvement. To be sure, White wrote that even though "the government under which Jesus lived was corrupt and oppressive" "the Savior attempted no civil reforms." Moreover, "He who was our example kept aloof from earthly governments" (DA 509). Yet these statements were never meant to silence Adventists relative to social issues. Instead, they were intended to challenge the immoderate pursuits of the social gospel movement of White's era, pursuits that included the establishment of a perfect society on earth.

Shortly before the death of her husband Ellen White attended a camp meeting at which delegates debated the temperance issue. The result was a resolution urging ministers "to use their influence among our churches and with the people at large to induce them to put forth every consistent effort by personal labor, and at the ballot box, in favor of the prohibitory amendment of the constitution, which the friends of temperance are seeking to secure" (RH, July 5, 1881). Awakened from her sleep one night to respond to some who wanted to delete the phrase "the ballot box," Ellen White dressed and spoke for 20 minutes (Te 255). "'Shall we *vote* for prohibition?' she asked. 'Yes, to a man, everywhere,' she replied, 'and perhaps I shall shock some of you if I say, If necessary, *vote* on the *Sabbath* day for prohibition if you cannot at any other time.'"— In DF 274, "The Des Moines, Iowa, Temperance Experience" (3Bio 160; italics supplied).

Just prior to her death Ellen White reminded Adventists of their responsibility to exercise every influence within their power, including their vote, to work for temperance and virtue.

She asserted that "every voter has some voice in determining what laws shall control the nation," and asked: "Should not that influence and that vote be cast on the side of temperance and virtue?" (RH, Oct. 15, 1914).

The evidence is clear that Ellen White deplored the wrongs in society and challenged Adventists to exercise their right to vote and thus influence the direction the United States was taking on several of these issues. Yet one issue she did not agitate for or lobby on behalf of was the right of women to vote or hold office (3T 565; DG 252).

The society into which Ellen White was born was plagued by the race issue, a perplexing matter over which she struggled and wrote prolifically. On March 21, 1891, Ellen White took the pulpit of the Battle Creek Tabernacle to address the assembled General Conference delegates, beginning a series of pointed admonitions on the race issue.

Ellen White asserted the intrinsic equality of Blacks, saying that in heaven's records the names of Whites are juxtaposed with those of Blacks. Arguing that God's love for His creation knows no division or preference based on race, nationality, or gender, she said that because the soul of the African is as precious in God's sight as that of any of His covenant people of ancient biblical Israel, those who speak ill or harshly of Blacks are guilty of misappropriating the blood of Jesus. White reminded Adventists that contrary to popular practice at the time, there would be no segregated neighborhoods in heaven (SW 11-15, 55).

Ellen White strongly supported the development of indigenous Black leadership, holding that Blacks were intelligent, competent people whose abilities could be honed and sharpened should they be given the same opportunities as Whites. She believed that even though slavery had degraded and corrupted the Black race, many African-Americans possessed "decided ability" and "more intelligence than do many of their more favored brethren among the white people" (RH, Jan. 28, 1896). Even so, White did not condone the penchant among some Blacks of aspiring to preach to White audiences. Believing that such a move was a mistake, she encouraged Black preachers to focus on their own race, saying that such an emphasis would inevitably result in contact with White gatherings, too (SW 15, 16).

Ellen White's counsels on the race issue during the 1890s were consistent with views she had earlier expressed on the subject. White had opposed the Fugitive Slave Law of 1850, which demanded the return of runaway slaves, encouraging church members to disobey the law and suffer the consequences. As the nation was becoming embroiled in its Civil War, White received a watershed vision about slavery. She called slavery a horrible curse and a "high crime," asserting that through the Civil War God would punish the South for perpetuating slavery and the North for allowing it (1T 202, 264). She claimed that slavery had been originated by Satan, and informed the American nation that it owed a "debt of love" to Blacks (RH, Jan. 28, 1896; RH, Jan. 21, 1896).

Notwithstanding her pointed statements condemning slavery and racism, Ellen White did make statements about the race issue that to some come across as contradictory and confusing. For example, while encouraging Whites to work for the rights of Blacks, she cautioned against "fanaticism," and specifically said that interracial marriage should neither be taught nor practiced (SW 15). Furthermore, White seemed to give tacit sanction to "separate but equal" facilities and operations for Blacks, her reasoning ostensibly driven by social realities and private concerns for the growth of the Black work (*ibid.* 15, 16). "In regard to

white and colored people worshiping in the same building, this cannot be followed as a general custom with profit to either party," wrote White, who argued that "the best thing will be to provide the colored people who accept the truth with places of worship of their own." This practice was to be continued until "the Lord shows us a better way" (9T 206, 207). When these statements are read in the context of all that Ellen White said and wrote on the race issue, however, they are seen for what they are—declarations prompted by the expediency and difficulty of the moment.

Nineteenth- and early-twentieth-century social issues, as delicate, complex, divisive, and potentially explosive as some were, did not drive Ellen White to despair or confusion. White decried the lack of progress the United States was making on some of these issues, and generally challenged Adventists to do what they could to bring about a change for the better. She was a veritable social reformer whose conscience prevented her from remaining silent on the social issues of her day.

See also: African-Americans, Adventism Among; Race Relations; Slavery.

Further reading: WM; GW 391-396; 2SM 336, 337; SW; Te; 7T 220-230; 9T 199-226; H. E. Douglass, *Dramatic Prophecies of Ellen White* (PPPA, 2007), pp. 45-57; G. Land, ed., *The World of Ellen G. White* (RHPA, 1987), pp. 47-60; G. R. Knight, *Ellen White's World* (RHPA, 1998).

R. Clifford Jones

SOCIAL MEETING. During most of Ellen White's lifetime Adventist Church members met together weekly for the purpose of conducting a Bible study and social meeting. Rarely was preaching heard in most early Adventist congregations. In the absence of pastors, these Adventists maintained their weekly worship times together without a paid minister to "entertain" them. Instead they practiced what they called "social meetings."

Social meetings appear to be an outgrowth of the early Methodist class meetings instituted by John Wesley. These were meetings during which a layperson led the group and focused on accountability. Ellen White's Methodist upbringing appears to have been the main influence in her strong support of this methodology for nurturing existing Adventists. By the mid-nineteenth century the Methodist class meeting had moved away from the strictness of the early days, but still maintained its emphasis on Christians sharing their life in Christ together.

Ellen White and early Adventists borrowed this concept from the Methodists, made their own innovations, and then advocated it as the primary way for Adventists to sustain the worship of God. As a result Adventists of that day would usually meet together on Sabbath for Bible study (the forerunner of the modern Sabbath school) and for the social meeting. This was the normal way the church worshipped in the absence of settled pastors (J. Hoffer, in RH, July 2, 1861).

These early Adventists did not feel they needed two cognitively oriented worship experiences on Sabbath morning. Instead the Bible study or Sabbath school served to meet their cognitive needs, while the social meeting served to meet their emotional/spiritual needs. Thus the social meetings referred to by Ellen White were not primarily Bible studies, but meetings during which believers shared with each other their spiritual journeys.

These occurred in almost all early Adventist gatherings. In addition to the local church, social meetings were conducted during evangelistic meetings, camp meetings (ST, May 17, 1883), and even General Conference sessions, during which they divided into smaller groups (RH, Nov. 12, 1889). It was by meeting often in this setting that the believers developed close ties and a strong trust in each other. This mutual trust and recognition that they were traveling together toward the kingdom enabled them to confront each other in love when they saw a fellow believer not living correctly. This was done without malice as a tool to hold each other accountable for their life in Christ.

Understanding the early Adventist social meeting helps one understand the many times Ellen White would openly reveal the sins of a fellow believer in a social meeting. Such openness is so strange to twenty-first-century Christians that her testimonies appear to be an invasion of privacy. Yet seen in the context of the community that existed in the Adventist circles of that time, they appear to be one more indication of the mutual trust of early Adventists.

What occurred during these social meetings? The content seems to have varied. Many times they appear to be like a testimony service, yet not dry and boring (FW 82). There were short testimonies—sometimes more than 100 occurred within an hour. Other times they openly addressed sin in a fellow believer or confronted people with attitude problems, such as at the 1888 General Conference session, where a breakthrough in attitude occurred in a social meeting at 5:30 a.m. (1888 Materials 284).

Social meetings were the expected activity when the church members gathered together. They happened in almost all Adventist churches. The Battle Creek church had the benefit of several of the church's clergy living in Battle Creek, so had the "blessing" of a sermon most of the time. Yet there were times that all the preachers would be gone from Battle Creek, and the church had to have a social meeting instead of a sermon. They usually reported that they were much better off spiritually as a result (RH, July 22, 1862).

When Ellen White went to Europe in 1885, she discovered that the European church had been started without conducting social meetings. She traveled throughout Europe showing these European Adventists how they were to do church the Adventist way—not with sermons, but in social meetings (16MR 251). J. N. Loughborough, in describing how to form a new Adventist church, suggests that a church should not be organized immediately after people accept the Adventist message, but instead the group of new believers should first meet and participate in social meetings to build social-spirited relationships. Only when they had begun to know each other in the social meeting would they be organized into an Adventist church (*The Church: Its Organization, Order, and Discipline* [PPPA, 1906], p. 126).

Social meetings were so critical to the Adventist way of life that one element of Ellen White's definition of a Christian is one who is active in social meetings (7BC 935). Social meetings were a vital part of the mutual care that early Adventists shared during the nineteenth and early twentieth centuries. Eventually they degenerated into the prayer meeting, and their original intent was lost. The modern small-group movement is an attempt to restore the relational element that existed in the early Adventist social meeting.

See also: Ministry.

Further reading: R. Burrill, *Recovering an Adventist Approach to Life and Mission in the Local Church* (Hart, 1998); R. Burrill, *The Revolutionized Church of the 21st Century* (Hart, 1997).

Russell Burrill

SOLEMN APPEAL RELATIVE TO SOLITARY VICE AND ABUSES AND EXCESSES OF THE MARRIAGE RELATION, A (RHPA, 1870, 272 pp.). Book edited by James White including

articles from several authors, some Adventist and some non-Adventist. Portions were written by James White and five sections by Ellen White. The overall theme of *A Solemn Appeal* deals with sexual morality and sinful behavior. Thinking that some of his readers may have felt the subject was approached too openly and bluntly, James White pointed out in the preface that personal feelings must be put aside "to call attention to those sins of youth, and the abuses and excesses, even in the married life, which are ruining the souls and bodies of tens of thousands" (p. 3). The first of the sections written by Ellen White (pp. 49-80) is a reprint of *An Appeal to Mothers* on the physical, mental, and moral effects of masturbation. Her second section (pp. 102-139) is a reprint of her second article in *Health: or How to Live*. It deals with sexuality between husband and wife, causes for unhappy marriages, differences in age of partners, and responsibilities of husbands and wives in regard to family activities and raising of children. Ellen White's third section (pp. 140-147) deals with obedience to the law of God and addresses the evils of lust, fornication, and adultery. The fourth section (pp. 147-157) contains instructions on female modesty and the avoidance of evil in dress and behavior. The last section is titled "Sentimentalism" and considers the evils of lust and inappropriate sexual passions. The last three of these sections were drawn from an article titled "An Appeal to the Church," found in *Testimonies for the Church*, volume 2 (pp. 439-489). Ellen White supervised some editorial changes to the original article in *Testimonies* before republishing it in this volume. Parts of *A Solemn Appeal* were later republished in *The Adventist Home* (pp. 99-128), *Child Guidance* (pp. 439-468), and *Selected Messages* (book 2, pp. 420-440).

SOLUSI MISSION. Established in 1894, some 32 miles (51 kilometers) west of Bulawayo, Zimbabwe, its direct relation to Ellen G. White stems from a controversy about its founding.

The General Conference session of 1893 accepted the recommendation of Pieter Wessels of South Africa that the church accept a free offer of land in Mashonaland from the British South Africa Company for African missions. Subsequently, Wessels and A. T. Robinson visited Cecil John Rhodes, prime minister of Cape Colony and chair of the company, and asked for a grant of land. Rhodes handed them a sealed letter to give to Dr. Leander Starr Jameson, Rhodes' representative in Bulawayo. In Bulawayo they met with Dr. Jameson and discovered that Rhodes had told Jameson to give them all the land they could use. They asked for 12,000 acres (4,860 hectares), which cost $60 a year, about 32 miles (51 kilometers) west of Bulawayo. This land became known as the Solusi Mission Project.

In Battle Creek, Michigan, this news was received with mixed emotions. Some saw in it a financial blessing. Others saw it as a violation of the separation of church and state. A. T. Jones, editor of the *American Sentinel,* and others opposed such gifts, as well as tax exemption for church or other ecclesiastical property. Adventist leaders in South Africa argued that the land gift was from the South Africa land company and not from the colonial government; hence the Solusi Mission Project did not violate the separation of church and state. Jones, however, disagreed, equating the company with the colonial government, and he published his views in the *Sentinel.*

The consensus in Battle Creek was that the land should be purchased, not received as a gift, but S. N. Haskell, then in South Africa, wrote to W. C. White, seeking advice from his mother, E. G. White, who was with him in Australia (4Bio 183-186).

Haskell's letter was read to Ellen White by W. C. White on January 30, 1895. Her reply to Haskell consisted of 14 pages (Lt 11, 1895, in 16MR 157-170). The first seven pages dealt with the question of unkind and sharp thrusts in denominational papers, such as had appeared in the *American Sentinel.* The last seven pages dealt with the question of the land grant as well as actions that had been taken on tax exemption. Copies of this letter were sent to F. M. Wilcox at the Foreign Mission Board and to O. A. Olsen, General Conference president, and later that year most of it was published in a pamphlet entitled *Special Instruction to Ministers and Workers.*

In the matter of receiving gifts from government leaders, Ellen White raised the question as to who is the real owner of the world, of houses and lands. God, of course. She stated that God has placed wealth in the hands of men to feed the hungry, to clothe the naked, and to house the homeless. The Lord moves upon the hearts of worldly men, even idolaters, to give of their abundance for the support of the work. We should approach them wisely and give them the privilege of contributing to God's cause, at the same time not sacrificing one principle of truth, while taking advantage of every opportunity to advance the cause of God (16MR 163).

She further stated that the movements being made in Battle Creek to "pay taxes on the property of the Sanitarium and Tabernacle have manifested a zeal and conscientiousness that in all respects is not wise or correct. Their ideas of religious liberty are being interwoven with suggestions that do not come from the Holy Spirit," she wrote. She was distressed to see leading men taking positions that were extreme and burdening themselves over matters that should not be taken up or worried over, but left in the hands of God for Him to adjust (*ibid.* 167, 168).

As the result of this counsel, the Foreign Mission Board voted to approve the acquisition of the land under certain broad principles, not including purchase.

From the opening of the elementary school in 1897, Solusi expanded to include secondary classes (1948) and college degrees (1954), and in 1994 received full accreditation as Solusi University.

Further reading: V. Robinson, *The Solusi Story* (RHPA, 1979); R. W. Schwarz, F. Greenleaf, *Light Bearers*, rev. ed. (PPPA, 2000), pp. 218, 219; E. Syme, *A History of SDA Church-State Relations in the United States* (PPPA, 1979); "Spirit of Prophecy Counsels Relating to Church-State Relationships" (EGWE, 2000, SDoc); L. F. Swanepoel, *The Origin and Early History of the Seventh-day Adventist Church in South Africa* (M.A. thesis, University of South Africa, 1972), pp. 66-77.

G. Ralph Thompson

SONS AND DAUGHTERS OF GOD (RHPA, 1955, 383 pp.). Fourth daily devotional book published by the Ellen G. White Estate. Materials selected for these meditations were drawn from Ellen White's published and unpublished writings. A special effort was made to select messages first addressed to young people in the *Youth's Instructor*. The selections were organized in different monthly topics emphasizing what it means for the Christian to be a child of God and how one can live a meaningful Christian life. The overall theme of the book is summarized in a quotation from Ellen White on the title page. She believed that "those who . . . connect their souls with God are acknowledged by Him as His sons and daughters" (4T 624).

SOUTH LANCASTER ACADEMY. Forerunner of Atlantic Union College. The central Massachusetts school that became South Lancaster Academy opened on April 19, 1882. *Stephen N. Haskell, the leading founder, corresponded frequently with Ellen White before and after the opening of the school, which was incorporated as South Lancaster Academy in 1883.

ACADEMY HALL AT SOUTH LANCASTER ACADEMY. BUILT IN 1884, IT IS THE OLDEST ADVENTIST EDUCATIONAL BUILDING IN CURRENT USE.

Ellen White first visited the school in the summer of 1883. Later that year she helped to raise funds to provide permanent facilities for the school and personally bought SLA stock. In the mid-1880s she stopped to see the new buildings that her investment had helped to make possible. One of her most memorable visits was in January 1889. Joining *Alonzo T. Jones in a revival series, she preached to the academy students and others about salvation by faith.

Between visits to South Lancaster Academy, Ellen White conferred with and corresponded with leaders of the academy, including principals *Goodloe Harper Bell and *Charles C. Ramsay, as well as Haskell. In those conferences and letters, as well as in her published writings and public presentations relating to the institution, Ellen White emphasized the importance of a broad, balanced education and sympathetic governance of the school.

After leaving for *Australia in 1891, Ellen White was not intensely involved in the affairs of SLA, although she would visit again following her return to the United States (1901).

Further reading: M. F. Wehtje, *And There Was Light: A History of South Lancaster Academy, Lancaster Junior College, and Atlantic Union College* (South Lancaster, Mass.: Atlantic Press, 1982).

Myron F. Wehtje

SOUTHERN MISSIONARY SOCIETY. Organization formed by J. Edson White in 1896 and incorporated in 1898, as an umbrella for his rapidly expanding work in the American South. The first president of the SMS was Edson White. Its first headquarters was on the *Morning Star* at Yazoo City, Mississippi, but eventually settled in Nashville, Tennessee. While the SMS was recognized by the General Conference as the agency largely responsible for the work of the church among African-Americans, it was largely a self-supporting work, carried on with approval of church leaders, but with minimal direct financial support.

The society's mission was "to carry the principles of Christian education to the people of the South" (GH, December 1899, p. 105). In 1896 Edson White was already operating four schools, with 10 teachers, and had requests to open three more schools. By 1908 the SMS administered 28 mission schools, with a combined enrollment of almost 1,000 students. Among other enterprises sponsored by the SMS were the Dixie Health Food Company, the Gospel Herald Publishing Company (forerunner of Southern Publishing Association), and the *Nashville Colored Sanitarium (1901-1903), which was replaced by the *Rock City Sanitarium in 1909.

In 1906, when Edson White retired, the SMS was attached to the Southern Union Conference and became responsible for the Black work in all the territory south of and including Kentucky and east of the Mississippi River, except the Oakwood Industrial School (now Oakwood University). In 1918 the SMS was absorbed into the Southern Union Mission, the forerunner of the present South Central and South Atlantic conferences.

Further reading: 5Bio 39, 189-197, 257, 258; R. D. Graybill, *Mission to Black America* (PPPA, 1971); R. S. Norman III, "Salvation and Social Action: Edson White's Southern Work Remembered," *Adventist World-NAD*, February 2008, p. 25; A. Robinson, "James Edson White: Innovator," in *Early Adventist Educators*, ed. G. R. Knight (AUP, 1983), p. 153; *SDA Encyclopedia* (1996), vol. 11, pp. 672-674.

Jerry Moon

SOUTHERN PUBLISHING ASSOCIATION. Adventist publishing house operated in Nashville, Tennessee, 1901-1980. A major part of James Edson White's evangelistic activities in the southern United States was the publication and distribution of books, some written for use in adult literacy education. In 1900 his Southern Missionary Society (SMS) set up printing facilities on a Nashville, Tennessee, estate rented by Louis A. Hansen to house his treatment-room staff. By December of that year the SMS had bought a two-story brick store at 1025 Jefferson Street, and the Herald Publishing Company moved there in March 1901. The Southern Publishing Association incorporated on June 4, 1901, as a stock company with capital stock of $25,000. Ellen White visited its site during that spring and several times afterward. Appeals in the *Review and Herald* during the summer raised enough money for the publishing institution to construct a larger building adjoining the original building.

Unfortunately the publishing house fell

$24,000 in debt despite soliciting commercial work, and it struggled with worn-out equipment. A General Conference committee including A. G. Daniells investigated the situation and recommended selling the equipment for junk and reducing the operation to a depository for the Review and Herald Publishing Association. But the committee wondered how Ellen White would react, since her son managed it. She had urged the church institutions to avoid debt and refrain from doing commercial work. Daniells took the report to her on October 19, 1902. Although deeply perplexed and sorely grieved by the loss, she reluctantly agreed that the publishing house be closed and her son Edson devote himself to the ministry and to writing. "I want [the committee] to act just as they would act if my son were not there" (Ms 123, 1902, in 17MR 270).

Before the committee could follow through with its decision, however, Ellen White received a series of visions. In one of them she found herself in the operating room of a large hospital. A voice said never to amputate a limb until everything possible had been done to save it. Then she seemed to be in a meeting in which E. R. Palmer, then secretary of the General Conference Publishing Department, urged that all denominational publishing be done by one institution to reduce expense. In response, another voice pointed out the danger of such consolidation. The vision also told her that SPA's situation had not been "correctly represented" and that she herself "had spoken unadvisedly" when she agreed to the closure (Lt 208, 1902, in SpM 282). She let her desire to avoid the appearance of favoring her son sway her decision. The Southern states should have their own publishing facility (Lt 162, 1902, in PM 193).

Although stunned by her change of mind, Daniells compared the situation to that of

Nathan receiving a vision after he had approved David's plan to build a temple in Jerusalem (1 Chron. 17:1-5). Even as they struggled to understand how to reconcile her new decision with her calls to avoid debt, and especially the meeting with her at Elmshaven, the General Conference president and the rest of the committee began to work to change SPA's financial condition.

The publishing house bought a seven-acre tract from Edson White on 24th Avenue North, constructed a new plant, and put into effect a series of reforms. By 1907 SPA was financially viable. It survived for 80 years. In 1980, as part of a series of mergers in the North American Division, SPA was absorbed into the Review and Herald.

Further reading: 5Bio 189-197; A. G. Daniells, *The Abiding Gift of Prophecy* (PPPA, 1936), pp. 322-329; L. A. Hansen, *From So Small a Dream* (SPA, 1968), pp. 101-106; *SDA Encyclopedia* (1996), vol. 11, pp. 677-680.

Gerald Wheeler

SOUTHERN WORK, THE (published by J. Edson White, 1898, 1901; RHPA, 1966, 96 pp.). The initial document in this compilation, "Our Duty to the Colored People," was an appeal from Ellen G. White to 30 Seventh-day Adventist leaders on March 21, 1891, at the General Conference session in Battle Creek, Michigan. Ellen White sought to stir the church to evangelistic and educational efforts on behalf of Southern Blacks who lacked the literacy necessary for Bible study. Discarded copies of this sermon, produced as a 16-page pamphlet, were "discovered" by Edson White in 1893. In response to its message, he and W. O. Palmer built a paddle-wheel steamboat, the *Morning Star,* and began work among Blacks in Vicksburg, Mississippi, in January 1895. Edson White, struggling to finance his missionary efforts in the face of limited denominational support, used publications such as *The Southern Work* to raise funds and recruit missionaries for the Southern field. In addition to "Our Duty to the Colored People," it contained nine articles, written by Ellen White from Australia and published in the *Review and Herald* between November 26, 1895, and February 4, 1896. The first article in the *Review and Herald* series, "Work Among the Colored People," published April 2, 1895, was apparently overlooked by Edson White, for it did not appear in either the 1898 or 1901 editions of *The Southern Work*. It is included in the 1966 edition. The 1898 edition, a 115-page booklet, also contained a letter to A. O. Tait, "Proper Methods of Work in the Southern Field" (Lt 73, 1895, in SW 72-78), and a manuscript, "Words of Precaution Regarding Sunday Labor" (Ms 22a, 1895, in SW 66-71).

In 1901 Edson White compiled additional letters and manuscripts by Ellen White regarding the work in the South into a supplement to *The Southern Work*. First circulated as a separate document, it was paged to follow the 1898 edition of *The Southern Work,* and subsequently bound to the original document, making a 147-page publication. Not until 1966 did the Review and Herald Publishing Association issue the first official edition of *The Southern Work* in response to long-standing requests. It contains all the material in the 1898 and 1901 editions, and includes the overlooked *Review and Herald* article from April 2, 1895.

Ellen White's intent in the original document, "Our Duty to the Colored People," was to enunciate guiding biblical principles regarding the church's response to the "color line." The following themes, in summary, pervade *The Southern Work*. God values each soul based on the infinite price paid for his or her salvation, not on race, class, rank, or caste; humans should not draw lines of distinction based on these factors. Slavery, an evil originated by Satan, was used by Whites to degrade the Black race and rob them of their time and education. Emancipation gave America an opportunity to repay the debt owed to Blacks by providing educational and material assistance. White compared the experience of Blacks with the Hebrew enslavement by the Egyptians and their subsequent liberation. While other denominations entered the Southern field to provide education for freed Blacks, the Seventh-day Adventist Church neglected this responsibility to the extent that the work had become difficult. Over time the prejudice of Southern Whites made the mixed worship of Blacks and Whites, initially encouraged by White, inadvisable because it might imperil workers' lives. White advised against establishing a colony of Black believers and White workers in the South, and explained that Sabbath observance did not require Sunday labor, a practice that incited Southern prejudice against Adventists (SW 66-71). She encouraged self-sacrifice on the part of missionary families who would teach Blacks to read the Bible, engage in various trades, and build houses and schools. Many Blacks possessed superior intellectual capacities and, if educated, could work effectively for others of their race. White directed that resources from fields already established be devoted to the great needs of the Southern field, and decried the misappropriation to other purposes of funds intended for the Southern field. She described this practice as poor stewardship.

The first two editions of *The Southern Work* were produced in the context of the progressive national retreat from the policies of Reconstruction that began as early as 1877 and continued through the beginning of the twentieth century. During this period the political and social stance of the nation regarding Black Americans underwent significant change; however, the implicit notion of inherent Black inferiority, the "color line," remained a pervasive aspect of White national consciousness. Although important legislation following the Civil War sought to establish a new social and political order for Blacks, by 1877 the Republican Party withdrew its support for civil rights, initiating a period of disfranchisement, victimization, and violence against Blacks. Legal restrictions against Black male suffrage began in Mississippi in 1890, and in the Southern states the new segregated social arrangement known as "Jim Crow" was legislated, modified, and expanded up until the 1950s. Segregation was given its most significant support by the Supreme Court's *Plessy* v. *Ferguson* decision of 1896 that established the "separate but equal" doctrine in public facilities and allowed states to use police power to enforce segregation law.

Edson White's work on the *Morning Star* was conducted under the threat and actuality of arson and violence to workers, necessitating extreme caution in relationships between Blacks and Whites. The growing problem of White prejudice explains the growing cautionary tone in Ellen White's statements over time.

After the 1901 edition of *The Southern Work* went out of print, Ellen White's 1909 testimony on race relations (9T 199-226) was taken out of historical context by some. This misunderstanding, compounded with the absence of an official publication of *The Southern Work* until 1966, led many Black members to be suspicious of the church and even to make charges of racism against Ellen White. To the contrary, it was in view of racial attitudes and tensions of the time that she had urged caution in race relations, especially in the South, "until the Lord shows us a better way" (*ibid.* 206, 207).

The period between 1909 and 1966 was marked by a growing separation of White and Black members at the local church level and the eventual organization of Black conferences beginning in the 1940s. The racial integration of church educational and health institutions did not begin until the 1950s, and many were still segregated as late as the 1960s. The first official publication of *The Southern Work* in 1966 took place at the height of the civil rights movement in America.

The Southern Work represents another attempt by Ellen White to reconcile the real and the ideal in addressing one of the central issues of her time. It gives a picture of someone struggling to apply the gospel in a real-life situation. In context she addresses the church during a period of resurgent institutional racism enforced by violence. She calls the church to service for "the least of these." Her premise was simple but profound: God is the Father of all; enslavement and its aftermath was part of Satan's plot to degrade and destroy all of humankind; Christ died to deliver sinners; and the body of Christ must do His work compassionately, serving all humanity in spite of circumstances and consequences. Ellen White recognized that particular situations would demand modification of approach, but she did not compromise the essential principle: all humanity is created in the image of God, and the good news of salvation through Jesus Christ alone must go to all.

Further reading: C. Crowe, ed., *The Age of Civil War and Reconstruction, 1830-1900: A Book of Interpretative Essays* (Homewood, Ill.: Dorsey Press, 1966); T. E. Frazier, ed., *Afro-American History: Primary Sources* (New York: Harcourt, Brace & World, 1970); R. E. Graham, *Ellen G. White, Co-Founder of the Seventh-day Adventist Church* (New York: P. Lang, 1985); R. D. Graybill, *Mission to Black America: The True Story of Edson White and the Riverboat Morning Star* (PPPA, 1971);

N. K. Miles, "Tension Between the Races," in G. Land, ed., *The World of Ellen G. White* (RHPA, 1987), pp. 47-60; A. L. White, "Survey of the E. G. White Writings Concerning the Racial Question" (1961, DF 42); C. Vann Woodward, *The Strange Career of Jim Crow*, 2nd rev. ed. (New York: Oxford University Press, 1966).

Gregory J. Allen

SPALDING AND MAGAN'S UNPUBLISHED MANUSCRIPT TESTIMONIES OF ELLEN G. WHITE (A. W. Spalding and Percy T. Magan, 1915-1916, 498 pp.). Compilation of heretofore-unpublished letters and manuscripts of Ellen White taken from the private collections of *E. A. Sutherland, *Percy T. Magan, *David Paulson, *O. A. Johnson, and *A. W. Spalding. Often referred to as the *Spalding-Magan Collection*, this compilation contains numerous testimonies of Ellen White written mainly from 1892 to 1915 and addressing a variety of subjects pertaining to the Adventist work in the southern United States, educational reform, and health-care institutions. The collection was published shortly after Ellen White's death.

SPECIAL TESTIMONIES, SERIES A AND B. Two series of pamphlets consisting of various counsels Ellen White wrote between 1892 and 1913. While she lived in Australia (1891-1900), she addressed many letters of counsel to O. A. Olsen, president of the General Conference (1888-1897), and to other church leaders in Battle Creek. These letters had to do mainly with the work of pastors, the standards of ministry, and the general welfare of the church. As Olsen received these letters, he sensed that the materials would be of real service to other ministers and arranged to have them printed in small pamphlets. Eleven of such pamphlets were published during the

1890s, and most were called "Special Testimonies for Ministers and Workers." Each of these pamphlets, after the first, had a number, and the later numbers carried the title *Special Testimonies, Series A*. These were circulated free of charge. (Number 12 of the series, published in 1905, was a testimony related to the medical work.) Most of this series was republished in 1923 in *Testimonies to Ministers and Gospel Workers*.

Special Testimonies, Series B, is a second series of 19 pamphlets written by Ellen White after she returned from Australia (1903-1913). These pamphlets dealt with various issues and local concerns. Portions of these pamphlets with more permanent interest and value have been incorporated in such volumes as *Testimonies for the Church*, volumes 8 and 9, *Counsels on Health*, *Testimonies to Ministers and Gospel Workers*, *Counsels on Stewardship*, and *Selected Messages*.

Further reading: EGWE, *Notes and Papers Concerning Ellen G. White and the Spirit of Prophecy*, pp. 304-310.

SPECIAL TESTIMONIES ON EDUCATION (1897, 240 pp.). Compilation of Ellen White's instruction on Christian education written between 1893 and 1896, subsequent to the publication of *Christian Education* (1893). Nearly all of *Special Testimonies on Education* was later republished in *Counsels to Teachers, Parents, and Students* (1913) and in *Fundamentals of Christian Education* (1923).

SPIRIT OF PROPHECY. Ellen White used the phrase "Spirit of Prophecy" in several ways, all derived from Revelation 19:10, "The testimony of Jesus is the spirit of prophecy." The Spirit of Prophecy is first the Spirit of God, who inspired the prophets and who speaks through the Scripture. "It was Christ that spoke to His people through the prophets.

The apostle Peter, writing to the Christian church, says that the prophets 'prophesied of the grace that should come unto you: searching what, or what manner of time the *Spirit of Christ* which was in them did signify, when it testified beforehand the sufferings of Christ and the glory that should follow.' 1 Peter 1:10, 11. It is the voice of Christ that speaks to us through the Old Testament. 'The testimony of Jesus is the spirit of prophecy.' Revelation 19:10" (PP 366, 367). Following Peter's insights, she applied the phrase to the Spirit that impressed Enoch, who "faithfully rehearsed to the people all that had been revealed to him by the spirit of prophecy" (ST, Feb. 20, 1879; cf. SR 59). In describing Jacob's parting words to his sons, she said that "God by the spirit of prophecy elevated the mind of Jacob above his natural feelings" (3SG 172). In the New Testament, aged Simeon, "just and devout," cradled the infant Jesus in his arms and "the spirit of prophecy was upon this man of God" (DA 55; Luke 2:25-32). Silas, Paul's faithful companion, "was a tried worker, gifted with the spirit of prophecy" (AA 203). Hence, the Agent who inspires the human prophet to tell the truth about God and Jesus is the Holy Spirit—the "Spirit" of prophecy: "The Holy Ghost is the author of the Scriptures and of the Spirit of Prophecy. These are not to be twisted and turned to mean what man may want them to mean, to carry out man's ideas and sentiments, to carry forward man's schemes at all hazards" (3SM 30).

In another sense, "the Spirit of prophecy" is also the testimony *about* Christ, the chief purpose for the gift of prophecy is indeed the story of Jesus Christ, the core theme of the gospel, and has always been the message of those who were given the spirit of prophecy. Ellen White's own ministry is marked by her intense devotion to Jesus about whom she wrote with remarkable sensitivity and insight.

Millions of people have opened their lives to Jesus as they read her messages about Him and messages from Him such as found in *The Desire of Ages* and *Steps to Christ*. By extension also, she entitled her four-volume set (produced between 1870 and 1884) that embraced the *great controversy theme from the beginning of sin to the new earth—*The Spirit of Prophecy*.

Because of the circumstances surrounding her visions, from the first when she was 17 to her last in her 80s, Ellen White was convinced that God had been using her as His messenger and thus applied the phrase "Spirit of prophecy" to her own ministry and writings. The powerful witness of her messages, especially personal ones, became a source of immense confidence to a growing world church. For that reason she was bold to defend her role as God's messenger, even though she did not "claim" the specific title *prophet. As in biblical times, not everyone could be persuaded that even Jesus was who He said He was. At times she had to be candid, as, for example, in this letter, written in 1906 and quoting an 1882 article: "Yet now when I send you a testimony of warning and reproof, many of you declare it to be merely the opinion of Sister White. You have thereby insulted the Spirit of God. You know how the Lord has manifested Himself through the Spirit of prophecy. Past, present, and future have passed before me. I have been shown faces that I had never seen, and years afterward I knew them when I saw them. I have been aroused from my sleep with a vivid sense of subjects previously presented to my mind and I have written, at midnight, letters that have gone across the continent, and arriving at a crisis, have saved great disaster to the cause of God. This has been my work for many years. A power has impelled me to reprove and rebuke wrongs that I had not thought of" (1SM 27).

And from material written in 1907: "A wealth of moral influence has been brought to us in the last half century. Through His Holy Spirit the voice of God has come to us continually in warning and instruction, to confirm the faith of the believers in the Spirit of prophecy. Repeatedly the word has come, Write the things that I have given you to confirm the faith of My people in the position they have taken. Time and trial have not made void the instruction given, but through years of suffering and self-sacrifice have established the truth of the testimony given. The instruction that was given in the early days of the message is to be held as safe instruction to follow in these its closing days" (*ibid.* 41).

Ellen White's relentless commitment to fulfill her role as God's messenger cannot be separated from the history and development of the Seventh-day Adventist Church. Many have been her contemporaries who have endorsed her timeless counsel. *J. A. Burden summarized these formative years in the introduction to *Loma Linda Messages*: "The question naturally arises: Whence comes this wisdom revealed through this gift, which is more than the combined wisdom of all the church besides? As the message developed and grew, it was this gift that urged the extension of the work, and from that day to this has done more than all other influences combined to push the message into the regions beyond. In every development of the message—evangelical, education, medical, and publishing, the spirit of prophecy has not only led the way, but given light on how to conduct these different departments in such a way as to bring success in the spread of the message. Again and again as the wisdom of men has failed and the work became hedged about or tangled up in any of its departments, the wisdom of this gift has always been shown in setting it free. The clear-cut missionary policy laid out for all departments of this great work by the spirit of prophecy in contrast with the mercenary policy oft times worked into it by men to whom the care and keeping of the message has been entrusted shows that the wisdom of this gift is from above" (LLM 34). So long as branches need the trunk, so security and strength will be found in the enduring value of her writings. In 1907 Ellen White wrote: "Whether or not my life is spared, my writings will constantly speak, and their work will go forward as long as time shall last. My writings are kept on file in the office, and even though I should not live, these words that have been given to me by the Lord will still have life and will speak to the people" (1SM 55).

Herbert E. Douglass

SPIRIT OF PROPHECY, THE (RHPA, 1870-1884; reprint 1969). Four-volume set of Ellen White's writings on the *great controversy between Christ and Satan. After receiving her *great controversy vision in 1858, Ellen White wrote extensively on the biblical theme of the struggle between good and evil. Her first account appeared in 1858 in *Spiritual Gifts*, volume 1. In its 219 pages this volume spans the story from the fall of Lucifer to the end of the millennium but omits almost all references to the Old Testament history, which was supplied in volumes 3 and 4 (1864).

The four-volume *Spirit of Prophecy* series provided for the growing church a much more detailed presentation of the great controversy story in 1,700 pages. In time this series was replaced by the still further expanded five-volume and 3,700-page *Conflict of the Ages Series. While the title page of each of the four books carries a double title—*The Spirit of Prophecy* and *The Great Controversy Between Christ and Satan*—in the early years the covers might be stamped with either of the two.

Today, to avoid confusion with the well-known and currently circulated fifth volume of the Conflict of the Ages Series, *The Great Controversy*, the White Estate uses the distinctive *Spirit of Prophecy* title in referring to each of these four books.

The Spirit of Prophecy, volume 1, bears the second title, *The Great Controversy Between Christ and His Angels and Satan and His Angels* (1870, 414 pp.), and covers the biblical story from the fall of Satan to the construction of Solomon's Temple. This volume also contains a brief introduction on the biblical gift of prophecy written by James White (pp. 7-16). The content of volume 1 was an expansion of *Spiritual Gifts*, volumes 3 and 4, and was later expanded to become *Patriarchs and Prophets* (1890).

The Spirit of Prophecy, volumes 2, 3, and 4, also bear the title *The Great Controversy Between Christ and Satan,* but have a different subtitle. Volume 2, *Life, Teachings and Miracles of Our Lord Jesus Christ* (1877, 396 pp.), covers the life of Christ from His birth to His riding into Jerusalem. Volume 3, *The Death, Resurrection and Ascension of Our Lord Jesus Christ* (1878, 442 pp.), covers Christ's ministry in Jerusalem to the martyrdom of Paul and Peter. (The first printing of this volume contained only 392 pages; five chapters were added by the author to the second printing.) In the 1880s, while Ellen White was in Europe, volumes 2 and 3 formed the basis for the publication of a book that was published only in European languages (Danish-Norwegian, Swedish, German, French, Finnish) under the title *The Life of Christ*. The desire for an English publication of this book led Ellen White to revise and expand its content into what became known as *The Desire of Ages* (1898). The section of volume 3 on the apostles Peter and Paul was expanded first into *Sketches From the Life of Paul* (1883) and later into *The Acts of the Apostles* (1911).

Volume 4, *From the Destruction of Jerusalem to the End of the Controversy* (1884, 506 pp.), relates the working of the great controversy during the dispensation of the Christian church until the end of time. This volume was the first to be expanded by Ellen White to form the fifth volume of the Conflict of the Ages Series. While traveling in Europe (1885-1887), Ellen White visited many sites of the Protestant Reformation and received many historical insights that she wished to include in a revised and expanded version of this volume. This revision is now known as *The Great Controversy*. First published in 1888, it was again revised in 1911.

Denis Fortin

SPIRIT OF PROPHECY CORRESPONDENCE COURSE, see **PROPHETIC GUIDANCE CORRESPONDENCE COURSE.**

SPIRITISM, see **SPIRITUALISM.**

SPIRITUAL GIFTS. One of the clearest and most extensive discussions of spiritual gifts by Ellen White is found in her presentation of Jesus' parable of the talents (Matt. 25:13-30). Here she appears to distinguish two types of gifts. First, Ellen White considers those talents—"gifts of the Holy Spirit"—which Christ imparts to the church as representing "especially the gifts and blessings imparted by the Holy Spirit" (COL 327). These may be understood as purely spiritual in nature. On the other hand, there are other talents, natural or acquired, which, upon surrendering to God, "He returns to us purified and ennobled, to be used for His glory in blessing our fellow men" (*ibid.* 328).

From the perspective of these two types of spiritual gifts, Ellen White's account of gifts extends to include those, such as ready speaking and writing, singing, and the power to explain God's Word, that are not usually found in such scriptural lists as 1 Corinthians 12:28-31; Romans 12:6-8; Ephesians 4:11, 12; and 1 Peter 4:11. Although no one person receives all the gifts, some are imparted to each believer, including even the poorest and most ignorant. Christ received these spiritual gifts for the church after His resurrection. Each is precious in its proper place and should be employed in Christ's service, for lack of use makes them feeble. The true value of a gift is seen in the wholesome fruit it bears in edifying the body of Christ, not in the excitement it creates in its manifestation.

The diversity of gifts leads to different operations, but "the Lord desires His chosen servants to learn how to unite together in harmonious effort" (9T 145). Indeed, because of the varied gifts of different people, some are better adapted to some aspects of God's work than others, yet "the work of each in his position is important" (4T 608, 609).

A more narrow usage of the expression "spiritual gifts" among early Adventists and by Ellen White focused on one of the spiritual gifts, namely the gift of prophecy. In this sense the phrases "spiritual gifts" and *"spirit of prophecy" came to be used interchangeably with reference to the gift of prophecy, especially, as evidenced in the writings of Ellen White.

Further reading: COL 325-333; 6T 291-293; 9T 144; DA 790, 823; 8T 22; GW 481; 1SM 127; GC 8; 1T 412; 4T 608, 609; G. E. Rice, "Spiritual Gifts," in R. Dederen, ed., *Handbook of Seventh-day Adventist Theology* (RHPA, 2000), pp. 644-650.

Kwabena Donkor

SPIRITUAL GIFTS (Steam Press, 1858-1864; reprint RHPA, 1995). Four-volume set of Ellen White's earliest writings on a variety of biblical, biographical, and health themes, still available in facsimile reprint. Volume 1 (1858, 219 pp.), subtitled *The Great Controversy Between Christ and His Angels and Satan and His Angels*, is the first printing of the great controversy story following her major vision on the subject in 1858 and highlights major events of the cosmic conflict surrounding Christ's life and ministry, the rise of the Adventist movement, and last-day events. This book also forms the last section of *Early Writings* (pp. 133-295).

Volume 2 (1860, 304 pp.), subtitled *My Christian Experience, Views, and Labors in Connection With the Rise and Progress of the Third Angel's Message*, is an autobiographical account of her labors to 1860. This volume was drawn upon for the publication of *Life Sketches of Ellen G. White* in 1915. Volume 3 (1864, 304 pp.), subtitled *Important Facts of Faith in Connection With the History of Holy Men of Old*, relates the biblical history from Creation to the giving of the law on Sinai. This book was later amplified as the first part of *The Spirit of Prophecy*, volume 1, in 1870.

Volume 4 (1864, 152 and 160 pp.), subtitled *Important Facts of Faith: Laws of Health, and Testimonies Nos. 1-10*, comprises two sections. The first section (vol. 4a) is an account of biblical history from Sinai to Solomon, with two chapters bridging to the advent of Christ, and a chapter entitled "Health," accompanied with related materials. The biblical history was later amplified as the last part of *The Spirit of Prophecy*, volume 1. The 32-page chapter "Health" is the first comprehensive presentation of the health message as given to Ellen White in a vision on June 6, 1863. This chapter was amplified in 1865 to become six chapters in six pamphlets entitled *Health: or How to Live*, edited by James White. The second section (vol. 4b) is a condensed reprint of *Testimonies for the Church*, numbers 1-10.

Denis Fortin

SPIRITUALISM. Ellen White employed the term *spiritualism* to refer to two different, unrelated phenomena that arose in the 1840s. Her initial use of the term was reserved for the movement that offered a "spiritual" interpretation of the experience of the Great Disappointment. This movement claimed that Christ came on October 22, 1844, to the earth spiritually, not physically, to the individuals who were genuinely prepared. The adherents of this view (who were simultaneously called "spiritualists" and "spiritualizers") believed that they had already entered the kingdom of heaven, and engaged in a number of practices that most considered fanatical.

Those who would become pioneers of the Seventh-day Adventist Church, including Ellen White, were among those who rejected this first brand of spiritualism. White described her early encounter with a group of spiritualists as follows: "In the period of disappointment after the passing of the time in 1844, fanaticism in various forms arose. Some held that the resurrection of the righteous dead had already taken place. I was sent to bear a message to those believing this. . . . I went into their meetings. There was much excitement, with noise and confusion. One could not tell what was piped or what was harped. Some appeared to be in vision, and fell to the floor. Others were jumping, dancing, and shouting. They declared that as their flesh was purified, they were ready for translation. . . . I bore my testimony in the name of the Lord, placing His rebuke upon these manifestations" (2SM 34).

Even while she was condemning spiritualism, some mistook White to be its adherent because she and other would-be Seventh-day Adventists continued to hold on to the significance of the October 22, 1844, date. The misunderstanding led her to make this strong statement against the spiritualist denial of the literal, bodily return of Christ: "I have often seen that the spiritual view took away all the glory of heaven, and that in many minds the throne of David and the lovely person of Jesus have been burned up in the fire of Spiritualism. I have seen that some who have been deceived and led into this error will be brought out into the light of truth, but it will be almost impossible for them to get entirely rid of the deceptive power of Spiritualism" (EW 77, 78).

In 1848, as the first phenomenon of spiritualism was fading, a new and completely unrelated movement also called spiritualism arose in the northeastern United States. On March 31, 1848, Margaret (age 15) and Kate (age 12) Fox, daughters of John and Margaret Fox, began communicating with what they believed to be the spirit of a man through a series of rapping or knocking sounds at their home in Hydesville, New York. The Fox sisters quickly became a sensation and gained a significant following among those who found the public demonstrations of the rapping convincing. These came to be known as spiritualists. They believed that the spirits of the dead existed on a higher plane than the world of human beings, that communication with the spirits was possible through mediums, and that such communication yielded important moral, ethical, and spiritual information.

In one of her earliest references to this second phenomenon called spiritualism, White cautioned that it was one of Satan's tools of deception. The devil "comes as an angel of light," she wrote, "and spreads his influence over the land," inciting "false reformations every where" (1SG 171). In another early work she also gave a stern warning against spiritualism: "[Satan] comes to poor, deceived mortals through modern spiritualism. . . . Some poor souls who have been fascinated with the eloquent words of the teachers of spiritualism, and have yielded to its influence, afterward find out its deadly character, and would renounce and flee from it, but cannot. Satan holds them by his power, and is not willing to let them go free" (1T 343).

The basis of White's objection to spiritualism lay in her staunch conviction that the dead are in a sleeplike, unconscious state, knowing nothing (Eccl. 9:5, 10) and thinking nothing (Ps. 146:4; GC 556). She believed that the doctrine of the immortality of the soul held by most Christians had paved the way for the rise of modern spiritualism (*ibid.* 551; SR 393). Though many Christian ministers and churches were embracing spiritualism as a godly phenomenon, White unequivocally condemned spiritualism as a "soul-destroying delusion" (1T 298) and as a continuation of Satan's lie to Adam and Eve—"Ye shall not surely die" (Gen. 3:4)—which was manifested throughout history in various forms, including ancient witchcraft condemned in the Old Testament (GC 561; PP 685; 1T 301). She believed that the rappings, séances, and different types of spirit channeling practiced by spiritualists were all manifestations of Satan impersonating the dead (AA 289, 290; Ev 603, 604; GC 551-553, 557, 560). Therefore, to accept and practice the teachings of spiritualism was akin to participating in demon worship (PP 688).

White also saw spiritualism as a force that would feature prominently in the end-time unfolding of the great controversy between Christ and Satan. She predicted that spiritualism "will become more and more pronounced as the professed Christian world rejects the plainly revealed truth of the Word of God" and that "[Satan] will show great signs and wonders as credentials of his divine claims, and through Spiritualism will work against Christ and His agencies" (ST, May 28, 1894). In a chapter in *The Great Controversy* devoted

to this end-time conflict White predicted that spiritualism in a Christian guise would unite with Roman Catholicism and American Protestantism to create an apostate "threefold union" whose mission would be to deceive and persecute God's saints. "Through the agency of spiritualism," she wrote, "miracles will be wrought, the sick will be healed, and many undeniable wonders will be performed," leading to heightened respect for the apostate religious power. The undiscerning people of the world would "accept the form of godliness without the power, and they will see in this union a grand movement for the conversion of the world and the ushering in of the long-expected millennium." It would be through spiritualism, she wrote, that "Satan appears as a benefactor of the race, healing the diseases of the people, and professing to present a new and more exalted system of religious faith." However, through all his efforts, Satan's goal would be to "divert the minds of the people from the work of preparation to stand in the day of God" (GC 588, 589).

If one is to clearly discern truth from error and combat the lure of spiritualism, White wrote, the people of God must remain faithful to the biblical teaching on the state of the dead and the true character of God: "God's Word, rightly understood and applied, is a safeguard against spiritualism. An eternally burning hell preached from the pulpit, and kept before the people, does injustice to the benevolent character of God. It presents Him as the veriest tyrant in the universe. This widespread dogma has turned thousands to universalism, infidelity, and atheism. The Word of God is plain. It is a straight chain of truth, and will prove an anchor to those who are willing to receive it, even if they have to sacrifice their cherished fables. It will save them from the terrible delusions of these perilous times" (1T 344, 345).

Further reading: H. E. Douglass, *Dramatic Prophecies of Ellen White* (PPPA, 2007), pp. 23-44; *SDA Encyclopedia* (1996), vol. 10, pp. 448-451; vol. 11, pp. 693-695.

Julius Nam

SPIRITUALITY. Ellen White's definition of spirituality differs from the primary meaning prevalent today. The word "spirituality" is used hundreds of times in her published writings (CD-ROM) and its meaning refers primarily to a life of piety, godliness, and sanctity. Today, however, the term *spirituality* is mostly used to "describe those attitudes, beliefs, and practices which animate people's lives and help them reach out toward super-sensitive realities" ("Spirituality," *Westminster Dictionary of Christian Spirituality*, p. 361). The study of spirituality according to this current definition examines the disciplines of prayer, meditation, Bible study, fasting, confession, worship, and related topics and how they affect our lives. While Ellen White's use of the specific term *spirituality* might suggest to some that she does not have a special interest in this area, a careful examination of her writings on the specific areas included in the present-day definition of the term reveals a deep and widespread interest in the topic.

Ellen White's understanding of spirituality is centered on Christ in at least two ways. First, Christ is the object of worship and the receiver and enabler of the believer's devotional life. Second, Jesus is an example of what the believer's spiritual/devotional life should be. Note that "Jesus is our example" (DA 74). "Every child may gain knowledge as Jesus did" (*ibid.* 70). Jesus' communion with God "revealed for us the secret of a life of power" (MH 51).

The fullest discussion of Jesus' devotional life comes in the chapter entitled "With Nature and With God" in *The Ministry of Healing* (pp. 51-58). This chapter and others make clear that spirituality, for Ellen White, was crucial to Jesus and to us. Devotional life is essential to Christian life. It was crucial for Jesus. Even Jesus, who was "wholly devoted" to serving others, found it "necessary" (MH 58) to seek solitude for "unbroken communion" with God. It was important for Jesus' disciples to do the same. The clear implication is that every believer has this identical need. "All who are under the training of God" need a quiet time for devotional communion with the Divine. "This is the effectual preparation for *all* labor for God" (*ibid.*; italics supplied).

What setting, practices, and disciplines constitute this time of communion with God? Although Jesus' time of devotional communion is often portrayed as being in a natural setting, this is not stated as a necessity. The "scenes of nature," such as "quiet valleys," "mountain-side," "forest," "fields," or "secluded place" (*ibid.* 52), are viewed as the ideal settings for communion. These locations not only are quiet and reminders of God's creation, but also furnish escape from distractions that may hamper unbroken fellowship. Five spiritual/devotional practices are specifically mentioned in this chapter, as well as in other places. The first is *meditation* (*ibid.*). For Ellen White, this is one form of communication with God. Unfortunately, neither in this chapter nor in any other place in her writings does she explain exactly what kind of meditation she has in mind. It is clear, however, that one form of meditation she endorses is that which takes Scripture and its themes and stories as a subject for reflection and meditation (SC 89-91). The second practice is *searching the Scriptures* (MH 52). The key here is *searching*. The nature of and methodology for this searching of Scripture is found in the book *Steps to Christ* (pp. 89-91). The search is an experiential search in which not merely the intellect, but the heart is filled with God's words. We are to meditate on, contemplate, and memorize the Word. A hasty reading will not do. Prayer must be offered to God so His Spirit and enlightenment can be present during the search. A true search will lead to a deep desire to follow God and experience His presence.

The third spiritual practice is *prayer* (MH 52). Ellen White defines prayer as "the opening of the heart to God as to a friend" (SC 93). This speaks both to the experiential nature of prayer and its intimacy as well as to its two-way nature. When people open their hearts to a friend, it means both speaking and listening. For Ellen White, prayer implies that when we are silent, God speaks to us.

The fourth of these practices is *singing*. Undoubtedly, the Psalms were the core of what was sung by Jesus. Specifically, Ellen White mentions "songs of thanksgiving" (MH 52) as a part of Jesus' activity during His hours of labor in the carpentry shop. Thus Jesus sang not only during His early-morning special time of communion, but during His time of work as well. We are called to do the same.

The fifth of these practices could best be called *guidance,* or *knowing God's will.* We are called to have a personal experience in obtaining knowledge of the will of God. "We must individually hear Him speaking to the heart" (*ibid.* 58). This can take place when in quietness we wait before God. In such a state we can "hear" God's voice (in thought, not usually audibly) and find practical daily guidance for our lives. The result of following such a spiritual path is a "life of power" (*ibid.* 51). Such power is blended with compassion and forms an atmosphere of spiritual life, which surrounds a person. Even though He toiled long, Jesus' time in prayer brought Him

freshness and vigor that enabled Him to minister to others. Believers who live a life undergirded by the practice of this Christlike spirituality become prepared for effective service to God. An atmosphere of light and peace will surround them, and they will receive both physical and mental strength. Their lives will manifest a divine power that reaches the hearts of people.

Further reading: G. R. Doss, "An Analytical Review of Christian Spirituality With Special Reference to the Seventh-day Adventist Church" (D.Min. project, AU, 1987); H. E. Douglass, *Dramatic Prophecies of Ellen White* (PPPA, 2007), pp. 163-188; J. L. Dybdahl, "Encounter With God: Steps Toward an Adventist Devotional Theology" (unpublished paper presented to the Andrews Society for Religious Studies, November 1988, CAR); J. L. Dybdahl, *Hunger: Satisfying the Longing of Your Soul* (Hagerstown, Md.: Autumn House, 2007); G. A. Schneider, *The Way of the Cross Leads Home: The Domestication of American Methodism* (Bloomington: Indiana University Press, 1993); R. Staples, "The Wesleyan Roots of Adventist Spirituality" (unpublished paper presented to the Andrews Society for Religious Studies, November 1988, CAR).

Jon L. Dybdahl

SPIRITUALITY OF ELLEN G. WHITE. Her personal relationship with God as evidenced in her practice of spiritual disciplines, such as Bible study, meditation, and prayer. Growing up in a devout Methodist home taught her to value the experiential aspects of a relationship with God in addition to an intellectual understanding of Him. From the time she found personal assurance of salvation about age 15, Ellen White placed primary emphasis on maintaining that relationship with God. As she matured she sought to live her entire life as a devotional experience. Central to her relationship with God was the experiential nature of her time spent with Him. She was daily in the presence of God. Her identity was rooted in her relationship with God. Ellen White did not have a set structure to her devotional life, because it encompassed all aspects of her life. Throughout her lifetime there is evidence that her life experiences, most notably her personal and physical suffering, led to increased spiritual maturity, and deeper trust in Jesus developed through trial.

As a young mother she faced severe bouts of depression as a result of overwork, travel, caring for the sick and needy, and raising a family. At times she struggled with feelings of inadequacy and abandonment by God. Once she prayed for God to restore the joy of salvation to her life (Ms 5, 1859). Another source of depression for her was writing personal testimonies. The duty of reproving others' sins weighed heavily on her. It seems the line between work and personal devotional time was blurred. Morning and evening family worship was structured, but her personal devotional time was less so. It appears that her spiritual work for others sometimes took precedence over maintaining her own spiritual well-being.

As she grew older she developed increased capacity for handling physical pain and depression. For most of 1892 she suffered from a combination of "malarial fever and inflammatory rheumatism" that wracked her with pain (4Bio 31). Similar trials in earlier days had caused bouts of depression, but she did not succumb to depression now. She called these the "happiest months" of her life, because God was so near (*ibid.* 32). She wrote, "I am so thankful that I had this experience, because I am better acquainted with my precious Lord and Savior" (Ms 75, 1893, in 4Bio 32).

Her sleepless nights caused by the pain were spent not in doubting but in communing with God. She wrote on May 9, "The past night has been a very long one. . . . I keep my mind as much as possible on the promises of God. I do not claim these promises because I deserve them, but because they are bestowed upon erring human beings as a free gift. . . . I am determined not to encourage feelings of despondency and gloom" (Ms 19, 1892, in 7MR 141).

Prayer was also crucial to Ellen White's spiritual experience. She spent extensive time in prayer. About the same time she wrote, "Prayer does not bring God down to us, but brings us up to Him" (SC 93). Besides her daily prayers, she lived in constant communion with God. "I praise the Lord that . . . I may have the light and love of Jesus. His presence is everything to me—comfort, hope, and soothing balm" (Ms 20, 1892, in 8MR 50).

Her improved health in later years had an impact on her spiritual life. Her practice was to go to bed early and awake by 2:00 a.m. She would spend the following hours communing with God and writing. In March 1906 she wrote, "These wakeful hours have been most refreshing. I have communed with my Savior. . . . Oh, how precious has this communion been to me! Thanksgiving and praise have been ascending to God and to Jesus my Savior" (Ms 123, 1906). An example of Ellen White's devotional experience is how she sometimes used the Lord's Prayer as a structure for her own prayers. For her it was comprehensive and "has efficiency because Christ composed that prayer, and there is not a useless word in it" (Ms 124, 1906).

Through the course of her life Ellen White went through spiritual struggles like everyone else. Though she was called to be a messenger for God at an early age, her early life was not marked with the same degree of spiritual maturity as her later years. She struggled with spiritual issues as a child, even questioning whether she was saved. In early adulthood she also struggled with depression, usually when she was overworked, physically exhausted, and in poor health. She sometimes felt that her life work was ended, and at other times her depression caused her to doubt whether she was in harmony with God (Ms 5, 1859). But through her struggles she never turned away from God.

Later in life Ellen White's journals reveal how she dealt with adverse circumstances in a more positive way. Knowing her own weaknesses, she determined not to fall into depression. Through praising God and claiming His promises she was able to keep her mind from sinking into depression. Her journal entries about her devotional experiences focus on staying on track with the work God had assigned her. She prayed for discernment to know God's will, and sought to make her daily life a continuous experience of devotion, defining her primary identity in terms of her relationship to God. It was because of these experiences that she could write such practical advice about spiritual growth: "It would be well for us to spend a thoughtful hour each day in contemplation of the life of Christ. . . . As we thus dwell upon His great sacrifice for us, our confidence in Him will be more constant, our love will be quickened, and we shall be more deeply imbued with His spirit" (DA 83).

Further reading: Mss 5-8, 1859; Mss 28-39, 1892; Mss 123-127, 1906; G. Doss, "An Analytical Review of Christian Spirituality With Reference to the Seventh-day Adventist Church" (D.Min. project, AU, 1987, CAR); H. E. Douglass, *Messenger of the Lord* (PPPA, 1998), pp. 68-92; E. Stubbert, "The Personal Spiritual Life of Ellen White" (research paper, AU, 2000, CAR); J. M. Wilson, "A Historical

Study of the Spiritual Lifestyle of Ellen White and Its Roots in Methodism" (research paper, AU, 1987, CAR).

Eric Stubbert

SPORTS, see **GAMES AND SPORTS; COMPETITION.**

STANDARDS OF CHRISTIAN BEHAVIOR. Postmodern society is permeated with the idea that humans are self-determined, and accountable only to themselves. Originating with Satan (Gen. 3:4, 5), this philosophy finds disciples among relativists, existentialists, and postmoderns alike. Accordingly, humans must reject any standards of conduct but their own, and obedience to any will but their own. In affirming the existence of standards of Christian behavior, Ellen White sought to respond to some perennial issues. This article looks at the reasons she gave for the need of standards; the right and legitimacy of God to claim human obedience; the nature of standards; how humans can know God's will; and finally, how love is related to obedience to God's standards.

According to Ellen White, human beings are finite and are sinners. This crucial fact, not to be overlooked, indicates that left alone, they exploit their environment, pollute water and air, and abuse their own organism, mind, and relationships to the point of self-destruction. Ellen White insists that the rationale for standards of Christian lifestyle and behavior must be grounded in the doctrine of creation and gives three reasons for this. In the first place, God created nature as an integrated system of interdependence. "The harmony of creation depends upon the perfect conformity of all beings, of everything, animate and inanimate, to the law of the Creator. . . . Everything is under fixed laws, which cannot be disregarded" (PP 52). Human beings are placed into this integrated system, and their happiness and survival depends on the degree of respect they show for these laws of nature.

Second, humans are more than natural beings; they are moral and spiritual beings created in the image of God, and their behavior is genuinely human only when it is governed by obedience to God's moral law. "To man, the crowning work of creation, God has given power to understand His requirements, to comprehend the justice and beneficence of His law and its sacred claims upon him; and of man unswerving obedience is required" (*ibid.*).

Third, God also remembers our limitations (Ps. 103:14) and the ignorance that ensues (Jer. 10:23). He knows how hard it is to be different and how easy it is to copy the practice of the prevailing culture. Thus standards are given to take us up and above the standards of society (3T 322) and to bring us into harmony with God's will.

But how can we be sure that these divine standards for human behavior are not an illegitimate divine intrusion against human nature, freedom, and dignity? Ellen White suggests several important factors to explain the legitimacy of God's claim on our behavior. First, all life belongs to Him and proceeds from Him (AH 280; Ed 99), and human beings are but God's stewards (7T 176). As rightful Owner of the whole of creation (Ps. 24:1, 2), God can require accountability for the way we treat His property, including ourselves (AH 368; 1T 169, 199; 2T 432; 4T 619).

Second, God has redeemed His creation from the hands of Satan; with the death of Jesus on the cross, He won the right to repossess His domain. In setting standards of behavior, God is protecting us from wrongful and harmful actions and their consequences, thus safeguarding the benefits of Christ's sacrifice. "What a God is our God! He rules over His kingdom with diligence and care, and He has built a hedge—the Ten Commandments—about His subjects to preserve them from the results of transgression. In requiring obedience to the laws of His kingdom, God gives His people health and happiness, peace and joy" (CT 454; cf. Ed 76, 77).

God's standards of behavior for His children are high, and we are called to elevate them (FE 288; 6T 146), rather than to lower them "to the very dust" (4T 37). But why would a loving God lay such expectations upon us?

God's high expectations reflect His unique insight into our potential. "Many who are qualified to do excellent work accomplish little because they attempt little. Thousands pass through life as if they had no great object for which to live, no high standard to reach. One reason for this is the low estimate which they place upon themselves. Christ paid an infinite price for us, and according to the price paid He desires us to value ourselves" (MH 498; cf. TM 121).

But the Christian believer is not left alone gazing at this high and lofty goal in discouragement and consternation. The attainment of God's highest goal for every individual is God's task as well. "Day by day God works with [the believer], perfecting the character that is to stand in the time of final test. And day by day the believer is working out before men and angels a sublime experiment, showing what the gospel can do for fallen human beings" (AA 483).

God-given standards reveal what is good and just, but also what is evil and unjust. In His Word God defines what sin is and warns, forbids, and disciplines His children as a supreme expression of His love. "Satan deceives many with the plausible theory that God's love for His people is so great that He will excuse sin in them; he represents that while the threatenings of God's Word are to serve a certain purpose in His moral government, they are never to be literally fulfilled. But in all His dealings with His creatures God has maintained the principles of righteousness by revealing sin in its true character—by demonstrating that its sure result is misery and death. The unconditional pardon of sin never has been, and never will be. Such pardon would show the abandonment of the principles of righteousness, which are the very foundation of the government of God. It would fill the unfallen universe with consternation. God has faithfully pointed out the results of sin, and if these warnings were not true, how could we be sure that His promises would be fulfilled?" (PP 522).

For Ellen White the Bible is the only source of standards. Culture, human preferences, or legislative authorities cannot ultimately define God's will for humans (Ed 260; 4T 312, 449; 5T 24). Every aspect of human life is to be governed by biblical precepts (CT 422; 5T 264; GC 521; Te 193). There is no better protection against temptations (3T 482), no better manual for character building (COL 60; GC 94), and no more reliable warning against sin and evil (SW, Apr. 23, 1907; Ed 76). The Bible "opens to man's understanding the great problems of life, and to all who heed its precepts it will prove an unerring guide, keeping them from wasting their lives in misdirected effort" (AA 506).

Ellen White perceived at least two levels of standards in Scripture. Frequently using the term *principles,* she referred to broad or general statements of God's Word that should be the foundation of character, from which all actions proceed (4T 562). These principles must not be compromised (GW 392; Ed 183; PK 548); they are fixed (CS 25; 2SG 261; MYP 102; 2T 488), fundamental (1SM 208), immutable (4T 312), immortal (7T 152), and exacting (DA 273). She identified the Ten Commandments

as principles of human conduct (Ed 69), which can be obeyed only if the two greatest principles of "supreme love to God and impartial love to man" permeate our motives (DA 498).

Beyond these broad and universal principles, humans need also more concrete rules or precepts. These rules and precepts are found in Scripture and stem from principles (4T 651, 652; FE 71), not from emotions alone (2SG 261; 1T 161), nor from unaided human wisdom (TM 192). They inform us of our immediate duties in particular situations (2SM 217; CG 66). An example of this is the prophet Daniel, who upheld the principle of healthful living by refusing to drink or eat anything that was not according to God's word (Dan. 1). "There are many among professed Christians today who would decide that Daniel was too particular, and would pronounce him narrow and bigoted. They consider the matter of eating and drinking as of too little consequence to require such a decided stand.... Those who accept and obey one of His precepts because it is convenient to do so, while they reject another because its observance would require a sacrifice, lower the standard of right, and by their example lead others to lightly regard the holy law of God" (FE 78; cf. CG 66; SD 78).

Ellen White urged her readers to "remember that a disciple is to do the will of his master. We are not to reason in regard to results" (MM 255). True love does not dispense with obedience (AA 563; SC 60, 61; PP 279; DA 126). Indeed, true love is obedience (1 John 5:3; DA 641). "If we abide in Christ, if the love of God dwells in the heart, our feelings, our thoughts, our actions, will be in harmony with the will of God. The sanctified heart is in harmony with the precepts of God's law" (AA 563). Such a response cannot be elicited by force. Only love can trust enough to leave the consequences with God (GC 460). "Christ does not drive but draws men unto Him. The only compulsion which He employs is the constraint of love" (MB 127). The genius of Christianity is that it embodies gentleness without compromise, patience without indifference, and forgiveness without excusing sin.

Ellen White reminds us that "Duty has a twin sister, Love; these united can accomplish almost everything, but separated, neither is capable of good" (4T 62; cf. 3T 108, 195).

Ever since God uttered His first standard of behavior to Adam and Eve—"But of the tree of the knowledge of good and evil, thou shalt not eat of it" (Gen. 2:17)—Satan has been waging war against the human race. The forces of evil discerned that the commands expressing God's will are the most vulnerable links in the divine-human relationship.

Further reading: M. M. Kiš, "Christian Lifestyle and Behavior," in R. Dederen, ed., *Handbook of Seventh-day Adventist Theology* (RHPA, 2000), pp. 675-723.

Miroslav M. Kiš

STEPS TO CHRIST (Chicago: Fleming H. Revell, 1892, 153 pp.; RHPA, 1896, 163 pp.). One of the most widely translated and distributed books of all time. The request for a small book on the Christian experience of salvation that could be sold for about 50 cents arose at a meeting in the summer of 1890. Ellen White was enthusiastic about the idea, and immediately she and *Marian Davis began sifting through her manuscripts and publications for suitable materials. She edited, rewrote, and arranged these into a coordinated account of the way and joys of the experience of salvation. The manuscript was presented to a group of workers attending the *Harbor Springs convention in July 1891. *G. B. Starr, who had previously worked with Dwight L. Moody, suggested that the manuscript be offered to Fleming Revell, a major nondenominational

Chicago publisher of religious works. It was felt that this would facilitate wide circulation (Revell's sister Emma was married to Moody, and it was Moody who had encouraged Revell to establish a press to publish his sermons and tracts and other Christian literature). Ellen White accepted the proposal, and *Steps to Christ* came off the press in 1892. The little book of 12 brief chapters was so enthusiastically received that it was reprinted seven times during the first year. Revell announced: " 'A Remarkable Book.' It is not often that a publisher has the opportunity of announcing a third edition of a new work *within six weeks of the first issue*. This, however, is the encouraging fact in connection with Mrs. E. G. White's eminently helpful and practical work, *Steps to Christ*. If you will read this work, it will *ensure* your becoming deeply interested in extending its circulation. *Steps to Christ* is a work to guide the inquirer, to inspire the young Christian, and to comfort and encourage the mature believer. The book is unique in its helpfulness."

Later that year Ellen White was requested by the International Tract Society in London to add to the book so that it could be copyrighted in the United Kingdom (Revell had waived publishing rights outside the U.S.). In response she added a beautiful introductory chapter "God's Love for Man." The copyright was purchased from Revell by the *Review and Herald in 1896 and the present preface added in the 1898 edition. *Steps to Christ* has since been translated into at least 160 languages and distributed in the hundreds of millions of copies.

The way of salvation so joyously presented in *Steps to Christ* is in harmony with the Wesleyan Arminian theological understanding. Both divine sovereignty and human responsibility, justification, and sanctification are affirmed. God does not force the human will, and there is a wonderful optimism about the possibilities open to "partakers of the grace of Christ" (SC 60, 78).

Further reading: 4Bio 11, 12, 36, 388; *Comprehensive Index to the Writings of Ellen G. White*, vol. 3, p. 3201; T. Poirier, "A Century of *Steps*," AR, May 14, 1992, pp. 14, 15.

Russell Staples

STEPS TO JESUS (RHPA, 1981, 125 pp.). *Steps to Christ*, adapted; also published under the title *Knowing Him Better*. This simplified edition of *Steps to Christ* was authorized by the White Estate board to meet the needs of youth and those having a limited knowledge of the English language. The preface states: "The author's thoughts have been retained, [but] hard-to-understand phrases have been restated in everyday language, the vocabulary has been simplified, and long sentences have been shortened." Scripture passages from Today's English Version were substituted for those from the King James Version.

Tim Poirier

STEWARDSHIP. The concept of stewardship is prominent throughout the writings of Ellen White. Her view of stewardship involved the total lifestyle of the individual from childhood to final estate distribution. In addition to financial stewardship, Ellen White spoke frequently of the stewardship of time, talents, body temples (healthful living), and the gospel of grace itself (CT 309).

White emphasized biblical principles of stewardship, beginning with the basic understanding that God is the owner of everything and humans are His stewards (Ed 137). She also gives much counsel to church leaders and families about avoiding debt and how to get out of debt (CS 257).

Ellen White gives considerable emphasis to family and personal finance, including living within the income, avoiding debt, saving a little from every income item, training children, faithfulness in *tithes and offerings, planning for the future, estate planning, and giving an account to God (AH 367-398; CG 131-133).

White strongly emphasizes that stewards be honest with God—the Owner, particularly regarding tithes and offerings. With regard to the tithe she wrote that Malachi 3:10, "'Bring ye all the tithe into the storehouse' . . . is God's command. No appeal is made to gratitude or to generosity. This is a matter of simple honesty. The tithe is the Lord's; and He bids us return to Him that which is His own" (Ed 138, 139). She understood the tithe to be holy and sacred and wrote that to withhold or misuse the tithe was robbery of God. She maintained that the tithe was 10 percent, and that it was to be returned to the Lord's treasury for the support of the gospel ministry. She did not leave the use of the tithe to the discretion of the individual, even if that individual was a minister. Other good causes have their place in stewardship, but are not to detract from the tithe. "Let the work no longer be hedged up because the tithe has been diverted into various channels other than the one to which the Lord has said it should go. Provision is to be made for these other lines of work. They are to be sustained, but not from the tithe. God has not changed; the tithe is still to be used for the support of the ministry" (9T 250).

Offerings, on the other hand, are discretionary, not related to a percentage of income. Rather they are proportioned to income, prompted by willingness of heart, and gratitude for God's blessings. From Ellen White's perspective, offerings were not to be given just to pay the bills, but as a response to experienced grace and with a desire to see the work of God advance throughout the world. She stated that the value of money was to be understood in relation to three factors: "providing for the necessities of life, in blessing others, and advancing the cause of Christ" (COL 351; cf. Lt 155, 1899, in 4Bio 441).

In addition to the wholistic view of stewardship involving all of life, Ellen White also addressed the stages of life as recognized today by professional financial planners. There is a time for learning—she recognized the value of a good education, a time for earning. She recognized the importance of diligence in work and planning for the future, and a time for returning—the time of life for distributing assets.

Ellen White emphasized individual stewardship responsibility and warned against shifting that responsibility to others. She wrote, "Parents should exercise the right that God has given them. He entrusted to them the talents He would have them use to His glory. The children were not to become responsible for the talents of the father" (3T 121). Some have criticized her counsel on estate planning as neglectful of children. However, when one reads her counsel in this area it is clear that the family should take a prominent place in early estate planning when the children are minors, needy and dependent. It was only when the parents were old and the children were grown and independent that she encouraged those settling their accounts to return the assets to God as the owner who lent them their property to begin with. To a man of some means who had grown children she wrote, "Your wife and children, of course, should not be left destitute; provision should be made for them if they are needy. But do not, simply because it is customary, bring into your will a long line of relatives who are not needy" (4T 482).

In keeping with the great controversy theme, Ellen White frequently wrote about financial management in the context of end-time living. For example, she noted that "money will soon depreciate in value very suddenly when the reality of eternal scenes opens to the senses of man" (Ev 63). With the end in mind she encouraged families to invest in the cause of God so that fewer of their possessions would be "consumed in the final conflagration" (CS 60). And for those who live to see the literal Second Coming she noted that it was imperative that they place their trust in God rather than in perishable possessions, because "the time is coming when we cannot sell at any price. The decree will soon go forth prohibiting men to buy or sell of any man save him that hath the mark of the beast" (5T 152).

There is nothing more certain in the Scriptures or the writings of Ellen White than the judgment. It will be a pleasant experience for those who have been faithful stewards. "As Christ's followers give back to the Lord His own, they are accumulating treasure which will be theirs when they hear the words: 'Well done, thou good and faithful servant: . . . enter thou into the joy of thy Lord' " (9T 59).

Further reading: CS; Ed 135-145; 3T 381-413; 9T 245-252; C. E. Bradford, "Stewardship," in R. Dederen, ed., *Handbook of Seventh-day Adventist Theology* (RHPA, 2000), pp. 651-674; G. Edward Reid, *It's Your Money! Isn't It?* (RHPA, 1993).

G. Edward Reid

STORY OF JESUS, THE (RHPA, 1949, 2003, 142 pp.). As Ellen White was working on *The Desire of Ages*, her son *Edson White adapted some of her writings that she had compiled for it into a 158-page book suitable for children titled *Christ Our Saviour*, which especially focused on the childhood of Christ. The book initially appeared in 1896 under the imprint of the *International Tract Society. After Edson founded the *Southern Publishing Association, he released it again in 1900. Eventually the book was expanded to 182 pages. In 1949 the Southern Publishing Association reissued the longer version under the title *Story of Jesus* with new illustrations and a new format. All three North American publishing houses printed the book.

Changing literary styles in children's literature made the book seem increasingly old-fashioned and difficult to read. The *Review and Herald Publishing Association simplified the vocabulary and sentence structure, replaced the Bible quotations with a modern translation (New King James Version), reillustrated the book with full color throughout, and added tables listing the events of Jesus' life, the miracles He performed, and the parables He told. The redesigned 142-page edition appeared in 2003 under the title *The Story of Jesus: From the Manger to the Throne*. In 2006 the Review and Herald released another version of this book under the title *Life of Jesus*.

Gerald Wheeler

STORY OF REDEMPTION, THE (RHPA, 1947, 445 pp.). A concise presentation of the *great controversy between good and evil drawn from the earlier writings of Ellen G. White. The theme of the great controversy was foremost among the many themes Ellen White wrote on and describes the conflict between good and evil, from the fall of Lucifer in heaven and the fall of humanity, down through the centuries to the second coming of Christ, and the setting up of the kingdom of God on the earth made new. *The Story of Redemption* is a reprint of various chapters taken from *Spiritual Gifts*, volume 1 (1858), and *The Spirit of Prophecy*, volumes 1 (1870), 3 (1878), and 4 (1884). The chapters are grouped in their natural order according to the biblical narrative. The text of these chapters has been edited to accommodate a shorter presentation

of the subject and "the deletions necessary to present this story in a minimum of space are not indicated in the text" (p. 10). Current standards of spelling, punctuation, and grammar were adopted. Aside from these adjustments, the original text is unchanged, still maintaining its original graphic and terse treatment of the theme it presents. The story of the redemption of humanity, as a theme, is further developed in the *Conflict of the Ages Series.

STUDENTS, COUNSELS TO. Ellen White wrote extensive counsels to students. Most of her messages to students were addressed to youth from middle school to college level. Counsels for the training of younger children were generally directed to parents. The nature of the messages allows classification into at least four categories—spiritual, academic, social/practical, and health.

Spiritual counsels are the most abundant. Students are encouraged to pray, to study the Bible systematically, to attend school worships, and to make the knowledge of God a primary goal in their lives. School life is such that prayer should be intensified even more than when one is at home (3T 224). Communion with God is a personal matter that needs continual development: "Let every student take his Bible and place himself in communion with the great Teacher. Let the mind be trained and disciplined to wrestle with hard problems in the search for divine truth" (COL 334).

Students are also advised to excel in the academic side of their school experience. They are encouraged to be thorough with the basic areas—language and arithmetic—as a foundation to nearly all forms of employment and to "never rest satisfied with a low standard" (CT 218).

Strong emphasis is placed on social interactions. Young people can be transformed, for better or for worse, through the influence of companions. In fact, White remarks that peer influence is strongest during the school years (FE 297). For this reason her advice is clear: "Seek the company of those who are sound in morals, and whose aim tends to that which is good" (CT 225). The purpose of wise social choices is not only for personal protection, but also to provide support to others (6T 172) and to lead them to salvation (*ibid.* 133, 134).

Ellen White gives frequent practical advice about finances. Students—both men and women—are warned to be careful in their expenses, including practicing self-sacrifice, and learning to wash, mend, and keep in order their own clothes (*ibid.* 208). Students are also encouraged to "work their way through college" in order to gain independence and avoid becoming "helpless burdens" (AH 387).

White's counsels to students to maintain excellent health are prolific. Physical well-being is advantageous—virtually essential—to attaining the highest standard of moral and intellectual accomplishment. "To secure a strong, well-balanced character," she wrote, "both the mental and the physical powers must be exercised and developed" (PP 601). Students' practical knowledge of how to keep their bodies healthy is among the most basic goals of education (3T 142; CD 450). Diet is of particular importance. Many students are ignorant of the relationship between diet and health, and this must be corrected to avoid failure in many areas (FE 147).

See also: Schools, Church.

See also: *Counsels to Parents, Teachers, and Students*; *Fundamentals of Christian Education*; *Education*; *Christian Education*.

Julian Melgosa

SUBSTITUTE AND SURETY, see **ATONEMENT**.

SUNDAY LEGISLATION. Persecution, experienced in the present and expected in the future, was the key reason for Seventh-day Adventist opposition to Sunday legislation during the late nineteenth and early twentieth centuries. At least as early as 1858 Ellen G. White had predicted that Sunday laws would be used to persecute Sabbathkeepers just before the Second Advent. By 1889 her prediction seemed to be coming true.

The statute books of nearly every American state included extremely strict Sunday legislation that outlawed Sunday business, labor, and even most forms of recreation. In Arkansas and Tennessee the law even threatened to punish parents who permitted their children to play on Sunday. Many of these provisions, however, were largely a dead letter, routinely ignored by the police and the general public. But as Adventism began penetrating the South, pastors and zealous laymen from the older denominations began demanding the arrests of SDAs who worked around their farms on Sunday.

Such Sunday labor, many Adventists believed, was demanded by the words "Six days shalt thou labour" (Ex. 20:9). In addition, they saw Sunday work as an economic necessity. Adventist farmers and artisans believed earning a living would be impossible if they were idle on one of the working days God had given them.

Although the Seventh-day Adventists had only 538 Southern members in 1885, within the next 11 years more than 100 Adventists (mostly in the South) were arrested for Sunday work. Law enforcement officials in a few Southern counties, by their statements and actions, clearly indicated their determination to eradicate Adventism in their territory. These zealous persecutions resulted in ruinous fines, imprisonment, chain gang labor, and—for at least one person—death. Samuel P. Mitchell died on February 4, 1879, from an illness he had contracted in a Georgia jail while serving time for a Sunday-law violation.

These persecutions coincided with a concerted effort by several religious organizations to strengthen and revitalize existing Sunday legislation and to obtain a national Sunday law. Such groups as the National Reform Association, the American Sabbath Union, and the Women's Christian Temperance Union claimed the backing of millions of petitioners in their campaign for congressional action.

In 1888 and 1889 H. W. Blair introduced national Sunday bills in the United States Senate. When they failed to pass, the activists unsuccessfully attempted to persuade Congress to enact Sunday legislation for the District of Columbia. Finally they succeeded in getting Congress to condition their appropriation to the 1893 Chicago World's Fair upon an agreement to close the exposition gates on Sunday. However, the fair operators violated their pledge, and the federal government ignored the violation.

Adventists responded to this dual set of circumstances by publicizing the persecution and agitating against the proposed legislation, circulating petitions and testifying before the relevant congressional committees. To broadcast their views, they established the *American Sentinel and also created a press committee to alert the nation's newspapers to the persecution in the South and to their reasons for objecting to Sunday legislation. The press committee was succeeded by the National and then the International Religious Liberty Association. They opposed all Sunday laws, even those exempting people who worshipped on Saturday, arguing that such legislation was unfair to unbelievers, forcing atheists and the irreligious to behave as if they were religious. Besides, they had learned from experience

that authorities didn't always respect such exemptions.

Seventh-day Adventists also defended themselves in the courts. One of their cases, *King v. the State* [of Tennessee] (Blakely, pp. 465-474) was on its way to the United States Supreme Court when it was aborted by the unexpected death of Robert M. King. King's neighbors had demanded that he change his religion or leave the area. When he did neither, they began watching him, looking for violations of the Sunday legislation they themselves often ignored. Consequently he was arrested and fined for hoeing his cornfield on Sunday, June 23, 1889. After he paid his fine, he was rearrested for the same incident, charged this time with public nuisance. The prosecution, blatantly appealing to religious bigotry, secured a second conviction. Rather than pay the exorbitant fine the court imposed, King spent 23 days in jail before being released pending his unsuccessful appeal to the Tennessee Supreme Court, after which he appealed to the United States district court, again unsuccessfully. Although Judge E. S. Hammond considered King's conviction to be unjust, he ruled that federal courts had no authority to interfere (Blakely, pp. 475-477; Johns, p. 55).

Expecting more sinister legislation in the future, Ellen White strongly supported Adventist efforts to defeat Sunday laws. "It is our duty to do all in our power to avert the threatened danger," she wrote in 1885. "We should endeavor to disarm prejudice by placing ourselves in a proper light before the people. We should bring before them the real question at issue, thus interposing the most effectual protest against measures to restrict liberty of conscience" (5T 452). In 1889, asserting that the Sunday movement was being propelled by "a satanic force," she urged, "Let not the commandment-keeping people of God be silent at this time, as though we gracefully accepted the situation" (RH, Jan. 1, 1889). In the same year she warned Adventists against voting for politicians who favored Sunday legislation (FE 475). Yet she also advised that defiance of existing Sunday legislation would only "strengthen in their persecution the religious zealots" seeking enforcement. She suggested that rather than defying the law, Adventists use Sundays as a day for "missionary work," including "religious services" (9T 232, 233).

The reason White took this issue with such seriousness is that she saw the enactment and enforcement of Sunday legislation on a national level as the "last act in the drama" (ChS 50), the "last great conflict of the controversy between truth and error" (5T 451), before the end of the world. She believed that "as the approach of the Roman armies was a sign to the disciples of the impending destruction of Jerusalem," so will national Sunday legislation be a signal to end-time believers, that "the limit of God's forbearance is reached, that the measure of our nation's iniquity is full, and that the angel of mercy is about to take her flight, never to return" (ibid.).

She recognized that "in every church" there are "true Christians" who "honestly believe that Sunday is the Sabbath of divine appointment," and she acknowledged that "God accepts their sincerity of purpose and their integrity before Him." But when the truth about the Sabbath becomes universally known, those who then choose to keep God's commandments can no longer observe a day that rests on merely human authority (GC 449).

See also: Church and State; Religious Liberty.

Further reading: 1 SG 201-204; 5T 449-454, 711-720; 9T 227-238; Ev 232-237; CT 550-552; GC 52-54, 573-581, 587, 588, 592, 603-610, 614-616; 3SM 383-402; 6Bio 263-266; W. A.

Blakely, American State Papers and Related Documents on Freedom in Religion, 4th rev. ed. (Washington, D.C.: Religious Liberty Association [RHPA], 1949); W. L. Johns, Dateline Sunday, U.S.A.: The Story of Three and a Half Centuries of Sunday-law Battles in America (PPPA, 1967); D. L. Pettibone, "Caesar's Sabbath: The Sunday-Law Controversy in the United States, 1879-1892" (Ph.D. diss., University of California, Riverside, 1979); D. Pettibone, "The Sunday Law Movement," in G. Land, ed., The World of Ellen G. White (RHPA, 1987), pp. 113-128.

Dennis Pettibone

SUNNYSIDE, see **HOMES OF JAMES AND ELLEN G. WHITE.**

SUPPLEMENT TO CHRISTIAN EDUCATION (Battle Creek, International Tract Society, 1894, 31 pp.). Pamphlet published to supplement Ellen White's book Christian Education (1893). The supplement consists of a reprint of five articles she published in the Review and Herald in November 1893 and January 1894, and later republished in Fundamentals of Christian Education. The articles are addressed particularly to students and present Jesus as the model teacher.

SUPPLEMENT TO THE EXPERIENCE AND VIEWS OF ELLEN G. WHITE (James White, 1854, 48 pp.). Ellen White's second booklet published as a follow-up to *A Sketch of the Experience and Views of Ellen G. White (1851). The Supplement presents an explanation of some misunderstood or misconstrued phrases in Experience and Views and additional counsels, some of which had appeared in the *Review and Herald. These counsels emphasized the need for "gospel order" (i.e., church organization) and spiritual preparation for Christ's coming. Along with the earlier work, the *Supplement* was republished in 1882 as part two of **Early Writings.*

SWEDEN. Fourth European country visited by Ellen White during her stay in Europe (1885-1887). During her first visit in October 1885 she visited Stockholm, Grythyttehed, and Örebro and, sensing some antinomianism among church members, preached on the necessity of a faithful observance of the Sabbath. Her second visit occurred in June 1886 in connection with a session of the Swedish Conference preceded by a weeklong workers' meeting in the town of Örebro. Behind the scenes at this conference people were discussing the shortcomings of the president, **J. G. Matteson. Supporting Matteson's work, she believed that he had done the best he could amid many sacrifices, yet she counseled him to accept the fact that he needed the help and strength of other capable workers, such as **O. A. Olsen. Ellen White's last visit to Sweden happened in June 1887 when tent meetings were held in Stockholm. During her three visits Ellen White noted the attractiveness and beauty of Stockholm, the charm of the people she met, and appreciated learning about the Protestant Reformation in Sweden and the ministry of the child preachers in 1842-1843. This information helped her describe in *The Great Controversy* the Reformation and the religious revivals in that country in connection with the worldwide Advent proclamation of the early 1840s (GC 242-244, 366-368).

Further reading: EGWEur 102-114, 192-198, 304, 305.

SWITZERLAND. Switzerland is considered to be the cradle of Seventh-day Adventism in Europe. In 1864 **M. B. Czechowski began to work there, followed by **J. N. Andrews in 1874.

After a vision on January 3, 1875, in which Ellen White saw printing presses running in many countries, she pledged to contribute $1,000 by the end of 1876 to establish a press in Basel, Switzerland. This press started to operate in the summer of 1885, shortly before her arrival in Europe. When Ellen White arrived in Basel on September 3, 1885, and was shown the new publishing house, she said: "I feel that I have seen this place before" (EGWEur, 48). In a vision 10 years before (*ibid*. 50), she had already become acquainted with the place where she would spend most of her time while in Europe. In no other European country did she do as much work

HOME OF J. N. ANDREWS IN SWITZERLAND

as in Switzerland. In September 1885 she encouraged the workers at the second annual meeting of the Swiss Conference, pointing out proper methods of labor. At the third European Missionary Council, which followed, she appealed for unity among the various national groups and called for a loving spirit in presenting the gospel message. Besides her continuing ministry in Basel, she visited almost all groups of Adventist believers in Switzerland. On one such trip Ellen White met the *Roth family, who were instrumental in establishing the first European Adventist chapel on their own property in Tramelan. She spoke at the chapel's dedication service in December 1886. Returning to Basel, Ellen White participated in a special Christmas service at the publishing house during which an evergreen tree was decorated with money gifts to help the colporteur work in Russia. On another occasion she was impressed by the Swiss discipline as she observed military drills performed in a public park across from the publishing house. She saw in the thoroughness of these army exercises a model worthy of imitation in the spiritual realm and asked: "Why should there not be in Basle a large army of Christian soldiers drilling for actual service in the battles to be fought in the different countries of Europe against tradition, superstition, and error?" (HS, 171). The unifying, admonishing, and motivating aspects of Ellen White's ministry in Switzerland set the course for the spiritual and organizational development of Adventism in Europe. Ellen White remained in Switzerland until May 26, 1887, when she embarked on her last tour across the European continent.

Further reading: HS; EGWEur; J. R. Zurcher, "Ellen G. White in Switzerland," in *Ellen G. White and Europe: Symposium Papers 1987* (Bracknell, Eng.: Ellen G. White Research Centre, Europe, 1987), pp. 7-47.

Daniel Heinz

SYDNEY SANITARIUM. Adventist medical institution in Wahroonga, New South Wales, Australia, that opened in January 1903, and now called Sydney Adventist Hospital. Ellen White's influence was decisive in the founding and development of what is currently the largest single-campus private hospital in the Australian state of New South Wales.

White ministered from 1891 to 1900 within the territory of what is now the South Pacific Division of Seventh-day Adventists, fostering numerous health-related initiatives, but a century later only the Sydney "San" and the international Sanitarium Health Food Company remain. Although she was supportive of preliminary ventures from 1896 in the Sydney suburbs of Ashfield and Summer Hill, White told the 46 delegates to the Australasian Union Conference session, on July 21, 1899, that "the grand and ennobling work we have to do for the Master" required a better and bigger institution. Almost spontaneously, immediate fund-raising began; White pledged (and borrowed to pay) £100 of the £905 ($4,500) raised that same day (AUCR, July 28, 1899). Thereafter she actively stimulated the search for land in a nonurban setting yet close to the significant population of the country's first city. She inspected the 80-acre (32-hectare) Wahroonga site with others during October 1899, fostered the gathering of funds (£8,453 [$42,300]) were spent on the building, its furniture and equipment by opening day), and vacationed on the property in January 1900. Her letters until 1907 demonstrated a sustained interest in the sanitarium.

The institution, extensively rebuilt and renamed Sydney Adventist Hospital in 1973, has changed from a rural "health home," with orchards, vegetable gardens, poultry and a dairy, to embrace scientific medicine. White's writings fostered this transformation as well as a continuing emphasis on the values of wholistic health care. The hospital's nurse-education program continues to enrich Adventist mission in many parts of the world, and since 1973 has expanded its outreach by sending surgical teams to the Pacific Islands, Asia, Africa, and elsewhere. By its centennial year the hospital of 415 beds was treating 175,000 outpatients, 18,000 day patients, and 38,000 inpatients annually.

Further reading: 4Bio 428-433; RH, Nov. 14, 1899; A. N. Patrick, *The San: 100 Years of Christian Caring, 1903-2003* (Wahroonga: Sydney Adventist Hospital, 2003); *SDA Encyclopedia* (1996), vol. 11, pp. 732, 733.

Arthur N. Patrick

SYSTEMATIC BENEVOLENCE, see **TITHE**.

TASMANIA, see **AUSTRALIA**; **LACEY, HERBERT CAMDEN**.

TEA, see **BEVERAGES**.

TEACHERS AND TEACHING. The character, aims, and work of teachers are essential parts of Ellen White's *educational philosophy, summarized as follows: "True education means more than the pursual of a certain course of study. It means more than a preparation for the life that now is. It has to do with the whole being, and with the whole period of existence possible to man. It is the harmonious development of the physical, the mental, and the spiritual powers. It prepares the student for the joy of service in this world and for the higher joy of wider service in the world to come" (Ed 13).

This educational philosophy reflects a biblical orientation, derived from the concept of the *imago Dei* (Gen. 1:26). White elaborates this concept as including individuality, creativity, and initiative. "Every human being, created in the image of God, is endowed with a power akin to that of the Creator—individuality, power to think and to do. The men in whom this power is developed are the men who bear responsibilities, who are leaders in enterprise, and who influence character. It is the work of true education to develop this power, to train the youth to be thinkers, and not mere reflectors of other men's thought" (*ibid.* 17).

The damage that sin brought to this image of God necessitated the Savior and plan of salvation, that the Eden lost might be restored. "To restore in man the image of his Maker, to bring him back to the perfection in which he was created, to promote the development of body, mind, and soul, that the divine purpose in his creation might be realized—this was to be the work of redemption. This is the object of education, the great object of life" (*ibid.* 15, 16).

White's close identification of education with redemption makes her philosophy of education virtually a restatement of her understanding of spiritual restoration through grace by faith. She can even say that "in the highest sense the work of education and the work of redemption are one" (*ibid.* 30). To achieve these goals is the purpose of teaching. "To aid the student in comprehending these principles, and in entering into that relation with Christ which will make them a controlling power in the life, should be the teacher's first effort and his constant aim" (*ibid.*). In view of this high purpose, White addresses six aspects of teachers and teaching: (1) character, (2) aims, (3) work, (4) methods, (5) health, and (6) circumstances.

First, because White saw the essence of education as transformation of character, she saw the teacher's own character as the most essential qualification. "To the teacher is committed a most important work—a work upon which he should not enter without careful and thorough preparation. . . . The more of true knowledge a teacher has, the better will be his work. . . . Natural ability and intellectual culture" "are indispensable, but without a spiritual fitness for the work he is not prepared to engage in it" (CT 229). "Parents and schoolteachers are certainly disqualified to educate children properly if they [themselves] have not first learned the lessons of self-control, patience, forbearance, gentleness, and love" (*ibid.* 73). "Unless the teacher realizes the need of prayer, and humbles his heart before God, he will lose the very essence of education" (*ibid.* 231). "The greatest of teachers are those who are most patient, most kind" (*ibid.* 269). Therefore to teachers especially applies the maxim "The greatest want [lack] of the world is the want [lack] of men . . . who will stand for the right though the heavens fall" (Ed 57).

It appears that the teaching profession calls for people who possess balanced minds and well-developed potentials—indeed, humans who are little lower than the angels. The expectations are high, but divine grace makes all things possible. However, the human responsibility of selecting the best teachers and then making them even better must not be overlooked.

Second, the teacher's qualifications are critical because the aims of teaching are so high. In White's words: "Higher than the highest human thought can reach is God's ideal for His children" (*ibid.* 18). "The great aim of the teacher should be the perfecting of Christian character in himself and in his students" (CT 68). With such a goal, the "true teacher is not satisfied with second-rate work," but seeks to inspire students with "principles of truth, obedience, honor, integrity, and purity—principles that will make them a positive force for the stability and uplifting of society" (Ed 29, 30). Such a teacher "will spare no pains to reach the highest standard of excellence" (*ibid.* 281).

Third, the work of the teacher involves three phases—(1) *saving encounter:* each student must be led to Christ; (2) *saving relationship:* through union with Christ (*ibid.* 30), each student develops toward his or her highest potential in character and ability for service; and (3) *saving restoration:* each student gains ultimate transformation and eternal life in Christ's kingdom. Because of its eternal results, White declares that "the management and instruction of children is the noblest missionary work that any man or woman can undertake" (6T 205).

Fourth, regarding methods, White advises: "Instead of confining their study to that which men have said or written, let students be directed to the sources of truth, to the vast fields opened for research in nature and revelation" (Ed 17). Even beyond that, the supreme example is Christ the Master Teacher. Christ drew principles and illustrations from nature, life experience, and Scripture. Through His experience He understood humanity, He lived what He taught; and He saw in His students infinite potential. Daily dependent on God for grace and wisdom, Christ taught students to behold God through His Word, works, and providences. Rather than teaching abstract theories, Christ constantly integrated His teaching with practical life. Some areas on which teachers need to focus include: the combination of holy character, literary attainments, and physical health; such qualities as enthusiasm, true dignity, orientation toward continuous growth, excellence, and necessary knowledge, plus life's essentials—sacrifice, sunny temper, punctuality, thoroughness, prayer interlocked with faith; repentance, conversion, and the power of Christ; stimulation of minds without coercion; and useful labor for all (Ed 41-47, 77-82, 257-281, summarized by Douglass).

Fifth, White also challenges teachers to carefully mind their physical health. Since in their work, "quality is so much more important than quantity," teachers "should guard against overlabor—against attempting too much" in their "own line of duty; against accepting other responsibilities that would unfit" them for their work; and "against engaging in amusements and social pleasures that are exhausting rather than recuperative" (Ed 278).

Finally, the serious observer of White's educational ideals should be aware of the need to interpret White's counsels in light of the times and circumstances in which they were written. She herself recognized that at times the ideal she upholds in some writings may not be situationally practical in all circumstances. For example, she frequently upheld the ideal of having schools in rural locations. "The very atmosphere of the city is polluted. Let your schools be established away from the cities, where agricultural and other industries can be carried on" (21MR 90). But she also recognized that circumstances may require establishing a school in a less-than-ideal situation. "*So far as possible* these schools should be established outside the cities. But in the cities there are many children who could not attend schools away from the cities; and for the benefit of these, schools should be opened in the cities as well as in the country" (9T 201; italics supplied).

In conclusion, teachers and teaching deserve the best advantages that can be obtained, for they are instrumentalities for the eternal salvation of the students. To a large extent, the quality of teachers determines the quality of the schools and the degree of their benefit to the students, the community, the society, and the world. In view of teachers' global and eternal impact, either positive or negative, schools need to regularly review educational practices from the standpoint of teacher retention, for quality education will not happen apart from quality teachers.

See also: Education, Ellen White's Role in Adventist; Education, Philosophy of.

Further reading: Counsels on Education; Ed; FE; CT; CG; E. M. Cadwallader, *Principles of Education in the Writings of Ellen G. White*

(Payson, Ariz.: Leaves-of-Autumn Books, 1988); H. E. Douglass, "Spirit of Prophecy Perspectives: Education's Grand Theme," *Journal of Research on Christian Education* 10 (Summer 2001): 268-272; G. R. Knight, "The Aims of Adventist Education in Historical Perspective," *Journal of Research on Christian Education* 10 (Summer 2001): 195-199; *idem*, "The Devil Takes a Look at Adventist Education," *Journal of Research on Christian Education* 10 (Summer 2001): 180, 181; *idem, Myths in Adventism: An Interpretive Study of Ellen White, Education, and Related Issues* (RHPA, 1985); A. N. Nelson and R. G. Manalaysay, *The Gist of Christian Education*, 6th ed. (Manila: Philippine Union College; Riverside, Calif.: Loma Linda University, 1971); J. A. Tucker, "Pedagogical Application of the Seventh-day Adventist Philosophy of Education," *Journal of Research on Christian Education* 10 (Summer 2001): 310-315.

Adelino T. Libato and Reuel Almocera

TEMPERANCE. Temperance was a favorite subject of Ellen White's (4T 290). She spoke to her largest crowds as a lecturer on temperance and wrote profusely on this subject throughout her lifetime. "The temperance question is of tremendous importance to each one of us. It is far-reaching. I have spoken twenty-one times in succession on this subject," she wrote in 1893 (Te 284). She believed that a part of her specific calling "as the Lord's appointed messenger" was "to speak on the subject of temperance" (*ibid.* 259).

She insisted that temperance can be understood only from a Bible standpoint (*ibid.* 151, 100, 239). She set forth temperance as God's answer to intemperance, in order to bring a restoration of moral power. She drew on many Bible stories and passages to teach the results of temperance and of intemperance. She especially liked to teach temperance from the Christian standpoint, beginning with the fall of Adam, when self-control and moral power were lost to the human race. Then she showed that through Jesus self-control and "moral power" are restored, enabling the believer to overcome "the slavery of habit and indulgence of perverted appetite" (*ibid.* 265). "Temperance alone," she wrote, "is the foundation of all the graces that come from God, the foundation of all victories to be gained" (*ibid.* 201). Temperance therefore has its foundation in Divine Law—the "law of temperance" (CH 42; Te 146), which includes both natural and moral law and operates according to the divine principle of cause and effect (Te 84, 23).

Through inciting human appetite and passion, Satan subtly used the principle of cause and effect to destroy humankind. But Jesus undertook "to bear the burden for man, and overcome the power of appetite in his behalf" (Con 37; Te 20, 267). This Christ did by taking on human nature and fasting in the wilderness to successfully resist and overcome the temptation to intemperance (Con 39; Te 20, 121).

Ellen White saw alcohol and tobacco as twin evils (Te 72) and other harmful foods and drinks as avenues that impair the mind and body. "True temperance," she wrote, "teaches us to dispense entirely with everything hurtful, and to use judiciously that which is healthful" (*ibid.* 138).

The importance of the mind for receiving and maintaining temperance was spotlighted in two major ways. First, she emphasized the importance of the brain and nervous system as "the only medium through which Heaven can communicate to man and affect his inmost life" (*ibid.* 13). Second, she insisted on the individual's power of choice and decision. "Everything depends on the right action of the will" (*ibid.* 112). She noted that humans are "in constant peril" until they understand "the true force of the will" (*ibid.* 113). Her understanding of the human *will was far more nuanced and perceptive than the common idea of "will power" (*ibid.*). She taught that by yielding up the will to Christ, humans ally themselves to divine power, receiving "strength from God" to live a "life of faith" (*ibid.*). "Subjection to the will of Christ means restoration to perfect [humanity]" (*ibid.* 110).

Contrary to popular opinion, temperance is not restriction, nor condemnation, but release and restoration. "The Word of God does not condemn or repress man's activity, but tries to give it a right direction" (*ibid.* 193). While "Jesus rebuked intemperance, self-indulgence, and folly; yet He was social in His nature." "Innocent happiness" was pleasing to the Son of man (*ibid.*).

Ellen White clearly identified intemperance as sin, the breaking of natural and divine law (*ibid.* 89). Intemperance was to be perceived as opposition to life, health, and character, for "intemperance lies at the foundation of all the evil in our world" (*ibid.* 165). Intemperance was clearly presented by Ellen White as a "highway" (*ibid.* 93, 96, 163, 182), a progressive path from habit to addiction to loss of self control when the end result of "self-indulgence is not only a moral sin, but a physical disease" (*ibid.* 127).

Repeatedly her message was of prevention, not by attacking bad habits, but by presenting "something better" (*ibid.* 132). Believers are to be reformers, unselfish, kind, and courteous always, realizing that "God's plan is first to reach the heart" (*ibid.* 133). She urged all to reason from cause to effect, with temperance as the cause, and life, health, and character the effects. Temperance, she declared, must not be narrowed but placed on a "broader" and "an elevated platform" (*ibid.* 141, 165) as part of education, social and family relationships, community witness, and health issues.

Her repeated use of the words "health and temperance" specifies the distinction, yet repeated relation between health and temperance—with temperance as the foundation of good health, and intemperance, in its various forms, a major cause of disease (*ibid.* 169, 237, 242-245, 248, 262). Further, temperance was to be a key ecumenical avenue and a means to reach out to people in other denominations. She entreated and urged efforts to arouse public sentiment, both for temperance and against intemperance, with the raising of "our voices against the curse of drunkenness" (*ibid.* 238), including voting in favor of prohibition (*ibid.* 47, 254). This was to be as a warfare—a part of the great controversy between good and evil and the giving of the three angels' messages of Revelation 14 (*ibid.* 244, 245, 110, 238). Directing her message to Seventh-day Adventist church leaders and members, she called them to be at "the head in the temperance reform" (*ibid.* 220, 233).

Ellen White recommended cooperation with the *Woman's Christian Temperance Union, organized in 1874. Later she expressed regret for the church's neglect in not recognizing "the great advantage to be gained by connecting with the W.C.T.U. workers" (*ibid.* 223).

In January 1879 Ellen White and General Conference leaders organized the American Health and Temperance Association (AHTA). J. H. Kellogg was elected president. Limited action by church leaders, however, prompted James and Ellen White to personally take up the task and travel extensively organizing temperance societies and holding many meetings (SHM 230-235). In 1893 the AHTA became part of the newly formed *Medical Missionary and Benevolent Association, which had charge of Adventist health work in general

(*ibid.* 235). After the passage of the national prohibition law in 1919, Adventists and other reform organizations relaxed their efforts, leading to the repeal of prohibition in the United States in 1933.

In 1932, paralleling 1879, Adventists revived their temperance work under the name American Temperance Society. Years of growth in the temperance work followed, climaxing in a "temperance year," 1979, which marked the centenary of the first Adventist temperance association. In 1980 the General Conference Temperance Department was again merged with the Health Department, and in 2000 the word "temperance" was dropped from the departmental name, as "Health and Temperance" became "Health Ministries." Perhaps a letter of Ellen White in 1911 could again be most relevant: "If our people can be made to realize how much is at stake, and will seek to redeem the time that has been lost, by now putting heart and soul and strength into the temperance cause, great good will be seen as the result" (Te 257).

Further reading: J. L. Clark, "The Crusade Against Alcohol," in Gary Land, ed., *The World of Ellen White* (RHPA, 1987), pp. 131-140; SHM 223-235; R. Whitaker, "Drying Up the Stream," AR, Jan. 22, 2004; *SDA Encyclopedia* (1996), vol. 10, pp. 60-63.

Ernest H. J. Steed

TEMPERANCE (PPPA, 1949, 309 pp.). A compilation of Ellen White's counsels on temperance, which she once called "my favorite subject" (Te 260). The volume sets forth key elements of White's philosophy in these areas: (1) disobeying the laws of health is as much a sin against God as transgression of His moral law; (2) only conversion and the power of Christ can produce true temperance; (3) temperance encompasses all areas of life, requiring healthful practices in diet, dress, and work, as well as abstinence from alcohol, tobacco, and stimulants; (4) Christians should work to prevent intemperance in their own homes and in society and should seek to rescue those caught in harmful habits. Perhaps her most frequently quoted statement on temperance is the following: "Our danger is not from scarcity, but from abundance. We are constantly tempted to excess. Those who would preserve their powers unimpaired for the service of God must observe strict temperance in the use of His bounties, as well as total abstinence from every injurious or debasing indulgence" (*ibid.* 101). Appendices provide examples of White's personal efforts to promote temperance, including the content of three temperance lectures she gave.

Rachel Whitaker

TEMPTATION. Throughout her writings Ellen White recognizes that temptations come from "inclinations of the natural heart" (5T 177), from placing ourselves needlessly in the way of temptation or conforming to worldly practices (MYP 82), and from Satan's constant effort to take our eyes off the Savior. Whether through "the pleasures of this world, life's cares and perplexities and sorrows, the faults of others," or by focusing on our faults and weaknesses instead of on Christ (SC 71), temptations aim at separating us from God. She urges her readers to "dart a prayer to heaven" when temptation comes and resist the temptation "in such a decided manner that it will never be repeated" (SD 164). In addition to the example of Christ, she points to Joseph, whose first thought was to be true to Him instead of yielding to temptation (PP 217). She also points to Daniel, to whom "approval of God was dearer to him ... than life itself" (PK 483). Those who would be joint heirs with Christ must through the grace that He provides do their part overcoming (4T 33).

To be tempted is not a sin, says Ellen White, but "sin comes in when temptation is yielded to" (4T 358). "Unless there is a possibility of yielding, temptation is no temptation" (3SM 132). Jesus was tempted, yet He remained pure and holy (5T 426). He did not yield, and so it can be with us (DA 123). From His example Christ shows that the only hope of victory is resistance to the devil's attacks by uniting human weakness to divine strength (MYP 50). To parley with Satan, Ellen White warns, is to give him an advantage (DA 121). Satan cannot force one to transgress; if that were so, sin could be excused (4T 623), but God has provided means for resisting every temptation, no matter how strong (1SM 82). Christ, in His humanity, resisted and overcame temptation by the Word of God. Ellen White maintains that Christians who "look not to circumstances or to the weakness of self, but to the power of the Word" of God, can do likewise (DA 123).

See also: Christ, Temptations of.

Jack J. Blanco

TEN COMMANDMENTS, see **LAW OF GOD**.

TENNIS, see **GAMES AND SPORTS; COMPETITION**.

TEN VIRGINS, PARABLE OF, see **MIDNIGHT CRY**.

TESTIMONIES FOR THE CHURCH (PPPA, RHPA, 1885-1909). Series of nine volumes containing Ellen White's messages of counsels to Seventh-day Adventists, to either individuals or groups (such as churches and institutions). These messages relate to specific situations or are more of a general character dealing with principles of Christian living and the mission of the church.

Very early in her ministry Ellen White

opposed and rebuked various phases of fanaticism and error that threatened the welfare of the small group of ex-Millerites who formed the nucleus of the future Seventh-day Adventist Church. Not only did she express her views on doctrinal errors and false interpretations of Scripture (which led to aberrant behaviors), but she also gave directions regarding the establishment and enlargement of the work of the church. At first many of her messages were given orally to small groups of believers as she traveled from place to place. As the Adventist work progressed and spread to new areas, it became increasingly difficult for her to reach all the scattered believers, and she began to write her messages, also called *testimonies, and sent them to the leaders or the individuals to whom they were originally addressed. At a meeting in Battle Creek, Michigan, in November 1855 church leaders agreed that Ellen White's messages of warning and instruction should be published for the benefit of all believers. Thus came about the publication of a 16-page pamphlet called "Testimony." One hundred fifty copies of this pamphlet were printed and sent to believers. This was the first of a series of 37 "Testimonies for the Church" that would, in the course of 55 years, amount to nearly 5,000 pages.

Many of the personal testimonies that were written out and sent to individuals dealt with dangers and problems that also confronted others in similar circumstances. It soon became evident that the instruction found in these messages would also be beneficial to the church members in general. Ellen White explained: "Since the warning and instruction given in testimony for individual cases applied with equal force to many others who had not been specially pointed out in this manner, it seemed to be my duty to publish the personal testimonies for the benefit of the church" (5T 658, 659). In the publication of these letters, names of individuals and places were usually omitted.

The publication of these consecutively numbered pamphlets occurred regularly through the 1850s and 1860s. By the time *Testimony for the Church*, number 10, was published early in 1864, the small editions of the earlier pamphlets were out of print. As requests for these increased, it was decided that the earlier numbers should be reprinted. The reprinted *Testimonies* formed part of *Spiritual Gifts*, volume 4. Another nine pamphlets (numbers 11 to 19) of the *Testimonies* appeared between 1865 and 1870. By then earlier numbers were again out of print and to meet this increasing demand, numbers 1 to 16 were reprinted and bound in two books of about 500 pages each. Numbers 20 to 30 appeared between 1871 and 1881, once more with the reprinting in black bound volumes of earlier pamphlets. By 1883 the publishers were again unable to furnish complete sets of the *Testimonies* either in pamphlet form or in bound volumes, and to meet the constant demand it was decided to republish all of numbers 1 to 30.

This decision, however, led to a close look into the Seventh-day Adventist understanding of inspiration in relation to Ellen White's prophetic ministry. Some of the early *Testimonies* had been written under very unfavorable circumstances, and in the haste to publish them for the people, numerous grammatical errors had been allowed to go uncorrected into the published works. In contrast to earlier republications, Ellen White decided that this time these errors should be corrected so as to present the message in better literary form. This decision was of such vital importance that the General Conference session of 1883 discussed it and decided to approve of the republication of these *Testimony* pamphlets following a more thorough editorial process. What caused the difficulty was the thought held by some that Ellen White's inspiration was of a verbal-dictation type and that every word she wrote was somehow dictated to her by the Holy Spirit. Given such a view of inspiration, many felt that editorial corrections were equivalent to a tampering with the very words of God. The majority of delegates at the General Conference session, however, did not agree with this view of inspiration but rather believed that "the light given by God to His servants is by the enlightenment of the mind, thus imparting the thoughts, and not (except in rare cases) the very words in which the ideas should be expressed." Hence it was agreed that earlier writings of Ellen White could be edited and perfected, as to grammar and syntax, without invalidating her gift of inspiration (RH, Nov. 27, 1883).

The delegates also decided to reprint the first 30 *Testimony* pamphlets into four volumes of about 700 or 800 pages each, volumes 1 to 4 of our present nine-volume series of *Testimonies for the Church*. Volume 1 contains pamphlet numbers 1 to 14 (originally published between 1855 and 1868) and a biographical sketch of Ellen White's life and ministry up to the death of her husband in 1881. Volume 2 includes numbers 15 to 20 (published between 1868 and 1871); volume 3, numbers 21 to 25 (published between 1872 and 1875); and volume 4, numbers 26 to 30 (published between 1876 and 1881). This new edition was heartily welcomed by church members and widely circulated. Later numbers were added to this set, and in 1889 volume 5 appeared containing numbers 31, 32, and 33. Volumes 6 (1900), 7 (1902), 8 (1904), and 9 (1909) appeared as complete volumes, but were also numbered consecutively to bring the total number of *Testimony* pamphlets to 37. Each current volume includes a brief

historical account of the times in which the pamphlets were published and the various themes, issues, and problems it addresses.

Further reading: A. L. White, *Ellen G. White: Messenger to the Remnant,* rev. ed. (RHPA, 1969), pp. 62-67; P. A. Gordon, *My Dear Brother M...: Why Ellen White Wrote the Letters in* Testimonies for the Church (PPPA, 1997); J. Moon, *W. C. White and Ellen G. White* (AUP, 1993), pp. 122-129; W. C. White, "Integrity of the Testimonies for the Church" (EGWE, SDoc).

Denis Fortin

TESTIMONIES ON SABBATH SCHOOL WORK (RHPA, 1900, 128 pp.). Compilation of Ellen White's counsels on the work of *Sabbath schools. Materials found in this book were selected largely from her periodical articles published in the *Sabbath School Worker* between 1885 and 1896, and other writings. Articles are presented in the chronological order of their original publication. Most of the contents of this booklet was later republished in *Counsels on Sabbath School Work* (1938). The many subjects presented in this book include the purpose and influence of Sabbath schools, the study of the Bible, and qualifications of teachers.

TESTIMONIES ON SEXUAL BEHAVIOR, ADULTERY, AND DIVORCE (EGWE, 1989, 271 pp.). Compilation of Ellen White's writings on sexual behavior and related moral problems. Materials selected for this book were drawn largely from her unpublished letters. This book was originally prepared for the benefit of church administrators and other ministers who must deal with questionable or immoral conduct.

Many of the letters cited in this volume were addressed to errant ministers. Since Ellen White corresponded largely with ministers and church administrators, this should come as no surprise. However, in spite of the faults and sins of those to whom she wrote, she had confidence in the ministry of the Seventh-day Adventist Church. Since contemporary moral problems are similar to those of past decades, the compilers believed that many letters written by Ellen White a century ago contain warnings and appeals that need to be heard today.

This compilation was not designed to serve as a manual of rules for dealing with immorality, infidelity, or unscriptural divorce and remarriage. Moral problems are complex, and no two situations are exactly alike. It was Ellen White's "intention that there should not go forth from her pen anything that could be used as a law or a rule dealing with these questions of marriage, divorce, remarriage, and adultery" (pp. 6, 7). Although many of the letters quoted in this book refer to difficult moral situations, she attempted in her correspondence to uphold the standards of the law of God and to approach each situation with pastoral care, compassion, and love. Perhaps more than any other book, *Testimonies on Sexual Behavior, Adultery, and Divorce* shows that the grace of God and the work of the Holy Spirit can change lives and provide hope for those whose complex moral problems seem beyond human solution.

TESTIMONIES TO MINISTERS AND GOSPEL WORKERS (PPPA, 1923, 1944, 1962, 544 pp.). One of the first posthumous books compiled by the trustees of E. G. White Estate, this volume contains counsels sent to General Conference officers and to the Battle Creek church between 1890 and 1900, the decade following the Minneapolis *General Conference session of 1888. These messages focused especially on the need for personal and corporate revival and reformation. Excerpts from other published materials relating to the work

of the ministry in its various phases are also included. Many of these counsels were initially published in pamphlets and periodical articles, particularly *Special Testimonies, Series A* (1892-1897), and *Special Testimonies, Series B* (1903-1913). Other related items were drawn from articles published in the *Review and Herald*.

The third edition carries a concise historical foreword clarifying the context of some denominational developments during the 1880s and 1890s to help readers better understand the circumstances that prevailed at the time the messages were written. Appendix notes have also been supplied. The source of each article, with date of first publication, is indicated in footnote references. In the third edition the lists of items "for further study" have been expanded to include references to related material appearing in other compilations published subsequent to 1923. The counsels are arranged in 15 chapters covering many issues related to the person, work, methods, integrity, and character of the minister.

S. Joseph Kidder

TESTIMONY, TESTIMONIES. General term for a believer's declaration or profession of faith, either *spoken* to one or more individuals, or *written*, or *lived*, from which are derived several more specialized meanings in Adventist usage. Ellen White's testimony originally meant simply her witness, like any other believer, about her own Christian experience (see 1T 32-38, 44). After she began receiving visions with messages for others, her communication of such messages to others was also called her "testimony." As these messages began to be published, the terms *Testimony*, *Testimonies*, and *Testimonies for the Church* became titles of pamphlets and books. Other variants of the general term "testimony" include straight testimony (with the connotation of direct, stringent, uncompromising), and "living" testimony, meaning vibrant, full of spiritual life (5T 229); current, contemporary (3T 360); and/or the testimony of one's life as complementing one's spoken testimony (TM 391).

An associated term is the "testimony of Jesus" (see Rev. 1:2, 9; 12:17; and 19:10; cf. Rev. 22:9), understood to mean especially the message of Jesus through prophets. As the Holy Spirit in the role of teaching truth is called the "Spirit of truth" (John 15:26) so the Holy Spirit in the role of inspiring prophets is called the *Spirit of prophecy.

Ellen White solemnly affirmed that the ultimate purpose of end-time "testimonies" is to enable all who will heed them to be ready for the second advent of Christ. "The very last deception of Satan [within the church] will be to make of none effect the testimony of the Spirit of God. 'Where there is no vision, the people perish' (Prov. 29:18). Satan will work ingeniously, in different ways and through different agencies, to unsettle the confidence of God's remnant people in the true testimony" (1SM 48). "There will be a hatred kindled against the testimonies which is satanic. The workings of Satan will be to unsettle the faith of the churches in them, for this reason: Satan cannot have so clear a track to bring in his deceptions and bind up souls in his delusions if the warnings and reproofs and counsels of the Spirit of God are heeded" (*ibid.* 48).

See also: Laodicean Message.

Further reading: 1T 186, 187; 2T 604-608; 3T 252-272; 4T 83-93; 5T 654-691.

Jerry Moon

TESTIMONY COUNTDOWN. A weekly program conducted in Seventh-day Adventist churches planned by the Ellen G. White Estate to promote the systematic study of the nine volumes of the *Testimonies for the Church*. The program was launched at the Takoma Park, Maryland, church in 1969, with more than 1,600 people attending each Wednesday night. It consisted of four parts: (1) a story from the time period under study, (2) a review of the historical background of each volume, (3) "discovery" time in which participants gave personal testimonies about their weekly study, and (4) a brief review from a study guide of assignments in each volume. It was later used in all of North America with special materials prepared for pastors and elders. Testimony Countdown II followed in 1976, with similar success. Testimony Countdown III was launched in 1991, using *Counsels for the Church* as its textbook.

Paul A. Gordon

TESTIMONY STUDIES ON DIET AND FOODS, see **COUNSELS ON DIET AND FOODS**.

TESTIMONY TREASURES (PPPA, 1949, 1771 pp.). Three-volume set of Ellen White's messages to the Seventh-day Adventist Church selected from the *Testimonies for the Church*. The 1,600 pages of text in these three volumes represent about one third of the content of the original nine volumes. Articles were selected on the basis of their appeal to a broad international readership, in order to serve as the basic edition for foreign language translations of the *Testimonies*. Not found in this set are messages of local and personal concern and counsels regarding certain institutions. Also, no articles were included that are closely paralleled in other publications. Most of the articles that had already appeared in the three volumes of *Selections From the Testimonies* (SPA, 1936) were included in *Testimony Treasures*. For each article the original source is given, and with few exceptions, articles appear in the same chronological order as in the full nine-volume set.

Texas. James and Ellen White lived in Texas from November 1878 through April 1879. Accompanied by their daughter-in-law, *Emma White, and *S. N. Haskell, they arrived by train in Dallas on November 6, 1878. While in Texas, Ellen White participated in the organization and strengthening of the Texas Conference and concentrated on her writing projects. For most of their stay in Texas the Whites made their headquarters in *J. F. Bahler's large new home on Morgan Street in southwest Denison.

Attending the state's first camp meeting on Job Huguley's farm in Plano, November 12-17, 1878, James and Ellen preached six sermons each, while S. N. Haskell preached 11 times. In a letter to her son Willie she remarked, "We have come on the ground only last night, and I have not been in meeting yet. Shall speak this afternoon, as the people are on the tiptoe of expectation." Recognizing her infirmities, she continued with a benchmark statement, "Might just as well let them feel at once that they have expected too much, that I am nothing but a weak, frail, imperfect woman at best, looking to and trusting in God alone to accomplish the work" (Lt 53, 1878).

Following *Robert M. Kilgore's election to the presidency of the conference, the Whites supported his evangelistic efforts and requested large amounts of literature to give away to individuals (Lt 58, 1878). They also held meetings in several surrounding country schoolhouses and at the Dallas church (ST, Mar. 6, 1879). Invited by prominent government officials, Ellen White held a week of evangelistic meetings in Dallas, followed by similar meetings in the Denison area. Perhaps their greatest accomplishment was their inadvertent meeting with a young couple who were attempting to enter gospel ministry work, *Arthur G. and Mary Daniells.

During the late months of 1878 Ellen White concentrated her efforts on the completion of *Testimony* number 28 (cf. 4T 271-383). While James White served as her copy editor for a time, *Marian Davis arrived in Texas on January 1, 1879, to begin a quarter century of editorial work for Ellen White. That winter, Ellen White's writing included work on *Testimony* number 29 (cf. *ibid.* 384-522), but seemed to focus mainly on an enlargement of *Spiritual Gifts*, volume 1, which was serialized in *Signs of the Times* before becoming *The Spirit of Prophecy*, volume 4. James reported to Willie in January, "Your mother astonishes us all in the amount and quality of her writing" (JW to WCW, Jan. 14, 1879).

Besides Ellen White's participation in the business of the church, her humanitarian lifestyle and attitude while in Texas are noteworthy. The Whites' first act in Texas was to come to the aid of the McDearmons (Emma White's family) living in Grand Prairie. Every member of that family, emigrants from Wright, Michigan, to Texas, two years earlier, had succumbed to a nationwide yellow fever epidemic. Emma's teenage brother had died, and the entire family then became too ill to care for themselves. James, Ellen, and Emma brought the McDearmons food, clothing, and two mattresses as well as financial assistance and personal care (Lt 54, 1878; JW to WCW, Nov. 12, 1878). Ellen arranged shelter for another family of destitute believers in north Texas, and provided furnishings, clothing, and groceries, and cooked meals to several other families (Lt 63, 1878, in 14MR 318-321). She often expressed concern for the tobacco users, the spiritually ignorant, and those who suffered physically, especially as a result of their own intemperance. She searched out remnants of cloth to sew for "so many poor children, half dead" (Lt 60, 1878) and confided, "I cannot see want and misery and enjoy the comforts of life" (Lt 63, 1878).

In spite of Ellen's accomplishments in Texas, her husband wrote to Willie in February 1879, "Your mother is determined not to like" Texas. She had complained of "hacking about in a lumber wagon," of chopping her false teeth out of ice during a "fearfully cold" spell, and of dreading the summer heat. She was frustrated by the lack of laborers, saying, "We feel there is much work to be done even here in Texas, but no one to do it. It is the most destitute field for help I know of anywhere" (JW to WCW, February 1879). Despite her disenchantment with conditions in the Lone Star State, Ellen concluded to A. G. Daniells, still in Texas, "We would not discourage those who can labor there from doing so" (Lt 32, 1879).

On April 22, 1879, the Whites set out by *wagon train from Denison to Colorado in an attempt to resettle some families in a more prosperous part of the country.

Further reading: 3Bio 98-108.

Mary Ann Hadley

THANKSGIVING, see **HOLIDAYS**.

THAT I MAY KNOW HIM (RHPA, 1964, 382 pp.). Seventh daily devotional book published by the Ellen G. White Estate. Selections for this devotional book were made largely from materials not in print at the time of publication. More than half the book is drawn from articles that appeared in Adventist periodicals and from unpublished letters and manuscripts. Although no central theme guided the selection of materials, of special interest are several pages of extracts from early-morning entries in Ellen White's diary that give insights into her personal prayer life. References to the materials selected are given at the end of the book.

THAT OTHER ANGEL, see ***COLPORTEUR MINISTRY***.

THEATER, see **DRAMA AND THEATER**.

THEATRICAL BEHAVIOR, see **DRAMA AND THEATER**.

THIRD ANGEL'S MESSAGE, see **THREE ANGELS' MESSAGES**.

THIS DAY WITH GOD (RHPA, 1979, 384 pp.). Twelfth daily devotional book published by the Ellen G. White Estate. The selection of materials in this book was made from letters and manuscripts written or orally presented by Ellen White on the same calendar day designated for that day's reading. No central theme guided the selection of these messages except that whenever possible the excerpts intended to bring inspiration and encouragement for daily living. A brief biographical chronology of Ellen White's life and ministry is found at the end of the book (pp. 375-381).

THOUGHTS FROM THE MOUNT OF BLESSING (PPPA, 1896, 1955, 172 pp.). Ellen White's presentation of the lessons Jesus taught in the Sermon on the Mount. Issued in several editions since 1896, the Ellen G. White Estate produced a standard reference edition in 1955. *Thoughts From the Mount of Blessing* is the first of three books—with *The Desire of Ages* (1898) and *Christ's Object Lessons* (1900)—on the life and ministry of Jesus that Ellen White prepared while living in Australia. The six chapters are a commentary on the Sermon on the Mount as found in the Gospel of Matthew and cover the Beatitudes (pp. 6-44), the spirituality of the law of God (pp. 45-78), the true motive in service (pp. 79-101), the Lord's Prayer (pp. 102-122), and not judging others (pp. 123-152). Her preface highlights that "the Sermon on the Mount is Heaven's benediction to the world—a voice from the throne of God. It was given to mankind to be to them the law of duty and the light of heaven, their hope and consolation in despondency, their joy and comfort in all the vicissitudes and walks of life.... Throughout all time the words that Christ spoke from the mount of Beatitudes will retain their power. Every sentence is a jewel from the treasure house of truth" (pp. vii, viii). A contemporary adaption of the book prepared by Jerry D. Thomas was published in 2008 under the title *Blessings* (PPPA, 142 pp.).

Thoughts on Revelation, see **Smith, Uriah**.

Three Angels' Messages. A reference to the angelic messages of Revelation 14:6-12, which Seventh-day Adventists regard as symbolizing their own message and mission to the world prior to the *second coming of Christ (Rev. 14:14-20). Foundational for the Adventist understanding of those messages are the notions that "no one hears the voice of these angels, for they are a symbol to represent the people of God who are working in harmony with the universe of heaven," and that the messages have "a direct bearing upon the people living in the last days of this earth's history" (LS 429).

Seventh-day Adventist authors, including Ellen G. White, refer to the preaching of the three angels as initiated by the nineteenth-century Millerite and Sabbatarian Adventist movements. The first message (verses 6, 7) has been identified as the Millerite proclamation in the late 1830s and early 1840s that "the hour of his judgment" would arrive in 1843-1844, at the end of the 2300 symbolic days of Daniel 8:14. The second message (verse 8) has been understood as the warnings by *Charles Fitch and a few others, from the summer of 1843 on, calling the Millerites out

of the churches that had rejected the message of the first angel. Some of those who left the churches eventually accepted the third angel's message (verses 9-12), preached since 1844, and embraced "the light of the Sabbath" and follow Jesus "by faith" into the Most Holy Place of the heavenly sanctuary (see 1SG 128-173). Seventh-day Adventists eventually enriched their understanding of the third angel's message by adding to it, in the 1860s, the health message and, in the 1880s, a clearer understanding of justification (righteousness) by faith.

One of the most insightful keys to understand Ellen White's concept of the missiological function of the three angels' messages is the analogy, in her 1858 great controversy vision, portraying those messages as "three steps" leading people up to the "solid, immovable platform" of present truth (see *ibid.* 168-173). She describes two classes of people who climbed up to the platform. First, she mentions a whole "company" of believers who had been led "step by step" by God up to the platform (*ibid.* 168, 169). That group was made up, evidently, of those who accepted all three messages at the time of their original preaching within Millerite circles. Speaking about the Millerite experience, Ellen White referred to "the close of the second angel's message" for those to whom it had been then preached (*ibid.* 140; cf. EW 238, 304). Out of that experience came the early notion that while the Millerites had announced, up to 1844, the first two messages, the Sabbatarian Adventists were proclaiming, since 1844, especially the third message. Consequently many Seventh-day Adventists have spoken over the years about their doctrinal system in terms of "the third angel's message."

But after describing the Millerite "company" on the platform, Ellen White speaks about other non-Millerite "individuals" who later on approached the platform, examined its foundation, and also stepped upon it. The existence of other "individuals" still climbing up to the platform unveils the need of a post-1844 ongoing proclamation of all three messages. Back in 1850 Ellen White had already seen that "the burden of the message should be the first, second, and third angels' messages, and those who had any hope in God would yield to the force of that truth" (5MR 203). Yet in 1858 she recognized more explicitly that "many who embraced the third message had not an experience in the two former messages," but they "saw the perfect chain of truth in the angels' messages, and gladly received it. They embraced them in their order, and followed Jesus by faith into the heavenly Sanctuary. These messages were represented to me as an anchor to hold the body. And as individuals receive and understand them, they are shielded against the many delusions of Satan" (1SG 165, 166).

During the 1890s Ellen White emphasized several times the enduring simultaneous preaching of all three messages. For instance, in 1892 she stated that "the first, second, and third angels' messages are all linked together," for "the same message that was given by the second angel" of Revelation 14:8 is repeated "in the loud cry of the third angel's message" of Revelation 18:1-5 (2SM 117, 118). In 1896 she explained that "the first and second messages were given in 1843 and 1844, and we are now under the proclamation of the third; but all three of the messages are still to be proclaimed. It is just as essential now as ever before that they shall be repeated to those who are seeking for the truth," because "there cannot be a third without the first and second" (ibid. 104, 105). In 1897 she added that "these messages are connected and bound together. One cannot be carried without the other" (1MR 56). And in 1900 she stated that the third angel's message "embraces the messages of the first and second angel" (ibid. 57). Therefore, "the three angels' messages are to be combined, giving their threefold light to the world." She viewed the angel of Revelation 18 as proclaiming "the last and threefold message of warning to the world" (7BC 985; cf. GC88 685).

Ellen White drew a strong link between the third angel's message and the message of righteousness by faith. "Some of our brethren have expressed fears that we shall dwell too much upon the subject of justification by faith, but I hope and pray that none will be needlessly alarmed; for there is no danger in presenting this doctrine as it is set forth in the Scriptures. If there had not been a remissness in the past to properly instruct the people of God, there would not now be a necessity of calling a special attention to it" (1SM 372).

Her understanding of the end-time missiological significance of the three angels' messages is highlighted in the following statements: "In a special sense Seventh-day Adventists have been set in the world as watchmen and light bearers. To them has been entrusted the last warning for a perishing world. On them is shining wonderful light from the word of God. They have been given a work of the most solemn import—the proclamation of the first, second, and third angels' messages. There is no other work of so great importance. They are to allow nothing else to absorb their attention" (9T 19). As the "testing message" for our time (UL 368), "the truth comprised in the first, second, and third angels' messages must go to every nation, kindred, tongue, and people; it must lighten the darkness of every continent and extend to the islands of the sea. Nothing of human invention must be allowed to retard this work" (6T 133).

Further reading: H. K. LaRondelle, "The

Remnant and the Three Angels' Messages," in R. Dederen, ed., *Handbook of Seventh-day Adventist Theology* (RHPA, 2000), pp. 857-892; A. R. Timm, *The Sanctuary and the Three Angels' Messages: Integrating Factors in the Development of Seventh-day Adventist Doctrines*, Adventist Theological Society Dissertation Series (Berrien Springs, Mich.: ATS Pub., 1995), vol. 5.

Alberto R. Timm

TIME MANAGEMENT. Two aspects of time are reflected in the Bible: quantitative time, which is the chronological measurement of time, and qualitative time, which is the significance of time in its content and meaning (Lake). Ellen White reflects both of these aspects in her understanding of time and its management. Her most significant statement on time is found in *Christ's Object Lessons* where she discusses the talents of Matthew 25:14-30. There she describes the talent of time first in terms of its theological, qualitative aspect: "Our time belongs to God. Every moment is His, and we are under the most solemn obligation to improve it to His glory. Of no talent He has given will He require a more strict account than of our time." As such, every moment is precious and "freighted with eternal consequences." These moments should be treasured and used wisely. While "time squandered can never be recovered," we can redeem the time "by making the most of that which remains" (COL 342, 343).

Next, she describes time in terms of its quantitative aspect: "It is the duty of every Christian to acquire habits of order, thoroughness, and dispatch. There is no excuse for slow bungling at work of any character." Thus, a person must work to overcome "fussy, lingering habits" which slow their work down. All should have a definite aim. "Decide how long a time is required for a given task, and then bend every effort toward accomplishing the work in the given time. The exercise of the will power will make the hands move deftly." Thus, a "resolute purpose, persistent industry, and careful economy of time will enable men to acquire knowledge and mental discipline which will qualify them for almost any position of influence and usefulness" (*ibid.* 344).

In the backdrop of this quantitative and qualitative approach to time, she encouraged Christians to implement basic time-management principles such as daily planning and scheduling (Hobbs). "As far as possible," she counseled, "it is well to consider what is to be accomplished through the day. Make a memorandum of the different duties that await your attention, and set apart a certain time for the doing of each duty. Let everything be done with thoroughness, neatness, and dispatch" (SD 114). She frequently encouraged Christians to discipline their time by rising early and carefully managing the moments spent traveling or waiting for appointments. If "these fragments of time were improved in study, reading, or careful thought," she emphasized, "what might not be accomplished" (COL 344; cf. MH 208). Consistent with her biblical focus, she frequently appealed to Paul's words in Romans 12:11 as a spiritual motivation to improve time-management habits: "Let those who are naturally slow of movement seek to become active, quick, energetic, remembering the words of the apostle, 'Not slothful in business; fervent in spirit; serving the Lord'" (SD 114; cf. COL 346). As such, her century-old writings on the use of time reflect the dual emphasis on personal effectiveness and efficiency found in contemporary time-management literature (Covey).

Her own practice of time management involved scheduling and a careful use of the hours in each day. *Willie recalls her writing schedule when they lived at *Battle Creek.

Without much variation, she began writing at 3:00 or 4:00 in the morning until breakfast at 6:30. After working in her flower garden for about 30 minutes with her children, she would devote three or four more hours to writing. The afternoon was then occupied with home responsibilities. She would also write while traveling. In later life she did most of her writing while others were asleep: "I build my fire, and then write uninterruptedly, sometimes for hours" (Douglass). Her literary output of some 100,000 pages over her 70-year ministry attests to her careful use of time.

Further reading: S. R. Covey, *First Things First: To Live, to Love, to Learn, to Leave a Legacy* (New York: Simon & Schuster, 1994); H. E. Douglass, *Messenger of the Lord* (PPPA, 1998), pp. 108, 109; C. R. Hobbs, *Time Power* (New York: Harper & Row, 1987); J. Lake, "Time Management in the Ministry: A Study of the Charles R. Hobbs Time Power System and Its Application to the Ministry" (D.Min. diss., Reformed Theological Seminary, 1994), pp. 149-159.

Jud Lake

TIME OF TROUBLE. Taken from Daniel 12:1, the phrase "time of trouble" describes the tribulations God's people will go through just before their deliverance and the establishment of God's everlasting kingdom. Ellen White uses two related expressions regarding the time of trouble that should not be confused: the "little time of trouble" and the "time of Jacob's trouble." She explains that the "little time of trouble" will be a short period of affliction and persecution just prior to the close of *probation and Christ's intercession in heaven. During this time, when "the nations will be angry," the *latter rain will fall on the sealed people of God in order to give power to the message of the third angel and prepare God's children for "when the seven last *plagues

shall be poured out" (EW 85, 86). Those who then choose to stay loyal to Christ at any cost will use the "little time of trouble" to proclaim the third angel's message to the world.

The Adventist understanding of the "time of Jacob's trouble" grows out of Jacob's experience at the brook Jabbok (Gen. 32:22-30) and is applied by Jeremiah to Israel prior to her deliverance from Babylonian captivity and return from exile (Jer. 30:3-11). As Jacob had to go through agony at Jabbok, so it will be with God's people during the time of Jacob's trouble. Jeremiah announces, "Alas! for that day is great, so that none is like it: it is even the time of Jacob's trouble, but he shall be saved out of it" (verse 7). Ellen White elaborates on this theme, explaining that God's people will experience something similar to Jacob in his struggle with the angel of the Lord. He had repented from his sin in obtaining his birthright by fraud, and the Lord forgave him and saved his life. The same will be with the people of God just prior to Christ's return. If they have unconfessed sins, they will be overwhelmed. Despair will cut off their faith, and they will not "have confidence to plead with God for deliverance" (GC 620). However, all those who have truly confessed their sins and have "a deep sense of their unworthiness" will be forgiven and saved. "Their sins have gone beforehand to judgment and have been blotted out, and they cannot bring them to remembrance" (*ibid.*). For Ellen White the "time of Jacob's trouble" corresponds to the "time of trouble" mentioned in Daniel 12:1 and refers to the very end-time developments on earth during the seven last plagues before the coming of Christ.

During the time of trouble the righteous will live without an intercessor but not without the Holy Spirit's empowerment (*ibid.* 610, 614). According to Daniel 12, the standing up of Michael refers to Christ finishing His high-priestly ministry in the heavenly sanctuary and closing the time of probation. Thus, this time of trouble refers to a brief period between the close of probation and the second coming of Christ. It coincides with the time allotted to the seven last plagues (Rev. 15:1), which are poured out upon those who have rejected God's mercy. When Christ finishes His intercessory work in behalf of sinners, the Holy Spirit is withdrawn from the inhabitants of the earth, and God's people are sealed. Then all the previously restrained powers of darkness are let loose, and unite to come down upon the world with indescribable ferocity. "There will be such a scene of strife as no pen can picture" (6T 408). At that time God's people will experience a period of utmost anguish and testing, from which Christ delivers them at His coming.

Ellen White provides a detailed description of the experiences through which God's people will go during this period (EW 282-285; GC 613-634). The righteous "shall be treated as traitors" (6T 394; cf. 5T 450). To escape persecution, they will have to leave cities and villages, and many will be put into prisons and sentenced to death (GC 626). The time of trouble will reach a climax in what is called the "time of Jacob's trouble," when the leaders of earth issue a universal decree against those who keep the Sabbath according to the fourth commandment, authorizing "to strike in one night a decisive blow" to God's people (*ibid.* 615, 616, 635). However, "the righteous will be preserved through the ministration of heavenly angels" (PP 256). God will miraculously protect them. "Some are assailed . . . but the swords raised against them break and fall powerless as a straw," while "others are defended by angels in the form of men of war" (GC 631). "It is at midnight," when God's people are surrounded and the death decree is about to be enforced, "that God manifests

His power for the deliverance of His people" (*ibid.* 636).

Further reading: GC 613-634; EW 36, 37, 71, 282-287; SR 406-411; P. G. Damsteegt, *Foundations of the Seventh-day Adventist Message and Mission* (Grand Rapids: Eerdmans, 1977; reprint, AUP, 1988), pp. 143-146; *SDA Encyclopedia* (1996), vol. 10, pp. 816, 934; vol. 11, p. 777.

Anna Galeniece

TIME SETTING. The attempt to predict either an exact or an approximate date for the *second coming of Christ. Throughout the Christian era students of the books of *Daniel and *Revelation have used the prophetic times of the 3½ times (Dan. 7:25; Rev. 12:14), 42 months (Rev. 11:2; 13:5), 1260 days (Rev. 11:3; 12:6), 1290 and 1335 days (Dan. 12:11, 12), and *2300 days (Dan. 8:14) to calculate the time of either the judgment, resurrection of the dead, or second advent of Christ. Although they were disappointed when these events did not take place, they discovered that the fulfillment of these prophetic time periods were milestones in prophetic history, revealing signs of the nearness of Christ's return.

For Ellen White, the last legitimate prophetic time setting to affect the whole Christian world was that of Daniel 8:14, about the cleansing of the *sanctuary at the end of the *2300 days. This prophetic message was proclaimed in connection with the message about "the hour of His judgment" (Rev. 14:7) during the first part of the nineteenth century, and resulted in the rise of the Second Advent movement.

Ellen White fully endorsed this proclamation of the 2300 prophetic days, stating, "The preaching of a definite time for the judgment, in the giving of the first message [Rev. 14:6, 7], was ordered by God. The computation of the prophetic periods on which that message was based, placing the close of the 2300 days in the autumn of 1844, stands without impeachment" (GC 457). Adventists hold that this prophecy marked the beginning of Christ's final atoning ministry of the antitypical day of atonement.

This prophetic proclamation included the announcement that "there should be time no longer" (Rev. 10:6), indicating "the end of the prophetic periods" (Mar 18). This meant that with the fulfillment of the 2300 prophetic days in 1844 there was to be no more preaching of definite prophetic time periods before the Second Advent.

In the middle of 1845, when some Adventists were involved in time setting, Ellen White received a vision warning that they would be disappointed (WLF 22). Again in 1851 she warned against time setting: "The Lord showed me that the message must go, and that it must not be hung on time; for time will never be a test again. I saw that some were getting a false excitement, arising from preaching time, that the third angel's message [of Rev. 14] can stand on its own foundation, and that it needs not time to strengthen it, and that it will go with mighty power, and do its work, and will be cut short in righteousness" (1SM 188).

Unfortunately, some early Adventists continued with time setting for the coming of Christ and experienced disappointment after disappointment. On the events following 1844 Ellen White commented: "Some were led into the error of repeatedly fixing upon a definite time for the coming of Christ. The light which was now shining on the subject of the sanctuary should have shown them that no prophetic period extends to the second advent; that the exact time of this advent is not foretold. But, turning from the light, they continued to set time after time for the Lord to come, and as often they were disappointed" (GC 456).

In 1884, 40 years after the Great Disappointment, Ellen White reacted strongly against another attempt at time setting and explained the damaging effect of this practice. She said that God had not given the knowledge of the time of the Second Advent because if He did, people "would not make a right use of it." "A condition of things would result from this knowledge among our people that would greatly retard the work of God in preparing a people to stand in the great day that is to come. We are not to live upon time excitement" (1SM 189). She pointed out that Jesus "told His disciples to 'watch,' but not for a definite time." Then she gave the following practical counsel: "You will not be able to say that He will come in one, two, or five years, neither are you to put off His coming by stating that it may not be for ten or twenty years" (*ibid.*).

"Our position," she added, "has been one of waiting and watching, with no time-proclamation to intervene between the close of the prophetic periods in 1844 and the time of our Lord's coming. We do not know the day nor the hour, or when the definite time is, and yet the prophetic reckoning shows us that Christ is at the door" (10MR 270).

She further warned that continued attempts to time-set "not only lead minds away from the present truth, but throw contempt upon all efforts to explain the prophecies. The more frequently a definite time is set for the second advent, and the more widely it is taught, the better it suits the purposes of Satan. After the time has passed, he excites ridicule and contempt of its advocates, and thus casts reproach upon the great advent movement of 1843 and 1844. Those who persist in this error will at last fix upon a date too far in the future for the coming of Christ. Thus they will be led to rest in a false security, and many will not be undeceived until it is too late" (GC 457).

Even more strongly she maintained that

those who continue to set definite time "are advancing infidelity rather than Christianity. They produce Scripture and by false interpretation show a chain of argument which apparently proves their position. But their failures show that they are false prophets, that they do not rightly interpret the language of inspiration. The Word of God is truth and verity, but men have perverted its meaning. These errors have brought the truth of God for these last days into disrepute" (4T 307).

To discourage time setting, Ellen White called attention to 2 Thessalonians 2, where believers evidently expected the Second Advent while major prophecies had yet to be fulfilled. This was a deception. Applying "the apostle's admonition" to "those who live in the last days," she observed, "Many Adventists have felt that unless they could fix their faith upon a definite time for the Lord's coming, they could not be zealous and diligent in the work of preparation. But as their hopes are again and again excited, only to be destroyed, their faith receives such a shock that it becomes well-nigh impossible for them to be impressed by the great truths of prophecy" (GC 457).

A major reason that time setting continues in the present is the apparent delay of the Second Advent. The longer the delay, the greater the temptation to some to question the correctness of the prophecies that brought about the Advent movement. These impatient believers seem to have missed Ellen White's observation that a major cause for the delay is the failure of God's people to proclaim the third angel's message of Revelation 14, which is "the gospel message for these last days" (6T 241).

She compares Israel's 40 years of wilderness wanderings because of unbelief (Heb. 3:19) with conditions among Adventists: "It was not the will of God that the coming of Christ should be so long delayed and His

people should remain so many years in this world of sin and sorrow. But unbelief separated them from God" (GC 458). She says also: "If all who had labored unitedly in the work in 1844 had received the third angel's message and proclaimed it in the power of the Holy Spirit, the Lord would have wrought mightily with their efforts. A flood of light would have been shed upon the world. Years ago the inhabitants of the earth would have been warned, the closing work completed, and Christ would have come for the redemption of His people" (*ibid.*). Instead of being occupied with prophetic time settings, Adventists should focus on "present truth," particularly the three angels' messages of Revelation 14 (1MR 57), for until these have been preached to the whole world, the end will not come (Matt. 24:14; Ev 697).

See also: Prophetic Interpretation; Second Coming of Christ, Delay of.

Further reading: Ev 694-697; P. G. Damsteegt, "Early Adventist Timesettings and their Implications for Today," JATS 4, no. 1 (1993): 151-168.

P. Gerard Damsteegt

TITHE. The tenth of one's increase that belongs to God (Lev. 27:30; Deut. 14:22). In the early years of the Seventh-day Adventist organization, the church struggled with the issue of regular financial support of the ministry. The plan of Systematic Benevolence was adopted, and proposed different ways to calculate the amount that should be given. Already in 1861 Ellen White commended the tithe system by referring to Malachi 3:8-11 (1T 221, 222). James White and other pioneers supported a tithing system that was adopted in the 1870s and defined as a tenth of all income.

In her writings Ellen White stressed the spiritual blessing of *stewardship and in particular of tithing (3T 404, 405; CS 90), especially for character development (Ed 44; CS 74; 1T 237). "It has ever proved that nine tenths are worth more to [faithful tithers] than ten tenths" (3T 546). For her, the tithing system began in the days of Adam (3T 393). Tithing did not pass away with the sacrificial offerings that typified Christ (CS 67), but, on the contrary, was confirmed in the New Testament by passages such as Matthew 23:23 (DA 616) and 1 Corinthians 9:7-14 (AA 335, 336). In her concept of divine ownership and redemptive love the tithe belongs to God as Creator (PP 528, 529), and not to pay tithe is a serious offense and "robbery" toward God (Mal. 3:9; CS 77, 86). Ministers are duty-bound to teach congregations and new converts their responsibility to be faithful in tithes and offerings (CS 87, 105; 9T 250). Even those in debt are obligated to pay tithes (CS 92, 93). Ellen White acknowledged that mistakes in the management of God's cause can weaken confidence in those accountable, but nevertheless, tithe funds are God's property and are to be paid in the "storehouse" or "treasury" of God—that is, they should go to the conference (CS 93; 7MR 366) and not to various other channels or institutions (see 9T 247-251; 2T 518, 519; TM 53, 305).

Concerning the use of tithe funds Ellen White gave clear counsels. Tithe should be used primarily to pay the wages of ministers (9T 250), Bible instructors (Ev 492), and ministers' wives doing work "in the same line" as their husbands (5MR 29). Among the proper recipients of tithe she counts institutions involved in the proclamation of the gospel (4T 464), the printed truth (*ibid.* 472), missionary work (6T 447; 9T 52), Bible teachers in schools (1MR 189; 6T 215), mission fields in America and overseas (1MR 182, 184, 192), medical missionaries (MM 245), and retirement benefits for ministers and their families (1MR 189).

Ellen White's rather broad understanding of the question of tithe use is underscored by her willingness to make exceptions to the rules under certain circumstances. Thus, in rare instances, tithe funds could be used for church buildings (1MR 191). Although she normally "paid her tithes in the regular way into the conference treasury" (5Bio 392), at a time when there was inadequate funding for ordained ministers working among African-Americans she paid some of her own tithe directly to their employer, the Southern Missionary Society (see *ibid.* 389-397). And apparently Ellen White agreed to pay a partial salary for some literature evangelists in difficult territories (as done in Australia according to a letter from W. C. White to J. B. Blosser, June 11, 1902). These exceptions were not, however, her regular practice.

On the other hand, she specifically disapproved of using tithe for: care of the poor and sick (CS 103; 3MR 218), general support of students (1MR 193, 194) or schools (9T 248, 249), regular church operating expenses (CS 103), construction of churches and institutional buildings (1MR 191), or wages of regular colporteurs who were to earn their own commissions (9T 248, 249). She seems, however, to have approved the support of directors of publishing departments (WCW to W. S. Lowry, May 10, 1912). The reason Ellen White opposed church members assigning their tithe to projects of their own choosing was not that these causes were undeserving; rather, she was emphasizing the sacredness of the tithe, and the seriousness of diverting resources from the direct support of gospel ministry (9T 247, 248).

Further reading: CS 65-108; R. W. Coon, "Tithe: Ellen G. White's Counsel and Practice" (RHPA, 1991); R. W. Olson, "Ellen G. White Comments on the Use of Tithe Funds" (1986, rev. 1990), p. 50; G. E. Reid, "In Search of the Storehouse" (SDoc); Á. M. Rodríguez, "Tithing in the Writings of Ellen G. White" (April 2001, SDoc); A. L. White, "Ellen G. White and the Tithe" (1959, rev. 1990, SDoc); A. L. White, "Highlights of the Beginning of the Tithing System" (1975, rev. 1990, SDoc).

Johannes Kovar

To Be Like Jesus (RHPA, 2004, 383 pp.). Nineteenth devotional book published by the Ellen G. White Estate. The title depicts a favorite theme in Ellen White's writings; she often invited her readers to "talk as Christ talked. Work as Christ worked. We must look to Christ and live. Catching sight of His loveliness, we long to practice the virtues and righteousness of Christ" (p. 5). This devotional book was "designed to help readers fix their eyes on Jesus, noting how He lived, studying His attitudes and practices, and encouraging them to follow His example" (*ibid.*). Selections from the writings of Ellen White were taken from her articles, books, and letters, and inclusive language was used where appropriate.

"To the Little Remnant Scattered Abroad" (Portland, Maine, Apr. 6, 1846). The first of three "broadsides" on which were printed Ellen Harmon's earliest visions. A broadside is a large sheet of paper printed on only one side. Broadsides were an economical and convenient way to disseminate information because they could be easily printed, folded, addressed, sealed, and sent to potentially interested readers. In this particular case the broadside contained several of Ellen Harmon's earliest visions largely paralleling the accounts now printed in *Early Writings* (pp. 13-22). Otis Nichols wrote a letter on April 20, 1846, on the back side of one of these broadsides describing Ellen Harmon's experience to William Miller. It is located at Aurora University, west of Chicago in Aurora, Illinois. A reprint of the broadside is available through Adventist Heritage Ministry.

Tobacco. "Tobacco is a slow, insidious poison, and its effects are more difficult to cleanse from the system than those of liquor" (3T 569; cf. MH 327), wrote Ellen White in 1875. She first warned against the dangerous effects of tobacco after she received her first health vision in the fall of 1848. She recognized that tobacco affects not only physical health but the nervous system as well (CH 81; MH 327, 328). She wrote of tobacco's impact on the immune system, that it reduces the body's natural capacity for healing itself (MM 11) and that the body slowly gives up the struggle to expel the poisonous intruder (Ms 3, 1897, in Te 57). Her counsels on tobacco are noted for their broad conception of the physical, mental, social, and spiritual dimensions of tobacco use, in an era when some physicians still prescribed inhaling cigar smoke as a therapy for lung disease (SHM 22). Her warning about tobacco in *Health: or How to Live* (1864) came just a century before the U.S. surgeon general's report, *Smoking and Health*, in 1964.

Regarding the characteristics of the tobacco addiction, she taught that the craving for tobacco was stimulated by the use of tea and coffee (ST, Sept. 1, 1887) and that the use of tobacco "excites a thirst for strong drink and in many cases lays the foundation for the liquor habit" (MH 327; cf. 3T 564). She recognized the hereditary dimension of the tobacco problem, that unnatural cravings for tobacco are transmitted from one generation to another (Te 56). She noted that "tobacco using is a habit which frequently affects the nervous system in a more powerful manner than does the use of alcohol. It binds the victim in stronger bands of slavery than does the intoxicating cup; the habit is more difficult to overcome. Body and mind are, in many cases, more thoroughly intoxicated with the use of tobacco than with spirituous liquors, for it is a more subtle poison" (3T 562). The earlier in life that such a habit is formed, the more damaging to health and the more difficult to overcome (*ibid.* 564, 567).

She warned about the danger of second-hand smoke, that wives and children of smokers "become diseased by inhaling the atmosphere of a room poisoned by the tobacco user's tainted breath" (Te 58) and that infants are especially susceptible to the poisoning of their brain, heart, liver, and lungs (*ibid.*). Tobacco also affects the mind, diminishing the user's decision-making ability (Ms 38½, 1905, in Te 59). Spiritually, it benumbs "the finer sensibilities of the soul" (3SG 116; ST, Apr. 24, 1879).

Yet in spite of the damaging effects of tobacco, she did not sanction harsh dealing with persons struggling with this addiction. In 1878, regarding a physician who had used tobacco "for many years" (15MR 140), she observed that "this habit was not as offensive in the sight of God" as the "censorious, condemning spirit" of those who "dealt with him." She recognized that for one of his age to change the habits of a lifetime "may not be expected in a day or a week or a month." She acknowledged that the "indulgence of tobacco is an evil which God would have him overcome," but she also insisted that he "can do this in the name and strength of Jesus" (12MR 285). Then she summarized her personal policy toward church members who used tobacco: "Some have taken the position that those who use tobacco should be dealt with and turned out of the church at once; but with some who would engage in this work there are greater defilements of the soul-temple than tobacco can make. In all our experience for many years, not a case of this kind has

been thus treated. We have borne for years with those in the slavery of habit, and unless there was some other cause for such action, we have not felt at liberty to deal with them or separate them from the church. We have prayed and labored with them, and in many cases have after a time succeeded in winning them fully. Those who did not reform, became lax in other things, and gave up their efforts to overcome, so that offenses of a grievous character occurred that required action on the part of the church" (15MR 139; cf. 12MR 286; 9MR 195). "The worth of a soul cannot be fully estimated by finite minds," she concluded. "How gratefully will the ransomed and glorified ones remember those who were instrumental in their salvation! No one will then regret his self-denying efforts and persevering labors, his patience, forbearance, and earnest heart-yearnings for souls that might have been lost had he neglected his duty" (15MR 144).

Further reading: 9MR 193-197; 12MR 274-295; 15MR 134-144; SHM 22, 23, 65-72.

Paul Z. Gregor and Jerry Moon

TONGUES, UNKNOWN, see **ECSTATIC EXPERIENCES**.

TOPSHAM, MAINE, see **HOWLAND, STOCKBRIDGE**.

TRACT AND MISSIONARY SOCIETIES. Organizations (1870-1901) that promoted distribution of Adventist books and tracts, evangelistic letter writing and visitation, and service to the poor. Their forerunner was the Vigilant Missionary Society, formed in Massachusetts in 1869, of which *Mary Haskell was the vice president and likely instigator. Her husband, *S. N. Haskell, president of the New England Conference in 1870, organized the first conference-wide T. and M. Society and was soon asked by the General Conference to promote that work throughout the denomination. In 1874 this endeavor was organized at the General Conference level, being named in 1882 the International Tract and Missionary Society. By 1901 the Tract and Missionary Societies were said to have won more converts to the Adventist faith than had the professional ministers (*SDA Encyclopedia* [1996], vol. 11, pp. 786-788).

Ellen White highly recommended this work, especially evangelistic letter writing.

She challenged ministers that if they would teach church members how to conduct missionary correspondence successfully, it would be a major stimulus to other forms of evangelism (ChS 131). Doing this work "successfully" seems to have depended on two dynamics: providing appropriate reading material and then following up with letters, not of instruction or admonition, but of "inquiry." The biblical exposition was left to the printed material. The letters were sensitive inquiries, "drawing out the true feelings of friends who have received our papers and tracts" (ChS 28). "This is a work you may all engage in successfully," she assured, "if you will but connect with God. Before writing letters of inquiry, always lift up your heart to God in prayer that you may ... bear fruit to the glory of God. All who with humble hearts take part in this work will be continually educating themselves as workers in the vineyard of the Lord" (ChS 131).

Jerry Moon

TRANSLATIONS OF ELLEN G. WHITE BOOKS. In her last will and testament Ellen White charged the trustees of her estate with the task of "the securing and printing of new translations" of her books and manuscripts. Her interest in seeing her works translated for non-English readers around the globe

was not an afterthought, but mission-driven, as evidenced by her close involvement with the translation effort dating from the mid-1880s.

Ellen White's first non-English book appears to have been *Aandelige Erfaringer* (*Christian Experience*), published in 1884 in the Danish language. It included material from Ellen White's autobiographical accounts in *Testimonies for the Church* and *Spiritual Gifts,* volume 1. Soon to follow were translations into other European languages of her writings on the life of Christ (adaptations of volumes 2 and 3 of *The Spirit of Prophecy*) and *The Great Controversy.*

As of 2008 Ellen White's books have been translated into more than 165 languages, with *Steps to Christ* being her most translated work—more than 160 languages. Spanish has been the leading non-English language for translations of Ellen White's books, followed closely by Portuguese.

The General Conference Spirit of Prophecy Committee gives subsidies to the church's world divisions and publishing houses for the publication of new translations based on the size of church membership and local economic conditions. Translators are chosen by, and work closely with, the church entities that serve the constituencies in a given language area. This helps to ensure that the translation is accurate and unbiased and that the translated work will be distributed through existing church channels.

In parts of the world in which it is not economically practical to translate and publish entire books, selections or abridgments are often produced. For example, the three-volume set *Testimony Treasures* (1949) enables translations to be made of the principal messages of the nine *Testimonies for the Church* volumes, while reducing the overall size by two thirds.

In 2005 the General Conference launched

"Connecting With Jesus," the largest global book distribution project in the history of the Seventh-day Adventist Church. Its goal was to provide 10 Ellen White books to 2 million Adventist families around the world during a five-year period, published in all the major languages at affordable, subsidized prices.

Further information regarding the policies governing the translation of Ellen White's books may be found in the General Conference *Working Policy,* section GE.

Tim Poirier

TRAVELS AND TRANSPORTATION. Ellen White was one of the most widely traveled of the early Sabbatarian Adventist pioneers. During her lifetime she experienced the transportation revolution firsthand as she took advantage of just about every commonly available form of transportation on three continents.

As a girl Ellen Harmon had little means available to her to travel very far from *Portland, Maine. She traveled with a small group of friends on roads using a small carriage or, in the wintertime, a sled. Her travels broadened after her first vision, when she began to share her "testimony" about what she had seen in vision to small groups of Advent believers. These early journeys used primitive modes of transportation that were quite often dangerous. She was furthermore dependent upon the generosity of family and friends who traveled with her within about 200 miles of Portland so that she could share her testimony. As it was considered improper in those days for a young woman to travel alone, she was accompanied by a female traveling companion, often her older sister *Sarah, or another family friend such as *Clarissa Bonfoey (2SG 138, 143, 161). From the spring of 1845 James White took upon himself the responsibility of assisting her in meeting her appointments

to speak at various Adventist gatherings. They were married in 1846, and until his death in 1881 he remained her most steadfast supporter and traveling companion.

Among the Whites' earliest and most significant travels were the *Sabbatarian Bible Conferences of 1848-1850. These conferences began unintentionally when *Albert Belden invited them to visit his home in Connecticut where the first of these small gatherings was held. With the invitation he enclosed $10, which was enough money to cover half of their train fare. The Whites left Maine, stopping first in Dorchester, Massachusetts, where *Otis and Mary Nichols gave them an additional $10 to complete their journey. Once they arrived at the Belden home, James White mowed hay to earn their travel expenses to another conference in New York, and to purchase badly needed clothing and supplies. This journey west would be the farthest from Maine the two had ever traveled before.

In preparation for this journey they left their oldest son, Henry, in the care of their close friend, Clarissa Bonfoey. Over the next few years they would often leave their children in the care of trusted friends. Reflecting back on this period, Ellen White wrote that this was one of the most difficult sacrifices she was ever called to make (2SG 96, 107, 128).

Travel during the 1850s was primitive by modern standards. On these trips the Whites would travel by walking, stagecoach (*ibid.* 127, 128), "packet" (boat) along the Erie Canal (*ibid.* 104, 141), horse-drawn hack (small carriage) (*ibid.* 149), and in the wintertime a horse-drawn sleigh (*ibid.* 145). Roads were often across rough "log-ways" (also called corduroy road, made by laying logs crosswise of the line of travel to keep vehicles out of the mud) and "mud-sloughs" that made travel something that one "endured" (*ibid.* 188). Occasionally as train routes became more common, the Whites were able to take advantage of this mode of transportation. Yet railroad travel could be perilous, and on at least one occasion the Whites narrowly avoided being killed in a train wreck (*ibid.* 188-191). In addition to the perils encountered while traveling, they barely received enough donations to offset expenses, so they often suffered from hunger and exposure to the elements, especially in winter (*ibid.* 146, 147).

During the late 1840s and early 1850s the Whites lived in a number of *homes (none of which they owned) and gradually moved westward. In 1855 they moved from *Rochester, New York, to *Battle Creek, Michigan (*ibid.* 203), where they helped to establish the publishing work and other church institutions. From Battle Creek their travels tended to be less nomadic and featured shorter itineraries that were restricted to specific destinations. During these short trips they organized churches, settled personal and theological disputes, and spoke at Advent gatherings. This work expanded during the 1860s with the development of monthly or quarterly meetings, and such meetings drew a large attendance when it was announced ahead of time in the *Review and Herald* that the Whites would be present. By 1868 *camp meetings began to feature prominently in their travels with one or both of them often as featured speakers. Occasionally the two would diverge on their itineraries so that at least one of them might be present at camp meetings held simultaneously. Their influence spread and the fledgling denomination grew.

Only three years after the first transcontinental railroad service began in 1869 the Whites made their first continental venture across the United States to *California. They rented and eventually purchased a home in California and for much of the following decade crisscrossed the country for speaking appointments alternated by short periods of time at either one of their homes to rest, recuperate, write, and take care of administrative duties. By the 1870s, while traveling could still be difficult, it had become much safer and in spite of nuisances, such as rough roads and smoke-filled train cars, Ellen White enjoyed seeing various parts of the country. She personally owned a number of travel guides, and some of her letters and diaries contain fascinating descriptions of the geographical scenery she saw during her travels. During this period, in 1879, Ellen White lived a unique experience as she accompanied her husband and other church members on a *wagon train from Denison, Texas, to Emporia, Kansas (3Bio 107-117, 272, 273).

Ellen White's first transatlantic journey was to *Europe, where from 1885 to 1887 she nurtured the development of the Adventist work on that continent. A description of her travels, including engravings of places she visited, was published in *Historical Sketches* (1886). Only a decade earlier (1874) the denomination had sent its first official missionary, *J. N. Andrews, to organize a small group of believers who had begun to keep the Sabbath through the leadership of *M. B. Czechowski. Ellen White was fascinated with the charm and lure of the Old Country. She was enraptured by the beautiful scenery and visited many of the tourist sites, including the royal gardens and royal palaces in several of the countries she visited. In typical fashion she traveled by steamboat from Boston to Liverpool, and from there made her way across the English Channel. Once she arrived on the continent, she traveled by train and on more localized trips by horse and carriage. She was usually accompanied by a translator and by one or more of her *literary assistants, who served as traveling companions.

Ellen White returned to the United States

in 1887 and spent the next few years alternating between her homes in *California and *Michigan. Much of her time was taken up with writing, interspersed with speaking itineraries across the United States.

Her travels during the 1890s would be characterized by more severe hardships as she aged and suffered from severe arthritis. In 1891 she made her third transoceanic trip, this time to *Australia. Only a few days after boarding a steamer in San Francisco, she turned 64. The journey across the Pacific Ocean took about a month, with stopovers in Honolulu, Samoa, and *New Zealand. While living in the South Pacific, she traveled across Australia by carriage and train, and made an extended trip to New Zealand.

In 1900 Ellen White returned to the United States. In January 1902 she had her first ride in an automobile—a Worth—when she arrived in Chicago, on her way to California. During that first decade of the twentieth century she made several cross-country trips to attend General Conference sessions, and one final trip to her hometown in Portland, Maine, in 1909. But with advancing age she increasingly felt that she was not obligated to attend as many church meetings, and stayed closer to her *home at Elmshaven.

Throughout her life Ellen White did a large amount of her traveling. Those who had an opportunity to travel with her often recounted how it was a highlight of their lives. Ellen White loved meeting people, and her diary frequently describes the many different people she met. She looked for opportunities to talk with people about their spiritual lives and showed a genuine interest in other people. On some occasions, while traveling by boat or train, she was asked to address her fellow passengers, and song services were conducted, with many passengers joining in the singing (cf. Lt 139, 1905).

Further reading: R. R. Butler II, "Overland by Rail, 1869-1890," in G. Land, ed., *The World of Ellen G. White* (RHPA, 1987), pp. 63-76; P. Anderson, *The Course of Empire: The Erie Canal and the New York Landscape, 1825-1875* (Rochester, N.Y.: Memorial Art Gallery of University of Rochester, 1984); J. F. Davidson and M. S. Sweeney, *On the Move: Transportation and the American Story* (Washington, D.C.: National Geographic Press, 2003); H. E. Douglass, *Messenger of the Lord* (PPPA, 1998), pp. 102-107, 544-546; T. F. Howard, *Sierra Crossing: First Roads to California* (Berkeley: University of California Press, 1998); B. W. Labaree et al., *America and the Sea: A Maritime History* (Mystic, Conn.: Mystic Seaport, 1998); R. E. Shaw, *Canals for a Nation: The Canal Era in the United States, 1790-1860* (Lexington: University Press of Kentucky, 1990); R. E. Shaw, *Erie Water West: A History of the Erie Canal, 1792-1854* (Lexington: University of Kentucky Press, 1966); J. F. Stover, *American Railroads* (Chicago: University of Chicago Press, 1961); G. R. Taylor, *The Transportation Revolution 1815-1860* (New York: Rinehart, 1951); W. L. Withuhn, ed., *Rails Across America: A History of Railroads in North America* (New York: Smithmark, 1993); J. A. Miller, *Fares, Please! From Horse-Cars to Streamliners* (New York: D. Appleton-Century, 1941); Jerry Stevens, "O Zion, Haste," AR, Jan. 17, 2008, pp. 22-24.

Michael W. Campbell

TRIBULATION, see **TIME OF TROUBLE**.

TRINITY, see **GODHEAD**.

TRIUMPH OF GOD'S LOVE, THE (SPA, 1957, 429 pp.). Reprint of *The Great Controversy* (1911 edition) for subscription sale. Along with the change of title, titles of some chapters were changed, subtitles added, and the format of the volume modernized with the addition of drawings. The text remains the same as in the 1911 edition.

TRUE EDUCATION, see *EDUCATION.*

TRUTH ABOUT ANGELS, THE (PPPA, 1996, 314 pp.). Statements on angels drawn from virtually the whole range of Ellen White's writings (1846-1914) arranged largely in biblical-chronological order. The first chapter gives a brief overview of the activity of good and evil angels; the second, the relationship of angels to individuals today. Chapter 3 begins with the Godhead in eternity past, before angels were created. Subsequent chapters cover the activity of angels in the great controversy from the origin of evil until the restoration of the new earth, and beyond into eternity future. This material seems to divide itself naturally into three main sections: (1) the events relating to the origin of evil and the early history of this earth up to Israel's entrance into Canaan; (2) the events surrounding Christ's earthly ministry and the period of the early Christian church; and (3) the events related to the Second Coming, the close of the millennium, and the hereafter.

Further reading: D. E. Mansell and V. W. Mansell, *Angels and the Unseen Conflict* (PPPA, 1996).

Donald E. Mansell

2300 DAYS, see **INVESTIGATIVE JUDGMENT; KARAITE CALENDAR.**

TYNDALE, WILLIAM (c. 1494-1536). A central figure in the English Reformation of the sixteenth century, whom Ellen White ranked with *Wycliffe, *Huss, *Luther, and *Wesley (GC 609; Ed 254). Tyndale is best known for his masterful English translations of the New Testament and portions of the Old Testament that are heavily reflected in later translations

(in segments he translated, some 80 percent of the King James Version may be traced to him). Tyndale advocated positions on the state of humankind in death, the resurrection (see GC 547), and the covenants, that became important to Seventh-day Adventists.

To translate the Bible into English, he mastered Greek and Hebrew, adding to the six languages he spoke. In 1523 he sought the patronage and protection of Cuthbert Tunstall,

bishop of London, for his translation work. Failing in the bid, he became a fugitive on the Continent, moving from printing center to printing center, to publish the Bible in English. His first edition of the New Testament came out in 1526, followed by sections

WILLIAM TYNDALE, EARLY ENGLISH REFORMER AND TRANSLATOR OF THE BIBLE INTO ENGLISH

of the Old Testament in the next few years. Thousands of Tyndale's New Testaments (and counterfeit copies) were smuggled into England, mostly through the textile trade, and reached a hungry audience. He often worked on the run, suffering a police raid and a shipwreck in which all his manuscripts were lost.

During a time of relative calm in Antwerp, Belgium, he wrote important works, including *The Obedience of a Christian Man* (1528). He was betrayed there in 1535 by a man he had befriended, Henry Phillips. Held for 16 months in extreme conditions in Vilvoorde Castle, Tyndale endured an extended trial carried out in writing and was executed at the stake in October 1536. According to Foxe, his last words were "Lord, open the king of England's eyes." A few scant months later Henry VIII authorized publication of "Matthew's Bible" (1537), which bears the ornamental initials "WT" in acknowledgment of the martyr.

In volume 4 of *The Spirit of Prophecy* (pp.

170-172), Ellen White introduced Tyndale as doing for England what Luther had done for Germany in "opening a closed Bible," and she shared the story of his famous retort to a learned ecclesiastical opponent, "I will cause a boy who driveth the plow to know more of the Scriptures than you do." Following a summary of Tyndale's early work, she told of the purchase of Tyndale's "whole stock of Bibles, for the purpose of destroying them" by Tunstall (called "the bishop of Durham"), a strategy that had the opposite effect. Narrating Tyndale's death, she concluded that "the weapons which he prepared have enabled other soldiers to do battle through all the centuries even to our time."

Between the publication of volume 4 of *The Spirit of Prophecy* and the 1888 edition of *The Great Controversy, Ellen White traveled in Europe, including visits to Hamburg, Cologne, and Worms. In each case, it is the connection to Tyndale's story that holds most meaning. Out of Worms, she commented, "went forth Tyndale's Bible, the most powerful agent in the Reformation of England" (HS 225). Likely inspired by her travels, Ellen White expanded Tyndale's story in the 1888 edition of *The Great Controversy*. She set his story in the context of Wycliffe and Erasmus and shared additional vignettes of quarrels with priests and prelates, conflicts that only toughened Tyndale's resolve to offer the Bible as an antidote for error. All of this passed more or less unchanged into the 1911 edition of *The Great Controversy* (pp. 245-248), in which three of the stories are attributed to D'Aubigné's *History of the Reformation of the Sixteenth Century* and one to Anderson's *Annals of the English Bible*.

For Ellen White, Tyndale played a key role in the story of the *great controversy by doggedly articulating the supremacy of the Bible and by providing it to the English-speaking world, so offering a foil to the opposing practices of church authorities. "The grand principle maintained by Tyndale . . . was the divine authority and sufficiency of the Sacred Scriptures" (4SP 173).

Further reading: D. Daniell, *William Tyndale: A Biography* (New Haven, Conn.: Yale University Press, 1994); *idem, Let There Be Light: William Tyndale and the Making of the English Bible* (London: British Library, 1994); M. Galli, "What the English Bible Cost One Man," *Christian History* 13 (1994): 12-15; W. Tyndale, *The Obedience of a Christian Man*, ed. with an introduction and notes by David Daniell (London: Penguin, 2000); W. Tyndale, *Tyndale's New Testament*, modern-spelling edition with an introduction by David Daniell (New Haven, Conn.: Yale University Press, 1989).

John K. McVay

UNCLEAN FOOD. Ellen White's knowledge regarding clean and unclean food expanded progressively, and her understanding of the food regulation as presented in Leviticus 11 and Deuteronomy 14 changed over time—from a tolerance of eating pork to a position against the consumption of all unclean food.

On October 21, 1858, she reproved *Stephen N. Haskell for teaching that it was wrong to eat pork; but it is important to note that contrary to some allegations, Ellen White did not advocate eating pork. She said Haskell was wrong to make abstaining from pork a criterion for church membership, and advised him not to push the matter because if it were God's will for Christians not to eat pork, He would reveal it to the church as a whole. She stated: "If God requires His people to abstain from swine's flesh, He will convict them on the matter. . . . If it is the duty of the church to abstain from swine's flesh, God will discover it to more than two or three. He will teach

His *church* their duty" (1T 207). This advice was written five years before her major health reform vision of June 6, 1863, in which she saw that people should not consume pork and that vegetarianism is the preferred diet.

By 1864 Ellen White concluded that "God never designed the swine to be eaten under any circumstances" (4aSG 124; CD 392). The rationale behind the prescription of not eating pork was not a merely arbitrary prohibition, but was related to health principles. She stated explicitly: "God did not prohibit the Hebrews from eating swine's flesh merely to show His authority, but because it was not a proper article of food for man" (2SM 417; cf. 4aSG 124). Later she asserted: "God forbade the eating of unclean beasts . . . to preserve the life and health of His people. In order for them to retain their faculties of mind and body, it was necessary that their blood should be kept pure, by eating simple, healthful food. He therefore specified the animals least objectionable for food" (ST, Mar. 21, 1878). Furthermore, this prohibition was more than a mere ceremonial law: "The distinction between articles of food as clean and unclean was not a merely ceremonial and arbitrary regulation, but was based upon sanitary principles" (PP 562).

Even though Ellen White was a strong advocate of vegetarianism, and wrote only sporadically about clean and unclean food, her standpoint on the topic, especially on the prohibition of eating pork, became clear fairly early in her ministry. Her most elaborate explanation on pork as unfit and injurious for human consumption is in her article on health entitled "Disease and Its Causes," written in 1865 (2SM 417; cf. DA 617; 3SP 63, 64). Yet she grew in her understanding of what it means to abstain from the consumption of unclean food, particularly in regard to what animals belong to that category (e.g.,

squirrels [Lt 3, 1866, in 20MR 204] and shellfish [Lt 16, 1882]).

Ellen White understood that Peter's vision in Acts 10 did not abolish the ordinance regarding unclean food. "Some have urged that this vision was to signify that God had removed His prohibition from the use of the flesh of animals which He had formerly pronounced unclean; and that therefore swine's flesh was fit for food. This is a very narrow, and altogether erroneous interpretation, and is plainly contradicted in the scriptural account of the vision and its consequences" (3SP 327, 328; for the purpose of the vision, see SR 285, 286 and AA 193). She also interpreted God's permission of eating meat in Genesis 9:3 as referring to clean animals only (PP 107) and stressed that Samson's parents abstained from "every unclean thing" (*ibid.* 562).

Her most elaborate and comprehensive explanation of prohibited food was published in 1905: "The Israelites were permitted the use of animal food, but under careful restrictions which tended to lessen the evil results. The use of swine's flesh was prohibited, as also of other animals and of birds and fish whose flesh was pronounced unclean. Of the meats permitted, the eating of the fat and the blood was strictly forbidden" (MH 311, 312). "The tissues of the swine swarm with parasites. Of the swine God said, 'It is unclean unto you: ye shall not eat of their flesh, nor touch their dead carcase.' Deuteronomy 14:8. This command was given because swine's flesh is unfit for food. Swine are scavengers, and this is the only use they were intended to serve. Never, under any circumstances, was their flesh to be eaten by human beings. It is impossible for the flesh of any living creature to be wholesome when filth is its natural element and when it feeds upon every detestable thing" (*ibid.* 313, 314).

Further reading: 2SM 410-419; MH

311-317; R. Coon, *Ellen G. White and Vegetarianism: Did She Practice What She Preached?* (PPPA, 1986); R. Graybill, "The Development of Adventist Thinking on Clean and Unclean Meats" (EGWE, 1981, SDoc); J. Moskala, *The Laws of Clean and Unclean Animals in Leviticus 11: Their Nature, Theology, and Rationale* (Berrien Springs, Mich.: ATS Pub., 1998); A. L. White, "Dietary Witness of the Ellen G. White Household" (unpublished paper, 1978).

Jiří Moskala

UNION COLLEGE. A coeducational baccalaureate college in Lincoln, Nebraska. In the spring of 1889 Adventists in Kansas and Minnesota were both considering expanding a *conference school into a college. *W. W. Prescott cautioned that too-rapid multiplication of schools could weaken the entire Adventist educational program, and suggested that rather than every conference attempting to fund its own college, several conferences unite to maintain a college. In response, Adventists from Minnesota, Wisconsin, Iowa, Nebraska, and the Dakota Territory began to make plans for a united school. At the Kansas camp meeting a few weeks later Prescott further proposed that all the Adventists west of the Mississippi River and east of the Rocky Mountains unite to sustain a single strong college. Ellen White was present and on May 25, 1889, endorsed Prescott's plan, arguing that the limited resources of Midwestern Adventists would be stretched to the limit to maintain one college with high standards in both religion and science. Kansas voted the concept, and other conferences soon threw their influence behind the idea of "the union college" (Dick, pp. 11, 19, 381). The school opened in September 1891—just weeks before Ellen and W. C. White left for nine years in Australia.

In 1900 Ellen White donated the proceeds of her book *Christ's Object Lessons* to reducing the debts on Adventist educational institutions. Ministers, teachers, students, and church members joined in a great sales campaign that in the Union College territory alone raised $58,000 for debt reduction (Dick, pp. 90-92).

In 1905 she visited the college briefly, lodging overnight in the Nebraska *Sanitarium on campus (5Bio 354). In November of that year, near the climax of the *Kellogg crisis, the General Conference held a medical missionary convention at Union College, during which W. C. White gave an address entitled "The Integrity of the Testimonies to the Church."

In May 1909, on her way to the 1909 General Conference session in Washington, D.C., Ellen White stopped long enough to speak four times at Union College, which then had more than 500 students. One of the questions discussed at the conference was how the church could better serve the educational needs of its immigrant constituency. Besides the courses in English, Union College had a Swedish Department, a German Department, and a Danish-Norwegian Department, each offering Bible and history classes in its own language. In 1908 Ellen White advised, "The Lord is certainly opening the way for us as a people to divide and subdivide the companies that have been growing too large to work together to the greatest advantage." She urged that "to establish another school will be better than further enlargement of the school at Lincoln" (Lt 253, 1908, in SpM 440). The issue was debated at length.

At the 1909 session four church leaders asked Ellen White to comment further. Their burden was that the church was losing the immigrant young people because the foreign language departments were not working very well. Ellen White responded, "I have light on that topic, and my response to you is that the foreign departments in Union College should now be moved out of that school." W. C. White, knowing that his mother was somewhat hard of hearing, feared she had not heard the question, and asked her again. She gave the same answer. He repeated the question a third time, and she gave the same reply. When he began to explain it further, she said firmly, "I have heard all you people have said from the beginning, and I am repeating that I have light that the foreign departments of Union College should move out into separate schools" (Christian, pp. 176, 177). After several days of study and prayer, it was decided to separate the foreign departments of Union College into three new schools: Clinton German Seminary, Clinton, Missouri; Danish-Norwegian Seminary, Hutchinson, Minnesota; and Broadview Swedish Seminary, west of Chicago, Illinois. While the drop in enrollment created temporary financial difficulties, the college recovered, reaching an enrollment of 1,200 in 1967. In that year Southwestern Junior College in Keene, Texas, became a four-year college, ending a half-century of affiliation with Union College. As in 1909, progress elsewhere temporarily reduced enrollment at Union, but by 2008 Union College again enrolled 1,000 students.

Further reading: "Instruction to Students and Teachers of Union College," quoted in PH113 19, 20; 5Bio 354; 6Bio 191; L. H. Christian, *Sons of the North* (PPPA, 1942), pp. 170-182; E. D. Dick, *Union: College of the Golden Cords* (Lincoln, Nebr.: Union College Press, 1967), pp. 10-12, 90-92, 381-395; W. C. White, "The Integrity of the Testimonies to the Church: Remarks at College View, Nebraska, Nov. 25, 1905" (SDoc).

Jerry Moon

UNIONS, LABOR, see **LABOR UNIONS**.

UNITED STATES IN PROPHECY. In the mid-1880s, as momentum for putting the power and authority of the federal government behind a quasi-Protestant cultural dominance grew, the role of the United States in apocalyptic prophecy became a major theme in Ellen White's writings. She challenged Americans to grapple with the prophetic revelation that forces already converging were leading their own nation's government to betray the liberties for which it had been the greatest beacon in the world's history. In so doing, she made specific, vivid, and inescapable the general Christian principle that loyalty to God must be placed above earthly governments.

Though not directly addressed in Ellen White's writings prior to the 1880s, belief that the two-horned beast of Revelation 13:11-18 symbolized the emergence and destiny of the United States became a crucial component of the sabbatarian Adventist movement's sense of identity and vocation in the 1850s. The interpretation first set forth in 1851 by John N. Andrews in the *Review and Herald* won rapid, enthusiastic, and lasting acceptance. Ellen White's incorporation of the main lines of Andrews' interpretation in *The Great Controversy* (1888) gave it an authoritative and enduring presence in the Adventist Church.

Andrews and the other Adventist expositors of the 1850s and 1860s used a vast and intricate array of exegetical arguments within the then-prevalent "historicist" tradition of interpretation to buttress the claim that this beast that had two horns like a lamb but spoke like a dragon pointed to the United States. The two horns, they concluded, stood for two centerpieces of the American "fair experiment": "Republicanism," or the civil liberty comprised of constitutional rights, representative government, and political equality; and "Protestantism," referring not to a specific creed but to religious liberty—freedom from government interference against the right to follow the dictates of individual conscience. However, in its support for slavery and in repressing religious liberty through Sunday laws, among other ways, Protestant America was on the way to forming an "image to the beast"—that is, the first beast mentioned in Revelation 13, long and widely understood as a symbol of the Papacy. All of this would lead to the final apocalyptic crisis before the return of Christ.

The possibility of *Sunday legislation becoming a major issue in a great social crisis dividing the nation would not have strained the credulity of nineteenth-century Americans. Sunday observance was a critical measure of the influence of Christianity in a national culture that had implemented the radical concept of disestablishment of religion at the federal level. Not satisfied with the uneven legislative bolstering at the state and local levels, Protestant moral reformers launched a major effort to gain federal government recognition of Sunday as a religious day of rest through a Congressional ban on Sunday mail delivery. The bill had been defeated in 1830 after extensive debate in Congress. But in 1857 Adventist pioneer J. N. Loughborough proposed that successful implementation of a *national* Sunday law would signal the point at which support for religious coercion in America constituted an "image to the beast" as depicted in prophecy.

Thus Adventists believed they were seeing a new progression in the fulfillment of prophecy in 1879 when the National Reform Association, which for more than a decade had been gathering support for a constitutional amendment declaring the United States to be a "Christian nation," made a national Sunday law an explicit part of its agenda. Several measures for implementing that agenda were introduced and debated in the national Congress between 1888 and 1893, supported by an array of reform organizations. The imprisonment of scores of Adventists for violating Sunday laws, mainly in the South, during the final quarter of the nineteenth century also signaled a building national crisis.

The accelerating support for recognition of Sunday by the national government in the 1880s was part of an effort to strengthen and formalize the Protestant establishment's hold on American culture that was in fact being weakened by rapidly advancing secularization and diversity in the post-Civil War decades. Sunday legislation was one attractive means of saving "Christian civilization" from the onslaught of poverty, crime, drunkenness, labor strife, immorality, and infidelity that came with the immense social changes made by the combined forces of urbanization, industrialization, and immigration.

In volume 4 of *The Spirit of Prophecy* (1884), where the first exposition of America in prophecy in her writings appears, Ellen White pointed out the widely held diagnosis attributing the "fast-spreading corruption" in society "to the desecration of the so-called 'Christian Sabbath,'" and the corresponding claims "that the enforcement of Sunday observance would greatly improve the morals of society" (4SP 404). She crystallized her analysis of these developments in a single paragraph in 1885 in *Testimony* number 32: "By the decree enforcing the institution of the papacy in violation of the law of God, our nation will disconnect herself fully from righteousness. When Protestantism shall stretch her hand across the gulf to grasp the hand of the Roman power, when she shall reach over the abyss to clasp hands with spiritualism, when, under the influence of this threefold union, our country shall repudiate every principle of its Constitution as a Protestant and republican government, . . . then we may know . . . that the end is near" (5T 451).

Sunday legislation was an issue of momentous consequence for America in Ellen White's view because, in the first place, it represented an arrogant assertion of the authority of human government against God's law and government. Its defiance is directed specifically against that portion of the law of God—the fourth commandment—that "is the sign of His creative power and the witness to His claim upon man's reverence and homage" (GC88 446; cf. 4SP 400). Laws exalting and enforcing a "spurious sabbath" thus raise the ultimate issue of loyalty to earthly governments or loyalty to the laws of God's kingdom (RH, Feb. 6, 1900; 1MR 296, 297).

Second, Sunday legislation constitutes reversion from the constitutional principles of religious and civil liberty (Protestantism and Republicanism), wherein lies the republic's "righteousness"—a level of virtue unique in the history of human governments. The nation would revert to the papal system of the church employing the "strong arm of civil power" (4SP 425) to advance its ends and suppress dissent. The defiance of God's law entailed in Sunday legislation thus has to do not merely with upholding a different day but with repression of the freedom that God's sovereignty confers on all human beings. "Force is the last resort of every false religion," Ellen White commented (ST, May 6, 1897). Compelling the conscience for observance of the genuine Sabbath would be equally illegitimate (RH, Apr. 15, 1890).

Third, this apocalyptic repudiation of liberty will come about as the very different religious forces in America's uniquely pluralistic society align in a coalition of expedience to defend the status quo in a time of national crisis. Protestantism, though divided into numerous denominations, represented an imprecise yet very real collective ethos that made it still the most powerful of the collaborators in the "threefold union" (GC88 588), as well as the initiator of the handclasps bringing the three together. By working through transdenominational organizations such as the National Reform Association, the Protestant majority would make an "image to the beast" in America by gaining controlling influence for religious power over civil government (*ibid.* 442-445). It would also clasp hands with Rome in a second and more direct sense of cultivating political cooperation with the growing Catholic presence in America (4SP 425). The nation's leading Catholic prelate, Cardinal James Gibbons of Baltimore, did in fact endorse the national Sunday rest bill introduced in Congress in 1888. Spiritualism meanwhile was bolstering the coalition by fascinating the popular imagination with a source of religious revelation that undercut the authority of the Scriptures and supported theological errors at the heart of the final attack on God's truth—Sunday sacredness and immortality of the soul.

Suppression of dissenters against the broad threefold union—already evident in the jailings of Sabbath observers in the South—would be justified on grounds of national security and harmony: "Those who honor the Bible Sabbath will be denounced as enemies of law and order, as breaking down the moral restraints of society, causing anarchy and corruption" (4SP 409). In the face of such repression, Ellen White sought to arm Adventists with martyrlike resolve to stand for the truth "at any cost, even tho[ugh] gaping prisons, chain-gangs, and banishment stare us in the face" (ST, May

6, 1897). To those who, citing Romans 13, ask if Christians are not required to obey the "powers that be," her response was: "Yes, when they are in harmony with the higher powers that be" (RH, Apr. 15, 1890).

Ellen White's stark and startling prognosis of the direction of American society could be treated as primarily a sensational forecast or reason for disengagement from society. But that is not how she used it. Instead she used it as a basis for appeals to fidelity and unity in the cause of God and, paradoxically, for activism on behalf of human rights and societal well-being. In a testimony published in 1889 entitled "The Impending Conflict," she warned believers against the passivity that merely charted fulfillment of prophecy rather than taking an aggressive public stand for liberty. "We are not doing the will of God if we sit in quietude, doing nothing to preserve liberty of conscience," she wrote (5T 714). She saw the onset of religious persecution in America not as a signal for retreat but a wake-up call for Adventists to shake out of their "listless attitude" and bear their witness to the world (*ibid.* 711-718).

Liberty itself was an intrinsic part of that witness for "present truth." In proclaiming "the message which is present truth for this time," she exhorted, Adventists were to "show the people where we are in prophetic history and seek to arouse the spirit of true Protestantism, awaking the world to a sense of the value of the privileges of religious liberty so long enjoyed" (*ibid.* 716). Because God still "has His agents among the leading men of the nation," effective action in the public arena was possible (4SP 429). Such action to fight back the forces of repression would make it possible for the work of the "third message" and the wholistic redemption it brings to go forward. The apocalyptic crisis and renewal to which the gospel message pointed was still

soon to come. However, in the meantime, some of the "leading men through whom the Lord is now working" in the governmental realm would be among those who would accept the saving message (*ibid.*).

The ambiguity of the two-horned beast of Revelation 13 was itself part of what made it such a rich metaphor for navigating the challenging course required to live faithfully as citizens of the soon-victorious kingdom of God in the midst of the greatest but still-human government in history. While the dragon voice seemed louder at some times than others, such as during the slavery crisis of the 1850s and 1860s and the Sunday law crisis of the 1880s and 1890s, the lamblike virtues, in Ellen White's view, were never completely lost or unsustainable. Faithfulness to the Adventist cause in the run-up to the very final apocalyptic crisis thus meant being at the same time a prophetic minority bearing radical witness against the nation's hypocrisies and pretensions and a world-engaging people fostering the lingering good in American democracy. Throughout the 1880s and 1890s particularly, much of Ellen White's ministry involved guiding the church toward judicious, discerning, and principled appropriations of both principles.

See also: Sunday Legislation; Seal of God; Mark of the Beast; Revelation, Book of.

Further reading: J. M. Butler, "Adventism and the American Experience," in E. S. Gaustad, ed., *The Rise of Adventism: Religion and Society in Mid-Nineteenth-Century America* (New York: Harper & Row, 1974), pp. 173-206; J. M. Butler, "The World of E. G. White and the End of the World," *Spectrum* 10, no. 2 (August 1979): 2-13; H. E. Douglass, *Dramatic Prophecies of Ellen White* (PPPA, 1998), pp. 109-136; G. R. Knight, *Ellen White's World* (RHPA, 1998); D. Morgan, *Adventism and the American Republic: The Public Involvement of a Major*

Apocalyptic Movement (Knoxville, Tenn.: University of Tennessee Press, 2001); D. L. Pettibone, "The Sunday Law Movement," in Gary Land, ed., *The World of Ellen G. White* (RHPA, 1987), pp. 113-128; E. D. Syme, *A History of SDA Church-State Relations in the United States* (PPPA, 1973).

Douglas Morgan

UNITY IN DIVERSITY. Ellen White frequently used the phrase "unity in diversity" or "diversity in unity" (8MR 66, 67) to describe the profound union that should always characterize those who love Christ, despite their differences in virtually every other aspect. Scriptures she referred to most frequently in this connection include Matthew 23:8; John 13:35; 15:1-5; 17:20, 21; Acts 10:34; 17:26; 1 Corinthians 6:19, 20; 12:4-6, 12; 13:1-13; Galatians 6:2; Ephesians 4:3-14; 5:30; 1 Peter 3:8; and Revelation 2:4 (6T 422; 7BC 956-958).

Her theology of unity in diversity was grounded in the nature of God, the natural universe, and the composition of Scripture. First, she saw the unity among diverse believers as analogous to the unity of one *God in different persons. "Christ prayed [John 17:21, 22] that His disciples might be one, even as He and His Father are one" (15MR 149; cf. TDG 88). "The unity that exists between Christ and His disciples does not destroy the personality of either. In mind, in purpose, in character, they are one, but not in person" (SD 286). Second, she saw "unity in diversity" as "a principle that pervades the whole creation," even "the entire universe" (5BC 1143; GCB, Feb. 27, 1895).

Third, she found unity in diversity in the varied composition of Scripture. "Why do we need a Matthew, a Mark, a Luke, a John, a Paul, and all the writers who have borne testimony in regard to the life and ministry of the Savior? Why could not one of the disciples have written a complete record and thus have given us a connected account of Christ's earthly life? Why does one writer bring in points that another does not mention? Why, if these points are essential, did not all these writers mention them? It is because the minds of men differ. Not all comprehend things in exactly the same way. Certain Scripture truths appeal much more strongly to the minds of some than of others" (CT 432).

This article will consider the necessity, basis, and marks of unity; the necessity, power, and beauty of diversity in unity; and the means to attaining unity in diversity. The necessity of unity among believers is that this is the proof to the world of the truth of Christianity (John 13:35; 17:20, quoted in PP 520). "Unity in diversity among God's children—the manifestation of love and forbearance in spite of difference of disposition—this is the testimony that God sent His Son into the world to save sinners" (SD 286). Beyond all "sermons and arguments," unity among diverse believers is the clearest proof of grace (Ev 342).

The basis of unity is that *no* external characteristic—not "caste," nor nationality, nor social class, nor "color, race, position, wealth, birth, or attainments"—makes any person better or worse in the eyes of Jesus. "With God there is no respect of persons" (1SM 259; RH, Dec. 22, 1891). Under the reign of sin virtually all individual differences have been made reasons for either pride and preferment, or of shame and exclusion, but in Christ all are equally of infinite value. "The secret of unity is found in the equality of believers in Christ" (1SM 259). In Christ every kind of social, intellectual, racial, national, or cultural difference becomes intrinsically advantageous, essential to spiritual growth, and in a diverse world absolutely essential to the successful mission of the church (9T 195-197; RH, Dec. 22, 1891).

In view of the unique talents—and universal defects—of humanity, White viewed unity in diversity as indispensable to social, intellectual, and spiritual power. No individual is "a complete whole in himself" (6BC 1090). "There is no person, no nation," she wrote, "that is perfect in every habit and thought. One must learn of another. Therefore God wants the different nationalities to mingle together, to be one in judgment, one in purpose" (HS 137). "Our minds do not all run in the same channel, and we have not all been given the same work" (5BC 1148). But the Lord can use "differently constituted characters" to do a better work and "much larger" than any of them could do alone; "for in their diversity of talent, yet unity in Christ," is "the power of their usefulness" (3MR 11).

White also saw beauty in diversity. "A life consecrated to the service of God will be developed and beautified in its individuality. No person can sink his individuality in that of another. . . . The great Master Artist has not made two leaves of the same tree precisely alike" (2MCP 426). "Yet this variety adds to the perfection of the tree as a whole" (1SM 21). So God's "creative power does not give to all minds the same likeness. They are created to live through ceaseless ages, and there is to be complete unity, mind blending with mind; but no two are to be of the same mold" (2MCP 426). Likewise there is beauty in the diversity of the Bible writers. Their thoughts do not have "a set uniformity, as if cast in an iron mold, making the very hearing monotonous. In such uniformity there would be a loss of grace and distinctive beauty" (1SM 21).

Thus White viewed all the differences of mind (5BC 1148; 6BC 1083; 2MCP 426; PM 100, 101), temperament, disposition, intelligence (15MR 149; TSA 21), plans, and ideas (RH, Feb. 6, 1908), as so many valuable tools for God's use. "In the work of soul saving, the Lord calls together laborers who have different plans and ideas and various methods of labor. But with this diversity of minds, there is to be revealed a unity of purpose" (RH, Feb. 6, 1908).

Within this unity of purpose, even different ways of understanding and expressing truth are seen as not only valuable but necessary. "The Creator of all ideas may impress different minds with the same thought, but each may express it in a different way, yet without contradiction. The fact that this difference exists should not perplex or confuse us. It is seldom that two persons will view and express truth in the very same way. Each dwells on particular points which his constitution and education have fitted him to appreciate" (1SM 22). Similarly, one speaker "dwells at considerable length on points that others would pass by quickly or not mention at all. The whole truth is presented more clearly by several than by one" (CT 432).

For this reason she recommended that "the work of teaching the Scriptures to the youth is not to be left wholly with one teacher for a long series of years" (*ibid.*), and where possible, schools employ several Bible teachers, for "one man's mind is not to mold and fashion the work according to his special ideas" (Ev 104; cf. 1888 Materials 133). "Often through unusual experiences, under special circumstances, [God] . . . gives to some Bible students views of truth that others do not grasp. It is possible for the most learned teacher to fall far short of teaching all that should be taught" (CT 433).

Even in scriptural interpretation there will be diversity. "One man may be conversant with the Scriptures, and some particular portion of the Scripture is especially appreciated by him because he has seen it in a certain striking light; another sees another portion as very important; and thus one and another presents the very points to the people that appear of highest value. This is all in the order of God. One man blunders in his interpretation of some portion of the Scripture, but shall this cause diversity and disunion? God forbid. *We cannot then take a position that the unity of the church consists in viewing every text of Scripture in the very same shade of light.*" Lest anyone think she condoned doctrinal pluralism, she continued: "The great truths of the Word of God are so clearly stated that none need make a mistake in understanding them" (Lt 29, 1889, in 15MR 149, 150; italics supplied).

An example of her distinction between the great truths on which there is a broad, firm consensus, and minute points on which there may be legitimate differences of opinion, is the practical exposition of *righteousness by faith. "Many commit the error," she wrote, "of trying to define minutely the fine points of distinction between justification and sanctification. Into the definitions of these two terms they often bring their own ideas and speculations. Why try to be more minute than is Inspiration on the vital question of righteousness by faith? Why try to work out every minute point, as if the salvation of the soul depended upon all having exactly your understanding of this matter? *All cannot see in the same line of vision*" (Ms 21, 1891, in 6BC 1072 and FW 14; italics supplied). At the same time, she maintained that the cardinal doctrines of Scripture were beyond dispute (4T 446, 447; GC 582-584).

While she advocated forbearance regarding minor differences of opinion, she did not condone doctrinal pluralism (GC 582-584). "God is leading a people out from the world upon the exalted platform of eternal truth, the commandments of God and the faith of

Jesus. . . . They will not be at variance, one believing one thing, and another having faith and views entirely opposite; each moving independently of the body. Through the diversity of the gifts and governments that He has placed in the church, they will all come to the unity of the faith. If one man takes his views of Bible truth without regard to the opinion of his brethren, and justifies his course, alleging that he has a right to his own peculiar views, and then presses them upon others, how can he be fulfilling the prayer of Christ? And if another and still another arises, each asserting his right to believe and talk what he pleases, without reference to the faith of the body, where will be that harmony which existed between Christ and His Father, and which Christ prayed might exist among His brethren?" (CET 201, 203).

"Though we have an individual work and an individual responsibility before God, we are not to follow our own independent judgment, regardless of the opinions and feelings of our brethren; for this course would lead to disorder in the church. It is the duty of ministers to respect the judgment of their brethren; but their relations to one another, as well as the doctrines they teach, should be brought to the test of the law and the testimony; then, if hearts are teachable, there will be no divisions among us. Some are inclined to be disorderly, and are drifting away from the great landmarks of the faith; but God is moving upon His ministers to be one in doctrine and in spirit" (*ibid.* 203).

In conclusion, the chief obstacle to unity is not individual diversity, but the sinful *self, which must be overcome. "One great hindrance to the advancement of the work has been, and will be, that those placed in [positions] of trust feel that of themselves they could manage the work; that they have ability and they want to sway everything their way. Among the workers there is much of self, that lives, and refuses to die." If "this self" is "cherished" and "allowed to rule," the workers "will just as surely work at cross purposes, as they are different in character, unless they are daily-converted men" (Lt 31, 1892, in 3MR 10, 11). "There is to be only one master spirit—the Spirit of Him who is infinite in wisdom, and in whom all the diverse elements meet in beautiful, matchless unity" (Lt 78, 1894, in OHC 169).

"The reason [for] all division, discord, and difference is found in separation from Christ. Christ is the center to which all should be attracted; for the nearer we approach the center, the closer we shall come together in feeling, in sympathy, in love, growing into the character and image of Jesus" (RH, Dec. 22, 1891).

Further reading: 3MR 10-19; 8MR 64-71; 15MR 149-151; 9T 179-198.

Jerry Moon

UNIVERSE. Although Ellen White was not an astronomer, nor does she seem to have read a lot about the subject, she wrote much about the universe. What she wrote was based on her study of the Scriptures and what was shown to her in visions. While the emphasis of her statements is primarily on spiritual and moral aspects of the universe, many remarks have a bearing on the physical nature of the universe.

That God is the Creator, Sustainer, and Governor of the universe is fundamental to Ellen White. "Men need to recognize God as the Creator of the universe, One who commands and executes all things" (DA 606). She refers to God as "the great moral Governor of the universe" (1MR 62) and to the law of God as "the law of the universe" (ST, June 15, 1891). For her our relationship to the universe is determined by our relationship to the

Creator of the universe. "Our allegiance to the King of kings must ever be made a matter of paramount importance. We cannot afford to be out of harmony with the Creator of the universe" (RH, Sept. 27, 1906). It is not surprising, therefore, that practically all her statements on the physical aspects of the universe are correlated to moral or spiritual observations.

Early in Ellen White's prophetic ministry she was given a vision of other inhabited worlds (EW 39). One of those worlds she describes as "a place that was bright and glorious.... The inhabitants of the place were of all sizes; they were noble, majestic, and lovely. They bore the express image of Jesus," and she was told that they had never disobeyed God's law like the inhabitants of the earth (*ibid.*). Later statements suggest that she was made aware of the immensity of God's creation and of His care for that creation. She wrote, "Every world throughout immensity engages the care and support of the Father and the Son; and this care is constantly exercised for fallen humanity" (RH, Jan. 11, 1881). God "controls the heavens with their numberless worlds. He preserves in perfect harmony the grandeur and beauty of the things which He has created." In the same article, she refers to "the starry hosts of heaven, the millions of worlds above" that testify to the greatness and majesty of the Creator (RH, Mar. 1, 1881).

That God is a God of order is a basic truth of Scripture, stressed by Ellen White in a variety of contexts. There is perfect order in heaven among the angels loyal to God (1T 649; 4T 429). "The sequence of nature is under God's jurisdiction. God works by His own laws, for He is a God of order" (15MR 220). God displays His wisdom "in maintaining perfect order in the vast universe" (LHU 54; cf. SL 76). "From the stars that in their trackless courses through space follow from age to age their appointed path, down to the minutest atom, the things of nature obey the Creator's will" (SC 86). The "glory of creation" consists of "suns and stars and systems, all in their appointed order circling the throne of Deity," and in all things "are the riches of His power displayed" (GC 677, 678). Ellen White contrasts the order that characterizes God's created works with the disorder resulting from rebellion and disobedience. While "the will of God is the sole law to which the sun, moon, and stars in the firmament of heaven yield obedience" and while at "the mandate of Jehovah, they move in perfect order," it is the human race who sets up its "will against the will of the omniscient One," and enters "into conflict with Him who rules the universe" (ST, Aug. 24, 1888).

Narrow ideas about the magnitude of the universe are refuted by Ellen White. In an article entitled "The Government of God" she wrote: "Many seem to have the idea that this world and the heavenly mansions constitute the universe of God. Not so. The redeemed throng will range from world to world, and much of their time will be employed in searching out the mysteries of redemption" (RH, Mar. 9, 1886). She shows how the great controversy between God and Satan affected the entire universe and that the only world in which Satan succeeded to introduce sin and rebellion was our world. Consequently, this world "because of sin . . . was struck off from the continent of heaven, and Satan claimed it as his" (*ibid.*).

There is a significant emphasis in Ellen White's writings on the fact that Christ's sacrifice on the cross secures not only the salvation of the human race but also the eternal peace and harmony of the universe. While through Christ's incarnation and His cross the human race is reconciled with God and this world reunited with the "continent of heaven" (e.g., 1BC 1084, 1095; RH, June 10, 1890; YI, Feb. 22, 1900), Christ's atoning work also makes the whole loyal universe eternally secure against another rise of rebellion, apostasy, and sin. "The atonement will never need to be repeated; and there will be no danger of another rebellion in the universe of God. That which alone can effectually restrain from sin in this world of darkness [i.e., the cross of Christ] will prevent sin in heaven" (ST, Dec. 30, 1889). The cross of Christ benefits "not only the inhabitants of this speck of a world, but the whole universe, every world which God had created" (RH, July 5, 1887; cf. BE, July 15, 1893).

For Ellen White there is no thought that the universe will ever end up in some eternal darkness or terrible conflagration. Rather, the universe will exist forever as the theater of God's love and power. She describes this in simple yet lofty words at the end of her book *The Great Controversy*: "The great controversy is ended. Sin and sinners are no more. The entire universe is clean. One pulse of harmony and gladness beats through the vast creation. From Him who created all, flow life and light and gladness, throughout the realms of illimitable space. From the minutest atom to the greatest world, all things, animate and inanimate, in their unshadowed beauty and perfect joy, declare that God is love" (GC 678).

Peter M. van Bemmelen

UPWARD LOOK, THE (RHPA, 1982, 383 pp.). Thirteenth daily devotional book published by the Ellen G. White Estate. Selections from the writings of Ellen White in this book were made from letters and manuscripts written or orally presented by her on the same calendar day designated for that day's reading. No central theme was followed in the selection of these messages except that whenever possible the excerpts are intended to bring encouragement. Much of the material in this volume had either appeared in journals or never been published before. A brief biographical outline of Ellen White's life and ministry is given at the beginning of the book (pp. 7-13).

VEGETARIANISM. Ellen White's writings urge adoption of a vegetarian diet. She held that "by meat eating, the physical, mental, and moral powers are weakened" (CD 269): meat shortens the life span (*ibid.* 373), diminishes intellectual activity (*ibid.* 389), enfeebles perception and thought regarding God and truth (*ibid.* 384), deteriorates the moral powers (*ibid.* 382, 383), creates an appetite for liquor (*ibid.* 268, 269), and strengthens animal propensities (*ibid.* 382-384, 390).

She described the ideal vegetarian diet: "Fruits, grains, and vegetables, prepared in a simple way, free from spice and grease of all kinds, make, with milk or cream, the most healthful diet" (*ibid.* 355). She emphasized foods from the plant kingdom: "Vegetables, fruits, and grains should compose our diet" (*ibid.* 380) and also included nuts in some lists of recommended foods, while warning against making them too large a part of the diet (MH 296, 298). Though she stressed plant foods, she offered caution regarding the risks of eliminating all animal products: "Some, in abstaining from milk, eggs, and butter, have failed to supply the system with proper nourishment, and as a consequence, have become weak and unable to work. Thus health reform is brought into disrepute" (CD 207, 208). Vitamin B_{12}, found in its physiologically active form in milk and eggs but not in plant foods, may be a key factor in this counsel.

While stressing a plant-based diet, White never referred to milk and eggs as inherently bad, and she did not class them with meat (*ibid.* 351). However, she warned of a time during which disease in the animal kingdom could make products from those animals unsafe for food. "The time will come when we may have to discard some of the articles of diet we now use, such as milk and cream and eggs; but my message is that you must not bring yourself to a time of trouble beforehand, and thus afflict yourself with death" (*ibid.* 206). Her view seems to connect the nonuse of milk and eggs with a time of trouble, not to be brought on prematurely. Regarding the time to lay aside these products, she wrote, "God will reveal this" (*ibid.*). She taught that in preparation for that time, one should learn how to cook without these foods (*ibid.* 349).

Her views on the vegetarian diet are broad in scope. She felt it is a "sacred duty" to accept the information God has given and to keep ourselves in the very best health (2T 70). White wrote of "the danger of meat eating" to "the physical, mental, and spiritual health" (CD 382). Vegetarianism is a goal, and God leads His people away from eating "the flesh of dead animals" (*ibid.* 411); people should return to the diet given to humanity at the beginning (MH 317). The church's health institution workers should "use less and less meat, until it is not used at all" (CD 407). "Among those who are waiting for the coming of the Lord, meat eating will eventually be done away; flesh will cease to form a part of their diet" (*ibid.* 380, 381). Health reformers "are to make no prescriptions that flesh meats shall never be used," but through education the individual conscience will be guided from a "perverted appetite" into better choices (*ibid.* 291). She warned that "many who are now only half converted on the question of meat eating will go from God's people to walk no more with them" (*ibid.* 382).

People were not to discard meat before they could make adequate nutritional replacement. They were not to adopt a "poverty-stricken diet. Place enough on the table to nourish the system" (*ibid.* 489). "Should health reform in its most extreme form be taught to those whose circumstances forbid its adoption, more harm than good would be done" (9T 163).

White consistently held that the vegetarian diet, while clearly a "teaching" of the church, was not to be a "test" of church membership among Seventh-day Adventists (*ibid.* 159). She presented the vegetarian diet as a part of a larger health message. She often spoke of the health message as the "right arm" in relation to the "body" of the three angels' messages of Revelation 14, and she warned against making the health message itself the "body" of the church's teachings.

As strongly as Ellen White advocated the vegetarian diet, she did not insist on it for all people everywhere. With the Christian's responsibility to care for the health for spiritual as well as physical reasons, she taught that one should adopt the best diet available. "We do not mark out any precise line to be followed in diet; but we do say that in countries where there are fruits, grains, and nuts in abundance, flesh food is not the right food for God's people" (*ibid.*).

White endeavored to carry out these principles of the vegetarian diet in her own life. She adopted a meatless diet as her customary eating pattern when she first began to teach it. However, over the years her practice of vegetarianism became more complete as conditions made this easier to attain and her own convictions deepened, as the following brief review of her experience indicates.

Before White received her health reform instruction she was "weak and feeble, subject to frequent fainting spells" (*ibid.* 158). She had thought of meat as a strengthening, indispensable food. However, despite her heavy use of it, she continued to grow weaker (CD 487). Her comprehensive health reform vision of June 6, 1863, repeated some of the earlier

health instruction and added more. Among other things, the vision urged abstinence from flesh food. Her response was prompt and positive: "I at once cut meat out of my bill of fare," even as she indicated that this did not mean total abstinence from then on (*ibid.*).

She wrote in 1870 that no "flesh meats of any kind come on my table" (2T 487). This was her customary practice, but a temporary departure from her vegetarian diet could occur for various reasons, such as when a new cook did not know how to prepare vegetarian meals. W. C. White wrote that at times "our table showed some compromises between the standard which Sister White was aiming at and the knowledge and experience and standard of the new cook" (WCW, "The Use of Meat in the White Family" [n.d.], Q&A File 22-F-1, EGWE-GC). Sometimes meat was used because of travel hardships—limited money, dependence on church members who were often poor and using meat by necessity, or when fruits and vegetables were not in season. White also made allowance for departure from a vegetarian pattern in cases in which meat might temporarily serve therapeutic purposes. Some people with "feeble digestive organs" might tolerate some meat or chicken broth when they could not tolerate other foods (CD 395). In such situations it was important to use only the flesh of healthy animals (*ibid.* 394).

W. C. White wrote of their dietary practice prior to the mid-1890s, "For years the White family had been vegetarians, but not 'teetotalers'" (WCW to G. B. Starr, Aug. 24, 1933, cited in *The Fannie Bolton Story* [EGWE, 1990], p. 119). In 1894, in answer to an inquiry from a non-Adventist woman, Ellen White wrote optimistically of Seventh-day Adventists, "All are vegetarians, many abstaining wholly from the use of flesh food, while others use it in only the most moderate degree" (Lt 99, 1894, in 4Bio 119). For her, a vegetarian was one whose customary practice was not to eat meat but who was not necessarily a total abstainer ("teetotaler").

White also seemed to distinguish between "meat" and fish or poultry. She wrote to her traveling husband in 1876, "We have not had a particle of meat in the house since you left and long before you left. We have had salmon a few times" (14MR 336). In 1894 she determined that she would no longer eat meat even occasionally (CD 488). Conditions that had made this more difficult in earlier years (lack of trained cooks, lack of meat substitutes, primitive travel conditions, etc.) had abated, at least to some degree. Evidence indicates that she also discontinued the use of fish before the end of the 1890s (Coon, pp. 21, 22). Many of her strongest statements against meat eating come from her later years, beyond the turn of the twentieth century.

In describing White's commitment to the vegetarian diet, W. C. White declared her to have been "steadfast but not fanatical" ("The Use of Meat in the White Family"). She credited adherence to health reform principles with having greatly improved her quality of life. At 81 she could declare, "I have better health today, notwithstanding my age, than I had in my younger days" (9T 159).

Over the years accusations have arisen that White was inconsistent and even hypocritical in regard to her vegetarian practice. An understanding of her concept of a vegetarian, the conditions of the times, and of her own personal journey allow for a more charitable assessment. She stated her own view of the matter in 1909: "It is reported by some that I have not followed the principles of health reform as I have advocated them with my pen; but I can say that I have been a faithful health reformer. Those who have been members of my family know that this is true" (*ibid.*).

Further reading: CD 481-494; 9T 153-166; R. W. Coon, *Ellen White and Vegetarianism: Did She Practice What She Preached?* (PPPA, 1986); H. E. Douglass, *Messenger of the Lord* (PPPA, 1998), pp. 279-299, 310-342; R. Graybill, "The Development of Adventist Thinking on Clean and Unclean Meats" (EGWE, 1981); R. L. Numbers, *Prophetess of Health: A Study of Ellen G. White,* third ed. (Grand Rapids: Eerdmans, 2008); *A Critique of Prophetess of Health* (EGWE, 1976).

Sylvia M. Fagal and Roger W. Coon

VINDICATION OF THE BUSINESS CAREER OF ELDER JAMES WHITE (Steam Press of the SDA Publishing Association, 1863, 39 pp.). Prior to the establishment of a legal *church organization the key institutions of the Seventh-day Adventist Church were registered under James White's name. This situation greatly concerned White, who began to push for a legal organizational structure. Instances had already occurred with church members who had built meetinghouses, or bought an evangelistic tent, only to lose possession of those facilities when the members in whose name the property was held died or left the movement. During the early 1860s rumors began to circulate that James White was becoming rich by registering under his name such church entities as the *Review and Herald. In order to alleviate these concerns, an action was taken at the 1863 General Conference session to establish a committee of three respected church leaders, *Uriah Smith, chair; *G. W. Amadon; and E. S. Walker, to examine these charges. The committee circulated announcements for anyone who had information or a charge to make against James White to come forward. When no one came forward, an appeal was made for testimonials about White's integrity. The resulting pamphlet includes 39 testimonials (pp. 9-36), with a list of 58 others who sent in testimonials that the committee was unable to print for lack of space (pp. 37, 38). As a result the committee commended "Bro. White to the confidence and sympathy of Christians everywhere" (p. 39).

Further reading: C. M. Maxwell, *Tell It to the World* (PPPA, 1982), pp. 137, 143, 144; G. R. Knight, *Organizing to Beat the Devil* (RHPA, 2001), pp. 50, 51.

Michael W. Campbell

VISIONS OF ELLEN G. WHITE. It is estimated that during her 70 years of ministry Ellen White received approximately 2,000 visions. Visions came to her in a variety of ways and varied greatly in duration. In the early years of her ministry many visions were accompanied by physical phenomena similar to those of biblical prophets (cf. Dan. 10:5-10). In the later years, visions happened mainly during the night. While some of the visions were long, at times lasting more than an hour and on one occasion four hours, there were other times during which the visions were very brief in duration—only a few minutes or, in some cases, seconds. There were times visions were instantaneous views about certain situations or conditions. At such times the vision usually related to only one subject or one phase of a subject, while the longer visions might deal with many subjects or events occurring over a long period of time. The visions of the early years were more comprehensive in their content, longer in duration, and less frequent. In later years they were more frequent but often limited in scope. Ellen White's first vision occurred in December 1844. Her last public vision happened either in 1879 or 1884 (there are two different accounts of when this last public vision occurred). Her last vision, or prophetic dream, was received in March 1915, shortly after her accident.

There are several eyewitness accounts of what usually took place in connection with the visions accompanied by physical phenomena in her early years of ministry. At the beginning of a vision she uttered an exclamation of "Glory!" or "Glory to God!" at times repeated. She appeared to lose her physical strength and did not breathe, although the heartbeat continued normally, and her facial complexion appeared natural. Witnesses claim that the most critical tests were done on her physical body to reveal any hoax or change to the circulatory system. Occasionally there would be exclamations indicative of the scene being presented to her. Her eyes were open, not with a vacant stare, but as if she were intently watching something. Her physical position might vary. At times she was seated; at times reclining; sometimes she walked about the room and made graceful gestures as she spoke of matters presented to her. There seemed to be an absolute unconsciousness of what was occurring about her. She neither saw, heard, felt, nor perceived in any way her immediate surroundings. The close of the vision was indicated by a deep inhalation, followed in about a minute by another, and very soon natural breathing was resumed. Immediately after the vision all seemed very dark to her, but within a short time natural strength and abilities were regained. One example of these phenomena relates how Ellen White is said to have held at arm's length a large Bible for several minutes and walked around a room, pointing to Bible passages in this Bible (1Bio 92). Although Ellen White made no reference to the experience, it was witnessed by many people who later wrote accounts of the events (*ibid.* 92, 101-105).

Such intriguing physical phenomena provided tangible and convincing evidence to early Adventist believers at a time when her work was not well known. Although not a proof of the divine authenticity of her visions, these phenomena nonetheless provided substantiation of the supernatural nature of her experience. Ellen White rarely spoke of the physical phenomena that attended her visions given in public, perhaps because she herself had no firsthand knowledge of these experiences. She made one reference to her experience in 1906: "Sometimes while I was in vision, my friends would approach me and exclaim, 'Why, she does not breathe!' Placing a mirror before my lips, they found that no moisture gathered on the glass. It was while there was no sign of any breathing that I kept talking of the things that were being presented before me. These messages were thus given to substantiate the faith of all, that in these last days we might have confidence in the spirit of prophecy" (RH, June 14, 1906).

During the last 30 years or so of her ministry, Ellen White received her visions mainly through what she called "visions of the night," or dreams. She made a distinction, however, between normal dreams and supernatural visions, which she attributed to God. In 1868 she stated, "Dreams from the Lord are classed in the Word of God with visions and are as truly the fruits of the spirit of prophecy as visions. Such dreams, taking into the account the persons who have them, and the circumstances under which they are given, contain their own proofs of their genuineness" (5T 658). Answering an inquiry from her son W. C. White as to how she could distinguish between a natural dream and a supernatural vision, she said that she could tell the difference because "the same angel messenger stands by my side instructing me in the visions of the night, as stands beside me instructing me in the visions of the day." Natural dreams did not have the angel messenger while visions did (in A. L. White, *Messenger to the Remnant*, p. 7). It was not too uncommon also for Ellen White to be given a vision while praying, either in private or in public (e.g., 5Bio 53, 54).

Some have assumed wrongly that Ellen White wrote her manuscripts and books while receiving visions, or that some mechanical force guided her pen while her mind was in some kind of ecstatic state or trance. Or that when she wrote she was recording words dictated to her by an angel. Except in rare instances when short, direct quotations are given of what the angel said, these views of her experience are not accurate. She herself, her family members, and others in her immediate circle of friends and acquaintances stated many times that Ellen White did not write her books while receiving visions and that in fact she was exercising her full mental abilities while writing, being fully cognizant of her task and the words she penned. In 1860 she wrote this brief description of how matters were revealed to her: "As inquiries are frequently made as to my state in vision, and after I come out, I would say that when the Lord sees fit to give a vision, I am taken into the presence of Jesus and angels, and am entirely lost to earthly things. I can see no farther than the angel directs me. My attention is often directed to scenes transpiring upon earth. At times I am carried far ahead into the future and shown what is to take place. Then again I am shown things as they have occurred in the past" (2SG 292).

But perhaps more important than how visions were given to Ellen White is the question of why she received visions. White's visions served a number of purposes. She believed that the role of her visions consisted in the enlightening of her mind upon a wide range of subjects that God wanted her to communicate to the Adventist people. Often the matters revealed were of general interest and concern, but frequently specific messages were given for individuals. And then when she was not in vision it was her responsibility to pass on to others instruction, admonition, and information that she had received. Her ministry, therefore, born from her prophetic gift, not only involved providing counsels on a variety of matters impacting the development of the Seventh-day Adventist Church, but also included writing on biblical and historical themes for the spiritual edification of people.

In many visions the events of the past, present, and future were opened up to Ellen White in panoramic view. It seemed to her that she witnessed in rapid succession the vivid enactment of various scenes of history. Many of these visions were the foundation of her writings on the cosmic conflict between good and evil as found in the *Conflict of the Ages Series. In her introduction to *The Great Controversy* she gives a glimpse of what she meant by the enlightenment of her mind while receiving visions and the reason for receiving these visions.

"Through the illumination of the Holy Spirit [i.e., visions], the scenes of the long-continued conflict between good and evil have been opened to the writer of these pages. From time to time I have been permitted to behold the working, in different ages, of the great controversy between Christ, the Prince of life, the Author of our salvation, and Satan, the prince of evil, the author of sin, the first transgressor of God's holy law. . . . As the Spirit of God has opened to my mind the great truths of His Word, and the scenes of the past and the future, I have been bidden to make known to others that which has thus been revealed—to trace the history of the controversy in past ages, and especially so to present it as to shed a light on the fast-approaching struggle of the future" (GC x, xi).

Oftentimes while in vision Ellen White would see events transpiring at some Adventist institutions; at times she would seem to be attending committee meetings. She would witness the actions of individuals, hear the words spoken, and observe the surroundings in general (e.g., CH 412, 413; Lt 30, 1887, in 8MR 315). Sometimes institutions or buildings were shown to Ellen White before they were erected, even before they were planned (e.g., Lt 135, 1903, in 3SM 55; 9T 28, 29; Lt 140, 1906, in HFM 77-82).

One last point to consider is the often-repeated charge that Ellen White's visions were the result of a nervous disorder (such as a form of temporal lobe epilepsy) as a result of the accident she suffered to her head at the age of 9. This charge first appeared around 1887 after a close friend of Ellen White's, Dudley M. Canright, left Adventism to become a bitter opponent of the movement. Although Canright was not a physician, the charge has been made by physicians since then.

Adventists have responded to this charge in two different ways. A first response has been a careful study of the medical evidences of Ellen White's head injury. In 1988 D. I. Peterson, professor of neurology at Loma Linda University School of Medicine and chief of neurology at Riverside General Hospital, in California, did a detailed analysis of the evidences available regarding Ellen White's head injury after her accident and her state of mind and physical phenomena while in vision. He concluded his study by stating that she did not suffer from "some form of epilepsy." "Abundant evidence supports the belief that 'something supernatural' *was indeed* happening when Ellen White experienced her visions" (Peterson, p. 27).

A second response to the charge of neurological disorder has been done from an experiential perspective, as showcased in F. D.

Nichol's *Ellen G. White and Her Critics*. If Ellen White's visions were a result of epilepsy, so goes the argument, then how could she have such a major influence on a young denomination and on many aspects of life, such as personal spirituality, health principles, educational reform, and administrative insights? After describing Ellen White's lifelong accomplishments, Nichol concluded, "In the light of this life sketch, brief though it is, one is tempted to dispose of the mental-malady charge here and now with one sentence in comment: If such mental illness as Mrs. White is supposed to have suffered from will produce a life of sacrificial service and ardor, of far mission planning, of counsel to holy living and high standards, of selfless love for the needy, and all the other Christian graces that radiated from her life, then we would say solemnly, God give us more mentally malad-justed people" (p. 50). Nichol's conclusion is perhaps the strongest argument Adventists have used against any critique of Ellen White's prophetic gift—the fruits of her labor speak for themselves.

See also: Great Controversy Vision; Iceberg Vision; Salamanca Vision.

Further reading: H. E. Douglass, *Messenger of the Lord* (PPPA, 1998), pp. 134-169; F. D. Nichol, *Ellen G. White and Her Critics* (RHPA, 1951), pp. 26-86; D. I. Peterson, *Visions or Seizures: Was Ellen White the Victim of Epilepsy?* (PPPA, 1988); A. L. White, *Ellen G. White— Messenger to the Remnant* (RHPA, 1969), pp. 5-8; A. L. White, "Variation and Frequency of the Ellen G. White Visions" (Apr. 5, 1982, SDoc); W. C. White, "The Visions of Ellen G. White" (EGWE, 1905, SDoc). A chronological listing of Ellen White's published visions is found in the *Comprehensive Index to the Writings of Ellen G. White*, vol. 3, pp. 2978-2984.

Denis Fortin

VOCATIONAL EDUCATION. "In order to have well developed, well-balanced men and women," Ellen White urged that "moral, intellectual, and physical culture should be combined" (FE 42). The combination of the theoretical studies with practical experience produces incalculable benefits.

Ellen White grounded her advocacy of vocational education on the biblical premise that at Creation, before the entrance of sin, labor "meant development, power, happiness." Even after millennia of sin, labor is "still a source of happiness and development," and a "safeguard against temptation." God, who is a "constant worker," has endowed human beings with creativity, a degree of power over the forces of nature, the ability to bring order and beauty out of confusion, and, like God at the close of Creation, to experience joy in work well done (Ed 214, 215). She pointed out that in Israel "it was regarded a crime to allow children to grow up in ignorance of useful labor," and "every child was taught some trade" (FE 97). She also made multiple references to Christ's mastery of the carpenter's trade, and how that experience shaped His character (DA 72; FE 142, 417; MH 399; 3T 566).

In White's educational paradigm, vocational training is among the most essential subjects taught in school. As far as possible, every school should offer manual training in "as many as possible of the most useful trades," so that "every youth, on leaving school," has the "knowledge of some trade or occupation by which, if need be, he may earn a livelihood." And "since both men and women have a part in home-making, boys as well as girls should gain a knowledge of household duties" (Ed 216, 218).

She attributed to vocational education both immediate and long-term values for students. One immediate value is "relaxation from study," for which "useful employment"—especially when it involves outdoor, whole-body exercise—carries greater benefits than sports. Besides physical exercise, useful work combines discipline, responsibility, and service, producing a greater sense of real accomplishment. Another immediate value is the opportunity for the student to be self-sustaining and avoid the accumulation of debt (*ibid.* 215, 219, 221).

Long-term benefits of vocational education include insights that help students select their lifework, and development of "that practical wisdom which we call common sense." "Practical work . . . develops ability to plan and execute, strengthens courage and perseverance, and calls for the exercise of tact and skill" (*ibid.* 220). The most highly educated professionals gain increased influence when it is evident that they have not only theoretical knowledge, but skill in practical areas. In emergencies, practical skills often make "the difference between success and failure" in the lifework (*ibid.* 221).

Because it combines whole-body exercise in the open air, with the rewarding purpose of producing a sustainable food supply, White held that "no line of manual training is of more value than agriculture" (*ibid.* 219). Indeed, she taught that "agriculture is the ABC of industrial education" (2MR 74). Many missionaries and founders of institutions have proved the value of that counsel by being able to grow their own food in situations in which they could not have survived otherwise (Mittleider and Nelson).

Further reading: CT 273-293; Ed 214-222; FE 71-76, 310-327, 416-420, 512-515; J. R. Mittleider and A. N. Nelson, *Food for Everyone: The Mittleider Method* (College Place, Wash.: Color Press, 1973).

Jerry Moon

VOICE IN SPEECH AND SONG, THE, see *COUNSELS ON SPEECH AND SONG*.

VOICE OF GOD, GENERAL CONFERENCE AS THE. A recurring theme in Ellen White's writings regarding ecclesiastical authority, from 1870 to 1913. While Ellen White elsewhere identified a number of concepts, such as God's word and providence (PP 126), conscience (5T 120), and the voice of duty (CH 562), God's created works, and God's judgments (PP 587), as the "voice of God," it was a series of sharp critiques of the General Conference that brought the expression "voice of God" to prominence in the context of church organization and authority.

The concept of the voice of God must be understood within the context of three factors: (1) the development of the Seventh-day Adventist organization; (2) Ellen White's understanding of the General Conference as the highest ecclesiastical authority on earth; and (3) the emergence in 1888 of the message of *righteousness by faith as a guiding theological doctrine. Shortly after the successful formation of the General Conference in 1863, Ellen White wrote, with reference to the authority of local and traveling elders, that there was "no higher tribunal upon earth than the church of God" (5MR 296). Later she revealed that her understanding of the General Conference as the highest authority on earth was based on the authority of the Jerusalem Council as described in Acts 15 (3SP 375, 376; LP 69).

Ellen White's earliest statements on the General Conference as the "voice of God" occur in a lengthy letter to *G. I. Butler. She told Butler (a former and future General Conference president) that the "principles in regard to leadership" that he had published in 1873 were mostly "right." "But you greatly err," she wrote, "in giving to one man's mind and judgment that authority and influence which God has invested in His church in the judgment and voice of the General Conference"—"the highest organized authority" both in the church and upon the earth (3T 493; cf. *ibid.* 417).

Consequently, the delegates to the 1877 General Conference session repudiated their 1873 acceptance of Butler's views on centralized leadership and instead voted an expression maintaining the authority of the General Conference as the highest authority among Seventh-day Adventists, to be submitted to by all unless found in conflict with the Word of God and individual conscience (RH, Oct. 4, 1877). Yet for most of the years between 1863 and 1888 Butler and James White, both strong personalities, presided over the General Conference, making it hard for centralizing tendencies to be resisted. Also, by 1885 only one of the five-member General Conference Executive Committee lived in Battle Creek, making consultation almost impossible. These dynamics made it increasingly difficult for the 1877 view on the authority of the General Conference to be realized in practice.

By the time of the *General Conference session of 1888, Ellen White's frustration with centralizing tendencies had reached a peak. This session marked a turning point in her attitude toward the authority of the General Conference. She wrote that Butler had been in office three years too long, that he was no longer a humble person, and that he believed that "his voice is infallible" (1888 Materials 183). For this and other reasons, Butler was replaced by *O. A. Olsen as president—who affirmed at the 1889 session that "we acknowledge the General Conference to be the highest authority recognized by God on the earth" (GCDB, Oct. 28, 1889).

By 1891 Ellen White had completely changed her views on the authority of the General Conference. That year she bluntly wrote: "I was obliged to take the position that there was not the voice of God in the General Conference management and decisions. Methods and plans would be devised that God did not sanction, and yet Elder Olsen made it appear that the decisions of the General Conference were as the voice of God. Many of the positions taken, going forth as the voice of the General Conference, have been the voice of one, two, or three men who were misleading the [General] Conference" (17MR 167). More such statements were to follow.

In 1895 she wrote of the General Conference that "there is no voice from God through that body that is reliable" (*ibid.* 178; cf. *ibid.* 221, 222). The next year her sentiments, while largely unchanged, became more intense. "The sacred character of the cause of God is no longer realized at the center of the work," she wrote. "The voice from Battle Creek, which has been regarded as authority in counseling how the work should be done, is no longer the voice of God; but it is the voice of—whom? From whence does it come, and where is its vital power? This state of things is maintained by men who should have been disconnected from the work long ago. These men do not scruple to quote the Word of God as their authority, but the god who is leading them is a false god" (*ibid.* 185, 186). Two years later she appealed directly to *E. J. Waggoner and his wife to come to Australia, instead of placing a request through the General Conference, giving as her reason that "it has been some years since I have considered the General Conference as the voice of God" (*ibid.* 216).

During the 1899 General Conference session *A. T. Jones quoted from the above letter to Waggoner and called for corporate repentance. Eleven leaders (including *G. A. Irwin, *O. A. Olsen, and *A. F. Ballenger) prayed for repentance, with *L. A. Hoopes and *A. J. Breed in particular specifically praying that the General Conference might once again become the voice of God (GCDB, Feb. 22, 1899). Nine months later, however, Ellen White had not changed her mind: she implied that those in America "who suppose the voice of the General Conference to be the voice of God" were not "one with God" (13MR 291).

This negative assessment of the General Conference as no longer being the voice of God reflected conditions among leadership that were not substantially rectified until the *General Conference sessions of 1901 and 1903. The centralization of authority and *kingly power, combined with financial mismanagement and a lack of true spirituality among some in high positions, were some of the reasons she gave for these sharp statements. Thus her writings during the decade of 1891-1901 not only denied that the General Conference represented the voice of God, but repeatedly rebuked its leaders for their persistent "disregard of right principles" (17MR 209; cf. 13MR 192; 17MR 240, 250).

It is important to note that at the same time she was critiquing General Conference authority as not representing the voice of God, she still submitted to its authority. In regard to her move to Australia in 1891, she wrote that she had received no "clear light" that she should go to Australia but had followed the "voice of the [General] Conference" (19MR 288). In 1896 she wrote to her son Edson, "I had not one ray of light that He [the Lord] would have me come to this country [Australia]. I came in submission to the voice of the General Conference, which I have ever maintained to be authority" (1MR 156).

Her attitude toward the authority of the General Conference during this era was not, however, always submissive. In 1894, for example, regarding suggestions that she travel

to Europe or Africa, she responded: "I have not the slightest inclination to go to Europe or to visit Africa, and I have not one ray of light that I should go. I am willing to go wherever the Lord indicates my duty, but I am not willing to go at the voice of the [General] Conference unless I see my own way closer to do so" (1888 Materials 1263).

The 1899 General Conference session brought into sharp focus the problems of a rapidly growing denomination still governed by an overly centralized administrative structure. After returning to the United States, Ellen White explicitly stated at the 1901 General Conference session that the General Conference was no longer the voice of God: "That these men should stand in a sacred place, to be as the voice of God to the people, as we once believed the General Conference to be,—that is past. What we want now is a reorganization. We want to begin at the foundation, and to build upon a different principle" (GCB, Apr. 3, 1901).

Ellen White was initially encouraged by the major structural and personnel changes made in 1901 (LDE 54). She reprimanded her son Edson for using, in the changed context after 1901, critical statements she had made before to 1901 regarding the General Conference as not the voice of God (19MR 146-148). "Great changes" had been made since the conference, she explained, and "many more changes will be made and great developments will be seen" (*ibid.* 146, 147).

But she later realized that the reforms of 1901 had been incomplete. Toward the end of 1902 she wrote that because "the leading men" "act without wisdom" and "do not obey the Word," she had "lost confidence" in them to the point that she was tempted to return to Australia (Lt 263, 1902). She was also particularly agitated regarding the neglect of the Southern field, and she wrote to her son

Willie that "the leading men are blind," that she had "but little courage" and feared greatly, and that she could not ever remember "having such a hopeless presentation in regard to the future" (Lt 288, 1903).

In the burning of the Review and Herald printing plant in Battle Creek in December 1902, she saw God's disapproval of the past leadership of the General Conference and "[marveled] that judgment has not fallen" on the General Conference itself. With dictatorial power still in play, God's statutes set aside, and His authority insulted, she wrote that "the General Conference has fallen into strange ways"; no longer could "the representatives of the [General] Conference" say "the temple of the Lord are we" (14MR 280).

By the 1909 General Conference session, however, much had changed. Addressing the session, she reiterated her past counsel: "At times when a small group of men entrusted with the general management of the work have, in the name of the General Conference, sought to carry out unwise plans and to restrict God's work, I have said that I could no longer regard the voice of the General Conference, *represented by these few men*, as the voice of God. But this is not saying that the decisions of a General Conference composed of *an assembly of duly appointed, representative men from all parts of the field* should not be respected. God has ordained that the representatives of His church from all parts of the earth, when assembled in a General Conference, shall have authority. The error . . . is in giving to the mind and judgment of *one man*, or of *a small group* of men, the full measure of author- ity and influence that God has vested in His church in the judgment and voice of the General Conference assembled to plan for the prosperity and advancement of His work" (9T 260, 261; italics supplied).

But after the session she wrote to the president and vice president, *A. G. Daniells and *W. W. Prescott, that "grave perils" faced the church unless "there was a decided change in the spiritual discernment of the men at the head of the work" (Lt 47, 1909). Not all of the delegates at the 1909 General Conference session had responded to the influence of the Holy Spirit, and she was in "much distress" over the spiritual condition of "some who are bearing grave responsibility" (Lt 162, 1909). Specifically she saw that the reelection of Daniells by the General Conference after nine years already as president "was a hasty move," a "mistake" made "without due consideration" (Lt 153, 1910).

Nevertheless, in 1911 White reprinted her words from the 1870s: "God has invested His church with special authority and power which no one can be justified in disregarding and despising, for he who does this despises the voice of God" (AA 164; cf. 3T 417; RH, May 11, 1911). She also reiterated her 1878 view that the Acts 15 council was a model for the General Conference as the voice of highest spiritual authority on earth (AA 195, 196; cf. 3SP 375, 376). She seems to have come full circle to her earlier high view of the authority of the General Conference (cf. 2SM 400-402).

Five observations may be drawn from this study. First, Ellen White's statements on the General Conference as the voice of God changed in relation to time and historical context. No one statement can be considered absolute, for each statement reflected an evaluation at a specific time. Second, while she severely criticized some church leaders, she did not include *all* of its leaders in her rebukes. Furthermore, it should be noted that her references to the General Conference as the voice of God were directed at the leaders of the church in between General Conference sessions. Third, not every rebuke to an individual General Conference leader implied a loss of confidence in all of its leaders. Statements regarding the General Conference as the "voice of God" pertained particularly to the period of organizational breakdown, c. 1888-1903. Fourth, despite her criticisms, she did not abandon the church, but continued to write, rebuke, and exhort from within the church. Finally, while her rebukes often focused on "kingly power" and overly centralized authority, she also mentioned spiritual reasons for her objections. Consequently, organizational changes alone did not alleviate her concerns. Several post-1901 statements continue to mention such pre-1901 concerns as centralization of authority, the dictatorial spirit of some leaders, unspirituality and spiritual blindness, the rejection of light, and the need for leaders to be converted. Thus Ellen White's criticisms regarding "kingly power" and other leadership problems were often linked with her emphasis on righteousness by faith and the need to trust Christ rather than humans for support.

Further reading: 5Bio 70-110, 198-258; B. Haloviak, "SDAs and Organization: 1844-1907" (1987, CAR); G. R. Knight, *Organizing for Mission and Growth: The Development of Adventist Church Structure* (RHPA, 2006); B. D. Oliver, *SDA Organizational Structure: Past, Present, and Future* (AUP, 1989); G. E. Rice, "The Church: Voice of God?" *Ministry*, December 1987, pp. 4-6; R. W. Schwarz and F. Greenleaf, *Light Bearers: A History of the Seventh-day Adventist Church* (PPPA, 2000), pp. 248-257; A. L. White, "The Story of the General Conference of 1901" (EGWE, 1962, SDoc).

Ross E. Winkle

VOTING, see **POLITICS AND VOTING**.

WAGON TRAIN, ELLEN WHITE'S EXPERIENCE WITH. A unique travel experience from Denison, Texas, to Emporia, Kansas, in May 1879. Having spent the winter of 1878-1879 organizing and strengthening the Texas Conference, James and Ellen White prepared for their colorful wagon train trip with a trial run, when a party of 15 traveled from Dallas to Denison in March 1879. James and Ellen were pleased with the success of this short trip.

Several years earlier James had dreamed of a wagon train experience, driving cattle, horses, and mules from Texas to Colorado for a profit. In the ensuing months, however, those plans had been tempered. Reacting to adverse experiences with the Texas weather and economics, the Whites decided to move the McDearmon family to Colorado. Two other families, also Michigan emigrants, too impoverished to afford public transportation, also expressed a desire to make the trip. Recognizing an opportunity to help these families and other single individuals, James sold most of the livestock he had acquired, investing the money in covered wagons. A group of 31 individuals, instead, would make the four-state trip in eight covered wagons and the Whites' two-seated surrey.

The wagon train set out from Denison on April 22, 1879, only to be stalled for several days at the Red River as they waited for one of the party to recover from an illness and searched for a ferry to cross the river swelled by spring rains (PC 26, 27).

Though not a treacherous journey, still it had many inconveniences. The travelers navigated the unfamiliar terrain admirably enough, moving northward through quicksand, then through dense timber, and finally across a prairie glen with large, hairy tarantulas. Several larger rivers were crossed by ferry. Smaller rivers and streams they forded with the assistance of Native Americans, who usually charged 25 cents for such favors.

J. O. Corliss had been elected trailmaster. Inexperienced at the task, he served better as scout, messenger, and special assistant to the Whites. Corliss' lack of experience called forth heavy criticism from several of the Whites' traveling guests. Ellen would later remonstrate the inappropriateness of their complaints.

Ever careful to keep the communication lines open with church headquarters in Battle Creek, the Whites sent a rider some 40 miles eastward to Atoka to telegraph their whereabouts and to pick up the latest mail. They informed friends and family in Battle Creek of their next stop, Old Stonewall (now called Frisco), some 20 miles southeast of the present Ada, Oklahoma.

To supplement a staple of jerky and crackers, for which James had made provision, Ellen, with Marian Davis and two young girls on the journey, foraged for wild berries and edible greens as opportunity permitted, and Ellen deplored this duty, regretting there was not a cook in the group.

Although frantically busy, Ellen did take a little time to observe the spring beauty of native Oklahoma wildflowers and forest as well as the Arbuckle Mountains to their west and the Shawnee Hills to their east, which the travelers carefully avoided. She also took charge of the spiritual welfare of the travelers, conducting worship services while on the trail.

After arriving at Old Stonewall, a Chickasaw town, the traveling party found a willing audience at the Chickasaw boarding school, located on the highest point in that area. Ellen addressed a congregation of about 100 Native Americans, who responded graciously to the gospel message.

Avoiding the nearly impenetrable ancient oak forests that extended from central Texas up to eastern Kansas, the wagon train made its way across the Canadian River near the southern boundary of the Seminole Nation, then traversed the Creek Nation, and viewed that tribe's impressive council house near Okmulgee. There James and Ellen spoke to the handsome ruddy citizens.

Writing of his idea to turn back northwest and follow the Chisholm Trail, James noted that they had traveled 160 miles from Denison and had yet 200 miles to their Kansas camp meeting destination—at least 10 days away, since a wagon train would normally do well to travel about 20 miles per day.

While their traveling companions looked forward to a "better life" in Colorado, the Whites were more anxious to meet their Kansas camp meeting appointment. It seems that James' zigzagging travel plans were immediately adjusted, because the party continued northeast. During the final days of the journey, their course paralleled the MKT (Missouri-Kansas-Texas) Railroad northward through the Cherokee Nation.

Finally, after crossing Kansas' southern border, they intersected the railway. The Whites, not willing to pass up a good opportunity, boarded the speedier mode of travel to the camp meeting at Emporia. Had they taken the northbound steam locomotive at Denison, the entire journey would have consumed parts of two days, in contrast to the monthlong wagon train journey.

Ellen arrived at the Emporia campground thoroughly exhausted and 12 pounds lighter, but happy to be back into her camp meeting circuit. For months she had feared she was not using her time and energies efficiently. Never again would she return to Texas or Oklahoma.

The remainder of the wagon train arrived at the campground several days later, then completed their journey westward to Boulder, Colorado. The Whites, meanwhile, made several camp meeting stops through the summer of 1879. Some weeks later all the wagon train traveling companions were reunited near the Whites' summer cabin in Colorado.

Further reading: 3Bio 107-117, 272, 273 (photo).

Mary Ann Hadley

WAHROONGA SANITARIUM, see **SYDNEY SANITARIUM**.

WALDENSES. Christian believers who, generally, inhabited the valleys of the mountainous area in southeastern France and northern Italy for many centuries and became in the twelfth century a well-known reform movement whose influence was increased by the leadership of Peter Waldo, a rich merchant of Lyon, who adopted a life of strict gospel simplicity and poverty. Although at first the movement did not intend to challenge the authority of the Roman Catholic Church, their belief in the supreme authority of the Bible for personal and social conduct and their anticlericalism led Pope Lucius III to condemn them as heretics in 1184. Thereafter, the Waldenses were subject to periodic persecutions and found refuge in the Piedmont valleys of northern *Italy. The Scripture was central to their lives of faith. Men, women, and children committed large passages of the Bible to memory. Not content to keep the truth found in Scripture to themselves, and adopting the occupation of traveling merchants as a cover, they went as missionaries to many parts of Europe. Wherever they found hearts open to the gospel they shared their faith at the risk of persecution and death.

Ellen White visited the Piedmont valleys on three different occasions during her stay in Europe (1885-1887). In her second visit, April 1886, she visited small groups of Adventist Sabbathkeepers in the Piedmont and, in the company of *A. C. Bourdeau and W. C. White,

also visited some of the noted places where the Waldenses had been tortured and slain by their persecutors (EGWEur 179, 180; LS 289, 290). They saw the site where thousands were thrown to their death into a deep ravine below. While standing on the very precipice and looking down onto the jagged rocks where so many lost their lives simply because they would not adhere to the Roman faith, she reflected on what a sight it will be when the Life-giver, with the voice of the archangel and the trump of God, shall call them forth from the rocky caverns, dungeons, caves, and clefts of the rocks (2MR 303, 304). Many of the places she visited looked familiar to her, for in vision she had been shown the travails and persecutions of these people.

The story of the Waldenses occupies a prominent place in Ellen White's writings. Her heart appreciated the sacrifices they accepted in order to keep their faith in Christ and the Scriptures, which they translated into their native tongue hundreds of years before the Reformation (GC 65). She placed them at the beginning of a long list of faith heroes who stood faithfully on the Word of God (AA 598).

On visiting the Piedmont Valley, White expressed "mingled feelings of joy and sorrow"—of joy because there existed, many years before the Reformation, a people who were not afraid to "stand in defense of Bible truth; of sorrow because so few of their descendants manifest a desire to continue to walk in the light as it shines from the Word of God" (HS 249). She predicted that God would again work for this people, and restore many of them to their former purity and fidelity to His service.

Further reading: GC 61-78; 2MR 303-308; 3Bio 334-336; HS 239-249; Jan Voerman, "Errors in Inspired Writings," *Adventist Affirm* 15, no. 1 (Spring 2001): 25-43.

Kathleen Demsky

WALLA WALLA COLLEGE. A Seventh-day Adventist educational institution founded to serve the Pacific Northwest, located in College Place, near Walla Walla in southeastern Washington. The college emerged after a bitter feud between the supporters of North Pacific Academy in Portland and Milton Academy in Milton, Oregon. In early 1890 W. W. Prescott, the education secretary of the General Conference, tried unsuccessfully to bring the rival regions to consensus. On July 14, 1890, Ellen White wrote a letter to John E. Graham,

WALLA WALLA COLLEGE, C.1895

the president of the North Pacific Conference, that paved the way for both regions to accept a "union" school. The college opened on December 7, 1892, with W. W. Prescott listed as president and Edward A. Sutherland serving as principal. In 1895 E. A. Sutherland cited Ellen White's writings as the motivation for his new curriculum emphasizing practical, Bible-based education. In 1904, as the young college struggled under a burden of debt, the WWC board chair, A. J. Breed, wrote to Ellen White for counsel, wondering if the college should be abandoned or relocated. Ellen White responded, in February 1905, that the college should continue: "Do not give up," she

counseled (Lt 61, 1905). Ellen White's influence on the Seventh-day Adventist educational system ultimately led to the full accreditation of Walla Walla College in 1935. In 2007 the institution was renamed Walla Walla University.

Further reading: Lt 25a, 1890; Ellen White, "August 1, 1901: Walla Walla College," PUR, Aug. 1, 1901; T. Aamodt, *Bold Venture: A History of Walla Walla College* (College Place, Wash.: Walla Walla College, 1992); C. Thurston, *60 Years of Progress: Walla Walla College* (College Place, Wash.: College Press, 1952).

Terrie Aamodt

WASHINGTON SANITARIUM. Adventist health facility in Washington, D.C. As early as 1903 plans were made for a sanitarium in the United States capital, but when the decision was made to move the denominational headquarters to Washington, D.C., plans for a sanitarium were quickly overshadowed by the search for land for the headquarters. When a suitable piece of property was found in Takoma Park, Maryland, one mile (1.6 kilometers) north of Washington, D.C., Ellen White reiterated to church leaders the importance of having a sanitarium near the denomination's headquarters (5Bio 318). As a result the western portion of the land was set aside for a sanitarium. On February 1, 1904, the sanitarium enterprise was incorporated and medical work began in a temporary clinic. Ellen White continued to encourage church leaders to push ahead with a new building for the sanitarium (Ms 86, 1905, in 2MR 53). Appeals were made to church members to contribute funds, and Ellen White devoted a portion of her royalties from *The Ministry of Healing to the project. She continued to counsel those who were making plans for the sanitarium (Ms 83, 1906) until its opening on June 13, 1907 (RH, Aug. 15, 1907). Drs. *Daniel H. and Lauretta Kress served as the first medical director and surgeon, respectively, of the new sanitarium. In 1973 the institution's name was changed to Washington Adventist Hospital.

Further reading: SDA Encyclopedia (1996), vol. 11, pp. 856-858.

Michael W. Campbell

WASHINGTON TERRITORY, see **OREGON; WALLA WALLA COLLEGE.**

WASHINGTON TRAINING COLLEGE. School established in Takoma Park, Washington, D.C., when the General Conference moved there from Battle Creek, Michigan, in 1904. Ellen White had a temporary residence nearby and took an interest not only in the students and faculty, but in the workers who were constructing the buildings and campus. A short discourse addressed to the "stewards

WASHINGTON MISSIONARY COLLEGE, TAKOMA PARK, MARYLAND

and matrons, accountants and clerks, foremen and laborers" and students may have been a morning worship talk. From this college, she declared, "missionaries are to be sent forth to many distant lands" ("Instruction for Helpers and Students at Takoma Park, D.C.," RH, Apr. 27, 1905). That purpose became even more focused in 1907, when the General Conference formally selected the Washington school as the denominational center for missionary training and orientation, changing its name to Washington

Foreign Mission Seminary. As it grew into a four-year liberal arts college, it was renamed Washington Missionary College in 1914, and in 1961 became Columbia Union College. The school was renamed Washington Adventist University in 2009. The 1905 and 1909 General Conference sessions, both of which Ellen White attended, were held at the Washington Training College.

Further reading: SDA Encyclopedia (1996), vol. 10, pp. 395-398.

WATER, see **BEVERAGES; HYDROTHERAPY.**

WEDDING RING. Many of the earliest Adventists came from a Puritan and Methodist background that promoted modesty, economy, and simplicity in all areas of life and consequently banned jewelry (along with card playing, gambling, dancing, etc.) as worldly and contrary to Scripture. They cited 1 Timothy 2:9 and 1 Peter 3:3 as clear prohibitions against "wearing of gold" (for examples in Ellen White's writings, see AA 523; CG 416; Ev 270, 271; GC 462; 2SG 100, 228, 229; 1T 20, 21). Most of them did not practice the wearing of the wedding ring.

During the last half of the nineteenth century, immigrants arriving in the United States brought with them their own national customs, including that of the wedding ring. Some of these became Seventh-day Adventists, and removed the ring, as they wanted nothing to mar the unity of the believers. As the church began to send out missionaries to all the world, they often came in contact with local customs, including the wedding ring. In order to fit in with those they were working for, some adopted the wedding ring. Then when they returned home, they continued the practice, much to the concern and disapproval of their fellow church members.

During the 1890s, while living in Australia,

Ellen White wrote her only statement on the subject of the wedding ring. It was written August 3, 1892, in a letter addressed to "My Dear Brethren and Sisters"—primarily Australian Adventists, but also to the church in general—and was subsequently published under the heading "Economy to Be Practiced in All Things" (TM 180, 181). This statement discouraged the wearing of the wedding ring except in countries in which it was obligatory, and in which Adventists—in that setting— could wear it in good conscience. The statement addresses four major issues: influence, "leavening" of the church, stewardship of finances, and individual conscience (see Coon, p. 7).

Ellen White also met the wedding band issue during the two years she was in Europe. One minister was quite adamant in denouncing the wedding ring as jewelry. In Europe this was seen not as adornment, but as a sign of marital fidelity. When asked about it, she said that "where the wearing of the wedding ring was demanded by custom as a matter of loyalty, our preachers should not press the matter of its being laid aside" (W. C. White to D. C. Babcock, Aug. 6, 1913).

When *W. C. White accompanied his mother to Australia in 1891, he was a widower. After several years he married *Ethel May Lacey, a young British woman born in India, educated in England, and now living in Tasmania. The culture of these three countries recognized the wedding ring as a sign of marital fidelity. Ellen White made no objection to her new daughter-in-law's wearing the ring. However, Ellen White herself never wore a wedding band in America, Europe, or Australia. (May Lacey White wore her wedding ring for only a few months. She took it off while having her hands in sudsy water, laid it on a shelf, and never put it back on.)

Ellen White's statements about jewelry in general make it clear that she did not equate a simple, nonjeweled wedding band with rings for ornamentation. In both Europe and in Australia she advised ministers not to insist that the women in their congregations put away their wedding rings. But when some of the American wives of ministers put on the wedding ring, she felt it was not necessary. It was not considered obligatory in North America.

Further reading: R. W. Coon, "The Wedding Band, Ellen G. White, and the Seventh-day Adventist Church" (EGWE, SDoc); C. Morgan, *The Wedding Ring and Adornment: An Analysis and Appeal* (Roseville, Calif.: Amazing Facts, 2002); A. M. Rodriguez, *Jewelry in the Bible* (Silver Spring, Md.: Ministerial Associate of the General Conference, 1999).

Norma Collins

WELFARE MINISTRY (RHPA, 1952, 349 pp.). A compilation of Ellen White's counsels on how to reach people and win souls for Christ through neighborly kindness. The 42 chapters of *Welfare Ministry: Instruction in Christian Neighborhood Service* are subdivided into 11 sections dealing with such topics as "the divine philosophy of suffering and poverty," "neighborhood evangelism," "relieving suffering humanity," and "financial resources for welfare work." In this book Ellen White sets Christ's ministry as an example to follow in relieving suffering in the world. God's program for the church, also patterned after the ministry of the early Christians in the New Testament, seeks to minister to those who are poor, unfortunate, widowed, orphaned, and aged. While all Christians are to engage in this type of work for the welfare and benefit of their communities, she also invites those with financial means to support such a work in local churches. Finally, Ellen White believes that all those who participate in this ministry will be richly blessed in the present and will receive a reward when the Lord returns.

Wellington S. Chapi

WESLEY, JOHN (1703-1791). Probably the most well-known leader of the English Evangelical Revival of the eighteenth century, John Wesley, along with his brother, Charles Wesley (1707-1788), headed up the Arminian (emphasis on free will) wing of what became known as Methodism. While mostly recognized for his fearless, sustained itinerant evangelism, small group nurture, and founding  of the United Societies, or the Wesleyan Connection, he also made a very strong contribution to Protestant theological developments. Though Wesley never wrote a systematic theology (like Calvin's *Institutes*), there was a sustained core to his theology around which revolved a number of key themes that he elaborated in oral and published sermons, commentaries on Scripture, published journals, occasional pamphlets, and periodical articles and letters.

JOHN WESLEY, ENGLISH REVIVALIST AND FOUNDER OF METHODISM

PHOTO CREDIT: UNKNOWN

Broadly Arminian in his outlook, Wesley strongly accented God's gracious initiative in salvation (prevenient grace), which elicits a freely chosen response on the part of the convicted sinner. Strongly opposed to the "irresistible grace" themes of Calvinism, Wesley proclaimed both justifying and sanctifying grace in pursuit of his central theological theme—sinners are *pardoned* in order to *participate*. His strong emphasis on the importance of sanctification and perfection led him to oppose antinomian tendencies, especially those coming out of the Calvinistic wing of English evangelicalism. While influenced by the classic Anglican doctrinal standards (especially the Thirty-Nine Articles, the Book of Common Prayer, and the Edwardsean homilies), with their mild affirmations of the role of Christian Tradition (the famed *via media* between Rome and Puritan Protestantism), Wesley always sought biblical foundations for his theological convictions.

Ellen White did comment on Wesley in an affirmative but brief manner in a number of her published works (AA 598; COL 78, 79; Ed 254; GW 34, 35; PP 404). However, her only sustained treatment of his life, ministry, and theological convictions is found in *The Great Controversy* (1911), pages 253-264. After briefly reviewing the rise of Oxford Methodism (in both Britain and colonial Georgia), Wesley's struggles with legalism, his frantic search for "holiness of heart" (GC 254), his evangelical conversion, and the beginnings of the English Evangelical Revival, Ellen White approvingly notes a number of his key theological emphases.

The lead factor for Ellen White was Wesley's hard-won understanding (both theological and experiential) of the proper relationship between justification and sanctification: "He continued his strict and self-denying life, not now as the *ground*, but the *result* of faith; not the *root*, but the *fruit* of holiness. The grace of God in Christ is the foundation of the Christian's hope, and that grace will be manifested in obedience. Wesley's life was devoted to the preaching of . . . justification through faith in the atoning blood of Christ, and the renewing power of the Holy Spirit upon the heart, bringing forth fruit in a life conformed to the example of Christ" (*ibid.* 256). This exposition of law and grace was understood by her as the center around which all else orbited.

Other key theological planets in the

Wesleyan solar system of grace which Ellen White affirmed were (a) universal election and free will (*ibid.* 261, 262), in opposition to the limited atonement and irresistible election doctrine of Calvinism, (b) prevenient grace (*ibid.* 262), (c) the full affirmation of the authority of the "moral law, contained in the Ten Commandments" (*ibid.*), and (d) the "perfect harmony of the law and the gospel" (*ibid.* 263): "Thus while preaching the gospel of the grace of God, Wesley, like his Master, sought to 'magnify the law, and make it honorable'" (*ibid.* 264).

While Ellen White might have been negative on American Methodism (which disfellowshipped her and her family because of their Millerite views) and the Holiness movement because of their rejection of numerous doctrines held by the emerging Seventh-day Adventists, she was always affirmative of the core of Wesley's theology, especially the main outlines of his teachings on salvation. Thus it seems safe to conclude that the most important influence of Wesley on Ellen White was the core of his theology of salvation, which emerged in a setting of free grace and called for the response of human faith in God's offer of grace (both justifying and sanctifying). While Ellen White did go on to reject Wesley's teaching that sanctifying grace would lead to a moment of instantaneous perfection (in which original sin, with its inherited and cultivated tendencies to evil, would be purged away before glorification), she was in essential agreement with the basic thrust of his teachings on transforming grace.

In fact, it could be persuasively argued that the Adventist doctrine of the "investigative judgment" (strongly affirmed by Ellen White) could emerge only in a setting mentored by the Wesleyan/Arminian tradition. If salvation is irresistible as the fruit of God's predetermined election, judgment becomes superfluous, as there is no freely chosen response of faith in God's offer of salvation. If God, however, seeks the freely chosen response of faith to His grace, and our response can necessarily include either a reception or rejection of saving grace (both justifying grace, the *"root"* of faith, and sanctifying grace, the *"fruit"* of obedience), then there is the strong implication that sinners are responsible to God and there can be a judgment according to works. And these works will witness to the justice of God in His just judgments of human reception or rejection. While Wesley did not understand such a judgment as "pre-Advent," he clearly taught a judgment of investigation for the professed believers in Christ at the end of the age.

While it is true that the theology of Ellen White is not exclusively indebted to any one of the major Protestant theological traditions, the way Wesley understood the issues of personal salvation (and the closely related issues of election, free will, grace, heart-felt religion, law, sin, perfection and judgment according to works) seems to have most profoundly influenced Ellen White. While not wanting to exclude formative issues such as theological method (Bible authority and its relationship to reason, experience, and tradition), Trinity, church organization, and Ellen White's own Methodist-nurtured experience of conversion and sanctification, it appears that the heart of Wesley's influence on Ellen White and subsequent Adventist theological developments came mainly through his expositions on personal salvation.

Further reading: R. P. Heitzenrater, *Wesley and the People Called Methodists* (Nashville: Abingdon Press, 1995); F. Baker and R. P. Heitzenrater, gen. eds., *The Bicentennial Edition of the Works of John Wesley* (Nashville: Abingdon Press, 1984ff.); K. Collins, *The Scripture Way of Salvation: The Heart of John Wesley's Theology*

(Nashville: Abingdon Press, 1997); K. Collins, *A Real Christian: The Life of John Wesley* (Nashville: Abingdon Press, 1999); R. L. Maddox, *Responsible Grace: John Wesley's Practical Theology* (Nashville: Kingswood Books, 1994); W. W. Whidden, *Ellen White on Salvation* (RHPA, 1995); *idem*, "Sola Scriptura, Inerrantist Fundamentalism, and the Wesleyan Quadrilateral: Is 'No Creed But the Bible' a Workable Solution?" AUSS 35 (Autumn 1997): 211-226; *idem*, "Ellen White and John Wesley," *Spectrum* 25, no. 5 (September 1996): 48-54.

Woodrow W. Whidden

WESTERN HEALTH REFORM INSTITUTE, see **BATTLE CREEK SANITARIUM; HEALTH REFORM INSTITUTE**.

WHITE ESTATE, see **ELLEN G. WHITE ESTATE, INCORPORATED**.

WHITE MEMORIAL MEDICAL CENTER. The *College of Medical Evangelists (CME) opened an outpatient clinic in Los Angeles, California, on September 29, 1913, to provide on-site field experience for medical students. By 1916

WHITE MEMORIAL HOSPITAL, LOS ANGELES, CALIFORNIA

church leaders had begun to implement new standards from the Council on Medical Education, the medical-education accrediting body of the American Medical Association,

which mandated that every medical college must have an adjoining hospital in a large city (RH, Sept. 21, 1916). The year before, *E. E. Andross and *G. B. Starr wrote to Ellen White outlining plans to upgrade the clinic in order to meet the new requirement. *W. C. White, her son, recorded her response: "I am glad you [W. C. White] told me this. I have been in perplexity about Loma Linda, and this gives me courage and joy" (RH, Sept. 28, 1916). Initially referred to as the Los Angeles Hospital, the facilities were moved to another part of town in 1917 and built as funds came in. When the hospital was dedicated on April 21, 1918, it was named the Ellen G. White Memorial Hospital in recognition of her pivotal role in developing the Seventh-day Adventist *medical work. Soon after the dedication the Council on Medical Education raised CME's rating to "B" class, which granted it the status to confer medical degrees recognized by the state (RH, May 2, 1918). On January 1, 1964, the hospital was renamed the White Memorial Medical Center, Inc.

Further reading: D. L. Bell and G. A. Hein, "The Persistence of the Possible," AR, Aug. 28, 2003; *SDA Encyclopedia* (1996), vol. 11, pp. 896, 897.

Michael W. Campbell

WICKED, FATE OF THE. The fate of the wicked involves two aspects: their punishment according to their deeds, as determined in the records God keeps; and the second death, a final and total separation from life and from God. These two aspects meet in what the Bible calls "the lake of fire" (Rev. 20:10, 14, 15).

Although the wicked who live through the final days before the *second coming of Christ have to endure the *seven last plagues and are destroyed by the glory of Christ at His coming, this is not their ultimate fate or punishment (GC 544), for they must still face the fate of all the wicked, including Satan and his hosts (DA 763), which is the second death. There will yet be a "resurrection of damnation" (John 5:29), in which the wicked will be raised at the end of the *millennium to receive their reward "according to their works" (Rev. 20:12). This is the punishment aspect. They will be arraigned before the bar of infinite justice, and Christ Himself will render the verdict for their rejection of His sacrifice for their salvation, their treason against the government of heaven, and their oppression of God's faithful people (FLB 356; EW 221).

"At the close of the thousand years, all who have refused to accept him shall be destroyed with fire from heaven. . . . God declares that this shall be so" (GCB, Apr. 1, 1897; cf. Ps. 11:6; Jude 7; Rev. 20:9). Fire comes not only from heaven but also from within the earth. "The earth's surface seems one molten mass—a vast, seething lake of fire. It is the time of the judgment and perdition of ungodly men—'the day of the Lord's vengeance, and the year of recompenses for the controversy of Zion.' Isaiah 34:8" (GC 672, 673). The wicked "suffer punishment varying in duration and intensity, 'according to their works,' but finally ending in the second death" (ibid. 544). "Some are destroyed as in a moment, while others suffer many days" (ibid. 673). Satan will "suffer not only for his own rebellion, but for all the sins which he has caused God's people to commit" (ibid.). He will live and suffer on after all the others have perished, until he also is finally destroyed. Thus the demands of justice are met, and heaven and earth unite in proclaiming the righteousness of Jehovah (ibid.).

The second death is brought about by what the Bible describes as the "lake of fire" (Rev. 20:14; 21:8). The fire that consumes the wicked is the same fire that engulfs and purifies the earth (ibid. 673, 674). Nothing survives this conflagration. There is "no eternally burning hell" (ibid. 674), "no lost souls to blaspheme God, as they writhe in never-ending torment" (ibid. 545). The wicked end in "eternal oblivion" (ibid.).

Questions have been raised about the concept of God punishing His children by fire. Ellen White replies, "The plea may be made that a loving Father would not see His children suffering the punishment of God by fire while He had the power to relieve them. But God would, for the good of His subjects and for their safety, punish the transgressor. God does not work on the plan of man. He can do infinite justice that man has no right to do before his fellow man" (LDE 241). "Those who flatter themselves that God is too merciful to punish the sinner have only to look to Calvary to make assurance doubly sure that vengeance will be visited upon every transgressor of his righteous law" (ST, Apr. 3, 1884). At the same time, White is clear that the destruction of the wicked "is not an act of arbitrary power on the part of God," but is the direct result of the choices they have made (DA 764). "Those who do not choose to accept of the salvation so dearly purchased must be punished" (SR 391). "The extermination of sin will vindicate God's love and establish His honor" before the universe (DA 764).

Further reading: GC 542-545, 671-674; LDE 240-243; FLB 356-358; SR 391, 392, 425-429; GCB, Apr. 1, 1897; N.-E. A. Andreasen, "Death: Origins, Nature, and Final Eradication," in R. Dederen, ed., *Handbook of Seventh-day Adventist Theology* (RHPA, 2000), pp. 314, 340-346.

Edwin E. Reynolds

WIGS, see general article: **CURRENT SCIENCE AND ELLEN WHITE: TWELVE CONTROVERSIAL STATEMENTS**

WILL, HUMAN. In Ellen White's writings the nature, role, and status of the human will receive significant attention. Theologically, it has been debated wether the will is an abstract, discrete faculty, or an attribute that pertains to the total person in its capacity to act as an individual person. Although Ellen White notes that the will "brings all the other faculties under its sway" (5T 513), it seems quite clear in her work that the will is identified with the essence of what it means to be human (see TM 518, quoted below). God implanted the will in men and women's nature for high and holy purposes. "The will is the governing power in the nature of man, the power of decision, or choice" (Ed 289); "it is the choice, the deciding power, the kingly power, which works in the children of men unto obedience to God or to disobedience" (ML 318); it "is the spring of all . . . actions" (MYP 153). The essence of human nature is the power to choose, to will, which runs contrary to any mechanical theories of human personality, or any external control of the will.

As the spring of all human actions, the will has an important role to play in the Christian life. There is in Ellen White a clear anti-Pelagian bent (i.e., denying any ability of humans to please God on their own), when she notes that the will "cannot change the heart" or "purify the springs of life" (SC 18). Nevertheless, the exercise of the will, the power of choice, is important, both in conversion and in forming character. Significantly, Ellen White observes that "it is not an abundance of light and evidence that makes the soul free in Christ; it is the rising of the powers and the will and the energies of the soul to cry out sincerely, 'Lord, I believe; help Thou mine unbelief' "(TM 518). It is through the act of choice that faith is exercised. Thus the will is needed in the warfare against inclinations and propensities, in overcoming

sin, and in remedying defects of character.

The human will performs its role correctly when it is united with God's will. Unfortunately, the will is depraved and weakened (MH 173), and every act of sin depraves it further (ST, Mar. 30, 1904). She never uses the expression "prevenient grace," but the idea is present as she notes that God's Spirit works with all people, including the heathen (DA 638; cf. PP 66). At the Fall the will was given in to Satan's control, but through Christ's sacrifice a person may choose to resist Satan by the power of the Holy Spirit (Rom. 8:13), take the will from Satan's control, and surrender it to God. Thus sinners can have the mind of Christ and make God's will their own (5T 515).

This transformation takes place through a voluntary surrender to God, for He will not coerce the will. But when in response to the Holy Spirit the human disciple freely chooses to resist Satan and yield the will to God, the will can be strengthened and controlled through the power of the Holy Spirit (*ibid.* 514). God's desire is that "our will . . . be yielded to Him, that we may receive it again, purified and refined, and so linked in sympathy with the Divine that He can pour through us the tides of His love and power" (MB 62).

See also: Self, Overcoming.

Further reading: 3T 84; SC 33, 51; COL 94, 327, 331; 5T 513-515, 675; MYP 153, 154; 4T 215; Te 110-114; MB 142, 143.

Kwabena Donkor

WILL AND TESTAMENT, ELLEN G. WHITE'S LAST, AND SETTLEMENT OF HER ESTATE. The last will and testament of Ellen G. White (printed in its entirety in H. E. Douglass, *Messenger of the Lord*, pp. 569-572), probated after her death on July 16, 1915, had been signed by her on February 9, 1912. It was the culmination of several previous attempts by

Ellen White to provide for her literary estate and property rights after her death.

Although no longer extant, the earliest known will was prepared in 1891 shortly before Ellen White went to Australia. In it she is said to have left "very heavy responsibilities to her son W. C. White" (WCW, "A Statement to Those Members of the General Conference Committee Assembled at Mountain View Regarding the Proposed 'Joint Bill of Sale and Agreement,' to Be Entered Into by the White Estate Trustees and the General Conference Corporation," Jan. 27, 1933, p. 5, DF 821 and DF 823). Sometime around 1898 Ellen White was given a vision that led her to believe that she would not live until the Lord's return, a fact that doubtless prompted her later actions to keep refining drafts of her will until achieving one that was satisfactory to her.

After returning to the United States in 1900, Ellen White signed a new will on October 6, 1901. In it all her literary and property rights were left to her two sons, Edson and W. C. White. In addition, Edson was to receive his mother's library, while Willie was to get $5,000 to help educate his children. Half of all future royalties were to be used to support various church mission, social, and education projects, as well as to fund the translation, publication, and circulation of their mother's books. The executors were to be her two sons. The first hint of a trustee concept was appended in a note suggesting that her literary assets should be held in trust by her two sons and S. N. Haskell as a "perpetual trust" for the various uses specified in her will. This will was drawn by Mrs. N. H. Druillard, without the knowledge of either of Ellen White's sons.

Ellen White's next attempt at preparing a will was signed August 14, 1906. However, this one was not acceptable to the General Conference officers, according to a hand-written note on it. In this document her literary estate was to be controlled by a committee of five persons, elected by the General Conference. Four named individuals were to receive $500 each. Her personal property was to be divided between her two sons. Half of the assets from her literary estate were initially to go to liquidate her indebtedness, 30 percent was to be divided between her two sons, and 20 percent was to be used to translate and publish her books. After the debt was liquidated, the 50 percent specified for debt reduction was then also to be used for improving her books. W. C. White was named sole executor of his mother's estate. Many years later W. C. White said that he thought that the plan of the General Conference choosing replacement trustees was a good idea, and he urged his mother to accept the plan. Apparently she thought otherwise. The reason this will was not acceptable to the General Conference officers is not known.

In 1909 Ellen White tried again. The same four named individuals were to receive $500 each. Her two sons were to receive some specified items, but her literary estate was entrusted to a committee of five, including W. C. White; the president and secretary of the General Conference; and two others to be named by the General Conference in session. From her literary estate, 70 percent of the profits were to be used to liquidate her indebtedness, after which the money was to be used to improve her books and to support the general missionary work of the church. The remaining 30 percent was to be divided between her two sons. As with the 1906 will, this draft will, which was never signed, included none of the social or education projects listed in the 1901 will. In this document W. C. White was named sole executor of his mother's estate.

What was to become Ellen White's last

will and testament was signed by her on February 9, 1912. A San Francisco attorney, Theodore A. Bell, prepared it for a fee of $25.85. Apparently Ellen White never met with the attorney, her intentions being communicated to him via W. C. White. Besides including the provisions desired by Ellen White for the handling of her estate after her death (see also *Ellen G. White Estate), the attorney also included a provision instructing that if the trust was ever terminated, the remainder of her literary estate would revert directly to W. C. White or his heirs.

Despite A. G. Daniells' obvious interest in the disposition of Ellen White's literary estate, it appears that the General Conference president had no input whatsoever in the will that was finally signed. W. C. White and Charles H. Jones, manager of the Pacific Press, were named as executors of Ellen White's estate.

This will contained many of the same provisions as in the previous ones. Five named individuals were each to receive a $500 bequest. Ellen White's son, Edson, was to receive $3,000. The rights to several of her books, including *Education*, were willed to Ellen White's other son, Willie, as were her rights to two of Edson's books that she had received in exchange for money she had lent her elder son. Willie was also to receive his mother's personal library, as well as all manuscripts, letters, diaries, and other writings not given to her five literary estate trustees. Her personal property was to be divided between her two sons.

The trusteeship established in her will specified five individuals by name: W. C. White, her son; Clarence C. Crisler, her secretary; Charles H. Jones, manager of the Pacific Press; Francis M. Wilcox, editor of the *Review and Herald*; and Arthur G. Daniells, president of the General Conference. To these trustees were left all the rights to the copyrights and book plates for most of her 24 books then in print. In addition, they were given her general manuscript file, and all the indexes for it, plus her office furniture and her office library. The responsibilities of the trustees specifically included authority to promote and care for her writings in English, make new translations into other languages, and make new compilations from her existing published and unpublished manuscripts. (See *Ellen G. White Estate.)

Although "self-perpetuating" is not mentioned in the will, provision was made for filling any future vacancies among her trustees, or their successors, by a majority of the remaining trustees. If ever the surviving trustees could not agree upon someone to fill a vacancy, the executive committee of the General Conference was to appoint the new trustee.

Royalty income was to be divided as follows by the trustees: (1) 20 percent of the net proceeds were to be divided equally between each of her sons; (2) 5 percent was to be used as an education trust for her grandchildren and great-grandchildren, or other worthy individuals. The balance was to be used to pay her debts. If there was any remaining income, it was to be used to improve the publication of her books then in print, produce additional translations, print new compilations from her manuscript file, assist with the general missionary work of the denomination, and support mission schools operated by the Negro Department of the General Conference, as well as to support mission schools for illiterate Whites in the Southern states of the United States.

Less than a month before Ellen White's death, three of her trustees, plus two others, met at Ellen White's Elmshaven home to consider her forthcoming estate. Among other things, they concluded that there were negotiable assets worth $91,633, considerably more than her outstanding liabilities.

Ellen White died Friday afternoon, July 16, 1915. Funerals were held the following Sunday at her Elmshaven home, with about 500 in attendance; on Monday afternoon at the camp meeting then in progress at Richmond (near Oakland), California, with about 1,000 in attendance; and the following Sabbath in the Dime Tabernacle in Battle Creek, Michigan, with about 3,500 in attendance. At their request, the $820.65 cost for the three funerals was shared equally between the General Conference, North American Division, Pacific Press Publishing Association, and Review and Herald Publishing Association.

On Auguest 9, 1915, Ellen White's will was filed with the probate court. Also soon after her death several of her former employees were let go in an effort to cut expenses. Also, work on settling the estate began, including a court-appointed appraisal of all her assets and outstanding debts. According to the probate court appraisal, based upon what the estate's assets could reasonably be expected to bring if sold immediately, the value of her estate was appraised at $65,721.87. (The higher valuation shown by her accountant was based upon the amount things had originally cost to produce, rather than upon what could be expected to bring in an estate sale.) Contrasted to her assets, she had $87,250 in liabilities, leaving an overall deficit balance of $21,528.13.

The origin of Ellen White's indebtedness is now often forgotten. Besides the cost of publishing her various books, the expense of which she totally bore but for which royalties would eventually repay, Ellen White also borrowed money at interest in order to give to various church projects. In addition, she occasionally lent money to her sons, but especially to Edson, who perpetually seemed to face financial problems. To support these various expenses, Ellen White borrowed from individual church members who wanted to invest money with her. In addition, she also borrowed from the church's publishing institutions and the General Conference, pledging her future book royalties as collateral. Actually, funds continued to be borrowed in Ellen White's name nearly to the time of her death. Presumably this was because of the instruction to her trustees in her will that compilations were to be made from her writings, the cost of producing which would be covered by her estate. Doubtless it was thought that people would be more willing to lend money to her than to her estate after she died. Even so, the royalties from the future sale of her books was projected to repay these costs.

Although Ellen White requested in her will that her creditors allow time for the royalties from the sale of her books to repay their loans, the court would not allow such. In accordance with California law, the court ruled that before any other provisions of the will could be carried out, all of Ellen White's outstanding debts had to be repaid. This forced changes in the way Ellen White's estate had to be settled.

At the 1915 Fall Council held in Loma Linda, California, Ellen White's will was read in executive session to the assembled church leaders. W. C. White was specifically instructed not to be present. At the meeting A. G. Daniells reported on the total assets and liabilities of Ellen White's estate, including the deficit. A plan was developed whereby the General Conference would assume the liabilities of the estate, with the estate in turn assigning its "real and personal property" to the General Conference as security "until such time as the obligations are fully discharged." Although the proposed agreement was shared with W. C. White (he was in Loma Linda), details of the legal arrangements and how they were to be implemented were not fully presented to him until a few weeks later.

During this time Edson, who was living in Michigan and did not have sufficient finances to travel to California to investigate his rights, was writing to various ones, including his brother, trying to discover what was happening. This put W. C. White in an awkward position because he himself was not privy to exactly all that was being decided, despite being urged by the General Conference treasurer to get his brother to sign the proposed settlement.

Eventually both Edson and Willie accepted what was proposed, there being little other choice under the circumstances. When on October 2, 1916, Ellen White's estate was sold by the court to the General Conference, her estate legally ceased to exist. And in so doing, Willie forfeited the proposed education trust to be established for his children and grandchildren, as well as royalties to several books that his mother had willed him. In place of those provisions in his mother's will, W. C. White was given a cash settlement, plus the $1,500 that he owed his mother when she died was forgiven. Edson owed his mother about $10,000 at the time of her death; in essence his indebtedness was forgiven.

As a trustee of his mother's proposed literary estate, W. C. White watched as everything that could be sold to the General Conference was sold at the court-appointed sale. Although not exactly what Ellen White had envisioned in her will, this arrangement seemed to church leaders to be the best way to handle the indebtedness of her estate. Legally the General Conference now owned Ellen White's complete estate, though it appears that as far as many church leaders were concerned, the money advanced for its purchase was in effect considered to be a loan to Ellen White's literary trustees. That "loan" was to be repaid at 4 percent interest from future royalty income, plus from the quick sale of Elmshaven and other tangible assets not otherwise specifically described in her will. The loan was finally fully repaid in the 1930s.

Because the only bid received by the court was from the General Conference, the entire estate, including the literary portion originally left to the trustees, was sold to the church for $87,250 (later increased to $89,371.02), which also included $11,500 for Elmshaven. Shortly afterward, on February 13, 1917, Ellen White's estate was closed and her two executors discharged. Attorney Bell's fees for handling the estate totaled $1,000.

Although the General Conference now legally owned Ellen White's entire estate, including the literary portion of it, following the previously agreed-upon plan, the General Conference quickly turned over to Ellen White's five trustees her literary properties purchased as part of the court sale. By handling the estate in this manner, two things happened. First, since Ellen White's entire estate belonged to the General Conference by virtue of the court-appointed sale, no financial assets remained in her estate for anyone in the future to try to claim. Second, because of the court sale, the provision of Ellen White's will in relation to her literary estate and its potential reversion to her heirs if not honored was extinguished.

Further reading: J. Nix, "History of the Ellen G. White Estate" (EGWE); G. Valentine, *The Struggle for the Prophetic Heritage: Issues in the Conflict for the Control of the Ellen G. White Publications, 1930-1939* (Muak Lek, Thailand, Institute Press, 2006); *SDA Encyclopedia* (1996), vol. 10, pp. 503-506.

James R. Nix

WILL OF GOD. According to Ellen White, it is God's will that people should love Him because of their admiration of His attributes (GC 541). He takes no pleasure in forced obedience and gives everyone freedom to serve Him voluntarily (PP 34). Variance from God's will would make the will of humanity supreme, says Ellen White, and God's will—His purpose of love toward us—would not be respected (MB 51, 52). It was not God's will that sin should exist, but He foresaw its existence, and made provision for it through His Son (DA 22). God has also given us the Holy Scriptures, she says, as a perfect standard of truth to know of His will and His ideal for His children (Ed 17, 18). In Christ, who is the Word of God, God's thought was even made audible (DA 19).

Ellen White points out that in the divine arrangement humanity's will must be given totally to the Lord, for the potter cannot mold that which has never been placed in His hands (TMK 55). God requires us to prove our loyalty to Him by actions that are in harmony with His will, and by relying on Him for strength to carry it out (*ibid.* 252). But Christ will not use coercion to bend the human will to the will of God (ML 340). If it were possible to force us to do God's will, that would not make us Christians, but if we are willing to be made willing, the Holy Spirit will do it for us (MB 142). It is God's intention, says Ellen White, not that our will should be destroyed, but that it should be yielded to Him, to receive it back, purified and refined (*ibid.* 62). Then He will so identify His will with ours that when obeying Him, we are simply carrying out the thoughts of our own minds (UL 187). God never leads us otherwise than we would choose if we could see His purpose for us from beginning to end (DA 224, 225). She says that to understand God's will expands the mind, elevates the thoughts, and brings the faculties in touch with the divine (HP 133). We do the greatest injury to ourselves when we think and act contrary to God's will (PP 600). Christ made no plans for Himself, but day by day accepted God's plans for Him; so should we depend on God, that our lives may be the outworking of His will (DA 208).

Jack J. Blanco

WILLIAM MILLER: HERALD OF THE BLESSED HOPE (RHPA, 1994, 94 pp.). Compilation of Ellen White's writings on *William Miller (1782-1849), Second Advent preacher in the 1830s and 1840s, prepared for the 150th anniversary of the *Millerite disappointment in 1844. After an intense search of the Bible, Miller believed that Christ would return to earth about 1843 or 1844. His numerous lectures in the northeastern United States and Canada gave birth to a widespread Second Advent movement and, in time, to the Seventh-day Adventist Church. In March 1840 Ellen Harmon (White) attended a series of lectures by Miller that changed her life. Years later she wrote about how God had used him to warn the world. Relying upon Miller's own biographical sketch for many details, she wrote of his early life, conversion, in-depth study of the Bible, and preaching ministry. Ellen White believed that God had raised up Miller to preach the doctrine of the second coming of Christ and that angels accompanied him in his mission. "Under his preaching, thousands of sinners were converted, backsliders were reclaimed, and multitudes were led to study the Scriptures and to find in them a beauty and glory before unknown" (p. 28). She explained also how many Millerite teachings guided early Sabbatarian Adventists in the development of their doctrines.

WINE, see **BEVERAGES; TEMPERANCE.**

WITH GOD AT DAWN (RHPA, 1949, 367 pp.).

Second daily devotional book published by the Ellen G. White Estate. Materials selected for these meditations were drawn from Ellen White's published writings and were arranged to match monthly themes, including the love of God, salvation, repentance, the new-birth experience, and consecration to God.

WITNESSING. Witnessing is testifying to one's own experience with God, His teachings, and His prescribed manner of living. While Ellen White used the term more broadly to include other aspects of soul winning and evangelism, its basic meaning focuses primarily on sharing one's experience rather than on teaching doctrine. She often engaged in such witnessing, and she both described the activity and encouraged it in her writings.

In her youth, after her own conversion and an ensuing intense period of doubt and despair (LS 20-40), Ellen Harmon shared with others the joy she had found in Jesus' love and forgiveness. In public meetings her testimony moved others to accept Jesus (*ibid.* 41). She also became concerned for her friends, witnessing to and praying for them individually until everyone was converted to God (*ibid.* 42). She witnessed to her Methodist "class meeting" of her deliverance from guilt and of her joy over Jesus' soon return, but they were not receptive to talk of Jesus' imminent coming (*ibid.* 43-46).

Ellen White welcomed opportunities to share her witness, as two examples from her life, one early and one late, illustrate. In 1854, when she and her party lost their way on a wilderness journey and were refreshed by a woman at a remote cabin, she spoke to the woman fervently of Jesus and the beauties of heaven and gave her a copy of her first book. Twenty-two years later she learned that the woman and many of her neighbors had accepted the Advent message as a result (Ev

448, 449). Long after Ellen White died in 1915, neighbors near her northern California home remembered her as "the little white-haired lady who always spoke so lovingly of Jesus" (6Bio 374).

In Ellen White's view, witnessing is foundational to fulfilling Christ's commission. "Our confession of His faithfulness is Heaven's chosen agency for revealing Christ to the world. . . . That which will be most effectual is the testimony of our own experience. . . . God desires that our praise shall ascend to Him, marked with our own individuality. These precious acknowledgments to the praise of the glory of His grace, when supported by a Christlike life, have an irresistible power that works for the salvation of souls" (MH 100).

Ellen White believed that witnessing is a natural outgrowth of a genuine experience with Christ. "No sooner does one come to Christ than there is born in his heart a desire to make known to others what a precious friend he has found in Jesus; the saving and sanctifying truth cannot be shut up in his heart" (SC 78). She noted that witnessing, as an expression of one's experience, does not depend upon acquiring extensive training or theological knowledge. As an example of this, she cited the two restored demoniacs, who "were the first missionaries whom Christ sent to preach the gospel in the region of Decapolis. For a few moments only these men had been privileged to hear the teachings of Christ. Not one sermon from His lips had ever fallen upon their ears. They could not instruct the people as the disciples who had been daily with Christ were able to do. But they bore in their own persons the evidence that Jesus was the Messiah. They could tell what they knew; what they themselves had seen, and heard, and felt of the power of Christ. This is what everyone can do whose heart has been touched by the grace of God" (DA 340).

Ellen White described the kind of content that a verbal witness might include: "Strive to arouse men and women from their spiritual insensibility. Tell them how you found Jesus and how blessed you have been since you gained an experience in His service. Tell them what blessing comes to you as you sit at the feet of Jesus and learn precious lessons from His Word. Tell them of the gladness and joy that there is in the Christian life. Your warm, fervent words will convince them that you have found the pearl of great price. Let your cheerful, encouraging words show that you have certainly found the higher way. This is genuine missionary work, and as it is done, many will awake as from a dream" (9T 38).

Ellen White held that every Christian is called to witness. "Every member should be a channel through which God can communicate to the world the treasures of His grace, the unsearchable riches of Christ" (AA 600). "To everyone who becomes a partaker of His grace the Lord appoints a work for others. ... It is our work to reveal to men the gospel of their salvation. Every enterprise in which we engage should be a means to this end" (MH 148).

While in some cases people may ask direct questions on spiritual things, Ellen White observed that witnessing need not be limited to such occasions. "Wherever we are, we should watch for opportunities of speaking to others of the Saviour" (COL 339). The very talent of speech, Ellen White taught, "was given to us that we might present Christ as the sin-pardoning Saviour" (ibid.). Doing so blesses the witness, not just the hearer. "The effort to bless others will react in blessings upon ourselves. This was the purpose of God in giving us a part to act in the plan of redemption" (SC 79).

Ellen White recognized that one's witness was comprised of more than direct verbal testimony. Avoiding what is "vain or frivolous in conversation, in dress, or in deportment," by a sober and contemplative demeanor one may be "constantly exerting an influence to attract souls to the Redeemer. ... God enjoins upon all His followers to bear a living testimony in unmistakable language by their conduct, their dress and conversation, in all the pursuits of life, that the power of true godliness is profitable to all in this life and in the life to come; that this alone can satisfy the soul of the receiver" (4T 580, 581).

The Christian may further prepare the way for an effective verbal witness by performing deeds of loving service for others. "If we follow Christ's example in doing good, hearts will open to us as they did to Him" (COL 339). Personal efforts, undergirded by a selfless interest in others, will bear fruit. "Christ's method alone will give true success in reaching the people. The Saviour mingled with men as one who desired their good. He showed His sympathy for them, ministered to their needs, and won their confidence. Then He bade them, 'Follow Me'" (MH 143).

Witnessing, Ellen White noted, is often done for one person. Individual labor "was Christ's method. ... He had a faithful regard for the one-soul audience. Through that one soul the message was often extended to thousands." "The Lord desires that His word of grace shall be brought home to every soul. To a great degree this must be accomplished by personal labor" (COL 229).

According to Ellen White in *The Great Controversy*, the closing events of this world will elicit a powerful witness from God's people—a warning message, direct and confrontational, that they would not bear so openly and boldly under more normal circumstances. "God's Spirit, moving upon their hearts, has constrained them to speak," which they have done "without coldly calculating the consequences of speaking to the people the word which the Lord had given them. . . . Yet when the storm of opposition and reproach bursts upon them, some, overwhelmed with consternation, will be ready to exclaim: 'Had we foreseen the consequences of our words, we would have held our peace.'" In that time of persecution and extreme difficulty, "they remember that the words which they have spoken were not theirs, but His who bade them give the warning. God put the truth into their hearts, and they could not forbear to proclaim it." They bear witness to the power of God's warnings and pleadings. God "commands His servants to present the last invitation of mercy to the world. They cannot remain silent, except at the peril of their souls" (GC 608, 609).

According to Ellen White, witnessing, accompanied by the Holy Spirit and the work of angels, will fulfill God's purposes for it. "In many places consecrated men and women may be seen communicating to others the light that has made plain to them the way of salvation through Christ. And as they continue to let their light shine, . . . they receive more and still more of the Spirit's power. Thus the earth is to be lightened with the glory of God" (AA 54). "In working for perishing souls, you have the companionship of angels . . . [who] are waiting to cooperate with members of our churches in communicating the light that God has generously given, that a people may be prepared for the coming of Christ" (9T 129).

Further reading: AH 484-490; CC 249; CT 243-245; Mar 99-117, 121-123, 253; MYP 192-207; ML 61-63; PaM 151-154; 8T 53-56; UL 264; VSS 23-29; WM 59-65; YI, May 4, 1893.

William A. Fagal

WOLFF, JOSEPH (1795-1862). Missionary, explorer, and herald of Christ's advent. Wolff was born in Germany and converted to Christianity from Judaism at an early age. As a young man he studied abroad, where he finally became a Catholic at the age of 17, adopted the name "Joseph," and entered the College of Propaganda in Rome to become a missionary. Here he made the acquaintance of Henry Drummond, who was presumably visiting Rome on business. During his studies Wolff became dissatisfied with the papal claim to infallibility, which eventually led to his dismissal. He left for England and one year later became reacquainted with Drummond, who sponsored his training in Protestant schools. This time Wolff specialized in how to win Jewish people to Christ. In 1821, before *William Miller, Wolff began teaching the soon return of Christ based on the 2300-day prophecy of Daniel 8:14. This became a convincing argument for Wolff to share with his fellow Jews the imminent return of the Messiah, who would soon set up His kingdom again. It was to this end that he began the first of three extensive missionary tours (1821-1826, 1828-1834, 1836-1838) aimed initially at finding scattered Jews. These journeys took him to Greece, Malta, the Crimea, Palestine, Turkey, Egypt, Central Asia, Abyssinia, Yemen, India, and other lands. In 1837 Wolff addressed the Congress of the United States. Ellen White saw Wolff's proclamation of the Advent message as evidence of the hand of God simultaneously stirring people around the world with the message that the end was near. It was through Wolff and others like him that "the Advent message was carried to a large part of the habitable globe" (*Southern Watchman*, Jan. 24, 1905; cf. GC 357-362).

Further reading: J. Wolff, *Travels and Adventures of the Rev. Joseph Wolff* [autobiography] (London: Saunders, Oatley, and Co., 1861); Y. Davy, *Trail of Peril: The Story of Joseph Wolff* (RHPA, 1984); C. M. Maxwell, "Joseph Wolff: Missionary Extraordinaire"

Dialogue 9, no. 2 (1997): 9-11; M. W. Campbell, "Joseph Wolff: A Bibliography" (2001, CAR).

Michael W. Campbell

WOMAN'S CHRISTIAN TEMPERANCE UNION (WCTU). Interdenominational women's *temperance organization founded in 1874 to promote alcohol abstinence and prohibition laws. The group grew to 150,000 members and spread overseas by 1900, proving highly influential in the temperance movement.

The Woman's Christian Temperance Union received Ellen White's hearty support because of its Christian underpinnings. White urged Adventists to cooperate with the work of the WCTU whenever they could do so without compromise. She believed such cooperation should be a two-way street. The WCTU workers, she wrote, were more advanced in their methods than Adventists and thus should be invited to camp meetings to train their Adventist sisters; Adventists should reciprocate by accepting invitations to speak at WCTU events. Ever eager to spread Adventism's unique message, White emphasized that working with the WCTU would expose these fellow temperance workers to "the truth for this time" (Te 225).

White herself spoke at meetings held by the WCTU and other temperance groups, whether in the United States, Europe, or Australia. She noted that such contacts helped break down prejudice against Adventists.

See also: S.M.I. Henry.

Further reading: R. Bordin, *Woman and Temperance: The Quest for Power and Liberty, 1873-1900* (New Brunswick, N.J.: Rutgers University Press, 1990); A. Dubbs Hays, *Heritage of Dedication: One Hundred Years of the National Woman's Christian Temperance Union, 1874-1974* (Evanston, Ill.: Signal Press,

1973); I. Tyrrell, *Woman's World, Woman's Empire: The Woman's Christian Temperance Union in International Perspective, 1880-1930* (Chapel Hill, N.C.: University of North Carolina Press, 1991).

Rachel Whitaker

WOMEN, MINISTRY OF. Students of Ellen White hold two main views regarding the ministry of women. The "egalitarian" view emphasizes the equality of men and women from Creation (Gen. 1:26, 27; cf. 4T 484; PP 58) and in the gospel (Gal. 3:27, 28), and that leadership roles are determined by spiritual gifts and God's call, regardless of gender (Joel 2:28, 29; 1 Cor. 12:7-11; cf. 6T 322 and 19MR 55, 56).

The "male-headship complementarian" view holds that male and female persons are uniquely diverse, but complementary (interdependent) in such a way that their roles are ideally noninterchangeable. Within this intentional diversity of roles, the Creator designed men to be the primary spiritual leaders and women to be associate leaders in both home and church.

Both views support the active involvement of women in a wide variety of leadership roles in home and church. But they differ over whether women may be ordained as clergy. Ellen White vigorously promoted women in evangelistic ministry, and their support from the tithe, but she never gave a comprehensive theological rationale on the *ordination of women. For that, she pointed her readers to the Bible, insisting that "the Scriptures are plain upon the relations and rights of men and women" (1T 421). In harmony with this position, a large number of scholars were, at the time of publication (2013-2014), involved in a major international study, seeking clear biblical conclusions on the question of ordaining women as clergy. The present article focuses primarily on White's statements about the roles of women in the church.

Both Scripture (Gal. 6:10; Eph. 5:32; 1 Tim. 3:5) and Ellen White draw close parallels between home and church (1NL 77; PaM 88, 89; 1T 307, 308; FLB 259), but neither sees leadership in either home or church as absolutely restricted to males (19MR 55, 56). For instance, while she clearly saw the father as "head of the household" (AH 119, 211, 213; PP 176), she could also refer to the mother as "head teacher" of the family (CG 119, 549). While she called the father "the highest priest of the family" (RC 170; cf. AH 212; CG 521; MH 392), she also recognized the mother as a priest, giving spiritual leadership in the father's absence (AH 212).

She consistently taught the equality of wives to their husbands (AH 231; CCh 143; DG 43, 151; Ev 494) and condemned the tyrannical, controlling spirit of some husbands (AH 119, 215, 227). She cited Abigail's initiative with David (1 Sam. 25) as an example of "circumstances under which it is proper for a woman to act promptly and independently, moving with decision in the way she knows to be the way of the Lord" (DG 43). At the same time, she taught wives to respect their husbands and support them in their spiritual leadership. "We women must remember that God has placed us subject to the husband. He is the head and our judgment and views and reasonings must agree with his if possible. If not, the preference in God's Word is given to the husband where it is not a matter of conscience. We must yield to the head" (Lt 5, 1861, in 6MR 126). Yet the wife is *not* to surrender her "identity," her "individuality," or "her judgment and conscience" to the "control of her husband" (10MR 179; AH 47). A wife's "entire submission is to be made only to the Lord Jesus Christ" (AH 115, 116).

Proponents of both views mentioned above have produced significant publications in support of their positions (see *further reading*). One indication of Ellen White's influence on Adventist thought is the degree of common ground between these views, on the need, legitimacy, and divine mandate for women in ministry. Even on the debated question of roles, the area of agreement is broader than the area of disagreement. This article will not resolve all disagreements on the subject, but it does present an inductive examination of the primary data that must be taken into account by all who seek a balanced understanding of the writings of Ellen G. White on (1) the need and divine mandate for women in ministry, (2) appropriate roles for women in ministry, and (3) appropriate recognition and encouragement for women in ministry.

Concerning *the divine mandate for the ministry of women,* many Ellen White statements show that she considered the participation of women in gospel ministry as essential for the highest success in preaching the gospel. "If there were twenty women where now there is one, who would make this holy mission their cherished work," she wrote in 1879, "we should see many more converted to the truth. The refining, softening influence of Christian women is needed in the great work of preaching the truth" (Ev 471, 472; cf. DA 568).

She taught that women are indispensable in ministry because they can minister in ways that men cannot. "They can do in families a work that men cannot do, a work that reaches the inner life. They can come close to the hearts of those whom men cannot reach" (WM 145). "There is a great work for women to do in the cause of present truth," she affirmed elsewhere. "Through the exercise of womanly tact and a wise use of their knowledge of Bible truth, they can remove difficulties that our brethren cannot meet. We need women workers to labor in connection with their husbands, and should encourage those who wish to engage in this line of missionary effort" (Ev 491).

All of these counsels are based on the premise that neither males nor females can do alone the quality of work that the two can do together. "When a great and decisive work is to be done, God chooses men and women to do this work, and it will feel the loss if the talents of both are not combined" (Ev 469; cf. CH 544, 547).

Further, Ellen White advocated that women who devote their time and talents to ministry should receive wages just as male ministers do. "The method of paying men laborers, and not paying their wives who share their labors with them, is a plan not according to the Lord's order, and if carried out in our conferences, is liable to discourage our sisters from qualifying themselves for the work they should engage in" (GW 452, 453; Ev 492). Asking women to do regular ministerial work without pay, she calls "exaction," "partiality," "selfishness," and "robbery," and liable to discourage women from devoting themselves to ministry as a vocation. She believed large numbers of women should be encouraged to "qualify themselves" for gospel ministerial work (Ev 492; cf. ibid. 472).

White also asserted the legitimacy of paying women ministers from the tithe, which she elsewhere maintained is to be sacredly reserved for the support of the gospel ministry (CS 81, 101-103; 9T 247-250). "The tithe should go to those who labor in word and doctrine, be they men or women," she averred (Ev 492).

Several of the pertinent quotations mention "wives" of ministers, indicating Ellen White's particular endorsement of husband-and-wife ministerial teams. Other references, however, apply the same concept to young women not specified as minister's wives, and

to widowed women, showing that Ellen White saw some form of ministry as an appropriate career choice for women, whether or not they were married to ministers. "Women who work in the cause of God should be given wages proportionate to the time they give to the work.... As the devoted minister and his wife engage in the work, they should be paid wages proportionate to the wages of two distinct workers, that they may have means to use as they shall see fit in the cause of God. *The Lord has put His spirit upon them both.* If the husband should die, and leave his wife, *she is fitted to continue her work in the cause of God, and receive wages* for the labor she performs" (5MR 323, 324; italics supplied).

It is clear from the foregoing that Ellen White considered the ministry of women to be not merely an option but a divine mandate, the neglect of which would result in diminished ministerial efficiency (Ev 491), fewer converts (*ibid.* 472), and "great loss" to the cause (*ibid.* 493, 469), compared to the fruitfulness of the combined gifts of men and women in ministry.

The second major area of consideration concerns *specific roles that Ellen White envisioned for ministering women.* The most frequently mentioned vocations in which Ellen White called women to minister are those of house-to-house ministry to families (Ev 459, 464, 470, 471, 478, 491), giving evangelistic Bible studies (*ibid.* 491-493; cf. *ibid.* 456, 469, 470, 475, 477), teaching in various capacities (*ibid.* 469, 473-477; 5MR 325), door-to-door sales of Adventist literature (*colporteur ministry) (2T 322, 323; 6T 469, 470; 8T 229, 230), and pastoral or evangelistic work (2T 322, 323; 8T 229, 230; Ev 467-473, 491-493). Also mentioned are medicine (specifically obstetrics and gynecology [CH 365]), chaplains for medical and other institutions (8T 143, 144), personal counseling with women (Ev

460), and temperance leadership, particularly in connection with the *Woman's Christian Temperance Union (1MR 125).

The largest group of Ellen White statements regarding women in ministry are set in the context of a team ministry in which women ministers employ their gifts largely, but not exclusively, in teaching and counseling individuals and small groups, especially families. These women are called "self-sacrificing" because this work with individuals and families is seen as a supporting rather than a leading role in the ministerial team. Yet it is precisely in this supporting role that women are promised "a power that exceeds that of men," to "do in families a work that men cannot do," and "come close to the hearts of those whom men cannot reach" (WM 145).

In addition, women are mentioned as teaching in schools, Sabbath schools, and camp meeting Bible classes, as well as in public pulpit ministry (Ev 469, 473-477; CSW 90-96). During her ministry in Australia she spoke approvingly of two Bible instructors, Sister Robinson and Sister Wilson, who were "doing just as efficient work as the ministers." She reported that at "some meetings when the ministers are all called away, Sister [Wilson] takes the Bible and addresses the congregation" (Lt 169, 1900, in Ev 473; cf. Ms 43a, 1898, in 5MR 323-327).

One of the objections sometimes raised against Ellen White's own ministry was that women were not to "teach" men (1 Tim. 2:12). This her colleagues consistently refuted, not by pleading that she as a prophet constituted a special category, but by arguing that the verse was wrongly applied to prohibiting women ministers in general (cf. Lt 17a, 1880, in 10MR 70). J. N. Andrews cited Paul's female coworkers (Phil. 4:3), Phoebe the deaconess (Rom. 16:1), Priscilla's role in "instructing Apollos," and the leadership roles of other

New Testament women to prove that Paul's "*general* rule with regard to women as public teachers" did not constitute a rigid or universal prohibition. Andrews argued that Romans 10:10 requires public confession of the faith as integral to salvation, and therefore "must apply to women equally with men" (J. N. Andrews, "May Women Speak in Meeting?" RH, Jan. 2, 1879). J. H. Waggoner agreed, with one clarification: "A woman may pray, prophesy, exhort, and comfort the church, but she cannot occupy the position of a pastor or a ruling elder. This would be looked upon as usurping authority over the man, which is here [1 Tim 2:12] prohibited" (J. H. Waggoner, "Woman's Place in the Gospel," ST, Dec. 19, 1878).

While Ellen White did not often refer to the Pauline passages on women as teachers, she did cite the work of Aquila and Priscilla in teaching Apollos as an example of "a thorough scholar and brilliant orator" being taught by two laypersons, one of whom was a woman (LP 119). Thus she rejected the traditional interpretation of 1 Timothy 2:12 as prohibiting all women in all circumstances from having a teaching ministry that included men.

While Ellen White specifically commended women who serve in supporting ministerial roles, she also encouraged women with gifts for public leadership to fully exercise those gifts. When *Mrs. S. M. I. Henry, national evangelist for the Woman's Christian Temperance Union (WCTU), became a Seventh-day Adventist, she corresponded with Ellen White regarding her connection with the WCTU (4Bio 346-348). Ellen White replied, "We believe fully in church organization, but in nothing that is to prescribe the precise way in which we must work; for all minds are not reached by the same methods. . . . You have many ways opened before you. Address the crowd whenever you can; hold every jot of influence you can by an association that can be made the means of introducing the leaven to the meal" (Lt 54, 1899, in DG 130 and Ev 473).

Up to this point, there is broad agreement among most students of Ellen White's writings. Only concerning roles traditionally reserved for "clergy" do the sharpest disagreements arise, because Scripture itself does not draw the line between clergy and laity in the way that later became traditional in the Christian church. Scripture teaches the ministry of every believer (Ex. 19:6; 1 Peter 2:9), the special ministry of congregational leaders (Acts 14:23), and that some are given leadership authority above the local congregation (Ex. 29:1-37; Eph. 4:11). There are likewise rituals of appointment and spiritual empowerment (*ordination) for every member (Acts 19:1-7; 1 John 2:20, 27), for congregational leaders (Acts 6:3-6), and for leadership beyond the congregation (2 Tim. 1:6), as well as for special ministries, such as those of missionaries (Acts 13:2, 3). While each of these ministries seems to have had a distinctive function, the boundaries between them were not sharply drawn. In Acts 6:2-6 seven men were set apart by the laying on of hands to "serve tables." But almost immediately Stephen and Philip began preaching, teaching, and baptizing—clearly exceeding the job description for which they had been ordained (Acts 6:8-7:60; 8:5, 12, 14, 35-58).

Following Scripture, Ellen White also uses such key words as "ministry," "pastor," and "laying on of hands" in ways and contexts capable of being applied to appointed leaders or to every member or both. She speaks of "unselfish ministry" in the broadest sense as the privilege and obligation of every Christian (7T 50). "Ministry" can also denote the verbal communication of the gospel by either laity or clergy. Thus she saw pastors and teachers, physicians and nurses, *colporteurs, Bible instructors, and parents as all being engaged in aspects of gospel ministry. She also speaks of "the ministry," referring to the specific vocation of clergy. For an example that shows how these categories overlap in her thought, she declares that "medical missionaries who labor in evangelistic lines are doing a work of as high an order as are their ministerial fellow laborers." Since they are "engaged in the same work," they should be "as sacredly set apart" as is the gospel minister, by the "laying on of hands" (Ev 546). This, she says, will help to fortify the medical evangelist against the temptation to leave the evangelistic work to engage in purely medical work. Thus she recognizes a diversity of ministries in which lay ministry and clergy ministry cannot always be sharply distinguished.

For instance, she wrote that "young men and young women who should be engaged in the ministry, in Bible work, and in the canvassing work should not be bound down to mechanical employment" (8T 229, 230). Are the young women invited into "the ministry" in the same sense as the young men, or only in the roles of Bible work and canvassing work? Some parallel statements may imply the former (Lt 33, 1879, in 19MR 55, 56) and other statements the latter (5T 60 [1882]; RH, Dec. 19, 1878; RH, Jan. 2, 1879).

Another statement speaks of women as "pastors." "All who desire an opportunity for *true ministry,* and who will give themselves unreservedly to God, will find in the canvassing work opportunities to speak upon many things pertaining to the future, immortal life. The experience thus gained will be of the greatest value to those who are *fitting themselves for the ministry. It is the accompaniment of the Holy Spirit of God that prepares workers, both men and women, to become pastors to the flock of God"* (6T 322; italics supplied).

Thus she goes directly to the theological core of the matter—that calling and equipping are supremely the work of Christ through the Holy Spirit (Eph. 4:7-13), who distributes "to each one individually *as He wills*" (1 Cor. 12:11, NASB).

Part of the difficulty in understanding this passage stems from the fact that while many today use "pastor" to denote an ordained minister, Adventists in the nineteenth century did not generally have settled pastors. "Pastoral care" was a responsibility more often carried out by laypersons than by ordained ministers.

In context, the quoted sentence (from 6T 322) make three points. 1. The canvassing work is one form of "true ministry." 2. The verbs "fitting" and "prepares" are parallel; and the objects, "the ministry" and "pastors," are also parallel; hence the canvassing work is a valuable training experience for those, "both men and women," who are "fitting themselves for the ministry," i.e., "[preparing] . . . to become pastors." 3. The fundamental qualification to be a pastor is not any external characteristic (such as gender), but the "accompaniment of the Holy Spirit" (cf. 1 Cor. 12:11), who is given to both men and women.

This interpretation is confirmed by what follows two paragraphs later. "The *preaching* of the word is a means by which the Lord has ordained that His warning message shall be given to the world. In the Scriptures the faithful *teacher* is represented as a *shepherd* of the flock of God" (*ibid.* 323; italics supplied). "Shepherds of the flock of God" stands directly parallel to the expression "pastors to the flock of God" on the previous page. From these parallel statements it is clear that the Holy Spirit "prepares workers, both men and women, to become pastors," i.e., preachers and teachers, "to the flock of God." This is in harmony with the context of the chapter and with her

statement a year earlier that women as well as men are to "labor in word and doctrine" and be supported from the tithe (Ms 149, 1899, in Ev 492). The references to the "Holy Spirit," "gifts," "pastor," "teacher," and "shepherd" (6T 322, 323) imply that the spiritual gift of pastor-teacher (Eph. 4:11) is given to both men and women.

That Ellen White saw both women and men as eligible for church leadership is shown by her scathing rebuke to a man who had "a disposition to dictate and control matters" in a certain local church, but who had only "sneers" for the work of certain women in the congregation. "Jesus is ashamed of you," she wrote. "You are not in sympathy with the great Head of the church. . . . This contemptible picking, faultfinding, seeking spot and stain, ridiculing, gainsaying, that you with some others have indulged in, has grieved the Spirit of God and separated you from God. *It is not always men who are best adapted to the successful management of a church* [a work typically assigned to pastors or elders]. If *faithful women* have more deep piety and true devotion than men, they could indeed by their prayers and their labors do more than men who are unconsecrated in heart and life" (Lt 33, 1879; 19MR 55, 56; italics supplied). The words "best adapted" point to personal talents and spiritual gifts, which, along with "deep piety and true devotion," constitute the essential qualifications for spiritual leadership.

Yet to be examined is the statement in which White explicitly calls for setting women apart by the laying on of hands. The main concern of the passage is that the majority of church members were inactive in the work of spreading the gospel. "A few" officers were "spiritual burden bearers," but "the talent of other members has remained undeveloped." To remedy this, White urged ministers to involve the congregation both in "planning" and in "executing the plans," so that every member has a definite part in the work of the church.

In this context White advises that "women who are willing to consecrate some of their time to the service of the Lord should be *appointed* to visit the sick, look after the young, and minister to the necessities of the poor. *They should be set apart to this work by prayer and laying on of hands.* In some cases they will need to counsel with the church officers or the ministers; but if they are devoted women, maintaining a vital connection with God, they will be a power for good in the church. This is another means of strengthening and building up the church. We need to branch out more in our methods of labor. Not a hand should be bound, not a soul discouraged, not a voice should be hushed; let every individual labor, privately or publicly, to help forward this grand work" (RH, July 9, 1895; italics supplied; cf. DG 249, 250).

This passage speaks of laywomen who will give "some of their time," not their full time, to church work. This is not a career choice by which they will earn their livelihood, but a part-time volunteer ministry. On one hand, the words "appointed" and "set apart . . . by prayer and the laying on of hands" were Ellen White's characteristic expressions for a ceremony of ordination (AA 160, 161; GW 15, 452; 2MR 32; 5MR 29, 323; 8MR 189; MYP 226; RH, May 11, 1911; 6T 444; TM 188). On the other hand, these terms could also be used for bestowal of the Holy Spirit for other kinds of service.

Three responses to this appeal are known. Shortly after this was written, the Ashfield church in Sydney, *Australia, not far from where Ellen White was then working, held an ordination service for newly elected church officers. "Pastor Corliss and McCullagh of the Australian conference set apart the elder, deacons, [and] deaconesses by prayer and the laying on of hands" (minutes of the Ashfield SDA Church, Sydney, Australia, Aug. 10, 1895, cited by A. Patrick; cf. DG 249). Notice that identical terminology is used for all three offices. Another record from the same church five years later reports the ordination of two elders, one deacon, and two deaconesses. This time the officiating minister was *W. C. White, whose diary corroborates the church records (see Patrick).

A third example comes from early 1916, when E. E. Andross, then president of the Pacific Union Conference, officiated at a women's ordination service and cited Ellen White's 1895 *Review* article as his authority (DG 253-255). Both the internal evidence of Ellen White's 1895 article and the responses of those close to her at the time—the Ashfield church; her son W. C. White; and *E. E. Andross, president of the Pacific Union Conference during her *Elmshaven years—confirm that Ellen White here approved the ordination of women to a role then associated with the office of deaconess in the local church.

This evidence suggests that Ellen White viewed the "laying on of hands" as a ceremony of consecration appropriate for both clergy and laity, and thus for both women and men.

In summary, Ellen White maintained that (1) women's participation in ministry is "essential," and without it the cause will "suffer great loss" (Ev 493); (2) women in ministry should receive just wages; (3) these wages may appropriately come from the tithe; (4) a woman's call to ministry can sometimes take priority over even child care (*ibid.* 492, 493); (5) some women should make ministry a vocation in which they earn their livelihood; and (6) conferences should not "discourage" women from "qualifying themselves" for ministerial work (*ibid.* 492). Regarding roles, she further taught that (7) all Christians, women and men, who possess gifts for bringing others to a knowledge of Christ should employ those gifts in ministries suited to their gifts; (8) the gifts of evangelism and pastoring-teaching are given to both men and women (Eph. 4:11); (9) some women possess gifts for the "successful management of a church" (10MR 70); (10) women as well as men who are called to a specific ministry, whether preaching, teaching, or serving "the sick," "the young," and "the poor," may be consecrated to that ministry by the laying on of hands. Regarding headship, White supports a careful, defined male leadership in the home (MB 64, 65; 1T 307-309) but denounces the common abuses and perversions of male "headship" (AH 215, 216; FLB 259), and quotes Colossians 3:18 to show that the wife's "entire submission is to be made only to the Lord Jesus Christ" (AH 115, 116).

Thus Ellen White strongly affirms the need, legitimacy, and divine mandate for women in ministry. She sees women as receiving and exercising a wide range of spiritual gifts, and filling an indispensable place on the ministerial team. She does not specify any particular role in ministry as categorically inappropriate for women.

Further reading: DG 248-256; S. Bacchiocchi, *Women in the Church* (Berrien Springs, Mich.: Biblical Perspectives, 1987); R. T. Banks, ed., *A Woman's Place* (RHPA, 1992); B. Beem and G. Harwood, "'Your Daughters Shall Prophesy': James White, Uriah Smith, and the 'Triumphant Vindication of the Right of the Sisters' to Preach," AUSS 43 (Spring 2005): 41-58; B. Beem and G. Harwood, "'It Was Mary That First Preached a Risen Jesus': Early Seventh-day Adventist Answers to Objections to Women as Public Spiritual Leaders," AUSS 45 (Autumn 2007): 221-245; J. Benton, *Called by God: Stories of Seventh-day Adventist Women Ministers* (Smithsburg, Md.: Blackberry Hill

Publishers, 1990); M. H. Dyer, ed., *Prove All Things: A Response to* Women in Ministry (Berrien Springs, Mich.: Adventists Affirm, 2000); P. A. Habada and R. F. Brillhart, eds., *The Welcome Table: Setting a Place for Ordained Women* (Langley Park, Md.: TEAM Press, 1995); C. R. Holmes, *The Tip of an Iceberg: Biblical Authority, Biblical Interpretation, and the Ordination of Women in Ministry* (Berrien Springs, Mich.: Adventists Affirm and Pointer Publications, 1994); S. Koranteng-Pipim, *Searching the Scriptures: Women's Ordination and the Call to Biblical Fidelity* (Berrien Springs, Mich.: Adventists Affirm, 1995); A. N. Patrick, "The Ordination of Deaconesses," AR, Jan. 16, 1996, pp. 18, 19; R. W. Pierce, R. M. Groothuis, and Gordon Lee, eds., *Discovering Biblical Equality: Complementarity Without Hierarchy* (Downers Grove, Ill.: InterVarsity Press, 2004); *The Role of Women in the Church* (GC of SDA, 1984; PPPA, 1995), pp. 138-155, 194; N. J. Vyhmeister, ed., *Women in Ministry: Biblical and Historical Perspectives* (AUP, 1998).

Jerry Moon

WOMEN'S ISSUES. Forming and guiding the Seventh-day Adventist Church during a 70-year public ministry, Ellen White repeatedly addressed issues affecting women. Her counsel cut a wide swath. She commented on the minutia of nineteenth-century domestic life as well as the broad themes of health, temperance, and educational reform. She upheld motherhood as the "greatest mission ever given to mortals" (DG 193) and called on fathers to lighten the drudgery of household tasks and become partners in parenting. In addition, White urged women to cherish the inner life and connect personally with Christ. She also challenged them to gain training, education, and experience so that they might use their gifts productively in God's service.

As Adventist women entered church leadership and employment, White spoke approvingly of them and admonished administrators to provide equitable pay.

Early-nineteenth-century American society confined and defined women. The ideal woman was expected to stay in the private world of homemaking and child rearing. Endless work characterized domestic life. Many women did hard physical labor as they cooked over woodstoves, carried water, washed laundry by hand, gardened, preserved food, sewed, scrubbed, and cleaned house. In rural areas they often helped with farmwork. The dictates of fashion—including tightly cinched corsets and heavy, street-length skirts—not only restricted normal movement but also caused physical harm. Death in childbirth was not uncommon. For those exhausted by repeated pregnancies and the care of young children, life was marginal.

Doors to advanced education and professions were closed to women. They could not vote and did not speak in public. Married women could not hold legal title to property. These societal norms began to change, but slowly. One impulse that moved women into the public arena sprang from Christian revivals known as the Second Great Awakening (1790-1840). When Ellen Harmon experienced her first vision in 1844, Wesleyan Methodists were among the few denominations that allowed women to speak to "promiscuous," or mixed, groups of men and women. Ellen's family came from this branch of Methodists.

Early in her ministry, however, one of her brothers recoiled at the thought of Ellen doing public work. "I beg of you do not disgrace the family. I will do anything for you if you will not go out as a preacher," he wrote. She replied, "Disgrace the family! Can it disgrace the family for me to preach Christ and Him crucified! If you would give me all the gold your house could hold, I would not cease giving my testimony for God" (ST, June 24, 1889). Throughout her life she made God's call paramount. At the same time—by her words, her explication of Scripture, and her personal actions—she persistently entreated the church to use and value women's talents.

Addressing issues of the private realm, Ellen White wrote about women in marriage, homemaking, parenting, healthful living, and devotional life. Married at 18 and a mother at 19, Ellen White was pressed by poverty and illness while pursuing a traveling ministry with James. Personal experiences became the seedbed for hundreds of pages of counsel on marriage, parenting, and homemaking.

She promoted a lifelong commitment to one's partner, mutuality in marriage, and the dual responsibility of mother and father in rearing children. Citing the Eden home as a pattern, she taught that Eve was created as an equal with Adam. Sin drastically disrupted this harmony, and women, in particular, often suffered abuse and misery. White believed husbands were leaders of the home and family, but not masters. "Entire submission is to be made only to the Lord Jesus Christ" and a wife's "individuality cannot be merged into that of her husband" (AH 116; cf. 2MCP 426). She imbued the humble, routine tasks of child rearing with dignity. She equated a mother with an artist, sculptor, author, musician, missionary, and minister of the word. A husband, she said, should share a wife's burdens and provide whatever laborsaving devices possible.

Sexual excess dismayed White. Marital relations intended by God as a blessing could become a debasing curse. At the time, birth control and family size depended entirely on abstinence. When passion was uncontrolled, women bore most of the consequences—pain, suffering, and "a miserable existence, with children in their arms nearly all the time" (2T 380). She condemned flirtation and sexual indiscretion by both sexes and taught that divorce was justified only by infidelity.

White longed for happy homes where families would thrive on love and tender affection. She appealed to couples to relate to each other in the spirit of Christ, to be kind and forbearing, and to make home "a little heaven upon earth" (3T 539).

Poor health plagued the Whites as it did most nineteenth-century Americans. In 1830 life expectancy for both men and women was about 35 years. Two of the Whites' four sons died young—John Herbert as an infant in 1860; and Henry at age 16 in 1863. Ellen's health was fragile, and James suffered extended illnesses from overwork and strokes.

Following her health vision in 1863, Ellen White began validating health practices that were new to many Americans—water treatments for those suffering from diphtheria; fresh air, sunshine, rest, and recreation to reduce stress; and new eating and exercise patterns to increase well-being. She promoted, contrary to prevailing notions, a diet of fruits and vegetables, and urged Adventists to eschew meat, tobacco, alcohol, and other stimulants. She also began to see health as a religious duty.

White pinpointed women as major players in health reform. She felt it was a woman's right to understand the human body, principles of hygiene, dress, diet, and other matters that concerned her household. Nineteenth-century fashion especially victimized women. In addition to being expensive, tight corsets, heavy fabrics, hoops, and bulky ornaments combined to deform their bodies and drain their vitality. Dress reform became inseparable from health reform.

Good health improves one's ability to discern God's will and to do God's work, but salvation is the highest priority. White pleaded with women and men to savor a life-empowering devotional life. Only a direct connection to Christ through meditation, Bible study, and prayer brings eternal life.

In the public realm Ellen White encouraged women in lay ministry, evangelism, education, and careers in the church. Ever expecting the Second Advent, Ellen White rallied all—men and women, young and old—to announce Jesus' soon return. "Some can do more than others; but all can do something," she emphasized (ST, Sept. 16, 1886).

She sanctioned women working outside their homes as lay evangelists—holding church offices, visiting neighbors, giving Bible studies, and distributing tracts. Husbands and children need not be neglected, and "all have not these responsibilities," she said pointedly. She added that it was appropriate, at times, for women to place their children in the care of others while they continued ministry. White encouraged women to mentor other women in Christian grace, sell literature door to door, and assist the needy. As the temperance movement gained momentum, she commended those in the cause. She directed S.M.I. Henry to "address the crowd whenever you can; hold every jot of influence you can by any association that can be made the means of introducing the leaven to the meal" (DG 130). A sought-after speaker herself, White spoke to some of the largest crowds of her career at temperance meetings.

When Adventists founded their first college in 1874, they admitted young women with young men. Ellen White asserted that God gifted both males and females with intellectual ability. "Every human being . . . is endowed with a power akin to that of the Creator—individuality, power to think and to do. . . . It is the work of true education to develop this power" (Ed 17).

Students prepared for careers as teachers, nurses, doctors, missionaries, church leaders, and gospel ministers. Both Ellen and James White recommended that women consider teaching careers. As sanitariums and hospitals were established, Ellen urged women to train as nurses and physicians; she felt keenly that gynecologists should be women. Both single and married women became overseas missionaries. Several of her women contemporaries were elected to high church office: three as treasurer of the General Conference, some as executive secretaries or treasurers of local conferences, and a host of others as heads of conference Sabbath school and education departments (*The Welcome Table,* pp. 51, 52).

White championed fair wages for women, vigorously protested injustice, and stipulated that financial sacrifices should not be forced on a few. "A great work is to be done in our world, and every talent is to be used in accordance with righteous principles. If a woman is appointed by the Lord to do a certain work, her work is to be estimated according to its value," she stated in 1898 (Ev 491). "When self-denial is required because of a dearth of means . . . let all unite in the sacrifice" (7T 207, 208).

Women engaged in gospel ministry during Ellen White's lifetime, some as public evangelists. The *SDA Yearbook* lists more than 30 who were licensed to preach between 1878 and 1910 (DG 249, 250). Recognizing the success she and James usually had in working together, she endorsed team ministry, observing that a wife could reach some people that her husband could not. Emphasizing that "Mary . . . first preached a risen Jesus," she yearned to see twenty women where there was then one engaged in "this holy mission," adding that the "refining, softening influence

of Christian women is needed in the great work of preaching the truth" (RH, Jan. 2, 1879).

Despite Ellen White's endorsement of women as effective workers in private and public ministries, the twentieth-century church favored domestic roles for women. Responding to a proposal that women be ordained to ministry, the 1973 Annual Council agreed to conduct more studies, but voted that "the primacy of the married woman's role in the home and family, as repeatedly emphasized in the Scriptures and the Spirit of Prophecy, continue to be recognized and emphasized at all levels of the church" (RH, Dec. 6, 1973). The two quotations that the council cited from Ellen White praised motherhood and home duties. Subsequently, in 1975 the church *discontinued* its 100-year practice of granting ministerial licenses to women.

Later Annual Council actions authorized ordination services for deaconesses and women elders, if divisions also approved it. Ordaining deaconesses actually provoked spirited debate until 1986, when research showed that William White had participated in such a ceremony while he and his mother were in Australia in the 1890s (RH, Jan. 16, 1986).

Ellen White believed she was ordained of God and did not need human hands laid upon her. Following her husband's death, however, she often carried the same credentials as ordained ministers. In 1881 a resolution to ordain women to gospel ministry was discussed in General Conference session, referred to committee, but never acted on. The implications of White's statements validating women as preachers and gospel ministers, and those stating that such women could be paid with tithe, are interpreted differently by those opposing or favoring women's ordination to the gospel ministry (DG 250-252).

White's outspoken campaign for women's

fair wages faded from the church's memory after her death in 1915. An employee lawsuit filed against the Pacific Press in the early 1970s eventually resulted in equal pay for women employed in North America. Many parts of the world church have yet to adopt the policy.

Although women's rights and the right to vote were much agitated during her lifetime, White scarcely addressed them (cf. *ibid.* 18). In the 1860s the women's movement attracted extremists, including those flaunting a "reform dress." Seeing the dress publicly derided, she steered away from it. "There is a great work for us to do in the world, and God would not have us take a course to lessen or destroy our influence" (1T 422). When reform styles later moderated, she joined in decrying the ills caused by fashion and promoted plain, sensible dress (*ibid.* 717, 718).

Ellen White cared deeply about women and issues that affected them. She sought to improve relationships in marriage, the home, and child rearing by calling for mutuality between husband and wife, family planning, and shared household responsibilities. Neither spouse should try to control the other, she said. Because women managed the home, she directed counsels to them about diet, exercise, temperance, dress, and simple treatments for the sick. But nothing exceeded her concern for eternal life. She constantly urged men and women to prize a personal relationship with Christ.

White said little about women's rights per se. Yet her actions demonstrated a powerful commitment to righting wrongs and expanding women's opportunities. Societal norms to the contrary, she prodded women to earn an education, develop their talents, and work in every aspect of the church's mission, private or public. She approved of women contemporaries who were teachers, physicians,

evangelists, missionaries, and elected church leaders. When administrators paid women poor wages or failed to pay them at all, she confronted the injustice, insisting that women be treated according to righteous principles. Overall Ellen White improved women's lives by her counsel and personal example.

Further reading: R. T. Banks, ed., *A Woman's Place: Seventh-day Adventist Women in Church and Society* (RHPA, 1992); J. Benton, *Called by God: Stories of Seventh-day Adventist Women Ministers* (Smithsburg, Md.: Blackberry Hill, 1990); Malcolm Bull and Keith Lockhart, *Seeking a Sanctuary: Seventh-day Adventism and the American Dream* (San Francisco: Harper & Row, 1989), pp. 186-188; R. W. Coon, "The 'Role-of-Women-in-the-Church' Message" (lecture, Berkeley Springs, West Virginia, SDA Church, Mar. 19, 1996); K. Flowers, "The Role of Women in the Church: An International Survey of Seventh-day Adventist Women in Leadership" (GC Women's Ministries Advisory, 1989); R. D. Graybill, "The Power of Prophecy: Ellen G. White and the Women Religious Founders of the Nineteenth Century" (Ph.D. diss., Johns Hopkins University, 1983); P. Habada and R. Brillhart, eds., *The Welcome Table: Setting a Place for Ordained Women* (Langley Park, Md.: Team Press, 1995); B. Haloviak, "Longing for the Pastorate: Ministry in the 19th Century" (unpublished manuscript, GCAr); C. R. Holmes, *The Tip of an Iceberg: Biblical Authority, Biblical Interpretation, and the Ordination of Women in Ministry* (Berrien Springs, Mich.: Adventists Affirm and Pointer Publications, 1994); Rosalie Haffner Lee, "Is Ordination Needed to Women's Ministry?" in S. W. Bacchiocchi, *Women in the Church: A Biblical Study on the Role of Women in the Church* (Berrien Springs, Mich.: Biblical Perspectives, 1987), pp. 239-254; L. E. Morales-Gudmundsson, ed., *Women and the Church: The Feminine Perspective* (AUP, 1995); A. Patrick, "The Ordination of Deaconesses," AR, Jan. 16, 1986; M. Pearson, *Millennial Dreams and Moral Dilemmas: Seventh-Day Adventism and Contemporary Ethics* (Cambridge: Cambridge University Press, 1990), pp. 134-161; R. A. Tucker and W. L. Liefield, *Daughters of the Church* (Grand Rapids: Zondervan, 1987), pp. 235-241; M. S. Van Leeuwen, ed., *After Eden: Facing the Challenge of Gender Reconciliation* (Grand Rapids: Eerdmans, 1993), pp. 34, 35, 389, 390, 416, 417, 437; N. Vyhmeister, ed., *Women in Ministry: Biblical and Historical Perspectives* (AUP, 1998); K. Watts, "Why Did Women Begin to Preach?" AR, Mar. 30, 1995; K. Watts, "Our Forgotten Heritage," AR, May 4, 1995; K. Watts, "Moving Away From the Table: A Survey of Historical Factors Affecting Women Leaders," in P. Habada and R. Brillhart, eds., *The Welcome Table*, pp. 45-59.

Kit Watts

WOOD STREET HOME, see **HOMES OF JAMES AND ELLEN G. WHITE**.

WORD TO THE "LITTLE FLOCK," A (James White, 1847, 24 pp.). The first synopsis of Sabbatarian Adventist thought that established a baseline perspective on the issues most important to them. It prepared the way for additional ideas and a united movement that would begin to come together during 1848 to 1850. Compiled and published by James White, the 24-page paper was as much a pastoral epistle as it was a doctrinal presentation. It contained a series of articles by James White, Ellen White, and Joseph Bates.

The tract supported the Midnight Cry as a true fulfillment of Bible prophecy and had at least three major objectives: to trace events from October 1844 to the end of sin after the

millennium, to feature and promote their teaching on the Sabbath and shut door, and to present and explain Ellen White's visions and prophetic gift.

The broad overview of end-time events as given in *A Word to the "Little Flock"* provided a framework to understand "present truth." Central to "present truth" was the linkage of the Sabbath to the work of Jesus in the Most Holy Place of the heavenly sanctuary. Because Jesus had moved from the holy place to the Most Holy Place of the heavenly sanctuary, a new revelation of the Sabbath appeared as the law of God was revealed in the ark of the covenant (Rev. 11:19). This gave the Sabbath unique eschatological significance.

Vitally connected to this view was an extensive three-phase understanding of the time of trouble that encompassed the period from October 22, 1844, to the voice of God at the second coming of Jesus. First, as a lesser "time of trouble" increased in intensity, the Sabbath would be proclaimed more fully. Second, Michael would stand up (Dan. 12:1) and probation would close, leading to the seven last plagues and the greater *time of trouble. Third, near the end of the great time of trouble, the "time of Jacob's trouble" would climax with a proclamation of the voice of God announcing the deliverance of His people.

Ellen White's visions were prominently featured in *A Word to the "Little Flock."* James White and Joseph Bates give a considered presentation on the relationship of Ellen White's visions to the Bible, a scriptural rationale for modern prophetic manifestation, and a reasoned response to the questions that many had concerning Ellen White's experience. The tract had the effect of increasing awareness and acceptance of her visions among Sabbatarian Adventists. This allowed her to give support to particular ideas or expand on them and give influential advice on a wide variety of issues.

A Word to the "Little Flock" was reprinted in facsimile format by the Review and Herald in 1944. It was also reprinted in its entirety in the appendix to F. D. Nichol's *Ellen G. White and Her Critics* (RHPA, 1951), pp. 560-584.

Merlin D. Burt

WORLD WAR I. Seventh-day Adventists first defined their attitude toward *military service by a resolution of the newly organized General Conference in August 1864. The Adventist declaration of noncombatancy took advantage of a United States government draft law with special provisions for conscientious objectors. The principle is to cooperate with military authorities (e.g., medical corps) without compromising the law of God. No major conflict ever arose between Adventists and American military authorities.

In *Europe, however, most governments did not recognize the Adventist position of noncombatancy. During World War I church officials on the continent normally left it to the individual's conscience to decide whether or not to bear arms or perform duty on Sabbath. It was not until 1923 that European Adventists took an official stand on noncombatancy (RH, Mar. 6, 1924).

Ellen White was first confronted with European military service laws during her stay in *Switzerland (1885-1887). Referring to the Swiss Adventist draftees in Basel, she wrote, "They [governmental authorities] demand that young men . . . shall not neglect the exercise and drill essential for soldier service. We were glad to see that these men with their regimentals had tokens of honor for faithfulness in their work. . . . [They] did not go from choice, but because the laws of their nation required this. We gave them a word of encouragement to be found true

soldiers of the cross of Christ . . . that the angels of God may go with them and guard them from every temptation" (Ms 33, 1886, in 2SM 335). Thus, in a general manner, Ellen White counseled against defying military authority. She encouraged Adventist draftees to be loyal to the government, and at the same time faithful to God and His commandments.

At the outbreak of World War I in the summer of 1914, European Adventists were not prepared for the trials the war would bring to the church. Ellen White was well advanced in years and gave no written instruction concerning the duty of Adventists in military service. In a conversation with her son, W. C. White, in May 1915, shortly before her death, she asked him how the war was impacting Adventists. W. C. White reported that many had been "pressed into" military service, and that some church members thought they should refuse military service, even if such refusal led them to be shot. Her reply was "I do not think they ought to do that." "I think they [European Adventists] ought to stand to their duty as long as time lasts" (6Bio 426, 427). It is not clear whether by "their duty" she meant their military duty or their duty to God. Arthur White suggests that her statement, whatever its precise meaning, "was based on her general understanding of avoiding rash positions" (*ibid.* 427). An interpretation that agrees with her earliest counsels would be that she simply meant both. She always maintained that one's loyalty to God took priority over every obligation, but that the precise course to be followed would be a matter of individual conscience.

Further reading: J. M. Barbour, "World War I Military Crisis in SDA Church—Did God Reject or Unite His People?" (unpublished paper, DF 320, CAR); J. M. Patt, "The History of the Advent Movement in Germany" (Ph.D. diss., Stanford University, 1958), pp. 241-276;

R. W. Schwarz and F. Greenleaf, *Light Bearers* (PPPA, 2000), pp. 364-384; A. L. White, "Ellen G. White and World War I" (DF 350-b, CAR).
Daniel Heinz

WORSHIP. Ellen White's thought on worship integrates a number of Christian doctrines. God deserves our worship by virtue of His attributes and actions, and a proper understanding of His character gives way to worship and praise. The divine qualities of infinity, eternity, majesty, perfection, goodness, mercy, power, sovereignty, sanctity, love, and justice provide the motivation for worship. God is worthy of worship for His actions as Creator, Sustainer, and Revealer. Ellen G. White's concept of worship shows a balance between the transcendence and the immanence of God, and in consequence, a balance between the formal and informal aspects of worship. Worship, then, moves between awe and joyful fellowship. Worship is inevitably Trinitarian because it recognizes the divine dignity of Christ and the leading role of the Holy Spirit. Therefore, worship is a theocentric experience, motivated and guided by a God who at the same time is sovereign and is present in the community.

For Ellen White, worship is the answer of humankind to the divine Being and His work. This answer must be characterized not only by reverence and humility but also by gratitude, praise, joy, and love. Before the divine reality, humanity is made conscious of its indignity. Worship is a positive and an integral answer of the human being to God.

There is a close relationship between worship and soteriology, for worship focuses on the redemptive work of Christ in the plan of salvation. Human worship is possible only by divine grace and Christ's righteousness and constitutes a response of living and saving faith. Such a faith is made manifest in good works, obedience, and ministry. Therefore

worship is christocentric and is expressed through faith and commitment.

Ellen White gives vital importance to worship in the church community. She considers true worship as a blessing, and a sacred and precious moment. On the one hand, it requires order and rules in regard to time, place, and way of worship. She is concerned about the decorum, promptness, serenity, and dignity of the act of worship. She rejects negligence, indifference, dryness, noise, confusion, disorder, and the extremes of formalism and fanaticism. On the other hand, she insists on spiritual, interesting, and attractive worship, in which the whole congregation participates, and gratitude and fellowship are cultivated. She uplifts the value of elements such as prayer and the reading and preaching of the Word. In this way, worship honors God and builds the church.

Her writings also highlight the eschatological dimension of worship. At the end of time she foresees a great reform movement with a remarkable spirit of worship. Worship is at the heart of the cosmic conflict between good and evil that began in heaven. The eschatological conflict will prove the loyalty of the people of God to the only One who deserves worship. The final controversy between true and false worship is related to the attitude of human beings to the law of God and will divide them in two great groups. Worship is central in this eschatological conflict and has to do with the eternal destiny of believers.

For Ellen White worship is a vital subject. Worship has a divine objective: it begins, focuses, and concentrates on God, who is at the same time transcendent and immanent. Its subject is the human or angelic creature who responds actively to the divine calling. It is generated and validated by the redemption mediated by Jesus Christ, to whom human beings respond in fidelity and commitment. It is manifested in personal and communal ways in harmony with the dynamic and the order of the church. Finally, it looks forward to the eschatological moment when God's children will be reunited with Christ.

Further reading: ST, June 24, 1886; COL 150-163; 5T 491-500; DA 188, 189; PK 661-668; C. R. Holmes, *Sing a New Song! Worship Renewal for Adventists Today* (AUP, 1984).

Daniel Oscar Plenc

WRATH OF GOD. For Ellen White the wrath of God is no contradiction to His great love. The same God who is "merciful and gracious, longsuffering and abundant in goodness and truth, forgiving iniquity and transgression and sin" (Ex. 34:6, 7), is "slow to anger" but "will not leave the guilty unpunished" (Nahum 1:3, NIV). Just as God is active in His love, He is active in His wrath. God's wrath flows from His holiness and is an expression of justice against sin (cf. GC 627). It is God's holy reaction against every sin and the transgression of His law (1SM 218). In a general sense the Fall of Adam and Eve brought the wrath of God upon the whole human race (1SP 49) so that we are "by nature the children of wrath" (Eph. 2:3). Yet the wrath of God was also at work in specific judgments, such as the Flood (PP 338; AA 572) and the 10 plagues in Egypt (ST, Apr. 1, 1880); it was aroused through Israel's unfaithfulness and the breaking of the covenant (cf. PP 455; EW 162). The persistent rejection of light awakens the wrath of God (PP 97). It is also aroused by the stubborn obstinacy of those who defy God's forgiveness and mercy and with determination repeat their sins of the past and do not want to be forgiven (ST, Sept. 27, 1899). Therefore God's anger is just (RH, June 2, 1885; 3SP 344) and righteous (ST, Feb. 15, 1899) and has a retributive dimension (GW92

87; 4T 185). Yet it is not vindictive, for God Himself provides the means to avoid His wrath. Reconciliation is initiated by God (2 Cor. 5:19; Rom. 2:4; Acts 5:31).

God's wrath is His necessary reaction against all sin and evil, yet it remains God's strange work (Isa. 28:21; 2SM 372; GC 627), for God is love! No one is made to suffer the *judgment of divine wrath until God's will has been clearly understood and truth is rejected (GC 605). Thus the principles of eternal justice will have full control in the day of God's wrath (YI, June 8, 1893). Christ took upon Himself, on the cross voluntarily, the wrath of God, which sinful humans should have suffered (DA 686, 753; 1SM 313; 5BC 1103). Thus Christ's substitutionary death is a propitiation for human sin (RH, June 23, 1896).

For Ellen White the wrath of God has a strong future connotation. After the close of *probation God's anger will be poured out without mercy at the great day of His wrath (Rev. 6:17). Already now a few drops of God's wrath have begun to fall upon the children of disobedience (3MR 304; CH 134), but until probation is closed God's wrath is still mingled with His mercy, because God desires that sinners come to their senses, turn from their evil conduct (Isa. 42:25), and receive eternal life (Eze. 33:11; 18:30-32). The results of those first signs of God's wrath are but a faint representation of what will take place in the future (3SM 391). During the seven last *plagues God withdraws His protection, and the *wicked, who have rejected God's mercy, will suffer the wrath of God without shelter (EW 44). At the same time, the death of Christ is hope and eternal life to all who believe in Him (TM 139). The good news is that the wrath of God will not fall upon anyone who has taken refuge in Christ (AG 70).

In perhaps her most poignant illustration of the wrath of God, she declared that "heaven stands indignant at the neglect shown to the souls of men. . . . How would a father and mother feel, did they know that their child, lost in the cold and the snow, had been passed by, and left to perish, by those who might have saved it? Would they not be terribly grieved, wildly indignant? Would they not denounce those murderers with wrath hot as their tears, intense as their love? The sufferings of every man are the sufferings of God's child, and those who reach out no helping hand to their perishing fellow beings provoke His righteous anger. This is the wrath of the Lamb" (DA 825).

The final wrath of God will not come until Jesus has finished His work in the Most Holy Place of the heavenly *sanctuary. According to Ellen White the anger of the nations, the wrath of God and the time to judge the dead are separate and distinct and follow each other (EW 36; LS 116). With eternal death, when the *wicked exist no longer and every sin is eradicated, the wrath of God comes to an end (ST, Aug. 28, 1879).

Even though Ellen White did take seriously the reality of the wrath of God in her writings, she also strongly urged believers not to threaten others with the idea of the wrath of God if they do wrong (CG 253). Instead of dwelling upon the wrath of God, we should think of God's abundant mercy, His great compassion, and His willingness to save sinners (HP 119).

Further reading: F. M. Hasel, "The Wrath of God," *Ministry*, November 1991, pp. 10-12; F. V. Leamon, "The Wrath of God" (unpublished paper, AU, 1975, CAR).

Frank M. Hasel

WRITING AND SENDING OUT OF THE TESTIMONIES TO THE CHURCH, THE (PPPA, n.d., 32 pp.). Compilation of four letters and manuscripts from Ellen White and one statement from W. C. White regarding the preparation of her testimonies to individuals and churches. Ellen White wrote letters to answer questions about how she wrote her testimonies and to refute suspicions that people near her influenced her to write these testimonies. W. C. White comments that he often witnessed his mother in vigorous discussions with church leaders and that she was the one who influenced them in taking certain positions, not the other way around. Sections of this pamphlet can be found in F. D. Nichol, *Ellen G. White and Her Critics* (RHPA, 1951), pp. 644-651.

WYCLIFFE, JOHN (c. 1320-1384). Early English reformer. She perceived Wycliffe, as one among many great persons, the "morning star of the Reformation" (GC 80), whose love for the Scripture and truth led him to be used by God in the recovery of long-forgotten or obscured teachings of the Bible. Wycliffe's acceptance of the Bible as "a sufficient rule of faith and practice" (*ibid.* 93) shaped his character, educated his mind, and convinced him to obey God rather than human beings. Ellen White notes that Wycliffe taught salvation through faith in Christ and the sole infallibility of the Scriptures. Some of his teachings provoked the indignation of church leaders and brought him difficulties and persecution.

PHOTO CREDIT: UNKNOWN

JOHN WYCLIFFE, EARLY ENGLISH REFORMER

Particularly displeasing were his rejection of the temporal authority of the Papacy over England and the payments of tributes to Rome, and his requests for the abolishment of mendicant orders. Wycliffe also did not hesitate to contrast the pompous and pleasure-loving lifestyle of popes and bishops with the humble life of Christ. Comparable to John the Baptist, Wycliffe "was the herald of a new era" (*ibid.* 93). The greatest work of his life, however, was, according to Ellen White, the first translation of the Bible into the English language, which she saw as "a light which should never be extinguished" and "the most powerful of all weapons against Rome" (*ibid.* 88). As the first of the Protestant Reformers, Wycliffe's writings also influenced *John Huss and *Jerome in Bohemia, and their successors.

Further reading: GC 79-96, 249; G. R. Evans, *John Wyclif: Myth and Reality* (Downers Grove, Ill.: InterVarsity Press, 2005).

Denis Fortin

Ye Shall Receive Power (RHPA, 1995, 382 pp.). Seventeenth daily devotional book published by the Ellen G. White Estate. Materials selected for these meditations were drawn from Ellen White's books, periodical articles, and unpublished letters and manuscripts. Each month follows a different theme that highlights the person, presence, and work of the Holy Spirit in a Christian's life. These daily readings emphasize how the Holy Spirit transforms and guides the Christian, brings about the fruit of the Spirit, and gives spiritual gifts to the church. Although a compilation, this book gives a balanced but compact presentation of her thought on the Holy Spirit and His work.

Your Home and Health (PPPA, 1943, 304 pp.). Abridgment of Ellen White's book *The Ministry of Healing* (1905). Most chapters from the original edition have been included, although their order is rearranged and some have been abridged to better serve the purpose of presenting the subject in a more popular form. *Your Home and Health* was a book sold by Seventh-day Adventist *colporteurs. A similar abridgment of *The Adventist Home*

appeared in 1971 under the title *Happiness Homemade*.

Youth Ministry. Although the Bible does not specifically mention "youth ministry" as a special area of ministry either in Old Testament times or within the Christian church, this does not mean that Scripture is silent on the topic. It was God's intention that parents be responsible for the nurture of their children and that they paint the portrait of God upon the canvas of their children's lives (Deut. 6:4-9). Jesus Himself challenged His disciples to "feed my lambs" (John 21:15), and reserved His harshest judgment for those who caused a young person to stumble (Matt. 18:6). With the breakdown of families in modern society, and widespread abdication of parental responsibilities, the church ministry specifically to young people has become more imperative than ever.

Youth ministry can be viewed from a number of angles—first *ministry for youth*. Ellen White was well ahead of her peers when she described relational ministry and incarnational ministry for youth. "Ministers of the gospel should form a happy acquaintance with the youth of their congregations. . . . Why should not labor for the youth in our borders be regarded as missionary work of the highest kind?" (GW 207). "The youth need more than a casual notice, more than an occasional word of encouragement. They need painstaking, prayerful, careful labor. He only whose heart is filled with love and sympathy will be able to reach those youth who are apparently careless and indifferent" (*ibid.* 208). "Jesus did not remain in heaven, away from the sorrowing and sinful; He came down to this world, that He might become acquainted with the weakness, the suffering, and the temptations of the fallen race. He reached us where we were, that He might lift us up. In our work for the youth, we must meet them where they are, if we would help them" (*ibid.* 209).

Another area of youth ministry in which Ellen White led the field was *ministry by the youth*. She foresaw young people taking the lead as missionaries to the world. "The church is languishing for the help of [young men and young women] who will bear a courageous testimony, who will with their ardent zeal stir up the sluggish energies of God's people, and so increase the power of the church in the world" (MYP 25).

Ellen White believed that youth can sway a mighty influence not only with their peers but also with the rest of society. "Preachers, or layman advanced in years, cannot have one-half the influence upon the young that the youth, devoted to God, can have upon their associates" (*ibid.* 204). "With such an army of workers as our youth, rightly trained, might furnish, how soon the message of a crucified, risen, and soon-coming Saviour might be carried to the whole world!" (*ibid.* 196).

Ministry by young people was a prominent factor in the early Adventist Church. Ellen White was only 17 when she received her first vision; *James White was a successful public evangelist at the age of 21; *Uriah Smith was only 21 when he joined the editorial staff of the *Review and Herald*; John N. Andrews began evangelistic preaching at 21. Publications for Sabbatarian Adventist young people began at least by 1852, when James White, then 31, founded a periodical, *The Youth's Instructor*.

The first Adventist young people's society was founded by 14-year-old *Luther Warren and 17-year-old Harry Fenner at Hazelton, Michigan, in 1879. In 1891 Meade MacGuire, 16, organized another youth group at Antigo, Wisconsin. Ellen White was very supportive of this new work, and when A. G. Daniells

started a youth ministry program in Adelaide, Australia, in 1892, Ellen White called for young people's groups to be organized in every church (ST, May 29, 1893). She saw this ministry as both essential and vital to the health of the church and lived to see the adoption of a new department of the General Conference called the Young People's Missionary Volunteer Department. It took only a short time for young people to become known as MVs and their meetings, MV programs. Although the name has since changed to Adventist Youth (AY), the aim and motto remain the same: "The Advent message to all the world in this generation" and "The love of Christ constraineth us."

Ellen White advocated special Sabbath schools for children and youth and described some of the approaches that work best with these age groups. She encouraged small-group work and intimate ministry with young people. "We should seek to enter into the feelings of the youth, sympathizing with them in their joys and sorrows, their conflicts and victories" (GW 209). She encouraged pastors to meet in small groups with the young people of their churches and said that by so doing they would begin to see potential even in some of the youth who might otherwise be ignored. She encouraged those involved in youth ministry not to be unduly influenced by the outward appearance, but to look beyond it to the potential that lies in each young person.

"Often those whom we pass by with indifference, because we judge them from outward appearance have in them the best material for workers, and will repay the efforts bestowed on them. There must be more study given to the problem of how to deal with the youth, more earnest prayer for the wisdom that is needed in dealing with minds" (*ibid.* 208). Ministry of youth for youth—or Youth to Youth, as some call it—was also a prominent theme in her writings, and she called for training to be provided in this area (6T 115).

As a specialized ministry within the Seventh-day Adventist Church, youth ministry has been divided into a number of areas—Adventurers, ages 6-9, Pathfinders, ages 10-15, and Youth Ministry for 16- to 30-year-olds. The mighty army Ellen White dreamed of is making an enormous contribution to the preaching of the gospel to "every kindred, and tongue, and people" (Rev. 5:9).

In March 1915 Ellen White received her last vision, which was addressed to the youth of the church (FE 547-549; MYP 287-289; cf. 6Bio 425, 426).

Further reading: MYP; GW 207-212; *SDA Encyclopedia* (1996), vol. 11, pp. 924-926.

Barry Gane

YOUTH'S INSTRUCTOR ARTICLES, THE, ELLEN G. WHITE (RHPA, 1986, 640 pp.). One-volume facsimile reproduction of Ellen White's articles published in *The Youth's Instructor* from 1852 to 1914. In 1852 James White, then editor of the **Review and Herald*, sensed a need for a periodical dedicated to the youth of the church. In August of that year he launched a monthly journal titled *The Youth's Instructor*, which became a weekly in 1879. In her lifetime Ellen White authored approximately 500 articles for this paper, the majority published between 1892 and 1903. In her articles in *The Youth's Instructor* she attempted to simplify the gospel and the Adventist message; to explain God's Word so that young people could easily understand it. From 1852 to 1859 her articles often took the form of letters addressed to "Dear Young Friends" and often included personal recollections of her life as a youth.

From 1872 to 1874 she published a series of 12 articles on the life of Christ, presenting Jesus as the example for young people, a recurrent theme in her writings and especially in *The Youth's Instructor* in the 1880s and 1890s.

Z FILE. A file of Ellen White's original letters and manuscripts that no longer exists. It once contained about 100 letters that dealt with the sins of erring church leaders. After Ellen White's death in 1915 her son W. C. White became increasingly concerned about how to handle Ellen White's letters of counsel that dealt with moral lapses on the part of Adventist ministers or other church workers, some of whom were still living. Probably in the early 1930s he withdrew these "sensitive" letters from the regular manuscript and letter files and put them in two separate drawers that were given the name "Z File." The Z file was off-limits to most scholars and researchers. However, with the passage of time, the people addressed in these letters all died. The White Estate trustees recognized that the publication of the counsels contained in these letters could help others, so in 1987 the decision to eliminate this special file, return the letters to their original places in the letter file, and publish some of the counsels in a form designed to minimize embarrassment to descendants of the original recipients was made. Excerpts from many of these letters may now be found in the book *Testimonies on Sexual Behavior, Adultery, and Divorce*, published in 1989.

Further reading: R. W. Coon, "What's the White Estate Attempting to Hide?" AR, July 2, 1987; see also DF 828-a-3, CAR.

Robert Olson

Appendices

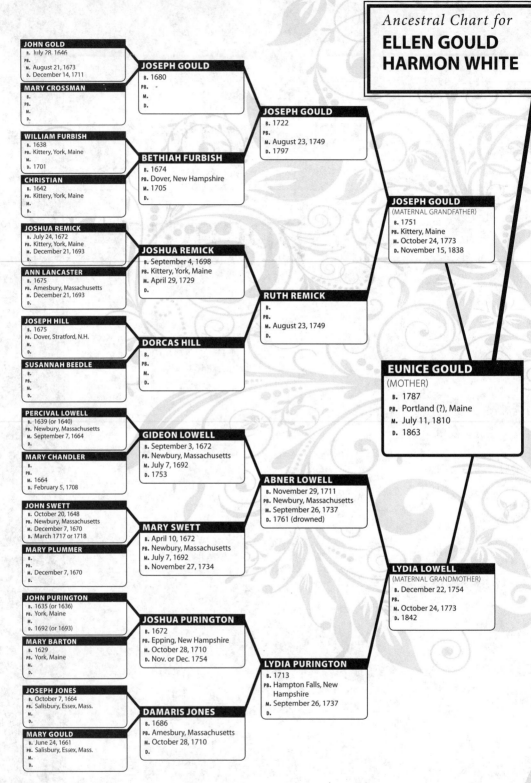

Ancestral Chart for
ELLEN GOULD HARMON WHITE

JOHN GOLD
B. July 28, 1646
PB.
M. August 21, 1673
D. December 14, 1711

MARY CROSSMAN
B.
PB.
M.
D.

JOSEPH GOULD
B. 1680
PB.
M.
D.

WILLIAM FURBISH
B. 1638
PB. Kittery, York, Maine
M.
D. 1701

CHRISTIAN
B. 1642
PB. Kittery, York, Maine
M.
D.

BETHIAH FURBISH
B. 1674
PB. Dover, New Hampshire
M. 1705
D.

JOSEPH GOULD
B. 1722
PB.
M. August 23, 1749
D. 1797

JOSHUA REMICK
B. July 24, 1672
PB. Kittery, York, Maine
M. December 21, 1693
D.

ANN LANCASTER
B. 1675
PB. Amesbury, Massachusetts
M. December 21, 1693
D.

JOSHUA REMICK
B. September 4, 1698
PB. Kittery, York, Maine
M. April 29, 1729
D.

JOSEPH GOULD
(MATERNAL GRANDFATHER)
B. 1751
PB. Kittery, Maine
M. October 24, 1773
D. November 15, 1838

JOSEPH HILL
B. 1675
PB. Dover, Stratford, N.H.
M.
D.

SUSANNAH BEEDLE
B.
PB.
M.
D.

DORCAS HILL
B.
PB.
M.
D.

RUTH REMICK
B.
PB.
M. August 23, 1749
D.

EUNICE GOULD
(MOTHER)
B. 1787
PB. Portland (?), Maine
M. July 11, 1810
D. 1863

PERCIVAL LOWELL
B. 1639 (or 1640)
PB. Newbury, Massachusetts
M. September 7, 1664
D.

MARY CHANDLER
B.
PB.
M. 1664
D. February 5, 1708

GIDEON LOWELL
B. September 3, 1672
PB. Newbury, Massachusetts
M. July 7, 1692
D. 1753

JOHN SWETT
B. October 20, 1648
PB. Newbury, Massachusetts
M. December 7, 1670
D. March 1717 or 1718

MARY PLUMMER
B.
PB.
M. December 7, 1670
D.

MARY SWETT
B. April 10, 1672
PB. Newbury, Massachusetts
M. July 7, 1692
D. November 27, 1734

ABNER LOWELL
B. November 29, 1711
PB. Newbury, Massachusetts
M. September 26, 1737
D. 1761 (drowned)

JOHN PURINGTON
B. 1635 (or 1636)
PB. York, Maine
M.
D. 1692 (or 1693)

MARY BARTON
B. 1629
PB. York, Maine
M.
D.

JOSHUA PURINGTON
B. 1672
PB. Epping, New Hampshire
M. October 28, 1710
D. Nov. or Dec. 1754

LYDIA LOWELL
(MATERNAL GRANDMOTHER)
B. December 22, 1754
PB.
M. October 24, 1773
D. 1842

JOSEPH JONES
B. October 7, 1664
PB. Salisbury, Essex, Mass.
M.
D.

MARY GOULD
B. June 24, 1661
PB. Salisbury, Essex, Mass.
M.
D.

DAMARIS JONES
B. 1686
PB. Amesbury, Massachusetts
M. October 28, 1710
D.

LYDIA PURINGTON
B. 1713
PB. Hampton Falls, New Hampshire
M. September 26, 1737
D.

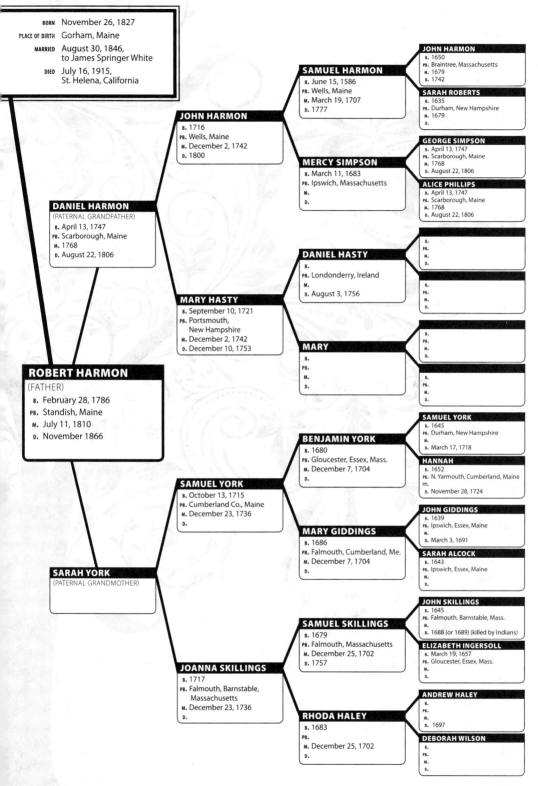

	SAMUEL HARMON B. June 15, 1586 PB. Wells, Maine M. March 19, 1707 D. 1777	**JOHN HARMON** B. 1650 PB. Braintree, Massachusetts M. 1679 D. 1742
		SARAH ROBERTS B. 1635 PB. Durham, New Hampshire M. 1679 D.

BORN November 26, 1827
PLACE OF BIRTH Gorham, Maine
MARRIED August 30, 1846,
to James Springer White
DIED July 16, 1915,
St. Helena, California

JOHN HARMON
B. 1716
PB. Wells, Maine
M. December 2, 1742
D. 1800

SAMUEL HARMON
B. June 15, 1586
PB. Wells, Maine
M. March 19, 1707
D. 1777

MERCY SIMPSON
B. March 11, 1683
PB. Ipswich, Massachusetts
M.
D.

JOHN HARMON
B. 1650
PB. Braintree, Massachusetts
M. 1679
D. 1742

SARAH ROBERTS
B. 1635
PB. Durham, New Hampshire
M. 1679
D.

GEORGE SIMPSON
B. April 13, 1747
PB. Scarborough, Maine
M. 1768
D. August 22, 1806

ALICE PHILLIPS
B. April 13, 1747
PB. Scarborough, Maine
M. 1768
D. August 22, 1806

DANIEL HARMON
(PATERNAL GRANDFATHER)
B. April 13, 1747
PB. Scarborough, Maine
M. 1768
D. August 22, 1806

DANIEL HASTY
B.
PB. Londonderry, Ireland
M.
D. August 3, 1756

B.
PB.
M.
D.

B.
PB.
M.
D.

MARY HASTY
B. September 10, 1721
PB. Portsmouth,
New Hampshire
M. December 2, 1742
D. December 10, 1753

MARY
B.
PB.
M.
D.

B.
PB.
M.
D.

B.
PB.
M.
D.

ROBERT HARMON
(FATHER)
B. February 28, 1786
PB. Standish, Maine
M. July 11, 1810
D. November 1866

BENJAMIN YORK
B. 1680
PB. Gloucester, Essex, Mass.
M. December 7, 1704
D.

SAMUEL YORK
B. 1645
PB. Durham, New Hampshire
M.
D. March 17, 1718

HANNAH
B. 1652
PB. N. Yarmouth, Cumberland, Maine
m.
D. November 28, 1724

SAMUEL YORK
B. October 13, 1715
PB. Cumberland Co., Maine
M. December 23, 1736
D.

MARY GIDDINGS
B. 1686
PB. Falmouth, Cumberland, Me.
M. December 7, 1704
D.

JOHN GIDDINGS
B. 1639
PB. Ipswich, Essex, Maine
M.
D. March 3, 1691

SARAH ALCOCK
B. 1643
PB. Ipswich, Essex, Maine
M.
D.

SARAH YORK
(PATERNAL GRANDMOTHER)

SAMUEL SKILLINGS
B. 1679
PB. Falmouth, Massachusetts
M. December 25, 1702
D. 1757

JOHN SKILLINGS
B. 1645
PB. Falmouth, Barnstable, Mass.
M.
D. 1688 (or 1689) (killed by Indians)

ELIZABETH INGERSOLL
B. March 19, 1657
PB. Gloucester, Essex, Mass.
M.
D.

JOANNA SKILLINGS
B. 1717
PB. Falmouth, Barnstable,
Massachusetts
M. December 23, 1736
D.

RHODA HALEY
B. 1683
PB.
M. December 25, 1702
D.

ANDREW HALEY
B.
PB.
M.
D. 1697

DEBORAH WILSON
B.
PB.
M.
D.

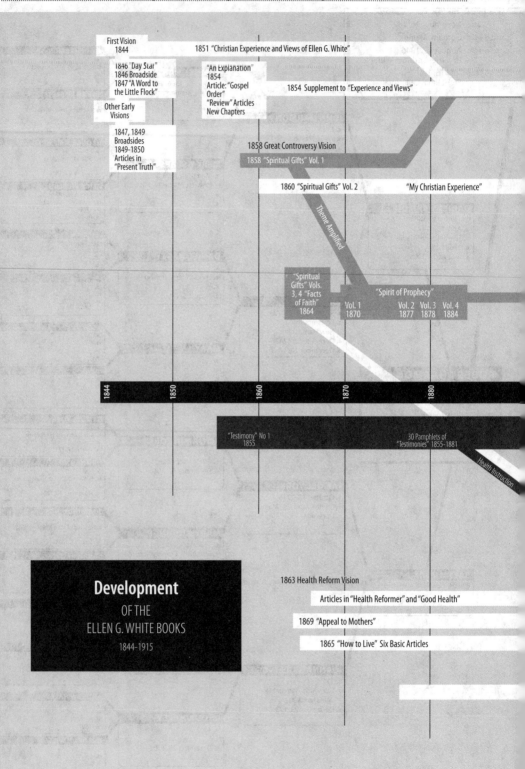

First Vision
1844

1851 "Christian Experience and Views of Ellen G. White"

1846 "Day Star"
1846 Broadside
1847 "A Word to
the Little Flock"

"An Explanation"
1854
Article: "Gospel
Order"
"Review" Articles
New Chapters

1854 Supplement to "Experience and Views"

Other Early
Visions

1847, 1849
Broadsides
1849-1850
Articles in
"Present Truth"

1858 Great Controversy Vision

1858 "Spiritual Gifts" Vol. 1

1860 "Spiritual Gifts" Vol. 2

"My Christian Experience"

Theme Amplified

"Spiritual
Gifts" Vols.
3, 4 "Facts
of Faith"
1864

Vol. 1
1870

"Spirit of Prophecy"

Vol. 2   Vol. 3   Vol. 4
1877   1878   1884

1844   1850   1860   1870   1880

"Testimony" No 1
1855

30 Pamphlets of
"Testimonies" 1855-1881

Health Instruction

Development
OF THE
ELLEN G. WHITE BOOKS
1844-1915

1863 Health Reform Vision

Articles in "Health Reformer" and "Good Health"

1869 "Appeal to Mothers"

1865 "How to Live" Six Basic Articles

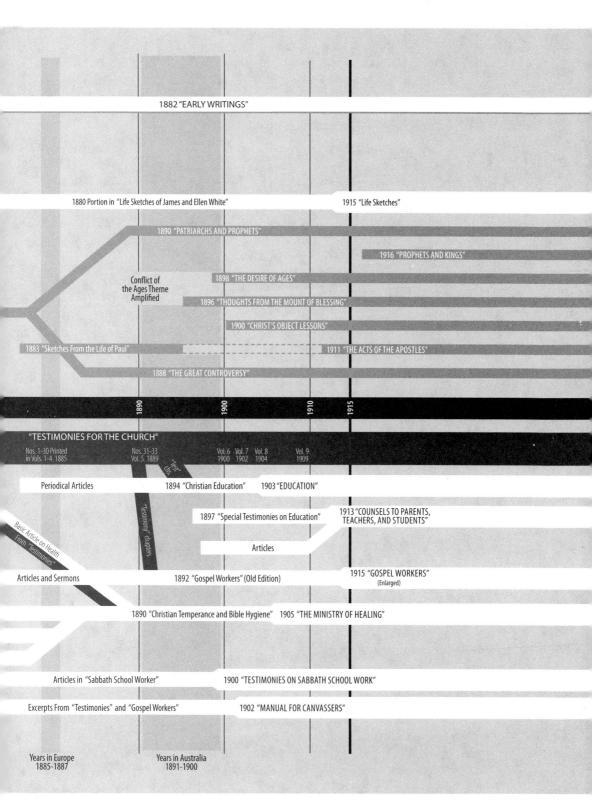

1882 "EARLY WRITINGS"

1880 Portion in "Life Sketches of James and Ellen White"   1915 "Life Sketches"

1890 "PATRIARCHS AND PROPHETS"

1916 "PROPHETS AND KINGS"

Conflict of
the Ages Theme
Amplified   1898 "THE DESIRE OF AGES"

1896 "THOUGHTS FROM THE MOUNT OF BLESSING"

1900 "CHRIST'S OBJECT LESSONS"

1883 "Sketches From the Life of Paul"   1911 "THE ACTS OF THE APOSTLES"

1888 "THE GREAT CONTROVERSY"

1890   1900   1910   1915

"TESTIMONIES FOR THE CHURCH"

| Nos. 1-30 Printed in Vols. 1-4 1885 | Nos. 31-33 Vol. 5 1889 | Vol. 6 1900 | Vol. 7 1902 | Vol. 8 1904 | Vol. 9 1909 |

Periodical Articles   1894 "Christian Education"   1903 "EDUCATION"

1897 "Special Testimonies on Education"   1913 "COUNSELS TO PARENTS, TEACHERS, AND STUDENTS"

Articles

Articles and Sermons   1892 "Gospel Workers" (Old Edition)   1915 "GOSPEL WORKERS"
(Enlarged)

Basic Article on Health From "Testimonies"   1890 "Christian Temperance and Bible Hygiene"   1905 "THE MINISTRY OF HEALING"

Articles in "Sabbath School Worker"   1900 "TESTIMONIES ON SABBATH SCHOOL WORK"

Excerpts From "Testimonies" and "Gospel Workers"   1902 "MANUAL FOR CANVASSERS"

Years in Europe
1885-1887

Years in Australia
1891-1900

APPENDIX C
List of Ellen G. White's Letters

ADDRESSEE	FILE #	DATE	PLACE	WHERE PUBLISHED
				Bold italics indicates complete letter
		1845		
Jacobs, Enoch	J-001	45/12/20	Portland, Me.	*From DS 1/24/1846*
		1846		
Jacobs, Enoch	J-001	46/02/15	Falmouth, Ma.	*From DS 3/14/1846*
		1847		
Bates, Joseph	B-001	47/04/07	Topsham, Me.	*From WLF 18-20*
Curtis, Eli	C-002	47/04/21	Topsham, Me.	*From WLF 11-12*
Bates, Joseph	*B-003	47/07/13	Gorham, Me.	*5MR 95-98*
Hastings, Sr.	*H-004	47/08/25	Gorham, Me.	
		1848		
Scattered Remnant	B-002	48/12/18	Rocky Hill, Ct.	Cf. EW 41
		1849		
Hastings, Sr.	*H-002	49/03/00	Boston, Ma.?	
Hastings, Br-Sr.	*H-004	49/03/22	Topsham, Me.	1Bio 159
Hastings, Br-Sr.	*H-005	49/04/21	Milton, Ma.	1MR 390;5MR 93-94,200
Collins, Gilbert/Deborah	*C-007	49/09/00		*3MR 174-175*
Hastings, Br-Sr.	*H-008	49/05/29	Rocky Hill, Ct.	4MR 323-326;5MR 248-249
		1850		
Collins, Br-Sr.	*C-004	50/02/18	Oswego, NY	1MR 31;5MR 91;6MR 339
Hastings, Arabella	*H-008	50/08/04	Centerport, NY	*19MR 129-132*
Hastings, Br.	*H-010	50/03/18	Oswego, NY	*14MR 52-54*
Howland, Br-Sr.	H-012	50/08/15	Centerport, NY	*15MR 207-209*
Bates, Sr.	*B-014	50/09/01	Port Byron, NY	7MR 351-352;8MR 221-222
Hastings, Br-Sr.	H-018	50/01/11	Oswego, NY	*19MR 128*
Loveland, Br-Sr. [Reuben]	*L-026	50/11/01	Paris, Me.	*15MR 210-213*
Church in Br. Hastings' House	*H-028	50/11/27	Paris, Me.	*16MR 206-209*
Loveland, Br-Sr.	*L-030	50/12/13	Paris, Me.	1MR 31-32;4MR 270;5MR 226;6MR 252; 8MR 223;9MR 98-99
Nichols, Br-Sr.	N-031	50/12/00		
		1851		
Preston, Br-Sr.	*P-001	51/10/19	Saratoga Spgs., NY	5MR 226-227;8MR 223-224
Hastings, Harriet	*H-003	51/08/11	Saratoga Spgs., NY	3SM 260-261;LDE 286-287
Dodge, Br-Sr.	*D-004	51/07/21	Ballston Spa, NY	*5MR 99-101*
Barnes, Br.	*B-005	51/12/14	Saratoga Spgs., NY	1Bio 224;8MR 225
Loveland, Br-Sr.	*L-006	51/04/01	Paris, Me.	3SM 63;6MR 252
Hastings, Br-Sr.	*H-007	51/07/27	Ballston Spa, NY	6MR 253;8MR 339-340
Howland, Br-Sr.	H-008	51/11/12	Waterbury, Vt.	3MR 242-245,401-403;5MR 239-240; 6MR 118,253;8MR 225-227;1Bio 219-222

Dodge, Br-Sr.	D-009	51/12/21	Saratoga Spgs., NY	RC 350;2MR 248;6MR 253;8MR 228
Rhodes, Br.	R-010	51/05/18	Paris, Me.	

1852

Brn.-Srs. in Jackson	B-002	52/06/02	Rochester, NY	*17MR 341-343*
Dear Friends	*F-004	52/10/25	Rochester, NY	6MR 253-254

1853

White, Anna	W-002	53/05/26	Plymouth, Mi.	1Bio 274
Church in Jackson	B-003	53/06/29	Rochester, NY	1Bio 281
Pearsall, Br-Sr.	*P-004	53/06/30	Rochester, NY	
Dodge, Br-Sr.	D-005	53/07/05	Rochester, NY	1Bio 282
Dodge, Br-Sr.	D-006	53/08/03	Rochester, NY	7MR 351
Smith, Br-Sr.	*S-007	53/08/24	Rochester, NY	1Bio 282
Kellogg, Sr.	*K-009	53/12/05	Rochester, NY	EW 115-117;5MR 205,240-241;6MR
Chase, Mary	*C-010	53/05/00		
Pierce, Br.	*P-011	53/12/03		1Bio 404

1854

Stevens, Harriet	*S-001	54/03/10	Rochester, NY	5MR 436
Pierce, Br-Sr.	*P-002	54/04/11	Rochester, NY	
Pearsall, Br-Sr.	*P-003	54/07/12	Rochester, NY	*7MR 208*
Brn-Srs.	*B-005	54/12/16	Rochester, NY	6MR 297;7MR 259-260
Loughborough, Sr.	*L-006	54/00/00		10MR 20
Loughborough, Br-Sr.	*L-007	54/07/12	Rochester, NY	7MR 259,352
Brn-Srs. at Bedford	*B-008	54/07/00		*21MR 364-366*

1855

Andrews, John	*A-001	55/08/26	Topsham, Me.	9MR 313-314
Stevens, Harriet	*S-002	55/08/00	Paris, Me.	

1856

Howland, Br-Sr.	H-001	56/07/15	Battle Creek, Mi.	1Bio 341-342
Loveland, Br-Sr.	*L-002a	57/01/24	Battle Creek, Mi.	RC 351;1Bio 335-336;10MR 21
Friends at Home	*W-004	56/12/24	Volney, Ia.	1Bio 347-348
Children	W-005	56/12/24	Volney, Ia.	*From AY 40-41*
Cornell, M.E./Palmer, D./Kellogg, J.P.	*C-006	56/00/00		5MR 237
Stevens, Harriet	*S-008	56/01/21	Battle Creek, Mi.	
Below, Sr. E.P.	*B-009	56/01/01	Battle Creek, Mi.	HP 352;1Bio 332-334;3MR 225;7MR
Lamson, David	*L-010	56/01/00		

1857

Burwell, Br-Sr. A.	*B-001	57/01/28	Battle Creek, Mi.	
Burwell, Br.	*B-002	57/10/21	Battle Creek, Mi.	1Bio 363
Smith, Br-Sr.	*S-003	57/10/08	Battle Creek, Mi.	*PH016 28-30*
Everts, Br.	*E-005	57/11/22	Battle Creek, Mi.	
Smith, Uriah	*S-006	57/10/08	Battle Creek, Mi.	*PH016 25-28*
Rhodes, S.W.	*R-008	57/07/19	Battle Creek, Mi.	
Rumery, Br.	*R-009	57/10/00	Battle Creek, Mi.	
Stevens, Harriet	*S-012	57/01/30	Battle Creek, Mi.	
Everts, Br.	*E-014	57/07/12	Battle Creek, Mi.	6MR 130

Pierce, Br.	P-015	57/00/00		*18MR 248-253*

1858

Loughborough, Mary	*L-001	58/03/03	Green Springs, Oh.	*21MR 252-257*
Woodruff, Br.	*W-002	58/00/00		*21MR 258-259*
White, Henry/White, J.E.	W-003	58/03/02	Green Springs, Oh.	*From AY 42-44*

1859

T., Brother	*T-001	59/01/01		
Hastings, Amelia/Hastings, Emma	*H-001a	59/01/04	Battle Creek, Mi.	
Byington, Br.	*B-002	59/06/21	Battle Creek, Mi.	5MR 290
Harmon, Robert and Eunice/Parents	*H-003	59/09/01	Berlin, Ct.	
Peabody, Br.	*P-004	59/09/02		
White, Henry	*W-005	59/09/06	Somerville, Ma.	*AY 44-47*
White, W.C.	*W-006	59/09/15	Dartmouth, Ma.	3MR 120
Graham, Br.	*G-007	59/09/24	Topsham, Me.	
Fraser, Jenny	*F-008	59/09/15	Dartmouth, Ma.	
White, W.C.	*W-009	59/09/06	Somerville, Ma.	3MR 121
White, W.C.	*W-010	59/09/00		3MR 121-122
White, J.E.	*W-011	59/10/15	Enosburg, Vt.	*AY 52-53*
Friends	*B-013	59/01/05	Battle Creek, Mi.	5MR 291
White, W.C.	W-014	59/10/22	Mannsville; missing	
M., Br-Sr.	*M-015	59/00/00		
Rhodes, Br.	*R-016	59/10/28	Hubbardsville, NY	
Friends at Roosevelt	*B-017	59/10/28	Hubbardsville, NY	
Naramore, Dr.	*N-018	59/04/14	Battle Creek, Mi.	OHC 9,201;2MR 248;see RH 04/28/1859
Chamberlain, Sr.	*C-019	59/10/04	Newport, NH	
Bean, Br.	*B-020	59/09/00		
Evans, Br.	*E-021	59/09/00		
Phillips, Br.	*P-022	59/10/10	Roxbury, Vt.	
Children	W-023	59/09/20	Topsham, Me.	*From AY 47-48*
White, W.C.	W-024	59/09/20	Topsham, Me.	*From AY 48-49*
White, Henry	W-025	59/10/04	Newport, NH	*From AY 50-51*
White, Henry/White, J.E.	W-026	59/10/30	Brookfield, NY	*From AY 53-56*
Peabody, William	P-027	59/00/00		*PH016 35-38*
Byington, Br.	B-028	59/00/00	Battle Creek, Mi.	MRmnt 110;2Bio 98
Children	W-029	59/09/15	Dartmouth, Ma.	*From AY 65-66*
Friends	F-030	59/10/12	Enos, Vt.	5MR 231
Pierce, Br-Sr.	P-031	59/02/21	Battle Creek, Mi.	
Smith, Br-Sr. [Cyrenius]	*S-032	58/07/09	Battle Creek, Mi.	

1860

White, Henry/White, J.E.	*W-001	60/03/03	Iowa City, Ia.	*From AY 57-60*
White, W.C.	*W-002	60/03/03	Anamosa, Ia. ?	*AY 60-61*
White, W.C.	*W-003	60/03/14	Iowa City, Ia.	*AY 61-63*
Waggoner, J.H.	*W-004	60/04/14	Battle Creek, Mi.	
Pratt, Sr.	*P-005	60/04/15	Battle Creek, Mi.	1Bio 416
Loughborough, Br-Sr.	*L-006	60/04/15	Battle Creek, Mi.	1Bio 416-417
Loughborough, Br-Sr.	*L-006a	60/04/17	Battle Creek, Mi.	variant of Lt 6
Smith, Harriet	*S-007	60/06/00	Battle Creek, Mi.	*PH016 5-25*
Smith, Harriet	*S-007a	60/06/00	Battle Creek, Mi.	variant of Lt 7
Andrews, J.N.	*A-008	60/06/11	Battle Creek, Mi.	1Bio 417;1MR 306-307;7MR 315
Frisbie, Br.	*F-009	60/06/17	Battle Creek, Mi.	
White, J.S.	*W-010	60/10/12	Battle Creek, Mi.	1Bio 426

White, J.S.	*W-011	60/10/22	Battle Creek, Mi.	1Bio 426-427
White, J.S.	*W 012	60/10/28	Battle Creek, Mi.	6MR 189
White, J.S.	*W-012a	60/10/00	Battle Creek, Mi.	2MR 248-249;6MR 298
White, J.S.	*W-013	60/11/07	Battle Creek, Mi.	6MR 189
White, J.S.	*W-014	60/11/19	Battle Creek, Mi.	2MR 249;5MR 175;6MR 189-190
White, J.S.	*W-015	60/11/21	Battle Creek, Mi.	
Green, Deloss B.	*G-016	60/00/00	Battle Creek, Mi.	
Hall, Lucinda	*H-017	60/10/24	Battle Creek, Mi.	5MR 428
Hall, Lucinda	*H-018	60/11/02	Battle Creek, Mi.	*8MR 15-16*
Ross, Sr.	*R-019	60/00/00		
Friends in Mansville & Vicinity	*B-020	60/00/00		5MR 290

1861

Jones, Victory	*J-001	61/01/00	Battle Creek, Mi.	5MR 378;1Bio 465
C., Br-Sr.	*C-001a	61/01/24		*1T 240-243*
William	*W-002	61/02/23		OHC 230,288
White, Henry/White, J.E./White, W.C.	*W-003	61/03/18	Marion, Ia.	4MR 98;AY 63-64
White, Henry/White, J.E./White, W.C.	W-003a	61/03/18	Marion, Ia.;missing	
H., Mrs.	*H-004	61/03/00		*19MR 30-34*
Sperry, Br-Sr.	*S-004b	61/04/00	Battle Creek, Mi.	
Loughborough, Mary	*L-005	61/06/06	Battle Creek, Mi.	1Bio 468-469
Hall, Lucinda	*H-005a	61/04/05	Battle Creek, Mi.	1Bio 441-442
Hall, Lucinda	*H-005b	61/04/05	Battle Creek, Mi.	
Loughborough, Mary	*L-006	61/06/17	Battle Creek, Mi.	1Bio 448,469-470;5MR 379
Friends at Home	*W-006a	61/07/26	Eagle Harbor, NY	3MR 122-123
Children	*W-007	61/08/00	Grass River, NY	*AY 74-75*
Sperry, Sr.	*S-008	61/09/26	Battle Creek, Mi.	
Glover, Br-Sr. [Charles]	*G-009	61/10/12	Battle Creek, Mi.	TDG 294
Daigneau., Br-Sr. [John]	*D-010	61/10/18	Battle Creek, Mi.	
Friends	*B-011	61/12/00	Orleans, Mi.	5MR 291-292
Church at Caledonia	*C-012	61/12/00	Orleans, Mi.	
Kellogg, Br.	*K-015	61/00/00		
Church at Roosevelt, NY	*B-016	61/08/03		5MR 60-62;7MR 113-114;15MR 124-125
Church at Roosevelt, NY	B-016a	61/08/03		5MR 60-62;7MR 113-114;15MR 124-125
Ingraham, W.S.	*I-017	61/01/17	Battle Creek, Mi.	10MR 22
Buck, Br.	*B-018	61/01/19	Battle Creek, Mi.	5MR 292-293
Lyon, Mary	*L-019	61/10/13	Battle Creek, Mi.	UL 300;TDG 295
Wheeler, Br.	*W-020	61/08/00	Battle Creek, Mi.	
White, Henry/White, J.E./White, W.C.	*W-021	61/03/25	Plum River, Il.	*13MR 34-36*
White, Henry/White, J.E.	*W-023	61/07/26	Eagle Harbor, NY	*From AY 68-71*
White, W.C.	W-024	61/07/26		*From AY 71-72*
White, Henry/White, J.E.	W-025	61/07/00	Rochester, NY	*From AY 72-74*
Hall, Lucinda	*H-026	61/05/04	Battle Creek, Mi.	1Bio 444;5MR 432-433;
Hall, Lucinda	*H-027	61/06/19	Battle Creek, Mi.	1Bio 470;5MR 433-434;
				9MR 192;10MR 23
Hall, Lucinda	*H-028	61/09/21	Battle Creek, Mi.	
Hall, Lucinda	*H-029	61/11/13	Battle Creek, Mi.	
Shortridge, Br.	S-030	61/11/22	Battle Creek, Mi.	*From RH Supp. 08/00/1862*
Czechowski, Br.	*C-031	61/00/00		*8MR 414-421*
Czechowski, Br.	*C-031a	61/00/00		*8MR 72-73*
Ingraham, W.S.	*I-032	61/00/00	Battle Creek, Mi.	
Ingraham, W.S.	*I-032a	61/00/00	Battle Creek, Mi.	

1862

Phillips, Br.	*P-002	62/01/20	Battle Creek, Mi.	
Friends in Caledonia	*C-003	62/01/22	Battle Creek, Mi.	1Bio 466;5MR 293
Friends at Home	*W-004	62/03/05	Lodi, Wi.	
Banks, Br.	*B-005	62/05/08	Battle Creek, Mi.	
White, J.E./White, W.C.	W-006	62/07/25		*From AY 77-78*
Steward, Sr.	*S-007	62/08/19	Battle Creek, Mi.	2Bio 43-44
Davis, Br-Sr.	D-008	62/12/07	missing	
Frisbie, Br.	F-009	62/12/31	missing	
Andrews, J.N.	*A-011	62/11/09	Monterey, Mi.	2Bio 55-58;6MR 98-100;7MR 113; 9MR 315
Munsel, Jarvis	*M-012	62/00/00		
Wheeler, Br.	*W-013	62/01/13	Battle Creek, Mi.	
Lyon, Mary	*L-014	62/01/13	Battle Creek, Mi.	
Ingraham, W.S.	*I-015	62/02/28	Lodi, Wi.	
Ingraham, W.S.	*I-015a	62/02/28	Lodi, Wi.	
Wood, Br.	*W-016	62/00/00		
Russell, Sr.	*R-017	62/12/07	Battle Creek, Mi.	HP 119
Steward, T.M.	*S-018	62/00/00		*1T 311-325*
Marks, Allen	*M-019	62/00/00		
Hull, Sr.	*H-020	62/00/00		6MR 100-101
Friends	*F-021	62/00/00		
King, S.H. and Family	*K-023	62/00/00		
Ross, Alexander	*R-024	62/00/00		1T 359-360

1863

Friends at Home	*W-001	63/06/12	Monterey, Mi.	*20MR 145*
Cornell, Br.	*C-002	63/01/20	Battle Creek, Mi.	5MR 436;11MR 352-353
King, Br-Sr.	*K-003	63/03/02	Battle Creek, Mi.	2Bio 95
Scott, Br-Sr.	*S-005	63/07/06	Battle Creek, Mi.	5MR 296-297;15MR 125
White, Henry/White, J.E./White, W.C.	*W-007	63/11/05	Adams Centre, NY	
Sawyer, Br.	*B-008	63/00/00		3MR 261-262
Cornell, Sr.	*C-010	63/11/28	Topsham, Me.	5MR 386
Children	*W-011	63/10/23	Newport, N.H.	
Friends at Hanover	*H-012	63/02/18	Battle Creek, Mi.	2MCP 632-633;15MR 125-126
Jones, Charles	*J-013	63/06/21	Battle Creek, Mi.	
Ministers in Minnesota	*B-014	63/05/00		5MR 294
Noise, Br-Sr.	*N-015	63/01/24	Battle Creek, Mi.	
Andrews, J.N.	*A-016	63/01/00		
Fish, Emery	*F-017	63/00/00		

1864

Bates, Br-Sr.	*B-001	64/00/00		
Phillips, Br.	*P-004	64/01/12	Battle Creek, Mi.	1T 455
Phillips, Br.	*P-004a	64/01/00	Battle Creek, Mi.	
Phillips, Br.	*P-004b	64/12/23	Battle Creek, Mi.	UL 93;1T 455
Hutchens, Br.	*H-005	64/02/22	Battle Creek, Mi.	2Bio 77;ChL 68-69
Hutchens, Br.	*H-005a	64/02/23	Battle Creek, Mi.	
Lockwood, Br-Sr.	*L-006	64/09/00	Dansville, NY	*5MR 379-384;6MR 346*
Folsom, Br-Sr.	*F-007	64/10/14	Topsham, Me.	
Chase, Maria	*C-008	64/10/14	Topsham, Me.	
Howland, Sr.	*H-009	64/03/20	Battle Creek, Mi.	UL 93;10MR 24-25
Frisbie, Br.	*F-010	64/00/00		

EGW Letters File—Page 5

Mears, Br.	*M-011	64/00/00		
Munsel, Mrs.	*M-012	64/00/00		*TSB 130-132*
Kellogg, Br-Sr. [J.P.]	K-017	64/00/00		5MR 385-386
Kellogg, Br-Sr. [J.P.]	*K-017a	64/00/00		
Folsom, Paul	*F-018	64/00/00		

1865

Hall, Br.	*H-001	65/05/09	Battle Creek, Mi.	
Chase, Maria	*C-002	65/06/12	Wisc.	*DG 120-122*
White, J.E./White, W.C.	*W-003	65/06/13	Monroe, Wi.	5MR 384
White, J.E.	*W-004	65/06/20	Cranes Grove, Il.	4MR 173-177;6MR 298-299
White, J.E./White, W.C./Patten, Adelia/Anna	*W-005	65/09/18	Rochester, NY	5MR 384;10MR 26-27
White, J.E.	*W-005a	65/09/00	To Dansville, NY	
White, J.E./White, W.C./Patten, Adelia	*W-006	65/09/22	Dansville, NY	5MR 385
Children	*W-006a	65/00/00	Dansville, NY	3MR 175
White, J.E.	*W-007	65/10/19	Dansville, NY	4MR 95;5MR 385
White, J.S.	*W-008	65/11/21	Rochester, NY	5MR 385
White, J.S.	*W-009	65/11/22	Rochester, NY	5MR 387;10MR 27
White, J.S.	*W-010	65/11/24	Rochester, NY	5MR 387;10MR 28
Cornell, Angeline	*C-011	65/00/00		
Br. [Re Public Prayer]	B-012	65/06/15	Jaynesville, Wi.	

1866

White, J.E.	*W-002	66/09/12	Olcott, NY	6MR 299
White, J.E.	*W-003	66/09/21	Olcott, NY	*20MR 204*
White, J.E.	*W-004	66/09/22	Olcott, NY	11MR 28
White, W.C.	*W-004a	66/10/00	Kensington, Ct.	
White, J.E.	*W-005	66/10/07	Hubbardsville, NY	*2Bio 155*
White, J.E.	*W-006	66/12/08	Battle Creek, Mi.	2Bio 156
White, J.E.	*W-007	66/12/13	Battle Creek, Mi.	5MR 387-388
White, J.E.	*W-009	66/00/00		
Garget, Sr.	*G-010	66/00/00		
White, J.E.	*W-011	66/00/00		
Andrews, J.N.	*A-012	66/00/00	Battle Creek, Mi.	
White, J.E.	*W-016	66/10/14	Kensington, Ct.	6MR 300;10MR 28-29

1867

White, J.E.	*W-001	67/01/07	Wright, Mi.	
McPherson, Br.	*M-001a	67/01/02	Wright, Mi.	
White, J.E.	*W-002	67/01/29	Wright, Mi.	
Higley, Br.	*H-003	67/01/29	Wright, Mi.	
White, J.E.	*W-004	67/02/13	Greenville, Mi.	
Belden, Stephen/Belden, Sarah	*B-005	67/09/24	Davenport, Ia.	11MR 106
Lay, Br-Sr.	*L-006	67/05/06	Greenville, Mi.	5MR 388-389
Aldrich, Br.	*A-008	67/08/20	Greenbush, Mi.	5MR 389
White, W.C.	*W-009	67/09/19	Johnstown, Wi.	
Sanborn, Br-Sr.	*S-010	67/10/04	Mt. Pleasant, Ia.	*1T 707-710*
White, W.C.	*W-011	67/10/22	Battle Creek, Mi.	3MR 123-124
White, W.C.	*W-012	67/10/31	Topsham, Me.	3MR 125-126
White, W.C.	*W-013	67/11/07	Fairfield, Me.	3MR 126-127;5MR 62
White, J.E.	*W-014	67/11/09	Norridgewock, Me.	5MR 62-63,389
White, J.E./White, W.C.	*W-015	67/11/09	Norridgewock, Me.	3MR 127-128;5MR 390
White, W.C.	*W-016	67/12/10	Topsham, Me.	3MR 50-52
Maynard, Br-Sr.	*M-017	67/11/00		

EGW Letters File—Page 6

Davis, Br.	*D-018	67/12/11	Topsham, Me.	
White, J.E.	*W-019	67/12/14	Topsham, Me.	
Morrell, Br.	*M-020	67/12/28	Enosburg, Vt.	UL 376;5MR 298-299
Children	*W-021	67/12/29	Enosburg, Vt.	HP 362;3MR 128-129;5MR 392
Alchin, Br.	*A-022	67/00/00		*1T 543-549*
Smith, Br./Amadon, Br./Cornell, Br.	*S-023	67/01/06	Battle Creek, Mi.	

1868

Maynard, Br.-Sr.	*M-001	68/10/01	Pilot Grove, Ia.	
White, J.E.	*W-001a	68/01/19	Greenville, Mi.	
White, J.E.	*W-002	68/01/29	Greenville, Mi.	
White, J.E.	*W-003	68/02/11	Greenbush, Mi.	
White, W.C.	*W-004	68/02/17	Tittebewassee, Mi.	2Bio 227-228
White, J.E.	*W-005	68/02/27	Watrousville, Mi.	5MR 392-393
White, J.E.	*W-006	68/03/02	Tuscola, Mi.	2Bio 228-229
White, J.E.	*W-007	68/03/08	Greenville, Mi.	
White, J.E.	*W-008	68/03/09	Greenville, Mi.	2Bio 221-222;11MR 201
Clarke, Br.	*C-009	68/03/22		
White, J.E.	*W-010	68/03/22	Greenville, Mi.	
White, J.E.	*W-011	68/03/30	Greenville, Mi.	2MR 154
White, J.E.	*W-012	68/04/03	Greenville, Mi.	
White, J.E.	*W-015	68/06/17	Greenville, Mi.	3MR 129-130;10MR 30
Taylor, Br.	*T-016	68/06/20	Greenville, Mi.	See 2T 156-161
White, J.E.	*W-017	68/07/27	Greenville, Mi.	*2T 261-268*
King, Seneca	*K-018	68/07/00	Orleans, Mi.	4MR 258
White, J.E.	*W-019	68/08/11	Greenville, Mi.	
White, J.E.	*W-020	68/08/11	Greenville, Mi.	CTr 97
Farnsworth, J.P.	*F-021	68/10/07	Pilot Grove, Ia.	TSB 23-24
Lockwood, Sr.	*L-022	68/10/20	Battle Creek, Mi.	2Bio 251-252
Friends in Burlington	*B-023	68/04/27	Battle Creek, Mi.	9MR 280-281
White, J.E./White, W.C.	*W-024	68/10/00	Adams Center, NY	
Children	*W-025	68/12/02	Richmond, Me.	4MR 38;5MR 63
White, J.E./White, W.C.	*W-026	68/12/16	Rochester, NY	2Bio 253;3MR 48-49
White, J.E./White, W.C.	*W-026a	68/12/16	Rochester, NY	
Smith, Hanna/Smith, Mary	*S-027	68/12/18	Attica, NY	
White, J.E./White, W.C.	*W-028	68/11/04	Albany-Springfield	3MR 175-176;2Bio 252-253
Wicks, Br.-Sr.	*W-029	68/03/17	Greenville, Mi.	
Rogers, Br.-Sr.	*R-030	68/04/06	Greenville, Mi.	*2T 50-55*
Aldrich, J.M.	*A-031	68/00/00		
Smith, Harriet	*S-032	68/03/00		

1869

Stickney, Br.-Sr.	*S-001	69/03/22	Battle Creek, Mi.	*2T 431-436*
White, J.E.	*W-002	69/04/29	Greenville, Mi.	
Smith, Br./Amadon, Br.	*S-003	69/04/23	Greenville, Mi.	5MR 164-168;2Bio 267-268
White, J.E.	*W-004	69/04/28	Greenville, Mi.	
White, J.E.	*W-005	69/05/25	Battle Creek, Mi.	14MR 312-314
White, J.E.	*W-006	69/06/10	Battle Creek, Mi.	5MR 393-394
White, J.E./McDearmon, Emma	*W-007	69/06/27	Wright, Mi.	TSB 17;7MR 241-242
White, J.E.	*W-008	69/07/06	Greenville, Mi.	3MR 295-296;9MR 383
Amadon, Br.-Sr.	*A-009	69/07/07	Greenville, Mi.	
Loughborough, J.N.	*L-010	69/08/15	Greenville, Mi.	
Lockwood, Sr.	*L-011	69/09/01	S. Lancaster, Ma.	
Children	*W-012	69/09/00	Ma.	2Bio 276
Smith, Harriett/Cornelia/Amadon, Martha	*S-013	69/09/24	Chicago, Il.	6MR 114-115

White, J.E.	*W-014	69/06/17	Orange, Mi.	
Fargo, Br-Sr.	*F-015	69/00/00		See 2T 327-334
White, J.E.	*W-016	69/12/11	Battle Creek, Mi.	
Russell, William	R-017	69/03/00	Battle Creek, Mi.	*From PH107 2-7*

1870

King, Br.	*K-001	70/02/19	Battle Creek, Mi.	11MR 201
Chase, Mary	*C-002	70/03/02	Battle Creek, Mi.	OHC 312
Shields, Br.	*S-003	70/03/15	Battle Creek, Mi.	
Rhodes, S.W.	*R-004	70/03/23	Battle Creek, Mi.	TSB 28-31
Sister	*S-005	70/04/03	Battle Creek, Mi.	2Bio 302-304
Waggoner, Br.	*W-006	70/04/08	Battle Creek, Mi.	
White, J.E.	*W-008	70/05/17	Battle Creek, Mi.	
McDearmon, Emma	*M-009	70/06/09	Marion, Ia.	2Bio 290-292
Dayton, Sr.	*D-010	70/08/05	Oneida, NY	UL 231
Howard, Br.	*H-011	70/09/05	Skowhegan, Me.	
White, W.C.	*W-012	70/09/06	Fairfield, Me.	11MR 108
White, W.C.	*W-013	70/09/23	Clyde, Oh.	2Bio 293-294
White, W.C.	*W-014	70/09/27	Clyde, Oh.	3MR 130-131
White, W.C.	*W-015	70/10/06	La Cross, In.	
White, W.C.	*W-016	70/10/17	Pleasanton, Ks.	
White, J.E./White, Emma	*W-016a	70/10/17	Pleasanton, Ks.	6MR 301,315
White, W.C.	*W-017	70/10/24	Hamilton, Mo.	VSS 398-399;2Bio 294
White, J.E./White, Emma	*W-018	70/11/09	Battle Creek, Mi.	2Bio 294;3MR 296;9MR 383
White, J.E./White, Emma	*W-019	70/11/27	Battle Creek, Mi.	4MR 38-39
Cousin Reed	*R-020	70/00/00	Battle Creek, Mi.	
Children	*W-021	70/12/02	Battle Creek, Mi.	
White, J.E./White, Emma	*W-022	70/12/16	Battle Creek, Mi.	3MR 296-297
Rogers, Br-Sr.	*R-023	70/11/25	Battle Creek, Mi.	OHC 318
White, J.E./White, Emma	*W-024	70/09/00	Clyde, Oh.	*20MR 331-334*
Lay, Br-Sr.	*L-030	70/02/13	Battle Creek, Mi.	5MR 394-397
Sister	*S-031	70/00/00		*20MR 12-13*
White, W.C./Hall, Lucinda	*H-032	70/09/05	Skowhegan, Me.	
Hall, Lucinda	*H-033	70/04/07	Battle Creek, Mi.	

1871

Bailey, Br-Sr.	*B-001	71/01/03	Battle Creek, Mi.	*DG 208-210*
Children	*W-002	71/01/30	Greenville, Mi.	10MR 29
Children	*W-003	71/02/22	Battle Creek, Mi.	10MR 30-31
Alexander	*A-004	71/03/16	Battle Creek, Mi.	
White, J.E./White, Emma	*W-005	71/03/23	Greenville, Mi.	
White, J.E.	*W-006	71/04/02	Battle Creek, Mi.	
White, J.E.	*W-008	71/05/06	Battle Creek, Mi.	
White, J.E.	*W-009	71/05/24		
White, J.E.	*W-010	71/06/08	Washington, Ia.	
White, J.E./White, Emma	*W-011	71/06/16	La Porte City, Ia.	
White, John	*W-011a	71/06/29	Medford, Mn.	
White, W.C.	*W-011b	71/06/29	Medford, Mn.	
White, J.S.	*W-012	71/08/27	Amherst, Ma.	
White, J.S.	*W-013	71/09/02	Skowhegan, Me.	ChL 20;13MR 32
White, J.E.	*W-014	71/10/26	Potterville, Mi.	
White, J.E./White, Emma	*W-015	71/11/15	S. Boston, Ma.	5MR 397
White, J.E./White, Emma	*W-015a	71/11/15	S. Boston, Ma.	TDG 328;5MR 397
White, W.C.	*W-016	71/11/03	S. Lancaster, Ma.	
White, W.C.	*W-017	71/11/10	S. Boston, Ma.	

EGW Letters File—Page 8

White, W.C.	*W-018	71/11/18	S. Boston, Ma.	
White, W.C.	*W-020	71/11/23	Portland, Me.	
White, J.E./White, Emma	*W-021	71/11/29	Skowhegan, Me.	
White, J.E.	*W-021a	71/00/00	fragment	10MR 386
Kellogg, H.W.	*K-022	71/12/27	Battle Creek, Mi.	
Cornell, M.E.	*C-023	71/12/27	Battle Creek, Mi.	TSB 166-168
Wells, Sr.	*W-025	71/07/00	Battle Creek, Mi.	
White, W.C.	*W-026	71/11/25	Richmond, Me.	
White, J.E./White, Emma	*W-027	71/06/02	Ashland Crossing, Ia	*19MR 189-193*
Friends at Home	*W-028	71/06/02	Ashland Crssing, Ia	5MR 429
Hall, Lucinda	*H-029	71/06/17	La Porte, Ia.	
Francisco, Br.	F-030	71/12/10		*From PH159 94-97*

1872

Maynard, Sr.	*M-001	72/06/23	Washington, Ia.	2SM 302;2Bio 341
Lay, Br.	*L-001a	72/01/11	Battle Creek, Mi.	OHC 93;5MR 294-295;CTr 212
Bates, Br.	*B-002	72/02/12	Grand Rapids, Mi.	*RY 126-127*
White, J.E.	*W-002a	72/01/14	Battle Creek, Mi.	
Waggoner, J.H.	*W-003	72/02/01	Battle Creek, Mi.	
Ball, W.H.	*B-004	72/04/11	Battle Creek, Mi.	
White, J.E./White, Emma	*W-005	72/06/19	Washington, Ia.	2Bio 340
White, W.C.	*W-005a	72/05/15	Battle Creek, Mi.	
White, W.C.	*W-006	72/05/20	Washington, Ia.	2Bio 339
White, W.C.	*W-007	72/05/22	Washington, Ia.	*19MR 194*
Curtis, Mary	*C-008	72/06/02	Aledo, Ill.	
White, J.E./White, Emma	*W-009	72/07/05	Ottawa, Kan.	
White, J.E./White, Emma	*W-010	72/07/04	Ottawa, Kan.	9MR 80;15MR 129
White, J.E./White, Emma	*W-011	72/07/23	Denver, Co.	
White, J.E./White, Emma	*W-012	72/07/31	Central City, Co.	UL 226;7MR 214;8MR 120-121; 11MR 115-117
White, J.E./White, Emma	*W-013	72/08/18	Livingston, Co.	
White, J.E./White, Emma	*W-013a	72/08/22	Walling's Mills, Co.	2Bio 349
White, J.E./White, Emma	*W-014	72/09/07		3MR 159;5MR 397-398
White, W.C.	*W-015	72/09/30	Santa Rosa, Ca.	
White, J.E./White, Emma	*W-016	72/09/27	San Francisco, Ca.	OHC 242;2Bio 356-357
White, J.E.	*W-017	72/09/28	Santa Rosa, Ca.	TDG 280;2Bio 357
White, J.E./White, Emma	*W-018	72/10/10	San Francisco, Ca.	2Bio 359-361
White, J.E./White, Emma	*W-019	72/10/25	Woodland, Ca.	5MR 398
White, J.E./White, W.C.	*W-020	72/12/07	San Francisco, Ca.	*21MR 239-240*
White, J.E./White, W.C.	*W-021	72/12/13	San Francisco, Ca.	
Diggings, Br.	*D-022	72/12/18	San Francisco, Ca.	2Bio 369-370
White, J.E./White, W.C.	*W-023	72/12/24	Bloomfield, Ca.	
White, J.E./White, Emma	*W-025	72/08/05	Walling's Mills, Co.	2Bio 342
White, J.E./White, Emma	W-026	72/09/23	Denver to Calif.	*11MR 117-119*
Burton, Br.	*B-027	72/11/22	San Francisco, Ca.	1MCP 157-158,275;2MCP 381,394;HP 193; TDG 335
Ball, W.H.	*B-028	72/02/27	Battle Creek, Mi.	
Cornell, M.E.	*C-029	72/10/00		See 3T 227-243
Cornell, M.E.	*C-029a	72/10/00	Co.	See 3T 227-243
White, J.E./White, Emma	*W-030	72/08/00		2Bio 342-344
Andrews, J.N.	*A-031	72/00/00		*13MR 341-347*
White, J.E.	*W-032	72/10/23	Woodland, Ca.	

1873

Canright, Br.-Sr.	*C-001	73/11/12	Battle Creek, Mi.	*15MR 231-249*

EGW Letters File—Page 9

Children	*W-001a	73/01/02	Santa Rosa, Ca.	
Children	*W-001b	73/01/07	Santa Rosa, Ca.	2MCP 782;OHC 25;TMK 304
Church in Monterey	*B-002	73/01/00		1MCP 229
Harmon, John	*H-002a	73/01/21	Santa Rosa, Ca.	
White, J.E.	*W-003	73/01/21	Santa Rosa, Ca.	
White, W.C.	*W-004	73/01/25	San Francisco, Ca.	
Chittenden, Br-Sr.	*C-005	73/02/05	Santa Rosa, Ca.	
Children	*W-006	73/02/06	Santa Rosa, Ca.	5MR 399-400
Children	*W-007	73/02/13	Bloomfield, Ca.	3SM 79;2Bio 371
Diggings, Br-Sr.	*D-008	73/03/29	Battle Creek, Mi.	OHC 17,22,33,34,196;CTr 90
Billet, Sr.	*B-009	73/04/05	Battle Creek, Mi.	DG 230-233;OHC 149,186
Smith, Br.	*S-010	73/05/14	Potterville, Mi.	5MR 313
White, J.E.	*W-011	73/08/09	Black Hawk, Co.	
White, J.E./White, Emma	*W-012	73/08/09	Black Hawk, Co.	TDG 230
White, J.E./White, Emma	*W-013	73/09/28	Grand Lake, Co.	3MR 166-167
White, W.C.	*W-013a	73/10/22	Black Hawk, Co.	
White, W.C.	*W-013h	73/10/14	Black Hawk, Co.	
White, J.E.	*W-014	73/10/28	Black Hawk, Co.	
White, J.E.	*W-015	73/11/22	Battle Creek, Mi.	
Cramer, Br-Sr.	*C-016	73/11/25	Battle Creek, Mi.	
Children	*W-017	73/11/17	Battle Creek, Mi.	
White, J.E./White, Emma	*W-018	73/12/27	Ogden-Sacramento	*11MR 125-127*
White, J.E./White, Emma	*W-019	73/12/27	Ogden-Sacramento	*11MR 127-129*
White, J.E./White, Emma	*W-020	73/12/27	Ogden-Sacramento	*10MR 377-378*
White, W.C.	*W-021	73/12/30	Santa Rosa, Ca.	
White, J.E./White, Emma	*W-023	73/12/24	Omaha, Ne.	TDG 367;OHC 44;11MR 125
White, J.E./White, Emma	*W-024	73/03/00		11MR 121-122
Woolsey, Br.	*W-025	73/00/00		
Ferguson, Br.	*F-026	73/02/17	Bloomfield, Ca.	
Hall, Lucinda	*H-027	73/11/27	Battle Creek, Mi.	5MR 430-431
Hall, Lucinda	*H-028	73/12/17	Battle Creek, Mi.	5MR 428-429
Hall, Lucinda	*H-029	73/12/19	Chicago, Il.	
Stockton, Br-Sr.	*S-030	73/03/28	Battle Creek, Mi.	*6MR 344-345*

1874

White, J.S.	W-001	74/06/03	Sacramento, Ca.	
Loughborough, J.N.	*L-002	74/08/24	Battle Creek, Mi.	*8MR 228-243*
Children	*W-002a	74/02/00	Santa Rosa, Ca.	
White, W.C.	*W-002b	74/01/11	Santa Rosa, Ca.	*11MR 357-359*
Loughborough, J.N.	*L-002c	74/08/24	Battle Creek, Mi.	
Temple, Sr.	T-003	74/07/06	Battle Creek, Mi.	
White, W.C.	*W-003a	74/01/12	Santa Rosa, Ca.	
White, W.C.	*W-004	74/01/13	Santa Rosa, Ca.	2Bio 402
White, W.C.	*W-005	74/01/23	Santa Rosa, Ca.	2Bio 402,405
White, J.E./White, Emma	*W-006	74/01/27	Santa Rosa, Ca.	
White, W.C.	*W-007	74/01/27	Santa Rosa, Ca.	2Bio 405
White, J.E./White, Emma	*W-008	74/02/07	Santa Rosa, Ca.	2Bio 404-405
White, W.C.	*W-009	74/02/07	Santa Rosa, Ca.	2Bio 404-405
White, W.C.	*W-010	74/02/10	Santa Rosa, Ca.	2Bio 403-404
Littlejohn, W.H.	*L-010a	74/02/24	Santa Rosa, Ca.	
Smith, Br-Sr.	*S-011	74/02/15	Santa Rosa, Ca.	
White, W.C.	*W-012	74/02/15	Santa Rosa, Ca.	*14MR 322-323*
White, W.C.	*W-013	74/02/16	Santa Rosa, Ca.	
Salie, Br.	*S-014	74/02/17	Santa Rosa-S.F., Ca	
White, W.C.	*W-016	74/02/24	Santa Rosa, Ca.	2Bio 407;4MR 237-238
White, W.C.	*W-017	74/03/20	Santa Rosa, Ca.	2Bio 406-407

White, W.C.	*W-018	74/03/25	Napa, Ca.	
White, W.C.	*W-018a	74/03/00	Napa, Ca.	
White, J.E./White, Emma	*W-019a	74/04/28	Santa Rosa, Ca.	
White, J.E./White, Emma	*W-019b	74/04/27	Bloomfield, Ca.	2Bio 411-412;5MR 313-315
White, W.C.	*W-019c	74/04/20	San Francisco, Ca.	UL 124;4MR 340-341
White, W.C.	*W-019d	74/02/24	Santa Rosa, Ca.	
White, W.C.	*W-019e	74/04/22	Cloverdale, Ca.	
White, J.E./White, Emma	*W-019f	74/05/06	Oakland, Ca.	2Bio 413
White, W.C.	*W-019g	74/05/11	Oakland, Ca.	
White, W.C.?	*W-019h	74/05/19	Oakland, Ca.	
White, W.C.	*W-021	74/04/22	Santa Rosa, Ca.	
White, W.C.?	*W-022	74/04/28	Santa Rosa, Ca.	2Bio 412
White, W.C./White, J.E.	*W-023	74/04/00	Bloomfield, Ca.	2Bio 410-411
Children	*W-024	74/05/05	Santa Rosa, Ca.	UL 139
Smith, Br-Sr.	*S-025	74/05/06	Oakland, Ca.	2Bio 413-414;5MR 315
White, W.C.	*W-026	74/05/11	Oakland, Ca.	2Bio 412-415
White, W.C.	*W-027	74/05/15	Oakland, Ca.	2Bio 430;5MR 315-316
Littlejohn, Br.	*L-028	74/05/23	Oakland, Ca.	2Bio 415-417
White, J.E./White, Emma	*W-029	74/05/23	Oakland, Ca.	2Bio 418
Children	*W-030	74/05/26	Oakland, Ca.	*19MR 185-188*
White, J.S.	*W-032	74/06/15	Sheridan, Il.	
White, J.S.	*W-033	74/06/20	Lodi, Wi.	
White, J.S.	*W-034	74/06/21	Lodi, Wi.	2Bio 421,430-431
White, J.S.	*W-035	74/06/22	Lodi, Wi.	
White, J.S.	*W-036	74/06/26	Medford, Mn.	
White, J.S.	*W-037	74/06/29	Medford, Mn.	UL 194;
White, J.S.	*W-038	74/07/02	Washington, Ia.	2Bio 432-434
Temple, Sr.	*T-039	74/07/06	Battle Creek, Mi.	
White, J.S.	*W-040	74/07/08	Battle Creek, Mi.	2Bio 435-437;9MR 319
White, J.S.	*W-040a	74/07/10	Battle Creek, Mi.	2Bio 437-438;10MR 69-70
White, J.S.	*W-041	74/07/11	Battle Creek, Mi.	*19MR 366-369*
Abbey, Br-Sr.	*A-041a	74/07/11	Battle Creek, Mi.	OHC 227
White, J.S.	*W-042	74/07/13	Battle Creek, Mi.	2Bio 441
White, J.S.	*W-043	74/07/15	Battle Creek, Mi.	2Bio 422-423,441
White, J.S.	*W-044	74/07/17	Battle Creek, Mi.	2Bio 441;5MR 427;6MR 302;10MR 31
Abbey, Br./Doctors	*A-045	74/07/18	Battle Creek, Mi.	7MR 347
White, J.E./White, Emma	*W-046	74/07/22	Battle Creek, Mi.	
White, J.E./White, Emma	*W-046a	74/08/05	Battle Creek, Mi.	
White, J.S.	*W-047	74/07/23	Battle Creek, Mi.	2Bio 442;6MR 302;10MR 31
White, J.E./White, Emma	*W-047a	74/08/21	Battle Creek, Mi.	OHC 266;7MR 347
White, J.S.	*W-049	74/08/28	Lancaster, Ma.	2Bio 450;6MR 302
White, J.S.	*W-049a	74/09/01	Saco Depot, Me.	
Children	*W-050	74/09/02	Gorham, Me.	
Walling, Addie/Walling, May	*W-050a	74/09/00		
White, J.E./White, Emma	*W-050b	74/09/00		2Bio 450
White, J.S.	*W-051	74/09/10	Kirkville, NY	2Bio 450;5MR 437;6MR 302-303; 10MR 31-32
White, J.E./White, Emma	*W-051a	74/09/11	Kirkville, NY	3MR 427-428;11MR 30
White, J.E./White, Emma	*W-052	74/09/25	Kokomo, In.	TDG 277
Children	*W-052a	74/09/25	Kokomo, In.	
Ball, Br.	*B-053	74/10/10	Battle Creek, Mi.	
Lee, Charles	*L-054	74/10/24	Battle Creek, Mi.	*3T 414-434*
Butler, G.I.	*B-055	74/10/28	Battle Creek, Mi.	*7MR 36-42*
White, J.E.	*W-056	74/10/28	Battle Creek, Mi.	TDG 310
White, J.E.	*W-057	74/10/28	Battle Creek, Mi.	
Littlejohn, Br.	*L-058	74/11/04	Battle Creek, Mi.	
White, J.E./White, Emma	*W-059	74/11/06	Battle Creek, Mi.	

White, J.E.	*W-060	74/11/10	Battle Creek, Mi.	
Littlejohn, Br.	*L-061	74/11/11	Battle Creek, Mi.	2Bio 430,464-465;4MR 37;5MR 400
Bangs, Lizzie	*B-062	74/11/19	Battle Creek, Mi.	
Children	*W-063	74/11/16	Battle Creek, Mi.	2Bio 454-455
Steward, Sr.	*S-063a	74/11/16	Battle Creek, Mi.	
Brn-Srs in Allegan and Monterey	*B-064	74/12/24	Battle Creek, Mi.	
Abbey, Br-Sr.	*A-065	74/07/00		
White, J.E.	*W-066	74/00/00		
White, W.C.	*W-067	74/04/00	Cloverdale, Ca.	2Bio 409;11MR 129-130
White, J.S.	*W-068	74/07/08	Battle Creek, Mi.	2Bio 421-422
Hall, Lucinda	*H-069	74/09/25	Kokomo, In.	DG 233-234;5MR 431
Hall, Lucinda	*H-070	74/10/08	Battle Creek, Mi.	5MR 427
Hall, Lucinda	*H-071	74/10/14	Battle Creek, Mi.	5MR 427-428;10MR 32
Hall, Lucinda	*H-071a	74/10/14	Battle Creek, Mi.	
Hall, Lucinda	*H-072	74/10/20	Battle Creek, Mi.	
Hall, Lucinda	*H-073	74/11/01	Battle Creek, Mi.	
Hall, Lucinda	*H-074	74/11/03	Battle Creek, Mi.	
Hall, Lucinda	*H-075	74/11/09	Battle Creek, Mi	
Hall, Lucinda	*H-076	74/11/23	Battle Creek, Mi.	5MR 430
Hall, Lucinda	*H-077	74/11/30	Battle Creek, Mi.	
Hall, Lucinda	*H-078	74/12/02	Battle Creek, Mi.	5MR 429
Hall, Lucinda	*H-079	74/12/14	Battle Creek, Mi.	5MR 430;10MR 32-33
Walling, Mr.	W-080	74/07/24	Battle Creek, Mi.	

1875

Haskell, S.N.	B-001	75/10/12	Oakland, Ca.	CW 140-141;Ev 129,159,194-195,216 236-237,329,514-515;TSB 120;4MR 108
White, W.C.	*W-002	75/01/28	Chicago, Il.	11MR 131
Smith, Br-Sr.	*S-003	75/11/12	San Francisco, Ca.	
Belden, F.E.	*B-004	75/01/31	To Ogden, Ut.	4MR 190-192
White, W.C./Hall, Lucinda	*W-005	75/01/29	To Omaha, Ne.	
White, W.C.	*W-005a	75/01/31?	To Oakland, Ca.	11MR 131-132
White, W.C.	*W-006	75/02/10	Oakland, Ca.	
Abbey, Br-Sr.	*A-007	75/02/23	Oakland, Ca.	
White, W.C.	*W-008	75/02/00	Oakland, Ca.	
White, W.C.	*W-009	75/02/01	Elko, Nv.	
Hall, Lucinda	*H-010	75/02/00	To Ca.	
White, J.S.	*W-011	75/03/27	Oakland, Ca.	
White, W.C.?	*W-011a	75/05/03	to Sydney, Ne.	3MR 131
White, W.C.	*W-012	75/05/10	Battle Creek, Mi.	
Hall, Sr.	*H-014	75/05/26	Chicago, Il.	
White, W.C./White, J.E.	*W-015	75/05/04	To Chicago, Il.	7MR 339-340;11MR 132
Butler, G.I.	*B-016	75/06/06	Newton, Ia.	TDG 166;2Bio 442;5MR 232
White, W.C.	*W-018	75/06/08	Newton, Ia.	
Cook, Mr.	*C-019	75/06/14	Sheridan, Il.	8MR 214
White, J.E./White, Emma	*W-019a	75/06/24	Sparta, Wi.	3MR 177-178;4MR 181-186;11MR 132-133
White, W.C./Mary	*W-020	75/06/27	to Wyoming, Mn.	5MR 232-233
White, W.C./Mary	*W-021	75/06/27	to Wyoming, Mn.	
White, W.C.	*W-021a	75/06/27	Eagle Lake, Mn.	11MR 134
White, W.C.	*W-022	75/06/30	Eagle Lake, Mn.	4MR 205-207
White, J.E./White, Emma	*W-023	75/07/13	Battle Creek, Mi.	UL 208;2Bio 475
White, W.C.	*W-024	75/07/13	Battle Creek, Mi.	2Bio 475-476
White, W.C.	*W-025	75/07/20	Battle Creek, Mi.	2Bio 475-477
White, W.C.	*W-026	75/07/22	Goguac Lake, Mi.	
White, W.C.	*W-027	75/07/26	Battle Creek, Mi.	
White, W.C.	*W-029	75/08/08	Battle Creek, Mi.	

Mary	*M-030	75/08/22	Essex Junction, Vt.	LYL 53-55;TDG 243
White, W.C.	*W-031	75/09/03	Richmond, Me.	10MR 280-281
White, J.E./White, Emma	*W-032	75/09/10?		
Children	*W-033	75/09/22	To Sacramento, Ca.	11MR 134-135
Haskell, S.N.	*H-034	75/10/12	Oakland, Ca.	LDE 22;8MR 215
Nichols, Br.	*N-035	75/10/22	Oakland, Ca.	2Bio 479
Ross, Br.	*R-036	75/11/10	Oakland, Ca.	UL 328
White, J.E.	*W-038	75/12/30	Oakland, Ca.	
Abbey, Br.	*A-039	75/00/00		
White, W.C./White, J.E.	*W-040	75/05/00	Battle Creek, Mi.	
Johnson, Br-Sr.	*J-041	75/05/20	Battle Creek, Mi.	
Johnson, Sr.	*J-042	75/07/04	Sparta	TDG 194
White, W.C.?	*W-043	75/00/00	fragment	HP 9
Hall, Lucinda/Rasmussan, Anna	*H-044	75/05/16	Battle Creek, Mi.	*13MR 400-404*
Hall, Lucinda	*H-045	75/06/05	Newton, Ia.	
Hall, Lucinda	*H-046	75/06/17	MacConnell' Grove	10MR 33
Hall, Lucinda	*H-047	75/07/07	Battle Creek, Mi.	
Hall, Lucinda	*H-048	75/07/14	Battle Creek, Mi.	10MR 33
Butler, G.I./re Bourdeau, Br-Sr.	*B-049	75/00/00	Battle Creek, Mi.	*19MR 5-15*

1876

White, J.S.	*W-001	76/03/31	Oakland, Ca.	3Bio 23-24;8MR 29-30
White, J.S.	*W-001a	76/03/24	Oakland, Ca.	3Bio 23;8MR 76
White, J.S.	*W-002	76/04/00	Oakland, Ca.	
White, J.S.	*W-003	76/04/04	Oakland, Ca.	7MR 279,281;8MR 76;9MR 28-29; 11MR 201-202
White, J.S.	*W-004	76/04/07	Oakland, Ca.	7MR 277-278;9MR 29
White, J.S.	*W-004a	76/04/08		3SM 104;7MR 279-280
White, J.S.	*W-005	76/04/11	Oakland, Ca.	TDG 110;3Bio 26-27;7MR 280-281; CTr 242
White, J.S.	*W-006	76/04/13	Oakland, Ca.	3Bio 27-28;7MR 278;10MR 33-34
White, J.S.	*W-007	76/04/14	Oakland, Ca.	3SM 105;3Bio 28;7MR 278
White, J.S.	*W-008	76/04/16	to Brooklyn, Ca.	3SM 105;3Bio 28-29;5MR 194;7MR 284
White, J.S.	*W-009	76/04/18	Oakland, Ca.	3SM 105-106;3Bio 28-29;9MR 31
White, J.S.	*W-010	76/04/19	Oakland, Ca.	
White, J.S.	*W-011	76/04/20	Oakland, Ca.	2Bio 443;7MR 230,280;9MR 31-32
White, J.S.	*W-012	76/04/21	Oakland, Ca.	3SM 106;8MR 77
White, J.S.	*W-013	76/04/24	Oakland, Ca.	*14MR 335-338*
White, J.S.	*W-014	76/04/25	Oakland, Ca.	3SM 107;7MR 283-284
White, J.S.	*W-015	76/04/27	Oakland, Ca.	8MR 77;9MR 33
White, J.S.	*W-016	76/04/28	Oakland, Ca.	
White, J.S.	*W-016a	76/04/28	Oakland, Ca.	9MR 34
White, J.S.	*W-017	76/04/31	Oakland, Ca.	8MR 77
White, J.S.	*W-018	76/04/00	Oakland, Ca.	7MR 279;9MR 34
Children	*W-019	76/06/02	Holden	
White, J.S.	*W-020	76/05/01	Oakland, Ca.	TDG 130
White, J.S.	*W-021	76/05/05	Oakland, Ca.	3SM 107;3Bio 31;8MR 77;8MR 124
White, J.S.	*W-022	76/05/06	Oakland, Ca.	7MR 276,280;8MR 124-125
White, J.S.	*W-023	76/05/10	Oakland, Ca.	6MR 303
White, J.S.	*W-024	76/05/11	Oakland, Ca.	9MR 35
White, J.S.	*W-025	76/05/12	Oakland, Ca.	3Bio 34
White, J.S.	*W-025a	76/05/12	Oakland, Ca.	
White, J.S.	*W-026	76/05/14	Oakland, Ca.	3Bio 35
White, J.S.	*W-027	76/05/16	Oakland, Ca.	*20MR 24-34*
White, Mary	*W-027a	76/05/22	to Ks.	9MR 35

Children	*W-028	76/05/23	Ogden, Ut.
Children	*W-028a	76/05/24	Laramie Plains	*14MR 315-317*
White, W.C./White, Mary	*W-029	76/05/25	Kansas City	7MR 282-283;11MR 136-137
White, W.C./White, Mary	*W-030	76/05/28	Melvern, Ks.	3Bio 37-38
White, J.E.	*W-030a	75/12/00?	in 76	
White, J.E./White, Emma	*W-031	76/06/07	to Council Bluffs	3Bio 38
White, W.C.	*W-031a	76/06/07	to Council Bluffs	*11MR 137-138*
White, J.E./White, Emma	*W-032	76/06/14	to Dubuque, Ia.	TDG 174;7MR 285-286
Children	*W-033	76/07/07	Battle Creek, Mi.	3Bio 42
White, W.C./White, Mary	*W-034	76/07/11	Battle Creek, Mi.	3Bio 41-42;7MR 287
Children	*W-035	76/07/30	Wilmington, De.	UL 225;3Bio 43;7MR 287
White, J.E./White, Emma	*W-036	76/08/10	Columbus, Oh.	
White, W.C./White, Mary	*W-037	76/08/15	to Rome, NY	
White, W.C./White, Mary	*W-038	76/08/16	Rome, NY	
White, W.C.	*W-039	76/08/17	Milton, Vt.	10MR 34
White, W.C.	*W-040	76/08/22	Milton, Vt.	
White, W.C./White, Mary	*W-041	76/08/24	Groveland, Ma.	6MR 303-304
White, J.E./White, Emma	*W-042	76/08/30	Gorham, Me.	3Bio 46
White, W.C./White, Mary	*W-044	76/09/02	Richmond, Me.	7MR 288
White, W.C./White, Mary	*W-045	76/10/19	Battle Creek, Mi.	9MR 35-36
Children	*W-046	76/10/26	Battle Creek, Mi.	3SM 108;3Bio 48-50,53-54
White, W.C./White, Mary	*W-047	76/07/00	Auburn, Me.	
Van Horn, Br-Sr.	*V-048	76/00/00		*DG 138-140*
White, J.S.	*W-049	76/00/00		PM 103-104;6MR 303
White, J.S.?	*W-050	76/00/00	Oakland, Ca.	
White, J.E.	*W-051	76/01/00		
Cornell, M.E.	*C-052	76/00/00		TSB 168-171;3SM 53
Cornell, M.E.	*C-053	76/00/00		TSB 171-172
Cornell, M.E.	*C-054	76/00/00		
Cornell, M.E.	*C-055	76/00/00		
Bangs, Elizabeth	*C-057	76/00/00		
Hall, Lucinda	*H-058	76/04/06	Oakland, Ca.	10MR 35-36
Hall, Lucinda	*H-059	76/04/08	Oakland, Ca.	5MR 431-432;9MR 29-30
Hall, Lucinda	*H-060	76/04/20	Oakland, Ca.	
Hall, Lucinda	*H-061	76/04/27	Oakland, Ca.	5MR 432;7MR 282;
Hall, Lucinda	*H-062	76/09/29		
White, J.S.	*H-063	76/03/25	Oakland, Ca.	3SM 103;10MR 34-35
Hall, Lucinda	*H-064	76/05/10	Oakland, Ca.	*DG 266-268*
Hall, Lucinda	*H-065	76/05/12	Oakland, Ca.	*DG 268*
Hall, Lucinda	*H-066	76/05/16	Oakland, Ca.	*DG 268-270*
Hall, Lucinda	*H-067	76/05/17	Oakland, Ca.	*DG 271-272*

1877

Br-Sr.	B-001	77/12/17	Oakland, Ca.	AH 353-356,359;CG 544;6MR 40-41,47-49
Children	*W-002	77/05/17	Battle Creek, Mi.	3Bio 65
White, J.E.	*W-003	77/05/12		UL 146;OHC 224
White, J.E./White, Emma	*W-004	77/06/05	Battle Creek, Mi.	CS 257
Chittenden, Charles	*C-005	77/05/09	Oakland, Ca.	TDG 138;1BC 1094-1095;2SM 329-330; CTr 85
Children	*W-005a	77/06/09	Battle Creek, Mi.	
Clough, Mary	*C-006	77/11/03	Oakland, Ca.	MRmnt 119
White, J.E.	*W-006a	77/06/20	Battle Creek, Mi.	
White, J.E./White, Emma	*W-007	77/07/22	Battle Creek, Mi.	TDG 212;3Bio 66
White, J.S.	*W-008	77/08/10	Michigan City, Mi.	
White, J.E./White, Emma	*W-009	77/08/21	Battle Creek, Mi.	
Clough, Mary	*C-010	77/08/29	S. Lancaster, Ma.	

White, J.E./White, Emma	*W-010a	77/08/30	S. Lancaster, Ma.	
Children	*W-011	77/08/31	S. Lancaster, Ma.	5MR 241-242;10MR 36
White, W.C./White, Mary	*W-012	77/08/31	S. Lancaster, Ma.	
White, W.C./White, Mary	*W-013	77/09/03	Ashley, Ma.	2Bio 445
White, W.C./White, Mary	*W-014	77/09/05	Cornish, NH	
Children	*W-015	77/09/06		
White, J.E./White, Emma	*W-016	77/09/07	Morrisville, Vt.	6MR 304;10MR 36
Children	*W-017	77/09/10	Morrisville, Vt.	*11MR 106-107*
White, W.C./White, Mary	*W-018	77/09/11	Carthage	
White, J.E./White, Emma	*W-019	77/09/28	Battle Creek, Mi.	10MR 36-37
Children	*W-020	77/10/10	to Omaha, Ne.	
Children	*W-021	77/10/11	past Sidney, Ne.	11MR 138
Children	*W-022	77/10/12	to Ca.	*11MR 139-140*
Children	*W-023	77/10/13	Carlin, Nv.	*11MR 140*
Children	*W-024	77/10/14	Oakland, Ca.	
Children	*W-025	77/10/16	Oakland, Ca.	3Bio 73
Children	*W-026	77/10/18	Oakland, Ca.	3Bio 74
White, Mary	*W-027	77/10/21	Oakland, Ca.	3Bio 74
Chase, Mary	*W-028	77/10/26	Healdsburg, Ca.	3Bio 73
White, W.C./White, Mary	*W-029	77/10/26	Healdsburg, Ca.	3Bio 75
Walling, Addie/Walling, May	*W-030	77/10/27	Healdsburg, Ca.	
White, Mary	*W-031	77/11/01	Oakland, Ca.	
White, W.C./White, Mary	*W-032	77/11/03	Oakland, Ca.	
White, Mary	*W-033	77/11/04		
White, W.C./White, Mary	*W-034	77/11/04	Oakland, Ca.	
Clough, Caroline	*C-035	77/11/06	Oakland, Ca.	TDG 319
Clough, Caroline	*C-035a	77/11/06	Fragment	CTr 317-318
Clough, Caroline	*C-035b	77/11/06	Fragment	CTr 77-78
Clough, Mary	*C-036	77/11/10	Oakland, Ca.	4MR 228-233
Children	*W-037	77/11/11	Oakland, Ca.	
White, W.C./White, Mary	*W-038	77/11/16	Oakland, Ca.	
White, W.C./White, Mary	*W-039	77/11/27	Healdsburg, Ca.	3Bio 76-77
White, W.C./White, Mary	*W-040	77/12/05	St. Helena, Ca.	3Bio 78-79
Belden, F.E.	*B-041	77/12/07	St. Helena, Ca.	2SM 330;OHC 80,193;FLB 26;TDG 350
Children	*W-042	77/12/19	Healdsburg, Ca.	3Bio 79
White, W.C./White, Mary	*W-043	77/12/25	Healdsburg, Ca.	3Bio 79-81
White, J.E./White, Emma	*W-045	77/06/01	Battle Creek, Mi.	3Bio 62
Hall, Sr.	*H-046	77/12/06	St. Helena, Ca.	
Hall, Lucinda	*H-047	77/00/00		*10MR 37-38*

1878

White, J.S./Children	*W-001	78/08/24	Battle Creek, Mi.	9MR 317-318
Brn. in Switzerland	B-002	78/08/29	Ballardvale, Ma.	TDG 249
Brn. in Switzerland	B-002a	78/08/29	Ballardvale, Ma.	*16MR 316-327*
Olmstead, Br.	O-003	78/11/24	Plano, Tx.	PM 279-280;1MCP 103;2MCP 437-438
White, W.C./White, Mary	*W-004a	78/01/01	To Healdsburg, Ca.	
White, W.C.	*W-004b	78/01/12	Healdsburg, Ca.	
White, Mary	*W-004c	78/01/14	Healdsburg, Ca.	3Bio 81
White, W.C./White, Mary	*W-004d	78/01/22	Healdsburg, Ca.	3Bio 81;10MR 12
White, W.C.	*W-005	78/01/24	Healdsburg, Ca.	
Children	*W-006	78/01/25	Healdsburg, Ca.	
Children	*W-007	78/02/10	Oakland, Ca.	
White, W.C.	*W-007a	78/00/00	Fragment	8MR 412
White, W.C.	*W-008	78/02/13	Oakland, Ca.	
White, W.C.	*W-009	78/02/19	Oakland, Ca.	
White, W.C./White, Mary	*W-010	78/02/21	Oakland, Ca.	

White, W.C./White, Mary	*W-011	78/02/23	Oakland, Ca.	
White, W.C.	*W-012	78/02/25	Oakland, Ca.	
White, W.C.	*W-013	78/02/27	Oakland, Ca.	
White, W.C.	*W-014	78/03/08	Oakland, Ca.	
White, W.C./White, Mary	*W-015	78/03/10	Oakland, Ca.	
White, W.C./White, Mary	*W-016	78/03/13	Healdsburg, Ca.	
Belden, F.E.	*B-017	78/03/14	Healdsburg, Ca.	*20MR 70*
White, W.C.	*W-018	78/03/20	Healdsburg, Ca.	6MR 305
White, W.C.	*W-019	78/03/31	Oakland, Ca.	
White, W.C./White, Mary	*W-020	78/03/00	San Francisco, Ca.	
White, W.C.	*W-021	78/04/05	Oakland, Ca.	
White, J.S.	*W-022	78/04/05	Oakland, Ca.	3Bio 82-83
White, W.C./White, Mary	*W-023	78/04/11	Oakland, Ca.	
White, W.C./White, Mary	*W-024	78/04/30	Healdsburg, Ca.	
Healey, Br.	*H-025	78/04/00	Healdsburg, Ca.	
Children	*W-026	78/05/02	Healdsburg, Ca.	
White, W.C./White, Mary	*W-027	78/05/05	Healdsburg, Ca.	
Hall, Sr.	*H-029	78/06/19	Salem, Or.	3Bio 85;5MR 178
White, J.E.	*W-030	78/06/20	Salem, Or.	OHC 32;5MR 178
White, J.S.	*W-031	78/06/20	Salem, Or.	3Bio 85;5MR 179
White, J.S.	*W-032	78/06/24	Salem, Or.	UL 189;3Bio 85,88;5MR 180-181; 10MR 38
White, J.E./White, Emma	*W-034	78/06/26	Salem, Or.	
White, J.S.	*W-035	78/06/27	Salem, Or.	*21MR 241-244*
White, W.C.	*W-036	78/06/28	Salem, Or.	5MR 181-182
White, J.S.	*W-037	78/06/28	Salem, Or.	UL 193;5MR 234;15MR 132
White, J.S.	*W-037a	78/07/08	Salem, Or.	
White, J.S.	*W-038	78/07/01	Salem, Or.	
White, J.S.	*W-039	78/07/08	Salem, Or.	3Bio 88;5MR 182;6MR 305
Kilgore, R.M.	*K-039a	78/07/08	Salem, Or.	*4T 321-330*
White, J.S.	*W-040	78/07/03	Salem, Or.	3Bio 86-89
White, J.S.	*W-040a	78/07/11	Steamer Idaho	5MR 182-183
White, W.C.	*W-041	78/07/22	Oakland, Ca.	
White, J.S.	*W-042	78/07/27	Oakland, Ca.	UL 222;3Bio 89
White, J.S.	*W-042a	78/07/00	Fragment	OHC 232
Hall, Sr.	*H-043	78/08/13	Rollinsville, Co.	3Bio 93
White, J.S.	*W-045	78/08/21	Cheyenne, Co.	11MR 56
White, J.S./Children	*W-046	78/08/26	Battle Creek, Mi.	
White, J.S.	*W-047	78/08/28	to Syracuse, NY	
White, J.S.	*W-048	78/08/28	Shawsheen Grove, Ma	
Smith, Uriah	*S-048a	78/00/00		
White, J.S.	*W-049	78/08/30	Ballardvale, Ma.	
White, J.S.	*W-049a	78/08/30	Ballardvale, Ma.	TDG 251
White, J.S.	*W-050	78/08/31	Ballardvale, Ma.	
Cook, Br-Sr.	*C-051	78/10/02	Battle Creek, Mi.	
Van Horn, Br-Sr.	*V-051a	78/00/00		
White, Mary	*W-052	78/11/08	Grand Prairie, Tx.	3Bio 102-103
White, W.C./White, Mary	*W-052a	78/11/09	Grand Prairie, Tx.	
White, W.C./White, Mary	*W-053	78/11/14	Plano, Tx.	
White, J.E.	*W-054	78/11/15	Plano, Tx.	3Bio 99-100
White, Mary	*W-055	78/11/20	Denison, Tx.	3Bio 103
White, Mary	*W-056	78/11/21	Denison, Tx.	3Bio 103
Children	*W-057	78/11/27	Dallas, Tx.	4MR 39-40
White, W.C.	*W-057a	78/12/03	Plano, Tx.	
White, W.C./White, Mary	*W-058	78/12/04	Denison, Tx.	3Bio 104-105
White, Mary	*W-058a	78/12/06	Denison, Tx.	
White, Mary	*W-059	78/12/07	Denison, Tx.	3Bio 106

White, Mary	*W-060	78/12/08	Denison, Tx.	
White, W.C.	*W-061	78/12/11	Denison, Tx.	
Children	*W-062	78/12/19	Denison, Tx.	
Family at Battle Creek/White, W.C./Mary	*W-063	78/12/26	Denison, Tx.	*14MR 318-321*
White, Emma	*W-064	78/12/03	Denison, Tx.	
White, W.C.	*W-065	78/04/02	Oakland, Ca.	6MR 305
White, J.E.	W-065a	78/12/05	Denison, Tx.	
Kellogg, J.H.	*K-066	78/02/08	Oakland, Ca.	HP 54
Andrews, J.N.	*A-071	78/12/05	Denison, Tx.	TDG 348;HP 272,371;5MR 437
White, J.S.	*W-072	78/09/20	Battle Creek, Mi.	

1879

Haskell, S.N.	H-001	79/01/27	Denison, Tx.	Ev 323-324;3MR 19-20;6MR 33-34,114; 16MR 68
White, J.E.	*W-001a	79/01/01	Denison, Tx.	
White, W.C./White, Mary	*W-002	79/01/02	Denison, Tx.	
Harris, Chapin	H-003	79/08/00	Ballardvale, Ma.	4MR 214-226;9MR 384
White, J.E.	*W-003a	79/01/06	Denison, Tx.	3Bio 104
White, W.C./White, Mary	*W-004	79/01/06	Denison, Tx.	3Bio 104
Fairfield, Br./Sprague, Br.	*F-004a	79/01/12	Denison, Tx.	TDG 20
King, Br.	K-005	79/07/00		OHC 225-226;4MR 99
White, W.C.	*W-005a	79/01/13	Denison, Tx.	3Bio 104
White, W.C.	*W-006	79/01/14	Denison, Tx.	
White, W.C./White, Mary	*W-007	79/01/16	Denison, Tx.	
White, W.C.	*W-008	79/01/19	Denison, Tx.	
White, J.E./White, Emma	*W-008a	79/01/20	Denison, Tx.	UL 34
White, W.C.	*W-009	79/01/22	Denison, Tx.	
Andrews, J.N.	*A-010	79/01/22	Denison, Tx.	HP 271
Children	*W-011	79/01/26	Denison, Tx.	
White, W.C./White, Mary	*W-012	79/02/11	Denison, Tx.	
Children	*W-013	79/02/11	Denison, Tx.	
White, J.E./White, Emma	*W-013a	79/02/11	Denison, Tx.	OHC 174,184;2MCP 663
White, J.E./White, Emma	*W-014	79/02/16	Denison, Tx.	
White, W.C./White, Mary	*W-015	79/02/20	Denison, Tx.	16MR 69
Matteson, Br.	*M-016	79/02/21	Denison, Tx.	TDG 60;4MR 207-210
Tay, Br.	*T-017	79/02/27	Denison, Tx.	
White, W.C./White, Mary	*W-018	79/02/25	Denison, Tx.	3Bio 104;10MR 7
White, J.E.	*W-019	79/03/22	Denison, Tx.	10MR 379
White, Mary	*W-020	79/05/20	Emporia, Ks.	3Bio 116-11760
White, W.C./White, Mary	*W-020a	79/05/03	Johnson Ranch	3Bio 110,112
Bourdeau, Br-Sr.	*B-021	79/06/28	Dunlap, Ia.	
White, J.E.	*W-022	79/07/01	Dunlap, Ia.	VSS 391-392;8MR 77
Walling, Addie/Walling, May	*W-022a	79/07/14	Sioux Falls, SD	5MR 191;11MR 140
White, J.E./White, Emma	*W-023	79/08/05	White's Ranch, Co.	4MR 210-214
Witham, Br.	*W-024	79/08/23	missing	
Morrison, Charlie and Emma	*B-026	79/09/12	Carthag, NY	TDG 264
Cornell, Br-Sr.	*C-027	79/09/25	Lyons, Mi.	
Walling, Mr.	*W-028	79/10/26	Battle Creek, Mi.	
White, J.E.	*W-029	79/11/10	fragment	2MCP 649-650;OHC 81;TDG 323
Mt. Pleasant Church	*B-031	79/09/00	Greenville, Mi.	
Daniells, A.G.	*D-032	79/07/17	Swan Lake	11MR 61-62
Johnson, Br.	*J-033	79/00/00		*19MR 55-61*
Children	*W-036	79/05/04	Stone Wall	3Bio 111
Cornell, Br-Sr.	*C-037	79/00/00		
Cornell, James	*C-038	79/01/16	Tx.	
Brn. [re Cornells]	*B-039	79/00/00		

Loughborough, J.N.	*L-040	79/00/00		ChL 68;8MR 105-106
Children	*W-041	79/01/29	Denison, Tx.	
White, J.E.	*W-042	79/11/21	Battle Creek, Mi.	TDG 334
White, W.C.	*W-043	79/00/00		
Glenn, W.N.	*G-044	79/00/00		
Donaldson, Edith	*D-045	79/03/22	Denison, Tx.	3Bio 108
Canright, Lucretia	*C-046	79/02/21	Denison, Tx.	*DG 217-219*
Walling, Mr.	W-047	79/11/12	Battle Creek, Mi.	
Stillman, Br-Sr.	*S-048	79/06/00		

1880

Canright, D.M.	C-001	80/10/15	Battle Creek, Mi.	*2SM 162-170*
Fairfield, W.	*F-001a	80/01/05	Battle Creek, Mi.	
Haskell, S.N.	*H-002	80/11/08	Battle Creek, Mi.	PM 332-333,335;3Bio 155
Haskell, S.N./Butler, G.I./Whitney, B.	H-002a	80/11/08	Battle Creek, Mi.	Variant of B-002-1880
Haskell, S.N.	H-003	80/11/17	Battle Creek, Mi.	3Bio 154-155
White, J.E.	*W-003a	80/02/03	Battle Creek, Mi.	3Bio 133
Haskell, S.N.	H-004	80/08/26	Boylston, Ma.	3MR 279
Brigs, Sr.	*B-004a	80/02/08	Battle Creek, Mi.	TDG 47;11MR 30-31
White, J.S.	W-005	80/03/18	Oakland, Ca.	7BC 903;3Bio 138-139;4MR 259-260; 11MR 24-27
White, J.S.	W-005a	80/02/14	Ligonier, In.	
Cornell, M.E.	*C-006	80/09/28		TSB 172-182;CTr 148
Bangs, Lizzie	*B-006a	80/02/26	To Ca.	*20MR 291-298*
Bangs, Lizzie	*B-006b	80/02/26	To Ca.	*20MR 299-306*
White, J.S.	*W-007	80/02/27	To Ogden, Ut.	
White, J.S.	*W-009	80/03/11	Oakland, Ca.	
White, J.S.	*W-010	80/03/12	Oakland, Ca.	
White, J.S.	*W-011	80/03/15	Oakland, Ca.	TDG 83
White, J.S.	*W-012	80/03/15	Boat Donohue	
White, J.S.	*W-013	80/03/17	Oakland, Ca.	11MR 63
White, J.S.	*W-016	80/03/24	Oakland, Ca.	TDG 92;OHC 296
White, W.C./White, Mary	*W-017	80/03/29	Woodland, Ca.	3MR 404;11MR 63
White, J.S.	*W-017a	80/04/01	Oakland, Ca.	10MR 70
White, J.S.	*W-018	80/04/02	Oakland, Ca.	
White, J.S.	*W-019	80/04/06	Oakland, Ca.	3Bio 133,136
White, J.S.	*W-020	80/04/07	Oakland, Ca.	*Test. of Jesus*, by F.M. Wilcox, *149-151*
White, J.S.	*W-020a	80/04/13	Oakland, Ca.	
White, J.S.	W-021	80/04/15	Oakland, Ca.	9MR 97
White, J.S.	*W-022	80/04/16	Oakland, Ca.	UL 120;3Bio 140
White, J.S.	*W-023	80/04/17	Oakland, Ca.	3Bio 137
White, J.S.	*W-024	80/04/19	Oakland, Ca.	3Bio 136,140;5MR 236
White, J.S.	*W-025	80/04/23	Hanford/Lemoore	UL 127;11MR 63-64
White, J.S.	*W-026	80/04/23	Hanford/Lemoore	OHC 134,162;11MR 64
White, J.S.	*W-027	80/05/02	Lemoore	3Bio 135
White, J.S.	*W-027a	80/05/16	Walla Walla, Wa.	
White, J.S.	*W-028	80/05/20	Walla Walla, Wa.	UL 154
White, J.S.	*W-029	80/05/20	Milton, Or.	*21MR 206-212*
White, J.S.	*W-030	80/05/26	Milton, Or.	*21MR 245-251*
White, W.C.	*W-031	80/05/27	Milton, Or.	
Foss, Samuel/Foss, Mary	*F-032	80/06/01	to Portland, Or.	3Bio 140
White, J.E./White, Emma	*W-032a	80/06/14	Salem, Or.	16MR 210-211
White, J.S.	*W-033	80/06/06	Portland, Or.	
White, J.S.	*W-033a	80/06/23	Tto San Francisco	*16MR 149-151*
White, J.E.	*W-034	80/07/13	Auburn, Ca.	
White, J.S.	*W-035	80/07/23	Oakland, Ca.	11MR 65

Brn-Srs. at Woodland	*B-036	80/07/00	Oakland, Ca.	
Children	*W-037	80/07/28	Humboldt, Nv.	11MR 65-66
White, W.C./White, Mary	*W-038	80/08/01	Cheyenne, Nv.	*11MR 66-68*
Children	*W-039	80/08/19	Waterville, Me.	5MR 57-58
Children	*W-039a	80/08/26	Boylston, Ma.	
Children	*W-040	80/09/18	Clyde, Oh.	
White, W.C./White, Mary/Haskell, S.N.	*W-041	80/09/16	Buffalo, NY	3Bio 146-147
White, W.C./White, Mary	*W-042	80/09/22	Battle Creek, Mi.	3Bio 146-147;5MR 58-60;9MR 267
Children	*W-043	80/10/14	Battle Creek, Mi.	3Bio 148-149
Children	*W-044	80/10/20	Battle Creek, Mi.	
Children	*W-045	80/10/27	Battle Creek, Mi.	
White, W.C./White, Mary	*W-045a	80/10/30	Battle Creek, Mi.	
White, W.C./White, Mary	*W-045b	80/11/03	Battle Creek, Mi.	3Bio 149,154
White, W.C./White, Mary	*W-045c	80/11/07	Battle Creek, Mi.	3Bio 152
Sanborn, Br-Sr.	*S-046	80/10/30	Battle Creek, Mi.	
White, W.C./White, Mary	*W-048	80/11/22	Battle Creek, Mi.	
White, J.S.	*W-049	80/03/25	Oakland, Ca.	3Bio 136-137
Harris, Chapin	*H-050	80/09/00		4MR 226-228;9MR 384
Children	*W-051	80/12/20		3Bio 149
White, J.S.	*W-053	80/07/00		3Bio 137
Lily	*L-054	80/01/24	Battle Creek, Mi.	
Haskell, S.N.	*H-055	80/10/29	Battle Creek, Mi.	
White, J.E.	*W-056	80/01/29	Battle Creek, Mi.	3Bio 150-151
White, W.C.	*W-057	80/11/00	Battle Creek, Mi.	
Harris, Chapin	*H-058	80/01/12	Battle Creek, Mi.	LYL 68-69
Levitt, James	*L-059	80/06/08	Salem, Or.	TSB 19-23;LYL 36-37
Walling, Mr.	*W-060	80/00/00		
Harris, Chapin	H-061	80/09/09	Hornellsville, NY	4MR 223-226;9MR 384

1881

Haskell, S.N.	H-001	81/04/22	Battle Creek, Mi.	PM 328-329,352;3Bio 155-157;12MR 56
White, W.C./White, Mary	*W-001a	81/01/06	Battle Creek, Mi.	7MR 230-231
Haskell, S.N.	H-002	81/06/28	Battle Creek, Mi.	3Bio 153,161
Children	*W-002a	81/04/06	Battle Creek, Mi.	
Walling, Addie/Walling, May	*W-003	81/04/15	Battle Creek, Mi.	DG 196-198
White, J.E.	*W-003a	81/04/22	Battle Creek, Mi.	3Bio 157
White, W.C./White, Mary	*W-003b	81/04/19	Newton, Mi.	3Bio 156-157;6MR 306;14MR 282
Bourdeau, D.T.	*B-004	81/05/14	Battle Creek, Mi.	
Children	*W-004a	81/05/15	Battle Creek, Mi.	3Bio 158;6MR 306
Bourdeau, Br-Sr. A.C.	*B-005	81/05/21	Spring Arbor, Mi.	
White, W.C./White, Mary	*W-005a	81/06/14	Des Moines, Ia.	3Bio 158-159;6MR 306;9MR 99
White, J.E./White, Emma	*W-006	81/06/16	Hampton, Ia.	TDG 176;4MR 96
Butler, G.I./Haskell, S.N.	*B-008	81/06/20	Neenah, Wi.	3Bio 161;6MR 117
White, W.C./White, Mary	*W-008a	81/07/27	Charlotte, Mi.	3Bio 165,167
Br-Sr.	*B-009	81/10/20	Sacramento, Ca.	TDG 302;3Bio 173,180;2MR 249-250; 6MR 306-307
Brother	*B-010	81/10/26	Oakland, Ca.	
White, W.C.	*W-011	81/11/09	Healdsburg, Ca.	
White, W.C.	*W-012	81/11/09	Healdsburg, Ca.	
Smith, Uriah	*S-014	81/00/00		2MR 250
White, W.C./White, Mary	*W-015	81/03/15	Grand Ledge, Mi.	
White, W.C.	*W-016	81/09/08	White's Ranch, Co.	
White, W.C.	*W-017	81/09/12	White's Ranch, Co.	RY 161-163;3Bio 182-183
White, W.C.	*W-018	81/12/06	Healdsburg, Ca.	
White, W.C.	*W-019	81/12/07	Healdsburg, Ca.	
White, W.C.	*W-020	81/12/11	St. Helena, Ca.	

White, W.C	*W-020a	81/12/14	St. Helena, Ca.	
White, W.C./White, J.E./White, Emma	*W-021	81/12/19	Napa, Ca.	

1882

Test. for Monterey Church	*B-001	82/00/00		Te 217-220;OHC 255,260
White, W.C.	*W-001a	82/02/07	Santa Rosa, Ca.	3Bio 194
Children	*W-001b	82/02/22	Santa Rosa, Ca.	
White, W.C.	*W-001c	82/02/23	Healdsburg, Ca.	
Children	*W-001d	82/02/24	Healdsburg, Ca.	
Chapman, Sr.	*C-001e	82/03/03	Oakland, Ca.	*DG 220-221*
White, W.C.	*W-002	82/03/10	Woodland, Ca.	
Smith, Uriah	S-002a	82/03/28	Healdsburg, Ca.	*PH117 19-41*
Brn-Srs. in Battle Creek	B-002b	82/06/20	Healdsburg, Ca.	*PH117 41-66*
Gage, Br.	*G-003	82/04/01	Healdsburg, Ca.	ChL 12
White, W.C./White, Mary	*W-003a	82/04/01	Healdsburg, Ca.	
White, W.C./White, Mary	*W-004	82/04/02	Healdsburg, Ca.	3Bio 195
Children	*W-005	82/04/03	Healdsburg, Ca.	2MR 250
White, W.C.	*W-006	82/04/04	Healdsburg, Ca.	
Brn-Srs. in Battle Creek	*B-007	82/04/08	Healdsburg, Ca.	
Children	*W-008	82/04/10	Healdsburg, Ca.	3Bio 195
White, W.C.	*W-009	82/04/16	Healdsburg, Ca.	3Bio 195
White, Mary	*W-010	82/05/02	Healdsburg, Ca.	
Butler, G.I./Stone, C.W./Oyen, A.B./Kellogg, J.H.	*B-011	82/05/05	Hanford, Ca.	11MR 202-203
Ings, Br-Sr.	*I-011a	82/05/08	Hanford, Ca.	
White, W.C.	*W-012	82/05/19	St. Helena, Ca.	
White, W.C./White, Mary	*W-013	82/05/21	St. Helena, Ca.	
White, W.C./White, Mary	*W-014	82/05/22	St. Helena, Ca.	2MR 250
White, W.C.	*W-015	82/05/23	St. Helena, Ca.	8MR 77
White, Mary	*W-016	82/05/31	Healdsburg, Ca.	
White, W.C.	*W-017	82/06/07	Healdsburg, Ca.	
White, W.C.	*W-018	82/06/13	Healdsburg, Ca.	
White, J.E.	*W-019	82/07/02	Oakland, Ca.	
Marshmeyer, Br-Sr.	*M-020	82/07/00	Healdsburg, Ca.	2SM 302-303
Ings, Br-Sr.	*I-020a	82/07/28	Oakland, Ca.	
Brn-Srs. in Battle Creek	*B-021	82/08/03	Oakland, Ca.	*PH155 1-12*
Children	*W-022	82/09/25	Healdsburg, Ca.	
White, W.C.	*W-023	82/12/01	Santa Rosa, Ca.	4MR 40;9MR 97
White, W.C.	*W-024	82/12/18	Healdsburg, Ca.	TDG 361;3Bio 220
Brownsberger, Sr.	*B-024a	82/10/00	Healdsburg, Ca.	
Brownsberger, Sr.	*B-025	82/10/00	St. Helena, Ca.	*DG 164-170*
White, W.C.	*W-026	82/12/04	Healdsburg, Ca.	
Edwards, W.H.	*E-027	82/04/20	Oakland, Ca.	
Edwards, W.H.	*E-028	82/09/00		
Edwards, W.H.	*E-029	82/06/14	Healdsburg, Ca.	10MR 386-387
Butler, G.I.	*B-030	82/07/12	Oakland, Ca.	3Bio 201;9MR 104-105
Davis, Marian	*D-031	82/03/16	Oakland, Ca.	
Review and Herald (Telegram)	*R-032	82/00/16	Oakland, Ca.	

1883

Andrews, J.N.	*A-001	83/03/29	Healdsburg, Ca.	TSB 34-35;2MCP 461,463;UL 102; OHC 363;Ev 96;3MR 318,337; 9MR 370;10MR 8
Whitney, B.L.	*W-002	83/03/30	Healdsburg, Ca.	10MR 8
Smith, Uriah	*S-003	83/07/31	Healdsburg, Ca.	3SM 350-351;8MR 64-65
Smith, Uriah	*S-003a	83/07/31	Healdsburg, Ca.	3MR 318-319

EGW Letters File—Page 20

Brethren	B-005	83/11/00	Battle Creek, Mi.	*13MR 329-333*
Andrews, R.F.	*A-006	83/00/00		9MR 165-168
Kellogg, H.W.	K-007	83/00/00		3BC 1163;7BC 935;SD 271
White, W.C.	*W-008	83/01/04	Oakland, Ca.	3Bio 209
Andrews, J.N.	*A-009	83/03/17	Healdsburg, Ca.	TSB 34;3Bio 215
Bangs, Lizzie	*B-010	83/04/08	Oakland, Ca.	
Torr, Br.	*T-011	83/05/12	Lemoore, Ca.	TDG 141
Ings, Sr.	*I-013	83/07/03	Oakland, Ca.	3Bio 215
Smith, Br-Sr.	*S-014	83/08/08	Healdsburg, Ca.	*14MR 1-7*
Davis, Marian	*D-015	83/11/02	Battle Creek, Mi.	
Whalin, Br.	W-015a	83/11/18	Battle Creek, Mi.	3Bio 235,239
Butler, G.I./Members of the Board	*B-016	83/11/29	S. Lancaster, Ma.	
Morton Children	*M-017	83/00/00		OHC 264
White, W.C.	*W-019	83/02/06	Healdsburg, Ca.	
White, W.C.	*W-020	83/06/11	San Jose, Ca.	TDG 171
White, W.C.	*W-021	83/06/13	San Jose, Ca.	TDG 173
Children	*W-022	83/08/15	Laramie	11MR 68-70
Children	*W-023	83/08/18	Battle Creek, Mi.	3Bio 227
White, W.C./White, Mary	*W-024	83/08/23	Worcester, Ma.	ChL 43-44;2MR 250-251;10MR 339
White, W.C./White, Mary	*W-025	83/08/29	S. Lancaster, Ma.	
White, W.C./White, Mary	*W-026	83/09/03	Montpelier, Vt.	
White, W.C./White, Mary	*W-027	83/09/04	Montpelier, Vt.	2MR 251
Bourdeau, Mrs. A.C.	B-028	83/09/03	Montpelier, Vt.	

1884

Br-Sr.	B-002	84/02/17	Healdsburg, Ca.	*KC 68-70*
Friends at the Health Retreat	F-003	84/02/05	Healdsburg, Ca.	CD 173,405-409;2SM 283;4MR 383
Maxson, Br-Sr.	M-004	84/02/06	Healdsburg, Ca.	7MR 43;7MR 349
Sister	S-005	84/00/00		*CG 213 with 8MR 388-392*
Butler, G.I./Haskell, S.N.	B-006	84/01/20	St. Helena, Ca.	*21MR 325-328*
Smith, Br-Sr.	*S-007	84/06/17	Portland, Or.	3Bio 252;7MR 54;*LS 273*
Van Horn, I.D.	*V-008	84/02/26	Healdsburg, Ca.	
Haskell, S.N.	H-009	84/00/00	To San Francisco	9MR 9-10
Matteson, Br.	M-010	84/05/03	San Jose, Ca.	TDG 132;ChL 48-49;7MR 314-315; 3SM 96-98
Smith, Uriah	*S-011	84/02/19	Healdsburg, Ca.	
Smith, Uriah	*S-011a	84/02/19	Healdsburg, Ca.	*19MR 77-80*
Brownsberger, Br-Sr.	*B-012	84/00/00	Healdsburg, Ca.	3SM 293-294;7MR 3-6
Butler, G.I.	*B-013	84/01/02	Healdsburg, Ca.	
Newton, Br-Sr.	*N-014	84/01/18	St. Helena, Ca.	UL 32
Rue, Br-Sr.	*R-015	84/01/20	Healdsburg, Ca.	
St. John, Br.	*S-016	84/03/26	Healdsburg, Ca.	
Hemstreet, Br-Sr.	*H-017	84/04/29	Oakland, Ca.	
Hemstreet, Br-Sr.	*H-018	84/04/30	Oakland, Ca.	
Smith, Br-Sr.	*S-019	84/06/15	Walla Walla, Wa.	*21MR202-205*
Haskell, S.N.	*H-019a	84/06/10	Walla Walla, Wa.	*21MR 198-201*
Smith, Uriah	*S-020	84/06/27	E. Portland, Or.	*20MR 356-360*
Haskell, S.N./Butler, G.I.	*H-021	84/07/10	Healdsburg, Ca.	3Bio 248;9MR 136
Ings, Sr.	*I-022	84/07/30	Oakland, Ca.	
Ings, Sr.	*I-022a	84/07/30	Oakland, Ca.	3Bio 244
Ings, Sr.	*I-023	84/08/04	Oakland, Ca.	
Jones, Br-Sr.	*J-024	84/08/10	Kansas City, Mo.	
Whitney, B.L.	*W-025	84/08/11	Kansas City, Mo.	
Bell, G.H.	*B-026	84/09/11	Portland, Me.	
Ings, Sr.	*I-027	84/09/17	S. Lancaster, Ma.	3Bio 261
Brisbin, W.L.	*B-028	84/11/18	Battle Creek, Mi.	
Salisbury, Br.	*S-029	84/11/20	Battle Creek, Mi.	2SM 329;OHC 317

Savage, Adeline	*S-030	84/11/21	Battle Creek, Mi.	*DG 198-200*
Children	*W-036	84/01/15	St. Helena, Ca.	
McEnterfer, Sara?	*M-037	84/02/14	Healdsburg, Ca.	3Bio 241
White, W.C.	*W-038	84/02/14	Healdsburg, Ca.	
White, W.C.	*W-039	84/02/21	Healdsburg, Ca.	
White, W.C.	*W-040	84/02/29	St. Helena, Ca.	
White, W.C.	*W-041	84/02/29	St. Helena, Ca.	
White, W.C.	*W-042	84/03/16	Healdsburg, Ca.	
White, W.C.	*W-043	84/03/18	Healdsburg, Ca.	
Children	*W-044	84/03/27	Healdsburg, Ca.	3Bio 242
White, W.C.	*W-045	84/03/27	Healdsburg, Ca.	
White, W.C.	W-046	84/04/26		
Children	*W-047	84/05/15	Los Angeles, Ca.	3Bio 246
White, W.C.	*W-048	84/07/07	Healdsburg, Ca.	
Children	*W-049	84/08/10	Kansas City, Mo.	11MR 145-146
White, W.C./White, Mary	*W-050	84/08/13	Kansas City, Mo.	
White, W.C./White, Mary	*W-051	84/08/16	Marshalltown, Ia.	
White, W.C.	*W-052	84/08/20	Syracuse, NY	
White, W.C./White, Mary	*W-053	84/08/20	Syracuse, NY	TSB 202;12MR 269
White, W.C./White, Mary	*W-054	84/08/22	Syracuse, NY	
Children?	*W-054a	84/05/09	Benecia, Ca.	*19MR 283-286*
White, W.C./White, Mary	*W-055	84/08/24	Syracuse, NY	
White, W.C./White, Mary	*W-056	84/08/24	Syracuse, NY	
Children	*W-057	84/09/01	Worcester, Ma.	3SM 112-113
Children	*W-058	84/09/09	Burlington, Vt.	
White, W.C.	*W-059	84/09/11	Portland, Me.	3SM 111;3Bio 262
Children	*W-060	84/09/16	S. Lancaster, Ma.	3Bio 262
White, John	*W-061	84/11/27	Battle Creek, Mi.	3Bio 270;6MR 307
White, W.C.	*W-062	84/12/18	Healdsburg, Ca.	
White, W.C./White, Mary	*W-063	84/08/00	To Reno, Nv.	*11MR 146-148*
Osborn, Br.	*O-065	84/02/07	St. Helena, Ca.	HP 305;12MR 42
Brn-Srs. in Monterey	*B-066	84/00/00		*5T 341-348*

1885

Directors of the Sanitarium at Battle Creek	B-001	85/11/03	Christiania, Norway	MM 211;11MR 78-79
Andrews, Edith	*A-004	85/11/21	Basel, Switz.	OHC 158;2MCP 632;TMK 95
Butler, G.I.	B-005	85/10/31	Christiana, Norway	*TM 297-300*
Andrews, Edith	A-006	85/00/00		*10MR 53-58*
Bourdeau, Daniel	B-007	85/02/10	Healdsburg, Ca.	UL 55;VSS 216
Starr, G.B.	S-008	85/03/13		
Waggoner, Br. [J.H.]	*W-010	85/11/04	Christiania, Norway	TSB 182-184;5MR 243,245
A, Br.	A-010a	85/00/00		
Butler, G.I./Haskell, S.N.	B-012	85/10/28	Orebro, Sweden	*SpTA #6 61-67*
Church at St. Claire, Nevada	B-014	85/03/13		OHC 34,94;TDG 81;1MCP 321;2MCP 691
Waggoner, J.H./Jones, C.H.	W-015	85/03/07	Healdsburg, Ca.	*20MR 48-50*
Andrews, Edith	*A-016	85/01/15	Healdsburg, Ca.	
Andrews, Edith	*A-017	85/02/10		
Burgis, Br.	*B-018	85/01/20	Healdsburg, Ca.	
Smith, Br-Sr.	*S-019	85/03/23	Healdsburg, Ca.	5MR 175
Friends at Healdsburg	*B-020	85/07/14	Modesto, Ca.	
Waggoner, Sr. [E.J.?]	*W-021	85/08/20	Great Grimsby, Eng.	
Gibbs, Dr.	*G-022	85/09/05	Basel, Switz.	EGWE 35,40,43-44,46
Butler, G.I.	*B-023	85/10/01	Basel, Switz.	*15MR 345-370*
Bourdeau, Daniel	*B-024	85/11/23	Basel, Switz.	8MR 106-107
Vaucher, Jules Alfred	*V-025	85/12/16	Geneva, Switz.	LYL 47-48;8MR 429-430

n.a. [re Edith Andrews]	*B-026	85/12/24	Basel, Switz.	EGWE 89
Walling, Addie	*W-028	85/11/03	Christiania, Norway	*DG 159-160*
White, W.C.	*W-029	85/02/15	St. Helena, Ca.	
White, W.C./White, Mary	*W-030	85/02/16	Healdsburg, Ca.	
White, W.C./White, Mary	*W-031	85/02/17	Healdsburg, Ca.	
White, W.C.	*W-032	85/02/19	St. Helena, Ca.	
White, W.C.	*W-033	85/02/20	St. Helena, Ca.	
White, W.C.	*W-034	85/02/22	St. Helena, Ca.	
White, W.C.	*W-035	85/11/17	Gytteborg, Sweden	3Bio 327-328
White, W.C.	*W-036	85/11/20	Basel, Switz.	*20MR 45-47*
White, W.C.	*W-037	85/11/23	Basel, Switz.	*17MR 323-328*
White, J.E./White, W.C.	*W-038	85/12/22	Basel, Switz.	3Bio 337-338;8MR 445
White, W.C.	*W-039	85/12/30	Basel, Switz.	
Davis, Marian	*D-040	85/07/30	Rome, NY	

1886

White, J.E./White, Emma	*W-002	86/06/24	Orebro, Sweden	TDG 184;3MR 393-399
Vaucher, Br.	V-003	86/00/00		*18MR 303-320*
Oviatt, Br.	O-005	86/09/09	Basel, Switz.	*17MR 140-145*
Kellogg, J.H.	K-006	86/12/30		Ev 69;6MR 256-260
Kellogg, J.H.	K-007	86/04/26	Torre Pellice	ChL 45-48;3Bio 342
Ings, Br-Sr.	I-007a	86/08/11	Basel, Switz.	*21MR 306-309*
Kellogg, J.H.	K-008	86/07/16	to Copenhagen	UL 211;11MR 299-300
Harmon, Br-Sr.	H-009	86/02/08	Basel, Switz.	*21MR 329-331*
Gibbs, Dr.	G-010	86/12/01		
Gibbs, Dr.	G-011	86/04/05	Basel, Switz.	TDG 104;3Bio 341
Daniels, Br-Sr. E.P.	D-011a	86/08/06	Basel, Switz.	*21MR 332-335*
Daniels, Br-Sr. E.P.	D-011b	86/08/06	Basel, Switz.	
Chapman, Sr.	C-012	86/12/27	Basel, Switz.	4BC 1161;6MR 256
Bourdeau, Br-Sr.	B-013	86/08/22	Basel, Switz.	Ev 646-647
Gibbs, Dr./Burke, Dr.	B-016	86/05/15	Basel, Switz.	SD 82,331;TDG 144
n.a.	B-017	86/12/01		TMK 301;TDG 349;1MCP 104
Rice, J.D.	*R-018	86/03/12	Basel, Switz.	3Bio 340-341
Haskell, S.N.	*H-019	86/07/12	Christiania, Norway	EGWE 206;4MR 327-328;6MR 92-94
White, Mary	*W-019a	86/07/12	Christiania, Norway	EGWE 203
Bourdeau, A.C.	B-020	86/01/25	Basel, Switz.	
Brn-Srs. in Healdsburg	B-021	86/07/09	Christiania, Norway	See 5T 477-490;5MR 242
Gibbs, Dr.	G-022	86/09/19	Great Grimsby, Eng.	UL 276
Albert [Vuilleumier?]	A-023	86/09/23	Great Grimsby, Eng.	AH 46;LYL 21-22
White, Mary	*W-023a	86/09/23	Great Grimsby, Eng.	EGWE 224
Managers of the Health Retreat	*B-024	86/09/19	Great Grimsby, Eng.	
Bourdeau, D.T.	B-025	86/01/10	Basel, Switz.	
Vuilleumier, Br.	V-028	86/02/09	Basel, Switz.	
Hanson, Br-Sr.	H-029	86/02/07	Basel, Switz.	EGWE 153
Brownsberger, Br.	*B-029a	86/02/07	Basel, Switz.	
Bourdeau, D.T.	*B-030	86/02/10	Basel, Switz.	
Bourdeau, Augustin	B-031	86/02/11	Basel, Switz.	EGWE 174
Kellogg, J.H.	K-032	86/02/17		3Bio 340;EGWE 153
Bourdeau, A.C.	B-033	86/02/27	Basel, Switz.	1MCP 101;2MCP 399,592,656,801; VSS 323-324
Butler, G.I.	B-034	86/03/01	Basel, Switz.	PM 230;PH102 15-17;SpM 132-134
Butler, G.I.	B-034a	86/03/01	Basel, Switz.	PC 364-379
Bourdeau, D.T.	B-035	86/03/07	Basel, Switz.	EGWE 171
Lockwood, Br-Sr.	L-036	86/03/16	Basel, Switz.	
Bourdeau, A.C.	B-037	86/03/18	Basel, Switz.	
White, J.E./White, Emma	*W-038	86/03/28	Basel, Switz.	EGWE 172-173

EGW Letters File—Page 23

White, Mary	*W-038b	86/06/27	Orebro, Sweden	3Bio 346;5MR 190
Henry, A.R.	*II-039	86/03/28	Basel, Switz.	5MR 441-442;PH102 17-18
Bourdeau, Br-Sr.	B-040	86/04/04	Basel, Switz.	
Sharp, Br.	S-041	86/04/07	Basel, Switz.	TSB 203
Ramsey, Br.	*R-042	86/04/07	Basel, Switz.	5T 651-654;UL 111;3SM 228
Matteson, Br.	M-043	86/04/13	Basel, Switz.	*17MR 98-106*
Littlejohn, Br-Sr.	L-044	86/05/10	Basel, Switz.	5MR 275-276
Vuilleumier, Br-Sr.	V-045	86/05/12	Basel, Switz.	
Bourdeau, Br. [D.T.]	B-047	86/06/05	Basel, Switz.	*6MR 178-188*
Bourdeau, Br. [D.T.]	B-047a	86/06/05	Basel, Switz.	8MR 328-330
Brn. Engaged in Labor in Nimes	B-048	86/08/24	Basel, Switz.	*17MR 67-74*
Conradi, L.R.	C-049	86/08/30	Basel, Switz.	*21MR 219-221*
Ertzenberger, Br.	*E-050	86/09/05	Basel, Switz.	
Butler, G.I.	B-051	86/09/06	Basel, Switz.	*21MR 378-387*
Bourdeau, A.C.	B-052	86/11/20	Lausanne, Switz.	AH 307;3SM 53
White, W.C.	*W-052a	86/11/20	Lausanne, Switz.	
Babcock, Br-Sr.	B-053	86/11/22	Lausanne, Switz.	
Stewart, Sr.	S-054	86/04/04		TDG 103
Butler, G.I./Haskell, S.N.	B-055	86/12/08	Basel, Switz.	*12MR 318-328*
Butler, G.I.	*B-056	86/12/13	Basel, Switz.	Ev 373-375
Rice, Br./Gibbs, Br.	*R-057	86/12/17	Basel, Switz.	CD 211-212;7MR 370;9MR 113-114;
Loughborough, J.N.	L-058	86/12/20		
Smith, Hubbel	S-059	86/12/20		Ev 449-451
Corliss, John/Corliss, Julia	C-060	86/12/25	Tramelan	Ev 84-85,340;UL 373;EGWE 249;5MR 328-329;
				6MR 64,196
Church, Br.	C-061	86/12/20		CD 289;7MR 296-297
Kellogg, J.H.	K-062	86/08/02	Basel, Switz.	14MR 26-30;CTr 354
Brn. Having the Responsibilities of the Work of God	B-063	86/11/28	Basel, Switz.	*16MR 136-142*
Kellogg, J.H.	K-064	86/00/00		ChL 55;11MR 300-301
Chapman, Sr.	C-065	86/12/31		*5T 542-549*
Laborers at Lausanne	B-066	86/00/00		3SM 24-25
Laborers at Lausanne	B-066a	86/00/00		
Bourdeau, Br-Sr.	B-068	86/03/28	Basel, Switz.	
Brn. in New York	B-070	86/12/27	Basel, Switz.	*PH039 3-13*
Matteson, Br-Sr.	*M-072	86/01/02	Basel, Switz.	EGWE 79
White, W.C.	*W-072a	86/01/04	Basel, Switz.	EGWE 149-150
Butler, G.I.	*B-073	86/01/16	Basel, Switz.	TSB 184-185;10MR 388
Chittenden, Sr.	*C-074	86/01/25	Basel, Switz.	
Brethren	*B-075	86/02/23	Basel, Switz.	
Loughborough, J.N./Jones, A.T./Waggoner, E.J./J.H.	*B-076	86/04/00		*21MR 147-149*
Butler, G.I.	*B-077	86/04/05	Basel, Switz.	
Ings, Br-Sr.	*I-078	86/05/26	Chaux-de-Fonds	*21MR 312-314*
Littlejohn, Br-Sr.	*L-079	86/06/28	Orebro, Sweden	
Church at Healdsburg	*B-080	86/07/09	Christiania, Norway	
Oyen, Br.	*O-081	86/07/23	Copenhagen	
Decker, Br.	*D-082	86/02/10	Basel, Switz.	TSB 204-206
Charles	*C-083	86/00/00		
Butler, G.I./Haskell, S.N.	*B-084	86/09/14	Basel, Switz.	6MR 94;10MR 267-268
Children	*W-084a	86/09/16	Great Grimsby, Eng.	
Smith, Uriah	*S-085	86/07/24	Copenhagen	UL 219;6MR 144
Walling, Addie	*W-091	86/01/01	Basel, Switz.	EGWE 148
Walling, Addie	*W-092	86/01/29	Basel, Switz.	TDG 37
Smith, Uriah	*S-092a	86/03/00		
Children	*W-093	86/08/02	Basel, Switz.	
n.a.	*W-094	86/01/31		3Bio 339
Walling, Addie	*W-095	86/02/16	Basel, Switz.	DG 189-190;3Bio 340;EGWE 153;9MR 383
Walling, Addie	*W-096	86/03/23	Geneva, Switz.	3Bio 341

EGW Letters File—Page 24

White, J.E./White, Emma	*W-097	86/04/29	Turin, Italy	LDE 42,278;EGWE 186-187
White, J.E./White, Emma	*W-098	86/05/09	Basel, Switz.	
White, J.E./White, Emma	*W-099	86/06/18	Orebro, Sweden	TDG 178;3MR 399
White, J.E./White, Emma	*W-100	86/06/28	Orebro, Sweden	
Walling, Addie	*W-101	86/07/21	Copenhagen	EGWE 209;8MR 79;10MR 380
White, J.E./White, Emma	*W-102	86/07/25	Copenhagen	6MR 143;8MR 104-105;10MR 380-381
White, J.E./White, Emma	*W-103	86/07/27	Cologne, Germany	
White, J.E./White, Emma	*W-104	86/07/28	Basel, Switz.	
White, J.E./White, Emma	*W-105	86/08/11	Basel, Switz.	EGWE 211-212;5MR 184
Walling, Addie	*W-106	86/08/16	Basel, Switz.	EGWE 212
Walling, Addie	*W-107	86/09/10	Basel, Switz.	
Foss, Br-Sr.	*F-108	86/10/28	Nimes, France	*17MR 75-82*
Children	*W-108a	86/10/00	Fragments	3MR 64
Walling, Addie	*W-109	86/11/01	Nimes, France	
White, W.C./White, Mary	*W-110	86/11/04	Torre Pellice	EGWE 237-238;8MR 354
Meyrat, Adolphe	*M-111	86/00/00		
Bourdeau, A.C./Bourdeau, D.T.	*B-112	86/00/00		
White, J.E./White, Emma	*W-113	86/07/11	Fragment	*21MR 340-345*
Butler, G.I.	*B-114	86/10/12	London, Eng.	3Bio 353-355
Butler, G.I.	*B-115	86/11/24	Basel, Switz.	3Bio 358
n.a./Butler, G.I.?	*B-116	86/12/00	Fragment	
Butler, G.I.	*B-117	86/06/25	Orebro, Sweden	EGWE 197;ChL 44
Vuilleumier, Br-Sr.	*V-118	86/06/03	Basel, Switz.	
Walling, Addie	*W-119	86/05/30	Chaux-de-Fonds	
Butler, G.I.	B-120	86/01/02	Basel, Switz.	
California Conference	B-121	86/07/07	Christiania, Nor.	*PUR 9/4/1913*
Children	W-122	86/08/11		

1887

n.a.	S-001	87/06/03	Copenhagen	LYL 83-84
White, Mary	*W-001a	87/06/03	Copenhagen	
White, Mary	*W-001b	87/06/05	London, Eng.	
Rice, Br./Gibbs, Br./Loughborough, J.N.	R-002	87/03/16	Basel, Switz.	
Oyen, Sr.	O-003	87/06/09	Moss, Norway	
Maxson, Br-Sr.	M-004	87/02/25	Basel, Switz.	
Maxson, Br-Sr.	M-005	87/03/24	Basel, Switz.	
Maxson, Br-Sr.	M-006	87/05/20	Basel, Switz.	
Maxson, Br-Sr.	*M-007	87/04/16	Basel, Switz.	3SM 52-53
Lockwood, Br-Sr.	L-008	87/02/11	Basel, Switz.	TDG 50
Kellogg, J.H.	*K-009	87/04/15	Basel, Switz.	CD 105-106,345;2MR 142-144;5MR 23-25
Kellogg, J.H.	K-010	87/02/23	Basel, Switz.	CW 127-128;TDG 62;BCL 8-10
Burke, Dr.	B-011	87/03/10	Basel, Switz.	OHC 177
Boyd, Br.	B-012	87/06/25	Stockholm, Sweden	TSA 14-20;CD 309;6MR 308;7MR 322-323
Butler, G.I./Smith, Uriah	B-013	87/04/05	Basel, Switz.	*16MR 281-286*
Robinson, Br./Boyd, Br.	*B-014	87/06/18	Moss, Norway	*TSA 7-13*
Brn. in Europe	B-015	87/08/06	Atlantic Ocean	*3MR 5-10*
White, Mary/White, Emma	*W-015a	87/08/14	New Bedford, Ma.	
Butler, G.I.	*B-016	87/04/21	Basel, Switz.	TSB 239-242
Butler, G.I.	B-016a	87/04/21	Basel, Switz.	*16MR 338-339*
Andrews, Br-Sr.	A-017	87/09/06	Battle Creek, Mi.	3SM 64-66
Brn-Srs. in St. Helena	B-019	87/10/24	St. Helena, Ca.	
Haskell, S.N.	H-020	87/01/14	Basel, Switz.	*21MR 315-318*
Canright, D.M.	*C-022	87/04/20		5T 621-628
Haskell, S.N.	H-023	87/12/08		3Bio 377;12MR 210-211
White, Mary	*W-023a	87/12/11	Healdsburg, Ca.	FBS 2
White, W.C.	*W-023b	87/12/12	Healdsburg, Ca.	3Bio 378

EGW Letters File—Page 25

Haskell, S.N.	H-024	87/02/07	Tramelan, Switz.	
Underwood, Br.	U-025	87/03/24	Basel, Switz.	
Covert, Br./Indiana Conference	C-026d	87/09/27	Grand Rapids, Mi.	CM 66;HP 172,195-197,199;1MCP 104-105, 226-227,235-237;6MR 165
Ballou, George	*B-027	87/04/03	Basel, Switz.	
Rice, Br.	*R-030	87/06/11	Norway	3SM 43-44;ML 235,242;MM 166,172,207, 212-213;TSB 147;WM 168
Bourdeau, Martha	B-031	87/01/01	Basel, Switz.	TDG 9
Jones, C.H.	J-032	87/01/31	Basel, Switz.	
Loughborough, J.N.	L-034	87/02/05	Tramelan, Switz.	PM 226-227;LDE 34-35;3Bio 359
Loughborough, J.N.	*L-034a	87/02/11	Basel, Switz.	
Bourdeau, Martha	B-035	87/02/06	Basel, Switz.	DG 145-149
Frey, Henri	*F-036	87/02/10	Basel, Switz.	*18MR 254-262*
Waggoner, E.J./Jones, A.T.	W-037	87/02/18	Basel, Switz.	*15MR 18-28*
n.a. [Sister]	S-038	87/02/24	Basel, Switz.	TDG 63
Bourdeau, D.T.	B-039	87/00/00		*20MR 132-139*
Bourdeau, D.T.	B-039a	87/00/00	Chaux de Fonds	
Underwood, Br./Farnsworth, Br.	*U-040	87/04/13	Basel, Switz.	
Wilcox, Br-Sr.	*W-041	87/04/12	Basel, Switz.	
Butler, G.I.	*B-042	87/04/13	Basel, Switz.	
Brown, Br.	B-043	87/04/15	Basel, Switz.	*21MR 412-413*
Trustees of the Pacific Publishing House	B-044	87/04/19	Basel, Switz.	2SM 209;4MR 117-118;see 5T 580-586
Kellogg, J.H.	K-046	87/04/22	Basel, Switz.	TDG 121;LDE 173;11MR 302
Frey, Henri	F-047	87/05/07	Basel, Switz.	
Frey, Henri [edited copy]	F-047a	87/05/07	Basel, Switz.	
Frey, Henri	F-048	87/07/19	Grimsby, Eng.	
Frey, Henri	F-049	87/07/21	Grimsby, Eng.	See 5T 508-516
Haskell, S.N.	H-050	87/09/01	Battle Creek, Mi.	3MR 20-21;6MR 34-35,123-125; 7MR 244-245
Rice, Br./Gibbs, Br.	B-051	87/10/28		
White, Mary	*W-051a	87/10/30	Oakland, Ca.	
White, Mary	*W-051b	87/11/06	Los Angeles, Ca.	
White, Mary	*W-051c	87/11/19	Oakland, Ca.	3Bio 376
Rice, J.D.	*R-051d	87/10/28	Oakland, Ca.	
Rice, J.D.	R-051e	87/11/20	Oakland, Ca.	
Brn-Srs. Attending April Meeting at Oakland	B-053	87/03/01	Basel, Switz.	3SM 154-155;CG 234;5MR 124;6MR 11-13; see 5T 532-541
Gibbs, Dr.	*G-055	87/06/00	Stockholm	
Durland, Br./John, Br.	B-057	87/07/23	Grimsby, Eng.	*21MR 301-303*
Brn-Srs.	B-058	87/00/00		
Jones, Charles	*J-060	87/02/12	Basel, Switz.	
Butler, G.I.	*B-061	87/04/05	Basel, Switz.	
Gibbs, Dr.	*G-062	87/04/07	Basel, Switz.	
Oyen, Br.	*O-063	87/05/31	Vohwinkel, Prussia	*16MR 254-255*
Ings, Jenny	*I-064	87/08/03	Hotel Liverpool	
Ings, Sr.	*I-065	87/08/04	Atlantic Ocean	3Bio 373
Ings, Sr.	*I-066	87/08/17	New Bedford, Ma	
Patchen, D.H.	*P-067	87/08/21	New Bedford, Ma.	
White, Mary/White, Emma	*W-067a	87/08/25	Springfield, Il.	
Ings, Br-Sr.	*I-068	87/00/00		
Gilmore, Br.	*G-069	87/09/14	Battle Creek, Mi.	
White, J.E./White, Emma	*W-081	87/01/19	Basel, Switz.	TDG 27
White, J.E./White, Emma	*W-082	87/04/18	Basel, Switz.	TDG 117;3Bio 362
Children	*W-083	87/05/28	Vohwinkel, Germany	*16MR 251-253*
White, W.C./White, Mary	*W-084	87/06/24	Stockholm, Sweden	
Children	*W-085	87/06/30	Kittering, Eng.	*21MR 310-311*
Belden, Hattie	*B-086	87/08/26	Springfield, Il.	

Ketchum, Br-Sr.	*K-088	87/12/22	Healdsburg, Ca.	
n.a.	*B-089	87/05/27	Cologne, Germany	*16MR 250*
White, W.C./White, Mary	*W-090	87/07/20	Grimsby, Eng.	3Bio 372
Kellogg, Br-Sr. [J.H.]	K-091	87/01/01		UL 15;OHC 10; HP 245;ML 338
Brn-Srs. in California	B-092	87/04/13	Basel, Switz.	

1888

Walling, Fred	W-001	88/05/28	Reno, Nv.	
Walling, Fred	*W-001a	88/05/20	St. Helena, Ca.	*11MR 149-150*
Walling, Fred	W-002	88/04/13	Healdsburg, Ca.	8MR 109-110
Prescott, Br-Sr.	P-004	88/09/10	Healdsburg, Ca.	5MR 18;10MR 345
Morse, Br.	*M-005	88/12/26	Battle Creek, Mi.	*19MR 300-305*
Knight, Br-Sr.	K-006	88/01/18	Healdsburg, Ca.	
Healey, Br.	H-007	88/12/09	Battle Creek, Mi.	*1888 186-189*
Gibbs, Dr.	G-008	88/00/00		TSB 158-163;8MR 431-433;9MR 370
Daniels, Br-Sr. [E.P.]	*D-009	88/08/10	Healdsburg, Ca.	*PH096 57-63*
Daniels, Br-Sr. [E.P.]	D-010	88/04/00	Healdsburg, Ca.	*PH096 8-22*
Daniels, E.P.	D-011	88/07/06	Fresno, Ca.	*PH096 46-53*
Daniels, E.P.	D-012	88/07/01	Burrough Valley	*PH096 53-56*
Rice, Br.	*R-012a	88/03/00	Selma, Ca.	2BC 1013;CTr 142
Daniels, E.P.	D-013	88/07/03	Burrough Valley	*PH096 39-46*
Burke, Dr.	B-014	88/03/19	Fresno, Ca.	
Brn-Srs. in Illinois	B-015	88/12/14	Battle Creek, Mi.	See RH 12/18/1888
Rice, Br.	R-016	88/04/30	Oakland, Ca.	*21MR 157-170*
Butler, Br-Sr.	B-018	88/12/11	Battle Creek, Mi.	*1888 190-195*
Brn. Assembling in General Conference	B-020	88/08/05	Healdsburg, Ca.	*1888 38-46*
Brn. Assembling in the Week of Prayer	B-020a	88/08/05	Healdsburg, Ca.	*1888 196-202*
Butler, G.I.	B-021	88/10/14	Minneapolis, Mn.	*1888 85-106*
Butler, G.I.	B-021a	88/10/15	Minneapolis, Mn.	*1888 107-116*
Daniels, Br-Sr. [E.P.]	D-023	88/04/24	Oakland, Ca.	*PH096 22-39*
Haskell, S.N.	H-024	88/01/24	Healdsburg, Ca.	OHC 82;HP 107;3MR 21-22,279-280
White, Mary	*W-024a	88/02/06	Healdsburg, Ca.	
Haskell, S.N./Ings, Br-Sr.	H-025	88/02/13	Healdsburg, Ca.	*21MR 321-324*
Rice, Br.	R-026	88/02/20	Healdsburg, Ca.	MM 171
Haskell, S.N.	H-027	88/05/29	Reno, Nv.	TSB 155;VSS 344;3Bio 383
White, Mary	W-027a	88/05/29	Reno, Nv.	3Bio 383
Burke, Br.	B-028	88/04/05	Fresno, Ca.?	3SM 63-64;1MCP 45,271-272;2MCP 643; 8MR 107-109
Butcher, Br-Sr.	B-030	88/03/01	St. Helena, Ca.	*18MR 321-330*
Butcher, Br-Sr.	B-031	88/03/02	Healdsburg, Ca.	
Butler, G.I.	*B-032	88/03/08	Lemoore, Ca.	
Church, Br.	*C-033	88/03/21	Fresno, Ca.	*20MR 363-372*
Church, Br.	C-033a	88/03/21	Fresno, Ca.	See 20MR 363-372
Belden, Charlie	*C-034	88/06/08	Fresno, Ca.	
Snook, Edward	*S-035	88/06/09	Fresno, Ca.	
Cody, Br.	*C-036	88/06/28	Burrough Valley	WM 218-219
n.a. [Sister]	*S-038	88/08/11	Healdsburg, Ca.	*16MR 174-179*
Harper, Sr.	H-039	88/08/29	Healdsburg, Ca.	*19MR 217-221*
Harper, Br.	H-040	88/08/29	Healdsburg, Ca.	*13MR 296-298*
Brn-Srs. at Fresno	*B-041	88/07/07	Burrough Valley	*13MR 232-237*
Brn-Srs. at Fresno	*B-041a	88/07/07	Burrough Valley	10MR 71
Kellogg, J.H.	K-042	88/09/12	Healdsburg, Ca.	
Carpenter, Br-Sr.	C-043	88/11/15	Battle Creek, Mi.	
Frisbie, Br.	F-046	88/12/30	Battle Creek, Mi.	5MR 349
n.a. [Brother]	B-047	88/03/00		6MR 150-152
Lamson, D.H.	L-048	88/12/13	Battle Creek, Mi.	CS 254-255;2MCP 767;OHC 335;UL 361;

				CG 135-136
n.a. [Sister]	B-049	88/00/00		OHC 119
Ballou, George	*B-051	88/01/01	Healdsburg, Ca.	OHC 140;1MCP 32-33
White, Mary	*W-051a	88/01/04	Healdsburg, Ca.	
Butler, G.I.	*B-053	88/02/10	Healdsburg, Ca.	*20MR 373-377*
Butler, G.I.	*B-054	88/03/23	Salmar, Ca.	
Maxson, Dr.	*M-055	88/04/03	Burrough Valley	
Friends at St. Helena	*W-055a	88/04/04	Burrough Valley	3Bio 379
Burke, Br.	*B-056	88/05/28	Reno, Nv.	UL 162
Harper, Sr.	*H-057	88/06/08	Fresno, Ca.	*TSB 54-57*
Kellogg, Br-Sr. [J.H.?]	*K-058	88/06/22	Borrough Valley	
Butler, Br-Sr.	*B-059	88/08/01	Healdsburg, Ca.	FBS 2
Daniels, E.P.	*D-060	88/08/12	Healdsburg, Ca.	
Daniels, Br-Sr. [E.P.]	*D-061	88/08/24	Healdsburg, Ca.	
Roth, Mary	*R-062	88/09/00	Healdsburg, Ca.	
Lucas, Br.	*L-063	88/10/15	Minneapolis, Mn.	
Collie, Br-Sr. [Joseph]	*C-064	88/11/05	Minneapolis, Mn.	OHC 239;12MR 42
White, Mary	*W-071	88/01/08	Healdsburg, Ca.	
Walling, Fred	*W-072	88/03/02	Healdsburg, Ca.	
White, Mary	*W-072a	88/03/06	Healdsburg, Ca.	
White, W.C.	*W-073	88/04/08	Fresno, Ca.	
Scott, Sr.	*S-074	88/04/00	Oakland, Ca.	OHC 239
Scott, Sr.	*S-075	88/05/04	St. Helena, Ca.	3Bio 383
Lockwood, Br-Sr./Bolton, F./Davis, M./Walling, M.	*L-076	88/05/24	Reno, Nv.	DG 175-179
White, Mary/McComber, Sr.	*M-078	88/07/27	Healdsburg, Ca.	3Bio 383
White, Mary	*W-078a	88/07/22	Fresno, Ca.	
White, W.C./White, Mary	*W-079	88/08/17	Healdsburg, Ca.	
White, Mary	*W-080	88/10/08	Kansas City	3Bio 387
White, Mary	*W-081	88/10/09	Minneapolis, Mn.	*1888 66-68*
White, Mary	*W-082	88/11/04	Minneapolis, Mn.	*1888 182-185*
White, Mary	*W-082a	88/11/29	Battle Creek, Mi.	3Bio 419
Caldwell, Dr./Gibbs, Dr.	C-085	88/05/10	Healdsburg, Ca.	7MR 224-225;8MR 330-331;13MR 371-372
White, Mary	*W-086	88/05/11	Healdsburg, Ca.	
Maxson, Br-Sr.	M-087	88/01/21	Healdsburg, Ca.	

1889

White, W.C.	W-001	89/04/07	Chicago, Il.	*1888 286-291*
White, Mary	W-002	89/12/29	Battle Creek, Mi.	UL 377;OHC 318;FLB 99;7BC 911-912
Underwood, R.A.	U-003	89/01/25	Washington, D.C.	*1888 251-256*
Miller, Howard/Miller, Madison	M-004	89/07/23	Battle Creek, Mi.	*1888 388-428*
Miller, Howard	*M-005	89/06/01		*1888 330-335*
Loughborough, Sr.	L-006	89/11/14	Battle Creek, Mi.	
Daniels, E.P.	D-007	89/07/28	Battle Creek, Mi.	*PH096 64-65*
Daniels, E.P.	D-008	89/11/05	Battle Creek, Mi.	*PH096 65-80*
Daniels, Br-Sr. [E.P.]	D-009	89/07/25	Battle Creek, Mi.	VSS 275;2MCP 768
Daniels, Br-Sr. [E.P.]	D-009a	89/05/12	Ottawa, Ks.	
Craig, Br-Sr.	C-010	89/04/02	Chicago, Il.	AH 109-110;10MR 72-73
Burke, Dr.	B-011	89/11/30	Battle Creek, Mi.	
Daniels, Paul	D-012	89/07/04	Battle Creek, Mi.	*4MR 164-165*
Kellogg, M.G.	K-013	89/07/14		missing
Children of the Household	*C-014	89/05/12	Ottawa, Ks.	*1888 307-325*
White, J.E.	*W-014a	89/04/07	Chicaco, Il.	*1888 292-293*
Burke, Dr.	*B-015	89/12/20	Battle Creek, Mi.	2MR 30
H., Br.	H-018	89/01/05		
White, John	W-019	89/01/08		
Giles, Charles	G-020	89/01/11		See 5T 629-635

Underwood, R.A.	U-022	89/01/18	Battle Creek, Mi.	*1888 230-242*
Underwood, R.A.	U-022a	89/01/18		*1888 243-250*
Underwood, R.A.	*U-023	89/02/08	Battle Creek, Mi.	*1888 263-266*
General Conference	B-024	89/00/00		*1888 439-446*
Eldridge, Br.	E-025a	89/09/08	Denver, Co.	*21MR 432-435*
Maxson, Br-Sr.	M-026a	89/03/02	Battle Creek, Mi.	*13MR 174-178*
Maxson, Br-Sr.	M-026b	89/03/02	Battle Creek, Mi.	variant of M-026a
Gotzian, Sr.	G-028	89/03/28	Battle Creek, Mi.	WM 326-327
Buckner, Br-Sr.	B-029	89/11/08	Battle Creek, Mi.	*15MR 144-153*
Fulton, Br.	F-030	89/11/27	Battle Creek, Mi.	7MR 54
Brn. in Fresno	B-031	89/06/13	Rome, NY	
Tyszkiewicz, Br.	T-032	89/03/03	Battle Creek, Mi.	
Brn-Srs.	B-034	89/01/04	Battle Creek, Mi.	1MCP 38;5T 642-650
Strong, Br-Sr.	*S-035	89/12/06	Battle Creek, Mi.	
Brn. in Healdsburg	*B-046	89/01/10	Battle Creek, Mi.	5T 696-698;8MR 346
Harper, Laura	*H-047	89/03/01	Battle Creek, Mi.	TSB 58-61
Bell, Br.	*B-048	89/03/08	Battle Creek, Mi.	
Morrison, Br.	*M-049	89/04/04	Chicago, Il.	*1888 274-276*
Morrison, Br./Nicola, L.	*M-049a	89/04/00		
Fargo, Br.	*F-050	89/05/02	Canton, Pa.	*1888 294-301*
Harper, Laura	*H-051	89/05/19	Ottawa, Ks.	TSB 61-63;LYL 43-44
Harper, Laura	*H-052	89/05/28	Battle Creek, Mi.	
Church, M.J.	*C-054	89/06/06	Williamsport, Pa.	3MR 237,408
Smith, Uriah	*S-055	89/06/14	Rome, NY	*1888 336*
Hall, W.H.	*H-056	89/10/25	Battle Creek, Mi.	9MR 41
Brn-Srs.	*B-057	89/11/20	Battle Creek, Mi.	*1888 498-500*
Loughborough, J.N./McClure, Br./Owen, Br.	*L-058	89/12/10	Battle Creek, Mi.	
Brn-Srs.	*B-059	89/12/10	Battle Creek, Mi.	TSB 199
Ings, Sr.	*I-061	89/01/26	Battle Creek, Mi.	
White, Mary	*W-062	89/02/05	missing	
White, Mary	*W-063	89/02/00	Indianapolis, In.	
White, Mary	*W-064	89/03/20	missing	
White, Mary	*W-064a	89/03/00		3SM 92-93;10MR 383
Ings, Sr./White, Mary/McComber, Sr.	*I-065	89/03/28	Battle Creek, Mi.	
White, J.E.	*W-066	89/04/09	Chicago, Il.	FBS 2
White, Mary/McComber, Sr.	*W-067	89/06/01	to Williamsport, Pa.	3MR 237
White, Mary	*W-068	89/06/12	Williamsport, Pa.	3MR 238
White, Mary	*W-069	89/06/28	Wexford, Mi.	
White, Mary	*W-070	89/07/15	Battle Creek, Mi.	*1888 382-385*
White, Mary	*W-071	89/11/04	Battle Creek, Mi.	2SM 246
White, Mary	*W-072	89/07/19	Battle Creek, Mi.	3Bio 452-453
White, Mary	*W-074	89/10/03	Oakland, Ca.	9MR 44-45
White, Mary	*W-075	89/12/06	Battle Creek, Mi.	2SM 247
White, Mary	*W-076	89/10/29	Battle Creek, Mi.	*1888 450-451*
White, Mary	*W-077	89/10/31	Battle Creek, Mi.	*1888 469-470*
White, Mary	*W-078	89/11/20	Battle Creek, Mi.	
White, Mary	*W-080	89/12/18	Battle Creek, Mi.	
Walling, Fred	*W-081	89/00/00		
Giles, Br.	*G-082	89/01/09	Battle Creek, Mi.	OHC 86,119
White, Mary	*W-083	89/01/05	Battle Creek, Mi.	1SM 150-151;3MR 189-190;3Bio 423
White, W.C.	*W-084	89/04/05	Chicago, Il.	
n.a. [Brethren]	*B-085	89/04/00		*1888 277-285*
Wheeler, Br-Sr.	*W-086	89/07/19	Battle Creek, Mi.	
Smith, Uriah	S-087	89/09/00	Denver, Co.	*1888 437-438*
Kellogg, M.G.	K-088	89/06/01	to Williamsport, Pa.	
Olsen, O.A.	*O-089	89/08/25	Battle Creek, Mi.	

1890

Brethren	B-001	90/05/14	St. Helena, Ca.	*1888 651-664*
Abbey, Sr.	A-001a	90/07/06	Battle Creek, Mi.	
Atwood, Br./Pratt, Br.	A-001c	90/05/28	Crystal Springs, Ca.	6MR 55-56;15MR 153-157
Abbey, Ira	A-001d	90/01/28	Battle Creek, Mi.	TSB 142-145
Abbey, Ira	A-001e	90/01/14	Battle Creek, Mi.	TSB 133-137
Brn. in Responsible Positions	B-001f	90/11/00	Salamanca, NY	*1888 720-731*
Burnett, Br.	B-002	90/01/15	Battle Creek, Mi.	
Dunlap, Br.	D-003a	90/10/28	S. Lancaster, Ma.	
Missionaries in Africa	B-004	90/03/09	Battle Creek, Mi.	*TSA 21-27*
Baker, Br.	*B-005	90/05/24		TSB 155-158;Ev 507
Baker, Br.	B-005a	90/05/24	Crystal Springs, Ca	variant of Lt 5
Managers of the Health Inst./Crystal Springs	B-006a	90/04/00	Healdsburg, Ca.	MM 144-147,193-194,205-206,217, 259-260;TSB 16,145-147;VSS 422; 8MR 382-383
Brn-Srs. in Africa	*B-006b	90/00/00		*TSA 28-35*
Cody, Br.	*C-007	90/01/06	Battle Creek, Mi.	
Church, Br.	C-008	90/07/07	Battle Creek, Mi.	
Church, Br.	C-008a	90/07/07	Battle Creek, Mi.	*20MR 93-98*
Fulton, Br./Burke, Br.	*F-009c	90/10/23	S. Lancaster, Ma.	
Fulton, John	F-010	90/01/02	Battle Creek, Mi.	1MR 374-382
Garmire, Br-Sr.	G-011	90/08/06		*15MR 12-17*
Garmire, Br-Sr.	G-012	90/08/12	Petoskey, Mi.	2SM 56,73-79,82-84;Ev 247-248,256, 368,682;OHC 214;10MR 310-312; 12MR 116-119;CTr 332
Gibbs, Br-Sr.	G-013	90/10/01	Battle Creek, Mi.	
Hutchings, Br-Sr.	H-013a	90/10/28	S. Lancaster, Ma.	
Hutchings, George	H-013b	90/01/15	Battle Creek, Mi.	MRmnt 123
Irwin, Br.	I-015	90/08/12	Petoskey, Mi.	Ev 642-644;8MR 338
Jones, Edwin	J-015a	90/05/19	Crystal Springs, Ca.	*1SM 176-184 with 6MR 222*
Kellogg, J.H.	K-018	90/10/18	S. Lancaster, Ma.	*8T 133-144*
Larson, Matthew	*L-018d	90/03/06		*1888 584-589*
Lindsay, Br-Sr.	L-018e	90/02/05	Battle Creek, Mi.	*21MR 429-431*
Lindsay, Charley	L-018f	90/02/05	Battle Creek, Mi.	
Olsen, O.A.	*O-020	90/10/07	Battle Creek, Mi.	*1888 714-719*
Olsen, O.A.	O-021	90/12/13	Danvers, Ma.	missing
Physicians and Health Institutions	P-022	90/05/20	St. Helena, Ca.	*20MR 378-390*
Rogers, Br.	R-022a	90/02/09	Battle Creek, Mi.	
Paddock, Mr.	P-022b	90/03/08		
Place, Br.	P-022c	90/03/28	Springdale, Ar.	
Stone, Br.	S-023	90/01/06	Battle Creek, Mi.	1888 520;ChL 23;HP 60;9MR 127
Saterlee, Annie	*S-023a	90/01/14	Battle Creek, Mi.	*TSB 137-140*
Saxby, Br.	S-024	90/08/13	Petoskey, Mi.	1MCP 228;4MR 450;9MR 160
Saterlee, Annie	S-024a	90/01/28	Battle Creek, Mi.	TSB 140-142
Graham, Br.	G-025a	90/07/14	Battle Creek, Mi.	*21MR 457-462*
Abbey, Sr./Rosetta/Arthur	A-027	90/07/06	Battle Creek, Mi.	TMK 371;CG 188,506
Van Horn, Amanda	V-028	90/07/01	Battle Creek, Mi.	TSB 39-43;AH 36,348;CG 219
Van Horn, Br.	V-029	90/08/05	Petoskey, Mi.	Ev 283,441-442;9MR 173
White, W.C./White, Mary	*W-030	90/03/10	Battle Creek, Mi.	*1888 622-626*
Fulton, Samuel	*F-031	90/04/23	Oakland, Ca.	*16MR 242-244*
Smith, Uriah	S-032	90/12/09	Lynn, Ma.	3BC 1146
Brn-Srs. in Norwich	B-033	90/12/04	Lynn, Ma.	2MCP 639;5MR 231;9MR 132-135
Craig, Br.	C-034	90/03/23	Chicago, Il.	*16MR 301-315*
Wessels, Br.	W-035	90/02/16	Battle Creek, Mi.	*PC 28-29*
Gray, Br-Sr.	G-036	90/05/11	St. Helena, Ca.	

Washburn, J.S.	W-036a	90/09/18	Battle Creek, Mi.	*1888 708-713*
Foss, Mary	*F-037	90/12/22	Washington, D.C.	*A Prophet Among You, 487-489*
Church, Br./Bell, Br./Church in Fresno	B-038	90/02/21	Battle Creek, Mi.	*PH028 20-28*
Smith, Uriah	S-040	90/12/31	Battle Creek, Mi.	*1888 790-801*
Kellogg, J.H.	K-041	90/12/24	Washington, D.C.	*1MR 197-221*
Burke, Br-Sr.	B-042	90/10/01	Battle Creek, Mi.	OHC 124,303;2MCP 687
Olsen, O.A.	O-043	90/12/18	Lynn, Ma.	*1888 743-749*
Olsen, O.A.	O-043a	90/12/18	Lynn, Ma.	*1888 750-757*
Brn-Srs. in California	B-044	90/07/02	Battle Creek, Mi.	
Olsen, O.A.	O-046	90/05/08	St. Helena, Ca.	*1888 645-650*
Loughborough, J.N.	*L-051	90/01/06	Battle Creek, Mi.	
Loughborough, J.N.	*L-052	90/01/07	Battle Creek, Mi.	
Ballenger, Br./Smith, Leon	*B-053	90/01/17	Battle Creek, Mi.	*1888 528-532*
Loughborough, J.N.	*L-054	90/02/11	Battle Creek, Mi.	
Jones, A.T.	*J-055	90/02/17	Battle Creek, Mi.	
White, Mary	*W-056	90/02/12	Battle Creek, Mi.	2SM 248
White, Mary	*W-057	90/02/13	Battle Creek, Mi.	2SM 249
Rogers, Br.	*R-058	90/03/01	Battle Creek, Mi.	
Smith, Uriah	*S-059	90/03/08	Battle Creek, Mi.	*1888 599-605*
Colcord, W.A.	*C-060	90/03/10	Battle Creek, Mi.	*1888 620-621*
Daniells, Br-Sr.	*D-061	90/04/00	Oakland, Ca.	
Fulton, John	*F-062	90/05/05	St. Helena, Ca.	
Thomson, Sr.	*T-063	90/05/22	St. Helena, Ca.	
Jones, E.R.	*J-064	90/07/04	Battle Creek, Mi.	
Olsen, O.A./Jones, Dan	*O-065	90/07/27	Petoskey, Mi.	
Olsen, O.A./White, W.C.	*O-066	90/07/29	Petoskey, Mi.	*13MR 166*
Brn. in the Ministry	*B-067	90/09/17	Battle Creek, Mi.	*1888 706-707*
Fulton, John	*F-068	90/09/19	Battle Creek, Mi.	
Review Office	*B-069	90/10/08	Battle Creek, Mi.	
Daniels, E.P.	*D-070	90/10/30	Salamanca, NY	
Jones, Charles	*J-071	90/11/01	Salamanca, NY	
Harris, Albert	*H-072	90/11/10	Sands, Va.	
Harris, Albert	*H-072a	90/11/12	New York, NY	2MR 332
Smith, Uriah	*S-073	90/11/25	Brooklyn, NY	*1888 732-734*
General Conference	*B-074	90/12/09	Lynn, Ma.	
Appley, Sr.	*A-075	90/12/09	Lynn, Ma.	
Children	*W-077	90/05/28	St. Helena, Ca.	2SM 249-250
White, W.C.	*W-078	90/06/16	Battle Creek, Mi.	2SM 250
White, Mary	*W-079	90/01/10	Battle Creek, Mi.	
White, W.C.	*W-080	90/03/07	Battle Creek, Mi.	*1888 590-592*
White, Mary	*W-081	90/03/07	Battle Creek, Mi.	
White, W.C./White, Mary	*W-082	90/03/09	Battle Creek, Mi.	*1888 617-619*
White, W.C./White, Mary	*W-083	90/03/13	Battle Creek, Mi.	*1888 627-635*
White, W.C./White, Mary	*W-084	90/03/19	Battle Creek, Mi.	*1888 642-644*
Children	*W-085	90/03/23	Chicago, Il.	
White, W.C.	*W-086	90/03/24	Chicago, Il.	
White, W.C./White, Mary	*W-087	90/04/14	Fresno, Ca.	
White, W.C.	*W-088	90/04/21	Oakland, Ca.	
Children	*W-089	90/04/29	Oakland, Ca.	
White, W.C.	*W-090	90/04/30	Oakland, Ca.	
White, W.C./White, Mary	*W-091	90/05/02	St. Helena, Ca.	
White, W.C./White, Mary	*W-092	90/05/15	St. Helena, Ca.	
White, W.C./White, Mary [May Walling ?]	*W-093	90/05/20	St. Helena, Ca.	
White, W.C.	*W-094	90/06/17	Battle Creek, Mi.	
White, W.C./Household	*W-095	90/07/17	Petoskey, Mi.	8MR 125
White, W.C.	*W-096	90/07/24	Petoskey, Mi.	
White, W.C.	*W-097	90/07/27	Petoskey, Mi.	*1888 683-687*

White, W.C.	*W-098	90/07/31	Petoskey, Mi.	
White, W.C.	*W-099	90/08/08	Petoskey, Mi.	
White, W.C.	*W-100	90/08/11	Petoskey, Mi.	
White, W.C.	*W-101	90/08/15	Petoskey, Mi.	
White, W.C.	*W-102	90/08/15	Petoskey, Mi.	
White, W.C.	*W-103	90/08/19	Petoskey, Mi.	*1888 688-694*
White, W.C.	*W-104	90/08/23	Petoskey, Mi.	
White, W.C.?	*W-105	90/08/25		
White, W.C.	*W-106	90/08/28	Petoskey, Mi.	
White, W.C.	*W-107	90/09/02	Petoskey, Mi.	
Davis, Marian	*D-108	90/10/23	S. Lancaster, Ma.	
White, W.C./White, J.E./White, Emma	*W-109	90/12/06	Lynn, Ma.	*1888 735-742*
White, W.C.	*W-110	90/12/12	Denver, Co.	
White, W.C.	*W-111	90/12/18	Lynn, Ma.	
White, W.C./White, J.E./White, Emma	*W-112	90/12/22	Washington, D.C.	*1888 758-763*
Children/Workers in my Home	*W-113	90/12/30		
Olsen, O.A.	*O-114	90/06/09	Denver, Co.	*18MR 374-379*
Olsen, O.A.	*O-115	90/06/21	Battle Creek, Mi.	*1888 675-682*
Olsen, O.A.	*O-116	90/08/27	Petoskey, Mi.	*1888 703-705*
Olsen, O.A.	*O-117	90/08/03		
Olsen, O.A.	*O-118	90/09/03	Harbor Springs, Mi.	
General Conference Committee	*B-119	90/00/00		
Loughborough, J.N.	*L-120	90/02/21	Battle Creek, Mi.	
Olsen, Andrew D.	O-121	90/07/11	Battle Creek, Mi.	

1891

Fulton, John/Burke, Br.	*B-003	91/03/20	Battle Creek, Mi.	3Bio 489-490;3MR 194-195
Ferrell, Br-Sr.	F-004	91/05/01	Grand Rapids, Mi.	
Bliss, C.H.	B-005	91/01/18	Battle Creek, Mi.	TSB 218-219
n.a. [Afflicted Brother]	*B-005a	91/02/13	Battle Creek, Mi.	RY 74-75
Burke, W.P.	B-005b	91/05/30	Harbor Springs, Mi.	OHC 32,147,216
Brn. in the RH Office	B-006	91/03/16	Battle Creek, Mi.	*19MR 16-18*
Chapman, Br.	C-007	91/06/11	Petoskey, Mi.	*14MR 175-180*
Craig, Br.	*C-008	91/02/04	Battle Creek, Mi.	1MCP 22,29,237-238;2MCP 802
Evans, Br-Sr. [William]	E-008b	91/06/10	Petoskey, Mi.	RY 178-180;2BC 1039;CC 197
Ferrell, Br-Sr.	F-009	91/05/15	Petoskey, Mi.	
Gilbert, Sr. [D.S.]	G-009a	91/06/03	Petoskey, Mi.	OHC 163;6MR 18-19,31
Kellogg, J.H.	*K-010	91/05/15	Petoskey, Mi.	CD 334;6MR 390;3Bio 491-492
White, W.C.	*W-011	91/06/29	Petoskey, Mi.	
Haskell, S.N.	H-014	91/12/11	Sidney, Aus.	*1888 964-976*
Harper, Laura	H-014a	91/03/08	Battle Creek, Mi.	*TSB 63-67*
Irwin, Br-Sr.	I-016	91/06/09	Petoskey, Mi.	
Irwin, Br-Sr.	I-016a	91/06/09	Petoskey, Mi.	
Irwin, G.A.	I-017	91/07/20	Harbor Spgs., Mi.	3SM 54-55;4MR 63;12MR 40-41
Ings, Br-Sr./Fulton, John	I-017a	91/11/18	Steamer Alameda	*18MR 237-247*
Irwin, Br-Sr.	I-018	91/06/29	Petoskey, Mi.	1MCP 237;8MR 244
Kynett, Br-Sr.	K-018a	91/04/13	Battle Creek, Mi.	AH 106,112,119
Kynett, Br-Sr.	K-018b	91/02/15	Battle Creek, Mi.	*13MR 74-91*
Miller, H.C.	M-018c	91/06/04	Petoskey, Mi.	
Miller, H.C.	M-019a	91/04/02	Battle Creek, Mi.	AH 225-226;CG 262;CD 494;5MR 401-403
Smith, Uriah	S-020	91/01/06	Battle Creek, Mi.	*1888 846-849*
Olsen, O.A.	O-021	91/12/13	Syndey, Aus.	4Bio 22
Sisley, Br.	S-025	91/01/12	Battle Creek, Mi.	
Smith, Leon	S-026	91/10/09	St. Helena, Ca.	3SM 232-233;4MR 47-51
Steward, Mary	S-026a	91/08/01	Harbor Springs, Mi.	*DG 136-138*
Workers in the Office at Oakland	W-031	91/12/19	N. Fitzroy, Aus.	*PH152 26-48*

Washburn, Br-Sr.	W-032	91/01/08	Battle Creek, Mi.	*1888 850-853*
White, J.E./White, Emma	W-032a	91/12/07	Alameda	4Bio 19-21;3MR 250,376;4MR 43
Brn-Srs. Assembled in Campmeeting	B-033	91/09/15	Colorado Spgs., Co.	
Workers at the Health Retreat	B-034	91/05/31	Harbor Springs, Mi.	1MCP 297;2MCP 760,784
Burke, Dr.	B-035	91/11/06	Oakland, Ca.	
Webber, Emma	W-037	91/02/12	Battle Creek, Mi.	*12MR 104-111*
Daniels, E.P.	D-038	91/11/10	Oakland, Ca.	3SM 301-302
Burke, Dr.	B-040	91/10/08	Healdsburg, Ca.	
Burke, Dr.	B-041	91/10/24	St. Helena, Ca.	1MCP 23-24;2MCP 421
Gates, Elsie	G-042	91/10/25	Healdsburg, Ca.	
Gates, Elsie	G-044	91/09/29	Healdsburg, Ca.	
n.a. [Brother]	B-045	91/12/28		LDE 237;6MR 321
Gates, Elsie	G-046	91/12/15	Sydney, Aus.	
Burke, Dr.	*B-047	91/01/06	Battle Creek, Mi.	
Burke, Dr.	*B-048	91/10/00	date uncertain	9MR 72
Jones, Charles	*J-049	91/01/26	Battle Creek, Mi.	
Place, Dr.	*P-050	91/04/27	Greenville, Mi.	
Van Horn, Br.	*V-051	91/05/01	Grand Rapids, Mi.	
n.a. [Brother]	*B-052	91/05/03	Grand Rapids, Mi.	
Fulton, John	*F-053	91/06/02	Petoskey, Mi.	
Jones, Charles	*J-054	91/07/07	Petoskey, Mi.	
Burke, Dr.	*B-055	91/09/29	Healdsburg, Ca.	
Ings, Sr.	*I-056	91/09/30	Healdsburg, Ca.	
Children/Olsen, Br-Sr.	*W-057	91/10/12	St. Helena, Ca.	4Bio 18
Kellogg, J.H.	*K-058	91/11/05	Healdsburg, Ca.	
Bangs, Lizzie	*B-061	91/02/21	Battle Creek, Mi.	3MR 193
White, W.C.	*W-062	91/04/30	Greenville, Mi.	
White, W.C.	*W-063	91/04/22	Greenville, Mi.	
White, W.C.	*W-064	91/04/25	Greenville, Mi.	
White, W.C.	*W-065	91/04/27	Greenville, Mi.	3Bio 490
White, W.C.	*W-066	91/04/27	Greenville, Mi.	
McEnterfer, Sara	*M-067	91/05/04	Grand Rapids, Mi.	
White, W.C.	*W-068	91/05/04	Grand Rapids, Mi.	
White, W.C.	*W-069	91/05/19	Petoskey, Mi.	
White, W.C.	*W-070	91/05/00	Petoskey, Mi.	
White, W.C.	*W-071	91/05/26	Petoskey, Mi.	
White, W.C.	*W-072	91/05/26	Petoskey, Mi.	
White, W.C.	*W-073	91/05/26	Petoskey, Mi.	
White, W.C.	*W-074	91/05/28	Petoskey, Mi.	
White, W.C.	*W-075	91/05/29	Petoskey, Mi.	
White, W.C.	*W-076	91/05/31	Petoskey, Mi.	
White, W.C.	*W-077	91/06/01	Petoskey, Mi.	
White, W.C.	*W-078	91/06/02	Petoskey, Mi.	
White, W.C.	*W-079	91/06/05	Petoskey, Mi.	
White, J.E./White, Emma	*W-080	91/06/16	Petoskey, Mi.	
White, W.C.	*W-081	91/06/23	Petoskey, Mi.	
White, W.C.	*W-082	91/06/03	Petoskey, Mi.	
White, W.C.	*W-083	91/07/03	Petoskey, Mi.	9MR 72-73
White, W.C.	*W-084	91/07/13	Petoskey, Mi.	*18MR 153-154*
Starr, J.A.	S-085	91/09/22	Healdsburg, Ca.	*13MR 148-152*
Olsen, O.A.	*O-086	91/03/20	Battle Creek, Mi.	
Olsen, O.A.	*O-087	91/04/21	Greenville, Mi.	
General Conference Committee	*B-088	91/08/11		
Olsen, O.A.	*O-089	91/08/14	Harbor Springs, Mi.	
Colcord, W.A.	*C-090	91/06/11	Petoskey, Mi.	
Olsen, O.A.	O-091	91/11/27	Steamer *Alemda*	

1892

Brn. who stand in Responsible Positions	B-001	92/01/12	N. Fitzroy, Aus.	*20MR 391-394*
Belden, Frank/Belden, Hattie	B-002a	92/11/05	Adelaide, Aus.	*14MR 104-113*
Brn-Srs.	B-002b	92/08/03	Preston, Aus.	See TM 177-181
Brn-Srs. in Battle Creek	B-002c	92/12/21	Melbourne, Aus.	See GCDB 01/28/1893
Brn. of the General Conference	*B-002d	92/12/23	George's Terrace	*GCDB 02/27/1893*
Curtis, Br.	C-003	92/01/16	N. Fitzroy, Aus.	6MR 68-69,199;PH118 1-10
Daniells, Sr.	D-004	92/09/19	Preston, Aus.	RC 108;6MR 41-42;9MR 210,375-376
Eldridge, C.	E-005	92/09/02	N. Fitzroy, Aus.	PM 242-243;1MR 267-268
Haskell, S.N.	H-006	92/05/01	Preston, Aus.	9MR 156-157
Grainger, Br-Sr.	G-007	92/10/24	Adelaide, Aus.	2SM 240-245
Health Retreat	H-008	92/03/14	N. Fitzroy, Aus.	
Hare, Br-Sr. [Robert]	H-009	92/12/01		1BC 1106;3BC 1163
Haskell, S.N.	H-010	92/04/06	Preston, Aus.	4Bio 35,38
Haskell, S.N.	H-010a	92/04/06	Preston, Aus.	Ev 344-345;1MR 16;6MR 376-377
Haskell, S.N.	H-011	92/03/18	N. Fitzroy, Aus.	5BC 1097;TMK 19
Haskell, S.N.	H-011b	92/07/17	Preston, Aus.	2MR 36-37
Haskell, S.N.	H-011c	92/02/11	Melbourne, Aus.	5MR 130;6MR 54
Haskell, S.N.	H-012	92/11/05	Adelaide, Aus.	AH 472-473;7BC 912-913;WM 76,105,166
Haskell, S.N.	H-013	92/08/22	N. Fitzroy, Aus.	*1888 993-1003*
Haskell, S.N.	H-014	92/09/02	Preston, Aus.	*1888 1033-1035*
Haskell, Sr.	*H-014b	92/10/26	Adelaide, Aus.	2SM 231-232
Haskell, S.N.	H-015	92/06/25	Preston, Aus.	1SM 158;SD 248;6BC 1116;LDE 92,173; 1MR 176;5MR 334-335
Holland, Br-Sr.	H-016	92/11/10	Adelaide, Aus.	1BC 1092;9MR 347-348
Jones, Br-Sr. [C.H.]	J-016a	92/07/04	Preston, Aus.	CTr 11
Haskell, S.N.	H-016c	92/05/12	Preston, Aus.	4Bio 37
Haskell, S.N.	H-016d	92/05/07	Preston, Aus.	ChL 36;GCDB 02/04/1893
Haskell, S.N.	H-016e	92/02/06	Preston, Aus.	Ev 443;4MR 242;GCDB 02/04/1893
Haskell, S.N.	H-016f	92/05/09	Preston, Aus.	*12MR 329-338*
Haskell, S.N.	H-016g	92/05/29	Preston, Aus.	*1888 987-990*
Haskell, S.N.	H-016i	92/11/23	Adelaide, Aus.	
Jones, A.T.	J-016j	92/09/02	Preston, Aus.	*1888 1036-1039*
Kellogg, J.H.	K-017	92/03/11	N. Fitzroy, Aus.	*19MR 225-228*
Kellogg, J.H.	K-018	92/04/15	Preston, Aus.	*1888 977-986*
Kellogg, Br-Sr. [J.H.]	K-018a	92/07/05	N. Fitzroy, Aus.	2SM 233-234
Kellogg, J.H.	K-019	92/08/05	N. Fitzroy, Aus.	*16MR 57-67*
Olsen, O.A.	O-019a	92/04/12	Melbourne, Aus.	12MR 103
Olsen, O.A.	O-019b	92/06/19	Preston, Aus.	TM 159-167;4MR 345;5MR 137; 6MR 19-21;8MR 452
Olsen, O.A.	O-019c	92/01/00		CD 259-260,487;7MR 346;8MR 49
Olsen, O.A.	O-019d	92/09/01	N. Fitzroy, Aus.	*1888 1018-1032*
Olsen, O.A.	O-019e	92/10/26	Adelaide, Aus.	ML 10;2MCP 492;8MR 186
Kellogg, J.H.	K-020	92/10/17	Adelaide, Aus.	*19MR 88-100*
Kellogg, J.H.	K-021	92/09/28	Adelaide, Aus.	
Maxson, Br-Sr.	M-021a	92/07/03	Preston, Aus.	
Kellogg, Br-Sr. [J.H.]	K-021b	92/12/23	George's Terrace	*20MR 158-163*
Maxson, Br-Sr.	M-021c	92/01/08	N. Fitzroy, Aus.	*20MR 119-122*
Olsen, O.A.	O-022	92/11/23	Adelaide, Aus.	*PH002 23-28*
Olsen, O.A.	O-023	92/09/20	N. Fitzroy, Aus.	*5MR 9-14*
Prescott, Br-Sr.	P-023a	92/09/25	George's Terrace	OHC 280
Robinson, A.T.	R-023c	92/07/20	N. Fitzroy, Aus.	TSA 63-66
Olsen, O.A.	O-023d	92/11/23	Adelaide, Aus.	
Smith, Uriah	S-024	92/09/19	N. Fitzroy, Aus.	*15MR 80-94*
Scazighini, Br-Sr.	S-025	92/10/12	Adelaide, Aus.	OHC 320
Tenney, G.C.	T-025a	92/12/23	George's Terrace	6MR 122

EGW Letters File—Page 34

Smith, Uriah	S-025b	92/08/30	N. Fitzroy, Aus.	*1888 1004-1017*
White, J.E./White, Emma	W-027	92/05/29	Preston, Aus.	HP 147,155;OHC 241
Waggoner, E.J.	W-027a	92/12/27	George's Terrace	3SM 26;Ev 580-581
Wessels, P.W.B.	W-028	92/07/00	N. Fitzroy, Aus.	TSA 36-39;TMK 283
Wessels, Br-Sr.	W-029	92/08/01		TSA 39-40
White, W.C.	W-029a	92/11/20	Adelaide, Aus.	8MR 454-455
Haskell, S.N.	H-030a	92/09/06	Preston, Aus.	4Bio 46;HP 48;Mar 197;UL 262; 7BC 964-965;3SM 326-327;LDE 147
Waggoner, Br.	W-031	92/05/00	N. Fitzroy, Aus.	*3MR 10-19*
Brn. of the General Conference	B-032	92/12/19	Melbourne, Aus.	*GCDB 01/29/1893*;see TM 24-32
Brn. of the General Conference	B-032a	92/12/19	Melbourne, Aus.	Similar to Lt 32, 1892
Kellogg, Br-Sr.	K-034	92/09/16	Preston, Aus.	MM 300-301;5MR 130-131;7MR 46; see CH 503-508
White, J.E./White, Emma	W-036	92/05/05	Preston, Aus.	TMK 56
White, J.E./White, Emma	W-037	92/03/09	N. Fitzroy, Aus.	OHC 134
Smith, Br-Sr.	S-038	92/06/29	Preston, Aus.	7MR 145-147
Olsen, O.A.	O-040	92/07/15	Preston, Aus.	TM 167-173;3SM 115;3MR 248; 8MR 452-454;10MR 66-67;4Bio 28
Olsen, O.A.	O-041	92/08/00		ChL 76-77
Ings, Br-Sr.	O-042	92/08/11	N. Fitzroy, Aus.	
Haskell, S.N.	H-043	92/09/18	Preston, Aus.	3BC 1150;7BC 927,937;1SM 106-107; 11MR 363-364; CTr 164
Wessels, Br-Sr. [P.B.W.]	W-044	92/11/07	Adelaide, Aus.	TSA 41-45
Robinson, A.T.	*R-045	92/11/07	Adelaide, Aus.	ML 304,307;8MR 266
Olsen, O.A.	O-046	92/12/13	George's Terrace	3SM 84-85;5MR 454;4Bio 45,48,50
Morrison, Br.	M-047	92/12/22	Melbourne, Aus.	*1888 1081-1086*
Haskell, S.N.	H-048	92/00/00		2MCP 725
Gates, Br-Sr.	*G-049	92/12/23	George's Terrace	
Gates, Br-Sr.	G-049a	92/06/14	Preston, Aus.	CD 162
Olsen, O.A.	O-050	92/03/12	Preston, Aus.	PH002 17-20;10MR 73
Children	*W-051	92/06/15		
Children	*W-052	92/07/17	Preston, Aus.	
White, J.E.	*W-053	92/07/26	Preston, Aus.	
White, J.E.	*W-054	92/09/22	Melbourne, Aus.	9MR 339;4Bio 45
White, J.E.	*W-055	92/10/05	Adelaide, Aus.	
White, J.E.	*W-056	92/10/26	Adelaide, Aus.	
White, J.E.	*W-057	92/10/00		
Children	*W-058	92/11/24	Adelaide, Aus.	
Children	*W-059	92/12/27	Melbourne, Aus.	
White, W.C.	*W-061	92/10/04	Adelaide, Aus.	
White, W.C.	*W-062	92/03/21	Preston, Aus.	4Bio 35-36
White, W.C.	*W-063	92/03/25	Preston, Aus.	
White, W.C.	*W-064	92/03/27	Preston, Aus.	4Bio 34
White, W.C.	*W-065	92/03/29	Preston, Aus.	4Bio 34
White, W.C.	*W-066	92/04/00	Preston, Aus.	
White, W.C.	*W-067	92/05/02	Preston, Aus.	
White, Ella May	*W-068	92/06/10	Preston, Aus.	
White, Mabel	*W-069	92/06/10	Preston, Aus.	
White, Ella May	*W-070	92/07/07	Preston, Aus.	
White, Mabel	*W-071	92/07/07	Preston, Aus.	
White, W.C.	*W-072	92/10/05	Adelaide, Aus.	
White, W.C.	*W-073	92/10/07	Adelaide, Aus.	
White, W.C.	*W-074	92/10/10	Adelaide, Aus.	FBS 8
White, W.C.	*W-075	92/10/13	Adelaide, Aus.	
White, W.C.	*W-076	92/10/16	Adelaide, Aus.	
White, W.C.	*W-077	92/10/21	Adelaide, Aus.	FBS 8;3MR 410
White, W.C.	*W-078	92/10/21	Adelaide, Aus.	

White, W.C.	*W-079	92/10/25	Adelaide, Aus.	
White, W.C.	*W-080	92/10/27	Adelaide, Aus.	
Davis, Marian	*D-081	92/10/28	Adelaide, Aus.	3MR 410
White, W.C.	*W-082	92/11/06	Adelaide, Aus.	
White, W.C.	*W-083	92/11/08	Adelaide, Aus.	
White, W.C.	*W-084	92/11/09	Adelaide, Aus.	8MR 454
White, W.C.	*W-085	92/11/16	Adelaide, Aus.	
White, W.C.	*W-086	92/11/18	Adelaide, Aus.	3MR 411
White, W.C.	*W-087	92/11/23	Adelaide, Aus.	
White, W.C.	*W-088	92/11/30	Ballarat, Aus.	
White, W.C.	*W-089	92/12/27	Melbourne, Aus.	
Hall, Sr.	*H-090	92/01/23	N. Fitzroy, Aus.	4Bio 30
Hall, Sr.	*H-091	92/11/23	Adelaide, Aus.	
n.a.	B-092	92/05/09	Preston, Aus.	4Bio 30
Brn-Srs. in Battle Creek /All Who Need These Words	B-093	92/01/21	N. Fitzroy, Aus.	GCB 4th Q, 1896, 764-768
White, J.E.	W-094	92/05/05	Preston, Aus.	
Olsen, O.A.?	O-095	92/00/00		
Olsen, O.A.	O-096	92/10/14	Adelaide, Aus.	
Olsen, O.A.	O-097	92/10/22	Adelaide, Aus.	
Olsen, O.A.	O-098	92/11/16	Adelaide, Aus.	
Olsen, O.A.	O-099	92/11/23	Adelaide, Aus.	
Olsen, O.A.	O-100	92/11/12		

1893

Brown, Sr.	*B-001	93/08/04	Paremata, N.Z.	*20MR 51-58*
Brown, Sr.	B-002	93/08/07	Paremata, N.Z.	
Brown, Martha	*B-003	93/08/23	Hastings, N.Z.	
Brn-Srs.	B-004	93/12/23	Sydney, Aus.	*14MR 189-199*
Bell, Susan	B-005	93/09/03	Napier, N.Z.	
Brown, Sr.	B-006	93/09/04	Napier, N.Z.	OHC 49,98,317
Belden, Byron	B-006a	93/04/23	Wellington, N.Z.	VSS 144
Haskell, S.N.	H-006b	93/02/22	Kaeo, N.Z.	3MR 325
Brn-Srs. in Australia	B-007	93/11/00		*BE 12/08/1893*
Hare, Joseph	H-008	93/03/08	Kaeo, N.Z.	Te 63,193;6MR 261-262;8MR 308
Brn-Srs. in New Zealand	B-008a	93/10/31	Gisborne, N.Z.	*11MR 7-12*
Belden, F.E./Belden, Hattie	B-009	93/07/12		*1888 1185-1191*
Brn. in America	B-009a	93/08/01	Wellington, N.Z.	5MR 232;11MR 1-7;HM 11/1893
Corkham, D.A.	C-010	93/05/30	Wellington, N.Z.	HP 126;OHC 58
Caro, Eric	C-011	93/10/26	Gisborne, N.Z.	See FE 297-306
Christie, Louis	C-012	93/08/01	Paremata, N.Z.	
Christie, Louis	C-012a	93/00/00		CC 157;1BC 1114;5BC 1136;TMK 62; 7MR 172-173;CTr 125
Christie, Louis	C-012b	93/00/00		Var. of Lt 12a, 1893
General Matter re the Christie Case	C-013	93/00/00		2BC 997;7BC 938,950-951;OHC 142; 10MR 282-283;YI 1/25-2/15/1894
To Whom It May Concern re Christie Case	C-014	93/07/23		
Re Christie Case	C-014a	93/07/23		VSS 145-146
Caldwell, W.F.	*C-015	93/06/09	Wellington, N.Z.	
Caldwell, W.F.	C-016	93/06/11	Wellington, N.Z.	2SM 63-69
Caro, Edgar/Caro, Eric	C-017	93/09/05	Hastings, N.Z.	
Caro, Edgar	*C-017a	93/10/02	Napier, N.Z.	2SM 279-280,321-324;7MR 274-275
Colcord, W.A.	C-017b	93/02/23	Kaeo, N.Z.	
Daniells, Br-Sr. [A.G.]	D-018	93/05/11	Wellington, N.Z.	Ev 439-440
Daniells, A.G.	D-018a	93/01/30	Parramatta, Aus.	
Daniells, Br-Sr. [A.G.]	D-019	93/09/08	Ormondville, Aus.	
Bolton, Fannie/Davis, Marian	B-020	93/11/02	Gisborne, N.Z.	Ev 122-123,291

Eldridge, C.	E-020a	93/01/09	Melbourne, Aus.	*1888 1096-1117*
Faulkhead, Br-Sr.	*F-021	93/10/08	Napier, N.Z.	Ev 622
Faulkhead, Br.	F-021a	93/01/11		*14MR 9-16*
Gage, Br-Sr. [William]	G-022	93/10/22	Gisborne, N.Z.	CTr 171
Gribble, Carrie	G-023	93/09/13	Hastings, N.Z.	LYL 76-77;1MCP 300-302;AH 53
Gates, E.H.	G-023a	93/01/10	Melbourne, Aus.	VSS 400-401;TDG 18;ML 163;Ev 277,582, 621-622;CS 96-97;PM 166;5MR 156, 161-162;6MR 71-72;12MR 7-9;4Bio 58
Gage, Fred	*G-024	93/10/04	Napier, N.Z.	
Haskell, S.N.	H-026	93/02/19	Auckland, N.Z.	
Hare, Br-Sr. [Samuel]	H-027	93/03/07		
Hare, Br-Sr. [Senior]	H-028	93/10/24	Gisborne, N.Z.	
Hare, Br-Sr. [E.]	H-028a	93/07/21	Wellington, N.Z.	
Heady, S.D.	H-029	93/11/03	Gisborne, N.Z.	
Hare, Samuel	H-030	93/03/07	Kaeo, N.Z.	HP 126,127,366
Haskell, S.N.	H-031	93/06/02	Wellington, N.Z.	OHC 41
Haskell, S.N.	H-031a	93/04/19	Wellington, N.Z.	
Haskell, S.N.	H-031b	93/03/21	Napier, N.Z.	
Hare, Br-Sr. [Joseph Senior]	H-032	93/07/00	Wellington, N.Z.	2SM 260-261
Haskell, S.N.	H-032b	93/03/17	Auckland, N.Z.	4Bio 76
Ings, Jennie	*I-033	93/09/26	Napier, N.Z.	WM 330;7MR 86-87;9MR 25
Ings, Br-Sr.	I-033a	93/03/21	Napier, N.Z.	
Kellogg, Br-Sr. [J.H.]	K-035	93/02/19	Auckland, N.Z.	6MR 222-227
Kellogg, Br-Sr. [J.H.]	*K-036	93/10/02	Napier, N.Z.	2MR 239-240;7MR 127;14MR 88
Kellogg, J.H.	K-036a	93/07/09	Wellington, N.Z.	
Lons, Sr.	L-037	93/09/04	Napier, N.Z.	*DG 223-224*
McKnight, Br.	M-038	93/12/11	Wellington, N.Z.	OHC 101,102,235
Maxson, Br-Sr.	M-039	93/03/20	Napier, N.Z.	*20MR 156-157*
McCullagh, Br-Sr.	M-040	93/09/00	Hastings, N.Z.	*12MR 339-344*
Corkham, D.A.	C-041	93/05/16	Wellington, N.Z.	UL 150;2MCP 456,480
Haskell, S.N.	H-041a	93/05/12	Wellington, N.Z.	*1888 1183-1184*
Olsen, O.A.	O-042	93/07/13	Wellington, N.Z.	1MR 265-266;FLB 84;PM 132-133
Olsen, O.A.	O-043	93/02/17	Auckland, N.Z.	
Jones, A.T.	J-044	93/04/09	Napier, N.Z.	*1888 1164-1166*
Prescott, W.W.	P-045	93/12/22	Sydney, Aus.	2SM 361;CL 25-28
Prescott, W.W.	P-046	93/09/05	Hastings, N.Z.	1SM 132-133;2MR 60;8MR 392-393
Prescott, W.W.	P-047	93/10/25	Gisborne, N.Z.	6BC 1094;2MR 217-220;6MR 127-128; 10MR 345-347
Prismall, Br.	P-048	93/01/15	Melbourne, Aus.	
Prescott, Br-Sr.	*P-049	93/10/02		
Prescott, Br-Sr.	*P-050	93/11/14	Napier, N.Z.	FE 277-284;5MR 403-404
Rousseau, Sr.	R-051	93/04/09	Napier, N.Z.	
Rousseau, Sr.	R-051a	93/05/29	Wellington, N.Z.	
Rousseau, Sr./Walling, May	R-052	93/04/24	Wellington, N.Z.	2MCP 772
Roth, Mary	R-053	93/10/22	Gisborne, N.Z.	
Rice, Br-Sr.	R-054	93/11/01	Gisborne, N.Z.	*14MR 181-183*
Foss, Mary	F-055	93/02/21	N.Z.	TMK 203;4Bio 73-74
Stephens, Br-Sr.	S-056	93/11/18	Ormondville, N.Z.	
Stanton, Br.	S-057	93/03/22	Napier, N.Z.	*TM 58-62*
Smith, Uriah	S-058	93/11/30	Wellington, N.Z.	*1888 1210-1213*
Rousseau, Sr.	*R-058a	93/07/24	Wellington, N.Z.	
Tuxford, Sr.	T-059	93/09/04	Napier, N.Z.	
Tenney, G.C.	T-059a	93/08/03	Wellington, N.Z.	
Van Horn, I.D.	V-060	93/07/20	Wellington, N.Z.	*1888 1197-1203*
Van Horn, I.D.	V-061	93/01/20	Melbourne, Aus.	*1888 1136-1146*
Wilson, Br-Sr.	W-062	93/05/04	Wellington, N.Z.	Ev 497-498
Wessels, P.W.B.	W-063	93/03/17	Auckland, N.Z.	TSA 45-47;RH 08/08/1893;

				RH 08/15/1893
Wessels, P.W.B.	W-063a	93/03/17	Auckland, N.Z.	variant of Lt 63, 1893
Wessels, Sr.	W-064	93/06/08	Wellington, N.Z.	
Wessels, Brn.	W-065	93/05/16	Wellington, N.Z.	4Bio 45
White, W.C.	*W-066	93/08/18	Hastings, N.Z.	
Wessels, Philip W.B.	W-067	93/05/30	Wellington, N.Z.	
Walling, Addie	W-068	93/10/23	Gisborne, N.Z.	Te 264;4Bio 106-107
Walling, May	W-068a	93/05/15	Wellington, N.Z.	
Nicola, Leroy	N-069	93/07/19	Wellington, N.Z.	*1888 1192-1194*
Tuxford, Sr. [M.H.]	T-069a	93/08/16	Hastings, N.Z.	incomplete
Forest, Br./Stevens, Br.	F-070	93/12/00	to Sydney, Aus.	
Lyndon, Sydney	L-071	93/09/21	Napier, Aus.	HP 171,172;3BC 1147;TMK 57,309; ML 103
Wade, J.W.	*W-072	93/11/14	Napier, Aus.	Ev 242-243
Haskell, S.N.	H-073	93/11/29	Wellington, N.Z.	
Brown, Sr. and Household	B-074	93/11/28	Wellington, N.Z.	*11MR 12-13*
Smith, Br-Sr.	S-075	93/11/30	Wellington, N.Z.	*11MR 13-15*
Ings, William	I-077	93/01/09	Melbourne, Aus.	*15MR 294-311*
Waggoner, E.J.	W-078	93/01/22	Melbourne, Aus.	UL 36;9MR 209
Lindsay, Harmon	L-079	93/04/24	Wellington, N.Z.	*1888 1171-1182*
Caro, Margaret	C-080	93/04/27	Wellington, N.Z.	incomplete
Wessels, P.W.B.	*W-082	93/04/28	Wellington, N.Z.	
Davis, Marian	D-083	93/05/04	Wellington, N.Z.	
Wilson, Br.	W-084	93/05/09	Wellington, N.Z.	
Kellogg, Br-Sr. [J.H.]	K-085	93/05/16	Wellington, N.Z.	3MR 247
Kellogg, Br-Sr. [J.H.]	K-085a	93/05/16	Wellington, N.Z.	
Kellogg, Br-Sr. [J.H.]	K-086a	93/05/16	Wellington, N.Z.	*1888 1147-1163*
Haskell, S.N.	H-087	93/06/13	Wellington, N.Z.	
Custer, John	C-088	93/06/05	Wellington, N.Z.	
Olsen, O.A.	O-089	93/06/08	Wellington, N.Z.	
Hare, Edward	H-091	93/06/12	Wellington, N.Z.	
Kellogg, J.H.	K-092	93/06/14	Wellington, N.Z.	
Harris, Br-Sr. [J.]	H-093	93/06/00	Wellington, N.Z.	
Hare, Elsie	H-094	93/07/17	Wellington, N.Z.	ML 283
Waterman, Cora B.	W-095	93/07/20	Wellington, N.Z.	*TSB 163-166*
Piper, Br-Sr. [I.]	P-096	93/09/27	Napier, N.Z.	
Friends in Hastings	B-097	93/10/16	Gisborne, N.Z.	
Vickers, George T.	V-098	93/10/21	Gisborne, N.Z.	2MCP 452
Rousseau, L. J.	R-100	93/11/21	Wellington, N.Z.	*WM 329*
Brn. of the Napier Church	B-101	93/00/00		
Wilson, Br-Sr. [G.T.]	W-102	93/04/27	Wellington, N.Z.	
Amadon, Br-Sr.	*A-103	93/06/15	Wellington, N.Z.	5MR 168-169
Starr, G.B.	S-104	93/06/09	Wellington, N.Z.	
Hare, Joseph	H-105	93/03/17		AH 119-120,214-215,280,439; 6BC 1086,1101
Starr, Br-Sr. [G.B.]	S-107	93/05/22	Wellington, N.Z.	
Davis, Marian/Walling, May	*D-108	93/02/14	Auckland, N.Z.	
Hare, Joseph	*H-109	93/03/12		OHC 310
Robinson, A.T.	*R-110	93/04/24	Wellington, N.Z.	OHC 352;TMK 173,345;HP 86; 2MR 161-164
White, W.C.	*W-111	93/08/25	Hastings, N.Z.	
Faulkhead, Br.	*F-113	93/01/02	N. Fitzroy, Aus.	*20MR 282-290*
White, J.E./White, Emma	*W-115	93/03/00	Napier, N.Z.	
White, J.E./White, Emma	*W-116	93/04/18	Wellington, N.Z.	
White, J.E./White, Emma	*W-117	93/07/12	Wellington, N.Z.	12MR 299
White, J.E./White, Emma	*W-118	93/09/06	Hastings, N.Z.	
Children	*W-119	93/09/27	Napier, N.Z.	TMK 47,80

White, J.E./White, Emma	*W-120	93/10/15	Gisborne, N.Z.	TMK 235;4Bio 107
Children	*W-121	93/12/15	Auckland, N.Z.	11MR 15-19
White, Emma	*W-122	93/06/14	Wellington, N.Z.	
White, J.E.	*W-123	93/06/21	Wellington, N.Z.	4Bio 95-97
White, J.E.	*W-124	93/07/18	Wellington, N.Z.	TMK 137;GH 07/1898
Hall, Sr.	H-125	93/07/31	Wellington, N.Z.	
n.a. [Brother]	*B-126	93/00/00		
White, W.C.	*W-127	93/01/29	Parramatta, Aus.	4Bio 70
White, W.C.	*W-128	93/06/02	Wellington, N.Z.	
Starr, Br-Sr. [G.B.]	*S-129	93/06/02	Wellington, N.Z.	
White, W.C.	*W-130	93/06/07	Wellington, N.Z.	11MR 32;FBS 14
White, W.C.	*W-131	93/06/15	Wellington, N.Z.	3SM 116;4Bio 94
White, W.C.	*W-132	93/07/02	Wellington, N.Z.	3SM 116;4Bio 98
White, W.C.	*W-133	93/07/05	Wellington, N.Z.	3SM 116
White, W.C.	*W-134	93/07/17	Wellington, N.Z.	
White, W.C.	*W-135	93/07/19	Wellington, N.Z.	
White, W.C.	*W-136	93/07/19	Wellington, N.Z.	
White, W.C.	*W-137	93/07/27	Wellington, N.Z.	
White, W.C.	*W-138	93/08/13	Wellington, N.Z.	12MR 136-138;4Bio 101
Rasmussen, Annie	*R-138a	93/10/02	Napier, N.Z.	
White, W.C.	*W-139	93/10/11	Gisborne, N.Z.	
White, W.C.	*W-140	93/10/16	Gisborne, N.Z.	3MR 411;4Bio 106-107
White, W.C.	*W-141	93/10/24	Gisborne, N.Z.	
White, W.C.	W-142	93/08/07	Paremata, N.Z.	
Davis, Marian/Bolton, Fannie/Walling, May	*D-143	93/04/17	Wellington, N.Z.	
Ings, Br-Sr.	I-144	93/02/02	Auckland, N.Z.	
Haskell, S.N.	H-145	93/03/08	Kaeo, N.Z.	
Smith, Br-Sr. [Uriah]	*S-146	93/08/10	Wellington, N.Z.	
Olsen, O.A.	O-147	93/07/12	Wellington, N.Z.	

1894

Walling, May	W-001	94/09/27	Granville, Aus.	
Gates, Br-Sr.	*G-001a	94/01/01	Melbourne, Aus.	TMK 45;Ev 630-631;SD 191
Brn. Assembling in General Conference	B-002	94/10/21	Ashfield, Aus.	*17MR 170-176*
General Conference	B-003	94/07/19	Granville, Aus.	FBS 36-37
Buster, J.R.	B-004	94/08/03	Granville, Aus.	
Bolton, Fannie	B-006	94/02/10	Melbourne, Aus.	*FBS 34-36*
Brn-Srs.	B-006a	94/03/16	Melbourne, Aus.	*PC 127-130*
Bolton, Fannie	B-007	94/02/06	Melbourne, Aus.	*FBS 20-28*
Brownsberger, Br.	B-007a	94/05/17	Granville, Aus.	TSB 222-223
Corliss, J.O.	C-008	94/11/14	Granville, Aus.	VSS 260
Corliss, J.O.	C-009	94/12/28	Granville, Aus.	
Corliss, J.O.	C-009a	94/12/08	Fairlight, Aus.	GCB 04/00/1895 501-502
Corliss, J.O.	C-010	94/10/27	Ashfield, Aus.	UL 314;SD 224,298;HP 164;ChL 48-49
Corliss, Br-Sr.	C-010a	94/05/17	Granville, Aus.	
Colcord, Br-Sr.	C-011	94/01/16	Brighton, Aus.	Ev 303;3SM 29-30
Christiansen, Captain	C-011a	94/01/02	Melbourne, Aus.	*14MR 76-87*
Cornell, Sr.	C-012	94/05/10	Granville, Aus.	2SM 48-49
Childs, Br-Sr.	C-013	94/09/27	Granville, Aus.	TMK 78,270
Clausen, Sr.	C-013a	94/06/14	Granville, Aus.	4Bio 137
Davis, Marian	D-014	94/08/27	Cooranbong, Aus.	8MR 125;11MR 53;4Bio 154
Daniells, A.G.	D-015	94/04/04	Granville, Aus.	GCB 02/04/1895 2-3
Daniells, A.G.	D-016	94/03/11	Melbourne, Aus.	
Daniells, Br-Sr.	D-017	94/03/06	Melbourne, Aus.	
Daniells, Sr.	D-018	94/03/23	Melbourne, Aus.	
Daniells, Sr./Rousseau, Sr.	D-019	94/03/07	Melbourne, Aus.	

EGW Letters File—Page 39

Eldridge, Br-Sr.	E-020	94/04/14	Granville, Aus.	*1888 1227-1232*
Eldridge, Sr.	F-021	94/04/00	Granville, Aus.	2SM 185-186;3MR 302;9MR 371
Eldridge, C.	E-022	94/08/12	Granville, Aus.	3MR 302;9MR 371;10MR 389-390
Edwards, W.H.	E-023	94/09/18	Granville, Aus.	
Evans, I.H./Battle Creek	E-023b	94/07/20	Granville, Aus.	*8T 48-53*
Evans, I.H./Battle Creek	E-023c	94/07/20	Granville, Aus.	*PH084 1-5*
Haskell, S.N.	H-024	94/04/00		6MR 134-135
Haskell, S.N.	H-025	94/08/03	Granville, Aus.	
Haskell, S.N.	H-026	94/11/22	Granville, Aus.	SD 44;8MR 249
Haskell, S.N.	H-027	94/06/01	Granville, Aus.	*1888 1240-1255*
Haskell, S.N.	H-028	94/05/09	Granville, Aus.	12MR 77-82
Haskell, S.N.	H-029	94/09/02	Granville, Aus.	8MR 140-144
Haskell, S.N.	H-030	94/08/13	Granville, Aus.	4Bio 164-165
Harper, Br.	H-030a	94/07/08	Granville, Aus.	12MR 94;4Bio 141,163-164
Harper, Br.	H-031	94/09/23	Granville, Aus.	6MR 21-22;RH 07/21/1896;4Bio 164
Henry, A.R.	H-031a	94/10/27	Ashfield, Aus.	*1888 1295-1315*
Hartman, Sr.	H-032	94/01/28	Brighton, Aus.	UL 42
Hall, Sr.	H-033	94/08/23	Cooranbong, Aus.	10MR 11
Hardy, Br.	H-034	94/12/20	Granville, Aus.	OHC 179,262
Innes, Lizzie	I-035	94/08/09	Granville, Aus.	*10MR 174-178*
Ings, Jennie L.	I-036	94/08/04	Granville, Aus.	TMK 351
Jones, A.T.	J-037	94/01/14	Melbourne, Aus.	TM 227-229;VSS 401-402;14MR 200-202; 4Bio 117-119
Jones, A.T.	J-038	94/04/14	Granville, Aus.	1MCP 29;2MCP 633-634
Jones, A.T.	J-039	94/06/07	Granville, Aus.	*6MR 199-207*
Jones, A.T.	J-040a	94/11/00	Granville, Aus.	TM 256-258
Jones, C.H.	J-040b	94/05/14	Granville, Aus.	7MR 52
Jones, C.H.	J-041	94/05/06	Granville, Aus.	*1888 1233-1239*
Kellogg, H.W.	K-042	94/10/24	Ashfield, Aus.	WM 330;16MR 68;4Bio 168-169
Kellogg, H.W.	K-043	94/11/04	Granville, Aus.	4Bio 170-171
Kellogg, H.W.	K-044	94/08/03	Granville, Aus.	PC 134-139
Kellogg, H.W.	K-045	94/05/14	Granville, Aus.	WM 23-24
Kellogg, J.H.	K-046	94/05/17	Granville, Aus.	8MR 386;4Bio 140,148
Kellogg, J.H.	K-046a	94/10/25	Granville, Aus.	3SM 117-118;16MR 69-70;MRmnt 122; FBS 41
Kellogg, Br-Sr. [J.H.]	K-047	94/04/18	Granville, Aus.	MM 243-245;TMK 216;Te 263;8MR 95-96; 12MR 91-92;4Bio 148;CTr 85
Littlejohn, Br.	L-048	94/06/03	Granville, Aus.	*13MR 269-280*
Littlejohn, Br.	L-049	94/08/03	Granville, Aus.	CW 152-157;10MR 12-13;13MR 287-288
Lacey, Br. [not H.C.]	L-049a	94/04/30	Granville, Aus.	
Lindsay, Harmon	L-050	94/06/14	Granville, Aus.	9MR 94;12MR 92-94;4Bio 142
Lockwood, Br.	L-050a	94/05/18	Granville, Aus.	
Leininger, Br-Sr.	L-050b	94/05/17	Granville, Aus.	4Bio 141
Martin, Chrissie	M-051	94/08/09	Granville, Aus.	OHC 206,300;4MR 193-198
Mills, Br.	M-051a	94/05/17	Granville, Aus.	
Olsen, O.A.	O-051b	94/01/00		OHC 43
McCoy, Br.	M-052	94/01/05	Melbourne, Aus.	*15MR 265-268*
Minsters of the Australian Conference	M-053	94/11/11	Granville, Aus.	9MR 177-180
Olsen, O.A.	O-054	94/06/10	Granville, Aus.	2BC 1004;5MR 349-350;6MR 57; 10MR 283-284
Olsen, O.A.	O-054a	94/06/24	Granville, Aus.	PM 300;8MR 386
Olsen, O.A.	O-055	94/08/00	Granville, Aus.	*1888 1280-1285*
Olsen, O.A.	O-056	94/10/26	Ashfield, Aus.	4MR 414;4Bio 167
Olsen, O.A.	O-057	94/06/10	Granville, Aus.	*1888 1256-1267*
Olsen, O.A.	O-058	94/11/26	Granville, Aus.	*1888 1316-1321*
Olsen, O.A.	O-059	94/02/05	Melbourn, Aus.	*FBS 19-20*
Olsen, O.A.	O-060	94/04/03	Granville, Aus.	TMK 306;YI 01/03/1895 & 01/10/1895

Olsen, O.A.	O-062	94/05/04	Granville, Aus.	OHC 221;4Bio 141
Olsen, O.A.	O-063	94/07/19	Granville, Aus.	
Olsen, O.A.	O-064	94/05/06	Granville, Aus.	1MR 29;7MR 82
Pitcairn Crew	P-065	94/01/06	Middle Brighton	*7MR 198-206*
Friends on Pitcairn Island	P-065a	94/01/01	Melbourne, Aus.	*2SM 269-274*
Prescott, W.W.	P-066	94/04/10	Granville, Aus.	OHC 309;2SM 92-93;3SM 403-405; 7BC 962,964;LDE 21-22,77;10MR 347; CTr 131
Prescott, Br-Sr.	P-067	94/01/18	Middle Brighton	3SM 90;2MR 211;10MR 42-43,67,347-349
Prescott, W.W./Jones, A.T.	P-068	94/04/16	Granville, Aus.	*14MR 184-188*
Conference Men/Review and Herald Office	R-069	94/10/01	Granville, Aus.	MRmnt 59;10MR 13
Review and Herald Office	R-070	94/01/13	Brighton, Aus.	*PC 389-395*
Gen. Conf. Comm/Review & Herald/Pacific Press	R-071	94/04/08	Granville, Aus.	PH150 18-22;PM 147-148;11MR 273; CTr 179
Review and Herald Office	R-071a	94/09/20	Granville, Aus.	
Rousseau, Sr.	R-072	94/01/00	Middle Brighton	
Rousseau, Sr.	R-073	94/03/02	Melbourne, Aus.	
Rousseau, Br-Sr.	R-074	94/04/19	Granville, Aus.	
Rousseau, Sr.	R-075	94/03/00	Melbourne, Aus.	
Rousseau, Sr.	R-076	94/03/00	Melbourne, Aus.	*13MR 137-147*
Scazighini, Br.	S-077	94/08/03	Granville, Aus.	
Starr, Br-Sr. [G.B.]	S-078	94/03/20	Melbourne, Aus.	OHC 169,183;2MCP 800
White, J.E./White, Emma	W-079	94/05/02	Granville, Aus.	4Bio 132,144-145
White, J.E.	W-080	94/11/06	Granville, Aus.	4MR 262-263;11MR 28
White, J.E./White, Emma	W-081	94/11/16	Granville, Aus.	
White, J.E./White, Emma	W-082	94/05/01	Granville, Aus.	8MR 133-140
White, J.E./White, Emma	W-083	94/10/27	Ashfield, Aus.	
White, J.E./White, Emma	W-084	94/11/14	Granville, Aus.	10MR 127-128;16MR 37-38;HM 08/1896
White, J.E./White, Emma	*W-085	94/07/27	Granville, Aus.	4Bio 137,156-157
White, J.E./White, Emma	W-086	94/01/12	Middle Brighton	4Bio 115,117,119
White, J.E./White, Emma	W-087	94/06/28	Granville, Aus.	1BC 1111;7BC 947-948;4MR 263
White, W.C.	*W-088	94/02/06	Melbourne, Aus.	*FBS 28-32,123*
White, J.E./White, Emma	W-088a	94/02/10	Melbourne, Aus.	4Bio 118
White, J.E./White, Emma	W-089	94/09/18	Granville, Aus.	*20MR 75-79*
White, J.E./White, Emma	W-089a	94/08/22	Cooranbong, Aus.	WM 328-329;6MR 135-136;4Bio 153-154
Walling, Addie	W-089b	94/08/27	Cooranbong, Aus.	
White, J.E./White, Emma	W-090	94/05/29	Granville, Aus.	2MR 319-320;CTr 176
Jones, C.H.	J-093	94/05/09	Granville, Aus.	8MR 249
Bond, Br-Sr.	B-095	94/09/08	Granville, Aus.	
Jones, C.H.	J-096	94/09/30	Granville, Aus.	
O'Kavanagh, Mrs. M.M.J.	M-099	94/01/08		4Bio 119
O'Kavanagh, Mrs. M.M.J.	M-099a	94/01/11	Middle Brighton	
Caro, Sr.	C-100	94/01/12	Middle Brighton	4Bio 116-117
White, J.E./White, Emma	W-102	94/02/06	Melbourne, Aus.	*PC 101-107*
Jones, A.T.	J-103	94/03/15	Melbourne, Aus.	2SM 85-88;7ABC 466-467;4MR 119-120; 4Bio 128
White, J.E./White, Emma	*W-105	94/07/27	Granville, Aus.	
Martin, Chrissie	M-108	94/09/13	Granville, Aus.	
Wales, William	W-109	94/09/18	Granville, Aus.	
Corliss, J.O.	C-113	94/12/16		8MR 24-25
Wessels, Philip	*W-116	94/09/13	Granville, Aus.	
n.a. [Brother]	*B-117	94/10/00	Granville, Aus.	
White, J.E./White, Emma	*W-118	94/09/17	Granville, Aus.	
White, J.E.	*W-119	94/09/18	Ashfield, Aus.	
White, J.E./White, Emma	*W-120	94/09/30	Granville, Aus.	
White, J.E./White, Emma	*W-121	94/10/01	Granville, Aus.	
White, J.E./White, Emma	*W-122	94/12/13	Fairlight	*8MR 144-146*

EGW Letters File—Page 41

White, J.E.	*W-123	94/12/20	Granville, Aus.	4Bio 172-175
White, J.E./White, Emma	*W-124	94/12/20		3MR 409;4Bio 178,181
White, J.E./White, Emma	*W-125	94/01/12	Brighton	4Bio 116
White, J.E./White, Emma	*W-126	94/01/14	Melbourne, Aus.	
White, Emma	*W-127	94/03/16	Melbourne, Aus.	
White, J.E./White, Emma	*W-128	94/04/04	Granville, Aus.	4Bio 139-140
White, J.E./White, Emma	*W-129	94/11/26	Granville, Aus.	
White, J.E./White, Emma	*W-130	94/11/14	Granville, Aus.	4Bio 173-174
White, J.E./White, Emma	*W-131	94/06/11	Granville, Aus.	
White, J.E./White, Emma	*W-132	94/06/00		
White, J.E./White, Emma	*W-133	94/07/09	Granville, Aus.	TMK 284;3MR 410;4Bio 156
White, W.C.	*W-134	94/08/30		
White, W.C.	*W-135	94/08/06	Granville, Aus.	16MR 69;4Bio 157-158
White, W.C.	*W-136	94/01/08	Melbourne, Aus.	FBS 18-19
White, W.C.	*W-137	94/00/00	Fragment	FBS 19;7MR 87
White, W.C.	*W-138	94/02/12	Melbourne, Aus.	
White, W.C.	*W-139	94/02/13	Melbourne, Aus.	
White, W.C.	*W-140	94/02/15	Melbourne, Aus.	3MR 411;4BIO 138
White, W.C.	*W-141	94/02/15	Melbourne, Aus.	4Bio 125
White, W.C.	*W-142	94/02/21	Melbourne, Aus.	
White, W.C.	*W-143	94/02/25	Melbourne, Aus.	
White, W.C.	*W-144	94/03/01	Melbourne, Aus.	
White, W.C.	*W-145	94/03/27	Granville, Aus.	4Bio 139
White, W.C.	*W-146	94/03/29	Granville, Aus.	FBS 36
White, W.C.	*W-147	94/06/00	Granville, Aus.	4Bio 141-142
White, W.C.	*W-148	94/07/03	Granville, Aus.	
White, W.C.	*W-149	94/07/30	Granville, Aus.	FBS 37
White, W.C.	*W-150	94/08/02	Granville, Aus.	
White, W.C.	*W-151	94/08/09	Granville, Aus.	
White, W.C.	*W-152	94/09/20	Granville, Aus.	FBS 37
White, W.C.	*W-153	94/11/05		*20MR 238-240*
n.a. [Brethren]	*W-154	94/11/05	Granville, Aus.	8MR 363;4Bio 177
White, Ella/White, Mabel	*W-155	94/00/00	Fragment	
Hall, Sr.	*H-156	94/01/14	Melbourne, Aus.	
Mortensen, Mary	*M-157	94/01/19	Middle Brighton	

1895

Aubrey, Sr.	A-001	95/00/00		
Austin, Sr.	A-001a	95/01/17	Cooranbong, Aus.	
Those who work at Cooranbong	B-002	95/03/04	Granville, Aus.	FLB 220,235,236;OHC 292,295;4Bio 251
Men in Responsible Positions in Battle Creek	B-004	95/09/00	Granville, Aus.	*PC 409-416*
Brethren in Responsible Positions in America	B-005	95/07/24	Granville, Aus.	SpM 13-19;4MR 1-5;11MR 360; see 8T 56-61
Bollman, C.P.	B-007	95/10/20	Granville, Aus.	*19MR 101-107*
Baker, Br-Sr. [W.L.H.]	B-008	96/02/09	Filed in 1895	*13MR 13-30*
Bolton, Fannie	B-009	95/11/07		*FBS 46-48*
Bolton, Fannie	B-009a	95/11/11	Armadale, Aus.	*FBS 48-49*
Belden, Frank	B-010	95/06/09		*1888 1392-1393*
Haskell, S.N.	H-011	95/01/30	Granville, Aus.	*16MR 157-170*
Belden, Frank	B-013	95/11/13	Armadale, Aus.	*1888 1469-1475*
Bolton, Fannie	B-014	95/11/23	Armadale, Aus.	*TSB 208-209*
Belden, Frank	B-015	95/06/08	Granville, Aus.	*17MR 107-118*
Bollman, C.P.	B-016	95/06/18	Granville, Aus.	5MR 65-66
n.a. [Brother]	B-016a	95/02/08	Granville, Aus.	*21MR 178-182*
Caldwell, W.F.	C-017	95/09/06	Cooranbong, Aus.	TSB 206-207;1MCP 157;Te 32; CD 131,137-138,333;FBS 40;

EGW Letters File—Page 42

				3MR 307-308;4MR 364-365
Corliss, J.O.	C-018	95/09/13	Granville, Aus.	*13MR 310-317*
Caro, Dr.	C-019	95/06/01	Granville, Aus.	OHC 116
Campbell, Emily C.	C-019a	95/02/11	Granville, Aus.	
Corliss, J.O.	C-020	95/09/13	Granville, Aus.	TMK 52
Corliss, J.O.	C-021	95/09/13	Granville, Aus.	TM 245-251
Corliss, J.O.	C-021a	95/08/20	Cooranbong, Aus.	Ev 166-167;8MR 254;4Bio 173,251
Daniells, Br-Sr.	D-022	95/04/01	Granville, Aus.	
Davis, Marian	D-022a	95/11/29	Hobart	FBS 53-54;7MR 83
Daniells, A.G.	D-023	95/03/05	Granville, Aus.	
Eckman, Sr.	E-024	95/05/19	N. Fitzroy, Aus.	*12MR 33-39*
Haskell, S.N.	H-025	95/11/06	Armadale, Aus.	4Bio 232
Haskell, S.N.	H-025a	95/05/31	Granville, Aus.	HP 66
Hare, Br-Sr.	H-025b	95/04/28		3MR 188-189
Haskell, S.N.	H-025c	95/11/06	Armadale, Aus.	4Bio 233
Haskell, S.N.	H-026	95/10/11	Granville, Aus.	3SM 324
Howe, F.	H-027	95/05/21	Granville, Aus.	11MR 160-161
Haskell, S.N.	H-028	95/06/25	Granville, Aus.	VSS 402-403;4Bio 259
Hare, Robert	H-029	95/03/22	Granville, Aus.	VSS 283-285,321,329,340-341,345
Hardy, Br.	H-030	95/01/29	Granville, Aus.	UL 43;LDE 60-61
Harper, Walter	H-031	95/01/17	Cooranbong, Aus.	
Himes, J.V.	H-031a	95/01/17	Cooranbong, Aus.	4Bio 180
Harper, Walter	H-031b	95/03/07	Granville, Aus.	WM 332
Harper, Walter	H-031d	95/01/01	Granville, Aus.	
Israel, Sr.	I-032	95/07/24	Granville, Aus.	
Israel, Sr.	I-033	95/07/22	Granville, Aus.	ML 184,313;7BC 916,948;4Bio 251
Ings, Sr.	I-034	95/05/16	N. Fitzroy, Aus.	
Jones, A.T.	J-035	95/11/21	Melbourne, Aus.	*RH 4/13/1911 with SpTA #7 59-64 and 11MR 33*
Jones, A.T.	J-035a	95/07/08	Cooranbong, Aus.	*1888 1408-1411*
Jones, A.T.	J-036	95/10/13	Granville, Aus.	See 6T 394-401;LDE 90,216;VSS 240-242
Johnson, Lewis	J-037	95/06/13	Granville, Aus.	3MR 352-353
Jones, C.H.	J-038	95/02/17	Granville, Aus.	
Kellogg, J.H.	K-039	95/02/03	Granville, Aus.	WM 330-331;FBS 38;4Bio 173
Kellogg, J.H.	K-040	95/12/01	Newtown, Tasmania	*8T 153-157*
Kellogg, J.H.	K-042	95/08/28	Cooranbong, Aus.	8MR 92-94
Kellogg, J.H.	K-043	95/06/14	Granville, Aus.	MM 252;ChL 6;FLB 66;4BC 1153; PCP 45-49;5BC 1094,1095,1133,1144; 6BC 1117;7BC 942,943;4MR 131; 9MR 371;12MR 120;17MR 308-309; YI 10/24/1895 & 10/31/1895; RH 10/22/1895 & 10/29/1895
Kellogg, J.H.	K-044	95/08/29	Cooranbong, Aus.	FBS 39
Kellogg, J.H.	K-045	95/07/15	Cooranbong, Aus.	*1888 1412-1420*
Kellogg, J.H.	K-046	95/04/15	N. Fitzroy, Aus.	10MR 273-275;12MR 299;4Bio 183
Kellogg, J.H.	K-047	95/03/21	Granville, Aus.	*FE 334-367*; see Ms 10a, 1895
Kellogg, Br-Sr. [J.H.]	K-047a	95/08/27	Cooranbong, Aus.	TM 239-245
Kellogg, H.W.	K-048	95/02/15	Granville, Aus.	
Kellogg, H.W.	K-049	95/07/01	Granville, Aus.	
Ketring, Sr.	K-050	95/08/26	Cooranbong, Aus.	*TSB 67-74*
McCullagh, S.	M-051	95/11/07	Armadale, Aus.	2BC 995-996;4Bio 233;CTr 136
Lindsay, Harmon	L-051a	95/05/01	Tasmania	*1888 1344-1355*
McCullagh, S.	M-052	95/12/06	Hobart, Tasmania	UL 354;6MR 391-393
Olsen, O.A.	O-053	95/09/10	Granville, Aus.	*1888 1421-1424*
Olsen, O.A.	O-054	95/09/19	Granville, Aus.	*PH080 25-51*
Olsen, O.A.	O-055	95/09/19	Granville, Aus.	*1888 1425-1454*
Olsen, O.A.	O-056	95/05/27	N. Fitzroy, Aus.	*RH 07/30/1895*

EGW Letters File—Page 43

Olsen, O.A.	O-057	95/05/01	Hobart, Tasmania	*14MR 114-135*
Olsen, O.A.	O-058	95/05/07	Glenorchy, Tasmania	SpTA #3 42-59;2MR 257-259
Olsen, Br-Sr.	*O-059	95/05/12	Launceston, Tasmania	*19MR 267-278*
Olsen, Br-Sr.	O-059a	95/05/12	Launceston, Tasmania	variant of Lt 59, 1895
Olsen, O.A.	O-060	95/04/22	Bismark, Tasmania	*FE 368-372*
Olsen, O.A.	O-061	95/02/02	Granville, Aus.	TM 204-208;Ev 355;7MR 52-53;11MR 161
Olsen, Br-Sr.	O-062	95/04/11	Granville, Aus.	4Bio 189
Olsen, O.A.	O-063	95/05/07	Glenorchy, Tasmania	See TM 210-227
Olsen, O.A.	O-064	95/06/20	Granville, Aus.	
Olsen, Br-Sr.	O-064a	95/09/01	Cooranbong, Aus.	TM 230-238;SpTA #4 11-12
Olsen, O.A.	O-065	95/06/19	Granville, Aus.	*1888 1394-1407*
Pomare, Maui	P-066	95/09/26	Granville, Aus.	
Prescott, W.W.	P-067	95/06/12	Granville, Aus.	*FE 381-389*
Prismall, Br.	P-068	95/05/27	N. Fitzroy, Aus.	
Rousseau, Br.	R-069	95/03/20	Granville, Aus.	
Review and Herald	R-070	95/06/09	Granville, Aus.	
Review and Herald	R-071	95/02/12	Granville, Aus.	VSS 303;7BC 933,934
Tait, A.O.	T-073	95/11/20	Armadale, Aus.	*SW 72-78*
Tait, A.O.	T-074	95/11/21	Armadale, Aus.	
Tait, A.O.	T-075	95/06/10	Granville, Aus.	PM 130-131;PH102 18-21
Tait, A.O.	T-076	95/06/06	Granville, Aus.	*1888 1369-1378*
Workers in Sydney	B-077	95/11/14		PCP 51;Ev 228,299,485,633,687-688; 1MR 20
White, Ella/White, Mabel	W-080	95/11/11	Armadale, Aus.	3MR 132
White, J.E./White, Emma	*W-080a	95/08/16	Cooranbong, Aus.	4MR 5-7,264;6MR 173
White, J.E.	W-082	95/11/00	Armadale, Aus.	VSS 219,390,403-404;TMK 275,297,318; 4Bio 234
White, J.E.	W-083	95/11/18	Armadale, Aus.	*21MR 388-393*
White, J.E.	W-084	95/10/22	Armadale, Aus.	PM 209;TMK 215,217,337,343
White, J.E.	W-085	95/10/07	Granville, Aus.	4MR 265
White, J.E.	W-086	95/09/25	Granville, Aus.	*1888 1455-1468*
White, J.E./White, Emma	W-087	95/06/19	Granville, Aus.	4MR 263
White, J.E./White, Emma	W-088	95/04/04	Granville, Aus.	Ev 471;11MR 278-279;4Bio 187,189
White, J.E./White, Emma	*W-088a	95/07/07	Cooranbong, Aus.	11MR 185
White, W.C.	W-089	95/03/11	Armadale, Aus.	FBS 38
White, W.C.	W-089a	95/03/13	Granville, Aus.	Ev 445,452-453
Wessels, Sr.	W-090	95/01/15	Cooranbong, Aus.	4BC 1184;UL 29;RC 266;WM 267
Wessels, Henry	W-091	95/01/30	Granville, Aus.	TDG 38;4Bio 251
White, J.E./White, Emma	W-092	95/02/17	Granville, Aus.	*19MR 202-216*
White, W.C.	W-092a	95/03/21	Granville, Aus.	4Bio 188
White, J.E./White, Emma	W-092b	95/04/11	Granville, Aus.	FBS 39;4Bio 188
White, J.E.	W-093	95/06/18	Granville, Aus.	
White, J.E.	W-093a	95/10/17	Granville, Aus.	
Wessels, Sr. and Children	W-094	95/01/31	Granville, Aus.	TDG 39
Wessels, Henry	W-095	95/06/26	Granville, Aus.	
Young Friend [McCann, William?]	Y-096	95/11/12	Armadale, Aus.	TMK 41
Wessels, Henry	W-097	95/10/08	Granville, Aus.	OHC 196,340;TMK 230,278;4MR 158-164
Jones, C.H.	J-098	95/01/15	Cooranbong, Aus.	
Olsen, O.A.	O-099	95/05/07	Glenorchy, Tasmania	*20MR 164-166*
Haskell, S.N.	H-100	95/10/11	Granville, Aus.	TMK 79;OHC 114;6MR 1
Children/Family at Granville	C-101	95/11/02	Armadale, Aus.	1MR 346-347
Davis, Marian	*D-102	95/10/29	Armadale, Aus.	*FBS 41-44*
Davis, Marian	*D-103	95/11/12	Armadale, Aus.	FBS 49
Walling, Addie/Walling, May	*W-104	95/12/11	Hobart, Tasmania	*FBS 56-57*
Campbell, Emily	*C-105	95/12/09	Hobart, Tasmania	FBS 54
Kellogg, J.H.	*K-106	95/12/20	Granville, Aus.	FBS 59-62
Starr, Br-Sr. [G.B.]	S-107	95/01/27	Granville, Aus.	4Bio 194

EGW Letters File—Page 44

Olsen, O.A.	*O-108	95/01/18	Cooranbong, Aus.	
Brethren who are acting an important part in our Inst.	*B-109	95/02/10	Granville, Aus.	
Prescott, W.W.	*P-110	95/04/10	Granville, Aus.	
Wessels, Philip	*W-111	95/09/01	Cooranbong, Aus.	
Brethren at Battle Creek	*B-112	95/09/01	Cooranbong, Aus.	
Kellogg, Br-Sr. [J.H.]	*K-113	95/11/17	Armadale, Aus.	*2MR 165-167*
White, J.E.	*W-114	95/10/18	Armadale, Aus.	4Bio 228-229;CTr 241
Bolton, Fannie	*B-115	95/11/26	Armadale, Aus.	*FBS 51-53*
Olsen, O.A.	*O-116	95/05/24	N. Fitzroy, Aus.	
White, J.E./White, Emma	*W-117	95/01/15	Cooranbong, Aus.	3MR 298-299;7MR 87;4Bio 182,193-194
White, J.E./White, Emma	*W-118	95/01/23	Granville, Aus.	3MR 408-409;FBS 38
White, J.E./White, Emma	W-119	95/02/18	Granville, Aus.	SpTA #3 39-41;14MR 17-25;PC 398-400
White, J.E./White, Emma	*W-120	95/05/15	N. Fitzroy, Aus.	4Bio 195,198
Brn. Connected with the Review and Herald	*B-122	95/06/19	Granville, Aus.	From Lt 65, 1895
White, J.E./White, Emma	*W-123	95/12/09	Hobart, Tasmania	
White, J.E.	*W-123a	95/12/09	Hobart, Tasmania	*FBS 54-55*
White, J.E./White, Emma	*W-124	95/06/07		4Bio 198
White, J.E./White, Emma	*W-125	95/08/04	Cooranbong, Aus.	4Bio 221-222
White, J.E./White, Emma	*W-126	95/08/19	Cooranbong, Aus.	RC 119;TMK 268;8MR 146-150; 4Bio 215-218
White, J.E./White, Emma	*W-127	95/12/11	Hobart, Tasmania	FBS 55-56;4Bio 236
White, J.E./White, Emma	*W-128	95/12/22	Granville, Aus.	UL 370;TMK 214;4Bio 236
White, J.E.	W-128a	95/12/22	Granville, Aus.	
White, J.E.	*W-129	95/11/18	Armadale, Aus.	
White, J.E./White, Emma	*W-130	95/01/21	Cooranbong, Aus.	
White, W.C.	*W-131	95/07/11	Cooranbong, Aus.	
White, W.C.	*W-132	95/01/08	Granville, Aus.	
White, W.C.	*W-133	95/01/10	Granville, Aus.	
White, W.C.	*W-134	95/01/11	Granville, Aus.	
White, W.C.	*W-135	95/01/13	Granville, Aus.	
White, W.C.	*W-136	95/01/14	Cooranbong, Aus.	
White, W.C.	*W-137	95/01/20	Cooranbong, Aus.	3MR 410
White, W.C.	*W-138	95/01/21	Cooranbong, Aus.	
White, W.C.	*W-139	95/02/05	Granville, Aus.	3MR 411
White, W.C.	*W-140	95/02/13	Granville, Aus.	
White, W.C.	*W-141	95/02/18	Granville, Aus.	
White, W.C.	*W-142	95/02/19	Granville, Aus.	
White, W.C.	*W-143	95/02/28	Granville, Aus.	
White, W.C.	*W-145	95/03/15	Granville, Aus.	3MR 405;4Bio 194
White, W.C.	*W-146	95/04/05	Granville, Aus.	
White, W.C.	*W-147	95/08/02	Cooranbong, Aus.	3MR 406
White, W.C.	*W-148	95/08/06	Cooranbong, Aus.	
White, W.C.	*W-149	95/08/06	Cooranbong, Aus.	4Bio 222-223
White, W.C./White, May	*W-150	95/08/07	Cooranbong, Aus.	
White, W.C.	*W-151	95/08/15	Cooranbong, Aus.	
White, May	*W-152	95/08/26	Cooranbong, Aus.	3MR 407
White, W.C.	*W-153	95/08/26	Cooranbong, Aus.	3MR 407
White, W.C.	*W-154	95/08/27	Cooranbong, Aus.	
White, May	*W-155	95/08/28	Cooranbong, Aus.	
White, W.C.	*W-156	95/08/28	Cooranbong, Aus.	
White, W.C.	*W-157	95/10/04	Granville, Aus.	3MR 410
White, W.C.	*W-158	95/10/06	Granville, Aus.	
White, W.C.	*W-159	95/00/00	Fragment	
Hall, Sr.	*H-160	95/04/15	N. Fitzroy, Aus.	
Hall, Sr./Walling, Addie	*H-161	95/06/20	Granville, Aus.	
Kellogg, J.H.	K-162	95/06/13		
Kellogg, J.H.	K-163	95/11/19		

White, J.E.	W-164	95/11/00		

1896

Anderson, Mrs. R.	A-001	96/06/08	Cooranbong, Aus.	SD 167
Anderson, Br-Sr./Belden, Br-Sr.	A-001a	96/01/14	Cooranbong, Aus.	*10MR 129-134*
Anderson, C.	A-002	96/01/03	Cooranbong, Aus.	
Anderson, Br-Sr.	A-002a	96/02/16	Cooranbong, Aus.	
Blombery, Mrs. S.	B-003	96/12/29	Cooranbong, Aus.	
Men who occupy Responsible Positions	B-004	96/07/01	Cooranbong, Aus.	*17MR 181-195*
Those in Responsible Positions in Battle Creek	B-005	96/12/18		*1888 1628-1635*
Brethren who occupy Responsible Positions	B-006	96/01/16	Cooranbong, Aus.	*1888 1476-1486*
My Brethren in Battle Creek	B-007	96/05/11	Granville, Aus.	*17MR 196-207*
My Brethren in America	B-008	96/02/06	Cooranbong, Aus.	*1888 1493-1501*
n.a. [Brother and Sister]	B-008a	96/04/01	Cooranbong, Aus.	AH 308,317,439-440;CG 219
n.a. [Brother]	*B-009	96/02/05	Cooranbong, Aus.	3MR 313-314
Belden, Br-Sr.	B-010	96/02/03	Cooranbong, Aus.	1BC 1109;4Bio 261
Belden, Sarah	B-011	96/09/28	Cooranbong, Aus.	
Belden, F.E.	B-012	96/11/24	fragment	10MR 134-135
Burham, Sr.	B-013a	96/01/05	Cooranbong, Aus.	
Corliss, J.O.	C-015	96/07/20	Cooranbong, Aus.	8MR 331
Corliss, Burr	*C-015a	96/04/14	Cooranbong, Aus.	4MR 198-205
Cady, Br-Sr.	C-016	96/11/17	Ashfield, Aus.	*12MR 302-306*
Caldwell, W.F.	C-017	96/05/07		*10MR 190-194*
Caldwell, W.F.	C-018	96/04/09	Cooranbong, Aus.	TSB 210-214
Caldwell, W.F.	C-019	96/06/07		TSB 207-208;3MR 306
Colcord, W.A./Daniells, A.G./Faulkhead, Br.	C-020	96/08/25	Cooranbong, Aus.	5MR 374
Colcord, W.A.	*C-021	96/01/07	Cooranbong, Aus.	9MR 272-273
Colcord, W.A.	C-022	96/06/22	Cooranbong, Aus.	UL 187;OHC 104;5MR 348-349
Collins, Br.	C-023	96/12/14	Cooranbong, Aus.	4MR 385-386;7MR 338
Church at Cooranbong	C-024	96/05/23	Cooranbong, Aus.	10MR 115-118;CTr 112
Conference Presidents/"God gave to Moses..."	C-024a	96/08/00	Cooranbong, Aus.	TM 340-346;9MR 157
Daniells, A.G./Colcord, W.A.	D-025	96/06/01	Cooranbong, Aus.	2SM 207;1MR 264-265
Daniells, A.G.	D-026	96/07/19	missing	
Daniells, A.G./Colcord/Faulkhead/Salisbury	D-027	96/09/20	Cooranbong, Aus.	PM 42-44,77,112,114;3BC 1154
Eldridge, Captain	E-028	96/08/30	Cooranbong, Aus.	PM 247;5Bio 231
General Conference of 1897	G-029	96/12/27		*TM 331-340*
Hickox, Br-Sr.	H-030	96/10/13	Adelaide, Aus.	OHC 126
Hughes, Br-Sr.	H-032	96/03/07	Cooranbong, Aus.	AH 416-417;6MR 262;CTr 343
Hawkins, Harry	H-033	96/11/27	Cooranbong, Aus.	UL 345
Hare, Br-Sr.	H-034	96/12/19	Cooranbong, Aus.	Ev 169,178;2MR 93-95;CTr 247
Hardy, Br.	H-035	96/07/14	Cooranbong, Aus.	
Haskell, S.N.	H-036	96/04/26	Cooranbong, Aus.	5MR 147;4Bio 264
Haskell, S.N.	H-037	96/02/02	Extract	BTS 08/1905 and 05/1915
Haskell, S.N.	H-038	96/05/30	Cooranbong, Aus.	*1888 1536-1555*
Haskell, S.N.	H-039	96/04/26	Cooranbong, Aus.	10MR 63
Haskell, S.N.	H-040	96/05/04	Cooranbong, Aus.	*TM 387-391*
Israel, Sr.	I-041	96/07/30	Cooranbong, Aus.	
Israel, Sr.	I-042	96/08/14	Cooranbong, Aus.	VSS 161
Israel, Sr.	I-043	96/08/06	Cooranbong, Aus.	5BC 1141
Israel, Sr.	I-044	96/07/01	Cooranbong, Aus.	
Israel, Sr.	I-045	96/04/27	Cooranbong, Aus.	
Israel, Sr.	I-046	96/04/07	Cooranbong, Aus.	
Israel, Sr.	I-047	96/08/28	Cooranbong, Aus.	
Israel, Sr.	I-048	96/06/15	Cooranbong, Aus.	*UL 180*
Israel, Sr.	I-049	96/07/17	Cooranbong, Aus.	*TSB 257-260*
Workers in the Echo Office	B-049a	96/09/00		SD 15,33,34;13MR 362-363

Israel, Sr.	I-050	96/07/24	Cooranbong, Aus.	
Israel, Sr.	I-051	96/03/28	Cooranbong, Aus.	
Israel, Sr.	I-052	96/06/22	Cooranbong, Aus.	
Israel, Sr.	I-052a	96/04/21	Cooranbong, Aus.	
Ings, Sr.	I-052b	96/05/07	Cooranbong, Aus.	FBS 71
Johnson, Br.	J-053	96/06/29	Cooranbong, Aus.	Ev 499
Kellogg, J.H.	K-054	96/07/10	Cooranbong, Aus.	CD 110,291-292;SpM 30-33
Kellogg, Br-Sr. [J.H.]	K-055	96/11/14	Ashfield, Aus.	1MR 146-150
Kellogg, J.H.	K-056	96/01/19	Cooranbong, Aus.	*1888 1487-1492*
Kellogg, J.H.	K-057	96/05/27	Cooranbong, Aus.	*16MR 332-337*
Kellogg, J.H.	K-058	96/05/07	Cooranbong, Aus.	*21MR 394-397*
Kellogg, J.H.	K-059	96/11/22	Ashfield, Aus.	*18MR 14-21*
Lacey, Herbert	L-060	96/12/20	Cooranbong, Aus.	8MR 284-285;CS 272
Friends of the School [Avondale]	L-060a	96/12/20	Cooranbong, Aus.	*8MR 150-155*
Lane, S.N.	L-061	96/04/12	Cooranbong, Aus.	Ev 209-210,494;VSS 274-275
Lindsay, Sr.	L-062	96/05/20	Cooranbong, Aus.	
Lindsay, Harmon	L-063	96/04/20	Cooranbong, Aus.	*1888 1502-1512*
Lindsay, Harmon	L-064	96/05/08	Cooranbong, Aus.	*1888 1516-1519*
Miller, Br./Woods, Br.	M-065	96/11/08	Cooranbong, Aus.	
McCullagh, Br-Sr.	M-066	96/03/25	Cooranbong, Aus.	4Bio 278
McCullagh, Br-Sr.	M-067	96/03/30	Cooranbong, Aus.	*18MR 42-53*
McCullagh, S.	M-068	96/07/12	Cooranbong, Aus.	2MR 27-28;5MR 342-343
McCullagh, S.	M-069	96/07/11	Cooranbong, Aus.	AH 241,310;CD 425;CG 261,390; 1MCP 169;2MCP 407,579-580;3SM 290; Te 149-150;VSS 123;4Bio 276-277
Maxson, Br-Sr.	M-069a	96/11/05	Cooranbong, Aus.	
Maxson, Br-Sr.	M-071	96/08/12	Cooranbong, Aus.	1MR 286-287
Maxson, Br-Sr.	M-072	96/11/05	Cooranbong, Aus.	CD 113,232-233,259,319,386-387,396,437; MM 276-278;PC 45-48;1MR 66;SpM 45-48
Maxson, Br-Sr.	M-073	96/10/12	Adelaide, Aus.	*20MR 104-118*
Maxson, Br-Sr.	M-073a	96/08/30	Cooranbong, Aus.	*SpM 38-45*
Managers and Workers in our Institutions	M-074	96/06/09 93/01/00?		*PH088 3-24*
Nobbs, Alred	N-075	96/11/24	Ashfield, Aus.	Ev 489;9MR 351-352
Gilbert, Lillie	G-076	96/08/01	Cooranbong, Aus.	TSB 47-49;AH 350
Olsen, O.A.	O-077	96/07/05	Cooranbong, Aus.	TM 374-386
Olsen, O.A.	O-078	96/07/06	Cooranbong, Aus.	*TM 279-297*
Olsen, Br-Sr.	O-080	96/10/00	Ballarat, Aus.	9MR 349-351
Olsen, O.A.	O-080a	96/04/01	Cooranbong, Aus.	PM 153-154;4MR 439-440
Olsen, O.A.	O-081	96/05/31	Cooranbong, Aus.	*1888 1556-1573*
Olsen, O.A.	O-082	96/09/10	Cooranbong, Aus.	TM 305-308
Olsen, O.A.	O-082a	96/09/00		
Olsen, O.A.	O-083	96/05/22	Cooranbong, Aus.	*1888 1520-1535*
Olsen, O.A.	O-084a	96/01/14	Cooranbong, Aus.	
Olsen, O.A.	O-085	96/03/16	Cooranbong, Aus.	UL 89;WM 202
Olsen, O.A.	O-086	96/05/26	Cooranbong, Aus.	*PH080 1-8*
Olsen, O.A.	O-087	96/08/25	Cooranbong, Aus.	ChL 58;Ev 20-21,195-196;SD 68
Olsen, O.A.	O-087a	96/05/25	Cooranbong, Aus.	FBS 72;12MR 57;4Bio 254-255
Prescott, Br-Sr.	P-088	96/09/01	Cooranbong, Aus.	*1888 1616-1620*
Prescott, W.W.	P-089	96/09/02	Cooranbong, Aus.	9MR 165
Palmer, W.O.	P-090	96/01/24	Cooranbong, Aus.	PM 217-218;3SM 118;8MR 349; 9MR 268-269
Brn-Srs. on Pitcairn Island	P-091	96/05/12	Cooranbong, Aus.	*RH 08/04/1896*
Robinson, A.T.	R-092	96/09/02	Cooranbong, Aus.	TSA 66-68
Robinson, A.T.	R-093	96/09/30	Cooranbong, Aus.	TSA 69-71
Starr, Br-Sr. [G.B.]	S-094	96/06/14	Cooranbong, Aus.	*TM 309-318*
Starr, G.B.	S-095	96/08/11	Cooranbong, Aus.	Ev 158-159,445,457-458,463-464;4MR 36;

				6MR 194-195;8MR 196-197
Smith, Uriah	S-096	96/06/06	Cooranbong, Aus.	*1SM 234-235*
Shannan, J.G.	S-097	96/12/26	Cooranbong, Aus.	Ev 685
Shannan, Br-Sr.	S-098	96/12/26	Cooranbong, Aus.	
Semmens, Br.	S-098a	96/12/29	Cooranbong, Aus.	
n.a. [Sister]	S-098b	96/05/21	Cooranbong, Aus.	SD 53;ML 100;HP 116;2MR 98
n.a. [Sister]	S-098c	96/05/20	Cooranbong, Aus.	
n.a. [Sister]	S-098d	96/05/12	Cooranbong, Aus.	
n.a. [Sister]	S-098e	96/05/07	Cooranbong, Aus.	
Tait, A.O.	T-100	96/08/27	Cooranbong, Aus.	*1888 1607-1615*
Tait, A.O.	T-101	96/02/17		
Tait, A.O.	T-102	96/03/00	Cooranbong, Aus.	*7MR 420-424 and CD 462*
Tait, A.O.	T-102a	96/03/09	Cooranbong, Aus.	PM 218;UL 82
Workers in Sydney	W-103	96/07/17	Cooranbong, Aus.	CD 310;4MR 385;5MR 220
Williams, I.N.	W-104	96/04/12	Cooranbong, Aus.	*TSB 214-216*
Wessels, Peter	W-106	96/06/26	Cooranbong, Aus.	4BC 1148;5BC 1123-1124;9MR 109,266
Wessels, Peter	W-106a	96/06/01	Cooranbong, Aus.	TSB 124-128
Wessels, Brothers	W-107	96/04/29	Cooranbong, Aus.	*21MR 5-7*
Wessels, Philip	W-108	96/10/14	Adelaide, Aus.	*19MR 385-392*
Wessels, Philip	W-109	96/07/00	Cooranbong, Aus.	
Wessels, John	W-110	96/10/29	Northcote, Aus.	3SM 248;TMK 289;1MCP 248
Wessels, Sr.	W-111	96/05/03	Cooranbong, Aus.	4Bio 266
Wessels, Sr. and Children	W-112	96/10/16	S. Australia	9MR 118,348-349
Wessels, Sr.	W-113	96/10/20	Victoria, Aus.	
Wessels, Sr.	W-114	96/07/16	Cooranbong, Aus.	3SM 119;8MR 251;4Bio 265-266
Wessels, Sr.	W-115	96/12/14	Cooranbong, Aus.	8MR 56,251;9MR 352
Wilson, Br-Sr.	W-116	96/01/01	Cooranbong, Aus.	TMK 22,275;3SM 420-421;FBS 62
Woods, Br-Sr.	W-117	96/11/03	Northcote, Aus.	2MCP 624,676;HP 201
Walling, Addie/Walling, May	W-118	96/11/17	Ashfield, Aus.	9MR 99
White, J.E./White, Emma	W-119	96/07/31	Cooranbong, Aus.	TMK 170;2MR 48;4MR 265;4Bio 265
White, J.E./White, Emma	W-121	96/04/11	Cooranbong, Aus.	4MR 265;8MR 251;4Bio 265
White, J.E./White, Emma	*W-122	96/08/21	Cooranbong, Aus.	
White, J.E./White, Emma	W-123	96/08/30	Cooranbong, Aus.	12MR 218
White, J.E.	W-124	96/08/09	Cooranbong, Aus.	*1888 1816-1821*
Young Friend	Y-125	96/05/27	Cooranbong, Aus.	
Olsen, O.A.	O-127	96/12/01	Cooranbong, Aus.	*1888 1621-1627*
Watson, Mary Clough	W-128	96/07/09	Cooranbong, Aus.	*14MR 327-334*
Miller, Sr.	M-129	96/09/10	Cooranbong, Aus.	
Workers in the Publishing House	M-129a	96/09/10		From M-129-96
White, J.E./White, Emma	*W-131	96/03/21	Croydon, Aus.	FBS 124-125
Caro, Sr.	*C-132	96/08/30	Cooranbong, Aus.	
Wessels, Peter	*W-133	96/06/21	Cooranbong, Aus.	
Belden, Sarah	*S-134	96/07/19	Cooranbong, Aus.	
Colcord, Charlie	*C-135	96/00/00		
Kellogg, Henry	*K-136	96/02/27	Cooranbong, Aus.	*2MR 170-176*
Kellogg, Br-Sr. [J.H.]	K-137	96/04/06	Cooranbong, Aus.	TMK 356;SpM 80;4Bio 265
White, J.E./White, Emma	*W-139	96/01/16	Cooranbong, Aus.	*18MR 274-275*
White, J.E./White, Emma	*W-140	96/01/23	Cooranbong, Aus.	
White, J.E./White, Emma	*W-141	96/01/30	Cooranbong, Aus.	UL 44;1MCP 358;6MR 262-263
White, J.E./White, Emma	W-141a	96/01/30		Extract of W-141-96
White, J.E./White, Emma	*W-142	96/02/14	Cooranbong, Aus.	
White, J.E./White, Emma	*W-143	96/02/14	Cooranbong, Aus.	
White, J.E./White, Emma	*W-144	96/02/16	Cooranbong, Aus.	11MR 109;4Bio 387
White, J.E./White, Emma	*W-145	96/02/25	Cooranbong, Aus.	
White, J.E.	*W-146	96/03/01	Cooranbong, Aus.	
White, J.E./White, Emma	*W-147	96/03/13	Cooranbong, Aus.	TMK 212,341;4Bio 263
White, J.E./White, Emma	*W-148	96/04/07	Cooranbong, Aus.	

EGW Letters File—Page 48

White, J.E./White, Emma	*W-149	96/05/01	Cooranbong, Aus.	
White, J.E./White, Emma	*W-150	96/05/06	Cooranbong, Aus.	4Bio 389
White, J.E./White, Emma	*W-151	96/06/10	Cooranbong, Aus.	
White, J.E./White, Emma	*W-152	96/07/05	Cooranbong, Aus.	TMK 328;4Bio 255,268
White, J.E./White, Emma	*W-153	96/07/09	Cooranbong, Aus.	FBS 72;4Bio 255-257
White, J.E./White, Emma	*W-154	96/08/02		FBS 72-73
White, J.E.	*W-155	96/08/10	Cooranbong, Aus.	
White, J.E./White, Emma	*W-156	96/09/07	Ashfield, Aus.	5MR 138
White, J.E./White, Emma	*W-157	96/09/09	Cooranbong, Aus.	
White, J.E./White, Emma	*W-158	96/10/00	Adelaide, Aus.	8MR 252;SpTA #7 64
White, J.E./White, Emma	*W-159	96/10/24	Melbourne, Aus.	
White, J.E./White, Emma	*W-160	96/11/10	Cooranbong, Aus.	
White, J.E./White, Emma	*W-161	96/11/23	Ashfield, Aus.	
White, J.E./White, Emma	*W-162	96/12/16	Cooranbong, Aus.	8MR 252-253;4Bio 271
McCullagh, S.	*M-163	96/02/13	Cooranbong, Aus.	
Corliss, Br-Sr.	*C-164	96/04/06	Cooranbong, Aus.	FBS 67-68
Corliss, Br-Sr.	*C-165	96/04/06	Cooranbong, Aus.	
Olsen, O.A.	*O-166	96/04/24	Cooranbong, Aus.	*1888 1513-1515*
Haskell, S.N.	*H-167	96/06/01	Cooranbong, Aus.	4Bio 388
Kellogg, Henry	*K-168	96/06/07	Cooranbong, Aus.	4Bio 264
Corliss, Br-Sr.	*C-169	96/04/00		
White, W.C.	*W-170	96/03/13	Cooranbong, Aus.	
White, W.C.	*W-171	96/03/13	Cooranbong, Aus.	
White, W.C.	*W-172	96/09/17	Cooranbong, Aus.	
White, W.C.	*W-173	96/12/29	Cooranbong, Aus.	
Farnsworth, Br-Sr.	*F-174	96/12/20	Cooranbong, Aus.	
Durland, Br-Sr.	D-175	96/03/26	Cooranbong, Aus.	1BC 1089;5BC 1086;7MR 367
Tailt, A. O.	*T-176	96/11/09	Cooranbong, Aus.	
Olsen, O.A.	O-177	96/03/16	Cooranbong, Aus.	

1897

Church in Adelaide	A-001	97/04/22	Cooranbong, Aus.	*9MR 358-364*
Brn-Srs. in Adelaide	A-003	97/05/06	Cooranbong, Aus.	9MR 364-366;CTr 202
Brn-Srs. in Adelaide	A-004	97/04/05	Cooranbong, Aus.	*9MR 353-357*
My Brethren in America	B-005	97/03/02	Cooranbong, Aus.	SpTA #10 2-12
Brethren in Battle Creek	B-007	97/09/13	Cooranbong, Aus.	
Evans, I.H.	E-007a	97/12/22	Stanmore, Aus.	PM 235
Brethren/Sisters	B-009	97/04/18	Cooranbong, Aus.	
Brethren	B-010	97/09/02	Cooranbong, Aus.	*19MR 19-29*
n.a.	B-011	97/12/14	Cooranbong, Aus.	*21MR 20-26*
Brethren/Sisters	B-012	97/08/01	Cooranbong, Aus.	CTr 166-168
Brethren	B-013	97/08/27	Cooranbong, Aus.	Ev 125;4Bio 335
Brethren	B-014	97/03/30	Cooranbong, Aus.	3SM 74-75;4Bio 281
Wessels, Peter	B-015	97/02/08	Cooranbong, Aus.	
n.a. [Br-Sr.]	B-016	97/06/11	Cooranbong, Aus.	1BC 1086-1087;CTr 36
n.a.	B-017	97/04/07	Cooranbong, Aus.	ChL 64
Those in Resp. Positions in our Publ. Houses	B-018	97/01/00	Cooranbong, Aus.	PM 215,217
Haughey, J.H.	H-019	97/07/04	Cooranbong, Aus.	3SM 252-255;VSS 65-66;SpM 90-92
My Brethren in Battle Creek	B-019a	97/07/27	Cooranbong, Aus.	2SM 147-153;5MR 413-414
Brethren in California	B-020	97/11/22	Stanmore, Aus.	*16MR 45-56*
My Ministering Brethren	B-021	97/12/19	Cooranbong, Aus.	OHC 236;LDE 233;2MR 30-31
Brn-Srs. in Cooranbong	B-022	97/12/23	Stanmore, Aus.	4MR 104-105
Bolton, Fannie	B-024	97/06/25	Cooranbong, Aus.	*FBS 76-78*
Bolton, Fannie	B-025	97/04/11	Cooranbong, Aus.	*FBS 73-75*
Belden, Frank	B-026	97/12/10	Cooranbong, Aus.	1MR 269-270
Belden, Br-Sr.	B-027	97/11/10	Cooranbong, Aus.	Ev 335-336

Belden, Br.-Sr.	B-028	97/07/29	Cooranbong, Aus.	HP 245;2SM 84;LDE 33,76;10MR 275
Those in Resp. Positions in our Publ. Houses	B-028a	97/01/09	Cooranbong, Aus.	CW 172;PM 216-217;8MR 349
Belden, Frank/Belden, Hattie	B-029	97/01/01	Cooranbong, Aus.	2MCP 376-377;8MR 293-294
Barren, Br.-Sr.	B-030	97/12/30	Cooranbong, Aus.	
Colcord, W.A.	C-031	97/02/28	Cooranbong, Aus.	*19MR 378-384*
Collins, Gilbert	C-033	97/06/09	Cooranbong, Aus.	WM 332-333;2BC 1010;7BC 918-919; CG 41-42;7MR 252-255;4Bio 295-296; CTr 310
Collins, Gilbert	C-034	97/06/08	Cooranbong, Aus.	
Chapman, Br./Bell, Br.	C-035	97/01/22	Cooranbong, Aus.	
Davis, N.A.	*D-036	97/08/16	Cooranbong, Aus.	*13MR 1-5*
Davis, Marian	D-037	97/11/19	Stanmore, Aus.	*12MR 345-362*
Daniells, A.G.	D-038	97/01/10	Cooranbong, Aus.	BTS 03/1909
Daniells, A.G.	D-039	97/08/31	Cooranbong, Aus.	*15MR 338-344*
Daniells, A.G.	D-040	97/03/16	Cooranbong, Aus.	*13MR 281-286*
Daniells, A.G.	D-040a	97/01/14	Cooranbong, Aus.	
Daniells, A.G.	D-041	97/02/24	Cooranbong, Aus.	
Daniells, A.G.	D-042	97/09/28	Cooranbong, Aus.	*15MR 1-5*
Daniells, A.G.	D-043	97/09/24	Cooranbong, Aus.	
Daniells, A.G.	D-044	97/01/01	Cooranbong, Aus.	3MR 249;4Bio 287-288
Daniells, A.G./Church in Melbourne	D-045	97/11/15	Cooranbong, Aus.	UL 333;15MR 271
Daniells, A.G./Palmer, E.R.	D-046	97/06/30	Cooranbong, Aus.	
Daniells, A.G./Palmer, E.R.	D-047	97/06/28	Cooranbong, Aus.	VSS 126;8MR 285
Daniells, A.G./Salisbury, W.D.	D-048	97/01/21	Cooranbong, Aus.	UL 35;ML 157,162,217;CTr 231
Daniells/Colcord/Faulkhead/Palmer/Salisbury	D-049	97/09/01	Cooranbong, Aus.	*21MR 336-339*
Workers in our Institutions	L-049a	97/09/00		*SpM 87-90*
Daniells, A.G./Palmer, E.R./Colcord, W.A.	D-050	97/03/12	Cooranbong, Aus.	SpM 60-69
Daniells, A.G./Palmer, E.R./Colcord, W.A.	D-050a	97/03/12	Cooranbong, Aus.	Variant of Lt 50, 1897
Evans, Br.	E-051	97/11/21	Stanmore, Aus.	15MR 6-9
Judge/Jones/Redwood/Simpson [students]	F-051a	97/07/08	Cooranbong, Aus.	10MR 307
Farnsworth, Br.-Sr.	F-052	97/01/18	Cooranbong, Aus.	HP 300;CS 259-260
Farnsworth, Br.-Sr.	F-053	97/03/19	Cooranbong, Aus.	
Farnsworth, Br.-Sr.	F-054	97/12/15	Cooranbong, Aus.	
Brn.-Srs. Assembling in General Conference	B-055	97/01/10	Cooranbong, Aus.	6MR 381-382
Hare, Br.	H-056	97/08/17	Cooranbong, Aus.	*13MR 355-358*
Hare, Br.-Sr.	H-057	97/01/20	Cooranbong, Aus.	ML 184;2BC 1023;4Bio 288
Hare, Sr. [Wesley]	H-058	97/12/18	Cooranbong, Aus.	*12MR 350-353*
Hare, Br./Hughes, Br.	H-059	97/09/09	missing	
Hickox, Br.-Sr.	H-060	97/10/25	Stanmore, Aus.	
Hickox, Br.-Sr.	H-061	97/04/12	Cooranbong, Aus.	
Hickox, Br.-Sr.	H-063	97/09/07	Cooranbong, Aus.	AH 392;CS 256
Hickox, Br.-Sr.	H-064	97/09/03	Cooranbong, Aus.	CTr 169
Hawkins, Br.-Sr.	H-065	97/04/06	Cooranbong, Aus.	3SM 349-350;1MR 56
Henry, A.R.	H-066	97/08/00	Cooranbong, Aus.	3SM 84;7MR 300
Henry, A.R.	H-067	97/11/08	Cooranbong, Aus.	
Hardy, Br.	H-068	97/02/07	Cooranbong, Aus.	
Hardy, Br.	H-069	97/02/07	Cooranbong, Aus.	4BC 1146;5BC 1103;3SM 134-136; 8MR 447;9MR 213-214
Haskell, S.N.	H-070	97/01/03	Cooranbong, Aus.	TMK 227;4Bio 289-290,315
Haskell, Br.-Sr.	H-071	97/11/05	Cooranbong, Aus.	
Haskell, Br.-Sr.	H-072	97/12/01	Cooranbong, Aus.	9MR 371
Haskell, Br.-Sr.	H-072a	97/12/14	Cooranbong, Aus.	
Humphries, Br.	H-074	97/02/07	Cooranbong, Aus.	TDG 46;TMK 94
Haskell, Br.-Sr.	H-074a	97/03/01	Cooranbong, Aus.	3SM 338-339;7MR 386-387;CTr 357
Haskell, Br.-Sr./Starr, Br.-Sr./Wilson, Br.-Sr.	H-074b	97/12/16	Cooranbong, Aus.	
Ings, Sr.	I-075	97/07/03	Cooranbong, Aus.	*7MR 76-77*
Irwin, G.A.	I-076	97/07/22	Cooranbong, Aus.	8MR 56-57,191;SpM 95-96

Jones, C.H.	J-077	97/07/09	Cooranbong, Aus.	4Bio 294,313
Jones, C.H.	J-077a	97/07/09	Cooranbong, Aus.	
Jones, C.H.	J-078	97/12/07	Cooranbong, Aus.	
Jones, Mr. [student]	J-079	97/07/14	Cooranbong, Aus.	SD 241
Jones, A.T.	J-080	97/12/09	Cooranbong, Aus.	PH146 8-15
Jones, C.H.	J-081	97/05/27	Cooranbong, Aus.	CS 263;1MR 184-186,189-191
Jones, C.H.	*J-081a	97/12/20	Stanmore, Aus.	8MR 456-457
Kellogg, J.H.	K-082	97/08/01	Cooranbong, Aus.	*21MR 289-291*
Kellogg, Br-Sr.	K-082a	97/02/10	Sydney, Aus.	*21MR 188-192*
Kellogg, J.H.	K-083	97/02/14	Sydney, Aus.	
Kellogg, J.H.	K-084	97/08/29	Cooranbong, Aus.	
Kerr, Sr.	K-085	97/10/21	Stanmore, Aus.	
Lawrence, Br.	L-086	97/12/21	Cooranbong, Aus.	
Lacey, Br-Sr.	L-087	97/03/19	Cooranbong, Aus.	
Lacey, Herbert/Lacey, Lillian	L-088	97/03/18	Cooranbong, Aus.	
Lacey, Herbert	L-089	97/06/30	Cooranbong, Aus.	
Lacey, Herbert/Lacey, Lillian	L-089a	97/03/16	Cooranbong, Aus.	
Lacey, Herbert/Lacey, Lillian	L-089b	97/03/22	Cooranbong, Aus.	2MR 31-32
Lacey, Herbert/Lacey, Lillian	L-089c	97/03/23	Cooranbong, Aus.	7BC 967-968
Lindsay, Br-Sr.	L-090	97/08/18	Cooranbong, Aus.	1MCP 327;12MR 218-221;4Bio 316-317
Lindsay, Br-Sr.	L-091	97/11/29	Cooranbong, Aus.	
Lindsay, Br-Sr.	L-092	97/01/31	Cooranbong, Aus.	8MR 368-369;4Bio 290
Loughborough, J.N.	L-092a	97/12/19	Stanmore, Aus.	
Miller, Walter	M-093	97/09/01	Cooranbong, Aus.	
Miller, Sr.	M-094	97/09/01	Cooranbong, Aus.	
Miller, Sr.	M-095	97/08/31	Cooranbong, Aus.	
Miller, Walter (telegram)	M-096	97/08/00	Cooranbong, Aus.	
Martin, Mr-Mrs.	M-097	97/01/16	Cooranbong, Aus.	
Martin, Mr-Mrs.	M-098	97/03/31	Cooranbong, Aus.	
McCullagh, S.	M-098a	97/04/09	Cooranbong, Aus.	3SM 348-349;7MR 174;10MR 166-172
Olsen, Br-Sr.	O-099	97/08/19	Cooranbong, Aus.	3MR 274;6MR 265;4Bio 294
Pallant, Br. [J.]	P-100	97/12/09	Cooranbong, Aus.	
Rogers, Sanford	R-101	97/11/08	Cooranbong, Aus.	4Bio 322
Robinson, A.T.	R-102	97/03/05	Cooranbong, Aus.	TSA 72-74
Robinson, Br-Sr. [A.T.]	R-102a	97/12/22	Stanmore, Aus.	Ev 439;Te 58,239
Sutherland, E.A.	S-103	97/07/23	Cooranbong, Aus.	*13MR 254-259*
Sutherland, E.A.	S-104	97/12/15	Cooranbong, Aus.	*PH086 40-48*
Skinner, Br.	S-105	97/03/19	Cooranbong, Aus.	
Starr, Br-Sr. [G.B.]	S-106	97/05/14	Cooranbong, Aus.	*15MR 286-293*
Starr, Br-Sr. [G.B.]	S-107	97/05/07	Cooranbong, Aus.	
Starr, Br-Sr. [G.B.]	S-108	97/12/14	Cooranbong, Aus.	
Shannan, Br.	S-110	97/02/05	Cooranbong, Aus.	ML 331;CTr 83
Steed, Br./Haskell, S.N./Farnsworth, Br.	S-112	97/01/18	Cooranbong, Aus.	
Semmens, Br.	S-112a	97/03/10	Cooranbong, Aus.	*20MR 278-281*
Slocum, Sr. [Booth]	S-113	97/06/09	Cooranbong, Aus.	WM 333-334;PH048 16
Tuxford, Sr.	T-113a	97/09/24	Cooranbong, Aus.	Ev 633
Tenney, Br-Sr.	T-114	97/07/01	Cooranbong, Aus.	*FBS 78-80*
Tenney, Br.	T-114a	97/06/00		
Tenney, Br.	T-115	97/07/05	Cooranbong, Aus.	*FBS 80-81*
Wessels, Peter	W-116	97/02/17	Cooranbong, Aus.	
Wessels, Peter	W-117	97/01/26	Cooranbong, Aus.	ML 25,263
Wessels, Peter	W-118	97/02/00	Syndey, Aus.	
Wessels, Peter	W-119	97/03/08	Cooranbong, Aus.	6BC 1073
Wessels, Peter	W-120	97/03/10		TSB 128-129
Wessels, Br-Sr. [Peter]	W-121	97/02/20	Cooranbong, Aus.	TMK 291,363
Wessels, Philip	W-123	97/03/08	Cooranbong, Aus.	TSA 47-53
Wessels, Sr. [Philip]	W-124	97/03/07	Cooranbong, Aus.	*DG 183-185*

EGW Letters File—Page 51

1353

Wessels, Br-Sr. [John]	W-126	97/05/18	Cooranbong, Aus.	7MR 174-175;8MR 367-368;4Bio 305,307
Wessels, John	W-127	97/01/01	Cooranbong, Aus.	6MR 78-81
Wessels, Br-Sr. [John]	W-128	97/06/25	Cooranbong, Aus.	*13MR 153-156*
Wessels, Br-Sr. [John]	W-129	97/05/18	Cooranbong, Aus.	3SM 58-59;6BC 1112
Wessels, John	W-130	97/02/17	Sydney, Aus.	TSA 54-55;4Bio 291
Wessels, Sr.	W-131	97/06/24	Cooranbong, Aus.	*17MR 57-60*
Wessels, Sr.	W-132	97/06/24	Cooranbong, Aus.	3MR 250,274;4Bio 314
Wessels, Sr.	W-133	97/03/07	Cooranbong, Aus.	
Wessels, Sr.	W-134	97/02/08	Cooranbong, Aus.	
Wessels, Sr.	W-135	97/02/20	Cooranbong, Aus.	SD 342;TMK 118;1SM 117-118;CC 353
Winslow, Br-Sr.	W-136	97/11/07	Cooranbong, Aus.	4Bio 335-338
White, W.C.	W-137	97/12/14	Cooranbong, Aus.	5MR 190
White, W.C.	W-138	97/06/10	Cooranbong, Aus.	*20MR 213-218*
White, W.C.	W-139	97/04/11	Cooranbong, Aus.	
White, W.C.	W-140	97/06/06	Cooranbong, Aus.	4Bio 306-307
White, W.C.	W-141	97/05/05	Cooranbong, Aus.	5MR 186;8MR 365-367;11MR 206-207; 4Bio 295-296,301-302
White, W.C.	W-142	97/12/09	Cooranbong, Aus.	
White, W.C.	W-143	97/05/06	Cooranbong, Aus.	7MR 175-177;9MR 366
White, W.C.	W-144	97/12/01	Cooranbong, Aus.	
White, W.C.	W-145	97/08/15	Cooranbong, Aus.	PC 88-90;2MR 177;11MR 174
White, J.E.	W-146	97/06/21	Cooranbong, Aus.	
White, J.E.	W-147	97/09/12	Cooranbong, Aus.	1MR 41;4MR 361
White, J.E./White, Emma	W-147a	97/09/26	Cooranbong, Aus.	Ev 646
White, J.E./White, Emma	W-148	97/10/23	Stanmore, Aus.	7ABC 468;4Bio 336-337
White, J.E./White, Emma	*W-148a	97/10/25	Stanmore, Aus.	
White, J.E./White, Emma	*W-149	97/05/30	Cooranbong, Aus.	*20MR 228-237*
White, J.E./White, Emma	*W-149a	97/05/30	Cooranbong, Aus.	
White, J.E./White, Emma	W-150	97/11/06	Cooranbong, Aus.	TMK 126;4MR 361
White, J.E./White, Emma	W-151	97/08/29	Cooranbong, Aus.	1MR 177-178
White, J.E./White, Emma	W-151a	97/08/29	Cooranbong, Aus.	4Bio 319
White, J.E./White, Emma/White, W.C.	W-152	97/04/06	Cooranbong, Aus.	7MR 83-84;9MR 357-358;4Bio 294-298
White, J.E./White, Emma	W-153	97/04/06	Cooranbong, Aus.	*14MR 273-277*
White, J.E./White, Emma	W-153a	97/08/24	Cooranbong, Aus.	*21MR 367-372*
Weber, Sr. [R.]	W-154	97/12/08	Cooranbong, Aus.	
To Whom It May Concern [re Power of Attorney]	B-155	97/00/00	Cooranbong, Aus.	
To Whom It May Concern [re Power of Attorney]	B-155a	97/00/00	Cooranbong, Aus.	
Haskell, S.N.	H-156	97/04/08	Cooranbong, Aus.	1BC 1115;4BC 1163-1164;7MR 177-178
Starr, Br-Sr. [G.B.]	S-157	97/04/14	Cooranbong, Aus.	10MR 293
Starr, Br-Sr. [G.B.]	S-158	97/05/19	Cooranbong, Aus.	*9MR 366-368*
Haskell, Br-Sr./Starr, Br-Sr. [G.B.]	B-159	97/12/07	Cooranbong, Aus.	
Haskell, Br-Sr.	H-160	97/12/00		
Caro, Sr.	*C-161	97/00/00		
White, J.E./White, Emma	*W-162	97/10/16	Cooranbong, Aus.	4Bio 320-322
Kellogg, Br-Sr.	*K-163	97/12/20	Stanmore, Aus.	4Bio 339
White, J.E./White, Emma	*W-164	97/07/04	Cooranbong, Aus.	4Bio 305,308,324-325
Farnsworth, Br-Sr.	*F-165	97/12/06	Stanmore, Aus.	
White, J.E./White, Emma	*W-166	97/01/14	Cooranbong, Aus.	TDG 22;4Bio 289
White, W.C.	*W-166a	97/01/11	Cooranbong, Aus.	
White, W.C.	*W-167	97/01/14	Cooranbong, Aus.	8MR 256
White, W.C.	*W-168	97/01/17	Cooranbong, Aus.	
White, W.C.	*W-169	97/01/18	Cooranbong, Aus.	4Bio 323-324
White, J.E.	*W-170	97/01/00	Cooranbong, Aus.	
White, J.E./White, Emma	*W-171	97/02/15	Sydney, Aus.	TMK 198,330;4Bio 291;CTr 45
White, J.E./White, Emma	*W-172	97/03/15	Cooranbong, Aus.	
White, W.C.	*W-174	97/07/05	Cooranbong, Aus.	
White, J.E.	*W-175	97/07/09	Cooranbong, Aus.	

White, J.E./White, Emma	*W-176	97/07/19	Cooranbong, Aus.	
White, J.E./White, Emma	*W-177	97/08/16	Cooranbong, Aus.	8MR 257
White, J.E./White, Emma	*W-178	97/10/18	Cooranbong, Aus.	3MR 275;4Bio 321
White, J.E.	*W-179	97/12/06	Cooranbong, Aus.	
Starr, Br-Sr. [G.B.]	*S-180	97/01/20	Cooranbong, Aus.	
White, W.C.	*W-181	97/03/15	Cooranbong, Aus.	*21MR 183-187*
White, W.C.	*W-182	97/05/06	Cooranbong, Aus.	4Bio 305
Edwards, Sr.	*E-183	97/05/06	Cooranbong, Aus.	
Robinson, Br-Sr.	*R-184	97/12/23	Stanmore, Aus.	
Daniells, A.G./Palmer, E.R.	*D-185	97/06/27	Cooranbong, Aus.	4Bio 305-306
White, W.C.	*W-186	97/02/04	Cooranbong, Aus.	4Bio 289-290
White, W.C.	*W-187	97/02/10	Sydney, Aus.	4Bio 326
White, W.C.	*W-188	97/02/15	Sydney, Aus.	4Bio 291
White, W.C.	*W-189	97/03/11	Cooranbong, Aus.	4Bio 292-293,324
White, W.C.	*W-190	97/04/09	Cooranbong, Aus.	4Bio 293-294
White, W.C.	*W-192	97/07/20	Cooranbong, Aus.	
White, W.C.	*W-193	97/07/23	Cooranbong, Aus.	4Bio 311-312
White, W.C.	*W-194	97/08/01	Cooranbong, Aus.	
White, W.C.	*W-195	97/08/05	Sydney, Aus.	*20MR 35-36*
White, W.C.	*W-196	97/08/06	Sydney, Aus.	
White, W.C.	*W-197	97/08/30	Cooranbong, Aus.	
White, W.C.	*W-198	97/09/21	Cooranbong, Aus.	
White, W.C.	*W-199	97/11/06	Cooranbong, Aus.	
White, W.C.	*W-200	97/11/26	Cooranbong, Aus.	4MR 44;11MR 271
White, W.C.	*W-201	97/12/01	Cooranbong, Aus.	
White, W.C.	*W-202	97/12/02	Cooranbong, Aus.	
White, W.C.	*W-203	97/12/02	Cooranbong, Aus.	
White, W.C.	*W-204	97/12/04	Stanmore, Aus.	
White, W.C.	*W-205	97/12/06	Cooranbong, Aus.	4Bio 339
White, W.C.	*W-206	97/12/07	Cooranbong, Aus.	4Bio 340-341
White, W.C.	*W-207	97/12/08	Cooranbong, Aus.	
White, W.C.	*W-208	97/12/10	Cooranbong, Aus.	4Bio 341
White, W.C.	*W-209	97/12/12	Cooranbong, Aus.	4Bio 391
White, W.C.	*W-210	97/12/16	Stanmore, Aus.	
White, W.C.	*W-211	97/12/31	Cooranbong, Aus.	
Starr, Br-Sr. [G.B.]	*S-212	97/04/30	Cooranbong, Aus.	
Hall, Sr.	*H-213	97/05/05	Cooranbong, Aus.	
Farnsworth, Br-Sr.	*F-214	97/06/16	Cooranbong, Aus.	
Farnsworth, Br-Sr.	*F-215	97/08/18	Cooranbong, Aus.	
Farnsworth, Br-Sr.	*F-216	97/09/07	Cooranbong, Aus.	
Brethren	B-217	97/12/10	Cooranbong, Aus.	*1888 1652*
Tait, A.O.	T-218	97/09/12	Cooranbong, Aus.	
Children [White, J.E. and White, Emma]	W-219	97/09/27		
White, J.E.	W-220	97/09/27	Cooranbong, Aus.	

1898

Austin, Sr.	A-001	98/01/14	Cooranbong, Aus.	4Bio 342
Leading Men in our Churches [Fitzroy/Echo]	B-002	98/03/17		*PH162*
Brethren	B-003	98/02/02		Ev 475;7BC 989
Brethren	B-004	98/02/20		2SM 336-337;1BC 1095;8MR 352
Michaels, Br./N. Fitzroy Church/Echo Office	B-005	98/04/12		OHC 105;3MR 320-321
Avondale School Board	B-005a	98/04/28	Cooranbong, Aus.	8MR 257
Campbell, Emily	C-006	98/01/12	Cooranbong, Aus.	*12MR 353-357*
Gotzian, Sr.	G-008	98/02/14	Cooranbong, Aus.	*21MR 292-299*
Henry, S.M.I.	H-009	98/01/02	Cooranbong, Aus.	7MR 155
Hare, J.	H-010	98/01/26	Cooranbong, Aus.	TDG 34

Hare, M	H-011	98/01/21		
Hare, M.	H-012	98/01/21		8MR 155-156
Hare, M.	H-013	98/01/19	Cooranbong, Aus.	
Haskell, Br-Sr.	H-014	98/03/27	St. Kilda, Aus.	
Haskell, Br-Sr.	H-014a	98/03/03	Balaclava, Aus.	
Henry, A.R.	H-015	98/04/20	Stanmore, Aus.	*1888 1653-1662*
Jones, C.H.	J-016	98/01/17	Cooranbong, Aus.	
Jones, C.H.	J-017	98/02/04	Cooranbong, Aus.	
Jones, C.H.	J-018	98/03/23	Balaclava, Aus.	Ev 432-433,437,446-447
Jones, C.H.	J-019	98/03/25	Balaclava, Aus.	8MR 457
Kelsey, Sr.	K-020	98/01/16	Cooranbong, Aus.	UL 30
Kellogg, J.H.	K-021	98/02/13	Cooranbong, Aus.	AH 367-368,383;4Bio 395
Kellogg, J.H.	K-022	98/03/25	Balaclava, Aus.	8T 177-179;HP 77
Kellogg, J.H.	K-023	98/04/28	Cooranbong, Aus.	
Merrill, Br.	M-024	98/03/25	Balaclava, Aus.	WM 33,244
Peck, Sr.	P-026	98/03/03	Balaclava, Aus.	8MR 56
Robinson, Br-Sr. [D.A.]	R-028	98/01/24	Cooranbong, Aus.	
Sisley, Br.	S-029	98/01/11	Cooranbong, Aus.	12MR 221-222
Sanderson, Dr.	S-030	98/04/28	Cooranbong, Aus.	
Smith, Uriah	S-031	98/01/12	Cooranbong, Aus.	*PH086 25-40*
Tripp, Mary	T-032	98/04/27	Cooranbong, Aus.	TSA 75-76
Wessels, Br-Sr. [John]	W-033	98/01/25	Cooranbong, Aus.	WM 193;8MR 57
Wessels, Sr.	W-034	98/02/21	Cooranbong, Aus.	
White, J.E.	W-035	98/01/01	Cooranbong, Aus.	*19MR 171-178*
White, J.E./White, Emma	W-036	98/01/11	Cooranbong, Aus.	4Bio 342
White, J.E./White, Emma	W-037	98/02/13	Cooranbong, Aus.	
White, J.E./White, Emma	W-038	98/02/02	Stanmore, Aus.	12MR 357-359
Woods, H./Miller, W.H.B.	W-039	98/03/27		ChL 12;1MR 264;4Bio 344
Advisers of Medical Students	B-039a	98/10/26	Brisbane, Aus.	*8T 163-165*
Wilson, Br-Sr. [G.T.]	W-040	98/05/10	Cooranbong, Aus.	
Henry, A.R.	H-041	98/05/16	Cooranbong, Aus.	*1888 1663-1678*
Irwin, G.A.	I-042	98/05/19	Cooranbong, Aus.	SpM 122-124
Gage, W.C.	G -043	98/05/19	Cooranbong, Aus.	
Evans, I.H.	E-044	98/05/20	Cooranbong, Aus.	
Gage, Br-Sr.	G-045	98/05/19	Cooranbong, Aus.	11MR 272
Hardy, E.	H-046	98/05/24	Cooranbong, Aus.	TMK 53,209;3MR 320
Haskell, S.N.	H-047	98/06/01	Cooranbong, Aus.	*GH 08/00/1898*
Gorick, Br.	G-048	98/06/01	Cooranbong, Aus.	*20MR 61-63*
Daniells, A.G.	D-050	98/06/03	Cooranbong, Aus.	8MR 257-258
Daniells, A.G.	D-050a	98/06/06	Cooranbong, Aus.	4Bio 351
Brethren in Battle Creek	B-051	98/06/06	Cooranbong, Aus.	11MR 217-218
Smith, Uriah/Irwin, G.A.	*S-051a	98/06/06	Cooranbong, Aus.	7MR 366;11MR 218
Brethren in Battle Creek	B-051b	98/06/06	Cooranbong, Aus.	*SpTA #11 20-28*
Daniells, A.G.	D-052	98/06/13	Cooranbong, Aus.	8MR 156;4Bio 355
Teachers and Students in our Schools	T-053	98/06/12		CD 334,340;5MR 222-224
Brethren in the Ministry	B-054	98/06/15		*SpTA #11 13-20*
Ministers in our Conferences	B-054a	98/06/00	Cooranbong, Aus.	4MR 371-372
Brethren in Battle Creek	B-055	98/06/15		See 8T 76-80
Appeal to our Brethren in Battle Creek	B-055a	98/06/16		*8T 76-80*
Wessels, Br-Sr. [John]	W-056	98/06/28		4Bio 355
Prescott, Br-Sr.	P-057	98/06/19	Cooranbong, Aus.	11MR 279;4Bio 353
White, J.E./White, Emma	W-058	98/07/13	Cooranbong, Aus.	3MR 316-317;8MR 258;4Bio 355
Gorick, Sr.	*G-058a	98/07/00	Cooranbong, Aus.	*11MR 334-342*
Kellogg, J.H.	K-059	98/07/26	Stanmore, Aus.	*18MR 352-357*
To Whom It May Concern	*B-060	98/07/29	Cooranbong, Aus.	PM 223;2MCP 560
Jones, A.T.	J-061	98/08/01	Cooranbong, Aus.	3MR 340-341;5MR 414-415
White, W.C.	W-062	98/08/10	Cooranbong, Aus.	4Bio 359

White, W.C.	W-063	98/08/11	Cooranbong, Aus.	OHC 335;4BC 1154
White, W.C.	W-063a	98/08/12	Cooranbong, Aus.	4Bio 358-360
Griggs, F./Howe, Br.	G-065	98/08/23	Cooranbong, Aus.	*20MR 194-203*
White, J.E.	W-066	98/08/28	Cooranbong, Aus.	TMK 89,293
Sanderson, Br.	S-068	98/08/29	Cooranbong, Aus.	MRmnt 105;WM 39
Burden, J.A.	*B-069	98/08/29	Cooranbong, Aus.	PC 31
Hare, Br.	H-070	98/08/31	Cooranbong, Aus.	TSB 32-33
Prescott, Br-Sr.	P-071	98/08/27	Cooranbong, Aus.	*17MR 208-215*
Smith, Uriah	S-072	98/09/05	Cooranbong, Aus.	
Churches in America	B-073	98/08/05	Cooranbong, Aus.	
Kellogg, Henry	K-074	98/09/09	Cooranbong, Aus.	
Sutherland, E.A.	S-075	98/09/24	Cooranbong, Aus.	*13MR 92-104*
Wessels, Philip	W-076	98/10/02	Cooranbong, Aus.	
Weber, E.	W-076a	98/09/28	Cooranbong, Aus.	
Waggoner, Br-Sr. [E.J.]	W-077	98/08/26	Cooranbong, Aus.	*17MR 216-220*
Salisbury, Br./Faulkhead, Br.	S-078	98/10/03	Cooranbong, Aus.	
Lindsay, Harmon	L-079	98/10/03	Cooranbong, Aus.	SD 14;3SM 316;3MR 204-205
Lacey, Herbert	L-079a	98/04/28	Cooranbong, Aus.	
Waggoner, E.J.	W-080	98/09/24	Cooranbong, Aus.	*11MR 367-374*
Wessels, John	W-081	98/10/05	Cooranbong, Aus.	
Wessels, Sr. [Philip]	W-082	98/10/05	Cooranbong, Aus.	DG 185-186
White, W.C.	W-083	98/08/17	Cooranbong, Aus.	TMK 88;UL 243;VSS 15
Starr, Br-Sr. [G.B.]	S-083a	98/09/29	Cooranbong, Aus.	
Kellogg, J.H.	K-084	98/10/05	Cooranbong, Aus.	CD 293-294,412-414;8MR 258-259; 11MR 185-186
Jones, C.H.	J-085	98/10/07	Cooranbong, Aus.	2MR 38
Kellogg, J.H.	K-086	98/10/17	Cooranbong, Aus.	4Bio 363-364
Faulkhead, Br./Salisbury, Br./Robinson, Br.	F-087	98/10/20	Brisbane, Aus.	3MR 247-248;9MR 9
Irwin, G.A.	I-088	98/10/30	Brisbane, Aus.	
White, J.E.	W-089	98/10/30	Brisbane, Aus.	1SM 174;1BC 1105;5MR 305;CTr 66
Kellogg, J.H.	K-090	98/10/20	Brisbane, Aus.	CG 558;HP 192,357-358;5MR 64
Haskell, Br-Sr.	*H-091	98/11/11	Cooranbong, Aus.	Ev 657-658;CD 95,321,333
Pallant, J.	P-092	98/11/11	Cooranbong, Aus.	
Salisbury, W.D.	S-093	98/11/05	Rockhampton, Aus.	CD 52
Robinson, Br-Sr. [A.T.]	R-094	98/11/16	Cooranbong, Aus.	
Hubbard, G.	H-095	98/11/18	Cooranbong, Aus.	10MR 231
Robinson, A.T.	R-096	98/11/18		Ev 498;BTS 10/1916 and 11/1916
Brethren in N. Fitzroy	B-097	98/11/18		2MCP 436,673-674;OHC 42; 6BC 1100-1101;7BC 925-928
Walling, Addie/Walling, May	W-098	98/11/03	Rockhampton, Aus.	
King, Br.	K-099	98/11/20	Cooranbong, Aus.	
Wilson, G.T./Pallant, J./Chapman, T.A.	W-100	98/11/03	Rockhampton, Aus.	2MCP 407;3MR 164;9MR 284
Pallant, J./Chapman, T.A.	P-101	98/11/20		KC 20-21
Kellogg, J.H.	K-102	98/11/20	Cooranbong, Aus.	3MR 366-367
Peck, Sr.	P-103	98/11/21	Cooranbong, Aus.	2SM 264;7MR 411;8MR 57-58
Haskell, Br-Sr.	H-104	98/11/25	Cooranbong, Aus.	
Haskell, Br-Sr.	H-105	98/11/28	Cooranbong, Aus.	3SM 200-201;TMK 226;7MR 388-389; BTS 06/1915
Chapman, T.A.	C-106	98/11/29		*PC 44-49*
Brn-Srs. in Rockhampton	*B-107	98/11/06	Rockhampton, Aus.	CG 509;AH 164,226;5MR 371
Starr, Br-Sr. [G.B.]	*S-107a	98/11/06	Rockhampton, Aus.	
Brn-Srs. in Rockhamton	*B-108	98/11/25		*2SAT 130-134*
Moon, A.	M-109	98/11/29	Cooranbong, Aus.	4Bio 363;8MR 244
Miller, Walter	M-109a	98/00/00		OHC 245
Lindsay, Br-Sr.	L-110	98/11/06	Rockhampton, Aus.	
Wessels, Sr.	W-111	98/12/01	Cooranbong, Aus.	WM 334-335
Kellogg, J.H.	K-112	98/12/01	Cooranbong, Aus.	

EGW Letters File—Page 55

Rousseau, Sr.	R-113	98/12/01	Cooranbong, Aus.	TMK 277
Kellogg, J.H.	K-114	90/11/30	Cooranbong, Aus.	
Kellogg, J.H.	K-115	98/12/01	Cooranbong, Aus.	
Kellogg, J.H.	K-116	98/12/01		MM 79-81;MM Extra 05/1899
Griggs, F.	G-117	98/12/01	Cooranbong, Aus.	CG 473;11MR 40-41;12MR 267-268
Henry, S.M.I.	H-118	98/12/01	Cooranbong, Aus.	3SM 57;7MR 155-158;MRmnt 118
Henry, S.M.I.	H-119	98/12/02	Cooranbong, Aus.	1NL 35-36
Haskell, Br-Sr.	H-120	98/12/05	Cooranbong, Aus.	1NL 31-32
Haskell, Br-Sr.	H-120a	98/12/00	Cooranbong, Aus.	variant of H-120-1898
Haskell, Br-Sr.	H-121	98/12/12	Cooranbong, Aus.	3MR 280;6MR 57;7MR 389
Lucas, L.	L-122	98/12/13	Cooranbong, Aus.	
Kellogg, J.H.	K-123	98/02/03?	Balaclava, Aus.	8T 158-165
Those on the Avondale School Ground	B-123a	98/12/14		*16MR 278-280*
Kellogg, J.H.	K-124	98/12/18	Cooranbong, Aus.	*15MR 250-252*
Irwin, G.A.	I-125	98/12/18	Cooranbong, Aus.	4Bio 370-371
Irwin, G.A.	I-125a	98/12/18	Cooranbong, Aus.	variant of Lt 125, 1898
Kellogg, J.H.	K-126	98/12/00		*21MR 51-58*
Wilson, Br-Sr. [G.T.]	W-127	98/12/27	Hamilton, Aus.	UL 375
Brethren in California	B-128	98/12/28	Hamilton, Aus.	
White, J.E./White, Emma	W-129	98/12/28	Hamilton, Aus.	6BC 1112;4Bio 371-373
Haskell, Br-Sr.	H-130	98/12/26	Hamilton, Aus.	*21MR 227-236*
Smouse, Br-Sr. [C.]	S-131	98/12/31		4Bio 371-372,374
Kellogg, J.H.	K-132	98/12/29	Hamilton, Aus.	3SM 419-420;Ev 150,500-501;4Bio 398
Henry, S.M.I.	H-133	98/04/12		*RH Supp. 12/06/1898*
Haskell, Br-Sr.	H-133a	98/12/22	Cooranbong, Aus.	
Starr, G.B.	S-135	98/00/00		HP 27;1MCP 350;2MR 34-35,46; 6MR 14-15;10MR 331-332
White, J.E./White, Emma	W-136	98/08/14	Cooranbong, Aus.	*21MR 265-268*
White, J.E.	W-136a	98/08/14		2SM 14-15;6BC 1064-1065;4MR 267; 5MR 354-355;12MR 206
Irwin, G.A./Evans, I.H./Smith, U./Jones, A.T.	I-137	98/04/21	Stanmore, Aus.	*21MR 355-363*
Smith, Uriah/Jones, A.T./Evans, I.H.	S-137a	98/04/21	Stanmore, Aus.	
Smith, Uriah/Jones, A.T.	S-137b	98/04/22	Sydney, Aus.	
Kellogg, J.H.	K-138	98/12/14		7MR 6-7;4Bio 397
Jones, A.T.	J-139	98/12/16	Cooranbong, Aus.	WM 122;Ev 522;2MCP 377,412,792; 5BC 1108;2MR 26-27;4MR 349-350,365
Kellogg, J.H.	K-140	98/12/20		Ev 58;13MR 405-406;4Bio 427
Wessels, Philip	W-141	98/03/00	Balaclava, Aus.	
Haskell, Br-Sr.	*H-142	98/03/02	Balaclava, Aus.	
Farnsworth, Br-Sr.	*F-144	98/03/22	Balaclava, Aus.	HP 139
White, J.E.	*W-145	98/09/22	Cooranbong, Aus.	
White, W.C.	*W-170	98/03/25	Balaclava, Aus.	
Clough, J.C.	*C-171	98/04/27	Cooranbong, Aus.	
Smith, Uriah/Jones, C.H.	*S-172	98/05/07	Cooranbong, Aus.	4Bio 344
Olsen, Br-Sr.	*O-173	98/08/26	Cooranbong, Aus.	
Salisbury, W.D.	*S-174	98/11/09	Cooranbong, Aus.	
n.a.	*B-175	98/01/11	Cooranbong, Aus.	
White, W.C./White, May	*W-176	98/03/21	Geelong, Aus.	4Bio 343
White, W.C./White, May	*W-177	98/03/22	Balaclava, Aus.	4Bio 344
White, W.C.	*W-178	98/04/14	Stanmore, Aus.	
White, W.C.	*W-179	98/04/15	Stanmore, Aus.	
White, J.E./White, Emma	*W-180	98/07/29	Cooranbong, Aus.	4Bio 357
White, J.E./White, Emma	*W-181	98/07/31	Cooranbong, Aus.	4Bio 357
White, W.C.	*W-182	98/08/11	Cooranbong, Aus.	
White, W.C.	*W-183	98/08/00	Cooranbong, Aus.	
Smith, Uriah/Jones, A.T.	S-184	98/07/07	Stanmore, Aus.	
Davis, Marian	*D-185	98/03/22	Balaclava, Aus.	

Kellogg, J.H./wife	*K-186	98/07/04	Cooranbong, Aus.	
Wilson, Br-Sr.	W-187	98/11/11	Cooranbong, Aus.	
Wilson, Br-Sr.	W-188	98/11/18	Cooranbong, Aus.	
Starr, Br-Sr. [G.B.]	*S-189	98/07/31	Cooranbong, Aus.	
Starr, Br-Sr. [G.B.]	*S-190	98/07/31c		
Proper Persons to Whom These Lines Should be ...	*B-191	98/00/00		
Farnsworth, Br-Sr.	*F-192	98/03/00		
Workers in the Echo Publishing House	B-193	98/05/16		

1899

Haskell, Sr.	H-001	99/01/02		7MR 390
Sanitarium Board	S-002	99/01/03	Hamilton, Aus.	Ev 582-583
Kellogg, J.H.	K-003	99/01/05		2MR 239;9MR 81
Kellogg, J.H.	K-004	99/01/06	Hamilton, Aus.	Ev 264-265;4MR 414-415
Brn-Srs. in Camp-Meeting at Ballarat	B-006	99/01/14	Cooranbong, Aus.	3SM 351-352;UL 28
Haskell, Br-Sr.	H-007	99/01/22	Cooranbong, Aus.	4MR 362
Kellogg, J.H.	K-008	99/01/23		TDG 31;11MR 276
Kellogg, J.H.	*K-008a	99/01/15	Cooranbong, Aus.	
Brn. in the General Conference	B-009	99/01/24		WM 275;TDG 32;FLB 138;Ev 682-683
Kellogg, J.H.	K-010	99/01/14	Cooranbong, Aus.	Te 258;2MR 32-33;10MR 296
Brethren	B-011	99/01/25	Cooranbong, Aus.	TDG 33;ML 358
Walling, Addie/Walling, May	W-012	99/01/26	Cooranbong, Aus.	*13MR 105-110*
Wessels, Br-Sr. [John]	W-014	99/01/00	Cooranbong, Aus.	HFM 44;3MR 23-24
Children of Sr. Wessels, A.E./Wessels, Daniel	W-015	99/02/03		ML 54,158
Wessels, Daniel	W-016	99/02/02	Cooranbong, Aus.	
Children of Sr. Wessels	W-017	99/02/02	Cooranbong, Aus.	
Rousseau, Sr.	R-018	99/02/03	Cooranbong, Aus.	
Caro, E.R.	C-019	99/02/03	Hamilton, Aus.	
Wessels, Philip	W-020	99/02/03	Cooranbong, Aus.	LDE 236-237;2MR 12;4MR 362
Wessels Family	W-021	99/02/04	Cooranbong, Aus.	AH 401
Wessels, J.J.	W-022	99/02/03	Cooranbong, Aus.	6MR 382-384
Wessels, Sr. [A.E.]	W-023	99/02/06	Cooranbong, Aus.	
Men in Responsible Positions in the Work	B-026	99/02/10		*1888 1679-1686*
Kellogg, J.H.	K-028	99/02/11	Cooranbong, Aus.	
Waggoner, E.J.	W-029	99/02/12	Cooranbong, Aus.	
Boyd, Maud	B-030	99/02/12	Cooranbong, Aus.	
Sisley, W.C.	S-031	99/02/12	Cooranbong, Aus.	12MR 47-49
Muckersey, Br-Sr.	M-032	99/02/14		4BC 1169,1171;5BC 1130;5MR 139; *Problems in Bible Translation* 70
McCullagh, S.	M-033	99/02/12	Cooranbong, Aus.	4Bio 285-286
n.a. [Br-Sr.]	B-034	99/02/14	Cooranbong, Aus.	3BC 1142;4BC 1154-1156;ChL 13; 12MR 301;CTr 188
Loughborough, J.N.	L-035	99/02/19	Cooranbong, Aus.	*21MR 74-78*
Loughborough, J.N.	L-035a	99/02/19	Cooranbong, Aus.	variant of L-35-1899;PC 140
Irwin, G.A./Prescott/Waggoner, E.J./Jones, A.T.	I-036	99/02/21		
Brn. in the General Conference	B-037	99/02/01	Cooranbong, Aus.	8T 166-171
Prescott, W.W./Irwin/Jones, A.T./Smith/Waggoner, E.J	B-038	99/02/22		*BCL 14-18*
Brn. in Responsible Positions in the Work	B-039	99/02/22		1BC 1113;PM 354-355;PH139 25-29; CTr 122
Kellogg, J.H.	K-040	99/02/23		*21MR 40-50*
Caro, E.R.	C-041	99/03/03	Cooranbong, Aus.	Ev 425-426;WM 101-102
Irwin, G.A./Sisley, W./Smith, U./Jones, A.T.	I-043	99/03/11	Cooranbong, Aus.	*PH079*
James, G.	J-044	99/03/17		OHC 104
Brn-Srs. in Battle Creek	B-045	99/03/17		2SM 17
Wessels, Philip W.	W-047	99/03/00	Cooranbong, Aus.	*17MR 133-139*
n.a. [Brother]	B-048	99/03/20	Cooranbong, Aus.	WM 335-336;PM 394

Wessels, Peter	W-049	99/01/01	Hamilton, Aus.	4Bio 420
Wessels, Br-Sr. [J.J.]	W-050	99/03/23	Cooranbong, Aus	
Wessels, Br-Sr. [Peter]	W-051	99/03/23	Cooranbong, Aus.	*18MR 276-280*
Prescott, Amos	P-052	99/03/23	Cooranbong, Aus.	
Craw, Br.	C-053	99/03/23	Cooranbong, Aus.	*RY 96-98*
Henry, S.M.I.	H-054	99/03/24	Cooranbong, Aus.	RH 05/09/1899;6T 114-116
Kellogg, J.H.	K-055	99/03/24	Cooranbong, Aus.	*BCL 19-20*
James, Br-Sr.	J-057	99/03/28	Cooranbong, Aus.	
Haskell, Br-Sr./Tenney, G.C.	H-059	99/03/29	Cooranbong, Aus.	
Haskell, Br-Sr.	H-061	99/04/02	Cooranbong, Aus.	9MR 50;11MR 92-93;4Bio 412,438-439
n.a. [Sister]	S-062	99/04/02	Cooranbong, Aus.	
Wessels, Br-Sr. [John]	W-063	99/04/04	Cooranbong, Aus.	UL 108;PM 28;11MR 93-95
Wessels, Henry	W-066	99/04/05	Cooranbong, Aus.	
Kellogg, J.H.	K-067	99/04/06	Cooranbong, Aus.	*16MR 287-294*
Wessels, Br-Sr. [John]	W-068	99/04/10	Cooranbong, Aus.	WM 232;9MR 236
Wessels, John	W-069	99/04/12	Cooranbong, Aus.	
Haskell, Br-Sr.	H-070	99/04/14	Cooranbong, Aus.	11MR 95-96;4Bio 415,417
Anthony, R.S.	A-071	99/04/17	Cooranbong, Aus.	
Tenney, Br-Sr. [G.C.]	T-072	99/04/20	Cooranbong, Aus.	Ev 557-558,561
Kellogg, J.H.	K-073	99/04/17	Cooranbong, Aus.	8T 172-176;2SM 285;2MR 339-342; 7MR 325;10MR 15;11MR 307;4Bio 438
Kellogg, J.H. [edited from K-073-99]	K-073a	99/04/17	Cooranbong, Aus.	*From 8T 172-176*
Butler, G.I.	B-074	99/04/21	Cooranbong, Aus.	Ev 427;8MR 262;4Bio 406-407,437
Kellogg, J.H.	K-075	99/04/20	Cooranbong, Aus.	11MR 96-97;4Bio 423
Brethren in America	B-076	99/04/26	Cooranbong, Aus.	*GCB 2nd Quarter, 1899, 35-36*
Wessels, Br-Sr. [John]	W-077	99/05/01	Cooranbong, Aus.	7BC 969;MM 11-12;3MR 367
Lindsay, H.	L-078	99/02/20	Cooranbong, Aus.	
Hyatt, W.S.	H-079	99/03/03	Cooranbong, Aus.	Ev 426-427;3MR 293-294;4MR 395
Belden, Frank	B-081	99/05/08	Cooranbong, Aus.	*10MR 135-137*
Brethren	B-082	99/05/08		See 6T 326-328
Norman, Captain	N-083	99/05/04	Cooranbong, Aus.	*DG 106-110*
Jones, A.T.	*J-084	99/04/28	Cooranbong, Aus.	3BC 1164;7MR 149
Editors "The Christian Educ."/"Youth's Inst."	*B-085	99/05/14	Cooranbong, Aus.	CW 115-122
Editors "The Christian Educ."/"Youth's Inst."	B-085a	99/05/14	Cooranbong, Aus.	
Kellogg, J.H.	*K-086	99/06/05	Cooranbong, Aus.	CG 75;1MR 235-236
Hickox, Br-Sr. [A.S.]	H-087	99/05/18	Hamilton, Aus.	
Haynes, Br.	H-088	99/05/01	Summer Hill, Aus.	
Jones, C.H.	J-089	99/06/04	Cooranbong, Aus.	CW 112-114
Ballenger, A.F.	B-090	99/06/05	Cooranbong, Aus.	SW 83-87;11MR 48
Ballenger, A.F.	B-090a	99/06/05	Cooranbong, Aus.	Variant of Lt 90, 1899
Jones, A.T.	J-091	99/05/01	Cooranbong, Aus.	*19MR 195-201*
Brethren [Sisley, W.C./Jones, C.H.]	*B-092	99/06/16	Cooranbong, Aus.	3MR 41
Brethren in America	B-093	99/06/19	Cooranbong, Aus.	6MR 319-320
Brethren in Responsible Positions	B-094	99/06/16	Cooranbong, Aus.	3BC 1132;1MR 277
Teachers and Managers of our Schools	*B-095	99/06/16	Cooranbong, Aus.	*FE 475-484*
Henry, S.M.I.	H-096	99/06/21	Cooranbong, Aus.	3SM 51,79-80;7MR 159-161
Henry, S.M.I.	*H-096a	99/07/19	Cooranbong, Aus.	*21MR 154-156*
Chick, Sr.	C-097	99/06/26	Cooranbong, Aus.	11MR 162
Jones, C.H./Pacific Press	*J-098	99/02/20	Cooranbong, Aus.	*21MR 143-146*
Kellogg, H.W.	K-099	99/06/10	Cooranbong, Aus.	
Ballenger, A.F.	B-100	99/07/02	Cooranbong, Aus.	*SW 88-90*
Responsible Men in our Institutions	B-101	99/07/03		6MR 270-271
White, J.E.	W-102	99/07/03		TMK 117;OHC 174
White, J.E./White, Emma [part of W-102b-99]	W-102a	99/06/21	Cooranbong, Aus.	*SW 91-93*
White, J.E./White, Emma	*W-102b	99/06/16	Cooranbong, Aus.	*PC 112-116*
Caro, Dr./Morse, Dr.	C-103	99/07/03	Cooranbong, Aus.	
Haskell, S.N.	H-104	99/08/01	Cooranbong, Aus.	*15MR 47-53*

EGW Letters File—Page 58

Haskell, Br-Sr.	H-105	99/07/30	Cooranbong, Aus.	7MR 390
Managers of Pacific Press	B-106	99/08/01	Cooranbong, Aus.	
Managers of the Colorado Sanitarium	B-107	99/08/01	Cooranbong, Aus.	
Those Working in Educational Lines	B-108	99/07/27		3SM 227;5BC 1102;6BC 1088
Brn-Srs. in the Faith in Africa	B-109	99/08/08		1BC 1092;12MR 42;CTr 72
Wessels, Sr. [A.E.]	W-110	99/08/08	Cooranbong, Aus.	UL 234
Lindsay, Harmon	L-111	99/08/04	Cooranbong, Aus.	
Lindsay, Br-Sr. [H.]	L-112	99/08/08	Cooranbong, Aus.	
Lindsay, Kate	L-113	99/08/09	Cooranbong, Aus.	*19MR 144*
Lindsay, Harmon	L-114	99/08/09	Cooranbong, Aus.	
Wessels, Peter	W-115	99/08/08	Cooranbong, Aus.	
Wessels, Philip	W-116	99/08/10	Cooranbong, Aus.	1SM 94-97
White, J.E.	W-117	99/08/11	Cooranbong, Aus.	OHC 174,184,274
White, J.E./White, Emma	W-117a	99/07/18	Cooranbong, Aus.	
Jones, C.H.	J-118	99/08/10	Cooranbong, Aus.	
White, J.E./White, Emma	W-119	99/08/13	Cooranbong, Aus.	UL 239;5BC 1099-1100
Those at the Head of the Work	*B-120	99/08/14		Ev 375-376;2SM 188
Jones, A.T.	J-121	99/08/14	Cooranbong, Aus.	
Haskell, Br-Sr.	H-122	99/08/14	Cooranbong, Aus.	*BE Supp. 09/18/1899*
Faulkhead, Br./Salisbury, W.D.	F-123	99/08/17	Cooranbong, Aus.	BE Supp. 09/18/1899
Brethren in Victoria	B-124	99/08/18		BE Supp. 09/18/1899
Daniells, A.G./Robinson, A.T.	D-125	99/08/17	Cooranbong, Aus.	
Jones, C.H.	J-127	99/05/11	Cooranbong, Aus.	
Leininger, Br-Sr. [J.]	L-128	99/08/23	Cooranbong, Aus.	MRmnt 105
Kellogg, J.H.	K-129	99/08/29	Cooranbong, Aus.	11MR 308
Kellogg, J.H.	K-129a	99/08/29	Cooranbong, Aus.	11MR 308
Irwin, G.A.	I-130	99/08/29	Cooranbong, Aus.	
White, J.E.	W-131	99/09/12		
Wessels, Br-Sr. [J.J.]	W-132	99/09/12	Cooranbong, Aus.	
White, J.E./White, Emma	W-133	99/09/10	Strathfield, Aus.	PM 218;10MR 98-99
Brethren in America	B-134	99/09/08	Strathfield, Aus.	7BC 933;TMK 260
Kellogg, J.H.	K-135	99/08/29	Cooranbong, Aus.	4MR 131-133;11MR 308
Kellogg, J.H.	K-136	99/08/29	Cooranbong, Aus.	
White, J.E.	W-137	99/09/08	Strathfield, Aus.	PM 219
Henry, S.M.I.	H-138	99/09/13	Cooranbong, Aus.	7MR 164-165,228;BTS 05/1913
Gotzian, Sr. [J.]	G-139	99/09/11	Strathfield, Aus.	*17MR 119-124*
Wessels, John	W-140	99/09/14	Cooranbong, Aus.	
Daniells, A.G./White, W.C./Palmer, E.R.	D-141	99/09/15	Wallsend, Aus.	8MR 372-373
Sisley, W.C.	S-142	99/08/14	Cooranbong, Aus.	
Claremont Sanitarium/Wessels Family/S. Africa	B-143	99/09/24	Cooranbong, Aus.	
Wessels, Henry	W-144	99/09/24		
Irwin, G.A.	I-145	99/09/08	Strathfield, Aus.	*15MR 114-117*
Sisley, W.C./Jones, C.H.	S-146	99/09/25	Cooranbong, Aus.	
Haskell, Br-Sr.	H-147	99/09/25	Cooranbong, Aus.	PM 215-216
Managers of our Publishing Houses	B-148	99/09/24	Cooranbong, Aus.	MM 199
Kellogg, J.H.	K-149	99/09/25	Cooranbong, Aus.	1MR 231-232
Review and Herald Office	B-150	99/09/26	Cooranbong, Aus.	PM 59-60,157-158,213-214;WM 25-26; 9MR 372
Wessels Family	W-151	99/00/00		AH 378
Morse, G.W.	M-152	99/10/02	Cooranbong, Aus.	
Haskell, Br-Sr.	H-153	99/10/04	Cooranbong, Aus.	
Carle, Sr.	C-154	99/10/06	Cooranbong, Aus.	Ev 381
Wilson, Elsie	W-155	99/10/06	Cooranbong, Aus.	4Bio 441
White, J.E.	W-156	99/09/12	Cooranbong, Aus.	*17MR 129-132*
Irwin, G.A.	I-157	99/10/11	Cooranbong, Aus.	
Lindsay, Kate	L-158	99/10/12	Cooranbong, Aus.	*19MR 145*
Lindsay, Harmon	L-159	99/10/11	Cooranbong, Aus.	9MR 372

Wessels, Sr. [A.E.]	W-160	99/08/03	Cooranbong, Aus.	
Bicknall, Br-Sr.	B-161	99/10/12	Cooranbong, Aus.	
Anthony, R.S.	A-162	99/10/12	Cooranbong, Aus.	
Magan, P.T.	M-163	99/10/21	Toowoomba, Aus.	SpM 151-153
White, J.E./White, Emma	W-164	99/10/20	Toowoomba, Aus.	GH 12/00/1894;8MR 10-14
Belden, F.E.	B-165	99/10/22	Toowoomba, Aus.	PH151 81-82;4MR 13-16;8MR 336-337
Irwin, G.A.	I-166	99/10/24	Cooranbong, Aus.	11MR 52
Irwin, G.A.	I-166a	99/10/24		11MR 52
Anthony, Sr. [R.S.]	A-167	99/10/12	Cooranbong, Aus.	
Mountain, A.	M-168	99/10/25	Cooranbong, Aus.	Ev 660-661;6MR 47;7MR 391
Hickox, Br-Sr. [A.S.]	H-169	99/10/25	Cooranbong, Aus.	
Wessels Family	W-170	99/10/25	Cooranbong, Aus.	
Lindsay, Br-Sr. [H.]	L-171	99/11/02	Cooranbong, Aus.	2MR 9
Lacey, Br-Sr. [H.C.]	L-172	99/10/31	Cooranbong, Aus.	
Wessels, Peter	W-173	99/11/04	Maitland, Aus.	7MR 149
Lacey, Br-Sr. [H.C.]	L-174	99/10/30	Cooranbong, Aus.	7MR 149
Wessels, Philip	W-175	99/11/04	Maitland, Aus.	12MR 85-86
Irwin, G.A./Jones, A.T./Smith, Uriah	*I-176	99/04/11	Cooranbong, Aus.	
Haskell, Br-Sr.	H-177	99/11/02	Maitland, Aus.	
White, J.E./White, Emma	W-178	99/11/06	Maitland, Aus.	GH 01/00/1899;TMK 129;HP 162;ChL 19
White, J.E./White, Emma	W-179	99/11/03	Maitland, Aus.	
Irwin, G.A.	I-180	99/11/07	Maitland, Aus.	
Wessels, Philip	W-181	99/11/06	Maitland, Aus.	
Wessels, Peter	W-182	99/11/06	Maitland, Aus.	*PC 26-27*
Hyatt, W.S.	H-183	99/11/09	Maitland, Aus.	*1888 1693-1705*
Hyatt, W.S.	H-184	99/11/10	Maitland, Aus.	
Wessels, Br-Sr. [J.J.]	W-185	99/11/15	Cooranbong, Aus.	5MR 357-358
Haskell, Br-Sr.	H-186	99/11/12	Maitland, Aus.	
Haskell, S.N.	H-187	99/11/16	Cooranbong, Aus.	TSA 96-97;13MR 291
Haskell, Br-Sr.	H-188	99/11/13	Maitland, Aus.	TSA 97
Lacey, Br-Sr. [H.C.]	L-189	99/11/19	Maitland, Aus.	Ev 142,462;3SM 228
Gotzian, Sr. [J.]	G-190	99/11/01	Cooranbong, Aus.	3MR 240-241
Irwin, G.A./Haskell, S.N.	B-191	99/11/00	Maitland, Aus.	*16MR 84-88*
Directors of the Sanitarium	B-192	99/11/21		*6MR 397-400*
Wessels, Sr. [A.E.]	W-193	99/11/28	Cooranbong, Aus.	
Lindsay, Br-Sr. [H.]	L-194	99/11/27	Cooranbong, Aus.	
Colcord, W.A./Starr, G.B./Hickox, A.S.	S-195	99/11/29	Cooranbong, Aus.	1BC 1102;4MR 245;11MR 274;CTr 53
Robinson, Sr. [A.H.]	R-196	99/11/27	Cooranbong, Aus.	2SM 258-259;DG 225-226
Andre, Hattie	A-197	99/12/01	Cooranbong, Aus.	8MR 262;9MR 307-308
Kellogg, J.H.	K-198	99/11/26	Maitland, Aus.	Ev 512;4Bio 436-437
Haskell, Br-Sr.	H-199	99/12/03	Cooranbong, Aus.	TMK 305
Brn-Srs. Laboring in Maitland	B-200	99/12/04	Cooranbong, Aus.	2MCP 440
Ministering Brethren	B-201	99/12/05		*11MR 98-104*
Jones, C.H.	J-202	99/12/03	Cooranbong, Aus.	
White, J.E./White, Emma	W-203	99/12/03	Cooranbong, Aus.	DG 226-227
Kellogg, J.H.	K-204	99/12/12	Cooranbong, Aus.	BCL 28
Kellogg, J.H.	K-205	99/12/19	Cooranbong, Aus.	*20MR 249-255*
Kellogg, J.H.	K-206	99/12/10	Maitland, Aus.	5MR 406;9MR 82-83
Haskell, S.N./Irwin, G.A.	H-207	99/12/15		*14MR 55-65*
Members of the Book Committee	*B-208	99/12/18		CW 160-161
Daniells, A.G./Farnsworth, Br.	D-209	99/12/19	Cooranbong, Aus.	VSS 329-330;Ev 230;3MR 344; 8MR 191-192
Brethren in the Work of God	B-210	99/12/20	Cooranbong, Aus.	5BC 1139
Rand, S.	B-211	99/12/21	Cooranbong, Aus.	
Lacey, Br-Sr. [H.C.]	L-212	99/12/22	Cooranbong, Aus.	
Wilson, Sr. [G.T.]	W-213	99/12/22	Cooranbong, Aus.	
Tenney, Br-Sr. [G.C.]	T-214	99/12/22	Cooranbong, Aus.	

EGW Letters File—Page 60

Kellogg, J.H.	K-215	99/12/12	Cooranbong, Aus.	*KC 87-94;*(8T 180-191)
Kellogg, J.H.	K-215b	99/12/14	Cooranbong, Aus.	*BCL 29-36*
Irwin, G.A.	I-216	99/05/09	Cooranbong, Aus.	
Irwin, G.A.	I-217	99/11/21	Cooranbong, Aus.	Ev 259-260;9MR 307
Haskell, Br-Sr.	H-218	99/11/29	Cooranbong, Aus.	PM 344;3MR 275;7MR 391
Irwin, G.A./Haskell, S.N.	H-219	99/09/12	Cooranbong, Aus.	
Haskell, Br-Sr.	H-220	99/10/24	Cooranbong, Aus.	PH139 17-18
Haskell, Br-Sr.	H-221	99/08/00	Cooranbong, Aus.	13MR 135-136
White, J.E./White, Emma	W-222	99/08/22	Cooranbong, Aus.	
White, J.E./White, Emma	W-223	99/06/22	Cooranbong, Aus.	*20MR 85-86*
Jones, C.H./Sisley, W.C./Tait, A.O./Belden, F.E.	J-225	99/05/08	Cooranbong, Aus.	
Haskell, Br-Sr.	H-226	99/03/15	Cooranbong, Aus.	
Haskell, S.N.	H-227	99/01/07	Hamilton, Aus.	
Haskell, S.N.	H-228	99/05/11	Cooranbong, Aus.	
Starr, G.B.	S-230	99/12/03	Cooranbong, Aus.	VSS 325;2MR 24
Henry, S.M.I.	H-231	99/12/00	Cooranbong, Aus.	7MR 165-167
Kellogg, J.H.	*K-232	99/11/10		7BC 983;Ev 132;4MR 423-426
n.a./Brother	B-233	99/09/10	Cooranbong, Aus.	*21MR 398-401*
Starr, Br-Sr. [G.B.]	S-234	99/10/15	Toowoomba, Aus.	4Bio 435
Kellogg, J.H.	*K-235	99/09/00	Strathfield, Aus.	
White, J.E.	W-236	99/10/11	Cooranbong, Aus.	
Henry, S.M.I.	*H-237	99/12/10	Maitland, Aus.	
White, J.E./White, Emma	*W-238	99/04/10	Cooranbong, Aus.	
White, J.E./White, Emma	*W-239	99/07/04	Cooranbong, Aus.	
White, J.E./White, Emma	*W-240	99/07/30	Cooranbong, Aus.	11MR 346
White, J.E./White, Emma	*W-241	99/07/30	Cooranbong, Aus.	
White, J.E./White, Emma	*W-242	99/09/00	Cooranbong, Aus.	
White, J.E./White, Emma	*W-243	99/06/05	Cooranbong, Aus.	14MR 281;4Bio 417,449
Haskell, S.N.	*H-244	99/10/00	Fragment	
White, W.C.	*W-245	99/08/00		
Belden, Br-Sr. [S.T.]	*B-246	99/00/00		
n.a./Sister	*S-247	99/10/12	Cooranbong, Aus.	
Davis, Marian	*D-248	99/10/20	Toowoomba, Aus.	
Kellogg, Br-Sr. [J.H.]	*K-249	99/06/03	Cooranbong, Aus.	4Bio 396-397
n.a.	*B-250	99/01/15	Cooranbong, Aus.	
Haskell, Br-Sr.	*H-251	99/01/07	Hamilton, Aus.	
Kellogg, Br-Sr. [J.H.]	*K-252	99/04/27		4Bio 416,440
Ings, Sr.	*I-253	99/11/08	Maitland, Aus.	
Wessels, Sr.	*W-254	99/12/22	Cooranbong, Aus.	*20MR 10-11*
Butler, G.I.	*B-255	99/05/22	Hamilton, Aus.	
White, W.C.	*W-256	99/10/15	Toowoomba, Aus.	
Kellogg, J.H.	K-257	99/12/00	Cooranbong, Aus.	5MR 235-236;1MR 242;11MR 309; 12MR 1
Henry, S.M.I.	*H-258	99/05/22	Hamilton, Aus.	
Jones, C.H.	*J-259	99/06/20	Cooranbong, Aus.	
Wellman, Br-Sr.	W-260	99/10/11	Cooranbong, Aus.	
Hickox, Br-Sr.	*H-261	99/12/22	Cooranbong, Aus.	

1900

Sisley, Br-Sr. [W.C.]	S-002	00/01/03	Cooranbong, Aus.	*12MR 44-47*
Irwin, Br-Sr. [G.A.]	I-003	00/01/01	Cooranbong, Aus.	3MR 403-404;4MR 133,426-429;
Tenney, Br-Sr. [G.C.]	T-004	00/01/04	Summer Hill, Aus.	5MR 162-163
Colcord, W.A.	C-005	00/01/04	Thornleigh, Aus.	TDG 12;5BC 1134;6BC 1086,1088; 7BC 926
Tenney, Br-Sr. [G.C.]	T-006	00/01/04	Thornleigh, Aus.	
Lacey, Br-Sr. [H.C.]	L-006a	00/01/04	Thornleigh, Aus.	UL 18

Kellogg, W.K.	K-007	00/01/25	Thornleigh, Aus.	UL 39;CTr 191
Murphet, E.	M-008	00/01/29	Cooranbong, Aus.	
Brn. in the Review and Herald Office	B-009	00/01/16	Hornsby Jct., Aus.	
White, J.E./White, Emma	W-011	00/01/23	Cooranbong, Aus.	WM 258;1MR 225;4Bio 432
Haskell, Br-Sr.	H-012	00/02/05	Cooranbong, Aus.	7BC 980;5MR 336;BTS 12/1903
Kellogg, H.W.	K-013	00/02/01	Cooranbong, Aus.	
Haysmer, Br-Sr.	H-014	00/02/05	Cooranbong, Aus.	VSS 15;ML 284,291
Lay, George	L-015	00/02/01	Cooranbong, Aus.	3MR 378
Belden, F.E.	B-016	00/01/27	Cooranbong, Aus.	*18MR 22-25*
Jones, A.T.	J-017	00/02/06	Cooranbong, Aus.	Ev 554,558;1MR 123-124
White, J.E./White, Emma	W-018	00/02/06	Harnsby Jct., Aus.	
Haskell, S.N./Irwin, G.A.	H-019	00/02/07	Cooranbong, Aus.	
White, J.E./White, Emma	W-020	00/01/31	Cooranbong, Aus.	1BC 1086;1MR 57
Haskell, S.N.	H-021	00/02/12	Cooranbong, Aus.	
Hare, Br-Sr. [Joseph]	H-022	00/02/13	Cooranbong, Aus.	1BC 1085-1086;7ABC 469
Hare, Br-Sr. [Wesley]	H-023	00/02/13	Cooranbong, Aus.	5MR 177
Wessels, Sr.	W-024	00/02/15	Cooranbong, Aus.	TSA 57-58;12MR 164-165
Wessels, Sr. [A.E.]	W-025	00/02/15		LDE 237
Hyatt, W.S.	H-026	00/02/15	Cooranbong, Aus.	*TSA 85-91*
Lindsay, Br-Sr. [H.]	L-027	00/02/16	Cooranbong, Aus.	
Prescott, Br-Sr. [W.W.]	P-028	00/02/17	Cooranbong, Aus.	*14MR 158-167*
Fellow-workers in Maitland	B-029	00/02/17	Cooranbong, Aus.	SD 194,239;Ev 355
Hickox, Br-Sr. [A.S.]	H-030	00/02/25	Cooranbong, Aus.	*19MR 262-266*
Hart, Br-Sr.	H-031	00/02/19	Cooranbong, Aus.	
White, J.E./White, Emma	W-032	00/02/27		3MR 378-379
Kellogg, J.H.	K-033	00/02/27	Cooranbong, Aus.	2MR 241;4MR 138-144
Brn-Srs. in Australasia	B-034	00/02/24	Cooranbong, Aus.	4MR 127-129;8MR 156-157;11MR 163; CTr 174
General Conference Committee	B-035	00/02/13	Cooranbong, Aus.	PM 79,134
Tatum, Lettie H.	T-036	00/02/18	Cooranbong, Aus.	*3SM 324-326*
Colcord, Sr. [M.R.]	C-037	00/03/04	Cooranbong, Aus.	2SM 328
Mangers of the Review and Herald Office	B-037a	00/02/26	Cooranbong, Aus.	4MR 17;6MR 173-175
Wilson, Sr. [G.T.]	W-038	00/03/04	Cooranbong, Aus.	
Wilson, Sr. [G.T.]/Robertson, Sr.	W-039	00/03/07	Cooranbong, Aus.	
Steed, D.	S-040	00/03/24		
Kellogg, J.H.	K-041	00/03/10	Geelong, Aus.	WM 260;1MR 224-225;2MR 241
Haskell, Br-Sr.	H-042	00/03/00	Geelong, Aus.	OHC 10,117,144;Te 265;8MR 303
Sisley, W.C.	S-043	00/03/00	Cooranbong, Aus.	
Farnsorth, Br-Sr. [E.W.]	F-044	00/03/29	Cooranbong, Aus.	Ev 494;2MCP 797,799;1MR 19
Kellogg, J.H.	K-045	00/03/12	Geelong, Aus.	WM 336-337;4MR 429-433;9MR 85-90
Steed, D.	S-046	00/03/22	Geelong, Aus.	TDG 90
Baker, Br-Sr. [W.L.H.]	B-047	00/03/23	Geelong, Aus.	
Steed, D.	S-048	00/03/23	Geelong, Aus.	
Steed, D.	S-048a	00/03/00	Geelong, Aus.	
McCullagh, S.	M-049	00/03/25	Geelong, Aus.	CS 262
White, J.E./White, Emma	W-049a	00/03/00	Geelong, Aus.	
Murphet, E.	M-050	00/03/29	Cooranbong, Aus.	*KC 85-87*
Starr, Br-Sr. [G.B.]	*S-050a	00/03/29	Cooranbong, Aus.	
Caro, E.R.	C-051	00/03/29	Cooranbong, Aus.	MM 167-168;HFM 45-46
Caro, E.R.	C-052	00/03/31	Cooranbong, Aus.	
Haskell, S.N.	H-053	00/04/04	Cooranbong, Aus.	1SM 21-22;Ev 379-380;1MR 20; 5MR 361-362;8MR 66-71
Haskell, S.N.	H-054	00/04/05	Cooranbong, Aus.	
White, J.E./White, Emma	W-055	00/04/08	Cooranbong, Aus.	BTS 06/1910
Borland, Sr.	B-056	00/04/10	Cooranbong, Aus.	2SM 266-267
Haskell, S.N.	H-057	00/04/09		
Starr, Br-Sr. [G.B.]	S-058	00/04/11	Cooranbong, Aus.	7BC 905-906,918;5Bio 180

EGW Letters File—Page 62

Jones, A.T.	J-059	00/04/18	Cooranbong, Aus.	7MR 167-170
McDaniel, Charles	M-060	00/04/21	Cooranbong, Aus.	UL 125;1MCP 219;TDG 120
Irwin, G.A.	I-061	00/04/23	Cooranbong, Aus.	*FBS 94-96*
Irwin, G.A. [revised from I-061-00]	I-061a	00/04/23	Cooranbong, Aus.	*FBS 92-94*
Jones, A.T./Wilcox, M.C./Irwin, G.A.	B-062	00/04/18	Cooranbong, Aus.	*KC 106-108*
Barnes, Sr. [Edward] and Son	B-063	00/04/24	Cooranbong, Aus.	
Steed, Br-Sr. [D.]	S-064	00/05/02	Cooranbong, Aus.	UL 136;5BC 1135
Covell, W.	C-065	00/03/00	Geelong, Aus.	Ev 379;2MR 15-16;7MR 150
Baker, W.L.H.	B-066	00/05/02	Cooranbong, Aus.	5MR 123;6MR 386-387
Haskell, Br-Sr.	H-067	00/04/26	Hamilton, Aus.	*KC 127-131*
White, J.E./White, Emma	W-068	00/05/04	Maitland, Aus.	*20MR 188-193*
Jones, C.H.	J-069	00/05/09	Cooranbong, Aus.	
Scobi, Br.	S-070	00/05/09	Cooranbong, Aus.	CD 324
Daniells, A.G.	D-070a	00/05/17		4Bio 455
Wessels, John	W-071	00/05/17	Cooranbong, Aus.	UL 151
Farnsworth, E.W.	F-072	00/05/17	Cooranbong, Aus.	
Kellogg, J.H.	K-073	00/05/00	Cooranbong, Aus.	
Kellogg, J.H.	K-074	00/05/20	Cooranbong, Aus.	CG 489
Irwin, G.A.	I-075	00/05/21	Cooranbong, Aus.	PM 212,215-216;TDG 150;CM 121, 126-127;6MR 274-275
Irwin, G.A.	I-076	00/05/22	Cooranbong, Aus.	PM 219;7BC 970;6MR 275
Haysmer, Br-Sr.	H-078	00/01/20	Maitland, Aus.	TDG 28
Kerr, William	K-079	00/05/10	Cooranbong, Aus.	OHC 28;UL 144;7BC 922,967,978-979; 1MR 113,145,388-389
Lamont, Br.	L-080	00/05/24	Cooranbong, Aus.	TDG 153
Baker, Br.	B-081	00/05/25	Cooranbong, Aus.	*19MR 306-307*
Atkins, Elsie/Children	C-082	00/05/31	Cooranbong, Aus.	TDG 160
Irwin, G.A.	I-083	00/06/05	Cooranbong, Aus.	
Morse, Sr. [O.A.]	M-084	00/06/07	Cooranbong, Aus.	5BC 1087;5MR 173;8MR 263
Kellogg, J.H.	K-085	00/05/00	Cooranbong, Aus.	4MR 418;12MR 1
Daniells, A.G.	D-086	00/06/18	Cooranbong, Aus.	*KC 120-125*
White, J.E./White, Emma	W-087	00/06/20	Cooranbong, Aus.	3SM 119-120;UL 185
Managers and Teachers in the Avondale School	B-088	00/04/13	Cooranbong, Aus.	*8MR 157-163*
Those in Resp. Positions in Avondale School	B-089	00/06/26	Cooranbong, Aus.	
Haskell, Br-Sr.	H-090	00/06/12	Cooranbong, Aus.	4MR 420;CTr 26
Brethren .	B-091	00/06/24	Maitland, Aus.	1BC 1082-1083;CC 20;4MR 137;9MR 237
Kellogg, J.H.	K-092	00/07/02	Cooranbong, Aus.	TDG 192;2MR 189;4MR 136-137
Irwin, G.A.	I-093	00/07/03	Cooranbong, Aus.	*16MR 15-19*
Smith, Br-Sr. [Uriah]	S-094	00/07/03	Cooranbong, Aus.	LDE 220
Brethren of the Illinois Conference	B-095	00/07/03	Cooranbong, Aus.	
Haskell, Br-Sr.	H-096	00/07/03	Cooranbong, Aus.	*13MR 323-328*
Gotzian, Sr. [J.]	G-097	00/07/03	Cooranbong, Aus.	
Brother	*B-098	00/07/10		*KC 146-153*
Caro, E.R.	C-099	00/07/09	Cooranbong, Aus.	2SM 199-200;TDG 199
Wessels, John	W-100	00/06/16	Cooranbong, Aus.	
Hyatt, W.S.	H-101	00/07/12	Cooranbong, Aus.	
Brethren	*B-102	00/07/13		*KC 43-44*
Robinson, Dores	R-103	00/07/13	Cooranbong, Aus.	*20MR 341-345*
Robinson, Dores [edited from R-103-00]	R-103a	00/07/00	Cooranbong, Aus.	*SpTB #1 28-32*
Wessels, Sr./Anthony, Sr.	W-104	00/07/16	Cooranbong, Aus.	8MR 192-193
Haskell, Br-Sr.	H-105	00/07/04	Cooranbong, Aus.	*KC 125-127*
To Whom It May Concern	B-106	00/07/17	Cooranbong, Aus.	*BCL 37-39*
Braucht, F.E.	B-107	00/07/04	Cooranbong, Aus.	Te 221
Braught, F.E.	B-107a	00/03/21	Geelong, Aus.	
Brandstater, Br.	B-107b	00/03/22	Geelong, Aus.	4MR 67
Haskell, S.N.	H-108	00/05/00	Cooranbong, Aus.	*20MR 361-362*
Irwin, G.A.	I-109	00/06/27	Cooranbong, Aus.	

White, J F./White, Emma	W-110	00/07/17	Cooranbong, Aus.	*KC 82-85*
Jones, C.H.	J-111	00/07/17	Cooranbong, Aus	
Piper, A.H.	P-112	00/07/16	Cooranbong, Aus.	
Caro, E.R.	C-113	00/07/18	Cooranbong, Aus.	
Lane, Sr. [S.H.]	L-114	00/07/18	Cooranbong, Aus.	
Caro, E.R.	C-115	00/07/19	Cooranbong, Aus.	
Hall, Sr.	*H-118	00/08/02	Cooranbong, Aus.	3SM 317-319
Tenney, Br-Sr. [G.C.]	T-119	00/08/02	Cooranbong, Aus.	VSS 304-307
Bolton, Fannie [Collected letters to]	B-120	00/00/00		*From Lt 6, 1894 and Lt 9, 1895*
Haskell, Br-Sr.	H-121	00/08/13	Cooranbong, Aus.	*1888 1706-1713*
Irwin, G.A.	I-122	00/08/12	Cooranbong, Aus.	7BC 946;6MR 52-53
White, J.E./White, Emma	W-123	00/08/14	Cooranbong, Aus.	Ev 547;12MR 309;5Bio 14-15
Caro, Sr. [E.R.]	C-124	00/08/19	Cooranbong, Aus.	7ABC 457
James, Br-Sr.	J-125	00/08/24	Cooranbong, Aus.	TDG 245;6MR 25-26
Hickox, A.S.	H-126	00/08/05	Cooranbong, Aus.	6MR 46
Irwin, Br-Sr. [G.A.]	I-127	00/10/16	St. Helena, Ca.	5Bio 34
Kress, Br-Sr.	K-128	00/10/16	St. Helena, Ca.	
Magan, P.T.	M-129	00/10/16	St. Helena, Ca.	*6MR 402-404*
Murphey, E.	M-130	00/10/16	St. Helena, Ca.	*11MR 224-226*
Daniells, A.G.	D-131	00/10/14	St. Helena, Ca.	*21MR 346-354*
Haskell, Br-Sr.	H-132	00/10/10	St. Helena, Ca.	*21MR 126-133*
Kellogg, J.H.	K-133	00/10/06?	Oakland, Ca.	5Bio 23
Jones, C.H.	J-134	00/10/27	St. Helena, Ca.	
Robinson, Br-Sr. [A.T.]	R-135	00/10/24	St. Helena, Ca.	CM 19
Sharp, Br./Caro, E.R./Kellogg, M.G.	B-136	00/10/29	St. Helena, Ca.	1MR 72-73
Crothers, W.M.	C-137	00/10/30	St. Helena, Ca.	CW 128-129
Palmer, E.R./Robinson, Br./Hughes/Farnsworth, Br-Sr	B-138	00/10/30	St. Helena, Ca.	
Officers of the General Conference	B-139	00/10/24	St. Helena, Ca.	*1888 1714-1724*
Kellogg, H.W.	K-140	00/11/01	St. Helena, Ca.	
Magan, P.T./Sutherland, E.A.	B-141	00/10/00	St. Helena, Ca.	PH68 19-23;6MR 404-406
McClure, N.C.	M-142	00/11/02	St. Helena, Ca.	CD 102,112,317,334-335,339; 2MCP 392-393
McClure, N.C.	*M-143	00/11/05c	Granville, Aus.	TDG 318
Kerr, Sr.	K-145	00/11/08	St. Helena, Ca.	AH 349;2MCP 435;SD 245;8MR 440-441
Farnsworth, Br-Sr. [E.W.]	F-146	00/10/06	St. Helena, Ca.	7MR 185-186;5Bio 34
Rice, Anna C.	R-147	00/11/11		
Kerr, Sr.	K-148	00/11/11	St. Helena, Ca.	UL 329;5Bio 44
Kellogg, Br-Sr. [H.W.]	K-149	00/11/11	St. Helena, Ca.	5Bio 17
Irwin, G.A.	I-150	00/10/26	St. Helena, Ca.	6BC 1062,1086;CTr 309
Larson, H.	L-151	00/11/20	St. Helena, Ca.	1MR 393-394
Cottrell, R.F.	C-152	00/11/20	St. Helena, Ca.	6MR 308-309
White, J.E./White, Emma	W-153	00/11/20	St. Helena, Ca.	
Ottosen, Br.	O-154	00/11/25	Healdsburg, Ca.	*13MR 226-229*
Waggoner, E.J.	W-154a	00/10/20	St. Helena, Ca.	CM 134
General Conference Committee	B-155	00/12/04	St. Helena, Ca.	Ev 145;5Bio 45
White, J.E./White, Emma	W-156	00/12/10	St. Helena, Ca.	LHU 134;6BC 1091,1112;4MR 17-18
Farnsworth/Robinson/Starr/Palmer/Caro/Sharp	B-157	00/12/12	St. Helena, Ca.	CD 309;5MR 65,135
Wilson, Sr. [G.T.]	W-158	00/11/12	St. Helena, Ca.	1MR 306;5Bio 29,31
Irwin, G.A.	I-159	00/12/16	St. Helena, Ca.	5Bio 45-46
Kellogg, J.H.	K-160	00/10/18	Pacific Ocean	
Druillard, Br-Sr.	D-161	00/12/20		TDG 363
White, J.E./White, Emma	W-162	00/07/13	Cooranbong, Aus.	WM 254-255;4BC 1164
Haskell, S.N.	H-163	00/12/30	St. Helena, Ca.	5Bio 25
Caro, Sr. [E.R.] [Edith]	C-164	00/09/01	Steamer "Moana"	FLB 30;MM 10;5Bio 18
Magan, P.T./Sutherland, E.A.	*B-165	00/09/00	St. Helena, Ca.	6MR 401-402
Haskell, Br-Sr./Irwin, G.A.	*B-166	00/04/25	Cooranbong, Aus.	FBS 96
Irwin, G.A.	I-167	00/03/23	Geelong, Aus.	10MR 9-10;12MR 159

Irwin, G.A.	*I-168	00/06/20	Cooranbong, Aus.	
Irwin, G.A./Haskell, S.N.	I-169	00/07/17	Cooranbong, Aus.	Ev 472-473;7MR 89-90
Irwin, G.A.	*I-170	00/01/00		4Bio 400
Haskell, Br-Sr.	H-174	00/03/21	Geelong, Aus.	Ev 61;3MR 248;4Bio 454-455
Kellogg, J.H.	K-175	00/10/14	St. Helena, Ca.	5Bio 36
Kellogg, J.H.	K-176	00/10/16	St. Helena, Ca.	
Kellogg, J.H.	*K-177	00/01/21	Cooranbong, Aus.	1MR 233-235;11MR 309-310
Starr, Br-Sr. [G.B.]	S-178	00/02/15	Cooranbong, Aus.	
Starr, G.B.	S-179	00/02/16	Cooranbong, Aus.	Ev 690
Kellogg, Br-Sr. [J.H.]	*K-185	00/01/01	Cooranbong, Aus.	
White, J.E./White, Emma	*W-186	00/07/01	Cooranbong, Aus.	8MR 263;4Bio 456
White, J.E./White, Emma	W-187	00/02/27	Cooranbong, Aus.	
Haskell, Br-Sr.	H-188	00/06/20	Cooranbong, Aus.	
White, J.E./White, Emma	*W-189	00/01/01	Cooranbong, Aus.	UL 23;4Bio 448
Friends in Cooranbong	*F-190	00/09/06	Steamer "Moana"	*AUCR 11/01/1900*
White, J.E./White, Emma	*W-191	00/04/30	Cooranbong, Aus.	
White, W.C./White, May	*W-192	00/01/14	Hornsby Jct., Aus.	
White, W.C./White, May	*W-193	00/01/18	Hornsby Jct., Aus.	
Colcord, W.A.	*C-194	00/01/22	Cooranbong, Aus.	
Colcord, W.A.	*C-195	00/01/22	Cooranbong, Aus.	
White, W.C./White, May	*W-196	00/03/07	Melbourne, Aus.	4Bio 454
Jones, C.H.	*J-197	00/03/09	Geelong, Aus.	
White, W.C.	*W-198	00/03/09	Geelong, Aus.	4Bio 454
Steed, D.	*S-199	00/03/21	Geelong, Aus.	
McCullagh, S.	*M-200	00/03/24	Melbourne, Aus.	
Farnsworth, Br-Sr. [E.W.]	*F-201	00/04/01	Cooranbong, Aus.	
McCullagh, S.	*M-202	00/08/25	Cooranbong, Aus.	
Sharp, Br.	*S-203	00/09/10	Steamer "Moana"	5Bio 22
n.a./Sister	*S-204	00/12/14	St. Helena, Ca.	
White, W.C./White, May	*W-205	00/12/21	San Francisco, Ca.	
White, W.C.	*W-206	00/12/26	Oakland, Ca.	
Davis, Marian	*D-207	00/01/10	Hornsby Jct., Aus.	
Davis, Marian	*D-208	00/01/00	Summer Hill, Aus.	
White, Ella May	*W-209	00/12/20	St. Helena, Ca.	
Irwin, G.A.	*I-210	00/01/00	Hornsby, Jct., Aus.	
White, Mabel	*W-211	00/11/02	St. Helena, Ca.	
Wellman, George O./wife	W-212	00/04/27	Cooranbong, Aus.	
Haskell, Br-Sr. [S.N.]	H-213	00/01/00		

1901

Conference Officers/Managers of our Schools	B-001	00/12/30	Filed in 1901	*19MR 1-4*
White, J.E./White, Emma	W-002	01/01/02		5Bio 51
Caro, E.R.	C-003	01/01/03	St. Helena, Ca.	*17MR 87-94*
Caro, E.R. [variant]	C-003a	01/01/03	St. Helena, Ca.	Variant;5Bio 52
Roysten, Grant	R-004	01/01/08	St. Helena, Ca.	2SM 482,484
Kellogg, J.H.	K-005	01/01/09	St. Helena, Ca.	
Brethren in Positions of Responsibility	B-006	01/01/16	St. Helena, Ca.	
Brethren Who Occupy Positions of Trust	B-007	01/01/17	St. Helena, Ca.	*16MR 68-75*
Kress, Br-Sr.	K-008	00/11/00	Filed in 1901	HP 318;SD 272;3BC 1151-1152,1160
Farnsworth, Br-Sr. [E.W.]	F-009	01/01/18	St. Helena, Ca.	
Palmer, Br-Sr. [E.R.]	B-010	01/01/21	St. Helena, Ca.	PM 298-299;5Bio 36
Kellogg, M.G.	K-011	01/01/21	St. Helena, Ca.	TDG 29;2MR 182-183,187;
Brn-Srs. in Australia	B-012	01/01/21	St. Helena, Ca.	*AUCR 04/00/1901*
Burden, Br-Sr. and Family	B-013	01/01/22		
Rand, S.	R-014	01/01/22	St. Helena, Ca.	*21MR 285-288*
Starr, Br-Sr. [G.B.]	S-014a	01/01/22	St. Helena, Ca.	5Bio 51

James, Br-Sr. [G.]	J-015	01/01/22	St. Helena, Ca.	
Jones, C.H.	J-016	01/01/23	St. Helena, Ca.	12MR 139
Reaser, G.W./Nichols, G.A.	R-017	01/01/23	St. Helena, Ca.	
Henry, A.R.	*H-018	01/01/20	St. Helena, Ca.	5MR 443-445
Franke, E.E.	*F-019	01/01/00	St. Helena, Ca.	*21MR 269-279*
Kellogg, J.H.	K-020	01/01/28	St. Helena, Ca.	*14MR 139-149*
Franke, E.E.	*F-021	00/10/05	Filed in 1901	HP 286;ML 74;TDG 287;OHC 117;
				1MCP 324;2MCP 792;3MR 277-278;
				4MR 350
Brn-Srs. in California	B-022	01/02/03	Healdsburg, Ca.	7BC 986;3MR 434-435
Mills, Br-Sr. [G.W.]	M-023	01/02/02	Healdsburg, Ca.	
White, J.E./White, Emma	W-024	01/02/07	St. Helena, Ca.	
Starr, Br-Sr. [G.B.]/Sisley, Sr.	S-025	01/02/13	St. Helena, Ca.	*15MR 10-11*
Colcord, W.A.	C-026	01/02/13	St. Helena, Ca.	
Pearce, Srs.	P-027	01/02/13	St. Helena, Ca.	1MCP 249-250
Caro, E.R.	C-028	01/02/13	St. Helena, Ca.	
Church in Barbados	B-029	01/02/21	St. Helena, Ca.	*3MR 55-60*
Kellogg, J.H.	K-030	01/02/14	St. Helena, Ca.	
Kellogg, J.H.	K-031	01/02/16	St. Helena, Ca.	CD 323-324
Kellogg, J.H.	K-032	01/02/20	St. Helena, Ca.	5Bio 48
Kellogg, J.H.	*K-033	01/02/23	St. Helena, Ca.	5Bio 53-54
Minchin, Sr.	M-034	00/12/12	Filed in 1901	6MR 31-32
Brn-Srs. at Crystal Springs	B-035	01/03/07	St. Helena, Ca.	1BC 1119;5MR 219
Leadsworth, Br.	L-035a	01/00/00	undated	
Brown, M.H./Wilcox/Jones	B-035b	01/03/06c		
White, Ella	W-036	01/04/25	Battle Creek, Mi.	OHC 279;1MCP 15
Kress, Br-Sr. [D.H.]	K-037	01/05/29	St. Helena, Ca.	*12MR 168-178*
Caro, E.R.	*C-038	01/05/28	Battle Creek, Mi.	MM 130-132;1MR 265
Farnsworth, Br-Sr. [E.W.]	F-039	01/05/29	St. Helena, Ca.	CD 210-211;1MR 291-292
Brn-Srs. in the Iowa Conference	B-040	01/06/01	St. Helena, Ca.	5BC 1101-1102;7BC 937;ML 111
White, J.E./White, Emma	W-041	01/05/10	Denver, Co.	
Rand, H.F.	R-042	01/06/12	Oakland, Ca.	SD 193
Kellogg, Br-Sr. [J.H.]	K-043	01/06/13	Oakland, Ca.	1NL 15-16;8T 192-194
Brn-Srs. in Portland, Or.	B-044	01/06/11	Oakland, Ca.	
Burden, Br-Sr. and their sisters	B-045	01/06/13		UL 178
Caro, E.R.	C-046	01/06/12	Oakland, Ca.	MM 127-128
Palmer, Br-Sr. [W.O.]	P-047	01/06/16		
White, J.E.	W-048	01/06/16		6MR 275-276
Kellogg, M.G.	K-049	01/06/16	Oakland, Ca.	5Bio 119
White, J.E.	W-050	01/06/14	Oakland, Ca.	
Caro, E.R.	C-051	01/06/17	Oakland, Ca.	WM 49-50
Caro, E.R.	C-052	01/06/20	Oakland, Ca.	
Farnsworth, Br-Sr. [E.W.]	F-053	01/06/12	Oakland, Ca.	
White, J.E.	W-054	01/06/00	St. Helena, Ca.	*19MR 146-151*
Daniells, A.G.	D-055	01/06/24	St. Helena, Ca.	PM 132;5Bio 378
Jones, C.H.	J-056	01/06/26		Ev 382;6MR 62-63
Mangers of the Pacific Press	B-057	01/06/25		
Sisley, W.C.	S-058	01/06/13		
Daniells, A.G.	D-059	01/06/05	Oakland, Ca.	UL 170
Daniells, A.G.	D-060	01/06/28		*14MR 203-208*
Daniells, A.G.	D-061	01/06/28	St. Helena, Ca.	4MR 261
White, J.E./White, Emma	W-062	01/06/26	St. Helena, Ca.	4MR 18
Daniells, A.G.	D-063	01/06/00	St. Helena, Ca.	
Jones, A.T.	J-064	01/06/30		*1888 1755-1756*
Daniells, A.G.	D-065	01/06/24	St. Helena, Ca.	*20MR 140-144*
Kilgore, R.M.	K-066	01/06/26	St. Helena, Ca.	2SM 346-347;OHC 134;PM 297-298;
				7MR 376;10MR 388;11MR 343;MR311 44

Palmer, W.O.	P-067	01/07/02	St. Helena, Ca.	
Kilgore, R.M.	K-068	01/07/02	St. Helena, Ca.	*14MR 50-51*
Directors of the Medical Missionary Work	*B-069	01/04/10	Battle Creek, Mi.	LLM 339;2MR 95
Kellogg, Br-Sr. [J.H.]	K-070	01/05/01	Indianapolis, In.	7MR 12-13;5Bio 111
Lane, M.H.	L-071	01/05/12	Boulder, Co.	
Those in Resp. Positions in Battle Creek	B-073	01/07/07	St. Helena, Ca.	*13MR 215-225*
Evans, I.H.	E-074	01/07/08	Oakland, Ca.	SpM 177-180
Farnsworth, E.W./Robinson, A.T./Kress, D.H.	B-075	01/07/10	St. Helena, Ca.	
Davis, N.A.	D-076	01/07/10	Oakland, Ca.	ML 28
Palmer, E.R.	P-077	01/07/10	St. Helena, Ca.	
Burden, Br-Sr. [J.A.]	B-078	01/07/10	St. Helena, Ca.	CG 170,562-563;4Bio 1154
Daniells, A.G.	D-079	01/07/11	St. Helena, Ca.	TDG 201;UL 206;4MR 261
Managers of the Review and Herald Office	B-080	01/07/12	St. Helena, Ca.	SpM 181-182
Brn-Srs. in the Faith	B-081	01/07/13	St. Helena, Ca.	
Brethren and Sisters	B-082	01/07/15	St. Helena, Ca.	TDG 205
Brethren and Sisters	B-083	01/07/15	St. Helena, Ca.	*PC 1-2*
Brethren in Denver	B-084	01/07/16	St. Helena, Ca.	Ev 402-403;4MR 18-19
Haskell, Br-Sr.	H-085	01/07/18	St. Helena, Ca.	
Those Working in the South	B-086	01/07/18	St. Helena, Ca.	
Hoover, W.L.	H-087	01/07/22		CS 267-270;5Bio 115
Taylor, Br-Sr. [C.L.]	T-088	01/07/21	St. Helena, Ca.	
Magan, P.T./Sutherland, E.A.	M-089	01/07/21	St. Helena, Ca.	8MR 28
Shireman, Br-Sr. [D.T.]	S-090	01/07/21	St. Helena, Ca.	
White, J.E./White, Emma	W-091	01/07/21	St. Helena, Ca.	
Craig, J.	C-092	01/07/22	St. Helena, Ca.	
Sharp, Smith	S-093	01/07/23	St. Helena, Ca.	1MCP 44
Belden, F.E.	B-094	01/07/10	St. Helena, Ca.	
Belden, F.E.	B-095	01/07/23	St. Helena, Ca.	9MR 372-373
Haskell, Br-Sr.	H-096	01/07/18	St. Helena, Ca.	
White, J.E./Palmer, W.O.	W-097	01/05/11	Denver, Co.	*19MR 141-143*
White, J.E./White, Emma	W-097a	01/05/21	Waitsburg, Wa.	Ev 106;8MR 118-119
Kress, Br-Sr. [D.H.]	K-098	01/06/19	Oakland, Ca.	HFM 50-51;1MR 281-282;7MR 327-328; 9MR 177
Belden, F.E.	B-099	01/07/24	St. Helena, Ca.	
Mills, Br.	M-100	01/07/29	St. Helena, Ca.	15MR 167-168
McElhaney, S.	M-101	01/07/27	St. Helena, Ca.	
Church at Healdsburg	B-102	01/07/21	St. Helena, Ca.	OHC 235;TMK 114;15MR 167
Hindson, J.	H-103	01/07/28	St. Helena, Ca.	*10MR 138-139*
Braman, Br-Sr. [C.K.]	B-104	01/08/04	St. Helena, Ca.	*21MR 134-137*
Marsh, W.	M-105	01/07/28	St. Helena, Ca.	6BC 1106-1107
Managers of the St. Helena Sanitarium	B-106	01/08/06	St. Helena, Ca.	AH 285;2MCP 665
Johnston, J.O.	J-108	01/07/27	St. Helena, Ca.	*SpM 191-193*
Johnston, J.O.	J-109	01/08/06	St. Helena, Ca.	*SpM 194-196*
White, J.E./White, Emma	W-110	01/08/07	St. Helena, Ca.	
Hoover, W.L.	H-111	01/08/13		
Kellogg, J.H.	K-112	01/07/00	St. Helena, Ca.	12MR 1-2
White, J.E./White, Emma	W-113	01/08/13	Los Angeles, Ca.	WM 49,169-170;4MR 19-21;5Bio 124-125
Hopkins, H.E.S.	H-114	01/08/19	Los Angeles, Ca.	
Santee, C.	S-115	01/08/22	St. Helena, Ca.	
Healey, W.	H-116	01/08/21	Los Angeles, Ca.	*1888 1757-1761*
Sanderson, Sr. [A.J.]	S-117	01/08/23	St. Helena, Ca.	1MCP 27,200,316;2MCP 412,596;5Bio 128
Sanderson, Sr. [A.J.]	S-118	01/08/24	St. Helena, Ca.	5Bio 128
Sanderson, Sr. [A.J.]	S-119	01/08/26	St. Helena, Ca.	5Bio 128
Sanderson, A.J.	S-120	01/08/26	St. Helena, Ca.	MM 39,49;2MCP 409,720
Sanderson, A.J.	S-121	01/09/12	St. Helena, Ca.	MM 111-115;1SM 22;HP 75;7BC 939
Kellogg, J.H.	K-122	01/09/11	St. Helena, Ca.	5MR 87;LHU 229;12MR 59-60
Sanderson, Br-Sr. [A.J.]	S-123	01/09/00	Healdsburg, Ca.	*18MR 79-82*

Sanderson, Br-Sr. [A.J.]	S-124	01/09/00	St. Helena, Ca.	2MR 24-25
Haskell, Br-Sr.	H-125	01/09/01	Healdsburg, Ca.	UL 258;12MR 82-83;5Bio 98,125
Santee, C.	S-126	01/09/03	St. Helena, Ca.	Ev 315,BTS 03/1903;MRmnt 121
Sanderson, A.J.	S-127	01/09/01	St. Helena, Ca.	
Hoover, W.L.	H-128	01/05/12		
Hoover, W.L.	H-129	01/09/25		
Sanderson, Br-Sr. [A.J.]	S-130	01/09/27	St. Helena, Ca.	OHC 109;3SM 29;2MCP 710,783; 5MR 344-345
Kellogg, J.H.	K-130a	01/09/29	St. Helena, Ca.	1MCP 46
Kellogg, J.H.	K-131	01/10/09	St. Helena, Ca.	
Haskell, Br-Sr.	H-132	01/10/07	St. Helena, Ca.	Ev 87-88;7MR 393;10MR 227-228
Sanderson, A.J.	S-133	01/10/06	St. Helena, Ca.	*18MR 263-273*
Teachers/Students of the Healdsburg School	B-134	01/10/11	St. Helena, Ca.	TDG 293;SD 207,315;CTr 175
Directors of Pacific Press	B-136	01/10/15	St. Helena, Ca.	
White, J.E.	W-137	01/09/14	St. Helena, Ca.	
Managers of Review and Herald Office	*B-138	01/10/16		8T 90-96;5MR 1-2
Sanderson, A.J.	S-139	01/10/16		
Mangers of our Publishing Houses	B-140	01/10/16		PM 101,255,259;2SM 350;6MR 276
Haskell, Br-Sr.	H-141	01/09/16	St. Helena, Ca.	4MR 319-320
Sutherland, E.A.	S-142	01/10/16	St. Helena, Ca.	4MR 299-300;SpM 196-198
Santee, C./Moran, Br.	S-143	01/09/06	St. Helena, Ca.	5Bio 125
Students in our School	B-144	01/10/11	St. Helena, Ca.	4MR 167-173
Jones, A.T.	J-145	01/10/19	St. Helena, Ca.	CD 177
Sanderson, A.J.	S-146	01/10/22	St. Helena, Ca.	
Gilson, Anna J.	G-147	01/09/25	St. Helena, Ca.	*13MR 251-253*
Riley, W.H.	R-148	01/10/24	St. Helena, Ca.	3MR 339
Jayne, J.E.	J-149	01/10/25	St. Helena, Ca.	Ev 89;4MR 312-313
Haskell, Br-Sr.	H-150	01/10/02	St. Helena, Ca.	Ev 385;7MR 393-394
Boeker, Br.	B-151	01/02/03	Healdsburg, Ca.	CD 359
Brethren in Iowa	B-152	01/10/29	St. Helena, Ca.	*20MR 326-330*
Brn-Srs. in Australia	B-153	01/10/26	St. Helena, Ca.	TDG 308;5Bio 132;CTr 369
Daniells, A.G./White, W.C.	B-154	01/10/28	St. Helena, Ca.	Ev 388-389
Palmer, E.R.	P-155	01/09/15	St. Helena, Ca.	5MR 1
Hoover, W.L.	H-156	01/05/12	Boulder, Co.	2SM 329;5Bio 114-115
Franke, E.E.	F-157	01/10/31	St. Helena, Ca.	*6MR 232-237*
Haskell, Br-Sr.	H-158	01/10/31	St. Helena, Ca.	6MR 237-239
Haskell, S.N.	H-159	01/11/03	St. Helena, Ca.	TSB 119-120;6MR 239
Haskell, Br-Sr.	H-160	01/11/03	St. Helena, Ca.	Ev 489;4MR 298;7MR 393-394
Magan, P.T./Sutherland, E.A.	M-161	01/11/05	St. Helena, Ca.	*SpM 198-200*
White, W.C.	W-162	01/11/05	St. Helenca, Ca.	
Daniells, A.G.	D-163	01/09/26	St. Helena, Ca.	
Daniells, A.G.	D-164	01/01/23	St. Helena, Ca.	Ev 79;4MR 420-421
Brn-Srs. of the Iowa Conference	B-165	01/11/06	Des Moines, Ia.	*1888 1762-1771*
McClure, Br-Sr.	M-166	01/10/00	St. Helena, Ca.	CG 249-250
Druillard, Br-Sr.	D-167	01/11/10	Chicago, Il.	
Carlyle, Sr.	C-168	01/03/00		1MR 161
Those Heading the Medical Missionary Work	B-169	01/07/24		WM 181;SpTB #18 4
Brn. Bearing Responsibilities	B-170	01/02/16		
Daniells, A.G.	D-171	01/09/17		
Sutherland, E.A./Magan, P.T.	S-172	01/11/14		
Hoover, W.L.	H-173	01/11/14		
Friends at Home	B-174	01/11/14	To Chicago, Il.	5Bio 138
White, J.E.	W-175	01/11/04	St. Helena, Ca.	2SM 341-342;TSB 225-227
Daniells, A.G.	D-176	01/09/22	St. Helena, Ca.	
Brn-Srs. of the Iowa Conference	B-177	01/05/07	Des Moines, Ia.	CD 364;7BC 986;TDG 136;8MR 384; 5Bio 116
Sanderson, A.J.	S-178	01/08/00	Los Angeles, Ca.	1MR 71

Sanderson, A.J.	S-178a	01/12/03	S. Lancaster, Ma.	5Bio 141-142
Parritt, Br.	P-179	01/12/03	S. Lancaster, Ma.	
Kellogg, J.H.	K-180	01/07/28	St. Helena, Ca.	2MR 242;5MR 407
Burden, Br-Sr. [J.A.]	B-181	01/07/29	St. Helena, Ca.	*18MR 347-349*
Haskell, Br-Sr.	H-182	01/11/04	St. Helena, Ca.	SD 22,331;7MR 395
n.a.	B-183	01/11/26	S. Lancaster, Ma.	4MR 314-316;5MR 364;5Bio 140
Magan, P.T.	M-184	01/12/07	S. Lancaster, Ma.	*20MR 310-314*
Franke, E.E.	F-185	01/12/27	Nashville, Tn.	
Ministers/Friends of Berrien Springs School	B-186	01/12/27	Nashville, Tn.	*RH 01/28/1902*
Haskell, Br-Sr.	H-187	01/12/29	Nashville, Tn.	6MR 239-241;7MR 395-396;9MR 17
Kellogg, J.H.	K-188	01/12/30	Nashville, Tn.	2BC 993;HFM 54;11MR 310-311
Hoover, W.L.	H-191	01/05/16	To Ogden, Ut.	TDG 135
Leaders in the Medical Missionary Work	B-192	01/07/03	St. Helena, Ca.	8T 232-234;HFM 51-52;5MR 307
White, J.E./White, Emma	W-193	01/07/31		TDG 221
Franke, E.E.	*F-194	01/09/23	St. Helena, Ca.	
Haskell, Br-Sr.	*H-195	01/09/23	St. Helena, Ca.	Ev 387;4MR 322;6MR 229-231; 7MR 394-395;BTS 01/1904
Boeker, Br.	*B-196	01/09/18	St. Helena, Ca.	UL 270;9MR 176
Haskell, Br-Sr.	*H-197	01/09/29	St. Helena, Ca.	UL 286;6MR 231
Nelson, L.C.	N-198	01/09/00	St. Helena, Ca.	AH 178-179
Kellogg, J.H.	K-199	01/10/15	St. Helena, Ca.	CS 273-274;12MR 3
Corliss, J.O./Brown, Br.	B-202	01/11/08	To New York, NY	TMK 46
Farnsworth, Br-Sr. [E.W.]	*F-203	01/01/01	St. Helena, Ca.	
Kellogg, M.G.	*K-204	01/01/03	St. Helena, Ca.	
Evans, I.H.	*E-205	01/06/00		
White, W.C.	*W-206	01/09/00	St. Helena, Ca.	
Jones, A.T.	*J-207	01/00/00		
Brethren	*B-208	01/05/21	Waitsburg, Wa.	
White, J.E./White, Emma	*W-209	01/05/00		
White, J.E.	*W-210	01/05/26	Portland, Or.	
White, J.E.	*W-211	01/00/00		
Haskell, S.N.	*H-212	01/10/31	Fragment	
White, J.E.	*W-213	01/07/00	Fragment	5Bio 118,123-124
Farnsworth, Br-Sr. [E.W.]	*F-214	01/00/00	St. Helena, Ca.	
White, J.E./White, Emma	*W-215	01/07/01	St. Helena, Ca.	
Crisler, C.C.	*C-216	01/05/12	Boulder, Co.	
Lacey, Herbert/Lacey, Lillian	*L-217	01/11/12	New York, NY	4MR 316
Brethren and Sisters	B-218	01/11/25	New York, NY	*AU Gleaner, 01/08/1902*
Kellogg, J.H.	K-219	01/12/01	S. Lancaster, Ma.	
Kellogg, J.H.	K-220	01/12/25	Nashville, Tn.	
White, W.C.	*W-221	01/08/00	St. Helena, Ca.	
White, W.C.	*W-222	01/10/27	St. Helena, Ca.	
White, W.C.	*W-223	01/10/30	St. Helena, Ca.	
White, W.C.	*W-224	01/11/04	St. Helena, Ca.	4MR 317-318
Kellogg, J.H.	K-225	01/12/26	Nashville, Tn.	
Peck, Sarah	*P-226	01/12/24	Nashville, Tn.	
n.a.	*B-227	01/12/08		
White, Edson	*W-228	01/05/28		
Kress, D.H.	*K-229	01/00/00		
Kress, Br-Sr.	*K-230	01/07/29	St. Helena, Ca.	
Kress, Br-Sr.	*K-231	01/00/00		
Hare, Br-Sr. [Robert]	H-232	01/22/01		
White, W.C. [telegram]	W-233	01/10/30	St. Helena, Ca.	

1902

Haskell, Br-Sr.	H-001	02/01/18	St. Helena, Ca.	TDG 26;10MR 222-224;BTS 10/1902

Haskell, Br-Sr.	H-003	02/01/01	Nashville, Tn.	7MR 396-397
White, Ella May/White, Mabel	W-004	02/01/01	Nashville, Tn.	PM 291;3MR 424
Caro, Br-Sr.	C-004a	02/01/03	Nashville, Tn.	AH 381-382;MM 133
White, May/White, Ella/White, Mabel	W-005	02/01/01	Nashville, Tn.	
Collins, Gilbert	C-006	02/01/03	Nashville, Tn.	4MR 320-321
White, J.E./White, Emma	W-008	02/01/22	St. Helena, Ca.	5Bio 146
White, J.E.	W-009	02/01/29	St. Helena, Ca.	*17MR 252-256*
White, J.E./White, Emma	W-010	02/01/27	St. Helena, Ca.	CD 324;3MR 263-264
Kellogg, H.W.	K-011	02/01/28	St. Helena, Ca.	6MR 255;5Bio 143-144
Caro, Br-Sr.	C-013	02/02/03	St. Helena, Ca.	MM 46-47,135;Ev 347;3SM 80;6MR 63
Irwin, Br-Sr. [G.A.]	I-014	02/02/04	St. Helena, Ca.	CM 140-141;10MR 224-225
Kellar, Br-Sr. [P.M.]	K-015	02/02/05	St. Helena, Ca.	KC 21-22
Burden, Br-Sr. [J.A.]	B-016	02/02/05	St. Helena, Ca.	Ev 135
Haskell, Br-Sr.	H-017	02/02/06	St. Helena, Ca.	Ev 95,130-131,136-139;1MCP 46,49; 7MR 398
Sanderson, Sr. [A.J.]	S-018	02/02/16	St. Helena, Ca.	5Bio 130
Sanderson, A.J.	S-019	02/02/16		
Sanderson, Br-Sr. [A.J.]	S-020	02/02/16		2MCP 715-716;OHC 108;MM 31-32,189
Daniells, A.G./Palmer, E.R.	B-021	02/02/16	St. Helena, Ca.	CM 20;11MR 354-356;5Bio 147
White, J.E./White, Emma	W-022	02/02/01	St. Helena, Ca.	4MR 333,336;5MR 216;5Bio 144-145
White, J.E./White, Emma	W-022a	02/02/11	St. Helena, Ca.	
Palmer, Br-Sr. [W.O.]	P-023	02/01/27	St. Helena, Ca.	*17MR 257-258*
White, J.E./Palmer, W.O.	P-024	02/01/27	St. Helena, Ca.	
Leaders in the Southern Field	B-025	02/02/05	St. Helena, Ca.	CL 19-20;HFM 55-57;MM 268,323;Te 29; 2MR 64-65;10MR 265,388
Butler, G.I.	B-027	02/02/26	St. Helena, Ca.	HFM 57-58;5Bio 145
Druillard, Br-Sr. [N.H.]	D-029	02/02/23	St. Helena, Ca.	AH 17,440;CG 319;5Bio 151
Sanderson, Sr. [A.J.]	S-030	02/03/05	St. Helena, Ca.	5Bio 132
Zelinsky, Br.	*Z-031	02/03/09	St. Helena, Ca.	
Franke, E.E.	F-038	02/03/02	St. Helena, Ca.	3MR 277
Franke, E.E.	F-039	02/03/12	St. Helena, Ca.	UL 85;Ev 331;1BC 985-986
White, J.E.	W-040	02/03/18	St. Helena, Ca.	3SM 45
Palmer, Br-Sr. [W.O.]	P-041	02/03/18	St. Helena, Ca.	7MR 341;5Bio 147
Brethren in Australia	B-042	02/03/19	St. Helena, Ca.	*AUCR 06/15/1902*
Hart, J.S.	H-043	02/03/19	St. Helena, Ca.	Ev 17-18;CM 77;3MR 310-311
White, W.C.	W-044	02/03/23	St. Helena, Ca.	
White, W.C.	W-045	02/03/23	St. Helena, Ca.	
Santee, C./Moran, F.B.	S-046	02/03/22	St. Helena, Ca.	
Haskell, Br-Sr.	H-047	02/02/05	St. Helena, Ca.	*20MR 219-222*
Nelson, Mary	N-047a	02/03/19	St. Helena, Ca.	AH 253;CG 110;DG 186-189,206-208
Franke, Br-Sr. [E.E.]	F-048	02/03/19	St. Helena, Ca.	Ev 148,169;1NL 113-115
Haskell, Br-Sr.	H-049	02/02/05	St. Helena, Ca.	Ev 63,89-90,264-265,501,509,672; MM 275;3MR 279;8MR 331;9MR 387-388 BTS 06/1902
Franke, E.E.	F-051	02/03/20	St. Helena, Ca.	Ev 127,203,250,509,558-560,658;3MR 277
Jones, Br./Brown, M.H.	J-053	02/03/28		
Prescott, Br-Sr. [W.W.]	P-054	02/03/30	St. Helena, Ca.	PM 83-84;MRmnt 110;10MR 352
Zelinsky, Br-Sr. [F.]	Z-055	02/04/06	St. Helena, Ca.	AH 118-119;CG 211-212,301-302
Magan, P.T.	M-056	02/04/06	St. Helena, Ca.	5MR 216
Zelinsky, Br-Sr. [F.]	*Z-057	02/04/07	St. Helena, Ca.	AH 94-96
Manager of the Sanitarium and Food Factory	B-058	02/04/09	St. Helena, Ca.	MM 171-172,182-185
Shireman, Br-Sr. [D.T.]	*S-061	02/04/17	St. Helena, Ca.	UL 121
Caro, E.R.	C-062	02/04/20		
Shireman, Br-Sr. [D.T.]	S-063	02/04/22	St. Helena, Ca.	RY 75-78
White, J.E.	*W-064	02/04/24	St. Helena, Ca.	UL 128
Jones, Br-Sr. [C.H.]	J-065	02/04/23	St. Helena, Ca.	5Bio 166-167
n.a. [Brother]	B-066	02/04/24	St. Helena, Ca.	

Brethren at the Pacific Press	*B-067	02/04/25	St. Helena, Ca.	MM 180-182;7ABC 468;UL 129; 9MR 161;5Bio 167
Kress, Br-Sr. [D.H.]	K-068	02/04/28	St. Helena, Ca.	5MR 453;5Bio 177
Burden, Br-Sr. [J.A.]	B-069	02/04/28	St. Helena, Ca.	
Moran, F.B.	M-070	02/05/01	Oakland, Ca.	
Magan, P.T.	M-071	02/05/07	St. Helena, Ca.	MM 231-232;5Bio 154
Churches in America	B-072	02/05/18		*RH 05/27/1902*
Brethren in the Review and Herald Office	B-073	02/05/19	St. Helena, Ca.	
Brethren who are Working in the South	B-074	02/05/02	St. Helena, Ca.	*SW 05/29/1902*
Brn-Srs. in Australia	B-075	02/05/02	St. Helena, Ca.	*From B-074-1902*
Exec. Comm. of M.M. & B. Assoc./San. Managers	B-076	02/01/25	St. Helena, Ca.	4BC 1149,1151
Keck, Br-Sr.	K-077	02/05/00	St. Helena, Ca.	*RY 115-118*
Keck, Br-Sr.	K-078	02/05/23	St. Helena, Ca.	RY 118-119
Franke, E.E.	F-079	02/05/23	St. Helena, Ca.	3MR 277;6MR 241;9MR 44-45
White, J.E.	W-080	02/05/25	St. Helena, Ca.	TDG 154;5MR 368-369
White, J.E.	W-081	02/05/20	St. Helena, Ca.	
Butler, Hiland	B-082	02/06/02	St. Helena, Ca.	
Butler, G.I./Burden-Bearers in the South	B-083	02/06/03	St. Helena, Ca.	LHU 263;WM 18,177,243;5MR 216; 13MR 305-306
Stone, W.J.	S-084	02/06/03	St. Helena, Ca.	
Medical Workers in Southern California	B-085	02/05/01	Oakland, Ca.	
Brethren	B-085a	02/00/00		Ev 19
Kilgore, R.M.	K-086	02/06/11	Petaluma, Ca.	BTS 12/1910 and 01/1911
Kilgore, R.M.	K-087	02/06/11	Petaluma, Ca.	*14MR 45-49*
Shireman, Br-Sr. [D.T.]	S-088	02/05/29	Petaluma, Ca.	
Haskell, Br-Sr.	H-089	02/05/25	St. Helena, Ca.	2SM 21
Johnson, Br.	J-090	02/05/23	St. Helena, Ca.	TDG 152;10MR 220
Jones, A.T./Brethren	J-091	02/06/22	St. Helena, Ca.	
Brn. in Medical Missionary Work	*B-092	02/04/08	St. Helena, Ca.	WM 329-330;UL 112;TDG 107;1MR 228
Butler, G.I.	B-093	02/06/27	St. Helena, Ca.	*SpM 230-232*
Palmer, W.O.	P-094	02/06/26	St. Helena, Ca.	
Kilgore, R.M./Jacobs, Br.	K-095	02/06/26	St. Helena, Ca.	*SpM 228-230*
Magan, P.T./Sutherland, E.A.	B-096	02/07/04	St. Helena, Ca.	Ev 327-328;see 7T 267-274
Waggoner, E.J.	W-097	02/07/07	St. Helena, Ca.	*12MR 212-216*
Churches and Companies in Greater New York	B-098	02/07/08	St. Helena, Ca.	*7MR 93-102*
Prescott, W.W.	P-099	02/07/10	St. Helena, Ca.	5Bio 174
Prescott, Br-Sr. [W.W.]	P-100	02/07/07	St. Helena, Ca.	SW 08/14/1902;WM 175-176; 10MR 352-353
Waggoner, E.J.	W-101	02/06/30	St. Helena, Ca.	*21MR 72-73*
Prescott, W.W.	P-102	02/06/30	St. Helena, Ca.	*15MR 118-123*
Teachers at Berrien Springs	*B-103	02/07/06	St. Helena, Ca.	*RH 09/09/1902*
Warren, Luther	W-104	02/07/08	St. Helena, Ca.	*RH 09/16/1902*
Managers of our Work in Avondale	B-105	02/07/14	St. Helena, Ca.	WM 333
Managers of the Signs of the Times	B-106	02/07/15	St. Helena, Ca.	*CW 172-176*
Those Connected with the Work at Nashville	B-107	02/04/05	St. Helena, Ca.	
Faulkhead, Br-Sr. [N.D.]	F-108	02/07/14	St. Helena, Ca.	2MR 251;5MR 450
Starr, Br-Sr. [G.B.]	S-109	02/06/12	Petaluma, Ca.	8MR 305
Paulson, David	P-110	02/07/07	St. Helena, Ca.	CW 108-109; 2SM 384;MM 328-329; 1MR 372-373;4MR 374-376;10MR 1-2,4-6; 5Bio 152,156
Ryan, Br.	R-111	02/07/22	St. Helena, Ca.	OHC 126
Rice, Br-Sr. [J.D.]	R-112	02/07/20	St. Helena, Ca.	Ev 177-178,293;1BC 1118-1119;3BC 1153
Irwin, Br-Sr. [G.A.]	I-113	02/06/15	Petaluma, Ca.	Ev 245-246,404-405;3MR 282; 7MR 255-258
Burden, Br-Sr. [J.A.]	B-114	02/07/23	St. Helena, Ca.	*17MR 259-262*
Those Laboring in the Southern States	B-115	02/07/25	St. Helena, Ca.	PM 93,94,131-132
Druillard, Br-Sr.	D-116	02/07/19	St. Helena, Ca.	5Bio 171-172,180-181

Butler, Hiland	B-117	02/07/28	St. Helena, Ca.	*21MR 105-107*
Keck, Dr-Sr.	K-118	02/07/31	St. Helena, Ca.	
Brethren in the Southern Union Conference	B-119	02/06/28	St. Helena, Ca.	4MR 101
White, J.E./Palmer, W.O.	W-120	02/06/28	St. Helena, Ca.	
German Brethren and Sisters in America	B-121	02/08/07	St. Helena, Ca.	Ev 292,413-414;PM 367;6MR 415-416
White, J.E.	W-122	02/06/12	Petaluma, Ca.	*SpM 223-228*
Kellogg, J.H.	K-123	02/08/05	St. Helena, Ca.	*BCL 55-58*
Kellogg, J.H.	K-124	02/08/06	St. Helena, Ca.	SpTB #6 35-40;CM 20-21;3SM 56
Kellogg, J.H.	K-125	02/05/01	St. Helena, Ca.	5Bio 153-154
Franke, Br-Sr. [E.E.]	F-126	02/08/07	St. Helena, Ca.	UL 233;6MR 377-378
Irwin, Br-Sr. [G.A.]	I-127	02/07/18	St. Helena, Ca.	2MR 157
Gen. Conf. Committee/Med. Missionary Board	*B-128	02/07/06	St. Helena, Ca.	*KC 70-75*
Gen. Conf. Committee/Med. Missionary Board	B-129	02/08/11	St. Helena, Ca.	*KC 95*
White, J.E.	W-130	02/08/14	St. Helena, Ca.	UL 241;7BC 966;SpTB # 19 29-31
White, Emma	W-131	02/08/18	St. Helena, Ca.	UL 244
Irwin, G.A.	I-132	02/08/17	St. Helena, Ca.	9T 232-236;Ev 60-61;7MR 251
Foss, Mary	F-133	02/08/10	St. Helena, Ca.	3SM 90-91;6MR 412
Brn-Srs. of the Iowa Conference	B-134	02/08/27	St. Helena, Ca.	*7MR 232-238*
Brn-Srs. of the Iowa Conference	B-135	02/08/28	St. Helena, Ca.	MM 261-262,273-274;Ev 262;CD 39-40,58
Iowa Conference	B-136	02/08/28	St. Helena, Ca.	*16MR 340-349*
Magan, P.T.	*M-137	02/08/29	St. Helena, Ca.	*2MR 310-312*
Daniells, A.G.	D-138	02/09/05	St. Helena, Ca.	*BCL 59-60*
White, J.E.	W-139	02/09/09	St. Helena, Ca.	4MR 22
Haskell, Br-Sr.	H-140	02/09/11	Santa Barbara, Ca.	BTS 11/1902
Haskell, Br-Sr.	H-141	02/09/10	Oakland, Ca.	TDG 262;OHC 170;4BC 1174;6BC 1106;
				3MR 359-360;7MR 343;8MR 345
				BTS 11/1902 and 12/1902 and 02/1903
Jones, W.H.	J-142	02/09/15	Los Angeles, Ca.	
Foss, Mary	F-143	02/09/12	Los Angeles, Ca.	*16MR 20-25*
Kress, Br-Sr. [D.H.]	K-144	02/09/18	Los Angeles, Ca.	CC 49;9MR 211
Burden, Br-Sr. [J.A.]	B-145	02/09/21	Los Angeles, Ca.	2MR 251;8MR 397-398
Burden, Br-Sr. [J.A.] [extract of B-145-02]	B-145a	02/09/21	Los Angeles, Ca.	
Belden, Br-Sr. [S.T.]	B-146	02/09/22	Los Angeles, Ca.	10MR 140-144
Pallant, J.	P-147	02/09/22	Los Angeles, Ca.	
Farnsworth, Br-Sr. [E.W.]	F-148	02/09/22	Los Angeles, Ca.	
Starr, Br-Sr. [G.B.]	B-149	02/09/22	Los Angeles, Ca.	10MR 64
Irwin, C.W.	I-150	02/09/22	Los Angeles, Ca.	Ev 220;2MR 252;10MR 383
S.D.A. Mission Board	B-151	02/09/25	San Diego, Ca.	
Butler, Hiland	B-152	02/09/26	San Diego, Ca.	
Haskell, Br-Sr.	H-153	02/09/27	San Diego, Ca.	3SM 201-203;OHC 254;5MR 342;7MR 401
				BTS 02/1904 and 05/1904 and 04/1905
Whitelock, T.S.	W-154	02/10/06	Fresno, Ca.	5MR 216
Arthur, Br-Sr. [Jesse]	A-155	02/09/05	St. Helena, Ca.	CH 302-303;ML 49,250,340;TDG 257;
				7MR 151
Dir. of Los Angeles Med. Miss. Ben. Assn.	B-157	02/10/13	St. Helena, Ca.	*4MR 280-290*
Burden, Br-Sr. [J.A.]	B-158	02/10/08	Fresno, Ca.	CS 274-275;CL 8;HFM 60;1MR 394
Kellogg, M.G.	K-159	02/10/09	Fresno, Ca.	*13MR 167-173*
Irwin, Br-Sr. [G.A.]	I-160	02/10/14	St. Helena, Ca.	3MR 282;15MR 270
Kress, Br-Sr. [D.H.]	K-161	02/10/15	St. Helena, Ca.	
Brethren	B-162	02/10/20	St. Helena, Ca.	*SpM 267-269*
Palmer, W.O.	P-163	02/06/26	St. Helena, Ca.	*14MR 209-213*
Jones, A.T.	J-164	02/09/00	Los Angeles, Ca.	*21MR 95-100*
Cornell, Myron	C-165	02/10/23	St. Helena, Ca.	5Bio 186
Whitelock, T.S.	W-166	02/10/23	St. Helena, Ca.	
Evans, Br-Sr. [I.H.]	E-167	02/10/26	St. Helena, Ca.	3MR 240
Ross, Sr.	*R-168	02/10/23	St. Helena, Ca.	ML 226;5MR 84
Butler, G.I.	B-169	02/09/15	Los Angeles, Ca.	2MCP 578,634

Franke, E.E./Haskell, Br-Sr.	F-170	02/11/10	St. Helena, Ca.	6MR 241-242;BTS 4/1903 and 05/1903
Haskell, S.N.	H-171	02/07/00		3MR 278-279;7MR 398-400
Haskell, S.N.	H-172	02/11/09	St. Helena, Ca.	2MR 101-102
Those Assembled in Council at Battle Creek	*B-173	02/11/13	St. Helena, Ca.	TDG 326;5Bio 194-195
Kellogg, J.H.	K-174	02/11/11	St. Helena, Ca.	*BCL 61-67*
Bollman, C.P.	B-174a	02/07/29	St. Helena, Ca.	SD 84,193
Daniells, A.G.	D-175	02/11/16	St. Helena, Ca.	
Daniells, A.G.	D-175a	02/11/17	St. Helena, Ca.	
Butler, G.I.	B-176	02/11/15	St. Helena, Ca.	
Butler, G.I.	B-177	02/11/16	St. Helena, Ca.	
Palmer, W.O.	P-178	02/07/00	St. Helena, Ca.	6MR 138-139
Bollman, C.P.	B-179	02/11/19	St. Helena, Ca.	*1888 1787-1798*
Kellogg, W.K.	K-180	02/10/15	St. Helena, Ca.	HP 153
White, W.C.	W-181	02/11/21	St. Helena, Ca.	
Brethren	B-182	02/09/20	Los Angeles, Ca.	1MR 250-254
Moran, Br-Sr.	M-183	02/09/20	Los Angeles, Ca.	
White, W.C.	W-184	02/11/21	St. Helena, Ca.	
Lane, Sands	L-185	02/11/26	St. Helena, Ca.	3MR 334
White, J.E./White, W.C.	W-186	02/12/02	St. Helena, Ca.	*17MR 63-66*
Brethren in the Southern Field	B-187	02/12/02	St. Helena, Ca.	HP 237
Cady, M.E.	C-188	02/12/04	St. Helena, Ca.	
Brethren in the Work of God in Europe	B-189	02/12/07	St. Helena, Ca.	*21MR 304-305 (8T 38-40)*
Franke, E.E.	*F-190	02/12/11		Ev 126-127,304,509;4MR 275-276
White, J.E.	*W-191	02/12/06	St. Helena, Ca.	
Palmer, Br-Sr. [W.O.]	*P-192	02/12/01	St. Helena, Ca.	UL 348
McDearmon, Sr.	M-193	02/12/08	St. Helena, Ca.	
Daniells, A.G.	D-194	02/12/07	St. Helena, Ca.	3MR 251;5Bio 194-196
Bollman, C.P.	*B-195	02/12/08	St. Helena, Ca.	
Brethren and Sisters	B-196	02/12/06	St. Helena, Ca.	*RH 01/20/1903 and 01/27/1903*
White, W.C.	W-197	02/12/09	St. Helena, Ca.	Ev 629;5MR 142
Whitelock, T.S.	W-198	02/12/14	St. Helena, Ca.	
White, W.C.	W-199	02/12/14	St. Helena, Ca.	9MR 47-48
Kress, Br-Sr. [D.H.]	K-200	02/12/15	St. Helena, Ca.	SpM 212-214;1MR 289-290;2MR 23; 6MR 167
Burden, Br-Sr. [J.A.]	B-201	02/12/15	St. Helena, Ca.	*7MR 55-62*
Brethren and Sisters	B-202	02/12/15	St. Helena, Ca.	*PUR 01/15/1903*
Farnsworth, Br-Sr. [E.W.]	F-203	02/12/17	St. Helena, Ca.	*13MR 373-376*
White, W.C.	W-204	02/12/21	St. Helena, Ca.	
Brethren and Sisters	B-205	02/12/20	St. Helena, Ca.	
White, W.C.	W-206	02/12/13	St. Helena, Ca.	4MR 21;6MR 175
White, W.C.	W-207	02/12/24	St. Helena, Ca.	
Brn. in Positions of Responsibility	*B-208	02/12/26		*SpM 282-293*
Medical Missionary Workers	*B-208a	02/04/00	St. Helena, Ca.	Ev 109
White, J.E.	W-209	02/12/26	St. Helena, Ca.	
Jones, A.T.	J-210	02/12/26	St. Helena, Ca.	
Lane, Sands	L-211	02/12/24	St. Helena, Ca.	10MR 220-222
Daniells, A.G./Palmer, E.R.	P-212	02/12/30	St. Helena, Ca.	PM 122-123
Brn. at the St. Helena Sanitarium	B-213	02/11/03	St. Helena, Ca.	CD 282-283;MM 283-284;Ev 149,537,539; 1MR 290-291
White, J.E.	W-214	02/12/31	St. Helena, Ca.	5Bio 225
Jones, A.T.	J-215	02/05/07	St. Helena, Ca.	*11MR 208-210*
White, J.E./White, Emma	*W-253	02/01/20	St. Helena, Ca.	
Daniells, A.G./Evans, I.H.	*D-254	02/01/22	St. Helena, Ca.	
White, J.E.	*W-255	02/01/28	St. Helena, Ca.	
Van Horn, Sr.	*V-256	02/04/14	St. Helena, Ca.	
Baker, Br-Sr. [W.L.H.]	*B-257	02/04/27	Oakland, Ca.	
White, J.E.	*W-258	02/05/13		

Review and Herald	*B-259	02/06/13	Petaluma, Ca.	
White, J.E.	*W-260	02/06/26	St. Helena, Ca.	5Bio 166
White, J.E.	*W-261	02/07/26	St. Helena, Ca.	
White, J.E./White, Emma	*W-262	02/10/23	St. Helena, Ca.	5Bio 396
White, W.C.	*W-263	02/11/27	St. Helena, Ca.	
White, W.C.	*W-264	02/11/00	St. Helena, Ca.	
White, J.E.	*W-265	02/12/30	St. Helena, Ca.	
White, Emma	*W-266	02/12/15	St. Helena, Ca.	
White, W.C.	*W-267	02/11/17	St. Helena, Ca.	
Wilber, Br-Sr.	*W-268	02/02/20	St. Helena, Ca.	
Kellogg, J.H.	K-269	02/02/05	St. Helena, Ca.	

1903

White, W.C./White, J.E.	W-001	02/12/28	Filed in 1903	PM 313-314
White, J.E.	W-002	03/01/01	St. Helena, Ca.	PM 176;ML 52
White, J.E.	W-003	03/01/01	St. Helena, Ca.	
Caro, Br-Sr. [E.R.]	*C-004	03/01/03	St. Helena, Ca.	
Daniells, A.G.	D-005	03/01/05	St. Helena, Ca.	OHC 85,132;TMK 351;8T 97-101
Caro, E.R.	C-006	03/01/04	St. Helena, Ca.	5MR 455
Daniells, A.G.	D-007	03/01/05	St. Helena, Ca.	8T 104-106
Burden, Br-Sr. [J.A.]	B-008	03/01/05	St. Helena, Ca.	*17MR 280-283*
Burden, Br-Sr. [J.A.]	B-009	03/01/06	St. Helena, Ca.	3SM 93;5MR 185
Palmer, E.R./Daniells, A.G.	B-010	03/01/08	St. Helena, Ca.	ChL 27-28
White, J.E.	W-011	03/01/03	St. Helena, Ca.	PC 18-19
White, J.E.	W-012	03/01/11	St. Helena, Ca.	TDG 19
Knox, W.T.	K-013	03/01/13	St. Helena, Ca.	
Kellogg, H.W.	K-014	03/01/13	St. Helena, Ca.	
Kellogg, H.W.	K-015	03/01/13	St. Helena, Ca.	
Haskell, Br-Sr.	H-016	03/01/01	St. Helena, Ca.	1SM 163;1MR 40-41,58-59;7MR 401
				BTS 06/1903 and 07/1903
Arthur, Judge Jesse	A-017	03/01/14	St. Helena, Ca.	*13MR 120-128*
Brn-Srs. in America	B-018	03/01/23	St. Helena, Ca.	*Medical Missionary 01/00/1903*
Daniells, A.G.	D-019	03/01/23	St. Helena, Ca.	
Kress, Br-Sr. [D.H.]	K-020	03/01/24	St. Helena, Ca.	HP 179;7ABC 468-469;7MR 123-124
Those Who Chose Australia as Their Field	B-021	03/01/26	St. Helena, Ca.	Ev 116;1MR 18-19;6MR 67;BTS 11/1909
Starr, Br-Sr. [G.B.]	S-022	03/01/25	St. Helena, Ca.	
Members of the North Fitzroy Church	B-023	03/01/25	St. Helena, Ca.	
Faulkhead, N.D.	F-024	03/01/27	St. Helena, Ca.	
Faulkhead, N.D.	F-025	03/01/27	St. Helena, Ca.	TMK 128,196,202,210;ML 28
Burden, Br-Sr. [J.A.]	B-026	02/12/10	Filed in 1903	*4MR 74-78*
Jones, A.T./Jones, C.H./Wilcox, M.C.	B-027	03/01/27	St. Helena, Ca.	*PC 124-125*
Burden, Br-Sr. [J.A.]	B-028	02/07/21	Filed in 1903	
Churches in Australia and New Zealand	B-029	03/01/25	St. Helena, Ca.	6MR 30-31;9MR 238
Murphet, E.	M-030	03/01/28	St. Helena, Ca.	CD 178;3MR 329-330
Robinson, Br-Sr. [A.T.]	R-031	03/01/28	St. Helena, Ca.	
Farnsworth, Br-Sr. [E.W.]	F-032	03/01/28	St. Helena, Ca.	1SM 83-85;9MR 303
White, J.E./White, Emma	W-033	03/01/29	St. Helena, Ca.	
White, J.E./White, Emma	W-034	03/02/01	St. Helena, Ca.	
Hall, L.M.	H-035	03/02/25	St. Helena, Ca.	TDG 64
Brethren and Sisters	B-036	03/02/22	St. Helena, Ca.	*RH 03/10/1903*
Haskell, Br-Sr.	H-037	03/02/28	St. Helena, Ca.	PM 172-173;5Bio 225
Burden, Br-Sr. [J.A.]	*B-037a	03/04/01?	Oakland, Ca.	TDG 100
White, J.E./White, Emma	W-038	03/03/02	St. Helena, Ca.	TDG 70;12MR 254
Wessells, John J.	W-039	03/02/28	St. Helena, Ca.	TDG 67;UL 73
Haskell, S.N.	H-039a	03/11/26	St. Helena, Ca.	
Braucht, F.E.	B-040	03/02/22	St. Helena, Ca.	MM 44-46

Braucht, F.E.	B-041	03/02/24	St. Helena, Ca.	MM 47-48;UL 69
Friend	B-042	03/03/10	St. Helena, Ca.	
Hall, L.M.	H-043	03/03/06	St. Helena, Ca.	PM 28,175,358,366-367;WM 132; Ev 402;UL 79
Burden, Br-Sr. [J.A.]	B-044	03/03/09	St. Helena, Ca.	SpM 259-260;TDG 77;7BC 943,963; OHC 32
Kress, Br-Sr. [D.H.]	K-045	03/03/10	St. Helena, Ca.	*13MR 37-43*
Evans, I.H.	E-046	01/06/00	Filed in 1903	
Gilbert, F.C.	G-047	03/03/28	Oakland, Ca.	*20MR 152-155*
Kress, Br-Sr. [D.H.]	K-048	03/04/01	Oakland, Ca.	HP 72;7BC 958;4MR 451
Daniells, A.G. and his Fellow-workers	D-049	03/04/12	St. Helena, Ca.	Ev 98;4MR 293;8MR 194-196; 10MR 355-356;5Bio 254,263-264
Kellogg, J.H.	*K-051	03/11/03	St. Helena, Ca.	
Kellogg, J.H.	*K-052	03/04/05	Oakland, Ca.	4MR 292-293;11MR 313-314;5Bio 292
Physicians and Managers of our Medical Work	B-053	03/04/15	St. Helena, Ca.	*SpM 297-300*
Those in Council at Battle Creek, Mi.	B-054	03/04/16	St. Helena, Ca.	*SpM 301-303*
Kellogg, J.H.	K-055	03/04/15	St. Helena, Ca.	UL 119;2MR 242-243;13MR 303; 17MR 284-285;5Bio 268
White, J.E.	W-056	01/05/00?	Filed in 1903	3MR 337,353
Brethren in Council at Battle Creek	B-058	03/04/17	St. Helena, Ca.	*SpM 303-304*
Jones, A.T.	J-059	03/04/19	St. Helena, Ca.	5Bio 263-265
Rice, Br-Sr. [J.D.]	R-060	03/04/19	St. Helena, Ca.	Ev 444,552-553
Kellogg, M.G.	K-061	03/04/18	St. Helena, Ca.	
Burden, Br-Sr. [J.A.]	B-062	03/04/21	St. Helena, Ca.	CD 490-491;8MR 399-400
Brethren at the Medical Missionary Council	*B-063	03/04/19	St. Helena, Ca.	7MR 262-266;MM 129-130
Kress, Br-Sr. [D.H.]	K-064	03/04/22	St. Helena, Ca.	
Kellogg, J.H.	*K-065	03/04/19	St. Helena, Ca.	*BCL 68-71*
Jones, A.T.	J-066	03/04/22	St. Helena, Ca.	
Brethren at the Medical Missionary Council	B-067	03/04/23	St. Helena, Ca.	PM 142
Butler, Hiland	*B-068	03/05/0c		
Van Horn, Charles	V-069	03/04/23	St. Helena, Ca.	TDG 122;3BC 1154
Walling, Addie/Walling, May	W-070	03/04/27	St. Helena, Ca.	ML 42;5Bio 259-262
Haskell, Br-Sr.	H-071	03/04/24	St. Helena, Ca.	TSB 49-52;UL 132
Watson, Addie S.	W-072	03/04/28	St. Helena, Ca.	TSB 49-52;UL 132
Brn. in the Ministry and Med. Miss. Work	B-073	03/04/24	St. Helena, Ca.	1SM 41-42;PM 359;MRmnt 92
Brethren in Battle Creek	B-074	03/05/01	St. Helena, Ca.	*RH 05/19/1903*
Christenson, C.	C-074a	03/05/05	St. Helena, Ca.	
Drier, Marian	D-075	03/05/07	St. Helena, Ca.	
Drier, Br.	D-076	03/05/07	St. Helena, Ca.	
Drier, Br-Sr.	D-077	03/05/08	St. Helena, Ca.	
Burden, Br-Sr. [J.A.]	B-078	03/03/00	Oakland, Ca.	2MR 156
Burden, Br-Sr. [J.A.]	B-079	03/05/07	St. Helena, Ca.	*17MR 289-293*
Kellogg, J.H.	K-080	03/05/08	St. Helena, Ca.	TDG 1375Bio 269
Kress, Br-Sr. [D.H.]	K-081	03/05/08	St. Helena, Ca.	*21MR 70-71*
Burden, Br-Sr. [J.A.]	B-082	03/05/10	St. Helena, Ca.	MM 267;3MR 326
Kellogg, H.W.	K-083	03/05/13	St. Helena, Ca.	HFM 66-67;MRmnt 124
White, J.E./White, Emma	W-084	03/05/12	St. Helena, Ca.	
Santee, Clarence	S-085	03/05/15	St. Helena, Ca.	
Exec. Committee of Southern Calif. Conf.	B-086	03/05/17	St. Helena, Ca.	
Students of the Fernando School	B-087	03/05/17	St. Helena, Ca.	*SpM 296-297*
Those in Charge of the Fernando School	B-088	03/05/17	St. Helena, Ca.	*SpM 295-296*
Teachers of the Fernando School	B-089	03/05/17	St. Helena, Ca.	*SpM 293-294*
Santee, Clarence	S-090	03/05/18	St. Helena, Ca.	
Faith, Elizabeth	F-091	03/05/18	St. Helena, Ca.	
Palmer, E.R.	P-092	03/05/21	St. Helena, Ca.	*21MR 17-19*
Arthur, Sr.	A-093	03/05/21	St. Helena, Ca.	
Hall, L.M.	H-094	03/05/21	St. Helena, Ca.	4BC 1184;10MR 279

EGW Letters File—Page 75

Daniells, A.G.	D-095	03/05/19	St. Helena, Ca.	5Bio 272-273
Hall, L.M.	H-096	03/05/22	St. Helena, Ca.	PM 344-345;WM 339
Kellogg, J.H.	K-097	03/05/22	St. Helena, Ca.	
Morton, Eliza	*M-098	03/05/25	St. Helena, Ca.	2SM 261
Nichols, Henry	*N-099	03/05/24	St. Helena, Ca.	
Kress, Br-Sr. [D.H.]	K-100	03/05/25	St. Helena, Ca.	PC 37-38
Irwin, Sr. [G.A.]	I-101	03/05/12	St. Helena, Ca.	
Burden, Br-Sr. [J.A.]	B-102	03/06/03	St. Helena, Ca.	2MCP 375-376
Starr, Br-Sr. [G.B.]	S-103	03/06/03	St. Helena, Ca.	TDG 163
Faulkhead, Br-Sr. [N.D.]	F-104	03/06/03	St. Helena, Ca.	
Butler, G.I.	B-105	03/06/01	St. Helena, Ca.	*17MR 344-347*
General Conference Committee	*B-106	03/05/30	Healdsburg, Ca.	2SM 384;Ev 21;1MR 275; RH 08/11/1903, 09/17/1903
Kellogg, J.H.	*K-107	03/05/08	St. Helena, Ca.	
Palmer, Br-Sr. [W.O.]	P-108	03/06/06	St. Helena, Ca.	
White, J.E./White, Emma	W-109	03/06/00	St. Helena, Ca.	10MR 356
Richardson, Edwin	R-110	03/06/20		
Magan, P.T.	M-111	03/06/16	St. Helena, Ca.	CS 278;6MR 106-109
Burden, Br-Sr. [J.A.]	B-112	03/06/21	St. Helena, Ca.	TDG 181;8MR 58
Brn. in the Medical Missionary Work	B-113	03/05/00	St. Helena, Ca.	2MCP 559;Ev 23-24;HFM 71;2BC 1033
Leaders in our Work	B-114	03/05/23	St. Helena, Ca.	*7MR 62-70*
Wessels, John	W-115	03/06/20	St. Helena, Ca.	TSA 58-59;1MR 383;7MR 151
Kress, Br-Sr. [D.H.]	K-116	03/06/24	St. Helena, Ca.	Ev 103;PC 16-17
Caro, E.R.	C-117	03/06/24	St. Helena, Ca.	MM 19-21;TMK 54
Irwin, Sr. [G.A.]	I-118	03/06/24		
Santee, Br./Whitelock, Br.	B-119	03/06/12	St. Helena, Ca.	
Daniells, A.G.	D-120	03/06/26	St. Helena, Ca.	5Bio 274
Hall, L.M.	H-121	03/06/25	St. Helena, Ca.	UL 190;7BC 970;MRmnt 105
Kellogg, H.W.	K-122	03/06/28	St. Helena, Ca.	MRmnt 114
White, J.E./White, Emma	*W-123	03/06/25	St. Helena, Ca.	TDG 185
McClure, N.C.	M-124	03/06/25	St. Helena, Ca.	
Brn. in the Med. Miss. Work & Review & Herald	B-125	03/06/11	St. Helena, Ca.	Ev 102;7BC 969
Brn. in Battle Creek, Mi. and in other States	B-126	03/07/01		PM 176-177,181-182,184
Haskell, S.N.	H-127	03/07/01	St. Helena, Ca.	6BC 1106;TDG 191;7MR 186,402; BTS 11/1903
Daniells, A.G./Prescott, W.W.	B-128	03/07/01	St. Helena, Ca.	
Arthur, Judge Jesse	*A-129	03/07/02	St. Helena, Ca.	CH 316-318;Ev 54,307-308
White, Ella	W-130	03/07/05	St. Helena, Ca.	3MR 178
Foss, Mary	F-131	03/07/01	St. Helena, Ca.	
Butler, G.I.	B-132	03/07/03	St. Helena, Ca.	Ev 395;SpTB #18 8-9
Brn-Srs. in America	B-133	03/07/05	St. Helena, Ca.	*RH 07/28/1903*
Butler, G.I.	B-134	03/07/01	St. Helena, Ca.	1NL 141-142;PM 177
Haskell, Br-Sr.	H-135	03/03/08	St. Helena, Ca.	3SM 55;7MR 401-402;6Bio 96-97
White, W.C.	W-136	03/07/08	St. Helena, Ca.	5MR 438
Brethren and Sisters	B-137	03/07/06	Healdsburg, Ca.	*RH 08/11/1903*
White, W.C.	W-138	03/07/10	St. Helena, Ca.	
Brn. in Responsible Positions in the Work	B-139	03/07/02	St. Helena, Ca.	3BC 1154
Brethren	B-140	03/07/05	St. Helena, Ca.	*RH 08/11/1903*
White, W.C.	W-141	03/07/12	St. Helena, Ca.	
White, J.E.	W-142	03/07/12	St. Helena, Ca.	
Palmer, E.R.	P-143	03/03/10	St. Helena, Ca.	2SM 262-263
White, J.E.	W-144	03/07/12	St. Helena, Ca.	TDG 202
Palmer, Br-Sr. [W.O.]	P-145	03/07/14	St. Helena, Ca.	
Friends in Australia	B-146	03/07/15	St. Helena, Ca.	VSS 285-286
Farnsworth, Br-Sr. [E.W.]	F-147	03/07/14	St. Helena, Ca.	3SM 409
Faulkhead, Br-Sr. [N.D.]	F-148	03/07/15	St. Helena, Ca.	
Belden, Br-Sr. [S.T.]	B-149	03/07/15	St. Helena, Ca.	*10MR 82-85*

White, J.E.	W-150	03/07/19	St. Helena, Ca.	CD 490;2MCP 470,506;HP 120; 6MR 139-140
White, J.E.	W-151	03/07/23	St. Helena, Ca.	VSS 156;Ev 431
To All Whom It May Concern/Work of Pioneers	B-152	03/07/22	St. Helena, Ca.	RY 35-38
White, J.E./White, Emma	W-153	03/07/15	St. Helena, Ca.	PM 89
White, J.E.	W-154	03/07/26	St. Helena, Ca.	
Christenson, C.	C-155	03/07/25	St. Helena, Ca.	
Magan, P.T.	M-156	03/07/27	St. Helena, Ca.	*SpM 305-306*
Harper, Walter	H-157	03/07/28	St. Helena, Ca.	*12MR 242-245*
Magan, Br-Sr. [P.T.]	M-158	03/07/29	St. Helena, Ca.	
Magan, P.T.	M-159	03/07/30	St. Helena, Ca.	*21MR 8-12*
Hart, Br-Sr. [R.A.]	H-160	03/03/00	Oakland, Ca.	Ev 447
Daniells, A.G./Prescott, W.W.	B-161	03/07/30	St. Helena, Ca.	*15MR 227-230*
Lane, Sands	L-162	03/04/12	St. Helena, Ca.	UL 116;1MCP 320;SpTB #6 60-61
White, W.C.	W-163	03/08/03	St. Helena, Ca.	
Those in Charge of the Wahroonga Sanitarium	B-164	03/07/29	St. Helena, Ca.	10MR 300
White, W.C.	W-165	03/08/03	St. Helena, Ca.	SpM 306-307
Kress, Br-Sr. [D.H.]	K-166	03/08/04	St. Helena, Ca.	*20MR 80-84*
Members of our Churches in Every Place	B-167	03/08/04	St. Helena, Ca.	
Stickney, Sr. [A.S.]	S-168	03/08/04	St. Helena, Ca.	
Daniells, A.G.	D-169	03/08/04	St. Helena, Ca.	PM 278,288;1BC 1087
Daniells, A.G. [variant of D-169]	D-169a	03/08/04	St. Helena, Ca.	*8MR 298-301*
Irwin, Sr. [G.A.]	I-170	03/08/04	St. Helena, Ca.	
Burden, Br-Sr. [J.A.]	B-171	03/08/04	St. Helena, Ca.	CD 295-296
White, W.C.	*W-172	03/08/04	St. Helena, Ca.	*BCL 72-75*
Brethren	B-173	03/08/05	St. Helena, Ca.	TDG 226
Harper, Walter	H-174	03/08/05	St. Helena, Ca.	PM 297
Wessels, J.J.	W-175	03/08/07	St. Helena, Ca.	
Kellogg, H.W.	K-176	03/08/09	St. Helena, Ca.	Ev 387-388;LS 411-412;PM 280-281
White, J.E.	W-177	03/08/09	St. Helena, Ca.	TDG 229;Ev 143
Jones, A.T.	J-178	03/08/02	St. Helena, Ca.	LLM 62-63
Jones, A.T.	J-179	03/08/02	St. Helena, Ca.	
Kellogg, J.H.	*K-180	03/05/05?	St. Helena, Ca.	11MR 313;LLM 73
Kellogg, J.H.	*K-181	03/09/02	St. Helena, Ca.	4BC 1144;LLM 62;5Bio 270
Belden, F.E.	B-182	03/08/13	St. Helena, Ca.	PM 173
Harper, Walter	H-184	03/08/28	St. Helena, Ca.	
Haskell, Br-Sr.	H-185	03/08/17	St. Helena, Ca.	TDG 238;4MR 300
White, W.C.	W-186	03/08/18	St. Helena, Ca.	PC 15-16
White, W.C.	W-187	03/08/17	St. Helena, Ca.	*17MR 316-322*
White, W.C.	W-188	03/08/25	St. Helena, Ca.	3MR 38
Griggs, F.	G-189	03/08/26	St. Helena, Ca.	*11MR 41-47 and KC 11-12*
Daniells, A.G.	D-190	03/08/27	St. Helena, Ca.	*SpM 316-318*
Crothers, William	C-191	03/08/27	St. Helena, Ca.	
Jones, A.T.	J-192	03/08/28	St. Helena, Ca.	4MR 354-355
Franke, E.E.	F-193	03/09/01	St. Helena, Ca.	Ev 331;1MR 16;3MR 278;1Bio 33
Cady, M.E.	C-194	03/09/02	St. Helena, Ca.	*14MR 168-171*
White, W.C.	W-195	03/09/06	St. Helena, Ca.	UL 263;BCL 76-78
Wessels, J.J.	W-196	03/09/03	St. Helena, Ca.	TDG 255;TSA 98
Cady, M.E.	C-197	03/09/07	St. Helena, Ca.	*14MR 171-173*
Healdsburg College Board	B-198	03/09/07	St. Helena, Ca.	*14MR 173*
Brn. in Positions of Responsibility	*B-199	03/09/08	St. Helena, Ca.	*8T 9-13 (RH 10/01/1903)*
Butler, G.I.	B-200	03/09/10	St. Helena, Ca.	SpM 260-261;2MR 66-67
White, J.E./White, Emma	W-201	03/09/10	St. Helena, Ca.	*7MR 117-122*
White, J.E./White, Emma	W-202	03/09/11	St. Helena, Ca.	7MR 116;LLM 73
Nashville Publishing House	B-203	03/09/14	St. Helena, Ca.	SD 321;TDG 266
White, J.E.	W-204	03/09/14	St. Helena, Ca.	
Brn-Srs. in Australia	B-205	03/09/14	St. Helena, Ca.	UL 271

Kress, Br-Sr. [D.H.]	K-206	03/09/16	St. Helena, Ca.	
Brethren and Sisters	B-207	03/08/13	St. Helena, Ca.	SpTB #6 44-45;6Bio 57
Brethren and Sisters	*B-208	03/05/20	St. Helena, Ca.	2MCP 466,492
Kellogg, H.W.	K-209	03/09/20	St. Helena, Ca.	5Bio 378
Teachers in Emmanuel Missionary College	B-210	03/09/21	St. Helena, Ca.	*1NL 96 and LLM 56-58*
Teachers in Emmanuel Missionary College	B-211	03/09/22	St. Helena, Ca.	*RH 10/22/1903*
Teachers in Emmanuel Missionary College	B-212	03/09/23	St. Helena, Ca.	SpM 324-325
Friends at Berrien Springs	B-213	03/10/09	St. Helena, Ca.	ML 61;2MR 44-45
Magan, P.T./Sutherland, E.A.	M-214	03/10/09	St. Helena, Ca.	*SpM 328-330*
White, J.E./White, Emma	W-215	03/10/09	St. Helena, Ca.	
Leaders in our Medical Work	B-216	03/08/04	St. Helena, Ca.	*12MR 64-71*
Tenney, Br-Sr. [G.C.]	T-217	03/10/13	St. Helena, Ca.	5Bio 304
Wessels, Andrew	W-218	03/10/19	St. Helena, Ca.	SpTB #18 9
Butler, G.I.	B-219	03/10/13	St. Helena, Ca.	*17MR 310-315*
Paulson, David	P-220	03/10/14	St. Helena, Ca.	*SpM 331-338*
Leaders in our Work	B-221	03/10/12	St. Helena, Ca.	
Leaders in our Work	B-222	03/10/15	St. Helena, Ca.	*BCL 84-85*
Daniells, A.G./Prescott, W.W.	B-223	03/10/14	St. Helena, Ca.	2MCP 429
Prescott, W.W./Daniells, A.G.	B-224	03/10/11	St. Helena, Ca.	5Bio 304
Prescott, W.W./Daniells, A.G.	B-225	03/10/14	St. Helena, Ca.	*SpM 330-331*
Wessels, Andrew	W-226	03/10/09	St. Helena, Ca.	Te 103-104;TSA 59-60
Daniells, A.G./Prescott, W.W.	D-227	03/10/09	St. Helena, Ca.	*15MR 214-216*
Jones, W.H.	J-228	03/10/18	St. Helena, Ca.	MM 41-44;LLM 58-59
White, J.E./White, W.C.	W-229	03/09/27	St. Helena, Ca.	*21MR 439-441*
Waggoner, E.J.	*W-230	03/10/02	St. Helena, Ca.	*21MR 171-173*
Waggoner, E.J.	*W-231	03/10/05	St. Helena, Ca.	*TSB 199-200 and 10MR 185-187*
Kellogg, J.H.	K-232	03/10/06	St. Helena, Ca.	3MR 344;11MR 314;3Bio 303-304
Palmer, E.R.	*P-233	03/10/26	St. Helena, Ca.	
Wessels, Sr. [A.E.]	*W-234	03/10/12	St. Helena, Ca.	
Lindsay, Annie Wessels	*L-235	03/10/12	St. Helena, Ca.	
Wessels, Andrew	*W-236	03/10/00	St. Helena, Ca.	TSA 60-61
Daniells, A.G.	D-237	03/11/01	St. Helena, Ca.	
Daniells, A.G.	D-238	03/11/01	St. Helena, Ca.	PM 175-176;5Bio 301
Kellogg, J.H.	K-239	03/10/28	St. Helena, Ca.	1MR 26-27;2MR 156;12MR 60;6Bio 97-98
Medical Students and Nurses	B-240	03/11/05		UL 323;MM 94-96
Medical Missionaries	B-241	03/10/17	St. Helena, Ca.	*CH 369-372*
Physicians and Ministers	B-242	03/10/00	St. Helena, Ca.	*SpTB #7 36-42*
Hall, L.M.	H-243	03/05/11	St. Helena, Ca.	*17MR 294-297*
Sanitarium Managers/Parents	B-244	03/11/05		7MR 229
Kellogg, J.H.	K-245	03/10/05	St. Helena, Ca.	
Kellogg, J.H. [variant of K-245]	K-245a	03/10/05	St. Helena, Ca.	
Sanitarium Family/Battle Creek Church	B-246	03/10/12	St. Helena, Ca.	3MR 38-39;SpTB #6 20
Leaders in our Medical Missionary Work	B-247	03/11/12	St. Helena, Ca.	MM 96
White, J.E.	W-248	03/11/13	St. Helena, Ca.	
Magan, P.T./Sutherland, E.A.	B-249	03/11/11	St. Helena, Ca.	*SpM 339-341*
White, J.E.	W-250	03/11/16	St. Helena, Ca.	UL 334
Wessels, John	W-251	03/11/01	St. Helena, Ca.	
Burden, Br-Sr. [J.A.]	B-252	03/11/16	St. Helena, Ca.	Ev 103
Kellogg, J.H.	K-253	03/11/20	St. Helena, Ca.	4MR 57-61;11MR 314-315
Kellogg, J.H.	*K-253a	03/11/18	St. Helena, Ca.	SpTB #7 46-51
Medical Missionaries/Christ Our Example (#1)	B-254	03/10/30	St. Helena, Ca.	*8T 201-205*
Medical Missionaries/Christ Our Example (#2)	*B-255	03/10/30	St. Helena, Ca.	*8T 206-212*
Intern. Med. Miss. & Benev. Assoc.	*B-256	03/10/25	St. Helena, Ca.	*BCL 86-91*
Kellogg, J.H.	K-257	03/11/26	St. Helena, Ca.	OHC 102;TDG 339;7MR 151-152; 12MR 61
Hall, L.M.	H-258	03/11/23	St. Helena, Ca.	RY 60
Hall, L.M.	H-259	03/11/23	St. Helena, Ca.	TDG 336;UL 341;1BC 1103

Hare, George A.	H-260	03/12/02	St. Helena, Ca.	PC 12-13
Waggoner, E.J.	W-261	03/11/30	St. Helena, Ca.	
Ministers and Other Workers in the South	*B-262	03/11/24	St. Helena, Ca.	MM 102-103;6BC 1067;SpTB #18 9; 5MR 164
Physicians and Nurses	*B-263	03/11/12	St. Helena, Ca.	TDG 325;1MR 116
Wessels, John	W-264	03/12/07	St. Helena, Ca.	*20MR 87-92*
Kellogg, J.H. and associates	K-265	03/11/26	St. Helena, Ca.	*11MR 247-253*
Tenney, G.C./Jones, A.T.	B-266	03/12/03	St. Helena, Ca.	*BCL 92-96*
Brunson, John A.	B-267	03/12/16	St. Helena, Ca.	
Paulson, David	P-268	03/12/17	St. Helena, Ca.	UL 365
Daniells, A.G.	D-269	03/12/14	St. Helena, Ca.	10MR 356-357
White, J.E.	W-270	03/12/21	St. Helena, Ca.	UL 369
Haskell, Br-Sr.	H-271	03/12/17	St. Helena, Ca.	2MCP 771
Daniells, A.G.	D-271a	03/09/18	St. Helena, Ca.	5Bio 302-303
Daniells, A.G.	D-271b	03/09/18	St. Helena, Ca.	5Bio 303
Brn-Srs. Gathered in Council at Nashville	B-272	03/12/20	St. Helena, Ca.	*SW 01/19/1904*
Wessels, Peter and Family	*W-272a	03/10/00	St. Helena, Ca.	
n.a./Brother	B-274	03/12/30	St. Helena, Ca.	
Brn. Laboring in Battle Creek	*B-275	03/11/00	St. Helena, Ca.	*19MR 356-365*
Haskell, Br-Sr.	H-283	03/11/26	St. Helena, Ca.	
White, W.C.	*W-288	03/01/23	St. Helena, Ca.	
Belden, F.E.	*B-289	03/03/01	St. Helena, Ca.	
Leaders in the Medical Work	*B-291	03/08/04		TMK 199,281
White, W.C.	*W-292	03/08/06	St. Helena, Ca.	
White, W.C.	*W-293	03/08/16	St. Helena, Ca.	
Magan, P.T.	*M-294	03/11/10	St. Helena, Ca.	*13MR 157-158*
White, Emma	*W-296	03/01/11	St. Helena, Ca.	
Daniells, A.G.	*D-297	03/08/05	St. Helena, Ca.	
White, W.C.	*W-298	03/08/18	St. Helena, Ca.	
White, W.C.	*W-299	03/08/00	Healdsburg, Ca.	
Kellogg, J.H.	*K-300	03/03/16	St. Helena, Ca.	5Bio 292
Kellogg, J.H.	*K-301	03/04/05		5Bio 292
Kress, Br-Sr.	*K-302	03/11/22	San Diego, Ca.	
Kellogg, J.H.	K-303	03/08/29	St. Helena, Ca.	CTr 227
Hughes, Br-Sr.	*H-304	03/08/01	St. Helena, Ca.	*PCO 87-91*

1904

Brethren and Sisters	B-001	03/12/31	Filed in 1904	HP 83,176,226,242;TDG 374;11MR 29
Druillard, Sr. [N.H.]	*D-003	04/01/07	St. Helena, Ca.	
Brn-Srs. in the Medical Work in Southern Ca.	B-005	04/01/08	St. Helena, Ca.	*19MR 229-232*
Daniells, A.G.	D-007	04/01/10	St. Helena, Ca.	
White, Mabel	W-009	04/01/09	St. Helena, Ca.	*19MR 81-87*
Brn-Srs. at Nashville	B-011	04/01/07	St. Helena, Ca.	*SW 03/01/1904*
Butler, G.I.	B-013	04/01/12	St. Helena, Ca.	ML 185
Butler, G.I.	B-015	04/01/12	St. Helena, Ca.	*17MR 298-299*
Butler, G.I.	B-017	04/01/12	St. Helena, Ca.	
White, J.E./White, Emma	W-019	04/01/13	St. Helena, Ca.	2MCP 508
Kellogg, J.H.	K-021	04/01/02	St. Helena, Ca.	*SpM 344-345*
Kellogg, J.H.	*K-023	03/12/00	Filed in 1904	*SpM 341-343*
Brn-Srs. in the Southern Union Conference	B-025	04/01/12	St. Helena, Ca.	AH 18-19;MM 96-97; 9MR 239-240;RH 09/07/1905
Irwin, Br-Sr. [G.A.]	I-027	04/01/18	St. Helena, Ca.	
Burden, Br-Sr. [J.A.]	B-029	04/01/17	St. Helena, Ca.	SD 191;8MR 351
Burden, Br-Sr. [J.A.]/Kress, Br-Sr. [D.H.]	B-031	04/01/17	St. Helena, Ca.	UL 31
Faulkhead, N.D./Salisbury, W.D.	B-033	04/01/19	St. Helena, Ca.	2MR 243
Farnsworth, Br-Sr. [E.W.]	F-035	04/01/19	St. Helena, Ca.	PC 34

EGW Letters File—Page 79

Kress, Br-Sr. [D.H.]	*K-037	04/01/18	St. Helena, Ca.	*21MR 103-104*
Butler, G.I.	B-043	03/12/14	Filed in 1904	12MR 112
Harper, Walter	H-045	04/01/19		1MCP 322 323
Harper, Walter	H-047	03/07/00	Filed in 1904	AH 378
Harper, Sr. [F.]	H-049	04/01/24	St. Helena, Ca.	2MCP 501-502
Haskell, S.N.	H-051	03/11/26	Filed in 1904	*BCL 101-102*
Prescott, W.W.	P-053	04/01/26	St. Helena, Ca.	Ev 395-396;1NL 105-106;7BC 944;
				1MR 383-384;4MR 368-369;6MR 26-27
White, W.C.	W-055	04/01/29	St. Helena, Ca.	1MR 384
Leading Medical Workers	B-057	03/11/12	Filed in 1904	*BCL 6-7*
Brn-Srs. in the South	B-059	04/01/22	St. Helena, Ca.	
Brethren Bearing Responsibilities	B-061	04/02/01	St. Helena, Ca.	TDG 40;MM 33
Hall, L.M.	H-063	04/02/05	St. Helena, Ca.	ChL 18-19;ML 128
Burden, Br-Sr. [J.A.[	B-064	04/02/09	St. Helena, Ca.	
Harper, Walter	H-065	04/02/06	St. Helena, Ca.	AH 378
White, Mabel	W-067	04/02/06	St. Helena, Ca.	3MR 133
White, J.E./White, Emma	W-069	04/02/08	St. Helena, Ca.	5MR 451
Irwin, Br-Sr. [G.A.]	I-071	04/02/06	St. Helena, Ca.	
Irwin, Br-Sr. [G.A.]	I-073	04/02/09	St. Helena, Ca.	
Brunson, J.A.	B-075	04/02/08	St. Helena, Ca.	VSS 248
White, W.C.	W-077	04/02/12	St. Helena, Ca.	
Whitelock, T.S.	W-079	04/02/12	St. Helena, Ca.	
Those Connected with the Potts Sanitarium	B-081	04/02/15	St. Helena, Ca.	5MR 320-322
Daniells, A.G./Prescott, W.W./Hare, Br.	B-083	04/02/15	St. Helena, Ca.	9T 12-13;PC 328-330
White, W.C.	W-085	04/02/16	St. Helena, Ca.	
White, W.C.	W-087	04/02/15	St. Helena, Ca.	1MR 324-325
Ballenger, E.S.	B-089	04/02/18	St. Helena, Ca.	
White, W.C.	W-091	04/02/18	St. Helena, Ca.	TDG 57;1SM 79-82;MRmnt 105
White, W.C.	W-093	04/02/21	St. Helena, Ca.	4MR 89
Whitelock, T.S.	W-095	04/02/22	St. Helena, Ca.	
Hall, L.M.	H-097	04/02/23	St. Helena, Ca.	PC 41
White, J.E./White, Emma	W-099	04/02/23	St. Helena, Ca.	4MR 23,90
White, J.E./White, Emma	W-101	03/09/30	St. Helena, Ca.	
Craw, Hiram A.	C-103	04/02/24	St. Helena, Ca.	*13MR 390-394*
White, J.E.	W-105	04/03/01	St. Helena, Ca.	1MR 397;4MR 24;LLM 51;5Bio 319
Butler, G.I.	B-107	04/02/28	St. Helena, Ca.	6BC 1106;7BC 905;CC 342
White, W.C.	W-109	04/03/03	St. Helena, Ca.	
Butler, G.I.	B-111	04/03/13	St. Helena, Ca.	UL 86;VSS 341-342;2MCP 539
Butler, G.I.	B-111a	04/05/09		RY 23-24
Butler, G.I.	B-113	04/03/14	St. Helena, Ca.	
White, J.E./White, Emma	W-115	04/03/14	St. Helena, Ca.	GH 03/01/04
White, J.E.	W-117	04/03/15	St. Helena, Ca.	
Wessels, J.J.	*W-119	04/03/01	St. Helena, Ca.	2SM 54-55
White, J.E./White, Emma	W-121	04/03/29	St. Helena, Ca.	*1888 1803-1810*
White, J.E.	W-123	04/03/29	St. Helena, Ca.	1MCP 103-104,235,318;2MCP 466-467;
				HP 74,164,186,231;MM 101-102;
				8MR 334;12MR 40;CTr 170
Craw, Hiram A.	*C-125	04/03/02	Healdsburg, Ca.	
Irwin, Br-Sr. [G.A.]	I-127	04/04/11	St. Helena, Ca.	CD 288-289,491
Irwin, G.A./Starr, G.B.	B-129	04/04/12	St. Helena, Ca.	
Sharp, Br./Caro, E.R.	*B-131	04/04/11	St. Helena, Ca.	HP 245;9MR 373-374
White, J.E./White, Emma	W-133	04/04/12	St. Helena, Ca.	TDG 111;5Bio 319
Cady, Br./Lucas, Br.	B-135	04/04/15	St. Helena, Ca.	
Hizerman, H.	H-137	04/04/11	St. Helena, Ca.	4MR 165-167;7MR 328
Vickery, Robert	V-139	04/04/17	St. Helena, Ca.	PM 209-210;TDG 116
White, J.E./White, Emma	W-141	04/04/27	Washington, D.C.	LDE 106;1MR 325;3MR 44-45;8MR 165

Davis, Marian	D-143	04/04/28	Washington, D.C.	Ev 568;8MR 165;9MR 386
n.a./Brother	B-145	04/04/15	St. Helena, Ca.	LLM 39-43;CD 311;Te 248;2SM 180; SpTB #19 26-29
Bowles, Br.	B-147	04/04/26	Takoma Park, Md.	1MR 254-256
Butler, G.I.	B-149	04/05/02	Takoma Park, Md.	SpTB #6 3
Butler, G.I.	B-151	04/05/04	Takoma Park, Md.	SpTB #6 25
Fellow Workers	B-153	04/05/10	Takoma Park, Md.	*ST 06/15/1904*
Butler, G.I.	B-155	04/05/08	Takoma Park, Md.	3MR 354;8MR 97
Nelson, Sr. [M.J.]	N-157	04/04/28	Takoma Park, Md.	4MR 24;5MR 119;5Bio 324
James, Iram	J-159	04/05/10	Takoma Park, Md.	*16MR 185-187*
Butler, G.I.	B-161	04/05/18	Berrien Springs, Mi.	5Bio 320
Hall, L.M.	H-163	04/05/15	Elkhart, In.	MRmnt 121;5Bio 330
Daniells, A.G./Prescott, W.W.	B-165	04/05/20	Berrien Springs, Mi.	*SpTB #2 30-35*
Santee, Br./Owen, Br.	B-167	04/04/27	Takoma Park, Md.	SpTB #3 14-15;7MR 138
Ministers in Southern California	B-169	04/04/27	Takoma Park, Md.	1MCP 178;2MCP 633;Ev 382;1MR 256; 6MR 62
Hizerman, H.	H-171	04/05/10	Takoma Park, Md.	
Prescott, W.W./Daniells, A.G.	B-173	04/05/20	Berrien Springs, Mi.	
Ministers and Teachers	B-175	04/05/21	Berrien Springs, Mi.	Ev 623-624;2MCP 718;12MR 61-62
Medical Men at Battle Creek	B-177	04/05/21	Berrien Springs, Mi.	*BCL 106-107*
Editors of our Periodicals	B-179	04/05/21	Berrien Springs, Mi.	
Hall, L.M.	H-181	04/05/26	Nashville, Tn.	OHC 280;4MR 377
White, W.C.	*W-183	04/06/01	Nashville, Tn.	5Bio 341
White, W.C.	*W-185	04/06/02	Nashville, Tn.	
Butler, G.I./Haskell, S.N.	B-187	04/06/03	Nashville, Tn.	9MR 97
White, May Lacey	W-189	04/06/06	Nashville, Tn.	3MR 52-54
White, Mabel	W-191	04/06/07	Nashville, Tn.	SpTB #18 10;3MR 265
Druillard, Sr. [N.H.]	D-193	04/06/09	Edgefield Jct., Tn.	3MR 265-267
Daniells, A.G.	D-195	04/06/13	Morning Star	SpTB #11 5-7;5Bio 339,345;6Bio 110
Evans, I.H.	E-197	04/06/15	Nashville, Tn.	*21MR 425-428*
Burden, J.A.	B-199	04/06/15	Nashville, Tn.	12MR 43
Brethren Who Are Assembled in Council	B-201	04/06/22	Huntsville, Al.	*PCO 97-98*
Franke, E.E.	F-203	03/10/01	Filed in 1904	6MR 243-244
Franke, E.E.	F-205	03/10/09	Filed in 1904	2MCP 383-384,768;Ev 139
Sperry, Byron	S-207	04/06/28	Nashville, Tn.	TDG 188
Henry, A.R.	H-209	04/06/24	Nashville, Tn.	5MR 445-446
Ministers in Southern California	B-211	04/06/30	Nashville, Tn.	*LLM 43-47*
Richart, Br-Sr.	R-213	04/06/30	Nashville, Tn.	3MR 267
Hare, G.A.	H-214	04/08/00	Washington, D.C.	
Davis, Marian	D-215	04/06/30	Nashville, Tn.	*14MR 35-44*
Young, W.R.	Y-217	04/07/03	Nashville, Tn.	9T 28-29
n.a./Sister	B-219	04/07/06	Nashville, Tn.	
n.a./Sister	*B-220	04/07/06	Nashville, Tn.	
n.a./Brother	B-220a	04/07/06	Nashville, Tn.	
Foote, Frank	F-221	04/07/06	Nashville, Tn.	Ev 469;2MR 69
Daniells, A.G./Prescott, W.W./Hare, G.A.	B-223	04/06/15	Nashville, Tn.	4BC 1184
White, J.E.	W-225	04/01/29	St. Helena, Ca.	
Huntsville School Board and Faculty	B-227	04/07/06	Nashville, Tn.	*PCO 98-99*
White, J.E.	W-229	04/07/08	Takoma Park, Md.	
Crawford, M.	C-231	04/07/11	Takoma Park, Md.	5Bio 379
Palmer, Br-Sr. [E.R.]	P-233	04/07/08	Takoma Park, Md.	*14MR 215-218*
Burden, J.A.	B-235	04/07/15	Takoma Park, Md.	*LLM 48*
Butler, G.I.	B-237	04/07/14	Takoma Park, Md.	*19MR 308-312*
Walling, Addie/Walling, May	W-239	04/07/11	Takoma Park, Md.	
White, J.E.	W-241	04/07/18	Takoma Park, Md.	
Union Conference Presidents	B-243	04/06/15	Huntsville, Al.	*PCO 94-96*

McClure, N.C.	M-245	04/07/12	Takoma Park, Md.	3MR 268-269
Young, W.P.	Y-247	04/07/19	Takoma Park, Md.	5MR 118-119;5Bio 379
Arthur, Br-Sr. [Judge Jesse]	A-249	04/07/19	Takoma Park, Md.	UL 214
Arthur, Br-Sr. [Judge Jesse]	*A-249a	04/06/27	Nashville, Tn.	5Bio 346
Simpson, Abbie Winegar	S-251	04/07/22	Takoma Park, Md.	*AUCR 09/01/1904*
Hart, R.A.	*H-253	04/07/18	Takoma Park, Md.	UL 213
Magan, P.T./Sutherland, E.A.	B-255	04/07/23	Takoma Park, Md.	7ABC 466;SpM 361-365
Kellogg, J.H.	*K-256	04/10/00	St. Helena, Ca.	
Kellogg, J.H.	K-257	04/07/27	Takoma Park, Md.	HP 101;11MR 317-318
Union Conf. Presidents/Med. Missionaries	*B-259	04/06/23	Nashville, Tn.	*BCL 108-110*
Physicians and Ministers	*B-261	04/06/00	Nashville, Tn.	
Our Leading Physicians	*B-263	04/07/24	Washington, D.C.	*1SM 193-198*
White, J.E./White, Emma	W-265	04/07/21	Washington, D.C.	
Hayward, Br. [O.M.]	H-267	04/07/24	Washington, D.C.	2MR 50
Kellogg, J.H.	K-269	04/05/22	Berrien Springs, Mi.	11MR 316-317
Kellogg, J.H.	K-271	04/07/29	Washington, D.C.	12MR 62;5Bio 349
Sutherland, E.A./Magan, P.T.	B-273	04/07/28	Takoma Park, Md.	2MR 50
Davis, Marian	D-275	04/08/07	Washington, D.C.	9MR 269
Paulson, David	*P-276	04/07/30	Takoma Park, Md.	TMK 299;HP 41
Read, A.J.	R-277	04/07/31	Washington, D.C.	1SM 199-200;1MR 53
Paulson, D./Sadler, W./Jones, A.T./Waggoner, E.J.	B-279	04/08/01	Takoma Park, Md.	*21MR 174-177*
Ministers, Physicians, and Teachers	*B-280	04/09/03	Middletown, Ct.	UL 260;LHU 76
Ministers, Physicians, and Teacher	*B-280a	04/09/03	Middletown, Ct.	*21MR 416-420*
Riley, W.H.	R-281	04/08/03	Washington, D.C.	*15MR 258-264*
Kellogg, J.H.	K-283	04/09/10	Omaha, Ne.	VSS 21-22;11MR 318
Kellogg, Sr. [W.K.]	K-285	04/09/25		
Kellogg, J.H.	K-287	04/09/21	College View, Ne.	5Bio 353
Kellogg, J.H.	K-289	04/09/23	College View, Ne.	5MR 136
Hayward, O.M.	H-291	04/10/12	St. Helena, Ca.	MM 292-293;LLM 49-50
Belden, Br-Sr. [S.T.]	B-293	04/10/17	St. Helena, Ca.	5Bio 350-352
Ford, Br./Spire, Br.	B-295	04/10/21	St. Helena, Ca.	
Daniells, A.G./Prescott, W.W.	B-296	04/10/00		Ev 35-36;1MR 168
Palmer, W.O.	P-297	04/10/28	St. Helena, Ca.	CD 354;2MCP 387-388
Hare, Sr.	H-299	04/10/31	Armona, Ca.	TDG 313;RY 144-145;7MR 154
Haskell, Br-Sr.	H-301	04/11/02	Armona, Ca.	TDG 315;BTS 01/1905 and 02/1905 and 03/1905
Hayward, Br./Hansen, Br.	B-303	04/11/08	Los Angeles, Ca.	SpTB #18 14-15;5Bio 379
Brethren Throughout America	*B-304	04/11/11	San Diego, Ca.	2MR 69-70
Collins, Gilbert	C-305	04/08/00	Melrose, Ma.	1MR 226-227;5Bio 350
White, J.E./White, Emma	W-307	04/11/05	Los Angeles, Ca.	4MR 26
Porter, Br-Sr. [C.W.]	P-309	04/11/20		
Simpson, W.W.	*S-310	04/11/27	San Diego, Ca.	TDG 340
Kellogg, J.H.	K-311	04/11/25	National City, Ca.	*14MR 224-240*
Brethren and Sisters/A Needy Field	B-313	04/11/02	Armona, Ca.	SpTB #12 11-12;8MR 129
Wilcox, F.M.	W-315	04/11/22	San Diego, Ca.	9MR 285-286
Grey, Sr.	G-317	04/11/23	San Diego, Ca.	*14MR 218-220*
Gage, Frank	G-317a	04/11/20		
White, May/White, Henry/White, Herbert/Gracie	W-319	04/12/04	Los Angeles, Ca.	*14MR 230-235*
Druillard, Sr. [N.H.]	D-321	04/12/10	Redland, Ca.	*14MR 235-240*
Palmer, Br-Sr. [E.R.]	P-323	04/12/12	Glendale, Ca.	
Brn-Srs. in Southern California	*B-325	04/12/12	Los Angeles, Ca.	*LLM 79-82*
Starr, G.B.	S-327	04/12/20	St. Helena, Ca.	
Simpson, Sr.	S-329	04/12/20	St. Helena, Ca.	3SM 56;AH 160,270
Kress, Br-Sr. [D.H.]	K-331	04/12/21	St. Helena, Ca.	*14MR 244-249*
Butler, G.I.	B-333	04/03/14	St. Helena, Ca.	3MR 309
Hare, G.A. and his associate Physicians	B-335	04/08/22	Melrose, Ma.	Ev 86;3BC 1156
Nicola, Ben	N-337	04/12/25		*PCO 103-104*

Harper, Walter	H-339	04/12/26	St. Helena, Ca.	
Collins, Gilbert	C-341	04/12/22	St. Helena, Ca.	*16MR 26-29*
Simpson, Br-Sr. [W.W.]	S-343	04/12/27	St. Helena, Ca.	*PC 3-5*
Rogers, F.R.	R-345	04/12/27	St. Helena, Ca.	*SpTB #12 12-16*
Ballenger, E.S.	B-347	04/12/27	St. Helena, Ca.	
Crawford, Marian Stowell	C-349	04/12/29	St. Helena, Ca.	*14MR 249-254*
Conference Officers	*B-351	04/12/00	St. Helena, Ca.	*PH160 1-4*
Kellogg, J.H.	K-353	04/07/29	Washington, D.C.	
Ashley, L.A.	A-355	04/08/04	Melrose, Ma.	HP 104
White, J.E.	W-357	04/08/08	Washington, D.C.	3MR 133-135
Foss, Mary	F-359	04/08/10	Philadelphia, Pa.	8MR 165
Kellogg, J.H.	K-361	04/08/25	Melrose, Ma.	11MR 318
White, J.E.	W-363	04/09/15	College View, Ne.	UL 272
Davis, Marian	D-365	04/09/16	College View, Ne.	TDG 268;9MR 270
Davis, Marian	D-366	04/08/29	Melrose, Ma.	9MR 269-270
Simpson, W.W.	S-367	04/09/18	College View, Ne.	*9MR 13-17*
Kellogg, J.H.	K-368	04/08/31	Melrose, Ma.	*BCL 115-117*
Hayward, Br./Hansen, Br.	B-369	04/09/21	College View, Ne.	11MR 166-167
Brethren	*B-377	04/05/21	Berrien Springs, Mi.	
Davis, Marian	*D-378	04/08/17	Melrose, Ma.	2SM 251
Davis, Marian	*D-379	04/08/24	Melrose, Ma.	2SM 251-253
Davis, Marian	*D-380	04/09/04	Middletown, Ct.	
Davis, Marian	*D-381	04/09/06	Battle Creek, Mi.	
Davis, Marian	*D-382	04/09/26	College View, Ne.	2SM 254
Prescott, Br-Sr. [W.W.]	*P-383	04/06/09	Nashville, Tn.	
Kellogg, J.H.	*K-384	04/00/00		
Kellogg, J.H.	*K-385	04/00/00	Fragment	
Crisler, C.C.	*C-386	04/09/16	College View, Ne.	
White, J.E./White, W.C.	*W-387	04/03/08	St. Helena, Ca.	
White, W.C.	*W-388	04/03/14	St. Helena, Ca.	
White, W.C.	*W-389	04/08/18	Melrose, Ma.	
White, W.C.	*W-390	04/08/29	Melrose, Ma.	*21MR 414-415*
White, W.C.	*W-391	04/09/01	Melrose, Ma.	
Brn-Srs. in Australia	B-392	04/12/21	St. Helena, Ca.	*14MR 241-244*
White, Ella/White, Mabel	W-393	04/11/18	San Diego, Ca.	*14MR 263-266*
White, Ella/White, Mabel	W-394	04/11/23	San Diego, Ca.	*14MR 266-268*
Kress, Br-Sr.	*K-395	04/02/09	St. Helena, Ca.	
Kress, Br-Sr.	*K-396	04/04/12	St. Helena, Ca.	
Battle Creek Church	B-397	04/11/24	National City, Ca.	
Druillard, Sr.	*D-398	04/10/27	St. Helena, Ca.	
Medical Missionaries	B-399	04/06/00	Nashville, Tn.	
Hall, Lucinda	*H-400	04/04/07	St. Helena, Ca.	

1905

Students in the Huntsville School	B-001	05/01/01	St. Helena, Ca.	SF Echo 04/1910
Jones, C.H.	J-003	05/01/04	St. Helena, Ca.	1BC 1110
Church in Reno	B-005	05/01/04	St. Helena, Ca.	CS 276
Workmen in the Pacific Press Publishing House	B-007	05/01/05	St. Helena, Ca.	
Leading Men of the Pacific Press	B-009	05/01/05	St. Helena, Ca.	
Those Assembled in Council at Nashville	B-011	05/01/10		UL 24;2MCP 522;6MR 281-282
Haskell, S.N./Butler, G.I.	B-013	05/01/10	St. Helena, Ca.	
Leaders in our Work at Takoma Park	*B-015	05/01/11	St. Helena, Ca.	*RH 04/13/1905 and 04/27/1905*
Our Workers in Washington, D.C.	B-017	05/01/11	St. Helena, Ca.	*RH 02/02/1905*
Workers in the Washington Publishing House	B-019	05/01/11	St. Helena, Ca.	
Prescott, W.W./Colcord, W.A.	B-021	05/01/16	St. Helena, Ca.	PM 211;10MR 358;RH 02/16/1905; 5Bio 418

Nicola, Br-Sr. [C.C.]	N-023	05/01/17	St. Helena, Ca.	5Bio 382-383
Place, A.E.	P-025	05/01/17	St. Helena, Ca.	SpTB #13 8
Evans, T.J.	*E-027	05/01/18	St. Helena, Ca.	5Bio 383-384
Bradford, Sr.	B-029	05/01/01	St. Helena, Ca.	Ev 392-393;1MR 256;5Bio 358
Haskell, Br-Sr.	H-031	05/01/25	Mountain View, Ca.	*15MR 200-202*
Groves, Mildred	G-033	05/01/23	Mountain View, Ca.	LLM 51;5Bio 384-385
White, Ella May/White, Mabel	*W-035	05/01/26	St. Helena, Ca.	
Butler, G.I.	B-037	05/01/30	St. Helena, Ca.	
Belden, Br-Sr. [S.T.]	B-039	05/01/30	St. Helena, Ca.	3SM 72-73
Belden, Br-Sr. [S.T.]	B-041	05/02/01	St. Helena, Ca.	*RY 60-62*
Brethren and Sisters	B-043	05/01/29	St. Helena, Ca.	Ev 24;5MR 137;6MR 242
Washburn, Br-Sr. [F.A.]	W-045	05/02/03	St. Helena, Ca.	2SM 255
Pallant, Jesse	P-047	05/02/01	St. Helena, Ca.	
Anderson, C.J.	A-049	05/02/01	St. Helena, Ca.	
Anderson, Sr. [C.J.]	A-051	05/02/01	St. Helena, Ca.	
Ballenger, E.S./Palmer, E.R.	B-053	05/02/02	St. Helena, Ca.	*18MR 227-231*
Olsen, O.A.	O-055	05/01/30	St. Helena, Ca.	1MR 140-142
Breed, Sr. [A.J.]	B-057	05/02/05	St. Helena, Ca.	TDG 44
Burden, Br-Sr. [J.A.]	B-059	05/02/04	St. Helena, Ca.	MM 174-175;7MR 378-379;LLM 77-78; 5Bio 387-389
Breed, A.J.	B-061	05/02/05	St. Helena, Ca.	11MR 164
Farnsworth, Br-Sr. [E.W.]	F-063	05/02/05	St. Helena, Ca.	OHC 89;5Bio 385-387
Jones, A.T.	J-065	05/02/13	St. Helena, Ca.	Ev 187;UL 58;5Bio 417-418
Brethren and Sisters	B-067	05/02/18	St. Helena, Ca.	15MR 168-171
Brown, M.H.	B-069	05/02/18	St. Helena, Ca.	
White, J.E.	W-071	05/02/18	St. Helena, Ca.	
Kress, Br-Sr. [D.H.]	K-073	05/02/01	St. Helena, Ca.	CD 296;UL 46;7MR 152;5Bio 379; 6Bio 262
Palmer, E.R./Ballenger, E.S.	B-075	05/02/20	St. Helena, Ca.	*15MR 312-317*
White, J.E.	W-077	05/02/21	St. Helena, Ca.	
Kress, D.H.	K-079	05/02/17	St. Helena, Ca.	3SM 98;Ev 425,594-595;CD 303
Faulkhead, N.D.	F-081	05/02/21	St. Helena, Ca.	MRmnt 124
Ballenger, E.S.	B-083	05/02/26	St. Helena, Ca.	*PC 322-325*
Gotzian, J.	G-085	05/02/26	St. Helena, Ca.	PM 358-359
Haskell, Br-Sr.	H-087	05/02/25	St. Helena, Ca.	8MR 17;BTS 03/1915
White, W.C.	*W-088	05/02/25	St. Helena, Ca.	
Ballenger, E.S.	*B-089	05/03/01	St. Helena, Ca.	PH094 16;8MR 17
Williams, Jennie	*W-091	05/03/01	St. Helena, Ca.	
White, J.E.	*W-093	05/03/05	St. Helena, Ca.	CW 135
Gotzian, J.	G-094	05/03/11	St. Helena, Ca.	UL 79
Kress, Br-Sr. [D.H.]	*K-095	05/03/14	St. Helena, Ca.	*10MR 44-48*
Workers in the Glendale Sanitarium	*B-097	05/03/14	St. Helena, Ca.	*PC 326-328*
White, W.C.	*W-099	05/04/06	St. Helena, Ca.	PM 31
Packham, James	*P-101	05/04/07	St. Helena, Ca.	
White, J.E.	*W-102	05/04/04	St. Helena, Ca.	
Ballenger, E.S.	*B-103	05/04/09	St. Helena, Ca.	TDG 108;7MR 139
White, W.C.	*W-104	05/04/04	St. Helena, Ca.	
White, W.C.	*W-105	05/04/10	St. Helena, Ca.	
Burden, Br-Sr. [J.A.]	B-106	05/04/10	St. Helena, Ca.	
Brethren and Sisters	*B-107	05/04/09	St. Helena, Ca.	Ev 85
Walling, Addie/Walling, May	W-109	05/04/11	St. Helena, Ca.	*14MR 254-258*
White, W.C.	W-111	05/04/11	St. Helena, Ca.	5Bio 35,399
Gotzian, J.	G-113	05/04/11	St. Helena, Ca.	MM 208-209
Burden, J.A.	B-115	05/04/12	St. Helena, Ca.	*PC 231-234*
Kellogg, J.H.	*K-116	05/04/22		*20MR 346-351*
White, W.C.	W-117	05/04/14	St. Helena, Ca.	5Bio 35
Members of the Nashville Church	B-119	05/04/14	St. Helena, Ca.	TDG 113;4MR 26-28

EGW Letters File—Page 84

White, J.E.	W-121	05/03/15	St. Helena, Ca.	UL 88
Lane, S.H.	L-123	05/04/16	St. Helena, Ca.	TDG 115
White, J.E./White, Emma	W-125	05/04/10	St. Helena, Ca.	GH 04/00/1905
Brethren and Sisters	B-127	05/03/26	St. Helena, Ca.	
Hare, G.A.	H-128	05/06/08	Washington, D.C.	MM 34,192-193
White, J.E./White, Emma	W-129	05/03/28	St. Helena, Ca.	
Brethren and Sisters	B-130	05/03/30	St. Helena, Ca.	*Indiana Reporter 04/26/1905*
McEnterfer, Sara	M-131	05/04/02	St. Helena, Ca.	*13MR 230-231*
White, J.E.	W-133	05/04/30	St. Helena, Ca.	UL 134;5Bio 400
White, J.E./White, Emma	W-135	05/05/10	Washington, D.C.	Ev 503;PM 394;5Bio 401
Irwin, Sr. [G.A.]	I-137	05/05/18	St. Helena, Ca.	2MR 199
Burden, J.A.	B-139	05/05/14	Takoma Park, Md.	*PC 235-237*
Butler, G.I.	B-141	05/00/00		7MR 190
Burden, Br-Sr. [J.A.]	B-143	05/05/23	Takoma Park, Md.	PC 234
Burden, J.A.	B-145	05/05/24	Takoma Park, Md.	*PC 234-235*
Olsen, O.A.	O-146	05/05/24	Takoma Park, Md.	*KC 19-20*
White, Mabel	W-147	05/05/24	Takoma Park, Md.	3MR 45-46
Collins, Gilbert	C-149	05/05/27	Takoma Park, Md.	5Bio 414
Corliss, J.O.	C-151	05/05/27	Takoma Park, Md.	
Burden, J.A.	B-153	05/05/28	Takoma Park, Md.	*PC 240-241*
Burden, J.A.	B-155	05/05/31	Takoma Park, Md.	*PC 239-240*
Collins, Gilbert	C-157	05/05/31	Takoma Park, Md.	
Daigneau, Sr. [J.E.]	D-159	05/06/11	New Mexico	UL 176
Burden, Br-Sr. [J.A.]	B-161	05/06/25	San Jose, Ca.	*PC 250-253*
Burden, J.A.	B-161a	05/07/05	St. Helena, Ca.	*PH094 33*
Wilcox, F.M.	W-163	05/06/29	San Jose, Ca.	
Radley Children	R-165	05/06/29	San Jose, Ca.	*2SM 265-266*
Radley, Sr.	R-167	05/06/29	San Jose, Ca.	*2SM 264-265*
Harper, Sr. [Walter]	H-169	05/06/29	San Jose, Ca.	
White, J.E./White, Emma	W-171	05/06/29	San Jose, Ca.	TDG 189
White, J.E.	W-173	05/06/01	Takoma Park, Md.	
Fitzgerald, W.J.	F-175	05/06/08	Atlanta, Ga.	
Bourdeau, Patience	B-177	05/06/08	Atlanta, Ga.	*DG 98-99*
White, J.E.	W-179	05/06/09	Train to Ca.	
White, J.E.	W-179a	05/06/11	Train to Ca.	
White, J.E.	W-179b	05/07/07	St. Helena, Ca.	
White, J.E.	W-179c	05/07/21	St. Helena, Ca.	
Butler, G.I.	B-181	05/06/22	Glendale, Ca.	
Butler, G.I.	B-183	05/06/23	Glendale, Ca.	*PC 253-257*
White, J.E.	W-185	05/06/26	Takoma Park, Md.	ML 52
White, J.E.	W-186	05/06/00	Takoma Park, Md.	
Jones, A.T.	J-187	05/02/26	St. Helena, Ca.	Ev 401-402;4MR 276
White, J.E.	W-188	05/07/00	St. Helena, Ca.	CTr 198
Rand, H.F.	R-189	05/07/01	San Jose, Ca.	
Brethren in Battle Creek	*B-190	05/07/03	St. Helena, Ca.	1BC 1092-1093,1099
Haskell, S.N.	H-191	05/07/05	St. Helena, Ca.	1MCP 41;LLM 54
Harris, Stonewall Jackson	H-192	05/07/06	San Jose, Ca.	
Reaser, G.W.	R-193	05/07/07	St. Helena, Ca.	Ev 406,689-690
Ballenger, E.S.	B-195	05/07/09	St. Helena, Ca.	CD 312,323
Burden, Br-Sr. [J.A.]	B-197	05/07/10	St. Helena, Ca.	*LLM 107-108*
Brethren in Nashville	B-199	05/07/11	St. Helena, Ca.	RC 203
Evans, I.H.	E-200	05/07/19	St. Helena, Ca.	
Officers of the Southern Missionary Society	B-201	05/07/17	St. Helena, Ca.	3MR 269-270
Kress, Br-Sr. [D.H.]	K-203	05/07/18	St. Helena, Ca.	MM 324-325;LLM 52-54;9MR 369
Evans, I.H./Washburn, J.S.	B-205	05/07/19	St. Helena, Ca.	*SpM 377-381*
General Conference Committee	B-207	05/07/20	St. Helena, Ca.	SpM 381-382
Hare, Br-Sr. [G.A.]	H-208	05/07/20	St. Helena, Ca.	TDG 210

Haskell, S.N.	H-209	05/07/21	St. Helena, Ca.	
White, J.E.	W-211	05/07/22	St. Helena, Ca.	
Butler, G.I.	B-213	05/07/22	St. Helena, Ca.	Sp1B #18 15-16
Haskell, Br-Sr.	H-215	05/07/24	St. Helena, Ca.	SpTB #18 16
Place, O.G.	P-217	05/05/30	Takoma Park, Md.	
Place, O.G.	P-219	05/06/11	Train to Ca.	
Place, O.G.	P-221	05/07/12	St. Helena, Ca.	
Burden, J.A.	B-223	05/06/02	Takoma Park, Md.	UL 167;MM 87;PC 237-239;3MR 343
Butler, G.I.	B-225	05/07/24	St. Helena, Ca.	
Brn-Srs. in the Southern Union Conference	B-226	05/07/25	St. Helena, Ca.	*SW 09/05/1905*
Belden, F.E.	B-227	05/07/27	St. Helena, Ca.	PM 248
Board of Managers of the Huntsville School	B-229	05/07/30	St. Helena, Ca.	*PCO 109-112*
Kress, Br-Sr. [D.H.]	K-231	05/07/11	St. Helena, Ca.	CD 292-293;2MCP 682-683;3MR 331,368
Kress, Br-Sr. [D.H.]	K-233	05/08/09	St. Helena, Ca.	*20MR 256-263*
Daniells, A.G.	D-235	05/05/31	Takoma Park, Md.	
Hall, L.M.	H-237	05/09/04	Glendale, Ca.	6Bio 26-27
Walling, Addie/Walling, May	W-239	05/09/04	Glendale, Ca.	*PC 185-186*
White, J.E.	W-239a	05/09/22	St. Helena, Ca.	
White, W.C./White, May	*W-240	05/09/07	Glendale, Ca.	
Brethren and Sisters	B-241	05/06/26	San Jose, Ca.	SpTB #3c 20-22
White, W.C.	W-241a	05/08/13	Los Angeles, Ca.	*15MR 61-64*
White, W.B.	W-243	05/00/00		
Stowell, L.O.	S-243a	05/08/13	Los Angeles, Ca.	Te 66,255
White, W.C.	*W-244	05/09/08	Glendale, Ca.	
Holden, W.B.	H-245	05/09/00	Glendale, Ca.	*PC 196-198*
White, May Lacey	W-245a	05/08/20	Loma Linda, Ca.	
Morse, John F.	M-247	05/08/24	Loma Linda, Ca.	*PC 241-244*
Wessels, Andrew	W-248	05/08/09	St. Helena, Ca.	
Stone, W.J.	S-249	05/08/22	Loma Linda, Ca.	
Wessels, Sr. [A.E.]	W-250	05/08/09	St. Helena, Ca.	
Bourdeau, Patience	B-251	05/08/27	Loma Linda, Ca.	*LLM 121-122*
Kress, Br-Sr. [D.H.]	K-253	05/08/29	Loma Linda, Ca.	PC 244-247
White, W.C./White, May	W-255	05/09/12	National City, Ca.	
Baldridge, J.W.	B-257	05/09/13	National City, Ca.	
Hare, Br-Sr. [G.A.]	H-259	05/09/14	National City, Ca.	
Exec. Comm. of the Southern California Conf.	B-261	05/09/14	National City, Ca.	*15MR 59-60*
White, J.E.	W-263	05/09/15	National City, Ca.	1MR 394-395;6Bio 26-27
Peck, Sarah	P-265	05/09/15	National City, Ca.	*DG 92-93*
Watson, G.F.	W-267	05/01/22	Mountain View, Ca.	*2MR 99-100*
Haskell, S.N./Butler, G.I./Ford, I.A.	B-269	05/09/15	National City, Ca.	8MR 401
Burden, Br-Sr. [J.A.]	B-271	05/09/27	St. Helena, Ca.	*PC 187-189*
Burden, Br-Sr. [J.A.]	*B-272	05/09/27	St. Helena, Ca.	*LLM 130-131*
White, Mabel	W-273	05/09/28	St. Helena, Ca.	
Farnsworth, E.W.	F-275	05/10/05	St. Helena, Ca.	
Haskell, Br-Sr.	H-277	05/00/00	St. Helena, Ca.	*PC 108-111 and 198-203*
Santee, Clarence	S-279	05/10/04	St. Helena, Ca.	Ev 367;6MR 283;7MR 139;9MR 96-97; 6Bio 52-53
Kress, Br-Sr. [D.H.]	K-281	05/10/10	St. Helena, Ca.	CM 127;UL 297;2BC 1040
Wade, Br./Hill, Br.	B-283	05/10/10	St. Helena, Ca.	6Bio 42-43
Wade, Br.	W-285	05/10/02	St. Helena, Ca.	ChL 63;6Bio 40-41
Promoters of the Canon City Sanitarium	*B-287	05/10/02	St. Helena, Ca.	SpTB 45 43-52;7MR 131-132;6Bio 41
Brethren in the Ministry	B-289	05/09/13	National City, Ca.	TDG 265
White, Julia A.	W-291	05/09/15	National City, Ca.	*DG 100*
White, J.E.	W-293	05/09/26	St. Helena, Ca.	3MR 271-272
Baldwin, J.H.	B-295	05/10/18	St. Helena, Ca.	SpTB #18 22-26
Simpson, W.W. and the San Diego Church	B-297	05/10/14	St. Helena, Ca.	
Helpers at Paradise Valley Sanitarium	B-299	05/10/22	St. Helena, Ca.	*7MR 46-50*

Belden, F.E.	B-301	05/10/20	St. Helena, Ca.	3SM 63;5MR 418-422
Merrill, I.L.	M-303	05/10/26	St. Helena, Ca.	
Harper, Walter	H-305	05/10/27	St. Helena, Ca.	8MR 401;PC 190
Harper, Walter	H-307	05/10/27	St. Helena, Ca.	9MR 227-228
Burden, Br-Sr. [J.A.]	*B-309	05/11/01	St. Helena, Ca.	MM 7;LLM 137-138;PC 190-192
Daniells, A.G./Prescott, W.W. and associates	B-311	05/10/30	St. Helena, Ca.	*BCL 122-128*
White, Mabel	W-313	05/11/02	St. Helena, Ca.	UL 320
Burden, J.A.	B-315	05/11/03	St. Helena, Ca.	
Brn. in the Ministry and Med. Miss. Work	B-317	05/04/10	St. Helena, Ca.	PC 11
Brn. in the Ministry and Med. Miss. Work	B-317a	05/04/10	St. Helena, Ca.	TDG 109
Kellogg, J.H.	K-319	05/06/02	Takoma Park, Md.	*BCL 118-121*
Kellogg, J.H.	*K-320	03/11/21	Filed in 1905	5MR 439
White, J.E./White, Emma	W-321	05/11/27	St. Helena, Ca.	2MR 252-253
Belden, Br-Sr. [S.T.]	B-322	05/11/26	St. Helena, Ca.	*PC 5-7*
Daniells, A.G./Irwin, G.A./Butler, G.I./Haskell, S.N.	B-323	05/11/27	St. Helena, Ca.	
Burden, Br-Sr. [J.A.]	B-325	05/12/10	St. Helena, Ca.	PC 203-204
White, W.C.	*W-326	05/12/04	St. Helena, Ca.	UL 352
White, W.C.	W-327	05/12/10	St. Helena, Ca.	1NL 45-46
Burden, J.A.	B-329	05/12/11	St. Helena, Ca.	*PC 204-209*
White, Mabel	W-329a	05/11/16	St. Helena, Ca.	3SM 52;6BC 1073;TDG 329
Brn-Srs. in Nashville	B-331	05/12/14	St. Helena, Ca.	
Prescott, W.W./Daniells, A.G.	B-333	05/12/16	St. Helena, Ca.	6Bio 72
White, W.C.	W-334	05/12/28	St. Helena, Ca.	Te 236
White, W.C.	W-335	05/12/19	St. Helena, Ca.	2MCP 606-607
Christiansen, Jessie	C-337	05/12/19	St. Helena, Ca.	PC 209-211
Kellogg, J.H.	*K-338	05/12/22	St. Helena, Ca.	6MR 378-379;5Bio 423
White, Mabel	W-339	05/12/01	St. Helena, Ca.	OHC 276;2MCP 669;3MR 135-136
White, W.C.	W-341	05/12/27	St. Helena, Ca.	
Brethren in Nashville	B-343	05/00/00		
Amadon, George	*A-345	05/12/29	St. Helena, Ca.	
White, W.C.	*W-346	05/11/29	St. Helena, Ca.	
White, W.C.	*W-348	05/12/07	St. Helena, Ca.	
White, W.C.	*W-349	05/12/18	St. Helena, Ca.	
White, J.E.	*W-350	05/03/07	St. Helena, Ca.	
White, J.E./White, Emma	*W-351	05/01/00	St. Helena, Ca.	
White, W.C.	*W-352	05/12/29	St. Helena, Ca.	6Bio 67-68
Crisler, C.C. & wife & mother/White, May	*W-353	05/08/27	Loma Linda, Ca.	
Vincent, Br.	*V-354	05/06/11	New Mexico	11MR 105
Zelinsky, Br.	*Z-356	05/11/06	St. Helena, Ca.	
Robinson, Br-Sr. [D.E.]	*R-358	05/12/24	St. Helena, Ca.	
White, W.C.	*W-359	05/12/07	St. Helena, Ca.	
Kellogg, J.H.	K-360	05/03/20		
Druillard, Sr.	*D-361	05/12/14	St. Helena, Ca.	
White, W.C.	*W-362	05/03/01	St. Helena, Ca.	
Irwin, Sr.	*I-363	05/02/22	St. Helena, Ca.	
Olsen, Sr.	*O-364	05/08/09	St. Helena, Ca.	

1906

Kellogg, Br-Sr. [W.K.]	K-010	06/01/01	St. Helena, Ca.	6Bio 74
Olsen, Br-Sr. [O.A.]	O-012	06/01/02	St. Helena, Ca.	
Kress, Br-Sr. [D.H.]	K-014	06/01/03	St. Helena, Ca.	UL 17
Workman, Mabel E.	W-018a	06/11/15	St. Helena, Ca.	*21MR 79-82*
White, W.C.	*W-022	06/01/08	St. Helena, Ca.	3SM 352;13MR 363-364
White, W.C.	W-024	06/01/09	St. Helena, Ca.	
White, W.C.	W-026	06/01/15	St. Helena, Ca.	
Robinson, T.H.	R-026a	06/01/02	St. Helena, Ca.	

EGW Letters File—Page 87

White, J.E.	W-027	06/01/15	St. Helena, Ca.	
Amadon, G.W.	A-028	06/01/15	St. Helena, Ca.	*PC 93*
Brn-Srs. in Battle Creek	B-030	06/01/12	St. Helena, Ca.	*13MR 318-322*
White, W.C.	W-032	06/01/16	St. Helena, Ca.	ML 311;9MR 172
White, J.E.	W-033	06/01/19	St. Helena, Ca.	
Burden, Br-Sr. [J.A.]	B-034	06/01/19	St. Helena, Ca.	*LLM 154-158*
Brn-Srs. in Battle Creek	B-036	06/01/23	St. Helena, Ca.	
Wahroonga Sanitarium Family	B-038	06/01/23	St. Helena, Ca.	3MR 39;9MR 40;6Bio 76-77
Hughes, Br-Sr. [C.B.]	H-040	06/01/23	St. Helena, Ca.	MR760 20-21
White, W.C.	W-042	06/01/23	St. Helena, Ca.	VSS 347
Olsen, Br-Sr. [O.A.]/Kress, Br-Sr. [D.H.]	O-044	06/01/23	St. Helena, Ca.	
Brethren	B-046	06/01/25	St. Helena, Ca.	
Irwin, G.A.	I-048	06/01/26	St. Helena, Ca.	
Simpson, W.W.	S-050	06/01/30	St. Helena, Ca.	*MR760 21-23*
Farnsworth, Br-Sr. [E.W.]	F-052	06/01/29	St. Helena, Ca.	1MR 28;7BC 922;7ABC 465;6Bio 101
Farnsworth, Br-Sr. [E.W.]	F-054	06/01/30	St. Helena, Ca.	*21MR 436-438*
Robinson, Br-Sr. [D.E.]	R-056	06/02/01	St. Helena, Ca.	
White, W.C.	*W-057	06/02/07	St. Helena, Ca.	
Washburn, J./Prescott/Daniells/Colcord, W.A.	B-058	06/01/16	St. Helena, Ca.	PM 222;TDG 24;9MR 125
Haskell, Br-Sr.	H-060	06/02/08	St. Helena, Ca.	7MR 266-267
White, W.C.	*W-061	06/02/09	St. Helena, Ca.	
Palmer, W.O.	P-062	06/01/21	St. Helena, Ca.	
Rand, H.F.	R-064	06/02/15	St. Helena, Ca.	
Haskell, Br-Sr.	H-066	06/02/10	St. Helena, Ca.	TDG 49;7MR 403
Haskell, Br-Sr.	H-068	06/02/17	St. Helena, Ca.	
Amadon, Br-Sr. [G.W.]	A-070	06/01/30	St. Helena, Ca.	5MR 169
Farnsworth, Br-Sr. [E.W.]	F-072	06/02/19	St. Helena, Ca.	UL 64;8MR 310;11MR 365-366
Jones, C.H.	J-074	06/01/28	St. Helena, Ca.	
Squires, George	S-076	06/02/22	St. Helena, Ca.	
Haskell, Br-Sr.	H-078	06/02/25	St. Helena, Ca.	SD 196;PM 225-226;2SM 230-231
Wilcox, F.M.	W-080	06/02/15	St. Helena, Ca.	TDG 54
Capehart, Fannie Ashurst	C-082	06/02/28	St. Helena, Ca.	*DG 219-220,274-275*
Farnsworth, Br-Sr. [E.W.]	F-084	06/02/17	St. Helena, Ca.	TDG 56
Butler, G.I.	B-086	06/03/08	St. Helena, Ca.	*3SM 71-72 with TDG 76 and 10MR 343-344*
Butler, G.I.	B-088	06/03/09	St. Helena, Ca.	RY 123-124;3BC 1141
Brn. Assembled in council at Graysville, Tn.	B-090	06/03/06	St. Helena, Ca.	3SM 122;TDG 74;7BC 931;7MR 192-193
Officers of the Southern Union Conference	B-092	06/03/05	St. Helena, Ca.	*SpM 387*
McPherson, Addie Walling	M-094	06/03/01	St. Helena, Ca.	PC 211-213
Haskell, Br-Sr.	H-096	06/03/11	St. Helena, Ca.	7MR 403
Farnsworth, Br-Sr. [E.W.]	F-098	06/03/12	St. Helena, Ca.	*PC 122-123*
Belden, Br-Sr. [S.T.]	B-100	06/03/23	St. Helena, Ca.	TDG 91
Druillard, N.H.	D-102	06/03/25	St. Helena, Ca.	5MR 92-93;6Bio 78
Haskell, Br-Sr.	H-104	06/04/01	St. Helena, Ca.	
Robinson, Br-Sr. [D.E.]	R-106	06/03/30	St. Helena, Ca.	
White, Mabel	W-108	06/03/30	St. Helena, Ca.	
Wilson, Sr. [J.]	W-110	06/03/30	St. Helena, Ca.	
Foss, Mary	F-112	06/04/02	St. Helena, Ca.	*14MR 258-262*
Brn. Assembled in Council at Washington	B-114	06/04/02	St. Helena, Ca.	*SpM 388-389*
Paulson, Br-Sr. [D.]	P-116	06/04/02	St. Helena, Ca.	5Bio 414,416-417,420
Sadler, Br-Sr. [W.S.]	S-118	06/04/02	St. Helena, Ca.	
Those Who Are Perplexed Re the Testimonies	B-120	06/03/30	St. Helena, Ca.	6Bio 90
Jones, A.T.	*J-121	05/04/09	Filed in 1906	13 Crisis Years 323
Robinson, Br-Sr. [D.E.]	R-122	06/04/11	St. Helena, Ca.	
White, J.E./White, Emma	W-124	06/04/10	St. Helena, Ca.	
Butler, G.I.	B-126	06/04/11	St. Helena, Ca.	UL 115;2MCP 793
Butler, G.I.	B-128	06/04/11	St. Helena, Ca.	

EGW Letters File—Page 88

Lunt, Sr./Winslow, Sr.	L-130	06/02/23	St. Helena, Ca.	
Andre, Rosa	A-132	06/06/26	St. Helena, Ca.	
Paulson/Read/Edwards/Morse/Riley/Arthur	B-134	06/05/08	St. Helena, Ca.	
Butler, G.I./Daniells, A.G./Irwin, G.A.	B-136	06/04/27	Loma Linda, Ca.	2SM 53;3SM 54;5MR 154
White, J.E./White, Emma	W-137	06/04/26	Loma Linda, Ca.	
Farnsworth, Br-Sr. [E.W.]	F-138	06/05/15	St. Helena, Ca.	
Burden, J.A.	B-140	06/05/06	Mountain View, Ca.	*LLM 165-171*
White, J.E./White, Emma	W-141	06/05/10	St. Helena, Ca.	*21MR 83-84*
Burden, Br-Sr. [J.A.]	B-142	06/05/17	St. Helena, Ca.	*LLM 174-176*
White, J.E./White, Emma	*W-143	06/05/21	St. Helena, Ca.	4MR 240;6Bio 101
Church in Mountain View	B-144	06/05/04	Mountain View, Ca.	UL 138;CG 272;CC 143
Jones, C.H.	J-146	06/05/23	St. Helena, Ca.	
Nicola, C.C.	N-148	06/05/14	St. Helena, Ca.	*LLM 172-174*
Nicola, Br-Sr. [C.C.]	N-150	06/05/15	St. Helena, Ca.	SpTB #13 14-16
Butler, G.I.	B-152	06/05/22	St. Helena, Ca.	
White, J.E./White, Emma	W-154	06/05/12	St. Helena, Ca.	*21MR 85-89*
Faulkhead, N.D.	F-156	06/05/29	St. Helena, Ca.	11MR 164
Kress, Br-Sr. [D.H.]	K-158	06/05/10	St. Helena, Ca.	*21MR 90-92*
Olsen, O.A.	O-160	06/05/30	St. Helena, Ca.	
Kress, Br-Sr. [D.H.]	K-162	06/05/29	St. Helena, Ca.	3SM 349;4BC 1143
King, Martha/Nicola, Br-Sr. [C.C.]	K-164	06/05/28	St. Helena, Ca.	PC 215
Harper, Walter	H-166	06/05/30	St. Helena, Ca.	
McDearmon, Sr.	M-168	06/05/30	St. Helena, Ca.	UL 164
Stewart, C.E.	S-170	06/06/13	St. Helena, Ca.	*SpM 462-265*
Paulson, David/Sadler, W.S.	B-172	06/06/14	St. Helena, Ca.	*PC 32-34*
Nicola, Br-Sr. [C.C.]	N-174	06/06/07	St. Helena, Ca.	
Prescott, W.W.	P-176	06/06/15	St. Helena, Ca.	
Prescott, Br-Sr. [W.W.]	P-178	06/06/13	St. Helena, Ca.	
Nicola, Br-Sr. [C.C.]	N-180	06/06/15	St. Helena, Ca.	6Bio 95
Haskell, Br-Sr.	H-182	06/06/15	St. Helena, Ca.	Ev 84
Faulkhead, N.D.	F-184	06/06/10	St. Helena, Ca.	
Salisbury, W.D./Olsen, O.A.	S-186	06/05/31	St. Helena, Ca.	*20MR 167-169*
Olsen, O.A./Kress, D.H.	O-188	06/06/18	St. Helena, Ca.	*20MR 170-174*
Taylor, C.L.	T-190	06/06/22	St. Helena, Ca.	
Haskell, Br-Sr.	H-192	06/06/08	St. Helena, Ca.	*LLM 179-180*
Morse, John F.	M-194	06/06/26	St. Helena, Ca.	
Place, O.G. and associates at Boulder, Co.	P-196	06/06/26	St. Helena, Ca.	6Bio 36
Place, A.E.	P-198	06/06/26	St. Helena, Ca.	6Bio 36
Amadon, Br-Sr. [G.W.]	A-200	06/06/26	St. Helena, Ca.	*PC 125-126*
Place, A.E.	P-202	06/06/26	St. Helena, Ca.	Ev 392
Burden, J.A.	B-204	06/06/17	St. Helena, Ca.	SpM 389-391
Paulson, David	P-206	06/06/14	St. Helena, Ca.	1SM 24-31;5BC 1083
Tenney, G.C.	T-208	06/06/29	St. Helena, Ca.	PM 314;MR760 27-28
Reaser, G.W.	R-210	06/06/29	St. Helena, Ca.	
Read, A.J.	R-212	06/07/02	St. Helena, Ca.	*10MR 162-163*
Ministers and Physicians/Aggressive Work	B-214	06/07/03	St. Helena, Ca.	*PC 81-83*
n.a./Brother	B-216	06/07/02	St. Helena, Ca.	8MR 31
Elders of the Battle Creek Church/Ministers	B-218	06/06/28	St. Helena, Ca.	Ev 220;4MR 417-418
White, J.E./White, Emma	W-222	06/07/01	St. Helena, Ca.	
Sadler, W.S.	S-224	06/07/06	St. Helena, Ca.	1MR 35
Sadler, Br-Sr. [W.S.]	*S-224a	06/07/00	St. Helena, Ca.	
Brother/Writing and Sending Out of the Test.	B-225	06/07/08	St. Helena, Ca.	1SM 49-53
Brother/Writing and Sending Out of the Test.	B-225a	06/07/08	St. Helena, Ca.	See 1SM 49-53
Brother/Writing and Sending Out of the Test.	B-225b	06/07/08	St. Helena, Ca.	See 1SM 49-53
Sadler, W.S. [variant]	B-225c	06/07/08	St. Helena, Ca.	See 1SM 49-53
Sadler, Br-Sr. [W.S.]	S-225d	06/06/28	St. Helena, Ca.	
Butler, G.I.	B-226	06/07/08	St. Helena, Ca.	TDG 198

EGW Letters File—Page 89

Scott, Br./Ballenger, E.S./Buchanan, R.A.	B-228	06/07/08	St. Helena, Ca.	
Elders of the Battle Creek Church/Ministers	B-230	06/07/05	St. Helena, Ca.	*PC 73-76*
n.a./Brother	B-232	06/07/09	St. Helena, Ca.	
Sadler, W.S./Brother	S-234	06/07/09	St. Helena, Ca.	9MR 205-206
Gibbs, Br.	G-236	06/07/10	St. Helena, Ca.	
Gilbert, Lily Belden	G-238	06/07/04	St. Helena, Ca.	
White, Emma	W-240	06/07/09	St. Helena, Ca.	
Jones, A.T.	J-242	06/07/03	St. Helena, Ca.	KC 33-40
Elders of the Battle Creek Church	B-244	06/07/17	St. Helena, Ca.	1SM 36;12MR 87-88
To My Brethren in Battle Creek	B-244a	06/06/06c		variant of B-244-1906
Buchanan, R.A.	B-246	06/07/27	Oakland, Ca.	
Kress, Br-Sr. [D.H.]	K-248	06/07/27	Oakland, Ca.	
Starr, Br-Sr. [G.B.]	S-250	06/08/01	St. Helena, Ca.	6Bio 106
Olsen, Br-Sr. [O.A.]	O-252	06/07/25	Oakland, Ca.	*21MR 138-140*
Haskell, Br-Sr.	H-254	06/07/30	Oakland, Ca.	6Bio 110
Ministering Brethren in Australia	B-256	06/08/01	St. Helena, Ca.	TDG 222;5MR 351
Kress, Br-Sr. [D.H.]	K-258	06/08/01	St. Helena, Ca.	
Workers in Oakland	*B-260	06/07/29	Oakland, Ca.	PM 182-183
Haskell, Br-Sr.	H-262	06/08/02	St. Helena, Ca.	
Daniells, A.G.	D-264	06/08/07	St. Helena, Ca.	
White, J.E./White, Emma	W-266	06/08/05	St. Helena, Ca.	7MR 193
Kress, Br-Sr. [D.H.]	K-268	06/08/20	Oakland, Ca.	TMK 210;LDE 114;ChL 12
Cobb, S.M.	C-270	06/08/22	St. Helena, Ca.	
Simpson, W.W.	S-272	06/08/20	Oakland, Ca.	6Bio 110
Reaser/Burden/Exec. Comm. of S. Cal. Conf.	B-274	06/08/19	Oakland, Ca.	*PC 218-220*
Brn. Engaged in Medical Work in Colorado	B-276	06/08/20	Oakland, Ca.	
White, W.C.	W-278	06/08/27	St. Helena, Ca.	Ev 29
Brn-Srs. in Denver and Boulder	B-280	06/08/27	St. Helena, Ca.	TDG 248;5MR 151
White, W.C.	W-282	06/08/22	St. Helena, Ca.	
Place, O.G.	P-284	06/08/29	St. Helena, Ca.	
Logan, Roy	L-286	06/09/03	St. Helena, Ca.	PC 220-221
White, J.E.	W-288	06/09/04	St. Helena, Ca.	6Bio 109
Kress, Br-Sr. [D.H.]	K-290	06/09/02	St. Helena, Ca.	OHC 16
Kress, Br-Sr. [D.H.]	K-292	06/09/04	St. Helena, Ca.	TDG 256
Olsen, Sr. [O.A.]	O-294	06/09/09	St. Helena, Ca.	1MCP 68;2MCP 400-401
Olsen, O.A.	O-296	06/09/09	St. Helena, Ca.	UL 266
Belden, Br-Sr. [S.T.]	B-298	06/09/11	St. Helena, Ca.	
White, Emma	W-300	06/09/17	St. Helena, Ca.	
Washburn, J.S.	W-302	06/09/30	St. Helena, Ca.	
Burden, Br-Sr. [J.A.]	B-304	06/09/14	St. Helena, Ca.	*LLM 185-187*
Kress, Br-Sr. [D.H.]	K-306	06/07/27	Oakland, Ca.	PC 331-332;6Bio 109
Starr, Br-Sr. [G.B.]	S-308	06/10/03	St. Helena, Ca.	Ev 540
Salisbury, W.D./Echo Publishing Co.	S-310	06/10/06	St. Helena, Ca.	*20MR 175-177*
White, J.E.	W-311	06/10/05	St. Helena, Ca.	
White, J.E.	W-311a	06/11/28	St. Helena, Ca.	
White, J.E.	W-311b	06/05/10	St. Helena, Ca.	
Belden, Br-Sr. [S.T.]	B-312	06/10/03	St. Helena, Ca.	2SM 256
Olsen, O.A.	O-314	06/10/02	St. Helena, Ca.	UL 289
Brn-Srs. in Nashville and in Madison	B-318	06/10/15	St. Helena, Ca.	TDG 297;SpTB #11 17-18;SpM 391-393
Haskell, Br-Sr.	H-320	06/10/14	St. Helena, Ca.	ML 152;7MR 404
Olsen, Sr. [O.A.]	O-322	06/10/23	St. Helena, Ca.	TDG 305
Sisley, Sr.	S-324	06/10/23	St. Helena, Ca.	
Belden, Br-Sr. [S.T.]	B-326	06/10/22	St. Helena, Ca.	Ev 204
Kress, Br-Sr. [D.H.]	K-328	06/10/23	St. Helena, Ca.	
Cobb, S.M.	*C-330	06/10/23	St. Helena, Ca.	2SM 198-199
Cobb, S.M.	*C-331	06/10/24	St. Helena, Ca.	
Olsen, O.A.	O-332	06/10/23	St. Helena, Ca.	9MR 147

EGW Letters File—Page 90

Faulkhead, Br-Sr. [N.D.] and children	F-334	06/10/24	St. Helena, Ca.	
Brn. in Responsible Positions in Australia	B-336	06/10/25	St. Helena, Ca.	1MR 80-81;4MR 355
Salisbury, W.D.	S-338	06/10/24	St. Helena, Ca.	
Washburn, J.S.	W-340	06/10/17	St. Helena, Ca.	
White, J.E./White, Emma	W-342	06/10/16	St. Helena, Ca.	3SM 266
Simpson, W.W.	S-344	06/10/27	St. Helena, Ca.	7MR 193-194
Cornell, M.E.	C-346	06/10/25	St. Helena, Ca.	
Butler, G.I.	B-348	06/10/30	St. Helena, Ca.	RY 62;2MR 71;SpTB #11 18-19; PH116 19-24;PC 332-333
Burden, J.A.	*B-349	06/11/02	St. Helena, Ca.	*PC 223-224*
Belden, F.E.	B-350	06/11/06	St. Helena, Ca.	Ev 204-205;PM 359
Washburn, J.S.	W-352	06/11/06	St. Helena, Ca.	Ev 76,577;SpTB #11 19-20
Harper, Walter	*H-353	06/11/09	San Francisco, Ca.	5MR 287;11MR 199
Amadon, G.W.	A-354	06/09/19	St. Helena, Ca.	HFM 82-84;10MR 62
Olsen, O.A.	O-356	06/11/14	St. Helena, Ca.	Ev 211
Workers at the Madison School	B-358	06/11/15	St. Helena, Ca.	*SpM 393*
Olsen, O.A.	O-360	06/11/15	St. Helena, Ca.	4BC 1178-1179
Lane, Sr. [S.H.]	L-362	06/11/15	St. Helena, Ca.	DG 222-223
Hopkins, Hannah Sawyer	H-364	06/11/16	St. Helena, Ca.	
Hibbard, E.J.	H-366	06/12/03	St. Helena, Ca.	Ev 184,304
Belden, Br-Sr. [S.T.]	B-368	06/12/04	St. Helena, Ca.	
Belden, F.E.	B-370	06/12/06	St. Helena, Ca.	
Olsen, O.A./Kress, D.H.	B-372	06/12/04	St. Helena, Ca.	Ev 283-284;TDG 347;MRmnt 110
Haskell, Br-Sr.	H-374	06/12/09	St. Helena, Ca.	
Simpson, W.W.	S-376	06/12/04	St. Helena, Ca.	Ev 76,438,470;13MR 304
Butcher, Br-Sr. [William]	B-378	06/12/10	St. Helena, Ca.	
Haskell, Br-Sr.	H-380	06/12/13	St. Helena, Ca.	Ev 327;6Bio 112-113
Haskell, Br-Sr.	H-382	06/12/14	Oakland, Ca.	
Leaders in the Oakland and Berkeley Churches	B-384	06/12/17	Berkeley, Ca.	
Haskell, Br-Sr.	*H-385	06/12/17	Berkeley, Ca.	
Haskell, Br-Sr.	*H-386	06/12/17	Berkeley, Ca.	
White, J.E./White, Emma	W-388	06/12/17	Berkeley, Ca.	Ev 257
White, J.E.	*W-390	06/12/19	St. Helena, Ca.	
White, J.E.	*W-391	06/00/00		6Bio 100-101
Beerman, Marie	B-392	06/12/16	St. Helena, Ca.	6Bio 117
Belden, Vina	B-393	06/12/16	St. Helena, Ca.	*10MR 145-146*
Haskell, S.N.	H-394	06/12/21	St. Helena, Ca.	
Cobb, S.M.	C-395	06/12/25	St. Helena, Ca.	11MR 153
Belden, Sr. [S.T.]	B-396	06/12/26	St. Helena, Ca.	RY 164-165
Those Bearing Responsibilities in Wash., D.C.	B-397	06/12/27	St. Helena, Ca.	
Kress, Br-Sr. [D.H.]	K-398	06/12/26	St. Helena, Ca.	TDG 369
Olsen, O.A.	O-400	06/12/26	St. Helena, Ca.	*PC 98-100*
Magan, P.T.	*M-403	06/02/10	St. Helena, Ca.	*SpM 385-387*
Jones, A.T.	*J-404	06/10/26	St. Helena, Ca.	
n.a./Sister	B-406	06/00/00		TMK 174,290;6BC 1074
Kress, Br-Sr.	K-407	06/01/22	St. Helena, Ca.	

1907

Brn-Srs. in Avondale	B-004	07/01/17	St. Helena, Ca.	8MR 263
Church Members in Australasia	B-006	07/01/17	St. Helena, Ca.	*AUCR 03/11/1907*
Olsen, O.A. and his fellow-workers	O-008	07/01/17	St. Helena, Ca.	*AUCR 03/18/1907*
Members of the Oakland Church	*B-010	07/01/18	St. Helena, Ca.	*21MR 93-94*
Nicola, Br-Sr. [C.C.]	N-012	07/01/23	St. Helena, Ca.	UL 37;1MR 135
Taylor, E.G.	T-014	07/01/25	St. Helena, Ca.	
Haskell, Br-Sr.	H-016	07/01/30	St. Helena, Ca.	Ev 366
Belden, Vina	B-018	07/02/03	St. Helena, Ca.	10MR 86

Olsen, O.A.	O-020	07/02/02	St. Helena, Ca.	KC 166-167
Kress, D.H.	K-022	07/02/03	St. Helena, Ca.	
Daniells, A.G.	D-024	07/02/04		2MR 106;6Bio 120
Salisbury, W.D.	S-026	07/02/05	St. Helena, Ca.	2SM 357;2MCP 709;8MR 1
Olsen, O.A.	O-028	07/02/05	St. Helena, Ca.	3SM 42;HP 248
Faulkhead, N.D.	F-030	07/02/05	St. Helena, Ca.	*19MR 35-37*
Members of our Churches in Melbourne	B-032	07/02/05	St. Helena, Ca.	*19MR 233-238*
Olsen, Sr. [O.A.]	O-034	07/02/06	St. Helena, Ca.	TDG 45
Irwin, C.W. and others in the Avondale School	I-036	07/02/06	St. Helena, Ca.	8MR 369-371
Hart, Russell	H-038	07/02/04	St. Helena, Ca.	UL 49;11MR 213-215;CTr 32
Hayes, E.G.	H-040	07/02/05	St. Helena, Ca.	*SpM 398-399*
Wilcox, F.M.	W-042	07/02/08	St. Helena, Ca.	OHC 36
Sheafe, L.C.	S-044	07/02/04	St. Helena, Ca.	*13MR 159-165*
Daniells, A.G.	D-046	07/01/25	St. Helena, Ca.	
Cal. Conf. Comm./Brn-Srs. in Berkeley/Oakland	B-048	07/02/01	St. Helena, Ca.	Ev 690-691;3SM 408;1MR 263
Belden, F.E.	B-050	07/02/06	St. Helena, Ca.	7MR 271-272
Belden, F.E.	B-052	07/02/09	St. Helena, Ca.	
Gotzain, J.	G-054	07/02/23	St. Helena, Ca.	CD 295;6Bio 144
Workers in the Paradise Valley Sanitarium	B-056	07/02/12	St. Helena, Ca.	*PC 226-228*
Board of Paradise Valley Sanitarium	B-058	07/02/13	St. Helena, Ca.	
Southern Union Conference Committee	B-060	07/02/24	St. Helena, Ca.	*SpTB #11 24-26*
Brethren in Graysville, Tn.	B-062	07/02/11	St. Helena, Ca.	*SpM 397-398*
Wessels, J.J.	W-064	07/02/21	St. Helena, Ca.	
Palmer, E.R.	P-066	07/02/21	St. Helena, Ca.	PM 124,314;7MR 194
Haskell, S.N.	H-068	07/02/24	St. Helena, Ca.	
Haskell, S.N.	H-070	07/02/26	St. Helena, Ca.	*1MR 168-170*
Palmer, E.R.	*P-072	07/02/25	St. Helena, Ca.	CM 141;PM 124;1MR 170-171
Members of the Berkeley Churches	B-078	07/03/05	St. Helena, Ca.	TDG 73
Members of the Australasian Churches	B-080	07/03/05	St. Helena, Ca.	*AUCR 04/29/1907*
Olsen, O.A.	O-082	07/03/05	St. Helena, Ca.	UL 78
Kress, D.H.	K-084	07/03/05	St. Helena, Ca.	
Churches in the Large Cities	B-086	07/03/04	St. Helena, Ca.	UL 77;TDG 72;WM 161-162
Our People in Washington, D.C.	B-088	07/03/04	St. Helena, Ca.	
White, J.E./White, Emma	W-090	07/03/10	St. Helena, Ca.	3SM 51;5MR 111,282
Workers in the Boulder Sanitarium	B-094	07/03/14	St. Helena, Ca.	UL 87
Haskell, S.N.	H-096	07/03/06	St. Helena, Ca.	
Haskell, Br-Sr.	H-098	07/03/15	St. Helena, Ca.	3BC 1134
Campbell, M.N.	C-100	07/03/13	St. Helena, Ca.	3BC 1134;CTr 185
Haskell, Br-Sr.	H-102	07/03/17	St. Helena, Ca.	2MR 252-254
Those making Large Gifts to the Cause	B-104	07/03/19	St. Helena, Ca.	*NUR 04/16/1907*
Rasmussan, Sr.	R-106	07/03/19	St. Helena, Ca.	3SM 32
Cottrell, H.W.	C-107	07/03/19	St. Helena, Ca.	
Brethren in Graysville	B-108	07/03/18	St. Helena, Ca.	UL 91
White, J.E.	W-110	07/03/22	St. Helena, Ca.	
Nashville Sanitarium/Southern Union Conf.	B-112	07/03/10	St. Helena, Ca.	*SpM 402-405*
Daniells, A.G./Kress, D.H./Irwin, G.A.	B-114	07/04/02	St. Helena, Ca.	2MR 49-50
Campbell, M.N.	C-116	07/03/23	St. Helena, Ca.	*PC 119-122*
Daniells, A.G.	D-118	07/01/19	St. Helena, Ca.	*SpM 395-396*
Burden, J.A.	B-120	07/04/03	St. Helena, Ca.	*LLM 201-203*
Crawford, Marian Stowell	C-122	07/04/01	St. Helena, Ca.	9MR 119-120
Nicola, Sr. [C.C.]	N-124	07/04/04	St. Helena, Ca.	
Crawford, Marian Stowell	C-126	07/04/03	St. Helena, Ca.	
Haskell, Br-Sr.	H-128	07/04/04	St. Helena, Ca.	
White, J.E.	W-130	07/04/05	St. Helena, Ca.	
Ballenger, J.F.	B-132	07/04/04	St. Helena, Ca.	
Gotzain, J.	G-134	07/04/05	St. Helena, Ca.	
McDearmon, Sr.	M-136	07/03/25	St. Helena, Ca.	

EGW Letters File—Page 92

Simpson, W.W.	S-138	07/04/09	St. Helena, Ca.	
White, J.E./White, Emma	W-140	07/04/08	St. Helena, Ca.	8MR 103
Wilcox, F.M.	W-142	07/04/09	St. Helena, Ca.	
Brn-Srs. in Battle Creek	B-144	07/04/11	St. Helena, Ca.	
Haskell, Br-Sr.	H-146	07/04/16	St. Helena, Ca.	
Harper, Sr. [Walter]	H-148	07/04/16	St. Helena, Ca.	*TSB 74-75*
Workers at Pardise Valley Sanitarium	B-150	07/04/17	St. Helena, Ca.	
Brethren in Battle Creek	B-152	07/04/17	St. Helena, Ca.	*PC 77-80*
Washburn, J.S.	W-154	07/04/17	St. Helena, Ca.	*SpM 408-409*
Washburn, J.S.	W-156	07/04/18	St. Helena, Ca.	*SpM 410-411*
Friends who are Caring for Elder Simpson	B-158	07/04/26	Loma Linda, Ca.	
Starr, Br-Sr. [J.A.]	*S-160	07/04/30	Loma Linda, Ca.	TDG 129
White, W.C.	W-162	07/05/08	National City, Ca.	3SM 60
White, J.E.	W-164	07/05/07	National City, Ca.	PC 228
White, W.C.	W-166	07/05/13	Loma Linda, Ca.	
Magan, P.T.	M-168	07/05/14	Loma Linda, Ca.	*SpM 411-412*
Campbell, M.N./Amadon, G.A.	C-170	07/05/06	National City, Ca.	*PC 117-119*
Magan, P.T.	M-172	07/05/15	Loma Linda, Ca.	*21MR 463-464*
White, J.E.	*W-173	07/05/16	Loma Linda, Ca.	
Brethren and Sisters/An Open Letter	B-174	07/05/19	Loma Linda, Ca.	*PC 228-230*
Haskell, Br-Sr.	H-176	07/05/20	St. Helena, Ca.	PC 230-231
White, J.E.	W-178	07/05/17	Loma Linda, Ca.	2MR 15
Brethren at the Merced Camp-Meeting	B-180	07/05/29	St. Helena, Ca.	5BC 1100
Robinson, A.T.	R-182	07/05/22	Glendale, Ca.	*PC 285-286*
Wolfsen, Br.	W-184	07/06/04		
Butler, G.I.	B-186	07/05/29	St. Helena, Ca.	Ev 97;PC 286-288
Friend	B-188	07/05/30	St. Helena, Ca.	LDE 107;1MR 127-128
Brethren	B-190	07/05/06	National City, Ca.	RC 204
Caro, E.R.	C-192	07/06/12	St. Helena, Ca.	
White, Emma	W-194	07/06/13	St. Helena, Ca.	7MR 50
Belden, Hattie	B-196	07/06/12	St. Helena, Ca.	
White, J.E.	W-198	07/06/11	St. Helena, Ca.	
Belden, Vina/Believers on Norfolk Island	B-200	07/06/10	St. Helena, Ca.	10MR 146-149
Brethren who are Laboring in Merced	B-202	07/06/13	St. Helena, Ca.	5MR 345-346
n.a./A Pioneer	B-204	07/06/06	St. Helena, Ca.	Ev 106-107,332,633;OHC 16
Tenney, J.E.	T-206	07/06/03	St. Helena, Ca.	5MR 358
Teachers in the Graysville Academy	B-208	07/06/18	St. Helena, Ca.	
Amadon, G.W.	A-210	07/06/19	St. Helena, Ca.	
Starr, Lillis Wood	S-212	07/06/15	St. Helena, Ca.	
Sawyer, Robert/Hopkins, Hannah Sawyer	H-216	07/07/08	St. Helena, Ca.	
Workers in Nashville	B-218	07/06/18	St. Helena, Ca.	
Nicola, Br-Sr. [C.C.]	N-220	07/07/09		incl. 07/06/20
Nicola, Br-Sr. [C.C.]	N-221	07/07/20	St. Helena, Ca.	
Battle Creek Church	B-222	07/07/02	St. Helena, Ca.	*PC 71-72*
Cottrell, H.W.	C-224	07/07/10	St. Helena, Ca.	4Bio 1165;6Bio 133
Churches in San Francisco, Oakland, Berkeley	B-226	07/06/23	St. Helena, Ca.	
Officers of the General Conference	B-228	07/06/14	St. Helena, Ca.	2MR 72-73;4MR 29-30
White, J.E./White, Emma	W-230	07/07/22	St. Helena, Ca.	SD 228;LDE 115
Burden, J.A.	B-232	07/08/01	St. Helena, Ca.	
Nicola, Br-Sr. [C.C.]	N-234	07/08/02	St. Helena, Ca.	
Baird, A.S.	B-236	07/07/26	St. Helena, Ca.	
Baird, Br-Sr. [A.S.]	B-238	07/07/29	St. Helena, Ca.	2MCP 558
Olsen, O.A.	O-240	07/08/04	St. Helena, Ca.	
Nicola, Mary	N-242	07/08/06	St. Helena, Ca.	*LLM 226-227*
Burden, J.A.	B-244	07/08/08	St. Helena, Ca.	*LLM 227-229*
Laborers in Southern California	B-246	07/07/29	St. Helena, Ca.	6Bio 148,151
Colorado Conference	B-248	07/08/13	St. Helena, Ca.	1MCP 22-23

Haskell, Br-Sr.	H-250	07/08/15	St. Helena, Ca.	6Bio 134
Colorado Conf. Comm./Place, Br.	B-252	07/08/15	St. Helena, Ca.	
Kress, D.H.	K-254	07/08/15	St. Helena, Ca.	
Rice, Br-Sr. [J.D.]	R-256	07/08/15	St. Helena, Ca.	
White, J.E.	W-258	07/08/16	St. Helena, Ca.	Mar 283;5BC 1083-1084;7BC 946; OHC 23;TDG 237;LDE 27;6Bio 134
Burden, Br-Sr. [J.A.]	B-260	07/08/29		*PC 280-281*
White, W.C.	*W-261	07/08/25	St. Helena, Ca.	
White, J.E.	W-262	07/08/21	St. Helena, Ca.	3SM 57
Haskell, Br-Sr.	H-264	07/08/27	St. Helena, Ca.	
White, W.C.	*W-265	07/08/26	St. Helena, Ca.	3SM 51-52
White, Emma	W-266	07/09/03	St. Helena, Ca.	*21MR 101-102*
White, J.E.	W-268	07/09/03	St. Helena, Ca.	
White, J.E.	W-270	07/08/30	St. Helena, Ca.	7BC 969;2MR 40
Knox, W.T.	K-271	07/08/00	St. Helena, Ca.	
Wilcox, F.M.	W-272	07/09/04	St. Helena, Ca.	
Burden, J.A.	B-274	07/09/02	St. Helena, Ca.	*LLM 258-260*
Burden, J.A.	B-276	07/09/05c		*PC 288-290*
Starr, Lillis Wood	S-278	07/09/05	St. Helena, Ca.	LLM 262-264
Bree, Maggie Hare	B-282	07/09/04	St. Helena, Ca.	
White, Emma	W-284	07/09/16	St. Helena, Ca.	8MR 62-63;6Bio 136
Wessels, Br-Sr. [J.J.]	W-286	07/09/17	St. Helena, Ca.	
White, J.E./White, Emma	W-288	07/09/23	St. Helena, Ca.	
Butler, G.I. and co-laborers	B-289	07/09/10	St. Helena, Ca.	2MR 73-75
Reaser, G.W./Ministers in Southern Cal.	R-290	07/08/29	St. Helena, Ca.	*SpM 412-413*
White, J.E./White, Emma	W-292	07/09/21	St. Helena, Ca.	3SM 358-359;4MR 92-93;9MR 93
Ministers/Physicians/Teachers in Southern Ca.	B-294	07/09/12	St. Helena, Ca.	*LLM 266-270*
Butler, G.I.	B-296	07/09/22	St. Helena, Ca.	
White, J.E./White, Emma	W-298	07/09/26	St. Helena, Ca.	
Olsen, O.A.	O-300	07/09/29c		TDG 281
Starr, Lillis Wood	S-302	07/09/19	St. Helena, Ca.	LLM 274-275
Rasmussan, Sr. [M.]	R-304	07/09/28	St. Helena, Ca.	
Nicola, Br-Sr. [C.C.]	N-306	07/09/30	St. Helena, Ca.	*PC 291-292*
Foss, Mary	F-308	07/09/30	St. Helena, Ca.	LDE 23;10MR 150
Workman, Mabel White	W-310	07/10/02	St. Helena, Ca.	
Burden, Br-Sr. [J.A.]	B-312	07/10/02c		*PC 292-293*
Daniells, A.G./Evans, I.H.	B-314	07/09/23	St. Helena, Ca.	*8MR 201-207*
Ford, Br.	F-315	07/09/24	St. Helena, Ca.	
Starr, Br-Sr. [G.B.]	S-316	07/10/01	St. Helena, Ca.	Te 222
Nashville Church	B-317	07/09/24	St. Helena, Ca.	4MR 30-31
Olsen, O.A.	O-318	07/10/08	St. Helena, Ca.	TDG 290
Haskell, Br-Sr.	H-320	07/10/04	St. Helena, Ca.	
Officers of the General Conference	B-322	07/10/02	St. Helena, Ca.	*2MR 76-78*
Reaser, G.W.	R-324	07/10/03	St. Helena, Ca.	*SpM 414-417*
Wessels, Br-Sr. [J.J.]	W-326	07/09/25	St. Helena, Ca.	
Daniells, A.G./Palmer, E.R.	D-328	07/09/26	St. Helena, Ca.	*13MR 387-389*
Workers in Nashville	B-330	07/10/05	St. Helena, Ca.	
Workers in Nashville	B-332	07/10/09	St. Helena, Ca.	6BC 1084;7MR 272-273
Workman, Mabel White	W-334	07/10/17	St. Helena, Ca.	
Hopkins, Hannah E. Sawyer	H-336	07/10/17	St. Helena, Ca.	6Bio 135
Wessels, Br-Sr. [J.J.]	W-338	07/10/14	St. Helena, Ca.	
Workers in Southern California	*B-340	07/10/03	St. Helena, Ca.	*9T 277-280*
Workers in Southern California	*B-342	07/09/02	St. Helena, Ca.	*LLM 255-258*
Daniells, A.G./Irwin, G.A./Prescott, W.W.	B-344	07/10/01	St. Helena, Ca.	ChL 28
Ministers and Teachers	*B-346	07/10/12	St. Helena, Ca.	*NPU Gleaner 12/18/1907*
Our Churches	*B-347	07/10/12	St. Helena, Ca.	
Ministering Brethren	B-348	07/10/00	St. Helena, Ca.	

EGW Letters File—Page 94

Ministering Brethren [from B-348]	B-348a	07/10/00	St. Helena, Ca.	*AUCR 12/30/1907*
White, J.E./White, Emma	W-350	07/10/22	St. Helena, Ca.	15MR 54-58;6Bio 141
Scott, J.R.	S-354	07/10/24	St. Helena, Ca.	
Members of the Battle Creek Church	B-356	07/10/24	St. Helena, Ca.	AH 187,388;CG 66,321;PC 139
Haskell, Br-Sr.	H-358	07/11/03	St. Helena, Ca.	PC 274-276
Workman, Mabel White	W-360	07/10/30	Loma Linda, Ca.	PC 295-296
Kress, Br-Sr. [D.H.]	K-361	07/12/03	Loma Linda, Ca.	
Baird, Br-Sr. [A.S.]	B-362	07/11/05	Loma Linda, Ca.	
Kress, Br-Sr. [D.H.]	K-363	07/11/05	Loma Linda, Ca.	CD 321,324,466;1MR 293-294;2MR 187
Haskell, Br-Sr.	H-364	07/11/10	Loma Linda, Ca.	LLM 321-322
White, J.E.	W-366	07/11/10	Loma Linda, Ca.	5MR 373
Salisbury, H.R.	S-368	07/11/08	Loma Linda, Ca.	
Kress, Br-Sr. [D.H.]	K-370	07/10/23	St. Helena, Ca.	2SM 197-198
Wilcox, F.M./My Work and My Helpers	W-371	07/10/23	St. Helena, Ca.	*PH116 10-16*
Kress, Br-Sr. [D.H.]	K-372	07/10/24	St. Helena, Ca.	2SM 201
Faulkhead, N.D.	F-374	07/11/10	Loma Linda, Ca.	LDE 107
Ballenger, E.S.	B-376	07/11/13	Loma Linda, Ca.	
Leading Men in the Southern California Conf.	B-378	07/11/11	Loma Linda, Ca.	*LLM 322-325*
Reaser, G.W.	R-380	07/11/11	Loma Linda, Ca.	ChL 24
Reaser, G.W.	R-382	07/11/09	Loma Linda, Ca.	
Davison, Sr. [L.E.]	D-384	07/11/18	Loma Linda, Ca.	
Caro, E.R.	C-386	07/11/15	Loma Linda, Ca.	
Hirschmiller, Charles I.	H-388	07/11/19	Loma Linda, Ca.	UL 337
Butler, G.I.	B-390	07/11/29	National City, Ca.	11MR 168
Workman, Mabel White	W-391	07/11/25	National City, Ca.	
White, J.E./White, Emma	W-392	07/12/01	National City, Ca.	PC 257-258
Workman, Mabel White	W-393	07/11/00	Loma Linda, Ca.	4MR 356
White, J.E./White, Emma	W-394	07/11/24	National City, Ca.	
Wessels, Br-Sr. [J.J.]/Cummings, Br-Sr. [R.]	B-396	07/12/01	National City, Ca.	
Wessels, Andrew	W-398	07/12/03	National City, Ca.	
Amadon, G.W.	A-400	07/11/03	National City, Ca.	
Mason, Paul C.	M-402	07/12/17	Loma Linda, Ca.	
White, W.C.	W-404	07/12/30c		Ev 105-106
Belden, Vina	B-406	07/12/29	St. Helena, Ca.	
Olsen, O.A.	P-408	07/12/30	St. Helena, Ca.	
White, J.E.	W-410	07/08/26	St. Helena, Ca.	*19MR 371-375*
Brn-Srs. of the California Conference	B-412	07/01/27	St. Helena, Ca.	1MCP 274
White, J.E.	W-412a	07/01/27	St. Helena, Ca.	
Haskell, Br-Sr.	H-414	07/08/27	St. Helena, Ca.	
Daniells, A.G./White, W.C.	B-416	07/12/30	St. Helena, Ca.	ChL 34-35;3SM 427;3MR 220
Simpson, R.W./Simpson, A.W.	S-418	07/12/13	Loma Linda, Ca.	
White, W.C.	W-419	07/12/00	St. Helena, Ca.	
White, W.C.	*W-420	07/08/29	St. Helena, Ca.	
Druillard, Sr.	*D-421	07/12/30	St. Helena, Ca.	
Rice, Br-Sr.	*R-422	07/02/18		

1908

Reaser, G.W.	R-004	08/01/01	St. Helena, Ca.	7BC 956;6Bio 162-163
Haskell, S.N.	H-006	08/01/03	St. Helena, Ca.	
White, J.E.	W-008	08/01/03	St. Helena, Ca.	
Haskell, Br-Sr.	H-010	08/01/05	St. Helena, Ca.	
Burden, J.A.	B-012	08/01/05	St. Helena, Ca.	*LLM 330-332*
Wilcox, F.M.	W-014	08/01/05	St. Helena, Ca.	
Gotzian, J.	G-016	08/01/05	St. Helena, Ca.	
White, W.C.	W-018	08/01/06	St. Helena, Ca.	
White, W.C.	W-020	08/01/08	St. Helena, Ca.	

EGW Letters File—Page 95

Kress, Br-Sr. [D.H.]	K-026	07/11/00	Filed in 1908	SpM 418-419
Reaser, G.W.	P-028	08/01/10	St. Helena, Ca.	
Caro, Edith	C-030	08/01/10	St. Helena, Ca.	
Brethren in Positions of Responsibility	B-032	08/01/06	St. Helena, Ca.	*SpM 419-424*
Brethren in Positions of Responsibility	B-032a	08/01/06	St. Helena, Ca.	*20MR 99-103*
Reaser, G.W.	R-034	08/01/13	St. Helena, Ca.	
Place, Br.	P-038	08/01/12	St. Helena, Ca.	Ev 30
White, J.E.	W-040	08/01/16	St. Helena, Ca.	
Reaser, G.W.	R-044	08/01/18	St. Helena, Ca.	
Burden, J.A./Reaser, G.W.	B-046	08/01/13	St. Helena, Ca.	*LLM 333-335*
Washburn, J.S.	W-048a	08/02/04	St. Helena, Ca.	4MR 31-32
White, J.E.	W-050	08/02/05	St. Helena, Ca.	CD 491-493;1MR 241;7MR 329;6Bio 165
Corliss, J.O.	C-052	08/01/28	St. Helena, Ca.	
n.a./Re Elder Knox	B-054	08/01/21	St. Helena, Ca.	2SM 397;OHC 317
Knox, W.T.	K-056	08/01/28	St. Helena, Ca.	
Burden, Br-Sr. [J.A.]	B-058	08/01/12	St. Helena, Ca.	*LLM 332-333*
Haskell, Br-Sr.	H-060	08/02/03	St. Helena, Ca.	9MR 18-19
Reaser, G.W.	R-062	08/02/02	St. Helena, Ca.	9MR 18
Reaser, G.W.	R-064	08/02/04	St. Helena, Ca.	
Haskell, Br-Sr.	H-066	08/02/03	St. Helena, Ca.	
Haskell, Br-Sr.	H-068	08/02/05	St. Helena, Ca.	7MR 404
Cottrell, H.W.	C-070	08/02/05	St. Helena, Ca.	
Reaser, G.W./Burden, J.A.	B-072	08/02/06	St. Helena, Ca.	*LLM 347-348*
Harper, Walter	H-074	08/02/13	St. Helena, Ca.	
Burden, J.A.	*B-075	08/02/16	St. Helena, Ca.	
Foss, Mary	F-076	08/01/00	St. Helena, Ca.	
Gotzian, J.	G-078	08/02/18	St. Helena, Ca.	
Cummings, Br-Sr. [R.S.]	C-080	08/02/18	St. Helena, Ca.	
Physicians and Manager at Loma Linda	*B-082	08/02/20	St. Helena, Ca.	LLM 353-355
Workman, Mabel White	*W-084	08/03/03	St. Helena, Ca.	
Campbell, M.N.	*C-085	08/03/13	Oakland, Ca.	
Knox, W.T.	K-086	08/02/07	St. Helena, Ca.	
Cottrell, H.W./Haskell, S.N.	B-088	08/02/16	St. Helena, Ca.	7MR 404-405
Burden, J.A. and others at Loma Linda	B-090	08/03/24	St. Helena, Ca.	*LLM 364-367*
Burden, J.A.	*B-091	08/03/24	St. Helena, Ca.	
White, J.E.	W-092	08/03/31	St. Helena, Ca.	6Bio 165
Haskell, S.N.	H-094	08/03/29	St. Helena, Ca.	PM 121-122
Gilmore, Alexander	G-096	08/03/31	St. Helena, Ca.	
Gotzian, J.	G-098	08/04/01	St. Helena, Ca.	
Rasmussan, Sr.	R-100	08/02/11	St. Helena, Ca.	
Terwilliger, Br.	T-102	08/02/11	St. Helena, Ca.	PM 394
Haskell, Br-Sr.	H-104	08/03/30	St. Helena, Ca.	
Haskell, Br-Sr.	H-106	08/04/02	St. Helena, Ca.	PM 208,234-235;3SM 204;1MR 172-174
Kress, Br-Sr. [D.H.]	*K-108	08/04/06c		
Kress, Br-Sr. [D.H.]	K-110	08/04/08	St. Helena, Ca.	
Knox, W.T.	K-112	08/04/10	St. Helena, Ca.	
Irwin, Br-Sr. [G.A.]	I-114	08/04/15	St. Helena, Ca.	
Workman, Br-Sr. [W.]	W-116	08/04/15	St. Helena, Ca.	
White, J.E./White, Emma	W-118	08/04/23	St. Helena, Ca.	*12MR 262-266*
White, J.E./White, Emma	W-120	08/04/03	St. Helena, Ca.	
Haskell, Br-Sr.	H-122	08/04/26	St. Helena, Ca.	7MR 405-406;6Bio 168
Irwin, C.W.	I-124	08/04/23	St. Helena, Ca.	
Simpson, Br-Sr. [W.]	S-126	08/04/23	St. Helena, Ca.	
Brethren in Southern California	B-132	08/04/23	St. Helena, Ca.	*PC 263-265*
Starr, J.A.	S-136	08/05/05	Lodi, Ca.	
Cummings, Br-Sr. [R.S.]	C-138	08/05/06	Lodi, Ca.	
White, J.E.	W-140	08/05/06	Lodi, Ca.	WM 85-86,312-313

White, J.E./White, Emma	W-142	08/05/10	Lodi, Ca.	
White, J.E./White, Emma	W-144	08/05/15c		
Bree, Maggie Hare	B-146	08/05/09	Lodi, Ca.	1MR 325;6Bio 165
Caro, E.R.	C-148	08/05/12	Lodi, Ca.	5MR 357
Caro, M.	C-150	08/05/09	Lodi, Ca.	
Hall, L.M.	H-152	08/05/12	St. Helena, Ca.	12MR 262
Haskell, Br-Sr.	H-154	08/05/19	St. Helena, Ca.	*1MR 325-326*
Hare, Br-Sr. [Metcalfe]	H-156	08/05/14	St. Helena, Ca.	
White, J.E.	W-158	08/05/14	St. Helena, Ca.	TDG 143;3SM 295-296
Hare, Br-Sr. [Metcalfe]	H-160	08/05/13	St. Helena, Ca.	
Daniells, A.G.	D-162	08/03/29	St. Helena, Ca.	*SpM 426-429*
Workman, Br-Sr. [W.D.]	W-164	08/05/22	St. Helena, Ca.	
Prescott, W.W.	P-166	08/05/22	St. Helena, Ca.	TDG 151;10MR 361
White, J.E./White, Emma	W-168	08/05/26	St. Helena, Ca.	11MR 182-183
Evans, I.H.	E-170	08/05/22	St. Helena, Ca.	
Officers of the General Conference	B-172	08/05/26	St. Helena, Ca.	*SpM 435-437*
Gotzian, J.	G-174	08/05/28c		
Gilmore, Alexander	G-176	08/05/24	St. Helena, Ca.	
Scriver, Sr.	S-178	08/05/24	St. Helena, Ca.	
Irwin, G.A./Hare, M.	B-180	08/05/26	St. Helena, Ca.	
Wessels, Br-Sr. [J.J.]	W-182	08/05/29	St. Helena, Ca.	
Hurlbutt, Br-Sr.	H-184	08/06/02	St. Helena, Ca.	3MR 428-429
Stafford, M.G.	S-186	08/06/13	Melrose, Ca.	
Haskell, Br-Sr.	H-188	08/06/17	St. Helena, Ca.	
Simpson, Br-Sr.	S-190	08/06/15	St. Helena, Ca.	5MR 54
Lindsay, Harmon	L-192	08/06/16	St. Helena, Ca.	
Teachers in the Washington School	B-194	08/06/02	St. Helena, Ca.	
Daniells, A.G.	D-196	08/06/20	St. Helena, Ca.	*LLM 388*
Brethren in Oakland	B-198	08/06/16	St. Helena, Ca.	1MR 120,261
Churches Near Camp-Meetings Have Been Held	B-200	08/06/17	St. Helena, Ca.	
Belden, F.E.	*B-201	08/06/00	St. Helena, Ca.	
Haskell, Br-Sr.	H-202	08/06/23	St. Helena, Ca.	UL 188
Haskell, Br-Sr.	H-204	08/07/16	St. Helena, Ca.	
Hirschmiller, Charles I.	H-206	08/07/14	St. Helena, Ca.	*17MR 83-86*
Hibbard, E.J.	H-210	08/07/01	St. Helena, Ca.	
Haskell, Br-Sr.	H-212	08/07/15	St. Helena, Ca.	*7MR 406*
Workman, Br-Sr. [W.D.]	W-216	08/07/17	St. Helena, Ca.	4MR 186-187
Stone, W.J./Pres. of the Indiana Conference	B-218	08/07/16	St. Helena, Ca.	*12MR 311-314*
Parmele, R.W./Pres. of the Florida Conference	B-220	08/07/23	St. Helena, Ca.	*12MR 310-311*
Kress, Br-Sr. [D.H.]	K-222	08/07/23	St. Helena, Ca.	VSS 95;7MR 196
Prescott, W.W.	P-224	08/06/24	St. Helena, Ca.	10MR 358-359;6Bio 248-249
Prescott, W.W.	P-226	08/07/01	St. Helena, Ca.	*12MR 223-226*
White, J.E./White, Emma	W-228	08/07/27	St. Helena, Ca.	
Jones, A.T.	J-230	08/07/25	St. Helena, Ca.	*9MR 278-279*
Hare, Br-Sr. [M.]	H-232	08/07/26	St. Helena, Ca.	TDG 216
Haskell, Br-Sr.	H-234	08/08/03	St. Helena, Ca.	6Bio 169-170
Haskell, Br-Sr.	H-236	08/08/13	Los Angeles, Ca.	7BC 974
Wilcox, F.M.	W-238	08/07/31	St. Helena, Ca.	
Jones, A.T.	*J-239	08/07/00	St. Helena, Ca.	*20MR 352-355*
Haskell, Br-Sr.	H-240	08/08/16	Los Angeles, Ca.	8MR 19;6Bio 179
Haskell, S.N.	H-242	08/08/23	Los Angeles, Ca.	UL 249;ML 361
Those Assembled at the Oakwood School	B-244	08/08/23	Los Angeles, Ca.	2MR 81-82
Strother, W.R.	S-246	08/08/13	Los Angeles, Ca.	*PCO 114-115*
Wilcox, F.M.	W-248	08/08/20	Los Angeles, Ca.	
Haskell, S.N.	H-250	08/08/28	Loma Linda, Ca.	*9MR 106-107*
Underwood, R.A.	U-252	08/09/10	St. Helena, Ca.	*SpM 1-2*
Shireman, D.T.	S-254	08/09/12	St. Helena, Ca.	SpM 376-377

Haskell, S.N.	H-256	08/09/13	St. Helena, Ca.	6Bio 180
White, J.E.	W-258	08/09/11	St. Helena, Ca.	6Bio 170
Warren, Luther	W-260	08/08/22	Los Angeles, Ca.	GW 163-164
Cottrell, H.W./Pres. of Pac. Union Conf.	C-262	08/09/17	St. Helena, Ca.	
White, Emma	W-264	08/09/20	St. Helena, Ca.	
Haskell, Br-Sr.	H-266	08/09/22	St. Helena, Ca.	
Scriver, Sr.	S-268	08/09/22	St. Helena, Ca.	
Reaser, G.W.	R-270	08/09/23	St. Helena, Ca.	*LLM 389-390*
Haskell, Br-Sr.	H-272	08/09/24	St. Helena, Ca.	
Workman, Br-Sr. [W.D.]	W-274	08/09/23	St. Helena, Ca.	CD 101,107,126;6Bio 171,189
Ferguson, D.C.	F-276	08/09/22	St. Helena, Ca.	
Kerr, Sr.	K-278	08/02/21	St. Helena, Ca.	7MR 381
Kress, Br-Sr. [D.H.]	K-280	08/09/28	St. Helena, Ca.	6Bio 171
Members of the Fresno Church	B-282	08/09/28	St. Helena, Ca.	
Haskell, Br-Sr.	H-284	08/09/28	St. Helena, Ca.	
Haskell, Br-Sr.	H-286	08/10/02	St. Helena, Ca.	
Reaser, G.W.	R-288	08/09/29	St. Helena, Ca.	OHC 275;6MR 284-285
White, J.E.	W-290	08/09/29	St. Helena, Ca.	
White, J.E.	W-292	08/10/05	St. Helena, Ca.	2BC 994;6Bio 171
White, J.E.	W-302	08/10/16	St. Helena, Ca.	
Churches in Washington, D.C.	*B-304	08/10/19c		Ev 397;4MR 32-33
Those Interested in Paradise Valley Sanit.	B-308	08/10/20	St. Helena, Ca.	
White, J.E.	W-310	08/10/01	St. Helena, Ca.	6MR 153-154;6Bio 261-262
Haskell, Br-Sr.	H-312	08/07/28	St. Helena, Ca.	CD 112-113
Haskell, Br-Sr.	H-314	08/10/27	St. Helena, Ca.	
Daniells, A.G. and associates	B-316	08/10/25	St. Helena, Ca.	1MCP 352;2MCP 523;3MR 220
Underwood, R.A.	U-318	08/10/21	St. Helena, Ca.	Ev 47
Underwood, R.A.	U-320	08/10/26	St. Helena, Ca.	*SpM 438-439*
Members in the California Conference	B-322	08/11/01	St. Helena, Ca.	*1MR 326-330*
White, J.E.	W-324	08/11/03	St. Helena, Ca.	1MR 330-331
Sawyer, Robert/Sawyer-Hopkins, Hanna	S-326	08/11/04	St. Helena, Ca.	*RY 68-70*
Crawford, Marion Stowell	C-328	08/11/04	St. Helena, Ca.	6Bio 175
Haskell, Br-Sr.	H-330	08/11/11	St. Helena, Ca.	1MR 331-332;7MR 196
Burden, J.A.	B-332	08/11/25	St. Helena, Ca.	*LLM 391-392*
White, J.E./White, Emma	W-334	08/11/25	St. Helena, Ca.	6Bio 189
Sawyer, Br-Sr. [Robert]	S-336	08/12/02	St. Helena, Ca.	*RY 70-72*
Haskell, S.N.	H-338	08/11/26	St. Helena, Ca.	*2SM 41-42*
Haskell, S.N.	H-340	08/12/09	St. Helena, Ca.	8MR 21
Rice, Br-Sr. [J.D.]	R-342	08/11/23	St. Helena, Ca.	*13MR 384-386*
Gotzian, J.	G-344	08/12/12	St. Helena, Ca.	6Bio 182
Washburn, Br-Sr. [J.S.]	W-346	08/12/11	St. Helena, Ca.	
Hare, Br-Sr. [Metcalfe]	H-348	08/12/15	St. Helena, Ca.	*14MR 339-342*
Starr, J.A.	S-350	08/12/16	St. Helena, Ca.	
Haskell, S.N.	H-352	08/12/16	St. Helena, Ca.	*6MR 59-62*
Our Brethren in California	B-354	08/12/11	St. Helena, Ca.	*PUR 12/31/1908*
Crawford, Marion Stowell	C-356	08/12/13	St. Helena, Ca.	7MR 196-197;8MR 21,103;6Bio 182
Mackin, Br-Sr. [Ralph]	M-358	08/12/11	St. Helena, Ca.	*3SM 376-378*
Mackin, Br-Sr. [Ralph] [variant of M-358]	M-358a	08/12/11	St. Helena, Ca.	*2SM 44-45 and 3SM 376-378*
Cummings, Sr. [R.S.]	C-360	08/12/16	St. Helena, Ca.	
Rice, Br-Sr. [J.D.]	R-362	08/12/16	St. Helena, Ca.	
Haskell, Br-Sr.	H-364	08/12/17	St. Helena, Ca.	*19MR 376-377*
Haskell, S.N.	H-366	08/12/18	St. Helena, Ca.	
Cottrell, H.W./Haskell, S.N./Knox, W.T.	B-368	08/12/17	St. Helena, Ca.	4MR 110
Haskell, S.N.	H-370	08/12/24	St. Helena, Ca.	
Review and Herald/Southern Publ. Assn.	B-372	08/10/06	St. Helena, Ca.	*PM 71-72*
Haskell, S.N.	H-374	08/12/27	St. Helena, Ca.	
Irwin, G.A.	I-382	08/12/23	St. Helena, Ca.	1MCP 41-42;3BC 1145-1146;11MR 165

EGW Letters File—Page 98

Brethren in Washington, D.C.	*B-383	08/05/29	St. Helena, Ca.	
Hulbert, Br-Sr.	H-384	08/04/20	Clear Lake, Ca.	
Hadfield, James A.	H-385	08/02/27	St. Helena, Ca.	

1909

Gotzian, J.	G-002	09/01/01	St. Helena, Ca.	1MR 332-333;5MR 111
White, J.E./White, Emma	W-004	08/12/29	Filed in 1909	6Bio 182
White, W.C.	W-006	09/01/01	St. Helena, Ca.	*20MR 395-397*
McReynolds, C.	M-008	09/01/05	St. Helena, Ca.	Ev 463
McReynolds, C.	M-010	09/01/05	St. Helena, Ca.	
Haskell, Br-Sr.	H-014	09/01/12	St. Helena, Ca.	
Peck, Sara	P-016	09/01/11	St. Helena, Ca.	8MR 60-62
White, J.E./White, Emma	W-018	09/01/13c	St. Helena, Ca.	8MR 21;11MR 167
Hare, Metcalfe	H-020	09/01/14	St. Helena, Ca.	2SM 301
Belden, Vina	B-022	09/01/11	St. Helena, Ca.	
Scriver, Sr.	S-024	09/01/19	St. Helena, Ca.	
White, W.C.	W-026	09/01/24	St. Helena, Ca.	
Rasmussan, Anna	R-028	09/01/15	St. Helena, Ca.	11MR 166
Haskell, Br-Sr.	H-030	09/01/27	St. Helena, Ca.	
Lindsay, H.W.	L-032	09/01/21	St. Helena, Ca.	
Crawford, Marion Stowell	C-034	09/02/14	St. Helena, Ca.	
Cummings, Br-Sr. [R.S.]	C-036	09/01/27	St. Helena, Ca.	
Haskell, Br-Sr.	H-038	09/02/11	St. Helena, Ca.	7MR 407
Those in Charge of the Colored Orphanage	B-040	09/02/16	St. Helena, Ca.	SpTB #12x 2;8MR 129
Haskell, Br-Sr.	H-042	09/02/21	St. Helena, Ca.	4BC 1142-1143,1148;7MR 197
White, J.E./White, Emma	W-044	09/02/24	St. Helena, Ca.	
Haskell, Br-Sr.	H-046	09/02/26	St. Helena, Ca.	*19MR 62-66*
Brethren	B-047	09/06/09	Washington, D.C.	MM 304
Gotzian, J.	G-048	09/02/28	St. Helena, Ca.	6Bio 189
Sanderson, A.J.	S-050	09/03/03	St. Helena, Ca.	TDG 71;MM 25
Rice, Br-Sr. [J.D.]	R-052	09/03/02	St. Helena, Ca.	
Haskell, S.N.	H-054	09/03/07	St. Helena, Ca.	Ev 472;TDG 75
Cummings, Br-Sr. [R.S.]	C-056	09/03/20	St. Helena, Ca.	
Payne, Sarah H.	P-058	09/03/14	St. Helena, Ca.	1NL 59
Washburn, J.S.	W-060	09/03/29	St. Helena, Ca.	
Parsons, D.A.	D-062	09/03/28	St. Helena, Ca.	1SM 128;1NL 60
Haskell, Br-Sr.	H-064	09/04/05	St. Helena, Ca.	OHC 35;1MCP 351-353
Those Assembled at Camp-Meeting	B-066	09/04/10	Loma Linda, Ca.	*PUR 05/06/1909*
Haskell, S.N.	H-068	09/04/10	Loma Linda, Ca.	
Morton, Eliza	M-070	09/04/12	Loma Linda, Ca.	PC 267
Those Buying and Selling Land Near Sonoma, Ca.	B-072	09/04/04	St. Helena, Ca.	CS 240-241
Haskell, Br-Sr.	H-074	09/04/27	Huntsville, Al.	*PCO 116-117*
Those Gathered for Council at Asheville	B-076	09/05/02	Asheville, N.C.	
Rasmussan, Anna	R-078	09/05/03	Takoma Park, Md.	
Cottrell, H.W.	C-080	09/04/11	Loma Linda, Ca.	
White, J.E.	W-082	09/05/05	Takoma Park, Md.	
Teachers in Union College	B-084	09/05/07	Washington, D.C.	*LLM 404-409*
White, J.E.	W-086	09/05/11	Takoma Park, Md.	
Belden, Vina	B-088	09/05/11	Washington, D.C.	
Atkinson, Ellen F.	A-090	09/06/07	Washington, D.C.	
Anderson, Sr.	A-092	09/06/10	Takoma Park, Md.	
Kress, Br-Sr. [D.H.]	K-094	09/01/14	St. Helena, Ca.	1MR 257;LLM 403-404
Brethren and Sisters in Washington	B-094a	09/06/06	Washington, D.C.	*2SAT 305-313*
Parsons, D.A.	P-096	09/06/13	Philadelphia, Pa.	3SM 51
White, J.E./White, Emma	W-098	09/06/16	Philadelphia, Pa.	TMK 188;MM 88;3MR 223
Burden, J.A.	B-100	09/06/09	Washington, D.C.	*PC 267-269*

Sutherland, E.A./Magan, P.T.	B-102	09/06/08	Washington, D.C.	TDG 168;SpM 447-449
Stillman, Br.-Sr.	S-104	09/08/17	Madison, Wi.	
Churches in Oakland and Berkeley	B-106	09/09/26	St. Helena, Ca.	*18MR 232-236*
Irwin, G.A.	I-108	09/09/25	St. Helena, Ca.	
White, J.E.	W-110	09/09/17	St. Helena, Ca.	*1MR 338-342*
Board of Managers of the Melrose Sanitarium	B-112	09/07/04	Portland, Me.	*7MR 301-312*
Workman, Mabel	W-114	09/09/30	Angwin, Ca.	8MR 114-116;6Bio 185
Read, A.J.	R-116	09/07/22	Three Rivers, Mi.	
Marrow, James	M-118	09/06/24	S. Lancaster, Ma.	*8MR 19*
Haskell, Br.-Sr.	H-120	09/10/12	St. Helena, Ca.	DG 224-225
Haskell, S.N.	H-121	09/08/09	Hinsdale, Il.	
Spaulding, Br.	S-122	09/08/13	Hinsdale, Il.	11MR 165
Laborers in Indiana	B-124	09/08/12	Hinsdale, Il.	RH 12/23/1909;4MR 377-378
Cummings, Br.-Sr. [R.S.]	C-126	09/09/19	St. Helena, Ca.	MM 28-29
Kress, D.H.	K-128	09/10/03	St. Helena, Ca.	MM 241-242
Gotzian, Josephine	G-130	09/10/07	St. Helena, Ca.	
Burden, J.A.	B-132	09/10/11	St. Helena, Ca.	*PC 302-304*
Starr, G.B.	S-136	09/10/14	St. Helena, Ca.	*10MR 232-233*
Brethren and Sisters/An Appeal	B-138	09/10/19	St. Helena, Ca.	6Bio 211
Burden, J.A.	B-140	09/11/05	St. Helena, Ca.	*MM 84-85*
Daniells, A.G.	D-142	09/10/27	St. Helena, Ca.	*17MR 33-37*
Daniells, A.G.	D-143	09/11/00	St. Helena, Ca.	
White, J.E./White, Emma	W-144	09/11/22	St. Helena, Ca.	6Bio 268
Kress, Br.-Sr. [D.H.]	K-146	09/11/28	St. Helena, Ca.	*7MR 102-106*
Starr, Br.-Sr. [G.B.]	S-148	09/12/01	St. Helena, Ca.	*7MR 107-109*
Irwin, Br.-Sr. [G.A.]	I-150	09/11/26	St. Helena, Ca.	Ev 37
Hannaford, Mary	H-152	09/12/03	St. Helena, Ca.	
Cummings, Br.-Sr. [R.S.]	C-154	09/11/29	St. Helena, Ca.	
Simpson, Br.-Sr. [W.W.?]	S-156	09/12/05	St. Helena, Ca.	
Kress, D.H.	K-158	09/11/18	St. Helena, Ca.	*KC 163-166*
Cottrell, H.W.	C-160	09/12/06	St. Helena, Ca.	
Responsible Men in Washington	B-162	09/12/01	St. Helena, Ca.	2MR 50-51
Workers in Washington and Mountain View	B-164	09/11/30	St. Helena, Ca.	PM 63;143-144;TDG 343;7BC 970
Hansen, Lars	B-166	09/12/05	St. Helena, Ca.	
Officers of the General Conferencew	B-168	09/12/01	St. Helena, Ca.	MM 300,308-310;4MR 278-279;
				10MR 362;LLM 459-461
Starr, Br.-Sr. [G.B.]	S-170	09/12/08	St. Helena, Ca.	
White, J.E./White, Emma	W-172	09/12/22	St. Helena, Ca.	2MR 182;4MR 279
Rumbough, Sr.	R-174	09/12/21	St. Helena, Ca.	Ev 306;6MR 29-30;6Bio 213,269
Leading Ministers in California	B-178	09/12/06	St. Helena, Ca.	PC 296-300
Kress, D.H.	*K-182	09/12/27	St. Helena, Ca.	6Bio 269
White, J.E./White, Emma	*W-183	09/03/17	St. Helena, Ca.	6Bio 189-190
White, J.E./White, Emma	*W-184	09/05/00	Takoma Park, Md.	
White, J.E./White, Emma	*W-185	09/11/01		
n.a./Sister	*S-186	09/12/00	St. Helena, Ca.	
n.a./Brethren?/Our Schools; The Angwin Property	*B-187	09/11/27		6Bio 183-187
Evans, I.H.	E-188	09/09/15c	St. Helena, Ca.	

1910

Haskell, S.N.	H-002	10/01/10	St. Helena, Ca.	
Kress, D.H.	K-004	10/01/13	St. Helena, Ca.	Ev 544-545;CME 42;KC 168
White, J.E./White, Emma	W-006	10/01/15	St. Helena, Ca.	
Brethren	B-008	10/01/13	St. Helena, Ca.	Ev 79;6Bio 270-271,290
Workman, Br.-Sr. [W.D.]	W-010	09/12/10	Filed in 1910	
Leaders in the Maine Conference	B-012	10/01/17	St. Helena, Ca.	
Cottrell, H.W. [from C-018]	B-012a	10/01/27	Mountain View, Ca.	LLM 487-489

EGW Letters File—Page 100

Our Brethren in Portland, Maine	B-014	10/01/20	St. Helena, Ca.	
Managers of the St. Helena Sanitarium	B-016	10/01/10	St. Helena, Ca.	
Cottrell, H.W.	C-018	10/01/27	Mountain View, Ca.	PC 305-306;6Bio 282
Starr, Br-Sr. [G.B.]	*S-019	10/01/00	St. Helena, Ca.	
Kress, D.H.	K-020	10/02/09	St. Helena, Ca.	Ev 390;KC 169
Butler, Br-Sr. [G.I.]	*B-021	10/02/16	St. Helena, Ca.	
Ford, S.H.	F-024	10/03/17	St. Helena, Ca.	
Burkhardt, Sr. [M.C.]	B-026	10/02/24	St. Helena, Ca.	*TSB 37-38*
Daniells, A.G./Prescott, W.W.	B-028	10/02/22	St. Helena, Ca.	Ev 390;10MR 362
Daniells, A.G. and others in Washington	B-030	10/03/19	Oakland, Ca.	
Daniells, A.G./Prescott, Br-Sr. [W.W.]	B-032	10/03/18	Oakland, Ca.	6BC 1055;6Bio219
Daniells, A.G./Prescott, Br-Sr. [W.W.]	B-032a	10/03/18	Oakland, Ca.	variant of Lt 32, 1910
Simpson, Abbie Winegar	S-034	10/03/29	Loma Linda, Ca.	
White, J.E./White, Emma	W-036	10/04/03	Loma Linda, Ca.	8MR 19-20;4Bio 8
White, J.E./White, Emma	W-038	10/04/20	Loma Linda, Ca.	
White, W.C.	*W-039	10/04/20	Loma Linda, Ca.	
Ford, Br.	F-040	10/04/18	Loma Linda, Ca.	
Parsons, D.A.	P-042	10/04/29	Loma Linda, Ca.	TDG 128
My Fellow-Workers in the Ministry	B-044	10/04/20	Loma Linda, Ca.	9MR 148
White, W.C.	W-048	10/04/02	Loma Linda, Ca.	9MR 145
Haskell, Br-Sr.	H-050	10/05/24	St. Helena, Ca.	*20MR 223*
White, J.E.	W-052	10/06/06	St. Helena, Ca.	
Workman, Br-Sr. [W.D.]	W-054	10/06/16	St. Helena, Ca.	
Brownsberger, Br-Sr.	B-056	10/06/13	St. Helena, Ca.	TSB 223;MM 303-304
Daniells, A.G./Prescott, W.W.	B-058	10/06/15	St. Helena, Ca.	6MR 73-77;10MR 362-364;6Bio 225
Irwin, G.A.	I-058a	10/06/30	Napa, Ca.	9MR 153
Rasmussen, Anna	R-058b	10/07/10	St. Helena, Ca.	
Daniells, A.G./Prescott, W.W	*B-059	10/06/00		fragment;not on file
McReynolds, C.	M-060	10/07/13	St. Helena, Ca.	*15MR 43-46*
Burden, J.A.	B-061	10/04/27	St. Helena, Ca.	*LLM 542-546*
My Brethren in the Ministry	B-062	10/08/03	St. Helena, Ca.	1SM 167-168
Kress, Br-Sr. [D.H.]	K-064	10/07/16	St. Helena, Ca.	*PC 42-44*
Kress, Br-Sr. [D.H.]	K-066	10/07/31	St. Helena, Ca.	*15MR 76-79*
Daniells, A.G.	D-068	10/08/11	St. Helena, Ca.	*19MR 123-124*
Daniells, A.G.	D-070	10/08/11c		7MR 45;10MR 49-51,336-337,364-366
White, J.E.	W-072	10/09/03		
Amadon, G.W.	A-074	10/09/12	St. Helena, Ca.	*PC 91-92*
Burden, J.A.	B-076	10/09/04	Angwin, Ca.	*LLM 558-559*
Those in our Sanitariums	B-077	10/09/10	St. Helena, Ca.	*LLM 559-560*
White, J.E.	W-078	10/09/18	St. Helena, Ca.	
Parsons, D.A.	P-080	10/09/16	St. Helena, Ca.	
Rumbough, Martha	R-082	10/09/20	St. Helena, Ca.	Ev 36
Daniells, A.G.	D-084	10/07/26	St. Helena, Ca.	Ev 75,473-474;HFM 71-72;3MR 223
White, J.E.	W-086	10/09/23	St. Helena, Ca.	
Daniells, A.G.	D-088	10/09/30	St. Helena, Ca.	TDG 282;1MR 308;5MR 128-129
Reaser, W.A.	R-090	10/09/22	St. Helena, Ca.	
White, J.E.	W-092	10/10/02	St. Helena, Ca.	VSS 200-201
Duce, William	D-094	10/07/12	St. Helena, Ca.	8MR 21-22;6Bio 264
Daniells, A.G.	D-096	10/10/05	St. Helena, Ca.	9MR 310-312
Daniells, A.G.	D-098	10/10/10	St. Helena, Ca.	1MR 307-308
Rumbough, Martha	R-100	10/10/05	St. Helena, Ca.	
White, J.E.	W-102	10/10/12	St. Helena, Ca.	RY 2;CM 111;6Bio 229-230
Haskell, Br-Sr.	H-104	10/10/18	St. Helena, Ca.	UL 305;7MR 407
Kress, Br-Sr. [D.H.]	K-106	10/10/23	St. Helena, Ca.	Ev 96;7MR 312-313
Daniells, A.G.	D-108	10/09/01	St. Helena, Ca.	MM 140
Morton, Eliza	M-112	10/10/31	St. Helena, Ca.	
Daniells, A.G.	D-114	10/10/27	St. Helena, Ca.	*19MR 393-395*

EGW Letters File—Page 101

Workman, Mabel	W-116	10/11/02	St. Helena, Ca.	
White, W.C.	W-118	10/11/06	St. Helena, Ca.	
White, W.C.	W-120	10/11/07	St. Helena, Ca.	
White, J.E./White, Emma	W-122	10/11/07	St. Helena, Ca.	
Kress, Br-Sr. [D.H.]	K-124	10/11/08	St. Helena, Ca.	
Haskell, Br-Sr.	H-126	10/11/09	St. Helena, Ca.	
White, W.C.	*W-127	10/11/22	St. Helena, Ca.	3SM 32;10MR 313
Daniells, A.G.	D-128	10/11/23	St. Helena, Ca.	
Butler, G.I.	B-130	10/11/23	St. Helena, Ca.	*1888 1811-1812*
Cottrell, H.W.	C-132	10/12/01	St. Helena, Ca.	
White, W.C.	W-134	10/12/01	St. Helena, Ca.	
White, J.E.	W-136	10/11/26	St. Helena, Ca.	2SM 397;6Bio 338
Starr, Br-Sr. [G.B.]	S-138	10/12/12	St. Helena, Ca.	TDG 355
Lindsay, Harmon	L-140	10/09/10	St. Helena, Ca.	
Haskell, Br-Sr.	H-142	10/03/04	St. Helena, Ca.	
Bree, Maggie Hare	B-144	10/01/13	St. Helena, Ca.	
White, W.C.	W-146	10/04/26	Loma Linda, Ca.	6Bio 296
Magan, P.T.	M-148	10/10/09	St. Helena, Ca.	
White, W.C.	*W-150	10/04/01	Loma Linda, Ca.	6Bio 290,295
White, W.C.	*W-151	10/04/00	Loma Linda, Ca.	6Bio 296-297
Daniells, A.G.	*D-152	10/00/00	Fragment	
Brethren and Sisters	*B-153	10/00/00	St. Helena, Ca.	
Kress, Br-Sr. [D.H.]	*K-154	10/00/00	Fragment	
Cottrell, H.W.	*C-155	10/00/00		
Cottrell, H.W.	*C-156	10/00/00		*20MR 224-227*
Cottrell, H.W.	*C-157	10/00/00		
Cottrell, H.W.	*C-158	10/00/00		
Crisler, C.C.	*C-159	10/02/00	Loma Linda, Ca.	6Bio 297
n.a.	*B-160	10/00/00		
White, J.E./White, Emma	*W-161	10/00/00		
Prescott, Br-Sr. [W.W.]	*P-162	10/00/00		
Daniells, A.G./Prescott, W.W.	*D-163	10/00/00		
Ministering Brethren	*B-164	10/00/00		
Mason, Paul C.	M-165	10/03/17		

1911

White, W.C.	W-004	11/02/15	St. Helena, Ca.	CG 134;UL 60;6Bio 340,344
Paulson, David	*P-006	11/02/06	St. Helena, Ca.	4MR 378
Haskell, Br-Sr.	H-008	11/03/05	St. Helena, Ca.	
Palmer, E.r.	P-010	11/03/05	St. Helena, Ca.	3MR 272-273
Cottrell, H.W.	C-012	11/03/03	St. Helena, Ca.	3BC 1161
Harper, Walter	H-014	11/03/09	St. Helena, Ca.	
Haskell, S.N./Leaders in Washington	*H-015	11/03/00	St. Helena, Ca.	6Bio 344
Kellogg, Sr. [H.W.]	K-016	11/05/02	St. Helena, Ca.	
Burden, J.A.	B-018	11/05/18	St. Helena, Ca.	LLM 573
Burden, Br-Sr. [J.A.]	B-020	11/04/30	St. Helena, Ca.	*LLM 568-569*
Ruble, Br./Burden, J.A./Evans, I.H.	B-022	11/05/07	St. Helena, Ca.	*SpTB #15 1-11*
Irwin, Sr.	I-024	11/04/03	Loma Linda, Ca.	6Bio 345
Piper, J.F.	P-026	11/06/07	St. Helena, Ca.	
Harris, Stonewall Jackson	H-028	11/06/07	St. Helena, Ca.	*SpTB #17 23-29*
White, J.E.	W-030	11/06/06	St. Helena, Ca.	2SM 303;Ev 458,535-536; 10MR 208-209;6Bio 341
Kress, D.H.	K-032	11/06/05	St. Helena, Ca.	LLM 573
Burden, J.A.	B-034	11/06/07	St. Helena, Ca.	*LLM 573-574*
Harris, Stonewall Jackson/Covell, Br.	B-036	11/06/07	St. Helena, Ca.	2SM 28
White, J.E.	W-040	11/06/08	St. Helena, Ca.	

Haskell, S.N.	H-041	11/06/04	St. Helena, Ca.	
White, J.E.	W-044	11/06/13	St. Helena, Ca.	RC 248
Leading Men in our California Conferences	B-046	11/06/15	St. Helena, Ca.	SpTB #17 29-39
Believers at the Stockton Camp-Meeting	B-048	11/06/08	St. Helena, Ca.	
White, J.E.	W-050	11/06/11	St. Helena, Ca.	
Laird, Br-Sr./Hurlbutt, Br-Sr./Black, Br.	L-052	11/07/09	Oakland, Ca.	
Kress, Sr. [L.]	K-054	11/07/28	St. Helena, Ca.	5MR 86
Wilcox, F.M.	W-056	11/07/25	St. Helena, Ca.	*Test. of Jesus, by F.M. Wilcox, 115-117*
Wilcox, F.M.	*W-057	11/07/27	St. Helena, Ca.	
Haskell, Br-Sr.	H-058	11/08/02	St. Helena, Ca.	
White, J.E.	W-060	11/08/04c		3MR 181-182;11MR 20
Daniells, A.G.	D-062	11/08/25	St. Helena, Ca.	
Haskell, Br-Sr.	H-064	11/08/31	St. Helena, Ca.	CG 555-556;3MR 326;7MR 407-408; 11MR 20
Haskell, Br-Sr.	H-066	11/08/28	Long Beach, Ca.	UL 254;7MR 408;8MR 334-335
Sanderson, Sr. [A.J.]	S-070	11/09/08	St. Helena, Ca.	CD 484-485
Workman, Mabel	W-072	11/09/18	St. Helena, Ca.	
Haskell, Br-Sr.	H-074	11/09/10	St. Helena, Ca.	6Bio 357
United Laborers in Portland	B-076	11/09/10	St. Helena, Ca.	
Haskell, Br-Sr.	H-078	11/09/28	St. Helena, Ca.	Te 257,259;PC 314
Burden, J.A.	*B-079	11/10/04	St. Helena, Ca.	
Haskell, Br-Sr.	H-080	11/10/06	St. Helena, Ca.	8MR 216-217
Workman, Mabel	W-082	11/10/06	St. Helena, Ca.	
White, J.E./White, Emma	W-084	11/10/06	St. Helena, Ca.	
Rand, Howard	R-086	11/10/09	St. Helena, Ca.	
White, J.E./White, Emma	W-088	11/10/15	St. Helena, Ca.	MRmnt 61
Haskell, Br-Sr.	H-090	11/10/25	St. Helena, Ca.	AH 321;TDG 307;7MR 408-409
Roth, Br-Sr. [L.]	R-092	11/11/09	Loma Linda, Ca.	TDG 322
Belden, Vina	B-094	11/11/19	Loma Linda, Ca.	
Gravelle, Sr. [J.J.]	G-096	11/12/29	St. Helena, Ca.	*12MR 271-273*
Kellogg, J.H.	K-100	11/11/21c		*13MR 366-370*
Jones, A.T.	J-104	11/11/19c		13 Crisis Years 319-320
Mason, Paul C.	M-106	11/07/31	St. Helena, Ca.	
Coon, Br.	C-108	11/10/10	St. Helena, Ca.	*20MR 16*
Nicola, Mary	*N-110	11/02/28		
Those in Charge of the Nashville Sanitarium	*B-112	11/07/09		
Harris, Sr.	H-114	11/06/13		
White, W.C.	W-116	11/11/26	Los Angeles, Ca.	

1912

Haskell, Br-Sr.	H-002	11/12/28	Filed in 1912	SD 215;6Bio 377
White, J.E./White, Emma	W-004	12/01/08	St. Helena, Ca.	6Bio 360
Ernston, Br-Sr./Members of San Jose Church	E-006	12/02/22	St. Helena, Ca.	
Haskell, S.N.	H-008	12/02/14	St. Helena, Ca.	TDG 53;3MR 182
Rand, Howard	R-010	12/02/23c		AH 434;CG 489
Haskell, Br-Sr.	H-012	12/02/26	St. Helena, Ca.	
Workman, Br-Sr. [W.D.]	W-014	12/02/25	St. Helena, Ca.	
Board of Trustees of Loma Linda College	B-016	12/04/09	Loma Linda, Ca.	
Haskell, Br-Sr.	H-018	12/05/12	St. Helena, Ca.	7MR 409-410
Rossiter, F.M.	R-020	12/05/14	St. Helena, Ca.	11MR 22
Burden, Br-Sr. [J.A.]	B-022	12/05/16	St. Helena, Ca.	
White, J.E./White, Emma	W-024	12/05/24	St. Helena, Ca.	SD 189;3MR 323
Haskell, Br-Sr.	H-028	12/06/11	St. Helena, Ca.	11MR 21
Haskell, Br-Sr.	H-030	12/06/27	St. Helena, Ca.	2BC 1037;3MR 182
Sanitarium Family at St. Helena	B-032	12/07/05	St. Helena, Ca.	*AUCR 09/30/1912*
Workman, Br-Sr. [W.D.]	W-034	12/07/17	St. Helena, Ca.	

EGW Letters File—Page 103

Friend	F-036	12/08/07	St. Helena, Ca.	*2SM 344*
White, J.E.	W-040	12/01/28	St. Helena, Ca.	6Bio 377
Brethren	B-042	11/11/06	Filed in 1912	*6MR 375 with 1MR 315-316*
Amadon, G.W.	A-044	12/12/15	St. Helena, Ca.	*5MR 170-171*
Mason, Paul	M-046	12/01/01	St. Helena, Ca.	

1913

Our Bookmen	B-003	13/01/23	St. Helena, Ca.	*PH122*
Workers in the Message	B-005	13/02/20	St. Helena, Ca.	*RH 06/19/1913*
Those Assembled in General Conference	B-007	13/05/04	St. Helena, Ca.	*TM 513-515*
White, J.E./White, Emma	W-009	13/05/07	St. Helena, Ca.	11MR 23
White, W.C.	*W-010	13/06/00	St. Helena, Ca.	
White, J.E./White, Emma	W-011	13/08/28	St. Helena, Ca.	2MR 254;11MR 23;6Bio 393-394,396
White, J.E./White, Emma	W-013	13/12/04	St. Helena, Ca.	2MR 255;6Bio 380-381,401

1914

Sister	B-002	14/06/14	St. Helena, Ca.	*TM 516-520*

APPENDIX D

List of Ellen G. White's Manuscripts

TITLE	FILE #	DATE	PLACE	WHERE PUBLISHED
				Bold italics indicates complete manuscript
		1848		
EGW Utterances During Vision	MS-001	48/11/18		*From Seal of the Living God, pp. 24-26,32*
		1849		
Vision of the Open and Shut Door	MS-001	49/03/24	Topsham, Me.	See PT 08/00/1849
The Sealing	*MS-002	49/01/17	Topsham, Me.	1Bio 157-158; see EW 36-39
Duty in Time of Trouble	MS-003	49/01/18	Topsham, Me.	5MR 200; see EW 56-58
Remarks in Vision	*MS-005	49/09/23	Topsham, Me.	
Synopsis of E.G. White's Vision at Rocky Hill, Ct.	*MS-006	49/06/30	Rocky Hill, Ct.	
Affliction of Mrs. Hastings	MS-007	49/03/11		
		1850		
The Call Out of Babylon	MS-001	50/04/15		Unauthenticated
Need of Present Truth	*MS-002	50/01/09	Oswego, NY	*1Bio 172*
To the Little Flock	*MS-004	50/01/26	Oswego, NY	*16MR 30-35*
Vision at Oswego	MS-005	50/07/29	Oswego, NY	*18MR 10-13*
Testimony to a Church	*MS-005a	50/07/00	E. Hamilton, NY	*21MR 237-238*
Dream	*MS-006	50/08/22		*16MR 171-172*
Vision at Br. Harris'	*MS-007	50/08/24		6MR 250-251;8MR 220;1Bio 183-184
Vision at Br. Harris'	MS-007a	50/08/24		Variant of Ms 7, 1850;7MR 318
Vision of Aug. 24, 1850	MS-008	50/08/24		**Refer to Ms 5, 1850 and EW 59-60**
Copy of an Early Vision	MS-009	50/10/23	Dorchester, Ma.	**Refer to Ms 15, 1850**
Utterances in Vision	*MS-010	50/12/24	Paris, Me.	1Bio 201
Vision at Paris, Maine	*MS-011	50/12/25	Paris, Me.	*13MR 299-302*
Vision at Sutton, Vt.	*MS-014	50/09/00	Sutton, Vt.	*12MR 246-252*
Vision at Dorchester, Mass.	*MS-015	50/10/23	Dorchester, Ma.	6MR 249
		1851		
Time Setting	*MS-001	51/06/21	Camden, NY	RH July 21, 1851
Camden Vision	MS-001a	51/06/29	Camden, NY	Unauthenticated
Test. re Company at Camden	*MS-002	51/06/23	Camden, NY	
Test. re Company at Camden	*MS-002a	51/06/23	Camden, NY	variant of Ms 2, 1851
Exclamations while in Vision	MS-003	51/04/27	Paris, Me.	Unauthenticated
Opposition to Sabbath	*MS-005	51/05/18	Paris, Me.	6MR 168-172
Test. to Believers at Paris, Maine	*MS-009	51/00/00	Paris, Me.	*PH016 31-32*
		1852		
The Nations	*MS-001	52/03/18		*SpM 2a-3*
General Conference at Ballston	MS-002	52/03/14	Ballston, NY	
Latter Rain	MS-004	52/09/00	Washington, NH	*SpM 4*
		1853		
Vision at Jackson, Mi.	*MS-001	53/06/02	Jackson, Mi.	13MR 359-360
Vision for Ministers	*MS-002	53/03/01		See EW 103

EGW Manuscripts File—Page 1

Vision for Commandment-Keepers	*MS-003	53/07/02	Rochester, NY	*5MR 424-426*
Extract From a Vision Given at Rochester, NY	*MS-004	53/07/02	Rochester, NY	
Extract From a Vision re James White	*MS-005	53/07/00		

1854

Reproof for Adultery and Neglect	MS-001	54/02/12	Brookfield, NY	CG 540;1MR 33-34;6MR 217-219; 7MR 1;1Bio 290-292;
Test. for Churches in New York State	*MS-003	54/02/12	Brookfield, NY	TSB 247-249;3SM 257,273-275; 5MR 230-231;7MR 368-370; 9MR 321-323
Testimony	*MS-004	54/04/00		*PH016 32-33*
Gather the Children	*MS-005	54/06/00	Sylvan, Mi.	5MR 205-206
Courtesy and Kindness	MS-006	54/02/19	Lincklaen, NY	
Vision Conc. Children of Jackson Church	*MS-007	56/06/00		

1855

Fragments/"At the Conference at Sylvan..."	MS-001	55/00/00		AH 177;6MR 297;9MR 196-197
Vision at Paris, Me.	*MS-002	55/08/26	Paris, Me.	PH016 33-35;MRmnt 40
Fragments re James White	MS-003	55/05/05		1Bio 318

1856

Vision at Round Grove	*MS-001	56/12/09	Round Grove, Il.	See 1T 149-153
Test. for Brn. Arnold and Ross	*MS-002	56/05/27		

1857

Lack of Appreciation of the Ministry	*MS-001	57/06/00	Vermont	LDE 234-235
Church Trials	*MS-002	57/07/06	Ulysses, Pa.	See 1T 164-168

1858

Test. re Work in Vt., N.H.	*MS-002	58/12/27	Battle Creek, Mi.	*21MR 373-377*
Test. re John & Mary Loughborough	*MS-003	58/03/00		10MR 281

1859

Proof of the Call to the Ministry	MS-001	59/09/24	Topsham, Me.	*21MR 13-16*
Vision for Vermont	MS-001a	59/08/00		
Diary	*MS-002	59/01/01		
Vision for James White	*MS-003	59/00/00		
The Case of Sister Cranson	*MS-004	59/07/00		
Diary [Jan. 1 - Mar. 31]	*MS-005	59/01/01		2SM 337;3SM 261-262;WM 322-325; 3MR 136-142;4MR 437;7MR 216-217; 1Bio 396-400
Diary [Mar. 10,17]	MS-005a	59/03/10		*From The Good Samaritan, 12/00/1859*
Diary [Apr. 1 - June 30]	*MS-006	59/04/01		3SM 262-263;WM 325;3MR 142-143; 5MR 218;7MR 217-218;1Bio 404-406
Diary [July 1 - Sept. 30]	*MS-007	59/07/01		3MR 143
Diary [Oct. 10 - Nov. 20]	*MS-008	59/10/10		3MR 144-145;7MR 218
Early Experiences in Meeting Fanaticism	*MS-009	59/00/00		See 2SG 49-52
Early Experiences in Meeting Fanaticism	*MS-010	59/00/00		See 2SG 46-50

1860

Diary [Jan. 1, 2]	*MS-001	60/01/01	1Bio 410-411
"I was shown that a heavy cloud hangs..."	*MS-002	60/00/00	
Test. for Monterey	*MS-004	60/12/00	*15MR 326-337*
Pure Religion	MS-005	60/00/00	*From The Good Samaritan, 02/00/1860*
Western Missionary Field	MS-006	60/00/00	*From The Good Samaritan, 02/00/1860*

1861

The Case of Hiram Rich	*MS-001	61/01/00	Battle Creek, Mi.	*19MR 222-224*
Diary--Western Tour	*MS-002	61/03/21	Dubuque, Ia.	
Test. for Mill Grove Church	*MS-003	61/00/00		OHC 230;5MR 295
The Review Office	*MS-005	61/00/00		

1862

The Case of Br. Mackey	*MS-002	62/04/30	Battle Creek, Mi.	
The Cause in Wisconsin	*MS-003	62/00/00		See 1T 326-340
Re the Civil War	*MS-005	62/00/00	Battle Creek, Mi.	*7MR 111-112*
Test. re Moses Hull and Wife/Br. Whitney	*MS-006	62/00/00		
Test. re Br. Shepley and Sr. Rickford	*MS-007	62/00/00	Battle Creek, Mi.	
Test. re James and Ellen White's Family	*MS-008	62/00/00	Battle Creek, Mi.	
Diary/Labors in Monterey, Allegan, etc.	*MS-009	62/11/00		3MR 145-148;1Bio 481-484
Test. re Brn. Merril and Gravel	*MS-010	62/11/26	Orleans, Mi.	

1863

Test. re James and Ellen White	*MS-001	63/06/06		3SM 279-280;10MR 23-24;2Bio 18-20
Test. re Monterey Church	*MS-002	63/06/06	Otsego, Mi.	*17MR 153-161*
Vision concerning Caledonia Church	*MS-003	63/07/22	Battle Creek, Mi.	
Early Trials and Labors	*MS-005	63/00/00		
The Case of Asa Green	*MS-006	63/00/00	Battle Creek, Mi.	
For Ministers	*MS-007	63/00/00		*9MR 207-208*
Test. re Work in Ohio	*MS-008	63/05/00	Battle Creek, Mi.	*21MR 260-264*
Test. re the Young	*MS-009	63/06/00		HP 218
Temptations of the Young	*MS-010	63/00/00		HP 218
Test. re J.N. Andrews	*MS-011	63/00/00		
Test. re Sr. Noise	*MS-012	63/01/24	Battle Creek, Mi.	
Death of Henry White	*MS-013	63/12/00		
Test. re Br. Fuller	*MS-014	63/06/06		
Test. re Br-Sr. Wheeler	*MS-015	63/06/06		
Test. re Church at Mansville, NY	*MS-016	63/00/00		

1864

1865

Rebellion Within the Ranks	*MS-001	65/00/00	5MR 297;CTr 115
Test. re Work in Maine	*MS-002	65/12/25	
Test. re James White	*MS-003	65/12/25	
Test. for church at Convis, Michigan	*MS-004	65/00/00	
Importance of Consecration	*MS-005	65/00/00	

EGW Manuscripts File—Page 3

Vision of Sister Orton's Affliction	*MS-006	65/04/09	Battle Creek, Mi.	

1866

Our Late Experience	MS-001	66/00/00	*From RH 02/20/1866 and 02/27/1866*
Concerning "Our Home," Dansville, NY	*MS-005	66/00/00	*1T 615-620*
Surmisings at Battle Creek	*MS-006	66/00/00	*1T 526-528*
Test. re Br-Sr. Wicks	*MS-007	66/00/00	
Proper Observance of the Sabbath	*MS-008	66/00/00	*1T 531-533*

1867

Account of James White's Sickness/Recovery	*MS-001	67/00/00	written in 1880's	OHC 318;5MR 390-391; 6MR 90,300-301;11MR 108; 2Bio 122
"I saw that Brother Alonzo and Diana Abbey"	*MS-002	67/00/00		
Re Elder Waggoner	*MS-004	67/00/00		
Re Br. Howard	*MS-005	67/00/00		*2T 695-711*
Writing out the Light on Health Reform	*MS-007	67/00/00		*3SM 280-282*
Test. re Brn. McPherson and Cramer	*MS-008	67/00/00		5MR 437
Vision for the Abbey Family	*MS-009	67/01/19	Brookfield, NY	

1868

Test. re Br. Dennis	*MS-001	68/02/28	Watrousville, Mi.	
Test. to Washington, N.H. Brethren	*MS-002	68/00/00		*2T 93-111*
Long Praying and Preaching	*MS-003	68/06/12		
Laying Burdens on Others	*MS-004	68/06/12		*2T 118-124*
Test. re the Battle Creek Church	*MS-005	68/06/30	Battle Creek, Mi.	
Our Travels	*MS-006	68/05/00		7MR 220-221
Test. re L.L. Howard	*MS-007	68/10/25		
Test. to Bushnell Church	*MS-008	68/00/00	Greenville, Mi.	
Test. to Bushnell Church	*MS-008a	68/00/00		
Counsel to Wife of Unbelieving Husband	*MS-009	68/00/00	Battle Creek, Mi.	*TSB 44-47*
Caledonia	*MS-010	68/00/00		
Test. to Sr. Doud	*MS-011	68/02/28		*18MR 368-371*
Diary [Jan. 1-31]	*MS-012	68/01/00		3MR 148-150;7MR 218-219
Diary [Feb. 1-29]	*MS-013	68/02/00		3MR 150-152;10MR 29-30; 2Bio 228-229
Diary [Mar. 1-31]	*MS-014	68/03/00		3MR 152-154;2Bio 224
Diary [Apr. 1-30]	*MS-015	68/04/00		3MR 154-155;7MR 219-220
Diary [May 1-10]	*MS-016	68/05/00		3MR 155
Test. re Br. Smith and Family	*MS-017	68/00/00		
Test. re Br. Covey's Family	*MS-018	68/00/00		
Test. re Br. Cramer	*MS-019	68/00/00		
Counsel to Ministers	*MS-020	68/00/00		*2T 498-522*
Appeal to Ministers	*MS-021	68/00/00		*2T 334-346*
Test. re Sr. Wilson and Br-Sr. Maynard	*MS-022	68/00/00		*2T 73-77*

1869

Remarks/Remarks by Sr. White in Battle Creek	MS-001	69/03/26	Battle Creek, Mi.	*2SAT 1-9*
Test. to Mt. Pleasant Church	*MS-002	69/05/00	Battle Creek, Mi.	4MR 339

1870

Activity a Blessing	MS-002	70/00/00	1MCP 117-119

EGW Manuscripts File—Page 4

1871

Youth in Battle Creek	*MS-002	71/00/00	OHC 222;2MCP 604;TSB 25
Elder White's Labors/Errors of His Brethren	*MS-003	71/00/00	See 3T 88-95

1872

Orphan Children	*MS-003	72/00/00	
Diary [July 14-Sept. 4]	*MS-004	72/07/00	3SM 263-264;3MR 155-158;7MR 231
Diary [Oct. 2-Dec. 13]	*MS-005	72/10/00	2Bio 361-362,367-368
Joy in Christ's Service	*MS-006	72/00/00	

1873

Two Dreams that Illustrate Unity of Action	*MS-001	73/01/20	*1SAT 1-3*
Diary [Jan. 1-31]	*MS-003	73/01/00	3SM 90;3MR 173;6MR 290-291; 10MR 65-66
Diary [Feb. 1-28]	*MS-004	73/02/00	TSB 19;3MR 174;6MR 291-292; 11MR 119-120
Diary [Mar. 1-31]	*MS-005	73/03/00	11MR 120-121;2Bio 377-379
Diary [Apr. 1-30]	*MS-006	73/04/00	3SM 264;8MR 448;2Bio 379,381
Diary [May 1-31]	*MS-007	73/05/00	3SM 264;4MR 436;2Bio 382
Diary [Jun. 1-30]	*MS-008	73/06/00	3SM 264;3MR 159-160; 11MR 122-124;2Bio 383-384
Diary [Jul. 1-31]	*MS-009	73/07/00	3MR 161;2Bio 386
Diary [Aug. 1-31]	*MS-010	73/08/00	3MR 161-162;6MR 293;2Bio 387
Diary [Sep. 1-30]	*MS-011	73/09/00	*20MR 205-212*
Diary [Oct. 1-26]	*MS-012	73/10/00	3MR 168-172;6MR 294;2Bio 388-389
Diary [Nov. 5-18]	*MS-013	73/11/00	3SM 265;3MR 172;5MR 295; 11MR 124-125

1874

Methods of Labor/Work in the Cities	MS-001	74/04/01		*SpTA #7 2-19*
Work in California	*MS-001a	74/00/00		5MR 300-301
Diary [Jan. 1-Feb. 16]	*MS-002	74/01/00		4MR 339-340
Diary [Feb. 17-28]	*MS-003	74/02/00		
Diary [Jun. 4-20]	*MS-004	74/06/00		11MR 130-131
Test. re Br. Stockings	*MS-005	74/00/00		3SM 332-335;9MR 21-22
Test. to Wisconsin Workers	*MS-006	74/06/00		4MR 341-342
Temperance Test. in Battle Creek	*MS-007	74/00/00		Te 200-202;7MR 347-348
Sermon/"The words which I have selected..."	MS-008	74/00/00	Washington, Ia.	*1SAT 4-9*
The Spirit of Sacrifice	MS-009	74/01/00		*From The True Missionary, 01/00/1874*
The Work for this Time	MS-010	74/02/00		*From The True Missionary, 02/00/1874*

1875

Educational, Health, and Temperance Work	MS-001	75/10/12		CW 123-126
Re Families in the San Francisco Church	*MS-002	75/01/03		
Test. re Br. Littlejohn	*MS-003	75/01/15	Battle Creek, Mi.	
Trials of James White	*MS-004	75/00/00		
Parents as Reformers	MS-005	75/00/00		See 3T 560-570;2MCP 394

1876

Diet	MS-001	76/06/12	CD 179;CG 386-387,399;7MR 1-2
Diary [Jan. 1-12]	MS-002	76/01/00	3Bio 15-17
Diary [Jun. 14-21]	*MS-003	76/06/00	
Testimony to E.H. Gaskill and Wife	*MS-004	76/00/00	7MR 3
The Days of Noah	*MS-005	76/00/00	*10MR 265-266,371-374 with*
			12MR 207-209
On Jonah	*MS-006	76/00/00	
Statement Regarding Israel Dammon	*MS-007	76/00/00	

1877

Simplicity in Dress	MS-001	77/10/23	Oakland, Ca.	*RH 03/20/1958*
Proper Dress	MS-002	77/00/00		ML 146;See 1877 HR articles
Talk/"When we engage with all"	MS-003	77/00/00		*18MR 281-285*

1878

Church Difficulties	MS-001	78/10/09		FLB 92,138;TDG 291;Ev 691;
				12MR 113-116;15MR 134-144
Sermon/The Duties and Dangers of our Time	*MS-002	78/08/25	Battle Creek, Mi.	
Camp meeting at Plano, Tx.	*MS-003	78/11/00		3Bio 100
Visit to Oregon State Prison	MS-004	78/00/00		5MR 178
Diary [Oct. 23-Nov. 3]	*MS-005	78/10/00		11MR 57-58
Test. to Oakland Church	*MS-006	78/00/00		TMK 196,313,325

1879

The Publishing Work/"My husband has seen...	*MS-001	79/06/06		PM 331-333
A View of the Judgment	*MS-002	79/10/23	Battle Creek, Mi.	
Sermon/How to Keep the Sabbath	MS-003	79/05/23	Emporia, Ks.	HP 152;CG 533--534
Diary [Apr. 30-May 19]	*MS-004	79/05/00		11MR 58-61;3Bio 115
Diary [May 20-Jun. 14]	*MS-005	79/05/00		7MR 348-349
The Judgment	MS-006	79/10/23		*From PH043*
The Publishing House in California	*MS-007	79/00/00		
A Dream re Pacific Press Office	*MS-008	79/00/00		

1880

Church Difficulties	MS-001	80/02/18	Battle Creek, Mi.	*12MR 274-295*
A Dream	MS-002	80/00/00		*12MR 10-11*
The Bible and the School	*MS-004	80/00/00		FLB 20,222
Test. to Publishing House Workers	*MS-005	80/01/28	Battle Creek, Mi.	
The Needs of California	*MS-006	80/04/04	Ca.	
Diary [Feb. 24-Mar. 21]	*MS-007	80/03/00		11MR 62-63;3Bio 132-133
How Shall We Celebrate Christmas and New Year	*MS-008	80/00/00		*21MR 222-226*
Agents of Satan	*MS-009	80/09/00		TSB 104-107;7MR 209-210;5T 137-148
Proper Training in Our Schools	MS-010	80/00/00		
Our Sabbath Schools	MS-011	80/00/00		

1881

Our College	MS-002	81/00/00		*20MR 182-187*
Remarks/At Funeral of James White	MS-003	81/08/00		*From LS88 448-451*
Test. re James White	*MS-004	81/07/08	Battle Creek, Mi.	

Proper Use of the Test. on Health Reform	MS-005	81/03/23	Battle Creek, Mi.	*3SM 283-288*
Sketch of Last Sickness and Death of J. White	MS-006	81/09/00		*From "In Memoriam" 44-57*

1882

Test. to Battle Creek Sanitarium	MS-002	82/00/00		*12MR 129-135*
God in Nature	MS-004	82/00/00	Rome, NY	*GCDB 02/18/1897*
With Believers at Ukiah, California	*MS-005	82/00/00		3Bio 220-221
Diary [Nov. 26]	*MS-006	82/11/26		4MR 40
Test. re Battle Creek	*MS-007	82/12/00		*PH155 12-24*
Camp-meeting Hygiene	MS-008	82/05/05		*Gospel of Health, 04/00/1898*

1883

Sermon/Doubting the Testimonies	MS-001	83/11/00	Battle Creek, Mi.	*1SM 45-48*
Sermon/Words to Ministers	MS-002	83/11/00	Battle Creek, Mi.	1MR 19;5MR 156
Sermon/Genuine Faith and Holiness	MS-003	83/11/00	Battle Creek, Mi.	*From GW92 226-229*
Suppression and the Shut Door	MS-004	83/00/00	Healdsburg, Ca.	*1SM 59-73*
Sermon/At 1883 Gen. Conf.	*MS-005	83/11/20	Battle Creek, Mi.	*2SAT 10-19*
Test. re G.A. Carlsbadt	*MS-008	83/09/03		
Walk in the Light	*MS-009	83/09/03	Montpelier, Vt.	See ST 09/27/1883;HP 36
Christ Our Counselor	MS-011	83/00/00		ChL 63

1884

Remarks/Temperance	MS-001	84/09/26	Jackson, Mi.	*From RH 10/21/1884*
Sermon	*MS-002	84/05/13	Los Angeles, Ca.	UL 147
Sermon/Parental Responsibility	*MS-003	84/05/14	Los Angeles, Ca.	
Sermon/Los Angeles Campground	*MS-004	84/05/15	Los Angeles, Ca.	
Sermon/Los Angeles Campground	*MS-005	84/05/16	Los Angeles, Ca.	*1SAT 10-12*
Sermon/Los Angeles Campground	*MS-006	84/05/17	Los Angeles, Ca.	
Sermon/Oakland, Cal.	*MS-007	84/05/24	Oakland, Ca.	
"In the Sunday School lessons..."	*MS-008	84/06/12		
Visit to Multnomah Falls	*MS-009	84/06/20	E. Portland, Or.	TDG 180;3Bio 252-253
Sermon/Portland, Oregon	*MS-010	84/06/29	Portland Or.	Notes only. Not on file.
Proper Breathing and Good Speaking	*MS-011	84/00/00		
The Fruit of Persecution and Suffering	*MS-012	84/00/00		
The Ladder to Heaven	*MS-013	84/00/00		*19MR 338-355*
Message of the Autograph	*MS-014	84/00/00		*In YI 05/05/1959*
The Ohio Camp Meeting	MS-015	84/09/00		
Satan's Last Deception	*MS-016	84/00/00		LDE 164-165

1885

Sermon/Battle Creek Tabernacle	MS-002	85/07/25	Battle Creek, Mi.	2MR 211;9MR 42-43
The Obedience of the Sabbath	MS-003	85/10/08	Christiania, Norway	3SM 259-260;HP 150,151;
				1BC 1099-1100;6BC 1102;
				5MR 3-6;CTr 109
Sermon/Christian Fellowship	MS-004	85/11/09	Christiania, Norway	*2SAT 20-25*
Counsel to Physicians and Medical Students	MS-004a	85/07/27		*PH167*
Words of Counsel to Young Physicians	MS-004b	85/07/27		See Ms 4a, 1885
Sermon/Hearing and Doing	MS-005	85/03/07	Santa Rosa, Ca.	*1SAT 13-24*
The Spirit of Service	MS-006	85/00/00	Basel, Switz.	
Come Out From Among Them	MS-007	85/07/27		See Ms 4a, 1885
Sermon/Soldiers of Christ	MS-008	85/10/24	Grythytthed, Sweden	OHC 326;6MR 50-51;CTr 205
Sermon/God's Purpose For Us	MS-009	85/10/24	Grythytthed, Sweden	
Sermon/The Price of Eternal Life	MS-010	85/10/27	Orebro, Sweden	

Sermon/Waiting & Watching for Christ's Appearing	MS-011	85/10/28 Orebro, Sweden	HP 42,233,355
Statement re Mr. Garmire	MS-012	85/08/0? S. Lancaster, Ma.	*PH050 9-12*
Talk/Before the European Council	*MS-014	85/09/21 Basel, Switz.	1MR 151-153;5MR 308-311
Influence of Unconsecrated Workers	*MS-015	85/07/17 Winslow, Az.	TDG 207;OHC 303
Diary [Jul. 7]	*MS-016	85/07/07	EGWE 25
Diary [Jul. 7-Sep. 24]	*MS-016a	85/07/00	3MR 179-180;5MR 268-269; 11MR 148-149;3Bio 289-293, 297-300;EGWE 27,88
Shipboard Meditations	*MS-017	85/08/14 "Cephalonia"	TDG 235;EGWE 28-29
Remarks/European Council	*MS-018	85/09/20 Basel, Switz.	*21MR 300*
Talk?/European General Council	*MS-019	85/09/21 Basel, Switz.	4MR 408-409;6MR 130-133
Diary [Sep. 25]	*MS-020	85/09/25 Basel, Switz.	3Bio 310-313;EGWE 83
Diary [Oct. 15]	*MS-021	85/10/15 Steamer for Malmo	3Bio 318
Re Miles Grant in Italy	*MS-022	85/11/30 Italy	5MR 269
Re Miles Grant	*MS-023	85/00/00 Italy	
Diary [Sep. 25-Oct. 5]	*MS-024	85/09/00 Basel, Switz.	2MR 112-116;3Bio 313;EGWE 83,86
Diary [Oct. 6-14]	*MS-025	85/10/00	5MR 157-160;6MR 143,295; EGWE 99-100
Diary [Oct. 15-30]	*MS-026	85/10/00	TDG 299;3SM 313-316;2MR 153; 3MR 373,383-389;6MR 94;9MR 99-100; 3Bio 320;EGWE 100,105,108-109
Diary [Oct. 31-Nov. 19]	*MS-027	85/11/00	2MR 116-121;3Bio 328-329; EGWE 124-126
Diary [Nov. 20-25]	*MS-028	85/11/00	*17MR 329-335*
Diary [Nov. 26-Dec. 15]	*MS-029	85/12/00	3Bio 333-336;3MR 214-216;4MR 41; 5MR 270;10MR 379-380
Report of Meeting in Torre Pellice	*MS-029a	85/11/28	
Diary [Dec. 16-31]	*MS-030	85/12/00	5MR 183,270-271;3Bio 337; EGWE 89-90,145-146
Purity	*MS-031	85/00/00	TSB 92
God's Purpose for Israel	*MS-032	85/00/00	CTr 111
Sermon/Christiania, Norway	MS-033	85/11/10 Christiania, Norway	HP 289;5MR 435
Ministers' Families	MS-034	85/02/15 Healdsburg, Ca.	Unverified extracts
Ministers' Families	MS-034a	85/02/15 Healdsburg, Ca.	Unverified extracts
Ministers' Families	MS-034b	85/10/22 Kopparberg, Sweden	Unverified extracts
Sermon?/The Use of Means	MS-035	85/10/19 Stockholm, Sweden	*19MR 133-140*
Lessons from the Training and Character of Moses	MS-036	85/12/13 Torre Pellice, Italy	See YI 01/29/1903;CTr 100,116,135
Sermon/Address to Ministers	MS-037	85/00/00?	

1886

Sermon/Striving to Enter In	MS-005	86/06/19 Orebro, Sweden	HP 118,263;CTr 220
Talk/Beginnings of Work in Scandinavia	MS-006	86/06/23 Orebro, Sweden	Ev 420-421;11MR 76-77
Sermon/Preparation for the Judgment	MS-006a	86/06/27 Orebro, Sweden	*1SAT 25-38*
Remarks/Reproof for Sabbath-Breaking	MS-007	86/07/11 Christiania, Norway	*10MR 89-95*
Sermon/Christ's Agony over Jerusalem	MS-007a	86/07/11 Christiania, Norway	
Talk/Overcoming Self	MS-008	86/07/19 Copenhagen, Denmark	TDG 209;CTr 126
Sermon/Having Our Conversation in Heaven	MS-009	86/07/24 Copenhagen, Denmark	*1SAT 39-47*
Sermon/Preparation for Christ's Coming	MS-010	86/07/24 Copenhagen, Denmark	*2SAT 26-30*
Sermon/Christ's Controversy With the Devil	MS-011	86/07/25 Copenhagen, Denmark	CTr 216,288
Talk/Christian Brotherhood	MS-013	86/09/22 Grimsby, England	TDG 274;2MR 145
Christian Integrity in the Ministry	MS-015	86/00/00 Basel, Switz.	*11MR 82-91*
Labors in Italy	MS-015a	86/04/18 Torre Pellice, Italy	5MR 272-273
Visit to Copenhagen	MS-015b	86/07/00 Copenhagen, Denmark	LDE 232;6MR 143-144
Sermon/The Privilege of Being a Christian	MS-016	86/09/16 Grimsby, England	*2SAT 31-38*
God's Building	MS-017	86/00/00 missing	
Sermon/Lessons from the Life of Abraham	MS-019	86/03/13	HP 112;10MR 118-121;CTr 73,75

EGW Manuscripts File—Page 8

Sermon/Lessons from the Life of Abraham	MS-019a	86/03/27	Basel, Switz.	1BC 1093-1094;TDG 95;6MR 5-6; CTr 76,80
Sketch of Journey	MS-020	86/06/20	Basel, Switz.	5MR 18-23;3Bio 342;EGWE 190
Healdsburg College	MS-022	86/00/00		*1MR 317-322*
Building a House for God	MS-023	86/00/00		Ev 377-378;CG 542-543;CTr 364
Objections to the Bible	*MS-024	86/00/00		*1SM 19-21*
Talk/Sanctification	MS-025	86/06/20	Orebro, Sweden	5MR 123-124
Sermon/Evil Speaking	MS-026	86/07/15	Christiania, Norway	UL 210;OHC 234;Ev 244-245
Sermon/Building on the Rock	MS-027	86/07/25	Copenhagen, Denmark	TDG 215;Ev 595-596
Sermon/The Hope Set Before Us	MS-028	86/10/24	Nimes, France	*3MR 104-107*
Talk/Gaining a Fitness for Heaven	MS-029	86/10/31	Nimes, France	*3MR 113-116*
Sermon/The Christian Pathway	MS-030	86/11/07	Villar Pellice, Italy	*5MR 250-253*
Sermon/Giving Up Our Will for God's Will	MS-031	86/11/07	Torre Pellice, Italy	*5MR 253-256*
Travels in Switzerland	*MS-033	86/09/02	Basel, Switz.	2SM 335;5MR 194;EGWE 214-215
A Christ-like Character	*MS-035	86/07/00		OHC 176;TSB 261
Counsel to Church Members	*MS-037	86/00/00		
Counsel to Chaux-des-Fonds Church	*MS-037a	86/00/00		
Sermon/Whom are we Following?	*MS-038	86/11/11	St. Germain, Italy	*5MR 256-262*
Sermon/"If Thou Wilt Enter Into Life"	*MS-039	86/10/16	Nimes, France	*3MR 66-70*
Sermon/Come Unto Me	*MS-040	86/10/17	Nimes, France	*3MR 70-75*
Sermon/Walk in the Light	*MS-041	86/10/18	Nimes, France	*3MR 75-81*
Sermon/The Ladder to Heaven	*MS-042	86/10/20	Nimes, France	*3MR 81-88*
Sermon/Search the Scriptures	*MS-043	86/10/21	Nimes, France	*3MR 88-93*
Sermon/The Cross Before the Crown	*MS-044	86/10/22	Nimes, France	*3MR 93-99*
Sermon/God's Law the Standard of Character	*MS-045	86/10/23	Nimes, France	*3MR 99-104*
Sermon/The Two Standards	*MS-046	86/10/30	Nimes, France	*3MR 107-113*
The Battle Following Conversion	*MS-046a	86/11/11	Nimes, France	*3MR 117-119*
Sermon/Keep My Commandments	*MS-047	86/11/14	Torre Pellice, Italy	*5MR 262-267*
Sermon/At Lausanne	*MS-048	86/11/21	Lausanne, Switz.	
Sermon/Church Dedication	*MS-049	86/12/25	Tramelan, Switz.	*3MR 230-236*
Economy	*MS-050	86/06/00	Christiania, Norway	3SM 330-331
Human Lips to Give the Message	*MS-051	86/00/00		
Visit to Bienne	*MS-052	86/03/19	Bienne, Switz.	CTr 326
At Bienne	*MS-053	86/03/22	Lausanne, Switz.	EGWE 172
Diary [Apr. 18-May 19]	*MS-054	86/04/00	Torre Pellice, Italy	OHC 245;EGWE 177,187
Visit to Bobbio	*MS-055	86/04/25	Villa Pellice, Italy	VSS 400;2MR 303-304;5MR 273;CTr 29
Traveling in Switzerland	*MS-056	86/05/20	Laufen, Switz.	TMK 146,360,361;10MR 367-370; 3Bio 343
Diary [Jul. 8]	*MS-057	86/07/08	Christiania, Norway	3Bio 347-349;EGWE 203
Visit to Hansen Home	*MS-058	86/07/00	Christiania, Norway	8MR 122-123
Sketch of Journey to England	*MS-059	86/09/00		3Bio 354;EGWE 216-217
Sermon/The Mission of Christ	*MS-060	86/12/26	Tramelan, Switz.	HP 370;UL 374
Diary [Mar. 21]	*MS-061	86/03/21	Basel, Switz.	EGWE 148
Diary [Apr. 15-29]	*MS-062	86/04/00		OHC 34,139,253;1MR 309-310; 2MR 307-309;5MR 274;6MR 295; 10MR 370-371;EGWE 176,179-184; CTr 248,322
Journey from Italy to Switzerland	*MS-063	86/04/29		
Diary [Apr. 30-May 23]	*MS-064	86/05/00		3MR 228-229,373-374;5MR 27-28
Diary [Jun. 15-Jul. 1]	*MS-065	86/06/00		OHC 139,212;3MR 389-390;4MR 99; 9MR 92,94;3Bio 345;EGWE 193-195
Diary [Jul. 2-15]	*MS-066	86/07/00	Christiania, Norway	8MR 123-124;3Bio 347,349,351-352; EGWE 199,202,204-205
Diary [Jul. 16-27]	*MS-067	86/07/00		3Bio 352
Diary [Jul. 28-Aug. 11]	*MS-068	86/08/00	Basel, Switz.	
Diary [Sep. 14-Oct. 13]	*MS-069	86/09/00		
Diary [Oct. 14-Nov. 2]	*MS-070	86/10/00		3MR 61-64;5MR 317-319;3Bio 355

EGW Manuscripts File—Page 9

Diary [Nov. 3-12]	*MS-071	86/11/00		
Diary [Dec. 24-31]	*MS-072	86/12/00		3MR 229 230;5MR 25 27
Descriptive Items from Travels	*MS-073	86/00/00		OHC 252;3MR 216-217;EGWE 237-238
Record of Writing	*MS-074	86/00/00		
Visit to Paris and Versaille, France	*MS-075	86/10/00		HP 40,44;CTr 292
Recollections of Early Days of the Message	*MS-076	86/11/00		4MR 402-403;EGWE 266
Labors in Tramelan, Switzerland	*MS-077	86/12/00		See RH 04/15/1887
Nearing the Judgment	*MS-078	86/00/00		HP 218
Sermon/At Orebro, Sweden	MS-079	86/06/24	Orebro, Sweden	HP 331
Sermon/At Grimsby, England	MS-080	86/09/21	Grimsby, England	HP 353,354;9MR 249-251
Sermon/At Grimsby, England	MS-081	86/09/21	Grimsby, England	*1SAT 48-51*
Sermon/At Grimsby, England	MS-082	86/09/00	Grimsby, England	9MR 253-256
Sermon/At Grimsby, England	MS-083	86/09/00	Grimsby, England	3SM 420;8MR 104;9MR 256-259;CTr 42
Sermon/At Grimsby, England	MS-084	86/09/26	Grimsby, England	HP 369;9MR 259-264
Important Test. to our Brn. and Srs. in NY	MS-085	86/12/27	Basel, Switz.	*PH039*
Sermon/Noah	MS-086	86/02/27	Basel, Switz.	CTr 39,55,57-60
Preparing for the Time of Testing	MS-087	86/00/00	Copenhagen, Denmark	

1887

High Standard of Gospel Ministry	*MS-003	87/03/01	Basel, Switz.	
Sermon/The Need of Earnest, Intelligent Workers	MS-014	87/03/07	Basel, Switz.	*2SAT 39-47*
Sermon/Behold What Manner of Love	MS-016	87/05/22	Zurich, Switz.	CC 29;8MR 406-407
Sermon/Practical Godliness	MS-017	87/06/11	Moss, Norway	6MR 13,196-197;8MR 32
Sermon/Christian Temperance	MS-018	87/06/19	Moss, Norway	CC 130;9MR 232-234
Sermon/A Practical Education	MS-019	87/08/19	New Bedford, Ma.	AH 88,299;CG 124,126,254-255,358; 4MR 96;11MR 155
Sermon/Morning Talk at Grand Rapids	MS-020	87/09/25	Grand Rapids, Mi.	UL 282
Sermon/At Oakland	MS-021	87/10/14	Oakland, Ca.	
Sanitariums	MS-022	87/09/12	Battle Creek, Mi.	*15MR 272-285*
Equality in Distribution of Means	MS-023	87/00/00	Battle Creek, Mi.	
Investing Means in Building Sanitariums	MS-023a	87/00/00	Battle Creek, Mi.	Variant of Ms-023-1887
Test. for Workers of Publ. House at Basel	MS-024	87/02/14		AH 308;Ev 94,650-651;OHC 175,240; UL 59;1BC 1108,1113;3BC 1159-1162; 4BC 1144;8MR 325-328;9MR 374
Sermon/A Peculiar People	*MS-025	87/07/14	Wellingborough, Eng.	UL 209;EGWE 311
Sermon/A Living Sacrifice	*MS-026	87/02/06	Tramelan, Switz.	4MR 445-446;CTr 215
Storm at Sea	*MS-027	87/08/00	En route to USA	EGWE 317
Diary [Jan. 1-May 15]	*MS-029	87/01/00	Switz.	1SM 147;3MR 374-375;6MR 193; 8MR 445-446;9MR 94-95; 3Bio 361-363;EGWE 267-269,271-274
Diary [May 13-22]	*MS-031	87/05/00	France	5MR 319
Diary [May 26-31]	*MS-032	87/05/00	Germany	*2MR 121-130*
Diary [Jun. 1-8]	*MS-033	87/06/00	Denmark	6MR 145;EGWE 298-299
Diary [Jun. 9-22]	*MS-034	87/06/00	Norway	2MR 130-138
Diary [Jun. 23-28]	*MS-035	87/06/00	Sweden	3MR 390-393
Diary [Jun. 29-Jul. 10]	*MS-036	87/07/00	England	2MR 138-142;6MR 123; EGWE 307-308,311
Cooperating With God	*MS-037	87/06/07	Copenhagen, Denmark	TDG 167
The Witness of John Huss	*MS-038	87/00/00		*9MR 275-277*
"I have been unable to sleep much..."	MS-039	87/07/23	Grimsby, Eng.	*3MR 1-4*
"I have been unable to sleep much..."	MS-039a	87/07/23	Grimsby, Eng.	variant of Ms 39, 1887
Peril of Doubt and Unbelief	MS-040	87/00/00		HP 105;See ST 06/23/1887
The Value of Redemption/"In order to..."	MS-041	87/00/00		CC 325;SD 249;1BC 1107;5BC 1149; 7ABC 487

1888

Our Health Institutions	MS-001	88/02/01	Healdsburg, Ca.	1MR 278-281;SpM 208-210
Engaging in Worldly Speculation	MS-002	88/09/07		*1888 47-65*
Sermon/Living for God	MS-003	88/09/25	Oakland, Ca.	Te 158,192,256;2SM 301-302;
				4MR 363-364;9MR 374-375;
				10MR 71;MRmnt 123
Sermon/How to Become True Ministers for Christ	MS-004	88/10/08	Kansas City	2SAT 48-56
Talk/A Living Connection with God	MS-006	88/10/11	Minneapolis, Mn.	*1888 69-73*
Sermon/Tell of His Love and Power	MS-007	88/10/13	Minneapolis, Mn.	*1888 74-84*
Sermon/Advancing in Christian Experience	MS-008	88/10/20	Minneapolis, Mn.	*1888 121-128*
Sermon/Counsel to Ministers	MS-008a	88/10/21	Minneapolis, Mn.	*1888 132-145*
Talk/At Minneapolis	MS-009	88/10/24	Minneapolis, Mn.	*1888 151-153*
Remarks/On Missionary Work	MS-010	88/10/23	Minneapolis, Mn.	*1888 146-150*
Treatment of the Erring	MS-011	88/00/00		*15MR 172-199*
Test. to Dr. Burke	MS-012	88/04/00	Oakland, Ca.	5MR 337;10MR 121,287-289
Sermon/At Des Moines	MS-013	88/12/01	Des Moines, Ia.	1SAT 61-77;ML 29;AH 319,528-529;
				CG 272;9MR 98
How Can Institutions Be Made a Success?	MS-014	88/02/01		AH 53-54;TSB 115-117;7MR 128-130
A Call to a Deeper Study of the Word	MS-015	88/11/00	Minneapolis, Mn.	*1888 163-175*
The Guide Book	*MS-016	88/00/00	Minneapolis, Mn.	*1SM 15-18*
Sermon/A Chosen People	MS-017	88/10/21	Minneapolis, Mn.	*1888 129-131*
Religious Liberty	MS-018	88/00/00		*1SAT 78-92*
Who Shall Be Saved?	MS-019	88/00/00		
Sermon/Abide in Me	*MS-020	88/11/25	Potterville, Mi.	TDG 338;10MR 381-382
Distressing Experiences of 1888	*MS-021	88/00/00		*1888 176-181*
Diary [Jan. 1-30]	*MS-022	88/01/00		TSB 54
Diary [Feb. 1-14]	*MS-023	88/02/00		
Looking Back at Minneapolis	*MS-024	88/11/00		*12MR 179-205*
Diary [Dec. 16-31]	*MS-025	88/12/00	Battle Creek, Mi.	3Bio 421-423
Remarks/At Minneapolis	MS-026	88/10/00	Minneapolis, Mn.	*1SAT 52-60*
Living the Truth	MS-027	88/00/00		7MR 331
Diary [May-June]	*MS-028	88/05/00		

1889

Sermon/The Quality of Faith	MS-001	89/05/11	Ottawa, Ks.	*FW 63-80*
Talk/Picking Flaws	MS-002	89/05/12	Ottawa, Ks.	*1SAT 93-97*
Talk/Morning Talk	MS-003	89/05/14	Ottawa, Ks.	*1SAT 98-101*
Talk/Preparation for Christ's Coming	MS-004	89/05/14	Ottawa, Ks.	*1SAT 102-104*
Sermon/Christ and the Law	MS-005	89/06/19	Rome, NY	*1SAT 105-119*
Counsels Regarding Matters at Gen Conf.	MS-006	89/11/04	Battle Creek, Mi.	*1888 471-497*
Neatness and Order at Camp meetings	MS-007	89/00/00		1BC 1119
Advancing in Christ's Training School	MS-008	89/00/00	Kalamazoo, Mi.	
The Excellence of Christ	MS-010	89/10/00		*1888 447-449*
Test. to Leaders	MS-011	89/08/10	Harbor Heights, Mi.	
Establish the Work in Many Places	*MS-012	89/00/00		*PH151 6-8*
Standing by the Landmarks	MS-013	89/00/00		*1888 516-519*
The Elevating Character of True Religion	MS-014	89/00/00		*HM 12/00/1889*
Counsels to Our Colporteurs re Diet	*MS-015	89/00/00		*16MR 173*
The Discernment of Truth	*MS-016	89/01/00		*1888 257-262*
Diary [Jan. 1-31]	*MS-017	89/01/00		3Bio 423,425,427;FBS 2
Diary [Feb. 1-25]	*MS-018	89/02/00		9MR 93-94
Diary [Mar. 2-28]	*MS-019	89/03/00		*1888 269-273*
Diary [Jun. 15-28]	*MS-020	89/06/00		
Diary [Sep. 6-29]	*MS-021	89/09/00		Mar 197;OHC 99;TDG 261,279;

				11MR 150-152
Diary [Oct. 16-31]	*MS-022	89/10/00	Battle Creek, Mi.	*1888 452-468*
Diary [Nov. 1-23]	*MS-023	89/11/00	Battle Creek, Mi.	OHC 211;3SM 360;11MR 109-113;
				12MR 57
Diary [Dec. 4-27]	*MS-024	89/12/00	Battle Creek, Mi.	TDG 364,368
Resume of Travels and Labors	*MS-025	89/00/00		*3Bio 417-418*
Unity and Harmony Among Ministers	*MS-026	89/09/11	Denver, Co.	RC 277;UL 268
True Concept of Righteousness by Faith	*MS-027	89/09/13	Denver, Co.	*3SM 183-189*
A Significant Dream	*MS-028	89/11/18	Battle Creek, Mi.	TDG 331
Love and Consideration in Worker Relationship	*MS-029	89/11/18	Battle Creek, Mi.	
Experiences Following the Minneapolis Conf.	*MS-030	89/06/00		*16MR 212-241*
Diary/Paragraphs on various subjects	MS-031	89/00/00		3SM 43;VSS 77-78,131-132;1BC 1092;
				3BC 1156;4BC 1147;5BC 1083,1089,
				1135-1136;6BC 1076,1111,1118-1119;
				7BC 988;17MR 32;CTr 234
Sermon/At Kansas Camp-meeting	MS-032	89/05/10	Ottawa, Ks.	*From Topeka Daily Capital,*
				05/11/1889
Sermon/At Kansas Camp-meeting	MS-033	89/05/14	Ottawa, Ks.	*From Topeka Daily Capital,*
				05/15/1889
Sermon/At Kansas Camp-meeting	MS-034	89/05/15	Ottawa, Ks.	*From Topeka Daily Capital,*
				05/16/1889
Sermon/Progress in the Work of Christ	MS-035	89/11/16	Battle Creek, Mi.	
Ministry of Angels	MS-036	89/00/00		
Resisting Doubt	MS-037	89/00/00		

1890

Sermon/Heaven's Part in Life's Conflict	MS-001	90/02/01	Battle Creek, Mi.	*2SAT 57-70*
A Consecrated Ministry	MS-001a	90/02/13	Battle Creek, Mi.	*PH028 1-20*
Sermon/The Spirit of Discernment	MS-002	90/03/09	Battle Creek, Mi.	*1SAT 139-142*
Sermon/Faith	MS-002	90/03/16	Battle Creek, Mi.	*1SAT 143-149*
The Work in Michigan	MS-003	90/08/10		*2SAT 71-79*
Sermon/"Yesterday morning before I went..."	MS-004	90/03/08		*1888 593-598*
"Wherewithal shall a young man cleanse..."	MS-005	90/00/00	Battle Creek, Mi.	*19MR 73-76*
"John to the seven churches..."	MS-006	90/11/25	Brooklyn, NY	*PC 385-389*
Remarks/"We have the exhortation..."	MS-007	90/02/05		7BC 937
Sr. White's Test. Through the *Review*	MS-008	90/00/00		*From RH*
Remarks/At the Bible School	MS-009	90/02/03		*1SAT 120-128*
Remarks/At the Bible School	MS-010	90/02/06		*1SAT 129-138*
"The true Witness speaks through John..."	MS-016	90/10/01	Lynn, Ma.	2SM 19-21;PM 67,79;Ev 593-594;
				CW 94-95;MM 98-99;VSS 315-316;
				5BC 1126;6BC 1097;7BC 907,934,941,
				949,979;1MR 109-110;2MR 197;
				5MR 164;CTr 124,238
"Dr. ----'s great success is largely due..."	MS-017	90/10/01	Battle Creek, Mi.	From Lt 13, 1890;MM 51-53,147-151
To the Ministers and Churches in Ohio Conf.	MS-019	90/08/20	Petoskey, Mi.	TM 147-158
"Missions are essential..."	MS-019a	90/05/01	St. Helena, Ca.	*GCDB 02/06/1893 162-163*
Sermon/"I have felt that there is too..."	MS-019b	90/07/14	Lake Goguac, Mi.	*2SAT 80-91*
"But ye shall receive power..."	MS-021	90/10/11	Adam's Center, NY	See RH 08/16/1898
Diary [Jan. 10-Mar. 1]	MS-022	90/01/00	Battle Creek, Mi.	*1888 568-583*
Diary [Nov. 24]	MS-023	90/11/24	Brooklyn, NY	UL 342;PM 356;CM 129
"In the beginning was the Word..."	MS-024	90/05/18		*1888 665-672*
Diary [Jan. 7-9]/"I arise at half past..."	MS-025	90/01/07	Battle Creek, Mi.	*13MR 238-244*
Diary/"Dealing in mining stocks..."	MS-026	90/01/07	Battle Creek, Mi.	*15MR 68-71*
Warning Against Financial Speculation	MS-026a	90/01/07	Battle Creek, Mi.	*15MR 71-75*
Rules for Christian Workers	MS-027	90/11/10	Sands, Va.	

EGW Manuscripts File—Page 12

Diary [Dec.]	MS-028	90/12/00	Norwich-Boston, Ma.	*2SM 387-389*
Diary [Nov. 20-24]/"I spoke this evening"	MS-029	90/11/20	Brooklyn, NY	*21MR 446-456*
Diary [Nov. 20-24]/"I spoke this evening"	MS-029a	90/11/20	Brooklyn, NY	variant of Ms-029-1890
"God's servants are to impress..."	MS-030	90/00/00	Battle Creek, Mi.	*1888 906-916*
Circulation of The Great Controversy	MS-031	90/00/00		*1888 802-809*
The Source of the Church's Power	MS-032	90/00/00		*From HM 11/00/1890*
To Rise Up and Call Them Blessed	*MS-033	90/10/11		2SM 223-224
Loyalty of Daniel and his Three Companions	*MS-035	90/00/00		
Danger of False Ideas on Justification by Faith	*MS-036	90/00/00		*FW 15-28 and 6MR 147-148*
Light in God's Word	*MS-037	90/00/00		*1888 825-838*
Diary [Jan. 2]	*MS-038	90/01/02	Battle Creek, Mi.	TDG 10
The Vision at Salamanca	*MS-040	90/11/03	Salamanca, NY	*1888 917-949*
The Vision at Salamanca	MS-040a	90/11/03	Salamanca, NY	variant of Ms 40, 1890
Diary [Oct. 9-13]	*MS-041	90/10/00	Adam's Center, NY	OHC 146,297,299;2SM 223-224; HP 329;UL 296;MR1033 5-7
Diary [Oct. 14-29]	*MS-042	90/10/00	S. Lancaster, Ma.	OHC 20,42,91,136,281,285,286; UL 312;MR1033 7-16;CTr 127
Review of Experiences at S. Lancaster, Ma.	*MS-043	90/10/30	En route to NY	MR1033 16-17
Diary/Exp. at Salamanca, NY [Oct. 30-Nov. 4	*MS-044	90/11/00		9MR 73-75;MR1033 17-20
Diary [Nov. 4-11]	*MS-045	90/11/00	Sands, Va.	*2MR 322-331 with MR1033 21*
Diary [Nov. 13-20]	*MS-046	90/11/00	Washington, D.C.	MR1033 24-26,28-29
Reflections on Labors in Brooklyn, NY	*MS-048	90/11/26	Steamer	UL 344;4MR 41,309-311;13MR 31
Diary [Nov. 26-Dec. 3]	*MS-049	90/11/00	Norwich, Ct.	MR1033 32-36
Diary/Visit to Lynn, Ma. [Dec. 4-9]	*MS-050	90/12/00	Lynn, Ma.	MR1033 36-40
Diary/Labors at Danvers, Ma. [Dec. 10-14]	*MS-051	90/12/00	Danvers, Ma.	MR1033 41-44
Second Visit to Lynn, Ma. [Dec. 15-18]/Diary	*MS-052	90/12/00	Lynn, Ma.	MR1033 45
Visit to Washington, D.C. [Dec. 19-29]/Diary	*MS-053	90/12/00	Washington, D.C.	*1888 766-786*
In Battle Creek Again [Dec. 30-31]/Diary	*MS-054	90/12/00	Battle Creek, Mi.	*1888 787-789*
Peril of Trusting in the Wisdom of Men	*MS-055	90/00/00		*1888 839-845*
Remarks/Lessons From the Vine	*MS-056	90/02/07		*1888 561-567*
Christ's Humiliation	*MS-057	90/00/00		*16MR 180-184*
General Hygiene	MS-058	90/00/00		See CTBH 96-108;CTr 20,113
Hygienic Reform: Our Present Work	MS-059	90/00/00		3SM 292;Te 169;See CTBH 117-122
Our Institutions	*MS-060	90/00/00		
Danger in Adopting Worldly Policy in the Work	MS-061	90/00/00		*PH133*
Devotion to God Needed in the Publishing House	MS-062	90/00/00		
Comments Concerning 4T	*MS-063	90/00/00		

1891

Sermon/"I am the true vine..."	MS-001	91/01/11	Pine Creek, Mi.	ML 289
"I have been laboring two months..."	MS-002	91/01/09	Battle Creek, Mi.	*1888 854-860*
"Home again..."	MS-003	91/01/09	Battle Creek, Mi.	*14MR 66-69*
"The Lord will bless those who..."	MS-004	91/01/09	Battle Creek, Mi.	MRmnt 109
Sermon/Comments on Isaiah 58	MS-005	91/01/10	Pine Creek, Mi.	Ev 244;1BC 1095;5MR 34-35;CTr 86
Our Duty to the Colored People	MS-006	91/03/20		*SW 9-18*
"What are God's plans and purposes..."	MS-007	91/06/10	Petoskey, Mi.	4BC 1159;Ev 338;TDG 170; 6MR 65-66;9MR 158,375
Remarks/"Today as I have been writing..."	MS-008	91/07/24	Harbor Heights, Mi.	*9MR 51-55*
Talk/The Proper Way to Deal with Students	MS-008a	91/07/21	Harbor Heights, Mi.	*9MR 55-64*
Talk/Talk to Teachers	MS-008b	91/07/27	Harbor Heights, Mi.	*9MR 65-71 with 4MR 46-47*
"A spirit of independence has been..."	MS-008c	91/07/26	Harbor Heights, Mi.	*OHC 333 with 1MR 333-339 and 7MR 71-73*
Sermon/"O there is trading to be done..."	MS-009	91/08/22	Battle Creek, Mi.	3SM 192-193;10MR 272-273
Sermon/"And as Moses lifted up..."	MS-010	91/08/02	Harbor Heights, Mi.	TDG 223;RC 356;6MR 51
Remarks/At Michigan Conf. Meeting	MS-011	91/09/03		*1SAT 162-170*
Diary/"At the seven o'clock meeting..."	MS-012	91/12/28	Melbourne, Aus.	VSS 302-303,314-315,317;OHC 178

"In connection with our publishing work..."	MS-013	91/12/29	Melbourne, Aus.	AH 180,279-280;4Bio 26-27
"In connection with our publishing work..."	MS-013a	91/12/29	Melbourne, Aus.	variant with additional material
"I have been instructed by the Lord..."	MS-014	91/12/23	Melbourne, Aus.	*PH152 17-26*
"Wives, submit yourselves..."	MS-017	91/00/00		*21MR 213-218*
"The condition of children who do not..."	MS-018	91/00/00		AH 177-178,360-363;CG 237-238; ML 200
Diary/"I attended the ministerial..."	MS-019	91/03/03	Battle Creek, Mi.	PM 70;3MR 193-194; 13 Crisis Years 150-151
Diary [Mar. 7-8]	MS-019a	91/03/07	Battle Creek, Mi.	3Bio 479-480
Diary [Dec. 28-31]/"After addressing the..."	MS-020	91/12/28	Melbourne, Aus.	1SM 156-157;MRmnt 116
Diary/Christ Our Righteousness	*MS-021	91/02/27	Battle Creek, Mi.	*9MR 293-302*
Diary/"Nearly the entire day I have..."	*MS-023	91/03/12	Battle Creek, Mi.	PM 213;18MR 380;5Bio 227-229
Diary/Circulation of Great Controversy	*MS-024	91/01/01	Battle Creek, Mi.	*19MR 239-261*
"When Christ died to begin in redeeming..."	MS-025	91/00/00		*18MR 54-56*
"The publishing institution was arranged..."	MS-025a	91/00/00		2SM 191-194;OHC 116;1MR 263-264
The Orphan's Home	MS-026	91/00/00		*MM 06/00/1891 and 07/00/1891*
Sermon/"But ye shall receive power..."	*MS-027	91/04/18	Greenville, Mi.	*2SAT 92-98*
"There is much talk in regard to..."	*MS-029	91/08/20	Harbor Heights, Mi.	*1SAT 155-161*
"I am burdened for the Rural Health..."	*MS-030	91/11/00	Oakland, Ca.	
"The ship cannot come into port..."	*MS-032	91/11/27	Samoan Islands	*10MR 59*
Board and Council Meetings	*MS-033	91/00/00		*17MR 166-169*
The Case of the Walling Children	MS-034	91/09/12	Colorado Springs, Co.	4Bio 17
Sermon/Work & Baptism of the Holy Spirit Needed	MS-035	91/09/26	Healdsburg, Ca.	*1SAT 171-193*
Sermon/Fruits of Conversion	MS-036	91/09/19	Healdsburg, Ca.	*1SAT 194-213*
Counsel and Warning	MS-039	91/11/17	Steamer "Alameda"	*TM 264-278*
Diary [Jan.]	*MS-040	91/01/00	Battle Creek, Mi.	*1888 865-889*
Diary [Feb.]	*MS-041	91/02/00	Battle Creek, Mi.	
Diary [Mar.]	*MS-042	91/03/00	Battle Creek, Mi.	MR1033 64-65
Diary [Jun.]	*MS-043	91/06/00	Petoskey, Mi.	OHC 34,170;3Bio 492
Diary [Aug.]	*MS-044	91/08/00	Harbor Springs, Mi.	*18MR 155*
Diary [Dec.]	*MS-045	91/12/00	Melbourne, Aus.	8MR 358;4Bio 23-26
Justified by Faith	*MS-046	91/01/06	Battle Creek, Mi.	*8MR 355-357*
Arrival in Australia	MS-047	91/12/00		*From BE 01/01/1892*
Our Present Dangers	MS-048	91/03/24		*GCDB 04/13/1891 256-261*
Sermon/Importance of Exercising Faith	MS-083	91/07/22	Harbor Heights, Mi.	*1SAT 150-154*
A Message to the Churches	*MS-084	91/11/08	Sydney, Aus.	
Talk/At Battle Creek Tabernacle	MS-085	91/01/00	Battle Creek, Mi.	Notes only;not on file
Talk/At Battle Creek Tabernacle	MS-086	91/01/26	Battle Creek, Mi.	Notes only;not on file
Talk/At Battle Creek Tabernacle	MS-087	91/01/27	Battle Creek, Mi.	Notes only;not on file
Talk/At Battle Creek Tabernacle	MS-088	91/02/15	Battle Creek, Mi.	Notes only;not on file
Talk/At Battle Creek Tabernacle	MS-089	91/03/14	Battle Creek, Mi.	Notes only;not on file
Talk/At Battle Creek Tabernacle	MS-090	91/03/17	Battle Creek, Mi.	Notes only;not on file
Remarks at Presidents' Council	MS-091	91/02/25	Battle Creek, Mi.	

1892

"The world's Redeemer passed over..."	MS-001	92/11/15		*6MR 334-343*
Diary/"We left Adelaide Nov. 28th..."	*MS-002	92/12/13	George's Terrace	TDG 346
"In the starting of the work in this..."	MS-006	92/01/05	N. Fitzroy, Aus.	AH 459-461;TDG 13;OHC 99;3MR 380; PC 141-143;CTr 123,370
"I am now in Adelaide..."	MS-007	92/10/11	Adelaide, Aus.	
Christ Our Sufficiency	MS-008	92/11/25	Adelaide, Aus.	UL 343;HP 73;7BC 914;ChL 66-67; 2MR 24;9MR 164
Test. to Battle Creek Church	MS-010	92/06/10		*18MR 156-161*
Stewards of God's Gifts	MS-011	92/06/00		OHC 190;1MCP 245-246;2MR 98
Call to a Deeper Experience	MS-013	92/00/00		*RH 04/04/1893, 04/11/1893, and 04/18/1893*

Love for Brethren	MS-016	92/12/22	TDG 365
Diary [Apr.-Jul.]/"I am deeply grieved..."	*MS-019	92/04/00 Preston, Aus.	*21MR 108-125*
Diary/"The Lord has brought me through..."	*MS-020	92/07/15 Preston, Aus.	SD 19,124;7MR 143-144;8MR 49-51;
			12MR 140-141
Diary [Sep. 28-Nov.27]	*MS-021	92/10/00 Adelaide, Aus.	1MR 385;Ev 453-455
Re President of Australian Conference	MS-022	92/07/25	
Love, The Need of the Church	MS-024	92/00/00	*11MR 261-269*
Address to Physicians	MS-025	92/07/18	CH 340-343
"During my sickness I have thought much..."	MS-026a	92/08/05	1SM 379-381;SpM 5-7
The Crisis Imminent	MS-027	92/02/18 Melbourne, Aus.	*SpTA #1 37-40*
Diary [Jan.]	*MS-028	92/01/00 Melbourne, Aus.	8MR 44;4Bio 29
Diary [Feb.]	*MS-029	92/02/00 Melbourne, Aus.	TDG 61;OHC 368;3MR 377;MR728 22
Diary [Mar.]	*MS-030	92/03/00 Melbourne, Aus.	3MR 377
Diary [Apr.]	*MS-031	92/04/00 Melbourne, Aus.	3MR 376
Diary [May]	*MS-032	92/05/00 Melbourne, Aus.	2SM 235;3MR 376-377
Diary [Jun.]	*MS-033	92/06/00 Melbourne, Aus.	4Bio 38;See 21MR 112-121
Diary [Jul.]	*MS-034	92/07/00 Melbourne, Aus.	*19MR 287-299*
Diary [Aug.]	*MS-035	92/08/00 Melbourne, Aus.	8MR 358
Diary	*MS-035b	92/08/09 Melbourne, Aus.	variant of Ms-35-1892
Diary [Sep.]	*MS-036	92/09/00 Melbourne, Aus.	
Diary [Oct.]	*MS-037	92/10/00 Adelaide, Aus.	3MR 377-378;9MR 339-341
Diary [Nov.]	*MS-038	92/11/00 Adelaide, Aus.	Ev 453-455;1MR 385;4MR 43;
			9MR 347;4Bio 47
Diary [Dec.]	*MS-039	92/12/00 Ballarat/Melbourne	8MR 51-55;14MR 8
Diary	*MS-040	92/02/13 Melbourne, Aus.	HP 121;4Bio 34
God's Love For Man	MS-041	92/00/00	*BTS 12/00/1907, 02/00/1908,*
			03/00/1908, 11/00/1908, 12/00/1908,
			and 01/00/1909
Treatment of Erring Pupils/"God has given"	MS-043	92/00/00	*SSW 12/00/1892 and 01/01/1893*
The Bible School Privileges Unappreciated	MS-044	92/12/00	
The Sufferings of Christ	MS-045	92/00/00	
Talk/Address at George's Terrace	MS-046	92/08/24 Melbourne, Aus.	

1893

Sermon/"This is a wonderful and important..."	MS-002	93/01/29 Parramatta	6BC 1105;SD 57
Sermon/At Parramatta	MS-003	93/01/29	Missing
Diary/"We left Melbourne Thursday..."	MS-005	93/02/01 Parramatta	8MR 80-81
Sermon/Isaiah 58:1-3	MS-006	93/02/11 Auckland	OHC 45;2MCP 520,583
Sermon/"Now we have the rich promises..."	MS-008	93/02/09 Auckland	
"But Daniel purposed in his heart..."	MS-009	93/03/05 Kaeo, N.Z.	CG 93,186;AH 18;Te 56,105;3MR 365;
			6MR 262;8MR 381;10MR 74
Sermon/"Our blessed Saviour said..."	MS-011	93/03/28 Napier, N.Z.	*2SAT 99-103*
Sermon/"My mind has been much exercised..."	MS-012	93/03/28 Napier, N.Z.	CC 120;9MR 3-6;MRmnt 13
Sermon/Diligence in Service	MS-013	93/04/07 Napier, N.Z.	3MR 302-303
Sermon/"Here is the test..."	MS-014	93/04/22 Petone, N.Z.	HP 254
Sermon/"Here John has a view of the..."	MS-016	93/02/12 Auckland, N.Z.	CTr 209
Sermon/"The most important question ever..."	MS-017	93/03/26 Napier, N.Z.	CG 208;1MCP 26;TMK 108;5BC 1083;
			6BC 1105;7BC 922;3MR 424
Sermon/"This brings us to when Jesus..."	MS-018	93/04/06 Napier, N.Z.	
"Those that have published the Loud Cry..."	MS-021	93/06/12 Wellington, N.Z	*RH 11/08/1956.*
Diary/"Last Wednesday, July 5..."	MS-022	93/07/12 Wellington, N.Z.	9MR 25
Sermon/Temperance	MS-027	93/10/15 Gisborne, N.Z.	*Te 283-292*
"Since coming to New Zealand..."	MS-029	93/04/20 Palmerston, N.Z.	VSS 322-323;TDG 119
"There is a subject that urges..."	MS-032	93/02/16 Auckland, N.Z.	PM 91;6MR 376
"I was a few nights since in my dreams..."	MS-034	93/05/14	See FE 260-276 and SpM 104-113
Publishing Work	MS-035	93/01/08 Melbourne, Aus.	UL 22

Diary/"We left Sydney at two..."	MS-036	93/02/14	Auckland, N.Z.	
Diary	MS-037	93/03/01	Kaeo, N.Z.	*8MR 81-84*
Labors in Kaeo	MS-038	93/03/08	Kaeo, N.Z.	8MR 84-85
Diary	MS-039	93/05/20	Wellington, N.Z.	OHC 131;TMK 357
Diary	MS-040	93/06/16		
Maori Boys Interested in the Truth	MS-041	93/07/13	Wellington, N.Z.	
Educational Advantages Not Centered in B.C.	MS-045	93/00/00		1SM 129-130;10MR 345
New Zealand Camp Meeting	MS-046	93/00/00		*RH 06/06/1893*
Notes of Travel and Labor	MS-047	93/00/00		*RH 05/30/1893*
Diary/Christ and the Law	MS-048	93/05/06	Wellington, N.Z.	TMK 292;FLB 114;HP 38
"My mind is exercised in regard to..."	MS-049	93/10/28	Gisborne, N.Z.	*1NL 81-84 with 15MR 157*
"Know ye not that they which run..."	MS-050	93/09/00		*1SAT 214-226*
To Teachers and Students in our College in B.C.	MS-051	93/10/00		FE 220-230;5MR 247-248
Labors in Gisborne/"I have worked very hard"	MS-055	93/10/30	Gisborne, N.Z.	Te 264-265
Dependence and Trust/"The more our faith"	*MS-056	93/00/00		TMK 231
Visit to Paremata	*MS-059	93/08/08	Wellington, N.Z.	12MR 72-76;4Bio 100-104
Dedication of the Ormondville Church	*MS-060	93/11/20	Wellington, N.Z.	
Review and Herald Office	*MS-061	93/00/00		*1888 1813-1815*
The Mine of Truth	*MS-062	93/00/00		TMK 195
Diary [Jan.]	*MS-063	93/01/00		2MR 155
Diary [Feb.]	*MS-064	93/02/00	Parramatta	7MR 87-88
Diary	*MS-065	93/07/22	Wellington, N.Z.	
Diary [Aug.]	*MS-066	93/08/00	Napier, N.Z.	
Diary/Dedication of Ormondville Church	*MS-067	93/11/00	Napier, N.Z.	
Abundant Holidays	*MS-068	93/00/00	N.Z.	
Parables	*MS-073	93/07/00		*15MR 97-104*
Early Labors in Australia [1891-1892]	MS-075	93/00/00		OHC 120;4Bio 31-33
Diary [Feb. 2-20]	*MS-076	93/02/00		3SM 265
Diary [Feb. 20-Mar. 15]	*MS-077	93/03/00	Kaeo, N.Z.	4Bio 73,75
Diary [Mar. 15-Apr. 12]	*MS-078	93/03/00	Napier, N.Z.	4MR 104-105;4Bio 79
Diary [Apr. 13-17]	*MS-079	93/04/00	Palmerston, N.Z.	4Bio 89-90
Diary [Apr. 18-May 31]	*MS-080	93/05/00	Wellington, N.Z.	UL 137;TDG 156,158;3SM 115-116;
				1888 1167-1170;8MR 359;17MR 301-
				302; 4Bio 92-93
Diary [Jun. 1-Jul. 26]	*MS-081	93/06/00	Wellington, N.Z.	TDG 208;1888 1195-1196;8MR 85-86;
				10MR 385;4Bio 94,100
Diary [Jul. 27-Aug. 7]	*MS-082	93/07/00	Long Point, N.Z.	3MR 210-211
Diary [Aug. 8-14]	*MS-083	93/08/00	Wellington, N.Z.	TDG 233
Diary [Aug. 15-23]	*MS-084	93/08/00	N.Z.	4MR 102;4Bio 104-105
Diary [Sep. 1-Oct. 7]	*MS-085	93/09/00	N.Z.	8MR 86-89
Diary [Oct. 8-Nov. 11]	*MS-086	93/10/00	Gisborne, N.Z.	4MR 97,103
Diary [Nov. 12-20]	*MS-087	93/11/00	Napier/Ormondville, N.Z.	4Bio 108
Diary [Nov. 20-Dec. 19]	*MS-088	93/12/00	Wellington, N.Z.	8MR 89-92;4Bio 109
Diary [Dec. 20-30]	*MS-089	93/12/00	Sydney/Melbourne, Aus.	15MR 95-96;4Bio 112
Our Attitude Toward Powers That Be	*MS-090	93/08/29	Hastings, N.Z.	*TDG 250*
The Mother A Teacher	*MS-091	93/00/00		
Liquor Saloons a Curse	*MS-092	93/00/00		
Privileges and Responsibilities of Sons of God	*MS-093	93/00/00		*20MR 323-325*
Could Christ Have Yielded to Temptation?	*MS-094	93/00/00		*6MR 110-112*
S.D.A. Church Not Babylon [Fragment]	*MS-095	93/00/00		
Respect is Due to God's Instrumentalities	MS-096	93/00/00		*RH 10/10/1893*
Words to the Young	MS-097	93/00/00		*YI 08/31/1893*
Our Duty in Ministering to the Poor	MS-098	93/00/00		*RH 06/20/1893 and 06/27/1893*
Liberality the Fruit of Love	MS-099	93/00/00		*RH 05/09/1893 and 05/16/1893*
Christ Our Helper in the Great Crisis	MS-100	93/00/00		*HM 11/011893*
"This is a beautiful place...."	*MS-101	93/11/00		
"Walk in the Spirit."	MS-102	93/00/00		*ST 12/25/1893*

EGW Manuscripts File—Page 16

Bought With a Price   *MS-103   93/12/00   Wellington, N.Z.   AH 464;5MR 339;8MR 249;9MR 376

1894

"I address my dear brethren..."/Pitcairn	MS-001	94/01/05	Melbourne, Aus.	*14MR 70-75*
"Sabbath January 20th, has passed..."	MS-003	94/01/21	Middle Brighton, Aus.	
"Tents were first pitched..."	MS-004	94/01/29	Middle Brighton, Aus.	4Bio 124-125
"Yesterday, Sunday, in company with..."	MS-005	94/02/00		10MR 74-76
To Friends in America	MS-006	94/02/16	Melbourne, Aus.	*21MR 280-284*
Sermon/"And one of the elders answered..."	MS-007	94/01/28	Brighton, Aus.	*7MR 78-81*
Where Shall We Locate Our School?	*MS-008	94/02/00	Melbourne, Aus.	*FE 310-327*
The Kind of Schools Needed	MS-008a	94/02/00		
"I am constantly burdened in regard to..."	MS-009	94/02/10	Melbourne, Aus.	*SpTEd 164-170*
Sermon/Keep the Commandments	MS-010	94/02/11	Williamstown, Aus.	*1SAT 227-238*
Sermon/Isaiah 58	MS-011	94/02/10	Brighton, Aus.	*5MR 36-48*
Sermon/Isaiah 58	MS-011b	94/02/10	Brighton, Aus.	Variant of Ms-11-1894
Sermon/"As thou has given him power..."	MS-012	94/02/18	Prahan, Aus.	*1SAT 239-249*
Talk/Australian Bible School	MS-013	94/02/20	Melbourne, Aus.	1MCP 324
Talk/Australian Bible School	MS-014	94/02/22	Melbourne, Aus.	1MCP 53-54;CG 98;ML 291;5BC 1095
Talk/Address to Students	MS-015	94/02/23	Melbourne, Aus.	2MCP 724;10MR 113
Sermon/"Therefore being justified..."	MS-016	94/02/25	N. Brighton, Aus.	3SM 34-35;2MCP 675,803-804
Sermon/"Peter, an apostle of Jesus..."	MS-017	94/03/03	N. Brighton, Aus.	OHC 334;2MCP 578-579,670,794-795
Sermon/"And you hath he quickened..."	MS-018	94/03/04	Williamstown, Aus.	TDG 72;6BC 1093
"Friday was a very busy day..."	MS-019	94/03/17	Melbourne, Aus.	1MCP 22;2MCP 764-765;EV 238-239
Sermon/"Lay not up for yourself..."	MS-020	94/03/18	Williamstown, Aus.	Ev 243-244;TDG 86;Te 30;SD 59,141
Testimony to Ministers	MS-021a	94/04/02		Ev 102,104,116,336-337;1NL 127-130; 11MR 278
Diary/"I thank the Lord it is as well..."	MS-023	94/04/09	Granville, Aus.	WM 184-185;10MR 194-196;4Bio 133
Testimony to Canvassers	MS-024	94/04/23	Granville, Aus.	CG 124
Testimony to Canvassers	MS-024a	94/04/23	Granville, Aus.	variant of MS-024, 1894;CM 95-97
Test. Concerning Idleness	MS-024b	94/04/30	Granville, Aus.	AH 317;CG 88,110-111,345,355; 6MR 47
"Last night I seemed to be in an assembly"	MS-025	94/04/23	Granville, Aus.	*HM 12/1894*
Sermon	MS-026	94/05/13	Parramatta, Aus.	*2SAT 104-109*
Dear Brethren in the SDA Faith	MS-027	94/06/07	Granville, Aus.	PM 225;2MR 7-8;5MR 286-287; 13MR 361-362;4Bio 133-134,135-137; CTr 186
"In company with my son W.C. White..."	MS-028	94/06/25		6BC 1103
Meeting at Seven Hills	MS-032	94/07/29	Granville, Aus.	TDG 219;OHC 168;4BC 1183; 9MR 91-92;CTr 187;RH 09/10/1895
Diary/"Last Sabbath, July 28, my son..."	MS-032a	94/07/30	Granville, Aus.	*ST 06/06/1895*
Test. to Battle Creek	MS-033	94/08/03	Granville, Aus.	7BC 961;8MR 189;12MR 217
"I have recieved a letter from Brother..."	MS-034	94/08/03	Granville, Aus.	*1888 1268-1279*
Diary/Letter to S.N. Haskell	MS-035	94/08/27	Cooranbong, Aus.	*13MR 355-358*
Sermon/Dedication at Prospect Church	MS-037	94/09/16	Prospect, Aus.	*BE 10/01/1894 and 10/08/1894*
Sermon/"Christ said to his disciples..."	MS-038	94/10/09		*HM 04/00/1895*
"The great controversy between the Prince"	MS-039	94/10/09		*RH 04/14/1896*
Sanctification and Repentance	MS-040	94/10/10		*RH 08/27/1901 and 09/03/1901*
Diary/"I was present in morning meeting..."	MS-041	94/10/19	Ashfield, Aus.	CC 358;2BC 1036;3MR 249; 6MR 247-248;4Bio 168-169,277
Talk/Look and Live	MS-041a	94/10/20	Ashfield, Aus.	
Ashfield Camp Meeting	MS-041b	94/10/16		Missing
Talk/Morning Talk	MS-042	94/10/22	Ashfield, Aus.	Ev 299-300,339,488
Talk/Morning Talk	MS-042a	94/10/26	Ashfield, Aus.	
Sermon/The Vine and the Branches	MS-043	94/10/27	Ashfield, Aus.	RC 247,285,355;5MR 333-334
Sermon	MS-043a	94/10/28	Ashfield, Aus.	*1SAT 250-270*

EGW Manuscripts File—Page 17

"Last night in my sleeping hours..."	MS-044	94/10/30	Ashfield, Aus.	*GCB 02/25/1895 337-340 and 1M 194-197*
"Because iniquity shall abound..."	MS-045	94/11/00		
"Beloved, let us love one another..."	MS-046	94/11/00		
"All day the people pressed about Jesus..."	MS-047	94/11/26		*SSW 06/1895 & 07/1895*
Talk/Morning Talk	MS-048	94/11/03	Ashfield, Aus.	
Sermon	MS-049	94/11/03	Ashfield, Aus.	OHC 62;CG 565;7BC 989,944; 5MR 234-235;10MR 308-309;CTr 206
Talk/Morning Talk	MS-050	94/11/10		1MCP 205
Diary/"There is a great work to be done..."	MS-051	94/11/14	Granville, Aus.	*HM 08/00/1896*
Seeking to Save the Lost	MS-052	94/00/00		*8MR 189-191*
Should Christians Be Members of Secret Societies?	MS-053	94/00/00		*2SM 121-139*
"Salt is good: but if the salt..."	MS-054	94/12/17		*ST 11/07/1895*
"After these things the Lord appointed..."	MS-055	94/12/10		
Sermon/"There were present at that..."	MS-056	94/12/30		3BC 1140
Beneficent Action a Proof of Sincere Love	MS-060	94/00/00		CG 124;OHC 268;TMK 63;AH 494; 11MR 194
Walk in the Light of the Cross	MS-061	94/09/16	Granville, Aus.	*10MR 77-80*
Home Missionary Work	MS-062	94/08/18		*RH 01/08/1895 and 01/15/1895 and 01/22/1895*
Diary/"During the past night matters..."	MS-064	94/10/27	Ashfield, Aus.	WM 306;6MR 228
Help in God	MS-065	94/00/00		*RH 02/05/1895*
Missionary Work	MS-066	94/00/00		Ev 556-557,564
"The light of the body is the eye..."	MS-067	94/00/00		1MCP 250,324;2BC 998
We Shall Reap As We Sow	MS-068	94/00/00		*RH 08/21/1894*
Regarding Fern Hill Farms	*MS-069	94/00/00		
Importance of Maintaining Personal Integrity	*MS-070	94/00/00		TMK 199,248
Diary [Jan.]	*MS-071	94/01/00	Brighton, Aus.	
Diary [Feb. 22-23]	*MS-072	94/02/22	Melbourne, Aus.	
Diary [Mar.]	*MS-073	94/03/00	Melbourne, Aus.	
Diary [Apr.]	*MS-074	94/04/00	Granville, Aus.	10MR 13;4Bio 144
Diary [May]	*MS-075	94/05/00	Granville, Aus.	
Diary	*MS-076	94/06/14	Granville, Aus.	2MR 154
Diary [Aug.]	*MS-077	94/08/00	Granville, Aus.	8MR 361-362;4Bio 160-161
Diary [Sep.]	*MS-078	94/09/00	Granville, Aus.	
Diary [Oct.]	*MS-079	94/10/00	Ashfield, Aus.	
Diary [Nov.]	MS-080	94/11/00	Ashfield, Aus.	From Ms 41, 1894
Intelligence in the Practice of Health Reform	*MS-081	94/00/00		ML 132;See ST 09/30/1897
Fanaticism and Side Issues	MS-082	94/01/14		*3MR 25-36*
Christ the Center of the Message	MS-084	94/00/00		*RH 03/20/1894 (1SM 383-388)*
Diary/"On Sabbath Willie accompanied me..."	*MS-085	94/04/22	Granville, Aus.	UL 126
Sermon/Christ's Mission of Love	MS-086	94/10/21	Ashfield, Aus.	*BE 11/12/1894 and 11/19/1894*
Our Duty to the Poor and Afflicted	MS-087	94/00/00		*RH 12/18/1894 and 12/25/1894 and 01/01/1895*
Words to the Young	MS-088	94/00/00		*YI 06/07/1894*
Self-Discipline Necessary to Parents	MS-089	94/00/00		*ST 05/07/1894*
Sustainers of the Liquor Traffic Responsible for its	MS-090	94/00/00		*RH 05/22/1894*
A Perpetual Memorial	MS-091	94/00/00		*ST 11/12/1894*
Delusions of the Last Days	MS-092	94/00/00		*ST 05/28/1894*
Uphold Ministers	MS-093	94/00/00		See RH 07/17/1894
Experience with Fannie Bolton	MS-094	94/00/00		*FBS 123-124*
Presenting the Truth in New Areas	*MS-095	94/02/00		Ev 227-228;RH 10/14/1902 and 10/21/1902
Talk/"I want to say a few words to..."	MS-096	94/00/00		
"Emily and I rode about three miles..."	*MS-097	94/08/28	Cooranbong, Aus.	
"This day at noon..."	*MS-098	94/09/03	Granville, Aus.	
For Zion's Sake	MS-099	94/12/16		

Danger of Men Usurping the Place of God	MS-100	94/12/17		
Offending Christ's Little Ones, No. 1	MS-101	94/00/00		
Offending Christ's Little Ones, No. 2	MS-102	94/00/00		

1895

Diary/"The Australian campmeeting..."	MS-001	95/01/14	Ashfield, Aus.	2MR 45-46;4MR 103-104;9MR 146; 4Bio 167-168,170,176-177
"The Lord has a work for each individual"	MS-002	95/01/14	Granville, Aus.	
"I wish to make a brief statement..."	MS-002a	95/01/16	Cooranbong, Aus.	
Statement re Walling Case	MS-002b	95/01/26	Granville, Aus.	
Testimony regarding Br. Humphrey	MS-003	95/02/01	Granville, Aus.	7BC 928;LDE 68-69
Diary/"Sunday has been a busy day..."	MS-004	95/02/02	Sydney, Aus.	WM 331-332
By Many Infallible Proofs	MS-005	95/02/15		*YI 11/18/1897*
Are We Genuine Christians?	MS-006	95/02/15		*RH 04/09/1895*
"I must speak to my brethren..."	MS-007	95/03/08		*TM 347-359*
Diary/"Saturday, March 16..."	MS-009	95/03/16		
Speedy Preparation for Work	MS-010a	95/03/21	Granville, Aus.	*FE 334-367*
"God is a God of justice..."	MS-011	95/04/10	Granville, Aus.	4MR 441;5MR 454-455;11MR 77
"He that will love life..."	MS-011a	95/04/14		See YI 06/27/1895 and 07/11/1895
Sermon	MS-012	95/05/19	Williamstown, Aus.	1MCP 154,184-185;AH 32; CG 172,567-568
"Christ came to seek the lost pearl..."	MS-013	95/06/10	Granville, Aus.	10MR 225-227;see RH 04/21/1896
Diary/"This day has been a most precious..."	MS-014	95/08/10	Cooranbong, Aus.	Ev 278;6MR 4
An Earnest Admonition/"I do not find rest"	MS-015	95/09/19	Granville, Aus.	TM 359-364
Sermon/"And you hath he quickened..."	MS-016	95/10/20	Armadale, Aus.	UL 307;CG 54-55,494;CC 35; ML 91,361
"I was in a council meeting where many..."	MS-017	95/10/17	Granville, Aus.	2MCP 577,771-772
Sermon/"When therefore the Lord knew..."	MS-018	95/10/19	Armadale, Aus.	TDG 301;VSS 123
True Education	MS-020	95/11/10		8MR 250,280-283
Sermon/"Behold what manner of love..."	MS-021	95/11/00	Armadale, Aus.	*2SAT 110-114*
Appeal for Southern Field	MS-021a	95/00/09		*SW 25-30*
The Bible the Most Important Book for Study	MS-022	95/01/09		FE 444-452
Interview re Work Among the Colored People	MS-022a	95/11/20	Armadale, Aus.	*SpM 19-26*
"The Australian campmeeting..."	MS-023	95/11/19	Melbourne, Aus.	See RH 01/07/1896
Sermon/"Lay not up for yourselves..."	MS-024	95/11/00	Armadale, Aus.	
Diary/"On Christmas day..."	MS-025	95/12/29		Ev 95,652
The Essential Education	MS-025a	95/12/00		6MR 77-78
Tasmanian Camp Meeting	*MS-027	95/12/00		*RH 02/11/1896*
Education	MS-028	95/12/09	Hobart, Tasmania	
Converted Men Needed in all Departments	MS-029	95/00/00		PM 58-59;3MR 37-38;MRmnt 123
Consolidation of the Publishing Work	MS-031	95/00/00		*PH150 6-11*
Relation of G.C. Committee to Business Interests	MS-033	95/00/00		*14MR 278-279*
"The sufferings of humanity ever touched..."	MS-035	94/09/13	Filed in 1895	*BTS 09/00/1915 and 10/00/1915*
To the Church in Hobart	MS-038	95/05/00	Glenorchy, Tasmania	*2MR 264-285*
Education	MS-040	96/01/09	Filed in 1895	2MR 96;8MR 296
"Solemn, serious times are upon us..."	MS-041	95/01/31	From B-11-1895	*TM 200-203*
Diary/"On Sabbath, Jan'y 5th..."	MS-042	95/01/16		
Overbearing Control Reproved	MS-043	95/03/17		*PC 398-400*
To Every Man His Work	MS-044	95/00/00		*RH 06/25/1895 and 07/02/1895*
Go Ye Into All the World	MS-045	95/00/00		*RH 06/11/1895 and 06/18/1895*
Parable of the Ten Virgins	MS-047	95/10/26	From W-86-1895	*1888 1455-1456*
"Give Us This Day Our Daily Bread"	MS-048	95/01/19	Cooranbong, Aus.	OHC 209
No Other Gods Before Me	MS-049	95/00/00		See RH 05/14/1901
"Education as conducted in the schools..."	MS-050	95/00/00		OHC 209
God to Control His Heritage	MS-051	95/08/01	Granville, Aus.	*18MR 223-226*

Regarding Children	MS-053	95/00/00		*1NL 80*
Visit to Bismark, Tasmania	MS-054	95/04/26	Glenorchy, Tasmania.	2MR 259-260,4Bio 191-192
Labors in Bismark	*MS-055	95/04/26		TMK 42;2MR 261-263
The G.C. and the Publishing Work	*MS-056	95/09/01	Cooranbong, Aus.	
Concerning the Review and Herald	*MS-057	95/10/12	Granville, Aus.	*17MR 177-180*
Diary	*MS-058	95/12/11	Hobart, Tasmania	
Diary [Feb.]	*MS-059	95/02/00	Granville, Aus.	15MR 217-226;4Bio 183,187
Diary [Mar.]	*MS-060	95/03/00	Granville, Aus.	
Diary [Jul.]	*MS-061	95/07/00	Cooranbong, Aus.	4Bio 220-221
Reminiscences of Early Days in California	*MS-062	95/00/00	N.S.W., Aus.	*2Bio 419-420*
Sanctified Humility	MS-064	95/00/00		*RH 02/18/1896*
Prejudice Blinds To Truth/"In all their..."	MS-065	95/00/00		*ST 04/25/1895*
What Atmosphere Surrounds the Soul?	MS-066	95/00/00		*ST 05/02/1895*
Personal Labor Required of the Ministers	MS-067	95/00/00		*RH 03/05/1895*
Sermon/Address at Armadale Campmeeting	MS-068	95/11/00	Armadale, Aus.	
Sermon/Address to the Leading Brethren	MS-070	95/00/00		

1896

"Take heed, brethren, lest there be..."	MS-001	96/01/12	Cooranbong, Aus.	
"The less that children shall become..."	MS-002	96/02/09		UL 54
"And they brought young children to him..."	MS-003	96/02/11		
"We have also a more sure word..."	MS-004	96/02/04		*3BC 1149 with 4MR 55-56*
"O how I love thy law!"	MS-005	96/02/10		CG 31,494-495,499,510;AH 189
"How little of the spirit of Christ..."	MS-007	96/02/03		*4MR 8-9 with 2SM 343*
"Whatsoever a man soweth, that shall he..."	MS-007a	96/02/27		*14MR 89-98*
True Education	MS-008	96/03/26		*FE 405-415*
"Those who are daily learning of Jesus..."	MS-009	96/03/23		*FE 397-404*
Sermon	MS-011	96/03/04	Cooranbong, Aus.	
"Before me is the light..."	MS-012	96/03/11		
Higher Education	MS-012b	96/03/17		AH 183;CG 224;6MR 15-16;10MR 301
"Friday, March 20, I arose early..."	MS-012c	96/03/20	Sydney, Aus.	*FBS 65-67*
Diary/"I awakened this morning at..."	*MS-012d	96/03/20	Sydney, Aus.	*FBS 63-64*
Faithfulness in Confessing Christ	MS-013	96/04/25		*12MR 227-231*
Qualifications Essential for the Work of God	MS-014	96/04/28		*PC 395-398*
"The word revelation means all that..."	MS-015	96/04/27		*13MR 59-73*
Let Him that Thinketh He Standeth Take Heed	MS-016	96/05/10		*19MR 108-122*
"In the night season I was listening..."	MS-017	96/05/13		*TM 319-330*
The Danger of Self-sufficiency in God's Work	MS-018	95/05/30	Filed in 1896	*1888 1356-1368*
"On our trip to Tasmania..."	MS-019	96/00/00		
"He that is faithful in that which is least"	MS-020	96/06/01		TDG 161
"This morning I will state the matters..."	MS-021	96/06/06	Cooranbong, Aus.	
"If it be possible, as much as..."	MS-023b	96/07/25		UL 220;15MR 158-161
"We are of good courage in the Lord..."	MS-024	96/09/09	Cooranbong, Aus.	1SM 175
"Blessed is he that readeth..."	MS-025	96/09/28	Cooranbong, Aus.	*16MR 256-266*
Systematic Benevolence	MS-026	96/09/25		*RH Supp. 12/01/1896*
"Yesterday Sr. McEnterfer accompanied..."	MS-027	96/09/04	Ashfield, Aus.	*RH 11/17/1896*
To Those Concerned in Publ. Mount of Blessing	MS-028	96/10/04	Ashfield, Aus.	PM 70-71,151-152;TDG 286;UL 291
"I fear greatly for the church at North Fitzroy..."	MS-029	96/10/31	North Fitzroy. Aus.	OHC 131,209;4MR 411-412
"There is a great deficiency in our schools"	MS-030	96/10/03		3SM 311;2MR 220-221
"According to appointment, I met with..."	*MS-030a	96/10/04	Ashfield, Aus.	*HM 11/00/1897*
Test. Re Views of Prophecy of John Bell #1	MS-031	96/11/08	Cooranbong, Aus.	*17MR 1-5*
Test. Re Views of Prophecy of John Bell #2	MS-032	96/12/06	Cooranbong, Aus.	*17MR 6-23*
Prepare to Meet the Lord	MS-032a	96/00/00		*18MR 57-64*
"I was awakened at half past eleven..."	MS-033	96/11/27		*SpTA #9 63-67*
"I was unable to sleep after eleven..."	MS-034	96/11/27	Cooranbong, Aus.	
Adopting Infant Children	MS-035	96/12/16		*14MR 301-310*

EGW Manuscripts File—Page 20

"The strength of nations and of individuals"	MS-036	96/12/09	TDG 352;3MR 186-187;CTr 180
"Will a Man Rob God?"	MS-037	96/08/00	*PH087*
Shall I Be Clothed with Immortality?	MS-038	96/12/15	
"Make Straight Paths for your Feet"	MS-039	96/12/31	OHC 53;3BC 1142,1161;6BC 1086; 7BC 921;10MR 296-297;11MR 49-51
The Workers Needed in Cooranbong	MS-040	96/12/31	2MCP 572;5MR 448-449;9MR 377
"In the night season some things..."	MS-041a	96/12/20	Cooranbong, Aus.	*1SAT 278-291*
"In the night season some things..."	MS-041b	96/12/20	Cooranbong, Aus.	variant of Ms-041a-1896;6MR 136-137
"On Wednesday night I had a dream..."	MS-042	96/12/30	Cooranbong, Aus.	*18MR 286-287*
Political Controversy	MS-043	96/12/27	Cooranbong, Aus.	*GCDB 02/17/1897 58-59*
Diary/"Today I picked the first ripe peach"	MS-044	96/12/04	Cooranbong, Aus.	Te 88-89;CD 425;4Bio 271
"The kingdom of heaven is like unto..."	MS-046	96/00/00	
The Lack of Unity a Cause of Failure	MS-047	96/00/00	*14MR 289-300*
"Better far would be the cross..."	MS-052	96/00/00	4MR 358;9MR 91
A Knowledge of Physiology Necessary	MS-053	96/04/24c	TDG 123;10MR 299
True Education	MS-054	96/05/07	Cooranbong, Aus.	8MR 251
Diary/"On October 1, 1896, we assembled..."	*MS-055	96/10/01	Cooranbong, Aus.	8MR 365;12MR 95
Diary Fragments/A Beautiful Dream	*MS-056	96/07/10	Cooranbong, Aus.	See LS 360-362
The Great Controversy	MS-057	96/12/30c	*18MR 358-367*
The Least of These My Brethren	MS-058	96/00/00	17MR 25
God's Claim on His Stewards	*MS-060	96/10/00	Sydney, Aus.	SpTA #9 67-74
Diary [Jan. 1-11]	*MS-061	96/01/00	Cooranbong, Aus.	4Bio 260
Diary [Feb.]	*MS-062	96/02/00	Cooranbong, Aus.	TMK 133,147,266,349;3MR 407-408; 11MR 114;12MR 58;4Bio 255, 261-263,387;FBS 63
Diary [Mar.]	*MS-063	96/03/00	Cooranbong, Aus.	FBS 64-65
Diary [Apr.]	*MS-064	96/04/00	Cooranbong, Aus.	
Diary [Jun.]	*MS-065	96/06/00	Cooranbong, Aus.	7MR 86;4Bio 388
Diary [Jul.]	*MS-066	96/07/00	Cooranbong, Aus.	TMK 127
Diary fragment	*MS-067	96/12/21	Ashfield, Aus.	
Criticising, Condemning, and All Evil Speaking To	MS-068	96/12/26c	*PC 356-360*
Upholding the Law of God	MS-069	96/00/00	1SM 115;3BC 1133,1152; 4BC 1143-1144
Systematic Benevolence	MS-070	96/09/27c	
Higher Education	MS-071	96/03/14c	
Amusements	MS-072	96/02/09c	
The Manifest Working of the Holy Spirit at BCC	MS-073	96/04/30c	*SpTEd 77-83*
God in Nature	MS-074	96/05/20	*CT 185-188*
Foreign Mission Work	MS-075	96/11/12	

1897

Forgetfulness	MS-001	97/01/11	*PH086 1-13*
"The Lord is speaking to men today..."	MS-002	97/01/11	Cooranbong, Aus.	
"I was awakened at 11:30 last night..."	MS-003	97/01/11	Cooranbong, Aus.	*PC 160-168*
"Be Ye Therefore Perfect"	MS-004	97/01/12	VSS 201-202;258-260;
Talk/Remarks at a Counsel Meeting	MS-005	97/01/17	
"Then the power of the Lord came upon me..."	MS-006	97/01/01	Cooranbong, Aus.	*HM 11/00/1897*
"Again and again the Lord has sent..."	MS-007	97/01/27	Cooranbong, Aus.	*1888 1636-1642*
"And, behold, a certain lawyer stood up..."	MS-008	97/02/02	Ev 275,278
"I feel greatly burdened over the case..."	*MS-012	97/02/11	Cooranbong, Aus.	
"My heart is troubled..."	MS-013	97/02/20	HP 142,161;1MCP 124-125;2MCP 663
"God so loved the world..."	MS-014	97/02/21	*ST 06/24/1897*
"The Lord has made known the duty..."	MS-014a	97/02/14	Sydney, Aus.	EV 567-568;4BC 11481 1MR 156
"Side by side, wearing the yoke of Christ"	MS-015	97/03/14	*HM 06/00/1897*

"The heavens declare the glory of God..."	MS-016	97/03/25	3BC 1144-1145;UL 98;8MR 286; 9MR 379
"Letters have come to me from Oakland..."	MS-017	97/03/14 Cooranbong, Aus.	*SpTA #10 16-25*
The Work for Today	MS-018	97/03/12	*RH 05/25/1897*
The Ordinance of Feet Washing	MS-019	97/03/29	*RH 06/14/1898 and 06/21/1898 and 06/28/1898 and 07/05/1898*
"I have not been able to sleep past twelve"	MS-020	97/03/05 Cooranbong, Aus.	*12MR 232-238*
"What Shall We Have for Sabbath Dinner?"	MS-021	97/03/17 Cooranbong, Aus.	*RH 06/01/1897 and 06/08/1897*
Go Ye Into All the World, and Preach	MS-022	97/03/05	5BC 1137;SpTA #10 33-39
"The Word of God must be our authority..."	MS-023	97/03/13	GCB 2nd Quarter, 1897 80-81
"There are exceptional cases..."	MS-024	97/03/15	*PH157 10-21*
"The Lord has aggressive work to be done..."	MS-025	97/03/02	*HM 06/00/1897*
"The Lord has made his people..."	MS-027	97/03/30	*HM 07/00/1897*
Judas	MS-028	97/04/22	SD 300;5BC 1101;2MCP 598; 4MR 359-360;see RH 10/05/1897 and 10/12/1897;CTr 252
"I feel deeply over the sudden apostacy..."	MS-029	97/04/06 Cooranbong, Aus.	CD 493;3MR 337;5MR 143;FBS 73
"The position which Dr. Burk insisted..."	MS-031	97/02/20 Cooranbong, Aus.	AH 381;1MR 69-71
"This is God's own world..."	MS-032	97/04/13 Cooranbong, Aus.	
"I am awakened at half past twelve..."	MS-033	97/04/06 Cooranbong, Aus.	UL 110;VSS 325-326;6BC 1092-1093; 7ABC 467
"We are nearing the close of this..."	MS-034	97/04/16	3SM 422-423;OHC 88;FLB 35; 5MR 78-80
"Then came the day of unleavened bread..."	MS-035	97/04/06	*RH 05/31/1898 and 06/07/1898*
"But I have a baptism to be baptised with"	MS-036	97/04/01	*ST 12/23/1897*
"The object of conversion is twofold..."	MS-038	97/04/01	1BC 1087;see ST 05/05/1898 and 05/12/1898
Christ or Barabbas?	MS-040	97/00/00	6BC 1107;3SM 415-418;10MR 338; see RH 01/23/1900 and 01/30/1900
Words of Comfort	MS-041	97/04/29c	HM 07/00/1897
In Gethsemane	MS-042	97/05/16c	11MR 345;CTr 266-268
Ministry	MS-043	97/05/21c	5BC 1138-1139;2MR 59-60; 6MR 23-24;17MR 24
Christ's Representatives	MS-044	97/05/13c	TDG 142;Southern Review 09/13/1898 and 10/25/1898;CTr 260
"Now the chief priests and elders..."	MS-045	97/05/14c	5BC 1137,1149
The Entrance of Thy Word Giveth Light	MS-046	97/05/02c	TDG 131
Judas	MS-047	97/05/20c	*20MR 146-149*
"When thou saidst, Seek ye my face..."	MS-049	97/05/19 Cooranbong, Aus.	*KC 44-49*
The Work of Christ	MS-050	97/05/31c Adelaide, Aus.	UL 165
In the Judgment Hall	MS-051	97/05/20c	5BC 1148
The Crucifixion of Christ	MS-052	97/05/03c	5BC 1124-1125;7ABC 458
The Ordinance of Humility	MS-054	97/05/20c	Similar to MS-035-1897
"God calls upon helpers..."	MS-055	97/06/03c	9MR 151-152
"I am of good courage in the Lord..."	MS-056	97/06/24c	
Remember the Sabbath Day to Keep It Holy	MS-057	97/06/09c	*Lake Union Herald 03/31/1909 and 04/07/1909 and 04/14/1909*
The Truth as it is in Jesus	MS-058	97/06/21c	1BC 1104;3BC 1166;4BC 1184; 5BC 1147;8MR 290
Sanctify Them Through Thy Truth	MS-059	97/06/24c	OHC 106,227,280;ML 189;2MCP 436; 1BC 1097
True Christianity	MS-060	97/06/28c	WM 83,154,297-298
Our School Work	MS-061	97/06/08c	
"My mind has been strongly exercised..."	MS-062	97/06/03 Cooranbong, Aus.	2MR 10;8MR 289
The Sabbath of the Lord	MS-063	97/06/28c	ST 03/31/1898 and 04/07/1898
"When he saw the multitude, he was moved..."	MS-064	97/06/06c	
Tradition	MS-065	97/06/06c	5MR 81

EGW Manuscripts File—Page 22

The Vine and the Branches	MS-066	97/06/00c	6MR 104
The Vine and the Branches	MS-067	97/00/00c	*RH 11/02/1897*
Correct School Discipline	MS-068	97/06/21c	*FE 454-466*
The Bible in our Schools	*MS-069	97/06/17c	CG 200;7ABC 469;6MR 263-265;
			8MR 254,287;9MR 116
Diary [Jul. 29;Sep. 7,8,24,25;Nov. 6]	*MS-070	97/07/29 Cooranbong, Aus.	3SM 118-119;TDG 220;UL 324;
			VSS 121;HP 326;8MR 254
Words of Comfort	MS-070a	97/07/12c	*RH 10/26/1897*
Denouncing the Pharisees	MS-071	97/07/11c	4BC 1139;5BC 1098;Ev 496-497
"In common with the Jewish teachers..."	MS-072	97/07/00	
Our Words	MS-073	97/07/02c	*RH 01/18/1898 and 01/25/1898*
Our Words	MS-074	97/07/04c	VSS 30-32,34-35,42,43,66,127,149,
			189-190;3MR 360-361;6MR 265
The Position God's People Should Occupy	MS-075	97/07/29c	1MR 37-38
Sermon/"The words of truth..."	MS-075a	97/00/00	variant of MS-075-1897
True Education	MS-076	97/07/08c	*SpM 56-59*
On Which Side Will You Stand?	MS-077	97/07/18c	CC 26;VSS 30,47;1BC 1086;9MR 379
The Blessing of Obedience	MS-078	97/07/28c	*ST 09/22/1898 and 02/08/99 and*
			RH 12/13/1898 and 12/20/1898 and
			12/27/1898
Christ's Second Coming	MS-079	97/07/29c	4MR 115-116
Diary/"At three o'clock my sleep is ended"	MS-080	97/07/04 Cooranbong, Aus.	MRmnt 124
"I have a burden that I must communicate..."	MS-081	97/07/07 Cooranbong, Aus.	8MR 254;11MR 156-157;SpM 75-77
"I must speak to the students at our school"	MS-082	97/07/18 Cooranbong, Aus.	KC 95-99
The Need of Missionary Effort	MS-083	97/07/22c	Ev 343;9MR 200-201
Study for Time and for Eternity	MS-084	97/07/30c	1BC 1085;SpM 93-94
Christ on the Cross	MS-084a	97/00/00	TDG 236;11MR 345
The Attitude in Prayer	MS-084b	97/08/01c	*21MR 59-63*
"I desire that the book..."	MS-085	97/08/29 Cooranbong, Aus.	
"I have many things to say..."	MS-086	97/08/25 Cooranbong, Aus.	*20MR 1-9*
All That Will Live Godly in Christ Jesus Shall Suffer	MS-087	97/08/19c	*RH 04/19/1898*
As It Was in the Days of Noah	MS-088	97/08/20c	*19MR 179-184*
"Looking for that blessed hope..."	MS-089	97/08/20c	*RH 04/12/1898*
God's Chosen People	MS-090	97/08/02c	*ST 05/26/1898 and 06/02/1898*
The Crucifixion	MS-091	97/08/11c	*12MR 385-387*
God's Messengers	MS-092	97/08/12c	*TM 404-415*
The Arrest	MS-093	97/08/16c	
The Lord is Risen Indeed	MS-094	97/09/29c	5BC 1114;OHC 315
The Condemnation	MS-095	97/09/22c	
The Jews' Rejection of Christ	MS-096	97/09/23c	TDG 275
"The Lord has moved upon us here..."	MS-097	97/09/12 Cooranbong, Aus.	
"I have written many things for our youth"	MS-098	97/09/13 Cooranbong, Aus.	8MR 255
The Truth Revealed in Jesus	MS-099	97/09/14c	*RH 02/08/1898*
The Arrest of Christ	MS-100	97/09/15c	TDG 267
The True High Priest	MS-101	97/09/26c	*12MR 387-399*
Caiaphas	MS-102	97/09/26c	5BC 1105
Prophecy Fulfilled in Christ	MS-103	97/09/19c	CC 325
Condemned by the Jews	MS-104	97/09/00c	*19MR 162-170*
"That which is of great interest to all..."	MS-105	97/09/28c	
Christ and the Law	MS-106	97/09/22c	*18MR 70-78*
Search the Scriptures	MS-107	97/09/15c	8MR 413
"Last night I was troubled and anxious..."	MS-108	97/09/01 Cooranbong, Aus.	
"And when the servant of the man of God..."	MS-109	97/10/00c	*16MR 295-300*
"And I will put enmity..."	*MS-110	97/10/10c	CTr 93
Our Substitute and Surety	*MS-111	97/10/07c	*12MR 399-421*
Before Pilate and Herod	MS-112	97/10/00c	CTr 270-273
The Walk to Emmaus	MS-113	97/10/14c	CTr 295-298

EGW Manuscripts File—Page 23

"I attended meeting, and spoke..."	MS-114	97/10/07	Cooranbong, Aus.	6BC 1065;7ABC 466;TDG 289
The Risen Saviour	M3-115	97/10/14c		5BC 1110;6BC 1092;CTr 283-286
"I have been listening to the words..."	MS-115a	97/10/27c		SD 30;3MR 249,308-309;9MR 163-164
The Building of the Lord's House	MS-116	97/10/03c		3BC 1133-1134;4BC 1175-1176; 3MR 346;10MR 122-126
Judas	MS-120	97/10/27		See DA 716-722
Daniel	MS-122	97/03/10		UL 83;6BC 1108-1109;4MR 125-127; 5MR 210;7MR 333-334;CTr 173
Christ's Commission	*MS-123	97/11/17c		TDG 330
Go, Preach the Gospel	*MS-124	97/11/17c		*RH 03/15/1898 and 03/22/1898*
"We are living amid the perils of..."	MS-125	97/11/12		Ev 565
The Training of Children	MS-126	97/11/15c		CG 27,86-87,151,213-214,232,272; AH 187,283,287,432;OHC 143; 4MR 99-100,360-361;8MR 380-381
"Here we are at Stanmore..."	MS-127	97/11/22	Stanmore, Aus.	3SM 311-312;LDE 111;3MR 314-315
The Only True Mediator	*MS-128	97/11/28c		FLB 76;TMK 73;TDG 341;6BC 1115; 7BC 913-914;7ABC 470;17MR 24; CTr 293-294
Condemnation of Christ	MS-129	97/00/00		
The Truth as it is in Jesus	*MS-130	97/11/23		OHC 32,208;HP 142;1MCP 324-325; 2MCP 656-657;5MR 210-211
I am the Resurrection and the Life	MS-131	97/00/00		5BC 1113
Holiday Presents	MS-132	97/00/00		*RH 11/21/1878*
The Wrath of the Lamb	MS-133	97/11/26		*BE 05/30/1898*
"God is gone up with a shout..."	MS-134	97/00/00		6BC 1053
"The reasons for the transgression..."	MS-134a	97/11/24c		
The Judgment	MS-137	97/12/16c		LDE 276;see RH 09/20/1898
The Gospel Message	MS-138	97/12/02c		7ABC 478;VSS 339-340;Ev 291-292; 10MR 290-291
The Work Before God's People	MS-139	97/12/09		Ev 430;9MR 129;BTS 09/1908
God's Claim on Us	MS-140	97/12/14c		CG 482-483;ML 102;AH 35-36
"Yesterday was a hard day for me..."	MS-141a	97/12/17	Stanmore, Aus.	
God's Care for his Workers	MS-142	97/12/16c		6BC 1057,1105;UL 364
Christ's Mission to Earth	MS-143	97/12/09		*16MR 115-125*
"I would now speak..."	MS-144	97/12/30		
"I have a deep interest for every..."	MS-145	97/12/30	Cooranbong, Aus.	*21MR 193-197*
"I very much desire the presence..."	MS-146	97/12/05	Stanmore, Aus.	
All Power is Given Unto Me	MS-147	97/12/09c		VSS 233-234;see RH 07/19/1898 and 07/26/1898
The Christian Life	*MS-148	97/12/05c		*12MR 50-55*
The Remission of Sins	MS-149	97/12/01c		See RH 06/13/1899
Our Reasonable Service	MS-150	97/00/00		Not on file;same as CTBH 15-24
An Appeal to our Churches in Behalf of Home	MS-151	97/00/00		*PH007 3-21*
The Church Must be Quickened	MS-152	97/00/00		*PH007 21-27*
Every Individual Member Should Be An Active	MS-153	97/00/00		*PH007 27-29*
Laborers Together With God	MS-161	97/12/16	Cooranbong, Aus.	*RH 03/10/1904*
How To Conduct Sanitariums	MS-162	97/00/00		MM 141,163-164,199-201,207,214-216, 227-229
"We are laborers together with God..."	MS-163	97/12/17	Stanmore, Aus.	7BC 981;7ABC 471;LDE 136; 5MR 102-103
The Southern Field	*MS-164	97/03/02	Cooranbong, Aus.	SW 79-82
Hopeful Words for Stanmore	MS-166	97/12/00		2MR 38-39
"In answer to the questions..."	MS-167	97/07/00		OHC 40,43;*Story of Our Health Message* 441-445
The Avondale School	*MS-168	97/11/00		
God, Not Men, To Be Our Counselor	*MS-169	97/00/00		
Great in the Sight of the Lord	*MS-170	97/04/21	Cooranbong, Aus.	

EGW Manuscripts File—Page 24

Diary [Mar. 5-7]	*MS-171	97/03/00	Cooranbong, Aus.	
Diary [Apr. 6-28]	*MS-172	97/04/00	Cooranbong, Aus.	4Bio 293,302
Diary [Jun. 18-30]	*MS-173	97/06/00	Cooranbong, Aus.	5MR 187;8MR 368;10MR 342
Diary [Jul.]	*MS-174	97/07/00	Cooranbong, Aus.	TMK 141,143;5MR 187;
				4Bio 304,306-311,327-329,391
Diary [Aug.]	*MS-175	97/08/00	Cooranbong, Aus.	3MR 274-275,292;5MR 187-188;
				13MR 407-408;20MR 39;
				4Bio 317-320,326
Diary [Sep.]	*MS-176	97/09/00	Cooranbong, Aus.	20MR 37-38;4Bio 329-330
Diary [Oct.]	*MS-177	97/10/00	Cooranbong, Aus.	4Bio 333,337-338
Diary [Nov. 1-28]	*MS-178	97/11/00	Cooranbong, Aus.	4Bio 338
Diary [Dec. 3-28]	*MS-179	97/12/00	Cooranbong, Aus.	
"I appeal to the teachers in our school..."	*MS-180	97/00/00		
"There is a work to be done here..."	*MS-181	97/09/08		
"For we are laborers together with God..."	*MS-182	97/09/24	Cooranbong, Aus.	TDG 276;11MR 37-39
The Two Classes	MS-183	97/03/09	Cooranbong, Aus.	*RH 06/15/1897*
"Believe in Me"	MS-184	97/00/00		7BC 989
Apostasies	MS-185	97/00/00		*2SM 392-395*
Apostasy of McCullagh and Hawkins	MS-186	97/00/00		
An Appeal for Sydney	MS-187	97/12/20	Cooranbong, Aus.	
"Be Ye Therefore Perfect"	MS-188	97/02/03		

1898

Matthew's Feast	MS-003	98/01/09c	*ST 06/23/1898 and 07/07/1898 and*
			07/14/1898
The Christian's Duty	MS-004	98/01/09c	*RH 08/23/1898*
"Sunday, May 18, 1895, with Elder Corliss"	MS-004a	98/01/09c	RH 08/09/1898
True Education in our Churches	MS-007	98/01/14c	*TM 120-131*
The Necessity of Studying the Word	MS-008	98/01/16c	*20MR 178-181*
Our Talents	*MS-009	98/01/25c	ST 08/18/1898;RH 01/24/1899
The Necessity of Establishing Schools	MS-010a	98/02/01c	2MR 212;3MR 364;CTr 348
The Word of God as a Study Book	MS-011	98/02/04c	9MR 379-380;11MR 157;
			YI 06/30/1898 and 07/07/1898
A God-given Work	MS-012	98/02/09c	AH 265,324;CG 52-53,69,175-176,205,
			223-224,259,482,520;7MR 207
Seed Sown Among Thorns	MS-013	98/02/09c	4BC 1161;7MR 178-179
Like Unto Leaven	MS-014	98/02/09c	TDG 48
The Fear of the Lord is the Beginning of Wisdom	MS-015	98/02/10c	HP 137;1MCP 92,194-195,357-358;
			5MR 359-360;CTr 251
Wholehearted Service	MS-016	98/02/10c	CC 34;8MR 291
The Work for Today	MS-017	98/02/13c	Ev 565;2BC 1035;Te 30,36,34,62;
			GH 09/1898
One That is Mighty	MS-018	98/02/18c	TMK 48,67;YI 12/29/1898
The Unjust Steward	MS-019	98/02/18c	6MR 25
His Wonderful Love	MS-020	98/02/18c	*8MR 39-41*
Ye Are Not Your Own	MS-021	98/02/20c	HP 165,170;CTr 244
Christ the Great Missionary	MS-022	98/02/20c	TMK 39,43;TDG 59;3BC 1140;
			WM 19-20,172-173
The Character of God Revealed in Christ	MS-023	98/02/20c	
Christ's Life on Earth	MS-024	98/02/22c	UL 67
The Man of Sorrows	MS-025	98/02/24c	3MR 425-426
The Parable of the Sower	MS-026	98/02/28c	RH 09/26/1899
The Pure in Heart Shall See God	MS-027	98/02/18c	5BC 1114
Teaching From Nature	MS-028	98/03/02c	2MCP 423,465,564;3BC 1143-1144
The Great Supper	MS-029	98/03/03c	RH 01/17/1899
The Seed is the Word	MS-030	98/03/04c	3MR 343;RH 10/03/1899

Ask, and It Shall Be Given Unto You	MS-031	98/03/04c	
"At that time Jesus went on the Sabbath..."	MS-031a	98/03/07c	UL 80;CC 34;12MR 307
The Barren Fig-Tree	MS-032	98/03/08c	ST 02/15/1899;CTr 256
The Unjust Judge	MS-033	98/03/09c	2BC 1013-1014;ST 09/08/1898 and
		09/15/1898	
Seed-Sowing	MS-034	98/03/09c	
"After Christ had talked with the..."	MS-035	98/03/09c	
Christ's Mission	MS-036	98/03/10c	*KC 159-163*
And the Grace of God was Upon Him	MS-037	98/03/10c	YI 09/08/1898
Lessons From Israel	MS-038	98/03/11c	CD 375
The Day of Reckoning	MS-039	98/03/11c	UL 84;6BC 1100;5MR 353-354;
			8MR 348;12MR 308;RH 11/22/1898
"Because of transgression, Adam and Eve..."	MS-040	98/03/13c	CC 193;CTr 159
"How many are seeking earthly treasures..."	MS-041	98/03/16c	TDG 84
To Every Man His Work	MS-042	98/03/17c	KC 153-159;RH Supp. 06/21/1898
Remember the Former Things of Old	MS-043	98/03/22 Orange Grove, Aus.	2MCP 533-534728;UL 95;5MR 2
The Laborer is Worthy of His Hire	MS-043a	98/03/22c	5MR 162,323-327;15MR 161-163
The Pearl of Great Price	MS-044	98/03/29c	7BC 907;5MR 423;CTr 301
Hidden Treasure	MS-045	98/03/30c	1MCP 194;UL 103;3MR 347
"There is a work to be done in our cities"	MS-046	98/03/31c	TDG 99;WM 199-200,311-312;
			2MR 193-196
The Echo Office and Commercial Work	MS-047	98/03/31	CC 200;OHC 254;Ev 491-492;
			3BC 1158;4MR 123-124;6MR 266-270;
			7MR 74;CTr 352
Our Relation to Commercial Work	MS-047a	98/05/16c	3MR 40
Treasure Hid in a Field	MS-048	98/04/03c	*13MR 129-134*
The Lack of Spirituality in our Churches	MS-049	98/04/09c	*21MR 27-39*
The Jews Require a Sign	MS-050	98/04/28c	TDG 127;5BC 1095-1096;6MR 81
The Hebrew Captives	MS-051	98/05/01c	*12MR 120-123*
The Work Required of God's People	MS-052	98/05/01c	WM 273;7BC 941;1MR 14;
			15MR 163-164;see RH 11/29/1898
The Source of All Truth	MS-053	98/05/11c	3MR 367
Our School	MS-054	98/05/02c	11MR 157-158,169-170
Union with Christ and with Each Other	MS-055	98/05/04c	11MR 170-171
The Need of Harmonious Action	MS-056	98/04/27c	3SM 26;OHC 26;8MR 283-284;
			MR311 25;SpM 119-122
Our School at Avondale	MS-057	98/05/08c	8MR 260
The Mistake of a Low Fee for Tuition	MS-058	98/04/17 Stanmore, Aus.	11MR 178;SpM 128-131;5Bio 199-200
Notes on the Work	MS-059	98/05/10c	1SM 116-117;12MR 360-362
How the Echo Office Should be Regarded	MS-060	98/05/12c	
True Greatness	MS-061	98/05/08c	HP 173;7BC 962
Selection of the School Land at Cooranbong	MS-062	98/06/28	*16MR 152-156*
Home Missionary Work	MS-063	98/05/18c	TDG 147
The Danger of Rejecting Light	MS-064	98/05/19c	*20MR 315-322*
"I have a word to speak to all who are..."	MS-065	98/05/19c	
Words of Instruction to Ministers and People	MS-065a	98/05/22c	variant of MS 42, 1898
The Poor Have the Gospel Preached Unto Them	MS-065b	98/05/21c	WM 22,170-172
To the General Conference & our Publishing	MS-066	98/05/24c	*17MR 221-235*
Search the Scriptures	MS-067	98/06/09c	1MCP 188-189;OHC 35;TDG 169;
			1BC 1083;7BC 904-905,989;3MR 433;
			11MR 172-173;17MR 25;CTr 33
The Leaven of Truth	MS-068	98/06/09c	5MR 346-347;see RH 07/25/1899
"I have not been able to sleep much..."	MS-069	98/06/02c	12MR 161-162
The Need of Missionary Effort	MS-070	98/06/13c	*Christian Educator 10/1898*
"On Monday afternoon I met with those..."	MS-071	98/06/14c	7BC 989;11MR 177-178
Shall Not God Avenge His Own Elect?	MS-072	98/06/14c	5MR 416-418
Extracts From Personal Letters re W.C.T.U.	MS-074	98/12/01	WM 164

Come Out From Among Them, and Be Ye Separate	MS-075	98/06/16c	4MR 449;5MR 418;9MR 129-131
"During the week of prayer we appointed..."	MS-076	98/06/16 Cooranbong, Aus.	4MR 129-130;4Bio 354
Notes of the Work During the Week of Prayer	MS-077	98/06/16 Cooranbong, Aus.	3MR 302;12MR 144
I am the True Vine	MS-078	98/06/17c	UL 182
Missionary Work a Means of Education	MS-079	98/06/22c	8MR 258
Love as Brethren	MS-080	98/06/23c	AH 217,311
The Rich Man and Lazarus	MS-081	98/06/23c	TDG 183
The Leaven of Truth	MS-082	98/06/26c	*2SAT 115-122*
"All who are led by the Spirit of God..."	MS-083	98/06/28c	
Notes on the Work During the Week of Prayer	MS-084	98/07/03c	8MR 259;11MR 177
Notes of the Week of Prayer--3	MS-085	98/07/03c	
Notes of the Week of Prayer--5	MS-086	98/07/03c	UL 198;3MR 347-349;see RH 11/08/1898
Go, Work Today in My Vineyard	MS-087	98/07/07c	Te 232-235,243,354-355;6MR 25
The Parable of the Householder	MS-088	98/07/10c	UL 205;TDG 200;see ST 03/01/1899
How Oft Shall I Forgive My Brother?	MS-089	98/07/13c	see RH 01/03/1899
"We find that we have much to be..."	MS-091	98/06/17 Cooranbong, Aus.	*16MR 39-44*
The Revelation of God	MS-092	98/07/06c	7MR 371
The Parable of the Ten Virgins	*MS-092a	98/07/22c	*16MR 267-276*
"July 21, W.C. White, Sister Sara..."	MS-093	98/07/22 Stanmore, Aus.	
The Unity of the Spirit	MS-094	98/07/28c	
Meat in Due Season	MS-095	98/08/08c	PM 222-224;3BC 1144;7BC 989
Christ Our Portion	MS-096	98/08/10c	MM 161;Ev 139;TDG 231;
			2MCP 557-558;5BC 1144-1145
The Necessity of a Close Walk with God	MS-097	98/08/11 Cooranbong, Aus.	*13MR 6-12*
God's Promises Our Plea	MS-098	98/08/11 Cooranbong, Aus.	
Through Nature to Nature's God	*MS-100	98/08/20c	TDG 241
Draw With Christ	*MS-101	98/08/23c	4MR 11
Doers of the Word	MS-102	98/08/23c	
A Word to our Ministers in Regard to Health	MS-103	98/08/23c	4MR 372-373
Christ's Manner of Teaching	*MS-104	98/08/24c	*20MR 241-248*
The Education Our School Should Give	MS-105	98/08/26c	HFM 38-42;PM 149-150;1MR 392;
			2MR 212;4MR 244;SpM 134-140
The Ministry	MS-107	98/08/28c	*1SAT 292-299*
Higher Education	MS-108	98/09/01c	TDG 253
Peter's Fall and Restoration	MS-109	98/09/08c	TDG 260
"Why is it a great advantage..."	MS-110	98/09/08c	
"During the night I slept well..."	*MS-111	98/07/22	1BC 1087;2MR 26;5MR 121;CTr 54
Believe	MS-112	98/09/08c	5BC 1135
Present your Bodies a Living Sacrifice	MS-113	98/09/08c	2MCP 388,694;5MR 360-361;
			7MR 133;10MR 306
Not in Man's Wisdom	MS-114	98/09/12c	See RH 07/16/1899
The Avondale School Farm/"I have words..."	MS-115	98/09/14c	6T 181-192;8MR 265
The Two Great Principles of the Law	MS-116	98/09/16	*18MR 1-9*
A Personal God	*MS-117	98/09/21c	3MR 326-327,335-336,355-356;
			7MR 371-376
The Lost Sheep	*MS-118	98/09/22c	
The Word of God our Study Book	*MS-119	98/09/22c	Te 75;4MR 97-98
The Need of Simplicity and Consecration	MS-120	98/09/24	*20MR 268-270*
An Example of Faithfulness	*MS-121	98/10/02c	2MCP 688-689;TDG 284;12MR 255;
			1NL 100;CTr 180;see RH 05/02/1899 and
			05/09/1899
Danger of Restricting the Work	MS-121b	98/10/01	2MR 19;From Lt 5, 1885
Prepare ye the Way of the Lord	MS-121c	98/05/03c	*RH 08/02/1898*
An Appeal for Help II/"The obligations which"	MS-122	98/10/04c	CTr 349
An Appeal for Help I/"I arose at half past..."	MS-123	98/10/03 Cooranbong, Aus.	Ev 249-250
An Appeal for Help III/"God's people have a..."	MS-124	98/10/05	
Education in the Home	MS-125	98/10/06c	TDG 288

Search the Scriptures	*MS-126	98/10/17c	
Words to Parents	MS-127	98/10/17c	AII 197;CG 216
Self-Culture	*MS-128	98/10/17c	OHC 219
Words to Parents	*MS-129	98/10/17c	AH 196,295;CG 352-353
Moses as a Shepherd	MS-130	98/10/17c	
True Education	*MS-131	98/10/17c	
The Bible the Foundation of Education	MS-132	98/10/17c	
Parents and Children	*MS-133	98/10/17c	AH 310-311;CG 197-198;10MR 112
The Youth to Improve their Capabilities	MS-134	98/10/19c	LDE 242;Te 236;Ev 24;PH136 9
True Education	MS-135	98/10/19c	4MR 121-122
Fragments on Religion in the Home	*MS-136	98/10/20c	*1NL 92*
Labor and Amusement	*MS-137	98/10/20c	
Words to Parents	*MS-138	98/10/20c	*1NL 91*
An Appeal for Missions	MS-139	98/10/21c	*PH004*
Christ's Teaching	*MS-140	98/10/22c	
Education	*MS-141	98/10/24c	
Ye are the Salt of the Earth	*MS-142	98/10/17c	AH 174;CG 240,484-485
The Parable of the Wedding Feast	*MS-143	98/10/17c	UL 304
The Ten Virgins	*MS-144	98/10/19c	
"Last evening Bro. Daniels spoke..."	MS-145	98/10/18 S. Brisbane, Aus.	
"I must make an appeal to our brethren..."	MS-147	98/10/24c Brisbane, Aus.	
"I have just been reading the article..."	MS-148	98/10/26c	10MR 350
He Spoke to Them by Parables	MS-149	98/10/26c	
How Shall We Use Our Lord's Goods?	MS-150	98/10/27c	Te 17
"On Wednesday evening, Oct. 12..."	*MS-151	98/11/02c Brisbane, Aus.	HP 175;2MCP 637; 2SM 331;3MR 218;10MR 275-276
Notes of Travel	*MS-152	98/11/20c	Ev 634;HP 101;4MR 257-258,412
"We all feel very grateful to..."	MS-153	98/10/28 Brisbane, Aus.	Ev 296;TMK 70,340;4Bio 368
The Pearl of Great Price	MS-154	98/11/22c	HP 49;7MR 180-181
"Let not your heart be troubled..."	MS-155	98/12/02c	
The Need of Self-Sacrificing Effort	MS-156	98/12/05c	5MR 370-371;1NL 99-100
Be Ye Therefore Perfect	MS-157	98/12/05c	5MR 369;6MR 5
The Gift of the Holy Spirit	*MS-158	98/12/07c	11MR 158,178-179;12MR 144-145; MR311 36
Speak Evil of No Man	MS-159	98/12/08c	TDG 351;ChL 60;HFM 42-43
"The ways of man are before the Lord..."	*MS-160	98/12/08c	5BC 1140
"The ways of man are before the Lord..."	*MS-160a	98/12/08c Cooranbong, Aus.	Edited copy of Ms 160, 1898
"I speak to the students who come..."	MS-161	98/12/10c	7MR 320
Be Ye Kind One to Another	MS-162	98/12/10c	
Talk/Address to Echo Employees	MS-163	98/04/14	*2SAT 123-129*
The Two Great Principles of the Law	*MS-163a	98/12/10c	
"Be Ye Therefore Perfect"	*MS-164	98/12/14c	TDG 357;6MR 5
Unity a Test of Discipleship	MS-165	98/12/13c	TDG 356;5MR 370;15MR 165-166
The Lord's Vineyard	MS-166	98/12/15c	6BC 1079;17MR 26
The Good Samaritan	MS-167	98/12/16c	6BC 1116
Fragments	MS-168	98/00/00c	CS 255;OHC 245;CM 95-96;7BC 933-934; 5MR 371
The Character and Work of Avondale School	MS-172	98/12/20 Cooranbong, Aus.	11MR 168,180-181
Go Forward	*MS-173	98/12/20 Newcastle, Aus.	*13MR 395-399*
Diary/"We, Sara, W.C. White..."	*MS-174	98/11/02 Gladstone, Aus.	
Diary/Medical Missionary Work & the Minister	*MS-175	98/01/00	*BCL 11-13*
Test. to the Members of the Prahran Church	MS-176	98/04/04 Ballarat, Aus.	*21MR 1-4*
Test. to Metcalf Hare/"It would be an..."	*MS-177	98/00/00	17MR 26
Test. re Metcalf Hare and C.B. Hughes	*MS-179	98/00/00	
Diary [Jan.]	*MS-180	98/01/00	
Diary [Feb.-Mar.]	*MS-181	98/02/00	
Diary [May 9-31]	*MS-182	98/05/00	5MR 188;4Bio 348-350

Diary [Jun.]	*MS-183	98/06/00	5MR 188-189;4Bio 351
Diary [Jul.]	*MS-184	98/07/00	5MR 189;4Bio 353-357,360
Diary [Aug.]	*MS-185	98/08/00	5MR 189;8MR 260-261
Diary [Sep.]	*MS-186	98/09/00	5MR 190;4Bio 353
Diary [Oct.]	*MS-187	98/10/00	TDG 298,300;4Bio 367-368,371
Diary [Nov. 1,6,7]	*MS-188	98/11/00	
Diary [Dec. 18-31]	*MS-189	98/12/00	
Church Members/"We are living in a most..."	*MS-190	98/01/01	Cooranbong, Aus.
Evils of Tobacco/"I have been wakened..."	*MS-191	98/10/21	Brisbane, Aus.
Diary/"I will write a few lines more..."	*MS-192	98/00/00	
"Our first meeting in the chapel..."	*MS-193	98/04/00	Stanmore, Aus.	HP 283;17MR 26
"Slept well last night but all..."	*MS-194	98/12/00	Newcastle, Aus.	HP 55,84,277
Week of Prayer in Australia	MS-195	98/06/00	*RH 09/27/1898*
Appealing to Lawyers	MS-196	98/00/00	*3SM 299-301*
"In the parable of the call..."	MS-197	98/00/00	
Talk/Thoughts from Talks to the Students	MS-198	98/00/00	Cooranbong, Aus.
Re Elder Haskell	*MS-199	98/07/04	

1899

"And he gave some apostles..."	MS-001	99/01/19c	UL 33;OHC 176;Te 32;9MR 320
The Need of Greater Consecration	MS-002	99/01/24c	UL 38;BTS 10/1908
The Work for this Time	MS-003	99/01/25c	*GCDB 03/02/1899*
The Effective Use of Means in Missionary	MS-004	99/01/25c	*GCDB 03/02/1899*
The Need for Consecrated Workers	MS-005	99/01/26c	4MR 98
The Poor Rich Man	MS-006	99/01/31c	UL 45
Home-Training	MS-007	99/01/31c	*1NL 93-95*
Talk/Talk at School Opening/"There is a great..."	MS-008	99/02/01c	OHC 19;1MCP 190;2MCP 806; 8MR 261
God's Purpose for His People	MS-009	99/02/08c	OHC 21
Words of Warning	MS-010	99/02/16c	TDG 55
The Work at Newcastle	MS-011	99/02/21c	Ev 501,529;VSS 302;see RH 04/24/1900 and 05/01/1900
The Need of a Knowledge of God's Word	*MS-012	99/02/22c	3SM 21
Christian Perfection	MS-013	99/02/23c	5BC 1110;CTr 52;see ST 10/25/1899
To Every Man His Work	MS-014	99/02/23c	UL 68;6MR 384-385
"In the third chapter of Malachi..."	MS-015	99/02/23c	4BC 1182
The Marriage at Cana at Galilee	MS-016	99/02/19c	*10MR 197-203*
Cooperation	MS-016a	99/03/01c	*RH 05/28/1908*
The New Commandment	MS-017	99/03/02c	OHC 24,231;SD 101;2MCP 579
The Call to the Feast	MS-018	99/03/06c	
Compel Them to Come In	MS-019	99/03/06c	WM 286-288
The Second Advent	*MS-020	99/03/08c	FLB 288;HP 34
Give Unto the Lord the Glory Due Unto His Name	MS-021	99/03/08c	1MCP 271;UL 81;VSS 14
"And it came to pass..."	MS-023	99/03/09c	OHC 18,36,82,130;1MCP 262-263; 6BC 1058;7BC 942-943;CTr 140; 12MR 255-256;17MR 27
Faithfulness in the Work of God	MS-025	99/03/12c	Ev 354;TDG 80;5MR 358-359;9MR 102
"When anyone heareth the word..."	MS-026	99/03/14c	
The Great Standard of Righteousness	MS-027	99/03/19c	1BC 1088;2BC 994;3BC 1152; 7BC 951,970,980-981;see RH 04/23/1901 and 05/07/1901
Think Not That I am Come to Destroy the Law	MS-028	99/03/19c	TDG 87
Sacrificed for Us	MS-029	99/03/17c	UL 90;5BC 1085;7BC 914-915;6MR 2
Do All to the Glory of God	MS-031	99/03/19c	11MR 279;see ST 10/18/1899
Home-Training	MS-032	99/03/20c	AH 236,245-246;CG 106-107,205, 247-248,251;see RH 12/05/1899

"The Lord accepts those who will accept..."	MS-033	99/03/20c	
The Home-Life	MS-034	99/03/21c	UL 94,CD 315,3DC 1129;5BC 1085
Teaching From Nature	MS-035	99/03/21c	*13MR 335-338*
The Marriage at Cana	MS-036	99/03/21c	*10MR 187-190*
The Need of Consecrated Workers	MS-037	99/03/21c	8MR 287-288;10MR 319
The Will of God Concerning You	MS-038	99/03/26c	*1SAT 300-303*
Loyalty or Disloyalty	MS-039	99/03/23c	*RH 02/06/1900*
I Will Have Mercy and not Sacrifice	MS-040	99/03/26c	WM 24;9MR 160;10MR 95-96
The Religion of Christ	MS-041	99/03/28c	
Kept in Trial	MS-042	99/03/28c	*RH 06/19/1900*
Sabbath-School Work	MS-045	99/03/29c	
The Pearl of Great Price	MS-046	99/03/29c	
God Loveth a Cheerful Giver	MS-047	99/03/29c	TDG 97;WM 279-280
Work in Christ's Lines	MS-048	99/03/29c	See ST 12/20/1899 and 12/27/1899
The Seal of God	MS-051	99/04/02c	*ST 11/01/1899 and 11/08/1899*
The Danger of Self-Sufficiency	MS-052	99/04/02c	
Words of Instruction to those Connected with the...	MS-053	99/04/03c	TDG 102;Ev 539,542-543;VSS 52
"After the closing exercises of..."	MS-054	99/04/04c	PM 84-85,93;4Bio 53
Following Christ	MS-056	99/04/07c	*GCB 2nd Quarter 1899 33-35*
Words of Gratitude	MS-057	99/04/11c	*GCB 2nd Quarer 1899 36-38*
The Duty of Parents to Children	MS-058	99/04/13c	AH 172-173,389-390;7MR 7
The Perfect Standard	MS-059	99/04/13c	
The Teacher Sent from God	MS-061	99/04/20c	*16MR 89-96*
Judge Not	MS-062	99/04/18c	8MR 309
"Yesterday Miss McEnterfer and Miss Maggie"	MS-063	99/04/22c Hamilton, Aus.	*15MR 29-42*
Words to Parents	MS-064	99/04/25c	CG 27,80,97,101,194;1MR 112-113
"At a counsel meeting held last Thursday..."	MS-065	99/04/25c	*16MR 245-249*
Talk/"School work is a work of partnership"	MS-066	99/04/13 Cooranbong, Aus.	*2SAT 135-139*
"I must write in regard to the way in..."	MS-067	99/04/25c	2SM 284-285,347-348;8MR 258
Diary [Apr. 14-25]/"This is the preparation..."	*MS-068	99/04/25c	2SM 299-300;1MR 392;3MR 425;PC 15
Words of Counsel in Regard to the Publishing	MS-069	99/05/08	
Laborers Together with God	MS-070	99/02/26	TDG 65;7BC 906
Abide in Me	MS-073	99/05/11c	TDG 140
"The third chapter of first Corinthians..."	MS-074	99/05/11c	6BC 1082,1086
"Those who have been separating from..."	MS-075	99/05/11c	*1888 1687-1692*
God's Law Immutable	MS-077	99/05/14c	LDE 18,217;1BC 1102;4BC 1147-1148; 5BC 1131
He Casteth Out Devils	MS-078	99/05/15c	5BC 1092-1093
How Much Owest Thou Unto My Lord?	*MS-079	99/05/01 Cooranbong, Aus.	
The Selection of Articles for our Papers	*MS-080	99/05/16c	*CW 17-19 with PH070*
The Parable of the Talents	MS-081	99/05/21c	WM 245
In the Master's Service	*MS-082	99/05/21c	4BC 1172;RH 04/17/1900
That They All May Be One	*MS-083	99/05/17c	6MR 331
The Sanitarium--Where Shall It Be Located?	MS-085	99/06/05c	*10MR 234-248*
The Review & Herald and the College Debt	MS-086	99/06/06c	*SpM 147-150*
The Last Shall Be First And the First Last	*MS-087	99/06/13c	2SM 182
Lessons from the Christ-Life	MS-088	99/06/14c	See RH 02/13/1900
Shall We Erect Homes for Consumptives	MS-089	99/06/19c	*9MR 281-284*
"I cannot sleep past eleven o'clock..."	*MS-090	99/04/27	SW 94-96
Words of Counsel Regarding the Management	MS-091	99/06/19	*13MR 179-191*
The Importance of Christ's Lessons to His	*MS-092	99/07/12c	CG 79-80;7BC 932-933,936; 7ABC 460;4MR 245
"Know ye not, Paul asks,..."	*MS-093	99/07/13c	6BC 1089;7BC 912,924;TDG 203
Sermon/"These words spake Jesus..."	MS-093a	99/07/23	*1SAT 304-311*
To Do Justly, to Love Mercy, and to Walk Humbly	*MS-094	99/07/18c	HP 236;1MR 272-273; GCB 4th Q. 1899 99-103
The Apostle Paul and Manual Work	MS-095	99/07/20c	6BC 1065

EGW Manuscripts File—Page 30

The Bible as our Study-Book	*MS-096	99/07/20c	*13MR 260-268*
The Minister and Physical Work	MS-097	99/07/24c	TDG 214;2SM 196-197
The Need of Liberality	*MS-098	99/07/24c	6BC 1103-1104
Talk/"I want to say that I am very..."	MS-099	99/07/20	11MR 158-159
An Appeal for Help	MS-100	99/07/24c	*AUCR 07/28/1899*
The [Avondale] School and Its Work	MS-101	99/07/24c	*AUCR 07/28/1899*
Talk/"I desire that we shall know the very"	MS-102	99/07/09 Cooranbong, Aus.	UL 204;5MR 339-340
Remarks/"The first I knew anything about this"	MS-103a	99/07/25 Cooranbong, Aus.	
Battle Creek Sanitarium/Large Buildings	MS-103b	99/00/00	Compiled from other letters/ms
The Board of Directors	*MS-104	99/07/30c	
Words of Instruction to Responsible Men	*MS-105	99/07/30c	WM 123,228-229
Remarks/Report of Committee Meeting	MS-106	99/07/26	CS 275-276
The Debt on Battle Creek College	MS-107	99/08/02c	
He That Loveth Not His Brother Abideth in Death	MS-108	99/08/02	7BC 962-963;11MR 274
The Need of Equalizing the Work	MS-109	99/08/03c	1MR 229-231;3MR 324
The Unfaithful Husbandmen	*MS-110	99/08/06c	UL 232
Talk/Our Sanitarium and Its Work	MS-111	99/07/21c	*AUCR 07/21/1899*
The Wages of Unrighteousness	*MS-113	99/08/11c	1BC 1111-1112;1MR 271-272
"And there came a man from..."	*MS-114	99/08/13c	LHU 62;5MR 305-306
Words of Exhortation to the Workers	*MS-115	99/08/15c	1MR 236-241
The Sin of Jezebel	MS-116	99/08/15c	2BC 1038;10MR 384
The Medical Missionary Work	MS-117	99/08/15c	*BCL 25-27*
The Work in the South	MS-118	99/08/21c	4MR 12-13
Words to Parents	MS-119	99/08/21c	AH 320,526;CG 210,237,277, 303,334-336;5MR 338-339
Go, Work Today in My Vineyard	*MS-120	99/08/23c	TDG 244
Lessons from Israel	*MS-121	99/08/24c	1BC 1112;1MCP 241;3MR 347; 6MR 394;16MR 277
The Canvasser and His Work	MS-122	99/07/02c	Collection of extracts largely taken from 5T 396-407;see also 1MCP 51; 6MR 271-273
The Vineyard	*MS-123	99/08/25c	*16MR 328-331*
Words of Warning	MS-126	99/08/28c	2BC 998;CM 29;3MR 239
The Parable of the Two Sons	MS-127	99/09/05c	OHC 81;HP 42;CG 248;5BC 1097; RH 02/20/1900 and 02/27/1900
Christ's Entry Into Jerusalem	MS-128	99/09/07c	CTr 253-255
The Wicked Husbandmen	MS-129	99/09/06c	
The Test of Obedience	MS-130	99/09/08c	SD 313,314;Te 65,79-80,195-196; 5BC 1121;4MR 410;11MR 274-275; 15MR 166
The Danger of Extravagance in Illustrating our...	MS-131	99/09/12c	*15MR 105-113*
Diary/"Last night was a night of great..."	*MS-132	99/09/13	
The Importance of the Law of God	MS-133	99/09/20c	*21MR 408-411*
The Unfaithful Husbandmen	*MS-134	99/09/20c	2BC 998-999;CTr 133
Joshua's Last Words	MS-135	99/09/20c	
The True and the False	*MS-136	99/09/20c	5BC 1107,1136;CTr 35
Notes of the Work/"Sept. 22, 1899 we drove"	MS-137	99/09/22	
Parables of the Vineyard	MS-138	99/09/27c	
A Call for Help	MS-138a	99/09/25c	*RH 11/14/1899*
Lessons from the Vineyard	MS-139	99/09/27c	Te 29
What Do Ye More Than Others?	MS-141	99/10/02c	Ev 46
God's Care for His Church	MS-142	99/10/03c	7BC 922,930-931;see ST 02/14/1900
Co-Workers with Christ	MS-143	99/10/04c	ChL 7-8,26;4MR 365-367;6MR 105-106
Give, and It Shall be Given Unto You	MS-145	99/10/06c	4BC 1143,1151
"The question was asked by Christ..."	MS-146	99/10/07 Cooranbong, Aus.	
The Yoke of Restraint and Obedience	MS-147	99/10/09c	8MR 266-267;17MR 27

EGW Manuscripts File—Page 31

The Need of Self-Surrender	MS-148	99/10/08c	Southern Review 12/05/1899; BTS 10/1910
"I was instructed in America..."	MS-149	99/10/24 Cooranbong, Aus.	*18MR 65-69*
"The revelation of Jesus Christ..."	MS-150	99/10/26c	CG 310;7BC 954;4MR 416;CTr 312
A Lesson from Israel's Disobedience	MS-151	99/10/30c	2BC 1017;4BC 1144,1146,1156
The Temple of God Must be Holy	MS-152	99/10/31c	TSB 15;3SM 419;4MR 380-381,398
Victory Over Temptation	MS-153	99/10/31c	Ev 591;1BC 1105;CTr 200
Restitution Due to the Southern Field	MS-154	99/11/18c	3MR 262-263
Temperance from a Christian Standpoint	MS-155	99/11/17c	1BC 1101;Te 162,196;CG 391
Diary/"Yesterday, although it had been..."	MS-156	99/11/17 Maitland, Aus.	
A Message to the Battle Creek Church	MS-157	99/12/04c	HP 283;Ev 512
Diary/"Today is my birthday..."	MS-158	99/11/26 Maitland, Aus.	4MR 44
The Privileges and Duties of a Christian	MS-159	99/12/13c	2SM 284;MM 41;CS 66-67;5MR 133-134
God's Design in Establishing Sanitariums	MS-160	99/12/15c	
Notes of the Work	MS-161	99/12/17c	
This Do, and Thou Shalt Live	MS-162	99/12/17c	
Our Need of Faith	MS-163	99/12/18c	
Faithful or Unfaithful Stewards	MS-164	99/12/26c	2SM 183-185
Words of Counsel to Ministers and Physicians	MS-165	99/12/26c	TMK 304;1BC 1113;6BC 1084-1085, 1087;7ABC 461,476;1MR 223-224; 5MR 114,134-135
God's Design in Establishing Sanitariums	MS-166	99/12/22c	*KC 12-14*
The Medical Missionary Work and the Gospel	MS-167	99/12/22c	*KC 15-18*
The Physician's Work a Cure of Souls	MS-168	99/12/22c	*KC 49-53* (see 6T 229-234)
Dangers and Duties of the Physician	MS-169	99/12/22c	*KC 53-61*
Exorbitant Fees	MS-169a	99/00/00 From 1899/1900 Lts/Ms	MM 125-127,169-171
The Avondale School Farm	MS-170	99/07/22	*AUCR 07/31/1898*
Diary/"I have slept until half past two..."	*MS-172	99/00/00c	MM 159-161,166-167;CD 75; 7BC 982,985
Diary/"The canvassing work is one of the..."	MS-174	99/00/00c	*1MR 60-65*
Diary/"I attended the morning service..."	*MS-175	99/00/00 Summer Hill, Aus.	*19MR 157-161*
Diary/"I thank the Lord for his great..."	*MS-176	98/11/04 Rockhampton, Aus.	Filed in 1899;*21MR 402-407*
The Medical Missionary Work	*MS-177	99/05/10	WM 253-254;Ev 523;4MR 412; 9MR 129;MR311 47
"I may soon be called to lay off..."	MS-178	99/11/11 Maitland, Aus.	TSA 56-57
Experiences in Medical Missionary Work	MS-181	99/08/00	*From GH 10/1899*
Diary [Jan. 1-5]	*MS-182	99/01/00	
Diary [Feb. 13-28]	*MS-183	99/02/00	
Diary [Mar.]	*MS-184	99/03/00	4Bio 416-417
Diary [Apr. 1-25]	*MS-185	99/04/00	
Diary [May 12-30]	*MS-186	99/05/00	
Diary [Jun. 14-30]	*MS-187	99/06/00	
Diary [Jul. 1-26]	*MS-188	99/07/00	
Diary [Aug. 12-19]	*MS-189	99/08/00	4Bio 400
Diary [Sep. 29,30]	*MS-190	99/09/00	
Diary [Oct. 1-16]	*MS-191	99/10/00	
Diary [Nov. 3-14]	*MS-192	99/11/00	
Helping Needy Families at Cooranbong	*MS-193	99/00/00	
Diary	*MS-194	99/11/23 Cooranbong, Aus.	
Royalties--Robbery Toward God	*MS-195	99/00/00	
"As the head of humanity..."	MS-196	99/00/00	incomplete

1900

The Need of a Reformation	*MS-002	00/01/02c	UL 16;6MR 39-40;9MR 229-230; MR311 45-46
The Death of Sr. S.M.I. Henry	MS-003	00/02/28c	*RH 04/03/1900*

The Unjust Steward	MS-004	00/01/02c	
The Work for this Time	MS-005	00/01/02c	*GCB 1st Q. 1900 108-109*
Words of Instruction Regarding the Medical	MS-006	00/01/12c	Ev 289-290,581-582;4MR 416
The Importance of Camp Meeting Work	MS-007	00/01/15c	Ev 137,151;CTr 236
Last Words of Instruction to the Disciples	*MS-007a	00/01/25c Toowooba, Aus.	Ev 647-648
The Ministry of Angels	MS-008	00/01/25c	ML 88;6BC 1109,1120
Our Duty Under Persecution	MS-009	00/01/26c	UL 40;3SM 400-402;12MR 149
Help to be Given to our Schools	MS-010	00/01/22c	PH139 5-13
Good and Evil Agencies	MS-011	00/01/28c	ML 67;CTr 307-308
Who Will Help?	MS-012	00/01/31c	Te 89;6BC 1102-1103;11MR 221-223
The Necessity for Immediate Action	MS-012a	00/01/00c	*Sanitarium Announcement 01/01/1900*; Edited from Ms 12, 1900
Words to Students	MS-013	00/02/02c	*1SAT 312-317*
Offer Unto God Thanksgiving	*MS-014	00/02/11c	9MR 265
Whoso Offereth Praise Glorifieth God	MS-015	00/02/14c	Compiled from Scripture
The Work for This Time/"The third angel's..."	MS-016	00/02/20c	Ev 230;WM 258-259;7BC 974,980
Diary/"We left Geelong, Friday..."	MS-018	00/03/25 Geelong, Aus.	
A Perfect Ministry	MS-019	00/03/05c	*AUCR 06/01/1900*
God's Love Manifested	MS-021	00/02/16c	*AUCR 06/01/1900*
Witnessing for Christ	MS-022	00/03/08c	
Unfaithful Servants	MS-023	00/04/01c	
Words of Instruction to Physicians	MS-024	00/04/03c	SpTB #15 16-23
A Physician's Opportunities	MS-025	00/04/08c	*KC 41-43*
Diary/"To spend money..."	MS-026	00/04/18	In Ms 92, 1900
Obedience or Disobedience	MS-027	00/05/06c	UL 140;1MCP 321
God's Purpose for His People	MS-027a	00/04/19c	Ev 273;UL 123;6BC 1075
Obedience or Disobedience	MS-028	00/05/10c	4BC 1148-1149;5MR 82
Faithful Stewardship	MS-029	00/05/21c	UL 155;OHC 114;ML 304;6BC 1065; 7BC 922-924
Diary/"Some things have been presented..."	MS-030	00/06/18c	*KC 75-80*
Diary/"This has been a trying day for me..."	MS-031	00/06/18c Summer Hill, Aus.	*KC 80-82*
Dangers in Amusements	MS-032	00/06/26c	6BC 1068-1069,1120;12MR 257-258
Unfaithful Shepherds	*MS-033	00/06/25c	CG 513;5MR 82;10MR 106-107
Faithful Stewardship	MS-034	00/06/26c	*KC 108-120*
Our Work for this Time	MS-035	00/06/28c	Ev 225
Diary--The Canvassing Work	*MS-036	00/07/05c	*19MR 152-156*
The Revelations of the Judgment	*MS-037	00/07/08c	UL 203
Diary--The Canvassing Work	*MS-038	00/07/08c	
Words of Instruction Re the Building of the San.	MS-039	00/07/13c	
A Work to be Done for God	MS-040	00/07/16c	7BC 971-972;
Fragments/Commandment-keeping	MS-041	00/07/23c	MM 211-212;Ev 610-611;2MR 244-246
Words of Instruction Regarding the Sanitarium	MS-042	00/07/23c	ML 54;1BC 1087-1088;1NL 48; 11MR 223-224;CTr 49,56
Fragments B/The Prophet, Enoch	MS-043	00/08/02c	AH 28,197,202,245,255;CG 92,123,195, 216-217,230,433-434;UL 228; 1BC 1088;3MR 218;6MR 146-147,274; 7MR 8;CTr 50-51
Jots and Tittles/The Last Days	*MS-044	00/07/24c	CG 113;Ev 18;WM 232-233,238; 2MR 41;11MR 196-197;19MR 370
What is the Chaff to the Wheat?	MS-045	00/04/28 Hamilton, Aus.	UL 221;4BC 1157;5MR 88-89,340-342
The Temperance Work	MS-046	00/07/25c	AH 394;4MR 133-136
Christian Liberality	MS-047	00/08/06c	
A Warning for this Time	MS-048	00/00/00c	4BC 1150,1152;5MR 32-33
Christ Our High Priest	MS-050	00/03/28c	*1SM 340-344*
Knowledge, Spurious and Genuine	MS-051	00/00/00c	*20MR 40-44*
The Work to be Done	MS-052	00/02/28c	Te 203,242-243;Ev 584;7BC 985
The Simplicity of Christ's Teaching	MS-053	00/04/03c	*16MR 97-99*

EGW Manuscripts File—Page 33

The First Love	MS-055	00/00/00c	4BC 1154
Preparation for Baptism I	MS 056	00/08/12c	*6MR 155-165*
Preparation for Baptism II	*MS-057	00/08/12c	FLB 143;6BC 1074,1114-1115;6T 93-95
The Law and the Gospel	MS-058	00/08/14c	FLB 104;OHC 46;1BC 1107-1108;
			2BC 1005;6BC 1099-1100;
			10MR 328-331
Jots and Tittles/Dishonesty among Canvassers	MS-059	00/08/16c	*19MR 313-332*
The Transgression of God's Law	MS-060	00/08/20c	LDE 248;4BC 1155;12MR 145-146
"I have been passing through..."	MS-061	00/10/11 St. Helena, Ca.	UL 298;ML 152,178
Talk/Medical Missionary Work and the Gospel	MS-062	00/11/13 St. Helena, Ca.	*2SAT 140-144*
"The Lord is soon to come..."	MS-063	00/10/02 St. Helena, Ca.	2MCP 786;2MR 28;
			10MR 100
An Appeal in Behalf of our Work in Scandinavia	MS-065	00/11/20c	*PH008 7-16*
"I make an appeal to our brethren..."	MS-065a	00/11/19 St. Helena, Ca.	variant of Ms 65, 1900
An Appeal in Behalf of our Sanitarium in Denmark	MS-066	00/12/03c	*PH008 18-24*
An Appeal in Behalf of our Sanitarium in Denmark	MS-066a	00/12/03c	variant of Ms 66, 1900
Words of Instruction to the Church	MS-067	00/11/29c	TDG 342;3MR 40-41;5MR 449
God's People to be Living Epistles	*MS-068	00/11/30c	
Regarding the Heating of Churches	MS-069	00/12/03c	
What God Expects From Us	MS-070	00/12/03c	CG 510;5MR 83-84
Children to be the Lord's Helpers	MS-071	00/12/03c	*7MR 8-10*
Instruction for Those Planning to Attend the Conf.	MS-072	00/12/03c	
Bring an Offering Unto the Lord	MS-073	00/12/12c	UL 360
Our Life-Work	MS-073a	00/12/18c	2SM 154-157
Our Camp-Meetings	MS-074	00/12/12c	AH 422-423;CG 143;7MR 10-11
Regarding the Journey to Battle Creek	MS-074a	00/12/18c	
A Call to Young Men	MS-075	00/12/12c	Ev 686;CM 105
Judge Not	MS-075a	00/12/18c	UL 366;HP 34
Fragments C/Words to Ministers	MS-076	00/12/14c	1MCP 169-170,289;2MCP 656;Ev 277;
			6BC 1093
Fragments/"It is a solemn thing to live..."	MS-076a	00/12/19c	
God's Sign	MS-077	00/12/19c	*RH 10/28/1902*
"I Know Thy Works"	*MS-078	00/12/19c	Ev 155;2MR 181-182;13MR 339-340
Diary/"Some work has been done..."	*MS-079	00/12/23 San Francisco, Ca.	CD 274-275;Ev 403,545-546;MM 329;
			HFM 49;TDG 366
A Holy People	*MS-080	00/07/04 Cooranbong, Aus.	5MR 347;9MR 121-122
Diary/Solomon's Reign	*MS-081	00/00/00	WM 101;CM 18;3BC 1129,1131;CTr 156;
			7BC 944,955,959;1MR 372;3MR 316
Diary [Aug. 29-Sep. 14]/"We are on our way"	*MS-082	00/08/29 To Ca.	*20MR 24-34*
The Law in Galatians	*MS-087	00/00/00 Oakland, Ca.	*1SM 233,234*
Sabbath Meeting in West Maitland	*MS-088	00/01/00	17MR 27
Caution re Over-Illustrating of Books	*MS-088a	00/01/20	1Bio 91-92
Diary [Jan. 1-28]	*MS-089	00/01/00	2MR 167-169;17MR 28;4Bio 404-405
Diary [Feb.]	*MS-090	00/02/00	7MR 84-85
Diary [Mar. 1-25]	*MS-091	00/03/00	
Diary [Apr. 7-28]	*MS-092	00/04/00	8MR 74,75,262-263;
			4Bio 442,444-445,455
Diary [May 9-29]	*MS-093	00/05/00	4Bio 383
Diary [Jun. 1-20]	*MS-094	00/06/00	4Bio 445
Diary [Jul. 1-Aug.20]	*MS-095	00/07/00	5Bio 15
Diary [Aug. 29-Sep. 30]	*MS-096	00/09/00	TMK 219,296;3MR 379;13MR 33;
			5Bio 16,18,21,29,32-33
Diary [Dec. 20]	*MS-097	00/12/20	
True Soldiers of Christ	*MS-098	00/08/04 Cooranbong, Aus.	UL 230
Canvassing for Christ's Object Lessons	MS-099	00/00/00	*PH153*
Working for our Neighbors	*MS-100	00/10/11 Crystal Springs, Ca	
Diary Fragment	*MS-101	00/03/22 Geelong, Aus.	

EGW Manuscripts File—Page 34

Instruction re the Work of Dr. Caro	*MS-102	00/03/13	Geelong, Aus.	2SM 201-202

1901

Notes of Work	MS-001	01/01/01		*17MR 38-46*
Notes of Work	MS-002	01/01/12		*4MR 251-254*
Notes of Work	MS-003	00/12/20	Filed in 1901	*17MR 47-49*
The Need and Importance of Voice Culture	MS-004	01/01/15		AH 435
A Very Present Help	MS-005	01/01/15		Ev 524;TDG 23
Words of Teachers	MS-006	01/01/16		
Camp Meetings	MS-007	01/01/21		
"We are sorry that..."	*MS-010	01/01/04	St. Helena, Ca.	
Words of Instruction to the Church	MS-011	01/02/05	St. Helena, Ca.	AH 37;6BC 1102;7BC 968;ML 341; 1MR 323-324
The Living Water	*MS-012	01/02/07		Ev 267-268;UL 52;3MR 431-433
To Those Who Are Worried over Minor Matters	MS-012a	01/02/12	St. Helena, Ca.	5MR 343
Diary/"The Lord has appointed his work..."	*MS-014	01/02/21		2SM 158-160;CD 271;Te 245-246; 6BC 1078;2MR 41-42;1NL 62
Diary/"Last night in a meeting..."	*MS-015	00/05/00	Filed in 1901	12MR 150
Testimony to the Battle Creek Church	MS-016	01/02/25		1SM 112-115;UL 70;ChL 15
Testimony to the Battle Creek Church	MS-017	01/02/26		UL 71;WM 255;8MR 302
Canvassing for Christ's Object Lessons	MS-018	01/02/27		OHC 306;UL 72;8MR 263
"I have been instructed that all..."	MS-018a	01/00/00		CM 89
Help for Our Scandinavian Institutions	MS-019	01/02/27		
Diary/"I am awakened this morning..."	MS-021	01/03/03		1SM 43-45
Diary/"I thank my heavenly Father that..."	*MS-022	01/03/03		Ev 516-517;UL 76
"This afternoon I had a conversation..."	MS-024	01/03/04		1MCP 327-328;OHC 106
The Canvassing Work and the Scandinavian	MS-026	01/03/05		CM 31,32,47;LDE 76;1SM 174-175; 7MR 315-316
Talk/"I will present to you..."	MS-027	01/03/16	Vicksburg, Ms.	*GH 03/00/1901*
Talk/"I am thankful to the Lord..."	MS-028	01/03/27	Battle Creek, Mi.	*2SAT 145-150*
Talk/"I feel an intense desire..."	MS-029	01/03/28	Battle Creek, Mi.	*2SAT 151-155*
Reply to H.T. Nelson	MS-030	01/03/00		*RH 07/30/1901*
Sermon/The Christian Life	MS-031	01/04/14	Battle Creek, Mi.	*1SAT 318-329*
Medical Missionary Work	MS-032	01/04/16		MM 315-318
Diary/"I am not able to sleep past..."	*MS-033	01/04/19		MM 33-34,240-241,249-250,312; Ev 518;1MR 228
Our Aged Workers	MS-034	01/04/20		RY 34-35;ChL 18
Consumers, but not Producers	MS-035	01/04/25		*17MR 244-251*
Diary/"Last night I spoke in the College..."	MS-036	01/04/26		Ev 333
Talk/Regarding the Southern Work	MS-037	01/04/00	Battle Creek, Mi.	*2SAT 156-162*
Sermon/The Unity of the Spirit	MS-038	01/05/06	Des Moines, Ia.	HP 321
Sermon/Living for Christ	MS-039	01/05/00	Denver, Co.	TMK 149
An Appeal for the Southern Field	MS-040	01/04/02	Battle Creek, Mi.	PM 194;Ev 88
Instruction to those who are working in the	MS-041	01/00/00		
Revealing the Christlikeness	MS-042	01/06/02		TMK 199;1BC 1110;3BC 1149; 4BC 1148;7BC 928-930;Ev 653-654; 6MR 119-121;7MR 183;8MR 192
Talk/"I would prefer not to speak today..."	MS-043	01/04/01	Battle Creek, Mi.	*13MR 192-207*
Talk/"Elder A.G. Daniells in the Chair..."	MS-043a	01/04/01	Battle Creek, Mi.	Variant of MS-043-1901
Talk/"I would prefer not to speak today..."	MS-043b	01/04/01	Battle Creek, Mi.	Variant of MS-043-1901
Talk/"I would prefer not to speak today..."	MS-043c	01/04/01	Battle Creek, Mi.	Variant of MS-043-1901
Talk/"I would prefer not to speak today..."	MS-043d	01/04/01	Battle Creek, Mi.	Variant of MS-043-1901
Instruction to Believers	MS-044	01/06/04		*15MR 253-257*
"Comfort ye, comfort my people..."	*MS-045	01/00/00		
"This Conference is an important..."	MS-046	01/04/00	Battle Creek, Mi.	

EGW Manuscripts File—Page 35

"Then opened he their understanding..."	MS-047	01/06/12		See RH 01/07/1902
Bring an Offering to the Lord	MS-048	01/06/23	St. Helena, Ca.	See RH 11/26/1901
Work Out Your Own Salvation	MS-049	01/06/26		AH 201-202,235-236,268;
				CG 79,276-277,498;6MR 16-18;7MR 11-12
"What shall we render to God..."	MS-050	01/06/09		4BC 1182;UL 174;3MR 333
The Need of Self-Examination	MS-051	01/06/26		*1SM 89-93*
Watch and Pray	MS-052	01/06/26		SD 13
"Christ, the Majesty of heaven..."	MS-053	01/06/30		UL 195
Go Work Today in My Vineyard	MS-054	01/07/01		1MR 262-263;See RH 08/26/1902
Go, Work Today in My Vineyard	MS-054a	01/07/01		Variant of MS-054-1901
Words of Instruction	*MS-055	01/07/01		*13MR 208-214*
The Need of Missionary Effort	MS-056	01/07/03		See RH 12/24/1901
Robbing God	*MS-057	01/07/04		*RH 12/03/1901 and 12/10/1901*
A Union of Ministerial & Medical Missionaries	*MS-058	01/07/07		*14MR 269-272*
Diary/"Today I spoke both in the..."	*MS-060	01/04/23	Battle Creek, Mi.	OHC 209,255
Diary/"I praise the Lord this morning..."	*MS-061	01/04/28	Battle Creek, Mi.	
Sermon/"Simon Peter, a servant..."	MS-062	01/07/09	Battle Creek, Mi.	CG 120,489-490,561;5MR 17
Diary/"I have passed another sleepless..."	MS-063	01/04/30		HP 283,302;6MR 166;
				See RH 06/13/1907
Physicians and Meat-eating	MS-064	01/07/17		*CD 290-291*
Sermon/"To every one in this room..."	MS-065	01/07/28		VSS 45,144-145;Ev 498;4MR 130
Fragments/Work in the South	MS-066	01/07/28		2MCP 390;UL 223
The Church School	MS-067	01/07/29		*SpM 183-191*
The Unity of the Spirit	MS-069	01/07/29		11MR 276-277
Diary/What is the Chaff to the Wheat?	*MS-070	01/07/30		*20MR 335-340*
The Blood of Jesus Christ His Son Cleanseth	MS-071	01/07/31		
True Obedience to the Commandments of God	MS-072	01/08/02		1BC 1086;5BC 1084;6BC 1115-1116;
				9MR 235-236
"Thus saith the Lord, Go down..."	MS-073	01/08/02		*14MR 343-352*
Parental Responsibility	MS-075	01/08/05		AH 246-247;7MR 13-14
Diary/Words of Instruction	*MS-076	01/08/08		*21MR 442-445*
Regarding the late movement in Indiana	MS-076a	01/04/17		*GCB 04/23/1901*
Diary/The Southern Work	*MS-077	01/08/08		
Sermon/"I have words to speak to our..."	MS-078	01/06/00	Oakland, Ca.	LHU 292;1BC 1081;9MR 380
Testimony to the Parents of the Los Angeles	MS-079	01/08/18		CG 107,110,251,259;AH 174,220-
				221,314;7MR 14-16,75
A Message to the Los Angeles Church	MS-080	01/08/19		AH 174;CG 500-501
Talk/To Board of Directors of Pacific Press	MS-081	01/08/21		PM 61,91-94,195-196;9MR 95
Talk/The Work in England	MS-081a	01/04/19	Battle Creek, Mi.	*GCB Extra 04/19/1901*
Interview/With Dr. and Mrs. Sanderson	MS-082	01/08/25	St. Helena, Ca.	CG 85-86,253-254;CD 489-490;
				1MR 71-72,282-283;1Bio 21
Interview/With Dr. and Mrs. Sanderson [variant]	MS-082a	01/08/25	St. Helena, Ca.	
God's Purpose for His Sanitariums	MS-083	01/08/26		Ev 210-211;1MR 227
Talk/Teachers To Have a Living Experience	MS-084	01/08/28	Healdsburg, Ca.	6BC 1083-1084;11MR 159-160
Talk/Teachers to Have an Abiding Christ	MS-085	01/08/30	Healdsburg, Ca.	5BC 1092,1095,1142-1143;6BC 1075;
				UL 256
The Need of Medical Missionary Work	MS-086	01/09/12		RH 03/04/1902;CH 575-579
"Many temptations will come..."	MS-087	01/00/00		
"I am instructed to say..."	MS-088	01/00/00		8MR 394-396
"The Lord would have all who are..."	MS-089	01/00/00		*SW 10/09/1901*
The Southern California Conference	MS-090	01/09/17		*PUR 09/26/1901*
Talk/Teachers to Make the Lord Their	MS-091	01/09/04	Healdsburg, Ca.	OHC 325;HP 78;2MCP 650-651;
				LHU 185
Talk/"And unto the angel of the church..."	MS-092	01/09/05	Healdsburg, Ca.	SD 351;5BC 1110;7BC 937-938,
				957,959-961;7MR 125-126
Care to be Shown in the Establishment of	MS-093	01/09/23		MM 153-154;CD 136,281,297;
				1MCP 179;2MCP 391-392;VSS 64;

				CG 548
The Importance of Care and Faithfulness in	MS-094	01/09/23		See PUR 12/19/1901
Regarding the Importance of Cooking	MS-095	01/09/29		MM 269-271;3MR 324
Instruction to Church-Members	MS-096	01/09/24	Healdsburg, Ca.	
Sin and Its Result	MS-097	01/09/24		CTr 19;See RH 02/11/1902
Fragments/The Need of Church Schools	MS-098	01/09/25		*10MR 107-111*
The Southern California Conference	MS-099	01/09/25		13MR 408-410
Talk/Parents to Cooperate with Church School	MS-100	01/09/08	Healdsburg, Ca.	
The Need of the Grace of Christ	MS-101	01/04/00	Battle Creek, Mi.	2SM 24
Sermon/"We give thanks to God..."	MS-102	01/09/21	St. Helena, Ca.	HP 246,247;2MCP 579;AH 323;CG 95;
				7MR 130,376-377
"I have a most earnest desire for..."	*MS-103	01/10/08	St. Helena, Ca.	7MR 226-227
The Need of a Reform	MS-104	01/10/08		5MR 449-450;7MR 131
Sermon/"God, who at sundry times..."	MS-105	01/09/28	St. Helena, Ca.	1MCP 128;2MCP 539;MM 115-117;
				4BC 1171;5BC 1095,1135
Instruction Regarding the Publishing Work	MS-107	01/10/16		
Diary/"I had an interview with Brethren..."	MS-108	01/08/14	Los Angeles, Ca.	UL 240;4MR 447
Work for the Higher Classes	MS-109	01/10/22		
Sermon/The Christian's Hope	MS-110	01/10/05	St. Helena, Ca.	*2SAT 171-179*
Sermon/"I beseech you therefore..."	MS-111	01/10/19	St. Helena, Ca.	VSS 392;UL 306
Make Ready a People Prepared for the Lord	MS-112	01/11/03		5BC 1077,1115
Canvassers Needed	MS-113	01/11/04		CM 7,14-15,23-24,90,132,139;CD 402;
				4MR 129;7MR 377
Lessons from the Experience of Elisha	MS-114	01/11/13		UL 331
Be Ye Therefore Sober	*MS-115	01/11/13		
Regarding Dr. Sanderson's Work	MS-116	01/11/14		
The Need of Aggressive Effort	MS-117	01/11/14		Ev 387;4MR 322
Fragments/Respect for Aged Workers	MS-117a	01/11/14		RY 32-33;6BC 1112;7BC 918;Ev 173
The Teacher's Work	MS-118	01/11/21		
The Church in the Home	MS-119	01/11/24		*16MR 143-148*
Fidelity to Principle	MS-120	01/11/24		
The Debt of the Healdsburg Church	MS-120a	01/00/00		
Physical Labor	MS-121	01/11/28		CG 355
The Law	MS-122	01/11/23		*8MR 98-100*
Injurious Effects of Wrong Habits	MS-123	01/11/28		Te 68-69
Satanic Literature	MS-124	01/12/09		*17MR 236-243*
The Unchangeable Law of God	MS-125	01/12/09		SD 55,325;LDE 155;1SM 107-108;
				UL 357;4BC 1178;7MR 334;
				8MR 346;17MR 28
The Giving of the Law	MS-126	01/12/10		*2SAT 180-189*
Fragments/"This is my seventy-fourth..."	MS-127	01/11/26	S. Lancaster, Ma.	Ev 75,378;4MR 44;5MR 331;
				6MR 320;10MR 14-15;5Bio 140-141
The Principles that should Control	MS-128	01/12/24		AH 283,388,488;SD 312;Ev 42,86;
				4MR 297;11MR 276
Continuation of the Situation in the South	MS-129	01/12/07	S. Lancaster, Ma.	CD 52;LHU 321;VSS 151-152
Training Children for God's Service	MS-129a	01/12/24		
A Call to Service	MS-129b	01/00/00		*SW 02/27/1902, 03/06/1902,*
				03/13/1902
"Sunday the 24th was a rainy..."	MS-130	01/11/27	S. Lancaster, Ma.	*16MR 188-205*
"Our school interest are important..."	MS-131	01/12/29	Nashville, Tn.	5BC 1115
Extracts from Testimonies on Daniel 1	MS-132	01/00/00		CG 166-167;BTS 11/1912;4MR 123
Proper Books and Literature to Read	MS-133	01/00/00		*Extracts from published sources.*
Music	MS-134	01/00/00		Extracts from 1T,2T,3T,4T,RH,PP, and
				Ms 157, 1899
Union and Organization	MS-135	01/00/00		*Extracts from published sources.*
Organization	MS-139	01/00/00		*Extracts from published sources.*
Letters Regarding the Publishing Work	MS-140	01/00/00		4BC 1179;10MR 389-390

The Divine and Human Nature of Christ	MS-141	01/00/00		*17MR 336-340*
Extracts on Daniel and the Revelation	MS-142	01/00/00		Extracts
Testimonies on the Book of Revelation	MS-143	01/00/00		*7MR 78-81 and RH sources*
Talk/"I thank the Lord that so many..."	MS-144	01/04/03	Battle Creek, Mi.	*2SAT 163-170*
Talk/"The Lord God is our helper..."	MS-146	01/04/04	Battle Creek, Mi.	*GCB 04/05/1901 83-86*
Talk/Will a Man Rob God?	MS-147	01/04/06	Battle Creek, Mi.	*GCB 04/08/1901 124-128*
Talk/The Need of Missionary Effort	MS-148	01/04/09	Battle Creek, Mi.	*GCB 04/10/1901 182-184*
Talk/	MS-149	01/04/15	Battle Creek, Mi.	*GCB 04/16/1901 267-269*
Talk/Give the Medical Missionary Work Its Place	MS-150	01/04/11	Battle Creek, Mi.	*GCB 04/12/1901 203-205 and*
				GCB 04/23/901 424
Diary/The Reward of the Obedient	*MS-151	01/09/07		1BC 1118;3BC 1150;LHU 160;8MR 193
Diary/A Message to our Brethren and Sisters in Ca.	MS-152	01/10/10	St. Helena, Ca.	1BC 1105;LHU 139,145;1MR 246-247
Growing in Grace	*MS-153	01/04/00	Battle Creek, Mi.	
Diary/Unheeded Admonitions	*MS-156	01/11/27	S. Lancaster, Ma.	CD 268-269,271-272;2MR 101;
				MRmnt 118
Unheeded Warnings I.	MS-156a	01/11/27	S. Lancaster, Ma.	*BCL 43-47*
Unheeded Warnings II.	MS-156b	01/11/27	S. Lancaster, Ma.	UL 177
Settling in America	*MS-166	01/02/10	St. Helena, Ca.	
An Appeal for the Work in the South	*MS-167	01/04/21	Battle Creek, Mi.	
Diary Fragments [Jan.-Jun.]	*MS-168	01/01/00		
Diary Fragments [Aug.-Nov.]	*MS-169	01/08/00		4MR 313
Individuality in Educational Work	*MS-170	01/05/00		10MR 302-305
Regarding Christ's Object Lessons	*MS-171	01/00/00		
Use and Misuse of Means	*MS-172	01/00/00		
Shall the Work at Nashville Go Forward?	MS-173	01/07/19		
Morning Lesson from Hebrews Two	MS-174	01/11/14		UL 332
How to Study the Bible	MS-175	01/00/00		*2MR 89-92*
"All Ye Are Brethren"	MS-176	01/00/00		
Remarks at Meeting of Cal. M. M. & B. Assn.	MS-177	01/08/20	Oakland, Ca.	
Remarks at Meeting of Cal. M. M. & B. Assn.	MS-178	01/10/01	San Francisco, Ca.	
Sermon/Ephesians 3	MS-179	01/09/07	Healdsburg, Ca.	
Sermon/On the Twelfth of Romans	MS-180	01/12/01	S. Lancaster, Ma.	RH 01/07/1902

1902

God's Justice	MS-001	02/01/06		TDG 14;CTr 289-291
Rivalry in the Publishing Work	MS-002	02/01/12		
Diary/Neglected Duties and Privileges	*MS-004	01/06/20	Oakland, Ca. (1902)	
Diary/The Need of an Awakening	*MS-005	01/06/21	Oakland, Ca. (1902)	UL 186
Diary/A Call to Service	*MS-006	01/06/22	Oakland, Ca. (1902)	*20MR 123-131*
Ministerial Work	MS-006a	02/02/26		*AUCR 07/15/1902*
"In carrying on the different lines..."	MS-007	02/01/26		
God's Law	MS-008	02/01/27c		
Christian Ministry	MS-011	02/02/04c		17MR 28
Remember Therefore from Whence Thou Art	MS-012	02/02/03c		PM 111
God's People to be Light-Bearers	MS-013	01/06/08	Filed in 1902	UL 173
Regarding Health Foods	MS-014	02/02/10c		
The Need of Self-Denial	MS-015	02/02/10c		
The Payment of Workers	MS-016	02/02/11c		MM 275
Parents' Work	MS-017	02/02/11c		*20MR 275-277*
Lessons from the First Chapter of Ephesians	MS-018	02/02/12c		
Evidences of Discipleship	MS-019	01/12/17	Nashville, Tn. (1902)	
Our Elder Brother	MS-020	02/02/12c		*2SAT 190-192*
Fragments/Christ's Filial Love	MS-021	02/02/13c		7BC 946-947;1NL 26,95-96
"I wish to make some statements..."	MS-022	02/02/14		
A Call to Service	MS-022a	02/02/26c		
A Word of Explanation	MS-023	02/02/19	St. Helena, Ca.	

EGW Manuscripts File—Page 38

These Things Ought Not So To Be	MS-024	02/02/20c	*PUR 10/09/1902*
The Sin of Withholding Tithes and Offerings	MS-025	02/02/20c	
The Location and Management of New Sanitariums	MS-026	01/05/00 Des Moines, Ia. (1902)	MM 34-35;151-152
Instruction Regarding Sanitarium Work	MS-027	02/02/23c	MM 175-179
Medical Missionary Work to be Recognized	MS-028	02/02/26c	
The Journey to the General Conference	MS-029	01/01/31 Filed in 1902	5Bio 57-58,60,64,67,69
Christlikeness in Business Dealing	MS-030	02/03/02c	UL 75
Fragments/God's Purpose in Trial	MS-031	02/03/02c	
"And it shall come to pass..."	MS-032	02/03/02c	
The Waste Places in the Lord's Vineyard	MS-034	02/03/04c	
Christ the Redeemer of Both Soul and Body	MS-035	02/03/04c	
Make Full Proof of thy Ministry	MS-036	02/03/05c	CTr 48
Of Some Have Compassion	MS-037	02/03/09c	12MR 96-97
Faithful in Every Good Work	MS-038	02/03/10c	
The Location of the Sanitarium in Southern	MS-041	02/03/14 St. Helena, Ca.	*17MR 348-362*
The Health Food Question	*MS-042	02/03/17c	
The Southern California Sanitarium	MS-043	02/03/17 St. Helena, Ca.	MM 232-233;LLM 476
Diary/God's Plan for the Location of Our Sanitarium	*MS-044	02/03/12	LLM 475-476
Laborers Together with God	MS-045	02/03/23	
Unity a Sign of Discipleship	MS-046	02/03/31c	UL 104
Lessons from the Eighteenth of Matthew	MS-047	02/04/02c	UL 106
What the Sale of Christ's Object Lessons	MS-048	02/04/06 St. Helena, Ca.	*RH 06/17/1902*
Noble Service for the Master	MS-049	02/04/17c	
On Various Phases of Medical Missionary Work	MS-050	02/04/13 St. Helena, Ca.	2SM 306-308;5MR 177
God's Unchangeable Law	*MS-051	02/04/17c	*18MR 133-136*
Fragments/Go Forward	MS-052	02/04/18c	*18MR 146-152*
Fragments/The Work of God's Servants	MS-053	02/04/18c	*18MR 137-145*
How to Solve Perplexing Problems	MS-054	02/04/29c	UL 133
Diary/The Long-Sufferance of God	*MS-055	01/01/27 St. Helena, Ca. (1902)	UL 41;PH050 9-10
Written for our Admonition	MS-056	02/05/09c	4BC 1156-1157;UL 143;TMK 270
Sermon/"If ye then be risen with Christ..."	MS-057	02/04/19 St. Helena, Ca.	
The Making of Wills	MS-058	02/05/26c	
Our Attitude Toward the Southern Field	MS-059	01/12/00 Nashvile, Tn. (1902)	SpTB #18 5-6
Fragments/The Sermon on the Mount	MS-060	02/05/12c	*18MR 83-91*
Instruction Regarding Church Discipline	MS-061	02/05/13 St. Helena, Ca.	
Christ's Sacrifice Our Inspiration	MS-062	02/05/14c	TMK 81,344
A Partial Outline of the Beginnings of J.E. White's	MS-063	01/12/04 Nashville, Tn. (1902)	
Diary/Execute True Judgment	*MS-064	01/04/28 Battle Creek, Mi. (1902)	
A Warning Against Coveteousness	MS-065	02/05/18c	
Words to Christians	MS-066	02/05/23c	
The Southern Work	*MS-067	02/05/20c	SW 06/19/1902;SpTB #18 6
The Misappropriation of Gifts	*MS-068	02/05/20c	
The Grace of Courtesy	MS-069	02/05/26c	*3SM 237-240*
Instruction Regarding the Southern Work	MS-070	02/05/28 St. Helena, Ca.	SpM 219-223
Fragments/Satan's Work	MS-071	02/05/29c	UL 163
As It Was in the Days of Noah	MS-072	02/06/04c	*18MR 92-100*
The Value of Out-Door Life	MS-073	02/06/09c	
The Establishment of Sanitariums	MS-076	02/06/10c	*MM 154-156*
Sermon/Lessons from the First Chapter of	MS-077	02/06/07 Petaluma, Ca.	*2SAT 193-203*
The Health Food Question	MS-078	02/06/16c	*KC 132-133*
The Manufacture of Health Foods I.	*MS-079	00/03/10 Cooranbong, Aus. (02)	*KC 133-135;* see 7T 124-126
The Manufacture of Health Foods II.	MS-080	01/02/16 St. Helena, Ca. (1902)	*KC 135-137;* see 7T 127-131
Medical Missionary Work in the Cities of California	MS-081	00/12/12 San Francisco, Ca (02)	*KC 138-140* ; see 7T 110-114
On the Location of Sanitariums	MS-082	02/06/11c	*From MS-041-1902 and MS-043-1902*
Locating Sanitariums	MS-083	02/06/11c	7T 88-89
Report of Council Re Medical Missionary Work	MS-085	02/04/13 St. Helena, Ca.	From MS-050-1902;*KC 140-146*
Report of Council Re Medical Missionary Work	MS-086	02/04/13 St. Helena, Ca.	From MS-050-1902;7T 78-79,82-83

EGW Manuscripts File—Page 39

Sermon/On The Training of Children	MS-087	02/06/08 Petaluma, Ca.	BE 02/16/1903 and 02/23/1903 and 03/02/1903 and 03/09/1903 and 03/16/1903 and 03/23/1903
A World-Wide Work	*MS-088	02/06/18c	MM 252-253,322;UL 183
Choosing a Site for a Sanitarium	MS-089	02/06/26c	
Christ's Sacrifice for Us	MS-091	02/06/26c	UL 191
Report of Council Meeting	MS-092	02/06/22 St. Helena, Ca.	
Report of Council Meeting	MS-093	02/06/22 St. Helena, Ca.	
God's Purpose for His People	MS-094	02/06/27c	
Ye Are Clean Through The Word	MS-095	02/06/30c	4BC 1176-1177
Talk/"Conformity to the world..."	MS-096	02/06/19 St. Helena, Ca.	*2SAT 204-212*
Talk/Medical Dispensary Work	MS-097	02/06/12 Petaluma, Ca.	LLM 72-72b
Consideration to be Shown to Those Who in their	MS-098	02/07/10c	*SpM 232-238*
Fragments/A Holy People	MS-099	02/07/12c	SD 68,112,286,333;HP 232;UL 207; MM 221;OHC 294;1BC 1104;7BC 941-942,955;5MR 15,53-54
Talk/On the Church School Question	MS-100	02/07/14 St. Helena, Ca.	*SpM 239-246*
Ministers and Teachers to Take Time to Talk With	*MS-101	02/07/21c	2SM 187-188;VSS 304
The Relation That Should Exist Between Teacher &	MS-102	02/07/27c	12MR 146-147
Doing God's Will	*MS-103	02/07/29c	UL 224;OHC 208;5BC 1141;CG 23
Report of Meeting	MS-104	02/07/14 St. Helena, Ca.	*17MR 50-56*
Instruction to Workers	MS-105	02/07/16 St. Helena, Ca.	Ev 196-197,404-406,654;HFM 59; MM 32-33;17MR 263-265
An Aggressive Work	MS-106	02/07/21 St. Helena, Ca.	7T 18-19
The Outlook	MS-107	02/07/07 St. Helena, Ca.	See 7T 270-272
The Object of Establishing Hygienic Restaura	MS-108	02/08/07	4MR 107-108;See 7T 121-123
The Favor of God of More Value Than Worldly	MS-109	02/08/11c	WM 239-240;MM 157-158; 11MR 186-187
Test. on the Establishment of Sanitariums	MS-110	02/08/12c	Compiled from earlier manuscripts
Testimonies on the Health Food Question	MS-111	02/08/12c	Compiled from earlier manuscripts
The Relation that the Medical Miss. Work	MS-112	02/08/12c	Compiled from earlier manuscripts
Tempted In All Points LIke as We Are	MS-113	02/09/07c	OHC 87;Ev 58;7BC 908;17MR 28; CTr 217-218
Instruction Regarding Sanitarium Work	MS-114	02/09/01c	*10MR 209-214*
The Danger of Self-Sufficiency	MS-115	02/09/07c	TDG 259;WM 116;6MR 24-25;17MR 29; CTr 276
Sermon/"Cry aloud, spare not..."	MS-116	02/08/30 St. Helena, Ca.	3BC 1143;4BC 1144,1151;Ev 240
"I can not sleep after half past ten..."	MS-117	02/09/18 Los Angeles, Ca.	7BC 963-964
Christ's Method of Imparting Truth	MS-118	02/10/06c	*21MR 150-153*
An Appeal for the Work in Southern Cal.	MS-119	02/10/08 Fresno, Ca.	HFM 84
Report of Ministers' Meeting	MS-120	02/10/06 Fresno, Ca.	Ev 282;
The Results of Genuine Conversion	MS-121	02/10/15c	1MCP 10;2MCP 781;HP 28;6MR 58
Our Restaurant Work	MS-122	02/10/16c	See 7T 115-120
Report of Council Meeting	MS-123	02/10/19 St. Helena, Ca.	MM 83;5Bio 162,191,200-201;4MR 146; 17MR 266-275
The Work in Nashville	MS-124	02/05/00 St. Helena, Ca.	*1888 1772-1779*
Talk/Words to Students	MS-125	02/10/01	*1SAT 334-339*
Talk/The Student's Privilege	MS-125a	02/10/01	*1SAT 330-333*
Sermon/"And they, when they had..."	MS-126	02/10/11 Fresno, Ca.	HP 322;PM 303,368;Ev 172;3MR 375; 4MR 294-296;see RH 11/11/1902
Talk/Words to Ministers	MS-127	02/09/16 Los Angeles, Ca.	Ev 91,146,174,346,663,685-686; 6MR 63-64
The Work in Nashville	MS-128	02/10/28c	*17MR 276-279*
Consideration for the Colored Race	MS-129	02/11/11c	*9T 223-224*
Diary/Christ Our Example in Every Line of Work	*MS-130	02/10/27 St. Helena, Ca.	*18MR 101-111*
Diary/Words of Counsel to Students	*MS-131	01/12/03 S. Lancaster, Ma. 1902	Ev 666
The Saviour's Characteristics	MS-132	02/10/30c	*18MR 112-117*

Fragments/Is Not This the Carpenter's Son?	MS-133	02/10/30c	MM 280-281,310;4MR 275
His Own Received Him Not	MS-134	02/10/30c	
Instruction to the Churches	*MS-135	02/10/31c	*14MR 150-157*
The Message of Revelation	*MS-136	02/10/22c	7BC 956;MM 37-38,189-190
Diary/"During the past night I have..."	*MS-137	02/10/26 St. Helena, Ca.	5Bio 203
Diary/The Formation of Character	*MS-138	02/07/07 St. Helena, Ca.	*18MR 162-167*
Words of Counsel	MS-139	02/09/15 Los Angeles, Ca.	*18MR 168-173*
Principles for the Guidance of Men in Positions of	MS-140	02/11/03c	*SpM 279-282*
Instruction to Workers	*MS-141	02/10/19 St. Helena, Ca.	
To Every Man His Work	MS-143	02/11/06c	Ev 633-634;MR311 31-32
The Results of Following Human Wisdom	MS-144	02/11/09 St. Helena, Ca.	CS 281-282;5Bio 198-199
Diary/"I thank the Lord with heart..."	*MS-145	02/09/02 St. Helena, Ca.	*SpM 246-250*
Diary/Prayer	*MS-146	02/08/02 St. Helena, Ca.	*20MR 271-274*
An Appeal for More Earnest Effort	MS-147	02/11/12c	UL 330
Diary/Be Ye Therefore Perfect	*MS-148	02/09/05 St. Helena, Ca.	TMK 130;MM 253-256;10MR 161
Diary/"In the visions of the night..."	MS-149	02/10/00 Fresno, Ca.	
Diary/Our Attitude Toward the Work and Workers in	*MS-150	02/11/17c	*SpM 274-278*
The Work in the South	*MS-151	02/11/07 St. Helena, Ca.	*SpM 269-274*
Establishing Schools in the South	*MS-152	02/11/16c	*SpM 253-256*
Calamities	*MS-153	02/11/05c	*19MR 279-282*
Instruction to Men in Positions of Responsibility	MS-154	02/10/24c	Ev 42;MM 165;2BC 1026;SpTB #13 3; 1MR 228;4MR 274-275;7MR 211-213; 9MR 172
Sermon/The Study of the Book of Revelation	MS-155	02/11/22 St. Helena, Ca.	*2SAT 213-224*
Diary/Gather Up the Fragments That Remain	*MS-156	02/12/03c	
The Canvassing Work	MS-157	02/12/03c	
Fragments/Go Forward	MS-158	02/12/14c	UL 362
Fragments/The Food Work	MS-159	02/12/15c	UL 363;HFM 51
Words to Parents	*MS-160	02/12/15c	*18MR 118-120*
The Home Life	MS-161	02/12/15c	*18MR 121-123*
Diary/The Ministry is Ordained of God	*MS-162	02/12/11c	
David's Testimony to God's Goodness	MS-163	02/12/15c	2BC 1018;3BC 1128;CTr 146
Solomon's Dream	MS-164	02/12/15c	2BC 1025-1026;3BC 1128;CTr 158
Diary/The Christ-Life	*MS-165	02/08/31 St. Helena, Ca.	*18MR 174-184*
The Need of Earnest Effort	MS-166	02/12/17c	*18MR 185-196*
Diary/Regarding the Work in Nashville	MS-167	02/10/00 Fresno, Ca.	
Diary/Regarding the Work in Nashville	MS-167a	02/10/00 Fresno, Ca.	variant of MS-167-1902
The Sin of Evil-Speaking	MS-168	02/12/24c	*18MR 197-207*
The Work of the St. Helena Sanitarium	MS-169	02/07/14 St. Helena, Ca.	*19MR 38-54*
On the Establishment of a Restaurant in L.A.	MS-172	02/05/07 St. Helena, Ca.	
Medical Missionary Work in Southern Cal.	MS-173	02/09/15 Los Angeles, Ca.	*10MR 248-252*
Talk/School Discipline	MS-174	02/10/10	
Justice in Sanitarium Management	*MS-175	02/00/00	
God's Church the Light of the World	*MS-176	02/00/00	*18MR 208-210*
Cousels Regarding the Review and Herald Publ.	*MS-216	02/11/11 St. Helena, Ca.	
Cautions Regarding Restaurant Work	*MS-217	02/00/00	
Methods of Labor--E.E. Franke	MS-218	02/00/00	Missing
True Medical Missionary Work	*MS-219	02/00/00	
Diary Fragment	*MS-220	02/01/01 Nashville, Tn.	*18MR 124-126*
Diary Fragments [Feb. 2-May 10]	*MS-221	02/02/00 St. Helena, Ca.	*18MR 211-216*
Diary Fragments [Aug. 1-Sep. 29]	*MS-222	02/08/00	5MR 453;8MR 295
Diary [Nov. 12-30]	*MS-223	02/11/00 St. Helena, Ca.	*18MR 217-222*
To God Be The Glory	*MS-224	02/00/00	*18MR 127-132*
"We have had rain, rain..."	*MS-225	02/12/12 St. Helena, Ca.	
Our Denominational Book Work	MS-226	02/00/00	
I Stand Alone	*MS-227	02/07/00 St. Helena, Ca.	*3SM 66-67*
Bible Writers Inspired, Not Extinguished	*MS-228	02/00/00	*11MR 347*

EGW Manuscripts File—Page 41

Sermon/1 John 3	MS-229	02/09/13	Los Angeles, Ca.
Sermon/Matthew 6:19	MS-230	02/09/14	Los Angeles, Ca.
Remarks/Report of Council Meeting	MS-231	02/09/25	San Diego, Ca.
Remarks/Report of Council Meeting	MS-232	02/10/01	Fernando, Ca.

1903

An Appeal	MS-001	03/01/07		*RH 01/27/1903*
Following Christ	MS-002	03/01/16c		1BC 1095;5BC 1096;AH 386-387;
				CG 151,193,249,271-272,487-488;
				2MCP 453-454;13MR 364-365;CTr 89
To Every Man His Work	MS-003	03/03/01c		UL 74;8MR 332
The St. Helena Sanitarium	MS-003a	03/01/23	St. Helena, Ca.	CD 414-415;1MR 284
Adonijah's Rebellion	MS-006a	03/02/17		2BC 1024;CTr 104-105;RH 10/08/1903
Words of Counsel to Burden-Bearers	MS-007	03/10/08c		*HFM 62-63;8T 140-142,190*
Written for our Admonition	*MS-009	03/00/00		OHC 81;17MR 29
Sermon/Lessons from the Sending Out of the	MS-010	03/03/28		*GCB 03/30/1903 7-11*
Talk/Words of Counsel	MS-011	03/03/26		PM 170-171;1BC 1099,1117;
				4MR 353-354,367-368
Instruction Regarding the Publishing Work	MS-012	02/11/26	Filed in 1903	
A Division of Responsibilities	MS-013	03/04/20c		PM 145-146
Talk/Lessons From Josiah's Reign	MS-014	03/03/30		*GCB 04/01/1903 29-33*
Talk/How to Receive God's Blessing	MS-015	03/03/31		*GCB 04/02/1903 55-57*
Talk/Unity of Effort	MS-016	03/04/01		*GCB 04/02/1903 57-59*
Talk/Unity of Spirit	MS-017	03/04/02		1BC 1087
A Call to Repentance	*MS-018	02/11/10	Filed in 1903	4MR 321;6MR 217
Unselfishness in Service	*MS-019	03/04/08c		*SpTB #19 18-20*
Talk/Our Duty to Leave Battle Creek	MS-020	03/04/03		*GCB 04/06/1903 84-88*
Talk/A Call to Repentance	MS-021	03/04/04		*GCB 04/06/1903 88-91*
Talk/The Work Before Us	MS-022	03/04/05		*GCB 04/07/1903 104-106*
Prove All Things	*MS-023	03/04/08c		
The Trial Volume of the Review	MS-024	03/04/24c		PM 221-222;Ev 15,565;1SM 118;
				1NL 95
Words of Counsel	MS-025	03/04/09c		LLM 68-69
Regarding Work of General Conference	MS-026	03/04/03	Oakland, Ca.	*14MR 279-280*
Talk/Our Helper	MS-027	03/03/25		
The Southern Work	MS-028	03/04/19c		
The Southern Work	MS-029	03/04/19c		3MR 264-265
Instruction Re the Establishment of Institutions	MS-030	03/04/20c		*2SAT 225-227*
Lessons From the Third Chapter of First John	*MS-031	03/08/22		RC 28;UL 248
Found Wanting	MS-032	03/04/21		8T 247-251
Instruction for Men in Positions of Responsibility	*MS-033	03/04/27c		*14MR 99-103*
The Two Great Principles of the Law	MS-034	03/04/27c		
False Repentance: What Is It?	MS-035	03/04/27c		*RH 08/19/1971*
Directions for Work	MS-037	03/05/01	Oakland, Ca.	UL 135
Talk/The Southern Work	MS-038	03/04/09		*GCB 04/14/1903 202-205*
Perseverance in the Work of God	MS-040	03/05/04c		6BC 1051;PM 281;8MR 26
Less Preaching; More Teaching	MS-041	03/05/05c		VSS 235-237;CG 531;ML 194
The Training of Children	MS-042	03/05/04c		RC 179;CG 261,280;7MR 16
The Result of Self-Denying Effort	MS-043	03/03/06		7MR 336
Dangers in the Health Food Business	MS-044	03/04/28	St. Helena, Ca.	HFM 61-66
Make the Health Food Work a Blessing	MS-045	03/05/17c		HFM 67-71
Christ's Object Lessons	MS-046	03/05/15c		RH 06/02/1903
A Call for Repentance	*MS-048	03/01/02	St. Helena, Ca.	SpTB #6 56
Prayer	MS-049	03/05/19c		
A Sermon, By Paul	MS-050	03/05/19c		6BC 1080;2SM 360
Our Duty to Needy Fields	MS-051	03/05/19c		3BC 1153;17MR 29

Diary/"This morning, I feel thankful..."	*MS-052	03/01/02	1BC 1108
Memorials in Many Places	MS-053	03/05/20c	*17MR 286-288*
Talk/The Work of Our Fernando School	MS-054	02/09/17 Filed in 1903	*8MR 2-7 and CT 205-210*
A Cause of Spiritual Weakness	MS-055	03/05/22c	*SW 06/18/1903 and 07/09/1903*
A Present Help	MS-056	03/05/22c	1MR 115-116
An Appeal for Consecration and Service	MS-057	03/05/27c	CG 549;1MR 21;CTr 360
Nehemiah's Prayer	MS-058	03/06/16c	3BC 1136;CTr 182-184
A Call to Repentance	*MS-059	03/07/02c	
Unity in the Home and in the Church	MS-060	03/06/24c	*19MR 67-72*
Learn of Me	MS-061	03/07/02c	*SW 06/11/1903*
Diary/That They All May Be One	*MS-062	02/11/28 Filed in 1903	Ev 31
Diary/Feeding Upon the Word of God	*MS-063	02/12/01 Filed in 1903	6MR 37
God's Covenant with Israel	*MS-064	03/07/02c	1MR 104-109
Diary/The Need of Repentance	*MS-065	02/11/08 Filed in 1903	9MR 380
Our Duty Toward the Lord's Institution	MS-066	03/07/15c	*RH 08/04/1903*
Sermon/Fishers of Men	MS-067	03/05/30 Healdsburg, Ca.	RC 237,255;CG 21,435;PM 283; 4MR 109
Answering Christ's Prayer for Us, By Obeying His	MS-068	03/07/06 Healdsburg, Ca.	
Talk/Instruction Regarding School Work	MS-069	03/07/07	2MR 213-216
Sermon/"Behold, what manner of love..."	MS-070	03/06/07 Calistoga, Ca.	RH 09/03/1903
Talk/To Every Man His Work	MS-071	03/06/18	MM 293;Ev 109,687;3SM 303;ML 47; 1MR 27;4MR 87;LLM 66-67
The Color-Line	MS-073	03/07/27c	Compiled from earlier manuscripts.
Lessons From Paul's Ministry	MS-074	03/07/27c	6BC 1088-1089,1106
Practical Christianity	*MS-075	03/08/01c	
Diary/The Color-Line	*MS-075a	03/07/29	
The Burning of the Sanitarium	*MS-076	02/02/20 Filed in 1903	SpTB #6 5-10;6BC 1074;7BC 904; HP 10;3MR 358
The Color-Line	MS-077	03/08/02c	See 9T 213-221
A Worldwide Message	MS-078	03/07/24	*RH 08/20/1903*
How God Trains His Workers	MS-079	03/08/04c	*8MR 422-424*
Sermon/Whoso Offereth Praise Glorifieth God	MS-080	03/08/01 St. Helena, Ca.	*2SAT 228-237*
God's Chosen People	MS-081	03/08/04c	
Diary/The Promise of the Spirit	*MS-082	02/09/25 Filed in 1903	5MR 126-127;11MR 219-220
Diary/Christ Our Example in Medical Missionary	*MS-083	02/10/29 Filed in 1903	MM 21-22;TDG 311;8T 206-212
Diary/The Restaurant Work	*MS-084	03/08/03c	*MM 306-308*
Diary/"I am grateful for the sleep..."	*MS-085	02/09/29 Filed in 1903	8MR 398
The Work at Yountville	*MS-086	03/08/09c	*12MR 315-317*
The Hour of Satan's Triumph	*MS-087	03/08/11c	
Be Not Weary in Well-Doing	*MS-088	03/08/09 St. Helena, Ca.	UL 235;SpM 314-315
First Be Reconciled To Thy Brother	MS-089	03/08/12c	UL 238;6BC 1115;7BC 905
A Time of Peril	*MS-090	03/06/11	
Talk/Self-Improvement	MS-091	03/08/20 Healdsburg, Ca.	*2SAT 238-248*
Honor to be Shown to Our Pioneer Workers	MS-092	03/07/24 St. Helena, Ca.	RY 32;7BC 947
Concerning the Signing of Contracts	*MS-093	03/08/31c	UL 257
Lessons From the Past	MS-094	03/08/27c	*KC 1-9*
Lessons From the Past [edited]	MS-094a	03/08/27c	Edited copy of MS-094-1903
The Contending Forces of Good and Evil	MS-095	03/08/28c	6BC 1119;SD 100,105
Christian Education in our Schools	*MS-099	03/09/01c	3SM 141-142
Diary/Temperate in All Things	*MS-101	03/09/01c	6MR 37
Co-Laborers With Christ	*MS-102	02/11/17 Filed in 1903	6BC 1087,1098;10MR 323-327; 17MR 29
Instruction to Ministers and Physicians	MS-103	02/09/15 Filed in 1903	2SM 396
The Last Supper	MS-106	03/09/14c	CTr 261-264
Diary/Unity With The Father	*MS-107	02/10/31 Filed in 1903	ML 58;17MR 29-30
Diary/Instruction Concerning Wages	*MS-108	02/08/15 Filed in 1903	2SM 186-187;Ev 636
Diary/Notes of Travel	*MS-109	02/09/11 Filed in 1903	

Diary/Blessed With All Spiritual Blessings	*MS-110	03/06/10	St. Helena, Ca.	6BC 1113
That They May Be One	*MS-111	03/10/22		5BC 1148
The Work to be Done in Battle Creek	*MS-112	03/08/22	Healdsburg, Ca.	*SpTB #6 16-19*
That They All May Be One	MS-113	03/10/08c		OHC 226
Talk/Duties and Privileges of the Christian	MS-114	03/06/14	Calistoga, Ca.	CG 98,246,499;AH 197,536;UL 179
Diary/Instruction Regarding Sanitarium Work	*MS-115	02/09/04	Filed in 1903	MM 306;CG 486;3BC 1148; 10MR 164-165;PC 38-40;SpM 256-259
Lessons from the Story of Cornelius	MS-116	03/10/08c		
A Neglected Work	MS-117	03/09/24	St. Helena, Ca.	WM 36-37,43,48,217-218,242;8MR 197
Decided Action to be Taken Now	MS-117a	03/10/00	St. Helena, Ca.	*SpTB #7 36-42*
What a Medical Missionary Leader Should Be	MS-118	03/08/13	St. Helena, Ca.	
Lessons From Israel	*MS-119	03/10/07c		UL 294;6BC 1081
Lessons from the Epistle of John	*MS-120	03/10/08c		UL 295;RH 06/30/1910
A Solemn Warning	MS-121	03/10/08c		*PH058*
The Time of the End	MS-122	03/10/09c		3SM 76-77;2MR 21-22;RH 10/13/1904
The Battle Creek College Debt	MS-123	03/10/08c		*SpM 325-327*
A Personal God	MS-124	03/10/14c		5BC 1145;6BC 1079-1080; 9MR 122-124
The Workers Needed Now	MS-125	03/10/16c		*RH 11/05/1903 and 11/19/1903*
Christ at the Marriage Feast	MS-126	03/10/26c		CD 436-437;Te 18;10MR 204-207;CTr 229
A Call to Service	MS-127	03/10/27		*BSL #181 3-9*
Wrong-Doing to be Condemned	MS-128	03/10/04c		*16MR 1-14*
Wrong-Doing to be Condemned	MS-128a	03/10/04c		variant of Ms 128, 1903
Lessons from the Past--3	MS-129	03/10/28c		*10MR 252-259*
Christ Stilling the Tempest	*MS-130	03/11/03c		UL 321
Genuine Conversion	*MS-131	03/11/06c		
God's Chosen People	*MS-132	03/11/08c		7BC 981;MM 91-94;UL 326
A View of the Conflict	MS-134	03/11/03c		*8T 41-47*
Establishing the Foundation of our Faith	MS-135	03/11/04c		3MR 412-414
Extracts/The Need of an Awakened Church	MS-136	03/00/00		Compiled from earlier manuscripts.
The Personality of God	*MS-137	03/11/12c		
How We Can Help the Southern Work	MS-138	03/11/17	St. Helena, Ca.	*Southern Missionary, 1903 #4*
The Message in Revelation	MS-139	03/10/23c		*18MR 26-41*
The Fall of our First Parents	MS-140	03/09/27	Healdsburg, Ca.	5BC 1129-1130;LHU 235;6MR 102
"We are nearing the closing scenes..."	MS-141	03/08/17	St. Helena, Ca.	Ev 525;see SpTB #6 46-48
A Collection of Mss. on Auditing	MS-142	03/00/00		Compiled from earlier manuscripts.
Unity	*MS-143	03/00/00		UL 358
Leadership	*MS-144	03/11/17	St. Helena, Ca.	8T 236-238;1BC 1117-1118
Beware of Fanciful Doctrines	MS-145	03/12/02c		*RH 01/21/1904*
Abiding in Christ	MS-146	03/12/20	St. Helena, Ca.	WM 272;1NL 40-41
The Narrow Way	MS-147	03/12/31c		UL 379;3Bio 1147
Diary/The Need of Humility and Unity	*MS-148	03/03/00	Oakland, Ca.	
One With Christ in God	MS-149	03/12/31c		*SW 02/02/1904*
The Blessing of Service	MS-150	03/12/20	St. Helena, Ca.	RC 202
Through Nature to Nature's God	MS-151	03/11/20c		*Compiled from published sources*.
A Collection of Mss re Living Temple	MS-152	03/11/17c		Compiled from earlier manuscripts.
A Collection of Mss re the Personality of God	MS-153	03/11/09c		Compiled from earlier manuscripts and printed sources.
Talk/Words of Counsel to Educators	MS-154	03/09/25	Healdsburg, Ca.	
Our Youth to be Shielded from Evil Influence	MS-155	03/10/25c		
Christ, Our Divine-Human Example	MS-156	03/10/26c		UL 313
The Reception of the Holy Spirit	MS-157	03/10/27c		*AUCR 06/01/1904*
A Message to Leading Physicians	MS-159	03/09/04c		UL 261;5BC 1146;6BC 1118
The Peril of Rejecting Light	*MS-161	03/07/01	St. Helena, Ca.	UL 196
Written for our Admonition	*MS-162	03/06/29	St. Helena, Ca.	Ev 233;5MR 83
Josiah's Mistake	*MS-163	03/05/15		2BC 1039-1040

EGW Manuscripts File—Page 44

Words of Warning Against Present Dangers	MS-169	03/10/12c		UL 299
Coming Destruction of Cities	*MS-170	03/00/00		
Diary [Jan. 3-31]	*MS-171	03/01/00		5MR 453;12MR 83
Diary [Feb. 2-17]	*MS-172	03/02/00		
Diary [Apr. 17-Jun. 30]	*MS-173	03/04/00		12MR 83-84
Diary [Jul. 5-31]	*MS-174	03/07/00		3SM 76;3MR 211;6MR 102
Diary [Aug. 1-22]	*MS-175	03/08/00		11MR 200
Diary [Sep. 12-Nov. 1]	*MS-176	03/09/00		
Diary [Dec. 2-17]	*MS-177	03/12/00		UL 350;12MR 84
Who are Subjects of the Kingdom of God?	*MS-178	03/00/00		
If I Should Be Removed by Death	*MS-179	03/00/00		
Dangers in Overemphasis of Health Food	*MS-180	03/03/16		
Warning in Regard to Food Factories	*MS-181	03/00/00		
Humility Above Reputation	*MS-182	03/00/00		HP 220
The Child Jesus in the Temple	*MS-183	03/00/00		
The Gospel to be Lived	*MS-184	03/00/00		
The Gospel Invitation & the Great Commissio	*MS-185	03/00/00		
Economy in our School Work	MS-186	03/00/00		
Diary/"The Lord is my helper..."	*MS-187	03/08/09	St. Helena, Ca.	UL 236;5BC 1084-1085;10MR 299-300
Sermon/John 14	MS-188	03/06/13	Calistoga, Ca.	
Sermon/On Ephesians Chapter Two	MS-189	03/06/20	St. Helena, Ca.	incomplete
Sermon/Matthew 6:19-21	MS-190	03/07/11	St. Helena, Ca.	
Talk/"This is the first time..."	MS-191	03/11/03	St. Helena, Ca.	
Talk/"Never was there a time..."	MS-192	03/00/00	St. Helena, Ca.	
Stand Firm for the Right	MS-193	03/00/00		
Remarks at Ca. M. M. & B. Assn. Board	MS-194	03/02/09	St. Helena, Ca.	
Interview/Between E. G. White and A. T. Jones	MS-195	03/08/15		incomplete;filed in DF 151

1904

A Message of Warning	*MS-002	03/12/15	St. Helena, Ca.	Filed in 1904
True Repentance	*MS-004	04/01/15c		
Diary/"The past night has been one of..."	*MS-005	04/01/20	St. Helena, Ca.	*13MR 377-383*
Interview/Counsel on Age of School Entrance	MS-007	04/01/14	St. Helena, Ca.	*6MR 348-374* (3SM 214-226)
Sermon/Lessons from the Fifty-Eighth of Isa.	MS-008	04/01/23	St. Helena, Ca.	*2SAT 249-259*
Instruction Re the Medical Missionary Work	MS-010	04/01/29c		*BCL 103-105*
The Blessing of Obedience	MS-012	04/01/11	St. Helena, Ca.	CW 109
Duties and Privileges of the Physician	MS-014	04/02/03c		MM 40-41
Working for Christ	MS-016	04/02/03c		MM 319-320
The World to be Warned	MS-018	03/02/03	St. Helena, Ca. (1904)	RH 07/28/1904
Instruction to Canvassing Agents	MS-020	04/02/18c		*PM 258-259*
Co-operation Between School and Home	MS-022	04/01/00	St. Helena, Ca.	CG 260-261,557-558;SD 321;CC 49
Words of Instruction	MS-024	04/03/08c		CG 420-421;1SM 86-88
Persecution Not To Be Needlessly Encountered	MS-026	04/03/11c		LDE 151-152
Unwise Speculations	MS-028	04/03/11c		1SM 172-174
Redeem the Time	MS-030	03/10/29	St. Helena, Ca. (1904)	CG 328-329;UL 316;1SM 169-170
The New Life in Christ	MS-036	04/04/13c		6BC 1115;UL 117
Our Work in Washington	*MS-038	04/05/03	Washington, D.C.	6 articles used in various publications
Shall We Colonize Around Our Institutions?	MS-040	04/04/20c		*RH 06/02/1904*
The Power of the Word of God	MS-042	04/05/22		MM 88-89;OHC 132;RH 11/10/1904
Preach the Word	*MS-044	04/00/00		*RH 11/03/1904*
That They May Be One	*MS-045	04/05/14	Washington, D.C.	UL 149;1MR 15;6MR 389;5Bio 326-327
Talk/The Foundation of our Faith	MS-046	04/05/18	Berrien Springs, Mi.	*1SAT 340-348*
Talk/Lessons from the 1st and 2nd Chap. of Col.	MS-048	04/05/20	Berrien Springs, Mi.	6MR 39
Talk/Lessons from the Third Chapter of Rev.	MS-050	04/05/21	Berrien Springs, Mi.	OHC 19;2MCP 436-437;5MR 407-408
Sermon/A Plea for Unity	MS-052	04/05/22	Berrien Springs, Mi.	*2SAT 260-269*
Talk/"We may find valuable instruction..."	MS-054	04/05/23	Berrien Springs, Mi.	*SpM 352-355*

Talk/"I therefore, the prisoner of..."	MS-056	04/05/23	Berrien Springs, Mi	UL 157;Ev 398,2MCP 727
"Last night matters were presented..."	MS-058	04/05/24	Berrien Springs, Mi.	6MR 414;10MR 357-358;5Bio 338
Talk/The Work of the Huntsville School	MS-060	04/06/21	Huntsville, Al.	*6MR 208-216*
"The converting power of God..."	MS-062	04/06/25	Nashville, Tn.	
"Before leaving Washington..."	*MS-064	04/06/23	Nashville, Tn.	SpTB #6 41-44;see Lt 259, 1904
"I praise the Lord for the good..."	MS-066	04/06/30	Nashville, Tn.	
General Conference Men Unduly Burdened	MS-068	04/06/30	Nashville, Tn.	2MR 199
The Huntsville School	MS-070	04/00/00		*RH 09/01/1904*
The Great Controversy	MS-072	04/07/25	Washington, D.C.	*SpTB #2 1-11*
The Berrien Springs Meeting	MS-074	04/07/25	Washington, D.C.	*SpTB #2 25-29*
Freedom or Bondage	MS-076	04/00/00		*SpTB #2 44-48*
Our Work	MS-078	04/00/00		MM 89-90
Lessons from the Chronicles	MS-080	04/00/00		
The Use of the Tithe	MS-082	04/00/00		*7MR 135-138*
Revealing Christ to the World	*MS-083	04/08/20	Melrose, Ma.	UL 246
The Melrose Sanitarium	MS-084	04/08/21	Melrose, Ma.	1MR 134-135;see RH 09/29/1904
The New England Sanitarium	MS-086	04/08/21	Melrose, Ma.	see RH 09/29/1904
Notes of Travel	MS-090	04/09/00		*RH 10/06/1904*
"The great need of efficient helpers..."	MS-092	04/09/21	College View, Ne.	MM 97;7BC 979
The Sin of Evil-Speaking	MS-094	04/09/23	College View, Ne.	VSS 146;UL 280
A Tribute to Marian Davis	MS-095	04/09/26		3SM 93
An All-Sufficient Saviour	MS-096	04/00/00		7MR 187
Talk/Self-Denial Boxes	MS-098	04/09/20	College View, Ne.	*AU Gleaner 10/05/1904*
Our Duty Toward the Huntsville School	MS-100	04/08/11c		
Sermon/"Now before the feast of the..."	MS-102	04/07/02	Nashville, Tn.	RC 243,250,261,283;Ev 274
"My mind is weighed down by perplexities..."	MS-104	04/03/00	St. Helena, Ca.	
Sermon/Words of Encouragement	MS-106	04/04/30	Washington, D.C.	5MR 116-118
Sermon/"Simon Peter, a servant..."	MS-108	04/04/30	Washington, D.C.	variant of Ms 106, 1904
Sermon/Lessons from the First Chapter of Daniel	MS-110	04/03/19	Healdsburg, Ca.	17MR 30;CTr 177-178
Watchman, What of the Night?	MS-112	04/10/25	St. Helena, Ca.	
Directions Regarding Work for Colored People	MS-114	04/09/17	College View, Ne.	*PCO 124-127*
Let This Mind Be In You	MS-116	04/04/14	St. Helena, Ca.	
Talk/Union With Christ	MS-118	04/12/11	Riverside, Ca.	*PC 314-319*
Counsel Regarding the Work at Huntsville	*MS-139	04/07/06	Nashville, Tn.	*PCO 122-123*
Diary [Jan. 30-Mar. 22]	*MS-140	04/01/00		
Diary [Apr. 1-30]	*MS-141	04/04/00		5MR 119-120;8MR 165;5Bio 319-320
Diary [May 4-26]	*MS-142	04/05/00		5Bio 319,326-327
Diary [Jun. 8-29]	*MS-143	04/06/00		5Bio 342-344
Diary [Jul. 14-20]	*MS-144	04/07/00		5Bio 378
Our Work in the Washington Area	MS-144a	04/07/20	Takoma Pk., Md.	
Diary [Aug. 5-Sep. 4]	*MS-145	04/08/00		*21MR 421-424*
Diary [Oct. 9]	*MS-146	04/10/09	St. Helena, Ca.	3SM 91
Diary [Nov. 23-Dec. 27]	*MS-147	04/11/00		*14MR 221-224*
Fragments/"Nevertheless I have somewhat..."	*MS-149	04/12/14	Redfield, Ca.	
Need of the Work in the Nashville Area	MS-150	04/07/23	Washington, D.C.	
Sermon/"We want to give..."	MS-151	04/03/27	Healdsburg, Ca.	
Interview/With Huntsville School Board	MS-152	04/07/05	Nashville, Tn.	*PCO 135-146*
Sermon/"This is the only definition..."	MS-153	04/08/13	Philadelphia, Pa.	
Sermon/Abide With Me	MS-154	04/08/14	Philadelphia, Pa.	
Sermon/"The first day of the week..."	MS-155	04/09/04	Middletown, Ct.	
Sermon/1 John 2:3	MS-156	04/09/07	Battle Creek, Mi.	
Sermon/"If ye be therefore..."	MS-157	04/09/08	Battle Creek, Mi.	
Sermon/"These words spake Jesus..."	MS-158	04/09/10	Omaha, Ne.	
Sermon/Rev. 1:1-3	MS-159	04/09/11	Omaha, Ne.	
Talk/To College Students	MS-160	04/09/15	College View, Ne.	
Sermon/"The revelation of Jesus Christ..."	MS-161	04/09/17	College View, Ne.	CTr 101

EGW Manuscripts File—Page 46

A Solemn Charge	MS-162	04/00/00		
The Melrose Sanitarium	*MS-163	04/09/02		
Sermon/Micah 6:1-8	MS-164	04/05/19	Berrien Springs, Mi.	incomplete
Talk/"My mind is greatly stirred..."	MS-165	04/04/00	Washington, D.C.	c. April to July, 1904
Sermon/Lessons from the Fifteenth Chap. of John	MS-166	04/06/25	Nashville, Tn.	Notes only;filed in DF 151
Sermon/"Christ did not forget..."	MS-167	04/08/27	Melrose Ma.	incomplete
Interview on School Verandah; Berrien Springs Meeting	MS-168	04/00/00		

1905

New Years' Day Jottings	*MS-001	05/01/01		
Talk/The work in the Southern States	MS-002	04/09/25	College View, Ne. (1905)	*SpM 372-374*
"I am afraid that sufficient..."	MS-004	04/12/27c	Filed in 1905	1MCP 327;2MR 181;3MR 319-320; 9MR 287
The Nebraska Sanitarium	MS-006	04/09/26	College View, Ne. (1905)	*Nebraska Reporter, 02/28/1905*
Talk/Growing in Grace	MS-008	04/09/23	College View, Ne. (1905)	HP 99;4MR 369
Non-Essential Subjects to be Avoided	*MS-010	04/09/12	Omaha, Ne. (1905)	*17MR 303-307*
Instruction Regarding the Huntsville School	*MS-012	04/06/10	"Morning Star" (1905)	*PCO 118-122*
Holy and Without Blame	MS-014	05/02/01c		AH 17,436;CH 260
Regarding the Work of Mrs. E.G. White	MS-016	05/02/07c		
The Reign of King Solomon	MS-018	05/02/20c		2BC 1026,1029-1030
Go Ye Into all the World, and Preach	MS-020	05/02/20c		Ev 285,644-646;2MCP 426-427
Christ Our Only Hope	*MS-022	04/03/07	St. Helena, Ca. (1905)	17MR 31
A Call to Reach a Higher Standard	MS-024	05/02/22c		
A Great Work Before Us	MS-026	05/02/27	St. Helena, Ca.	Ev 686-687;7BC 960-961;CM 88-89
The Result of Repentance	MS-028	04/08/13	Philadelphia, Pa. (1905)	6BC 1068,1071;7MR 292-293
A Visit to Redlands	*MS-030	05/03/06c		*RH 03/30/1905 and 04/06/1905*
An Open Letter	MS-032	05/03/06	St. Helena, Ca.	*RH 03/23/1905*
A Call to the First Love	*MS-034	05/02/09	St. Helena, Ca.	7BC 958
Be Not Weary in Well-Doing	MS-036	05/00/00		PUR 03/16/1905
Be of Good Cheer	*MS-038	05/03/27c		UL 100;Ev 193;3BC 1142-1143, 1146-1147
Sermon/Who May Abide the Day of His Coming?	MS-038a	05/04/01	St. Helena, Ca.	UL 105;Te 29,59,119,130-131,163
Faithful Stewardship	MS-040	05/04/09c		UL 113
God's Word to Be Our Study	*MS-041	05/04/09	St. Helena, Ca.	
Not With Outward Show	MS-042	05/04/13c		Ev 79,160,203-204,530-531
An Appeal for Faithful Stewardship	MS-044	05/03/29		CS 96;8MR 310;MR760 5-7
Lessons from Paul's Ministry	MS-046	05/04/14	St. Helena, Ca.	6BC 1082-1084
Making Up the One Hundred Thousand Dollar	MS-050	05/02/15	St. Helena, Ca.	CD 281
Talk/"I want to say a few words at..."	MS-052	05/05/11	Takoma, Pk., Md.	*RH 05/18/1905*
Unto Seventy Times Seven	*MS-053	05/05/11	Takoma Pk., Md.	HP 297;UL 145;8MR 187-188
Talk/Lessons from the Third Chapter of Phil.	MS-054	05/05/13	Takoma Pk., Md.	*RH 06/15/1905*
Talk/Lessons from the First Epistle of John	MS-056	05/05/16	Takoma Pk., Md.	*RH 07/13/1905 and 07/20/1905*
Talk/The Work in Washington	MS-058	05/05/19	Takoma Pk., Md.	*RH 06/01/1905*
Diary/The Sabbath Truth in the Sentinel	*MS-059	05/05/20	Takoma Pk., Md.	*MR760 2-5*
"I have been able to sleep only a very..."	MS-060	05/05/21	Takoma Pk., Md.	1MCP 29-31
"I am bidden to bear a message to our..."	MS-062	05/05/24	Takoma Pk., Md.	*MR760 7-12*
"A question has been brought to me..."	MS-064	05/05/24	Takoma Pk., Md.	2SM 97-98
Talk/The Need of Home Religion	MS-066	05/05/25	Takoma Pk., Md.	*RH 06/22/1905 and 06/29/1905*
Talk/The Ladder of Progress	MS-068	05/05/25	Takoma Pk., Md.	*RH 07/06/1905*
Talk/A Message of Warning	*MS-070	05/05/30	Takoma Pk., Md.	5MR 278-279;6Bio 58-59
Talk/A Message of Warning [variant]	MS-070a	05/05/30	Takoma Pk., Md.	
Talk/The Boulder Sanitarium	MS-072	05/05/29	Takoma Pk., Md.	*SpTB #5 39-43*
Talk/Our Duty Toward the Jews	MS-074	05/05/29	Takoma Pk., Md.	*9MR 309-310*
Building the Waste Places	*MS-075	05/05/00	Takoma Pk., Md.	*MR760 13-14*
"The Lord has given me a message..."	MS-076	05/06/29	San Jose, Ca.	*19MR 333-337*
"During the night impressions..."	*MS-077	04/06/30	Nashville, Tn. (1905)	

A Message to Believers	MS-078	05/00/00		OIIC 92;2MCP 559;7BC 973; 6MR 27-28
"I am awakened at two o'clock to..."	MS-080	04/08/25	Melrose, Ma. (1905)	UL 251
A Change of Heart Needed	MS-082	04/08/08	Washington, D.C. (1905)	
That Your Joy May Be Full	MS-084	04/08/00	Washington, D.C. (1905)	RC 124;Ev 121
The Washington Sanitarium	MS-086	05/07/14	St. Helena, Ca.	1MCP 11;2MCP 713;2MR 53
One, Even as We Are One	MS-088	05/00/00		*BTS 02/1906*
An Appeal in Behalf of the Work in Nashville	MS-088a	05/00/00		2MR 11
Collection of Matter re the Colorado Sanitarium	MS-090	05/00/00		*SpTB #5 20-43*
The Loma Linda Sanitarium	MS-092	05/00/00		*SpTB #3b 3-17*
Test. re Our General Publishing Work	MS-094	05/00/00		*SpTB #4*
Words of Counsel/The Health Food Work	MS-096	05/09/07	Glendale, Ca.	HFM 72-75
A Message of Warning	MS-098	05/07/15	St. Helena, Ca.	*SpTB #7 32-33*
Ask, and Ye Shall Receive	*MS-098a	05/00/00		
A Solemn Warning	MS-100	05/06/28	San Jose, Ca.	*SpTB #7 30-32*
"During the past night we were in..."	MS-101	05/11/07	St. Helena, Ca.	*BCL 3*
Co-Operation Between Schools and Sanitariums	MS-102	05/11/14		*SpTB #11 11-16*
A Message to our Physicians	MS-104	05/06/02		*SpTB #7 24-30*
A Plea for Loyalty	MS-106	05/11/20	St. Helena, Ca.	UL 338;3MR 226-227;7MR 190; Nebraska Reporter 11/30/1905
A Warning and an Appeal	*MS-108	05/11/20	St. Helena, Ca.	*SpTB #7 8-18*
Sermon/Education in the Home	MS-110	04/08/07	Takoma Park, Md. (1905)	
Standing the Way of God's Messages	MS-111	05/12/04	St. Helena, Ca.	*SpTB #7 57-60*
Test. re the Youth Going to Battle Creek	MS-112	05/00/00		*SpTB #6*
Talk/Unwise Investments	MS-114	05/08/15	Los Angeles, Ca.	*SpTB #17 8-13*
Diary/"Last evening I was deeply..."	*MS-115	05/08/00	Los Angeles, Ca.	10MR 333
An Entire Consecration	MS-116	05/12/19	St. Helena, Ca.	UL 367
The Result of a Failure to Heed God's	*MS-120	04/01/01	St. Helena, Ca. (1905)	*SpTB #7 51-57*
A Solemn Appeal	*MS-122	03/08/00	St. Helena, Ca. (1905)	SpTB #7 19-23
Hold Fast That Which is Good	MS-124	05/00/00		*RH 08/31/1905*
A Warning Against Present Dangers	*MS-126	03/11/27	St. Helena, Ca. (1905)	SpTB #7 3-7
Take Heed to Thyself and to the Doctrine	*MS-127	05/00/00		
Our Possibilities	*MS-128	05/12/19c		Ev 468
Steadfast Unto the End	*MS-129	05/12/24c		*20MR 150-151*
Extracts on Medical Missionary Work	MS-130	05/00/00		Compiled from published and unpublished sources
Our Substitute and Surety	MS-134	05/03/08		2MCP 464-465;ST 08/09/1905
A Prayer for Help	*MS-136	05/03/03		
"We had a very pleasant journey..."	MS-140	05/01/30	St. Helena, Ca.	1MR 140-142
Talk/Words of Thanksgiving	MS-142	05/11/26		6Bio 54-55
How to Deal With the Erring	MS-143	04/10/26	St. Helena, Ca. (1905)	
"The good work that has been begun..."	MS-144	05/08/03	St. Helena, Ca.	LLM 338
Diary/"I awake at three o'clock..."	*MS-145	05/10/31	St. Helena, Ca.	*MR760 15-18*
"This morning I arise at four o'clock..."	*MS-146	05/07/25	St. Helena, Ca.	8MR 130
Diary/"This morning I rise at four..."	*MS-146a	05/07/25	St. Helena, Ca.	Cf. MS 146, 1905
Sermon/"After the resurrection..."	MS-148	05/02/21	Mountain View, Ca.	CL 23,29
Diary/"This morning I can not sleep..."	*MS-149	05/09/27	St. Helena, Ca.	12MR 84
Talk/The Restaurant Work	MS-150	05/09/23	St. Helena, Ca.	*8MR 171-181*
Should Our Youth Go to Battle Creek?	*MS-151	05/10/28	St. Helena, Ca.	*15MR 203-206*
Diary/"I thank the Lord for a good..."	*MS-153	05/11/02	St. Helena, Ca.	Mar 270
Our Work	*MS-162	05/12/25c		Ev 18-19;10MR 228-230
Diary/"If any man serve me..."	*MS-164	05/12/28c		
Aggressive Work to be Done	*MS-166	04/12/03	Filed in 1905	TDG 373
Warnings Re Binding Our Medical Instit. Together	MS-168	05/00/00		
Talk/Marriage and the Christian Home	MS-170	05/05/01	St. Helena, Ca.	*2SAT 270-273*
Methods of Labor	*MS-171	05/00/00		
Test. re Estab. the Publishing Work in Mt. View	*MS-172	05/01/26	Oakland, Ca.	

EGW Manuscripts File—Page 48

Diary [Jan. 1-25]	*MS-173	05/01/00		TDG 15;5Bio 381
Diary [Feb. 8-Mar. 6]	*MS-174	05/02/00		
Diary [Apr. 10- Jul. 15]	*MS-175	05/04/00		8MR 427
Diary [Aug. 1-25]	*MS-176	05/08/00		
Diary [Sep. 1- Oct. 31]	*MS-177	05/09/00		6Bio 62
Diary [Nov. 2- Dec. 20]	*MS-178	05/11/00		
Problems of the Work in Berkeley	*MS-179	05/07/01	San Jose, Ca.	
Christ's Object Lessons	MS-180	05/00/00		
"Never was there a time when..."	MS-181	05/00/00		*1NL 123-124*
The Christian Life	MS-182	05/00/00		5MR 343-344
The Nashville Sanitarium	*MS-183	05/00/00		
A Message to our Leading Physicians	MS-184	05/00/00		
Interview re Canon City Sanitarium	MS-185	05/09/24	St. Helena, Ca.	
Remarks/At Los Angeles	MS-186	05/06/20	Los Angeles, Ca.	
Sermon/"I have been in..."	MS-187	05/01/20	Mountain View, Ca.	
Sermon/Acts 1:1-4	MS-188	05/01/21	Mountain View, Ca.	
Sermon/Mark 1:1-4	MS-189	05/01/22	Mountain View, Ca.	
Talk/Remarks at Pacific Press Stockholders Meeting	MS-190	05/01/23		
Sermon/Rev. 7	MS-191	05/08/12	Los Angeles, Ca.	
Sermon/Isaiah 58:1-3	MS-192	05/08/13	Los Angeles, Ca.	
Sermon//Rev. 1:1-3	MS-193	05/09/18	National City, Ca.	

1906

Take Heed That Ye Be Not Deceived	MS-001	05/12/24	St. Helena, Ca. (1906)	7BC 957
Search the Scriptures	MS-003	06/01/06c		*RH 03/22/1906*
Be Guarded	*MS-005	06/01/11	St. Helena, Ca.	
Unity in Christ	*MS-009	05/04/11	St. Helena, Ca. (1906)	SpTB #7 42-46
On the Health Food and Restaurant Work	MS-010	06/00/00		CD 277;3MR 342;8MR 402-403;TSDF 107
Growing in Grace	MS-011	05/11/27	St. Helena, Ca. (1906)	*2SAT 274-278*
Israel's Apostasy at Sinai	*MS-013	05/12/11	St. Helena, Ca. (1906)	1BC 1113-1114;6MR 6-7
It is Time for Thee, Lord, to Work	*MS-015	04/01/18	St. Helena, Ca. (1906)	3BC 1153
The United States an Asylum for Religious Liberty	*MS-017	04/01/00	Filed in 1906	Mar 193;4BC 1171;7BC 975;9MR 1-4
Ahab--A Wicked King	MS-019	06/02/07c		2BC 1033
Preach the Word	MS-020	06/02/07c		*20MR 64-69*
Come Out and be Separate	*MS-021	05/11/00	St. Helena, Ca. (1906)	SpTB #7 60-64;BTS 03/1906
A God of Knowledge	MS-023	06/02/08c		*RH 03/08/1906*
It is Required in Stewards That a Man...	MS-025	06/02/14c		
Sermon/Instr. to Sanitarium & Restaurant Workers	MS-027	05/09/09	Los Angeles, Ca. (1906)	*1SAT 349-359*
That They All May Be One	MS-029	06/03/08	St. Helena, Ca.	5BC 1145;7ABC 681-682,684;8MR 292
Be Vigilant	MS-031	06/04/02	St. Helena, Ca.	*RH 04/19/1906*
The Chicago Work/"During the general..."	MS-033	06/03/20	St. Helena, Ca.	*PC 49-52*
A Message to A.T. Jones and Others in B.C.	*MS-034	06/03/23	St. Helena, Ca.	
The Judgments of God	MS-035	06/04/27c		*21MR 64-69*
A Solemn Warning and Appeal	*MS-036	06/03/24	St. Helena, Ca.	3SM 427;UL 976Bio 78
To Ministers and Physicians	MS-037	06/05/01	Loma Linda, Ca.	*PC 214*
The Law of God	MS-039	06/05/01c		*20MR 14-15*
Universal Guilt During the Time of the End	MS-041	06/00/00		RH 10/11/1906
Gratitude to God for His Goodness and Mercy	MS-043	05/09/11	San Diego, Ca. (1906)	
A Visit to Mountain View, Cal.	MS-045	06/05/06	Mountain View, Ca.	5MR 110
The San Francisco Earthquake	MS-047	06/00/00		*RH 05/24/1906*
Sermon/Lessons from the First Chapter of 2 Peter	MS-049	06/04/14	Loma Linda, Ca.	RH 06/14/1906
Conversion	MS-051	06/00/00		4MR 92
The Reward of Fidelity	MS-053	06/00/00		LDE 219
Talk/The Work at Mountain View	MS-057	06/05/03	Mountain View, Ca.	PM 165-166;5MR 193
Visit to Paradise Valley	MS-059	06/04/27	Loma Linda, Ca.	LHU 181;3MR 349
Hold Fast the Beginning of your Confidence	MS-061	06/06/03	St. Helena, Ca.	*PC 66-68*

God's Judgments on the Cities	MS-061a	06/06/03		*2SAT 279-284*
A Messenger	MS-063	06/05/26	St. Helena, Ca.	*RH 07/26/1906*
God's Messenger	MS-063a	06/05/26		variant of MS 63, 1906
Teachers as Examples of Christian Integrity	MS-065	06/07/04c		CS 271-272;1BC 1088,1092
The Work in Oakland	MS-067	06/08/06	St. Helena, Ca.	1MR 258;8MR 353;9MR 38-39
The Medical work in Boulder	*MS-069	06/08/30	St. Helena, Ca.	
Words of Counsel	MS-071	06/09/11	Mountain View, Ca.	PM 120-121
The Work in Mountain View	MS-073	06/09/10	Mountain View, Ca.	*5MR 70-77*
A Caution Against Heavy Investment in Food	MS-075	06/09/19	St. Helena, Ca.	*15MR 318-325*
Christ, the Bread of Life	MS-077	06/09/28c		1NL 41-42
Leave Your Nets and Follow Me	MS-079	06/10/01	St. Helena, Ca.	TDG 283;UL 288;17MR 300;
The Object of Health Food Work	MS-081	06/09/27	St. Helena, Ca.	SD 70;4BC 1160;HFM 88-91
Interview/Re Washington Sanitarium	MS-083	06/06/12	St. Helena, Ca.	
Perfect Through Sufferings	MS-085	06/08/22		*SpTB #9 8-14*
And What Shall This Man Do?	MS-087	06/00/00		7MR 153
Humility, An Essential Qualification	MS-089	06/10/22	St. Helena, Ca	7MR 152.
Praise Ye The Lord	MS-091	06/08/00	Berkeley, Ca.	
Sermon/Lessons from the Fifteenth of Romans	MS-095	06/10/20	Oakland, Ca.	*1SAT 360-383*
Sermon/A New Commandment	MS-097	05/07/02	San Jose, Ca. (1906)	CTr 214
Our Need of the Holy Spirit	*MS-099	06/12/01	St. Helena, Ca.	*RH 01/03/1907*
The Lord Loveth a Cheerful Giver	*MS-101	06/12/03	St. Helena, Ca.	OHC 198,200;UL 351;6BC 1104
Gifts and Offerings	MS-103	06/12/06	St. Helena, Ca.	TDG 349;2SM 187;WM 171
The Work in Oakland and San Francisco	MS-105	06/12/26c		Ev 205,284,315;MRmnt 113;PC 140
Sermon/Behold, What Manner of Love	MS-107	06/07/25	Oakland, Ca.	*RH 09/27/1906*
Sermon/Love Toward God and Man	MS-109	06/07/21	Oakland, Ca.	*RH 09/13/1906 and 09/20/1906*
A Warning Against Formalism	MS-111	06/10/22	St. Helena, Ca.	UL 309;10MR 391
Emphasize Bible Subjects	*MS-112	06/10/25	St. Helena, Ca.	
The Use of the Testimonies	MS-113	06/07/25c		
"I am bidden to warn our people..."	MS-115	06/09/19	St. Helena, Ca.	
"When the light that God gives..."	MS-117	06/10/30	St. Helena, Ca.	
Talk/"I have a chapter before me..."	MS-119	06/05/05		6MR 283-284
The Long-Sufferance of God	MS-120	06/00/00		
Working for Souls	*MS-121	06/00/00		
Justice in Deal in the Southern Publ. Assn.	*MS-122	06/00/00		
Diary [Jan. 1-Apr. 15]	*MS-123	06/01/00		6Bio 29
Diary [May 17-Jun. 19]	*MS-124	06/05/00		6Bio 104
Diary [Jul. 5-25]	*MS-125	06/07/00		6Bio 113
Diary [Aug. 11-27]	*MS-126	06/08/00		11MR 361-362
Diary [Sep. 1-26]	*MS-127	06/09/00		
Diary [Oct. 1-Dec.15]	*MS-128	06/10/00		
Test. re Work in San Francisco Area	*MS-129	06/00/00		
Counsel to Students	*MS-130	06/00/00	Los Angeles, Ca.	
Interview/William Foy--A Statement by EGW	MS-131	06/08/13		17MR 95-97
Interview/Narrative of Early Experiences	MS-131a	06/00/00		5MR 192
Remarks/At California Conf. Committee	MS-132	06/11/13	St. Helena, Ca.	
Diary/"The past night..."	*MS-133	06/04/06	St. Helena, Ca.	
Diary/"I wish this morning..."	MS-134	06/06/26	St. Helena, Ca.	
"In the night season..."	MS-135	06/00/00		
Remarks/Abstract of a conversation	MS-136	06/06/25		
Relieving the Debt of Our Schools	MS-137	06/00/00		
Sermon/2 Peter 1	MS-138	06/03/24	St. Helena, Ca.	
Sermon/Matthew 4:13-25	MS-139	06/07/24	Oakland, Ca.	
Sermon/Col. 1:1-5	MS-140	06/07/28	Oakland, Ca.	
Sermon/"I want to give you some reasons..."	MS-141	06/08/11	St. Helena, Ca.	
Sermon/"We have met together..."	MS-142	06/08/18	Oakland, Ca.	
Sermon/1 Cor. 2:1	MS-143	06/09/01	Oakland, Ca.	incomplete
Sermon/Rev. 7:1-4	MS-144	06/09/22	Oakland, Ca.	

EGW Manuscripts File—Page 50

Sermon/Lessons from the Fifteenth of John	MS-145	06/11/03	San Francisco, Ca.	
Sermon/"Remember the Sabbath Day"	MS-146	06/11/10	San Francisco, Ca.	
Sermon/"Behold, What Manner of Love"	MS-147	06/12/15	Oakland, Ca.	
Sermon/"The Word testifies..."	MS-148	06/07/30	Oakland, Ca.	fragment;not on file
Interview/The Work in Oakland and Berkeley	MS-149	06/12/16	Oakland, Ca.	

1907

A Practical Faith	MS-025	07/01/18c		6MR 284
Extracts re the New England Sanitarium	MS-027	07/01/22c		Compiled from earlier published and unpublished sources
Individual Responsibility & Christian Unity	MS-029	07/01/16	St. Helena, Ca.	TM 485-505
Awake! Awake! Awake!	MS-031	07/01/24c		*SpTB #9 3-8*
Faithful Stewardship	MS-033	07/01/24		9T 245-251
Counsel to Conference Presidents	MS-035	06/09/27	Filed in 1907	
Erroneous Teaching Regarding Holy Flesh	MS-039	07/00/00		
Encourage the Workers	MS-041	07/03/04	St. Helena, Ca.	*SpTB #11 3-4*
Exhortation to Faithfulness	MS-043	07/03/12c		*7MR 353-361*
The Misappropriation of Gifts	*MS-045	07/03/20c		From MS 67, 1902 and Ms 68, 1902
A Broader Work	MS-047	07/04/01c		*SpM 405-408*
The Work in New Orleans	MS-049	07/04/08c		Ev 399-400;SD 42,47;17MR 31
An Expression of Gratitude	MS-051	06/09/10	Berkeley, Ca.	Filed in 1907
The Work of Christian Physicians	MS-053	07/06/03	St. Helena, Ca.	*CH 361-366*
The Work in Washington, D.C.	MS-055	07/05/30	St. Helena, Ca.	*PH147*
Make a Covenant by Sacrifice	MS-057	07/05/20c		SD 15,265;7BC 921-922
A Missionary Education	MS-059	07/06/18c		*SpTB #11 27-32*
Sermon/Address to Young People	MS-061	07/06/27	St. Helena, Ca.	*2SAT 285-288*
Individual Responsibility	MS-063	07/06/18	St. Helena, Ca.	*LLM 211-212*
Sowing Beside All Waters	MS-065	07/06/18	St. Helena, Ca.	*AUCR 12/16/1907*
God's People to be Living Epistles	MS-067	07/07/06c		CG 148-149;6BC 1117-1118; 1MR 117-118
The High Standard for Sanitarium Workers	MS-069	07/07/12	St. Helena, Ca.	
Sermon/Clear the King's Highway	MS-071	07/02/16	Berkeley, Ca.	1MR 119-120
Jehovah Is Our King	MS-073	07/08/15c		*TM 477-484*
God's Wisdom to be Sought	MS-075	07/07/29	St. Helena, Ca.	*LLM 220-223*
Extracts from Letters to Mrs. S.M.I. Henry	MS-077	07/08/15c		*LLM 232-234*
Extracts/The Temperance Work	MS-079	07/08/15c		*LLM 236-239*
Extracts/To Seek and to Save That Which was Lost	MS-081	07/08/15c		From 5T and Lt 17, 1900
The Colorado Conference and the Boulder San.	MS-083	07/08/14	St. Helena, Ca.	
The Work in Boulder, Colorado	MS-085	07/08/14	St. Helena, Ca.	
Our Duty Toward the Jews	MS-087	07/08/16c		*6MR 323-330*
Extracts/Workers in the Cause	MS-089	07/00/00		*From 5T 721-729*
The Work to be Done for the W.C.T.U.	MS-091	07/08/15		*LLM 235-236*
Report of Berkeley Church Meeting	MS-093	07/02/17	Oakland, Ca.	
Arise, Shine!	MS-095	07/08/29		*SpTB #10 5-12*
In Humility and Faith	*MS-097	07/09/19c		*PC 281-285*
The Essential in Education	MS-099	07/09/25c		
A Message to Teachers	MS-101	07/09/25c		*FE 516-519*
The Sale of "Object Lessons"	MS-103	07/10/03c		2MR 78
Interview/The Resp. of a Conf. President	MS-105	07/10/05	St. Helena, Ca.	*LLM 288-295*
Interview/The Glendale Sanitarium	*MS-107	07/10/06	St. Helena, Ca.	
Interview/The Management of Conference Affairs	MS-109	07/10/06	St. Helena, Ca.	*LLM 295-300*
I Am But A Little Child	MS-111	07/10/15c		*9T 281-284*
Judge Not	*MS-113	07/10/21c		UL 308
Sermon/Why We Have Sanitariums	MS-115	07/10/20	St. Helena, Ca.	*2SAT 289-291*
The Work Hindered by Lack of Faith	*MS-117	07/10/11	St. Helena, Ca.	PC 293-295;MR311 33-34;9MR 176;

Words of Encouragement to Workers	MS-119	07/10/09	St Helena, Ca.	*AU Gleaner 12/25/1907*
The Work of Elder W.C. White	MS-121	07/00/00		*PH116 17-24*
Our Duty to the W.C.T.U. Workers	MS-123	07/10/23		*From Lt 274, 1907*
Sermon/Lessons From the Visions of Ezekiel	*MS-125	06/07/04	Filed in 1907	*1SAT 384-390*
Lessons for Sanitarium Workers	MS-126	07/11/11c		*KC 24-31*
The Work in Southern California	MS-127	07/11/03	Loma Linda, Ca.	*LLM 310-314*
Diary/"On Sabbath day, Elder Haskell..."	*MS-129	06/10/00	Filed in 1907	
Sermon/Preaching The Word of the Living God	MS-131	07/12/21	Loma Linda, Ca.	
One Is You Master, Even Christ	MS-133	07/01/16	St. Helena, Ca.	
Exalting Christ	MS-137	07/06/17	St. Helena, Ca.	*Lake Union Herald 11/03/1909*
A Call to Consecration	MS-139	07/06/18	St. Helena, Ca.	Lake Union Herald 11/17/1909
Words to Church-Members	MS-141	07/06/19	St. Helena, Ca.	*AUCR 10/07/1907*
An Address to the Young	MS-143	07/06/27		*Lake Union Herald 10/20/1907*
A Call to Service	MS-145	07/06/20	St. Helena, Ca.	*AUCR 10/14/1907*
An Experience in Divine Healing	MS-147	07/11/12		
"I have a message to speak to the..."	MS-149	07/05/03	National City, Ca.	*RH 07/18/1907*
Talk/The High Order of the Loma Linda School	MS-151	07/10/30	Loma Linda, Ca.	*LLM 303-304*
Sermon/Behold, What Manner of Love	MS-153	07/10/29	Loma Linda, Ca.	2MCP 789
Diary [Jan. 1-Mar. 30]	*MS-154	07/01/00		6Bio 122-123
Diary [Apr. 5-Jun. 30]	*MS-155	07/04/00		
Diary [Jul. 22-Oct. 29]	*MS-156	07/07/00		*16MR 126-135*
Fairness in Wage-Setting	*MS-157	07/08/14	St. Helena, Ca.	
Unity in Council Meetings	*MS-158	07/12/00	Loma Linda, Ca.	
Does Sister White Work Miracles?	*MS-159	07/00/00		18MR 372-373
Sermon/God's Goodness	*MS-160	07/06/22		
Our Health Institution	*MS-161	07/00/00		
To Church Members	*MS-162	07/00/00		
The Lord Loveth a Cheerful Giver	MS-163	07/03/08	St. Helena, Ca.	SpTB #8 3-6
Sermon/God's Plan of Addition	MS-164	07/04/21	San Fernando, Ca.	
God's Work in the World	*MS-165	07/00/00		
Testimony Regarding Elder and Mrs. Rice	*MS-166	07/00/00		
"It may strike us..."	MS-167	07/00/00		
Stand Firm for the Right	MS-168	07/00/00		
Words of Counsel to Camp-Meeting Laborers	MS-169	07/06/15		
A Message to Parents	MS-170	07/00/00		
Paradise Valley Sanitarium--Early History	MS-171	07/00/00		
All God's Children Indebted to Him	MS-172	07/00/00		
Counsel Against Large Wages	MS-173	07/00/00		
Dangerous Familiarity Between the Sexes	MS-174	07/00/00		
The Sabbath a Day of Praise	MS-175	07/11/11	Loma Linda, Ca.	
Shall We Take Up Collections on the Sabbath?	MS-176	07/00/00		
Sermon/Hebrews 1:1,2	MS-177	07/04/27	Loma Linda, Ca.	
Talk/"We are very glad to have..."	MS-178	07/05/03	National City, Ca.	
Sermon/Hebrews 1:1	MS-179	07/05/04	San Diego, Ca.	
Sermon/1 Peter 2:1-5	MS-180	07/05/05	San Diego, Ca.	
Remarks/To Helpers at Paradise Valley San.	MS-181	07/05/06	National City, Ca.	
Sermon/John 15:1,2	MS-182	07/05/11	San Pasqual, Ca.	
Sermon/2 Peter 1:1	MS-183	07/05/12	Escondido, Ca.	
Talk/Address to Students	MS-184	07/05/14	Loma Linda, Ca.	
Talk/Talk to Students	MS-185	07/05/15	Loma Linda, Ca.	
Sermon/Isaiah 58:1-3	MS-186	07/05/18	Loma Linda, Ca.	
Sermon/Exodus 19:1-6	MS-187	07/05/19	Los Angeles, Ca.	
Sermon/Rev. 22:1-5	MS-188	07/05/22	Glendale, Ca.	
Sermon/2 Peter 1:1-11	MS-189	07/05/28	Merced, Ca.	
Sermon/Daniel 1:1-8	MS-190	07/06/26	St. Helena, Ca.	Fragment;not on file
Sermon/"I have been awake since..."	MS-191	07/10/31	Loma Linca, Ca.	
Sermon/2 Peter 1:1,2	MS-192	07/11/02	Loma Linda, Ca.	

Prayer of E. G. White	MS-193	07/11/08	Loma Linda, Ca.	
Sermon/"We are glad to hear..."	MS-194	07/11/09	Loma Linda, Ca.	
Interview/"I was very tired..."	MS-195	07/03/03		Fragments;filed in DF 151
Interview/On Our Work in the Southern States	MS-196	07/04/29	Loma Linda, Ca.	
Interview/Meeting at Paradise Valley Sanitarium	MS-197	07/05/02	National City, Ca.	

1908

Work Among the Jews	MS-001	08/02/03c		*14MR 136-138*
The Work in Southern California	*MS-003	08/02/21c		PC 259-260
The Medical Missionary Work	MS-005	08/02/23		*20MR 264-267*
Enter the Cities	MS-007	08/02/24c		Ev 32-33,46-47,64-65;MM 263
A Message to the Churches	MS-009	08/02/10	St. Helena, Ca.	*17MR 162-165*
The Regions Beyond	MS-011	08/02/15	St. Helena, Ca.	Ev 19-20,60,428;MM 322-323;
				6BC 1104;1MR 192-193
An Appeal for the Madison School	MS-013	08/03/25		PM 31;7MR 195
The Need of Watchfulness	*MS-015	08/03/30		HP 256;ML 32-33;7MR 45;CTr 219
Arbitrary Control	*MS-016	08/03/00	St. Helena, Ca.	
The Work in California	MS-017	08/02/15	St. Helena, Ca.	Ev 307;ML 42;6BC 1059;MR311 20
A Broader View	MS-019	08/04/17c		*9T 76-80*
To Ministers, Physicians, and Teachers	MS-021	08/00/00		Ev 397-398;SpTB #10 42-48
Circulate the Publications	MS-023	08/05/04c		*9T 65-75*
A Plea for Aggressive Work	MS-025	08/05/05c		Ev 70;5MR 111;6MR 58
Truth to be Maintained	MS-027	08/05/05c		2MR 96
The Aim of Our School Work	MS-029	08/05/15c		*Educational Messenger 08/07/1908*
Deeper Consecration	MS-031	08/05/17c		*CT 248-252*
Home Schools	MS-033	08/05/17c		*7MR 19-22*
Sermon/Conflict and Victory	MS-035	08/03/07	Oakland, Ca.	*RH 07/09/1908*
Sermon/Abiding in Christ	MS-037	08/03/10	Oakland, Ca.	*2SAT 292-298*
Sermon/Let Us Glorify God	MS-039	08/03/11	Oakland, Ca.	VSS 121-122,132-133,148;8MR 343
Sermon/Lessons from the First Chap. of 2 Peter	MS-041	08/03/12	Oakland, Ca.	2MCP 387,389-390,434-435,
				493-494,673;Te 139,162
Sermon/Lessons from the Fifty-Eighth of Isa.	MS-043	08/03/14	Oakland, Ca.	OHC 15;CD 309;4BC 1151-1154;
				5MR 82-83;11MR 188
Sermon/That Ye Should Go and Bring Forth	MS-045	08/05/05	Lodi, Ca.	
Sermon/As Little Children	MS-047	08/05/07	Lodi, Ca.	*2SAT 299-304*
Sermon/Lessons from the Exper. of Pentecost	MS-049	08/05/09	Lodi, Ca.	*1SAT 391-396*
An Appeal to Ministers	MS-051	08/05/21c		*RH 07/23/1908*
Our Publications	MS-053	08/05/24c		*9T 61-64*
The Temperance "Watchman"	MS-055	08/05/24c		*RH 06/18/1908*
An Appeal for the Madison School	MS-057	08/01/06		*PH119*
The New England Sanitarium	MS-059	08/00/00		*SpTB #13 3-16*
Collection of Mss. re the Huntsville School	MS-061	08/00/00		*SpTB #12x 3-16*
Instruction to Sanitarium Workers	MS-063	08/06/03c		*LLM 379-382*
Labor to be Given to Lakeport	MS-065	08/06/09c		CG 76;Ev 46,50-52;PC 8-9
Modern Reflections	MS-067	08/06/20c		*PUR 07/02/1908*
Teacher, Know Thyself	MS-069	08/06/19c		FE 525-527
To Workers in Washington	MS-071	08/06/19c		3SM 80-81;CD 381
Counsels Repeated	MS-073	08/06/19c		*PC 2-3*
Words to Students	MS-075	08/06/19c		
Lamps Without Oil	MS-077	08/06/19c		*RH 09/17/1908*
Build On a Sure Foundation	MS-079	08/06/19	St. Helena, Ca.	*RH 09/24/1908*
Words of Exhoration and Warning	MS-081	08/06/26c		*Educational Messenger 09/04/1908*
				and 09/11/1908
"I wish to make some statements regarding"	MS-083	08/06/25	St. Helena, Ca.	PC 34-35
"In company with Dr. Rand..."	MS-085	08/06/30	St. Helena, Ca.	*10MR 259-264*
Our Camp Meetings an Object-Lesson	MS-087	08/07/17	St. Helena, Ca.	CD 329-330

EGW Manuscripts File—Page 53

Co-Operation Between Our Schools & Sanitariums	MS-089	08/07/24c	Extracts from earlier published and
			unpublished sources
A Revival Needed	MS-091	08/08/20 Los Angeles, Ca.	*Lake Union Herald 11/04/1908*
Talk/Lessons from the Fifteenth of John	MS-092	08/08/22 Glendale, Ca.	7BC 982;8MR 290;9MR 381
Sermon/The Sabbath of the Fourth Commandment	MS-093	08/08/23 Los Angeles, Ca.	Te 224
Sermon/Lessons From Christ's Labors	MS-095	08/09/05	*RH 01/21/1909*
Extracts/Dress	MS-097	08/00/00	From Lt 19, 1897 and Lt 45, 1899
The Buena Vista Property	MS-099	08/09/23c	2SM 359;Te 252;5MR 89;17MR 31
Sermon/Called to Glory and Virtue	MS-099a	08/08/29 Loma Linda, Ca.	*RH 01/14/1909*
Sermon/Parting Words of Instruction	MS-101	08/08/26 National City, Ca.	*RH 01/07/1909*
Proclaiming the Truth Where There is Race	*MS-103	08/10/19c	*9T 204-212*
Words of Counsel to our Colored People	MS-105	08/10/19c	*PCO 128-130*
The Color Line	MS-107	08/10/21c	9T 213-222;OHC 287;4MR 33
A Call for Colored Laborers	MS-109	08/10/21c	*9T 199-203*
The Paradise Valley Sanitarium	MS-111	08/10/21c	SpTB #14 15-16
Sermon/Lessons From the Sixtieth of Isaiah	MS-113	08/10/28 St. Helena, Ca.	*3MR 284-291*
Interview/Regarding Ralph Mackin	MS-115	08/11/12 St. Helena, Ca.	*RH 08/10/1972 and 08/17/1972 and*
			08/24/1972 (see 3SM 363-378)
A Message To Our Churches in California	MS-117	08/12/17 St. Helena, Ca.	*1SM 221-225*
Regarding the Work of Publication	MS-119	08/05/06 St. Helena, Ca.	
Instruction re the Work of the Head Physician	MS-121	08/12/22c	*SpTB #19 14-17*
Mss. on the Huntsville School	MS-123	08/00/00	*SpTB #12 4-16*
Diary Fragments [Jan.-Dec.]	*MS-126	08/00/00	6Bio 167
Concerning E.G.W.'s Donation of Books	*MS-127	08/00/00	
Individual Responsibility	*MS-128	08/00/00	
Warning Against Lending Aid to the Enemy	*MS-129	08/00/00	
Words to Believers	*MS-130	08/00/00	
"I awoke this morning at twelve o'clock..."	*MS-131	08/00/00	
Test. re Elder Reaser	*MS-132	08/00/00	
Proclaiming the Sabbath in the Last Days	*MS-133	08/00/00	
Arbitrary Control	*MS-134	08/00/00	
The Work in the California Conference	MS-135	08/03/03	
The Needs of Paradise Valley Sanitarium	*MS-136	08/00/00	
Honoring God By Obedience	MS-137	08/00/00	
On Soliciting Means From Unbelievers	MS-138	08/00/00	
Sermon/"There are some things..."	MS-139	08/01/22 St. Helena, Ca.	Fragments only;not on file
Sermon/"I wanted to read a little to you..."	MS-140	08/11/14 Healdsburg, Ca.	
Sermon/John 15:1	MS-141	08/11/15 Healdsburg, Ca.	

1909

What is Higher Education?	MS-001	09/01/19 St. Helena, Ca.	10MR 295
Higher Education Revealed in Co-Operating	MS-003	09/01/28	CT 397-400
Sermon/Two Kinds of Service	MS-005	09/02/06 Oakland, Ca.	*RH 03/18/1909 and 03/25/1909*
Sermon/The Need of the Holy Spirit	MS-007	09/02/08 Oakland, Ca.	*RH 04/01/1909 and 04/08/1909*
Talk/The Buena Vista School Property	MS-009	09/02/06 Oakland, Ca.	*1MR 333-338*
That They All Might Be One	MS-011	09/00/00	*RH 09/23/1909 and 09/30/1909*
To the Workers and Students at Hill Crest	MS-013	09/04/26	UL 130
Talk/Words of Encouragement to Self-Supporting	MS-015	09/04/26 Madison, Tn.	WM 72-73,77-78;Ev 45;4MR 34-35
Sermon/A Holy Calling	MS-017	09/04/25 Nashville, Tn.	4MR 33;6Bio 191-192
Sermon/Abiding in Christ	MS-019	09/05/15 Takoma Park, Md.	*GCB 05/17/1909 37-39*
Sermon/A Call to Service	MS-021	09/05/17 Takoma Park, Md.	*GCB 05/18/1909 56-58*
Sermon/The Work Before Us	MS-023	09/05/19 Takoma Park, Md.	*GCB 05/21/1909 105*
The Hillcrest School	MS-025	09/05/17 Washington, D.C.	*PH037 33-36*
Talk/Words of Encouragement	MS-027	09/04/29 Huntsville, Al.	*2MR 82-86*
Sermon/A Risen Saviour	MS-029	09/05/22 Takoma Park, Md.	*GCB 05/24/1909 137-138*
Sermon/Individual Co-Operation	MS-031	09/04/17 College View, Ne.	AH 206;7BC 988;8MR 62;11MR 190

EGW Manuscripts File—Page 54

Sermon/A Lesson in Health Reform	MS-033	09/05/26	Takoma Park, Md.	*GCB 05/30/1909 213-215*
Talk/Let Us Publish Salvation	MS-035	09/05/27	Takoma Park, Md.	*GCB 05/31/1909 225-226*
Talk/Faithfulness in Health Reform	MS-037	09/05/30	Takoma Park, Md.	*9T 153-166*
Talk/God's Plan	MS-037a	09/05/30	Takoma Park, Md.	*From GCB 06/01/1909 236-237*
Work the Cities	*MS-038	09/05/00	Takoma Park, Md.	
Talk/The Spirit of Independence	MS-038a	09/05/30	Takoma Park, Md.	*From 9T 257-261*
The Loma Linda College of Evangelists	MS-039	09/06/01	Takoma Park, Md.	*9T 173-178*
A Message to Responsible Men and Church Mem.	MS-041	09/06/03		3MR 222;10MR 359-360
Sermon/Get Ready!	MS-043	09/05/29	Takoma Park, Md.	*GCB 06/06/1909 344-346*
A Message to the Responsible Men in the S.P.A.	MS-045	09/06/03	Washington, D.C.	
Words Addressed to the Workers at Rock City San.	MS-047	09/04/30c		
Sermon/Partakers of the Divine Nature	MS-049	09/06/06	Takoma Park, Md.	HP 280;17MR 32;6Bio 197
The High Standard to be Maintained in Nash. Publ.	MS-051	09/07/23		
Talk/Proclaiming the Third Angel's Message	MS-053	09/06/11	Takoma Park, Md.	Ev 38-40,61-62;3MR 220-222; 10MR 360-361;PC 269;6Bio 208-209
Talk/Lessons from the Sermon on the Mount	MS-055	09/08/16	Madison, Wi.	*Wisconsin Reporter 09/08/1909 and 09/15/1909*
Talk/Words of Counsel to Madison San.	MS-057	09/08/16	Madison, Wi.	MM 173-174,201-202,212; RH 12/30/1909;2MR 42
Talk/Educational Advantages of the Angwin	MS-059	09/09/13	Fruitvale, Ca.	*PUR 09/23/1909*
Words of Instruction	MS-061	09/09/17c		*10MR 214-219*
Talk/Words of Counsel	MS-063	09/09/05	Boulder, Co.	
Talk/If Thou Wilt Walk in My Ways	MS-065	09/09/29	Angwin, Ca.	*PUR 10/07/1909*
A High Standard	MS-067	09/10/07c		CG 80-81;HP 216
The Helpers in our Sanitariums	MS-069	09/09/12	St. Helena, Ca.	*MM 172-173 and UL 269*
Interview/The Relation of Loma Linda to	MS-071	09/09/20	St. Helena, Ca.	*LLM 424-428*
Interview/The Relation of Loma Linda to	MS-072	09/09/20	St. Helena, Ca.	*PC 269-274 (variant of Ms 71, 1909)*
Sermon/Lessons from the First of Daniel	MS-073	09/08/27	Council Grove, Ks.	*2SAT 314-321*
Sermon/Labor for the Unconverted	MS-075	09/08/29	Boulder, Co.	10MR 111-112
Talk/Words of Counsel and Encouragement	MS-077	09/08/26	Council Grove, Ks.	Ev 629
Sermon/That It May Bring Forth More Fruit	MS-079	09/08/26	Council Grove, Ks.	UL 252
Sermon/An Extended Work	MS-081	09/08/23	Nevada, Ia.	
Sermon/Seek Ye the Kingdom of God	MS-083	09/08/29	Council Grove, Ks.	Ev 237-238;3SM 248-249
Sermon/Lessons of Self-Denial, Trust	MS-085	09/08/21	Nevado, Ia.	UL 247;VSS 220;SD 268;8MR 291
Words Addressed to the Workers at Boulder	MS-087	09/09/03	Boulder, Co.	SD 268,365;6MR 286
Talk/A Work of Preparation	MS-089	09/08/18	Madison, Wi.	
Sermon/"These words spake Jesus..."	MS-091	09/09/04	Boulder Co.	RH 01/13/1910
Talk/Address to Church Members at Salt Lake City	MS-093	09/09/07	Salt Lake City, Ut.	CG 244-245;AH 323;1MCP 170; 1MR 120-121;10MR 320-322
Sermon/A Message to the Churches	MS-095	09/09/05	Boulder, Co.	VSS 150;6MR 287
Sermon/I Am The True Vine	MS-097	09/10/16	San Jose, Ca.	*1SAT 397-405*
Extracts/The Work of the Pioneers	MS-099	09/00/00		Compiled from earlier published and
			unpublished sources	
A Message to our Ministers and Fellow-laborers	MS-101	09/12/01	St. Helena, Ca.	
Sermon/Partakers of the Divine Nature	MS-103	09/11/07	Lodi, Ca.	*2MR 286-291*
A Confusion of the Sacred and the Common	*MS-107	09/03/05	St. Helena, Ca.	1SM 38-39;7MR 290-291
Foundation Principles of Healthful Dressing	MS-109	09/00/00		
Aged Ministers to Have a Part in the Work	*MS-110	09/00/00		
Sermon/"And I, brethren, when..."	MS-111	09/11/06	Lodi, Ca.	
Sermon/"Therefore we ought to give..."	MS-112	09/11/08	Lodi, Ca.	
The Work in Portland, Maine and the East	*MS-113	09/07/03	Portland, Me.	10MR 16-19
Sermon/John 15	MS-114	09/06/12	Philadelphia, Pa.	
Sermon/"One week ago..."	MS-115	09/06/19	New York, NY	
Sermon/Matthew 13:1-12	MS-116	09/06/20	Newark, NJ	
Sermon/Exodus 20:1-6	MS-117	09/06/26	Nashua, NH	
Sermon/2 Peter 2:1-5	MS-118	09/06/27	Nashua, NH	
Sermon/John 15	MS-119	09/06/29	Nashua, NH	

EGW Manuscripts File—Page 55

Sermon/Deut. 4:1,2	MS-120	09/07/03	Portland, Me.	
Sermon/Acts 2.1-3	MS-121	09/07/05	Portland, Me.	
Sermon/Isaiah 56:1-10	MS-122	09/07/07	Portland, Me.	
Sermon/Luke 17:11	MS-123	09/07/17	Buffalo, NY	
Sermon/Isaiah 55:1,2-6	MS-124	09/07/18	Buffalo, NY	
Sermon/Genesis 2:1-3	MS-125	09/07/24	Three Rivers, Mi.	
Sermon/Isaiah 52:1-8	MS-126	09/07/25	Three Rivers, Mi.	
Sermon/Rev. 22:1	MS-127	09/07/27	Three Rivers, Mi.	
Prayer of E. G. White	MS-128	09/07/29	Battle Creek, Mi.	
Talk/To Workers and Inmates at the Rescue Home	MS-129	09/08/04	Hinsdale, Il.	
Sermon/John 14	MS-130	09/08/07	Elgin Il.	Northern Illinois Recorder, 08/17/1908
Talk/Isaiah 55	MS-131	09/08/08	Elgin, Il	incomplete
Talk/To Patients and Workers at Hinsdale San.	MS-132	09/08/10	Hinsdale, Il	
Talk/To Heads of Departments at Hinsdale San.	MS-133	09/08/13	Hinsdale, Il.	
Sermon/2 Peter 2:1	MS-134	09/09/15	Fruitvale, Ca.	
Sermon/John 17	MS-135	09/10/17	San Jose, Ca.	
Sermon/Deut. 5:1-3,4	MS-136	09/11/05	Lodi, Ca.	fragment only;not on file
Sermon/Isaiah 55:1-5	MS-137	09/11/13	Lodi, Ca.	fragment only;not on file
Sermon/Isaiah 42:1-3	MS-138	09/12/11	Mountain View, Ca.	incomplete
Sermon/Fruit-Bearing Branches	MS-139	09/12/12	Mountain View, Ca.	
Sermon/John 15:1	MS-140	09/12/18	Oakland, Ca.	
The Needs of the Cities	MS-141	09/06/00		

1910

An Appeal to our Brethren in the Atlantic U. Conf.	MS-001	10/01/24c		*AU Gleaner 06/08/1910*
Portland, Buffalo, and Rochester	MS-001a	10/00/00		variant of Ms 1, 1910
An Appeal to our Churches Throughout the US	MS-003	10/01/20	St. Helena, Ca.	*RH 05/18/1910*
Talk/Words of Counsel to Advanced Students	MS-005	10/02/05	Lodi, Ca.	*2MR 291-296*
A Statement re the Training of Physicians	MS-007	10/01/27		*LLM 486-487*
Talk/Words of Counsel to Workers	MS-009	10/01/27	Mountain View, Ca.	MM 304
Our Attitude Toward Doctrinal Controversy	MS-011	10/07/31	St. Helena, Ca.	*PH020 5-10*
A Call to the Watchmen	MS-013	10/08/08c		*PH020 1-5*
Go, Preach the Gospel	MS-015	10/00/00		*RH 11/17/1910*
Regarding Representations in our Papers	MS-017	10/00/00		6MR 287
Theatrical Methods of Work to be Discouraged	MS-019	10/00/00		*19MR 125-127*
A Call to Labor in the Great Cities	MS-021	10/06/22	St. Helena, Ca.	*MM 302-303 and 3SM 50 and PC 69-70*
Talk/A Promise of Life Eternal	MS-023	10/01/29	Mountain View, Ca.	NPU Gleaner 03/09/1910
Talk/An Address to the Workers Assembled	MS-025	10/01/28	Mountain View, Ca.	*2SAT 322-328*
The Lodi School	MS-026	10/08/24	Berkeley, Ca.	*2MR 296-298*
Let Your Light So Shine Before Men	MS-027	10/11/13c		*RH 12/15/1910 and 12/22/1910*
The Work Before Us	MS-029	10/11/14c		
The Home School	*MS-031	10/00/00c		*RH 01/12/1911*
Lessons from Esther	MS-039	10/12/14c		3BC 1139
The Principles of Christianity	*MS-041	10/12/27c		
Talk/A Call to Consecrated Effort	MS-043	10/01/29	Mountain View, Ca.	*NPU Gleaner 03/16/1910*
Talk/Mission Fields at Home	MS-045	10/01/28	Mountain View, Ca.	*NPU Gleaner 04/13/1910*
Talk/Come Into Line	MS-047	10/01/27	Mountain View, Ca.	*NPU Gleaner 03/23/1910*
Warning the Cities	MS-049	10/00/00		*From RH 04/17/1910*
The East and the West	MS-051	10/00/00		*NPU Gleaner 03/30/1910*
Wake up the Watchmen	MS-053	10/01/28	Mountain View, Ca.	Ev 29,71,114,482;6MR 195-196
True Conversion	*MS-055	10/00/00		*Ev 286-287*
True Conversion [variant]	MS-055a	10/00/00		*Ev 286-287*
Test. Concerning the School at Lodi, Ca.	*MS-057	10/00/00		
Temperance	*MS-059	10/00/00		
Diary Fragment	*MS-060	10/11/26	St. Helena, Ca.	*4MR 44-45*

EGW Manuscripts File—Page 56

Practical Sympathy for the Afflicted	*MS-061	10/09/27	St. Helena, Ca.	
A Call to Work the Cities	*MS-062	10/01/00	Mountain View, Ca.	
Fragments/Extension of the Work	*MS-063	10/00/00		
Sermon/"I want to say that the..."	*MS-064	10/02/02	Lodi, Ca.	
Interview/At Paradise Valley Sanitarium	MS-065	10/04/17	National City, Ca.	
Our Appointed Work	MS-066	10/10/19	St. Helena, Ca.	
Errors and Dangers of Prescott and Daniells	*MS-067	10/00/00		20MR 17-22
An Appeal for Greater Earnestness	MS-068	10/10/24	St. Helena, Ca.	
The Family As An Educational Agency	MS-069	10/00/00c		*PUR 08/18/1910*
Interview/Discussion with Mr. Tufts	Ms-070	10/00/00?		
Sermon/Daniel 1:1-21	MS-071	10/02/19	Angwin, Ca.	
Sermon/"I want to read a few verses..."	MS-072	10/03/08	Angwin, Ca.	
Sermon/Acts 1	MS-073	10/03/19	Oakland, Ca.	
Sermon/"I have words to speak..."	MS-074	10/03/20	Oakland, Ca.	
Sermon/1 Timothy 4:1	MS-075	10/03/21	Oakland, Ca.	
Talk/2 Peter 2:1-9	MS-076	10/03/23	Oakland, Ca.	
Sermon/John 15:1	MS-077	10/03/26	Los Angeles, Ca.	
Sermon/2 Peter 1:1-15	MS-078	10/04/02	Loma Linda, Ca.	
Talk/Luke 13:11	MS-079	10/04/05	Loma Linda, Ca.	*LLM 533-542*
Talk/Rev. 19:1-5	MS-080	10/04/07	Loma Linda, Ca.	incomplete
Talk/"As I look at this company..."	MS-081	10/04/09	San Fernando, Ca.	
Talk/Rev. 21:1-6	MS-082	10/04/10	San Fernando, Ca.	
Sermon/Deut. 4:1-7	MS-083	10/04/16	San Diego, Ca.	
Sermon/"I have chosen my subject..."	MS-084	10/04/23	Los Angeles, Ca.	
Sermon/Lessons from the First Chap. of Daniel	MS-085	10/08/20	Berkeley, Ca.	
Sermon/Lessons from the Fifteenth Chap. of John	MS-086	10/08/21	Berkeley, Ca.	
Interview/On the Work in the Cities	MS-087	10/06/19	St. Helena, Ca.	Filed in DF 151

1911

Talk/A Deeper Consecration	MS-001	11/04/16	National City, Ca.	*SpTB #15 6-11*
Talk/Men and Women Physicians	MS-002	11/04/04	Loma Linda, Ca.	*13MR 113-119*
Interview/Re S. J. Harris	MS-003	11/05/29	St. Helena, Ca.	SpTB #17 13-20
City Work	MS-007	11/06/13c		
Talk/Aggressives Moves at Loma Linda	MS-009	11/04/20	Loma Linda, Ca.	*LLM 563-568*
Talk/Conformity to Christ's Example	MS-011	11/06/10	Angwin, Ca.	HP 278
Re the Purchase of Land Adjoining Loma Linda	MS-013	11/08/29c		*LLM 579-580*
An Appeal in Behalf of our Medical College	MS-015	11/08/29	St. Helena, Ca.	*LLM 580-582*
Sermon/"If there be any consolation..."	MS-017	11/08/19	Long Beach, Ca.	UL 245
Fragments/"We should make decided..."	MS-019	11/10/09c		MM 320;8MR 402
Fragments/"Fathers and mothers..."	MS-021	11/10/09c		HP 58
Regarding the Testimonies	MS-023	11/10/10c		*PC 9-19*
Sermon/"Simon Peter, a servant..."	MS-025	11/08/16	Long Beach, Ca.	
Sermon/The Responsibility of Parents	MS-027	11/08/18	Long Beach, Ca.	*10MR 101-106*
Fragments on Old Testament History	MS-029	11/11/17c		CC 36;2SM 300;PM 142,148;2BC 1033; 3BC 1139;4BC 1137;7BC 947; 7MR 381;10MR 76;CTr 162
Diary Fragments/Praising God	*MS-031	11/11/19c		*18MR 331-346*
Sermon/"Simon Peter, a servant..."	MS-045	11/11/06	Loma Linda, Ca.	7MR 22-27
On the Attitude of Some of our Leaders...	MS-049	11/11/21c		
What is the Chaff to the Wheat?	MS-053	11/11/21c		OHC 277;ML 89;6MR 287-289
Fragments/"Our ministers and teachers..."	MS-055	11/11/19c		
Work of J.E. and W.C. White	*MS-056	11/00/00		*21MR 141-142*
Work of J.E. and W.C. White	*MS-056a	11/00/00		6Bio 355-356;From Ms 56, 1911
"I attended the camp meeting held..."	*MS-057	11/07/26	St. Helena, Ca.	
An Appeal to Fathers and Mothers	*MS-058	11/00/00		
Work to be Done at Riverside	*MS-059	11/00/00		

To Fathers and Mothers	*MS-060	11/00/00		
Individual Responsibility of Fathers and Mothers	*MS-061	11/10/15	St. Helena, Ca.	UL 302
Counsels on Discipline	*MS-062	11/07/04		
A Message to Parents and Ministers	*MS-063	11/00/00		
Parents to be Teachers	*MS-064	11/00/00		
Fragments/Messages to Parents	*MS-065	11/00/00		
Sermon/Parents and Preparation for Heaven	MS-066	11/04/15	San Diego, Ca.	
A Statement Regarding Dr. Coon's Pamphlet	MS-067	11/10/00		
Sermon/John 17:1-6	MS-068	11/04/08	Riverside, Ca.	
Sermon/1 Peter 4:1	MS-069	11/04/14	National City, Ca.	
Sermon/John 15:1,2	MS-070	11/04/22	Los Angeles, Ca.	
Sermon/Isaiah 55:1-3	MS-071	11/04/23	Glendale, Ca.	
Sermon/Luke 9:1	MS-072	11/04/24	San Fernando, Ca.	
Sermon/2 Peter 1:1-8	MS-073	11/07/08	Oakland, Ca.	
Sermon/Acts 2:1-47	MS-074	11/07/11	Oakland, Ca.	
Sermon/John 14:1-31	MS-075	11/07/15	Oakland, Ca.	
Interview/On Men and Women Physicians	MS-076	11/11/07	Loma Linda, Ca.	Filed in DF 151

1912

Jereboam	MS-001	12/01/09c		2BC 1032-1033;CTr 161
Be Not Discouraged	MS-003	12/01/14	St. Helena, Ca.	*SpTB #18 32-36*
Diary/Sacrificing in High Places	MS-005	12/00/00c	To Washington	2BC 1025,1030
Of Such Is The Kingdom of Heaven	MS-007	12/00/00		
Interview/Re Purchase of Land at Loma Linda	MS-011	12/03/28	Loma Linda, Ca.	*Medical Practice and the Educational Program at Loma Linda 128-131*
Talk/Not Division, But Unity	MS-013	12/03/28	Loma Linda, Ca.	*LLM 598-601*
Advice to Loma Linda Board	MS-014	12/04/04	Loma Linda, Ca.	*Medical Practice and the Educational Program at Loma Linda 133-134*
Discussions at Loma Linda	MS-014a	12/04/04		
Sermon/An Appeal for Unity	MS-015	12/04/16	Loma Linda, Ca.	*LLM 601-606*
Sermon/Accepting the Promise	MS-017	12/03/16	Los Angeles, Ca.	
The Rebuilding of the Melrose Sanitarium	MS-021	12/00/00c		
The Washington Sanitarium	MS-023	12/00/00		
The Wages of Faithful Ministers	MS-033	12/00/00c		Compiled from earlier published and unpublished sources
Freely Ye Have Received; Freely Give	MS-039	12/00/00		*RH 06/06/1912*
Extracts re the Caring of Tourists in Medical Inst.	MS-041	12/00/00		From Lt 244, 1903 and RH 12/17/1903
Moving Out Into New Places	MS-043	12/00/00c		Extracts from earlier published and unpublished sources
Good Samaritan Work	MS-047	12/00/00c		Compiled from earlier sources
Talk/Timely Instruction	MS-049	12/07/06	St. Helena, Ca.	6Bio 370-372
Sermon/Seeking for Heaven	MS-051	12/04/13	Loma Linda, Ca.	OHC 284
Talk/A Neglected Work	MS-053	12/03/18	Los Angeles, Ca.	1NL 85-88
A Call to Awake	MS-055	12/08/13	Loma Linda, Ca.	*13MR 44-48*
The Privilege of Ministry	MS-057	12/08/13c		MM 194-196;7MR 132
Fragments/Need of Greater Effort	MS-059	12/08/13c		CD 199-200;MM 128;HFM 72; 4MR 279-280,448;MRmnt 93
The Sermon on the Mount	MS-063	12/08/29c		HP 315
The Fruitless Fig-Tree	MS-065	12/09/02		*2SAT 329-333*
The Sin and Death of Moses	MS-069	12/09/10c		1BC 1102,1115-1116;4BC 1146, 1173-1174;7BC 1134;10MR 151-160
"Last Friday I accepted an invitation..."	MS-070	10/09/12	Filed in 1912	MM 128
Talk/Be of Good Cheer	MS-071	12/11/09	Loma Linda, Ca.	*LLM 611-614*
The Danger in Amusements	MS-073	12/08/05c		*CT 348-354*
Fragments/Wages	MS-075	12/09/16c		1MR 262
"I am charged..."	MS-077	12/08/05	St. Helena, Ca.	

EGW Manuscripts File—Page 58

Repent and Be Converted	MS-078	12/07/03	St. Helena, Ca.	
Sermon/2Peter 1	MS-079	12/02/03	St. Helena, Ca.	
Sermon/John 17:1-26	MS-080	12/03/20	Los Angeles, Ca.	
Sermon/Isaiah 58:1-3	MS-081	12/03/23	Los Angeles, Ca.	
Sermon/Romans 6:1-5	MS-082	12/08/10	St. Helena, Ca.	
Interview/The Nashville Sanitarium	MS-083	12/01/14		Filed in DF 151
Interviews/Feb. 13,25, and 28, 1912	MS-084	12/02/13		Statement by C. C. Crisler;filed in DF 151
Interview/Regarding Br. Burden	MS-085	12/04/08		Filed in DF 151
Interview/Regarding Loma Linda	MS-086	12/00/00		Filed in DF 151

1913

Statement re W.C. Wales	MS-002	13/00/00c		*TSB 233-235*
Courage in the Lord	MS-004	13/00/00c		*2SM 402-408*
The Work of Elder W.C. White	MS-006	13/00/00c		*PH116 17-24*
Interview/Regarding Wages	MS-012	13/12/04	St. Helena, Ca.	*LLM 614-621*
Interview/With E.E. Andross	MS-014	13/12/12	St. Helena, Ca.	1MR 86-88
Talk/Following On to Know the Lord	MS-016	13/06/15		*2SAT 334-336*
Sermon/I Am The True Vine	MS-018	13/06/07	St. Helena, Ca.	
Sermon/I Will Not Leave You Comfortless	MS-020	13/09/27	St. Helena, Ca.	*2SAT 337-339*
Interview/With E.E. Andross	MS-022	13/10/02	St. Helena, Ca.	
Remarks/A Visit of the Bookmen of PPPA to EGW	MS-023	13/01/23	St. Helena, Ca.	

1914

Consecrated Efforts to Reach Unbelievers	MS-002	14/06/05		*Church Officers' Gazette 09/1914*
Untitled	MS-004	14/00/00		Missing
Fragments/Look Unto Jesus	MS-008	14/00/00c		HP 19
Interview/With Dr. Thomason	MS-010	14/09/08	St. Helena, Ca.	
Interview/With W.C. White	MS-012	14/08/15	St. Helena, Ca.	
Statement at end of J.N.L. Letter	*MS-013	14/01/18		
EGW Comments on The Value of Organization	*MS-014	14/08/03	St. Helena, Ca.	*13MR 111-112*
Let This Work Go Forward	*MS-015	14/05/00		
Interview/EGW Comments	MS-016	14/08/05		Filed DF 151

1915

Testimony of Ellen G. White	MS-001	15/02/24		
Interview/Between Dr. Paulson and E. G. White	MS-002	15/01/24		Filed in DF 151
Prayer of E. G. White	MS-003	15/01/00		Filed in DF 151
Interview/Comments to C. C. Crisler	MS-004	15/03/07		Filed in DF 151
Interview/Comments to C. C. Crisler	MS-005	15/03/10		Filed in DF 151